ss Information

Northern California High Technology Directory

32nd Edition

A prospecting database of high-technology companies in Northern California

Published by Rich's Business Information

Rich's Business Information

Pearline Jaikumar, *Editor*

* * *

Rich's Business Information is in business to provide the most comprehensive up-to-date information on the high technology industry. This directory is part of a larger database and directory group covering all of California.

While every effort has been made to ensure that the information published in this directory is accurate, Rich's Business Information cannot be held liable or responsible for any errors, omissions or inaccuracies, typographical or otherwise. The companies and information featured in this directory was chosen and researched based on the creative judgement of Rich's staff.

Published Annually

**ISBN 978-0-7808-1839-2
Rich's Business Information
615 Griswold St., Ste. 520
Detroit, MI 48226
Tel: 800-207-4103**

www.richsdata.com

Table of Contents

Statistics for 2021

4,646 Listings

406 New Listings

By Size (Number of employees)

Between 1 and 10	*1*
Between 11 and 25	*2*
Between 26 and 50	*3*
Between 51 and 100	*2*
Between 101 and 250	*6*
Between 251 and 500	*4*
Between 501 and 1000	*5*
1000+ employees	*3*

By Size (Number of employees)

10 or more Employees	*26*
25 or more Employees	*24*
50 or more Employees	*21*
100 or more Employees	*18*
500 or more Employees	*8*

Misc. Statistics:

Fax Number Count	*2,896*
Email Count	*3,412*
Addressess Count	*4,646*
Web	*4,618*
New Listing	*406*

Companies by Function:

HQ-Headquarters	*4,083*
DH-Division Headquarters	*66*
BR-Branch	*418*
LH-Local Headquarters	*17*
RH-Regional Headquarters	*62*

Companies by Year Established:

2016 – 2020	*10*
2010 – 2015	*370*
2000 – 2009	*1,048*
1990 – 1999	*1,015*
1980 – 1989	*732*
1970 – 1979	*411*
Before 1970	*483*

By Department Head:

President	1,766
Vice President	9
General Manager	413
CEO	1,909
COO	503
CFO	760
CTO	3,777
Owner	400
Engineer	2,784
Marketing	955
Marketing/Sales	0
Sales	1,648
Purchasing	94
MIS	88
Director	3,163
Manager	5,144
Facility Manager	4
Board Member	3
Designer	117
Controller	215

By County (Alphabetically)

Alameda	816	Placer	73
Amador	3	Riverside	9
Butte	24	Sacramento	173
Calaveras	3	San Benito	9
Contra Costa	231	San Bernardino	21
El Dorado	37	San Diego	20
Fresno	58	San Francisco	335
Glenn	2	San Joaquin	59
Humboldt	5	San Luis Obispo	2
Inyo	1	San Mateo	429
Kern	2	Santa Barbara	7
Kings	2	Santa Clara	1,575
Lake	2	Santa Cruz	67
Los Angeles	131	Shasta	19
Madera	8	Siskiyou	3
Marin	76	Solano	51
Mariposa	2	Sonoma	121
Mendocino	10	Stanislaus	35
Merced	6	Sutter	6
Mono	1	Tehama	2
Monterey	24	Tulare	14
Napa	19	Tuolumne	6
Nevada	20	Ventura	11
Orange	68	Yolo	45
Orange	1	Yuba	2

Companies by Product:

Aerospace/Aircraft & Equipment	87
Analytical & Testing Equipment	114
Biotechnology	432
Business Management Services	78
Chemicals	116
Communications Equipment/Services	575
Components	655
Computer Systems (Hardware)	189
Computer Peripherals/Accessories	161
Electronics Production Equipment	108
Energy	123
Environmental	260
Industrial Equipment & Services	625
Lasers/Optics/Photonics	160
Material Handling Equipment	49
Medical Equipment/Devices & Services	681
Microelectronics	776
Military Equipment/Services	21
Monitoring/Controlling Equipment	97
Non-Industrial Electrical Products	127
Pharmaceuticals	308
Plastics/Advanced Materials	93
Power Devices/Systems	135
Research, Development & Testing	285
Robotics/Factory Automation	52
Software Development/Services	416
Software - Related Services	2,082

Cities

City	#	County	City	#	County	City	#	County
Acampo	1	San Joaquin	Cotati	1	Sonoma	Gold River	3	Sacramento
Alameda	30	Alameda	Cottonwood	1	Tehama	Granite Bay	3	Placer
Alamo	4	Contra Costa	Crows Landing	1	Stanislaus	Grass Valley	17	Nevada
Albany	3	Alameda	Cupertino	38	Santa Clara	Graton	1	Sonoma
American Canyon	2	Napa	Daly City	3	San Mateo	Groveland	1	Tuolumne
Anderson	1	Shasta	Danville	10	Contra Costa	Half Moon Bay	6	San Mateo
Angels Camp	2	Calaveras	Davis	24	Yolo	Hanford	3	Kings
Antioch	3	Contra Costa	Diamond Springs	5	El Dorado	Hayward	100	Alameda
Aptos	4	Santa Cruz				Healdsburg	2	Sonoma
Arcata	3	Humboldt	Dinuba	1	Tulare	Hercules	6	Contra Costa
Auburn	22	Placer	Dixon	3	Solano	Hollister	7	San Benito
Belmont	8	San Mateo	Dublin	15	Alameda	Hughson	1	Stanislaus
Ben Lomond	1	Santa Cruz	East Palo Alto	1	Santa Clara	Huntington Beach	1	Orange
Benicia	21	Solano	El Dorado Hills	21	El Dorado			
Berkeley	62	Alameda	El Granada	1	San Mateo	Irvine	3	Orange
Biola	1	Fresno	El Macero	1	Yolo	June Lake	1	Mono
Bishop	1	Inyo	El Sobrante	1	Contra Costa	Kerman	1	Fresno
Brentwood	4	Contra Costa	Elk Grove	6	Sacramento	La Mesa	1	Placer
Brisbane	13	San Mateo	Emerald Hills	1	San Mateo	Lafayette	8	Contra Costa
Browns Valley	1	Yuba	Emeryville	35	Alameda	Lake Forest	1	Lake
Burbank	1	Los Angeles	Escalon	2	San Joaquin	Lakeport	2	Lake
Burlingame	30	San Mateo	Escondido	1	Santa Clara	Lincoln	5	Placer
Byron	1	Contra Costa	Eureka	2	Humboldt	Lindsay	1	Tulare
Cameron Park	4	El Dorado	Exeter	2	Tulare	Livermore	75	Alameda
Campbell	47	Santa Clara	Fair Oaks	3	Sacramento	Lodi	12	San Joaquin
Carlsbad	3	San Diego	Fairfax	1	Marin	Lone	1	Amador
Carmel	1	Monterey	Fairfield	12	Solano	Loomis	2	Placer
Carmichael	1	Sacramento	Felton	2	Santa Cruz	Los Altos	29	Santa Clara
Castro Valley	2	Alameda	Folsom	21	Sacramento	Los Altos Hills	5	Santa Clara
Ceres	3	Stanislaus	Forestville	1	Sonoma	Los Gatos	28	Santa Clara
Chico	21	Butte	Fort Bragg	3	Mendocino	Madera	6	Madera
Chowchilla	1	Madera	Foster City	21	San Mateo	Manteca	3	San Joaquin
Citrus Heights	4	Sacramento	Fountain Valley	1	Orange	Marina	3	Monterey
Cloverdale	1	Sonoma	Fowler	1	Fresno	Marinez	1	Contra Costa
Clovis	3	Fresno	Freedom	2	Santa Cruz	Mariposa	2	Mariposa
Colfax	1	Placer	Fremont	269	Alameda	Martinez	12	Contra Costa
Comptche	1	Mendocino	Fresno	46	Fresno	McClellan	1	Sacramento
Concord	47	Contra Costa	Georgetown	1	El Dorado	Menlo Park	62	San Mateo
Corte Madera	3	Marin	Gilroy	8	Santa Clara	Merced	6	Merced
			Glen Ellen	1	Sonoma	Mesa	1	Maricopa

Cities

City	#	County	City	#	County	City	#	County
Mill Valley	8	Marin	Portola Valley	1	San Mateo	Seaside	1	Monterey
Millbrae	2	San Mateo	Rancho Cordova	34	Sacramento	Sebastopol	3	Sonoma
Milpitas	106	Santa Clara				Selma	2	Fresno
Mission Viejo	1	Orange	Red Bluff	1	Tehama	Shingle Springs	1	El Dorado
Modesto	17	Stanislaus	Redding	16	Shasta	Sonoma	5	Sonoma
Moffett Field	2	Santa Clara	Redwood City	90	San Mateo	Sonora	7	Tuolumne
Monte Sereno	1	Santa Clara	Redwood Shores	6	San Mateo	Soquel	4	Santa Cruz
Monterey	14	Monterey				Soulsbyville	1	Tuolumne
Moraga	4	Contra Costa	Redwood Valley	2	Mendocino	South Lake Tahoe	2	El Dorado
Morgan Hill	48	Santa Clara	Reedley	1	Fresno			
Moss Beach	1	San Mateo	Richmond	24	Contra Costa	South Sacramento	1	Sacramento
Moss Landing	1	Monterey	Rio Vista	1	Solano			
Mount Shasta	1	Siskiyou	Ripon	4	San Joaquin	South San Francisco	88	San Mateo
Mountain View	110	Santa Clara	Rocklin	19	Placer			
Napa	13	Napa	Rodeo	2	Contra Costa	St. Helena	4	Napa
Nevada City	1	Nevada	Rohnert Park	13	Sonoma	Stockton	24	San Joaquin
Newark	39	Alameda	Roseville	19	Placer	Suisun	1	Solano
Newcastle	1	Placer	Sacramento	101	Sacramento	Suisun City	1	Solano
Newport Beach	1	King	Salida	3	Stanislaus	Sunnyvale	173	Santa Clara
Novato	19	Marin	Salinas	3	Monterey	Sutter	1	Sutter
Oakdale	3	Stanislaus	San Anselmo	5	Marin	Tiburon	3	Marin
Oakland	76	Alameda	San Bruno	7	San Mateo	Tollhouse	1	Fresno
Oakley	1	Contra Costa	San Carlos	45	San Mateo	Torrance	1	Los Angeles
Orangevale	3	Sacramento	San Diego	1	San Diego	Tracy	9	San Joaquin
Oregon House	1	Yuba	San Francisco	362	San Francisco	Truckee	3	Nevada
Orinda	5	Contra Costa	San Jose	584	Santa Clara	Tulare	1	Tulare
Orland	2	Glenn	San Juan Bautista	1	San Benito	Turlock	4	Stanislaus
Oroville	3	Butte				Ukiah	2	Mendocino
Pacheco	1	Contra Costa	San Leandro	39	Alameda	Union City	26	Alameda
Pacifica	2	San Mateo	San Martin	1	Santa Clara	Vacaville	13	Solano
Palo Alto	107	Santa Clara	San Mateo	80	San Mateo	Vallejo	3	Solano
Paradise	2	Butte	San Pablo	1	Contra Costa	Visalia	7	Tulare
Parlier	1	Fresno	San Rafael	30	Marin	Vista	1	San Diego
Petaluma	34	Sonoma	San Ramon	45	Contra Costa	Walnut Creek	34	Contra Costa
Piedmont	1	Alameda	Sanger	1	Fresno	Watsonville	11	Santa Cruz
Pine Grove	1	Amador	Santa Ana	1	Salt Lake	West Sacramento	12	Yolo
Pinole	2	Contra Costa	Santa Clara	345	Santa Clara			
Pittsburg	9	Contra Costa	Santa Cruz	28	Santa Cruz	Willits	1	Mendocino
Placerville	3	El Dorado	Santa Rosa	60	Sonoma	Windsor	4	Sonoma
Pleasant Grove	1	Sutter	Santra Clara	1	Santa Clara	Woodland	11	Yolo
Pleasant Hill	4	Contra Costa	Saratoga	8	Santa Clara	Yreka	2	Siskiyou
Pleasanton	85	Alameda	Sausalito	7	Marin	Yuba City	4	Sutter
Point Richmond	1	Contra Costa	Scotts Valley	20	Santa Cruz			
Porterville	1	Tulare	Seal Beach	1	Orange			

Sample Entry

Listing data include the following, as applicable and available:

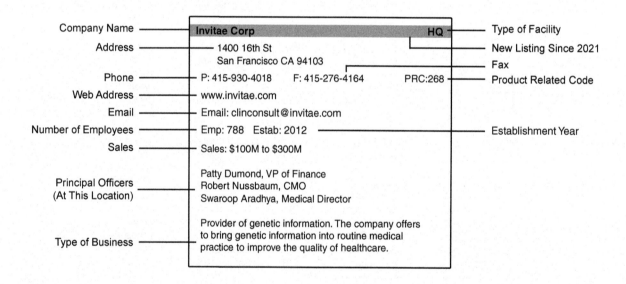

Company Name	Invitae Corp — HQ	Type of Facility
Address	1400 16th St / San Francisco CA 94103	New Listing Since 2021 / Fax
Phone	P: 415-930-4018 F: 415-276-4164 PRC:268	Product Related Code
Web Address	www.invitae.com	
Email	Email: clinconsult@invitae.com	
Number of Employees	Emp: 788 Estab: 2012	Establishment Year
Sales	Sales: $100M to $300M	
Principal Officers (At This Location)	Patty Dumond, VP of Finance / Robert Nussbaum, CMO / Swaroop Aradhya, Medical Director	
Type of Business	Provider of genetic information. The company offers to bring genetic information into routine medical practice to improve the quality of healthcare.	

FACILITY CLASSIFICATION

HQ = Headquarters
BR = Branch
RH = Regional Headquarters
DH = Division Headquarters
LH = Local Headquarters

MAIN INDEX

10X Genomics Inc   HQ
6230 Stoneridge Mall Rd
Pleasanton CA 94588-3260
P: 925-401-7300   PRC:34
www.10xgenomics.com
Email: info@10xgenomics.com
Estab: 2012

Ben Hindson, Chief Scientific Officer & President
& Co-Founder
Serge Saxonov, CEO & Co-Founder

Provider of gemcode, instruments, software,
and applications technology for RNA and DNA
analysis.

15five Inc   HQ
12 Gallagher Ln Ste 279
San Francisco CA 94103
P: 415-967-3483   F: 601-510-3274   PRC:326
www.15five.com
Estab: 2011

David Hassell, CEO & Founder
Shane Metcalf, Chief Culture Officer
Bill MacAitis, Advisor
Jason Calacanis, Advisor
Cameron Herold, Advisor

Provider of services that allow you to question
and start conversations that matters to elevate
performance of employees, managers, and entire
organizations.

21Tech LLC   BR
1330 Broadway Ste 1530
Oakland CA 94612
P: 415-355-9090   PRC:326
21tech.com
Email: contact@21tech.com
Estab: 1996

Linda Short, VP of Professional Services
Brad Baker, Director of Sales
Azhar Mahmood, Partner
Bill Carrick, Director of EAM Services
Dilraj Kahai, Managing Partner

Provider of business and technology solutions
such as technology consultancy, strategic sourc-
ing/placement, and branding and creative services
practice.

23andme Inc   HQ
223 N Mathilda Ave
Sunnyvale CA 94086
P: 800-239-5230   PRC:34
23andme.com
Email: privacy@23andme.com
Estab: 2006

Anne Wojcicki, CEO & Founder
Andy Page, President
Kathy Hibbs, Chief Legal & Regulatory Officer
Mike Polcari, Chief Architect
Arnab Chowdry, VP of Genetic Technology

Provider of genetic information. The company
specializes in DNA analysis technologies and
web-based interactive tools.

2K Games Inc   HQ
10 Hamilton Landing
Novato CA 94949
P: 415-479-3634   PRC:317
www.2k.com
Estab: 2005

Matt Gorman, VP of Marketing
Scott Sanford, Quality Assurance Director
Tim Holman, Senior Director of Business Devel-
opment
Jack Scalici, Director of Creative Production
Jonathan Tilden, Technical Director

Developer of interactive entertainment for console
systems. The company also focuses on handheld
gaming systems and personal computers.

2ndEdison Inc   HQ
11 El Gavilan Rd
Orinda CA 94563
P: 844-432-8466   PRC:316
www.2ndedison.com
Estab: 2000

Chris Bradley, Founder & CEO

Provider of e-Commerce applications. The company also offers business process consulting and
design services.

314e Corp   HQ
6701 Koll Center Pkwy Ste 340
Pleasanton CA 94566
P: 510-371-6736   F: 510-255-4534   PRC:194
314e.com
Email: info@314e.com
Estab: 2004

Abhishek Begerhotta, Founder & CEO
Alok Sharma, COO
Kesav Kolla, CTO
Gaurav Mundra, VP of Operations
Kat Mako, Regional VP of Sales

Provider of IT skills, methodologies, and cost-ef-
fective managed services for healthcare application and technical support services.

37 Degrees Inc   HQ
PO Box 411163
San Francisco CA 94141
P: 415-315-9380   F: 415-765-9201   PRC:322
37degrees.com
Email: info@37degrees.com
Estab: 1999

Jacob Pipe, Director

Provider of technology and management consulting services for publishing, media, software
technology, and beverage industries.

3D Robotics Inc   HQ
1608 Fourth St Ste 410
Berkeley CA 94710
P: 858-225-1414   PRC:311
3dr.com
Email: support@3dr.com
Estab: 2009

Chris Anderson, Co-Founder & CEO
Jordi Munoz, Co-Founder & Director
Lorena Diaz, Director of Operations
Michael Wiener, IT Director
Lauren Howell, Director of Sales Operations &
Strategy

Manufacturer of drone systems for exploration
and business applications. The company offers
autopilot controllers and flight controllers.

3DTL Inc   HQ
1243 Reamwood Dr
Sunnyvale CA 94089
P: 408-541-8550   F: 408-541-8555   PRC:53
www.3dtl.com
Email: info@3dtl.com
Estab: 1996

Elizabeth Downing, President & CEO
Robert Rewick, Research Chemist

Provider of authentication technology services.
The company develops 3D displays for medical,
industrial, and military applications.

3K Technologies LLC   HQ
1114 Cadillac Ct   [N]
Milpitas CA 95035
P: 408-716-5900   F: 408-884-2420   PRC:322
www.3ktechnologies.com
Estab: 2002

Krish K. Chittabathini, CEO

Provider of IT services to finance, government
and high-tech industries.

3Q Digital Inc   BR
301 Howard St 11th Fl
San Francisco CA 94105
P: 650-539-4124   PRC:45
3qdigital.com
Estab: 2008

David Rodnitzky, Founder
Rob Murray, President
Ellen Corrigan, CRO
Laura Rodnitzky, Chief Human Resource Officer
Brian Grabowski, Chief Growth Officer

Performance and digital marketing agency that
provides digital media services.

3rd Stone Design Inc   HQ
30 Castro Ave
San Rafael CA 94901
P: 415-454-3005   PRC:13
www.3rdstonedesign.com
Email: info@3rdstonedesign.com
Estab: 2005

Robert Miros, CEO
Li Jin, Supply Chain Manager
Chris Holscher, Quality & Regulatory Manager
Keith Payea, Electrical Engineer
Alex Fraser, Quality Engineer

Provider of design, product development, and
engineering services. The company serves the
consumer products and healthcare industries.

3Scan Inc   HQ
2122 Bryant St
San Francisco CA 94110
P: 415-851-5376   PRC:34
www.3scan.com
Email: info@3scan.com
Estab: 2011

Megan Klimen, Founder & COO
Terri Hnatyszyn, VP of Marketing
Dylan Jutt, Creative Director

Provider of automated microscopy services and
supporting software for the 3D analysis of cells,
tissues, and organs.

4D Inc DH
95 S Market St Ste 240
San Jose CA 95113
P: 408-557-4600 PRC:323
www.4d.com
Email: info@4d.com
Estab: 1984

Laurent Esnault, VP of Engineering
Asmae Benkirane, EVP
Dominique Coste, Distribution Sales Manager

Developer of web and Internet applications. The company serves universities, corporations, governments, and individuals.

4D Molecular Therapeutics LLC HQ
5858 Horton St Ste 455
Emeryville CA 94608
P: 510-505-2680 PRC:34
4dmoleculartherapeutics.com
Email: information@4dmoleculartherapeutics.com
Estab: 2013

David Kirn, CEO & Co-Founder & Chairman
David Schaffer, Co-Founder & Chief Scientific Advisor
Theresa Janke, COO & Co-Founder
Peter Francis, CMO
August Moretti, CFO

Provider of gene therapy product research and development for the treatment of genetic diseases such as diabetes, arthritis, and heart failure.

6connect Inc HQ
548 Market St Ste 39313
San Francisco CA 94104-5401
P: 650-646-2206 PRC:324
www.6connect.com
Email: support@6connect.com
Estab: 2009

Aaron Hughes, CEO & CTO & Co-Founder
Pete Sclafani, COO & Co-Founder
Anna Claiborne, VP

Provider of network resource provisioning and automation products and services such as data normalizer, pro services, and provision jumpstart.

6connex HQ
425 Soledad St Ste 500
San Antonio CA 78205
P: 800-395-4702 PRC:326
6connex.com
Email: sales@6connex.com
Estab: 2008

Michael Nelson, CEO
Henry Tran, CTO
Michael Goodell, EVP of Product Engineering
Marc Goodell, EVP
Jennifer Kidwell, Director of Sales

Provider of virtual environment space and powering virtual destinations for career fairs, corporate universities, product launches, and user conferences.

6WIND USA Inc RH
2445 Augustine Dr Ste 150
Santa Clara CA 95054
P: 408-816-1366 PRC:97
www.6wind.com
Email: 6wind-contact@6wind.com
Estab: 2000

Aymeric Pintaud, CFO
Jean-Mickael Guerin, CTO
Roland Rodriguez, VP of Sales for EMEA & APAC
Yann Rapaport, VP of Product Management
Kelly LeBlanc, VP of Marketing

Manufacturer of virtual accelerators, routers, and related accessories. The company offers network security and network appliance solutions.

8minute Solar Energy HQ
4370 Town Center Blvd Ste 110
El Dorado Hills CA 95762
P: 916-608-9060 F: 916-608-9861 PRC:135
www.8minute.com
Email: info@8minutenergy.com
Estab: 2010

Mario Ricci, VP of Corporate Finance
Ali Chowdhury, VP
Dennis Harper, VP
Benjamin New, SVP of EPC
Betsy Engle, SVP of Finance

Developer of solar PV projects. The company specializes in project development, financing, utility engineering, and business development.

8x8 Inc HQ
675 Creekside Way
Campbell CA 95008
P: 408-727-1885 PRC:68
8x8.com
Email: ro-recruitment@8x8.com
Estab: 1987
Sales: $300M to $1 Billion

Bryan R. Martin, CTO & Chairman
Kim Niederman, President
Vikram Verma, CEO
Steven Gatoff, CFO
Marge Breya, Executive VP & CMO

Provider of cloud communications and computing solutions. The company sells IP phones, IP conference, soft, video and analog phones and accessories.

A & A Machine & Development Company Inc HQ
16625 Gramercy Pl [N]
Gardena CA 90247
P: 310-532-7706 F: 310-532-7626 PRC:80
www.aamach.com
Email: eric@aamach.com
Estab: 1972

Arlene Hymovitz, President
Guy Falkner, General Manager

Manufacturer of CNC equipment for airspace and commercial industries.

A A Networks HQ
111 Anza Blvd Ste 130
Burlingame CA 94010
P: 650-872-1998 F: 650-548-1999 PRC:59
aanetwork.com
Email: service@aanetworks.net
Estab: 1996

Bill Lui, Manager

Provider of Internet, networks and cabling, computer hardware and software, remote and on-site technical support services.

A J Edmond Co BR
1717 Solano Way Ste 38
Concord CA 94520
P: 925-521-1555 F: 925-521-1556 PRC:51
ajedmondco.com
Estab: 1965

Jignesh Panchal, Director of Technology
Robert Llerena, Director of Field Operations
Douglas Schug, Field Operations Manager
Esther Iniguez, Lab Technician

Provider of sampling and analytical services to petroleum refineries. The company's service areas include petroleum coke, coal, and gypsum.

A Step Above HQ
1064 Horizon Dr Ste 5
Fairfield CA 94533
P: 707-421-2917 PRC:180

Anthony E. Lewis II, Owner & Technician
Lindsey Lewis, Owner & Office Manager
Tatiana Lewis, Executive Administrative Assistant

Provider of elevator services. The company offers escalators, walks, manlifts, and traction cars and related troubleshooting, testing and service.

A TEEM Electrical Engineering HQ
3841 N Freeway Blvd Ste 145
Sacramento CA 95834
P: 916-457-8144 F: 916-457-7876 PRC:144
www.ateem.com
Estab: 1988

Sharon Kimizuka, Owner
Erik Burns, Controls Engineer

Provider of outreach safety training, electrical design and construction management, and control system programming services.

A&D Engineering Inc RH
1756 Automation Pkwy
San Jose CA 95131
P: 408-263-5333 F: 408-263-0119 PRC:189
andonline.com
Email: info@andonline.com
Estab: 1982

Terry Duesterhoeft, President & CEO
Fred Lau, Director of Finance & Information Technology
Jerry Wang, Director of Engineering & QA

Supplier of electric scale balancers and blood pressure monitors. The company offers services to the business sector.

A&D Precision Inc   HQ
  4155 Business Center Dr
  Fremont CA 94538
P: 510-657-6781   PRC:80
www.adprecision.com
Estab: 1978

Andy Dreifort, CEO
Caprice Dreifort, Marketing Manager
Jimmy Ying, Quality Control Lead
Conni Chandler, Office Administrator
Helen Tu, Senior Sales Representative

Provider of contract manufacturing, program
management, electro-mechanical assembly, and
precision machining services.

A&L Western Labs Inc   HQ
  1311 Woodland Ave Ste 1
  Modesto CA 95351
P: 209-529-4080   F: 209-529-4736   PRC:139
www.al-labs-west.com
Estab: 1971

Robert Butterfield, Owner & President
Kathryn Butterfield-Byrne, Operations Manager

Provider of analytical services to agricultural sector. The company's services include soil analysis,
pathology, microbiology, and water analysis.

A'n D Cable Products Inc   HQ
  1460 Washington Blvd Ste A-102
  Concord CA 94521
P: 925-672-3005   F: 925-672-0317   PRC:62
www.andcable.com
Email: sales@andcable.com
Estab: 1989

Louis Chompff, Owner

Manufacturer, installer, and reseller of cable
accessories. The company focuses on cable management and labeling solutions.

A-1 Jay's Machining Inc   HQ
  2228 Oakland Rd
  San Jose CA 95131
P: 408-262-1845   F: 408-262-4561   PRC:80
a1jays.com
Email: info@a1jays.com
Estab: 1991

Shanmuga C. Ganesan, Senior Manager
Thomas Abraham, Manager
Vasant Shetty, Tool Design Engineer

Provider of machining, product assembly, and
finishing services. The company is engaged in
vertical milling, laser Micro-machining and waterjet
cutting.

A-Laser   HQ
  675 Trade Zone Blvd
  Milpitas CA 95035
P: 408-954-8582   PRC:80
a-laser.com
Email: norcalorders@a-laser.com
Estab: 1994

Joe Azevedo, Sales Manager

Provider of precision parts manufacturing services. The company specializes in laser cutting
and caters to a wide range of industries.

A3 Solutions Inc   HQ
  1 Market Plz Spear Twr 36th Fl
  San Francisco CA 94105
P: 415-356-2300   PRC:325
a3solutions.com
Email: info@a3solutions.com
Estab: 1988

Rob Lautt, CEO & Founder
Stuart Ratner, COO
Del Valle Lola, Director
James Williamson, IT Administrator

Developer and marketer of enterprise modeling
software. The company is also engaged in unified
budgeting and consolidation services.

A10 Networks Inc   HQ
  2300 Orchard Pkwy
  San Jose CA 95131
P: 408-325-8668   F: 408-325-8666   PRC:97
www.a10networks.com
Estab: 2004
Sales: $100M to $300M

Dhrupad Trivedi, President & CEO
Raj Jalan, CTO
Andrew Kim, VP of Worldwide Human Resources
Gunter Reiss, VP of Worldwide Marketing
Eric Kwok, VP of Worldwide Support & Services

Provider of networking and security solutions
such as cloud computing and virtualization and
bandwidth management.

AA Portable Power Corp   HQ
  825 S 19th St
  Richmond CA 94804
P: 510-525-2328   F: 510-439-2808   PRC:288
www.batteryspace.com
Email: sales@batteryspace.com
Estab: 2000

Jing Chen, Manager
Po-Feng Chen, Battery Engineer

Manufacturer of lithium-ion batteries. The company serves the mobile, consumer electronics,
energy storage, and light electric vehicle markers.

AAT Bioquest Inc   HQ
  520 Mercury Dr
  Sunnyvale CA 94085
P: 408-733-1055   F: 408-733-1304   PRC:34
www.aatbio.com
Email: info@aatbio.com
Estab: 2006

Jack Diwu, President
George Yi, Organic Chemistry Manager
Jixiang Liu, Manager
Zhen Luo, Staff Scientist & Manager
Xing Han, Scientist

Developer and manufacturer of bioanalytical
research reagents and kits. The company focuses
on photometric detections including absorption.

AB Medical Technologies Inc   HQ
  20272 Skypark Dr
  Redding CA 96002
P: 530-605-2522   PRC:189
www.abmedtech.com
Email: sales@abmedtech.com
Estab: 2009

Ken Brown, President of Operations
Dwight Abbott, President of Regulatory & Sales

Manufacturer of electronic medical systems and
powered surgical instruments such as surgical
pumps, arthroscopy shavers and lab equipment.

AB&I Foundry   HQ
  7825 San Leandro St
  Oakland CA 94621
P: 510-632-3467   F: 510-632-8035   PRC:53
abifoundry.com
Email: info@mcwane.com
Estab: 1906

Kurt Winter, EVP
Dave Robinson, VP of Operations
Ted Ray, VP of Trading
Paul Quezada, Compliance Director
Michael Lowe, General Manager

Provider of casting products and accessories. The
company's products include pipes and fittings, custom castings, foundry, and recyclable materials.

Abacus Solutions Inc   HQ
  24704 Voorhees Dr
  Los Altos Hills CA 94022
P: 650-941-1728   PRC:319
www.abacussolutionsinc.com
Email: info@abacussolutionsinc.com

Salim J. Jabbour, CEO
Vadim Nazaryants, Chief System Architect

Developer of SATURN, an integrated enterprise ETRM system and focuses on generation
optimization, parameters estimation, and credit
management.

Abaxis Inc   HQ
  3240 Whipple Rd
  Union City CA 94587
P: 510-675-6500   F: 510-441-6150   PRC:303
www.abaxis.com
Estab: 1995

Ross Taylor, CFO
Donald P. Wood, COO
Kenneth P. Aron, CTO
Craig Tockman, VP of Sales & Marketing
My Ha, Technical Support Director

Provider of on-site patient testing, leading-edge
point-of-care technologies for veterinary practices
and laboratory services for medical professionals.

Abbomax Inc   HQ
  2528 Qume Dr Ste 8
  San Jose CA 95131
P: 408-573-1898   F: 408-573-1858   PRC:249
abbomax.com
Email: info@abbomax.com
Estab: 2005

Yuan Zhou, CSO
Ma Li, Scientist

Provider of antibody, peptide, and assay products
and services. The company offers antibody production, fragmentation, assay development, and
other services.

Abbott Diabetes Care   BR
  1420 Harbor Bay Pkwy
  Alameda CA 94502
P: 510-749-5400   F: 510-749-5401   PRC:34
abbott.com
Email: ruitservice@abbott.com

Robert Ford, President
Jared Watkin, SVP
Kelly Duffy, DVP of Global Quality Assurance
Duncan Williams, Divisional VP of New Analyte
Ventures
Udo Hoss, Director of Sensor Chemistry

Provider of healthcare solutions. The company
specializes in diagnostics, diabetes care, vision technologies, nutrition, pharmaceuticals & animal health.

ABBYY USA HQ
890 Hillview Ct Ste 300
Milpitas CA 95035
P: 408-457-9777 F: 408-457-9778 PRC:323
www.abbyy.com
Email: sales@abbyyusa.com
Estab: 1999

Jupp Stoepetie, CMO
Konstantin Anisimovich, CTO
Vitaliy Tyshchenko, Chief Customer Officer
Anthony MacCiola, Chief Innovation Officer
Bodo Wagener, Chief Sales Officer

Provider of optical character recognition solutions.
The company offers scanners, screenshot readers, document converters, and linguistic solutions.

ABCO Laboratories Inc HQ
2450 S Watney Way
Fairfield CA 94533
P: 707-432-2200 F: 707-432-2240 PRC:272
www.abcolabs.com
Estab: 1964

David Baron, President
Adrian Cesana, CIO
Eric Whitaker, EVP
Rich Hale, Director of QA & QC
Vanessa Montiel-Quiles, Accounts Receivable Manager

Provider of turnkey solutions. The company also offers contract manufacturing, product development and private labeling.

ABCO Wire & Metal Products BR
4061 E Castro Valley Blvd
Castro Valley CA 94552-4840
P: 510-909-5626 F: 510-581-0889 PRC:88
www.abcowire.com
Email: sales@abcowire.com

Mike Hopper, General Manager
Dale Silva, National Accounts Manager

Designer and manufacturer of display racks. The company focuses on roller grill, drying racks, and POP displays.

AbGenomics International Inc HQ
555 Twin Dolphin Dr Ste 310
Redwood City CA 94065
P: 650-453-3462 PRC:249
www.abgenomics.com
Email: info@altrubio.com
Estab: 2000

Patrick Y. Yang, Executive Chairman of the Board & Audit Committee Member & Compensation Committee Member
Ron Lin, CEO
Hsiao-Wen Tuan, Associate VP of Finance
Leewen Lin, VP of Administration
Hazel T.Y. Cheng, VP of Clinical & CMC Project Management

Specializes in the development of drug candidates for immune-mediated inflammation and cancer therapies.

Able Design Inc HQ
2267 Old Middlefield Way
Mountain View CA 94043
P: 650-961-8245 F: 650-961-8246 PRC:159
abledesigninc.com
Email: sales@abledesigninc.com
Estab: 1978

John Meadows, Owner

Provider of design services that involves specialization in automated handling of small high technology devices.

Able Health Inc HQ
1516 Folsom St Unit C
San Francisco CA 94103
P: 805-288-0240 PRC:194
ablehealth.com
Email: hello@ablehealth.com

Rachel Katz, CEO

Provider of value-based reimbursements under MACRA, MIPS, PQRS, medicaids, and commercial programs.

Ablesys Corp HQ
8407 Central Ave Ste 1882
Newark CA 94560
P: 510-265-1883 F: 510-265-1993 PRC:322
wintick.com
Email: sales@ablesys.com
Estab: 1994

John Wang, CEO
Yi Fan, VP & CTO

Provider of financial trading software and web applications. The company focuses on portfolio and algorithmic trading solutions.

ABM-USA Inc HQ
305 Piercy Rd
San Jose CA 95138
P: 408-226-8722 F: 408-226-8775 PRC:124
www.abmusainc.com
Email: po@abmusainc.com
Estab: 1986

Anhvu Vu, VP
Jessica Do, Office Manager & Executive Assistant

Manufacturer and seller of mask aligner and exposure systems. The company also provides vacuum chucks, intensity meters, and probes.

Aborn Electronics Inc HQ
2108 E Bering Dr
San Jose CA 95131
P: 408-436-5445 F: 408-436-0969 PRC:203
www.abornelectronicsinc.com
Estab: 1978

Vijay Lumba, President

Manufacturer of fiber optic systems. The company specializes in the design and manufacture of fiber optic receivers and transmitters.

Abrisa Industrial Glass Inc HQ
200 S Hallock Dr [N]
Santa Paula CA 93060
P: 805-525-4902 F: 805-525-8604 PRC:277
abrisatechnologies.com
Email: info@abrisatechnologies.com
Estab: 2005

Maarten Oostendorp, CFO

Provider of full-service custom glass fabrication.

ABT-TRAC HQ
517 A Martin Ave
Rohnert Park CA 94928
P: 707-586-3155 F: 707-586-3159 PRC:155
abttrac.com
Email: info@abttrac.com
Estab: 1986

D'Milo Hallerberg, Founder
David Catterson, Product Manager

Provider of yacht and boat stabilizers and bow and stern thrusters. The company also offers integrated hydraulic products.

Abtech Technologies HQ
2042 Corte Del Nogal [N]
Carlsbad CA 92009
P: 760-827-5100 PRC:104
abtechtechnologies.com

Jill H. Twombly, Controller

Provider of IT consulting and enterprise-wide solutions specializing in Hewlett-Packard, IBM, Sun Microsystems, and storage hardware and services. Professional services include: On-site support services, technical consulting, hardware and software rentals and leasing, asset recovery and disposal services.

ABX Engineering Inc HQ
875 Stanton Rd
Burlingame CA 94010-1503
P: 650-552-2300 F: 650-259-8750 PRC:86
www.abxengineering.com
Email: sales@abxengineering.com
Estab: 1980

Brian Helm, SVP
Joe Gotisar, Sales Program Manager
John Turner, Sales Program Manager
Henry Deng, Engineer

Manufacturer of printed circuit board assemblies and electromechanical products for medical devices, agriculture, and military electronics industries.

AC Photonics Inc HQ
2701 Northwestern Pkwy
Santa Clara CA 95051
P: 408-986-9838 F: 408-986-0188 PRC:170
www.acphotonics.com
Email: sales@acphotonics.com
Estab: 1995

Henry Chang, Account Manager
Tony Cortez, Sales Manager
Sunny Chen, Engineer

Manufacturer of custom-made precision optical components. The company also offers fiber optic components and modules.

Acadia Technology Inc HQ
1021 Helena Dr
Sunnyvale CA 94087
P: 408-737-9528 PRC:101
www.globalwinusa.com
Email: sales@globalwinusa.com
Estab: 1996

Chung Bao, Manager

Dealer of power supplies, water cooling kits, cases, fans and fan ducts, and digital temperature displayers.

ACC Environmental Consultants　　HQ
　7977 Capwell Dr Ste 100
　Oakland CA 94621
P: 510-638-8400　F: 510-638-8404　　PRC:139
www.accenv.com
Email: general@accenv.com
Estab: 1986

Mark Sanchez, President
Jim Wilson, CEO
Chris Yama, Project Manager
Ian Sutherland, Project Manager
Sarah Wilson, Marketing Coordinator

Provider of environmental consulting services. The company's services include moisture testing, site assessment, mold testing, and asbestos consulting.

Accela Inc　　HQ
　2633 Camino Ramon Ste 500
　San Ramon CA 94583-2539
P: 925-659-3200　F: 925-659-3201　　PRC:323
www.accela.com
Email: info@accela.com
Estab: 1999

Gary Kovacs, CEO
Renato Mascardo, CTO
Tom Nieto, COO
Bobby Wilson, CFO
Dennis Michalis, CRO

Provider of licensing, asset and land management, and public health and safety solutions. The company offers technical support services.

Accelerance Inc　　HQ
　303 Twin Dolphin Dr Ste 600
　Redwood City CA 94065
P: 650-472-3785　　PRC:325
www.accelerance.com
Email: info@accelerance.com
Estab: 2001

Rod McCowan, Founder & Chief Catalyst
Steve Mezak, CEO
Scott Pollov, CFO
Michael J. Kimball, Managing Director

Provider of software design, development, and deployment services. The company focuses on web hosting and programming solutions.

Accelerate Learning & Development Inc　　HQ
　One Victor Square Ste 8003
　Scotts Valley CA 95066
P: 831-291-3770　　PRC:322
www.accelerate-ld.com

John Boring, CEO

Provider of design, live training, and performance support tools such as the influencer app that helps assess working style for managers.

AccelerATE Solutions Inc　　HQ
　2033 Gateway Pl Ste 500
　San Jose CA 95110
P: 408-573-6066　　PRC:86
acceler-ate.com
Email: info@acceler-ate.com
Estab: 2006

Tom Nulsen, Founding Partner

Provider of test engineering services. The company offers device characterization, applications support, and test program development services.

Accellion　　HQ
　1804 Embarcadero Rd Ste 200
　Palo Alto CA 94303
P: 650-485-4300　F: 650-485-4308　　PRC:325
www.accellion.com
Email: info@accellion.com
Estab: 1999

Jonathan Yaron, Chairman & CEO
Kurt Michael, CRO
Cliff White, CTO
Joel York, CMO
Glen Segal, CFO & COO

Provider of web-based file transfer applications. The company also focuses on data management solutions.

Accenture　　BR
　415 Mission St Ste 3300
　San Francisco CA 94105
P: 415-537-5000　F: 415-537-5042　　PRC:45
www.accenture.com
Estab: 1989

David Rowland, Executive Chairman
Julie Sweet, CEO
K.C. McClure, CFO
Paul Daugherty, CTO & Group Chief Executive of Technology
Jo Deblaere, COO

Provider of management consulting and technology services. The company also offers application outsourcing and IT consulting services.

Access Business Technologies　　HQ
　850 Iron Point Rd
　Folsom CA 95630
P: 888-636-5426　　PRC:323
myabt.com
Email: info@myabt.com
Estab: 1998

Chris Schwartz-Edmisten, VP of Sales & Marketing

Provider of cloud-based software and hosting solutions for government agencies, banks, credit unions, accounting firms, and servicing companies.

Access Communications Inc　　HQ
　976 Rincon Cir
　San Jose CA 95131-1313
P: 800-342-4439　F: 408-970-0941　　PRC:62
www.access-comm.net
Email: info@access-comm.net
Estab: 1997

Allen Davis, Owner

Provider of telecommunications cabling and audio visual solutions. The company offers audio visual integration, installation, and design services.

Access Softek Inc　　HQ
　727 Allston Way Ste C
　Berkeley CA 94710-2229
P: 510-848-0606　F: 510-848-0608　　PRC:323
www.accesssoftek.com
Email: sales@accesssoftek.com
Estab: 1986

Chris Doner, CEO
Mark Barish, VP of Business Development
William Raymer, VP of Product
Evan Barale, Senior Product Manager
Weston Thornburg, Implementation Manager

Developer of mobile banking software solutions. The company focuses on software and product development, QA testing, user interface, and graphic design.

Access Video Productions　　HQ
　1442A Walnut St Ste 480
　Berkeley CA 94709
P: 510-528-6044　　PRC:60
www.accessvideoproductions.com
Estab: 1980

Dave Karp, Videographer

Provider of production, editing, and duplication services for small and large companies, and individuals.

Acco Semiconductor Inc　　HQ
　1290 Oakmead Pkwy Ste 201
　Sunnyvale CA 94085
P: 408-524-2600　F: 408-524-2626　　PRC:68
Estab: 2008

Ron Das, Founder & CEO
Minh Dao, Manager of Test Development Engineering

Provider of outsourced operations and engineering services. The company serves fabless semiconductor companies.

Accounting Micro Systems　　HQ
　1700 Montgomery St Ste 220
　San Francisco CA 94111
P: 415-362-5100　F: 415-276-5875　　PRC:322
www.accountingmicro.com
Email: sales@accountingmicro.com
Estab: 1988

John Kearns, President
Raynes White, Senior Consultant

Developer of accounting and business management software products. The company offers MAS500, MAS90 and MAS200, FAS Asset solutions, and SalesLogix.

Accsys Technology Inc　　HQ
　1177 A Quarry Ln
　Pleasanton CA 94566
P: 925-462-6949　F: 925-462-6993　　PRC:152
www.accsys.com
Email: info@linacs.com
Estab: 1985

Marjan Zand, Manufacturing Manager
Keenan Moore, Mechanical Engineer
Glenn James, Senior Electronics Engineer
Sean Ireland, Sales Engineer
Kazuko Omoto, Accounting Supervisor

Manufacturer of ion linear accelerator systems used in medical imaging devices, industrial applications and in research.

Accton Technology Corp　　DH
　1200 Crossman Ave Ste 130
　Sunnyvale CA 94089
P: 408-747-0994　F: 408-747-0982　　PRC:97
www.accton.com
Estab: 1988

Raul Lozano, Senior Engineering Director
Joanne Hsu, Corporate Marketing Manager

Distributor of network connectivity products and ethernet hubs. The company focuses on home security, cloud, data center switch, and other needs.

Accu-Image Inc HQ
2360 Owen St
Santa Clara CA 95054-3210
P: 408-736-9066   F: 408-736-9065   PRC:324
www.accu-image.com
Email: support@accu-image.com
Estab: 1988

Larry Bennett, CEO
Mai Chiem, Operations Manager
Greg Johnson, Senior Project Manager
Nikki Lacey, iOS Engineer
Anna Mae Cantoria, Data Entry Specialist

Supplier of transfer document image processing
equipment. The company is engaged in business
process consulting and document management.

Accu-Sembly Inc HQ
1835 Huntington Dr   [N]
Duarte CA 91010
P: 626-357-3447   F: 626-357-0778   PRC:211
www.accu-sembly.com
Email: info@accu-sembly.com
Emp: 51-200   Estab: 1983

John Doe, President & Founder
Jane Doe, CEO

Manufacturer of electronic assemblies for flight
control electronics, navigation systems, and mechanical control components.

Accu-Swiss Inc HQ
544 Armstrong Way Hi-Tech Pk
Oakdale CA 95361
P: 209-847-1016   F: 209-847-8362   PRC:80
www.accuswissinc.com
Email: info@accuswissinc.com
Estab: 1977

Millie Namowicz, Office Manager
Bill Bradford, Applications Engineer
Ali Gabajiwala, Manufacturing Engineer
Furqan Ahmed, Contact

Manufacturer of precision CNC and screw machined products. The company's services include
engineering, milling, and threading.

Accurate Always Inc HQ
127 Ocean Ave
Half Moon Bay CA 94019
P: 650-728-9428   F: 650-331-3511   PRC:68
www.accuratealways.com
Email: sales@accuratealways.com
Estab: 2003

Kate Haley, Founder & VP of Strategic Alliances
Yousef Shemisa, CTO
Alex Ford, Federal Account Manager
Elaine Frankovic, Service Delivery Manager
Sarah Layton, Software Developer

Provider of digital voice and video recording
services. The company also offers radio and
telephone call monitoring service.

Accuray Inc HQ
1310 Chesapeake Ter
Sunnyvale CA 94089
P: 888-522-3740   F: 408-716-4601   PRC:34
www.accuray.com
Estab: 1999
Sales: $300M to $1 Billion

Joshua H. Levine, President & CEO
Shigeyuki Hamamatsu, CFO
Holly Grey, SVP of Finance
Chris Janko, Manager of Imaging Systems
Vicky Ross, Facilities Manager

Provider of oncology treatment solutions. The
company develops, manufactures and sells precise and innovative tumor treatment solutions.

Accusilicon USA Inc HQ
2901 Tasman Dr Ste 107
Santa Clara CA 95054
P: 408-256-0858   PRC:200
www.accusilicon.com
Email: info@accusilicon.com
Estab: 2010

Yi Zhou, Founder
Jingjing Tong, Volunteer

Manufacturer of TCXO IC chips and designer and
developer of high frequency oscillators for the
industrial sector.

Accusplit Inc HQ
1262 Quarry Ln Ste B
Pleasanton CA 94566
P: 800-935-1996   PRC:14
accusplit.com
Email: sales@accusplit.com
Estab: 1972

W. Ron Sutton, Founder
Barbara Jacobs, Contact

Provider of digital stopwatches and pedometer
products. The company is also engaged in technical support services.

Ace Seal LLC HQ
23 Las Colinas Ln Ste 112
San Jose CA 95119
P: 408-513-1070   F: 408-513-1074   PRC:163
www.aceseal.com
Estab: 1982

Barbara Gallaty, President
Gina Gallaty, Sales & Marketing Manager
Cindy Graver, Sales & Marketing Manager

Manufacturer of molded rubber, seals, and o-rings.
The company serves the aerospace, semiconductor, oil and gas, medical, and biotechnology
sectors.

AcelRx Pharmaceuticals Inc HQ
351 Galveston Dr
Redwood City CA 94063
P: 650-216-3500   F: 650-216-6500   PRC:268
www.acelrx.com
Email: info@acelrx.com
Estab: 2005
Sales: $1M to $3M

Pamela Palmer, CMO & Founder
Vincent J. Angotti, CEO
Raffi Asadorian, CFO
David H. Chung, Chief Commercial Officer
Larry Hamel, Chief Development Officer

Manufacturer of pharmaceuticals. The company
provides therapies for treatment of acute and
breakthrough pain.

Acer America Corp HQ
1730 N First St Ste 400
San Jose CA 95112
P: 408-533-7700   F: 408-533-4555   PRC:93
acer.com
Email: ama.acercare@acer.com
Estab: 1976

Kevin Kuo, Director of Finance
Rich Black, Director of Marketing
Elaine Tam, Tax Director
Irene Chan, Director
Aj Wang, Senior Director

Supplier of desktops, notebooks, tablets, monitors
and projectors. The company also offers application and support services.

Acesis Inc HQ
2047 Old Middlefield Way
Mountain View CA 94043
P: 650-396-7540   PRC:319
www.acesis.com
Email: info@acesis.com
Estab: 2006

Kevin Chesney, Founder & CEO

Provider of web-based platform for overseeing
healthcare quality improvement and compliance
documentation, workflow, and analytics.

Achaogen Inc HQ
1 Tower Pl Ste 300
S San Francisco CA 94080
P: 650-800-3636   PRC:34
www.achaogen.com
Email: info@achaogen.com
Estab: 2002

Kenneth J. Hillan, CEO
Derek A. Bertocci, CFO
Ian R. Friedland, CMO
Dennis Hom, VP of Finance & Corporate Devel-
opment
Jim Kirchner, Senior Director of CMC

Developers of antibacterial. The company discovers and develops antibacterial for the treatment of
serious bacterial infections.

Achronix Semiconductor Corp HQ
2903 Bunker Hill Ln
Santa Clara CA 95054
P: 408-889-4100   PRC:212
www.achronix.com
Email: info@achronix.com
Estab: 2004

John Lofton Holt, Founder & Chairman
Robert Blake, President & CEO
Virantha N. Ekanayake, CTO
Howard S. Brodsky, VP of Business Operations
& CFO
Raymond Nijssen, VP & Chief Technologist

Manufacturer of semiconductor devices. The
company's products are used for networking,
edge networking, and test and measurement
applications.

ACI Alloys Inc   HQ
1458 Seareel Pl
San Jose CA 95131
P: 408-259-7337   F: 408-729-0277   PRC:80
www.acialloys.com
Estab: 1985

Paul Albert, Founder
Larry Albert, Owner

Manufacturer of purity alloys for thin film applications. The company offers evaporation and thin film materials.

ACIES Engineering   HQ
3371 Olcott St
Santa Clara CA 95054
P: 408-522-5255   F: 408-522-5260   PRC:304
www.acies.net
Email: info@acies.net
Estab: 1999

Wilson Lee, Founder & Owner
Tomislav Gajic, Owner
Srdjan Rebraca, CEO
Gary Pham, Project Director
Alexander Petrovic, Project Manager

Provider of engineering and design development solutions. The company caters to retail, restaurant, residential and commercial sectors.

Acionyx   HQ
PO Box 701013
San Jose CA 95170
P: 408-366-2908   F: 408-366-2909   PRC:322
www.acionyx.com
Email: opr@acionyx.com
Estab: 1997

Umesh Hiriyannaiah, Founder & CTO
Kiran Mundkur, Director of Product Marketing
Ramprasad Tandle, Senior Manager
Acionyx Recruiter, Recruiter

Provider of systems development and engineering consulting services. The company also deals with testing and quality assurance.

Acon Builders Construction Inc   HQ
2302 Tripaldi Way
Hayward CA 94545
P: 408-980-1388   F: 408-827-9559   PRC:304
www.aconbuilders.com
Email: info@aconbuilders.com
Estab: 1989

Danny Chan, President
Jennifer Chan, Project Manager

Provider of scheduling, planning, change management, status reporting, zoning, and code compliance services.

Acosta Sheet Metal Manufacturing Inc   HQ
930 Remillard Ct
San Jose CA 95122
P: 408-275-6370   F: 408-297-0130   PRC:157
www.acostamfg.com
Email: help@acostamfg.com
Estab: 1972

Michelle Acosta, Marketing Director & Project Manager

Manufacturer of HVAC and architectural products, and sheet metal building materials. The company provides gutter profile caps and conductor heads.

Acoustic Emission Consulting Inc   HQ
5000 San Juan Ave Ste D
Fair Oaks CA 95628
P: 916-965-4827   PRC:87
Estab: 1991

John Rodgers, President

Specializes in acoustic emission inspection services and testing, and acoustic emission instrumentation, sensors, and probes.

Acree Technologies Inc   HQ
1980 Olivera Rd Ste D
Concord CA 94520
P: 925-798-5770   F: 510-588-4046   PRC:47
www.acreetech.com
Email: info@acreetech.com
Estab: 2004

Tanya Kavka, Research Scientist

Provider of PVD thin film coating services for medical, defense, and other sectors. The company also specializes in R&D and sell coating systems.

Acronics   HQ
2102 Commerce Dr
San Jose CA 95131
P: 408-432-0888   F: 408-884-2418   PRC:104
acronics.com
Email: sales@acronics.com
Estab: 1994

Michael Nguyen, Engineering Project Manager
Kiem Vo, Product Manager
Tri Thanh Nguyen, PCB Manager
Long Nguyen, Principal Engineer

Provider of engineering services. The company is involved in systems and mechanical design services.

Acrylic Art   HQ
1290 45th St
Emeryville CA 94608
P: 510-654-0953   F: 510-654-8003   PRC:80
acrylicart.com
Email: info@acrylicart.com
Estab: 1986

Ronald Coleman, Owner
Jeff Schnur, President
Arthur Goosen, Director
Manish Bhalodiya, Managing Director
Marielena Markakou, Finance Manager

Provider of fabrication and machining services. The company focuses on painting, product finishing, anodizing, and vapor polishing.

Actagro LLC   HQ
PO Box 309
Biola CA 93606
P: 559-369-2222   F: 559-843-2845   PRC:42
www.actagro.com
Email: info@actagro.com
Estab: 1990

Jerel Kratt, Senior Regional Agronomist Manager
David Davis, National Sales Manager
Jason Rudstrom, Advisor of Field Product Development
Jeff Palmbach, Technical Sales Representative
Nichole Cagle, Purchasing Agent & Purchasing & Supply Chain Clerk

Manufacturer of agricultural products for crops such as alfalfa, almonds, blueberries, corn, tomatoes, onions, rice, strawberries, and wine grapes.

Actelis Networks Inc   HQ
47800 Westinghouse Dr
Fremont CA 94539
P: 510-545-1045   F: 510-657-8006   PRC:64
actelis.com
Email: info@actelis.com
Estab: 1999

Kamran Elahian, Founder
Eric Vallone, VP of Marketing
Joe Manuele, SVP of Worldwide Sales & Customer Support
Bruce Hammergren, EVP of Sales

Provider of carrier Ethernet over copper networking equipment. The company serves government, service operators, and utilities.

Actian Corp   HQ
2300 Geng Rd Ste 150
Palo Alto CA 94303
P: 650-587-5500   F: 650-587-5550   PRC:315
www.actian.com
Email: sales@actian.com
Estab: 2005

Robin Abrams, Chairman
Lewis Black, CEO
Marc Potter, CRO
Melissa Ribeiro, Chief Human Resource Officer
Jeff Veis, CMO & SVP of Marketing

Provider of on-premises applications and cloud data management solutions.

Actinix   HQ
6060 Graham hill Rd
Felton CA 95018
P: 831-440-9388   PRC:34
www.actinix.com
Email: sales@actinix.com
Estab: 1999

Jim Jacob, CEO

Developer of ultraviolet light generation, long-coherence-length pulsed fiber laser systems, high energy laser systems and optical tools/methods.

Actiontec Electronics Inc   HQ
3301 Olcott St
Santa Clara CA 95054
P: 408-752-7700   F: 408-541-9003   PRC:97
actiontec.com
Email: broadband-sales@actiontec.com
Estab: 1993

Brian Paul, CFO
Bo Xiong, CTO
Brian Henrichs, Chief Business Development Officer
Mike Ehlenberger, VP & General Manager
Gin-Pao Lu, VP Of Software Development

Provider of Internet modems, networking adapters, and routers. The company offers fiber routers, powerline network kits and wireless display products.

Active Video Networks   HQ
333 W San Carlos St Ste 900
San Jose CA 95110
P: 408-931-9200   F: 408-931-9100   PRC:324
www.activevideo.com
Email: info@activevideo.com

Jeff Miller, President & CEO
Brian Sereda, CFO
Murali Nemani, CMO
Ronald Brockmann, CTO
Ivan Dowling, Engagement Manager

Designer and developer of advertising solutions.
The company also provides mosaic, guide, and
navigation enablement services.

Acu Spec Inc   HQ
990 Richard Ave Ste 103
Santa Clara CA 95050-2828
P: 408-748-8600   F: 408-748-8605   PRC:80
www.acuspecinc.com

Amy Budde, CFO
Dominic Mathis, Operations Manager

Manufacturer of engineering products. The
company offers horizontal and vertical machining,
CNC turning, CAD software, and CMM inspection
services.

Acumen Pharmaceuticals Inc   HQ
4435 N First St Ste 360
Livermore CA 94551
P: 925-368-8508   F: 925-605-3813   PRC:34
www.acumenpharm.com
Email: info@acumenpharm.com
Estab: 1996

Franz Hefti, President & CEO
William Goure, COO

Specializes in the discovery and development of
therapeutics and diagnostics related to soluble A~
oligomers.

Acutherm   HQ
6379 Clark Ave Ste 280
Dublin CA 94568
P: 510-785-0510   PRC:78
www.acutherm.com
Email: info@acutherm.com
Estab: 1978

Kurt Herzog, VP & Managing Director
James Totten, VP
Renae Bell-Costello, Customer Relations Director
Mark Saguindel, Sheet Metal Worker
Mark Alan, Sheet Metal Worker

Manufacturer of components for heating and air
conditioning systems. The company offers therma-fuser variable air volume diffusers.

Acutrack Inc   HQ
350 Sonic Ave
Livermore CA 94551
P: 925-579-5000   F: 925-579-5001   PRC:116
acutrack.com
Email: sales@acutrack.com
Estab: 1992

Brian Schmille, COO
Scott Donovan, VP of Sales Operation
Erica Chipres, Project Manager
Chris Vogt, Business Development Manager &
Business Development Manager
Stephen Sideris, Digital Media Manager

Provider of CD and DVD duplication and production services. The company is also engaged in
kitting, assembly, and USB fulfillment.

Ad Art Inc   HQ
150 Executive Park Blvd Ste 2100
San Francisco CA 94134
P: 800-675-6353   PRC:316
www.adart.com
Email: info@adart.com
Estab: 2003

Terry Long, Owner
Dana Long, VP & General Counsel
Neal Tibbs, EVP of Operations
Abigail Wendel Hall, Project Manager
Andrew Garabedian, Account Executive

Provider of digital signage solutions. The company
also offers graphic designs, animation, commercial lighting, and maintenance services.

Adamas Pharmaceuticals Inc   HQ
1900 Powell St Ste 1000
Emeryville CA 94608
P: 510-450-3500   F: 510-428-0519   PRC:268
www.adamaspharma.com
Email: info@adamaspharma.com
Estab: 2002
Sales: $30M to $100M

David L. Mahoney, Chairman
Alfred G. Merriweather, CFO
Jennifer J. Rhodes, Chief Business Officer &
General Counsel
Vijay Shreedhar, CCO
Jeffrey H. Knapp, Chief Commercial Officer

Manufacturer of health care products. The
company offer products for patients with chronic
disorders of the central nervous system.

Adaptive Engineering   HQ
PO Box 2330
San Ramon CA 94583
P: 415-518-7131   F: 925-828-3140   PRC:212
www.adaptiveengineering.com

Matthew Hasel, Owner
Graham Smith, President & CEO
Jay Patel, Director
Terry Clarke, General Manager
Chirag Soni, Managing Director

Provider of engineering products such as
automatic mixture control, talking telemetry, and
telephone-based microclimate monitors.

Adaptive Insights   HQ
2300 Geng Rd Ste 100
Palo Alto CA 94303
P: 650-528-7500   PRC:322
www.adaptiveinsights.com
Email: sales@adaptiveinsights.com
Estab: 2003

Tom Bogan, CEO
Connie DeWitt, CMO
Fred Gewant, CRO
David Pefley, CFO
Bhaskar Himatsingka, Chief Product Officer

Provider of training, consulting, and related support services. The company serves the healthcare,
insurance, and manufacturing industries.

Adax Inc   HQ
2900 Lakeshore Ave
Oakland CA 94610
P: 510-548-7047   F: 510-548-5526   PRC:68
adax.com
Email: sales@adax.com
Estab: 1982

Javier Kim, Director of Integration
Christopher Benson, Software Engineer

Provider of packet processing, security, and
telecom network infrastructure components.
The company's products include gateways and
controllers.

ADCO Manufacturing   HQ
2170 Academy Ave
Sanger CA 93657
P: 559-875-5563   F: 559-875-7665   PRC:311
www.adcomfg.com
Email: info@adcomfg.com
Estab: 1958

Michael May, President & COO
Kate King, CEO
Paul Kessock, VP of Sales
Darwin Rhodes, Service Manager
Ann Davern, Western Regional Sales Manager

Provider of consumer packaged goods. The
company's solutions include cartoners, top load
systems, case packers, sleevers, and robotic
packaging.

Addepar Inc   HQ
303 Bryant St
Mountain View CA 94041
P: 855-464-6268   PRC:322
addepar.com
Email: inquiries@addepar.com
Estab: 2009

Eric Poirier, CEO
Nick Kochanski, Managing Director & CFO
Jeff Ramseyer, VP of Sales
Caroline O'Mahony, Senior Director of Product
Marketing

Provider of investment management solutions and
technology platform for data aggregation, powerful
analytics, and empowering clients to excel.

Addison Engineering Inc   HQ
150 Nortech Pkwy
San Jose CA 95134
P: 408-926-5000   F: 408-956-5111   PRC:86
www.addisonengineering.com

George McMaryion, Materials Manager

Supplier of silicon wafers and semiconductor
process components. The company's products
include ceramic packages and semiconductor
equipment.

Addonics Technologies Inc   HQ
1918 Junction Ave
San Jose CA 95131
P: 408-573-8580   F: 408-573-8588   PRC:95
www.addonics.com
Estab: 1998

Jacqueline Wong, Sales Administrator

Manufacturer of storage systems and products.
The company's products include drive cartridge
system, host controller, converter, and adapter.

Adelphi Technology Inc HQ
2003 E Bayshore Rd
Redwood City CA 94063
P: 650-474-2750   F: 650-474-2755   PRC:152
www.adelphitech.com
Email: info@adelphitech.com
Estab: 1984

Melvin Piestrup, President
Charles K. Gary, CEO
J. Theodore Cremer, Chief Scientist
Michael Fuller, VP of Marketing
David Williams, VP

Developer and manufacturer of X-ray optics. The
company serves the medical, industrial, and
scientific sectors.

Adem LLC HQ
1040 Di Giulio Ave Ste 160
Santa Clara CA 95050
P: 408-727-8955   F: 408-727-2055   PRC:80
www.ademllc.com
Estab: 1997

Val Sokolsky, Owner
Jacob Obolsky, Owner
Yusef Wright, Founder & CEO
Boris Kesil, Managing Partner
Yury Nikolenko, Electrical Engineer

Designer and manufacturer of special and
automated fixtures for assembly lines, and also
provides turnkey production solutions.

Adhesive Products Inc HQ
520 Cleveland Ave
Albany CA 94710
P: 510-526-7616   F: 510-524-0573   PRC:47
www.adhesiveproductsinc.com
Email: sales@adhesiveproductsinc.com
Estab: 1878

Trish Shattuck, Owner & Executive Director
Paul Shattuck, President
Tom Bell, VP
Tim Shattuck, National Accounts Manager
Cecilia Viera, Manager of Customer Service

Manufacturer of glues, adhesives, tapes, labels,
and coatings. The company is engaged in sales
and delivery services.

Aditazz HQ
2000 Sierra Point Pkwy
Brisbane CA 94005
P: 650-492-7000   F: 650-684-1145   PRC:304
www.aditazz.com
Email: info@aditazz.com
Estab: 2010

Deepak Aatresh, CEO
Aditazz Admin, Marketing Manager
Agnessa Todorova, Architect
Anatoly Kaplan, Software Delivery Management
Pujuan Huang, Translator

Designer, manufacturer, and assembler of building
components. The company is engaged in operational modeling.

ADLINK Technology Inc LH
5215 Hellyer Ave Ste 110
San Jose CA 95138
P: 408-360-0200   F: 408-360-0222   PRC:96
www.adlinktech.com
Email: info@adlinktech.com
Estab: 1995

Steve Marks, Director of Quality
Brandon Chen, Sales Director
Lawrence Shen, Hardware Manager

Designer and manufacturer of products for embedded computing, test and measurement, and
automation applications. The company serves
various sectors.

Admecell Inc HQ
883 Island Dr Ste 212
Alameda CA 94502
P: 510-522-4200   F: 510-522-4203   PRC:196
www.admecell.com
Email: info@admecell.com
Estab: 2008

Sandy Koshkin, President
Matt Pourfarzaneh, CEO
Barbara Levin, CFO
Dokhi Nargessi, Chief Scientific Officer & VP of
R&D

Manufacturer of ready to use products such as
cell based, TRANSIL, and ELISA based assays
for in-vitro therapeutic modeling and re-profiling.

Adobe Systems Inc HQ
345 Park Ave
San Jose CA 95110-2704
P: 408-536-6000   F: 408-537-6000   PRC:319
www.adobe.com
Estab: 1982
Sales: Over $3B

Charles M. Geschke, Co-Founder
John E. Warnock, Co-Founder & Director
Shantanu Narayen, President & CEO & Chairman
Ann Lewnes, EVP & CMO
David Welch, VP of Solution Leader Microsoft
Solutions & Senior Director Solution Leader AEM
Forms & Adobe Connec

Developer of software solutions for digital media
creation and editing, multimedia authoring, and
web development.

ADPAC Corp HQ
1996 Holmes St
Livermore CA 94550
P: 415-777-5400   F: 415-374-8505   PRC:319
www.adpac.com
Email: sales@adpac.com
Estab: 1963

Ed Severs, President & CEO

Provider of software to improve productivity and
value of current application software focusing on
business rule extraction, M&A, and documentation.

ADR Environmental Group Inc HQ
225 30th St Ste 202
Sacramento CA 95816
P: 916-921-0600   F: 916-648-6688   PRC:139
adreg.com
Estab: 1995

Kevin Gallagher, Account Manager
Ron Kern, Principal

Provider of risk management services and due
diligence services. The company's due diligence
service includes engineering and structural
services.

Adtec Technology Inc HQ
48625 Warm Springs Blvd
Fremont CA 94539
P: 510-226-5766   PRC:292
www.adtecusa.com
Email: info@adtecusa.com
Estab: 1996

Shuitsu Fujii, President
Taras Bodrouk, VP

Manufacturer of RF plasma generators, matching
units, and power measurement devices. The company serves semiconductor and solar processing
tool needs.

Adtech IT Solutions HQ
1571 E Whitmore Ave [N]
Ceres CA 95307
P: 209-541-1111   F: 209-541-1401   PRC:322
adtech-it.com/contact
Email: support@adtech-it.com
Estab: 1986

James Lawson, President & CEO

Provider of IT solutions and services.

Advance Carbon Products Inc HQ
2036 National Ave
Hayward CA 94545
P: 510-293-5930   F: 510-293-5939   PRC:80
advancecarbon.com
Estab: 1956

William J. Crader, Founder

Manufacturer of carbon. The company offers
equipment such as CNC lathes, grinders, lappers,
and diamond saws.

Advance Research Associates HQ
2350 Mission College Blvd Ste 825
Santa Clara CA 95054
P: 650-810-1190   F: 650-810-1195   PRC:191
www.advanceresearch.com
Estab: 1996

Peter Shabe, Founder & President
Michelle Stoddard, Senior Director of Clinical Data
Management
Lauren Intagliata, Senior Director of Clinical Data
Management
Tami Crabtree, Director of Biostatistics
Simon Read, Account Manager

Developer of human bio-therapeutic platform
technology solutions, drug discovery, and related
support services.

Advanced Cell Diagnostics Inc HQ
7707 Gateway Blvd
Newark CA 94560
P: 510-576-8800 F: 510-576-8801 PRC:34
www.acdbio.com
Email: info@acdbio.com
Estab: 2006

Xiao-Jun Ma, CSO
Tom O'Lenic, Chief Commercial Officer
Christopher Bunker, VP of Business Development
Jessie Qian Wang, Senior Scientist

Developer of biotechnological diagnostic tests.
The company specializes in the identification and
validation of RNA biomarkers for cancer diagnosis.

Advanced Component Labs HQ
990 Richard Ave Ste 118
Santa Clara CA 95050-2828
P: 408-327-0200 F: 408-327-0202 PRC:86
www.aclusa.com
Email: acl1@aclusa.com
Estab: 1994

Mike Oswald, President
Pat Smith, Operations Manager
Winston Labucay, Purchasing Manager
Nerissa de Ramos, Sales Manager
Don Bentley, Engineering Manager

Manufacturer of flip chips, thermal vias, build ups,
and related supplies. The company's services
include drilling, lamination, and engineering.

**Advanced Digital Solutions
International Inc** HQ
7026 Koll Center Pkwy
Pleasanton CA 94566
P: 510-490-6667 PRC:93
adsii.com
Email: quote@adsii.com
Estab: 1989

Shahid H., CEO

Provider of information technology solutions. The
company provides backup media tapes, barcode
labels, tape drives, and data center supplies.

Advanced Fabrication Technology HQ
31154 San Benito St
Hayward CA 94544
P: 510-489-6218 F: 510-489-6686 PRC:80
www.aftmetal.com
Email: custser@aftmetal.com
Estab: 1983

Todd Morey, VP
Linda McKibbin, Customer Service Manager

Provider of metal fabricating services for the
electronics, manufacturing, and semiconductor
industries.

Advanced Geoenvironmental Inc BR
122 Calistoga Rd Ste 325
Santa Rosa CA 95409
P: 800-511-9300 PRC:142
advancedgeo.biz
Email: info@advgeoenv.com

Robert Marty, President
Dennis Delaney, Director of Air Quality Division
Arthur Deicke, Project Manager
Rebecca Natal, Project Scientist
Rene Toth, Contact

Provider of environmental consulting services. The
company services include soil and groundwater
remediation and water and wastewater services.

Advanced Integrated Solutions Inc BR
5072 Hillsdale Cir Ste 100
El Dorado Hills CA 95762
P: 714-572-5600 F: 714-572-5655 PRC:301
www.aisconsulting.net
Email: info@aisconsulting.net
Estab: 1994

Hagop Belekdanian, President

Provider of enterprise systems management, call
center, and information technology infrastructure
library based service management solutions.

**Advanced Laser & Waterjet Cutting
Inc** HQ
48607 Warm Springs Blvd
Fremont CA 94539
P: 408-486-0700 F: 510-252-1123 PRC:157
www.adv-laser.com
Email: info@adv-laser.com
Estab: 1996

Lester Gragg, President

Provider of precision cutting services for all types of
materials. The company's services include electronic shielding, fabrivision, and overnight shipping.

Advanced Lease Systems Inc HQ
7658 Avianca Dr [N]
Redding CA 96002
P: 530 378 6868 F: 530-378-3433 PRC:319
www.advancedlease.com
Estab: 1984

Dennis Szody, Contact

Provider of design, development and other services in IT sector.

Advanced Linear Devices Inc HQ
415 Tasman Dr
Sunnyvale CA 94089
P: 408-747-1155 F: 408-747-1286 PRC:208
www.aldinc.com
Email: sales@aldinc.com
Estab: 1985

Robert Chao, President

Designer and manufacturer of precision CMOS analog integrated circuits. The company serves industrial
control, computer, automotive, and other sectors.

Advanced Micro Devices Inc HQ
2485 Augustine Dr
Santa Clara CA 95054
P: 408-749-4000 PRC:93
www.amd.com
Estab: 1969
Sales: Over $3B

Lisa T. Su, President & CEO
Mark D. Papermaster, CTO & SVP of Technology
& Engineering
Devinder Kumar, SVP & CFO & Treasurer
Forrest E. Norrod, SVP & General Manager of Da-
tacenter & Embedded Solutions Business Group

Provider of products such as desktops, notebooks,
servers, workstations, and embedded systems. The
company also offers a variety of software.

Advanced Microtechnology Inc HQ
480 Vista Way [N]
Milpitas CA 95035
P: 408-945-9191 F: 408-945-3548 PRC:65
www.advancedmicrotech.com
Estab: 1977

Prabath Mohottige, Deputy General Manager

Provider of burn-in systems, burn-in boards,
burn-in board testers, custom test equipment and
fixtures and system design services.

Advanced Microwave Inc HQ
333 Moffett Park Dr
Sunnyvale CA 94089
P: 408-739-4214 F: 408-739-4148 PRC:206
www.advmic.com
Email: sales@advmic.com
Estab: 1995

Susan Ghandehari, Owner
Rene Magana, QA & Sales Engineer

Manufacturer of military electronic components
and subsystems. The company offers amplifiers, mixers, threshold detectors, and converter
products.

Advanced Power Solutions HQ
5936 Las Positas Rd
Livermore CA 94551
P: 925-456-9890 F: 925-456-9050 PRC:290
www.advpower.com
Email: sales@advpower.com
Estab: 1982

Bob Vieira, President
Yvonne Marquez, Account Manager

Provider of power supplies. The company is
involved in manufacturing, sales, and related
support services.

Advanced Radiation Corp HQ
2210 Walsh Ave
Santa Clara CA 95050
P: 408-727-9200 F: 408-727-9255 PRC:243
www.arc-lamps.com
Email: rcpaquette@arc-lamps.com
Estab: 1971

John Paquette, VP

Manufacturer of mercury-xenon, and capillary
lamps. The company's services include design,
installation, and delivery.

Advanced Rotorcraft Technology Inc HQ
635 Vaqueros Ave
Sunnyvale CA 94085
P: 408-523-5100 F: 408-732-1206 PRC:3
www.flightlab.com
Email: info@flightlab.com
Estab: 1982

Ronald Du Val, President
Dooyong Lee, Senior Aerospace Engineer

Designer of fixed-wing and helicopter simulation
productivity tools. The company services include
avionics testing and simulator integration.

Advanced Semiconductor Engineering Inc DH
1255 E Arques Ave
Sunnyvale CA 94085
P: 408-636-9500 PRC:212
www.aseglobal.com
Email: ase_antitrust@aseglobal.com

Elvira Rebano, Accounts Receivable Representative

Manufacturer of integrated circuits and semiconductor packaging products. The company is involved in delivery, installation, and sales.

Advanced Software Design Inc HQ
1371 Oakland Blvd Ste 100
Walnut Creek CA 94596
P: 925-975-0694 F: 925-975-0696 PRC:326
asdglobal.com
Email: admin@asdglobal.com
Estab: 1982

Sonali Singh, President
Salig Chada, Division Head & VP of Public Sector
Sharron Scott, Capture Manager
Kathleen Lonero, Accounting Associate

Provider of knowledge based engineering software and industry focused business solutions. The company offers services to the public sector.

Advanced Systems Group LLC HQ
1226 Powell St [N]
Emeryville CA 94608
P: 510-654-8300 F: 510-654-8370 PRC:322
www.asgllc.com
Estab: 1997

Dave Van Hoy, President
Amy Zeno, CFO

Provider of design, consulting, value added reseller, large scale integration, software development, and much more services.

Advanced Vision Science Inc HQ
5743 Thornwood Dr [N]
Goleta CA 93117
P: 805-683-3851 F: 805-964-3065 PRC:189
www.advancedvisionscience.com
Emp: 51-200 Estab: 1998

Akira Kurokawa, Chairman
Shigeo Taniuchi, CEO & President
Takeshi Ito, Executive Corporate Officer & Head of Japan Business & Head of Japan Sales & Marketing Division
Yasuyuki Miyasaka, Outside Auditor
Hiroshi Isaka, Standing Corporate Auditor

Manufacturer of ophthalmic medical devices including intraocular lenses and lens material.

Advanced Witness Series Inc HQ
910 Bern Ct Ste 100
San Jose CA 95112
P: 408-453-5070 F: 408-453-5199 PRC:169
www.awitness.com
Email: sales@awitness.com

Craig Vossbrinck, President
Huy Huynh, Software Developer

Designer of electrical and mechanical components and tools. The company caters to various applications.

M-12

Advancing Ideas LLC HQ
570 Hayes St Ste 4
San Francisco CA 94102
P: 415-625-3338 PRC:325
advancingideas.net
Email: hello@advancingideas.net
Estab: 2006

Samuel K. Ackerman, Executive Producer

Provider of market research and analysis, application branding, and user interface development services.

Advansta Inc HQ
1505 Adams Dr Ste B1
Menlo Park CA 94025
P: 650-325-1980 F: 650-325-1904 PRC:53
advansta.com
Estab: 2005

Rosar Vitug, Operations Manager
Advansta Marketer, Marketing Manager
Tony Li, Product Specialist

Developer and manufacturer of bioresearch agents. The company focuses on protein staining, purification, and electrophoresis.

Advantage Electric Supply Inc HQ
31857 Hayman St
Hayward CA 94544
P: 510-324-9070 F: 510-324-9073 PRC:124
www.advantageelectricsupply.com
Email: sales@advantageelectricsupply.com

Sandra Sorce, VP
Krystle Garrity, Office Manager & Inside Sales

Distributor of electrical and electronic components for OEM's, industrial automation, solar, and renewable energy industries.

Advantage Metal Products HQ
7855 Southfront Rd
Livermore CA 94551
P: 925-667-2009 PRC:88
www.advantagemetal.com
Email: customerservice@advantagemetal.com
Estab: 1988

Phil Segundo, Owner
Lisa Levan, Accounting Manager

Provider of sheet metal and machining services. The company offers painting and silk screening, forming, welding, and machine shop services.

Advantage Pharmaceutics Inc HQ
4351 Pacific St
Rocklin CA 95677
P: 916-630-4960 F: 916-624-2088 PRC:266
www.custom-meds.com
Estab: 2004

Corey Whitney, Partner

Provider of pharmaceuticals specializing in compounding. The company provides compounded medicines in dosage forms for human and veterinary needs.

Advantec MFS Inc HQ
6723 Sierra Ct Ste A
Dublin CA 94568
P: 925-479-0625 F: 925-479-0630 PRC:304
advantecmfs.com
Email: sales@advantecmfs.com
Estab: 1995

Koichi SHIODE, CFO & Secretary
Alex Rockwell, Assistant Logistics Manager
Katsuaki Tanaka, Manager
Yukio Aida, Assistant Manager
Debby Leglu, Senior Manager of Sales & Tech

Producer of filtration media and related scientific products. The company focuses on laboratory instruments and filtration products.

Advantech Inc DH
380 Fairview Way
Milpitas CA 95035
P: 408-519-3898 F: 408-519-3899 PRC:91
www.advantech.com
Email: ags.usa@advantech.com
Estab: 1983

Chaney Ho, Founder
K.C. Liu, Chairman
Miller Chang, Division President
Allan Yang, CTO
James Yang, VP of Cloud-IoT Group

Provider of system integration, hardware, software, embedded systems, automation products, and logistics support.

Advantek Inc BR
20969 Cabot Blvd
Hayward CA 94545
P: 510-623-1877 F: 510-623-1886 PRC:209
advantek.com
Email: sales@veridicon.com
Estab: 1978

Alex Lim, Director of Engineering
Arlene Clarice Tan, Materials Science Engineer
Anita Eramela, Controller

Provider of packaging products. The company offers carrier and cover tapes, and tape and reel packaging products.

Advantest America Inc LH
3061 Zanker Rd
San Jose CA 95134
P: 408-456-3600 F: 408-456-5174 PRC:212
www.advantest.com
Email: support-americas@advantest.com
Estab: 1954

Keith Hardwick, Director & CFO
Kimiya Sakamoto, EVP of Sales Group
Sanjeev Mohan, EVP of Sales & Support
Soichi Tsukakoshi, EVP of Production Group
Mani Balaraman, VP of Marketing

Provider of measurement systems and solutions. The company offers electronic measuring instruments, and optical sensing and imaging analysis systems.

Advantiv Technologies Inc DH
46781 Fremont Blvd
Fremont CA 94538
P: 510-490-8260 PRC:212
www.advantivtech.com
Email: sales@advantivtech.com
Estab: 2002

Rich Furuya, COO

Manufacturer and supplier of semiconductor
components. The company offers wafers, solar,
materials, and vacuum components.

Advantrics LLC HQ
1477 Drew Ave Ste 103
Davis CA 95618
P: 530-297-3660   F: 530-297-3661 PRC:324
www.advantrics.com
Estab: 1998

Eric Overfield, Co-Founder & President
Greg Snow, Co-Founder & CEO
Jason Reckers, COO
Vic Bucher, CFO
Corrie Haffly, Senior Multimedia Developer

Designer and developer of Internet technologies. The company also specializes in multime-
dia-based products.

Advenira Enterprises Inc HQ
320 Soquel Way
Sunnyvale CA 94085
P: 408-732-3950   F: 408-732-3965 PRC:47
advenira.com
Email: info@advenira.com
Estab: 2010

Elmira Ryabova, CEO & CTO
Val Ryabov, VP of Operations

Provider of equipment and provision of services
for multi functional coating deposition using nano-
composite technology solution.

Advisor Software Inc HQ
2185 N California Blvd Ste 290
Walnut Creek CA 94596
P: 925-299-7782   F: 925-962-0658 PRC:323
www.advisorsoftware.com
Email: sales@advisorsoftware.com
Estab: 1995

Steve Bradley, EVP of Operations & Client Implementation
Michael Granger, EVP of Product Development

Provider of planning, proposal generation, portfolio construction, rebalancing, and investment
analytics services.

Adynxx Inc HQ
100 Pine St Ste 500
San Francisco CA 94111
P: 415-512-7740 PRC:249
www.adynxx.com
Email: info@adynxx.com
Estab: 2007

Julien Mamet, Founder & Chief Scientific Officer
Rick Orr, President & CEO
William Martin, EVP of Corporate Development &
Operations
Dina Gonzalez, SVP of Finance
Kimberley Hebert, Senior Director of Clinical
Operations

Developer of drugs to prevent acute post-surgical
pain and the transition to persistent or chronic pain.

Aechelon Technology Inc HQ
888 Brannan St Ste 210
San Francisco CA 94103
P: 415-255-0120   F: 415-255-0129 PRC:323
aechelon.com
Email: support@aechelon.com
Estab: 1998

Nacho Sanz-Pastor, President & CEO
Vishal Nayak, Software Technology Director
Lucas Fritz, Automation Engineer
Elliot Wilen, Senior System Administrator

Developer of real time computer graphics applications in the training, simulation, and entertainment
markers.

Aegea Medical Inc HQ
4055-A Campbell Ave
Menlo Park CA 94025
P: 650-701-1125   F: 650-701-1126 PRC:187
maratreatment.com
Email: info@aegeamedical.com
Estab: 2008

Alexis Dineen, Acting Vice President of Regulato-
ry Affairs
Maria Sainz, President & CEO
John Beck, Acting CFO
Don Gurskis, CTO
Hiram Chee, EVP of Research & Development

Developer of women healthcare solutions. The
company develops a system for the treatment of
excessive menstrual bleeding.

AEHR Test Systems HQ
400 Kato Ter
Fremont CA 94539
P: 510-623-9400   F: 510-623-9450 PRC:15
www.aehr.com
Estab: 1977
Sales: $10M to $30M

Gayn Erickson, President & CEO
Rhea Posedel, Chairman
Dave Hendrickson, CTO
Ken Spink, VP of Finance & CFO
Don Richmond, VP of Engineering

Designer and manufacturer of dynamic burn in
and test systems. The company is engaged in
troubleshooting and maintenance services.

AEI Consultants BR
1900 Point West Way Ste 142
Sacramento CA 95815
P: 916-333-4568 PRC:139
aeiconsultants.com
Email: info@aeiconsultants.com
Estab: 1992

Craig Hertz, Founder & Chairman
Holly Neber, CEO
Paul Hinkston, COO
Mark Nobler, Chief Business Development Officer
Adam Bennett, VP

Provider of environmental and engineering
services. The company's services also include
industrial hygiene and construction.

Aelan Cell Technologies Inc HQ
655 Third St
San Francisco CA 94107
P: 415-991-9915 PRC:34
aelanct.com
Email: contact@aelanct.com
Estab: 2015

Victoria Lunyak, Founder & CEO
James Tollervey, Director
Meenakshi Gaur, Director

Provider of research, discovery, development, and
commercialization of biomedical technologies for
the advancement of human health.

Aemetis Inc HQ
20400 Stevens Creek Blvd Ste 700
Cupertino CA 95014
P: 408-213-0940   F: 408-252-8044 PRC:34
www.aemetis.com
Emp: 53
Sales: $100M to $300M

Eric A. McAfee, CEO & Chairman
Sanjeev Gupta, President
Todd Waltz, CFO & EVP
Jeffrey Welch, VP of Strategic Projects
Andy Foster, EVP

Producer of biochemicals, renewable fuels, food,
and feed products. The company's products
include Z-Microbe, Glycerin, and edible oils.

AEMTEK Laboratories HQ
466 Kato Terrace
Fremont CA 94539
P: 510-979-1979   F: 510-668-1980 PRC:41
www.aemtek.com
Email: lab@aemtek.com
Estab: 2002

Florence Qiuxin Wu, President
Feifei Han, Director of Food Testing

Provider of testing, research, training and consulting services and sampling products for the food,
environmental and pharmaceutical industries.

Aero Chip Inc HQ
13563 Freeway Dr [N]
Santa Fe Springs CA 90670
P: 562-404-6300   F: 562-404-6322 PRC:80
www.aerochip.com
Emp: 11-50 Estab: 1988

Liviu Pribac, Accountant

Designer and developer of complex components
for the aerospace industry through machining,
forming and assembling.

Aero Precision HQ
201 Lindbergh Ave
Livermore CA 94551
P: 925-455-9900 PRC:219
www.aeroprecision.com
Email: info@aeroprecision.com
Estab: 1993

Evren Ergin, Founder
Frank Cowle, President
Scott Dover, CEO
Denzil Thies, CFO
Tiffany Walden, VP of Sales

Supplier of military aircraft parts for the aerospace
industry. The company's services include repair,
replacement, and maintenance.

Aero Turbine Inc   HQ
  6800 S Lindbergh St
  Stockton CA 95206
  P: 209-983-1112   PRC:150
  Estab: 1978

Douglas R. Clayton, President
James Simpkins, CEO
Ken Thrasher, COO
Alex Thagard, SVP
Steve Hutchings, General Manager

Provider of overhaul, repair, and testing services
for turbine engines and accessories. The company
also sells engine components and accessories.

Aero-Environmental Consulting   HQ
  1426 Via Isola
  Monterey CA 93940
  P: 831-394-1199   F: 831-394-1627   PRC:139
  aero-enviro.com
  Estab: 2002

Jorge Vizcaino, Certified Industrial Hygienist

Provider of environmental consulting solutions.
The company's services include air quality
assessment, regulatory compliance, and health
planning.

Aerojet Rocketdyne   RH
  PO Box 13222
  Sacramento CA 95813-6000
  P: 916-355-4000   F: 916-351-8667   PRC:7
  www.rocket.com
  Email: comments@rocket.com
  Estab: 1942
  Sales: $1B to $3B

Eileen P. Drake, CEO & President
Mark Tucker, COO
Natalie Schilling, Chief Human Resource Officer
Paul Lundstrom, VP of Finance & CFO
Arjun L. Kampani, VP & General Counsel &
Secretary

Provider of propulsion and energetic to its space,
missile defense, strategic, tactical missile. and
armaments customers.

Aerojet Rocketdyne   HQ
  PO Box 13222
  Sacramento CA 95813-6000
  P: 916-355-4000   F: 916-351-8667   PRC:5
  www.rocket.com
  Email: comments@rocket.com
  Estab: 1945

Warren M. Boley, President
Eileen P. Drake, CEO
Mark Tucker, COO
Natalie Schilling, Chief Human Resource Officer
Paul Lundstrom, VP of Finance & CFO

Manufacturer of missile and space propulsion
components. The company also offers defense
weapons and armaments.

Aerometals   HQ
  3920 Sandstone Dr
  El Dorado Hills CA 95762
  P: 916-939-6888   F: 916-939-6555   PRC:5
  www.aerometals.aero
  Email: pmasales@aerometals.aero
  Estab: 1998

Rex Kamphefner, Owner
Lorie Symon, President
David Postema, COO
George Azzam, Director
Jerry Moore, General Manager

Manufacturer of heater control valve assembly,
gear shafts, and fuel filler caps. The company
offers water jet cutting, milling, and lathe services.

AerospaceComputing Inc   HQ
  465 Fairchild Dr Ste 224
  Mountain View CA 94043
  P: 650-988-0388   F: 650-988-0389   PRC:36
  www.aerospacecomputing.com
  Email: acihq@aerospacecomputing.com
  Estab: 1989

Nathanial Smith, Research Engineer

Provider of computer technology application services to aerospace sciences. The company also
focuses on business development services.

Aethlabs   HQ
  1640 Valencia St Ste 1C
  San Francisco CA 94110
  P: 415-529-2355   PRC:138
  aethlabs.com
  Estab: 2011

Jeff Blair, President & CEO & Co-Founder
Steven Blair, COO & Co-Founder

Provider of black carbon monitoring equipment.
The company also deals in manufacturing and
assembly services.

AFC Finishing Systems   HQ
  250 Airport Pkwy
  Oroville CA 95965
  P: 800-331-7744   F: 530-533-0179   PRC:159
  www.afc-ca.com
  Email: sales@afc-ca.com
  Estab: 1967

Carl Lee Hagan, President
Nicky Trevino, VP & CFO
Jeremy Hagan, Manager of Sales
Scott Nail, Production Manager
Joshua Freeman, Sales Engineer

Developer of air filter and spray booth products.
The company offers auto and truck spray booths,
air make-up units, and powder coating products.

AG Microsystems Inc   HQ
  3194 De La Cruz Blvd Ste 14
  Santa Clara CA 95054
  P: 408-834-4888   PRC:204
  www.agmicrosystems.com
  Email: info@agmicrosystems.com
  Estab: 2005

Asif A. Godil, CEO & Chairman

Provider of testing and development in the areas
of micro electro mechanical systems and micro
optics.

Agari Data Inc   HQ
  950 Tower Ln Ste 2000
  Foster City CA 94404
  P: 650-627-7667   F: 650-242-4999   PRC:325
  www.agari.com
  Email: info@agari.com
  Estab: 2009

Ravi Khatod, CEO
Raymond Lim, CFO
John Wilson, CTO
Armen Najarian, CMO & Chief Identity Officer
John Giacomini, CRO

Provider of email security and social engineering
solutions. The company serves the healthcare,
financial services, and government industries.

Agile Global Solutions Inc   HQ
  193 Blue Ravine Rd Ste 160
  Folsom CA 95630
  P: 916-655-7745   F: 916-848-3659   PRC:323
  agileglobalsolutions.com
  Email: info@agileglobal.com
  Estab: 2003

Nathan Stewart, Business Development Manager
Jaswinder Singh, Talent Acquisition Specialist
Evan Privett, Geologist

Provider of business and IT solutions such as
custom and enterprise application management
and mobile business solutions.

Agilis Software LLC   HQ
  548 Market St Ste 95777
  San Francisco CA 94104
  P: 415-458-2614   PRC:326
  agilis-sw.com
  Estab: 2002

Vinay Sabharwal, CEO & CTO
Matt Teter, VP of Customer Experience

Developer of software licensing and software
license management solution for enterprise
software, embedded systems, and cloud software
industries.

Agiloft Inc   HQ
  460 Seaport Ct Ste 200
  Redwood City CA 94063
  P: 650-587-8615   F: 650-745-1209   PRC:319
  www.agiloft.com
  Email: sales@agiloft.com
  Estab: 1991

Colin Earl, CEO
Patricia Pritts, VP of Sales

Provider of contract, work flow, change, and asset
management services. The company offers services to armed forces and universities.

Agnitus   HQ
  120 Hawthorne Ave
  Palo Alto CA 94301
  P: 877-565-1460   PRC:322
  www.agnitus.com
  Estab: 2011

Azhar Khan, CEO & Co-Founder
Haris Khan, Chief Product Officer & Co-Founder
Lance Vikaros, Executive Director of Education
Jillian OrRico, Director of Educational Partner-
ships
Heather Browning, STEM Game Designer

Developer of touch enabled learning applications
for iPad. The company specializes in educational
games such as little bo peep and ABC hide n seek.

Agra Tech Inc HQ
2131 Piedmont Way
Pittsburg CA 94565
P: 925-432-3399   F: 925-432-3521   PRC:137
agratech.com
Email: agratech@agratech.com
Estab: 1973

John Pound, CEO
Anita Pound, COO
Adam Pound, Sales Manager
Erik Klug, Order Coordinator
James Roberts, Contact

Manufacturer of greenhouses and accessories for commercial, horticultural, and agricultural growers. The company offers heating and cooling equipment.

Agri-Analysis LLC BR
950 W Chiles Rd
Davis CA 95618
P: 800-506-9852   F: 530-757-4655   PRC:43
agri-analysis.com
Email: info@agri-analysis.com
Estab: 1981

Alan Wei, Owner & President
Andrew Zinkl, Senior Research Specialist
Robert Metz, Lab Technician

Provider of agricultural diagnostic laboratory services. The company specializes in grapevine virus testing services.

Agricultural Manufacturing Company Inc HQ
4106 S Cedar Ave
Fresno CA 93725
P: 559-485-1662   F: 559-485-6408   PRC:159
agmanco.com

John Cabrera, President
Sabino Mendez, Contact

Manufacturer of sprayers. The company specializes in engineering agricultural spraying equipment and other products such as pumps and tanks.

AGS Inc HQ
5 Freelon St
San Francisco CA 94107
P: 415-777-2166   F: 415-777-2167   PRC:41
www.agsinc.com
Email: info@agsinc.com
Estab: 1983

David Mahaffy, Founder
Bahram Khamenehpour, President
Tina Wong, EVP
Nemanja Milosavljevic, Electrical Package Manager
Meenakshi Satyavolu, Project Controls Manager

Provider of civil, structural, and geotechnical engineering services. The company serves the water and transportation infrastructure markers.

AGS Plasma Systems Inc HQ
3064 Kenneth St
Santa Clara CA 95054
P: 408-855-8686   PRC:165
www.agsplasma.com
Email: info@agsplasma.com
Estab: 1991

Allen Guastavino, President & CEO

Manufacturer and distributor of vacuum plasma systems. The company serves microelectronics and optoelectronics industries.

AGTEK Development Company Inc HQ
396 Earhart Way
Livermore CA 94551
P: 925-606-8197   PRC:323
www.agtek.com
Email: sales@agtek.com

Michael Clapp, CTO
Victoria Swingle, CFO
Bill Cope, VP of Corporate Sales
Theresa Clarke, Order Processing Renewals Manager

Developer of high tech surveying, analysis, and control solutions for residential, commercial, transportation, water, energy, and government.

Aheadtek HQ
6410 Via Del Oro
San Jose CA 95119
P: 408-226-9800   F: 408-226-9195   PRC:60
aheadtek.com

Ed Soldani, CFO
Patrick Johnston, VP
Hristo Mishkov, Director of Manufacturing
Yolanda Verdugo, Director of Human Resources
Hui Xiao, Engineering Manager

Supplier of magnetic head solutions. The company specializes in television broadcast, video production, and computer and data storage.

Ahram Biosystems Inc HQ
1549 Ilikai Ave
San Jose CA 95118-1943
P: 408-645-7300   PRC:34
www.ahrambio.com
Email: info@ahrambio-us.com
Estab: 2001

William Lee, Manager

Developer of new life science tools. The company provides battery-powered, palm-size portable PCR machine.

Aimer Corp HQ
3250 McKinley Dr
Santa Clara CA 95051
P: 408-260-8588   F: 408-260-9539   PRC:80
aimercorp.com
Estab: 1994

John Tchiang, CEO

Provider of thermal management products. The company also offers connectors, PCB boards, cables, and mechanical parts.

Aimmune Therapeutics RH
8000 Marina Blvd Ste 200
Brisbane CA 94005-1884
P: 650-614-5220   F: 650-616-0075   PRC:34
www.aimmune.com
Email: info@aimmune.com
Estab: 2011

Stephen Dilly, CEO
Jeffrey Knapp, COO
Warren DeSouza, CFO
Jerome Pinkett, Senior Director of Operations
Sukhi K. Thethy, Director of Accounting & External Reporting

Developer of desensitization treatments. The company is engaged in clinical trials and it serves the healthcare sector.

Air Exchange Inc HQ
495 Edison Ct Ste A
Fairfield CA 94534
P: 800-300-2945   F: 707-864-2705   PRC:125
www.airexchange.com
Email: info@airexchange.com
Estab: 1982

Dick Bertani, President
Carl Sciortino, Supply Chain Manager
Steve Harris, Operations Manager
Leif Neuman, Sales Engineer
James Fox, Sales Engineer

Supplier of air purification and clean air machines, and fans. The company serves commercial facilities and public institutions.

Air Hollywood HQ
13240 Weidner St   [N]
Pacoima CA 91331
P: 818-890-0444   F: 818-890-7041   PRC:316
www.airhollywood.com
Emp: 11-50   Estab: 1998

Norm Jones, EVP

Provider of aviation-themed production solutions to the motion picture, television, and commercial production industry.

Air Monitor Corp HQ
1050 Hopper Ave
Santa Rosa CA 95403
P: 707-544-2706   F: 707-526-9970   PRC:233
www.airmonitor.com
Estab: 1967

Dean DeBaun, President
Andrew Chew, Project Manager of Engineering
Paresh Dave, Manager of Applications Engineering
Dawson Rambo, IT Manager
Andrew Ward, Operations Manager

Manufacturer of airflow and space pressurization control systems and offers airflow traverse probes, pressure sensors, and electronic transmitters.

Air Worldwide Corp   BR
388 Market St Ste 750
San Francisco CA 94111
P: 415-912-3111   F: 415-912-3112   PRC:322
www.air-worldwide.com
Email: info@air-worldwide.com

Bill Churney, President
Jayanta Guin, EVP & Chief Research Officer of Research & Modeling
Boris Davidson, SVP & Chief Software Architect of Software Research & Development
David Lalonde, SVP of Consulting & Client Services
Milan Simic, EVP & Managing Director of Global Business Development

Provider of software development and consulting services. The company focuses on risk modeling software and risk assessment and management consulting.

Air-O-Fan Products   HQ
507 E Dinuba Ave
Reedley CA 93654
P: 559-638-6546   F: 559-638-9262   PRC:159
airofan.com
Email: info@airofan.com
Estab: 1987

Brent Davis, Sales & Marketing Manager
Paul Mariscal, Welder

Developer of spray application machinery solutions. The company manufactures engine and PTO drives for orchard, vineyard, and herbicide sprayers.

Aircraft Xray Laboratories Inc   HQ
5216 Pacific Blvd   [N]
Huntington Park CA 90255
P: 323-587-4141   F: 323-588-6410   PRC:306
www.aircraftxray.com
Estab: 1938

Gary Newton, President & CEO
James Newton, VP of Corporate Development
Jose Delgadillo, Manager
Juan Perez, Quality Control Manager
Sandi Spelic, Controller & Office Manager

Provider of NDT and surface treatment services.

Airdex International Inc   BR
4675 MacArthur Court Ste 1470
Newport Beach CA 92660
P: 702-575-0625   PRC:2
www.airdex.com
Estab: 2002

Eugene Lin, Operation Manager

Manufacturer of air freight products. The company offers lightweight, air pallets for perishables and pharmaceuticals.

Aire Sheet Metal   HQ
1973 E Bayshore Rd
Redwood City CA 94063
P: 650-364-8081   PRC:88
www.airesm.com
Email: pm@airesm.com
Estab: 1971

Eugene Bramlett, Founder & CEO
Bob Bramlett, President
Marlo Bramlett, VP
Tim McEntee, Project Manager & Architectural Estimator
Jason Canen, Estimator & Project Manager

Provider of mechanical and architectural sheet metal services. The company is involved in the design and construction of commercial projects.

Airgard Inc   HQ
2190 Paragon Dr
San Jose CA 95131
P: 408-573-0701   PRC:133
www.airgard.net
Email: info@airgard.net
Estab: 1988

Dan White, Chairman & CEO
Mark Johnsgard, CTO
Martin Johnson, CFO & Secretary
Kevin McGinnis, VP of sales & Marketing
Joe Ploshay, VP of Operations

Manufacturer of gas scrubbers servicing epitaxial, metal etch, poly etch, and CVD process abatement applications.

Airnex Communications Inc   HQ
PO Box 11357
Pleasanton CA 94588-1357
P: 800-708-4884   PRC:64
www.airnex.com
Email: info@airnex.com
Estab: 1995

Arnold Marasigan, Manager
Dennis Duran, Head of Network Operations
Zara Arev, Bilingual Customer Service Representative

Provider of digital wireless telecommunications and Internet access services. The company also focuses on web hosting.

Airpoint Precision Inc   HQ
6221 D Enterprise Dr
Diamond Springs CA 95619
P: 530-622-0510   PRC:80
www.airpointinc.com
Email: accounting@airpointinc.com
Estab: 2001

Clem Fanning, Contact

Provider of precision machining services. The company serves the industrial needs of the community in a cost efficient and timely manner.

Airtronics Metal Products Inc   HQ
140 San Pedro Ave
Morgan Hill CA 95037
P: 408-977-7800   F: 408-977-7810   PRC:88
www.airtronics.com
Email: info@airtronics.com
Estab: 1960

Jim Ellis, VP of Engineering & Owner
Jeffrey Burke, President & CEO
Mike Nevin, Director of Sales & Marketing
Aaron Lahann, Customer Engineering Manager
Fermin Rodriguez, Process Engineer

Manufacturer of sheet metal fabrication and machining. The company provides custom sheets for the electronics, telecommunications and other markers.

Airxpanders Inc   HQ
3047 Orchard Pkwy
San Jose CA 95134
P: 650-390-9000   PRC:11
www.airxpanders.com
Estab: 2005

Belinda Pinedo, Director of Regulatory Affairs
Thavy C. Dy, Production Supervisor
Nelida Vazquez, Quality Assurance Technician

Provider of controlled tissue expander and small handheld wireless controller of breast cancer reconstructive surgery.

Aitech International Corp   HQ
1288 Kifer Rd Ste 203
Sunnyvale CA 94086
P: 408-991-9699   F: 408-991-9691   PRC:208
aitech.com
Email: aitech-sales@aitech.com
Estab: 1987

Michael J. Chen, Founder & Chairman & CEO

Provider of video conversion technology solutions. The company provides scan converters, wireless products, HDTV tuners, HDMI switches, and cables.

Aja Video Systems Inc   HQ
180 Litton Dr
Grass Valley CA 95945
P: 530-274-2048   F: 530-274-9442   PRC:60
www.aja.com
Email: sales@aja.com
Estab: 1993

Nick Rashby, President
Bill Bowen, CTO
Stephanie Camp, Creative Director
Eric Gysen, Director of Engineering
Gerard Tassone, Product Manager-Converters

Provider of video systems and routers. The company also offers broadcast and mini converters and recording equipment.

AKM Semiconductor Inc   HQ
226 Airport Pkwy Ste 470
San Jose CA 95110
P: 408-436-8580   PRC:208
www.akm.com
Estab: 1995

Paul Werner, VP of Business Development
Masao Awatsu, RF Application Engineering
Manager
Jun Tokunaga, Reference Design Manager
Alice Yen, Senior Accountant

Designer and manufacturer of mixed signal
integrated circuits. The company serves consumer
electronics, industrial, and automotive sectors.

AKMI Corp   HQ
19240 Cabot Blvd
Hayward CA 94545
P: 510-670-9550   F: 510-670-9540   PRC:150
www.akmicorp.com
Email: inquiry@akmicorp.com
Estab: 1981

Mitra Ashraf, President
Charles Harvey, Purchasing Manager
Pat Johnson, Sales Manager
Kenneth Kling, Sales Representative

Distributor of aftermarket diesel engine parts. The
company provides accessory drive units, cam-
shafts, flywheels, and exhaust manifolds.

Akon Inc   HQ
2135 Ringwood Ave
San Jose CA 95131
P: 408-432-8039   F: 408-432-1089   PRC:209
www.akoninc.com
Email: sales@akoninc.com
Estab: 1980

Steven Pekarthy, CFO & Consultant
Avinash Ratra, VP
Ajay Dalal, Project Manager
Richard Sanders, Senior Program Manager
Lynette Ovalle, Accounting Assistant

Supplier of microwave products. The company focuses on airborne, ground, shipboard, and space
applications.

Akra Plastic Products Inc   HQ
1504 E Cedar St   [N]
Ontario CA 91761
P: 909-930-1999   F: 909-931-1948   PRC:189
www.akraplastics.com
Emp: 1-10   Estab: 1972

Alex Semeczko, CEO
Bentley Callaway, COO
Brian Fuerbach, R&D Manager
Lupita Ruiz, Office Manager

Manufacturer of plastics products.

Akribis Systems Inc   RH
780 Montague Expy Ste 508
San Jose CA 95131
P: 408-913-1300   PRC:150
www.akribis-sys.com
Estab: 2004

Joseph Blake, Application Engineer
Wenhan Tang, Application Engineer

Designer and manufacturer of motors, stages, and
precision systems. The company's products are
used in inspection and testing applications.

Aktana Inc   HQ
207 Powell St 8th Fl
San Francisco CA 94102
P: 888-707-3125   PRC:323
www.aktana.com
Estab: 2008

Derek Choy, Founder & COO
David Ehrlich, President & CEO
Clay Hausmann, CMO
Colm Callan, CFO
Kate Terrell, CPO

Provider of decision support engine that pores
through multiple data services and delivers insights and suggestions right in the rep's workflow.

Al & L Crop Solutions   HQ
7769 N Meridian Rd
Vacaville CA 95688
P: 530-387-3270   F: 707-693-3050   PRC:41
www.allcropsolutions.com
Email: info@allcropsolutions.com

Anna-Liisa Fabritius, Plant Pathologist

Provider of solutions for crops. The company specializes in disease testing services for grapevine
diseases and soil pathogens.

Alacrinet Consulting Services Inc   HQ
530 Lytton Ave 2nd Fl
Palo Alto CA 94301
P: 650-646-2670   PRC:324
www.alacrinet.com
Email: info@alacrinet.com
Estab: 2002

Brian Bouchard, President & CEO
Daniel Duhaime, VP of Sales
Marykay Michaels, Director of Professional
Services

Developer of software solutions. The company offers enterprise search, web content management,
business intelligence, and analytics services.

Alchemic Solutions Group Inc   HQ
1720 S Amphlett Blvd Ste 168
San Mateo CA 94030-2710
P: 510-919-8105   PRC:323
www.alchemicsolutions.com
Email: info@alchemicsolutions.com

Jane Chen, Partner
Mark Trinh, Partner
Peter Trinh, Partner
Ray Taylor, Partner

Provider of technology marketing solutions for wireless sectors. The company focuses on product management, software development, and consultation.

Alcon Entertainment LLC   HQ
10390 Santa Monica Blvd Ste 250 [N]
Los Angeles CA 90025
P: 310-789-3040   F: 310-789-3060   PRC:37
www.alconent.com
Estab: 1997

Andrew Kosove, CEO & Founder
Scott Parish, COO & CFO
Carl Rogers, SVP of Development
Ryan Dornbush, SVP of Operations & Human
Resources

Provider of finance, produce, market, and distributor of entertainment that delights both its creators
and its audience.

Aldelo LP   HQ
6800 Koll Center Pkwy Ste 310
Pleasanton CA 94566
P: 925-621-2410   PRC:323
www.aldelo.com
Email: sales@aldelo.com

Harry Tu, President
Jeff Moore, VP of Operations
Jerry Wilson, VP of Merchant Services
Leonard Tacla, Director of Support Services
Brenden Carney, Information Technology Support
Manager

Provider of software solutions. The company offers
solutions for the hospitality, retail, and payment
processing industries.

Aldetec Inc   HQ
3560 Business Dr Ste 100
Sacramento CA 95820
P: 916-453-3382   F: 916-453-3384   PRC:60
www.aldetec.com
Email: aldetec@aldetec.com
Estab: 1999

Teresa Robertson, Office Manager
Dan Almond, Engineering Technician

Manufacturer of microwave amplifier products.
The company provides low noise amplifiers, down
converters, and octave band amplifiers.

Aldo Ventures Inc   HQ
7370 Viewpoint Rd
Aptos CA 95003
P: 831-662-2536   PRC:324
www.aldo.com
Email: info@aldo.com

Avron Barr, Principal
Shirley Tessler, Principal

Provider of studies such as software technology,
markers, companies, platforms, products, and
investment strategies of the software industry.

Alector LLC   HQ
131 Oyster Point Blvd Ste 600
S San Francisco CA 94080
P: 415-231-5660   PRC:268
www.alector.com
Email: info@alector.com
Estab: 2013
Sales: $10M to $30M

Arnon Rosenthal, Founder & CEO
Tillman Gerngross, Chairman
Robert Paul, CMO
Robert King, Chief Development Officer
Sabah Oney, Chief Business Officer

Developer of therapeutics. The company specializes in cutting edge antibody technologies for
treating alzheimer's disease.

Alert Technologies Corp   HQ
4847 Hopyard Rd Ste 160
Pleasanton CA 94588
P: 925-461-5934   PRC:323
www.alerttech.com
Estab: 1996

Jim Paulson, CEO

Developer of emergency management software.
The company offers professional services to
assist customers in solving their information management challenges.

Alertenterprise Inc   HQ
   4350 Starboard Dr
   Fremont CA 94538
P: 510-440-0840   F: 510-440-0841   PRC:327
www.alertenterprise.com
Email: info@alertenterprise.com
Estab: 2007

Jasvir Gill, CEO
Kaval Kaur, CFO
Ruby Deol, COO
Azizur Rahman, VP of Global Business Development & Sales
Imran Rana, SVP of Professional Services

Developer of information and operational technology solutions such as identity intelligence, and enterprise access, and incident management.

Alger Precision Machining LLC   HQ
   724 S Bon View Ave   [N]
   Ontario CA 91761
P: 909-983-3351   PRC:80
www.alger1.com
Estab: 2007

Jim Hemingway, President
Duane Femrite, CEO
Danny Hankla, VP of Operations
Debbie Miller, Executive Director
Carl Boyd, Executive Director

Manufacturer of screw machine products.

Algo-Logic Systems   HQ
   172 Component Dr
   San Jose CA 95131-1132
P: 408-707-3740   F: 408-618-8953   PRC:322
algo-logic.com
Email: solutions@algo-logic.com
Estab: 2009

John W. Lockwood, CEO
John Hagerman, VP of Marketing & Business Development
Mark Crockett, Director of Operations
Kevin O'Connor, Sales Director
Marina Slutsker, Senior Product Manager

Specializes in building networking solutions. The company also offers technological and data handling services to firms.

AlgoMedica Inc   HQ
   440 N Wolfe Rd
   Sunnyvale CA 94085
P: 516-448-3124   PRC:194
www.algomedica.com
Email: info@algomedica.com

Ramesh Neelmegh, President
Jagdish Vij, CEO

Developer of medical imaging software based on artificial neural networks for abdomen/pelvis, head, and liver and pediatrics CT scans.

Alien Technology Corp   HQ
   845 Embedded Way
   San Jose CA 95138-1030
P: 408-782-3900   F: 408-782-3908   PRC:61
www.alientechnology.com
Estab: 1994

Zhongrui Xia, Chairman
Leiping Lai, President
Glenn R. Haegele, CFO
David A. Aaron, CLO & VP of Business Development
Terrel Pruett, VP of Marketing & Global Reader Sales

Provider of UHF radio frequency identification products and services to customers in retail, consumer goods, logistics, and pharmaceutical industries.

Align Technology Inc   HQ
   2820 Orchard Pkwy
   San Jose CA 95134
P: 408-470-1000   F: 408-470-1010   PRC:189
www.aligntech.com
Email: corporateinfo@aligntech.com
Estab: 1997
Sales: $1B to $3B

Joseph M. Hogan, President & CEO & Director
John F. Morici, CFO & SVP of Global Finance
Raphael S. Pascaud, Chief Marketing Portfolio & Business Development Officer & SVP of iTero Scanner & Services
Stuart Hockridge, SVP of Global Human Resources
Wendy Chen, Director of Ortho Channel Marketing

Provider of medical devices such as invisalign clear aligners, itero intraoral scanners and ortho CAD digital services for orthodontic industry.

Alisto Engineering Group Inc   HQ
   2737 N Main St Ste 200
   Walnut Creek CA 94597
P: 925-279-5000   F: 925-279-5001   PRC:142
www.alisto.com
Email: subcontracts@alisto.com
Estab: 1992

Nancy Valero, CFO
Rinaldo Veseliza, Senior Program Manager & Director of Sustainability & Marketing
Clem Holst, Program Manager
Mark Young, Senior Project Engineer & Manager
Stanley Hill, Senior Project Manager & Engineer

Provider of engineering and environmental consulting services. The company serves the private industry and government agencies.

All Fab Precision Sheetmetal Inc   HQ
   1015 Timothy Dr
   San Jose CA 95133
P: 408-279-1099   F: 408-297-3803   PRC:80
www.allfabprecision.com
Estab: 1999

Son Ho, President & CEO

Provider of contract manufacturing services for metal formed products. The company is involved in laser cutting, deburring, bending, and welding activities.

All Power Labs   HQ
   1010 Murray St
   Berkeley CA 94710
P: 510-845-1500   F: 510-550-2837   PRC:142
www.allpowerlabs.com
Estab: 2008

Jim Mason, Founder & CEO
Alejandro Abalos, COO
Bear Kaufmann, CTO
James Reischutz, Chief Testing Engineer
Nick Bindbeutel, Director

Manufacturer of biomass fueled power generators. The company is a global leader in small scale gasification.

All Sensors Corp   HQ
   16035 Vineyard Blvd
   Morgan Hill CA 95037
P: 408-225-4314   F: 408-225-2079   PRC:236
www.allsensors.com
Email: info@allsensors.com
Estab: 1999

Dale Dauenhauer, VP of Operations
Jason Paiva, Strategic Sourcing Manager
Jim Brownell, Sales Manager
Katie Dauenhauer, Production Control Manager
Stephen Johnson, Quality Manager

Manufacturer of MEMS piezoresistive pressure sensors and pressure transducers. The company serves the medical, industrial, and HVAC markers.

All Weather Inc   HQ
   1165 National Dr
   Sacramento CA 95834
P: 800-824-5873   F: 916-928-1165   PRC:13
www.allweatherinc.com
Email: marketing@allweatherinc.com
Estab: 1977

Mauricio Garcia, President
Neal Dillman, CTO
Steve Glander, Sales Manager
Barbara Baca, Sales Manager
Maria Gustafson, Office Manager

Manufacturer of meteorological instruments and systems. The company is also engaged in the development of air traffic management solutions.

Allaccem Inc   HQ
   1001 Center St
   San Carlos CA 94070
P: 650-593-8700   F: 650-593-8705   PRC:268
www.allaccem.com
Estab: 2005

Jeffery Whiteford, President & CEO

Manufacturer of pharmaceutical products such as dermatology, optic, and dental products for goats, dogs, and cats.

Allakos Inc   HQ
   975 Island Dr Ste 201
   Redwood City CA 94065
P: 650-597-5002   PRC:30
www.allakos.com
Estab: 2012

Adam Tomasi, President & COO
Robert Alexander, CEO
Leo Redmond, CFO
Henrik Rasmussen, CMO
Tim Varacek, CCO

Developer of therapeutic antibodies for the treatment of inflammatory and proliferative diseases such as asthma, nasal polyposis, and fibrosis.

Allcells LLC   HQ
1301 Harbor Bay Pkwy Ste 200
Alameda CA 94502
P: 510-726-2700   F: 510-521-7600   PRC:36
allcells.com
Email: info@allcells.com
Estab: 1998

Jay Tong, President & CEO
Jack Zhai, VP of Sales & Marketing
Anh Lo, Lab Manager
Laurie Ho, Senior Procurement Supervisor
Charlynn Young, Inventory Specialist

Provider of medical services for human primary cells. The company focuses on fields such as cell biology, oncology, and virology.

Allegro Consultants Inc   HQ
PO Box 4049
Menlo Park CA 94026-4049
P: 408-252-2330   F: 408-200-4488   PRC:323
www.allegro.com
Email: info@allegro.com
Estab: 1984

Donna Hofmeister, Senior Support Specialist & VP of Technical Support

Provider of operating system technical support for third party maintenance and multi-vendor service community.

Allergy Research Group LLC   BR
2300 N Loop Rd
Alameda CA 94502
P: 510-263-2000   F: 510-263-2100   PRC:250
www.allergyresearchgroup.com
Email: info@allergyresearchgroup.com
Estab: 1979

Stephen Levine, Founder
Fred Salomon, President & Vice Chairman
Jason Lui, Senior Accountant & Analyst

Provider of nutritional products for blood sugar, brain, cardiovascular, metabolic, hormone, liver, and immune support.

Alliacense   HQ
20883 Stevens Creek Blvd Ste 100
Cupertino CA 95014
P: 408-446-4222   PRC:304
alliacense.com
Email: customerservice@alliacense.com

Mac Leckrone, President
Mike Davis, SVP of Licensing
Dung Nguyen, Technology Analyst
Parag Desai, Microprocessor Systems Analyst

Provider of intellectual property solutions. The company's services include broad spectrum, reverse engineering, and product reports.

Alliance Support Partners Inc   HQ
5036 Commercial Cir Unit C
Concord CA 94520
P: 925-363-5382   F: 925-363-7882   PRC:316
www.asp-support.com
Email: sales@asp-support.com
Estab: 2004

Chuck Eyerly, President
Harold Ng, CEO

Provider of test solutions, instrumentation engineering, test system design, and turnkey outsourcing support services.

Allied Crane Inc   HQ
855 N Parkside Dr
Pittsburg CA 94565
P: 925-427-9200   F: 925-427-9107   PRC:179
www.alliedcrane.us
Email: mail@alliedcrane.us
Estab: 1976

Dave Costa, President
Sandy Cariel, Accounting Analyst

Provider of crane services. The company offers crane repair, installation and removal, and preventive maintenance programs.

Allied Environmental Inc   HQ
26291 Production Ave Ste 1
Hayward CA 94545
P: 510-732-1300   F: 510-732-1386   PRC:139
alliedenv.com
Estab: 1995

Allen Wellborn, CEO
Alan Salmen, VP
Steve Whittington, General Manager
Jamie Falgoust, Office Manager & Accounts Payable
Jason Standley, Project Manager & Safety Officer

Provider of asbestos and load abatement services. The company specializes in commercial, residential, and industrial contracting services.

Allied Fire Protection   HQ
555 High St
Oakland CA 94601
P: 510-533-5516   F: 510-533-0913   PRC:159
www.alliedfire.com
Email: sales@alliedfire.com

Alan Hertz, Owner
J.D. Locklear, President
Tina Tiller, CAO
Kevin Thomas, Chief Estimator
Derek Peterson, VP

Designer and manufacturer of fire protection sprinkler systems. The company also offers installation services.

Allied Security Alarms   HQ
130 Produce Ave Ste D
S San Francisco CA 94080
P: 650-871-8959   F: 650-871-8973   PRC:59
www.allied24.com
Email: contactus@allied24.com
Estab: 1971

Rudy Alva, Owner
Patricia Alva, Manager

Provider of security products such as fire and burglar alarms, video surveillance systems, motion detectors, and access controls.

Allied Telesis Inc   BR
3041 Orchard Pkwy
San Jose CA 95134
P: 408-519-8700   PRC:67
www.alliedtelesis.com
Estab: 1987

Keith Southard, CEO
Bob Blackmer, Director of Compliance Engineering
Kafong Siek, Project Manager
Diana Tran, Materials Planning Manager
Dennis Duchmann, Manager of Components Engineering

Developer of network solutions for Internet protocol surveillance. The company focuses on web hosting and programming solutions.

Allmotion Inc   HQ
30097 Ahern Ave
Union City CA 94587
P: 510-471-4000   F: 510-400-8001   PRC:292
www.allmotion.com
Email: support@allmotion.com

Jamie Rodriguez, Operations Manager
Jessica Suto, Production & Operations Manager
Olga Akopian, Technician & Operation Manager
Brad Douglas, Engineer

Manufacturer and distributor of stepper drives, stepper controllers, servo drives, and servo controllers.

Alloy Metal Products   HQ
7801 Las Positas Rd
Livermore CA 94551
P: 925-371-1234   F: 925-371-2367   PRC:80
www.alloymp.com
Email: info@alloymp.com
Estab: 1977

Fred Matter, Founder
Gary Pardini, Operations Manager

Provider of precision CNC machining, tumbling, annealing, cutting, and packaging services. The company serves aerospace and medical device fields.

Alloy Tool Steel Inc   HQ
13525 E Freeway Dr   [N]
Santa Fe Springs CA 90670
P: 562-921-8605   F: 562-802-1728   PRC:62
www.alloytoolsteel.com
Emp: 1-10   Estab: 1973

Tom Hardy, Manager of Sales

Distributor of stainless steel, alloy tool steel, and titanium alloys.

Allstar Microelectronics Inc   HQ
30191A Avenida de las Banderas   [N]
Rancho Santa Margarita CA 92688
P: 949-546-0888   F: 949-546-0898   PRC:322
www.allstarshop.com
Email: service@allstarshop.com
Estab: 1995

Ming-Chyi Chiang, Contact

Distributor of computer storage devices.

Allterra Environmental Inc   HQ
207 McPherson St Ste B
Santa Cruz CA 95060
P: 831-425-2608   F: 831-425-2609   PRC:142
allterraenv.com
Email: info@allterraenv.com

James Allen, President & CEO
Micah Breeden, CFO
Nathaniel Allen, COO
Joe Mangine, Environmental Division Director
Samantha Willis, Staff Engineer

Provider of environmental site remediation and compliance services. The company offerings include permitting, geologic hazards, and sustainable solutions.

Alltronics LLC   HQ

2761 Scott Blvd   [N]
Santa Clara CA 95050
P: 408-778-3868   F: 408-778-2558   PRC:80
www.alltronics.com
Email: warehouse@alltronics.com
Emp: 1-10

Andy Franklin, Contact

Distributor of electrical and electro-mechanical parts such as automotive, computer, capacitors and more.

Allvia Inc   HQ
657 N Pastoria Ave
Sunnyvale CA 94085
P: 408-212-3200   F: 408-720-3334   PRC:79
www.allvia.com
Email: info@allvia.com
Estab: 1997

Sergey Savastiouk, CEO
Nagesh V.K., VP of Technology Development & Manufacturing
Biswajit Sur, Director of Technology & Manufacturing
Jim Hewlett, Test & Equipment Manager

Provider of silicon interposer and through-silicon via foundry services to the semiconductor and optoelectronics industries.

Allwin21 Corp   HQ
220 Cochrane Cir
Morgan Hill CA 95037
P: 408-778-7788   F: 408-904-7168   PRC:86
allwin21.com
Email: sales@allwin21.com
Estab: 2000

Zhengming Chen, Owner
Peter Chen, Market Manager
David Chang, Senior Service Engineer & R&D
Qing Zhou, Engineer
Jian Xu, Staff Engineer

Provider of high-tech equipment, related services, and technical support for the semiconductor and biomedical industries.

Allwire Inc   HQ
16395 Avenue 24 1/2
Chowchilla CA 93610
P: 559-665-4893   F: 559-665-7389   PRC:202
allwire.com
Email: info@allwire.com
Estab: 1967

Dana Oyler, VP of Sales

Provider of design, analysis, and programming services for businesses. The company is also involved in web hosting and technical support.

Alpha & Omega Semiconductor   HQ
475 Oakmead Pkwy
Sunnyvale CA 94085
P: 408-830-9742   F: 408-830-9749   PRC:212
www.aosmd.com
Email: inquiries@aosmd.com
Estab: 2000
Sales: $300M to $1 Billion

Sik Kwong Lui, Co-Founder & VP of Silicon Technology
Yueh-Se Ho, Co-Founder & COO & Director
Mike F. Chang, Founder & Chairman & CEO
Yifan Liang, CFO & Corporate Secretary
Hamza Yilmaz, EVP

Designer, developer, and supplier of power semiconductors. The company's applications include notebook PCs and power supplies.

Alpha Networks Inc   HQ
1551 McCarthy Blvd Ste 201
Milpitas CA 95035
P: 408-844-8850   PRC:97
www.alphanetworks.com

Yuchin Lin, President
John Lee, CEO
Colin Hsu, Sales Director
Claire Yu, Manager of Investor Relations & Deputy Spokesperson
Vanessa Lan, Associate Project Manager of Investor Relations

Designer and manufacturer of networking products. The company also focuses on computers and computer peripherals.

Alpha Omega Wireless Inc   BR
5710 Auburn Blvd Ste 2
Sacramento CA 95841
P: 800-997-9250   F: 512-298-1646   PRC:63
aowireless.com
Email: info@aowireless.com
Estab: 2003

Joe Wargo, President & Visionary

Provider of broadband wireless network technology integration solutions. The company also focuses on wireless backhaul solutions.

Alpha Orthotics Corp   HQ
PO Box 1107
Tiburon CA 94920
P: 415-389-8980   F: 415-389-1063   PRC:190
www.alphaorthotics.com
Email: info@alphaorthotics.com
Estab: 1998

Gaby Federal, Owner
Donna Egeberg, Office Manager

Distributor of non-invasive orthotic products. The company provides products for catalogs, specialty foot retailers, and medical distributors.

Alpha Research & Technology Inc   HQ
5175 Hillsdale Cir
El Dorado Hills CA 95762-5708
P: 916-431-9340   F: 916-431-9360   PRC:327
www.artruggedsystems.com
Email: busdev@artruggedsystems.com
Estab: 1993

Deann Kerr, Co-Founder & CEO & President
Donne Smith, CTO & VP & Co-Founder
Kathy Gudel, Human Resources Manager
Steve Totah, Systems Engineer
Sherrie Zeitler, Buyer

Designer and manufacturer of airborne systems for command, communications, intelligence, surveillance, and other needs and focuses on installation.

Alphaems Corp   HQ
44193 S Grimmer Blvd
Fremont CA 94538
P: 510-498-8788   F: 510-498-4484   PRC:91
www.alphaemscorp.com
Estab: 2003

Eric Chang, President & CEO & Co-Founder
Shulin Chen, Co-Founder & VP of Material
Elton Li, CFO
Ben Wang, VP of Engineering
Bill Yee, VP of Operations

Provider of printed circuit board prototyping and PCB assembly production services. The company also involves in material purchasing and warehousing.

Alphalyse Inc   HQ
299 California Ave Ste 200
Palo Alto CA 94306
P: 650-543-3193   PRC:36
alphalyse.com
Email: info@alphalyse.com
Estab: 2002

Thomas Kofoed, CEO

Provider of protein analysis services. The company focuses on support research, manufacturing, and clinical development activities.

Alstem Inc   HQ
2600 Hilltop Dr Bldg B Ste C328
Richmond CA 94806
P: 510-708-0096   PRC:36
www.alstembio.com
Email: info@alstembio.com
Estab: 2012

Gang Li, Founder
Patrick Hop, Director of AI Research
Scott Ezell, Senior Data Scientist

Provider of virus concentration and transduction solutions. The company's offerings include assay kits, antibodies etc.

Alta Design & Manufacturing Inc   HQ
885 Auzerais Ave
San Jose CA 95126
P: 408-450-5394   F: 408-450-5395   PRC:80
alta-eng.com
Estab: 1999

Steven Hernandez, President

Manufacturer of precision-machined components. The company is engaged in production manufacturing, prototype services, and electromechanical assembly.

Alta Devices   HQ
    545 Oakmead Pkwy
    Sunnyvale CA 94085
    P: 408-988-8600   PRC:212
    www.altadevices.com
    Email: info@altadevices.com
    Estab: 2008

Jeff Zhou, Executive Chairman
Jian Ding, CEO
Rich Kapusta, CMO & Head of Sales
Thomas Giap, VP of Finance
Ray Milano, VP of Technology

Provider of mobile power technology services. The
company offers unmanned systems, consumer
devices, and Internet technology services.

Alta Manufacturing Inc   HQ
    47650 Westinghouse Dr
    Fremont CA 94539
    P: 510-668-1870   F: 510-668-1877   PRC:211
    www.altamfg.com
    Email: info@altamfg.com
    Estab: 1998

Billy Thach, Production Manager
Will Ziakas, Account Manager
Sean Chandler, National Sales Manager

Manufacturer of printed circuit board assemblies
and offers program management, testing, material
procurement, and optical inspection solutions.

Altaflex   HQ
    336 Martin Ave
    Santa Clara CA 95050
    P: 408-727-6614   PRC:211
    altaflex.com
    Email: sales@altaflex.com
    Estab: 2000

Michele Cannito, General Manager Production
Ferdie Robancho, Manager of Production
Wita Kawi, Finance Manager
James Cao, Program Manager
Francisco Duarte, CAD & CAM Programmer
Manager

Developer and fabricator of touch panels and
component assemblies, and circuits. The company
serves the electronic sector.

Altair Technologies Inc   HQ
    41970 Christy St
    Fremont CA 94538
    P: 650-508-8700   PRC:157
    www.altairusa.com
    Email: info@altairusa.com
    Estab: 1991

Curtis Allen, President
Chris Ferrari, CEO
Christopher Ferrari, Director of Engineering
A.L. Luna, Director of Sales
Greg Shouse, Production Manager

Provider of precision furnace brazing services.
The company serves the medical, defense, and
semiconductor industries.

Altamont Manufacturing Inc   HQ
    241 Rickenbacker Cir
    Livermore CA 94551
    P: 925-371-5401   PRC:86
    www.altamontmfg.com
    Estab: 2003

Rick Stivers, Owner

Provider of precision CNC machining, welding,
and fabrication services. The company offers
semiconductor, aerospace, medical, and robotics
components.

Altemp Alloys Inc   HQ
    330 W Taft Ave   [N]
    Orange CA 92865
    P: 714-279-0249   F: 714-279-3991   PRC:62
    www.altempalloys.com
    Email: info@altempalloys.com
    Emp: 11-50   Estab: 1979

Connie Mayhill, President

Distributor of high-temperature alloys such as
inconel, hastelloy steel, and other materials.

Alten Calsoft Labs   HQ
    2903 Bunker Hill Ln Ste 107
    Santa Clara CA 95054
    P: 408-755-3000   F: 925-249-3031   PRC:324
    www.altencalsoftlabs.com
    Email: business@acldigital.com
    Estab: 1992

Ramandeep Singh, CEO
Sai Satyam, CFO
Narendra Dhara, CTO
Mrinmoy Purkayastha, VP
Suresh Kumar M., Associate Director

Provider of breed consulting, enterprise IT, and
product engineering services for enterprises in
healthcare, telecom, and high-tech and retail
industries.

Alterflex Corp   HQ
    1717 Oakland Rd
    San Jose CA 95131
    P: 408-441-8688   PRC:80
    www.alterflex.com
    Email: pcb@alterflex.com
    Estab: 1983

Kennth Wong, President

Designer and manufacturer of printed circuit
boards. The company also provides engineering
support services.

Alterg Inc   HQ
    48438 Milmont Dr
    Fremont CA 94538
    P: 510-270-5900   F: 510-225-9399   PRC:196
    www.alterg.com
    Email: info@alterg.com
    Estab: 2005

Charles Remsberg, CEO
Kevin Davidge, COO
Fran Hackett, VP of Global Sales
Michael McGirr, VP of Engineering
Bryan Cass, Accounting Manager

Provider of new technologies and products such
as anti-gravity treadmills and bionic leg for physical therapy and athletic training.

Altergy Systems   HQ
    140 Blue Ravine Rd
    Folsom CA 95630
    P: 916-458-8590   F: 916-200-0488   PRC:129
    www.altergy.com
    Email: info@altergy.com
    Estab: 2001

Gary Watson, Chairman
Eric S. Mettler, President & CEO
James Oros, SVP of Deployment & Field Opera-
tions
Jayson J. Watson, VP of Supply Side Manage-
ment
Rick Burant, VP of Sales

Designer and manufacturer of fuel cell power
systems. The company serves telecommunication, emergency response, data center, and other
fields.

Altest Corp   HQ
    898 Faulstich Ct
    San Jose CA 95112
    P: 408-436-9900   PRC:207
    www.altestcorp.com
    Email: info@altestcorp.com

Joe Corcoran, Director of Business Relations

Provider of PCB assembly and engineering
colutions. The company offers services to the
aerospace and commercial industries.

Altierre Corp   HQ
    1980 Concourse Dr
    San Jose CA 95131
    P: 408-435-7343   F: 408-544-2323   PRC:324
    Estab: 2002

Sunit Saxena, CEO
Anurag Goel, CTO & VP Software Development
Dave Diffenderfer, VP Operations
Ravi Bhatnagar, VP Digital Systems & Digital IC
Development
Rob Crane, SVP of Global Sales

Provider of digital retail services. The company
offers retail integration, software support, and
consulting services.

Altigen Communications Inc   HQ
    670 N McCarthy Blvd Ste 200
    Milpitas CA 95035
    P: 408-597-9000   F: 408-597-9020   PRC:68
    www.altigen.com
    Email: sales@altigen.com
    Estab: 1994

Jeremiah J. Fleming, CEO
Shirley Sun, VP of Research & Development
David Tang, VP of Cloud Solutions
Mike Plumer, VP of Sales
Scott Lee, Director of DevOps

Manufacturer of voice and data telecommunication
equipment. The company specializes in hosted
business communication solutions.

Alumawall Inc   HQ
1701 S Seventh St Ste 9
San Jose CA 95112
P: 408-292-6353   F: 408-275-6225   PRC:80
www.alumawall.com
Estab: 1984

Ken Matarazzo, Chief Estimator
Maureen Sullivan, Project Manager
Jason Askins, Architectural Design Engineer
Reena Naidu, Architectural Designer

Manufacturer of metal panel and fabricator and erector of aluminum and metal composite panel systems.

Alzeta Corp   HQ
2343 Calle Del Mundo
Santa Clara CA 95054
P: 408-727-8282   F: 408-727-9740   PRC:154
www.alzeta.com
Estab: 1982

Angela Kendall, Owner
John D. Sullivan, President
John E. Kendall, Chairman
Stephen G. Egli, CFO
Guadalupe Aguilera, Production Manager

Provider of clean air solutions and related research and development services. The company offers services to the industrial and commercial sectors.

AM Fitzgerald & Associates LLC   HQ
700 Airport Blvd Ste 210
Burlingame CA 94010
P: 650-347-6367   F: 650-347-6366   PRC:209
www.amfitzgerald.com
Email: info@amfitzgerald.com
Estab: 2003

Carolyn D. White, Associate

Provider of MEMS solutions. The company's products include piezoresistive cantilevers, ultrasound transducers, and infrared imagers.

Amag Technology Inc   HQ
20701 Manhattan Pl   [N]
Torrance CA 90501
P: 310-518-2380   PRC:109
www.amag.com
Email: international@amag.com
Emp: 51-200   Estab: 1998

Jason Schimpf, VP of Partner Programs & Education
Jeanne Imbrogno, VP of Customer Services
Jeff Leblanc, VP of Client Services
Jody Ross, VP of Sales
Jonathan Moore, VP of Product Management

Designer and manufacturer of access control and video security solutions.

Amaranth Medical Inc   HQ
1145 Terra Bella Ave Ste A
Mountain View CA 94043
P: 650-965-3830   PRC:251
Estab: 2006

Kamal Ramzipoor, President & CEO
Eveleen Tang, Principal Engineer
Sandy Liu, Controller

Specializes in proprietary polymer structure and processing technology. The company's products are used in vascular and nonvascular applications.

Amasco   HQ
6017 Snell Ave Ste 319
San Jose CA 95123
P: 408-360-1300   PRC:293
amasco.com
Email: sales@amasco.com
Estab: 1974

Trevor Nicholaidis, General Manager
Canute Dsouza, Marine Manager
Fausto Palma, Diving Manager
Murali Ambala Kolliyil, Finance Manager
Jan Fichera, Office Manager

Distributor of products for the telecommunications, commercial, industrial, medical, and military electronics markers.

Amax Information Technologies Inc   HQ
1565 Reliance Way
Fremont CA 94539
P: 510-651-8886   F: 510-651-4119   PRC:116
www.amax.com
Email: sales@amax.com
Estab: 1979

Jean Shih, President
Julia Shih, VP of Business Development
Edgardo Evangelista, Senior Solution Engineer

Manufacturer and seller of custom servers and storage solutions. The company focuses on platform design, custom branding, and supply chain management.

Ambarella Inc   HQ
3101 Jay St
Santa Clara CA 95054
P: 408-734-8888   F: 408-734-0788   PRC:86
www.ambarella.com
Emp: 165 Estab: 2004
Sales: $100M to $300M

Fermi Wang, CEO
George Laplante, CFO
Chan Lee, VP of VLSI
Didier Legall, EVP
David Young, Director of Business Development

Developer of high-definition video compression and image processing solutions. The company's products are used in security IP cameras and sports cameras.

Amber Precision Instruments Inc   HQ
101 Bonaventura Dr
San Jose CA 95134
P: 408-752-0199   F: 408-752-0335   PRC:110
www.amberpi.com
Email: amberpi@amberpi.com
Estab: 2006

Harris Park, Director
Hamed Kajbaf, EMC Engineer

Provider of scanner products. The company specializes in electromagnetic immunity scanners and near field scanners.

Amdocs Ltd   BR
1100 Investment Blvd Ste 250
El Dorado Hills CA 95762
P: 916-934-7000   F: 916-934-7221   PRC:68
www.amdocs.com
Estab: 1982

Michal Zuk, Global Travel Manager
Omri Yaniv, Head of Tax
Velmurugan Sankaranarayanan, Principal Software Engineer & Principal Software Engineer

Provider of customer management and billing solutions software. The company offers services to the industrial sector.

Amerex Instruments Inc   HQ
3951C Industrial Way
Concord CA 94520
P: 925-299-0743   F: 925-299-0745   PRC:195
www.amerexinst.com
Email: marketing@amerexinst.com
Estab: 1991

Saw Ewe Lee, Secretary

Provider of lab equipment. The company provides shakers, top-loading autoclaves, incubators, hybridization and convection ovens and water baths.

America Aopen Inc   HQ
2150 N First St Ste 400
San Jose CA 95131
P: 408-586-1200   PRC:105
www.aopen.com
Estab: 1996

Dale Tsai, President

Specializes in the manufacture and marketing of personal computer (PC) components and peripherals. The company also offers speakers and bare systems.

American Broadband Services   HQ
5718 E Shields Ave
Fresno CA 93727
P: 866-827-4638   F: 559-272-5266   PRC:68
www.americanbroadbandservices.com
Estab: 1999

Julie Coltrinari, Owner
Jeremy Hall, President
Daryl C. Plummer, Managing VP & Gartner Fellow
Jay Davis, IT Recruiter

Provider of web, Internet connectivity, VoIP, spam and virus filtering, and technical support services.

American Cylinder Head Inc   HQ
499 Lesser St
Oakland CA 94601
P: 800-356-4889   F: 510-536-6620   PRC:159
www.americancylinderheads.com
Email: sales@americancylinderheads.com

Arvid Elbeck, President

Provider of diesel and gas cylinder head repair and remanufacturing services. The company focuses on automotive, heavy duty, and CNG cylinder heads.

American Die & Rollforming Inc   HQ
3495 Swetzer Rd Ste 300
Loomis CA 95650
P: 916-652-7667   F: 916-647-0477   PRC:80
www.americandieandrollforming.com
Estab: 2008

Chris Tatasciore, President
Sherri Wandell, Office Manager

Manufacturer of metal roofing, siding, and structural products. The company also specializes in canopies and decking.

American Integrated Services Inc   HQ
1502 E Opp St   [N]
Wilmington CA 90744
P: 310-522-1168   F: 310-522-0474   PRC:45
www.americanintegrated.com
Emp: 51-200   Estab: 1998

David Herrera, President

Provider of comprehensive environmental solutions through construction, remediation, demolition, abatement, industrial services, emergency and disaster response, specialty transportation, and waste management services.

American Metal Bearing Co   HQ
7191 Acacia Ave   [N]
Garden Grove CA 92841
P: 714-892-5527   F: 714-898-3217   PRC:159
www.ambco.net
Emp: 11-50   Estab: 1960

Michael Litton, President
Mimosa Diep, Secretary

Designer and manufacturer of plain bearings for all industrial applications.

American Micro Detection Systems Inc   HQ
2800 W March Ln
Stockton CA 95219
P: 209-985-1705   PRC:230
www.amdsinc.com
Estab: 2003

Robert Keville, CEO
Lynn Essman, COO
Daniel Dietrich, Chief Science Officer

Provider of water analysis treatments. The company deals with research, development, and monitoring services.

American Portable Welding   HQ
3329 Baumberg Ave
Hayward CA 94545-4411
P: 510-887-4279   F: 510-887-0505   PRC:80
www.americanportablewelding.com
Email: apweld@sbcglobal.net
Estab: 1974

Lew Larimer, Owner
Alan Klepatsky, Office Manager

Provider of welding, fabrication, and engineering services. The company offers services to the industrial sector.

American Portwell Technology Inc   DH
44200 Christy St
Fremont CA 94538
P: 510-403-3399   F: 510-403-3184   PRC:93
www.portwell.com
Email: info@portwell.com
Estab: 1993

Allen Lee, CEO
Kevin Lee, VP of Operations
Aaron Tong, Senior Director of QA
Robert Feng, Product Marketing Director
Sandy Wen, Purchasing Director

Designer and manufacturer of industrial PC products. The company also offers embedded computing, network appliances, and human machine interfaces.

American Power Systems   BR
1627 Industrial Dr Ste C
Stockton CA 95206
P: 209-467-8999   PRC:68
ampowersys.com
Estab: 1994

Gary Hughes, President
Brett Cooke, Director of Sales
Albert Cuellar, Service Manager
Deborah Thornton, Service Coordinator
Tom Treacy, Contact

Provider of power management products and services. The company's offerings include UPS, DC power, and battery testing.

American Precision Spring Corp   HQ
1513 Arbuckle Ct
Santa Clara CA 95054
P: 408-986-1020   F: 408-986-1012   PRC:80
www.americanprecspring.com
Email: sales@americanprecspring.com
Estab: 1979

Kathy Chu, CEO

Designer of electronic circuits. The company specializes in the design and fabrication of printed circuit boards.

American Probe & Technologies Inc   HQ
1795 Grogan Ave
Merced CA 95341
P: 408-263-3356   F: 408-263-3797   PRC:189
www.americanprobe.com
Email: sales@americanprobe.com
Estab: 1984

Kenneth Chabraya, President
Kim Merrill, VP
David Chabraya, VP
Kim Chabraya, VP
Dawn Fleming, Production Coordinator & Plant Manager

Manufacturer of analytical probes and accessories for the semiconductor test and measurement industry.

American Prototype and Production Inc   HQ
555 Bragato Rd
San Carlos CA 94070
P: 650-595-4994   PRC:80
www.americanprototype.com

Blaine D. Bolich, President & Owner
Cheri Perez, Operations Manager

Manufacturer of industrial laser cutting machines. The company focuses on industries such as CNC milling, CNC turning, and laser engraving.

American Relays Inc   HQ
15537 S Blackburn Ave   [N]
Norwalk CA 90650
P: 562-944-0447   F: 562-944-0590   PRC:290
www.americanrelays.com
Email: sales@americanrelays.com
Emp: 1-10   Estab: 1985

Hyo Lee, CEO
Soo Lee, Secretary

Designer and manufacturer of reed relay.

American Telesource Inc   HQ
1311 63rd St Ste B
Emeryville CA 94608
P: 800-333-8394   PRC:325
www.ati-cti.com
Estab: 1983

Fred Schwartz, Field Service Engineer
Tenzin Passang, Accountant

Provider of voice and data communication applications. The company offers unified communications, wireless, and process automation solutions.

American Voice Mail Inc   HQ
2310 S Sepulveda Blvd   [N]
Los Angeles CA 90064
P: 310-478-4949   F: 310-478-5171   PRC:62
www.americanvoicemail.com
Email: sales@americanvoicemail.com
Emp: 11-50   Estab: 1977

Mark Gordon, President

Provider of electronic voice mail, pager, messaging, toll and long distance services.

Ameriflex Inc   HQ
2390 Railroad St   [N]
Corona CA 92880
P: 951-737-5557   F: 951-737-3992   PRC:82
www.ameriflex.net
Emp: 201-500   Estab: 1981

Dawn Segovia, Controller

Manufacturer of precision bellows, flanges, flexible metal hose and much more products for vacuum applications.

Amerimade Technology Inc   HQ
449 Mountain Vista Pkwy
Livermore CA 94551
P: 925-243-9090   F: 925-243-9266   PRC:86
amerimade.com
Estab: 1994

Greg Rondeau, Manager
Armando Garil, Field Service Engineer
Jay Patel, Senior Account Executive

Manufacturer of wet processing equipment. The company's equipment include fully and semi automated benches, chemical handling equipment, and process tanks.

Ameritech Industries Inc HQ
20208 Charlanne Dr
Redding CA 96002
P: 530-221-4470 F: 530-221-5201 PRC:8
www.americanpropeller.com
Estab: 1976

Kathleen Dawes, Owner
James Bridgeman, General Manager
Robert Honig, Corporate Sales Manager

Provider of aircraft engines and certified and ex-
perimental engines and propellers and also offers
overhaul and exchange services.

Ameritechnology Group HQ
PO Box 60155
Sacramento CA 95860
P: 916-395-6776 PRC:323
ameritechnologygroup.com
Email: info@amtgi.com
Estab: 1999

Tom McNabb, Owner
Matt Macbride, Technician

Provider of IT consulting, asset tracking, auditing,
telecom connectivity logistics, relocation, and data
recovery solutions for businesses.

AmeriTel Inc HQ
8910 Quartz Ave [N]
Northridge CA 91324
P: 818-734-7400 F: 818-734-7444 PRC:68
www.ameritelinc.com
Email: info@ameritelinc.com
Emp: 11-50 Estab: 1983

Chaz Chahal, CEO

Provider of system design, installation and servicing of business voice and data communications
systems and offers voice processing, voice over
IP, video security systems, and network services
and serves the healthcare, education, hospitality,
legal, financial, and manufacturing industries.

Amgen Inc BR
1120 Veterans Blvd
S San Francisco CA 94080
P: 650-244-2000 F: 650-837-9421 PRC:34
www.amgen.com
Estab: 1980

Robert A. Bradway, CEO & Chairman
David W. Meline, CFO
Jonathan P. Graham, EVP & General Counsel &
Secretary
Steven K. Galson, SVP of Global Regulatory
Affairs & Safety
Sasha Kamb, SVP of Research & Development

Provider of scientific applications services. The
company's services include clinical trials, ethical
research, biosimilars, and web resources.

M-24

Amimon Inc HQ
2025 Gateway Pl Ste 450
San Jose CA 95110
P: 408-490-4686 PRC:212
www.amimon.com
Email: contact@amimon.com
Estab: 2004

Ram Ofir, President & CEO
Efrat Birav, Director of Human Resources

Developer and manufacturer of HD wireless video
modules. The company's products include Studio
Link, Live Link, and View Link.

Amind Solutions LLC HQ
3201 Danville Blvd Ste 155
Alamo CA 94507
P: 925-804-6139 PRC:322
www.amindsolutions.com
Email: marketing@amindsolutions.com
Estab: 2005

Billy Hunt, President
Robert Wing, CTO
Sharad Mitra, COO

Provider of technology and services. The company offers enterprise mobility, quoting and ordering,
product configuration, and e-Commerce services.

Amobee Inc HQ
901 Marshall St Ste 200
Redwood City CA 94063
P: 650-353-4399 F: 650-802-8951 PRC:322
www.amobee.com
Estab: 2005

Kim Reed Perell, President
Mark Strecker, CEO

Provider of marketing intelligence and cross
channel, cross device advertiser, and publisher
solutions for marketers, publishers, and operators.

AMPAC Fine Chemicals DH
PO Box 1718
Rancho Cordova CA 95741-1718
P: 916-357-6880 F: 916-353-3523 PRC:53
www.ampacfinechemicals.com
Email: afcbusdev@apfc.com

Aslam Malik, President
Larry Zeagler, VP of Contracts & Commercial
Products & General Manager
James Pilney, VP of Manufacturing Operations
Chris Conley, VP of Safety & Health & Environ-
ment
Mark Silber, Director of Procurement

Manufacturer of active pharmaceutical ingredients (APIs) and registered intermediates. The
company's services include product development
and scale-up.

Ampex Data Systems HQ
26460 Corporate Ave Ste 200
Hayward CA 94545-3914
P: 650-367-2011 PRC:95
ampex.com
Email: info@ampex.com
Estab: 1944

Phat Ly, Senior Technician

Manufacturer of digital storage systems. The
company also offers airborne and ground systems
and related video solutions.

Amprius Inc HQ
1180 Page Ave
Fremont CA 94538
P: 800-425-8803 PRC:140
www.amprius.com
Email: info@amprius.com
Estab: 2008

Kang Sun, CEO
Aaron Bakke, Senior Director of Quality
Weijie Wang, Senior Director of Technology
Development
Chentao Yu, Senior Director of Operations
Yi-Lei Chow, Engineering Operations Manager

Developer and manufacturer of lithium-ion batteries. The company offers services to the industrial
sectors.

Ampro Systems Inc RH
1000 Page Ave
Fremont CA 94538
P: 510-624-9000 F: 510-624-9002 PRC:207
www.amprosystems.com
Email: sales@amprosystems.com
Estab: 1997

Ting Ya Wang, CEO & CFO & Secretary

Manufacturer of printed circuit board assemblies.
The company deals with procurement services
and serves the government and military industries.

Ampteks Inc HQ
265 Rickenbacker Cir
Livermore CA 94551-7216
P: 925-493-7150 F: 925-493-7151 PRC:85
ampteks.com
Estab: 2005

Mike Clark, CEO

Provider of engineering solutions. The company
provides alternatives for dichromate plating and
electro silver plating.

AMtec Industries Inc BR
7079 Commerce Cir
Pleasanton CA 94588
P: 510-887-2289 PRC:290
www.amtec1.com

Robert Bradley, President
Brian Pessano, VP
Tom Willis, Director of Sales
David Getty, Project Manager
Dante Kabiling, Quality Assurance Manager

Manufacturer of industrial custom control panels.
The company is engaged in design, fabrication,
and installation services.

AmTECH Microelectronics Inc HQ
485 Cochrane Cir
Morgan Hill CA 95037
P: 408-612-8888 PRC:207
www.amtechmicro.com
Email: info@amtechmicro.com
Estab: 1993

Walter Chavez, CEO
Clifford Mihalyfi, Senior Executive

Provider of manufacturing solutions. The company
deals with PCB fabrication, machining, and assembly services.

Amulet Technologies LLC   HQ
1475 S Bascom Ave Ste 111
Campbell CA 95008
P: 408-374-4956   F: 408-374-4941   PRC:204
www.amulettechnologies.com
Email: info@amulettechnologies.com
Estab: 1998

Paul Indaco, President & CEO
Kimberly Cope, Contact

Provider of embedded graphical user interface solutions. The company also specializes in modules and chips.

Amunix Pharmaceuticals Inc   HQ
500 Ellis St
Mountain View CA 94043
P: 650-428-1800   PRC:252
www.amunix.com
Email: bd@amunix.com
Estab: 2006

Volker Schellenberger, President & CTO
Angie You, CEO
Bryan Irving, CSO
Darcy Mootz, Chief Business Officer

Developer of biomolecular therapy. The company specializes in the development of protein and peptide based therapeutic products.

Amyris Inc   HQ
5885 Hollis St Ste 100
Emeryville CA 94608
P: 510-450-0761   F: 510-225-2645   PRC:52
www.amyris.com
Email: info@amyris.com
Estab: 2003
Sales: $100M to $300M

Joel Cherry, President of Research & Development
John Melo, CEO
Jonathan Wolter, Interim CFO
Chris Paddon, Technical Liaison Director
Yue Yang, Director of Program Management

Provider of renewable products. The company delivers cosmetic emollients and fragrances, fuels and lubricants, and even biopharmaceuticals.

Analatom Inc   HQ
4655 Old Ironsides Dr Ste 130
Santa Clara CA 95054
P: 408-980-9516   F: 408-980-9518   PRC:87
www.analatom.com
Email: info@analatom.com
Estab: 1997

Bernard C. Laskowski, President
Tyrell Black, CEO
Jeffrey Morse, Director of Advanced Research
Peter Steiniger, Accounting Manager
Stella Zhu, Accountant

Provider of materials science research services focusing on product development in the field of micro electrical mechanical systems.

Analog Bits Inc   HQ
945 Stewart Dr Ste 250
Sunnyvale CA 94085
P: 650-314-0200   F: 650-618-1976   PRC:212
analogbits.com
Email: sales@analogbits.com
Estab: 1995

Mahesh Tirupattur, EVP
Will Wong, Director of Customer Support
Jimmy Lam, Engineer
Amit Kumar, Circuit Design Engineer
Mary Lee, IC Mask Layout Designer

Supplier of low-power, customizable analog IP for modern CMOS digital chips. The company also offers interfaces and converters.

Analogix Semiconductor Inc   HQ
3211 Scott Blvd Ste 100
Santa Clara CA 95054
P: 408-988-8848   F: 408-988-8686   PRC:86
www.analogix.com
Email: info@analogixsemi.com
Estab: 2002

Kewei Yang, CEO
Ning Zhu, CTO
Mike Seifert, CFO
Hing Chu, VP of WW Operations
Andre Bouwer, VP of Marketing

Designer of mixed-signal semiconductors. The company offers input-output display translators, timing controllers, and accessory display converters.

Analytical Sciences LLC   HQ
110 Liberty St
Petaluma CA 94952
P: 707-769-3128   PRC:303
analyticalsciences.net
Estab: 1995

Joe Furlong, General & Sales Manager

Provider of laboratory services. The company specializes in environmental testing and analytical chemistry.

Anamet Inc   HQ
26102 Eden Landing Rd Ste 3
Hayward CA 94545
P: 510-887-8811   F: 510-887-8427   PRC:142
www.anametinc.com
Email: info@anametinc.com
Estab: 2002

William Cady, President
Kenneth R. Pytlewski, Director of Engineering & Laboratories
Harold R. Harlan, Director
Edward A. Foreman, Quality Control Manager
Dilip Bhandarkar, Testing Manager & Senior Materials Engineer

Provider of materials engineering analysis and lab testing services. The company focuses on product testing, failure analysis, and forensic engineering.

Anand Systems Inc   HQ
35 E Tenth St Ste F
Tracy CA 95376
P: 209-830-1484   F: 209-830-0593   PRC:323
www.anandsystems.com
Email: info@anandsystems.com
Estab: 1998

Pratic Patel, President & CEO
Smita Surti, HR Manager
Anil Patel, Project Manager
Pratik Vakil, System Analyst

Designer of custom software solutions for the hotel industry. The company also offers related hardware, website design, and surveillance systems.

Anaspec Inc   HQ
34801 Campus Dr
Fremont CA 94555
P: 510-791-9560   F: 510-791-9572   PRC:50
anaspec.com
Email: service@anaspec.com
Estab: 1993

Anita Hong, President
Masatoshi Yoshimatsu, CFO
Xiaowei Zhang, Director of Production
Alice Wen, QC Analyst
Deepa Mohan, Scientist

Provider of integrated proteomics solutions for life science research. The company offers peptides, detection reagents, and combinatorial chemistry.

Anatech USA   HQ
2947 Whipple Rd
Union City CA 94587
P: 510-401-5990   F: 510-401-5994   PRC:165
anatechusa.com
Email: info@anatechusa.com
Estab: 2006

Tracy Watts, President
Robert Misata, Sales & Marketing Manager
Melissa Watts, Administrator
Jason Hokett Wright, Manufacturing Technician

Provider of high vacuum systems with plasma technology. The company's applications include flip chips, multichip modules, and photoresist strips.

Anchor Orthotics & Prosthetics   HQ
1828 Tribute Rd Ste G
Sacramento CA 95815
P: 877-977-0448   F: 916-484-0682   PRC:190
anchorot.com

Terry McDonald, President

Provider of orthotics and prosthetics. The company offers personal ankle bionic systems, braces and support and artificial limbs for amputees.

Anchor Semiconductor Inc   HQ
3235 Kifer Rd Ste 200
Santa Clara CA 95051
P: 408-986-8969   F: 408-986-8999   PRC:212
www.anchorsemi.com
Email: info@anchorsemi.com
Estab: 2000

Zhijin Chen, Principle Engineer & Manager of Research & Development

Developer of software to improve IC manufacturing efficiency and chip yield. The company specializes in semiconductor hotspot pattern management.

Anderson Pacific Engineering Construction Inc HQ
 1390 Norman Ave
 Santa Clara CA 95054
 P: 408-970-9900   F: 408-970-9975   PRC:304
 www.andpac.com
 Email: accounting@andpac.com
 Estab: 1960

Karen Thayer, Director of Finance
Andrew Sullivan, Project Manager
Michael Gossett, Project Manager

Provider of constructing and retrofitting pump stations, lift stations, bridges, reservoirs, treatment plants, and seismic retrofit projects.

Andes Technology USA Corp RH
 2860 Zanker Rd Ste 104
 San Jose CA 95134
 P: 408-809-2929   PRC:110
 www.andestech.com
 Email: america@andestech.com
 Estab: 2002

Emerson Hsiao, SVP

Provider of infrastructural solutions for embedded system applications. The company serves the semiconductor industry.

Andover Consulting Group Inc HQ
 1029 S Claremont St
 San Mateo CA 94402
 P: 415-537-6950   PRC:97
 www.andovercg.com
 Email: sales@networktigers.com
 Estab: 1996

Michael Syiek, President & Founder

Supplier of network components. The company offers data center liquidation, network security, and network equipment services.

Andrew Ndt Engineering Corp HQ
 1253 Fleming Ave
 San Jose CA 95127
 P: 408-710-0342   PRC:202
 www.andrewndt.com

Cuong Le, President

Manufacturer of probes, ultrasonic transducers, diamond cutting tools, proximity sensors, cables, and offers calibration services.

Angels Sheet Metal Inc HQ
 2502 Gun Club Rd
 Angels Camp CA 95222
 P: 209-736-4541   PRC:88
 www.angelssheetmetalinc.com
 Estab: 1968

Ron Dwelley, Sales Manager

Provider of sheet metal fabrication services. The company focuses on heating and air conditioning systems.

M-26

Angular Machining Inc HQ
 2040 Hartog Dr
 San Jose CA 95131
 P: 408-954-8326   F: 408-954-0440   PRC:157
 angularmachining.com
 Email: sales@angularmachining.com
 Estab: 1999

Yen Nguyen, Senior Production Planner
Phi Hung Nguyen, Operator

Provider of product manufacturing services for aerospace, telecom, and biomedical sectors and focuses on mechanical assembly and quality control.

Anki Inc HQ
 55 Second St 15th Fl
 San Francisco CA 94105
 P: 415-670-9488   PRC:322
 anki.com
 Email: info@anki.com
 Estab: 2010

Boris Sofman, Co-Founder & CEO
Hanns Tappeiner, Co-Founder & President
Mark Palatucci, Co-Founder & Chief Product Officer
Craig Rechenmacher, CMO
Gabriel Hebert, VP of Operations

Provider of robotic racing products such as drive and expansion cars, starter, bottleneck and cross-road tracks, and accessories for consumers.

Anmar Metrology Inc HQ
 7726 Arjons Dr   [N]
 San Diego CA 92126
 P: 858-621-2630   F: 858-621-6019   PRC:306
 www.anmar.com
 Emp: 11-50   Estab: 1987

Martin Bakker, President

Firm is a provider of calibration, testing and repair laboratory services and calibration software.

Annexon Inc HQ
 180 Kimball Way 2nd Fl Ste 200
 S San Francisco CA 94080
 P: 650-822-5500   F: 650-636-9773   PRC:268
 www.annexonbio.com
 Email: info@annexonbio.com

Douglas Love, President & CEO
Jennifer Lew, EVP & CFO
Sanjay Keswani, EVP & CMO
Ted Yednock, EVP & Chief Scientific Officer

Focuses on the development of therapeutic products. The company serves patients with complement-mediated neurodegenerative disorders.

Anomali RH
 808 Winslow St
 Redwood City CA 94063
 P: 844-484-7328   PRC:325
 www.anomali.com
 Email: general@anomali.com
 Estab: 2013

Colby Derodeff, Co-Founder
Greg Martin, Co-Founder
Hugh Njemanze, CEO
Wei Huang, CTO
Dan Maier, CMO

Specializes in the delivery of cyber security solutions. The company services to big and small organizations.

Anotek Inc HQ
 2349 Hill St   [N]
 Santa Monica CA 90405
 P: 310-450-5027   F: 310-450-0867   PRC:319
 www.anotek.com
 Email: georgeb@anotek.com
 Estab: 1986

George N. Balanis, Contact

Developer of software and books to teach the Greek language to English speaking people.

Anova Microsystems Inc HQ
 173 Santa Rita Court
 Los Altos CA 94022
 P: 408-941-1888   PRC:209
 www.anova.com
 Estab: 1990

Raymond Chuang, President

Provider of rackmount server cabinets and system components. The company deals with storage and GPU solutions.

Anresco Laboratories HQ
 1375 Van Dyke Ave
 San Francisco CA 94124
 P: 415-822-1100   F: 415-822-6615   PRC:47
 www.anresco.com
 Email: info@anresco.com
 Estab: 1943

David Eisenberg, President
Hingman Mang, Section Supervisor of Gas Chromatography
Cathy Cheng, Section Supervisor of High Performance Liquid Chromatography
Zachary Eisenberg, VP
Vu Lam, Co-Laboratory Director

Provider of analysis and research to food and food-related industries. The company also offers solutions to support the business and analytical specifications.

Anritsu Co DH
 490 Jarvis Dr
 Morgan Hill CA 95037-2809
 P: 408-778-2000   PRC:18
 www.anritsu.com
 Email: marketing-communications@anritsu.com
 Estab: 1895

Hirokazu Hamada, Representative Director & President & Group CEO & Measurement Business Group President
Masumi Niimi, Director & SVP & PQA Group President
Takeshi Shima, Director & SVP & Test & Measurement Company President
Yukihiro Takahashi, Senior Executive Officer & Measurement Business Group Vice President & Chief Service Assurance Busin
Akifumi Kubota, Director & EVP & CFO & Chief Corporate Officer

Provider of test solutions for telecommunication applications. The company also caters to microwave applications.

Ansari Structural Engineers Inc HQ
300 Montgomery St Ste 860
San Francisco CA 94104
P: 415-348-8948 PRC:304
www.ansariinc.com
Email: info@ansariinc.com
Estab: 1999

Mehri Ansari, President & Principal

Provider of structural consulting services. The
company focuses on remodeling, due diligence
studies, equipment anchorage, and structural peer
review.

Ansync Labs HQ
5090 Robert J Mathews Pkwy
El Dorado Hills CA 95762
P: 916-933-2850 PRC:159
www.ansync.com
Estab: 2001

Sam Miller, CEO

Provider of engineering and design services. The
company specializes in electrical engineering,
mechanical engineering, and industrial design.

ANSYS Inc BR
2855 Telegraph Ave Ste 501
Berkeley CA 94705
P: 844-462-6797   F: 510-841-8523 PRC:326
www.ansys.com
Estab: 1970

Ajei S. Gopal, President & CEO & Director
Maria T. Shields, CFO & SVP of Finance & Admin-
istration
Shane Emswiler, VP & General Manager of Me-
chanical Fluids & Electronics Business Units
Dipankar Choudhury, VP of Research

Provider of engineering solutions. The company
serves the aerospace, defense, and construction
industries.

Antagene Inc HQ
3350 Scott Blvd Bldg 46 Ste 4602
Santa Clara CA 95054
P: 408-588-1998 PRC:257
www.antageneinc.com
Email: info@antageneinc.com

Ming Mao, CEO

Provider of custom antibody and peptide synthesis. The company is engaged in animal and
histology services.

Antec Inc HQ
47681 Lakeview Blvd
Fremont CA 94538
P: 510-770-1200   F: 510-770-1288 PRC:110
antec.com
Email: customersupport@antec.com
Estab: 1986

Jack Chiu, Sales Account Manager
Katie Chang, Contact

Supplier of computer components and accessories. The company provides enclosures, power
supplies, accessories, and mobile products.

Antech Diagnostics HQ
17620 Mt Herrmann St
Fountain Valley CA 92708
P: 800-872-1001 PRC:23
www.antechdiagnostics.com
Estab: 1994

Rhett Carlin, Group Vice President Sales
Drake Josh, President
Jeffrey L. Edwards, Chief of Anatomic Pathology
Scott Moroff, VP & CSO
Scott Fitzpatrick, Group VP

Provider of diagnostic and laboratory testing
services for chemistry, pathology, endocrinology,
serology, hematology, and microbiology.

Antedo Inc HQ
21952 Lindy Ln
Cupertino CA 95014
P: 408-253-1870 PRC:45
www.antedo.com
Email: ctaysi@antedo.com
Estab: 1994

Candan Taysi, Financial Officer

Provider of consulting services. The company
offers international engineering and management
consulting services.

Anthera Pharmaceuticals Inc HQ
25801 Industrial Blvd Ste B
Hayward CA 94545
P: 510-856-5600   F: 510-856-5597 PRC:257
www.anthera.com
Email: info@anthera.com
Estab: 2004

James E. Pennington, CMO
Philip Sager, Group VP
Paul Adams, SVP of Global Regulatory Affairs &
Compliance
John Craig Thompson, Director
Nicole Ramza, Clinical Program Manager

Manufacturer of biopharmaceuticals that treat
serious diseases like lupus, lupus with glomerulo-
nephritis, IgA nephropathy and cystic fibrosis.

Antibodies Inc HQ
PO Box 1560
Davis CA 95617-1560
P: 530-758-4400   F: 530-758-6307 PRC:249
www.antibodiesinc.com
Email: info@antibodiesinc.com
Estab: 1962

Will Fry, President
Shawna Wicks, CEO
Kim Gressard, VP
Rick Gould, Manager Biochemistry
Ricardo Rodarte, Manager of OEM Manufacturing

Manufacturer of monoclonal and polyclonal antibodies, diagnostic reagents, diagnostic kits, and
developer of immunoassays.

Antibody Solutions HQ
1130 Mountain View Alviso Rd
Sunnyvale CA 94089
P: 650-938-4300   F: 408-734-0400 PRC:26
www.antibody.com
Email: solutions@antibody.com
Estab: 1995

Judith Lynch-Kenney, CFO & Co-Founder
John S. Kenney, Co-Founder & President
Joshua Lowitz, Project Manager
Michael Trang, Project Manager
John Nichols, Project Manager

Provider of antibody products and services. The
company serves biotechnology, diagnostic and
pharmaceutical companies.

Anvato Inc HQ
1600 Amphitheatre Pkwy
Mountain View CA 94043
P: 866-246-6942 PRC:318
www.anvato.com
Email: info@anvato.com
Estab: 2007

Alper Turgut, Contact

Provider of video software platform to television
broadcasters and offers live and on-demand video
management, analytics, and tracking features.

Anybots 20 Inc BR
6341 San Ignacio Ave
San Jose CA 95119-1202
P: 877-594-1836   F: 650-745-2487 PRC:68
anybots.com
Email: support@anybots.com
Estab: 2001

April Buchheit, Office Assistant

Provider of robotic device that acts as a personal
remote avatar which can be operated remotely
thus creating a virtual presence.

Apex Envirotech Inc HQ
11291 Pyrites Way Ste B
Gold River CA 95670
P: 800-242-5249   F: 916-851-0177 PRC:142
apexenvirotech.com
Estab: 1993

Tom Landwehr, President
Brandon Poteet, Field Services Department
Manager
Lisa Nicodemus, Contact

Provider of environmental management and
remediation technology. The company also offers
engineering services.

Apex Technology Management Inc HQ
310 Hemsted Dr Ste 300
Redding CA 96002
P: 530-248-1000   F: 530-243-9184 PRC:326
apex.com
Email: info@apex.com
Estab: 1991

Scott Putnam, President & CEO
Tom Grisell, Virtual CIO
George Passidakis, Director of Sales & Marketing
Daniel Langenberg, Project Manager
Tiffany Chipley, Finance Clerk II

Provider of information technology services such
as business continuity planning, virtualization, and
email protection.

Apex Testing Labs HQ
1790 Yosemite Ave
San Francisco CA 94124
P: 415-550-9800   F: 415-550-9880   PRC:306
www.apextestinglabs.com
Email: info@apextestinglabs.com

Weimin Jiang, Manager
Norbu Dhonyo, Marketing Manager
Josh Sircy, Construction Inspector

Provider of testing and inspection services. The
company engages in the geotechnical engineering
and inspection of construction materials.

Apexigen HQ
75 Shoreway Rd Ste C
San Carlos CA 94070
P: 650-931-6236   F: 650-931-6235   PRC:34
www.apexigen.com
Email: info@apexigen.com
Estab: 2010

Xiaodong Yang, President
Kenneth Fong, Chairman of the Board
Mark Nevins, VP of Business Development
Jamie Grayson, Director of Project Management
Christine Tan, Antibody Discovery Manager

Specializes in document management and
managed print solutions. The company serves the
business sector.

Apixio Inc HQ
1850 Gateway Dr 3rd Fl
San Mateo CA 94404
P: 877-427-4946   PRC:194
www.apixio.com
Estab: 2009

Darren Schulte, CEO
John Schneider, CTO
Mark Scott, CMO
Meg Holland, COO
Tom McNamara, Chief Growth Officer

Provider of cognitive computing platform that
enables the analysis of unstructured healthcare
data at individual level, providing groundbreaking
insights.

Aplena Inc HQ
1500 E Hamilton Ave Ste 213
Campbell CA 95008
P: 408-256-0030   F: 408-273-6993   PRC:40
aplena.com

Norm Shockley, CEO
Larkin Ryder, Director of Process & Compliance

Provider of technology solutions for data center
services. The company offers relocation, installation, and managed services.

APLEX Technology Inc BR
2065 Martin Ave Ste 107
Santa Clara CA 95050
P: 669-999-2500   F: 669-999-2499   PRC:110
www.aplextec.com
Email: sales@aplextec.com
Estab: 2004

David Kok, General Manager
Siddhartha Khadka, Production Engineer

Manufacturer of industrial displays, heavy-duty
expendables, industrial panels, and related accessories. The company serves the healthcare sector.

Apneos Corp HQ
2033 Ralston Ave Ste 41
Belmont CA 94002
P: 650-591-2895   F: 501-694-9807   PRC:268
apneos.com
Email: info@apneos.com
Estab: 2001

William Howard Taft, President

Developer of services for healthcare professionals. The company detects and manages sleep
breathing disorders.

Apogee Software Inc HQ
19039 Overlook Rd
Campbell CA 95030
P: 408-369-9001   F: 408-369-9018   PRC:319
apogee.com
Email: info@apogee.com
Estab: 1988

George Malek, President & CEO
Yuko Malek, CFO

Provider of integrated development environment
for Java and C. The company offers industrial
monitors and controllers.

Apolent Corp HQ
2570 N First St Ste 200
San Jose CA 95131
P: 408-203-6828   F: 408-262-4783   PRC:325
apolent.com
Email: info@apolent.com
Estab: 2006

Dinesh Kumar, VP
Chetan Sharma, Business Development Manager
Gary Winblad, Staff Engineer
Ed Chang, System Architect

Provider of business process and software
technology outsourcing services focusing on niche
market segments.

Apollomics Inc HQ
989 East Hillsdale Blvd Ste 220
Foster City CA 94404
P: 925-272-4090   F: 925-272-4094   PRC:196
www.apollomicsinc.com
Estab: 2016

Sanjeev Redkar, President & Founder
Tillman Pearce, CMO
Gavin Choy, EVP & COO

Developer of oncology therapeutics. The company
focuses on discovering therapeutics for the
immune system and molecular pathways to treat
cancer.

AppEnsure HQ
111 N Market St Ste 300
San Jose CA 95113
P: 408-418-4602   F: 408-418-4603   PRC:40
appensure.com
Email: info@appensure.com
Estab: 2012

Sri Chaganty, COO, CTO & Founder
Colin Macnab, CEO
Subha Chaganty, Director of fshore Operations

Provider of cloud application performance and
infrastructure management such as applica-
tion-aware infrastructure performance management solution.

APPL Inc HQ
908 N Temperance Ave
Clovis CA 93611
P: 559-275-2175   F: 559-275-4422   PRC:306
www.applinc.com
Estab: 1982

BJ Watrous, VP & Chief IP Counsel
Priya Balasubramaniam, VP of Operations
Mark Steinberg, Automation Manager

Provider of analytical testing services. The
company specializes in analysis of environmental
samples for chemical pollutants.

Apple Inc HQ
One Apple Pkwy
Cupertino CA 95014
P: 408-996-1010   PRC:209
www.apple.com
Estab: 1976
Sales: Over $3B

Steve Wozniak, Founder
Tim Cook, CEO
Jeff Williams, COO
Luca Maestri, CFO & SVP
Michael Tchao, VP of Product Marketing

Designer and marketer of consumer electronics.
The company also focuses on computer software
and personal computers.

Applian Technologies Inc HQ
20 Vineyard Ave
San Anselmo CA 94960
P: 415-480-1748   F: 415-373-0558   PRC:322
www.applian.com
Estab: 1997

Bill Dettering, CEO
Tom Mayes, COO
Leslie Bee, Director of Marketing

Provider of solutions for the capture and conversion of web video, streaming audio, and song and
radio program software for Windows users.

Applied Aerospace Structures Corp HQ
3437 S Airport Way
Stockton CA 95206
P: 209-983-3314   F: 209-983-3375   PRC:8
www.aascworld.com
Email: marketing@aascworld.com
Estab: 1954

John Rule, President
Patrick Hart, Director of Business Development
Mike Guthmiller, Director of Quality Assurance
Harry Davis, Materials Manager
John Regan, Marketing Manager

Designer of space and aircraft metal structures.
The company also specializes in fabrication and
other services.

Applied Ceramics Inc HQ
48630 Milmont Dr
Fremont CA 94538
P: 510-249-9700   F: 510-249-9797   PRC:212
www.appliedceramics.net
Estab: 1994

David Kolaric, General Manager
Rick Le, Chemical Manager

Manufacturer of custom ceramics, quartz silicon,
stainless steel, and sapphire for the semiconductor industries.

Applied Computer Solutions   BR
    3825 Hopyard Rd Ste 220
    Pleasanton CA 94588
P: 925-251-1000   F: 925-467-1937   PRC:324
acsacs.com
Email: info@acsacs.com
Estab: 1989

Elaine Bellock, President
Mark Andrion, Director of Professional Services
Joey Mendoza, Senior Account Manager
Dennis DiPietro, Manager of Sales Operations
Cheryl Heslington, Inside Sales Manager

Provider of information technology solutions.
The company offers solutions for virtualization,
storage, security, and networking.

Applied Earthworks Inc   HQ
    1391 W Shaw Ave Ste C
    Fresno CA 93711-3600
P: 559-229-1856   PRC:142
appliedearthworks.com
Email: info@appliedearthworks.com
Estab: 1995

Barry A. Price, Chairman of the Board & Principal
Archaeologist
Mary Clark Baloian, President & Principal Archae-
ologist
Jennifer Barbee, CAO
Ann Munns, Regional Manager & Senior Archae-
ologist & Laboratory Director
Brian Kellogg, Accounting Manager

Provider of history, archaeology, paleontology,
and cultural resources management and related
services.

Applied Engineering   HQ
    6341 San Ignacio Ave Ste 10
    San Jose CA 95119
P: 408-286-2134   F: 408-971-0776   PRC:209
www.appliedengineering.com
Email: sales@appliedengineering.com
Estab: 1979

Jack Yao, President & CFO
Jerry Cutini, Chairman
John Villadsen, COO
Mark Danna, VP of sales & Marketing
Colleen Sweeney, VP of Operations & General
Manager

Provider of contract electronics manufacturing
services. The company also specializes in clean
room assembly services.

Applied Engineering   HQ
    991 Montague Expy Ste 207
    Milpitas CA 95035
P: 408-263-5900   F: 408-263-5915   PRC:304
www.appliedse.com
Email: info@appliedse.com
Estab: 1991

Sasson Rajabi, Owner
Jinken Cho, Structural Design Engineer

Provider of structural analysis and seismic evaluation services. The company is involved in specialty
engineering and project management.

Applied Expert Systems Inc   HQ
    PO Box 50927
    Palo Alto CA 94303
P: 650-617-2400   F: 650-617-2420   PRC:322
www.aesclever.com
Email: info@aesclever.com
Estab: 1991

David Cheng, VP of Engineering
Candy Tyner, Business Development Manager

Developer of networking solutions for business
service management. The company provides
virtualization and cloud computing services.

Applied Fusion Inc   HQ
    1915 Republic Ave
    San Leandro CA 94577
P: 510-351-8314   F: 510-351-0692   PRC:80
www.appliedfusioninc.com
Email: sales@appliedfusioninc.com
Estab: 1972

Kirk Campbell, Chief Strategic Officer
George Silva, VP of Manufacturing
John Kuhl, General Manager
Steve Lockert, Safety Manager
Jim Warner, Project Engineering Manager

Provider of precision metal fabrication, electron beam
and laser welding, and CNC machining services.

Applied Interconnect Inc   HQ
    1262 Lawrence Station Rd
    Sunnyvale CA 94089-2218
P: 408-749-9900   F: 408-734-9770   PRC:62
onlinecables.com
Email: sales@onlinecables.com

John Claras, CEO & Founder

Supplier of cables and electro mechanical assemblies. The company also specializes in microwave
sub-assemblies.

Applied Materials & Engineering Inc   HQ
    980 41st St
    Oakland CA 94608
P: 510-420-8190   PRC:304
www.appmateng.com
Email: info@appmateng.com
Estab: 1988

Dushyant Manmohan, Principal & Founder
Tae Kyung Won, Director of Engineering
Nadine Alexis, Application Engineer
Mohammed Faiyaz, Senior Engineer
Armen Tajirian, Principal

Provider of construction materials consulting
services. The company focuses on petrographic
and laboratory testing services.

Applied Materials Inc   HQ
    3050 Bowers Ave
    Santa Clara CA 95054-3299
P: 408-727-5555   F: 760-436-4774   PRC:212
appliedmaterials.com
Email: staffing_inquiries@amat.com
Estab: 1967
Sales: Over $3B

Gary E. Dickerson, President & CEO
Jay Kerley, CIO
Dan Durn, CFO
Gino Addiego, SVP of Engineering, Operations &
Quality
Prabu G. Raja, SVP

Provider of equipment, services, and software
for the manufacture of semiconductor, flat panel
display, and solar photovoltaic products.

Applied Membranes Inc   HQ
    2450 Business Park Dr   [N]
    Vista CA 92081
P: 800-321-9321   PRC:144
www.appliedmembranes.com
Email: sales@appliedmembranes.com
Estab: 1983

Gil Dhawan, President

Manufacturer of water treatment membranes and
systems.

Applied Motion Products Inc   HQ
    404 Westridge Dr
    Watsonville CA 95076
P: 831-761-6555   F: 831-761-6544   PRC:98
www.applied-motion.com
Email: customerservice@applied-motion.com
Estab: 1978

Jeff Kordik, CTO
Sally Lovejoy, VP of Administration & Accounting
Julie Georgiana, Director of Manufacturing
Dennis Joyce, Manager of East Regional Sales
Jim Amos, Applications Engineer

Manufacturer of stepper drives and motors, gearheads, power supplies, and related accessories.
The company offers technical support services.

Applied Optics Inc   HQ
    3349 Vincent Rd
    Pleasant Hill CA 94523
P: 925-932-5686   F: 925-932-2502   PRC:173
www.applied-optics.com
Email: service@applied-optics.com
Estab: 1973

Gery Koch, President & CFO & COO
Annette Hurst, CNC Operator & Optical Technician
Milton Biagas, Optic Polisher

Provider of precision optical components and custom optics. The company is engaged in delivery
and installation services.

Applied Photon Technology Inc   HQ
    3346 Arden Rd
    Hayward CA 94545
P: 510-780-9500   F: 510-780-1798   PRC:243
www.appliedphoton.com
Email: info@appliedphoton.com
Estab: 2002

Len Goldfine, President & CEO
Barry Smith, VP of Sales & Marketing
Rodney Romero, VP of Engineering
Rafael Olano, VP of Manufacturing
Tian Liu, Business Development Manager

Provider of precision flash lamps. The company's
products include Krypton arc lamps, OEM's and
APT's laser flash lamps, and specialty lamps.

Applied Physics Systems   HQ
    425 Clyde Ave
    Mountain View CA 94043
P: 650-965-0500   F: 650-965-0404   PRC:87
appliedphysics.com
Email: info@appliedphysics.com
Estab: 1976

Tim Pletschet, Senior Mechanical Engineer &
Chief Mechanical Engineer

Supplier of magnetic measure and other electronic equipment. The company specializes in
measurement while drilling systems and magne-
tometers.

Applied Process Cooling Corp HQ
4812 Enterprise Way
Modesto CA 95356
P: 209-578-1000   F: 209-578-1021   PRC:159
apcco.net
Estab: 1981

Gary Dunn, President
Dave Hill, North Coat Division Manager
Jim Helsel, Project Engineer
Jodi Smith, Service Engineer
Josh Hill, Project Engineer

Provider of refrigeration solutions. The company's
services include laser alignment, control panel
retrofits, valve exercising, and condenser cleaning.

Applied Spectra Inc HQ
46665 Fremont Blvd
Fremont CA 94538
P: 510-657-7679   PRC:172
www.appliedspectra.com
Email: contact@appliedspectra.com
Estab: 2004

Jong Yoo, President & CEO
Richard Russo, Executive Chairman
Chunyi Liu, SVP
Steve Shuttleworth, VP of Global Sales Management
Zhenhuan Chi, Director of Sales

Manufacturer of analytical instrumentation. The
company's products include J200 Tandem, J200
Femtosecond, Laser Ablation System, and Aurora
LIBS Spectrometer.

Applied Stemcell Inc HQ
521 Cottonwood Dr Ste 111
Milpitas CA 95035
P: 408-773-8007   F: 650-800-7179   PRC:34
www.appliedstemcell.com
Email: info@appliedstemcell.com
Estab: 2008

Ruhong Jiang, Co-Founder & President & CEO
Ruby Yanru Chen-Tsai, Co-Founder & CSO
Michael Cleary, Co-Founder & Associate Chair
Guo-Liang Yu, Executive Chairman & CTO
Maki Ogawa, Marketing Director

Provider of stem cell characterization, gene targeting, teratoma formation, and embryoid body (EB)
formation services.

Applied Systems Engineering Inc HQ
1671 Dell Ave Ste 200
Campbell CA 95008
P: 408-364-0500   F: 408-364-0550   PRC:5
www.ase-systems.com
Email: sales@ase-systems.com
Estab: 1981

Prasanth Gopalakrishnan, President & CEO
Jack Verson, VP

Provider of consulting, software, design, and
testing services. The company's products cater to
communication applications.

**Applied Wireless Identifications
Group Inc** HQ
18300 Sutter Blvd
Morgan Hill CA 95037
P: 408-825-1100   F: 408-782-7402   PRC:68
awid.com
Email: support@awid.com
Estab: 1997

Elizabeth Wei, Senior SW Engineer

Provider of communication systems for engineering applications. The company also offers
modules, antennas, and accessories.

Applozic Inc HQ
Stanford Financial Sq 2600 El Camino Real
Ste 415
Palo Alto CA 94306
P: 310-909-7458   PRC:315
www.applozic.com
Email: contact@applozic.com
Estab: 2015

Devashish Mamgain, Co-Founder & CEO
Adarsh Kumar, Co-Founder & CTO
Vigil Vishwanathan, Director of Sales & Marketing
Monamie Reddy, HR Manager

Empowers businesses with in-app messaging
solutions and all-in-one customer support solution.

Appro Technology Inc BR
1180 Miraloma Way Ste E
Sunnyvale CA 94085
P: 408-720-0018   F: 408-720-0019   PRC:59
appro-us.com
Email: info@appro-us.com

Spencer Tsai, President
Wang Bao Luo, VP
Jeffrey Yang, Hardware Manager
Charlie Liu, Sales Manager

Manufacturer of network surveillance systems.
The company's products include dome cameras,
LCD monitors, and cables.

Apptimize Inc HQ
330 Townsend St Ste 234
San Francisco CA 94107
P: 415-926-5398   PRC:315
apptimize.com
Email: contact@apptimize.com
Estab: 2013

Scott Ings, VP of Product
Craig Gering, VP of Engineering

Providers of robust mobile experimentation and
optimization solution to improve an user's mobile
experience through A/B testing.

Apptology HQ
2260 E Bidwell St
Folsom CA 95630
P: 877-990-2777   PRC:322
www.apptology.com
Email: information@apptology.com
Estab: 2009

Rich Foreman, Co-Founder & CEO
Dana Smith, Co-Founder & CMO
Gary Dalal, CTO
Michelle Bocchicchio, Director of Sales
Robin Foreman, Account Manager

Provider of mobile application development, training, marketing, iPhone application development,
and Android application development services.

Apt Electronics Inc HQ
241 N Crescent Way   [N]
Anaheim CA 92801
P: 714-687-6760   F: 714-687-6900   PRC:209
www.aptelectronics.com
Emp: 51-200   Estab: 1999

Dale Robertson, VP of Operations
Michael Sprague, General Manager
Ernie Calderon, Manager of Materials
Imran Ahmad, Manager

Manufacturer of automated electronics contract
products and specializes in surface mount.

Aptible Inc HQ
548 Market St Ste 75826
San Francisco CA 94104
P: 866-296-5003   PRC:68
www.aptible.com
Email: hello@aptible.com
Estab: 2013

Chas Ballew, Co-Founder & CEO
Frank MacReery, Co-Founder & CTO
Caroline Lau, VP of People
Henry Hund, VP of Operations
Skylar Anderson, VP of Design

Developer of secure, private cloud deployment
platform built to automate HIPAA compliance for
digital health.

Apttus Corp HQ
1400 Fashion Island Blvd Ste 100
San Mateo CA 94404
P: 650-445-7700   PRC:315
apttus.com
Estab: 2006

Neehar Giri, Co-Founder
Kent Perkocha, Co-Founder
Frank Holland, CEO
Praniti Lakhwara, CIO
Sam Zayed, CRO

Developers of AI revenue intelligence software.

APX Power Markets Inc BR
2150 N First St Ste 200
San Jose CA 95131
P: 408-517-2100   PRC:142
apx.com
Email: intellectualproperty@apx.com
Estab: 1996

Jason Brome, CTO
Carl Schlemmer, Demand Response product
Manager
Lars Kvale, Head of Business Development
Nino Mijares, East Desk Supervisor
Crystal Baird-Martowski, Research Analyst

Provider of e-commerce services for the electrical
sector. The company serves residential, commercial, and industrial properties.

AQS Inc   DH
47817 Fremont Blvd
Fremont CA 94538
P: 510-249-5800   F: 510-249-5810   PRC:189
www.aqs-inc.com
Email: info@aqs-inc.com
Estab: 1991

Ali Shareef, Owner & CEO
Amir Nosrati, Quality Engineer

Provider of electronic manufacturing solutions.
The company offers electronic assembly, test
engineering, system integration and final test
services.

Aqua Metrology Systems Ltd   HQ
1225 E Arques Ave
Sunnyvale CA 94085
P: 408-523-1900   PRC:11
www.aquametrologysystems.com
Email: info@aquametrologysystems.com
Estab: 2007

Rick Bacon, CEO
Jim Garvey, Director of Engineering & Customer
Service

Developer of online and offline analytical instrumentation for determination of water contaminants
and trace metals for municipal and industrial
markers.

Aqua Sierra Controls Inc   HQ
1650 Industrial Dr
Auburn CA 95603
P: 530-823-3241   F: 530-823-3476   PRC:159
aquasierra.com
Email: service@aquasierra.com
Estab: 1979

Les Watson, President
Josh Lane, Manager of SCADA

Provider of instrumentation and electrical contract
services. The company specializes in process
control automation for industrial installations.

Aquantia Corp   HQ
91 E Tasman Dr Ste 100
San Jose CA 95134
P: 408-228-8300   PRC:208
www.aquantia.com
Email: info@aquantia.com
Estab: 2004

Phil Delansay, Founder & SVP of Business
Development
Linda Reddick, CFO
Nick Shamlou, VP of Sales
Shelley Hu, Tax Director
John Bray, Supply Chain Manager

Provider of software solutions such as signal
processing, agile management, and technical
support. The company serves the IT sector.

Aquifer Sciences Inc   HQ
3520 Golden Gate Way
Lafayette CA 94549
P: 925-283-9098   PRC:142
www.aquifer.com
Estab: 1988

Becky Sterbentz, President
Duncan Knudsen, Contact

Provider of environmental assessment and remediation services. The company is also engaged in
remedial design and implementation.

Aquifi Inc   HQ
2225 E Bayshore Rd Ste 110
Palo Alto CA 94303
P: 650-213-8535   PRC:316
www.aquifi.com
Email: info@aquifi.com
Estab: 2011

Jason Trachewsky, CEO
Abbas Rafii, CTO
Thomas Sawyer, CFO
Tony Zuccarino, VP
Bin An, Director of Business Development

Developer of fluid technology solutions. The company is involved in computer vision and machine
learning algorithms.

Arable Corp   HQ
10061 Bubb Rd Ste 200
Cupertino CA 95014
P: 408-825-4755   F: 408-659-3732   PRC:269
www.arablecorp.com
Email: info@arablecorp.com
Estab: 2010

Richard K. Williams, President
Ary Sarkar, CEO & Chairman
Brian Fahle, EVP
Daniel Schell, Scientist

Provider of products and services to health care,
pharmaceutical, biotechnology and medical
device companies.

Aragen Bioscience   HQ
380 Woodview Ave
Morgan Hill CA 95037
P: 408-779-1700   F: 408-779-1711   PRC:34
www.aragenbio.com
Email: info@aragenbio.com
Estab: 1993

Oren Beske, President
Axel Schleyer, CEO
Malavika Ghosh, VP
Steven Lang, VP of Biologics
Deepika Kurl, Director of Finance & Corporate
Controller

Provider of services such as protein expression
and purification, molecular biology, immunology,
and in vivo services to the biotech and pharma
industries.

Aragon Consulting Group Inc   HQ
19925 Stevens Creek Blvd Ste 100
Cupertino CA 95014
P: 415-869-8818   PRC:45
www.krugle.com
Email: enterprise-support@krugle.com

Mel Badgett, VP of Product Marketing

Provider of software development services. The
company also offers authoring, coding, consulting,
and technical support solutions.

Aras Power Technologies   HQ
371 Fairview Way
Milpitas CA 95035
P: 408-935-8877   F: 408-935-9177   PRC:76
araspower.com
Email: sales@araspower.com
Estab: 2002

Cf Chu, VP
Kevin Fread, Account Manager
David Greenfield, Application Engineer

Provider of power delivery solutions. The company
offers conventional, alternating current solutions,
and custom power supply design services.

Arasan Chip Systems Inc   RH
2150 N First St Ste 240
San Jose CA 95131
P: 408-433-9633   F: 408-282-7800   PRC:212
arasan.com
Estab: 1996

A.K. Ganesan, President & CEO
Padamunnur Rao, CFO
Prakash Kamath, CTO
Ron Mabry, VP of Worldwide Sales
Chari Santhanam, VP of Engineering

Provider of total IP solutions such as digital IP
cores, protocol analyzers, and traffic generators
for mobile storage and connectivity applications.

Aravo Solutions Inc   HQ
88 Kearny St 12th Fl
San Francisco CA 94108
P: 415-835-7600   F: 415-835-7610   PRC:45
www.aravo.com
Email: info@aravo.com
Estab: 2000

Tim Albinson, Founder & Chairman
Michael Saracini, CEO
Eric Hensley, CTO & CSO
Kimberley Allan, CMO
David Rusher, Chief Customer Officer

Provider of risk and performance management,
Supplier Information Management (SIM), and
related services.

ARBOR Solution Inc   RH
46539 Fremont Blvd
Fremont CA 94538
P: 408-452-8900   F: 408-452-8909   PRC:68
us.arborsolution.com
Email: info1@arborsolution.com
Estab: 1993

Eric Lee, President
Long Hoang, Director of Engineering
Steven Fong, Operations Manager

Provider of embedded computing and networking
solutions for the transportation, medical, automation, and military segments.

Arbor Vita Corp   HQ
48371 Fremont Blvd Ste 101
Fremont CA 94538
P: 408-585-3900   F: 408-585-3901   PRC:28
www.arborvita.com
Email: info@arborvita.com
Estab: 1998

Peter S. Lu, Founder & CEO
Charles R. Trimble, Chairman
Bryan Beacraft, Materials Manager
Pedro Caceres, Facilities Manager
Thuy Tran-Lam, Human Resources Assistant

Provider of protein-based molecular diagnostics
that is used for the management of infectious
diseases and cancer.

ARC HQ
12657 Alcosta Blvd Ste 200
San Ramon CA 94583
P: 925-949-5100 PRC:67
www.e-arc.com
Email: communications@e-arc.com
Estab: 1988
Sales: $300M to $1 Billion

Denis Le Bosse, President
Suriyakumar Kumarakulasingam, CEO & Chairman
Jorge Avalos, CFO
Rahul Roy, CTO
Dilo Wijesuriya, COO

Provider of document management services to the architectural, engineering, and construction industries.

Arcadia Biosciences Inc HQ
202 Cousteau Pl Ste 105
Davis CA 95618
P: 530-756-7077 F: 530-756-7027 PRC:34
www.arcadiabio.com
Email: info@arcadiabio.com
Estab: 2002
Sales: $1M to $3M

Matthew Plavan, President & CEO
Pam Haley, CFO
Randall Shultz, CTO
Roger Salameh, VP of Business Development
Wendy Neal, VP & CLO

Developer of agricultural products with enhanced traits. The company uses technological tools, genetic screening and genetic engineering to achieve this.

ArcherHall HQ
2081 Arena Blvd Ste 200
Sacramento CA 95834
P: 855-839-9084 F: 916-449-2821 PRC:322
www.capitol-digital.com
Estab: 1997

Tristan Hopkins, President
Thon Kong, Production Manager
Karl Rozak, Production Manager
Tim Peregoy, E-Discovery Project Manager
Vang Lor, Production Coordinator

Provider of litigation support services. The company offers forensic data collection, online document review, and e-discovery processing services.

Architectural Cathode Lighting Inc HQ
5301 Pacific Blvd [N]
Huntington Park CA 90255
P: 323-581-8800 F: 323-581-7971 PRC:243
www.cathodelighting.com
Email: aclinfo@cathodelighting.com
Estab: 1970

Eric Zimmerman, Owner

Manufacturer and distributor of neon, cold cathodes and LED lightings.

M-32

Architectural Lighting Works HQ
1035 22nd Ave Unit 1
Oakland CA 94606
P: 510-489-2530 F: 650-249-0412 PRC:243
www.alwusa.com
Email: talktous@alwusa.com
Estab: 2005

Jim Prior, President
Andreas Dankelmann, VP of Operations
Ricardo Vargas, General Manager
Dale Patterson, Finance Manager
Marco Zarate, Purchasing Manager

Manufacturer of suspended, wall, and ceiling lighting products and related accessories. The company also deals with installation services.

Arcscale LLC HQ
PO Box 20621
San Jose CA 95160
P: 408-476-0554 F: 408-267-7980 PRC:68
arcscale.com
Email: info@arcscale.com
Estab: 2005

Sheri Fliss, CFO & Owner

Provider of colocation, technology integration, hosting, implementation, and telecommunication services. The company also deals with procurement.

Arcsoft Inc HQ
46605 Fremont Blvd
Fremont CA 94538
P: 510-440-9901 F: 510-440-1270 PRC:323
www.arcsoft.com
Estab: 1994

Michael Deng, CEO
Mike Ling, VP
Bill Chen, VP & GM of CPSG
Frank Feng, VP
Lisa Zulueta-Rapo, Senior Sales Manager

Developer of multimedia technologies and applications. The company serves both desktop and embedded platforms.

Arcus Technology Inc HQ
3159 Independence Dr
Livermore CA 94551
P: 925-373-8800 F: 925-373-8809 PRC:94
www.arcus-technology.com
Email: info@arcus-technology.com
Estab: 2002

Thomas Judge, Engineering Manager

Provider of motor controllers, stepper motors, and related accessories such as cables, encoders, and gearboxes.

Ardelyx Inc HQ
34175 Ardenwood Blvd Ste 200
Fremont CA 94555
P: 510-745-1700 F: 510-745-0493 PRC:268
www.ardelyx.com
Email: info@ardelyx.com
Estab: 2007
Sales: $3M to $10M

Mike Raab, President & CEO
David Mott, Chairman
Mark Kaufmann, CFO
Reginald Seeto, COO & EVP
David Rosenbaum, Chief Development Officer

Developer of non-systemic and small molecule therapeutics that work in the GI tract to treat cardio-renal, GI, and metabolic diseases.

Ardent Systems Inc HQ
2040 Ringwood Ave
San Jose CA 95131
P: 408-526-0100 PRC:211
ardentsi.com
Email: info@ardentsi.com
Estab: 1989

Thomas Han, President
Seonae Lee, Software Engineer

Provider of electronics manufacturing services and storage device test solutions. The company is engaged in material management services.

Ardica Technologies HQ
2325 Third St Ste 424
San Francisco CA 94107
P: 415-568-9270 PRC:288
ardica.com
Email: info@ardica.com
Estab: 2004

Daniel Braithwaite, Chief Product Officer & Co-Founder
Tibor Fabian, CTO & Co-Founder
Kris Lichter, CEO
John Hardman, CFO
Joe Coury, VP & Fuel Production

Provider of integrated power and fuel cell technology solutions for commercial and military applications.

Area West Environmental Inc HQ
6248 Main Ave Ste C
Orangevale CA 95662
P: 916-987-3362 PRC:142
areawest.net
Email: frontdesk@areawest.net
Estab: 2000

Becky Rozumowicz, President
Cay Goude, Senior Conservation Specialist
Aimee Dour-Smith, Senior Environmental Planner

Provider of environmental assessment services. The company is also engaged in planning, permitting, and regulatory compliance management services.

Areias Systems Inc HQ
5900 Butler Ln Ste 280
Scotts Valley CA 95066
P: 831-440-9800 F: 831-439-9295 PRC:78
www.areiasys.com
Email: sales@areiasys.com
Estab: 2000

Michael Nunns, VP of Quality Assurance
Jonathan Lee, Controls Engineer
George Scott, Supervisor

Provider of services to the technology sector. The company focuses on design, engineering, manufacturing, and prototyping.

ARES Corp HQ
1440 Chapin Ave Ste 390
Burlingame CA 94010
P: 650-401-7100 F: 650-401-7101 PRC:304
www.arescorporation.com
Email: areshq@arescorporation.com
Estab: 1992

Doug Schmidt, CFO
Stanley Lynch, SVP
Jane Stuart, VP of Marketing
Bruce Anich, Deputy Director
Joyce Grant, Controller

Provider of engineering, risk assessment, project
management, and other services and focuses on
nuclear, clean technology, space, and defense
fields.

Aria Technologies Inc HQ
102 Wright Brothers Ave
Livermore CA 94551
P: 925-447-7500 F: 925-447-7511 PRC:62
ariatech.com
Email: sales@ariatech.com
Estab: 1991

Joe McGuinness, President
Paula McGuinness, CEO
David Dickens, VP of Manufacturing
Stash McGuinness, VP of Business Development
Justin Tidd, Manufacturing Manager

Provider of fiber optic cable assemblies and
connectivity products to the data, telecom, and
operator market places.

Aridis Pharmaceuticals LLC HQ
5941 Optical Ct
San Jose CA 95138
P: 408-385-1742 F: 408-960-3822 PRC:248
www.aridispharma.com
Email: info@aridispharma.com
Estab: 2003
Sales: $1M to $3M

Eric J. Patzer, Founder & Chairman
V.U. Truong, CEO
Fred Kurland, CFO
Paul Mendelman, Interim CMO
Steven Chamow, VP of Research & Development

Focuses on anti-infective alternatives to conventional antibiotics. The company offers services to
the pharmaceutical sector.

Arista Corp HQ
40675 Encyclopedia Cir
Fremont CA 94538
P: 510-226-1800 F: 510-405-8437 PRC:93
www.goarista.com
Email: sales@goarista.com
Estab: 1994

Wei Wang, Accounting Manager
Arlinda Nguyen, Western Regional Sales Manager
Zhichen Zhao, Product Material Controller
Dean Kirk, Contact

Manufacturer of industrial computer products
such as industrial rack mounts, touch screen
displays, and fanless, embedded, and wall mount
computers.

Arista Networks Inc HQ
5453 Great America Pkwy
Santa Clara CA 95054
P: 408-547-5500 F: 408-538-8920 PRC:68
arista.com
Email: sales@aristanetworks.com
Estab: 2004
Sales: $1B to $3B

Andy Bechtolsheim, Co-Founder & Chief Develop-
ment Officer & Chairman
Kenneth Duda, Co-Founder
Jayshree Ullal, CEO & President
Anshul Sadana, COO
Ita Brennan, CFO

Provider of cloud networking, network virtualization, high frequency trading, and government
solutions for data center needs.

ARK Diagnostics Inc HQ
48089 Fremont Blvd
Fremont CA 94538
P: 877-869-2320 F: 510-270-6298 PRC:186
www.ark-tdm.com
Email: salesinquiries@ark-tdm.com
Estab: 2003

Byung Moon, VP of Operations
Ryan Olandria, Sales Consultant
Mitchell Low, Research Scientist II
Leopoldo Guerrero, Scientist
Melody Chao, Controller

Manufacturer of in vitro diagnostic products for the
treatment of cancer, veterinary, HIV/AIDS, antifun-
gal drugs, and epilepsy and pain management.

Arm Ltd RH
150 Rose Orchard Way
San Jose CA 95134-1358
P: 408-576-1500 F: 408-576-1501 PRC:212
www.arm.com
Estab: 1990

Dipesh Patel, President IoT Services Group
Graham Budd, President & COO
Rene Haas, President of IP Products Group
Simon Segars, CEO
Jason Zajac, CSO

Manufacturer of digital products and offers wireless, networking, and consumer entertainment
solutions to imaging, automotive, and storage
devices.

Armageddon Energy Inc HQ
949 Hamilton Ave
Menlo Park CA 94025
P: 650-641-2899 PRC:135
www.armageddonenergy.com
Email: info@armageddonenergy.com
Estab: 2008

Mark Goldman, CEO & Founder

Designer and manufacturer of rooftop solar
systems. The company is engaged in installation
services and serves homeowners.

Armite Laboratories Inc HQ
1560 Superior Ave Ste A4 [N]
Costa Mesa CA 92627
P: 949-646-9035 F: 949-646-8319 PRC:54
armitelabs.com
Email: support@armite.com
Estab: 1923

Mike Sandstrum, President & Owner
Megan Sandstrum, Director of Quality Systems

Provider of lubricating oil and grease products.

Armorstruxx HQ
850 Thurman St
Lodi CA 95240-3131
P: 209-365-9400 F: 209-224-0959 PRC:80
www.armorstruxx.com
Email: info@armorstruxx.com
Estab: 2006

Ray Harper, Shipping Receiving Manager
Frank Koukis, Facilities Manager
Leah Arnold, Purchasing Agent

Provider of ballistic and blast protection solutions.
The company offers armor systems design and
integration services.

Array Networks Inc HQ
1371 McCarthy Blvd
Milpitas CA 95035
P: 408-240-8700 F: 408-240-8754 PRC:63
www.arraynetworks.com
Email: info@arraynetworks.com
Estab: 2000

Michael Zhao, President & CEO
Robert Shen, Board Chairman
Vinod Pisharody, CTO & VP Engineering
Sameena Ahmed, CFO
Fara Zarrabi, VP of HW Engineering & Operations

Developer of integrated web traffic management
technology. The company focuses on load balancing and application acceleration solutions.

Arrayit Corp HQ
927 Thompson Pl
Sunnyvale CA 94085
P: 408-744-1331 F: 408-744-1711 PRC:191
www.arrayit.com
Email: arrayit@arrayit.com
Estab: 1999

Mark Schena, President
Todd Martinsky, SVP
William L. Sklar, Financial Consultant

Focuses on the discovery, development and manufacture of proprietary life science technologies
and consumables for disease prevention.

Arrgh!! Manufacturing Company Inc HQ
831 Vallejo Ave
Novato CA 94945-2430
P: 415-897-0220 F: 415-898-0831 PRC:13
www.arrgh.com
Email: sales@arrgh.com
Estab: 1972

Tom Graham, President & CEO
Alan Dedier, Chief Engineer
Allen Coddington, VP
Marc Wilson, General Manager

Manufacturer of battery chargers, controls, battery
discharge alarms, microcomputer charger controls, and gas detectors.

Art's Sheet Metal Manufacturing Inc HQ
16075 Caputo Dr
Morgan Hill CA 95037
P: 408-778-0606 F: 408-778-0879 PRC:88
www.artssheetmetal.com
Email: sales@artssheetmetal.com

Shawn Chizanskos, Owner

Manufacturer of flashings, vents, drainage products, tie plates, and hangers. The company also focuses on distribution aspects.

Artcraft Welding Inc HQ
781 E McGlincy Ln
Campbell CA 95008
P: 408-377-2725 PRC:121
www.artcraftwelding.com

Dan Ammon, Owner

Designer and manufacturer of ultrasonic cleaning equipment. The company specializes in precision cleaning fixtures.

Artec Group Inc BR
2880 Lakeside Dr Ste 135
Santa Clara CA 95054
P: 669-292-5611 PRC:159
www.artec3d.com
Email: info@artec-group.com
Estab: 2007

Anna Galdina, Sales Channel Director

Developer and distributor of 3D scanners and 3D cameras. The company's products include Artec iD, Artec 3D, Viewshape, and Shapify.

Artech Industries Inc HQ
1966 Keats Dr [N]
Riverside CA 92501
P: 951-276-3331 F: 951-276-4556 PRC:209
www.artechloadcell.com
Email: info@artechloadcell.com
Estab: 1985

Girish R. Bera, CFO

Manufacturer and distributor of strain gauge load cells or force transducers.

Arteris Inc HQ
595 Millich Dr Ste 200
Campbell CA 95008
P: 408-470-7300 PRC:86
arteris.com
Estab: 2003

K. Charles Janac, Chairman & CEO & President
Nick Hawkins, CFO
Benoit de Lescure, CTO
Kurt Shuler, VP of Marketing
David Mertens, VP of Worldwide Sales

Provider of interconnect semiconductor IP solutions to system-on-chip makers and serves networking, automotive, video and mobile-phone processors.

Arterys Inc HQ
51 Federal St
San Francisco CA 94107
P: 650-319-7230 PRC:194
arterys.com
Email: info@arterys.com
Estab: 2007

Fabien Beckers, Co-Founder & CEO
John Cilies, Co-Founder & CTO

Developer of medical imaging cloud platform. The company specializes in diagnostic platform to make healthcare more accurate and data driven.

Articulate Solutions Inc HQ
65 Fifth St Ste 100
Gilroy CA 95020
P: 408-842-2275 F: 408-852-0384 PRC:323
www.articulate-solutions.com
Email: info@articulate-solutions.com
Estab: 1991

Katherine Filice, CEO & Executive Creative Director
Jason Raby, Director of Communications
Chi Nguyen, Associate Art Director
Jenny Arellano, Marketing Communication Manager
Dakota Filice, Head of Security

Provider of branding services such as website development, identity design, social media marketing, and search engine optimization.

Artifex Software Inc HQ
1305 Grant Ave Ste 200
Novato CA 94903
P: 415-492-9861 F: 415-492-9862 PRC:323
www.artifex.com
Email: info@artifex.com
Estab: 1993

Miles Jones, President
Scott Sackett, VP of Sales & Licensing

Provider of software solutions for host based applications. The company also focuses on embedded printer markers.

Artium Technologies Inc HQ
470 Lakeside Dr Unit C
Sunnyvale CA 94085
P: 408-737-2364 PRC:172
www.artium.com
Email: info@artium.com
Estab: 1998

William D. Bachalo, CEO & President
Khalid Ibrahim, Senior Design Engineer

Developer of products for spray diagnostics, particulate monitoring, and cloud research applications.

ArtNet Pro Inc HQ
2315 Paragon Dr
San Jose CA 95131
P: 408-954-8383 F: 408-954-8380 PRC:172
www.artnetpro.com
Email: sales@artnetpro.com

Meir Polack, President
Tal Hod, Online Sales Manager
Eddie Bernal, Operations Manager

Provider of reused equipment. The company offers direct imaging systems, laser photo plotters, and scanners.

Artwork Conversion Software Inc HQ
417 Ingalls St
Santa Cruz CA 95060
P: 831-426-6163 PRC:316
www.artwork.com
Email: info@artwork.com
Estab: 1987

Steve Dibartolomeo, President & Founder
Hagai Pettel, Sales Manager
Felix Lev, Senior Scientist

Developer of CAD translation programs and CAD viewers software. The company also offers plotting software and IC packaging software.

Aruba HQ
3333 Scott Blvd
Santa Clara CA 95054
P: 408-227-4500 F: 408-752-0626 PRC:63
www.arubanetworks.com
Email: corporate.compliance.hpe@hpe.com
Estab: 2002

Keerti Melkote, President & Founder
Dominic Orr, CEO
Chris Kozup, CMO
Partha Narasimhan, CTO
Vishal Lall, COO

Manufacturer of enterprise network infrastructure equipment. The company serves healthcare, government, education, and other sectors.

ARX Networks Corp HQ
37100 Central Ct
Newark CA 94560
P: 650-403-4000 PRC:325
arxnetworks.com
Email: info@arxnetworks.com
Estab: 1998

Ray Marmash, Founder & President

Provider of IT support and maintenance and cloud services. The company also focuses on unified communications and procurement.

ARX PAX Labs Inc HQ
105 Cooper Ct
Los Gatos CA 95032
P: 408-335-7630 PRC:304
arxpax.com
Estab: 2014

Greg Henderson, Co-Founder & CEO
Jill Henderson, Co-Founder & CCO

Developer of magnetic field architecture technology for structural isolation, recreation and entertainment, industrial automation, and transportation.

Aryaka Networks Inc HQ
1800 Gateway Dr Ste 200
San Mateo CA 94404
P: 888-692-7925 F: 408-273-8430 PRC:325
aryaka.com
Email: info@aryaka.com
Estab: 2008

Ashwath Nagaraj, Founder & CTO
Ram Gupta, Non-Executive Chairman
Matt Carter, CEO
Karen Freitag, CRO
Kelly Hicks, CFO

Provider of cloud-based WAN optimization services. The company focuses on application performance, data protection, and bandwidth reduction.

ASA Computers Inc   HQ
645 National Ave
Mountain View CA 94043
P: 650-230-8000   PRC:92
www.asacomputers.com
Email: sales@asacomputers.com
Estab: 1989

Anu Bhargava, Co-Founder & CFO
Arvind Bhargava, Co-Founder & CEO
Joel Wineland, CTO
Chris Terry, VP of Sales of Racklive Systems
Division
Abhi Shah, VP of Sales of Servers Division

Manufacturer of full service custom servers and
storage systems. The company also focuses on
integration.

Asani Solutions LLC   HQ
2060 Walsh Ave Ste 115
Santa Clara CA 95050
P: 408-330-0821   F: 408-330-0822   PRC:324
www.asani.com
Email: info2@asani.com
Estab: 1999

Ryan Nelson, Senior Systems Administrator

Provider of networking solutions and system
integration services. The company also focuses on
Internet and corporate consulting.

Asap Systems   HQ
355 Piercy Rd
San Jose CA 95138
P: 408-227-2720   F: 408-227-2721   PRC:325
www.asapsystems.com
Email: sales@asapsystems.com
Estab: 1990

Eric Fombona, Owner
Elie Jean Touma, CEO
Megan Swanson, Support & Sales Manager
Joel Segovia, Channel Accounts Manager
Chafic Aouad, Regional Manager

Developer of inventory management and asset
tracking software. The company also offers barcode scanners and printers and RFID tags.

Asbestech Laboratory   HQ
6825 Fair Oaks Blvd Ste 103
Carmichael CA 95608
P: 916-481-8902   F: 916-481-3975   PRC:306
asbestechlab.com
Email: asbestech@sbcglobal.net
Estab: 1987

Tommy G. Conlon, Laboratory Director & Asbestos Lab Manager

Provider of asbestos and lead testing services.
The company also offers transmission electron
microscopes.

Asbestos Tem Laboratories Inc   HQ
3431 Ettie St
Oakland CA 94608
P: 510-704-8930   F: 510-704-8429   PRC:138
asbestostemlabs.com
Estab: 1989

Mark Bailey, President
Chase Aquino, Lab Operations Manager
Dorothea Rastegar, Accounting Manager
Tom Suess, Quality Manager
Gabriela Mondar, Administrative Assistant

Provider of laboratory services including asbestos
and lead testing. The company serves geologists,
contractors, and homeowners.

Asbury Graphite Incorporated of CA   BR
2855 Franklin Canyon Rd
Rodeo CA 94572
P: 510-799-3636   F: 510-799-7460   PRC:278
asbury.com
Email: asburyinfo@asbury.com
Estab: 1895

Noah Nichelson, President
Stephen Riddle, CEO
Sue Rish, VP & CFO
Lew Fish, VP of Sales
Marc Stassen, General Manager Asbury Graphite
& Carbons

Supplier of carbon and graphite products for the
chemicals, cement, rubber, and metal industries.
The company's products include coals, cokes, and
carbon fiber.

ASC Profiles LLC   HQ
2110 Enterprise Blvd
West Sacramento CA 95691-3428
P: 916-372-0933   F: 253-896-8471   PRC:82
ascprofiles.com
Email: ar@ascprofiles.com
Estab: 1971

Susan Nahlen, Senior Accountant
John Fitch, Outside Sales Representative

Supplier of building products such as panels, roofing products, and standing seams. The company
serves the commercial and residential markers.

Ascendance Wireless LLC   HQ
11760 Atwood Rd Ste 6
Auburn CA 95603
P: 530-887-8300   F: 530-889-1255   PRC:61
www.ascendancewireless.com
Email: sales@ascendancewireless.com
Estab: 2004

Mark Cederloff, President & CEO

Designer and manufacturer of fixed wireless networks. The company finds application in security
and surveillance needs.

Ascendis Pharma A/S   BR
500 Emerson St
Palo Alto CA 94301
P: 650-352-8389   F: 650-618-1592   PRC:34
www.ascendispharma.com
Email: info@ascendispharma.com
Estab: 2006

Jan Moller Mikkelsen, President & CEO
Michael Wolff Jensen, Chairman & SVP & CLO
Scott T. Smith, SVP & CFO
Thomas A. Larson, SVP & CCO
Lars Waehrens, VP

Focuses on the creation of drug candidates,
proteins, peptides and small molecules, suitable
for either local or systemic treatment.

Ascentool   HQ
3711 Yale Way
Fremont CA 94538
P: 510-683-9332   PRC:165
www.ascentool.net/home.html
Estab: 2005

George Guo, Chairman & CEO
Miya Yang, Finance Manager
Efrain A. Velazquez, Electrical Engineer

Designer, manufacturer, and marketer of vacuum
thin-film deposition systems for making solar
photovoltaic devices.

ASCENX Technologies Inc   HQ
41900 Christy St
Fremont CA 94538
P: 408-945-1997   F: 408-945-1999   PRC:202
www.ascenx.com
Email: info@ascenx.com
Estab: 2003

Tung Bach, President & CEO

Provider of engineering services to the semiconductor industry. The company is also engaged in
contract manufacturing and repair services.

Asepco Corp   HQ
1161 Cadillac Ct
Milpitas CA 95035
P: 650-691-9500   F: 650-691-9600   PRC:78
www.watson-marlow.com
Email: info.asepco@wmftg.com
Estab: 1989

Mark Embury, EVP
Barry Hoffman, Customer Service Lead
Terry Flanders, Designer

Manufacturer of valves and magnetic mixers. The
company also offers diaphragms, connectors, and
actuators.

ASF Electric Inc   HQ
76 Hill St
Daly City CA 94014-2504
P: 650-755-9032   F: 650-755-2975   PRC:245
www.asfelectric.net
Estab: 1971

Cathy Lagomarsino, President
Caren Ferrari, Director of Human Resource &
Payroll Director
John A. Ferrari, Senior Estimator & Project
Manager
Nicole Lagomarsino, Marketing Communication
Manager & Website content
David Mills, Project Manager

Provider of electrical contracting services. The
company installs fire safety systems for the retail,
health care and public entities.

Ashby Communications   HQ
10642 Industrial Ave Ste 120
Roseville CA 95678
P: 916-960-0701   PRC:71
www.ashbycommunications.com
Email: sales@ashbycommunications.com
Estab: 1991

Brian Ashby, Founder & CEO
Charlie Ashby, President
Ron Reeder, Sales Manager
Abigail Joy, Office Manager
Michael Bird, IT Manager

Provider of voice and data cabling solutions. The
company's services include network installation,
support, spam blocking, and cloud computing.

Ashlock Co   HQ
855 Montague Ave
San Leandro CA 94577
P: 510-351-0560   F: 510-357-0329   PRC:153
www.ashlockco.com
Email: info@ashlockco.com

Karen Hallett, Office Manager & Financial Book-
keeping

Provider of pitting equipment. The company offers
equipment such as cherry pitting, date pitting, and
olive pitting machines.

ASI Controls HQ

5111 Johnson Dr
Pleasanton CA 94588
P: 925-866-8808 F: 925-866-1369 PRC:154
www.asicontrols.com
Email: info@asicontrols.com
Estab: 1986

Paul Chapman, President
Francis Chapman, CEO
Jack Floyd, VP of Sales
Mashuri Warren, Director of Product Development
Bill Chapman, Account Manager

Manufacturer of direct digital controls for HVAC
and light industrial marketplace. The company also
offers networking products and unitary controls.

Asian Pacific Environmental Network HQ

426 17th St Ste 500
Oakland CA 94612
P: 510-834-8920 F: 510-834-8926 PRC:142
apen4ej.org
Email: info@apen4ej.org

Amee Raval, Director of Research
Laiseng Saechao, Political Director
Miya Yoshitani, Executive Director
Ratha Lai, Coordinator
Chiravann Uch, Operations Coordinator

Provider of environmental services. The company
engages in membership of low income immigrant
and refugee communities.

Asmeix Corp HQ

PO Box 5188
Concord CA 94524
P: 877-977-7999 F: 925-930-8223 PRC:320
www.cspec.com
Email: service@cspec.com
Estab: 1985

Mike Bernasek, CEO & President
Fredrik Nilsson, Manager of Sales

Provider of welding procedure software services
such as technical support, installation, maintenance, and demo services.

ASML Silicon Valley BR

399 W Trimble Rd
San Jose CA 95131
P: 669-265-3200 PRC:159
www.asml.com

Martin van den Brink, President & CTO
Peter Wennink, CEO
Roger Dassen, EVP & CFO
Frederic Schneider-Maunoury, EVP & COO
Frits van Hout, CSO & EVP

Manufacturer of lithography systems for semiconductor industries. The company also offers
customized imaging solutions.

M-36

Aspen Environmental Group BR

235 Montgomery St Ste 640
San Francisco CA 94104
P: 415-955-4775 F: 415-955-4776 PRC:139
www.aspeneg.com
Email: business@aspeneg.com
Estab: 1991

Hamid Rastegar, Founder
Jon Davidson, EVP
Tom Murphy, VP
Susan Lee, VP
Chris Huntley, Senior Biologist & Biological Group
Manager

Provider of environmental compliance, impact
assessment, and mitigation services. The company's services include construction monitoring and
project management.

Aspera Inc HQ

5900 Hollis St Ste E
Emeryville CA 94608
P: 510-849-2386 F: 510-868-8392 PRC:323
www.asperasoft.com
Email: info@asperasoft.com
Estab: 2004

Richard Heitmann, VP of Marketing
Chris Markle, Director of Engineering
Scott Burger, Demand Generation Manager
Charles Shiflett, Software Engineer

Developer of file transport technologies. The
company provides client and server software,
consoles, and mobile uploaders.

Aspire Systems Inc BR

1735 Technology Dr Ste 260
San Jose CA 95110
P: 408-260-2076 F: 408-904-4591 PRC:325
www.aspiresys.com
Email: info@aspiresys.com
Estab: 1996

Gowri Shankar Subramanian, CEO
Sridhar Ps, SVP of Finance & Administration
Sunil J N V, EVP of Delivery
Andy Chadha, Director
Prathap Valliyatil Achuthan, Head of North Ameri-
ca Retail Sales

Provider of product engineering, infrastructure
and application support, and testing services. The
company serves healthcare and education fields.

Assay Technology Inc HQ

1382 Stealth St
Livermore CA 94551
P: 925-461-8880 F: 925-461-7149 PRC:233
www.assaytech.com
Email: custservice@assaytech.com
Estab: 1981

Rena Kirkpatrick, Chief Marketing Advisor
Steve Green, Director of Laboratories & General
Manager
Beth Hager Green, Marketing Manager of Product
Specialist
Veronica Liebowitz, Quality Control Technician

Provider of personal monitoring badges to monitor chemicals in worker's breathing zone. The
company also analyzes the contents of returned
samplers.

Assembly Biosciences Inc RH

331 Oyster Point Blvd 4th Fl
S San Francisco CA 94080
P: 833-509-4583 PRC:34
www.assemblybio.com
Email: info@assemblybio.com
Estab: 2014

Derek A. Small, Co-Founder & President & CEO
& Director
Uri Lopatin, Co-Founder & CMO & VP of Re-
search & Development
Richard Colonno, CSO
Qi Huang, VP
Jennifer Troia, SVP

Developer of therapeutics for the treatment of
hepatitis B virus (HBV) infection. The company
specializes in clinical trials.

Assembly Tek HQ

175 El Pueblo Rd Ste 27
Scotts Valley CA 95066
P: 831-439-0800 PRC:62
assemblytek.com
Estab: 1987

Glenn Smith, CEO

Manufacturer of custom cables. The company
offers services like design, laminating, JIT programs, and wire preparation.

Assia Inc HQ

203 Redwood Shores Pkwy Ste 100
Redwood City CA 94065
P: 650-654-3400 F: 650-654-3404 PRC:326
assia-inc.com
Email: info@assia-inc.com
Estab: 2003

John M. Cioffi, CEO
Tuncay Cil, SVP of Product Management
Assia Cioffi, EVP of Operations
Jarrett Miller, VP
Sina Zahedi, Director of System Engineering

Provider of broadband solution such as cloud
check, technology licensing, DSL expresse, and
expresse products and solution.

**Associated Lighting Representatives
(ALR) Inc** HQ

7777 Pardee Ln
Oakland CA 94621
P: 510-638-3800 F: 510-638-2908 PRC:245
www.alrinc.com
Estab: 1961

Margaret Porpora, Manager
Dave Ruth, Principal of Information Technology
Dennis Davis, Contractor & Distributor - East Bay

Provider of lighting services. The company offers
controls, emergency, indoor, LED, outdoor and
pole lighting from several manufacturers.

Associated Pathology Medical Group Inc   HQ

105A Cooper Ct
Los Gatos CA 95032
P: 408-399-5050   PRC:303
apmglab.com
Email: services@apmglab.com
Estab: 1956

Julia S. Chan, President & Medical Director
Werner J. Stamm, Director of Cytopathology
Leonard A. Valentino, Pathologist
Jeffrey F. Young, Pathologist
Katharine A. Brady, Pathologist

Provider of medical care services. The company focuses on women's health, dermatopathology, family practice, and urology areas.

Associated Production Music LLC   BR

6255 W Sunset Blvd Ste 900   [N]
Hollywood CA 90028
P: 323-461-3211   F: 323-461-9102   PRC:60
www.apmmusic.com
Email: info@apmmusic.com
Estab: 1984

Adam Taylor, President
Adam Weitz, Executive Director
Bob Frymire, Executive Director
Bruce Amdur, Executive Director
Caron Nightingale, Director of Sales

Provider of music such as various genres and categories.

Associated Television International   HQ

4401 Wilshire Blvd   [N]
Los Angeles CA 90010
P: 323-556-5600   PRC:60
www.associatedtelevision.com
Email: info@associatedtelevision.com
Emp: 51-200   Estab: 1982

Ron Braverman, Director of Marketing

Provider of television production and syndication services.

Assurx Inc   HQ

18525 Sutter Blvd Ste 150
Morgan Hill CA 95037
P: 408-778-1376   F: 408-776-1267   PRC:326
www.assurx.com
Email: info@assurx.com
Estab: 1993

John Kielty, VP of Sales

Provider of quality management and regulatory compliance software solutions for biotechnology, medical devices, pharmaceutical, and energy industries.

Asteelflash   BR

4211 Starboard Dr
Fremont CA 94538
P: 510-440-2840   PRC:200
www.asteelflash.com
Email: info@asteelflash.com
Estab: 1999

Albert Yanez, EVP
Veronique Danciu, Director of Import Export
Peter Wang, Director of Information Technology
Mathieu Kury, Manager of Business Development & Marketing
Johnson Wu, Information Technology Manager

Provider of electronic manufacturing services. The company offers engineering design, contract manufacturing, and delivery services.

Astex Pharmaceuticals   HQ

4420 Rosewood Dr Ste 200
Pleasanton CA 94588
P: 925-560-0100   F: 925-560-0101   PRC:257
www.astx.com
Estab: 1991

Mohammad Azab, President & CMO
David Rees, CSO
Martin Buckland, Chief Corporate Officer
Harold Keer, SVP of Clinical Development
Yong Hao, VP of Biostatistics & Data Management

Developer of small-molecule therapeutics. The company focuses on products for treatment of cancer and central nervous system disorders.

Astreya   HQ

2099 Gateway Pl Ste 140
San Jose CA 95110
P: 800-224-1117   PRC:324
www.astreya.com
Email: sales@astreya.com
Estab: 2001

Jeffrey Freeland, Founder
Andrea Bendzick, CFO
Anita Nunes, SVP of Strategic Sales
Brandon Curry, SVP of Solution Sales
Steve Shaffer, VP of COE & Marketing

Provider of staffing services. The company specializes in recruitment of systems administrators, network engineers, system, and network architects.

Astronic   HQ

2 Orion   [N]
Aliso Viejo CA 92656
P: 949-900-6060   PRC:211
www.astronic-ems.com
Email: info@astronic-ems.com
Estab: 1981

Sang Choi, Contact

Manufacturer of electronic manufacturing devices.

ASUSTeK Computer Inc   HQ

48720 Kato Rd
Fremont CA 94538
P: 510-739-3777   F: 510-608-4555   PRC:105
www.asus.com.tw
Estab: 1989

L. Y. Chen, Senior Director
Lillian Lin, Marketing Director
Isaac Ho, Senior Hardware Engineer

Manufacturer of computer systems and hardware components such as desktops, notebooks, peripherals, motherboards, and graphic cards.

AT&T Inc   BR

1040 Grant Rd
Mountain View CA 94040
P: 650-938-9479   PRC:68
www.att.com
Estab: 1876

Juan Contreras, Director of Content & Programming

Provider of smartphones, TV services, business solutions, wireless networks, and broadband services.

AT&T Inc   BR

1410 E Hatch Rd
Modesto CA 95351
P: 209-556-9042   PRC:64
att.com
Estab: 1876

Sorabh Saxena, President & Business Operations

Provider of IP based communication solutions. The company offers services in the areas of broadband, Wi-Fi, wireless networks, and mobile phones.

ATAC Corp   HQ

2770 De La Cruz Blvd
Santa Clara CA 95050-2624
P: 408-736-2822   F: 408-736-8447   PRC:6
www.atac.com
Estab: 1979

Scott Simcox, President
Wink Winkleman, VP & CFO
Eric Boyajian, Director

Developer of products and services like decision aids, analysis tools, and expert consulting for aviation modeling and simulation.

Atara Biotherapeutics Inc   HQ

611 Gateway Blvd Ste 900
S San Francisco CA 94080
P: 650-278-8930   PRC:254
atarabio.com
Email: office@atarabio.com
Estab: 2012

Christopher Haqq, CMO
John F. McGrath, CFO

Provider of biotherapeutic services. The company focuses on the treatment of cancer, kidney disease, and other illnesses.

Atech Flash Technology Inc   HQ
46045 Warm Springs Blvd
Fremont CA 94539
P: 510-824-6868   F: 510-824-6869   PRC:110
atechflash.com
Email: sales@atechflash.com
Estab: 2001

Hsien-Rong Liang, CEO

Provider of commercial and consumer products
that include drive bay multiple flash card reader,
portable card readers, and iPod accessories.

Athana International Inc   HQ
602 Faye   [N]
Redondo Beach CA 90277
P: 310-539-7280   F: 310-539-6596   PRC:95
www.athana.com
Email: info@athana.com
Estab: 1997

John Wright, Contact

Provider of computer storage devices.

Atheer Inc   HQ
2350 Mission College Blvd Ste 1200
Santa Clara CA 95054
P: 650-933-5004   PRC:319
www.atheerair.com
Estab: 2011

Soulaiman Itani, Founder & CTO
Alka Patel, Accounting Manager

Developer of 3D smart glasses and productivity
application for aerospace, insurance, field maintenance, oil and gas, and healthcare.

ATI North America   HQ
11281 Pyrites Way Ste B
Gold River CA 95670
P: 916-518-1445   PRC:20
www.conquipinc.com
Email: info@wxati.us
Estab: 1994

Bruce Ballard, CEO
Yayun Zhang, Project Manager & Project Manager
Les Hite, Production Manager & Production
Manager
John Dill, Controls Engineer
John Penman, Lead

Manufacturer of converting equipment. The company specializes in volume manufacturing solutions, and also offers repair and upgrade services.

Atlantis Software Inc   HQ
34740 Blackstone Way   [N]
Fremont CA 94555
P: 510-796-2180   PRC:324
www.atlantissoftware.com
Email: asinfo@atlantissoftware.com
Emp: 11-50   Estab: 1991

Sandip Pandey, PHP Developer

Provider of network management solutions.

M-38

Atlas Engineering Services Inc   HQ
135 Spring St
Santa Cruz CA 95060
P: 831-426-1440   PRC:142
atlasengineeringservices.com
Email: atlasengr@calcentral.com

Frederick A. Yukic, President & Principal Engineer
Joshua G. East, Associate Geologist

Provider of environmental consulting services. The
company offers services for aquifer testing, onsite
wastewater disposal, and groundwater sanitary
surveys.

Atlas Testing Laboratories Inc   HQ
9820 Sixth St   [N]
Rancho Cucamonga CA 91730
P: 909-373-4130   F: 909-373-4132   PRC:306
www.atlastesting.com
Emp: 11-50   Estab: 1982

Leo Norton, CEO & Owner
Pete Salazar, VP of Special Projects
Angie Rojas, VP of Sales
Alan Hambley, Technical Director
Sharon Norton, Director of Quality Assurance

Operator of testing laboratories.

Atlassian   BR
350 Bush St 13th Fl
San Francisco CA 94104
P: 415-701-1110   F: 415-449-6222   PRC:323
atlassian.com

Mike Cannon-Brookes, Founder & CEO
Jay Simons, President
Cameron Deatsch, CRO
Jurgen Spangl, Chief Experience Officer
Sid Suri, VP of Marketing

Provider of software development and collaboration tools. The company offers software for
chats, tracking, repository management, and code
hosting.

Atlona Inc   HQ
70 Daggett Dr
San Jose CA 95134
P: 877-536-3976   F: 408-743-5622   PRC:61
www.atlona.com
Email: support@atlona.com
Estab: 2003

Ilya Khayn, Founder & CEO
Michael Khain, VP of Engineering
Harsha Avunoori, Network Engineer
Robert Johnson, Technical Support Engineer
Mark Alain Ramos, Customer Support Supervisor

Provider of technology products for classrooms,
large corporations and small businesses, hospitality venues, and residences.

ATN Corp   HQ
1341 San Mateo Ave
S San Francisco CA 94080
P: 650-989-5100   F: 650-875-0129   PRC:168
www.atncorp.com
Email: info@atncorp.com
Estab: 1995

James Munn, CEO

Developer and manufacturer of precision night optics and thermal imaging solutions. The company
serves law enforcement and military clients.

Atomwise Inc   HQ
717 Market St Ste 800
San Francisco CA 94103
P: 650-449-7925   PRC:268
www.atomwise.com
Email: hello@atomwise.com

Abraham Heifets, CEO
Izhar Wallach, CTO

Developer of artificial intelligence systems for
the discovery of drugs. The company serves the
healthcare sector.

ATP Electronics Inc   RH
2590 N First St Ste 150
San Jose CA 95131
P: 408-732-5000   F: 408-732-5055   PRC:96
www.atpinc.com
Email: sales@atpinc.com
Estab: 1991

Mike McClimans, VP of Sales
Jeff Hsieh, SVP
Eunice Chen, Sales & Marketing Manager
Liwei Liao, Operations Manager
Louis Lau, R & D Manager

Provider of NAND flash and DRAM memory
modules. The company specializes in telecom,
medical, automotive, and enterprise computing.

ATS Inc   HQ
2785 Goodrick Ave
Richmond CA 94801
P: 510-234-3173   F: 510-234-3185   PRC:166
www.atsduct.com
Estab: 1978

Jeff Shea, President & CEO
Doug Williams, Sales Manager
Lou Flores, Engineer
Kathleen Passalacqua, Accounting Analyst

Manufacturer of fiberglass ductwork for fume
exhaust systems. The company offers installation
and other related services.

Attention Control Systems Inc   HQ
650 Castro St Ste 120-197
Mountain View CA 94041
P: 888-224-7328   PRC:323
www.brainaid.com
Email: info@brainaid.com
Estab: 1996

David Halper, VP

Manufacturer of cognitive aids. The company also
offers technical assistance solutions and serves
the healthcare sector.

Atypon Systems LLC   HQ
5201 Great America Pkwy Ste 215
Santa Clara CA 95054
P: 408-988-1240   F: 408-988-1070   PRC:320
www.atypon.com
Email: info@atypon.com
Estab: 1996

Georgios Papadopoulos, CEO
Gordon Tibbitts, EVP of Corporate Development
Marty Picco, General Manager
Mayank Varia, Software Engineer
Kendall Shaw, Software Engineer

Provider of service content delivery software
for publishers. The company serves information
discovery, e-commerce, and business intelligence
needs.

Aubin Industries Inc HQ
23833 S Chrisman Rd
Tracy CA 95304
P: 209-833-7592   F: 209-833-7594   PRC:159
www.aubinindustries.com
Email: info@aubinindustries.com

Philip Aubin, Owner & President
Shanda O'Donnell, Marketing Manager
Dee Silveira, Office Administrator
Stefanie Price, Operations Officer

Designer and manufacturer of mobile wheel systems. The company serves the material handling industry.

Audible Magic Corp HQ
985 University Ave Ste 35
Los Gatos CA 95032
P: 408-399-6405   PRC:60
www.audiblemagic.com
Email: info@audiblemagic.com
Estab: 1999

Vance Ikezoye, President & CEO
Doug Keislar, Senior Engineer
Michael Perkins, Senior Software Engineer
Carol Murphy, Marketing Consultant

Developer of media identification and synchronization, content registration, and copyright compliance solutions.

Augmedix Inc HQ
1161 Mission St Ste 210
San Francisco CA 94103
P: 888-669-4885   PRC:194
www.augmedix.com
Email: info@augmedix.com
Estab: 2012

Ian Shakil, Founding Chairman & CSO
Manny Krakaris, CEO
Jonathan Hawkins, CRO
Matteo Marchetta, CFO
Sriram Vaidyanathan, CTO

Provider of technology enabled documentation services for health systems and doctors.

Augmentum Inc HQ
1065 E Hillsdale Blvd Ste 413
Foster City CA 94404
P: 650-578-9221   PRC:319
augmentum.com
Email: info@augmentum.com
Estab: 2004

Leonard Liu, Chairman & CEO
Wayne Hom, CTO & EVP
Yuen Lee, EVP of Worldwide Sales & Applications

Provider of software development and solution implementation services. The company focuses on Internet applications and product development outsourcing.

Auriga Corp HQ
890 Hillview Ct Ste 130
Milpitas CA 95035
P: 408-946-5400   F: 408-942-9625   PRC:323
www.aurigacorp.com
Email: info@aurigacorp.com
Estab: 1990

Ramesh Daryani, CTO
Willy Dommen, Director of Technology Services
Fred Perry MacHiya, Director
Soham Mookerjea, Project Manager
Nischit Doshi, Senior Program Manager

Provider of technology consulting services for electric power, telecommunications, transportation, and information technology systems.

Aurionpro Solutions Inc DH
4000 Executive Pkwy Ste 250
San Ramon CA 94583
P: 925-242-0777   F: 925-242-0778   PRC:322
www.aurionpro.com
Email: info@aurionpro.com

Paresh Zaveri, Chairman & Managing Director
Samir Shah, CEO
Dusan Jovanovic, CFO
Raj Biyani, VP of Delivery Banking & Payments
Amit R. Sheth, Managing Director

Provider of solutions to streamline corporate banking, treasury, fraud prevention, risk management, governance and compliance needs.

Aurostar Corp HQ
46560 Fremont Blvd Ste 201
Fremont CA 94538
P: 510-249-9422   PRC:85
www.aurostar.net
Email: sales@aurostar.net
Estab: 2002

Vasudeva Kamath, President & Founder

Provider of technology products and services focusing on home theater systems, consumer electronics, desktops and notebooks, and networking solutions.

AuSIM Inc HQ
1110 La Avenida Ste C
Mountain View CA 94043-1424
P: 650-322-8746   PRC:207
ausim3d.com
Email: info@ausim3d.com
Estab: 1998

William Chapin, President

Developer of audio simulation technology and products for auditory displays for mission-critical applications.

Austin Precision Inc HQ
4382 Contractors Common
Livermore CA 94551
P: 925-449-1049   F: 925-449-5176   PRC:80
austinprecisioninc.com
Estab: 1991

Chanler Gross, ERP Project Manager
Andy McCorkle, Supervisor

Provider of precision machined parts. The company offers parts made from aluminum, plastics, stainless steel, and other metals.

Auto Parts Warehouse HQ
16941 Keegan Ave   [N]
Carson CA 90746
P: 801-214-2997   PRC:359
www.autopartswarehouse.com
Email: corporate@autopartswarehouse.com
Emp: 11-50   Estab: 1954

Warren B. Phelps, Chairman
Lev Peker, CEO & Director
Nanxi Liu, Director
Sol Khazani, Director
Jim Barnes, Director

Distributor of auto parts and accessories.

AutoCell Electronics Inc HQ
9370 Studio Ct Ste 188
Elk Grove CA 95758
P: 888-393-6668   F: 916-393-6871   PRC:243
www.autocell.net
Email: info@autocell.net

Richard Ng, CEO

Manufacturer and distributor of energy efficient lighting products. The company offers compact fluorescent lamps, LED flashlights, and showerheads.

Autodesk Inc BR
1 Market Ste 500
San Francisco CA 94105
P: 415-356-0700   PRC:323
www.autodesk.com
Estab: 1982

Andrew Anagnost, President & CEO
Richard Scott Herren, CFO
Steven M. Blum, SVP of Worldwide Field Operations
Pascal W. Di Fronzo, SVP of Corporate Affairs & CLO & Corporate Secretary
Brian Pene, Director of Emerging Technology

Provider of 3D design, engineering, and entertainment software solutions. The company also offers technical support services.

Autoflow Products Inc HQ
3860 Cincinnati Ave
Rocklin CA 95765
P: 916-626-3058   F: 916-626-3068   PRC:230
autoflowproducts.com
Email: admin@pfc.io
Estab: 1982

Peggy Stevens, Owner
Miranda King, Contact

Manufacturer of flow switches. The company specializes in designing switches for chemical analyzers, chemical injectors, and chromatographic systems.

AutoGrid Systems Inc HQ
255 Shoreline Dr Ste 350
Redwood City CA 94065
P: 650-461-9038 PRC:323
auto-grid.com
Email: info@auto-grid.com
Estab: 2011

Amit Narayan, CEO & Founder
Rajeev Singh, CTO
Om Moolchandani, CSO
Quique Schwarz, Chief Data Scientist
Tommer Wizansky, Chief Architect

Provider of grid-sensing technologies. The company focuses on energy data platform and optimized demand management services.

Automate Scientific Inc HQ
812 Page St
Berkeley CA 94710
P: 510-845-6283 F: 510-280-3795 PRC:122
autom8.com
Email: info@autom8.com
Estab: 1992

Joe Cordes, President
Ryan Arant, Application Scientist
Gong Cheng, Senior Application Scientist

Manufacturer and distributor of biomedical equipment. The company offers amplifiers, manipulators, software, and accessories.

Automated Inspection Systems HQ
1870 Arnold Industrial Pl Ste 1055
Concord CA 94520
P: 925-335-9206 PRC:19
www.ais4ndt.com
Email: ais@slip.net
Estab: 1996

Randy Fong, Senior Software Engineer, Architecture
Steve Madera, Software Engineer

Designer and builder of inspection equipment. The company caters to the oil and gas pipeline inspection needs.

Automatic Bar Controls Inc HQ
2060 Cessna Dr
Vacaville CA 95688
P: 707-448-5151 F: 707-448-1521 PRC:19
www.wunderbar.com
Estab: 1971

Bret Baker, VP

Provider of beverage and liquor dispensers. The company's products include beverage and food and sauce dispensers, and food preparation systems.

Automation Partners Inc HQ
6115 State Farm Dr Unit A2
Rohnert Park CA 94928
P: 707-665-3980 PRC:94
www.automationpartners.com
Email: info@automationpartners.com
Estab: 1990

Larry Tausch, President
Mihir Shukla, CEO

Manufacturer of controls for control systems and regulators. The company specializes in products for fabric density measurement.

Automattic Inc HQ
60 29th St Ste 343
San Francisco CA 94110
P: 877-273-3049 PRC:326
www.automattic.com
Estab: 2005

Matt Mullenweg, CEO & Founder
Peter Slutsky, Director of Platform Services
George Ng, Director of Finance
Paul Sieminski, General Counsel
Holly Hogan, Associate General Counsel

Provider of blogging services. The company specializes in handling non-profit and open source projects.

Autonet Mobile Inc HQ
3636 N Laughlin Rd Ste 150
Santa Rosa CA 95403
P: 415-223-0316 F: 707-284-4458 PRC:68
autonetmobile.com
Email: support@autonetmobile.com
Estab: 2005

Faiza Qadri, Software Engineer
Danny Gomez, Junior Software Engineer
Krysteen Hopkins, Operations Analyst
Neena Bonetti, Controller

Provider of Internet based telematics and applications service platform for the automotive transportation market.

Autonomic Software Inc HQ
381 Hartz Ave Ste A
Danville CA 94526
P: 925-683-8351 PRC:325
autonomic-software.com
Email: info@autonomic-software.com
Estab: 2004

Tony Gigliotti, President & CEO
Alexander Gigliotti, Director of Sales
Harish Rao, Principal Software Engineer

Developer of software for endpoint and security management, imaging, and other needs. The company serves government, finance, and other sectors.

Avalanche Technology HQ
3450 W Warren Ave
Fremont CA 94538
P: 510-897-3300 F: 510-438-0143 PRC:95
www.avalanche-technology.com
Email: info@avalanche-technology.com
Estab: 2006

Rajiv Ranjan, Chief Technologist & Co-Founder
Petro Estakhri, CEO & President & Co-Founder & Director
Bob Netter, CFO
Sam Nemazie, VP of Operations
Yiming Huai, VP of Technology

Provider of programmable storage solutions. The company offers services to the consumer electronics industry.

Avalent Technologies Inc HQ
920 Hillview Ct Ste 195
Milpitas CA 95035
P: 408-657-7621 F: 408-727-6940 PRC:126
avalent.com
Email: info@avalent.com
Estab: 1999

DuenShun Wen, President & CEO
Mazin Khurshid, VP of Engineering
Mike Rhoades, Senior IC Design Engineer
Kanoon Chalabi, Quality Control & Welding Inspector

Provider of fabless semiconductor devices. The company's services include platform development, processor development, and analog design services.

Avantec Vascular Corp HQ
870 Hermosa Ave
Sunnyvale CA 94085
P: 408-329-5400 F: 408-329-5499 PRC:189
www.avantecvascular.com
Email: info@avantecvascular.com
Estab: 1999

Jack Hoshino, CEO & President
Vivian Chen, Senior Director of Finance
Sandeep Kaur, Quality Engineer
Cisco Miranda, Process Engineer
Boni Estrada, Senior Production Supervisor

Manufacturer of therapeutic medical devices such as cardio and peripheral vascular devices for cardiovascular, neurovascular, and peripheral disease.

AvantPage HQ
132 E St Ste 370
Davis CA 95616
P: 530-750-2040 F: 530-750-2024 PRC:325
avantpage.com
Email: info@avantpage.com
Estab: 1996

Luis Miguel, CEO
Joanna Oseman, Director of Business Development

Provider of foreign language translation services for the medical, technical, healthcare, financial industries.

Avatier Corp HQ
4733 Chabot Dr Ste 201
Pleasanton CA 94588
P: 925-217-5170 F: 925-275-0853 PRC:323
avatier.com
Email: sales@avatier.com
Estab: 1995

Nelson Cicchitto, CEO & Chairman & Founder
Christopher Arnold, VP of Development
Corey Merchant, VP of Sales
Richard Darrell, VP of Strategic Alliances
James Swan, Global Sales Manager

Provider of identity management consulting, software development, password management, and user provisioning solutions.

Avaya Inc HQ
4655 Great America Pkwy
Santa Clara CA 95054-1233
P: 908-953-6000 PRC:64
www.avaya.com
Estab: 2000
Sales: $1B to $3B

Jim Chirico, President & CEO
Darwin Thusius, SVP & CTO
Dave Vellequette, SVP & CFO
Bernard Gutnick, Senior Director of Engagement
Evangelist Organization

Provider of PBX solutions, IVR applications,
IP telephony solutions, voice messaging, and
consulting.

AverLogic Technologies Inc HQ
2635 N First St Ste 243
San Jose CA 95134
P: 408-526-0400 F: 408-526-0500 PRC:94
www.averlogic.com
Email: sales@averlogic.com
Estab: 1996

Kyle Chang, President
Becker Sze, Director of IC Design
Bo Luo, Principal Engineer of ASIC Design &
Verification

Designer and seller of integrated ICs. The company primarily caters to multimedia and video
applications.

Avermedia Technologies Inc DH
47358 Fremont Blvd
Fremont CA 94538
P: 510-403-0006 F: 510-403-0022 PRC:110
www.avermedia.com
Email: avtsales.usa@avermedia.com
Estab: 1990

Michael Kuo, Chairman
Ted Dai, SVP & CTO
Jesse Lin, Director of Accounting & Director of
Finance

Designer and manufacturer of multimedia, Internet TV, and electronic products. The company
provides USB, TV box, streaming server, and
accessories.

Aviat Networks Inc HQ
860 N McCarthy Blvd Ste 200
Milpitas CA 95035
P: 408-941-7100 F: 408-941-7110 PRC:70
www.aviatnetworks.com
Email: aviatcareeducate@aviatnet.com
Estab: 2007
Sales: $100M to $300M

Walter Stanley Gallagher, VP & COO & Principal
Financial Officer
Eric Chang, SVP & CFO
Ola Gustafsson, SVP & CPO
Heinz H. Stumpe, SVP & Chief Sales Officer
Shaun McFall, SVP of Corporate Development

Provider of microwave networking solutions. The
company's products are interactive 3D product
models, trunking microwaves, and dual hybrid/
packet microwaves.

Aviation Design HQ
20166 Pine Mountain Dr
Groveland CA 95321
P: 209-962-0415 F: 209-962-0418 PRC:8
www.aviationdesign.com
Email: thallock@aviationdesign.com
Estab: 1979

Tim Hallock, Owner
Thomas Miller, President

Designer of aircraft interiors for commercial and
private aircrafts. The company offers services to
the aviation industry.

Avid Technology Inc BR
2903 Bunker Hill Ln Ste 100
Santa Clara CA 95054
P: 800-955-0960 PRC:60
www.avid.com
Estab: 1987

Jeff Rosica, President & CEO
Ken Gayron, CFO & EVP
Melissa Puls, CMO & SVP
Diana Brunelle, Chief Human Resource Officer
& VP
Jason Duva, Chief Legal & Administrative Officer
& EVP

Manufacturer of computer automated audio mixing
consoles. The company offers audio product registration and software activation services.

Avinger Inc HQ
400 Chesapeake Dr
Redwood City CA 94063
P: 800-208-2988 PRC:187
www.avinger.com
Estab: 2007

Jeff Soinski, President & CEO
Himanshu Patel, CTO
Jay Sundaram, VP of Quality
Elmar Horn, VP of International
Jeff Dolin, Machine Shop Manager

Designer and developer of precision medical
device technology solutions. The company is
engaged in manufacturing services.

Aviram Networks Inc HQ
1175 Saratoga Ave Ste 11
San Jose CA 95129
P: 408-624-1234 PRC:59
www.nevisnetworks.com
Estab: 2002

Ajit Shelat, Founder
Radha Shelat, CEO
Raghu Iyer, CTO

Provider of wire-speed IPS for recognition and visualization, access control, and other needs. The
company offers consulting and training services.

Avision Labs Inc DH
6815 Mowry Ave
Newark CA 94560
P: 510-739-2369 F: 510-739-6060 PRC:176
www.avision.com
Email: sales@avision-labs.com
Estab: 1991

Jun Huang, General Manager

Designer and manufacturer of network and document scanners. The company specializes in sales
and installation services.

Aviso Inc HQ
805 Veterans Blvd Ste 300
Redwood City CA 94063
P: 650-567-5470 PRC:322
www.aviso.com
Email: sales@aviso.com
Estab: 2012

Michael Lock, CEO
Ravi Suryanarayan, VP
Roxanna Farshchi, Director of Solution Engineer-
ing & Customer Experience

Creator of software to change how enterprises
make critical revenue decisions and automate
sales forecasting process with data science for
enterprises.

Avocet Sales & Marketing Inc HQ
737 Second St Ste 305
Oakland CA 94607-3007
P: 510-891-0093 PRC:80
www.avocetsales.com
Email: avocet@avocetsales.com
Estab: 1989

Zachary J. Makowsky, Owner & CEO
Anthony Esposo, Manager of Accounting & Office
Jeff Briggs, Professional Sales Representative

Provider of custom engineered mechanical component parts and sub assemblies. The company
offers contract manufacturing and automation
services.

Avontus Software Corp DH
2150 Shattuck Ste 750
Berkeley CA 94704
P: 800-848-1860 PRC:323
www.avontus.com
Email: sales@avontus.com
Estab: 1998

Brian Webb, CEO & Founder
Andrew Smith, VP of Operations
Ali Hajighafouri, Director of Sales
Susie Sargent, Manager of Operations & Finance
Tracey Williams, Manager of Implementation

Creator of software for formwork, scaffolding, and
shoring industries, both custom development for
enterprises and packaged software for public.

Avp Technology LLC HQ
4140 Business Center Dr
Fremont CA 94538-6354
P: 510-683-0157 F: 510-683-0176 PRC:207
avptechnologyllc.com
Estab: 2005

Zhicheng Wang, Skills For Engineers

Provider of thin film equipment services. The company provides custom designing, remanufacturing, and field services.

AW Die Engraving Inc HQ
8550 Roland St [N]
Buena Park CA 90621
P: 714-521-0842 F: 714-521-2709 PRC:80
www.awdie.com
Estab: 1972

Arturo Chavez, President
Marcos Chavez, VP
Marco Silva, General Manager
Gloria Chavez, Office Manager
Jose Castaneda, Manager of Production

Manufacturer of precision rotary and flat dies for labeling, printing and die cutting.

Axelsys LLC HQ
177 Park Ave Ste 200
San Jose CA 95113
P: 408-600-0871 PRC:2
www.axelsys.com
Email: sales@axelsys.com
Estab: 2009

Jay Aggarwal, CEO

Provider of electronic design and manufacturing services. The company's offerings include LED and AC to DC industrial power supplies.

Axsen LLC HQ
5472 Black Ave Ste 1000
Pleasanton CA 94566
P: 925-398-0112 F: 866-380-2189 PRC:325
www.axsen.com
Email: sales@axsen.com
Estab: 2002

Shane Workman, Owner

Developer of web designs and provider of online marketing solutions. The company serves the industrial sector.

AXT Inc HQ
4281 Technology Dr
Fremont CA 94538
P: 510-438-4700 F: 510-353-0668 PRC:86
www.axt.com
Email: sales@axt.com
Estab: 1986
Sales: $30M to $100M

Morris Young, CEO
Gary Fischer, VP & CFO
Liming Zhu, VP of Sales
Raj Shetty, Director of Crystal Technology
Shun Sit, Director of Information Technology

Designer, developer, manufacturer, and distributor of high performance compound semiconductor substrates.

M-42

Ayantra Inc HQ
47873 Fremont Blvd
Fremont CA 94538
P: 510-623-7526 F: 510-623-7839 PRC:17
www.ayantra.com
Email: info@ayantra.com

Ashok Teckchandani, Chairman & CEO
Andy Rogers, VP of Business Development
Ram Charan, VP of Operations
Ravi Koppula, VP of Engineering

Provider of wireless communication technology services. The company is engaged in monitoring and asset tracking.

Ayasdi Inc HQ
4400 Bohannon Dr Ste 200
Menlo Park CA 94025
P: 650-704-3395 PRC:322
www.ayasdi.com
Estab: 2008

Ishan Manaktala, CEO
Peter Downs, CFO
Jennifer Kloke, CTO
Michael Sanders, Chief Medical Information Officer of Flagler Hospital
Ajith Warrier, SVP of Engineering

Provider of software applications that discovers critical intelligence in company data for right operational decisions quickly.

Ayla Networks Inc HQ
4250 Burton Dr Ste 100
Santa Clara CA 95054
P: 408-830-9844 F: 408-716-2621 PRC:40
www.aylanetworks.com
Email: marketing@aylanetworks.com
Estab: 2010

Jonathan Cobb, CEO
Craig Payne, Security Privacy Officer

Provider of Ayla's IoT cloud platform that brings connected products to market quickly and securely for manufacturers and service providers.

Azbil North America Inc BR
2334 Walsh Ave
Santa Clara CA 95051
P: 408-245-3121 F: 408-245-3151 PRC:87
azbil.com
Estab: 1996

Gary Johnson, President
Fumitaka Nozawa, VP Human Resources

Designer, manufacturer, and supplier of medical devices. The company offers automation products, control products, and industrial automation systems.

Azimuth Industrial Company Inc HQ
30593 Union City Blvd Ste 110
Union City CA 94587
P: 510-441-6000 F: 510-441-6008 PRC:208
www.azimuthsemi.com
Email: questions@azimuthsemi.com
Estab: 1972

David Lee, General Manager

Provider of integrated circuit assembly and packaging services. The company specializes in prototyping and production.

Aziyo Biologics Inc BR
880 Harbour Way S Ste 100
Richmond CA 94804
P: 855-416-0596 F: 510-307-9896 PRC:34
aziyo.com
Estab: 2015

Kevin Rakin, Executive Chairman
Ronald Lloyd, President & CEO
Tom Englese, CCO
Andrew M. Green, EVP of Regulatory & Scientific Affairs
Jeff Hamet, VP of Finance

Manufacturer of allograft tissue products for use in orthopedic, spinal, sports medicine, and dermal applications.

Azul Systems Inc HQ
385 Moffett Park Dr Ste 115
Sunnyvale CA 94089-1306
P: 650-230-6500 F: 650-230-6600 PRC:319
azul.com
Email: info@azul.com
Estab: 2002

Gil Tene, Co-Founder & CTO & VP of Technology
Scott Sellers, Co-Founder & CEO & President
George W. Gould, VP of Business Development & Partner Alliances
Elias Atmeh, VP of Systems Engineering
Anya Barski, VP of Engineering

Provider of Java applications for real time businesses. The company's Zing is a JVM enterprise application.

B & J Specialties Inc HQ
321 Ingalls St
Santa Cruz CA 95060
P: 831-454-0713 F: 831-454-0743 PRC:212
bandjspecialties.com
Email: bjamrus@aol.com
Estab: 1989

Brian Jamrus, Owner

Manufacturer of nanometrics film thickness and CD measurement equipment. The company offers nanometrics equipment, Nanoline, and Nanospec.

B&H Engineering HQ
1725 Old County Rd
San Carlos CA 94070
P: 650-594-2861 F: 650-594-0278 PRC:80
www.bhengineering.com
Email: info@bhengineering.com
Estab: 1972

Bakir Begovic, CEO
Hamida Begovic, CFO
Robert Gizatullin, Projects Manager
Jurica Jurkic, Purchasing Manager
Martin Villegas, Quality Manager

Supplier of assemblies, process kits, and individual parts. The company caters to the semiconductor equipment industry.

B&Z Manufacturing Company Inc   HQ

1478 Seareel Ln

San Jose CA 95131

P: 408-943-1117   F: 408-943-1067   PRC:80

bzmfg.com

Email: info@bzmfg.com

Estab: 1960

Dennis Kimball, Owner

Provider of multi-axis milling and turning services. The company offers ultra precision components for electronic, aerospace, and computer fields.

B-K Lighting Inc   HQ

40429 Brickyard Dr

Madera CA 93636

P: 559-438-5800   F: 559-438-5900   PRC:243

www.bklighting.com

Email: info@bklighting.com

Estab: 1984

Douglas W. Hagen, CEO & Founder

Nathan Sloan, Manufacturing Manager

Justin Perez, Manufacturing Manager

Ryan Berrios, National Sales Manager

Becky Carlson, Marketing Manager

Provider of architectural outdoor landscape lighting products. The company serves residential and commercial properties.

B-Metal Fabrication Inc   HQ

318 S Maple Ave

S San Francisco CA 94080

P: 650-615-7705   PRC:80

www.bmetalfabrication.com

Email: bmfab@bmetalfabrication.com

Robert Steinebel, CEO

Provider of metal fabrication services. The company offers services for the commercial, residential, retail, and bio pharmaceutical industries.

BK Thorpe Co   HQ

1811 E 28th St   [N]

Signal Hill CA 90755

P: 562-595-1811   F: 562-426-6016   PRC:212

bkthorpe.com

Estab: 1965

Jerry Priest, VP of Operations

Distributor of valves and fittings for commercial and industrial application such as brass appliances, ball-plex and duplex, grooved end, tilting disc check, sampling and much more.

Babbitt Bearing Company Inc   HQ

1170 N Fifth St

San Jose CA 95112

P: 408-298-1101   F: 408-998-4134   PRC:80

www.bbcmachine.com

Email: info@bbcmachine.com

Estab: 1945

Rick Valencia, Manager of Flame Spray Department

Provider of repair and manufacturing services. The company deals in hard chrome plating, non-destructive testing, and machinery repair.

Babcock Laboratories Inc   HQ

6100 Quail Valley Ct   [N]

Riverside CA 92507

P: 951-653-3351   F: 951-653-1662   PRC:306

www.babcocklabs.com

Email: info@babcocklabs.com

Emp: 51-200   Estab: 1978

Allison Mackenzie, CEO

Tiffany Gomez, CFO

Brad Meadows, VP

Caroline Sangari, Manager

Cindy Waddell, Project Manager

Provider of environmental and food product testing services including the analysis of food, beverages, drinking water, wastewater, groundwater, storm water and hazardous materials.

Backproject Corp   HQ

170 N Wolfe Rd

Sunnyvale CA 94086

P: 408-730-1111   F: 408-404-8100   PRC:196

www.backproject.com

Email: info@backproject.com

Estab: 2001

Steve Hoffman, CEO

Manufacturer of physical therapy equipment. The company specializes in vertical physical therapy equipment for musculoskeletal pain relief.

Backshop Inc   HQ

85 Liberty Ship Way Ste 201

Sausalito CA 94965

P: 415-332-1110   F: 415-289-3802   PRC:323

backshop.com

Email: info@backshop.com

Estab: 2000

Jim Flaherty, President & CEO

Michelle Link, CTO

Jack Gao, VP & Chief Architect

Katherine Geis, VP of Client Services

Jeff Holder, VP of Client Services

Provider of commercial real estate software for full deal-stack modeling, loan origination, asset management, and data library for customers.

Bactrack   HQ

300 Broadway Ste 26

San Francisco CA 94133

P: 415-693-9756   F: 415-358-8030   PRC:124

www.bactrack.com

Email: info@bactrack.com

Estab: 2001

Keith Nothacker, CEO

Shawn Casey, VP of Marketing

Pauline Basaran, VP of Operations

Hazel Chen, Customer Success Manager

Charly Mejia, Accounting Manager

Provider of breathalyzers. The company provides products for a wide range of personal, professional and smartphone use.

Badger Maps Inc   HQ

539 Broadway

San Francisco CA 94133

P: 415-592-5909   PRC:322

www.badgermapping.com

Steve Benson, CEO

Gady Pitaru, CTO & VP of Engineering

Christina Wong, VP of Sales

Sophie Lhoutellier, Operations Manager

Anna Bolender, Head of Public Relations

Provider of easy to use interface to manage our daily call routes, track visits, and update records.

Balance Hydrologics Inc   HQ

800 Bancroft Way Ste 101

Berkeley CA 94710-2227

P: 510-704-1000   F: 510-704-1001   PRC:139

balancehydro.com

Email: office@balancehydro.com

Estab: 1988

Barry Hecht, Founder & Founder

Edward Ballman, VP & CFO & Principal Engineer & Civil Engineer

Rachel Boitano, Accounts Manager

Colleen Haraden, Marketing Manager & Geoscientist

Denis Ruttenberg, Engineer & Hydrologist

Provider of hydrologic services. The company offers geomorphology, restoration design, watershed management, and wetland inspection services.

Balance Therapeutics Inc   HQ

1250 Bayhill Dr Ste 125

San Bruno CA 94066

P: 650-741-9100   PRC:268

www.balance-therapeutics.com

Email: info@balance-therapeutics.com

Lyndon Lien, Founder & Advisor

Developer of pharmaceuticals. The company develops therapeutics to address neurological disabilities resulting from excess inhibition of the brain.

Baldor   BR

21056 Forbes St

Hayward CA 94545

P: 510-785-9900   F: 510-785-9910   PRC:245

www.baldor.com

Ronald Tucker, CEO & President

Jeff Hines, VP & Director of Information Services

Randy Colip, EVP & Sales Manager

Jason Green, VP & Director of Human Resources

Scott Fullbright, VP & Director of Manufacturing Operations

Manufacturer of electric drives. The company also offers bearings, electric motors, drives, gear assemblies, and transmission systems.

Baltimore Aircoil Company Inc   BR

15341 Road 28 1/2

Madera CA 93638

P: 559-673-9231   F: 559-673-5095   PRC:154

www.baltimoreaircoil.com

Email: info@baltimoreaircoil.com

Estab: 1938

Mark Giltmier, Plant Engineering Manager

Provider of assembled evaporative heat rejection and thermal storage equipment. The company also offers circuit cooling towers.

Bandai Namco Entertainment America Inc   HQ

2051 Mission College Blvd
Santa Clara CA 95054
P: 408-235-2000   PRC:317
www.bandainamcoent.com

Hide Irie, EVP & COO
Chris Gilbert, SVP
Denny Chiu, Director of Communications & Social Media
Karim Farghaly, Director of Business Development
Terry Kim, Director of 360 Product Management

Provider of gaming solutions. The company is engaged in technical support and it serves the entertainment industry.

Bandwidth10 Inc   BR

2150 Kittredge St Ste 250
Berkeley CA 94704
P: 203-561-0769   PRC:213
www.bandwidth10.com
Email: info@bandwidth10.com
Estab: 2011

Phil Worland, Founder & President & CEO

Developer of tunable, singlemode, 1550 nm long-wavelength VCSELs, and transceivers for datacom applications.

Banks Integration Group   HQ

600 E Main St Ste 100
Vacaville CA 95688
P: 707-451-1100   PRC:159
banksintegration.com
Estab: 1994

Greg Banks, President
Stan Reyna, Director of Operations
Cassy Gardner, Group Engineering Manager & Lead Automation Engineer
Avo Stepanian, Project Manager
Bessida Taonda, Automation Engineer

Developer and provider of control systems and plant automation software. The company serves biotech, food, brewery, oil and gas, and other sectors.

Banpil Photonics Inc   HQ

4800 Patrick Henry Dr Ste 120
Santa Clara CA 95054
P: 408-282-3628   PRC:87
www.banpil.com
Email: info@banpil.com
Estab: 2003

Rabi Sengupta, Research & Development Manager

Developer and manufacturer of image sensors for automotive and medical imaging systems, security and surveillance, and machine vision applications.

M-44

Barco Inc   RH

11101 Trade Center Dr
Rancho Cordova CA 95670-6119
P: 888-414-7226   PRC:323
www.barco.com
Estab: 1979
Sales: $1B to $3B

Mike Jones, VP & General Manager
Andreas Yerocostas, R&D Director of Projection & Image Processing
Neil Wittering, Director of Strategic Marketing
Kent Vogel, Quality Manager
Scott Nipper, Training Manager

Manufacturer of digital scan conversion equipment and radars. The company serves healthcare, defense, media, simulation, and other needs.

Barracuda Networks Inc   HQ

3175 Winchester Blvd
Campbell CA 95008
P: 408-342-5400   F: 408-342-1061   PRC:322
www.barracuda.com
Email: sales@barracuda.com
Estab: 2002

Zach Levow, EVP & Founder & CTO
B.J. Jenkins, President & CEO
Hatem Naguib, SVP & COO
Simon Yeo, SVP & CIO
Michael Perone, EVP & CMO

Developer of solutions for IT problems primarily focusing on security and storage. The company also focuses on application delivery and productivity.

Barrington Consultants Inc   HQ

2239 Valdes Ct
Santa Rosa CA 95403
P: 707-527-8254   F: 707-542-9730   PRC:289
www.barringtoninc.com
Email: ghb@barringtoninc.com
Estab: 1995

Gary Barrington, President

Manufacturer of transformer monitors and temperature monitors for testing high voltage circuit breakers and offers circuit breaker simulators.

Baseline Environmental Consulting   HQ

5900 Hollis St Ste D
Emeryville CA 94608
P: 510-420-8686   PRC:139
www.baseline-env.com
Email: info@baseline-env.com
Estab: 1985

Mengzhu Luo, Environmental Engineer
Patrick Sutton, Environmental Engineer III
Bruce Abelli-Amen, Principal
Monika Krupa, Environmental Scientist
Todd Taylor, Environmental Associate

Provider of environmental consulting services including remediation, investigations, data management, and surveys.

BASF Venture Capital America Inc   RH

46820 Fremont Blvd
Fremont CA 94538
P: 510-445-6140   PRC:42
www.basf.com

Teressa Szelest, President
Wayne Smith, CEO

Manufacturer of basic chemicals and intermediates such as solvents, plasticizers, and monomers. The company serves the agriculture market.

Basics Environmental Inc   HQ

655 12th St Ste 126
Oakland CA 94607
P: 510-834-9099   F: 510-834-9098   PRC:142
basicsenvironmentalinc.com
Email: basicsenvironmental@gmail.com
Estab: 1994

Donavan G. Tom, Principal

Provider of environmental engineering consulting services. The company focuses on environmental site assessments for real estate transactions.

Bat Gundrilling Services Inc   HQ

2730 Scott Blvd
Santa Clara CA 95050
P: 408-727-1220   F: 408-727-1217   PRC:157
www.batgundrilling.com
Email: batgundrilling@gmail.com
Estab: 1993

Max Gomez, President

Provider of manufacturing services. The company specializes in engineering, tap extraction, gun drill tool sharpening, and deburring services.

Batchtest Corp   HQ

2118 Walsh Ave Ste 240
Santa Clara CA 95050
P: 408-454-8378   PRC:207
www.batchtest.com
Estab: 2005

Dinesh Patel, President
Silvia Castellini, Business Development Manager

Provider of embedded solutions. The company specializes in the design and manufacturing of industrial PC products.

Bauer Engraving Company Inc   HQ

11290 Sunrise Gold Cir Ste G
Rancho Cordova CA 95742
P: 916-631-9800   PRC:157
www.bauerengraving.com
Email: artwork@bauerengraving.com
Estab: 1900

Bauer Engraving, Owner
William Bratt, President

Provider of engraving services. The company offers foil stamping dies, embossing dies, wood branding dies, and letterpress printing plates.

Baumbach & Piazza Inc   HQ

323 W Elm St
Lodi CA 95240
P: 209-368-6618   F: 209-368-6610   PRC:304
www.bpengineers.net
Email: contact@bpengineers.net
Estab: 1961

Josh Elson, Principal

Provider of design, engineering, and boundary and topography surveying, and construction staking services.

Bay Advanced Technologies HQ
8100 Central Ave
Newark CA 94560
P: 510-857-0900   F: 510-857-1400   PRC:189
www.bayat.com
Email: sps-docs@bayat.com
Estab: 1961

Dennis R. Hansen, VP of Strategic Business
Development
Pat Collins, Senior Account Manager
Bob Rogers, Account Manager
John Herne, Corporate Quality Manager
Matt Shea, Sales Manager

Provider of solutions for automation and control
applications. The company offers precision automation, fluid controls and fabricated materials.

Bay Area Circuits Inc HQ
44358 Old Warm Springs Blvd
Fremont CA 94538
P: 510-933-9000   F: 510-933-9001   PRC:76
bayareacircuits.com
Email: support@bacircuits.com
Estab: 1975

Stephen Garcia, President
Brian Paper, COO
Ron De Franco, Business Development Manager
Ron Charfauros, Sales Account Manager
Michael Millor, Sales Manager

Provider of engineering services that include fabrication, layout, and design services to the original
equipment manufacturers.

**Bay Associates Wire Technologies
Corp** HQ
46840 Lakeview Blvd
Fremont CA 94538
P: 510-933-3800   F: 510-933-3870   PRC:62
baycable.com
Email: bayinfo@baycable.com
Estab: 1962

Mitzy Butte, Purchasing Manager
Strato Han, Manufacturing Engineer
Barbara Scott, Contact

Provider of cable and cable assembly solutions.
The company serves the medical, navigation,
audio, and automotive markers.

Bay Materials LLC HQ
48450 Lakeview Blvd
Fremont CA 94538
P: 650-566-0800   PRC:306
baymaterials.com
Email: info@baymaterials.com
Estab: 1999

Ray Stewart, Founder
Chris Vogdes, Laboratory Manager
Klaus Dahl, Principal Scientist
John Lahlouh, Senior Polymer Scientist

Manufacturer of polymer products. The company
offers services for spectroscopy, osmometry,
viscosity, and surface measurement.

Bay Standard Manufacturing Inc HQ
24485 Marsh Creek Rd
Brentwood CA 94513
P: 800-228-8640   F: 925-634-1925   PRC:80
www.baystandard.com
Email: sales@baystandard.com
Estab: 1959

Wally Gross, President
Michael Davis, Sales Manager

Manufacturer of machinery components. The
company offers thread, foundation bolts, u-bolts,
and specialty fasteners.

BayFab Metals Inc HQ
870 Doolittle Dr
San Leandro CA 94577
P: 510-568-8950   PRC:80
bayfabmetals.com
Estab: 1968

Paul Tavares, Project Manager
Marcella Witt, Project Manager
Jim Bava, Contact

Manufacturer of custom and production parts.
The company's products include Trumpf TruLaser,
Trumpf Laser Cutter, and AMADA.

BayNODE LLC HQ
4 Embarcadero Ctr Ste 3350
San Francisco CA 94111
P: 415-274-3100   F: 415-274-3119   PRC:326
baynode.com
Estab: 1998

Sener Akyol, Senior Solutions Architect

Provider of data network solutions, outsourcing,
and network security services. The company
caters to the IT sector.

Bayometric HQ
1743 Park Ave
San Jose CA 95126
P: 408-940-3955   PRC:320
bayometric.com
Email: sales@bayometric.com
Estab: 2007

Danny Thakkar, Senior Product Manager

Supplier of fingerprint scanners, single sign-on
solution and access control systems. The company serves the business and industrial markers.

BaySand Incorporated BR
6203 San Ignacio Ave Ste 110
San Jose CA 95119
P: 408-669-4992   PRC:86
www.baysand.com
Email: info@baysand.com
Estab: 2009

Salah M. Werfelli, President & CEO & Founder
Avi Zakai, SVP of Sales & Business Development
Worldwide
George N. Alexy, Marketing Research Analyst
Advisor
Seiji Miwa, Strategic Business Advisor
Sam L. Appleton, Contact

Developer of metal only configurable ASIC. The
company uses disruptive metal configurable standard cell technology for its products.

Bayspec Inc HQ
1101 McKay Dr
San Jose CA 95131
P: 408-512-5928   F: 408-512-5929   PRC:176
www.bayspec.com
Email: sales@bayspec.com
Estab: 1999

Jeff MacCubbin, Business Development &
Founder
BaySpec Inc, Manager Management
Masayuki Kamata, Senior Engineer

Manufacturer of mass spectrometers, microscopes, hyperspectral imagers, and OEM spectral
engines for biomedical, pharmaceuticals, and food
industries.

Baystar Electrument Inc HQ
1903 Concourse Dr
San Jose CA 95131
P: 408-272-3669   PRC:87
baystar-inc.com
Email: info@baystar-inc.com

John Bai, Manager
Meiyin Wu, Sales Administrator

Manufacturer of pressure sensors, pressure transducers and transmitters. The company deals with
digital signal processing services.

Bazell Technologies Corp HQ
5066 Commercial Cir
Concord CA 94520
P: 925-603-0900   F: 925-603-0901   PRC:156
www.bazell.com
Email: info@bazell.com
Estab: 1983

Helen Bazell, Office Administrator & Manager

Manufacturer of solid wall basket centrifuges.
The company also focuses on centrifugal fluid
processing systems.

BBI Engineering Inc HQ
241 Quint St
San Francisco CA 94124
P: 415-695-9555   F: 415-695-9276   PRC:60
bbinet.com
Email: sales@bbinet.com
Estab: 1984

Sarah Roos, CFO
Jim Sallee, Project Manager
Steven Ramsey, Engineer
Kevin McKereghan, Lead
Tony Paredes, Administrator

Designer and installer of audiovisual, multimedia,
teleconferencing and data systems for museums,
aquariums, zoos, schools, and universities.

BCG Management Resources Inc HQ
1320 Willow Pass Rd Ste 600
Concord CA 94520
P: 800-456-8474   PRC:326
www.beckconsulting.com
Email: sales@beckconsulting.com
Estab: 1986

Dirk Manders, President
Cheryl Irons, Account Executive

Provider of enterprise software solutions and professional services such as dynamics NAV and BC
solutions for food and manufacturing industry.

BCL Technologies HQ
3031 Tisch Way Ste 1000
San Jose CA 95128
P: 408-557-2080   F: 408-249-4046   PRC:322
www.bcltechnologies.com
Email: info1@bcltechnologies.com
Estab: 1993

Hassan Alam, Co-Founder
Frankie Tsoi, Co-Founder
Yenny H., MIS Manager
Jeremy Chan, Account Manager
Tamas Demjen, Senior Software Engineer

Developer of document creation, conversion, and extraction solutions. The company offers BCL easyPDF Cloud, a cloud-based PDF conversion platform.

BCT Consulting Inc HQ
7910 N Ingram Ave Ste 101
Fresno CA 93711
P: 559-579-1400   F: 559-472-7300   PRC:325
www.bctconsulting.com
Email: info@bctconsulting.com
Estab: 1996

Mike Rosa, Business Development Engineer
Thomas Buehner, Systems Administrator
Grant Robison, Senior Network Administrator
Alysse Dyer, Accounting Assistant

Provider of computer network support, web design, application programming, and other technology services.

BD Biosciences BR
2350 Qume Dr
San Jose CA 95131
P: 877-232-8995   PRC:186
www.bdbiosciences.com
Email: bdbcustomerservice@bd.com

Robert Balderas, VP of Research & Development
Vishal Lokhande, Staff Mechanical Engineer

Manufacturer of medical devices. The company provides a broad range of medical supplies, devices, laboratory equipment and diagnostic products.

Beachhead Solutions Inc HQ
1150 S Bascom Ave 1st Fl Ste 7
San Jose CA 95128
P: 408-496-6936   F: 408-246-3026   PRC:327
www.beachheadsolutions.com
Email: info@beachheadsolutions.com
Estab: 2003

Tim Lavelle, VP of Sales & Founder
Jim Obot, President & CEO
Rob Weber, Director of Product & Support
Cam Roberson, Director of Marketing

Provider of web-based console to enforce encryption, manage security, and give providers the ability to change policy on iPhones and android devices.

Beahm Designs Inc HQ
1502 Gladding Ct
Milpitas CA 95035
P: 408-395-5360   F: 408-871-8295   PRC:159
www.beahmdesigns.com
Email: sales@beahmdesigns.com
Estab: 1990

Anita Butterfield Beahm, CEO

Provider of tailor made manufacturing equipment. The company focuses on tube processing machines for catheter manufacturing.

Bear River Associates Inc HQ
436 14th St Ste 300
Oakland CA 94612
P: 510-834-5300   F: 510-834-5396   PRC:325
www.bearriver.com
Email: info@bearriver.com
Estab: 1985

Anthony Meadow, President
Randall Matamoros, CEO
Val Perry, QA Lead Engineer

Provider of enterprise mobile computing products and services. The company serves business services, government, high-tech, and life science sectors.

Bearing Engineering Company Inc HQ
667 McCormick St   [N]
San Leandro CA 94577
P: 510-596-4150   F: 510-658-1646   PRC:80
www.bearingengineering.com
Email: corp@bearingengineering.com
Estab: 1936

William D. Seagren, President

Distributor of power transmission products such as bearings, belts, bushings, chains and chain drives and more.

Bearing Engineers Inc HQ
27 Argonaut   [N]
Aliso Viejo CA 92656
P: 949-586-7442   PRC:212
motionsolutions.com/WpPNZ
Email: sales@motionsolutions.com
Estab: 1956

Scott Depenbrok, President & CEO
Elizabeth Gordon, CFO
Bill Lackey, VP of Automation
Bill Saunders, VP of Sales
Wally Logan, VP of Engineering

Manufacturer of semiconductor fabrication equipment, medical equipment, aerospace and robotics components.

Beganto Inc HQ
4800 Patrick Henry Dr
Santa Clara CA 95054
P: 510-280-0554   F: 408-492-1772   PRC:323
www.beganto.com
Email: sales@beganto.com
Estab: 2002

Yamamoto Masami, CEO
Ryan Scott Saunders, Financial Analyst

Provider of web-based applications and support services. The company specializes in application, component, design, and sales engineering.

Bell Biosystems Inc HQ
626 Bancroft Way Ste A
Berkeley CA 94710
P: 877-420-3621   PRC:24
www.bellbiosystems.com

Daniel Bell, Agent

Provider of biotechnology services. The company develops proteins targeted to kill specific bacteria but cause minimal collateral damage.

Bema Electronics Inc HQ
4545 Cushing Pkwy
Fremont CA 94538
P: 510-490-7770   F: 510-490-6598   PRC:211
www.bemaelectronics.com
Email: info@bemaelectronics.com
Estab: 2000

Helen Kwong, President
Suju Kwong, VP of Finance & CFO
Wayne Yu, General Manager
Bud Kwan, Procurement Manager
Luis Medina, Account Manager

Provider of manufacturing, supply chain management, material procurement, prototyping, and surface mount technology of electronic appliances.

Benchling Inc HQ
555 Montgomery St Ste 1100
San Francisco CA 94111
P: 415-980-9932   F: 732-858-1337   PRC:34
benchling.com
Email: contact@benchling.com
Estab: 2012

Sajith Wickramasekara, Founder & CEO

Developer of integrated software solution for experiment design, note-taking, and molecular biology for industry and academia.

Benchmark Electronics Inc BR
4041 Pike Ln
Concord CA 94520
P: 925-363-1100   PRC:211
www.bench.com
Estab: 1979

Gayla J. Delly, President
Jeff Benck, CEO
Rhonda Turner, Chief Human Resource Officer
Robert Gifford, COO
Jan Janick, CTO

Provider of electronic manufacturing services to OEMs of telecommunication, computers, and related products.

Benchmark Home Elevator Inc HQ
145 Berna Ave
Napa CA 94559
P: 707-255-4687   F: 707-254-7859   PRC:180
www.benchmarklift.com
Email: questions@benchmarklift.com
Estab: 1991

Brian Hofacre, General Partner
Scott Britton, General Partner

Provider of elevator products. The company's products include curved rail stairlifts, straight rail stairlifts, home elevators, and wheelchair lifts.

Benchmark Thermal Corp HQ
13185 Nevada City Ave
Grass Valley CA 95945
P: 530-477-5011 PRC:153
www.benchmarkthermal.com
Email: thermal@benchmarkthermal.com
Estab: 1984

Carol Vanidestine, Manager
Jim Gaines, Project Coordinator

Manufacturer of custom semiconductor products, drum and cartridge heaters, controls, and related accessories.

Benevity Inc BR
32 W 25th Ave Ste 203
San Mateo CA 94403-2266
P: 855-237-7875 PRC:315
www.benevity.com
Email: support@benevity.com

Bryan de Lottinville, Founder & CEO
Ryan Courtnage, Co-Founder & VP of Products
& Insights
Jason Becker, Co-Founder & VP of Technology
Operations
Kelly Schmitt, CFO & President
Trey Yost, SVP of Sales

Specializes in corporate social responsibility employee engagement software.

Benicia Fabrication & Machine Inc HQ
101 E Channel Rd
Benicia CA 94510
P: 707-745-8111 F: 707-745-8102 PRC:80
beniciafab.com
Email: info@beniciafab.com
Estab: 1983

Tom Cepernich, President
Randy Reffner, Manufacturing Manager
Janet Saladino, Controller
James Taylor, Estimator

Manufacturer of industrial equipment and provider of repair and maintenance services. The company develops pressure vessels and heat exchangers.

Bentek Corp HQ
1991 Senter Rd
San Jose CA 95131
P: 408-954-9600 F: 408-954-9688 PRC:291
www.bentek.com
Email: info@bentek.com
Estab: 1985

Mitchell Schoch, President & CEO
Michal Hoppner, CFO
Wayne Erickson, VP of Sales Manufacturing
Services
John Buckley, Executive Sales & VP of Marketing
Wesley DeLap, Director of Operations

Provider of manufacturing and engineering services. The company's offerings include power distribution system design and mechanical manufacturing.

Benvenue Medical Inc HQ
4590 Patrick Henry Dr
Santa Clara CA 95054
P: 408-454-9300 F: 408-982-9023 PRC:195
www.benvenuemedical.com
Email: info@benvenuemedical.com
Estab: 2004

Laurent Schaller, Founder & CTO
Robert Weigle, CEO
Victor Barajas, VP of Operations
Ophie Myint, Customer Service Manager
Jeff Stibling, Manufacturing Application Engineer

Developer of expandable implant systems for the spine. The company focuses on cylindrical implant design.

Beranek Inc HQ
2340 205th St [N]
Torrance CA 90501
P: 310-328-9094 F: 310-328-2764 PRC:4
www.beranekinc.com
Estab: 1978

Douglas Beranek, General Manager
George Beranek, General Manager

Manufacturer of precision machined components for aerospace, military, space and communication industry.

Berkeley Analytical Associates LLC HQ
815 Harbour Way S Ste 6
Richmond CA 94804-3614
P: 510-236-2325 F: 510-236-2335 PRC:306
www.berkeleyanalytical.com
Email: info@berkeleyanalytical.com
Estab: 1989

Raja S. Tannous, Founder & Laboratory Director

Provider of specialized chemical and flame retardant analysis and formaldehyde testing services. The company serves the flooring and textile industries.

Berkeley Design Technology Inc HQ
1646 N California Blvd Ste 220
Walnut Creek CA 94596
P: 925-954-1411 F: 925-954-1423 PRC:322
www.bdti.com
Email: info@bdti.com
Estab: 1991

Jeremy Giddings, Director of Business Development

Provider of analysis, advice, and engineering solutions for embedded processing technology and applications.

Berkeley Forge & Tool Inc HQ
1331 E shore Hwy
Berkeley CA 94710
P: 510-526-5034 F: 510-525-9014 PRC:158
www.berkforge.com
Email: sales@berkforge.com

Paul Bierwith, Owner & Partner

The company is engaged in the design, engineering, manufacture, and marketing of mining and commercial forging products.

Berkeley Nucleonics Corp HQ
2955 Kerner Blvd
San Rafael CA 94901
P: 415-453-9955 F: 415-453-9956 PRC:293
www.berkeleynucleonics.com
Email: info@berkeleynucleonics.com
Estab: 1963

Mel Brown, CEO & Founder
Allan Gonzalez, Director of Sales & Marketing
Juan Espinoza, Product Manager
Mark Slattery, Applications Manager
Bernadette Jamieson, Customer Service Manager

Designer and manufacturer of precision test, measurement, and nuclear instrumentation. The company mainly offers generators and analyzers.

Bernell Hydraulics Inc HQ
8810 Etiwanda Ave [N]
Rancho Cucamonga CA 91739
P: 909-899-1751 PRC:150
www.bernellhydraulics.com
Email: info@bernellhydraulics.com
Emp: 11-50 Estab: 2012

Sandy Kinnee, Office Manager

Provider of fluid power distributor, manufacturer, and systems designer, hydraulic repair, and services.

Bess Mti Inc BR
991 George St
Santa Clara CA 95054
P: 408-988-0101 F: 408-988-0103 PRC:304
besstestlab.com
Email: info@besstestlab.com
Estab: 1964

Jose Bohorquez, President

Provider of subsurface utility engineering services. The company engages in utility locating and structural concrete scanning services.

BESST Inc HQ
50 Tiburon St Ste 7
San Rafael CA 94901-4762
P: 415-453-2501 PRC:160
besst-inc.com
Estab: 1999

Noah Heller, President
Sheldon Hanft, VP
Miles Koehler, Operations Manager
Ansel McClelland, Project Geologist

Provider of groundwater sampling technology solutions. The company also offers customized packages for specialized applications.

Bestek Manufacturing Inc HQ
675 Sycamore Dr Ste 170
Milpitas CA 95035
P: 408-321-8834 F: 408-321-8670 PRC:306
www.bestekmfg.com

Tyler Dang, Director of Materials

Provider of supply chain services. The company engages focuses on systems manufacturing, materials management, and prototype support areas.

Bestronics HQ
2090 Fortune Dr
San Jose CA 95131
P: 408-385-7777 F: 408-432-3455   PRC:207
www.bestronicsinc.com
Email: sales@bestronicsinc.com

James Choe, Owner
Ron Menigoz, President & CTO
Steve Yetso, VP of Commercial Operations &
Supply Chain
Chuck Hong, Director of Manufacturing
Myung Yun, Director of Commercial Operations

Provider of electronics manufacturing services.
The company deals with product development,
system integration, and prototyping services.

Beta Breakers Software Quality HQ
7665 Redwood Blvd Ste 100
Novato CA 94945
P: 415-878-2990 F: 415-878-2989   PRC:306
betabreakers.com
Email: info@betabreakers.com

Evan Domingo, President & CEO
Robert Chrum, VP
Greg Masada, IT Manager
Jeremy Spear, Project Manager
Damon Perdue, Project Manager

Provider of software and application testing services. The company offers functionality, compatibility, website, and mobile device testing services.

Beta Circuits Inc HQ
1200 Norman Ave
Santa Clara CA 95054
P: 408-980-9938   PRC:211
www.betacircuits.com
Email: sales@betacircuits.com
Estab: 1989

John Huang, Sales Manager

Manufacturer of printed circuit board. The
company offers all solutions from designing to
prototyping.

Betatron Inc HQ
1722 Ringwood Ave
San Jose CA 95131
P: 408-453-1880   PRC:209
www.betatron.net/home.html
Estab: 1999

Mike Young, CEO & Manufacturing Manager

Designer and manufacturer of PC board assemblies for the medical, telecommunication, industrial, commercial, and semiconductor markers.

Better World Group Inc BR
980 Ninth St 16th Fl
Sacramento CA 95814
P: 916-498-9411   PRC:142
betterworldgroup.com
Estab: 1999

Wendy James, Founder
Sharon Wrathall, CFO

Provider of environmental strategy consulting
services. The company offers political strategy, co-
alition management, media, and communications.

M-48

BetterDoctor Inc HQ
945 Bryant St Ste 350
San Francisco CA 94103
P: 844-668-2543   PRC:322
betterdoctor.com
Email: support@betterdoctor.com
Estab: 2011

Ari Tulla, CEO & Co-Founder
Tapio Tolvanen, CTO & Co-Founder
Paul Whitaker, VP of Business Development
Matt Levy, VP of Engineering
Joel Enquist, Director of Operations

Provider of mobile apps for iPhone to find primary
care, OBGYN, pediatricians, dentist, eye, and all
specialties doctors.

Betts Spring Inc HQ
2843 S Maple Ave
Fresno CA 93725
P: 559-498-3304   F: 559-445-9129   PRC:159
www.bettsspring.com
Estab: 1868

Bill Betts, President
Mike Betts, CEO
Jonathan Lee, CTO
Dan Flores, CFO
Don Devany, SVP

Manufacturer of custom precision spring products.
The company offers coil and leaf springs and
serves the mining, military, and trucking industries.

Beyond Lucid Technologies Inc HQ
1220 Diamond Way Ste 240
Concord CA 94520
P: 650-648-3727   PRC:194
www.beyondlucid.com
Estab: 2009

Christian C. Witt, CTO & Co-Founder & President
Jonathon Feit, Co-Founder & CEO
David P. Saylor, Chief Engineer
Michael R. Onkst, Director of Training & Process
Improvement
Bruce Graham, Director of Operations

Developer of cloud-based software platform.
The company offers services to the emergency
medical, disaster management, and first response
industries.

Beyond Oil Solar HQ
49 Morning Sun Ave
Mill Valley CA 94941
P: 415-388-0838   PRC:135
beyondoilsolar.com
Email: sales@beyondoilsolar.com
Estab: 1998

Daniel Rivest, Owner
Alex Leason, Manager

Provider of energy equipment products. The
company offers solar panels, inverters, charge
controllers, mounting systems, and water pumps.

Bhatia Associates Inc HQ
44 Montgomery St Ste 3030
San Francisco CA 94104
P: 415-646-0050   PRC:304
www.bhatiaassociates.com
Estab: 1984

Sat S. Bhatia, President

Provider of design and electrical engineering consulting services to the institutional, commercial,
residential, and light industrial buildings.

Bibbero Systems Inc HQ
1300 N McDowell Blvd
Petaluma CA 94954
P: 800-242-2376   PRC:189
www.bibbero.com
Email: info@bibbero.com
Estab: 1953

Michael Buckley, President
Buz Buckley, VP
Sharon Hamernick, Manager of Accounts Receiv-
able

Manufacturer of filing and office supplies including
custom chart and index tab dividers, and color
coded and pressboard classification file folders.

Big Bear Visitors Bureau HQ
630 Bartlett Rd   [N]
Big Bear Lake CA 92315
P: 909-866-7000   F: 909-866-8034   PRC:24
www.bigbear.com

Rebecca Hrabia, Director of Operations

Publisher of newsletters and magazines.

Big Joe Handling Systems HQ
25932 Eden Landing Rd
Hayward CA 94545
P: 510-785-6900   F: 510-785-0908   PRC:181
www.bigjoelift.com
Estab: 2003

Rod Kiefus, VP of Sales
Juan Reyes, Supervisor

Supplier of warehouse storage and material
handling equipment. The company specializes in
pallet and product storage systems.

Bigfoot Biomedical Inc HQ
1561 Buckeye Dr
Milpitas CA 95035
P: 408-716-5600   PRC:194
www.bigfootbiomedical.com
Email: info@bigfootbiomedical.com
Estab: 2014

Jeffrey Brewer, Founder & CEO
Brett Hale, CFO
Ian Hanson, CTO
Jyoti Palaniappan, CCO

Developer of biomedical solution to improve the
lives of people with diabetes through the application of smart technology.

Billington Welding & Manufacturing Inc   HQ
1442 N Emerald Ave
Modesto CA 95352
P: 209-526-9312   F: 209-521-4759   PRC:82
www.billington-mfg.com
Email: info@billington-mfg.com
Estab: 1969

Chris Hendryk, Manufacturing Engineer

Manufacturer of food process equipment and custom products. The company serves the construction, automotive, and food processing industries.

Bio Medical Forensics   HQ
1660 School St Ste 103
Moraga CA 94556
P: 925-376-1240   PRC:304
biomedicalforensics.com

Laura Liptai, Principal Scientist & Director
Adrianne Lee, Bookkeeper

Provider of engineering and applied science. The company specializes in mechanism and causation of trauma and impact biomechanics.

Bio Plas Inc   HQ
4380 Redwood Hwy Ste C-16
San Rafael CA 94903
P: 415-472-3777   F: 415-472-3758   PRC:189
www.bioplas.com
Email: info@bioplas.com
Estab: 1977

Bill Slattery, National Marketing Manager

Manufacturer of laboratory disposables such as foam tube racks, biopsy bags, bacti cell spreaders, and siliconized products.

Bio Rad Laboratories Inc   BR
1000 Alfred Nobel Dr
Hercules CA 94547
P: 510-741-1000   F: 510-741-5800   PRC:28
www.bio-rad.com
Email: support@bio-rad.com
Estab: 1952

Norman Schwartz, Chairman & CEO & President
Annette Tumolo, EVP & President of Life Science Group
John Hertia, EVP of President of Clinical Diagnostics Group
Andrew Last, COO
Ilan Daskal, CFO

Provider of life science research and clinical diagnostics products and services for pharmaceutical manufacturers and biotechnology researchers.

Bio Rad Laboratories Inc   HQ
1000 Alfred Nobel Dr
Hercules CA 94547
P: 510-724-7000   F: 510-741-5817   PRC:28
www.bio-rad.com
Estab: 1952
Sales: $1B to $3B

Annette Tumolo, EVP & President
Christine Tsingos, EVP & CFO
Scott Jenest, SVP of Global Supply Chain
Giovanni Magni, CSO & EVP
John Hertia, SVP of Global Technology & Systems

Provider of medical products and services that advance scientific discovery and improve healthcare for life science research and clinical diagnostic.

Bioassay Systems   HQ
3191 Corporate Pl
Hayward CA 94545
P: 510-782-9988   F: 510-782-1588   PRC:261
bioassaysys.com
Email: info@bioassaysys.com

Frank Huang, CEO

Developer and marketer of assay solutions. The company focuses on solutions for research and drug discovery.

Biocardia Inc   HQ
125 Shoreway Rd Ste B
San Carlos CA 94070
P: 650-226-0120   F: 650-631-3731   PRC:187
www.biocardia.com
Email: info@biocardia.com
Estab: 2002
Sales: Under $1 Million

Peter A. Altman, President & CEO
Eric Duckers, CMO
David McClung, CFO
Ian McNiece, CSO
Phil Pesta, VP of Operations

Developer of clinical stage regenerative therapeutic products for the treatment of cardiovascular diseases.

Biocare Medical LLC   HQ
60 Berry Dr
Pacheco CA 94553
P: 925-603-8000   F: 925-603-8080   PRC:41
www.biocare.net
Estab: 1997

Gene Castagnini, CFO
Mark Castagnini, Director of Sales
Carla Cayson, Human Resource Manager
Leah Smith, Payroll Coordinator

Developer of automated immunohistochemistry instrumentation, reagents for IHC lab testing. The company also offer tissue diagnostic products for cancer.

Biochain Institute Inc   HQ
39600 Eureka Dr
Newark CA 94560
P: 510-783-8588   F: 510-783-5386   PRC:24
www.biochain.com
Email: info@biochain.com
Estab: 1994

Grace Tian, CEO
Sean Han, Partner
Bingfang Huan, General Manager
Xiaoshan Wang, Facility Manager
Jenny Weng, Production Manager

Provider of bio-sample preparation, analysis, and application assays accelerating the development of personalized diagnostics, therapeutics, and medicine.

Biocheck Inc   HQ
425 Eccles Ave
S San Francisco CA 94080
P: 650-573-1968   F: 650-573-1969   PRC:187
www.biocheckinc.com
Email: info@biocheckinc.com
Estab: 1997

Christine Kuo, Director of RA & Quality Assurance
David Herbert, Client Service Director
Anna Pao, Director of Administration
Cathleen Wong, Research & Development Manager

Provider of custom immunoassay development, antibody conjugation and purification, and contract manufacturing services.

Bioclinica Inc   HQ
7707 Gateway Blvd 3rd Fl
Newark CA 94560
P: 415-817-8900   F: 415-817-8999   PRC:188
www.bioclinica.com
Estab: 1990

Humaira Qureshi, President
William Hogan, EVP & CFO
Michael J. O'Neal, CMO
Thomas Fuerst, Chief Science Officer & Head of Musculoskeletal
Todd Kisner, VP

Developer of medical therapies. The company specializes in medical imaging services, cardiac safety, and enterprise eClinical platforms.

BioConsortia Inc   HQ
1940 Research Park Dr Ste 200
Davis CA 95618
P: 530-564-5570   PRC:24
www.bioconsortia.com
Email: info@bioconsortia.com
Estab: 2014

Marcus Meadows-Smith, CEO
Christina Huben, SVP of Operations & Administration
Hong Zhu, SVP of Research & Development
Jorge Santiago Ortiz, Director of Process Development
Tristan Mueller, Director of Global Field Development

Focuses on the discovery, development, and commercialization of microbial consortia seed treatment and soil additive products.

Biofuel Oasis   HQ
1441 Ashby Ave
Berkeley CA 94702
P: 510-665-5509   PRC:134
biofueloasis.com
Estab: 2003

Sarahope Smith, Owner

Producer of biodiesel and seller of urban farm supplies, poultry feed and equipment. The company specializes in biodiesel made from waste oil.

Biogenex Laboratories Inc   HQ
48810 Kato Rd Ste 200E
Fremont CA 94538
P: 510-824-1400   F: 510-824-1490   PRC:187
www.biogenex.com
Email: customer.service@biogenex.com
Estab: 1981

Krishan Kalra, CEO

Manufacturer of automated slide-based staining instruments and histology products for cancer diagnosis, prognosis, and therapy selection.

Biokey Inc HQ
44370 Old Warm Springs Blvd
Fremont CA 94538
P: 510-668-0881   F: 510-252-0188   PRC:41
www.biokeyinc.com
Email: info@biokeyinc.com

George Lee, VP
Christina Mi, Regulatory Affairs & Quality Assurance Associate

Provider of API characterization, pre-formulation studies, formulation development, and analytical method development services.

Bioluminate Inc HQ
3371 Melendy Dr
San Carlos CA 94070
P: 650-743-0240   PRC:186
www.bioluminate.com
Estab: 2000

Richard Hular, President & CEO

Developer of probes that provide breast cancer detection data to physicians. The company serves the medical sector.

Biolytic Lab Performance Inc HQ
5680 Stewart Ave
Fremont CA 94538
P: 510-795-1142   F: 510-795-1149   PRC:31
biolytic.com
Email: sales@biolytic.com
Estab: 1993

Thomas Demmitt, President
Kim Edmonds, Director of Finance & Administration
Nicole Parnala, Technical Support Engineer
Jeffery Demmitt, Manufacturing Supervisor

Provider of instrumentation and accessories for oligonucleotide, DNA synthesis and oligo purification. The company specializes in rebuilt instruments.

Biomarin Pharmaceutical Inc HQ
770 Lindaro St
San Rafael CA 94901
P: 415-506-6700   PRC:254
www.biomarin.com
Email: support@biomarin-rareconnections.com
Estab: 1997
Sales: $1B to $3B

Henry J. Fuchs, President of Worldwide Research & Development
Eric Davis, President of Global Manufacturing & Technical Operations
Jean-Jacques Bienaime, Chairman & CEO
Daniel Spiegelman, EVP & CFO
Jeff Ajer, EVP & Chief Commercial Officer

Developer of biopharmaceutical products for treatment of morquio A, phenylketonuria, mucopolysaccharidosis VI and I, and lambert-eaton myasthenic syndrome.

Biomarker Pharmaceuticals Inc HQ
5941 Optical Ct
San Jose CA 95138
P: 408-257-2000   F: 408-356-6661   PRC:254
www.biomarkerinc.com
Email: contactus@biomarkerinc.com
Estab: 2002

Xi Zhao-Wilson, Chairman & Co-Founder
Saul Kent, Director & Co-Founder
Charles Garvin, CEO
Victor V. Vurpillat, VP of Corporate Affairs of Director
Paul C. Watkins, VP of Business Development

Developer of scientifically-based aging intervention products for slowing the process of aging and delaying the onset of age-related diseases.

Biomarker Technologies Inc HQ
638 Martin Ave
Rohnert Park CA 94928
P: 707-829-5551   F: 707-586-9618   PRC:24
biomarker-inc.com
Email: info@biomarker-inc.com
Estab: 1993

Mike Moldowan, CEO
Jaime J. Moldowan, CFO
Shaun M. Moldowan, COO
Fred Fago, Technical Consultant

Provider of geochemical technology services. The company offers asphaltene analysis, diamondoids, and gas chromatography analysis services.

Biomax Environmental Inc HQ
775 San Pablo Ave
Pinole CA 94564-2631
P: 510-724-3100   PRC:142
biomaxenvironmental.com
Estab: 1996

Michael A. Polkabla, Owner & Senior Certified Industrial Hygienist

Provider of indoor air quality assessment, sampling, industrial hygiene monitoring, auditing, and assessment services.

Biomedecon LLC HQ
PO Box 129
Moss Beach CA 94038
P: 650-563-9475   F: 650-563-9485   PRC:300
biomedecon.com
Email: media@biomedecon.com
Estab: 1904

Amy Bronstone, Director of Medical Writing

Provider of health economics and outcomes research. The company caters to pharmaceutical and medical industries.

Biomertech HQ
1047 Serpentine Ln Ste 200
Pleasanton CA 94566
P: 925-931-0007   F: 925-931-0300   PRC:271
www.biomertechnology.com
Email: info@biomertech.com

Jerry Chou, Manager

Provider of tailor-made peptide and antibody solutions such as pepdyes and polyclonal antibody advantage for the scientific community.

Biometrix Inc HQ
2435 Ocean Ave
San Francisco CA 94127
P: 415-333-0522   F: 415-333-0532   PRC:306
www.biometrixinc.com
Email: info@biometrixinc.com
Estab: 1998

John Ademola, President
Shilpa Goel, Clinical Research Manager

Manufacturer of pathway analysis and variant analysis products. The company specializes in web-analysis.

Biomicrolab HQ
2500-A Dean Lesher Dr
Concord CA 94520
P: 925-689-1200   PRC:160
www.biomicrolab.com
Email: sales@biomicrolab.com
Estab: 2004

David Miller, President
William Hess, VP of Products
Lisa Simmons, Director of Sales & Marketing
Jaime Maldonado, Manager
Christina Gonzalez, Sales Manager

Manufacturer of robotics based sorting and weighing systems sample management automation. The company serves bio-lab purposes.

Bioneer Inc BR
155 Filbert St Ste 216
Oakland CA 94607
P: 877-264-4300   F: 510-865-0350   PRC:38
us.bioneer.com
Email: order.usa@bioneer.us.com

Edgar Elenes, Director of Business Operations & Title Customer Operations Manager

Developer of molecular biology products and technologies for life science researchers in academia, biotech, and pharmaceutical companies.

Bionexus Inc HQ
222 Madison St
Oakland CA 94607
P: 510-625-8400   F: 510-625-8419   PRC:191
www.bionexus.net
Email: info@bionexus.net
Estab: 1996

Arman Berloui, Director of Operations
Azita Berloui, Technical Director
Thomas Quinto, Engineering Manager
Athena Berloui, Contact

Provider of biomedical products and services for research areas such as genomics, proteomics, immunology, protein expression, and cell biology.

BioQ Pharma Inc HQ
1325 Howard St
San Francisco CA 94103
P: 415-336-6496   PRC:267
www.bioqpharma.com
Email: admin@bioqpharma.com

Josh Kriesel, CEO
Ronald Pauli, CFO
Walter Cleymans, CCO
Christopher Vega, VP of Controller
Ralph McNall, VP & Engineering

Manufacturer of proprietary products. The company is involved in the sale of infusion pharmaceuticals.

Bioscience Advisors   HQ
    2855 Mitchell Dr Ste 103
    Walnut Creek CA 94598
P: 925-954-1397   PRC:40
www.biosciadvisors.com
Estab: 2011

Mark G. Edwards, Managing Director

Provider of consulting services. The company
serves the pharmaceutical and biotechnology
industries concerning commercialization agree-
ments.

Biosearch Technologies Inc   RH
    2199 S McDowell Blvd
    Petaluma CA 94954-6904
P: 415-883-8400   PRC:34
www.biosearchtech.com
Email: info@biosearchtech.com
Estab: 1993

Ron Cook, Chief Scientific Officer
Chad Gerber, Director of IVD Oligonucleotide
Manufacturing
Mikey Songster, Director of Information Technol-
ogy
Jason Erickson, Director of Quality
Luan Le, Research & Development Scientist

Manufacturer of nucleic acid based products
that accelerate the discovery and application of
genomic information.

Biotium Inc   HQ
    46117 Landing Pkwy
    Fremont CA 94538
P: 510-265-1027   F: 510-265-1352   PRC:268
biotium.com
Email: btinfo@biotium.com
Estab: 2001

Vivien Chen, VP of Business Development &
Marketing & Co-Founder
Fei Mao, CEO & CSO & Co-Founder
Wai-Yee Leung, VP of R&D
Lori Roberts, Director of Bioscience
Patrick McGarraugh, Director of Manufacturing

Supplier of glowing products. The company offers
enzyme substrates and kits for labeling proteins
and antibodies.

BioTrace Medical Inc   HQ
    3925 Bohannon Dr Ste 200
    Menlo Park CA 94025
P: 650-779-4999   F: 650-779-4746   PRC:198
www.biotracemedical.com
Email: info@biotracemedical.com
Estab: 2013

Kevin Tausend, VP of Marketing & Commercial-
ization
Kirk Li, Director of Operations
Cory White, Field Clinical Manager
Chris Foster, R&D Manager
Nami Landavazo, Sales Manager

Manufacturer of medical devices. The company
specializes in cardiac pacing device which can
treat reversible symptomatic bradycardia.

Bioved Pharmaceuticals Inc   HQ
    1929 O'Toole Way
    San Jose CA 95131
P: 408-432-4020   PRC:261
www.bioved.com
Email: sales@bioved.com

Deepa Chitre, Chairman & CEO
Deben Dey, CSO
Sadanand Bajekal, SVP of BIO-VED India
Alfred Grigsby, VP of Sales
Ajit Chitre, Director of India Operations

Manufacturer of health care products. The company specializes in ayurvedic pharmaceutical,
nutraceutical and OTC drugs from plant extracts.

BioVentrix Inc   HQ
    12647 Alcosta Blvd Ste 400
    San Ramon CA 94583
P: 925-830-1000   PRC:189
bioventrix.com
Email: info@bioventrix.com
Estab: 2003

Kenneth Miller, President & CEO
Lon S. Annest, CMO
Kevin Van Bladel, SVP of Product & Therapeutic
Development
David Schickling, VP of Sales & Marketing
Noel Messenger, VP of Quality & Regulatory
Affairs & and Clinical Affairs

Provider of medical devices. The company offers
treatment for congestive heart failure by catheter
based approaches.

Biovision Inc   HQ
    155 S Milpitas Blvd
    Milpitas CA 95035
P: 408-493-1800   F: 408-493-1801   PRC:189
www.biovision.com
Email: sales@biovision.com

Grigoriy Tchaga, Senior Director of Research
Development
Nick Chacos, Director of Operations

Developer of medical products such as assay kits,
antibodies, and research tools for studying apop-
tosis, metabolism, diabetes, and gene regulation.

Biozone Laboratories Inc   HQ
    580 Garcia Ave
    Pittsburg CA 94565
P: 925-473-1000   F: 925-473-1001   PRC:261
www.biozonelabs.com
Email: info@biozonelabs.com
Estab: 1987

Bob Stoddard, Manager of Engineering

Manufacturer of over the counter drugs, cosmetics, personal care, and nutritional supplements
such as creams, gels, drops, syrups, and sun
protection.

Birdsall Interactive   HQ
    3527 Mt Diablo Blvd Ste 427   [N]
    Lafayette CA 94549
P: 510-385-4714   PRC:322
www.birdsallinteractive.com
Email: info@birdsallinteractive.com
Emp: 1-10   Estab: 1991

Maureen Birdsall, Owner & Creative Force &
Social Strategist

Provider of website design.

Birst Inc   HQ
    45 Fermont St 18th Fl
    San Francisco CA 94105
P: 415-766-4800   PRC:322
birst.com
Email: birstteam@infor.com
Estab: 2005

Paul Staelin, Founder & VP of Customer Success
Brad Peters, Chief Product Officer & Chairman
Rick Spickelmier, CTO & VP of Technology, BI &
Analytics
Stefano Acerbetti, Director of Mobile Engineering
& Product
Steven Hom, Information Technology Manager

Provider of supply chain, marketing, human
resources, financial, and sales analytics solutions
for businesses.

Bishop-Wisecarver Corp   HQ
    2104 Martin Way
    Pittsburg CA 94565
P: 925-439-8272   F: 925-439-5931   PRC:159
www.bwc.com
Email: info@bwc.com
Estab: 1950

Pamela Kan, President
Kelly Walden, VP of Manufacturing
Leslie Lui, Mechanical Design Engineer
Benjamin Domingo, Applications Engineer
Ariol Oriol, Applications Engineer

Manufacturer of guide wheels and guided motion
products for the medical, aerospace, electronic,
and packaging industries.

Bitglass Inc   HQ
    675 Campbell Technology Pkwy Ste 225
    Campbell CA 95008
P: 408-337-0190   PRC:319
www.bitglass.com
Email: info@bitglass.com
Estab: 2013

Nat Kausik, CEO
Anurag Kahol, CTO
Anoop Bhattacharjya, Chief Scientist
Chris Chan, SVP of Engineering
Andrew Urushima, SVP of Finance

Provider of data protection solutions. The company focuses on cloud encryption, mobile security,
and discovery solutions.

BiTMICRO Networks Inc   HQ
    47929 Fremont Blvd
    Fremont CA 94538
P: 888-723-0123   F: 510-623-2342   PRC:95
www.bitmicro.com
Email: sales@bitmicro.com
Estab: 1995

Hazel Tolosa, Account Executive

Developer and manufacturer of flash-based SSD
technology, products, and solutions. The company
focuses on cloud computing and gaming applications.

BitPusher LLC   HQ
100 Pine St Ste 460
San Francisco CA 94111
P: 415-751-1055   PRC:325
bitpusher.com
Email: info@bitpusher.com
Estab: 1999

Adam Quigley, System Engineer
Ilya Gershov, Business Developer & Junior
DevOps Engineer
Amy Squires, Contact

Provider of IT infrastructure management services. The company also focuses on consulting and hosted IT services.

Bitscopic   HQ
255-B Constitution Dr Ste 106
Menlo Park CA 94025
P: 650-503-3120   PRC:40
bitscopic.com
Email: info@bitscopic.com
Estab: 2012

Payam Etminani, Co-Founder & CEO
Farshid Sedghi, COO & Co-Founder
Joel Mewton, CTO
Russell Ryono, Clinical Application Director
Steven Phelps, Director of Data Science

Provider of consulting and computer-related services. The company serves businesses and industrial customers.

Bitsculptor   HQ
901 S Main St
Lakeport CA 95453
P: 707-263-5241   F: 707-993-4924   PRC:325
www.bitsculptor.com
Email: support@bitsculptor.com

Eric Schlange, Owner
Sloan Reynolds, Web Developer

Provider of web design, hosting, branding and search engine positioning solutions. The company also offers SEO, photography, and consulting services.

BitTorrent Inc   HQ
301 Howard St Ste 2000
San Francisco CA 94105
P: 415-568-9000   PRC:322
www.bittorrent.com
Email: adsales@bittorrent.com
Estab: 2004

David Chao, Co-Founder
Bram Cohen, Co-Founder
Eric Klinker, CEO
Jascha Kaykas-Wolff, CMO
Dipak Joshi, CFO

Provider of download software solutions. The company offers design, data and content management, and installation services.

M-52

Bivio Networks Inc   HQ
4457 Willow Rd Ste 240
Pleasanton CA 94588
P: 925-924-8600   F: 925-924-8650   PRC:62
www.bivio.net
Email: info@bivio.net
Estab: 2000

Keith Glover, President
Ronak Shukla, Manager of Engineering
Tim Skelton, Hardware Engineer

Provider of cyber security and network control solutions. The company offers cyber defense systems, surveillance, flow analysis, and monitoring tools.

BizeeBee Inc   HQ
661 Channing Ave
Palo Alto CA 94301
P: 650-489-6233   PRC:325
bizeebee.com
Email: support@bizeebee.com
Estab: 2010

Poornima Vijayashanker, CEO & Founder
Samihah Azim, Product Manager

Provider of lightweight software solution designed to help fitness studios and other membership based businesses.

Bizlink Technology Inc   HQ
47211 Bayside Pkwy
Fremont CA 94538
P: 510-252-0786   F: 510-252-1178   PRC:62
www.bizlinktech.com
Email: sales@bizlinktech.com
Estab: 1996

Annie Kuo, Founder & General Manager & Director
Roger Liang, Chairman
Felix Teng, CEO
Rita Chen, Chief Finance Officer
Ted Hsiao, VP of Product Development

Manufacturer and assembler of cables and harnesses. The company serves the medical devices, solar energy, and fiber optics industries.

BKF Engineers   BR
1730 N First St Ste 600
San Jose CA 95112
P: 408-467-9100   F: 408-467-9199   PRC:304
www.bkf.com
Estab: 1915

Roland Haga, VP
Jason White, VP
Chris Rideout, VP
Simon North, VP
Jim McCurdy, VP

Provider of civil engineering, design, surveying, design, transportation, and entitlement support services.

BKF Engineers   BR
1646 N California Blvd Ste 400
Walnut Creek CA 94596
P: 925-940-2200   F: 925-940-2299   PRC:304
www.bkf.com
Estab: 1915

David LaVelle, President & CEO
Dan Schaefer, Principal & VP & Principal & VP
David Richwood, VP
Natalina Bernardi, VP

Provider of civil engineering consulting, and land surveying services. The company serves business organizations.

BlackBag Technologies Inc   HQ
300 Piercy Rd
San Jose CA 95138
P: 408-844-8890   F: 408-844-8891   PRC:323
www.blackbagtech.com
Email: sales@blackbagtech.com
Estab: 2002

Derrick Donnelly, Co-Founder & Chief Scientist
Ben Charnota, Co-Founder & Chief Customer Officer
Ken Basore, CEO
Paul Jordan, CFO
Drew Fahey, VP of Product Development

Provider of Mac-based data forensic and eDiscovery solutions. The company is involved in data processing and related services.

Blackburn Consulting   HQ
11521 Blocker Dr Ste 110
Auburn CA 95603
P: 530-887-1494   F: 530-887-1495   PRC:139
blackburnconsulting.com
Estab: 1998

Thomas W. Blackburn, President
Bryce W. Moore, Director of Construction Services
Daniel Blackburn, Director
Donald Blackburn, Business Manager
Ken Raney, Field Service Manager

Provider of geotechnical engineering, geo environmental engineering, design materials engineering, forensic, and construction services.

Blackhawk Network Inc   HQ
6220 Stoneridge Mall Rd
Pleasanton CA 94588
P: 925-226-9990   PRC:45
blackhawknetwork.com
Email: pr@bhnetwork.com
Estab: 2001

Talbott Roche, President & CEO
Jerry Ulrich, CFO & CAO
David Tate, SVP of Products & Marketing

Provider of employee engagement and customer engagement services such as gift cards, reloadable prepaid debit cards, and cash-based payment products.

Blacksquare   HQ
  501 Greenwich St
  San Francisco CA 94133
  P: 415-640-6339   PRC:325
  www.blacksquare.com
  Email: hello@blacksquare.com
  Estab: 1997

Dan Jobber, Founder & Managing Director
Julia Ogrydziak, Founding Partner
Sunil Sharma, COO
Chris O'Brien, Managing Director
Alejandro Nunez, Investment Advisor

Provider of location-based, social, m-commerce, game, and video applications. The company serves Fortune 500 companies.

Blackstone Technology Group Inc   HQ
  33 New Montgomery St Ste 850
  San Francisco CA 94105
  P: 415-837-1400   F: 415-837-1474   PRC:322
  bstonetech.com
  Estab: 1998

Casey Courneen, Co-Founder & President
David Mysona, Co-Founder & CEO
Rakesh Agrawal, Co-Founder & EVP
Ken Hans, Partner & Divisional VP of Sales
Korrie Courneen, Director of Human Resources

Provider of IT solutions, commercial, and government consulting, staffing services, and trellis natural gas transaction management web solution.

Blade Therapeutics Inc   HQ
  442 Littlefield Ave S
  S San Francisco CA 94080
  P: 650-278-4291   PRC:25
  www.blademed.com
  Estab: 2015

Wendye Robbins, President & CEO
Brad Buckman, SVP of Drug Discovery & Medicinal Chemistry

Developer of biopharmaceutical products. The company specializes anti-fibrotic drug discovery and development for treatment of fibrotic disease.

Blair Electric Services Inc   HQ
  1829 Thunderbolt Dr
  Porterville CA 93257
  P: 559-784-8658   PRC:94

Bruce Blair, Owner

Provider of electrical contracting services. The company offers pump and well controls, PLC controls, and surveillance systems.

Blankinship & Associates Inc   HQ
  1615 Fifth St Ste A
  Davis CA 95616
  P: 530-757-0941   PRC:304
  h2osci.com
  Email: info@h2osci.com
  Estab: 2000

Kenneth Tanaka, Project Engineer
Kelly Phang, Associate Environmental Specialist
Lindsey Curley, Staff Scientist
David Bonnar, Environmental Scientist
Stephen Burkholder, Senior Biologist

Provider of environmental science and engineering services focusing on biological resources, stormwater and nitrogen management, and other needs.

Blast Analytics & Marketing   HQ
  6020 W Oaks Blvd Ste 260
  Rocklin CA 95765
  P: 916-724-6701   F: 916-724-6714   PRC:325
  www.blastam.com
  Email: solutions@blastam.com
  Estab: 1999

Kayden Kelly, CEO
Charles Davis, VP of Solutions Director
Alexei Kulberg, Director of Strategic Solutions
Olaf Calderon, Director of Implementation
Nick Mannon, Director of Data Solutions

Provider of web design, e-commerce, and brand design services. The company is involved in hosting and technical support.

Blentech Corp   HQ
  2899 Dowd Dr
  Santa Rosa CA 95403
  P: 707-523-5949   PRC:159
  www.blentech.com
  Estab: 1986

Darrell Horn, Founder & Chairman
Daniel Voit, CEO
Keith Weerts, Chief Digital Officer
Kevin Jesch, Western Regional Sales Manager
Drew Moug, Mechanical Engineering Manager

Manufacturer of custom processing systems. The company serves the food production, pharmaceuticals, chemical, and biochemical industries.

Bloom Energy Corp   HQ
  4353 N First St
  San Jose CA 95134
  P: 408-543-1500   F: 408-543-1501   PRC:293
  bloomenergy.com
  Email: info@bloomenergy.com
  Estab: 2001

K.R. Sridhar, Founder & Chairman & CEO
Sonja Wilkerson, EVP & CPO
Susan Brennan, COO
Venkat Venkataraman, EVP of Engineering & CTO
Chris White, EVP & Chief Sales Officer

Provider of power generation systems. The company focuses on solid oxide fuel cells and mission critical systems.

Blue Danube Systems Inc   BR
  3131 Jay St Ste 201
  Santa Clara CA 95054
  P: 650-316-5010   PRC:71
  www.bluedanube.com
  Email: info@bluedanube.com
  Estab: 2006

Mihai Banu, CTO & Founder
Mark Pinto, President & CEO
David Poticny, VP of Business Development
John Shelnutt, VP of Global Sales
Adam Grosser, Group Head & Managing Director of Silver Lake Kraftwerk

Designer and developer of mobile wireless access solutions that increase network capacity. The company serves the industrial sector.

Blue Harbors   HQ
  803 South Humboldt St
  San Mateo CA 94402
  P: 415-799-7769   PRC:328
  blueharbors.com
  Estab: 2001

Thorsten Raab, CFO & Founder
Rahul V., Director of SAP SCM
Josh Riff, Project Manager & SAP Supply Chain Logistics Consultant
Carl Edwards, SAP Logistics Consultant

Provider of warehouse and transportation management, and shipping solutions. The company serves the industrial sector.

Blue Jeans Network Inc   HQ
  3098 Olsen Dr FL 2
  San Jose CA 95128
  P: 408-550-2828   F: 408-550-2829   PRC:322
  bluejeans.com
  Estab: 2009

Alagu Periyannan, Founder & CTO
Quentin Gallivan, CEO
Debbie Murray, CPO
Matt Collier, VP of Strategic Alliances & Business Development
Oded Gal, VP of Product Management

Provider of cloud-based video conferencing solutions. The company also offers mobile video collaboration and cloud video bridging solutions.

Blue Oak Energy   HQ
  1560 Drew Ave
  Davis CA 95618
  P: 530-747-2026   F: 530-747-0311   PRC:135
  www.blueoakenergy.com
  Email: information@blueoakenergy.com
  Estab: 2003

Tobin Booth, Founder & CEO
Danny Lee, VP of Business Development
Ryan Zahner, VP of Operations
Cherie Garrett, VP of Finance
Dan Noren, Director of Engineering

Designer of photovoltaic solar energy systems. The company is engaged in designing, building, and maintenance of solar energy systems.

Blue Sky Environmental Inc   HQ
  624 San Gabriel Ave
  Albany CA 94706
  P: 510-525-1261   PRC:306
  blueskyenvironmental.com
  Email: info@blueskyenvironmental.com
  Estab: 1999

Guy Worthington, Owner & Senior Project Manager
Jeramie Richardson, Project Manager
Adam Ashlin, Project Manager & CEMS Maintenance Specialist
Chuck Arrivas, Project Manager

Provider of air emissions source testing services. The company's services include alternative monitoring and validation testing.

Blue Sky Research Inc   HQ
510 Alder Dr
Milpitas CA 95035
P: 408-941-6068   F: 408-941-0406   PRC:83
www.blueskyresearch.com
Email: sales@blueskyresearch.com
Estab: 1989

Chris Gladding, President & CEO
Sandip Basu, CFO
Joe Kulakofsky, VP of Applications & Product
Engineering
Bin Li, Director of Manufacturing
Bill Chang, Principal Optic Engineer

Manufacturer of laser products and micro optics.
The company designs and fabricates semiconductor based lasers and fiber optic cables.

Blue Source LLC   BR
528 Market St Ste 1505
San Francisco CA 94104
P: 415-399-9101   PRC:142
www.bluesourcecan.com
Email: info@bluesource.com

Bill Townsend, Chairman & Chief Strategy Officer
Yvan Champagne, President of Bluesource
Methane
Roger Williams, President
Eric Townsend, CEO
Kevin Townsend, CCO

Provider of services for the mining industry. The
company offers project development, offset sales
and marketing, consulting, and other related
services.

Blue Star Electronics   HQ
6748 Preston Ave Ste G
Livermore CA 94551
P: 925-420-5593   PRC:140
www.bluestarco.com
Email: recycle@bluestarco.com

Louis Sarkis, CFO

Focuses on the resale, recycling and end of life
programs for electronic equipment and components. The company offers e-waste solutions.

Blue Turtle Bio Technologies Inc   HQ
479 Jessie St
San Francisco CA 94103
P: 313-806-2774   PRC:34
blueturtlebio.com
Email: info@blueturtlebio.com
Estab: 2014

Adham Aljahmi, CEO & Co-Founder
Nilesh Joshi, Co-Founder

Creator of therapeutic products. The company
specializes in microbiome to recruit genetically
malleable and easily replenishable organ in the
human body.

M-54

BlueChipTek Inc   HQ
3030 Olcott St
Santa Clara CA 95054
P: 408-731-7700   F: 408-731-7701   PRC:326
bluechiptek.com
Email: bct-sales@bluechiptek.com
Estab: 2002

Cindy Kennedy, President
Jessica Geis, CEO
Marc Farmer, Director of Sales
Jay Ratford, Network Security Engineer
Jason Geis, Principal

Provider of data management and protection,
information life cycle management, networking,
security, and data center solutions.

BlueLight Therapeutics Inc   HQ
170 Harbor Way Ste 100
S San Francisco CA 94080
P: 650-871-8716   PRC:42
www.biodesy.com
Email: info@biodesy.com
Estab: 2013

Ariel Notcovich, CEO
Gayle Kuokka, CFO
Heather Meeks, Senior Office Manager
Erick Tu, Product Development Manager
Julia Okrut, Senior Scientist

Developer of proteins and biological molecules for
the treatment of cancer, cardiovascular, Alzheimer's, and Parkinson's diseases.

Blunk Microsystems LLC   HQ
3626 Fair Oaks Blvd Ste 400
Sacramento CA 95826
P: 408-323-1758   F: 408-323-1757   PRC:322
www.blunkmicro.com
Email: sales@blunkmicro.com
Estab: 1995

Tim Stoutamore, Principal Engineer

Provider of turnkey packages for embedded
development to customers around the world. The
company also offers development tools.

Blymyer Engineers Inc   HQ
1101 Marina Village Pkwy Ste 100
Alameda CA 94501
P: 510-521-3773   F: 510-865-2594   PRC:129
www.blymyerengineers.com
Email: info@blymyer.com
Estab: 1961

Michael Rantz, President
Michael Lewis, VP & Principal
Bjorn Enstrom, Project Manager
Robin Davis, Manager

Provider of solar engineering, facility design, and
related services. The company serves the food
and beverage and glass manufacturing industries.

BMC Software Inc   BR
2755 Great America Way Ste 501
Santa Clara CA 95054-1170
P: 800-793-4262   F: 408-965-0353   PRC:324
bmc.com
Email: customer_support@bmc.com

Bill Miller, President of Solutions
Bob Beauchamp, Chairman
Nayaki Nayyar, President of Digital Service &
Operations Management
Ayman Sayed, CEO
Kia Behnia, SVP & CTO

Provider of cloud management, workforce automation, and IT service management solutions.
The company serves business enterprises and
service providers.

BMI Imaging Systems Inc   BR
749 W Stadium Ln
Sacramento CA 95834
P: 800-359-3456   F: 408-736-4397   PRC:171
bmiimaging.com
Email: info@bmiimaging.com
Estab: 1958

Bill Whitney, President
Brad Penfold, VP
Jim Modrall, VP
Brad Gilbert, VP of Software Development &
Project Manager
Michael Aufranc, Direct Sales Manager

Provider of document management services. The
company offers document scanning and hosting,
system integration, and microfilm conversion
services.

Bmw Precision Machining Inc   HQ
2379 Industry St   [N]
Oceanside CA 92054
P: 760-439-6813   F: 760-439-5940   PRC:80
www.bmwprecision.com
Emp: 11-50   Estab: 1981

Romel Leacock, Manager of Manufacturing
Orlando Soulivong, Senior Quality Engineer
Sara Wolleson, Administrative Assistant
Oscar Munguia, CNC Machinist

Provider of full service fabrication and assembly for the medical, electronics and commercial
industries.

Boardwalktech Inc   HQ
10050 N Wolfe Rd Ste SW1-276
Cupertino CA 95014
P: 650-618-6200   PRC:325
www.boardwalktech.com
Email: info@boardwalktech.com
Estab: 2004

Andrew Duncan, CEO & Chairman
Charlie Glavin, CFO & Director
Ravi Krishnan, CTO
Glenn Cordingley, SVP of Sales
Dharmesh Dadbhawala, SVP of Enterprise

Provider of enterprise collaboration software specializing in tax planning, cash management, and
revenue forecasting solutions.

Bodhtree Solutions Inc BR
210 Hammond Ave
Fremont CA 94539
P: 408-954-8700 PRC:320
bodhtree.com
Email: business@bodhtree.com
Estab: 1999

Rama Krishna, Sales Manager
Chandana Reddy, Accounts Manager

Provider of information technology consulting services. The company deals with product engineering, application development, and training.

Bold Data Technology Inc HQ
47540 Seabridge Dr
Fremont CA 94538
P: 510-490-8296 F: 510-490-7981 PRC:120
www.boldata.com
Estab: 1984

Andrew Kretzer, Director

Provider of computer components and services. The company offers desktop computers, servers, notebooks, and workstations.

Boldfocus Inc HQ
1900 S Norfolk St Ste 350
San Mateo CA 94403
P: 650-212-2653 F: 650-212-2654 PRC:325
www.boldfocus.com
Estab: 1995

Caly Lam, Art Director
Eddy Mejia, Application Developer

Provider of digital communications and technology services focusing on development, content management, and search engine optimization.

Bolsa Analytical HQ
6950 Santa Teresa Blvd Ste C
San Jose CA 95119
P: 831-637-4590 F: 831-634-1854 PRC:306
www.bolsalab.com
Estab: 1993

Tomas Moreno, Director of Laboratories

Provider of reliable chemical and microbiological analysis and testing of water, soil, plants and food.

Boly Media Communications Inc HQ
3235 Kifer Rd Ste 260
Santa Clara CA 95051
P: 408-533-0207 PRC:168
www.bolymedia.com
Email: us_sales@bolymedia.com
Estab: 2000

Xiaoping Hu, CEO & Co-Founder
David Tsang, Co-Founder
Michelle Lin, Accounting & HRD Manager
Jie Shen, Stockholder

Supplier of trail cameras and security cameras. The company also specializes in ultrasonic motors and optical zooms.

Boracchia & Associates HQ
3920 Cypress Dr
Petaluma CA 94954
P: 800-826-1690 F: 707-765-3113 PRC:189
bormed.com
Email: customerservice@bormed.com
Estab: 1978

Edward J. Boracchia, Founder & CEO
Brianna Frey, Finance Manager
Helene Tienda, Accounting Manager

Provider of consultant services and products to surgeons and medical facilities. The company offers operating room products, post-operative, and cast room products.

Borden Lighting HQ
460 Roland Way
Oakland CA 94621
P: 510-357-0171 F: 510-357-3832 PRC:243
www.bordenlighting.com

Randy Borden, Owner
Allen Reaves, Senior Project Manager
Barry Gould, Production Manager
David Berks, Manager of National Sales
Karla Paredes-Perez, Office & Project Manager

Provider of lighting solutions. The company provides table and floor lamps, architectural lighting, and louvers.

Border Collie Solutions Inc HQ
433 Airport Blvd Ste 316
Burlingame CA 94010
P: 650-343-2400 F: 650-343-9707 PRC:322
www.bcsii.net
Email: support@bcsii.com

Howard A. Neckowitz, Founder

Provider of security surveillance software products. The company focuses on security panel, energy management, and medical monitoring.

Borsting Laboratories Inc HQ
14 Commercial Blvd Ste 105
Novato CA 94949
P: 415-883-1337 F: 415-883-3842 PRC:303
borstinglabs.com
Email: info@borstinglabs.com
Estab: 1961

Chris Oatman, General Manager
Jeff Morris, Quality Assurance Manager

Provider of histology services. The company specialize in processing skin biopsies and expert second-opinion dermato pathological interpretation.

Boster Biological Technology HQ
3942 B Valley Ave
Pleasanton CA 94566
P: 888-466-3604 F: 925-215-2184 PRC:24
www.bosterbio.com
Email: support@bosterbio.com
Estab: 1993

Steven Xia, Owner & President
C.J. Xia, VP of Marketing & Sales

Provider of antibodies and ELISA kits. The company serves customers in the biochemicals and molecular biology areas.

Boston Scientific Corp BR
150 Baytech Dr
San Jose CA 95134
P: 408-935-3400 PRC:195
www.bostonscientific.com

Michael F. Mahoney, CEO & Chairman
Kevin Ballinger, SVP & President of Interventional Cardiology
Art Butcher, EVP & President of Asia Pacific
David A. Pierce, EVP & President of Medical Surgical
Eric Th'paut, SVP & President of Europe, Middle East & Africa

Manufacturer of baskets, forceps, imaging systems, needles, pacemakers, CTO and direct visualization systems.

Boston Scientific BR
47215 Lakeview Blvd
Fremont CA 94538-6530
P: 510-440-7700 PRC:195
bostonscientific.com

Michael F. Mahoney, CEO & Chairman
Daniel J. Brennan, CFO & EVP

Provider of forceps, imaging systems, needles, pacemakers, snares, probes, and other related accessories.

Bowsmith Inc HQ
131 Second St
Exeter CA 93221
P: 559-592-9485 F: 559-592-2314 PRC:166
www.bowsmith.com
Email: Info@bowsmith.com
Estab: 1974

Allan Smith, President
Ken Berg, General Manager & COO
Kari Grove, Inside Sales Manager
Victor Gonzalez, Manufacturing Manager
Lee Gipson, Sales Manager

Provider of micro-irrigation equipment for agriculture, landscape, greenhouse, and heap leach mining. The company offers drip emitters and sprinklers.

Boyd Lighting HQ
30 Liberty Ship Way Ste 3150
Sausalito CA 94965
P: 415-778-4300 F: 415-778-4319 PRC:243
www.boydlighting.com
Estab: 1921

Jason Boyd, Owner
Jay Sweet, Owner
James Boyd, President
Dennis Boyd, COO
Lincoln Lee, Credit Manager

Manufacturer of lighting devices. The company offers its products in white glass, clear ribbed glass, and gloss ivory acrylic product finishes.

Bracesox The Original HQ
5161 Soquel Dr Ste E
Soquel CA 95073
P: 831-479-7628 F: 831-479-3621 PRC:190
www.bracesox.com
Estab: 1980

Anne Adams, President

Manufacturer of bracesox, a brace cover with undersleeves and oversleeves to give brace comfort for patients.

Bradford Technologies Inc　　HQ
302 Piercy Rd
San Jose CA 95138
P: 408-360-8520　F: 408-360-8532　　PRC:323
www.bradfordsoftware.com
Email: support@bradfordsoftware.com
Estab: 1987

Ladonna Batterson, Product Manager

Developer of appraising software solutions for the real estate sector. The company offers backup and storage and digital signature scanning services.

Braigo Labs Inc　　HQ
3260 Hillview Ave
Palo Alto CA 94304
P: 408-850-0614　　PRC:115
www.braigolabs.com
Email: info@braigolabs.com
Estab: 2014

Shubham Banerjee, Founder
Malini Banerjee, President

Developer of humanely optimized technologies such as research, design, and creation of technology-based innovations and services for marketplace.

Brakeley Briscoe Inc　　BR
322 West Bellevue Ave　　[N]
San Mateo CA 94402
P: 650-344-8883　F: 650-344-3387　　PRC:45
www.brakeleybriscoe.com
Emp: 11-50

George A. Brakeley, Executive Chairman of the Board

Provider of creative and comprehensive solutions to the fundraising, strategic planning, and executive search needs.

Bramasol Inc　　BR
3979 Freedom Cir Ste 620
Santa Clara CA 95054
P: 408-831-0046　F: 408-831-0047　　PRC:322
www.bramasol.com
Estab: 1996

Dave Fellers, CEO
Mina Farahmand, CFO
Patrick Kelliher, SVP & Chief Accounting Officer
Mike Curry, SVP Sales
Christine Molinaro, VP of Finance

Provider of SAP-based solution for high tech software, life science, industrial machinery and components, and Telco, wireless, and Internet services.

Branch Metrics　　HQ
1400 Seaport Blvd Blgd B 2nd Fl
Redwood City CA 94063
P: 650-209-6461　　PRC:315
branch.io
Email: info@branch.io
Estab: 2014

Mike Molinet, Founder & COO
Alex Austin, CEO
Eric Stein, EVP & General Manager
Colin Behr, VP of Discovery Partnerships
Stephen Daniels, Director of Sales Operations

Provides deep link solutions that unify user measurement across different devices, platforms, and channels.

Brandt Electronics Inc　　HQ
1971 Tarob Ct
Milpitas CA 95035
P: 408-240-0004　F: 408-240-0014　　PRC:209
www.brandtelectronics.com
Email: info@brandtelectronics.com
Estab: 1979

Phil Duvall, CEO
Shawn Tran, Operations Manager
John Ross, Design Engineer
Kevin Berg, Senior Design Engineer

Manufacturer of power supplies. The company specializes in the design and maintenance of power equipment used in military applications.

Bravo Communications Inc　　HQ
3463 Meadowlands Ln
San Jose CA 95135
P: 408-270-1547　F: 408-270-4500　　PRC:62
www.bravobravo.us
Email: sales@bravobravo.us
Estab: 1985

Dennis Mozingo, President

Supplier of network surge and lightning protection products. The company also offers data line extenders and related accessories.

Breathing Color Inc　　HQ
18552 MacArthur Blvd　　[N]
Irvine CA 92612
P: 866-722-6567　　PRC:283
www.breathingcolor.com
Email: info@breathingcolor.com
Emp: 11-50　　　　Estab: 2003

Nick M. Friend, President

Designer and supplier of digital inkjet media and post-print protective coatings.

Brechtel Manufacturing Inc　　HQ
1789 Addison Way
Hayward CA 94544
P: 510-732-9723　F: 510-732-9153　　PRC:165
www.brechtel.com
Email: bmi_info@brechtel.com
Estab: 1986

Fred Brechtel, CEO & Owner
Gloria Tabarez, Office Manager
Andy Corless, Senior Design Engineer
Lorenzo Gamero, Senior Welding Specialist
Tom Johnson, Material Handling Specialist

Provider of aerosol solutions to the government, academic, and corporate sectors. The company also supplies vacuum brazing furnaces and leak valves.

Brekeke Software Inc　　HQ
1730 S El Camino Real Ste 400
San Mateo CA 94402
P: 650-401-6633　　PRC:325
brekeke.com
Estab: 2002

Mitu S. Mitsumata, CTO
Dane Turner, Account Executive

Developer of session initiation protocol software products for Internet protocol network communication needs.

Brelje & Race Laboratories Inc　　HQ
425 S East St
Santa Rosa CA 95404
P: 707-544-8807　F: 707-544-5736　　PRC:142
www.brlabsinc.com
Email: contact@brlabsinc.com
Estab: 1967

Hal Race, General Manager
Jill Brodt, Laboratory Director
Linda Adams, Project Manager
Jaime Lynch, Principal Analyst
Lisa Surber, Principal Analyst

Provider of water and wastewater testing services. The company analyses process include nitrate, arsenic, and volatile organics compounds.

Bridgepoint Systems Inc　　HQ
2607 Seventh St Ste C
Berkeley CA 94710
P: 510-346-1510　F: 510-346-2410　　PRC:209
www.bridgepointsystems.com
Email: customerservice@bridgepointsystems.com
Estab: 1995

Tom Corder, President & CEO
Jim Mullin, VP of Engineering

Provider of security solutions such as CAC card readers, PIV card readers, and access control experts for government contractors and security integrators.

Bright Computing Inc　　HQ
2880 Zanker Rd Ste 203
San Jose CA 95134
P: 408-300-9448　F: 408-715-0102　　PRC:323
www.brightcomputing.com
Email: info@brightcomputing.com
Estab: 2009

Dave Maples, SVP
Panos Labropoulos, Support Engineer
Brian Cassidy, Independent Investor

Provider of software solutions for provisioning and managing HPC clusters, Hadoop clusters, and openstack private clouds.

Bright Pattern Inc　　HQ
611 Gateway Blvd Ste 810
S San Francisco CA 94080
P: 650-529-4099　　PRC:326
www.brightpattern.com
Email: sales@brightpattern.com
Estab: 2010

Alexei Vovenko, VP of Engineering
Ivan Malyshkin, Director of Business Development
Nikolay Anisimov, Director of Research
Aleksandr Lobastov, Director of Engineering
Sergey Menshikov, Product Manager

Provider of enterprise contact center application for blended multi-channel interactions. The company offers products based on modern technology.

BrightEdge Technologies Inc　　HQ
989 E Hillsdale Blvd Ste 300
Foster City CA 94404
P: 800-578-8023　　PRC:325
www.brightedge.com
Estab: 2007

Jim Yu, CEO & Co-Founder
Lemuel Park, CTO & Co-Founder
Joseph Russell, CFO
Krish Kumar, CRO & COO
Sammy Yu, Chief Architect

Developer of mobile web applications, websites, and publishing platforms. The company specializes in SmartPath technology.

Brighterion Inc HQ
123 Mission St 17th Fl
San Francisco CA 94105
P: 415-986-5600 F: 415-986-5694 PRC:325
www.brighterion.com
Email: info@brighterion.com
Estab: 2000

Jason Revelle, VP & CTO
Jeff Muschick, VP of Business Development
Sudhir Jha, Mastercard SVP & Head of Brighterion
Kurt Schwabe, Marketing Manager
David Wang, Software QA Engineer

Provider of products for fraud prevention, predictive intelligence, risk management, and homeland security. The company focuses on adaptive analytics.

Brightidea Inc HQ
25 Pacific Ave
San Francisco CA 94111
P: 415-692-1912 PRC:323
brightidea.com
Email: support@brightidea.com
Estab: 1999

Matthew Greeley, CEO
Vincent Carbone, COO
David Carter, VP of Finance & People
Gretchen Hoffman, VP of Marketing
Genevieve Wang, VP of Product

Provider of innovative management software solutions. The company's products include WebStorm, Switchboard, and Pipeline modules.

Brightsign LLC HQ
983-A University Ave
Los Gatos CA 95032
P: 408-852-9263 PRC:323
www.brightsign.biz
Email: sales@brightsign.biz
Estab: 2002

Anthony Wood, Founder & Chairman
Jeff Hastings, CEO
Sarah Dryden, CFO
Bryan Kennedy, VP of Business Development
Ann Holland, VP of Marketing

Provider of digital sign media players, software, and networking solutions for the commercial digital signage industry.

Brightsource Energy Inc HQ
1999 Harrison St Ste 2150
Oakland CA 94612
P: 510-550-8161 F: 510-550-8165 PRC:129
www.brightsourceenergy.com
Estab: 2006

David H. Ramm, Chairman & CEO
Eitan Abramovitch, CFO & Chief Administrative Officer
Tom Wray, VP of Business Development
Danny Eytani, SVP of Project Engineering
Mathew Brett, SVP of Business Development

Developer of solar thermal technology for electric power, petroleum, and industrial-process markers.

Broadcom Inc HQ
1320 Ridder Park Dr
San Jose CA 95131
P: 408-433-8000 PRC:61
www.broadcom.com
Estab: 1991

Hock E. Tan, President & CEO
Tom Krause, CFO
Charlie Kawwas, SVP & Chief Sales Officer
Mark Brazeal, CLO
Kirsten Spears, VP & Corporate Controller & Principal Accounting Officer

Developer of digital and analog semiconductors. The company also specializes in optical communication semiconductors.

Broadway Sheet Metal & Mfg HQ
133 Starlite St
S San Francisco CA 94080-6313
P: 650-873-4585 F: 650-873-4582 PRC:157
www.broadwaysheetmetal.com
Email: bsmmfg@broadwaysheetmetal.com
Estab: 1971

Alex Merzel, President

Manufacturer of sheet metals. The company's products include hoods cartridge, sinks, tables, and mixer stands.

Bromium Inc HQ
20883 Stevens Creek Blvd Ste 100
Cupertino CA 95014
P: 408-213-5668 PRC:323
www8.hp.com
Estab: 2010

Ian Pratt, Co-Founder & President
Simon Crosby, Co-Founder & CTO & Advisor
Gregory Webb, CEO
Kevin Mosher, CRO
Aarij Khan, CMO

Provider of enterprise security solutions. The company focuses on security software development, technical support, and task introspection.

Broncus Medical Inc HQ
125 Nicholson Ln
San Jose CA 95134
P: 650-428-1600 F: 650-428-1542 PRC:28
www.broncus.com
Email: info@broncus.com
Estab: 2012

Todd Cornell, President
Henky Wibowo, Consulting CTO
Tom Keast, VP of Product Development & Operations
Vince Chung, Materials Manager

Provider of navigation, diagnostic and therapeutic technology solutions for treating patients with lung disease.

Brooks Automation Inc BR
46702 Bayside Pkwy
Fremont CA 94538
P: 510-661-5000 F: 510-661-5166 PRC:121
www.brooks.com
Email: sales@brooks.com
Estab: 1978

Stephen S. Schwartz, President & CEO
Lindon G. Robertson, EVP & CFO
William T. Montone, SVP of Human Resources
Jason W. Joseph, SVP & General Counsel & Corporate Secretary
Barbara Culhane, Corporate Marketing Manager

Provider of automation, vacuum, and instrumentation solutions for the semiconductor manufacturing, life sciences, and clean energy industries.

Brown and Caldwell BR
75 E Santa Clara Ste 375
San Jose CA 95113
P: 408-703-2528 PRC:142
brownandcaldwell.com
Email: info@brwncald.com
Estab: 1947

Jay Patil, SVP & Director of sales strategy & marketing
Susy Pepper, SVP of Corporate HR
Michael Puccio, Senior Associate

Provider of engineering consulting services. The company specializes in contracting, pumping station design, project management, and odor control.

Brown Metals Co HQ
8635 White Oak Ave [N]
Rancho Cucamonga CA 91730
P: 909-484-3124 PRC:62
www.brownmetals.com
Emp: 1-10 Estab: 1970

Carolyn Brown, CEO
Justin Lasley, CIO
Amy Blanes, Manager of Internal Operations
Krista Lane, Administrative Assistant

Manufacturer and distributor of stainless steel strip, sheet, copper strip and much more.

BRS Media Inc HQ
350 Townsend St Ste 321
San Francisco CA 94107-1696
P: 415-677-4027 F: 415-677-4025 PRC:318
brsmedia.com
Email: investor@brsmedia.com
Estab: 1995

George T. Bundy, Founder & Chairman & CEO
Junaid Siddiqui, Operations & Business Development Manager

Provider of multimedia e-commerce services. The company specializes in radio and Internet applications.

Bryan World Productions HQ
PO Box 74033 [N]
Los Angeles CA 90004
P: 323-856-9256 PRC:60
www.graffitiverite.com

Bob Bryan, Executive Producer

Retailer of Design CDs and DVDs, books and instruction manuals.

BSK Associates BR
3140 Gold Camp Dr Ste 160
Rancho Cordova CA 95670
P: 916-853-9293   F: 916-853-9297   PRC:140
bskassociates.com
Email: olau@bskassociates.com
Estab: 1966

Richard Johnson, President
Mike Vartanian, CFO
Kris Morton, CIO
Sherri Petro, Director of Human Resources
Elizabeth Bunger, Lab Director

Provider of geotechnical and environmental testing services. The company also offers materials testing services.

BT Laser & Manufacturing Inc HQ
425 Reed St
Santa Clara CA 95050
P: 408-566-0135   F: 408-562-3999   PRC:80
btlaser.com
Estab: 1995

Kirk Rossman, Founder & CEO

Provider of custom design, laser and water jet cutting, fabrication, and welding services for solar, semiconductor, and communication sectors.

Buckles-Smith BR
540 Martin Ave
Santa Clara CA 95050
P: 408-280-7777   PRC:245
buckles-smith.com
Email: info@buckles-smith.com

Art Cook, CEO
Eric Peschke, VP of Operations
Kevin Machi, Director of Industrial Sales
Michele Sauvadon, Director of Organizational
Development
Peter Fenyes, Account Manager

Supplier of industrial automation equipment. The company offers signaling devices, wires and cables, enclosures, and fasteners.

Bugcrowd HQ
921 Front St 1st Fl
San Francisco CA 94111
P: 888-361-9734   PRC:326
bugcrowd.com
Email: hello@bugcrowd.com
Estab: 2012

Casey Ellis, Chairman & Founder & CTO
Nick Telford, CFO
Jason Pitzen, Director of Sales
Drew Lebeau, Senior Director Enterprise Sales
Sam Houston, Senior Community Manager

Provider of security solutions. The company is engaged in pre-launch consulting, research, and testing services.

Buglab LLC HQ
3600 Clayton Rd Ste B
Concord CA 94521
P: 925-208-1952   F: 925-208-1917   PRC:187
www.buglab.com
Email: info@buglab.com
Estab: 2003

Martin Debreczeny, Founder
John Gwynn, Manufacturing Engineer

Developer of biomass measuring equipment such as sensors, biomass monitor, and biomass multiplier involved in fermentation and microbial cultures.

Buildera HQ
570 El Camino Real Ste 150 PMB 415
Redwood City CA 94063-1262
P: 650-587-6738   PRC:319
www.buildera.com
Estab: 1999

Greg Lowitz, CEO
Kamrul Hasan, Director

Focuses on structural crack monitoring solutions. The company deals with installation services and serves the industrial sector.

BuildingIQ Inc HQ
2121 S El Camino Real Ste 200
San Mateo CA 94403
P: 888-260-4080   PRC:326
www.buildingiq.com
Estab: 2009

Steve Nguyen, VP
Scott McCormick, VP

Provider of software-as-a-service solution to optimize energy use in commercial buildings such as hospitality, healthcare facilities, and utilities.

Bullet Guard Co HQ
3963 Commerce Dr
West Sacramento CA 95691
P: 916-373-0402   F: 916-373-0208   PRC:137
www.bulletguard.com
Email: sheila@bulletguardmail.com
Estab: 1976

Karlin Lynch, President
Ken Brumbaugh, VP

Designer and manufacturer of bullet resistant and bullet proof products. The company serves the banking, government, and law enforcement sectors.

Bulling Metal Works Inc HQ
459 Hester St
San Leandro CA 94577
P: 510-351-2073   PRC:82
www.bullingmetalworks.com
Estab: 1977

Walter Bulling, President
Kara Bulling, Office Manager
James Knoll, Design & Programming Manager

Manufacturer of pressure vessels and laser cutting machinery. The company also offers other custom fabrication products.

Burleson Consulting Inc HQ
950 Glenn Dr Ste 245
Folsom CA 95630
P: 916-984-4651   F: 916-984-8261   PRC:142
www.burlesonconsulting.com
Email: info@burlesonconsulting.com
Estab: 1985

Nadia Burleson, President & Principal Engineer
Jacque Thompson, Business Manager & CFO
Allison Nunes, Greenhouse Manager
Alex Henson, Environmental Engineer
Gregory Reller, Principal Geologist

Provider of environmental compliance and engineering services for the clients in Southern Oregon, Northern California, and Nevada.

Burlington Safety Laboratory Inc BR
7087 Commerce Cir Ste B
Pleasanton CA 94588
P: 925-251-1412   PRC:306
www.burlingtonsafety.com
Email: info@burlingtonsafety.com
Estab: 1971

Michael Senin, General Manager
Justin White, Western Regional Safety Manager
Bill Sherwood, Laboratory Manager

Designer and manufacturer of laboratory and electrical safety equipment. The company's customers include electric utilities and contractors.

Burstorm Inc HQ
355 Hartz Ave Ste D
Danville CA 94526
P: 650-610-1480   PRC:323
burstorm.com
Email: info@burstorm.com
Estab: 2009

Brandon Abbey, CEO

Provider of cloud design tools application. The company specializes in design, collaborate, quote, and implement of cloud architecture.

Busse Design USA Inc HQ
5857 Chabot Ct
Oakland CA 94618
P: 415-689-8090   PRC:323
bussedesign.com
Estab: 1997

Joy A. Busse, CEO & Director of User Experience

Provider of interface design services. The company's services include website design and application user interface.

Butterfly Sciences HQ
PO Box 2363
Davis CA 95617
P: 415-518-8153   PRC:24
bf-sci.com
Email: info@bf-sci.com
Estab: 2009

Brian Hanley, Founder & Chief Scientist

Developer of gene therapies for HIV and aging. The company also provides consulting services for biotech investment evaluations.

BuyerLeverage   HQ
 2225 E Bayshore Ave Ste 200
 Palo Alto CA 94303
 P: 650-320-1608   PRC:320
 www.buyerleverage.com
 Email: corp-info@buyerleverage.com

Mark Landesmann, Developer

Provider of technologies and services that allow consumers and businesses to profit and control their communications and information.

C & G Plastics   HQ
 12729 Foothill Blvd   [N]
 Sylmar CA 91342
 P: 818-837-3773   F: 818-837-3770   PRC:189
 www.cgplastics.net
 Email: info@cgplastics.net
 Estab: 1994

Greg Leighton, President

Manufacturer of plastic products and also provides services including, injection molding, shipping and packaging, and assembly.

C & H Testing Service LLC   HQ
 6224 Price Way   [N]
 Bakersfield CA 93308
 P: 661-589-4030   F: 661-589-5390   PRC:149
 www.candhtesting.com
 Estab: 1981

Ken Dickinson, General Manager
Michael Sears, Manager of Safety & Dispatcher & Local HR
Carrie Rickels, Administrative Accounting Technician

Provider of services to oil and gas production industry specializing in pressure testing and magnetic flux testing to verify pipe and tubing integrity.

C L Hann Industries Inc   HQ
 1020 Timothy Dr
 San Jose CA 95133
 P: 408-293-4800   F: 408-293-5858   PRC:80
 clhann.com
 Email: info@clhann.com
 Estab: 1971

Pete Hann, CEO
Cheyne Hann, CFO & Project Manager
Arthur Korp, VP
Billy Haynes, Procurement Manager
Georgette Hann, Office Manager

Provider of contract manufacturing services including CNC machining, welding, assembly and testing, and conditioning.

C Sys Labs Inc   HQ
 3030 Thorntree Dr Ste 6
 Chico CA 95973
 P: 530-894-7954   PRC:211
 www.csyslabs.com
 Estab: 1987

Thomas Mroz, President

Designer and manufacturer of test printed circuit boards. The company is engaged in cable fabrication and failure analysis services.

C&C Machining Inc   HQ
 28424 Century St
 Hayward CA 94545
 P: 510-876-8139   F: 510-876-8913   PRC:80
 candcmachininginc.com
 Email: sales@candcmachininginc.com

Steve Claesson, Owner

Provider of machining services. The company specializes in magnetic alloys, expansion alloys, and shielding alloys.

C&D Semiconductor Services Inc   HQ
 2031 Concourse Dr
 San Jose CA 95131
 P: 408-383-1888   F: 408-383-1889   PRC:126
 www.cdsemi.com
 Email: contactus@cdsemi.com
 Estab: 1989

Rick Acaba, Global Sales Manager

Manufacturer of cleaner systems, wafer sorters, and wafer inspection systems. The company deals with inspection and processing.

C&M Biolabs   HQ
 2600 Hilltop Dr Ste B-C147
 Richmond CA 94806
 P: 510-691-7160   PRC:272
 cmbiolabs.com
 Email: info@cmbiolabs.com
 Estab: 2011

Dao-Yao He, Founder & President

Provider of products and services to scientists. The company offers cloning and sequencing and antibody services.

C&P Microsystems LLC   HQ
 1260 Holm Rd Ste C
 Petaluma CA 94954
 P: 707-776-4500   F: 707-776-4555   PRC:159
 microcutsystems.com
 Estab: 2003

Wayne Smith, VP

Manufacturer and seller of paper cutter control systems. The company offers microcip, cutternet, and micro facts.

C&S Telecommunications Inc   HQ
 3105 Fite Cir Ste 104
 Sacramento CA 95827
 P: 916-364-8636   F: 916-363-6280   PRC:68
 www.cstelecommunications.com
 Estab: 1994

Chuck Smith, Owner

Supplier of telephone systems and data networks. The company offers installation, training, and other services.

C-Scan Corp   HQ
 14125 Capri Dr Ste 8A
 Los Gatos CA 95032
 P: 800-953-7888   PRC:12
 www.cscan.com
 Email: customersupport@cscan.com
 Estab: 1988

Ata Khojasteh, CEO
Karen Mattson, Sales Administrator

Manufacturer and designer of thermal recorders and printers for medical applications and the healthcare sector.

CW Cole & Company Inc   HQ
 2560 Rosemead Blvd   [N]
 South El Monte CA 91733
 P: 626-443-2473   F: 626-443-9253   PRC:243
 www.colelighting.com
 Estab: 1911

Steve Cole, President
Katy Cole, VP
Matthew Goslin, Light Rail Project Manager
Alma Loza, Manager of Human Resources
Dan Wilkins, Manager of Design & Engineering

Manufacturer and distributor of lighting products.

C3Nano Inc   HQ
 3988 Trust Way
 Hayward CA 94545
 P: 510-259-9650   PRC:87
 c3nano.com
 Email: info@c3nano.com
 Estab: 2010

Ajay Virkar, Founder & CTO
Cliff Morris, CEO
Xiqiang Yang, Director of Research & Development
Yadong Cao, Application Engineerings & Technical Marketing Manager
Vicki Luo, Quality Manager

Developer of transparent conductive ink and film such as touch sensors, OLED lighting and displays, EMI shielding for touch sensor and display industry.

Caban Resources LLC   HQ
 130 Arena St   [N]
 El Segundo CA 90245
 P: 877-880-1600   PRC:130
 www.cabanresources.com
 Estab: 2001

Robert Caban, Contact

Provider of health information management services and solutions, and coding services.

Cable Connection Inc   HQ
 1035 Mission Ct
 Fremont CA 94539
 P: 510-249-9000   F: 510-354-8000   PRC:211
 cable-connection.com
 Email: sales@cable-connection.com

William Parrette, VP
Patrick McQuade, Director
Vince Truong, Manager

Provider of premium PCB assemblies and turnkey OEM/ODM product. The company also specializes in cable and wire harness services.

Cable Labs BR
400 W California Ave
Sunnyvale CA 94086
P: 669-777-9020 PRC:62
cablelabs.com

Phil McKinney, President & CEO
Belal Hamzeh, CTO & SVP
Rachel Beisel, CMO & SVP
Anju Ahuja, VP
Martha Lyons, Director of Market Development

Provider of cable services. The company is engaged in virtualization and network evaluation services.

Cable Moore Inc HQ
4700 Coliseum Way
Oakland CA 94601
P: 510-436-8000 F: 510-436-8010 PRC:159
www.cablemoore.com
Estab: 1986

Sandra Moore, President
Tino Faaumu, Purchasing Agent

Manufacturer and distributor of safety and construction equipment and guy and bridge strands. The company offers wire ropes, cables, railings, and slings.

CAD Masters Inc HQ
201 N Civic Dr Ste 182
Walnut Creek CA 94596
P: 925-939-1378 F: 925-939-1380 PRC:316
cadmasters.com
Estab: 1994

Michelle Self, CEO & Founder
Neil Bondy, VP of Technical Services
John Catoline, Account & Sales Manager
Artem Chulikanov, IT Manager
Dwayne Tindall, Account Manager

Designer and developer of software and hardware solutions. The company focuses on drafting, engineering, plotting, and on-site project assistance.

CAD PROS PCB Design Inc HQ
PO Box 54289
San Jose CA 95154
P: 408-734-9600 PRC:124
www.cadpros.com
Estab: 1997

John Koehne, General Manager of Sales

Designer and manufacturer of printed circuit boards. The company offers services to the residential and commercial sectors.

Cadence Design Systems Inc HQ
2655 Seely Ave
San Jose CA 95134
P: 408-943-1234 F: 408-428-5001 PRC:155
www.cadence.com
Estab: 1988
Sales: Over $3B

Anirudh Devgan, President
Lip-Bu Tan, CEO
Neil Kole, SVP & CIO
John M. Wall, CFO
Jim Cowie, SVP & General Counsel & Secretary

Provider of semiconductor IP and electronic design automation services. The company offers tools for logic and RF design, IC packaging, and other needs.

Cairn Biosciences HQ
455 Mission Bay Blvd S
San Francisco CA 94158
P: 415-503-1185 PRC:34
www.cairnbio.com
Email: info@cairnbio.com
Estab: 2013

Mary Ludlam, Founder & CEO
Duncan Parsons-Karavassilis, VP of Finance & Operations

Provider of therapeutic solutions for treating cancer. The company is involved in biotechnical research and commercial business.

Cal Semi LLC HQ
175 Bernal Rd Ste 100
San Jose CA 95119
P: 510-687-9960 PRC:212
www.calsemi.com

Mark Martin, President

Provider of semiconductor equipment remanufacturing services. The company specializes in products such as furnaces, cantilever, and wet sinks.

Cal-Disc Grinding Company Inc HQ
1741 Potrero Ave [N]
South El Monte CA 91733
P: 626-444-9576 F: 626-444-9683 PRC:24
caldisc.com
Estab: 1999

Steve Kimbrough, Contact

Provider of disc grinding, flat lapping and much more services.

Cal-Tron Corp HQ
2290 Dixon Ln
Bishop CA 93514
P: 760-873-8491 F: 760-873-8431 PRC:84
www.caltroncorp.com
Email: info@caltroncorp.com
Estab: 1939

Scott Lasley, Operations Supervisor

Developer and manufacturer of cell reagent tools. The company's products find application in proteomic research.

Cal-West Specialty Coatings Inc HQ
1058 W Evelyn Ave
Sunnyvale CA 94086
P: 408-720-7440 F: 408-720-7450 PRC:47
cal-west.net
Email: info@cal-west.net
Estab: 1988

Brian Wong, VP

Supplier of liquid masking and surface preparation products. The company also offers temporary protective coatings.

Cala Health Inc HQ
875 Mahler Rd Ste 168
Burlingame CA 94010
P: 415-890-3961 PRC:196
www.calahealth.com
Email: info@calahealth.com

Kate Rosenbluth, Founder & Chief Scientific Officer
Renee Ryan, CEO
Kristie Burns, CMO
Manish Gupta, VP of Clinical & Regulatory Affairs
John Colombo, VP of Product Development & Operations

Provider of therapeutic solutions. The company focuses on the development of neuro peripheral therapy to treating chronic diseases.

Calabazas Creek Research Inc HQ
690 Port Dr
San Mateo CA 94404-1010
P: 650-312-9575 F: 650-312-9536 PRC:2
calcreek.com
Email: rlives@calcreek.com
Estab: 1994

Julie Givens, CFO
George Collins, Operations Manager

Specializes in the research and development of high power RF sources, and components. The company offers software development services.

Calchemist HQ
220 South Linden Ave Ste L
S San Francisco CA 94080
P: 650-551-1495 PRC:80
www.calchemist.com
Email: info@calchemist.com
Emp: 29 Estab: 2007

Marc Schrier, Owner

Provider of contract research services. The company specializes in chemical, material science and laboratory equipment testing.

Calcoast-Itl HQ
683 Thornton St
San Leandro CA 94577
P: 510-924-7100 F: 510-878-9251 PRC:306
www.calcoast-itl.com
Email: sales@calcoast-itl.com
Estab: 1949

Mark Evans, Laboratory Director & Owner

Provider of testing services for automotive and roadway lightings. The company offers consultation, assistance, and laboratory installation services.

Calcon Systems Inc HQ
12919 Alcosta Blvd Ste 9
San Ramon CA 94583
P: 925-277-0665 F: 925-277-9647 PRC:228
www.calconsystems.com
Email: sales@calcon.com
Estab: 1987

Pete Schratz, President
Ryan Smith, General Manager
Ana Springer, Office Manager
Frank Ortega, Manager
John Perotti, Project Manager

Provider of process control, instrumentation, and automation solutions specializing in turnkey design-build system integration and support.

Calcula Technologies HQ
959 Peralta Ave
San Francisco CA 94110
P: 650-724-8696 PRC:189
www.calculatech.com
Estab: 2012

Buzz Bonneau, CEO

Developer of medical devices for the treatment of
kidney stones. The company serves the healthcare sector.

Calex Manufacturing Company Inc HQ
2401 Stanwell Dr
Concord CA 94520-4841
P: 925-687-4411   F: 925-687-3333   PRC:209
calex.com
Email: sales@calex.com
Estab: 1962

Susan Benker, Quality Assurance Manager

Supplier of electrical instrument modules. The
company also specializes in power supplies and
converters.

**California Brazing & Nevada Heat
Treating** HQ
37955 Central Ct
Newark CA 94560
P: 510-790-2300   F: 510-791-9300   PRC:159
www.californiabrazing.com
Email: info@californiabrazing.com

Jeff Ager, General Manager

Provider of brazing services. The company
specializes in machining and heat treatment of
components for the aviation industry.

**California Clinical Laboratory
Association** HQ
1127 11th St Ste 820
Sacramento CA 95814
P: 916-446-2646   F: 916-446-6095   PRC:191
www.ccla.info
Estab: 1976

Christine S. Sabol, President
Michael J. Arnold, Legislative Advocate & Execu-
tive Director
Traci Y. Hundley, Executive Legislative Secretary
Kristian E. Foy, Legislative Advocate

Provider of an Association for small and large
laboratories in California. The company files suits
to prevent medicare from denying coverage for
lab tests.

California Contract Company HQ
1900 Seventh St Unit D
Richmond CA 94801
P: 510-654-9375   F: 510-631-4669   PRC:82
californiacontractco.com
Email: railings@prodigy.net
Estab: 1973

Micheal O. Stang, Owner

Provider of metal fabrication and installation
services. The company focuses on aluminum,
stainless steel and glass, and bronze.

California Eastern Laboratories HQ
4590 Patrick Henry Dr
Santa Clara CA 95054-1817
P: 408-919-2500   F: 408-988-0279   PRC:61
www.cel.com
Estab: 1959

Gretchen King, Director of Human Resources
Mouqun Dong, QA Manager
Sam Yacoub, Senior Product Marketing Manager

Provider of RF, microwave, and optoelectronic
semiconductors. The company also offers lasers,
detectors, and other products.

California Electric Supply HQ
3301 N Sillect Ave [N]
Bakersfield CA 93308
P: 661-324-6727   F: 661-323-6547   PRC:245
royalbakersfield.com
Estab: 1971

Alex Nolan, Manager
Andrew Combs, Manager
Jake Walters, Manager
Arash Goodarzi, Consultant
Chris Harrison, Consultant

Distributor of electrical products such as cable
ties, enclosures, hole cutting and much more.

**California Hydroforming Company
Inc** HQ
850 S Lawson St [N]
City Of Industry CA 91748
P: 626-912-0036   F: 626-965-5944   PRC:159
californiahydroforming.com
Estab: 1988

David Wickey, President
Richard Robles, VP & Operations Manager
Shaun Vail, Procurement Manager & Production
Manager
Juan Figueroa, Quality Manager

Provider of metal forming using hydroforming
presses.

**California Integration Coordinators
Inc** HQ
6048 Enterprise Dr
Diamond Springs CA 95619
P: 530-626-6168   F: 530-626-7740   PRC:211
www.cic-inc.com
Email: cic@cic-inc.com
Estab: 1988

Cherie Snyder-Myers, President
William Yu, Director
Debby Verry, Lab Manager
Harry Rehder, Project Coordinator
Justin Cary, Project Coordinator

Manufacturer of custom turnkey printed circuit
boards. The company's services include repairs,
component sourcing, fabrication, and assembly.

California Laboratory Services HQ
3249 Fitzgerald Rd
Rancho Cordova CA 95742
P: 800-638-7301 PRC:306
www.californialab.com

Scott J. Furnas, President
Zhonqwen Liang, Laboratory Director
Mark Smith, Operations Manager
Tyler Gustafsson, Business Development Manager
Mark Dingman, Accounting Manager

Provider of analytical testing services. The company offers a comprehensive range of soil and water
testing for government and private agencies.

California Motor Controls HQ
3070 Bay Vista Ct
Benicia CA 94510
P: 707-746-6255   F: 707-746-6165   PRC:228
www.cmcontrols.com
Email: sales@cmcontrols.com
Estab: 2004

Tom Duling, President & CEO
Jarrod Slate, COO
Mike Loden, Manager of Customer Service

Manufacturer of electrical control panels. The
company offers pump controls and communication
systems for municipal and commercial applications.

California Seed & Plant Lab Inc HQ
3556 Sankey Rd
Pleasant Grove CA 95668
P: 916-655-1581   F: 916-655-1582   PRC:31
calspl.com
Estab: 1992

Sukhi Pannu, Director of Research & Business
Development
Ashlee Bednorski, Testing Coordinator

Provider of pathological and genetic testing services. The company provides services for the vege-
table seed, grapevine, and strawberry industries.

California Software Systems HQ
1791 San Juan Canyon Rd
San Juan Bautista CA 95045
P: 831-477-6843   F: 831-265-4553   PRC:322
californiasoftwaresystems.com
Email: sales@californiasoftwaresystems.com

Russell W. Walton, Founder

Provider of graphics software solutions. The company products include DNC file server for windows
and graphics software.

California Solar Systems BR
2780 N Miami Ave Ste 102
Fresno CA 93727
P: 855-227-6527 PRC:135
855casolar.com
Email: info@855casolar.com

Barry Wardak, President
Patti Pueschel, Operations Manager
Nancy McLaughlin, Marketing Manager
Ryan Lien, Regional Sales Manager
Derek Patterson, Marketing Manager

Provider of grid-tied turn key solar electric systems. The company caters to both residential and
commercial sectors.

California Steel Industries   HQ

14000 San Bernardino Ave   [N]
Fontana CA 92335
P: 909-350-6300   F: 909-350-6398   PRC:141
www.californiasteel.com
Email: communications@californiasteel.com
Emp: 501-1000   Estab: 1984

Ricardo Bernardes, EVP
Scott Starr, EVP of Operations
John Walburg, Manager of Sales & Marketing
Kyle Schulty, Manager of Communications
Pete Broderick, Regional Manager

Manufacturer of steel products.

California Transport Enterprises Inc   HQ

2610 Wisconsin Ave   [N]
South Gate CA 90280
P: 323-357-1720   F: 323-357-1724   PRC:142
www.cteinc.com
Email: sales@cteinc.net
Estab: 1978

Philippe Shepnick, CEO

Provider of transportation and trucking services.

Calithera Biosciences Inc   HQ

343 Oyster Point Blvd Ste 200
S San Francisco CA 94080
P: 650-870-1000   PRC:191
www.calithera.com
Estab: 2010

Susan M. Molineaux, President & CEO & Founder
Keith Orford, CMO
Sumita Ray, SVP & General Counsel & Chief
Compliance Officer
Curtis C. Hecht, Chief Business Officer
Eric B. Sjogren, SVP of Drug Discovery

Developer of small molecule drugs directed
against tumor metabolism and tumor immunology
targets for the treatment of cancer.

Calix Inc   HQ

1435 N McDowell Blvd Ste 200
Petaluma CA 94954
P: 707-766-3000   F: 707-283-3100   PRC:68
www.calix.com
Email: info@calix.com
Estab: 1999
Sales: $300M to $1 Billion

Carl Russo, CEO
Jill Von Berg, VP & CIO
Cory J. Sindelar, CFO
Michael Weening, EVP & COO
Matt Collins, CMO

Provider of broadband communications access
systems and software. The company offers business, fiber access, and mobile backhaul solutions.

Callouette Fabricators Inc   HQ

320 W Channel Rd Unit E
Benicia CA 94510
P: 707-746-0962   F: 707-746-6429   PRC:80
callouettefabricators.com

Barry Callouette, President

Developer of machining components for automotive, process control, biotech, plasma, instrumentation, and aviation industries.

M-62

Calmar Laser   HQ

951 Commercial St
Palo Alto CA 94303
P: 650-272-6980   F: 650-272-6988   PRC:172
www.calmarlaser.com
Email: contacts@calmarlaser.com
Estab: 1996

Claire Chen, Sales Manager
William Shao, Operations Manager
Kai You, Electronic Engineer
Shenghong Huang, Senior Optical Engineer

Manufacturer of ultrafast fiber laser and fiber amplifier solutions for the needs of industry, research
institutions, and universities.

Calmax Technology Inc   HQ

526 Laurelwood Rd
Santa Clara CA 95054
P: 408-748-8660   PRC:80
www.calmaxtechnology.com
Email: customerservice@calmaxtechnology.com
Estab: 1987

Boguslaw Marcinkowski, Owner
George Marcinkowski, President
Scott Shimada, Director of Operations
Gary Keppers, Account Manager
Manny Adame, Business Development Manager

Provider of precision machined components and
electro-mechanical assemblies. The company
serves semi-conductor and medical industries.

Calolympic Safety   HQ

1720 Delilah St   [N]
Corona CA 92879
P: 951-340-2229   F: 951-340-3337   PRC:80
www.caloly-safety.com
Estab: 1958

Dale C. Bermond, CEO & President

Distributor of bandages and health-conscious
ergonomic products.

Calpico Inc   HQ

1387 San Mateo Ave   [N]
S San Francisco CA 94080
P: 650-588-2241   F: 650-873-6952   PRC:202
www.calpicoinc.com
Emp: 1-10   Estab: 1959

Carey Wilson, President

Manufacturer and distributor of underground
piping products.

Calsoft Inc   HQ

1762 Technology Dr Ste 229
San Jose CA 95110-1385
P: 408-834-7086   PRC:323
www.calsoftinc.com
Email: marcom@calsoftinc.com
Estab: 1998

Bo Shao, President
Anupam Bhide, CEO
Kiran S. Kotian, Senior Manager

Designer and developer of storage, networking,
and operating systems. The company deals with
design, delivery, and installation.

Caltest Analytical Lab   HQ

1885 N Kelly Rd
Napa CA 94558
P: 707-258-4000   F: 707-226-1001   PRC:306
www.caltestlabs.com
Email: info@caltestlabs.com
Estab: 1974

Todd Albertson, VP
Shawna Rees, Laboratory Director
Sonya Allahyari, Project Manager
Mike Hamilton, Project Manager
Ricky Dy, Information Technology Manager

Provider of analyses services of wastewater,
groundwater, non-radioactive water, and hazardous waste samples.

Caltron Components Corp   HQ

3350 Scott Blvd Bldg 31
Santa Clara CA 95054
P: 408-748-2140   PRC:84
www.caltroncomponents.com
Email: sales@caltroncomponents.com
Estab: 1964

Bob Roumimper, President
Arnold Moore, VP
Brian Maguire, Director of Engineering
Kenny Kumar, Account Manager
Elton Kong, Territory Account Manager

Distributor of electronic capacitors and resistors.
The company also focuses on semiconductor
products.

Caltron Industries Inc   HQ

43436 Mission Siena Cir
Fremont CA 94539
P: 510-440-1800   PRC:112
www.caltronind.com
Estab: 1997

Jim Wang, General Manager
Andrew Leung, Account Executive

Manufacturer of digital signage products and touch
screen monitors. The company specializes in digital
video signage and media advertising services.

Calypso Systems Inc   HQ

2255 O'Toole Ave Ste 60
San Jose CA 95131
P: 408-982-9955   PRC:15
www.calypsotesters.com
Email: info@calypsotesters.com
Estab: 1991

Eden Kim, CEO

Developer of solid state storage test and measurement. The company specializes in test results
automatically stored in the CTS MySQL database.

Calypso Technology Inc   HQ
595 Market St Ste 700
San Francisco CA 94105
P: 415-530-4000   PRC:323
www2.calypso.com
Estab: 1997

Didier Bouillard, CEO
Helene Koutsoudakis, CFO
Tej Sidhu, CTO
Laurent Jacquemin, Chief Customer Officer
Jonathan D. Walsh, CAO

Provider of front-to-back technology solutions
for the financial markers. The company offers
technology platform for cross asset trading risk
management.

Calysta   HQ
1140 O'Brien Dr
Menlo Park CA 94025
P: 650-492-6880   PRC:268
www.calysta.com
Email: info@calysta.com
Estab: 2011

Alan Shaw, President, CEO & Founder
Lynsey Wenger, CFO & Chief Sustainability
Officer
Josh Silverman, Chief Product & Innovation
Officer
Blake Campbell, VP of Administration & General
Counsel
Lori Giver, VP of Research & Development

Focuses on the development and manufacture of
protein for commercial aquaculture and livestock
feed.

Calyx Technology Inc   HQ
6475 Camden Ave Ste 207
San Jose CA 95120
P: 214-252-5610   F: 214-252-5650   PRC:320
www.calyxsoftware.com
Email: sales@calyxsoftware.com
Estab: 1991

Doug Chang, President
Ted Hicks, Director of Product Management
Sung Park, Director of Product Development
Max Youm, Director of Systems & QA Group
Mitra Eslami, Director of Program Management
Office

Provider of mortgage solutions for banks and
credit unions. The company also serves mortgage
bankers and brokers.

**Campbell/Harris Security Equipment
Company**   HQ
875-A Island Dr Ste 356
Alameda CA 94502-6768
P: 510-864-8010   F: 510-864-8013   PRC:58
www.cseco.com
Email: info@cseco.com
Estab: 1984

Tony Harris, President & CEO

Manufacturer of busters, fiberscopes, probe kits,
and personal radiation detectors. The company
also focuses on distribution.

Canary Instruments   HQ
1385 Eighth St Ste 205
Arcata CA 95521
P: 707-506-6611   PRC:131
canaryinstruments.com
Email: info@canaryinstruments.com
Estab: 2013

Kimberli Hudson, CEO
Lonny Grafman, CPO
Gabriel Krause, CTO

Provider of home energy monitor with colorful
LED lights that provide instant feedback on the
electricity use.

Cannon Water Technology   HQ
233 Technology Way Ste 9
Rocklin CA 95765
P: 916-315-2691   PRC:50
cannonwater.com
Email: csd@cannonwater.com
Estab: 1985

Richard Cannon, Owner
David Cannon, President
Janis Cannon, VP & CFO
Paula Gallegos, Inside Sales Representative

Manufacturer of chemical pumps, water treatment
chemicals, and water treatment equipment. The
company offers services to the industrial sector.

Cantabio Pharmaceuticals Inc   HQ
2225 E Bayshore Rd
Palo Alto CA 94303
P: 844-200-2826   PRC:34
www.cantabio.com
Email: info@cantabio.com
Estab: 2009

Gergely Toth, Founder & CEO
Simon Peace, CFO

Provider of therapeutic solutions. The company
specializes in developing therapeutic proteins to
prevent degenerative brain diseases.

Capax Technologies Inc   HQ
24842 Avenue Tibbitts   [N]
Valencia CA 91355
P: 661-257-7666   F: 661-257-4819   PRC:200
www.capaxtechnologies.com
Estab: 1988

Hiran Patel, EVP
Kira Patel, VP of Marketing & Customer Relations

Designer and manufacturer of capacitors for
commercial and military RF and Microwave
applications.

Capcom USA   LH
185 Berry St Ste 1200
San Francisco CA 94107
P: 650-350-6500   PRC:317
www.capcom.com
Email: privacy@capcom.com
Estab: 1985

Kazuhiko Abe, President
Kenzo Tsujimoto, CEO
Kazuo Kano, CFO
Ikuo Hirano, Director of Corporate Planning
Estela Lemus, Corporate Counsel

Manufacturer and distributor of electronic game
machines. The company specializes in resident
evil, monster hunter, lost planet, and devroom
games.

Capella Microsystems Inc   HQ
2201 Laurelwood Rd
Santa Clara CA 95054
P: 408-988-8000   F: 408-969-0894   PRC:87
www.capellamicro.com.tw
Email: mycapella@vishay.com
Estab: 2002

Jim Kung, VP of Sales
Peter G. Henrici, SVP of Corporate Communications

Developer of integrated technology solutions for
IC design. The company is involved in installation
and technical support.

**Capital Asset Exchange & Trading
LLC**   HQ
5201 Great America Pkwy Ste 272
Santa Clara CA 95054
P: 650-326-3313   PRC:86
www.caeonline.com
Email: info@caeonline.com
Estab: 1982

Ryan Jacob, CEO & Chairman
Jeff Robbins, President
Ricky Vij, Director
Andrew Hung, Director

Provider of secondary capital equipment. The
company offers evaporators, spectrometers,
residual gas analyzers, and electronic testing
equipment.

Capital Engineering Consultants Inc   HQ
11020 Sun Center Dr Ste 100
Rancho Cordova CA 95670
P: 916-851-3500   F: 916-631-4424   PRC:142
www.capital-engineering.com
Email: office@capital-engineering.com
Estab: 1947

Chuck Shinneman, Director of Sustainability &
Optimization
Aaron Wintersmith, Project Manager
Steve Magennis, Project Manager & Senior
Associate
Matthew Hamilton, Project Manager
Ryan Celaya, Project Manager

Provider of mechanical engineering, sustainable
design and green engineering, building commissioning, energy modeling, and other related
services.

Capital Machine HQ
83 N 17th St
Sacramento CA 95814
P: 916-443-6671 F: 916-443-6675 PRC:290
www.capmachine.com
Estab: 1936

John Collier, President
Eugene Spyksma, VP

Provider of machining, welding, fabrication, and design services. The company also distributes steel and power transmission products.

Capital Management Group HQ
934 S Flintridge Way [N]
Anaheim CA 92808
P: 714-439-9600 PRC:325
cm-group.com
Email: cm-group@sbcglobal.net
Estab: 2000

Ray Shah, President

Provider of management consulting service for small businesses.

Capital Network Solutions Inc HQ
8950 Cal Center Dr Ste 341
Sacramento CA 95826
P: 916-366-6566 PRC:326
cns-service.com
Email: help@cns-service.com
Estab: 1989

Don Thompson, CEO
John Guarienti, VP of Sales
Thom Scott, Service Engineer I
Shareef Huddle, Senior Systems Architect

Provider of Internet security systems, phone systems, and off-site encrypted backup for small and medium sized businesses.

Capital Sheet Metal HQ
500 N 16th St
Sacramento CA 95811
P: 916-443-3761 F: 916-443-3610 PRC:80
www.capitalsheetmetal.net
Email: info@capitalsheetmetal.net
Estab: 1945

Ken Hammill, President
Sam Gordon, CEO
Lindsey Heidrick, Assistant VP
Scott Johnson, Project Manager
Marcus Pantoja, Estimator

Manufacturer of custom countertops. The company deals with shearing, welding, laser cutting, and polishing services.

Capitol Communications Inc HQ
480 Ninth St
San Francisco CA 94103
P: 415-861-1727 F: 415-861-8537 PRC:63
capitolcommunications.com
Estab: 1994

Ronald J. Burgess, President
Freddie Little, Project Manager

Provider of infrastructure communication solutions for business operations. The company caters to electronics, media, and manufacturing industries.

Capnia HQ
1235 Radio Rd Ste 110
Redwood City CA 94065
P: 650-213-8444 F: 650-213-8383 PRC:186
www.capnia.com
Email: info@capnia.com

David O'Toole, CFO
Gerard Pereira, Chief Business Officer
Tony Wondka, SVP & General Manager
Scott Gilbert, VP of Engineering
Ding Hong Bin, General Manager

Focuses on the development and commercialization of therapeutic and diagnostic products to address significant unmet healthcare needs.

Capriza Inc HQ
3000 El Camino Real Ste 5-800
Palo Alto CA 94306
P: 650-600-3661 PRC:326
www.capriza.com
Estab: 2011

Oren Ariel, Founder & Chief Products & Strategy Officer
Yuval Scarlat, Chairman

Provider of codeless enterprise mobility platform. The company offers mobile-enabling business applications such as design, zaaps, manage, and security.

CapsoVision HQ
18805 Cox Ave Ste 250
Saratoga CA 95070-6615
P: 408-624-1488 F: 408-370-4795 PRC:186
www.capsovision.com
Email: info@capsovision.com
Estab: 2006

Srini Muthuswamy, Senior Director of Global Sales & Marketing
David Chung-Ta Lee, Director of ASIC
Chenyu Wu, Director of Software R&D
Chun Jia, Manager of Senior Software Engineer
Honeylette Barros, Quality Engineer Manager

Specializes in the diagnostic imaging of the gastrointestinal systems. The company offers services to hospitals and patients.

Carando Technologies Inc HQ
345 N Harrison St
Stockton CA 95203
P: 209-948-6500 F: 209-948-6757 PRC:159
carando.net
Email: sales@carando.net
Estab: 2003

Shannon Crawford, Office Manager

Manufacturer of container closing tools and dies. The company fabricates drums, water heater tanks, spare parts, appliances, and container closing tools.

Carbon Five Inc HQ
585 Howard St 2nd Fl
San Francisco CA 94105
P: 415-546-0500 PRC:323
www.carbonfive.com
Email: info@carbonfive.com
Estab: 2000

Don Thompson, COO
Christian Nelson, Partner & Director of Engineering
Courtney Hemphill, Partner & Technical Lead
David Hendee, Partner & Director of Design
Erik Ingenito, Partner

Provider of software development services such as lean design and agile development for the web and mobile sectors.

Carbon3D Inc HQ
1089 Mills Way
Redwood City CA 94063
P: 650-285-6307 PRC:275
carbon3d.com
Email: info@carbon3d.com
Estab: 2013

Joseph DeSimone, Executive Chairman
Luke Kelly, SVP of Customer Success
Craig Carlson, VP of Engineering
Jason Rolland, VP of Materials
John Norwood, Product Support Manager

Provider of hardware and software engineering and molecular science. The company specializes in continuous liquid interface production technology.

Cardiva Medical Inc HQ
1615 Wyatt Dr
Santa Clara CA 95054
P: 408-470-7170 F: 408-470-7134 PRC:189
www.cardivamedical.com
Email: customerservice@cardivamedical.com
Estab: 2002

John Russell, President & CEO
Lisa Garrett, CFO & VP of Human Resources
Justin Ballotta, COO
Zia Yassinzadeh, CTO
Roger R. Owens, Chief Commercial Officer

Developer of vascular access management products such as vascade and catalyst to facilitate rapid hemostasis following diagnostic procedures.

Caredx Inc HQ
3260 Bayshore Blvd
Brisbane CA 94005
P: 415-287-2300 F: 415-287-2450 PRC:41
caredx.com
Email: customercare@caredx.com
Estab: 2000
Sales: $100M to $300M

Peter Maag, CEO
Sasha King, CMO
Michael Bell, CFO
John J. Sninsky, CSO
Robert Woodward, Senior Director of Research

Provider of genomics technologies for the development of molecular diagnostic assays. The company specializes in molecular diagnostics.

Caribou Biosciences Inc   HQ
2929 Seventh St Ste 105
Berkeley CA 94710
P: 510-982-6030   PRC:34
cariboubio.com
Email: info@cariboubio.com
Estab: 2011

Rachel Haurwitz, President & CEO
Steven Kanner, CSO
Barbara McClung, CLO

Developer of cellular engineering and analysis solutions. The company is involved in applied biological research.

Carl Group Inc   HQ
282 Dry Creek Rd   [N]
Aptos CA 95003
P: 831-708-2610   PRC:322
www.thecarlgroup.com
Email: info@thecarlgroup.com
Estab: 1985

Tim Carl, Contact

Provider of technical writing services, technical training, web development, web design and much more.

Carlson and Beauloye   HQ
2141 Newton Ave   [N]
San Diego CA 92113
P: 619-234-2256   F: 619-234-2095   PRC:80
www.cbmachineandair.com
Email: info@cbmachineandair.com
Estab: 1924

Valerie Beauloye, Parts & Sales Manager

Manufacturer of the motorless water pump that generates its horsepower from water weight and gravity.

Carlson Wireless Technologies Inc   HQ
3134 Jacobs Ave Ste C
Eureka CA 95501
P: 707-443-0100   F: 707-443-3449   PRC:61
www.carlsonwireless.com
Email: sales@carlsonwireless.com
Estab: 1999

James R. Carlson, Founder & CEO
John Zott, CFO
Sebastien Amiot, CTO
Ken Garnett, Group VP
Shamus Jennings, Technical Support Manager

Manufacturer of wireless communication products. The company also provides broadband and related services.

Carmot Therapeutics Inc   BR
409 Illinois St
San Francisco CA 94158
P: 510-828-0102   PRC:268
carmot-therapeutics.us
Email: info@carmot.us
Estab: 2008

Stig Hansen, Founder & CEO
Roman Dvorak, VP of Clinical Development
Johan Enquist, Scientist

Provider of drug discovery to address unmet chemical needs for the treatment of oncology, inflammation, and metabolic disease.

Carroll Engineering Inc   HQ
1101 S Winchester Blvd Ste H 184
San Jose CA 95128-3903
P: 408-261-9800   PRC:304
www.carroll-engineering.com
Email: info@carroll-engineering.com
Estab: 1993

Bryce Carroll, Founder
Robert Henry, President
Matthew Martus, VP
Kim Murray, Engineer
Drew Spencer, Assistant Engineer

Provider of civil engineering and surveying services focusing on boundary and topographic surveys, civil engineering design, and construction support.

Carter Contact Lens Inc   HQ
105 W Dakota Ave Ste 109
Clovis CA 93612
P: 559-294-7063   F: 559-294-8851   PRC:173
cartercl.com
Email: carterlens@sbcglobal.net
Estab: 1997

Bill Carter, Co-Founder
John Carter, Co-Founder

Manufacturer of contact lenses. The company product range include crescent bifocal, target bifocal, front bifocal, and keratoconic designs.

Casahl Technology Inc   HQ
2400 Camino Ramon Bldg K Ste 355
San Ramon CA 94583
P: 925-328-2828   F: 925-328-1188   PRC:326
www.casahl.com
Email: info@casahl.com
Estab: 1993

Wesley Wong, VP of Engineering
Karim Senussi, Technical Sales Support Engineer

Provider of collaboration and content environment optimization services. The company focuses on cloud integration and content management.

Cascadia Labs   HQ
1140 Bel Arbres Dr
Redwood Valley CA 95470
P: 855-800-6890   PRC:34
www.cascadia-labs.com
Email: info@cascadia-labs.com
Estab: 2011

Jeremy L Sackett, Founder & CSO

Provider of analytical services. The company specializes in analytical, pharmaceutical, horticulture, and food science.

Casella Lighting   HQ
10183 Croydon Way Ste C
Sacramento CA 95827
P: 888-252-7874   PRC:243
www.casellalighting.com
Email: info@casellalighting.com
Estab: 1930

Chuck Bird, Manager
Darrell Currie, Fabricator

Retailer of lamps and chandeliers. The company also sells floor lamps, wall lamps, picture lights, and ceiling fixtures.

Casetrakker   HQ
990 Reserve Dr Ste 200
Roseville CA 95678
P: 916-757-1444   F: 916-781-0168   PRC:323
www.casetrakker.com
Email: sales@casetrakker.com
Estab: 1990

Joseph Donovan, Business Systems Analyst
Melissa Ruddick, Business Systems Analyst

Developer of Windows-based case management software. The company is engaged in programming and hosting solutions.

Casetronic Engineering Group   HQ
1126 Yosemite Dr
Milpitas CA 95035
P: 408-262-8588   PRC:79
www.casetronic.com
Email: sales@casetronic.com
Estab: 2000

Ed Huang, VP
Stella Zhou, Accountant

Designer and manufacturer of electronic enclosures, DC converters, AC adapters, flash readers, and IPC rackmount solutions.

Caseware International Inc   DH
2425B Channing Way Ste 590
Berkeley CA 94704
P: 416-867-9504   F: 416-867-1906   PRC:319
www.caseware.com
Email: info@caseware.com
Estab: 1998

Dwight Wainman, CEO

Supplier of software solutions to accountants and auditors worldwide. The company offers working papers to accounting firms.

Caspio Inc   HQ
2550 Great America Way Ste 325
Santa Clara CA 95054
P: 650-691-0900   F: 650-403-0701   PRC:315
www.caspio.com
Email: support@caspio.com
Estab: 2000

Frank Zamani, Founder & CEO & President
Ioannis Kritikopoulos, VP of Engineering & Operations
Brian Metzger, VP of Global Marketing
Sabina Tuladhar, VP of Technical Support & Customer Care
Napoleon Valdez, Director of Sales

Builds online database applications without coding.

Castagnolo Dental Laboratory Inc   HQ
10055 Miller Ave Ste 102
Cupertino CA 95014
P: 408-446-1466   F: 408-446-9571   PRC:302
www.castagnolo-lab.com
Estab: 1977

David Castagnolo, President

Provider of custom packed columns, empty synthesis columns, empty synthesis plates, and related supports.

Castle Rock Computing Inc   HQ
12930 Saratoga Ave
Saratoga CA 95070
P: 408-366-6540   PRC:322
www.castlerock.com
Email: sales@snmpc.com
Estab: 1987

John Maytum, VP of Sales

Designer and manufacturer of SNMPC network management software. The company's product caters to a wide range of sectors.

Catalia Health Inc   HQ
118 Second St 2nd Fl
San Francisco CA 94105
P: 415-660-9264   PRC:194
www.cataliahealth.com
Email: info@cataliahealth.com
Estab: 2014

Cory Kidd, Founder & CEO
Gary Arnold, CTO

Provider of medical solutions for pharmaceuticals, healthcare systems, and home care. The company specializes in robotic aides for an aging population.

Catalyst Biosciences   HQ
611 Gateway Blvd Ste 710
S San Francisco CA 94080
P: 650-871-0761   PRC:34
www.catalystbiosciences.com
Email: info@catbio.com
Estab: 2002

Nassim Usman, President & CEO
Ed Madison, CSO
Howard Levy, CMO
Anju Chatterji, SVP
Arwa Shurrab, VP

Developer of catalytic biopharmaceutical products based on engineering human proteases for hemostasis, age-related macular degeneration, and inflammation.

Catalyst Business Solutions   HQ
6203 San Ignacio Ave Ste 110
San Jose CA 95119
P: 408-281-7100   F: 408-281-7101   PRC:323
www.catalyst-us.com
Estab: 2002

Amol Awasthi, Co-Founder
Anupam Awasthi, Co-Founder & CEO
Jay Kalra, EVP of Technology
Muhammad Raza, Manager

Provider of technology consulting services in business applications, data center, and machine-to-machine/Internet of things.

Catalyst Environmental Inc   HQ
170 Glenn Way Ste 7
San Carlos CA 94070
P: 650-642-6583   F: 650-622-9881   PRC:142
catenv.com
Email: info@catenv.com

Ray Villanueva, Project Manager
Joseph Berkshire, Principal
Kurt Soto-Gambini, Principal

Provider of environmental services. The company's services comprise tank cleaning and hydro blasting services and soil and groundwater sampling.

Cavendish Kinetics Inc   HQ
2960 N First St
San Jose CA 95134
P: 408-457-1940   PRC:86
www.cavendish-kinetics.com
Email: info@cavendish-kinetics.com
Estab: 1994

Paul Dal Santo, President & CEO
Luis Arzubi, Chairman
Patrick Murray, CFO
Dan Smith, CMO
Richard Knipe, VP of Engineering & CTO

Supplier of tunable components for RF circuit applications. The company offers antennas, power amps, filters, and other products.

CBS Local Media   HQ
855 Battery St   [N]
San Francisco CA 94111
P: 415-765-8144   PRC:325
cwsanfrancisco.cbslocal.com
Email: feedback@kbcwtv.com

Tom Spitz, Director of Operations

Operator of TV broadcasting network.

Ccintegration   HQ
2060 Corporate Ct
San Jose CA 95131
P: 408-228-1314   F: 408-228-1315   PRC:325
ccintegration.com
Email: sales@ccintegration.com
Estab: 1985

Hank Ta, Founder
Anna Hung, CEO
Kelly Styskal, CFO
Kevin Schoonover, VP of Engineering
Michael Johnson, VP of Operations

Provider of business engagement models such as OEM and virtual OEM. The company services include design, integration, and logistics.

CCS Associates Inc   HQ
2001 Gateway Pl Ste 350W
Mountain View CA 95110
P: 650-691-4400   F: 650-691-4410   PRC:268
www.ccsainc.com
Email: info@ccsainc.com
Estab: 1985

Caroline C. Sigman, President & CEO & Founder
Daniel Milgram, Chief of Technology & Bioinformatics & Senior Director of IT & Data Management
Beverly D. Smolich, Senior Director of Clinical Research & Regulatory Affairs
Donya Bagheri, Executive Director & Senior Director of Research & Development
Meena Navidi, Senior Director of Preclinical Research & Development Projects

Provider of scientific services in product discovery and development for government agencies, pharmaceutical, and biotech industries.

CCS Inc   HQ
400 China Rose Ct
Lincoln CA 95648
P: 949-855-9020   PRC:323
ideaweb.com
Email: pay@ideaweb.com
Estab: 1970

Michael O'Brien, CEO
Casey O'Brien, CTO & VP of Operations

Provider of business accounting software solutions. The company is also engaged in web integration and custom software development.

CEA Consulting   HQ
235 Montgomery St Ste 950
San Francisco CA 94104
P: 415-421-4213   F: 866-496-7098   PRC:139
www.ceaconsulting.com
Estab: 1984

Kirk Marckwald, Founder & Principal
Kelly Solari, CFO
Darcy Wheeles, Director
Max Levine, Director
Mark Michelin, Director

Provider of environmental consulting services. The company's services include recruiting and organizational design services.

Cedaron Medical Inc   HQ
1644 Da Vinci Ct
Davis CA 95618
P: 800-424-1007   F: 530-759-1699   PRC:194
www.cedaron.com
Email: info@cedaron.com
Estab: 1990

Malcolm Bond, Founder & Chief Scientist
Karen Bond, President & CEO
Lucas Collins, Customer Support Manager & Director
Loran Kelley, Customer Support Manager
Vikram Singh, Software Engineer

Provider of entrepreneurial, medical, technological, marketing, and documentation software solutions for healthcare providers.

Cederdahl Consulting and Coaching   HQ
4109 Nabal Dr   [N]
La Mesa CA 91941
P: 619-670-1122   F: 619-670-9363   PRC:45
www.cederdahl.com
Estab: 1985

Bob Cederdahl, Consultant

Provider of profitable business and management experience to serious individuals, quality driven companies, and future-directed government identities to improve their bottom lines, their services include planning-creating foresighted paths for financial success, financing-finding rewarding resources for spirited growth, human resources-developing meaningful relationships for additional dividends.

Ceecon Testing Inc HQ
434 N Canal St Ste 6
S San Francisco CA 94080
P: 650-827-7474   F: 650-827-7476   PRC:129
www.ceecon.com
Email: info@ceecon.com

Michael Hodges, Chief Adventure Officer

Provider of soil and groundwater remediation services. The company services also include regulatory compliance and remediation equipment.

Celadon Inc HQ
58 Paul Dr Ste D
San Rafael CA 94903
P: 415-472-1177   F: 415-472-1179   PRC:61
www.celadon.com
Email: sales@celadon.com
Estab: 1990

Michael Griswold, VP of Sales

Provider of OEM products and services. The company's products include OEM remote controls, infrared receivers, and backlighting systems.

Celestix Networks Inc HQ
215 Fourier Ave Ste 140
Fremont CA 94539
P: 510-668-0700   PRC:322
www.celestix.com
Email: info@celestix.com
Estab: 1999

Bobby Chen, Director of Finance & Operation

Provider of security appliances and solutions for healthcare, legal and financial, education, commercial, small business, and public sector industries.

Celestron LLC HQ
2835 Columbia St   [N]
Torrance CA 90503
P: 310-328-9560   F: 310-212-5835   PRC:31
www.celestron.com
Estab: 1950

Corey Lee, CEO
Paul Roth, CFO
Ben Hauck, SVP of Sales
Eric Kopit, Director of Product Development
Amir Cannon, Director of Operations

Manufacturer of telescopes, binoculars, spotting scopes, microscopes and accessories.

Celigo Inc HQ
1820 Gateway Dr
San Mateo CA 94404
P: 650-579-0210   F: 650-240-0143   PRC:323
celigo.com
Email: info@celigo.com
Estab: 2005

Jan Arendtsz, Founder & CEO
Scott Henderson, CTO
Rula Kallas, VP of Customer Success
Matt Graney, VP of Product
Mark Simon, VP of Strategy & Operations

Provider of cloud computing products and solutions. The company offers NetSuite consulting services that include implementation and optimization.

Cell Marque Corp HQ
6600 Sierra College Blvd
Rocklin CA 95677
P: 916-746-8900   F: 916-746-8989   PRC:249
www.cellmarque.com
Email: service@cellmarque.com
Estab: 1994

Nora Lacey, President
David Zembo, CFO
Anh Ngo, VP of Strategic Initiatives
Jeff Gordon, Director of Sales & Marketing
Nora Minasyan, Manufacturing Manager

Producer of primary antibodies, buffers and pre-treatment, ancillary reagents, and lab equipment for pathology laboratories and research facilities.

Cell Technology HQ
48820 Kato Rd Ste 400B
Fremont CA 94538
P: 650-960-2170   F: 650-960-0367   PRC:36
www.celltechnology.com
Email: info@celltechnology.com
Estab: 1998

Sumant Dhawan, CSO & Founder

Developer of assays to study cellular functions by researchers using cell preamble agents for academic, biotechnology, and pharmaceutical industries.

CellarStone Inc HQ
80 Cabrillo Hwy Ste Q216
Half Moon Bay CA 94019
P: 650-242-0008   PRC:326
www.cellarstone.com
Email: info@cellarstone.com
Estab: 2000

Gopi Mattel, CEO & Founder
Ajoop Kalavath, VP of Customer Success
Sanal K. Sankar, Director of Technology
Srinivasa Rao Rekapalli, Director of Operations
Mohamed Basha, Senior Project Manager

Provider of sales commissions and incentive compensation software and solutions. The company offers version upgrades and re-engineering services.

Cellecta Inc HQ
320 Logue Ave
Mountain View CA 94043
P: 650-938-3910   F: 650-938-3911   PRC:34
cellecta.com
Email: info@cellecta.com
Estab: 2006

Alex Chenchik, President
Paul Diehl, COO
Donato Tedesco, Director of Research & development
Costa Frangou, Head of Genomics
Mikhail Makhanov, Scientist

Provider of custom and contract solutions for high-throughput genetic screening needs and also develops therapeutic targets and drugs.

Cellerant Therapeutics Inc HQ
1531 Industrial Rd
San Carlos CA 94070
P: 650-232-2122   F: 650-595-2268   PRC:34
www.cellerant.com
Email: info@cellerant.com
Estab: 2003

Ram Mandalam, President & CEO
Rodney Young, CFO
William Reed, VP of Clinical Development
Jagath Reddy Junutula, VP of Antibody Discovery & Development
Steve Greenberg, Managing Director

Developer of novel innate and adaptive immunotherapies for oncology and blood-related disorders, including cell-based and antibody therapeutics.

Cellmax Life HQ
1271 Oakmead Pkwy
Sunnyvale CA 94085
P: 650-564-3905   PRC:41
cellmaxlife.in
Email: support@cellmaxlife.com
Estab: 2013

Ben Hsieh, Founder & R&D Director
Atul Sharan, CEO
Rui Mei, CSO
Prabhat Goyal, CFO
Padma Sundar, VP of Marketing & Business Development

Provider of personalized multi-biomarker technologies for non-invasive saliva and blood tests. The company is also involved in drug discovery.

CellSight Technologies Inc HQ
185 Berry St Ste 350
San Francisco CA 94107
P: 650-799-1589   F: 650-267-6023   PRC:194
cellsighttech.com
Email: contact@cellsighttechnologies.com
Estab: 2009

Sam Quezada, Founder & COO
Aruna Gambhir, CEO
Jelena Levi, Director of Research & Development

Provider of imaging tools to assess immunotherapy for the clinicians. The company focuses on the development of polyethylene terephthalate tracers.

Celltheon HQ
32980 Alvarado Niles Rd Ste 826
Union City CA 94587
P: 510-306-2355   PRC:36
www.celltheon.com
Email: info@celltheon.com
Estab: 2012

Amita Goel, Founder & CEO
Rene Pagila, Director

Developer of customized solutions for preclinical studies of the biotechnology and pharmaceutical industries.

Celsia Inc HQ
3287 Kifer Rd
Santa Clara CA 95051
P: 650-667-1920 PRC:154
celsiainc.com
Email: engineering@celsiainc.com
Estab: 2001

George Meyer, CEO
Wen Xing Hua, VP
Zoe Ho, Customer Service Director
Emily Liu, Purchasing Director
Erin Chen, QC Director

Designer and manufacturer of heat sinks. The
company provides thermal solutions using vapor
chamber, heat pipe, and hybrid designs.

Cemex USA BR
5180 Golden Foothills Pkwy
El Dorado Hills CA 95762
P: 916-941-2800 PRC:47
cemexusa.com
Estab: 1906

Jaime Muguiro, President
Jeff Bobolts, Regional President of Florida Region
Scott Ducoff, Regional President of Texas Region
Marc Tyson, Regional President of Mid-South
Region
Eric Wittmann, Regional President of West Region

Supplier of bulk cement, sand, aggregates, ready
mix materials, and architectural products. The
company serves the construction industry.

Cenergy Power HQ
1520 W Main St
Merced CA 95340
P: 209-233-9777 F: 209-668-5726 PRC:135
www.cenergypower.com
Email: info@cenergypower.com
Estab: 2006

Andrew Goldin, SVP of EPC Operations
Doan Vo, VP of O&M & Quality
Nader Yarpezeshkan, VP of Sales & Corporate
Development
Ryan Kretschmer, Project Manager
Eilroma Sarkis, Senior Project Manager

Developer and installer of solar for the agricultural,
commercial, industrial, and utility scale markers.

Ceniom Inc HQ
333 University Ave Ste 200
Sacramento CA 95825
P: 800-403-3204 PRC:67
www.ceniom.com
Email: info@ceniom.com
Estab: 2004

Yan Kit Chan, Director

Provider of security, network design, and data recovery services. The company is engaged in web
design, hosting, and technical support.

CenterVue Inc BR
979 Corporate Way
Fremont CA 94539
P: 408-988-8404 F: 408-716-3271 PRC:11
www.centervue.com
Email: infous@centervue.com
Estab: 2008

Stefano Gallucci, CEO

Designer and manufacturer of medical devices
for the diagnosis and management of ocular
pathologies.

Centric Software Inc HQ
655 Campbell Technology Pkwy Ste 200
Campbell CA 95008
P: 408-574-7802 F: 408-377-3002 PRC:322
centricsoftware.com
Email: centric@centricsoftware.com
Estab: 1998

Chris Groves, CEO
Ravi Rangan, CTO
Fabrice Canonge, COO
James Horne, VP of Marketing
Alice Gerbel, VP of Finance & Administration

Provider of product lifecycle management solution
to apparel, consumer goods, luxury good, and
footwear industries.

Centrify HQ
3300 Tannery Way
Santa Clara CA 95054
P: 669-444-5200 PRC:319
centrify.com
Email: support@centrify.com
Estab: 2004

Adam Au, Co-Founder & SVP of engineering
Paul Moore, Co-Founder & CTO
Tom Kemp, CEO
Tim Steinkopf, CFO
Gary Taggart, SVP Worldwide Sales

Provider of identity and access management
solutions. The company offers services to pharma
companies and financial institutions.

Centrillion Technologies HQ
2500 Faber Pl
Palo Alto CA 94303
P: 650-618-0111 F: 650-618-0121 PRC:34
centrilliontech.com
Email: info@centrillionbio.com
Estab: 2009

Wei Zhou, President & CEO
James Zhang, CSO
Jeremy Edwards, VP of Sequencing Technology
Glenn McGall, SVP of Technology
Janet Warrington, SVP of Research & Develop-
ment

Provider of genomic and bioinformatics solution.
The company offers genomic technology to improve sequencing performance.

Centrillion Technology Holdings Ltd HQ
2500 Faber Pl
Palo Alto CA 94303
P: 650-618-0111 F: 650-618-0121 PRC:38
www.centrilliontech.com
Email: info@centrilliontech.com
Estab: 2009

Wei Zhou, President & CEO
James Zhang, CSO
Janet Warrington, SVP of Research & Develop-
ment
Jeremy Edwards, VP of Sequencing Technology
Michael Henry, SVP & General Manager Consum-
er Genomics

Developer of genomics solutions for the researchers, physicians, and consumers. The company
also offers clinical testing and consumer genomics
services.

Century Technology Inc HQ
225 Harris Ct
S San Francisco CA 94080
P: 650-583-8908 PRC:207
century-technology.com
Email: info@century-technology.com

Henry Ho, Owner

Provider of PCB assembly services. The company
also offers distribution, testing, and wire harness
services.

Cepheid HQ
904 Caribbean Dr
Sunnyvale CA 94089
P: 408-541-4191 F: 408-541-4192 PRC:186
www.cepheid.com
Email: info@cepheidbenelux.com
Estab: 1996

John L. Bishop, CEO & Chairman
David Persing, EVP & CMO & CTO
Yi-Wei Tang, CMO
Srikanth Kalluri, CIO
Russel Enns, Chief Regulatory Officer

Provider of molecular diagnostic testing of patient
specimen on a centralized basis enabling medical
providers identify and treat disease early.

Ceramic Tech Inc HQ
46211 Research Ave [N]
Fremont CA 94539
P: 510-252-8500 F: 510-252-8700 PRC:80
www.ceramictechinc.com
Email: info@ceramictechinc.com
Estab: 1989

Parth Patel, Manufacturing Engineer

Manufacturer and fabrication of ceramic parts.

Ceras Health Inc BR
995 Market St 2nd Fl
San Francisco CA 94103
P: 415-477-9908 PRC:40
cerashealth.com
Email: info@cerashealth.com

Anita Waxman, Founder & Director
Kevin Murphy, CEO

Focuses on mobile application development. The
company serves patients, hospitals, and related
healthcare organizations.

Ceridian Corp   BR
   17390 Brookhurst St   [N]
   Fountain Valley CA 92708
P: 714-963-1311   PRC:319
www.ceridian.com
Email: marketingops@ceridian.com
Estab: 1957

David Ossip, CEO & Chairman of the Board
Larry Dunivan, CRO
Ozzie Goldschmied, CTO
Paul Elliott, COO
Scott Kitching, EVP & General Counsel

Firm is a provider of human capital management
solutions.

Cermetek Microelectronics   HQ
   374 Turquoise St Ste 2
   Milpitas CA 95035
P: 408-942-2200   F: 408-942-1346   PRC:97
www.cermetek.com
Email: info@cermetek.com
Estab: 1968

Henry Cermetek, President & CEO
Frank Stempski, Sales Manager
Steven Clary, Marketing Manager

Manufacturer of communication modules for
embedded systems. The company caters to power
generation, irrigation control, and medical monitoring fields.

Cernex Inc   HQ
   1710 Zanker Rd Ste 103
   San Jose CA 95112-4219
P: 408-541-9226   F: 408-541-9229   PRC:209
www.cernex.com
Email: sales@cernex.com
Estab: 1988

Bill Yu, VP of Technology
Lam Huynh, Business Development Manager
Anh Hai Nguyen, Production Manager
Michael Nghia Nguyen, Mechanical Engineer
Duc Nguyen, Tester

Manufacturer of microwave and millimeter-wave
components and sub-assemblies. The company's
products include amplifiers, converters, detectors,
and cables.

CERONIX Inc   HQ
   13350 New Airport Rd
   Auburn CA 95602-2055
P: 530-886-6400   PRC:112
www.ceronix.com
Email: sales@ceronix.com
Estab: 1984

Don Whitaker, Founder
Nathan Jay, Warehouse Manager
Sheri Bomhoff, Sales & Service Manager
Kay Whitaker, Office Manager & Human Resource
Brian Looper, Electronic Engineer

Manufacturer of color video touch display monitors
and printed circuit boards. The company offers
LCD and CRT monitor assemblies and spare
parts.

Certain Inc   DH
   75 Hawthorne St Ste 550
   San Francisco CA 94105
P: 888-237-8246   PRC:320
www.certain.com
Email: help@certain.com
Estab: 1994

Peter Micciche, CEO
Kristen Logan Alexander, CMO
Aleks Rabrenovich, CFO
Gerard Larios, VP of Development Operations &
Information Technology
Betsy Zikakis, VP of Marketing

Provider of enterprise event management solutions that include e-mail marketing, event reporting, registration, and consulting services.

Certent Inc   HQ
   1548 Eureka Rd
   Roseville CA 95661
P: 925-730-4300   F: 925-730-4045   PRC:322
certent.com
Email: privacy@certent.com
Estab: 2002

Michael Boese, CEO
Mobeen Bajwa, Chief Product & Technology
Officer
Don Gillotti, SVP of Sales
Joanie Creger, VP of Human Resources
Aaron Bolshaw, VP of Marketing

Provider of equity compensation management,
equity compensation reporting, and disclosure
management solutions.

Certified Medical Testing   HQ
   7600 N Ingram Ste 234
   Fresno CA 93711
P: 559-960-8756   F: 559-435-8827   PRC:189
cmtmedgas.com
Email: cmt@cmtmedgas.com

Roland Lamer, Owner & Managing Executive
Jake Granger, Manager of Sales & Service

Provider of engineering services. The company
provides services for healthcare organizations related to piped medical gas and vacuum systems.

Cerus Corp   HQ
   1220 Concord Ave
   Concord CA 94520
P: 925-288-6000   F: 925-288-6001   PRC:36
www.cerus.com
Estab: 1991
Sales: $30M to $100M

William M. Greenman, President & CEO
Dan Swisher, Chairman
Richard J. Benjamin MBChB, CMO
Kevin D. Green, VP of Finance & CFO
Laurence M. Corash, CSO

Manufacturer of biomedical products such as the
intercept blood system and pathogen reduction
system, focused in the field of blood safety.

Cesco Magnetics Inc   HQ
   PO Box 6359
   Santa Rosa CA 95406
P: 877-624-8727   PRC:159
cescomagnetics.com
Estab: 1946

Steve Blackwell, Engineer
James Heinmiller, Staff Scientist

Provider of magnetic separators. The company
offers magnetic filters, magnetic plates, and
sanitary valves.

Cetecom Inc   BR
   411 Dixon Landing Rd
   Milpitas CA 95035
P: 408-586-6200   F: 408-586-6299   PRC:68
www.cetecom.com
Email: contact@cetecom.com
Estab: 1993

Peter Nevermann, Director of Radio Communica-
tions & EMC
Wilfried Klassmann, Director
Rami Saman, Senior Engineering Project Man-
ager
Issa Ghanma, EMC Engineer
Ali Taba, Test Engineer

Provider of consulting and testing services. The
company focuses on the telecommunications and
information technology industries.

Ceva Inc   HQ
   1174 Castro St Ste 210
   Mountain View CA 94040
P: 650-417-7900   F: 650-417-7995   PRC:61
www.ceva-dsp.com
Email: sales@ceva-dsp.com
Estab: 2002
Sales: $30M to $100M

Gideon Wertheizer, CEO
Michael Boukaya, COO
Erez Bar-Niv, CTO
Yaniv Arieli, CFO
Issachar Ohana, EVP of World Wide sales

Provider of digital signal processor technology.
The company also specializes in offering consulting services.

CGI Technical Services Inc   HQ
   1612 Insight Pl
   Redding CA 96003
P: 530-244-6277   F: 530-244-6276   PRC:142
www.cgitechnical.com
Email: sales@currygroup.com
Estab: 1999

Clifford D. Curry, President
Jose Corrales, Project Manager
Sherrie Curry, Business Resource Manager
Vikram Kyatham, Operations Manager
Ashton Erickson, Laboratory Manager

Provider of technical services. The company offerings include geotechnical engineering, engineering geology, and pavement design services.

CHA Corp   HQ
1170 National Dr Ste 70
Sacramento CA 95834
P: 916-550-5380   F: 916-550-5342   PRC:139
chacorporation.com
Email: ccha@chacorporation.com

Chang Cha, President

Developer and marketer of microwave technologies. The company offers carbon regeneration, hypergolic destruction, and emission control solutions.

Chai   HQ
990 Richard Ave Ste 110
Santa Clara CA 95050
P: 650-779-5577   F: 650-779-5606   PRC:34
www.chaibio.com
Email: sales@chaibio.com
Estab: 2013

Josh Perfetto, Founder
Ellen Antonucci, HR Manager of Operations

Specializes in DNA diagnostics. The company offers services to clinics, patients, and the medical sector.

Champ Systems Inc   HQ
6060 Freeport Blvd
Sacramento CA 95822
P: 916-424-4066   F: 916-424-3844   PRC:319
champsystems.com
Estab: 1979

Norm Champ, President
Denise Maglinte, Senior System Analyst
Diana Reiff, Senior System Analyst
Kyle Kumasaki, Systems Analyst
Doug Warner, Systems Analyst

Provider of business management and accounting software. The company offers ERP programming, training, software, and hardware services.

Champion Industrial Contractors Inc   HQ
1420 Coldwell Ave   [N]
Modesto CA 95350
P: 209-524-6601   F: 209-524-6931   PRC:63
www.championindustrial.com
Estab: 1965

Darrell Champion, President
Ashveen Singh, CFO
John Walter, COO
Eli Champion, VP
Rob Moga, Project Manager

Provider of industrial HVAC, plumbing and electrical services.

Champion Microelectronic Corp   RH
960 Saratoga Ave Ste 125
San Jose CA 95129
P: 408-985-1898   F: 408-985-1683   PRC:212
www.championmicro.com.tw

Jeffrey Hwang, CTO & COO

Designer and manufacturer of semiconductor devices. The company's products include battery management IC, fan controller, and interface products.

Chander Software Solutions Inc   HQ
1622 Saint Regis Dr   [N]
San Jose CA 95124
P: 408-406-5624   PRC:319
www.chandersoft.com
Email: info@chandersoftware.com
Estab: 1992

Harish Chander, Founder

Provider of marketing, call center, project management and technical support software and technical staffing augmentation solutions.

Channel Medsystems Inc   HQ
5858 Horton St Ste 200
Emeryville CA 94608
P: 510-338-9301   PRC:188
www.channelmedsystems.com
Email: info@channelmedsystems.com
Estab: 2006

Ric Cote, President & CEO
Bill Malecki, COO
Witney McKiernan, VP
Rhonda Bracey, VP of Finance

Developer of cryothermic technology and streamlined delivery system for women with heavy menstrual bleeding.

ChannelNet   BR
1 Harbor Dr Ste 106
Sausalito CA 94965
P: 415-332-4704   PRC:319
www.channelnet.com
Estab: 1985

Paula George Tompkins, CEO & Founder
ERIC V. PETERSEN, CFO
CHRIS SIMS, CTO
Molly Smith, VP of Operations
Joe Karle, VP of Account Management

Provider of digital solutions to connect brands and customers. The company specializes in strategy development, design, and content optimization.

Chartware Inc   HQ
PO Box 3137
Rohnert Park CA 94927
P: 800-642-4278   F: 707-544-2712   PRC:194
www.chartware.com
Estab: 1995

David Tully-Smith, President & CEO
Reg Green, VP
Dana Tully-Smith, VP

Manufacturer of scheduler and practice management interfaces and systems. The company serves the medical sector.

Check Point Software Technologies Inc   HQ
959 Skyway Rd Ste 300
San Carlos CA 94070
P: 800-429-4391   PRC:322
www.checkpoint.com
Estab: 1993
Sales: $1B to $3B

Marius Nacht, Co-Founder & Chairman
Gil Shwed, Co-Founder & CEO
Amnon Bar-Lev, President
Jerry Ungerman, Vice Chairman
Tal Payne, CFO & COO

Developer of software technology solutions such as mobile security and next generation firewalls for retail/point of sale and financial services.

CHECKPOiNT Technologies   HQ
66 Bonaventura Dr
San Jose CA 95134
P: 408-321-9780   PRC:172
www.checkpointtechnologies.com
Email: sales@checkpointtechnologies.com
Estab: 1995

Robert Hand, Director of Sales and Marketing
Gil Mishal, Channel Manager
Kee Yang, Product Engineer
Hai Tran, Senior Technician
Audrey Laurin, Recruiting Human Resources

Manufacturer of optical failure analysis tools such as laser scanning microscopy, photon emission, infrascan, and solid immersion lens objectives.

Chelsio Communications   HQ
209 N Fair Oaks Ave
Sunnyvale CA 94085
P: 408-962-3600   F: 408-962-3661   PRC:95
chelsio.com
Email: sales@chelsio.com
Estab: 1997

Kianoosh Naghshineh, CEO & President
Asgeir Eiriksson, CTO
William Delaney, CFO
Danny Gur, VP of Worldwide Sales
Kun Yim, VP of Operations

Provider of Ethernet adapters. The company offers storage routers, wire adapters, virtualization and management software, and accessories.

Chemical Safety Technology Inc   HQ
2461 Autumnvale Dr
San Jose CA 95131
P: 408-263-0984   F: 408-263-2640   PRC:143
kemsafe.com
Email: info@kemsafe.com
Estab: 1987

Lincoln Bejan, President & CEO
Jackie Bejan, EVP & CFO

Supplier of chemical processing machines. The company also offers design, manufacturing, and sheet metal fabrication services.

Chemocentryx Inc HQ
850 Maude Ave
Mountain View CA 94043
P: 650-210-2900   F: 650-210-2910   PRC:268
www.chemocentryx.com
Email: info@chemocentryx.com
Estab: 1997
Sales: $300M to $1 Billion

Thomas J. Schall, CEO, Chairman & President
Susan M. Kanaya, CFO & CAO & EVP & Secretary
Juan Jaen, SVP of Drug Discovery & Chief Scientific Officer
Markus J. Cappel, Chief Business Officer & Treasurer
Rajinder Singh, SVP of Research & Head of Pharmaceutics

Manufacturer of biopharmaceutical products and orally-administered therapeutics to treat autoimmune diseases, inflammatory disorders, and cancer.

ChemSoft HQ
1101 S Winchester Blvd Ste P299
San Jose CA 95128
P: 408-615-1001   F: 408-615-1073   PRC:319
www.chemsoft.com
Email: sales@chemsoft.com

John Rather, VP of IS
Clare Reynolds, Managing Director
Lorrie Conklin, Software Developer

Provider of software consulting services. The company specializes in custom business solutions, access, excel, PowerPoint, word, and visual basic.

Chesapeake Technology Inc HQ
4906 El Camino Real Ste 206
Los Altos CA 94022
P: 650-967-2045   F: 650-903-4500   PRC:322
chesapeaketech.com
Email: info@chesapeaketech.com
Estab: 1995

Eileen Gann, President
John Gann, VP of Software Development
David Finlayson, VP of Engineering
Ashley Chan, Marketing & Sales Manager
Stephen D'Andrea, Business Manager

Provider of sonar mapping software as well as consulting services to the marine, geophysical, and geological survey industries.

Chess com HQ
PO Box 60400
Palo Alto CA 94306
P: 800-318-2827   PRC:317
www.chess.com
Email: support@chess.com
Estab: 2005

Erik Allebest, CEO

Provider of unlimited chess games and free tournaments that can be played by challenging friends and meet new players.

Chevron Corp HQ
6001 Bollinger Canyon Rd
San Ramon CA 94583
P: 925-842-1000   PRC:133
www.chevron.com
Email: chvcips@chevron.com
Estab: 1879
Sales: Over $3B

Pierre R. Breber, CFO
Jay R. Pryor, VP
Jeanette Ourada, Corporate VP & Controller
Joseph C. Geagea, EVP of Technology Projects & Services
Nancy Smith, General Manager of HR

Provider of mobile asset tracking and management solutions. The company serves the marine, chemicals, and aviation industries.

Chiapas Edi Technologies Inc HQ
1405 Birch Ln
Davis CA 95618
P: 415-298-8166   PRC:322
chiapas-edi.org
Email: support@chiapas-edi.org
Estab: 2010

Alden Richard Temps, CEO & Founder

Developer of electronic data interchange software for health insurance exchange brokers, MSOs, HMOs, and healthcare business data analytics services.

Chico Environmental Science & Planning HQ
333 Main St Ste 260
Chico CA 95928
P: 530-899-2900   PRC:142
chicoenvironmental.com
Email: info@chicoenvironmental.com

John Lane, Principal Scientist & Owner
Jess Kolstad, Staff Environmental Scientist

Provider of environmental consulting services. The company offers site assessments, storm water pollution prevention plans, and environmental forensics.

China Custom Manufacturing Ltd HQ
44843 Fremont Blvd
Fremont CA 94538
P: 510-979-1920   F: 510-979-1930   PRC:280
www.pacificbusinessco.com
Email: info@ccmfg.com
Estab: 1993

Bonnie Chen, Account Manager

Provider of tooling, plastic injection molding, and sheet metal stamping services. The company focuses on the aerospace and electronics industries.

Chris French Metal Inc HQ
2500 Union St
Oakland CA 94607
P: 510-238-9339   F: 510-238-9373   PRC:82
cfrenchmetal.com
Estab: 2007

Richard Lovato, Project Manager & Designer
Chris French, Principal
David Hinman, Lead Fabricator & Designer

Provider of fabrication services. The company offers design, installation, prototyping, and repair services.

Chrometa LLC HQ
1029 H St Ste 103
Sacramento CA 95814
P: 916-546-9974   PRC:322
www.chrometa.com
Email: sales@chrometa.com
Estab: 2008

Brett Owens, CEO

Provider of time keeping management software and services. The company offers products for PC, Mac, iPhone, and Android platforms.

Chromeworks Inc HQ
252 Lockheed Ave
Chico CA 95973
P: 530-343-2278   F: 530-343-2287   PRC:185
chromeworksinc.com
Estab: 1985

Jerry Robinson, Owner
Kathy Robinson, Founder & CFO
Debbie Garcia, General Manager

Manufacturer of chrome frames for the dental lab industry. The company's services include shipping and delivery.

Chronix Biomedical Inc HQ
5941 Optical Ct Ste 201
San Jose CA 95138
P: 408-960-2306   F: 408-960-2305   PRC:187
www.chronixbiomedical.com
Email: info@chronixbiomedical.com
Estab: 1997

Bill Boeger, Founder & Director of Business Development
Howard Urnovitz, CEO
John DiPietro, CFO
Julia Beck, VP of Research

Provider of molecular diagnostics laboratory services such as second opinion tests and delta dot test for screening and monitoring cancer.

Chrontel Inc HQ
2210 O'Toole Ave Ste 100
San Jose CA 95131
P: 408-383-9328   F: 408-383-9338   PRC:208
www.chrontel.com
Email: sales@chrontel.com
Estab: 1986

David Soo, President & CEO
James Lin, CFO
Sidney Yen, Director of Applications
Rod Jarrar, Manager of Test & Product Engineering
Joseph Wong, Design Engineer

Designer of mixed-signal IC products. The company's products find application in personal computer and telecom sectors.

CHS Consulting Group HQ
177 Maiden Ln 5th Fl
San Francisco CA 94108
P: 415-392-9688 F: 415-392-9788 PRC:304
www.chsconsulting.net
Estab: 2000

Chi-Hsin Shao, President
Chris Hopper, Director
Soroush Khadem, Senior Engineer
William Lieberman, Transportation Planning
Coordinator

Provider of transportation planning and traffic
signal design services. The company also focuses
on traffic safety.

CHT Global HQ
2107 N First St Ste 580 [N]
San Jose CA 95131
P: 408-988-1898 F: 408-573-7168 PRC:68
www.chtglobal.com
Email: info@chtglobal.com
Emp: 11-50 Estab: 2002

Joe Yang, CEO & President
Shan-Yun Chung, Manager of Product

Developer and provider of global telecommunication solutions.

Cibiem Inc HQ
5150 El Camino Real Ste E30
Los Altos CA 94022
P: 650-397-6685 F: 650-386-6125 PRC:189
www.cibiem.com
Email: info@cibiem.com

Ken Martin, President & CEO
Mark Gelfand, CTO
Howard R. Levin, Chief Scientific Officer
Xian Wei, Research & Development Engineer

Manufacturer of medical devices. The company
provides solutions to treat sympathetic nervous
system-mediated diseases.

Ciena Corp BR
3939 N First St
San Jose CA 95134
P: 408-904-2100 F: 408-944-9290 PRC:97
ciena.com

Rick Dodd, SVP of Marketing
John Marson, VP of Product & Industry Marketing
Rob Meier, VP
Prasad Kotta, Lead Engineer
Joseph Forsythe, Lead Engineer

Provider of cloud networking, network transformation, and packet network solutions for multi-data
center environments.

Cinema Libre Studio HQ
8328 De Soto Ave [N]
Canoga Park CA 91304
P: 818-349-8822 F: 818-349-9922 PRC:60
www.cinemalibrestudio.com
Email: info@cinemalibrestudio.com
Emp: 11-50

Rick Rieger, Department Head

Provider and distributor of independent film
production.

Cinnabar Bridge Communications HQ
41 Sutter St Ste 1368
San Francisco CA 94104
P: 415-975-0950 F: 415-704-3212 PRC:45
www.cinnabarbridge.com

Paula Hendricks, Founder

Provider of writing, book publishing, book design,
consulting, and project and process management
services.

Ciphercloud Inc DH
2581 Junction Ave
San Jose CA 95134
P: 855-524-7437 PRC:323
ciphercloud.com
Email: info@ciphercloud.com
Estab: 2010

Pravin Kothari, Founder & Chairman & CEO
Varun Badhwar, VP of Product Strategy & Solution
Engineering
Sreekar Nagubadi, Software Engineer

Provider of comprehensive cloud application
discovery and risk assessment, data protection,
data loss management, key management, and
malware detection.

Circle Internet Services Inc HQ
201 Spear St Ste 1200
San Francisco CA 94105
P: 800-585-7075 PRC:322
circleci.com
Email: sayhi@circleci.com
Estab: 2011

Paul Biggar, Founder
Jim Rose, CEO
Rob Zuber, CTO
Erich Ziegler, CMO
Rishi M. Kumar, Director of Strategy

Provider of continuous integration and delivery
solution. The company offers apps for docker,
enterprise, and mobiles.

Circle Pharma HQ
280 Utah Ave Ste 100
S San Francisco CA 94080
P: 650-392-0363 PRC:25
www.circlepharma.com
Email: info@circlepharma.com
Estab: 2012

Matthew Jacobson, Co-Founder
Scott R. Lokey, Co-Founder
David J. Earp, President & CEO
James Aggen, VP of Chemistry
Pablo D. Garcia, Senior Director of Biology
Research

Focuses on the development of cell permeable
macrocyclic peptide therapeutics. The company
serves the pharmaceutical sector.

Circle Video Productions HQ
630 N San Mateo Dr
San Mateo CA 94401
P: 650-619-7367 F: 650-340-7391 PRC:318
www.circlevideo.com
Email: support@circlevideo.com
Estab: 1984

Rob Delantoni, Owner

Provider of video production and multimedia
solutions. The company offers video dispositions,
editing, and duplication services.

CIRCOR Aerospace Inc HQ
2301 Wardlow Cir [N]
Corona CA 92880
P: 951-270-6200 F: 951-270-6201 PRC:166
www.circoraerospace.com
Email: sales_cai_ca@circoraerospace.com
Emp: 501-1000

Vincent Sandoval, Group President
Tony Najjar, VP of Sales & Marketing
Chris Reuther, Group VP of Finance
Don Stinnett, General Manager
Robert Lenardi, General Manager

Distributor of fluidic control and undercarriage
components and subsystems in the aerospace
and defense markers.

Circuit Automation Inc HQ
5292 System Dr [N]
Huntington Beach CA 92647
P: 714-763-4180 PRC:209
s585017606.onlinehome.us/en
Estab: 2003

Chuck Hughes, Manager

Designer and manufacturer of dual-sided solder
mask coating and vertical drying equipment.

Circuit Therapeutics Inc HQ
1505 O'Brien Dr
Menlo Park CA 94025
P: 650-324-9400 F: 650-324-9403 PRC:191
www.circuittx.com
Email: info@circuittx.com
Estab: 2011

Karoly Nikolich, Founder
Fred Moll, CEO & Chairman
Michael Kaplitt, CSO
Dan Andersen, VP of Engineering
Chris Towne, Director of Gene Therapy

Focuses on drug discovery and development as
well as forging direct therapeutic applications of
optogenetics.

Cirexx International Inc HQ
791 Nuttman St
Santa Clara CA 95054
P: 408-988-3980 F: 408-988-4534 PRC:211
www.cirexx.com
Email: info@cirexx.com
Estab: 1980

Philipp Menges, President & CEO
Kurt Menges, VP & CFO
Don Angulo, Quality Systems Manager & ISO
Management Rep & ITAR Compliance Officer
Al Wasserzug, Business Development Manager
Don Kaufman, Business Development Manager

Provider of PCB design layout, fabrication, and
assembly services. The company serves customers in the aerospace, military, semiconductor, and
medical sectors.

Cirius Group Inc HQ
2300 Contra Costa Blvd Ste 250
Pleasant Hill CA 94523
P: 925-685-9300 F: 925-685-6526 PRC:320
www.ciriusgroup.com
Email: sales@ciriusgroup.com
Estab: 1984

Paul Bartlett, President
Greg Delucchi, VP of Software Development
Erin Fernandez, Director of Compliance
Mark Ehnen, Senior Director of Sales & Marketing
& Account Manager
Adriana Munoz, Office Manager

Designer and marketer of financial and medical
software. The company serves hospitals and
healthcare providers.

Cirrus Digital Systems HQ
2077 Centro E
Tiburon CA 94920
P: 415-608-9420 PRC:168
cirrus-designs.com
Email: sales@cirrus-designs.com

John Arvesen, Principal Engineer

Developer of single and multi-camera mapping
systems for NASA applications and high altitude
manned and unmanned aircraft needs.

Cirtec Medical HQ
101 B Cooper Ct
Los Gatos CA 95032
P: 408-395-0443 PRC:187
www.cirtecmed.com
Estab: 1986

Brian Highley, CEO
John Mulvihill, VP of Sales & Marketing
Tim Binder, Director of Supply Chain
Erik Morgan, Director of Information Technology
Kim Dickey, Human Resources Manager

Manufacturer of complex implantable device manufacturing, medical device solutions, and smart
solutions for highly complex miniaturization.

Cisco Systems Inc HQ
170 W Tasman Dr
San Jose CA 95134
P: 408-526-4000 PRC:64
www.cisco.com
Estab: 1984
Sales: Over $3B

Chris Dedicoat, Advisor Office of the Chairman
& CEO
Joseph M. Bradley, Global Vice President of IoT
Blockchain AI & Incubation Businesses
Francine Katsoudas, EVP & CPO
Padmasree Warrior, SVP of Engineering & CTO
Kelly A. Kramer, EVP & CFO

Designer and manufacturer of IP-based networking products. The company also offers security
solutions and architectures.

Citilabs Inc HQ
2005 N St
Sacramento CA 95811
P: 888-770-2823 PRC:40
www.citilabs.com

Michael Clarke, President & CEO
Arthur Leung, CFO
Austen Duffy, CTO
Katie Brinson, Director of Global Accounts
Jacob Asplund, Director of Streetlytics Engineer-
ing & Support

Provider of software development services. The
company designs and develops products for transportation planning.

Citrix Systems Inc BR
4988 Great America Pkwy
Santa Clara CA 95054
P: 408-790-8000 PRC:322
www.citrix.com
Estab: 1989

David J. Henshall, CEO & President
Donna Kimmel, EVP & CPO
Mark J. Ferrer, EVP & CRO
Mark M. Coyle, Manager of Product Design

Provider of transition to software-defining the
workplace, uniting virtualization, mobility management, networking, and SaaS solutions.

CitrusBits HQ
5994 W Las Positas Blvd Ste 219
Pleasanton CA 94588
P: 925-452-6012 PRC:315
citrusbits.com
Email: sales@citrusbits.com
Estab: 2005

Breann Johnson, Product Owner
Harry Lee, CEO
James Hsu, VP of Growth & Strategy
Chandler Faye, Art Director
Simon Hanan, Project Manager

Designs and develops impactful mobile apps for
businesses of all sizes by using augmented/virtual
reality, artificial intelligence, blockchain, and The
Internet of Things (IoT).

Cityspan Technologies Inc HQ
2054 University Ave Ste 5F
Berkeley CA 94704
P: 510-665-1700 PRC:323
cityspan.com
Email: info@cityspan.com
Estab: 1996

Mark Chuang, CTO
Kara Johnson, Director of Business Development
Hayley Cole, Project Manager
Navdeep Sheena, Project Manager
Ariel Hollie, Project Manager

Developer of software for social services. The
company offers software to manage grants, track
clients, and evaluate outcomes.

Civil Maps HQ
2720 Taylor St Ste 320
San Francisco CA 94133
P: 415-287-9977 PRC:227
www.civilmaps.com
Email: info@civilmaps.com
Estab: 2013

Scott Harvey, CTO & Founder
Satya Vakkaleri, VP of Product Management
Venkata Kolla, Director of Engineering
Anuj Gupta, Director of Map Expansion
Melody Li, Product Manager

Developer of autonomous vehicles and cognitive
perception systems. The company specializes in
localization technology and artificial intelligence.

CJS Labs HQ
57 States St
San Francisco CA 94114-1401
P: 415-923-9535 PRC:304
cjs-labs.com
Email: cjs@cjs-labs.com
Estab: 2006

Christopher J. Struck, CEO & Chief Scientist

Provider of electronic design, consulting,
engineering, and test automation programming
assistance services.

CK Associates HQ
33 Hammond Ste 204 [N]
Irvine CA 92618
P: 949-457-7800 F: 949-457-7801 PRC:45
www.ckassoc.com
Email: info@ckassoc.com
Emp: 11-50 Estab: 1991

Gary Caito, President
Jeffrey Davidson, CEO & Manager
Bryan Hennes, CTO
Cheri Lowery, Product Manager
Mari Denton, Product Manager

Provider of sales and marketing strategy for product demands to customers.

CKC Engineering LLC HQ
6617 San Leandro St
Oakland CA 94621
P: 415-494-8225 PRC:81
ckcengineering.com
Email: info@ckcengineering.com
Estab: 2005

Chris Duggan, President & Co-Founder
Carl Dipietro, VP & Co-Founder
Kenji Sytz, Co-Founder & VP
Glen Garcia, Senior Technician

Provider of custom equipment solutions for clinical, manufacturing, pharmaceutical, medical device, and drug delivery industries.

CKC Laboratories Inc HQ
5046 Sierra Pines Dr
Mariposa CA 95338
P: 209-299-5240 F: 858-300-5341 PRC:306
ckc.com
Estab: 1973

Bonnie Robinson, President & CEO
Steve Behm, Director of Engineering
William Brandle, Information Technology Manager
Christine Nicklas, Principal Consultant
Gina Buskeness, Service Advisor

Provider of electromagnetic compatibility testing, safety testing, design development and agency certification services for industries.

CKC Laboratories Inc BR
1120 Fulton Pl
Fremont CA 94539
P: 510-249-1170 PRC:306
ckc.com
Estab: 1973

Bonnie Robinson, President & CEO
Steve Behm, Director of Engineering Services
Todd Robinson, Director of Administration & Marketing
Dawniele Oliphant, Project Manager

Provider of design and testing consultation services. The company offers design consultation, testing, training, and support services.

Clare Computer Solutions HQ
2400 Camino Ramon Ste 195
San Ramon CA 94583
P: 925-277-0690 F: 925-277-0694 PRC:325
clarecomputer.com
Email: info@clarecomputer.com
Estab: 1990

Ralph Lawhorn, President
Bruce Campbell, VP of Marketing
John Isaac, VP of Sales & Project Manager
Abbie Stenson, Account Manager
Kyle Lawhorn, Marketing Manager

Provider of information technology services. The company offers computer network, software consultation, visualization, and cloud computing solutions.

Claresco Inc HQ
2342 Shattuck Ave Ste 504
Berkeley CA 94704
P: 510-528-0238 F: 510-549-2298 PRC:322
www.claresco.com
Email: info@claresco.com
Estab: 1997

Brett D'Ambrosio, CEO
Daniel Pearson, Quality Assurance Manager
John Moore, Project Manager
Loren D'Ambrosio, Lead Programmer
Matthew Allen-Goebel, Linux System Administrator

Provider of design and implementation services for customized business software. The company serves multi-national firms.

Claret Medical Inc HQ
1745 Copperhill Pkwy Ste 1
Santa Rosa CA 95403
P: 707-528-7253 F: 707-528-9302 PRC:189
www.claretmedical.com
Estab: 2009

Dan Fifer, VP of Research and Development

Manufacturer of catheters to protect the patient's brain during Transcatheter Aortic Valve Implantation (TAVI) and other endovascular procedures.

Clari Inc HQ
1154 Sonora Ct
Sunnyvale CA 94086
P: 650-265-2111 PRC:315
www.clari.com
Email: hello@clari.com
Estab: 2012

Andy Byrne, CEO
Venkat Rangan, CTO
Cornelius Willis, CMO
Alyssa Filter, CFO
Kevin Knieriem, CRO

Developers of an AI-based data capturing software that helps the marketing, sales, and customer success teams.

Claris International Inc HQ
5201 Patrick Henry Dr
Santa Clara CA 95054
P: 408-987-7000 F: 408-987-7447 PRC:323
www.claris.com
Email: claris_sales@claris.com
Estab: 1998

Brad Freitag, CEO
Heping Shang, Cloud Architect
Scott Lewis, VP of Operations & Information Systems
Simon Thornhill, VP of Engineering
Rick Kalman, Director of Product Management

Provider of database software which assists organizations in the management, analysis, and sharing of information.

Clarizen HQ
2755 Campus Dr Ste 300
San Mateo CA 94403
P: 866-502-9813 F: 650-227-0308 PRC:325
www.clarizen.com
Email: info@clarizen.com
Estab: 2006

Boaz Chalamish, CEO
Rao Adavikolanu, CMO
Viken Eldemir, CFO
Tamir Dresher, Chief Architect
Angela Bunner, VP of Customer Experience

Provider of collaborative online project management software. The company offers work management, time tracking, and project scheduling solutions.

Clayborn Lab HQ
40173 Truckee Airport Rd
Truckee CA 96161-4110
P: 530-587-4700 F: 530-587-5255 PRC:151
www.claybornlab.com
Email: claybornlab@claybornlab.com
Estab: 1963

Maureen Horvath, Owner
Justin Horvath, Owner & President
Mo Horvath, Owner
Tim Edge, Outside Sales Manager
David Millholen, Production Manager & Engineer

Developer of heat tapes, hot tubes, and custom tape heaters. The company serves the medical, transportation, and pharmaceutical sectors.

Clean Earth BR
30677 Huntwood Ave
Hayward CA 94544
P: 510-429-1129 F: 510-429-1498 PRC:139
aerc.com
Estab: 1990

Chris Dods, President & CEO
Sandra Coelho, Inside Sales Manager
Rick Rudd, Outside Sales Representative

Provider of recycling solutions. The company acts as regulated and permitted electronics and universal waste recycler.

Clean Energy Systems Inc HQ
3035 Prospect Park Dr Ste 120
Rancho Cordova CA 95670
P: 916-638-7967 F: 916-244-0709 PRC:152
www.cleanenergysystems.com
Email: info@cleanenergysystems.com
Estab: 1993

Keith L. Pronske, President & CEO
Joshua Perron, CRS Director of Business Development
Bill Hayes, Director of Manufacturing
Heath Evenson, Plant Manager
Patrick Skutley, Project Engineer & Process Engineer

Developer and manufacturer of steam and drive gas generator units. The company is engaged in design, delivery, and installation services.

Clean Power Research   HQ
1541 Third St
Napa CA 94559
P: 707-258-2765   PRC:319
www.cleanpower.com
Email: privacy@cleanpower.com
Estab: 1998

Jeff Ressler, CEO
Alan Saunders, Director of Business Development
Skip Dise, Product Manager
Brian Boler, Lead Product Manager
William Molinari, Controller

Provider of program automation, customer engagement, and solar data and intelligence solutions. The company offers services to the solar industry.

CleanAir Solutions Inc   HQ
826 Bayridge Pl
Fairfield CA 94534
P: 707-864-9499   F: 707-864-9399   PRC:125
www.cleanroomspecialists.com
Email: info@cleanroomspecialists.com
Estab: 1998

Kathie Kalafatis, President & CEO

Provider of stainless steel furniture and ESD curtain systems. The company serves pharmaceutical and medical device manufacturing companies.

Cleangrow   DH
3734 Bradview Dr Ste A
Sacramento CA 95827
P: 415-460-7295   PRC:87
www.cleangrow.com
Email: info@cleangrow.com
Estab: 2009

Roy O'Mahony, Founder & CTO
Lacey Macri, Director of Business Development
Donald Ormandy, Managing Director
Breeanna Ford, Operations Manager
Iain Aspley, Electrochemist

Manufacturer of sensors for the measurement of calcium, potassium, ammonium, magnesium, and fluoride ions.

Cleantec   HQ
4120 Douglas Blvd
Granite Bay CA 95746
P: 916-791-8478   PRC:56
www.gocleantec.com
Email: info@gocleantec.com

Aaron Tartakovsky, Founder & CEO
Bob Nelson, Contact

Provider of solutions for greenhouse gas emissions, air pollution, water conservation, and waste management.

Clear-Com LLC   HQ
1301 Marina Village Pkwy Ste 105
Alameda CA 94501
P: 510-337-6600   F: 510-337-6699   PRC:61
www.clearcom.com
Email: salessupportus@clearcom.com
Estab: 1968

Robert Cruz, Director of Finance
Albert Weber, Accountant I

Manufacturer of wireless and digital matrix intercom products and related accessories. The company serves the broadcasting and commercial markers.

ClearCare Inc   HQ
150 Spear St Ste 1550
San Francisco CA 94105
P: 800-449-0645   PRC:323
www.clearcareonline.com
Estab: 2010

Geoff Nudd, CEO & Founder
David Cristman, COO
Michael Cavan, VP of Sales
Ed Chuang, VP of Marketing & Business Development
Balki Nakshatrala, VP of Engineering

Provider of front and back office software solution such as billing, payroll, and marketing management for private duty home care agencies.

CLEARink Displays Inc   RH
4020 Clipper Ct
Fremont CA 94538
P: 510-624-9305   PRC:124
www.clearinkdisplays.com
Estab: 2012

Robert Fleming, VP of Research & Development
Scott Ferguson, VP of Engineering & Operations

Developer of reflective display modules for wearables, smartphones/tablets, electronic shelf labels, and outdoor signage.

ClearStory Data Inc   HQ
4300 Bohannon Dr Ste 100
Menlo Park CA 94025
P: 650-322-2408   PRC:325
www.clearstorydata.com
Email: info@clearstorydata.com
Estab: 2011

Carol Kimura, Director of Corporate Marketing & Marketing Operations

Provider of data analysis and collaboration solutions for food and beverage, healthcare and life services, media and entertainment, and financial services.

Cleasby Manufacturing Company Inc   HQ
1414 Bancroft Ave
San Francisco CA 94124
P: 415-822-6565   F: 415-822-1843   PRC:159
www.cleasby.com
Email: info@cleasby.com
Estab: 1949

John Cleasby, President

Provider of roofing services. The company also offers single ply, cold process, and built up roofing services.

Clickatell (pty) Ltd   HQ
900 Island Dr Ste 202
Redwood City CA 94065
P: 650-641-0011   F: 650-440-4961   PRC:323
www.clickatell.com
Estab: 2000

Pieter De Villiers, CEO & Co-Founder
Casper De Villiers, Co-Founder & SVP of Data Compliance & Shared Services Operations
Patrick Lawson, Co-Founder
Michael Jordan, Chairman
Nirmal Nair, CMO

Provider of SMS solutions such as SMS alerts, reminders, call centers, reservations and bookings for healthcare, marketing, and IT/software industries.

Clicktime Com Inc   HQ
282 Second St 4th Fl
San Francisco CA 94105
P: 415-684-1180   F: 415-684-1099   PRC:325
www.clicktime.com
Email: info@clicktime.com
Estab: 1997

Alex Mann, CEO
Yulia Delnik, Accounting Manager
Anthony Severo, Customer Education & Senior Support Manager
Allen Liu, Technology Lead

Provider of web-based tools, software, and IT consulting services. The company serves the aerospace, defense, automotive, and construction industries.

Climate Earth   HQ
137 Park Pl Ste 204
Point Richmond CA 94801
P: 415-391-2725   PRC:324
climateearth.com
Email: support@climateearth.com
Estab: 2008

Andy Miller, Founder
Chris Erickson, CEO

Provider of environmental product declarations and supply chain solutions such as supply chain, climate change risk, and natural capital management.

Climax Laboratories Inc   HQ
1939 Monterey Rd Ste 10
San Jose CA 95112
P: 408-298-8630   PRC:303
www.climaxlabs.com
Email: info@climaxlabs.com
Estab: 2009

Yeping Zhao, President

Provider of contract research services. The company offers bioanalytical and analytical testing services.

Clinisense Corp   HQ
15466 Los Gatos Blvd Ste 109-355
Los Gatos CA 95032
P: 408-348-1495   PRC:189
clinisense.com
Email: admin@clinisense.com
Estab: 2001

Stephen E. Zweig, Founder & CEO

Developer of technology for shelf-life monitoring. The company offers applications such as diagnostics, medical supplies, and RFID tags.

Clinovo Inc   HQ
4010 Moorpark Ave Ste 226
San Jose CA 95117
P: 866-994-3121   PRC:194
www.clinovo.com
Estab: 2013

Vamsi Maddipatla, President
Ritesh Patel, CEO & COO

Provider of resourcing solutions for pharmaceutical, biotechnology, diagnostic, medical device, and CRO customers.

Cloudera Inc   HQ
5470 Great America Pkwy
Santa Clara CA 94306
P: 650-362-0488 F: 888-789-1488   PRC:323
www.cloudera.com
Email: info@cloudera.com
Estab: 2008
Sales: $300M to $1 Billion

Amr Awadallah, Founder & CTO
Mike Olson, Chief Strategy Officer & Board
Chairman
Tom Reilly, CEO
Jim Frankola, CFO
Scott Aronson, CRO

Provider of professional services that include
cluster certification, descriptive analytics pilot, and
security integration pilot.

CloudFlare Inc   RH
101 Townsend St
San Francisco CA 94107
P: 650-319-8930   PRC:325
www.cloudflare.com
Estab: 2009

Michelle Zatlyn, Founder & Head of User Expe-
rience
Chris Merritt, CRO
Rachele Gyorffy, Contact
Wanda Lee, Customer Success Manager
Dani Grant, Product Manager

Provider of load balancers, traffic controllers,
and web optimization products. The company is
engaged in analytics services.

Cloudmark Inc   HQ
128 King St 2nd Fl
San Francisco CA 94107
P: 415-946-3800 F: 415-543-1233   PRC:323
www.cloudmark.com
Email: cm-sales@proofpoint.com
Estab: 2001

Vipul Ved Prakash, Owner
Hugh McCartney, CEO
Neil Cook, CTO
Kevin San Diego, VP of Product Management
Dave Kelly, Director of Technical Support

Provider of messaging infrastructure and security
solutions. The company delivers scalable messaging platform, security intelligence, and filtering.

Cloudpassage Inc   HQ
44 Tehama St Ste 412
San Francisco CA 94105
P: 415-886-3020   PRC:324
www.cloudpassage.com
Estab: 2010

Carson Sweet, Co-Founder & CEO
Vitaliy Geraymovych, Co-Founder & VP of Eng.,
Sami Laine, Principal Technologist

Developer of software solutions. The company
also offers account management, configuration
security monitoring, and alerting services.

Cloudshare Inc   HQ
351 California St Ste 1600
San Francisco CA 94104
P: 888-609-4440 F: 800-848-2854   PRC:326
cloudshare.com
Email: info@cloudshare.com
Estab: 2007

Zvi Guterman, Founder & CEO
Muly Gottlieb, VP of Research & Development
Annie Reiss, VP of Marketing
Ariel Fattal, VP of Finance
Tzvika Zitzman, VP of Cloud Operations

Provider of flexible and cloud-computing platform
for developing and testing IT applications, software, and systems.

Cloudtc   HQ
555 Bryant St Ste 337
Palo Alto CA 94301
P: 650-238-5203   PRC:319
cloudtc.com
Email: info@cloudtc.com
Estab: 2007

Anthony Gioeli, President & CEO

Designer and developer of voice communications
platform. The company specializes in business
applications.

Cloudwords Inc   HQ
201 California St Ste 1350
San Francisco CA 94111
P: 415-394-8000   PRC:325
www.cloudwords.com
Email: info@cloudwords.com
Estab: 2010

Michael Meinhardt, Founder & CEO
Steve Baggerly, CTO
Kevin Benson, Head of Sales

Provider of translation management systems and
content localization solutions to manage translation process, vendors, and content systems.

Clover Machine & Manufacturing   HQ
800 Mathew St Ste 101
Santa Clara CA 95050
P: 408-727-3380 F: 408-727-7015   PRC:80
clovermachine.com
Email: quotes@clovermachine.com
Estab: 1978

Bill Traill, Owner

Provider of contract manufacturing and machining services. The company supplies tooling and
fixtures to its customers.

Cloverleaf Solutions Inc   HQ
333 University Ave Ste 200
Sacramento CA 95825
P: 916-484-4141   PRC:324
www.cloverleafsolutions.com
Email: info@cloverleafsolutions.com

Christopher Bodine, President
Carlos Hinojosa, Maintenance Manager

Provider of data validation and information processing computer solutions. The company caters
to businesses.

Clovis Oncology   BR
499 Illinois St Ste 230
San Francisco CA 94158
P: 415-409-5440 F: 415-552-3427   PRC:254
clovisoncology.com
Email: medinfo@clovisoncology.com
Estab: 2009

Patrick Mahaffy, President & CEO & Director
Daniel W. Muehl, CFO
Lindsey Rolfe, EVP of Clinical Preclinical Develop-
ment & Pharmacovigilance & CMO
Gillian C. Ivers-Read, EVP & Chief Regulatory
Officer
Ann Bozeman, EVP of Human Resources

Developer of targeted therapies for the treatment
of patients with cancer. The company is involved
in clinical trials.

Clustered Systems Company Inc   HQ
3350 Scott Blvd Bldg 30-01
Santa Clara CA 95054
P: 408-327-8100 F: 408-327-8101   PRC:209
www.clusteredsystems.com

Phillip Hughes, CEO & Co-Founder
Robert Lipp, COO & Co-Founder

Provider of cooling technology services. The company's resources include data sheets, technology,
deployment, and white papers.

Clustrix Inc   HQ
201 Mission St Ste 1400
San Francisco CA 94105-1855
P: 415-501-9560   PRC:327
mariadb.com
Estab: 2006

Michael Howard, CEO
Michael Monty Widenius, CTO
Franz Aman, CMO
Jon Bakke, CRO
Kenneth Paqvalen, CFO

Provider of a SQL database with no limits to
database size, table size, query complexity, and
performance.

CMD Products   HQ
1410 Flightline Dr Ste D
Lincoln CA 95648
P: 916-434-0228 F: 916-434-0214   PRC:159
www.cmdproducts.com
Email: info@cmdproducts.com
Estab: 2003

Monique Harris, President
Thamara Z. Quintero, Operations Manager
Mary Powers, Warehouse Manager
Georgina Ramirez, Assembly Manager
Yareli Reyes, Assistant Manager

Manufacturer of replacement heads and accessories. It's products find application in gas and
electric weed trimmers.

CMI Manufacturing Inc   HQ
414 Umbarger Rd
San Jose CA 95111
P: 408-982-9580 F: 408-982-9583   PRC:157
www.cmi-mfg.com
Estab: 2011

Maria Baez-Moreno, President

Provider of prototype machining services. The
company also focuses on 3D surfacing, production, and manufacturing engineering support.

CMOS Sensor Inc HQ
20045 Stevens Creek Blvd Ste 1A
Cupertino CA 95014
P: 408-366-2898   F: 408-366-2841   PRC:87
www.csensor.com
Email: sales@csensor.com
Estab: 1997

Bill Wang, Founder
Simon Lin, Engineer

Designer and manufacturer of electro-optical
image acquisition and also surveillance solutions
for the medical market.

Coadna Photonics Inc HQ
733 Palomar Ave
Sunnyvale CA 94085
P: 408-736-1100   F: 408-736-1106   PRC:124
www.coadna.com
Email: sales@coadna.com
Estab: 2000

Jim Yuan, President & CEO
Jack Kelly, VP & CTO
Oliver Lu, Chief Commercial Officer
Jeff Tseng, Director of Quality Assurance
Maurice Chin, Director of Operations

Provider of tunable fiber optic solutions for optical
networks. The company's products are used in
high broadband applications.

Coast Aluminum and Architectural Inc HQ
10628 Fulton Wells Ave   [N]
Santa Fe Springs CA 90670
P: 562-946-6061   F: 562-946-4188   PRC:62
www.coastaluminum.com
Estab: 1991

Charley Holton, Branch Manager
Rick Abina, Sales Manager
Seth Olsen, Branch Manager
Thomas Stevenson, Operation Manager

Manufacturer and installer of switchgear control
panels, test stands and specialized electrical
equipment.

Coast Appliance Parts Co HQ
2606 Lee Ave   [N]
South El Monte CA 91733
P: 626-579-1500   PRC:31
www.coastparts.com
Email: parts@coastparts.com
Estab: 1958

Robin Georgian, Owner

Distributor of heating, ventilating, and air conditioning equipment.

Coast Metal Cutting HQ
2500 Bay Rd
Redwood City CA 94063
P: 650-369-9837   F: 650-369-1488   PRC:80
coastmetal.com
Email: sales@coastmetal.com
Estab: 1967

Brian Kottmeier, President

Provider of machining and metal cutting services.
The company's services include production, turning, drilling, and tapping.

Coast Sign Inc HQ
1500 W Embassy St   [N]
Anaheim CA 92802
P: 714-520-9144   F: 714-520-5847   PRC:316
www.coastsign.com
Emp: 201-500   Estab: 1985

Ernie Rivas, SVP of Business Development
Fred Siavoshi, VP of Sales
Melinda Washington, Manager of Human Re-
sources

Provider of project management, turnkey brand
conversions and re-branding manufacturing specialized services, leasing, engineering, installation
and much more services.

Coastside Net HQ
525-B Obispo Rd
El Granada CA 94018
P: 650-712-5900   PRC:325
coastside.net
Email: info@coastside.net
Estab: 1994

Rob Genovesi, Owner
Coastside Net, Owner
Steve Dennis, Senior Technician

Provider of Internet access and technology solutions. The company also offers website services
including website hosting, design, and development.

Cobalt Polymers Inc HQ
421 S Cloverdale Blvd
Cloverdale CA 95425
P: 800-337-0901   PRC:281
www.cobaltpolymers.com
Email: sales@cobaltpolymers.com

Robert Foley, President

Manufacturer of polymer tubing for medical device
and high technology applications, with polymer
chemistry, radiation science, and process engineering.

Cobham Defence Electronics BR
5300 Hellyer Ave
San Jose CA 95138
P: 888-310-0010   F: 408-624-3913   PRC:8
www.cobham.com
Estab: 1994

John Ries, Program Manager
Roger Smith, Senior Engineering Manager &
Member of Technical Staff

Manufacturer and designer of electrical components. The company caters to the military and
commercial sectors.

Codar Ocean Sensors Ltd HQ
1914 Plymouth St
Mountain View CA 94043
P: 408-773-8240   F: 408-773-0514   PRC:68
www.codar.com
Email: info@codar.com
Estab: 1960

Don Barrick, President
Chad Whelan, CTO
Pederson Laura, Director of Marketing
Allison Mendes, Assistant Operations Manager
Bonnie Ngai, Product & Test Manager

Designer and manufacturer of radar systems for
ocean current and wave monitoring. The company
specializes in sea state monitoring.

Code-N Technology Inc HQ
1370 Willow Rd
Menlo Park CA 94025
P: 650-234-8400   PRC:315
www.code-n.com
Email: info1@code-n.com
Estab: 2012

Marketta Silvera, Founder & Executive Chairman
of the Board
Randy Haldeman, CEO & President

Leverages advanced semantic web technology to
provide software solutions to businesses.

Codeobjects Inc HQ
490 N McCarthy Blvd
Milpitas CA 95035
P: 408-432-1180   PRC:322
www.codeobjects.com
Email: info@codeobjects.com
Estab: 2006

Anil Annadata, CEO
Cathy Takahashi, Director of Business Analysis
Navnika Wason, Product Manager
Chad Gurung, Product Manager
John Laverty, Technical Account Manager

Developer of insurance process management and
business intelligence solutions. The company also
offers claims management services.

Codexis Inc HQ
200 Penobscot Dr
Redwood City CA 94063
P: 650-421-8100   PRC:34
www.codexis.com
Emp: 132 Estab: 2002
Sales: $30M to $100M

John Nicols, President & CEO
Ross Taylor, CFO
Doug Sheehy, EVP & Chief Administrative Officer
& General Counsel & Secretary
Joseph Sarret, SVP & Chief Business Officer
Scott Watson, VP of Sales & Marketing

Provider of biocatalysts products such as screening kits and other accessories. The company
serves the food and nutrition industries.

Cofan USA Inc HQ
48664 Milmont Dr
Fremont CA 94538
P: 510-490-7533   F: 510-490-7931   PRC:88
www.cofan-usa.com
Email: info@cofan-usa.com
Estab: 1994

Allen Ong, VP
Valerie Ramos, People Operations Manager
Joe Cabe, Head of Global Talent

Developer and manufacturer of products for thermal engineering. The company specializes in fans,
heat sinks, and custom products.

Coffer Group LLC   HQ
268 Bush St Ste 4324
San Francisco CA 94104
P: 415-963-4382   PRC:40
coffergroup.com
Email: info@coffergroup.com
Estab: 2007

Jason Coffer, Founder
Brian Valadez, Information Technology Support
Engineer
Ehsan Alahdad, Network Engineer

Provider of information technology solutions. The
company specializes in private equity, venture
capital, and hedge funds.

Cogco Inc   HQ
PO Box 1310
Woodland CA 95776-1310
P: 530-666-1716   F: 530-666-1942   PRC:133
cogcowireline.com
Email: info@cogcowireline.com
Estab: 1977

James Cogbill, President
Nancy Goyet, Office Manager

Provider of gas and oil well services such as per-
forating, thru tubing, case logging, and jet cutting.

Cognex Corp   BR
20380 Town Center Ln Ste 195 and 250
Cupertino CA 95014
P: 858-481-2469   F: 858-792-0470   PRC:159
cognex.com
Estab: 1981

Robert J. Shillman, Chairman & Founder
Robert Willett, President & CEO
John J. Curran, EVP of Finance & Administrative
& Treasurer & CFO
Sheila DiPalma, SVP of Corporate Employee
Services & Corporate Officer
Patrick A. Alias, SVP

Supplier of barcode readers and sensor products.
The company offers vision sensors, fixed mount
readers, handheld readers, and mobile computers.

Cognizant Technology Solutions   BR
5000 Executive Pkwy Ste 295 296 & 298
San Ramon CA 94583
P: 925-790-2000   PRC:323
cognizant.com
Email: inquiry@cognizant.com

Malcolm Frank, President of Cognizant Digital
Business
Dharmendra Kumar Sinha, President
Ganesh Ayyar, President of Cognizant Digital
Operations
Gregory Hyttenrauch Greg, President of Cogni-
zant Digital Systems & Technology
Brian Humphries, CEO

Provider of business consulting, enterprise
application development, IT infrastructure, and
outsourcing services.

CohBar Inc   HQ
1455 Adams Dr
Menlo Park CA 94025
P: 650-446-7888   PRC:303
www.cohbar.com
Email: info@cohbar.com
Estab: 2007

Albion J. Fitzgerald, Chairman
Simon Allen, CEO
Jeffrey Biunno, CFO
Jon Stern, COO
Kenneth Cundy, Chief Scientific Officer

Developer of treatments for metabolic dysfunction
that includes NASH, obesity, cancer, neurodegenerative diseases, and more.

Cohere Technologies Inc   HQ
2550 Walsh Ave Ste 150
Santa Clara CA 95051
P: 408-246-1277   PRC:68
cohere-technologies.com
Estab: 2013

Ronny Hadani, Co-Founder & Chief Scientific
Officer
Shlomo Rakib, Co-Founder & CTO
Raymond P. Dolan, Chairman & CEO
Ram Prasad, COO
Ronny Haraldsvik, CMO

Developers of wireless technology solutions. The
company offers solutions for orthogonal time
frequency space.

Coherent Inc   HQ
5100 Patrick Henry Dr
Santa Clara CA 95054
P: 408-764-4000   PRC:172
www.coherent.com
Email: coherent.europe@coherent.com
Estab: 1966
Sales: $1B to $3B

John R. Ambroseo, President & CEO
Kevin S. Palatnik, EVP & CFO
Luis Spinelli, CTO
Bret DiMarco, EVP & General Counsel
Mark S. Sobey, EVP & General Manager of OEM
Laser Sources

Manufacturer of optics and laser instruments.
The company serves the medical and research
industries.

Coherus Biosciences   HQ
333 Twin Dolphin Dr Ste 600
Redwood City CA 94065
P: 800-794-5434   PRC:253
www.coherus.com
Estab: 2010

Denny Lanfear, CEO
Barbara Finck, CMO
Peter Watler, CTO
Jean-Frederic Viret, CFO
Vladimir Vexler, CSO

Developer of biosimilars and it serves the global
marketplace. The company is engaged in delivery
services.

Colabo Inc   HQ
751 Laurel St Ste 840
San Carlos CA 94070
P: 650-288-6649   F: 650-240-0281   PRC:322
colabo.com
Email: info@colabo.com
Estab: 2010

Naama Halperin, Co-Founder & COO
Yoav Dembak, Co-Founder & CEO
Asaf Wexler, CTO
Nofar Neuberg, QA Manager

Provider of multi-functional software that enables
professionals across all industries to achieve a
number of business objectives.

Cold Ice Inc   HQ
9999 San Leandro St
Oakland CA 94603
P: 510-568-8129   F: 510-568-2355   PRC:159
www.coldice.com
Email: info@coldice.com
Estab: 1982

Ray Wilhelm, President
Phil Deckard, General Manager
Melissa Malana, Office Supervisor

Manufacturer of refrigerants, insulated shipping
containers and temperature monitors. The company serves the agricultural and gourmet food
industries.

Cold Room Solutions Inc   HQ
4695 Chabot Dr Ste 200
Pleasanton CA 94566
P: 925-462-2500   F: 925-462-2502   PRC:159
www.coldroomsolutions.com
Email: sales@coldroomsolutions.com
Estab: 2001

Brad Bidwell, President

Provider of walk-in cold rooms, freezers, and
warm rooms. The company focuses on preventive
maintenance programs.

Colema Boards Of California Inc   HQ
PO Box 1879
Cottonwood CA 96022
P: 530-347-5700   F: 530-347-3122   PRC:189
colema.com
Email: info@colema.com
Estab: 1975

Victor Earl Irons, Founder

Manufacturer of home enema board kits. The
company's products include colema boards and
cleansing kits.

Colfax International   HQ
750 Palomar Ave
Sunnyvale CA 94085
P: 408-730-2275   F: 408-730-2274   PRC:323
www.colfax-intl.com
Email: sales@colfax-intl.com
Estab: 1987

Gautam Shah, CEO
Michael Fay, VP of Sales
Achim Wengeler, Director of SW Development
Richard Jackson, Director of Technical
Manish Shah, Manager of Marketing Communi-
cations

Provider of workstations, servers, clusters, storage, and personal supercomputing solutions to
accelerate business and research outcomes.

Collaborative Drug Discovery Inc   HQ
  1633 Bayshore Hwy Ste 342
  Burlingame CA 94010
P: 650-242-5259   PRC:324
www.collaborativedrug.com
Email: info@collaborativedrug.com
Estab: 2004

Barry A. Bunin, CEO
Krishna Dole, CTO & Security Officer
Sean Ekins, CSO
Kellan Gregory, Director of Product Excellence
Sylvia Ernst, Head of Sales & Sales Operations

Provider of drug discovery research informatics.
The company offers hosted biological and chemical database that securely manages private and
external data.

Collidion Inc   HQ
  1770 Corporate Cir
  Petaluma CA 94954
P: 707-668-7600   PRC:189
collidion.com
Email: info@collidion.com
Estab: 2015

Hoji Alimi, CEO & Chairman & Founder

Provider of healthcare products. The company
specializes in antibiotic resistance, specific drugs
to eradicate biofilms, and delivery systems.

Collimated Holes Inc   HQ
  460 Division St
  Campbell CA 95008
P: 408-374-5080   F: 408-374-0670   PRC:84
www.collimatedholes.com
Email: contact@collimatedholes.com
Estab: 1975

Richard W. Mead, President
Matt Fate, Director of Sales & Manufacturing

Designer and manufacturer of fiber optic components, sub-assemblies, and imaging systems. The
company also provides design and manufacturing
services.

Columbia Machine Works   HQ
  934 75th Ave
  Oakland CA 94621
P: 510-568-0808   F: 510-568-0810   PRC:80
www.columbiamachine.net
Estab: 1955

John Sol, General Manager

Provider of coining equipment and contracting
services. The company offers coining presses,
rimming machines, and consumable tooling.

Comit Systems Inc   HQ
  1246 Gainsborough Dr
  Sunnyvale CA 94087
P: 408-988-2988   PRC:212
sites.google.com/comit.com
Email: info@comit.com
Estab: 1992

Venkat Iyer, President & CEO

Provider of full service contract engineering for
wireless and cleantech, methodology consulting,
Soc design and verification, board design, and
software.

CommerceNet   HQ
  5050 El Camino Real Ste 215
  Los Altos CA 94022
P: 650-289-4040   PRC:325
commerce.net
Email: info@commerce.net
Estab: 1994

Jay M. Tenenbaum, Founder
Allan M. Schiffman, Executive Director
Anne Ferris, Director of Operations
Jeff Shrager, Consulting Professor

Provider of Internet based research and piloting
services such as Internet business, open trading
networks, and Internet-user demographic surveys.

**Commodity Resource &
Environmental Inc**   BR
  493 Reynolds Cir
  San Jose CA 95112
P: 408-501-0691   F: 408-436-5578   PRC:142
www.creweb.com
Email: info@creweb.com
Estab: 1980

Stacy Aesoph, President
Charles Yohn, VP of Sales

Producer of silver. The company engages in silver
recovery, photo solution waste disposal, and other
activities.

**Common Interest Management
Services**   BR
  1720 S Amphlett Blvd Ste 130
  San Mateo CA 94402
P: 650-286-0292   F: 650-286-0296   PRC:45
commoninterest.com
Estab: 1990

Mike Archer, CEO
Lisa Marrone, Senior Director
Leonard Ataide, Property Manager
Adrianne Bretao, Association Manager
Ann Naviaux, Manager of Community Association

Provider of homeowner association management
solutions such as escrow and disclosure, maintenance, online and community services.

**Communications & Power Industries
LLC**   HQ
  811 Hansen Way
  Palo Alto CA 94304
P: 650-846-2900   F: 650-846-3276   PRC:61
www.cpii.com
Email: mppmarketing@cpii.com
Estab: 1948

Joe O. Caldarelli, CEO
Joel A. Littman, CFO
Lindsey Kemp, West Coast Regional Sales
Manager
Mike Bayless, Operations Manager
Marina Remmel, Senior Human Resources
Representative

Developer and manufacturer of microwave, radio
frequency, power, and control solutions. The company serves medical and critical defense fields.

CommWorld of San Francisco   HQ
  4336 Jessica Cir
  Fremont CA 94555
P: 650-358-8700   F: 650-585-2174   PRC:45
www.commworldsf.com
Email: sales@commworldsf.com
Estab: 1979

Carmelo Vazquez, Operations Manager
Terri Nubla, Manager
Mark Mandrik, Manager of National Accounts

Provider of telecommunication services such as
computer networking, structured cabling, project
management and repair.

Comp Pro Med Inc   HQ
  3418 Mendocino Ave
  Santa Rosa CA 95403
P: 707-578-0239   PRC:41
comppromed.com
Email: info@comppromed.com
Estab: 1983

Hal Petersen, Operations Manager
Daniel Best, Senior Developer

Provider of laboratory information systems for
clinical laboratories. The company offers services
to the healthcare sector.

Compact Imaging Inc   HQ
  897 Independence Ave Ste 5B
  Mountain View CA 94043
P: 650-694-7801   F: 650-694-4972   PRC:187
compactimaging.com
Email: info@compactimaging.com

Carol Wilson, Founder & Head of Engineering &
Vice President
Don Bogue, CEO
Josh Hogan, CTO
Michael R. Hee, CMO

Developer of miniature optical sensor technology. The company specializes in mobile health
applications.

Compandent Inc   HQ
  26666 Birch Hill Way
  Los Altos Hills CA 94022
P: 650-241-9231   F: 425-790-0949   PRC:62
www.compandent.com
Email: sales@compandent.com
Estab: 2001

Oded Gottesman, CEO & CTO

Developer of customized algorithms. The company
offers digital sign processing services to telecommunications and semiconductor companies.

Comparative Biosciences Inc   HQ
  786 Lucerne Dr
  Sunnyvale CA 94085
P: 408-738-9260   F: 408-738-9278   PRC:34
www.compbio.com
Estab: 1996

Carol Meschter, CEO
James Christenson, SVP
Robin Dean, Senior Scientist & Director of Tox
Study
Hongqing Du, Pharmacology & Study Director
Douglas Crowder, Business Development Man-
ager

Provider of research and development support
services. The company serves the biotechnology
and pharmaceutical industries.

Compass & Anvil Sales and Engineering Inc HQ
118 El Olivar
Los Gatos CA 95032
P: 408-205-1319   F: 408-866-5150   PRC:159
www.compass-anvil.com
Estab: 2005

Charlie Lawton, Owner

Provider of engineering services. The company focuses on metal prototypes, forgings, castings, and metal stampings.

Compass Made HQ
48133 Warm Springs Blvd
Fremont CA 94539-7498
P: 510-656-4700   F: 510-656-4682   PRC:202
www.ccicms.com
Estab: 1979

Thomas Maurer, VP
Bill Turner, Director of Strategic Projects

Manufacturer of custom cables and harnesses and distributor of electronic components. The company also manufactures electromechanical products.

Compatible Cable Inc HQ
5046 Commercial Cir Ste B
Concord CA 94520
P: 888-415-1115   PRC:62
www.compatiblecable.com
Email: sales@compatiblecable.com
Estab: 2009

Angela Trantham, Office Manager
Bill Calkins, Sales Manager

Manufacturer of custom cable assemblies and off-the shelf cables. The company offers services to the automotive, broadcast, and electronics industries.

Complete Genomics Inc HQ
2904 Orchard Pkwy
San Jose CA 95134
P: 408-648-2560   PRC:25
www.completegenomics.com
Email: info@completegenomics.com
Estab: 2006

Radoje Drmanac, CSO
Avanindra Chaturvedi, CFO
Brock Peters, Senior Director of Research
Jody Beecher, Senior Director of Fluidic Devices
Yuan Jiang, Director of Research

Developer of human genome sequencing technology, research and development, clinical and consumer applications.

ComplianceEase HQ
111 Anza Blvd Ste 200
Burlingame CA 94010-1823
P: 650-373-1111   F: 650-373-7844   PRC:326
complianceease.com
Email: sales@complianceease.com
Estab: 2001

Anita Kwan, CEO
Chris Rodskog, CFO
Sanjay Tibrewal, CPO
Al Ogrodski, SVP of Solution Strategy
Katrina Chang Ouano, Sales Director

Provider of intelligent business solutions to financial service institutions. The company offers automated compliance and risk management solutions.

Comptech USA HQ
5437 Stationers Way
Sacramento CA 95842
P: 916-338-3434   PRC:80
www.comptechusa.com
Estab: 1979

Fred Penney, President & CEO

Manufacturer and fabricator of race engines. The company also offers R&D and road racing track maintenance services.

Compton Enterprises HQ
2434 Dayton Rd
Chico CA 95928
P: 530-895-1942   F: 530-895-0760   PRC:179
www.comptonenterprises.com

Jason Compton, Owner
Wes Compton, President
Laura Compton, CEO
Chris Compton, Manager

Manufacturer of moving equipment. The company specializes in rail-cars, conveyors, and truck loaders.

Compudata Inc HQ
855 Folsom St Apt 122
San Francisco CA 94107
P: 415-495-3422   F: 415-495-1962   PRC:224
www.compu-data.net
Email: sales@compu-data.net

Angela Nadeau, President & CEO
Ed Guarrieri, VP of Technology
Bessie Lee-Cham, VP of Operations
Paul Thompson, Director of Support
Roula Daniel, Manager of Sales

Provider of sales, accounting, and manufacturing software. The company especially caters to businesses.

Compugraphics USA Inc BR
43455 Osgood Rd
Fremont CA 94539
P: 510-249-2600   PRC:77
www.compugraphics-photomasks.com
Email: us@compugraphics.com

Craig Durgy, Eastern Regional Sales Manager
Laurie Sullivan, Account Manager
Farzan Hakami, Engineering Section Head

Designer and developer of photomasks for semiconductor, optoelectronic devices, MEMs, nanotechnology, and renewable energy sectors.

Computer Deductions Inc HQ
8680 Greenback Ln Ste 210
Orangevale CA 95662
P: 916-987-3600   F: 916-987-3606   PRC:323
www.cdi-hq.com
Email: info@cdi-hq.com
Estab: 1971

Tom Calabro, VP & CIO
Matthew Iskra, Senior Technical Analyst & Database Administrator
Christopher Hadtrath, Senior Application Developer

Provider of software development services as a subcontractor to corporations. The company also offers management consulting services.

Computer Logistics Corp HQ
1135 Pine St Ste 202
Redding CA 96001
P: 530-241-3131   PRC:159
compulog.com
Estab: 1986

Bob Andrews, CEO & Principal
Rafe Spaulding, CIO & Principal
Damien Owen, Service Manager
Greg Bromley, Senior Consultant
Staphanie Marain, Technician

Provider of system and Internet integration, system design, custom programming, web design, and hosting services.

Computer Methods HQ
1660 W Linne Rd Ste H
Tracy CA 95377
P: 510-824-0252   F: 510-824-0254   PRC:324
computer-methods.com
Estab: 1986

David Lieberman, Owner & President
Frank Monzo, COO
Mike Parratt, Account Manager

Manufacturer of physical therapy testing equipment. The company's products include WebExam, PP004, WinHand, and ActivitySuite.

Computer Plastics Inc HQ
1914 National Ave
Hayward CA 94545
P: 510-785-3600   F: 510-785-3229   PRC:163
www.computerplastics.com
Email: cpi-sales@computerplastics.com
Estab: 1969

Timalex Gina, Manager

Provider of molding services. The company offers custom plastic injection molding, engineering, assembly, and tooling services.

Computer Presentation Systems Inc HQ
3035 Prospect Park Dr Ste 90
Rancho Cordova CA 95670
P: 916-635-3487   F: 916-635-1809   PRC:323
www.cpsusa.com
Email: info@cpsusa.com
Estab: 1985

Zoe Miller, Owner & Principal
Robert Musa, President
Lisa Meylor, Marketing Manager

Designer and developer of hardware and software solutions for home builders ranging from local entrepreneurs to regional builders.

Computer Software For Professionals Inc HQ
5346 College Ave
Oakland CA 94618
P: 510-547-8085   F: 510-547-8159   PRC:319
www.legalmaster.com
Email: csp@legalmaster.com
Estab: 1977

Phillip Rubin, Director of Design

Provider of law office management software and related tools. The company offers services to the legal industry.

Computerland Of Silicon Valley HQ
482 W San Carlos St
San Jose CA 95110
P: 408-519-3200 F: 408-519-3260 PRC:68
www.cland.com
Email: info@cland.com
Estab: 1991

Ken Chang, IT Technician

Provider of hardware, software, and networking services. The company serves government and educational institutions.

Computers & Structures Inc HQ
1646 N California Blvd Ste 600
Walnut Creek CA 94596
P: 510-649-2200 PRC:322
csiamerica.com
Email: feedback@csiamerica.com
Estab: 1975

Ashraf Habibullah, President & CEO
Syed Hasanain, EVP
Faisal Habib, Software Support Manager
Umer Haroon, Software Engineer

Provider of integrated design, analysis, assessment, drafting of building systems, and related support services.

CompuTrust Software HQ
18625 Sutter Blvd Ste 500
Morgan Hill CA 95037
P: 800-222-7947 PRC:323
www.computrustcorp.com
Email: sales@computrustcorp.com
Estab: 1982

Lily Yee, Technical Support & Projects Manager
Paula Lomanto, Manager of Project

Developer and seller of software for public administrators. The company offers services to businesses and enterprises.

Comtech Xicom Technology Inc HQ
3550 Bassett St [N]
Santa Clara CA 95054
P: 408-213-3000 F: 408-213-3001 PRC:68
xicomtech.com
Email: info@xicomtech.com
Estab: 1991

John Branscum, President
Kevin Kirkpatrick, VP of Marketing & Sales

Supplier of amplifiers to the satellite communications sector.

Concentric Analgesics Inc HQ
101 California St Ste 1210
San Francisco CA 94111
P: 415-484-7921 F: 707-313-7200 PRC:303
www.concentricanalgesics.com
Email: medinfo@concentricanalgesics.com
Estab: 2014

John Donovan, Co-Founder & President
Craig Husfeld, Co-Founder & VP of Chemistry
Frank Bellizzi, CEO
Mike Royal, CMO

Developer of therapeutic solutions. The company focuses on discovery and development of novel, non opioid therapeutics for treating acute and chronic pain.

Concept Models Inc HQ
2127 Research Dr Ste 9
Livermore CA 94550
P: 925-606-6743 PRC:80
www.cmodelz.com

Bob Hallock, Contact

Provider of prototyping devices. The company specializes in surgical devices, CNC programming, tap burning, and rubber molding.

Concepts 2 Industries HQ
2829 S Rodeo Gulch Rd Ste 6
Soquel CA 95073
P: 831-464-1111 F: 831-464-1100 PRC:163
www.concepts2.com
Email: molding@concepts2.com
Estab: 1990

Michael Lodico, VP of Sales & Administration & Founder
Kayla Gammino, Customer Service Manager

Manufacturer of custom injection molded plastic parts. The company serves computer, medical, telecom, and other sectors.

Concord Sheet Metal HQ
1666 Willow Pass Rd
Pittsburg CA 94565
P: 925-680-8723 F: 925-680-6569 PRC:80
concordsheetmetal.com
Estab: 1986

Ron Wessels, President
Sean Murphy, Production Manager
Marcia Wessels, Office Manager
Randy Smith, Estimator

Provider of architectural metal products. The company focuses on fasteners, copper gutters, and decorative chimney tops.

Condor Country Consulting HQ
815 Estudillo St
Martinez CA 94553-1617
P: 925-335-9308 F: 925-231-0571 PRC:142
condorcountry.com
Email: info@condorcountry.com
Estab: 2001

Wendy Dexter, President
Christian Knowlton, Biological Technician
Denise Wight, Biological Technician
Ted Robertson, Contact
Samantha Weber, Senior Biologist

Provider of natural and cultural resource supporting services. The company also provides ecological, natural resource, and cartographic services.

Condor Reliability Services Inc HQ
3400 De La Cruz Blvd Unit R [N]
Santa Clara CA 95054
P: 408-486-9600 F: 408-486-9606 PRC:204
www.crsigroup.com
Emp: 51-200 Estab: 1980

Brian Travers, Aviation Weather Observer
Frank Acropolis, Meteorological Tech
Greg Morrissey, Weather Observer

Provider of innovative solutions to government and industry.

Configure Inc HQ
1800 Hamilton Ave Ste 100
San Jose CA 95125
P: 877-408-2636 PRC:67
configureinc.com
Email: sales@configureinc.com
Estab: 1996

RUDAIN ARAFEH, Founder & President & CEO
A.J. VERDECCHIA, COO & CFO
Dina Fernandes, Project Manager
Debby McLaurin, Project Manager

Provider of communication consulting services. The company specializes in network design, transport service implementation, and project management.

Confometrx HQ
3070 Kenneth St
Santa Clara CA 95054
P: 408-496-6276 PRC:34
confometrx.com

Brian Kobilka, Founder
Tong Sun Kobilka, CEO
Xichen Li, Manager of Lab & Research Associate
Shane Li, Lab Manager
Bingfa Sun, Scientist

Developer of a platform of drug development tools. The company specializes in drug discovery technologies.

Conformiq HQ
14435 C Big Basin Way Ste 271
Saratoga CA 95070
P: 408-898-2140 PRC:322
www.conformiq.com
Email: conformiq@conformiq.com
Estab: 1998

Mark Creamer, CEO
Stephan Schulz, CTO
Kimmo Nupponen, VP of Engineering & Chief Scientist
Jani Koivulainen, VP of Customer Success Services
Clark Cochran, VP of Field Operations Americas

Provider of automated test designing services. The company focuses on training, project implementation, change management, and executive consulting.

Connectance Inc HQ
38 Miller Ave Ste 315
Mill Valley CA 94941
P: 415-891-8872 PRC:194
www.connectance.com
Email: sales@connectance.com

Nabil W. Moukheibir, CEO
Rick Beberman, COO

Provider of software for diagnosis in health care industry. The company offer online access too to detect a disease and offer treatment suggestion.

Connectec Company Inc   HQ

1701 Reynolds Ave   [N]
Irvine CA 92614
P: 949-252-1077   F: 949-252-1299   PRC:202
www.connectecco.com
Email: corp@connectecco.com
Estab: 1988

Marnie Primmer, Founder & CEO
John Rus, QA Manager

Manufacturer of modeling, fabrication and tooling services.

Connected Io Inc   HQ

573 University Ave
Los Gatos CA 95032
P: 669-221-6100   PRC:63
www.connectedio.com
Email: info@connectedio.com
Estab: 2013

Yakov Temov, CEO
David Hargis, COO
Barakha Shah, Software Quality Assurance Engineer
Nishima Mohan, Lead Software Quality Assurance Engineer

Developer of altair-based cellular module for Internet of Things applications. The company provides hardware design and development services.

Connected Marketing   HQ

1340 S De Anza Blvd Ste 201
San Jose CA 95129
P: 408-647-2198   PRC:324
connectedmarketing.com
Email: info@connectedmarketing.com

Tricia Hart, Director
Robert Beckman, Sales Director
Carol Francavilla, Principal & Account Manager
Rebecca Seggel, Project Manager
Tammy Brooks, Project Manager & Research Specialist

Provider of marketing services. The company also offers web development, branding, and lead generation services.

Connekt LLC   HQ

15844 Norlene Way
Grass Valley CA 95949
P: 530-604-5821   PRC:78
connektllc.com
Email: scott@connektllc.com
Estab: 1992

Scott Raitt, CEO

Developer and manufacturer of mechanical engineering design solutions. The company's services include CAD, reverse engineering, and sheet metal design.

Connor Manufacturing Services Inc   HQ

1710 S Amphlett Blvd Ste 318
San Mateo CA 94402
P: 800-968-7078   PRC:157
www.connorms.com
Email: sales@connorms.com
Estab: 1913

Robert Sloss, CEO & Chairman

Provider of customized solutions for precision metal stamping, wire forms, springs, and integrated assembly needs.

M-82

Consensus Orthopedics Inc   HQ

1115 Windfield Way Ste 100
El Dorado Hills CA 95762
P: 916-355-7100   F: 916-355-7190   PRC:190
consensusortho.com
Email: info@consensusortho.com

Colleen Gray, CEO
Curt Wiedenhoefer, VP of Global Sales & Marketing
Michael Droege, Senior Director of Global Business & Market Development
Carol Hermans, Materials Manager
Kathy Toy, Accounting Manager

Manufacturer of orthopedic medical devices. The company's products include consensus hip systems, revision knee systems, mobile bearing knee systems, and others.

ConSol Consulting & Solutions Corp   HQ

201 Spear St Ste 1100
San Francisco CA 94105
P: 925-479-1370   F: 925-479-1371   PRC:325
consol.com
Email: info@consol.com
Estab: 2001

Ulrich Schwanengel, Founder & Owner
Michael Beutner, CEO
Markus Mayer, COO

Provider of information technology services. The company offers software, networking, outsourcing, and monitoring solutions.

Construction Electrical Products   HQ

7800 Las Positas Rd
Livermore CA 94551
P: 925-828-9420   F: 925-828-3416   PRC:243
www.cepnow.com
Email: sales@cepnow.com
Estab: 1976

Rob Larrabee, CEO
Emily Thompson, Manager

Provider of electrical products for the construction sector. The company offers temporary power products, extension cords, and portable lighting.

Continental Motors Inc   HQ

840 W Brockton Ave   [N]
Redlands CA 92374
P: 909-793-3131   F: 909-793-5818   PRC:288
www.teledyne.com
Email: communications@teledyne.com
Estab: 1920

Melanie S. Cibik, SVP & General Counsel & Chief Compliance Officer & Secretary
Cynthia Y. Belak, VP & Controller
Jason VanWees, SVP

Manufacturer of aircraft batteries, ground power batteries, and standby power batteries.

Contract Room Inc   HQ

1670 S Amphlett Blvd Ste 140
San Mateo CA 94402
P: 800-950-9101   PRC:315
www.contractroom.com
Email: sales@contractroom.com
Estab: 2012

Emil Stefanutti, Co-Founder & CEO
Peter Thomson, Co-Founder & COO
Charlene Dickey, VP of Enterprise Sales
Cesar Soto, Head of Engineering

Provides contract management software.

Contrast Media Labs   HQ

388 Market St Ste 1300
San Francisco CA 94111
P: 415-471-1323   PRC:319
contrastmedialabs.com
Email: info@contrastmedialabs.com
Estab: 2010

Arvin Tehrani, Founder
Edwin Tehrani, Marketing Director

Provider of graphic design and software development services. The company services include android applications and digital and print media design.

Contrast Security   HQ

240 Third St 2nd Fl
Los Altos CA 94022
P: 888-371-1333   PRC:325
www.contrastsecurity.com
Email: support@contrastsecurity.com
Estab: 2014

Jeff Williams, Founder & CTO
Alan Naumann, Chairman & CEO & President
Surag Patel, Chief Strategy Officer
Mark Hodgson, VP of Corporate Marketing
Mike Keating, VP of Worldwide Sales & Operations

Designer and developer of self-protection software. The company is also engaged in operations support services.

Control Laboratories Inc   HQ

42 Hangar Way
Watsonville CA 95076
P: 831-724-5422   F: 831-724-3188   PRC:41
www.controllabs.com

Mike Galloway, Director of Lab

Provider of agricultural analytical services such as compost, water, soil, plant, remediation and bio-fuel testing.

Control Systems West Inc   HQ

1150 Industrial Ave Ste F
Petaluma CA 94952
P: 707-763-1108   F: 707-763-9324   PRC:143
www.controlwest.com
Email: info@controlwest.com
Estab: 1970

Richard Borders, VP & Industrial Engineer
Joseph Perry, Engineering Manager

Designer and fabricator of a broad variety of custom electrical controls for industrial applications.

Controlco HQ
3451 Vincent Rd Ste C
Pleasant Hill CA 94523
P: 800-800-7126 PRC:304
www.controlco.com
Email: sales@controlco.com
Estab: 1958

Brian Turner, President

Provider of automation and solutions to address
the Internet of Things for commercial buildings,
(BIoT).

Convaid Products LLC HQ

2830 California St [N]
Torrance CA 90503
P: 310-618-0111 F: 310-618-2166 PRC:189
www.convaid.com
Estab: 1976

Chris Braun, CEO
Nanneke Dinklo, Director of Marketing
Ro Octave, Director of Finance
Steve Ricker, Manager of Sales
Nick Chan, Manager of Production

Manufacturer of compact folding wheelchairs.

Conval Inc BR
6006 Kibler Rd
Paradise CA 95969
P: 530-877-5172 PRC:166
conval.com
Email: convalwest@sbcglobal.net

Scott Hilke, US Western Regional Manager

Manufacturer of pressure forged steel valves.
The company products include globe valves, ball
valves, and strainers.

Convergent Laser Technologies HQ
1660 S Loop Rd
Alameda CA 94502
P: 510-832-2130 F: 510-832-1600 PRC:189
www.convergentlaser.com
Email: sales@convergentlaser.com
Estab: 1984

Sarah Weld, Product Manager & Junior Executive

Provider of medical laser systems and fiber optic
devices. The company deals with training and
product support services.

Conversion Devices Inc HQ

15481 Electronic Ln [N]
Huntington Beach CA 92649
P: 714-898-6551 F: 714-894-9248 PRC:189
www.cdipower.com
Email: sales@cdipower.com
Emp: 11-50 Estab: 1981

Alan Augusta, VP of Marketing
Harish Khatter, Engineering Director
Roland Roth, Manager of Sales
Joy Kennelly, Technician

Provider of medical power supply solutions.

Cooling Source Inc HQ
2021 Las Positas Ct Ste 101
Livermore CA 94551
P: 925-292-1293 F: 925-292-5061 PRC:129
www.coolingsource.com
Email: info@coolingsource.com
Estab: 2009

Michel Gelinas, President & CEO
Son Trinh, Program Manager

Provider of thermal design solution for LED
lighting, medical, military/aero, and test equipment
industries.

Copypro Inc HQ
2500-A Dean Lesher Dr
Concord CA 94520
P: 925-689-1200 F: 925-689-1263 PRC:110
www.copypro.com
Email: copypro@copypro.com
Estab: 1993

Bob Klein, General Manager

Manufacturer and seller of heavy-duty desktop
duplication systems such as duplicators, printers,
and analyzers.

Corad Technology Inc BR
3080 Olcott St Ste B200
Santa Clara CA 95054
P: 408-496-5511 PRC:126
www.corad.com
Email: ate@corad.com
Estab: 1987

Michael Lugay, Senior Applications Engineer

Manufacturer of load boards, probe cards, instrumentation systems, and related components. The
company deals with installation services.

Corcept Therapeutics Inc HQ
149 Commonwealth Dr
Menlo Park CA 94025
P: 650-327-3270 F: 650-327-3218 PRC:261
www.corcept.com
Email: info@corcept.com
Estab: 1998
Sales: $300M to $1 Billion

Joseph K. Belanoff, Founder & CEO & President
& Director
Hazel Hunt, CSO
Charlie Robb, CFO
Sean Maduck, SVP of Commercial
Carl Wilson, Director of Quality Assurance

Focuses on the discovery of drugs. The company
offers services to patients, physicians, and also
hospitals.

Cordis A Cardinal Health Co HQ
5452 Betsy Ross Dr
Santa Clara CA 95054
P: 408-273-3700 F: 844-279-2752 PRC:189
www.cordis.com
Email: gmb-cordis-customer-support@cardinal-
health.com

Gerry Prather, VP of Sales
Ernest Estrada, National Sales Manager
Esteban Peralta, Chemist

Provider of diagnostic and interventional products
for healthcare devices such as catheters, balloons, stents, wires and vascular closure.

Cordova Printed Circuits Inc HQ
1648 Watson Ct
Milpitas CA 95035
P: 408-942-1100 F: 408-946-3252 PRC:207
cordovaprintedcircuits.com
Estab: 1978

Josel Buada, VP
Lisa Luna, Executive

Provider of flex circuits and printed circuit boards.
The company focuses on sculptured flex circuits
and multilayer flex circuits.

Corecess Global Inc BR
3080 Olcott St Ste 125-A
Santa Clara CA 95054
P: 408-567-5300 PRC:61
www.corecess.com
Email: sales@corecess.com
Estab: 1997

Hon S. Yi, Contact

Designer, developer, and manufacturer of
telecommunication equipment for the broadband
access network.

Coretest Systems Inc HQ
400 Woodview Av
Morgan Hill CA 95037
P: 408-778-3771 F: 408-779-9418 PRC:19
www.coretest.com
Email: sales@coretest.com
Estab: 1984

David Lynch, President
Matthew Lynch, Manager of Production
Scelina Guel, Administrative Assistant

Designer and manufacturer of core analysis
equipment for the oil and gas, hydrothermal, and
environmental segments.

Corium International Inc HQ
235 Constitution Dr
Menlo Park CA 94025
P: 650-298-8255 F: 650-298-8012 PRC:159
www.coriumintl.com
Estab: 1995

Sophie Kornowski, Chairman
Adrian Faasse, CEO
Bobby Singh, CTO & VP of Research & Develop-
ment
John Miller, CFO
Christina Dickerson, VP of Corporate Development

Provider of transdermal delivery systems and
related technology solutions. The company is also
engaged in therapeutic product development.

Corman Technologies Inc HQ
1060A Fourth St
Santa Rosa CA 95404
P: 707-575-7800 PRC:322
cormtech.com

Roger Corman, President
Frances Corman, CFO
Joseph Chenoweth, Software Engineer

Provider of software development and consulting
services for a variety of clients in the software
industry.

Corning Technology Center BR
680 W Maude Ave
Sunnyvale CA 94085
P: 650-846-6000 PRC:86
www.corning.com
Estab: 1851

Wendell Weeks, Chairman & CEO
David L. Morse, EVP & CTO
Donnell Walton, Research Director

Provider of specialty glass and ceramics services
and sells keystone components to electronics, mobile emissions control, and life science industries.

Cornucopia Tool & Plastics Inc HQ
448 Sherwood Rd [N]
Paso Robles CA 93447
P: 805-369-0030 F: 805-369-0033 PRC:189
www.cornucopiaplastics.com
Email: info@cornucopiaplastics.com
Estab: 1972

Jason Montello, President & Business Development
Shannon Montello, VP & CFO
Thomas Pendley, Quality Assurance Manager
John Cromwell, Operations Manager
Jonathan Greer, Plant Manager

Manufacturer and supplier plastics for medical and
dental items, electronic components, business
machines, food processing equipment, house
ware products, and much more.

Corona Labs Inc HQ
611 Mission St 7th Fl
San Francisco CA 94105
P: 415-996-6877 PRC:319
www.coronalabs.com
Email: info@coronalabs.com
Estab: 2008

Vlad Shcherban, Engineering Lead

Developer of games, e-books, and other interactive content. The company offers services to the
educational sector.

Corona Labs Inc HQ
611 Mission St 7th Fl
San Francisco CA 94105
P: 415-996-6877 PRC:315
coronalabs.com
Email: info@coronalabs.com
Estab: 2008

Rob Miracle, Developer Relations Manager

A cross-platform framework for creating apps and
games for mobile devices and desktop systems.

Corrigo Inc BR
1900 S Norfolk St Ste 100
San Mateo CA 94403
P: 877-267-7440 PRC:324
www.corrigo.com
Email: info@corrigo.com
Estab: 1999

David Rainton, EVP of Technology
Lyle Newkirk, EVP of Finance & Administration
Deanna Gallentine, Director of Finance
John Dynes, Director of Partner Sales
Alex Bendikov, Engineering Director

Developer of facilities management platforms. The
company offers services to business organizations.

M-84

Corsair Inc HQ
47100 Bayside Pkwy
Fremont CA 94538
P: 510-657-8747 F: 510-657-8748 PRC:96
www.corsair.com
Email: support@corsair.com
Estab: 1994

Andrew Paul, CEO & President
Michael Potter, CFO
Terri Stynes, Chief Human Resource Officer
Thi La, COO
Bertrand Chevalier, SVP of Worldwide Sales

Designer of high-speed modules for mission-critical servers. The company also caters to high-end
workstations.

Corvus Pharmaceuticals Inc HQ
863 Mitten Rd Ste 102
Burlingame CA 94010
P: 650-900-4520 PRC:268
www.corvuspharma.com
Estab: 2014

Richard Miller, Co-Founder & President & CEO
Joseph J. Buggy, Co-Founder & EVP of Discovery
Research
Leiv Lea, CFO
Daniel W. Hunt, SVP & Chief Business Officer
Erik Verner, VP of Chemistry Research

Focuses on the development of first-in-class
agents that target the immune system. The company serves the healthcare industry.

Cosmed USA HQ
1850 Bates Ave
Concord CA 94520
P: 925-676-6002 F: 925-676-6005 PRC:189
www.cosmed.com
Email: info@cosmed.com
Estab: 1980

Orla May, Owner
Steve Roberts, Director of Finance
Becky Keehn, Sales Manager of Health & Well-
ness
Nathan Miller, Customer Service Manager
Michael Bryazki, Service Manager

Developer and manufacturer of medical devices
for accurate body composition assessments for
infants, children, and adults.

Cosmo Bio USA Inc HQ
2792 Loker Ave W Ste 101 [N]
Carlsbad CA 92010
P: 760-431-4600 F: 760-431-4604 PRC:53
cosmobiousa.com
Email: info@cosmobiousa.com
Emp: 1-10 Estab: 1986

Haruhisa Sakurai, President & CEO
Edward M. Rosen, VP & General Manager

Manufacturer and distributor of antibodies, biochemical, reagents, and instruments.

Couchbase Inc HQ
3250 Olcott St
Santa Clara CA 95054
P: 650-417-7500 PRC:323
www.couchbase.com
Email: info@couchbase.com
Estab: 2009

Matt Cain, President & CEO
Peter Finter, CMO
Ravi Mayuram, Engineering & CTO
Chris Galy, CPO
Denis Murphy, CRO

Developer of products and technology to meet the
elastic scalability, always-on availability, and data
mobility requirements of critical applications.

Countis Laboratories HQ
12295 Charles Dr
Grass Valley CA 95945
P: 530-272-8334 F: 530-272-6702 PRC:70
www.countis.com
Email: tcountis@countis.com
Estab: 1964

Michelle Baker, Contact

Manufacturer of microwave components. The company also offers custom machined components for
space, defense, medical and telecommunication
industries.

Countryman Associates Inc HQ
195 Constitution Dr
Menlo Park CA 94025
P: 650-364-9988 F: 650-364-2794 PRC:60
www.countryman.com
Email: support@countryman.com
Estab: 1978

Preston Countryman, CEO
Gabriela Sucher, Office Administrator

Manufacturer of direct boxes and ultra-miniature
microphones. The company's products include ear
sets, hanging, and podium microphones.

Coupa Software Inc HQ
1855 S Grant St
San Mateo CA 94402
P: 650-931-3200 PRC:315
www.coupa.com
Email: contact@coupa.com
Emp: 728 Estab: 2006
Sales: $300M to $1 Billion

Rob Bernshteyn, CEO
Todd Ford, CFO
Steve Winter, CRO
Chandar Pattabhiram, CMO
Ray Martinelli, CPO

Global technology platform for Business Spend
Management (BSM) to deliver measurable value.

Cozad! Trailers HQ
4907 Waterloo Rd
Stockton CA 95215
P: 209-931-3000 F: 209-931-0239 PRC:179
www.cozadtrailers.com
Email: sales@cozadtrailers.com
Estab: 1955

Delores Pistacchio, President
Mark Westcott, Corporate Controller

Manufacturer of trailers. The company serves
small and large construction companies and the
military and aerospace industries.

CP Communications LLC HQ
2010 Crow Canyon Pl Ste 100
San Ramon CA 94583
P: 951-694-4830 PRC:324
www.cpcom.com

Robb Capielo, President

Provider of audio visual production, website development and hosting, social media marketing, and related services.

CP Lab Safety HQ
14 Commercial Blvd Ste 113
Novato CA 94949
P: 415-883-2600 F: 415-532-1662 PRC:20
www.calpaclab.com
Email: info@cplabsafety.com
Estab: 1996

Farideh Kelly Farhangi-Najafi, President & CEO
Carel Thomas, Marketing Manager
Michelle Walters, Web Manager & Graphic Designer
Jordan Leigh, Web Specialist

Manufacturer of laboratory safety equipment to prevent fire, reduce waste emission and exposure to toxic fumes.

CP Manufacturing Inc HQ
6795 Calle de Linea [N]
San Diego CA 92154
P: 619-477-3175 F: 619-477-2215 PRC:159
www.cpmfg.com
Estab: 1977

Dirk Kantak, Director of Sales

Manufacturer of special industry machinery.

CP Software Group HQ
716 Figueroa St
Folsom CA 95630
P: 916-985-4445 F: 916-985-3557 PRC:326
cpsoftwaregroup.com
Estab: 1991

David Saykally, President

Provider of capital formation, fund raising, management consulting, technical and marketing, and incubator services for startup and established companies.

Cpacket Networks HQ
2130 Gold St Ste 200
San Jose CA 94043
P: 650-969-9500 PRC:97
www.cpacket.com
Estab: 2007

Edward Barr, Chairman
Brendan O'Flaherty, CEO
Ron Nevo, CTO
Hari Miriyala, VP of Software Engineering
Nadeem Zahid, VP of Product Management & Marketing

Provider of solutions for network traffic monitoring and data center performance management. The company specializes in traffic monitoring switches.

CPC Scientific Inc HQ
160 E Tasman Dr Ste 200
San Jose CA 95134
P: 408-734-3800 F: 408-734-3810 PRC:251
www.cpcscientific.com
Email: sales@cpcscientific.com
Estab: 2001

Shawn Lee, CEO & Founder
Theresa Cheng, President
Irvine Skeoch, COO
Xiaohe Tong, CTO
Howard Huang, VP of Sales

Provider of amino acids, cGMP, generic, catalog, modified, FRET and TR- FRET, and custom peptides to researchers and pharmaceutical companies.

CPI International HQ
5580 Skylane Blvd
Santa Rosa CA 95403
P: 707-525-5788 F: 707-545-7901 PRC:31
www.cpiinternational.com
Email: sales@cpiinternational.com
Estab: 1986

Tommy Mitchell, President
Joe Caldarelli, Vice Chairman
Chris Woodruff, VP of Business Development
Emanuel Moshi, Director of Operations
Ryan Vice, Director of Client Relations

Manufacturer of microbiological testing products and analytical instrument supplies. The company serves the semi-conductor industry.

Cpp Inc HQ
185 N Wolfe Rd [N]
Sunnyvale CA 94086
P: 650-969-8901 F: 650-969-8608 PRC:319
www.cpp.com
Email: custserv@cpp.com
Estab: 1956

Carl E. Thoresen, Chairman of the Board
Bill Chapman, SVP & CIO
Calvin W. Finch, CFO & SVP & Treasurer
Dennis Diligent, SVP of Sales
Nicole Trapasso, VP of Human Resources

Publisher of books on psychology and distributes publications of Jossey-Bass, Harper and Row, and B and D book and reaches market through direct mail, trade sales, and distributors.

Crane Consulting HQ
11052 Picaza Pl [N]
San Diego CA 92127
P: 858-487-9017 F: 858-592-0689 PRC:45
www.craneconsulting.com
Email: tgcrane@craneconsulting.com
Emp: 1-10 Estab: 1995

Thomas G. Crane, Consultant

Publisher of books on management leadership and offers consulting services.

CRCdj LLC HQ
1462 Seareel Pl Ste F
San Jose CA 95131
P: 408-855-8909 PRC:163
www.crcdj.com
Email: dj@crcdj.com

Didier deGery, President

Provider of shaped bags and pouches. The company's services include rotary die cutting, steel rule die cutting, and micro-form and fill.

Credence MedSystems Inc HQ
1430 O'Brien Dr Ste D
Menlo Park CA 94025
P: 844-263-3797 PRC:248
www.credencemed.com
Email: info@credencemed.com
Estab: 2013

John Merhige, CCO

Provider of pharmaceutical products. The company specializes in single-dose injectable medications in pre-filled syringes.

Creganna Medical BR
1353 Dell Ave
Campbell CA 95008
P: 408-364-7100 PRC:194
www.creganna.com
Estab: 1979

Chip Hance, CEO
Pat Duane, VP & GM Interventional
Jack Clarke, Manager of Production
Garry Murphy, Value Stream Manager
Susan Engelking, Manager II Customer Support

Provider of medical devices. The company offers services that ranges from clinical and regulatory support to design and manufacturing services.

Crestpoint Solutions Inc HQ
4900 Hopyard Rd Ste 100
Pleasanton CA 94588
P: 925-828-6005 F: 925-828-6022 PRC:322
www.crestpt.com
Email: info@crestpt.com
Estab: 2000

Erick Domingo, VP of Operations & Technology
Jose Medina, Senior Software Engineer

Provider of project planning, programming, web hosting, and wireless and records management services.

CRI Design Inc HQ
48834 Kato Rd Ste 101A
Fremont CA 94538
P: 510-770-4925 F: 510-770-4930 PRC:211
cridesign.com
Email: sales@cridesign.com
Estab: 1996

Leo Jiang, Director of System Design Ario Data
Shenglei Yang, Senior PCB Design Engineer
Christine Yeh, Supply Chain Buyer

Provider of PCB layout design, fabrication, assembly and turnkey services. The company offers services to the industrial sector.

Crime Alert HQ
690 Lenfest Rd
San Jose CA 95133
P: 800-367-1094 F: 408-254-9813 PRC:63
www.crimealert.com
Email: info@crimealert.com

Shanaaz Bux, Founder
Ed Flowers, Owner
Julie A. Buller, CEO
Jim Maruca, General Manager
Bongani Daniel Shabangu, Managing Director

Provider of residential, industrial, and commercial security monitoring solutions. The company focuses on IP monitoring and disaster recovery.

Criterion Network Services Inc HQ
763 Parma Way
Los Altos CA 94024
P: 650-947-7755 PRC:67
www.criter.com
Email: info@criter.com

Srinivas Vegesna, Founder & CEO

Provider of network design, system integration, configuration, and remote network management services.

Crmantra Inc HQ
6425 Christie Ave Ste 290
Emeryville CA 94608
P: 415-839-9672 F: 415-738-6345 PRC:322
www.crmantra.com
Email: info@crmantra.com
Estab: 2005

Amit Garg, Founder & CEO

Developer of software for customer relationship management needs. The company also focuses on business intelligence and analysis.

CRMIT Solutions Pvt Ltd HQ
1525 McCarthy Blvd Ste 1000
Milpitas CA 95035
P: 408-372-5379 PRC:326
www.crmit.com
Estab: 2003

Vinod Reddy, Founder & CEO

Provider of customer experience cloud solutions for banking, insurance education, retail, life science, energy, telecom, and financial services.

Crocus Technology HQ
2380 Walsh Ave
Santa Clara CA 95051
P: 408-380-8300 F: 408-732-8250 PRC:86
www.crocus-technology.com
Email: info@crocus-technology.com

Jeff Childress, VP of Magnetic Devices
Anuraag Mohan, VP
Mihai Lita, Senior CAD Manager
Lucas Pannell, Corporate Accounting Manager

Manufacturer of magnetic switches, current sensors, and embedded memory products. The company serves the automotive and industrial sectors.

Cross-Circuit Networks Inc HQ
5655 Silver Creek Valley Rd Ste 545
San Jose CA 95138
P: 408-654-9637 F: 408-654-9657 PRC:326
www.cross-circuit.com
Estab: 1997

Arthur Xu, CEO

Provider of networking solutions specializing in information technology infrastructure design, systems virtual environment and consolidation.

Crossbar Inc HQ
3200 Patrick Henry Dr Ste 110
Santa Clara CA 95054
P: 408-884-0281 F: 408-884-0283 PRC:212
www.crossbar-inc.com
Email: info@crossbar-inc.com
Estab: 2010

Hagop Nazarian, VP & Co-Founder
George Minassian, CEO & Co-Founder
Mark Davis, President
Sung Hyun Jo, CTO
Mehdi Asnaashari, Chief System Architect

Provider of 3D resistive RAM technology. The company serves customers in the automotive, connected devices, consumer, and enterprise segments.

CrowdANALYTIX HQ
440 N Wolfe Rd
Sunnyvale CA 94085
P: 866-333-4515 PRC:315
www.crowdanalytix.com
Email: connect@crowdanalytix.com
Estab: 2012

Divyabh Mishra, CEO & Founder
Amit Nagpal, COO
Aravind Venugopalan, VP of Solutions

Develops and deploys AI and Data Science solutions.

Crown Bioscience Inc HQ
16550 West Bernardo Dr Bldg 5 Ste 525
San Diego CA 92127
P: 858-622-2900 PRC:305
www.crownbio.com
Estab: 2006

Alex Wu, CEO
Henry Li, CSO
Eva Ho, CFO
Jim Wang, SVP Cardiovascular & Metabolic Disease Research
Leon Hall, Senior Scientific Director of Global Oncology

Specializes in drug discovery, clinical trials, and cardiovascular and metabolic disease research programs.

Crown Lift Trucks Ltd BR
1420 Enterprise Blvd
West Sacramento CA 95691
P: 916-373-8980 F: 916-373-8990 PRC:179
crown.com
Email: info@crown.com
Estab: 1960

Jim Mozer, SVP
Tim Quellhorst, SVP
Dave Brown, Sales Manager
Kevin McCarthy, Branch Manager

Manufacturer of industrial lift trucks. The company offerings include C-5 Series IC Trucks, Hand Pallet Trucks, Tow Tractors, and Walkie Stackers.

Crown Manufacturing Company Inc HQ
37625 Sycamore St
Newark CA 94560
P: 510-742-8800 F: 510-742-8500 PRC:157
www.crown-plastics.com
Estab: 1959

Aziz Shariat, President & CEO
John Coffman, Plant Manager & Tooling Manager

Provider of plastic and injection molded products. The company offers insert and over molding, drilling, tapping, and heat stamping services.

CryptoForensics Technologies Inc HQ
14895 E 14th St Ste 440
San Leandro CA 94578
P: 510-483-1933 PRC:26
www.cryptoforensics.com
Email: enquiries@cryptoforensics.com

Austine Ohwobete, Cyberstrategist

Provider of cybersecurity solutions to businesses, organizations, and the government. The company focuses on cyberforensics and compliance services.

Crystal Dynamics Inc HQ
1400A Seaport Blvd Ste 300
Redwood City CA 94063
P: 650-421-7600 PRC:317
crystald.com
Estab: 1992

Gary Snethen, CTO
James Loe, Technical Director
Chad Queen, Director of Production
Noah Hughes, Studio Creative Director
Chris Hudson, Director of Operations

Designer and developer of animated videos. The company also specializes in mobile gaming software products.

Crystal River Optics HQ
2127 Research Dr Ste 8
Livermore CA 94550
P: 925-371-1309 F: 925-454-0875 PRC:173
www.crystalriveroptics.com
Email: krystalriv@aol.com
Estab: 1994

Ted Judd, Owner

Provider of custom fabrication services of optical components. The company is engaged in prototyping and offers technical support.

Crystal Solar Inc   HQ
3050 Coronado Dr
Santa Clara CA 95054
P: 408-490-1340 F: 408-727-1705   PRC:135
www.xtalsolar.com
Email: info@xtalsolar.com
Estab: 2008

Ashish Asthana, Co-Founder & Adviser
T.S Ravi, Co-Founder & CEO
David Bostwick, CFO
V. Siva, EVP of Engineering
Somnath Nag, SVP of Product Development

Developer of solar cells and modules. The company focuses on the conversion of feedstock gas to mono-crystalline silicon wafers.

Crystallume Pvd   HQ
3300 Nicolaus Rd
Lincoln CA 95648
P: 916-645-3560 F: 916-645-0146   PRC:47
www.crystallumepvd.com
Email: sales@crystallumepvd.com
Estab: 1984

David Baker, President

Provider of PVD coatings for functional applications. The company also specializes in infinium coatings.

CSBio   HQ
20 Kelly Court
Menlo Park CA 94025
P: 650-322-1111   PRC:15
www.csbio.com
Email: peptides@csbio.com
Estab: 1993

Jason Chang, CEO
Zoe Liang, Director of Operations
Hanson Chang, Senior Director of Instrumentation

Provider of automated peptide synthesis instrumentation, peptide synthesizers, and custom peptides to the life science community.

CSI Forensic Supply   HQ
418 N Buchanan Cir
Martinez CA 94553
P: 925-686-6667 F: 925-686-6696   PRC:233
www.csiforensic.com
Email: sales@csiforensic.com
Estab: 1978

Bob Cellucci, President

Manufacturer and supplier of products for law enforcement for crime scene and crime laboratory applications.

CSRware Inc   HQ
100 Shoreline Hwy Ste 100B
Mill Valley CA 94941
P: 855-277-9273   PRC:323
www.csrware.com
Email: info@csrware.com
Estab: 2006

Karen Alonardo, CEO
Adam Escobar, Environmental Sustainability Manager

Developer of sustainability resource management software. The company specializes in supply chain, enterprise ERP solutions, and consulting services.

CSS Corp   HQ
1900 McCarthy Blvd Ste 210
Milpitas CA 95035
P: 650-385-3820 F: 408-429-9232   PRC:67
www.csscorp.com
Email: info@csscorp.com
Estab: 1996

Manish Tandon, CEO
Sundararajan Sampath, EVP & CFO
Sunil Mittal, EVP & Chief Sales & Marketing Officer
Nishikant Nigam, EVP & Chief Delivery Officer
Vivian Gomes, SVP & Head of Marketing & Inside Sales

Provider of enterprise level support solutions for IT products. The company is involved in virtualization, storage, and archiving solutions.

CTI Controltech   HQ
22 Beta Ct
San Ramon CA 94583
P: 925-208-4250 F: 925-208-4251   PRC:148
cti-ct.com
Email: contactus@cti-ct.com
Estab: 1976

Adam Pennell, Sales Manager
Jeff Podesto, Manager of Technical Sales
John Constas, Manager of Sales Account
Steve Briggs, Inside Sales Manager
Rency Ignacio, Control Systems Engineer

Provider of industrial process control and emission solutions. The company's services include engineering, sales, and support.

CTT Inc   HQ
5870 Hellyer Ave Ste 70
San Jose CA 95138
P: 408-541-0596 F: 408-541-0794   PRC:209
www.cttinc.com
Email: sales@cttinc.com
Estab: 1981

Tom Roe, President
Thanh Thai, VP of Operations
Gordon Graham, Regional Sales Manager
Junghui Chen, Manager of Engineering
Michael Roden, Manager of Quality Assurance

Manufacturer and supplier of power amplifiers, frequency converters and multipliers, and transmitters and receivers. The company serves military purposes.

Cubus Solutions Inc   HQ
3049 Independence Dr Ste A
Livermore CA 94551
P: 925-344-5195   PRC:326
www.cubussolutions.com
Email: info@cubussolutions.com
Estab: 2006

John-Ashley Paul, President & CEO

Provider of online banking solutions to seamlessly integrate with core system while delivering real-time, and secure, banking services to members.

Cultivate Systems   HQ
1040 Main St Ste 301
Napa CA 94559
P: 707-690-9425 F: 707-944-1733   PRC:326
www.cultivatesystems.com
Email: info@cultivatesystems.com
Estab: 1998

Eric Binau, Founder & Owner

Provider of construction services. The company offers civil site work, construction, demolition, and general contracting services.

Cummings Transportation   HQ
19605 Broken Ct   [N]
Shafter CA 93263
P: 661-746-1786   PRC:149
www.cummings2.com
Estab: 1981

Pam Cummings, President & Owner
Ted Cummings, VP & Owner
Tom Pruitt, General Manager

Provider of trucking services.

CUneXus Solutions Inc   HQ
50 Old Courthouse Sq Ste 300
Santa Rosa CA 95404
P: 877-509-2089   PRC:323
cunexusonline.com
Email: info@cunexus.com
Estab: 2008

Haans Galassi, VP of Product Development

Provider of pre-screening lending strategy that pre-approves entire loan product portfolio for customers.

Cupertino Signal Processing   HQ
PO Box 631
Cupertino CA 95015-0631
P: 408-725-0846   PRC:207
www.cupertinosignal.com
Email: info@cupertinosignal.com

John Wincn, Owner

Specializes in analog circuit analysis and evaluation services. The company offers technical documentation.

Cureline Biopathology LLC   HQ
150 N Hill Dr Ste 24
Brisbane CA 94005
P: 415-468-6400 F: 415-468-2248   PRC:306
curelinebiopathology.com
Estab: 2003

Olga Potapova, President & CEO
Kathleen Talmadge, VP of Finance & Operations
Lita DeLeon, Director of Histology Laboratory

Provider of human and animal tissue processing services. The company also focuses on preservation and biospecimen management.

Curiox Biosystems Inc HQ
735 Industrial Rd Ste 109
San Carlos CA 94070
P: 650-226-8420   F: 650-590-5406   PRC:34
www.curiox.com
Email: sales@curiox.com

Namyong Kim, CEO

Developer of assay platforms. The company specializes in surface chemistry and engineering. It focuses on automation of bioassays.

Current Controls Inc HQ
4110 Citrus Ave Ste 5
Rocklin CA 95677
P: 916-630-5507   F: 916-630-5570   PRC:323
www.currentcontrols.net
Email: gcook@currentcontrols.net

Gary Cook, Partner

Designer and manufacturer of control panels for OEMs in many sectors. The company also offers PLC programming, system integration, and other services.

Curtis Instruments Inc BR
235 E Airway Blvd
Livermore CA 94551
P: 925-961-1088   PRC:94
www.curtisinstruments.com
Estab: 1960

Mike Bachman, Executive Director
Phil Surrena, Engineering Manager
Anders Hultman, Regional Manager
Gilbert Mink, Senior Technician
Steven Lambert, Senior PCB Designer & Senior PCB Designer

Manufacturer of hydraulic pump controllers. The company also specializes in electric steering controllers.

Custom Alloy Corp BR
2337 California Ave
South Lake Tahoe CA 96150
P: 530-544-2836   F: 530-544-2888   PRC:81
www.customalloy.us
Estab: 1968

Adam M. Ambielli, Chairman
Bruce Nagel, Quality Director
Lisa Nigrelli, IT Manager
Mike Parker, Project Manager

Manufacturer of metals for seamless and welded pipe fittings and forgings. The company's products are in alloy steels, nickel alloys, and carbon steels.

Custom Coils Inc HQ
4000 Industrial Way
Benicia CA 94510
P: 707-752-8633   F: 707-752-8637   PRC:214
www.ccoils.com
Email: info@ccoils.com
Estab: 1978

Thomas Quinn, President
Deanna Larson, Human Resource Coordinator

Manufacturer of coils, coil assemblies, and solenoids. The company also offers other electro-magnetic devices.

M-88

Custom Gear & Machine HQ
6459 Brisa St
Livermore CA 94550
P: 925-455-9985   F: 925-455-9925   PRC:80
www.cgmgear.com
Email: info@cgmgear.com
Estab: 1983

Anthony Castruccio, President
Jane Castruccio, VP

Manufacturer of custom gears. The company also offers overhaul services for gearboxes and caters to industries like food and steel processing.

Custom Micro Machining Inc HQ
707 Brown Rd
Fremont CA 94539
P: 510-651-9434   F: 510-351-9437   PRC:80
www.cmmusa.com
Estab: 1990

Victor Nguyen, Founder

Manufacturer of precision housing carriers and microwave assemblies. The company is involved in design, installation, and delivery services.

Custom Microwave Components Inc HQ
44249 Old Warm Springs Blvd
Fremont CA 94538
P: 510-651-3434   F: 510-651-1054   PRC:86
www.customwave.com
Estab: 1982

Greg Mau, President
Nam Nguyen, Microwave Technician

Manufacturer of microwave components. The company also specializes in providing attenuators with control devices.

Custom Product Development Co HQ
4603A Las Positas Rd
Livermore CA 94551
P: 925-960-0577   PRC:80
www.cpd-corp.com
Estab: 1974

Gerald J. Ammirato, President

Developer and manufacturer of mechanical components and turnkey assembly solutions. The company specializes in developing customized products.

Customweather Inc HQ
271 Miller Ave
Mill Valley CA 94941
P: 415-777-3303   F: 415-777-3003   PRC:325
customweather.com
Email: sales@customweather.com
Estab: 2000

Geoff Flint, President & CEO
Agustin Diaz, Chief Meteorologist
Kevin Levey, VP of Operations
Susan Flint, Business Manager
Jared Lovell, Systems Administrator

Provider of industry solutions. The company offers hurricane tracking, developer tools, and marine forecasts.

Cutera Inc HQ
3240 Bayshore Blvd
Brisbane CA 94005
P: 415-657-5500   PRC:13
www.cutera.com
Email: info@cutera.com
Estab: 1998
Sales: $100M to $300M

David H. Mowry, CEO
Fuad Ahmad, Interim CFO
Michael Karavitis, EVP & CTO
Lukas Hunziker, SVP of Research & Development
Amogh Kothare, VP of Clinical & Regulatory Affairs

Manufacturer of aesthetic solutions such as face and body laser, light, and other energy-based aesthetic systems for hair removal and pigmented lesions.

Cutting Edge Machining Inc HQ
100 San Lucar Ct
Sunnyvale CA 94086
P: 408-738-8677   F: 408-738-3684   PRC:5
www.cemachining.com
Email: info@cemachining.com
Estab: 1922

Ron Gokan, Owner

Provider of contract manufacturing solutions for the medical, aerospace, and telecommunication sectors.

CVM Inc HQ
7066-D Commerce Cir
Pleasanton CA 94588
P: 925-847-8808   PRC:80
cvmcvm.com
Email: info@cvmcvm.com
Estab: 1980

Bob Switek, Founder & CEO
Toby Switek, President
Glen Garrettson, VP of Engineering
Paul Widergren, Fabrication Project Manager
Garrett Gersten, Senior Mechanical Engineer

Provider of custom machine tools. The company also offers electrical fabrication, machining, and robotic services.

Cyagen Biosciences Inc HQ
2255 Martin Ave Ste E
Santa Clara CA 95050-2709
P: 408-969-0306   F: 408-969-0336   PRC:34
www.cyagen.com
Email: service@cyagen.com
Estab: 2005

Xiao Xu, Contact

Manufacturer of cell culture products. The company also focuses on animal models and molecular biology tools.

Cyberdata Corp HQ
3 Justin Ct
Monterey CA 93940
P: 831-373-2601   F: 831-373-4193   PRC:62
www.cyberdata.net
Email: sales@cyberdata.net
Estab: 1974

Phil Lembo, President
Paul Towber, RMA Manager
Ken Chitpanich, Purchasing Manager
Allyn Donigian, Marketing Manager

Designer and manufacturer of USB cables. The
company also offers VoIP and printed circuit board
design services.

CyberGlove Systems LLC HQ
2157 O'Toole Ave Ste 20
San Jose CA 95131
P: 408-943-8114   F: 408-943-8119   PRC:316
www.cyberglovesystems.com
Estab: 1990

Faisal Yazadi, CEO

Provider of data glove technology. The company
offers system installation and integration and
custom software and hardware services.

Cybermanor HQ
610 University Ave
Los Gatos CA 95032-4416
P: 408-399-3331   F: 408-399-3341   PRC:329
www.cybermanor.com
Email: info@cybermanor.com
Estab: 1999

Gordon Van Zuiden, Founder
PATRICK ROSENGARTEN, VP of Sales & Design
Jim Kohl, Director of Operations
Ed Lalosh, Senior Installer

Designer of Internet connected home electronic
and networking solutions. The company also
offers installation services.

Cybersoft BR
165 Glenview Dr
San Francisco CA 94131
P: 415-449-7998   PRC:324
www.cybersoftbpo.com
Email: info@cyberconversion.com
Estab: 1998

Pawan Chalasani, CEO
Roger Ramos, IT Infrastructure Manager
Devet Soriano, Software Solutions Manager

Provider of offshore business and knowledge
process outsourcing services. The company specializes in title, financial, and document processing services.

**Cybosoft General Cybernation Group
Inc** HQ
2868 Prospect Park Dr Ste 300
Rancho Cordova CA 95670
P: 916-631-6313   F: 916-631-6312   PRC:99
www.cybosoft.com
Email: info@cybosoft.com
Estab: 1994

George Cheng, ISA President

Provider of control technology solutions for the
process control, building control, and equipment
control markers.

Cyclos Semiconductor HQ
1995 University Ave Ste 375
Berkeley CA 94704
P: 510-649-3741   F: 510-665-1331   PRC:86
www.cyclos-semi.com
Estab: 2004

Marios C. Papaefthymiou, President
Alexander T. Ishii, VP of Engineering

Provider of resonant mesh semiconductor IP,
design automation tools, and design consulting
services to mobile, wireless, and medical sectors.

Cygna Energy Services Inc HQ
1600 S Main St
Walnut Creek CA 94596
P: 925-930-8377   F: 925-930-8375   PRC:322
cygna.net
Estab: 2003

Glenn Smith, President & CEO

Provider of application development, data integration, systems integration, consulting, and web
services.

Cymabay Therapeutics Inc HQ
7575 Gateway Blvd Ste 110
Newark CA 94560
P: 510-293-8800   F: 510-293-9090   PRC:249
www.cymabay.com
Email: info@cymabay.com

Sujal Shah, CEO & President
Pol Boudes, CMO
Janet Dorling, CCO
Klara Dickinson, Chief Regulatory & Compliance
Officer
Daniel Menold, VP of Finance

Developer of therapies for the treatment of
metabolic diseases. The company serves the
healthcare industry.

Cymed HQ
1123 N Market Blvd Ste 5
Sacramento CA 95834
P: 800-582-0707   PRC:187
cymed.us
Email: customerservice@cymed.us
Estab: 1986

Shaun Gill, Manager
Nicholas Gritzai, Manager of Marketing

Provider of ostomy pouching systems. The company specializes in skin care products and serves
individuals and hospitals.

Cypress Digital Media HQ
650 Castro St Ste 120-500
Mountain View CA 94041
P: 650-257-0741   F: 650-268-8636   PRC:324
www.cypressdigitalmedia.com
Email: info@cypressdigitalmedia.com
Estab: 2010

John Ghashghai, Founder & Managing Partner
James Yokota, Director of Client Operations

Provider of web design, mobile development,
and online marketing for interactive agencies and
marketing campaigns.

Cypress Envirosystems Inc HQ
5883 Rue Ferrari Ste 100
San Jose CA 95138
P: 800-544-5411   F: 888-681-8319   PRC:124
www.cypressenvirosystems.com
Email: info@cypressenvirosystems.com
Estab: 2006

Harry Sim, CEO

Provider of solutions to retrofit existing commercial buildings and industrial facilities for improved
asset utilization and lower maintenance costs.

Cypress Systems Inc HQ
40365 Brickyard Dr Ste 101
Madera CA 93636
P: 559-229-7850   F: 559-225-9007   PRC:272
selenoexcell.com
Email: info@selenoexcell.com
Estab: 1995

Paul A. Willis, CEO & President
Mark Whitacre, Chief Science Officer
Roland Geiger, Business Operations Manager

Provider of natural food forms of organically
bound minerals and nutritional yeast products and
related supplies.

Cyrun Corp HQ
2125 Delaware Ave Ste C
Santa Cruz CA 95060
P: 831-458-0949   F: 831-459-9406   PRC:319
www.cyrun.com
Estab: 1993

Glen Haimovitz, Co-Founder & CEO
John Roevekamp, Co-Founder & CTO
Darrell Luera, VP of Client Services
Gary Powell, Director of Business Development
Gaming

Developer of windows-based integrated software
system. The company caters to public safety
organizations.

Cytoculture International Inc HQ
249A Tewksbury Ave
Point Richmond CA 94801
P: 510-233-0102   F: 510-233-3777   PRC:34
www.cytoculture.com
Estab: 1986

Alexa Davis, Administrative Assistant

Provider of technical consulting and microbiological laboratory services. The company specializes
in biofuel project.

Cytokinetics Inc HQ
280 E Grand Ave
S San Francisco CA 94080
P: 650-624-3000   PRC:34
www.cytokinetics.com
Estab: 1997
Sales: $10M to $30M

Robert I. Blum, President & CEO
David W. Cragg, Chief Human Resource Officer
& CAO
Ching W. Jaw, SVP & CFO
Fady I. Malik, EVP of Research & Development
Andrew A. Wolff, SVP & Senior Fellow of Clinical
Research & Development

Developer of cancer treatment programs for
cancer and also cardiovascular patients. The company specializes in therapeutic programs.

Cytomx Therapeutics Inc HQ
151 Oyster Point Blvd Ste 400
S San Francisco CA 94080-1913
P: 650-515-3185 F: 650-351-0353 PRC:249
www.cytomx.com
Estab: 2008

Sean McCarthy, CEO
Michael Kavanaugh, Chief Scientific Officer &
Head of Research & Early Development
Danielle Olander, VP of Human Resources
Marc Besman, Director of Program
James West, Director of Research

Developer of biomolecular therapeutics. The company specializes in antibody drug development, cancer study, clinical and translational medicine.

Cytosport Inc HQ
1340 Treat Blvd Ste 350
Walnut Creek CA 94597
P: 888-298-6629 PRC:272
www.musclemilk.com
Estab: 1998

Chris Kildow, Senior Director
Ralph Knights, Director of Innovation
Brandon Hagy, Sports Marketing Manager
Frank Povich, Sales Manager
Jake Opperud, Inventory Control Manager

Manufacturer of health care supplements. The company specializes in fitness supplements for athletes, to strengthen muscles and bones.

D & T Fiberglass Inc HQ
8900 Osage Ave Ste D
Sacramento CA 95828
P: 916-383-9012 F: 916-383-1851 PRC:280
www.dtfiberglass.com
Email: info@dtfiberglass.com
Estab: 1987

Donny Stommel, President & CEO

Manufacturer of fiberglass reinforced plastic bulk containers. The company's products are used for water and chemical treatment applications.

D Danz & Sons Inc HQ
6741 N Willow Ave Ste 101
Fresno CA 93710
P: 559-252-1770 F: 559-252-1781 PRC:190
www.ddanzandsons.com
Email: customerservice@ddanzandsons.com
Estab: 1927

Antonio Alcorta, President & Ocularist
Angie Burke, CFO

Specializes in the custom fitting, designing, and manufacturing of ophthalmic prosthetics. The company deals with patient care.

D-EYE BR
6097 Rocky Point Cir
Truckee CA 96161
P: 401-473-6323 PRC:186
www.d-eyecare.com
Email: info@d-eyecare.com
Estab: 2014

Alberto Scarpa, CEO

Designer and manufacturer of diagnostic instruments. The company offers smartphone based retinal imaging systems for clinical assessments.

D-Tools Inc HQ
1850 Gateway Blvd Ste 1060
Concord CA 94520
P: 925-681-2326 F: 925-681-2900 PRC:318
www.d-tools.com
Email: sales@d-tools.com
Estab: 1998

Adam Stone, President
Steve Collard, COO & CFO
Corey Krehel, CTO
Tim Bigoness, VP of Sales & Marketing
David Sylvester, Creative Director

Developer and marketer of software to streamline processes which accompany the integration and installation of low-voltage systems.

d2m Interactive HQ
309 Westhill Dr
Los Gatos CA 95032
P: 408-315-6802 PRC:325
www.d2m.com
Email: d2m@d2m.com
Estab: 1996

David Rose, Owner

Provider of web development, management, and e-commerce services. The company also focuses on marketing.

D2s Inc HQ
4040 Moorpark Ave Ste 250
San Jose CA 95117
P: 408-781-9017 PRC:323
www.design2silicon.com
Email: contact@design2silicon.com
Estab: 2007

Aki Fujimura, Owner & CEO
Ryan Pearman, Chief Scientist of TrueModel
P. Jeffrey Ungar, Chief Scientist of TrueMask ILT
James Fong, VP of Operations
Shone Lee, Director of Application Engineering

Supplier of a computational design platform to maximize eBeam technology. The company's products include TrueMask MDP and DS.

Daihen Advanced Component Inc RH
1223 E Arques Ave
Sunnyvale CA 94085
P: 408-736-2000 F: 408-736-2010 PRC:209
www.daihen-ac.com
Email: sales@daihen-ac.com
Estab: 1996

William Brown, VP of Business Operations
Brian Haines, VP
Rick Tanaka, Manager

Supplier of vacuum environment material handling and RF transmission products to semiconductor, flat panel display and solar, and equipment manufacturers.

Dakota Ultrasonics HQ
1500 Green Hills Rd Ste 107
Scotts Valley CA 95066
P: 831-431-9722 F: 831-431-9723 PRC:19
www.dakotaultrasonics.com

Teresa Engel, COO
Russ Vogel, Software Engineer

Manufacturer of industrial ultrasonic testing equipment. The company serves the aerospace, power generation, and petrochemical industries.

Dali Wireless Inc RH
535 Middlefield Rd Ste 280
Menlo Park CA 94025
P: 408-481-9400 F: 408-481-9420 PRC:63
daliwireless.com
Email: information@daliwireless.com
Estab: 2006

Albert Lee, CEO
Shawn Stapleton, CTO
Basem Anshasi, COO
Sasa Trajkovic, VP of Engineering
Andrew Leung, VP of Operations

Provider of RF router platform for healthcare, airport, education, hospitality, stadium, residential and MDU, and metros and train industries.

DAM Good Engineering & Manufacturing Inc HQ
2720 Aiello Dr Ste A
San Jose CA 95111
P: 408-224-6494 F: 408-224-5394 PRC:80
www.damgood.com
Email: contact@damgood.com
Estab: 1988

Adan Giron, Front Desk Receptionist

Manufacturer of parts for microwave, telecom, and industrial sectors. The company offers gaming devices, model engine parts, and other products.

Danco Machine HQ
950 George St
Santa Clara CA 95054
P: 408-988-5235 PRC:157
dancomachine.com
Email: info@dancomachine.com
Estab: 1979

Dan Mothena, Owner
Jim Herget, Chief Engineer
Jesse Kuhn, Manager of Engineering, Estimating & Planning
Juan Sanchez, Contact
Carlos Ocana, Contact

Developer of machined components and assemblies. The company is involved in EDM, welding, sheet metal, and precision grinding.

Daniel B Stephens & Associates Inc BR
1300 Clay St Ste 600
Oakland CA 94612
P: 800-933-3105 F: 510-645-1532 PRC:140
www.dbstephens.com

Nicole T. Sweetland, Principal Hydrogeologist & DBS&A & President of Geo-Logic Associates
Stephen J. Cullen, SVP of California Operations
Eric Hendrix, VP & Principal Hydrogeologist
John J. Dodge, Principal Hydrogeologist
Gregory Schnaar, Senior Environmental Scientist

Provider of services in hydrology, environmental engineering, and science. The company services include water resources and soil testing.

Dantel Inc HQ
4210 N Brawley Ave Ste 108
Fresno CA 93722
P: 800-432-6835   F: 559-292-9355   PRC:59
www.dantel.com
Email: info@dantel.com
Estab: 1971

Al Hutcheson, CEO & President
Mary Jane Papadopoulos, CFO
Frank Martinez, SVP of Sales & SVP of National Accounts
Ifty Husain, Director of Product Development
Denny Frazier, Firmware Engineer

Manufacturer of telecommunications instrumentation equipment. The company offers documentation support and upgrading services.

Darcoid Nor-Cal Seal HQ
950 Third St
Oakland CA 94607
P: 510-836-2449   F: 510-836-2675   PRC:162
www.darcoid.com
Estab: 1947

Bill Sharratt, Director of Sales
Yamita Anderson, Inside Sales Manager
Nang Tom, QA Manager
Jason Hainer, Sales Engineer
James Wojna, Production Supervisor

Provider of rubber based products. The company offers gaskets, composite and dynamic seals, molded shapes, and thermal products.

Data Distributing LLC HQ
220A Fern Ste
Santa Cruz CA 95060
P: 831-457-3537   F: 831-425-1186   PRC:95
www.datadistributing.com
Email: info@datadistributing.com
Estab: 1984

Nancy Buell, COO
Jennifer King, Regional Account Manager
Robert Medina, National Sales Account Manager
Jason Smith, Shipping Manager
Gordon Lilley, Executive Assistant

Provider of solutions such as mass storage, peripheral, storage management software, import, archive, and images and data distribution.

Data ID Systems HQ
286 E Hamilton Ave Ste F
Campbell CA 95008
P: 408-371-5764   F: 408-626-7066   PRC:103
dataid.com
Email: sales@dataid.com
Estab: 1982

Mark Fitchjian, Director of Sales & Marketing

Provider of identification management solutions. The company offers passport readers, barcode scanners, and fixed asset tracking products.

Data Path Inc HQ
1415 J St
Modesto CA 95354
P: 209-521-0055   PRC:323
mydatapath.com
Email: info@mydatapath.com
Estab: 2005

James Bates, Founder & VP Operations, Strategic Partnerships & Research & Development

Provider of IT services such as IT management, web design, software development, and education related data services.

Data Physics Corp HQ
2480 N First St Ste 100
San Jose CA 95131
P: 408-437-0100   F: 408-456-0100   PRC:209
dataphysics.com
Email: sales@dataphysics.com
Estab: 1984

Sabine Castagnet, COO
Kalyan Vitta, Applications Engineer
Leonard Kandt, Product Development Engineer
Raman Sridharan, Applications Engineer
Wes Christner, Service Engineer

Provider of high performance test and measurement solutions for noise and vibration applications. The company offers drop testing services.

Data Scale HQ
42430 Blacow Rd
Fremont CA 94539
P: 510-651-7350   PRC:159
www.datascale.com
Email: sales@datascale.com
Estab: 1973

Terry Lowe, Business Owner

Manufacturer of liquid net weight filling equipment. The company offers services to the food and chemical industries.

Data Tech HQ
4910 E Clinton Way Ste 103
Fresno CA 93727
P: 800-833-8824   F: 559-226-5418   PRC:322
www.datatechag.com
Email: sales@datatechag.com
Estab: 1980

Isaac Davidian, President
Matthew Davidian, VP
Hannah Tarrats, Contact

Developer of specialized accounting software. The company primarily caters to the agricultural industry.

Data Trace Information Services LLC HQ
200 Commerce   [N]
Irvine CA 92602
P: 800-221-2056   PRC:64
www.datatracetitle.com
Email: customersuccess@datatracetitle.com

Robert Karraa, President
Jim Portner, SVP
Mark Johnson, VP of Sales
Darren Chinn, Director of Sales

Provider of technology services related to real estate services and solutions.

Data-Com Solutions HQ
8413 Washington Blvd Ste 140
Roseville CA 95678
P: 916-331-2377   PRC:64
www.data-comsolutions.com

Rick Gewerth, President

Designer of data communication networks, national equipment roll outs, and network hardware installation services.

Database International HQ
1301 McKenzie Ave
Los Altos CA 94024
P: 650-965-9102   PRC:325
www.databaseinternational.com
Email: consulting@databaseinternational.com
Estab: 1998

Vladimir Rubashevsky, Database Administration

Provider of database application development and database administration services and also offers project management and event coordination services.

Database Republic HQ
8712 Marysville Rd
Oregon House CA 95962
P: 530-692-2500   PRC:324
databaserepublic.com
Estab: 2002

Anthony Williams, Programmer & Analyst

Provider of enterprise analysis and strategy modeling services. The company also focuses on DB design and implementation.

Databricks Inc HQ
160 Spear St 13th Fl
San Francisco CA 94105
P: 866-330-0121   PRC:326
databricks.com
Email: info@databricks.com
Estab: 2013

Ion Stoica, Co-Founder & Executive Chairman
Matei Zaharia, Co-Founder & Chief Technologist
Ali Ghodsi, Co-Founder & CEO
Rick Schultz, CMO
Ron Gabrisko, CRO

Provider of platform for big data processing solutions. The company offers exploration and visualization, production pipelines, and third party apps.

DataDirect Networks Inc   BR
   2929 Patrick Henry Dr
   Santa Clara CA 95054
P: 408-419-2800   PRC:95
www.ddn.com
Email: info@ddn.com
Estab: 1998

Randy Kreiser, Chief Architect

Provider of storage array, file system, and object storage appliances to broadcast, biopharma, supercomputing, and financial service sectors.

DataGlance Inc   HQ
   42840 Christy St Ste 106
   Fremont CA 94538-3154
P: 510-656-0500   PRC:322
www.dataglance.com
Email: sales@dataglance.com
Estab: 2001

Ashok Shetty, President & CEO
Martin Pyne, Software Engineer

Provider of data management software that support LIVE data conversion/migration, electronic document generation and processing, and web services.

Dataguise   HQ
   39650 Liberty St Ste 400
   Fremont CA 94538
P: 877-632-0522   PRC:324
dataguise.com
Estab: 2007

Manmeet S. Bhasin, Founder & CEO
JT Sison, VP
Jim Emmons, VP of Sales
Ben Kam, Creative Director & Senior Designer
Umesh Kundi, Software Quality Assurance Manager

Provider of cloud migration, auditing, and monitoring solutions. The company serves the healthcare, consumer, and retail industries.

Datalab   HQ
   1893 Concourse Dr
   San Jose CA 95131
P: 408-943-1888   PRC:53
datalabsj.com

Helen Ham, Director

Provider of analysis and certification of process tanks and printed circuit board sections. The company also offers chemical process control software.

Datameer Inc   HQ
   535 Mission St Ste 2602
   San Francisco CA 94105
P: 800-874-0569   PRC:323
www.datameer.com
Email: info@datameer.com
Estab: 2009

Stefan Groschupf, CEO
Peter Voss, CTO
John Morrell, Senior Director of Product Marketing
Pablo Redondo, Engineer
Shirley Liu, Controller

Provider of data analytics solution for business users. The company also focuses on integration, business analytics consulting, and training.

Dataray Inc   HQ
   1675 Market St
   Redding CA 96001
P: 530-395-2500   F: 530-255-9062   PRC:172
www.dataray.com
Email: corporate@dataray.com
Estab: 1988

Steve Garvey, Owner
Kevin Garvey, COO
Rocco Dragone, VP of Engineering
Jack Moore, Acting National Director of Sales
Natalia Tjandra, Operations Manager

Supplier of performance beam profiling products to the photonics community. The company provides BladeCam, Beam Scope, Phase Pro, and UV converters.

DataSafe Inc   HQ
   574 Eccles Ave
   S San Francisco CA 94080
P: 650-875-3800   PRC:324
www.datasafe.com
Email: info@datasafe.com
Estab: 1946

Rob Reis, President
Tom Reis, CEO
Scott Reis, Director of Sales
Daryl Savage, Director of Operations
Amy Magni, Director of Corporate Services

Provider of digital solutions. The company's services include records storage, document shredding and imaging, and rotation.

Datastax Inc   RH
   3975 Freedom Cir 4th Fl
   Santa Clara CA 95054
P: 650-389-6000   PRC:324
www.datastax.com
Email: info@datastax.com
Estab: 2010

Jonathan Ellis, CTO & Founder
Billy Bosworth, CEO
Martin Van Ryswyk, EVP of Engineering
Robin Schumacher, VP of Products
Charlotte Crouch, Manager of Accounts Payable

Distributor of database management system for Internet enterprise. The company offers training and certification, expert support, and consulting services.

Datavision Inc   HQ
   3018 Knollwood Dr
   Cameron Park CA 95682
P: 530-387-3575   F: 530-387-3587   PRC:319
www.datvsn.com
Email: support@datvsn.com
Estab: 1978

Teri Christiansen, Software Design & Development

Provider of software solutions for accounting, supply chain, and water and utility applications. The company also offers hosting and support.

Datest Corp   HQ
   47810 Westinghouse Dr
   Fremont CA 94539
P: 510-490-4600   F: 510-490-4111   PRC:306
www.datest.com
Email: info@datest.com
Estab: 1984

Robert Boguski, President

Provider of testing and inspection services. The company specializes in engineering testing and counterfeit inspection for industrial products.

Datum Technologies Inc   HQ
   327 Ohair Ct Ste D
   Santa Rosa CA 95407
P: 707-738-3914   PRC:80
www.datumtech-cnc.com
Email: info@datumtechnologiesinc.com
Estab: 2003

Richard F. Hunt, President & Owner
Analisa Hunt, CFO

Manufacturer of precision machining services. The company serves customers in the aerospace, medical device, and energy industries.

David J Powers & Associates Inc   HQ
   1871 The Alameda Ste 200
   San Jose CA 95126
P: 408-248-3500   F: 408-248-9641   PRC:142
davidjpowers.com
Email: info@davidjpowers.com
Estab: 1972

Akoni Danielsen, President
Martha Silveira, CFO
John Hesler, VP | Principal Project Manager
Judy Shanley, VP & Principal Project Manager
Zachary Dill, Creative Director

Provider of environmental consulting services. The company focuses on transportation, parks, and recreation projects.

Davlin Coatings   HQ
   700 Allston Way
   Berkeley CA 94702
P: 510-848-2863   F: 510-848-1464   PRC:275
www.davlincoatings.com
Estab: 1968

Jim Hofmeister, CEO
Janie Hofmeister, Director of Sales & Marketing
Matthew Jeffries, Manager of Sales
Jonathan Baker, Operations Manager

Manufacturer of coatings for architectural and industrial purposes. The company offers elastomeric waterproof coatings.

Davtron Inc   HQ
   427 Hillcrest Way
   Emerald Hills CA 94062
P: 866-369-5588   F: 650-369-9988   PRC:5
davtron.com
Email: sales@davtron.com
Estab: 1960

Kevin Torresdal, President
Rod Walker, Engineer

Designer and manufacturer of avionic instruments. The company's portfolio comprises volt meters, clocks, probes, and more.

Dawn Reis Ecological Studies   HQ
  38 Lower Cutter Dr
  Watsonville CA 95076
P: 831-588-7550   F: 831-761-9496   PRC:34
ecologicalstudies.com
Email: moreinfo@ecologicalstudies.com

Jessica Wheeler, Assistant Ecologist & GIS
Specialist
Kaia Colestock, Wildlife Ecologist
Kim Glinka, Wildlife Ecologist
Dawn Reis, Senior Wildlife & Aquatic Ecologist
Eric Scott, Wildlife Ecologist

Provider of wildlife research and biological
consulting services. The company is specialized
in aquatic systems and endangered species
population.

Dawn Sign Press   HQ
  6130 Nancy Ridge Dr   [N]
  San Diego CA 92121
P: 858-625-0600   F: 858-625-2336   PRC:323
www.dawnsign.com
Email: info@dawnsign.com
Estab: 1976

Joe W. Dannis, Contact

Publisher of books and DVD"s for deaf peoples.

Dawn VME Products   HQ
  47915 Westinghouse Dr
  Fremont CA 94539
P: 510-657-4444   F: 510-657-3274   PRC:79
www.dawnvme.com
Email: sales@dawnvme.com
Estab: 1985

Barry Burnsides, CEO
Nelson Carney, SVP of Corporate Development
Eddie Chin, Regional Sales Manager
Tim Collins, Program Manager
Sharnjit Sekhon, Quality Manager

Designer and manufacturer of enclosures, back-
planes, chassis and card cage. The company also
offers design services and power supplies.

Day Wireless Systems   BR
  4728 E Second St Ste 10
  Benicia CA 94510
P: 707-746-5920   F: 707-746-5924   PRC:60
www.daywireless.com
Email: support@daywireless.com
Estab: 1969

Gordon Day, President & Owner
Brent McGraw, EVP
Marty Gant, VP of Rentals
Mike Ishida, VP of Sales
Heather James, Licensing Manager

Supplier of RF, wireless, and radio communication equipment. The company's services include
rentals, system integration, and marketing.

Dazeworks Inc   HQ
  649 Mission St 5th Fl   [N]
  San Francisco CA 94105
P: 415-818-8069   F: 415-818-8068   PRC:104
dazeworks.com
Email: info@dazeworks.com
Emp: 51-200   Estab: 2015

Shivanath Devinarayanan, CEO

Provider of solutions to help clients innovate and
stand out from their competition.

DB Control Corp   HQ
  1120 Auburn St
  Fremont CA 94538-7328
P: 510-656-2325   F: 510-656-3214   PRC:70
dbcontrol.com
Email: marketing@dbcontrol.com
Estab: 1990

Steve Walley, VP of Business Development
Jacob Thampan, VP of Engineering
Steven Olson, Marketing Manager

Provider of high-power solutions for mission-critical applications. The company's services include
repairs and contract manufacturing.

DB Design Group   HQ
  48507 Milmont Dr
  Fremont CA 94538
P: 408-834-1400   PRC:19
www.dbdesign.com
Email: info@dbdesign.com
Estab: 1989

Mark Stenholm, President
Rennie Bowers, CEO
John Love, Manager of Worldwide Sales Account

Supplier of technology solutions. The company
caters to the semiconductor, solar, and medical
industries.

DCL Inc   HQ
  48641 Milmont Dr
  Fremont CA 94538
P: 510-651-5100   PRC:326
dclcorp.com
Email: info@dclcorp.com
Estab: 1982

David Tu, Founder
Dave Tu, President
Norman Tu, CEO
Brian Tu, CRO
Mike Schneider, VP of Operations

Provider of fulfillment and supply chain management services. The company offers e-Commerce,
retail fulfillment, and reverse logistics services.

DCM Infotech Limited   RH
  39159 Paseo Padre Pkwy Ste 303
  Fremont CA 94538
P: 510-494-2321   F: 510-494-2330   PRC:322
www.dcmds.com
Email: sales@dcmusa.com
Estab: 1972

Ashok Rai Choudhury, President
A. C. Biji, Specialist

Provider of managed IT services. The company
focuses on system administration, storage, enterprise management, and staffing services.

Dcx-Chol Enterprises Inc   HQ
  12831 S Figueroa St   [N]
  Los Angeles CA 90061
P: 310-516-1692   PRC:209
www.dcxchol.com
Email: sales@dcxchol.com
Estab: 1997

Neal Castleman, President
Jack Cate, CIO
Mike Jamison, VP & General Manager
Brian Gamberg, VP
Travis Cooper, Manager of Sales

Manufacturer of cable assemblies, wire harnesses, electromechanical devices and pneumatic
signal and control mechanisms.

DDRdrive LLC   HQ
  384 Madeline Ct
  Palo Alto CA 94306
P: 650-804-8227   PRC:126
www.ddrdrive.com
Email: sales@ddrdrive.com
Estab: 2007

Christopher George, Founder & CTO

Provider of solid-state storage system. The company specializes in ZFS and ZIL acceleration.

De Anza Manufacturing Services Inc   HQ
  1271 Reamwood Ave
  Sunnyvale CA 94089
P: 408-734-2020   F: 408-734-2580   PRC:62
www.deanzamfg.com
Estab: 1978

Art Takahara, President & CEO
Mike Takahara, VP of marketing & Sales

Provider of manufacturing services. The company
specializes in cable, harness, wiring, and mechanical assemblies.

De Leon Enterprises   HQ
  11934 Allegheny St   [N]
  Sun Valley CA 91352
P: 818-252-6690   PRC:211
www.deleonenterprises.com
Emp: 1-10   Estab: 1994

Miguel de Leon, Contact

Manufacturer of PCB assembly, harness assembly
and chassis build.

Decco Graphics Inc   HQ
  24411 Frampton Ave   [N]
  Harbor City CA 90710
P: 310-534-2861   F: 310-534-4529   PRC:80
www.deccographics.com
Estab: 1979

Phil Kielty, Customer Service Representative

Manufacturer of steel rule dies and hand assembly for printing industry.

Decker Electric Company Inc HQ

1282 Folsom St [N]
San Francisco CA 94103
P: 415-552-1622   F: 415-861-4257   PRC:245
www.deckerelectric.com
Estab: 1896

Evelyn Sobejana Robinson, Controller

Provider of comprehensive commercial, industrial, and institutional electrical services.

Del Mar Trade Shows Inc HQ

5724 La Jolla Hermosa Ave [N]
La Jolla CA 92037
P: 858-459-1682   PRC:24
www.mfgshow.com

Julie Bodenstab, Contact

Provider of electronic components, fabrication, design and most aspects of electronics manufacturing.

Del Paso Pipe & Steel Inc HQ

5519 Raley Blvd [N]
Sacramento CA 95838
P: 916-992-6500   F: 916-992-2828   PRC:62
www.delpasopipeandsteel.com
Email: sales@delpasopipeandsteel.com
Estab: 1939

Donna Karnofsky, VP & Owner
Bob Burdick, Manager of Sales
Jordan Karnofsky, Administrative Assistant

Manufacturer of pipes, steel products such as channel iron, angle and square tubing.

Delmar Pharmaceuticals Inc DH

3475 Edison Way Ste R
Menlo Park CA 94025
P: 604-629-5989   PRC:254
www.delmarpharma.com
Email: info@delmarpharma.com

Robert E. Hoffman, Chairman
Scott Praill, CFO

Developer of pharmaceutical products. The company specializes in treatment of various cancer such as lung, brain, cervical, ovarian tumors and leukemia.

Delong Manufacturing Company HQ

967 Parker Ct
Santa Clara CA 95050
P: 408-727-3348   F: 408-727-7615   PRC:80
www.delongmfg.com
Email: delongmfg@aol.com
Estab: 1966

Dave Delong, CEO & Owner

Provider of machining services. The company focuses on prototype development, production, engineering design, and kitting and assembly.

Delphix HQ

1400A Seaport Blvd Ste 200
Redwood City CA 94063
P: 650-494-1645   PRC:323
www.delphix.com
Email: sales@delphix.com
Estab: 2008

Jedidiah Yueh, CEO & Founder
Chris Cook, President
Adam Leventhal, CTO
Monika Saha, CMO
Marc Aronson, SVP of Engineering

Developer of software, database, and database virtualization. The company focuses on website design and hosting and software application development.

Delphon Industries LLC HQ

31398 Huntwood Ave
Hayward CA 94544
P: 510-576-2220   F: 510-576-2282   PRC:86
delphon.com
Email: info@delphon.com
Estab: 1980

Jeanne Beacham, CEO
Raj Varma, CTO
Diana Morgan, CFO
Darby Davis, VP of Sales & Marketing
Philip Haseltine, VP of Manufacturing Operations

Provider of materials and services to the semiconductor, medical, photonics, telecommunications, and military markers.

Delpor Inc HQ

150 N Hill Dr Ste 250
Brisbane CA 94005
P: 415-480-6870   F: 415-480-6871   PRC:257
www.delpor.com
Email: info@delpor.com
Estab: 2009

Tassos Nicolaou, President & CEO
Frank Martin, CSO
Carl Spetzler, Director
Brian Liu, R&D Engineer
Lana Ho, Associate Scientist

Developer of next generation drug delivery systems which improve the clinical and commercial value of new and existing drugs and biopharmaceuticals.

Delta Machine HQ

2180 Oakland Rd
San Jose CA 95131
P: 408-955-9140   F: 408-955-9141   PRC:80
www.deltamachine.com
Email: customerservice@deltamachine.com
Estab: 1989

Dave Swatridge, Company Owner
Debra Kessler, Owner
Janos G., President
Heidi Holmes, Technology Director
Ben Van Wyhe, Director

Provider of precision machine components and custom parts. The company specializes in CNC milling, CNC turning, and turn key mechanical assemblies.

Delta Pacific Products Inc HQ

33170 Central Ave
Union City CA 94587
P: 510-487-4411   F: 510-487-5511   PRC:84
www.deltapacificinc.com
Email: info@deltapacificinc.com
Estab: 1988

Fred Betke, President
Yi Wang, Project Manager
Pat Dooley, Manager
Ajeya Singh, Senior Manufacturing Engineer
Louie Cabrera, Shipping Supervisor

Provider of plastics injection molding and mold making services. The company serves the automotive, agriculture, aerospace, and recreational sectors.

Delta Star Inc BR

270 Industrial Rd
San Carlos CA 94070
P: 800-892-8673   PRC:296
www.deltastar.com
Estab: 1908

Jason Greene, President & CEO
Ray Glover, COO
Michael Fayngersh, VP of Quality & Test
Ben Magana, General Manager
Abdulmajid Shaikh, Test Manager

Manufacturer of devices for the electrical sector. The company offers devices for the generation, transmission, and distribution of electrical energy.

Delta Turnstiles LLC HQ

1011 Detroit Ave Ste C
Concord CA 94518
P: 925-969-1498   PRC:82
www.deltaturnstile.com
Email: sales@deltaturnstile.com
Estab: 2005

Vanessa Howell, Project Manager

Manufacturer of optical turnstiles. The company mainly caters to the corporate sector and the government.

Deltatrak Inc HQ

PO Box 398
Pleasanton CA 94566
P: 925-249-2250   F: 925-249-2251   PRC:233
www.deltatrak.com
Email: salesinfo@deltatrak.com
Estab: 1989

Frederick Wu, President & Founder
Fred Wu, CEO
Ray Caron, COO
Cecilia Sun, VP
Brian Edwards, VP of Sales of Cold Chain Solutions

Manufacturer of cold chain management systems. The company provides data loggers, chart recorders, thermometers, and timers and pH meters.

Demtech Services Inc   HQ
6414 Capitol Ave
Diamond Springs CA 95619
P: 530-621-3200   F: 530-621-0150   PRC:157
www.demtech.com
Estab: 1999

Dave McLaury, CEO
Gus Fauci, Production & Development Manager

Manufacturer of welding machines. The company also specializes in the manufacture of testing instruments for geosynthetic installers.

Denali Therapeutics Inc   HQ
161 Oyster Point Blvd
S San Francisco CA 94080
P: 650-866-8548   PRC:268
www.denalitherapeutics.com
Email: contact@dnli.com
Estab: 2015
Sales: $10M to $30M

Robert Nelsen, Managing Director & Founder of Arch Venture Partners
Vicki Sato, Chairman of Denail Therapeutics
Ryan Watts, CEO
Carole Ho, CMO
Cindy Dunkle, CPO

Provider of therapeutic solutions for the treatment of neurodegenerative diseases. The company also specializes in blood brain barrier programs.

Dendreon Pharmaceuticals LLC   HQ
1700 Saturn Way
Seal Beach CA 90740
P: 877-256-4545   PRC:188
www.dendreon.com
Estab: 1992

Linda Staley, VP of Information Technologies & VP of Information Technologies
Nadeem Sheikh, Senior Director
Ngoc Vu, Accounts Payable Supervisor
Bryan Boyd, Supervisor
Randall Chu, Senior Scientist

Provider of biotechnology services. The company provides therapeutics for the treatment of cancer employing active cellular immunotherapy.

Denele Analytical Inc   HQ
1232 South Ave
Turlock CA 95380
P: 209-634-9055   F: 209-634-9057   PRC:139
www.denelelabs.com
Email: info@denelelabs.com
Estab: 1978

Brando Gonzalez, Laboratory Manager

Provider of agriculture and environmental support services. The company offers analytical services for plant tissue, manure, and wastewater needs.

Denise Duffy & Associates Inc   HQ
947 Cass St Ste 5
Monterey CA 93940
P: 831-373-4341   F: 831-373-1417   PRC:37
ddaplanning.com
Estab: 1984

Denise Duffy, Owner & Principal
Josh Harwayne, Senior Project Manager

Provider of environmental sciences, planning, and biological consulting services. The company is also focused on land use and contract planning.

DenMat Holdings LLC   HQ
1017 W Central Ave   [N]
Lompoc CA 93436
P: 805-346-3700   F: 805-736-1829   PRC:185
www.denmat.com
Email: info@denmat.com

Robert Cartagena, COO

Manufacturer of dental products that includes curing and bleaching lights, impressions, instruments, restoratives, and more.

Denodo Technologies Inc   HQ
525 University Ave Ste 31
Palo Alto CA 94301
P: 650-566-8833   F: 650-566-8836   PRC:67
www.denodo.com
Email: info.us@denodo.com
Estab: 1999

Angel Vi, CEO & Founder
Ravi Shankar, SVP & CMO
Paul Moxon, SVP of Data Architectures & Chief Evangelist
Suresh Chandrasekaran, Executive VP
Richard Walker, VP

Provider of enterprise data virtualization, data federation, and cloud data integration middleware solutions.

Dentoni's   HQ
801 S Airport Way
Stockton CA 95205
P: 209-464-4930   PRC:80
www.dentoni.com
Estab: 1980

David B. Dentoni, President

Provider of services for trucks and trailers. The company specializes in welding, machining, ornamental iron, and springs.

Dependable Plastics   HQ
4900 Fulton Dr
Fairfield CA 94534
P: 707-863-4900   PRC:280
www.dependableplastics.com
Email: info@dependableplastics.com
Estab: 1983

Harry Marquez, Owner
Emil Eger, Owner
Abe Lubinsky, Owner
Kathy Nunan, CFO
Marc Strum, Sales Manager

Provider of vacuum and pressure forming, plastic fabrication, and turnkey operations that involve assembly, conductive coating, and painting.

Dependable Precision Manufacturing Inc   HQ
1111 S Stockton St
Lodi CA 95240
P: 209-369-1055   PRC:80
www.dependableprecision.com
Estab: 1978

Cliff Mc Bride, President

Provider of precision sheet metal fabrication services. The company serves the government and high tech sectors.

Deplabs Inc   HQ
755 Baywood Dr Ste 165
Petaluma CA 94954
P: 415-456-5600   PRC:323
www.deplabs.com
Email: info@deplabs.com
Estab: 2004

Huw Roberts, Founder & CTO
Martin Spiek, Chief Search Solutions Officer
Shideh Derakhshani, Software Engineer
Merrell Maschino, Senior Information Architect & Lead of UX & UI

Provider of eCommerce projects. The company involves in eCommerce co-development, application development, third party integration, and back-end integration.

Deposition Sciences Inc   HQ
3300 Coffey Ln
Santa Rosa CA 95403
P: 707-573-6700   PRC:175
www.depsci.com
Email: solutions@depsci.com
Estab: 1985

Stephanie Ferguson, Human Resource Business Partner
Robert Crase, Assistant Director of Manufacturing
Lisa Russell, Project & Program Manager & Project & Program Manager
Evan Craves, Program Manager
Justin Mosier, Manager of Program & Engineer

Manufacturer of heat resistant, optical thin film coatings, including color control, metal, optical mirror, and beam splitter coatings.

Dermira Inc   HQ
275 Middlefield Rd Ste 150
Menlo Park CA 94025
P: 650-421-7200   PRC:34
www.dermira.com
Email: info@dermira.com
Estab: 2010

Luis Pena, Co-Founder & VP of Product Development
Eugene A. Bauer, CMO & Co-Founder
Thomas G. Wiggans, CEO
Andrew Guggenhime, CFO & Chief Business Officer
Janice Drew, VP of Project Management

Developer of biopharmaceutical products for the treatment of dermatology diseases such as acne, plaque psoriasis, and hyperhidrosis.

Desaware Inc   HQ
4750 Almaden Expy Ste 124-390
San Jose CA 95118
P: 408-404-4760   F: 408-404-4780   PRC:323
www.desaware.com
Email: info@desaware.com
Estab: 1991

Dan Appleman, Founder
Franky Wong, VP
Marian Kicklighter, Editor

Developer of tools and components for visual studio programmers. The company offers documentation and professional services.

Designerx Pharmaceuticals Inc   HQ
4941 Allison Pkwy Ste B
Vacaville CA 95688
P: 707-451-0441   PRC:254
www.drxpharma.com
Estab: 2002

Robert Randolph, Information Technology Manager
Jonathan Ngai, Associate Production Scientist
Kunal Patel, Production Scientist
David Sitty, Production Scientist
Larry Dunham, Staff Accountant

Provider of pharmaceutical products for treatment of cancer cells from tumors such as melanoma, hepatocellular carcinoma, pancreatic, and mesothelioma.

DesignMap   HQ
700 Alabama St
San Francisco CA 94110
P: 415-357-1875   PRC:323
www.designmap.com
Email: info@designmap.com
Estab: 2006

Ryan Cornwell, VP of UX Design
Chuck Moore, Partner
Nathan Kendrick, Partner
Gregory Baker, Partner
Kana Knaak, Senior Director of UX

Provider of web site and application design services. The company also specializes in research, usability studies, and visual design.

Destiny Tool   HQ
3233 De La Cruz Blvd Ste C
Santa Clara CA 95054-2604
P: 408-988-8898   F: 408-988-8927   PRC:157
www.destinytool.com
Email: sales@destinytool.com
Estab: 1982

Guy Calamia, Owner
Anabel Duarte, Manager of Inside Sales
Brandon Latzke, Manager of Inside Sales
Nettie Calamia, Office Manager
Daniel Wagner, Manager of Outside Sales

Developer of end mills. The company offers technical support to customers in Philadelphia, Akron, Dayton, and Iowa regions.

Detention Device Systems   HQ
25545 Seaboard Ln
Hayward CA 94545
P: 510-783-0771   F: 510-783-5409   PRC:13
www.detentiondevicesystems.com
Email: sales@dds-group.com
Estab: 1985

Dan Breuner, Quality Assurance Manager
Ron Blair, Plant Superintendent

Provider of design and manufacturing services for detention equipment metal fabrications. The company offers sliding door locking and other devices.

Development Planning and Financing Group   BR
4380 Auburn Blvd   [N]
Sacramento CA 95841
P: 916-480-0305   F: 916-480-0499   PRC:45
www.dpfg.com

Chris Austin, Principal

Provider of real estate consulting, compliance, entitlement analysis, cash flow feasibility analysis, engineering, project management, capital markets solutions and property tax appeals.

Device Authority Ltd   RH
12677 Alcosta Blvd Ste 250
San Ramon CA 94583
P: 650-603-0997   PRC:324
deviceauthority.com
Email: info@deviceauthority.com
Estab: 2014

Darron Antill, CEO
James Penney, CTO
Rao Cherukuri, CSO

Provider of IoT security solutions for industrial, automotive, transportation, healthcare, utilities, and smart cities.

Devicelock Inc   HQ
111 Deerwood Rd Ste 200
San Ramon CA 94583
P: 925-231-4400   PRC:317
devicelock.com
Email: us.sales@devicelock.com
Estab: 1996

Ashot Oganesyan, Founder
Vitaly Shipitsin, CEO
Vladimir Chernavsky, EVP
David Matthiesen, Director of Strategic Accounts
Flavio Sangalli, General Manager Italy

Developer of device control software solutions. The company offers contextual and content-based control for data leak prevention.

DevonWay   HQ
601 California St Ste 210
San Francisco CA 94108
P: 415-904-4000   F: 415-904-0440   PRC:322
www.devonway.com
Email: info@devonway.com
Estab: 2005

Chris Moustakas, President & CEO
Steve Johnson, CTO
Matthew Sacks, VP of Sales
Robert Lentz, VP of Technical Operations
Scott Brenner, VP

Provider of enterprise software solutions for utilities and process industries. The company specializes in enterprise asset management solutions.

Deweyl Tool Inc   HQ
959 Transport Way
Petaluma CA 94954
P: 707-765-5779   F: 707-765-0327   PRC:80
www.deweyl.com
Email: info@deweyl.com
Estab: 1969

William Cline, President

Manufacturer of bonding, large and double flat wire, and small wire bonding wedges. The company's products are used in ultrasonic applications.

DG Industries   HQ
226 Viking Ave   [N]
Brea CA 92821
P: 714-990-3787   F: 714-990-6541   PRC:80
www.dgindustries.com
Email: sales@dgindustries.com
Emp: 11-50   Estab: 1978

David Gillanders, CEO & Director

Manufacturer and distributor of fastener products.

Dhap Digital Inc   HQ
1501 Mariposa St Ste 317
San Francisco CA 94107
P: 415-962-4900   PRC:323
dhapdigital.com
Email: hello@dhapdigital.com
Estab: 1998

Dave McKew, Operations Manager
Tim Irvin, Consultant & Corporate IT

Provider of interface that translates a desktop experience to a smartphone and go through Scion vehicle configurations without app download.

DHV Industries Inc   HQ
3451 Pegasus Dr   [N]
Bakersfield CA 93308
P: 661-392-8948   F: 661-392-8947   PRC:212
www.dhvindustries.com
Email: sales@dhvindustries.com
Emp: 11-50

David Huang, Sales President
Sonny S., VP of USA, LAC & APAC
Lee Davies, General Manager of Europe, Middle East & South Africa

Distributor of carbon steel, cast iron, stainless steel, and alloy gate valve products.

DI-NO Computers Inc   HQ
2817 E Foothill Blvd   [N]
Pasadena CA 91107
P: 626-795-6674   PRC:324
di-no.com
Emp: 51-200   Estab: 1978

Larry D. Moon, VP

Retailer of computer hardware and offers computer repair services.

Diablo Analytical Inc   HQ
5141 Lone Tree Way
Antioch CA 94531
P: 925-755-1005   F: 925-755-1007   PRC:329
www.diabloanalytical.com
Email: info@diabloanalytical.com
Estab: 1993

Scott Hein, Founder

Provider of system integration for analytical measuring instruments. The company is engaged in custom software development and laboratory analysis.

Diablo Clinical Research   HQ
2255 Ygnacio Valley Rd Ste M
Walnut Creek CA 94598
P: 925-930-7267   F: 925-930-7392   PRC:268
diabloclinical.com
Email: studies@diabloclinical.com
Estab: 1995

Emily Galdes, VP & COO
Lori Vitti, Director of Finance
Leonard Chuck, Co-Medical Director
Mark P. Christiansen, Co-Medical Director & Endocrinologist
Richard L. Weinstein, Executive Medical Director

Provider of clinical research services specializing in endocrinology, internal medicine, cardiology, and neurology.

Diablo Green Consulting Inc   HQ
696 San Ramon Valley Blvd Ste 208
Danville CA 94526
P: 925-365-0730   F: 925-365-0729   PRC:142
www.diablogreen.com
Email: contact@diablogreen.com
Estab: 2005

Chad Simmons, Account Manager
Anindya Kar, Environmental Consultant

Provider of environmental consulting services. The company specializes in site assessments, geophysical survey, and cultural resource management.

Diablo Precision Inc   HQ
500 Park Center DR Ste 8
Hollister CA 95023
P: 831-634-0136   F: 831-634-0103   PRC:80
www.diabloprecision.com
Email: info@diabloprecision.com
Estab: 2004

Conor Kelly, President
Michael David, Account Manager

Manufacturer of metal and plastic parts. The company also provides machining, milling, turning, and contract inspection services.

Diablo Solar Services   HQ
5021 Blum Rd Ste 2
Martinez CA 94553
P: 925-313-0600   PRC:135
www.diablosolar.com
Email: info@diablosolar.com
Estab: 1984

Phil Deatsch, Owner
Bryan Raymond, President & Sales of Design & Marketing
Dave Hampton, Solar System Designer
John Snyder, Contact
Linda Monroe, Contact

Provider of solar pool heating and solar power photovoltaic systems. The company also offers installation services.

DiaCarta Inc   HQ
2600 Hilltop Dr
Richmond CA 94806
P: 800-246-8878   F: 510-735-8636   PRC:34
www.diacarta.com
Email: information@diacarta.com
Estab: 2012

Aiguo Zhang, President & CEO & Founder
Michael Powell, CSO
Michael Sha, SVP of R&D
Nitin Udar, SVP of Diagnostics & Regulatory
Jinwei Du, Associate Director of R&D

Provider of molecular diagnostics tools such as genotyping tests, colon cancer tests, DNA sample card, and gene mutation detection kits.

Diagnostic Biosystems Inc   HQ
6616 Owens Dr
Pleasanton CA 94588
P: 925-484-3350   F: 925-484-3390   PRC:34
www.dbiosys.com
Email: customersupport@dbiosys.com
Estab: 1994

Bipin Gupta, Founder & CEO & CSO

Developer of primary and monoclonal antibodies, ancillaries, chromogens, and multiplex kits. The company serves the healthcare sector.

Diagnostic Pathology Medical Group Inc   HQ
3301 C St Ste 200E
Sacramento CA 95816
P: 916-446-0424   F: 916-446-9330   PRC:303
www.dpmginc.com

Carol Smalley, Director of Operations
Ryan Kenery, Histotechnician
David R. Guillen, Contact
Cynthia Gasper, Pathologist

Specializes in identifying enzymes extracted from extremophiles for molecular biology, diagnostics, and industrial applications.

Dial Precision Inc   HQ
17235 Darwin Ave   [N]
Hesperia CA 92345
P: 760-947-3557   F: 760-947-7746   PRC:80
www.dialprecision.com
Email: info@dialprecision.com
Emp: 11-50   Estab: 1981

Jeff Marousek, VP & COO
April Ferguson, Manager of Human Resources

Manufacturer of precision components.

Dialog Semiconductor Inc   BR
2560 Mission College Blvd
Santa Clara CA 95054
P: 408-845-8500   F: 408-727-3205   PRC:207
dialog-semiconductor.com
Email: na_sales_enquiries@diasemi.com
Estab: 1986

Jalal Bagherli, CEO
Vivek Bhan, SVP of Engineering
Judy Sha, Analog Group Manager

Creator of mixed-signal integrated circuits. The company offers products such as audio, backlight LED, wireless audio, and home automation.

Dialog Semiconductor   RH
675 Campbell Technology Pkwy Ste 150
Campbell CA 95008
P: 408-374-4200   F: 408-341-0455   PRC:208
www.dialog-semiconductor.com

Jalal Bagherli, CEO
Wissam Jabre, CFO & SVP of Finance
Sean McGrath, SVP & General Manager Connectivity & Audio Business
Vivek Bhan, SVP & General Manager & Custom Mixed Signal Business Segment
Mark Tyndall, SVP of Corporate Development & Strategy

Manufacturer of AC/DC and LED SSL products. The company's products include home appliances, smart meters, power adapters, and backlighting devices.

Diamond Systems Corp   HQ
158 Commercial St
Sunnyvale CA 94086
P: 650-810-2500   F: 650-810-2520   PRC:329
www.diamondsystems.com
Email: sales@diamondsystems.com
Estab: 1989

Jonathan D. Miller, President
Jeanne L. Gale, Outsourcing Manager
Joshil O., Senior Hardware Engineer

Supplier of SBCs, embedded-ready subsystems, and system expansion modules targeting real-world applications.

Diamond Tech Inc   HQ
4347 Pacific St
Rocklin CA 95677
P: 916-624-1118   F: 916-624-1285   PRC:159
www.dtiinnovations.com

Sean Ward, General Manager of Sales
Ingo Pfeiffer, Manufacturing Manager

Provider of drilling equipment and services. The company specializes in electric, core drills, hydraulic, and drill stands.

Diamond Tool & Die Inc   HQ
508 29th Ave
Oakland CA 94601
P: 510-534-7050   F: 510-534-0454   PRC:80
dtdjobshop.com
Email: rfq@dtdjobshop.com
Estab: 1968

Darrell Holt, President
Dan Welter, VP
Naya Pillazar, Accounting Assistant

Provider of general machine services for the high tech industry. The company serves the aerospace, construction, and food processing industries.

Dicom Systems Inc   HQ
1999 S Bascom Ave Ste 700
Campbell CA 95008
P: 415-684-8790   PRC:189
www.dcmsys.com
Email: info@dcmsys.com
Estab: 2008

Dmitriy Tochilnik, President & CTO
Josh Baker, Technical Project Manager

Provider of enterprise imaging, interoperability, and teleradiology solutions. The company offers services to patients.

Dicon Fiberoptics Inc   HQ
1689 Regatta Blvd
Richmond CA 94804
P: 510-620-5000   F: 510-620-4100   PRC:19
www.diconfiberoptics.com
Email: sales@diconfiber.com
Estab: 1986

Hoffman Cheung, Director of Quality & Reliability
Hsiao-Mei Yu, Manager of Accounting

Supplier of optical components, integrated modules, and test equipment for the fiber optics industry.

Diener Precision Pumps LP   DH
935 E Turner Rd
Lodi CA 95240
P: 209-365-0405   F: 209-365-0667   PRC:160
dpp.swiss
Email: usa@dpp.swiss
Estab: 1993

Audrey Roberts, USA Sales & Business Development Director

Developer of gear and piston pumps, and valves for cooling and fleshing, refrigeration, medical, biotech, and pharmaceutical industries.

Dieselcraft Fluid Engineering   HQ
PO Box 4625
Auburn CA 95604
P: 530-613-2150   PRC:159
www.dieselcraft.com
Email: sales@dieselcraft.com
Estab: 2002

John T. Nightingale, Chief Engineer

Provider of oil and fuel cleaning technology. The company offers services for pickup trucks, loaders, boats, and gen sets.

DIGICOM Electronics Inc   HQ
7799 Pardee Ln
Oakland CA 94621
P: 510-639-7003   F: 510-639-7090   PRC:91
www.digicom.org
Email: info@digicom.org
Estab: 1982

Mo Ohady, General Manager
Norma Criglar, Controller

Provider of electronics manufacturing services. The company also deals with packing, shipping, and labeling services.

DigiLens Inc   HQ
1276 Hammerwood Ave
Sunnyvale CA 94089
P: 408-734-0219   PRC:176
www.digilens.com
Email: information@digilens.com
Estab: 2003

Jonathan D. Waldern, Founder
Alastair Grant, SVP of Optical Engineering
Shibu Abraham, Senior Materials Director
Tiffany Pham, Manufacturing Manager
Thanh Le, Senior Material Engineer

Provider of optical design, software development, electrical engineering, and illumination design services.

Digipede Technologies LLC   HQ
3527 Mt Diablo Blvd Ste 343
Lafayette CA 94549
P: 510-834-3645   F: 510-834-8632   PRC:323
www.digipede.net
Estab: 2003

Robert W. Anderson, CTO
Daniel Ciruli, Director of Products

Provider of distributed computing solutions for academic research, entertainment, financial services, and manufacturing business applications.

Digital Anarchy   HQ
226 Tulare St
Brisbane CA 94005
P: 415-287-6069   PRC:316
www.digitalanarchy.com
Email: sales@digitalanarchy.com
Estab: 2001

Garrick Meeker, CTO
Jim Tierney, Chief Executive Anarchist
Maggie Percell, Customer Support & Anarchist

Provider of photography and video plugins for Photoshop, elements, after effects, and final cut pro.

Digital Artforms Inc   HQ
264 Los Gatos-Saratoga Rd
Los Gatos CA 95030
P: 408-356-6169   F: 408-395-3444   PRC:198
digitalartforms.com
Email: info@dartforms.com
Estab: 1998

Paul Mlyniec, President
Jason Jerald, Chief Scientist
Arun Yoganandan, Lead Architect

Provider of immersive 3D interaction for specialized markers and applications including medicine, security, and military/command and control.

Digital Canvas   HQ
3731 Sunset Ln Ste 210
Antioch CA 94509
P: 925-706-1700   F: 925-405-0950   PRC:325
www.digitalcanvas.com
Email: support@digitalcanvas.com
Estab: 1997

Jeff Shaikh, CEO & Co-Founder
James Rogowy, Business Owner
Tony Ash, Co-Founder
Kanchanmala Ghosh, Owner
Nitya Singbal, Managing Director

Provider of web design and web application development services. The company also offers web hosting, security solutions, and services.

Digital Dynamics Inc   HQ
5 Victor Sq
Scotts Valley CA 95066
P: 831-438-4444   F: 831-438-6825   PRC:207
digitaldynamics.com
Email: info@digitaldynamics.com
Estab: 1974

Daryl A. Gault, President & CEO
Bill Murvihill, SVP & COO
Ray Gorski, Director of Sales & Marketing
Steve Grube, Quality Assurance Manager
Rhiannon Hecht, DevOps Specialist

Supplier of embedded process control products. The company is also engaged in manufacturing OEM control system products.

Digital Keystone Inc   HQ
21631 Stevens Creek Blvd Ste A
Cupertino CA 95014
P: 650-938-7300   PRC:319
www.digitalkeystone.com
Email: sales@dkeystone.com
Estab: 2001

Luc Vantalon, CTO & Founder
Paolo Siccardo, President & CEO
Mike Jones, Release Engineer

Provider of solutions enabling content distribution to tablets, connected TVs, and other entertainment platforms with suite of software and tools.

Digital Loggers Inc   HQ
2695 Walsh Ave
Santa Clara CA 95051
P: 408-330-5599   F: 408-970-3491   PRC:295
www.digital-loggers.com
Email: sales@digital-loggers.com
Estab: 1980

Rick Lebherz, Sales Engineer

Manufacturer of recording systems and power switches. The company offers call center recorders, radio logging systems, and recording accessories.

Digital Mountain Inc   HQ
4633 Old Ironsides Dr Ste 401
Santa Clara CA 95054
P: 866-344-3627   F: 408-845-9455   PRC:323
www.digitalmountain.com
Email: info@digitalmountain.com
Estab: 2003

Julie Lewis, President & CEO & Founder
Kevin Fagalde, Director of Computer Forensics
Valerie Karty, Accounting Manager
David Dang, Senior Manager
Wansin Ounkeo, Computer Forensics Examiner

Provider of electronic discovery and computer forensic services focusing on reduplication, data management, ESI planning, and cybersecurity.

Digital Power Corp   HQ
1635 S Main St
Milpitas CA 95035
P: 510-657-2635   F: 510-657-6634   PRC:98
www.digipwr.com
Email: sales@digipwr.com
Estab: 1969

Amos Kohn, President & CEO
William B. Horne, CFO & Director
Fernando Sandoval, Director of Sales
Jake Moir, Managing Director

Designer and manufacturer of switching power supplies. The company serves the industrial, military, and medical markers.

Digital Products Co   HQ
134 Windstar Cir
Folsom CA 95630-4929
P: 916-985-7219   F: 916-985-8460   PRC:68
www.digitalproductsco.com
Email: info2009@digitalproductsco.com

T. Black, Owner

Provider of telephone line simulators. The company offers two-line telco and party-line simulators and real phone line products.

Digital View Inc HQ
18440 Technology Dr Bldg 130
Morgan Hill CA 95037
P: 408-782-7773   F: 408-782-7883   PRC:94
www.digitalview.com
Estab: 1998

Neil Wood, President
James Henry, CEO
Luka Mucic, CFO
Juergen Mueller, CTO
Stefan Ries, Chief Human Resource Officer

Developer and manufacturer of flat panel-related
products. The company's offerings include media
players, video flyers, and accessories.

Digite Inc HQ
21060 Homestead Rd Ste 220
Cupertino CA 95014
P: 408-418-3834   PRC:325
www.digite.com
Email: support@digite.com

Mahesh Singh, Co-Founder & SVP of Marketing
A. V. Sridhar, Founder & President & CEO
Ram Subramanian, Co-Founder & VP of Sales
Ramesh Patil, CTO
Raghunath Basavanahalli, SVP & Head of
Business Development, Professional Services &
Customer Support

Provider of collaborative enterprise application
software. The company's product finds application
in process and portfolio management.

Dinucci Corp HQ
1057 Shary Cir
Concord CA 94518
P: 925-798-3946   F: 925-798-3896   PRC:80
www.dinuccicorp.com
Email: shipping.receiving@dinuccicorp.com
Estab: 1978

Jerome Ramos, Quality Control Manager
Kitten Nash, Manager Shipping & Receiving

Provider of computerized manufacturing and
prototyping services. The company offers services
to the business sector.

Diodes Inc BR
1545 Barber Ln
Milpitas CA 95035
P: 408-232-9100   F: 408-434-1040   PRC:212
www.diodes.com
Email: inquiries@diodes.com
Estab: 1959

Keh-Shew Lu, Chairman of the Board & President
& CEO
Brett Whitmire, CFO
Joseph Liu, SVP of Operations
Hans Rohrer, SVP of Business Development
Julie Holland, VP

Provider of electronic components for communications, lighting, motor control, and audio applications.

Direct Mail Center HQ
1099 Mariposa St
San Francisco CA 94107
P: 415-252-1600   F: 415-252-9100   PRC:324
directmailctr.com
Email: dmc@directmailctr.com

Pierre Smit, General Manager
Ray Leung, Account Manager
Wendy Wang, Accounting Manager

Provider of data processing, fulfillment, digital
and offset printing, mail production, and logistics
services.

Direct Technology HQ
3009 Douglas Blvd Ste 300
Roseville CA 95661
P: 916-787-2200   PRC:323
directtechnology.com
Email: info@directtechnology.com
Estab: 1996

Daniel Konieczny, CEO
Damion Walkup, CTO
Kristen Long, VP of Human Resources
Davood Ghods, VP of Government Solutions
Tim Oxley, Director

Provider of software application design and hosting services. The company is engaged in software
application development.

Directed Light Inc HQ
74 Bonaventura Dr
San Jose CA 95134
P: 408-321-8500   F: 408-321-8466   PRC:171
www.directedlight.com
Email: info@directedlight.com
Estab: 1983

Neil Ball, President
Michael McCourt, CEO
Karen Croom, Customer Service Manager
Pia Concepcion, Financial Controller

Manufacturer of industrial and scientific laser
components. The company offers laser welding,
cutting, drilling, ablation, and marking services.

DirectGov Source Inc HQ
39 Bellarmine Ct
Chico CA 95928
P: 530-899-3327   F: 530-809-0372   PRC:188
www.directgovsource.com
Estab: 2007

Jonathan Johnson, President

Manufacturer of personal protection kits. The
company offers disposable clothing, biohazard
disposal, antimicrobial sanitizers, and hand protection gloves.

Directnu Energy Corp HQ
189 W Santa Clara St
San Jose CA 95113
P: 408-657-3314   F: 408-790-2038   PRC:135
www.directnuenergy.com
Email: info@directnuenergy.com
Estab: 2009

David Curtin, President
Hamid Saadat, VP of Operations
Randal Abraham, Manager of Product & Business
Development
Keegan Wada, Engineer
Stefano Falomi, Senior Design Engineer

Provider of wind-solar energy solutions with integrated storage and control systems for businesses
and government entities.

Discoverx Corp HQ
42501 Albrae St Ste 100
Fremont CA 94538
P: 510-979-1415   F: 510-979-1650   PRC:24
www.discoverx.com
Email: info@discoverx.com
Estab: 2000

Jagdish Saini, VP of Operations
Theresa Schaub, SVP of Commercial Operations
Neil Charter, VP of Cell-Based Assay Operations
Stephanie Fong, Associate Project Manager
Philip Achacoso, Scientist

Developer and marketer of innovative solutions to
study major drug target classes such as GPCRs
and kinases.

DisplayLink Corp HQ
480 S California Ave Ste 305
Palo Alto CA 94306
P: 650-838-0481   F: 650-838-0482   PRC:212
www.displaylink.com
Email: sales@displaylink.com
Estab: 2003

John Cummins, SVP of Sales & Marketing

Provider of solutions for virtual graphics connectivity between computers and displays. The company
makes use of USB, wireless USB, and ethernet.

Distribution Technologies Inc HQ
19 Juno Rd
Tiburon CA 94920
P: 415-999-1191   PRC:179
www.distribution-technologies.com
Email: fulfillment@distribution-technologies.com
Estab: 2003

Scott Sims, Founder & President

Provider of design, analysis, simulation, automation, and project implementation solutions. The
company also deals with technical support.

DiTom Microwave Inc HQ
7592 N Maroa Ave
Fresno CA 93711
P: 559-255-7045   F: 559-255-1667   PRC:70
www.ditom.com
Email: sales@ditom.com
Estab: 1987

Mark Weisz, President & CEO
Aram Cooper, Manufacturing Manager
John Molina, Manager of Inside Sales
Doug Waggoner, Manager of Inside Sales

Provider of microwave components for both military and commercial applications. The company
offers products such as isolators and circulators.

Dix Metals Inc HQ
14801 Able Ln   [N]
Huntington Beach CA 92647
P: 714-677-0800   PRC:62
www.dixmetals.com
Estab: 1972

Jon-David Nutter, General Manager

Provider of precision-ground, machine-ready
metal blanks and other materials.

DKW Precision Machining Inc HQ
17731 Ideal Pkwy
Manteca CA 95336
P: 209-456-5709   F: 209-824-7889   PRC:80
dkwmachine.com
Estab: 1984

Kurt Franklin, Owner

Manufacturer of precision machined parts and components. The company offers CNC milling and turning, prototype, and production services.

DNA Bridges Inc HQ
55 New Montgomery St Ste 605
San Francisco CA 94105
P: 415-362-0442   F: 415-536-2871   PRC:268
www.dnabridges.com

L. Gene Burton, VP of Process, Manufacturing & Product Development
Cori Gorman, Principal
Greg Landes, Biotechnology Consultant

Provider of corporate development services. The company offers market analysis, business plan development, patent research, and other services.

DNAmito Inc HQ
2225 E Bayshore Rd Ste 200
Palo Alto CA 94303
P: 650-687-0899   PRC:34
dnamito.com
Email: info@dnamito.com
Estab: 2015

Syed Hamdani, CEO

Provider of DNA technology and cloud platform to enable cancer treatment and early prediction of chronic disease thus vastly improving patient care.

Dnanexus Inc HQ
1975 W El Camino Real Ste 204
Mountain View CA 94040
P: 415-857-0158   PRC:40
dnanexus.com
Email: info@dnanexus.com
Estab: 2009

Richard Daly, CEO
Omar Serang, Chief Cloud Officer
Tim O'Brien, VP of Sales
Bill Agee, Software Developer in Test

Provider of genome informatics and data management platform. The company provides a global network to share and manage genomic data.

DNH Industries Inc HQ
24100 Frampton Ave Bldg B   [N]
Harbor City CA 90710
P: 310-517-1769   F: 310-517-0875   PRC:290
www.dnhindustries.com
Estab: 1974

David Hitt, Contact

Manufacturer of electrical and electronic control products.

M-100

DNN Corp HQ
155 Bovet Rd Ste 201
San Mateo CA 94402
P: 650-288-3150   PRC:319
www.dnnsoftware.com
Email: sales@dnnsoftware.com
Estab: 2006

Lee McGrath, CFO
Will Morgenweck, VP of Product Management
John Kelly, Product Manager

Provider of software solutions for content management. The company also offers marketing and eCommerce and product development services.

Docker Inc HQ
318 Cambridge Ave
Palo Alto CA 94306
P: 415-941-0376   PRC:325
www.docker.com
Email: info@docker.com
Estab: 2013

Scott Johnston, CEO
David Messina, VP
Vivek Saraswat, Senior Product Manager
Karen Bajza, Community Marketing Manager
Andrea Luzzardi, Software Engineer

Provider of docker platform and docker ecosystem of contributors, partners, and adopters the way distributed applications are built, shipped, and run.

DOCOMO Innovations Inc HQ
3301 Hillview Ave
Palo Alto CA 94304
P: 650-493-9600   PRC:68
www.docomoinnovations.com
Email: inquiries@docomoinnovations.com
Estab: 2011

Takashi Suzuki, CEO
Kumi Ishiguro, Associate VP
Sanae Muranaka, AVP of Human Resources
Satoko Izumi, Business Development Manager
Hiroki Nishikawa, Assistant Manager

Provider of products and services for businesses. The company focuses on business development, network solutions, and mobile network technology.

Docsend Inc HQ
351 California St Ste 1200
San Francisco CA 94104
P: 888-258-5951   PRC:319
docsend.com
Email: sales@docsend.com
Estab: 2013

Russ Heddleston, Co-Founder & CEO
Tony Cassanego, Co-Founder & CTO
Frances Le, Director of Engineering
Justine DiPrete, Software Engineer

Provider of service that makes documents more effective communication tool with intelligence to track, optimize, and control the business documents sent.

Doctor on Demand HQ
275 Battery St Ste 650
San Francisco CA 94111
P: 800-997-6196   PRC:188
www.doctorondemand.com
Email: support@doctorondemand.com
Estab: 2013

Hill Ferguson, CEO
Christina Hwang Smith, Marketing Director
Natasha Pillay, Marketing Manager

Provider of urgent care doctors. The company offers lab screens for the treatment of mental health and chronic conditions.

DocuSign Inc HQ
221 Main St Ste 1550
San Francisco CA 94105
P: 877-720-2040   PRC:323
www.docusign.com
Estab: 2003
Sales: $300M to $1 Billion

Dan Springer, CEO
Joan Burke, CPO
Kirsten Wolberg, CTO & Operations Officer
Loren Alhadeff, CRO
Scott Olrich, COO

Provider of digital transaction management platform helps to accelerate transactions, reduce costs, and delight customers, suppliers, and employees.

Doering Machines Inc HQ
1000 N Burke St Ste D
San Francisco CA 94124
P: 415-526-2131   F: 415-526-2136   PRC:159
www.doeringmachines.com
Email: sales@doeringmachines.com
Estab: 1884

Richard Doering, President

Manufacturer of food processing equipment. The company also offers pumping systems, extruders, and conveyors.

Dogpatch Technology Inc HQ
548 Market St Ste 66918
San Francisco CA 94104
P: 415-663-6488   PRC:322
Estab: 2011

Jean Truelson, Co-Founder & CEO
Palmer Truelson, Co-Founder & CTO

Provider of digital strategy and mobile development solutions for game design and research, global media and communications, and grant writing projects.

Dohmen Capital Research Institute HQ
PO Box 49-2433   [N]
Los Angeles CA 90049
P: 310-476-6933   PRC:305
www.dohmencapital.com
Email: office@dohmencapital.com
Estab: 1997

Bert Dohmen, Founder

Provider of investment, economic research, analysis and guidance.

Dolby Laboratories Inc   BR
432 Lakeside Dr
Sunnyvale CA 94085
P: 408-330-3300   F: 408-330-3200   PRC:60
www.dolby.com
Estab: 1965

Kevin Yeaman, President & CEO
Lewis Chew, EVP & CFO
Todd Pendleton, SVP & CMO
Dean Drougas, CIO
Andy Sherman, EVP & General Counsel & Corporate Secretary

Provider of speech recognition and voice identification products. The company also offers voice control services.

Dolcera Corp   BR
155 Bovet Rd Ste 302
San Mateo CA 94402
P: 650-425-6772   PRC:325
dolcera.com
Email: info@dolcera.com
Estab: 2004

Samir Raiyani, CEO & Co-Founder
Ed Rozenberg, Co-Founder & Managing Director
Lakshmikant Goenka, Co-Founder & Managing Director
Anil Sharma, Lead of Biomedical Practice
Sateesh Thipirisetti, Lead of High tech practice

Provider of business research, analytics, collaboration, IP patent licensing, and related support services.

Dolphin Graphics   HQ
17200 Foothill Blvd
Castro Valley CA 95377
P: 510-881-0154   PRC:115
www.dolphingraphics.com
Estab: 1986

Nilesh Sharma, Owner
Dolphin Graphics Andre, President
Linda Luis, Director of Marketing
Bebe Duarte, Promotions Director
Gretchen Elliott, Bindery Manager

Provider of branding and marketing solutions. The company also offers graphics design and web design services.

Dolphin Technology Inc   DH
333 W Santa Clara St Ste 920
San Jose CA 95113
P: 408-392-0012   F: 408-392-0090   PRC:126
www.dolphin-ic.com
Email: corp@dolphin-ic.com
Estab: 1996

Mo Tamjidi, Founder
Ta-Ke Tien, Senior Technical Staff Engineer

Provider of silicon-proven Internet protocol for memory, standard cells, input and output, memory controllers, and memory test and repair.

Domico Software   HQ
1220 Oakland Blvd Ste 300
Walnut Creek CA 94596
P: 510-841-4155   F: 510-644-3156   PRC:319
www.domico.com
Email: sales@domico.com
Estab: 1984

Rosie Austin, Office Coordinator

Supplier of management and accounting software for managing self storage units, tenants, and accounts.

Dominar Inc   HQ
734 Aldo Ave
Santa Clara CA 95054
P: 408-496-0508   F: 408-496-0910   PRC:175
www.dominar-inc.com
Email: sales@dominar-inc.com
Estab: 1987

John Ellis, President

Provider of optical and semiconductor thin-film coating services. The company serves customers in Europe, Asia, and Australia.

Domino Data Lab Inc   HQ
548 Fourth St
San Francisco CA 94107
P: 415-570-2425   PRC:191
www.dominodatalab.com
Email: support@dominodatalab.com
Estab: 2013

Chris Yang, Co-Founder & CTO
Matthew Granade, Co-Founder
Nick Elprin, Co-Founder & CEO
Madhavan Thirumalai, VP of Engineering

Provider of premise and cloud-based enterprise data science platform for analysis applications. The company serves the business sector.

Donal Machine Inc   HQ
591 N McDowell Blvd
Petaluma CA 94954
P: 707-763-6625   PRC:80
www.donalmachine.com
Estab: 1969

Chris Bergstedt, President
Donna Bergstedt, CFO
Norm Booth, Quality Assurance Manager
Robert Alleman, Machinist

Provider of precision machining and sheet metal services. The company focuses on CNC machining, precision laser cutting, and welding and fabrication.

Donald P Dick Air Conditioning   HQ
1444 N Whitney Ave
Fresno CA 93703
P: 559-255-1644   PRC:147
mrcool4ac.com
Estab: 1970

David Dick, VP
Nick Scott, VP
Bill Hanner, Sales Manager
John Calandri, Sales Manager
Doug Galvani, Estimator

Provider of air conditioning services. The company's offerings include sheet metal fabrication, ductless heating, energy recovery ventilators, and solar water heaters.

Dorado Software Inc   HQ
4805 Golden Foothill Pkwy
El Dorado Hills CA 95762
P: 916-673-1100   PRC:329
doradosoftware.com
Email: sales@doradosoftware.com
Estab: 1999

Tim Sebring, CEO
Chris Simon, CSO
Jayson Hotell, Director of Channel Sales
Erika Davis, Operations Manager
Julia Ou, Build & Release Engineer

Provider of inventory, monitoring, storage management, network configuration, and mobile back hauling solutions.

Douglas Electronics Inc   HQ
2777 Alvarado St
San Leandro CA 94577
P: 510-483-8770   F: 510-995-7897   PRC:209
douglas.com
Email: info@douglas.com
Estab: 1953

Steve Vierra, Production Manager

Provider of CAD/CAM tools for personal computers. The company specializes in custom board manufacturing and electronic design software products.

Douloi Automation Inc   HQ
3517 Ryder St   [N]
Santa Clara CA 95051
P: 408-735-6942   PRC:319
www.douloiautomation.com
Email: sales@douloiautomation.com
Estab: 1991

Randolph Andrews, Founder
Randy Andrews, Owner

Developer of prepackaged motion control software.

Dowd & Guild Inc   HQ
14 Crow Canyon Ct Ste 200
San Ramon CA 94583
P: 925-820-7222   F: 925-820-7225   PRC:275
www.dowdandguild.com
Email: info@dowdandguild.com
Estab: 1986

Patrick Kelly, President
Tim Fetters, CEO
Jeff Moore, VP of Commercial Development
Tina Onderbeke, EVP
Caryl Caskey, Account Manager

Distributor of chemicals and containers. The company supplies resins, grinding media, oils and waxes, rheological products, and pigments.

DPS Telecom   HQ
4955 E Yale Ave
Fresno CA 93727
P: 559-454-1600   F: 559-454-1688   PRC:59
www.dpstele.com
Email: support@dpstele.com
Estab: 1986

Eric Storm, President
Bob Berry, CEO
Ron Stover, Corporate VP
Andrew Erickson, Director of Marketing
Sergey Dub, Director of Engineering

Developer of network alarm monitoring solutions. The company also focuses on publishing the SNMP Tutorial.

DPSS Lasers Inc HQ

2525 Walsh Ave
Santa Clara CA 95051
P: 408-988-4300   F: 408-988-4305   PRC:159
www.dpss-lasers.com
Email: sales@dpss-lasers.com
Estab: 1998

Alex Laymon, President
Randy Kimball, VP of Business Development
Oscar Varela, Director of Engineering
Allie Constantino, Marketing Manager
Karen M. Wheeler, Manager of Human Resource

Manufacturer of high power, short wavelength solid state lasers for industrial, scientific, and research applications.

Dr Revenue HQ

1700 Mandeville Canyon Rd   [N]
Los Angeles CA 90049
P: 310-476-3355   F: 310-471-7721   PRC:45
www.drrevenue.com
Email: drrevenue@drrevenue.com
Estab: 1974

John Haskell, Owner

Provider of consumer durables and services, electronics, computers, information technology, education, publishing, and professional and financial services worldwide.

Drawbridge Health Inc HQ

2882 Sand Hill Rd
Menlo Park CA 94025
P: 650-714-6791   PRC:24
www.drawbridgehealth.com
Email: info@dbhealth.com
Estab: 2015

Lee McCracken, CEO
Greg Nagy, CMO

Provider of diagnostic testing solutions. The company offers blood testing solutions for a range of biomarker.

DrChrono Inc HQ

328 Gibraltar Dr
Sunnyvale CA 94089
P: 844-569-8628   PRC:40
www.drchrono.com
Email: sales@drchrono.com
Estab: 2009

Daniel Kivatinos, Co-Founder & COO
Michael Nusimow, CEO & Co-Founder
Craig Silverman, VP of Sales & Customer Success
Barbara Gerke, Office Manager
Vishal Kuber, Product Manager

Provider of electronic health record and practice management solution which includes scheduling and clinical documentation.

DreamFactory Software Inc HQ

1999 S Bascom Ave Ste 928
Campbell CA 95008
P: 415-993-5877   PRC:320
www.dreamfactory.com
Email: info@dreamfactory.com
Estab: 2005

Eric Rubin, Founder
Bill Appleton, CEO
Ben Busse, VP of Product Management
Tom Appleton, VP of Customer Success
Jennifer Mercer, Director of Business Operations

Provider of software development services. The company offers hosting, external integration, SQL, and user management services.

DreamHost HQ

417 Associated Rd   [N]
Brea CA 92821
P: 714-671-9098   PRC:323
www.dreamhost.com
Email: abuse@dreamhost.com
Emp: 51-200   Estab: 1997

Michael Rodriguez, CEO
Tyler Lampella, VP of Marketing
Andrea Silas, VP of Technical Support
Brett Dunst, VP of Corporate Communications
Chris Ghazarian, Secretary & General Counsel

Provider of web hosting and domain name registration; flash-based multimedia products.

Dripless Inc HQ

527 Mendocino Ave Ste E
Santa Rosa CA 95401
P: 707-568-5081   F: 707-568-5085   PRC:148
www.dripless.com
Email: dripless@sonic.net

Tom Allen, Director

Manufacturer of utility spatulas, caulking guns, holsters, and related accessories. The company serves the painting industry.

Drivers License Guide Co HQ

1492 Oddstad Dr   [N]
Redwood City CA 94063
P: 650-369-4849   F: 650-364-8740   PRC:323
www.driverslicenseguide.com
Emp: 11-50

Linda Arata, Account Manager
Lynn Hawthorne, Account Manager

Provider of risk management and compliance programs.

Drivesavers Inc HQ

400 Bel Marin Keys Blvd
Novato CA 94949-5650
P: 415-382-2000   F: 415-883-0780   PRC:325
drivesaversdatarecovery.com
Estab: 1985

Jay Hagan, CEO
Mike Cobb, Director of Engineering

Provider of data recovery services for financial institutions, healthcare providers, major film studios, government agencies, and small businesses.

Drobo Inc HQ

1289 Anvilwood Ave
Sunnyvale CA 94089
P: 408-454-4200   F: 408-276-8401   PRC:95
www.drobo.com
Email: sales@drobo.com
Estab: 2004

Mihir Shah, CEO
John Apps, VP of Operations
Tom Wong, VP of Sales
Samina Subedar, Director of Marketing
Phat Ta, Senior Manufacturing Manager & Test Engineer

Provider of virtualization and backup and archiving services. The company also offers disaster recovery and cloud storage solutions.

Droisys Inc HQ

4800 Patrick Henry Dr
Santa Clara CA 95054
P: 408-874-8333   F: 408-493-4533   PRC:323
droisys.com
Email: sales@droisys.com
Estab: 2003

Amit Kumar, CEO
Shum Mukherjee, CFO
Rahul Agarwal, VP of Engineering
Preeti Agrawal, Product Manager
Amish Srivastava,, Manager

Provider of business solutions and offers services such as content management, enterprise resource planning, and business efficiency consulting.

Dropbox Inc HQ

1800 Owens St
San Francisco CA 94158
P: 415-857-6800   PRC:325
www.dropbox.com
Estab: 2007

Arash Ferdowsi, Co-Founder
Drew Houston, Co-Founder & CEO
Ajay Vashee, CFO
Quentin Clark, CTO
Yamini Rangan, Chief Customer Officer

Provider of data transfer and sharing services that involves sharing of files, documents, and pictures from anywhere.

Druva Inc RH

150 Mathilda Pl Ste 450
Sunnyvale CA 94086
P: 650-238-6200   PRC:319
druva.com
Estab: 2008

Jaspreet Singh, Co-Founder & CEO
Milind Borate, Co-Founder & CTO
Mahesh Patel, CFO
Abhay Ghaisas, VP of Engineering
Dave Packer, VP of Corporate & Product Marketing

Provider of cloud based data protection products. The company offers services to the manufacturing, healthcare, and education industries.

DSP Concepts Inc HQ
3235 Kifer Rd Ste 100
Santa Clara CA 95051
P: 408-747-5200 PRC:322
www.dspconcepts.com
Email: info@dspconcepts.com
Estab: 2003

Chin Beckmann, Co-Founder & CEO
Paul Beckmann, Co-Founder & CTO
Tim Eun, CFO
Steven Isabelle, VP of Engineering
Jim Warngier, VP of Sales & Marketing

Provider of embedded audio processing tools and services. The company offers system design, embedded software development, and optimization services.

DST Controls HQ
651 Stone Rd
Benicia CA 94510
P: 800-251-0773 PRC:228
www.dstcontrols.com
Email: info@dstcontrols.com
Estab: 1975

William Southard, President & CEO
Greg Dumas, CTO
Read Hayward, VP
Conn McLean, Director of Engineering
Bill VanDervoort, Director

Provider of control systems integration, industrial data management, and related enterprise solutions. The company serves the industrial sector.

Dt Research Inc HQ
2000 Concourse Dr
San Jose CA 95131
P: 408-934-6220 F: 408-934-6222 PRC:323
www.dtresearch.com
Email: sales@dtri.com
Estab: 1995

Jeffrey Johnston, Director of Channel Sales West
Perry Kao, Director of Product Management
Carmino Rosa, Operations Manager
Mario Gosalvez, Business Development Manager
Hoan Q. Ho, Technical Support Engineer

Developer and manufacturer of embedded computing systems. The company serves hospitality, healthcare, and digital signage needs.

Du Pont EKC Technology Inc BR
2520 Barrington Ct
Hayward CA 94545
P: 501-784-9105 PRC:53
www.dupont.com

Elaine Masser, Quality Manager
Charles Chen, Project Engineering Consultant
Paul Bernatis, Principal Investigator

Provider of science and technology solutions. The company engages in product line such as food, personal care and industrial biotechnology.

Dualsonic Inc HQ
2294 Walsh Ave
Santa Clara CA 95050
P: 408-457-8585 F: 408-748-1567 PRC:79
www.dual-sonic.com
Email: info@dual-sonic.com

Michael Chao, VP of Manufacturing

Provider of technology solutions for electronic and precision CNC machining. The company designs and manufactures PCMCIA cards and RFID housings.

Dubberly Design Office HQ
2501 Harrison St Ste 7
San Francisco CA 94110
P: 415-648-9799 F: 415-648-9899 PRC:325
www.dubberly.com
Email: hello@dubberly.com
Estab: 2000

Knut Synstad, Visual Designer

Developer of software related solutions. The company offers user interface and visual design, brand development, and usability testing services.

Duda HQ
577 College Ave
Palo Alto CA 94306
P: 866-776-1550 PRC:325
www.duda.co
Email: support@duda.co
Estab: 2009

Amir Glatt, Co-Founder & CTO
Itai Sadan, Co-Founder & CEO & President
Stephanie Hsiung, CFO
Alan Keller, Chief Enterprise Sales Officer
Oded Ouaknine, Chief Customer Officer

A web design platform offering web design services to small businesses.

Dudek HQ
605 Third St [N]
Encinitas CA 92024
P: 760-942-5147 F: 760-632-0164 PRC:45
dudek.com
Email: hello@dudek.com
Emp: 501-1000 Estab: 1980

Frank Dudek, Chairman of the Board & CEO
Joe Monaco, President

Provider of environmental planning and engineering services.

Duke Empirical HQ
2829 Mission St
Santa Cruz CA 95060
P: 831-420-1104 F: 831-420-1196 PRC:189
www.dukeempirical.com
Email: info@dukeempirical.com
Estab: 2000

Robert LaDuca, CEO
Michael Stramowski, VP of Operations
Tyler Starkman, Director of IT
Bridgette Blotz, Manager of Production
Ryan Drake, Purchasing Manager

Provider of product development, catheter design, and manufacturing services to medical manufacturers.

Duniway Stockroom Corp HQ
48501 Milmont Dr
Fremont CA 94538
P: 650-969-8811 F: 650-965-0764 PRC:165
www.duniway.com
Email: info@duniway.com
Estab: 1976

Robert Reid, VP of Operations
Michael Ricks, General Manager

Supplier of vacuum equipment. The company offers ion, diffusion, and mechanical pumps, and valves to the industrial sector.

Dunlop Manufacturing Inc HQ
150 Industrial Way
Benicia CA 94510
P: 707-745-2722 F: 707-745-2658 PRC:245
www.jimdunlop.com
Email: customerservice@jimdunlop.com
Estab: 1965

Graham Shaw, Art Director
Stephen A. Goodrich, Director of Sales
Joey Tosi, Creative Director
Samuel McRae, Director of R&D
Joe Lam, Electronic Manufacturing Manager

Manufacturer of musical instruments and accessories. The company also designs amplifiers, guitar pedals, picks, capos, and strings.

Durabook Americas Inc BR
48329 Fremont Blvd
Fremont CA 94538
P: 510-492-0828 F: 510-492-0820 PRC:93
www.durabook.com
Email: sales@durabookamericas.com
Estab: 1984

Steven Gau, President
Julie Meng, Executive Assistant for Administration & Manager of Human Resource
Kuo Claire, Inside Sales Manager
Emily Tang, Sales Assistant

Manufacturer of portable notebook computers. The company offers rugged notebook and tablet PC, parts, and accessories.

Durabrake Co HQ
2311 Calle Del Mundo
Santa Clara CA 95054
P: 408-748-0400 F: 408-748-0410 PRC:81
www.durabrake.com
Email: info@durabrake.com
Estab: 1998

Rita Shroff, CFO & Controller
Caroline Siegel, Office Manager

Manufacturer of automotive products. The company's products include brake drums, rotors, and hubs for the aftermarket and OEMs.

Duravent Inc   HQ
877 Cotting Ct
Vacaville CA 95688
P: 800-835-4429   PRC:134
www.duravent.com
Email: customerservice@duravent.com
Estab: 1956

Ron Weissmann, Human Resource Manager
Mark Palmatier, Operations Manager
Pat Woods, Information Technology Manager
Linda Hanson, Senior Human Resource Administrator & Senior Payroll Specialist
Cheryl Curnow, Senior Accountant

Manufacturer of pellets, pressure stacks, and special gas vents. The company is involved in condensing application installation.

Durect Corp   HQ
10260 Bubb Rd
Cupertino CA 95014-4166
P: 408-777-1417   F: 408-777-3577   PRC:269
www.durect.com
Email: busdev@durect.com
Estab: 1998
Sales: $10M to $30M

Felix Theeuwes, CSO & Chairman
James E. Brown, CEO & President
Mike Arenberg, CFO
Steven Helmer, Chief Patent Counsel
Jian Li, VP of Finance & Corporate Controller

Developer of products for the treatment of chronic debilitating disease. The company specializes in biotechnology products.

DVK Integrated Services Inc   HQ
1570 The Alameda Ste 216
San Jose CA 95126
P: 408-436-0100   F: 408-436-0321   PRC:207
www.dvk.com
Email: dvk@dvk.com
Estab: 1984

Karl Varsanyi, VP
Deb Albert, Partner
Richard Nadeau, Designer

Provider of turnkey services that include prototyping services, printed circuit board design, and engineering services.

DyAnsys Inc   HQ
300 N Bayshore Blvd
San Mateo CA 94401
P: 888-950-4321   PRC:186
www.dyansys.com
Email: customer.contact@dyansys.com
Estab: 2001

Srini Nageshwar, CEO

Provider of medical diagnostic and monitoring systems to clinicians and hospitals for patients. The company deals with research services.

Dynamic Graphics Inc   HQ
1015 Atlantic Ave
Alameda CA 94501
P: 510-522-0700   F: 510-522-5670   PRC:319
dgi.com
Email: sales@dgi.com
Estab: 1969

Tamara Paradis, Owner
Arthur Paradis, President
Roy Burlingame, Director of Business Development
Carol Mann, Project Manager
Susan Brooks, Manager of Human Resource

Provider of geospatial software solutions such as earth modeling, well planning, and visualization for the petroleum industries.

Dynamic Test Solutions America Inc   BR
1762 Technology Dr Ste 115
San Jose CA 95110
P: 408-264-8880   PRC:211
www.dynamic-test.com
Email: saleusa@dynamic-test.com
Estab: 2003

Kevin Hesse, CFO
Chandra Quibilan, Application Engineer

Provider of design services. The company deals with gold and nickel plating, stub drilling and mixed dielectric fabrication.

Dynamic Ventures Inc   HQ
10366 Avenida Ln
Cupertino CA 95014
P: 408-343-0234   PRC:323
www.dyve.com
Email: info@dyve.com
Estab: 1986

Yitzchak Ehrlich, CTO & Managing Director
Quang Nguyen, Project Manager

Provider of onsite and offsite custom software development services. The company also focuses on maintenance.

Dynatex International   HQ
5577 Skylane Blvd
Santa Rosa CA 95403-1048
P: 707-542-4227   F: 707-579-8590   PRC:47
www.dynatex.com
Email: customerservice@dynatex.com
Estab: 1958

Dharmendra Jani, Owner
Kate Henry, President
John Tyler, VP of Sales
Matt Acker, Manager of DP Product Group
Richard Gaona, Software Engineer

Manufacturer of semiconductor, dicing equipment, and supplies. The company also offers dicing and wafer bonding services.

Dynavax Technologies Corp   HQ
2100 Powell St Ste 900
Emeryville CA 94608
P: 510-848-5100   F: 510-848-1327   PRC:268
www.dynavax.com
Email: contact@dynavax.com
Emp: 169   Estab: 1996
Sales: $30M to $100M

David Novack, President & COO
Dino Dina, CEO
Michael S. Ostrach, CFO & Chief Business Officer & SVP
Robert Janssen, CMO & SVP of Clinical Development
Steven N. Gersten, SVP & General Counsel & Chief Ethics & Compliance Officer & Secretary

Developer of clinical-stage biopharmaceutical company committed to discovering and developing products to prevent and treat infectious diseases.

DynEd International Inc   HQ
1350 Bayshore Highway Ste 850
Burlingame CA 94010
P: 650-375-7011   PRC:323
www.dyned.com
Email: info@dyned.com
Estab: 1987

Lance Knowles, Founder
Hoa Tran, CFO
Douglas Crane, SVP of Engineering

Provider of computer-based English language teaching solutions. The company offers mobile solutions, analytics, testing, and monitoring tools.

Dysert Environmental Inc   HQ
955 E San Carlos Ave Ste B
San Carlos CA 94070
P: 650-799-9204   PRC:142
dysertenvironmental.com
Email: info@dysertenvironmental.com
Estab: 2005

Mark Dysert, President

Provider of environmental solutions. The company's services include wastewater sampling, project management, soil sampling, and decontamination confirmation.

E Enterprise Tech   HQ
3010 N First St
San Jose CA 95134
P: 408-844-8176   F: 408-844-8269   PRC:80
www.e-enterprisetech.com

Phan Pham, Owner
Rhonda Botros, Administrative Assistant
Edwin Escobar, Machinist
Abraham Najar, Purchaser

Manufacturer of machined components. The company offers CNC machining, sheetmetal, cabling, electrical, and mechanical assembly services.

E la Carte Inc HQ
810 Hamilton St
Redwood City CA 94063
P: 530-377-3786 PRC:326
presto.com
Email: info@presto.com
Estab: 2008

Rajat Suri, CEO & Founder
Bill Healey, CTO
Ashish Gupta, CFO
Daniel Dreymann, Chief Product Officer
Stacy Rademacher, VP of Customer Success

Provider of digital restaurant services. The
company specializes in operations, engineering,
business development, and marketing.

E&F Plastics Inc HQ
2742 Aiello Dr
San Jose CA 95111
P: 408-226-6672 F: 408-226-6673 PRC:80
enfplastics.com
Email: sales@enfplastics.com
Estab: 1980

Eddie Seijas, President

Provider of plastic fabricated products. The
company offers bonded PVC, vapor polished
polycarbonates, and vacuum formed Kydex.

E*Healthlinecom Inc HQ
2450 Venture Oaks Way Ste 100
Sacramento CA 95833
P: 916-924-8092 F: 916-924-8209 PRC:194
ehealthline.com
Email: contactus@ehealthline.com
Estab: 1999

Georgette Smart, CEO

Provider of integrated health care information
management software such as administration
discharge transfer, bed management, and patient
billing.

E-3 Systems Inc HQ
1220 Whipple Rd
Union City CA 94587
P: 510-487-7393 F: 510-487-7794 PRC:63
www.e3systems.com
Estab: 1989

Andres Carrasco, Transport Division Manager &
Project Manager

Provider of data center design and installation
services. The company focuses on engineering,
cable plant analysis and documentation, and
maintenance.

E-Fab Inc HQ
1075 Richard Ave
Santa Clara CA 95050
P: 408-727-5218 F: 408-988-3342 PRC:68
www.e-fab.com
Email: eng@e-fab.com
Estab: 1981

Jerry Banks, Owner
Rick Espino, President
Ed Hinson, General Manager
Carol Spicker, Accounting Manager

Provider of precision manufacturing and fabrication solutions. The company offers mesh screens,
etched antennas, encoder strips, and PCB
jumpers.

E-Health Records International Inc HQ
6800 Palm Ave Ste D
Sebastopol CA 95472
P: 707-284-4300 F: 707-284-4302 PRC:194
harmonimd.com
Email: sales@harmonimd.com
Estab: 2014

Nick Smith, CTO

Provider of electronic medical record system that
can manage all aspects of clinical care in a busy
hospital environment.

E-M Manufacturing Inc HQ
1290 Dupont Ct
Manteca CA 95336
P: 209-825-1800 F: 209-825-1855 PRC:80
www.emmanufacturing.com
Email: sales@emmanufacturing.com

Scott Hicken, VP

Provider of prototyping and short run production
machining services. The company is engaged in
sheet metal design.

E-N-G Mobile Systems Inc HQ
2245 Via De Mercados
Concord CA 94520
P: 925-798-4060 F: 925-798-0152 PRC:68
www.e-n-g.com
Email: info@e-n-g.com
Estab: 1977

Dick Glass, President
Claudia Cannata, Office Manager
Mary O'Hern, Inside Sales Manager
Jason Ramos, Construction Technician

Manufacturer of specialty vehicles. The company focuses on TV vans and trucks, emergency
response trailers, mobile labs, and other vehicles.

E-Scape Bio HQ
4000 Shoreline Ct Ste 400
S San Francisco CA 94080
P: 650-431-0100 PRC:34
www.e-scapebio.com
Email: info@escapebio.com
Estab: 2015

Leon Chen, CEO
Anthony M. Rimac, CFO
Ann Kapoun, SVP of Research & Development
Al Garofalo, Chemistry Director
Raquel Andrade, Office Manager

Provider of therapeutic solutions. The company
focuses on discovery and development of small
molecule drugs for the treatment of neurodegenerative diseases.

E-Z Tel Inc HQ
510 N L St
Livermore CA 94551-2808
P: 925-449-1504 PRC:61
www.e-ztel.com
Email: sales1@e-ztel.com
Estab: 1973

Brenda Leavy, Sales Manager

Provider of basic and unified communication
solutions. The company serves small and medium-sized organizations and enterprises.

EB Stone Organics HQ
PO Box 550
Suisun CA 94585
P: 707-426-2500 F: 707-429-8960 PRC:48
ebstone.org
Estab: 1979

Larry Byers, Territory Manager
Lisa Scott, Sales Representative

Supplier of garden fertilizers. The company also
offers lawn maintenance, composite maker, soil,
and plant aid services.

E2C Remediation HQ
1020 Winding Creek Rd Ste 100
Roseville CA 95678
P: 916-782-8700 PRC:140
e2cr.net
Email: atyourservice@e2cr.net

Philip Goalwin, President
Michael George, General Counsel
Aiguo Xu, Principal Engineer

Provider of environmental remediation services.
The company services also include soil and
groundwater remediation and civil and geological
engineering.

EA Machining Inc HQ
3390 De La Cruz Blvd Unit W
Santa Clara CA 95054-2631
P: 408-727-4962 F: 408-727-4970 PRC:8
eamachining.com
Email: aamaro@eamachining.com

Ann Marie Amaro, CEO & Owner

Provider of CNC turning and milling services. The
company offers services to the semiconductor
manufacturing equipment industry.

Eagle Roofing Products HQ
3546 N Riverside Ave [N]
Rialto CA 92377
P: 909-822-6000 PRC:358
www.eagleroofing.com
Emp: 501-1000 Estab: 1989

Hans Matheus, National Components Manager
Josh Bartlett, Regional Sales Manager
Mario Villaneda, Senior Regional Sales Manager
Annette Sindar, Technical & Marketing Adminis-
trator
Jimmy Mallonee, Sales Associate

Distributor of concrete tile roof products.

Eagle Shield Inc HQ
4115 Blackhawk Plaza Cir Ste 100
Danville CA 94506
P: 800-408-2375 PRC:129
eagleshield.com
Estab: 2003

Garrett Harwood, CEO

Provider of energy conservation and renewable
energy solutions. The company offers services to
homes and businesses.

Eargo Inc   HQ
1600 Technology Dr 6th Fl
San Jose CA 95110
P: 650-351-7700   PRC:188
eargo.com
Email: sales@eargo.com
Estab: 2010

Raphael Michel, Founder & Advisor
Christian Gormsen, CEO
Wilson On, Senior Staff Design Engineer
Ron Gill, Hearing Instrument Specialist
Joe Pistorio, Producer

Creator of medical device. The company specializes in virtually invisible in-ear hearing device that is comfortable, natural sounding, and rechargeable.

Earlens Corp   HQ
4045-A Campbell Ave
Menlo Park CA 94025-4745
P: 650-366-9000   PRC:195
earlens.com
Email: customercare@earlens.com
Estab: 2005

Mark Bishop, VP of Operations & Quality
Chris Writer, Area VP
Ketan Muni, Senior R&D Director
Andy Atamaniuk, Director of R&D
Kyle Imatani, Staff R&D Engineer

Manufacturer of medical devices such as contact hearing devices and sensorineural and conductive hearing impairment.

Earthquake Protection Systems   HQ
451 Azuar Ave Bldg 759
Vallejo CA 94592
P: 707-644-5993   F: 707-644-5995   PRC:159
www.earthquakeprotection.com
Email: eps@earthquakeprotection.com
Estab: 1985

Victor Zayas, President
Julie Robinson, CFO
Anoop Mokha, VP
Esteban Sevilla, Director

Supplier of seismic isolators for earthquake bearings. The company offers single and triple pendulum bearings and related supplies.

Earthquake Sound Corp   HQ
2727 McCone Ave
Hayward CA 94545
P: 510-732-1000   F: 510-732-1095   PRC:60
www.earthquakesound.com
Email: us-sales@earthquakesound.com
Estab: 1984

Joseph Sahyoun, President
Abraham Sahyoun, Director of Marketing
Rani Sentana, Assistant Export Manager
Carlos Frias, Sales Manager

Manufacturer and seller of sound equipment for mobile audio, marine audio, gaming, and home audio sectors.

East Bay Machine   HQ
1030 Shary Ct
Concord CA 94518
P: 925-689-2421   F: 925-689-2837   PRC:80
www.eastbaymachine.com
Email: info@eastbaymachine.com

Sean McLellan, President & CEO

Provider of machining services including welding and fabrication. The company offers services to the business sector.

East West Investment Services   HQ
135 N Los Robles Ave 7th Fl   [N]
Pasadena CA 91101
P: 626-768-6000   PRC:325
www.eastwestbank.com
Estab: 2004

Shirley Wang, VP
Mimy Luc, Branch Manager
Johnny Leung, Assistant Branch Manager
Jun Liu, Customer Service Supervisor
Emily Wong, Mortgage Loan Officer

Provider of investment brokerage services.

Eastar Chemical Corp   HQ
1215 K St Ste 1700
Sacramento CA 95814
P: 800-898-2436   PRC:50
www.eastarchem.com
Email: info@eastarchem.com
Estab: 1984

Tony Chu, President
Charles Chu, Chairman
George Chu, CEO
Howard Brainard, VP of Sales
David A. Roberts, Director

Manufacturer of chemicals and pharmaceuticals. The company offers Venlafaxine, Usnic acid, Pentaerythritol, and Octanedinitrile.

Eastern Research Group Inc   BR
8950 Cal Center Dr Ste 230
Sacramento CA 95826
P: 916-635-6592   PRC:142
www.erg.com
Estab: 1984

John Koupal, Principal Engineer

Provider of performance measurement, risk assessment, event planning and facilitation, and training services.

Eastridge Workforce Solutions   HQ
2355 Northside Dr   [N]
San Diego CA 92108
P: 800-778-0197   PRC:319
www.eastridge.com
Emp: 201-500   Estab: 2007

Adam Svet, CEO
Brandon Stanford, CFO
Erin Medina, CLO
Kasey Hadjis, Chief Administrative Officer
Jairo Carrion, EVP

Provider of workforce management, workforce recruitment, workforce technology and staffing solutions.

Ebara Technologies Inc   HQ
51 Main Ave
Sacramento CA 95838
P: 916-920-5451   F: 916-830-1900   PRC:212
www.ebaratech.com
Email: info@ebaratech.com
Estab: 1912

Naoki Ando, President & CEO
Corum Stan, CFO
Brian Lutolf, VP of Operations Division
Sachin Paradkar, VP & General Manager of Strategic Global Components Division
Mark Perry, VP & General Manager of Global Components Division

Manufacturer of vacuum pumps for the semiconductor industry. The company offers repair, training, and field and system services.

EBR Systems Inc   HQ
480 Oakmead Pkwy
Sunnyvale CA 94085
P: 408-720-1906   F: 408-720-1996   PRC:186
www.ebrsystemsinc.com
Email: info@ebrsystemsinc.com
Estab: 2003

Rick Riley, VP of Field Engineering & Founder
John McCutcheon, President & CEO
Allan Will, Chairman of the Board
Suzanne Pilkington, CFO & VP of Finance & Admin
Parker Willis, CTO

Designer and developer of implantable systems for wireless tissue stimulation. The company focuses on the treatment of heart failure.

Ebusinessdesign   HQ
900 E Hamilton Ave Ste 100
Campbell CA 95008
P: 408-654-7900   F: 408-654-7907   PRC:323
www.ebusinessdesign.com
Email: info@ebusinessdesign.com
Estab: 1995

Amardeep Misha, Co-Founder
Pardeep Boparai, Co-Founder

Provider of technology consulting services, specializing in business analysis, architecture design, and open source development.

Echopixel Inc   HQ
4677 Old Ironsides Dr Ste 445
Santa Clara CA 95054
P: 844-273-7766   PRC:187
www.echopixeltech.com
Email: info@echopixeltech.com
Estab: 2012

Sergio Aguirre, Founder & CTO
Ron Schilling, CEO & Chairman

Provider of 3D medical visualization software for radiologists, cardiologists, pediatric cardiologists, and interventional neuroradiologists.

Eckhart Corp   HQ

7110 Redwood Blvd Ste A
Novato CA 94945
P: 415-898-9528   PRC:268
www.eckhartcorp.com
Email: info@eckhartcorp.com
Estab: 1989

Deepak Chopra, CEO
Sandeep Chopra, CFO
Eric Lim, VP of Sales
Usama Hammad, Sales & Marketing Director
Andrey Prokofiev, Director

Manufacturer of nutritional supplements. The
company is engaged in product development and
packaging services.

Eclipse Metal Fabrication Inc   HQ

2901 Spring St
Redwood City CA 94063
P: 650-298-8731   F: 650-298-8747   PRC:80
www.eclipsemf.com
Estab: 1999

Joe Anaya, Owner

Provider of metal fabrication services. The company provides CNC machining, laser, and waterjet
cutting services in the San Francisco Bay area.

Eco Sound Medical Services   HQ

1865 N Macarthur Dr
Tracy CA 95376-2820
P: 800-494-6868   F: 209-835-7554   PRC:189
e-ecosound.com
Email: sales@e-ecosound.com

Don Huhn, Owner & Co-Founder of Eco Sound
Medical Services
Mark Hineser, Owner & Co-Founder of Eco Sound
Medical Services
Patrick Meadows, COO
Paula Stinyard, Medi-Cal Department Director

Distributor of healthcare products and medical
supplies. The company is focused on incontinence
products, medical nutrients, and nursing supplies.

Ecodomus Inc   HQ

1203 Union St
San Francisco CA 94109
P: 571-277-6617   PRC:323
ecodomus.com
Email: info@ecodomus.com
Estab: 2008

Igor Starkov, CEO

Provider of information technology software for
improved design and construction data collection,
facility management, operation, and maintenance.

Ecomicron Inc   HQ

2161 O'Toole Ave Ste 30
San Jose CA 95131
P: 408-526-1020   F: 408-526-1040   PRC:86
www.ecomicron.com
Email: info@ecomicron.com
Estab: 2008

Justin Hong, CEO & President
Malcolm B., Account Sales Manager
Bryan Kirby, Senior Account Manager
Patrick Wilson, Software Engineer
Uladzislau Lekhtsikau, Software Quality Assur-
ance Engineer

Manufacturer of semiconductor equipment. The
company caters to semiconductor, photovoltaic,
and hybrid industries.

Economic & Planning Systems   BR

400 Capitol Mall 28th Fl   [N]
Sacramento CA 95814
P: 916-649-8010   F: 916-649-2070   PRC:305
www.epsys.com
Emp: 11-50   Estab: 1983

Amy Lapin, EVP
Ellen Martin, EVP
Russ Powell, SVP
Victoria Allensworth, Manager of Production
Anya Tamagni, Office Manager

Provider of real estate development services for
the public and private sector.

Econugenics Inc   HQ

396 Tesconi Ct
Santa Rosa CA 95401
P: 800-521-0160   PRC:272
www.econugenics.com
Email: sales@econugenics.com
Estab: 1995

Isaac Eliaz, Founder & Formulator
Barry Wilk, Director of Quality Assurance & Re-
search & Development
Bonnie Frese, Sales Manager
Kristina Young, Accounting & Sales Analyst
Elaine Weil, Medical Research Specialist

Manufacturer and distributor of dietary supplements and healthcare products. The company
serves the medical sector.

Ecoshift Consulting LLC   HQ

126 Bonifacio Pl Ste G
Monterey CA 93940
P: 831-277-0167   PRC:142
www.ecoshiftconsulting.com

Kristin Cushman, CEO
Chris Sentieri, Manager of Climate Division
Benjamin Fordham, Climate & Energy Analyst
Alexander Gershenson, Advisor
James Barsimantov, Advisor

Provider of consulting services. The company
offers consulting for alternative fuels, climate
change, carbon reduction strategies, and carbon
trading.

Ecrio Inc   HQ

19925 Stevens Creek Blvd Ste 100
Cupertino CA 95014
P: 408-973-7290   F: 408-973-7292   PRC:326
www.ecrio.com
Email: info@ecrio.com
Estab: 1998

Michel Gannage, Founder & CEO
Krishnakumar Narayanan, VP of Engineering
Vikram Karmarkar, VP of Product Marketing &
Business Development
Lina Martin, VP of Finance
Hide L. Tanigami, Director of Investor

Provider of wireless messaging applications. The
company offers video telephony, content sharing,
social communications, and enterprise solutions.

Ed Fagan Inc   HQ

10537 Humbolt St   [N]
Los Alamitos CA 90720
P: 562-431-2568   F: 562-598-7122   PRC:62
www.edfagan.com
Email: sales@edfagan.com
Estab: 1965

Jeffrey Hopkins, General Manager

Manufacturer of metals and alloys for aerospace,
aviation, defense, electronics, telecommunications
and other sectors.

EDA Direct Inc   HQ

4701 Patrick Henry Dr Ste 1301
Santa Clara CA 95054
P: 408-496-5890   F: 408-684-8854   PRC:319
edadirect.com
Email: sales@edadirect.com
Estab: 1997

Heather Cox, Office Manager
Kate Vu, Sales Account Manager
Natalie Chan, Digital Marketing Manager
Mario Rocha, Sales Account Manager
Jack Lee, Contact

Provider of EDA software products and services.
The company's products include Cliosoft, MunE-
DA, and Mentor Graphics.

EDC Biosystems Inc   HQ

49090 Milmont Dr
Fremont CA 94538
P: 510-257-1500   F: 510-257-1186   PRC:159
www.edcbiosystems.com
Email: info@edcbiosystems.com

Greg Stephens, President
Charles Reichel, VP of Engineering
Ron Jones, Senior Director
Linna Lee, Purchasing Manager
Michael Forbush, Physicist

Provider of technology solutions for biotech
liquid transfer applications. The company serves
the electronics, precision mechanics, and other
sectors.

Edeniq Inc HQ
6910 West Pershing Ct
Visalia CA 93291
P: 559-302-1777 PRC:24
www.edeniq.com
Email: info@edeniq.com
Estab: 2007

Randy Asher, Section Head of Analytical Chemistry
Aubrey Zigler, Human Resource Generalist
Denmark Antolin, Analytical Chemist

Focuses on the production of ethanol, other biofuels, and/or biochemicals. The company combines mechanical and biological processes.

Edgewater Networks Inc HQ
5225 Hellyer Ave Ste 100
San Jose CA 95138
P: 408-351-7200 F: 408-727-6430 PRC:97
info.rbbn.com
Estab: 2002

John Macario, VP of Marketing
Gernot Scheichl, VP of Support & Services
Ben Pons, Senior Systems Engineer
Yun-Fong Loh, Principal Engineer
Mohan Kumar Kannekanti, Software Engineer

Provider of enterprise session controllers for business purposes. The company also offers security and policy management services.

Edmar Engineering Inc HQ
340 Industrial Way Ste H & I
Dixon CA 95620
P: 707-693-0390 F: 707-693-0395 PRC:80
www.edmarengineering.net
Estab: 1978

Ed Martinelli, VP

Manufacturer of precision machined products. The company's products include CNC mills and lathes, inspection equipment, and lathe and mill software.

Edwards Lifesciences Corp HQ
1 Edwards Way
Irvine CA 92614
P: 949-250-5070 F: 949-250-2625 PRC:184
www.edwards.com
Email: tech_support@edwards.com
Estab: 2010
Sales: Over $3B

Cory Fackiner, Quality Engineering Manager
Quinn Lavender, Quality Manager Internal Audit
Shreyas Hoskere, Principal Engineer of Quality

Manufacturer of medical devices. The company specializes in technologies for structural heart diseases and critical care monitoring.

Eeonyx Corp HQ
750 Belmont Way
Pinole CA 94564
P: 510-741-3632 PRC:129
eeonyx.com
Email: info@eeonyx.com
Estab: 1989

Jamshid Avloni, President
Jimmy Holliman, CEO
Mahemuti Abula, CTO
Kanwar Ali, Product Developer

Manufacturer and provider of knitting services. The company focuses on textiles, foams, felts, and powders.

Eezer Products Inc HQ
4734 E Home Ave
Fresno CA 93703
P: 559-255-4140 F: 559-255-4907 PRC:53
www.eezer.com
Email: sales@eezer.com
Estab: 1964

Leighton Sjostrand, President & General Manager

Designer and manufacturer of sanding tools. The company also offers handles and various finishing tools.

Efficient Drivetrains Inc HQ
1181 Cadillac Ct
Milpitas CA 95035
P: 408-624-1231 PRC:150
www.efficientdrivetrains.com
Email: info@efficientdrivetrains.com

Andy Frank, CTO
Mario Miranda, Mechanical Design Engineer

Provider of vehicle developer equipment. The company also offers PHEV and CVT solutions, and hybrid vehicles.

Effone Software Inc HQ
4701 Patrick Henry Dr Bldg 16
Santa Clara CA 95054
P: 408-830-1010 PRC:325
effone.com
Email: info@effone.net
Estab: 1996

Hemanth Kumar, President

Provider of IT consulting services including software development, application integration, and staff augmentation.

Efinix Inc HQ
900 Lafayette St Ste 406
Santa Clara CA 95050
P: 408-789-6917 PRC:110
www.efinixinc.com
Email: sales-na@efinixinc.com
Estab: 2012

Sammy Cheung, CEO & Co-Founder & President
Tony Ngai, Co-Founder & CTO
Jay Schleicher, SVP of Software Engineering
Ming Ng, SVP of Operations & Applications

Focuses on the building of programmable devices. The company serves the industrial, medical, and automotive markers.

EG Systems LLC HQ
6200 Village Pkwy
Dublin CA 94568
P: 408-528-3000 F: 408-528-3500 PRC:86
www.electroglas.com
Email: sales@electroglas.com

Thomas E. Brunton, VP of Finance & CFO & Treasurer & Secretary
Richard J. Casler, VP of Engineering
Wes Highfill, VP of Global Sales & Marketing
Wayne E. Woodard, VP of Service & Operations
Rohit Chokshi, Senior Accountant

Provider of test equipment such as wafer probers, prober-based test handlers, and test floor management solutions.

eGain Corp HQ
1252 Borregas Ave
Sunnyvale CA 94089
P: 408-636-4500 F: 408-636-4400 PRC:323
www.egain.com
Email: info@egain.com
Estab: 1997
Sales: $30M to $100M

Ashutosh Roy, CEO & Chairman & Co-Founder
Gunjan Sinha, Co-Founder & Director
Eric Smit, CFO
Promod Narang, SVP of Products & Technologies
Anand Subramaniam, SVP of Marketing

Provider of custom engagement software solutions. The company offers co-browsing, email management, web self-service, and analytics services.

EGeen Inc HQ
1949 Landings Dr
Mountain View CA 94043
P: 650-967-5010 PRC:257
www.egeeninc.com
Email: info@egeeninc.com
Estab: 2001

Kalev Kask, CEO & Founder

Provider of drug development for biotech and pharmaceutical clients. The company serves clinics, hospitals, and the healthcare sector.

Egnyte Inc HQ
1350 W Middlefield Rd
Mountain View CA 94043
P: 650-968-4018 PRC:325
www.egnyte.com
Email: support@egnyte.com
Estab: 2006

Vineet Jain, CEO
Steve Sutter, CFO
Amrit Jassal, CTO
David Spitz, CMO
Eric Cross, CRO

Provider of online storage, cloud computing, and file sharing services. The company serves the financial, banking, and pharmaceutical industries.

EGS Inc HQ
2777 Yulupa Ave Ste 604
Santa Rosa CA 95405
P: 707-595-8760 F: 707-544-4127 PRC:139
envgeo.com
Email: info@envgeo.com
Estab: 1995

Paul Brophy, President
Gene Suemnicht, CEO & Chief Geologist

Provider of geothermal exploration development services. The company's services include remote sensing, geologic mapping, and subsurface visualization.

Eigen HQ
13366 Grass Valley Ave
Grass Valley CA 95945
P: 530-274-1240 PRC:196
www.eigen.com
Email: sales@eigen.com
Estab: 1975

Mahtab Damda, President
Syed Arsal Zaidi, CFO
William Mandel, VP of Regulatory Affairs & Quality
Assurance & Operations
Michael Ahmadi, EVP of Global Marketing &
Sales
Rajesh Venkataraman, R&D Manager

Manufacturer of cardiology and radiology imaging
products. The company serves urologists and
radiation oncologists.

Eigenstate Consulting LLC HQ
PO Box 411607 [N]
San Francisco CA 94141
P: 415-225-6703 PRC:104
www.eigenstate.net

Matisse Enzer, CEO

Creator and provider of customized presentations
for companies and groups, consulting services
through the Internet and related technologies.

Eiger Biopharmaceuticals Inc HQ
2155 Park Blvd
Palo Alto CA 94306
P: 650-282-6138   F: 650-618-1621   PRC:249
www.eigerbio.com
Email: info@eigerbio.com
Estab: 2008

David A. Cory, CEO & President
Joanne Quan, CMO
Sri Ryali, CFO
Stephana Patton, General Counsel & Corporate
Secretary & Chief Compliance Officer
James P. Shaffer, Chief Business Officer

Developer of antiviral therapy and treatments for
rare disease therapeutics. The company specializes in treatment for Hepatitis Delta.

Einfochips HQ
2025 Gateway Pl Ste 270
San Jose CA 95110
P: 408-496-1882   F: 801-650-1480   PRC:86
www.einfochips.com
Estab: 1994

Pratul Shroff, Founder & CEO
Shashank Waman Khare, CTO
Sumit Sethi, COO
Parag Mehta, Chief Business Development Officer
Vilesh Shah, Program Manager

Provider of product design services and solutions.
The company offers product engineering and
semiconductor services.

EIQ Energy Inc HQ
294 Brokaw Rd
Santa Clara CA 95050
P: 408-643-0020 PRC:124
eiqenergy.com
Email: info@eiqenergy.com
Estab: 2007

William Reed, CTO
James Allen, Chief Power Designer

Designer and manufacturer of power electronics.
The company provides solar cells, panels, and
monitoring systems.

EKM Metering Inc HQ
122 Benito Ave
Santa Cruz CA 95062
P: 831-425-7371 PRC:233
ekmmetering.com
Email: info@ekmmetering.com
Estab: 2007

Jonathan Park, CTO & EVP & Founder
Jameson Brouwer, CEO
Adam Brouwer, Chief Design Officer
Seth B., VP of Customer Support
Lydia Mugalu, Client Liaison Manager

Provider of submetering hardware and services.
The company's solutions include revenue metering and data monitoring.

Eko Devices Inc HQ
2600 Tenth St Ste 260
Berkeley CA 94710
P: 844-356-3384 PRC:186
ekodevices.com

Connor Landgraf, Co-Founder & CEO
Jason Bellet, Co-Founder & Chief Customer
Officer
Tyler Crouch, Co-Founder & Product Development

Developer of digital stethoscope/electronic stetho-
scope to help confidently and quickly assess
patient's heart, lung, and body sounds.

Ekso Bionics Holdings Inc HQ
1414 Harbour Way S Ste 1201
Richmond CA 94804
P: 510-984-1761 PRC:25
eksobionics.com
Email: support@eksobionics.com
Estab: 2005

Darrell Musick, VP of Clinical Research

Developer and manufacturer of powered exoskel-
eton bionic devices. The company is engaged in
distribution services.

El Portal Imaging Center HQ
3365 G St Ste 100
Merced CA 95340
P: 209-384-4250   F: 209-384-4269   PRC:198
www.elportalimaging.com

Brian Amfahr, COO

Specializes in diagnostic imaging solutions. The
company serves hospitals, clinics, and the healthcare sector.

El Teatro Campesino HQ
705 Fourth St [N]
San Juan Bautista CA 95045
P: 831-623-2444 PRC:60
www.elteatrocampesino.com
Estab: 1965

Louisa Casarez, Business Manager & Secretary

Publisher of theatrical material.

Elasticsearch Inc HQ
800 W El Camino Real Ste 350
Mountain View CA 94040
P: 650-458-2620 PRC:315
www.elastic.co
Email: info@elastic.co
Estab: 2012
Sales: $300M to $1 Billion

Shay Banon, Co-Founder & CEO
Steven Schuurman, Co-Founder
Uri Boness, Co-Founder
Simon Willnauer, Co-Founder
Aaron Katz, CRO

A software company that builds self-managed and
SaaS offerings that make data usable in real time.

Eldex Laboratories Inc HQ
30 Executive Ct
Napa CA 94558-6278
P: 707-224-8800   F: 707-224-0688   PRC:20
www.eldex.com
Email: sales@eldex.com
Estab: 1972

Stephen Amendola, President
Robert Larsen, Manufacturing Manager

Manufacturer of instruments for analytical chemistry laboratories and chemical process control. The
company also creates customized products.

Eldridge Products Inc HQ
465 Reservation Rd
Marina CA 93933
P: 831-648-7777   F: 831-648-7780   PRC:14
www.epiflow.com
Email: sales@epiflow.com
Estab: 1988

Mark Eldridge, President
Ryan Eldridge, General Manager

Manufacturer of thermal mass flow meters and
flow switches. The company focuses on sales,
installation, and inspection.

Elecraft Inc HQ
125 Westridge Dr
Aptos CA 95076
P: 831-763-4211   F: 831-763-4218   PRC:71
www.elecraft.com
Email: info@elecraft.com
Estab: 1998

Wayne Burdick, CTO
Paul Giannini, Materials Manager
Michael Mistor, Production Control Bench Tech-
nician
Ed Muns, Field Tester

Provider of transceivers and accessories. The
company also offers auto antenna tuners, antenna
systems, microphones, wattmeter, and other
products.

Electric Cloud Inc BR
4 N Second St Ste 1270
San Jose CA 95113
P: 408-419-4300 PRC:323
www.cloudbees.com
Email: info@cloudbees.com
Estab: 2002

Carmine Napolitano, CFO
Rohit Jainendra, Chief Product Officer
Samuel D. Fell, Director of Product Marketing
Atanu Majumdar, Senior Director of Engineering
Tim Johnson, Director of Product Marketing

Provider of software development, information technology consulting, test automation, virtualization, and cloud computing solutions.

Electric Power Research Institute Inc HQ
3420 Hillview Ave
Palo Alto CA 94304
P: 650-855-2000 PRC:131
www.epri.com
Email: askepri@epri.com
Estab: 1973

Michael W. Howard, President & CEO
Arshad Mansoor, SVP of Research & Development Group
Naresh Kumar, Senior Program Manager
Manuel Morales, Software Quality Assurance Lead
Christine Lee, Senior Statistical Analyst

Provider of research and development services related to the generation, delivery, and use of electricity for the benefit of the public.

Electro Adapter Inc HQ
20640 Nordhoff St [N]
Chatsworth CA 91311
P: 818-998-1198 F: 818-709-5773 PRC:202
www.electro-adapter.com
Email: sales@electro-adapter.com
Emp: 51-200 Estab: 1983

Ray Fish, President
Lori Fish, General Manager & Director of Operations
Jim Alderson, Director of Marketing
Marty Partridge, Manager
Ken Ivers, Controller

Manufacturer of connector accessories and adapters.

Electro Diagnostic Imaging Inc HQ
200F Twin Dolphin Dr
Redwood City CA 94065-1402
P: 650-631-0120 F: 650-631-0122 PRC:78
www.veris-edi.com
Email: sales@veris-edi.com
Estab: 1989

Susan Martin, Operations Manager
Kenny Noble, Assistant Office Manager

Developer and manufacturer of products for electrophysiology. The company's services include research, sales, and marketing.

Electro Magnetic Test Inc HQ
1547 Plymouth St
Mountain View CA 94043-1229
P: 650-965-4000 F: 650-965-3000 PRC:142
emtlabs.com
Email: info@emtlabs.com

Jay Gandhi, Owner

Provider of testing and consulting services. The company focuses on engineering services in wireless, wireline telecom, and safety certifications.

Electro Plating Specialties Inc HQ
2436 American Ave
Hayward CA 94545
P: 510-786-1881 F: 510-786-1060 PRC:159
www.eps-plating.com
Email: eps@eps-plating.com

Mary L. Hall, President
Robert Hall, General Manager

Provider of electroplating services. The company offers parts cleaning, anodizing, electropolishing, and rust removal services.

Electro-Coatings of California Inc BR
893 Carleton St
Berkeley CA 94710
P: 510-849-4075 F: 510-849-1817 PRC:80
www.electro-coatings.com

Aaron Plechaty, Production Manager

Provider of electroless nickel coating services. The company also offers industrial hard chrome and nickel metal finishing services.

Electrochem Solutions Inc HQ
32500 Central Ave
Union City CA 94587
P: 510-476-1840 F: 510-323-7200 PRC:80
www.electro-chem.com
Estab: 1982

David Rossiter, President & CEO
Francisco Ruiz, General Manager
Janet Nielsen, Sales Manager
Onur Guner Bakirman, Process Engineer
S. Dean Novy, Senior Technician

Provider of plating, anodizing, parts cleaning services. The company caters to high technology industries.

Electromax Inc HQ
1960 Concourse Dr
San Jose CA 95131
P: 408-428-9474 F: 408-428-9475 PRC:211
www.electromaxinc.com
Estab: 1991

Aaron Wong, President & General Manager
Benny Lee, Director of Marketing & Business Development
Ken Wong, Director of Engineering
Alan Haywood, Regional Sales Manager
Linda Yue, Senior Manager of Human Resources & Administration

Manufacturer of heavy machinery. The company offers engineering support, materials management, prototyping and testing services.

Electronic Arts Inc HQ
209 Redwood Shores Pkwy
Redwood City CA 94065
P: 800-314-3291 F: 650-628-1422 PRC:317
www.ea.com
Email: info@ea.com
Estab: 1982
Sales: Over $3B

Andrew Wilson, CEO
Chris Bruzzo, CMO
Ken Moss, CTO
Mala Singh, CPO
Ken Barker, SVP & Chief Accounting Officer

Developer, publisher, and distributor of software for video game systems, personal computers, wireless devices, and Internet.

Electronic Carbide Inc HQ
13005 Loma Rica Dr Ste 1
Grass Valley CA 95945-9382
P: 530-272-6154 F: 530-272-3179 PRC:80
electroniccarbide.com
Email: ecpmichelle@sbcglobal.net
Estab: 1978

Michelle Harris, CFO & Office Manager
Gordon C. Mulay, VP of Operations & Manager

Provider of CNC precision machining, fabrication, and wire EDM services. The company serves the industrial sector.

Electronic Surface Mounted Industries Inc HQ
6731 Cobra Way [N]
San Diego CA 92121
P: 858-455-1710 F: 858-455-6745 PRC:211
www.esmiinc.com
Estab: 1986

Henry Kim, Founder

Provider of electronic manufacturing services to original equipment and manufacturer in aerospace, military, industrial, education, telecommunication and consumer products.

Electronics Cooling Solutions Inc HQ
2344B Walsh Ave Bldg F
Santa Clara CA 95051
P: 408-738-8331 F: 408-738-8337 PRC:124
ecooling.com
Email: info@ecooling.com
Estab: 1998

Bharath Nagendran, Thermal Engineer
Ceferino Sanchez, Consulting Engineer

Provider of thermal management consulting services. The company serves customers in the avionics, medical, and telecommunications industries.

Elegrity Inc   HQ
160 Pine St Ste 720
San Francisco CA 94111
P: 855-353-4462   F: 415-826-7758   PRC:325
www.elegrity.com
Email: info@elegrity.com
Estab: 1998

Joy E. Spicer, President & CEO & Founder
Craig A. Mason, Chief Architect
Kandace Donovan, VP of Sales & Marketing
Timothy J. Conlon, Secretary of the Board
Jeffrey Wolk, Treasurer of the Board

Provider of law business management software, SharePoint, virtualization, and unified communication solutions.

Element Science Inc   HQ
200 Kansas St Ste 210
San Francisco CA 94103
P: 415-872-6500   PRC:189
www.elementscience.com
Estab: 2011

Uday Kumar, Founder & President & CEO
Sidney Negus, Senior Director of Manufacturing & Operations
Tim Bahney, Senior Director of Research & Development

Developer of wearable platform solution. The company offers wearable cardioverter defibrillator for monitoring the heart of the patient.

Elemental LED Inc   HQ
1195 Park Ave Ste 211
Emeryville CA 94608
P: 510-379-4200   PRC:209
www.elementalled.com
Email: answers@elementalled.com
Estab: 2007

Randy Holleschau, President & CEO
Preet Khangura, CFO
Andrew Yanev, VP of Sales
Jeff Johnson, CAO & EVP
Craig Anderson, VP of Infrastructure & Technology

Provider LED lighting accessories and products. The company's products include LED strip lights, kits, light fixtures, and dimmable lighting products.

Elementum   HQ
1825 S Grant St Floor 9
San Mateo CA 94402
P: 650-318-1491   PRC:322
www.elementum.com
Estab: 2012

Nader Mikhail, CEO
David Blonski, Head of Operations

Provider of apps to manage your global supply chain. The company offers manufacturing operations, mission control, supplier, and logistics management.

Elevator Controls Corp   HQ
6150 Warehouse Way
Sacramento CA 95826
P: 916-428-1708   F: 916-428-1728   PRC:86
www.elevatorcontrols.com
Email: sales@elevatorcontrols.com
Estab: 1986

Fernando Ortiz, President & CEO
Francisco Ortiz, VP of Product Engineering & Support
Ron Ishimoto, Director of Operations
Steve Randall, Director of Sales
Diane Ellis, Human Resources Business Partner

Manufacturer of non-proprietary microprocessor based elevator controllers. The company offers technical support and field services.

Elevator Technology Inc   HQ
2050 Arroyo Vista Way
El Dorado Hills CA 95762
P: 916-939-4323   F: 916-369-8260   PRC:180
www.elevatortechnologyinc.com
Email: elevatortec@att.net
Estab: 1991

Leonard Bates, Founder

Provider of elevator repair and installation services. The company specializes both in residential and commercial elevators.

Elite E/M Inc   HQ
340 Martin Ave
Santa Clara CA 95050
P: 408-988-3505   F: 408-988-3540   PRC:80
eliteem.com
Email: sales@eliteem.com
Estab: 1988

Igor Brovarny, President

Provider of precision machining services. The company offers prototyping, tooling, shearing, and cutting services.

Elixir Medical Corp   HQ
920 N McCarthy Blvd Ste 100
Milpitas CA 95035
P: 408-636-2000   PRC:189
www.elixirmedical.com
Email: info@elixirmedical.com
Estab: 2005

Motasim Sirhan, CEO
John Yan, CTO
Andrew Kramer, EVP of Operations
Erin Mazzone, Senior Director of Regulatory Affairs

Provider of pharmaceuticals for drug-device treatment solutions to patients. The company is engaged in drug delivery.

Elk Antennas   HQ
2308 Lomond Ln
Walnut Creek CA 94598-3705
P: 925-330-0049   PRC:61
www.elkantennas.com
Estab: 1995

Jim Siemons, Owner

Provider of log periodic antennas made of aluminum elements and stainless steel hardware and with gain, directivity, and front-to-back ratio.

Elkay Plastics Inc   HQ
6000 Sheila St   [N]
Commerce CA 90040
P: 323-722-7073   F: 323-869-3911   PRC:284
www.elkayplastics.com
Estab: 1968

Louis Chertkow, President & CEO

Distributor of flexible packaging products for food, healthcare and various other sectors.

Ellex iScience Inc   BR
41316 Christy St
Fremont CA 94538
P: 510-291-1300   PRC:172
ellex.com
Estab: 1985

Victor Previn, Chairman
Maria Maieli, Interim CEO
Cynthia Kendall, VP of Clinical Applications
Mike Southard, Executive Director
Alex Sundich, Non Executive Director

Developer and provider of technology solutions for the treatment of eye conditions. The company products include tango, eye one, eye cubed, tango reflex, and more.

Ellie Mae Inc   HQ
4420 Rosewood Dr Ste 500
Pleasanton CA 94588
P: 925-227-7000   F: 925-227-9030   PRC:322
www.elliemae.com
Email: info@elliemae.com
Estab: 1997
Sales: $300M to $1 Billion

Jonathan H. Corr, President & CEO
Limin Hu, EVP & CTO
Joe Tyrrell, COO
Dan Madden, EVP & CFO
Linh Lam, SVP & CIO

Focuses on mortgage compliance services. The company offers services to banks and other financial institutions.

Elliot Manufacturing   HQ
2664 S Cherry Ave
Fresno CA 93706
P: 559-233-6235   F: 559-233-9833   PRC:159
www.elliott-mfg.com
Email: elliottmfg@elliott-mfg.com
Estab: 1929

Mike Tilly, Sales Manager

Manufacturer of case erectors, case sealers, cartoners, and case packers. The company is engaged in sales and delivery services.

Ellison Fluid Systems Inc   HQ
23052H Alicia Pkwy Ste 395
Mission Viejo CA 92692
P: 877-339-3412   F: 909-906-1473   PRC:8
ellison-tbi.com
Email: info@ellison-fluid-systems.com

Ben Ellison, President

Provider of fluid systems that includes throttle body injector. The company offers fuel metering for aircrafts engines and throttle response.

ELMA Electronic Inc HQ
44350 S Grimmer Blvd
Fremont CA 94538
P: 510-656-3400 F: 510-656-3783 PRC:93
www.elma.com
Email: sales@elma.com
Estab: 1960

Urs Hess, VP of Information Technology
Peter Brunner, EVP of Finance & Administration
Badri Rajan, VP of Operations
Troy Lauritsen, Director of Enclosures & Components
Mostafa Gardizi, Regional Sales Manager

Designer and manufacturer of electronic components and enclosures. The company is involved in design, installation, and delivery services.

Elmech Inc HQ
195 San Pedro Ave [N]
Morgan Hill CA 95037
P: 408-782-2990 PRC:209
www.elmechinc.com
Emp: 51-200 Estab: 1980

Lori A. Balog, VP

Manufacturer of cables, harnesses, fan and power supply modification.

Elo Touch Solutions Inc HQ
670 N McCarthy Blvd
Milpitas CA 95035-7920
P: 408-597-8000 PRC:93
www.elotouch.com
Email: elosales.na@elotouch.com
Estab: 1971

Craig Witsoe, CEO
Jay Delatte, CFO
John Lamb, CMO
Chris Sullivan, SVP
Corbett Wood, VP

Designer, developer, and manufacturer of touch products and technologies. The company's products include tablets, touchscreens, and touch monitors.

Elucit Inc HQ
31575 Misty Ln
Fort Bragg CA 95437
P: 707-961-1016 PRC:323
www.elucit.com
Email: lee@elucit.com
Estab: 1999

Karthikeyan V, Assistant Manager

Provider of hardware and software development services. The company also offers data recorders and calibration services.

EM Lab P&K BR
880 Riverside Pkwy
West Sacramento CA 95605
P: 916-374-4483 F: 650-742-8191 PRC:139
emlab.com

Kamash Ramanathan, Regional Director
Amber Engle, Marketing Coordinator

Provider of indoor air quality testing services. The company offers culturable air fungi, spore trap analysis, and yeast identification services.

Emagined Security Inc HQ
2816 San Simeon Wy
San Carlos CA 94070
P: 415-944-2977 PRC:67
www.emagined.com
Email: info@emagined.com
Estab: 2002

David Sockol, CEO
Paul Underwood, COO
David Zuckerman, SVP of Sales & Marketing

Provider of professional services for information security solutions. The company also focuses on compliance.

Emanio Inc HQ
832 Bancroft Way
Berkeley CA 94710
P: 510-849-9300 F: 510-849-9302 PRC:323
www.emanio.com
Email: info@emanio.com
Estab: 1994

Knut Oygardslia, Chief Scientist

Developer of products for data management, dashboarding, and reporting and predictive analysis needs. The company focuses on consulting and training.

Embedur Systems Inc HQ
42808 Christy St Ste 102
Fremont CA 94538
P: 510-353-9111 F: 510-353-9986 PRC:71
embedur.com
Estab: 2004

Rajesh C. Subramaniam, CEO & Co-Founder
Samir Virmani, Co-Founder
Abhishek Sharma, VP of Engineering
Pervez Mohta, Director of Engineering
Rajas Mohile, Software Engineer

Developer of software solutions. The company also offers technical and management services for the embedded market.

Emboline Inc HQ
2811 Mission St
Santa Cruz CA 95060
P: 831-900-5020 F: 831-900-5019 PRC:189
emboline.com
Email: info@emboline.com
Estab: 2011

Scott Russell, CEO & President
Stephen Kleshinski, VP of Research & Development

Developer of cardiovascular embolic protection devices for transcatheter and surgical cardiac procedures.

EME Systems HQ
2229 Fifth St
Berkeley CA 94710
P: 510-848-5725 F: 510-848-5748 PRC:11
www.emesystems.com
Email: info@emesystems.com
Estab: 1985

Teri Piccolo, Owner
Thomas Tracy Allen, Founder
Tracy Allen, President

Designer and manufacturer of instruments for environmental science. The company also offers signal conditioners, sensors, enclosures, and batteries.

EMED HQ
1262 Hawks Flight Ct Ste 200
El Dorado Hills CA 95762
P: 916-932-0071 F: 916-932-0074 PRC:189
www.emedtc.com
Email: info@emedtc.com
Estab: 1990

Hoda Aref, Owner
E-Med Helathcare, CEO
Joseph Barbrie, VP of Sales & Marketing
Julie Schoenstadt, VP of Ad sales
Grace Yip, Sales Manager

Manufacturer of safety medical products and specialty medical devices with a focus on infusion therapy.

Emkay Manufacturing Inc HQ
815 Sweeney Ave Unit D
Redwood City CA 94063
P: 650-365-3010 F: 650-365-9135 PRC:80
www.emkaymfg.com
Estab: 1978

Anne Feher, Owner

Provider of precision milling and turning services. The company serves the medical, electrical, aerospace, and defense sectors.

Emlinux HQ
1240 McKendrie St
San Jose CA 95126-1408
P: 408-249-5574 PRC:224
www.emlinux.com
Email: sales@emlinux.com
Estab: 1999

Joel Williams, Principal Owner & Engineer

Developer of embedded Linux designs. The company provides marketing level definition and system architecture services.

Emotiv HQ
490 Post St Ste 824
San Francisco CA 94102
P: 415-801-0400 PRC:209
emotiv.com
Estab: 2011

Tan Le, Founder & CEO

Provider of neuroengineering products and services. The company offers algorithms to detect subconscious emotional states and facial expressions.

Emotive Brand HQ
580 Second St Ste 245
Oakland CA 94607
P: 510-496-8888 PRC:45
www.emotivebrand.com
Estab: 2009

Tracy Lloyd, Co-Founder & Chief Strategy Officer
Bella Banbury, Co-Founder & CEO
Giovanna Keren, Director of Strategy
Jonathan Fisher, Director of Production
Robert Saywitz, Design Director

Brand strategy and design firm that helps to transform the businesses.

Empire Magnetics Inc HQ
5830 Commerce Blvd
Rohnert Park CA 94928
P: 707-584-2801 F: 707-584-3418 PRC:292
www.empiremagnetics.com
Email: sales@empiremagnetics.com
Estab: 1987

Rick Halstead, President

Manufacturer of specialty, cryogenic, dust proof, high temperature, water proof, and radiation hardened motors.

Empire West Inc HQ
PO Box 511
Graton CA 95444
P: 707-823-1190 F: 707-823-8531 PRC:284
www.empirewest.com
Email: info@empirewest.com
Estab: 1968

Ed Davis, President
Rich Yonash, CEO
Sonya Yonash, Controller
Susan Skocypec, Web Developer & Web Developer

Designer and developer of envelope handling trays, custom thermoformed ceiling tiles and panels, and optic packaging solutions.

EMSL Analytical Inc BR
464 McCormick St
San Leandro CA 94577
P: 510-895-3675 F: 510-895-3680 PRC:18
www.emsl.com
Email: sanleandrolab@emsl.com
Estab: 1981

Peter Frasca, President
Ron Smith, VP of Sales

Provider of laboratory analytical testing services. The company specializes in a wide range of environmental, material and forensic testing.

Emtec Engineering HQ
16840 Joleen Way Bldg F1
Morgan Hill CA 95037
P: 408-779-5800 F: 408-778-2850 PRC:80
www.emtec.cc
Email: info@emtec.cc
Estab: 1987

Chris Fontaine, President

Provider of precision machining and precision sheet metal fabrication services to the computer, telecommunication, and medical industries.

Emtrain HQ
2 Embarcadero 9th Fl
San Francisco CA 94111
P: 916-481-7474 F: 866-513-7171 PRC:326
emtrain.com
Estab: 2000

Janine Yancey, CEO & Founder
Robert Todd, Chief Product Officer
Hennie Farrow, VP of Design & UX
Bob Benedict, VP of Engineering
Scott Barbour, VP of Sales & Strategy

Provider of learning management system such as online training platform for all levels of HR professionals, trainers, and administrators.

Enablence Technologies Inc DH
2933 Bayview Dr
Fremont CA 94538
P: 510-226-8900 F: 510-226-8333 PRC:64
www.enablence.com
Email: info@enablence.com
Sales: $1M to $3M

Jacob Sun, President
Tao Zhang, CFO

Manufacturer of silicon products for communication needs. The company's offerings include optical splitters and channel filters.

Encore Industries Inc HQ
597 Brennan St
San Jose CA 95131-1202
P: 408-416-0501 F: 408-416-0511 PRC:80
www.encoreindustries.com
Estab: 1997

Mark Hacker, President & CEO

Provider of technical services to engineering and procurement. The company's domain includes medical and science, consumer products, and structural.

Endicia HQ
278 Castro St
Mountain View CA 94041-1204
P: 800-576-3279 F: 650-321-0356 PRC:323
www.endicia.com
Email: support@endicia.com
Estab: 1989

Harry Whitehouse, CTO
Amino Khoohfo, General Manager
Emma Johnson, Director of Marketing
Jeanney Kim, Product Marketing Manager
Loryll DeNamur, Associate Manager of Public Relations & Marketing Content

Provider of electronic postage software solutions and offers shipping and mailing services to online sellers, warehouse shippers, and office mailers.

Endo Gastric Solutions Inc HQ
1900 Ofarrell St Ste 235
San Mateo CA 94403
P: 650-578-5100 F: 650-578-5101 PRC:188
endogastricsolutions.com
Email: info@endogastricsolutions.com
Estab: 2003

Skip Baldino, President & CEO
Michael Burke, CFO
Adrian Lobontiu, CMO
Darren Crow, VP & R&D of Operations
Martin Reid, VP of Sales

Provider of treatment services for gastroesophageal reflux disease. The company also focuses on training and education.

Endologix Inc HQ
3910 Brickway Blvd
Santa Rosa CA 95403
P: 707-543-8800 F: 855-569-7763 PRC:189
www.trivascular.com
Email: customerservice@trivascular.com
Estab: 1999

Dan Lemaitre, Chairman
John Onopchenko, CEO
Matthew Thompson, CMO
Reyna Fernandez, Chief Human Resource Officer
Jeff Brown, COO

Developer of endovascular grafts for the treatment of aneurysmal disease in the abdominal aorta and the thoracic aorta.

Endpoint Clinical Inc HQ
55 Francisco St Ste 200
San Francisco CA 94133
P: 415-229-1600 PRC:194
www.endpointclinical.com
Email: info@endpointclinical.com
Estab: 2009

Christine Oliver, CEO
Ryan Harrison, Director of Business Development

Designer of response technology platforms to access data through phones, the web, and mobile devices. The company is engaged in engineering services.

Enea Openwave Inc DH
400 Seaport Ct Ste 104
Redwood City CA 94063
P: 650-480-7200 PRC:322
owmobility.com
Email: info@owmobility.com

John Giere, CEO
Indranil Chatterjee, VP of Products Sales & Marketing

Provider of mobile media optimization solutions. The company is engaged in the mediation of encrypted traffic streams.

Enel X e-Mobility HQ
846 Bransten Rd
San Carlos CA 94070
P: 844-584-2329 PRC:209
emotorwerks.com
Estab: 2010

Val Miftakhov, CEO
Alexander Gurzhi, Chief Software Architect of Cloud
Vincent Schachter, SVP of Energy Services
Daniel Feldman, VP of Product Management
Vinay Krishnan, VP of Embedded Systems

Developer of electric vehicle charging technologies such as smart grid EV charging networks for residential, workplace, and commercial installation.

Energous Corp HQ
3590 N First St Ste 210
San Jose CA 95134
P: 408-963-0200 PRC:288
www.energous.com
Estab: 2012
Sales: Under $1 Million

Stephen R. Rizzone, President & CEO & Director
Cesar Johnston, COO
Howard Yeaton, Interim CFO
Brian Sereda, SVP
Gordon Bell, VP of Marketing

Provider of energy solutions. The company offers a wire-free charging system for portable electronic devices.

Energy Recovery HQ
1717 Doolittle Dr
San Leandro CA 94577
P: 510-483-7370   F: 510-483-7371   PRC:134
www.energyrecovery.com
Email: support@energyrecovery.com
Estab: 1992
Sales: $30M to $100M

Robert Mao, Chairman of the Board of Directors &
President & CEO
Farshad Ghasripoor, CTO
Joshua Ballard, CFO
David Barnes, CSO
Audrey Bold, CMO

Manufacturer of energy recovery devices. The
company offers pressure exchangers, chargers,
pumps for desalination processes, oil and gas
applications.

energyOrbit Inc HQ
1 Market St Spear Twr Ste 3600
San Francisco CA 94105
P: 866-628-8744   PRC:322
energy-orbit.com
Estab: 2007

Udi Merhav, CEO & Founder
Alex Zeltser, CTO
John Fruin, CFO
Jim Murray, VP of Professional Services
Jason Adge, VP of Business Development

Provider of cloud based platform and solution for
streamline demand side management programs,
projects, and relationship management for customers.

Enerparc Inc DH
1999 Harrison St Ste 830
Oakland CA 94612
P: 844-367-7272   PRC:135
www.enerparc.de
Email: info@enerparc.us
Estab: 2008

Florent Abadie, CEO
Donald Miller, General Counsel of Americas &
Director of Project Finance
Nikolaus Mainka, Associate Director of Finance
Thomas Houghton, Director of Engineering &
Construction
Patrick Schaufelberger, Associate Director of
Project Finance

Developer and designer of photovoltaic systems.
The company services include EPC work, EPC
management, operation, and maintenance.

Eneura Inc HQ
715 N Pastoria Ave
Sunnyvale CA 94085
P: 408-245-6400   F: 408-245-6424   PRC:186
www.eneura.com
Estab: 2000

Terese Baker, President
Donald Pearl, CEO
Vince Nguyen, Senior Director of Operations
Tom Brooks, Venture Partner of Camden Partners
Nexus
Jacob Vogelstein, Partner & Portfolio Manager &
Camden Partners Holdings

Provider of medical technology solutions. The
company offers transcranial magnetic stimulation
devices for the treatment of migraine.

M-114

Enfos Inc HQ
2929 Campus Dr Ste 415
San Mateo CA 94403
P: 650-357-0007   PRC:325
enfos.com
Email: sales@enfos.com
Estab: 2000

Craig Modesitt, CEO
Roger Well, COO
Sandeep Digra, CTO
Ryan Eric Well, Manager of Asia Region

Provider of business software solutions for environmental management. The company specializes
in financial, compliance, and GIS data management.

Engage Communication Inc HQ
9565 Soquel Dr
Aptos CA 95003
P: 831-688-1021   F: 831-688-1421   PRC:97
www.engageinc.com
Email: sales@engageinc.com
Estab: 1989

Mark Doyle, CEO & President
Steve Corriveau, Technical Sales Engineer

Developer and manufacturer of telecommunications equipment. The company focuses on encryption, mobile, and cellular backhauling solutions.

Engagio Inc HQ
181 Second Ave Ste 200
San Mateo CA 94401
P: 650-487-2050   PRC:315
www.engagio.com
Email: sales@engagio.com
Estab: 2015

Jon Miller, Co-Founder & CEO
Brian Babcock, Co-Founder & CTO
Cheryl Chavez, Chief Product Officer
Megan Heuer, VP of Marketing
Inger Rarick, VP of Customer Experience

B2B Marketing Engagement Software that enables marketers and sellers to work as a team.

Engineering By Design HQ
2157-G O'Toole Ave Ste 40
San Jose CA 95131
P: 408-324-1500   F: 408-324-1501   PRC:159
www.ebdesign.com
Email: info@ebdesign.com
Estab: 1985

Dale Henson, President & Founder
Judy Henson, CFO

Provider of engineering and support services. The
company's products include laminators, coil and
fiber winders, motors, and extrusion pullers.

Engineering Design Industries Inc HQ
9649 E Rush St   [N]
South El Monte CA 91733
P: 626-443-7741   F: 626-443-9651   PRC:80
www.edimfg.com
Email: sales@edimfg.com
Estab: 1988

Loc Tran, CEO
Oscar Flores, Contact
Duc Le, Contact

Manufacturer and distributor of industrial machines.

**Engineering/Remediation Resources
Group Inc** HQ
4585 Pacheco Blvd Ste 200   [N]
Martinez CA 94553
P: 925-969-0750   F: 925-969-0751   PRC:304
www.errg.com
Emp: 201-500   Estab: 1997

Brad Hall, CTO & VP
Brad Kordic, VP of Business Development
Doug Bielskis, Regional Manager
Rowan Tucker, Manager
David Tang, Principal

Provider of construction engineering and construction material testing services and environmental and remediation construction including
contaminated soil excavation, landfill capping
and closure, storage tank removal and slope
stabilization and hazardous waste transportation,
decontamination, and disposal.

Enlighta HQ
111 Deerwood Rd Ste 200
San Ramon CA 94583
P: 510-279-5820   PRC:326
www.enlighta.com
Email: info@enlighta.com
Estab: 2002

Gaurav Bhatia, Manager
Callistus Chui, Lead Technologist of User Experience

Provider of software solutions to service organizations grappling with governance and management
of global services delivery.

Enlighted Inc HQ
3979 Freedom Cir Ste 210
Santa Clara CA 95054
P: 650-964-1094   PRC:130
www.enlightedinc.com
Email: sales@enlightedinc.com
Estab: 2009

Tanuj Mohan, Founder & CTO & Chief Product
Officer
Joe Costello, CEO
Ramki Ramakrishnan, COO
Dirk Rauber, CFO
Stan Shparberg, EVP of Sales

Provider of lighting control systems to commercial buildings, office workspaces, and garages.
The company serves facilities and development
companies.

Enocean Alliance Inc   HQ
5000 Executive Pkwy Ste 302
San Ramon CA 94583
P: 925-275-6601   PRC:227
www.enocean-alliance.org
Email: info@enocean-alliance.org
Estab: 2008

Graham Martin, CEO & Chairman

Manufacturer of wireless switches, sensors, and controls for building automation and residential property needs.

Enovity Inc   HQ
100 Montgomery St Ste 600   [N]
San Francisco CA 94104
P: 415-974-0390   F: 415-974-0399   PRC:304
enovity.com
Emp: 51-200   Estab: 2002

Dan Morelock, Technical Manager
Stephen Casey, Manager of Engineering
Zhan Wang, Technical Manager
Greg Cunningham, Principal
Jonathan Soper, Principal

Designer and developer of building facilities.

Enphase Energy Inc   HQ
1420 N McDowell Blvd
Petaluma CA 94954
P: 877-797-4743   PRC:151
enphase.com
Estab: 2006
Sales: $300M to $1 Billion

Martin Fornage, Co-Founder & CTO
Raghu Belur, Co-Founder & Chief Products Officer
Badri Kothandaraman, CEO
Bill Rossi, CMO
Eric Branderiz, CFO

Distributor of electronic products. The company offers services to the solar, telecom, networking, and software industries.

Enplan   HQ
3179 Bechelli Ln Ste 100
Redding CA 96002
P: 530-221-0440   PRC:142
enplan.com
Estab: 1980

Femi Sonuga, President
Randall Hauser, CEO

Provider of environmental and geospatial technology services. The company focuses on wetland delineation and permit processing activities.

Enplas Tech Solutions Inc   RH
3211 Scott Blvd Ste 103
Santa Clara CA 95054
P: 669-243-3600   F: 669-243-3696   PRC:86
enplas.co.jp
Email: info@enplas-ets.com
Estab: 1993

Jaime Bernal, Coordinator of Sales Administration

Distributor of engineering plastic products. The company also offers optical devices, semiconductor peripherals, and related supplies.

Enpro Solutions Inc   HQ
6500 Dublin Blvd Ste 215
Dublin CA 94568-3152
P: 925-803-8045   PRC:142
enprosolutionsinc.com
Estab: 1998

R. Maqbool Qadir, Principal & Founder

Provider of environmental remediation, management, permitting, and construction services. The company also deals with process safety consulting.

Ens Technology LLC   HQ
3145 & 3165 Molinaro St
Santa Clara CA 95054-2424
P: 408-496-0740   PRC:280
www.enstechnology.com
Estab: 1970

Brett Dawson, President
Leo Baltazar, Operations Manager

Provider of plating services. The company plates materials such as common metals, alloys, and refractory metals.

Ensemble Designs Inc   HQ
PO Box 993
Grass Valley CA 95945
P: 530-478-1830   F: 530-478-1832   PRC:60
www.ensembledesigns.com
Email: info@ensembledesigns.com
Estab: 1989

David Wood, President
Mondae Hott, Director of Sales
Deb Locker, Shipping Manager
Michael Sauter, Customer Service Manager
Cindy Zuelsdorf, Marketing Manager

Manufacturer of audio embedders, video converters, routers, and related products. The company serves post production, education, and other sectors.

Ensenta Corp   HQ
303 Twin Dolphin Dr Ste 201
Redwood Shores CA 94065
P: 866-219-4321   PRC:323
www.ensenta.com
Email: support@ensenta.com
Estab: 2001

Morgan Wilson, System Administrator

Developer of software solutions. The company is involved in development of cloud-based imaging and self-service technology.

ENT Networks Inc   HQ
240 Spring St Ste A
Pleasanton CA 94566
P: 925-462-7125   PRC:326
www.entnetworks.com
Email: info@entnetworks.com
Estab: 1985

Billy Buckley, CEO
Theresa Buckley, Office Manager
Emilio Martin, Network Engineer

Provider of custom system manufacturing, database management, hardware sales, business consulting, and repair services.

Entech Electronics   BR
5201 Great America Pkwy Ste 320
Santa Clara CA 95054
P: 408-730-2650   F: 408-562-5745   PRC:91
entechelectronics.us
Email: service@entechelectronics.us

Wayne Hoffman, CEO
Jason Reeves, Global Sales & Marketing Manager

Supplier of electronic equipment. The company also offers laser cut stencils, graphic decals, LCD screens, and engineering services.

Envestnet   BR
160 W Santa Clara Ste 850
San Jose CA 95113
P: 866-924-8912   F: 408-962-7850   PRC:322
www.envestnet.com
Email: marketing@envestnet.com
Estab: 1999

James Lumberg, Founder & EVP
Babu Sivadasan, Group President
Bill Parsons, Group President Data Analytics & International Operations
Frank Coates, Executive Managing Director Group President Envestnet Analytics
Bill Crager, Interim CEO

Provider of application software for financial service firms. The company is involved in practice and portfolio management.

Enview Inc   HQ
164 Townsend St Unit 11
San Francisco CA 94107
P: 415-483-5680   PRC:323
enview.com
Estab: 2015

Krassimir Piperkov, Co-Founder & COO
San Gunawardana, Co-Founder & CEO
Eleanor Crane, CTO
Damond Hedley, Senior Director of Engineering
Brendan Ray, Director of Business Development

Specializes in threat prevention systems. The company deals with data analytics and remote sensing services.

Enviro Safetech Inc   HQ
2160 B Oakland Rd
San Jose CA 95131
P: 408-943-9090   F: 408-943-9292   PRC:136
envirosafetech.com
Email: info@envirosafetech.com
Estab: 1990

Jay Jamali, Environmental Health & Safety Director

Provider of environmental, health, and safety consulting services. The company deals with auditing and inspections.

Enviro Survey Inc   HQ
82 Mary St
San Francisco CA 94103
P: 415-882-4549   F: 415-882-1685   PRC:142
envirosurvey.net
Estab: 1991

Alex Zebarjadian, President
Mahsa Hakimi, Contact

Provider of environmental consulting and technical services. The company provides soil and groundwater remediation and environmental safety services.

Enviro Tech Chemicals Inc HQ
500 Winmoore Way
Modesto CA 95358
P: 209-581-9576   F: 209-581-9653   PRC:51
www.envirotech.com
Email: customerservice@envirotech.com
Estab: 1991

Mike Harvey, President & CEO
Brent Bankosky, COO
Jon Howarth, SVP of Technology
Steve Jacobs, VP of Sales
Joseph E. Donabed, Director of Research & Business Development

Manufacturer of peracetic acid. The company focuses on the development of EPA and FDA regulated chemistries and novel solutions.

Enviro-Tech Services Co HQ
4851 Sunrise Dr Ste 101
Martinez CA 94553
P: 800-468-8921   F: 925-370-8037   PRC:138
envirotechonline.com
Estab: 1987

Fred Ousey, Owner
Charles Lawton, President
Steve Jacobs, VP of Sales
Sue Koepp-Baker, Principal

Designer and manufacturer of environmental products. The company offers water sampling equipment, air monitoring equipment, and general field supplies.

Envirocare International HQ
507 Green Island Rd
American Canyon CA 94503
P: 707-638-6800   F: 707-638-6898   PRC:151
www.envirocare.com
Email: info@envirocare.com
Estab: 1980

John Tate, Owner
Reid Thomas, Manager of Parts & Service
Jim Whitten, Project Engineer
John Fosgate, Project Engineer

Designer of pollution control appliances. The company also specializes in manufacturing gas cooling and gas conditioning systems.

EnviroKinetics Inc HQ
101 S Milliken Ave   [N]
Ontario CA 91761
P: 909-621-7599   F: 909-621-7899   PRC:45
www.envirokinetics.com
Email: sales@envirokinetics.com
Estab: 2001

James Mosley, Owner & CEO
Cheryl Fogarty, VP & Purchasing & Admin
Don Turner, Director of Business Development
Shannon Homan, Coordinator
Michael Payne, Electronic Tech

Manufacturer and supplier of excellent equipment and engineering services such as incinerators for gases and liquids with or without waste heat recovery, SCR systems for NOx reduction, catalytic oxidation, and scrubbers for entrained solids and contaminant gases and manufactures burner management systems and other skid-mounted instrument and control systems.

Environmental Incentives LLC HQ
3351 Lake Tahoe Blvd Ste 2
South Lake Tahoe CA 96150
P: 530-541-2980   PRC:142
enviroincentives.com
Email: info@enviroincentives.com
Estab: 2004

Jeremy Sokulsky, CEO
Andrew Alexandrovich, Director of Finance & Operations
Chad Praul, Partner
Eoin Doherty, Senior Associate
Katie Riley, Senior Associate

Provider of environmental conservation services. The company projects include Nevada conservation credit system and Colorado habitat exchange.

Environmental Micro Analysis Inc HQ
460 N East St
Woodland CA 95776
P: 530-666-6890   F: 530-666-2987   PRC:306
emalab.com
Email: customerservice@emalab.com

Hardik Amin, Senior Chemist

Provider of food safety consulting services. The company specializes in pesticide residue analysis in agricultural products, processed foods and other matrices.

Environmental Products & Technologies Corp HQ
4216 S Mooney Blvd Ste 131
Visalia CA 93277
P: 559-201-6484   PRC:140
www.eptcorp.com
Estab: 1983

Marvin Mears, President & CEO
John F Graham, Chief Knowledge Officer
Bruce Andersen, VP of Administration
Scott Mears, VP of Marketing & Corporate Secretary
Kris Schulthies, VP of Field Operations

Developer of closed-loop, short hydraulic retention time anaerobic digesters. The company specializes in biogas technology solutions.

Environmental Remedies Inc HQ
1999 Alpine Way
Hayward CA 94545
P: 925-461-3285   PRC:142
environmentalremediesinc.com
Email: Info@environmentalremediesinc.com
Estab: 2004

Jaime Tamayo, Owner
Melisa Christensen, Project Coordinator

Provider of asbestos abatement services. The company engages in mold remediation, lead removal, and biological containment radiation service.

Environmental Risk Communications Inc BR
2121 Tunnel Rd
Oakland CA 94611
P: 510-548-5570   PRC:139
erci.com
Email: info@erci.com
Estab: 1994

John Rosengard, President

Provider of consulting services in environmental liabilities management. The company's services include site strategic planning and project controls.

Environmental Sampling Services LLC HQ
6680 Alhambra Ave Ste 102
Martinez CA 94553
P: 925-372-8108   PRC:142
www.envsampling.com

Stephen Penman, Manager

Provider of technical services for environmental assessments needs. The company also focuses on investigation and remediation.

Environmental Science Associates HQ
550 Kearny St Ste 800
San Francisco CA 94108
P: 415-896-5900   PRC:139
www.esassoc.com
Estab: 1969

Albert Cuisinot, CFO
Deanna Hansen, VP
Annette Bonilla, Director of Human Resources
Jill Hamilton, Director
Adrian M. Jones, Director

Provider of restoration and mitigation, regulatory permitting, compliance monitoring, and community planning services.

Environmental Stress Systems Inc HQ
21089 Longeway Rd
Sonora CA 95370
P: 209-588-1993   F: 209-588-1997   PRC:153
www.essproducts.com
Email: ess@essproducts.com
Estab: 1989

Neil Johnson, Machinist & Production Leader

Manufacturer of mechanically refrigerated, cryogenically cooled, and liquid cooled thermal platforms.

Eon Technologies Inc HQ
1226 Lincoln Ave
Alameda CA 94501
P: 510-523-3832   PRC:40
eontech.com
Email: support@eontech.com
Estab: 1990

Robert Cullmann, CEO

Provider of IT and computer support services. The company's services include malware and virus removal tools and printer repair services.

EoPlex Inc   BR
1925 Zanker Rd
San Jose CA 95112
P: 408-638-5100   F: 408-638-5101   PRC:203
www.eoplex.com
Email: info@eoplex.com
Estab: 2001

Ali Modjtahedi, Engineer

Creator of HVAM technology and process for
advanced 3D-printed components for mobile
devices, IoT, automotive, medical, and wearable
applications.

Epiphotonics Corp   HQ
832 Jury Ct Unit 3
San Jose CA 95112
P: 408-920-7019   F: 408-920-7021   PRC:124
www.epiphotonics.com
Email: info@epiphotonics.com
Estab: 2007

Keiichi Nashimoto, President & CEO

Manufacturer of photonic components and
subsystems. The company is engaged in design,
delivery, and installation services.

EPIX Orthopaedics Inc   HQ
445 Lambert Ave
Palo Alto CA 94306
P: 844-710-9105   PRC:190
epixortho.com
Email: info@epixortho.com

Amir Matityahu, Founder
Ben Clawson, Consultant & CTO
Debra Matityahu, Director

Developer of orthopaedic devices that improve
patient outcomes, surgeon accuracy and efficiency, and reduce costs to patients and health care
system.

Epsilon Strategic Systems   HQ
Saint Mathew Sta
San Mateo CA 94401
P: 650-579-5515   PRC:45
www.epsilon-systems.com
Email: sales@epsilon-systems.com
Estab: 1988

Roy Erickson, President

Provider of management consulting and information technology services. The company offers
customization, advisory, and staff development
services.

Epylon Corp   HQ
630 San Ramon Valley Blvd Ste 210
Danville CA 94526
P: 925-407-1020   F: 925-407-1021   PRC:323
www.epylon.com
Email: service@epylon.com
Estab: 1999

Kelly Blanton, Owner
Tim Blanton, CEO & President
Ted Witt, VP of Strategic Sourcing
Howard Chung, IT Manager

Developer of e-procurement software and services. The company serves the government and
education sectors.

Equilar Inc   HQ
1100 Marshall St
Redwood City CA 94063
P: 877-441-6090   PRC:319
www.equilar.com
Email: info@equilar.com
Estab: 2001

David Chun, CEO & Co-Founder
Steven Borden, Co-Founder & President
Lanny Baker, CFO
Julie Fletcher, Chief Talent Officer
Michele Lau, SVP of Corporate Secretary &
Associate GC

Developer of industry-leading data and tools for
public and private companies, compensation
consultants, attorneys, and corporate governance
leaders.

Equinix   HQ
1 Lagoon Dr 4th Fl
Redwood City CA 94065
P: 866-378-4649   F: 650-598-6900   PRC:324
equinix.com
Email: info@equinix.com
Estab: 1998
Sales: $300M to $1 Billion

Charles J. Meyers, President & CEO
Karl Strohmeyer, President of Americas
Peter F. Van Camp, Executive Chairman
Keith D. Taylor, CFO
Ihab Tarazi, CTO

Provider of interconnection data center and global
colocation services focusing on cloud, business
continuity, financial, and digital media.

Equipment Solutions Inc   HQ
1098 W Evelyn Ave Ste 102
Sunnyvale CA 94086
P: 408-245-7162   F: 408-245-7160   PRC:176
equipsolutions.com
Email: info@equipsolutions.com
Estab: 1990

Jeff Knirck, CEO

Manufacturer and provider of actuators and motion control systems. The company offers optical
scanners, servo amplifiers, and digital autocolli-
mators.

Ergo Direct Com   HQ
1601 Old County Rd
San Carlos CA 94070
P: 650-654-4300   PRC:60
ergodirect.com
Email: customerservice@ergodirect.com

Nick Moshiri, Founder

Provider of adjustable desks, arms, and mounts.
The company offers ergonomic keyboards, monitor arms, and mounting adapters.

Eritech International   HQ
1515 W Glenoaks Blvd   [N]
Glendale CA 91201
P: 818-244-6242   F: 818-500-7699   PRC:322
www.eritech.com
Email: sales@eritech.com
Estab: 1994

Andranik Issagholian, CEO & CFO & Secretary &
Director

Wholesaler of computer hardware, digital cameras
and TVs.

Errigal Inc   HQ
3 Embarcadero Ctr Ste 1440
San Francisco CA 94111
P: 415-523-9245   PRC:322
errigal.com
Email: sales@errigal.com
Estab: 1996

Padraig Tobin, Founder & CEO
Patrick Gary, Customer Operations Project
Manager
Shea Lawrence, Software Engineer

Designer and developer of software products and
services. The company also deals with configuration management and ticketing.

Erthbound Entertainment Inc   HQ
PO Box 40011   [N]
Studio City CA 91614
P: 818-884-3033   F: 818-376-1042   PRC:60
www.erthbound.com
Estab: 1998

Jeffrey Willerth, President

Publisher of racing school directory, as well as
CD-ROMs, DVDs and software titles.

Escalera Inc   HQ
PO Box 1359
Yuba City CA 95992
P: 530-673-6318   F: 530-673-6376   PRC:180
www.escalera.com
Email: info@escalera.com
Estab: 1968

Bryan Miller, Sales Manager

Manufacturer of stair climbing trucks. The company's products include forklifts, handtrucks, and
load movers.

Escend Pharmaceuticals Inc   HQ
3475 Edison Way Ste R
Menlo Park CA 94025
P: 650-241-9128   PRC:268
www.escendpharma.com
Email: info@escendpharma.com
Estab: 1997

Dennis Brown, Co-Founder
Saira Bates, Co-Founder & CEO

Provider of therapeutic solutions. The company
focuses on cancer stem cells in acute myeloge-
nous leukemia and hematologic malignancies for
drug development.

Ese Consulting Engineers Inc　　　　HQ
　1060 Grant St Ste 3D
　Benicia CA 94510
P: 707-747-1755　F: 707-747-6538　　PRC:304
eseweb.com
Email: mail@eseweb.com
Estab: 1988

Hadieh Elias, President
Amir Firouz, VP

Provider of structural engineering design, seismic analysis and retrofitting, and peer review services.

eShares Inc　　　　HQ
　333 Bush St 23rd Fl Ste 2300
　San Francisco CA 94104
P: 650-669-8381　　　PRC:325
carta.com
Email: support@carta.com
Estab: 2012

Henry Ward, CEO
Charly Kevers, CFO
Jerry Talton, CTO
Sumeet Gajri, CSO

Specializes in capitalization table management and valuation software.

ESI Bio　　　　HQ
　1010 Atlantic Ave Ste 102
　Alameda CA 94501
P: 510-521-3390　F: 510-648-3255　　PRC:34
www.esibio.com
Email: orders@esibio.com
Estab: 2000

Jeffrey Janus, CEO

Provider of stem cell solutions. The company's products are used in bioprinting, stem cell analysis, and stem cell reprogramming.

ESOP Services Inc　　　　BR
　PO Box 420563　　　[N]
　San Diego CA 92142
P: 858-292-4819　　　PRC:45
www.esopservices.com

Ronald J. Gilbert, President & Founder

Provider of preliminary assessments, decision package, and turnkey implementation solutions.

Esp Interactive Solutions Inc　　　　HQ
　1223 Solano Ave Ste 8
　Albany CA 94706
P: 510-526-2592　F: 510-526-2692　　PRC:325
www.espinteractivesolutions.com
Email: info@espis.com
Estab: 2001

Tariq Khan, President & CEO
Salman Sethi, Manager of Business Development

Provider of web design and development services such as web video creation, content management system, and social networks marketing.

M-118

Esp Safety Inc　　　　HQ
　555 N First St
　San Jose CA 95112
P: 408-886-9746　　　PRC:13
www.espsafetyinc.com
Email: info@espsafetyinc.com
Estab: 1973

Frank Paulsen, Sales Manager
Fabian Martinez, Applications Engineer

Manufacturer of combustible gas and flame detectors, test lamps, and multi-channel controllers for custom applications.

ESS Technology Inc　　　　HQ
　237 South Hillview Dr
　Milpitas CA 95035
P: 408-643-8800　F: 408-643-8801　　PRC:60
www.esstech.com
Estab: 1984

Bob Blair, CEO
Dan Christman, VP & CMO
John Marsh, CFO
Patrick Yeto, VP of Operations
Duat Tran, Director of Hardware Engineering

Designer and marketer of video and audio semiconductors for the home, automotive, and entertainment markers.

Essai Inc　　　　HQ
　48580 Kato Rd
　Fremont CA 94538
P: 510-580-1700　F: 510-580-1810　　PRC:209
essai.com
Email: info@essai.com
Estab: 2003

Linh Nguyen, Manager of Purchasing
Kurt Sanfilippo, Manufacturing Manager
Kristina Ngo, Junior Buyer

Provider of engineering services. The company provides solutions for the semiconductors, telecom, computer components, and automotive sectors.

ET Solar Inc　　　　DH
　4900 Hopyard Rd Ste 290
　Pleasanton CA 94588
P: 925-460-9898　F: 925-460-9929　　PRC:135
www.etsolar.com
Email: sales@etsolar.com
Estab: 2005

May Khasem, Director of Operations

Provider of solar inverters and modules. The company offers design, installation, maintenance, and repair services.

ETA-USA　　　　HQ
　16170 Vineyard Blvd Ste 180
　Morgan Hill CA 95037
P: 408-778-2793　F: 408-779-2753　　PRC:98
www.eta-usa.com
Email: sales@eta-usa.com
Estab: 1994

Amir Safakish, President
Phil Silverstein, Chief Engineer
Dave Lemberger, VP of Sales
Nari Safa, Web Manager
Sousan Manteghi-Safakish, Manager

Provider of power supplies and manufacturer of battery chargers. The company serves the communication, gaming, and computing industries.

Ethylene Control Inc　　　　HQ
　8232 E Dinuba Ave
　Selma CA 93662
P: 559-896-1909　　　PRC:53
www.ethylenecontrol.com
Email: info@ethylenecontrol.com
Estab: 1986

Dave Biswell, General Manager of Sales
Norma Hollnagel, Production Manager

Manufacturer of ethylene and gas removal products. The company's products include filters, filtration systems, and sachets.

Etm Electromatic Inc　　　　HQ
　35451 Dumbarton Ct
　Newark CA 94560
P: 510-797-1100　F: 510-797-4358　　PRC:138
www.etm-inc.com
Email: supportetm@etm-inc.com
Estab: 1973

Tom Hayse, CEO & Chairman
John Capovilla, Vice-Chairman & Executive Advisor
Ryan Pollace, VP of High Power Microwave
Bill Nighan, VP of High Energy X-Ray
Ramesh Garg, VP of Supply Chain

Manufacturer of custom high voltage power supplies and amplifiers. The company is engaged in troubleshooting, repairs, and maintenance services.

Eton Corp　　　　HQ
　1015 Corporation Way
　Palo Alto CA 94303
P: 650-903-3866　F: 650-903-3867　　PRC:209
www.etoncorp.com
Email: info@etoncorp.com
Estab: 1986

John R. Smith, COO

Manufacturer of solar energy products. The company offers products for weather alert radios, backup battery packs, and sound systems.

Etouch Systems Corp　　　　BR
　6627 Dumbarton Cir
　Fremont CA 94555
P: 510-795-4800　F: 510-795-4803　　PRC:323
www.virtusa.com
Estab: 1998

Kris Canekeratne, Chairman & CEO
Samir Dhir, President & Head of Americas
Sundararajan Narayanan, EVP & CPO
Madu Ratnayake, EVP & CIO & GM
Ranjan Kalia, EVP & CFO

Provider of design web engineering services. The company focuses on business process management and enterprise application integration services.

Etrigue Corp HQ
6399 San Ignacio Ave 2nd Fl
San Jose CA 95119
P: 408-490-2900   F: 408-490-2901   PRC:326
www.etrigue.com
Estab: 2005

Jim Meyer, VP & General Manager
David Drach, Director IT SaaS Operations
Ewing Clay Parton, Technical Lead

Provider of marketing automation solutions such
as email marketing, event management, derived
data, 3-D leading scoring, and marketing database management.

Etron Technology America Inc RH
3375 Scott Blvd Ste 128
Santa Clara CA 95054
P: 408-987-2255   F: 408-987-2250   PRC:208
etronamerica.com
Email: invest@etron.com
Estab: 1991

Nicky Lu, CEO & Chairman

Provider of integrated circuits for applications,
such as storage device, display, handset, PDA,
and multimedia device.

ETS Laboratories HQ
899 Adams St Ste A
St. Helena CA 94574
P: 707-963-4806   F: 707-963-1054   PRC:306
www.etslabs.com
Email: info@etslabs.com
Estab: 1978

Gordon Burns, Founder & Technical Director
Jim Welsh, IT Director
Sedonia Yoshida, Team Lead
Kingsley Burns, Business Analyst
John Masyczek, Logistics Specialist

Specializes in analytical tools. The company
focuses on export analysis, harvest, and fuel
ethanol services.

Ettus Research LLC DH
4600 Patrick Henry Dr
Santa Clara CA 95054
P: 408-610-6399   PRC:63
www.ettus.com
Estab: 2004

Michael West, Senior Software Design Engineer

Provider of software defined radio systems for
research, academic, industrial, and defense
applications.

Eureka Chemical Co HQ
234 Lawrence Ave
S San Francisco CA 94080
P: 650-761-3536   F: 650-589-1943   PRC:52
www.fluid-film.com
Email: info@fluid-film.com
Estab: 1953

Gen Hess, President
James Crosby, Sales & Marketing Manager

Provider of corrosion control services. The company is involved in creating products that offers
corrosion protection and lubrication for all metals.

Eurofins E&E North America BR
3162 Belick St
Santa Clara CA 95054
P: 408-748-3585   F: 510-489-6372   PRC:306
www.metlabs.com
Email: info@metlabs.com
Estab: 1959

Asad Bajwa, Director of EMC Lab
Camilo Obana, EMC Technical Manager
Lauren Foster, Project Engineer
Randy Hoopai, EMC Engineer

Provider of electrical testing services focusing on
product safety, RF testing, and others. The company serves medical, RFID, and other sectors.

Evans Analytical Group HQ
810 Kifer Rd [N]
Sunnyvale CA 94086
P: 408-530-3500   F: 408-530-3501   PRC:306
www.eag.com/locations
Estab: 1978

Dan Tilley, CIO
Stefan Karnavas, CFO
Tomoya Aoyama, SVP
Patricia M. Lindley, EVP
Amanda Halford, EVP

Provider of materials characterization surface
analysis and much more services.

Everest Consulting Group Inc BR
39650 Mission Blvd [N]
Fremont CA 94539
P: 510-494-8440   PRC:104
www.everestconsulting.net
Emp: 201-500   Estab: 1997

Rajaganesh Kamalnathan, VP
Shoban Rao, Manager of Human Resources
Carla Sridharan, Manager of Operations
Nancy Robert, Manager of Development
Prabhakar Pamula, Manager of Business Devel-
opment, Sales & Technical Recruiting

Provider of customer solutions in IT project and
staff augmentation areas offers technology due
diligence, new application development, and
product engineering.

Evergreen (CP) USA Inc HQ
338 N Canal St Ste 8
S San Francisco CA 94080
P: 650-952-8091   F: 650-952-3629   PRC:288
www.evergreencpusa.com
Email: sales@evergreencpusa.com
Estab: 1986

Stacy Li, Account Executive

Manufacturer of batteries. The company offers
lithium coin cells, nickel cadmium batteries, man-
ganese button cells, and silver oxide button cells.

Evernote Corp HQ
305 Walnut St
Redwood City CA 94063
P: 650-257-0885   F: 650-386-1571   PRC:319
evernote.com

Phil Libin, CEO
Dave Engberg, CTO
Philip Constantinou, VP of Products
Alex Pachikov, VP of Partnerships
Andrew Sinkov, VP of Marketing

Provider of note management and digital link
services. The company also offers handwriting
recognition services.

EverString Technology HQ
1850 Gateway Dr Ste 400
San Mateo CA 94404
P: 650-425-3937   PRC:315
www.everstring.com
Email: contact@everstring.com
Estab: 2012

J.J. Kardwell, Co-Founder & CEO
Vincent Yang, Co-Founder & Executive Chairman
Jeff Stephens, CFO
Amit Rai, COO
Rakesh Gowda, CTO

Provider of AI SaaS solution for B2B sales and
marketing professionals.

Evidation Health Inc HQ
167 Second Ave
San Mateo CA 94401
P: 650-727-5557   PRC:191
evidation.com
Email: press@evidation.com
Estab: 2012

Christine Lemke, Co-Founder & President
Luca Foschini, CDS & Co-Founder
Mikki Nasch, Co-Founder & VP of Business
Development
Deborah Kilpatrick, CEO

Provider of digital health solutions for healthcare
providers, payers, pharma/biotech, and digital
health companies.

Evolphin Software Inc HQ
2410 Camino Ramon Ste 228
San Ramon CA 94583
P: 888-386-4114   PRC:322
evolphin.com
Email: info@evolphin.com
Estab: 2007

Brian Ahearn, CEO
Rahul Bhargava, CTO
Silvia C., Director of Marketing

Provider of digital and media asset management
software for video production, game developers,
media, television broadcasters, and eLearning
groups.

Evolve Biosystems HQ
  2121 Second St Ste C108
  Davis CA 95618
P: 530-747-2012 PRC:42
www.evolvebiosystems.com
Email: info@evolvebiosystems.com
Estab: 2012

David Kyle, Chairman & Chief Scientific Officer
Timothy B. Brown, CEO
Sandy Argabrite, CFO
Christie Fleming, SVP of Sales & Marketing
Rodney Hicks, Director of Supply Chain

Focuses on the development and marketing of probiotic-based biotherapeutics. The company serves the pharmaceutical industry.

Evolve Manufacturing Technologies Inc HQ
  47300 Bayside Pkwy
  Fremont CA 94538
P: 510-690-8959 PRC:159
www.evolvemfg.com
Email: services@evolvemfg.com
Estab: 1999

Sarvar Samia, Director of Human Resources
James Han, Director of NPI & Industrial Engineering
Trang Tran, Director of Program & Service

Designer and manufacturer of electro-mechanical, optical, and prototyping products. The company offers testing, logistics, and documentation services.

Evolveware Inc HQ
  3375 Scott Blvd Bldg 224
  Santa Clara CA 95054
P: 408-748-8301 PRC:322
www.evolveware.com
Email: infous@evolveware.com
Estab: 2001

Miten Marfatia, CEO

Developer of products to automate and modernize IT infrastructure focusing on assessment, documentation, impact analysis, and other solutions.

Exabeam Inc HQ
  2 Waters Pk Ste 200
  San Mateo CA 94403
P: 844-392-2326 PRC:326
www.exabeam.com
Email: info@exabeam.com
Estab: 2013

Domingo Mihovilovic, CTO & Co-Founder
Nir Polak, CEO & Co-Founder
Sylvain Gil, VP of Products & Co-Founder
Ralph Pisani, EVP of Field Operations

Provider of software to discover attackers impersonating users and to protect against cyber attacks.

Exacta Tech Inc HQ
  378 Wright Brothers Ave
  Livermore CA 94551
P: 925-443-8963 F: 925-443-6296 PRC:21
www.exacta-tech.com
Email: exacta@exacta-tech.com
Estab: 1961

Carlos Manrique, President
Stacey Lopez, COO & Director of Operations
Elena Chirimele, Administrative Assistant

Manufacturer of custom machine components and parts and provider of design, inspection and engineering services for industries.

Exadel Inc HQ
  1340 Treat Blvd Ste 375
  Walnut Creek CA 94597
P: 925-363-9510 PRC:315
exadel.com
Email: info@exadel.com
Estab: 1998

Fima Katz, Founder & CEO & President
Lev Shur, President of Exadel Solutions
Igor Landes, CTO
Lynne Walter, CFO
Mikhail Andrushkevich, VP of Delivery

Custom software agency that produces software and mobile solutions.

Exadel Inc HQ
  1340 Treat Blvd Ste 375
  Walnut Creek CA 94597
P: 925-363-9510 PRC:322
exadel.com
Email: info@exadel.com
Estab: 1998

Fima Katz, Founder & President & CEO
Lev Shur, President of Exadel Solutions
Igor Landes, CTO
Lynne Walter, CFO
Gregory Katzman, VP of Global Operations

Provider of software using technologies including mobile, cloud, and web user interfaces. The company also delivers tools and products for users.

Exagen Inc HQ
  1261 Liberty Way Ste C
  Vista CA 92081
P: 888-452-1522 PRC:41
www.exagen.com
Email: info@exagen.com
Estab: 2002

Ron Rocca, President & CEO
Kamal Adawi, CFO
Arthur Weinstein, CMO
Dale Olson, VP & General Manager
Brian Littlefield, SVP of Information Services

Developer of laboratory technology solutions. The company offers services to hospitals, clinics, and the healthcare sector.

Exatron Inc HQ
  2842 Aiello Dr
  San Jose CA 95111-2154
P: 800-392-8766 F: 408-629-2832 PRC:171
www.exatron.com
Email: info@exatron.com
Estab: 1974

Robert Howell, President & Co-Founder
Jim Mori, Machine Shop Manager
Bob Garcia, Sales Manager
Gloria Matson, System Sales Manager
Adam Nomura, System Engineer

Manufacturer of automatic test equipment and IC handlers. The company also specializes in open short testers.

Excel Precision Corp HQ
  3255 Scott Blvd Ste 1-101
  Santa Clara CA 95054
P: 408-727-4260 F: 408-727-1026 PRC:87
www.excelprecision.com
Email: info@excelprecisionusa.com
Estab: 1986

Annie Yang, Office Manager
Andrew Shu, Electrical Engineer

Designer and manufacturer of laser interferometer systems for measurement and calibration. The company's products include level sensors and angular sensors.

Excelchem Laboratories Inc HQ
  1135 W Sunset Blvd Ste A
  Rocklin CA 95765
P: 916-543-4445 F: 916-543-4449 PRC:142
www.ssalabs.com
Estab: 1991

Brian Garcia, Lab Technician
Ajay Virk, Laboratory Technician

Provider of analytical consultation, on-site analysis, custom reporting, and mobile laboratory services.

Excelfore HQ
  3155 Kearney St
  Fremont CA 94538
P: 510-868-2500 PRC:323
excelfore.com
Email: sales@excelfore.com
Estab: 2008

Shrinath Acharya, CEO
Subhash Nair, VP of Business Development
Pawel Veselov, Development Engineer
Danielle McCown, Technical Support Engineer
Harry Rothenberg, Corporate Controller

Provider of cloud applications. The company offers infotainment and telematics products for insurance, financing, and logistics sectors.

Excelitas Technologies Corp BR
6701 Koll Center Pkwy Ste 400
Pleasanton CA 94566
P: 510-979-6500 PRC:124
www.excelitas.com
Estab: 1931

David Nislick, CEO
Jim Rao, EVP & CFO
Joel Falcone, EVP & COO
Marc Reuss, EVP & Chief Human Resource
Officer
Paul Igoe, EVP & General Counsel & Chief Compliance Officer & Secretary

Provider of opto-electronics solutions. The company serves the medical, industrial, aerospace, and defense markers.

Exclara Inc HQ
4701 Patrick Henry Dr Bldg 17
Santa Clara CA 95054
P: 408-492-1009 PRC:212
www.exclara.com
Email: sales@exclara.com
Estab: 2004

Anatoly Shteynberg, CTO
Tony Suzer, VP of Sales
Anwar Aslam, Senior Applications Engineer

Designer and manufacturer of high-voltage LED drivers which provide integrated-circuit and module-based solutions.

Exelixis Inc HQ
1851 Harbor Bay Pkwy
Alameda CA 94502
P: 650-837-7000 F: 650-837-8300 PRC:34
www.exelixis.com
Email: druginfo@exelixis.com
Estab: 1994
Sales: $300M to $1 Billion

Stelios Papadopoulos, Founder & Chairman
Michael M. Morrissey, President & CEO
Gisela M. Schwab, EVP & CMO
Christopher J. Senner, EVP & CFO
Peter Lamb, EVP of Discovery Research & Chief Scientific Officer

Focuses on the development and commercialization of small molecule therapies. The company is also engaged in clinical trials.

Exit445 Group HQ
817 Marin Dr
Mill Valley CA 94941
P: 415-381-1852 PRC:325
exit445.com

Jonathan Schwartz, Owner

Provider of information architecture, e-Commerce, email marketing, search engine optimization, website hosting, and other services.

Expandable Software Inc HQ
900 Lafayette St Ste 400
Santa Clara CA 95050
P: 408-261-7880 F: 408-247-2160 PRC:323
www.expandable.com
Email: sales@expandable.com
Estab: 1983

Jerry Lass, VP of Research & Development & Co-Founder & Director
David M. Kearney, CFO & Director & Co-Founder
Bob Swedroe, President & CEO
Clint Taylor, VP of Sales
Patti Hales, VP of Finance

Developer of enterprise software for manufacturers. The company is engaged in medical technology and general manufacturing solutions.

Expedite Precision Works Inc HQ
931 Berryessa Rd
San Jose CA 95133
P: 408-573-9600 PRC:80
www.expediteprecision.com
Email: epwi@expediteprecision.com
Estab: 1995

Orlando Teixeira, Owner
Huy Nguyen, Quality Assurance Manager
Chiho Choi, Scientist

Manufacturer of diverse products involving micro and custom machining and fabrication of metal and plastic. The company also manufactures vessels and tanks.

Experexchange Inc HQ
46751 Fremont Blvd
Fremont CA 94538
P: 510-623-7071 F: 510-623-9290 PRC:326
www.experexchange.com
Email: it_consulting_team@experexchange.com
Estab: 1989

Bo Yan, VP
Marina Zhao, VP

Provider of software and professional IT solutions such as web based applications, software life cycle service, embedded systems, and software testing.

Expertech HQ
10 Victor Sq Ste 100
Scotts Valley CA 95066
P: 831-439-9300 PRC:124
www.exper-tech.com
Email: service@exper-tech.com
Estab: 1992

Jonathan George, Owner
Mark Cooper, President

Provider of custom, new and re-manufactured thermal processing solutions. The company offers diffusion furnaces for semiconductor and solar devices.

Exploramed HQ
2570 W El Camino Real Ste 310
Mountain View CA 94040
P: 650-472-0300 F: 650-472-0330 PRC:187
www.exploramed.com
Email: info@exploramed.com
Estab: 1995

Joshua Makower, Founder & Executive Chairman
Karen Nguyen, Director of Finance & HR
Jonathan Podmore, Project Architect

Developer of novel medical devices with cutting edge medical technology for use by major medical device manufacturing companies.

Exponent Partners HQ
One Market St 36th Fl
San Francisco CA 94105
P: 800-918-2917 PRC:323
www.exponentpartners.com
Estab: 2005

Rem Hoffmann, CEO
Michael Hassid, VP of Finance & Operations
Mary Lynn Antush, Assistant Director
Michelle Reiss-Top, Technology & Data Systems Manager
Peter Bender, Senior Consultant

Provider of performance and outcomes management solutions. The company's services include systems integration and custom application development.

Extend Inc HQ
4847 Hopyard Rd Ste 4
Pleasanton CA 94588
P: 925-484-0395 F: 925-397-6722 PRC:323
www.extendinc.com
Email: info@extendinc.com
Estab: 1993

Joe Ciolek, Owner

Developer of business software. The company also provides Internet and marketing consulting services.

ExThera Medical Corp HQ
757 Arnold Dr Ste B
Martinez CA 94553
P: 925-839-2060 F: 925-839-2075 PRC:187
www.extheramedical.com
Email: info@extheramedical.com
Estab: 2007

Robert Ward, President & CEO
Vidur Sahney, COO
George Pitarra, EVP & CDO
Keith Mccrea, VP of Research & Development & CSO
Lynn Krekemeyer, Director of Administration

Developer of medical devices that address unmet clinical needs in the treatment of bloodstream infections and pathogen-reduction in blood banking.

Extractable Inc HQ
44 Montgomery St 3rd Fl
San Francisco CA 94104
P: 415-426-3600 PRC:322
www.extractable.com
Email: hello@extractable.com
Estab: 1999

Craig McLaughlin, CEO
Alex Jimenez, CSO
Mark Ryan, Chief Analytics Officer
Christine Meginness, VP of Project Management
Joel Oxman, VP of Business Development

Provider of websites, applications, social and mobile experiences for transactional, educational, lead generation, and entertainment purposes.

Exxact Corp HQ
46221 Landing Pkwy
Fremont CA 94538
P: 510-226-7366 F: 510-226-7367 PRC:91
www.exxactcorp.com
Email: sales@exxactcorp.com
Estab: 1992

Jason Chen, VP
Nicholas Chen, Director of Business Development
Andrew Nelson, Director of Engineering
Mike Sucharew, Senior Account Manager
Kevin Wong, Manager of Production Engineering

Supplier of workstation graphic cards and solutions. The company also offers servers, HPC clusters, and computing software.

EXXIM Computing Corp HQ
5165 Johnson Dr Ste 100
Pleasanton CA 94588
P: 925-416-1900 F: 925-369-0385 PRC:318
www.exxim-cc.com
Email: info@exxim-cc.com
Estab: 2002

Horst Bruning, President & CEO
Sergei Gouzeev, VP
Irene Bruning, VP
Larry Israel, General Counsel

Manufacturer of cutting-edge radiological imaging technology and equipment designed for dental, medical, and scientific and industrial industries.

Eyefinity Inc HQ
10875 International Dr Ste 200
Rancho Cordova CA 95670
P: 877-448-0707 F: 877-790-8162 PRC:323
www.eyefinity.com
Email: customercare@eyefinity.com
Estab: 2000

Troy Eberlein, SVP of Product Management
Lara Cone, Account Manager of Strategic Services

Provider of software solutions for the eyecare industry. The company focuses on practice and revenue cycle management and electronic health records.

EZB Solutions HQ
1400 Coleman Ave Ste D22
Santa Clara CA 95050
P: 408-988-8760 PRC:325
www.ezbsolutions.com
Email: info@ezbsolutions.com
Estab: 2003

Ruben Fernandes, Managing Partner

Provider of software, hardware, and installation services. The company also deals with training, consulting, and technical support.

M-122

eze System HQ
785 Orchard Dr Ste 100
Folsom CA 95630
P: 716-393-9330 PRC:87
ezesys.com
Email: contact@ezesys.com
Estab: 2009

Anders Rehnvall, CEO
John Parman, Senior Technician

Provider or monitoring and measuring solutions. The company's products include controllers, controller expansions, and sensors.

FDS Manufacturing Co HQ
2200 S Reservoir St [N]
Pomona CA 91766
P: 909-591-1733 F: 909-591-1571 PRC:283
www.fdsmfg.com
Email: sales@fdsmfg.com
Estab: 1950

Sam Stevenson, Co-Founder & CEO
Dan Dayton, Co-Founder
Fritz Fernstrom, Co-Founder
Kevin Stevenson, VP of Engineering
Susan Lindgren, Manager of Purchasing

Manufacturer of packaging products for industrial and agricultural markers.

F5 Networks Inc BR
3545 N First St
San Jose CA 95134
P: 408-273-4800 F: 408-273-4925 PRC:319
www.f5.com
Email: info@f5.com
Estab: 1996

Francois Locoh-Donou, President & CEO & Director
Frank Pelzer, EVP & CFO
Geng Lin, EVP & CTO
Mika Yamamoto, EVP & CMO & Customer Experience Officer
Steve McMillan, EVP of Global Services

Provider of strategic points of control throughout the IT infrastructure for organizations to scale, adapt, and align with changing business demands.

Fab 7 Designs HQ
2748 Ross Rd
Palo Alto CA 94303
P: 650-462-9745 PRC:325
fab7.com
Email: business@fab7.com
Estab: 1993

Peter Lonsky, Owner

Provider of graphic designing services. The company offers website, multimedia, editorial, and package designing services.

FAB-9 Corp BR
5400 Hellyer Ave
San Jose CA 95138
P: 408-791-6462 F: 408-791-6757 PRC:211
www.fab-9.com
Estab: 2003

Quin Vo, Manager of Business Development

Provider of printed circuit board fabrication, design, assembly, and manufacturing services. The company serves the business sector.

FABNexus Inc HQ
660 Arboleda Dr [N]
Los Altos CA 94024
P: 650-207-8235 F: 650-276-7456 PRC:319
fabnexus.com

Jerry W. Rice, President & CTO

Provider of application-specific machine control and SEMI-standards conformant network automation software to the semiconductor manufacturing and support industry.

Facebook Inc HQ
1 Hacker Way
Menlo Park CA 94025
P: 650-543-4800 PRC:322
www.facebook.com
Email: facebookinc@usa.com
Estab: 2004
Sales: Over $3B

Eduardo Saverin, Co-Founder
Dustin Moskovitz, Co-Founder
Mark Zuckerburg, President
Sheryl Kara Sandberg, COO

Designer and developer of technologies to communicate with their family, friends, and also coworkers.

FactoryWiz HQ
6920 Santa Teresa Blvd Ste 201
San Jose CA 95119
P: 408-224-9167 PRC:319
factorywiz.com
Estab: 1983

Richard Hefner, VP of Engineering

Provider of CNC Machine Tool monitoring and data collection products. The company is also involved in preventive maintenance services.

Fafco Inc HQ
435 Otterson Dr
Chico CA 95928-8207
P: 530-332-2100 F: 530-332-2109 PRC:135
www.fafco.com
Email: sales@fafco.com
Estab: 1969

Bob Leckinger, President & CEO
Freeman A. Ford, Chairman
Brian Smith, VP of Operations
Alex Ward, Director of Engineering & Operations
J.D. Tenuta, Operations Manager

Manufacturer of polymer heat exchangers. The company also specializes in thermal energy storage systems.

Fair Isaac Corp   HQ
181 Metro Dr
San Jose CA 95110
P: 408-817-9100   F: 408-535-1776   PRC:319
www.fico.com
Email: info@fico.com
Estab: 1956
Sales: $1B to $3B

Claus Moldt, EVP & CTO & Chief Product Officer
Stuart C. Wells, EVP & Chief Product & Technology Officer
James M. Wehmann, EVP of Scores
Michael Leonard, VP & CAO
Allen Strand, Principal

Provider of analytical, software installation, and integration services. The company serves business enterprises.

Fairbanks Scales   BR
8240 Belvedere Ave Ste D
Sacramento CA 95826
P: 916-384-1394   PRC:233
www.fairbanks.com
Estab: 1830

Richard Norden, President & CEO
Nick Cillino, Area Sales Manager
Kevin Oliver, Area Service Manager

Provider of scales and weighing systems. The company serves the agriculture, parcel shipping, transport, and waste management Industries.

Fairchild Imaging Inc   DH
1841 Zanker Rd Ste 50
San Jose CA 95112
P: 650-479-5749   F: 408-433-2604   PRC:87
www.fairchildimaging.com
Email: cams.sales@baesystems.com
Estab: 2001

Will Chen, Information Technology Manager
Carol Zhao, Senior Engineer
Bliss Ron, Financial Analyst

Developer and manufacturer of solid-state electronic imaging components, cameras, and systems. The company's products include image sensors and cameras.

Fall Creek Engineering Inc   HQ
1525 Seabright Ave
Santa Cruz CA 95062
P: 831-426-9054   PRC:304
www.fallcreekengineering.com
Email: info@fallcreekengineering.com
Estab: 1994

Robyn Cooper, Senior Engineer & Engineering Director
Vicki Miller, Office Manager
Carina Chen, Senior Associate Engineer
Samantha Sharp, Senior Associate Engineer
Peter Haase, Principal Engineer

Provider of civil, environmental, and water resources engineering and consulting services. The company engages in site planning and design services.

Famsoft   HQ
1762 Technology Dr Ste 108
San Jose CA 95110
P: 408-452-1550   PRC:326
famsoft.com
Email: info@famsoft.com
Estab: 1997

Mohammed Ilyas, Office Manager
Jamila Hassan, Recruitment Manager
Fahad Rahman, Business Analyst
Gaurav Bahal, Infrastructure Analyst

Provider of ERP consulting and infrastructure management services such as managed support, IBM products, enterprise solution, and migration services.

Farallon Geographics Inc   HQ
601 Montgomery St Ste 1095
San Francisco CA 94111
P: 415-227-1140   F: 415-227-1148   PRC:325
fargeo.com
Email: info@fargeo.com
Estab: 1997

Dennis Wuthrich, CEO & Founder
Alexei Peters, Director of Web Development
Ryan Anderson, Geospatial Developer
Adam Lodge, Geospatial Systems Developer

Provider of strategic planning, spatial data processing, training, and web application development services.

Farasis Energy Inc   HQ
21363 Cabot Blvd
Hayward CA 94545
P: 510-732-6600   F: 510-887-1211   PRC:288
www.farasis.com
Email: sales@farasis.com.cn
Estab: 2002

Keith Kepler, Co-Founder & CTO
Yu Wang, Co-Founder & CEO
Madhuri Thakur, Senior Scientist & Manager of Cell Technology Development
Anita Pai, Technical Project Manager
Colvin Wang, Program Manager

Designer and developer of energy storage solutions. The company serves the transportation, consumer electronics, and power distribution markers.

Farlow's Scientific Glassblowing Inc   HQ
962 Golden Gate Ter Ste B
Grass Valley CA 95945
P: 530-477-5513   F: 530-477-9241   PRC:189
www.farlowsci.com
Estab: 1981

Charlotte Farlow, President & CEO

Provider of precision drilling, boring, cutting, grinding, salvage and repair, custom tooling, metal-to-glass bonding, and related services.

Farpointe Data Inc   HQ
2195 Zanker Rd
San Jose CA 95131
P: 408-731-8700   F: 408-731-8705   PRC:63
www.farpointedata.com
Email: support@farpointedata.com
Estab: 2003

Scott Lindley, President
Kirk Bierach, Director of Engineering
Stephen Sheppard, Key Accounts Sales Manager
Tom Piston, Sales Manager
Rudolph Regidor, Customer Service Manager

Provider of RFID electronic access control technologies for electronic access control professionals around the world.

Fast Trak Fabrication   HQ
3011 W Dakota Ave
Fresno CA 93722
P: 559-222-4450   F: 559-222-4453   PRC:80
www.fasttrakfab.com
Email: info@fasttrakfab.com
Estab: 2008

Ferol Garcia, Partner

Provider of metal fabrication services. The company's services include laser cutting, machining, forming, and welding.

Fastening Systems International Inc   HQ
1206 E Mac Arthur St
Sonoma CA 95476
P: 707-935-1170   F: 707-935-1828   PRC:157
fsirivet.com
Email: sales@fsirivet.com
Estab: 1983

Roger Nikkel, President
Kathryn Nikkel, CFO
Mark Herand, VP
Nolund Kowalski, Operations Manager

Supplier of blind fasteners and blind rivet installation tools. The company offers rivet guns, rivet nuts, pop rivets, and more.

FCS Software Solutions Ltd   HQ
2375 Zanker Rd Ste 250
San Jose CA 95131
P: 408-324-1203   PRC:326
www.fcsltd.com
Email: info@fcsltd.com
Estab: 1993

Anil Sharma, CFO

Provider of consulting, product development, e-learning, digital content, and product support services.

Feeney Inc   HQ
2603 Union St
Oakland CA 94607-2423
P: 510-893-9473   F: 510-893-9484   PRC:157
www.feeneyinc.com
Email: sales@feeneyinc.com
Estab: 1948

Katrina Ralston, President
Andrew Penny, VP of Marketing
Andrew Toimil, VP of Operations
George Shevchuk, Operations Specialist

Provider of architectural and garden products. The company specializes in products such as rail kits, lighting, and accessories.

Femtochrome Research Inc HQ
2123 Fourth St
Berkeley CA 94710
P: 510-644-1869   F: 510-644-0118   PRC:172
www.femtochrome.com
Email: sales@femtochrome.com

Zafer Yasa, Research Director

Manufacturer of instruments for characterization of ultrafast laser pulses focusing on nonlinear crystal and two-photon conductivity autocorrelators.

Fenix International HQ
30 Cleveland St
San Francisco CA 94103
P: 415-754-9222   PRC:135
www.fenixintl.com
Email: press@fenixintl.com
Estab: 2009

Allegra Fisher, Director of Strategic Projects
Emma Frederick, Director of Hardware Engineering

Provider of affordable power generation, smart-storage, and distribution solutions for the 1.6 billion people living off the electricity grid.

Ferreira Service Inc HQ
2600 Old Crow Canyon Rd Ste 100
San Ramon CA 94583
P: 800-522-6064   F: 800-784-6727   PRC:151
ferreira.com
Email: service@ferreira.com

Susan Ferreira, CEO

Provider of energy engineering services. The company offers heating, ventilation, and air conditioning maintenance and repair services.

Ferrotec USA Corp RH
3945 Freedom Cir Ste 450
Santa Clara CA 95054
P: 408-964-7700   F: 408-964-7775   PRC:80
www.ferrotec.com
Email: info@ferrotec.com
Estab: 1968

Bob Otey, Chief of Technology - Thermal Solutions
Rik Michaud, Director of Sales
Scott Libby, Operation's Manager
Susan Hwang, Customer Service Coordinator
Maria Ho, International Sales Administrator

Manufacturer and distributor of quartz solutions and fluid sealants. The company serves business organizations and enterprises.

FET Test Inc HQ
6292 San Ignacio Ave Ste G
San Jose CA 95119
P: 408-778-0234   F: 408-778-0822   PRC:212
www.fettest.com
Email: info@fettest.com
Estab: 1976

Helge Krystad, CTO
Wayne Pearson, Operations Manager

Manufacturer of automated test equipment. The company also offers modular analog/mixed-signal testers and test system controller software.

M-124

Fiber Optic Cable Shop HQ
136 S Second St
Richmond CA 94804
P: 510-234-9090   F: 510-233-8888   PRC:62
fiberopticcableshop.com
Email: sales@fibermailbox.com
Estab: 1976

Mark Wieber, Sales Manager
Paul Fletcher, Accounting Manager

Provider of fiber optic cable products. The company's products include fiber optic media inverters, adapters, aerial cables, and fiber optic switches.

Fibera Inc HQ
3255 Scott Blvd 1-101
Santa Clara CA 95054
P: 408-492-9555   F: 408-492-9559   PRC:235
fiberausa.com
Email: info@fiberausa.com
Estab: 2001

John Tsai, CEO

Manufacturer and designer of wavelength management products. The company also specializes in fiber optic products.

Fiberoptic Systems Inc HQ
60 Moreland Rd   [N]
Simi Valley CA 93065
P: 805-583-2088   F: 805-583-4018   PRC:62
www.fiberopticsystems.com
Emp: 11-50   Estab: 1982

Kathy Hanau, Controller

Manufacturer of OEM products used to measure chemical compositions, perform medical procedures, measure color properties, and quantify radiance in the UV, visible, and IR regions of the spectrum.

Fibrogen Inc HQ
409 Illinois St
San Francisco CA 94158
P: 415-978-1200   F: 415-978-1902   PRC:34
www.fibrogen.com
Email: info@fibrogen.com
Estab: 1993

Pat Cotroneo, CFO
Mike Martinelli, VP of Technical Development
R. Wayne Frost, VP of Regulatory Affairs
Carl Drinkwater, VP of Information Technology
Gail Walkinshaw, VP of Research

Developer of therapeutic products. The company is engaged in commercialization and clinical trial programs.

Fictiv Inc HQ
168 Welsh St
San Francisco CA 94107
P: 415-580-2509   PRC:280
www.fictiv.com
Email: info@fictiv.com

Dave Evans, Co-Founder
Nathan Evans, Co-Founder
Jim Ruga, Chief Architect
Andy Sherman, Director of Production
Madelynn Martiniere, Director of Community

Provider of tooling services for hardware engineers. The company specializes in distributed manufacturing of idle 3D printers from single platform.

Fiduciary Management Technologies Inc HQ
1 Capitol Mall Ste 200
Sacramento CA 95814
P: 916-930-9900   F: 916-930-9902   PRC:322
efmt.com
Email: info@efmt.com
Estab: 1990

Scott M. Sackett, President & Co-Founder
Marilyn R. Bessey, Co-Founder & EVP & CFO

Provider of insolvency case, fiduciary case, and estate management solutions. The company offers SEC distribution fund administration services.

Fidus Systems Inc BR
927 Corporate Way
Fremont CA 94539-6118
P: 408-217-1928   PRC:326
fidus.com
Estab: 2001

Michael Wakim, CEO

Specializes in electronic product development and consulting services. The company also deals with hardware design.

Fil-Tech West Inc BR
5673 W Las Positas Blvd
Pleasanton CA 94588
P: 925-251-8200   F: 925-251-8205   PRC:86
www.filtech.com
Email: paula@filtech.com
Estab: 1969

Douglas P. Becker, President

Distributor of semiconductor parts and vacuum components. The company is engaged in troubleshooting and maintenance services.

FileOpen Systems Inc HQ
1010 Fair Ave Ste A
Santa Cruz CA 95060
P: 831-706-2170   PRC:323
www.fileopen.com
Email: info@fileopen.com
Estab: 1997

Diana Holm, Founder & CMO
Sanford Bingham, President
Malcolm Ellis, CTO
Michel Coste, Chief Engineer
Bob Koche, VP of Business Development

Provider of digital rights management and document security solutions for corporations and governments.

Filtration Group LLC BR
498 Aviation Blvd
Santa Rosa CA 95403
P: 707-525-8633   PRC:156
filtrationgroup.com
Email: cc-inquiry@filtrationgroup.com
Estab: 1942

Tom Gebhardt, President
Matt Huser, CMO
Estela Prado, Human Resource Manager

Provider of filtration solutions. The company supplies filtration products for the HVAC, turbine, cleanroom, and filter media markers.

Filtration Solutions Inc HQ
6372 Lower Wyandotte Rd
Oroville CA 95966
P: 530-534-1000 PRC:143
www.filtrationsolutions.us

Klaus Franz, Owner

Provider of water treatment systems. The company focuses on engineering, manufacturing, installation, and more.

Financial Oxygen Inc HQ
4620 Fortran Dr Ste 101
San Jose CA 95134
P: 925-465-1225 F: 408-945-9533 PRC:319
financialoxygen.com
Email: info@financialoxygen.com
Estab: 1999

Pssmurthy Kruthiventi, Java Technical Lead
Satya Pati, Senior Systems Analyst

Provider of cash management and fixed income products and it serves individual banks and broker-dealers.

FinancialContent Services Inc HQ
195 Glenn Way Ste 250
San Carlos CA 94070
P: 888-688-9880 PRC:325
www.financialcontent.com
Estab: 2000

Mark Dierolf, Founder & CEO

Provider of stock market information. The company deals with advertising, newspaper, and consulting services.

Financialforce Com HQ
595 Market St Ste 2000
San Francisco CA 94105
P: 866-743-2220 PRC:325
www.financialforce.com
Email: info@financialforce.com
Estab: 2009

Andrew Fawcett, CTO
Johnny Ola, VP of Global Alliances & Business Development
Debbie Ashton, VP of Products & Customer service
Jim Carney, VP of Finance
Kevin Roberts, VP of Business Development

Developer of automation software solutions. The company also deals with cloud accounting and resource planning solutions.

Fine-Line Circuits Ltd BR
11501 Dublin Blvd Ste 328
Dublin CA 94568
P: 877-876-3660 PRC:211
www.finelineindia.com
Email: finelineus@aol.com

Abhay B. Doshi, Managing Director

Manufacturer of printed circuit boards. The company specializes in models such as single sided, double sided, and standard multilayer.

Finelite Inc HQ
30500 Whipple Rd
Union City CA 94587-1530
P: 510-441-1100 F: 510-441-1510 PRC:243
www.finelite.com
Estab: 1991

Terry Clark, Founder & Chairman
Jerry Mix, CEO
David Aziz, VP of Engineering
Vickie Lauck, Director of Applications
Marc McMillan, Director of Marketing

Manufacturer of lighting products. The company's services include design, installation, repairs and replacement, and maintenance.

Fingerprint Digital Inc HQ
240 Stockton St 6th Fl
San Francisco CA 94108
P: 855-543-4263 PRC:317
www.fingerprintplay.com
Estab: 2010

Nancy MacIntyre, CEO & Founder

Designer and developer of mobile kids network solutions. The company offers services to kids of all ages.

Finishline Advanced Composites LLC HQ
3820 Industrial Way Ste H
Benicia CA 94510
P: 707-747-0788 F: 707-747-0780 PRC:157
finishlinecomposites.com
Email: info@finishlinecomposites.com

James Porreco, President & CEO

Provider of composite repair services for production projects. The company is involved in design, development, prototyping, testing, and production.

Finjan Holdings Inc HQ
2000 University Ave Ste 600
East Palo Alto CA 94303
P: 650-282-3228 PRC:304
www.finjan.com
Email: info@finjan.com
Estab: 1997
Sales: $10M to $30M

Phil Hartstein, President & CEO
Jevan Anderson, CFO
Julie Mar-Spinola, Chief Intellectual Property Officer & VP & Legal Ops
Atreyee Dhar, Director of Patent Analysis
John Garland, Director of Business Development

Specializes in the research and development of transformative technologies for the securing of information.

Fire2wire HQ
5462 Pirrone Rd
Salida CA 95368
P: 209-543-1800 F: 209-545-1469 PRC:67
www.fire2wire.com
Email: info@fire2wire.com
Estab: 2000

Kristian Hoffmann, President
Duane Severson, CEO
William Moreno, VP of Sales
Bill Moreno, VP
Marlene Sosa, Sales Manager

Provider of network consulting, server colocation, website hosting and design, wireless Internet, and content management services.

FireEye Inc HQ
601 McCarthy Blvd
Milpitas CA 95035
P: 408-321-6300 F: 408-321-9818 PRC:323
www.fireeye.com
Email: info@fireeye.com
Estab: 2004
Sales: $300M to $1 Billion

Travis Reese, President
Kevin Mandia, CEO
Vasu Jakkal, EVP & CMO
Frank E. Verdecanna, EVP & CFO & Chief Accounting Officer
Barbara Massa, EVP & Chief Business Operations

Focuses on cyber security solutions. The company serves the utilities and pharmaceutical industries.

First Class Plus LLC HQ
214 Ryan Way
S San Francisco CA 94080
P: 650-589-8346 PRC:324
www.firstclassplus.com
Estab: 1986

Fernando Balazs, Founder & Direct Mail Design Consultant & Postal Regulations Expert

Provider of fundraising and marketing solutions. The company deals with print production, design assistance, and pre-press services.

First Databank Inc HQ
701 Gateway Blvd Ste 600
S San Francisco CA 94080
P: 650-588-5454 PRC:40
fdbhealth.com
Email: cs@fdbhealth.com
Estab: 1977

Charles Tuchinda, President
Patrick Lupinetti, SVP
Julie Suko, VP of Editorial Content Services
Bob Katter, EVP & CCO
Tracy Lofland, VP of Quality Management

Provider of healthcare solutions to hospitals, retail pharmacies, payers, drug manufacturers, and healthcare providers.

Fischer Custom Communications Inc HQ
20603 Earl St [N]
Torrance CA 90503
P: 310-303-3300 PRC:65
www.fischercc.com
Email: sales@fischercc.com
Emp: 11-50 Estab: 1971

Joe Fischer, Founder

Designer, developer, and manufacturer of transient protection devices and RF test equipment.

Fisher Manufacturing HQ
1900 S O St
Tulare CA 93274
P: 800-421-6162 F: 800-832-8238 PRC:159
www.fisher-mfg.com
Estab: 1936

Ray Fisher, President

Manufacturer of advanced plumbing systems. The company's products include faucets, valves, sprays, and fillers.

Fit Bearings HQ
47881 Fremont Blvd
Fremont CA 94538
P: 510-623-1688 F: 510-226-6104 PRC:158
www.fitbearings.com
Estab: 1988

Dong Yili, CEO
Will Horng, SVP of Sales & Business Operations
Ken Lee, Manager

Designer and manufacturer of bearings. The company's products include seals, drive components, and agricultural and industrial wheel hubs.

Five Prime Therapeutics Inc HQ
111 Oyster Point Blvd
S San Francisco CA 94080
P: 415-365-5600 F: 415-365-5601 PRC:34
www.fiveprime.com
Email: pr@fiveprime.com
Estab: 2001
Sales: $10M to $30M

William R. Ringo, CEO & Chairman
David Smith, EVP & CFO
Francis W. Sarena, CSO & Secretary
Helen Louise Collins, SVP & CMO
Amy Collins, VP of Legal Affairs

Developer and discovery of therapeutics products for the enhancement of lives of patients with serious diseases.

Five9 Inc HQ
4000 Executive Pkwy Ste 400
San Ramon CA 94583
P: 925-201-2000 F: 925-480-6202 PRC:322
www.five9.com
Email: info@five9.com
Estab: 2001
Sales: $300M to $1 Billion

Dan Burkland, President
Rowan Trollope, CEO
Ryan Kam, CMO
Jonathan Rosenberg, CTO
Barry Zwarenstein, CFO

Seller of call center software focusing on IVR System, an interactive voice response software, Outbound Call Center software, and Auto Dialer.

Five9 Network Systems LLC HQ
368 A Calcaterra Pl
Palo Alto CA 94306
P: 650-494-2220 PRC:97
www.five9network.com
Estab: 2008

Souheil Saliba, Founder & CEO
Annie Lin-Johnson, VP of Business & Corporate Operations

Provider of server and storage solutions. The company serves the government, printing, cloud infrastructure, and energy markers.

Flamort Company Inc HQ
2368 Alvarado St
San Leandro CA 94577
P: 510-357-9494 PRC:47
flamort.com
Email: info@flamort.com
Estab: 1965

Dean Narahara, General Manager

Provider of fire retardant coatings. The company's products are used in restaurants, trade shows, amusement parks, and theaters.

Flashline Electronics Inc HQ
2149-20 O'Toole Ave
San Jose CA 95131
P: 408-988-4722 F: 408-988-4724 PRC:211
flashlineelectronics.com
Email: sales@flashlineelectronics.com

Tom Hanighen, VP of Sales & Marketing

Manufacturer of printed circuit boards. The company develops blind and buried vias, rigid flex, and flex PCB.

Flashpoint Machining HQ
517 Aldo Ave
Santa Clara CA 95054-2205
P: 408-213-0071 F: 408-213-0073 PRC:157
www.flashpointmachining.com
Email: info@flashpointmachining.com

Eric David, Owner
Karen Mesa, Office Manager

Provider of precision prototype, R&D, and detail and production machining services. The company also offers industrial machined parts.

Flashtalking BR
110 Sutter St 7th Fl
San Francisco CA 94104
P: 628-207-8080 PRC:325
www.flashtalking.com
Estab: 2001

Joe Sabol, CRO
Betsy Adelstein, SVP of Midwest Sales
Chris Winburn, VP of Sales & East
Adam Smith, VP of Sales & West
Dan Rosler, VP

Provider of online advertising technologies. The company is also engaged in analytics and reporting services.

Flex Interconnect Technologies Inc HQ
1603 Watson Ct
Milpitas CA 95035
P: 408-635-3540 F: 408-956-8278 PRC:211
www.fit4flex.com
Email: sales@fit4flex.com
Estab: 1998

Dean Matsuo, VP
Meet Shah, Solutions Provider

Developer of printed circuit technologies which provide solutions to organizational inter connectivity problems.

Flex Logix Technologies Inc HQ
2465 Latham St
Mountain View CA 94040
P: 650-851-1411 PRC:212
www.flex-logix.com
Email: info@flex-logix.com
Estab: 2014

Geoffrey Tate, CEO & Founder
Abhijit Abhyankar, VP
Andy Jaros, VP of Sales
Cheng Wang, SVP of Engineering
Tony Kozaczuk, Director of Solutions Architecture

Developer of reconfigurable RTL IP cores and software.

Flexline LLC HQ
1394 Tully Rd Ste 201
San Jose CA 95122
P: 408-295-3901 F: 408-295-7341 PRC:235
flexlinellc.com
Email: sales@flexlinellc.com

John Oldham, President & Owner
Juan Hagen, Project Manager
Ron Garman, Purchasing & Logistics Manager
Hong Li, Software & Firmware Engineer
Florence Usita, Principal Engineer

Provider of custom solutions for manufacturing and test problems. The company also deals with automation, engineering, and production tooling.

Flickerbox Inc HQ
739 Bryant St Ste 202
San Francisco CA 94107
P: 415-436-9383 PRC:319
flickerbox.com
Email: hello@flickerbox.com
Estab: 1999

Aretoula Arvanitidis Hickson, General Manager
Paul J. Martinez, Director of Technology
Kathy Stewart, Office Manager
Ben Bridge, Senior Full Stack Developer
Todd J. Collins, Senior Designer

Provider of marketing, design, and technology support services. The company also deals with lead generation campaigns.

Flight Light Inc HQ
2708 47th Ave
Sacramento CA 95822-3806
P: 916-394-2800 F: 916-394-2809 PRC:243
www.flightlight.com
Email: sales@flightlight.com
Estab: 1993

Kyle Owens, Founder & CEO
Isabel Martin, President
Isabel Perez-Martin, General Manager
Steven Graham, Supply Chain Manager

Supplier of airport lighting products. The company is a manufacturer of runway lights, taxiway lights, wind cones, and approach systems.

Flory Industries HQ
4737 Toomes Rd [N]
Salida CA 95368
P: 209-545-1167 F: 209-543-7646 PRC:179
www.floryindustries.com
Emp: 51-200 Estab: 1939

Stuart Layman, Owner
Julie Dugo, Director of Sales & Marketing
Darin Denlinger, Director of Manufacturing Systems
Darren Harper, Sales representative

Provider of nut-harvesting equipment for harvesting almonds, cashews, chestnuts, figs, hazelnuts, macadamia, pecans, tung nut and walnuts.

Flostor Engineering HQ

21371 Cabot Blvd
Hayward CA 94545
P: 800-500-8256   F: 510-785-7463   PRC:159
www.flostor.com
Email: information@flostor.com
Estab: 1983

Robert Weeks, President
Chuck Ireland, VP of System Sales
Eric Landtbom, Director of Sales
Sam Weeks, Director of Operations
David Almquist, Manager of Engineering

Developer of automation solutions for inventory, distribution, fulfillment, and manufacturing systems.

Fluid Inc HQ

1611 Telegraph Ave 4th Fl
Oakland CA 94612
P: 877-343-3240   F: 415-263-7701   PRC:326
www.fluid.com
Email: sales@www.fluid.com
Estab: 1998

Mark Belanger, CTO & Co-Founder
Kent Deverell, CEO & Co-Founder
Sara Arias, Product Manager
Edison Zuluaga, QA Engineer
Laura Orozco, Software Engineer

Provider of software solutions. The company's services include automated retail planning and content strategy.

Fluidigm Corp HQ

2 Tower Pl Ste 2000
S San Francisco CA 94080
P: 650-266-6000   F: 650-871-7152   PRC:36
fluidigm.com
Sales: $100M to $300M

Stephen Christopher Linthwaite, President & CEO
Fred Walder, COO
Vikram Jog, CFO
Mai Chan Yow, Managing Director of Fluidigm Singapore Pte Ltd & EVP of Worldwide Manufacturing
Nick Khadder, SVP & General Counsel & Corporate Secretary

Manufacturer of life-science tools. The company's technologies are focused on microfluidics and mass cytometry.

Fluidigm Sciences Inc HQ

7000 Shoreline Ct Ste 100
S San Francisco CA 94080
P: 650-871-7152   PRC:34
www.dvssciences.com
Estab: 1999

Chris Linthwaite, President & CEO
Vikram Jog, CFO
Sudhakar Chilukuri, SVP & CIO
Colin McCracken, Chief Commercial Officer
Angela Peters, VP of Global Human Resources

Developer and creator of technologies for life science tools designed to revolutionize biology. The company is involved in research programs.

FLYTECH Technology Company Ltd BR

271 E Brokaw Rd
San Jose CA 95112
P: 510-257-5180   F: 510-257-5181   PRC:91
www.flytech.com
Email: sales@flytech.com

Thomas Lam, Founder & Chairman

Developer and manufacturer of touch screen, LCD, and other peripherals. The company also designs motherboard.

FM Industries Inc HQ

221 Warren Ave
Fremont CA 94539
P: 510-668-1900   F: 510-490-1647   PRC:80
www.fmindustries.com
Estab: 1989

Musaud Yawar, RMA & MRB Coordinator
Leslie Busch-Wilson, Planner

Designer and manufacturer of precision machined components. The company also offers electro mechanical assemblies.

Foam Molders and Specialties HQ

11110 Business Cir   [N]
Cerritos CA 90703
P: 800-378-8987   PRC:281
www.foammolders.com
Email: info@foammolders.com
Estab: 1973

Dan Doke, President

Manufacturer of polyurethane, polyethylene, and EVA foams.

Foamlinx LLC HQ

1248 Birchwood Dr
Sunnyvale CA 94089
P: 408-454-6163   F: 408-212-8348   PRC:157
foamlinx.com
Email: info@foamlinx.com
Estab: 2002

Tal Barnea, Owner

Provider of foam cutting computer numerical control machines. The company offers cutters, shredders, compactors, and cutting services.

Fochon Pharmaceuticals Ltd DH

1933 Davis St Ste 270
San Leandro CA 94577
P: 510-638-8080   PRC:268
fochon.com
Estab: 2009

Jacob Plattner, Co-Founder & CSO
Jiemin Fu, Co-Founder & Vice Chairman
Weibo Wang, Co-Founder & CEO

Provider of therapeutic solutions. The company focuses on research and development of small molecule drugs for health care.

Foodpro International Inc BR

11 S San Joaquin St 9th Fl   [N]
Stockton CA 95202
P: 209-943-8400   F: 209-946-1753   PRC:45
www.foodpro.net
Email: info@foodpro.net

Bill Washburn, President
Joel Svendsen, Contact

Distributor of food products.

Foodtools Inc HQ

315 Laguna St   [N]
Santa Barbara CA 93101
P: 805-962-8383   F: 805-966-3614   PRC:159
www.foodtools.com
Email: info@rvo.com.au
Emp: 11-50   Estab: 1985

Martin Grano, President & CEO
Doug Petrovich, VP
Mike Hodgson, Director

Manufacturer of food products equipment.

FoothillNet Inc HQ

24388 Main St   [N]
Foresthill CA 95631
P: 530-820-1031   F: 530-367-4140   PRC:24
www.foothill.net
Email: info@foothill.net
Estab: 1995

Devin Koch, Director of Business Development

Provider of computer and technology services to companies.

Force Flow Inc HQ

2430 Stanwell Dr
Concord CA 94520
P: 925-686-6700   F: 925-686-6713   PRC:159
forceflowscales.com
Email: info@forceflow.com
Estab: 1967

Michael Donn, Manager of Product Development

Provider of chemical monitoring scales. The company exclusively caters to the water and wastewater industry.

Foreal Spectrum Inc HQ

2370-A Qume Dr
San Jose CA 95131
P: 408-436-5558   F: 408-436-5557   PRC:175
forealspectrum.com
Email: salesteam@forealspectrum.com
Estab: 2003

Dan Cifelli, VP
Ronggui Shen, Engineer

Provider of coating services for laser, biotech, and medical industries. The company also offers LED illumination and optical components.

Forecross Corp   HQ
   505 Montgomery St 11th Floor
   San Francisco CA 94111
P: 415-543-1515   F: 415-543-6701   PRC:325
www.forecross.com
Email: info@forecross.com
Estab: 1982

Bonnie Castello, SVP

Provider of automated migration of legacy systems. The company specializes in XML solutions, migration solutions, and integrity solutions.

Forell/Elsesser Engineers Inc   HQ
   160 Pine St Ste 600
   San Francisco CA 94111
P: 415-837-0700   F: 415-837-0800   PRC:304
www.forell.com
Email: recruiting@forell.com
Estab: 1960

Simin Naaseh, CEO & President
Paul Rodler, COO & Senior Principal
Mason Walters, Senior Principal & Technical Director
Carolynn Smith, Office Manager
Shaun Peppers, CAD Manager

Provider of structural engineering, design build, earthquake engineering, research and development, and seismic design services.

Forensic Analytical Consulting Services Inc   HQ
   3777 Depot Rd Ste 413
   Hayward CA 94545
P: 866-637-9924   PRC:306
forensicanalytical.com
Email: sales@forensicanalytical.com
Estab: 1986

Gustavo Delgado, CEO
Lily K.S. Yee, Program Manager of LIMS & Data Solutions

Provider of analytical testing services. The company specializes in a wide array of material testing, forensic and environmental testing.

Forensic Logic Inc   HQ
   1255 Treat Blvd Ste 610
   Walnut Creek CA 94597
P: 833-267-5465   PRC:326
www.forensiclogic.com
Email: info@forensiclogic.com
Estab: 2003

Bob Batty, Executive Chairman & Co-Founder
Ron Mayer, CTO & Co-Founder
Bradford J. Davis, President & CEO
Dave Dunlap, COO
Mike Romano, SVP of Sales

Provider of software-as-a-service information technology to local, state and federal government workers and private sector organizations.

Forescout Technologies Inc   HQ
   190 W Tasman Dr
   San Jose CA 95134
P: 408-213-3191   F: 408-371-2284   PRC:325
www.forescout.com
Email: info@forescout.com
Estab: 2000

Mike DeCesare, CEO
Christopher Harms, CFO
Ori Naishtein, VP of Research & Development
Nitin Yenigalla, Manager of Corporate Strategy

Provider of network access control and policy compliance management solutions. The company serves the business sector.

ForgeRock   HQ
   201 Mission St Ste 2900
   San Francisco CA 94105
P: 415-599-1100   PRC:319
forgerock.com
Email: privacy@forgerock.com
Estab: 2010

Mike Ellis, CEO
Robert Humphrey, CMO
John Fernandez, CFO
Peter Barker, EVP & CPO
Grant Fengstad, Director of Information Technology & CIO

Provider of identity solutions. The company serves the digital health, financial services, communication, and media industries.

Forio Corp   HQ
   2601 Mission St Ste 800
   San Francisco CA 94110
P: 415-440-7500   F: 415-529-5984   PRC:323
www.forio.com
Email: info@forio.com
Estab: 2001

Michael Bean, Founder
Will Glass-Husain, Chief Software Architect
Andrew Northrop, VP of Operations
Federico Pasumbal, Quality Assurance Manager
Amber Christiansen, Customer Experience Manager

Provider of software products for simulations, data explorations, and predictive analysis needs. The company caters to universities and corporations.

Form & Fusion MFG Inc   HQ
   11261 Trade Center Dr
   Rancho Cordova CA 95742
P: 916-638-8576   F: 916-638-2205   PRC:47
form-fusion.com/contact.php
Email: info@form-fusion.com

Dave Lewis, Founder & Owner

Provider of metal fabrication services. The company mainly focuses on powder coating, metal fabrication, and assembly and packaging.

Formfactor Inc   HQ
   7005 Southfront Rd
   Livermore CA 94551
P: 925-290-4000   F: 925-290-4010   PRC:86
www.formfactor.com
Email: info_usa@formfactor.com
Emp: 1188   Estab: 1993
Sales: $300M to $1 Billion

Mike Slessor, President & CEO
Amy Leong, CMO & SVP of Mergers & Acquisitions
Mike Ludwig, CFO
Benjamin Eldridge, CIO & SVP of New Business Initiatives
January Jarek Kister, CTO & SVP of Technology Research & Development

Provider of product and professional services to semiconductor manufacturers. The company also offers sales and support services.

Formula Consultants Inc   HQ
   222 S Harbor Blvd Ste 650   [N]
   Anaheim CA 92805
P: 714-778-0123   F: 714-778-6364   PRC:319
www.formula.com
Email: info@formula.com
Estab: 1978

R. Joseph Dale, President
Bud Schultz, VP of Sales & Marketing
Tony Sapienza, Contact

Provider of software development and consulting services.

Formulation Technology Inc   HQ
   571 Armstrong Way
   Oakdale CA 95361
P: 209-847-0331   F: 209-847-1975   PRC:272
formulationtech.com
Email: info@formulationtech.com
Estab: 1982

Keith Hensley, President
Ron Bahadur, Production Manager

Manufacturer of custom dietary supplements and OTC medications. The company focuses on contract manufacturing services.

Formumax Scientific Inc   HQ
   1230 Bordeaux Dr
   Sunnyvale CA 94089
P: 408-400-0108   F: 408-465-5338   PRC:34
formumax.com
Email: service@formumax.com

Robert Abra, Principal Scientist

Provider of contract drug delivery to pharmaceutical and biotech industries. The company specializes in injectables, liposomes, and microemulsions.

Formurex Inc   HQ
   2470 Wilcox Rd
   Stockton CA 95215
P: 209-931-2040   F: 209-931-2177   PRC:268
www.formurex.com

Bhaskara Jasti, Co-Founder
Xiaoling Liang, Co-Founder & CSO
Sunny Sun, Management Analyst

Provider of services to the biotech industry in preformulation, formulation development, stability and clinical trial materials manufacturing.

Forsgren Associate Inc   DH
3110 Gold Canal Dr Ste C
Rancho Cordova CA 95670
P: 916-638-1119 F: 916-638-1129   PRC:137
forsgren.com
Estab: 1962

Richard Noll, President
Alan Driscoll, VP & Director of Environmental
Services

Provider of civil and environmental engineering
consulting services. The company specializes
in planning, design, survey, and construction
management.

ForteBio   LH
47661 Fremont Blvd
Fremont CA 94538
P: 650-322-1360 F: 650-322-1370   PRC:34
www.fortebio.com
Email: fortebio_info@sartorius.com

Susan Murphy, President
Joe Keegan, CEO
Steven Qian, CFO & VP of Finance
Martin Verhoef, VP of Strategy & New Product
Generation
Poonam Taneja, VP & General Manager of Asia
Commercial Operations & Global Distribution

Provider of dip and read assay kits. The company's products are used in the application of kinetic
characterization.

Fortemedia Inc   HQ
4051 Burton Dr
Santa Clara CA 95054
P: 408-861-8088   PRC:204
www.fortemedia.com
Email: info@fortemedia.com
Estab: 1996

Paul Huang, CEO
Quintin Liu, VP of Engineering
Xiao Lin, Senior Director & Principal Engineer
Weldon Huang, Sales Director
Yan-Chen Lu, Senior Manager of SW Engineering

Provider of voice processing integrated circuits.
The company also offers related hardware and
software components.

Fortinet Inc   HQ
899 Kifer Rd
Sunnyvale CA 94086
P: 408-235-7700 F: 408-235-7737   PRC:323
www.fortinet.com
Estab: 2000
Sales: $1B to $3B

Ken Xie, Co-Founder & Chairman & CEO
Michael Xie, Co-Founder & CTO & President
Amanda Mallow, EVP & CPO
John Maddison, CMO & EVP of Products
Keith F. Jensen, CFO

Provider of network security appliances and threat
management solutions such as network security
platform and reporting and authentication.

Fortrend Engineering Corp   HQ
2220 O'Toole Ave
San Jose CA 95131
P: 408-734-9311 F: 408-734-4299   PRC:138
www.fortrend.com
Email: sales@fortrend.com
Estab: 1979

Chris Wu, CEO
Harriet West, Materials Manager
Ruihan Zhao, Account Manager
Kelin Ko, Manager
Donna Cheng, Controller

Designer and manufacturer of mechanical handling equipment. The company also specializes in
distribution services.

Foster Brothers Security Systems Inc   HQ
555 S Murphy Ave
Sunnyvale CA 94086
P: 408-736-4500 F: 408-736-0468   PRC:59
fosterbrothers.com
Email: locks@fosterbrothers.com
Estab: 1955

Jeff Sanchez, Sales Manager

Provider of security systems. The company offers
locks and keys, access control systems, and tools
and accessories.

Foundation Constructors Inc   HQ
81 Big Break Rd
Oakley CA 94561
P: 925-754-6633   PRC:304
www.foundationpiledriving.com
Estab: 1971

Dermot Fallon, President
Nikki Sjoblom, CFO
Earl Robbins, VP of Operations
Wyatt Gregory, Director of Engineering & Precon-
struction
Chris Kinley, Safety Director

Provider of pile solutions and shoring systems.
The company also offers pile, H-beams, sheets,
and concrete pile types.

Four Dimensions Inc   HQ
3140 Diablo Ave
Hayward CA 94545
P: 510-782-1843 F: 510-786-9321   PRC:212
www.4dimensions.com
Email: info@4dimensions.com
Estab: 1978

James Chen, President
Chen-Fan Huang, Application Engineer

Manufacturer of semiconductor probing systems.
The company offers Four Point Probe, Mercury
Probe CV maps, and Mercury Four Imaging
systems.

Foxit Corp   HQ
41841 Albrae St
Fremont CA 94538
P: 510-438-9090 F: 510-405-9288   PRC:322
foxitsoftware.com
Email: sales@foxitsoftware.com
Estab: 2001

Eugene Xiong, Founder & Chairman
Susana De Abrew, President of Foxit SDK BU
George Gao, CEO
Frank Kettenstock, CMO
Phil Lee, CRO

Developer of software. The company offers
software such as Foxit Reader, Enterprise, and
Mobile Reader.

Franz Inc   HQ
2201 Broadway Ste 715
Oakland CA 94612
P: 510-452-2000 F: 510-452-0182   PRC:323
franz.com
Email: info@franz.com
Estab: 1984

Kevin Layer, COO & Co-Founder
John Foderaro, Co-Founder & Chief Scientist
Sheng-Chuan Wu, VP of Asia & Corporate Devel-
opment
Craig Norvell, VP of Global Sales & Marketing
David Margolies, Manager

Provider of information technology solutions. The
company offers web technology and enterprise
development tools, and professional services.

Free Hot Water   HQ
2023 O'Toole Ave
San Jose CA 95131
P: 408-432-9900 F: 408-872-4142   PRC:135
www.freehotwater.com
Email: info@freehotwater.com
Estab: 1998

Gal Moyal, Founder & CEO & CTO

Manufacturer and distributor of solar thermal products. The company serves engineers, architects,
developers, and business owners.

Freetech Plastics Inc   HQ
2211 Warm Springs Ct
Fremont CA 94539
P: 510-651-9996 F: 510-651-9917   PRC:84
www.freetechplastics.com
Email: sales@freetechplastics.com
Estab: 1976

Richard Freeman, CEO
Judy Nguyen, Materials Manager

Manufacturer of pressure thermoforming products.
The company's products include medical, scientific, and telecommunication enclosures.

FreeWire Technologies Inc   HQ
1933 Davis St Ste 301A
San Leandro CA 94577
P: 415-779-5515   PRC:288
www.freewiretech.com
Estab: 2014

Arcady Sosinov, CEO

Provider of mobile distributed power solutions.
The company serves the business and industrial
sectors.

Frequentis California Inc   DH
2511 Garden Rd Ste A-165
Monterey CA 93940
P: 831-392-0430   PRC:66
www.frequentis.com
Estab: 1978

Norbert Haslacher, CEO
Dieter Eier, VP
Vince Campanella, VP

Provider of air traffic management and other
e-services. The company serves the defense and
public transport sectors.

Frequentz LLC   HQ
12667 Alcosta Blvd
San Ramon CA 94583
P: 925-824-0300   PRC:326
frequentz.com
Email: hello@rfxcel.com
Estab: 2003

Byron S. Lee, CTO

Designer and developer of product tracking software. The company serves the life sciences and
industrial sectors.

Fresenius Medical Care   BR
365 Lennon Ln Ste 160
Walnut Creek CA 94598
P: 925-947-4545   F: 925-947-4547   PRC:186
www.freseniuskidneycare.com

Janet Voss, Project Manager
Thomas Merics, Senior Software Engineer
Kelly Yik, Electrical Engineer

Focuses on the treatment of patients with renal
and other chronic conditions. The company serves
the healthcare industry.

Freshwater Environmental Svc   HQ
78 Sunnybrae Ctr
Arcata CA 95521
P: 707-839-0091   PRC:139
freshwaterenvironmentalservices.com
Estab: 2007

Orrin Plocher, Geologist & Project Manager

Provider of environmental services. The company's services include soil investigation work plans,
soil sampling reporting, sediment sampling, and
monitoring.

Fresno Valves & Castings Inc   HQ
7736 E Springfield Ave
Selma CA 93662
P: 559-834-2511   F: 559-834-2017   PRC:147
www.fresnovalves.com
Email: info@fresnovalves.com
Estab: 1952

Kelvin Kerst, Regional Manager
Leonor Lopez, Human Resource Manager
Rich Korbe, Fabricated Gates Sales Manager
Renee Moore, Territory Sales Manager
Craig Linder, IS Manager

Provider of water control devices used in irrigation
applications. The company's products include
valves, filters, air vents, fittings, gates, and lifts.

Frey Environmental Inc   BR
1336 Brommer St Ste A6
Santa Cruz CA 95062
P: 831-464-1634   F: 831-464-1644   PRC:139
freyinc.com
Email: freyinc@freyinc.com
Estab: 1989

Uyen Le, Manager of Accounts
Walter Bell, Engineer
Ed Rands, Senior Project Engineer
Brian Finkelstein, Staff Engineer
Joe Frey, Principal

Provider of geological and engineering consulting
services. The company offers stormwater management, methane assessments/mitigation, and
asbestos-related services.

Frontier Analytical Laboratory   HQ
5172 Hillsdale Cir
El Dorado Hills CA 95762
P: 916-934-0900   F: 916-934-0999   PRC:303
www.frontieranalytical.com
Email: info@frontieranalytical.com
Estab: 2001

Tom Crabtree, Director of Mass Spectrometry
Brad Silverbush, Director of Operations
Dan Vickers, Director Of Air Toxics & Quality
Assurance Officer

Provider of testing services for analysis of poly-
chlorinated dibenzo dioxins and furans polychlori-
nated biphenyls and polyaromatic hydrocarbons.

Fruit Growers Laboratory Inc   BR
2500 Stagecoach Rd
Stockton CA 95215
P: 209-942-0182   F: 209-942-0423   PRC:140
fglinc.com
Estab: 1925

Kelly Dunnahoo, President & Laboratory Director
Glenn Olsen, Marketing Director
David Terz, Quality Assurance Director
Richard Hawkins, Lab Manager
Belen Castaneda, Lab Manager

Provider of testing and analytical services. The
company performs drinking and waste water
analysis, agriculture testing, and hazardous waste
analysis.

FTG Circuits Inc   HQ
20750 Marilla St   [N]
Chatsworth CA 91311
P: 818-407-4024   PRC:211
www.ftgcorp.com
Email: info@ftgcorp.com
Estab: 2016

Hitesh Talati, VP & General Manager

Manufacturer and supplier of printed circuit
boards.

FUEL Creative Group   HQ
5001 24th St
Sacramento CA 95822
P: 916-669-1591   PRC:325
fuelcreativegroup.com

Steve Worth, Owner
Brent Rector, Creative Director & Principal
Nicolette Countryman, Project Manager
Kelina Orozco, Designer
Brittany Baledio, Production Designer

Provider of graphic design, branding, and signage
services. The company also focuses on packaging
and printing.

Fuji Electric Corp of America   BR
47520 Westinghouse Dr
Fremont CA 94539
P: 510-440-1060   F: 510-440-1063   PRC:86
americas.fujielectric.com
Estab: 1970

Steve Snyder, Western Regional Sales Manager

Provider of electric technology services. The company offers solutions for disk media, power supply,
industrial systems, and radiation.

Fujikin of America Inc   RH
454 Kato Ter
Fremont CA 94539
P: 408-980-8269   F: 408-980-0572   PRC:166
www.fujikin.com
Email: sales@fujikin.com
Estab: 1930

Ayami Botkin, Senior Manager
Masayo Miyauchi, Human Resource Coordinator

Manufacturer of fluid and gas flow valves and fittings. The company also offers process equipment
control systems.

Fujikura America Inc   BR
920 Stewart Dr Ste 150
Sunnyvale CA 94085
P: 408-748-6991   F: 408-727-3415   PRC:209
www.fujikura.com

Jason Peng, President & CEO
Kazuhiro Sato, Director
Tetsuya Noda, General Manager
Yuji Saito, General Manager
Bill Seki, Senior Manager

Manufacturer of fiber optics flexible printed circuits
and cables. The company also offers membrane
switches and printed circuit board assemblies.

Fujitsu Components America Inc   HQ
2290 N First St Ste 212
San Jose CA 95131
P: 408-745-4900   F: 408-745-4970   PRC:78
www.fujitsu.com
Email: components@us.fujitsu.com

Bob Thornton, President

Provider of computing products and services. The
company's products include servers, storage,
scanners, and displays.

Full Circle Crm Inc   HQ
1800 Gateway Dr Ste 130
San Mateo CA 94404
P: 650-641-2766   PRC:326
fullcircleinsights.com
Estab: 2011

Bonnie Crater, President & CEO & Co-Founder
Dan Appleman, Co-Founder & CTO
Rochelle Richelieu, VP of Customer Success

Specializes in response management and it offers management products. The company serves businesses.

Full Circle Insights Inc   HQ
1800 Gateway Dr Ste 130
San Mateo CA 94404
P: 650-641-2766   PRC:315
fullcircleinsights.com
Email: success@fullcircleinsights.com
Estab: 2011

Dan Appleman, Founder & CTO
Bonnie Crater, CEO & President
Rochelle Richelieu, VP of Customer Success
Bob Teplitsky, VP of Engineering

Delivers marketing and sales performance measurement solutions to optimize a company's marketing automation solutions.

Fuller Manufacturing Inc   HQ
130 Ridge Rd   [N]
Sutter Creek CA 95685
P: 209-267-5071   F: 209-267-9338   PRC:159
www.fullermfg.com
Emp: 11-50   Estab: 1979

Martin Nmi Fuller, General Manager

Provider of precision products such as grinding, milling, cutting, turning, and drilling services.

Funambol Inc   HQ
1065 E Hillsdale Blvd Ste 250
Foster City CA 94404
P: 650-701-1450   F: 650-701-1484   PRC:324
www.funambol.com
Email: info@funambol.com
Estab: 2002

Amit Chawla, CEO
Ata Rasekhi, VP of Product
Steve Tomasini, VP of Sales of Americas & APAC

Provider of open source mobile application server software. The company offers training and technical support services.

Function Engineering   HQ
163 Everett Ave
Palo Alto CA 94301
P: 650-326-8834   PRC:304
www.function.com
Email: info@function.com
Estab: 1987

Stan Brigham, Senior Managing Engineer
Michelle Deng, Mechanical Engineer
Joel Jensen, Principal Engineer
Gary Gehrke, Product Designer
Sonya Fagan, Contact

Provider of mechanical design and engineering services for product development. The company serves the consumer electronics and robotics industries.

Funmobility Inc   HQ
2430 Camino Ramon
San Ramon CA 94583
P: 925-598-9700   F: 925-598-9770   PRC:316
www.funmobility.com
Email: info@funmobility.com
Estab: 1999

Adam Lavine, CEO
Ken Nowak, VP of Content & Operations
Brian Dana, VP of Development & Operations
Hudson George, VP of User Experience
Kai Yung, VP of Platform Engineering

Provider of solutions for mobile engagement and mobile marketing. The company also offers content marketing, digital strategy, and other services.

Furaxa Inc   HQ
808 Gilman St
Berkeley CA 94710
P: 925-253-2969   F: 925-253-4894   PRC:15
www.furaxa.com
Email: support@furaxa.com
Estab: 2001

Joel Libove, CEO
Steve Chacko, VP
Mike Ingle, VP of Engineering

Designer and supplier of signal synthesis, sampling, and pulse generating technologies and products.

Furukawa Sangyo North America Inc   LH
1871 The Alameda Ste 350
San Jose CA 95126
P: 408-496-0051   F: 408-496-0052   PRC:212
www.furukawa.co.jp

Mitsuyoshi Shibata, President

Provider of electric products for telecommunications and automotive needs. The company also serves energy, construction, and other sectors.

Futronix Inc   HQ
855 Mathew St
Santa Clara CA 95050
P: 408-735-1122   PRC:94
www.futronix-inc.com
Email: admin@futronix-inc.com
Estab: 1974

Tony Erlund, Administrator

Designer and developer of energy management systems. The company provides computer line clocks, electronic cam systems, and energy control systems.

Future Facilities Inc   BR
2055 Gateway Pl Ste 110
San Jose CA 95110
P: 408-436-7701   F: 408-436-7705   PRC:322
www.futurefacilities.com
Email: info@futurefacilities.com
Estab: 2004

Sherman Ikemoto, Director

Developer of engineering simulation software for the design and operation of electronics products. The company serves the industrial sector.

Future Fibre Technologies (US) Inc   HQ
800 W El Camino Real Ste 180
Mountain View CA 94040
P: 877-650-8900   F: 435-417-6671   PRC:59
www.fftsecurity.com
Email: sales@fftsecurity.com
Estab: 1994

Rob Broomfield, COO

Provider of fiber optic based intrusion detection systems for perimeter protection and pipeline security.

Futuredial Inc   HQ
392 Potrero Ave
Sunnyvale CA 94085
P: 408-245-8880   F: 408-245-8885   PRC:64
www.futuredial.com
Email: sales@futuredial.com
Estab: 1999

George C. Huang, CEO & Chairman
Dan Kikinis, CTO
Jason Li, VP of Engineering
Clarice Liao, Executive Director of Operations
Rae Jin, Product Manager

Developer of carrier-grade solutions and tools for mobile device recyclers, wireless operators, and mobile device manufacturers.

FutureWei Technologies Inc   BR
2330 Central Expy
Santa Clara CA 95050
P: 408-330-5000   PRC:63
huawoi.com
Email: tac.usa@huawei.com
Estab: 1987

Guo Ping, Deputy Chairman & Rotating Chairman
Liang Hua, Chairman
Wang Tao David Wang, Executive Director & Chairman of the Investment Review Board
Xu Wenwei William Xu, Director of the Board & President of the Institute of Strategic Research
Xu Zhijun Eric Xu, Deputy Chairman & Rotating Chairman

Provider of information and communications technology solutions. The company focuses on products such as transport network and data communication.

G Fred Lee & Associates   HQ
27298 E El Macero Dr
El Macero CA 95618-1005
P: 530-753-9630   PRC:142
www.gfredlee.com

G. Fred Lee, President

Provider of surface and groundwater evaluation services. The company focuses on landfill impacts, eutrophication, watershed studies, and other needs.

G&R Labs   HQ
2395 De La Cruz Blvd
Santa Clara CA 95050
P: 408-986-0377   F: 408-986-0416   PRC:13
www.grlabs.com
Estab: 1995

George Richardson, Founder

Manufacturer, seller, and calibrator of light measurement equipment. The company is engaged in design, delivery, and installation services.

g2 Engineering BR
16991 McGill Rd
Saratoga CA 95070
P: 650-605-4500   F: 650-887-2332   PRC:159
www.g2-engineering.com
Email: inbox@g2-engineering.com
Estab: 2005

Dave Reeder, VP of Marketing

Manufacturer of engineering products such as
bead mounts and related accessories. The company's applications include industrial automation
and controls.

G4s Secure Solutions (USA) Inc BR
100 Century Center Ct Ste 200
San Jose CA 95112
P: 408-453-4133   F: 408-453-6440   PRC:322
www.g4s.com
Email: sfr_info@usa.g4s.com
Estab: 1901

Mel Brooks, Regional President
John Connolly, Chairman of the Board
John Kenning, Regional CEO
Tim Weller, CFO
Stephane Verdoy, Group Sales & Marketing
Director

Provider of security management solutions such
as compliance and investigations, disaster and
emergency, and fraud abatement.

Galil Motion Control HQ
270 Technology Way
Rocklin CA 95765
P: 916-626-0101   F: 916-626-0102   PRC:94
www.galilmc.com
Email: support@galil.com
Estab: 1983

Jacob Tal, Co-Founder
Wayne Baron, Co-Founder & President
Kaushal Shah, VP
John Thompson, VP of Operations
Mark Middleton, Manager of Worldwide Sales

Manufacturer and supplier of motion controllers
and software tools. The company also offers drives
and power supplies.

Gallery Systems Inc BR
3200 College Ave Ste 6
Berkeley CA 94705
P: 510-652-8950   PRC:323
www.gallerysystems.com

Heather Lake, Manager of EmbARK Client
Services
Armen Baghdasaryan, IC Layout Engineer

Provider of collection management systems. The
company offers procedures consulting, project
management, and strategic planning services.

Gambit Corp HQ
586 Martin Ave Ste 7
Rohnert Park CA 94928
P: 707-588-2797   F: 707-588-2799   PRC:212
www.gambitcorp.com
Email: sales@gambitcorp.com
Estab: 1962

George Weise, President

Provider of engineering parts and services. The
company specializes in designing and building
tools and dies.

M-132

Game Your Game Inc HQ
653 Bryant St
San Francisco CA 94107
P: 888-245-3433   PRC:322
www.gamegolf.com
Email: support@gameyourgame.com
Estab: 2011

John McGuire, CEO

Developer of digital tracking system such as automatic shot tracking and hands-free game tracking
device to get the insights to improve the game.

GangaGen Inc HQ
3279 Emerson
Palo Alto CA 94306
P: 650-856-9642   PRC:34
www.gangagen.com
Email: info@gangagen.com
Estab: 2001

Janakiraman Ramachandran, Chairman
Amy Percy, President

Provider of proprietary recombinant protein for the
topical prevention and treatment of Staphylococ-
cal infections.

Gara Inc HQ
1730 Industrial Dr
Auburn CA 95603
P: 530-887-1110   F: 530-887-0807   PRC:243
www.1stsourcelighting.com
Email: sales@1stsourcelight.com
Estab: 1993

Greg Cooper, Sales Manager
Robert Brown, Sales & Business Development
Manager

Designer and manufacturer of energy efficient
lighting technologies. The company also focuses
on supply aspects.

Garcia and Associates HQ
2601 Mission St Ste 600
San Francisco CA 94110
P: 415-642-8969   F: 415-642-8967   PRC:133
garciaandassociates.com
Estab: 1994

Gus Garcia, Owner
Pat Moyer, CFO
Joe Drennan, VP of Wildlife Ecologist & Wetlands
Specialist & Regional Manager
David Kelly, VP of Environmental Compliance
Specialist & Regional Manager
John McCarthy, VP of Environmental Compliance
Specialist & Regional Manager

Provider of natural and cultural resource consultant services. The company's services include
permit acquisition, agency consultation, and
ecological research.

Garratt-Callahan Co HQ
50 Ingold Rd
Burlingame CA 94010
P: 650-984-5126   F: 650-692-6098   PRC:233
garrattcallahan.com
Estab: 1904

Jeffrey L. Garratt, President
Cesar Zabala, Territory Manager
Manny Chargualaf, Marketing Manager
Charles Burkland, Territory Manager
Matthew R. Garratt, SW Regional Sales Manager

Provider of water treatment services. The company's solutions include cooling water treatment and
safer chemical cleaning.

GarrettCom Inc HQ
47823 Westinghouse Dr   [N]
Fremont CA 94539
P: 510-438-9071   F: 510-438-9072   PRC:109
www.garrettcom.com
Email: sales@garrettcom.com
Emp: 51-200   Estab: 1989

John Stroup, Executive Chairman
Roel Vestjens, President & CEO
Henk Derksen, SVP of Finance & CFO
Ashish Chand, EVP of Industrial Automation
Brian Anderson, SVP of Legal & General Counsel
& Corporate Secretary

Manufacturer of land products hubs, repeaters,
concentrators, transceivers and media converters.

Gasket Specialties Inc HQ
6200 Hollis St
Emeryville CA 94608
P: 510-547-7955   F: 510-547-8242   PRC:162
www.gasketspecialties.com
Email: emeryville@gsimfg.com
Estab: 1925

Louise Barbee, Branch Manager
Paul Gutierrez, Manager
Erna Cariaso, Contact

Manufacturer of gaskets. The company engages
in adhesives, assembly, and bar coding services.

Gatan Inc HQ
5794 W Las Positas Blvd
Pleasanton CA 94588
P: 925-463-0200   PRC:20
www.gatan.com
Email: info-gatan@ametek.com
Estab: 1964

Jennifer McKie, VP of Global Marketing
Paolo Longo, Director of Global Applications
Paul Mooney, Director of Imaging R&D
Bob Buchanan, Director of Bus Development
Daniel Ray, Director of Technical Support Group

Manufacturer of instrumentation and software
used to enhance and extend the operation and
performance of electron microscopes.

Gateway Precision Inc HQ
2300 Calle De Luna
Santa Clara CA 95054
P: 408-855-8849 F: 408-855-9004 PRC:80
gatewayprecision.com
Email: sales@gatewayprecision.com
Estab: 1998

Chi To, Materials Manager
Jim Harrigan, Project Manager

Manufacturer of precision-machined components
and assemblies for image equipment manufacturers, telecom, food processing, and semiconductor
sectors.

Gauss Surgical Inc HQ
334 State St Ste 201
Los Altos CA 94022
P: 650-949-4153 PRC:189
www.gausssurgical.com
Email: info@gausssurgical.com
Estab: 2011

Siddarth Satish, Founder & CEO
Griffeth Tully, CMO
Mac Farnsworth, CFO
Steve Scherf, CTO
Douglas R. Carroll, CCO

Manufacturer of mobile devices. The company is
engaged in research and development services
and it serves the healthcare sector.

GC Micro Corp HQ
3910 Cypress Dr
Petaluma CA 94954
P: 707-789-0600 F: 707-789-0700 PRC:207
gcmicro.com
Email: info@gcmicro.com
Estab: 1986

Belinda Guadarrama, CEO
Chris Wilcox, Account Manager
Blaise Dunn, IT Manager
Eric Grumley, Account Manager
Joseph Whitson, Deputy Program Manager

Provider of IT hardware, software, and related
products to corporate and government accounts.
The company specializes in information technology.

GCT Semiconductor Inc HQ
2121 Ringwood Ave
San Jose CA 95131
P: 408-434-6040 F: 408-434-6050 PRC:61
www.gctsemi.com
Email: sales@gctsemi.com
Estab: 1998

John Schlaefer, CEO
Jeongmin Jeemee Kim, CTO & VP of Engineering
Gene Kulzer, Chief Financial & Administrative
Officer
David Yoon, VP International Finance & Treasurer
Alex Sum, VP of sales & Marketing

Designer and supplier of 4G mobile semiconductor solutions. The company also offers wireless
solutions for its clients.

GCX Corp HQ
3875 Cypress Dr
Petaluma CA 94954-5635
P: 707-773-1100 F: 707-773-1180 PRC:94
www.gcx.com
Email: sales@gcx.com
Estab: 1971

John Kruger, President & CEO
Del France, VP of Operations
Clint Thompson, VP
Mark Ross, General Manager
Ryan Boland, Director of OEM Sales

Provider of mounting solutions, application specific solutions, on-site services, and also technical
support.

GDCA Inc HQ
1799 Portola Ave
Livermore CA 94551
P: 925-456-9900 F: 925-456-9901 PRC:211
www.gdca.com
Email: sales@gdca.com
Estab: 1987

Ethan Plotkin, CEO
Bill Spain, Director of Legacy Solutions
Lynn McFarland, Director of Special Product
Services
Anne Bennedsen, Director of Quality
Christa Williams, Human Resource Manager

Manufacturer of legacy embedded computers and
single boards. The company also specializes in
assurance, planning, and engineering.

GDM Electronic Medical HQ
2070 Ringwood Ave
San Jose CA 95131
P: 408-945-4100 F: 408-945-4070 PRC:189
www.gdm1.com
Email: sales@gdm1.com
Estab: 1982

Grant Murphy, President
Shawn Gorham, VP
Karen Guerrero, Director of Operations
Diego Martinez, Customer Service Manager
Susie Perches, Business Manager

Manufacturer of devices, electrical and electronics for medical, manufacturing and engineering
industries.

GDR Engineering Inc HQ
3525 Mitchell Rd
Ceres CA 95307-9479
P: 209-538-3360 PRC:304
gdrengineering.com
Email: info@gdrengr.com
Estab: 1978

Rick Ringler, Civil Engineer
Jason Andrews, Engineering Technician
Max Garcia, Principal

Provider of land development and infrastructure
engineering services. The company also focuses
on land planning and surveying.

Geiger Manufacturing Inc HQ
1110 E Scotts Ave [N]
Stockton CA 95205
P: 209-464-7746 F: 209-464-0536 PRC:80
www.geigermfg.com
Estab: 1969

Roger Haack, Contact

Provider of industrial equipment, fabrication, CNC
milling and welding services.

Gel-Pak DH
31398 Huntwood Ave
Hayward CA 94544
P: 510-576-2220 F: 510-576-2282 PRC:285
www.gelpak.com
Email: support@gelpak.com
Estab: 1980

Raymund Abiera, National Sales Manager
Ginger DeMello, Production Manager
Ted Villavicencio, Shipping Team Lead
Joey Flores, Automation Specialist
Linda Lou, Accountant

Provider of safety transport and product handling
services from bare die to medical components,
and other fragile parts.

Gemini Bio-Products HQ
930 Riverside Pkwy
West Sacramento CA 95605
P: 800-543-6464 F: 916-273-5222 PRC:24
www.gembio.com
Email: customerservice@gembio.com
Estab: 1985

Bert Polan, President
Dale Gordon, CEO
Rob Perry, COO
Scott Kantor, CFO
Ted Ayliffe, CTO

Provider of supplements, reagents, and human
products. The company is involved in medical
research and development.

Gen-9 Inc HQ
800 W El Camino Real
Mountain View CA 94040
P: 650-903-2235 PRC:325
www.gen-9.net
Email: info@gen-9.net
Estab: 2005

Mark A. Fauci, Founder & President & CEO

Provider of personal information management
services. The company offers services to the
industrial and commercial markers.

Genapsys Inc HQ
200 Cardinal Way 3rd Fl
Redwood City CA 94063
P: 650-330-1096 PRC:34
genapsys.com
Email: info@genapsys.com
Estab: 2010

Hesaam Esfandyarpour, Founder & CEO

Developer of DNA sequencing to enable a paradigm shift in genomic diagnostics. The company
specializes in GENIUS system that has footprint
of Apple iPad.

Genbook Inc HQ
548 Market St
San Francisco CA 94104
P: 415-227-9904 PRC:325
www.genbook.com
Email: bizdev@genbook.com
Estab: 2006

Rody Moore, Founder & CEO

Developer of online appointment scheduling software. The company is engaged in social media marketing services.

Genemed Biotechnologies Inc HQ
458 Carlton Ct
S San Francisco CA 94080-2012
P: 650-952-0110 F: 650-952-1060 PRC:39
www.genemed.com
Email: order@genemed.com
Estab: 1987

Dean Tsao, Chairman
Peter Luu, President
Rina Wu DeCamillis, VP of R&D & Operations
Frank Ling, Operations Manager
Erik Hasal, Technical Support Manager

Manufacturer of diagnostic reagents. The company caters to the pharmaceutical and diagnostic sectors.

Genentech Inc HQ
1 DNA Way
S San Francisco CA 94080-4990
P: 650-225-1000 F: 650-225-4630 PRC:34
www.gene.com
Email: busdev@gene.com
Estab: 1976

Bob Swanson, Founder
Julia Edwards, Chief of Staff & Advisor & Pharma Technical Regulatory
Sara Kenkare-Mitra, SVP of Development Sciences
Puneet S. Arora, VP of Clinical Development at Principia Biopharma
Mary Cromwell, VP of Pharma Technical Quality Drug Substance

Focuses on the treatment of breast cancer. The company offers services to patients and medical professionals.

Genentech Inc BR
1000 New Horizons Way
Vacaville CA 95688
P: 707-454-1000 F: 707-454-4390 PRC:34
www.gene.com
Email: supplierrelations@gene.com

Alexander Hardy, CEO
Ed Harrington, CFO
Levi Garraway, EVP & CMO
Cynthia Burks, SVP of Human Resources
Michael Varney, EVP

Provider of biotechnology services. The company uses human genetic information to develop medicines for life-threatening medical conditions.

Genepharm Inc HQ
1237 Midas Way
Sunnyvale CA 94085
P: 408-773-1082 F: 408-773-1018 PRC:268
www.genepharminc.com
Email: info@genepharminc.com
Estab: 2000

Xinfan Huang, CEO & President
George J. Lee, Chairman
Hanafi Tanojo, Vice President of Research & Development

Developer and commercialization of therapeutics for skin-related problems. The company is engaged in pre-clinical research.

General Foundry Service HQ
1390 Business Center Pl
San Leandro CA 94577
P: 510-297-5040 F: 510-614-2171 PRC:34
www.genfoundry.com
Email: data@genfoundry.com
Estab: 1946

John Fehringer, Quality Manager
E. John Ritelli, Project Manager
Rundong Zhu, Software Engineer
Dhivya Chandrasekaran, US IT Recruiter

Provider of foundry services. The company engages in pattern making, precision sand casting, and rubber plastic mold.

General Grinding Inc HQ
801 51st Ave
Oakland CA 94601
P: 510-261-5557 F: 510-261-5567 PRC:157
www.generalgrindinginc.com
Estab: 1943

Michael Bardon, President
Lynne Fone, Office Manager

Provider of precision, centerless, and surface grinding services. The company serves the medical and military industries.

General Hydroponics Inc HQ
2877 Giffen Ave
Santa Rosa CA 95407
P: 707-824-9376 F: 707-824-9377 PRC:43
www.generalhydroponics.com
Estab: 1976

Kristina Haley, VP
Keith Evans, Operations Manager
Terry Neider, Technical Sales Officer

Providers of Hydroponics. The company offer solution for commercial producers especially in non arable areas.

General Lasertronics Corp HQ
1520 Montague Expy Ste 5
San Jose CA 95131-1408
P: 408-947-1181 PRC:159
www.lasertronics.com
Email: info@lasertronics.com
Estab: 1996

Ray J. Noel, President & CEO
Mitchell Wool, VP of Programmer
Robert L. Cargill, VP of Technology Development
Ralph Miller, Director of Marketing Communications
Haresh Patel, Electronics Engineer

Developer of scanning and control technologies that make laser ablation an alternative to traditional abrasives and solvents for removing coatings.

General Networks Corp HQ
3524 Ocean View Blvd [N]
Glendale CA 91208
P: 818-249-1962 PRC:104
gennet.com
Email: info@gennet.com
Emp: 51-200 Estab: 1984

Todd Withers, President

Provider of consulting and managed services for customers who need to manage and process business-critical information.

General Vision HQ
1150 Industrial Ave Ste A
Petaluma CA 94952
P: 707-765-6150 PRC:189
www.general-vision.com
Estab: 1987

Guy Paillet, President & CEO

Provider of hardware and software products. The company specializes in artificial intelligence and image analytics.

Genesys Logic America Inc BR
2860 Zanker Rd Ste 105
San Jose CA 95134
P: 408-435-8899 F: 408-435-8886 PRC:110
www.genesyslogic.com
Email: sales@genesysamerica.com
Estab: 2002

Simon Lou, Sales Manager

Developer of electric circuits, semiconductors, digital communications products, computer peripherals, and other related products.

Genmark Automation Inc HQ
46723 Lakeview Blvd
Fremont CA 94538
P: 510-897-3400 F: 510-897-3401 PRC:309
www.genmarkautomation.com
Email: mktg-sales@genmarkautomation.com
Estab: 1985

Victor Sales, President
Bill Harrell, VP of Operations
Marius Avram, Global Sales Director
Brian Paiva, RMA Service Department Technician in Test & Calibration

Provider of robotics for automated manufacturing applications. The company offers services to the data storage and related industries.

Genomic Health Inc HQ
301 Penobscot Dr
Redwood City CA 94063-4700
P: 650-556-9300 F: 650-556-1132 PRC:34
www.genomichealth.com
Email: customerservice@genomichealth.com
Estab: 2000

Steven Shak, Founder
Kimberly J. Popovits, CEO & President & Chairman
Dean L. Schorno, CFO
Brad Cole, COO
James J. Vaughn, Chief U.S. Commercial Officer

Specializes in the treatment of cancer. The company is engaged in patient management software development.

Genstor Systems Inc HQ
1501 Space Park Dr
Santa Clara CA 95054
P: 408-980-0121 F: 408-980-0127 PRC:91
www.genstor.com
Email: info@genstor.com

Michael Ko, Production Manager

Provider of customized hardware solutions for server, storage, clusters, personal computers, and workstations.

Gentec Manufacturing Inc HQ
2241 Ringwood Ave
San Jose CA 95131
P: 408-432-6220 F: 408-435-1757 PRC:80
gentecmfg.com
Email: sales@gentecmfg.com
Estab: 1976

Mark Diaz, President
Mike Elder, Manager of Production

Provider of machining services. The company also offers measuring, testing, turning, and engineering services.

Geo M Martin Co HQ
1250 67th St
Emeryville CA 94608
P: 510-652-2200 F: 510-652-6447 PRC:80
www.geomartin.com
Email: info@geomartin.com
Estab: 1929

Robert A. Morgan, President
George R. Martin, EVP & COO
Greg Gargalikis, Production Manager
Jon Ames, Mechanical Engineering R&D Manager
Edwina Figueras, Payroll Accounting Manager

Developer of equipment for corrugated container industry. The company offers training, field support, and technical services.

Geo Semiconductor Inc HQ
101 Metro Dr Ste 620
San Jose CA 95110
P: 408-638-0400 F: 408-638-0443 PRC:86
geosemi.com
Email: sales@geosemi.com
Estab: 2009

Paul M. Russo, Founder & Director & Chairman & CEO
Raphael Hananel, Owner
Hiro Ito, VP
Ronald Allard, VP of Worldwide Sales
Kent Goodin, VP

Provider of imaging solutions. The company specializes in the design and fabrication of image sensors and multimedia processing engines.

Geo-Tech Information Solutions HQ
PO Box 418150
Sacramento CA 95841
P: 916-941-8300 F: 916-941-6578 PRC:142
geo-techsolutions.com
Email: geo-tech@comcast.net

Keith Betchley, Principal

Provider of concierge services in the environmental and natural hazard disclosure risk management field.

Geochemical Research Laboratory HQ
20 Portola Green Cir
Portola Valley CA 94028-7833
P: 650-851-1410 PRC:131
www.geochemicalresearch.com
Estab: 1986

Richard E. Hughes, Founder & Director of Laboratory

The company uses energy dispersive x-ray fluorescence spectrometry to determine the element composition of volcanic rocks. The company specializes in archaeological geochemistry.

Geofusion Inc HQ
2830 Smith Grade
Santa Cruz CA 95060
P: 831-458-1418 PRC:316
www.geofusion.com
Email: sales@geofusion.com
Estab: 2001

Alexander Matiyevsky, Founder & VP

Specializes in virtual reality and 3D visualization services. The company offers software development kits.

Geometrics Inc HQ
2190 Fortune Dr
San Jose CA 95131
P: 408-954-0522 F: 408-954-0902 PRC:13
www.geometrics.com
Email: sales@geometrics.com
Estab: 1969

Mark Prouty, President
Ron Royal, VP of Operations
Craig Lippus, VP of Seismic Division
Douglas Groom, Director of Electromagnetic Products
Steve Rosen, Director of Marketing

Manufacturer of geophysical instruments and equipment. The company also focuses on the sales and distribution.

Georg Fischer Signet LLC HQ
3401 Aero Jet Ave [N]
El Monte CA 91734
P: 626-571-2770 F: 626-573-2057 PRC:235
www.gfps.com
Email: info@georgfischer.com
Estab: 2007

Mads Joergensen, CFO & SVP

Manufacturer of piping systems and components.

Geosyntec Consultants Inc BR
3043 Gold Canal Dr Ste 100
Rancho Cordova CA 95670
P: 916-637-8048 PRC:138
www.geosyntec.com
Email: contact@geosyntec.com
Estab: 1983

Ken Susilo, VP
Sam Williams, Principal Hydrogeologist & VP
Thierry Sanglerat, EVP
Chuck Raymond, Marketing Manager
Avery Blackwell, Senior Staff Engineer

Provider of consulting and engineering services. The company serves customers in the oil and gas, refining, petrochemical, and waste management industries.

GeoTrust Inc HQ
350 Ellis St [N]
Mountain View CA 94043
P: 520-477-3110 F: 650-429-7367 PRC:104
www.geotrust.com
Email: support@geotrust.com
Estab: 1998

Jorge Sauri, Founder & CTO

Provider of digital certificates for secure online transactions and business over the Internet.

Gerlinger Steel & Supply Company HQ
1527 Sacramento St
Redding CA 96001
P: 530-243-1053 F: 530-246-4736 PRC:80
www.gerlinger.com
Email: sales@gerlinger.com
Estab: 1929

Jo Gerlinger, CFO & Owner
Jason Bahr, Manager
Judy Waldear, Outside Sales Representative

Provider of metal products and industrial services. The company offers metalworking machinery and supplies.

Geron Corp HQ
149 Commonwealth Dr Ste 2070
Menlo Park CA 94025
P: 650-473-7700 F: 650-473-7750 PRC:268
www.geron.com
Email: info@geron.com
Estab: 1990
Sales: Under $1 Million

John A. Scarlett, President & CEO & Chairman
Olivia K. Bloom, EVP of Finance & CFO & Treasurer
Andrew J. Grethlein, EVP
Leslie Mooi, VP of Intellectual Property
Melissa A. Kelly Behrs, EVP

Developer of telomerase inhibitors, imetelstat, in hematologic myeloid malignancies. The company is engaged in clinical trials.

GestureTek Inc HQ
5255 Stevens Creek Blvd Ste 162
Santa Clara CA 95051
P: 408-506-2206   F: 408-732-3977   PRC:322
gesturetekmobile.com
Email: support@gesturetekmobile.com
Estab: 1986

Yoshitaro Kumagai, SVP
Patti Jordan, Director of Marketing & Communications

Provider of gesture-based user interfaces for
mobile devices. The company offer services to the
gaming and entertainment industries.

Gevicam Inc HQ
691 S Milpitas Blvd Ste 115
Milpitas CA 95035
P: 408-262-5772   F: 408-262-0962   PRC:68
gevicam.com
Email: info@gevicam.com
Estab: 2006

Toshi Hori, President

Developer and manufacturer of industrial cameras
based on Gigabit Ethernet Technology for the industrial, scientific, and homeland security markers.

Giga Test Labs HQ
2324 Walsh Ave
Santa Clara CA 95051
P: 408-524-2700   F: 408-524-2777   PRC:209
www.gigatest.com
Estab: 1989

Harry Christie, VP of Sales

Provider of measurement and probing products
for the electronics industry. The company offers
test equipment and fixtures for modeling and
simulation.

GigaGen Inc HQ
1 Tower Pl Ste 750
S San Francisco CA 94080
P: 415-978-2101   PRC:34
www.gigagen.com
Estab: 2010

Everett Meyer, Founder
David Johnson, CEO
Adam Adler, CSO
Carter Keller, COO
Erica Stone, VP of Oncology

Provider of biotherapeutics solutions. The company offers recombinant polyclonal hyperimmune
gammaglobulin.

Gigamat Technologies HQ
47269 Fremont Blvd
Fremont CA 94538
P: 510-770-8008   PRC:159
www.gigamat.com
Email: sales@gigamat.com
Estab: 2002

Edmond Abrahamians, President & CEO

Provider of polishers, sorters, grinders, crystal
pullers, and related accessories. The company
offers services to the industrial sector.

Gigamon HQ
3300 Olcott St
Santa Clara CA 95054-5455
P: 408-831-4000   F: 408-831-4001   PRC:324
www.gigamon.com
Email: inside.sales@gigamon.com
Estab: 2004

Shane Buckley, President & COO
Paul Hooper, CEO
Shehzad Merchant, CTO
Christel Ventura, CPO
Karl Van den Bergh, CMO

Provider of traffic visibility solutions for enterprises, data centers, and the education, financial, and
healthcare industries.

Gigwalk HQ
539 Bryant St Ste 401
San Francisco CA 94107
P: 888-237-5896   PRC:323
www.gigwalk.com
Email: sales@gigwalk.com
Estab: 2010

Sriram Yadavalli, CEO
Molly Glover Gallatin, VP of Marketing

Provider of analytics and collaboration tools and
they are used in the management of mobile work
force.

Gigya Inc HQ
2513 E Charleston Rd
Mountain View CA 94043
P: 650-353-7230   PRC:322
www.sap.com

Christian Klein, CEO
Juergen Mueller, CTO
Luka Mucic, CFO
Stefan Ries, Chief Human Resource Officer
Thack Brown, COO

Provider of widget distribution, content sharing,
and advertising platform. The company caters to
the needs of social web.

Gilead Sciences Inc HQ
333 Lakeside Dr
Foster City CA 94404
P: 650-574-3000   F: 650-578-9264   PRC:268
www.gilead.com
Email: corporate_development@gilead.com
Estab: 1987
Sales: Over $3B

Andrew Dickinson, CFO
Johanna Mercier, CCO
John G. McHutchison, EVP of Research, Clinical
Research & Development & Chief Scientific
Officer
Jyoti Mehra, EVP of Human Resources
Taiyin Yang, EVP of Pharmaceutical Development
& Manufacturing

Provider of medicines for the treatment of liver
diseases, hematology, oncology, and other cardiovascular diseases.

Gilmour Craves HQ
455 Irwin St Ste 201
San Francisco CA 94107
P: 415-431-9955   F: 415-431-9905   PRC:325
gilmourcraves.com
Email: info@gilmourcraves.com
Estab: 1996

Bill Craves, Founding Partner
David Gilmour, Creative Director
Matt Browne, Art Director & Senior Visual De-
signer
Joanne Walker, Production Manager
Nathan Craves, Site Support Manager

Provider of graphic design, advertising, media
planning, strategic marketing, and print management services.

Gilsson Technologies HQ
2576 Barrington Ct
Hayward CA 94545
P: 510-940-7777   F: 510-740-3459   PRC:68
www.gilsson.com
Estab: 2001

Ming Ho, President

Manufacturer of GPS systems and accessories.
The company offers external GPS antenna
mounts and GPS antenna network splitter kits.

GiS Planning Inc HQ
1 Hallidie Plz Ste 760
San Francisco CA 94102
P: 415-294-4775   F: 415-294-4770   PRC:325
gisplanning.com
Email: sales@gisplanning.com
Estab: 1998

Pablo Monzon, Managing Director & Founder
Jeff Suneson, Director of Client Services
Bryan Beatty, Director of Sales
David Battles, Regional Director

Provider of geographic information systems. The
company is engaged in the building of patent-pro-
tected site selection website.

GitHub Inc HQ
88 Colin P Kelly Jr St
San Francisco CA 94107
P: 877-448-4820   PRC:315
github.com
Email: support@github.com
Estab: 2008

Nat Friedman, CEO
Erica Brescia, COO
Carrie Olesen, Chief Human Resource Officer
Mike Taylor, CFO
Jason Warner, CTO

Provider of an online platform that allows users to
learn, store and share codes with individuals.

Glacier Microelectronics Inc HQ
990 Richard Ave Ste 105
Santa Clara CA 95050
P: 408-244-0778   PRC:212
glaciermicroelectronics.com
Email: info@glaciermicroelectronics.com

Paul McCambridge, CEO & President
Dave Byrd, CTO

Developer of mixed signal semiconductor devices.
The company's products include synthesizers and
RFIC devices.

Glaser & Associates Inc HQ
4808 Sunrise Dr
Martinez CA 94553
P: 925-228-3200   F: 925-228-3220   PRC:80
www.glaserbolt.com
Email: customerservice@glaserbolt.com
Estab: 1964

William Glaser, Founder

Manufacturer and distributor of fastening solutions.
The company offers bolts, screws, rods and studs,
and anchors.

Glassbeam Inc HQ
2350 Mission College Blvd Ste 777
Santa Clara CA 95054
P: 408-740-4600   F: 408-740-4601   PRC:322
www.glassbeam.com
Email: info@glassbeam.com
Estab: 2009

Puneet Pandit, Founder & CEO
Ashok Agarwal, VP of Engineering
Pramod Sridharamurthy, VP of Products & India
Operations
John Ferraro, VP of Sales
Dinesh Katiyar, Senior Director of Strategic
Accounts

Provider of support solutions and it serves the medical, storage, and wireless networking industries.

Glasspoint Solar Inc HQ
47669 Fremont Blvd
Fremont CA 94538
P: 415-778-2800   PRC:135
www.glasspoint.com
Email: info@glasspoint.com
Estab: 2009

David Allsworth, CFO
John O'Donnell, VP of Business Development
Ali Zaabi, Information Technology Manager
Manish Chandra, Senior Mechanical Engineer

Manufacturer of solar steam generators for the
oil and gas industry. The company is engaged in
design and installation services.

Glenmount Global Solutions BR
600 E Main St Ste 100
Vacaville CA 95688
P: 707-258-8400   F: 707-258-8465   PRC:323
www.glenmountglobal.com
Estab: 1986

Tom Nelson, EVP of Western Region of Glen-
mount Global Solutions
Brant Jorgenson, Senior Project Manager
Kristin Worrell, Scientist

Provider of industrial equipment control, energy
management, and other systems. The company
serves automotive, food, chemical, and other
sectors.

GLF Integrated Power Inc HQ
4500 Great America Pkwy Rm 1045
Santa Clara CA 95054
P: 408-239-4326   PRC:126
glfipower.com
Email: info@glfipower.com
Estab: 2013

Stephen W. Bryson, VP of Engineering

Manufacturer of power switch devices for smartphones, mobile health devices, laptops, remote
sensors, wearables, SSD modules, and off
batteries.

Gliamed Inc HQ
1072 S De Anza Blvd Ste A107-538
San Jose CA 95129
P: 408-457-8828   PRC:333
www.gliamed.com
Email: info@gliamed.com
Estab: 2001

Barry Dickman, CEO
John McCartney, Senior Director of Project Management

Provider of drugs for the regeneration of skin,
cardiac muscle, cartilage, bone, brain and other
tissues.

Global Cybersoft Inc HQ
5994 West Las Positas Blvd Ste 20
Pleasanton CA 94588
P: 424-247-1226   F: 424-247-1201   PRC:322
www.globalcybersoft.com
Estab: 2000

Chris Nguyen, VP
Toan Ngo, Director

Provider of software development and IT outsourcing services, such as systems integration
and maintenance.

Global Infotech Corp HQ
2890 Zanker Rd Ste 202
San Jose CA 95134
P: 408-567-0600   PRC:323
www.global-infotech.com
Email: info@global-infotech.com
Estab: 1996

Alka Singh, Account Manager
Praful Sharma, Staffing & Operations Manager
Rhea Kapoor, Technical Recruiter
Manish Sharma, Recruiter

Provider of software services. The company's
software solutions focuses on staff augmentation,
telecom, systems integration, chip design, ERP,
and CRM domains.

Global Marketing Associates Inc HQ
751 N Canyon Pkwy
Livermore CA 94551
P: 510-887-2462   F: 510-887-1882   PRC:42
www.gmaherbs.com
Email: operation@gmaherbs.com

Jack Klein, Founder & Product Development &
Strategic Marketing
Kenneth Yeung, Chairman
Clement Yu, President & CEO

Providers of nutrition supplements to health care
industry. The company supply innovative and
quality ingredients to health care industry.

Global Presenter BR
728 Charcot Ave
San Jose CA 95131
P: 408-526-0221   F: 408-526-0212   PRC:316
www.globalpresenter.com
Email: sales@globalpresenter.com
Estab: 2000

John Miles, VP
Laurie Smith, Accounting Manager
David Marsac, Engineering Manager
Ed Goldman, Sales Manager
Pat Kelley, Area Sales Manager

Designer and builder of meeting room communication systems. The company is a provider of
design, delivery, and system integration solutions.

Global Software Resources HQ
4447 Stoneridge Dr
Pleasanton CA 94588
P: 925-249-2200   F: 925-249-2203   PRC:323
www.gsr-inc.com
Email: corporate@gsr-inc.com
Estab: 1992

Fred Valdez, Information Technology Manager

Provider of application development, business
intelligence, testing and mobile computing, and
collaboration services.

Global Unichip Corp HQ
2851 Junction Ave Ste 101
San Jose CA 95134
P: 408-382-8900   F: 408-321-8299   PRC:208
www.globalunichip.com
Email: sales@ip-semantics.com

Ken Chen, President
Vincent W. Li, Chief Human Resource Officer & VP
Daniel Chien, CFO & SVP
Louis Lin, SVP of Design Service
Chiang Fu, SVP

Provider of technology and embedded CPU
design services. The company's services include
package engineering, test engineering, and supply chain management.

GlobalFluency HQ
1494 Hamilton Way   [N]
San Jose CA 95125
P: 408-677-5300   F: 408-677-5301   PRC:45
www.globalfluency.com
Email: donovan@globalfluency.com
Emp: 11-50   Estab: 1987

Donovan Neale-May, President
Bryan DeRose, VP of Business Development
Dave Murray, EVP
Kevin Sugarman, Director of Relations

Provider of communications services that helps
clients in shaping perceptions, developing and
growing markers, expanding customer relationships and building valued brands.

Globalfoundries Inc   BR
2600 Great America Way
Santa Clara CA 95054
P: 408-462-3900   PRC:86
www.globalfoundries.com
Estab: 2009

Thomas Caulfield, CEO
Doug Devine, SVP & CFO
Emily Reilly, SVP & Chief Human Resource
Officer
Cary Haggard, Chief Audit Executive
Gregg Bartlett, SVP of Technology, Engineering
& Quality

Provider of semiconductor foundry services. The
company deals with design tools, IP suppliers and
ASIC partners.

GlobalSoft Inc   HQ
255 N Market St Ste 285
San Jose CA 95117
P: 408-564-0307   PRC:325
www.globalss.com
Email: info@globalss.com
Estab: 1998

Raj Lohia, CEO
Robert Caplan, COO

Provider of software consultancy services. The
company offers application development, training
program management, and engineering services.

Globant   BR
875 Howard St 3rd Fl Ste 320
San Francisco CA 94103
P: 877-215-5230   PRC:323
www.globant.com
Email: info@globant.com

Andres Angelani, Chief Solutions Officer
Andrew Burgert, General Manager
Juan Pedro Pereyra, Solutions Partner

Provider of software products and solutions for
cloud computing, mobile, gaming, enterprise
consumerization, and data visualization.

Globavir Biosciences Inc   HQ
5150 El Camino Real Ste A-32
Los Altos CA 94022
P: 650-351-4495   PRC:34
www.globavir.com
Email: info@globavir.com
Estab: 2011

Shalabh Gupta, Founder & President & CEO

Developer of biotechnology products. The company specializes in small molecule drugs to treat
cancer and infectious diseases.

Glooko Inc   HQ
303 Bryant St
Mountain View CA 94041
P: 650-720-5310   PRC:194
www.glooko.com
Email: support@glooko.com
Estab: 2010

Yogen Dalal, Founder
Rick Altinger, CEO
Vikram Singh, Director of Product Management
Sam Wynbrandt, Director of Product Management
Erica Ceballos, Associate Marketing Manager

Provider of diabetes management solution. The
company offers platform to allow patients manage
diabetes data and collaborate with their doctors.

M-138

**Glowlink Communications Technology
Inc**   HQ
1215 Terra Bella Ave
Mountain View CA 94043
P: 650-237-0220   F: 650-237-0225   PRC:68
Estab: 2000

Chris Vo, Manager of Product Testing
Harry Zhu, Engineer

Provider of emitters, global monitoring, and uplink
power control devices. The company also offers
alignment and commissioning services.

Glycomine Inc   HQ
733 Industrial Rd
San Carlos CA 94070
P: 650-401-2016   PRC:196
glycomine.com
Email: info@glycomine.com

Peter McWilliams, CEO
Teppei Shirakura, Scientific Director of Chemistry
Kathlene Powell, Senior Director CMC & Quality
Operations
Lisa Koch-Hulle, Senior Director of Regulatory
Affairs
Mary Jo Bagger, Senior Director of Clinical
Operations

Developer of therapy solutions for the treatment
of orphan diseases of glycosylation. The company
focuses on genetic disorders of lipid glycosylation
and protein.

Glyphic Technology   HQ
156 E Dana St
Mountain View CA 94041-1508
P: 650-964-5311   F: 650-967-4379   PRC:323
www.glyphic.com
Email: frontdesk2@glyphic.com
Estab: 1992

Mark Lentczner, Chief Architect & CEO
Leslie Smith, COO
Regan Bauman, Director of Marketing

Provider of software design and architecture solutions. The company focuses on Internet, server,
desktop, mobile, and embedded systems.

GM Associates Inc   HQ
9824 Kitty Ln
Oakland CA 94603
P: 510-430-0806   PRC:286
www.gmassoc.com
Email: sales@gm-quartz.com
Estab: 1974

Terri Hartman, VP
Karen Beato, VP
Deborah Camp, VP
Deacon French, CNC Manager
Bryan Casiano, Materials Engineer

Manufacturer of quartz fabricated products and
etch chalmers. The company offers machining,
slicing, cutting, and other services.

GM Nameplate Inc   BR
2095 O'Toole Ave
San Jose CA 95131
P: 408-435-1666   F: 408-435-8121   PRC:163
www.gmnameplate.com
Estab: 1954

David Fabris, General Manager
David Woodard, Prepress Manager

Manufacturer of die cut components. The company offers components for shielding, insulators,
adhesives, and fabricated parts.

Go!Foton Corp   RH
100 Century Center Ct Ste 203
San Jose CA 95112
P: 408-831-0131   F: 732-469-9654   PRC:63
gofoton.com
Estab: 1918

Simin Cai, Founder & President & CEO
Michael Zammit, VP & General Manager of Connectivity Solutions

Supplier of optical materials and components. The
company focuses on markers such as industrial,
image and scanning, and biomedical research.

GoEngineer   BR
3350 Scott Blvd Bldg 44
Santa Clara CA 95054
P: 408-213-1580   F: 408-213-1581   PRC:224
www.goengineer.com
Email: info@goengineer.com
Estab: 1984

Phillip Hughes, CEO & Co-Founder
Robert Lipp, COO & Co-Founder
Bruce Gale, Branch Manager
Drew Davis, Manufacturing Application Engineer
Andrew Berwald, Application Engineer

Provider of solid works engineering and Oracle
agile PLM products. The company offers services
to the business sector.

Gold Standard Diagnostics Corp   HQ
2851 Spafford St
Davis CA 95618
P: 530-759-8000   F: 530-759-8012   PRC:20
goldstandarddiagnostics.com
Email: info@gsdx.us
Estab: 2006

John Griffiths, President
Jennifer Roth, VP of Product Development
Sarah Freligh, Buyer & Operations Supervisor

Provider of laboratory diagnostic solutions. The
company specializes in diagnosis of autoimmune
diseases, bacterial and viral diseases.

Gold Standard Productions   HQ
12952 Miriam Pl   [N]
Santa Ana CA 92705
P: 714-544-7000   PRC:60
www.goldstandardproductions.com
Email: gkstone@earthlink.net
Estab: 1982

Gary Stone, Director

Provider of video production, editing, DVD authoring, business meetings services.

Gold Star Web HQ
2499 Bruce Rd
Chico CA 95928
P: 530-891-1841 F: 530-891-4025 PRC:67
www.gs-web.com
Email: design@gs-web.com
Estab: 1995

Sherry Gillis, Owner

Provider of website design and hosting, development and web marketing, technical support, and programming services.

Golden Altos Corp HQ
402 S Hillview Dr
Milpitas CA 95035
P: 408-956-1010 F: 408-956-1212 PRC:211
goldenaltos.com
Email: sales@goldenaltos.com
Estab: 1984

Arlen Chou, President
Ben Mendoza, VP & General Manager
Rosa Ho, Manager
Roger Soroten, Equipment Engineer
Winston Kuok, Contact

Designer and manufacturer of burn-in boards. The company also provides post wafer fabrication services.

Golden Pacific Laboratories LLC HQ
4720 W Jennifer Ave Ste 105
Fresno CA 93722
P: 559-275-9091 PRC:303
www.gplabs.com
Email: info@gplabs.com

Sami Selim, President
Thomas Moate, General Manager

Provider of state of the art independent contract research services for agricultural, residential and occupational exposure assessments.

Golden Plastics Corp HQ
8465 Baldwin St
Oakland CA 94621
P: 510-569-6465 F: 510-569-9741 PRC:280
goldenplasticscorp.com
Email: sales@goldenplasticscorp.com
Estab: 1953

Robert Pardee, Plastic Technician

Provider of thermoforming services. The company specializes in part trimming, part design, and tooling.

Golden State Assembly LLC HQ
47823 Westinghouse Dr
Fremont CA 94539
P: 510-226-8155 PRC:62
gsassembly.com
Email: customerservice@gsassembly.com
Estab: 2006

Cesar Madrueno, President

Provider of turnkey engineered solutions for wiring, harnessing and custom cable assembly requirements. The company serves the industrial sector.

Golden Valley Systems Inc HQ
1605 S Main St Ste 113
Milpitas CA 95035
P: 408-934-5898 F: 408-934-5896 PRC:325
gvsystems.com
Email: sales@gvsystems.com
Estab: 1989

Irene Lee, Accounting Manager

Provider of enterprise integration solutions. The company offers technical, IT consulting, and green energy services.

Golden West Technology HQ
1180 E Valencia Dr [N]
Fullerton CA 92831
P: 714-738-3775 F: 714-738-7727 PRC:211
www.goldenwesttech.com
Emp: 51-200 Estab: 1974

Mike Kutzle, Director

Manufacturer of electronic equipment.

Golder Associates Inc BR
425 Lakeside Dr
Sunnyvale CA 94085
P: 408-220-9223 F: 408-220-9224 PRC:142
golder.com
Estab: 1960

Anna-Lena Oberg-Hogsta, President Europe Middle East
Greg Herasymuik, President
Hisham Mahmoud, Global President & CEO
Mark Brightman, President of Mining
Tom Logan, COO

Provider of ground engineering and environmental services. The company serves business organizations and the industrial sector.

Gongio HQ
814 Mission St 4th Fl
San Francisco CA 94103
P: 650-276-3068 PRC:315
www.gong.io
Estab: 2015

Amit Bendov, Co-Founder & CEO
Eilon Reshef, Co-Founder & CTO
Eran Aloni, COO
Ryan Longfield, CRO
Tim Riitters, CFO

Developers of revenue intelligence platform that delivers insights at scale.

Gonsel'S Machine Shop HQ
8710 G St
Oakland CA 94621
P: 510-569-8086 F: 510-569-0433 PRC:233
gonsels.com
Estab: 1953

Jim Gonsalves, Owner

Provider of CNC and millwork, inspection, fabrication, and re-machining services. The company serves the food and beverage industry.

Gooch & Housego BR
44247 Nobel Dr
Fremont CA 94538
P: 650-300-5744 PRC:212
www.goochandhousego.com
Estab: 1948

Mark Webster, CEO
Chris Jewell, CFO
Murray Reed, CTO
Jon Fowler, EVP of Commercial Development
Kathy Sarna, Customer Service Manager

Manufacturer of precision optical components. The company also focuses on related subsystems and systems.

Good Dog Design HQ
21 Corte Madera Ave Ste 2
Mill Valley CA 94941
P: 415-383-0110 PRC:325
gooddogdesign.com
Email: info_us@gooddogdesign.com
Estab: 1992

Ken Hodgson, Owner
Gini Gooden, Manager
Laurie Chu, Project Manager
Wesley Huang, Software Engineer
Jerry Chai, Software Engineer

Provider of digital designing services. The company offers web development and designing and mobile application services.

Goodman Ball Inc HQ
3639 Haven Ave
Menlo Park CA 94025
P: 650-363-0113 F: 650-363-8294 PRC:152
www.goodmanball.com
Email: sales@goodmanball.com
Estab: 1983

Tom Krpan, Controller
Emmett Summers, Buyer & Planner

Manufacturer of spare military equipment for the U.S. Government. The company's in-house capabilities include CNC machining and structural welding.

Googleplex HQ
1600 Amphitheatre Pkwy
Mountain View CA 94043
P: 650-253-0000 PRC:322
www.google.com
Estab: 1998

Sergey Brin, Co-Founder
Ragi Burhum, Co-Founder & CEO
Patrick Pichette, SVP & CFO
Catherine Lacavera, VP of Legal
Iris Chen, VP of Legal

Provider of search engine to make world's information universally accessible. The company specializes in Internet-related services and products.

Gorilla Circuits Inc HQ
1445 Oakland Rd
San Jose CA 95112
P: 408-294-9897 F: 408-297-1540 PRC:211
www.gorillacircuits.com
Email: info@gorillacircuits.com

Hershel Petty, President
Karl Rauch, VP of Sales
Jaime Gutierrez, VP of Operations
Ted Nguyen, General Manager of Assembly
Operations
Crescencio Gutierrez, General Manager

Provider of printed circuit engineering and fabrication solutions. The company caters to electronic companies.

Grabber Construction Products Inc BR
205 Mason Cir
Concord CA 94520
P: 800-869-1375 F: 407-295-9305 PRC:80
www.grabberman.com
Email: deckmaster@deckmaster.com

Roland Snyder, President & CFO
Tracy Yoder, Operations Manager
Terry Boswell, National Accounts Manager
Shawn Rogers, Outside Sales Representative

Manufacturer of fasteners and machine tools. The company also specializes in distribution and other services.

Grabit Inc HQ
751 Laurel St Ste 534
San Carlos CA 94070
P: 408-642-1830 PRC:311
www.grabitinc.com
Email: info@grabitinc.com
Estab: 2011

Harsha Prahlad, Founder & CTO & Product Officer
Greg Miller, CEO & President
Ron Wilderink, CFO
Dave Pap Rocki, VP of Engineering
Bob Roy, VP of Engineering

Inventor of electroadhesion technology. The company specializes in parts handling, package handling, and each pick applications.

Gracenote Inc HQ
2000 Powell St Ste 1500
Emeryville CA 94608
P: 510-428-7200 PRC:323
www.gracenote.com
Estab: 1998

Karthik Rao, President
John Batter, CEO
Amilcar Perez, CRO
Kay Johansson, CTO
Simon Adams, Chief Product Officer

Provider of music, video, and automotive solutions. The company focuses on television businesses and entertainment products.

GRAIL Inc HQ
1525 O'Brien Dr
Menlo Park CA 94025
P: 650-542-0372 PRC:25
grail.com
Email: bd@grail.com
Estab: 2016

George Golumbeski, President
Jennifer Cook, CEO
Angela Lai, CTO
Alex Aravanis, VP

Provider of research services and clinical study programs for the detection of cancer at an early stage.

Granberg International HQ
1051 Los Medanos St
Pittsburg CA 94565
P: 925-380-9400 PRC:159
www.granberg.com
Email: info@granberg.com
Estab: 1954

Erik Granberg, President
John Mahley, General Manager
Sylvia Mahley, Office Manager
Ben Hawkins, Sales Manager
Brian Mohr, Project Manager

Manufacturer of saw chain maintenance tools to repair and sharpen saw chain and attachments. The company offers brush attachments and cutting bars.

Grandflow Inc HQ
135 Lindberg Ave Ste D
Livermore CA 94551
P: 925-443-0855 F: 925-443-9428 PRC:323
www.grandflow.com
Email: support@grandflow.com
Estab: 1973

Matt Rusca, President
Tom Allen, COO & CTO
John Rusca, VP
Jack Vallerga, Contact
Jack Parker, Contact

Provider of e-cataloging and marketing automation solutions. The company offers print production, warehousing, and document management services.

Grandt Line Products HQ
2965 Minert Rd Ste B
Concord CA 94518
P: 925-671-0143 PRC:84

Phyllis G. Nishimori, Secretary & Treasurer

Manufacturer and wholesaler of model railroad miniatures in plastics. The company's services include design and installation.

Granite Digital HQ
3101 Whipple Rd
Union City CA 94587
P: 510-471-6442 F: 510-471-6267 PRC:62
www.granitedigital.com
Email: info@granitedigital.com

Frank Gabrielli, President
Conor Buckley, CEO
Mark Rodgers, EVP of Sales
Jonathan Callan, Creative Director
Sean Byrne, Director

Manufacturer of external diagnostic peripherals. The company is engaged in troubleshooting and maintenance services.

Granite Horizon LLC HQ
8153 Elk Grove Blvd Ste 20
Elk Grove CA 95758-5965
P: 916-647-6350 PRC:320
www.granitehorizon.com
Estab: 2007

Greg McAvoy-Jensen, CEO

Provider of content management solutions. The company offers design, development, project management, and user and developer training services.

Graybug Vision Inc HQ
275 Shoreline Dr Ste 450
Redwood City CA 94065
P: 650-487-2800 PRC:34
graybug.com
Email: info@graybug.vision
Estab: 2011

Frederic Guerard, CEO
Dan Salain, CTO
Daniel Geffken, Interim CFO
Charles Semba, CMO
Karl G. Trass, VP of Global Regulatory Affairs

Developer of pharmaceutical products for the treatment of blindness, including neovascular, glaucoma, and corneal graft rejection.

Grayland Environmental HQ
1807 Valdora St
Davis CA 95618-6315
P: 530-756-1441 PRC:139
graylandenvironmental.com
Email: grayland@prodigy.net
Estab: 1993

Jeffrey A. Clayton, Principal Geologist

Provider of environmental and natural resources protections services. The company offers environmental engineering, geological and geophysical services.

Great Circle Associates Inc HQ
2608 Buena Vista Ave [N]
Alameda CA 94501
P: 415-861-3588 F: 415-552-2982 PRC:322
www.greatcircle.com
Email: info@greatcircle.com
Estab: 1989

Brent Chapman, Founder & Principal

Provider of enterprise information technology infrastructure and networking services.

Greatlink International Inc   RH
44168 S Grimmer Blvd
Fremont CA 94538
P: 510-657-1667   F: 510-445-1588   PRC:97
www.greatlink.com
Email: ussales@greatlink.com
Estab: 1979

Herbert Hou, Operation Manager

Manufacturer of cable assemblies and related products for the medical, aerospace, and automotive industries.

Green Plug   HQ
Bishop Ranch 2, 2694 Bishop Dr Ste 209
San Ramon CA 94583
P: 925-867-2781   PRC:212
www.greenplug.us
Email: info@greenplug.us
Estab: 2006

Kathleen Harrison, Personal Assistant to CEO

Developer and provider of digital controller technology solutions and products to the consumer electronics markers.

Green Source Automation LLC   HQ
3506 Moore Rd
Ceres CA 95307
P: 209-531-9163   F: 209-531-9171   PRC:311
www.greensourceautomation.com
Email: info@greensourceautomation.com
Estab: 2009

Jim Frias, President
Chad Myers, Manager
Cliff Olson, Senior Service Engineer

Provider of redefining solutions for dairy industry. The company also offers technology for milking process.

Greenliant Systems   HQ
3970 Freedom Cir Ste 100
Santa Clara CA 95054
P: 408-200-8000   F: 408-200-8099   PRC:212
www.greenliant.com
Email: media@greenliant.com
Estab: 2010

Bing Yeh, CEO & Chairman
Arthur Kroyan, VP of Business Development & Marketing
Danny Ma, Senior Director
Dongsheng Xing, Director
Liu Heng Xiu, Senior Director of Product Engineering

Developer of storage solutions for the embedded systems. The company offers solid-state storage, controllers, and specialty flash memory.

Greenvity Communications Inc   HQ
5655 Silver Creek Valley Rd Ste 798
San Jose CA 95138
P: 408-935-9358   F: 408-273-6597   PRC:212
greenvity.com
Email: info@greenvity.com
Estab: 2011

Hung Nguyen, President & CEO
John Tero, VP
Edward Inyoung Cho, VP of Sales & Marketing
Jenny Lin, Senior RF System Engineer

Designer and developer of semiconductor solutions for home gateways, electric vehicles, and lighting products.

Greenwood Machine & Fabrication Inc   HQ
2517 Railroad Ave
Ceres CA 95307-1099
P: 209-538-2277   F: 209-538-3065   PRC:80
www.greenwoodmachine.net
Email: info@greenwoodmachine.net
Estab: 1976

Todd Greenwood, Owner
Kristin L. Willis, Office Manager

Provider of repair and fabrication services for commercial and industrial equipment. The company's customers include private companies and military contractors.

Grey San Francisco   BR
1001 Front St
San Francisco CA 94111
P: 415-403-8000   PRC:63
www.grey.com

Owen Dougherty, Chief Communications Officer
Don Lee, Payroll Manager

Provider of advertising, planning, sports marketing solutions. The company also focuses on customer relationship management.

Greytrix   RH
350 Rhode Is Ste 240
San Francisco CA 94103
P: 888-221-6661   PRC:323
greytrix.com
Email: us.sales@greytrix.com
Estab: 1997

Jiten Somani, COO
Rohit S. Greytrix, SVP
Pooja Singh, Project Manager
Harshil Rasputra, Regional Sales Manager
Francis Rodrigues, Products Head

Provider of integration and migration solutions. The company deals in analytics, cloud, mobility, and ERP/CRM consulting.

GridGain Systems Inc   HQ
1065 E Hillsdale Blvd Ste 220
Foster City CA 94404
P: 650-241-2281   F: 925-369-7193   PRC:325
www.gridgain.com
Email: info@gridgain.com
Estab: 2007

Nikita Ivanov, CTO & Founder
Abe Kleinfeld, President & CEO
Eoin O. Connor, CFO
Elena Schtein, VP of Finance
Terry Erisman, VP of Marketing

Developer of a Java and Scala-based cloud computing middleware for a wide range of multimedia applications.

Grio   HQ
201 Post St 11th Fl
San Francisco CA 94108
P: 415-395-9525   PRC:315
grio.com
Email: info@grio.com
Estab: 2008

Douglas Kadlecek, President & Founder
Brad Johnson, Partner
Brooks Mason, Managing Director
Adam Keating, Director of Engineering & Web
Chris Aldama, Managing Director

Specializes in web, iOS, and Android development.

Ground Hog Inc   HQ
1470 S Victoria Ct   [N]
San Bernardino CA 92408
P: 909-478-5700   F: 909-478-5710   PRC:159
www.groundhoginc.com
Email: sales@groundhoginc.com
Estab: 1948

Ed Carlson, Contact

Provider of earth drills and trenchers.

Groundwater & Environmental Services Inc   BR
882 Dover Cir
Benicia CA 94510
P: 866-507-1411   PRC:142
gesonline.com
Estab: 1985

Ann Downey, President & COO
Anthony Kull, Chairman
Edward Van Woudenberg, CEO
Michael Lemon, CFO
Rich Evans, SVP of Engineering & Technical Functions

Provider of environmental consulting services. The company serves customers in the oil and gas, government, and petroleum markers.

Group Manufacturing Services Inc   HQ
1928 Hartog Dr
San Jose CA 95131
P: 408-436-1040   F: 408-436-7967   PRC:80
www.groupmanufacturing.com
Email: sales@groupmanufacturing.com
Estab: 1981

Don Bader, Quality Assurance Manager

Manufacturer of precision sheet metal fabrication, precision machining, and design support services.

Group Seven Corp   HQ
930 Rincon Cir
San Jose CA 95131
P: 408-435-7477   F: 408-435-7478   PRC:209
www.group7.net
Email: info@group7.net
Estab: 1984

Jerry O'Connor, President

Producer of turnkey solutions to support high mix and low volume needs. The company also offers Vendor Managed Inventory (VMI) services.

Growing Energy Labs Inc   HQ
111 New Montgomery St Ste 500
San Francisco CA 94105
P: 415-857-4354   PRC:323
geli.net
Email: info@geli.net
Estab: 2010

Ryan Wartena, Founder

Developer of software to integrate, network, and economically operate energy storage systems. The company is engaged in analysis services.

GS Cosmeceutical USA Inc   HQ
131 Pullman St
Livermore CA 94551
P: 925-371-5000   F: 925-960-1400   PRC:251
gscos.com
Estab: 1998

Gogi Sangha, Founder
Gurkirpal Sandhu, COO
Sandhya Singh, Director of Research & Business
Development
Ronald Brooks, Associate Director of Operations
Norman Poon, IT Manager

Provider of custom contract manufacturing services. The company offers skin and personal care products.

GSI Technology   HQ
1213 Elko Dr
Sunnyvale CA 94089
P: 408-331-8800   F: 408-331-9795   PRC:96
www.gsitechnology.com
Email: apps@gsitechnology.com
Estab: 1995
Sales: $30M to $100M

Lee-Lean Shu, Chairman
Douglas Schirle, CFO
Patrick Chuang, SVP of Design Engineering
Ping Wu, VP of U.S. Operations
Robert Yau, VP of Engineering

Provider of telecommunication and networking services. The company is also engaged in sales and distribution.

GT Nexus Inc   HQ
1111 Broadway 7th Fl
Oakland CA 94607
P: 510-808-2222   F: 510-808-2220   PRC:325
gtnexus.com
Email: information@gtnexus.com
Estab: 1998

Greg Johnsen, CMO
Kurt Cavano, SVP & General Manager
Ron Park, Director of Product Management

Provider of supply chain, transportation, and investment management solutions. The company serves retailers and manufacturers.

Guardant Health Inc   HQ
505 Penobscot Dr
Redwood City CA 94063
P: 855-698-8887   F: 888-974-4258   PRC:44
guardanthealth.com
Email: clientservices@guardanthealth.com
Emp: 454 Estab: 2012
Sales: $100M to $300M

AmirAli Talasaz, President & COO
Helmy Eltoukhy, CEO
Derek Bertocci, CFO
Michael Wiley, CLO

Provider of sequencing and rare-cell diagnostics services focusing on cancer. The company serves the healthcare sector.

M-142

Guardian Analytics   HQ
2465 Latham St Ste 200
Mountain View CA 94040
P: 650-383-9200   PRC:325
guardiananalytics.com
Email: success@guardiananalaytics.com
Estab: 2005

Laurent Pacalin, CEO
Hue Harguindeguy, CFO
Prashanth Shetty, VP of Global Marketing
Luis Rojas, VP
Stephen Walsh, VP of Global Sales

Provider of enterprise and community banking solutions. The company is engaged in training and applied fraud analysis services.

Guerra Technologies Inc   HQ
5205 Prospect Rd 135-157
San Jose CA 95129
P: 408-526-9386   PRC:61
Estab: 1993

Maria Guerra, Owner
Jorge Guerra, CFO

Designer and manufacturer of RF technology related products. The company also offers consulting and evaluation services.

Guided Wave Inc   HQ
3033 Gold Canal Dr
Rancho Cordova CA 95670
P: 916-638-4944   F: 916-635-8458   PRC:11
www.guided-wave.com
Estab: 1983

Roger Schirmer, Owner
Susan Foulk, President
Justin Stirrat, Manufacturing & Facilities & Quality Manager
Ryan Lerud, Product Manager
Ken Gruessing, Electronic Engineer

Provider of online optical measurements services. The company caters to process analytical chemistry needs.

Guidetech   HQ
1300 Memorex Dr
Santa Clara CA 95050
P: 408-733-6555   PRC:19
www.guidetech.com
Email: sales@guidetech.com
Estab: 1988

Freddy Ben-Zeev, CTO

Developer of time measurement instruments. The company mainly caters to the semiconductor test industry.

Gumas Advertising   HQ
99 Shotwell St   [N]
San Francisco CA 94103
P: 415-621-7575   F: 415-255-8804   PRC:325
www.gumas.com
Email: jgumas@gumas.com
Estab: 1984

Craig Alexander, President
John Gumas, CEO
Janice Herwegh, SVP of Media
Frosene Phillips, Director of Operations
Kyle Gosselin, Digital Marketing Manager

Provider of strategic marketing, creative development and media planning and placement.

Guntert & Zimmerman Const Div Inc   HQ
222 E Fourth St
Ripon CA 95366
P: 209-599-0066   F: 209-599-2021   PRC:159
www.guntert.com
Email: gz@guntert.com
Estab: 1942

Ronald M. Guntert, CEO & President
Rolf C. Guntert, EVP of Sales
R.K. Shaw, VP of International Sales & Service
John Eisenhour, Sales Manager

Manufacturer of canal lining equipment, concrete batch plants, and other special equipment. The company serves the industrial sector.

Guzik Technical Enterprises   HQ
2443 Wyandotte St
Mountain View CA 94043
P: 408-752-5840   F: 650-625-9325   PRC:95
www.guzik.com
Email: sales@guzik.com
Estab: 1982

Nahum Guzik, CEO
Edmond Yip, Director of Product
Shelley Ortega, Purchasing Manager
Mikhail Konstantinov, Senior RF Engineer
Sergey Konshin, Senior Electronics Engineer

Manufacturer of test equipment for the computer industry. The company is involved in sales, training, and software downloads.

Gynesonics   HQ
600 Chesapeake Dr
Redwood City CA 94063
P: 650-216-3860   F: 650-299-1566   PRC:187
gynesonics.com
Estab: 2005

Chris Owens, President & CEO
Jordan Bajor, COO
Diane King, VP of Regulatory Affairs & Quality Assurance
Taraneh G. Farazi, VP of Clinical Affairs
James Sparks, VP of Manufacturing

Manufacturer and developer of therapeutic devices and related supplies for the treatment of uterine fibroids in women.

H & M Precision Machining   HQ
504 Robert Ave
Santa Clara CA 95050
P: 408-982-9184   F: 408-982-9186   PRC:80
h-mprecisionmachining.com
Estab: 1960

Bruce Harvey, President

Provider of precision manufacturing solutions. The company offers screw machines, CNC turning, CNC milling, and sawing services.

H J Hirtzer & Associates Inc   HQ
570 Valdry Ct Unit C-4
Brentwood CA 94513
P: 925-931-1450   PRC:179
www.hjhirtzer.com
Email: info@hjhirtzer.com

Jay Hirtzer, President

Manufacturer of steel links. The company specializes in the fabrication of insulated links for shipping and defense industries.

H P Machine & Engineering Inc HQ
2150 Oakland Rd
San Jose CA 95131
P: 408-383-9075 F: 408-383-9027 PRC:80
hpmachine.com
Estab: 1974

Nicole Peisker, Office Manager

Provider of job shop, prototype machining, CNC, and wire EDM services. The company offers services to the industrial sector.

H-Square Corp HQ
3100 Patrick Henry Dr
Santa Clara CA 95054-0701
P: 408-982-9108 F: 408-982-9183 PRC:209
www.h-square.com
Email: info@h-square.com
Estab: 1975

Myron Moreno, General Manager
Tony Newton, Manager & Manager
Caroline Montojo, Customer Service Manager
Paul Vierhus, Production Manager
Gary Lee, Machinist

Designer and manufacturer of tools and equipment. The company caters to the wafer fabrication industry.

H5 HQ
595 Market St Ste 610
San Francisco CA 94105
P: 415-625-6700 PRC:40
h5.com
Email: info@h5.com
Estab: 1999

Josh Simms, Founder & CEO
Todd Barber, Owner
Lionel Barrere, CTO
Carlos Oliveira, VP
Jason Richard, VP of Products

Provider of investigation solutions. The company offers hosting, case preparation, and keyword consulting services.

HackerRank HQ
700 E El Camino Real Ste 300
Mountain View CA 94041
P: 415-900-4023 PRC:315
www.hackerrank.com
Email: support@hackerrank.com
Estab: 2012

Vivek Ravisankar, Co-Founder & CEO
Harishankaran Karunanidhi, Co-Founder & CTO
Harishankaran K., Co-Founder
Jennifer Stagnaro, CMO
Juan Herrera, CRO

Technology recruiting tool that helps tech recruiters and hiring managers to identify and hire talents.

Hahnemann Laboratories Inc HQ
1940 Fourth St
San Rafael CA 94901
P: 415-451-6978 F: 415-451-6981 PRC:306
www.hahnemannlabs.com
Email: info@hahnemannlabs.com
Estab: 1985

Michael Quinn, Founder & President & CEO

Manufacturer of homeopathic medicines. The company offers dispensing kits, first aid kits, and also professional kits.

Haig Precision Manufacturing Corp HQ
3616 Snell Ave
San Jose CA 95136
P: 408-378-4920 F: 408-629-3459 PRC:80
www.haigprecision.com
Estab: 1960

Karl-Heinz Lachnit, Agent

Manufacturer of precision parts and assemblies. The company focuses on sheet metal, CNC milling and turning, stamping, welding, and powder coating.

Hallock Coin Jewelry HQ
2060 W Lincoln Ave [N]
Anaheim CA 92801
P: 714-635-8247 PRC:82
www.hallockjewelry.com
Email: hallock2@hotmail.com
Estab: 1970

Brett Hallock, Owner

Manufacturer of coin jewelry products.

Halo Electronics Inc HQ
2933 Bunker Hill Ln Ste 200
Santa Clara CA 95054
P: 650-903-3800 F: 650-903-9300 PRC:209
www.haloelectronics.com
Email: info@haloelectronics.com
Estab: 1991

Jeffrey Heaton, VP of Technical Marketing
Sharon Pickard, EU Sales Manager

Manufacturer of electromagnetic components. The company's products include DC/DC transformers, inductors, and RF transformers.

Halo Neuro Inc HQ
735 Market St 4th Fl
San Francisco CA 94103
P: 415-851-3338 PRC:189
www.haloneuro.com
Email: support@haloneuro.com
Estab: 2013

Brett Wingeier, CTO & Co-Founder
Daniel Chao, CEO & Co-Founder
Mark Mastalir, CMO

Developer of neurotech platform. The company offers services to athletes, elite teams, and organizations.

Halus Power Systems HQ
2539 Grant Ave
San Leandro CA 94579
P: 510-278-2212 F: 510-278-2211 PRC:297
www.halus.com
Email: office@halus.com
Estab: 2000

Louis Rigaud, General Manager
Kenneth Fries, Technical Services Manager
Lindsey K. Kendall, Engineering Manager
Sean Scarlett, Production Manager

Manufacturer of renewable energy products specializing in wind turbines and controls. The company offers design and remanufacturing services.

Hamamatsu Corp BR
2875 Moorpark Ave
San Jose CA 95128
P: 408-261-2022 F: 408-261-2522 PRC:13
www.hamamatsu.com
Email: usa@hamamatsu.com

Reji Samuel, VP
Connie Lazarus, Sales Manager
Michael Nguyen, Sales Engineer
Mai Idzkowski, Customer Service Representative

Manufacturer of devices for the generation and measurement of infrared, visible, and ultraviolet light.

Hammett & Edison Inc HQ
470 Third St W
Sonoma CA 95476
P: 707-996-5200 PRC:304
h-e.com
Estab: 1952

William F. Hammett, President
Rajat Mathur, VP
Brian Palmer, Staff Engineer
Neil Olij, Staff Engineer
Andrea L. Bright, Staff Engineer

Provider of engineering and related services to the wireless telecommunications and broadcasting industries.

Hammon Plating Inc HQ
890 Commercial St
Palo Alto CA 94303
P: 650-494-2691 PRC:53
www.hammonplating.com
Email: sales@hammonplating.com

Glenn Phinney, VP-General Manager
Dil Jeer, Quality Manager

Supplier of metal plating applications. The company also provides supply chain management solutions.

Hamrock Inc HQ
12521 Los Nietos Rd [N]
Santa Fe Springs CA 90670
P: 562-944-0255 PRC:202
www.hamrock.com
Email: info@hamrock.com
Emp: 1-10 Estab: 1976

Stephen R. Hamrock, President
Michael E. Hamrock, EVP

Provider of fabricated wire products.

Hana Microelectronics Inc BR
3140 De La Cruz Blvd Ste 101
Santa Clara CA 95054
P: 408-452-7474 PRC:212
www.hanagroup.com
Email: info-request@hanaus.com

Richard Han, CEO

Provider of electronic manufacturing services. The company focuses on PCBs, circuit assembly, RFID devices, LEDs, coil windings, and other products.

Hand Biomechanics Lab Inc HQ
77 Scripps Dr Ste 104
Sacramento CA 95825
P: 916-923-5073 F: 916-920-2215 PRC:303
www.handbiolab.com
Email: info@handbiolab.com
Estab: 1979

John Agee, President
Kim Sutton, Accountant

Provider of Biomechanics treatment devices. The company offers products like Agee Turnkey FCS, Wrist Jack, and Digit Widget.

Hanger Prosthetics & Orthotics Inc BR
1248 32nd St
South Sacramento CA 95816
P: 916-452-5724 F: 916-452-2715 PRC:190
hangerclinic.com
Estab: 1861

Vinit Asar, President & CEO

Provider of prosthetic and orthotic components and services. The company serves hospitals, patients, and the healthcare industry.

Hanger Prosthetics & Orthotics Inc BR
436 E Yosemite Ave Ste C
Merced CA 95065
P: 209-725-1295 F: 209-725-1769 PRC:189
hangerclinic.com
Estab: 1861

Rick Taylor, President
Richard Mason, Area Clinic Manager

Provider of orthotic and prosthetic services and products. The company also offers clinically differentiated programs to its clients.

Hantronix Inc HQ
10080 Bubb Rd
Cupertino CA 95014-4132
P: 408-252-1100 F: 408-252-1123 PRC:169
www.hantronix.com
Estab: 1975

Richard Choi, Director
Andrew Kim, Sales Manager
Ali Mosiemi, Sales Manager
Ali Moslemi, Area Sales Manager
Richard Kim, Regional Sales Manager

Producer of standard character and graphic modules, notebook displays, and custom liquid crystal displays.

Harkness Pharmaceuticals Inc HQ
4401 Eastgate Mall   [N]
San Diego CA 92121
P: 858-550-6061 F: 858-677-0800 PRC:268
www.harknesspharmaceuticals.com
Email: info@harknesspharmaceuticals.com
Estab: 2003

Byron Rubin, Co-Founder & Chief Scientific Officer & VP of Research
Edward Dennis, Co-Founder
Timothy J. Wollaeger, CEO
Peter C.M. McWilliams, Director of Business Development

Provider of research and development of therapies dealing with obesity.

Harmonie HQ
691 S Milpitas Blvd
Milpitas CA 95035
P: 408-907-1339   PRC:322
www.harmon.ie
Email: sales@harmon.ie
Estab: 1993

Yaacov Cohen, Founder & CEO
David Lavenda, VP of Product Strategy
Alyssa Franklin, Sales Manager

Provider of SharePoint applications for Outlook, mobile, and desktop platforms. The company offers records and knowledge management services.

Harmonic Inc HQ
4300 N First St
San Jose CA 95134
P: 408-542-2500 F: 408-542-2511 PRC:60
www.harmonicinc.com
Email: support@harmonicinc.com
Emp: 375 Estab: 1988
Sales: $300M to $1 Billion

Patrick Harshman, President & CEO
Carolyn V. Aver, CFO
Shahar Bar, SVP of Corporate Development
Charles Bonasera, SVP of Operations & Quality
Thierry Fautier, VP

Provider of production and delivery solutions. The company serves the broadcast, media, service providers, and post production markers.

Harris & Bruno International HQ
8555 Washington Blvd
Roseville CA 95678
P: 916-781-7676 F: 916-781-3645 PRC:159
www.harris-bruno.com
Email: info@harris-bruno.com
Estab: 1948

Nick Bruno, President
Jim Riga, VP of Operations
Leandra Wilson, Director of Human Resources & Strategic Operations
Joe Rodriguez, Project Manager
Kevin Kelley, Purchasing Manager

Provider of printing and coating solutions. The company offers web coaters, chalmers, offline coaters, pumps, and other products.

Harris & Lee Environmental Sciences LLC HQ
120 Ross Valley Dr
San Rafael CA 94901
P: 415-287-3007   PRC:142
www.hlenv.com
Email: request@hlenv.com
Estab: 1992

Elaine Everest, Manager
Cathy Neumann, Senior Environmental Specialist
Robert Harris, Senior Scientist

Provider of environmental consulting services. The company's services include environmental risk management, and preliminary environmental assessment.

Harris Industrial Gases HQ
8475 Auburn Blvd
Citrus Heights CA 95610
P: 916-725-2168 F: 916-725-2117 PRC:51
www.harrisgas.com
Estab: 1936

Aaron Haupt, COO of Contract Negotiations
Tim Lettich, General Manager
Mark Stavig, Branch Manager
Scott Rosenberg, Account Manager
Nancey Holland, Account Manager

Provider of specialty gases welding equipment. The company also offers services for welding supplies and safety equipment.

Harvest Moon Studio HQ
3516 Dover St   [N]
Los Angeles CA 90039
P: 323-660-3444   PRC:60
www.harvestmoonstudio.com
Email: m@nullharvestmoonstudio.com

Mark Lindquist, Founding Partner & Creative Director
Heather Lindquist, Contact

Publisher of books and interactive media.

Hawk Ridge Systems BR
4 Orinda Way Ste 100B
Orinda CA 94563
P: 510-482-6110   PRC:316
hawkridgesys.com
Email: info@hawkridgesys.com
Estab: 1996

Gabriel Rapisardo, CRO
Sheree Carlson, Partner
Nick Weirens, Director of Marketing
Tim Fulton, CAMWorks Manager
Brian DeLuca, Account Manager

Provider of 3D design software solutions. The company offers CAD, analysis consulting, product data management, and solid works services.

Hawk Ridge Systems BR
575 Clyde Ave Ste 420
Mountain View CA 94043
P: 877-266-4469 F: 650-428-1868 PRC:319
www.hawkridgesys.com
Email: info@hawkridgesys.com
Estab: 1996

Dale Ford, President & COO
Gabriel Rapisardo, CRO
Kimberly Enright, VP
Cameron Carson, VP of Engineering
Bryan Wakehouse, Director of Sales

Provider of parametric 3D product design and analysis services. The company also offers data management tools.

Hayward Quartz Technology Inc HQ
1700 Corporate Way
Fremont CA 94539
P: 510-657-9605 F: 510-657-6404 PRC:80
www.haywardquartz.com
Email: sales@haywardquartz.com
Estab: 1984

Ken Jacoby, VP of Operations
Hoang Nguyen, Quality Control Manager
Dean Gehrman, Sales Manager
Bac Le, Manager
Rafik Ayvazyan, Senior Research Developer

Manufacturer of machined and fabricated parts. The company exclusively caters to the semiconductor industry.

Hazelcast Inc HQ
350 Cambridge Ave Ste 100
Palo Alto CA 94306
P: 650-521-5453 PRC:323
hazelcast.com
Email: sales@hazelcast.com
Estab: 2008

Enes Akar, Founder & CTO
Kelly Herrell, CEO
Marion Smith, CFO
Steve Wooledge, CMO
Chris Wilson, CRO

Provider of training, consulting, and technical support services. The company serves the logistics and healthcare industries.

HB Fuller BR
10500 Industrial Ave
Roseville CA 95678
P: 916-787-6000 PRC:47
www.hbfuller.com
Estab: 1887

Jim Owens, President & CEO
Ted Clark, EVP & COO
Abe Rezai, CTO
John J. Corkrean, EVP & CFO
Traci L. Jensen, SVP of Global Construction Products

Manufacturer of adhesives and sealants. The company also specializes in paints and other specialty chemical products.

HBR Industries Inc HQ
2261-B Fortune Dr
San Jose CA 95131
P: 408-988-0800 F: 408-432-0104 PRC:209
www.hbrindustries.com
Estab: 1979

Mike Ryssemus, President
Karl Ryssemus, Director of Operations
Karl Steinkraus, Quality Control Manager

Provider of electronics manufacturing services. The company offers coil solutions and services for the medical, military, and semiconductor industry.

HCL America Inc LH
330 Potrero Ave
Sunnyvale CA 94085
P: 408-733-0480 F: 408-733-0482 PRC:323
www.hcltech.com
Estab: 1988

Ajay Dhankhar, General Manager
Vasant Shejwal, General Manager
Apurva Bhargava, Director Sales
Pankaj Gupta, General Manager
Satish Singh, General Manager

Provider of software and IT solutions, infrastructure, engineering, research and development, and outsourcing services.

Headsets Com Inc BR
211 Austin St
San Francisco CA 94109-4519
P: 800-432-3738 PRC:71
www.headsets.com
Email: info@headsets.com
Estab: 1998

Mike Faith, CEO
Chris Bentley, Marketing Coordinator

Provider of office telephone headsets. The company also offers cellphone, computer, and cordless phone headsets.

Headway Technologies Inc HQ
682 S Hillview Dr
Milpitas CA 95035
P: 408-934-5300 F: 408-942-6916 PRC:95
www.headway.com
Email: info@headway.com
Estab: 1994

Wenjie Chen, President
Moris Dovek, SVP Product Development & CTO
David Wagner, VP of Operations
Edward Zawada, Senior Director of Operations
Grace Gorman, Senior Director

Designer and manufacturer of hard-disk drives. The company is engaged in installation and technical support services.

Healfies HQ
180 Sansome St 4th Fl
San Francisco CA 94104
P: 415-312-4525 PRC:270
healfies.com
Estab: 2015

Helyson Velasco, Co-Founder
Denis Avdic, Co-Founder
Alvin Yip, COO

Developer and provider of software platform to manage health information. The company serves the healthcare sector.

Health Advances LLC BR
101 Second St Ste 800
San Francisco CA 94105
P: 415-834-0800 F: 781-392-1484 PRC:191
healthadvances.com
Email: info@healthadvances.com
Estab: 1992

Balazs Felcsuti, VP
Carrie Jones, VP
Claudia Graeve, VP
Darcy Krzynowek, VP
Kate McLaughlin, VP

Provider of consulting services to the healthcare industry. The company offers clinical development, product positioning, lifecycle management, and more.

Health Fidelity Inc HQ
4 W Fourth Ave Ste 501
San Mateo CA 94402
P: 650-727-3300 PRC:324
healthfidelity.com
Email: info@healthfidelity.com
Estab: 2011

Steve Whitehurst, CEO
Brian McDonald, CFO
Bill Zahn, COO
Craig Gomulka, Chief Development Officer
Robin Lloyd, Chief Commercial Officer

Provider of natural language processing technology and inference platform to analyze vast amounts of unstructured data for clinical and financial insights.

Health Gorilla Inc HQ
185 N Wolfe Rd
Sunnyvale CA 94085
P: 844-446-7455 PRC:326
www.healthgorilla.com

Andrei Zudin, CTO & Co-Founder
Steve Yaskin, CEO & Co-Founder
Sergio Wagner, Chief Strategy Officer
Ali Zaman, VP of Marketing
Vladimir Davydenko, VP of Technology

Focuses on diagnostic tests. The company offers services to clinics, patients and healthcare organizations.

Healthcare Systems & Technologies LLC HQ
3675 Mt Diablo Blvd Ste 100B
Lafayette CA 94549
P: 800-290-4078 PRC:326
www.hstpathways.com
Email: hstsales@hstpathways.com
Estab: 2005

Tom Hui, Founder & CEO
Harry Yee, CTO
Karlene Ochoa, VP of Operations
Chris Beavor, SVP of Strategic Development

Designer and developer of AC surgery software. The company offers services to corporate management companies.

Healthline Media HQ
660 Third St
San Francisco CA 94107
P: 415-281-3100 PRC:315
www.healthline.com
Estab: 2006

David Kopp, CEO
Cheryl Kim, CFO
Andy Atherton, SVP of Revenue Operations & General Manager of Programmatic
Jeff Bernstein, SVP & General Manager of Provider Services
Tracy Stickler, SVP of Content

Provider of health information.

Healthstar Laser Services Inc HQ
  PO Box 806
  Lafayette CA 94549
  P: 415-937-1942 PRC:172
  www.healthstarlaser.com
  Estab: 1991

  Allen S. Kent, Founder & President

  Provider of web-based scheduling and mobile
  laser services. The company serves the healthcare sector.

HeartFlow Inc RH
  1400 Seaport Blvd Bldg B
  Redwood City CA 94063
  P: 650-241-1221 PRC:270
  www.heartflow.com
  Email: info@heartflow.com
  Estab: 2007

  Charles A. Taylor, Founder & CTO
  Dana G. Mead, President & CEO
  Renata Naoumov, VP & CPO
  Baird Radford, EVP & CFO
  Auston Davis, VP & Chief Information Security
  Officer

  Provider of analysis technology that creates a
  personalized 3D model of the coronary arteries
  and analyzes the impact that blockages have on
  blood flow.

HeartVista Inc HQ
  4984 El Camino Real Ste 102
  Los Altos CA 94022
  P: 650-800-7937 PRC:189
  www.heartvista.com
  Email: info@heartvista.com

  William R Overall, CTO & Founder
  Juan M Santos, President

  Developer of magnetic resonance imaging (MRI)
  applications and development tools to aid in the
  diagnosis of cardiovascular disease.

Heat & Control Inc HQ
  21121 Cabot Blvd
  Hayward CA 94545
  P: 510-259-0500 PRC:159
  www.heatandcontrol.com
  Estab: 1950

  Eric Brick, General Manager
  Alex Caridis, Designer

  Manufacturer of food processing and packaging
  equipment systems. The company offers inspection system, product handling equipment, and
  coating system.

Heatscape Inc HQ
  318 Digital Dr
  Morgan Hill CA 95037
  P: 408-778-4615   F: 408-778-4616 PRC:159
  heatscape.com
  Email: info@heatscape.com
  Estab: 1999

  Ali Mira, President & CEO & Principal
  Yashar Mira, Principal & VP of Global Sales &
  Marketing
  Michael Mira, Global Manager

  Designer and manufacturer of thermal solutions.
  The company engages in thermal analysis, thermal testing, and finite element analysis.

M-146

HECO Inc HQ
  2350 Del Monte St
  West Sacramento CA 95691
  P: 916-372-5411   F: 916-373-0952 PRC:163
  www.hecogear.com
  Email: info@hecogear.com
  Estab: 1974

  Mike Jacobs, President
  Allen Rasmussen, VP
  John Woodhouse, Director of Sales

  Manufacturer of planetary speed reducers. The
  company's applications include swing drives,
  wheel drives, conveyor drives, winch drives,
  mixers, and augers.

Heco Pacific Manufacturing Inc HQ
  1510 Pacific St
  Union City CA 94587
  P: 510-487-1155   F: 510-487-4466 PRC:183
  www.hecopacific.com
  Estab: 1961

  Allan Alarab, President & CEO
  Rita Kachhia, Accounting Manager
  Dwight Chew, Project Engineer
  German Morales, Project Engineer

  Manufacturer and seller of industrial cranes and
  overhead cranes. The company offers custom
  engineering, maintenance, testing, and other
  services.

Heinzen Manufacturing International HQ
  405 Mayock Rd
  Gilroy CA 95020
  P: 408-842-7233   F: 408-842-6678 PRC:159
  www.heinzen.com
  Estab: 1978

  Alan Heinzen, Founder
  Jeffrey Goulding, Sales Manager
  Courtney Knutson, Sales Engineer

  Designer and manufacturer of custom food
  processing equipment. The company specializes
  in shakers, bin dumpers, fruit equipment, and
  trimlines.

Heirloom Computing Inc HQ
  3000 Danville Blvd
  Alamo CA 94507
  P: 510-573-3579 PRC:322
  heirloomcomputing.com
  Estab: 2010

  Gary Crook, President & CEO
  Kevin Moultrup, COO
  Mark Haynie, CTO

  Focuses on the transformation of enterprise
  applications. The company offers services to the
  industrial sector.

Heliodyne Inc HQ
  4910 Seaport Ave
  Richmond CA 94804
  P: 510-237-9614   F: 510-237-7018 PRC:151
  heliodyne.com

  Ole Pilgaard, President
  David Stampfli, Contact

  Manufacturer of solar water heating systems
  for the residential and commercial sectors. The
  company focuses on installation, repair, and
  replacement.

HelioWorks Inc HQ
  1275 Fourth St Ste 614
  Santa Rosa CA 95404
  P: 707-578-7200 PRC:243
  www.helioworks.com
  Email: info@helioworks.com
  Estab: 2003

  Don Wood, CEO

  Manufacturer of infrared lamps. The company's
  products are used in non-dispersive infrared gas
  detectors for medical and industrial applications.

Helium Systems Inc HQ
  1663 Mission St Ste 250
  San Francisco CA 94103
  P: 415-510-2110 PRC:68
  www.helium.com
  Email: sales@helium.com
  Estab: 2013

  Marc Nijdam, CTO

  Provider of connectivity solutions for smart devices. The company offers services to individuals and
  businesses.

Helix Environmental Planning Inc HQ
  7578 El Cajon Blvd
  La Mesa CA 91942
  P: 619-462-1515   F: 619-462-0552 PRC:142
  www.helixepi.com
  Estab: 1995

  David Bise, Senior Project Manager & Wildlife
  Biologist
  Dianne Ransby, Senior Project Operations
  Manager
  Kelly Bayne, Senior Biologist & Regulatory
  Specialist
  Michael Brewer, GIS Specialist

  Provider of landscape architecture, planning, environmental consulting, restoration, and regulatory
  permitting services.

Hellwig Products Company Inc HQ
  16237 Ave Ste 296
  Visalia CA 93292
  P: 559-734-7451   F: 559-734-7460 PRC:80
  www.hellwigproducts.com
  Email: customerservice@hellwigproducts.com
  Estab: 1946

  Mark Hellwig, President
  Ben Knaus, Director of Engineering
  Nancy Souza, Director of Business

  Provider of sway control and load control products
  for trucks and SUV's. The company also offers
  fleet solution services.

Hemostat Laboratories HQ
  PO Box 790
  Dixon CA 95620
  P: 800-572-6888   F: 707-678-1150 PRC:250
  hemostat.com
  Email: info@hemostat.com
  Estab: 1980

  Jim McElligott, President
  Kate Murphy, General Manager
  Andy Bouwens, Lab Manager

  Provider of defibrinated sheep blood and other
  animal blood products for cell culture, diagnostic
  and veterinary applications.

Hench Control Inc   HQ
3701 Collins Ave Ste 8C
Richmond CA 94806
P: 510-741-8100 F: 510-307-9804   PRC:130
www.henchcontrol.com
Email: sales@henchcontrol.com
Estab: 1989

Alex Daneman, President & CEO
Tyler Winters, Software Developer

Manufacturer of modular energy management systems. The company's products find application in industrial refrigeration.

Hepco Inc   HQ
150 San Lazaro Ave
Sunnyvale CA 94086-5209
P: 408-738-1880 F: 408-732-4456   PRC:159
www.hepcoblue.com
Email: info@hepcoblue.com
Estab: 1970

Tim Hoffman, President
Blair Kummer, Senior Recruiter

Manufacturer of electronic components. The company offers design, fabrication, analysis, and testing tools for semiconductor industries.

Hera Systems Inc   HQ
7013 Realm Dr
San Jose CA 95119
P: 844-437-2797   PRC:9
www.herasys.com
Email: info@herasys.com
Estab: 2013

Bobby Machinski, CEO
David Squires, VP of Space Systems
Jolyon Thurgood, VP of Corporate Development & Marketing
Jim Opfer, Senior Advisor

Provider of satellite information and analytics that collects images of Earth, for commercial and government organizations to monitor and make decisions.

Hero Digital   HQ
55 Francisco st Ste 350
San Francisco CA 94133
P: 415-409-2400   PRC:325
herodigital.com
Estab: 2006

Patrick Frend, President
David Kilimnik, CEO
Kenneth Parks, CMO
Tony Rems, CTO
Carl Agers, EVP of Strategic Planning

Provider of website and mobile design and development services. The company specializes in mobile marketing programs.

Heroku Inc   HQ
415 Mission St Ste 300
San Francisco CA 94105
P: 866-278-1349   PRC:323
www.heroku.com
Email: pr@heroku.com
Estab: 2007

Mike Pyle, CTO

Designer and developer of cloud application platforms. The company offers services to software developers.

Heron Innovators   HQ
1025 Nichols Dr
Rocklin CA 95765
P: 916-408-6601 F: 916-408-6991   PRC:144
www.heroninnovators.com
Email: info@heroninnovators.com
Estab: 1975

John Barsotti, President & Founder
Boguslaw Marcinkowski, Owner
Jeff Knollenberg, VP of Sales
Jennifer Barsotti, Manager

Provider of suspended air flotation systems. The company offers products for processing tomato, food, meat, and others.

Hesco   HQ
693 Whitney St
San Leandro CA 94577
P: 510-568-1380   PRC:198
www.hescoxray.com
Estab: 1990

Michael A. Depinna, President
Roger Owen, Director of Business

Provider of portable x-ray imaging services. The company offer services for power plants, bridges, dams, refineries, and more.

Hesse Mechatronics Inc   LH
225 Hammond Ave
Fremont CA 94539
P: 408-436-9300 F: 484-231-3232   PRC:159
www.hesse-mechatronics.com
Email: info@hesse-mechatronics.com
Estab: 1986

Kristian Oftebro, Senior Process Development Engineer

Developer of equipment for heavy wire and thin wire wedge bonders. The company also focuses on the marketing aspects.

Hexcel Corp   BR
11711 Dublin Blvd
Dublin CA 94568-2832
P: 800-444-3923   PRC:4
www.hexcel.com
Estab: 1948

Tim Swords, President of Industrial
Nick L. Stanage, Chairman & CEO
Colleen Pritchett, President
Paul Mackenzie, SVP & CTO
Don Morrison, SVP & CIO

Provider and manufacturer of advanced material solutions. The company manufactures everything from a carbon fiber to finished aircraft structures.

HFE Consulting   BR
PO Box 111874   [N]
Campbell CA 95011
P: 408-234-6903 F: 408-521-1931   PRC:45
www.hfeconsulting.com

Kenneth Nemire, Consultant

Provider of consulting services on human factors engineering and ergonomics issues.

Hi Rel Connectors Inc   HQ
760 W Wharton Dr   [N]
Claremont CA 91711
P: 909-626-1820 F: 909-399-0626   PRC:202
www.hirelco.net
Email: info@hirelco.net
Estab: 1967

Sheila Bragole, Manager of Sales
Wesley Beauvais, Manager of Facilities
Richard Hoang, Manager of Information Technology
Saul Ibarra, Lead Design Engineer
Ray Figueroa, Design Engineer

Designer, manufacturer and distributor of electrical connectors, interconnect systems, cables and connector accessories.

Hiebert Sculpture Works   HQ
540 47th St
Oakland CA 94609
P: 510-654-7488 F: 510-654-2723   PRC:163
www.hieberts.com
Email: hsw@hieberts.com
Estab: 1966

Billy Hiebert, Owner

Provider of plastic injection molding products. The company also offers composite epoxy tooling, design assistance, and custom molds.

Higgins Analytical Inc   HQ
1166 Independence Ave
Mountain View CA 94043
P: 650-988-8930 F: 650-988-8931   PRC:20
www.higanalyt.com
Email: info@higanalyt.com
Estab: 1994

Steve Jones, General Manager
Dale Miller, Office Manager & Office Manager

Manufacturer and marketer of laboratory equipment and supplies. The company specializes in HPLC columns, cartridges, and separations consumables.

High Connection Density Inc   HQ
820A Kifer Rd
Sunnyvale CA 94086-5200
P: 408-743-9700 F: 408-743-9701   PRC:206
hcdcorp.com
Email: sales@hcdcorp.com
Estab: 1997

Charlie Stevenson, COO & CFO
Nitin Gupta, Sales Operations Manager
Shengjie Wang, Product Development Engineer

Supplier of electronic packaging solutions and connection technologies. The company serves communications, medical, military, and aerospace fields.

Highfive   HQ
500 Arguello St Ste 300
Redwood City CA 94063
P: 844-464-4445   PRC:323
highfive.com
Email: sales@highfive.com
Estab: 2012

Jeremy Roy, Founder

Focuses on video conferencing and re-imaging solutions. The company offers services to business organizations.

Highland Technology Inc   HQ
650 Potrero Ave
San Francisco CA 94100
P: 415-551-1700   F: 415-551-5129   PRC:65
www.highlandtechnology.com
Email: info@highlandtechnology.com
Estab: 1984

Elizabeth Larkin, VP
Kevin Brown, Director of Business Development
Karla Vega, Test Engineer Head of Test Department & Test Engineer & Head of Test Department
Rob Gaddi, Engineer
Paul Bailey, Embedded Systems Engineer

Designer and manufacturer of precision analog instrumentation. The company serves laboratory research purposes.

Highwired Inc   HQ
PO Box 420
Redwood Valley CA 95470
P: 516-785-6197   PRC:322
www.highwiredinc.com
Estab: 1998

David Levine, Consultant & CTO

Developer of multimedia and supporting products and services. The company focuses on branding, billing, and delivery solutions.

Hildy Licht Company Inc   HQ
897 Independence Ave Bldg 3-B
Mountain View CA 94043
P: 650-962-9300   F: 650-254-1855   PRC:207
hildy.com
Estab: 1971

Keri MacKey, President
Cheryl Spears, Director of Operations

Provider of electric assembly and manufacturing services. The company is engaged in engineering and prototyping.

Hill Brothers Chemical Co   BR
410 Charcot Ave
San Jose CA 95131
P: 408-599-5041   F: 408-435-1104   PRC:51
hillbrothers.com
Email: infomail@hillbrothers.com
Estab: 1923

Tom James, CFO
Matt Thorne, EVP of Sales & Marketing
Darlene Harrison, Executive Secretary
Kathy Waters, Secretary Treasurer
Adam Hill, Manager of Customer Service Administration

Provider of industrial and construction chemicals. The company also offers decking systems and seaters.

Hillstone Networks   RH
5201 Great America Pkwy Ste 420
Santa Clara CA 95054
P: 408-508-6750   PRC:325
www.hillstonenet.com
Email: inquiry@hillstonenet.com
Estab: 2006

DongPing Luo, CEO & Co-Founder
Tim Liu, CTO & Co-Founder
Zhong Wang, VP of New Technologies
Zhou Yan, Director of Global Sales Engineer
Shu Lin Yang, R&D engineering director

Provider of security solutions for enterprises and data center networks. The company serves Fortune 500 companies and educational institutions.

Hilti Inc   BR
180 Pennsylvania
San Francisco CA 94107
P: 800-879-8000   F: 800-879-7000   PRC:300
www.hilti.com
Email: us-sales@hilti.com
Estab: 1941

Christoph Loos, CEO

Developer and manufacturer of construction equipment. The company's services include trainings, engineering, administration, and tools.

Hirose Electric USA Inc   BR
2841 Junction Ave Ste 200
San Jose CA 95134
P: 408-253-9640   F: 408-253-9641   PRC:76
www.hirose.com
Estab: 1937

Kazunori Ishii, President
Jeff Combs, Director of Sales
Alicia Lalonde, Accounts Receivable Manager

Manufacturer of connectors. The company provides couplers, dividers, terminators, coaxial switches, and memory cards.

Histo path   HQ
961 N Emerald Ave Ste D
Modesto CA 95351
P: 209-522-8240   F: 209-522-2486   PRC:36
histo-path.com
Email: kathy@histo-path.com
Estab: 1974

Michael Garcia, Owner & Lab Manager
Dan Garcia, President
Kathy Cruz, Office Manager

Provider of histotechnology services. The company specializes in providing tissue culture slides for dermatologists.

Hitachi Chemical Diagnostics Inc   HQ
630 Clyde Ct
Mountain View CA 94043
P: 650-961-5501   F: 650-969-2745   PRC:186
hcdiagnostics.com
Email: info@hcdiagnostics.com
Estab: 1983

Hideki Itaya, VP

Provider of in vitro allergy diagnostics products. The company offers alternative means of diagnosing allergy.

Hitachi High Technologies America Inc   BR
5960 Inglewood Dr
Pleasanton CA 94588-3355
P: 925-218-2814   F: 925-218-3230   PRC:11
www.hitachi-hightech.com
Email: iot.dg@hitachi-hightech.com
Estab: 2002

Masahiro Miyazaki, President & CEO & Representative Executive Officer
Lorena Ferry, VP & General Manager Semiconductor Metrology Division
Steve Joens, Nanotechnology Marketing Manager
Dan Becker, Northwestern Sales Manager
Frank Fales, Senior Manager

Seller of semiconductor manufacturing equipment and analytical instrumentation and also offers electronic devices, bio-related, and other products.

Hitachi Metals America Ltd   BR
1920 Zanker Rd
San Jose CA 95112
P: 408-467-8900   F: 408-467-8901   PRC:157
www.hitachimetals.com
Estab: 1965

Joedel Dizon, Managing Director

Manufacturer and marketer of metal products. The company offers cable systems, cutting tools, ceramics, sensors, and other materials.

HMS Electronics Inc   HQ
5711 Marsh Hawk Dr
Santa Rosa CA 95409
P: 707-584-8760   PRC:189
www.hms-electronics.com
Estab: 1985

Richard Harkey, Owner & CEO

Manufacturer of medical device components. The company offers custom made specialty component parts for x-ray machines.

Hof Machining Inc   HQ
2290 Ringwood Ave Unit B
San Jose CA 95131
P: 408-526-1155   F: 408-744-0443   PRC:80
hofmachining.com

Saju Kooplicat, President

Provider of exotic geometry and prototype machining services. The company's offerings include machine shop services and machining materials.

Hoffmeyer Company Inc   HQ
1600 Factor Ave   [N]
San Leandro CA 94577
P: 510-895-9955   F: 510-895-9014   PRC:212
www.hoffmeyerco.com
Email: sales@hoffmeyerco.com
Emp: 51-200   Estab: 1986

Niels Rifbjerg, General Manager
Jeff Little, Manager of Sales & Service
Randy Lewis, Manager of Shop
Vince Borja, Inside Sales Representative
Nikki Mercado, Accounting Assistant

Manufacturer and distributor of conveyor belting and components, couplings, industrial and hydraulic hoses.

Hogan Manufacturing Inc   HQ
1704 First St
Escalon CA 95320
P: 209-838-2400   F: 209-838-8648   PRC:80
www.hoganmfg.com
Email: information@hoganmfg.com
Estab: 1944

Mark Hogan, President
Joe DeBiasio, CFO
Zach Hogan, Operations Manager

Provider of steel manufacturing fabrication services. The company's products include plate weldments, alloy specialties, and waste separation equipment.

Holland Communications Inc HQ

7866 Deering Ave [N]
Canoga Park CA 91304
P: 818-854-6136 PRC:325
www.holland-comm.com
Estab: 1974

Bill Holland, President & Founder
Jill Lovell, General Manager

Provider of advertising and public relations firm.

Holman Group HQ

9451 Corbin Ave Ste 100 [N]
Northridge CA 91324
P: 818-704-1444 F: 818-704-9339 PRC:196
www.holmangroup.com
Emp: 51-200 Estab: 1978

Ron Holman, Founder
Linda Holman, VP & CFO
Marcus Sola, SVP & Chief Compliance Officer
Elizabeth Holman, VP of Sales & Marketing &
EVP of Finance & Business Development
Jane L. Snowden, VP

Provider of behavioral healthcare programs and
other services for employers and others.

Hologic Inc BR

2520 Mission College Blvd Ste 202
Santa Clara CA 95054
P: 669-224-6420 PRC:186
hologic.com
Email: info@hologic.com

Jay A. Stein, Founder & SVP & CTO
Peter J. Valenti, Division President of Breast &
Skeletal Health Solutions
Stephen P. MacMillan, Chairman & CEO &
President
Sean S. Daugherty, Group President
Kevin R. Thornal, Division President of Diagnos-
tics Solutions

Provider of healthcare and diagnostics. The company offers breast and skeletal healthcare and
diagnostics, and GYN surgical solutions.

Holz Rubber Company Inc HQ
1129 S Sacramento St
Lodi CA 95240
P: 209-368-7171 PRC:57
www.holzrubber.com
Email: sales@holzrubber.com
Estab: 1935

Dave Smith, President

Provider of custom molded services. The company's offerings include pump parts, slide-lag
traction pads, and related supplies.

Home Medix Inc HQ

3811 Atlantic Ave [N]
Long Beach CA 90807
P: 888-553-0051 PRC:189
www.homemedix.com
Email: homemedix@homemedix.com
Emp: 11-50 Estab: 1983

Mastaneh Moradfar, Contact

Provider of wheelchairs, power chairs, scooters,
walking aids and other medical equipment for
patients, hospitals and others.

Honda Research Institute USA Inc HQ
70 Rio Robles
San Jose CA 95134
P: 650-314-0400 PRC:304
www.honda-ri.com
Email: hri_contact@honda-ri.com
Estab: 2003

Kikuo Fujimura, Project Director
Chihiro Suga, Research Engineer
Joel Wormer, Senior Engineer
Paul Cummings, Principal
Soshi Iba, Principal Scientist

Manufacturer of engines. The company focuses
on material science research, computer science
research, and academic outreach activities.

Hopelab HQ
100 California St Ste 1150
San Francisco CA 94111
P: 650-569-5900 PRC:268
www.hopelab.org
Email: communications@hopelab.org
Estab: 2001

Dan Cawley, COO
Chris McCarthy, VP of Strategy & Design
Brian Rodriguez, Director of People & Culture
Fred Dillon, Director
Jana Haritatos, Director

Developer of technology to improve human health
and well-being. The company provides online
games to help young people fight cancer.

Horiba Instruments Inc BR
430 Indio Way
Sunnyvale CA 94085
P: 408-730-4772 F: 408-730-8975 PRC:235
www.horiba.com

Atsushi Horiba, Chairman & Group CEO
Amy Hou, Applications Scientist

Provider of instruments and systems for automotive research and development, and process and
environmental monitoring needs.

Horizon Water and Environment LLC HQ
266 Grand Ave Ste 210
Oakland CA 94610
P: 510-986-1850 F: 510-350-3592 PRC:139
horizonh2o.com
Email: info@horizonh2o.com
Emp: 25 Estab: 2008

Janis Offermann, Director
Laura Prickett, Director
Sandy Wieder, Manager of Business & Contracts
Thomas Engels, Principal
Kenneth Schwarz, Founding Principal

Provider of environmental consulting services.
The company specializes in watershed science,
environmental compliance, and water resources
management.

Horn Machine Tools Inc HQ
40455 Brickyard Dr
Madera CA 93636
P: 559-431-4131 F: 559-431-4431 PRC:80
hornmachinetools.com
Email: info@hornmachinetools.com
Estab: 1991

Kent Horn, President
James Moffatt, Senior Service Technician

Supplier of CNC and semi-automatic tube
benders. The company offers new tube benders,
rebuilt tube benders, and bender rebuilding and
retro-fitting.

Hospital Systems Inc HQ
750 Garcia Ave
Pittsburg CA 94565
P: 925-427-7800 F: 925-427-0800 PRC:189
hsiheadwalls.com
Email: info@hsiheadwalls.com
Estab: 1970

Becca Teutle, President
David Miller, CEO
Cameron Ross, Draftsman

Manufacturer of lighting, electrical and architectural products, and related supplies. The company is
engaged in installation services.

HotLava Systems Inc HQ
1300 Clay St Ste 600
Oakland CA 94612
P: 510-531-1169 F: 855-468-4834 PRC:64
www.hotlavasystems.com
Email: hotinfo@hotlavasystems.com
Estab: 2003

Bill Young, President

Provider of board-level solutions for servers and
appliances that operates in virtualized environments.

House of Batteries HQ

10910 Talbert Ave [N]
Fountain Valley CA 92708
P: 714-962-7600 F: 714-962-7644 PRC:31
www.houseofbatteries.com
Email: sales@houseofbatteries.com
Emp: 11-50 Estab: 1965

Don West, President

Manufacturer of battery assembly and battery
pack.

Howard Wire Cloth Co HQ
28976 Hopkins St Ste A
Hayward CA 94545-5096
P: 510-887-8787 F: 510-786-4167 PRC:80
www.howardwire.com
Email: sales@howardwire.com
Estab: 1938

Tim Curren, President

Provider of screening and wire fabrication products. The company offers wire cloth, stainless
steel netting, security screening, and perforated
metals.

Howlett Machine Works HQ
746 Folger Ave
Berkeley CA 94710
P: 510-845-2759 F: 510-841-1018 PRC:80
www.howlettmachine.com
Email: howlettmachine@sbcglobal.net
Estab: 1921

Mike Young, Owner

Manufacturer of machine works and custom made tools. The company also offers custom test fixtures and test machines.

HP Development Company LP HQ
1501 Page Mill Rd
Palo Alto CA 94304
P: 650-857-1501 PRC:102
www.hp.com
Estab: 1939

Meg Whitman, CEO
Cathie Lesjak, EVP & CFO
Todd Bradley, EVP of Strategic Growth
Dion Weisler, EVP of Printing & Personal Systems
Tony Sumpster, VP & General Manager

Provider of computer products that include desktops, monitors, printers and scanners, ink, toner and papers, and laptops.

HP Inc BR
1501 Page Mill Rd
Palo Alto CA 94304
P: 650-857-1501 PRC:108
www.hp.com

Dion Weisler, CEO & President
Enrique J. Lores, President of Imaging & Printing
Jon Flaxman, COO
Linh Ho, Senior Accountant

Provider of laptops, tablets, desktops, printers, and related accessories. The company specializes in business solutions.

HPM Systems Inc HQ
70 Saratoga Ave Ste 200
Santa Clara CA 95051-7301
P: 408-615-6900 PRC:231
hpmsystems.com
Email: hpm@hpmsystems.com
Estab: 1997

Bert Buehler, President
Don Stevenson, Project Manager

Provider of gas monitoring control systems. The company's services include design, integration, installation, and maintenance.

HS&S Inc HQ
2185 Ronald St
Santa Clara CA 95050-2838
P: 408-980-8909 PRC:80
www.hsands.com
Email: info@hsands.com
Estab: 1979

John Servin, President

Designer and manufacturer of machine tool and custom machine manufacturing. The company offers services like CNC conversion and contract inspection.

HSQ Technology HQ
26227 Research Rd
Hayward CA 94545-3725
P: 510-259-1334 F: 510-259-1391 PRC:212
www.hsq.com
Email: sales@hsq.com
Estab: 1979

Chris Maynard, President
Gustavo Jimenez, Director of Projects & Operations
Peter Polissky, Director of Engineering
Hugh Carter, Project Manager
Peter Waenink, Project Manager

Provider of control system and energy management services, specializing in data and SCADA monitoring.

HT Harvey & Associates HQ
983 University Ave Bldg D
Los Gatos CA 95032
P: 408-458-3200 F: 408-458-3210 PRC:142
www.harveyecology.com
Email: marketing@harveyecology.com
Estab: 1970

Karin Hunsicker, CEO
Daniel Stephens, VP
Brian Boroski, VP
Scott Terrill, VP
Michael MK Wong, Information Technology Service Desk Manager

Provider of ecological consulting services that include ecological research, impact analysis, restoration design, and park planning.

HT Precision Inc HQ
2284 Trade Zone Blvd
San Jose CA 95131
P: 408-719-1826 F: 408-719-1827 PRC:80
www.htprecision.com
Email: sales@htprecision.com

Steven Nguyen, General Manager

Provider of prototype, research, and production parts and equipment. The company serves electronics, medical, wireless, and semi-conductor industries.

HTA Photomask HQ
1605 Remuda Ln
San Jose CA 95112
P: 408-452-5500 F: 408-452-5505 PRC:86
www.htaphotomask.com
Email: sales@htaphotomask.com
Estab: 1982

Ken Caple, Chairman & CEO
James Campi, President
Mykola Kulishov, VP of Business Development
Luda Kuleshova, CAD Designer

Manufacturer of photo imaged products such as precision scales, resolution targets, and micro detectors.

HTD Biosystems Inc HQ
1061 Serpentine Ln Ste E
Pleasanton CA 94566-4800
P: 510-367-0528 F: 509-267-1491 PRC:269
www.htdcorp.com
Email: info@htdcorp.com
Estab: 2001

Rajiv Nayar, President

Focuses on the development of parenteral drugs. The company is engaged in design and product formulation services.

Hub Strategy and Communication BR
39 Mesa St Ste 212
San Francisco CA 94129
P: 415-561-4345 PRC:45
hubsanfrancisco.com
Email: get@hubsanfrancisco.com
Estab: 2002

Mike Reese, President
DJ O'Neil, CEO & Creative Director
Jason Rothman, Creative Director
Ryan Scheiber, Creative Director
Jess D'Elia, Director of Brand

Provider of web design and digital advertising.

HumanAPI HQ
1825 S Grant St Ste 450
San Mateo CA 94402
P: 650-542-9800 PRC:326
humanapi.co
Email: support@humanapi.co
Estab: 2014

Andrei Pop, CEO
Greg Enriquez, SVP & CRO

Focuses on the integration of health data and it specializes in retrieval of health data and other healthcare applications.

Hunter Micro Kitting and Turnkey HQ
1861 Little Orchard St
San Jose CA 95125
P: 408-977-7000 F: 408-977-7005 PRC:209
huntermicro.com
Email: sales@huntermicro.com
Estab: 2001

Scott Boyd, CEO & President
Bob Boyd, VP of Inside Sales

Provider of electronic solutions for emerging technology companies. The company offers design, distribution, and contract manufacturing services.

Huntington Mechanical Laboratories Inc HQ
13355 Nevada City Ave
Grass Valley CA 95945
P: 530-273-4135 F: 530-273-4165 PRC:209
www.huntvac.com
Email: vacman@huntvac.com
Estab: 1969

Kyle Lind, Engineering Manager
Tami Isaacson, Accounting Controller

Manufacturer and designer of bellows, chalmers, motion positioning products, and roughing accessories.

Hurd & Associates Design HQ
1343 Locust St Ste 209
Walnut Creek CA 94596
P: 925-930-8580 PRC:325
www.ihurd.com

Joan Hurd, Owner & Designer

Provider of print, logo, and web design, branding, marketing, advertising, and identity management services.

Hybrid Circuits Inc HQ
1391 Geneva Dr Ste 4
Sunnyvale CA 94089
P: 408-744-9080 F: 408-744-0800 PRC:209
www.hybridcircuits.com
Email: info@hybridcircuits.com

Mike Loskutoff, Owner & Owner

Provider of contract manufacturing services. The company focuses on design, prototyping, contract manufacturing, and delivery.

Hydra-Electric Co HQ
3151 Kenwood St [N]
Burbank CA 91505
P: 818-843-6211 F: 818-843-1209 PRC:290
hydraelectric.com
Emp: 201-500 Estab: 2009

Allen V.C. Davis, Founder
David Schmidt, CEO
Bob Guziak, VP of Engineering

Manufacturer of switches and other related products.

Hydratech LLC HQ
1331 S West Ave
Fresno CA 93706
P: 559-233-0876 F: 559-233-1754 PRC:159
www.hydratechcylinders.com
Estab: 1977

Itamar Kandel, CEO
Bob S Hu, CMO
Robert Morgan, Quality Assurance Manager
Dwight Nishimura, Contact
John Pauly, Contact

Manufacturer of cylinder component, hydraulic, and pneumatic cylinder with engineering capabilities needed to build superior cylinder solutions.

Hydratight BR
14504 Garfield Ave
Paramount CA 90723
P: 562-531-0973 F: 562-531-0976 PRC:80
www.hydratight.com

Mark Brenon, VP of North American Operations
Peter Griffiths, Director of UK Operations
Elmir Ibrahimov, Base Manager
Scott Mccloud, Quality Manager
Dustin Ishikura, Project Manager

Manufacturer of flanges and mechanical connectors. The company focuses on the subsea, nuclear, wind, and mining industries.

Hydraulic Controls Inc HQ
4700 San Pablo Ave
Emeryville CA 94608
P: 510-658-8300 F: 510-658-3133 PRC:155
www.hydraulic-controls.com

Aaron Piper, President
Rob Hulse, EVP
Angela Figgs, Branch Manager
Chuck Hranac, Corporate IT Manager
David Madden, Branch Manager

Distributor of fluid power systems. The company specializes in hydraulics, pneumatics, automation, and extrusion.

Hydrofarm Inc HQ
2249 S McDowell Ext
Petaluma CA 94954-5561
P: 800-634-9990 PRC:159
www.hydrofarm.com
Estab: 1977

Bill Toler, Chairman & CEO
Robert Clamp, COO
Kelly Calapp, Director of Procurement
Joe George, Director of Operations
Zoanne Kuhlman, National Director of Customer Service

Manufacturer of hydroponics equipment. The company also supplies plant care products and garden accessories.

Hydropoint Data Systems Inc HQ
1720 Corporate Cir
Petaluma CA 94954
P: 800-362-8774 F: 707-769-9695 PRC:324
hydropoint.com
Email: info@hydropoint.com
Estab: 2002

Chris Spain, CEO & President
Al Sonntag, VP of Operations
Chris Manchuck, SVP of Sales
Joni Moss, Senior Director of Customer Success
Jennifer Kohn, Senior Project Manager

Provider of irrigation solutions. The company specializes in site evaluations, upgrade planning, deployment, and optimization services.

Hygeia Laboratories Inc HQ
1253 Commerce Ave
Woodland CA 95776
P: 530-661-1442 F: 530-661-1663 PRC:23
hygieialabs.com
Email: info@hygieialabs.com
Estab: 1991

Jim Wallis, President

Developers of vaccines using novel technology for animals. The company offers animal pharmaceuticals for dairy cattle, sheep and poultry.

Hyperarts Web Design Development & Maintenance HQ
201 Fourth St Ste 404
Oakland CA 94607
P: 510-339-6084 PRC:323
www.hyperarts.com
Estab: 1998

Tim Ware, Owner
Bill Dailey, Project Manager

Provider of web design, development, and consulting services. The company performs SEO, SEM services, and web application development.

Hypersurf Internet Services HQ
1929 Concourse Dr
San Jose CA 95131
P: 408-325-0300 F: 408-325-0301 PRC:63
hypersurf.com
Estab: 1995

Richard Chen, Technical Support Manager

Provider of Internet access and Internet presence solutions such as dial-up, residential DSL, business DSL, fiber Ethernet, and web and email hosting.

HyPower Hydraulics HQ
1240 S First St
Turlock CA 95380
P: 209-632-2275 F: 209-634-6606 PRC:159
www.hypowerhydraulics.com
Email: sales@hypowerhydraulics.com
Estab: 1911

Perry Fick, General Manager
Fick Perry, General Manager

Manufacturer of hydraulic cylinders and related accessories. The company offers repair/rebuilding services.

HyTrust Inc HQ
1975 W El Camino Real Ste 203
Mountain View CA 94040
P: 650-681-8100 F: 650-681-8101 PRC:317
www.hytrust.com
Email: sales@hytrust.com
Estab: 2007

Eric Chiu, Founder & President

Provider of security, compliance, and control software for virtualization of information technology infrastructure.

Hyve Solutions HQ
44201 Nobel Dr
Fremont CA 94538
P: 510-668-3877 PRC:95
hyvesolutions.com
Email: sales@hyvesolutions.com

Steve Wei, Senior Director of Software Engineering
Roy Lee, Senior Director of Hardware Engineering
Shou Lin Chua, Senior Director of Sales
Sarkis Mekhjian, Senior Director of Program Management
Erica Ye, Product Manager

Designer of data center serve, storage, networking and appliance solutions. The company specializes in rack integration services.

I-Tech Company LLC HQ
42978 Osgood Rd
Fremont CA 94539
P: 510-226-9226 F: 510-372-2736 PRC:169
www.i-techcompany.com
Email: info@itechlcd.com
Estab: 1998

Alan Chung, Owner

Manufacturer of panel mounts, server racks, industrial computers, touch screen displays, and related accessories.

IAR Systems Software Inc RH
1065 E Hillsdale Blvd Century Plz
Foster City CA 94404
P: 650-287-4250 F: 650-287-4253 PRC:319
www.iar.com
Email: info@iar.com
Estab: 1983

Robert DeOliveira, Director of Global Strategic
Sales
Anders Lundgren, Product Manager

Provider of software tools and embedded systems.
The company's products include state machine
tools, starter kits, and compiler and debugger tool
suite.

Ibase Technology (USA) Inc BR
1050 Stewart Dr
Sunnyvale CA 94085
P: 408-992-0888 PRC:91
www.ibase-usa.com
Email: sales@ibase-usa.com
Estab: 2000

Jeff Hsu, President & CEO
Jacky Chen, Business Development Manager
Eric Chung, Account Manager

Developer of embedded products such as
industrial motherboards, CPU modules, barebone
systems, network appliances, and digital surveillance systems.

IBM Research - Almaden BR
650 Harry Rd
San Jose CA 95120-6099
P: 408-927-1080 PRC:300
www.research.ibm.com
Estab: 1957

C. Narayan, Director of Science & Technology
Heiko Ludwig, Manager of Cloud Management
Services
Brent Hailpern, Head of Computer Science IBM
Research
Rama Akkiraju, Distinguished Engineer
Lucian Popa, Research Scientist

Provider of computer technology services. The
company engages in cloud, mobility, and security
services.

Ibus Corp HQ
3350 Scott Blvd Bldg 54
Santa Clara CA 95054
P: 408-450-7880 F: 408-450-7881 PRC:92
www.ibus.com
Email: contact@ibus.com
Estab: 1982

Johni Chan, President & CEO

Manufacturer and provider of industrial computers.
The company also specializes in prototyping and
quality control.

M-152

IC Engineering Inc HQ
2603 Camino Ramon Ste 418
San Ramon CA 94583
P: 925-415-0074 F: 877-266-8959 PRC:304
www.ic-engineering.com
Email: info@ic-engineering.com
Estab: 2000

Frederick Foote, President & CEO
Ryan McCollum, Control Systems Engineer

Provider of design and engineering services to
industrial and commercial clients. The company
serves food, oil, parts manufacturing, and other
sectors.

ICC Instrument Company Inc HQ
1483 E Warner Ave [N]
Santa Ana CA 92705
P: 714-540-4966 F: 714-540-5327 PRC:188
www.iccinstrument.com
Email: sales@iccinstrument.com
Estab: 1964

Erica Sanchez, Manager
Mark Halloran, Manager

Provider of instrument calibration and repair
services.

ICO Rally HQ
2575 E Bayshore Rd
Palo Alto CA 94303
P: 650-856-9900 F: 650-856-8378 PRC:285
www.icorally.com
Estab: 1950

Edwina M. Cioffi, President
Brian Cioffi, VP of Sales & Marketing
Betty Klanda, Strategic Accounts Manager of Gov-
ernment Sales
Jason Cioffi, Quality Manager
Rita David, Strategic Account Manager

Manufacturer and supplier of heat shrinkable
materials, wiring accessories, and insulation
products. The company serves automotive and
marine sectors.

ICON Aircraft Inc HQ
2141 ICON Way
Vacaville CA 95688
P: 707-564-4100 PRC:3
iconaircraft.com
Estab: 2004

Kirk Hawkins, Founder
Thomas Wieners, President & COO
David Crook, EVP of Revenue
Tina Rulo, VP of Human Resources
Veronica Rubio Malo, VP of Supply Chain &
Manufacturing

Manufacturer of consumer aircraft. The company
specializes in giving the freedom, fun, and adventure of flying to all who have dreamed of flight.

Iconic Therapeutics Inc HQ
701 Gateway Blvd Ste 100
S San Francisco CA 94080
P: 650-437-1000 F: 650-246-9011 PRC:251
iconictherapeutics.com
Email: info@iconictherapeutics.com

William Greene, CEO
Brandon Smith, COO
Gabriela Burian, CMO

Provider of tissue factor therapeutics. The company focuses on the solid tumors and wet age
related macular degeneration.

Iconix Inc HQ
255 W Julian St Ste 302
San Jose CA 95110
P: 408-727-6342 F: 408-727-6249 PRC:325
spguard.wpengine.com
Estab: 2011

Robert Zager, CFO
Bob Zager, VP of Business Development

Provider of business solutions such as email
identity software. The company caters to brand
and customer security needs.

ICS Electronics HQ
2415 Radley Ct Ste 1
Hayward CA 94545
P: 925-416-1000 F: 925-416-0105 PRC:94
icselect.com
Email: sales@icselect.com
Estab: 1978

Denise Romandia, Customer Service Manager
Jerry Mercola, Manager

Provider of interfaces and controllers for assembling systems, interfacing devices, and legacy
systems.

ICU Eyewear HQ
1900 Shelton Dr
Hollister CA 95023
P: 800-435-5747 PRC:173
icueyewear.com
Email: info@icueyewear.com
Estab: 1997

Patricia Kesten, Founder
Christine Roach, CFO
Mel Raymond, VP of Sales & Planning
Dave Bibbey, VP of Supply Chain
Kelley Williams, Director of Distribution

Manufacturer of reading eyewear and sunglasses.
The company provides metal half rim, polarized
oval, and metal full aviator sunglasses.

Icube Information International HQ
200 Brown Rd Ste 114
Fremont CA 94539
P: 510-683-8928 F: 510-683-8607 PRC:320
www.icubeinfo.com
Email: info@icubeinfo.com
Estab: 1993

Herman Li, President

Publisher of software work flow based management systems, documentation, inventory processing, and revision tracking services.

Id Technology LLC BR
7447 N Palm Bluffs Ave
Fresno CA 93711
P: 559-436-8401 PRC:79
www.idtechnology.com
Estab: 1993

Bob Barnard, General Manager
Charles Shepherd, National Accounts Manager
Scott Pepin, National Accounts Manager
Joe Clear, National Integrator Manager
Wayne Moore, Regional Manager

Designer and manufacturer of custom identification systems. The company offers labeling, coding, and marketing equipment services.

IdeaBlade HQ
21C Orinda Way Ste 327
Orinda CA 94563-2534
P: 510-596-5100 F: 510-450-0379 PRC:322
www.ideablade.com
Email: info@ideablade.com
Estab: 2001

Jay Traband, Founder & CTO
Ward Bell, VP
Marcel Good, Senior Director of Professional Services
Josh Otis, Manager of Information Technology
Silvio Belini, Software Engineer

Provider of database application services. The company's products include DevForce, Coctail, and Breeze.

IDEAYA Biosciences HQ
7000 Shoreline Ct Ste 350
S San Francisco CA 94080
P: 650-443-6209 PRC:34
www.ideayabio.com
Email: info@ideayabio.com
Estab: 2015

Yujiro Hata, CEO
Julie Hambleton, SVP & CMO & Head of Development
Michael P. Dillon, SVP & Chief Scientific Officer & Head of Research
Paul Stone, SVP & General Counsel
Mark Lackner, VP

Provider of synthetic lethality medicines for the immuno oncology therapies. The company specializes in cancer biology, small molecule drug discovery, and immunology.

Idec Corp BR
1175 Elko Dr
Sunnyvale CA 94089-2209
P: 408-747-0550 F: 408-744-9055 PRC:314
www.idec.com
Email: opencontact@idec.com

Tomoko Noya, Marketing & Communications Manager
Masae Fukuda, Accounting Manager
Ed Moran, Human Resource Manager
Roger Aubuchon, Regional Sales Manager
John DeLand, Automation Sales Engineer

Designer and manufacturer of automated machines for various sectors. The company also offers products for environment, safety, and other needs.

Identiv Inc HQ
2201 Walnut Ave Ste 100
Fremont CA 94538
P: 888-809-8880 PRC:325
www.identiv.com
Email: sales@identiv.com
Estab: 1996
Sales: $30M to $100M

Jim Ousley, Chairman
Steven Humphreys, CEO & Director
Manfred Mueller, COO & General Manager
Calaimany Bhoopathi, Senior Engineer of CTO Office
Sandra Wallach, CFO

Provider of security technology services. The company's products include desktop readers, terminals, modules, and development kits.

IDEX Health & Science LLC BR
600 Park Ct
Rohnert Park CA 94928
P: 707-588-2000 F: 707-588-2020 PRC:13
www.idex-hs.com
Email: ihsdegassers-valves@idexcorp.com
Estab: 2002

Betsy Schaffer, Director of Human Resources
Audrey Schrock, Senior Product Manager

Provider of precision equipment for the health care industry. The company also offers detectors, fittings, and filters.

IEH JL Analytical Services HQ
217 Primo Way
Modesto CA 95358
P: 209-538-8111 F: 209-538-3966 PRC:306
iehinc.com
Email: info@iehinc.com
Estab: 1972

Mike Wolf, Laboratory Director

Provider of laboratory and consulting services for food microbiology, allergens, virology, and parasitology, forensics, and agricultural products.

Igenex Inc HQ
556 Gibraltar Dr
Milpitas CA 95035
P: 650-424-1191 F: 650-424-1196 PRC:34
igenex.com
Email: customerservice@igenex.com
Estab: 1983

Akhila Poruri, Research Associate

Provider of immunology laboratory services. The company offers service to private practice physicians, hospitals, and clinical reference laboratories.

iHEAR Medical Inc HQ
15250 Hesperian Blvd Ste 102
San Leandro CA 94578
P: 510-276-4437 F: 510-662-7900 PRC:191
ihearmedical.com
Email: info@ihearmedical.com
Estab: 2010

Adnan Shennib, Founder & CEO
Michael Potter, Consulting CFO
Varun Bhardwaj, VP of Operations
Marika Berkley, Director of Quality & Regulatory Affairs

Provider of hearing technology. The company specializes in web-enabled hearing device to fulfill the unmet needs of the hearing impaired.

Iksanika LLC HQ
60 S Market St Ste 1200
San Jose CA 95113
P: 408-490-0777 PRC:322
www.iksanika.com
Email: info@iksanika.com
Estab: 2000

Vital Volosiuk, EVP

Provider of custom software development, testing, quality assurance, porting, and re-engineering services.

Illumina Inc BR
25861 Industrial Blvd
Hayward CA 94545
P: 510-670-9300 F: 510-670-9302 PRC:34
www.illumina.com
Email: info@illumina.com
Estab: 1998

Francis deSouza, President & CEO
Mostafa Ronaghi, SVP & CTO
Phil Febbo, CMO
Sam Samad, SVP & CFO
Aimee Hoyt, SVP & CPO

Developer, manufacturer, and marketer of integrated systems for the analysis of genetic variation and biological function.

Illumio Inc HQ
920 De Guigne Dr
Sunnyvale CA 94085
P: 669-800-5000 PRC:323
www.illumio.com
Estab: 2013

P.J. Kirner, CTO & Co-Founder
Andrew Rubin, CEO & Co-Founder
Anup Singh, CFO
Bobby Guhasarkar, CMO
Suresh Pottur, Staff Engineer

Developer of security platform and it is also involved in data encryption and technical support services.

Illustris Pharmaceuticals Inc HQ
131 Innovation Dr Ste 150
Irvine CA 92617
P: 650-334-2090 PRC:268
www.illustris.com
Email: info@illustris.com
Estab: 2016

Jacob Waugh, Founder & CSO
Jonah Shacknai, Chairman
Mark Prygocki, CEO

Developer and provider of technology solutions for the delivery of large molecules through the tissue structures.

ILM Tool Inc HQ
23301 Clawiter Rd
Hayward CA 94545
P: 510-782-0100 F: 510-782-5475 PRC:80
ilmtool.com
Email: sales@ilmtool.com
Emp: 30 Estab: 1981

Joe Ilmberger, Owner
John Aldrete, Quality Manager

Provider of engineering and CNC machining services. The company offers precision machining services for the biotech and semiconductor industries.

Imageteq Technologies Inc   HQ
533 Airport Blvd Ste 400
Burlingame CA 94010
P: 650-403-4806   F: 650-403-0876   PRC:325
imageteq.com
Email: info@imageteq.com
Estab: 1999

Len Goldberg, Co-Founder & General Manager
Nancy Gaehwiler Goldberg, Co-Founder & Sales
Manager
Rajan Jena, CTO
Jim Pavlovcak, Development Manager

Provider of IT consulting and services. The company focuses on consulting, enterprise application, and staff augmentation.

Imagine IT!   HQ
21730 Nordhoff St   [N]
Chatsworth CA 91311
P: 818-368-2604   F: 818-322-1322   PRC:104
www.imagineit.com
Email: info@imagineit.com
Estab: 1992

Grant George, Manager
Jared D. Gerber, Consultant

Producer of customized interactive multimedia application developments for CD-ROM and corporate intranets. CD-ROMs produced are for employee training, business presentations, trade shows and conferences and also offers digital audio and video and DVD authoring.

Imagine That Inc   HQ
6830 Via Del Oro Ste 230
San Jose CA 95119
P: 408-365-0305   F: 408-629-1251   PRC:322
www.extendsim.com
Email: info@extendsim.com
Estab: 1987

Bob Diamond, Founder & CEO

Developer of simulation software. The company offers services to the retail, healthcare, insurance, and financial services industries.

Imaging Visions   HQ
15850 Orange Blossom Ln
Los Gatos CA 95032
P: 408-358-6427   F: 408-348-2436   PRC:316
www.imagingvisions.com

Rod Juncker, Designer & Manager

Provider of design, prototyping, and visualization services that include architectural and lighting, exterior and landscape, and furnishing design.

Imaja   HQ
1244 Hearst Ave Ste 7
Berkeley CA 94702
P: 510-526-4621   PRC:320
www.imaja.com
Email: support@imaja.com
Estab: 1985

Greg Jalbert, Owner
Margreet Hindriks, Owner
Ed Roseman, Manager
Imanuel Widjaja, Construction Administrator
Sebastian Sola Cuesta, Educator Social

Developer of computer applications. The company specializes in the development of educational tools for Macs.

M-154

iMaxsoft Corp   HQ
PO Box 1222
Cupertino CA 95015
P: 408-253-1987   PRC:326
www.imaxsoft.com
Estab: 1984

Lee Tsai, Founder & CEO

Provider of database and application migration services. The company offers services to government agencies.

IMC Power Sources   HQ
1272 Alma Ct
San Jose CA 95112
P: 408-924-0800   F: 408-494-0804   PRC:288
www.imcpower.com

Ron Evans, Owner
Kendra Latimore, Administrative Assistant

Supplier of SLA batteries, power test equipment, and test loads. The company serves the industrial market.

iMiners Inc   HQ
6894 Brookview Ct
Livermore CA 94551
P: 925-447-6073   F: 925-447-6074   PRC:325
iminers.com
Email: info@iminers.com
Estab: 2005

Sandesh Prabhu, Chief Architect

Provider of investor relations management tools and web-based communication platforms. The company offers website plug-ins and shareholder message boards.

Immecor   HQ
1650 Northpoint Pkwy Ste C
Santa Rosa CA 95407
P: 707-636-2550   F: 707-636-2565   PRC:224
www.immecor.com
Email: support@immecor.com
Estab: 1993

Nhon Tran, VP
James Foley, Director of National Sales

Provider of industrial computers, custom cables, and PCB assembly services. The company serves entertainment, medical, and telecom sectors.

Immersion Corp   HQ
50 Rio Robles
San Jose CA 95134
P: 408-467-1900   F: 408-467-1901   PRC:112
www.immersion.com
Estab: 1993
Sales: $30M to $100M

Vic Viegas, CEO
Christophe Ramstein, CTO
Nancy Erba, CFO
Chris Ullrich, VP
Dennis Sheehan, SVP of Sales & Marketing

Developer and marketer of haptic (touch feedback) technology. The company serves mobile device, wearable, automotive, medical, and other sectors.

Immuno Concepts Na Ltd   HQ
9825 Goethe Rd Ste 350
Sacramento CA 95827
P: 916-363-2649   F: 916-363-2843   PRC:31
www.immunoconcepts.com
Email: technicalsupport@immunoconcepts.com
Estab: 1979

Bert Williams, Owner
Harmeet Boparai, VP & General Manager
Natalie Zelenov, Quality Assurance Manager

Manufacturer and distributor of diagnostic assays. The company's products are used for systemic rheumatic diseases.

Immunoscience Inc   HQ
6670 Owens Dr
Pleasanton CA 94588
P: 925-828-1000   F: 925-397-2114   PRC:34
www.immunoscience.com
Email: info@immunoscience.com
Estab: 1995

Sateesh Apte, President & CEO & Founder
Paul Oken, CFO
Victor Martin, VP of Manufacturing
Geeta Kalbag, Product Development Specialist

Provider of biotechnology research and development for diagnosis and treatment of AIDS and HIV infection. The company also offers therapeutic vaccines.

Imosphere Inc   BR
71 Forest View Dr
San Francisco CA 94132
P: 800-802-1884   PRC:194
imosphere.com
Email: info@imosphere.com
Estab: 1993

Aidan Morris, CEO
Mark Rogers, CTO
Natalie Kenneison, COO
Mark Robinson, Chief Innovation Officer & Solution Architect
Kiran Padda, Manager of Delivery Team

Developer of healthcare analytics platform. The company offers services to healthcare professionals.

Impekable LLC   HQ
99 S Almaden Blvd Ste 600
San Jose CA 95113
P: 650-733-6006   PRC:315
impekable.com
Email: sales@impekable.com
Estab: 2012

Pek Pongpaet, CEO
Sara Gallagher, Director of Business Development & Partnerships

UI design and mobile development studio that helps organizations to create human-centric mobile experiences.

Imperva Inc HQ
3400 Bridge Pkwy Ste 200
Redwood Shores CA 94065
P: 650-345-9000 F: 650-345-9004 PRC:322
imperva.com
Email: privacy@imperva.com
Estab: 2002

Christopher S. Hylen, President & CEO & Director
Kunal Anand, CTO
Jim Dildine, CFO
David Gee, CMO
James Lok, SVP of Global Product Development

Provider of application and data security solutions. The company's products include database firewalls, management server, and monitoring software.

Importio HQ
12980 Saratoga Ave Ste B
Saratoga CA 95070
P: 650-935-4336 PRC:315
import.io
Email: hello@import.io
Estab: 2012

Matthew Painter, Co-Founder & CTO
Yaw Boakye, Business Owner
Andrew Fogg, Co-Founder
Gary Read, CEO & Chairman
Carol Manchester, CFO

Enables organizations to gain intelligence, abilities, and competing advantages from the vast amount of data on the web.

Impression Technology Inc HQ
1777 N California Blvd Ste 240
Walnut Creek CA 94596
P: 925-280-0010 F: 925-280-0092 PRC:323
www.impression-technology.com
Email: sales@impression-technology.com
Estab: 1997

Bruce Lechner, VP of Business Development
Charles Hou, VP of Engineering
Noel Ong, Senior Software Engineer

Provider of automated data capture solutions that meet the business objectives. The company primarily offers scanners.

Imprint Energy HQ
1320 Harbor Bay Pkwy Ste 110
Alameda CA 94502
P: 510-748-0233 PRC:288
www.imprintenergy.com

Christine Ho, CEO
Konstantin Tikhonov, VP of R&D
Jesse Smithyman, Director of Technology
Chaojun Shi, Materials Manager

Developer of zinc-based rechargeable batteries. The company is engaged in energy management solutions.

Impulse Semiconductor Inc HQ
111 North Market St 300
San Jose CA 95113
P: 408-355-5018 PRC:86
impulsesemi.com
Email: design@impulsesemi.com
Estab: 1994

Rosario Consiglio, Founder & President

Provider of electrostatic discharge and electrical overstress products and services. The company also provides virtual components and hardware.

Imra America Inc BR
48834 Kato Rd Ste 106A
Fremont CA 94538
P: 510-623-3507 F: 510-656-2093 PRC:172
imra.com
Email: lasers@imra.com

Fumiyo Yoshino, Applications Research Engineer
Mariko Yamaguchi, Application Development Scientist

Developer and manufacturer of fiber lasers. The company's products are used in cutting, drilling, welding, and thin-film removal applications.

IMT Precision Inc HQ
31902 Hayman St
Hayward CA 94544
P: 510-324-8926 F: 510-324-8943 PRC:80
www.imtp.com
Email: rfq@imtp.com
Estab: 1994

Jeff Nordloff, VP of Business Development
Zack Lemley, Director of Production & Planning
Peter Kunze, Quality Assurance Manager
Tim Ilario, Shareholder

Provider of sheet metal machining, fabrication, inspection and assembly services to semiconductor, aerospace, biotech, and education sectors.

Imtec Acculine Inc HQ
49036 Milmont Dr
Fremont CA 94538
P: 510-770-1800 F: 510-770-1400 PRC:159
www.imtecacculine.com
Email: sales@imtecacculine.com
Estab: 1972

Paul Mendes, President
Mark West, Sales Manager
Rich Tapia, Marketing Communication Manager
Richard Faria, Controller
Dick Grimsley, Mechanical Designer

Provider of wet process modules and systems. The company also supplies quartz constant temperature baths.

Inabyte Inc HQ
5 Betty Ln
Novato CA 94947
P: 415-898-7905 F: 415-898-1652 PRC:324
www.inabyte.com
Estab: 1996

P. Mark Hennessy, President
Myles Cagney, CEO

Manufacturer of developer tools. The company also offers solutions and services for developers and end users of PCs or workstations.

Inbus Engineering HQ
4771 Arroyo Vista Ste C
Livermore CA 94551
P: 925-454-2500 F: 925-454-2501 PRC:91
www.inbus.com
Email: sales@inbus.com
Estab: 1988

Jim Wright, Project Coordinator

Manufacturer and supplier of obsolete Intel boards emulators. The company offers repair and replacement and disk transfer services.

Incal Technology Inc HQ
46420 Fremont Blvd
Fremont CA 94538
P: 510-657-8405 PRC:15
www.incal.com
Email: sales@incal.com
Estab: 1988

Bruce Simikowski, VP & General Manager President & CEO
Stephen Tsun, Director of Sales & Marketing
Alberto Salamone, General Manager
Dennis Puddester, Sales Manager
Shalimar Rivera, Manager of Sales Account

Designer and manufacturer of test and burn in equipment and related hardware for board testing. The company serves the semiconductor industry.

InCarda Therapeutics Inc HQ
39899 Balentine Dr Ste 185
Newark CA 94560
P: 510-422-5522 PRC:261
www.incardatherapeutics.com
Email: info@incardatherapeutics.com
Estab: 2009

Carlos Schuler, Chief Operating & Technology Officer & Founder

Developer of drugs and inhaled therapy intended to treat paroxysmal atrial fibrillation and other cardiovascular diseases.

Incelldx Inc HQ
1541 Industrial Rd
San Carlos CA 94070
P: 650-777-7630 F: 650-587-1528 PRC:20
www.incelldx.com
Email: info@incelldx.com
Estab: 2010

Bruce Patterson, CEO
Daren Abe, Director of Financial Operations
Brian Francisco, Field Application Specialist

Provider of molecular diagnostics to detect and monitor cervical cancer, HIV/AIDS, hepatitis, and organ transplant rejection diseases.

Incentia Design Systems Inc HQ
3080 Olcott St Ste C250
Santa Clara CA 95054
P: 408-727-8988 F: 408-727-8008 PRC:325
www.incentia.com
Email: info@incentia.com
Estab: 1998

Al Lipinski, VP of Sales
Shing-Chong Chang, VP of Engineering

Provider of advanced timing and signal integrity analysis, design closure, and logic synthesis software for nanometer designs.

Inclin Inc BR
2655 Campus Dr Ste 100
San Mateo CA 94403
P: 650-376-4000 PRC:189
inclin.com
Email: busdev@inclin.com
Estab: 1998

Arnold Wong, Founder & CEO
Deb Manuel, VP of Clinical Data Management
Katherine Choy, Clinical Research Manager
Rhonda Asis, Human Resource Manager
Sandy Chen, Clinical Project Manager & QA
Manager

Provider of clinical, regulatory, and quality assurance services to pharmaceutical, biotechnology, and medical device companies.

Incotec Inc RH
1293 Harkins Rd
Salinas CA 93901-4408
P: 831-757-4367 F: 831-757-1512 PRC:39
www.incotec.com
Email: admin@incotec.com
Estab: 1968

Douwe Zijp, CEO
Shawna Castro, Customer Service Manager
Kathy Winn, Business Manager
Paul DeCarli, Account Manager
Kathy Townsend, Logistic Coordinator

Provider of solutions in the business areas such as vegetables, field crops, ornamentals, and analytical services.

Increv Corp HQ
1877 Austin Ave
Los Altos CA 94024
P: 408-689-2296 F: 650-625-9550 PRC:319
www.increvcorp.com
Email: info@increvcorp.com
Estab: 2006

Suthin Sadanandan, Senior Development Manager

Developer of business and information technology solutions. The company is engaged in consulting and product development services.

InCube Labs HQ
2051 Ringwood Ave
San Jose CA 95131
P: 408-457-3700 PRC:189
incubelabs.com
Email: inquiries@incubelabs.com
Estab: 1995

Mir Imran, CEO & Chairman
Mir Hashim, CSO
Svai Sanford, CFO
Stephanie McGrory, VP of Business Development
Angela Murch, VP of Intellectual Property

Provider of laboratory services. The company offers medical devices and pharmaceuticals to various therapeutic areas.

M-156

INDEC Medical Systems Inc HQ
4546 B-10 El Camino Real Ste 381
Los Altos CA 94022
P: 408-986-1600 F: 650-965-0264 PRC:325
www.indecmedical.com
Email: info@indecmedical.com

Carol Hubler, VP

Provider of hardware and software solutions for cardiovascular imaging applications such as intravascular ultrasound and angiography.

Individual Software Inc HQ
3049 Independence Dr Ste E
Livermore CA 94551
P: 925-734-6767 F: 925-734-8337 PRC:319
www.individualsoftware.com
Email: customercare@individualsoftware.com
Estab: 1981

Ken Wiens, VP
Diane Dietzler, EVP of Consumer Sales
Dwayne Tatum, VP of Information Technology &
Technical Services

Publisher and developer of education, business, and personal productivity software for consumers, schools, businesses, and government.

Indtec Corp HQ
3348 Paul Davis Dr Ste 109
Marina CA 93933
P: 831-582-9388 F: 831-582-9386 PRC:202
www.indtec.net
Email: sales@indtec.net
Estab: 1991

Pualani Visesio, Purchasing Manager

Manufacturer of printed circuit boards. The company specializes in assemblies, wires, cables, automated surface mounting, and harness services.

Inductive Automation HQ
90 Blue Ravine
Folsom CA 95630
P: 916-456-1045 F: 916-932-1194 PRC:319
inductiveautomation.com

Steve Hechtman, Founder & President & CEO
Don Pearson, CSO
Kristi Millard, Director of Human Resources
Colby Clegg, Co-Director of Software Engineering
Sandra Domerofski, Director of Finance

Supplier of web-based industrial automation software. The company offers solutions for end-users and integrators.

Industrial Control Links Inc HQ
1364 Blue Oaks Blvd
Roseville CA 95678
P: 530-888-1800 F: 530-888-7017 PRC:64
www.iclinks.com
Email: info@iclinks.com
Estab: 1986

Perry Spetz, Owner
Sarah Meyer, Account Manager
Joel Decker, Software Engineer

Designer and manufacturer of SCADA hardware and software solutions. The company focuses on monitoring, alarming, data collection, and other needs.

Industrial Electrical Co HQ
1417 Coldwell Ave
Modesto CA 95350
P: 209-527-2800 F: 209-527-4457 PRC:150
industrialelectricalco.com
Estab: 1935

Michelle Howell, Owner & VP
Paul Swanson, COO
Dave Jones, IT Director
Jim Wright, Territory Manager
Michael Crumley, Project Coordinator

Provider of electrical, manufacturing, and automation services for the commercial and industrial sectors.

Industrial Nuclear Co HQ
14320 Wicks Blvd
San Leandro CA 94577
P: 510-352-6767 F: 510-352-6772 PRC:159
ir100.com
Email: sales@ir100.com
Estab: 1972

Charles Bollinger, COO

Manufacturer of industrial gamma radiography equipment and radioactive sources. The company's services include calibration and repair and leak testing.

Industrial Optics Unlimited HQ
1680 S St
Anderson CA 96007
P: 530-365-1972 PRC:173
www.iouoptics.com
Email: mail@iouoptics.com
Estab: 1990

Kristie Fore, President

Provider of optical services. The company is involved in fabricating optical components for both commercial and laser applications.

Infin IT Consulting HQ
55 N Third St Ste 201
Campbell CA 95008
P: 866-364-2007 F: 408-361-8888 PRC:319
www.infinitconsulting.com
Email: helpdesk@infinitconsulting.com
Estab: 2006

Jerod Powell, Founder & President
Darrin Swan, CEO
Daniel Schneiderman, Director of IT Services &
CIO
Malu Septien Milan, Senior VP of Innovation
Alexis Nguyen, Support Engineer

Designer and developer of CNC machining and billet products. The company's products include fire extinguisher brackets, shift knobs, and boat accessories.

Infineon Technologies North American Corp BR
18225 Serene Dr Ste 100
Morgan Hill CA 95037
P: 866-951-9519 PRC:208
www.infineon.com

Johann Dechant, Deputy Chairman of General Works Council
Wolfgang Eder, Chairman
Reinhard Ploss, CEO
Dominik Asam, CFO
Hans Brueggemann, Director of Quality & Test

Provider of semiconductor and system solutions. The company focuses on mobile security, sensors, power management, and RF.

Infinera Corp HQ
140 Caspian Ct
Sunnyvale CA 94089
P: 408-572-5200 PRC:97
www.infinera.com
Email: techsupport@infinera.com
Estab: 2001
Sales: $1B to $3B

Dave Welch, Founder & Chief Strategy Officer
Tom Fallon, CEO & Director
Brett Hooper, Chief Human Resource Officer
David Heard, COO
Parthiban Kandappan, CTO

Provider of services and solutions in optical networks. The company serves cable operators and Internet content providers.

Infinite Technologies Inc HQ
1264 Hawks Flight Ct Ste 210
El Dorado Hills CA 95762
P: 916-987-3261 F: 916-987-3264 PRC:323
infintech.com
Estab: 1994

Michael Whittle, President
Don Petersen, Senior Lead Developer
Derik Harris, System Architect & Lead Technologist
Eric Jonsson, Programmer & Analyst
Nicolas Bailey, Senior Application Architect

Provider of information technology, strategic consulting, and engineering services. The company serves government and corporate entities.

Infiniti Solutions USA HQ
3910 N First St
San Jose CA 95134
P: 408-923-7300 F: 408-251-5431 PRC:124
infinitisolutions.com
Email: bi.sales@infinitisolutions.com
Estab: 2001

Vipul Panchal, COO
Selena Abebe, Manager of Purchasing & Administration

Provider of electronic manufacturing services. The company specializes in burn-in board and system design and manufacturing.

Infinity Quick Turn Material Inc HQ
4063 Clipper Ct
Fremont CA 94538
P: 510-661-0555 F: 510-661-0655 PRC:211
www.infinityquickturn.com
Estab: 2005

Jeff Carr, President

Provider of manufacturing solutions and services. The company deals with component distribution and PCB fabrication.

Inflection LLC HQ
555 Twin Dolphin Dr Ste 630
Redwood City CA 94065
P: 650-618-9910 F: 650-593-2799 PRC:325
inflection.com
Email: company@inflection.com
Estab: 2006

Brian Monahan, Founder
Mike Grossman, CEO
Nachi Sendowski, CTO & VP Engineering
Peter Chantel, CFO
Ellen Perelman, CMO

Provider of technology solutions and software products. The company develops search engines, cloud management, and web server applications.

Infobahn Softworld Inc HQ
2010 N First St Ste 470
San Jose CA 95131
P: 408-855-9616 F: 408-855-9490 PRC:325
www.infobahnsw.com
Email: info@infobahnsw.com
Estab: 1996

Nitin Chandra, President
Priti Sarma, Accounts Receivable Manager
Nick Kapur, IT Sales Manager & Manager of IT Sales
Naveen Pole, Recruiter
Sreeram Thattari, IT Recruiter

Provider of consulting, enterprise application integration, service oriented architecture, and systems integration solutions to fortune 500 companies.

Infoblox HQ
3111 Coronado Dr
Santa Clara CA 95054
P: 408-986-4000 F: 408-986-4001 PRC:97
www.infoblox.com
Email: info@infoblox.com
Estab: 1999

Jesper Andersen, President & CEO
Sammie Walker, EVP & CMO
Brad Bell, SVP & CIO
Hoke Horne, EVP & CFO
Liza Burns, VP of Business Operations

Provider of automated network control solutions. The company's services include training, implementation, migration, upgrade, repair, and maintenance.

Infoflex Inc HQ
PO Box 1596 [N]
Burlingame CA 94011
P: 650-270-1019 F: 650-433-8897 PRC:319
www.infoflex.com
Estab: 1986

Gerard Menicucci, CEO

Developer of accounting and 4GL software.

Infoimage Inc HQ
141 Jefferson Dr
Menlo Park CA 94025
P: 650-473-6388 PRC:324
infoimageinc.com
Estab: 1984

Howard Lee, President & CEO
Kim Mawla, CTO
Rose Lee, COO
Lenora Lee, CFO
Guy Mason, Director of Account Management & SVP of Sales & Marketing

Provider of technology solutions for job tracking and business continuity needs. The company also focuses on data integrity.

Infolane Inc HQ
3310 Powell St Ste B6
Emeryville CA 94608
P: 510-277-2399 PRC:323
www.infolane.com
Email: info@infolane.com
Estab: 1994

David Hillstrom, President

Provider of web design and development and support services that includes web content management, application development, and technical improvements.

Informatica Corp HQ
2100 Seaport Blvd
Redwood City CA 94063
P: 650-385-5000 F: 650-385-5500 PRC:324
www.informatica.com
Email: support@informatica.com
Estab: 1993

Anil Chakravarthy, CEO
Eric Brown, EVP & CFO
Erin Andre, SVP & Chief Human Resource Officer
Graeme Thompson, SVP & CIO
Margaret Breya, EVP & CMO

Provider of enterprise data integration and management solutions including data migration, warehousing, identity resolution, and other needs.

Informatica HQ
2100 Seaport Blvd
Redwood City CA 94063
P: 650-385-5000 F: 650-385-5500 PRC:315
www.informatica.com
Email: trainingsales@informatica.com
Estab: 1993

Tracey Newell, President of Global Field Operations
Amit Walia, President of Products & Marketing
Anil Chakravarthy, CEO
Eric Brown, EVP & CFO
Graeme Thompson, SVP & CIO

Provides data management software and services to help a company to achieve a competitive edge.

Informatix Inc HQ
  2485 Natomas Park Dr Ste 430
  Sacramento CA 95833
  P: 916-830-1400 PRC:323
  informatixinc.com
  Email: info@informatixinc.com
  Estab: 1999

  Raul Ocazionez, President
  Ronald Zuber, CFO
  Michele Blanc, COO
  Lisa Cruz, Director of BPO Services
  Ralph Petty, Director of PSG

  Provider of information technology and business
  solutions that include software development, document management, networking, and consulting
  services.

Infostretch Corp HQ
  3200 Patrick Henry Dr Ste 250
  Santa Clara CA 95054
  P: 408-727-1100 F: 408-716-2461 PRC:322
  www.infostretch.com
  Email: info@infostretch.com
  Estab: 2004

  Manish Mathuria, Co-Founder & COO
  Rutesh Shah, CEO & Co-Founder
  Pinakin Sheth, CFO
  Leila Modarres, CMO
  Avery Lyford, Chief Customer Officer

  Provider of mobile application development,
  quality assurance testing and automation, SaaS
  solutions, and ERP testing solutions.

InfoTech Spectrum Inc HQ
  2060 Walsh Ave Ste 120
  Santa Clara CA 95050
  P: 408-705-2237 F: 408-716-2625 PRC:224
  infotechspectrum.com
  Email: hr@infotechspectrum.com
  Estab: 2003

  Rajiv Pendyala, VP
  Rajkumar Jangirala, Account Manager
  Mahesh Mass Aron, Account Manager
  Shaik Saleem, IT Technical Recruiter
  Arun Putluru, Technical Recruiter

  Provider of integrated creative IT services including IT consulting, advanced technology deployment, and product development.

Infoyogi LLC HQ
  2320 Walsh Ave Ste A
  Santa Clara CA 95051
  P: 408-850-1700 F: 408-516-8945 PRC:323
  infoyogi.com
  Email: info@infoyogi.com
  Estab: 2004

  Rao Tallapragada, President

  Provider of information technology solutions for
  software application development and systems
  integration.

M-158

Infrared Industries Inc HQ
  25590 Seaboard Ln
  Hayward CA 94545
  P: 510-782-8100 F: 510-782-8101 PRC:11
  www.infraredindustries.com
  Email: info@infraredindustries.com
  Estab: 1959

  Mark Russell, CEO & VP of Research & Development
  Martha Rykala, CFO

  Developer of gas analyzer instrumentation for the
  automotive, oil and gas, industrial, environmental,
  and utility industries.

Ingenuus Software Inc HQ
  43575 Mission Blvd Ste 151
  Fremont CA 94539
  P: 510-824-5653 PRC:327
  www.ingenuus.com
  Email: sales@ingennus.com

  Vivek Prasad, President & CEO

  Provider of enterprise process orchestration solutions. The company develops business process
  management and process optimization software.

Inikosoft Inc HQ
  15495 Los Gatos Blvd Ste 4
  Los Gatos CA 95032
  P: 408-402-9545 PRC:318
  www.inikosoft.com
  Email: info@inikosoft.com
  Estab: 2003

  Zach Crawford, Creative Director
  Ryan Dedrick, Project Manager

  Provider of web, graphic, and print design services. The company is also engaged in e-commerce development and social media marketing.

Initio Corp LH
  910 Campisi Way Ste 2A
  Campbell CA 95008
  P: 408-608-0060 PRC:211
  www.initio.com
  Estab: 1994

  Jianjun Luo, Director
  Tong Chen, ASIC Design Manager

  Provider of integrated circuits and solutions for
  storage devices. The company is involved in
  design, installation, and delivery services.

Inland Metal Technologies HQ
  3245 Depot Rd
  Hayward CA 94545
  P: 510-785-8555 PRC:80
  www.inlandmetal.com
  Email: sales@inlandmetal.com
  Estab: 1964

  Moses Cardenas, Project Manager

  Provider of sheet metal fabrication, manufacturing,
  powder coating, silk-screening, and laser cutting
  services.

Inlite Corp HQ
  939 Grayson St
  Berkeley CA 94710
  P: 800-346-5932 F: 510-849-3230 PRC:243
  inlitelighting.com
  Email: info@inlitelighting.com
  Estab: 1974

  Craig Belle, President

  Manufacturer and distributor of directional lighting
  equipment. The company offers tracks and lighting
  components.

Inmon Corp HQ
  1 Sansome St 35th Fl
  San Francisco CA 94104
  P: 415-946-8901 F: 415-946-8903 PRC:323
  inmon.com
  Email: info@inmon.com
  Estab: 1999

  Peter Phaal, President
  Neil McKee, CTO & VP

  Developer of traffic management and monitoring
  products such as sFlow Trend, sFlow-RT, Hyper-V
  Agent, and others.

Innodisk USA Corp BR
  42996 Osgood Rd
  Fremont CA 94539
  P: 510-770-9421 F: 510-770-9424 PRC:95
  www.innodisk.com
  Email: usasales@innodisk.com
  Estab: 2005

  Victor K. Le, President
  David Wang, VP of Embedded Flash BU
  Kok Ten, Senior Director of Sales
  Wang Licheng, Deputy General Manager
  Johnny Vu, Product Manager

  Provider of embedded flash and dynamic random
  access memory storage products and technology
  solutions.

InnoMedia Inc RH
  1901 McCarthy Blvd
  Milpitas CA 95035
  P: 408-432-5400 F: 408-943-8604 PRC:61
  innomedia.com
  Email: sales_us@innomedia.com
  Estab: 1995

  Kai-Wa Ng, Chairman & CEO & Co-Founder
  Nan-Sheng Lin, Co-Founder & President
  Harprit Chhatwal, CTO
  Wymond Choy, Corporate VP of US
  Shailesh Patel, Senior Director & Broadband
  Product Management & Testing & Support

  Provider of broadband IP telephony products
  and solutions including TDM-PRI SIP gateways,
  enterprise SIP gateways cable, and element
  management systems.

Innominds Software Inc HQ
  2055 Junction Ave Ste 122
  San Jose CA 95131
  P: 408-434-6463 F: 408-434-7061 PRC:323
  www.innominds.com
  Estab: 1998

  Divakar Tantravahi, CEO & Chairman
  Krishna Guda, President & Chief Strategy Officer
  Sai Chintala, President of Quality Engineering
  Rajya Lakshmi Achanta, CPO
  Rao Yendluri, CTO

  Provider of product incubation services for the
  technology industries. The company focuses on
  app development, analytics, mobility, and testing.

Innosys Inc HQ
1555 Third Ave
Walnut Creek CA 94597
P: 510-222-7717 F: 510-222-0325 PRC:319
www.innosys.com
Email: techsupport@innosys.com
Estab: 1973

Jennifer Hwu, CEO
Julius Simon, Technical Director
Risa Baumrind, Programmer & Analyst

Provider of data communication solutions. The company serves airlines, travel agencies, and online travel services.

Innovative Concepts HQ
3440 Roberto Ct [N]
San Luis Obispo CA 93401
P: 805-545-9562 F: 805-545-5730 PRC:104
www.in-con.com
Email: sales@in-con.com
Emp: 11-50

Lonny W. Rollins, CEO
Keith Godfrey, Managing Director
Greg Whittington, Project Manager
Jarrett Prichard, Project Manager
Nick Yost, Project Manager

Provider of website design services.

Innovative Interfaces Inc HQ
1900 Powell St Ste 400
Emeryville CA 94608
P: 510-655-6200 F: 510-450-6350 PRC:322
www.iii.com
Email: info@iii.com
Estab: 1978

Marina Keating, VP of Professional Services
Jing Wang, Support Manager
Kevin Mitchell, Support Engineer
Joe Wojtowicz, Senior Consultant

Provider of technology solutions and services. The company deals with training and hosting, and technical support.

Innovion HQ
2121 Zanker Rd
San Jose CA 95131
P: 408-501-9100 F: 408-501-9110 PRC:211
innovioncorp.com
Email: sales@innovioncorp.com
Estab: 1981

Gary Holyoak, CEO
John Schuur, CTO
Douglas Gonelli, General Manager
Lisa Janello, Quality Manager
Dermot Cronin, Manager of Inside Sales

Provider of foundry and ion implantation services. The company serves the microelectronics industry.

Inovonics Inc HQ
5805 Highway 9
Felton CA 95018
P: 831-458-0552 F: 831-458-0554 PRC:61
www.inovonicsbroadcast.com
Email: info@inovonicsbroadcast.com
Estab: 1972

Ben Barber, President & CEO & COO
Wolfgang Rietz, CFO
Joshua McAtee, Senior Development Engineer

Manufacturer of a wide range of equipment for radio broadcasters. The company also focuses on the marketing aspects.

Inoxpa USA Inc HQ
3721 Santa Rosa Ave Ste B4
Santa Rosa CA 95407
P: 707-585-3900 PRC:160
www.inoxpausa.com
Email: inoxpa.us@inoxpa.com
Estab: 1972

Megan Hope, Technical Office Manager

Manufacturer and trader of pumps and components. The company caters to industries like food processing, dairy, wine-making, and cosmetics.

Inphenix Inc HQ
250 N Mines Rd
Livermore CA 94551
P: 925-606-8809 F: 925-606-8810 PRC:83
www.inphenix.com
Email: info@inphenix.com
Estab: 1999

Calin Moldovean, President of Business Assurance
Qinian Qi, VP of Subsystem & Module
David Lin, Assistant Manager of Quality Assurance
Chunyang Hu, Engineer of Senior product
Lisa Li, Engineer

Designer and manufacturer of active optoelectronic chips and modules. The company serves telecom, defense, biomedical, and industrial markers.

Inphi Corp HQ
2953 Bunker Hill Ln Ste 300
Santa Clara CA 95054
P: 408-217-7300 F: 408-217-7350 PRC:61
www.inphi.com
Email: sales@inphi.com
Estab: 2000
Sales: $300M to $1 Billion

Loi Nguyen, Founder & SVP of Optical Interconnect
Ford G. Tamer, President & CEO
Lawrence Tse, CTO
John Edmunds, CFO
Ron Torten, SVP of Operations & Information Technology

Provider of semiconductor solutions for the computing and telecom markers. The company's products include amplifiers, registers, buffers, and modulator drivers.

Inphora Inc HQ
1042 Country Club Dr Ste 1C
Moraga CA 94556
P: 925-322-5964 PRC:18
inphora.com
Email: info@inphora.com
Estab: 1989

Kathleen Muray, Founder & CTO
Murayk Kathleen, President
Lawrence Muray, CEO
Shelly Muray, Director of Operations
Ann Oeth, Controller

Supplier of high-precision photometric and radiometric instruments. The company's products include detectors, optical filters, and LED reference standards.

Input Optics Inc HQ
914 N Rengstorff Ave
Mountain View CA 94043
P: 650-969-3108 F: 650-969-3186 PRC:323
inputoptics.com
Email: info@inputoptics.com
Estab: 1971

Gary Selig, President
Mike McGillis, CEO

Provider of integration solutions for dental practice. The company also offers complimentary assessments and web services.

Inscopix Inc HQ
2462 Embarcadero Way
Palo Alto CA 94303
P: 650-600-3886 PRC:34
inscopix.com
Email: sales@inscopix.com
Estab: 2011

Kunal Ghosh, Founder & CEO
Pushkar Joshi, Director of Strategy & Business Development
Stephani Otte, Director of Application Development & Science
Vania Cao, Manager of Scientific Content & Training
Michael Wycisk, Manufacturing Engineering Manager

Provider of instrumentation and data analytics for next generation neuroscience. The company provides brain imaging solutions and data analysis suites.

Insight BR
19925 Stevens Creek Blvd Ste 136 137/138
Cupertino CA 95014
P: 877-776-0610 PRC:326
www.insight.com
Estab: 2011

Ken Lamneck, President & CEO
Jeff Shumway, CIO
Glynis Bryan, CFO
Dana A. Leighty, VP
Jen Vasin, SVP of Human Resources

Provider of mobility, network, and security solutions. The company is engaged in design, integration, and implementation services.

InsightRX Inc HQ
548 Market St Ste 88083
San Francisco CA 94104
P: 205-351-0574 PRC:40
insight-rx.com
Email: support@insight-rx.com
Estab: 2015

Ranvir Mangat, COO & Co-Founder
Sirj Goswami, CEO & Co-Founder

Developer of cloud-based platform for precision
medicine and clinical analytics. The company
serves individuals and healthcare organizations.

InSilixa Inc HQ
1000 Hamlin Ct
Sunnyvale CA 94089-1400
P: 408-809-3000 PRC:34
www.insilixa.com
Email: info@insilixa.com
Estab: 2011

Arjang Hassibi, Founder & CEO
Gary Schoolnik, CMO
Nader Gamini, COO
Patrick G., SVP of Commercial Development

Manufacturer of CMOS biosensor devices used
to identify multiple targets including nucleic acids
(DNA or RNA), peptides, or metabolites.

Inspection Services Inc HQ
1798 University Ave
Berkeley CA 94703-1514
P: 510-900-2100 F: 510-900-2101 PRC:304
www.inspectionservices.net
Email: info@inspectionservices.net
Estab: 1995

Leslie Sakai, President & CEO
Ed King, Principal & EVP

Provider of structural steel and welding, wood
framing, anchor and dowel installation, roofing,
and waterproofing services.

**Inspirisys Solutions North America
Inc** HQ
2975 Bowers Ave Ste 323
Santa Clara CA 95051
P: 408-514-5199 PRC:323
www.inspirisys.com/contact-us
Estab: 1991

Milind Kalurkar, President of Sales
John Rekesh, CTO

Provider of software development and technology
services for automotive, healthcare, life science,
networking, storage, and enterprise software
markers.

Inspironix Inc HQ
3400 Cottage Way Ste L
Sacramento CA 95825
P: 916-488-3222 F: 916-488-3210 PRC:323
inspironix.com
Email: info@inspironix.com
Estab: 1987

Cary Parkins, Founder
Matthew Grigas, CTO
Erika Friedman, CFO
Patrick Swayne, Senior Software Engineer
Matt Yamamoto, Consultant

Provider of information technology solutions. The
company offers software development, web application development, web design, and network services.

Instant Systems Inc HQ
39199 Paseo Padre Pkwy Ste A-1
Fremont CA 94538-1606
P: 415-682-6000 PRC:323
in.instantsys.com
Email: info@instantsys.com
Estab: 2004

Vipin Chawla, CEO
Uzay Takaoglu, VP of Product Development
David Esser, VP & Customer Evangelist
Nishant Anand, Director of Engineering
Vikas Sood, Director of Product Development

Provider of Internet based business software and
services. The company's services include distribution and technical support.

Instart Logic Inc HQ
450 Lambert Ave
Palo Alto CA 94306
P: 650-919-8856 PRC:322
www.instartlogic.com
Estab: 2010

Hariharan Kolam, CTO & Co-Founder
Manav Ratan Mital, Co-Founder
Sumit Dhawan, President & CEO
Jony Hartono, CFO
Natalie Lambert, CMO

Provider of software-defined application delivery
solutions. The company offers services to the
travel and hospitality industries.

InStyle Software Inc HQ
5249 Oak Meadow Dr
Santa Rosa CA 95401
P: 314-631-6982 PRC:323
www.instylesoft.com
Email: support@instylesoft.com
Estab: 1997

Sergio Prusky, CEO

Provider of Enterprise Resource Planning Software solutions. The company offers services to
the apparel industry.

Inszoom Inc HQ
5912 Stoneridge Mall Rd
Pleasanton CA 94588
P: 925-244-0600 PRC:323
www.inszoom.com
Email: sales@inszoom.com
Estab: 1999

Umesh Vaidyamath, Founder & CEO
Sunil Kolkur, Product Owner
Raj Vaidyamath, VP
Brian McNair, Director
Lawrence Dsouza, Head of Product Management

Focuses on immigration case management and
compliance automation solutions. The company
offers services to law firms.

Inta Technologies HQ
2281 Calle De Luna
Santa Clara CA 95054
P: 408-748-9955 F: 408-727-3027 PRC:80
www.intatech.com
Email: sales@intatech.com
Estab: 1978

Frank Kramer, CEO
Jim Lynch, General Manager
Lynch Jim, General Manager
Francis Honey, Engineering Manager
Pia Gronvaldt, Manager of Inventory I

Manufacturer of components used in instruments
for environmental analysis. The company also
offers ceramic-to-metal assemblies connectors.

Intake Screens Inc HQ
8417 River Rd
Sacramento CA 95832
P: 916-665-2727 F: 916-665-2729 PRC:159
www.intakescreensinc.com
Email: screens@intakescreensinc.com
Estab: 1996

Russell Berry, President
Dana Falvey, Operations Director & Project
Manager
Judy McAvoy, Office Manager
Jacob Chapin, Mechanical Design Engineer

Designer and manufacturer of intake screens for
fish protection and filtration. The company also
offers installation and maintenance services.

Intapp Inc HQ
3101 Park Blvd
Palo Alto CA 94306
P: 650-852-0400 F: 650-852-0402 PRC:322
www.intapp.com
Email: info@intapp.com
Estab: 2000

Daniel Harsell, SVP of Technology & Founder
John Hall, CEO
Thad Jampol, CTO
Jason Wood, VP of Business Operations
Sumit Garg, Director of Engineering

Provider of software and services for risk manage-
ment, time management, and box management.
The company's products include Intapp Time and
Wall Builder.

Intarcia Therapeutics Inc BR
24650 Industrial Blvd
Hayward CA 94545
P: 510-782-7800 F: 510-782-7801 PRC:268
www.intarcia.com
Estab: 1997

Kurt Graves, President & CEO & Chairman
James Ahlers, CFO
Thane Wettig, CMO
Andrew Young, CSO
Raymond T. Keane, CLO

Provider of therapeutic products and related supplies. The company is engaged in research and
development services.

Integral Development Corp HQ
3000 El Camino Real 2 Palo Alto Sq 6th Fl
Palo Alto CA 94306
P: 650-424-4500 PRC:322
www.integral.com
Estab: 1993

Harpal Sandhu, Founder & CEO
Al Yau, CFO
Vikas Srivastava, CRO
Udyan Kumar, Director of Engineering
Vishal Mahajan, QA Manager

Provider of customer-branded trading solutions
for brokers, dealers, banks, and fund investment
managers.

Integrated Communication Systems   HQ
6680 Via Del Oro
San Jose CA 95119
P: 408-491-6000   PRC:59
ics-integration.com
Estab: 2002

Aaron Colton, President & Principal
Justin Gamble, Director of Audio Visual Division
Mark Berlo, AV Project Manager
Nick Taylor, Project Manager
Vince Lacorte, Service Manager

Provider of communication and integration services. The company offers installation, space planning, project management, and maintenance services.

Integrated Engineering Services   HQ
70 Saratoga Ave Ste 200
Santa Clara CA 95051-7301
P: 408-261-3500   PRC:209
www.iesengineering.net
Email: ies@iesengineering.net
Estab: 1995

Tim Bancroft, Chemical Engineer
Leanne Cossairt, Associate Principal
Jeff Tarter, Principal

Provider of designs for complex high-tech micro-electronic needs. The company also serves the life science facilities.

Integrated Science Solutions Inc   HQ
1261 Locust St Ste 70
Walnut Creek CA 94596
P: 925-979-1535   PRC:304
issi-net.com
Email: info@issi-net.com
Estab: 1999

David C. Dobson, President
Cecelia McCloy, CEO
Carlin Gill, VP of Finance & Administration

Provider of professional services to federal and state clients. The company offers earth and environmental science and engineering services.

Integrated Silicon Solution Inc   HQ
1623 Buckeye Dr
Milpitas CA 95035-4216
P: 408-969-6600   F: 408-969-7800   PRC:208
www.issi.com
Email: sales@issi.com
Estab: 1988

Jian-Yue Pan, Partner & Founder
Jimmy Lee, Chairman
Seong Jun Jang, VP of Memory Design
Lou Yang, VP of Business Development
Ming Shiang Wang, Director of Memory Design

Designer and developer of high performance integrated circuits. The company also focuses on the marketing aspects.

Integrated Surface Technologies Inc   BR
3475-F Edison Way
Menlo Park CA 94025
P: 650-324-1824   PRC:209
www.insurftech.com
Email: info@insurftech.com
Estab: 2007

Jeff Chinn, Founder & CTO
Robert Ashurst, Chief Scientist of Auburn University Partnership
Mark Wiltse, VP
Fred Helmrich, VP of Sales
Zia Hassan, Manufacturing Manager

Provider of supramolecular ceramic coating for water saving electronics. The company offers stiction control and surface modification services.

Integrated Tooling Inc   HQ
1017 Pecten Ct
Milpitas CA 95035
P: 408-934-3862   F: 408-934-3863   PRC:80
www.integratedtoolinginc.com

Tony Silva, President

Developer and manufacturer of tools, dies, and molds. The company specializes in fabricating small intricate parts for machines.

Integrated Wave Technologies   HQ
4042 Clipper Ct
Fremont CA 94538
P: 510-353-0260   PRC:60
www.miltrans.com
Email: info@miltrans.com
Estab: 1995

Timothy McCune, President & Chief Technologist
Cindy Cook-Johnson, Business Manager

Provider of voice recognition technology services. The company offers printing calculators and electronic camera shutters.

Intel Corp   HQ
2200 Mission College Blvd
Santa Clara CA 95054-1549
P: 408-765-8080   PRC:91
www.intel.in
Sales: Over $3B

Andy D. Bryant, Chairman
Michael C. Mayberry, CTO
Sandra L. Rivera, EVP & CPO
Claire E. Dixon, Chief Communications Officer
Wendell M. Brooks, SVP

Designer, developer, and marketer of processors and motherboards. The company also focuses on tablets, laptops, desktops, and other devices.

IntelaMetrix Inc   HQ
2145 Elkins Way Ste G
Brentwood CA 94513
P: 925-606-7044   PRC:194
intelametrix.com
Email: webinfo@intelametrix.com
Estab: 2004

Luiz Da Silva, President & CEO
Heidi Stark, CFO
Daniel Watts, Accounts Manager
Patricia Bryan, Assembly Contractor

Specializes in ultrasound technology solutions. The company offers assessment tools for the health, fitness and wellness industries.

Intelepeer Cloud Communications   HQ
155 Bovet Rd
San Mateo CA 94402
P: 650-525-9200   PRC:68
www.intelepeer.com
Email: info@intelepeer.com
Estab: 2003

Frank M. Fawzi, President & CEO
Phil Bronsdon, CTO
Andre Simone, CFO
Robert Galop, CMO
Matt Edic, Chief Experience Officer

Provider of on-demand cloud-based communication services. The company offers media peering, SIP trunking, and direct inward dialing services.

Intelight ITS   HQ
5962 La Place Ct Ste 150
Carlsbad CA 92008
P: 520-795-8808   PRC:72
www.intelight-its.com
Email: info@intelight-its.com
Estab: 2006

Craig Gardner, Founder & President
Mike Gallagher, Senior Systems Engineer

Provider of electrical engineering solutions. The company offers expertise on systems, traffic products and software.

IntelinAir Inc   HQ
75 E Santa Clara St 6th Fl
San Jose CA 95113
P: 818-445-2339   PRC:324
www.intelinair.com
Email: contact@intelinair.com
Estab: 2015

Al Eisaian, CEO & Co-Founder
Greg Rose, SVP of Business Development & Strategy & Co-Founder
Naira Hovakimyan, Chief Scientist
Adrian Tudor, Chief Product Officer
Harold Reetz, Chief Agronomist

Provider of aerial imagery analytics such as image analysis and change detection and deep learning and neural networks for farmers.

Intellectsoft   HQ
721 Colorado Ave Ste 101
Palo Alto CA 94303
P: 650-300-4335   PRC:315
www.intellectsoft.net
Email: info@intellectsoft.net
Estab: 2007

Artem Kozel, Co-Founder & CSO
Alexander Skalabanov, Co-Founder
Vlad Vahromovs, CEO
Andriy Kashcheyev, CTO & Solution Architect
Iurii Odnorogov, VP of Sales

Provider of impactful digital engineering solutions with latest technologies.

Intelli-Touch Apps Inc HQ
2440 Camino Ramon Ste 155
San Ramon CA 94583
P: 925-884-1802 PRC:319
intelli-touch.com
Email: info@intelli-touch.com
Estab: 2011

William Westfall, CEO & Co-Founder
Barry Ford, COO & Co-Founder

Specializes in automating and simplifying the personal and business communications and it serves the legal industry.

Intellicon Solutions HQ
7 Windeler Ct Ste 700
Moraga CA 94556
P: 925-377-7925 F: 925-377-5035 PRC:322
intelliconsol.com
Email: info@intelliconsol.com

Doug Mosher, Co-Founder & COO
Todd Parsons, Co-Founder & President

Provider of intelligent consulting solutions for learning and development, performance management systems, and related social media communication.

Intelligent Computer Solutions Inc HQ
8968 Fullbright Ave [N]
Chatsworth CA 91311
P: 818-998-5805 F: 818-998-3190 PRC:322
www.ics-iq.com
Email: salesmail@ics-iq.com
Estab: 1990

Steven Katz, VP of Sales

Manufacturer and marketer of hard drive formatting and software pre-loading systems.

Intelligent Inference Systems Corp HQ
566-108 Nasa Research Pk
Moffett Field CA 94035
P: 408-390-1455 F: 408-730-1016 PRC:323
iiscorp.com
Email: admin@iiscorp.com
Estab: 1993

Hamid R. Berenji, CEO

Provider of computational intelligence services. The company primarily caters to high-tech companies.

Intelliswift Software Inc HQ
2201 Walnut Ave Ste 180
Fremont CA 94538
P: 510-490-9240 F: 510-490-9246 PRC:323
www.intelliswift.com
Email: info@intelliswift.com
Estab: 2001

Pat Patel, Founder
Deepesh Shah, Manager
Shafiq Mohammed, Senior Manager
Vinita Dujari, Human Resource Manager
Michelle Rose, Account Manager

Provider of application development services for enterprises. The company also focuses on big data, cloud, web solutions, and staffing services.

IntelliVision Technologies Corp HQ
6203 San Ignacio Ave Ste 112
San Jose CA 95119
P: 408-754-1690 PRC:318
intelli-vision.com
Email: info@intelli-vision.com
Estab: 2002

Whit Pritchett, President
Krishna Khadloya, VP of Engineering & Products & Delivery
Vaidhi Nathan, SVP of Cameras & Analytics
Sheri Becker, Controller

Provider of software and solutions for security, surveillance, traffic, automotive, robotics, drones, smart home, mobile, and retail analytics solutions.

Intematix Corp HQ
46410 Fremont Blvd
Fremont CA 94538
P: 510-933-3300 F: 510-668-0793 PRC:243
www.intematix.com
Email: sales@intematix.com
Estab: 2000

Yi-Qun Li, CEO & SVP of Sales & Marketing
Gang Wang, VP of Product Development
Benjamin Fan, Director of Manufacturing
Shengfeng Liu, Director of R&D Nitride Phosphors
Shifan Cheng, Phosphor R&D Director

Developer of microscopy metrology tools and electronic materials. The company offers services to commercial properties.

Intercom Inc HQ
55 Second St 4th Fl
San Francisco CA 94105
P: 877-595-5175 PRC:323
www.intercom.com
Email: team@intercom.com
Estab: 2011

David Barrett, Founder
Eoghan McCabe, CEO
Ciaran Lee, CTO
Darragh Curran, VP of Engineering
Paul Adams, VP of Products

Designer and developer of communication packages. The company also focuses on user intelligence solutions.

Interface Masters Technologies Inc HQ
150 E Brokaw Rd
San Jose CA 95112
P: 408-441-9341 F: 815-364-0888 PRC:324
interfacemasters.com
Email: sales@interfacemasters.com
Estab: 1995

Ben Askarinam, Founder & CEO
Jennifer Tam, Director of Operations
Matthew Butrimovitz, Marketing Manager

Developer of technology and networking solutions. The company's products include embedded switches, adapters, and related accessories.

Intergraphics HQ
667 Brighton Rd
Pacifica CA 94044
P: 650-359-3087 PRC:325
www.intergraphics.com
Email: kerstin@intergraphics.com
Estab: 1991

Kerstin Connelly, Owner
Pat Newman, Owner
Giorgos Papoutsakis, CEO
Shakir Ahmed, Manager of Accounts
Igor Shaklyar, Plant Manager

Developer of multilingual graphics. The company provides translation, typography, and other services.

Interloc Solutions HQ
340 Palladio Pkwy Ste 526
Folsom CA 95630
P: 916-817-4590 F: 916-817-4594 PRC:326
www.interlocsolutions.com
Email: info@interlocsolutions.com
Estab: 2005

Mike Watson, President & CEO
Gretchen Gallagher, EVP of Business Development & Marketing
Jason VenHuizen, EVP of Products & Technology
Joe Mendoza, VP of Technical Service
Brad Knowles, VP of Professional Services Canada

Provider of consulting services and mobile solutions. The company serves the oil and gas and transportation industries.

Intermedianet Inc HQ
100 Mathilda Pl Ste 600
Sunnyvale CA 94086
P: 650-641-4000 F: 646-225-7348 PRC:325
www.intermedia.net
Email: sales@intermedia.net
Estab: 1995

Michael Gold, CEO
Jason Veldhuis, CFO
Jonathan McCormick, COO & CRO
Scott Anderson, CMO
Jonathan Levine, CTO

Provider of UCaaS, CCaaS, and cloud business applications that helps businesses and partners with secure solutions for communication and collaboration.

Intermedianet Inc HQ
100 Mathilda Pl Ste 600
Sunnyvale CA 94086
P: 800-379-7729 F: 650-965-7791 PRC:67
intermedia.net
Email: sales@intermedia.net
Estab: 1995

Michael Gold, President
Jonathan McCormick, COO
Sarat Khilnani, VP of Product Management
Ryan Barrett, VP of Security & Privacy
Phil Koen, Senior Advisor

Provider of cloud services including VoIP telephony, instant messaging, and file management to small and mid-sized businesses.

Intermems Inc   HQ
  7370 Basking Ridge Ave
  San Jose CA 95138
  P: 408-241-0007   PRC:127
  intermems.com
  Email: info@intermems.com
  Estab: 2002

  Wendell E. McCulley, President & CEO
  Abhijeet D. Sathe, SVP of Research & Development
  Steven Repetto, Director of Sales & Marketing

  Provider of micromolding, plating, thin film deposition, anodic and wafer bonding, and related services.

InterMetro Communications Inc   HQ
  2685 Park Center Dr Bldg A   [N]
  Simi Valley CA 93065
  P: 805-433-8000   F: 805-582-1006   PRC:64
  www.intermetro.net
  Email: info@intermetro.net
  Emp: 11-50   Estab: 2003

  Charles Rice, Chairman of the Board & CEO & President
  Jon DeOng, CIO

  Provider of voice calling over the Internet.

Intermolecular Inc   HQ
  3011 N First St
  San Jose CA 95134
  P: 408-582-5700   F: 408-582-5401   PRC:212
  intermolecular.com
  Email: inquiry@intermolecular.com
  Estab: 2004

  Karl Littau, CTO
  Bill Roeschlein, CFO
  Milind Weling, SVP of Programs & Operations
  Sandeep Jaggi, General Counsel & SVP of Intellectual Property & Corporate Secretary
  Steve Kuhn, Director of Operations

  Provider of high productivity combinatorial technologies. The company serves solar device manufacturers.

Internap Corp   BR
  2151 Mission College Blvd
  Santa Clara CA 95054
  P: 877-843-7627   PRC:67
  inap.com
  Email: cloud-support@inap.com
  Estab: 1996

  Peter D. Aquino, Chairman & CEO
  Michael T. Sicoli, President & CFO
  Andrew Day, COO
  T.J. Waldorf, CMO & Head of Inside Sales & Customer Success
  John D. Filipowicz, CAO & Chief Governance Risk & Compliance Officer

  Provider of Internet network services, colocation, hosting, content delivery, and broadband solutions.

International Electronic Components Inc   RH
  809 Aldo Ave Unit 104
  Santa Clara CA 95054
  P: 408-496-0474   F: 408-496-0478   PRC:202
  www.ieccan.com
  Email: info@iecus.com
  Estab: 1966

  Jennifer Lewis, Customer Service Representative
  Geert Breesch, Contact

  Distributor of printed circuit boards, consumables, and inspection and measuring equipment. The company is engaged in installation services.

International Electronic Enterprises Inc   HQ
  110 Agate Ave   [N]
  Newport Beach CA 92662
  P: 949-673-2943   F: 949-673-0249   PRC:322
  www.ieei.com
  Email: sales@ieei.com
  Estab: 1976

  Summer Bailey, VP

  Distributor of computer spare parts, complete systems and peripheral devices including drives, controllers, SAN units and more and provider of digital storage solutions.

International Manufacturing   HQ
  1205 San Luis Obispo
  Hayward CA 94544
  P: 510-783-8872   F: 510-783-1430   PRC:80
  www.international-mfg.com
  Email: info@international-mfg.com
  Estab: 1981

  Clement C. Johnson, Owner & President

  Manufacturer of precision components for use in semiconductor equipment, medical devices, aerospace vehicles, and defense systems.

International Medcom Inc   BR
  103 Morris St Ste A-5
  Sebastopol CA 95472
  P: 707-823-0336   F: 707-823-7207   PRC:13
  medcom.com
  Estab: 1986

  Dan Sythe, CEO & Founder
  Steve Weiss, Chief Electronic Design Engineer
  Ross Randrup, Contact

  Provider of radiation detection instruments and systems. The company provides technology for nuclear medicine, health physics, and public safety products.

International Microsystems Inc   HQ
  48389 Fremont Blvd Ste 110
  Fremont CA 94538
  P: 408-813-9748   PRC:102
  www.imi-test.com
  Email: sales@imi-test.com

  Tho Nguyen, Software Engineer
  Wayne Chiu, Senior Software Engineer

  Designer and manufacturer of flash memory duplication equipment. The company also offers related test equipment.

International Power Technology Inc   HQ
  1042 W Hedding St Ste 100
  San Jose CA 95126
  P: 408-246-9040   F: 408-246-9036   PRC:293
  www.intpower.com
  Estab: 1974

  Robert J. Forgione, CFO

  Provider of operation and maintenance services for power plants. The company also focuses on engineering and field service.

International Process Solutions   HQ
  1300 Industrial Rd Ste 22
  San Carlos CA 94070
  P: 650-595-7890   F: 650-595-7899   PRC:31
  ips-us.com
  Email: sales-support@ips-us.com
  Estab: 1997

  John Doe, President

  Provider of calibration, maintenance, document generation and validation services of pharmaceutical and biotech process equipment.

International Sensor Technology Inc   HQ
  3 Whatney   [N]
  Irvine CA 92618
  P: 949-452-9000   F: 949-452-9009   PRC:13
  www.intlsensor.com
  Emp: 1-10   Estab: 1972

  Jack Chou, Founder & CEO

  Manufacturer and distributor of both the sensors and the instrumentations.

International Transportation Service Inc   HQ
  1281 Pier G Way   [N]
  Long Beach CA 90802
  P: 562-435-7781   PRC:34
  www.itslb.com
  Email: tmssupport@itslb.com
  Emp: 51-200   Estab: 1938

  John Miller, EVP
  Kiyoichi Kojitani, SVP
  Michael J. Shanks, SVP
  Philip Feldhus, SVP of Operations

  Provider of terminal services such as vessel stevedoring, container yard, maintenance, repair and much more.

Internet Brands Inc   HQ
  909 N Sepulveda Blvd 11th Fl   [N]
  El Segundo CA 90245
  P: 310-280-4000   PRC:24
  www.internetbrands.com
  Emp: 5001-10000   Estab: 1998

  Robert N. Brisco, CEO & President
  Scott A. Friedman, CFO
  Chuck Hoover, CMO
  Joe Rosenblum, CTO
  Lisa Morita, COO

  Operator of media and e-commerce sites for "large ticket" consumer purchases, such as cars and mortgages.

Internet Software Sciences HQ
13851 Fremont Pines Ln
Los Altos Hills CA 94022
P: 650-949-0942   F: 650-917-0913   PRC:325
www.inet-sciences.com
Email: sales@inet-sciences.com
Estab: 1995

Scott Vanderlip, President

Developer of web based applications for IT help
desk, customer support, asset tracking, and facilities management needs.

Internetspeech Inc HQ
5942 Foligno Way
San Jose CA 95138
P: 408-532-8460   F: 408-274-8151   PRC:67
www.internetspeech.com
Email: corporate@internetspeech.com
Estab: 1998

Emdad Khan, President & CEO
Jeff Griffin, VP of marketing & Sales
George Yan, Director of Applications

Provider of audio Internet technology services.
The company offers world-wide web and enabled
services.

Interphase Systems HQ
3565 Victor St Ste C
Santa Clara CA 95054
P: 408-315-8603   F: 408-516-9046   PRC:150
www.interphasesystems.us
Estab: 1995

Alex Cherkassky, VP of Engineering
Diane Reiseg, Office Manager
Bob Mullin, Consultant
Patty Gallagher, Team Leader

Manufacturer of test equipment for the disc drive
industry. The company offers consulting and build-
to-print services.

Interphasic LLC HQ
1621 Plumas Ave
Seaside CA 93955
P: 831-392-0708   F: 831-392-0710   PRC:211
www.interphasic.com
Email: sales@interphasic.com

Robert Engholm, President

Manufacturer of motion control systems. The company offers product support services and it serves
the industrial sector.

Interra Systems Inc HQ
1601 S De Anza Blvd Ste 212
Cupertino CA 95014
P: 408-579-2000   F: 408-579-2050   PRC:323
www.interrasystems.com
Email: info@interrasystems.com
Estab: 2001

Sunil Jain, CEO & President
Mark Brown, CFO
Vijeta Kashyap, VP of Operations
Ashish Basu, VP of Sales & Business Develop-
ment
Sanjay Mittal, Managing Director

Provider of diversified software products and
services for digital media and semiconductor
industries.

Intersect Ent Inc HQ
1555 Adams Dr
Menlo Park CA 94025
P: 650-641-2100   PRC:187
www.intersectent.com
Email: info@intersectent.com
Emp: 393
Sales: $100M to $300M

Monika de Martini, CFO
Amy Wolbeck, VP of Regulatory Affairs
James Stambaugh, VP of Clinical & Reimburse-
ment
Doug Rainforth, Senior Director of Finance
Brenda Lim, Senior Accounting Manager

Provider of steroid-releasing implants that props
open the sinuses for the treatment of common
cold and sinusitis.

Interson Corp HQ
7150 Koll Center Pkwy
Pleasanton CA 94566
P: 925-462-4948   F: 925-462-4833   PRC:198
www.interson.com
Estab: 1989

Roman Solek, President
Monica Solek, Director of Human Resources
Dale Mowery, Manufacturing Engineer
John Norberg, Manufacturing Lead
Nary Ong, Contact

Manufacturer of ultrasound products. The company offers services to offices, hospitals, and clinics
around the world.

Interstate Plastics Inc HQ
330 Commerce Cir
Sacramento CA 95815
P: 916-422-3110   F: 916-422-1608   PRC:284
www.interstateplastics.com
Email: info@interstateplastics.com
Estab: 1980

Galen Klokkevold, President
Mike Feld, Medical Sales Development Manager

Manufacturer and distributor of industrial plastics.
The company offers plastic sheets, rods, tubing,
and profiles.

Interstate Plastics BR
2065 Williams St
San Leandro CA 94577
P: 510-483-4341   F: 510-483-4350   PRC:284
interstateplastics.com
Email: info@interstateplastics.com

Mark Courtright, General Manager
Mike Feld, Medical Sales Development Manager
Gary Stelle, Sales Manager

Provider of plastic products. The company's
products include plastic sheets, rods, tubes, and
industrial accessories.

Intertek Group PLC BR
1365 Adams Ct
Menlo Park CA 94025
P: 650-463-2900   F: 650-463-2910   PRC:306
www.intertek.com
Estab: 1885

Wolfhart Hauser, CEO
Ross McCluskey, CFO
Diane Bitzel, Group CIO
Alex Buehler, EVP of Global Resources
Ian Galloway, SVP

Provider of advisory, business consulting, risk
management, outsourcing, validation, and training
services.

Intertrust Technologies Corp HQ
920 Stewart Dr
Sunnyvale CA 94085
P: 408-616-1600   F: 408-616-1626   PRC:325
www.intertrust.com
Estab: 1990

Talal G. Shamoon, CEO
David P. Maher, EVP & CTO
Matthew B. Glotzer, CFO & Head of Strategy
Robert E. Tarjan, Chief Scientist
Tim Schaaff, EVP & Chief Product Officer

Provider of security technology services such as
content protection, white label video distribution,
and software tamper resistance.

InterVene Inc HQ
415 Grand Ave Ste 302
S San Francisco CA 94080
P: 650-351-6725   PRC:186
www.intervene-med.com
Email: info@intervene-med.com
Estab: 2011

Fletcher Wilson, Founder
Jeff Elkins, CEO
Michi Garrison, VP of Research & Development
Tracy Roberts, VP of Clinical & Regulatory Affairs
Nancy Miceli, Quality Consultant

Provider of medical devices such as blueleaf en-
dovenous valve formation system to treat severe
venous disease in the legs.

Interworking Labs Inc HQ
PO Box 66190
Scotts Valley CA 95067
P: 831-460-7010   PRC:97
www.iwl.com
Email: info@iwl.com
Estab: 1993

Chris Wellens, President & CEO
Karl Auerbach, CTO
Judy Jones, Account Manager

Provider of network related services. The company focuses on testing, emulation, and also offers
network optimization products.

Intest Ems Products BR
47777 Warm Springs Blvd
Fremont CA 94539
P: 408-678-9167   PRC:208
www.intest.com
Email: info@intest.com

Dale Christman, General Manager
Leonard Torres, Operations Manager

Manufacturer of semiconductors to test integrated
circuits. The company also focuses on testing
wafer products.

Intevac Inc HQ
3560 Bassett St
Santa Clara CA 95054
P: 408-986-9888   F: 408-988-8145   PRC:95
intevac.com
Email: dpo@intevac.com
Estab: 1991
Sales: $100M to $300M

Wendell T. Blonigan, President & CEO
Jeff Andreson, CFO
Kimberly Burk, VP of Human Resources
Christopher Smith, EVP of Emerging Markets
Tim Justyn, VP of Operations

Supplier of magnetic media processing systems.
The company offers advanced equipment to the
hard disk drive, solar, and photonics industries.

Intilop Inc HQ
830 N Hillview Dr
Milpitas CA 95035
P: 408-791-6700   F: 408-496-0444   PRC:200
www.intilop.com
Email: info@intilop.com
Estab: 2004

Kelly Masood, CTO

Provider of engineering design services. The
company also develops and provides silicon IP
products.

Intool HQ
807 Aldo Ave Ste 109
Santa Clara CA 95054
P: 408-727-7575   PRC:80
intoolmachineshop.com
Estab: 1989

Doug Mooney, Owner
Courtney Mooney, Regional Sales Manager

Manufacturer and designer of the machine components. The company is involved in machining,
fabricating, casting and assembling services.

Intraop Medical Corp HQ
570 Del Rey Ave
Sunnyvale CA 94085
P: 408-636-1020   F: 408-636-0022   PRC:189
intraop.com
Email: info@intraopmedical.com
Estab: 1993

John Powers, CEO
Derek DeScioli, VP of Global Sales
Rick Belford, VP of QA & Regulatory Affairs

Manufacturer of mobetron for the treatment of
cancer. The company offers services to hospitals,
clinics, and patients.

Intrinsic-Id Inc HQ
710 Lakeway Dr Ste 150
Sunnyvale CA 94085
P: 408-933-9980   PRC:86
www.intrinsic-id.com
Email: info@intrinsic-id.com
Estab: 2008

Pim Tuyls, CEO
Luis Ancajas, SVP

Designer of security solutions. The company offers
services to semiconductor companies and device
manufacturers.

Intrinsyx Technologies Corp BR
350 N Akron Rd, NASA Research Park MS
19-102 Ste 2028
Moffett Field CA 94035
P: 650-210-9219   F: 650-210-9222   PRC:323
intrinsyx.com
Email: info@intrinsyx.com

Ghazala Mian, President
Ahsan Ali, CEO

Provider of information technology solutions. The
company caters to federal, state, and commercial
stakeholders.

Intuit Inc HQ
2700 Coast Ave
Mountain View CA 94043
P: 800-446-8848   PRC:324
intuit.com
Estab: 1983
Sales: Over $3B

Derek Tatman, Product Owner
Scott Cook, Founder & Chairman of the Executive
Committee
Brad Smith, Executive Chairman
Sasan Goodarzi, CEO
Tayloe Stansbury, CTO

Provider of financial management software
solutions. The company offers services to small
businesses and related organizations.

Intuity Medical Inc HQ
3500 W Warren Ave
Fremont CA 94538
P: 510-946-8800   F: 510-897-0603   PRC:187
www.presspogo.com
Email: support@presspogohelp.com
Estab: 2007

Emory V. Anderson, President & CEO
Robb Hesley, COO & SVP of Product Develop-
ment Manufacturing
Tammy Cameron, CFO
Timothy J. Buskey, CCO
Robin Gaffney, Senior Director Of Marketing

Provider of medical products such as blood
glucose monitoring system, meter, cartridge, and
data management for diabetes management.

Invensas Corp HQ
3025 Orchard Pkwy
San Jose CA 95134
P: 408-321-6000   F: 408-321-8257   PRC:212
www.invensas.com
Email: info@invensas.com
Estab: 2011

Scott F. McGrath, Senior Process Engineer

Provider of software solutions for computer applications. The company also offers semiconductor
technologies.

Inventive Resources Inc HQ
5038 Salida Blvd
Salida CA 95368
P: 209-545-1663   F: 209-545-3533   PRC:155
www.iriproducts.com
Email: info@iriproducts.com
Estab: 1984

John J. Paoluccio, Engineer

Manufacturer of products for the environmental
and contamination control industry. The company
also focuses on distribution.

Inverse Solutions Inc HQ
3922 Valley Ave Ste A
Pleasanton CA 94566
P: 925-931-9500   F: 925-931-9515   PRC:80
inversesolutionsinc.com
Email: info@inversesolutionsinc.com
Estab: 1999

David Jordan, Owner & CEO
Josh Jordan, VP of Manufacturing
Zach Jordan, Manager

Manufacturer of custom-made machines for commercial and government markers. The company
serves semiconductor, medical devices, and
aerospace fields.

Invitae Corp HQ
1400 16th St
San Francisco CA 94103
P: 415-930-4018   F: 415-276-4164   PRC:306
invitae.com
Email: clinconsult@invitae.com
Emp: 788   Estab: 2012
Sales: $100M to $300M

Robert Nussbaum, CMO
Patty Dumond, VP of Finance
Swaroop Aradhya, Medical Director
Randy Scott, Strategy Team Leader
Erynn Gordon, Genetic Counselor

Provider of genetic information. The company offers to bring genetic information into routine medical practice to improve the quality of healthcare.

Invoice2go Inc HQ
555 Bryant St Ste 263
Palo Alto CA 94301
P: 650-300-5180   PRC:315
invoice.2go.com
Email: support@invoice2go.com
Estab: 2002

Chris Strode, Founder
Greg Waldorf, CEO
Mark Bartels, CFO
Kyle Flowers, COO
Lisa Pritchard, VP of Marketing

A mobile and web app for micro and small business owners to create invoice, track expenses and
track time.

Invuity Inc HQ
444 De Haro St
San Francisco CA 94107
P: 415-655-2100   PRC:189
www.invuity.com
Estab: 2004

Philip Sawyer, CEO
Sham Shiblaq, VP
Susan Martin, VP of Marketing
Sam McCue, Director of Sales
Nancy Hargreaves, Director of Finance

Manufacturer of surgical devices with cutting edge
photonics technology to view surgical cavities
during open, minimally invasive procedures.

IO Informatics Inc   HQ
2550 Ninth St Ste 114
Berkeley CA 94710-2552
P: 510-705-8470   F: 510-705-8476   PRC:323
www.io-informatics.com
Email: info@io-informatics.com
Estab: 2003

Robert Stanley, President & CEO
Erich A. Gombocz, CSO
Kathy Gibson, Director
Jason Eshleman, Director of Informatics & Lead
Knowledge Engineer
Larry Benbow, Director of Systems Engineering

Provider of software and services for data integration applications in areas such as life science and medicine.

IO Integration Inc   HQ
20480 Pacifica Dr Ste 1C
Cupertino CA 95014
P: 408-996-3420   F: 408-996-3425   PRC:323
www.iointegration.com
Email: info@iointegration.com
Estab: 2001

Mike Holt, CEO
Bill Covington, CTO
Kevin Martorana, CIO
Arlie Andrews, CFO
Dean Holmes, Director of Development Services

Provider of marketing technology and digital media workflow solutions. The company offers marketing automation and cross-media publishing services.

Iometrix Inc   HQ
2 Embarcadero Ctr Fl 8
San Francisco CA 94111
P: 650-872-4001   PRC:306
www.iometrix.com
Email: info@iometrix.com
Estab: 2003

Thomas Mandeville, Director of Operations

Developer of next generation packet networks and solutions for telecom service providers and equipment manufacturers.

Ionix Internet   HQ
266 Sutter St
San Francisco CA 94108
P: 888-884-6649   F: 415-840-0658   PRC:67
www.ionix.net
Email: info@ionix.net
Estab: 1997

Russ Richardson, Founder & CIO

Provider of web hosting solutions. The company offers network security, research, high-speed access, and telecommuting services.

Ios Optics   HQ
3150 Molinaro St
Santa Clara CA 95054
P: 408-982-9510   F: 408-982-9513   PRC:175
www.iosoptics.com
Email: info@iosoptics.com
Estab: 1974

Derek Fitzpatrick, President
Douglas Fitzpatrick, Chairman
Dino Valencia, VP of Sales & Marketing
Keith Baldwin, Manufacturing Manager
Gener Gatmaitan, Coating Engineering Manager

Manufacturer of custom precision optical components. The company offers coating and filter glass services. It serves avionics and life sciences fields.

ioSafe Inc   HQ
10600 Industrial Ave Ste 120
Roseville CA 95678
P: 530-820-3090   PRC:95
iosafe.com
Email: info@iosafe.com
Estab: 2005

Robb Moore, CEO
Leif Watkins, Director of Sales
Chris Kruell, Director
Matthew Stojkovich, Manager of Technology
Linda Miller, Senior National Sales Manager

Provider of disaster proof hardware. The company provides SoloPRO SSD External and ioSafe Rugged Portable.

iota Computing Inc   HQ
2275 E Bayshore Rd Ste 108
Palo Alto CA 94303-3222
P: 888-440-4004   PRC:323
www.iotacomputing.com
Email: info@iotacomputing.com
Estab: 2010

Jeremy G. Walker, Founder & CEO

Specializes in turnkey architecture. The company is engaged in building core technology for tiny edge devices.

Ipdialog Inc   HQ
542 Lakeside Dr Ste 7
Sunnyvale CA 94085
P: 408-830-0800   PRC:71
www.ipdialog.com
Email: info@ipdialog.com
Estab: 1999

Hardish Singh, President & CEO
Gerry Smith, Director of Hardware Development

Developer of hardware and software technology. The company creates SIP stack, user interface, and media stream handling for phones.

Ipera Technology Inc   HQ
20660 Stevens Creek Blvd Ste 269
Cupertino CA 95014
P: 650-286-0889   F: 650-286-0890   PRC:323
iperatech.com
Email: info@iperatech.com
Estab: 2005

Johnson Yan, President & CEO

Provider of multi-format video transcoder solutions for broadcast and IP multi-screen video production.

IPG Photonics   BR
3930 Freedom Cir Ste 103
Santa Clara CA 95054
P: 408-492-8830   PRC:124
ipgphotonics.com
Email: salesus@ipgphotonics.com
Estab: 1990

Gregory Altshuler, President
Mark Cannata, Director & Sales & Marketing & Communications Products
Scott Christensen, Director of Advanced Applications
Mike Klos, General Manager
Toby Strite, Sales & Marketing Director

Provider of high power fiber lasers and amplifiers. The company's offerings include Q-switch lasers, multi-mode diodes, pulsed and direct-diode lasers.

Iridex Corp   HQ
1212 Terra Bella Ave
Mountain View CA 94043
P: 650-940-4700   F: 650-940-4710   PRC:186
www.iridex.com
Email: info@iridex.com
Estab: 1989
Sales: $30M to $100M

William Moore, CEO & Chairman
Atabak Mokari, CFO & VP of Corporate Development
George R. Marcellino, VP of Clinical & Regulatory Affairs
Ken Bice, VP of Aesthetic Sales
Naina Lalka, Director of Customer Service & Logistics

Provider of therapeutic based laser consoles, delivery devices, and consumable instrumentation. The company serves the healthcare industry.

Iris AO Inc   HQ
2930 Shattuck Ave Ste 304
Berkeley CA 94705-1883
P: 510-849-2375   F: 510-217-9646   PRC:200
www.irisao.com
Email: info@irisao.com
Estab: 2002

Pamela Caton, MEMS Engineer

Manufacturer of microelectromechanical based optical systems. The company's applications include biomedical imaging and portable laser communications.

Iris Biotechnologies Inc   HQ
5201 Great America Pkwy Ste 320
Santa Clara CA 95054
P: 408-867-2885   PRC:186
irisbiotechnologies.com
Email: simonchin@irisbiotech.com
Estab: 1999

Simon Chin, President & CEO
Ronald Mark Gemberling, CMO
James LeBlanc, VP of Operations
Ralph Sinibaldi, VP of Product Development
Gayle Murray, Manager of Business Development

Provider of medical informatics system. The company develops chips to precisely diagnose and identify actionable treatment choices for breast cancer.

Irislogic Inc HQ
2336 Walsh Ave Ste D
Santa Clara CA 95051
P: 408-855-8741 PRC:323
irislogic.com
Email: webadmin@irislogic.com
Estab: 1998

Lavita Dcruz, VP of Operations
Nick Boswell, Contact

Provider of global consulting services and solutions. The company specializes in custom software development, network security, cloud, and testing.

Iron Systems Inc HQ
980 Mission Ct
Fremont CA 94539
P: 408-943-8000 F: 408-943-8101 PRC:95
www.ironsystems.com
Email: info@ironsystems.com
Estab: 2002

Billy Bath, President & CEO
Harvey Bath, COO & VP of Operations & Finance
Robert Keith, CTO
Bob Sidhu, VP of Worldwide Sales
Vishal Sood, VP of Operations

Provider of network storage, hybrid cloud, and big data infrastructure solutions. The company offers OEM/ODM manufacturing services.

Ironmind Enterprises Inc HQ
PO Box 1228
Nevada City CA 95959
P: 530-272-3579 F: 530-272-3095 PRC:82
www.ironmind.com
Email: sales@ironmind.com
Estab: 1988

Chris Sheehan, Editor

Manufacturer of medical products with flower essences. The company's offerings also include gym equipment and training gears.

Irrometer Company Inc HQ
1425 Palmyrita Ave [N]
Riverside CA 92507
P: 951-682-9505 F: 951-682-9501 PRC:13
www.irrometer.com
Email: sales@irrometer.com
Emp: 11-50 Estab: 1951

Thomas C. Penning, President & CEO

Manufacturer of soil moisture measuring devices.

ISA Corp HQ
3213 Whipple Rd
Union City CA 94587
P: 510-324-3755 F: 510-324-3701 PRC:135
www.isa-corporation.com
Email: info@isa-corporation.com
Estab: 1997

Tony Zante, Owner
Francisco Ferre, Owner
John Feusner, Owner
Irvin Brombowitz, Chief of Operations
Brian Clarke, Sales Manager

Developer and manufacturer of solar mounting systems for commercial applications. The company also offers solar thermal systems.

ISE Labs Inc HQ
46800 Bayside Pkwy
Fremont CA 94538
P: 510-687-2500 F: 510-687-2513 PRC:208
www.iselabs.com
Estab: 1983

Mark Wang, Director of Organizational Development
Charles Watson, Laboratory Manager
Daniel Leung, Manager of Test Interface
Sara Wang, Account Manager
Ping Wong, Product Engineer

Provider of semiconductor services. The company offers services such as production test, test interface, and mechanical testing.

iSmart Alarm Inc HQ
120 San Lucar Ct
Sunnyvale CA 94086
P: 408-245-2551 PRC:59
www.ismartalarm.com
Email: customerservice@ismartalarm.com
Estab: 2012

Janine Wong, Customer Service & Tech Support Manager
Jerry Yu, Product Manager
Justin Chi, Product Manager
Joshua Proch, Customer Service Representative

Manufacturer of home security products. The company offers alarms, cameras, sirens, and related accessories.

iSOA Group Inc BR
1255 Treat Blvd Ste 100
Walnut Creek CA 94597
P: 925-465-7400 PRC:326
isoagroup.com
Email: commercesi@sisinc.com
Estab: 1997

Peter Ling, Founder & CTO
Cheryl Bertini, COO & Customer Relationship Executive & Principal
Taylor Kataoka, DataPower Engineer
Natalia Kataoka, Executive Administrative Assistant

Provider of business process management, service oriented architecture, and business analytics services to finance, energy, retail, and other sectors.

Isomorphic Software HQ
1 Sansome St Ste 3500
San Francisco CA 94104
P: 415-222-9902 F: 415-222-9912 PRC:322
www.smartclient.com
Estab: 1998

Charles Kendrick, CTO & Founder
Mabelene Ng, Software Engineer

Focuses on building web applications. The company is engaged in training, consulting, and technical support services.

ISSE Services HQ
9290 W Stockton Blvd Ste 100
Elk Grove CA 95758
P: 916-670-1082 PRC:323
isse-services.com

Angela Spease, Owner
Kevin D. Spease, President & CEO
Matthew Sahota, Sales Manager

Provider of security solutions principally focusing on supporting system implementation and security testing.

Issio Solutions Inc HQ
1485 Civic Ct Ste 1338
Concord CA 94520
P: 888-994-7746 PRC:323
www.issio.com
Estab: 2011

Arne Utne, CEO
Yorick Phoenix, CTO

Provider of workforce management software for surgical facilities. The company also serves ambulatory surgical centers.

IT Concepts LLC BR
1244-B Quarry Ln
Pleasanton CA 94566
P: 925-401-0010 F: 925-401-0011 PRC:316
www.itconceptsworld.com
Email: sales@itcworld.com

Alla Balashov, Director of Operations

Manufacturer of borescopes, videoscopes, fiberscopes, documentation solutions, and accessories for remote visual inspection needs.

IT Flux HQ
135 Camino Dorado Ste 12 A
Napa CA 94558
P: 408-649-5642 PRC:323
www.itflux.com
Email: info@itflux.com
Estab: 2003

Ram Panikath, President & CEO
Krishnanath Venkataraman, COO

Provider of custom software development services, outsourcing, and outsourced software testing services.

IT Pro Source HQ
2300 First St Ste 336E
Livermore CA 94550
P: 925-455-7701 PRC:325
www.itprosource.com
Email: info@itprosource.com
Estab: 2001

Mitch Pratt, Owner
Mark Becker, VP

Provider of on call plans, managed services, web based monitoring, and communication cabling services.

IT Systemworks HQ
7 Mt Lassen Dr Ste D-122
San Rafael CA 94903
P: 415-507-0123   F: 267-295-2542   PRC:323
www.itsystemworks.com
Estab: 2005

Keith Parker, President & Director of IT Consulting
Sean Maher, IT Consultant
Neicole Crepeau, Senior Technical Writer & Website Designer

Provider of networking and technological solutions. The company's services include installation, implementation, repair, and maintenance.

Italix Company Inc HQ
120 Mast St Ste 1
Morgan Hill CA 95037
P: 408-988-2487   PRC:80
italix.com
Email: sales@italix.com
Estab: 1977

Frank Fantino, President
Alyssa DePalma, Controller

Provider of chemical machining, etching, and metal finishing services. The company serves the aerospace, defense, and transportation markers.

ITC Service Group Inc HQ
7777 Greenback Ln Ste 201
Citrus Heights CA 95610
P: 877-370-4482   PRC:63
www.callitc.com
Email: info@callitc.com
Estab: 1999

Tim Sauer, Founder
Jim Rush, President
Jeremy Elmas, CFO
Anca Hoiland, Chief of Staff & VP of PMO
Doug Butz, VP of Business Development

Provider of personnel and managed services to IT, telecom, and the CATV industry. The company offers staffing and turnkey solutions.

Itradenetwork Inc HQ
4160 Dublin Blvd Ste 300
Dublin CA 94568
P: 925-660-1100   F: 925-660-1101   PRC:326
www.itradenetwork.com
Estab: 1999

Rhonda Bassett-Spiers, President & CEO
Ray Connelly, VP of Traceability & Merchandising
Venkat Pininty, Director of Engineering
Thao Tran, Data Manager
Jonathan E. Betts, Product Manager

Provider of supply chain management and intelligence solutions for procurement, order management, and data services.

Itrenew Inc HQ
7575 Gateway Blvd
Newark CA 94560
P: 408-744-9600   F: 408-744-1963   PRC:142
itrenew.com
Estab: 2000

Mostafa Aghamiri, Chairman on board
Aidin Aghamiri, CEO
Alan Miller, Director of Data Center Services
Matthew Mickelson, Principal System Architect

Provider of information technology services. The company focuses on data eradication, server application, logistics management, and configuration.

Itrezzo Inc HQ
333 W San Carlos St Ste 600
San Jose CA 95110
P: 408-540-5020   PRC:319
www.itrezzo.com
Estab: 2001

David Anderson, Manager of Customer Success
Lakeshia Hardy, Head of Content
Nikki Phung, Lead UI & UX Designer

Provider of unified contact management solutions and it serves schools, agencies, and healthcare organizations.

ITT BIW Connector Systems HQ
500 Tesconi Cir
Santa Rosa CA 95401
P: 707-523-2300   F: 707-523-3567   PRC:159
ittbiw.com
Email: santarosa.customerservice@itt.com
Estab: 1973

Pedro Andrade, Operations Director
Cal Wahhab, System Administrator

Supplier of connector systems and electrical feed-thru products. The company's products include wellhead feedthroughs and power interconnect products.

Ivalua Inc HQ
702 Marshall St Ste 520
Redwood City CA 94063
P: 650-930-9710   F: 650-365-5267   PRC:323
ivalua.com
Email: info@ivalua.com
Estab: 2000

Dan Amzallag, CEO
Laurence Mechali, Director of Customer Services & Support
Gabriel Pantic, Creative Director
Clark Kent, Senior Manager of Technical Project
Thomas Morel, R&D Software Engineer

Designer and developer of spend management solutions. The company offers services to medium and large sized companies.

IXL Learning HQ
777 Mariners Island Blvd Ste 600
San Mateo CA 94404
P: 650-372-4040   PRC:322
in.ixl.com
Email: info@ixl.com
Estab: 1998

Paul Mishkin, CEO
Joseph Kent, CTO
Jennifer Gu, COO
Suzanne Pelz, VP of Engineering
Kate Mattison, VP of Curriculum

Specializes in online maths practice and related lessons. The company serves educational institutions.

iXsystems Inc HQ
2490 Kruse Dr
San Jose CA 95131
P: 408-943-4100   F: 408-943-4101   PRC:95
www.ixsystems.com
Email: info@ixsystems.com
Estab: 2002

Mike Lauth, CEO
Brett Davis, Director of Sales & Business Development
Denise Ebery, Director of Public Relations & Marketing Consultant
Matt Finney, Director of Business Development
David Discher, Director of Information Technology

Provider of hardware, software, server, and storage solutions, and services such as software development and consultation.

Ixys Corp HQ
1590 Buckeye Dr
Milpitas CA 95035
P: 408-457-9000   F: 408-416-0223   PRC:208
www.ixys.com
Email: info@ixys.net
Estab: 1983

David W. Heinzmann, President & CEO
Meenal A. Sethna, EVP & CFO
Matthew J. Cole, SVP of Business Development & Strategy
Steve Darrough, VP of Marketing
Vladimir Tsukanov, VP of R&D Power MOS Products

Manufacturer of power semiconductor products. The company specializes in power semiconductors, integrated circuits, and radio frequency power.

J C Sales & Mfg Co HQ
414-C S Church St
Ione CA 95640
P: 800-527-6347   PRC:80
www.jcsalesmfg.com
Estab: 1992

Bill Irmer, Owner

Manufacturer of CNC machining metal and plastic parts. The company offers products for the semiconductor, electronics, military, aircraft, and other industries.

J&C Consulting Services   HQ
5 Thomas Mellon Cir Ste 155
San Francisco CA 94134
P: 415-935-4313   PRC:318
jandcconsultingservices.mystrikingly.com
Estab: 2004

Jaime Jones, CEO & President

Developer of consulting services. The company offers strategic planning, executive coaching, and leadership and team development solutions.

J&E Precision Machining   HQ
2814 Aiello Dr Ste A
San Jose CA 95111
P: 408-281-1195   F: 408-281-1197   PRC:80
www.jandeprecision.com
Estab: 1988

Eva Sousa, President
Jorge Sousa, VP of Programmer
Cyrus Yousefi, CMM Programmer

Manufacturer of electromechanical turnkey fixtures, prototype tooling, and EDM services. The company serves computer, medical, and other sectors.

J&M Manufacturing Inc   HQ
430 Aaron St
Cotati CA 94931
P: 707-795-8223   F: 707-795-6471   PRC:82
jmmfg.com
Estab: 2003

Jim Judd, Owner
Maria Patchin, Quality Manager

Provider of TIG, MIG and spot welding, silk-screening, contract manufacturing, and assembly services.

Jabil Circuit Inc   BR
30 Great Oaks Blvd
San Jose CA 95119
P: 408-361-3200   PRC:19
jabil.com

Tim L. Main, Chairman
Michael J. Loparco, EVP & CEO
Michael Dastoor, CFO
Bruce A. Johnson, EVP & Chief Human Resource Officer
Courtney J. Ryan, EVP Strategy & Corporate Development & Chief of Staff

Provider of global manufacturing solutions. The company serves the defense, aerospace, and industrial markers.

Jackrabbit Inc   HQ
471 Industrial Ave
Ripon CA 95366
P: 209-599-6118   F: 209-599-6119   PRC:159
jackrabbitequipment.com
Email: info@jackrabbit.bz
Estab: 1981

Danny Thomas, VP of Sales
Thomas Lenor, Senior Production Designer

Provider of nut harvesting systems including runner, elevator, reservoir cart, conditioner and pruning tower.

Jaguar Health   HQ
200 Pine St Ste 400
San Francisco CA 94104
P: 415-371-8300   PRC:268
jaguar.health
Email: hello@jaguar.health
Estab: 2013

Lisa Conte, Founder & CEO
Steven King, Chief Sustainable Supply, Ethnobotanical Research & IP Officer
Michael Guy, VP & Clinical Veterinarian
Ian Wendt, VP of Commercial Strategy
Kathy Rogers, HR Director

Provider of health solutions for the animals and humans. The company focuses on the development of gastrointestinal pharmaceuticals.

James Cox & Sons Inc   HQ
158 Whitcomb Ave Unit 10
Colfax CA 95713
P: 530-346-8322   F: 530-346-6854   PRC:159
jamescoxandsons.com
Email: info@jamescoxandsons.com

Linda Sullivan, CFO
Fred Cox, Project Manager
Garrett Wren, Head of Operations
Wyatt Yates, Technician

Developer of products for asphalt, concrete, and soil testing. The company is also engaged in calibration and remote support services.

JAMIS Software Corp   HQ
4909 Murphy Canyon Rd Ste 460
San Diego CA 92123
P: 800-655-2647   PRC:323
jamis.com
Email: info@jamis.com
Estab: 1987

Jeffrey N. Noolas, President & CEO
Steve Brander, VP of Sales & Business Development
Naomi May, VP of Product Development & Support
Dan Rusert, Director of Business Development & Marketing

Provider of job-cost, billing, and accounting systems and solutions. The company caters to the government contractors.

Jampro Antennas Inc   HQ
6340 Sky Creek Dr
Sacramento CA 95828
P: 916-383-1177   F: 916-383-1182   PRC:61
www.jampro.com
Email: jampro@jampro.com
Estab: 1954

Alex Perchevitch, President
Greg Montano, Regional Sales Manager
Val Munoz, Purchasing Manager
Aaron Callahan, Engineering Manager
David Houston, Production Manager

Supplier of antennas, combiners and filters, and radio frequency components for applications in the broadcast industry.

Jan Medical Inc   HQ
800 W El Camino Real Ste 180
Mountain View CA 94040
P: 650-316-8811   PRC:13
www.janmedical.com
Email: info@janmedical.com

Stephan Mittermeyer, VP of Research & Development
Julie Aguas, Software Engineer

Manufacturer of portable brain sensing devices for the detection of traumatic brain injuries, including concussions.

Jarvis Manufacturing   HQ
195 Lewis Rd Ste 36
San Jose CA 95111
P: 408-226-2600   F: 408-226-2650   PRC:80
www.jarvismfg.com
Email: info@jarvismfg.com
Estab: 1959

Tony Grewal, President
Harsimran Singh, Manufacturing Quality Engineer & VP of Operations

Manufacturer of precision machinery. The company offers CNC turning and milling, programming, and assembly and kitting services.

Jasper Ridge Inc   HQ
PO Box 151
San Mateo CA 94401-9991
P: 650-804-5040   PRC:187
jasperridge.net
Email: info@jasperridge.net
Estab: 2011

Peter Borden, President
Michele Klein, CEO

Manufacturer of tint and lighting exam systems. The company offers services to patients and hospitals.

Jatco Inc   HQ
725 Zwissig Way
Union City CA 94587
P: 510-487-0888   F: 510-487-1880   PRC:163
www.jatco.com
Estab: 1976

Steven Jones, President
Paul Appelblom, CEO
Eric Appelblom, VP of Sales & Marketing
Pat Martinez, Purchasing Manager
Steve Gelphman, Program Manager

Manufacture of plastic products. The company offers molding, tooling, quality control, and warehousing and distribution services.

Javad Electronic Manufacturing Services   HQ
900 Rock Ave
San Jose CA 95131
P: 408-770-1700   F: 408-770-1799   PRC:209
javad.com
Email: info@javadems.com

Gary Walker, VP
Pam Walke, Manufacturing Operations Manager

Provider of electronic components. The company specializes in products such as OEM, receivers, antennas, and accessories.

Jazz Pharmaceuticals BR
3170 Porter Dr
Palo Alto CA 94304
P: 650-496-3777 PRC:261
www.jazzpharma.com
Email: corpgiving@jazzpharma.com
Estab: 2003

Elmar Schnee, Chairman
Bruce C. Cozadd, Chairman & CEO
Daniel N. Swisher, President & COO
Matthew Young, SVP & CFO
Karen Smith, Global Head R&D & CMO

Developer and marketer of products for neurology and psychiatry. The company is engaged in clinical trials and research and development.

JB Precision Inc HQ
1640 Dell Ave
Campbell CA 95008
P: 408-866-1755 F: 408-866-2697 PRC:80
www.jesseebrothersinc.com
Estab: 1975

Kelley Mills, Office Manager

Manufacturer of precision machining services. The company's services also include inspection, production control, and management.

Jeda Technologies Inc HQ
2900 Gordon Ave Ste 100
Santa Clara CA 95051
P: 408-912-1856 F: 408-912-1855 PRC:319
www.jedatechnologies.net
Email: sales@jedatechnologies.net
Estab: 2003

Eugene Zhang, Founder
Atsushi Kasuya, CTO & Chief Architect
Teshager Tesfaye, Director of Product Development

Provider of chip based digital designs and semiconductor services. The company focuses on validation and automation solutions.

Jei HQ
3087 Alhambra Dr
Cameron Park CA 95682
P: 530-677-3210 F: 530-677-4714 PRC:68
jei-inc.com
Estab: 1967

Jei Millbrae, Director

Provider of communication recorders, voice logging recorders, and audio and custom products for public and military intelligence applications.

Jelli Inc HQ
703 S B St 2nd Fl
San Mateo CA 94401
P: 855-790-8275 PRC:325
www.jelli.com
Email: contact@jelli.com
Estab: 2009

Jateen Parekh, Co-Founder & CTO
Michael Dougherty, CEO & Co-Founder
Torsten Schulz, SVP of Product & Engineering
Dylan Hecklau, VP of Product Management
Delilah Brown, Senior Director of Operations

Developer of user-controlled radio used in iPhone and radio stations. The company's products are used in the automation of radio advertising.

JEM America Corp RH
3000 Laurelview Ct
Fremont CA 94538
P: 510-683-9234 F: 510-683-9790 PRC:86
www.jemam.com
Email: sales@jemam.com
Estab: 1987

Karen Wong, Manager of Sales & Marketing
Eric Wu, Product Engineer
Patrick Mui, Engineer
Trisha Quach, Engineering Technician
Lynn Nguy, Human Resource Generalist

Manufacturer and supplier of probe cards and tester interfaces. The company offers cantilever, vertical, and special-applications probe cards.

Jet Plastics HQ
941 N Eastern Ave [N]
Los Angeles CA 90063
P: 323-268-6706 F: 323-268-8262 PRC:189
www.jetplastics.com
Emp: 51-200 Estab: 1948

Lloyd Johnson, Founder

Supplier of plastic products.

Jetronics Co HQ
218 Roberts Ave
Santa Rosa CA 95401
P: 707-544-2436 F: 707-526-6612 PRC:298
www.jetronics.com
Estab: 1961

Frances Reilly, Manager of Service Group

Manufacturer of custom cable assemblies and harnesses, magnetics assemblies, sub-assembly components, front and rear panels, and chassis assemblies.

Jetway Computer Corp HQ
8058 Central Ave
Newark CA 94560
P: 510-857-0130 F: 510-857-0138 PRC:91
www.jetwaycomputer.com
Email: sales@jetwaycomputer.com
Estab: 1998

Alice Lo, Account Manager

Manufacturer of motherboards and LCD monitors. The company also specializes in graphic cards and barebones systems.

Jitterbit Inc HQ
1101 Marina Village Pkwy Ste 201
Alameda CA 94501
P: 877-852-3500 PRC:322
www.jitterbit.com
Email: info@jitterbit.com
Estab: 2004

Sharam Sasson, Chairman & Founder
George Gallegos, CEO
Allen Barr, CFO
Manoj Chaudhary, CTO & SVP of Engineering
Dan Moore, SVP of Services

Focuses on application integration solutions for aerospace and defense, life sciences, pharmaceuticals, and financial services.

Jiva Creative LLC HQ
909 Marina Village Pkwy Ste 139
Alameda CA 94501
P: 510-864-8625 F: 510-864-8626 PRC:322
jivacreative.com
Email: hello@jivacreative.com
Estab: 1996

Stacie Kizziar, Partner
Josh Carey, Interactive Developer

Provider of interactive design technology solutions. The company focuses on architecture, website hosting, and enterprise application development.

JN Biosciences LLC HQ
320 Logue Ave
Mountain View CA 94043
P: 650-967-9486 PRC:34
jn-bio.com
Email: info@jn-bio.com

J. Yun Tso, Managing Partner
Naoya Tsurushita, Managing Partner

Developer of antibody-based therapeutics and antibody engineered technologies. The company specializes in single homogenous molecular species.

Joe Kline Aviation Art HQ
6420 Hastings Pl
Gilroy CA 95020
P: 408-842-6979 PRC:325
www.joeklineart.com
Email: klinejd569@aol.com
Estab: 1949

Joe Kline, Founder & Owner

Provider of military aircraft painting services. The company offers customized prints, helicopter paintings, fixed wing paintings, and other prints.

Johansing Iron Works HQ
849 Jackson St
Benicia CA 94510
P: 707-361-8190 F: 709-361-2349 PRC:153
www.johansing.com
Email: sales@johansing.com
Estab: 1990

Alicia Miranda Emerson, Office Manager

Manufacturer of heat exchangers and metal tanks. The company also offers process equipment and pressure vessels.

Johnson Industrial Sheet Metal Inc HQ
2131 Barstow St
Sacramento CA 95815
P: 916-927-8244 F: 916-927-3319 PRC:88
www.johnson-ind.com
Email: curtiss@johnson-ind.com
Estab: 1972

Donna M. Johnson, Owner

Designer, fabricator, and installer of blowpipe systems, custom fabricated products, and packaged system projects.

Johnson Manufacturing   HQ
38574 W Kentucky Ave
Woodland CA 95695
P: 530-662-1788   F: 530-666-5585   PRC:159
jfmco.com
Email: sales@jfmco.com
Estab: 1943

Kirk Friedman, Owner
Alan Gickler, President
Morris Johnson, CEO
Steve Benson, Director
Hishab Israel, Manager

Developer of farm machinery equipment and utility
vehicles. The company offers trailers, air compressors, electric cars and golf car parts.

Jolly Technologies Inc   HQ
1510 Fashion Island Blvd Ste 102
San Mateo CA 94404
P: 650-594-5955   F: 650-989-2145   PRC:325
www.jollytech.com
Email: sales@jollytech.com
Estab: 2000

Ya-Lan Tsao, Junior Software Engineer

Provider of secure identification, visitor management, barcode and asset tracking software
services.

JON BRODY Structural Engineers   HQ
235 Montgomery St Ste 1040
San Francisco CA 94104
P: 415-290-9494   PRC:304
www.jonbrody.com
Email: inquiries@jonbrody.com

Jon Brody, Owner
David Ng, Project Manager

Provider of structural engineering services. The
company focuses on construction documentation,
reports and studies, and seismic retrofitting.

Josephson Engineering Inc   HQ
329A Ingalls St
Santa Cruz CA 95060
P: 831-420-0888   F: 831-420-0890   PRC:71
www.josephson.com
Email: info@josephson.com
Estab: 1988

David Josephson, Engineer & CEO
Connie Winton, Assembler & Test Technician &
Principal
David Gordon, Principal
Kelly Kay, Principal

Manufacturer of condenser microphones for
studio, stage, and field sound pickup, and audio
instrumentation.

Jova Solutions Inc   HQ
1402 18th St
San Francisco CA 94107
P: 415-816-4482   PRC:322
www.jovasolutions.com
Email: info@jovasolutions.com
Estab: 2000

Martin Vasey, VP of ISL Business Unit

Developer of systems for distributed process
control and data management for science and
industrial sectors. The company offers USB
instruments.

Joy Signal Technology LLC   HQ
1020 Marauder St
Chico CA 95973
P: 530-891-3551   F: 530-891-3599   PRC:206
www.joysignal.com
Email: customerservice@joysignal.com
Estab: 1987

John Joy, President

Developer of PCB and differential terminators,
MMCX plug assemblies, single signal carrier systems, Z-Trace connectors, and custom solutions.

Joyent Inc   HQ
655 Montgomery St Ste 1600
San Francisco CA 94111
P: 415-400-0600   PRC:325
joyent.com
Email: sales@joyent.com
Estab: 2004

Seong-Kook Shin, Compute Product Owner
Eric Hahm, CFO & VP
Angela Fong, VP of Engineering
Steve Tuck, SVP of Sales & Marketing
Bryan Cantrill, SVP of Engineering

Provider of cloud infrastructure services. The company's products include Compute service, Manta
storage, and Private Cloud.

JP Aerospace   HQ
2530 Mercantile Dr Ste I
Rancho Cordova CA 95742
P: 916-858-0185   PRC:2
jpaerospace.com

John Powell, President
Paul L. Turner, Associate

Developer of volunteer-based DIY space program.
The company provides the PongSat, MiniCube
and Airship to Orbit programs for space enthusiasts.

JP Machine Manufacturing   HQ
1600 Norman Ave
Santa Clara CA 95054
P: 408-988-1400   F: 408-988-0223   PRC:80
www.jpmachinemfg.com
Email: sales@jpmachinemfg.com
Estab: 1984

Young Pak, Founder

Manufacturer of machine parts. The company
offers medical, semiconductor capital equipment,
robotics, lasers, fiber optics, and test equipment.

Jr3 Inc   HQ
22 Harter Ave
Woodland CA 95776
P: 530-661-3677   F: 530-661-3701   PRC:87
www.jr3.com
Email: jr3@jr3.com
Estab: 1983

John Ramming, President & CTO
Eric Applebaum, Quality Assurance Manager

Designer and manufacturer of multi-axis force-
torque sensors. The company caters to robotics
and other applications.

JRH GoldenState Software Inc   HQ
29011 Golden Meadow Dr   [N]
Rancho Palos Verdes CA 90275
P: 310-544-1497   PRC:319
www.jrh-inc.com
Email: home@jrh-inc.com
Estab: 1998

Benjamin Pan, Contact

Developer and provider of software tools and solutions that supports complete DB2 catalog query
and object management.

JRP Historical Consulting LLC   HQ
2850 Spafford St
Davis CA 95618
P: 530-757-2521   PRC:142
www.jrphistorical.com
Estab: 1981

Christopher McMorris, VP & Principal
Heather Norby, Contact
Joseph Freeman, Contact
Scott Miltenberger, Senior Historian

Provider of resources management services. The
company's services include water use studies,
flood control, public access history, and legislative
history research.

JSK Associates   HQ
3561 Homestead Rd Ste 344
Santa Clara CA 95051
P: 408-980-8575   F: 408-980-8576   PRC:209
www.jskrep.com
Estab: 1979

Jerry Karp, President

Provider of electronics, medical, and semiconductor manufacturing services. The company also
offers assembly and research services.

JSR Micro Inc   HQ
1280 N Mathilda Ave
Sunnyvale CA 94089
P: 408-543-8800   PRC:79
jsrmicro.com
Email: info@jsrmicro.com
Estab: 1957

Ray Hung, Director of Manufacturing
Anthony Lee, Director
Isao Katayama, Director Product Management
Zhong Xiang, Account Manager
Jennifer Frey, Customer Service Manager

Provider of semiconductor, life sciences, and energy material solutions. The company specializes
in lithography materials and CMP consumables.

Juki Americas   BR
412 Kato Terrace Ste 101
Fremont CA 94539-7793
P: 510-249-6700   F: 510-249-6710   PRC:159
www.jukiamericas.com

Bill Astle, President
Bob Black, CEO
Carlos Eijansantos, Sales Manager

Provider of SMT assembly machines. The company offers inline selective soldering systems, mini-
wave soldering machines, and stamp soldering
products.

Junar Inc HQ
  111 N Market St Ste 300
  San Jose CA 95113
  P: 844-695-8627 PRC:322
  junar.com
  Email: support@junar.com
  Estab: 2010

  Chris Sayre, VP

  Provider of cloud-based open data platform. The
  company offers collaboration services to business
  organizations.

Juniper Networks Inc HQ
  1133 Innovation Way
  Sunnyvale CA 94089
  P: 408-745-2000 F: 408-745-2100 PRC:323
  www.juniper.net/us/en
  Estab: 1996
  Sales: $300M to $1 Billion

  Pradeep Sindhu, Founder & Chief Scientist
  Rami Rahim, CEO
  Lauren Flaherty, EVP & CMO
  Ken Miller, EVP & CFO
  Kireeti Kompella, SVP of Engineering

  Provider of network security solutions. The company serves the government, healthcare, utilities,
  and manufacturing industries.

JVD Inc HQ
  5346 Scotts Valley Dr Ste B
  Scotts Valley CA 95066
  P: 408-263-7704 PRC:86
  jvdinc.com
  Estab: 1982

  Michael VanDierendonck, President
  Gloria Reese, VP & CFO
  Bob Frostholm, VP of sales & Marketing
  Brian Harlanmoff, Director of Engineering

  Provider of custom integrated circuit design and
  test services. The company is also involved in
  wafer characterization.

Jway Group Inc HQ
  691 South Milpitas Blvd
  Milpitas CA 95035
  P: 408-247-5929 F: 408-247-5931 PRC:325
  jway.com
  Email: info@jway.com
  Estab: 1994

  Joe Choi, CEO
  Rex Mupas, CTO
  Ben Gomez, CFO
  Kelly Hemingway, CMO
  Ian Lopez, Chief of Staff

  Retailer of web consulting and service solutions
  such as web application development, web design, and mobile programming services.

Jwp Manufacturing HQ
  3500 De La Cruz Blvd
  Santa Clara CA 95054-2111
  P: 408-970-0641 F: 408-970-8612 PRC:80
  www.jwpmfg.com
  Email: info@jwpmfg.com

  Andy Eden, Sales Director
  Andrew Eden, Director of Sales
  Chris Heider, Manufacturing Manager
  Zai Rahim, Credit Manager
  Carl Madau, Operations Manager

  Provider of manufacturing solutions. The company
  offers CNC machining, engineering, and other
  services.

K&L Supply Co HQ
  2099 S Tenth St Unit 80
  San Jose CA 95112
  P: 408-727-6767 PRC:159
  www.klsupply.com
  Estab: 1968

  Joyce Perondi, Manager Office & Sales
  Michael Salvador, Manager of Sales & Marketing
  Grace Son, Accounting & HR Manager
  Paul Martin, Account Representative

  Manufacturer of specialty tools and shop equipment for motorcycle dealers. The company offers
  shop lift and wheel equipment, jacks, and other
  tools.

K-Pax Pharmaceuticals Inc HQ
  655 Redwood Hwy Ste 346
  Mill Valley CA 94941
  P: 415-381-7565 F: 415-381-7648 PRC:250
  kpaxpharm.com
  Email: ask@kpaxpharm.com
  Estab: 2005

  Jon Kaiser, CMO & Fatigue Specialist

  Provider of pharmaceutical grade vitamins and
  nutritional health supplements for kids, women,
  and men's health, joints and bones, and immune
  support.

Kahler Engineering Inc HQ
  8 Elm Ct
  San Anselmo CA 94960
  P: 415-453-8836 PRC:304
  www.ke-inc.com
  Email: erkahler@comcast.net
  Estab: 2009

  Marjorie Widmeyer, President

  Designer of instrumentation and power control
  systems. The company provides engineering
  services to power plant owners, operators, and
  constructors.

KaiserAir Inc BR
  8735 Earhart Rd
  Oakland CA 94621-4547
  P: 510-569-9622 F: 510-255-5017 PRC:2
  www.kaiserair.com
  Estab: 1954

  Rob Guerra, SVP of Operations
  Diane Hinds, Manager of Human Resources

  Provider of aircraft management services. The
  company also offers business aircraft chartering
  services.

Kal Machining Inc HQ
  18450 Sutter Blvd
  Morgan Hill CA 95037
  P: 408-782-8989 F: 408-782-9696 PRC:80
  kalmachining.com

  David Luong, CEO

  Manufacturer of medical, aeronautic, and military
  machine parts. The company offers CNC turning
  and milling services for plastic and metal parts.

KalioTek HQ
  19200 Stevens Creek Blvd Ste 110
  Cupertino CA 95014
  P: 408-550-8000 F: 408-550-8090 PRC:324
  www.kaliotek.com
  Email: sales@kaliotek.com
  Estab: 2002

  Mark Richards, CEO
  Bill Kim, VP of Infrastructure & Security Services
  Ben Fong, Director of Infrastructure Services
  Eric Joyce, Director of Hosting & Security
  Tom Lackovic, Director

  Provider of enterprise applications. The company
  also specializes in technical infrastructure for
  companies.

Kalman Manufacturing HQ
  780 Jarvis Dr Ste 150
  Morgan Hill CA 95037
  P: 408-776-7664 F: 408-776-3345 PRC:80
  www.kalman.com
  Estab: 1985

  Alan Kalman, CEO
  Freia Kalman, VP
  Rosa Esparza, Office Manager
  Jennifer Barbaglia, Human Resource Manager
  Mark Alberti, Quality Manager

  Provider of manufacturing and machining
  services. The company offers welding, shearing,
  cutting, and finishing services.

Kalytera Therapeutics Inc HQ
  4040 Civic Center Dr Ste 200
  San Rafael CA 94903
  P: 888-861-2008 PRC:268
  kalytera.co
  Email: info@kalytera.co
  Estab: 2014

  Robert Farrell, President & CEO
  Moshe Yeshurun, CMO
  Victoria Rudman, CFO
  Sari Prutchi-Sagiv, Chief Scientific Officer
  Ronen Raviv, Director of Finance

  Developer of cannabidiol and cannabinoid therapeutics for the treatment of life threatening human
  disease.

Kaman Industrial Technologies BR
30077 Ahern Ave
Union City CA 94587
P: 650-589-6800 PRC:163
ec.kamandirect.com
Email: kit511.sanfrancisco@kdgcorp.com
Estab: 1971

Steven J. Smidler, President
Roger S. Jorgensen, SVP of Finance & Administration
Robert F. Goff, VP of Human Resources & Organization Development
Carlos O. Ingram, VP of Business Systems
David H. Mayer, VP of Marketing

Provider of industrial technology solutions. The company's portfolio comprises bearings, gearing, linear motion, and power transmission products.

KAMET Precision Machining & Assembly HQ
1778 McCarthy Blvd
Milpitas CA 95035
P: 408-522-8000 F: 408-524-7884 PRC:80
www.kamet.com
Email: info@kamet.com
Estab: 1984

Ophelia Kwan, Account Manager
Pedavalli Anvesh Chowdary, Quality Engineer
Yolynar Boillet, Quality Management & Compliance Supervisor
Abel Nunez, Buyer
Jeff Hunter, Buyer

Provider of manufacturing solutions. The company offers engineering support, project management, and supply chain management solutions.

Kamper Fabrication Inc HQ
20107 N Ripon Rd [N]
Ripon CA 95366
P: 209-599-7137 PRC:179
www.kamperfab.com
Emp: 11-50 Estab: 1983

Brenda Kamper, Secretary & Treasurer

Designer of almond processing plants and manufactures equipment lines for almond shelling, hulling and finish processing.

Kan Herb Company HQ
380 Encinal St Ste 100
Santa Cruz CA 95060-2178
P: 831-438-9450 F: 831-438-9457 PRC:268
www.kanherb.com
Email: customer@kanherb.com
Estab: 1987

Robin Sigmann, Graphic Designer

Provider of Chinese herbal products and services.

Karius Inc HQ
975 Island Dr Ste 101
Redwood City CA 94065
P: 866-452-7487 F: 866-246-6567 PRC:25
www.kariusdx.com
Email: help@kariusdx.com
Estab: 2014

Timothy A. Blauwkamp, Founder & SVP
Mickey Kertesz, CEO
Sivan Bercovici, CTO
Brian Jung, CFO
David Hong, VP of Medical Affairs & Clinical Development

Provider of microbial genomics diagnostics. The company focuses on transforming infectious disease diagnostics with genomics.

Kaser Corp HQ
44240 Fremont Blvd
Fremont CA 94538
P: 510-894-6892 PRC:110
www.kasercorp.com
Estab: 1998

Steve Kaser, Manager
Rad Oyam, Emergency Medical Technician

Developer and marketer of Internet and communication equipment. The company offers Internet telephony, digital television, and accessories.

Kaseya International Ltd BR
2033 Gateway Pl Ste 512
San Jose CA 95110
P: 415-694-5700 PRC:319
kaseya.com

Prakash Khot, CTO

Provider of software solutions. The company offers cloud and network monitoring, asset management, and backup recovery services.

Kateeva Inc HQ
7015 Gateway Blvd
Newark CA 94560
P: 800-385-7802 PRC:243
www.kateeva.com
Email: info@kateeva.com
Estab: 2008

Conor Madigan, Founder & President
Alain Harrus, CEO & Chairman
Yan Xiaolin, CTO & SVP
Marc Haugen, COO
Monica Kaldani-Nasif, CPO

Manufacturer of LED and other display products. The company specializes in the design and fabrication of OLED displays.

Kaz & Associates Environmental Services HQ
4271 Park Rd
Benicia CA 94510
P: 707-747-1126 F: 925-871-5172 PRC:139
www.kazandassoc.com

Sean Kazemi, Principal
Patrick Murphy, Principal
Alex Kazemi, Environmental Inspector

Provider of water management consulting services. The company's services include enforcement response, and groundwater contamination investigation.

Kearneys Metals Inc HQ
2660 S Dearing Ave
Fresno CA 93725
P: 559-233-2591 F: 559-441-8055 PRC:159
www.kearneysaluminumfoundry.com
Estab: 1946

Michael Kearney, President
Bobby Kearney, Plant Manager & Master Pattern Maker
Bill Kearney, Sales Manager

Provider of foundry services. The company specializes in stainless steel and aluminium plates, sheets, structurals and bars.

Keck-Craig Inc HQ
PO Box 93966 [N]
Pasadena CA 91109
P: 626-584-1688 PRC:159
www.keckcraig.com
Email: info@keckcraig.com
Emp: 1-10 Estab: 1951

Warren Haussler, Owner
Bob Evans, Chief Engineer
Eric Vasquez, Design Engineer

Manufacturer of custom machinery and packaging machinery.

Keen Systems Inc HQ
1900 O'Farrell St Ste 145
San Mateo CA 94403
P: 888-506-5336 PRC:323
keenprint.com
Email: support@keenprint.com
Estab: 2008

Jim Dvorkin, Director

Provider of web-to print solutions. The company offers cloud-based services to small and medium sized printing companies.

Keep IT Simple HQ
48383 Fremont Blvd Ste 122
Fremont CA 94538
P: 510-403-7500 F: 510-403-7501 PRC:323
www.kiscc.com
Email: contactus@kiscc.com
Estab: 1988

Sean Canevaro, CEO
John Marciano, COO & Director of Sales
Craig Miller, Director of Engineering
Allan Hurst, Director of Enterprise Strategy
David Powell, Partner & Director of Cloud Service

Provider of virtualization and information technology services. The company focuses on virtualization assessment, cloud computing, and networking.

Keish Environmental PC HQ
6768 Crosby Ct
San Jose CA 95129
P: 408-359-7248 PRC:139
keishenv.com
Estab: 2014

Rachael Keish, CEO
Kristin Sideris, Office Manager

Provider of environmental and stormwater compliance services. The company also specializes in construction inspection services.

Kelly-Moore Paint Company Inc   HQ
  987 Commercial St
  San Carlos CA 94070
  P: 650-592-8337   F: 650-592-1215   PRC:47
  kellymoore.com
  Estab: 1946

Steve Devoe, President & CEO
Dan Stritmatter, CFO
Todd Wirdzek, VP of Product Development
James Alberts, VP of Sales
Audrey Gallagher, Corporate Network Manager

Developer and manufacturer of interior and exterior paints. The company also offers painting tools and related accessories.

Kelytech Corp   HQ
  1482 Gladding Court
  Milpitas CA 95035
  P: 408-935-0888   F: 408-935-0988   PRC:209
  www.kelytech.com
  Email: info@kelytech.com
  Estab: 1990

Bo Sun, Contact

Provider of assembly solutions for PCBs, chassis, cables, and magnetic products. The company serves defense, medical, industrial, and other sectors.

Kemet Electronics Corp   BR
  2350 Mission College Blvd Ste 972
  Santa Clara CA 95054
  P: 877-695-3638   F: 408-986-1442   PRC:214
  www.kemet.com
  Email: capmaster@kemet.com

Monica Highfill, VP of Sales & Americas

Provider of relays, EMI filters, transformers, capacitors, and ferrite products. The company serves the aerospace, defense, and automotive industries.

KEMPF Inc   HQ
  1245 Lakeside Dr Ste 3005
  Sunnyvale CA 94085
  P: 408-773-0219   F: 408-773-0524   PRC:159
  www.kempf-usa.com
  Email: info@kempf-usa.com
  Estab: 2007

Martine Kempf, CEO

Provider of driving solutions. The company offers digital hand controls and other handicap driving aids for paraplegic drivers.

Kennerley-Spratling Inc   HQ
  2116 Farallon Dr
  San Leandro CA 94577
  P: 510-351-8230   F: 510-352-9240   PRC:80
  www.ksplastic.com
  Email: sales@ksplastic.com
  Estab: 1955

Dick Spratling, President
Kevin Ahern, General Manager
Rob Lyneis, Manager of Engineering
Elvia Morales, Finishing Manager
Timothy Arambula, Plant Manager

Manufacturer of custom plastic injection and compression moldings. The company is involved in design, installation, and delivery services.

M-174

**Kensington Computer Products
Group**   DH
  1500 Fashion Island Blvd 3rd Fl
  San Mateo CA 94404
  P: 650-572-2700   PRC:108
  www.kensington.com
  Estab: 1981

Christine Coates, Director of Global Human Resources
Theresa Chavez, Financial Analyst

Provider of secure locking solution for laptops, portable laptop power, and mobile computing solutions.

Kensington Laboratories LLC   HQ
  6200 Village Pkwy
  Dublin CA 94568
  P: 510-324-0126   F: 510-324-0130   PRC:309
  www.kensingtonlabs.com
  Email: sales@kensingtonlabs.com

Anatoli Pavlov, Field Service Engineer

Provider of automation products for the semiconductor industry. The company is engaged in precision machining, automation, and system integration.

Kenzen Inc   HQ
  1663 Mission St Ste 520
  San Francisco CA 94103
  P: 650-384-5140   PRC:194
  www.kenzen.com
  Estab: 2014

Heidi Lehmann, CCO

Focuses on the manufacture of personal health monitors. The company serves individuals and healthcare organizations.

Keri Systems Inc   HQ
  302 Enzo Dr Ste 190
  San Jose CA 95138
  P: 408-435-8400   F: 408-577-1792   PRC:314
  www.kerisys.com
  Email: info@kerisys.com
  Estab: 1990

Dennis Geiszler, VP
Jorge Sanchez, VP of Operations
Tony Banwait, Manager of Operations
Dave Miller, Manager of Engineering
Maryann Gierke, Human Resource & Office Manager

Provider of access control and integrated security systems. The company offers technology support and training solutions.

Kespry Inc   HQ
  4040 Campbell Ave Ste 200
  Menlo Park CA 94025
  P: 203-434-7988   PRC:309
  kespry.com
  Estab: 2013

Jeff Palmer, President
Adam Rice, VP of Sales
John Laxson, Software Engineering Manager
Ilene Sempio, Office Manager
Jordan Croom, Lead Mechanical Engineer

Developer of automated drone system and cloud that automatically uploads data in cloud for aggregates, insurance, and construction industries.

Key Business Solutions Inc   HQ
  4738 Duckhorn Dr
  Sacramento CA 95834
  P: 916-646-2080   F: 916-646-2081   PRC:328
  www.keybusinessglobal.com
  Email: info@keybusinessglobal.com
  Estab: 1999

Rajan Gutta, President

Provider of software development and database management services. The company also specializes in business intelligence.

Key Performance Ideas Inc   BR
  268 Bush St Ste 2800
  San Francisco CA 94104
  P: 855-457-4462   PRC:322
  www.keyperformanceideas.com
  Email: info-web@keyperformanceideas.com
  Estab: 2005

Chris Werle, Owner
Nate Coate, Owner
Deanna Sunde, Director of Delivery
Selena Hira-Toth, Director of Corporate Operations

Provider of enterprise performance management and business intelligence solutions. The company offers Oracle Hyperion and OBIEE software for this need.

Key Solutions Inc   HQ
  2803 Lakeview Ct
  Fremont CA 94538
  P: 510-456-4500   F: 510-456-4501   PRC:323
  www.keyusa.com
  Email: contact@keyusa.com

Srinivas Kudaravalli, Owner
Swarupa Rani Mallipeddi, Manager of Operations

Provider of software development and database management services. The company also specializes in business intelligence.

Key Source International Inc   HQ
  7711 Oakport St
  Oakland CA 94621
  P: 510-562-5000   F: 510-562-0689   PRC:108
  ksikeyboards.com
  Email: info@ksikeyboards.com
  Estab: 1979

Phil Bruno, SVP of Sales & Marketing & President & CEO
Deanne VanKirk, National Sales Manager

Provider of disinfectant and germicidal wipes for keyboards. The company focuses on infection control and cross contamination.

Keysight Technologies Inc   HQ
  1400 Fountaingrove Pkwy
  Santa Rosa CA 95403-1738
  P: 800-829-4444   F: 800-829-4433   PRC:209
  www.keysight.com
  Estab: 2014
  Sales: Over $3B

Ronald S. Nersesian, CEO & President & Director
Soon Chai Gooi, SVP & President of Electronic Industrial Solutions Group
Neil P. Dougherty, CFO & SVP
Hamish Gray, SVP & Chief of Staff
Joseph DePond, VP & General Manager

Provider of electronic measurement services. The company products include oscilloscopes, network analyzers, and digital multimeters.

Kezar Life Sciences Inc HQ
4000 Shoreline Ct Ste 300
S San Francisco CA 94080
P: 650-822-5600 PRC:189
kezarlifesciences.com
Email: contact@kezarbio.com
Estab: 2015

Christopher Kirk, Co-Founder & President & Chief
Scientific Officer
John Fowler, CEO & Co-Founder
Marc L. Belsky, CFO
Celia Economides, SVP of Strategy & External
Affairs

Developer of small molecule therapeutics drugs
targeting protein homeostasis for transformative
treatments for autoimmune diseases.

KG Technologies Inc HQ
6028 State Farm Dr
Rohnert Park CA 94928
P: 888-513-1874 PRC:290
kgtechnologies.net
Email: info@kgtechnologies.net
Estab: 1999

Timothy Wells, VP of Engineering
David Ajo, Mechanical Design Engineer

Designer and developer of switching solutions.
The company's applications include welding,
brazing, and riveting.

Kidaptive Inc HQ
203 Redwood Shores Pkwy Ste 145
Redwood City CA 94065
P: 650-265-2485 PRC:326
www.kidaptive.com
Email: info@kidaptive.com
Estab: 2012

Dylan Arena, Co-Founder & Chief Learning
Scientist
P.J. Gunsagar, Co-Founder & CEO
Ashraf Jahangeer, VP of Engineering
Josine Verhagen, Director of Psychometrics
David Hatfield, Senior Director of Assessment &
Product

Provider of learning and integration solutions.
The company offers services to learners and the
educational sector.

Kiefer Consulting Inc HQ
13405 Folsom Blvd Ste 501
Folsom CA 95630
P: 916-932-7220 PRC:322
www.kieferconsulting.com
Email: info@kieferconsulting.com
Estab: 1988

Gregory Kiefer, CEO & President
Amy Hoffman, VP & CFO
Ben Cox, Director of Operations
Brian Wallace, Director of Marketing & Sales
Doug Robbins, Senior Project Manager

Provider of mobile application software services.
The company also offers SharePoint, Microsoft
Dynamics, and Microsoft.Net application services.

Kii Corp HQ
1900 S Norfolk St Ste 350
San Mateo CA 94403
P: 650-577-2340 PRC:325
www.kii.com
Email: sales@kii.com
Estab: 2010

Masanari Arai, Co-Founder & CEO
Naoshi Suzuki, Co-Founder & President
Phani Pandrangi, CPO

Provider of applications to device manufacturers
and mobile network operators. The company
serves enterprise, cross-platform games, and
other needs.

Kikusui America Inc HQ
3625 Del Amo Blvd Ste 160
Torrance CA 90503
P: 310-214-0000 F: 310-214-0014 PRC:293
www.kikusuiamerica.com
Email: kikusui@kikusuiamerica.com
Estab: 2004

Sunao Yamamoto, President & COO
Jun Liu, Technical Manager

Provider of electronic measuring instruments and
power supplies. The company's products include
electronic loads and power supply controllers.

Kimberlite Corp HQ
3621 W Beechwood Ave
Fresno CA 93711-0648
P: 559-264-9730 F: 559-233-5610 PRC:59
sonitrolsecurity.com
Estab: 1996

Joey Rao-Russell, President & CEO
Susie O'Hara, Director of Human Resources
Sonitrol Hr, Director of Human Resources
Mason Settlemoir, Regional Technical Manager
Dave Hill, Sales Manager

Dealer of security verification systems. The company offers access control, video surveillance, fire
detection, and intrusion detection systems.

Kimia Corp HQ
2102 Walsh Ave Ste B
Santa Clara CA 95050-2552
P: 408-748-1046 PRC:306
kimiacorp.com
Estab: 1994

Farbi Aria, President

Manufacturer of chemicals and custom synthesis services. The company offers amino acids,
vitamins, steroids, heptanes, and multifunctional
heterocycles.

Kindred Biosciences Inc HQ
1555 Bayshore Hwy Ste 200
Burlingame CA 94010
P: 650-701-7901 PRC:273
www.kindredbio.com
Estab: 2012
Sales: $3M to $10M

Richard Chin, Founder & CEO
Wendy Wee, CFO
Hangjun Zhan, CSO
Katja Buhrer, Chief of Staff & VP of Corporate
Development & Investor Relations
Kevin Schultz, Chief Scientific Officer & Head of
Research & Development

Provider of pharmaceutical products for treatment
of anemia, cancer, allergic, autoimmune, and gastrointestinal diseases in cats, dogs, and horses.

Kinematic Automation Inc HQ
21085 Longeway Rd
Sonora CA 95370
P: 209-532-3200 F: 209-532-0248 PRC:186
www.kinematic.com/index.html
Email: service@kinematic.com
Estab: 1980

Ted Meigs, Founder
Rory Kelly, Manufacturing Manager
Bob Hufman, Senior Mechanical Design Engineer
Lisa Hedges, Production Control Supervisor

Provider of manufacturing systems for the medical
industry. The company also offers automation,
strip cutting, rotary slitting services.

Kinetic Technologies HQ
6399 San Ignacio Ave Ste 250
San Jose CA 95119
P: 512-694-6384 F: 408-351-0338 PRC:212
www.kinet-ic.com
Email: americasales@kinet-ic.com
Estab: 2006

Brian North, VP of Engineering
Lu Chen, IC Design Director

Designer and developer of analog and mixed-signal power management semiconductors. The
company serves the consumer and communication markers.

King Sales & Engineering HQ
9 Jules Dr
Novato CA 94947
P: 415-892-7961 PRC:159
www.kingpac.com
Estab: 1930

David Rossman, CEO
Chip Barcus, Regional Manager
Craig Tabery, Sales Representative
Herb Olson, Representative of Pacific Northwest

Designer and seller of rotary fillers, labelers, and
case packers. The company offers products for the
tomato and fruit canning industry.

King Star Computer Inc HQ
855 Kifer Rd
Sunnyvale CA 94086
P: 408-736-8590 F: 408-736-4151 PRC:97
www.kingstarusa.com
Email: sales@kingstarusa.com
Estab: 1989

Jessie Chen, Sales Engineer
Lucy Yin, Sales Engineer
Sandy Kuo, Sales & Marketing Coordinator
Chengnan Zhang, Server Technician
John Wu, HPC Server & Storage Solution Pro-
vider

Provider of technology services to Fortune 500
companies, mid-size to small business, start-ups,
and government and educational organizations.

King-Solarman Inc   HQ
   48900 Milmont Dr
   Fremont CA 94538
P: 408-373-8800   PRC:130
king-solarman.com
Email: info@king-solarman.com
Estab: 2008

Michael Cung, CEO & Founder

Focuses on the sale of solar panels, power inverters, and related supplies. The company is involved in solar project financing services.

Kings River Conservation District   HQ
   4886 E Jensen Ave
   Fresno CA 93725
P: 559-237-5567   F: 559-237-5560   PRC:139
www.krcd.org
Email: comments@krcd.org
Estab: 1951

Randy Shilling, Deputy General Manager of Business Operations
David Merritt, Deputy General Manager of Power Operations
Rick Hoelzel, Director of Resources
Paul Peschel, General Manager
David Cone, Deputy General Manager

Provider of resource management solutions. The company focuses on flood protection, water supply, power generation, and other needs.

Kinnetic Laboratories Inc   HQ

   307 Washington St   [N]
   Santa Cruz CA 95060
P: 831-457-3950   PRC:268
www.kineticlabs.com
Emp: 11-50   Estab: 1972

Patrick Kinney, Principal

Provider of environmental and oceanographic science services including field and laboratory studies.

Kionix Inc   BR
   2323 Owen St
   Santa Clara CA 95054
P: 408-720-1900   PRC:87
www.kionix.com
Email: info.cal@kionix.com
Estab: 1993

Nader Sadrzadeh, President & CEO

Manufacturer of MEMS inertial sensors. The company offers accelerometers, gyroscopes, and combination sensors.

Kirby Manufacturing Inc   HQ
   484 S Hwy 59
   Merced CA 95340
P: 209-723-0778   F: 209-723-3941   PRC:159
kirbymanufacturing.com
Email: info@kirbymfg.com
Estab: 1946

Ric Kirby, President
Richard Wallace, General Manager
Brachen Millikan, Manager
Brett Baker, Sales Manager
Stephannie Sandoval, Controller

Provider of cattle feeding equipment such as horizontal and vertical mixers, manure spreaders, freestall wagons, scale systems, and haybusters.

M-176

KitApps Inc   HQ
   75 E Santa Clara St 6th Fl
   San Jose CA 95113
P: 866-944-8678   PRC:315
attendify.com
Email: support@attendify.com
Estab: 2012

Artyom Yaremchuk, Founder
Michael Balyasny, CEO
Anati Zubia, VP of Marketing
Jacob Wiggins, Director of Global Sales
Jessica Waggoner, Director of Client Experience

Provider of networking and other information-based tools to event organizers and attendees (end-users).

KKI Corp   HQ
   5300 Claus Rd Ste 10
   Modesto CA 95357
P: 209-863-8550   F: 209-863-8686   PRC:323
www.kkicorp.com
Email: support@kkicorp.com
Estab: 1975

Ken Iwahashi, President
Samantha Schonefeld, Operations Manager
Justin Payne, Systems Engineer II
Tom LaBarbera, Accounting Supervisor
James Buel, Systems Administrator

Provider of web and business services and software solutions. The company is also involved in design and technical support services.

KLA-Tencor Corp   HQ
   3 Technology Dr
   Milpitas CA 95035
P: 408-875-3000   F: 408-875-4875   PRC:212
kla-tencor.com
Estab: 1976
Sales: Over $3B

Rick Wallace, CEO & President
Bren Higgins, CFO
Ben Tsai, CTO
John Van Camp, Chief Human Resource Officer
Bobby Bell, CSO

Provider of inspection and metrology tools. The company also specializes in process control and yield management products.

KLC Enterprises   HQ
   6 Woodside Ct
   San Anselmo CA 94960
P: 415-485-0555   F: 415-485-0556   PRC:319
www.klcent.com
Email: info@klcent.com
Estab: 1988

Kit Christiansen, System Analyst

Provider of accounting software for the construction industry. The company offers services to the commercial and industrial sectors.

Kleenrite Equipment   HQ
   1122 Maple St
   Madera CA 93637
P: 800-241-4865   F: 559-673-5725   PRC:159
www.kleenritemfg.com
Email: sales@kleenritemfg.com
Estab: 1973

Jeremy Wheeler, Director of Operations

Developer and manufacturer of domestic and commercial cleaning devices. The company caters to commercial and constructional facilities.

KLH Consulting Inc   HQ
   2324 Bethards Dr
   Santa Rosa CA 95405
P: 707-575-9986   F: 707-575-8758   PRC:325
klhconsulting.com
Email: info@klhconsulting.com
Estab: 1980

Aaron Sternad, CIO & Account Manager
Hub Lampert, Principal & CTO
Casey Meister, Manager of Operations
Kavitha Selvaraj, Developer

Provider of IT consulting, cloud computing, and related business solutions. The company offers services to business executives and professionals.

Klippenstein Corp   HQ
   5399 S Villa Ave
   Fresno CA 93725
P: 559-834-4258   F: 559-834-4263   PRC:159
klippenstein.com
Email: sales@klippenstein.com
Estab: 1979

Ken Klippenstein, President
Wendy Klippenstein, Office Manager
Dennis Schramm, Project Engineer
Justin Carroll, Project Engineer
Alec Weins, Project Engineer

Manufacturer of packaging equipment. The company's products also include case formers, erectors, and sealers.

KMIC Technology Inc   HQ
   2095 Ringwood Ave Ste 10
   San Jose CA 95131
P: 408-240-3600   F: 408-240-3699   PRC:65
www.kmictech.com
Email: contact@kmictech.com
Estab: 1979

David Kim, President
Arthur Ignacio, Director of Sales & Marketing

Provider of amplifier products and solutions to the radio frequency, microwave, and millimeter wave markers.

Knightscope Inc   HQ
   1070 Terra Bella Ave
   Mountain View CA 94043
P: 650-924-1025   PRC:314
www.knightscope.com
Email: contact@knightscope.com
Estab: 2013

William Li, CEO & Chairman
Mercedes Soria, EVP & Chief Intelligence Officer
Aaron Lehnhardt, VP

Provider of security technology. The company specializes in monotonous, computationally heavy, and sometimes dangerous work for security operations.

Knowme Inc   HQ
   25 Taylor St
   San Francisco CA 94102
P: 800-713-9257   PRC:319
www.knowme.net
Email: info@knowme.net
Estab: 2005

Borris Medak, President & CEO
Austin E. Hills, Chairman
Dan Gregerson, Director
Dominic Johnson, Director
Fred Sakamoto, Project Manager

Provider of web based customer relationship management services. The company is also engaged in call routing and web and phone integration.

Knurr USA   BR
496 S Abbott Ave
Milpitas CA 95035
P: 510-353-0177   F: 408-809-9284   PRC:293
extroninc.com
Email: sales@extroninc.com
Estab: 1931

Sandeep Duggal, CEO
Dinesh Chatkara, VP of Operations & Quality
Kien Nguyen, VP of Customer Integration
Richard Rogers, Business Development Manager
Joyce Cheng, Controller

Provider of custom enclosures, mobile equipment
carriers and carts, outdoor cabinets, control room
consoles, and technical furniture.

Kodiak Precision Inc   HQ
444 S First St
Richmond CA 94804-2107
P: 510-234-4165   F: 510-232-5232   PRC:80
www.kodiakprecisioninc.com
Email: operations@kodiakprecisioninc.com
Estab: 2001

Neil Divers, VP & COO
Kristy Divers, Operations Manager
Chris Divers, Department Manager
David Divers, Manager of Production
Ed Cabrera, QA & QC Manager

Manufacturer of precision machine products. The
company's products include milling and turning
machines, fabricated parts, and machine support
equipment.

Kodiak Sciences Inc   HQ
2631 Hanover St
Palo Alto CA 94304
P: 650-281-0850   PRC:191
kodiak.com
Email: info@kodiak.com
Estab: 2009

Victor Perlroth, CEO & Co-Founder
Stephen A. Charles, Co-Founder
John Borgeson, SVP & CFO
Jason Ehrlich, CMO & Chief Development Officer
Joel Naor, VP of Clinical Science & Development
Operations

Manufacturer of medicines for the treatment of
patients with age-related macular degeneration
and diabetic eye disease, two leading causes of
blindness.

**Kokusai Semiconductor Equipment
Corp**   DH
2460 N First St Ste 290
San Jose CA 95131
P: 408-456-2750   F: 408-456-2760   PRC:212
www.ksec.com
Estab: 1992

Carl Lopez, Customer Support Engineer
Dinesh Patel, Controller
Anne Fresilli Panger, Human Resource Repre-
sentative

Provider of thermal processing solutions. The
company also provides technical, installation, and
retrofit services.

Kone Inc   BR
15021 Wicks Blvd
San Leandro CA 94577
P: 510-351-5141   PRC:180
www.kone.us

Larry Wash, EVP
Jeff Blum, Regional SVP
Ken Schmid, Regional EVP
Dennis Viehweg, SVP of Modernization
Corey Ward, SVP of Environment, Health & Safety

Manufacturer of moving solutions. The company
offers automatic building doors, elevators and
escalators, and accessories.

Konicom Inc   HQ
1819 J St
Sacramento CA 95811
P: 916-441-7373   F: 916-441-7577   PRC:325
www.konicom.com
Email: support@konicom.com
Estab: 2001

Bryan Wu, Owner
Roy Zhao, Technician

Provider of computer services to businesses and
individuals. The company offers Internet related
services such as wireless network and hotspot
setup.

KOR-IT Inc   HQ
1964 Auburn Blvd
Sacramento CA 95815
P: 916-372-6400   F: 877-767-3648   PRC:80
www.kor-it.com
Email: info@kor-it.com
Estab: 1958

Jessica Sandler, CEO

Manufacturer of diamond tools and core drill
machines. The company caters to the concrete
cutting industry.

Kortick Manufacturing   HQ
2230 Davis Ct
Hayward CA 94545
P: 510-856-3600   PRC:68
www.kortick.com
Email: sales@kortick.com

Gavin Frase, President
Martin Rich, General Manager
Jose Sanchez, Manager of Production
Ron Matthews, Sales & Purchasing Manager
Eugene Gaines, Assembly Supervisor

Manufacturer and distributor of pole line hardware.
The company primarily caters to the telecom
industry.

Kovair Software Inc   HQ
2410 Camino Ramon Ste 230
San Ramon CA 94583
P: 408-262-0200   PRC:319
www.kovair.com
Email: sales@kovair.com
Estab: 2000

Bipin A. Shah, CEO & Chairman

Provider of web-based document management
applications. The company offers product support
maintenance services.

Kovarus Inc   HQ
2000 Crow Canyon Pl Ste 250
San Ramon CA 94583
P: 800-454-1585   F: 650-952-2072   PRC:323
www.kovarus.com
Email: sales@kovarus.com
Estab: 2003

Alex Weeks, Regional Director of Consulting
Scott Wiele, Director of Public Sector
Jeremy Brown, Manager of Sales Operations
Joe Arauzo, Manager of Solutions Account
Jeremy Windeshausen, Senior Account Manager

Provider of integrated business IT solutions. The
company also deals with leasing, financing, project management, and related services.

KP LLC   BR
13951 Washington Ave
San Leandro CA 94578
P: 510-351-5400   F: 510-351-2555   PRC:325
www.kpcorp.com
Email: info@kpcorp.com
Estab: 1929

Joe Atturio, President & CEO
Matthew Stupfel, CFO
Paul Braverman, COO
Thomas Middleton, CIO
Aaron Hunt, Director of Information Security

Provider of marketing and outsourcing solutions
offering digital and offset printing and mailing
services.

Kraemer & Co Manufacturing Inc   HQ
3778 Road 99 W
Orland CA 95963
P: 530-865-7982   F: 530-865-5091   PRC:82
kraemermanufacturing.com

Jerry Kraemer, Owner

Provider of industrial equipment. The company
specializes in dyers, sprayers, storage units, and
heaters.

Kramer Metals Inc   HQ
1760 E Slauson Ave   [N]
Los Angeles CA 90058
P: 323-587-2277   F: 323-588-8007   PRC:145
www.kramermetals.com
Email: info@kramermetals.com
Emp: 1-10   Estab: 1930

Doug Kramer, Owner
Stanley Kramer, Chairman & CEO

Distributor of scrap metals to steel mills, aluminum
mills, non-ferrous foundries and vacuum filters.

Kreck Design Solutions   HQ
416 Aviation Blvd Ste E
Santa Rosa CA 95403
P: 707-433-6166   F: 707-433-6165   PRC:325
kreck.com
Email: info@kreck.com
Estab: 1997

Brian Kreck, Partner
Lydia Revelos, Manager

Provider of graphic design and Internet-related
services. The company focuses on corporate
identity and marketing, web design, SEO, content
management.

Krobach Manufacturing Corp   HQ
3504 Arden Rd
Hayward CA 94544
P: 510-783-9480 F: 510-783-9727 PRC:80
www.krobach.com
Email: info@krobach.com
Estab: 1959

Nathan Moore, Quality Manager

Provider of precision machine shop and general machining services. The company focuses on turning, milling, and grinding.

Krytar Inc   HQ
1288 Anvilwood Ave
Sunnyvale CA 94089
P: 408-734-5999 F: 408-734-3017 PRC:13
krytar.com
Email: sales@krytar.com
Estab: 1975

Michael Romero, Engineering Manager
Hilda Clayton, Buyer

Provider of broadband microwave components and test equipment. The company is engaged in troubleshooting and maintenance services.

KSD Inc   HQ
161 W Lincoln St   [N]
Banning CA 92220
P: 951-849-7669 F: 951-849-5913 PRC:80
www.ksdinc.net
Emp: 1-10 Estab: 1967

Robert Anderson, President

Manufacturer and distributor of flight safety parts.

KSM Corp   DH
1959 Concourse Dr
San Jose CA 95131
P: 408-514-2400 F: 408-514-2499 PRC:82
www.ksm.co.kr
Email: solutions@ksmusa.com
Estab: 1979

Tony Singh, Owner

Manufacturer of welded metal bellows for transportation, solar, pharmaceutical, and other sectors and provides build to print assembly services.

Kucklick Design   HQ
22700 Midpine Ct
Los Gatos CA 95033
P: 408-353-1508 PRC:191
kucklickdesign.com

Theodore Kucklick, CEO & Founder

Designer and developer of medical illustration products. The company's portfolio includes Nova-Som system, Starion devices, and Extravasate.

M-178

Kumu Networks   HQ
960 Hamlin Ct
Sunnyvale CA 94089
P: 408-786-9302 PRC:70
kumunetworks.com
Email: info@kumunetworks.com
Estab: 2011

Jeff Mehlman, Director of Engineering & Co-Founder
Mayank Jain, CTO & Co-Founder
Jung Il Choi, Co-Founder
David Cutrer, CEO
Jung-Il Choi, Chief System Architect

Developer of wireless technology that cancels self-interference, the unwanted energy that leaks into a radio's receiver while transmitting.

Kura MD Inc   HQ
130 Diamond Creek Pl
Roseville CA 95747
P: 855-587-2220 PRC:194
www.kura.md
Email: info@kura.md
Estab: 2013

Kevin Hamm, CEO

Provider of telemedicine platform enables convenient, secure, HIPAA compliant, and telehealth appointments between physicians and patients through tablet.

Kurz Instruments Inc   HQ
2411 Garden Rd
Monterey CA 93940
P: 831-646-5911 F: 831-646-8901 PRC:14
www.kurzinstruments.com
Email: sales@kurzinstruments.com
Estab: 1976

Tom Setliff, Director of International Sales
Marty Vandermolen, Sales Manager
Ricardo Martinez, Design Engineer
Scott Cooper, Engineering R&D
Frederico Dias, Marketing Coordinator

Designer and manufacturer of thermal mass flow transmitters. The company's products find application in industrial gases and liquids.

Kval Inc   HQ
825 Petaluma Blvd S   [N]
Petaluma CA 94952
P: 707-762-0621 PRC:159
www.kvalinc.com
Email: service@kvalinc.com
Emp: 51-200 Estab: 1961

Gavin Nielsen, System Engineer
Todd LaCasse, Electrician & CAD Designer
Barry Bunte, Technical Writer

Manufacturer of CNC door machinery for architectural and residential applications.

KWJ Engineering Inc   HQ
8430 Central Ave Ste C
Newark CA 94560
P: 510-794-4296 F: 510-574-8341 PRC:13
www.kwjengineering.com
Email: sales@kwjengineering.com
Estab: 1993

Joe Stetter, CTO & President
Tom Stetter, Marketing Director & Sales & Web & IT
Mike Carter, Director of Research
Vinay Patel, Director
Larry W. Johnson, Production Manager

Manufacturer of gas detection products. The company offers equipment to detect chlorine, carbon monoxide, ozone, and methane and propane.

Kycon Inc   HQ
305 Digital Dr
Morgan Hill CA 95037
P: 408-494-0330 F: 408-494-0325 PRC:159
kycon.com
Email: sales@kycon.com
Estab: 2005

Glen Pacheco, Regional Sales Manager
Kelli Huston, Manager of Sales
Allen Chen, Test Engineer
Barbara Piper, Controller

Provider of interconnect solutions. The company offers products such as audio jacks, card edge, and modular jacks.

Kyec USA   DH
101 Metro Dr Ste 540
San Jose CA 95110
P: 408-452-7680 F: 408-452-7689 PRC:86
www.kyec.com.tw
Estab: 1987

A. H. Liu, President
K. Lee, VP
Steven Chang, VP
Allen Tsai, Senior Director

Provider of testing services. The company offers services for testing integrated circuit (IC) packaging.

Kyosemi Opto America Corp   BR
4655 Old Ironsides Dr Ste 230
Santa Clara CA 95054
P: 408-492-9361 F: 408-492-9843 PRC:62
www.kyosemi.co.jp/en/contact/world/#usa

Kurt Kawabuchi, President

Manufacturer of opto-semiconductor devices. The company focuses on optical communication devices and photo devices for sensors.

L&T Precision Engineering Inc HQ
2395 Qume Dr
San Jose CA 95131
P: 408-441-1890 F: 408-441-1899 PRC:80
lt-engineering.com
Email: sales@lt-engineering.com
Estab: 1988

Lan Pham, Quality Assurance Manager
Steven Tran, Payroll & HR Supervisor
My Truong, Contact
Thang Dinh, Contact
Trung Nguyen, Contact

Provider of fabrication, precision engineering
assistance, and assembly services. The company
serves semiconductor, medical, and other sectors.

L-3 Narda Microwave-West HQ
107 Woodmere Rd
Folsom CA 95630
P: 916-351-4500 F: 916-351-4550 PRC:70
www.nardamicrowavewest.com
Email: smnmw-inside.sales@l3harris.com
Estab: 1997

Brad Morris, Senior Program Manager
Jason Baggett, Manager
Theresa Moreno, Calibration Administrator

Designer and manufacturer of RF microwave components and subsystems. The company products
include power dividers, filters, and linearizers.

La Belle Inc BR
174 E Fourth St
Ripon CA 95366
P: 209-599-6605 PRC:251
www.labelleinc.com
Email: sales@labelleinc.com
Estab: 1984

Mike Campbell, CSO
Mike Wiebe, COO
Gregg Whitley, VP of Sales & Marketing

Manufacturer of colostrum and chelated minerals.
The company also specializes in spray drying.

Lab Sensor Solutions Inc HQ
648 El Camino Real Ste P
Redwood City CA 94063
P: 650-275-3101 PRC:34
lsstracks.com
Email: forinfo@lsstracks.com
Estab: 2013

Geoff Zawolkow, CEO
Jarie Bolander, COO
Daniel Paley, EVP of Engineering

Provider of real-time sensor technology on
healthcare assets so customers can monitor,
report and act to assure items are in right place
and condition.

Labcon North America HQ
3700 Lakeville Hwy
Petaluma CA 94954
P: 707-766-2100 F: 707-766-2199 PRC:20
labcon.com
Email: custsupport@labcon.com
Estab: 1959

Ed Browning, Director of Business Development
Mark Bramwell, Director of Research & Develop-
ment
Tom Moulton, Director of Marketing
Mike Ford, Manager of Customer Service
Pete Owenson, Western Region Manager

Manufacturer of disposable plastic products for
laboratories. The company offers products for
liquid handling, culture, and molecular biology.

Labo America Inc HQ
920 Auburn Ct
Fremont CA 94538
P: 510-445-1257 F: 510-445-1317 PRC:174
www.laboamerica.com
Email: sales@laboamerica.com

Savita Aggarwal, Owner
Gautam Aggarwal, VP of Sales & Marketing
Asif Mushtaq, Operation Manager
Manish Anand, Regional Sales Manager

Manufacturer and distributor of stereo, compound,
surgical and digital microscopes, digital cameras
and measuring software.

Laboratory Equipment Co HQ
2506 Technology Dr
Hayward CA 94545
P: 510-887-4040 F: 510-887-4112 PRC:159
www.labequipco.com
Email: info@labequipco.com
Estab: 1948

Britta Johnson, Technical Sales Representative

Manufacturer of laboratory equipment. The company's products include alarm monitor systems,
bedding dispensers, dryers, and ovens.

Lacroix Davis LLC BR
3685 Mt Diablo Blvd Ste 210
Lafayette CA 94549
P: 925-299-1140 F: 925-299-1185 PRC:140
lacroixdavis.com

Gordon M. Bizieff, Director of Architectural Ser-
vices
Melinda Jones, Office Manager
James R. LaCroix, Principal

Provider of building and environmental forensics
and consulting services. The company provides
support for investigation, litigation, and education.

LakePharma Inc BR
520 Harbor Blvd
Belmont CA 94002
P: 650-288-4891 PRC:34
lakepharma.com
Email: inquiries@lakepharma.com
Estab: 2009

Hua Tu, CEO & Founder
Lisa Alexander, VP of Quality & Regulatory
Li Wang, Director
Bill Hermans, Senior Director of Production
Technology
Paula Criss, Director of Sales

Provider of contract research organization specializing in antibody and protein engineering, cell line
development, and protein production.

LAKOS Filtration Solutions HQ
1365 N Clovis Ave
Fresno CA 93727-2282
P: 559-255-1601 F: 559-255-8093 PRC:156
www.lakos.com
Email: info@lakos.com
Estab: 1972

Claude Laval, Owner
Craig Malsam, VP of Engineering
Ray Chatman, Welder
Leonardo Zepeda, Production Scheduler
Matthew Navarro, Strategic Buyer

Manufacturer of centrifugal separators and other
filtration solutions to remove sand and other solids
from water and liquids.

Lam Research Corp HQ
4650 Cushing Pkwy
Fremont CA 94538
P: 510-572-0200 PRC:212
www.lamresearch.com
Email: training.fremont@lamresearch.com
Estab: 1980

Timothy M. Archer, President & CEO
Douglas R. Bettinger, EVP & CFO
Sarah O'Dowd, SVP & CLO
Richard A. Gottscho, EVP of Technology &
Products
Harmeet Singh, Corporate VP

Manufacturer and distributor of single wafer
systems. The company primarily serves the semiconductor industry.

Lamar Tool & Die HQ
4230 Technology Dr
Modesto CA 95356
P: 209-545-5525 F: 209-545-5527 PRC:80
www.lamartoolanddie.com
Estab: 1982

Brian Kolsters, Director of Operations
Kelli Jones, Office Manager
Thomas Moore, Machine Operator
Shaheen Shamsavari, Senior Investment Manger

Manufacturer of die casting solutions. The company's offerings include machining and secondary
operations.

Lambda Research Optics Inc   HQ

1695 Macarthur Blvd   [N]
Costa Mesa CA 92626
P: 714-327-0600 F: 714-327-0610   PRC:31
www.lambda.cc
Email: sales@lambda.cc
Emp: 51-200   Estab: 1991

Mark Youn, President

Manufacturer of optical components.

Lamdagen Corp   BR

1455 Adams Dr Ste 1155
Menlo Park CA 94025
P: 650-571-5816 F: 650-571-5837   PRC:11
www.lamdagen.com
Email: info@lamdagen.com
Estab: 2005

Randy Storer, CEO & Founder
Daniele Gerion, Senior Scientist

Developer of nano technology based biosensors used in research and diagnostic equipment for human and animal health testing.

Lamek Industrial Corp   HQ

1254 Birchwood Dr
Sunnyvale CA 94089
P: 408-734-3363   PRC:80
www.lamekindustrial.com
Email: mail@lamekindustrial.com

Lamek Industrial, Owner
Tony Vattuone, Owner

Manufacturer of machined parts for the semiconductor, medical, and aeronautic sectors. The company focuses on bead blasting, tumbling and packaging.

Lamons   BR

189 Arthur Rd
Martinez CA 94553
P: 925-313-9080 F: 925-313-9348   PRC:162
www.lamons.com

Marc Roberts, CEO
Dave Metzer, VP of Sales
Larry Walls, Director Global Sourcing
Anthony Startz, Director of Human Resources
Bill Hinderman, District Manager

Manufacturer of industrial gaskets. The company caters to the refinery and packing industrial sectors.

Lamphier-Gregory   HQ

1944 Embarcadero
Oakland CA 94606
P: 510-535-6690 F: 510-535-6699   PRC:139
lamphier-gregory.com
Estab: 1979

Scott Gregory, President
Britt Hallquist, Principal & VP
Rebecca Gorton, Senior Planner
John Courtney, Senior Planner
Sharon Wright, Environmental Planner

Provider of urban planning services. The company provides environmental analysis, project management, and coordination services.

LAN-Power Inc   HQ

44240 Freemont Blvd
Fremont CA 94538-6000
P: 510-275-4572   PRC:59
www.lan-power.com
Email: sales@lan-power.com

Lance Rasmussen, VP of Marketing

Designer, developer, and manufacturer of break through technology for implementing surveillance and security systems.

Landel   HQ

175 Bernal Rd Ste 100-15
San Jose CA 95119
P: 408-360-0490   PRC:66
landel.com
Email: sales@landel.com
Estab: 1998

Steve Landry, President

Provider of telecommunication products such as MailBug, DataBug, and SurveyBug. The company is engaged in technical support services.

Langan Products Inc   HQ

2660 California St   [N]
San Francisco CA 94115
P: 415-567-8087 F: 415-398-7664   PRC:109
www.langan.biz/Site/Welcome.html
Estab: 1987

Leon Langan, Contact

Manufacturer of computer peripheral equipment and prepackaged software products.

Langill's General Machine Inc   HQ

7850 14th Ave
Sacramento CA 95826-4302
P: 916-452-0167 F: 916-452-2812   PRC:80
www.langills.com
Email: langills@sbcglobal.net
Estab: 1970

Benjamin Langill, Owner & VP

Manufacturer of precision machined components with a full array of state-of-the-art machines, operated by a highly trained workforce.

Langineers   HQ

1799 Bayshore Hwy Ste 230
Burlingame CA 94010
P: 650-692-2001 F: 650-692-2110   PRC:68
www.langineers.com
Email: sales@langineers.com
Estab: 1993

Lonnie Domnitz, President
Jason Baptista, Sales Manager
Micah Levine, Technician
Pete Askar, Accounting Associate

Provider of VoIP phone services, video conferencing, and hosting solutions. The company offers cordless DECT phones and video conferencing phones.

Langtech   HQ

733 Front St Ste 110
San Francisco CA 94111
P: 415-364-9600 F: 415-364-9650   PRC:323
langtech.com
Email: contact@langtech.com
Estab: 1987

Eivind Sukkestad, Principal & Owner
Brian Mott, President & CEO
Stephen Cheung, Company Director
Tracy Gribschaw, Director of IT & Client Services
Joe Hung, Managing Director

Provider of information technology services. The company provides software solutions, cloud services, system integration, and consulting.

Language Quest Traveler   HQ

309 N Mt Shasta Blvd
Mount Shasta CA 96067
P: 530-918-9540 F: 530-918-9541   PRC:323
www.languagequest.com
Email: info1@languagequest.com

Jim Havlice, Owner

Retailer of foreign language bibles, software, books, and dictionaries. The company also offers video/audio supplies.

Lanlogic   HQ

248 Rickenbacker Cir
Livermore CA 94551
P: 925-273-2300   PRC:328
lanlogic.com
Email: realpeople@lanlogic.com
Estab: 1995

Art Closson, Founder
Dan Ferguson, President & CEO
Wilma Smith, CFO
Marcus Solorio, General Manager
Eugene Worth, Hosted Services Manager

Provider of information technology services. The company offers network management and support services.

Lansmont Corp   HQ

17 Mandeville Court
Monterey CA 93940
P: 831-655-6600 F: 831-655-6606   PRC:235
www.lansmont.com
Estab: 1971

Dale Root, Software Development Manager
Peter Brown, Customer Service Manager
Keith Nordyke, Mechanical Engineering Manager
Jess Sumagang, Field Service Engineer
Lisa Chisman, AR Coordinator

Provider of products such as field instruments, shock machines, vibration systems, drop testers, and package shakers.

Lares Research HQ
295 Lockheed Ave
Chico CA 95973
P: 530-345-1767   F: 530-345-1870   PRC:185
www.laresdental.com
Email: world-sales@laresdental.com
Estab: 1956

Christian Godoy, Senior Executive Vice President
of Global Sales & Marketing
Craig J. Lares, President
Patti Kreitzer, Account Manager
Chuck Elton, Manufacturing Manager
Jason Orgain, Manager of Engineering

Developer and manufacturer of dental handpieces
and dental lasers. The company offers services to
the healthcare industry.

Larkin Precision Machining Inc HQ
175 El Pueblo Rd
Scotts Valley CA 95066
P: 831-438-2700   F: 831-438-2704   PRC:80
lpmachining.com
Estab: 1920

Rob Larkin, CEO & Founder
Seth Larkin, Managing Partner & Co-Owner-Lathe
Department Manager
Jon Larkin, Managing Partner & Co-Owner-Mill
Department Manager
Richard Larkin, Senior Programming Engineer &
General Manager
Henrik Ingesson, Quality Engineer & Manager of
Inspection Department

Manufacturer of machined parts of precision CNC
milling and turning devices specializing in assemblies, fixtures, flanges, grinding, and sawing.

Larry Walker Associates HQ
1480 Drew Ave Ste 100
Davis CA 95618
P: 530-753-6400   F: 530-753-7030   PRC:142
lwa.com
Email: infolwa@lwa.com
Estab: 1979

Larry Walker, Founder
Tom Grovhoug, President
Brian Laurenson, VP
Karen Ashby, VP
Malcolm Walker, VP

Provider of environmental engineering and
consulting services. The company provides water
quality solutions.

Larson Automation Inc HQ
960 Rincon Cir
San Jose CA 95131
P: 408-432-4800   PRC:19
www.larsonautomation.com
Email: info@larsonautomation.com
Estab: 1993

Wayne Larson, Founder
Cecilia Gold, Program Manager
Chris Reed, Production Manager

Developer of automated test solutions for telecommunication companies. The company offers board
test stations and level shifters.

Larson Electronic Glass HQ
2840 Bay Rd
Redwood City CA 94063
P: 650-369-6734   F: 650-369-0728   PRC:82
www.larsonelectronicglass.com
Email: sales@larsonelectronicglass.com
Estab: 1954

Chuck Kraft, Manager

Manufacturer of glass to metal sealing products.
The company offers vacuum flanges, viewports,
bellows, and electrical and fiber optics feedthroughs.

Laru Technologies HQ
400 Plaza Dr Ste 210
Folsom CA 95630
P: 916-458-6149   F: 916-404-7790   PRC:319
www.larutech.com
Email: sales@larutech.com
Estab: 2004

Carl Daniel, VP & CTO

Provider of ACH and Wire transaction monitoring
and control tools. The company focuses on risk
management and compliance solutions.

Laser Mark's LLC HQ
2109 O'Toole Ave Ste S
San Jose CA 95131
P: 408-433-9333   F: 408-433-9343   PRC:81
www.laser-marks.com
Email: lasermarks@gmail.com
Estab: 1988

Laser Mark, Manager

Provider of laser marking and engraving job shop
services. The company serves the agriculture,
food processing, automotive, and medical industries.

Laser Reference Inc HQ
151 Martinvale Ln
San Jose CA 95119
P: 408-361-0220   F: 408-361-3180   PRC:172
proshotlaser.com
Email: sales@proshotlaser.com
Estab: 1991

Lee Robson, President
David Kawano, Sales Manager

Supplier of laser level products for interior and
outdoor construction focusing on laser receivers
and accessories including telescopic laser tripods.

Laserline Inc BR
1800 Wyatt Dr Ste 9
Santa Clara CA 95054
P: 408-834-4660   F: 408-834-4671   PRC:171
www.laserline.com
Email: info-usa@laserline.com
Estab: 1997

Dave Matthews, Director of Customer Support

Manufacturer of diode lasers for welding metals
and plastics. The company also deals with cladding, hardening, and brazing.

Lasertec USA Inc HQ
2107 N First St Ste 210
San Jose CA 95131
P: 408-437-1441   F: 408-437-1430   PRC:68
www.lasertec.co.jp
Estab: 1960

Haruhiko Kusunose, EVP & Representative
Director

Developer and manufacturer of systems for
semi-conductor applications. The company also
offers systems for flat panel displays.

Lastline HQ
1825 S Grant St Ste 635
San Mateo CA 94402
P: 877-671-3239   PRC:325
www.lastline.com
Email: sales@lastline.com
Estab: 2011

Brian Laing, SVP
George Chitouras, SVP of Engineering
Clemens Kolbitsch, Director of Engineering
John Love, Director of Marketing
Paolo Milani Comparetti, Director of Engineering

Manufacturer of malware protection products. The
company serves schools, restaurants, and the
enterprise security inductry.

Lattice Engines Inc HQ
1820 Gateway Dr Ste 200
San Mateo CA 94404
P: 877-460-0010   PRC:322
lattice-engines.com
Email: partners@lattice-engines.com
Estab: 2006

Shashi Upadhyay, Founder & CEO
Gregory Haardt, CTO
Brian Kardon, CMO
Brett Dyer, CFO
Chitrang Shah, Chief Product Officer

Provider of business to business sales intelligence
software. The company is engaged in web design
and hosting and programming solutions.

Lattice Semiconductor BR
2115 O'Nel Dr
San Jose CA 95131
P: 408-826-6000   F: 408-826-6034   PRC:212
www.latticesemi.com
Estab: 1983

Jeff Richardson, Chairman
Jim Anderson, President & CEO & Director
Sherri Luther, CFO
Rick White, Corporate VP of Operations
Sunil Mehta, Director of Technology

Provider of design, development, and marketing
services for programmable logic devices. The
company also offers related software.

Lattice Technology Inc   BR
582 Market St Ste 1215
San Francisco CA 94104
P: 720-330-3197 F: 720-330-3198   PRC:319
www.lattice3d.com
Email: info@lattice3d.com
Estab: 1997

Bill Barnes, General Manager
Erik Freeman, Sales Manager
Masaru Hatakoshi, Solutions Engineer

Developer of 3D and 2D software for design review purposes. The company also focuses on 3D simulation and animation needs.

Laughter Works Seminars   HQ
PO Box 1220   [N]
Folsom CA 95763
P: 916-985-6570   PRC:45
www.laughterworks.com
Email: info@laughterworks.com
Emp: 1-10   Estab: 1982

Jim Pelley, Contact

Provider of seminars on the positive power of humor and creativity. Programs focus on selling, customer service, leadership, education, communication and health care. Industries served: healthcare, education, high-tech, manufacturing, service and government agencies.

Lavante Inc   HQ
5285 Hellyer Ave Ste 200
San Jose CA 95138-1081
P: 408-754-1410   PRC:322
www.lavante.com
Email: customerservice@lavante.com
Estab: 2001

Sam Klepper, CEO
Vinay Ambekar, VP of Engineering
Nina Pozegija, VP of Operations

Provider of on-demand strategic profit recovery solutions. The company also offers vendor information management software.

Lawson Mechanical Contractors   HQ
6090 S Watt Ave
Sacramento CA 95829-1302
P: 916-381-5000 F: 916-381-5073   PRC:80
lawsonmechanical.com
Estab: 1947

David Lawson, President
Rodney Barbour, EVP
Rod Lawson, VP
Stephen Humason, VP
Eric Fuchino, General Manager

Provider of mechanical construction services. The company offers plumbing, HVAC, industrial, and process piping services.

Lazestar Inc   HQ
6956 Preston Ave
Livermore CA 94551
P: 925-443-5293 F: 925-443-5262   PRC:80
www.lazestar.com

David Madrid, Laser Lab Manager
Gary Sickenger, Quality Manager

Provider of laser sealing, packing, precision fabrication, and welding services. The company serves the aerospace and commercial industries.

LCS Technologies Inc   HQ
11230 Gold Express Ste 310-140
Gold River CA 95670
P: 855-277-5527   PRC:326
lcs-technologies-inc.com
Email: sales@lcs-technologies-inc.com
Estab: 2006

Stephane Come, Co-Founder & CTO
Steve Simonetto, Co-Founder & President & CEO
Chris Wilson, COO
Ara Davis, Business Operations Manager

Provider of information services for customers with Oracle software and service needs using resources such as people, hardware, and software.

Leadman Electronics USA Inc   HQ
382 Laurelwood Rd
Santa Clara CA 95054
P: 408-380-4567 F: 408-738-2620   PRC:159
www.leadman.com
Email: sales@leadman.com
Estab: 1986

Jim Liang, VP
Eric Wang, Director of Power Supply BU

Provider of ODM/OEM, hardware engineering expertise, and custom solutions for a wide range of security, storage, server, and network applications.

Leaf Healthcare Inc   HQ
5994 W Las Positas Blvd Ste 217
Pleasanton CA 94588
P: 844-826-5323   PRC:189
leafhealthcare.com
Email: info@leafhealthcare.com
Estab: 2010

Annemari Cooley, VP of Market Development
Mark Smith, VP of Marketing & Strategic Business Development

Specializes in wearable healthcare technologies. The company deals with patient mobility programs and serves the medical industry.

LeapFILE Inc   HQ
19989 Stevens Creek Blvd
Cupertino CA 95014
P: 650-701-7241   PRC:323
www.leapfile.com
Email: clientservices@leapfile.com
Estab: 2004

Alex Teu, VP

Provider of on-demand file transfer, delivery, and collaboration solutions for businesses. The company serves the healthcare and advertising sectors.

Learning In Motion Inc   HQ
113 Cooper St 2nd Fl
Santa Cruz CA 95060-4526
P: 831-600-6606   PRC:319
www.learninginmotion.com
Email: helpdesk@learninginmotion.com
Estab: 1993

Marge Cappo, President

Provider of educational materials and services. The company offers content development, video production, and marketing collateral services.

Ledger Systems Inc   HQ
865 Laurel St
San Carlos CA 94070
P: 650-592-6211 F: 650-594-8453   PRC:224
www.ledgersys.com
Estab: 1983

Richard S. Wright, Co-Founder & Chairman & CEO
Stephen E. Kirby, Co-Founder & President & COO
Chris Monser, Director of Systems & Programming
Rick Hoelle, Director of Programming

Provider of network design and support services. The company also offers accounting and e-Commerce solutions.

LEE + RO Inc   BR
1550 Parkside Dr Ste 320
Walnut Creek CA 94596
P: 925-937-4050   PRC:304
www.lee-ro.com
Estab: 1979

Lee Badertscher, VP
Tony Park, VP
Daniel Park, Manager of Network & IT
Linda Tripp, Senior Project Manager
Charles Ro, Civil Engineer

Provider of environmental and infrastructure engineering solutions. The company is involved in design-build and construction management.

Lee Mah Electronics Inc   HQ
155 S Hill Dr
Brisbane CA 94005
P: 415-394-1288 F: 415-433-2560   PRC:209
leemah.com
Email: inquiry@leemah.com
Estab: 1971

Warren Gee, EVP

Provider of manufacturing solutions. The company serves customers in the medical, communications, and test and measurement industries.

Legend Design Technology Inc   HQ
2905 Stender Way Ste 50
Santa Clara CA 95054
P: 408-748-8888 F: 408-748-8988   PRC:211
www.legenddesign.com
Email: sales@legenddesign.com
Estab: 1996

You-Pang Wei, President & CEO

Provider of semiconductor IP characterization and verification tools and IC and PCB circuit simulators.

Leica Geosystems HDS LLC   RH
4550 Norris Canyon Rd
San Ramon CA 94583
P: 925-790-2300   PRC:172
hds.leica-geosystems.com
Estab: 1993

Tim Nolen, Southeast Regional Sales Manager

Manufacturer of surveying hardware and software solutions for measuring and modeling sites and structures with high accuracy, detail, speed, and safety.

LekasMiller Design HQ
1250 I Newell Ave Ste 340
Walnut Creek CA 94596
P: 925-934-3971 PRC:325
www.lekasmiller.com
Estab: 1985

Tina Lekas Miller, Owner & President & Creative Director
Ali Gencarelle, Studio Manager
Denise Fuller, Manager of Production

Provider of photography, printing, advertising, graphic design, mailing, and project management services.

Lemo USA Inc HQ
635 Park Ct
Rohnert Park CA 94928
P: 707-578-8811 F: 707-578-0869 PRC:76
www.lemo.com
Email: info@lemousa.com

Edna Isabel Limson, Territory Account Manager
Winfred Baerthel, Manager of Credit & Collection
Chris Van Nuys, Operations Manager
Bill Lee, Business Integration Manager
Julie Carlson, Marketing Manager

Designer and manufacturer of precision custom connectors, cable assemblies, and related accessories. The company serves the industrial sector.

Lendingclub Corp HQ
595 Market St Ste 200
San Francisco CA 94105
P: 415-632-5600 PRC:45
lendingclub.com
Email: info@lc-advisors.com
Emp: 1768 Estab: 2006
Sales: $300M to $1 Billion

Renaud Laplanche, Founder & CEO
Scott Sanborn, COO
Angela Loeffler, CPO
Carrie Dolan, CFO
John MacIlwaine, CTO

Provider of financial solutions. The company offers home improvement, business, pool, and consolidated debt loans.

Lenos Software HQ
312 Sutter St 5th Fl
San Francisco CA 94108
P: 415-281-8828 PRC:323
www.lenos.com
Email: support@lenos.com
Estab: 1999

Debra Chong, Founder & CEO
Patti H. Tackeff, President & CMO
Jacqueline Regalado, Manager of Professional Service
Matt Owens, QA Developer

Provider of enterprise resource management, development of motion graphics, and value-added management services.

Lenthor Engineering HQ
311 Turquoise St
Milpitas CA 95035
P: 408-945-8787 F: 408-956-1874 PRC:211
www.lenthor.com
Estab: 1985

Mark P. Lencioni, President & CEO
Dave Moody, Director of Sales Marketing
Rey Cervantes, Director of Quality
Rich Clemente, General Manager
Richard Clemente, General Manager

Designer and manufacturer of flexible and rigid printed circuit boards. The company serves the military, communications, medical, and other markers.

Lenz Precision Technology Inc HQ
355 Pioneer Way
Mountain View CA 94041
P: 650-966-1784 F: 650-966-1953 PRC:80
www.lenztech.com
Email: admin@lenztech.com
Estab: 1972

Eric Lenz, President
Steve Notti, Manager of Production

Manufacturer of precision machined components and sub assemblies. The company also focuses on the sales aspects.

Leoco USA Corp BR
4125 Business Center Dr
Fremont CA 94538
P: 510-429-3700 F: 510-429-3708 PRC:76
www.leoco.com.tw
Email: leocosales@leocousa.com
Estab: 1981

Alex Wang, VP

Manufacturer of interconnects. The company offers wire to board, wire to wire, board to board, and card and telecom connectors.

Leotek Electronics USA LLC HQ
1955 Lundy Ave
San Jose CA 95131
P: 408-380-1788 F: 408-518-8128 PRC:243
leotek.com
Estab: 1992

Chen Wu, CEO & Vice Chairman
Kenan Chen, Product Manager
Frank Soltani, Engineering Assistant

Manufacturer of light-emitting diodes and lights for traffic and transit, street and area, commercial, petroleum, and grocery and retail stores.

Lewiz Communications Inc HQ
738 Charcot Ave
San Jose CA 95131
P: 408-432-6248 F: 408-452-9805 PRC:97
www.lewiz.com
Email: info@lewiz.com
Estab: 2000

Chinh Le, CEO & CTO & Founder
John Floisand, VP & General Manager of Board Business Division
Steve Dowdell, VP of Sales
Ken Pope, VP of Marketing
Mary Le, VP of Operations

Provider of computer networking solutions. The company also offers data security, data management, and data streaming services.

Lexar Media Inc HQ
161 Baypointe Pkwy
San Jose CA 95134
P: 408-933-1088 F: 510-440-3499 PRC:96
www.lexar.com
Email: support@lexar.com
Estab: 1996

Donald Hills, Senior Pricing Manager

Provider of memory product lines such as USB drives, memory cards, card readers, and dram computer memory.

Lexicon Branding Inc HQ
30 Liberty Ship Way Ste 3360
Sausalito CA 94965
P: 415-332-1811 F: 415-332-2528 PRC:310
lexiconbranding.com
Email: info@lexiconbranding.com

David Placek, President
Alan Clark, Director of Trademark
Greg Alger, Director of Linguistics

Provider of services to develop, select and evaluate brand names. The company services include trademark evaluation, name development, and consumer research.

Lfw Manufacturing HQ
745 S Lincoln St
Stockton CA 95203
P: 209-465-0444 F: 209-465-6521 PRC:80
www.lfwmfg.com

Leo Wickham, President & Engineer
Rachelle D. Brown, Manager of Production & Office Manager

Manufacturer of gearboxes and gear sets. The company caters to a wide range of industrial applications.

LG Display America Inc BR
2540 N First St Ste 400
San Jose CA 95131
P: 408-350-0190 PRC:168
www.lgdisplay.com
Estab: 1987

Rok Park, Senior Manager & Project Leader

Manufacturer of thin-film transistor liquid crystal display panels. The company is also focused on OLEDs and flexible displays.

LGE Electrical Sales Inc HQ
650 University Ave Ste 218
Sacramento CA 95825
P: 916-563-2737 F: 916-563-2763 PRC:245
www.lgesales.com
Estab: 1987

Ray Landgraf, President
Dave Evans, VP
Terri Gierke, Outside Sales Manager
Daniel Iseman, Contact

Provider of electrical distribution and transmission products. The company's products include distran packaged substation products, G&W, MGM, and TIKA.

Libby Laboratories Inc HQ
1700 Sixth St
Berkeley CA 94710
P: 510-527-5400 F: 510-527-8687 PRC:264
www.libbylabs.com
Email: inquiries@libbylabs.com
Estab: 1959

Susan Libby, President

Manufacturer of cosmetics, OTC pharmaceuticals, drugs, and devices. The company offers skin and hair products, toiletries, natural and organic products.

Liberty Test Equipment HQ
1640 Lead Hill Blvd Ste 120
Roseville CA 95661
P: 916-625-4228 F: 916-782-0891 PRC:14
www.libertytest.com
Email: sales@libertytest.com
Estab: 2002

Mesut Koch, President & CEO
Panayiotis Frantzis, CTO
Jennifer DuMond, Account Manager
Patricia Phillimeano, Manager of Marketing & Operations
Rumi Sakaya, Accounting Manager

Provider of refurbished and new test equipment and related accessories. The company deals with sales, lease, and rental services.

LibraryWorld HQ
PO Box 231
San Jose CA 95103
P: 800-852-2777 F: 408-993-2147 PRC:322
www.libraryworld.com
Email: sales@libraryworld.com
Estab: 1987

Norman Kline, CEO
John McIntyre, CTO
William Kline, Manager of Quality Assurance
John Kline, Manager of Software Quality Assurance
Fred Zaccheo, Marketing Manager

Provider of library automation software solutions. The company serves schools, healthcare, law firms, museum, and architectural firms.

Lifescience Plus Inc HQ
2520-A Wyandotte St
Mountain View CA 94043
P: 650-565-8172 F: 650-336-1130 PRC:195
www.lifescienceplus.com
Email: sales@lifescienceplus.com
Estab: 2005

Vicky Feng, CEO & Founder
Shoba Viswanath, CSO
Audrey Vitale, Director of Regulatory Affairs
Cecilia Lin, Senior Accountant

Developer of wound care technology solutions and its applications include surgery, dentistry, and public safety.

Ligandal Inc HQ
650 Fifth St Ste 311
San Francisco CA 94107
P: 650-866-5212 PRC:191
www.ligandal.com
Estab: 2013

Andre Watson, Founder & CEO & Chairman

Developer of nanotechnology for precise and high-efficiency delivery of nucleic acids to specific cells and organelles for genetic medicine.

Light & Motion HQ
711 Neeson Rd
Marina CA 93933
P: 831-645-1538 PRC:243
www.lightandmotion.com
Estab: 1989

Daniel Emerson, CEO

Provider of light and motion personal lighting system for mountain, bike, foot, camera, water, and underwater activities.

Light Guard Systems Inc HQ
2292 Airport Blvd
Santa Rosa CA 95403
P: 707-542-4547 F: 707-525-6333 PRC:212
lightguardsystems.com
Email: office@lightguardsystems.com
Estab: 1994

Michael A. Harrison, President & CEO
Krista Kalemba, General Manager
Sher Paz, National Sales Manager
Jeannie Bartholdy, Executive Administrator

Provider of traffic safety products such as controllers, signal head and base plate modules, and LED signage products.

Light Polymers Inc HQ
347 Littlefield Ave
S San Francisco CA 94080
P: 650-678-7733 PRC:53
www.lightpolymers.com
Email: info@lightpolymers.com
Estab: 2013

Sergey Fedotov, Director of US Marketing & Operations

Developer of polymers and materials. The company formulates and develops solutions for lyotropic liquid crystals.

LightGuideOptics USA LLC RH
1101 S Winchester Blvd Ste L-238
San Jose CA 95128
P: 408-244-0686 F: 408-244-0714 PRC:62
lgoptics.com
Estab: 2008

Mick Speciale, CEO

Manufacturer of diameters, bundles and probes. The company's products are used in medical and high-tech applications.

Lighthouse Worldwide Solutions HQ
47300 Kato Rd
Fremont CA 94538
P: 510-438-0500 F: 510-438-3840 PRC:187
www.golighthouse.com
Email: info@golighthouse.com
Estab: 1982

Tae Yun Kim, CEO & Chairman
Paul Newman, SVP
Jason Kelly, VP of Sales
Thomas Saunders, SVP
Alvin Sojourner, Facilities Manager

Provider of dental supplies such as implants, dentures, partials, implant bars, and related accessories.

Lightning Bolt Solutions Inc HQ
323 Allerton Ave
S San Francisco CA 94080
P: 866-678-3279 F: 650-651-1637 PRC:194
www.lightning-bolt.com
Email: info@lightning-bolt.com
Estab: 2002

Suvas Vajracharya, CEO & Founder
Nirmal Govind, CTO
Kelly Challenger, Senior Director of Marketing
Jo Bhullar, Software Engineer
Connor Chin, Senior Application Consultant

Provider of medical staff scheduling software and solutions. The company's services include scheduling, keeping backups, technical support, and training.

Lightsand Communications BR
745 Emerson St
Palo Alto CA 94301
P: 619-865-6400 PRC:68
www.lightsand.com
Email: sales@lightsand.com
Estab: 1999

Richard Czech, CEO

Developer of SAN connectivity products. The company is engaged in troubleshooting and maintenance services.

Lightway Industries HQ
28435 Industry Dr [N]
Valencia CA 91355
P: 661-257-0286 F: 661-257-0201 PRC:243
www.lightwayind.com
Emp: 1-10 Estab: 1980

Jared Duncan, CEO
Larisa Duncan, CFO & Secretary

Designer, manufacturer and distributor of commercial, architectural lighting fixtures.

Lightwind Corp HQ
101 H St Ste E
Petaluma CA 94952
P: 707-981-4301 F: 925-820-2972 PRC:50
www.lightwindcorp.com
Email: info@lightwindcorp.com
Estab: 2001

Gary Powell, CTO
Robin Halloran, Accounts Manager

Provider of semiconductor manufacturing solutions. The company also deals with chemical analysis, process assessment, and refurbishment services.

Lilee Systems   HQ
91 E Tasman Dr Ste 150
San Jose CA 95134
P: 408-988-8672   F: 408-988-8813   PRC:61
lileesystems.com
Email: sales@lileesystems.com
Estab: 2009

Jia-Ru Li, CEO
Lele Nardin, VP of Engineering
Yale Lee, VP of Technology
Jessica Sweeney, Senior Director of Market &
Product Strategy
Sam Kanakamedala, Director of Product Management & Market Development

Provider of integrated services that include
system prediction modeling, project management,
and training services for the railroad industry.

LIM innovations Inc   HQ
424 Ninth St
San Francisco CA 94103
P: 844-888-8546   F: 415-651-9444   PRC:190
www.liminnovations.com
Email: info@liminnovations.com
Estab: 2012

Andrew Pedtke, CEO

Designer and manufacturer of prosthetic sockets
for amputees. The company offers custom-molded, adjustable, and modular prosthetic sockets.

LimFlow Inc   BR
2934 Scott Blvd
Santa Clara CA 95054
P: 888-478-7705   F: 408-898-1459   PRC:189
www.limflow.com
Email: info@limflow.com
Estab: 2012

Tim Lenihan, Founder & CTO
Dan Rose, CEO
Paul Limmer, VP of Finance & Administration
Thomas Engels, VP of Clinical & Regulatory
Affairs
Zachary Woodson, VP of Regulatory Affairs &
Quality

Designer and developer of LimFlow percutaneous
deep vein arterialization system to restore blood
flow to the ischemic foot.

Lin Engineering   HQ
16245 Vineyard Blvd
Morgan Hill CA 95037
P: 408-919-0200   F: 408-919-0201   PRC:150
www.linengineering.com
Email: sales@linengineering.com
Estab: 1987

Ted T. Lin, President
Richard Badgerow, Chief Technical Engineer
Ryan L., EVP
Melissa Filice, Director of Human Resources
Belal Azim, Director of Marketing & Sales

Manufacturer of step motors. The company's
products include BLDC motors, optical encoders,
gearheads, and accessories.

LinaTech USA   HQ
1294 Kifer Rd Ste 705
Sunnyvale CA 94086
P: 408-733-2051   F: 408-733-2045   PRC:189
www.linatech.com
Estab: 1998

Terry Lane, Director of Sales & Marketing

Manufacturer of medical devices and software for
the treatment of cancer through radiotherapy. The
company also supplies informatics software for
managing cancer clinics.

Linden Research Inc   HQ
945 Battery St
San Francisco CA 94111
P: 415-243-9000   F: 415-243-9045   PRC:323
www.lindenlab.com
Email: business@lindenlab.com
Estab: 1999

Rod Humble, CEO

Designer and developer of digital entertainment
solutions. The company's products include Desura, Patterns, and Versu.

Lindsley Lighting LLC   HQ
4871 Sunrise Dr Ste 101
Martinez CA 94553
P: 925-254-1860   F: 888-695-3699   PRC:243
www.lindsleylighting.com
Email: info@lindsleylighting.com
Estab: 1989

Karen Jess-Lindsley, CEO
Alan Lindsley, Chief Design Officer

Provider of lighting solutions focusing on design,
sales, installation, and delivery. The company
serves residential and commercial properties.

Lineage Cell Therapeutics Inc   HQ
2173 Salk Ave Ste 200
Carlsbad CA 92008
P: 510-871-4188   PRC:34
lineagecell.com
Email: contact@lineagecell.com
Estab: 1990
Sales: $3M to $10M

Brian Culley, CEO
Brandi Roberts, CFO
Derek Kelaita, VP of Business Development
Hal Sternberg, VP of Research
Francois Binette, SVP of Global Head of R&D

Provider of cell-based technologies and regenerative medicine for the treatment of chronic and
degenerative diseases.

Linear Industries Ltd   HQ
1850 Enterprise Way   [N]
Monrovia CA 91016
P: 626-303-1130   F: 626-303-2035   PRC:80
www.linearindustries.com
Email: linear@linearindustries.com
Estab: 1970

Tony Angelica, Owner
Jean Cade, CFO
Gary Wester, VP of Sales
Michael Brown, Specialist

Manufacturer and distributor of electronic and
mechanical automation control products.

Linear Integrated Systems   HQ
4042 Clipper Ct
Fremont CA 94538-6540
P: 510-490-9160   F: 510-353-0261   PRC:208
www.linearsystems.com
Email: sales@linearsystems.com
Estab: 1987

Will Hall, Founder
Timothy S. McCune, President
John Michael Hall, Chairman
Cindy L. Johnson, CEO

Manufacturer of semiconductor products. The
company offers bipolar transistors, input protection
diodes, resistors, and low leakage amplifiers.

Linguastat Inc   HQ
330 Townsend St Ste 108
San Francisco CA 94107
P: 415-814-2999   PRC:67
www.linguastat.com
Email: sales@linguastat.com
Estab: 2004

Linda Hayes, COO
Jacob Portnoff, Senior Content Architect & Lead
Engineer & Director of the Voise Center of Innovation

Provider of web based services to corporations
and government agencies. The company offers
optimized product descriptions for millions of
landing pages.

Linkbit Inc   HQ
3180 De La Cruz Blvd Ste 200
Santa Clara CA 95054-2434
P: 408-969-9940   F: 408-273-6009   PRC:97
www.linkbit.com
Email: contactus@linkbit.com
Estab: 2000

Tanya Sukhar, Senior Software Engineer

Manufacturer of network equipment. The company
primarily caters to service providers and network
operators.

Liqua-Tech Corp   HQ
3501 N State St
Ukiah CA 95482
P: 707-462-3555   F: 707-462-3576   PRC:159
www.liqua-tech.com
Email: ltc@liqua-tech.com
Estab: 1984

Marta Sligh, President
Ed Bruce, Director of Operations

Manufacturer of precision measurement systems.
The company offers flow meters, gear trains, and
measuring chalmers.

Lite-On Trading USA Inc   HQ
720 S Hillview Dr   [N]
Milpitas CA 95035
P: 408-946-4873   F: 408-941-4596   PRC:322
www.us.liteon.com
Estab: 1975

Sander Su, AVP

Manufacturer and distributor of power conversion
equipment, chassis, systems, keyboards and
much more.

Live Oak Associates Inc BR
6840 Via Del Oro Ste 220
San Jose CA 95119
P: 408-224-8300   F: 408-224-1411   PRC:142
loainc.com
Email: info@loainc.com
Estab: 1995

Davinna Ohlson, Director of Ecological Services
Tom Haney, Director of Cartography GIS
Pamela Peterson, Senior Project Manager & Plant
& Wetland Ecologist
Katrina Krakow, Project Manager & Staff Ecologist
Geoff Cline, Senior Project Manager

Provider of ecological and biological consulting
services. The company is also focused on environmental permitting and planning activities.

LiveAction HQ
3500 West Bayshore Rd
Palo Alto CA 94303
P: 408-217-6501   PRC:319
www.liveaction.com
Estab: 2007

John K. Smith, EVP & CTO & Founder
Stephen Stuut, CEO
Pete Tyrrell, CRO
Francine Geist, CFO
Joe O'Connor, SVP of Channels & Alliances

Provider of network visibility and performance
diagnostics products. The company focuses on
network and security forensics.

Livermore Software Technology Corp HQ
7374 Las Positas Rd
Livermore CA 94551
P: 925-449-2500   F: 925-449-2507   PRC:323
www.lstc.com
Email: support@lstc.com
Estab: 1970

John O. Hallquist, President
Guo Yong, Senior R&D Engineer
Todd Slavik, Engineer
Wei Hu, Senior Scientist
Ushnish Basu, Senior Scientist

Developer of software for automotive crashworthi-
ness, metal forming, aerospace, and other needs.
The company also offers training.

Livescribe Inc HQ
7677 Oakport St 12th Fl   [N]
Oakland CA 94621
P: 510-777-0071   PRC:322
Www.livescribe.com
Email: cs@livescribe.com
Emp: 51-200

James Marggraff, Contact

Provider and developer of mobile computing
platform.

Livevol Inc BR
220 Montgomery St Ste 360
San Francisco CA 94104
P: 312-786-7400   F: 415-358-5818   PRC:322
livevol.com
Email: sales@livevol.com
Estab: 1973

Edward T. Tilly, Chairman & CEO & President
Alex Klein, Senior System Engineer

Designer and developer of customized data solutions. The company's services include consulting
and technical support.

LiveVox Inc HQ
655 Montgomery St Ste 1000
San Francisco CA 94111
P: 415-671-6000   PRC:326
www.livevox.com
Email: info@livevox.com
Estab: 2001

Larry Siegel, Co-Founder & EVP of Product
Management
Louis Summe, Co-Founder & CEO
Dusty Whitesell, SVP of Marketing Services &
Chief Evangelist
Otis Siegel, Chief Culture Officer
Randy Nelson, SVP of Technical Operations

Specializes in business analytics and related
services. The company serves the telecom and
healthcare industries.

LMI Net HQ
1700 Martin Luther King Jr Way
Berkeley CA 94709
P: 510-843-6389   F: 510-843-6390   PRC:325
www.lmi.net
Email: info@lmi.net
Estab: 1992

Gary Morrell, Owner
Wyatt Atkinson, Customer Service Manager
Michael Kuntz, Manager
Doran Mori, Systems Engineer
Christopher Whitehorn, Computer Repair Tech-
nician

Provider of solar-assisted Internet connections.
The company offers computer repair, IT services,
web site development, and virus removal services.

Loadstar Sensors Inc HQ
48521 Warm Springs Blvd Ste 308
Fremont CA 94539
P: 510-274-1872   F: 510-952-3700   PRC:76
www.loadstarsensors.com
Email: info@loadstarsensors.com
Estab: 2004

Div Harish, CEO
Jesus Salcedo, Sales Manager

Manufacturer of sensors and load cells with wireless output, used in medical device, automotive,
aerospace, consumer and other industries.

Lobcom Inc HQ
185 Berry Ave Ste 1600
San Francisco CA 94107
P: 847-630-9275   PRC:315
lob.com
Email: support@lob.com
Estab: 2013

Harry Zhang, Co-Founder
Leore Avidar, Co-Founder & CEO

Builds an API toolkit that allows organizations
to innovate, move faster, and better differentiate
themselves.

Locus Technologies HQ
299 Fairchild Dr
Mountain View CA 94043
P: 415-360-5889   PRC:142
www.locustec.com
Email: info@locustec.com
Estab: 1997

Neno Duplan, Founder & CEO
Wes Hawthorne, President
Sandeep Khabiya, VP of Software Engineering
Dan Ducasse, Director of Automation Services
Amelia Anderson, Manager of SaaS Marketing

Provider of web based environmental information
management systems. The company's services
include field installation, training, and technical
support.

Lodi Iron Works Inc HQ
820 S Sacramento St
Lodi CA 95240
P: 209-368-5395   F: 209-339-1453   PRC:80
www.lodiiron.com
Email: sales@lodiiron.com
Estab: 1946

Kevin Van Steenberge, President
Lodi Paul, Quality Control Manager

Provider of machine shop services. The company
offers in-house pattern making, tooling, machining, and iron casting services.

Logen Solutions USA HQ
3003 N First St Ste 307
San Jose CA 95134
P: 408-519-5771   PRC:319
www.logensol.com

Andrew Chang, VP

Provider of truck, container, pallet and carton
loading and packaging software. The company
offers solutions for cargo load planning.

Logosol Inc BR
5041 Robert J Mathews Pkwy Ste 100
El Dorado Hills CA 95762
P: 408-744-0974   F: 408-744-0977   PRC:233
www.logosolinc.com
Email: info@logosolinc.com

Daniel Minkov, Customer Relations Manager
Violin Zlatanov, Electronics Engineer
Vladimir Mihaylov, Applications Engineer
Kroum Mihaylov, Mechanical Engineer
George Georgiev, Software Engineer

Manufacturer and designer of motion control
components. The company's products are used in
semiconductor material handling applications.

Longevity Welding HQ
23591 Foley St
Hayward CA 94545
P: 877-566-4462   PRC:152
www.longevity-inc.com
Email: sales@lwelds.com
Estab: 2001

Simon Katz, President

Manufacturer of welding equipment. The company
also offers filler rods, generators, plasma cutters,
and related accessories.

Loomis Industries Inc   HQ
1204 Church St
St. Helena CA 94574
P: 707-963-4111   F: 707-963-3753   PRC:127
loomisinc.com
Email: info@loomisinc.com
Estab: 1974

Diana Bustamante, COO
Rick Avidano, Mechanical Engineer
James Cook, Technical Advisor

Provider of fabrication services. The company
specializes in the design, print, and analysis of
semiconductor components.

Loprest Water Treatment Co   HQ
2825 Franklin Canyon Rd
Rodeo CA 94572-2195
P: 510-799-3101   F: 510-799-7433   PRC:144
www.loprest.com
Email: sales@loprest.com
Estab: 1928

Randy Richey, President & Owner of Loprest
Water Treatment

Provider of water treatment systems design and
fabricating services. The company focuses on
media analysis and filter inspection.

Lor-Van Manufacturing   HQ
3307 Edward Ave
Santa Clara CA 95054
P: 408-980-1045   F: 408-980-1047   PRC:80
www.lor-vanmfg.com
Email: chris@lor-vanmfg.com
Estab: 2005

James Hemphill, General Manager
Ismelda Lopez, Manager of Engineering
Jose Barajas, Manager of Quality Assurance
Lorena Lopez, Accounting Manager & Member
Moriah Fernandez, Human Resource Manager

Provider of precision sheet metal fabrication, laser
cutting, welding, and electronic chassis and card
cage assembly services.

Lorentz Solution Inc   HQ
3375 Scott Blvd Ste 105
Santa Clara CA 95054
P: 408-922-0765   F: 408-716-4934   PRC:323
www.lorentzsolution.com
Email: sales@lorentzsolution.com
Estab: 2003

Shun Lee, Administrative Manager
Genhua Guan, Research & Development Manager
Nick Karneyenka, Senior Software Engineer
Hyungon Kim, Senior R&D Engineer

Developer of electronic design automation
software services. The company is engaged in
modeling and electromagnetic shielding.

Lorom Industrial Company Ltd   BR
39650 Liberty St Ste 400
Fremont CA 94538
P: 919-535-5830   PRC:62
www.lorom.com
Email: info@lorom.com
Estab: 1988

YT. Yuan, President
Terry Tung, CFO

Designer and manufacturer of standard and be-
spoke cables and cable assemblies. The company
offers services to the industrial and commercial
sectors.

Lorom West   HQ
39650 Liberty St Ste 400
Fremont CA 94538
P: 919-535-5830   PRC:106
www.loromwest.com
Email: sales@cable-connection.com
Estab: 1988

Greg Gaches, President & CEO

Manufacturer of PCB assemblies, turnkey OEM/
ODM products and custom cable and wire harnesses. The company offers industry solutions.

Los Gatos Research Inc   HQ
3055 Orchard Dr
San Jose CA 95134
P: 650-965-7772   F: 650-965-7074   PRC:11
www.lgrinc.com
Email: icos.sales@ca.abb.com
Estab: 1993

Douglas Baer, President
Manish Gupta, CTO
Thomas Owano, VP of Engineering
Andrew Fahrland, Senior Scientist

Manufacturer of analyzers for the measurement
of trace gases and isotopes. The company serves
the industrial and environmental sectors.

Loudhouse Creative   HQ
2903 W Wyoming Ave   [N]
Burbank CA 91505
P: 818-643-1725   PRC:323
www.loudhousecreative.com
Email: francesca@loudhousecreative.com

Francesca Fuges, Founder

Publisher of hand-drawn and letterpress printed
greeting cards.

LP Glass Blowing Inc   HQ
2322 Calle Del Mundo
Santa Clara CA 95054
P: 408-988-7561   F: 408-988-8981   PRC:286
lpglassblowing.com
Email: sales@lpglassblowing.com
Estab: 1974

Ivan Katalinic, Quartz Welder

Provider of high-precision quartz ware and glass
products. The company offers research and development assistance services.

LS Biopath Inc   HQ
18809 Cox Ave Ste 140
Saratoga CA 95070
P: 408-464-4051   F: 408-963-6352   PRC:186
lsbiopath.com
Estab: 2007

Moshe Sarfaty, CEO

Developer of medical products and technologies
for the unmet need for real time imaging of ex-
cised tissue during breast cancer surgery.

LSA Associates Inc   BR
2215 Fifth St
Berkeley CA 94710
P: 510-540-7331   PRC:142
lsa.net
Estab: 1976

Les Card, Principal & CEO
Natalie Brodie, Cultural Resource Manager
Natalie Frey, Associate & Office Manager
Zhe Chen, Air Quality & Climate Change Manager
Patty Linder, Graphics Manager

Provider of consulting services. The company
focuses on environmental, transportation, and
planning services.

LSI Design & Integration Corp   HQ
2081 Forest Ave
San Jose CA 95124
P: 408-283-8540   F: 408-283-8544   PRC:204
www.ldic.com
Email: sales@ldic.com
Estab: 1996

Mehdi Bathaee, Market Leader

Designer and manufacturer of custom chips. The
company offers storage, communication, imaging,
and memory components.

LSVP International Inc   HQ
12755 Alto Verde Ln
Los Altos CA 94022
P: 650-969-1000   F: 650-969-2300   PRC:189
www.lsvpusa.com
Email: info@lsvpusa.com
Estab: 1992

Sophia Pesotchinsky, Owner

Manufacturer of flexible and semi-rigid endoscopic instruments. The company's services include
engineering and distribution.

LTX-Credence Corp   HQ
1355 California Cir   [N]
Milpitas CA 95035
P: 408-635-4300   F: 408-635-4985   PRC:65
www.ltxc.com
Email: info@ltxc.com
Estab: 1976

David G. Tacelli, CEO & President

Manufacturer of linear and digital test equipment.

Lucas Signatone Corp   HQ
393-J Tomkins Ct
Gilroy CA 95020
P: 408-848-2851   F: 408-848-5763   PRC:13
www.signatone.com
Email: sales@signatone.com
Estab: 1965

James Dickson, VP of Logistics
L. Brian Dickson, VP of Engineering
Marc Pinard, Sales Manager
Richard Dickson, Sales Manager
Loren Dickson, Sales Manager

Manufacturer of micro-probe stations, holders,
and accessories. The company's products are
used in resistivity test equipment.

Lucero HQ
193 Stauffer Blvd
San Jose CA 95125
P: 408-298-6001 F: 408-298-6002 PRC:78
www.luceromfg.com
Email: sales@luceromfg.com
Estab: 1978

Serjik Avanes, VP
Karen Schultz, Regional Sales Manager

Manufacturer of electronic products. The company's products include cables, harnesses, and electromechanical sub assemblies.

Lucidport Technology Inc HQ
19287 San Marcos Rd
Saratoga CA 95070
P: 408-720-8800 PRC:94
www.lucidport.com
Estab: 2004

Weiti Liu, President
Angel Chien, Business Analyst

Provider of semiconductor solutions. The company offers USB and wireless USB controllers for printers, scanners, digital cameras, and TV tuners.

Lucidworks HQ
235 Montgomery St Ste 500
San Francisco CA 94104
P: 415-329-6515 F: 650-620-9540 PRC:325
lucidworks.com
Email: contact-sales@lucidworks.com
Estab: 2008

Will Hayes, CEO
Reade Frank, COO
Grant Ingersoll, CTO
Gerald Kanapathy, VP of Products
Andy Wibbels, Director of Marketing

Provider of commercial foundation for architecture, design, development, and deployment of search solutions built with lucid works enterprise.

Luhdorff & Scalmanini Consulting Engineers HQ
500 First St
Woodland CA 95695
P: 530-661-0109 F: 530-661-6806 PRC:142
www.lsce.com
Email: admin@lsce.com
Estab: 1980

Vicki Kretsinger Grabert, President & Senior Principal Hydrologist
Jason Coleman, Project Engineer
Chris Curtis, Contact
Pavan Dhaliwal, Hydrogeologist

Provider of consulting and engineering services that include investigation, use, protection, development, and management of groundwater resources.

Lumasense Technologies Inc HQ
3301 Leonard Ct
Santa Clara CA 95054-2054
P: 408-727-1600 F: 408-727-1677 PRC:212
www.lumasenseinc.com
Email: info@lumasenseinc.com
Estab: 2005

Yuval Wasserman, CEO
Isabel Yang, CTO & SVP
Neil D. Brinker, COO & EVP
Paul Oldham, CFO & EVP
Stefan Warnke, Chief Technologist

Provider of temperature and gas sensing instruments for the energy, industrial, clean technology, and commercial markers.

M-188

Lumedx Corp HQ
555 Twelfth St Ste 2060
Oakland CA 94607
P: 800-966-0699 F: 510-419-3699 PRC:258
lumedx.com
Email: support@lumedx.com
Estab: 1990

Allyn McAuley, CEO & Founder
Chris Winquist, President & COO
Jay Soni, CFO
Laurel Shearer, EVP

Provider of cardiovascular information and imaging systems. The company specializes in cloud-powered healthcare solutions.

Lumen Therapeutics LLC HQ
325 Sharon Park Dr Ste 753
Menlo Park CA 94025
P: 650-450-4439 PRC:34
www.lumentherapeutics.com

Garrison Fathman, Director & Co-Founder
Paul McGrane, Director & Co-Founder
Michael Danaher, Director

Provider of therapeutic solutions. The company focuses on the proprietary drugs based on oligo-L-arginine.

Lumenetix Inc HQ
4742 Scotts Valley Dr
Scotts Valley CA 95066
P: 877-805-7284 PRC:243
lumenetix.com
Email: info@lumenetix.com
Estab: 2009

Yuko Nakazawa, Senior Optical Engineer
David Bowers, Senior Development Engineer
Linh Doan, QC Technician
Kellie Mages, Controller

Supplier of LED light engines, LED light modules, and LED components. The company also offers reflectors and surface mount LED light fixings.

Lumenis DH
2033 Gateway Pl Ste 300
San Jose CA 95110
P: 877-586-3647 F: 408-764-3999 PRC:187
www.lumenis.com
Email: information@lumenis.com
Estab: 1973

Brad Oliver, VP & Regional President of Americas
Tzipi Ozer-Armon, CEO
Hadas Padan, VP of Medical Business Group
Karen Smith, VP of Regulatory Affairs & Quality
Roy Ramati, SVP of EMEA & Business Development

Provider of minimally-invasive clinical solutions. The company develops and commercializes energy-based technologies.

Lumens Integration Inc RH
4116 Clipper Ct
Fremont CA 94538
P: 888-542-3235 F: 510-252-1389 PRC:60
www.lumens.com.tw
Estab: 1998

Rita Liu, VP of Operations

Designer and developer of visual presentation solutions. The company offers document cameras, video conferencing cameras, and charging carts.

Lumeras LLC HQ
207 McPherson St Ste C
Santa Cruz CA 95060
P: 650-575-7448 F: 831-425-1845 PRC:172
www.lumeras-labs.com
Email: info@lumeras-labs.com
Estab: 2006

Andrew Merriam, President

Developer and manufacturer of short-wavelength laser sources for materials characterization and chemical and biological analysis.

Lumina Decision Systems Inc HQ
26010 Highland Way
Los Gatos CA 95033-9758
P: 650-212-1212 F: 650-240-2230 PRC:316
www.lumina.com
Email: info@lumina.com
Estab: 1991

Max Henrion, CEO
Lonnie Chrisman, CTO
Kimberley Mullins, Senior Consulting Analyst

Provider of analytical training and consulting services. The company is engaged in technical support services.

Lumiphore Inc HQ
600 Bancroft Way Ste B
Berkeley CA 94710-2224
P: 510-898-1190 PRC:34
www.lumiphore.com
Email: info@lumiphore.com

Kenneth N. Raymond, President & Chairman
David Lund, CFO
Stephen H. Blose, Chief Business Development Officer
Nathaniel Butlin, Chief Intellectual Property Officer
Darren Magda, VP of Research & Development

Developer of proprietary lanthanide technology. The company develops and markers biological detection reagents.

Lumiquick Diagnostics Inc HQ
2946 Scott Blvd
Santa Clara CA 95054
P: 408-855-0061 F: 408-855-0063 PRC:186
lumiquick.co
Email: info@lumiquick.com

Charles Yu, Founder & President
Jeff Wang, Quality Systems Manager
Rongrong Zhao, Office Manager

Manufacturer of diagnostic products and other raw materials. The company is engaged in distribution services.

Luna's Sheet Metal Inc HQ
3120 Molinardo St
Santa Clara CA 95054
P: 408-492-1260 F: 408-492-1585 PRC:80
www.lunasheetmetal.com
Email: lunamtl@pacbell.net
Estab: 1995

Antonio Luna, President
Lupe Luna, CFO

Provider of metal fabrication and precision metal working services for the computer electronics, telecommunications, and automotive industries.

Lunagraphica Inc   HQ
720 S Wolfe Rd Ste 324
Sunnyvale CA 94086
P: 408-962-1588   PRC:325
lunagraphica.com
Email: info@lunagraphica.com
Estab: 2004

Cindy Couling, President & Creative Director
Robert Nicholson, VP of Technology
Falline Danforth, Office Manager

Provider of Internet marketing and consulting
solutions. The company offers services in graphic
design, website design, and web development.

Luthier's Mercantile International Inc   HQ
7975 Cameron Dr Bldg 1600   [N]
Windsor CA 95492
P: 707-687-2020   F: 707-687-2014   PRC:190
www.lmii.com
Estab: 1994

Chris Herrod, Manager of Sales

Distributor of exotic tone woods, professional tools
and parts to stringed instrument makers.

Luxience Technologies   HQ
2550 Zanker Rd
San Jose CA 95131
P: 669-235-5778   PRC:212
www.luxience.com
Email: info@luxience.com
Estab: 1988

Zoltan Albert, President

Provider of precision semiconductor equipment.
The company specializes in design, fabrication,
and supply of semiconductor equipment.

Lynch Marks LLC   HQ
2105 Bancroft Way
Berkeley CA 94720
P: 510-559-7200   PRC:322
www.psship.com
Estab: 1982

Ryan Emery, Director of Development
Jack P. Kern, Help Desk Lead
Roger Gibby, Senior Application Architect &
Developer

Provider of software development and technology
solutions focused on shipping applications. The
company focuses on consulting and package
tracking.

Lynx Media Inc   HQ
12501 Chandler Blvd Ste 202   [N]
Valley Village CA 91607
P: 800-451-5969   PRC:319
www.lynxmedia.us
Email: sales@lynxmedia.com
Estab: 1988

Len Latimer, President

Developer of inventory control and order entry
software.

Lynx Software Technologies   HQ
855 Embedded Way
San Jose CA 95138
P: 408-979-3900   F: 408-979-3920   PRC:322
www.lynx.com
Email: inside@lynx.com
Estab: 1988

Gurjot Singh, CEO
Will Keegan, CTO
Keith Shea, CRO
Ingrid Osborne, VP of Finance
Arun Subbarao, VP of Engineering

Developer of software technologies. The company
offers development tools, real-time monitoring
systems, and secure virtualization products.

Lytrod Software Inc   HQ
2573 Claybank Rd Ste 4
Fairfield CA 94533
P: 707-422-9221   F: 707-429-5179   PRC:323
www.lytrod.com
Email: sales@lytrod.com
Estab: 1985

Karen Lytle, EVP
Michael Lytle, Sales Operations Manager

Provider of variable data print software prod-
ucts. The company's products include VisionDP
Production and Automate, Proform Designer, and
Office Designer.

M & M Machine   HQ
10074 Ster Rd
Auburn CA 95602
P: 530-268-2112   F: 530-268-6720   PRC:80
www.mandmmachine.com
Email: sales@mandmmachine.com
Estab: 1972

Chris Duckett, Machine Shop Owner

Designer and manufacturer of machined parts and
components for automotive, laser, audio and video
and body building equipment manufacturers.

MAR's Engineering Company Inc   HQ
699 Montague Ave
San Leandro CA 94577
P: 510-483-0541   F: 510-483-1829   PRC:80
www.marseng.com
Email: info@marseng.com
Estab: 1964

Reine Ambrosio, Founder

Manufacturer of screw machines. The company
also offers prototyping, fabrication, and assembly
services.

M&L Precision Machining Inc   HQ
18665 Madrone Pkwy
Morgan Hill CA 95037
P: 408-224-2138   F: 408-224-2169   PRC:80
www.mlprecision.com
Email: sales@engbrecht.com
Estab: 1978

Karen Laisure, CFO
Mark Laisure, COO
Ross Laisure, VP of Sales
Harold Laisure, VP
Dave Gonzales, Director of Quality

Provider of machine shop services. The company
offers precision fabricated components, semiconductors, and related devices.

M-T Metal Fabrication Inc   HQ
536 A Lewelling Blvd
San Leandro CA 94579
P: 510-357-5262   F: 510-351-5506   PRC:88
www.mtmetalfab.com
Estab: 1950

Ross Bigler, Owner
Justin Bigler, VP

Provider of sheet metal solutions. The company
offers CNC laser cutting, precision welding, gain-
ing, PEM fastening, and silk screen.

M K Products Inc   HQ
16882 Armstrong Ave   [N]
Irvine CA 92606
P: 949-863-1234   F: 949-474-1428   PRC:209
www.mkprod.com/Contact-Us.html
Estab: 1966

Dana E. Paquin, Manager of Human Resources

Supplier of welding apparatus.

MIB Chock LLC   HQ
1048 24th St   [N]
Santa Monica CA 90403
P: 310-829-1612   PRC:45
www.mibchock.com
Estab: 1982

Margaret Chock, Principal

Provider of an objective, third-party view of information systems issues to support new development, due diligence review, or litigation.

M2 Antenna Systems Inc   HQ
4402 N Selland Ave
Fresno CA 93722
P: 559-432-8873   PRC:61
www.m2inc.com
Email: sales@m2inc.com
Estab: 1995

Mathew Staal, General Manager
Carrie Patton, Machinist

Manufacturer of antennas and systems. The
company specializes in computer aided antenna
design and simulation, and testing and prototyping
services.

MabPlex USA Inc   BR
4059 Clipper Ct
Fremont CA 94538
P: 510-830-1065   PRC:34
mabplexinc.com
Email: info@mabplexinc.com
Estab: 2013

Jianmin Fang, Chairman
Marie Zhu, CEO
Andrew Huang, CSO
James Ruan, SVP of Quality
Kenneth Meek, VP of Marketing & Business
Development

Developer and manufacture of biopharmaceuticals. The company also offers contract services
from DNA to finished drug product.

Mac Cal HQ
1737 Junction Ave
San Jose CA 95112
P: 408-441-1435 F: 408-441-1440 PRC:80
www.maccal.com
Email: documents@maccal.com
Estab: 1964

Michael Hall, President & CEO
Stacey Serio, Admin Assistant to President & IT
Justin Fontaine, Project Manager
Katrina England, Manager of New Business
Development
Jesus Contreras, Business Development Manager

Provider of sheet metals, assembly, cables and
harnesses and engineering tools. The company
deals with engineering services.

Machaon Diagnostics Inc HQ
3023 Summit St
Oakland CA 94609-3408
P: 510-839-5600 F: 510-839-6153 PRC:303
machaondiagnostics.com
Email: lab@machaondiagnostics.com
Estab: 2003

Michael Ero, Founder & CEO
Brad H. Lewis, Director of Medical
Bjorn Stromsness, Director of Client Services
Tamara Mihailovski, Technical Supervisor
Sheila Flaherty, Technical Supervisor

Provider of laboratory services in diagnosis, treatment and monitoring of hemostatic and thrombotic
conditions.

Machinist Group HQ
7200 Alexander St
Gilroy CA 95020
P: 408-842-8437 F: 408-842-0246 PRC:80
www.machinistcoop.com
Email: info@machinistgroup.com
Estab: 1980

Lloyd Hennessy, Founder & Co-Owner
Shawn Hennessy, VP & Co-Owner

Manufacturer of precision machined parts. The
company serves defense, IR, laser components,
prototype, and production industries.

Macken Instruments Inc HQ
3196 Coffey Ln Ste 604
Santa Rosa CA 95403
P: 707-566-2110 F: 707-566-2119 PRC:171
www.macken.com
Email: info@macken.com

Michael Gibbs, Operations Manager

Manufacturer of devices for measuring and
analyzing laser device power output. The company
offers laser power and beam probes and thermal
image plates.

Macro Plastics Inc HQ
2250 Huntington Dr
Fairfield CA 94533
P: 707-437-1200 PRC:280
macroplastics.com
Email: info@macroplastics.com

Warren MacDonald, CEO & President
Greg Sutton, CFO
Peter Piccioli, VP of Services
Jeff Mitchell, VP of Operations
Al Restaino, Director of New Business Development

Provider of agricultural, food processing, and
industrial bins. The company's services include
recycling, design, and business development.

MacroGenics Inc BR
3280 Bayshore Blvd Ste 200
Brisbane CA 94005
P: 650-624-2600 F: 650-624-2693 PRC:251
www.macrogenics.com
Email: info@macrogenics.com

James Karrels, SVP & CFO & Secretary
Eric Risser, SVP of Business Development & Port-
folio Management & Chief Business Officer
Lynn Cilinski, VP of Controller & Treasurer
Tom Spitznagel, SVP of BioPharmaceutical Devel-
opment & Manufacturing
Stanford Stewart, VP of Clinical Oncology Re-
search

Developer, manufacturer, and marketer of innovative antibody-based therapeutics for the treatment
of cancer and autoimmune disorders.

Macronix America Inc LH
680 N McCarthy Blvd Ste 200
Milpitas CA 95035
P: 408-262-8887 F: 408-262-8810 PRC:96
www.macronix.com
Estab: 1989

Mariano Bongulto, Quality Assurance Manager
& FAE
Fazail Khan, Manager of Marketing & Business
Development

Manufacturer of integrated device. The company
offers application driven system solutions and
non-volatile memory semiconductor solutions.

Macrotron Systems Inc HQ
44235 Nobel Dr
Fremont CA 94538
P: 510-683-9600 PRC:211
www.macrotronsystems.com
Email: macsales@macrotronsystems.com
Estab: 1984

Anita Ting, CFO
Debbie Chiu, Manufacture Manager
Pal Singh, Manufacturing Engineer
Vivian L. Lin, Accounting Analyst
Scott Blair, Business Developer

Designer and manufacturer of memory modules.
The company provides services such as electronics assembly and testing.

Magee Scientific Co HQ
1916A ML King Jr Way
Berkeley CA 94704
P: 510-845-2801 F: 510-845-7137 PRC:235
www.mageesci.com
Email: mail@mageesci.com
Estab: 1986

Tony Hansen, Owner & Principal Scientist
Sebastijan Marinic, General Manager

Provider of measurement instruments such as
aethalometers, transmissometers, and their
accessories for monitoring air quality and source
emissions.

Maggiora Bros Drilling Inc HQ
595 Airport Blvd
Watsonville CA 95076
P: 831-724-1338 F: 831-724-3228 PRC:144
www.maggiorabros.com
Estab: 1962

Mark Maggiora, Owner

Provider of water well drilling and pump installation services. The company specializes in hydrologic cycle such as evaporation and condensation.

Magnet Systems Inc HQ
435 Tasso St Ste 100
Palo Alto CA 94301
P: 650-329-5904 PRC:322
www.magnet.com
Estab: 2008

Alfred Chuang, Founder & Chairman
Hanju Kim, Director of Mobile Solutions
Nicole Laskowski, News Director
Susan Fogarty, Editorial Director
David Essex, Executive Editor

Provider of mobile apps with software, infrastructure and tools to build enterprise-grade mobile
apps. The company serves enterprises.

Magnetic Circuit Elements HQ
1540 Moffett St
Salinas CA 93905
P: 831-757-8752 F: 831-757-5478 PRC:214
www.mcemagnetics.com
Email: sales@mcemagnetics.com

Jedediah Koch, Design Engineer
Abigail Bufil, Purchasing & Electronic Assembly
Group Leader

Manufacturer of miniature transformers and inductors. The company's products include chokes,
inductors, transformers, and sine wave inverters.

Magnum Towers Inc HQ
9370 Elder Creek Rd
Sacramento CA 95829
P: 916-381-5053 F: 916-381-2144 PRC:61
www.magnumtowers.com
Estab: 1976

Jeff Styler, Project Manager

Provider of self-supporting and guy towers, and
accessories such as safety climbs, ice bridges,
antenna mounts, anti-climb devices, and insulators.

Magtech & Power Conversion Inc HQ
1146 E Ash Ave [N]
Fullerton CA 92831
P: 714-451-0106 F: 714-451-0111 PRC:214
www.magtechpower.com
Emp: 11-50 Estab: 1998

Tu Do, VP of Operation
Viet Pho, Magnetics Design Engineer
Tien Tran, Engineer

Designer and manufacturer of custom magnets.

Mailshell Inc   HQ
2336B Walsh Ave
Santa Clara CA 95051
P: 415-294-4242   F: 408-904-5079   PRC:325
www.mailshell.com
Email: info@mailshell.com
Estab: 1999

Tonny Yu, Founder & CEO
Manuel Mejia, CTO
Eytan Urbas, VP of Products & Business Development
Senate Taka, Software Engineer

Provider of traffic reputation software engines. The company also specializes in anti-spam and anti-phishing software engines.

Makel Engineering Inc   HQ
1585 Marauder St
Chico CA 95973
P: 530-895-2770   F: 530-895-2777   PRC:86
www.makelengineering.com
Email: info@makelengineering.com
Estab: 1995

Darby Makel, President

Developer and provider of products and services for aviation, space, military, and commercial applications.

Mako Industries   HQ
831 N K St
Livermore CA 94551
P: 925-209-7985   F: 925-396-6084   PRC:142
makoindustries.com

Gide Kouatchou, Founder
Mako Nesler, Owner
Gunnar Bredek, VP
Robert Larsen, VP
Eric Johnson, General Manager

Manufacturer of remediation systems for the environmental industry. The company is focused on field and carbon change out services.

Malaster Company Inc   HQ
3291 Edward Ave
Santa Clara CA 95054
P: 877-625-2783   F: 408-982-3295   PRC:212
malaster.com
Email: contact@malaster.com
Estab: 1988

Michael Cordingley, President
Melissa Hamro, Sales Manager

Provider of packing materials. The company specializes in offering package and shipping solutions for semiconductor industries.

Malcolm Drilling Company Inc   HQ
92 Natoma St Ste 400
San Francisco CA 94105
P: 415-901-4400   F: 415-901-4421   PRC:159
www.malcolmdrilling.com
Estab: 1962

Barry Kannon, EVP & CAO & Vice-Chairman of the Board
John M. Malcolm, CEO & Chairman of the Board
Al Rasband, President & COO
Derek Yamashita, VP & CFO & Secretary & Treasure
Peter Faust, VP of Business Development

Provider of specialty foundation industry services. The company is engaged in deep foundations, dewatering, and design build services.

Marathon Products Inc   HQ
14500 Doolittle Dr
San Leandro CA 94577-1109
P: 510-562-6450   F: 510-562-6408   PRC:189
www.marathonproducts.com
Email: web-inquiry@marathonproducts.com
Estab: 1991

Jon Y. Nakagawa, Founder & President & CEO
Greg Reel, Scientist & Chief Engineer
John Perry, VP of Sales & Marketing
Martin Thang, Calibration Engineer
Mikkel Ridley, Wireless & Network Specialist

Manufacturer of equipment for collecting data on temperature for use in packaging and shipping industries.

Marburg Technology Inc   HQ
304 Turquoise St   [N]
Milpitas CA 95035
P: 408-262-8400   PRC:109
www.glidewrite.com
Estab: 1988

Francis Burga, President

Designer and manufacturer of precision components and assemblies for the data storage and much more industries.

Marc Boogay   HQ
1584 Whispering Palm Dr   [N]
Oceanside CA 92056
P: 760-407-4000   F: 760-407-4004   PRC:139
www.boogay.com
Estab: 1988

Marc Boogay, Owner & Engineering Consultant
Claudia Padilla, Engineering Technician

Provider of phase I and II environmental site assessments, the design of remediation for contaminated soil or groundwater, monitoring progress in site remediation, asbestos surveys in buildings, designs asbestos abatements and asbestos operation management plans, building engineering inspection, seismic and probable maximum loss reports.

Marin Biologic Laboratories Inc   HQ
378 Bel Marin Keys Blvd
Novato CA 94949
P: 415-883-8000   F: 415-883-8011   PRC:34
www.marinbio.com
Email: marinbio378@marinbio.com
Estab: 1996

Tania Weiss, President & CEO
Peter Ralph, VP of Operations
Kevin Wilhelmsen, Senior Scientist

Provider of client research services. The company serves the pharmaceutical, biotechnology, diagnostic, agricultural, and legal markers.

Marin Software   HQ
123 Mission St 27th Fl
San Francisco CA 94105
P: 415-399-2580   PRC:319
www.marinsoftware.com
Email: info@marinsoftware.com
Estab: 2006
Sales: $30M to $100M

Christopher Lien, Co-Founder
Wister Walcott, Co-Founder & EVP of Products & Technology
David A. Yovanno, CEO
Matt Ackley, CMO
Bob Bertz, CFO

Developer of software products and provides software design and development for the architecture, engineering, and construction industries.

Mark-Costello Co   HQ
15351 Texaco Ave   [N]
Paramount CA 90723
P: 310-637-1851   F: 562-630-7960   PRC:319
www.mark-costello.com
Email: sales@mark-costello.com
Estab: 1956

Michael Kelleher, VP Partner

Wholesaler of waste compactors.

Market Vane Corp   HQ
PO Box 90490   [N]
Pasadena CA 91109
P: 626-395-7436   F: 626-795-7654   PRC:323
www.marketvane.net
Email: marketvane@earthlink.net
Estab: 1964

Richard Ishida, Contact

Provider of market sentiment analysis.

Marketo Inc   HQ
901 Mariners Island Blvd Ste 500
San Mateo CA 94404
P: 650-581-8001   F: 650-376-2331   PRC:322
www.marketo.com
Email: support@marketo.com
Estab: 2006

Shantanu Narayen, CEO
Abhay Parasnis, CTO
Ann Lewnes, CMO
Donna Morris, Chief Human Resource Officer & EVP
John Murphy, CFO

Provider of marketing automation software services. The company offers email and social marketing, marketing software, and digital marketing services.

Marki Microwave Inc   HQ
215 Vineyard Ct
Morgan Hill CA 95037
P: 408-778-4200   F: 408-778-4300   PRC:209
www.markimicrowave.com
Email: info@markimicrowave.com
Estab: 1991

Christopher Marki, CEO
Doug Jorgesen, Engineering Manager

Manufacturer of microwave mixers. The company offers adapters, amplifiers, couplers, diplexers, DC blocks, and other equipment.

MarkLogic Corp HQ
999 Skyway Rd
San Carlos CA 94070
P: 650-655-2300 F: 650-655-2310 PRC:319
www.marklogic.com
Estab: 2001

Christopher Lindblad, Founder
Michaline Todd, CMO
David Gorbet, SVP
Joe Pasqua, EVP
Linda Kato, VP of People

Provider of enterprise solutions. The company
serves the healthcare, legal, and insurance
industries.

Markmonitor Inc HQ
50 California St Ste 200
San Francisco CA 94111
P: 415-278-8400 F: 415-278-8444 PRC:326
www.markmonitor.com
Email: sales@markmonitor.com
Estab: 1999

Trina Schnapp, VP of Human Resources
Chandu K., Staff Engineer

Provider of brand protection, domain management, domain advisory, anti-piracy, and managed
services.

Marrone Bio Innovations Inc HQ
1540 Drew Ave
Davis CA 95618
P: 530-750-2800 PRC:34
marronebio.com
Email: info@marronebio.com
Estab: 2006

Jim Boyd, CFO
Keith Pitts, VP of Regulatory & Governmental
Affairs
Louis Boddy, Group Leader

Developer of naturally derived technologies of
pest management and plant health products used
in agricultural, ornamental, and water treatment.

Marseille Inc HQ
3211 Scott Blvd Ste 205
Santa Clara CA 95054
P: 408-855-9003 F: 408-855-9005 PRC:212
www.marseilleinc.com
Email: info@marseilleinc.com
Estab: 2005

Amine Chabane, Founder & CEO

Provider of video processing solutions. The
company's applications include home theaters and
audio and video receivers.

Martin Sprocket & Gear Inc BR
1199 Vine St
Sacramento CA 95811
P: 916-441-7172 F: 916-441-4600 PRC:78
www.martinsprocket.com
Estab: 1951

Ryan Davie, Manager of Western Regional

Manufacturer of industrial hand tools, convey-
or pulleys, and other products. The company
offers power transmission and material handling
products.

M-192

Martin Testing Laboratories HQ
4724 Arnold Ave
Mcclellan CA 95652
P: 916-920-4110 F: 916-920-4390 PRC:306
www.martintesting.com
Estab: 2000

Perry Martin, Owner

Provider of product assurance, failure analysis,
mechanical, metallurgical, electrical, and paint
and coating testing services.

**Martin's Metal Fabrication & Welding
Inc** HQ
7260 Lewis Rd
Vacaville CA 95687
P: 707-678-4117 F: 707-678-0251 PRC:159
www.martinsmetalfab.com
Email: info@martinsmetalfab.com
Estab: 1972

Carol Martin, Founder
David Martin, President & CEO
Chantelle Martin, VP & Secretary & Treasure
Tom Graef, General Manager

Provider of structural steel fabrication services
in Northern California. The company offers laser
cutting, beam line drilling, and other services.

Martinek Manufacturing HQ
42650 Osgood Rd
Fremont CA 94539-5627
P: 510-438-0357 F: 510-438-0359 PRC:80
www.martinek.com
Email: support@martinek.com
Estab: 2000

Mark Martinek, Owner
Charles Martinek, Owner
Jim Rumsey, Operations Manager

Provider of painting, plating, silk screening, sheet
metal fabrication, machining, and precision welding services.

Martinelli Environmental Graphics HQ
1829 Egbert Ave
San Francisco CA 94124
P: 415-468-4000 F: 415-468-4009 PRC:227
www.martinelli-graphics.com
Estab: 1989

Jack Martinelli, President & Owner
Jeff Osicka, VP
Kevin Hirst, Manager of Installation
Jake Wyatt, Installer & Fabricator

Provide of environmental graphic designing services. The company offers fabrication, installation,
and design build services.

Martinez and Turek Inc HQ
300 S Cedar Ave [N]
Rialto CA 92376
P: 909-820-6800 F: 909-873-3735 PRC:80
www.martinezandturek.com
Estab: 1980

Larry Tribe, President
John Romero, VP of Business Development

Provider of engineering and manufacturing
services.

Marvac Scientific Manufacturing Co HQ
3231 Monument Way Ste I
Concord CA 94518-2405
P: 925-825-4636 F: 925-825-4976 PRC:11
marvacscientific.com
Estab: 1959

Lori Stoos, Part Assembler

Provider of industrial grade belt drive vacuum
pumps. The company also offers cooling system
and other tools.

Marymonte Systems HQ
6630 Marymonte Court
San Jose CA 95120
P: 408-927-0606 PRC:68
www.marymonte.com
Email: sales@marymonte.com

John Lee, Owner

Provider of bar coding, wireless, time data collection, and RFID technology. The company offers
inventory control and material handling solutions.

Maselli Measurements Inc BR
7746 Lorraine Ave Ste 201
Stockton CA 95210
P: 209-474-9178 F: 209-474-9241 PRC:235
www.maselli.com
Email: maselliusa@maselli.com
Estab: 1948

Giovanni Maselli, CEO
Juan Pulido, Technical Sales Engineer

Provider of liquid measuring solutions. The company manufactures and distributes refractometers
and liquid analyzers for several industries.

Master Precision Machining HQ
2199 Ronald St
Santa Clara CA 95050
P: 408-727-0185 F: 408-727-0396 PRC:80
www.master-precision.com
Email: support@master-precision.com
Estab: 1969

Richard Rossi, Founder

Provider of precision machining services. The
company offers engineering, finishing, metrology,
and milling services.

Masterwork Electronics Inc HQ
891 Kuhn Dr Ste 216
Chula Vista CA 91914
P: 707-588-9906 F: 707-588-9908 PRC:209
www.masterworkelectronics.com
Email: sales@masterworkelectronics.com
Estab: 1994

L.J. Millick, Supply Chain Manager

Provider of printed circuit boards, cables, harness
assemblies, and wiring products. The company
is engaged in engineering and manufacturing
services.

Mateon Therapeutics Inc   HQ
701 Gateway Blvd Ste 210
S San Francisco CA 94080
P: 650-635-7000   F: 650-635-7001   PRC:254
www.mateon.com
Email: info@mateon.com
Estab: 1996

David Chaplin, CSO
Matthew Loar, CFO

Developer and provider of therapeutics. The company focuses on the treatment of acute myeloid leukemia.

Material Fabricators Inc   HQ
33 Commerce Dr   [N]
Buellton CA 93427
P: 805-686-5244   F: 805-686-5250   PRC:57
www.materialfabricators.com
Estab: 1946

Brian Brown, VP

Manufacturer of gaskets, shims, washers, metal stampings and die cut electrical insulators.

Materials Testing Inc   HQ
8798 Airport Rd
Redding CA 96002
P: 530-222-1116   F: 530-222-1611   PRC:140
mti-kcgeotech.com
Estab: 1996

Douglas G. King, Founder
Brian Nichols, Managing Partner
Lisa Peery, Office Manager
Andrew King, Principal Engineer
Genea Peery, Office Assistant

Provider of geotechnical engineering and materials testing services. The company offers geotechnical, environment, special inspection, and material testing services.

Materion Corp   BR
44036 S Grimmer Blvd
Fremont CA 94538
P: 510-623-1500   PRC:47
materion.com
Estab: 1931

Guido Beyss, President EMEA
Ian Tribick, Division President & CTO
John Grampa, SVP & CFO
Marc Kolanz, VP
Nic Baloi, VP

Provider of material solutions. The company deals with fabrication, analysis, research and development, and testing services.

Matheson Tri-Gas Inc   BR
6775 Central Ave
Newark CA 94560
P: 510-793-2559   F: 510-790-6241   PRC:133
mathesongas.com
Email: mtgnewark@matheson-trigas.com
Estab: 1926

Melanie Damrel, Office Manager

Provider of industrial, electronic, medical, and specialty gases. The company also offers gas detection, purification, and control equipment.

Matisse Software Inc   HQ
930 San Marcos Cir Ste 101
Mountain View CA 94043
P: 252-227-7013   PRC:319
www.matisse.com
Email: matisse.sales@matisse.com
Estab: 1998

Claude Ezran, VP of Marketing

Provider of database software and services. The company is also engaged in training, consulting, and technical support.

Matriscope   BR
601 Bercut Dr
Sacramento CA 95811
P: 916-375-6700   F: 916-447-6702   PRC:142
matriscope.com
Email: info@matriscope.com
Estab: 1995

Robert V. Tadlock, CEO & General Manager
David Palermo, CFO
Carla Collins, VP of Business Development & Project Manager
Prashant Gupta, Director
Joe Varella, Manager of Operations

Provider of geotechnical and environmental engineering services. The company also provides materials testing and special inspection services.

Matrix Computer Solutions Inc   HQ
3001 Bridgeway Ste K314
Sausalito CA 94965
P: 415-331-3600   F: 415-331-3655   PRC:323
www.matrixcomp.net
Email: support@matrixcomp.net

Jordan Gootnick, Founder & Chief Technologist
Aaron Powell, Technologist & Web Developer
Tom Zinn, Technologist
Anthony Kritikos, Technologist

Provider of computer and technology solutions for residential and business customers. The company also offers data backup, repair, and other services.

Matrix Logic Corp   HQ
1380 East Ave Ste 124-240
Chico CA 95973
P: 415-893-9897   PRC:323
www.matrix-logic.com
Email: sales@matrix-logic.com
Estab: 1994

Stephen Page, President
Jun Wen Du, Accounting Manager

Provider of enterprise content management solutions for law firms, businesses, and government agencies.

MatrixStream Technologies Inc   HQ
303 Twin Dolphin Dr 6th Fl
Redwood Shores CA 94065
P: 650-292-4982   PRC:67
Estab: 2004

Kate King, CEO
Robert Liu, COO

Provider of end-to-end enterprise, hospitality, embedded, and wireless Internet protocol television solutions.

Matronics   HQ
PO Box 347
Livermore CA 94551-0347
P: 925-606-1001   F: 925-606-6281   PRC:5
www.matronics.com
Email: sales@matronics.com

Matt Dralle, President

Provider of aircraft products. The company's products include return flow controllers, pulsation dampers, and governor MK III.

Mattermost Inc   HQ
530 Lytton Ave Ste 201
Palo Alto CA 94301
P: 650-866-5518   PRC:315
mattermost.com
Email: info@mattermost.com
Estab: 2015

Ian Tien, Co-Founder & CEO
Corey Hulen, Co-Founder & CTO
Alexis Schmidt, VP of Worldwide Sales
Alison Holmlund, VP of Customer Success
Aneal Vallurupalli, VP of Finance

Delivers open-source messaging tools for security-conscious enterprises and developers.

MATTERNET   HQ
3511 Edison Way
Menlo Park CA 94025
P: 650-260-2727   PRC:309
mttr.net
Email: contact@mattornet.us
Estab: 2011

Andreas Raptopoulos, Founder & CEO

Specializes in the creation of integrated delivery solutions. The company's products are used in healthcare, on-campus, and humanitarian applications.

Maverick Networks Inc   HQ
7060 Koll Center Pkwy Ste 318
Pleasanton CA 94566
P: 925-931-1900   F: 925-931-1919   PRC:63
www.mavericknetworks.net
Estab: 1986

Aaron Lee, CEO
Lillian Maeda, Sales Account Manager
David Ferris, Convergence Field Engineer
Darryl Pantonial, Convergence Engineer
Tyler Curcio, Convergence Engineer

Provider of VoIP telephone and related communication services. The company also provides design, implementation, and training solutions.

Maverick Therapeutics   HQ
3260 B Bayshore Blvd
Brisbane CA 94005
P: 650-338-1231   PRC:36
www.mavericktx.com
Email: info@mavericktx.com

James Scibetta, CEO
Robert DuBridge, EVP of Research & CTO
James Vasselli, VP
Chad May, VP

Provider of therapeutic solutions for the treatment of cancer. The company focuses on the research of cytotoxic T cells.

Mawi DNA Technologies LLC HQ
26203 Production Ave Ste 3
Hayward CA 94545
P: 510-256-5186 F: 510-576-2948 PRC:36
www.mawidna.com
Email: sales@mawidna.com
Estab: 2013

Jerome David, VP of Sales & Marketing

Provider of biosampling devices for non-invasive sample collection with the main objective of simplifying genomics and proteomics workflows.

Max Group Corp HQ
4841 Davenport Pl
Fremont CA 94538
P: 888-644-4629 F: 510-490-9942 PRC:91
maxgroup.com
Email: fremontsales@maxgroup.com
Estab: 1985

Johnny Tsai, President
Cecilia Hsu, Purchasing Manager
Iris Wu, Manager of Purchasing
Michael Chan, Product Manager

Distributor for computing devices. The company offers computer cases, fans and heatsinks, and hard drives.

Max Machinery Inc HQ
33A Healdsburg Ave
Healdsburg CA 95448
P: 707-433-2662 F: 707-433-1818 PRC:14
www.maxmachinery.com
Email: info@maxmachinery.com
Estab: 1967

Dan Turek, General Manager
Eric Baker, Marketing Manager
Peter Michenfelder, Operations Manager
Andrew Hiles, Operations Manager
Paul Hock, Marketing Manager

Manufacturer of precision flow meters. The company offers intermittent injection, low flow metering, and bi-directional flow measurement services.

Maxeler Technologies Inc HQ
1928 Old Middlefield Way Ste B
Mountain View CA 94043
P: 650-938-8818 PRC:110
www.maxeler.com
Email: info@maxeler.com
Estab: 2003

Oskar Mencer, Founder & CEO
Oliver Pell, VP of Engineering
James Spooner, VP of Acceleration

Developer of computing solutions. The company offers services to the oil and gas, analytical, and financial sectors.

M-194

MaxLinear BR
1060 Rincon Cir
San Jose CA 95131
P: 669-265-6100 PRC:209
maxlinear.com
Email: commsteam@maxlinear.com
Estab: 2003

Kishore Seendripu, CEO
Curtis Ling, CTO
Steven Litchfield, CFO & Chief Corporate Strategy Officer
Will Torgerson, VP & General Manager
Madhukar Reddy, VP of IC & RF Systems Engineering

Provider of integrated radio-frequency, analog, and mixed signal semiconductor SoC solutions. The company focuses on broadband communications applications.

Maxon Precision Motors Inc BR
1065 E Hillsdale Blvd Ste 210
Foster City CA 94404
P: 650-524-8822 F: 650-372-9395 PRC:80
maxongroup.us
Email: info.us@maxongroup.com
Estab: 1961

Deborah Mitchell, Office Manager
Biren Patel, Motion Control Engineering Manager
Sam Robinson, Marketing Manager
Scott Hamilton, Sales Engineer
Emmanuel Jimenez, Motion Control Applications Engineer

Provider of high-precision drives and systems. The company's products include brushed DC motors, brushless DC motors, spindle drives, and gearheads.

Maxta Inc HQ
2350 Mission College Blvd Ste 380
Santa Clara CA 95054
P: 669-228-2800 PRC:326
www.maxta.com
Email: marketing@maxta.com
Estab: 2009

Herb Schneider, VP of Engineering
Asad Bahou, Senior Director of Global Support
Kiran Sreenivasamurthy, Director of Product Management
Deepak Jagtap, Software Engineer

Provider of software-defined storage, disaster recovery, and also testing and development solutions.

MC Electronics HQ
1891 Airway Dr
Hollister CA 95023
P: 831-637-1651 F: 831-637-1309 PRC:202
www.mcelectronics.com
Email: info@mcelectronics.com
Estab: 1981

Marnix Claes, Owner
Alan Clark, President
Barrett Heywood, CEO
Angie Trujillo, VP
Ian Mathias, Director

Provider of turnkey solution for contract manufacturing. The company focuses on cable and harness assembly and full system integration.

MC Microwave Inc HQ
1777 Saratoga Ave Ste 205
San Jose CA 95129
P: 408-446-4100 F: 408-446-5430 PRC:159
www.mcmicrowave.net

Steve McCreddin, Application Engineer
Linda Eserini, Administrator

Provider of microwave and radio frequency components. The company's products are used in commercial and military applications.

Mcafee Inc HQ
2821 Mission College Blvd
Santa Clara CA 95054
P: 888-847-8766 PRC:319
www.mcafee.com
Email: sales@mcafee.com
Estab: 1987

John Giamatteo, President & CRO & Enterprise Business Group
Chris Young, CEO
Michael Berry, EVP & CFO
Steve Grobman, SVP & CTO
Allison Cerra, SVP & CMO

Provider of computer security solutions. The company specializes in database, web, email, network, endpoint, and mobile security services.

McCampbell Analytical Inc HQ
1534 Willow Pass Rd
Pittsburg CA 94565-1701
P: 925-252-9262 F: 925-252-9269 PRC:306
www.mccampbell.com
Email: main@mccampbell.com
Estab: 1991

Drew Gantner, Aquatic Toxicology Lab Director
Theresa Johnson, Quality Assurance & Control Manager
Elisa Venegas, Accounting Manager
Rosa Venegas, Sales Manager
Jennifer Lagerbom, Project Manager

Provider of analytical tests on drinking water, effluent, soils, solids, hazardous waste, air, soil vapor, and industrial materials.

McGuff Compounding Pharmacy Services Inc HQ
2921 W MacArthur Blvd Ste 142 [N]
Santa Ana CA 92704
P: 877-444-1155 PRC:261
www.mcguffpharmacy.com
Email: pharmacyanswers@mcguff.com
Estab: 1992

Cong Tran, Pharmacy Technician Supervisor
Clay Hammett, Compounding Pharmacist & Therapy Specialist
Mikayla Hoffmann, HR & Recruiting Assistant

Distributor of prescription and proprietary drugs, toiletries and more.

Mcintire Machine Inc HQ
22113 Hwy 33
Crows Landing CA 95313
P: 209-837-4409   F: 209-837-4413   PRC:80
www.mcintiremachineinc.com
Email: mcinmach@comcast.net
Estab: 1993

Ken McIntire, Owner

Provider of precision machining, welding, and
fabrication services. The company offers services
to the industrial sector.

McKenzie Machining Inc HQ
481 Perry Ct
Santa Clara CA 95054
P: 408-748-8885   F: 408-748-8887   PRC:80
www.mckenziemachining.com

Scott McKenzie, President

Provider of precision machining services of
pre-fabricated components. The company R&D,
manufacturing design, and other services.

MCLAB HQ
320 Harbor Way
S San Francisco CA 94080
P: 650-871-8771   F: 650-871-8796   PRC:306
www.mclab.com
Email: mclab@mclab.com
Estab: 1998

Nelda Knight, CEO
Mikheil Kvirikashvili, Marketing Manager
Giorgi Kelaptrishvili, Bar Manager
Zhejun Jia, Specialist
Shaukat Ali, Mobile Application Developer

Provider of DNA sequencing services. The company's products include enzymes and biochemical
reagents.

Mclellan Industries Inc HQ
13221 Crown Ave
Hanford CA 93230
P: 800-445-8449   F: 559-582-8155   PRC:158
www.mclellanindustries.com
Email: mclellan@mclellan-ind.com
Estab: 1965

Dale McLellan, Founder
Molly Mausser, President
Jim Ulery, Quality Control Manager
Nathan Sperling, Design Engineer
Adithya Katakam, Mechanical Design Engineer

Manufacturer of stainless steel and mild steel
tanks, hook lifts, tank kits, and related accessories.

MCM Engineering Inc HQ
845 Hinckley Rd
Burlingame CA 94010-4953
P: 650-259-9100   F: 650-259-9344   PRC:74
www.mcmeng.com
Email: sales@mcmeng.com
Estab: 1991

Patrick G. O'Brien, President & CEO
Paul M. Bade, Director of Engineering
Julie Smith, Full Charge Bookkeeper & HR
Manager

Provider of aircraft ground support systems. The
company offers products and services for airports
and aircraft manufacturers.

Mcneal Enterprises Inc HQ
2031 Ringwood Ave
San Jose CA 95131-1703
P: 408-922-7290   F: 408-922-7299   PRC:80
www.mcnealplasticmachining.com
Email: sales@mcneal.com
Estab: 1976

Ibrahim Ozturk, Quality Assurance Manager
Mike Rivera, Fabricator
Peter Smith, CNC Programmer
Paul Charland, CNC Programmer & Machinist

Provider of machined, fabricated, and thermoformed plastic components. The company serves
medical, semiconductor, solar, optics, and other
needs.

McWong International Inc HQ
1921 Arena Blvd
Sacramento CA 95834
P: 916-371-8080   F: 916-371-6666   PRC:243
www.mcwonginc.com
Email: support@mcwonginc.com
Estab: 1985

Blane Goettle, VP
Stephen Y. Zhou, VP

Designer and manufacturer of lighting control
equipment and related electrical components. The
company offers sensors and LED drivers.

MDA Precision HQ
360 Digital Dr
Morgan Hill CA 95037
P: 408-847-7790   PRC:80
www.mdaprecision.com
Email: info@mdaprecision.com
Estab: 2004

Markus Menig, Owner
Daniel Menig, Mechanical Engineer

Provider of benchtop milling machine and benchtop lathe systems. The company offers micro drilling machines, benchtop manual mills, and lathes.

Meadows Manufacturing HQ
545 Parrott St
San Jose CA 95112
P: 408-988-1252   F: 408-988-1126   PRC:80
www.meadowsmfg.com
Email: sales@meadowsmfg.com
Estab: 1958

Adam Gregorczuk, VP of Operations

Provider of engineering, design, and manufacturing solutions. The company serves the commercial
and industrial sectors.

Mean Well USA Inc HQ
44030 Fremont Blvd
Fremont CA 94538
P: 510-683-8886   F: 510-683-8899   PRC:293
www.meanwellusa.com
Email: mwsales@meanwellusa.com
Estab: 1999

Jerry Lin, Founder
Leo Cheong, General Manager
Joseph Taylor, Key Account Manager
Brian Lu, Application Engineer & Application
Engineer

Manufacturer of switching power supplies such as
AC to DC converters, DC to DC converters, DC to
AC inverters, and battery chargers.

MEC Aerial Work Platforms HQ
1401 S Madera Ave
Kerman CA 93630
P: 559-842-1500   F: 559-842-1520   PRC:180
www.mecawp.com

David White, President
Mike Liberto, Regional Manager
Jack Harwood, Sales Manager

Manufacturer of aerial work platforms. The company specializes in the design and manufacture of
scissors and booms.

Mecoptron Inc HQ
3115 Osgood Ct
Fremont CA 94539
P: 510-226-9966   F: 510-226-6750   PRC:80
www.mecoptron.com
Estab: 1986

Andy Law, Founder
Christine Law, Finance Manager

Provider of precision machining services. The
company's services include prototype machining,
production machining, and precision mechanical
assembly services.

Medallia Inc HQ
450 Concar Dr
San Mateo CA 94402
P: 650-321-3000   PRC:324
www.medallia.com
Estab: 2001

Borge Hald, Founder & CSO & Executive Chair-
man
Amy Pressman, President
John Abraham, General Manager
James Allworth, Director of Strategy
Chris Jackman, Senior Director of Solutions
Architecture

Provider of consulting, system configuration, user
training, and data warehouse integration services.

MedAutonomic Inc HQ
1235 Traud Dr
Concord CA 94518
P: 415-377-5653   PRC:34
medautonomic.com
Email: info@medautonomic.com

John Gonzales, Co-Founder & Chief Economist
Paolo Fabris, Co-Founder & CEO
Valerio Cigaina, Co-Founder & President
Alfredo Saggioro, Chief Medical Advisor
Simone Cigaina, VP of Operations

Developer of Brain NeuroModulator. The company
specializes in creating control action potentials in
individual neurons and in functional groups.

Meddev Corp HQ
730 N Pastoria Ave
Sunnyvale CA 94085
P: 408-730-9702   F: 408-730-9732   PRC:189
www.meddev-corp.com
Email: info@meddev-corp.com
Estab: 1971

Suzanne Grey, President

Developer, manufacturer, and marketer of medical
devices for niche market segments throughout the
world.

Medeanalytics Inc   HQ
4160 Dublin Blvd Ste 200
Dublin CA 94568
P: 510-379-3300   F: 510-647-1325   PRC:194
medeanalytics.com
Estab: 1993

Leigh Crawford, Associate VP of Product Ownership
Scott Hampel, President
Paul Kaiser, CEO
Melissa Green Dexter, Chief Human Resource Officer
Ping Zhang, SVP of Product Innovation & CTO

Provider of performance management, compliance, employer reporting, patient engagement, and satisfaction solutions.

Medeor Therapeutics   HQ
611 Gateway Blvd Ste 120
S San Francisco CA 94080
P: 650-627-4531   PRC:34
www.medeortx.com
Email: inquiry@medeortx.com

Scott Batty, CMO
Darin Weber, SVP & Chief Regulatory Officer
Iqbal Husain, SVP of Program Management
Michael Zdanowski, VP
Corinna X. Chen, VP of Corporate Development

Developer of personalized cellular immunotherapy for the organ transplant recipients. The company specializes in cellular immunotherapy, hematology, and transplantation product development.

MedGenome Inc   HQ
348 Hatch Dr
Foster City CA 94404
P: 888-440-0954   PRC:34
research.medgenome.com
Email: research@medgenome.com
Estab: 2013

Sam Santhosh, Founder & Global CEO & Chairman
Michael Nemzek, CCO
Amitabha Chaudhuri, VP of Research & Development
Hiranjith G.H., Senior Director & Corporate Marketing & Business Operations
Timothy Triche, Director of Laboratory

Provider of genomics based diagnostics and research services. The company specializes in bioinformatics, computing, genomics technologies, and big data analytics.

Media Flint   HQ
800 W El Camino Real Ste 180
Mountain View CA 94040
P: 888-592-2921   PRC:325
www.mediaflint.com
Email: info@mediaflint.com

Amin Haq, Founder & CEO
Ali Ghaznavi, CTO
Tom Jagger, VP of Account Services

Provides Internet marketing and advertising solutions to companies.

Media Net Link Inc   HQ
6114 La Salle Ave Ste 515
Oakland CA 94611
P: 866-563-5152   PRC:322
www.mnl.com
Email: info@mnl.com
Estab: 1994

Richard Kitamura, Project Manager
Mike Keller, Lead Designer

Provider of web business solutions. The company focuses on application development, systems integration, website design, and project management.

Media Specialty Resources Inc   HQ
61 Galli Dr Ste A
Novato CA 94949
P: 415-883-8053   F: 415-883-8147   PRC:60
www.msr-inc.com
Email: info@msr-inc.com
Estab: 2003

Anthony Grimani, President

Provider of acoustic panels for recording studios and home theaters. The company also offers noise control and soundproofing services.

Medical Design Solutions   HQ
1525 McCarthy Blvd Ste 1089
Milpitas CA 95035
P: 408-393-5386   PRC:189
www.medicaldesignsolutions.com
Email: rts@medicaldesignsolutions.com

Robert Stone, Founder & CEO
Darius A. Przygoda, VP of Electrical Engineering
Steve Sabram, Director of Wearable & Mobile Systems
Andrei Mariana, Manager
Larry J. Czapla, Senior Executive

Provider of medical design solutions. The company develops miniaturized sensors and systems used in medical device applications.

Medical Technology Stock Letter   HQ
PO Box 40460   [N]
Berkeley CA 94704
P: 510-843-1857   F: 510-843-0901   PRC:325
www.bioinvest.com
Email: admin@bioinvest.com
Estab: 1983

Jay Silverman, Partner
John McCamant, Editor

Publisher of medical technology stock letters.

Meditab Software Inc   HQ
1420 River Park Dr Ste 120
Sacramento CA 95815
P: 510-201-0130   F: 510-259-9731   PRC:323
www.meditab.com
Email: info@meditab.com
Estab: 1998

Paragi Patel, CEO
Darrin Luke, Project Manager
Feros Khan, Software Engineer
Mimi Keosakdy, VAR Support Team Lead

Developer of physical therapy, urology, cosmetic, and plastic surgery solutions. The company serves the healthcare industry.

Medland & Associates Inc   BR
PO Box 1275
San Martin CA 95046
P: 408-686-0460   F: 408-686-0462   PRC:83
www.medlandandassociates.com
Email: sales@medlandandassociates.com
Estab: 1994

David Medland, Owner & CEO
Sandy Medland, Manager of Sales & Accounting
John Mason, Field Applications & Design Engineer
Susan Kline, Sales Representative

Manufacturer of OEM products. The company's products include AC and DC converters, power supplies, switching regulators, and cable assemblies.

Medsoftware Inc   HQ
500 Cathedral Dr Ste 1780
Aptos CA 95001
P: 916-797-2363   PRC:323
www.medsoftware.com
Email: sales@medsoftware.com
Estab: 1990

Will Williams, Technical Director & Owner
Laurie Waters, Director of Sales

Provider of practice management software solutions. The company's services include data conversion and repair, training, and implementation.

Medtronic CardioVascular Inc   BR
3576 Unocal Pl Fountaingrove A
Santa Rosa CA 95403
P: 707-525-0111   F: 707-525-0114   PRC:188
medtronic.com
Email: rs.meniettinformation@medtronic.com
Estab: 1949

Geoff S. Martha, President
Michael J. Coyle, EVP & President of Cardiovascular
John Liddicoat, EVP & President of Americas Region
Brett Wall, EVP & President of Neuroscience
Bob White, EVP & President of Medical Surgical

Provider of disease management services. The company specializes in cardiovascular, diabetes, surgical technologies, and spinal and biologics.

Megaforce Corporation Inc   HQ
2035 O'Toole Ave
San Jose CA 95131
P: 408-956-9989   F: 408-956-9979   PRC:207
www.megaforcecorp.com
Email: info@megaforcecorp.com
Estab: 1994

Jason Trenh, CEO
Ray Woodfin, Director of Sales

Provider of supply chain, materials management, and test solutions. The company serves the industrial, commercial, and automotive sectors.

Megmeet USA Inc BR
4020 Moorpark Ave Ste 115
San Jose CA 95117
P: 408-260-7211 PRC:243
www.megmeetusa.com
Email: info@megmeetusa.com
Estab: 2003

Sandi Huang, Manager of Accounting & HR
Robert Staub, Business Development Executive

Manufacturer of electrical motors, general-used
converters, and optional devices. The company
offers industry automatic solutions.

Meiji Techno America BR
5895 Rue Ferrari
San Jose CA 95138
P: 408-226-3454 F: 408-226-0900 PRC:174
www.meijitechno.com
Email: admin@meijitechno.com
Estab: 1964

Anthony Rivero, General Manager
Rick McReynolds, Manager of Shipping and
Receiving

Manufacturer of optical microscope products.
The company offers gemological, biological, and
educational microscopes, and accessories.

Meivac Inc HQ
5830 Hellyer Ave
San Jose CA 95138
P: 408-362-1000 F: 408-362-1010 PRC:83
www.meivac.com
Email: support@meivac.com
Estab: 1993

David Meidinger, President & CFO
Jim Ritter, SVP & CTO
Alan Schauer, VP of Customer Support
Todd Johnson, Components Product Manager
Aditya Walimbe, Applications Engineer

Manufacturer of sputtering systems and components. The company offers throttle valves, integrators, OEM assemblies, and substrate heaters.

Mektec International Corp HQ
1731 Technology Dr Ste 840
San Jose CA 95110
P: 408-392-4000 F: 408-392-4077 PRC:209
www.mektec.com
Email: sales@mektecusa.com

Steve Decia, President & COO
Akio Yoshida, Director
Daniel Lien, Technical Sales Account Manager
Kunie Oda, Technical Manager of Sales
Brandon E., Sales Manager

Manufacturer of printed circuit boards. The
company deals with production, prototyping, and
application engineering services.

Meline Engineering Corp HQ
PO Box 276665
Sacramento CA 95827
P: 916-366-3458 PRC:135
www.meline.com
Email: me_info@meline.com
Estab: 1995

Lisa Meline, Principal Mechanical Engineer
Tom Santillan, Mechanical Designer

Provider of energy efficient mechanical system
design services. The company also offers mechanical engineering services.

Melrose Metal Products Inc HQ
44533 Grimmer Blvd
Fremont CA 94538
P: 510-657-8771 F: 510-657-7233 PRC:153
www.gomelrose.com
Email: mhoppe@gomelrose.com

Bob Lloyd, Contact

Manufacturer of melrose metal products. The
company offers design and installation services
for food processing and emission control systems.

Melrose Nameplate & Label Co HQ
26575 Corporate Ave
Hayward CA 94545
P: 510-732-3100 F: 510-732-3111 PRC:82
www.melrose-nl.com
Email: sales@melrose-nl.com
Estab: 1939

Jim Fritz, Manager of Purchasing & QC
Shannon Looper, Manager of Materials & Com-
pliance
Gabriella Cruz, Contact
Vanessa Hong, Contact

Developer and manufacturer of ID nameplates,
labels, and membrane switches. The company
offers touchscreen assembly and decorative
nameplates.

Meltwater Group HQ
465 California St 11th Fl
San Francisco CA 94104
P: 415-829-5900 F: 415-848-9190 PRC:323
www.meltwater.com
Estab: 2001

Jorn Lyseggen, Founder & Executive Chairman
Jens-Petter Glittenberg, Owner
Aditya Jami, CTO
Martin Hernandez, CFO
Curt McLeland, Chief Accounting Officer

Developer of software products such as Meltwater
BUZZ, Meltwater NEWS, and Meltwater DRIVE
to meet the specific needs of businesses around
the world.

Membrane Technology & Research HQ
39630 Eureka Dr
Newark CA 94560
P: 650-328-2228 F: 650-328-6580 PRC:54
www.mtrinc.com
Estab: 1982

Kaaeid Lokhandwala, VP of Commercial Opera-
tions
Alicia Breen, Director of Project Engineering
Doug Gottschlich, Director of Refining of Hydro-
gen & Syngas
Sachin Joshi, Director of Natural Gas
Priyanka Tiwari, Process Engineer

Developer and manufacturer of membrane-based
separation systems. The company serves the
petrochemical, natural gas, and refining industries.

Memsql Inc HQ
534 Fourth St
San Francisco CA 94107
P: 855-463-6775 PRC:323
www.memsql.com
Email: info@memsql.com
Estab: 2011

Adam Prout, CTO & Founder
Raj Verma, CEO
Manoj Jain, CFO
Gary Orenstein, CMO
Louis Yang, VP Finance

Provider of technology solutions and services. The
company serves the finance and digital advertising industries.

Menlo Security HQ
2300 Geng Rd Ste 200
Palo Alto CA 94303
P: 650-614-1705 PRC:325
www.menlosecurity.com
Email: info@menlosecurity.com
Estab: 2013

Amir Ben Efraim, CEO
David Eckstein, CFO
Scott Fuselier, CRO
Kowsik Guruswamy, CTO
Gautam Altekar, Chief Architect

Provider of security solutions. The company's
offerings include web isolation, document, and
phishing isolation services.

Menlo Therapeutics HQ
200 Cardinal Way 2nd Fl
Redwood City CA 94063
P: 650-486-1416 PRC:268
www.menlotherapeutics.com

Steve Basta, CEO
Kristine M. Ball, SVP of Corporate Strategy &
CFO
Mary Spellman, CMO
Paul Kwon, Chief Scientific Officer
Ron Krasnow, General Counsel & Chief Compli-
ance Officer

Developer and manufacture of biopharmaceuticals. The company focuses on the commercialization and development of serlopitant for treating
pruritus.

Mentor Graphics RH
46871 Bayside Pkwy
Fremont CA 94538
P: 510-354-7400 F: 510-354-7467 PRC:209
www.mentor.com
Email: sales_info@mentor.com
Estab: 1981

Walden Rhines, CEO
Mike Ellow, EVP of Mentor EDA
Scot Morrison, General Manager of Embedded
Runtime Solutions
Silvano Massimiani, Global Account Director
Laurent Remy, Strategic Account Director

Provider of electronic design automation software.
The company focuses on mechanical analysis,
system modeling, manufacturing, and verification.

Meraki LLC BR
  500 Terry A Francois Blvd
  San Francisco CA 94158
P: 415-432-1000   F: 415-255-9629   PRC:68
meraki.cisco.com
Email: sales@meraki.com
Estab: 2006

Paul Wolfe, Senior Software Engineer

Provider of branch networking solutions. The company offers services to the education, retail, and healthcare industries.

Meran Technology HQ
  8 Croydon Cir
  Piedmont CA 94611-3601
P: 510-530-5119   F: 510-482-2802   PRC:125
www.meran.net
Email: info1@meran.net
Estab: 1989

Jerry Herrick, Owner

Provider of process equipment for memory disk manufacturers. The company offers material handling equipment for fiber optic manufacturers.

Mercator Medsystems Inc HQ
  1900 Powell St Ste 800
  Emeryville CA 94608
P: 510-614-4550   F: 510-614-4560   PRC:196
www.mercatormed.com
Email: info@mercatormed.com

Kirk P. Seward, Founder & President & Chief Science & Technology Officer
Trent Reutiman, CEO
Steve Baker, CFO
Doug Wall, Director
Ned Scheetz, Director

Developer of therapeutics for vascular disease, oncology and regenerative medicine, and treatment of hypertension.

Meridian Surveying Engineering Inc HQ
  2958 Van Ness
  San Francisco CA 94109
P: 415-440-4131   F: 415-233-9671   PRC:304
www.meridiansurvey.com
Estab: 1989

Emily Thomas, Project Manager of LSIT
Rick Mather, Senior Project Manager
Kurt Kvam, Manager of IT & Office Operations
Stanley T. Gray, Principal

Provider or residential, commercial, and municipal surveys. The company also deals with claims litigation services.

Merieux Nutrisciences Corp BR
  5262 Pirrone Ct
  Salida CA 95368
P: 209-549-7508   PRC:19
www.merieuxnutrisciences.com
Estab: 1967

Jim Miller, President
Philippe Sans, CEO
John Marshall, General Manager

Provider of public health services. The company is focused on food and pharmaceutical products, cosmetics, and consumer goods.

Merit USA HQ
  620 Clark Ave   [N]
  Pittsburg CA 94565
P: 925-427-6427   PRC:62
www.meritsteel.com
Email: sales@meritsteel.com
Estab: 1999

Don Israel, Contact
Jason Brown, Contact

Provider of steel processing services for steel coils.

Meritronics Inc HQ
  500 Yosemite Dr Ste 108
  Milpitas CA 95035
P: 408-969-0888   F: 408-969-0801   PRC:211
meritronics.com
Email: sales@meritronics.com
Estab: 1995

Francis Rost, VP
Kiet Pham, VP of Quality & Engineering
Dennis Judd, Director of Business Development
Matthew O'Hare, Program Manager
Ramiro Equihua, Process Engineer

Provider of electronics assembly, and equipment assemblies. The company specializes in PCB assembly, cable assembly, and system assembly.

Merkle Inc BR
  49 Stevenson St 15th Fl
  San Francisco CA 94105
P: 415-918-2990   PRC:319
www.merkleinc.com
Estab: 2010

Geoffrey Smalling, CTO
Justin Yoshimura, SVP of Loyalty Services

Provider of omnichannel loyalty solution. The company offers service and technology to deliver seamless and powerful customer retention solutions.

Mesa/Boogie Ltd HQ
  1317 Ross St
  Petaluma CA 94954
P: 707-778-6565   F: 707-765-1503   PRC:60
mesaboogie.com
Email: info@mesaboogie.com
Estab: 1973

Randall Smith, President & Designer
Jim Aschow, EVP
Doug West, Director of Research & Development
Steve Mueller, General Manager of Sales
Andy Field, Partner

Provider of guitars, bass amplifiers, and cabinetry. The company provides pedals, speakers, guitars, and accessories.

MeshDynamics Inc HQ
  3555 Benton St
  Santa Clara CA 95051
P: 408-373-7700   F: 408-516-8987   PRC:63
www.meshdynamics.com
Email: info@meshdynamics.com
Estab: 2002

Francis daCosta, Founder

Provider of wireless mesh networking solutions focusing on wireless video surveillance, emergency response networks, and smart-grid multi use products.

Mesotech International Inc HQ
  4531 Harlin Dr
  Sacramento CA 95826
P: 916-368-2020   F: 916-368-2030   PRC:138
mesotech.com
Email: sales@mesotech.com
Estab: 1993

Christopher Swinehart, Director of Operations

Provider of weather monitoring and reporting systems and software solutions. The company serves airport, defense, and agriculture industries.

MessageSolution Inc HQ
  7080 Donlon Way Ste 216
  Dublin CA 94568
P: 925-833-8000   F: 925-833-8001   PRC:326
www.messagesolution.com
Email: techsupport@messagesolution.com
Estab: 2004

Jeff Liang, CTO
Josh Liang, VP of Marketing & Managing Director of Global Alliance Network
Kevin McInerney, Sales & Marketing Manager
Alan Zheng, Software Engineer
Ilya Levin, Senior iOS Developer

Provider of enterprise archiving, e-discovery, and migration solutions. The company deals with storage management solutions.

Meta Integration Technology Inc HQ
  700 E El Camino Real Ste 170
  Mountain View CA 94040
P: 650-273-6382   F: 650-307-6382   PRC:322
www.metaintegration.net
Email: info@metaintegration.net
Estab: 1997

Christian Bremeau, CEO
Volodymyr Vykhrushch, Senior Software Engineer
John O'Byrne, UI Architect

Provider of metadata components to data modeling, data integration, business intelligence, and metadata management tool vendors.

Metabiota Inc HQ
  425 California St Ste 1200
  San Francisco CA 94104
P: 415-398-4712   F: 415-398-4716   PRC:328
metabiota.com
Email: info@metabiota.com
Estab: 2008

Nathan Wolfe, Founder & Chairman
Nita Madhav, CEO
Mark Gallivan, Director of Data Science
Jaclyn Guerrero, Associate Director of Product, Policy & Partnerships
Jason Euren, Senior Scientist

Provider of risk analytics that help protect global health for governments and multinationals, food risk, and financial risk insights.

Metabyte Inc HQ
39300 Civic Center Dr Ste 260
Fremont CA 94538
P: 510-494-9700   F: 510-494-9100   PRC:323
www.metabyte.com
Email: info@metabyte.com
Estab: 1993

Manu Mehta, President & CEO

Provider of software solutions and related services to the government, healthcare, and retail industries.

MetaCert HQ
585 Bryant St 2nd Fl
San Francisco CA 94107
P: 415-529-2571   PRC:322
metacert.com
Estab: 2012

Paul Walsh, CEO
Liz Devine, CIO
Greg Johnson, COO
Mike Landis, CFO
David Rooks, Data Manager

Provider of security API for mobile app developers. The company offers content-based filtering services.

Metacrylics HQ
365 Obata Ct
Gilroy CA 95020
P: 408-280-7733   F: 408-280-6329   PRC:47
www.metacrylics.com
Email: sales@metacrylics.com
Estab: 1974

Mark Anthenien, Owner
Gary Rosenfield, Division President
Gary Anderson, Director of Operations
Steven Gruba, Office Manager
David Baez, Territory Sales Manager

Provider of coatings for commercial properties including material safety data sheets, data sheets, color chart, and test data.

Metal Fusion Inc HQ
425 Hurlingame Ave
Redwood City CA 94063-3407
P: 650-368-7692   F: 650-368-7691   PRC:80
www.metalfusioninc.com
Email: info@metalfusioninc.com
Estab: 1985

Mike Bourgeois, General Manager
Duane Linden, Manufacturing Engineer
Michael Olivio, Contact

Provider of thermal spray technology services. The company's portfolio includes shaft repair, roll repair, and mechanical seal.

Metal Surfaces Inc HQ
6060 Shull St   [N]
Bell Gardens CA 90201
P: 562-927-1331   F: 562-927-0692   PRC:280
www.metalsurfaces.com
Email: info@metalsurfaces.com
Emp: 51-200   Estab: 1981

Armando Celis, Manager

Provider of plating and polishing services.

Metalfx Inc HQ
200 N Lenore Ave
Willits CA 95490
P: 800-479-9451   F: 707-459-2046   PRC:82
www.metalfx.com
Email: info@metalfx.com
Estab: 1976

Gordon Short, President
Jill Porterfield, Controller
Carol Bartow, Contact

Provider of sheet metal fabrication services for metal and wood products. The company is engaged in engineering and quality assurance services.

MetalMart International Inc HQ
5828 Smithway St   [N]
Commerce CA 90040
P: 562-692-9081   F: 562-699-6868   PRC:280
www.metalmart.com
Email: salesmet@metal-mart.com
Estab: 1974

William A. Lippman, President

Distributor of metals and wrought magnesium.

Metaswitch Networks DH
399 Main St
Los Altos CA 94022
P: 415-513-1500   F: 415-513-1501   PRC:64
www.metaswitch.com

Martin Lund, CEO
Tom Cronan, CFO
Ian MacLean, CMO
Martin Taylor, CTO
Roger Heinz, CRO

Provider of service management solutions. The company offers original equipment manufacturer, multimedia subsystem, and hosted business services.

Methode Electronics BR
2025 Gateway Pl Ste 235
San Jose CA 95110
P: 510-610-5241   PRC:295
www.methode.com
Email: info@methode.com

Michael J. Hayward, VP & COO
Timothy R. Glandon, VP
Mehrdad Abtahi, Director of Engineering Technical Fellows
Duane Campbell, Manager of Business Development

Manufacturer of power management electronic products. The company is engaged in design, engineering, and technical support services.

Metis Technology Solutions Inc HQ
333 Cobalt Way Ste 105
Sunnyvale CA 94085
P: 650-967-3051   PRC:326
www.metis-tech.com
Estab: 2010

Hadi Mahdavi, CEO
Josh Puglise, CFO
James Theiss, VP of Space Programs
Jennifer Paulik, Executive Director of Human Resources
Ron Unruh, Executive Director of Contracts

Provider of technical services. The company engages in engineering, IT, aviation, space, and earth sciences fields.

MetricStream Inc HQ
2479 E Bayshore Rd
Palo Alto CA 94303
P: 650-620-2900   PRC:323
www.metricstream.com
Email: info@metricstream.com
Estab: 1999

Gunjan Sinha, Executive Chairman
Shellye Archambeau, CEO
Gaurav Kapoor, COO
Sanjay Sinha, CMO
Seema Iyer, Chief Human Resource Officer

Provider of enterprise risk, compliance, and internal audit management solutions. The company offers training services.

Metro-Med Inc HQ
1701 N San Fernando Blvd   [N]
Burbank CA 91504
P: 818-840-9090   PRC:189
www.metromed.com
Estab: 1980

Lauren Earley, Manager of Human Resources
Rick Atwood, Contact

Distributor of home respiratory systems and supplies.

Metrolaser Inc HQ
22941 Mill Creek Dr   [N]
Laguna Hills CA 92653
P: 949-553-0688   F: 949-553-0495   PRC:31
www.metrolaserinc.com
Email: sales@metrolaserinc.com
Emp: 11-50   Estab: 1988

Cecil Hess, Co-Founder
Jim Trolinger, Co-Founder & Owner
Tom Jenkins, President & CTO
Jacob George, CEO

Provider of optical and laser solutions.

Mettler-Toledo Rainin LLC BR
7500 Edgewater Dr
Oakland CA 94621
P: 800-472-4646   F: 510-564-1617   PRC:20
mt.com
Email: cs@rainin.com
Estab: 1963

Henri Chahine, COO
Ana Pan, Director of Human Resources
Brett Demshar, North American Lean Manager
Mark Richards, Head of Human Resources
David Greenwood, Head of Quality Systems

Provider of laboratory weighing and process analytics services. The company also focuses on industrial weighing.

Meyer Sound Laboratories Inc   HQ
    2832 San Pablo Ave
    Berkeley CA 94702
P: 510-486-1166   PRC:31
www.meyersound.com
Email: sales@meyersound.com
Estab: 1979

Cliff Eldridge, CFO
Brad Friedman, VP
Kim Sandholdt, Director of Service Worldwide
Patricia Chu, Senior Buyer

Manufacturer of loudspeakers, subwoofers, stage
monitors, and amplifiers. The company serves the
entertainment sector.

MG Technologies Inc   HQ
    11680 Regnart Canyon Dr
    Cupertino CA 95014-4830
P: 408-255-8191   PRC:323
www.mgtech.com
Email: info@mgtech.com

Mario M. Guzman, President

Provider of software services. The company
offers conversion, training, installation, and tuning
services.

MGE Engineering Inc   HQ
    7415 Greenhaven Dr Ste 100
    Sacramento CA 95831
P: 916-421-1000   F: 916-421-1002   PRC:304
www.mgeeng.com
Estab: 1990

Robert Sennett, Principal & VP
Kang Chen, Principal & VP
Darrel Huckabay, Senior Project Manager
Wesley Sennett, Project & Design Engineer
Peter Zhao, Engineer

Provider of civil/structural engineering and construction management services. The company
focuses on site development and construction
inspection.

MGM Transformer Co   HQ
    5701 Smithway St   [N]
    Commerce CA 90040
P: 323-726-0888   F: 323-726-8224   PRC:293
www.mgmtransformer.com
Email: management@mgmtransformer.com
Emp: 51-200   Estab: 1975

Sanju Kotbagi, Manager of Sales & Engineering

Manufacturer and dealer of transformers.

MiaSole Hi-Tech Corp   HQ
    2590 Walsh Ave
    Santa Clara CA 95051
P: 408-940-9658   PRC:135
www.miasole.com
Email: info@miasole.com
Estab: 2004

Jeff Zhou, CEO
Atiye Bayman, CTO
Shirlene Wang, Purchasing Manager
Suzy Berlant, Senior Benefits Analyst
Yana Qian, Senior Research Scientist

Manufacturer of copper indium gallium selenide
thin-film photovoltaic solar panels. The company
offers solar power plants for industrial needs.

Michael Patrick Partners   HQ
    388 Market St Ste 1300
    San Francisco CA 94111
P: 650-327-3185   PRC:326
www.michaelpatrickpartners.com
Estab: 1979

Dan O'Brien, President & Founder
Duane Maidens, CSO & Founding Partner & CEO
Robert Maidens, Creative Director & COO &
Associate Creative Director, Art & Copy & Chief
of Accounts
Laura Gross, Operations & Facility Manager

Provider of branding solutions. The company also
offers logo design, portfolio creation, web content,
and marketing services.

Micro Connectors Inc   HQ
    2700 Mccone Ave   [N]
    Hayward CA 94545
P: 510-266-0299   F: 510-266-0289   PRC:109
www.microconnectors.com
Emp: 1-10   Estab: 1986

Paul Lane, Sales Manager

Distributor of computer peripheral equipment.

Micro Dicing Services   HQ
    780 Montague Expy Ste 303
    San Jose CA 95131
P: 408-321-8840   F: 408-321-8843   PRC:173
www.microdicingtechnology.com
Email: info@microdicingtechnology.com

Peter Chiang, CEO
Janet Huang, Contact

Provider of sawing services. The company provides services to the microelectronic and optical
industries.

Micro Lambda Wireless Inc   HQ
    46515 Landing Pkwy
    Fremont CA 94538
P: 510-770-9221   F: 510-770-9213   PRC:15
www.microlambdawireless.com
Email: sales@microlambdawireless.com
Estab: 1990

John Nguyen, CEO
Rich Leier, VP of Sales & Marketing
Susan Sun, VP of Finance
David Suddarth, VP of Engineering
Linda Dimmers, Inside Sales Manager

Supplier of remote drivers, multipliers, bench test
filters, oscillators, synthesizers, and harmonic
generators.

Micro Lithography Inc   HQ
    1257 Elko Dr
    Sunnyvale CA 94089
P: 408-747-1769   F: 408-747-1978   PRC:36
www.mliusa.com
Estab: 1981

Qoang Bih, Manager
Kevin Duong, Customer Service Manager
David Wang, System Administrator
Julie Zhu, Senior Buyer

Manufacturer of pellicles using high end equipment for the production of frames and engineering
parts, automatic anodizing lines, and chemical
labs.

Micro Machine Shop   HQ
    743B Wakefield Ct
    Oakdale CA 95361
P: 209-848-8760   F: 209-848-8762   PRC:80
www.machining.us.com
Estab: 1984

Diane Resz, VP of Sales & Finance

Manufacturer of micro machines for telecommunications, microwave, semiconductor equipment,
valve, laser, medical, and other industries.

Micro Precision Calibration Inc   HQ
    22835 Industrial Pl
    Grass Valley CA 95949
P: 530-268-1860   PRC:306
www.microprecision.com
Email: calibrate@microprecision.com
Estab: 1969

Jerry Trammell, Owner
Jarrod Owen Trammell, President
Steve Joos, MPC Global Director of Sales
Enrique Hernandez, Quality Director
Danette Szymanski, Sales Manager

Provider of electrical and mechanical calibration
services. The company also offers optical and
temperature calibration services.

Micro Tech Systems   HQ
    2037 W Bullard Ave Ste 101
    Fresno CA 93711
P: 559-438-7580   F: 559-438-7585   PRC:104
microtechsys.com
Email: sales@microtech.com
Estab: 1980

Tino Sancetta, Manufacturing Manager
Joe Khoe, Principal & Consultant

Provider of cabling solutions. The company involves in the installation and repair of voice, data,
and video network systems.

Micro-Mechanics Inc   DH
    465 Woodview Ave
    Morgan Hill CA 95037
P: 408-779-2927   PRC:157
www.micro-mechanics.com
Email: mmusa@micro-mechanics.com
Estab: 1983

Chris Borch, CEO
Michael Maguire, Chief Engineer - Milling Devel-
opment & Technology
Andrew Eden, Director of Business Development
Colin Wojno, Operations Section Manager
Kathleen Edmiston, Manager of 24 & 7 Logistics
Section

Manufacturer of precision tools, assemblies, and
consumable parts used to manufacture and test
semiconductors. The company offers mold pots
and trims.

Micro-Vu HQ
7909 Conde Ln
Windsor CA 95492
P: 707-838-6272 PRC:13
www.microvu.com
Email: sales@microvu.com
Estab: 1959

Phil Dad, COO
Jerry Ding, Technology Development Manager
Mervin Buenaflor, Software Engineer
Jordan Trout, Firmware Engineer
Ian Davison, Mechanical Engineer

Designer and manufacturer of measuring machines, including automated and manual video systems, and optical comparators.

MicroCam Inc HQ
2597 Kerner Blvd
San Rafael CA 94901
P: 415-729-9391 PRC:189
microcam.co

Larry Gerrans, Founder & President & CEO

Provider of medical devices. The company focuses on commercializing the plug and play micro imaging system.

Microchek Inc HQ
922 Industrial Way Unit K
Lodi CA 95240
P: 209-333-5253 F: 209-339-1375 PRC:166
microchek.com
Email: sales@microchek.com
Estab: 1988

Susan Sinclair, CEO & General Manager
Yoshiko McDole, Secretary

Manufacturer of check valves and self-activating safety valves. The company's products include a diverse variety of valves.

Microchip Technology Inc BR
450 Holger Way
San Jose CA 95134
P: 408-961-6400 PRC:212
www.microchip.com
Estab: 1989

Milan Rai, Principal Electrical Design Engineer
Surjit Ghanta, Principal Engineer
Arpita Nigam, System Engineer
Roy Sasaki, Principal FAE

Provider of microcontroller and analog semiconductors. The company focuses on products such as amplifiers, data converters, and embedded controllers.

Microcube HQ
47853 Warm Springs Blvd
Fremont CA 94539
P: 510-651-5000 PRC:189
www.microcube.org
Email: support@microcube.org

Dinesh Mody, President
Mark Smith, Mechanical Engineer
Grason Ott, Designer
Amrish J. Walke, Medical Device Innovator

Provider of concept development, design, rapid prototyping and IP management, market mapping, clinical trials, and regulatory submissions.

MicroDental Laboratories HQ
5601 Arnold Rd
Dublin CA 94568
P: 925-829-3611 F: 925-828-0153 PRC:185
www.microdental.com
Email: info@microdental.com
Estab: 1964

Karsten Klimmek, Director of Operations
Dazia Bosworth, Director of Service Operations
Leonard Telesca, Dental Services Manager
Neil Dela Rosa, Account Manager

Provider of laboratory-fabricated restorations and related equipment. The company serves the healthcare sector.

Microelec Technical HQ
4633 Old Ironsides Dr Ste 110
Santa Clara CA 95054
P: 408-282-3508 F: 408-300-5780 PRC:126
www.microelecs.com
Email: sales@microelecs.com
Estab: 2006

K.Y Hwang, Manager of Engineering & Sales
Riani Dharma, Distribution Manager
Zafir Ahmad, Applications Engineer
Kevin Turner, OEM Customer Analyst

Manufacturer of semiconductor, micro-electronics, and mixed signal devices. The company specializes in switches, bridge rectifiers, and transistors.

Microform Precision LLC HQ
4244 S Market Ct Ste A
Sacramento CA 95834
P: 916-419-0580 F: 916-419-0577 PRC:82
www.mform.com
Email: info@mform.com
Estab: 1981

Bryan Wallace, Buyer & Purchaser
Manuel Buggs, Materials Handler

Provider of metal cutting, bending, fabrication, and coating services. The company offers shearing, punching, forming, and painting services.

MicroMed Laboratories HQ
1129 N McDowell Blvd
Petaluma CA 94954
P: 707-782-0792 PRC:306
www.micromedlabs.com
Email: info@micromedlabs.com
Estab: 1999

Kerri Sturtevant, QA Manager
Ann Hargens, Microbiology Tech II

Provider of regulatory consulting, microbial identification, environmental monitoring, and sterilization validation services.

Micromega Systems Inc HQ
2 Fifer St Ste 120
Corte Madera CA 94925-1134
P: 415-924-4700 F: 415-945-3301 PRC:324
www.micromegasystems.com
Estab: 1979

Charles Bornheim, President

Provider of database systems and e-business website design services. The company also focuses on training and installation.

Micron Technology Inc BR
Tasman Technology Pk 590 Alder Dr
Milpitas CA 95035
P: 408-855-4000 PRC:86
www.micron.com

Sanjay Mehrotra, President & CEO
April Arnzen, SVP of Human Resources & CPO
David Zinsner, SVP & CFO
Sumit Sadana, EVP & Chief Business Development Officer
Mike Bokan, SVP of Worldwide Sales

Designer and manufacturer of semiconductor systems for computing, networking, and communications applications.

Micropoint Bioscience Inc HQ
3521 Leonard Ct
Santa Clara CA 95054
P: 408-588-1682 F: 408-588-1620 PRC:186
www.micropointbio.com
Email: info@micropointbio.com
Estab: 2006

Nan Zhang, CEO & Founder
William Sumida, Manufacturing Supervisor
Wilson Zhang, Senior Research Associate

Developer of medical products and services for treatment of vascular disease such as peripheral artery disease and venous blood clots disorders.

Microsemi DH
3000 Oakmead Village Dr Ste 100
Santa Clara CA 95051
P: 408-986-8031 F: 408-986-8120 PRC:212
microsemi.com
Estab: 1960

Jim Ryan, Director WW Module Operations CMPG
Paul Quintana, Director Vertical Marketing
Tom Moore, Director of IP & Solutions Engineering
Paul O'Brien, Divisional Controller & Site Manager
Jeff Kuhn, Manager of Applications Group

Supplier of discrete military and aerospace components. The company's applications include embedded systems and power solutions.

Microsonic Systems Inc HQ
76 Bonaventura Dr
San Jose CA 95134
P: 408-844-4980 F: 866-404-4898 PRC:31
www.microsonics.com
Estab: 2004

Vibhu Vivek, President & CTO

Provider of ultrasonic fluid processing device built with MEMS technology to biotech and pharmaceutical industries.

Microvi Biotech Inc HQ
26229 Eden Landing Rd
Hayward CA 94545
P: 510-344-0668 PRC:24
www.microvi.com
Email: info@microvi.com

Fatemeh Shirazi, CEO & CTO
Norman L. Balme, SVP of IP & Legal
Karin Kidder, VP of Marketing
Ajay Nair, Global Director of Commercial & Technical Strategy
Ameen Razavi, Director of Innovation Research

Designer and developer of biotechnology solutions. The company commercializes biocatalytic solutions in the water, energy and chemical industries.

Microwave Technology Inc HQ
4268 Solar Way
Fremont CA 94538
P: 510-651-6700   F: 510-952-4000   PRC:70
www.mwtinc.com
Email: info@mwtinc.com
Estab: 1982

Greg Zhou, President
Don Apte, Director of Sales & Marketing
Jun Chen, Senior MMIC Designer
Hanh Nguyen, Contact
Tahrah Hunt, Contact

Manufacturer of RF and microwave discrete semiconductor products, GaAs and GaN RF power amplifiers, low noise pHEMT devices, and wireless amplifiers.

MicuRx Pharmaceuticals Inc HQ
950 Tower Ln Ste 390
Foster City CA 94404
P: 510-782-2022   PRC:249
www.micurx.com
Email: info@micurx.com
Estab: 2007

Zhengyu Yuan, President
Mikhail F. Gordeev, CSO

Provider of pharmaceuticals. The company develops antibiotics to combat drug-resistant bacterial infections.

Mid Labs Inc HQ
557 McCormick St
San Leandro CA 94577
P: 510-357-3952   F: 510-357-1582   PRC:195
www.midlabs.com
Email: info@midlabs.com
Estab: 1981

Angela Kent, Material Coordinator
Sheila Mayo, Purchasing Agent
Michelle Francis, Human Resource Generalist

Manufacturer of ophthalmic products such as vitreous cutters, titanium forceps, and related accessories.

Mikpower Technologies Inc HQ
800 Charcot Ave Ste 112
San Jose CA 95131
P: 408-493-5903   PRC:86
www.mikpowerinc.com
Email: info@mikpowerinc.com

Thomas Chao, President & CEO & Founder

Provider of lighting solutions. The company offers IC products for light bulbs, light tubes, and square lights.

Mikuni American Corp HQ
8910 Mikuni Ave   [N]
Northridge CA 91324
P: 818-885-1242   F: 818-993-6877   PRC:359
www.mikuni.com
Emp: 11-50   Estab: 1968

M. Ikuta, Chairman
S. Fujimori, President & CEO
Y. Fujii, CFO

Manufacturer of fuel injection systems, carburetors, pumps and much more.

Mil-Ram Technology Inc HQ
48009 Fremont Blvd
Fremont CA 94538
P: 510-656-2001   F: 510-656-2004   PRC:87
www.mil-ram.com
Email: sls@mil-ram.com
Estab: 1990

Cecile Snow, Accounts Payable Manager

Manufacturer of industrial gas and detection systems. The company serves the oil and gas, pulp and paper, and chemical industries.

Milagen Inc HQ
1255 Park Ave Ste B
Emeryville CA 94608
P: 510-597-1244   PRC:43
www.milagen.com
Email: info@milagen.com
Estab: 1997

Moncef Jendoubi, Founder & CEO & President & Chief Scientific Officer
Alfredo J. Quattrone, VP of Regulatory Affairs
Heinz Bodenmueller, VP of Business Development & Strategy
Rosaura P.C. Valle, VP of Operations & Strategic Alliances
Christine Chavany, Director of Immunoassay Development

Develops and manufactures healthcare products. The company offers immunohistochemistry and cytology products.

Milestone Inc HQ
3001 Oakmead Village Dr
Santa Clara CA 95051
P: 408-492-9055   F: 408-492-9053   PRC:325
milestoneinternet.com
Email: sales@milestoneinternet.com
Estab: 1998

Benu Aggarwal, Founder & President
Anil Aggarwal, CEO
Zulema Romero, Director of Client Services
Mike Supple, Director of Products & Social Media
Jeff Katz, Director of Enterprise Sales

Provider of hotel Internet marketing and website development services. The company focuses on website and social media marketing and ROI tracking.

Millennia Music & Media Systems HQ
6411 Capitol Ave
Diamond Springs CA 95619
P: 530-647-0750   F: 530-647-9921   PRC:209
www.mil-media.com
Email: sales@mil-media.com
Estab: 1992

John La Grou, Founder & President

Provider of music and media systems. The company also provides specialized tools for archival transfers and related applications.

Millennium Consulting Associates HQ
401 Roland Way Ste 250
Oakland CA 94621
P: 925-808-6700   F: 925-808-6708   PRC:140
mecaenviro.com
Email: hr@mecaenviro.com
Estab: 1998

Mike Noel, President

Provider of environmental and industrial hygiene services. The company offers environmental engineering, consulting, and compliance services.

Millennium Lapping & Grind Engineering HQ
3760 Yale Way Unit 3 & Unit 2
Fremont CA 94538
P: 510-438-9908   F: 510-438-9918   PRC:80
www.millenniumlapping.com
Email: millenniumlap@comcast.net

Dave Naicker, President
Joseph Naicker, Manager

Provider of lapping and grinding for CNC machining. The company specializes in single and double sided lapping diamond polishing of copper and silver.

Milner's Anodizing HQ
3330 McMaude Pl
Santa Rosa CA 95407
P: 707-584-1188   F: 707-584-1180   PRC:79
www.milnersanodizing.com
Email: info@milnersanodizing.com
Estab: 1983

Mike Marian, Owner
Vanessa Valentine, Manager

Provider of metal finishing solutions. The company's services include anodizing, anodizing, and passivation.

Miltenyi Biotec Inc DH
2303 Lindbergh St
Auburn CA 95602
P: 530-888-8871   F: 530-888-8925   PRC:43
www.miltenyibiotec.com
Email: macs@miltenyibiotec.com
Estab: 1990

Leonard Pulig, President & General Manager
Ira Marks, VP & General Manager
Kirt Braun, Marketing Manager
Rebecca McHugh, Customer Training Manager
Joan Blynn, Accounting Manager

Developer, manufacturer, and seller of products serving the fields of cell biology, immunology, regenerative medicine, and molecular biology.

Mindflash HQ
2825 El Camino Real Ste 200
Palo Alto CA 94306
P: 805-963-8417   F: 805-963-4020   PRC:319
www.mindflash.com
Estab: 1998

Julie Rieken, CEO
Mack Talcott, CTO
Michelle Bowman, Chief Customer Officer
Matt Smith, VP of Finance
Grant King, VP

Provider of online training and related solutions. The company offers services to the software industry.

Minerva Surgical Inc HQ
101 Saginaw Dr
Redwood City CA 94063
P: 855-646-7874   F: 866-465-2875   PRC:186
www.minervasurgical.com
Email: info@minervasurgical.com
Estab: 2008

Qiuyuan Liu, President
David Ferrito, VP of Sales & Customer Service
Akos Toth, Principal Engineer

Manufacturer of medical devices. The company
provides products for the treatment of abnormal
uterine bleeding.

Minimatics Inc HQ
3445 De La Cruz Blvd
Santa Clara CA 95054-2110
P: 650-969-5630   F: 408-496-0111   PRC:74
www.minimatics.com
Email: sales@minimatics.com
Estab: 1961

Mark Lentz, General Manager
Larry Hutnick, Information Technology Manager

Provider of precision machining solutions. The
company offers CNC milling, manual turning,
lapping, and honing services.

Minitool Inc HQ
1610 Doll Ave Ste H
Campbell CA 95008
P: 408-395-1585   F: 408-395-1605   PRC:80
www.minitoolinc.com
Email: info@minitoolinc.com

Renate Schaller, Advertising Manager

Manufacturer of precision instruments and small
tools for microscopic investigation. The company
also specializes in under-microscope precision
tools.

Minto Research & Development Inc HQ
20270 Charlanne Dr
Redding CA 96002-9223
P: 530-222-2373   F: 530-222-0679   PRC:189
sagersplints.com
Email: mintord@aol.com
Estab: 1979

Anne Borschneck, President

Supplier of emergency fracture response systems.

MIODx Inc HQ
5941 Optical Ct
San Jose CA 95138
P: 866-756-4639   PRC:186
www.miodx.com
Estab: 2014

Sean Givens, Founder & COO
Graeme McLean, CEO
Nhi Nguyen, Scientist

Provider of diagnostics and biomarker expertise in
a variety of cancer treatments including immu-
no-therapies.

Mirabilis Design Inc HQ
1159 Sonora Ct Ste 116
Sunnyvale CA 94086
P: 408-844-3234   F: 408-519-6719   PRC:323
www.mirabilisdesign.com
Email: info@mirabilisdesign.com
Estab: 2003

Deepak Shankar, Founder
Vaishnavi Shankar, CEO
Darryl Koivisto, CTO
S. Pradeep, Director of Sales

Provider of systems engineering solutions for
performance analysis and architecture exploration
of electronics and real-time software.

Miramar Labs Inc HQ
2790 Walsh Ave
Santa Clara CA 95051
P: 408-579-8700   F: 408-579-8795   PRC:186
www.miradry.com
Email: info@miramarlabs.com
Estab: 2006

Melinda Kolar, Director of Customer Service
Shannon Holt, HR Manager
Ramon Delacruz, Senior Lead Technician &
Trainer
Suryakant Devangan, Senior Tech Lead
Jason Rojas, Senior Manufacturing Technician

Provider of solutions for excessive sweat. The
company is engaged in clinical trials and research
programs.

Mirantis Inc HQ
900 E Hamilton Ave Ste 650
Campbell CA 95008
P: 650-963-9828   F: 650-968-2997   PRC:325
www.mirantis.com
Email: info@mirantis.com
Estab: 1999

Adrian Ionel, Co-Founder & CEO & Chairman
Boris Renski, Co-Founder & CMO
Alex Freedland, Co-Founder
Dave Van Everen, SVP of Marketing
Christian Nall, VP of West Region & AT&T

Specializes in the development and support of
Kubernetes and OpenStack.

Mirion Technologies Inc DH
3000 Executive Pkwy Ste 222
San Ramon CA 94583
P: 925-543-0800   PRC:189
www.mirion.com
Email: privacy@mirion.com
Estab: 2006

Bruno Morel, President of Detection & Measure-
ment Division
Iain Wilson, President of Sensing Systems
Division
Loic Eloy, President of Radiation Monitoring
Systems Division
Louis Biacchi, President of Dosimetry Services
Division
Thomas Logan, Chairman & CEO

Provider of solutions in radiation detection. The
company serves the healthcare, nuclear power,
and other industries.

Mission Bio HQ
6000 Shoreline Ct Ste 104
S San Francisco CA 94080
P: 415-854-0058   F: 650-763-4483   PRC:186
missionbio.com
Email: info@missionbio.com
Estab: 2014

Adam Sciambi, Co-Founder & Director of Engi-
neering
Charlie Silver, Co-Founder & CEO
Dennis Eastburn, Co-Founder & CSO
Darrin Crisitello, CCO
Rebecca Galler, SVP of Marketing

Developer and deliverer of precision medicine.
The company offers instruments, fixed panels,
custom panels, and software for the researchers
and clinicians.

**Mission Janitorial & Abrasive
Supplies** HQ
9292 Activity Rd   [N]
San Diego CA 92126
P: 858-566-6700   F: 858-271-5079   PRC:80
www.missionjanitorial.com
Email: sales@missionjanitorial.com
Emp: 11-50   Estab: 1939

Kevin Carlson, President & CEO
Ken Heck, Manager of Business Development

Manufacturer and distributor of chemicals, cleaners, and detergents.

Mission Peak Optics Inc HQ
46941 Rancho Higuera Rd
Fremont CA 94539
P: 510-438-0384   F: 510-438-9795   PRC:212
www.missionpeakoptics.com
Email: support@missionpeakoptics.com

Kent Lin, Operations Officer

Provider of measurement solutions for semiconductor industry. The company offers thin film
thickness measurement system.

Mission Rubber Co HQ
1660 Leeson Ln   [N]
Corona CA 92879
P: 951-736-1343   F: 800-637-4601   PRC:189
www.missionrubber.com
Emp: 201-500   Estab: 1958

Chris Vansell, VP & General Manager

Manufacturer of rubber coupling products.

**Mission Tool and Manufacturing
Company Inc** HQ
3440 Arden Rd
Hayward CA 94545
P: 510-782-8383   F: 510-785-0687   PRC:74
www.missiontool.com
Email: info@missiontool.com
Estab: 1968

Carol A. Smith, VP
John Jackson, Director of Operations

Manufacturer of precision stamped and machined
components. The company serves aerospace,
automotive, medical, telecom, defense, and commercial sectors.

Mistral Solutions Inc HQ
43092 Christy St
Fremont CA 94538
P: 408-705-2240   F: 408-987-9665   PRC:323
www.mistralsolutions.com
Email: usa@mistralsolutions.com
Estab: 1997

Anees Ahmed, President
Mujahid Alam, CEO
Anoop Agarwal, CFO
Ramanan J. V., VP of Engineering
Srinivas Panapakam, VP of Sales & Business
Development

Provider of technology design and systems
engineering solutions. The company's solutions
include hardware board design and embedded
software development.

Mitsui High-tec Inc BR
2001 Gateway Pl E Tower Ste 325
San Jose CA 95110
P: 408-980-0782   F: 408-727-8160   PRC:157
mitsuihightec.com

Kensuke Gondai, Finance Manager
Emerson Erazo, Senior Sales Manager of New
Business Development

Provider of grinder parts, precision tools, and
stamping products. The company is involved in
design, installation, and delivery services.

Mixbook HQ
726 Main St
Redwood City CA 94063
P: 855-649-2665   PRC:326
www.mixbook.com
Email: hello@mixbook.com
Estab: 2006

Andrew Laffoon, CEO & Founder
Tucker Taylor, Chief Marketing & Growth Officer
Scott Bonds, VP of Engineering
Allison Kreft, Art Director
Arun Vatturi, Director of WW Operations

Provider of customizable photo books, cards and
calendars, as well as creation of online scrap-
books on the web using design software.

Mixed Signal Integration HQ
2157-50 O'Toole Ave
San Jose CA 95131
P: 408-434-6305   F: 408-434-6417   PRC:59
mix-sig.com
Email: info@mix-sig.com
Estab: 1997

Levent Ozcolak, President
John Ambrose, VP of Applications & System
Engineering
Jeff Thompson, Director of Marketing & Sales

Specializes in the design, manufacture and sale
of turnkey analog and mixed-signal standard
products and custom ASICs.

Mixel Inc HQ
97 E Brokaw Rd Ste 250
San Jose CA 95112
P: 408-436-8500   F: 408-436-8400   PRC:204
www.mixel.com
Email: info@mixel.com
Estab: 1998

Scott Donnelly, Director of Process Development
Jintao Zang, Mixed Signal Design Engineer
Mandy Xu, Mixed-Signal IC Designer

Designer and developer of mixed-signal Internet
protocol cores for the semiconductor and electronics industries.

Mixonic HQ
3749 Buchanan St Unit 487
San Francisco CA 94147
P: 888-464-9664   PRC:95
www.mixonic.com
Email: customercare@mixonic.com
Estab: 2001

Daniel Weideman, Production Lead
Shimeel Sajid, Systems Analyst
Dai Akiyama, Accountant
Marianne Sampogna Jacobson, Contact
Greg Rivera, Sales Associate

Provider of design services. The company offers
custom CD and DVD duplication, disc packaging,
CD production, and printing services.

Mizuho OSI HQ
30031 Ahern Ave
Union City CA 94587-1234
P: 510-429-1500   F: 510-429-8500   PRC:189
www.mizuhosi.com
Email: custserv@mizuhosi.com
Estab: 1978

Steve Lamb, President
Greg Neukirch, VP of Sales & Marketing
Yosup Kim, VP of Finance
Patrick Rimroth, General Manager
Paul James, Director of Control Systems

Designs and manufactures medical components.
The company offers surgery tables, patient care
kits, trauma tables, and more.

MJB Precision Machining Inc HQ
715 E McGlincy Ln
Campbell CA 95008
P: 408-559-3035   F: 408-559-3037   PRC:80
mjbprecisionmachining.com
Email: mjbprec@aol.com

Mark Bamberg, President & CEO
Robert Roe, Manager of Sales Operations

Manufacturer of precision and prototype machining parts and components for the defense,
telecom, medical, and semiconductor manufacturing industries.

MLD Technologies LLC HQ
2672 Bayshore Pkwy Ste 701
Mountain View CA 94043
P: 650-938-3780   F: 650-938-3113   PRC:175
www.mldtech.com
Email: info@mldtech.com
Estab: 1997

Gary DeBell, Co-Founder
Len Mott, Co-Founder
Tony Louderback, Co-Founder
Ric Shimshock, Programming Manager
Linda Lingg, Senior Engineer

Supplier of optical coatings and components. The
company specializes in the design, development,
and manufacture of ion beam sputtered thin-films.

MMC AD Systems HQ
PO Box 12287
Pleasanton CA 94588
P: 925-485-4949   F: 925-485-4939   PRC:325
www.mmcad.com
Email: info@mmcad.com
Estab: 1975

Judy Louie, Senior Project Manager
Bill Sumerlin, Senior Consultant

Provider of architectural and consulting services.
The company focuses on strategic planning, market research, and business and web development.

MMR Technologies Inc HQ
41 Daggett Dr
San Jose CA 95134-1346
P: 650-962-9620   F: 650-962-9647   PRC:154
www.mmr-tech.com
Email: sales@mmr-tech.com
Estab: 1980

William Little, CEO
Ted M. Sanchez, Engineer
Jessica Jordan, Accounting Administrator &
Controller

Provider of micro-miniature refrigerator technology. The company offers hall measurement, optical
study systems, and temperature control services.

MobileFrame LLC HQ
101 Blossom Hill Rd
Los Gatos CA 95032
P: 408-885-1200   F: 408-280-0555   PRC:320
www.mobileframe.com
Email: sales@mobileframe.com
Estab: 2001

Lonny Oswalt, CEO
Glenn Wickman, CTO
Joseph Kliger, VP of Engineering
Patricia Oswalt, EVP of Sales & Marketing
Bruce Redke, Business Development Manager

Provider of enterprise mobility solutions that
include mobile application development, device
management, GPS tracking, and integration
features.

Mobileiron Inc HQ
490 East Middlefield Rd
Mountain View CA 94043
P: 650-919-8100   F: 650-919-8006   PRC:322
www.mobileiron.com
Email: info@mobileiron.com
Estab: 2007
Sales: $100M to $300M

Suresh Batchu, Co-Founder & CTO
Ajay Mishra, Co-Founder & Chief Customer
Officer
Simon Biddiscombe, President & CEO
Rhonda Shantz, CMO
Jared Lucas, CPO

Provider of mobile security, device, and application management solutions. The company focuses on technical support services.

Mobitor Corp HQ
1990 N California Blvd Ste 230
Walnut Creek CA 94596
P: 925-464-7700   PRC:319
Estab: 2001

Ahrhan Kim, Product Manager
Luke Hartsuyker, SQL Server Database Engineer
& Senior Software Engineer & Senior Technical
Lead

Provider of mobility software, connectivity, and information solutions. The company serves the aerospace, aviation, and manufacturing industries.

Mobitv HQ
1900 Powell St 9th Floor
Emeryville CA 94608
P: 510-450-5000   F: 510-450-5001   PRC:68
www.mobitv.com
Estab: 1999

Charlie Nooney, CEO & Chairman
Terri Stevens, CFO & GM of Mobile Business
Bill Routt, COO
Casey Fann, Operations Program Manager & VP
of Operations & Professional Services
Ankur Sharma, VP of Engineering

Provider of content delivery platforms. The company's products find application in mobile and broadband networks.

Mobiveil Inc HQ
890 Hillview Ct Ste 250
Milpitas CA 95035
P: 408-212-9512   F: 408-457-0406   PRC:323
www.mobiveil.com
Email: info@mobiveil.com
Estab: 2012

Ravi Thummarukudy, CEO
Gopa Periyadan, COO
Steven Shrader, Chief Architect
Dale Olstinske, VP of Sales
Amit Saxena, VP of Engineering

Provider of technology solutions. The company's products include Silicon IP and COTS Modules and offers IC design and embedded software services.

Modern Ceramics Manufacturing Inc HQ
2240 Lundy Ave
San Jose CA 95131
P: 408-383-0554   F: 408-383-0578   PRC:80
modernceramics.com
Estab: 1998

Julio Lung, Manufacturing Engineer

Supplier of ceramic materials and components. The company serves the semi-conductor and laser industries.

Modern Linear Inc HQ
75 Pelican Way Unit A
San Rafael CA 94901
P: 415-924-7938   F: 415-927-2360   PRC:80
www.modernlinear.com
Email: info@modernlinear.com
Estab: 2004

Steve Fulton, Founder

Manufacturer of guide roller products. The company mainly focuses on linear motion industry and serves commercial, packaging, and medical fields.

Modern Machine Company HQ
1633 Old Bayshore Hwy
San Jose CA 95112
P: 408-436-7670   F: 408-436-7674   PRC:159
www.modernmachine.com
Email: info@modernmachine.com

Ed Bauer, Owner
Brett Sherril, General Manager
Shelli Mazzone, Office Manager

Provider of machining services. The company focuses on robotic welding, automatic screw machines, and CNC machining centers.

Modern Systems Research Inc HQ
PO Box 62
Los Altos CA 94022
P: 650-940-2000   PRC:63
www.msr.com
Estab: 1960

Sam Wood, President

Provider of telecom design and voice and data networking services. The company also focuses on power systems and systems architecture.

Modified Plastics Inc HQ
1240 E Glenwood Pl   [N]
Santa Ana CA 92707
P: 714-546-4667   F: 714-546-0401   PRC:189
www.modifiedplastics.com
Emp: 1-10   Estab: 1976

Kevin Rodgers, Manager of Sales

Manufacturer of thermoplastic components.

Modius Inc HQ
71 Stevenson St Ste 400
San Francisco CA 94105
P: 415-655-6700   F: 415-655-6601   PRC:323
www.modius.com
Email: info@modius.com
Estab: 2004

Craig Compiano, CEO & President
Mark Stumm, VP of Marketing & Product Strategy
Scott Brown, VP of Engineering
Sean Gately, VP of Business Development
Mark Carberry, VP of Sales

Provider of performance management software. The company serves infrastructure monitoring applications.

Modules Technology Inc HQ
2526 Qume Dr Unit 28
San Jose CA 95131
P: 408-392-0808   PRC:124
www.modulestech.com
Email: syeh@modulestech.com
Estab: 1993

Henry Faun, President
Eve Duchene, Sales Administrator
Kevin To, International Sales Executive

Provider of custom module design solutions. The company's offerings include grinders, etching systems, and thermal recorders.

Modulus Data Systems HQ
386 Main St Ste 200
Redwood City CA 94063
P: 650-365-3111   F: 650-365-6111   PRC:196
www.modulusdatasystems.com
Email: info@modulusdatasystems.com
Estab: 1972

Kenji Tanaka, General Manager
Steve Waites, Engineering Manager
Mary Liviakis, Marketing Manager

Provider digital clinical cell (tally) counters. The company's products include Diffcount III, Comp-U-Diff, and Uro-Comp.

Modutek Corp HQ
6387 San Ignacio Ave
San Jose CA 95119
P: 408-362-2000   F: 408-362-2001   PRC:94
www.modutek.com
Estab: 1980

Doug Wagner, President & CEO
Robert Brody, Director of Operations & VP of
Operations
Joanne Turley, Director of Finance & Administration
Ruben Aguilar, Field Service Manager

Manufacturer of wet process equipment and environmental systems. The company serves the semiconductor sector and offers repair services.

Mojo Mobility Inc HQ
3350 Scott Blvd Bldg 37A
Santa Clara CA 95054
P: 650-446-0004 PRC:288
www.mojomobility.com
Email: sales@mojomobility.com
Estab: 2005

Afshin Partovi, CEO & Founder
Pouyan Shams, Hardware Systems Engineer

Provider of mobile recharge devices such as
batteries and pads for computer peripherals and
headsets for medical and commercial sectors.

Moldex-Metric Inc HQ
10111 W Jefferson Blvd [N]
Culver City CA 90232
P: 310-837-6500 F: 310-841-0171 PRC:189
www.moldex.com
Email: sales@moldex.com
Estab: 1960

Mark Magidson, CEO
Mark Meinecke, VP of Quality Assurance
Meiling Hsu, VP of Finance
James E. Hornstein, VP of Operations & General
Counsel
Jeffrey Birkner, VP of Technical Services & Quality
Assurance

Manufacturer and supplier of surgical appliances.

Molecular Devices LLC HQ
3860 N First St
San Jose CA 95134-1136
P: 800-635-5577 F: 408-747-3601 PRC:31
www.moleculardevices.com
Email: service.eu@moleculardevices.com
Estab: 1983

Susan Murphy, President
Steven Qian, CFO & VP of Finance
Laurent Claisse, VP & General Manager of Biolog-
ics Business Unit
Martin Verhoef, VP of Strategy & New Product
Generation
Poonam Taneja, VP & General Manager of Asia
Commercial Operations & Global Distribution

Manufacturer of bioanalytical measurement
systems. The company is engaged in life science
research, pharma, and bio therapeutic development.

Molecular Matrix Inc HQ
3410 Industrial Blvd Ste 103
West Sacramento CA 95691
P: 916-376-9404 PRC:24
molecularmatrix.com
Email: info@molecularmatrix.com
Estab: 2011

Charles Lee, Founder & CEO & Chairman of the
Board
Christopher Wink, CFO
Jim Keefer, COO
Steven I. Whitlock, CCO

Provider of research tools for cultivating and
studying stem cells. The company products provide solutions for growing cells.

Moller International Inc HQ
1855 N First St Ste C
Dixon CA 95620
P: 530-756-5086 PRC:4
www.moller.com
Email: dr.moller@moller.com
Estab: 1983

Paul Moller, President

Designer and developer of personal vertical take-
off and landing aircraft. The company specializes
in rotapower engines.

Momentum Design Lab HQ
300 Eighth Ave Ste 202
San Mateo CA 94401
P: 650-452-6290 PRC:323
momentumdesignlab.com
Email: hello@momentumdesignlab.com
Estab: 2002

David Thomson, CEO
Denis Lacasse, EVP
Matthew Wohl, Head of UX
Lydia Chang, Senior Product UX & UI Designer

Designer of enterprise-grade software products.
The company focuses on design, discovery, and
development of software.

Mondee Inc HQ
951 Mariners Island Blvd Ste 130
San Mateo CA 94404
P: 650-646-3320 PRC:323
www.mondee.com
Estab: 2011

William Gomes, President of Specialty & Global
Sales
Jagmit Soni, President of Sales
Prasad Gundumogula, CEO
Venkat Pasupuleti, CTO
Cho Tai, COO

Developer of technology for the generation of private fare distribution. The company offers services
to the travel industry.

Mondo Media Inc HQ
550 15th St Ste 31
San Francisco CA 94103
P: 415-865-2700 F: 415-865-2645 PRC:329
mondomedia.com
Email: customerservice@mondomedia.com
Estab: 1997

John Evershed, CEO & Founder
Douglas Kay, CFO
Aaron Simpson, VP of Animation & Business
Development
Dean MacDonald, Creative Director
April Pesa, Director of Development

Provider of gaming solutions. The company's store
features men's and women's T-shirts, smartphone
cases, and related supplies.

Monico Alloys Inc HQ
3039 Ana St [N]
Rancho Dominguez CA 90220
P: 310-928-0168 F: 310-928-0179 PRC:145
www.monicoalloys.com
Email: info@monicoalloys.com
Emp: 11-50 Estab: 1979

Jason Zenk, President
Saul Zenk, CFO
Ken Larson, EVP
Bruce Botansky, VP

Provider of scrap metal recycling services.

Monk & Associates Inc HQ
1136 Saranap Ave Ste Q
Walnut Creek CA 94595
P: 925-947-4867 F: 925-947-1165 PRC:142
monkassociates.com
Email: monkadmin@monkassociates.com
Estab: 1992

Chris Milliken, Office Manager

Provider of environmental consulting services.
The company specializes in biological constraints
analyses and mitigation plans.

Monogram Biosciences Inc HQ
345 Oyster Point Blvd
S San Francisco CA 94080
P: 650-635-1100 PRC:257
www.monogrambio.com
Email: pharmainfo@monogrambio.com
Estab: 1995

Christos J. Petropoulos, CSO
Gordon Parry, VP of Oncology, Research &
Development
Yolanda Lie, Clinical Research Program Manager
& Project Director & Sr. Manager Clinical & Re-
search Collaboration
Jackie Reeves, Director of Virology R&D
Weidong Huang, Senior Director of Clinical
research

Develops and commercializes diagnostic products.
The company offers products for the treatment
of human immunodeficiency virus and other viral
illnesses.

Monolith Materials Inc BR
662 Laurel St Ste 201
San Carlos CA 94070
P: 650-933-4957 PRC:51
monolithmaterials.com
Estab: 2012

Robert Hanson, Founder & CCO
Bill Brady, Executive Chairman
Tim Rens, CFO
Tom Maier, CTO
Chris Cornille, Chief Commercial & Supply Chain
Officer

Manufacturer of carbon black and hydrogen
for plastics, toner and printer ink, batteries and
conductive inks, and tires and industrial rubber
products.

Monolithic Power Systems Inc   HQ
79 Great Oaks Blvd
San Jose CA 95119
P: 408-826-0600   F: 408-826-0601   PRC:212
www.monolithicpower.com
Email: usinfo@monolithicpower.com
Estab: 1997
Sales: $300M to $1 Billion

Deming Xiao, President of Asia Operations
Michael R. Hsing, CEO & President & Chairman of the Board
Bernie Blegen, VP & CFO
Robert Nyberg, Chief Pilot
Saria Tseng, VP of Strategic Corporate Development & General Counsel & Corporate Secretary

Provider of analog semiconductor products. The company offers battery chargers, linear regulators and analog switches, voltage supervisors, and amplifiers.

Montavista Software LLC   HQ
5201 Great America Pkwy Ste 432
Santa Clara CA 95054
P: 408-520-1591   PRC:319
www.mvista.com
Email: info@mvista.com
Estab: 1999

Ravi Gupta, President & CEO
Hiroshi Someya, Director of APAC Sales
Mark Baker, Director of Sales
Armin Kuster, Lead Software Engineer
Vahe Sarrafian, Legal Counsel

Developer of embedded Linux system software, development tools, and related software products. The company's products include CGE and Dev-Rocket.

Monterey Bay Analytical Services   HQ
4 Justin Ct Ste D
Monterey CA 93940
P: 831-375-6227   F: 831-641-0734   PRC:41
mbasinc.com
Email: mweidner@mbasinc.com
Estab: 1999

David Holland, Principal Founder & Microbiologist & Chemist
Ben Sanchez, Principal Analyst
Mollie Wooden, Laboratory Supervisor
Hayden Maccagno, Lead Chemist
Linda Brown, Customer Relations Specialist & Sample Collector

Provider of laboratory testing services. The company services include sample collection, bacteria testing, and inorganic chemistry.

Monterey Computer Corp   HQ
501 Webster St
Monterey CA 93940
P: 831-646-1147   F: 831-646-1118   PRC:329
www.mccnet.com
Email: mcc@mccnet.com
Estab: 1979

Tary McConnell, Owner
Roy Weischadle, Chief IT Analyst

Provider of technology and integrated network services. The company offers networking, wireless Internet, server hosting, and surveillance services.

Monterey Regional Waste Management District   HQ
14201 Del Monte Blvd   [N]
Marina CA 93933
P: 831-384-5313   F: 831-384-3567   PRC:141
www.mrwmd.org
Emp: 51-200   Estab: 1951

Carrie Theis, Vice Chairman of the Board
Jeff Lindentha, Director of Communications
Peter K. Skinner, Director of Finance & Administration
Rick Downey, Manager
Kacey Christie, Manager

Dealer of solid waste management.

Moog Animatics   BR
2581 Leghorn St
Mountain View CA 94043
P: 650-960-4215   PRC:68
www.animatics.com
Email: animatics_sales@moog.com
Estab: 1987

Doug Parentice, President
Sean Brennan, Operations Manager
David Torrez, Shop Manager
Joe Ruf, Software Engineer
Keith Webster, Software Engineer

Provider of motion control devices. The company offers actuators, cables, power supplies, and peripherals.

Moog CSA Engineering   HQ
2581 Leghorn St
Mountain View CA 94043-1613
P: 650-210-9000   F: 650-210-9001   PRC:146
www.csaengineering.com
Email: infocsa@moog.com
Estab: 1982

Rainer N. Growitz, Business Manager
Christian Smith, Site Manager
Patrick Atkins, Laboratory Manager
Eric Austin, Site Engineering Manager
Jackson Smith, Mechanical Engineer

Designer and manufacturer of high precision systems. The company offers positioning systems, actuators, absorbers, and test systems.

Moogsoft Inc   HQ
1160 Battery St E 1st Fl
San Francisco CA 94111
P: 415-738-2299   PRC:323
www.moogsoft.com
Email: salesinfo@moogsoft.com
Estab: 2011

Phil Tee, Founder & Chairman & CEO & Herd Leader
Rob Harper, CSO
David Casper, CTO & CISO
Dixie Dunn, SVP of Customer Advocacy
Mike Silvey, EVP

Provider of collaborative situation management software solutions for Web-scale information technology (IT) operations.

Moon Valley Circuits   HQ
12350 Maple Glen Rd
Glen Ellen CA 95442
P: 707-996-4157   PRC:316
www.moonvalleycircuits.com
Estab: 1976

Mike Miller, Owner

Manufacturer of control systems for wineries. The company specializes in tank temperature, barrel-room, and refrigeration control systems.

Moonstone Interactive Inc   HQ
2010 Crow Canyon Pl Ste 100
San Ramon CA 94583-1344
P: 925-736-4178   PRC:323
www.msinteractive.com
Email: info@msinteractive.com
Estab: 1996

Stephen M. Herz, President & CEO
Jason Herz, QA Director & Senior Developer

Provider of website design services. The company offers web design and development, content management, and market visibility services.

Moore Twining Associates Inc   HQ
2527 Fresno St
Fresno CA 93721
P: 559-268-7021   F: 559-268-7126   PRC:139
mooretwining.com
Estab: 1898

Harry Moore, Owner
Ruthie Moore, Secretary & Treasurer
Read Andersen, Geotechnical Division Manager
Allen Bushey, Drilling Division Manager
Ken Clark, Engineering Geologist

Provider of geotechnical engineering, environmental, construction inspection, materials testing, analytical chemistry, and drilling services.

MORE Health Inc   HQ
999 Baker Way 5th Fl
San Mateo CA 94404
P: 888-908-6673   PRC:186
morehealth.com
Email: hello@morehealth.com
Estab: 2013

Bo Hu, Co-Founder & CTO
Hope Lewis, CEO & Co-Founder
Marc Shuman, CMO
Ted Bukowski, CRO
Robert Warren, Chief Medical Consultant

Specializes in collaborative diagnosis. The company serves patients, hospitals, and the medical industry.

Morgan Hill Plastics Inc   HQ
8118 Arroyo Cir   [N]
Gilroy CA 95020
P: 408-842-1322   F: 408-842-1335   PRC:189
www.morganhillplastics.net
Emp: 11-50   Estab: 1972

Jeffrey Hudson, VP of Manufacturing

Provider of vacuum forming, bending, polishing and much more services.

Morgan Industries Inc HQ

3311 E 59th St [N]
Long Beach CA 90805
P: 562-634-4074 PRC:159
www.morganindustriesinc.com
Emp: 1-10 Estab: 1968

Charles Land, President

Manufacturer of special industry machinery.

Morgan Manufacturing Inc HQ

PO Box 737
Petaluma CA 94953
P: 707-763-6848 F: 707-763-4507 PRC:81
www.morganmfg.com
Email: customerservice@morganmfg.com
Estab: 1952

Carl Palmgren, Owner

Manufacturer of auto body tools and tie-down
equipment. The company caters to the flat bed
trucking industry.

Morgan Royce Industries Inc HQ

49050 Milmont Dr
Fremont CA 94538
P: 510-440-8500 F: 510-440-0886 PRC:179
www.morganroyce.com
Email: mri@morganroyce.com
Estab: 1991

Carl Paxton, CEO
Emily Alvarez, Production control Manager

Developer and manufacturer of custom cables,
wire harness, and PCB assemblies. The company
offers project management and quality control
services.

Morgan Technical Ceramics BR

13079 Earhart Ave
Auburn CA 95602
P: 530-823-3401 PRC:53
www.morgantechnicalceramics.com
Estab: 2003

Zack Waddle, Engineering Manager

Manufacturer of cast and powder metal stainless steels. The company also focuses on other
specialty alloys.

Morley Manufacturing Inc HQ

14262 Meadow Dr
Grass Valley CA 95945
P: 530-477-6527 F: 530-477-0194 PRC:135
www.morleytanks.com
Email: morleymfg@att.net
Estab: 1984

Bob Pelton, President

Designer and manufacturer of drain back water
storage tanks for residential and commercial purposes. The company offers installation services.

Morrill Industries Inc HQ

24754 E River Rd
Escalon CA 95320
P: 209-838-2550 F: 209-838-3544 PRC:153
www.morrillinc.com
Estab: 1953

Michael Morrill, Corporate Manager

Manufacturer and supplier of irrigation equipment.
The company also offers custom built rotating
suction screens and industrial pipes.

MOS Plastics Inc HQ

2308 Zanker Rd
San Jose CA 95131
P: 408-944-9407 F: 408-944-9439 PRC:163
mosinc.com
Email: sales@mosinc.com
Estab: 1974

Deanna Musil, Program Manager
Ernest Harper, Production Control Manager
Judy Louie, Executive Assistant

Provider of precision injection-molding, contract
manufacturing, and assembly services for medical
and electronics OEMs.

Mosaic Industries Inc HQ

5437 Central Ave Ste 1
Newark CA 94560
P: 510-790-8222 PRC:208
www.mosaic-industries.com
Email: info@mosaic-industries.com
Estab: 1985

Paul Clifford, VP & COO
Elena Belkine, Production Manager
Kelcey Hein, Office Assistant

Developer and manufacturer of embedded
computers for instruments and automation. The
company serves sensor calibration and PID
control needs.

Moseley Associates Inc HQ

82 Coromar Dr [N]
Santa Barbara CA 93117
P: 805-968-9621 F: 805-685-9638 PRC:68
www.moseleysb.com
Email: info@moseleysb.com
Emp: 51-200 Estab: 1991

Jamal Hamdani, President & CEO
Bruce Tarr, CFO

Provider of broadband, carrier, broadcast technologies and designs, manufactures, and markers
digital transmission systems, radio and television
broadcast services.

**Motion Capture Camera & Software
Leader** HQ

6085 State Farm Dr Ste 100
Rohnert Park CA 94928
P: 707-579-6500 PRC:168
www.motionanalysis.com
Email: info@motionanalysis.com
Estab: 1982

Tom Whitaker, CEO
Rita Maloney, VP of Marketing
John Greaves, SVP
Shel Fung, SVP of Engineering
Bill Van Haaften, Production Manager

Provider of motion analyzers. The company specializes in engineering, animation, design, reality
augmentation, and simulation services.

Motion Control Engineering Inc HQ

11380 White Rock Rd
Rancho Cordova CA 95742
P: 916-463-9200 F: 916-463-9201 PRC:150
www.mceinc.com
Email: info@nidec-mce.com
Estab: 1983

Lawrence Vo, Director of Engineering
Richard Wagner, Technical Writer

Manufacturer of elevator control products. The
company's products include elevator and escala-
tor controls, complete elevators, and components
and peripherals.

Motiondsp Inc HQ

700 Airport Blvd Ste 270
Burlingame CA 94010
P: 650-288-1164 PRC:325
www.motiondsp.com
Email: sales@motiondsp.com
Estab: 2005

Sean Varah, CEO

Provider of software products. The company
serves the defense and intelligence, law enforcement, energy, and transportation markers.

Motive Medical Intelligence HQ

555 California St Ste 350
San Francisco CA 94104
P: 415-362-4007 F: 415-392-4067 PRC:188
motivemi.com
Email: info@motivepw.com
Estab: 1996

Jeanne Cohen, CEO
Leslie Kilgo, CFO
Rich Klasco, CMO
Nicholas Rains, Chief Solutions Officer
Jay Tyler, Chief Sales Officer

Developer of medical intelligence solutions. The
company also offers care plans for population
health management.

Motor Guard Corp HQ

580 Carnegie St
Manteca CA 95337
P: 209-239-9191 F: 209-239-5114 PRC:148
www.motorguard.com
Email: info@motorguard.com

David Barleen, President
Tim Keating, VP
Sandy Allen, Director
Brian Jacobson, National Sales Manager
Robert Rheinhart, PBE Sales Manager

Designer and developer of spray equipment and
tools for collision repairs. The company offers
services to the automotive sector.

Mountain View Pharmaceuticals Inc HQ

3475 Edison Way Ste S
Menlo Park CA 94025-1821
P: 650-365-5515 F: 650-365-5525 PRC:257
www.mvpharm.com
Email: busdev@mvpharm.com
Emp: 10 Estab: 1995

Merry Sherman, CEO
John French, Business Manager

Provider of pharmaceutical development, protein
biochemistry, immunology and polymer chemistry
solutions for delivery of therapeutic proteins.

Mountford Group Inc HQ
1486 Davis Ave
Concord CA 94518
P: 925-686-6613 F: 925-686-0226 PRC:323
www.mountfordgroup.com
Email: info@mountfordgroup.com

Gwaltney Mountford, Technical Communicator

Provider of system development and web application services. The company also focuses on technical communication.

Mountz Inc HQ
1080 N 11th St
San Jose CA 95112
P: 800-456-1828 F: 408-292-2733 PRC:159
www.mountztorque.com
Email: sales@mountztorque.com
Estab: 1965

Chris Morris, Marketing Manager
Rob Ralph, Sales Manager
Kevin Dockery, Territory Sales Manager
Alex Gregorios, Systems & IT Specialist

Manufacturer of torque analyzers, sensors, bits, sockets, and adapters. The company is engaged in installation and technical support services.

Moximed Inc BR
26460 Corporate Ave Ste 100
Hayward CA 94545
P: 510-887-3300 PRC:189
www.moximed.com

Anton Clifford, CEO & Founder
Christine Barcelos, VP of Corporate Operations
Keith Fong, VP of Marketing & Business Development
Nancy Isaac, Regulatory Counsel & VP of Quality
Luigi Bivi, Managing Director

Developer of joint preserving option for patients with knee osteoarthritis. The company serves the medical industry.

Mozilla Corp HQ
331 E Evelyn Ave
Mountain View CA 94041
P: 650-903-0800 F: 650-903-0875 PRC:323
www.mozilla.org/en-GB
Estab: 1998

Chris Beard, CEO
Jascha Kaykas-Wolff, CMO
Michael DeAngelo, CPO
Roxi Wen, CFO
Katharina Borchert, Chief Open Innovation Officer

Designer and developer of web application tools and browsers. The company serves individuals and businesses.

MPBS Industries HQ
2820 E Washington Blvd [N]
Los Angeles CA 90023
P: 323-268-8514 F: 323-386-4058 PRC:80
www.mpbs.com
Email: contact@mpbs.com
Emp: 11-50 Estab: 1938

Patty Hernandez, General Manager

Manufacturer and distributor of equipment and supplies for food processors and food packagers in the United States and around the globe.

Mphasis Corp BR
226 Airport Pkwy
San Jose CA 95110
P: 408-327-1240 PRC:322
www.mphasis.com
Email: whistleblower@mphasis.com
Estab: 1998

Davinder Singh Brar, Chairman
Dinesh Venugopal, President of Mphasis Direct & Digital
Elango R., President of DXC &HP SBU
Sundar Subramanian, President of Global Delivery
Nitin Rakesh, CEO & Executive Director

Provider of applications, infrastructure, and business process outsourcing services to the banking and healthcare sectors.

MSC Software BR
4675 MacArthur Ct
Newport Beach CA 92660
P: 714-540-8900 PRC:316
www.mscsoftware.com
Email: info-msc@mscsoftware.com
Estab: 1963

Doug Neill, VP

Developer of simulation software for acoustics, thermal analysis, and other needs. The company also offers software implementation and systems design services.

mscripts LLC HQ
445 Bush St Ste 200
San Francisco CA 94108
P: 888-672-7478 PRC:194
www.mscripts.com
Email: info@mscripts.com
Estab: 2007

Mark Cullen, CEO
Steve Brickman, VP of Engineering & CTO
Brian Davis, VP of Sales
Lara Loveman, VP of Business Strategy
Mahesh Srivastava, VP of Engineering

Specializes in clinical and manufacturer programs. The company offers services to patients and pharmacies.

MTI California Inc HQ
2890 N Main St Ste 300
Walnut Creek CA 94597
P: 925-937-1500 F: 925-937-8518 PRC:27
www.mti-ca.com
Email: sales@mti-ca.com
Estab: 1991

Scott McDonald, President

Specializes in designing and validating manufacturing controls. The company offers services to biotech companies.

Multi Metrics Inc HQ
865 Lemon St
Menlo Park CA 94025
P: 650-328-0200 F: 650-328-3586 PRC:319
multimetrics.com
Estab: 1975

Bill Tandler, President

Provider of geometric dimensioning and tolerance technology products and services and offers training and corporate implementation services.

Multibeam Corp HQ
3951 Burton Dr
Santa Clara CA 95054
P: 408-980-1800 F: 408-980-1808 PRC:212
www.multibeamcorp.com
Email: info@multibeamcorp.com

David K. Lam, Chairman & CEO
Lynn Barringer, President
David Liu, VP of Technology
Thanh Cao, Senior Systems Engineer

Producer of photomasks for optical lithography. The company's products are used in IC manufacturing and water defect inspection applications.

MultiDimension Technology Company Ltd BR
6000 Hellyer Ave Ste 100
San Jose CA 95138
P: 650-275-2318 F: 408-705-4588 PRC:86
www.dowaytech.com
Email: sales@dowayusa.com
Estab: 2010

Weifeng Shen, Founder & VP Engineering
Song Xue, CEO & President

Supplier of TMR magnetic sensors. The company mainly offers switch, linear, angle, and gear tooth sensors.

Multimedia Consulting Services Inc HQ
311 Grunion Ct
Foster City CA 94404
P: 650-578-8591 F: 650-649-2277 PRC:324
www.mmcs.net
Email: info@mmcs.net
Estab: 1991

Tony Bhanot, President

Provider of multimedia consulting services. The company offers design, implementation, and maintenance of the information technology infrastructure.

Multispan Inc HQ
26219 Eden Landing Rd
Hayward CA 94545
P: 510-887-0817 PRC:268
multispaninc.com
Email: info@multispaninc.com
Estab: 2004

Kishore HEMLANI, Chairman
Tiina Sepp, Director of Marketing
Jennifer Pham, Associate Scientist
Rebecca Wirth, Administrative Assistant

Provider of drug discovery services. The company also engages in compound profiling and antibody profiling services.

Murdoc Technology HQ
5683 E Fountain Way
Fresno CA 93727
P: 559-497-1580 F: 559-497-1587 PRC:91
www.murdoc.com
Email: sales@murdoc.com
Estab: 1999

Yee Vang, Production Manager
Greg Miller, Administrator

Manufacturer of electronics. The company primarily offers precision and wire harnesses and cables to various sectors.

Murigenics HQ
941 Railroad Ave
Vallejo CA 94592
P: 707-561-8900   F: 707-561-8943   PRC:24
murigenics.com

Henry Lopez, President & CSO
Steven Noonan, COO
Noy Vongphakham, VP Advanced Memory Solutions & VP Memory System Development
Chandra Khantwal, Senior Director

Provider of preclinical in-vivo and in-vitro contract drug discovery. The company is also focused on development services.

Murray Trailers HQ
1754 E Mariposa Rd
Stockton CA 95205
P: 209-466-0266   F: 209-466-0550   PRC:159
www.murraytrailer.com
Email: sales@murraytrailer.com
Estab: 1946

Doug Murray, President & CEO
Sue Smith, Contact

Designer and manufacturer of trailers. The company also offers related accessories and hauling services.

MusclePharm Corp HQ
4400 Vanowen St
Burbank CA 91505
P: 800-292-3909   PRC:272
www.musclepharm.com
Email: customer.service@musclepharm.com
Estab: 2006
Sales: $30M to $100M

Brian Casutto, EVP of Sales Operations & Director
David Garin, Controller

Provider of sports supplement and nutrition products such as fish oil, energy sport zero, and coco protein for weight loss, fitness, and athletes.

Mvinix Systems Inc HQ
2210 Lundy Ave
San Jose CA 95131-1816
P: 408-321-9109   F: 408-321-9110   PRC:211
www.mvinixsystems.com

Ronald Zuniga, Account Manager
Karma Dias, Account Executive
Xuan Vo, Buyer

Provider of electronic and manufacturing service provider for printed circuit board assemblies. The company deals with design and testing services.

MYCOM OSI Inc RH
2365 Iron Point Rd Ste 170
Folsom CA 95630
P: 916-467-1500   PRC:323
www.mycom-osi.com
Email: info@mycom-osi.com
Estab: 1997

Ian Meakin, Head of Marketing

Provider of performance management, compliance, employer reporting, patient engagement, and satisfaction solutions.

M-210

Mydax Inc HQ
12260 Shale Ridge Ln
Auburn CA 95602-8400
P: 530-888-6662   F: 530-888-0962   PRC:236
www.mydax.com
Email: sales@mydax.com
Estab: 1986

Tom Spesick, President & CEO
Brandon Hall, Engineering Manager & VP
Gary Kramer, VP of Engineering & Engineering Consultant
Justin Clark, Quality Assurance Manager
Sandie Rall-Smith, Accounting Manager

Designer and manufacturer of temperature control systems. The company offers the elite chiller system.

Myers Network Solutions HQ
1101 S Winchester Blvd Ste P-298
San Jose CA 95128
P: 408-483-1881   F: 408-244-1881   PRC:327
myersnetsol.com
Estab: 2002

Brad Myers, President & Co-Founder
Victoria Myers, Director of Operations & Marketing & Co-Founder
Rob Wallace, Network Engineer
Patti Boor, Marketing Assistant

Provider of network solutions. The company focuses on IT consulting, disaster recovery, network assessment, and cloud computing.

Myers Power Products Inc HQ
725 E Harrison   [N]
Corona CA 92879
P: 909-923-1800   PRC:200
www.myerspowerproducts.com
Emp: 5001-10000   Estab: 1968

Bruce Steigerwald, VP of Operations
Jon Waggener, EVP
Tom Rothenberger, EVP
Tony Williams, VP of Operations
Nancy Gordon-Brooks, Director of Marketing

Manufacturer of electrical distribution products, emergency power systems, medium voltage switchgear, powerhouses and much more.

MyoKardia Inc HQ
1000 Sierra Point Pkwy
Brisbane CA 94005
P: 650-741-0900   PRC:34
www.myokardia.com
Email: medinfo@myokardia.com
Estab: 2012
Sales: $30M to $100M

Tassos Gianakakos, CEO
Taylor Harris, CFO
Ingrid Boyes, Chief Human Resource Officer
Marc Semigran, CMO
Robert McDowell, CSO

Provider of precision medicine. The company focuses on developing and commercializing therapies for treating cardiovascular diseases.

MyVest Corp HQ
275 Battery St 17th Fl
San Francisco CA 94111
P: 415-369-9511   PRC:326
www.myvest.com
Email: info@myvest.com
Estab: 2001

Bill Harris, Co-Founder
Chuck Lewis, Co-Founder
Steve Warren, Co-Founder & Senior Technical Advisor
Anton Honikman, CEO
Josh Moats, CIO

Provider of enterprise wealth management solutions. The company offers services to business organizations.

N&K Technology Inc HQ
80 Las Colinas Ln
San Jose CA 95119
P: 408-513-3800   F: 408-513-3850   PRC:86
www.nandk.com
Email: inforequest@nandk.com
Estab: 1992

Iris Bloomer, Founder
Rahim Forouhi, President & CEO
Thomas Luong, Purchasing Manager

Manufacturer of metrology tools for the semiconductor, photomask, data storage, flat panel display, and solar cell industries.

NADA Technologies Inc HQ
4185 Blackhawk Plaza Cir Ste 220
Danville CA 94506
P: 650-678-4666   F: 650-401-7989   PRC:323
www.nadatechnologies.com

John Zuniga, Director of Global Customer Support

Provider of enterprise Oracle applications. The company also offers business intelligence solutions.

Nady Systems Inc HQ
870 Harbour Way S
Richmond CA 94804
P: 510-652-2411   F: 510-652-5075   PRC:68
www.nady.com
Email: support@nady.com
Estab: 1976

John Nady, CEO & President
Toby Nady, COO
Joy Ferrer, International Purchasing Manager

Designer and manufacturer of wireless microphones, and a full line of audio accessories. The company also focuses on marketing.

Naehas Inc HQ
3600 W Bayshore Rd Ste 104
Palo Alto CA 94303
P: 877-262-3427   PRC:323
naehas.com
Email: contact@naehas.com
Estab: 2006

Priti Lata Mondol, Senior UI Engineer
Alka Jain, Contact

Specializes in the automation of sales and marketing services. The company offers services to finance and insurance companies.

Nano Precision Medical Inc HQ
5858 Horton St Ste 280
Emeryville CA 94608
P: 415-506-8462 PRC:189
www.nanoprecisionmedical.com
Estab: 2007

Adam Mendelsohn, CEO & Co-Founder & Chairman
Kayte Fischer, CTO & Co-Founder
Lily Peng, VP of Clinical Development & Co-Founder
Tomoyuki Yoshie, VP of Device Research
Wouter Roorda, VP of Pharmaceutical Product Development

Developer of medical devices. The company specializes in rice-grain sized implant for the treatment of type II diabetes.

Nanolab Technologies Inc HQ
1708 McCarthy Blvd
Milpitas CA 95035
P: 408-433-3320 F: 408-433-3321 PRC:41
www.nanolabtechnologies.com
Email: pc@nanolab1.com
Estab: 2007

John Traub, President
Thomas Byrd, VP of Finance & Administration
Charlene Sun, Director of DB analysis operations
Xinyu Zhao, Technical Project Manager
Raymond Tang, Engineer

Provider of cutting edge technology and expertise for failure analysis, advanced microscopy and FIB circuit edit services.

Nanomix Inc HQ
5900 Hollis St Ste P
Emeryville CA 94608
P: 510-428-5300 F: 510-658-0425 PRC:186
www.nano.com
Email: info@nano.com
Estab: 2000

David Ludvigson, President & CEO
Sherrill Lavagnino, VP of Engineering
Bradley Johnson, Director of Engineering
Penny Hopkins, Manager of Finance & Administration
Cris Padilla, Associate Manufacturing Engineer

Manufacturer of diagnostic systems and supplies. The company is engaged in product development services.

Nanosyn HQ
3100 Central Expy
Santa Clara CA 95051
P: 408-987-2000 PRC:51
www.nanosyn.com
Email: info@nanosyn.com
Estab: 1998

Nikolai Sepetov, Owner
Olga Issakova, EVP
Wen Yang, Director of Synthetic Chemistry
Boris Pekelis, Director of Chemistry Technologies
Randy Scheuerman, Director of CGMP Operations

Provider of design, synthesis, and analysis of small organic compounds for the pharmaceutical and biotechnology industries.

Nanosys Inc HQ
233 S Hillview Dr
Milpitas CA 95035
P: 408-240-6700 F: 408-240-6900 PRC:288
www.nanosysinc.com
Email: info@nanosysinc.com
Estab: 2001

Jason Hartlove, President & CEO
Martin Devenney, SVP of Manufacturing & COO
Andrew Filler, VP of Intellectual Property
Jian Chen, VP of Research & Development
Noland Granberry, EVP

Developer of nanotechnology products for the LCD display and battery markers. The company focuses on display backlighting and energy storage devices.

Napajen Pharma Inc HQ
533 Airport Blvd Ste 527
Burlingame CA 94010
P: 650-685-2429 F: 650-401-2221 PRC:268
www.napajen.com
Email: info@napajen.com
Estab: 2004

Seiichi Okabe, CFO

Developer of novel drug delivery systems technologies for pharmaceutical and biotechnology industries.

Napo Pharmaceuticals Inc HQ
200 Pine St Ste 400
San Francisco CA 94104
P: 415-963-9938 F: 415-371-8311 PRC:269
www.napopharma.com
Email: hello@napopharma.com
Estab: 2001

Lisa Conte, Interim CEO & Director

Developer of pharmaceutical drugs. The company specializes in the development of patent pharmaceutical products.

Naprotek Inc HQ
90 Rose Orchard Way
San Jose CA 95134
P: 408-830-5000 F: 408-830-5050 PRC:209
www.naprotek.com
Email: info@naprotek.com
Estab: 1995

Najat El-Ayi Badriyeh, Founder & President & CEO
Larry Morrissey, VP of Operations
Paramajit Singh, Senior Director of Engineering & QMS
Amy Yin Chen, Director of Production
Arlis Greco, Quality Manager

Provider of electronics manufacturing services. The company serves customers in the satellites, industrial, medical, military, and other sectors.

Nasam Inc HQ
611 Gateway Blvd Ste 730
S San Francisco CA 94080
P: 650-872-1155 PRC:2
www.nasam.com

William Zimmerman, CFO
Wei Qian, GM & VP
Hiro Egawa, Deputy Director
Akira Yamamoto, Director of Space Programs
Kevin Townsend, Manager of Space Programs

Distributor of electronics products. The company offers military/defense equipment, aircraft support equipment, and other products.

Natera Inc HQ
201 Industrial Rd
San Carlos CA 94070
P: 650-249-9090 PRC:34
natera.com
Email: info@natera.com
Emp: 975
Sales: $300M to $1 Billion

Matthew Rabinowitz, Executive Chairman
Steve Chapman, CEO
Jonathan Sheena, CTO
Mike Brophy, CFO
Robert Schueren, COO

Provider of prenatal testing services. The company specializes in non-invasive prenatal testing, genetic carrier screening and paternity testing.

National Analytical Laboratories Inc HQ
10416 Investment Cir
Rancho Cordova CA 95670
P: 916-361-0555 F: 916-361-0540 PRC:142
nal1.com
Email: nal1@nal1.com
Estab: 1992

Paula Lee, President

Provider of environmental lab testing and consulting services. The company focuses on air monitoring, building inspection, and operations training.

National Center For Appropriate Technology BR
36355 Russell Blvd
Davis CA 95617
P: 530-792-7338 PRC:129
ncat.org
Email: rexd@ncat.org
Estab: 1976

Jeff Amerman, CFO
Jacqueline Hutchinson, VP of Operations
Carol Werner, Executive Director

Provider of information and access services. The company's offerings include weatherizing houses, monitoring energy applications, and testing products.

National Fabtronix Inc HQ
28800 Hesperian Blvd
Hayward CA 94545-5038
P: 510-785-3135 F: 510-785-1253 PRC:80
natfab.com
Estab: 1971

Knute Ream, President
Lauren Garcia, Purchasing Manager

Provider of custom fabrication and precision sheet metal services for the computer and medical industries.

National Vapor Industries Inc HQ
1811 Park St
Livermore CA 94551
P: 925-980-7341 F: 925-373-9692 PRC:152
www.nationalvapor.com
Email: davidjewell1@comcast.net
Estab: 2006

David Jewell, CEO
Terry Rice, Operations Director

Manufacturer of hydrogen generators. The company also offers marketing, installation, and other services.

Natron Resources Inc HQ
1480 Moraga Rd Ste I 229
Moraga CA 94556
P: 510-868-0701 PRC:135
www.natronresources.com
Email: info@natronresources.com
Estab: 2008

Jeff Ansley, Principal Solar Design Engineer

Provider of solar system, flat-plate photovoltaic, and solar thermal design and installations services.

Natural Logic HQ
PO Box 119
Berkeley CA 94701
P: 510-248-4940   F: 877-628-5644 PRC:325
natlogic.com
Email: info@natlogic.com
Estab: 1999

Jeremy Faludi, Director
Shana M. Gillis, Business Development & Operations Research

Provider of consulting, product development, e-learning, digital content, and product support services.

Nature's Cure HQ
4096 Piedmont Ave Ste 171
Oakland CA 94611
P: 877-469-9487 PRC:43
naturescure.com
Estab: 1994

Amy Baker, President & CEO & Owner

Provider of health and beauty solutions. The company offers over-the-counter products featuring natural ingredients.

Natus Medical Inc HQ
1501 Industrial Rd
San Carlos CA 94070
P: 650-802-0400   F: 650-802-0401 PRC:189
natus.com
Estab: 1987
Sales: $300M to $1 Billion

Jonathan Kennedy, President & CEO & Director
Drew Davies, EVP & CFO
Ivan Pandiyan, VP of Global Research & Development
Sean Langan, VP of Global Operations
Chris Chung, VP of Medical Affairs & Quality & Regulatory

Provider of medical devices, software, and services. The company offers products for neurology, newborn care, hearing diagnostics, and more.

Navire Pharma HQ
421 Kipling St
Palo Alto CA 94301
P: 650-391-9740 PRC:254
navirepharma.com
Email: info@navirepharma.com
Estab: 2017

Shafique Virani, CEO
Uma Sinha, CSO
Anna Wade, VP of Portfolio & Operations

Developer of novel therapies. The company focuses on developing SHP2 inhibitors for treating rare cancers.

Navis LLC HQ
55 Harrison St Ste 600
Oakland CA 94607
P: 510-267-5000   F: 510-267-5100 PRC:323
www.navis.com
Email: partners@navis.com
Estab: 1988

Benoit de la Tour, President & CEO
Bruce Jacquemard, CRO
Andy Barrons, CSO
Rob Dillon, SVP & CFO
Robert Inchausti, CTO

Provider of terminal operating solutions. The company offers solutions for container terminal operations, expert decking, and process automation.

Navlink LH
1001 Bayhill Dr Ste 200
San Bruno CA 94066
P: 650-616-4042 PRC:324
www.navlink.com
Estab: 1996

Richard Giugno, President & CEO
Antoine El-Am, CIO
Bassel Dbaibo, CCO
Bassem Soubra, VP of Global Market Development
Mansour Naufal, VP of Product Development & Service Enablement

Provider of managed data services, managed hosting services, and managed enterprise networking solutions.

NB Corporation of America BR
46750 Lakeview Blvd
Fremont CA 94538
P: 510-490-1420   F: 510-490-1733 PRC:146
www.nbcorporation.com
Email: info@nbcorporation.com
Estab: 2000

Larry Hansen, Director of Sales
Brian Pinkham, Director of Sales
Paul Morreale, Sales Manager
Kunmoon Koh, Branch Manager
Shoijro Oh, Operations Manager

Manufacturer of linear motion bearings, slides, ball splines, and related products. The company's products include slide guides, spindle shafts, and actuators.

NBA Engineering Inc HQ
897 Hyde St 2nd Fl
San Francisco CA 94109
P: 415-202-9840   F: 415-202-9838 PRC:154
www.nbaeng.com
Estab: 1994

Natalie Alavi, President
Jan Groupp, Marketing Coordinator

Provider of mechanical and electrical engineering design, energy conversion, and construction management services.

NComputing Company Ltd HQ
1875 S Grant St Ste 570
San Mateo CA 94402
P: 650-409-5959   F: 650-409-5958 PRC:110
www.ncomputing.com
Estab: 2003

Frank Pesek, Co-Founder & Chief Software Architect
Richard Sah, Co-Founder & CTO
Young Song, Co-Founder & CEO

Provider of desktop virtualization services. The company serves customers in the education, healthcare, enterprise, and enterprise sectors.

NDS Inc HQ
851 N Harvard Ave
Lindsay CA 93247
P: 888-825-4716   F: 559-562-4488 PRC:144
www.ndspro.com
Email: nds@ndspro.com

Mike Gummeson, President & CEO
Mike Fallon, VP of Sales
Steve de Kort, Director of Divisional Sales
Dan Nourian, Director of Research & Development
Shayna Burgess, Marketing Communication Manager

Provider of storm water management, efficient irrigation, and flow management solutions for residential and commercial applications.

NDS Surgical Imaging LLC HQ
5750 Hellyer Ave
San Jose CA 95138
P: 408-776-0085   F: 408-776-9878 PRC:169
www.ndssi.com
Email: info@ndssi.com
Estab: 1996

Karim Khadr, President & General Manager
Chad Chang, CTO
Jim Ciardella, VP & CFO
Gregg Young, VP of Corporate Sales
Rainer Scholl, VP of Engineering

Provider of medical imaging services. The company specializes in minimal invasive surgery viewing and diagnostic imaging.

Nearsoft Inc HQ
1854 Anne Way Ste 110
San Jose CA 95124
P: 408-691-1034 PRC:327
www.nearsoft.com
Estab: 2007

Roberto Martinez, CEO
Matt M. Perez, COO

Provider of services to grow development team in companies. The company exclusively caters to software product sectors.

Neato Robotics Inc   HQ
8100 Jarvis Ave
Newark CA 94560
P: 510-795-1351   PRC:209
www.neatorobotics.com
Estab: 2006

Holly Anderson, CFO
Allen Hollingshead, VP of Sales
Avril Murphy, General Manager
Aparna Aswani, Director of Global Communications
Rachel Lucas, Mechanical Engineer

Manufacturer of robots. The company manufactures robots for cleaning and other activities.

NEC Laboratories America Inc   BR
10080 N Wolfe Rd Ste SW3-350
Cupertino CA 95014
P: 408-863-6007   PRC:306
www.nec-labs.com

Ali Hooshmand, Contact

Provider of technology research services. The company specializes in research departments such as integrated systems, machine learning, and media analytics.

Nehanet Corp   HQ
5001 Great America Pkwy Ste 250
Santa Clara CA 95054
P: 888-552-4470   PRC:323
www.nehanet.com
Email: info@nehanet.com
Estab: 2000

Ankur Sharma, CEO
Mahesh Subramanyan, Director of Sales & Account Management & Director of Sales & Account Management
Ryan Williams, Marketing Manager
Ryan W., Inside Sales Representative

Provider of corporate responsibility management and sales and operation planning solutions to semiconductor and electronics component manufacturers.

Neil A Kjos Music Co   HQ
4382 Jutland Dr   [N]
San Diego CA 92117
P: 858-270-9800   F: 858-270-3507   PRC:323
www.kjos.com
Email: email@kjos.com
Emp: 11-50   Estab: 1936

Chris F. Callipari, Manager of Operations

Creator of books and educational materials.

Neill Aircraft Co   HQ
1260 W 15th St   [N]
Long Beach CA 90813
P: 562-432-7981   F: 562-491-0483   PRC:4
www.neillaircraft.com
Email: sales@neillaircraft.com
Emp: 11-50   Estab: 1956

Judy Carpenter, Contact

Provider of build-to-print parts, assemblies, and kitting services to the aerospace community.

Neilmed Pharmaceuticals Inc   HQ
601 Aviation Blvd
Santa Rosa CA 95403
P: 707-525-3784   F: 707-525-3785   PRC:261
www.neilmed.com
Email: questions@neilmed.com
Estab: 2000

Ketan Mehta, CEO & Founder
Nina Mehta, President
Ken Di Lillo, CFO
Dinesh Patel, VP of QA & RA
Srikanth Pai, Director of Global Marketing & Database

Manufacturer of large volume low pressure saline nasal irrigation systems for babies and children, first aid, dry noses, sterile saline spray, and ear care.

Nektar Therapeutics   HQ
455 Mission Bay Blvd S
San Francisco CA 94158
P: 415-482-5300   F: 415-339-5300   PRC:34
www.nektar.com
Email: nektarsf@nektar.com
Estab: 1990
Sales: $100M to $300M

Howard W. Robin, CEO & President
Robert B. Chess, Chairman
John Nicholson, SVP & COO
Gil M. Labrucherie, CFO & COO
Stephen K. Doberstein, Chief Scientific Fellow

Provider of therapeutic products for the treatment of opioid-induced constipation in adult patients with chronic non-cancer pain.

Nelson Biotechnologies Inc   HQ
16080 Caputo Dr Ste 150
Morgan Hill CA 95037
P: 408-778-2020   F: 408-778-7207   PRC:34
www.nelsonbiotech.com
Email: custserv@nelsonbiotech.com
Estab: 2000

Paul S. Nelson, President & CEO

Provider of oligonucleotide labeling and modification services. The company also specializes in contract research and manufacturing.

Neo Technology Inc   HQ
111 E Fifth Ave
San Mateo CA 94401
P: 855-636-4532   PRC:326
neo4j.com
Email: info@neo4j.com
Estab: 2007

Emil Eifrem, CEO
Johan Svensson, CTO
Lars Nordwall, COO
Philip Rathle, VP of Products

Developer of enterprise applications. The company focuses on technical support and related services.

Neo4j Inc   HQ
111 E Fifth Ave
San Mateo CA 94401
P: 855-636-4532   PRC:325
neo4j.com
Email: info@neo4j.com
Estab: 2007

Emil Eifrem, CEO & Founder
Lars Nordwall, President & COO
Mike Asher, CFO
Lance Walter, CMO
Jim Webber, Chief Scientist

Graph database platform that helps companies to access the business value of data connections.

Neoconix Inc   HQ
4020 Moorpark Ave Ste 108
San Jose CA 95117
P: 408-530-9393   F: 408-530-9383   PRC:206
neoconix.com
Email: info@neoconix.com
Estab: 2003

Lisa Lloyd, Sales Manager
Todd Bridges, HR Contractor Recruiter

Provider of electrical interconnect solutions. The company offers LGA sockets, board-to-board interposers, and standard products.

Neodyne Biosciences Inc   HQ
7999 Gateway Blvd Ste 110
Newark CA 94560
P: 800-519-7127   PRC:195
www.embracescartherapy.com
Email: info@embracescartherapy.com
Estab: 2007

Henry de Leon, Development Technician

Manufacturer of embrace devices and it helps in the concealment of scars. The company serves patients.

Neomagic Corp   HQ
830 Hillview Ct Ste 138
Milpitas CA 95035
P: 408-428-9725   F: 408-988-7036   PRC:86
www.neomagic.com
Email: sales@neomagic.com
Estab: 1993

Syed Zaidi, President & CEO
David Tomasello, VP of Strategic Planning & Chairman of the Board
Roderick Peterson, VP of Administration & Information
Benjamin Bolinguit, Director of Operations
Jo Beth Dietz, Executive Administrator

Developer of electronic device solutions. The company sells hardware, software, and microcontrollers for IP cameras and vehicle toll collection.

Neopeutics Inc USA   HQ
400 Oyster Point Blvd Ste 112
S San Francisco CA 94080
P: 650-624-4057   PRC:268
neopeutics.com
Email: info@neopeutics.com
Estab: 2009

Harlizawati Jahari, CEO
Anton Espira, COO

Provider of pre clinical contract research services and product development for the private and governmental regulatory agencies.

Neophotonics Corp   HQ
 3081 Zanker Rd
 San Jose CA 95134
P: 408-232-9200 F: 408-433-4898   PRC:209
www.neophotonics.com
Email: sales@neophotonics.com
Estab: 1996
Sales: $300M to $1 Billion

Tim Jenks, CEO
Chi Yue Cheung, COO & SVP
Elizabeth Eby, CFO
Wupen Yuen, SVP & General Manager
Ferris Lipscomb, VP of Marketing

Designer and manufacturer of photonic integrated
circuit based optoelectronic modules and subsystems for communications networks.

Neospeech Inc   HQ
 4633 Old Ironsides Dr Ste 200
 Santa Clara CA 95054
P: 408-914-2710 F: 408-890-4715   PRC:324
www.neospeech.com
Email: sales@neospeech.com
Estab: 2002

Trevor Jackins, Marketing Specialist
Brian Chiu, Sales & Marketing Project Specialist

Provider of text-to-speech software and applications for the mobile, enterprise, entertainment,
and education markers.

Neotech Products Inc   HQ
 28430 Witherspoon Pkwy   [N]
 Valencia CA 91355
P: 661-775-7466 F: 800-966-0585   PRC:189
www.neotechproducts.com
Estab: 1996

Craig McCrary, President & COO
Kathy Fetterman, Executive Director of Business
Administration
Cindy Cisneros, International General Manager
Leo Arya, QA & RA Manager
Sara Dimmitt, Manager of Business Development

Manufacturer of medical products.

Neotract Inc   HQ
 4473 Willow Rd Ste 100
 Pleasanton CA 94588
P: 925-401-0700 F: 925-401-0699   PRC:189
urolift.com
Email: info@neotract.com
Estab: 2004

Theodore C. Lamson, Founder
Dave R. Amerson, President & CEO & General
Manager
Wendy Sawyer, VP of Operations
Ann M. Decker, VP of Reimbursement & Health-
Care Policy
Brian R. DuBois, VP of Research & Development

Provider of medical devices for the treatment of
benign prostatic hyperplasia and its side effects
such as loss of productivity and sleep and depression.

Neova Tech Solutions Inc   BR
 4701 Patrick Henry Dr, Bldg 16 Ste 106
 Santa Clara CA 95054
P: 781-640-0588   PRC:323
neovasolutions.com
Email: sales@neovatechsolutions.com
Estab: 2007

Kalpesh Savla, Founder & CEO
Hemal Savla, Head of Finance

Provider of cloud solutions for web and mobile.
The company offers mobile development and QA
automation services.

Neptec Optical Solutions Inc   HQ
 48603 Warm Springs Blvd
 Fremont CA 94539
P: 510-687-1101 F: 510-687-0599   PRC:62
www.neptecos.com
Email: info@neptecos.com
Estab: 2001

David Cheng, CEO
Darlene Diaz, Customer Account Manager
Orlando Basco, Production Engineer

Provider of quick-turn fiber optic connectivity
solutions. The company also offers connector
reconditioning, switches, and fiber arrays.

Neptune Systems LLC   HQ
 15750 Vineyard Blvd Ste 150
 Morgan Hill CA 95037
P: 408-275-2205 F: 408-762-2042   PRC:159
www.neptunesystems.com
Email: support@neptunesystems.com
Estab: 1996

Terence Fugazzi, VP of Sales & Marketing
Paul Jansen, Customer Support Manager

Provider of aquarium controllers. The company
also offers expansion modules and accessories
and offers support services.

Net4site LLC   HQ
 3350 Scott Blvd Bldg 34B
 Santa Clara CA 95054
P: 408-427-3004   PRC:326
net4site.net
Email: info@net4site.net

Roger Diaz, Director

Provider of SAP solutions. The company serves
customers in the enterprise mobility, business
intelligence, and ERP arenas.

Netafim Irrigation Inc   HQ
 5470 E Home Ave
 Fresno CA 93727
P: 559-453-6800 F: 559-453-1043   PRC:159
www.netafimusa.com
Email: netafim.usa@netafim.com
Estab: 1965

Cori W., Director of Human Resources & Director
of Human Resources
Best Robert, District Sales Manager
Mark Jolles, Filtration Product Manager
Todd Rinkenberger, Western Region Sales Man-
ager - Ag Division
Jim McCarty, Technical Support Manager

Provider of drip and micro irrigation products for
agriculture, greenhouse and nursery, landscape
and turf, mining, and wastewater applications.

NetApp Inc   HQ
 1395 Crossman Ave
 Sunnyvale CA 94089
P: 408-822-6000 F: 408-822-4501   PRC:324
www.netapp.com
Email: info@netapp.com
Estab: 1992
Sales: Over $3B

Rob Salmon, President
Jay Kidd, CTO
Julie Parrish, SVP & CMO
Michael LiRocchi, Director of Legal
Matthew K. Fawcett, General Counsel

Provider of virtualization, mobile information
management, and cloud storage solutions. The
company serves the business sector.

Netblaze Systems Inc   HQ
 1299 Newell Hill Pl Ste 202
 Walnut Creek CA 94596
P: 925-932-1765   PRC:316
netblaze.biz
Email: info@netblaze.biz
Estab: 2005

Alan Kaplan, Founder
Igor Akkerman, Partner
Nicholas Dahlman, Systems Engineer

Provider of IT, integration, and network consulting
services. The company is also engaged in cloud
computing, web hosting, and hosted exchange.

Netease Inc   HQ
 PO Box 1610
 Forestville CA 95436
P: 800-580-0932   PRC:325
www.neteze.com
Email: support@neteze.com

Barbara Perdue, Owner
William Perdue, Owner

Provider of web hosting services. The company
offers domain registration, hosting, and dial-up
services.

Netformx Inc   HQ
 333 W Santa Clara St Ste 612
 San Jose CA 95113
P: 408-423-6600   PRC:326
www.netformx.com
Email: sales@netformx.com
Estab: 1994

Ittai Bareket, CEO
Tina Morarity-Breunig, Director of Corporate
Marketing
Mariquelle Lazaro, Executive Assistant

Designer and builder of solutions for the networking and service providers. The company specializes in desktop and cloud applications.

NETGEAR Inc HQ
350 E Plumeria Dr
San Jose CA 95134-1911
P: 408-907-8000   F: 408-907-8097   PRC:97
www.netgear.com
Email: sales@netgear.com
Estab: 1996
Sales: $300M to $1 Billion

Patrick Lo, CEO & Chairman
Mark Merrill, CTO
Christine M. Gorjanc, CFO
Michael F. Falcon, COO
Andrew Kim, SVP of Corporate Development &
General Counsel & Company Secretary

Provider of network solutions for home and
businesses. The company also offers home video
monitoring systems and storage products.

Netpace Inc HQ
5000 Executive Pkwy Ste 530
San Ramon CA 94583
P: 925-543-7760   F: 925-558-4015   PRC:322
www.netpace.com
Email: support@netpace.com
Estab: 1997

Rudy Aguirre, Creative Director
Hasnain Abidi, Software Engineer

Provider of consulting, cloud computing, database
management, and proprietary development
services.

Netscout BR
178 E Tasman Dr
San Jose CA 95134
P: 408-571-5000   PRC:322
www.netscout.com
Email: support@netscout.com
Estab: 2007

Anil Singhal, Founder & President & CEO &
Chairman of the Board
Richard Kenedi, President of Core Markets Busi-
ness Unit
Tom Raimondi, CMO
Jean Bua, CFO
Michael Szabados, COO

Developer of service assurance and applications,
service delivery management, network performance management software, and hardware
solutions.

Netskope HQ
2445 Augustine Dr Fl 3
Santa Clara CA 95054
P: 800-979-6988   PRC:323
netskope.com
Email: contact@netskope.com
Estab: 2012

Sanjay Beri, CEO
Krishna Narayanaswamy, CTO
Jason Clark, CSO & CMO
Drew Del Matto, CFO
David Wu, Chief Development Officer

Provider of cloud security brokering services. The
company offers services to the healthcare sector.

Network Design Associates Inc HQ
6060 Sunrise Vista Dr Ste 2440
Citrus Heights CA 95610
P: 916-853-1632   PRC:326
www.ndasacramento.com
Email: info@ndasacramento.com
Estab: 1992

Deborah Sackman, President
Gregory Nelson, VP of Engineering
Susan Gill, Engineer

Provider of engineering services for computer
systems. The company's services include network
design, implementation, support, and maintenance.

Network Environmental Systems Inc BR
1141 Sibley St   [N]
Folsom CA 95630
P: 800-637-2384   PRC:139
Nesglobal.Net
Email: office@nesglobal.net

Jerry Bucklin, President & CEO

Provider of occupational health and safety
training and environmental compliance consulting
services.

Network PCB Inc HQ
2360 Qume Dr Ste F
San Jose CA 95131
P: 408-943-8760   F: 408-943-8761   PRC:211
networkpcb.com
Email: sales@networkpcb.com
Estab: 1994

Hieu Tran, Account Manager
Kevin Le, Manager
Pauline Vo, Senior Account Manager
Charlie Nguyen, Production Manager
Lan Do, Controller

Provider of printed circuit board solutions. The
company's product line includes probe cards, high
density board, and impedance control board.

Netwoven Inc HQ
500 E Calaveras Blvd Ste 214
Milpitas CA 95035
P: 877-638-9683   PRC:323
www.netwoven.com
Email: info@netwoven.com
Estab: 2001

Niraj Tenany, President & CEO & & Co-Founder
Viraj Bais, Co-Founder & CTO
Pankaj Bose, VP of Engineering
Nicholas Simas, Client Relationship Director
Angira Dey, Client Relationship Director

Provider of enterprise content management and
business intelligence solutions. The company also
focuses on process management.

Netxperts Inc HQ
1777 Botelho Dr Ste 102
Walnut Creek CA 94596
P: 925-806-0800   PRC:317
netxperts.com
Estab: 1996

Gary Nordine, CEO & Founder
Jeremy Redman, Account Manager
Christen Schrepel, Human Resources Manager
Eric Gutierrez, Project Manager
Rondy Scippio, Network Operating Center Engi-
neer

Provider of unified communication solutions. The
company offers services to the healthcare and
transportation markers.

Neudesic LLC BR
200 Spectrum Ctr Dr Ste 2000
Irvine CA 92618
P: 949-754-4500   F: 949-788-0098   PRC:326
www.neudesic.com
Email: info@neudesic.com

Tim Marshall, Founder & President
Parsa Rohani, CEO & Founding Partner
Howard Dinet, VP of Sales
Wayne MacDonald, National Practice Director
Tim Corken, Director of Inside Sales

Provider of technology services. The company
focuses on social software, integration platform,
and CRM solutions and offers cloud computing
services.

Neuron Corp HQ
1777 Saratoga Ave Ste 104
San Jose CA 95129
P: 408-540-7959   PRC:323
www.neuroncorp.com

Ed Neubauer, President

Provider of computer and physical security products and services for the military, government, and
corporate sectors.

Neurona Therapeutics HQ
170 Harbor Way
S San Francisco CA 94080
P: 650-799-6465   PRC:34
www.neuronatherapeutics.com
Email: info@neuronatx.com
Estab: 2008

Cory Nicholas, Founder & CEO
Catherine Priest, VP of Preclinical Development
Estela Alvarez, VP of Quality Assurance & Control
Gautam Banik, VP of Manufacturing & Process
Sciences
John M. Centanni, Director of Global Regulatory
Affairs

Developer of neuronal stem cells to transplant
into the brain. The company offers services to the
healthcare industry.

Neuropace Inc HQ
455 N Bernardo Ave
Mountain View CA 94043
P: 650-237-2700 F: 650-237-2701 PRC:189
www.neuropace.com
Email: info@neuropace.com
Estab: 1999

Frank M. Fischer, CEO
Martha J. Morrell, CMO
Steve Archer, Senior Director of Electrical Dev
Roger Duguid, Senior Manager of Data Management
Kathy Miller, Clinical Trial Manager

Designer, developer, manufacturer, and marketer
of implantable devices for the treatment of neurological disorders.

Neurosky Inc HQ
100 Century Center Ct Ste 400
San Jose CA 95112
P: 408-200-6675 PRC:87
www.neurosky.com
Estab: 2004

KooHyoung Lee, Co-Founder & CTO
Jongjin Lim, President & Co-Founder
Stanley Yang, CEO
Rui Zou, Algorithm Development Scientist

Manufacturer of ECG biosensors and also EEG
biosensors for mobile solutions, wearable devices,
and service providers.

Neurotrack Technologies Inc HQ
399 Bradford St Ste 101
Redwood City CA 94063
P: 650-549-8566 PRC:34
neurotrack.com
Email: support@neurotrack.com
Estab: 2012

Elli Kaplan, CEO

Provider of computer-based cognitive tests. The
company offers services to Alzheimer's patients
and the medical industry.

Neutron Motorsports HQ
13435 S Main St [N]
Los Angeles CA 90061
P: 310-327-4981 F: 310-327-5078 PRC:359
www.neutronmotorsports.com

Josie G., General Manager

Manufacturer and retailer of automotive parts and
accessories.

Neutronix Inc HQ
385 Woodview Ave Ste 200
Morgan Hill CA 95037
P: 408-776-5190 F: 408-776-1039 PRC:212
www.neutronixinc.com
Email: sales@nxqinc.com
Estab: 1989

Brett Arnold, CEO & President
Lenore Arnold, COO
David Geder, VP of Sales
Curt Gamm, Director of Customer Support

Manufacturer of contact or proximity and projection mask aligners. The company is involved in
design, installation, and delivery services.

Nevarez Machining HQ
838 Jury Court Ste B
San Jose CA 95112
P: 408-279-1196 F: 408-279-1197 PRC:80
www.nevarezmachining.com

Jaime Nevarez, President
Gary Brusato, Programmer

Manufacturer of fabricated machined parts. The
company offers welding, machining, inspection,
and software machining services.

Nevro Corp HQ
1800 Bridge Pkwy
Redwood City CA 94065
P: 650-251-0005 PRC:196
www.nevro.com
Email: legal@nevro.com
Estab: 2006
Sales: $300M to $1 Billion

Rami Elghandour, President
Keith D. Grossman, Chairman & CEO
Andrew Galligan, CFO
Chris Christoforou, VP of Research & Development
Patrick Schmitz, VP of Operations

Developer of new high-frequency stimulation
technology for improving the role of spinal cord
stimulation in the treatment of chronic pain.

Nevtec Inc HQ
1150 S Bascom Ave Ste 12
San Jose CA 95128
P: 408-292-8600 PRC:224
www.nevtec.com
Email: sales@nevtec.com
Estab: 1996

Shawn Neverve, VP of Operations

Provider of networks implementation and maintenance services. The company also focuses on
workstations and the Internet.

New Faze Development Inc HQ
1825 Del Paso Blvd
Sacramento CA 95815
P: 916-929-6402 F: 916-929-0158 PRC:304
www.newfaze.com
Estab: 1990

Allen Warren, Founder
Mark T. Harris, President
Nick Pecha, CFO
Martin Harris, Chief of Staff

Provider of construction and management development services. The company also offers project
management and property management services.

New Generation Software Inc HQ
3835 N Freeway Blvd Ste 200
Sacramento CA 95834
P: 916-920-2200 F: 916-920-1380 PRC:322
www.ngsi.com
Email: marketing@ngsi.com
Estab: 1982

Bill Langston, Director of Marketing

Supplier of packaged data mart models with
analytical presentations and reports for wholesale
distribution, healthcare, and financial reporting.

New Power Technologies HQ
25259 La Loma Dr
Los Altos Hills CA 94022
P: 650-948-4546 PRC:130
newpowertech.com
Estab: 2004

Peter Evans, CEO

Provider of energy solutions. The company's offerings include energynet platform and energynet
solutions.

New Tech Solutions Inc HQ
4179 Business Center Dr
Fremont CA 94538
P: 510-353-4070 F: 510-353-4076 PRC:329
www.newtechsolutions.com
Email: info@ntsca.com
Estab: 1997

Rajesh Patel, President
Vijay Kumar, CEO
Satish Raina, VP of Sales
Vikram Kohli, VP of Operations
Anita Patel, Program Manager

Provider of technology solutions. The company
caters to networking, security, and communication
manufacturers.

New Vision Display Inc HQ
1430 Blue Oaks Blvd Ste 100
Roseville CA 95747-5156
P: 916-786-8111 F: 916-786-8121 PRC:169
newvisiondisplay.com
Email: sales@newvisiondisplay.com
Estab: 2012

Matthias Pfeiffer, CTO & President of Sales-Components Division
Jeff Olyniec, CEO
Alan Lefko, CFO
Y.K. Hoo, COO
David Kruse, Chief Sales Officer

Provider of display products. The company's
products include LCD modules, TFT LCD and
touch products.

New World Machining HQ
2799 Aiello Dr
San Jose CA 95111
P: 408-227-3810 F: 844-272-5214 PRC:80
newworldmachining.com
Email: contact@newworldmachining.com
Estab: 1973

Chris Elsten, VP of Operations & Estimator
Janice Flores, Customer Service Manager
Mary Guilbert, Manager
Norma Gonzalez, Purchasing Manager
Quang Le, Production Manager

Manufacturer of machined parts for the semiconductor, electronic, and security sectors specializing in prototype, production, and engineering
design.

New:Team SoftWare Inc HQ

PO Box 254807 [N]
Sacramento CA 95865
P: 415-461-8086 PRC:319
www.go2nts.com
Email: info@go2nts.com
Estab: 1985

Bjarne Winkler, Creator

Developer of software solutions.

Newby Rubber Inc HQ

320 Industrial St [N]
Bakersfield CA 93307
P: 661-327-5137 F: 661-327-8058 PRC:189
www.newbyrubber.com
Emp: 11-50 Estab: 1958

Kelly Howard Newby, President

Manufacturer and distributor of rubber products such as agriculture, food processing, waterworks, pump, and oilfield.

NewGen Surgical Inc HQ

41 Simms St Ste B
San Rafael CA 94901
P: 855-295-4500 F: 415-526-3742 PRC:195
newgensurgical.com
Email: info@newgensurgical.com
Estab: 2012

Rob Chase, Founder & President
Kimberlee Luedee-Chase, VP of Business Operations & Marketing
Peter Szyperski, Director of Engineering & Operations
Anne-Marie Regal, Medical Director
Barry Gardiner, Founding Medical Director

Designer of single use medical devices. The company offers skin staplers, needle counters, and procedure kit packaging trays.

NewGen Therapeutics Inc HQ

3475 Edison Way Ste R
Menlo Park CA 94025
P: 650-995-7508 PRC:268

Jeffrey Bacha, CEO & Secretary & CFO

Provider of therapeutic solutions. The company focuses on the development and discovery of small molecule drugs for cancer treatment.

Newland North America Inc HQ

46559 Fremont Blvd
Fremont CA 94538
P: 510-490-3888 F: 510-490-3887 PRC:59
www.newlandna.com
Email: info@nlscan.com
Estab: 2008

Wang Jing, President

Designer and developer of data collector and scanning systems. The company also offers customer information terminals.

Newnex Technology Corp HQ

3041 Olcott St
Santa Clara CA 95054
P: 408-986-9988 F: 408-986-8024 PRC:106
newnex.com
Email: information@newnex.com
Estab: 1993

Fuwen Xu, Senior Support Engineer

Developer of connecting cables, controllers, and repeaters. The company's services include design, installation, and technical support.

Newport-West Data Services Inc HQ

18120 Bollinger Canyon Rd Bldg 2 Ste A
San Ramon CA 94583
P: 925-855-1131 F: 925-855-1161 PRC:322
www.nwds.com
Email: info@nwds.com
Estab: 1979

Scott MacLean, Director of Programming

Designer and developer of minicomputer based business applications. The company specializes in installation.

Nexant Inc HQ

101 Second St Ste 1000
San Francisco CA 94105-3651
P: 415-369-1000 F: 415-369-9700 PRC:129
www.nexant.com
Email: sales@nexant.com
Estab: 2000

Basem Y. Sarandah, Founder & CEO
John Gustafson, President
Arjun Gupta, Executive Chairman
Sunil Bhardwaj, CFO
Josh Schellenberg, SVP of Advanced Analytics

Developer of software for utility, energy, chemical, and other sectors and also offers power grid consulting and energy advisory, and other services.

Nexb Inc HQ

735 Industrial Rd Ste 101
San Carlos CA 94070
P: 650-592-2096 PRC:325
www.nexb.com
Email: info@nexb.com
Estab: 2003

Michael Herzog, CEO & Founder
Dennis Clark, Product Manager
Pierre Lapointe, Customer Care Manager
Thomas Druez, Software Engineer
Jono Yang, Software Analyst & Developer

Designer and developer of software tools and services. The company offers services to business enterprises and related organizations.

Nexenta Systems Inc HQ

2929 Patrick Henry Dr
Santa Clara CA 95054
P: 408-791-3300 F: 408-791-3305 PRC:320
nexenta.com
Email: sales@nexenta.com
Estab: 2005

Dmitry Yusupov, CTO & Founder
Aditya Fotedar, CIO
Bridget Warwick, CMO
Rick Martig, CFO
Thomas Cornely, Chief Product Officer

Provider of enterprise class storage software solutions. The company is engaged in virtualization and business continuity planning.

Nexlogic HQ

2085 Zanker Rd
San Jose CA 95131
P: 408-436-8150 F: 408-436-8156 PRC:211
www.nexlogic.com
Email: support@nexlogic.com
Estab: 1995

Zulki Khan, Founder & CEO
Don Shell, Director of Business Development
Phillip Lerma, Fabrication Manager
Adrian Zuno, Account Manager
Alex Rosario, Manufacturing Manager

Designer of electronic circuits. The company specializes in the design and fabrication of printed circuit boards.

Nextaxiom Technology Inc HQ

600 Montgomery St Ste 2720
San Francisco CA 94111
P: 415-373-1890 F: 415-373-1899 PRC:322
www.nextaxiom.com
Email: info@nextaxiom.com
Estab: 2000

Ash Massoudi, CEO & Co-Founder
Sandy Zylka, VP of Products & Technology & Co-Founder
Dave Bakke, Senior Solutions Architect

Provider of testing, certification, and other professional services. The company offers work management and scheduling solutions.

Nextbus Inc BR

1800 Sutter St Ste 900
Concord CA 94520
P: 925-686-8200 PRC:319
www.cubic.com
Estab: 1997

Matt Cole, SVP & President of Cubic Transportation Systems
Mike Knowles, SVP & President of Cubic Global Defense
Bradley H. Feldmann, CEO & President & Chairman
Michael R. Twyman, SVP & President of Cubic Mission Solutions
Anshooman Aga, EVP & CFO

Provider of transit management solutions. The company also provides real-time passenger information solutions to organizations.

Nextec Microwave & Rf HQ
3010 Scott Blvd
Santa Clara CA 95054
P: 408-727-1189 F: 408-727-5915 PRC:70
www.nextec-rf.com
Email: sales@nextec-rf.com
Estab: 1996

Dongwook Lee, President

Provider of microwave amplifiers and integrated frequency multipliers. The company serves the aerospace, military, and defense sectors.

nexTier Networks Inc HQ
2953 Bunker Hill Ln Ste 400
Santa Clara CA 95054
P: 408-282-3561 F: 408-282-3501 PRC:84
www.nextiernetworks.com
Email: info@nextiernetworks.com
Estab: 2006

Tarique Mustafa, Founder & CEO & Chairman
John Racioppi, VP of Business Development
Mark Calomeni, SVP of Systems Engineering

Provider of data security services and solutions for vertical markers and original equipment manufacturers.

NextInput Inc HQ
980 Linda Vista Ave
Mountain View CA 94043
P: 650-963-9310 PRC:322
nextinput.com
Email: sales@nextinput.com

Ali Foughi, CEO & Founder
Ryan Diestelhorst, CTO

Provider of MEMS-based force sensing solutions for touch enabled devices in markers such as wearable, automotive, industrial, and medical applications.

NextLabs Inc HQ
2121 S El Camino Real Twr Plz Ste 600
San Mateo CA 94403
P: 650-577-9101 F: 650-577-9102 PRC:322
www.nextlabs.com
Email: info@nextlabs.com
Estab: 2004

Keng Lim, CEO & Founder
Jill Rubin, VP of Marketing
Andy Han, SVP of Products
Dennis Andrie, Director of Professional Services & Support
Navya Reddy, QA Engineer

Developer of software products. The company offers information risk management software products for enterprises.

Nextracker Inc HQ
6200 Paseo Padre Pkwy
Fremont CA 94555
P: 510-270-2500 F: 510-793-8388 PRC:131
nextracker.com
Email: info@nextracker.com

Mike Mehawich, Founder & Chief Strategy Officer
Dan Shugar, CEO
Alexander Au, CTO
Marco Miller, SVP of Global Operations
Allan Daly, VP of Software

Provider of horizontal tracking services. The company focuses on solar power plants and clean technology solutions.

Nextrials Inc HQ
2010 Crow Canyon Pl Ste 410
San Ramon CA 94583
P: 925-355-3000 F: 925-355-3005 PRC:326
www.nextrials.com
Email: info@nextrials.com
Estab: 1999

Jim Rogers, CEO
Robert Barr, CTO & SVP
Karmen Ghobrial, Quality Assurance Analyst

Provider of e-clinical and electronic health record tools. The company is engaged in clinical research and related services.

Nexusguard Ltd RH
548 Market St Ste 15269
San Francisco CA 94104
P: 415-299-8550 PRC:319
www.nexusguard.com
Email: media@nexusguard.com
Estab: 2008

Xenophon Giannis, VP of Sales

Provider of monitoring and DNA protection services. The company serves service providers and the entertainment sector.

NGM Biopharmaceuticals Inc HQ
333 Oyster Point Blvd
S San Francisco CA 94080
P: 650-243-5555 PRC:258
www.ngmbio.com
Email: info@ngmbio.com
Estab: 2008

Jeff Jonker, President
Alex DePaoli, CMO & VP of Translational Research
Zhonghao Liu, Director of Biology
Ruth Corbin, Director of Human Resources
Marc Learned, Director

Developer of novel and disease-altering biologics such as protein, peptide, and antibody drug for cancer, cardio-metabolic, and hepatic diseases.

NIC Components Corp BR
1650 Technology Dr Ste 200
San Jose CA 95110
P: 669-342-3960 F: 669-342-3969 PRC:203
www.niccomp.com
Email: sales@niccomp.com
Estab: 1982

Mary Ly, Global Business Development Manager

Designer, manufacturer, and supplier of passive components. The company offers ceramic capacitors, power inductors, and current sensing resistors.

Nice Touch Solutions Inc HQ
PO Box 1149
Alamo CA 94507
P: 925-385-8321 PRC:323
www.ewbills.com
Email: info@nicetouch.com
Estab: 1996

Arnold K. Young, CEO & President

Developer of software for the heavy highway construction industry. The company focuses on products for generating extra work bills.

Nichols Manufacturing Inc HQ
913 Hanson Ct
Milpitas CA 95035
P: 408-945-0911 F: 408-945-8127 PRC:157
www.nicholsmfg.com
Email: nichols@nicholsmfg.com
Estab: 1979

Lettie Nichols, President & Owner

Provider of product engineering and design, prototyping, and manufacturing services. The company serves the business sector.

Nidek Inc RH
47651 Westinghouse Dr
Fremont CA 94539
P: 800-223-9044 PRC:186
usa.nidek.com
Estab: 1971

Ron Kaiser, Director of Sales & Marketing
Naomi Nakayama, Controller & Office Manager
Jay Wollack, National Sales Manager
Devin Barshay, Territory Sales Manager
Hisako Ueno, QA Associate

Manufacturer of ophthalmic devices. The company also offers refractive systems and diagnostic products to the medical industry.

Nieco HQ
7950 Cameron Dr
Windsor CA 95492
P: 707-284-7100 F: 707-284-7430 PRC:159
nieco.com
Email: sales@nieco.com
Estab: 1905

Robert Nieman, Owner
Christopher Larkin, Business Owner
Korey Kohl, President
Tom Holmes, International VP
Matt Baker, VP of Research & Development

Manufacturer of automatic broilers. The company's applications include restaurants, fast food centers, and amusement parks.

Nikon Precision Inc HQ
1399 Shoreway Rd
Belmont CA 94002-4107
P: 650-508-4674 F: 650-508-4600 PRC:208
www.nikonprecision.com
Email: npicom@nikon.com
Estab: 1917

Toyohiro Takamine, President
Yoshiyuki Takabatake, CEO
Gregory Sasaki, VP of Finance & Corporate Services
Hamid Zarringhalam, EVP
Mohamad Zarringhalam, SVP of Engineering Services & Customer Support

Manufacturer of optical lenses and precision equipment. The company is also the supplier of step-and-repeat and step-and-scan lithography systems.

Nimbus Design HQ
611 Veterans Blvd Ste 214
Redwood City CA 94063
P: 650-365-7568   F: 650-365-3025   PRC:67
www.nimbusdesign.com
Estab: 1991

Karen Sparks, CFO & Account Executive
Arturo Samayoa, Partner & Chief Information
Executive
John Novicki, Director of Quality Assurance
Felipe Salazar, Operations Manager

Provider of design services. The company specializes in website design, content management, and e-commerce tools.

Nisene Technology Group Inc HQ
417-A Salinas Rd
Watsonville CA 95076
P: 831-761-7980   F: 831-761-2992   PRC:212
www.nisene.com

Lenna Wagner, President

Provider of automated decapsulator technology and plastic etching services. The company offers custom design services for nonstandard gaskets.

Nitinol Devices & Components Inc HQ
47533 Westinghouse Dr
Fremont CA 94539
P: 510-683-2000   PRC:235
www.nitinol.com
Email: sales@nitinol.com
Estab: 1991

Tom Duerig, CTO & Founder
Mark Lemma, CFO
Brian Adcock, Chief Human Resource Officer
Doug Hutchison, CCO
Brice de La Menardiere, SVP of Applied Technologies

Provider of rapid development and prototyping services. The company is also engaged in commercialization.

Nitto Denko America Inc HQ
48500 Fremont Blvd   [N]
Fremont CA 94538
P: 510-445-5480   PRC:170
www.nitto.com/in/en/contact
Estab: 1969

Hideo Takasaki, President & CEO & COO & Executive Director

Manufacturer of bonding, joining and surface protection products, sealants, anticorrosion and waterproofing, electrical insulating products, engineering plastics, medical-related, membrane, packaging, media-related, semiconductor-related, LCD-related and electronic components related products, industrial use barcode labels, flexible printed circuits, precision electronics materials.

NK Technologies HQ
3511 Charter Park Dr
San Jose CA 95136
P: 408-871-7510   F: 408-871-7515   PRC:87
www.nktechnologies.com
Email: sales@nktechnologies.com
Estab: 1982

Nitin Kelkar, Owner
Philip Gregory, President
Will Delsman, Manager of Inside & Technical Sales
Lila Harr, Office Manager
Michael Turner, Materials Manager

Manufacturer of current sensors and transducer products for the factory and industrial automation markers.

Nobix Inc HQ
PO Box 3592
San Ramon CA 94583
P: 925-659-3500   F: 925-659-3599   PRC:322
www.nobix.com
Email: sales@nobix.com
Estab: 1985

Pat Caster, Manager of Technology

Provider IT management products for job scheduling, problem alerting, and notification as well as provides software engineering services.

Noble Image Inc HQ
1507 Danbrook Dr
Sacramento CA 95835
P: 916-419-3570   F: 916-561-0542   PRC:318
www.nobleimage.com
Email: sales@nobleimage.com

Mark Ruff, President
Elly Callison, Web Designer
Ryan Stora, Senior Web Designer

Provider of website and graphic design, website development, hosting, programming, and technical support services.

Noel Technologies Inc HQ
1510-C Dell Ave
Campbell CA 95008
P: 408-374-9549   F: 408-374-4127   PRC:204
www.noeltech.com
Email: info@noeltech.com
Estab: 1996

Brenda Hill, VP

Provider of lithography, thin film deposition, and water recycling solutions. The company serves MEMS, defense, life science, and other sectors.

Noise and Vibration Technologies LLC HQ
17 Mandeville Ct
Monterey CA 93940
P: 831-655-6600   PRC:31
www.nvtgroup.com
Estab: 2014

Patti Monahan, VP of Finance

Provider of measuring, simulating, and analyzing the effects of vibration, noise, shock, and other environmental variables for various industries.

Nok Nok Labs Inc HQ
2100 Geng Rd Ste 105
Palo Alto CA 94303
P: 650-433-1300   PRC:325
www.noknok.com
Email: info@noknok.com
Estab: 2011

David Chao, Co-Founder & General Partner
Terry Opdendyk, Co-Founder
Richard Clarke, Chairman
Phillip M. Dunkelberger, President & CEO
Walter Beisheim, Chief Business Development Officer

Focuses on the development on online security solutions. The company is also involved in third party research services.

Nokia Corp BR
200 S Mathilda Ave
Sunnyvale CA 94086
P: 408-737-0900   PRC:71
www.nokia.com

Basil Alwan, President of IP & Optical Networks
Bhaskar Gorti, President of Nokia Software
Federico Guillen, President of Customer Operations
Kathrin Buvac, President of Nokia Enterprise
Marcus Weldon, Corporate CTO & President of Nokia Bell Labs

Specializes in mobile network infrastructure structure and services. The company is engaged in technology development.

Nomis Solutions Inc HQ
8000 Marina Blvd Ste 700
Brisbane CA 94005
P: 650-588-9800   PRC:322
www.nomissolutions.com
Estab: 2004

Robert L. Phillips, Founder & CSO
Frank Rohde, President & CEO
Ken Pulverman, CMO
Abhinav Mittal, CTO
Christopher Mondfrans, CFO

Provider of pricing and profitability management solutions. The company caters to the financial services.

Nor-Cal Metal Fabricators HQ
1121 Third St
Oakland CA 94607
P: 510-833-7157   F: 510-893-2940   PRC:82
nc-mf.com
Email: telsales@nc-mf.com
Estab: 1953

Michael Tran, President
Rick Turner, Information Technology Manager
Troy Nickles, Manufacturing Superintendent
Martin W. Hooey, Estimator
Steve Vickers, Estimator

Provider of general industrial metal fabrication and parts. The company is engaged in contract manufacturing and structural rolling.

Nor-Cal Perlite Inc HQ
2605 Goodrick Ave
Richmond CA 94801
P: 510-232-7337 F: 510-232-8127 PRC:53
www.norcalperlite.com
Email: info@norcalperlite.com
Estab: 1986

Justin Clarke, Manager

Manufacturer of perlite and perlite products. The company is involved in the development of specialty grades for individual customers.

Nor-Cal Products Inc HQ
1967 S Oregon St
Yreka CA 96097
P: 530-842-4457 F: 530-842-9130 PRC:165
n-c.com
Email: ncsales@n-c.com
Estab: 1962

Tom Deany, President & CEO
Ron Buracker, Production Manager
Jim Crowley, Product Manager

Provider of fabricating solutions for stainless steel flanges, fittings, and components. The company's services include welding, machining, and forming.

Norden Millimeter Inc HQ
5441 Merchant Cir Ste C
Placerville CA 95667
P: 530-642-9123 F: 530-642-9420 PRC:70
www.nordengroup.com
Email: sales@nordengroup.com
Estab: 2001

Duncan Smith, President
Lisa Schroeder, Purchasing Manager
Ross Ecker, Senior Engineer
Lorrie Hieb Hartsough, Assembly Supervisor
Stephen Sarver, Technician

Developer and manufacturer of amplifier products. The company specializes in millimeter wave amplifier products.

Nordic Naturals Inc HQ
111 Jennings Dr
Watsonville CA 95076
P: 831-724-6200 F: 831-724-6600 PRC:272
www.nordicnaturals.com
Email: info@nordicnaturals.com
Estab: 2002

Joar Opheim, CEO & Founder
Oscar Alaniz, Information Technology Coordinator
Todd Murphy, Financial Analyst

Specializes in the delivery of omega oil to consumers, veterinary professionals, pharmacists, and healthcare professionals.

Nordson MARCH HQ
2470-A Bates Ave [N]
Concord CA 94520
P: 925-827-1240 F: 925-827-1189 PRC:159
www.nordson.com/en/divisions/march
Emp: 51-200 Estab: 1983

James D. Getty, President
Gary Monahan, Director of Operations
John Guinn, Manager of Engineering & Product Manager

Manufacturer of plasma cleaning and treatment equipment, plasma applications and many more.

Noron Precision Machining Inc HQ
1245 Mt View Alviso Rd
Sunnyvale CA 94089
P: 408-739-6486 F: 408-739-2734 PRC:80
www.noronprecision.com
Estab: 1977

Debbie Hanks, Owner
Debbie Hanks Williams, President & COO
Jose Mendoza, Quality Assurance Manager
Trevor Hanks, Shop Assistant

Provider of machined parts for medical, microwave, aircraft, auto, computer peripheral, telecommunications, and biotech industries.

Norris Associates HQ
2534 Murrell Rd [N]
Santa Barbara CA 93109
P: 805-962-7703 F: 805-456-2169 PRC:45
www.norris-associates.com
Email: info@norris-associates.com
Estab: 1984

Wayne B. Norris, Principal

Publisher of books on humor and a catalog of jokes.

Nortek Security & Control LLC HQ
1950 Camino Vida Roble Ste 150 [N]
Carlsbad CA 92008
P: 760-438-7000 F: 800-468-1340 PRC:71
www.nortekcontrol.com
Email: linear.sales@nortekcontrol.com
Estab: 1961

Mike O"Neal, President
Tom Cummiskey, VP of Sales

Manufacturer and distributor of wired and wireless security and control systems for residential and commercial security markers.

North Coast Medical Inc HQ
780 Jarvis Dr Ste 100
Morgan Hill CA 95037
P: 408-776-5000 F: 877-213-9300 PRC:189
www.ncmedical.com
Email: custserv@ncmedical.com
Estab: 1974

Mark E. Biehl, President & CEO
Preston Kincaid, Creative Marketing Director
Laura Langton, Sales Administration Director
Becky Cohn, Product Labeling Coordinator
Sam Ramsey, Senior System Administrator

Manufacturer of medical and rehabilitation products such as castings, clinical supplies, and other wellness supplies.

Northgate Environmental Management Inc HQ
428 13th St 4th Fl
Oakland CA 94612
P: 510-839-0688 F: 510-839-4350 PRC:139
ngem.com
Email: contact@ngem.com
Estab: 1999

Deni Chambers, President & Owner
Randa Bitar, Office Manager
Alan Leavitt, Principal Engineer
Axel Rieke, Principal Engineer
Maile Smith, Principal Geologist

Provider of interdisciplinary technical solutions. The company focuses on results-oriented scientific and engineering investigation and analysis.

Northstar HQ
111 Mission Ranch Blvd Ste 100
Chico CA 95926
P: 530-893-1600 F: 530-893-2113 PRC:142
northstareng.com
Email: info@northstareng.com
Estab: 1983

Rommel Mijares, Business Owner
Jay Lowe, Owner
Mark Adams, President
Ross Simmons, Senior Engineer & CFO
Tony De Melo, Director of Engineering

Provider of land development services, municipal infrastructure design, onsite waste water systems, and environmental consulting services.

Nortra-Cables Inc HQ
570 Gibraltar Dr
Milpitas CA 95035
P: 408-942-1106 F: 408-942-1109 PRC:62
www.nortra-cables.com
Email: info@nortra-cables.com
Estab: 1985

Michelle Lateur, Sustainability Manager
Binhminh Le, Office Manager
Bill St. Clair, Sales Manager
Patrick Wilder, Quality Manager
Khai Do, Engineer

Provider of discrete and flat mechanical assembly cables. The company offers design, prototyping, and manufacturing services.

Nova Measuring Instruments Inc BR
3342 Gateway Blvd
Fremont CA 94538
P: 408-510-7400 PRC:159
www.novami.com
Email: info@novami.com

Michael Sendler, President of US Operations
Eitan Oppenhaim, President & CEO
Sharon Dayan, Chief Human Resource Officer
Shay Wolfling, CTO
Dror David, CFO

Provider of metrology solutions for semiconductor manufacturing industries. The company offers integrated and stand-alone metrology platforms.

Novabay Pharmaceuticals Inc HQ
2000 Powell St Ste 1150
Emeryville CA 94608
P: 510-899-8800   F: 510-474-1577   PRC:34
novabay.com
Estab: 2000
Sales: $3M to $10M

Justin M. Hall, General Counsel & CEO
Thomas Paulson, CFO
David W. Stroman, SVP of Ophthalmic Product
Development & Chair of Ophthalmology Advisory
Board
Lu Wang, Director
Lonnie Wong, Director of Regulatory Affairs &
Quality Assurance

Manufacturer of biopharmaceuticals. The company develops non-antibiotic anti-infective products to address the eye care market.

Novalynx Corp HQ
431 Crown Point Cir Ste 120
Grass Valley CA 95945
P: 530-823-7185   PRC:233
www.novalynx.com
Email: nova@novalynx.com
Estab: 1988

Joseph R. Andre, President
William Begg, Engineering Manager
Jon Carlson, Systems Design & Support Manager
Keith Andre, Sales Manager
Mary Sweetser, Sales Manager

Designer, manufacturer, and integrator of meteorological systems. The company's products are used in the industrial sector.

Novani LLC HQ
900 Kearny St Ste 388
San Francisco CA 94133
P: 415-731-1111   F: 415-731-4270   PRC:324
www.novani.com
Email: sales@novani.com
Estab: 1989

Francis Yiu, Founder & CEO
Nancy Perata, COO
Henry Dickinson, Systems Support Engineer
Aaron Yoffe, Senior Systems Engineer

Provider of disaster prevention and recovery solutions. The company also offers business continuity and virtualization solutions.

Novasentis Inc HQ
2560 Ninth St Ste 314
Berkeley CA 94710
P: 814-238-7400   PRC:209
www.novasentis.com
Estab: 2006

Francois Jeanneau, President & CEO
Michael Vestel, CTO
Linda Ara, CFO
John Jacobi, VP of Manufacturing
Christine Kittinger, VP of Human Resources

Creator of haptic actuator and sensor technology for the consumer electronics applications such as smart watches, jewelry, headbands, and smart glasses.

Novici Biotech LLC HQ
3333 Vaca Valley Pkwy Ste 400
Vacaville CA 95688
P: 707-446-5502   F: 707-446-3917   PRC:269
www.novicibiotech.com
Email: info@novicibiotech.com

Hal Padgett, CEO & CSO

Focuses on product development as well as protein engineering. The company serves the agriculture, industrial and pharmaceutical sectors.

Novozymes Inc BR
1445 Drew Ave
Davis CA 95616
P: 530-757-8100   F: 530-758-0317   PRC:25
www.novozymes.com
Email: info@novozymes.com
Estab: 1992

Alan Berry, Managing Director
Debbie Yaver, Director
Feng Xu, Staff Scientist
Hanshu Ding, Senior Scientist
Alfredo Lopez-De-Leon, Senior Scientist

Provider of industrial biotechnology solutions for the food and beverage, agriculture, textile, and pulp and paper industries.

NPI Solutions Inc HQ
685 Jarvis Dr
Morgan Hill CA 95037
P: 408-944-9178   F: 408-944-9644   PRC:202
www.npisolutions.com
Email: info@npisolutions.com
Estab: 2000

Kevin Andersen, President

Provider of design, engineering, and custom manufacturing solutions. The company offers on-site engineering services.

NQ Engineering Inc HQ
7470 Carmelo Ave
Tracy CA 95304
P: 209-836-3255   PRC:80
www.nqengineering.com
Email: nqengineering@att.net
Estab: 1985

Mike Quigg, Machinist

Provider of engineering services. The company specializes in fabricating, materials, inspection, and quality control.

NRC Environmental Services Inc BR
1605 Ferry Pt
Alameda CA 94501
P: 510-749-1390   F: 510-749-4150   PRC:140
nrcc.com
Email: sales@nrcc.com
Estab: 1922

Joe Peterson, CFO
Lou O'Brien, SVP of Sales & Marketing
Robert George, SVP
Mike Reese, SVP
Neil Challis, SVP & International

Provider of environmental, industrial, and emergency solutions. The company offers oil spill response, industrial cleaning, sediment remediation, and other services.

NRC Manufacturing Inc HQ
47690 Westinghouse Dr
Fremont CA 94539
P: 510-438-9400   PRC:211
Estab: 2008

Matt Davis, VP
Larry Wright, Account Manager
Ray Ung, Program Manager
David Sin, Technician

Provider of contract manufacturing and PCB assembly services. The company's services include cable assembly, box builds, and functional test.

Nsymbio Inc HQ
2330 Old Middlefield Way Ste 1
Mountain View CA 94043
P: 650-968-2058   PRC:327
www.nsymbio.com
Email: service@nsymbio.com
Estab: 1969

Mahesh Tank, Founder & CEO
Adam Mason, Solutions Manager

Provider of printing services. The company is engaged in project management, graphic design, print, and online ordering system services.

NTFB Combustion Equipment USA Inc HQ
950 Tower LN
Foster City CA 94404
P: 510-443-0066   F: 510-443-0069   PRC:159
www.ntfb.com
Email: info@ntfb.com

Edison Guerra, Director of Operations

Manufacturer of combustion equipment. The company offers mid to large size, single and multiple burner, water tube boiler, and furnace applications.

NTK Technologies Inc HQ
3979 Freedom Cir Ste 400
Santa Clara CA 95054
P: 408-727-5180   F: 408-727-5076   PRC:204
www.ntktech.com
Estab: 1936

Paul Furuya, President & CEO
Mariel Stoops, Senior Strategic Marketing Manager

Manufacturer of bio ceramics, oxygen sensors, ceramic heater, and transistor packages for the medical and telecommunication applications.

NTT Global Data Centers Americas HQ
PO Box 348060
Sacramento CA 95834
P: 916-286-3000   PRC:67
ragingwire.com
Estab: 2000

Douglas Adams, CEO
Joe Goldsmith, CRO
Meghan Krafka, VP of Finance
Jerry Gilreath, VP of Information Technology
Judi Lee, SVP of Human Resources

Provider of information technology services such as storage, backup services, monitoring, migration planning, and disaster recovery.

Nu-Concepts HQ

1737 S Vineyard Ave [N]
Ontario CA 91761
P: 909-930-6244 PRC:48
www.nuconcepts.com
Estab: 1978

Hilario Coelho, Area Manager

Publisher of lifestyle and interior decoration magazines.

Nu-Hope Laboratories Inc HQ

12640 Branford St [N]
Pacoima CA 91333
P: 818-899-7711 F: 818-899-2079 PRC:261
www.nu-hope.com
Email: info@nu-hope.com
Emp: 11-50 Estab: 1959

Bradley Galindo, President & CEO

Manufacturer of ostomy support belts and pouches to non-adhesive ostomy systems.

Nugen Technologies Inc HQ

201 Industrial Rd Ste 310
San Carlos CA 94070
P: 650-590-3600 F: 650-590-3630 PRC:28
www.nugen.com
Email: custserv@nugeninc.com
Estab: 2000

Doug Amorese, CSO
Luke Sherlin, Director of Global Technical Support
Bin Li, Senior Scientist

Provider of solutions for genomic analysis. The company focuses on DNA analysis and RNA analysis applications.

Nugentec HQ

1155 Park Ave
Emeryville CA 94608
P: 707-820-4080 F: 707-820-4079 PRC:56
nugentec.com
Email: salesteam@nugentec.com
Estab: 1997

Dane Shannon, National Sales Manager

Provider of chemicals and polymers. The company offers oilfield chemicals, cleaners, and lubricants.

NuMedii Inc HQ

66 Bovet Rd Ste 320
San Mateo CA 94402
P: 650-918-6363 PRC:34
numedii.com
Email: info@numedii.com
Estab: 2008

Gini Deshpande, Founder & CEO
Samuel Saks, Director
Atul Butte, Director

Provider of big data technology such as integrative genomics and chemoinformatics to discover and de-risk new indications for safe, existing drug.

Numenta Inc HQ

791 Middlefield Rd
Redwood City CA 94063
P: 650-369-8282 F: 650-369-8283 PRC:67
www.numenta.com
Estab: 2005

Jeff Hawkins, Founder
Donna Dubinsky, President & CEO
Subutai Ahmad, VP of Research
Christy Maver, VP of Marketing
Scott Purdy, Engineering Manager

Developer of biotechnology machine intelligence technologies for commercial and scientific applications.

Numerate Inc HQ

1501 Mariposa St Ste 426
San Francisco CA 94107
P: 650-472-0632 PRC:257
Estab: 2007

Brandon Allgood, CTO
John Griffin, CSO
Uwe Klein, VP of Biology
Simon Wilkinson, Director of Engineering

Provider of data analytics and drug design technology services for the pharmaceutical and biotechnology industries.

Numerify Inc HQ

1054 S De Anza Blvd Ste 203
San Jose CA 95129
P: 408-822-9611 PRC:323
numerify.com
Email: info@numerify.com
Estab: 2012

Gaurav Rewari, Founder & CEO

Provider of business, service, and asset analytics services. The company offers services to information technology organizations.

Nutanix Inc HQ

1740 Technology Dr Ste 150
San Jose CA 95110
P: 855-688-2649 F: 408-916-4039 PRC:322
www.nutanix.com
Estab: 2009
Sales: $300M to $1 Billion

Dheeraj Pandey, Founder & CEO & Chairman
Duston Williams, CFO
Rajiv Mirani, CTO
Howard Ting, SVP of Marketing
Venugopal Pai, VP

Focuses on the simplification of datacenter infrastructure by integrating server and storage resources into a turnkey hyper converged platform.

Nute Engineering HQ

907 Mission Ave
San Rafael CA 94901
P: 415-453-4480 F: 415-453-0343 PRC:304
www.nute.biz
Email: info@nute.biz
Estab: 1945

Edward W. Nute, Founder
Mark T. Wilson, President
Priscilla Mills, CAD Manager
Adrian Bartshire, Engineer
David Stier, Engineer

Developer of technologies for the water, wastewater treatment, and environmental protection projects.

Nutribiotic HQ

PO Box 238
Lakeport CA 95453
P: 707-263-0411 F: 707-263-7844 PRC:251
www.nutribiotic.com
Email: sales@nutribiotic.com
Estab: 1980

Vincent Cancilla, Independent Sales Representative
Carolyn Roberts, Administrative Assistant

Manufacturer of health, wellness, and fitness products. The company provides nutritional supplements and personal care products.

Nuvation Engineering HQ

1260 Birchwood Dr
Sunnyvale CA 94089
P: 408-228-5580 PRC:327
www.nuvation.com
Email: info@nuvation.com
Estab: 1997

Michael Worry, CEO

Provider of electronic engineering services. The company focuses on product design, embedded software development, and single integrity analysis.

Nuvolase Inc HQ

11 Ilahee Ln
Chico CA 95973
P: 530-809-1970 PRC:172
www.nuvolase.com
Email: customercare@nuvolase.com
Estab: 2011

Steve Duddy, President & CEO & Director
Maureen Brunner, Senior Marketing Consultant

Manufacturer of the pinpointed foot laser used for the treatment of nail fungus and in nail fungus procedures.

Nuvora Inc HQ

3350 Scott Blvd Ste 502
Santa Clara CA 95054
P: 877-530-9811 F: 408-727-1703 PRC:254
www.nuvorainc.com
Estab: 2007

Jerry Gin, Founder
Bolko Stolberg, Founding Partner & COO
Ben Ross, EVP

Focuses on dry mouth treatment and offers products for bad breath prevention. The company offers Dentiva and Sales.

Nuvoton Technology Corporation America DH

2727 N First St
San Jose CA 95134
P: 408-544-1718 PRC:209
www.nuvoton.com
Estab: 2008

Pei-Ming Chen, Chairman & CEO
Jou-Wei Fu, President
Erez Naory, VP & Nuvoton Technology Israel Ltd.
Hsin-Lung Yang, VP of Cloud & Computing Business Group
Aditya Raina, EVP of Engineering

Manufacturer of semiconductor products and applications. The company's offerings include microcontrollers, microprocessors and cloud computing.

NV5 BR
2525 Natomas Park Dr Ste 300
Sacramento CA 95833
P: 916-641-9100   F: 916-641-9222   PRC:304
www.nv5.com

Alexander A. Hockman, President
Dickerson Wright, CEO & Chairman
Edward H. Codispoti, CFO
Todd George, COO
Mary Jo O. Brien, CAO

Provider of technical consulting and certification
services. The company serves the infrastructure,
construction, and real estate markers.

NVIDIA Corp HQ
2788 San Tomas Expy
Santa Clara CA 95051
P: 408-486-2000   PRC:91
www.nvidia.com
Email: info@nvidia.com
Estab: 1993
Sales: Over $3B

Jensen Hsun Huang, Founder & CEO & President
& Director
Colette Kress, EVP & CFO
Shanker Trivedi, VP of Enterprise Sales & Business Development
Dan Vivoli, SVP
Greg Estes, VP of Marketing

Provider of visual computing solutions that include
video games, movie production, product design,
medical diagnosis, and scientific research.

Nvigen Inc HQ
1185 Campbell Ave Ste 015
San Jose CA 95126
P: 650-209-0268   PRC:24
www.nvigen.com
Email: info@nvigen.com
Estab: 2011

Qiuyuan Liu, President
Aihua Fu, CEO
Weiwei Gu, Lab Manager
Helen Zhou, Product Manager
Abdel Rahim Minalla, Senior Engineer

Developer of multifunctional and biodegradable
nanoparticles. The company is engaged in research and development services.

nVision Medical Corp HQ
1192 Cherry Ave
San Bruno CA 94066
P: 408-655-3577   PRC:186
nvisionmedical.com
Email: info@nvisionmedical.com
Estab: 2011

Surbhi Sarna, CEO & Founder
David Snow, VP of Research & Development

Developer of women's health products. The company offers services to clinicians and the medical
industry.

nWay HQ
301 Howard St Ste 1440
San Francisco CA 94105
P: 415-778-2866   PRC:317
nway.com
Email: info@nway.com
Estab: 2011

Taehoon Kim, Founder & CEO
Kyungtae Kim, HR Manager
Ivy Ye Jin Lee, Business Operations Manager
Liyue Shen, Software Engineer

Specializes in the development and publishing of
free-to-play online multiplayer games. The company offers services to individuals.

NXP Semiconductors BR
411 E Plumeria Dr
San Jose CA 95134
P: 408-551-2215   PRC:86
www.nxp.com
Estab: 2006

Jeff Miles, VP Global Business Development
Secure IOT & Cloud
Ruediger Stroh, EVP & General Manager
Janet Chou, VP
Saurin Choksi, Principal Design Engineer

Manufacturer of amplifiers, diodes, data converters, microcontrollers, and bipolar transistors
for the healthcare, automotive, and computing
sectors.

Nyad Inc HQ
1647 Willow Pass Rd Ste 509
Concord CA 94520
P: 925-270-3971   PRC:11
nyad.com
Email: sales@nyad.com
Estab: 1987

Claire Parrott, President
Carissa Harrild, Executive Operations Manager &
Executive Administrative Assistant

Supplier of gas analyzers. The company's product
line includes analyzers for moisture, oxygen,
carbon monoxide, carbon dioxide, hydrocarbon,
and transmitters.

Nyden Corp HQ
PO Box 640176
San Jose CA 95164
P: 510-894-3633   PRC:150
www.nydencorporation.com
Email: sales@nydencorporation.com

Clara Chien, VP of Sales

Supplier of stepper motors. The company deals
with the design of semiconductor equipment, laser
systems, and aerospace-related apparatus.

O&M Industries Inc HQ
5901 Ericson Way
Arcata CA 95521
P: 707-822-8800   F: 707-822-8995   PRC:80
omindustries.com
Email: info@omindustries.com
Estab: 1946

Kevin Williams, Operations Manager

Provider of industrial, mechanical, structural contractors, and fabrication services. The company
serves cement industries.

O'hara Metal Products HQ
4949 Fulton Ave
Fairfield CA 94534
P: 707-863-9090   F: 707-863-9006   PRC:80
www.oharamfg.com
Email: twives@oharamfg.com
Estab: 1964

Tim Ives, President

Manufacturer of metal products. The company's
products include springs, stampings, sheet metals, and wires EDM's.

O-Rings Inc HQ
3311 Pepper Ave   [N]
Los Angeles CA 90065
P: 323-343-9500   F: 323-343-9505   PRC:57
www.oringsusa.com
Email: sales@oringsusa.com
Estab: 1958

Sherin Lee, CEO & CFO & Secretary
Daniel Lee, Director

Manufacturer and distributor of rings and custom
molded rubber products.

O2micro USA LH
3118 Patrick Henry Dr
Santa Clara CA 95054
P: 408-987-5920   PRC:64
www.o2micro.com
Email: ir@o2micro.com
Estab: 1998

Sterling Du, President & CEO
Gary E. Abbott, Director of Investor Relations
Carl Durham, Senior Corporate Counsel

Provider of battery and power management
products. The company also offers LED general
lighting and backlighting products.

Objectivity Inc HQ
1980 Zanker Rd Ste 30
San Jose CA 95112
P: 408-992-7100   F: 408-992-7171   PRC:323
www.objectivity.com
Email: info@objectivity.com
Estab: 1988

Leon Guzenda, Founder & Chief Technical Mar-
keting Officer
John Jarrell, President & CEO
Gary Lewis, CFO
Brian Clark, VP of Product Management
Kim Wizer, Director of Sales & Marketing

Provider of distributed, real-time, SOA-enabled
service and offers embedded database management solutions.

OCAMPO-ESTA Corp HQ
1419 Tennessee St
Vallejo CA 94590
P: 707-642-8072 F: 707-552-6047 PRC:68
www.ocampo-esta.com
Email: oec@ocampo-esta.com
Estab: 1986

Oscar S.L. Ocampo, President
Russel B. Ocampo, VP of Administration &
Finance
Albert Palad, Substation Engineer
Bonifacio Rayala, Electrical Engineer
Tom Akin, Senior Design Engineer

Provider of engineering, design, construction
management, instrumentation and controls, and
project management services.

Occidental Power HQ
5982 Mission St
San Francisco CA 94112
P: 415-681-8861 F: 415-681-9911 PRC:135
www.oxypower.com
Email: sales@oxypower.com
Estab: 1989

Greg Kennedy, Co-Founder
Gregory Kennedy, Co-Founder
Keith Burkland, Field Supervisor
Kee-Fee Lim, Solar Technician
Carmine Garofalo, Designer

Designer and installer of commercial and residential solar electric, solar thermal, and natural gas
cogeneration systems.

Ocean Presence Technologies HQ
326 Pacheco Ave
Santa Cruz CA 95062
P: 831-426-4678 PRC:168
oceanpresence.com

Robert Aston, President

Manufacturer of underwater video monitoring
camera systems and offers cable systems, power
systems, lighting, wireless networks, and accessories.

Ocellus Inc HQ
450 Lindbergh Ave
Livermore CA 94551
P: 925-606-6540 PRC:191
www.ocellusinc.com
Email: information@ocellusinc.com
Estab: 1996

Zoran Savicic, President
Shannan Downey, Manager of Laboratory Operations

Provider of multidisciplinary technology and
services such as nanotechnology-based solutions
for aerospace, industrial, and medical applications.

OCSiAl BR
500 S Front St Ste 860
Columbus CA 43215
P: 415-906-5271 PRC:131
ocsial.com
Email: usa@ocsial.com

Oleg Kirillov, Co-Founder
Yuriy Zelvenskiy, Co-Founder
Yury Koropachinskiy, Co-Founder
Ian Fellows, CEO
Alexander Bezrodny, VP

Provider of technology and material solutions.
The company offers services to the nanomaterials
industry.

Ocumetrics Inc HQ
2224-C Old Middlefield Way
Mountain View CA 94043-2421
P: 650-960-3955 F: 650-960-0611 PRC:187
www.ocumetrics.com
Email: info@ocumetrics.com
Estab: 1993

Bruce Ishimoto, Owner

Manufacturer of Fluorotron Master Ocular Fluoro-
photometers. The company deals with research
services.

Odie Sheet Metal Shop HQ
375 Umbarger Rd
San Jose CA 95111
P: 408-281-2919 F: 408-281-2477 PRC:80
odiesheetmetal.com
Email: odiesheetmetal@sbcglobal.net
Estab: 1979

Michael Garcia, Shop Manager

Provider of sheet metal fabrication solutions. The
company also deals with manufacturing and prototype development.

Oea International Inc HQ
155 E Main Ave Ste 110
Morgan Hill CA 95037
P: 408-778-6747 F: 408-778-6748 PRC:323
www.oea.com
Email: info@oea.com
Estab: 1988

Ersed Akcasu, President
Jerry Tallinger, VP of Sales & Marketing

Developer of signal integrity software. The company serves the electronic design automation
industry.

Oepic Semiconductors Inc HQ
1231 Bordeaux Dr
Sunnyvale CA 94089
P: 408-747-0388 F: 408-747-5808 PRC:212
www.oepic.com
Email: sales@oepic.com
Estab: 2000

Majid Riaziat, President
Minh-Tam Nguyen, Controller

Provider of semiconductor fabrication services.
The company's products include optical and optoelectronic components.

Office Information Systems HQ
7730 Pardee Ln
Oakland CA 94621
P: 510-568-7900 PRC:329
www.ois-online.com
Estab: 1982

Richard Ozer, President

Provider of computer network design and consulting services. The company serves small and
medium sized organizations and law firms.

Ogletree's Inc HQ
935 Vintage Ave
St. Helena CA 94574
P: 707-963-3537 F: 707-963-8217 PRC:80
www.ogletreecorp.com
Estab: 1946

Matt Cia, President
Dennis Souza, Estimator & Project Manager
Sam Peers, Systems Design Engineer

Provider of metal and equipment fabrication services. The company focuses on design, detailing,
fabrication, and installation services.

Ohanae Inc HQ
16133 Hillvale Ave
Monte Sereno CA 95030
P: 888-617-7288 F: 413-691-1935 PRC:323
www.ohanae.com
Email: info@ohanae.com
Estab: 2007

Greg Hauw, Founder & Chairman & CEO

Provider of data and password protection and
data compliance solutions. The company offers
services to businesses.

OJO Technology Inc HQ
103 Hammond Ave
Fremont CA 94539
P: 877-306-4656 PRC:64
www.ojotech.com
Email: sales@ojotech.com
Estab: 2003

Angie Wong, CEO
Lai Wong, Project Manager
Derek Tokuda, Wireless Network Engineer
Kalyn Beery, Solution Engineer
Bob Bisetti, Security Solutions Advisor

Manufacturer of video surveillance systems. The
company offers services to the education, transportation, and utility sectors.

Okta Inc HQ
100 First St 6th Fl
San Francisco CA 94105
P: 800-219-0964 PRC:322
okta.com
Email: info@okta.com
Estab: 2009
Sales: $300M to $1 Billion

Frederic Kerrest, Executive Vice Chairperson &
COO & Co-Founder
Todd McKinnon, CEO & Co-Founder
Charles Race, President
Hector Aguilar, President of Technology
Ryan Carlson, CMO

Provider of identity and automated user management, administration, reporting, and application
integration solutions.

Olixir Technologies HQ
1525 McCarthy Blvd
Milpitas CA 95035
P: 408-719-0595 PRC:116
olixir.com
Email: sales@olixir.com
Estab: 2001

Darshan Shah, Founder & Head Product & Program Manager & CMO
Andrae Browne, Web Developer

Provider of external hard drives and racks and towers. The company also offers video surveillance and backup solutions.

Ologic HQ
3350 Scott Blvd Bldg 47
Santa Clara CA 95054
P: 408-663-6638 PRC:311
www.ologicinc.com
Email: info@ologicinc.com

Ted Larson, CEO
Brandon Blodget, VP of Technology Development
Ana Alcorn-Dominguez, Junior Project Manager
Lauren Hersh, Project Manager
Robert Garbanati, Robotics Engineer

Manufacturer of consumer electronics and toy products. The company specializes in defense and educational projects.

Omega Diamond Inc HQ
10125 Ophir Rd Ste A
Newcastle CA 95658-9504
P: 530-889-8977 F: 530-885-3785 PRC:80
omegadiamond.com
Estab: 1985

Sam Devai, CEO
Roneily Devai, Office Manager

Developer and manufacturer of diamond tools for the ultra precise semiconductor and optics industry. The company also offers power tools.

Omega Leads Inc HQ
1509 Colorado Ave [N]
Santa Monica CA 90404
P: 310-394-6786 PRC:209
www.omegaleads.com
Emp: 11-50 Estab: 1961

Cynthia Gonzalez, Manager of Account
Benjamin Gonzalez, Materials Handler

Manufacturer of commercial wire harness and cable assemblies.

OML Inc HQ
300 Digital Dr
Morgan Hill CA 95037
P: 408-779-2698 F: 408-778-0491 PRC:65
www.omlinc.com
Email: info@omlinc.com
Estab: 1991

Yuenie Lau, President & CEO

Provider of millimeter wave test instruments, calibration equipment and systems for radio astronomy, communication, imaging, and other sectors.

Omni Fab HQ
380 Martin Ave Ste 3
Santa Clara CA 95050
P: 408-492-1331 F: 408-492-1333 PRC:82
www.omnifab.com
Email: info@omnifab.com
Estab: 1977

Bruce Sunseri, Owner

Provider of precision sheet metal fabrication services. The company caters to the high technology industry.

Omni Pro Systems HQ
50 Mendell St Ste 2
San Francisco CA 94124
P: 415-648-1121 F: 415-648-1174 PRC:92
www.omnipro.com
Email: info@omnipro.com

Ran Jan, Owner
Edward Meyer, Sales Manager

Supplier and integrator of computer systems. The company offers custom logo engraving services and deployment ready solutions.

Omnicia Inc HQ
One Market St Spear Tower 36th Fl
San Francisco CA 94105
P: 415-293-8553 F: 650-588-2488 PRC:320
www.omniciainc.com
Email: info@omniciainc.com
Estab: 2001

Peachy Dimanlig, COO & Founder

Provider of electronic submissions for the life science sector. The company offers electronics and desktop publishing and document management services.

Omnicor HQ
1170 Foster City Blvd Ste 314
Foster City CA 94404
P: 650-572-0122 PRC:97
www.omnicor.com
Email: info@omnicor.com

Hafiz Muhammad Ali, Founder
Ivan Dubnov, CEO
Salman Aslam, CMO
Hilton Rudnick, Managing Director
Roman Porenta, Manager

Provider of network testing tools, vacuum capacitors, and interrupters and IP performance test systems.

Omnivision Technologies Inc HQ
4275 Burton Dr
Santa Clara CA 95054
P: 408-567-3000 F: 408-567-3001 PRC:212
www.ovt.com
Email: info@ovt.com
Estab: 1995

Henry Yang, President
Anson H. Chan, VP of Finance & CFO
Howard E. Rhodes, VP of Process Engineering
John Li, VP of System Technologies
Yuguo Ye, ASIC Design Director

Developer of digital imaging solutions for consumer and commercial applications, and automotive, medical, and security imaging sectors.

Omniyig Inc HQ
3350 Scott Blvd Bldg 66
Santa Clara CA 95054
P: 408-988-0843 PRC:212
Estab: 1973

Elaine O'B Capogeannis, Sales Manager
Tuan Ly, RF Design Engineer Manager
Michaela Pao Nieblas, Contracts Manager

Manufacturer of microwave devices for the defense industry. The company also offers limiters, drivers, and oscillators.

OMW Corp HQ
354 Bel Marin Keys Blvd
Novato CA 94949
P: 415-382-1669 F: 415-382-9069 PRC:80
www.omwcorp.com
Email: rfq@omwcorp.com
Estab: 1996

Joe Osborn, Founder
Geno Adoline, General Manager
Edgardo Oropeza Castillo, Director General
Matt Warr, Quality Assurance Manager
Michael Leeds, Machinist & Manager

Manufacturer of CNC machined parts. The company also deals with production machining, prototyping, and support services.

Onanon Inc HQ
720 S Milpitas Blvd
Milpitas CA 95035
P: 408-262-8990 PRC:76
www.onanon.com
Email: sales@onanon.com
Estab: 1979

Thomas Sahakian, Owner
Dennis Johnson, CEO
Jun Rimmer, CIO
Mohammad Younis, Manager of Production
John Mark Spadafora, Quality Manager

Manufacturer of connector components. The company offers pin connectors, cable assemblies, and machined plastics.

Onchip Devices Inc HQ
3054 Scott Blvd
Santa Clara CA 95054
P: 408-654-9365 PRC:126
onchip.com
Email: sales@onchip.com
Estab: 2007

Swamy Venkidu, Chairman
Ashok Chalaka, President & CEO

Provider of silicon and ceramic solutions and integrated passive devices for the computing and consumer electronics industries.

Onda Corp HQ
1290 Hammerwood Ave
Sunnyvale CA 94089
P: 408-745-0383   F: 408-745-0956   PRC:189
www.ondacorp.com
Email: info@ondacorp.com
Estab: 1990

Claudio Zanelli, Founder
Petrie Yam, VP of Sales & Marketing
Alfred Yue, Inside Sales Manager
Kimberly Sotelo, Procurement Manager

Manufacturer of medical devices. The company offers ultrasound measurement instrumentation and services for scientific applications.

Ondavia Inc HQ
26102 Eden Landing Rd Ste 1
Hayward CA 94545
P: 510-576-0476   F: 510-887-3180   PRC:138
www.ondavia.com
Email: info@ondavia.com
Estab: 2009

Mark Peterman, CEO
Merwan Benhabib, VP of Engineering

Provider of water analysis solutions. The company offers OndaVia analysis system that enables laboratory-grade water testing.

One Touch Systems HQ
2528 Qume Dr Unit 14
San Jose CA 95131
P: 408-660-8435   PRC:326
www.onetouchsys.com
Email: info@onetouchsys.com
Estab: 1989

Larry Speckels, President & CEO
Bob Wilkinson, VP & CFO
Gopinath Rebala, VP of Software Engineering

Provider of virtual distance learning, training and communication systems. The company offers services to the educational sector.

OneLogin HQ
848 Battery St
San Francisco CA 94111
P: 415-645-6830   PRC:325
www.onelogin.com
Email: press@onelogin.com
Estab: 2009

Christian Pedersen, Chief Architect & Founder
Danny Kibel, CEO
Courtney Harrison, Chief Human Resource Officer
Dayna Rothman, CMO
Bernard Huger, CFO

Provider of single sign-on and identity management for cloud-based applications. The company serves the industrial sector.

Oneto Metal Products Corp HQ
7485 Reese Rd
Sacramento CA 95828-3239
P: 916-681-6555   F: 916-681-6565   PRC:88
www.onetometal.com
Estab: 1988

Raymond Liberatore, President
Joe Liberatore, Controller
Catherine M. Liberatore, Controller
Paul T. Liberatore, Contact
Frank Yearsley, Contact

Manufacturer of fabricated sheet metal products. The company offers flashing, roof jacks, gravel stop and specialty architectural sheet metal.

Onfulfillment Inc HQ
8678 Thornton Ave
Newark CA 94560
P: 510-793-3009   PRC:325
www1.onfulfillment.com
Email: info@onfulfillment.com
Estab: 1999

Steve Friar, Founder & CEO
Dan Barnett, EVP & COO
Carolyn Lajoie, Customer Service Manager
Juan Rosales, Operational Manager
Veronica Price, Program Manager

Provider of printing solutions. The company offers order fulfillment, online delivery, and print management services.

Onque Technologies Inc HQ
281 Second St E
Sonoma CA 95476
P: 707-569-3000   PRC:320
www.onque.com
Email: sales@onque.com
Estab: 1997

Bret Andrews, President

Provider of software tools used for the management of human resources. The company serves business organizations and enterprises.

Onyx Optics Inc HQ
6551 Sierra Ln
Dublin CA 94568
P: 925-833-1969   F: 925-833-1759   PRC:172
www.onyxoptics.com
Email: sales@onyxoptics.com
Estab: 1992

Stephanie Meissner, President
Roberto Rodriguez, Plant Manager
Da Li, Electro-Optics Scientist & Engineer
Huai-Chuan Lee, Senior Optical Engineer
Dave Meissner, Production Supervisor

Manufacturer of laser and telecom composite crystals and glasses. The company also offers products for optical finishing and other needs.

Oomnitza HQ
414 Brannan St
San Francisco CA 94107
P: 650-417-3694   PRC:323
oomnitza.com
Email: team@oomnitza.com
Estab: 2012

Arthur Lozinski, Co-Founder & CEO
Ramin Ettehad, Co-Founder
Trent Seed, Co-Founder & Chief Architect
David Bercovich, COO
Udo Waibel, CTO

Provider of information technology asset management and related services. The company focuses on third party solutions.

Opac Consulting Engineers Inc HQ
315 Bay St 2nd Fl
San Francisco CA 94133
P: 415-989-4551   F: 415-989-4135   PRC:304
www.opacengineers.com
Estab: 1992

Kwong Cheng, President
Mark Ketchum, VP
Francis Drouillard, Principal
Vivian Chang, Principal

Provider of bridge and structural engineering services. The company's services are design, evaluation, and construction engineering.

Opal Soft Inc HQ
1288 Kifer Rd Ste 201
Sunnyvale CA 94086
P: 408-267-2211   F: 408-774-1451   PRC:68
opalsoft.com
Estab: 1997

Sharad Sharma, Director of Business Development

Provider of communications equipment installation and networking. The company's services include application development, network management, and maintenance.

Opamp Labs Inc HQ
1033 N Sycamore Ave   [N]
Los Angeles CA 90038
P: 323-934-3566   F: 323-462-6490   PRC:60
www.opamplabs.com
Email: opamplabs@gmail.com
Estab: 1965

Bela Losmandy, Founder & Chief Engineer

Manufacturer of audio and video products.

Open Five Inc   HQ
490 N McCarthy Blvd Ste 220
Milpitas CA 95035-5118
P: 408-240-5700   F: 408-240-5701   PRC:207
openfive.com
Email: info@openfive.com
Estab: 2003

Yunsup Lee, Founder & CTO
Stuart Ching, CRO
Steve Erickson, VP & General Manager of Platform Business Unit & VP & General Manager of Platform Business Unit
Steve Wong, Senior Product Engineering Manager & Senior Product Engineering Manager
Steve Eplett, Manager of DTA

Provider of IP, foundry, test, and packaging technologies. The company's services include system design, manufacturing, and program management.

Openclovis   HQ
765 Baywood Dr Ste 336
Petaluma CA 94954-5507
P: 707-981-7120   PRC:322
www.openclovis.com
Email: sales@openclovis.com
Estab: 2002

V.K. Budhraja, CEO

Provider of system infrastructure software platform. The company mainly serves the communication industry.

Opengov Inc   HQ
955 Charter St
Redwood City CA 94063
P: 650-336-7167   PRC:325
opengov.com
Email: pr@opengov.com.
Estab: 2012

Joe Lonsdale, Co-Founder & Chairman
Zac Bookman, Co-Founder & CEO
Nate Levine, Co-Founder
David Reeves, CRO
Matt Singer, CMO

Provider of financial transparency and business intelligence solutions. The company offers services to government agencies.

OpensourceCM   HQ
1098 Foster City Blvd Ste 106-725
Foster City CA 94404
P: 650-200-0506   F: 650-345-2098   PRC:323
www.opensourceinc.com
Email: info@opensourceinc.com
Estab: 1995

Zvi Margalit, CEO
Nathan Brand, CTO

Designer and developer of contract management software. The company also offers technical support services.

Openvpn Technologies Inc   HQ
7901 Stoneridge Dr Ste 540
Pleasanton CA 94588
P: 925-399-1481   PRC:323
openvpn.net
Email: privacy@openvpn.net
Estab: 2002

Francis Dinha, Co-Founder & CEO
James Yonan, Co-Founder & CTO
Elfredy Cadapan, Head of Engineering
Farhan Ul Haq, Senior Software Engineer

Specializes in deploying VPN access solutions. The company is engaged in marketing and communication services.

Oppo Digital Inc   HQ
162 Constitution Dr
Menlo Park CA 94025
P: 650-961-1118   F: 650-961-1119   PRC:110
www.oppodigital.com

Nan Yang, Product Manager
Tony Tang, Manager

Manufacturer of Blu-ray players and UP converting DVD players. The company's services include design, installation, and delivery.

Opsol Integrators Inc   HQ
1566 La Pradera Dr
Campbell CA 95008
P: 408-364-9915   F: 408-364-9916   PRC:326
www.opsol.com
Email: support@omnipayments.com
Estab: 1995

Yash Kapadia, CEO
Tojo Vilson, Principal Consultant
Rahul Gorse, Software Developer

Provider of universal messaging, data integration, and encryption products. The company serves banks, retail, telecom, and other sectors.

OPSWAT Inc   HQ
398 Kansas St
San Francisco CA 94103
P: 415-590-7300   PRC:323
www.opswat.com
Estab: 2002

Benny Czarny, Founder & CEO
Mike Spykerman, VP of Product Management
Tom Mullen, SVP of Business Development

Provider of endpoint software management, compliance, URL filtering, network monitoring, and related solutions.

Optical Structures Inc   HQ
11371 Pyrites Way Ste A
Rancho Cordova CA 95670
P: 877-623-4021   F: 916-671-5669   PRC:176
www.opticalstructures.com
Estab: 2006

Cary Chleborad, President

Provider of optical systems and services. The company's products find application in research and education sectors.

Optimal Synthesis Inc   HQ
95 First St Ste 240
Los Altos CA 94022
P: 650-559-8585   F: 650-559-8586   PRC:323
www.optisyn.com
Email: engineers@optisyn.com
Estab: 1992

Nicholas Niejelow, President & CEO
Vicky Lu, Director of Signal Processing Technologies
Jason Kwan, Research Engineer
Parikshit Dutta, Research Scientist

Provider of research, algorithm development, and software design services. The company caters to a variety of engineering and science applications.

Optimum Design Associates   HQ
1075 Serpentine Ln
Pleasanton CA 94566
P: 925-401-2004   F: 925-401-2010   PRC:211
www.optimumdesign.com
Email: sales@optimumdesign.com
Estab: 1990

Roger Hileman, CFO & Owner
Sherrie Hubbard, Director of Business Development
Brendon Parise, Senior PCB Design Manager
J. R. Reed, Engineering Manager
Benjamin Brown, Systems Administrator

Provider of printed circuit board design and layout services. The company also focuses on engineering and manufacturing services.

Optimum Processing Inc   HQ
55 Mitchell Blvd Ste 23
San Rafael CA 94903
P: 415-461-7033   PRC:268
opibioprocess.com
Email: info@opibioprocess.com
Estab: 1988

Peter Florez, Principal

Provider of filtration solutions and disposable bioprocess container systems. The company utilizes asymmetric morphology solutions.

Optiscan Biomedical Corp   HQ
24590 Clawiter Rd
Hayward CA 94545
P: 510-342-5800   PRC:187
www.optiscancorp.com
Email: info@optiscancorp.com
Estab: 1994

Peter Rule, CEO
Patrick Nugent, CFO
Chip Zimliki, VP of Regulatory & Quality & Clinical Affairs
Jim Causey, VP of Innovation
Mario P. Cervantes, VP of Operations

Provider of monitoring products for measuring glucose, plasma collection, and also detection of glucose among patients.

Optiworks Inc HQ
47211 Bayside Pkwy
Fremont CA 94538
P: 510-438-4560   F: 510-252-1178   PRC:170
www.optiworks.com
Email: sales@optiworks.com
Estab: 2000

Victor Yue, VP of Engineering
Dennis Ma, VP of sales & marketing
Mike Lin, General Manager
Ma Yanyan, Sales Manager

Manufacturer of fiber optic components. The
company's products include thin film filters, fused
components, sub components, and accessories.

Optoelectronix Inc HQ
111 W Saint John St Ste 588
San Jose CA 95113
P: 408-241-1222   PRC:243
www.optoelectronix.com
Email: sales@optoelectronix.com
Estab: 2006

Chuck Berghoff, CEO
Robert Kow, VP of Engineering
George Martin, VP of Engineering & IP Services
Jim Schenck, VP of Sales
Tom Thayer, SVP of Marketing & Business Devel-
opment

Designer, developer, and manufacturer of plug-
and-play and standardized LED-based landscape
lighting and engines.

Optoplex Corp HQ
48500 Kato Rd
Fremont CA 94538
P: 510-490-9930   F: 510-490-9330   PRC:62
optoplex.com
Email: info@optoplex.com
Estab: 2000

Vincent Chien, VP of Engineering
Lisa Cao, Accounting Manager
Carol Wu, Human Resource Manager
Tim Ngo, Optical Engineer
Xueyi Geng, Electrical Engineer

Supplier of cutting-edge photonic components and
modules for dynamic wavelength management
and signal conditioning.

Optovue Inc HQ
2800 Bayview Dr
Fremont CA 94538
P: 510-743-0985   F: 510-623-8668   PRC:186
www.optovue.com
Email: info@optovue.com
Estab: 2003

Jay Wei, Founder & CEO
David Voris, President & CFO
Paul Kealey, SVP of Product Development &
Business Strategy
Judy Bartlett-Roberto, VP of Marketing
John Hawley, SVP of Global Sales

Manufacturer of ophthalmic devices. The company
leads the commercialization of new imaging mo-
dalities to develop ophthalmic diagnosis.

Optowaves Inc HQ
6830 Via Del Oro Ste 200
San Jose CA 95119
P: 408-724-5888   F: 408-724-5889   PRC:170
www.optowaves.com
Estab: 2001

Jeffery Hsu, Account Manager
Angela Chung, Office Manager

Manufacturer and supplier of passive fiber optic
components, attenuator, coupler, and isolator for
the medical and communication industries.

Optumsoft Inc HQ
200 Middlefield Rd Ste 112
Menlo Park CA 94025
P: 844-361-8222   PRC:319
optumsoft.com
Email: info@optumsoft.com
Estab: 2004

David R. Cheriton, Founder & Chairman
Fusun Ertemalp, President & CEO
Xi Cheng, Software Engineer

Provider of distributed computing and technology
based software development that includes maintenance of structured software systems.

Oracle Corp BR
475 Sansome St 15th Fl
San Francisco CA 94111
P: 415-402-7200   F: 415-402-7250   PRC:322
www.oracle.com
Estab: 1977

Lawrence J. Ellison, Founder & Chairman & CTO
Thomas Kurian, President of Product Develop-
ment
Saeed Mirza, Group Vice President of Oracle
Cloud
Safra A. Catz, CEO
Douglas Kehring, EVP of Corporate Operations

Developer of hardware and software systems. The
company provides Oracle database, engineered
systems, and enterprise manager solutions.

**Orange County Industrial Plastics
Inc** HQ
4811 E la Palma Ave   [N]
Anaheim CA 92807
P: 714-630-6489   PRC:284
www.ocip.com
Emp: 11-50   Estab: 1982

Richard Weeks, Account Manager
Scott Cornogg, Production Manager

Manufacturer and distributor of plastic fabricator.

Orange Enterprises Inc HQ
2377 W Shaw Ste 205
Fresno CA 93711
P: 559-229-2195   F: 559-229-9348   PRC:323
tigerjill.com
Email: support@orangesoftware.com
Estab: 1984

Udi Sosnik, Owner
Shlomo Pleban, Research & Development
Director

Provider of software solutions. The company
mainly focuses on payroll tracking and agriculture
management.

Orbeon Inc HQ
3941 Pasadena Dr
San Mateo CA 94403
P: 650-762-8184   PRC:322
www.orbeon.com
Email: info@orbeon.com
Estab: 1999

Erik Bruchez, Software Architect
Alessandro Vernet, Software Architect

Provider of web form deployment services. The
company offers basic, gold, and platinum development support, and validation services.

Orbex Group HQ
46740 Lakeview Blvd
Fremont CA 94538
P: 408-945-8980   PRC:62
orbexgroup.com
Estab: 2007

Donna Sisk, Manager of Customer Service
Christy Hagenau, Compliance Manager

Manufacturer of electronic rings. The company
offers capsule slip rings, through-hole slip rings,
and harsh environment slip rings.

Orbotech LT Solar LLC BR
5970 Optical Ct
San Jose CA 95138
P: 408-226-9900   F: 408-226-9910   PRC:209
www.orbotech.com
Estab: 1981

Yair Alcobi, Corporate VP & President of the PCB
division
Eitan Judah, Corporate VP & President of the
FPD division
Kevin Crofton, Corporate EVP & President of
SPTS Technologies
Amichai Steimberg, CEO
Lior Maayan, Corporate VP of Business Develop-
ment & CMO

Manufacturer of electronic devices. The company
offers printed circuit boards, flat panel displays,
and touch screens.

Orbus Therapeutics Inc HQ
2479 E Bayshore Rd Ste 105
Palo Alto CA 94303
P: 650-656-9440   PRC:268
www.orbustherapeutics.com
Estab: 2012

Bob Myers, CEO & Co-Founder & President
Jason Levin, COO & Co-Founder
Noymi Yam, Head of Product Development

Developer of therapeutic products to treat rare
disease such as anaplastic astrocytoma.

Orchard Machinery Corp HQ
2700 Colusa Hwy
Yuba City CA 95993
P: 530-673-2822   F: 530-673-0296   PRC:159
shakermaker.com
Estab: 1961

Don Mayo, President & CEO
Brian Andersen, VP
Rodney Mayfield, Manager of Operations
John Krum, Territory Sales Manager
Brian Kaufman, Parts Manager

Manufacturer of tree shakers and material handling systems comprising shuttles, bin carriers,
conveyor carts, and elevators.

Ordinal Technology Corp HQ
20 Crestview Dr
Orinda CA 94563
P: 925-253-9204 F: 925-253-8502 PRC:324
www.ordinal.com
Email: enquiries@ordinal.com
Estab: 1994

Chris Nyberg, Founder

Provider of sorting services of massive and production data sets such as web logs for high-traffic
websites, phone logs, and government agency
data.

Organic Inc HQ
600 California St 7th Fl
San Francisco CA 94108
P: 415-581-5300 F: 415-581-5400 PRC:322
organic.com
Email: friends@organic.com

David Shulman, CEO

Provider of information technology services. The
company develops websites, mobile applications,
banner, and digital signage.

ORIC Pharmaceuticals Inc HQ
240 E Grand Ave 2nd Fl
S San Francisco CA 94080
P: 650-388-5600 PRC:268
oricpharma.com
Email: info@oricpharma.com
Estab: 2014

Jacob Chacko, CEO
Pratik Multani, CMO
Dominic Piscitelli, CFO
Valeria Fantin, CSO
Matthew Panuwat, Chief Business Officer

Provider of pharmaceutical research. The company specializes in discovering and developing novel
therapies for treatment-resistant cancers.

Oriental Motor USA Corp DH
570 Alaska Ave
Torrance CA 90503
P: 310-715-3301 F: 310-225-2594 PRC:146
orientalmotor.com
Estab: 1885

Kimberly Freisheim, Human Resource Manager

Provider of optimal motion systems. The company
focuses on producing fractional horsepower products for motion control applications.

Originate Inc DH
Two Embarcadero Ctr 8th Fl
San Francisco CA 94111
P: 800-352-2292 PRC:322
www.originate.com
Email: hello@originate.com
Estab: 2007

Darrell Mervau, President
Rob Meadows, CEO
Shahar Ben Hador, CIO

Developer of software to integrate, network, and
economically operate energy storage systems.
The company is engaged in analysis services.

Orion Labs HQ
208 Utah St Ste 350
San Francisco CA 94103
P: 415-800-2035 PRC:64
www.orionlabs.io
Email: info@orionlabs.io
Estab: 2013

Greg Albrecht, Founder & CTO
Jesse Robbins, CEO
Michael Schwartz, CMO
Craig Rankin, Director Sales Operations
Rob Cox, Marketing Director

Developer of wearable communication accessory
for instant voice conversations with many people,
across any distance.

Orion Wine Software HQ
2455 Bennett Valley Rd Ste C208
Santa Rosa CA 95404
P: 877-632-3155 F: 707-545-5298 PRC:323
orionwinesoftware.com
Email: info@orionwinesw.com
Estab: 2007

Jason Curtis, General Manager
Robert Chown, Support Manager

Developer of winery management solutions. The
company is also engaged in sales and inventory
management.

Ortho Group HQ
11431 Sunrise Gold Cir Ste B
Rancho Cordova CA 95742
P: 916-859-0881 PRC:190
www.orthogroup.com
Email: info@orthogroup.com
Estab: 2003

Henry Fletcher, CEO
Nizar Saidane, Industrial Director

Designer of devices for the medical industry.
The company specializes in orthopedic surgical
devices.

OrthoTrophix Inc HQ
303 Hegenberger Rd Ste 312
Oakland CA 94621
P: 510-488-3832 F: 510-567-8785 PRC:191
www.orthotrophix.com
Email: info@orthotrophix.com
Estab: 2011

Yoshi Kumagai, President & CEO
David M. Rosen, CSO
Dawn McGuire, CMO
Meghan Miller, Senior CRA & Project Lead

Developer of therapies for medical needs of patients. The company specializes in regeneration of
articular cartilage in knee and other joints.

Oryx Advanced Materials Inc HQ
46458 Fremont Blvd
Fremont CA 94538
P: 510-249-1157 F: 510-249-2008 PRC:80
www.oryxadv.com
Email: info@oryxadv.com
Estab: 1976

Norman Mills, President

Provider of thin film materials for PV cells. The
company also offers sputtering targets and bonding services to the magnetic data storage market.

Oscar Larson & Associates HQ
317 Third St 2nd Fl
Eureka CA 95501
P: 707-445-2043 F: 707-445-8230 PRC:304
olarson.com
Email: larson@olarson.com
Estab: 1945

Greg M. Hall, Project Civil Engineer
Tyler Duncan, Engineering Technician

Provider of environmental planning, permitting,
and related services and it specializes in residential and commercial projects.

Osel Inc HQ
320 Logue Ave
Mountain View CA 94043
P: 650-964-1420 F: 650-964-4679 PRC:34
www.oselinc.com
Email: info@oselinc.com

Peter P. Lee, Founder & Executive Chairman
Laurel A. Lagenaur, Director of Research
Tom Parks, Director of Product Development
Iwona Swedek, Research Associate

Developer of biotherapeutic products. The company focuses on treatment and prevention of conditions for women's health and infectious diseases.

Osisoft LLC HQ
1600 Alvarado St
San Leandro CA 94577
P: 510-297-5800 F: 510-357-8136 PRC:323
www.osisoft.com
Email: customerservice@osisoft.com
Estab: 1980

J. Patrick Kennedy, Founder & CEO
Jenny Linton, President
Richard Beeson, CTO
Bob Guilbault, CFO
Steve Nye, VP of Customer Services & Support

Developer of PI system software. The company
offers software such as PI Computing Engine,
Batch, Data Access, and Clients.

OtherWorld Enterprises Inc HQ
PO Box 1721 [N]
Simi Valley CA 93062
P: 805-768-4638 F: 203-779-4638 PRC:323
www.other-world.com
Estab: 1988

Ryan Perri Jones, President

Provider of web design, development and hosting
services.

OTRS Inc BR
19925 Stevens Creek Blvd
Cupertino CA 95014-2358
P: 408-549-1717 F: 408-512-1748 PRC:323
www.otrs.com
Email: sales@otrs.com
Estab: 2003

Andr' Mindermann, CEO & Founder
Christopher Kuhn, COO

Focuses on business solutions. The company
offers services to the hospitality, education, and
financial sectors.

Otsuka America Inc   HQ
1 Embarcadero Ctr Ste 2020
San Francisco CA 94111
P: 415-986-5300   F: 415-986-5361   PRC:261
www.otsuka-america.com

Mike Gehrke, VP of Internal Audit & Administration

Developer of pharmaceutical products for the treatment of central nervous system, ophthalmology, cardiovascular, and skin conditions.

Otter Computer Inc   HQ
3350 Scott Blvd Bldg 4   [N]
Santa Clara CA 95054
P: 408-982-9358   F: 408-982-9335   PRC:322
www.otterusa.com
Email: contact@otterusa.com
Emp: 1-10   Estab: 1989

Kin Tsai, President

Designer and provider of PCB layout and assembly Services.

Outformations Inc   HQ
939 61st St Ste 13
Oakland CA 94608-1304
P: 510-655-7122   PRC:326
outformations.com
Email: info@outformations.com
Estab: 1989

David Chilcott, President
Jill Kaplan, Office Manager
Don Robins, Principal
Eric Babinet, Business Consultant & Coach

Provider of consulting, application development, programming, technical support, and design services.

Outset Medical   HQ
3052 Orchard Dr
San Jose CA 95134
P: 669-231-8200   PRC:186
outsetmedical.com
Email: info@outsetmedical.com
Estab: 2010

Leslie Trigg, CEO
Jeff Mack, CFO
Michael Aragon, CMO
Dan Rogy, VP of Operations
Bhavesh Patel, VP

Developer of hemodialysis systems. The company offers services to patients, families, providers and physicians.

Outside Technology   HQ
PO Box 685
San Anselmo CA 94979
P: 415-488-4909   PRC:329
www.outsidetech.com
Email: support@outsidetech.com

Dan Katz, Owner

Provider of automated reservation systems. The company mainly caters to the outdoor recreation industry.

Owens Design   HQ
47427 Fremont Blvd
Fremont CA 94538
P: 510-659-1800   F: 510-659-1896   PRC:86
www.owensdesign.com
Email: sales@owensdesign.com
Estab: 1982

Thomas Owens, Owner
Jennifer Owens, Owner
Bob Fung, President
Etoli Wolff, VP of Sales
Paul Shufflebotham, VP of Engineering

Developer of advanced technology systems for semiconductor, hard disk drive, solar, medical device, and other sectors.

Owler Inc   HQ
800 S Claremont St Ste 203
San Mateo CA 94402
P: 650-242-9253   PRC:325
owler.com
Email: support@owler.com
Estab: 2011

Tim Harsch, Founder & CEO
Stephanie Vinella, CFO
John Duffy, Head of Engineering
Dhruv Gupta, Head of Product Development
Gretchen Vagharshakian, Head of Marketing

Provider of reliable and up-to-date business information.

Oxigraf Inc   HQ
238 E Caribbean Dr
Sunnyvale CA 94089
P: 650-237-0155   F: 650-237-0159   PRC:172
www.oxigraf.com
Email: sales@oxigraf.com
Estab: 1990

Bruce W. McCaul, Owner
Xing Chao, Chief Scientist
Jason Hoang, Test Supervisor

Supplier of oxygen analyzers and oxygen gas concentration measurement products. The company offers laser diode oxygen analyzers and OEM oxygen sensors.

Ozotech Inc   HQ
1015 South Main St
Yreka CA 96097
P: 530-842-4189   PRC:144
www.ozotech.com
Email: sales@ozotech.com
Estab: 1986

Nick Rouhier, General Manager
Lance Vogel, Head of Operations

Provider of water purification solutions. The company offers products such as bolted water systems, oxygen concentrators, air dries, and generators.

P&L Specialties   HQ
1650 Almar Pkwy
Santa Rosa CA 95403
P: 707-573-3141   F: 707-573-3140   PRC:80
www.pnlspecialties.com
Email: sales@pnlspecialties.com
Estab: 1984

Ed Barr, President
Lisa Hyde, VP
Jeff Sommers, Production Manager
Monte Springer, Mechanical Designer

Provider of engineering and fabrication services. The company's services include waterjet cutting and harvest lug washing.

PAC Integrations Inc   HQ
PO Box 6008
Concord CA 94524-1008
P: 800-479-4722   F: 925-687-7662   PRC:59
www.pacintegrations.com
Email: sales@pacintegrations.com
Estab: 1982

Harrison Farr, Director of Sales, Administration & Executive Management
Chad Custock, Director of Operations
John Matthies, Technical Support Manager
Corey Alexander, Purchasing Manager
Mike Ganguet, Sales Manager

Provider of security solutions. The company offers its solutions for residential, commercial, and fire and life safety applications.

PAC Machinery   HQ
25 Tiburon St
San Rafael CA 94901
P: 415-454-4868   F: 415-454-6853   PRC:79
www.pacmachinery.com
Email: info@pacmachinery.com

Johnny Pianka, Quality Assurance Lead

Manufacturer of heat sealing and packaging equipment such as tube sealers, shrink wrap systems, and skin packaging products.

PACE Engineering Inc   HQ
1730 South St   [N]
Redding CA 96001
P: 530-244-0202   PRC:70
www.paceengineering.us
Emp: 11-50   Estab: 1976

Paul Reuter, President

Provider of civil engineering services such as water and wastewater facilities, land development, structural, electrical, geotechnical, surveying and mapping.

Paceco Corp   HQ
25515 Whitesell St
Hayward CA 94545
P: 510-264-9288   F: 510-264-9280   PRC:183
pacecocorp.com
Email: email@pacecocorp.com
Estab: 1988

Yasuki Kishimoto, CEO
Sun Huang, GM & Chief Engineer
Rod Spires, Director
Troy Collard, General Manager of Sales
Trevin Freeman, Manager

Manufacturer of equipment to handle port cargo. The company also offers terminal operating systems and crane modification services.

Pacific Biodevelopment LLC   HQ
1900 Powell St Ste 600
Emeryville CA 94608
P: 510-858-5600   F: 510-858-5602   PRC:34
www.pacbiodev.com
Estab: 1997

Brian C. Rogers, Co-Founder
Jerome Moore, Co-Founder
Ira Wallis, VP of Regulatory Affairs

Provider of biotechnology services. The company
offers drug development services to allow timely
and cost efficient entry of drugs into the market.

Pacific Biolabs   HQ
551 Linus Pauling Dr
Hercules CA 94547
P: 510-964-9000   PRC:41
www.pacificbiolabs.com
Email: info@pacificbiolabs.com
Estab: 1982

Tom Spalding, President
Erik Foehr, VP
Aaron Burke, Director of Business Development &
Head of Sales & Marketing
Rick Shin, Director of Toxicology
Steve Guthrie, Equipment Manager

Provider of biological testing services. The company offers service to the pharmaceutical, biotechnology, and medical device industries.

Pacific Biosciences Of California Inc   HQ
1305 O'Brien Dr
Menlo Park CA 94025
P: 650-521-8000   PRC:34
www.pacb.com
Email: nasales@pacb.com
Sales: $30M to $100M

Michael Hunkapiller, President & CEO
Stephen Turner, CTO
Jonas Korlach, CSO
Kathy P. Ordonez, Chief Commercial Officer &
EVP & Director
Michael Phillips, SVP of Research & Development

Provider of targeted sequencing, base modifications, microbiology, and isoform sequencing
detection services.

Pacific Capacitor Co   HQ
288 Digital Dr
Morgan Hill CA 95037
P: 408-778-6670   F: 408-778-6680   PRC:203
www.pacific-capacitor.com
Email: info@pacific-capacitor.com
Estab: 1967

Mark Schiltz, Production Manager

Manufacturer of high voltage capacitors for the
electronics industry. The company is engaged in
sales and installation services.

Pacific Ceramics Inc   HQ
824 San Aleso Ave
Sunnyvale CA 94085
P: 408-747-4600   F: 408-745-6162   PRC:277
pceramics.com
Email: info@pceramics.com
Estab: 1969

Dennis Fleming, President
Nicholas Forney, Manager Assistant
Wolfram Schmedding, Head
Sehul Ahir, Quality Engineer

Manufacturer of microwave ceramic material. The
company's products include earth iron garnets, calcium vanadium garnets, lithium, and titanate dielectrics.

Pacific Coast Optics Inc   HQ
10604 Industrial Ave Ste 100
Roseville CA 95678
P: 916-789-0111   F: 916-789-0121   PRC:159
pcoptics.com
Estab: 2016

Shannon Rogers, President
Ignacio Ruvalcaba, Manager of Coatings

Provider of optical products, services and applications. The company offers prototype, polishing,
grinding, and coating.

Pacific Consolidated Industries LLC   HQ
12201 Magnolia Ave   [N]
Riverside CA 92503
P: 951-479-0860   PRC:156
www.pcigases.com
Estab: 2003

Bob Eng, CEO
Paul Stevens, CFO & VP & General Manager
Soeren Schmitz, VP & General Manager
Tarik Naheiri, VP of Engineering
Terry Wheaton, VP & General Manager

Manufacturer of general industrial machinery.

Pacific Crest   HQ
510 DeGuigne Dr
Sunnyvale CA 94085
P: 408-481-8070   F: 408-481-8984   PRC:64
pacificcrest.com
Email: info@pacificcrest.com
Estab: 1994

John F. Cameron, General Manager & Founder

Provider of communication solutions. The company specializes in the design and manufacture
of radio controlled and spotlight data transfer
systems.

Pacific Die Cut Industries   HQ
3399 Arden Rd
Hayward CA 94545
P: 510-732-8103   PRC:163
pacificdiecut.com
Email: sales@pacificdiecut.com
Estab: 1989

Mike Behnam, President & CEO
David Light, Program Manager
Gin Jei Chang, Business Development Manager
Koichi Aizawa, Account Manager
Andrew Wold, Account Manager

Provider of custom converting services that
include die cutting, laminating, and slitting. The
company also offers packaging solutions.

Pacific Dualies Inc   HQ
13637 Cimarron Ave   [N]
Gardena CA 90249
P: 310-516-9898   F: 310-516-8797   PRC:75
www.pacific-dualies.com
Emp: 11-50   Estab: 1979

Alan Wang, Contact

Designer, manufacturer, and distributor of truck
wheel simulators and accessories.

Pacific Ethanol Inc   HQ
400 Capitol Mall Ste 2060
Sacramento CA 95814
P: 916-403-2123   F: 916-446-3937   PRC:53
www.pacificethanol.com
Email: info@pacificethanol.com
Emp: 510   Estab: 2005
Sales: $1B to $3B

Neil M. Koehler, Founder & Director
Bryon McGregor, CFO
Michael D. Kandris, COO & Director
Tom Koehler, VP
Paul Koehler, VP

Producer and marketer of carbonated fuel and
corn oil. The company's services include ethanol
sales and distribution.

Pacific Gas & Electric Co   BR
77 Beale St 24th Fl Mail Code B24W
San Francisco CA 94105
P: 415-973-1000   F: 415-973-3582   PRC:130
www.pge.com
Estab: 1995

John Storm, Senior Customer Relationship
Manager

Provider of natural gas and electric services. The
company serves approximately 15 million people
throughout northern and central California.

Pacific Gas & Electric Co   BR
PO Box 997300
Sacramento CA 95899-7300
P: 800-743-5002   PRC:134
pge.com
Estab: 1905

Andrew M. Vesey, CEO & President
Kathleen B. Kay, SVP & CIO
David S. Thomason, VP & CFO & Controller
Mary K. King, VP of Human Resources & Chief
Diversity Officer
Stephen J. Cairns, VP of Internal Audit & Chief
Risk Officer

Provider of natural gas and electric services to the
areas in northern and central California. The company specializes in promoting renewable energy.

Pacific Instruments Inc   HQ
4080 Pike Ln
Concord CA 94520
P: 925-827-9010   F: 925-827-9023   PRC:68
www.pacificinstruments.com
Email: salesrequest@pacificinstruments.com
Estab: 1991

Moiz Balkhi, Owner
Patrick Rule, Senior Sales Manager
Morgan Butay, Marketing Coordinator

Manufacturer of computer-automated physical
measurement systems. The company specializes in signal conditioning and data acquisition
equipment.

Pacific Ozone Technology Inc HQ
6160 Egret Ct
Benicia CA 94510
P: 707-747-9600 F: 707-747-9209 PRC:159
pacificozone.com
Email: info@pacificozone.com
Estab: 1996

Brian Johnson, Director & CEO

Supplier of air-cooled, integrated ozone and oxygen systems and packaged controls for industrial ozone applications.

Pacific Pneumatic Tools Inc HQ
71 Glenn Way Ste 3
San Carlos CA 94070-6274
P: 650-592-6116 F: 650-802-9334 PRC:157
www.pacificpneumatic.com
Email: ppt@pacificpneumatic.com

Bruce Wernick, President

Manufacturer of air tools for industrial and automotive customers. The company offers wrenches, grinders, sanders, and other tools.

Pacific Powder Coating & Manufacturing HQ
8637 23rd Ave
Sacramento CA 95826
P: 916-381-1154 PRC:80
pacpowder.com
Estab: 1987

Jeff Rochester, President
Jolene Mark, Shipping & Receiving Manager

Provider of electrostatic powder coating and metal fabrication services. The company focuses on sandblasting and silkscreening services, and logistics.

Pacific Power Source Inc HQ
17692 Fitch [N]
Irvine CA 92614
P: 949-251-1800 F: 949-756-0756 PRC:209
www.pacificpower.com
Email: info@pacificpower.com
Emp: 51-200 Estab: 1971

Mitchel Orr, Manager of Sales

Designer, developer and dealer of both linear and high performance PWM AC power sources.

Pacific Precision Machine Inc HQ
21109 Longeway Rd Ste A
Sonora CA 95370
P: 209-588-9664 F: 209-588-9666 PRC:80
www.pacpre.com
Email: ppm@pacpre.com
Estab: 1984

Thomas Pellarin, President & Chairman
Linda Pellarin, Secretary & Treasurer

Provider of precision machining solutions. The company offers CNC turning and milling, procurement and assembly, and computer programming services.

Pacific Roller Die Company Inc HQ
1321 W Winton Ave
Hayward CA 94545
P: 510-782-7242 F: 510-887-5639 PRC:159
www.prdcompany.com
Email: prdsales@prdcompany.com
Estab: 1961

June Miller, Project Manager
Garrett Gersten, Senior Mechanical Engineer

Designer and manufacturer of corrugated metal pipes, coated and lined pipes, and duct products. The company offers installation and delivery services.

Pacific Rubber & Packing Inc HQ
1160 Industrial Rd Ste 3
San Carlos CA 94070
P: 650-595-5888 F: 650-591-8002 PRC:84
www.pacificrubber.com
Estab: 1979

Ashley Burfield, Owner
John Farcich, VP & General Manager

Provider of rubber seals, custom seals, rubber gaskets and o-ring products for medical/pharmacy, automotive, solar energy, and general industries.

Pacific Scientific Energetic Materials Company (California) LLC HQ
3601 Union Rd
Hollister CA 95023
P: 831-637-3731 PRC:4
psemc.com
Estab: 1975

Gary Churchman, Contracts Manager

Provider of energetic materials and services. The company offers services to the aircraft, missiles, space, and law enforcement industries.

Pacific States Felt & MFG Company Inc HQ
23850 Clawiter Rd Ste 20
Hayward CA 94545
P: 510-783-0277 F: 510-783-4725 PRC:162
www.pacificstatesfelt.net
Email: sales@pacificstatesfelt.net

Robert Perscheid, General Manager

Manufacturer of gaskets, seals, washers, pads, and molded bumpers. The company is engaged in lamination and fabrication.

Pacmold HQ
19707 Cabot Blvd
Hayward CA 94545
P: 510-785-9882 F: 510-785-9885 PRC:163
www.pacmold.com
Estab: 1979

Justin Liang, Chief Engineer
Rican Yu, Manager of Sales

Designer and manufacturer of plastic injection molds. The company has production facilities in Taiwan and China.

Pactech Inc HQ
2260 Trade Zone Blvd
San Jose CA 95131
P: 408-526-9363 F: 408-526-1233 PRC:170
www.pactech-inc.com
Email: sales@pactech-inc.com
Estab: 1994

Aaron Chui, Founder

Provider of computer cables, cooling items, and other components. The company also offers networking products.

Pactron/HJPC Corp HQ
3000 Patrick Henry Dr
Santa Clara CA 95054
P: 408-329-5500 F: 408-747-1239 PRC:211
www.pactroninc.com
Email: info@pactroninc.com
Estab: 1988

Sanjay Singh, VP of Sales
Kevin Dariani, Sales Account Manager

Provider of electronics design and design development services. The company is also involved in engineering and contract manufacturing.

Palantir Technologies Inc HQ
100 Hamilton Ave Ste 300
Palo Alto CA 94301
P: 650-815-0200 F: 650-618-2298 PRC:323
www.palantir.com
Estab: 2004

David Glazer, CFO
Shyam Sankar, Director of Forward Deployed Engineering
Peter Wilczynski, Product Manager & Product Quality Engineer
Shilpa Balaji, Engineering Manager
Clark Church, Business Operations & Strategy Manager

Provider of software for anti fraud, cyber security, intelligence, and other needs. The company serves government, commercial, and non-profit sectors.

Paleotechnics HQ
PO Box 876 [N]
Boonville CA 95415
P: 707-391-8683 PRC:316
www.paleotechnics.com
Email: ts@paleotechnics.com
Estab: 1992

Tamara Wilder, Contact

Publisher of how-to books on primitive technology and survival skills.

Palo Alto Networks Inc HQ
3000 Tannery Way
Santa Clara CA 95054
P: 408-753-4000 F: 408-753-4001 PRC:323
www.paloaltonetworks.com
Email: info@paloaltonetworks.com
Estab: 2000
Sales: Over $3B

Yuming Mao, Chief Architect & Co-Founder
Nir Zuk, Co-Founder & CTO
Rajiv Batra, Co-Founder
Mark D. McLaughlin, Vice Chairman
Rene Bonvanie, CMO

Provider of network and cyber security solutions. The company offers consulting and support, and solution assurance services.

Palo Alto Research Center Inc　　　DH
　3333 Coyote Hill Rd
　Palo Alto CA 94304
P: 650-812-4000　　　　　　　PRC:207
www.parc.com
Email: parcpr@parc.com
Estab: 1970

Mark Bernstein, CEO
Kyle Dent, Research Area Manager
David Phillips, Systems Engineer
John T. Maxwell, Principal Engineer of Knowledge
& Language & Interaction
David M. Johnson, Scientist

Provider of custom research services and intellectual property to global Fortune 500 companies
and government agency partners.

PalPilot International Corp　　　BR
　500 Yosemite Dr
　Milpitas CA 95035
P: 408-855-8866　F: 408-855-8868　PRC:211
www.palpilot.com
Estab: 1988

Eddy Niu, President
Fred Hillis, VP of Marketing
Derrick Wagner, Director of Sales
Jimmy Young, Director
Scott Trevino, Senior Director of Business Devel-
opment

Developer of interconnect solutions. The company
offers design, engineering, and manufacturing
support services.

Pan-International　　　LH
　48008 Fremont Blvd
　Fremont CA 94538
P: 510-623-3898　F: 510-623-3899　PRC:202
panintl.com
Email: sales@panintl.com
Estab: 1989

Michael Liu, CFO

Supplier of computer cables, wiring, switch boxes,
and connectors. The company is involved in design, installation, and delivery services.

Panasas Inc　　　HQ
　969 W Maude Ave
　Sunnyvale CA 94085
P: 408-215-6800　F: 408-215-6801　PRC:140
www.panasas.com
Email: info@panasas.com
Estab: 1999

Faye Pairman, President & CEO
Elliot Carpenter, CFO
Jim Donovan, Chief Sales & Marketing Officer
Jonathan Lister, VP of Global Sales Solutions
Ren Del Carlo, VP of Operations

Provider of scale-out NAS storage system for
most demanding workloads in life sciences,
media and entertainment, energy, and education
environments.

Pangea Environmental Services Inc　　　HQ
　1250 Addison St Ste 213
　Berkeley CA 94702
P: 510-836-3700　F: 510-836-3709　PRC:142
pangeaenv.com
Email: inquiry@pangeaenv.com

Bob Clark-Riddell, President & Principal Engineer

Provider of environmental consulting services. The
company's services include site assessment and
remediation, litigation support, and soil testing.

Panorama Environmental Inc　　　HQ
　717 Market St Ste 650
　San Francisco CA 94103
P: 650-373-1200　F: 650-373-1211　PRC:140
panoramaenv.com
Email: info@panoramaenv.com
Estab: 1983

Laurie Hietter, Principal
Tania Treis, Principal

Provider of environmental planning services. The
company engages in regulatory permitting and
geographic information systems.

PanTerra Networks Inc　　　HQ
　4655 Old Ironsides Dr Ste 300
　Santa Clara CA 95054
P: 800-805-0558　F: 408-980-9877　PRC:323
panterranetworks.com
Email: info@panterranetworks.com
Estab: 2001

Arthur G. Chang, President & CEO
Jeff Boucher, CFO
Jerome Friesenhahn, VP of Customer Success
Joel Stalder, Operations Manager

Provider of cloud-based communications software
solutions. The company is engaged in unified
communication and technical support.

Paradigm Strucural Engineers　　　HQ
　639 Front St 4th Fl
　San Francisco CA 94111
P: 415-362-8944　F: 415-362-8945　PRC:304
www.paradigmse.com
Email: info@paradigmse.com
Estab: 1999

Kurt Lindorfer, Founder & Principal
Kim Curry, Office Manager
Jake Avella, Staff Engineer
Brandon Dashwood, Structural Engineer
Aaron Blum, Project Engineer

Provider of structural engineering and consulting
services. The company offers schematic design,
planning, and construction documentation services.

Paragon Controls Inc　　　HQ
　2371 Circadian Way
　Santa Rosa CA 95407
P: 707-579-1424　F: 707-579-8480　PRC:236
www.paragoncontrols.com
Estab: 1984

Michelle Foszcz, General Manager
Adam Havner, Sales Engineer

Designer and manufacturer of air flow and
pressure measurement and control systems. The
company also offers airflow sensing elements.

Paragon Swiss Inc　　　HQ
　545 Aldo Ave Unit 1
　Santa Clara CA 95054
P: 408-748-1617　F: 408-748-0949　PRC:80
www.paragonswiss.com
Email: sales@paragonswiss.com
Estab: 1984

David Beatty, Owner
Kevin Beatty, President
Craig Kay, General Manager

Manufacturer of medical instruments, precision
shafts, optical bench fixtures, and related supplies.

Parallax Inc　　　HQ
　599 Menlo Dr Ste 100
　Rocklin CA 95765
P: 916-624-8333　F: 916-624-8003　PRC:212
www.parallax.com
Email: sales@parallax.com
Estab: 1987

Ken Gracey, CEO
Chuck Gracey, CFO
Andy Lindsay, Applications Engineer of Education
Department
Chip Gracey, Engineer
Jeff Martin, Senior Software Engineer

Manufacturer of electronic hardware and software
products. The company offers microcontrollers,
sensors, boards, and cables/converters.

Paramit Corp　　　HQ
　18735 Madrone Pkwy
　Morgan Hill CA 95037
P: 408-782-5600　F: 408-782-9991　PRC:196
www.paramit.com
Email: support@paramit.com
Estab: 1990

Billoo Rataul, CEO
Faiyaz Syed, COO
Jeff Johnson, VP Sales & Marketing
Francesco Grieco, VP of Operations
Merinda Do, Director of Human Resources

Manufacturer of medical devices. The company is
engaged in the planning and also implementation
of strategies.

Pariveda Solutions Inc　　　BR
　201 California St Ste 1250
　San Francisco CA 94111
P: 844-325-2729　F: 415-946-6101　PRC:322
parivedasolutions.com
Email: sanfrancisco@parivedasolutions.com
Estab: 2003

Lori Dipprey, CPO & Managing Vice President of
Capability
Bruce Ballengee, CEO
Kerry Stover, COO
Brian Orrell, CTO
James Kupferschmid, CFO

Provider of IT consulting services and technology
solutions such as custom application development, portals and enterprise content management.

Park Computer Systems Inc HQ
39899 Balentine Dr Ste 298
Newark CA 94560
P: 510-353-1700 F: 510-353-1900 PRC:326
www.parkcom.com
Email: info@parkcom.com
Estab: 1995

Pavan Kumar, Operations Manager
Pinky Kundu, Senior Talent Acquisition Specialist

Provider of mobile products and services. The
company also offers sales content automation and
staff augmentation services.

Parker Hannifin Corp DH
1640 Cummins Dr
Modesto CA 95358
P: 209-521-7860 F: 209-529-3278 PRC:74
www.parker.com
Email: c-parker@parker.com
Estab: 1969

Russ Sutherland, Research & Development
Engineer
Sheryle Knott, Administrator

Provider of fuel, air, oil, and coolant filtration
systems. The company serves the transportation,
marine, and oil and gas industries.

Parmatech Corp BR
2221 Pine View Way
Petaluma CA 94954
P: 707-778-2266 PRC:163
www.atwcompanies.com
Email: sales@parmatech.com
Estab: 1973

Rob Hall, President
Anita Shah, Manufacturing Manager
Keith Hanover, Senior Manufacturing Engineer
Lourdes Galapate, Senior Material Engineer
Damir Patino, Manufacturing Engineer

Supplier of metal injection molding components.
The company serves the automotive, medical,
industrial, and electronics industries.

Pasco Scientific HQ
10101 Foothills Blvd
Roseville CA 95747-7100
P: 916-786-3800 F: 916-786-7565 PRC:87
www.pasco.com
Email: sales@pasco.com
Estab: 1964

Richard Briscoe, President
Dave Mangelsdorf, VP of Manufacturing
Donna Amado, VP of Engineering
John DeLury, VP of Finance
Freda Husic, Director of Education Solutions

Provider of technology-based solutions for hands-
on science services. The company is engaged in
technical support.

M-234

Pass Laboratories Inc HQ
13395 New Airport Rd Ste G
Auburn CA 95602
P: 530-878-5350 F: 530-878-5358 PRC:318
www.passlabs.com
Email: info@passlabs.com
Estab: 1991

Desmond Harrington, President
Kent English, North American Sales Director

Developer of prototypes for amplifier design. The
company specializes in manufacturing amplifiers
and speakers.

Pasternack Enterprises Inc HQ
17802 Fitch [N]
Irvine CA 92614
P: 949-261-1920 F: 949-261-7451 PRC:62
www.pasternack.com
Email: sales@pasternack.com
Estab: 1972

Terry Jarnigan, CEO

Supplier of RF and microwave components.

Patriot Memory Inc HQ
47027 Benicia St
Fremont CA 94538
P: 510-979-1021 F: 510-979-1586 PRC:92
patriotmemory.com
Email: sales@patriotmem.com
Estab: 1985

Mai Kosla, Senior VP of Global Sales Operations
Meng J. Choo, Flash Product Manager

Developer of flash memory solutions. The company offers memory modules, flash cards, USB
drives, gaming memory cards, and accessories.

Patz Materials & Technologies HQ
4968 Industrial Way
Benicia CA 94510
P: 707-748-7577 F: 888-203-8791 PRC:34
patzmandt.com
Email: development@patzmandt.com
Estab: 2005

Gary Patz, Founder
Jez Talosig, Quality Assurance Manager
Tom Doolittle, Project Manager

Manufacturer of composite materials. The company portfolio includes unidirectional tapes, fabric
prepregs, composite armor systems, and cellular
developments.

Paul Graham Drilling And Service Co HQ
2500 Airport Rd
Rio Vista CA 94571
P: 707-374-5123 F: 707-374-6821 PRC:130
paulgrahamdrilling.com
Email: info@paulgrahamdrilling.com
Estab: 1968

Kevin Graham, CEO & President
Ted Coffey, Sales Manager

Provider of gas drilling services with over head
cranes and computer operated plasma cutting
machines for top notch drilling.

Pauli Systems Inc HQ
1820 Walters Ct
Fairfield CA 94533
P: 707-429-2434 F: 707-429-2424 PRC:8
paulisystems.com
Email: info@paulisystems.com
Estab: 1996

Robert Pauli, President

Manufacturer of custom finishing systems,
abrasive booths, and equipment including blast
rooms for aviation, automotive, and industrial
applications.

Pavilion Integration Corp HQ
2528 Qume Dr Ste 1
San Jose CA 95131
P: 408-453-8801 PRC:172
www.pavilionintegration.com
Email: sales@pavilionintegration.com
Estab: 2004

Lindsay Austin, Co-Founder & Chairman & CSO
Ningyi Luo, CEO & Co-Founder
Hui Fan, EE Manager

Designer and manufacturer of lasers, laser
modules and subsystems for instrumentation. The
company serves the industrial market.

PAX Scientific Inc HQ
PO Box 150840
San Rafael CA 94915-0840
P: 415-256-9900 F: 415-256-9901 PRC:159
paxscientific.com
Email: info@paxscientific.com
Estab: 1997

Francesca Bertone, COO
Leslie Miller, Administrative Manager
Robin Giguere, Principal Scientist

Provider of engineering research and product
design services. The company is also involved in
the design of industrial equipment.

Paxata Inc HQ
1800 Seaport Blvd 3rd Fl
Redwood City CA 94063
P: 650-542-7900 PRC:315
www.paxata.com
Email: info@paxata.com
Estab: 2012

Prakash Nanduri, Co-Founder & CEO
Nenshad Bardoliwalla, Co-Founder & Chief
Product Officer
Dave Brewster, Co-Founder & CTO
Christopher Maddox, Co-Founder & SVP of Busi-
ness Development & Strategic Alliances
Jonathan Barek, CFO

Enables business analysts to easily absorb,
analyze, and curate numerous raw data sets into
consumable information in a self-service manner.

Paxcell Group HQ
360 S Abbott Ave
Milpitas CA 95035
P: 408-945-8054 F: 408-945-8681 PRC:98
www.paxcell.com
Email: info@paxcell.com
Estab: 1993

Bill Cohune, Manager

Provider of electronic engineering and industrial
design services. The company also offers contract
manufacturing services.

Paxvax Inc　　　　　　　　　　　HQ
555 Twin Dolphin Dr Ste 360
Redwood City CA 94065
P: 650-847-1075　　　　　　　　　PRC:34
paxvax.com
Email: info@paxvax.com
Estab: 2007

Tom Yonker, VP
Yi Zhang, Research Associate

Provider of vaccines to protect from infectious diseases. The company offers treatments to diseases such as typhoid, cholera, and anthrax.

PBI Market Equipment Inc　　　　HQ
2667 Gundry Ave　　　　[N]
Signal Hill CA 90755
P: 562-595-4785　F: 562-426-2262　PRC:319
www.pbimarketing.com
Email: customerservice@pbimarketing.com
Emp: 1-10

Erik Everson, Contact

Distributor of meat wrappers, slicers, and digital scales.

PC Professional　　　　　　　　HQ
1615 Webster St
Oakland CA 94612
P: 510-874-5871　F: 510-465-8327　PRC:323
pcprofessional.com
Email: sales@pcprofessional.com
Estab: 1981

Paul Claahsen, Owner
Dan Sanguinetti, President & CEO
Matthew Powers, VP of Sales
Joe Santorsiero, VP

Provider of information technology solutions. The company focuses on cloud computing, application development, networking, and disaster recovery.

PCC Structurals Inc　　　　　　BR
414 Hester St
San Leandro CA 94577
P: 510-568-6400　　　　　　　　PRC:163
www.pccstructurals.com
Estab: 1953

Jim Collins, General Manager
Taylor Messner Schaack, Operations Manager
Simone Williams, Product Development Engineer
Brad Scott, Senior Project Engineer

Manufacturer of complex metal components and products. The company caters to industrial and aerospace applications.

PCT Systems Inc　　　　　　　　HQ
49000 Milmont Dr
Fremont CA 94538
P: 510-657-4412　F: 510-657-0112　PRC:86
www.pctsystems.com
Email: info@pctsystems.com
Estab: 1988

Susan Miranda, Owner
Sharyl Maraviov, President
Hank Miranda, CEO
Julie Garcia, Customer Service Manager
Mark Dye, Manager of Production

Manufacturer of semiconductor equipment and supplies. The company offers services to the semi-conductor industry.

PDF Solutions Inc　　　　　　　HQ
2858 De La Cruz Blvd
Santa Clara CA 95050
P: 408-280-7900　F: 408-280-7915　PRC:208
www.pdf.com
Email: info@pdf.com
Estab: 1991
Sales: $30M to $100M

Kimon Michaels, EVP of Products & Solutions & Director & Co-Founder
John K. Kibarian, Co-Founder & CEO & President & Director
Andrzej Strojwas, CTO
Christine Russell, EVP of Finance & CFO
Cornelius Hartgring, VP of Client Services & Sales

Provider of yield improvement technologies and services for the integrated circuit manufacturing process.

Peak Laboratories LLC　　　　　HQ
2330 Old Middlefield Way Ste 10
Mountain View CA 94043-2452
P: 650-691-1267　F: 650-691-1047　PRC:306
www.peaklaboratories.com
Email: sales_service@peaklaboratories.com
Estab: 2003

Steve Hartman, Owner
Heather Jones, Sales Account Manager

Designer and manufacturer of process gas chromatography systems. The company offers mercuric oxide, pulse discharge, and thermal conductivity detectors.

Pearl Lemon　　　　　　　　　　BR
3060 Fillmore St
San Francisco CA 94123
P: 628-214-1309　　　　　　　　PRC:325
pearllemon.com

Deepak Shukla, Founder

Digital marketing agency that offers results-oriented SEO services.

Pearson Electronics Inc　　　　HQ
4009 Transport St
Palo Alto CA 94303
P: 650-494-6444　F: 650-494-6716　PRC:214
www.pearsonelectronics.com
Email: sales@pearsonelectronics.com
Estab: 1955

Jeff Reed, President
David M. Ponce, Senior Engineer
Cathy Breton, Sales Assistant

Manufacturer of wide band current monitors. The company also offers high voltage pulse transformers and voltage dividers.

Peartech Inc　　　　　　　　　　HQ
1111 W El Camino Real Ste 109-354
Sunnyvale CA 94087
P: 408-542-9550　F: 408-716-2934　PRC:80
www.peartech.com
Estab: 1986

Bob Nordloff, President

Provider of solutions for electronic, computer, networking, and medical applications. The company offers solutions for precision machining and sheet metals.

PEC Manufacturing　　　　　　HQ
2110 Ringwood Ave
San Jose CA 95131
P: 408-577-1839　F: 408-577-1829　PRC:80
pecmfg.com
Estab: 2003

Dung Dinh, QC Engineer

Provider of customized electromechanical, electronic, and mechanical solutions such as cable and harness assemblies and electro-mechanical assemblies.

Peerless Lighting　　　　　　　HQ
2246 Fifth St　　　　　[N]
Berkeley CA 94710
P: 510-845-2760　F: 510-845-2776　PRC:243
www.acuitybrands.com/brands/lighting/peerless/contact-us
Estab: 1892

Vernon J. Nagel, Chairman & President & CEO
Richard K. Reece, EVP & CFO
Laurent J. Vernerey, EVP

Manufacturer of commercial and institutional lighting fixtures, linear and fluorescent.

PeerNova Inc　　　　　　　　　HQ
2055 Gateway Pl Ste 750
San Jose CA 95110
P: 669-400-7800　　　　　　　　PRC:327
peernova.com
Email: hello@peernova.com
Estab: 2013

Chris Mausler, CFO
Gangesh Ganesan, CTO

Provider of silicon valley-based technology such as distributed systems, networking solutions, big data, compiler technology, and financial services.

Pega Precision Inc　　　　　　　HQ
18800 Adams Ct
Morgan Hill CA 95037
P: 408-776-3700　F: 408-776-3707　PRC:88
www.pegaprecision.com
Estab: 1989

Aaron Fast, President
Manuel Gonzalez, Shipping Manager
Patricia Fast, Office Manager
John Cavanaugh, Quality Manager
Dennis Mattish, Quality Control Inspector

Manufacturer and marketer of precision sheet metal and machining components. The company serves the military, semiconductor, and solar industries.

Pegasus Design Inc　　　　　　HQ
3115 Independence Dr
Livermore CA 94551
P: 925-292-7567　　　　　　　　PRC:159
www.pegasus-design.com
Estab: 1994

Steve Calderon, CEO

Provider of machine design and contract manufacturing services. The company serves the pharmaceutical instrument industry.

Pelco By Schneider Electric   BR
625 W Alluvial Ave
Fresno CA 93711
P: 559-292-1981   PRC:209
www.pelco.com

Sharad Shekhar, CEO

Developer of video surveillance and security solutions. The company also involves in camera and video management.

Pelco Inc   HQ
625 W Alluvial
Fresno CA 93711
P: 559-292-1981   PRC:168
www.pelco.com
Estab: 1957

Timothy J. Jackson, Owner
Ronald Cadle, VP of operations

Manufacturer of closed circuit TV cameras and accessories. The company's services include training, engineering, and technical development.

Peloton Technology   HQ
1060 La Avenida St
Mountain View CA 94043
P: 650-395-7356   PRC:63
peloton-tech.com
Email: info@peloton-tech.com
Estab: 2013

Dave Lyons, Co-Founder & Chief Innovation Officer
Josh Switkes, Co-Founder & President
Oliver Bayley, VP
Esther Shon, Accounting Manager
Brian Silverman, Associate Software Engineer

Developer of truck platooning systems. The company offers services to the transportation, trucking, and railroad industries.

Pelvalon Inc   HQ
2880 Lakeside Dr Ste 201
Santa Clara CA 95054
P: 650-276-0130   F: 650-646-2213   PRC:196
eclipsesystem.com
Email: career@pelvalon.com
Estab: 2010

Miles Rosen, CEO
Jon Ward, VP of Sales

Provider of non-surgical therapy such as uninflated and inflated devices that offers immediate results for women experiencing loss of bowel control.

Pembroke Instruments LLC   HQ
120 Stanford Heights Ave
San Francisco CA 94127
P: 415-860-4217   PRC:19
pembrokeinstruments.com
Email: sales@pembrokeinstruments.com
Estab: 2008

Leslie Martin Tack, Founder & CEO

Manufacturer of products for scientific imaging applications. The company also focuses on optical spectroscopy needs.

Pencom   HQ
1300 Industrial Rd Ste 21
San Carlos CA 94070
P: 650-593-3288   F: 650-593-3299   PRC:80
pencomsf.com
Email: sales@pencomsf.com
Estab: 1982

Michael Gray, CCO
Oscar Tsai, General Manager
Gregg Summers, Director of Product Development
Blake Gardiner, Director of Marketing
Paula Elwell, Account Manager

Provider of component solutions to OEM design engineers. The company focuses on supply chain management, technical product support, and logistics.

Pendulum Therapeutics Inc   HQ
933 20th St
San Francisco CA 94107
P: 415-855-0940   PRC:34
pendulum.co
Email: hello@pendulum.co
Estab: 2012

Colleen Cutcliffe, Co-Founder & CEO
John Eid, CSO & Co-Founder
Jim Bullard, CTO & Co-Founder
Mohan Iyer, COO
Sangita Forth, CMO

Developer of microbiome interventions and diagnostics systems. The company is involved in research and development services.

Penguin Computing   HQ
45800 Northport Loop W
Fremont CA 94538
P: 415-954-2800   PRC:40
www.penguincomputing.com
Email: support@penguincomputing.com
Estab: 1999

Lisa Cummins, CFO
Daniel Dowling, VP of Engineering Services
Akila Senevirathne, Application Engineer
Rajeswari Natarajan, Senior Research & Development Engineer

Provider of Linux-based cloud and HPC solutions. The company's products include servers, network switches, and integrated rack solutions.

Penhall Company   BR
8416 Specialty Cir
Sacramento CA 95828
P: 916-386-1589   PRC:159
www.penhall.com
Estab: 1957

Gregory Rice, CEO & President
Lee Barnett, CFO
Brian Berger, SVP of Operations
Dave Myslenski, VP of Continuous Improvement
Terry Cooley, VP of Human Resources

Provider of concrete cutting services. The company specializes in core drilling, diamond saw cutting, and pavement repair methods.

Peninsula Engineering Solutions Inc   HQ
PO Box 1095
Danville CA 94526
P: 925-837-2243   F: 925-837-2298   PRC:129
www.peninsulaengineering.com
Email: info@peninsulaengineering.com
Estab: 2001

Frank Martens, President

Manufacturer of microwave RF repeaters. The company also specializes in cellular and PCS repeaters and related products.

Peninsula Spring Corp   HQ
6750 Silacci Way
Gilroy CA 95020
P: 408-848-3361   PRC:80
www.peninsulaspring.com
Estab: 1976

Laura Hampel, CFO & Office Manager

Provider of precision spring products. The company offers sheet metal stampings, electrical contacts, clips, and wire forms.

Pentagon Technologies   HQ
21031 Alexander Ct
Hayward CA 94545
P: 800-379-3361   F: 510-783-5055   PRC:86
www.pen-tec.com
Email: sales@pen-tec.com
Estab: 1998

David Christeson, CFO
Jeffrey Lupul, VP of CSG
Harley Mason, Director of Operations
Camilo Martinez, Production Manager
Kenny Aguiar, Plant Manager

Distributor of electromechanical components. The company offers shaft couplings, seals, and cable assemblies.

Penumbra Inc   HQ
One Penumbra Pl
Alameda CA 94502
P: 510-748-3200   F: 510-748-3232   PRC:189
www.penumbrainc.com
Email: info@penumbrainc.com
Estab: 2004
Sales: $300M to $1 Billion

Daniel Davis, President of North America
Adam Elsesser, CEO & Chairman
James Pray, President of International
Sri Kosaraju, President
Maggie Yuen, CFO

Manufacturer of interventional therapy devices. The company develops products to treat challenging medical conditions.

Perceptimed Inc   HQ
365 San Antonio Rd
Mountain View CA 94040
P: 650-941-7000   PRC:249
www.perceptimed.com
Email: info@perceptimed.com
Estab: 2011

Alan Jacobs, CEO
Ram Subramanian, CTO
Tom Lavin, Partner & CFO & New Science Ventures
Frank Maione, Chief Business Officer
Jim Mack, VP of Customer Services

Provider of medical technologies for dispensing and administration of prescription drugs safer, reducing injuries, and death.

Perfect World Company Ltd HQ
100 Redwood Shores Pkwy 4th Fl
Redwood City CA 94065
P: 650-590-7700   F: 650-591-1211   PRC:317
www.perfectworld.com
Email: dmca@perfectworld.com
Estab: 2008

Andrew Patrick, Quality Assurance Engineering
Manager
Fen Qin, Data Analyst
Alec Obert, Graphic Designer
Ben Rico, Customer Service Representative

Provider of gaming solutions. The company is
engaged in technical support and it serves the
entertainment industry.

Perforce Software Inc BR
2320 Blanding Ave
Alameda CA 94501
P: 510-864-7400   F: 510-864-5340   PRC:323
www.perforce.com
Email: info@perforce.com
Estab: 1995

Christopher Seiwald, Founder & President
Mike Goergen, CFO
Tim Russell, Chief Product Officer
Murtaza Amiji, Senior Director of Product Man-
agement

Developer of software management tools and
technology solutions. The company serves game
development, banking, healthcare, and other
sectors.

**Performance Polymer Technologies
LLC** HQ
8801 Washington Blvd Ste 109
Roseville CA 95678
P: 916-677-1414   F: 916-677-1474   PRC:57
www.pptech.com
Email: pptinfo@pptech.com
Estab: 1995

Ian MacAuley, VP
Bill Crawford, Quality Manager
Donald Fenton, Application Engineer

Manufacturer of elastomeric components for
material formulation, extruding, and stamping
applications.

Performex Machining Inc HQ
963 Terminal Way
San Carlos CA 94070
P: 650-595-2228   F: 650-595-0169   PRC:316
www.performexmachining.com
Email: performex963@gmail.com
Estab: 1977

Joey Iffla, President

Provider of machining services. The company
specializes in computer aided machining, designing, and fabrication.

Peridot Corp HQ
1072 Serpentine Ln
Pleasanton CA 94566-4731
P: 925-461-8830   F: 925-461-8833   PRC:80
www.peridotcorp.com
Email: pat@peridotcorp.com
Estab: 1996

Patrick Pickerell, President & Founder
Debra Van Sickle, VP
Ray Forbes, Quality Assurance Manager
Jojo Garcia, Purchasing Manager
Anthony Cano, Production Manager

Provider of design for manufacturing and packaging. The company also manufacturers of medical
components, miniature component and general
product prototypes.

PermaDri Inc HQ
4595 W Jacquelyn Ave
Fresno CA 93722
P: 559-275-9620   PRC:57

Richard D. Rosman, Agent

Provider of eco-friendly waterproofing and corrosion protection products. The company serves the
marine, landscape, and industrial markers.

Perry Tool & Research Inc HQ
3415 Enterprise Ave
Hayward CA 94545
P: 510-782-9226   F: 510-782-0749   PRC:80
www.perrytool.com
Email: info@perrytool.com
Estab: 1962

Ken Fusselman, Owner

Designer and manufacturer of powder metal parts
for OEMs. The company specializes in pulleys,
bearings, cams, sprockets, and fasteners.

Perryman Group Inc HQ
PO Box 6525
Folsom CA 95763
P: 916-630-7456   PRC:325
www.infostations.com
Email: support@infostations.com
Estab: 1998

Ray Perryman, President & CEO
Greg Munsill, Business Analyst

Provider of website design and hosting, e-commerce solutions, and networking services.
The company serves business and residential
customers.

Persistent Systems Inc BR
2055 Laurelwood Rd Ste 210
Santa Clara CA 95054
P: 408-216-7010   PRC:324
www.persistent.com
Estab: 1990

Sameer Bendre, CPO
Sunder Sarangan, CMO
Nitin Urdhwareshe, VP
Tom Klein, General Counsel & SVP of Corporate
Development
Pravin Tarde, General Manager of Human Re-
source

Developer of software and technology products for
life science, banking, and other sectors. The company offers big data, security, and cloud solutions.

Personal Data Systems Inc HQ
638 Sobrato Ln   [N]
Campbell CA 95008
P: 408-866-1126   PRC:322
www.personaldatasystems.com
Estab: 1987

Noel Runyan, Consultant

Provider of hardware and software development.

Personal Tex Inc HQ
722 Lombard St Ste 201
San Francisco CA 94133
P: 415-296-7550   F: 415-296-7501   PRC:320
www.pctex.com
Email: sales@pctex.com
Estab: 1985

Lance Carnes, Software Developer

Publisher of PCTeX software that enables mathe-
maticians to publish their formulas, equations, and
thoughts.

Personalis Inc HQ
1330 O'Brien Dr
Menlo Park CA 94025
P: 650-752-1300   F: 650-752-1301   PRC:39
www.personalis.com
Email: info@personalis.com

Jonathan MacQuitty, Chairman
John West, CEO
Richard Chen, CSO
Aaron Tachibana, CFO
Clinton Musil, CBO

Manufacturer of genome-guided medicine for
the treatment of cancer. The company deals with
research services.

Persys Engineering Inc HQ
815 Swift St
Santa Cruz CA 95060-5851
P: 831-471-9300   F: 831-471-9818   PRC:86
www.persyseng.com
Email: office@persyseng.com
Estab: 1988

Yitzhak Vanek, CEO

Provider of parts cleaning, refurbishing and manufacturing, decontamination, and maintenance of
assemblies and machine parts.

Pet Qwerks Inc HQ
9 Studebaker Dr   [N]
Irvine CA 92618
P: 949-916-3733   F: 949-916-3734   PRC:189
www.petqwerks.com
Email: sales@petqwerks.com
Emp: 11-50   Estab: 1958

Shane Gick, VP
John Miller, Partner

Distributor of pet supplies.

PFU America Inc BR
1250 E Arques Ave
Sunnyvale CA 94085
P: 408-992-2900   F: 408-992-2999   PRC:91
www.pfu.fujitsu.com
Email: inquire.pfu@us.fujitsu.com
Estab: 1997

Hasegawa Kiyoshi, President
Wilbur Tanaka, Project Coordinator & New Product
Development

Provider of technology solutions. The company
designs, develops, and sells computer hardware,
peripheral products, and systems.

PGH Wong Engineering Inc HQ
182 Second St
San Francisco CA 94105
P: 415-566-0800   F: 415-566-6030   PRC:304
pghwong.com
Email: info@pghwong.com
Estab: 1985

Jeffrey Katz, EVP
Roman Duarte, Senior Construction Manager
Tom McDermott, Communications Manager
Veronika Tan, Accounts Manager
Fiona Nguyen, Human Resource Manager

Provider of engineering, program and construction
management, and technology services for transit
projects.

Phage International Inc HQ
23 Railroad Ave Ste 355
Danville CA 94526
P: 925-984-9446   F: 925-937-6291   PRC:249
www.phageinternational.com
Estab: 2004

Christopher A. Smith, President & CEO
H. Fisher, Science Advisor

Provider of leverage bacteriophage therapy technologies. The company specializes in discovery
and rediscovery of effective health care solutions.

Pharmagenesis Inc HQ
303 Twin Dolphin Dr Ste 600
Redwood City CA 94065
P: 650-842-7060   PRC:257
Estab: 1991

John H. Musser, COO

Developer and manufacturer of prescription pharmaceuticals from plant extracts and other organic
products sourced from Chinese medical practice.

PharmaLogic Development Inc HQ
17 Bridgegate Dr
San Rafael CA 94903-1093
P: 415-472-2181   PRC:261
www.pharmalogic.com
Email: info@pharmalogic.com

Gary D. Novack, President

Focuses on planning, drug development, and
marketing services. The company serves the
pharmaceutical and biomedical industries.

M-238

Pharmedix HQ
3281 Whipple Rd
Union City CA 94587-1218
P: 800-486-1811   F: 800-783-2038   PRC:268
www.pharmedixrx.com
Estab: 1984

Veronica Salazar, Pharmacy Technician
Jaime Di Fiore, Pharmacy technician 2

Focuses on the repackaging of pharmaceutical
products. The company offers dispensing systems
and women's health products.

Pharmtak Inc HQ
30 W Montague Expy Ste 80
San Jose CA 95134
P: 408-954-8223   F: 408-954-8203   PRC:268
pharmtak.com
Estab: 2009

J.C. Lee, President & CEO
Shirley Zhang, Manager of Analytical
Raja Noel, Sales Regional Manager

Provider of pharmaceutical products and services.
The company focuses on developing novel
pharmaceuticals and cosmeceuticals utilizing
technology.

Phasespace Inc HQ
1933 Davis St Ste 304
San Leandro CA 94577
P: 510-633-2865   F: 925-945-6718   PRC:77
www.phasespace.com
Email: inquiries@phasespace.com
Estab: 1994

Betty Ho, Creative Director
Gregory D'Andrea, Senior Software Engineer
Lawrence Kwan, Software Engineer

Developer of technologies for motion tracking
markers. The company focuses on motion capture
for industrial research and graphic community.

Pherin Pharmaceuticals Inc HQ
PO Box 4081
Los Altos CA 94024-9991
P: 650-636-7064   PRC:268
www.pherin.com
Email: lmonti@pherin.com
Estab: 1991

Louis Monti, President & CEO

Developer of novel compounds for intranasal
spray delivery and also deals with the treatment of
neuro-psychiatric and neuroendocrine conditions.

Phihong USA Corp HQ
47800 Fremont Blvd
Fremont CA 94538
P: 510-445-0100   F: 510-445-1678   PRC:200
phihong.com
Email: usasales@phihongusa.com
Estab: 1972

Peter Lin, Chairman
Emily Tsai, Director of Finance & Operations
Jessica Fang, Director of Sales Operations
Kevin Hsu, Project Manager
Raymond Liu, Power Supply Design Engineer

Provider of power solutions in the telecom sector.
The company also offers data solutions in industrial and personal electronic markers.

Phil Wood & Co HQ
1125 N Seventh St Ste A
San Jose CA 95112
P: 408-569-1860   F: 408-298-9016   PRC:80
www.philwood.com
Email: sales@philwood.com
Estab: 1971

Garrett Enright, General Manager

Manufacturer of cycling and related recreation
oriented products. The company focuses to offer
maintenance-free hubs for cyclists.

Phoenix Pharmaceuticals Inc DH
330 Beach Rd
Burlingame CA 94010
P: 650-558-8898   F: 650-558-1686   PRC:268
www.phoenixpeptide.com
Email: info@phoenixpeptide.com
Estab: 1994

Rong M. Lyu, Senior Research & Development
Manager

Provider of peptide related products to researchers. The company specializes in obesity, cardiovascular, and diabetes.

Phoenix Technology Group LLC HQ
6630 Owens Dr
Pleasanton CA 94588
P: 925-485-1100   F: 925-485-1155   PRC:187
phoenixtech.com
Email: info@phoenixtech.com
Estab: 2007

Bert Massie, CEO & Chairman & Founder
Kirk Sadler, Senior Manufacturing Engineer

Provider of research laboratory services. The
company offers anterior segment imaging and
retinal imaging microscope services.

Photo Etch Technology BR
3014 Scott Blvd
Santa Clara CA 95054
P: 408-988-0220   F: 408-988-1422   PRC:88
www.stencil.com

Dan Latessa, EVP
Kevin Huynh, CAD & CAM Engineer
Maxey Lindsey, Contractor

Provider of stainless steel stencils. The company
offers epoxy stencils, precision metal parts, fixture
pallets, mesh screens, and artwork services.

Phynexus Inc HQ
3670 Charter Park Dr Ste A
San Jose CA 95136
P: 408-267-7214   F: 408-267-7346   PRC:31
www.phynexus.com
Email: phynexus.info@biotage.com
Estab: 2002

Douglas T. Gjerde, CEO
Lee Hoang, Director of Research & Business
Development
Mannix Mendoza, Director of Manufacturing
Carrie Huynh, Head of Sales
Shadie Nimri, Field Application Scientist

Provider of automated and scalable solutions for
the low volume protein and nucleic acid purification.

PhysioCue Inc HQ
1798 Technology Dr Ste 258
San Jose CA 95110
P: 408-524-1595 PRC:189
physiocue.com
Email: info@physiocue.com
Estab: 2015

Simon Yi, CEO
Rosh Kakubhai, VP of Clinical Research
Jieun Choi, Product Manager intern
Jaejung Lee, Business Development Manager

Developer of therapies and focuses on the
delivery of thermo-neurostimulation systems. The
company serves patients.

PianoDisc HQ
4111 N Freeway Blvd
Sacramento CA 95834
P: 916-567-9999 F: 916-567-1941 PRC:209
www.pianodisc.com
Email: sales@pianodisc.com
Estab: 1988

Les Cooper, Owner
Irene Chu, CFO
Tom Lagomarsino, EVP
David Honeywell, Engineering Director
Dave Huegel, Regional Sales Manager

Manufacturer of electronic reproducing systems
for acoustic pianos. The company is engaged in
design, delivery, and installation services.

Pica8 Inc HQ
1032 Elwell Ct Ste 105
Palo Alto CA 94303
P: 833-888-7422 PRC:97
www.pica8.com
Email: info@pica8.com
Estab: 2009

James Liao, CEO
Niraj Jain, COO
Lu Feng, VP of Finance & HR
Sharad Ahlawat, VP of Technology & Architecture
Jeff Paine, VP of Marketing

Manufacturer of white box switches. The company
specializes in traditional switches and routing
protocols.

Picarro Inc HQ
3105 Patrick Henry Dr
Santa Clara CA 95054
P: 408-962-3900 F: 408-962-3200 PRC:231
picarro.com
Email: info@picarro.com
Estab: 1998

Alex Balkanski, President & CEO
Eric Crosson, CTO
Betsy Kais, CFO
Jeff Braggin, Chief Quality Officer
Tom Dockery, VP of Marketing

Provider of environmental transformation solutions. The company provides isotope analyzers,
trace gas analyzers, accessories, and peripherals.

Pickering Laboratories Inc HQ
1280 Space Pkwy
Mountain View CA 94043
P: 650-694-6700 F: 650-968-0749 PRC:189
www.pickeringlabs.com
Email: sales@pickeringlabs.com
Estab: 1984

Jim Murphy, President
Tony McIsacc, Production Manager
Mike Gottschalk, Marketing Manager
Saji George, Quality Assurance Manager
Wendy Rasmussen, Sales Manager

Developer of post-column derivatization technology. The company specializes in manufacturing of
cation-exchange columns for amino acid analysis.

Pictron Inc HQ
1250 Oakmead Pkwy Ste 210
Sunnyvale CA 94085
P: 408-725-8888 F: 408-446-5552 PRC:320
www.pictron.com
Email: info@pictron.com
Estab: 2000

Sharon Huang, Senior Software Engineer

Provider of solutions for media applications in
corporate communications, eLearning, broadcast
production, and content based video search fields.

Pierce Washington HQ
Two Embarcadero Ctr 8th Fl
San Francisco CA 94111
P: 415-431-8300 PRC:325
piercewashington.com
Email: info@piercewashington.com
Estab: 2005

Austin Lowry, VP of E-Commerce
Ryan Akky, Director of Enterprise Sales
Faris Yamini, Partner
John Carey, Managing Partner
Rob Watters, Partner

Provider of systems integration and e-commerce
solutions. The company also deals with the development of software tools.

Piezo-Metrics Inc HQ
4509 Runway St [N]
Simi Valley CA 93063
P: 805-522-4676 F: 805-522-4982 PRC:204
www.microninstruments.com
Email: sensors@microninstruments.com
Estab: 1980

Robert A. Mueller, President & General Manager
Herbert Chelner, CEO
Franklin Wong, Manager of Production

Manufacturer and distributor of semiconductor
strain gages, pressure transducers, temperature
sensors and measuring systems.

Pindler & Pindler Inc HQ
11910 Poindexter Ave [N]
Moorpark CA 93021
P: 805-531-9090 F: 805-532-2020 PRC:46
www.pindler.com
Estab: 1947

Curt Pindler, President

Designer of fabrics.

Pinterest HQ
651 Brannan St
San Francisco CA 94107-1532
P: 415-762-7100 PRC:325
www.pinterest.com
Email: copyright@pinterest.com
Estab: 2010

Katharine Wang, Chief of Staff
Abby Maldonado, Human Resource Business
Partner
Matthew T. Lewis, Contact
Candice Morgan, Contact
Matt Bouret, Contact

Specializes in mobile application tools. The company focuses on pinning items, creating boards,
and interacting with other members.

Pionetics Corp HQ
151H Old County Rd
San Carlos CA 94070
P: 866-611-8624 PRC:144
linxdrinkingwater.com
Email: info@linxwater.com
Estab: 1995

Olivia Hensley, Consultant

Provider of water treatment products. The company's products include LNX 160 water filters, bottle-
less water coolers, and water treatment systems.

Pipe Shields Inc HQ
5199 Fulton Dr
Fairfield CA 94534
P: 800-538-7007 F: 707-447-4641 PRC:81
www.pipeshields.com
Email: info@pipeshields.com
Estab: 1971

Judith Betz, Sales Manager

Designer and manufacturer of pre-insulated pipe
supports, slides, guides, and anchors. The company's products include hanger types, shoes, and
riser clamps.

Pipsqueak Productions LLC HQ
120 El Camino Del Mar
San Francisco CA 94121
P: 415-668-4372 PRC:325
pipsqueak.com
Email: info@pipsqueak.com
Estab: 1994

Olga Werby, President
Christopher Werby, CEO

Provider of graphic design, photography, writing,
editing, animation, and website development
services.

Pivot Bio Inc HQ
2929 Seventh St Ste 120
Berkeley CA 94710
P: 877-451-1977 PRC:42
pivotbio.com

Karsten Temme, CEO
Alvin Tamsir, CSO

Provider of genome-scale programming of
microbes. The company offers services to farmers
and the agricultural sector.

Pivot Systems Inc HQ
4320 Stevens Creek Blvd Ste 174
San Jose CA 95129
P: 408-435-1000 F: 408-521-3322 PRC:322
www.pivotsys.com
Email: sales@pivotsys.com
Estab: 1997

Rajesh Nair, CEO

Provider of software development services and
related solutions for small, large and mid-size
companies.

Pivotal Labs HQ
875 Howard St 5th Fl
San Francisco CA 94103
P: 415-777-4868 PRC:323
pivotal.io
Estab: 1999

Bill Cook, President
Paul Maritz, Chairman
Rob Mee, CEO
Cynthia Gaylor, CFO
Joe Militello, CPO

Focuses on software development and related
services. The company serves start-ups and
Fortune 1000 companies.

Pivotal Systems HQ
48389 Fremont Blvd Ste 100
Fremont CA 94538
P: 510-770-9125 PRC:226
pivotalsys.com
Email: info@pivotalsys.com

Joseph Monkowski, President & CTO
John Hoffman, CEO
Kevin Landis, Chief Investment Officer

Provider of monitoring and process control technology solutions for the semiconductor manufacturing industry.

Pixami Inc HQ
6754 Bernal Ave Ste 740-106
Pleasanton CA 94566
P: 925-465-5167 PRC:325
pixami.com
Email: info@pixami.com
Estab: 1999

Tom Hodgens, President
Gary Wood, VP of Business Development
Rob Van Dell, Systems Engineer

Provider of imaging technologies. The company
caters to both photo-based and non-photo-based
businesses.

Pixelworks Inc HQ
226 Airport Pkwy Ste 595
San Jose CA 95110
P: 408-200-9200 F: 408-200-9201 PRC:61
www.pixelworks.com
Email: info@pixelworks.com
Estab: 1997
Sales: $30M to $100M

Indra Laksono, President
Todd DeBonis, CEO & Director
Steven L. Moore, CFO
Hongmin Bob Zhang, SVP & CTO
Ting Xiong, VP of Worldwide Sales

Designer and developer of video and pixel processing semiconductors and software for digital
video applications.

Planet Biotechnology Inc HQ
20980 Corsair Blvd
Hayward CA 94545
P: 510-887-1461 PRC:249
www.planetbiotechnology.com
Email: info@planetbiotechnology.com

Elliott L. Fineman, President & CEO
Jeffrey S. Price, Chairman
James W. Larrick, CSO & VP
Keith L. Wycoff, VP of Research
Don Cheema, Maintenance & Facilities Manager

Provider of biotechnology services. The company
develops antibody-based therapeutic and preventative products through plants to meet medical
needs.

Planetary Herbals HQ
PO Box 1760
Soquel CA 95073
P: 831-438-1700 F: 831-438-7410 PRC:34
www.planetaryherbals.com
Estab: 1980

Roy Upton, Herbalist

Provider of nutritional herbal healthcare products.
The company's products include Acai, Full Spectrum, Bacopa Extract, and Digestive Comfort.

Planeteria Media HQ
110 Stony Point Ste 225
Santa Rosa CA 95401
P: 707-843-3773 PRC:324
www.planeteria.com
Email: sales@planeteria.com
Estab: 1999

Renu Chadda, Managing Director
Sandeep Mehta, Director of Technical
Jessica Kane, Project Manager

Designer and developer of websites, applications,
e-commerce, content management systems,
video, and offers flash, and Internet marketing
services.

PlanGrid HQ
2111 Mission St Ste 400
San Francisco CA 94110
P: 800-646-0796 PRC:322
www.plangrid.com
Estab: 2011

Bill Smith, President
Michael Galvin, CFO
Kevin Halter, Regional VP of Sales
Emily Tsitrian, Director of Consulting Services
Shaya Fidel, Director of People

Developer of construction apps which automatically syncs notes, markups, and photos to all the
users' devices.

Planisware HQ
300 Montgomery St Ste 930
San Francisco CA 94104
P: 415-591-0941 PRC:328
planisware.com
Email: info@planisware.com
Estab: 1996

Pierre Demonsant, CEO
Nicolas Vilars, CMO
David Gustafson, VP of Business Development
Loic Sautour, SVP of North America
Dave Penndorf, VP of Life Sciences PPM Practice

Designer of portfolio management software solutions for product development and research and
development organizations.

Plant Sciences Inc HQ
342 Green Valley Rd
Watsonville CA 95076
P: 831-728-7771 F: 831-728-4967 PRC:41
www.plantsciences.com
Estab: 1985

Eric Levesque, General Manager
Vicki Nelson, Corporate Secretary
George D. Graff, Facilities Manager
Kendra Blaker, Manager
Rory Odegaard, Crop Manager

Provider of agricultural research services. The
company develops new technology to yield good
plant production.

Plantronics Inc HQ
345 Encinal St
Santa Cruz CA 95060
P: 831-426-5858 F: 831-426-6098 PRC:60
www.plantronics.com
Email: amerpartners@poly.com
Estab: 1961
Sales: $1B to $3B

Joseph B. Burton, President & CEO & Director
Tom Gill, VP & CIO
Mary Huser, EVP & Chief Legal & Compliance
Officer
Shantanu Sarkar, EVP of Headset Business Unit
Rich Pickard, VP

Provider of audio technology systems that
includes headsets, telephones, audio processors,
and speakerphones.

**Plasidyne Engineering &
Manufacturing Inc** HQ
3230 E 59th St [N]
Long Beach CA 90805
P: 562-531-0510 F: 562-531-1377 PRC:189
www.plasidyne.com
Estab: 1969

Michael Brown, CEO

Manufacturer of PTFE, Filled PTFE and precision-machined plastic parts for commercial and
aerospace.

Plasma Ruggedized Solutions HQ
2284 Ringwood Ave Ste A
San Jose CA 95131
P: 408-954-8405 F: 408-954-8401 PRC:47
www.plasmarugged.com
Email: sales@plasmarugged.com
Estab: 1990

Jim Stameson, President & CEO
Evan Persky, CFO
George Michael Forney, CTO
Hoang Nguyen, Operations Manager
Roger Adams, Technical Sales Manager

Provider of coating and related specialty engineering services. The company specializes in plasma
technologies and offers lab services.

Plasma Technology Systems LLC HQ
30695 Huntwood Ave
Hayward CA 94544
P: 650-596-1606 F: 650-596-1180 PRC:159
plasmatreat.com
Email: infoptna@plasmatreat.com
Estab: 1999

Jeff Leighty, Sales & Business Development
Manager

Provider of equipment and process development
services for plasma treatment of surfaces. The
company specializes in modification of polymers.

Plasmaterials Inc HQ
2268 Research Dr
Livermore CA 94550
P: 925-447-4030 F: 925-447-4031 PRC:79
www.plasmaterials.com
Email: info@plasmaterials.com
Estab: 1987

Don Sarrach, Owner

Provider of materials for thin film applications. The
company offers base metal alloys, backing plates,
and semiconductor alloys.

Plastech HQ
3555A Haven Ave
Menlo Park CA 94025
P: 650-568-9206 F: 650-568-9230 PRC:80
www.pmiplastech.com
Estab: 1985

Paul Molnar, Owner

Provider of machined and fabricated plastic
products for the semiconductor, biological, and
medical industries.

Plastikon Industries Inc HQ
688 Sandoval Way
Hayward CA 94544
P: 510-400-1010 F: 510-400-1133 PRC:80
www.plastikon.com
Estab: 1982

Guiv Soofer, VP of Manufacturing
John Yates, General Manager
Hany Botrous, Production Manager
James Orosco, Tooling Engineering Manager
Shirley Stapp, Corporate Senior HR Manager

Provider of contract manufacturing services for
custom designed plastic injection molding, for
medical, pharmaceutical and other industries.

Platina Systems Corp HQ
3180 De La Cruz Blvd Ste 110
Santa Clara CA 95054
P: 408-389-4268 PRC:97
www.platinasystems.com
Email: info@platinasystems.com
Estab: 2014

Frank Yang, Founder & CTO
Sharad Mehrotra, CPO
Scott Chandler, Chief Sales Officer
Meichi Lai, VP of Finance & Operations
Raj Venkatesan, VP of Engineering

Manufacturer of network equipment including
switches. The company serves industrial and
commercial customers.

Platron HQ
26260 Eden Landing Rd
Hayward CA 94545
P: 510-781-5588 F: 510-781-5589 PRC:80
www.platron.com
Estab: 1985

Bruce Garratt, Owner
James White, Operations Manager

Provider of selective plating services. The company caters to design engineering, electronics,
mechanical, and field service applications.

Pleasanton Garbage Service Inc HQ
3110 Busch Rd [N]
Pleasanton CA 94566
P: 925-846-2042 F: 925-846-9323 PRC:141
www.pleasantongarbageservice.com
Email: info@pleasantongarbageservice.com
Estab: 1969

Debbie Dugorepec, Accountant

Provider of garbage collection services for residential and commercial sectors.

Plethora HQ
1118 Harrison St
San Francisco CA 94103
P: 415-726-2256 PRC:316
www.plethora.com
Email: contact@plethora.com

Nick Pinkston, Co-Founder
Effi Baruch, CEO & Co-Founder
Michael Jeub, Director
Mark Mnich, Director of Business Operations
Jose Sanchez, Director

Focuses on CNC milling with automatic manufacturing analysis. The company is also involved in
prototyping services.

Plexxikon Inc HQ
91 Bolivar Dr
Berkeley CA 94710
P: 510-647-4000 F: 510-548-8014 PRC:34
www.plexxikon.com
Email: info@plexxikon.com
Estab: 2001

Gideon E. Bollag, CEO
Chao Zhang, CSO
Joseph Young, VP of Finance & Corporate Devel-
opment
Marguerite Hutchinson, SVP & General Counsel
Wayne Spevak, VP of Chemistry

Developer of pharmaceuticals. The company utilizes its proprietary discovery platform to produce
highly selective and targeted medicines.

Pliant Therapeutics Inc HQ
260 Littlefield Ave
S San Francisco CA 94080
P: 650-481-6770 PRC:28
pliantrx.com
Email: info@pliantrx.com
Estab: 2016

Bernard Coulie, CEO
Barbara Howes, Chief Human Resource Officer
Hans Hull, CBO
Scott Turner, VP of Translational Sciences
Bill Greenlee, Principal

Developer of therapeutics medicines for the
treatment of fibrosis in organs and conditions,
including liver, kidney, heart, and gastrointestinal
tract.

Plug-It Products HQ
940 E Pine St
Lodi CA 95240
P: 209-334-4904 F: 209-334-1671 PRC:166
plugitproducts.com
Estab: 1986

Steve Adolf, Shipping & Receiving Manager
Jon Smith, Contact

Provider of in-house products for the municipalities, maintenance contractors, underground
contractors, and rental companies.

Plumbing Wholesale Outlet HQ
520 N Fair Oaks Ave [N]
Pasadena CA 91103
P: 626-744-3170 F: 626-744-3175 PRC:135
www.pwooutlet.com
Emp: 11-50

Bobby Garcia, General Manager
Andrew Nava, Purchasing Manager
Susanna Acosta, Accounts Payable Specialist
Barbara Garcia, Contact
John Ramos, Sales Associate

Wholesaler of plumbing supplies and related
accessories.

PLX Devices Inc HQ
2526 Qume Dr Ste 23
San Jose CA 95131
P: 408-745-7591 PRC:209
www.plxdevices.com
Estab: 2003

Paul Lowchareonkul, Founder

Developer of high-tech measuring instruments.
The company is engaged in manufacturing, product testing, and technical support services.

PM Machining Inc HQ
8630 Argent St Ste C [N]
Santee CA 92071
P: 619-449-8989 F: 619-258-7958 PRC:80
www.pmmachining.com
Estab: 1977

Bill Parris, Owner

Provider of inspection equipment and processing
equipment for various sectors.

Pneu Design LLC HQ
3164 N Shingle Rd
Shingle Springs CA 95682
P: 530-676-4702   F: 530-676-4434   PRC:159
www.pneudesign.com
Email: sales@pneudesign.com
Estab: 1984

Mark Nagy, General Partner

Provider of electronic and pneumatic filling
machines for the petroleum and food processing
industry.

PNI Sensor BR
2331 Circadian Way
Santa Rosa CA 95407
P: 707-566-2260   F: 707-566-2261   PRC:87
www.pnicorp.com
Email: sales@pnicorp.com
Estab: 1987

Becky Oh, President & CEO
George Hsu, CTO
Joe Zils, Chief Legal Counsel
Eric Walters, VP of Finance
Betty Zhang, Software Engineer

Manufacturer of electronic sensors. The company
designs and fabricates processors, three-axis
controllers, and geomagnetic sensors.

POC Medical Systems Inc HQ
4659 Las Positas Rd
Livermore CA 94551
P: 925-331-8010   PRC:186
pocmedicalsystems.com
Estab: 2009

Sanjeev Saxena, CEO
Andrea Cuppoletti, VP

Provider of diagnostic medical devices for the
screening of life-threatening diseases like cancer,
cardiovascular disorders, and infectious diseases.

Poco Solar Energy Inc HQ
3345 Keller St
Santa Clara CA 95054
P: 408-970-0680   F: 408-987-0513   PRC:135
www.pocosolar.com
Email: info@pocosolar.com
Estab: 1984

Greg Cordero, Co-Founder
Paul Podesta, Co-Founder
Vern Johnson, Director of Sales
John McGuire, Solar Energy Consultant
Jesse Cordero, Solar Technician

Designer and installer of solar energy systems
that provide electricity and heat for swimming
pools.

Point of View Productions HQ
2477 Folsom St   [N]
San Francisco CA 94110
P: 415-821-0435   F: 415-821-0434   PRC:60
www.karildaniels.com
Estab: 1976

Karil Daniels, Producer & Editor & Director

Provider of film and video production services.

M-242

Polarity Inc HQ
11294 Sunrise Park Dr
Rancho Cordova CA 95742
P: 916-635-3050   F: 916-635-7866   PRC:290
www.polarity.net
Email: sales@polarity.net
Estab: 1999

David Chuang, President
Bogdan Svityashchuk, Electrical Engineer
Robby Beard, Electrical Engineer

Designer and manufacturer of power products for
commercial and government entities. The company also offers supply solutions.

Poly Seal Industries HQ
725 Channing Way
Berkeley CA 94710
P: 510-843-9722   F: 510-843-7316   PRC:284
www.polysealind.com
Email: info@polysealind.com
Estab: 1974

Daniel Baker, President & CEO

Manufacturer of molded rubber pipe gaskets for
water and sewage treatment applications. The
company serves the automotive and biomedical
industries.

Polycom Inc HQ
6001 America Center Dr
San Jose CA 95002
P: 408-586-3837   PRC:68
www.polycom.com
Email: polycomcapital@polycom.com
Estab: 2019

Alex Bustamante, EVP of Global Operations &
President of Plamex
Robert C. Hagerty, Director & Chairman of the
Board
Phil Sherburne, SVP & Chief of Staff to the Office
of the CEO
Anja Hamilton, EVP & Chief Human Resource
Officer
Chuck Boynton, EVP & CFO

Manufacturer and seller of teleconferencing equipment and provider of all other communications
solutions.

Polyfet RF Devices Inc HQ
1110 Avenida Acaso   [N]
Camarillo CA 93012
P: 805-484-4210   F: 805-484-3393   PRC:204
www.polyfet.com
Emp: 11-50   Estab: 1984

S.K. Leong, Contact

Provider of RF amplifier design assistance, and
RF mosfet transistors.

Polymath Research Inc HQ
827 Bonde Ct
Pleasanton CA 94566
P: 925-417-0609   F: 925-417-0684   PRC:323
www.polymath-usa.com

Bedros B. Afeyan, President

Developer of wave propagation and interaction, and photonic devices. The company offers
FEMLAB based photonics modeling package and
wavelet tools.

Polymeric Technology Inc HQ
1900 Marina Blvd   [N]
San Leandro CA 94577
P: 510-895-6001   PRC:189
www.poly-tek.com
Email: contact@poly-tek.com
Estab: 1963

Patrick Tool, Contact

Distributor of cast, molded and injected urethane,
polyurethane, plastic, silicone, and rubber parts.

Polyphenolics HQ
12667 Rd 24
Madera CA 93639
P: 559-661-5556   F: 559-661-5630   PRC:188
polyphenolics.com

James A. Kennedy, President
Steve Kupina, Director of Quality & Technology
Debra Cerda, Marketing Specialist
Jessica Ornelas, Customer Advocate

Supplier of grape seed, grape pomace, and whole
grape extracts. The company offers MegaNatu-
ral-BP, MegaNatural Red Wine Grape Extract, and
MegaNatural-GL.

POLYSTAK Inc HQ
2372 D Qume Dr
San Jose CA 95131
P: 408-441-1400   F: 408-441-1420   PRC:96
www.polystak.com
Email: info@polystak.com
Estab: 1999

Terry Chung, General Manager

Provider of silicon based multi chip package products as well as package stacking solutions and
repair services of components and modules.

Polywell Computers   HQ
1461-1 San Mateo Ave
S San Francisco CA 94080
P: 650-583-7222   PRC:93
www.polywell.com
Email: info@polywell.com
Estab: 1987

Jack Chen, Storage Product Sales Manager
Jerry Tighe, Technical Sales Manager
Jenny Lin, Manager
Jiaying Zhao, Administrative Assistant

Manufacturer of computer systems. The company
specializes in desktop PCs, workstations, and
servers.

Pomeranian Pictures   HQ
20236 Leadwell St   [N]
Winnetka CA 91306
P: 818-998-1983   PRC:60
www.pompixweb.com
Email: pompix@aol.com

Charles Domokos, Contact

Provider of production, post-production and distribution of independent film.

PONTiS Orthopaedics LLC   HQ
2299 Post St Ste 103
San Francisco CA 94115
P: 415-567-8935   F: 415-567-8934   PRC:189
www.pontisorthopaedics.com
Email: info@pontisorthopaedics.com
Estab: 2012

Tom Ross, COO
Jim Berman, VP of Sales & Marketing

Manufacturer of medical devices such as implants
and instrumentation for use in upper and lower
extremity bone and soft tissue repair.

Popcorn Press and Media   HQ
PO Box 3375   [N]
Rancho Santa Fe CA 92067
P: 858-759-2779   F: 206-984-3977   PRC:325
www.popcornpressandmedia.com
Estab: 1999

Janene Massieh, President

Creator of books and educational materials related to San Diego.

Portola Pharmaceuticals Inc   HQ
270 E Grand Ave
S San Francisco CA 94080
P: 650-246-7000   F: 650-246-7376   PRC:268
www.portola.com
Email: contact@portola.com
Emp: 324 Estab: 2003
Sales: $100M to $300M

Scott Garland, President & CEO
Ernie Meyer, EVP & Chief Human Resource
Officer
Mardi Dier, EVP & CFO & Chief Business Officer
Tao Fu, Chief Commercial & Business Officer &
EVP
Glenn Brame, EVP & Chief Technical Operations
Officer

Focuses on the development and commercialization of therapeutic products for the treatment of
hematologic disorders.

Portola Systems Inc   HQ
7064 Corline Court Ste B5
Sebastopol CA 95472
P: 707-824-8800   F: 707-824-8866   PRC:329
www.portolasystems.net
Email: info@portolasystems.net
Estab: 1994

Grant Smoot, President & CEO
Andrea Wills, Accounting Manager
Juan Pulido, Senior Engineer
Rich Coibion, Senior Engineer
James Brown, Information Technology Engineer

Provider of computer network engineering and
integration services. The company also specializes in IT consultation.

Portrait Displays Inc   HQ
6663 Owens Dr
Pleasanton CA 94588
P: 925-227-2700   F: 925-227-2705   PRC:323
portrait.com
Email: sales@portrait.com
Estab: 1996

J. Michael James, President & CEO
Derek Smith, CTO
Joao Pedras, CIO
Scott Anderson, CPO & EVP
James Lund, Chief Software Architect

Provider of extensible platforms supporting
embedded control of all display technologies and
monitors and operating system software.

POS Specialists   HQ
5051 Commercial Cir Ste F
Concord CA 94520
P: 925-626-3930   F: 925-626-3938   PRC:323
www.posspecialists.com
Email: sales@posspecialists.com
Estab: 1990

Doug Campbell, Owner
Bob Brockman, Owner
Alex Ugrin, CTO
David Bowers, Sales Manager
Denver Gaasch, Project Manager

Provider of digital dining solutions. The company
is engaged in business consultation, on-site training, and cloud services.

Posiflex Business Machines Inc   HQ
30689 Huntwood Ave
Hayward CA 94544
P: 510-429-7097   F: 510-475-0982   PRC:92
www.posiflexusa.com
Email: customer.service@posiflexusa.com
Estab: 1984

Dora Young, VP of Operations
Kenneth Fang, Regional Sales Manager

Provider of point of service hardware and platform
technology. The company caters to diverse
markers.

PosIQ Inc   HQ
189 W Santa Clara St
San Jose CA 95113
P: 408-676-7470   F: 408-831-3300   PRC:322
posiq.net
Email: info@posiq.net
Estab: 2008

Rick Onyon, CEO
Jeremy Maselko, Director of Quality Assurance

Provider of customer relationship management
and data solutions. The company offers services
to the hospitality sector.

PotBotics Inc   HQ
2225 E Bayshore Rd Ste 200
Palo Alto CA 94303
P: 650-837-0420   PRC:34
www.potbotics.com
Estab: 2013

Rick Andersson, Sales Manager

Developer of medical marijuana products such as
potbot, brainbot, and nanopot.

Potter Roemer- Fire Protection
Equipment   HQ
17451 Hurley St   [N]
City Of Industry CA 91744
P: 626-855-4890   F: 626-937-4777   PRC:156
www.potterroemer.com
Email: info@potterroemer.com
Estab: 1937

George Brown, VP of Sales

Manufacturer and distributor of interior hose,
standpipe equipment, cabinets, connections,
extinguishers, and valves.

Pottery Manufacturing and
Distributing Inc   HQ
18881 S Hoover St   [N]
Gardena CA 90248
P: 310-323-7754   F: 310-323-6613   PRC:163
www.potterymfg.com
Email: gotpots@potterymfg.com
Estab: 1971

Carol Shaw, President

Manufacturer and distributor of clay and glazed
pottery.

Power Industries   HQ
520 Barham Ave
Santa Rosa CA 95404
P: 707-545-7904   F: 707-541-2211   PRC:155
www.powerindustries.com
Estab: 1951

Rick Call, President

Supplier of ready-made solutions for industrial
applications. The company's products include
bearings and seals, hydraulics, and pneumatics.

Power Integrations HQ
5245 Hellyer Ave
San Jose CA 95138
P: 408-414-9200   F: 408-414-9201   PRC:208
power.com
Email: customerservice@power.com
Estab: 1998
Sales: $300M to $1 Billion

Balu Balakrishnan, President & CEO
Sandeep Nayyar, VP of Finance & CFO
Ben Sutherland, VP of Worldwide Sales
Douglas Bailey, VP of Marketing
Mike Matthews, VP of Product Development

Supplier of electronic components. The company's
products include AC-DC converters and LED
drivers.

Power Machinery Center HQ
3450 Camino Ave   [N]
Oxnard CA 93030
P: 805-485-0577   F: 805-983-2773   PRC:80
www.powermachinery.com
Emp: 51-200   Estab: 1950

Andres Diaz, Manager of Parts

Distributor of quality material handling and warehouse equipment.

Power Standards Lab HQ
980 Atlantic Ave
Alameda CA 94501
P: 510-522-4400   F: 510-522-4455   PRC:293
www.powerstandards.com
Email: info@powerstandards.com
Estab: 2000

Alex McEachern, Founder
Chris Hutter, Chairman & CEO
Barry Tangney, COO
Robert Pompeani, VP of Engineering
Marco Mancilla, VP of Sales

Manufacturer of precision electronic power instruments. The company is involved in testing and
calibration services.

PowerBeam Research LLC RH
704 Calderon Ave
Mountain View CA 94041
P: 408-933-9373   PRC:209
powerbeaminc.com

David Graham, Agent

Provider of firmware, hardware, and software
applications for video, optoelectronic systems
(lasers, LEDs, photodiodes, waveguides), and
robotics.

Powerlift Dumbwaiters Inc HQ
2444 Georgia Slide Rd
Georgetown CA 95634
P: 530-333-1953   F: 530-333-1055   PRC:179
www.dumbwaiters.com
Email: info@dumbwaiters.com
Estab: 1972

Larry Reite, VP of Operations

Provider of dumbwaiters that includes residential
powerlifts, commercial units, and mezzanine lifts.

Powerplant Consultants Inc HQ
1106 E Emporia St   [N]
Ontario CA 91761
P: 909-986-1141   F: 909-986-1147   PRC:45
www.gesco.org
Email: info@gesco.org
Estab: 1984

Christopher K. Lane, President

Provider of consulting services in industrial power
generation including co-generation, standby
emergency power, landfill and digester gas fueled
engines, geothermal, solar power, fuel cells, gas
turbine generators, power plant instrumentation
and control systems, economic analysis of power
generation systems and other energy processes.

Powertest Inc HQ
3719 Callan Blvd Ste 200
S San Francisco CA 94080-2431
P: 415-778-0580   F: 415-778-0599   PRC:322
www.powertest.com
Email: info@powertest.com
Estab: 1995

Teresa Fontanilla, VP of Operations

Provider of software-related professional services.
The company is also involved in load testing and
application performance management.

Powertronix Corp HQ
1120 Chess Dr
Foster City CA 94404
P: 650-345-6800   F: 650-345-7240   PRC:293
powertronix.com
Email: sales@powertronix.com
Estab: 1991

Carl Svensson, Owner
Raymond Soo, Electrical Design Engineer
Nettie Mah, Contact

Provider of in-house engineering and related
services. The company offers services to the
industrial sector.

PPBC HQ
2426 Sixth St
Berkeley CA 94710
P: 510-841-7242   F: 501-841-4313   PRC:288
polyplus.com
Email: info@polyplus.com
Estab: 1991

Steven Visco, CEO & CTO
Eugene Nimon, Director of Research & Business
Development

Engaged in the development of protected lithium
metal electrodes. The company's products include
lithium-sulfur batteries and protected lithium
anodes.

Practice Fusion Inc HQ
731 Market St Ste 400
San Francisco CA 94103
P: 415-346-7700   PRC:315
www.practicefusion.com
Estab: 2005

Ryan Howard, Founder
Matt Douglass, Co-Founder & SVP of Customer
Experience
Jonathan Malek, Co-Founder & CTO
Alan Wong, Co-Founder

Provider of cloud-based electronic health records
(EHR) platform in the U.S.

Praesum Communications Inc HQ
3558 Round Barn Blvd Ste 200
Santa Rosa CA 95403
P: 707-338-0946   PRC:97
www.praesum.com
Email: support@praesum.com
Estab: 2000

Kent Dahlgren, Owner & CEO

Provider of switching communication products.
The company offers IP cores, boards, and system
level products.

**Pragmatic Communications Systems
Inc** HQ
2340A Walsh Ave
Santa Clara CA 95051
P: 408-748-1100   F: 408-663-9783   PRC:60
www.wireless-experts.com
Email: sales@pragmatic1.com
Estab: 1994

Prasanna Shah, Founder & President
Karin Thompson, Senior Account Executive

Designer, developer, and manufacturer of pragmatic products. The company offers amplifiers, security cameras, speakers, and wireless products.

Pragmatics Technologies Inc HQ
100 Great Oaks Blvd Ste 140
San Jose CA 95119
P: 408-289-8202   F: 408-289-8109   PRC:200
www.pragmaticstech.com
Email: sales@pragmaticstech.com
Estab: 2000

Chris R. Mack, President & Founder

Provider of electromechanical interface solutions.
The company deals with the development of
custom and standard test interfaces.

Pre Plastics Inc HQ
12600-100 Locksley Ln
Auburn CA 95602
P: 530-823-1820   F: 530-823-1866   PRC:84
preplastics.com
Estab: 1986

Brian Miller, President
Linda Nelson, Office Manager
Katie Kuhl, Sales Manager
Allen Grim, Production Manager
Sam Ivey, Quality Assurance Manager

Provider of engineering and precision tooling
services. The company also offers plastic injection
molding and assembly services.

**Precise Aerospace Manufacturing
Inc** HQ
224 Glider Cir [N]
Corona CA 92880
P: 951-898-0500   F: 951-898-0600   PRC:189
www.precisemfg.com
Emp: 51-200   Estab: 1990

Ron Harwood, CEO
Michael Valeriano, General Manager
Devarsh Patel, Quality Control Manager

Manufacturer of plastics products.

Precise Automation Inc HQ
47350 Fremont Blvd
Fremont CA 94538
P: 408-224-2838   PRC:80
preciseautomation.com
Email: sales@preciseautomation.com
Estab: 2004

Betsy Lange, CFO
Mike Ouren, Chief Sales Engineer
Rajesh Kulkarni, Director of Electrical Engineering
Carl Lee, Engineer

Provider of industrial automation solutions. The
company's products include robots, guidance
controllers, and kinematics.

Precise Industries Inc HQ
610 Neptune Ave [N]
Brea CA 92821
P: 714-482-2333   F: 714-482-2332   PRC:48
preciseind.com
Emp: 11-50   Estab: 2005

Kenneth Stream, Contact

Manufacturer of sheet metal fab, CNC machining,
cables and electronic assemblies.

Precise Light Surgical HQ
310 W Hamilton Ave Ste 210
Campbell CA 95008
P: 831-539-3323   PRC:189
preciselightsurgical.com
Email: info@preciselightsurgical.com

Gerald Mitchel, Founder & CTO
Richard Nash, CEO

Provider of medical devices with vaporization
technology for the removal of delicate tissues,
reduce surgical risk, and down time in endoscopic
surgery.

Precision Asphere Inc HQ
48860 Milmont Dr Unit 105-C
Fremont CA 94538
P: 510-668-1508   F: 510-668-1595   PRC:173
precisionasphere.com
Email: sales@precisionasphere.com
Estab: 2002

John Kong, President & Founder

Provider of aspheric optical components fabrication services. The company offers optical surface
forming, polishing, and metrology services.

Precision Contacts Inc HQ
990 Suncast Ln
El Dorado Hills CA 95762
P: 916-939-4147   F: 916-939-4149   PRC:86
www.precisioncontacts.com
Email: sales@precisioncontacts.com
Estab: 1974

Dean Wroblewski, President
Jeremy Brittain, Material Manager

Provider of replacement contacts for handler
manufacturer. The company's products include
sockets, contacts, elements, and custom products.

Precision Identity Corp HQ
804 Camden Ave
Campbell CA 95008
P: 408-374-2346   PRC:80
precisionidentity.com
Email: info@precisionidentity.com
Estab: 1970

Roland Kamber, President
Pierre Kamber, VP

Manufacturer of machined components for the
medical device manufacturing industries. The
company offers inspection, cleaning, and support
services.

Precision Metal Tooling Inc HQ
5101 San Leandro St
Oakland CA 94601
P: 510-436-0900   F: 510-436-3030   PRC:163
www.precisionmetaltooling.com
Email: info@precisionmetaltooling.com
Estab: 1983

Margaret Carter, VP

Manufacturer of production tool and die manufacturing products. The company also focuses on
prototype tooling, tool engineering, and custom
tooling.

Precision Plastics Inc HQ
8456 Carbide Ct
Sacramento CA 95828
P: 916-689-5284   F: 916-689-5424   PRC:284
www.precisionplasticsinc.com
Email: info@precisionplasticsinc.com
Estab: 1984

David Freriks, VP
Justin Matisewski, Director of Sales

Provider of plastic fabrication services. The
company is engaged in fabrication, countertops,
machining, and consumer services.

Precision Swiss Products Inc HQ
1911 Tarob Ct
Milpitas CA 95035
P: 408-433-5880   F: 408-434-0764   PRC:80
precisionswiss.com
Email: sales@precisionswiss.com

Norbert Kozar, CEO
Peter Pichler, Chief Quality Officer
Melissa Kozar, EVP
Daniela Kozar, Director of Quality

Manufacturer of precision machined components.
The company serves medical, energy, and military
industries.

Precision Tool Distributors Inc HQ
46613 Fremont Blvd
Fremont CA 94538-6410
P: 408-774-1274   F: 408-774-1277   PRC:212
www.pretool.com
Estab: 1963

Frank Black, President
John Feuerhelm, Inspection Services Manager

Specializes in dimensional measurement products. The company offers inspection hand tools
and related accessories.

Precision Welding Technologies Inc HQ
6287 Viewridge Dr
Auburn CA 95602
P: 530-269-1826   F: 530-269-1827   PRC:82
www.pwt-online.com
Email: sales@pwt-online.com
Estab: 1993

Gregg Martsching, President

Provider of welding systems and components. The
company's service include equipment maintenance, planning and maintenance, and job shop.

Premier Biosoft International HQ
3786 Corina Way
Palo Alto CA 94303-4504
P: 650-856-2703   F: 650-618-1773   PRC:40
www.premierbiosoft.com
Email: support@premierbiosoft.com
Estab: 1994

Arun Apte, CEO

Specializes in software development, design,
testing and maintenance services. The company
serves life science companies and laboratories.

Premier Finishing Inc HQ
7910 Longe St
Stockton CA 95206
P: 209-982-5585   F: 209-983-4050   PRC:47
www.premierfinishing.com
Email: sales@premierfinishing.com
Estab: 1996

Craig Walters, President
Thom Foulks, VP
Carin Ribbens, VP
Jim Lowman, Office Manager
Ker Vang, Project Manager

Provider of precision services. The company
focuses on powder coating, liquid coating, pad
printing, and light mechanical assembly.

Premier Wireless Solutions   HQ
88 Bonaventura Dr
San Jose CA 95134
P: 650-230-1300   PRC:70
www.pws.bz

Vince Giacomini, CEO
Gregg Peterson, CTO
Mike Hoekstra, VP of Business Development
Roevic Garingan, VP of Business Development
Chris Mabee, Director of Engineering

Provider of wireless products, design and test /
certification services, network data plans, device
portals, and device management middleware.

Prescient Surgical   HQ
1585 Industrial Rd
San Carlos CA 94070
P: 650-999-0263   PRC:186
www.prescientsurgical.com
Email: info@prescientsurgical.com

Insoo Suh, Co-Founder
Jonathan Coe, Co-Founder & President & CEO

Developer of medical devices and technologies
to reduce the risk of surgical site infections in
patients undergoing abdominal gastrointestinal
surgery.

Prescript Pharmaceuticals Inc   HQ
39 California Ave Ste 104
Pleasanton CA 94566
P: 925-215-8608   F: 925-417-1413   PRC:270
www.prescript.net
Estab: 1992

William J. Hartig, President

Provider of repackaging services. The company
offers its products in sealed and tamper evident
containers.

Presentek Inc   HQ
987 University Ave Ste 11
Los Gatos CA 95032
P: 408-354-1264   F: 408-354-6261   PRC:224
www.presentek.com
Email: salessupport@presentek.com
Estab: 1987

Lee Mayfield, President

Designer of websites and web portals. The company also offers content management systems
and e-commerce handlers.

Presidio Inc   BR
5000 Hopyard Rd Ste 188
Pleasanton CA 94588
P: 415-501-9020   PRC:323
presidio.com

Rudy Casasola, President of Sales
Bob Cagnazzi, CEO
Dave Hart, COO
Jennifer Jackson, Chief Human Resource Officer
Neil Johnston, CFO

Provider of IP telephony and wireless networking
services. The company also deals with deployment, integration, and hardware and software
development.

M-246

Presidio Pharmaceuticals Inc   HQ
1700 Owens St Ste 184
San Francisco CA 94158
P: 415-655-7560   F: 415-986-2864   PRC:249
www.presidiopharma.com
Email: contact@presidiopharma.com
Estab: 2006

Leo Redmond, CFO

Developers of small-molecule antiviral therapeutics. The company is a clinical-stage pharmaceutical company.

Prestige Lens Lab   HQ
338 N Canal St Ste 14
S San Francisco CA 94080
P: 650-588-5540   F: 650-588-3322   PRC:306
prestigesafetyrx.com
Email: info@prestigesafetyrx.com
Estab: 1994

Steve Mori-Prange, Manager & Safety Optician
Richard Casey, Safety Rx Eyewear Specialist

Provider of optical laboratory services. The company specializes in prescription safety eyewear
programs.

Presto Engineering Inc   HQ
2635 N First St Ste 212
San Jose CA 95134
P: 408-372-9500   PRC:304
www.presto-eng.com
Email: sales-northamer@presto-eng.com
Estab: 2006

Michel Villemain, Founder & CEO
Daniel Lee, VP & GM of North America
Tim Lillie, VP & General Manager of North
America
Rick Vernor, Production Control Manager
Alok Savadatti, RF Engineer

Provider of semiconductor test and analysis
solutions. The company also offers engineering
services to the semiconductor market.

Prezi Inc   HQ
450 Bryant St
San Francisco CA 94107
P: 844-551-6941   PRC:322
prezi.com
Estab: 2008

Peter Arvai, Co-Founder & CEO
Adam Somlai-Fischer, Principal Artist &
Co-Founder
Jim Szafranski, COO
Nadjya Ghausi, CMO
Peter Hal, CTO

Provider of collaboration solutions. The company
offers strategy and technical consulting services.

Price Pump Co   HQ
21775 Eighth St E
Sonoma CA 95476-0329
P: 707-938-8441   F: 707-938-0764   PRC:160
www.pricepump.com
Email: sales@pricepump.com
Estab: 1932

Kurt Price, Owner
Karl Buder, CFO
Pawel Bankowski, VP of Engineering & Manufac-
turing
Jestin Plowright, VP of Sales & Marketing
John Armitage, Engineering & Manufacturing
Manager

Manufacturer of centrifugal and air operated dia-
phragm pumps. The company offers engineering
services and serves industrial and OEM users.

Prima Environmental Inc   HQ
5070 Robert J Mathews Pkwy Ste 300
El Dorado Hills CA 95762
P: 916-939-7300   F: 916-939-7398   PRC:140
primaenvironmental.com
Email: info@primaenvironmental.com
Estab: 1998

Cindy Schreier, President

Provider of laboratory testing services. The company specializes in treatability testing, technology
evaluation, and scientific consulting services.

Primary Instruments Inc   HQ
9553 Vassar Ave   [N]
Chatsworth CA 91311
P: 818-993-4971   F: 818-701-5516   PRC:306
www.primaryinstruments.com
Email: support@primaryinstruments.com
Estab: 1979

Allen Ganner, CEO & President
Brandon Ganner, VP of Business Development
Greg Ganner, VP & Marketing
Jun Bautista, Senior VP Operations
Peggy Ganner, EVP & Comptroller

Provider of metrology services.

Prime Engineering   HQ
4202 W Sierra Madre Ave
Fresno CA 93722
P: 559-276-0991   F: 559-276-3544   PRC:189
www.primeengineering.com
Email: info@primeengineering.com
Estab: 1984

Mary Wilson Boegel, President
Bruce Boegel, CFO
Mark Allen, VP
Greg Boyer, Director of Transportation
Dawn Smith, Customer Service Manager

Provider of standing systems products such as
grandstand, kidstand, symmetry mobile, uprite,
cindy lift, and the lift.

Primepay LLC   BR
5600 Mowry School Rd Ste 230
Newark CA 94560
P: 650-358-4555   F: 650-358-4559   PRC:45
primepay.com

William J. Pellicano, CEO
Ed Hughes, EVP & CFO
Todd Quarfot, EVP & Chief Business Development
Officer
Karen Cimorelli-Moor, EVP & Chief Experience
Officer
Rene Crawford, SVP & Executive Administrator &
Advisor

Provider of payroll processing services, HR
solutions, and insurance and benefit management
services.

Primity Bio Inc   HQ
48383 Fremont Blvd Ste 118
Fremont CA 94538
P: 510-210-0605   PRC:34
primitybio.com
Email: info@primitybio.com
Estab: 2010

Erika O'Donnell, Senior Scientist
Jason Vander Tuig, Research Assistant

Provider of assay platforms for biological relevance. The company specializes in cell biology, flow cytometry, and molecular biology.

Primus Power   HQ
3967 Trust Way
Hayward CA 94545
P: 510-342-7600   PRC:288
www.primuspower.com
Email: sales@primuspower.com
Estab: 2009

Tom Stepien, CEO
Mark Collins, Senior Director NPI Operations
Hossein Kazemi, Director of Systems Engineering
Jeffrey Bouchard, Electrical Engineer
Raymond Archer, Staff Scientist

Provider of energy storage solutions. The company develops EnergyPod, energy storage batteries, and EnergyCell for industrial and consumer applications.

Prism Inks Inc   HQ
824 W Ahwanee Ave
Sunnyvale CA 94085
P: 408-744-6710   PRC:53
www.prisminks.com
Email: orders@prisminks.com
Estab: 1999

Graham Dracup, Technical Support Department Manager
Rocky Road, Security Coordinator
Gul Kalal, Accountant
Griselda Quintero, Logistical Support Department
Amir Ajanee, Business Development Department

Manufacturer of inkjet printer inks to the proofing, signage, photography, arts and coding sectors. The company's products comprise UV curable and textile inks.

Pro Lab Orthotics   HQ
575 Airpark Rd
Napa CA 94558-7514
P: 707-257-4400   PRC:190
prolaborthotics.com

Paul R. Scherer, Founder
Jose Tirado, VPG Tech
Todd Izuhara, General Manager
Vicki Avila, Marketing Manager
Dan DeMars, Human Resource Manager

Manufacturer and supplier of orthoses products. The company's offerings include foot orthoses, pathology orthoses, and specialty orthoses.

Pro-Form Laboratories   HQ
PO Box 626
Orinda CA 94563
P: 707-752-9010   F: 707-752-9014   PRC:272
proformlabs.com
Email: info@proformlabs.com

Alex Gillespie, CEO & Co-Founder
Ryan Gillespie, Direction of Operations & Co-Founder
Jeff Mitchell, CFO & COO
Caryn David, VP of Supply Chains
JoAnn Gillespie, VP of Administration

Developer and producer of nutritional powders. The company also specializes in contract manufacturing services.

Pro-Tek Manufacturing Inc   HQ
4849 Southfront Rd
Livermore CA 94551
P: 925-454-8100   F: 925-454-8101   PRC:80
www.protekmfg.com
Email: protek@protekmfg.com
Estab: 1981

Ron Biela, Sales Account Manager
Wade Menard, Production Manager
Bill Ness, Manager of Estimating & Purchasing

Provider of sheet metal fabrication and machining services. The company is involved in prototyping and manufacturing.

Prob-Test Inc   HQ
364 W Tullock St   [N]
Rialto CA 92376
P: 909-421-4444   F: 909-421-4440   PRC:159
www.probtest.com
Emp: 11-50   Estab: 2005

Jeanne Lambeth, Office Manager

Designer and developer of military training equipment such as laser transmitters, man-worn detectors, vehicle detector assembles and etc.

Procept Biorobotics   HQ
900 Island Dr Ste 101
Redwood City CA 94065
P: 650-232-7200   F: 650-232-5782   PRC:189
procept-biorobotics.com
Email: info@procept-biorobotics.com
Estab: 2009

Reza Zadno, President & CEO
Kevin Waters, SVP & CFO
Surag Mantri, SVP of Research & Development
Eric Steuben, VP of Operations
Sham Shiblaq, Commercial SVP

Provider of healthcare services. The company primarily focuses on personalized image-guided waterjet tissue resection services.

Process Engineers Inc   HQ
26569 Corporate Ave
Hayward CA 94595
P: 510-782-5122   F: 510-785-8187   PRC:80
www.peiequipment.com

Gabriel Heredia, Production Manager
John Cortessis, Regional Sales Manager

Manufacturer of stainless steel equipment. The company also specializes in installation and other services.

Process Metrix Corp   BR
6622 Owens Dr
Pleasanton CA 94588
P: 925-460-0385   F: 925-460-0728   PRC:171
processmetrix.com
Estab: 1987

Tom Harvill, CTO
Donald Holve, Partner
Michel Bonin, Managing Partner

Supplier of instruments for industrial measurement and control. The company's products are used in molten metal applications.

Process Solutions Inc   HQ
550 Sycamore Dr
Milpitas CA 95035
P: 408-370-6540   F: 408-866-4660   PRC:144
4psi.net
Estab: 2003

Gunnar Thordarson, President

Provider of disinfection solutions. The company is engaged in facility management services and serves the commercial sector.

ProcessWeaver Inc   BR
5201 Great America Pkwy Ste 300
Santa Clara CA 95054
P: 888-932-8373   PRC:323
www.processweaver.com
Email: sales@processweaver.com
Estab: 2005

Kumar Vidadala, President & CEO
Don Spatola, COO
Bhavana Musuluri, SVP
Martin Garza, Senior Director
Prasad Chandra, Marketing Manager

Developer of multi-carrier shipping software and a provider of shipping solutions. The company also offers inbound and desktop shipping solutions.

Proco Products Inc   HQ
2431 N Wigwam Dr
Stockton CA 95205
P: 209-943-6088   F: 209-943-0242   PRC:159
www.procoproducts.com
Estab: 1980

Ed Marchese, CEO
Cal Hayes, General Manager

Manufacturer of expansion joints. The company serves the oil and gas, power generation, chemical, and steel industries.

Procurement Partners International Inc   HQ
133 30th Ave
San Mateo CA 94403-2712
P: 650-345-6118   F: 650-574-1081   PRC:88
www.thesourcepros.com
Email: info@thesourcepros.com
Estab: 1998

James Landi, Account Sales Manager

Provider of procurement services. The company offers mechanical components such as pins, rods, rollers, and sheet metal.

Prodigy Surface Tech Inc HQ
807 Aldo Ave Ste 103
Santa Clara CA 95054
P: 408-492-9390 F: 408-492-9391 PRC:157
www.prodigysurfacetech.com
Email: info@prodigysurfacetech.com
Estab: 2002

John Shaw, President

Provider of alternative to common electroplating shop. The company focuses on chem lab for analysis, blaster, and clean room.

Product Components Corp HQ
825 Arnold Dr Ste 7
Martinez CA 94553
P: 925-228-8930 F: 925-228-8933 PRC:84
www.product-components.com
Email: sales@product-components.com
Estab: 1962

Susan Lenz, Owner

Manufacturer of industrial plastic fasteners. The company offers screws, washers, pipe plugs, circuit board hardware, and other products.

Product Slingshot Inc HQ
2221 Rutherford Rd [N]
Carlsbad CA 92008
P: 760-929-9380 F: 760-929-9357 PRC:80
www.forecast3d.com
Email: hello@forecast3d.com
Estab: 1994

Guido Degen, CEO
Ulrich Wolf, CFO
Jason Goldman, Secretary

Provider of business services.

Production Robotics Inc HQ
562 Whitney St
San Leandro CA 94577
P: 510-777-0375 F: 510-777-9033 PRC:80
www.productionrobotics.com
Email: info@productionrobotics.com
Estab: 1986

Leonard Ginsburg, President
Greg Majewski, Machine Shop Manager
Jayaram Bhattarai, Quality Systems Manager
Shaon Ghosh, Office Manager
Marco Ginsburg, Automation Engineer

Designer and manufacturer of specialty engineered automation systems. The company serves biotech, diagnostics, microsurgery, and other sectors.

Professional Finishing HQ
770 Market Ave
Richmond CA 94801
P: 510-233-7629 F: 510-233-1359 PRC:47
www.professionalfinishing.com
Estab: 1979

Pat Ramnarine, VP
Gordon Zammit, Director
David Buchholz, General Manager
Jing Li, Director of Design Verification
Melissa Burks, Marketing Manager

Provider of liquid and powder coatings and finishing to the scientific and aerospace industries. The company focuses on sandblasting and silk screening.

M-248

Profusa Inc HQ
5959 Horton St Ste 450
Emeryville CA 94608
P: 415-655-9861 PRC:187
profusa.com
Email: info@profusa.com
Estab: 2009

Bill McMillan, Co-Founder & President & CSO
Natalie Wisniewski, Co-Founder & CTO
Ben Hwang, Chairman & CEO
Bruce Smith, Chief of Staff
Hesham Younis, VP of Products & VP of Business Development

Focuses on the development of biointegrated sensors. The company offers services to the environment sector.

Progenitor Cell Therapy BR
291 N Bernardo Ave
Mountain View CA 94043
P: 650-964-6744 PRC:34
www.pctcelltherapy.com
Estab: 1999

Brian Hanifin, VP of Technical Operations North America
J.O. Anne Valentino, VP of Head of Global Quality
Jacob Ceccarelli, Biotechnology Engineer
Thomas Heathman, Business Leader

Manufacturer of biotechnology products. The company develops cell therapy products on a contract basis.

Progent Corp HQ
2570 N First St 2nd Fl
San Jose CA 95131
P: 408-785-4781 PRC:323
www.progent.com
Email: information@progent.com
Estab: 2000

Les Kent, Founder & President
Tom Anderson, VP of Consulting Services
Beverly Katz, Controller

Provider of online technical support for small networks, and specializes in remote diagnosis, repair, and consulting services.

Progressive Concepts Machining HQ
1236 Quarry Ln Ste 104
Pleasanton CA 94566-4730
P: 925-426-0400 F: 925-426-0709 PRC:80
www.proconmach.com
Email: sales@proconmach.com
Estab: 1987

Chris Studzinski, President

Provider of welding, assembly, and machining services. The company also deals with inspection solutions and serves businesses.

Progressive Technology Inc HQ
4130 Citrus Ave Ste 17
Rocklin CA 95677
P: 916-632-6715 F: 916-632-9348 PRC:185
www.prgtech.com
Email: sales@prgtech.com

Shannon Rogers, President
Mike Fischer, Business Developer

Manufacturer of orthodontic braces. The company provides sapphire, alumina, zirconia, ceramic, and quartz braces.

Project Partners LLC HQ
520 Purissima St
Half Moon Bay CA 94019
P: 650-712-6200 F: 650-726-7975 PRC:326
projectp.com
Email: info@projectp.com
Estab: 1997

Randy Egger, President & CEO
Tamim Kulaly, VP of Oracle Primavera Solutions
David McNeil, VP of Oracle Services
Neeraj Garg, VP of Product Development

Provider of business solutions and information technology systems. The company offers NetSuite, Oracle Fusion Applications, and Primavera.

Prolynx LLC HQ
455 Mission Bay Blvd S Ste 145
San Francisco CA 94158
P: 415-552-5306 PRC:34
prolynxllc.com

Gary W. Ashley, Founder & Chief Scientific Officer
Daniel Santi, President
Louise Robinson, Senior Scientist
Eric Schneider, Senior Scientist II
Sam Pfaff, Scientist

Developer of technology solutions for releasable linkers. The company also specializes in injectable drugs.

ProMab Biotechnologies Inc HQ
2600 Hilltop Dr Bldg B Ste C320
Richmond CA 94806
P: 510-860-4615 F: 510-740-3625 PRC:34
promab.com
Email: info@promab.com
Estab: 2001

John Wu, CEO

Provider of cell isolation kits, custom antibodies, cancer stem cells, and recombinant protein products.

Promax Tools Lp HQ
11312 Sunrise Gold Cir
Rancho Cordova CA 95742
P: 916-638-0501 F: 916-638-0512 PRC:157
promaxtools.com
Estab: 1967

Nancy Owens, President

Manufacturer of solid carbide round tools. The company offers finishing end mills, die and mold tools, and solid carbide end mills.

ProMedia Audio & Video HQ
777 Arnold Dr Ste 100
Martinez CA 94553
P: 510-741-2925 F: 510-741-0790 PRC:209
www.promediaaudiovideo.com
Estab: 1978

Ted Leamy, SVP of Sales & Marketing
Mike Trimble, Engineer
Zachary Calhoun, Audio Engineer & Shop Assistant
Mike Chase, Sales Design Engineer

Focuses on the integration of audio/video and performance audio systems. The company serves educational facilities, concert halls, and auditoriums.

Promex Industries Inc HQ
3075 Oakmead Village Dr
Santa Clara CA 95051
P: 408-496-0222 PRC:209
promex-ind.com
Email: cpugh@promex-ind.com
Estab: 1975

Richard Otte, President & CEO
Annette Teng, CTO
Michael Lopez, COO
Yvonne Esquer, VP of Administration
Rosie Medina, Director of Sales & Marketing

Provider of packaging solutions. The company
is engaged in onshore production process flows
using process development.

Promise Technology Inc HQ
580 Cottonwood Dr
Milpitas CA 95035
P: 408-228-1400 F: 408-228-1100 PRC:95
www.promise.com
Email: sales@promise.com
Estab: 1988

James Lee, President
Heidi Tsui, Senior HR Manager
Nagendra Vadlakunta, Senior Firmware Engineer
Thanh Ngo, Logistics & Warehouse Specialist
Tiffany Chang, Controller

Provider of storage solutions such as cloud and
surveillance storage and virtual tape library for
digital home applications.

Promptu HQ
333 Ravenswood Ave Bldg 201
Menlo Park CA 94025
P: 650-859-5800 F: 650-859-6985 PRC:67
www.promptu.com
Estab: 2000

Giuseppe Staffaroni, President & CEO
Harry Printz, CTO & VP of Engineering
Jason Simpson, VP of Product Marketing
Daniele Poggetta, VP of Business Development
Wolfgang Appuhn, Director Business Development

Provider of voice-activated search and navigation
services. The company is also engaged in engineering and product marketing.

Pronto Networks HQ
1966 Tice Valley Blvd [N]
Walnut Creek CA 94595
P: 925-860-6200 F: 267-873-8803 PRC:319
www.prontonetworks.com
Email: info@prontonetworks.com
Emp: 51-200 Estab: 2001

Jasbir Singh, Chairman & Founder
Nisha Singh, CFO
Ravi Kasturi, Director of Engineering

Provider of Wi-Fi operation support system solutions for enterprises, wireless ISPs, WiMAX and
satellite networks.

Proofpoint Inc RH
892 Ross Dr
Sunnyvale CA 94089
P: 408-517-4710 F: 408-517-4711 PRC:324
www.proofpoint.com
Email: federalsales@proofpoint.com
Estab: 2002
Sales: $300M to $1 Billion

Gary Steele, CEO & Chairman
Blake P. Salle, CRO
Marcel DePaolis, CTO
Paul Auvil, CFO
David Knight, EVP & General Manger of Security
Products

Manufacturer of threat, email, social media, and
information protection products. The company
offers security and compliance solutions.

ProPlus Design Solutions Inc HQ
2025 Gateway Pl Ste 130
San Jose CA 95110
P: 408-459-6128 F: 408-459-6111 PRC:326
proplussolutions.com
Email: info@proplussolution.com
Estab: 2006

James Ma, President
Zhihong Liu, Chairman & CEO
Lianfeng Yang, SVP of Marketing & Business
Development
Hancheng Liang, VP of Research & Development
Yutao Ma, VP of Research & Development

Provider of electronic design automation solutions.
The company's products include NoisePro, Nano-
Spice, and NanoYield.

Prosoft Engineering Inc HQ
1599 Greenville Rd
Livermore CA 94550
P: 877-477-6763 PRC:322
www.prosofteng.com
Estab: 1985

Greg Brewer, CEO

Developer of data recovery software. The company provides Drive Genius, Data Rescue, and Data
Backup software.

Prosthetic Artists Inc HQ
1736 Professional Dr
Sacramento CA 95825
P: 916-485-4249 F: 916-485-4389 PRC:190
prostheticartists.com
Estab: 1931

Eric M. Lindsey, President & CEO
Paul Martin, Account Manager

Provider of impression-fitted, hand-sculpted,
hand-painted ocular prosthesis. The company also
fits thin shell prosthesis over disfigured eyes.

Prosthetic Solutions Inc HQ
191 San Felipe Rd Ste M1
Hollister CA 95023
P: 831-637-0491 PRC:190
www.prosthetic-solutions.com
Estab: 2001

Steve Geib, Owner
Wade Skardoutos, President & CEO
Susan Stenman, Clinic Director
Linda Ornelas, Office Manager
Stephanie Eden, Office Manager

Manufacturer of medical devices. The company
improves the lives of amputees by providing them
prosthesis.

Prosurg Inc HQ
2195 Trade Zone Blvd
San Jose CA 95131
P: 408-945-4044 F: 408-945-1390 PRC:195
www.prosurg.com
Email: mail@prosurg.com
Estab: 1989

Ashvin Desai, President
Twila Conner, Quality Assurance Manager

Manufacturer of medical devices. The company
offers products for women's and men's healthcare,
urological and gynecological disorders.

Protec Arisawa America Inc HQ
2455 Ash St [N]
Vista CA 92081
P: 760-599-4800 F: 760-597-4830 PRC:159
www.protec-arisawa.com

Rick Chacon, Manager
Stephane Kessaci, Manager

Designer and manufacturer of fiber reinforced
plastic pressure vessels for membrane filtration
systems.

Protection Plus Security Services Inc HQ
40543 Encyclopedia Cir
Fremont CA 94538
P: 510-770-9900 F: 510-770-9915 PRC:59
protectionplussecurity.com
Email: info@protectionplussecurity.com
Estab: 1990

Patrick Torpey, President

Provider of installation services to the electronic
security industry. The company's products include
access control, video surveillance, and fire alarm
systems.

Protein Research HQ
1852 Rutan Dr
Livermore CA 94551
P: 925-243-6300 F: 925-243-6308 PRC:268
www.proteinresearch.com
Estab: 1968

Ashley Matheson, President
Robert Matheson, CEO
Melissa Matheson, VP
Gary Troxel, VP of Business Development
Melissa Dethardt, VP

Manufacturer of nutritional products. The company
develops and formulates supplements for human
nutrition in capsules, tablets, powders and pre-
mixes.

ProteinSimple HQ
3001 Orchard Pkwy
San Jose CA 95134
P: 408-510-5500   F: 408-510-5599   PRC:31
www.proteinsimple.com
Email: info@proteinsimple.com
Estab: 2004

John Proctor, Director of Marketing & VP of Marketing
Robert Gavin, SVP
David Voehringer, Director of Sales
Tom Yang, Director of Engineering
Jessica Dermody, Director of R&D Science

Developer of proprietary systems, immunoassay system and consumables for protein analysis and purity of protein-based therapeutics.

Protemp Mechanical Inc HQ
3350 Scott Blvd Bldg 3
Santa Clara CA 95054
P: 408-244-9821   F: 408-980-9358   PRC:138
protemp.net
Email: info@protemp.net

Marty Reich, President

Provider of environmental test equipment calibration services. The company's services include preventative maintenance, chamber modifications, and consulting.

Proteus Digital Health Inc HQ
2600 Bridge Pkwy
Redwood City CA 94065
P: 650-632-4031   F: 650-632-4071   PRC:268
www.proteus.com
Email: press@proteus.com
Estab: 2001

David O'Reilly, CPO
Jafar Shenasa, VP-Head of Regulatory Affairs
Rob Duck, Director of Automation & Test
Peter Bjeletich, Director of Process Integration
Emily Fox, Head of Communications

Providers of health care service technology. The company offers health care products based on electronics technology.

Proteus Industries Inc HQ
340 Pioneer Way
Mountain View CA 94041
P: 650-964-4163   F: 650-965-9355   PRC:14
www.proteusind.com
Email: sales@proteusind.com
Estab: 1978

Jon Heiner, President
Grant Gower, Director of Marketing
Hamed Ershad, Automation Engineer
Alex Gahrahmat, Senior Sales Engineer
Wiki Fragiao, Customer Service Lead

Developer and manufacturer of rugged and sensitive flow sensing and control instruments. The company focuses on marketing.

Prothena RH
331 Oyster Point Blvd
S San Francisco CA 94080
P: 650-837-8550   F: 650-837-8560   PRC:24
www.prothena.com
Email: info@prothena.com

Gene G. Kinney, President & CEO & Director
Tran B. Nguyen, CFO & COO
Wagner M. Zago, CSO
Karin L. Walker, CAO
Tara Nickerson, Chief Business Officer

Focuses on the discovery, development and commercialization of protein immunotherapy programs for the treatment of diseases that involve amyloid.

Proto Services Inc HQ
1991 Concourse Dr
San Jose CA 95131
P: 408-719-9088   F: 408-719-9091   PRC:211
protoservices.com
Estab: 1998

Norman Lee, VP
Lan Tran, Program Manager

Provider of process verification, yield analysis, testing design, program management, and functional debugging services.

ProTrials Research Inc HQ
333 W San Carlos St Ste 800
San Jose CA 95110
P: 650-864-9180   F: 650-864-9190   PRC:37
protrials.com
Email: info@protrials.com
Estab: 1996

Inger Arum, Founder & CEO
Matthew Smith, CRO
Wendy Powers, Director of Business Development
Colette Tuttle, Director of Line Management
Jennifer Bui, Director of Finance

Provider of clinical research services. The company offers the ability to move a new drug or device from conception to FDA approval.

Proulx Manufacturing Inc HQ
11433 Sixth St   [N]
Rancho Cucamonga CA 91730
P: 909-980-0662   PRC:189
www.proulxmfg.com
Emp: 11-50   Estab: 1970

Richard A. Proulx, Contact

Manufacturer of trimmers.

Prousys Inc HQ
4700 New Horizon Blvd   [N]
Bakersfield CA 93313
P: 661-837-4001   F: 661-837-4004   PRC:304
www.prousys.com
Email: prousys@prousys.com
Emp: 51-200   Estab: 1999

Kevin Mueller, President
Mike Burton, EVP of Corporate Business Development
Mirek Kovalski, Eng. Manager
Christopher Diaz, Project Manager & Estimator
Scott Rupert, Sr. Project Engineer

Provider of computer programming services, custom-designed software, systems development, and integration.

Provectus IT Inc HQ
125 University Ave Ste 290
Palo Alto CA 94301
P: 877-951-2224   PRC:315
reinvently.com
Email: hello@reinvently.com
Estab: 2010

Olga Korchmar, Business Development Manager

Accelerates digital transformation by using Artificial Intelligence.

Providence Medical Technology Inc HQ
3875 Hopyard Rd Ste 300
Pleasanton CA 94588
P: 415-923-9376   F: 415-923-9377   PRC:188
www.providencemt.com
Email: providence@providencemt.com
Estab: 2008

Jeff Smith, CEO & Founder
Edward Liou, COO
Greg Curhan, CFO & SVP of Corporate Development
Rebecca Chung, VP of Human Resources
Jeremy Laynor, VP of Sales

Developer of medical devices and technologies such as dtrax spinal systems, cavux cervical cages, and ally screw systems for cervical spine care.

Prowess Inc HQ
1844 Clayton Rd
Concord CA 94520
P: 925-356-0360   F: 925-356-0363   PRC:194
www.prowess.com

John Nguyen, CEO & President
Rick Smith, Sales Marketing Manager & QA Manager
Vivi Tran, Project Manager & Software Engineer
Tan Pham, Software Engineer
Sharon Springorum, Contact

Focuses on Windows-based treatment planning systems for radiation therapy treatment and OIS software.

Proxim Diagnostics Corp HQ
325 E Middlefield Rd
Mountain View CA 94043
P: 408-391-6090   PRC:186
www.proximdx.com
Email: hello@proximdx.com
Estab: 2009

Mikhail Briman, CEO & Co-Founder
Vikram Joshi, Co-Founder

Manufacturer of diagnostics products and related supplies. The company deals with testing and research related services.

Proxim Wireless HQ
2114 Ringwood Ave
San Jose CA 95131
P: 408-383-7600   F: 408-383-7680   PRC:68
www.proxim.com

Fred Huey, CEO & CFO

Provider of Wi-Fi, point-to-point, and 4G wireless network technologies. The company's ORINOCO product is used by service providers and enterprises.

Proxio Inc — HQ
3945 Freedom Cir Ste 940
Santa Clara CA 95054
P: 415-723-1691 — PRC:326
www.proxio.com
Estab: 2007

Janet Case, CEO & Co-Founder
Peter Spicer, CTO & Co-Founder

Provider of digital real estate marketing solutions for agents, brokers and developers. The company serves businesses.

Prunella Enterprises Inc — HQ
986 Tower Pl
Santa Cruz CA 95062
P: 831-465-1818 — PRC:80
www.prunellaenterprises.com
Estab: 1983

Scott Prunella, President

Provider of custom machining and sub assembly services. The company serves the telecommunication and space sectors.

Prysm Inc — HQ
180 Baytech Dr Ste 200
San Jose CA 95134
P: 408-586-1100   F: 408-957-0364 — PRC:169
www.prysm.com
Email: support@prysm.com
Estab: 2005

Amit Jain, President & CEO & Co-Founder
Roger Hajjar, CTO & SVP of LPD Business Unit & Co-Founder
Jasbir Singh, CFO & SVP of Finance
Paige O'Neill, CMO
Patrick Finn, VP

Provider of large format digital display solutions and software for real-time visual communication applications.

PSC Electronics Inc — HQ
2307 Calle Del Mundo
Santa Clara CA 95054
P: 408-737-1333   F: 408-737-0502 — PRC:124
www.pscelex.com
Email: info@pscelex.com
Estab: 1985

Bob Gularte, VP of Sales & Engineering
Rick Maclaszek, VP
Charlie Colson, Branch Manager
Todd Derbique, Field Sales Engineer
Jena Craycroft, Sales Associate

Distributor of magnetic, interconnect, and electro-mechanical components. The company specializes in cable assembly and modification.

PTM & W Industries Inc — HQ
10640 S Painter Ave — [N]
Santa Fe Springs CA 90670
P: 562-946-4511   F: 562-941-4773 — PRC:280
www.ptm-w.com
Estab: 1959

Charles Owen, President
Bill Ryan, VP
John Kapadia, Technical Director
Pat Owen, Office Manager
Bud Turner, Manager of Sales

Manufacturer of laminated plastics plate and sheet.

PTR Manufacturing Inc — HQ
33390 Transit Ave
Union City CA 94587
P: 510-477-9654   F: 510-477-9653 — PRC:82
www.ptrmanufacturing.com

Sai La, President
Phong La, General Manager

Manufacturer of machining and sheet metals. The company offers manufacturing and manufacturing presentation services.

PubMatic Inc — HQ
3 Lagoon Dr Ste 180
Redwood City CA 94065
P: 650-331-3485 — PRC:325
www.pubmatic.com
Estab: 2006

Rajeev Goel, Co-Founder & CEO
Amar Goel, Chief Growth Officer & Co-Founder & Chairman
Cathie Black, President
Angela Pimentel, Assistant Controller & Senior Accounting Manager & Accounting Manager

Developer of marketing automation software. The company deals with the planning of media campaigns and offers services to publishers.

Pulmonx Corp — HQ
700 Chesapeake Dr
Redwood City CA 94063
P: 650-364-0400   F: 650-364-0403 — PRC:196
www.pulmonx.com
Email: liberate@pulmonx.com
Estab: 1995

Beran Rose, CCO
Marcee Maroney, VP
Lauren Cristina, VP of Finance & Administration
Sri Radhakrishnan, VP of Research & Development & Operations
Lisa Simmonds, Director of Supply Chain

Manufacturer of medical devices. The company focuses on developing both diagnostic and therapeutic technologies for Interventional Pulmonology.

Pulsar Vascular Inc — HQ
4030 Moorpark Ave
San Jose CA 95117
P: 408-260-9264 — PRC:186

Viet Le, Quality Director
Kevin Robert Costello, Contact

Manufacturer of endovascular diseases and it focuses on the treatment of complex aneurysms. The company is engaged in clinical trials.

Pulse Secure LLC — HQ
2700 Zanker Rd Ste 200
San Jose CA 95134
P: 408-372-9600 — PRC:319
www.pulsesecure.net
Email: info@pulsesecure.net
Estab: 2014

Sudhakar Ramakrishna, CEO
Jeffrey Key, CFO
Younus Aftab, VP of Product
Andreas Koch, VP
Yvonne Sang, Director of Software Engineering

Provider of product, hardware, partner, and enterprise solutions. The company offers services to the financial services and healthcare industries.

Pulver Labs Inc — HQ
320 N Santa Cruz Ave
Los Gatos CA 95031-2353
P: 408-399-7000   F: 408-399-7001 — PRC:41
pulverlabs.com
Email: information@pulverlabs.com
Estab: 1979

Lee Pulver, Founder & President & Chairman of the Board

Provider of equipment evaluation and testing services. The company also offers services for information technology, industrial and medical equipment.

Pump Engineering Co — HQ
9807 Jordan Cir — [N]
Santa Fe Springs CA 90670
P: 562-944-4768 — PRC:80
www.pumpengineering.net
Email: sales@pumpengineering.net
Emp: 51-200   Estab: 1946

Jim Soper, Manager of Sales
Rick Walsh, Manager of Sales

Distributor of pumps, fluid handling systems and much more.

Punchcut LLC — HQ
150 California St 9th Fl
San Francisco CA 94111
P: 415-445-8855 — PRC:325
punchcut.com
Email: business@punchcut.com
Estab: 2002

Jared Benson, Co-Founder & Executive Creative Director
Ken Olewiler, Principal & Managing Director & Co-Founder
Lonny Chu, Senior Director & Interaction Design
Nate Cox, Senior Director of Solutions
Jason Y. Siu, Senior Engineer

Provider of interface designs. The company offers mid, small, large, micro, and medium screen solutions.

Pure Storage Inc — HQ
650 Castro St Ste 400
Mountain View CA 94041
P: 833-371-7873   F: 650-625-9667 — PRC:95
purestorage.com
Email: info@purestorage.com
Estab: 2009
Sales: $1B to $3B

David Hatfield, President
Charles Giancarlo, Chairman & CEO
Scott Dietzen, Vice Chairman
Chadd Kenney, VP & CTO of Americas
Johanna Jackman, CPO

Provider of flash storage solutions. The company is focused on developing flash arrays for various enterprises.

Purigen Biosystems Inc   HQ
5700 Stoneridge Dr Ste 100
Pleasanton CA 94588
P: 877-787-4436   PRC:24
www.purigenbio.com
Email: info@purigenbio.com
Estab: 2012

Klint Rose, CSO & Founder
Peter V. Leigh, CEO
Pam Delucchi, SVP of Operations
Priyanka Agrawal, Analogs Manager
Gomathi Komanduru, Senior Analog

Provider of biotechnology such as isotachophoresis, an electric-field driven technique for extracting and quantifying DNA and RNA from biological samples.

Puronics Inc   HQ
5775 Las Positas Rd
Livermore CA 94551
P: 925-456-7000   F: 925-456-7010   PRC:144
puronics.com
Email: info@puronics.com
Estab: 2006

Scott A. Batiste, CEO
Joanne Wong, Operations Coordinator

Manufacturer of water treatment equipment. The company's products include drinking water systems, water softeners, and reverse osmosis systems.

Purple Communications Inc   HQ
595 Menlo Dr
Rocklin CA 95765
P: 877-885-3172   PRC:68
purplevrs.com
Estab: 1982

Francine Cummings, VP
Donald Cooler, District Manager
James Parker, Strategic Sales Manager
Pascal Lemke, Center Supervisor

Provider of communication services to deaf or hard of hearing people. The company serves the medical sector and clinics.

Pyramid Orthodontics   HQ
4328 Redwood Hwy Ste 100
San Rafael CA 94903
P: 877-337-3708   PRC:190
www.pyramidorthodontics.com
Estab: 1987

Rodney Schmitt, Owner
Greg De Boer, Owner
Sacha Laskar, Manager

Provider of orthodontics products. The company's products include clear brackets, bands, buccal tubes, and wire accessories.

Pyramid Semiconductor Corp   HQ
1249 Reamwood Ave
Sunnyvale CA 94089
P: 408-734-8200   F: 408-734-0962   PRC:208
www.pyramidsemiconductor.com
Email: info@pyramidsemiconductor.com
Estab: 2003

Joe Rothstein, President & CEO
Doug Beaubien, VP of Operations
Jagtar Sandhu, VP of Quality Assurance

Provider of assembly services. The company is focused in the assembly of monolithic ceramic products and multi-chip modules.

Pyxis Laboratories Inc   HQ
12499 Loma Rica Dr
Grass Valley CA 95945
P: 949-598-1978   PRC:41
www.pyxislabs.com
Email: orders@pyxislabs.com
Estab: 1997

Ines Moretti, President & Founder
Carolina Rojas, Director of Operations & Sales

Specializes in the research, development and production of specialty reagents for the diagnostics, pharmaceutical, and environmental industries.

Q Analysts LLC   HQ
4320 Stevens Creek Blvd Ste 130
San Jose CA 95129
P: 408-907-8500   F: 408-907-8515   PRC:326
www.qanalysts.com
Email: info@qanalysts.com
Estab: 2003

Ross Fernandes, CEO
Bob Long, Director of Talent Acquisition
Angelo Andriamalala, Local Director
Haran Kosambi, Talent Acquisition Manager
Piper Berge, Senior IT Project Manager & Kaiser

Provider of consulting, strategic advisory, and related compliance services. The company is also involved in mobile testing.

Qantel Technologies   HQ
3506 Breakwater Ct
Hayward CA 94545-3611
P: 510-731-2080   F: 510-731-2121   PRC:322
www.qantel.com
Estab: 1969

Michael Galvin, President & CTO
Jerry DeVries, VP of Application Development
Richard G. Morton, Director of Regional Sales
Carroll A. Bowen, Director of Customer Relations
Christy Garrelts, Regional Services Manager

Manufacturer of software systems. The company provides network connectivity and business software solutions.

Qarbon Inc   HQ
111 N Market St Ste 300
San Jose CA 95113
P: 408-430-5560   F: 408-430-5570   PRC:322
www.qarbon.com
Email: sales@qarbon.com
Estab: 1997

Jay Lucke, President & CEO
Jim Lynch, Secretary & Chairman
Dave Mosby, Director

Publisher of presentation software and the originator of patented Viewlet technology. The company serves business, government, and education markers.

Qardio Inc   HQ
115 Sansome St
San Francisco CA 94104
P: 855-240-7323   PRC:187
www.getqardio.com
Estab: 2012

Marco Peluso, Co-Founder & CEO
Rosario Iannella, Co-Founder
Alexis Zervoglos, Chief Business Officer
Betty Peng, Marketing Director

Creator of health monitoring devices such as blood pressure monitor, multiple-sensor EKG, and wireless scale and body analyzer.

QB3   HQ
1700 Fourth St Byers Hall Ste 214
San Francisco CA 94158
P: 415-514-9790   PRC:24
qb3.org
Estab: 2000

Nora Ke, Executive Assistant to the Director
Susan Marqusee, Director
Nevan Krogan, Director
Kaspar Mossman, Director of Communications & Marketing
Regis Kelly, Executive Director & Byers Family Distinguished Professor

Provider of life science services. The company focuses on research facilities, internships, mentoring, and seed-stage venture fund.

Qct LLC   HQ
1010 Rincon Cir
San Jose CA 95131
P: 510-270-6111   F: 510-270-6161   PRC:95
qct.io
Email: sales@quantaqct.com

Michael Quan, Director Sales Engineering

Provider of computer network services. The company also offers storage, database management, and data backup solutions.

Qi Medical Inc   HQ
13366 Grass Valley Ave Ste B
Grass Valley CA 95945
P: 530-272-8700   PRC:34
www.qimedical.com
Email: info@qimedical.com
Estab: 1992

Jan Hedman, Owner
Brady Schwarz, President

Manufacturer of fingertip testing, syringe filters, rinse fluids, incubators, and vial adaptors for pharmacists and nurses who handle sterile solutions.

Qool Therapeutics Inc   HQ
453 Ravendale Dr Ste G
Mountain View CA 94043
P: 650-328-1426   PRC:269
qooltherapeutics.com
Email: bhuss@qooltherapeutics.com
Estab: 2005

Amir Belson, Founder & CTO
Beverly Huss, CEO & President
Dalton W. Dietrich, Chair in Neurosurgery & Professor of Neurological Surgery of Neurology & Biology & Anatomy
Kim Tompkins, VP of Regulatory Quality & Clinical Affairs
Mike Horzewski, SVP of Research & Development & Operations

Developer of therapeutic hypothermia/temperature management therapies to preserve cells and tissues. The company serves the medical industry.

QSolv Inc HQ
440 N Wolfe Rd
Sunnyvale CA 94085
P: 408-962-3803 PRC:323
qsolv-inc.com
Estab: 1997

Sujaya S, Director
Pradeep P., Resource Manager
Sandy V., Business Development Manager
Son Nguyen, Software Engineer
Shiju Radhakrishnan, Technical Recruiter

Provider of cloud automation services. The
company provides network management, gap
analysis, tool evaluation, and framework implementation services.

Qspec Technology Inc HQ
1190 Mountain View Aliso Rd Ste J
Sunnyvale CA 94089
P: 408-541-1398 PRC:41
qspec.us
Email: analysis@qspec.us

Jack Sheng, Founder

Provider of surface analysis and materials characterization services. The company's applications
include device processing for microelectronics.

QT Ultrasound LLC HQ
3 Hamilton Landing Ste 180
Novato CA 94949
P: 415-842-7250 PRC:304
qtultrasound.com
Estab: 2011

John C. Klock, CEO & CMO
Mark Lenox, CTO
Ronald T LoVetri, COO
Rajni Natesan, CMO
Meg Donigan, CSO

Developer of ultrasound devices. The company
is involved in software development and clinical
testing services.

Quadbase Systems Inc HQ
275 Saratoga Ave Ste 105
Santa Clara CA 95050
P: 408-982-0835 F: 408-982-0838 PRC:323
www.quadbase.com
Email: sales@quadbase.com
Estab: 1988

Fred Luk, President

Designer of web-delivered and mobile enabled
business intelligence reporting, charting, and
dashboard tools.

Quail Electronics Inc HQ
2171 Research Dr
Livermore CA 94550-3805
P: 925-373-6700 F: 925-373-7099 PRC:200
www.quail.com
Estab: 1988

Denise Ruppert, CFO
Larrie Pimentel, Contact

Manufacturer of power cord supplies for the OEM
market. The company offers solutions for power
cords, current cords, and adapters, and traveler
kits.

Qualdeval International HQ
48837 Sauvignon Ct
Fremont CA 94539
P: 844-247-2523 PRC:80
qualdeval.com
Email: inquires@qualdeval.com

Ivy Lin, President
Gerry McFaull, CEO

Supplier of high-pressure fluid flow and special
core analysis equipment. The company offers
PCB fabrication and assembly, and other services.

Qualitau Inc HQ
5303 Betsy Ross Dr
Santa Clara CA 95054
P: 650-282-6226 F: 650-230-9192 PRC:86
www.qualitau.com
Email: sales@qualitau.com
Estab: 1991

Jacob Herschmann, President
Gadi Krieger, CEO
Mark McDonald, Chief Technologist
Nava Ben-Yehuda, VP of Finance & Control
Tony Chavez, Director of Sales

Supplier of test equipment and services. The company is involved in the development of electronic
equipment for semiconductor process reliability.

Quality Circuit Assembly HQ
1709 Junction Ct Unit 380
San Jose CA 95112
P: 408-441-1001 PRC:209
www.qcamfg.com
Email: sales@qcamfg.com
Estab: 1988

Timmy Nguyen, President

Manufacturer of printed circuit board and cable
assemblies. The company is also involved in box
build and turnkey solutions.

Quality Fabrication Inc HQ
9631 Irondale Ave [N]
Chatsworth CA 91311
P: 818-709-8505 F: 818-709-4530 PRC:159
www.quality-fab.com
Emp: 51-200 Estab: 1980

Pradeep Kumar, President

Manufacturer and dealer of precision sheet metal
fabrication and machining services.

Quality Grinding Company Inc HQ
6800 Caballero Blvd [N]
Buena Park CA 90620
P: 714-228-2100 PRC:157
www.qualitygrinding.net
Estab: 1946

Cornel Feceu, President & Owner
Yvonne Ramirez, Manager of Accounting

Manufacturer of precision grinding and machining
products.

Quality Machine Engineering Inc HQ
5600 Skylane Blvd
Santa Rosa CA 95403
P: 707-528-1900 PRC:80
www.qmeinc.com
Estab: 1991

Mark Hullinger, CFO

Provider of precision engineering solutions. The
company serves the medical, semiconductor,
aerospace, and other markers.

Quality Metal Spinning & Machining Inc HQ
4047 Transport St
Palo Alto CA 94303
P: 650-858-2491 F: 650-858-2494 PRC:80
qualitymetalspinning.us

Andrew Czisch, Quality Manager

Provider of metal spinning, sputtering shielding,
and purity coils. The company's services include
packing, shipping, and handling.

Quality Quartz Engineering Inc HQ
8484 Central Ave
Newark CA 94560
P: 510-745-9200 F: 510-745-7948 PRC:80
qqe.com
Email: info@qqe.com
Estab: 1995

Scott Moseley, CEO
Kevin Cordia, EVP
Kim Phippen, Office Manager
Mezhgan Karim, Office Manager
Tim Youngdale, Manager of Sales & Marketing

Designer and manufacturer of solid quartz
products for solar, fiber optic, semiconductor, and
lighting industries.

Quality Scales Unlimited HQ
5401 Byron Hot Springs Rd
Byron CA 94514
P: 925-634-8068 PRC:13
www.scalesu.com
Email: sales@scalesu.com
Estab: 1981

Rory Ward, President & General Manager
Courtney Ward, Operations Manager
Jesse Wetherell, Regional Sales Manager

Provider of mechanical and computer based
weighing systems. The company's services include repairs, replacement, and installation.

Quality Stainless Tanks HQ
510 Caletti Ave
Windsor CA 95492
P: 707-837-2721 F: 707-837-2733 PRC:153
www.qualitystainless.com

Justin George, Fabricator & Welder

Provider of ready-made tanks. The company
offers crafted tanks, stainless winery equipment,
and special application tanks.

Quality Transformer & Electronics HQ
963 Ames Ave
Milpitas CA 95035
P: 408-263-8444　F: 408-263-8448　PRC:293
www.qte.com
Email: sales@qte.com
Estab: 1964

Tony Clift, Sales & Marketing Manager
Emilie Ho, Accounting Manager

Manufacturer and seller of transformers. The
company also specializes in power supplies and
other components.

Qualtech Circuits Inc HQ
1101 Comstock St
Santa Clara CA 95054
P: 408-727-4125　F: 408-727-1411　PRC:211
qualtechcircuits.com
Email: info@qualtechcircuits.com

Jim Khosh, CEO

Producer of printed circuit boards. The company's
products include probe cards and edge plating.

Qualys Inc HQ
919 E Hillsdale Blvd 4th Fl
Foster City CA 94404
P: 650-801-6100　F: 650-801-6101　PRC:325
www.qualys.com
Email: info@qualys.com
Estab: 1999
Sales: $300M to $1 Billion

Philippe Courtot, CEO & Chairman
Sumedh Thakar, President & Chief Product Officer
Melissa Fisher, CFO
Nicolas Chaillan, Federal CTO
Rima Touma-Bruno, Chief Human Resource
Officer

Provider of security and compliance solutions. The
company also offers asset discovery and threat
protection solutions.

QuanDx Inc HQ
770 Charcot Ave
San Jose CA 95131
P: 650-262-4140　F: 866-928-7828　PRC:186
www.quandx.com
Email: info@quandx.com
Estab: 2012

Guo-Liang Yu, Co-Founder
Matthew Lei, Co-Founder & CTO
Hao Yu, CEO
Graeme Duncan, VP of European Sales & Mar-
keting
Tom Hayhurst, Business Development Consultant

Developer of molecular diagnostics for personalized cancer treatment. The company offers
detection kits and lung cancer assays.

Quanergy Systems Inc HQ
433 Lakeside Dr
Sunnyvale CA 94085
P: 408-245-9500　F: 408-245-9503　PRC:326
www.quanergy.com

Tianyue Yu, Founder & CDO
Enzo Signore, CMO
Gary Saunders, CRO
Patrick Archambault, CFO
Tomoyuki Izuhara, VP of Engineering

Developer of smart sensing solutions. The company offers solutions for real-time 3D mapping,
object detection, and tracking.

Quanta Computer USA Inc LH
45630 Northport Loop E
Fremont CA 94538
P: 510-226-1001　F: 510-226-1012　PRC:120
www.quantatw.com
Email: service@quantafremont.com
Estab: 1988

Elton Yang, CFO
Paul Tsang, Senior Manager of IT & Facility Man-
agement of Quanta Cloud Technology
Angelina Chew, Purchasing Manager
Lin Li, Process Engineer

Provider of design and manufacturing services for
technology products. The company specializes in
cloud computing solutions.

Quanta Laboratories HQ
3199 De La Cruz Blvd
Santa Clara CA 95054
P: 408-988-0770　PRC:139
quantalabs.com
Email: quantalabs@quantalabs.com
Estab: 1985

Hong-Sun Liu, President & Founder
Mike Hauf, General Manager
Robin Gardiner, Sales Manager
Terry Liu, Marketing Manager
Martin Nobre, Test Engineer

Provider of environmental testing and consulting
services. The company offers vibration test, shock
test, and chalmers test services.

Quantapore Inc HQ
815 Dubuque Ave
S San Francisco CA 94048
P: 650-321-2032　PRC:34
www.quantapore.com
Email: info@quantapore.com
Estab: 2009

Martin Huber, CEO
Brian Conn, CFO
Brett Anderson, Fellow & Director of Integration
Jena Derrick, Laboratory Manager

Developer of anopore based nucleic acid sequencing technology. The company's technology
is used to read human genomes.

Quantenna Communications Inc HQ
1704 Automation Pkwy
San Jose CA 95131
P: 669-209-5500　F: 669-209-5501　PRC:212
www.quantenna.com
Email: info@quantenna.com
Estab: 2006

Sam Heidari, CEO
Lionel Bonnot, SVP of Marketing & Business
Development
David Carroll, VP of Worldwide Sales
Kapil Gulati, Director of Systems
Huizhao Wang, Senior Director of Software

Developer of semiconductor solutions for the
Wi-Fi networks. The company serves retail, home
networking, consumer electronics, and enterprise
needs.

Quantitative Medical Systems Inc HQ
1900 Powell St Ste 810
Emeryville CA 94608
P: 510-654-9200　F: 510-654-1168　PRC:194
www.qms-us.com
Email: qms@qms-us.com
Estab: 1976

Jackie Wong, Engineering Manager & Lead Soft-
ware Engineer
Melissa Gabriel, R&D Manager
Pat Parra, Business Development Specialist
Janice Lau, Database Administrator & Architect

Provider of medical systems and dialysis billing
software products. The company is engaged in
clinical support.

Quantum Corp HQ
224 Airport Pkwy Ste 550
San Jose CA 95110
P: 408-944-4000　PRC:319
www.quantum.com
Estab: 1980
Sales: $300M to $1 Billion

Jamie Lerner, CEO & Chairman
Liz King, CRO
Natasha King Beckley, CMO
Shahid Khan, CIO
Jamie Girouard, Chief Human Resource Officer

Provider of software for backup, recovery, and
archiving needs. The company serves the healthcare, media, and entertainment industries.

Quantum Semiconductor LLC HQ
4340 Stevens Creek Blvd Ste 284
San Jose CA 95129-1162
P: 408-243-2262　F: 408-243-2272　PRC:212
quantumsemi.com
Email: info@quantumsemi.com
Estab: 2000

Carlos Augusto, Co-Founder & CTO
Lynn Forester, Co-Founder & CEO
Pedro Diniz, Co-Founder & VP of Design Engi-
neering

Manufacturer of semiconductor devices. The
company specializes in silicon photonic receivers
and solar cells.

Quantum3D Inc HQ
1759 McCarthy Blvd
Milpitas CA 95035
P: 408-600-2500　F: 408-600-2608　PRC:319
quantum3d.com
Email: sales@quantum3d.com
Estab: 1997

Mark Matthews, President
Murat Kose, COO & CFO
Tim Stewart, VP of Business Development
Edith Talamantes, Human Resource Manager
Joe Da Silva, Test & Manufacturing Manager

Developer and manufacturer of real-time visual
simulation and computing systems for fast-jet,
helicopter, refueling, and other needs.

QuantumScape Corp HQ
1730 Technology Dr
San Jose CA 95110
P: 408-452-2007 PRC:242
www.quantumscape.com
Email: info@quantumscape.com
Estab: 2010

Jagdeep Singh, CEO & Founder & Board Chairman

Provider of energy storage, electronics, and related solutions. The company offers services to the environmental sector.

Quarterwave Corp HQ
1300 Valley House Dr Ste 100
Rohnert Park CA 94928
P: 707-793-9105 F: 707-793-9245 PRC:70
www.quarterwave.com
Email: engineering@quarterwave.com
Estab: 1987

Steven Price, CEO
Paul R. Bradshaw, General Manager
Jade May, Marketing Director
Peggy Wise, Office Manager
Larry Kalder, Electronics Technician

Manufacturer of high power traveling wave-tube amplifiers, valves, and test equipment. The company deals with installation services.

Quartet Mechanics Inc HQ
1040 Di Giulio Ave Ste 100
Santa Clara CA 95050
P: 408-564-8901 F: 510-490-1887 PRC:80
quartetmechanics.com
Email: inquiry@quartetmechanics.com

Elik Gershenzon, Senior Mechanical Engineer
J.D. Hawk, Engineer

Provider of LED, MEMS, photovoltaics (PV) solar and medical/lab automation systems. The company also offers wafer sorting and packing products.

Qubell Inc HQ
4600 Bohannon Dr Ste 220
Menlo Park CA 94025
P: 888-855-9440 PRC:323
qubell.com
Email: info@qubell.com
Estab: 2012

Eugene Horohorin, VP
Dmitry Ornatsky, Director

Specializes in autonomic management solutions. The company focuses on e-commerce and other cloud applications.

Qubop Inc HQ
301 Folsom St Ste D
San Francisco CA 94105
P: 415-891-7788 F: 415-680-1721 PRC:322
www.qubop.com
Email: info@qubop.com
Estab: 2002

Chia Hwu, CEO

Developer of applications and games for mobile platforms. The company specializes in web applications, localization, IOS, and android development.

QuesGen Systems Inc HQ
851 Burlway Rd Ste 216
Burlingame CA 94010
P: 650-777-7617 PRC:326
www.quesgen.com
Email: info@quesgen.com
Estab: 2004

Michael Jarrett, Founder & CEO
Martin Jorgensen, Director of Operations & Finance
Vibeke Brinck, Director of Client Services
Bianca Byrne, Client Services Manager

Provider of data management solutions. The company is involved in clinical research and related support services.

Quest America Inc HQ
111 N Market St Ste 300
San Jose CA 95113
P: 408-492-1650 F: 408-492-1647 PRC:322
questam.com
Estab: 1995

Soundaran Natarajan, CEO
Melo Rajakumar, COO

Provider of information technology services. The company offers solutions through strategy, consulting, and outsourcing.

Quest Business Systems Inc HQ
PO Box 715
Brentwood CA 94513
P: 925-634-2670 PRC:325
www.questbusinesssystems.com
Email: sales@questbizsystems.com
Estab: 1983

Tom Elliott, Owner

Provider of solutions in police equipment tracking systems. The company also focuses on purchasing management.

Quest Diagnostics Inc BR
3714 Northgate Blvd
Sacramento CA 95834
P: 916-927-9900 PRC:186
www.questdiagnostics.com

Jay G. Wohlgemuth, SVP of R&D Medical & CMO
Gabrielle Wolfson, CDO & CIO
Mark J. Guinan, EVP & CFO
Cecilia McKenney, SVP & Chief Human Resource Officer
Manuel O. M'ndez, SVP & Chief Commercial Officer

Provider of diagnostic laboratory testing services. The company offers a wide range of test menu for diagnosing medical conditions.

Quest Inc HQ
9000 Foothills Blvd Ste 100
Roseville CA 95747-4411
P: 800-326-4220 PRC:326
www.questsys.com
Email: contact@questsys.com
Estab: 1982

Tim Burke, CEO
Mike Dillon, CTO
Barbara Klide, Director of Marketing

Provider of technology and infrastructure management services. The company caters to a wide range of businesses.

Quest Microwave Inc HQ
225 Vineyard Ct
Morgan Hill CA 95037-7121
P: 408-778-4949 F: 408-778-4950 PRC:200
questmw.com
Estab: 1996

Nabeel Khayat, Founder

Provider of ferrite products for the microwave electronics industry. The company offers both standard and custom designs.

Quicklogic Corp HQ
2220 Lundy Ave
San Jose CA 95131
P: 408-990-4000 F: 408-990-4040 PRC:86
www.quicklogic.com
Email: info@quicklogic.com
Estab: 1988
Sales: $10M to $30M

Andrew J. Pease, President & CEO
Timothy Saxe, CTO & SVP of Engineering
Sue Cheung, VP of Finance & CFO
Donald Alexander, VP of Worldwide Sales
Rajiv Jain, VP of Worldwide Operations

Provider of trading solutions for stock market investors. The company offers online trading platforms for mobiles, smartphones, and tablets.

Quid Inc HQ
1 California St 23rd Fl
San Francisco CA 94111
P: 415-813-5300 F: 415-400-5189 PRC:315
quid.com
Email: general@quid.com
Estab: 2010

Dan Buczaczer, CMO
Saravanan Subbiah, CTO
Shashi Reddy, Chief of Staff
Ryan Hilton, SVP of Global Head of Sales
Kate Wiggin, SVP of Customer Success & Operations

Developers of artificial intelligence to help organizations make important decisions.

Quint Measuring Systems Inc HQ
1541 Third Ave [N]
Walnut Creek CA 94597
P: 800-745-5043 PRC:13
quintmeasuring.com
Email: info@quintmeasuring.com
Estab: 1995

Carol Quint, Co-Founder
Richard Quint, Chairman & CEO & Co-Founder

Distributor of imported hand measuring and digital reading products and publisher of books, supplier of art and graphic supplies to various trades unions, and creator of sewing and quilting tools.

Quiq Labs HQ
8839 N Cedar Ave
Fresno CA 93720
P: 559-745-5511 PRC:322
www.quiqlabs.com
Email: team@quiqlabs.com

Curlen Phipps, Software Developer

Developer of tools and solutions. The company focuses on influencing consumer behavior and engagement.

Quisk Inc HQ
1183 Bordeaux Dr Ste 27
Sunnyvale CA 94089
P: 408-462-6800 PRC:322
www.quisk.co
Email: info@quisk.co
Estab: 2007

Steve Novak, Chairman
Praveen Amancherla, CTO

Specializes in the development of payment solutions. The company offers services to financial institutions.

Quizlet Inc BR
501 Second St Ste 500
San Francisco CA 94107
P: 510-495-6550 PRC:322
quizlet.com
Email: support@quizlet.com
Estab: 2005

Dave Margulius, CEO
Andrew Sutherland, CTO
Tim A. Miller, SVP of Engineering
Amanda Baker, Director of Product Analytics
Thompson Paine, General Manager

Provider of learning tools for students and teachers. The company offers services to the educational sector.

Qulsar Inc HQ
90 Great Oaks Blvd Ste 204
San Jose CA 95119
P: 408-715-1098 F: 408-392-0865 PRC:97
qulsar.com
Email: info@qulsar.com
Estab: 2010

Kishan Shenoi, CTO
Minoo Mehta, VP of Business Development & Marketing

Specializes in packaging, refinement, and distribution of precise time synchronization. The company serves the telecom and networking industries.

Qumu Inc BR
1350 Old Bayshore Hwy Ste 470
San Bruno CA 94010
P: 650-396-8530 PRC:326
www.qumu.com
Estab: 2002

Vern Hanzlik, President
Sherman Black, CEO
Jim Stewart, CFO

Provider of web casting, marketing, event, and other professional services. The company offers enterprise video solutions.

Quorum Technologies HQ
1755 Creekside Oaks Dr Ste 100
Sacramento CA 95833
P: 916-669-5577 PRC:322
quorumtech.net
Email: info@quorumtech.net
Estab: 2003

Binda Mangat, President & CEO
Bethanne Ponci, Senior Account Executive & Project Manager & IT Analyst
Mazhar Iqbal, Technical Support Analyst

Developer of recycling and waste disposal solutions for the automotive, industrial, municipal, hospitality, and food industries.

Qview Medical HQ
4546 El Camino Real Ste 215
Los Altos CA 94022
P: 650-397-5174 PRC:186
www.qviewmedical.com
Email: info@qviewmedical.com
Estab: 2006

Bob Wang, CEO
Bob Foley, VP
Tom Neff, Director of SW Development

Provider of assistance in the review of 3D automated breast ultrasound. The company offers services to the radiologists.

Qwilt Inc HQ
275 Shoreline Dr Ste 510
Redwood City CA 94065
P: 866-824-8009 F: 650-249-6521 PRC:318
qwilt.com
Email: hello@qwilt.com
Estab: 2010

Alon Maor, CEO & Founder
Greg Callanan, VP
Mark Fisher, VP
Nimrod Cohen, VP
Udi Lerner, VP

Developer of open caching, video intelligence, fixed, and mobile operators solutions. The company offers media analytics products.

R & R Rubber Molding Inc HQ
2444 Loma Ave [N]
South El Monte CA 91733
P: 626-575-8105 F: 626-575-3756 PRC:57
www.rrrubber.com
Estab: 1977

Rick Norman, President
Carmen Castillo, Manager of Quality Control
Lupe Frausto-Perez, Contact

Manufacturer of elastomeric, rubber parts, gaskets, seals and o-rings for aerospace, industry, commercial, aftermarket, military, and OEM design and specifications through the processes of injection, transfer, and compression.

R F Circuits Inc HQ
2299 Ringwood Ave Ste C-4
San Jose CA 95131
P: 408-324-1670 F: 408-324-1770 PRC:211
rfcircuitsinc.com
Email: kenny@rfcircuitsinc.com

Kenny Lee, Manager of Sales & Engineering Manager
Song Lim, Engineer
Sun Young, Contact
Liz Villa, Contact

Manufacturer of printed circuit boards and assemblies. The company is engaged in engineering and electronics manufacturing services.

R Systems Inc RH
5000 Windplay Dr Ste 5
El Dorado Hills CA 95762
P: 916-939-9696 F: 916-939-9697 PRC:322
rsystems.com
Email: rsi.marketing@rsystems.com
Estab: 1993

Chan Kum Ming, President ECNET & R Systems Singapore
Raj Gupta, President Digital Services
Mandeep Sodhi, COO
Nand Sardana, CFO
Sidhartha Dubey, VP of Analytics & Knowledge Services

Provider of information technology services and solutions. The company offers application, testing, BPO, and packaged services.

R&A Engineering Solutions Inc HQ
601 University Ave Ste 255
Sacramento CA 95825
P: 916-920-5965 F: 916-920-9239 PRC:304
www.ra-solutions.com
Email: info@ra-solutions.com
Estab: 1976

Amy Mountjoy, Office & Accounting Manager
Scott Crosby, Mechanical Engineer
Wayne Watts, Mechanical Engineer
Braden Bill, Principal
Harold A. Hougham, Principal

Provider of engineering consulting services. The company offers design, analysis, verification, and planning of HVAC, and plumbing system services.

R&D Logic Inc HQ
1611 Borel Pl Ste 2
San Mateo CA 94402
P: 650-356-9207 F: 650-571-1276 PRC:326
www.rdlogic.com
Estab: 2000

Wanda Ionescu, CEO & President
Joyce Bellomo, Chief Finance & Business Development Officer
Pierre Goldenstein, VP of Software Development

Developer of performance management software for R&D focused companies. The company offers implementation and training services.

R&D Tech HQ
500 Yosemite Dr Ste 108
Milpitas CA 95035
P: 408-761-5266 PRC:211
www.rdtechpcb.com
Email: sales@rdtechpcb.com

Dave Linebaugh, Founder & CFO
Richard Hernadez, Director of Operations
Larry Pilbin, Representative

Provider of prototyping services. The company specializes in fabrication and assembly services.

R&R Refrigeration And Air Conditioning Inc   HQ
1775 Monterey Rd Ste 66A
San Jose CA 95112
P: 408-297-0383 F: 408-453-5853   PRC:85
getcooled.com
Email: service@getcooled.com

Cindy Fairfield, President

Provider of environmental technological solutions. The company also offers maintenance and repair services for process systems.

R-Computer   HQ
3953 Industrial Way Ste A
Concord CA 94520
P: 925-798-4884 F: 925-798-4894   PRC:323
www.r-computer.com
Email: info@r-computer.com
Estab: 1986

Ed Roth, Owner
Dawn Roth, Founding Partner
Ethan Ting, Director of Managed Services
Rhonda Bigby, Front Office Manager
Stephen Haitch, Sales & Production Manager

Provider of computer solutions for small and medium-sized companies. The company also offers lifetime product guarantees and sales consultation.

R-Hub Communications Inc   HQ
4340 Stevens Creek Blvd Ste 282
San Jose CA 95129
P: 408-899-2830 F: 408-516-9612   PRC:97
www.rhubcom.com
Email: info@rhubcom.com
Estab: 2005

John Mao, Founder & CTO
Larry Dorie, CEO

Provider of web conferencing and remote support services. The company offers services for on-premise security, branding, and integration.

RL Shep Publications   HQ
PO Box 2706   [N]
Fort Bragg CA 95437
P: 707-964-8662   PRC:323
www.rlshep.com
Estab: 1980

R.L. Shep, Contact

Publisher of nineteenth-century costume, tailoring, and etiquette books.

RS Hughes Company Inc   HQ
1162 Sonora Ct   [N]
Sunnyvale CA 94086
P: 877-774-8443   PRC:212
www.rshughes.com
Estab: 1954

Pete Biocini, President & COO
Bob McCollum, CEO
Jon Baeder, VP of Operations
Justin Brown, Manager of Regional Operations
Dominic Smorto, Manager of Regional Operations

Distributor of industrial supplies such as abrasives, adhesives and sealants, chemicals and much more.

RW Smith & Co   HQ
8555 Miralani Dr   [N]
San Diego CA 92196
P: 800-942-1101   PRC:189
www.rwsmithco.com
Email: info@rwsmithco.com
Estab: 1935

Allan Keck, President
Drew Golley, Director of Business Development

Provider of foodservice products and solutions.

RackWare Inc   HQ
75 E Santa Clara St Unit 600
San Jose CA 95113
P: 408-430-5821   PRC:326
www.rackwareinc.com
Email: info@rackwareinc.com
Estab: 2009

Todd Matters, CTO & Founder
Ron Heinz, Chairman
Bryan Gobbett, CEO
Thomas G. Gannon, Regional Sales Director
Anup Bansod, Manager Software Development

Provider of disaster prevention and recovery solutions. The company also offers business continuity and virtualization solutions.

Raco Manufacturing & Engineering Company Inc   HQ
1400 62nd St
Emeryville CA 94608
P: 510-658-6713 F: 510-658-3153   PRC:59
www.racoman.com
Email: sales@racoman.com
Estab: 1948

Sam Siggins, VP of Engineering
James Garnett, Quality Assurance Manager & SQA Manager
Gene Cottom, Western Regional Sales Manager

Manufacturer of alarms and controllers. The company offers remote monitoring, reporting, datalogging, and control services.

Radian Thermal Products Inc   BR
2160 Walsh Ave
Santa Clara CA 95050
P: 408-988-6200   PRC:124
www.radianheatsinks.com
Email: sales@radianheatsinks.com
Estab: 1974

Thierry Sin, President & CEO
Phoebe Li, VP of Finance & Controller
Stuart Mitchell, Director of Sales & Marketing
Steve Johanson, Materials Manager
Alejandro Valle, Mechanical Engineer & Thermal Engineer

Manufacturer of custom and radiant heat sinks. The company's services include prototyping and engineering support.

Radiant Logic Inc   HQ
75 Rowland Way Ste 300
Novato CA 94945
P: 415-209-6800 F: 415-798-5697   PRC:324
radiantlogic.com
Email: info@radiantlogic.com
Estab: 1995

Michel Prompt, Founder & CEO
Leah Mazurette, Manager of Operations
Lauren Selby, Project Manager
Elsy Alvarado, Accounting Manager
Divya Kandi, Quality Assurance Engineer

Provider of identity and context virtualization solutions. The company caters to identity integration and management needs.

RadioMate   HQ
2954 Treat Blvd Ste A
Concord CA 94518
P: 925-332-8991   PRC:60
www.radiomate.com
Email: sales@radiomate.com
Estab: 1989

Harry Servidio, CFO

Provider of radio accessories specializing in headsets. The company also offers headsets for surveillance and fire and rescue applications.

Raditek Inc   HQ
1702L Meridian Ave Ste 127
San Jose CA 95125
P: 408-266-7404 F: 408-266-4483   PRC:68
www.raditek.com
Email: sales@raditek.com
Estab: 1993

Malcolm Lee, Founder
Hima Thakkar, Inside Sales Manager
Craig Madsen, IT Manager

Provider of solutions for the wireless and microwave telecom sector. The company offers passive components, active assemblies, and telecom systems.

RAF Electronics   HQ
10045 Nantucket Dr
San Ramon CA 94582
P: 925-551-5361   PRC:83
www.rafelectronics.com
Email: info@rafelectronics.com
Estab: 1989

Richard A. Flasck, Founder & CEO
Erik Van Der, Sales Manager

Provider of optical system design and related services. The company deals with sales and delivery solutions.

Rafi Systems Inc   HQ
750 N Diamond Bar Blvd Ste 224 [N]
Diamond Bar CA 91765
P: 909-861-6574 F: 909-396-7933   PRC:189
www.rafisystems.com
Email: rsi@rafisystems.com
Estab: 1996

Kusum Rafiquzzaman, Contact

Manufacturer of ophthalmic goods.

Rago & Son Inc HQ
1029 51st Ave
Oakland CA 94601
P: 510-536-5700 F: 510-536-3460 PRC:80
www.rago-son.com
Email: info@rago-son.com
Estab: 1945

Eddie Rago, Quality Manager
Alfonso Munoz, Supervisor

Provider of metal stamping and machining services. The company's services include stamping, complete welding, and perforated tubing.

Rainbow Electronics & Fasteners Corp HQ
30095 Ahern Ave
Union City CA 94587
P: 510-475-9840 F: 510-475-9845 PRC:124
www.rainbowelectronics.com
Estab: 1981

Hank Bombino, President

Distributor of electronic and mechanical hardware products. The company's products include fasteners, screws, standoffs, and spacers.

Rainier Therapeutics HQ
1040 Davis St Ste 202
San Leandro CA 94577
P: 925-413-6140 PRC:38
www.bioclintherapeutics.com
Email: info@bioclintherapeutics.com
Estab: 2010

Stephen Lau, CEO
Julie Eastland, CFO & Chief Business Officer
Valerie Fauvelle, VP & Advisor
Joseph Turner, Independent Director
Steve Abella, Advisor

Developer of biologic products for the treatment of metastatic bladder cancer (urothelial cell carcinoma) and achondroplasia (dwarfism).

Ralph E Ames Machine Works HQ
2301 Dominguez Way [N]
Torrance CA 90501
P: 310-320-2637 F: 310-320-6511 PRC:80
www.amesmachine.com
Email: mail@amesmachine.com
Estab: 1942

Mike Ames, President
Ron Ames, VP
Eric Anderson, General Manager
Kevin Esquivias, Manager
Alfonso Olivar, Manager

Manufacturer of industrial machinery.

Ralphs-Pugh Co HQ
3931 Oregon St
Benicia CA 94510
P: 707-745-6222 PRC:159
ralphs-pugh.com
Email: sales@ralphs-pugh.com
Estab: 1912

Tom Anderson, VP
Larry Bauer, Plant Manager
Mary Anderson, Manager of Customer Service
Amber Ricalday, Sales Manager
Casey Pugh, Industrial Tech & Marketing Executive

Manufacturer of conveyor rollers and related components. The company serves the agriculture, chemical, and food processing industries.

Rambus HQ
1050 Enterprise Way Ste 700
Sunnyvale CA 94089
P: 408-462-8000 F: 408-462-8001 PRC:64
www.rambus.com
Estab: 1990
Sales: $100M to $300M

Luc Seraphin, Interim CEO & Acting General Manager of Memory & Interface Division
Rahul Mathur, SVP & CFO
Jae Kim, SVP & General Counsel
Stefan Tamme, VP
Steven Woo, VP

Manufacturer of semiconductor, lighting, and IP products. The company serves the automotive and transportation markers.

Ramec Engineering HQ
1736 W 130th St [N]
Gardena CA 90249
P: 310-532-2573 F: 310-532-2576 PRC:4
www.ramec.net
Estab: 1972

Leonard Roberts, President

Designer, engineer, and manufacturer of aerospace parts.

Randal Optimal Nutrients Inc HQ
PO Box 7328
Santa Rosa CA 95407
P: 707-528-1800 F: 707-528-0924 PRC:272
www.randaloptimal.com
Email: customerservice@randaloptimal.com
Estab: 1947

Dan Brinker, President
Donna Coats, VP
Joseph Trejo, Production Specialist
Ellen Cruz, Controller

Manufacturer of consumer goods. The company produces dietary supplements and nutraceuticals to the health food and profession health care markers.

Range Networks HQ
2040 Martin Ave
Santa Clara CA 95050
P: 415-778-8700 PRC:325
rangenetworks.com
Email: info@rangenetworks.com
Estab: 2011

Brad Wurtz, CEO

Provider of mobile network solutions. The company is also engaged in software and hardware solutions and services.

Rani Therapeutics HQ
2051 Ringwood Ave
San Jose CA 95131
P: 408-457-3700 PRC:191
www.ranitherapeutics.com
Estab: 2012

Maulik Nanavaty, SVP & President of Neuromodulation
Svai Sanford, CFO
Mir Hashim, CSO
Arvinder Dhalla, Associate VP of Clinical & Regulatory Operations
Betsy Gutierrez, Associate VP of Quality Assurance

Developer of drug molecules including peptides, proteins and antibodies. The company offers services to the pharmaceutical industry.

Rantec Microwave Systems Inc HQ
31186 La Baya Dr [N]
Westlake Village CA 91362
P: 818-223-5000 PRC:17
www.rantecantennas.com
Email: marketing@rantecantennas.com
Emp: 11-50 Estab: 2000

Jim Soper, VP of Manufacturing
Dennis Lavelle, Director of Business Development

Manufacturer of microwave antennas for military and commercial applications.

Rapid Accu-Form Inc HQ
3825 Sprig Dr
Benicia CA 94510
P: 707-745-1879 F: 707-745-6219 PRC:80
www.rapidaccuform.com
Estab: 1975

Linda Brown, Accounting Analyst
Larry Brown, Contact

Provider of thermoforming and pressure forming services. The company specializes in tool and die and prototyping services.

Rapid Precision Manufacturing Inc HQ
1516 Montague Expy
San Jose CA 95131
P: 408-617-0771 F: 408-617-0772 PRC:80
www.rapidprecision.net
Email: rpm@rapidprecision.net
Estab: 1998

Paul Yi, CEO
Jane Yi, CFO

Provider of screw machining, surface grinding, sheet metal fabrication, tooling, and inspection services.

Rapidwerks Inc HQ
1257 Quarry Ln Ste 140
Pleasanton CA 94566
P: 925-417-0124 F: 925-417-0128 PRC:189
rapidwerks.com
Estab: 2004

Scott Herbert, President & Founder

Manufacturer of medical equipment and devices. The company also offers accessories and semiconductor products.

RAPT Therapeutics HQ
561 Eccles Ave
S San Francisco CA 94080
P: 650-489-9000 PRC:24
rapt.com
Estab: 2015

Brian Wong, CEO
William Ho, CMO
Dirk Brockstedt, CSO
Rodney Young, CFO
David Wustrow, SVP

Provider of immuno-oncology oral medicines designed to activate patients own immune system to eradicate cancer.

Rasilient Systems Inc   HQ
3281 Kifer Rd
Santa Clara CA 95051
P: 408-730-2568   PRC:60
rasilient.com
Email: info@rasilient.com
Estab: 2001

Sean Chang, CEO

Provider of technology products and services. The company offers a range of video surveillance and storage products.

Rasteroids Design   HQ
195 Jackson St
San Jose CA 95112
P: 408-979-9138   PRC:325
www.rasteroids.com
Estab: 2000

Miles Rast, Owner & Programming Lead

Provider of web designing, custom programming, implementation, custom software development, and hosting services.

Rathbun Associates   HQ
48890 Milmont Dr Ste 111D
Fremont CA 94538
P: 510-661-0950   F: 510-668-0369   PRC:200
rathbun.com
Email: sales@rathbun.com
Estab: 1967

Maria Camara, Administrative Assistant
Pam Biagio, Administrative Assistant

Distributor and reseller of converters. The company offers thermal management solutions, specialty tapes, and protective products.

Ray Carlson & Associates Inc   HQ
411 Russell Ave
Santa Rosa CA 95403
P: 707-528-7649   F: 707-571-5541   PRC:301
www.rcmaps.com
Email: rca@rcmaps.com
Estab: 1976

Ray C. Carlson, President
Walter Moody, GIS Manager
Bob Muollo, Land Surveyor

Provider of consulting, research, surveying, mapping, video branding, and related services. The company also offers data management products.

Ray L Hellwig   HQ
1309 Laurelwood Rd
Santa Clara CA 95054
P: 408-727-5612   F: 408-727-5409   PRC:80
www.rlhellwig.com
Email: info@hellwigmechanical.com
Estab: 1992

Jim Hadley, Project Manager
Chelsey Hadley, Assistant Project Manager
Nancy Lowe, Manager of Accounts Payable
Libby Sandoval, Manager of Construction Operations
Shari Bleeg, Controller

Designer and manufacturer of tools. It's products find application in mechanical, process piping, and plumbing needs.

Ray Morgan Co   BR
3131 Esplanade
Chico CA 95973
P: 530-343-6065   F: 530-343-9470   PRC:45
www.raymorgan.com
Email: info@raymorgan.com
Estab: 1956

Mike Morgan, VP & Owner
Chris Scarff, EVP & Owner
Sam Pulino, Founder
Greg Martin, President
Bob Quadros, CFO

Provider of document technology solutions. The company offers paperless, project management, and imaging system solutions.

Raymar Information Technology Inc   HQ
7325 Roseville Rd
Sacramento CA 95842
P: 916-783-1951   F: 916-783-1952   PRC:68
www.raymarinc.com
Email: sales@raymarinc.com
Estab: 1982

Gary Portellas, CEO & Managing Director
David Figueroa, CFO
Don Breidenbach, Managing Director
Michael Ellsworth, Account Manager
Calvin Soua Dao Vang, Lead

Provider of hardware supplies, network infrastructure, virtualization, disaster recovery, and managed services.

Rayteq LLC   HQ
PO Box 1343
Healdsburg CA 95448
P: 510-638-2000   PRC:151
www.rayteq.com
Email: information@rayteq.com

Frank B. Smith, President & CEO
Matthew Smith, EVP & Manager of Engineering

Manufacturer of energy-saving electric melting furnaces for the metal casting industry and offers electric heating systems and metal level sensors.

RCB Elevator Consulting LLC   HQ
16799 Estrella Dr
Sonoma CA 95476-3105
P: 415-350-0402   PRC:304
www.blaska.com
Estab: 1999

Richard C. Blaska, Owner

Provider of elevator design and structural engineering services to building owners, architects, and elevator companies and offers field surveys.

RCH Associates Inc   HQ
6111 Southfront Rd Ste C
Livermore CA 94551-5136
P: 510-657-7846   F: 510-657-6138   PRC:86
www.rchassociates.com
Email: info@rchassociates.com
Estab: 1990

Bob Hoelsch, President
Matthew Furlo, Engineer Manager
Willie Nono, Project Engineer

Provider of engineering solutions. The company specializes in equipment used in space, solar, and semiconductor industries.

RCM Industries Inc   HQ
110 Mason Cir Ste D
Concord CA 94520
P: 925-687-8363   F: 925-671-9636   PRC:14
www.flo-gage.com
Email: sales@rcmmeters.com
Estab: 1972

Vernon Reizman, CFO

Manufacturer of direct reading flow meters for liquid and gases. The company's products are used in chillers and satellite systems.

RDM Industrial Products Inc   HQ
1652 Watson Ct
Milpitas CA 95035
P: 408-945-8400   F: 408-945-8433   PRC:32
rdm-ind.com
Estab: 1977

Michele Gomez, VP
Lynn Tweedie, Administrative Assistant

Provider of laboratory and industrial furniture solutions. The company offers cabinets, counters, carts, and mobile tables.

Reaction Technology Inc   HQ
3400 Bassett St
Santa Clara CA 95054
P: 408-970-9601   F: 408-970-9695   PRC:47
www.reactiontechnology.com
Email: sales@reactiontechnology.com
Estab: 1991

Janis Ammirato-Terwilliger, Office Manager

Supplier of silicon epitaxy and silicon coatings. The company caters to the semiconductor and industrial sectors.

Readytech Corp   HQ
720 Second St Ste 111
Oakland CA 94612
P: 800-707-1009   PRC:319
readytech.com
Email: get-info@readytech.com
Estab: 1993

Miguel Palma, Marketing Manager

Provider of virtual labs for training, certification, and also sales demonstrations. The company deals with technology support.

Real Environmental Products LLC   HQ
1510 S State Hwy 49
Pine Grove CA 95642
P: 209-296-7900   F: 209-267-4018   PRC:134
www.realenvprod.com
Estab: 2000

Rodney Peoples, Owner

Provider of landfill gas products. The company products include LFG well heads and 1200 series monitoring well monuments.

Real Intent Inc　　　　　　　HQ
　932 Hamlin Ct
　Sunnyvale CA 94089
P: 408-830-0700　F: 408-737-1962　　PRC:323
www.realintent.com
Email: info@realintent.com
Estab: 1998

Prakash Narain, CEO & President
Pranav Ashar, CTO
Chris Morrison, Chief Architect
Oren Katzir, VP of Applications Engineering
Hamed Emami, VP of WW Sales

Provider of electronic design automation services. The company offers techniques for automatic design verification.

Real Sensors Inc　　　　　　　HQ
　20977 Cabot Blvd
　Hayward CA 94545-1155
P: 510-785-4100　F: 510-785-4400　　PRC:49
www.realsensors.com
Email: esales@realsensors.com

Ramesh Chand, Engineer

Manufacturer of chemical detection systems. The company also offers security solutions to government agencies and petrochemical industries.

REAL Software Systems LLC　　　HQ
　21255 Burbank Blvd Ste 220　　[N]
　Woodland Hills CA 91367
P: 818-313-8000　　　　　　　　PRC:319
www.realsoftwaresystems.com
Email: sales@realsoftwaresystems.com
Estab: 1993

Kent Sahin, CEO
Donald Venardos, Systems Engineering Manager
Jenny Gonzales, Project Manager
John Benoit, Manager of Sales
David Liptack, Talent Management Specialist

Developer of software solutions for the management of royalty, rights and revenue sharing contracts.

Real-Time Innovations Inc　　　HQ
　232 E Java Dr
　Sunnyvale CA 94089
P: 408-990-7400　F: 408-990-7402　　PRC:325
rti.com
Email: info@rti.com
Estab: 1991

Stan Schneider, CEO
Gerardo Pardo-Castellote, CTO
Catherine Mekler, VP of Operations
David Barnett, VP of Products & Markets

Provider for real-time infrastructure software solutions. The company also offers engineering and product development services.

ReaMetrix Inc　　　　　　　　HQ
　171 Main St Ste 670
　Los Altos CA 94022
P: 650-226-4144　　　　　　　　PRC:34
www.reametrix.com
Email: info@reametrix.com
Estab: 2003

Bala Manian, CEO

Provider of biotechnology services. The company develops innovative affordable diagnostic solutions.

M-260

Rearden LLC　　　　　　　　HQ
　211 S Whisman Rd Ste D
　Mountain View CA 94041
P: 415-947-5555　F: 415-947-5597　　PRC:318
rearden.com
Email: rearden7@rearden.com
Estab: 2000

Steve Perlman, Founder & CEO

Provider of cloud computing, motion picture, video game, consumer electronics, wireless, imaging, communications, and alternative energy technologies.

Recology Of The Coast　　　　HQ
　2305 Palmetto Ave
　Pacifica CA 94044
P: 650-355-9000　F: 650-359-9580　　PRC:141
www.recology.com
Estab: 1921

Michael J. Sangiacomo, President & CEO
Mark J. Arsenault, EVP & COO
Catherine Langridge, SVP & CFO
Julie Bertani-Kiser, SVP & Chief Human Resource Officer
Christine Crescio Porter, General Manager

Provider of resource recovery services. The company's services include urban cleaning services, collection, sorting, transfer, recovery and landfill management.

Recor Medical Inc　　　　　　RH
　1049 Elwell Ct
　Palo Alto CA 94303
P: 650-542-7700　　　　　　　　PRC:189
www.recormedical.com
Email: info@recormedical.com
Estab: 2009

Mano Iyer, Founder & COO
Andrew Weiss, President & CEO
Matthew Franklin, CFO
Leslie Coleman, VP

Manufacturer of ultrasound denervation products. The company is involved in clinical trials and research solutions.

Recortec Inc　　　　　　　　HQ
　2231-A Fortune Dr
　San Jose CA 95131-1871
P: 408-928-1480　F: 408-928-1489　　PRC:93
www.recortec.com
Email: sales@recortec.com
Estab: 1969

Edward Lee, Business Development Manager
Toni Tung, Assembler

Manufacturer of LCD monitors, KVM, keyboards, speakers, and computers. The company also offers customization services.

Red Hat Inc　　　　　　　　BR
　150 Mathilda Pl Ste 500
　Sunnyvale CA 94041
P: 650-567-9039　F: 650-567-9041　　PRC:319
www.redhat.com
Estab: 1993

Paul Cormier, President & CEO
Lee Congdon, CIO
Eric R. Shander, EVP & CFO
Michael R. Cunningham, EVP & General Counsel & Corporate Secretary
Mark Enzweiler, SVP of Global Channel Sales & Alliances

Provider of training, certification, consulting, cloud, application, and other technical support services.

Redbooth　　　　　　　　　HQ
　95 Third St Ste 231
　San Francisco CA 94103
P: 650-521-5459　　　　　　　　PRC:315
redbooth.com
Email: info@redbooth.com
Estab: 2008

John Gabaix, CEO
Callie Strawn, Director of Operations

A task and project management platform for team collaboration tasks, discussions, and file sharing.

Redis Labs Inc　　　　　　　HQ
　700 E El Camino Real Ste 250
　Mountain View CA 94040
P: 415-930-9666　　　　　　　　PRC:326
redislabs.com
Email: info@redislabs.com
Estab: 2011

Ofer Bengal, Co-Founder & CEO
Yiftach Shoolman, Co-Founder & CTO
Howard Ting, CMO
Rafael Torres, CFO
Alvin Richards, Chief Product Officer

Provider of zero management, infinite scalability, and other solutions for start-ups and business enterprises.

Redline Communications　　　BR
　1800 Wyatt Dr Ste 5
　Santa Clara CA 95054
P: 866-633-6669　　　　　　　　PRC:61
rdlcom.com
Email: info@rdlcom.com
Estab: 1999

Robert Williams, CEO
Philip Jones, CFO
Reno Moccia, EVP of Global Sales & Marketing
Abdelsalam Aldwikat, VP of Operations & Technology

Provider of networking and consulting solutions. The company serves the government, telecommunication, and military sectors.

Redline Solutions Inc　　　　HQ
　3350 Scott Blvd Ste 501 Bldg 5
　Santa Clara CA 95054
P: 408-562-1700　F: 408-562-1720　　PRC:304
www.redlinesolutions.com
Email: sales@redlinesolutions.com
Estab: 1997

Todd Baggett, Founder & CEO

Provider of produce traceability and barcode solutions, and warehouse and inventory management systems.

Redolent Inc　　　　　　　　HQ
　4620 Fortran Dr Ste 201
　San Jose CA 95134
P: 650-242-1195　　　　　　　　PRC:323
www.redolentech.com
Email: contact@redolentech.com
Estab: 1999

Samir Vyas, Director & Architect
Shubhada Ingole, Manager of Information Technology
Rahul Thakkar, Technical Recruiter

Provider of software solution in web, open source, e-commerce applications. The company also focuses on enterprise wide applications.

Redpark Product Development HQ
1555 Third Ave
Walnut Creek CA 94597
P: 510-594-1034   F: 510-222-0325   PRC:202
www.redpark.com
Email: info@redpark.com
Estab: 1995

Mike Ridenhour, President

Manufacturer of connectivity accessories for
iPhone and iPad. The company's products include
lightning cables and 30-pin cables.

Redpine Signals Inc HQ
2107 N First St Ste 680
San Jose CA 95131-2019
P: 408-748-3385   F: 408-705-2019   PRC:68
www.redpinesignals.com
Email: info@redpinesignals.com
Estab: 2001

Dhiraj Sogani, SVP of Marketing
Chandra Sekhar Abburi, VP of Systems & Software
David Shefler, SVP of Sales & Business Development
Narasimhan Venkatesh, VP of Advanced Technologies
Prabhashankar Shastry, VP of Engineering

Manufacturer of wireless systems. The company offers chipset and system level products for
wireless networks.

Redwhale Software Corp HQ
1755 E Bayshore Rd Ste 25B
Redwood City CA 94063
P: 650-312-1500   F: 650-285-6209   PRC:323
www.redwhale.com
Email: redwhale.info@redwhale.com
Estab: 1998

Jared Ho, Project Manager

Provider of software tools, technologies, and
professional services for the design, development,
and run-time management of user interfaces.

Redwood Renewables HQ
6 Endeavor Dr
Corte Madera CA 94925
P: 415-924-8140   F: 415-924-4041   PRC:135
www.redwoodrenewables.com
Email: tfaust@redwoodrenewables.com

Tom Faust, President

Developer and manufacturer of residential tiles
and solar roofing. The company also focuses on
the marketing aspects.

Redwood Toxicology Laboratory HQ
3650 Westwind Blvd
Santa Rosa CA 95403
P: 707-577-7959   F: 707-577-8102   PRC:306
www.redwoodtoxicology.com
Email: sales@redwoodtoxicology.com
Estab: 1994

Robert Mount, VP
Suman Rana, Director of Laboratory Operations &
Technology & SAMHSA Responsible Person
Lisa Downing, Human Resource Manager
Ellen Jones, Accounting Manager
Janee Gully, Regulatory Affairs & Quality Assurance Manager

Provider of drug and alcohol testing laboratories.
The company specializes in substance abuse
screening products to criminal justice and treatment markers.

Reel Solar Power Inc HQ
2219 Oakland Rd
San Jose CA 95131
P: 408-258-4714   PRC:135
reelsolar.com
Estab: 2009

Dori Gal, Founder & CTO
Scott Burton, CEO
Kuo-Jui Hsiao, Chief Scientist
Ariel Howard, Senior Process Technician

Provider of tools and materials to photovoltaic
manufacturing. The company also engages in the
manufacturing of cadmium telluride solar panels.

Reflektion Inc HQ
777 Mariners Island Blvd Ste 510
San Mateo CA 94404
P: 650-293-0800   PRC:326
reflektion.com
Email: sales@reflektion.com
Estab: 2012

Steve Papa, Entrepreneur & Founder & Executive
Chairman
Ray Villeneuve, President & COO
Sean Moran, CEO
Amede Hungerford, CMO
Rob Neibauer, SVP of Revenue & Marketing

Focuses on personalized site search, marketing,
analytics, and predictive product recommendation
solutions.

Regal Electronics Inc HQ
2029 Otoole Ave   [N]
San Jose CA 95131
P: 408-988-2288   PRC:209
www.regalusa.net
Estab: 1976

James Gaylard, Owner
Madeleine Lee, CEO
Lee Margaret, General Manager

Supplier of electronic components.

Regal Machine & Engineering Inc HQ
5200 E 60th St   [N]
Maywood CA 90270
P: 323-773-7462   F: 323-784-8500   PRC:80
www.regalmachine.com
Estab: 1985

Val Darie, President & Treasurer
Donna Darie, Director of Personnel
Felipe Pardo, Manager

Manufacturer of structural components for the
military and commercial aerospace industry.

Relay2 Inc HQ
1525 McCarthy Blvd Ste 209
Milpitas CA 95035
P: 408-380-0031   PRC:68
relay2.com
Email: sales@relay2.com
Estab: 2011

Suryakant Devangan, Senior Technical Lead

Provider of cloud Wi-Fi Services platform which
allows service providers to monetize value added
Wi-Fi services.

Relcomm Inc HQ
4868 Hwy 4 Ste G
Angels Camp CA 95222
P: 301-924-7400   F: 301-924-7403   PRC:64
www.relcomm.com
Email: sales@relcomm.com
Estab: 1989

Robert Henkel, Owner
Michael Shea, President
Paul Ungaro, Manager of Operations

Manufacturer of computer and data communication devices. The company offers data switches,
inline buffers, and current loop products.

Reliable Rubber Products HQ
815 D St
Modesto CA 95354
P: 888-525-9750   F: 209-521-7123   PRC:157
www.reliablerubber.com
Email: sales@reliablerubber.com

Marc Wilkins, President & CEO
Rahul Ranjan, Account Manager

Provider of rubber products. The company's products include dock bumpers, duty corner guards,
urethane wheel chocks, and street pads.

Reliant Labs Inc HQ
925 Thompson Pl
Sunnyvale CA 94085
P: 408-737-7500   PRC:306
reliantlabs.com
Email: info@reliantlabs.com
Estab: 2002

Roberto Carcamo, Lab Manager
Ken Duncan, Principal

Provider of environmental testing and reliability
services. The company is also engaged in power
supply evaluation.

Reltek LLC HQ
2345 Circadian Way
Santa Rosa CA 95407
P: 707-284-8808   F: 707-284-8812   PRC:47
www.reltekllc.com
Email: reltek@reltekllc.com
Estab: 1996

Robert E. Lindberg, Founder
Amy Huse, General Manager

Developer of analytical and empirical Accelerated
Life Testing technology for military, commercial,
and nuclear products.

Relucent Solutions LLC HQ
1415 N Dutton Ave Ste C
Santa Rosa CA 95401
P: 800-630-7704   PRC:188
www.relucent.com
Email: sales@relucent.com
Estab: 2007

Steve Parmelee, Founder
Tim Renaud, President
Stephen Endweiss, Director of Sales
Kurtis Rowell, Director of Process Development
Jennifer Griggs, Sales Manager

Manufacturer of medical devices. The company is
involved in laser cutting, precision manufacturing,
wire crimping, and related services.

Relypsa Inc HQ
100 Cardinal Way
Redwood City CA 94063
P: 650-421-9500   PRC:261
www.relypsa.com
Email: info@relypsa.com
Estab: 2007

Scott Garland, SVP & Chief Commercial Officer

Developer of polymer technology for the treatment
of patients with serious conditions. The company
is engaged in drug discovery.

Remote Sensing Systems HQ
444 Tenth St Ste 200
Santa Rosa CA 95401
P: 707-545-2904   F: 707-545-2906   PRC:304
www.remss.com
Email: support@remss.com
Estab: 1974

Frank Wentz, President & CEO
Marty Brewer, Manager of IT Services
Thomas Meissner, Scientist
Lucrezia Ricciardulli, Scientist

Processor of microwave data. The company
collects the data with the help of special satellite
microwave sensors.

Renegade Labs HQ
578 Sutton Way Ste 165
Grass Valley CA 95945
P: 530-273-7047   F: 530-271-0757   PRC:60
renegadelabs.com
Estab: 2004

Kirk Allen Bradford, CEO

Manufacturer of tools for the broadcast, video, and
film industries. The company's products include
digital audio mixers, metering and input and
output systems.

Renovorx Inc HQ
4546 El Camino Real Ste 223
Los Altos CA 94022
P: 650-284-4433   F: 650-397-4433   PRC:189
www.renovorx.com
Estab: 2012

Kamran Najmabadi, Co-Founder & Technical
Engineering Advisor
Ramtin Agah, Co-Founder & CMO
Shaun R. Bagai, CEO
Paul Manners, CFO
Nicole Lama, Associate Director of Clinical
Research

Manufacturer of medical devices. The company
develops solutions for targeted delivery of therapeutic and diagnostic agents.

Replicraft HQ
1400 Gomes Rd
Fremont CA 94539
P: 510-656-6039   PRC:5
replicraft.us.fm
Email: sopwithace@comcast.net

Jim Kiger, Owner

Provider of World War I aircraft plan sets for mod-
elers. The company provides plans for the aircrafts
in one-fifth, one-sixth and one-tenth scales.

Reprise Software Inc HQ
1530 Meridian Ave Ste 290
San Jose CA 95125
P: 781-837-0884   F: 408-404-0890   PRC:320
www.reprisesoftware.com
Email: info@reprisesoftware.com
Estab: 2006

Bob Mearns, Lead Developer

Provider of license management software solutions. The company's products include Exa, Arxan,
LMS, and Pace.

RES Environmental Services Inc HQ
2153 Martin Way
Pittsburg CA 94565
P: 925-432-1755   F: 925-432-1748   PRC:140
resenvironmentalservices.com
Estab: 1982

John Russo, President
Craig Joseph, General Manager

Provider of environmental services. The company
offers air-moving, contract safety, and vacuum
truck services.

Resilient Networks Systems Inc HQ
181 Second St
San Francisco CA 94105
P: 415-291-9600   PRC:323
www.resilient-networks.com
Email: info@resilient-networks.com
Estab: 2008

Richard Spires, Chairman
Ethan Ayer, CEO
Howard Bain, Director
Mark Hapner, Consulting Engineer
Ulagu Kumar, Principal Software QA Engineer

Developer of Internet software products. The company serves the healthcare, media, information
security, and government sectors.

Resilinc Corp HQ
890 Hillview Ct Ste 160
Milpitas CA 95035
P: 408-883-8053   PRC:325
www.resilinc.com
Estab: 2010

Bindiya Vakil, CEO & Founder & Chairman
Sumit Vakil, CTO
Daniel Biran, CSO
Pramod Akkarachittor, VP of Product Manage-
ment
Ranna Rose, VP of Operations

Provider of supply chain and risk management
solutions. The company serves the life science
and automotive industries.

Responsible Metal Fab Inc HQ
1256 Lawrence Station Rd
Sunnyvale CA 94089
P: 408-734-0713   F: 408-734-3006   PRC:80
www.responsiblemetal.com
Estab: 1985

Dan Martin, President
Rafael Grimaldo, VP of Sales & Engineering
Michael Paradice, Director of Business Develop-
ment
Ron Foster, Account Manager
Cande Arreola, Production Manager

Provider of precision sheet metal fabrication
services. The company offers machining, electro-
mechanical assembly, packaging, and delivery
services.

ResQ Manufacturing HQ
11365 Sunrise Park Dr Ste 200
Rancho Cordova CA 95742
P: 916-638-6786   F: 916-914-2075   PRC:78
resqmfg.com
Estab: 2012

Jim Chiodo, CEO
Kyle Varney, General Manager

Provider of contract manufacturing services. The
company offers cable assembly and electro-mechanical services.

Retail Pro International HQ
400 Plaza Dr Ste 200
Folsom CA 95630
P: 916-605-7200   PRC:322
www.retailpro.com
Email: moreinfo@retailpro.com

Harshad Palrecha, Business Owner
Kerry Lemos, CEO
Mike Bishop, COO
Peter LaTona, VP of Channel Sales, North
America
William Colley, VP & Managing Director

Provider of software solutions. The company's
services include automated retail planning and
content strategy.

RetailNext　　HQ
60 S Market St Ste 310
San Jose CA 95113
P: 408-884-2162　　PRC:325
retailnext.net
Email: info@retailnext.net
Estab: 2007

Mark Jamtgaard, Director of Technology
Lindsay Kelvie, Account Director
Dan Dixon, Mid Market Account Director
Maglaya Pajar, Global IT Director
Aaron Sorin, Account Director

Provider of in-store analytics solutions. The
company offers services to retail labs, marketing
departments, and shopping centers.

Retech Systems LLC　　HQ
100 Henry Station Rd
Ukiah CA 95482
P: 707-462-6522　　PRC:151
www.retechsystemsllc.com
Email: sales@retechsystemsllc.com
Estab: 1963

Bob Cook, Director of Casting Products
David Warren, Director of Special Projects
Joseph Ferraiuolo, Director of Business Develop-
ment
John McMenomey, Director of Electron Beam
Products
Terry Wickliffe, Manager of Information Technology

Designer and manufacturer of consumable electrode and furnaces, powder production, and other
thermal processing equipment.

Retrotope Inc　　HQ
4300 El Camino Real Ste 201
Los Altos CA 94022
P: 650-917-9256　　PRC:257
www.retrotope.com
Email: info@retrotope.com
Estab: 2006

Mikhail S. Shchepinov, Founder & CSO & Director
Peter G. Milner, CMO & Director
Anil Kumar, Chief Business Officer
Karsten Schmidt, SVP of Ophthalmology
Frederic Heerinckx, VP of Clinical Operations

Focuses on the discovery of drugs and platforms
for the treatment of regenerative diseases. The
company offers services to the healthcare sector.

Revance Therapeutics Inc　　HQ
7555 Gateway Blvd
Newark CA 94560-0303
P: 510-742-3400　F: 510-742-3401　PRC:268
www.revance.com
Emp: 170 Estab: 2002
Sales: Under $1 Million

Lauren Silvernail, CFO & EVP Corporate Develop-
ment
Arthur P. Bertolino, EVP & CMO
Roman Rubio, SVP of Clinical Development
Samir Gharib, Senior Director of Corporate
Controller
Ron Eastman, Director

Developers of botulinum toxin products. The company develops and manufactures botulinum toxin
products for aesthetic and therapeutic categories.

Revel Systems Inc　　BR
575 Market St Ste 2200
San Francisco CA 94105
P: 415-744-1433　　PRC:209
revelsystems.com
Email: info@revelsystems.com
Estab: 2010

Greg Dukat, CEO
Chris Lybeer, CSO & CMO
Arthur W. Beckman, SVP & CIO
Leslie Leaf, CCO
Tracy Caswell, SVP & General Counsel

Provider of POS systems and related services.
The company serves customers in the accounting,
security, reporting, and other industries.

Reviva Pharmaceuticals Inc　　HQ
1250 Oakmead Pkwy Ste 210
Sunnyvale CA 94085
P: 408-816-1470　F: 408-904-6270　PRC:257
www.revivapharma.com
Email: info.rp@revivapharma.com
Estab: 2006

Laxminarayan Bhat, President & CEO & Founder
Marc Cantillon, CMO
Partha R.R. Sarathy, CFO

Developer of therapy for CNS, cardiovascular,
metabolic and inflammatory diseases. The company is a clinical development pharmaceutical
company.

Revolution Medicines Inc　　HQ
700 Saginaw Dr
Redwood City CA 94063
P: 650-481-6801　　PRC:262
www.revolutionmedicines.com
Email: inquiries@revolutionmedicines.com
Estab: 2014

Kevan Shokat, Co-Founder & Scientific Advisory
Board Member
Michael Fischbach, Co-Founder & Scientific Advi-
sory Board Member
Mark A. Goldsmith, President & CEO & Chairman
of the Board
Peg Horn, COO & EVP & General Counsel
Luan Wilfong, SVP of Human Resources

Developer of medicines for the treatment of
serious diseases. The company is involved in the
synthesis of original compounds.

RevStream Inc　　HQ
100 Marine Pkwy Ste 310
Redwood Shores CA 94065
P: 888-738-0206　　PRC:325
www.revstreamone.com
Email: sales@revstreamone.com
Estab: 2008

Kai Wong, Director of Pre-Sales Consulting

Provider of enterprise revenue and billing
management solutions. The company also offers
advisory and technical support services.

Rex Key & Security　　HQ
1908 University Ave
Berkeley CA 94704
P: 510-527-7000　F: 510-848-0126　PRC:59
www.rexkey.com
Email: sales@rexkey.com
Estab: 1910

Toni Moreland, Dispatcher

Designer of security systems for automotive,
institutional, commercial, industrial, and residential
purposes.

Reynard Corp　　HQ
1020 Calle Sombra　　[N]
San Clemente CA 92673
P: 949-366-8866　F: 949-498-9528　PRC:83
www.reynardcorp.com
Email: info@reynardcorp.com
Emp: 11-50　　Estab: 1984

Randy Reynard, President
Todd Burr, Manager of Operations & Engineering
Andrew Beckman, Process Engineer
Marcus Gronberg, Thin Film Project Engineer
Christopher Karp, Business Development Exec-
utive

Manufacturer of custom optical thin film coatings.

RGB Spectrum　　HQ
950 Marina Village Pkwy
Alameda CA 94501
P: 510-814-7000　F: 510-814-7026　PRC:98
www.rgb.com
Email: sales@rgb.com
Estab: 1987

Bob Marcus, CEO
Scott Norder, COO
Iana Zemniakova, CFO
Andy Thompson, VP of Marketing & Product
Management
Bob Ehlers, VP of Marketing

Manufacturer of video and computer signal display
processors. The company serves security, oil and
gas, corporate, and military sectors.

RGS Industries　　HQ
445 Laurelwood Rd
Santa Clara CA 95054
P: 669-238-0632　　PRC:162
www.rgsindustries.com
Email: info@rgsind.com

Loren Briggs, President
Lisa Southard, CFO
Jane Morales, Marketing Manager

Manufacturer and supplier of gaskets. The company offers seals, shielding and related materials,
and die cutting services.

Rheosense Inc HQ
2420 Camino Ramon Ste 240
San Ramon CA 94583
P: 925-866-3801 F: 925-866-3804 PRC:13
www.rheosense.com
Email: info@rheosense.com
Estab: 2001

Garry Dauron, VP of sales
Eric Ng, International Sales Manager
Hua Han, Senior Production Manager
Angela Ng, Production Manager
Mahesh Gupta, Senior Staff Software Engineer

Designer and manufacturer of viscometers and extensional viscometers. The company offers calibration, sample testing, and maintenance services.

Rickard Metals Inc HQ
2043 Elm Ct [N]
Ontario CA 91761
P: 909-947-4922 PRC:62
www.rickardmetals.com
Estab: 1985

Peggy Rickard, Owner
John Rickard, SVP & CEO
Stacie Curcio, Production Supervisor

Provider of engineering and supply chain management services.

Ridge Communications Inc HQ
12919 Alcosta Blvd Ste 2
San Ramon CA 94583
P: 925-498-2340 F: 925-498-2341 PRC:63
www.ridgecommunicate.com
Estab: 2002

Wes Rigsby, General Manager
Rick Angkham, Manager of Project
Russ Patridge, Principal
Ron Roberts, Project Coordinator
Sherry Wiggins, Project Coordinator

Provider of network deployment and project management services. The company serves the wireless carrier industry.

Ridge to River HQ
1050 Cedar St
Fort Bragg CA 95437
P: 707-357-0857 PRC:140
ridgetoriver.com
Estab: 1995

Teri Jo Barber, Hydrologist & CEO

Provider of hydrologic analysis and modeling services. The company is also focused on ecological restoration, erosion control, and water quality analysis.

Riga Analytical Lab Inc HQ
3375 Scott Blvd Ste 132
Santa Clara CA 95054
P: 408-496-6944 F: 408-496-0981 PRC:306
sites.google.com/rigalab.com/rigalab
Email: info@rigalab.com
Estab: 1982

Lydia Vorgias, Analyst

Provider of laboratory services specializing in electrical failure analysis, circuit extraction, latch up evaluation, and parallel and angel lapping.

Rigel Pharmaceuticals Inc HQ
1180 Veterans Blvd
S San Francisco CA 94080
P: 650-624-1100 F: 650-624-1101 PRC:34
www.rigel.com
Email: ir@rigel.com
Estab: 1996
Sales: $30M to $100M

Raul R. Rodriguez, President & CEO
Anne-Marie Duliege, EVP & CMO
James Diehl, VP of Legal & Chief Patent Counsel
Tarek Sallam, VP of Marketing
Dolly Vance, EVP of Corporate Affairs & General Counsel

Developer novel, small-molecule drugs for the treatment of inflammatory and autoimmune diseases, immuno-oncology related diseases, and muscle disorders.

RightITnow HQ
101A Clay St Ste 150
San Francisco CA 94111
P: 415-350-3581 PRC:323
rightitnow.com
Email: info@rightitnow.com
Estab: 2013

Marc Ferrie, Founder & CEO
Devi Menon, Java Developer

Provider of information technology operations management software. The company offers services to government agencies and business organizations.

Rightpoint BR
1611 Telegraph Ave Ste 1550
Oakland CA 94612
P: 415-935-3390 PRC:45
www.rightpoint.com
Email: oakland@rightpoint.com
Estab: 2007

Ross Freedman, Co-Founder & CEO
Brad Schneider, Co-Founder & Advisor
Julie Lewis, CFO
Jobin Ephrem, Chief Growth Officer
Anamika Lasser, Chief Experience Officer

A digital consultancy firm that designs and engineers end-to-end digital experiences to help clients succeed at the speed of innovation.

Rightware Inc BR
470 Ramona St
Palo Alto CA 94301
P: 832-483-7093 PRC:322
www.rightware.com
Email: sales@rightware.com
Estab: 2009

Tero Sarkkinen, Founder & President
Ville Ilves, COO
Jussi Tammi, CFO

Provider of user interface technologies serving the mobile, automotive, and other embedded industries.

Riley Plastic Manufacturing Inc HQ
3551 Haven Ave Ste M
Menlo Park CA 94025
P: 650-366-5104 F: 650-366-2966 PRC:80
www.rileyplastic.com
Email: rileyplastic@yahoo.com

Richard Riley, President

Provider of vacuum forming, vapor polishing, and assembly services. The company serves the medical and biotech industries.

Rimnetics Inc BR
3141 Swetzer Rd
Loomis CA 95650
P: 916-652-5555 PRC:187
www.rimnetics.com
Estab: 1985

Siegfried Waaga, General Manager
Brena Winig, Office Manager
Suzanne Gonzales, Customer Service Manager
Katilin Jones, Quality Control Inspector
Vitaliy Khlystik, Finisher

Providers of RIM molded structural parts, enclosures, cosmetic housings, encapsulation and overmolding. The company makes molded polyurethane parts.

Rincon Broadcasting LLC HQ
414 E Cota St [N]
Santa Barbara CA 93101
P: 805-879-8300 PRC:63
www.ktyd.com
Email: lin@ktyd.com

Chip Ehrhardt, CRO
Darrin McAfee, EVP of Digital Sales
Brian Davis, Director of Program

Broadcaster of rock music.

Rincon Consultants Inc BR
449 15th St Ste 303
Oakland CA 94612
P: 510-834-4455 F: 510-834-4433 PRC:139
rinconconsultants.com
Email: info@rinconconsultants.com
Estab: 1994

Michael P. Gialketsis, President
Stephen Svete, VP
Jennifer Haddow, Principal & VP
Richard Daulton, EVP
Steve Hongola, Senior Ecologist & Biological Program Manager

Provider of environmental consulting services. The company specializes in land use planning, site assessment, remediation, and other services.

Ripon Manufacturing Company Inc HQ
652 S Stockton Ave
Ripon CA 95366
P: 209-599-2148 F: 209-599-3114 PRC:80
www.riponmfgco.com
Email: sales@riponmfgco.com
Estab: 1963

Ursula Navarro, Controller
Alana Navarro, Administrative Assistant

Fabricator of steel processing equipment. The company manufactures and installs peelers, sizers, hardshell crackers, hoppers, dryers, and sorters.

Riverbed Technology HQ
680 Folsom St
San Francisco CA 94107
P: 415-247-8800   F: 415-247-8801   PRC:68
www.riverbed.com
Email: info@riverbed.com
Estab: 2002

David M. Peranich, President of Worldwide Field
Operations
Rich McBee, CEO
Dan Smoot, COO
Ian Halifax, CFO
David Greene, CMO

Provider of WAN optimization, cloud, consolidation, disaster recovery, and network performance
management solutions.

Riverside Scrap Iron HQ
2993 Sixth St   [N]
Riverside CA 92507
P: 951-686-2129   F: 951-686-8933   PRC:145
www.riversidemetalrecycling.com
Estab: 1954

Danny Frankel, President
Raj Gandhi, EVP
Frank Cuthbert, Manager of Operations
Shar Bjork, Executive Assistant

Recycler of waste and scrap metals.

RIX Industries HQ
4900 Industrial Way
Benicia CA 94510
P: 707-747-5900   F: 707-747-9200   PRC:148
www.rixindustries.com
Email: info@rixindustries.com
Estab: 1878

Bert E. Otterson, President
Sheryl Sindt, CFO
Jerry Stultz, COO
Bryan Reid, CSO
Brad Klock, Chief Programs Officer

Manufacturer of air and gas compressors. The
company's products include industrial and commercial compressors, nitrogen generators, and
AMS parts.

RKI Instruments Inc HQ
33248 Central Ave
Union City CA 94587
P: 510-441-5656   F: 510-441-5650   PRC:13
www.rkiinstruments.com
Estab: 1994

Bob Pellissier, President
Sandra Gallagher, VP
Mike Johnson, Marketing Manager
Steve Peluffo, Technical Services Manager
Marty Schwartz, Technical Support Manager

Manufacturer of gas detectors and monitoring systems. The company caters to refineries, utilities,
and oil tankers.

RM King Co HQ
315 N Marks Ave   [N]
Fresno CA 93706
P: 559-266-0258   F: 559-266-1672   PRC:179
www.rmking.com
Email: info@rmking.com
Estab: 1953

Michael Dowling, Contact

Manufacturer of parts for cotton pickers overhauls
cotton pickers.

RM Machining Inc HQ
950 Terminal Way
San Carlos CA 94070
P: 650-591-4178   F: 650-591-4412   PRC:80
www.rm-machining.com
Email: sales@rm-machining.com
Estab: 1983

Robert Myhre, Owner
Michelle Myhre, Operations Manager & Operations Manager

Provider of precision machining services. The
company caters to the aerospace, defense, medical, and energy sectors.

RMC Engineering HQ
255 Mayock Rd
Gilroy CA 95020
P: 408-842-2525   F: 408-842-0670   PRC:80
www.rmcengineering.com
Email: info@rmcengineering.com
Estab: 1978

Kevin McKenzie, CEO
Blake Rider, VP
Shawna McKenzie, Manager
Joe Miranda, Supervisor
Justin Wheeler, Truck Driver

Provider of automated safety systems, resurfacing
tools, blowers, and related supplies. The company
offers repair and replacement services.

Robbjack Corp HQ
3300 Nicolaus Rd
Lincoln CA 95648
P: 916-645-6045   F: 916-645-0146   PRC:157
www.robbjack.com
Email: sales@robbjack.com
Estab: 1959

Mike MacArthur, VP of Engineering
Khadidja Norris, VP of Manufacturing
Kenneth Fickas, Maintenance Manager
Sherry Feightner, Manager Office
Steve Gregory, Manager

Provider of tools for aerospace, aluminum tools,
die mold and hard metal tools, custom end mills,
and custom saws.

Robertson Precision Inc HQ
325 Sharon Park Dr Unit 444
Menlo Park CA 94025
P: 650-363-2212   PRC:319
www.robertsonprecision.com
Email: rfq@robertsonprecision.com
Estab: 1984

Bill Robertson, President

Manufacturer of precision metals and plastic products. The company's services include engineering
support and process control.

ROBLOX Corp HQ
970 Park Pl
San Mateo CA 94403
P: 888-858-2569   PRC:317
www.roblox.com
Email: press@roblox.com
Estab: 2006

David Baszucki, Founder & CEO
Toby Teel, Software Engineer
Shailendra Rathore, Engineer

Specializes in game development, monetization,
and publishing services. The company serves
businesses.

Robson Technologies Inc HQ
135 E Main Ave Ste 130
Morgan Hill CA 95037
P: 408-779-8008   F: 408-782-7132   PRC:208
www.testfixtures.com
Email: rtisales@testfixtures.com
Estab: 1989

John Widmeyer, VP
Chris OConnor, Director of Applications of Sys-
tems
Kulia Lemus, Inside Sales Manager
Trevor Johnson, Applications Engineer
Nicklaus Schmidt, Mechanical Design Engineer

Provider of customizable hardware interfaces that
bridge the gap between the test device and the
measurement system.

Rock Systems Inc HQ
3250 Riverside Blvd
Sacramento CA 95818
P: 916-921-9000   F: 916-921-9070   PRC:80
www.rocksystems.com
Email: info@rocksystems.com
Estab: 1973

John Bruce, Founder
Mike Bruce, President

Provider of material handling solutions. The
company offers hoppers, feeders, conveyors,
separators, and related accessories.

Rocket Communications Inc HQ
81 Langton St Ste 12
San Francisco CA 94103
P: 415-863-0101   PRC:323
www.rocketcom.com
Email: info@rocketcom.com
Estab: 1992

Michal Anne Rogondino, Founder & CEO
Kevin Hause, COO
Mandy Wallace, CFO
Ty van Leuven, Visual Experience Director
Duncan McAlester, Astro Product Director

Developer of user interface, visual, and icon design services for software and related applications.

Rocket EMS Inc HQ
2950 Patrick Henry Dr
Santa Clara CA 95054
P: 408-727-3700 PRC:207
www.rocketems.com
Email: sales@rocketems.com
Estab: 2011

Michael Kottke, President
Chris Mak, CFO
Peter Chipman, VP
Scott Schaetzle, Director of Service Operations
Sheila Ramos, Executive Administrator & Manager of Program & Human Resource

Provider of electronic manufacturing services. The company caters to high growth technology sectors.

Rockliffe Systems Inc HQ
1901 S Bascom Ave Ste 1190
Campbell CA 95008
P: 408-879-5600 F: 408-879-5610 PRC:322
www.rockliffe.com
Email: sales@rockliffe.com
Estab: 1995

John Davies, Founder & CEO & President & Chairman

Provider of mobile communication software for service providers, enterprises, and consumers. The company offers design services.

Rocklin Hydraulics HQ
2304 Sierra Meadows Dr
Rocklin CA 95677
P: 916-624-8900 PRC:159
www.rocklinhydraulics.com
Email: info@rocklinhydraulics.com
Estab: 1995

Charlie Roberson, Owner

Manufacturer of hydraulic products. The company offers hydraulic hoses, caps and plugs, jaw couplers, and brass fittings.

Rockwell Automation Inc BR
3000 Executive Pkwy Ste 210
San Ramon CA 94583
P: 925-242-5700 PRC:311
Estab: 1903

Hedwig Maes, President
Sujeet Chand, SVP & CTO

Provider of control systems, sensing devices, security, and other products. The company offers asset management, network, and other services.

Rockyou Inc HQ
642 Harrison St Ste 300
San Francisco CA 94107
P: 415-580-6400 PRC:317
Estab: 2005

Lisa Marino, CEO
Scott McClellan, VP of Ad Operations & Ad Product
Brent Allard, Senior Director of IT & Operations
Robin Molt, Assistant Secretary

Provider of gaming solutions. The company's games include Poker, Bingo, Zoo World, and others and serves the entertainment sector.

ROD-L Electronics Inc HQ
935-F Sierra Vista
Mountain View CA 94043
P: 650-322-0711 F: 650-326-1993 PRC:209
www.rodl.com
Email: info@rodl.com
Estab: 1977

Roy Clay, Engineer

Provider of electrical safety testing equipment. The company also offers hipot test loads, test probes, bond testers, and ground testers.

Roettele Industries Inc HQ
15485 Dupont Ave [N]
Chino CA 91710
P: 909-606-8252 PRC:57
www.roetteleindustries.com
Emp: 1-10 Estab: 1979

Mark Roettele, Contact

Manufacturer of non-metallic washers and gaskets.

Roger K Sherman Co HQ
325 Los Altos Ave
Los Altos CA 94022
P: 650-941-8300 F: 650-949-3071 PRC:18
www.shermanstandards.com
Email: info@shermanstandards.com
Estab: 1962

Roger K. Sherman, President & Owner

Provider of microscope eyepiece reticles, calibration standards, and ruled master gages for the semiconductor and magnetic head industries.

ROHM Semiconductor USA LLC BR
2323 Owen St
Santa Clara CA 95054
P: 408-720-1900 F: 408-720-1918 PRC:207
www.rohm.com
Estab: 1958

Zachary Hunter, Director of IT & Logistics
Go Ezaki, System Architect
Desiree Doria, Human Resource Assistant

Manufacturer of amplifiers, clocks, modules, passive components, remote control receivers, and timers.

Rolepoint HQ
575 Market St Ste 401
San Francisco CA 94105
P: 888-571-2851 PRC:319
www.rolepoint.com
Email: inquiries@rolepoint.com
Estab: 2011

Kes Thygesen, Founder & CPO
Mark Price, VP of Business Development
Ryan Goetz, Customer Success Manager
Carl Henderson, Engineering Manager
Alessandra Williams, Marketing Development Lead

Focuses on talent acquisition services. The company serves small and medium businesses and Fortune 500 companies.

Rollbar Inc HQ
51 Federal St Ste 401
San Francisco CA 94107
P: 888-568-3350 PRC:322
rollbar.com
Email: team@rollbar.com
Estab: 2012

Cory Virok, Founder & CTO

Developer of error tracking software. The company is also engaged in coding and troubleshooting services.

Rollin J Lobaugh Inc HQ
1331 Old County Rd
Belmont CA 94002
P: 650-583-9682 PRC:80
www.rjlobaugh.com
Email: sales@rjlobaugh.com
Estab: 1922

Jack Corey, President

Manufacturer of machined components. The company mainly manufactures screws and offers supporting services.

Rollinson Advertising Design HQ
45 Janin Pl
Pleasant Hill CA 94523
P: 925-518-6698 PRC:318
rollinsonadvertising.com
Estab: 1990

Martin Rollinson, Owner

Provider of graphic design, traditional marketing, strategic planning, and e-mail blasting services.

Rolls-Royce Engine Services - Oakland Inc BR
7200 Earhart Rd
Oakland CA 94621
P: 510-613-1000 PRC:4
www.rolls-royce.com
Estab: 1960

John Rishton, CEO
Bilo Surdhar, VP of Customer Business
Tomas Lopez, Material Supervisor & Traffic Specialist
Raul Palma, Aircraft Technician

Designer, manufacturer, and marketer of power systems. The company offers engines for airliners and military aircraft.

Ron Witherspoon Inc HQ
1551 Dell Ave
Campbell CA 95008-6903
P: 408-370-6620 F: 408-370-4985 PRC:80
rwinc.com
Email: info@rwinc.com
Estab: 1977

Dave Arterburn, EDM Department Manager
Ken Nelson, Manager
Courtney Guetschow, Manager of Operations
Keshav Sharma, Quality & Manager of Business Development & Quality Systems Manager
Carol Andrews, Personnel Specialist

Manufacturer of high precision parts. The company offers milling, turning, electrical discharge machining, and grinding services.

Ronan Engineering Co HQ
28209 Ave Stanford [N]
Valencia CA 91355
P: 661-702-1344 F: 661-295-6063 PRC:235
www.ronan.com
Estab: 1962

John Hewitson, Founder

Manufacturer reliable and leading-edge instrumentation systems.

Roos Instruments Inc BR
2285 Martin Ave
Santa Clara CA 95050
P: 408-748-8589 F: 408-748-8595 PRC:212
www.roos.com
Email: support@roos.com
Estab: 1989

Mark Roos, Founder & CEO
Catherine Rossi Roos, COO
Don Ferris, Test & Fixturing Engineer
Mark Brown, Software Engineer
Devin Morris, Senior RF Applications Engineer

Manufacturer of automated test equipment. The company's products include MEMs devices, radars, amplifiers, and mixers.

Rootdesign LLC HQ
946 Noe St
San Francisco CA 94114
P: 415-282-2484 PRC:325
www.rootdesign.com
Email: info@rootdesign.com
Estab: 1997

Kevin Rogers, Founder & Lead Technical Director
Hien Phan, Programming Director

Provider of design solutions specializing in brand strategy, user interface design, and database development services.

Roplast Industries Inc HQ
3155 S Fifth Ave
Oroville CA 95965
P: 530-532-9500 F: 530-532-9576 PRC:280
www.roplast.com
Estab: 1990

Robert Berman, Owner
Michael Jobes, VP of Sales & Marketing
Mark Quillin, VP of Operations
Roxanne Vaughan, Director of Sales
Dean Squires, Plant Manager

Manufacturer of bags. The company specializes in custom designed bags made out of polyethylene films.

Rorze Automation Inc DH
41215 Albrae St
Fremont CA 94538
P: 510-687-1340 PRC:153
rorzeautomation.com
Estab: 1985

Bill Fyall, President
Keith Miyamoto, Senior Manager of Accounting & Human Resources
Jeze Acosta, Field Service Engineer
Trey Cherry, Mechanical Engineer
Jeff Aihara, Operation Coordinator

Manufacturer of automation products. The company's applications include displays, semiconductors, and laboratories.

Roscoe Moss Co HQ
4360 Worth St [N]
Los Angeles CA 90063
P: 323-263-4111 F: 323-263-4497 PRC:159
www.roscoemoss.com
Email: info@roscoemoss.com
Emp: 51-200 Estab: 1926

George E. Moss, Contact
Roscoe Moss, Contact

Manufacturer of water well casings and screens.

Rose Electronics Distributing Company Inc HQ
2030 Ringwood Ave
San Jose CA 95131-1728
P: 408-943-0200 F: 408-943-0360 PRC:201
www.rosebatteries.com
Email: sales@rose-elec.com
Estab: 1963

Katherine Mack, VP of Sales & Marketing

Provider of batteries and power solutions. The company primarily serves original equipment manufacturers such as VRLA batteries and lithium ion batteries.

Ross Engineering Corp HQ
540 Westchester Dr
Campbell CA 95008
P: 408-377-4621 F: 408-377-5182 PRC:78
www.rossengineeringcorp.com
Email: info@rossengineeringcorp.com
Estab: 1964

Cody Kulow, Quality Manager
Jim Ross, Sales Manager

Designer and manufacturer of high voltage electronic and electro-mechanical devices like relays, probes, voltmeters, switches, and breakers.

Rotometals Inc HQ
865 Estabrook St [N]
San Leandro CA 94577
P: 888-779-1102 PRC:80
www.rotometals.com
Email: sales@rotometals.com
Estab: 1939

Mike Hora, Contact

Distributor of non-ferrous metal elements and alloys such as aluminum, antimony, bismuth, indium and more.

Royal Circuit Solutions Inc HQ
21 Hamilton Ct
Hollister CA 95023
P: 831-636-7789 PRC:211
www.royalcircuits.com
Email: sales@royalcircuits.com
Estab: 1988

Milan Shah, CEO
Amber Marini, Regional Sales Manager

Manufacturer of printed circuit boards. The company's products are used in prototype and medium production runs and offers fabrication services.

Royce Instruments Inc HQ
480 Technology Way
Napa CA 94558
P: 707-255-9078 F: 707-255-9079 PRC:212
www.royceinstruments.com
Email: sales@royceinstruments.com
Estab: 1983

Malcolm Cox, Founder & Owner & CTO
Scott Newell, Technical Sales Manager
Sarah Parrish, Senior Sales Applications Engineer
Markus Liebhard, Senior Mechanical Engineer
Marci Sage Gillespie, Senior Quality Assurance Technician

Provider of bond testers and die sorters for the auto and medical electronics device manufacturers worldwide.

RS Software Inc BR
1900 McCarthy Blvd Ste 103
Milpitas CA 95035
P: 408-382-1200 F: 408-382-0083 PRC:323
rssoftware.com
Email: sales@rssoftware.com
Estab: 1991

Raj Jain, Managing Director & Chairman
Milind Kamat, COO
Vijendra Surana, CFO & Company Secretary
Sumit Misra, Associate VP
Bibok Das, EVP of Business Development

Provider of business payment solutions for the risk prediction, residual management, payment gateway, and merchant boarding areas.

Rucker Kolls Inc HQ
1064 Yosemite Dr
Milpitas CA 95035
P: 408-934-9875 F: 408-934-9720 PRC:211
ruckerkolls.com
Email: sales@ruckerkolls.com
Estab: 1968

Mark Waks, Regional Sales Manager
Jean Descanzo, Controller

Provider of solutions for ATE test interface products. The company's services include custom PCB design and card stiffeners and rings.

Ruckus Networks HQ
350 W Java Dr
Sunnyvale CA 94089
P: 650-265-4200 PRC:63
www.ruckuswireless.com
Estab: 2004

Victor Shtrom, Founder & Chief Wireless Architect
Alexander W. Pease, EVP & CFO
Karen K. Renner, SVP & CIO
Morgan C.S. Kurk, EVP & CTO
Robyn T. Mingle, SVP & Chief Human Resource Officer

Designer and manufacturer of Wi-Fi products and wireless LAN systems. The company also focuses on the marketing aspects.

Rudy's Commercial Refrigeration HQ
1660 Rumrill Blvd
San Pablo CA 94806-4305
P: 510-376-9163   F: 510-235-5556   PRC:154
rudysrefrigeration.com
Estab: 2009

Ben Plant, President

Provider of refrigeration products such as coolers and freezers, compressors, glass doors and strip curtains, and temperature alarms.

Runscope Inc HQ
548 Market St Ste 14137
San Francisco CA 94108-5401
P: 888-812-6786   PRC:325
www.runscope.com
Email: dmca@runscope.com
Estab: 2013

Troy Miller, API Product Manager

Specializes in automated performance monitoring and testing solutions. The company serves developers.

Runtime Design Automation HQ
2560 Mission College Blvd Ste 130
Santa Clara CA 95054-2904
P: 408-492-0940   F: 408-492-0941   PRC:322
runtimeinc.com
Email: info@rtda.com
Estab: 1995

Stuart Taylor, Director of Solutions Architecture
Yohan Bouvron, Technical Support Engineer

Provider of management system software for the IC design industry. The company is engaged in documentation and technical support.

RUSH PCB Inc RH
2149-20 O'Toole Ave
San Jose CA 95131
P: 408-496-6013   F: 408-854-8094   PRC:211
www.rushpcb.com
Email: sales@rushpcb.com
Estab: 1997

Akber Roy, CEO
Padma Dantu, Manager

Manufacturer of printed circuit boards and assemblies. The company is engaged in engineering and electronics manufacturing services.

Rutter Armey Inc HQ
2684 S Cherry Ave
Fresno CA 93706
P: 559-237-1866   F: 559-237-5806   PRC:80
www.rutterarmey.com
Email: rutterarmeyinc@yahoo.com
Estab: 1969

Henry Lopez, Contact
Kevin O'Neill, Service Department
David Fry, Shop Foreman
Al Smith, Shop Foreman

Provider of precision machining services. The company focuses on industrial hard chrome plating, welding, and metal spraying services.

Ryss Lab Inc HQ
29540 Kohoutek Way
Union City CA 94587
P: 510-477-9570   F: 510-477-0534   PRC:34
www.ryss.com
Email: info@ryss.com
Estab: 1997

Ming Lee, President
Joyce Wang, Revenue Accounting Supervisor

Provider of biotechnology and pharmaceutical development services. The company offers services to the healthcare sector.

S&C Electric Co BR
1135 Atlantic Ave
Alameda CA 94501
P: 510-864-9300   F: 510-864-6860   PRC:245
sandc.com
Estab: 1911

David W. Koepp, Regional VP of US Sales

Provider of equipment and services for electric power systems. The company is involved in design and installation services.

S2C Inc HQ
1762 Technology Dr Ste 209
San Jose CA 95110
P: 408-213-8818   F: 408-549-9948   PRC:323
www.s2cinc.com
Estab: 2003

Wendy Kuo, CFO
ChengLun Richard Chang, VP of Engineering
ShiYi Ma, Sales Manager

Provider of prototyping solutions. The company's customers include chip design and system design companies.

SA Photonics Inc HQ
120 Knowles Dr
Los Gatos CA 95032
P: 408-560-3500   F: 408-376-0950   PRC:177
www.saphotonics.com
Email: sales@saphotonics.com
Estab: 2002

Jim Coward, CEO
Dave Pechner, CTO
Toan Nguyen, Administrative Service Manager
Mark Koenig, Senior Software Engineer

Developer of photonic systems. The company offers solutions for head-mounted displays, microwave sensors, mirror sense, and control systems.

SACC Inc HQ
2903 Bunker Hill Ln Ste 107
Santa Clara CA 94054
P: 408-755-3000   F: 925-249-3031   PRC:324
www.saccinc.com
Email: salesinquiry@saccinc.com
Estab: 1998

Suhas Ahuja, Owner & CEO

Provider of enterprise resource planning, data warehousing, technology infrastructure, business process outsourcing, and staffing services.

SAE Engineering Inc HQ
365 Reed St
Santa Clara CA 95050
P: 408-987-9950   F: 408-987-9960   PRC:80
saeeng.com
Email: info@saeeng.com
Estab: 1963

James Millich, President
Alan Pats, CEO
Richard Lopez, Estimating Manager
Araceli Ramirez, Inside Sales Coordinator
Devon Hernandez, Executive Administrative Assistant

Provider of integrated turnkey assembly, precision machining, and sheet metal fabrication services to many sectors. The company also offers software.

SAES Pure Gas Inc HQ
4175 Santa Fe Rd   [N]
San Luis Obispo CA 93401
P: 805-541-9299   F: 805-541-9399   PRC:156
www.saespuregas.com
Estab: 1987

Tim Johnson, CEO

Manufacturer of gas purifiers for semiconductor industry.

Safe Hearing America Inc HQ
130 Allison Ct Ste G-1
Vacaville CA 95688
P: 707-446-0880   F: 707-446-9632   PRC:189
www.safehearingamerica.com

Willena Beyer, President
Susanne Schwartz, Data Systems Manager

Provider of mobile hearing testing services and products. The company offerings include AQ Solid Plug, Sleep Plug, and Solid Plug.

Safebridge Consultants Inc HQ
1924 Old Middlefield Way
Mountain View CA 94043-2503
P: 650-961-4820   F: 650-623-0096   PRC:142
www.safebridge.com
Email: susan.custer@safebridge.com
Estab: 1998

Teresa M. Bryning, VP & Principal Chemist
Bob Ku, VP
Allan W. Ader, Managing Director
Robert G. Sussman, Managing Director
Gail Baer, Administrative Office Manager

Provider of consulting services and analytical support. The company provides safety, health and environmental services.

Safety Equipment Corp HQ
1141 Old County Rd
Belmont CA 94002
P: 650-595-5422   F: 650-595-0143   PRC:159
www.safetyequipmentcorp.com
Email: info@safetyequipmentcorp.com
Estab: 1979

Ken Hettman, Manager

Designer and manufacturer of gas cabinets, valve boxes, leaker cabinets, exhausted enclosures, and related products.

SAGE Instruments Inc   RH
240 Airport Blvd
Freedom CA 95019
P: 831-761-1000   PRC:166
www.sageinst.com/contact.html
Email: sales@sageinst.com
Estab: 1984

Michael Groh, Engineering Director & Design Engineer
Dave Morris, Senior Hardware Engineer

Provider of wireless base station test products. The company offers battery operated handhelds, portables, bench tops, and rackmount test platforms.

Sage Metering Inc   HQ
8 Harris Ct Bldg D1
Monterey CA 93940
P: 831-242-2030   F: 831-655-4965   PRC:14
www.sagemetering.com
Email: info@sagemetering.com
Estab: 2002

Mark Crawford, VP of Operations
Gary Russell, VP of operations & Engineering
Myrna Thorson, Executive Assistant

Manufacturer of thermal mass flow meters. The company offers services to the environmental and industrial sectors.

Sagimet Biosciences   HQ
155 Bovet Rd Ste 303
San Mateo CA 94402
P: 650-561-8600   PRC:249
sagimet.com
Email: businessdevelopment@sagimet.com
Estab: 2006

George Kemble, CEO & CSO
Dennis Hom, CFO

Focuses on the discovery and development of therapeutic products for the treatment of oncology and infectious diseases.

Sai Technology Inc   HQ
2376 Walsh Ave
Santa Clara CA 95051
P: 408-727-1560   PRC:64
saitechnology.com
Email: info@saitechnology.com

Venkat Rayapati, Founder & Chairman & CEO
Xia Gao, Director of Technology

Designer and developer of wireless technology solutions. The company also deals with digital signage services.

Salter Labs   HQ
100 Sycamore Rd   [N]
Arvin CA 93203
P: 661-854-3166   F: 661-854-3850   PRC:189
www.salterlabs.com
Emp: 501-1000   Estab: 2010

Jane Kiernan, CEO

Manufacturer of surgical and medical instruments.

Salutron Inc   HQ
8371 Central Ave Unit A
Newark CA 94560
P: 510-795-2876   F: 510-657-7334   PRC:187
www.salutron.com
Email: sales@salutron.com
Estab: 1995

Mike Tsai, Co-Founder
Tom Lo, Co-Founder & CTO
Angela Cheng, Account Services Manager
May Lee, Program Manager

Providers of health care solutions. The company offers on-demand ECG accurate heart rate monitoring solutions.

Samax Precision Inc   HQ
926 W Evelyn Ave
Sunnyvale CA 94086
P: 408-245-9555   F: 408-245-0123   PRC:80
www.samaxinc.com
Email: info@samaxinc.com
Estab: 1963

Vicki Murray, President
Chris Hurrye, VP of Operations
Michael Tampier, CNC Prototype Machinist

Manufacturer and supplier of precision machined products. The company offers services like grinding and honing. It serves military and aerospace fields.

Samco Inc   RH
2302 Walsh Ave
Santa Clara CA 95051
P: 408-734-0459   F: 408-734-0961   PRC:126
www.samcointl.com
Email: info@samcointl.com
Estab: 1979

Peter Wood, Director of US Operations
Henry Chan, General Manager of Account Management

Manufacturer of deposition, etching, and surface treatment systems used in the manufacturing of LED, MEMS, power and RF device, and other products.

Samsara Networks Inc   HQ
350 Rhode Island St Ste 300
San Francisco CA 94103
P: 415-985-2400   PRC:325
www.samsara.com
Email: sales@samsara.com
Estab: 2015

John Bicket, CTO & Co-Founder
Sanjit Biswas, CEO & Co-Founder
Kiren Sekar, EVP of Product & Marketing
Ben Calderon, EVP of Hardware Engineering & Operations

Manufacturer of flexible sensors. The company is engaged in fleet monitoring, industrial sensing, cold chain monitoring, and fleet telematics.

Samsung Research America   DH
665 Clyde Ave
Mountain View CA 94043
P: 650-210-1001   PRC:306
sra.samsung.com
Email: sra-careers@sisa.samsung.com
Estab: 1988

Allan Devantier, VP of Audio Research & Development
Pascal BRUNET, Principal DSP Engineer

Provider of commercial, physical, and biological research services. The company is involved in testing and identification solutions.

Samsung Semiconductor Inc   HQ
3655 N First St
San Jose CA 95134
P: 408-544-4000   F: 408-544-4980   PRC:86
samsungsemiconductor-us.com
Email: phd.fellowship@ssi.samsung.com

Lifeng Zheng, Senior Engineer

Provider of electronics manufacturing and digital media products. The company also offers mobile services and PC software.

Samtec   BR
2323 Owen St Ste 120
Santa Clara CA 95054
P: 812-944-6733   F: 408-217-5171   PRC:76
www.samtec.com
Email: ecustomerservice@samtec.com

John Shine, President
Danny Boesing, Director of Product Marketing

Manufacturer of high-speed assemblies, connectors, edge cards, and jumpers. The company serves the industrial sector.

San Francisco Circuits   HQ
1660 S Amphlett Blvd Ste 200
San Mateo CA 94402
P: 800-732-5143   F: 650-655-7206   PRC:211
www.sfcircuits.com
Email: sales@sfcircuits.com
Estab: 2005

Alexander Danovich, President & CEO
Sam Danovich, VP of Sales
Robert Boten, Director of Quality

Provider and manufacturer of printed circuit boards. The company also offers services like PCB design and assembly and specializes in complex circuits.

San Joaquin Chemicals Inc   HQ
1236 N Sierra Vista
Fresno CA 93703
P: 559-725-1735   PRC:51
sjc-inc.com
Email: sales@sjc-inc.com
Estab: 1955

James Scott, Chemist

Provider of chemicals and services for condensers, boilers, closed loops, potable water, and waste water. The company serves the healthcare industry.

San-I-Pak Pacific Inc   HQ
23535 S Bird Rd
Tracy CA 95378
P: 209-836-2310   F: 209-836-2336   PRC:159
www.sanipak.com
Email: info@sanipak.com
Estab: 1978

Arthur McCoy, SVP
Mitch Alvillar, Director of Electronics & Technical Support

Manufacturer of compactors, shredders, and sterilizer supplies. The company serves the industrial sector and enterprises.

Sanah Inc   HQ
1104 Corporate Way Ste 127
Sacramento CA 95831
P: 888-306-1942   PRC:323
sanahinc.com
Email: info@sanahinc.com
Estab: 2003

Monica Tahiliani, Co-Founder & VP of Delivery
Rajnish Tahiliani, Co-Founder & CTO
Maher Madhat, President
Maj Gen L. Tahiliani, Partner of India Telecom Services
Avinash V., Assistant Manager

Provider of IT services such as IT strategy consulting, systems integration, and custom application development.

Sanbio Inc   HQ
231 S Whisman Rd
Mountain View CA 94041-1522
P: 650-625-8965   F: 650-625-8969   PRC:305
www.san-bio.com
Email: info@san-bio.com
Estab: 2001

Keita Mori, CEO & Founder
Michael P. McGrogan, VP of Process Development
Ernest W. Yankee, VP
Zuha Warraich, Research Scientist

Developer of regenerative therapies for neurological disorders. The company offers services to the healthcare sector.

Sancrosoft USA Inc   RH
4944 Sunrise Blvd Ste B4
Fair Oaks CA 95628
P: 916-671-5593   PRC:322
sankrosoft.com
Email: sankar@sancrosoftusa.com
Estab: 2008

Sonal Khunger, Director of Tabmiles
Sam Hunt, Recruitment Manager
Deepak Sancro, IT Recruiter
Arvind Reddy, Recruiter
Jatinder Chauhan, Recruiter

Provider of technology consulting, IT staffing, and recruiting services. The company offers systems integration and application development services.

Sanctuary Stainless   HQ
7532 Sandholdt Rd Ste 1
Moss Landing CA 95039
P: 831-633-3867   PRC:82
www.sancsta.com
Email: sancsta@redshift.com

David Jablonski, Owner

Provider of metal fabrication services. The company specializes in stainless and aluminum tubing and pipe fabrication.

Sandhu Products Inc   HQ
6052 Industrial Way Ste H
Livermore CA 94551
P: 510-996-7199   PRC:268
www.sandhuproducts.com
Email: info@sandhuproducts.com
Estab: 2004

Raman Sandhu, President
Bob Sandhu, CEO

Provider of ayurvedic herbal dietary supplements. The company offers products containing vitamins, amino acids, minerals and medicinal plant extracts.

SanDisk Corp   HQ
951 SanDisk Dr
Milpitas CA 95035
P: 408-801-1000   PRC:116
www.sandisk.com
Estab: 1988

Shuki Nir, SVP of Corporate Marketing & General Manager
Milo Azarmsa, SVP of Finance
Sumit Sadana, CSO & EVP
Tom Baker, SVP of Human Resources
Paul Alpern, Senior Director

Manufacturer of flash memory cards. The company's products include card readers, solid state drives, USB flash drives, and microSD cards.

Sandvik Thermal Process Inc   DH
19500 Nugget Blvd
Sonora CA 95370
P: 209-533-1990   F: 209-533-4079   PRC:159
www.mrlind.com
Estab: 1979

Tyke Johnson, General Manager of PC Components
Bjorn Larsson, Research & Development Manager
Richard Rosenberger, Service Engineer

Provider of thermal processing equipment. The company offers solar cells, semiconductors, and industrial heaters.

Sangamo Therapeutics   HQ
501 Canal Blvd
Richmond CA 94804
P: 510-970-6000   PRC:191
www.sangamo.com
Email: info@sangamo.com
Emp: 247 Estab: 1995
Sales: $100M to $300M

Edward R. Conner, SVP & CMO
Ward Wolff, EVP & CFO
Raphael Flipo, VP of COO Europe
Shirley Clift, VP of Regulatory Affairs
McDavid Stilwell, VP of Corporate Communications & Investor Relations

Developer of engineered DNA-binding proteins for the regulation of gene expression and for gene modification.

Sanovas Inc   HQ
2597 Kerner Blvd Ste 3320
San Rafael CA 94901
P: 415-729-9391   F: 415-729-9389   PRC:195
www.sanovas.com
Email: info@sanovas.com
Estab: 2009

Larry Gerrans, CEO
Charles N. Wang, CTO
Steve Goldsmith, VP of Marketing
Carlos Gonzalez, VP of RA & Quality Assurance
Alex Hsia, Director of Mechanical Engineering

Manufacturer of medical equipment. The company develops minimally invasive surgical tools and technologies.

SAP America Inc   BR
3410 Hillview Ave
Palo Alto CA 94304
P: 650-849-4000   F: 650-849-4200   PRC:319
www.sap.com

Eric Stine, Office of the President of Global Sales, Services & Customer Engagement
Jennifer Morgan, CEO
Juergen Mueller, CTO
Anthony Coletta, CFO
Thack Brown, COO

Developer of software applications. The company provides data and technology, custom development, and implementation services.

SAP Litmos   HQ
2700 Camino Ramon Ste 400
San Ramon CA 94583
P: 925-251-2220   PRC:324
www.litmos.com
Email: support@litmos.com
Estab: 2007

Dan Allen, VP of Engineering

Provider of learning management system solutions. The company serves the energy and engineering industries.

Sapphos Environmental Inc   BR
430 N Halstead St   [N]
Pasadena CA 91107
P: 626-683-3547   F: 626-683-1745   PRC:139
www.sapphosenvironmental.com
Email: mtejada@sapphosenvironmental.com
Emp: 11-50

Sarah Campbell, CFO

Provider of business consulting services.

Sardee Industries Inc   BR
2731 E Myrtle St
Stockton CA 95205
P: 209-466-1526   F: 209-466-1046   PRC:165
sardee.com
Email: sales@sardee.com
Estab: 1962

Thomas Hystad, Design Engineer
Bert Lum, Principal Scientist
Nancy Yu, Senior Research Associate

Provider of container manufacturing equipment. The company also offers engineering and repair services for packing and filling industries.

SAS Enterprises HQ

PO Box 21388 [N]
Concord CA 94521
P: 925-685-8968 PRC:45
sasenterprises.biz
Email: sashute@astound.net
Estab: 1990

Sally A. Shute, Principal

Provider of human resource management solutions.

Sasken Technologies Ltd BR

710 Lakeway Dr Ste 265
Sunnyvale CA 94085
P: 408-730-0100 PRC:63
www.sasken.com
Estab: 1989

Anjan Lahiri, CEO
Neeta Revankar, CFO & Whole-time Director

Provider of research and development consultation, wireless software products, and software services to automotive and health care sectors.

Satellite AV LLC HQ

4021 Alvis Ct Ste 5
Rocklin CA 95677
P: 916-677-0720 F: 916-644-6312 PRC:61
satelliteav.com
Email: support@satelliteav.com
Estab: 2005

Eugene Zaikin, Manager

Provider of broadcaster support and call center services. The company also deals with repairs, distribution, and sales.

Satori Labs Inc HQ

1800 Green Hills Rd Ste 203
Scotts Valley CA 95066
P: 831-457-9100 PRC:303
satorilabs.com
Email: info@satorilabs.com
Estab: 2003

Alan Copland, Director of Marketing

Provider of medical based software services. The company's offerings include FusionForm Desktop and FusionForm Mobile.

SatPath Systems Inc HQ

47971 Fremont Blvd
Fremont CA 94538
P: 510-979-1102 F: 510-979-1105 PRC:61
www.satpath.com
Estab: 2003

Herkea Jea, CEO
Cindy George, Office Manager

Provider of networking solutions. The company focuses on voice communication, video and video-conferencing, banking, and other applications.

Savari Inc HQ

2005 De La Cruz Blvd Ste 111
Santa Clara CA 95050
P: 408-833-6369 PRC:304
savari.net
Email: sales@savari.net
Estab: 2008

Ravi Puvvala, CEO & Founder
Paul Sakamoto, COO
Vibha Shrivastava, Human Resource Generalist

Provider of communications technology solutions. The company focuses on connecting cars to traffic lights, pedestrians, and smartphones.

SC Labs HQ

100 Pioneer St Ste E
Santa Cruz CA 95060
P: 866-435-0709 PRC:306
sclabs.com
Email: info@sclabs.com

Alec Dixon, Founder & Director of Client Relations
Josh Wurzer, President
Ian Rice, Director of Marketing & Development
MacKenzie Whitman, Laboratory Director
Jeff Dingman, Senior Technical Account Manager

Provider of medical quality assurance and safety testing services. The company's services include potency testing, pesticide testing, and microbial screening.

SC Mech Solution HQ

2241 Paragon Dr
San Jose CA 95131
P: 408-748-3380 PRC:80
www.sc-mechsolution.com
Estab: 2000

Edward Choi, Quality Assurance Manager
Jacqueline Nguyen, Coordinator

Manufacturer of electronic parts and components. The company provides CNC milling, tooling, design, and contract manufacturing services.

SC Solutions Inc HQ

1261 Oakmead Pkwy
Sunnyvale CA 94085
P: 408-617-4520 F: 408-617-4521 PRC:304
www.scsolutions.com
Email: sales@scsolutions.com
Estab: 1989

Abbas Emami, Director
Shawn Te, Information Technology Manager
Lydia Tallent, General Counsel
Vince Jacob, Principal Engineer & Structural Engineer
Harsh Nandan, Structural Engineer

Provider of control design and implementation services. The company also focuses on structural design and software development.

SCA Environmental Inc HQ

320 Justin Dr
San Francisco CA 94112
P: 415-882-1675 F: 415-962-0736 PRC:139
sca-enviro.com
Email: info@scasah.com
Estab: 1992

Glenn Cass, VP
Christina Codemo, Project Manager
Chuck Siu, Senior Consultant
Chaowen Huang, Environmental Scientist
Daniel Leung, Industrial Hygienist

Provider of environmental science, occupational health and safety, engineering, and laboratory analyses services.

Scandic HQ

700 Montague Ave
San Leandro CA 94577
P: 510-352-3700 PRC:82
www.scandic.com
Estab: 1969

Jia-Chwen Wu, Product Owner
Hale Foote, President
Jens Mathiesen, CEO
Magnus Berglund, Accessibility Director
Christian Borg, Commercial Director

Provider of machine tools. The company offers heat treatment, plating, engineering, and raw material guidance services.

Scepter Scientific Inc HQ

2021 Las Positas Ct Ste 129
Livermore CA 94551
P: 925-373-4802 F: 925-373-4807 PRC:87
scepter.net
Email: sales@scepter.net

Steven Harbaugh, President
Grant Schleiger, VP

Provider of feasibility evaluations, electronic, optical, and mechanical engineering, and prototype development services.

Schindler Elevator Corp BR

555 McCormick St
San Leandro CA 94577
P: 510-382-2075 PRC:180
www.schindler.com
Estab: 1874

Denis Davis, General Manager
Bradley Lay, General Manager
Troy Ferro, Business Unit Manager
Mike Relstab, Regional Field Engineer

Provider of elevators, escalators, and related services. The company creates and delivers urban mobility solutions.

Schmartboard Inc HQ
37423 Fremont Blvd
Fremont CA 94536
P: 510-744-9900 F: 510-744-9909 PRC:200
schmartboard.com
Email: info@schmartboard.com
Estab: 1863

Andrew Yaung, Co-Founder & President & CEO
Neal Greenberg, Co-Founder & VP of Sales &
Marketing
B. Schmart, CTO

Specializes in the production of hand soldering
components. The company's products are used in
sensor and USB technologies.

Schurter Inc DH
447 Aviation Blvd
Santa Rosa CA 95403
P: 707-636-3000 PRC:211
www.schurterinc.com
Email: info.sinc@schurter.com

Diane Cupples, VP of Marketing
Gisela Babb, Senior Quality Operations Analyst &
ISO Program Manager
Bill Cardoza, Facilities Administrator
Rhiannon Schwartz, Receptionist

Manufacturer of fuses, connectors, and circuit
breakers. The company also offers input systems
and EMC products.

SCHUTZE & Associates Inc HQ
44358 S Grimmer Blvd
Fremont CA 94538
P: 510-226-9944 F: 510-226-9948 PRC:140
www.schutze-inc.com
Email: js@schutze-inc.com
Estab: 2000

Jan Schutze, Founder

Provider of environmental consulting services. The
company's services include groundwater monitoring and dry cleaning remediation.

SciBac Inc HQ
1828 El Camino Real Ste 704
Burlingame CA 94010
P: 650-689-5343 F: 650-239-9160 PRC:34
www.scibac.com
Email: info@scibac.com
Estab: 2015

Derik Twomey, COO & Co-Founder
Anthony Cann, Co-Founder
Jeanette Mucha, CSO & Co-Founder & CEO
Maya Kuttan, Chief Counsel & Media Specialist
Stacy Townsend, Director of Pre-Clinical Devel-
opment

Developer of pharmaceuticals and medicinal
probiotics for the prevention and treatment of clos-
tridium difficile. The company serves the medical
sector.

Scientific Coating Labs HQ
350 Martin Ave
Santa Clara CA 95050-3112
P: 408-727-3296 F: 408-727-8775 PRC:127
www.scientificcoatinglabs.com
Email: customerservice@scientificcoatinglabs.com

Dick Rennolds, President
Tracie Rennolds, Front Office Manager

Provider of wafer coatings. The company specializes in coating components used in the semiconductor industry.

Scientific Specialties Inc HQ
1310 Thurman St
Lodi CA 95240
P: 209-333-2120 F: 209-333-8623 PRC:189
www.ssibio.com
Email: marketing@ssibio.com
Estab: 1990

Robbie Hovatter, Owner
Karen Ware, Director of Sales
Peter Cung, Business Development Manager
Cory Vohs, Production Manager

Manufacturer of injection molded plastic consumable and durable products such as tubes, pipette
tips, and racks for life science research industry.

Scigene Corp HQ
1287 Reamwood Ave
Sunnyvale CA 94089
P: 408-733-7337 F: 408-733-7336 PRC:31
www.scigene.com
Email: custserv@scigene.com
Estab: 2003

Jim Stanchfield, CEO
Terry Gill, Director of Manufacturing
Liz Robertson, Marketing Services Director
George Taylor, Director

Develops and commercializes solutions to
automate sample workflows. The company offers
reagents, microarray ovens, and arrays.

Scimage Inc HQ
4916 El Camino Real
Los Altos CA 94022
P: 866-724-6243 F: 650-694-4861 PRC:198
scimage.com
Email: corporate_sales@scimage.com
Estab: 1993

Sai Raya, Founder & CEO
Madvi Raya, CFO
Matthew Wolkenmuth, Program Manager
Vi Vo, UIUX Engineer
James Wong, Software Engineer

Provider of imaging solutions. The company also
deals with clinical and cloud solutions and business intelligence support.

Scimet LLC HQ
2745 Deer Meadow Dr
Danville CA 94506-2105
P: 925-736-2915 PRC:19
www.scimet.com
Estab: 2007

John W. Elmer, Founder

Provider of metallurgical consulting services. The
company specializes in welding, brazing, soldering, bonding, and heat treating.

Sciton Inc HQ
925 Commercial St
Palo Alto CA 94303
P: 650-493-9155 F: 650-493-9146 PRC:188
www.sciton.com
Email: info@sciton.com
Estab: 1997

Jim Hobart, CEO
Lars Isaacson, VP of Sales & Marketing
Jay Patel, VP
Jamie Isenhart, Area Sales Manager
Tony Rizzutti, Service Manager & Service Man-
ager

Provider of laser and light source solutions. The
company's products include JOULE, BBL, Clear-
Sense, Halo, and more.

Screw Conveyor Corp BR
7807 Doe Ave
Visalia CA 93291-9220
P: 559-651-2131 F: 559-651-2135 PRC:179
www.screwconveyor.com
Email: sales@screwconveyor.com
Estab: 1932

Randy Smith, General Manager Western Operations
Adolfo De La Rosa, Sales Engineer

Manufacturer of bulk material handling equipment
including screw conveyors, drag conveyors, and
bucket elevators.

Scribner Plastics HQ
11455 Hydraulic Dr
Rancho Cordova CA 95742
P: 916-638-1515 F: 916-638-2278 PRC:280
scribnerplastics.com
Email: info@scribnerplastics.com
Estab: 1978

Rick Scribner, Owner

Provider of shipping and packing solutions. The
company also deals with custom plastics design
and manufacturing services.

SCST LLC HQ
6280 Riverdale St [N]
San Diego CA 92120
P: 619-280-4321 F: 619-280-4717 PRC:306
www.scst.com
Estab: 2013

Laura Watts, Executive Director
Ron Baudour, Project Manager & Executive
Director
Scott J. Brockway, Project Manager
William Earle, Project Manager
Randy Hallmark, Project Manager

Provider of geotechnical engineering, environmental science and engineering, special inspection and material testing, and facilities consulting
services.

SDL USA BR
2550 N First St Ste 301
San Jose CA 95131
P: 408-743-3600 F: 408-743-3601 PRC:325
www.sdl.com
Estab: 1992

Tony White, Founder
Adolfo Hernandez, CEO
Roddy Temperley, Chief Human Resource Officer
Thomas Labarthe, CRO
Xenia Walters, CFO

Provider of web content and structured content
management, as well as e-commerce solutions,
and language technologies.

SE Ranking BR
228 Hamilton Ave
Palo Alto CA 94301
P: 415-704-4387 PRC:325
seranking.com
Estab: 2012

Artem Kozel, Partner & Advisor

SEO platform that allows individuals to optimize
and promote a website on the web.

Seagull Solutions Inc HQ
15105 Concord Cir Ste 100
Morgan Hill CA 95037-5487
P: 408-778-1127 F: 408-779-2806 PRC:5
www.seagullsolutions.net
Email: info@seagullsolutions.net

Donald Ekhoff, Owner & CTO
Carol Lawless, CFO & COO

Developer and manufacturer of air bearing spindles, clamps, and custom applications. The company mainly offers custom made services.

Searchforce HQ
3 Waters Park Dr Ste 211
San Mateo CA 94403
P: 650-235-8800 PRC:322
www.searchforce.com
Email: sales@searchforce.com
Estab: 2004

Dhiren Dsouza, Founder & President
Santhosh Nair, CTO
Henry Park, COO
Juan Lin, Chief Scientist
Angela Overhoff, VP of Client Services

Developer of automation software. The company offers software for automation, optimization, campaign management, and tracking.

Searchmetrics Inc HQ
1100 Park Pl Ste 150
San Mateo CA 94403
P: 866-411-9494 PRC:315
www.searchmetrics.com
Email: info@searchmetrics.com
Estab: 2005

Jordan Koene, CEO
Doug Bell, Global CMO

A Search and Content Marketing Platform that uncovers the opportunities and pitfalls of online marketing.

Seascape Lamps HQ
PO Box 810
Freedom CA 95019
P: 831-728-5699 F: 831-728-0658 PRC:243
www.seascapelamps.com
Email: sales@seascapelamps.com
Estab: 1980

Mike Shenk, President

Provider of contemporary and retro home lighting solutions. The company also specializes in printed drum lamp shades.

Seatec Lab Repair HQ
520 Woodstock Way
Santa Clara CA 95054
P: 408-828-1815 PRC:306
www.seatec-lab.com

Rich O'Neil, Owner
Deb O'Neil, Office Manager

Provider of services to analytical, biotech, and industrial laboratories. The company also focuses on equipment validation.

Sebastian HQ
7600 N Palm Ave
Fresno CA 93711
P: 559-432-5800 F: 559-432-5858 PRC:304
www.sebastiancorp.com
Email: customerservicefresno@sebastiancorp.com
Estab: 1946

Brandon Dukes, VP of Sales Marketing & Business Development

Provider of structured cabling and electrical contracting services. The company offers services to the residential and commercial sectors.

Seco HQ
4155 Oasis Rd
Redding CA 96003
P: 530-225-8155 F: 530-225-8162 PRC:19
www.surveying.com
Email: seco@surveying.com
Estab: 1977

Daniel Moller, Product Specialist of Holemaking

Manufacturer of surveying and positioning equipment and accessories. The company's products also finds application in site preparation.

Second Genome Inc HQ
341 Allerton Ave Ste 215
S San Francisco CA 94080
P: 650-440-4606 PRC:25
www.secondgenome.com
Email: info@secondgenome.com
Estab: 2009

Todd DeSantis, Co-Founder & VP of Informatics
Corey S. Goodman, Co-Founder & Chairman of the Board
Karim Dabbagh, President & CEO
Anu Hoey, Chief Business Officer
Andrew Han, Director

Focuses on the development of therapeutic products. The company serves pharmaceutical and nutritional companies.

Secret Builders HQ
1900 S Norfolk St Ste 219
San Mateo CA 94403-1172
P: 650-204-9098 PRC:317
www.secretbuilders.com
Email: info@secretbuilders.com
Estab: 2006

Umair Khan, CEO
Vladimir Soskov, CTO
Georgi Marinoff, Chief Architect

Provider of online games for children. The company also focuses on publishing writings, art, and videos.

Secugen Corp HQ
2065 Martin Ave Ste 108
Santa Clara CA 95050
P: 408-727-7787 F: 408-834-7762 PRC:319
www.secugen.com
Email: sales@secugen.com
Estab: 1998

Won Lee, CEO
M.J. Jin, VP of Finance
Jeff Brown, VP of Sales
Dan Riley, VP of Engineering

Manufacturer of fingerprint recognition devices. The company's products serve the purpose of integration into 3rd party hardware products.

Securematics Inc HQ
1135 Walsh Ave
Santa Clara CA 95050
P: 888-746-6700 F: 408-731-9124 PRC:59
www.securematics.com
Email: sales@securematics.com
Estab: 2002

Jon Bennett, Director
Keith H., Data Operations Manager
Anjum Khan, Senior Credit Financial Analyst
Ruby Ferguson, Marketing Assistant

Provider of secure networking, security, storage products and solutions. The company focuses on demand generation and e-commerce.

Seevider Inc HQ
4500 Great America Pkwy Ste 1054
Santa Clara CA 95054
P: 408-930-0852 PRC:87
www.seevider.com
Email: info@seevider.com
Estab: 2014

Hobin Kim, CEO

Manufacturer of smart vision devices. The company's products are used in light management, parking occupancy detection, and guiding.

SEG Inc HQ
1793 Lafayette St Ste 105
Santa Clara CA 95051
P: 408-260-8008 PRC:304
www.seg-corp.com
Email: hr@seg-corp.com
Estab: 2000

James Maggard, President
Wayne Johnson, Managing Partner
Jim Marsh, Senior Mechanical Engineer

Provider of consulting, design, engineering, project management, commissioning, and validation services.

Seiwa Optical America Inc HQ
3042 Scott Blvd
Santa Clara CA 95054
P: 408-844-8008 F: 408-844-8944 PRC:168
www.seiwaamerica.com
Email: info@seiwaamerica.com
Estab: 1947

Nobuteru Takashima, Manager
Megumi Morford, Contact

Manufacturer of optical components and photonic integrated circuits. The company offers network and access solutions.

Sekisui Diagnostics HQ
6659 Top Gun St [N]
San Diego CA 92121
P: 858-777-2600 F: 858-452-3258 PRC:268
www.sekisuidiagnostics.com
Email: medinfo@genzyme.com
Emp: 201-500 Estab: 1984

Bob Schruender, President & CEO
Raymond De Rise, General Counsel & Chief Compliance Officer
William Faranda, VP of Strategy & Business Development
Jason Bilobram, VP of Quality & Regulatory & Compliance
Alan Bauer, VP of Global Finance

Manufacturer of laboratories, biotechnology, and diagnostic healthcare products.

Selectiva Systems Inc   HQ
2051 Junction Ave Ste 225/215
San Jose CA 95131
P: 408-297-1336   F: 408-627-6484   PRC:325
www.selectiva.com
Email: info-sjc@selectiva.com

Ranjeet Jhala, Programmer Analyst
Vivek Sathe, Business Analyst

Provider of solutions for revenue reporting, customer service, and distributor management. The company serves high-tech, pharma, and other sectors.

Semi-Probes Inc   HQ
2075 Bering Dr Ste D
San Jose CA 95131
P: 408-866-6535   F: 408-866-0437   PRC:196
www.semi-probes.com
Estab: 1979

Marisela Valdez, Office Manager

Manufacturer and supplier of probe cards and tester interfaces. The company's services include design, installation, and delivery.

Semicat Inc   BR
47900 Fremont Blvd
Fremont CA 94538
P: 408-514-6900   F: 408-514-6901   PRC:126
www.semicat.com
Email: sales@semicat.com

Jin Kim, Marketing Director
Kenny Law, Field Service Manager
Tony Ham, Purchasing Manager
Adonis Sison, Senior Manager
Megan Park, Controller

Provider of refurbished equipment for semiconductors. The company deals in LED, and novel emerging applications.

Semicore Equipment Inc   HQ
470 Commerce Way
Livermore CA 94551-5215
P: 925-373-8201   F: 925-373-8202   PRC:212
www.semicore.com
Email: sales@semicore.com
Estab: 1996

Matthew Hughes, President
Trey Haight, Manufacturing & Engineering Manager
Jimmy Haight, Product Development Engineer
Matt Kuntz, Senior Mechanical Engineer
Alan Klaffke, Senior Electrical Engineer

Manufacturer of vacuum systems and equipment. The company's products include PVD coating systems, thermal evaporation, and sputtering equipment.

Semifab   HQ
150 Great Oaks Blvd
San Jose CA 95119
P: 408-414-5928   F: 408-414-5926   PRC:304
www.semifab.com
Estab: 1970

Humayun Kabir, President & CEO
Gerry Reynolds, Program Manager
Greg Krikorian, Contact
Showkot Hassan, Contact
John Tran, Contact

Supplier of process environment control systems for precise temperature, humidity, air flow, and airborne particulate management.

M-274

Sempac Inc   HQ
PO Box 3217
Los Altos CA 94024
P: 408-400-9002   F: 408-400-9006   PRC:86
www.sempac.com
Email: sales@sempac.com
Estab: 2000

Deborah Benando-Morris, VP of Operations

Developer of pre-molded open-cavity plastic packages for optoelectronic, telecom, RF, MEMS, and sensor applications.

Semprex Corp   HQ
782 Camden Ave   [N]
Campbell CA 95008
P: 408-379-3230   F: 408-374-1843   PRC:65
www.semprex.com
Estab: 1966

Lou Volk, CEO & Director
Rita Volk, CFO
Helga Volk, Secretary

Manufacturer of instruments that measure electricity.

Sendero Group LLC   HQ
PO Box 937
Rancho Cordova CA 95741
P: 888-757-6810   F: 888-757-6807   PRC:61
www.senderogroup.com
Email: info@senderogroup.com
Estab: 1993

Mike May, CEO & President
Charles Lapierre, CTO
Kim Casey, Director

Provider of GPS systems and products to the visually impaired. The company focuses on documentation and technical support services.

Sensifree   HQ
21631 Stevens Creek Blvd Ste B
Cupertino CA 95014
P: 669-230-5116   PRC:87
www.sensifree.com
Email: info@sensifree.com
Estab: 2012

Eran Agmon, CEO & Co-Founder
Llan Barak, CTO & Co-Founder
Moshe Kamar, CMO
Lior Haviv, COO & VP of R&D
Asaf Bar, VP of Business Development & Marketing

Manufacturer of contactless sensors for wearables. The company offers heart rate sensors, including fitness trackers, and activity monitors.

Sensoplex Inc   HQ
1735 E Bayshore Rd Ste 29B
Redwood City CA 94063
P: 408-391-9019   PRC:189
rover.health
Email: info@rover.health
Estab: 2012

Hamid Najafi, CEO & Founder
Adi Iyer, CMO
Gabriel Griego, VP of Sales & Marketing

Developer and manufacturer of wearable sensors. The company offers rechargeable batteries, displays, interfaces, and related accessories.

Sensor Concepts Inc   HQ
7950 National Dr
Livermore CA 94550
P: 925-443-9001   F: 925-443-9050   PRC:2
www.sensorconcepts.com
Email: sci@sensorconcepts.com
Estab: 1996

George Blenis, COO
Fiona Parken, Human Resource Manager
Vincent Varela, Manufacturing Engineer
John Meehan, Design Engineer
Seitu Barron, Mechanical Engineer & Team Lead

Developer of portable and integrated measurement systems. The company offers engineering, field measurement and software development services.

Sensor Systems Inc   HQ
8929 Fullbright Ave   [N]
Chatsworth CA 91311
P: 818-341-5366   F: 818-341-9059   PRC:68
www.sensorantennas.com
Emp: 201-500   Estab: 1961

Si Robin, VP & CEO
Christine Torres, Manager of Sales & Product Support
Craig Miller, Manager of EHS & Facilities

Manufacturer of airplane antennas.

Sensory Inc   HQ
4701 Patrick Henry Dr Bldg 7
Santa Clara CA 95054
P: 408-625-3300   F: 408-625-3350   PRC:325
www.sensoryinc.com
Email: sales@sensoryinc.com
Estab: 1994

Todd Mozer, CEO & Chairman
Pieter Vermeulen, VP of Technology
Mina Wong, Director of Finance
Johnny Chan, Senior Operations Manager
Erich Adams, Senior Field Apps Engineer

Provider of speech recognition and voice biometric ICs. The company's products are used in toys and home electronic products.

Sensys Networks Inc   HQ
1608 Fourth St Ste 200
Berkeley CA 94710
P: 510-548-4620   PRC:87
www.sensysnetworks.com
Estab: 2003

Amine Haoui, CEO
Brian Fuller, COO
Hamed Benouar, VP
David Sheahen, Director of Field Engineering
Vince Ferrinho, Director of Marketing

Manufacturer of wireless sensor cubes, repeaters, and related accessories. The company's services include training and technical support.

Sentek Dynamics Inc — HQ
2370 Owen St
Santa Clara CA 95054
P: 408-200-3100   F: 408-659-8229   PRC:159
www.sentekdynamics.com
Email: sales@sentekdynamics.com
Estab: 2011

Sentek Dynamics, Vibration Test Equipment Manufacturer

Manufacturer of vibration test equipment, shakers, power amplifiers, and related instruments. The company offers customer support solutions.

Sentient Energy Inc — HQ
880 Mitten Rd Ste 105
Burlingame CA 94010
P: 650-523-6680   F: 650-239-9048   PRC:130
www.sentient-energy.com
Email: info@sentient-energy.com
Estab: 2009

James Jim Keener, CEO
James Tracey, VP of Special Projects
Konda Ankireddyapalli, SVP of Engineering
George Asmus, SVP of Operations & Manufacturing
Mark Sloan, EVP of Engineering & Manufacturing Technology Operations

Provider of sensor devices for operational practices and engineering applications. The company also offers communication software.

Sentieon Inc — HQ
160 E Tasman Dr Ste 208
San Jose CA 95134-1619
P: 650-282-5650   PRC:40
www.sentieon.com
Email: info@sentieon.com
Estab: 2014

Jun Ye, President & CEO
Luoqi Chen, VP of Engineering
Rafael Aldana, Product Application Director
Zhipan Li, Principal Engineer
Don Freed, Bioinformatics Scientist

Supplier and developer of bioinformatics secondary analysis tools. The company offers precision data for precision medicine.

SentinelOne — HQ
605 Fairchild Dr
Mountain View CA 94043
P: 855-868-3733   PRC:63
sentinelone.com
Email: sales@sentinelone.com
Estab: 2013

Tomer Weingarten, CEO & Founder
Scott Gainey, CMO
Eran Ashkenazi, VP
Mark Danckert, VP of Sales - West
Yotam Gutman, Director of Marketing

Developer of endpoint protection software. The company serves the healthcare, oil and gas, and financial services industries.

Sentons USA Inc — HQ
627 River Oaks Pkwy
San Jose CA 95134
P: 408-732-9000   PRC:212
www.sentons.com

Sam Sheng, Founder & CTO

Provider of touch solutions. The company offers flat panel display, retail point of sale, and factory/industry automation products.

Sentreheart Inc — HQ
300 Saginaw Dr
Redwood City CA 94063
P: 650-354-1200   F: 650-354-1204   PRC:189
www.sentreheart.com
Email: info@sentreheart.com
Estab: 2005

Russell Seiber, President & CEO & Founder
Robert Strasser, VP
Greg Fung, VP of Research & Development
Pam Simons, VP of Clinical affairs

Developer of catheter technology solutions. The company is engaged in suture delivery and related services.

Sentry Products Inc — HQ
2378 B Walsh Ave
Santa Clara CA 95051
P: 408-727-1866   F: 408-727-2129   PRC:64
www.sentryproducts.net
Email: sentryscan@earthlink.net
Estab: 1974

Sam Stone, Contact

Provider of duress alarm systems. The company caters to judicial centers, emergency medical facilities, and schools.

Sepragen Corp — HQ
33470 Western Ave
Union City CA 94587
P: 510-475-0650   F: 510-475-0625   PRC:20
sepragen.com
Email: info@sepragen.com
Estab: 1985

Vinit Saxena, CEO & CTO
Renu Chabra, VP of Manufacturing & Engineering
Salah Ahmed, Director of Quality & Tech Support
George Martinez, Director
Dennis Gould, Manufacturing Manager

Provider of equipment, systems, and materials for the scale-up and purification of proteins, biopharmaceuticals, and nutraceuticals.

Sercomm USA Inc — BR
42808 Christy St Ste 231
Fremont CA 94538
P: 510-870-1598   F: 510-870-2320   PRC:323
www.sercomm.com
Email: market@sercomm.com
Estab: 1992

Ben Lin, CTO & Co-Founder
Paul Wang, Co-Founder & Chairman
James Wang, CEO & President
Arif Ahsan, Senior Director of Business Development

Provider of software and firmware for the development of broadband networking. The company also offers solutions for fixed mobile convergence.

Serpa Packaging Solutions — HQ
7020 W Sunnyview Ave
Visalia CA 93291
P: 559-651-2339   F: 559-651-2345   PRC:159
serpapackaging.com
Email: sales@serpapackaging.com
Estab: 1985

Fernando Serpa, President
Jim Muro, National Sales Manager
Aaron Metzler, Regional Sales Manager
Jon Gaiser, Engineering Manager
Pete Priebe, Service Manager

Provider of packaging solutions. The company's applications include pharmaceutical industry and bottles, vials, and ampules.

Sessco Technologies Inc — HQ
1701 Fortune Dr Ste A
San Jose CA 95131
P: 408-321-7437   PRC:19
www.sessco.com
Email: info@sessco.com
Estab: 1995

Ben Delavega, Founder & Test Handler System Architect
Vanessa Castro, Office Manager

Designer and manufacturer of tri-temperature test handlers for the commercial, industrial, automotive, and military grade circuit test applications.

SFJ Pharmaceuticals Group — HQ
5000 Hopyard Rd Ste 330
Pleasanton CA 94588
P: 925-223-6233   F: 925-425-0986   PRC:268
www.sfj-pharma.com
Estab: 2008

Robert Debenedetto, President & CEO
Alexandra Dilis, EVP & CCO

Focuses on the clinical development and registration of pharmaceutical products. The company is involved in clinical trials.

Shape Security — HQ
2755 Augustine Dr 8th Fl
Santra Clara CA 95054
P: 650-399-0400   PRC:326
www.shapesecurity.com
Email: security@shapesecurity.com
Estab: 2011

Derek Smith, Co-Founder & CEO
Sumit Agarwal, Co-Founder & COO
Shuman Ghosemajumder, CTO
Xinran Wang, Chief Security Scientist & VP of Security Research
Hasan Imam, VP of Sales

Provider of defense solutions against malicious automated cyber-attacks on web and mobile applications.

ShareThis Inc — HQ
3000 El Camino Real 5 Palo Alto Sq Ste 150
Palo Alto CA 94306
P: 650-323-1783   PRC:325
sharethis.com
Email: support@sharethis.com
Estab: 2007

Kurt Abrahamson, Executive Chairman
Dana Hayes, CEO
Chad Burns, CFO
Huanjin Chen, CTO
Rob Finora, CRO

Developers of social sharing solutions for website owners.

Sharp Dimension Inc   HQ
4240 Business Center Dr
Fremont CA 94538
P: 510-656-8938   F: 510-656-8940   PRC:80
www.sharpdimension.com
Email: contact@sharpdimension.com
Estab: 1993

Tracy Tran, Owner

Provider of production and prototype machining services. The company serves semiconductor, medical, robotics, solar, defense, and other sectors.

Sharp Electronics Corp   BR
1701 Junction Ct Ste 200
San Jose CA 95112
P: 408-452-6400   F: 408-436-0924   PRC:169
www.sharpsma.com
Estab: 1912

Mary Holland, Director of Human Resources

Provider of LCD, optoelectronics, imagers, and RF components. The company is involved in design and installation services.

Sharper Technology Inc   HQ
1032 Elwell Ct Ste 110
Palo Alto CA 94303
P: 650-964-4600   F: 650-964-4650   PRC:323
www.sharpertechnology.com
Email: info@sharpertechnology.com
Estab: 2003

Ronald Steffen, President & CEO
Kevin McCarthy, VP of Operations
Pat Glass, VP of Finance

Provider of network security solutions and services. The company also offers design, implementation, and training services.

Sharpesoft Inc   HQ
925 Market St
Yuba City CA 95991
P: 530-671-6499   F: 530-671-5739   PRC:319
www.sharpesoft.com
Email: sales@sharpesoft.com
Estab: 1986

Brent Hooton, Manager of Product Development
Kristopher Wilkins, IT Support Specialist

Provider of cost accounting, dispatching, and project management software. The company exclusively serves the construction sector.

SHASTA Electronic Manufacturing Services Inc   HQ
525 E Brokaw Rd
San Jose CA 95112
P: 408-436-1267   PRC:124
www.shastaems.com
Email: contact@shasta-ems.com
Estab: 2005

Rang N., VP of Operations

Provider of electronic manufacturing services. The company's services include prototype manufacturing, testing, materials, and quality control.

Shax Engineering Inc   HQ
44777 S Grimmer Blvd Ste C
Fremont CA 94538
P: 408-452-1500   F: 408-441-0634   PRC:124
shax-eng.com
Email: info@shax-eng.com
Estab: 1998

Isam Shakour, Founder

Provider of PCB fabrication and assembly services. The company serves original equipment manufacturers and technology companies.

Shen Milsom Wilke LLC   BR
351 California St Ste 810
San Francisco CA 94104-2406
P: 415-391-7610   F: 415-391-0171   PRC:304
www.smwllc.com
Estab: 1986

Tom Shen, President & CEO
Gary Lepkoski, Principal & CFO
Jerome Smith, Denver Office Director
Tyson Leonard, Director
Zane Au, Hong Kong Office Director

Provider of technology design and consulting solutions such as acoustics, medical equipment planning, audiovisual, and building security.

Shen Wei USA Inc   HQ
33278 Central Ave Ste 102
Union City CA 94587
P: 510-429-8692   F: 510-487-5347   PRC:195
shenweiusa.com
Email: info@shenweiusa.com
Estab: 1999

Belle Chou, Founder & President & CEO
Xie Jin Biao, Director

Manufacturer of disposable gloves and customizable products. The company offers services to the healthcare industry.

Sherrill-Lubinski Corp   HQ
871 Marlborough Ave Ste 100A
Riverside CA 92507
P: 415-927-8400   F: 415-927-8401   PRC:319
sl.com
Email: info@sl.com
Estab: 1983

Tom Lubinski, CEO
Nina Cartee, CFO
Ted Wilson, COO
Ed Koo, VP of Technical Services
Gia Lombardi-Hodges, Marketing Manager

Provider of monitoring and analytics solutions for middleware-powered applications. The company serves the electrical commodity market.

Shields Harper & Co   HQ
4591 Pacheco Blvd
Martinez CA 94553
P: 510-653-9119   F: 510-658-8448   PRC:133
www.shieldsharper.com
Email: martinez@shieldsharper.com
Estab: 1917

Dave Sarginson, President
Tim Roth, VP of Southern California - Shields Harper & Company
Doug DeLong, VP
Paul Chae, Manager of Information Technology
Jeff Nelson, Manager of Support Department

Provider of design assistance, testing, monitoring, fleet fuel control, and underground solutions to contractors, engineers, and designers.

Shifamed LLC   HQ
590 Division St
Campbell CA 95008
P: 408-560-2500   PRC:189
www.shifamed.com
Email: info@shifamed.com
Estab: 2008

Amr Salahieh, Founding President & CEO
Claudio Argento, CTO
David Voris, CFO
Jean Orth, CSO
Robert Edesess, VP of Intellectual Property

Manufacturer of medical technologies and products catheters, custom balloons, painted balloon electrodes, and diagnostic and therapeutic instrumentation.

Shimon Systems Inc   HQ
4984 El Camino Real Ste 200
Los Altos CA 94022
P: 650-461-9104   F: 650-461-9105   PRC:71
Estab: 2003

Ven Reddy, VP of Operations

Manufacturer of fingerprint authentication solutions. The company's services include research and development.

Shin-Etsu Polymer America Inc   HQ
5600 Mowry School Rd Ste 320
Newark CA 94560
P: 510-623-1881   F: 510-623-1603   PRC:78
www.shinpoly.com
Estab: 1960

Yoshio Akinaga, President
Akira Iwatsuki, Plant Manager
Richard Villanueva, Production Manager
Linda Ishiguro, Inside Sales Coordinator

Manufacturer of electro-mechanical components such as custom made keypads and inter-connectors, decorative films, and switch devices.

Shockwave Medical Inc   HQ
5403 Betsy Ross Dr
Santa Clara CA 95054
P: 877-775-4846   PRC:189
shockwavemedical.com
Email: info@shockwavemedical.com

Doug Godshall, CEO & President

Focuses on the production of highest performance personal submarines on the planet. The company is involved in research services.

Shotspotter Inc   HQ
7979 Gateway Blvd Ste 210
Newark CA 94560
P: 510-794-3144   PRC:59
shotspotter.com
Email: info@shotspotter.com
Estab: 1996

Robert L. Showen, Founder & Chief Scientist
Douglas A. McFarlin, VP
Joe Hawkins, SVP of Operations
Paul Ames, VP
Gary Bunyard, SVP

Provider of gunfire detection and location technology services. The company addresses gun violence in communities.

Shuttle Computer Group Inc   HQ

17068 Evergreen Pl   [N]
City Of Industry CA 91745
P: 626-820-9000   F: 626-820-5060   PRC:93
www.us.shuttle.com
Email: support@us.shuttle.com
Emp: 11-50   Estab: 1990

Marty Lash, Director of Sales & Marketing

Manufacturer and distributor of motherboards,
barebones computers, complete PC systems, and
monitors.

Si-Bone Inc   HQ

471 El Camino Real Ste 101
San Jose CA 95050
P: 408-207-0700   F: 408-557-8312   PRC:187
si-bone.com
Email: info@si-bone.com
Estab: 2008
Sales: $30M to $100M

Mark A. Reiley, CMO & Founder
Jeffrey Dunn, President & CEO & Chairman
Scott Yerby, VP & CTO
Laura Francis, CFO
Tony Recupero, Chief Commercial Officer

Developer of medical products and technologies
such as implants and titanium implant technology
for SI joint pain and sacroiliac joint fusion surgery.

Sicon International Inc   HQ

568 Charcot Ave
San Jose CA 95131-2201
P: 408-954-9880   F: 408-954-9886   PRC:202
sicon.com
Estab: 1989

Jack Wang, President
Russ Wiitala, VP
Louis Grijalva, Senior Sales Engineer
Alex He, Mechanical Engineer

Manufacturer of electronic components. The company specializes in the fabrication of connectors,
cables, circuit boards, and molded cables.

Sienna Corp   BR

41758 Christy St
Fremont CA 94538
P: 510-440-0200   F: 510-440-0201   PRC:70
siennagroup.com
Email: sales@siennagroup.com
Estab: 1995

Bruce Nimmer, Owner
Kunhamed Bicha, CEO
Jack McDonald, CFO
Mike Robinson, COO
Ron Greene, VP of Sales

Provider of electronic manufacturing services
including design and process engineering, prototyping, and electromechanical assembly services.

Sierra Chemical Company   HQ

788 Northport Dr
West Sacramento CA 95691
P: 916-371-5943   PRC:50
www.sierrachemicalcompany.com
Estab: 1946

Steve Gould, President
Jerry Eykelbosh, Manager of Sales
Nicholas Silva, Sales Manager
Tom Enos, Marketing Representative

Manufacturer of aquarium supplies, degreasers,
descalers, glass cleaners, and growing products.
The company deals with chemical consulting.

Sierra Circuits   HQ

1108 W Evelyn Ave
Sunnyvale CA 94086
P: 408-735-7137   F: 408-735-1408   PRC:211
www.protoexpress.com
Estab: 1986

Bala Bahl, Founder & VP
Ken Bahl, CEO
Steve Arobio, VP of Manufacturing Operations
Nilesh Parate, General Manager
Atar Mittal, General Manager of Design & Assem-
bly

Designer and manufacturer of printed circuit
boards. The company's manufacturing facilities
are located in California and Kansas.

Sierra Data Systems Inc   HQ

675 S Auburn St
Grass Valley CA 95959
P: 916-242-4604   PRC:324
www.sierradata.com
Email: support@sierradata.com
Estab: 1997

Keith Schneider, CEO
Steve Gallo, Account Manager
Scott French, Development Team Lead

Provider of data communication systems, Internet
related services, miscellaneous communications
equipment, telephone, and voice equipment.

Sierra Engineering Company Inc   HQ

35111 Lodge Rd
Tollhouse CA 93667
P: 559-855-2659   PRC:304
www.rvpartssierra.com
Email: sierraengineering@rvpartssierra.com
Estab: 1969

Jesus Sierra, President
Jim Piluso, VP

Manufacturer of recreational vehicles. The company offers rebuilding, repair, and maintenance
services.

Sierra Instruments Inc   HQ

5 Harris Ct Bldg L
Monterey CA 93940
P: 831-373-0200   F: 831-373-4402   PRC:14
www.sierrainstruments.com
Email: info@sierrainstruments.com
Estab: 1971

John Olin, Founder & Chairman
Jim O'Neill, VP of Operations
Scott Smitherman, Product Development & Asso-
ciate Project Manager
Daniel Durham, Purchasing Manager
Maryadine Washington, Marketing Communica-
tion Manager

Manufacturer of mass flow meters and mass flow
controllers. The company serves gas, liquid, and
steam applications.

Sierra Monitor Corp   HQ

1991 Tarob Ct
Milpitas CA 95035
P: 408-262-6611   F: 408-262-9042   PRC:138
www.sierramonitor.com
Email: info@sierramonitor.com
Estab: 1980
Sales: $1B to $3B

Tamara Allen, CFO
Michael Farr, VP
Mike Nugent, Director of Sales & Marketing
Richard Theron, Product Manager
Frank Baleto, Project Manager

Manufacturer and seller of safety and environmental instrumentation. The company offers hazardous gas detection systems and site management
products.

Sierra Precision Optics   HQ

12830 Earhart Ave
Auburn CA 95602
P: 530-885-6979   F: 530-885-1037   PRC:173
www.sierraoptics.com
Email: sales@sierraoptics.com

Michael Dorich, General Manager
Russell Lowe, Manager of Sales & Marketing
Stephen Bennion, Manager of Engineering
Karen Hartsfield, Senior Buyer
Stephen Elgin, Optician

Manufacturer of optical products. The company's
products include panels, mirrors, beam splitters,
and cylindrical lenses.

Sierra Tel   HQ

49150 Road 426   [N]
Oakhurst CA 93644
P: 559-683-4611   PRC:68
www.sierratel.com
Emp: 51-200   Estab: 1895

John Baker, VP
Michael Montgomery, Manager of Operations
Debbie Peters, Manager of Special Projects
Sandy Brinley, Manager of Human Resource
Robert Griffin, Controller

Provider of telecommunication, business solutions
and services.

Sierra Testing Service   HQ

9450 E Collier Rd
Acampo CA 95220
P: 209-333-3337   F: 209-339-9691   PRC:306
sierratestingservice.com
Estab: 1983

Stan Seifert, Founder

Provider of laboratory testing services. The company offers services such as grain testing, silage,
and grain samples.

Siesta Medical Inc HQ
101 Church St Ste 3
Los Gatos CA 95030
P: 408-320-9424   F: 408-399-7600   PRC:189
www.siestamedical.com
Email: info@siestamedical.com
Estab: 2009

Peter Martin, President & CEO & Director &
Co-Founder
Chris Feezor, VP of Research & Development &
Co-Founder
Erik Van Der Burg, Chairman & CTO & Co-Founder
Jay Shukert, CFO
Tedd Hinton, VP of Operations & Quality Assurance

Providers of medical devices. The company offers
surgical implants and tools for the treatment of
OSA.

Sight Sciences Inc HQ
4040 Campbell Ave Ste 100
Menlo Park CA 94025
P: 877-266-1144   PRC:176
www.sightsciences.com
Email: info@sightsciences.com
Estab: 2011

David Badawi, Co-Founder & CTO
Paul Badawi, Co-Founder & CEO
Jesse Selnick, CFO
Shawn O. Neil, CCO
Richard Rush, VP of Quality Assurance

Manufacturer and developer of surgical instruments and ophthalmic medical devices. The
company serves the medical sector.

Sightech Vision Systems HQ
1616 Culpepper Ave Ste A
Modesto CA 95351
P: 408-282-3770   PRC:168
www.sightech.com
Email: sales@sightech.com
Estab: 1983

Judy Gaffin, Owner
Art Gaffin, CEO
Judy Gaffom, Office Manager

Manufacturer of industrial vision systems. The
company offers quality vision systems, hard disk
inspection, and crimp verification services.

Sigma Designs Inc HQ
47467 Fremont Blvd
Fremont CA 94538
P: 510-897-0200   F: 510-897-0350   PRC:212
www.sigmadesigns.com
Email: sales@sigmadesigns.com
Estab: 1982
Sales: $30M to $100M

Elias N. Nader, Interim President & CEO & CFO
& Director
Jianbo Zhang, VP of HW Engineering & IP & Arch
Sal Cobar, VP of Worldwide Sales & Marketing
Jin Park, Director of Platform Engineering
Jimmy Nguyen, Director of Information Technology

Provider of system-on-chip solutions for media processing, smart TV, video encoding, AV
networking, video processing, and home control
systems.

Sigmatron International Inc BR
30000 Eigenbrodt Way
Union City CA 94587
P: 510-477-5000   PRC:211
www.sigmatronintl.com
Estab: 1994

Gary R. Fairhead, Chairman
Linda K. Frauendorfer, CFO
Yousef M. Heidari, VP of Engineering
Gregory A. Fairhead, EVP & Assistant Secretary
Curtis Campbell, VP of Sales

Provider of robust systems and program management support to track demand, material on order,
inventory, finished goods, and shipments.

Signal Hill Petroleum Inc HQ
2633 Cherry Ave   [N]
Signal Hill CA 90755
P: 562-595-6440   F: 562-426-4587   PRC:130
www.shpi.net
Email: recruiter@shpi.net
Emp: 51-200   Estab: 1979

Jerrel C. Barto, Chairman of the Board & Founder
Craig C. Barto, President & CEO
David L. Slater, EVP & COO
Jeffrey Ocheltree, CFO & SVP
Kevin Laney, VP

Producer and supplier of oil and gas.

Signosis Inc HQ
1700 Wyatt Dr Ste 10-12
Santa Clara CA 95054
P: 408-747-0771   F: 408-470-7719   PRC:34
signosisinc.com
Email: info@signosisinc.com
Estab: 2007

Jason Li, Owner
Reza Keikhaee, Research Scientist

Provider of bioassays. The company focuses on
the development and commercialization of plate-
based analysis products.

Siig Inc HQ
6078 Stewart Ave
Fremont CA 94538-3152
P: 510-657-8688   F: 510-657-5962   PRC:95
www.siig.com
Email: sales@siig.com
Estab: 1985

Mike Woodmansee, Director of Sales & Marketing
Steve Nguyen, Manager of Product
Edmund So, Material Planning Manager

Manufacturer of computer connectivity products.
The company is involved in increasing the bandwidth between a computer system and external
devices.

Silex Technology America Inc HQ
201 East Sandpointe Ste 245
Santa Ana CA 92707
P: 657-218-5199   F: 714-258-0730   PRC:104
www.silextechnology.com
Email: sales@silexamerica.com
Estab: 1973

Keith Sugawara, CEO & President

Manufacturer of print servers for network printers
and fingerprint readers. The company serves
security applications.

Silicon Frontline Technology Inc HQ
4030 Moorpark Ave Ste 249
San Jose CA 95117
P: 408-963-6916   F: 408-963-6906   PRC:126
www.siliconfrontline.com
Email: info@siliconfrontline.com
Estab: 2005

Yuri Feinberg, CEO
Dermott Lynch, COO

Provider of parasitic extraction and analysis
services for post layout verification. The company
specializes in electrostatic discharge analysis.

Silicon Genesis Corp HQ
145 Baytech Dr
San Jose CA 95134
P: 408-228-5858   F: 408-228-5859   PRC:126
sigen.net
Email: support@sigen.com
Estab: 1997

Theodore Fong, President & CEO
Marge Brandt, Executive Administrator

Manufacturer of semiconductor and solar fabrication tools. The company offers stand-alone plasma
tools and debond and cleave tools.

Silicon Laboratories BR
2708 Orchard Pkwy
San Jose CA 95134
P: 408-702-1400   PRC:326
www.silabs.com
Estab: 1996

Kevin Meehan, Director of Accounting & SEC
Reporting
Jim Parker, Design Manager
Shelley Buckner, Layout Manager
Gang Yuan, Design Manager
Henk de Ruijter, Principal Design Engineer &
Systems Engineering Manager

Provider of silicon, software, and system solutions.
The company focuses on Internet infrastructure,
industrial control, and consumer markers.

Silicon Light Machines HQ
820 Kifer Rd
Sunnyvale CA 94086
P: 408-240-4700   F: 408-456-0708   PRC:212
www.siliconlight.com
Email: sales@siliconlight.com
Estab: 1994

Lars Eng, President & CEO
Ken Fukui, SVP of Operations
Cindy Lott, Director of Finance
Clint Carroll, Production Manager
Yuen Wing Poon, Sales Manager

Provider of optical micro-electro-mechanical systems. The company's applications include mask-
less lithography and large format digital displays.

Silicon Microstructures Inc   HQ
1701 McCarthy Blvd
Milpitas CA 95035
P: 408-577-0100 F: 408-577-0123   PRC:163
www.si-micro.com
Email: info@si-micro.com
Estab: 1991

Friedrich Holz, CFO
Holger Doering, COO
Sandy Taylor, Human Resource Manager
Steve Rodriguez, Planning Manager
J. Fernando Alfaro, Design Engineer

Developer and manufacturer of MEMS-based pressure sensors. The company's products are used in medical, industrial, and automotive applications.

Silicon Mitus   BR
20370 Town Center Ln Ste 211
Cupertino CA 95014
P: 408-446-3151 F: 408-446-3285   PRC:98
siliconmitus.com

Harold Chang, CFO
Dong Chun Kim, EVP of Worldwide Sales & Marketing
Youngik Yoo, VP of Engineering
Kyunghwan Kim, VP of Operations
Francesco Rezzi, VP

Manufacturer and distributor of smart power management integrated chips solutions. The company focuses on power solutions.

Silicon Motion Inc   DH
690 N McCarthy Blvd Ste 200
Milpitas CA 95035
P: 408-519-7289 F: 408-519-7101   PRC:212
www.siliconmotion.com
Estab: 1995

Wallace Kou, CEO & President
Riyadh Lai, CFO
Arthur Yeh, VP of Sales
Frank Shu, VP of SSD Technology, Business Development & Verification
Kevin Yeh, VP of Research & Development, Algorithm & Technology

Designer of low-power semiconductor solutions. The company serves multimedia consumer electronic applications.

Silicon Publishing Inc   HQ
100 Pine St Ste 1250
San Francisco CA 94111
P: 925-935-3899   PRC:320
www.siliconpublishing.com
Email: sales@siliconpublishing.com
Estab: 2000

Max Dunn, President
Aaron Hodges, COO
Chris Jacobson, Business Development & Strategic Partnerships Manager

Provider of digital publishing solutions. The company deals with template designs and personalized communications.

Silicon Storage Technology Inc   HQ
450 Holger Way
San Jose CA 95134
P: 408-735-9110   PRC:86
www.sst.com
Email: info@sst.com
Estab: 1989

Toan Ly, Manager
Michael Doan, Senior Staff Engineer

Designer and manufacturer of memory and non-memory products. The company serves Internet computing markers.

Silicon Valley Mfg   HQ
6520 Central Ave
Newark CA 94560
P: 510-791-9450   PRC:80
www.svmfg.com
Email: sales@svmfg.com

Mark Serpa, President
Angie Ollendorf, Office Manager

Manufacturer and engineer of EDM prototype and production machining. The company's services include CNC milling, CNC turning, and manual machining.

Silicon Valley Precision Inc   HQ
5625 Brisa St Ste G
Livermore CA 94550
P: 925-373-8259 F: 925-373-6025   PRC:157
www.siliconvalleyprecision.com
Email: lara@siliconvalleyprecision.com
Estab: 1984

John Payne, Manager

Provider of custom vertical and horizontal CNC machining, fabrication and assembly of parts. The company offers powder coating, painting and grinding.

Silicon Wafer Enterprises LLC   HQ
3941 Park Dr Ste 20-726
El Dorado Hills CA 95762
P: 916-201-6675   PRC:212
siwaferenterprises.com

Linda Nathan, Owner

Provider of silicon wafers and other raw materials. The company's offerings include silicon, plate glass, pyrex, and sapphire.

Silicon360   HQ
1804 McCarthy Blvd
Milpitas CA 95035
P: 408-432-1790 F: 408-432-7350   PRC:212
www.silicon360.com
Email: sales@silicon360.com
Estab: 2009

Zef Malik, CEO

Supplier of semiconductors for the military, aerospace, industrial, medical, and commercial markers.

Silicondust USA Inc   RH
2150 Portola Ave Ste D 143
Livermore CA 94551
P: 925-443-4388 F: 925-443-3243   PRC:245
www.silicondust.com
Email: info@silicondust.com
Estab: 2007

Theodore Head, President & CEO
Nick Kelsey, CTO

Provider of network connected TV tuners. The company offers global solutions to Live TV streaming in businesses, hotels, and education facilities.

Silk Road Medical Inc   HQ
1213 Innsbruck Dr
Sunnyvale CA 94089
P: 408-720-9002 F: 408-720-9013   PRC:188
silkroadmed.com
Email: info@silkroadmed.com
Estab: 2007

Erica J. Rogers, President & CEO
Lucas Buchanan, CFO
Mark Page, VP of Strategic Initiatives
Richard Ruedy, EVP of RA & CA & QA
Shari Rideout, VP of Quality

Specializes in the treatment of carotid artery diseases. The company is engaged in clinical trials and related services.

Sillajen Inc   BR
450 Sansome St 2nd Fl
San Francisco CA 94111
P: 415-281-8886   PRC:34
www.sillajen.com
Estab: 2003

Eun Sang Moon, CEO
Myung Suk Song, CFO
Hyuk Chan Kwon, CMO
Robin Scully, VP of Product & Alliance Management
Terri Carroll Robertson, Director of Clinical Supply Chain

Developer of biotherapeutics specializing in cancer products. The company also focuses on marketing.

Silpac   HQ
1850 Russell Ave
Santa Clara CA 95054
P: 408-492-0011 F: 408-492-0022   PRC:133
www.silpac.net
Email: sales@silpac.net
Estab: 2000

Tom Vass, Owner
Ray Mendoza, President
Mark Thornberry, VP of Sales
Rusty McCullar, General Manager
Mark Dye, Business Manager

Distributor and manufacturer of specialty gas handling equipment. The company caters to markers like semiconductor, life science, and solar.

Silvaco Inc HQ
2811 Mission College Blvd 6th Fl
Santa Clara CA 95054
P: 408-567-1000 F: 408-496-6080 PRC:317
www.silvaco.com
Email: sales@silvaco.com
Estab: 1984

Hwang Mangyu, President of Asia Operations
David Dutton, CEO
Mark Maurer, VP of Business Development &
Foundry Relations
Eric Guichard, VP
Stan Jones, Director of Human Resources

Supplier of TCAD and EDA software for circuit simulation. The company also designs analog, mixed-signal, and RF integrated circuits.

Silver Creek Pharmaceuticals Inc HQ
409 Illinois St
San Francisco CA 94158
P: 415-978-2178 PRC:251
www.silvercreekpharma.com
Estab: 2010

Matt Onsum, President & CEO
Kris Kuchenbecker, Lead scientist & CTO
Sam Pfaff, Associate Director
Yan Zhang, Medical Director
Henry H. Chang, Scientist

Provider of pharmaceuticals. The company develops regenerative medicines with an initial focus on treating cardiovascular disease.

Silver Peak Systems Inc HQ
2860 De La Cruz Blvd
Santa Clara CA 95050
P: 408-935-1800 PRC:323
www.silver-peak.com
Email: info@silver-peak.com
Estab: 2004

Ian Whiting, President of Global Field Operations
Rick Tinsley, CEO
Eric Yeaman, CFO
John Vincenzo, SVP & CMO
Rick Valentine, Chief Customer Officer

Provider of miscellaneous communication equipment and services. The company focuses on WAN optimization, cloud networking, and replication acceleration.

Silveron Industries Inc HQ
182 S Brent Cir [N]
City Of Industry CA 91789
P: 909-598-4533 F: 909-594-9234 PRC:290
www.silveron.co.kr
Estab: 1977

James Lee, CEO & Secretary & CFO

Supplier of relays and industrial controls.

Silvestre Manufacturing HQ
1745 Grant St Ste 5
Santa Clara CA 95050
P: 408-988-0937 PRC:80
silvestremfg.com
Email: silvestremfg@gmail.com

Julian Silvestre, Owner

Provider of custom fabrication services. The company specializes in machining and prototype production.

M-280

Simco Electronics HQ
3131 Jay St
Santa Clara CA 95054
P: 408-734-9750 F: 408-734-9780 PRC:306
www.simco.com
Email: sales@simco.com
Estab: 1962

Brian Kenna, CEO
Marie-France Nelson, CFO
John Connelly, Chief Commercial Officer
Samuel Klooster, VP of Sales
Bradford Phillips, VP

Providers of services and software to medical device manufacturers. The company specializes in biotechnology.

Simco-Ion BR
1141 Harbor Bay Pkwy Ste 201
Alameda CA 94502
P: 510-217-0460 F: 510-217-0484 PRC:159
www.simco-ion.com
Email: info@simco-ion.com

Trevor Norman, Senior Director of Business Development
Steve Heymann, Senior Director of Technology Development
Marco Guarnieri, Manager of Cell
Veeresham Ramini, ERP System Manager
Mark Hogsett, Application Engineering Manager

Manufacturer of static control and process control products. The company is engaged in design and installation services.

Simonds Machinery Co HQ
259 Harbor Way
S San Francisco CA 94080
P: 650-589-9900 F: 650-589-5900 PRC:160
www.simondsmachinery.com
Email: pumps@simondsmachinery.com
Estab: 1905

Stephen Hipp, President
Kurt Hipp, VP

Distributor of portable pump carts, custom control panels, pressure booster systems, and related accessories.

Simplex Filler Co HQ
640-A Airpark Rd Ste A
Napa CA 94558
P: 707-265-6801 F: 707-265-6868 PRC:159
www.simplexfiller.com
Email: simplex@simplexfiller.com
Estab: 1947

Dennis Bertolucci, Director of Engineering

Manufacturer of liquid filling machines. The company offers volumetric fillers, pressure fillers, and accessories.

Simplicant Inc HQ
950 Page Mill Rd
Palo Alto CA 94304
P: 650-285-2394 PRC:315
www.simplicant.com
Email: info@simplicant.com
Estab: 2012

Zartash Uzmi, Founder
Sajjad Masud, CEO

Producer of modern recruitment software that also helps to track applicants.

Simplificare Inc HQ
480 S California Ave
Palo Alto CA 94306
P: 800-464-5125 PRC:40
www2.simplee.com
Estab: 2010

Roberto Rabinovich, Co-Founder & COO
Tomer Shoval, CEO & Co-Founder

Provider of software solutions for patient financial care (PFC). The company offers services to patients and clinics.

Simplion Technologies HQ
1525 McCarthy Blvd Ste 228
Milpitas CA 95035
P: 408-935-8686 F: 408-935-8696 PRC:322
www.simplion.com
Email: info@simplion.com
Estab: 2004

Neha Bhatia, Account Manager
Sandeep Kumar, Practice Head
S. Swain, Senior Analyst
Satyam Jha, Senior Technical Recruiter

Provider of consulting solutions. The company offers strategy development, implementation, deployment, and technical support services.

Sincere Design HQ
103 Santa Fe Ave [N]
Point Richmond CA 94801
P: 510-215-1139 PRC:24
www.sinceredesign.com
Email: sincere@pointrichmond.com
Estab: 1994

David Moore, Art Director & Owner

Provider of website design, Internet and traditional marketing, book design and production, computer graphics and communication services.

Single Cell Technology Inc HQ
6280 San Ignacio Ave Ste E
San Jose CA 95119
P: 408-265-9239 PRC:23
www.single-cell-technology.com
Email: info@singlecelltechnology.com

Chun-Nan Chen, CEO & CSO
Jim Bowlby, COO
Karen Mao, Scientist

Developer of cell technology solutions and also proportionary therapeutic antibody process for its clients.

Single Point Of Contact HQ
992 San Antonio Rd
Palo Alto CA 94303
P: 800-791-4300 F: 650-213-8327 PRC:324
singlepointoc.com
Email: sales@singlepointoc.com
Estab: 1999

Fernando Leon, VP of Sales & Marketing

Provider of IT management, enterprise, and planning services. The company is also engaged in cloud computing, web hosting, and hosted exchange.

Sios Technology Corp   HQ
155 Bovet Rd Ste 476
San Mateo CA 94402
P: 650-645-7000   F: 650-645-7030   PRC:324
us.sios.com
Email: info@us.sios.com

Jerry Melnick, COO
Sergey A. Razin, CTO
Tony Tomarchio, Director of Field Engineering

Provider of cloud virtualization protection solutions. The company also offers managed information technology services.

Sitepen Inc   HQ
530 Lytton Ave 2nd Fl
Palo Alto CA 94301
P: 650-968-8787   PRC:323
sitepen.com
Estab: 2000

Carrie Rice, COO
Aimee Busch, Director of Operations
Martin Klosi, Engineering Team Lead
Joel Chacon, Supervisor

Developer and provider of software products and services. The company also offers web application development and java support services.

SiteTech Inc   HQ
8061 Church St   [N]
Highland CA 92346
P: 909-864-3180   PRC:304
www.sitetechinc.com
Emp: 1-10

Bernie Mayer, President
Jason Mayer, VP & Director of Engineering

Provider of civil engineering, surveying, and land development related services.

Sitime Corp   HQ
5451 Patrick Henry Dr
Santa Clara CA 95054
P: 408-328-4400   F: 408-328-4439   PRC:86
www.sitime.com
Email: america-west-sales@sitime.com
Estab: 2005

Aaron Partridge, Founder & Chief Scientist
Rajesh Vashist, CEO
Arthur Chadwick, EVP & CFO
Piyush Sevalia, EVP of Marketing
Vinod Menon, EVP of Central Engineering

Provider of programmable oscillators and clock generators. The company also offers embedded resonators.

SiTune Corporation Inc   HQ
2216 Ringwood Ave
San Jose CA 95131
P: 408-324-1711   F: 408-521-3340   PRC:208
situne-ic.com
Email: sales@situne-ic.com
Estab: 2007

Marzieh Veyseh, CTO & Co-Founder
Vahid Toosi, Co-Founder & CEO
Sam Heidari, Chairman
Ben Runyan, VP of Sales & Marketing
Saeid Mehrmanesh, Director of RFIC

Provider of integrated circuits and systems. The company offers spectrum reception and concurrent tuners.

Siva Power Inc   HQ
5102 Calle Del Sol
Santa Clara CA 95054
P: 408-834-7400   PRC:135
www.sivapower.com
Email: info@sivapower.com

Mark Heising, Chairman
Bruce Sohn, CEO
Markus Beck, CTO
Chris McDonald, COO
BJ Stanbery, Chief Science Officer

Manufacturer of solar products. The company specializes in semiconductor, flat panel display, and solar devices.

SJ Amoroso Construction Co LLC   HQ
390 Bridge Pkwy
Redwood City CA 94065
P: 650-654-1900   F: 650-654-9002   PRC:304
www.sjamoroso.com
Estab: 1939

Dana C. Mcmanus, CEO
Laura Heckenberg, CFO
Jim Benson, Chief Estimator
Amy Trevisan, Project Manager
Dean Ramsay, Project Manager

Provider of construction contracting services. The company focuses on pre-construction consulting, design-build contracting and management.

SJ Die Casting & Machining Corp   HQ
600 Business Park Dr
Lincoln CA 95648
P: 408-262-6500   PRC:80
www.sjdiecasting.com

Mark Callaghan, President

Manufacturer of castings for computer, electronic, automotive, and military sectors specializing in sandblasting, deburring, and assembly services.

SJC Precision Inc   HQ
1811 Houret Ct
Milpitas CA 95035
P: 408-262-1680   F: 408-770-3737   PRC:157
www.sjcprecision.com
Email: jijo@sjcprecision.com
Estab: 1996

Jijo Chemmachel, CEO

Provider of precision machining and tool and die making services. The company designs and manufactures jigs, fixtures, and bookmolds.

SJK Company Ltd   BR
46715 Fremont Blvd
Fremont CA 94538
P: 510-573-4852   F: 510-573-6565   PRC:109
www.sejin.com
Email: info@sejin.com

Jong Lee, Business Development Manager

Manufacturer of automobile parts, smart grid products, input devices, and convergence products. The company offers customer support services.

SK hynix America Inc   BR
3101 N First St
San Jose CA 95134
P: 408-232-8000   F: 408-232-8103   PRC:126
www.hynix.com

Seok-Hee Lee, CEO
Junggeun Kim, Director

Manufacturer of DRAM products. The company focuses on consumer memory, graphics memory, mobile memory, and CMOS image sensors.

Skeletal Kinetics LLC   HQ
10201 Bubb Rd
Cupertino CA 95014
P: 408-366-5000   F: 408-366-1077   PRC:53
www.skeletalkinetics.com
Email: cs@skeletalkinetics.com
Estab: 2002

Christine Kuo, Director of RA & QA
Ken Weissel, Production Supervisor
Ricky Luong, Contact

Developer, manufacturer and marketer of bone fixation cement designed for the treatment of trauma fractures.

SKS Diecasting & Machining   HQ
1849 Oak St
Alameda CA 94501
P: 510-523-2541   PRC:163
www.sksdiecasting.com
Email: sales@sksdiecasting.com
Estab: 1946

Sean Keating, President
Richard Wieckowski, Chief Engineer
Jeff Ratto, Maintenance Supervisor
Jesusa JosonFusade, Controller

Manufacturer of aluminum die cast parts and related supplies. The company offers services to the high tech industry.

Skybox Security Inc   HQ
2077 Gateway Pl Ste 200
San Jose CA 95110
P: 408-441-8060   F: 408-441-8068   PRC:104
www.skyboxsecurity.com
Email: info@skyboxsecurity.com
Estab: 2002

Gidi Cohen, CEO & Founder
Lior Barak, CFO
Stewart Fox, EVP of Worldwide Sales & Applications
Albert Lozano, Corporate Account Manager
Jessica Le, Research & Development Engineer

Provider of risk analytics for cyber security. The company offers threat management and network security management solutions.

SkyRiver   HQ
7310 Miramar Rd Ste 600   [N]
San Diego CA 92126
P: 858-812-5280   PRC:62
www.skyriver.net
Email: info@skyriver.net
Estab: 2000

Saeed Khorami, President
Hugo Morales, VP of Operations

Provider of business Internet services.

Skyspares Parts Inc HQ
6640 View Park Ct [N]
Riverside CA 92503
P: 951-351-0770   F: 951-351-1741   PRC:4
Estab: 1975

Kevin Andrews, Contact

Manufacturer of CNC precision machined parts.

Sleepless Media HQ
2601 41st Ave Ste B
Soquel CA 95073
P: 831-427-1969   PRC:325
www.sleeplessmedia.com
Estab: 2001

Jon Cattivera, Owner & Creative Director &
Founder
Mark Anthony Serrano, Developer

Provider of website design and development
services. The company focuses on content management, e-commerce, SEO, hosting, and brand
identity.

Smaato Inc HQ
240 Stockton St 10th Fl [N]
San Francisco CA 94108
P: 650-286-1198   F: 650-240-0708   PRC:45
www.smaato.com
Email: support@smaato.com
Emp: 51-200   Estab: 2005

Petra Vorsteher, Co-Founder & Officer
Ragnar Kruse, Co-Founder & CEO
Georg Fiegen, COO
Gerry Louw, CTO
Glenn Fishback, CRO

Operator of mobile ad optimization platform.

Small Precision Tools Inc BR
1330 Clegg St
Petaluma CA 94954
P: 707-762-5880   F: 707-559-2072   PRC:80
www.smallprecisiontools.com
Email: info-usa@spt.net

Joe Gracia, CFO
Mark Hamilton, General Manager
Guangfu Wang, Mechanical Design Engineer
Michael Hutchison, Production Engineer
Juanita Flores, Electrical Engineer

Manufacturer of chip bonding tools, fine ceramic,
and machining parts. The company offers neces-
sary technical support and services.

Smart ERP Solutions Inc HQ
4683 Chabot Dr Ste 380
Pleasanton CA 94588
P: 925-271-0200   PRC:323
www.smarterp.com
Email: sales@smarterp.com
Estab: 2005

Raghu Yelluru, Co-Founder & COO
Ramesh Panchagnula, Co-Founder & President
Sreeni Muniswamy, Co-Founder & CTO
Doris Wong, CEO
Anand Kavatkar, CFO

Developer of enterprise class software. The company provides vendor management software and
support services.

M-282

Smart Modular Technologies HQ
39870 Eureka Dr
Newark CA 94560
P: 510-623-1231   F: 510-623-1434   PRC:96
www.smartm.com
Email: info@smartm.com
Estab: 1988
Sales: $1B to $3B

Ajay Shah, Executive Chairman of the Board
Hollie Smythe, Principal CEO
Jack Pacheco, COO & CFO & EVP
Bruce Goldberg, VP & CLO & CCO
Mike Rubino, VP of Engineering

Manufacturer of add on memory boards, flash,
and storage products. The company serves defense, gaming, storage, and other sectors.

Smart Monitor Corp HQ
6203 San Ignacio Ave Ste 113
San Jose CA 95119
P: 408-754-1695   F: 408-754-8629   PRC:187
www.smart-monitor.com
Email: support@smart-monitor.com
Estab: 2009

Anoo Nathan, CEO

Manufacturer of monitoring devices. The company
provides automated solution for detecting unusual
movements from chronic health conditions.

Smart Products Inc HQ
675 Jarvis Dr
Morgan Hill CA 95037
P: 408-776-3035   F: 408-776-3186   PRC:160
smartproducts.com
Email: sales@smartproducts.com
Estab: 1984

Mark Whittington, Operations Manager

Supplier of engineering products. The company
offers valves, fittings, and pumps for the automotive, medical, and water treatment markers.

Smart Wires Inc HQ
3292 Whipple Rd
Union City CA 94587
P: 415-800-5555   PRC:159
smartwires.com
Email: info@smartwires.com
Estab: 2010

Haroon Inam, CTO
Patricia Allen, Office Manager

Provider of grid optimization solutions. The company is involved in load and generation, alleviate
congestion, and network utilization services.

SMC Corporation of America BR
2841 Junction Ave Ste 110
San Jose CA 95134
P: 408-943-9600   PRC:146
smcusa.com
Estab: 1959

Kelley Stacy, President & COO
Timothy Kuchta, Director of Sales
John Moews, Account Manager
Eric McElroy, Account Manager
Scott Maurer, Product Manager

Provider of in pneumatic technology solutions
that are used in diverse range of industries from
automotive to life science.

SMC Ltd BR
3250 Brickway Blvd
Santa Rosa CA 95403
P: 707-303-3000   F: 707-303-3050   PRC:189
www.smcltd.com
Email: inquiry@smcltd.com
Estab: 1988

Paul LaFond, VP of Sales
Rajan Batra, Director
Meredith Canty, Director Drug Delivery Systems
Rick Walker, General Manager
Cory Lee, Project Manager

Provider of custom packing for product sterilization. The company is engaged in supply chain
management solutions.

Smith Food Machinery Inc HQ
1133 N Broadway Ave [N]
Stockton CA 95205
P: 209-465-3688   PRC:159
www.smithfoodmachinery.com
Estab: 2007

Grant Smith, Owner

Wholesaler of used food processing equipment
and paint liquidations and plant and equipment
appraisals, auction and plant liquidation services.

Smith Precision Products Co HQ
1299 Lawrence Dr [N]
Newbury Park CA 91320
P: 805-498-6616   F: 805-499-2867   PRC:156
www.smithpumps.com
Estab: 1939

Walter Smith, President

Manufacturer and distributor of pumps and fertiliz-
er injectors.

SMP Tech Inc HQ
17500 Depot St Ste 210
Morgan Hill CA 95037
P: 408-776-7776   PRC:186
www.smptech.com
Email: engineering@smptech.com
Estab: 1990

Alain Lacombe, Owner
Tom Roberts, CEO
Ann Roberts, CFO

Designer and builder of robotic DNA spotters, mi-
crofluidic devices, medical equipment, automated
machinery, and electro-mechanical products.

SMTC Corp BR
431 Kato Terr
Fremont CA 94539
P: 510-737-0700   F: 510-498-8525   PRC:86
www.smtc.com
Email: contact.us@smtc.com
Estab: 1985

Edward Smith, President & CEO & Director
Rich Fitzgerald, COO
Steven M. Waszak, CFO
Kenny Lai, VP & General Manager
Seth Choi, VP of Global Supply Chain Manage-
ment & Procurement

Provider of electronics manufacturing services for
the industrial, medical, computing, and communication markers.

SNA Electronics Inc HQ
3249 Laurelview Ct
Fremont CA 94538
P: 510-656-3903   F: 510-656-3909   PRC:68
www.sna-electronic.com
Estab: 1996

Chi Shin, CFO
Steve Hahn, Production Manager

Provider of electronic manufacturing services.
The company offers services to OEMs in the
networking, medical instruments, and aerospace
industries.

Snowline Engineering Inc HQ
4261 Business Dr
Cameron Park CA 95682
P: 530-677-2675   F: 530-677-9832   PRC:80
www.snowlineengineering.com
Email: sales@snowlineengineering.com
Estab: 1998

Cal Reynolds, President
Lee Block, EVP
Dave Greenacre, General Manager
Vern Holzer, Quality Assurance Supervisor

Provider of precision machining and fabrication
services. The company also engages in sheet
metal and assembly.

Socionext Inc HQ
2811 Mission College Blvd 5th Fl
Santa Clara CA 95054
P: 408-550-6861   PRC:63
www.socionext.com
Email: sna_inquiry@us.socionext.com
Estab: 2015

Vaidehi Sudhakar, CFO
Matt Hall, Senior Sales Manager

Designer and developer of System-on-Chip
products. The company's products are used in
imaging, networking, and computing fields.

Socket Mobile Inc HQ
39700 Eureka Dr
Newark CA 94560
P: 510-933-3000   F: 510-933-3030   PRC:176
www.socketmobile.com
Email: sales@socketmobile.com
Estab: 1992
Sales: $10M to $30M

Charlie Bass, Founder & Chairman
Kevin J. Mills, President & CEO
Leonard L. Ott, EVP of Engineering & CTO
Dave Dunlap, CFO
Vanessa Lindsay, Product Manager

Developer of wireless handheld and hands-free
barcode scanners and other products and serves
retail, logistics, automotive, and other sectors.

Soffa Electric Inc HQ
5901 Corvette St   [N]
Commerce CA 90040
P: 323-728-0230   F: 323-724-5513   PRC:304
www.soffaelectric.com
Emp: 51-200   Estab: 1971

Salib Mansour, Chief Engineer

Provider of engineering services.

Softjourn Inc HQ
39270 Paseo Padre Pkwy Ste 251
Fremont CA 94538
P: 510-744-1528   F: 815-301-2772   PRC:326
www.softjourn.com
Email: sales@softjourn.com
Estab: 2001

Emmy B. Gengler, CEO
Jeff Kreuser, CTO
Sergiy Fitsak, Managing Director & Director of
Technology
Bogdan Mykhaylovych, Engineering Manager &
Technical Director

Provider of outsource software development
services and focuses on offshore assessments,
application development, and quality assurance
testing.

SoftNet Solutions Inc HQ
940 Hamlin Ct
Sunnyvale CA 94089
P: 408-542-0888   PRC:326
softnets.com
Email: info@softnets.com
Estab: 1994

Kush Hathi, President & Co-Founder
Tehnaz Hathi, CFO & Co-Founder

Provider of enterprise solutions for high performance computing and network security. The
company specializes in IT consulting and cloud
services.

Softsol Inc HQ
42808 Christy St Ste 100
Fremont CA 94538
P: 510-824-2000   F: 510-217-3461   PRC:325
www.softsol.com
Email: info@softsol.com
Estab: 1993

Srini Madala, Chairman
Robert Hersh, CFO
Kumar Talluri, VP
R.K. Ghanta, VP
Priya Softsol, Team Lead

Provider of software solutions. The company offers
software such as Intelli Court Case Management,
Corporate Investigations, STIC, and PB Migration.

Software AG BR
2901 Tasman Dr Ste 219
Santa Clara CA 95054
P: 800-823-2212   PRC:325
www.softwareag.com
Email: sales@softwareagusa.com
Estab: 1969

Anneliese Schulz, President
Philippe La Fornara, President, EMEA
Renato Morsch, President, Latin America
Sanjay Brahmawar, CEO
Arnd Zinnhardt, CFO

Provider of enterprise management and business
solutions that include process intelligence and
automation, and enterprise architecture.

**Software Systems Quality
Consulting** HQ
2269 Sunny Vista Dr   [N]
San Jose CA 95128
P: 408-985-4476   F: 408-248-7772   PRC:45
www.ssqc.com
Estab: 1990

Robert Bamford, Co-Founder
William Deibler, Co-Founder

Provider of software process improvement,
software quality assurance and testing, CMMI implementation services. It also provides education
and training services for software and hardware
developers, manufacturers and service providers.

Solano Archaeological Services HQ
131 Sunset Ave Ste E120
Suisun City CA 94585-2064
P: 707-718-1416   F: 707-451-4775   PRC:135
solanoarchaeology.com
Email: admin@solanoarchaeology.com
Estab: 2005

Jason A. Coleman, Founder

Provider of archaeological services. The company
services also include cultural resource and artifact
analysis and curation.

Solar Design & Drafting HQ
149 Kentucky St Ste 5
Petaluma CA 94952
P: 415-305-3982   PRC:304
www.solardesignanddrafting.com

John Knueppel, Owner & Founder

Designer of solar devices. The company's services
include design considerations, flat rate permit
packages, and other services.

Solar Sense PV Inc HQ
7083 Commerce Cir Ste C
Pleasanton CA 94588
P: 888-786-4339   PRC:129
solarsensepv.com
Email: info@solarsensepv.com
Estab: 2010

Richard Hurst, CEO

Provider of solar power system installation
services. The company also focuses on design
and serves residential, commercial, and utility
applications.

Solarbos Inc HQ
310 Stealth Ct
Livermore CA 94551
P: 925-456-7744   PRC:135
www.solarbos.com
Email: sales@solarbos.com
Estab: 2004

Dustin Watson, VP of Sales
Jaimee Herschbach, Inside Sales Manager
Anthony Parsons, Manager of Operations
Rich Halket, Controller
Cole Snyder, CAD Designer

Designer and manufacturer of electrical products.
The company exclusively caters to the solar
industry.

Solarius Development Inc HQ
2360 Qume St
San Jose CA 95131
P: 408-435-2777 PRC:212
www.solarius-inc.com
Email: sales@solarius-inc.com
Estab: 2000

Hitendra Mistry, Project Manager
Amy Zullo, Office Manager
Clarence Tamargo, System Engineer
Kejul Patel, Application Engineer
Edgar Alvarez, Contact

Manufacturer of 3D metrology surface measurement systems. The company offers metrology services for surface form.

Solid State Optronics HQ
15 Great Oaks Blvd
San Jose CA 95119
P: 408-293-4600 F: 408-293-4848 PRC:86
ssousa.com
Estab: 1982

Juan Kadah, General Manager
Hemant Koria, Sales Manager

Manufacturer of miniature Solid State Relays. The company offers MOSFET drivers, specialty products, and optocouplers.

Soliton Systems Inc BR
2635 N First St Ste 213
San Jose CA 95134
P: 408-434-1923 PRC:325
solitonsys.com
Email: sales@solitonsys.com

Nobuo Kamada, President

Provider of information technology solutions. The company offers IT security, network infrastructure, cloud computing, and IT management services.

Solonics Inc HQ
31072 San Antonio St
Hayward CA 94544
P: 510-471-7600 F: 510-471-2168 PRC:63
www.solonics.com
Email: info@solonics.com
Estab: 1985

Bill O'Neil, Founder

Manufacturer of coded backboard systems and wire management products. The company focuses on design and delivery services.

Soltac Inc HQ
1630 Castilleja Ave
Palo Alto CA 94306
P: 650-327-7090 F: 650-327-7095 PRC:131
Estab: 2000

Jonathan A. Stoumen, Contact
Linda Swett, Bookkeeper

Designer and provider of solar devices. It's products find application in warming batteries, signaling, and radar locating.

M-284

Solution Architects Inc HQ
247 28th St
San Francisco CA 94131
P: 415-775-1656 F: 415-929-1118 PRC:322
www.solutionarchitects.com
Email: info@solutionarchitects.com
Estab: 1998

Asim Qadir, Founder & President

Provider of sophisticated IT solutions for complex systems. The company's services include analysis and product development.

Solutions Cubed LLC HQ
3045 Esplanade
Chico CA 95973
P: 530-891-8045 F: 530-891-1643 PRC:64
www.solutions-cubed.com
Email: sales@solutions-cubed.com
Estab: 1994

Frank Rossini, Design Engineer
Lon Glazner, Partner & Engineer

Provider of engineering solutions. The company is involved in early stage electronic prototyping to full production runs.

Solutionware Corp HQ
467 Saratoga Ave Ste 474
San Jose CA 95129
P: 408-249-1529 F: 408-371-3712 PRC:316
www.solution-ware.com
Email: info@solution-ware.com
Estab: 1980

Joe Baumgardner, Sales Manager

Provider of design solutions. The company offers computer aided design and computer aided manufacturing services.

SOMA Environmental Engineering Inc HQ
6620 Owens Dr Ste A
Pleasanton CA 94588
P: 925-734-6400 F: 925-734-6401 PRC:142
somaenv.com
Email: info@somaenv.com
Estab: 1992

Mansour Sepehr, President
Ruchi Mathur, Project Engineer

Provider of environmental engineering solutions. The company offers services for remediation and underground storage tanks.

Somagenics Inc HQ
2161 Delaware Ave
Santa Cruz CA 95060
P: 831-426-7700 F: 831-420-0685 PRC:252
www.somagenics.com
Email: infor@somagenics.com
Estab: 1997

Anne Scholz, VP of Administration
Sergei A. Kazakov, VP of Discovery Research
Anne Dallas, Principal Scientist
Sergio Barberan, Senior Scientist
Heini Ilves, Scientist

Developer of RNA-based therapeutics and diagnostics. The company's services include detection, monitoring, testing, and analysis.

Sonasoft Corp HQ
6920 Santa Teresa Blvd Ste 108
San Jose CA 95119
P: 408-708-4000 F: 408-946-5800 PRC:322
www.sonasoft.com
Estab: 2002

Andy Khanna, Founder
Mike Khanna, CEO
Bilal Ahmed, CTO & VP of Engineering
Rob Baumert, CFO
Vikas Agrawal, Chief Innovation Officer

Provider of software based solutions to simplify and automate replication, archiving, backup, recovery, and data protection operations.

Sonic Manufacturing Technologies HQ
47951 Westinghouse Dr
Fremont CA 94539
P: 510-756-5837 F: 510-492-0909 PRC:74
www.sonicmfg.com
Email: sales@sonicmfg.com
Estab: 1996

Henry Woo, Chief Process Engineer & Co-Founder
Kenneth Raab, President & CEO & Co-Founder & Chairman of the Board
Robert Pereyda, VP of Engineering & Co-Founder
Manmeet Wirk, VP of Sales & Marketing
David Ginsberg, VP of Supply Chain Management

Provider of contract manufacturing services. The company engages in supply chain, quality assurance, and design and engineering services.

Sonim Technologies Inc HQ
1875 S Grant St Ste 750
San Mateo CA 94402
P: 650-378-8100 F: 650-378-8109 PRC:71
www.sonimtech.com
Email: feedback@sonimtech.com
Estab: 2007

Bob Plaschke, CEO & Chairman
Richard Long, CFO
Peter Liu, EVP of Operations & General Manager of China

Designer and manufacturer of water-submersible mobile phones. The company's products are used in construction, security guarding, and oil and gas operations.

Sono Group Inc HQ
696 San Ramon Valley Blvd Ste 401
Danville CA 94526
P: 925-855-8552 PRC:323
www.sonogroup.com
Email: info@sonogroup.com
Estab: 1992

Carla Adcock, President

Provider of custom software and application development, training, social networking, and IT staffing services.

Sonoma Wire Works HQ
1049 El Monte Ave Ste C -73
Mountain View CA 94040
P: 650-948-2003 F: 650-948-0740 PRC:60
www.sonomawireworks.com
Email: info@sonomawireworks.com
Estab: 2003

Douglas Wright, President
Michelle Wright, VP of Sales & Marketing
Moses Abrego, Software Quality Assurance Engineer
Will Reichenthal, Software Developer

Provider of loop-based recording and collaboration software for musicians. It's products helps musicians to play, record, and share music.

Sootheze HQ
859 Washington St Ste 200
Red Bluff CA 96080
P: 844-576-6843 F: 530-727-6209 PRC:189
www.sootheze.com
Email: support@sootheze.com
Estab: 1995

Paul Losch, President

Manufacturer of aromatherapy products and other products that help relieve pain and provide comfort.

Soraa Inc HQ
6500 Kaiser Dr Ste 110
Fremont CA 94555
P: 510-456-2200 PRC:209
www.soraa.com
Email: support@soraahome.com
Estab: 2009

Steve Denbaars, Co-Founder
Shuji Nakamura, Co-Founder
Jeff Parker, CEO
Kieran Drain, COO
Michael Craven, VP of Epi Engineering

Provider of lighting design and fixture lamp solutions. The company serves hotels, restaurants, theaters, and private residences.

Sotcher Measurement Inc HQ
115 Phelan Ave Ste 10
San Jose CA 95112
P: 800-922-2969 F: 408-574-0116 PRC:19
www.sotcher.com
Email: sales@sotcher.com
Estab: 1969

Marc Sotcher, President & VP of Manufacturing

Provider of test equipment. The company provides test stations, service tags, generator test sets, and automatic test stations.

SoundHound Inc HQ
5400 Betsy Ross Dr
Santa Clara CA 95054
P: 408-441-3200 PRC:326
www.soundhound.com
Estab: 2005

Keyvan Mohajer, Founder & CEO
James Hom, Co-Founder & VP of Products
Majid Emami, Co-Founder & VP of Engineering
Tim Stonehocker, CTO
Amir Arbabi, VP of Business Development

Developer of a sound and speech responsive search engine. The company's product finds application in mobile and communication devices.

Soundvision Inc HQ
27 Commercial Blvd Ste M
Novato CA 94949
P: 415-456-7000 F: 415-883-7199 PRC:243
svsf.com
Email: info@svsf.com
Estab: 1998

Scott Sullivan, President
Erik Kelzer, Purchasing Manager
Brian Stang, Operations Manager
Kellie King, Office Manager
Andy Ross, Lead Programmer

Provider of home entertainment, home automation, house audio, lighting, and motorized window shades.

Source Engineering Inc HQ
3283-H De La Cruz Blvd
Santa Clara CA 95054
P: 408-980-9822 F: 408-980-1860 PRC:150
www.sei-automation.com
Email: rick@sei-automation.com
Estab: 1998

Scott Zimmer, President
Jim Walls, VP of Sales & Customer Service

Manufacturer of motors, cables, harnesses, and motion control products. The company also provides custom modification services on motors.

Source Naturals Inc HQ
23 Janis Way
Scotts Valley CA 95066
P: 831-438-1144 F: 831-438-7410 PRC:272
www.sourcenaturals.com
Estab: 1982

Ira Goldberg, CEO

Provider of vitamins, minerals, and nutritional supplements. The company deals with sales and delivery services.

South Bay Solutions Inc HQ
37399 Centralmont Pl
Fremont CA 94536
P: 650-843-1800 F: 650-843-1803 PRC:74
southbaysolutions.com
Email: info@southbaysolutions.com
Estab: 1992

Adam Drewniany, Founder
Parveen Johal, Quality Assurance Manager
German Avalos, Quotation Specialist
Beco Gutosic, QC Inspector

Provider of manufacturing services for the semiconductor, medical, aerospace, solar, and petroleum industries.

South Valley Internet Inc HQ
95 E San Martin Ave [N]
San Martin CA 95046
P: 408-683-4533 F: 408-681-1528 PRC:64
www.garlic.net
Email: sales@garlic.com
Emp: 11-50 Estab: 1994

Robert Brentnall, Founder

Provider of Internet and phone services.

Southall Environmental Associates Inc HQ
9099 Soquel Dr Ste 8
Aptos CA 95003
P: 831-661-5177 F: 831-661-5178 PRC:23
sea-inc.net

Brandon Southall, President & Senior Scientist
Joel Southall, Sustainability & Senior Scientist
Kristin Southall, Associate Scientist

Provider of science to support conservation management. The company specializes in marine and terrestrial ecosystems.

Southbay Foundry Inc HQ
9444 Abraham Way [N]
Santee CA 92071
P: 619-956-2780 F: 619-956-2788 PRC:62
www.southbayfoundry.com
Email: sales@southbayfoundry.com

Brian Elliott, VP & General Manager

Manufacturer of aerial platforms, scissor lifts, excavators, wheel loaders, crushers, crawlers and much more.

Southern Motorcycle Supply Inc HQ
3670 Ruffin Rd [N]
San Diego CA 92123
P: 858-560-5005 F: 858-560-4626 PRC:359
www.southernms.com
Email: southern@southernms.com
Emp: 11-50 Estab: 1967

Kyle Kassel, Director of Commercial Operations
Leonardo Orenday, Manager of Operations
Robert Schaufele, Manager of Information Services
Elizabeth Fernandez, Administrative Coordinator & Customer Service
Kiimon Kennedy, Shipping Receiving Specialist

Distributor of parts and accessories for motorcycles, personal watch-craft, small engines and much more.

SP Controls Inc HQ
930 Linden Ave
S San Francisco CA 94080
P: 650-392-7880 F: 650-392-7881 PRC:110
www.spcontrols.com
Email: info@spcontrols.com
Estab: 1995

Diane Peter, Operations Manager

Designer and manufacturer of projector control systems. The company also offers audio systems, mounting, signal distribution, and other products.

SP3 Diamond Technologies HQ
1605 Wyatt Dr
Santa Clara CA 95054
P: 408-492-0630 F: 408-492-0633 PRC:80
www.sp3diamondtech.com
Email: info@sp3diamondtech.com
Estab: 1993

Todd Lindseth, Materials Manager

Provider of electronics thermal management, diamond-on-silicon applications, and enhanced cutting surface solutions.

Space Machine Inc   HQ
303 Twin Dolphin Dr Ste 600
Redwood Shores CA 94065
P: 650-669-8629   PRC:328
www.spacemachine.net
Email: quant@spacemachine.net
Estab: 1999

John F.C. Cheong, CEO & Chief Scientist
Akinori Honda, VP of Innovation & Technology
Scott Jenkins, Head of Sales & Growth

Specializes in academic research. The company
focuses on the development of custom models
and trading strategies.

SPAP Company LLC   HQ
PO Box 680   [N]
Huntington Beach CA 92648
P: 714-960-0586   PRC:130
www.spapcompanyllc.com
Email: info@spapcompanyllc.com
Estab: 1987

Jeff Henderson, Contact

International manufacturer representative agency.

Sparkle Power Inc   HQ
48502 Kato Rd
Fremont CA 94538
P: 408-519-8888   F: 408-519-9999   PRC:290
www.sparklepower.com
Email: marketing@sparklepower.com
Estab: 1993

May Lai, Account Manager
John Luong, Senior Account Manager
David Hwang, Manager
Wendy Su, Credit Manager
Mike Huang, Account Manager

Manufacturer of switching power supply devices.
The company serves the PC, industrial PC, and
telecommunication industries.

Sparqtron Corp   HQ
5079 Brandin Ct
Fremont CA 94538
P: 510-657-7198   F: 510-683-0892   PRC:209
www.sparqtron.com
Email: info@sparqtron.com
Estab: 1999

Mitch Duh, Chairman
Johnny Chen, SVP
Gwei Hwaun, Director
Jerry Hsu, Engineering Manager
I. Chih Su, Program Manager

Provider of electronic contract manufacturing
services. The company focuses on prototyping,
inspection, PCB assembly, and materials and
logistics.

Specialty Precision Machining   HQ
1014 N Shaw Rd
Stockton CA 95215
P: 209-939-0546   F: 209-939-0617   PRC:80
www.specialtyprecisionmachining.com
Email: sales@specialtyprecisionmachining.com
Estab: 1991

Victor Gorecki, Owner
Jessica Mendosa, Office Manager

Provider of machining services. The company also
offers turning, contouring, milling, engraving, and
drilling services.

Specialty Products Design Inc   HQ
11252 Sunco Dr
Rancho Cordova CA 95742
P: 916-635-8108   F: 916-635-2970   PRC:80
spdexhaust.com
Email: info@spdexhaust.com

Chris Hill, Owner
Clea Talley, Principal Engineer

Provider of exhaust components. The company
focuses on exhaust fabricators, CNC header
flanges, stainless bellows, and sealing flanges.

Spectra 7 Microsystems Ltd   HQ
2550 N First St Ste 500
San Jose CA 95131
P: 408-770-2915   PRC:96
spectra7.com

Tony Stelliga, CEO
Andrew Kim, VP of Engineering & CTO
Robert Bosomworth, CFO

Manufacturer of analog semiconductor devices.
The company focuses on micro-thin interconnects
for consumer electronic products.

Spectra Watermakers Inc   HQ
20 Mariposa Rd
San Rafael CA 94901
P: 415-526-2780   F: 415-526-2787   PRC:53
www.spectrawatermakers.com
Email: sales@spectrawatermakers.com
Estab: 1997

Kelly Donahoe, Controller

Designer of energy recovery systems. The
company specializes in manufacturing of reverse
osmosis desalination systems for the ocean sailor.

Spectra-Mat Inc   HQ
100 Westgate Dr
Watsonville CA 95076
P: 831-740-0200   F: 831-722-4172   PRC:209
www.spectramat.com
Email: smi_sales@saes-group.com
Estab: 1963

John Paff, Manager of Quality Assurance

Manufacturer of products for electron emission
and controlled expansion of thermal management
materials for the microelectronics sector.

Spectra-Physics   HQ
3635 Peterson Way
Santa Clara CA 95054
P: 408-980-4300   F: 408-980-6921   PRC:172
www.spectra-physics.com
Email: sales@spectra-physics.com
Estab: 1999

Keith McCurdy, Director of Sales
Steve Utter, Senior Director of R&D
Victor David, Senior Account Manager
Klaus Reiter, Factory & Service Support Manager
Robert Wolf, International Sales Manager

Provider of precision laser technology services.
The company's products include ultrafast lasers,
fiber lasers, and tunable lasers.

Spectralus Corp   HQ
2953 Bunker Hill Ln Ste 205
Santa Clara CA 95054
P: 408-516-4870   PRC:172
www.spectralus.com
Email: info@spectralus.com
Estab: 2003

Stepan Essaian, President & CEO

Developer of green laser sources. The company
primarily caters to the need of mobile projection
applications.

Spectrex Corp   HQ
493 Seaport Ct Ste 105
Redwood City CA 94063
P: 650-365-6567   F: 650-365-5845   PRC:11
www.spectrex.com
Email: info@spectrex.com
Estab: 1966

John M. Hoyte, President
Stephen M. Figone, VP
Steve Figone, VP
Loan Tran, Corporate Secretary & Office Manager

Developer of environmental and analytical instruments. The company's offerings include detectors
and personal air samplers.

Spectros Corp   HQ
274 E Hamilton Ave Ste H
Campbell CA 95008
P: 650-851-4040   PRC:187
www.spectros.com
Email: info@spectros.com
Estab: 1995

David Benaron, Founder
Elizabeth van Thillo, VP of Operations
Michael Ohara, Director of Engineering
William Curnan, Contact
John C. Bagnatori, Contact

Manufacturer of tissue perfusion monitors and
they are used in plastic surgery, critical care, and
vascular surgery.

Spectrum Orthotics & Prosthetics   BR
1844 South St
Redding CA 96001
P: 530-243-4500   F: 530-243-4554   PRC:190
www.spectrumoandp.com
Estab: 1994

Tina Zeller, CFM & Office Manager
Jeff Zeller, Contact
Tyler Rowley, Prosthetist & Orthotist

Provider of orthotics and prosthetics products.
The company serves physicians and the medical
sector.

Speedinfo   HQ
100 W San Fernando St Ste 475
San Jose CA 95113
P: 408-446-7660   F: 408-289-9171   PRC:87
www.speedinfo.com
Email: info@speedinfo.com
Estab: 2002

Doug Finlay, Co-Founder & CEO & Chairman
Kailas Lunagariya, Co-Founder & Director
Glenn Harter, Director of Business Development
George Whitehill, Director
David Chang, Director

Developer of traffic measurement solutions for
broadcast media, government planning, and
mobile applications.

Spence Engineering Services Inc   HQ
1650 Borel Pl Ste 209
San Mateo CA 94402-3508
P: 650-571-6500   F: 650-571-6555   PRC:323
www.spenceengr.com
Email: info@spenceengr.com
Estab: 1999

Ellen Spence, VP of Finance & Operations

Provider of solutions for hardware and software
engineering problems. The company offers services to the technical sector.

Sperient Corporation Inc   HQ
1813 Rutan Dr
Livermore CA 94550
P: 925-447-3333   F: 925-447-9999   PRC:204
www.sperient.com
Email: info@sperient.com
Estab: 2003

E. Tom Rosenbury, President & CEO

Designer and developer of electronic systems.
The company's applications include telemedicine
and robotic sensing.

SPI Lasers LLC   BR
4000 Burton Dr
Santa Clara CA 95054
P: 408-454-1170   PRC:170
www.spilasers.com
Email: sales@spilasers.com
Estab: 2000

Mark Greenwood, CEO
Pete Fulford, SYNCHRO Specialist
Aaron Kentish, COO
Thomas Reinauer, CFO
Richard Hendel, VP of Sales

Designer and manufacturer of fiber lasers for systems integrators, factory automation specialists,
job shops, OEMs, and other academic institutions.

Spinal Kinetics Inc   HQ
501 Mercury Dr
Sunnyvale CA 94085
P: 408-636-2500   F: 408-636-2599   PRC:187
www.spinalkinetics.com
Email: info@spinalkinetics.com
Estab: 2003

Mike Gandy, CFO
Neal Defibaugh, VP of Clinical & Regulatory
Affairs
Larry Beeman, VP of RA, CA & Quality Assurance
Trudy Nichols, Director of Quality Assurance
Nick Koske, Director of Research & Development

Provider of preservation systems for treating
degenerative diseases of the spine. The company
serves the healthcare sector.

Spineguard Inc   DH
1388 Sutter St Ste 510
San Francisco CA 94109
P: 415-512-2500   F: 415-512-8004   PRC:189
www.spineguard.com
Email: contact@spineguard.com
Estab: 2009

Stephane Bette, Director & Founder & CEO

Specializes in spine surgery. The company offers
services to patients, hospitals, and healthcare
organizations.

Spintrac Systems Inc   HQ
690 Aldo Ave
Santa Clara CA 95054
P: 408-980-1155   F: 408-980-1267   PRC:159
www.spintrac.com
Email: info@spintrac.com
Estab: 1980

Alan Kukas, President

Manufacturer of automated resist coating equipment. The company is involved in repairs and
maintenance services.

Spiralinks Corp   HQ
900 E Hamilton Ave Ste 100
Campbell CA 95008
P: 408-608-6900   PRC:325
spiralinks.com
Email: info@spiralinks.com
Estab: 1994

Andrew Smith, Operations Director
Diana Mecum, Software Test Engineer

Provider of compensation management software
products. The company offers compensation
management, HR analytics, and payroll integration services.

Spire Manufacturing   HQ
49016 Milmont Dr
Fremont CA 94538
P: 510-226-1070   F: 510-226-1069   PRC:211
www.spiremfg.com
Estab: 2008

Christine Bul, President & CEO

Designer and manufacturer of printed circuit
boards. The company offers vertical probe cards,
test sockets, and mother boards.

Spirent Communications Inc   LH
2708 Orchard Pkwy Ste 20
San Jose CA 95134
P: 408-752-7100   PRC:17
www.spirent.com
Email: support@spirent.com
Estab: 1936

David DeSanto, Director of Products & Threat
Research
Patrick Johnson, General Manager
Abhitesh Kastuar, General Manager of Cloud & IP
Philip Joung, Senior Manager of Knowledge
Services
John Civitano, CRM Applications Manager

Provider of performance analysis technology
services. The company also offers network equipment and data center solutions.

Splunk Inc   HQ
270 Brannan St
San Francisco CA 94107
P: 415-848-8400   F: 415-568-4259   PRC:315
www.splunk.com
Email: info@splunk.com
Estab: 2003
Sales: $1B to $3B

Doug Merritt, President & CEO
Susan St. Ledger, President of Worldwide Field
Operations
Tim Tully, SVP & CTO
Carrie Palin, SVP & CMO
Dave Conte, CFO

Develops software for monitoring, searching, and
analyzing machine-generated big data through a
web-style interface.

Splunk Inc   HQ
250 Brannan St
San Francisco CA 94107
P: 415-848-8400   F: 415-568-4259   PRC:322
www.splunk.com
Email: partnersupport@splunk.com
Estab: 2004
Sales: $1B to $3B

Erik Swan, Founder
Douglas Merritt, CEO & President & Director
Graham V. Smith, Independent Chairman
Susan St Ledger, President of Worldwide Field
Operations
Stephen Sorkin, CSO

Provider of search engine services specializing
in IT data. The company serves the government,
healthcare, and telecommunication industries.

sPower   BR
201 Mission St Ste 540
San Francisco CA 94105
P: 415-692-7740   F: 415-362-4001   PRC:135
www.silveradopower.com
Email: info@spower.com
Estab: 2012

John Cheney, CEO

Provider of utility-scale solar generation and physical plant development services for landowners,
utilities, and communities.

Spracht   HQ
974 Commercial St Ste 108
Palo Alto CA 94303
P: 650-215-7500   F: 650-318-8060   PRC:92
www.spracht.com
Email: sales@spracht.com
Estab: 1993

Wytzke Triemstra, Owner
Margarita Kovats, VP

Designer and manufacturer of consumer electronic products. The company offers digital imaging, acoustics, LCD image displays, and other
products.

Spreadsheetworld Inc   HQ
PO Box 200
June Lake CA 93529
P: 818-995-3931   F: 760-648-1096   PRC:328
Estab: 1995

Janet S. Mincer, Director

Provider of services for application of MS Excel
and VBA tools in various fields. The company focuses on science, engineering, and management.

Springboard Biodiesel LLC   HQ
2323 Park Ave
Chico CA 95928
P: 530-894-1793   F: 530-894-1048   PRC:133
www.springboardbiodiesel.com
Estab: 2008

Mark Roberts, CEO

Manufacturer of automated biodiesel processors.
The company also offers fuel pumps, and tanks to
consumers, small businesses, and municipalities.

Sprint BR
4955 N Blackstone Ave
Fresno CA 93726
P: 559-244-3200 PRC:62
www.sprint.com

Marcelo Claure, Executive Chairman
Jan Geldmacher, President of Sprint Business
Rasel Hossain, Assistant to CEO
Nestor Cano, COO
John Saw, CTO

Provider of telephone and voice equipment, data
communication systems, and Internet related
services.

Sprintcom BR
2920 N Main St
Walnut Creek CA 94597
P: 925-933-0142 PRC:68
www.sprint.com

Mohamad Nasser, General Manager
Lavnya S, Java Developer

Provider of wireline and wireless communication
services. The company serves consumers, businesses, and government entities.

Sputnik Enterprises Inc HQ
1757 E Bayshore Rd Unit 16
Redwood City CA 94063
P: 650-363-7576 PRC:80
sputnikmodels.com
Estab: 2000

Val Kasvin, Founder

Provider of finishing, painting, casting, CNC
machining, model making, and custom product
development services.

Sputtering Components Inc BR
5625 Brisa St Ste B
Livermore CA 94550
P: 925-606-7241 F: 925-606-7243 PRC:209
www.sputteringcomponents.com
Email: sales@sputteringcomponents.com
Estab: 2001

Barry Nudelman, President & CEO
Julie Magdefrau, Human Resource Manager

Provider of rotating cathodes and magnet assemblies. The company's products find application in
industrial systems.

SPYRUS HQ
103 Bonaventura Dr
San Jose CA 95134
P: 408-392-9131 F: 408-392-0319 PRC:325
www.spyrus.com
Email: info@spyrus.com
Estab: 1992

Grant Evans, Chairman & CEO
Simon Blake-Wilson, CRO
Dan Turissini, CTO
Tom Dickens, COO
Tom Hakel, CFO

Developer and marketer of hardware encryption, authentication, and digital content security
products.

Square Inc HQ
1455 Market St Ste 600
San Francisco CA 94103
P: 415-375-3176 PRC:233
www.squareup.com
Estab: 2009
Sales: Over $3B

Jack Dorsey, CEO & Chairman
Amrita Ahuja, CFO
Sivan Whiteley, General Counsel

Builds tools to empower and enrich people and
help sellers of all areas to start, run, and grow
their businesses.

SRI International RH
333 Ravenswood Ave
Menlo Park CA 94025
P: 650-859-2000 PRC:34
www.sri.com
Email: privacy@sri.com
Estab: 1946

Steve Ciesinski, President
Diane Young, Managing Director
Dimitra Vergyri, Director of Speech Technology &
Research Lab
Laurie Menoud, Ventures Innovation Manager
William Brubaker, Research Scientist

Provider of consulting, research, and development
services. The company offers services to the
defense, security, and energy sectors.

SS Papadopulos & Associates Inc BR
45 Belden Pl 4th Fl
San Francisco CA 94104
P: 415-773-0400 F: 415-773-0401 PRC:323
www.sspa.com
Email: sanfrancisco@sspa.com
Estab: 1979

Michael Rafferty, VP & Principal
Mark de Wit, Construction Manager
Kinsley Binard, Project Engineer

Provider of web-based applications for customized online communities. The company serves
business enterprises.

SS&C Advent HQ
600 Townsend St 4th Fl
San Francisco CA 94103
P: 415-645-1000 PRC:323
www.advent.com
Email: info@advent.com
Estab: 1983

Karen Geiger, Chief Development Officer
Steve Leivent, SVP of Advisory
Bjorn Widerstedt, VP of Product Management for
Black Diamond
Brian Justice, VP of Advisory Sales & Business
Development
Holly Washington, VP of Marketing

Provider of data services, portfolio, performance,
research, client, margin and finance, and revenue
management solutions.

SSL Industries Inc HQ
PO Box 3113
Diamond Springs CA 95619
P: 530-644-0233 PRC:62
www.sslinc.net
Email: ssl@sslinc.net
Estab: 1975

John Russ, President

Designer and manufacturer of fiber optics and
networking products. The company is involved in
installation services.

SSP Data HQ
1304 S 51st St
Richmond CA 94804
P: 510-215-3400 F: 510-412-4343 PRC:316
www.ssp.com
Email: info@ssp.com
Estab: 1982

Jeff Westbrook, Senior Program Account Manager
Bill Guggemos, Systems Engineer
Anurag Jain, Network Architect
Donny Jackson, Account Representative

Developer of network solutions. The company also
offers design, deployment, and in-house management services.

SST Group Inc HQ
309 Laurelwood Rd Ste 20
Santa Clara CA 95054
P: 408-350-3450 F: 408-350-3100 PRC:189
www.sstgroup-inc.com
Email: sales@sstgroup-inc.com
Estab: 2004

Mike Sutherland, Director
Richard Murphy, Director & Managing Partner
Robert Riland, Director & Managing Partner
Paula Brogan, Account Manager
Achilles Martinez, Manager of Technical Support

Provider of medical displays, recorders, film
digitizers, and related accessories. The company
offers optical library support services.

SST Systems Inc HQ
1798 Technology Dr Ste 236
San Jose CA 95110
P: 408-452-8111 F: 408-452-8388 PRC:319
www.sstusa.com
Email: info@sstusa.com
Estab: 1983

P.B. Karthick, Chief Engineer of Engineering Auto-
mation & Products
R.P. Sudarsan, VP of Civil & Steel Structures
G.V. Ranjan, Director of Engineering Analyses &
Software Development
Mark Sutton, Sales Manager

Provider of solutions for piping design and analysis. The company's services include plant design
and engineering.

ST Johnson Co HQ
5160 Fulton Dr
Fairfield CA 94534
P: 510-652-6000 F: 510-652-4302 PRC:151
www.johnsonburners.com
Estab: 1903

Helen Friedland, Director of Engineering
Bob Nickeson, Engineer

Manufacturer of burners. The company specializes
in the design and fabrication of gas and nitrous
oxide burners for industries.

Stack Plastics Inc HQ
3525 Haven Ave
Menlo Park CA 94025
P: 650-361-8600 PRC:163
www.stackplastics.com
Estab: 1995

Mark Rackley, President
John Huynh, Production Manager
Scott Smith, Quality Manager
Carlene Duplan, Office Manager

Provider of plastic injection molding services. The company offers thermoplastics, elastomers, and resins.

Staco Systems Inc HQ
1139 Baker St [N]
Costa Mesa CA 92626
P: 714-549-3041 F: 714-549-0930 PRC:245
www.stacosystems.com
Email: sales@stacosystems.com
Emp: 51-200 Estab: 1958

Patrick Hutchins, President
Andy Bain, VP of Product Development & Engineering
Brett Meinsen, VP of Finance
Jeff Bowen, VP of Sales

Developer of illuminated panels, subsystems, switches and custom data entry solutions.

Stage 8 HQ
4318 Redwood Hwy Unit 200
San Rafael CA 94903
P: 415-485-5340 F: 415-485-0552 PRC:159
www.stage8.com
Email: info@stage8.com
Estab: 1986

Bruce Bennett, Founder & CEO

Designer and manufacturer of mechanical locking systems. The company has more than 78 patents and trademarks.

Standard Metal Products HQ
558 Bryant St
San Francisco CA 94107
P: 415-546-6784 PRC:156
www.smpmachine.com
Email: info@smpmachine.com
Estab: 1993

Kevin Binkert, President

Provider of prototype and production components and assemblies for transportation, bicycle builders, and medical device companies.

Stanfield Systems Inc HQ
718 Sutter St Ste 108
Folsom CA 95630
P: 916-608-8006 F: 916-608-0657 PRC:323
www.stanfieldsystems.com
Estab: 2000

Dave Doherty, CEO
Tim Jacobs, CTO
Bart Battaglia, VP of Technical Resources
Steve Hamilton, Partner
Chris Nail, Business Manager

Provider of system engineering and data management services. The company also focuses on web development and technical services.

Stanford Photonics Inc HQ
1032 Elwell Ct Ste 104
Palo Alto CA 94303
P: 650-969-5991 F: 650-969-5993 PRC:210
www.stanfordphotonics.com
Email: info@stanfordphotonics.com
Estab: 1989

Michael Buchin, Owner & Founder
David Callard, President

Provider of electronic imaging, digital microscope cameras, and photonics technology solutions for the industrial and military markers.

Stanford Research Systems HQ
1290 Reamwood Ave Ste D
Sunnyvale CA 94089
P: 408-744-9040 F: 408-744-9049 PRC:15
www.thinksrs.com
Email: info@thinksrs.com
Estab: 1980

John Willison, Founder
Greg Waters, Senior Mechanical Engineer
Judi Cushing, Software Engineer
Hoongsun Im, System Engineer

Manufacturer of electronic instruments, optical choppers, and temperature controllers for the research industry.

Stangenes Industries Inc HQ
1052 E Meadow Cir
Palo Alto CA 94303
P: 650-493-0814 F: 650-855-9926 PRC:78
www.stangenes.com
Email: info@stangenes.com
Estab: 1974

Lill Runge, VP
Charles Ingebretsen, Quality Manager
Paul Holen, Associate Mechanical Engineer
Connie Cabrera, Quality Administrator & Supervisor

Manufacturer of isolation transformers, current monitors, charging inductors, and magnetic components.

Stantec BR
376 Hartnell Ave Ste B
Redding CA 96002-1881
P: 530-222-5347 F: 530-222-4958 PRC:139
www.stantec.com
Estab: 1954

Gord Johnston, President & CEO
Theresa Jang, EVP & CFO
Stuart Lerner, EVP & COO
Emree Siaroff, SVP & Chief Human Resource Officer
Chris McDonald, SVP & CIO

Provider of environmental consulting services specializing in GIS mapping, remote sensing, permitting, and ecosystem restoration.

Stantec BR
3875 Atherton Rd
Rocklin CA 95765-3716
P: 916-773-8100 F: 916-773-8448 PRC:142
www.stantec.com
Email: media@stantec.com
Estab: 1954

Gord Johnston, President & CEO
Emree Siaroff, SVP & Chief Human Resource Officer
Stuart Lerner, EVP & COO
Theresa Jang, EVP & CFO
Tino DiManno, EVP & Chief Business Development Officer

Provider of civil construction services. The company also offers commercial program development and infrastructure management services.

Starch Medical Inc HQ
2150 Ringwood Ave
San Jose CA 95131
P: 408-428-9818 F: 408-383-9189 PRC:195
starchmedical.com
Email: info@starchmedical.com
Estab: 2007

Stephen Heniges, President

Provider of hemostatic solutions. The company offers services to patients and serves the healthcare industry.

StarDot Technologies HQ
6820 Orangethorpe Ave Building H [N]
Buena Park CA 90620
P: 714-228-9282 F: 714-228-9283 PRC:168
www.stardot-tech.com/contact.html
Estab: 1994

James Chan, Contact

Designer and manufacturer of digital cameras.

StarNet Communications Corp HQ
4677 Old Ironsides Dr Ste 210
Santa Clara CA 95054-1825
P: 408-739-0881 PRC:325
www.starnet.com
Email: sales@starnet.com
Estab: 1989

Steven Schoch, President

Developer of X Windows solutions for connecting computers to Unix and Linux desktops and applications.

Statico HQ
541 Taylor Way Ste 1
San Carlos CA 94070
P: 650-592-4733 F: 650-508-0761 PRC:212
statico.com
Email: sales2@statico.com

Fruhar Alavi, President & CEO
Elizabeth Paulsen, Office Manager
Micheal Byrd, Assembly Technician

Provider of ESD and static control products. The company offers test instruments, ionizers, and cleanroom products.

Stats Chippac Inc   DH
  46429 Landing Pkwy
  Fremont CA 94538
P: 510-979-8000   F: 510-979-8001   PRC:86
www.statschippac.com
Email: salescontact@statschippac.com

Vincent Shek, Technical Program Manager

Provider of semiconductor packaging design, bump, probe, assembly, test, and distribution solutions.

Stealth Network Communications Inc   HQ
  3350 Scott Blvd Bldg 47
  Santa Clara CA 94054
P: 925-846-7018   PRC:68
www.stealthnetwork.com
Email: sales@stealthnetwork.com
Estab: 1994

Margaret Nyswonger, CEO & President
Brad Berlin, General Manager

Provider of voice, data, security, network, and wireless solutions. The company also deals with consulting, design, and maintenance services.

Stella Technology Inc   HQ
  450 S Abel St Ste 360832
  Milpitas CA 95036
P: 844-278-3552   PRC:319
stellatechnology.com
Email: info@stellatechnology.com
Estab: 2012

Salim Kizaraly, SVP of Business Development & Founder
Lalo Valdez, President & CEO
Lin Wan, CTO
Jami Young, Senior Director of Client Services
Jeffrey Grant, Manager of Implementations

Provider of integration and collaboration solutions. The company deals with technology design, development, and consulting services.

Stellar Solutions   HQ
  250 Cambridge Ave Ste 204
  Palo Alto CA 94306
P: 650-473-9866   F: 650-473-9867   PRC:5
www.stellarsolutions.com
Email: info@stellarsolutions.com
Estab: 1995

Celeste Ford, CEO & Founder & Chairman of the board
Richard Rogers, EVP
Michael Abadjiev, Director of IT
Barry Stout, Program Manager
Dick Bowen, Project Manager

Provider of systems engineering, mission operations, and strategic planning services. The company focuses on commercial and government programs.

Stellartech Research Corp   HQ
  560 Cottonwood Dr
  Milpitas CA 95035
P: 408-331-3000   F: 408-331-3101   PRC:186
www.stellartec.com
Email: info@stellartec.com
Estab: 1988

Roger A. Stern, Founder & CEO & President
Jerome Jackson, VP of Research & Development
Mario Lopez, Director of Manufacturing & Service Operations
Mark Recob, Information Technology Manager
Tom Hussey, Senior Quality Engineer Supervisor

Designer, developer, and manufacturer of medical devices. The company specializes in surgical probes, balloon electrode catheters, and other products.

Stellarvue   HQ
  11802 Kemper Rd
  Auburn CA 95603
P: 530-823-7796   F: 530-823-8121   PRC:174
www.stellarvue.com
Email: orders@stellarvue.com
Estab: 1998

Vic Maris, Founder
C. Vic Maris, Owner

Designer and seller of refractor telescopes and telescope accessories. The company deals with design, delivery, and installation.

Stemexpress   HQ
  1743 Creekside Dr Ste 200
  Folsom CA 95630
P: 530-626-7000   PRC:250
stemexpress.com
Email: info@stemexpress.com
Estab: 2010

Cate Dyer, CEO
Laina Zarek Durbin, Chief of Staff
Art Romo, VP of Quality Operations
Heidi Steklis, Quality Manager
Megan Barr, Regional Site Manager

Provider of immunophenotyping, DNA quantitation and viability, tissue transplant verification, and related services.

Steven Engineering Inc   HQ
  230 Ryan Way
  S San Francisco CA 94080-6308
P: 800-258-9200   PRC:293
stevenengineering.com
Estab: 1975

Bonnie Walter, Chairman
Karen Mitts, Manager

Distributor of industrial controls and components. The company also provides contract manufacturing services.

Steven R Young Ocularist Inc   HQ
  411 - 30th St Ste 512
  Oakland CA 94609
P: 510-836-2123   F: 510-836-0383   PRC:190
stevenryoungocularist.com
Estab: 1975

Steven R. Young, Owner

Provider of ocular prosthetic services. The company engages in scleral cover shells and maxillo-facial prosthetics.

Stevens Creek Software   HQ
  PO Box 2126
  Cupertino CA 95015
P: 408-725-0424   PRC:322
www.stevenscreek.com

Steven L. Patt, President
Deborah Jamison, Director of Marketing
Eric Yeager, Assistant Service Manager

Provider of software solutions for the palm computing platform. The company is involved in custom development and technical support.

Stewart Audio Inc   HQ
  14335 Cuesta Ct Ste C
  Sonora CA 95370
P: 209-588-8111   F: 209-588-8113   PRC:60
www.stewartaudio.com
Email: sales@stewartaudio.com
Estab: 1982

Kevin Stone, General Manager
Debbie Bill Ulrey, Engineer

Provider of network amplifiers and sound systems. The company's products include digital signal processors, mixer amplifiers, and networked accessories.

Stewart Tool Company Inc   HQ
  3647 Omec Cir
  Rancho Cordova CA 95742
P: 916-635-8321   PRC:80
www.stewarttool.com
Email: quoting@stewarttool.com
Estab: 1972

Jeff Boyett, Engineering Manager
Stephen Shuman, Controller
Amber Stewart, Contact

Manufacturer of CNC precision machine components. The company specializes in manufacturing pressure vessels and provides field and assembly services.

STMicroelectronics   BR
  2755 Great America Way 3rd Fl
  Santa Clara CA 95054
P: 408-919-8400   PRC:208
www.st.com

Carlo Bozotti, President
Lorenzo Grandi, President of Finance & Infrastructure & Services & CFO
Marco Cassis, President of Sales, Marketing, Communications & Strategy Development
Orio Bellezza, President of Technology Manufacturing & Quality
Jean-Luc Decolle, CIO

Provider of analog, mixed signal ICs, transistor, and memories. The company also offers microcontroller products and services.

Stockton Tri Industries Inc HQ
2141 E Anderson St
Stockton CA 95205
P: 209-948-9701 F: 209-948-2310 PRC:80
stocktontri.com
Email: info@stocktontri.com
Estab: 1976

Fred Wells, Co-Owner
Ray Smith, Co-Owner
Denise Donahue, Sales Manager

Provider of custom rolling, bending, forming, machining, metal fabrication, and field erection services.

Stoll Metalcraft Inc HQ
24808 Anza Dr [N]
Valencia CA 91355
P: 661-295-0401 PRC:159
www.stoll-metalcraft.com
Emp: 11-50 Estab: 1973

Patrick Darrah, Manager of Sales

Fabricator of precision sheet metal parts and electro-mechanical assemblies.

Stonefly Inc HQ
26250 Eden Landing Rd
Hayward CA 94545
P: 510-265-1616 PRC:64
www.stonefly.com
Email: sales@stonefly.com
Estab: 2000

John Harris, Director of Technical Sales
Sam Malik, Managing Director
Viktor Nosov, Senior Software Engineer

Provider of storage optimization and disaster recovery protection for software solutions. The company also offers storage area networks.

Stopware Inc HQ
5000 Pleasanton Ave Ste 210
Pleasanton CA 94566
P: 408-367-0220 PRC:323
www.stopware.com
Email: info@stopware.com
Estab: 1997

Roberta Sosbee, Channel Sales Manager
Cha Yang, Development & Technical Support Manager
Bao Truong, Tech Support Engineer
Tito Cardoway, Sales Executive

Developer of visitor management security software. The company offers hardware, badge stock, and training services.

Storz & Bickel America Inc HQ
1078 60th St Ste A
Oakland CA 94608
P: 866-380-6278 PRC:159
www.storz-bickel.com
Estab: 2000

Markus Storz, Managing Director

Manufacturer of vaporizers. The company specializes in the design and fabrication of solid valve and easy valve systems.

Stracon Inc HQ
1672 Kaiser Ave [N]
Irvine CA 92614
P: 949-851-2288 F: 949-851-2299 PRC:159
www.straconinc.com
Emp: 11-50 Estab: 1986

Son Pham, CEO & CFO & Secretary

Manufacturer and distributor of electronic equipment.

Strataglass HQ
958 San Leandro Ave Ste 100
Mountain View CA 94043
P: 650-988-1700 F: 650-988-1739 PRC:300
strataglass.us
Email: info@strataglass.us
Estab: 1990

Dave Snow, President
Lisa Kerner, COO

Manufacturer of thin films. The company offers research and development, pilot production, and outsourced fabrication services.

Stratamet Inc HQ
46009 Hotchkiss St
Fremont CA 94539
P: 510-651-7176 F: 510-651-5936 PRC:84
www.stratamet.com
Email: sales@stratamet.com
Estab: 1982

Barbara Romero, CEO

Provider of precision ceramic components. The company offers engineering support, quick response, and customer support.

Stratedigm Inc HQ
6541 Via Del Oro Ste A
San Jose CA 95119
P: 408-512-3901 F: 408-351-7700 PRC:245
www.stratedigm.com
Email: info@stratedigm.com
Estab: 2004

Shervin Javadi, CEO
Alex Gordon, Systems Specialist Manager
Sirma Pandeva, Office Manager

Manufacturer of software products, consumables, and related accessories. The company deals with upgrades and installation.

Stratogent Corp HQ
1900 S Norfolk St Ste 245
San Mateo CA 94403
P: 650-577-2332 F: 650-641-2645 PRC:326
stratogent.com
Email: info@stratogent.com
Estab: 2008

Jishnu Mitra, President
Chetan Patwardhan, CEO
Ahmed Mohammed, Service Delivery Manager
Susan Kwok, Controller
Lydia Kim, Sales Representative

Provider of hosting and critical software systems operations. The company is engaged in design and programming solutions.

Stratovan Corp HQ
202 Cousteau Pl Ste 115
Davis CA 95618
P: 530-746-7970 F: 530-746-7974 PRC:323
www.stratovan.com
Email: support@stratovan.com
Estab: 2005

David F. Wiley, President & CTO
Jim Olson, CEO
Bernd Hamann, Director
Ryan Eberle, Program Manager
David Hinojosa, Senior Engineering Project Manager

Developer of visual analysis software. It's product finds application in 3D imaging and surgical planning research.

Streamline Electronics Manufacturing Inc HQ
4285 Technology Dr
Fremont CA 94538
P: 408-263-3600 F: 408-508-5638 PRC:211
www.sem-inc.com
Email: info@sem-inc.com
Estab: 1994

Shahab Jafri, President & CEO
Stephanie Broussard, Manager of Sales & Marketing
Syed Zaidi, Operational Control Manager
Ali Akber Jamal, Test Engineer & Operations Engineer

Provider of electronic manufacturing solutions and services. The company is engaged in product development and contract manufacturing.

Strike Technology Inc HQ
24311 S Wilmington Ave [N]
Carson CA 90745
P: 562-437-3428 F: 562-495-0904 PRC:209
www.wilorco.com
Emp: 11-50 Estab: 2001

Manouk Ohanesyan, Director of Operations
Raul Deanda, Manager

Manufacturer of custom power supplies, converters and inverters.

StrongKey HQ
20045 Stevens Creek Blvd Ste 2A
Cupertino CA 95014
P: 408-331-2000 PRC:326
strongkey.com
Estab: 2001

Arshad Noor, CTO
Brandon Hoe, CMO
David Irwin, VP of Engineering
Pushkar Marathe, Engineering Manager
Paula Shaffer, People & Ops Manager

Provider of enterprise key management solutions. The company serves the cloud computing, e-commerce, healthcare, finance, and other sectors.

Structural Integrity Associates Inc　　HQ

5215 Hellyer Ave Ste 210
San Jose CA 95138
P: 408-978-8200　F: 408-978-8964　　PRC:13
www.structint.com
Email: info@structint.com
Estab: 1983

Stager Dave, CFO
Jenny McGrew, Contracts Manager
Scott Chesworth, Senior Consultant
Shari Day, Senior Consultant
Afzal Ahmed, Staff Accountant

Provider of solutions for prevention and control
of structural and mechanical failures and serves
nuclear plants, oil and gas, and other sectors.

Sts Instruments Inc　　HQ

17711 Mitchell N　　[N]
Irvine CA 92614
P: 580-223-4773　　PRC:65
www.stsinstruments.com
Email: info@stsinstruments.com
Estab: 2004

Elmer Slaughter, Chief Engineer

Provider of off the shelf solutions for quality and or
defect testing of lead-acid batteries and systems
for electrical test and measurement of motors,
windings, electromechanical devices, coils and
lead-acid batteries.

STS International Inc　　HQ

4695 Chabot Dr Ste 102
Pleasanton CA 94588
P: 925-479-7800　F: 925-479-7810　　PRC:323
stsii.com
Estab: 1992

Kish Jha, VP of Operations
Tim Akers, Service Support Manager
Kristina Bennett, Human Resource Administrator

Provider of information technology solutions that
include infrastructure management, software application development, and systems integration.

SubrosasoftCom Inc　　HQ

5387 Diana Common
Fremont CA 94555
P: 510-870-7883　F: 510-868-3407　　PRC:325
subrosasoft.com
Email: support@subrosasoft.com
Estab: 2002

Mark Hurlow, General Manager

Developer of software for Mac operating systems.
The company offers software such as FileSalvage,
CopyCat, and ParentRemote.

SucceedNet　　BR

970 Reserve Dr Ste 160
Roseville CA 95678
P: 530-674-4200　F: 916-517-1647　　PRC:323
succeed.net
Email: sales@cwo.com
Estab: 1994

Robert Lavelock, CEO & Founder
Dale Karthauser, IT Manager & Field Engineer

Provider of Internet services. The company
specializes in metro Ethernet, wireless broadband, DSL service, national dial-up, and server
co-location.

Sumiden Wire Products Corp　　BR

1412 El Pinal Dr
Stockton CA 95205
P: 209-466-8924　F: 209-941-2990　　PRC:159
www.sumidenwire.com
Email: supportpcw@sumidenwire.com
Estab: 1979

Jeff Feitler, VP of Sales & Marketing

Supplier of wire products. The company offers
nickel plated wires, stainless spring wires, and
industrial alloys.

**Sumitomo Electric Device Innovations
USA Inc**　　LH

2355 Zanker Rd
San Jose CA 95131-1138
P: 408-232-9500　F: 408-428-9111　　PRC:62
www.sei-device.com
Estab: 2000

Peggy Chang, Corporate Controller

Developer of electronic devices that includes
wireless devices, optical data links, and optical
devices.

Summit Engineering Inc　　HQ

463 Aviation Blvd Ste 200
Santa Rosa CA 95403
P: 707-527-0775　F: 707-527-0212　　PRC:304
summit-sr.com
Email: info@summit-sr.com
Estab: 1978

Greg Swaffar, President
Jasper Lewis-Gehring, Principal & Civil Division
Manager
Paige Wray, Human Resource Manager
Kyle Moyer, Structural Division Manager
Zak Zakalik, Electrical & Lighting Design Division
Manager

Provider of facility planning, due diligence, design,
project management, and other services to wineries, resorts, food, education, and other sectors.

Summit Wireless Technologies Inc　　HQ

6840 Via Del Oro Ste 280
San Jose CA 95119
P: 408-627-4716　　PRC:208
www.summitwireless.com
Email: sales-americas-eu@summitsemi.com
Sales: $1M to $3M

Tony Ostrom, President of WiSA
Brett A. Moyer, CEO & Director & President &
Chairman
George Oliva, CFO
Keith Greeney, VP of Engineering
Gary Williams, VP of Finance & CAO

Developer of wireless audio integrated circuits.
The company specializes in semiconductors,
home entertainment, and pro-audio markers.

Sumo Logic　　HQ

305 Main St
Redwood City CA 94063
P: 650-810-8700　　PRC:324
sumologic.com
Email: info@sumologic.com
Estab: 2010

Christian Beedgen, CTO & Founder
B.J. Jenkins, President & CEO
Meagen Eisenberg, Strategic Advisor & CMO
Shea Kelly, CPO
Steve Fitz, CRO

Provider of compliance, security, monitoring, troubleshooting, and delivery solutions. The company
serves security, IT, and development teams.

Sun Enterprise Inc　　HQ

4010 Business Center Dr
Fremont CA 94538
P: 510-657-6507　　PRC:80
sun-enterprise.com
Email: sales@sun-enterprise.com
Estab: 2001

Myles Ly, Owner

Provider of ceramic and quartz machining products. The company specializes in the semiconductor, solar, laser, and structural industries.

Sun First! Solar　　HQ

136 Mitchell Blvd
San Rafael CA 94903
P: 415-458-5870　F: 415-458-5871　　PRC:135
www.sunfirstsolar.com
Email: info@sunfirstsolar.com
Estab: 1984

Aran Moore, Owner
Kim Fink, CEO

Provider of renewable energy services. The company offers residential and commercial solar PV
and swimming pool systems.

Sun-Net Inc　　HQ

2150 N First St Ste 550
San Jose CA 95131
P: 408-323-1318　F: 408-864-2064　　PRC:323
sunnetsoftware.com
Email: info@sncsw.com
Estab: 1999

Helen Hu, CEO & Founder
Sally Tan, Development Manager
Han Zhang, Software Engineer
Stella Chen, Software Engineer
Razieh Shamsedin, Senior Software Developer

Provider of enterprise software solutions supporting outage scheduling, logging, and reporting for
power, gas, and water utilities.

SunBurst Plant Disease Clinic Inc   HQ
677 E Olive Ave
Turlock CA 95380
P: 209-667-4442   F: 209-667-4443   PRC:306
www.sunburstpdcinc.com
Estab: 1998

Thomas T. Yamashita, Founder & Owner & Chief
Science Officer
Kathleen Yamashita, Owner
Susan Sallee, CEO
Theresa Borrelli, CFO
Sam Livingston, Lab Manager

Provider of solutions for pathological and phys-
iological problems in agriculture. The company
focuses on soil and tissue examination and
mineral analysis.

Suni Medical Imaging Inc   HQ
6840 Via Del Oro Ste 160
San Jose CA 95119
P: 408-227-6698   F: 408-227-9949   PRC:198
www.suni.com
Email: sales@suni.com
Estab: 1995

Al Bettencourt, COO
Yongjie Gan, Senior Software Engineer
Marty Rudnick, Senior Support Engineer
Julie Meneses, Technical Support Representative

Manufacturer of digital radiography. The company
designs, develops, manufactures and sell digital
sensors for the medical field.

Sunlink Corp   HQ
2 Belvedere Pl Ste 210
Mill Valley CA 94941
P: 415-925-9650   F: 415-276-8990   PRC:135
www.sunlink.com
Email: info@sunlink.com
Estab: 2004

John Eastwood, Founder
Tracy Hsieh, Project Manager
Mark Ginalski, General Counsel

Designer and manufacturer of roof and ground
mounted systems for commercial and utility-scale
installations.

Sunmedica Inc   HQ
1661 Zachi Way
Redding CA 96003
P: 530-229-1600   F: 530-229-9457   PRC:189
www.sunmedica.com
Email: service@sunmedica.com
Estab: 1988

Kimberly Mills, CFO
Dennis Haws, Contact

Specializes in surgical orthopaedics, wound management, cold therapy and sports medicine. The
company also offers surgical positioning devices.

Sunperfect Solar Inc   HQ
2570 N First St Ste 200
San Jose CA 95131
P: 510-573-6888   PRC:129
Estab: 2009

Willy Chow, CEO & President
Chung Wang, VP of Projects Engineering
Kevin Chan, VP of Operations
Yoshi Hoashi, Accounts Manager
Caroline Chow, Controller

Provider of energy solutions. The company
specializes in the design, manufacture, and installation of solar panels.

Sunrise Medical (US) LLC   HQ
2842 N Business Park Ave
Fresno CA 93727
P: 800-333-4000   F: 800-300-7502   PRC:190
www.sunrisemedical.com
Estab: 1983

Thomas Babacan, President & CEO
Pete Coburn, President of Commercial Operations
Adrian Platt, CFO
Bernd Krebs, CTO
Roxane Cromwell, COO

Distributor of folding wheelchairs, seating and
positioning systems, and other mobility products
to its customers.

Sunset Moulding Company   HQ
PO Box 326
Yuba City CA 95992
P: 530-700-2700   F: 530-605-2560   PRC:163
www.sunsetmoulding.com
Email: sales@sunsetmoulding.com
Estab: 1948

John Morrison, CEO & President
Mark Westlake, VP of Sales
Mike Morrison, Plant Manager

Provider of molding and millwork products. The
company offers products such as interior jambs,
board products, and shelving.

Sunsil Inc   HQ
3174 Danville Blvd Ste 1
Alamo CA 94507
P: 925-648-7779   F: 925-648-7749   PRC:86
www.sunsil.com
Email: sales@sunsil.com
Estab: 1999

Seth Alavi, President & CEO

Provider of total electronics manufacturing
solutions. The company offers wafer fabrication,
component assembly, testing, and wafer probing
services.

Sunterra Solar Inc   HQ
285 Bel Marin Keys Blvd Ste J
Novato CA 94949
P: 415-883-6800   F: 415-883-6804   PRC:135
www.sunterrasolar.com
Email: info@sunterrasolar.com
Estab: 2009

Chris Bunas, CEO & Founder
Rachel Hennessy, Office Manager
David Seiler, Program Manager

Designer of turnkey grid-connected solar power
systems for commercial, agricultural, and governmental customers.

Suntrek Industries Inc   BR
4851 Sunrise Dr Ste 102
Martinez CA 94553-4302
P: 925-372-8983   F: 925-269-2374   PRC:135
www.suntreksolar.com
Email: info@suntreksolar.com

Roy Heine, Founder
Scott Miner, Area Manager

Manufacturer, designer, and installer of solar
power systems for residential, commercial, and
agricultural solar power applications.

Sunverge Energy Inc   HQ
6665 Hardaway Rd
Stockton CA 95215
P: 209-931-5677   PRC:135
www.sunverge.com
Estab: 2009

Clinton Davis, SVP
Liem Truong, Software Engineer
Trisha Grobeck, Controller

Provider of power and energy services. The
company focuses on solar power and combines
batteries and power electronics.

Super Micro Computer Inc   HQ
980 Rock Ave
San Jose CA 95131
P: 408-503-8000   F: 408-503-8008   PRC:93
www.supermicro.com
Email: support@supermicro.com
Estab: 1993

Charles Liang, Co-Founder & CEO & Chairman
Sara Liu, Co-Founder & SVP & Director
Perry Hayes, President
Howard Hideshima, CFO
Alex Hsu, Chief Sales & Marketing Officer

Provider of server technology and computing solutions. The company offers networking, gaming,
micro cloud, and AMD services.

Super Talent Technology   HQ
2077 N Capitol Ave
San Jose CA 95132
P: 408-934-2560   F: 408-719-5020   PRC:95
www.supertalent.com
Email: support@supertalent.com
Estab: 1991

Sharon Wu, VP of Finance
Shimon Chen, VP of Engineering
Jen Wang, VP of Sales
Jin Kim, Director
James Lee, Director of Engineering

Designer and manufacturer of flash based storage
solutions for enterprise servers, portable devices,
personal computers, and consumer electronics.

Superior Automation   HQ
   47770 Westinghouse Dr
   Fremont CA 94539
P: 510-413-9790   F: 510-413-9984   PRC:311
superiorautomation.com
Email: sales@superiorautomation.com
Estab: 1994

Don Brosio, Owner
Roger Kessinger, President
James Wiseman, Chief Engineer
Kevin Johnson, VP
Chris Kieffer, Service Manager

Provider of custom automation solutions. The
company primarily caters to the semiconductor
industry.

SuperKlean   HQ
   1 Edwards Ct Ste 101
   Burlingame CA 94010
P: 650-375-7001   F: 650-375-7010   PRC:160
www.superklean.com
Email: sales@superklean.com
Estab: 1985

Joel Alvarez, Division Manager
Rajesh Raajaa, Civil Engineer
Adnan B., Accountant

Manufacturer of spray nozzles and swivel fittings.
The company also offers hot and cold water mixing stations and hose racks.

Supracor Inc   HQ
   2050 Corporate Ct
   San Jose CA 95131
P: 408-432-1616   F: 408-432-8985   PRC:189
www.supracor.com
Estab: 1982

Curtis Landi, Founder & President
Steven Landi, Contact

Developer of honeycomb products. The company's offerings include sandals, saddle pads, and
related supplies.

Surface Art Engineering Inc   HQ
   81 Bonaventura Dr
   San Jose CA 95134
P: 408-433-4700   F: 408-433-9988   PRC:207
surfaceart.com
Email: sales@surface-art.com
Estab: 1994

Paul Edwards, Director of Engineering
Angela Choi, Program Manager
Minji Kang, Program Manager
Jerry Woo, Program Manager
Richard Diep, Manufacturing Engineer

Provider of Printed Circuit Board Assembly (PCA)
and mechanical assembly for prototype, pre-pro-
duction and production assemblies.

Surplus Process Equipment Corp   HQ
   2526 Qume Dr Ste 19
   San Jose CA 95131
P: 408-654-9500   F: 408-654-9400   PRC:212
specequipment.com
Email: sales@specequipment.com
Estab: 1998

John B. Sardi, President & CEO
Kyle D. Willis, Operations Manager
Lee Stevens, Operations Manager
John R. Oncay, Project Manager
Linda M. Sardi, Controller

Provider of new, used, and refurbished semiconductor equipment. The company offers ashing and
etching systems.

Surtec Inc   HQ
   1880 N MacArthur Dr
   Tracy CA 95376
P: 209-820-3700   F: 209-820-3793   PRC:53
surtecsystem.com
Email: orderdesk@surtecsystem.com
Estab: 1975

Don C. Fromm, VP

Provider of technology solutions for maintenance
chemicals. The company is focused on services
for the commercial and industrial cleaning industry.

Surveillance Systems Integration Inc   HQ
   4465 Granite Dr Ste 700
   Rocklin CA 95677
P: 916-771-7272   F: 916-771-7297   PRC:159
www.ssicctv.com
Email: sales@ssicctv.com
Estab: 2002

Todd Flowers, President
Melissa Mount, VP
Don Mosbacher, Director of National Accounts
Darren Young, Director of Field Operations
Ruben Gamboa, Director of Field Operations

Provider of security products. The company
serves customers in the gaming, retail, education,
and healthcare industries.

SurveyMonkey Inc   HQ
   1 Curiosity Way
   San Mateo CA 94403
P: 650-543-8400   PRC:325
www.surveymonkey.com
Estab: 1999
Sales: $300M to $1 Billion

Tom Hale, President
Zander Lurie, CEO
Leela Srinivasan, CMO
Rebecca Cantieri, Chief Human Resource Officer
Robin Ducot, CTO

Provider of a cloud-based people-powered data
platform.

Sustainable Conservation   HQ
   98 Battery St Ste 302
   San Francisco CA 94111
P: 415-977-0380   F: 415-534-3480   PRC:142
suscon.org
Email: suscon@suscon.org
Estab: 1993

Bob Epstein, Co-Founder
Frank Boren, Co-Founder
Laura Hattendorf, Head of Investments & Mulago
Foundation & Co-Founder
Paula Daniels, Co-Founder & Chairman
Tina Quinn, Co-Founder

Provider of environmental protection services
and solutions. The company focuses on clean-air
farming and auto recycling projects.

Sutro Biopharma Inc   HQ
   310 Utah Ave Ste 150
   S San Francisco CA 94080
P: 650-392-8412   F: 650-872-8924   PRC:268
www.sutrobio.com
Email: general@sutrobio.com
Emp: 147 Estab: 2003
Sales: $30M to $100M

William J. Newell, CEO
Trevor Hallam, CSO
Arturo Molina, CMO
Henry Heinsohn, VP of Development & Manufac-
turing
Alexander Steiner, Senior Director of Business
Operations & Strategy

Developer of therapeutics for cancer therapy. The
company shares with select pharmaceutical and
biotech companies to develop new therapeutics.

Sutter Instrument Co   HQ
   1 Digital Dr
   Novato CA 94949
P: 415-883-0128   F: 415-883-0572   PRC:209
www.sutter.com
Email: info@sutter.com
Estab: 1977

Jack Belgum, Director of Research & Develop-
ment
Dan Carte, Product Manager
Ali Mahloudji, Product Manager DG4
Jan Dolzer, Product Manager of Patch Clamp
Systems
Adair Oesterle, Applications Engineer

Manufacturer of microprocessors and precision
electromechanical devices. The company offers
technical support services.

SWCA Environmental Consultants   BR
   60 Stone Pine Rd Ste 100
   Half Moon Bay CA 94019
P: 650-440-4160   PRC:138
www.swca.com
Estab: 1981

Steven W. Carothers, Director & Founder
Rich Young, President & COO
Joseph J. Fluder, CEO & Director
Deborah Owens, CPO
Denis Henry, CFO & EVP & Director

Provider of environmental consultant services.
The company focuses on environmental planning
and regulatory compliance activities.

Sweco Products Inc   HQ
2455 Palm St
Sutter CA 95982
P: 530-673-8949   F: 530-671-0110   PRC:159
www.swecoproducts.com
Estab: 1946

Ray Ziegenmeyer, President
Michael Ziegenmeyer, VP of Sales
Tim Towne, Sales Manager
Chris Souza, Purchasing Manager

Manufacturer of agricultural and construction equipment and hydraulic cylinders, and related supplies.

Swedcom Corp   HQ
1075 Old County Rd Ste C
Belmont CA 94002
P: 650-620-9420   F: 650-620-9281   PRC:70
www.swedcom.com
Email: info@swedcom.com
Estab: 1987

Hicham Chraibi, Senior Technician

Designer and manufacturer of log periodic antennas, channel banks, filters, and base stations for the telecommunication sector.

Swintek Enterprises Inc   HQ
5655 Silver Creed Valley Rd Ste 342
San Jose CA 95138
P: 408-727-4889   PRC:59
www.swintek.com
Email: sales@swintek.com

Bill William Swintek, CEO

Provider of transceivers, tactical repeaters, and surveillance solutions for the government agencies.

Swiss Productions Inc   HQ
2801 Golf Course Dr   [N]
Ventura CA 93003
P: 805-654-8525   F: 805-654-0315   PRC:280
www.swissproductions.com
Email: orders@swissproductions.com
Emp: 11-50   Estab: 1982

Michelle Rogers, CFO
Richard Petrash, COO
Timo Lunceford, General Manager

Provider of machining services for aerospace, electronic, automotive, defense and medical sectors.

Switchfly   HQ
500 Third St 17th Fl
Ste 215 CA 94107
P: 415-541-9100   PRC:325
www.switchfly.com
Email: marketing@switchfly.com
Estab: 2003

Bart Foster, Chairman
Craig Brennan, CEO
Ian Gillott, CIO
Scott Cross, CFO
Rick Cirigliano, CTO

Provider of software solutions such as travel commerce platforms, payments engines, mobile platforms, and social media solutions.

SwitchGear Genomics Inc   HQ
1914 Palomar Oaks Way Ste 150
Carlsbad CA 92008
P: 760-431-1263   F: 760-431-1351   PRC:34
www.switchgeargenomics.com
Email: sales@activemotif.com
Estab: 2006

Nathan D. Trinklein, Founder & CEO

Focuses on custom cloning, pathway screening, target validation, sequence variant assay, and custom mutagenesis services.

Swivl Inc   HQ
1450 El Camino Real
Menlo Park CA 94025
P: 888-837-6209   F: 650-362-1995   PRC:60
www.swivl.com
Email: info@swivl.com
Estab: 2010

Brian Lamb, Founder
Steve Clarence, VP of Sales

Provider of video tools for personalized teaching and learning. The company offers services to educators.

Sycard Technology   HQ
1484 Pollard Rd Ste 151
Los Gatos CA 95032
P: 408-399-8073   F: 408-354-1649   PRC:102
www.sycard.com
Estab: 1989

Mike T. Mori, President

Provider of 16-bit PC card and CardBus devices. The company also offers USB and smart media development services.

Symic Bio Inc   BR
5980 Horton St Ste 600
Emeryville CA 94608
P: 415-805-9005   PRC:36
www.symic.bio
Email: info@symic.bio
Estab: 2012

Ken Horne, CEO
Nathan Bachtell, CMO
Jocelyn Jackson, CFO
Glenn Prestwich, CSO
Grace Wong-Sarad, VP & Controller

Developer of proprietary bioconjugates. The company offers therapeutics focused on extracellular matrix biology.

Symplectic Engineering Corp   HQ
2901 Benvenue Ave
Berkeley CA 94705
P: 510-528-1251   F: 510-528-7102   PRC:323
www.symplectic.com
Email: info@symplectic.com

Jerome Sackman, Research Engineer

Provider of custom computational mechanics solutions. The company is involved in consulting services and it serves the industrial sector.

Symprotek Corp   HQ
950 Yosemite Dr
Milpitas CA 95035
P: 408-956-0700   F: 408-956-9400   PRC:211
www.symprotek.com
Email: sales@symprotek.com
Estab: 1994

Randy Hall, Contact

Provider of electronics manufacturing and engineering services. The company also focuses on procurement.

Synack   HQ
1600 Seaport Blvd Ste 170
Redwood City CA 94063
P: 855-796-2251   PRC:325
www.synack.com
Email: info@synack.com
Estab: 2013

Jay Kaplan, CEO
Mark Kuhr, CTO
Amit Sirdeshpandey, VP of Finance
Jonathan Diller, SVP of Operations
Ron Peeters, VP

Provider of security intelligence solutions. The company offers services to the commercial, industrial, and business sectors.

Synapse Design   HQ
2200 Laurelwood Rd
Santa Clara CA 95054
P: 408-850-9527   F: 408-645-5850   PRC:90
www.synapse-da.com
Email: sales@synapse-da.com
Estab: 2003

Devesh Gautam, COO & Co-Founder
Satish Bagalkotkar, President & CEO & Co-Founder
Tom King, VP of Business Development
Sundar Raman Ramani, Associate VP of Engineering
Hem Hingarh, VP of Engineering

Provider of embedded software design services. The company also offers test bench analysis and block and chip level verification services.

Synapsense Corp   HQ
340 Palladio Pkwy Ste 530
Folsom CA 95630
P: 916-294-0110   F: 916-294-0270   PRC:322
www.synapsense.com
Email: info@synapsense.com
Estab: 2006

Raju Pandey, CTO
Jeff Boone, SVP of Engineering
Pat Weston, VP of Engineering
Jeff Fitch, Director of Product Management
Dave Lemoine, Engineering Technician

Provider of wireless monitoring and cooling control solutions. The company also deals with data center infrastructure management.

Synaptics Inc   HQ
1251 McKay Dr
San Jose CA 95131
P: 408-904-1100   F: 408-904-1110   PRC:323
www.synaptics.com
Email: info@synaptics.com
Estab: 1986
Sales: $1B to $3B

Hing Chung Wong, VP of Worldwide Operations
Kevin D. Barber, SVP & General Manager of
Mobile Division
Godfrey Cheng, VP of Marketing
Kin Cheung, VP of Quality & Product Engineering
Phillip Kumin, SVP of WW Sales

Developer of human interface solutions. The
company's products find application in mobile
computing and entertainment devices.

Synchron Networks Inc   HQ
100 Enterprise Way C230
Scotts Valley CA 95066
P: 831-461-9735   F: 831-401-2359   PRC:323
www.synchronnetworks.com
Email: info@synchronnetworks.com
Estab: 1999

Carl Fravel, CEO & Chairman

Developer of application and file distribution software. The company focuses on system management and digital asset delivery services.

Syncplicity LLC   HQ
2811 Mission College Blvd
Santa Clara CA 95054
P: 888-997-9627   PRC:325
syncplicity.com
Email: sales@syncplicity.com
Estab: 2007

Leonard Chung, Founder & Chief Product Strat-
egist
Jeetu Patel, General Manager of Syncplicity
Business Unit

Provider of cloud-based file management solutions such as access, sync, backup and share of
files from anywhere for businesses and individuals.

Synder Filtration   HQ
4941 Allison Pkwy
Vacaville CA 95688
P: 707-451-6060   F: 707-451-6064   PRC:56
www.synderfiltration.com
Email: sales@synderfiltration.com
Estab: 1994

Jeff Yeh, President
Joseph Wang, Vice Chairman
Charles Jao, VP of Engineering
Kevin Carlson, General Manager
Gerard Bouchard, Privateer Manager

Manufacturer of membranes and systems. The
company offers training and performance evaluation services. It serves mining, biotech, and food
industries.

M-296

Synergenics LLC   HQ
1700 Owens St
San Francisco CA 94158
P: 415-554-8170   F: 415-864-6078   PRC:28
synergenics.net
Estab: 2002

William J. Rutter, CEO
Ella Zeltser, Accounting Manager

Provider of life science services. The company
also provides financial support and shared laboratory services.

Synergex International Corp   HQ
2355 Gold Meadow Way
Gold River CA 95670
P: 916-635-7300   F: 916-635-6549   PRC:322
synergex.com
Email: information@synergex.com
Estab: 1976

Kenneth Lidster, Synergex Founder & Chairman
of the Board
William Mooney, President & CEO
Roger Andrews, CTO & Professional Services
Manager
Daniela Calvitti, CFO
Rosanne Brill, VP of Software Development

Provider of business application optimization
solutions. The company serves the transportation,
retail, and manufacturing sectors.

Synergy Business Solutions   HQ
584 Castro St Ste 513
San Francisco CA 94114
P: 415-263-1843   F: 415-263-1846   PRC:323
www.synergybiz.com
Email: synergy@synergybiz.com
Estab: 1993

Bill Perrin, VP of Operations
Michael Bark, Director of Marketing
Jim Bruckner, Administration Director & Controller
Sophie O'Neal, Principal

Provider of technology evaluation, business
process improvement, and custom software development services to a wide range of sectors.

Syneron Inc   HQ
3 Goodyear Ste A   [N]
Irvine CA 92618
P: 949-716-6670   F: 949-716-8287   PRC:189
syneron-candela.com
Emp: 501-1000

Todd Van Horn, COO
Mary Trout, Chief Commercial Officer
Ty Guthaus, VP of Americas & EMEA
Greg Wallender, VP of Global Quality & Regula-
tory Affairs
Mary O'Connor, Director of Marketing

Manufacturer and distributor of aesthetic medical
products including hair removal and wrinkle
reduction.

Synopsys Corporate   HQ
690 E Middlefield Rd
Mountain View CA 94043
P: 650-584-5000   PRC:322
www.synopsys.com
Sales: Over $3B

Aart de Geus, CEO & Chairman
Yervant Zorian, Chief Architect Fellow & President
Hasmukh Ranjan, Corporate VP & CIO
Trac Pham, CFO
Deirdre Hanford, Chief Security Officer & Corpo-
rate Staff

Developer of synthesis technology solutions. The
company is also involved in design flow deployment, physical design assistance, and related
services.

Syntest Technologies Inc   HQ
4320 Stevens Creek Blvd Ste 100
San Jose CA 95129
P: 408-720-9956   F: 408-720-9960   PRC:323
www.syntest.com
Email: info@syntest.com
Estab: 1990

Shianling Wu, VP of Engineering

Provider of test solutions for the electronics industry. The company is involved in fault simulation
solutions and services.

Syntonic Microwave Inc   HQ
275 E Hacienda Ave
Campbell CA 95008
P: 408-866-5900   F: 408-866-5901   PRC:209
www.syntonicmicrowave.com
Email: syntonicsales@mrcy.com

Jay Goodfriend, President
Jerry McCoy, VP of Engineering

Manufacturer of wire-band receivers, generators,
translators, and related accessories. The company
specializes in customization.

Syrma Technology   BR
4340 Stevens Creek Blvd Ste 275
San Jose CA 95129
P: 408-404-0500   PRC:77
www.syrmatech.com
Email: syrma@syrmatech.com
Estab: 2006

Sreeram Srinivasan, CEO
Paul Dahl, Director of Business Development
Sathya Narayanan, Head of HR

Provider of entrepreneurial manufacturing services. The company's products include magnetics,
memory, and RFID.

System Biosciences LLC   HQ
2438 Embarcadero Way
Palo Alto CA 94303
P: 650-968-2200   F: 650-968-2277   PRC:34
systembio.com
Email: info@systembio.com

Paul Kao, SVP
Jacob Lesnik, VP of Sales & Marketing & Com-
mercial Development
Laurie Goldman, Sales Manager
Young Kim, Global Technical Support Manager

Provider of genome-wide analysis of the mechanisms that regulate cellular processes and
biological responses.

System General USA DH
6469 Almaden Expy Ste 80#377
San Jose CA 95035
P: 833-845-3900 PRC:212
www.sg.com.tw
Estab: 1983

Don Yang, Director of Finance & General Manager

Designer and manufacturer of device programmers and offers consultancy services in device programming and power management.

Systemacs HQ
616 Ramona St Ste 27
Palo Alto CA 94301
P: 650-329-9745 PRC:100
www.systemacs.com
Email: info@systemacs.com

Ken Easterby, Founder

Provider of solutions for upgrading or setting up networks which include hardware, software, and routers.

Systems Studies Inc HQ
2-1340 E Cliff Dr
Santa Cruz CA 95062
P: 831-475-5777 F: 831-475-9207 PRC:62
airtalk.com
Email: support@airtalk.com
Estab: 1979

Diane Bordoni, CEO

Supplier of cable pressurization products. The company is involved in training services and it serves the telephone industry.

SyTech Solutions Inc HQ
8930 Big Horn Blvd
Elk Grove CA 95758
P: 916-381-3010 PRC:323
www.sytechsolutions.com
Email: reply@sytechsolutions.com
Estab: 2001

Bryan Golden, President
Sam Velasquez, CTO
Jon Pritt, VP
Casey Morris, Account Manager

Provider of document management technology services. The company offers archive scanning, web-based document management, and data capture services.

T & K Machine HQ
257 Wright Brothers Ave
Livermore CA 94551
P: 925-344-7091 PRC:80
www.tk-machine.com
Estab: 1994

Tony Gallien, Owner

Designer and manufacturer of precision machines. The company also offers services like plating, labeling, powder coat, and silkscreen.

T&T Precision Inc HQ
1290 Pacific St
Union City CA 94587
P: 510-429-8088 F: 510-429-8488 PRC:80
www.ttprecision.com
Estab: 2012

Toan Tran, CEO
Thuan Nguyen, VP of Operations

Provider of precision machining services. The company specializes in electronics, automotive, and semiconductor equipment.

T&T Valve & Instrument Inc HQ
1181 Quarry Ln Ste 150
Pleasanton CA 94566
P: 925-484-4898 F: 925-484-4727 PRC:166
www.tt-valve.com
Email: sales@tt-valve.com
Estab: 1987

Todd Wolfe, President
Javier Cendejas, General Manager
Mike Harlan, Sales Engineer

Provider of manual and automated valves to industrial, municipal water, and wastewater industries. The company focuses on project assistance.

Tactus Technology Inc HQ
47509 Seabridge Dr
Fremont CA 94538
P: 510-244-3968 F: 650-641-2348 PRC:112
www.tactustechnology.com
Email: support@tactustechnology.com
Estab: 2008

Perry Constantine, CEO
Bob Pape, CFO
Justin Virgili, VP of Engineering
Ryosuke Isobe, Director of Process Engineering
Kang Liu, Technical Product Manager

Developer of tactile user interface for touchscreen devices. The company serves the industrial and technological sectors.

Takex America Inc DH
151 San Zeno Way
Sunnyvale CA 94086
P: 408-747-0100 F: 408-734-1100 PRC:233
www.takex.com
Email: sales@takex.com
Estab: 1982

Gary Buth, Director of Technical Sales
Rayman Ganap, Inside Sales & Application Engineer

Manufacturer of security and industrial sensor products. The company's products include photoelectric beams, outdoor and indoor PIR, and tower enclosures.

Talisman Systems Group Inc HQ
1111 Oak St
San Francisco CA 94117
P: 727-424-4261 PRC:323
www.talispoint.com
Email: inquiry@talisys.com
Estab: 1999

Monique Barkett, President & CEO
William Yu, Director of Technology
David Lovgren, Product Manager

Provider of document and panel management tools. The company serves insurance companies and managed care organizations.

TalkCycle LLC HQ
63 Bovet Rd Ste 208
San Mateo CA 94402
P: 888-400-2220 PRC:315
www.frontspin.com
Email: info@frontspin.com
Estab: 2015

Mansour Salame, Founder
Randy Rubingh, Chief Customer Officer
Aaron Browning, VP of Sales
V. Kate, Product Manager

Providers of innovative sales communication software.

Tamalpais Group Inc HQ
PO Box 2564
San Anselmo CA 94979
P: 415-455-5770 F: 415-455-5771 PRC:326
tamgroup.com
Email: contact@tamgroup.com
Estab: 1995

Christian Franklin, Founder & CTO
Jyll Cassidy, SVP of Operations

Provider of information technology solutions. The company offers data-centric delivery, infrastructure assessment, and IT performance services.

Tamura Corporation of America BR
1040 S Andreasen Dr Ste 100
Escondido CA 92029
P: 760-871-2009 F: 760-740-0536 PRC:200
www.tamuracorp.com

Jonathan Parker, COO

Manufacturer of DC power modules, current sensor products, telecom transformers, and LED products. The company is involved in distribution services.

Tangent Inc HQ
191 Airport Blvd
Burlingame CA 94010
P: 650-342-9388 F: 650-342-9380 PRC:120
www.tangent.com
Email: support@tangent.com
Estab: 1989

Kevin Bradley, Director of Healthcare Solutions

Provider of computer solutions. The company caters to healthcare, industrial, and military applications.

Tango Systems Inc HQ
1980 Concourse Dr
San Jose CA 95131
P: 408-526-2330 F: 408-526-2336 PRC:124
tangosystemsinc.com
Email: info@tangosystemsinc.com

Lee LaBlanc, Senior Mechanical Engineer

Supplier of cluster tools for dielectric films. The company's services include processing, thin film deposition, and quality analysis.

Tanium Inc HQ
2100 Powell St Ste 300
Emeryville CA 94608
P: 510-704-0202 PRC:327
tanium.com
Email: info@tanium.com
Estab: 2007

David Hindawi, Co-Founder & Executive Chairman
Orion Hindawi, Co-Founder & CEO
Thomas Stanley, CRO
Bina Chaurasia, CPO
Chris Pick, CMO

Provider of IT operations management, asset visibility, and security hygiene solutions. The company serves the healthcare and retail industries.

Tapemation HQ
13 Janis Way
Scotts Valley CA 95066
P: 831-438-3069 F: 831-438-2094 PRC:80
tapemation.com

John Stepovich, General Manager

Manufacturer of machined parts and tools for the aircraft, marine, electronic, solar, and space communication industries.

Tapjoy Inc HQ
111 Sutter St 12th Fl
San Francisco CA 94104
P: 415-766-6905 PRC:322
tapjoy.com
Estab: 2007

Steve Wadsworth, Chairman of the Board
Peter Dille, CMO
Jeff Drobick, Chief Product Officer
Paul Longhenry, VP & General Manager of Business & Corporate Development
Sarah Chafer, SVP of Global Performance Sales

Provider of advertising and targeting solutions. The company also deals with developer services such as consulting and real-time reporting.

Taracom Integrated Products HQ
1220 Memorex Dr
Santa Clara CA 95050
P: 408-691-6655 PRC:212
taracom.net
Email: info@taracom.net
Estab: 2000

Farhad Haghighi, CEO

Provider of multi-gigabit solutions for communications and storage applications. The company's solutions include backplane and fiber channel.

Tarana Wireless Inc HQ
590 Alder Dr
Milpitas CA 95035
P: 408-351-4085 PRC:61
www.taranawireless.com
Email: info@taranawireless.com
Estab: 2009

Rabin Patra, Founder

Provider of wireless performance solutions. The company serves the residential and enterprise markers.

Tavis Corp HQ
3636 Hwy 49 S
Mariposa CA 95338
P: 209-966-2027 F: 209-966-3563 PRC:5
www.taviscorp.com
Email: applications@taviscorp.com
Estab: 1969

Dina Lambert, Information Technology Manager
Carlo Sepe, Project Engineer
Scott Carpenter, Staff Electrical Engineer
Carrie Bonillas, Controller

Provider of custom pressure transducer sensor designs. The company offers services to measurement environments.

Tayco Engineering Inc HQ
10874 Hope St [N]
Cypress CA 90630
P: 714-952-2240 F: 714-952-2042 PRC:228
www.taycoeng.com
Email: international@taycoeng.com
Emp: 51-200 Estab: 1971

Charles H. Taylor, Founder & Chairman of the Board
Jay Chung, President & CEO
Ann Taylor, COO
Brent Taylor, VP of Production
Lisa Taylor, VP of Business Development

Designer and manufacturer of heating systems, temperature sensors, flexible cable, and other specialty products.

Tazmo Inc BR
42840 Christy St Ste 103
Fremont CA 94538
P: 510-438-4890 F: 510-226-4871 PRC:212
www.tazmoinc.com
Email: sales@tazmoinc.com

Toshio Torigoe, President
Kelly McCulley, Service Manager

Manufacturer of SOG and LCD color filter coaters. The company offers SOG, SOD, polyimide coaters and developers and LCD Resist coaters.

TCI International Inc DH
3541 Gateway Blvd
Fremont CA 94538
P: 510-687-6100 F: 510-687-6101 PRC:61
tcibr.com
Estab: 1968

Gene Lowe, President & CEO
Scott Sproule, CFO & VP & Treasurer
Tausha White, VP & Chief Human Resource Officer
Eric Fain, Director of Research & Development
James Miller, Director of Quality & Compliance

Provider of innovative radio frequency solutions. The company caters to spectrum monitoring and antenna applications.

TCS Healthcare Technologies HQ
11641 Blocker Dr Ste 200
Auburn CA 95603
P: 530-886-1700 PRC:194
tcshealthcare.com
Email: info@tcshealthcare.com
Estab: 1983

Robert Pock, CEO
Pat Stricker, SVP
Luis Luna, Director of Finance
Linda Killian, Manager of Client Services Operations

Provider of care management solutions. The company offers software implementation and training and workflow design services.

TCSN Inc HQ
1306 Pine St [N]
Paso Robles CA 93446
P: 805-227-7000 F: 805-237-0951 PRC:323
www.tcsn.net
Email: support@tcsn.net
Estab: 1991

JoEllen Fitton, Owner

Provider of Internet solutions, web hosting, website designing and much more.

TDK Corporation of America BR
1745 Technology Dr Ste 200
San Jose CA 95110
P: 408-467-5200 F: 408-437-9591 PRC:86
www.tdk.com
Estab: 1981

Christian Hoffman, Senior Chief Researcher
Rick Anderson, HEV & EV Ford Account Manager
Mitch Oda, Regional Sales Manager
Youli Yao, ICT Server Leader & Senior FAE & Technical Project Leader

Distributor of electronic products including capacitors, inductors, ferrites, factory automation system, transformers, magnets, and anechoic chalmers.

Tdn Electric Inc HQ
1071 Wright Ave
Mountain View CA 94043
P: 650-968-8000 F: 650-968-8222 PRC:124
tdnelectric.com
Estab: 1997

Tim Daniels, President

Retailer of electrical construction services for lighting, uninterruptible power supply, fire alarm, and photovoltaic systems.

Teamf1 Inc HQ
39270 Paseo Padre Pkwy Ste 153
Fremont CA 94538
P: 510-505-9931 F: 510-505-9941 PRC:319
www.teamf1.com
Estab: 1998

Hitesh Patel, Business Operations Manager

Provider of networking and security software for embedded devices. The company also offers technical support services.

Tecdia Inc HQ
2255 S Bascom Ave Ste 120
Campbell CA 95008
P: 408-748-0100 PRC:80
us.tecdia.com
Email: sales@tecdia.com
Estab: 1976

Shinn Wolfe, VP

Manufacturer of precision machine tools and
fixtures. The company also specializes in cutting
and scribing tools.

Tech Soft 3d HQ
2515 Ninth St
Berkeley CA 94710-2805
P: 510-883-2180 F: 510-883-2193 PRC:323
www.techsoft3d.com
Estab: 1996

Gavin Bridgeman, CTO
Eric Vinchon, VP of Product Strategy
Jennifer Ferello, Senior Director of Major Accounts
Ivan Lee, Director of Operations
Jennifer Gartz, Senior Marketing Manager

Provider of software solutions. The company offers
software for desktop visualization, modeling, cloud
and mobile solutions, and data exchange.

TechBIZ Inc RH
48501 Warm Springs Blvd Ste 101
Fremont CA 94539
P: 510-249-6800 F: 510-249-6808 PRC:67
techbizinc.com
Email: sales@techbizinc.com
Estab: 1998

Anthony Thia, President
Kristine Kim, VP

Provider of custom network and server solutions.
The company is involved in design and deployment services.

TechExcel Inc HQ
533 Airport Blvd Ste 400
Burlingame CA 94010
P: 925-871-3900 F: 925-871-3991 PRC:322
techexcel.com
Email: sales@techexcel.com
Estab: 1995

Jason Hammon, Director of Product Management
Prince Huang, Director of IT Operations
Lin Pan, QA Manager & Technical Support
Dan Randall, Inside Sales Manager
Hu Peng, Senior Development Manager

Provider of customer relationship management
software applications. The company is involved in
game development and hybrid agile management
solutions.

TechMD HQ
3750 S Susan St [N]
Santa Ana CA 92704
P: 888-883-2463 PRC:104
www.techmd.com
Email: info@techmd.com
Emp: 51-200 Estab: 2003

Mark Perez, President
Sebastian Igreti, CEO
David Bryden, CFO
Jason Gimeno, CTO

Provider of cloud solutions, cyber security services, strategic consulting, and managed services.

Technavibes Inc HQ
6518 Commerce Way Ste 4
Diamond Springs CA 95619
P: 530-626-8093 F: 530-626-6901 PRC:159
technavibes.com
Email: dub@technavibes.com
Estab: 1991

Dub Wilson, Owner

Manufacturer of feeder bowls. The company specializes in vibratory bowl feeders, vibratory feeder
in-line tracks, and vibratory feeder hoppers.

Techni-Glass Inc HQ
7846 Bell Rd
Windsor CA 95492
P: 707-838-3325 F: 707-838-3326 PRC:286
techni-glass.com
Email: thassur@techni-glass.com
Estab: 1979

Thomas Hassur, Principle Owner
Pat Murphy, President & CEO

Provider of glass blowing services. The company
specializes in glass used for research, laser, oil,
and medical services.

Technic Inc BR
1254 Alma Ct
San Jose CA 95112
P: 408-287-3732 F: 408-287-0763 PRC:53
www.technic.com
Email: info@technic.com
Estab: 1944

Steve Schaefer, COO
Gary Hemphill, GM & VP
George Federman, VP of Project Development
Paul Scorpio, Director of reel to reel technology
Jeff Ramirez, Director of Special Projects

Manufacturer of specialty chemicals, analytical
control tools, and surface finishing products. The
company offers electroplating and engineered
powders.

Technical Heaters Inc HQ
710 Jessie St [N]
San Fernando CA 91340
P: 800-394-9435 F: 818-361-2788 PRC:155
www.techheat.com
Estab: 1986

Margie Herrera, Sales Engineer

Manufacturer of rubber, plastics hose and beltings.

TechniQuip HQ
530 Boulder Ct Ste 103
Pleasanton CA 94566
P: 925-251-9030 F: 925-251-0704 PRC:198
techniquip.com
Email: orders@techniquip.com
Estab: 1970

David Wensley, President
Charles Mathewson, Director of Sales
George Gauer, Director of Operations
Robin Steingraf, Materials Controller

Supplier of lighting products. The company's offerings include illuminators, fiber optics, and video
equipment.

Tecma Co HQ
1812 Silica Ave
Sacramento CA 95815-3431
P: 916-925-8206 F: 916-925-2135 PRC:80
tecmacompany.com
Email: tecma@tecmacompany.com
Estab: 1957

Alfred Nohr, Co-Founder
Fred Schwarz, Co-Founder
Sonia Susac, President

Provider of CNC and conventional precision
machining solutions. The company serves the
aerospace, commercial, medical, and defense
industries.

Ted Levine Drum Co HQ
1817 Chico Ave [N]
South El Monte CA 91733
P: 626-579-1084 PRC:188
www.tldrumco.com
Emp: 11-50 Estab: 1983

Ozzie Levine, President
Sharon Levine, VP

Provider of repair services.

Ted Pella Inc HQ
PO Box 492477
Redding CA 96049-2477
P: 530-243-2200 F: 530-243-3761 PRC:31
www.tedpella.com
Email: sales@tedpella.com
Estab: 1968

Tom Pella, President
Ed Martinez, VP of Finance
David Rollings, VP of Marketing
Ken Cornyn, Director of Manufacturing
Wencui Zheng, TEM Lab Manager

Distributor of medical supplies and microscopy
products such as inverted microscope for science
and industry.

Teikoku Pharma USA Inc LH
1718 Ringwood Ave
San Jose CA 95131
P: 408-501-1800 F: 408-501-1900 PRC:268
teikokuusa.com
Email: info@teikokuusa.com
Estab: 1997

Ichiro Paul Mori, President & CEO
Junji Kachi, CFO & EVP
Jutaro Shudo, SVP & Chief Science Officer
Jack Wen, Senior Director of Research & Devel-
opment
Larisa Kalashnikova, Manager of Quality Assur-
ance & Quality Control

Focuses on the drug development and delivery of
treatments for CNS, pain management and oncology. The company serves the medical industry.

Teknika Strapping Systems   HQ
1650 Las Plumas Ave Ste F
San Jose CA 95133
P: 408-441-9071   F: 408-441-9037   PRC:159
teknika.com
Email: teknika@teknika.com
Estab: 1988

Dmitry Kondratyev, CEO
Lev Girshfeld, Sales Manager

Provider of hand tools for plastic stripping. The
company is engaged in repairs, replacement, and
maintenance services.

Teknova   HQ
2290 Bert Dr
Hollister CA 95023
P: 831-637-1100   F: 831-637-2355   PRC:271
www.teknova.com
Email: info@teknova.com
Estab: 1996

Ted Davis, CEO
Irene Davis, COO
Mari Davis, VP
Pablo Montero, Director of Quality Assurance
Ashley N. Holtz, Manager of Human Resource

Provider of agar plates and broths for growth of
bacterial, yeast, and microbiological applications
such as cloning, DNA sequencing, and immunology.

Tela Innovations Inc   HQ
475 Alberto Way Ste 120
Los Gatos CA 95032
P: 408-558-6300   PRC:208
www.tela-inc.com
Email: information@tela-inc.com
Estab: 2005

Scott Becker, President & CEO
Dhrumil Gandhi, COO
Peter Calverley, CFO
Neal Carney, VP of Marketing & Business Devel-
opment
Liz Stewart, VP & General Counsel

Provider of lithography optimized solutions. The
company's services include design, implementation, and technical support.

Teledesign Systems Inc   HQ
1729 S Main St
Milpitas CA 95035
P: 408-941-1808   F: 408-941-1818   PRC:111
www.teledesignsystems.com
Email: productsales@teledesignsystems.com
Estab: 1991

Bruce Delevaux, VP

Provider of wireless data solutions. The company
manufactures wireless industrial modems for commercial and industrial data collection applications.

Teledyne Technologies Inc   HQ
PO Box 359
Tracy CA 95378
P: 925-456-9700   PRC:47
www.teledynerisi.com
Email: tdemarketing@teledyne.com
Estab: 1984

Jim Varosh, General Manager
Sue Stowe, Purchasing Manager
Derek Hanton, Engineer
Gary Grigsby, EHS Coordinator

Manufacturer of exploding bridge wire detonators.
The company also manufactures electronic firing
systems.

Telemakus LLC   HQ
13405 Folsom Blvd Ste 502
Folsom CA 95630
P: 916-458-6346   F: 916-939-8713   PRC:87
www.telemakus.com
Email: mail@telemakus.com
Estab: 2004

Paul Clark, Owner & Member
Craig Walsh, CEO

Provider of USB controlled RF devices. The company devices include switches, vector modulators,
and digital attenuators.

Telemanagement Technologies Inc   HQ
2700 Ygnacio Valley Rd Ste 250
Walnut Creek CA 94598
P: 925-946-9800   F: 925-946-9801   PRC:319
www.telmantec.com
Estab: 1987

Lou Sandler, Chief Software Architect
Charles Coakley, VP of Sales & Marketing
Tej Bloom, Accounting Manager
Pablo Sanchez, Project Manager

Provider of telemanagement software products
and services. The company is engaged in troubleshooting and maintenance services.

Teleresults Corp   HQ
870 Market St Ste 556
San Francisco CA 94102
P: 415-392-9670   F: 415-392-9674   PRC:322
teleresults.com
Email: info@teleresults.com
Estab: 1995

John Moran, Product Manager
Tyler Charles, Support Engineer
James Jeha, Network Consultant
Darren Guan, Medical Software Developer

Provider of electronic medical record solutions
and transplant software. The company's services
include data conversion, interfaces, and training.

Telewave Inc   HQ
660 Giguere Ct
San Jose CA 95133
P: 408-929-4400   F: 408-929-4007   PRC:61
www.telewave.com
Email: sales@telewave.com
Estab: 1972

Robert Bagheri, CEO
Jeff Cornehl, Associate Systems Engineer
Brad Senge, Senior International Sales Engineer
Frank Amaral, Painter

Provider of wireless products such as transmitter
couplers and receiver multicouplers. The company
also offers antennas.

Telosa Software Inc   HQ
610 Cowper St
Palo Alto CA 94301
P: 800-750-6418   F: 650-853-1677   PRC:325
www.telosa.com
Email: info@telosa.com
Estab: 1986

David Blyer, Co-Founder & President & CEO
Susan Packard Orr, Co-Founder & Chairman
Sylvia Gastelbondo, CTO Online Fundraising
David Jost, CMO
Frank Horkey, CFO

Provider of CRM and fundraising software for
nonprofits. The company focuses on gift and grant
tracking, donor and volunteer management.

Tempo Automation   HQ
2460 Alameda St
San Francisco CA 94103
P: 415-320-1261   PRC:207
tempoautomation.com
Email: support@tempoautomation.com

Jeff McAlvay, Co-Founder & CEO
Jesse Koenig, Co-Founder & VP of Technology
Brady O. Bruce, VP of Marketing
Kathriona Murren, Director of Recruiting
Cole Kievit, Product Manager

Specializes in printed circuit board assemblies.
The company is engaged in design and delivery
services.

Ten Pao International Inc   HQ
333 W El Camino Real Unit 380
Sunnyvale CA 94087
P: 408-389-3560   F: 408-389-3564   PRC:200
www.tenpaoinc.com
Email: request@tenpaoinc.com
Estab: 1979

Etienne Finet, VP of Business Development

Manufacturer of power supply systems such as
switchings, displays, and traditional linear transformers.

Tenefit Corp HQ
2107 North First St Ste 660
San Jose CA 95131
P: 877-522-9464   F: 650-960-8145   PRC:322
tenefit.com
Estab: 2007

John Fallows, CTO & Founder
Bob Miller, CEO
Sue Liu, VP of Professional Services
Sidda Eraiah, VP of Cloud Services & Customer
Support
Jesse Selitham, Senior Support Engineer

Provider of software services. The company's IoT
gateway is used by mobile users, marketplaces,
and machines to connect and communicate in
real-time.

Tenera Environmental HQ
141 Suburban Rd Ste A2
San Luis Obispo CA 93401
P: 925-962-9769   F: 925-962-9758   PRC:142
tenera.com
Email: environmental@tenera.com
Estab: 1975

David L. Mayer, Owner & Principal Scientist
Doc Fish, President
Carol J. Raifsnider, VP & Principal Scientist
John Hedgepeth, Project Manager
Scott Kimura, Project Scientist & Manager

Provider of environmental consulting, stream restoration, power generation support, and minerals
management services.

Tenergy Corp HQ
436 Kato Ter
Fremont CA 94539
P: 510-687-0388   F: 510-687-0328   PRC:208
www.tenergybattery.com
Email: sales@tenergy.com
Estab: 2004

Jason Li, CEO
Judy Vo, Senior Account Sales Manager
Jane Xie, Purchasing Manager
Brian Qu, Warehouse Manager
Lena Beppu, Sales Account Manager

Designer and manufacturer of batteries and
chargers. The company serves medical, consumer
electronics, data management, military, and other
sectors.

Tennebaum-Manheim Engineers Inc HQ
165 Tenth St Ste 500
San Francisco CA 94103
P: 415-772-9891   PRC:304
tmesf.com
Email: info@tmesf.com
Estab: 1987

Nancy Tennebaum, Principal

Developer of engineering services. The company's
projects include residential housing, commercial
properties, and historical buildings.

Terabit Radios Inc HQ
1148 Cadillac Ct
Milpitas CA 95035
P: 408-431-6032   PRC:68
www.terabitradios.com
Email: info@terabitradios.com
Estab: 2012

Srinivas Sivaprakasam, Founder & CEO
Bruce Carpenter, VP of Global Sales

Manufacturer of wireless radios. The company
offers IP-centric (Gigabit and Multi-Gigabit) LoS
wireless IP transport technologies to its clients.

Teradyne Inc BR
875 Embedded Way
San Jose CA 95138
P: 480-777-7090   PRC:209
teradyne.com
Email: customercare@teradyne.com
Estab: 1960

Brad Robbins, President of LitePoint
Gregory Smith, President of Semiconductor Test
Division
Jurgen von Hollen, President of Universal Robots
Mark E. Jagiela, CEO & President
Sanjay Mehta, VP & CFO

Supplier of automatic test equipment. The company caters to semiconductor, electronics, and
automotive sectors.

**Terminal Manufacturing Company
LLC** HQ
707 Gilman St
Berkeley CA 94710
P: 510-526-3071   F: 510-526-3138   PRC:80
www.terminalmanufacturing.com
Email: tmci@terminalmanufacturing.com
Estab: 1918

Steve Mellinger, Owner

Designer and manufacturer of vacuum chalmers, pressure vessels, truck tanks, and assorted
fabrications.

Terrace Consulting Inc HQ
PO Box 597
San Francisco CA 94104
P: 415-848-7300   F: 415-848-7301   PRC:323
www.terrace.com
Estab: 1992

Todd P. Ziesing, CEO & Founder
Lisa Leung, VP of Project Management Office
Tracy Leung, Director of Finance & Operations &
Finance & HR & Operations Manager
Shinya Ito, Software Engineer

Provider of custom software development
services. The company focuses on eCommerce,
back office, business intelligence, cloud, and other
services.

Terradex Inc HQ
855 El Camino Real Ste 309
Palo Alto CA 94301
P: 650-227-3250   F: 650-227-3255   PRC:139
terradex.com
Email: sales@terradex.com
Estab: 2002

Bob Wenzlau, CEO & Founder
Peter Biffar, President
J. Michael Sowinski, VP of Environmental Protec-
tion Services
Sara Strojwas, Project Manager

Provider of web and consulting services. The
company offers dig clean, cleanup deck, and web
development services.

Terraphase Engineering HQ
1404 Franklin Ste 600
Oakland CA 94612
P: 510-645-1850   F: 510-380-6304   PRC:139
terraphase.com
Email: info@terraphase.com
Estab: 2010

William Carson, President & Principal Engineer
Andrew Romolo, VP & Principal & Geologist
Jen Otto, Business Manager
Doug Wolf, Principal Engineer
Alice Hale, Senior Project Engineer

Provider of environmental consulting services. The
company offers environmental due diligence, and
soil and groundwater remediation services.

Terrasat Communications Inc HQ
315 Digital Dr
Morgan Hill CA 95037
P: 408-782-5911   F: 408-782-5912   PRC:70
www.terrasatinc.com
Email: sales@terrasatinc.com
Estab: 1994

Jit Patel, President
Carl Hurst, VP of Operations
Jason Saffell, Technical Sales Manager
Mary Ann Convertino, Human Resource Admin-
istrator
Tony Morales, QC Inspector

Manufacturer of RF solutions. The company caters
to satellite communication and digital microwave
systems.

Tesco Controls Inc HQ
8440 Florin Rd
Sacramento CA 95828
P: 916-395-8800   PRC:65
www.tescocontrols.com
Email: sales@tescocontrols.com
Estab: 1972

Shain Thomas, CEO
Seth Robinson, CFO
Lyn Masterson, VP of Internal Operations
David Kubel, VP of Technical Services
Richard Haugh, Director of Project Management

Manufacturer of instrumentation, control systems,
and service pedestals for water and traffic sectors.
The company offers system integration services.

Tesla HQ
3500 Deer Creek Rd
Palo Alto CA 94304
P: 650-681-5000 PRC:130
www.tesla.com
Email: press@tesla.com
Estab: 2003
Sales: Over $3B

Elon Musk, CEO
Gilbert Passin, VP of Manufacturing
Doug Field, SVP of Engineering
Brad Buss, Director
Lina Osman, Associate Store Manager

Designer and manufacturer of electric sedans and electric SUVs. The company is engaged in the production of energy storage systems.

Test-O-Pac Industries Inc HQ
1188 Murphy Ave
San Jose CA 95131
P: 408-436-1117 PRC:139
www.testopac.com
Email: info@testopac.com
Estab: 1977

Sam Sohal, President
Oscar Joya, Quality & Test Engineer

Provider of environmental and package testing services. The company deals with component testing, product reliability, and medical package testing.

Test21 Inc HQ
48511 Warm Springs Blvd Ste 210
Fremont CA 94539
P: 510-438-0221 F: 510-438-0229 PRC:211
www.test21.com
Email: sales@test21.com

Bon Ho, President
Tatang Putra, Software Engineer

Designer and manufacturer of printed circuit boards including probe cards for semiconductor, ATE manufacturers, and silicon wafer foundries.

TestEdge Inc HQ
15930 Bernardo Center Dr [N]
San Diego CA 92127
P: 858-451-1012 F: 858-451-1018 PRC:306
www.testedgeinc.com
Email: sales@testedgeinc.com
Estab: 2002

Craig Bousquet, Contact

Provider of quality engineering testing of digital, analog, mixed-signal and RF devices.

Testmetrix Inc HQ
426 S Hillview Dr
Milpitas CA 95035
P: 408-730-5511 PRC:19
www.testmetrix.com

Christian Cojocneanu, President & CEO
Mike Bulat, VP of Engineering
Stephen Tseng, Director of Strategic Investment, Asia
Nick Balmez, Senior Hardware Engineer

Manufacturer of high-throughput AVTE systems, and offers official compliance certification test services.

Text Analysis International Inc HQ
10146 Alpine Dr Unit 1
Cupertino CA 95014
P: 650-308-9323 PRC:325
www.textanalysis.com
Email: info@textanalysis.com
Estab: 1998

Avi Meyers, CEO & President & Founder
Amnon Meyers, CTO
Keith Woods-Holder, COO

Provider of software development services for text analysis. The company focuses on project management, testing and implementation, and deployment.

TextDigger Inc HQ
12 S First St Ste 620
San Jose CA 95113
P: 408-416-3142 PRC:324
textdigger.com
Email: info@textdigger.com
Estab: 2005

Tim Musgrove, Founder & CEO

Developer of horizontal semantic solutions for search engines. The company focuses on content mining and analytics.

TFD Group BR
80 Garden Court Ste 240
Monterey CA 93940
P: 831-649-3800 PRC:322
www.tfdg.com
Estab: 1976

Robert Butler, CEO
Bill Blatch, Director
Anastacio Medina, Director Sales & Marketing
Jon Redfield, Director Technical Services
Joseph Radford, Marketing Director

Developer of analytical methods and software tools. The company caters to aerospace and defense sectors.

TG Service Inc HQ
PO Box 21225
El Sobrante CA 94820
P: 510-243-9931 PRC:326
genepilot.com
Email: sales@genepilot.com
Estab: 1998

Brett Miller, President

Producer of multimedia and Internet solutions. The company engages in microarray analysis on machines.

The Best Electrical Company Inc HQ
667 Walnut St
San Jose CA 95110
P: 408-287-2040 F: 408-287-0487 PRC:76
www.besteleco.com
Email: info@besteleco.com
Estab: 1954

Vic Giacalone, Owner

Provider of tenant improvement and maintenance services for the retail, commercial, industrial, and residential communities.

The Bit Shop Inc HQ
1646 Watson Ct [N]
Milpitas CA 95035
P: 408-262-0713 F: 408-945-0852 PRC:80
www.bsi-nc.com
Estab: 1978

Gary Clark, Owner
Richard Clark, Manager

Provider of plastics machining, drilling and other industrial services.

The Broach Masters Inc HQ
1605 Industrial Dr
Auburn CA 95603
P: 530-885-1939 F: 530-885-8157 PRC:80
www.broachmasters.com
Email: info@broachmasters.com

Jim Shaneyfelt, Gear Shop Manager

Manufacturer of broaches, disc shapers, disc shaper cutters, shank shapers, shank shaper cutters, gear shaper cutters, and spline broaches.

The Cohen Group HQ
1660 S Amphlett Blvd Ste 110
San Mateo CA 94402
P: 650-349-9737 F: 650-349-3378 PRC:136
thecohengroup.com
Email: admin@thecohengroup.com
Estab: 1980

Joel M. Cohen, Co-President & Founder
William Cohen, Owner
Robert Tyrer, Co-President
Megan Ortiz, COO
Timothy Bormann, VP

Provider of health and safety training, litigation support, indoor air quality, microbial contamination, and related services.

The Cooper Companies Inc HQ
6101 Bollinger Canyon Rd Ste 500
San Ramon CA 94583
P: 925-460-3600 PRC:173
coopercos.com
Email: info@cooperco.com
Estab: 1980

Daniel G. McBride, EVP & COO & President
Bob Weiss, CEO
Brian Andrews, SVP & CFO & Treasurer
Agostino Ricupati, CAO & SVP of Finance & Tax
Donald Press, Director

Provider of healthcare solutions. The company offers health and wellness programs for women, individuals, and communities.

The Detection Group Inc HQ
440 N Wolfe Rd Ste E211
Sunnyvale CA 94085
P: 650-215-7300 PRC:230
www.thedetectiongroup.com
Email: info@thedetectiongroup.com
Estab: 2006

Matt Barth, Founder & EVP
Laurie Conner, President & CEO
Mark Belinsky, COO
Cindy Anderson, VP of Marketing
Jens Rasmussen, VP of Engineering & Architecture

Provider of monitoring and alarming solutions. The company offers wireless water leak detection systems for commercial buildings.

The Ely Company Inc HQ
3046 Kashiwa St [N]
Torrance CA 90505
P: 310-539-5831   F: 310-530-3569   PRC:80
www.elyco.com
Estab: 1964

Walter Senff, Contact

Manufacturer and distributor of machined components for aerospace and commercial industries.

The Foundry LLC HQ
4040 Campbell Ave Ste 110
Menlo Park CA 94025
P: 650-326-2656 PRC:189
www.thefoundry.com
Email: info@thefoundry.com
Estab: 1998

Hanson Gifford, CEO

Focuses on product development, prototyping, market analysis, development, and pre-clinical and clinical support services.

The Igneous Group Inc HQ
PO Box 3702
Santa Cruz CA 95063
P: 831-469-7625 PRC:325
www.igneous.com
Email: info@igneous.com
Estab: 1991

Geoff Caras, General Manager

Provider of technology consulting services. The company focuses on web content, application development, and e-commerce.

The Lincoln Electric Co BR
5030 Hillsdale Cir Ste 106
El Dorado Hills CA 95762
P: 916-939-8788   F: 916-939-8789   PRC:159
www.lincolnelectric.com
Estab: 1895

Kevin Lowry, Senior Buyer

Provider of industrial control and automation solutions. The company's offerings also include torches, welding guns, and related accessories.

The Montague Co HQ
1830 Stearman Ave
Hayward CA 94545
P: 510-785-8822 PRC:159
montaguecompany.com
Email: domsales@montaguecompany.com
Estab: 1857

Tom Whalen, President
Joe Deckelman, VP of Sales & Marketing

Provider of commercial cooking equipment. The company's products include boilers, ovens, and refrigerated bases.

The Okonite Co BR
2440 Camino Ramon Ste 315
San Ramon CA 94583
P: 925-830-0801   F: 925-830-0954   PRC:62
www.okonite.com
Email: info@okonite.com
Estab: 1878

Gary Michalski, Director Purchasing
Aaron Cooper, District Manager
Dustin Banet, Plant Manager
Charlie Hagmaier, Plant Engineering Manager
Patrick Nash, District Manager

Manufacturer of electrical wire insulators. The company offers high and low voltage, instrumentation, and special purpose cables.

The Olander Company Inc HQ
144 Commercial St
Sunnyvale CA 94086
P: 408-735-1850   F: 408-735-6515   PRC:5
www.olander.com
Email: rfq@olander.com
Estab: 1962

Annie Olander, President & CEO
Michelle Richards, Director of Operations
John Butler, Director of New Business Development
Carl Ericsson, Manager of Business Development
Jeff Sablan, Account Manager

Distributor of standard and metric fasteners and electromechanical components. The company offers tools, adhesives, and wire management products.

The Thomas Kinkade Co HQ
18635 Sutter Blvd [N]
Morgan Hill CA 95037
P: 888-368-1336 PRC:189
www.thomaskinkade.com
Email: contact@thomaskinkade.com
Estab: 1990

Mark Mickelson, Owner
John Hasting, CEO
Thomas Kinkade, Art Director

Publisher of art works.

The Trinity Group Inc HQ
PO Box 810 [N]
Tracy CA 95378
P: 209-832-1293   F: 209-832-1376   PRC:45
www.trinitygrp.com
Emp: 11-50   Estab: 1993

John Moore, CEO & President

Provider of telecommunications, technology and data networking consulting services.

The Wecker Group HQ
462 Webster St Ste 1
Monterey CA 93940
P: 831-372-8377   F: 831-372-1353   PRC:325
www.weckergroup.com
Email: wecker@weckergroup.com
Estab: 1974

Robert Wecker, Owner & Founder
Ruth Minerva, Senior Designer

Provider of design studio and ad agency services. The company specializes in corporate identity, collateral, TV advertising, and event promotion.

The Wirebenders Orthodontic Lab HQ
2075 Lincoln Ave Ste A
San Jose CA 95125
P: 408-265-5576   F: 408-265-5579   PRC:185
thewirebenders.com
Email: info@thewirebenders.com
Estab: 1974

Gary Hawke, Owner

Provider of clinical support, research, and development services. The company specializes in appliance designs.

Theraject Inc HQ
39270 Paseo Padre Ste 112
Fremont CA 94538
P: 510-742-5832   F: 510-796-5732   PRC:261
www.theraject.com
Email: info@theraject.com

Sung-Yun Kwon, Founder & CEO

Developer of drug micro-needle technologies. The company is engaged in vaccine and also drug deliveries.

Theralife Inc HQ
650 B Fremont Ave Ste 218
Los Altos CA 94024
P: 650-949-6080 PRC:251
www.theralife.com
Email: info@theralife.com
Estab: 2000

Yang Lily, CEO

Manufacturer of botanical drugs. The company offer botanicals that provide symptom relief for problems related to eyes.

Theravance Biopharma US Inc HQ
901 Gateway Blvd
S San Francisco CA 94080
P: 650-808-6000 PRC:268
www.theravance.com
Estab: 2014
Sales: $30M to $100M

Ann B. Brady, President
Rick E. Winningham, Chairman & CEO
Brett K. Haumann, SVP of Clinical Development & CMO
Andrew A. Hindman, SVP & CFO
Frank Pasqualone, SVP & Chief Commercial Operations Officer

Provider of pharmaceuticals. The company develops new medicines with superior efficacy, convenience, tolerability and/or safety.

Therm-X   HQ
   3200 Investment Blvd
   Hayward CA 94545
   P: 510-606-1012   F: 510-441-2414   PRC:157
   www.therm-x.com
   Email: info@therm-x.com
   Estab: 1983

Dan Trujillo, CEO
Jim Gaiser, VP
Scott Sawicki, General Manager
Arturo L., IT Manager
Tejas Vaity, Quality Assurance Engineering
Manager

Provider of engineered solutions. The company
serves the semiconductor, petrochemical, life
sciences, and aerospace industries.

Therma   HQ
   1601 Las Plumas Ave
   San Jose CA 95133
   P: 408-347-3400   PRC:80
   www.therma.com
   Email: info@therma.com
   Estab: 1967

Steve Hansen, President
Mike Fisher, COO
Brooks Corcoran, Director of M&A & Strategy
Ronny Dominguez, Junior Project Manager
Mat Hayashi, Project Manager

Provider of mechanical contracting services. The
company also offers design and installation of
environmental systems.

Thermal Engineering Associates Inc   HQ
   3287 Kifer Rd
   Santa Clara CA 95051-0826
   P: 650-961-5900   F: 650-323-9237   PRC:212
   www.thermengr.net
   Email: info@thermengr.com
   Estab: 1997

Bernie Siegal, President
Bill Ribble, Director of Business Development

Provider of semiconductor thermal measurement
and modeling solutions. The company's products
include thermal test systems, test fixtures, and
test chips.

Thermal Press International Inc   HQ
   341 Stealth Ct
   Livermore CA 94551
   P: 925-454-9800   F: 925-454-9810   PRC:153
   www.thermalpress.com
   Estab: 1976

Ian McLean, Owner
Lance Crawford, VP of Sales
Tony Crabb, Manufacturing Manager
Nathan Zimmerman, Designer

Manufacturer of thermal presses and heat staking
machines. The company also offers heat sealing
and degating machinery.

Thermochem Inc   HQ
   3414 Regional Pkwy Ste A
   Santa Rosa CA 95403
   P: 707-575-1310   F: 707-575-7932   PRC:14
   thermochem.com
   Estab: 1985

Russell Kunzman, Senior Chemist & Lab Director
Mark Broaddus, Engineering Manager
Matt Broaddus, Field Service Manager
Joanna Collier, Team Leader
Lori Leigh, Office Administrator

Provider of chemical engineering, laboratory analysis, geochemistry and field testing services and
products to a wide range of energy industries.

ThermoGenesis Holdings Inc   HQ
   2711 Citrus Rd
   Rancho Cordova CA 95742
   P: 916-858-5100   PRC:31
   thermogenesis.com
   Email: customerservice@thermogenesis.com
   Estab: 1987
   Sales: $10M to $30M

Haihong Zhu, President
Chris Xu, CEO
Philip Coelho, CTO
Mindy Wilke-Douglas, VP of Operations
Jeff Cauble, VP of Finance & Principal Financial &
Accounting Officer

Manufacturer of therapeutic products and related
supplies. The company is involved in cellular bio-
processing and bone marrow transplants.

Theron Pharmaceuticals   HQ
   365 San Aleso Ave
   Sunnyvale CA 94085
   P: 408-792-7424   F: 408-744-6773   PRC:261
   www.theronpharma.com
   Email: info@theronpharma.com
   Estab: 2008

Xiaoming Zhang, Founder

Developer of long acting M3 muscarinic antago-
nist (LAMA) for the improved treatment of chronic
respiratory diseases.

Think Connected LLC   HQ
   365 Main St
   San Francisco CA 94105
   P: 877-684-4654   F: 510-291-3076   PRC:323
   www.thinkconnected.com
   Email: info@thinkconnected.com
   Estab: 2003

Tom Ivers, President & Founder
Joshua Demitro, Information Technology Service
Manager
Tristan Lucas, Information Technology Adminis-
trator
David Smart, System Administrator

Provider of data center, consulting, managed, and
supplemental information technology services for
small and medium-sized businesses.

Thinkify   HQ
   18450 Technology Dr Ste E1
   Morgan Hill CA 95037
   P: 408-782-7111   PRC:323
   thinkifyit.com
   Email: support@thinkifyit.com
   Estab: 2008

Peter Soule, Founder

Provider of radio frequency identification technology application services. The company provides
engineering services as well.

Third Pillar Systems   HQ
   577 Airport Blvd 8th Fl
   Burlingame CA 94010
   P: 650-372-1200   F: 650-240-0364   PRC:323
   www.thirdpillar.com
   Email: sales@thirdpillar.com
   Estab: 1999

Pankaj Chowdhry, President & CIO
Charles Stuard, Managing Director of Sales &
Marketing
Anil Chalamalasetti, Software Engineer

Developer of networks and software for the
commercial lending industry. The company offers
implementation and integration services.

**Thomas J Payne Market
Development**   BR
   865 Woodside   [N]
   San Mateo CA 94401
   P: 650-340-8311   F: 650-340-8568   PRC:45
   www.tjpmd.com

David Ropa, VP

Provider of food marketing consultancy services.

Thompson Gundrilling Inc   HQ
   13840 Saticoy St   [N]
   Van Nuys CA 91402
   P: 818-781-0973   PRC:53
   www.thompsongundrilling.com
   Emp: 11-50   Estab: 1973

Michael Thompson, President
Saul Aquirre, Supervisor
Salvador Leiva, Master Machinist

Provider of deep hole drilling for industries such
as nuclear, injections, military weapons, space,
special tubing, aircraft, oilfield, mold bases, and
dies.

Thor Electronics of California   HQ
   420 W Market St
   Salinas CA 93901
   P: 831-758-6400   F: 831-758-0162   PRC:206
   www.thorconnect.com
   Email: info@thorconnect.com
   Estab: 1966

Thor Cary, Owner
Stephen Abrams, President
Don Cole, Quality Assurance Manager
Romeo Centeno, Facilities Manager & Plant
Manager

Manufacturer of special connectors, molded cable
assemblies and covers, harness assemblies, and
electro-mechanical devices.

Thought Inc HQ

5 Third St Ste 1030
San Francisco CA 94103
P: 415-836-9199 F: 415-836-9191 PRC:322
www.thoughtinc.com
Email: sales@thoughtinc.com
Estab: 1993

Greg Baker, Director of Sales & Marketing

Provider of data management solutions. The company uses dynamic mapping and related software for this purpose.

Thoughtbot Inc BR

795 Folsom St
San Francisco CA 94107
P: 877-976-2687 PRC:315
thoughtbot.com
Estab: 2012

Kane Baccigalupi, Director of Development
Skipper Warson, Director of Design
Kate Tsunoda, Managing Director
Camille Baclay, Office Manager
Jessica Oceguera, Local Marketing Manager

Provider of web and mobile app design and development.

ThoughtSpot Inc HQ

910 Hermosa Ct
Sunnyvale CA 94085
P: 800-508-7008 PRC:315
www.thoughtspot.com
Email: marketing@thoughtspot.com
Estab: 2012

Ajeet Singh, Co-Founder & Executive Chairman
Amit Prakash, Co-Founder & CTO
Abhishek Rai, Co-Founder & VP of Engineering
Sanjay Agrawal, Co-Founder & VP of Engineering
Sudheesh Nair, CEO

A business intelligence platform that helps individuals to explore, analyze, and share real-time business analytics data.

Thoughtworks Inc BR

814 Mission St 5th FL
San Francisco CA 94103
P: 415-273-1389 F: 415-986-2964 PRC:323
www.thoughtworks.com
Email: info-us@thoughtworks.com
Estab: 1993

Roy Singham, Founder
Rebecca Parsons, CTO
Adam Monago, VP & Global Head of Digital Strategy
David Rice, Managing Director
Tim Brown, Principal Consultant

Provider of system design and e-business consulting services. The company is also involved in software design and delivery and support.

Thrasys Inc HQ

250 Executive Park Blvd Ste 2000
San Francisco CA 94134
P: 650-449-1000 PRC:325
thrasys.com
Email: info@thrasys.com

Randy Belknap, CTO
George He, VP of Application Systems
Weimin Shen, Staff Engineer
Mark Knapp, Software Developer & Architect
Ranjani Ramakrishna, Corporate Counsel

Provider of health networking solutions. The company serves patients, service centers, payers, and public health administrators.

Three Palm Software HQ

16 Yankee Point Dr
Carmel CA 93923
P: 408-356-3240 PRC:322
threepalmsoft.com
Email: info@threepalmsoft.com
Estab: 2007

Patrick Heffernan, CTO
Daoxian Zhang, Chief Scientist Manager

Designer and developer of software products for medical imaging and information. The company also deals with data processing services.

Threshold Enterprises Ltd HQ

23 Janis Way
Scotts Valley CA 95066
P: 831-438-6851 F: 831-438-6430 PRC:268
www.thresholdenterprises.com
Estab: 1978

Kevin Charries, Director of Quality Assurance

Distributor of nutritional supplements, healthcare, and beauty care products.

Thync Global Inc HQ

140 W Main St 2nd Fl
Los Gatos CA 95030
P: 408-484-4808 PRC:194
www.thync.com
Email: contact@thync.com
Estab: 2011

Anil Thakur, CTO & Co-Founder
Isy Goldwasser, CEO & Co-Founder
Sumon Pal, Co-Founder
Jwala Karnik, SVP of Clinical Development

Provider of wearable technology solutions. The company is involved in testing and related support services.

thyssenkrupp Elevator Corp BR

14400 Catalina St
San Leandro CA 94577
P: 510-476-1900 PRC:180
www.thyssenkruppelevator.com

Josh Fosson, Branch Manager

Provider of elevators and elevator solutions. The company offers MRL elevators, synergy elevators, momentum elevators, and freight elevators.

TIBCO Software Inc HQ

3307 Hillview Ave
Palo Alto CA 94304
P: 650-846-1000 F: 650-846-1005 PRC:319
www.tibco.com
Email: info@tibco.com
Estab: 1997

Scott Roza, President & Global Head of Customer Operations
Dan Streetman, CEO
Murray Rode, Vice Chairman
Matt Quinn, COO
Nelson Petracek, CTO

Provider of enterprise application integration software. The company serves the government, healthcare, and insurance industries.

Tiger Software HQ

PO Box 9491 [N]
San Diego CA 92169
P: 858-273-5900 PRC:319
www.tigersoft.com
Emp: 11-50 Estab: 1981

William Schmidt, Publisher

Developer of investment software.

Tintri Inc HQ

303 Ravendale Dr
Mountain View CA 94043
P: 650-810-8200 PRC:95
www.tintri.com
Email: info@tintri.com
Estab: 2008

Alex Bouzari, CEO & Chairman & Co-Founder
Paul Bloch, President & Co-Founder
Mario Blandini, CMO & Chief Evangelist
Ian Halifax, CFO
Kieran Harty, CTO

Developer of zero management storage systems. The company focuses on building storage for virtual environments.

Titan Pharmaceuticals Inc HQ

400 Oyster Point Blvd Ste 505
S San Francisco CA 94080-1958
P: 650-244-4990 F: 650-244-4956 PRC:268
www.titanpharm.com
Email: busdev@titanpharm.com
Emp: 23 Estab: 1992
Sales: $3M to $10M

Sunil Bhonsle, CEO
Kate DeVarney, EVP & Chief Scientific Officer
Dane D. Hallberg, EVP & CCO
Katherine L. Beebe, EVP & CDO

Provider of biopharmaceuticals. The company discovers proprietary therapeutics primarily for the treatment of serious medical disorders.

Tivix BR
600 California St
San Francisco CA 94108
P: 415-680-1299 PRC:315
www.tivix.com
Email: connect@tivix.com
Estab: 2008

Sumit Chachra, CEO & CTO
Bill Conneely, Senior Director of Finance &
Operations
Dariusz Fryta, Managing Director
John Hargan, Marketing Manager
Katarzyna Szostak, Administrative Manager

Focuses on the agile development of web, cloud,
and mobile applications.

TKO Video Communications HQ
1665 Willow St
San Jose CA 95125
P: 408-557-6900 F: 408-557-6901 PRC:60
www.tkoworks.com
Email: info@tkoworks.com
Estab: 1995

John Roensch, President & CEO
Mary Roensch, CFO
Craig Ortiz, Program Manager
Manmei Lam, Web Specialist Corporate Marketing

Provider of video communication services. The
company focuses on audio and video conferencing, satellite broadcasting, and telecommunications training.

TMT Enterprises Inc HQ
1996 Oakland Rd
San Jose CA 95131
P: 408-432-9040 F: 408-432-9429 PRC:142
tmtenterprises.net
Email: info@tmtenterprises.net
Estab: 1961

Ted Moore, President & CEO
Matt Moore, Operations Manager

Provider of baseball and softball playing surfaces
and supplier of agricultural mixes, construction
materials, organics, and aggregates.

TNT Plastic Molding Inc HQ
725 E Harrison St [N]
Corona CA 92879
P: 951-808-9700 PRC:189
www.tntplasticmolding.com
Email: info@tntplasticmolding.com
Emp: 51-200 Estab: 2001

Diane Mixson, President

Provider of plastic injection molding services.

TOA Electronics Inc DH
400 Oyster Point Blvd Ste 301
S San Francisco CA 94080
P: 650-452-1200 PRC:60
www.toaelectronics.com
Email: support@toaelectronics.com
Estab: 1974

Wynne Kwong, Account Manager
Robert McHale, Warehouse Coordinator

Developer and manufacturer of audio and security
products. The company is engaged in design,
delivery, and installation services.

M-306

Tobar Industries Inc HQ
912 Olinder Ct
San Jose CA 95122
P: 408-494-3530 PRC:82
tobarind.com
Estab: 1976

William Delaney, CFO
Ron Dias, Director of Engineering
David Jerger, Sales Manager
James Scripps, Quality Manager
Marianne Ryan, Human Resource Manager

Provider of contract manufacturing services. The
company offers services for computer chassis,
card cages, and frames.

Tolerion Inc HQ
131 Oyster Point Blvd Ste 400
S San Francisco CA 94080
P: 415-795-5800 PRC:266
tolerion.bio
Email: info@tolerion.bio
Estab: 2013

John R. Donovan, President & CEO
Michael Leviten, Director of Research

Provider of medical treatment solutions for
autoimmune diseases. The company focuses on
restoring the patient's immune system.

Tom Sawyer Software Corp HQ
1997 El Dorado Ave
Berkeley CA 94707
P: 510-208-4370 F: 510-527-1674 PRC:323
www.tomsawyer.com
Email: marketing@tomsawyer.com
Estab: 1992

Brendan Madden, CEO
Kevin Madden, Chief Software Engineer
Liangrong Yi, Senior Product Development
Engineer
Travis Cheng, Product Development Engineer

Developer of data relationship visualization and
analysis software for application developers. The
company offers training and consulting services.

TOMA Biosciences Inc HQ
303 Vintage Park Dr
Foster City CA 94404
P: 650-691-8662 PRC:24
tomabio.com
Estab: 2011

Wolfgang Daum, President & CEO

Provider of sequencing solutions. The company
serves laboratories and researchers to uncover
clinically meaningful genomic changes in tumors.

Tomi Engineering Inc HQ
414 E Alton Ave [N]
Santa Ana CA 92707
P: 714-556-1474 F: 714-979-8664 PRC:80
www.tomiengineering.com
Emp: 51-200 Estab: 1977

Mike Falbo, CEO
Nick Falbo, Manager of Sales & Estimating
John Castillo, Supervisor
Enrique Bejar, QC Administrator

Manufacturer of aerospace, medical, commercial
and electronic products.

Tomopal Inc HQ
1026 Florin Rd Ste 322
Sacramento CA 95831
P: 916-429-7240 F: 916-429-2701 PRC:156
www.tomopal.com
Email: sales@tomopal.com

Pal Sandhu, CEO
Nicoll Butterfield, Manager

Manufacturer and distributor of glass syringes,
scales and balances, gas filters, and other products for the laboratory and industrial markers.

Tooltek Engineering Corp HQ
4151 Business Center Dr
Fremont CA 94538
P: 510-683-9504 F: 510-683-9614 PRC:156
www.tooltek.com
Email: sales@tooltek.com
Estab: 1984

Roman Ruzhinsky, Systems Engineer
Jessie Zhu, Technician

Designer and fabricator of custom automated
equipment. The company is also engaged in
material handling and robotics solutions.

Toolwire Inc HQ
7031 Koll Center Pkwy Ste 200
Pleasanton CA 94566
P: 925-227-8500 F: 925-227-8501 PRC:323
toolwire.com
Estab: 1998

Joseph White, Manager of Technical Operations
Nancy Bissonnette, Office Manager

Designer and developer of experiential learning
solutions for higher education and corporate
training institutions.

Top Microsystems Corp HQ
1340 Norman Ave
Santa Clara CA 95054
P: 408-980-9813 F: 408-980-8626 PRC:288
www.topmicro.com
Email: infor@topmicro.com
Estab: 1989

Kevin Rea, Sales Manager
Kevin McCann, Sales Manager

Provider of conversion solutions and integration
services. The company offers blade, storage,
and rackmount servers, medical equipment, and
others.

Top Shelf BR
1851 E Paradise Rd Ste A
Tracy CA 95304
P: 866-592-0488 F: 209-834-8832 PRC:190
topshelfforthopedics.com

Scott Brougham, CEO
Bob McCune, General Manager & VP
Craig Koloske, Director of Manufacturing

Manufacturer of orthopedic bracing and appliances. The company offers products for knee,
shoulder, foot and ankle, and spine.

Toppan Printing Company Ltd BR
275 Battery St Ste 2600
San Francisco CA 94111
P: 415-393-9839   F: 415-393-9840   PRC:87
www.toppan.co.jp

Patrick Page, General Manager

Provider of printing solutions. The company serves customers in the food, beverage, and high barrier product industries.

Tora Trading Services Ltd BR
1440 Chapin Ave Ste 205
Burlingame CA 94010
P: 650-513-6700   PRC:319
www.tora.com
Email: pr@tora.com

Robert Dykes, CEO
Paul Catuna, CFO
Mihai Iosivas, CTO
Keith J. Ducker, Chief Investment Officer
Chris D. Jenkins, Managing Director of Sales & Operations

Provider of products such as Compass, Clearpool, and Crosspoint for buy-side traders to specifically address the trading challenges to Asia.

Toray Advanced Composites USA BR
18255 Sutter Blvd
Morgan Hill CA 95037
P: 408-465-8500   F: 408-776-0107   PRC:57
www.toraytac.com

Scott Unger, Group President
David Kapp, VP of Operations
Joseph Morris, Director of DOD Programs
Son Tran, Communications Manager
Susie Aguayo, Buyer

Manufacturer of advanced composites like adhesives, prepregs, and liquid resin systems. The company serves military, aerospace, and other sectors.

Toray International America Inc BR
411 Borel Ave Ste 520
San Mateo CA 94402
P: 650-341-7152   F: 650-341-0845   PRC:53
toray.com
Estab: 1988

Ken Irokawa, Office Manager

Provider of chemicals, plastics, textiles, and IT-related products. The company offers environment, engineering, life science, and other services.

Torian Group Inc HQ
519 W Center Ave
Visalia CA 93291
P: 559-733-1940   F: 559-532-0207   PRC:323
www.toriangroup.com
Email: support@toriangroup.com
Estab: 1983

Tim Torian, President
Jose Lucatero, Senior Network Engineer

Provider of computer, network, and web solutions such as virus removal, home network setup, and email.

Tosco - Tool Specialty Co HQ
1011 E Slauson Ave   [N]
Los Angeles CA 90011
P: 323-232-3561   F: 323-232-3429   PRC:157
www.toolspecialty.com
Email: info@toolspecialty.com
Estab: 1943

Jeff Tetzlaff, Contact

Manufacturer of carbide cutting tools.

Toshiba America Inc BR
2590 Orchard Pkwy
San Jose CA 95131
P: 408-526-2400   F: 408-526-2410   PRC:93
www.toshiba.com
Estab: 1965

Kenji Ito, VP
William Lam, VP of Engineering
Khalid Baig, Director of Strategic Sourcing
David Yun, Enterprise Architect & Manager
David Marsac, Engineering Manager

Manufacturer of LCD, laptop batteries, power adapters, laptop cases, and other laptop related accessories.

Tosk Inc HQ
2672 Bayshore Pkwy Ste 507
Mountain View CA 94043
P: 408-245-6838   F: 408-245-6808   PRC:261
www.tosk.com
Email: info@tosk.com
Estab: 1998

Brian D. Frenzel, President & CEO & Director & Founder
Stephen Yanofsky, VP of Research
Charles Garvin, Director
A. Lynne Moritz, Accounting Manager
Lawrence Marsh, Scientific Advisor

Manufacturer of drugs for the treatment of debilitating and life-threatening diseases such as cancer, arthritis, and psoriasis.

Tosoh Bioscience Inc BR
6000 Shoreline Ct Ste 101
S San Francisco CA 94080
P: 650-615-4970   F: 650-615-0415   PRC:19
www.tosohbioscience.com
Email: info.diag.am@tosohbioscience.com
Estab: 1989

Joseph Troche, Quality Assurance Project Manager
Randy Pietro, Regional Service Manager
Bill Christensen, Field Clinical Engineer
Beth Sumpter, Clinical Support Specialist

Provider of monitoring services for life threatening diseases and cancers. The company focuses on preventing epidemics and purifying water.

Total Environmental & Power Systems Inc HQ
2500 Bisso Ln Ste 500
Concord CA 94520
P: 925-681-2238   F: 510-217-2227   PRC:290
e-teps.net
Email: info@e-teps.net
Estab: 2002

Tom Masiewicz, President
Nicole Shipley, Senior Administrative Assistant

Provider of HVAC, electrical, and telecommunication services. The company's service areas include generators, radio frequency, and fabrication.

Total Resolution LLC HQ
20 Florida Ave
Berkeley CA 94707
P: 510-527-6393   F: 510-527-9151   PRC:319
www.totalresolution.com
Email: roar@totalresolution.com

Roar Kilaas, Owner

Developer of software for electron microscopy needs. The company provides MacTempasX and CrystalKitX.

Totango Inc HQ
1200 Park Pl Ste 200
San Mateo CA 94403
P: 800-634-1990   PRC:325
www.totango.com
Email: hi@totango.com
Estab: 2010

Guy Nirpaz, Co-Founder & CEO
Omer Gotlieb, Co-Founder & SVP of Business Development
Eric Benhamou, Chairman
Hamutal Anavi-Russo, CFO
Jamie Bertasi, COO

A customer success software helps to connect customer data, monitor health changes, and proactively engage the customers by using an integrated platform.

Totlcom Inc BR
4610 Northgate Blvd Ste 150
Sacramento CA 95834
P: 916-428-5000   F: 916-921-9767   PRC:64
totlcom.com
Email: info@totlcom.com

Sam Bishop, CEO
Brian Watters, CTO
Rod Belton, VP
Dale Hill, General Manager
Gloria Rodriguez, Branch Manager

Provider of IP voice and data services and products such as IP systems, VoIP systems, and mail systems for growing companies.

Totten Tubes Inc HQ
500 Danlee   [N]
Azusa CA 91702
P: 626-812-0113   PRC:62
www.tottentubes.com
Estab: 1955

Linda Ann Furse, CFO

Distributor of steel tubing and pipes.

Touchpoints Inc   DH
   3005 Douglas Blvd Ste 108
   Roseville CA 95661
P: 916-878-5940   F: 916-878-5951   PRC:326
touchpointsinc.com
Email: info@touchpointsinc.com
Estab: 2004

Pratima Mahato, Technical Recruiter
Satya Pravas Nanda, Talent Associate

Provider of application development, big data
engineering, and analytics solutions and it serves
the public and commercial sectors.

TPS Aviation Inc   HQ
   1515 Crocker Ave
   Hayward CA 94544-7038
P: 510-475-1010   F: 510-475-8817   PRC:5
www.tpsaviation.com
Email: admin@tpsaviation.com
Estab: 1961

Sue Bauer, Regional Sales Manager

Distributor of commercial and military aerospace
fasteners and electric components. The company
focuses on aerospace parts, components, and
logistics.

Trackdata Systems Corp   HQ
   21684 Granada Ave
   Cupertino CA 95014
P: 408-446-5595   PRC:322
trackinfo.com
Email: help@trackdatasystems.com
Estab: 1980

Michael Exley, Director of Operations

Provider of greyhound, thoroughbred, and harness racing information. The company features
up-to-date listing of racing schedules.

Trade Union International Inc   HQ
   4651 State St   [N]
   Montclair CA 91763
P: 909-628-7500   F: 909-628-0382   PRC:75
www.tradeunion.com.tw
Email: topline@tradeunion.com.tw
Estab: 1983

Mei Chang, VP
Angela Fox, Operations Manager & Warehouse
Manager
Felix Feng, Supply Chain Manager
Sarah Cervantes, Account Executive

Manufacturer and distributor of wheels and
accessories.

Trane   BR
   310 Soquel Way
   Sunnyvale CA 94085
P: 888-862-1619   F: 408-481-3666   PRC:154
trane.com
Estab: 1913

David Nation, Owner Direct Account Manager
Johnny Brown, VP & District General Manager
Al Fullerton, VP of Sales
Nick Hinz, VP & General Manager
Warren Michelsen, VP

Provider of heating, ventilation and air conditioning
(HVAC) systems, dehumidifying, and air cleaning
products.

M-308

Trans Bay Steel   HQ
   2601 Giant Rd
   Richmond CA 94806
P: 510-719-4613   F: 510-525-8027   PRC:80
www.transbaysteel.com

William Kavicky, General Manager

Provider of structural steel construction services.
The company offers heavy bridge piling and mechanical fabrication services.

Trans-Cal Industries Inc   HQ
   16141 Cohasset St   [N]
   Van Nuys CA 91406
P: 818-787-1221   F: 818-787-8916   PRC:212
www.trans-cal.com
Email: support@trans-cal.com
Estab: 1971

John Ferrero, President

Manufacturer of pressure altitude reporting equipment for general and military aviation markers.

Transcriptic Inc   HQ
   3565 Haven Ave Ste 3
   Menlo Park CA 94025
P: 650-763-8432   PRC:34
www.transcriptic.com
Email: team@transcriptic.com
Estab: 2012

Max Hodak, Founder & President
Scott Dillingham, Contract Administrator

Specializes in scientific research and the company
also supports an array of vitro molecular biology
and cell biology.

Transend Corp   HQ
   225 Emerson St
   Palo Alto CA 94301
P: 650-324-5370   PRC:322
www.transend.com
Email: sales.info@transend.com
Estab: 1978

Fred Krefetz, President & CEO
Joshua Krefetz, VP of Business Development
Jason Krefetz, VP of Sales

Provider of email migration and conversion solutions that support email systems. The company
serves business, education, reselling, and other
sectors.

**Transfer Engineering & Manufacturing
Inc**   HQ
   47697 Westinghouse Dr Ste 100
   Fremont CA 94539
P: 510-651-3000   F: 510-651-3090   PRC:165
www.transferengineering.com
Email: info@transferengineering.com
Estab: 1999

Judy Ackeret, Manager

Manufacturer and marketer of loadlocks and
transfer systems. The company offers precision
magnetic manipulators and transporters, and
other products.

Transfer Flow Inc   HQ
   1444 Fortress St
   Chico CA 95973
P: 530-893-5209   F: 530-893-0204   PRC:159
www.transferflow.com
Estab: 1983

Bill Gaines, Senior Engineer & Chairman
Gaines Jeanne, CEO
Ben Winter, Director of Business Development
Warren Johnson, Advertising & Marketing Director
Robert Green, Director of Sales

Manufacturer of fuel tanks. The company offers
axillary, replacement, and tanks with built-in
toolboxes.

Transgenomic Inc   BR
   2032 Concourse Dr
   San Jose CA 95131
P: 408-432-3230   F: 408-894-0405   PRC:39
www.transgenomic.com
Email: info@transgenomic.com
Estab: 1997

Paul Kinnon, President & CEO
Katherine A. Richardson, VP

Provider of patient testing and biomarker identification services. The company specializes in high
performance products.

**Transitional Systems Manufacturing
Inc**   HQ
   PO Box 359
   Browns Valley CA 95918
P: 530-751-2610   F: 530-751-2512   PRC:166
www.transitionalsystems.com
Email: info@transitionalsystems.com
Estab: 1985

Sean Siebern, CEO

Provider of products to repair landscape sprinkler
systems. The company also focuses on installation needs.

Translarity   HQ
   46575 Fremont Blvd
   Fremont CA 94538
P: 510-371-7900   PRC:212
translarity.com
Email: sales@translarity.com
Estab: 2003

Dominik Schmidt, President
Mark Gardiner, COO
Michael Chrastecky, VP of Business Development
Christopher Lane, VP of Engineering
Garry Crossland, VP of Sales & Marketing

Specializes in wafer translation technology. The
company offers device design and testing solutions to the semiconductor industry.

Transline Technology Inc HQ

1106 S Technology Cir [N]
Anaheim CA 92805
P: 714-533-8300 F: 714-533-8791 PRC:211
www.translinetech.com
Email: info@translinetech.com
Emp: 11-50 Estab: 1996

Chris Savalia, VP
Larry Padmani, VP

Manufacturer of printed circuit boards.

Transvision International HQ

550 Maulhardt Ave [N]
Oxnard CA 93030
P: 805-981-8740 PRC:64
www.txvision.com
Email: kvaughan@txvision.com
Emp: 51-200 Estab: 1986

Kimithy Vaughan, Contact

Provider of satellite network facilities and management solution services.

TRAXPayroll HQ
740 Alfred Nobel Dr
Hercules CA 94547
P: 866-872-9123 PRC:323
www.traxpayroll.com
Estab: 1997

Darcy Peluso, Business Development Manager
Kevin Kitani, Sales Executive
Sonja Stuart, Tax Payroll Admin

Specializes in payroll management solutions. The company also offers wage garnishment, worker's compensation, and tax filing solutions.

Trayer Engineering Corp HQ
1569 Alvarado St
San Leandro CA 94577
P: 415-285-7770 F: 415-285-0883 PRC:165
trayer.com
Email: sales@trayer.com
Estab: 1962

John Trayer, President & CEO
Adam Donoghue, Western Region Sales Manager
Ray Lemos, Press Operator
Buck Sherwin, Electrician
Brian Miller, Welder

Manufacturer of electronic distribution switchgears. The company's services include design, maintenance, and installation.

TRC Companies Inc BR
505 Sansome St Ste 1600
San Francisco CA 94111
P: 415-434-2600 F: 415-434-2321 PRC:68
trcsolutions.com
Estab: 1960

Christopher P. Vincze, CEO & Chairman
Ed Wiegele, President of Oil & Gas Sector
Jason S. Greenlaw, CFO
Laura Ramey, CPO
Marc Faecher, Chief Risk Officer

Provider of scientific and engineering software services. The company offers hydropower licensing, power delivery, and telecommunications engineering services.

Treasure Data Inc HQ
2565 Leghorn St
Mountain View CA 94043
P: 866-899-5386 PRC:315
www.treasuredata.com
Estab: 2011

Hiro Yoshikawa, Founder

Empower enterprises by unifying data from multiple sources such as online, offline, IoT and device-generated data.

Trellis Bioscience LLC HQ
702 Marshall St Ste 614
Redwood City CA 94063
P: 650-838-1400 PRC:34
www.trellisbio.com
Estab: 1998

Stote Ellsworth, COO & CTO & Co-Founder
Larry Kauvar, CSO-Co-Founder
Stefan Ryser, President & CEO
Tony Leighton, CMO
Mikhail Gishizky, VP of Research & Development

Developer of human antibody therapeutics as treatment for infectious disease and oncology indications.

Trench & Traffic Supply Inc HQ
2175 Acoma St
Sacramento CA 95819
P: 916-920-3304 F: 916-920-3305 PRC:227
www.trenchandtrafflc.com
Estab: 2003

John Harrah, President

Provider of traffic control equipment for rent and sale. The company offers equipment for traffic control, shoring, and pipe testing.

Trevi Systems HQ
1415 N McDowell Blvd
Petaluma CA 94954
P: 707-792-2681 F: 707-792-2684 PRC:306
www.trevisystems.com
Email: info@trevisystems.com
Estab: 2010

John Webley, CEO
Gary Carmignani, Chief Science Officer
Michael Greene, Director of Manufacturing
Victor Ivashin, Director of Engineering
Dave Zimkowski, Controller

Provider of desalination process services. The company focuses on osmosis system using proprietary membrane and draw solution using thermal heat.

TRI MAP International Inc HQ
119 Val Dervin Pkwy Ste 5
Stockton CA 95206
P: 209-234-0100 PRC:92
www.trimapintl.com
Email: info@trimapintl.com

Erika Jensen, Manager of Financial Services

Manufacturer of industrial grade rack mounts and desktop computers. The company is engaged in engineering and fabrication services.

Tri Tool Inc HQ
3041 Sunrise Blvd
Rancho Cordova CA 95742
P: 916-288-6100 F: 916-288-6160 PRC:80
tritool.com
Email: customer.service@tritool.com
Estab: 1972

George J. Wernette, Chairman of The Board
Christopher Belle, CEO
Chris Soriano, CFO
Scott Stanton, VP of Welding & Technical Director
Todd Fox, Senior Director of Global Sales & VP of Global Sales

Manufacturer of precision machine tools. The company also deals with products rentals, construction, and maintenance services.

Trianni Inc HQ
821 Irving St
San Francisco CA 94122
P: 866-374-9314 PRC:28
trianni.com
Email: info@trianni.com
Estab: 2010

Gloria Esposito, CTO
Maria Wabl, CFO
David Meininger, Chief Business Officer

Developer of humanized monoclonal antibody platform. The company offers services to pharmaceutical and biotechnology companies.

Tric Tools Inc HQ
1350 S Loop Rd Ste 104
Alameda CA 94502
P: 510-640-8933 F: 510-217-9493 PRC:142
www.trictools.com
Email: sales@trictools.com
Estab: 1996

Ward Carter, President & CEO
David Huff, National Sales Director
Steven Parfery, Director of Service Operations
Laura Servin, Assistant Office Manager

Provider of pipe-bursting systems. The company also offers installation, maintenance, and cleaning services for home-sewer systems.

Tricida Inc HQ
7000 Shoreline Ct Ste 201
S San Francisco CA 94080
P: 415-429-7800 PRC:34
www.tricida.com
Email: info@tricida.com
Estab: 2013

Claire Lockey, Chief Development Officer & SVP
David Skidmore, Director of Quality Assurance
Keerthini Manda, Scientist
Matthew Kade, Senior Scientist
Randi K. Gbur, Senior Scientist

Focuses on the discovery and clinical development of therapeutics to address renal, metabolic and cardiovascular diseases.

Tricontinent Scientific Inc BR
12740 Earhart Ave
Auburn CA 95602
P: 530-273-8888 F: 530-273-2586   PRC:186
www.gardnerdenver.com
Email: customerservice@tricontinent.com
Estab: 1975

Randy Dismukes, COO
Mik Bajka, Director of Business Development &
OEM Liquid Handling Solutions
John McDaniel, Materials Manager

Provider of liquid-handling products and instrument components for the medical diagnostics and biotechnology industries.

Tridecs Corp HQ
3513 Arden Rd
Hayward CA 94545-3907
P: 510-785-2620 F: 510-785-3146   PRC:80
www.tridecs.com
Email: sales@tridecs.com
Estab: 1969

Frank Schenkhuizen, President & CEO
Branden Schenkhuizen, Operations Manager
John Homa, Quality Control Manager
Rasheed Alhark, Accounting Analyst
Steve Koski, Materials Planner & Inspector

Manufacturer of machined metal and plastic parts. The company offers prototyping, product machining, engineering, and design and drafting services.

Trimble Inc HQ
935 Stewart Dr
Sunnyvale CA 94085
P: 408-481-8000   PRC:17
www.trimble.com
Email: mrmsales@trimble.com
Estab: 1978
Sales: Over $3B

Steven W. Berglund, President & CEO
Michael E. Scarpa, SVP & Chief Human Resource Officer
Rajat Bahri, CFO
Thomas S. Fansler, SVP & CTO
James A. Kirkland, SVP & General Counsel

Developer of positioning solutions for the agriculture, construction, mining, and surveying industries.

Trina Solar US Inc RH
100 Century Ctr Ste 501
San Jose CA 95112
P: 800-696-7114   PRC:135
www.trinasolar.com
Email: usa@trinasolar.com
Estab: 1997

Jim Day, Director of Sales & Marketing
Roy Shaw, Sales Manager
Chuck Rames, Inside Sales Leader
Mindy Hua, Staff Accountant

Manufacturer of mono and multicrystalline photovoltaic (PV) modules. The company serves residential, commercial, and utility purposes.

M-310

Trinapco Inc HQ
1101 57th Ave
Oakland CA 94621
P: 510-535-1082 F: 928-752-6271   PRC:51
www.trinapco.com
Email: sales@trinapco.com

Martin Johnson, President

Manufacturer of organic fine chemicals specializing in 1,8-naphthyridine compounds. The company offers custom synthesis services.

Trinity Broadcasting Network HQ
2442 Michelle Dr   [N]
Tustin CA 92780
P: 714-665-3619   PRC:63
www.tbn.org/publicfile/index.php?order=1&reverse=1
Email: comments@tbn.org
Emp: 501-1000

Jim Mittan, CFO
Larry Haley, Director of Broadcast Operations & Engineering
Emily Young, Station Manager
Juan Viola, Manager of Information Systems
Kristin Egan, Production Manager

Operator of a broadcasting network publishing religious content.

Trinity Consultants Inc BR
1901 Harrison St Ste 1590
Oakland CA 94612
P: 510-285-6351   PRC:138
www.trinityconsultants.com
Estab: 1974

Jay Hofmann, President & CEO
Dave Larsen, CFO
Chris Price, Director of Human Resources
Inaas Darrat, Director of Chemical Sector Services
Jason Schmitz, Director of Digital Solutions

Provider of environmental consulting services. The company engages in environmental outsourcing and litigation support services.

Trion Worlds Inc HQ
350 Marine Pkwy
Redwood City CA 94065
P: 650-273-9618   PRC:317
trionworlds.com
Estab: 2006

Deborah Davis, Community Coordinator & Marketing Coordinator
Len Williams, Lead Environment Artist

Publisher and developer of games. The company offers Defiance, RIFT, Archeage, and End of Nations games.

Triple O Systems Inc HQ
1550 Dell Ave Unit E
Campbell CA 95008
P: 408-378-3002 F: 408-378-7155   PRC:144
tripleo.com
Email: sales@tripleo.com
Estab: 1990

Larry Ramsauer, Founder

Designer and manufacturer of water treatment systems. The company also offers reverse osmosis product water tanks and water store water tanks.

Triple Ring Technologies Inc HQ
39655 Eureka Dr
Newark CA 94560-4806
P: 510-592-3000   PRC:189
www.tripleringtech.com
Email: info@tripleringtech.com
Estab: 2005

Phil Devlin, Chief Business Officer & SVP
Christina Goehrig, Director of Strategic Marketing

Manufacturer of in vitro diagnostics and life science tools. The company offer services to the medical devices, imaging, and industrial sectors.

TriReme Medical LLC RH
7060 Koll Center Pkwy Ste 300
Pleasanton CA 94566
P: 925-931-1300 F: 925-931-1361   PRC:196
qtvascular.com
Email: careers@qtvascular.com
Estab: 2005

Randal H. Farwell, CFO
Maria Pizarro, EVP & VP of Research & Development
Shiva Ardakani, VP
Tim Rooney, District Sales Manager

Developer of differentiated therapeutic solutions. The company manufactures and distributes the chocolate and glider families of angioplasty balloons.

Trivad Inc HQ
1350 Bayshore Hwy Ste 450
Burlingame CA 94010
P: 650-286-1086 F: 650-286-1686   PRC:64
www.trivad.com
Email: info@trivad.com

Jenna Lim, CEO
Hans Lim, Solutions VP
Zac Zuckerman, Senior Sales Consultant
Fil Gonzalez, Account Executive
Richard Yasumoto, Senior Account Executive

Developer of IT solutions. The company also offers training, implementation, and infrastructure assessment services.

Trivec-Avant Corp HQ
17831 Jamestown Ln   [N]
Huntington Beach CA 92647
P: 714-841-4976   PRC:68
www.trivec.com
Email: info@trivec.com
Emp: 51-200   Estab: 2011

Al Muesse, President
Mike Berberet, VP of Sales & Marketing
Darwyn Wolff, Program Manager
John Fenick, Operations Manager & Engineering Manager
Hugo Dimas, Production Lead

Designer and manufacturer of advanced antenna systems for U.S. and foreign militaries as well as commercial integrators and manufacturers.

Trofholz Technologies Inc   HQ
250 Technology Way
Rocklin CA 95765
P: 916-577-1903   F: 916-577-1904   PRC:326
www.trofholz.com
Email: info@trofholz.com
Estab: 2001

Yvonne Pire, CEO & Owner
Brenna Pedone, VP of Support
David Raymond, VP
Jesse Friedman, VP of Business Development
Cherise Raymond, Recruiter & Human Resource
Manager

Developer of IT information and security systems.
The company also specializes in communication
solutions.

Tronex Technology Inc   HQ
2860 Cordelia Rd Ste 230
Fairfield CA 94534
P: 909-627-2453   PRC:157
tronex.descoindustries.com
Email: service@tronextools.com
Estab: 1982

Arne Salvesen, President

Manufacturer of precision cutting tools and pliers.
The company offers hand cutters, hard wire cutters, and flat nose pliers.

Tru Technical Partners Inc   HQ
286 E Hamilton Ave Ste D
Campbell CA 95008
P: 408-559-2800   F: 408-559-2813   PRC:63
trutechnical.com
Email: sales@trutechnical.com

Truman R. Roe, CEO

Provider of information technology services on a
contract basis. The company's services include
managed desktops, workstation, anti-virus, and
others.

TruAdvantage   HQ
4950 Hamilton Ave Ste 212   [N]
San Jose CA 95130
P: 408-680-8389   PRC:104
www.truadvantage.com
Emp: 11-50   Estab: 2010

Iman Oskoorouchi, Co-Founder
Kayvan Yazdi, Co-Founder

Provider of support services ranging from consultation to design, support and training for small
and medium-sized companies and healthcare
practices. Services include managed IT services,
data backup and recovery, cloud services, VoIP
services, and data and network security.

True Circuits Inc   HQ
4300 El Camino Real Ste 200
Los Altos CA 94022
P: 650-949-3400   F: 650-949-3434   PRC:212
www.truecircuits.com
Email: sales@truecircuits.com
Estab: 1998

John Maneatis, President
Stephen Maneatis, CEO
Brian Gardner, VP of Business Development
Aldo Bottelli, Principal Design Engineer & Director
of Engineering

Developer and marketer of phase-locked loops,
delay-locked loops, and mixed-signal designs for
integrated circuits.

Trufocus Corp   HQ
468 Westridge Dr
Watsonville CA 95076
P: 831-761-9981   F: 831-761-9984   PRC:198
www.trufocus.com
Email: trufocus@trufocus.com
Estab: 1987

Goerge Howard, CEO
James Price, Mechanical Designer

Supplier of x-ray products. The company's products are used in industrial, medical, aerospace,
and analytical application.

Tschida Engineering Inc   HQ
1812 Yajome St
Napa CA 94559
P: 707-224-4482   F: 707-224-2406   PRC:80
tschidaeng.com
Email: info@tschidaeng.com
Estab: 1977

Bruce Tschida, Owner & Founder

Provider of CNC turning and milling, machining,
and fabrication services. The company serves
semiconductor, defense, medical, and environmental sectors.

TSMC North America   HQ
2851 Junction Ave
San Jose CA 95134
P: 408-382-8000   F: 408-382-8008   PRC:126
www.tsmc.com
Email: west@tsmc.com
Estab: 1987

David Keller, President & CEO
Roger Luo, President of TSMC Nanjing
Mark Liu, Chairman
Wendell Huang, CFO & VP of Finance
Rick Cassidy, SVP & Corporate Strategy Office

Manufacturer of products for the computer, communications, and consumer electronics market
segments.

TSS Consultants   HQ
5430 Carlson Dr Ste 100
Sacramento CA 95819-1720
P: 916-600-4174   PRC:142
tssconsultants.com
Estab: 1986

Tad Mason, CEO
Frederick Tornatore, CTO
Andrea L. Stephenson, Energy & Solid Waste
Consultant
David Augustine, Senior Environmental Consul-
tant
Steven J. Daus, Senior Planning & Regulatory
Compliance Consultant

Provider of energy resources management, environmental permitting, and financial assessment
services.

TTI Inc   BR
6611 Folsom Auburn Rd
Folsom CA 95630-2100
P: 916-987-4600   F: 916-987-4601   PRC:323
www.ttiinc.com
Email: information@ttiinc.com

Don Akery, President
Mike Morton, COO
Chris Goodman, CFO
Michael Kennedy, VP of Global Accounts
Mike Lynch, Product Manager

Distributor of passive, connector, electromechanical, and discrete components for the industrial,
military, and aerospace sectors.

TTI Medical   HQ
220 Porter Dr Ste 120
San Ramon CA 94583
P: 925-553-7828   F: 925-718-8225   PRC:195
www.ttimedical.com
Email: info@ttimedical.com
Estab: 1984

Allen Howes, Owner
Ross Howes, Director of Sales & Operations
Jason Botting, General Manager
Andrea Wong, Finance Manager
Karole Schatzman, Contact

Designer and marketer of surgical instruments
and medical devices. The company serves hospitals and the healthcare sector.

TTM Technologies Inc   BR
407 Mathew St
Santa Clara CA 95050
P: 408-486-3100   PRC:211
www.ttmtech.com

Douglas L. Soder, EVP & President & Commercial
Sector
Phil Titterton, EVP & President of Aerospace &
Defense & Specialty Business Unit
Thomas T. Edman, CEO
Todd B. Schull, EVP & CFO
Canice T.K. Chung, EVP of Business Develop-
ment & Asia Pacific

Manufacturer of printed circuit boards and backplane assemblies. The company's services include
design, installation, and delivery.

Turbo-Doc Medical Record Systems Inc HQ

6480 Pentz Rd Ste A
Paradise CA 95969
P: 530-877-8650 F: 530-877-8621 PRC:322
turbodoc.net
Email: turbodoc@turbodoc.com
Estab: 2007

Lyle B. Hunt, Owner

Provider of electronic medical record systems. The company offers walkout statements, drug information handouts, and medication rewrites.

Turley & Associates Mechanical Engineering Group Inc HQ

2431 Capitol Ave
Sacramento CA 95816
P: 916-325-1065 PRC:304
turleymech.com
Email: office@turleymech.com
Estab: 1975

Brian J. Provencal, President
John W. Thompson, Principal

Provider of engineering services to health care, education, industrial, public, and retail facilities.

Turner Designs Inc HQ

1995 N First St
San Jose CA 95112-4220
P: 408-749-0994 PRC:18
www.turnerdesigns.com
Email: sales@turnerdesigns.com
Estab: 1972

Jim Crawford, Owner
Pam Mayerfeld, VP of Marketing & Sales
Jake Vandenberg, VP of Finance
Karin Reed, Purchasing Manager

Provider of industrial fluorometers and rhodamine dyes. The company's applications include oil spill response and environmental monitoring.

Tusker Medical Inc HQ

155 Jefferson Dr Ste 200
Menlo Park CA 94025
P: 650-223-6900 PRC:189
www.tuskermed.com
Email: info@tuskermed.com
Estab: 2016

Amir Abolfathi, CEO
Eric Goldfarb, VP of Research & Development Operations
Sanaz Mirkhani, Director of Quality
Elmer Yee, Senior Manufacturing Engineer
Ari Kermani, R&D Engineer

Developer of pediatric-focused technologies. The company specializes in the placement of tubes without general anesthetics.

TUV Rheinland Of North America Inc DH

1279 Quarry Ln Ste A
Pleasanton CA 94566
P: 925-249-9123 F: 925-249-9124 PRC:211
www.tuv.com
Email: info@tuv.com
Estab: 1872

Balazs Bozsik, Technical Manager of Medical Audit
Sean Warnock, Data Center operations Manager
Nikolaus Wahl, Technical Program Manager
Keith Sinclair, Sales Executive of Medical Division

Provider of product testing, market access, specialty services, and management systems certification services.

TUV SUD America Inc BR

47460 Fremont Blvd
Fremont CA 94538
P: 510-257-7823 PRC:304
www.tuvsud.com
Email: info-us@tuvsud.com

Nancy Knap, Lead Office Administrator
Tiffany Long, Sales Account Executive
Johnny Wilson, Radiographer Technician

Provider of services for testing, certification, and engineering audits. The company is focused on medical devices and e-mobility.

TVU Networks Corp HQ

857 Maude Ave
Mountain View CA 94043
P: 650-969-6732 F: 650-969-6747 PRC:324
www.tvunetworks.com
Email: info@tvunetworks.com
Estab: 2005

Paul Shen, CEO
Chris Bell, VP of Technical Operations
Kap Shin, EVP of Business Development
Matthew McEwen, VP of Product Management
Dan Lofgren, SVP of Business Operations

Provider of wireless electronic news gathering services. The company offers TV broadcast, web streaming, and law enforcement services.

Twilio Inc HQ

375 Beale St Ste 300
San Francisco CA 94105
P: 415-390-2337 PRC:325
twilio.com
Email: sales@twilio.com
Estab: 2008
Sales: $1B to $3B

Jeff Lawson, CEO & Founder & Chairman
Lee Kirkpatrick, CFO
Lynda Smith, CMO
Ron Huddleston, Chief Partner Officer
Erin Reilly, Chief Social Impact Officer & General Manager of Social Impact Business

Provider of infrastructure APIs for businesses to build scalable, reliable voice, and text messaging apps.

Twist Bioscience HQ

681 Gateway Blvd
S San Francisco CA 94080
P: 800-719-0671 PRC:34
www.twistbioscience.com
Estab: 2013
Sales: $30M to $100M

Emily Leproust, CEO
Bill Peck, CTO
Bill Banyai, COO
Jim Thorburn, CFO
Mark Daniels, CLO & Chief Ethics & Compliance Officer & SVP & Secretary

Specializes in DNA synthesis programs. The company is engaged in genome editing and drug discovery services.

twoXAR Inc HQ

883 N Shoreline Blvd Ste A100
Mountain View CA 94043
P: 650-382-2605 PRC:25
www.twoxar.com
Estab: 2014

Andrew A. Radin, CEO & Founder
Brian Moriarty, CFO
Mark Eller, SVP of Research & Development
Allen Poirson, SVP of Biopharmaceutical Business Development

Developer of drug delivery platform. The company is involved in biological data extraction, automated model generation, and feature identification.

TY Lin International Group HQ

345 California St Ste 2300
San Francisco CA 94104
P: 415-291-3700 F: 415-433-0807 PRC:304
www.tylin.com
Email: tylininfo@tylin.com
Estab: 1954

Alvaro J. Piedrahita, Chairman of The Board
Tony Peterson, President
John Young, CIO
Bill Harnagel, CFO
David Goodyear, SVP & Chief Bridge Engineer of Americas

Provider of engineering services such as construction management, inspection, design and planning, and surveying.

Tyan Computer Corp DH

3288 Laurelview Ct
Fremont CA 94538
P: 510-651-8868 F: 510-651-7688 PRC:93
www.tyan.com
Estab: 1989

George Koivun, VP of Sales & Business Development
Jo Chang, Director of Sales

Designer and manufacturer of server/workstation platforms. The company's products are sold to OEMs, VARs, system integrators, and resellers.

Tymphany HK Ltd   HQ
1 Thorndale Dr Ste 200
San Rafael CA 94903
P: 415-887-9538   PRC:60
www.tymphany.com
Estab: 2004

Andrew Dielman, Director of Sales
Chris von Hellermann, Technology Research &
Implementation & Product Roadmap Development
& Senior Director of Technology M
Phil McPhee, Senior Director of Global Sales &
Marketing
Ed Boyd, Director

Manufacturer of acoustic products. The company's
products include consumers and Pro audio, OEM
transducers, and peerless catalogs.

UC Components Inc   HQ
18700 Adams Ct
Morgan Hill CA 95037
P: 408-782-1929   F: 408-782-7995   PRC:80
www.uccomponents.com
Email: sales@uccomponents.com
Estab: 1974

Rick Anderson, Sales Manager
John Leetch, Purchasing & Sales Manager

Manufacturer of RediVac coated and electro-pol-
ished vented screws. The company serves high
vacuum applications.

UHV Sputtering Inc   HQ
275 Digital Dr
Morgan Hill CA 95037
P: 408-779-2826   F: 408-776-3407   PRC:47
www.uhvsputtering.com
Email: info@uhvsputtering.com
Estab: 1990

John Cavanaugh, Quality Manager

Manufacturer of semiconductor devices and
vacuum equipment. The company is involved in
sputtering and bonding services.

Ulbrich Stainless Steels and Special
Metals Inc   BR
770 E Shaw Ave Ste 100
Fresno CA 93710
P: 559-456-2310   F: 559-456-2321   PRC:298
www.ulbrich.com
Email: info@ulbrich.com
Estab: 1924

Chris Ulbrich, CEO

The company manufactures and sells specialty
strip in stainless steel, and serves the industrial
sector.

Ultimate Index Inc   HQ
12122 Dry Creek Rd Ste 104
Auburn CA 95602
P: 530-878-0573   F: 530-878-0613   PRC:47
ultimateindexinc.com
Email: sales@ultimateindexinc.com
Estab: 2003

Gordon King, CEO

Manufacturer of E-beam deposition cones. The
company specializes in prepared coating materials for the precision thin film coating industry.

Ultra Clean Technology   HQ
26462 Corporate Ave
Hayward CA 94545
P: 510-576-4400   PRC:80
www.uct.com
Email: sales@uct.com
Estab: 1991
Sales: $1B to $3B

Bill Bentinck, President of Semiconductor Ser-
vices Business
Jim Scholhamer, CEO
Sheri Brumm Savage, CFO
David Speirs, VP of Operations
Joan Sterling, SVP of Human Resources

Manufacturer of gas panel delivery systems. The
company primarily caters to the semiconductor
industry.

Ultra Lift Corp   HQ
475 Stockton Ave Ste E
San Jose CA 95126
P: 408-287-9400   F: 408-297-1199   PRC:179
www.ultralift.com
Email: info@ultralift.com

Dabb George, President

Manufacturer of hand trucks. The company specializes in the fabrication of trucks that combine
hand-power and electric drives.

Ultra T Equipment Company Inc   HQ
41980 Christy St
Fremont CA 94538
P: 510-440-3909   F: 510-440-3920   PRC:86
www.ultrat.com
Email: sales@ultrat.com
Estab: 1991

Jack Williams, Electrical Engineer

Manufacturer of spin coaters, developer stations,
reionizers, and microelectronics cleaning systems.

Ultra-Flex Inc   HQ
169 Stanford Ave Ste 4
Half Moon Bay CA 94019
P: 650-728-6060   F: 650-728-6063   PRC:202
www.ultraflexinc.com
Estab: 1982

Rocky Raynor, Principal

Designer of component manufacturing solutions.
The company offers springs, fasteners, castings,
machined parts, and hardware items.

Ultra-X Inc   HQ
2075 De La Cruz Blvd Ste 101
Santa Clara CA 95050
P: 408-261-7090   F: 408-261-7077   PRC:68
www.uxd.com
Email: info@uxd.com
Estab: 1987

James Todd, International Sales Executive
Cory Grand, Sales Representative

Provider of personal computer diagnostic solutions for developers, manufacturers, system engineers, integrators, and computer professionals.

Ultracor Inc   HQ
2763 Boeing Way
Stockton CA 95206
P: 209-983-3744   PRC:5
www.ultracorinc.com
Estab: 1995

Asha Kai, CEO & Founder
Stan Wright, President
Walton Smith, Director of Operations
Sovanda Sing, Operations Manager
Thao Huynh, Quality Manager

Manufacturer of engineered specialty honeycomb
and related supplies. The company also deals with
custom designs.

Ultragenyx Pharmaceutical Inc   HQ
60 Leveroni Ct
Novato CA 94949
P: 415-483-8800   F: 415-483-8810   PRC:249
www.ultragenyx.com
Email: info@ultragenyx.com
Emp: 610 Estab: 2010
Sales: $100M to $300M

Emil D. Kakkis, CEO & President
Dennis Huang, CTO & EVP
John Pinion, Chief Quality Operations Officer &
EVP of Translational Sciences
Thomas Kassberg, Chief Business Officer & EVP
Tom Kassberg, Chief Business Officer

Developer of products for the treatment of rare
and ultra-rare diseases. The company is engaged
in commercialization of products.

Ultrasolar Technology Inc   HQ
1025 Comstock St
Santa Clara CA 95054
P: 408-499-6227   PRC:135
www.ultrasolartech.com
Email: peter@ultrasolartech.com

Santosh Kumar, CEO & CTO

Manufacturer of solar panel devices. The company
specializes in residential, commercial, and utility
solar arrays.

Ultrasound Laboratories Inc   HQ
305 South Dr Ste 7
Mountain View CA 94040
P: 408-829-6486   F: 408-890-4770   PRC:188
smarthealthscreening.com
Email: info@smarthealthscreening.com

Joseph Matthews, Technical Director
Nahid Kiani, Laboratory Technician

Provider of non-invasive ultrasound imaging
services. The company focuses on services such
as health screening, carotid artery, and kidney
screening.

Ultraview Corp   BR
808 Gilman St
Berkeley CA 94710
P: 925-253-2960   PRC:92
www.ultraviewcorp.com
Email: info@ultraviewcorp.com
Estab: 1987

Barbara Sacks, VP of Operations

Provider of data acquisition solutions, bus extenders, synthesizers, and direct digital synthesizers.

Uni-Fab Industries Inc HQ
1461 N Milpitas Blvd
Milpitas CA 95035
P: 408-945-9733   F: 408-945-1878   PRC:80
www.uni-fab.com

Bud Rogers, President
Don Cook, Manager of Account
Edwin Woo, Engineering Manager

Provider of precision sheet metal fabrication
services. The company's equipment services
include laser, punching and cutting, machining,
and sawing.

Uni-Flex Circuits Inc HQ
1782 Angela St
San Jose CA 95125
P: 408-998-5500   PRC:211
www.uniflexcircuits.com

Arnold Bulosan, Contact

Manufacturer of flexible circuits. The company
specializes in the design and fabrication of consumer electronic connectors.

Unico Mechanical Corp HQ
1209 Polk St
Benicia CA 94510
P: 707-745-9970   F: 707-745-9973   PRC:80
www.unicomechanical.com
Email: info@unicomechanical.com

Randall Potter, President & CEO
Amy Sterry, CFO
Shawn McNeil, VP
Ernie Trejo, Safety Manager
Randall Flulk, Manufacturing Supervisor

Provider of replacement machine parts. The company's services include welding, repairs, onsite
machining, welding, and millwright.

Uniform Industrial Corp DH
2901 Bayview Dr
Fremont CA 94538
P: 510-438-6799   F: 510-438-6790   PRC:153
www.uicworld.com
Email: info@uicusa.com
Estab: 2007

Edwin Young, Director of Product Management
Robin Tang, Director of Engineering
Carlos Sedano, Territory Manager Latin America
Cleo Chiang, Purchasing Manager
Kevin Chang, Software Engineering Manager

Provider of systems and components for banking
and retail solutions. The company also offers technology solutions and customer services.

Unigen Corp HQ
39730 Eureka Dr
Newark CA 94560
P: 510-896-1818   F: 510-623-1242   PRC:116
www.unigen.com
Email: sales@unigen.com
Estab: 1991

Sacha S. Heng, EVP
Simon Ip, VP of Finance
Gary Crafts, Senior Director & Global Supply
Chain Operations
Demitry Pinski, Director & Human Resources &
Sr. HR Business Partner
Vinay Shinde, Plant Operation Director

Manufacturer and designer of custom enterprise-grade flash storage and DRAM and AR-
MOUR product applications serving the telecommunications industry.

Unimicro Technologies Inc HQ
440 Boulder Coulte 100-C
Pleasanton CA 94566
P: 925-846-8638   F: 925-401-9548   PRC:13
unimicrotech.com
Email: info@unimicrotech.com
Estab: 1996

Chao Yan, President

Provider of chemical and biological separation
and analysis with micro separation technology
especially capillary electrochromatography.

Uniq Vision Inc HQ
2924 Scott Blvd
Santa Clara CA 95054
P: 408-330-0818   F: 408-330-0886   PRC:168
www.uniqvision.com
Email: info@uniqvision.com

Rex Siu, VP of Sales

Designer and manufacturer of high resolution
CCD cameras for medical, scientific, industrial,
and military applications.

Uniquify Inc HQ
2030 Fortune Dr Ste 200
San Jose CA 95131
P: 408-235-8810   PRC:126
www.uniquify.com
Email: sales@uniquify.com
Estab: 2005

Josh Lee, CEO & President
Sam Kim, COO
Graham Bell, VP of Marketing
J.H. Chen, VP of ASIC Engineering
Kevin Lau, VP of Engineering

Developer and manufacturer of SoC displays and
other semi-conductor products. The company
offers technical support services.

Unisec Inc HQ
2555 Nicholson St   [N]
San Leandro CA 94577
P: 510-352-6707   PRC:68
www.ultrabarrier.com
Email: info@ultrabarrier.com
Estab: 1971

Albert Hermans, Founder

Designer and manufacturer of security equipment.

Unisoft Corp HQ
10 Rollins Rd Ste 118
Millbrae CA 94030-3128
P: 650-259-1290   F: 650-259-1299   PRC:325
unisoft.com
Email: info@unisoft.com
Estab: 1981

Audrey Ruelas, Director
Jose Rodriguez, Director
Bern Ruelas, Project Manager

Provider of broadcast, development, and testing
tools specific to interactive TV standards. The
company focuses on US cable and broadcast
industries.

Unitech Tool & Machine Inc HQ
3025 Stender Way
Santa Clara CA 95054
P: 408-566-0333   PRC:80
unitechtool.com
Email: sales@unitechtool.com

Jeanne Lak, Owner & CFO
Ramin Lak, Owner & President

Manufacturer of custom finished parts, tooling,
and fixtures. The company is specialized in
milling and lathe fabrication, mechanical design
consulting.

United Manufacturing Assembly Inc HQ
44169 Fremont Blvd   [N]
Fremont CA 94538
P: 510-490-4680   F: 510-490-4380   PRC:306
www.umai.com
Estab: 1987

Ariene Chou, Contact

Provider of electronic manufacturing services to
OEMs nationwide.

United Mechanical Inc HQ
33353 Lewis Ave
Union City CA 94587
P: 510-537-4744   F: 510-537-9564   PRC:80
www.umec.net
Estab: 1982

Patty Middleton, Safety Director
Samantha Suriano, Project Manager
Dirk Durham, Senior Account Manager
Mark Swan, Senior Account Manager
Linda Congdon, Assistant Project Manager

Provider of precision sheet metal fabrication
services for semiconductor, disk drive, medical,
pharmaceutical, and aerospace equipment.

United Medical Instruments Inc HQ
832 Jury Ct
San Jose CA 95112
P: 408-278-9300   F: 408-278-9797   PRC:189
www.umiultrasound.com
Email: info@umiultrasound.com
Estab: 1996

Mansoor Ghanavati, CEO & President
Paul Werp, VP of Business Development & Gen-
eral Manager
Neil Walendy, National Director of Sales
Steven Kelley, Parts Sales Manager

Provider of ultrasound equipment. The company
focuses on pain management, breast imaging,
and pathology.

United Pro-Fab Manufacturing Inc   HQ
45300 Industrial Pl Unit 5
Fremont CA 94538
P: 510-651-5570   F: 510-651-5761   PRC:80
www.pfmfg.com
Email: quotations@pfmfg.com
Estab: 1984

Rajesh Gupta, President

Provider of machining and fabrication services. The company offers services for the aircraft, semiconductors, telecommunications, and biotechnology sectors.

United Security Products Inc   HQ
13250 Gregg St Ste B   [N]
Poway CA 92064
P: 858-413-0149   F: 858-413-0124   PRC:68
www.unitedsecurity.com
Email: sales@unitedsecurity.com
Emp: 11-50   Estab: 1971

Ted Greene, CEO
Marry Farrell, CFO
Alice Greene, Secretary

Manufacturer of security alarm products.

United Sheetmetal Inc   BR
44153 S Grimmer Blvd
Fremont CA 94538
P: 510-257-1858   F: 510-257-1850   PRC:88
www.unitedsheetmetal.com
Estab: 1964

Chay Mo, VP of Business Development
Paul Tsang, Business Development Manager
Jin Hu, Sales Engineer

Manufacturer of precision metal products. The company specializes in tooling, die casting, plastic injection, and sheet metal fabrication services.

United Sign Systems   HQ
5201 Pentecost Dr   [N]
Modesto CA 95356
P: 209-543-1320   F: 209-543-1326   PRC:316
www.unitedsign.net
Emp: 11-50   Estab: 1995

Brian Campbell, Contact
Darryl Johnson, Contact
Mike Noordewier, Contact

Provider of commercial sign services.

United States Thermoelectric Consortium   HQ
13267 Contractors Dr
Chico CA 95973
P: 530-345-8000   F: 678-821-4337   PRC:233
www.ustechcon.com
Estab: 1997

James Kerner, President & CEO

Manufacturer of thermal management and control systems. The company's offerings also include controllers and air and liquid cooling systems.

United Western Industries Inc   HQ
3515 N Hazel Ave   [N]
Fresno CA 93722
P: 559-226-7236   F: 559-226-3557   PRC:80
www.unitedwesternindustries.com
Emp: 1-10   Estab: 1971

Gale Pirtle, President
Rudy Neufeld, VP
Bruce Ketch, General Manager
Angela Pena, Office Manager

Provider of sheet metal fabrication, prototypes, tool and die, precision machining, CNC machining, welding, stamping, laser cutting and grinding.

Unitedlayer LLC   HQ
200 Paul Ave Ste 110
San Francisco CA 94124
P: 415-349-2100   F: 415-520-5700   PRC:67
unitedlayer.com
Email: sales@unitedlayer.com
Estab: 2001

Abhijit Phanse, CEO
Aaron Hughes, Chief Network Architect
Edward Buck, VP of Services & Support
Anas Alousi, Global Head of Operations

Provider of cloud hosting solutions. The company offers server clusters and routers, disaster recovery, infrastructure, and colocation services.

Unitek Inc   HQ
41350 Christy St
Fremont CA 94538
P: 510-623-8544   F: 510-623-8970   PRC:209
unitekinc.com
Estab: 1989

Paul Hyun, President
Joseph McCutchen, Business Development Manager
Ricardo Almada, Manager of Production
Dave Shin, Program Manager
Anyi Emelogu, Engineering Specialist

Provider of electronic manufacturing services. The company provides PCB assembly, material management, testing, and system integration services.

Universal Audio Inc   HQ
4585 Scotts Valley Dr
Scotts Valley CA 95066
P: 831-440-1176   PRC:148
www.uaudio.com
Email: info@uaudio.com
Estab: 1958

Bill Putnam, Owner
Kerwin Yuen, VP of Operations
Erik Hanson, Director of Marketing
Dan Freeman, Director of Hardware Engineering
Theo Lovejoy, Technical Publications Manager

Manufacturer of analog recording equipment. The company's products include audio interfaces, channel strips, plug-ins, and compressors.

Universal Light Source Inc   HQ
1553 Folsom St
San Francisco CA 94103
P: 415-864-2880   F: 415-864-3207   PRC:243
ulsi.net
Email: sales@ulsi.net
Estab: 1975

Douglas Ascher, CEO
Bryan Ascher, Technical Sales Manager

Provider of technical lighting applications. The company specializes in flash lamps and strobes, glass and window manufacturing, and PCBs.

Untangle   HQ
25 Metro Dr Ste 210
San Jose CA 95110
P: 408-598-4299   PRC:319
www.untangle.com
Email: info@untangle.com
Estab: 2003

Dirk Morris, Co-Founder
Emma Dutton, CTPO & Co-Founder
Angela McKinney, Co-Founder
Victoria Roberts, Owner
John Rizzo, President & COO

Designer and developer of network management software. The company specializes in firewall and Internet management application.

UpGuard Inc   HQ
723 N Shoreline Blvd
Mountain View CA 94043
P: 888-882-3223   PRC:325
upguard.com
Email: support@upguard.com
Estab: 2012

Alan Sharp-Paul, Founder & CEO
Hamish Hawthorn, COO
Spiro Spiroski, Chief Customer Officer
Jackie Ariston, Chief of Staff
Jon Hendren, Director of Strategy

Provider of integrity monitoring, vulnerability analysis, vendor risk assessment, and configuration differencing solutions.

Upsolar America Inc   BR
268 Bush St Ste 2919
San Francisco CA 94104
P: 415-263-9920   PRC:135
upsolaramerica.com
Email: support@upsolar.com
Estab: 2009

Stephane Dufrenne, CTO & President
Sebastian Wykeham, Director of Investor Relations
Jessy Li, Office Manager

Developer and producer of solar photovoltaic modules. The company's services include installation and maintenance and offers packing solutions.

Upwork Global Inc HQ
2625 Augustine Dr Ste 601
Santa Clara CA 95054
P: 650-316-7500 PRC:325
www.upwork.com
Estab: 2015
Sales: $300M to $1 Billion

Stephane Kasriel, CEO
Brian Kinion, CFO
Brian Levey, Chief Business Affairs & Legal Officer
Elizabeth Tse, SVP of Operations
Eric Gilpin, SVP of Sales

Web based platform for remote work.

**US Hydrotech Environmental
Solutions** HQ
1007 W College Ave Ste 461
Santa Rosa CA 95401
P: 707-793-4800 F: 888-473-3650 PRC:142
ushydrotech.com
Email: info@ushydrotech.com
Estab: 2007

Edward J. Bertain, President

Provider of hydro tech environmental solutions.
The company offers wash pads, containments,
pressure washers, and solar thermal products.

US Night Vision Corp HQ
1420 E Roseville Pkwy Ste 140-321
Roseville CA 95661
P: 800-500-4020 F: 916-788-1113 PRC:176
usnightvision.com
Email: sales@usnightvision.com
Estab: 2001

John Barbieri, President
Chris Byrd, VP of Sales
Steve Gibbons, Tactical Product Specialist

Provider of night vision, thermal imaging, infrared
and laser products. The company serves law
enforcement agencies and US military.

US Union Tool BR
2962 Scott Blvd
Santa Clara CA 95054
P: 714-521-6242 F: 714-521-8642 PRC:157
www.usuniontool.com
Estab: 1981

Dale Knealing, Regional Sales Manager
John McCandlish, Regional Manager

Designer and manufacturer of micro cutting
tools for the printed circuit industry. The company engages in mold and dies and medical and
aerospace parts.

USAPEX HQ
933-G La Mesa Ter
Sunnyvale CA 94086
P: 408-730-9800 F: 408-730-9808 PRC:206
usapex.com
Email: info@usapex.com

David Liu, President
Shirley Liu, Manager

Manufacturer of fiber optic products, metal and
plastic machined parts, lead free solder pastes,
liquid flux, power adapters, cables, and connectors.

USB Promos HQ
268 Bush St Ste 4302
San Francisco CA 94104
P: 800-515-3990 PRC:68
www.usbpromos.com
Estab: 2006

Cassey Xu, Director & Founder
Alex Rice, Director of Sales
Dan Westward, Director

Provider of USB flash drives, power banks, web
keys, video brochures and digital toys and promo-
tional items.

uSens Inc HQ
226 Airport Pkwy Ste 550
San Jose CA 95110
P: 408-564-0227 PRC:319
www.usens.com
Email: info@usens.com
Estab: 2013

Yue Fei, CTO & Co-Founder
Anli He, CEO & Co-Founder
Yiwen Rong, VP of Product Development
David Chiu, VP
Zhiyong Yang, Director of AI

Creator of 3D human computing interaction
software and hardware solutions. The company
focuses on artificial intelligence.

UserTesting HQ
690 Fifth St
San Francisco CA 94107
P: 888-877-1882 PRC:325
www.usertesting.com
Estab: 2007

Dave Garr, SVP of Customer Experience &
Co-Founder
Darrell Benatar, Executive Chairman & Co-Found-
er
Andy MacMillan, CEO
Michelle Huff, CMO
Carol MacKinlay, CPO

Deliver a human insight platform powered by customer experience for product teams, marketers,
and advertising companies.

Ushio America Inc HQ
5440 Cerritos Ave [N]
Cypress CA 90630
P: 714-236-8600 F: 714-229-3180 PRC:245
www.ushio.com
Email: customerservice@ushio.com
Emp: 51-200 Estab: 1967

Shinji Kameda, President
Frank Grobmeier, Manager

Manufacturer and distributor of lighting products.

USK Manufacturing Inc HQ
720 Zwissig Way
Union City CA 94587
P: 510-471-7555 F: 510-471-7554 PRC:80
www.uskmfg.com
Email: sales@uskmfg.com
Estab: 1987

Kendrick Kim, Operations Manager

Provider of precision sheet metal and machining
services. The company also focuses on mechanical assembly.

USWired Inc HQ
310 W Hamilton Ave Ste 200
Campbell CA 95008
P: 408-432-1144 F: 408-432-8660 PRC:323
www.uswired.com
Email: info@uswired.com
Estab: 1996

Robin Hau, President & CEO
Leonil Arce, Systems Engineer
Jon Schwartz, Desktop Technician

Provider of computer networking solutions that
include cloud hosting, network design and installation, and wireless networks.

Utstarcom Inc BR
2635 North First St Ste 148
San Jose CA 95134
P: 408-791-6168 F: 408-791-6167 PRC:63
www.utstar.com
Email: sales@utstar.com
Estab: 1991

Mickey Kwok Ming Yam, Senior Engineer
Matt Parker, Senior International Accountant

Manufacturer of IP based, end to end networking,
and telecommunications solutions. The company
also focuses on integration.

Uvexs Inc HQ
1287 Hammerwood Ave
Sunnyvale CA 94089
P: 408-734-4402 PRC:209
www.uvexs.com
Email: customerservice@uvexs.com
Estab: 1977

Brent Puder, President & CEO
Bruce Kennedy, Manager of Production
Lonnie Tillett, Engineer

Manufacturer of UV curing systems. The company's products find application in formulation of
UV-curable inks, adhesives, and coatings.

V&O Machine Inc HQ
17591 County Rd 97
Woodland CA 95695
P: 530-662-0495 F: 530-309-0395 PRC:80
vomachine.com
Email: vomachine@vomachine.com
Estab: 1974

Douglas Ostlind, Owner
Clifford Cooper, Contact

Manufacturer of machined parts for agri, hydraulics, food processing, and veterinary applications.
The company focuses on prototyping and CNC
milling.

V-Power Equipment Inc HQ
4201 W Capitol Ave
West Sacramento CA 95691
P: 916-266-6743 F: 916-266-6744 PRC:160
www.vpowerequip.com
Email: sales@vpowerequip.com
Estab: 2007

Melissa Reid, Director of Marketing
Chris Murray, Manager

Manufacturer and wholesaler of water well, wastewater, and construction dewatering pumps. The
company provides pump repair and diagnostic
services.

V-Soft Inc   HQ
888 Saratoga Ave Ste 203
San Jose CA 95129
P: 408-342-1700   F: 408-342-1705   PRC:322
www.v-softinc.com
Email: info@v-softinc.com
Estab: 1995

Ashwin Vora, CEO & Founder

Provider of product development services. The company also specializes in mobile application development.

V2plus Technology Inc   HQ
200 Brown Rd Ste 101
Fremont CA 94538
P: 510-226-6006   PRC:67
www.v2-plus.com
Email: admin@v2-plus.com

Ting Liu, President
Tom Lin, CTO

Provider of technology solutions. The company offers services for voice, data, and video over local wired and wireless communication networks.

V5 Systems   HQ
3191 Laurelview Ct
Fremont CA 94538
P: 844-604-7350   PRC:77
v5systems.us
Email: info@v5systems.us
Estab: 2014

Eddie Bedwan, Founder & VP
Mazin Bedwan, President & COO
Steve Yung, CEO & Chairman
Theodore Low, CFO
Frank Dere, Chief Architect

Provider of outdoor security and computing platforms. The company offers services to the government, military, and law enforcement industries.

Vacuum Engineering & Materials Co   HQ
390 Reed St
Santa Clara CA 95050
P: 408-871-9900   F: 408-562-9125   PRC:212
www.vem-co.com
Email: info@vem-co.com
Estab: 1987

Bob Kavanaugh, President
Stephanie McConnell, CFO
Jon Myers, VP of Sales & Marketing
Barry Henson, VP of Operations
Melvin Hirata, VP of Sales & Marketing & Technology

Manufacturer and supplier of PVD materials. The company also offers services like shield cleaning, material reclaim, and consignment programs.

Vacuum Process Engineering Inc   HQ
110 Commerce Cir
Sacramento CA 95815-4208
P: 916-925-6100   F: 916-925-6111   PRC:86
www.vpei.com
Email: info@vpei.com
Estab: 1976

Carl Schalansky, CEO
Ben Irani, Technical Sales Manager & Metallurgist
Tammy Volf, Purchasing Manager
Tom Bingham, Senior Manager
Brittany Wood, Project Engineer

Provider of engineering services. The company focuses on precision brazing, diffusion bonding, heat treating, and production of precision assemblies.

Valdor Fiber Optics Inc   RH
3116 Diablo Ave
Hayward CA 94545
P: 510-293-1212   F: 510-293-9996   PRC:170
www.valdor.com
Email: sales@valdor.com
Estab: 1985

Las Yabut, President
Elston Johnston, Chairman
Brian Findlay, CFO & Director
Ron Boyce, VP of Sales & Marketing & Director
Raj Kapany, Consultant

Provider of product design and development services of fiber optic products such as connectors, attenuators, couplers, splitters, and multiplexers.

Valent USA Corp   HQ
PO Box 8025
Walnut Creek CA 94596-8025
P: 800-682-5368   PRC:48
www.valent.com
Estab: 1988

David Nothmann, VP of Marketing
Eric Johnson, VP of Technology
Gary Schaefer, Director of Row Crops
Michael Tagle, Director of Finance
Trey Soud, Director of Seed Protection Business Unit

Provider of agricultural products. The company also deals with pest management solutions and serves the commercial agricultural sector.

Valiantica Inc   HQ
940 Saratoga Ave Ste 108
San Jose CA 95129
P: 408-725-2426   F: 408-580-8548   PRC:323
valiantica.com
Email: hr@valiantica.com
Estab: 2007

Peiwei Mi, Founder
Pratha Malhotra, Director of Sales
Reena Sah, Human Resource & Accounting Manager
Monisha Mitra, Account Manager
Shilpa Khandelwal, Account Manager

Provider of global IT solutions. The company's services include consulting, outsourcing, and mobile, enterprise and business application development.

Valimet Inc   HQ
431 Sperry Rd
Stockton CA 95206
P: 209-444-1600   F: 209-444-1636   PRC:50
www.valimet.com
Email: sales@valimet.com
Estab: 1965

Kurt Leopold, CEO
Valerie Waldon, VP of Sales & Marketing
Larry Elam, Quality Manager
Sifan Zhu, Process Engineer

Manufacturer of spherical atomized metal powders. The company also offers aluminum silicon and aluminum bronze and special alloys.

Valin Corp   HQ
5225 Hellyer Ave Ste 250
San Jose CA 95138
P: 800-774-5630   F: 408-730-1363   PRC:319
www.valin.com
Email: customerservice@valin.com
Estab: 1974

Joseph C. Nettemeyer, President & CEO
David Hefler, VP & CFO
Anne Vranicic, VP of Marketing
Robin Slater, Corporate VP of Sales
John Hill, VP

Provider of engineered solutions. The company serves the semiconductor, petrochemical, life sciences, and aerospace industries.

Valitor Inc   HQ
East Bay Innovation Ctr 820 Heinz Ave
Berkeley CA 94710
P: 510-545-6062   F: 510-647-8429   PRC:34
www.valitorbio.com
Email: info@valitorbio.com
Estab: 2010

Wesley Jackson, CSO

Developer of therapeutic protein drugs. The company's drugs are used in dermatology, ophthalmology, orthopedics, and stem cell therapy.

Valley Agricultural Software Inc   HQ
3950 South K St   [N]
Tulare CA 93274
P: 559-686-9496   F: 559-686-6253   PRC:322
www.vas.com
Email: info@vas.com
Estab: 1981

Kevin Callihan, VP of Engineering
Kirk Shrum, Sales Lead Specialist
Mike Tinker, Product Lead
Robert Bushnell, Product Lead
Ramon Gomez, Technician of Ag Software

Developer of software for the dairy industry.

Valley Communications Inc   HQ
6921 Roseville Rd
Sacramento CA 95842
P: 916-349-7300   F: 916-349-7329   PRC:62
www.valley-com.com
Email: info@valley-com.com
Estab: 1983

Kate DeWitt, VP of Finance & CFO
Bill Beban, Service Manager
Jami Walker, Project Manager
David Gross, Account Executive
Jared Carpenter, Marketing Admin

Provider of services for network cabling infrastructure needs. The company focuses on designing and installation.

Valley Tool & Manufacturing Co   HQ
2507 Tully Rd
Hughson CA 95326
P: 800-426-5615   PRC:159
valleytoolmfg.com
Email: info@valleytoolmfg.com
Estab: 1969

Fred Brenda, President
Luann Klann, Controller
John Wilkins, Sales Representative

Manufacturer of agricultural equipment like flail mowers, sprayers, and shredders. The company also manufactures skid steer and excavator attachments.

Valleytek Inc   HQ
930 Rincon Cir
San Jose CA 95131
P: 408-577-1218   F: 408-577-1299   PRC:209
valleytek.com
Email: info@valleytek.com
Estab: 2003

Thien Pham, Owner
Jolynn Ho, Sales Manager

Provider of expanded memory specification solutions, contract manufacturing services, and engineering services.

Valmark Interface Solutions   HQ
61 S Vasco Rd Ste L
Livermore CA 94551
P: 925-960-9900   F: 925-960-0900   PRC:209
nidec-vis.com
Email: vis@nidec-vis.com
Estab: 1976

Bill Canon, VP of Product Development & Engineering

Manufacturer of labels, panel overlays, and membrane switches. The company is engaged in engineering, assembly, and installation services.

Valqua America Inc   HQ
4655 Old Ironsides Dr Ste 380
Santa Clara CA 95054
P: 408-986-1425   F: 408-986-1426   PRC:86
www.valqua-america.com
Estab: 1998

Takafumi Sakurai, Technical Project Manager
Noriko Ishikawa, Information Technology Manager
Kaori Kawasaki, Sales Engineer

Seller and marketer of semiconductor related products. The company also offers R&D services for high performance elastomer seals.

M-318

Value Products Inc   HQ
2128 Industrial Dr
Stockton CA 95206
P: 209-983-4000   F: 209-983-4080   PRC:56
valueproductsinc.com
Email: graphics@valueproductsinc.com
Estab: 1970

Doug Hall, President
Erica Hall, Office Manager
Silverio Fernandez, Production Manager
June Guanzon, Lab Technician
Liz Maloney, Contact

Provider of chemical compounding and packaging solutions. The company services include silk screen printing and private labeling.

ValueLabs Inc   BR
1250 Oakmead Pkwy Ste 210
Sunnyvale CA 94085-4037
P: 408-475-2445   F: 408-716-2975   PRC:322
www.valuelabs.com

Venu Gangavarapu, Test Manager
Prakash Konakanchi, Module Lead
Amit Patel, Technical Lead
Nick Collins, Business Developer

Provider of technology solutions and services. The company's services include digital solutions, quality assurance, and application development.

Vanderhulst Associates Inc   HQ
3300 Victor Ct
Santa Clara CA 95054
P: 408-727-1313   PRC:80
vanderhulst.com
Estab: 1975

Hank Vanderhulst, Director of Human Resource & President
Alexandra Thompson, VP
Chris Hernandez, Production Manager
Kirk Dimulias, Production Manager

Provider of precision machining and manufacturing services. The company serves the medical, analytical, and semiconductor industries.

Vanderlans & Sons Inc   HQ
1320 S Sacramento St
Lodi CA 95240
P: 209-334-4115   F: 209-339-8260   PRC:159
www.lansas.com
Email: information@lansas.com
Estab: 1958

Eric Vander Lans, VP

Manufacturer of pipe and high pressure plugs, test equipment, hoses, gauges, ventilators, and related accessories.

Vandersteen   HQ
116 W Fourth St
Hanford CA 93230
P: 559-582-0324   F: 559-582-0364   PRC:60
www.vandersteen.com
Email: international@vandersteen.com

Richard Vandersteen, Founder

Manufacturer and distributor of loudspeakers. The company's products include VCC-5 Center, V2W Subwoofer, VLR, and 3a Signature.

Vantage Data Center Services & Solutionsÿ   HQ
2820 Northwestern Pkwy
Santa Clara CA 95051
P: 855-878-2682   PRC:290
www.vantagedatacenters.com
Email: info@vantage-dc.com
Estab: 2010

Sureel Choksi, CEO
Justin Thomas, CTO
Joe Goldsmith, CRO
Chris Yetman, COO
Sharif Metwalli, CFO

Provider of transformers, switches, generators, chillers, switch gears and security, and communication products.

Vantage Robotics LLC   HQ
1933 Davis St Ste 240
San Leandro CA 94577
P: 510-907-7012   PRC:311
vantagerobotics.com
Email: contact@vantagerobotics.com
Estab: 2013

Joe Van Niekerk, Co-Founder & CTO
Tobin Fisher, Co-Founder & CEO
Assaf Stoler, VP of Software
Aaron Breen, Director of Mechanical Engineering
Kaj Martin, Director of Operations

Developer and manufacturer of camera drones. The company serves the consumer electronics, automation, and robotics industries.

Vanton Research Laboratory LLC   HQ
3355 Clayton Rd
Concord CA 94517
P: 925-326-1802   F: 925-687-7815   PRC:268
www.vantonlab.com
Email: info@vantonlab.com
Estab: 1993

Eric Sheu, Director

Specializes in the development of non-conventional drug delivery systems and integrated pharmaceutical services.

Vapore LLC   HQ
1130 Burnett Ave Ste P
Concord CA 94520
P: 925-998-6116   PRC:189
www.mypurmist.com
Email: care@mypurmist.com
Estab: 2011

Lars Barfod, CEO & Owner
Brett MacKinnon, President
Kasia Kirkbride, Sales & Marketing Operations Manager
Graham Booth, Data Engineer

Manufacturer of personal steam inhalers. The company's products are used for relief from sinus congestion, allergies, and discomfort from sore throat.

Varentec Inc   HQ
3200 Patrick Henry Dr
Santa Clara CA 95054
P: 408-433-9900   F: 408-433-9919   PRC:290
varentec.com
Email: sales@varentec.com
Estab: 2012

Deepak Divan, President
Guillaume Dufosse, CEO
Erica Cowell Cronin, Chief of Staff
Damien Tholomier, EVP of Marketing
Sherman Lee, Director of Operations

Provider of grid control and monitoring solutions.
The company also offers asset management and
outage detection services.

Varian Medical Systems Inc   BR
660 N McCarthy Blvd
Milpitas CA 95035
P: 408-321-9400   PRC:195
www.varian.com
Email: info.europe@varian.com
Estab: 1940

Chris Toth, President of Oncology Systems
Gary E. Bischoping, President of Interventional
Oncology Solutions
Kevin O. Reilly, SVP & President
Kolleen T. Kennedy, President of Proton Solutions
& Chief Growth Officer
Dow R. Wilson, CEO

Provider of radiation therapies for cancer. The
company develops and markers different types of
radiation technologies to cure various cancers.

Varian Medical Systems Inc   HQ
3100 Hansen Way
Palo Alto CA 94304-1038
P: 650-493-4000   PRC:195
www.varian.com
Estab: 1948
Sales: Over $3B

Chris Toth, President & COO
Kolleen T. Kennedy, President of Proton Solutions
& Chief Growth Officer
Dow R. Wilson, CEO
Terilyn Monroe, CPO of SVP of People & Places
Thomas Rodden, SVP & CIO

Provider of radiation therapies for cancer. The
company develops and markers different types of
radiation technologies to cure various cancers.

Variant Microsystems   HQ
4128 Business Center Dr
Fremont CA 94538
P: 510-440-2870   F: 510-440-2873   PRC:120
www.variantusa.com
Email: sales@variantusa.com
Estab: 1994

Rajiv Chugh, President

Manufacturer and reseller of data collection
equipment such as barcode scanners, printers,
portables.

Varite Inc   HQ
111 N Market St Ste 730
San Jose CA 95113
P: 408-977-0700   F: 408-977-0760   PRC:323
www.varite.com
Email: contact@varite.com
Estab: 2000

Adarsh Katyal, President
Rahul Sharma, Director
Amarjeet Singh, Associate Account Manager
Swetha Reddy, Business Development Manager
Anubhav Sood, Strategic Account Manager

Provider of custom software development, integration, deployment, and implementation services in
the domains of core networking and virtualization.

vArmour Inc   HQ
270 Third St
Los Altos CA 94022
P: 650-564-5100   F: 650-564-5101   PRC:325
varmour.com
Email: info@varmour.com
Estab: 2011

Roger Lian, Founder & VP of Engineering
Timothy Eades, CEO
Marc Woolward, CTO

Provider of cloud security, segmentation, monitoring, and deception solutions. The company serves
banks and healthcare organizations.

Varna Products   HQ
4305 Business Dr
Cameron Park CA 95682
P: 530-676-7770   F: 530-676-7796   PRC:160
www.varnaproducts.com
Estab: 2005

Mark Ashurst, Operations Manager
Thomas Martin, Engineering Manager
Jordan Uggla, Embedded Software Developer

Manufacturer of pump and valve solutions. The
company offers oil pumps, pump controls, pressure relief valves, and check valves.

Vaxart Inc   HQ
385 Oyster Point Blvd Ste 9A
S San Francisco CA 94080
P: 650-550-3500   F: 650-871-8580   PRC:268
www.vaxart.com
Email: info@vaxart.com
Estab: 2004

Sean Tucker, Founder & Chief Scientific Officer
Wouter W. Latour, CEO & President & Chairman
David N. Taylor, CMO
Brant Biehn, SVP of Commercial Operations
David Ingamells, VP of Manufacturing

Manufacturer and developer of oral vaccines. The
company is engaged in drug development and
related services.

Vaxcyte Inc   HQ
353 Hatch Dr
Foster City CA 94404
P: 650-837-0111   PRC:268
www.sutrovax.com
Email: info@vaxcyte.com
Estab: 2003

Grant Pickering, CEO
Elaine Sun, CFO
Ash Khanna, Chief Business Officer
Jeff Fairman, VP of Research
Aym Berges, Senior Scientist

Developer of vaccines for the treatment of infectious diseases. The company is also engaged in
the production of vaccine antigens.

Vayusphere Inc   HQ
2685 Marine Way Ste 1305
Mountain View CA 94043
P: 650-960-2900   F: 650-960-2910   PRC:322
www.vayusphere.com
Email: sales@vayusphere.com
Estab: 2000

Pushpendra Mohta, CEO

Developer of instant messaging applications. The
company's customers include Morgan Stanley,
Deutsche Bank, and others.

VDx Veterinary Diagnostics and
Preclinical Research Services   HQ
215 C St Ste 301
Davis CA 95616
P: 530-753-4285   F: 530-753-4055   PRC:273
vdxpathology.com
Email: info@vdxpathology.com
Estab: 2001

John Peauroi, Founder & President
Jeffrey Lewis, Clinical Operations Manager
Robyn Mohr, Lab Assistant
Sonjia Shelly, Contact

Provider of histopathology and pathology support
to the medical device, biotech, pharmaceutical,
academic and veterinary communities.

Vector Fabrication Inc   HQ
1629 Watson Ct
Milpitas CA 95035
P: 408-942-9800   F: 408-942-9896   PRC:211
www.vectorfab.com
Email: info@vectorfab.com
Estab: 1995

Quang Luong, President

Manufacturer of printed circuit boards. The company offers circuit board assembly, drilling, solder
mask, plating, and testing services.

Vector Laboratories Inc   HQ
30 Ingold Rd
Burlingame CA 94010
P: 650-697-3600   F: 650-697-0339   PRC:306
vectorlabs.com
Email: vector@vectorlabs.com
Emp: 50   Estab: 1976

Erika Leonard, Director of Quality Control
Pamela James, Director of Research
Craig Pow, Director
Pam Williams, Business Manager & Director of
Human Resources
Darlene Ha, Production Scientist

Provider of labeling and detection services for
enzymes, antibodies and antigens, DNA and RNA
by using polymer reagents.

Veeco Instruments Inc BR
3050 Zanker Rd
San Jose CA 95134
P: 408-321-8835   PRC:209
www.veeco.com
Estab: 1945

William J. Miller, CEO
Shubham Maheshwari, EVP & CFO & COO
Peter Porshnev, SVP of Unified Engineering

Manufacturer of data storage, LED, and solar process equipment. The company serves solar, LED, data storage, wireless, optical, and other sectors.

Veeva Systems Inc HQ
4280 Hacienda Dr
Pleasanton CA 94588
P: 925-452-6500   F: 925-452-6504   PRC:323
veeva.com
Email: sales@veeva.com
Estab: 2007
Sales: $1B to $3B

Peter Gassner, Co-Founder & CEO
Matthew J. Wallach, Co-Founder
Tom Schwenger, President & COO
Nitsa Zuppas, CMO
Tim Cabral, CFO

Provider of cloud-based business solutions such as customer relationship management and content management for the life sciences industry.

VeEX Inc HQ
2827 Lakeview Ct
Fremont CA 94538
P: 510-651-0500   F: 510-651-0505   PRC:68
www.veexinc.com
Email: info@veexinc.com
Estab: 2006

Terence Leong, Director of Customer Care
Ildefonso Polo, Director of Product Marketing
Jim Keim, Senior Account Director
Simon Defayette, Technical Director
Eve Danel, Senior Product Manager

Developer of test and measurement solutions for next generation communication equipment and networks. The company serves the industrial sector.

Vektrex Electronic Systems Inc HQ
10225 Barnes Canyon Rd Ste A213   [N]
San Diego CA 92121
P: 858-558-8282   PRC:322
www.vektrex.com
Email: sales@vektrex.com
Estab: 1986

Brad Wise, Director

Provider of custom computer programming services.

M-320

Velano Vascular Inc HQ
221 Pine St Ste 200
San Francisco CA 94104
P: 844-835-2668   PRC:195
velanovascular.com
Email: support@velanovascular.com
Estab: 2012

Eric Ston, Co-Founder & CEO
Pitou Devgon, Co-Founder & President
Brian Funk, Research & Development Engineer

Manufacturer of needle-free devices for drawing blood from hospitalized patients. The company offers services to the medical industry.

Velocity Pharmaceutical Development LLC HQ
400 Oyster Point Blvd Ste 202
S San Francisco CA 94080
P: 650-273-5748   F: 650-745-8179   PRC:268
www.vpd.net
Email: info@vpd.net
Estab: 2011

David Collier, CEO
James Larrick, Managing Director & CMO
Matthew Kerby, Venture Partner
Leslie Loven, Office Manager
Sonia Kamal, Executive Assistant

Developer of drug candidates. The company specializes in clinical development programs and serves biotechnology and pharmaceutical companies.

Velos LLC HQ
42840 Christy St Ste 201
Fremont CA 94538
P: 510-739-4010   F: 510-739-4018   PRC:304
velos.com
Email: info@velos.com
Estab: 1996

John McIlwain, CEO
Sonia Abrol, VP of Development & Operations

Provider of clinical research solutions. The company offers services to hospitals, academic medical centers, and also cancer centers.

Vena Engineering Corp HQ
7 Hangar Way
Watsonville CA 95076
P: 831-724-5738   PRC:235
www.vena.com
Email: sales@vena.com
Estab: 1995

Jeff Greatorex, VP

Manufacturer of hard drive test equipment and environmental chalmers. The company also offers motors and power supplies.

Ventek International HQ
1260 Holm Rd Ste A
Petaluma CA 94954
P: 707-773-3373   F: 707-773-3381   PRC:238
www.ventek-intl.com
Email: info@ventek-intl.com
Estab: 1950

Gary A. Catt, President & Founder
Gareth Wheeler, Business Owner & CEO
Philip Wilkinson, COO
Craig Lewis, Chief of Production
Matthew Taylor, IT Director

Manufacturer of parking revenue control systems. The company offers recreation, commuter rail, and parking access control solutions.

Ventex Corp HQ
2153 Otoole Ave Ste 10
San Jose CA 95131
P: 408-436-2929   F: 408-436-2928   PRC:159
ventexcorp.com
Email: info@ventexcorp.com
Estab: 1994

James Docherty, Owner
Brett Pearson, CEO

Supplier of lithography equipment, spare parts, and services. The company also provides refurbishment and installation services.

Ventricle Software Systems Inc HQ
29205 Oceanridge Dr   [N]
Rancho Palos Verdes CA 90275
P: 310-948-2551   PRC:319
www.ventriclesoftware.com
Email: info@ventriclesoftware.com
Estab: 2006

David Finkel, Contact

Provider of software development for the healthcare industry.

Venturi Wireless Inc HQ
152 N Third St Ste 510
San Jose CA 95112
P: 408-982-1130   F: 408-638-0314   PRC:67
venturiwireless.com
Email: sales@venturiwireless.com
Estab: 1993

Uday Nagendran, President
Dan McEntee, VP of Finance & Administration & CFO
Ha Huynh, Senior Accountant

Provider of broadband optimization services. The company mainly caters to mobile and wireless operators.

Veolia Water BR
601 Canal Blvd
Richmond CA 94804
P: 510-412-2001   PRC:100
www.richmond.veolianorthamerica.com

Aaron Winer, Project Manager

Provider of water and wastewater treatment solutions. The company offers services for public authorities and industrial companies.

Veolia BR

8310 Umbria Ave
Sacramento CA 95828
P: 916-379-0872 PRC:142
veolianorthamerica.com

John Gibson, EVP & COO of Municipal & Commercial Business
Nisreen Bagasra, Chief Procurement Officer

Provider of complete environmental solutions. The company focuses on energy, water treatment, and waste management.

VeraCentra HQ

690 Airpark Rd
Napa CA 94558
P: 707-224-6161 PRC:326
www.veracentra.com
Estab: 1988

David Resnick, CIO of Technology & Client Solutions
Dan Plunkett, VP of Marketing Execution Services
Patti Arnold, Program Manager
Idalia Radillo, Supervisor
Adam Roberts, Account Executive

Provider of data leveraging services to brands for marketing needs and also focuses on customer intelligence, marketing execution, and consultation.

Veracyte Inc HQ

6000 Shoreline Ct Ste 300
S San Francisco CA 94080
P: 650-243-6300   F: 650-243-6301 PRC:268
www.veracyte.com
Email: info@veracyte.com
Estab: 2008
Sales: $100M to $300M

Bonnie Anderson, Chairman & CEO
Shelly D. Guyer, CFO
Neil Barth, CMO
John W. Hanna, Chief Commercial Officer
Ken Brunt, VP of Customer Operations

Focuses on molecular analysis and diagnostic tests. The company serves patients and the healthcare sector.

Verdafero Inc HQ

1012 Bent Oak Ln
San Jose CA 95129
P: 650-206-2441 PRC:315
www.verdafero.com
Estab: 2009

Alastair Hood, CEO
Terri Gilbert, Director of Information Technology
Christopher Hall, Director of Business Development

Offers a wide range of cloud-based software solutions that enable companies to manage their utility data and analytics.

Verge Analytics Inc HQ

Two Tower Pl Ste 950
S San Francisco CA 94080
P: 415-355-4737 PRC:257
www.vergegenomics.com
Email: hello@vergegenomics.com
Estab: 2015

Alice Zhang, CEO

Provider of treatment for brain diseases. The company is involved in drug development and research services.

Veridiam Inc HQ

1717 N Cuyamaca St [N]
El Cajon CA 92020
P: 619-448-1000   F: 619-562-5776 PRC:82
www.veridiam.com
Email: sales@veridiam.com
Emp: 51-200   Estab: 1889

Jonathan Iddings, VP of Operations

Manufacturer of tubing, special purpose tubular components, and nuclear components.

Verific Design Automation Inc HQ

1516 Oak St Ste 115
Alameda CA 94501
P: 510-522-1555   F: 510-522-1553 PRC:212
www.verific.com
Email: info@verific.com
Estab: 1999

Michiel Ligthart, COO
Rick Carlson, VP of Sales
Lawrence Neukom, Contact

Specializes in electronic design automation solutions. The company offers services to the semiconductor industry.

VeriSilicon Inc HQ

2150 Gold St Ste 200
San Jose CA 95002
P: 408-844-8560 PRC:208
verisilicon.com
Email: us-sales@verisilicon.com
Estab: 2002

Wayne Wei-Ming Dai, CEO & President & Chairman & Founder
Sam Shieh, Corporate VP of Technology
Yanjun Zhang, VP of Software Development
Shuangbei Li, Data Processing Engineer

Provider of IC design services specializing in custom silicon solutions. The company also offers SOC turnkey services.

Veritas Technologies LLC HQ

2625 Augustine Dr
Santa Clara CA 95054
P: 866-837-4827 PRC:315
www.veritas.com
Estab: 2016

Greg Hughes, CEO
Mark Dentinger, EVP & CFO
John Abel, SVP & CIO
Sophie Ames, SVP & Chief Human Resource Officer
Todd Forsythe, SVP & CMO

Empowers business with a multi-cloud data management solution.

Verix Inc HQ

4340 Stevens Creek Blvd Ste 166
San Jose CA 95129
P: 650-949-2700   F: 650-949-2722 PRC:325
www.verix.com
Email: info@verix.com
Estab: 2007

Amir Ashiri, Co-Founder
Haggay Tsaban, Co-Founder & VP of R&D & Products & WW Customer Solutions
Doron Aspitz, CEO

Designer and developer of precision tooling and equipment for performance engine builders and mechanists.

Versa Networks Inc HQ

6001 America Center Dr Ste 400
Santa Clara CA 95002
P: 408-385-7660   F: 888-498-5810 PRC:63
versa-networks.com
Email: info@versa-networks.com
Estab: 2012

Apurva Mehta, Founder & CTO
Kelly Ahuja, CEO
Rob Mustarde, SVP of Worldwide Sales
Tony Fallows, VP of Service Provider WW Sales
Atchison Frazer, Head of Marketing

Provider of networking solutions. The company specializes in virtualized network functions and services.

Versa Shore Inc HQ

1999 S Bascom Ave Ste 700
Campbell CA 95008
P: 408-874-8330 PRC:323
www.versashore.com
Estab: 2003

Shawn Rao, CEO & Founder
Donald Lightbody, CFO
Bruce Hobbs, Chief Architect
Bruce Dunn, Sales Manager
Roni Wu, Office Manager

Provider of data warehouse implementation, strategic blueprint creation, project management, and testing consulting services.

Versartis Inc HQ

4200 Bohannon Dr Ste 250
Menlo Park CA 94025
P: 650-963-8580 PRC:42
www.versartis.co/index.htm
Email: info@versartis.com
Estab: 2008

Scott Gorcey, Compliance Manager

Manufacturer and developer of therapeutic proteins for the treatment of endocrine disorders. The company develops recombinant human growth hormone.

Versatile Power   HQ
743 Camden Ave
Campbell CA 95008
P: 408-341-4600   F: 408-341-4601   PRC:129
www.versatilepower.com
Email: sales@versatilepower.com
Estab: 2002

Paul Burgess, Business Owner
Jerry Price, CEO
Mark Brown, Director of Sales & Marketing
Scott Jensen, Engineering Manager
Shad Schidel, Quality Manager

Designer and manufacturer of electronic subsystems
for manufacturers. The company focuses on application of radio frequency, ultrasonics, and lasers.

Verseon Corp   HQ
47071 Bayside Pkwy
Fremont CA 94538
P: 510-225-9000   F: 510-225-9001   PRC:269
www.verseon.com
Email: info@verseon.com
Estab: 2002

David Kita, Co-Founder & VP of Research &
Development
Eniko Fodor, COO & CFO & Co-Founder
Adityo Prakash, CEO
John Zhang, Senior Scientist
Douglas Pahel, Research Scientist & Research
Scientist

Focuses on the design of drug candidates. The
company offers services to the pharmaceutical
industry.

Versonix Corp   HQ
1175 Saratoga Ave Ste 4
San Jose CA 95129
P: 408-873-3141   F: 408-873-3139   PRC:323
www.versonix.com
Email: info@versonix.com
Estab: 1986

Victor Velton, President
Yuri Polissky, COO
Igor Vilenski, CTO
Vadim Evfimiou, Chief Architect
Jacob Dreyband, Director of Software Engineering

Provider of integrated and customized software
solutions. The company serves the travel and
leisure industries.

M-322

Vertical Systems Inc   HQ
3549 MacGregor Ln
Santa Clara CA 95054
P: 408-752-8100   F: 408-752-8102   PRC:322
ver-sys.com
Email: info@ver-sys.com
Estab: 2001

Saeed A. Kazmi, Chairman & CEO
Idris Kothari, CTO
Charlotte Williams, Account Manager
Saleem Kazmi, Controller

Provider of centric solutions for the hospitality
industry. The company is also engaged in mobile
application and custom solutions.

Vest Inc   HQ
6023 Alcoa Ave   [N]
Vernon CA 90058
P: 800-421-6370   PRC:159
www.vestinc.com
Email: sales@vestinc.com
Emp: 11-50   Estab: 1970

Yasuyuki Yuba, President
Mindy Kroman, General Manager of Finance &
Human Resources
Sean McCaughan, Manager
Dave Crepeau, Manager of Sales
Kaz Sawai, Manager of Sales

Producer of electric welded carbon steel tubing
products.

Vetequip Inc   HQ
1452 N Vasco Rd Ste 303
Livermore CA 94551
P: 925-463-1828   F: 925-463-1943   PRC:23
www.vetequip.com
Email: info@vetequip.com
Estab: 1990

Bob Schrock, Owner
Melinda Kolar, Director of Customer Service

Developer and manufacturer of drug delivery
systems. The company specializes in nasal anes-
thesia delivery systems.

VIA Licensing Corp   HQ
1275 Market St
San Francisco CA 94103
P: 415-645-4700   F: 415-645-4400   PRC:328
via-corp.com
Email: info@vialicensing.com
Estab: 2002

Joseph Siino, President
Zaynab Hararah, Senior Compliance Analyst
Khajal Cooper, Senior Analyst
Cindy Wong, Licensing Accountant
Cecilia Wong, Accountant

Provider of intellectual property programs and
business solutions. The company serves technology companies, entertainment companies, and
universities.

ViaCyte Inc   HQ
3550 General Atomics Ct   [N]
San Diego CA 92121
P: 858-455-3708   F: 858-455-3962   PRC:268
viacyte.com
Email: info@viacyte.com
Emp: 51-200   Estab: 1999

Fred A. Middleton, Chairman of the Board
Howard Foyt, VP & CMO
Kevin D"Amour, VP of Research & Chief Scientific
Officer
Liz Bui, VP
Mark Zimmerman, VP of Operations & Business
Development

Provider of biomedical research.

Vian Enterprises Inc   HQ
1501 Industrial Dr
Auburn CA 95603
P: 530-885-1997   F: 530-885-1998   PRC:160
vianenterprises.com
Email: info@vianenterprises.com
Estab: 1968

Sokheng Chheng, Design Engineer
Brian Wargala, Manufacturing Engineer

Manufacturer of gerotors, gears, and broached
hardware. The company also offers oil pump and
complete lubrication systems.

Vicom Systems Inc   HQ
2336 Walsh Ave Ste H
Santa Clara CA 95051
P: 408-588-1286   F: 650-560-6441   PRC:91
www.vicom.com
Email: info@vicom.com
Estab: 1996

Samuel Tam, CEO
Mark Egerton, VP of Sales & Partner Manage-
ment
Horatio Lo, VP of Systems & Professional Ser-
vices
Wei-Gung Wang, Director of Technical Marketing
Noel Hernandez, Project Manager

Provider of migration data services. The company
is involved in offering transparent wire-speed data
services for systems and storage.

Victorious   HQ
995 Market St
San Francisco CA 94301
P: 415-621-9830   PRC:325
victoriousseo.com
Email: hello@victoriousseo.com
Estab: 2012

Michael Transon, CEO
Dave Burton, VP of Finance
Houston Barnett-Gearhart, VP of Product
Kyle Wade, Director of Customer Success
Pete Tkachuk, Director of Sales

Search engine optimization agency that leverages a wealth of performance data and market
research to create scientifically-driven SEO
strategies.

Victory Foam Inc HQ

3 Holland [N]
Irvine CA 92618
P: 949-474-0690   F: 949-474-0663   PRC:212
www.victoryfoam.com
Emp: 51-200   Estab: 1985

Linda O'Donnell, Finance & Human Resource Manager

Provider of custom foam, plastic packaging and much more solutions for industry products and tools.

Vida Products Inc HQ

6147 State Farm Dr
Rohnert Park CA 94928
P: 707-541-7000   PRC:70
vidaproducts.com
Email: info@vidaproducts.com
Estab: 2003

Ronald Parrott, President & CTO

Supplier of radio frequency and microwave components and subsystems. The company provides magnetically tuned oscillators, filters, and synthesizers.

Vidado Inc HQ

130 Webster St Ste 200
Oakland CA 94067
P: 415-237-3676   PRC:315
vidado.ai
Estab: 2011

Nowell Outlaw, CEO
Bill Hoover, CFO
Elaine Zhou, CTO
Eng Lee, VP of Professional Services

Designed to help organizations collect and digitize inaccessible data.

Vidcrest HQ

PO Box 69642 [N]
Los Angeles CA 90069
P: 323-822-1740   PRC:60
www.vidcrest.net
Estab: 1981

Robert D. Weinbach, President

Creator of motion picture and special interest videos.

Video Clarity Inc HQ

1566 La Pradera Dr
Campbell CA 95008
P: 408-379-6952   PRC:60
videoclarity.com
Email: sales@videoclarity.com
Estab: 2005

Blake Homan, President
Adam Schadle, VP

Provider of real time and broadcast quality monitoring, perceptual analysis, recording, and automating services.

Videofax HQ

1750 Cesar Chavez St Unit G
San Francisco CA 94124
P: 415-641-0100   PRC:168
www.videofax.com
Email: rentals@videofax.com
Estab: 1987

Mona Marks, Rental Manager
Nick Schrader, Shop Manager
Sophie Aissen, Business Manager

Manufacturer of cameras, recorders, players, and related accessories. The company offers technical support services.

Vien Thao Media HQ

1982 Senter Rd [N]
San Jose CA 95112
P: 408-947-7517   F: 408-947-0463   PRC:325
www.vienthao.com
Email: info@vienthao.com

Do Van Tron, President

Operator of multiple Christian television stations.

View by View Inc HQ

1203 Union St [N]
San Francisco CA 94133
P: 415-359-4494   F: 415-359-4494   PRC:104
www.viewbyview.com
Email: lissette@viewbyview.com
Estab: 1990

France Israel, President

Provider of computer-generated architectural, medical modeling and simulations.

Viewics Inc HQ

2821 Scott Blvd
Santa Clara CA 95050
P: 415-439-0084   PRC:188
viewics.com
Email: info@viewics.com
Estab: 2009

Tim Kuruvilla, Founder & Head of Sales Marketing & Customer Success

Provider of consulting, custom development, and report authoring services. The company also offers packaged solutions.

Viking Enterprise Solutions HQ

2700 N First St
San Jose CA 95134
P: 408-964-3730   PRC:95
www.vikingenterprisesolutions.com
Email: info@vikingenterprise.com
Estab: 2000

Matt Babcock, Design Manager
Parker Boyce, Firmware Engineer
Nirmal Jain, Senior SI Engineer

Provider of solutions for data enterpriser centers. The company also offers storage expansion product platform.

Vindicia Inc HQ

2988 Campus Dr Ste 300
San Mateo CA 94403-2531
P: 650-264-4700   F: 650-264-4701   PRC:325
www.vindicia.com
Estab: 2003

Sharath Dorbala, CEO
Roy Barak, CFO & COO
Jack Bullock, CRO
Jesus Luzardo, VP & Head of Growth
Mark Elrod, EVP of Engineering

Developer of marketing and analytics solutions. The company offers customer acquisition and retention and customer relationship management services.

VinSuite HQ

1625 Trancas St Ste 2280
Napa CA 94558
P: 707-253-7400   PRC:326
www.vinsuite.com
Email: info@vinsuite.com
Estab: 2013

Carrie-Anne Wood, Enterprise Account Manager
Daniel Williams, Support Operations Manager
Erin Melugin Davis, Project Manager
Tom Gorton, Manager of Professional Services
Jon Trafton, Data & Integrations Manager

Developer of wine software and serves the consumer sector. The company offers support services to wineries and tasting rooms.

Vintara Inc HQ

1714 Franklin St Ste 100303
Oakland CA 94612
P: 877-846-8272   PRC:325
www.vintara.com
Email: info@vintara.com
Estab: 1997

Glenn Kohner, CEO & Chairman
Rob Power, Director of Engineering
Dawn Plaskon, Director of Consulting Services

Provider of web-based enterprise process management solutions and services. The company caters to a number of industries.

ViOptix Inc HQ

39655 Eureka Dr
Newark CA 94560
P: 510-226-5860   F: 510-226-5864   PRC:186
www.vioptix.com
Email: info@vioptix.com
Estab: 1999

Jack Lloyd, Executive Chairman
Scott E. Coleridge, CEO
Mark Lonsinger, VP & General Manager
Michael Glore, Account Manager
Derek Lee, Senior Engineer Technician

Manufacturer of medical support devices. The company specializes in devices used for respiratory support and oxygen supply.

VipeCloud   HQ
855 El Camino Real Ste 13A-302
Palo Alto CA 94301
P: 650-308-8473   PRC:325
vipecloud.com
Email: contact@vipecloud.com
Estab: 2011

Adam Peterson, CEO
Joseph Macias, CRO
Erica Lynne, COO
Drew Ross, Operations Manager

Developers of marketing CRM that helps small-
and mid-sized businesses accelerate the growth.

Virovek   HQ
22429 Hesperian Blvd
Hayward CA 94541
P: 510-887-7121   F: 510-887-7178   PRC:36
www.virovek.com
Email: info@virovek.com

Haifeng Chen, CEO
Leslie Duprey, Senior Manager of Marketing
June Song, Manager of Business Development
Courtney Jett, Buyer

Provider of adeno-associated virus production
and purification services. The company involves in
consulting and gene cloning services.

Virtual Driver Interactive   HQ
5137 Golden Foothill Pkwy Ste 150
El Dorado Hills CA 95762
P: 877-746-8332   PRC:329
www.driverinteractive.com
Email: support@driverinteractive.com
Estab: 2009

Bob Davis, CEO
Pam LeFevre, VP of Marketing
Van Burns, VP & General Manager
Andre Luongo, VP of Product Development
Dustin Davis, Account Executive

Manufacturer of virtual training simulators. The
company serves schools, corporations, schools,
and hospitals.

Virtual Instruments   HQ
2331 Zanker Rd
San Jose CA 95131
P: 408-579-4000   F: 408-579-4001   PRC:329
www.virtualinstruments.com
Email: sales@virtualinstruments.com
Estab: 2008

Ray Villeneuve, President
John W. Thompson, CEO
John Gentry, CTO
Len Rosenthal, CMO
Lisa Alger, COO

Developer of storage area network and virtual
infrastructure solutions. The company serves
healthcare, federal, and outsourcing and hosting
sectors.

Viscira LLC   HQ
200 Vallejo St
San Francisco CA 94111
P: 415-848-8010   PRC:322
www.viscira.com
Email: info@viscira.com
Estab: 2007

Dave Gulezian, Chairman & Founder
Rick Barker, President & CEO
Jeff Asada, CRO
Shan Jaffar, COO
Kimberly Davis-Wells, VP of Client Services

Manufacturer of software products. The company
deals with the development of animation technology solutions.

Vishay Intertechnology Inc   BR
3000 Bowers Ave
Santa Clara CA 95051
P: 408-727-2500   F: 408-727-5896   PRC:86
www.vishay.com
Estab: 1962

Gerald Paul, CEO & President & Director
Marc Zandman, Chief Business Development
Officer & Executive Chairman
Lori Lipcaman, EVP & CFO
Clarence Tse, EVP & Business Head of Semicon-
ductors
Matthew Carter, VP of Marketing

Manufacturer of electronic components. The company's products comprises of semiconductors and
passive components used across industries.

Vision3 Lighting   HQ
2850 San Antonio Dr
Fowler CA 93625
P: 559-834-5749   F: 559-834-4779   PRC:243
www.vision3lighting.com
Email: info@vision3lighting.com
Estab: 2001

Thomas Petrush, National Sales Manager

Manufacturer of landscape and exterior architectural lighting products. The company deals with
design and installation services.

**VisionCare Ophthalmic Technologies
Inc**   HQ
14395 Saratoga Ave Ste 150
Saratoga CA 95070
P: 408-872-9393   F: 408-872-9395   PRC:195
www.visioncareinc.net
Estab: 1997

Wolfgang Tolle, CEO
Richard P. Powers, EVP
Eli Aharoni, VP of Research & Development &
General Manager
Yona Katz, VP of Manufacturing
Doron Raz, VP of Finance & Administration

Manufacturer and marketer of implantable ophthalmic devices and technologies for improving
vision of individuals with untreatable retinal
disorders.

Visioneer Inc   HQ
5673 Gibraltar Dr
Pleasanton CA 94588
P: 925-251-6399   F: 925-416-8600   PRC:176
www.visioneer.com
Email: 2020@visioneer.com
Estab: 1992

Jon Harju, CTO
Dmitry Panich, Art Director

Marketer and distributor of digital imaging hardware devices. The company also offers related
tools and utilities and power tools.

Vistagen Therapeutics Inc   HQ
343 Allerton Ave
S San Francisco CA 94080
P: 650-577-3600   F: 888-482-2602   PRC:191
www.vistagen.com
Estab: 1998

H. Ralph Snodgrass, Founder & President & CSO
& Director
Jon S. Saxe, Chairman
Shawn K. Singh, CEO & Director
Jerrold D. Dotson, VP & CFO & Secretary
Mark A. Mcpartland, VP of Corporate Develop-
ment

Developer of medicine to treat depression, cancer
and diseases and disorders involving the central
nervous system.

Vistrian Inc   HQ
562 Valey Way
Milpitas CA 95035
P: 408-719-0500   F: 408-719-0505   PRC:323
vistrian.com
Email: info@vistrian.com
Estab: 2002

Ronald Allen, CEO
Doug Pagel, VP of Sales & Business Development

Developer of software products. The company's
services include escalation management, problem
isolation, and remote access.

VisualOn Inc   HQ
1475 S Bascom Ave Ste 103
Campbell CA 95008
P: 408-645-6618   F: 408-596-5495   PRC:323
www.visualon.com
Email: sales@visualon.com
Estab: 2003

Yang Cai, CEO
Jim Wang, Asia Sales VP
Judy Li, Director of Finance & Administration

Provider of software applications for the mobile
handset market enabling customers to access
multimedia content without dedicated hardware.

Visualware Inc HQ
937 Sierra Dr
Turlock CA 95381-0668
P: 209-262-3491 F: 916-273-3099 PRC:325
www.visualware.com
Email: sales@visualware.com
Estab: 2001

Henry Harris, Co-Founder
Julian Palmer, Co-Founder
Kevin Hahn, Senior Software Engineer
Dan Palmer, Software Architect Engineer

Provider of solutions to measure broadband
connection performance for enterprises, homes,
and offices. The company offers both hardware
and software.

Vital Connect Inc HQ
224 Airport Pkwy Ste 300
San Jose CA 95110
P: 408-963-4600 PRC:186
vitalconnect.com
Email: info@vitalconnect.com
Estab: 2011

Nersi Nazari, Executive Chairman
Peter Van Haur, CEO
Wenkang Qi, CTO
Joseph Roberson, CMO
Allison Herd, VP of Human Resources

Provider of healthcare solutions. The company
focuses on biosensors, clinical-grade biometric
measurements.

Vital Enterprises HQ
1355 Market St Ste 488
San Francisco CA 94103
P: 650-394-6486 PRC:194
vital.enterprises
Email: info@vital.enterprises
Estab: 2013

Ash Eldritch, CEO
Aaron Vargas, CTO

Provider of field service and manufacturing solutions. The company offers services to hospitals
and R&D laboratories.

VITEC BR
931 Benecia Ave
Sunnyvale CA 94085
P: 800-451-5101 F: 408-739-1706 PRC:60
www.vitec.com
Email: sunnyvale@vitec.com
Estab: 1988

Eli Garten, VP of Product Management
Matt McKee, VP of Broadcast Sales
Bryan Reksten, VP of Marketing
Pascal Barthares, VP of Operations
Michael Chorpash, VP of Sales

Provider of digital video products. The company
offers software for video encoding, decoding, and
conversion.

Vitriflex Inc HQ
2350 Zanker Rd
San Jose CA 95131-1115
P: 408-468-6700 PRC:209
www.vitriflex.com
Email: info@vitriflex.com

Ravi Prasad, CTO & Founder
Dave Pearce, CEO & Chairman
Martin Rosenblum, VP of Engineering
Mark George, Director
Rex Chang, Senior Process Development Engineer

Manufacturer of ultra-barrier films for electronic
applications. The company focuses on surface
science and engineering.

Vitron Electronic Services Inc HQ
5400 Hellyer Ave
San Jose CA 95138
P: 408-251-1600 PRC:207
www.vitronmfg.com
Estab: 1985

Daniel Tran, Manager

Provider of electronics manufacturing services.
The company deals with product development,
system integration, and prototyping services.

Vivante Corp HQ
2150 Gold St Ste 200
San Jose CA 95002
P: 408-844-8560 F: 408-844-8563 PRC:325
giquila.com
Email: info@vivantecorp.com
Estab: 2004

Mike Cai, CTO & Founder & Board Director
Wei-Jin Dai, President & CEO
Brian Hutsell, Chief GPU Architect
David Jarmon, SVP of Sales & Business Devel-
opment
Jeff Li, VP & General Manager

Provider of semiconductors for graphics and multimedia. The company focuses on image and video
processing services.

Vivax-Metrotech Corp HQ
3251 Olcott St
Santa Clara CA 95054
P: 408-734-1400 F: 408-734-1415 PRC:63
www.vivax-metrotech.com
Email: sales@vxmt.com
Estab: 1976

Mark Drew, President
Rich Jordan, Product Manager
Matt Manning, Regional Sales Manager
Jeff Fisher, Accountant & HR

Manufacturer of mapping tools. The company
specializes in tools used for underground cabling
and piping works.

Vivid Vision Inc HQ
424 Treat Ave Unit B
San Francisco CA 94110
P: 877-877-0310 PRC:317
www.seevividly.com
Email: contact@seevividly.com
Estab: 2013

James Blaha, Co-Founder & CEO
Manish Gupta, Co-Founder & CTO
Tuan Tran, Chief Optometrist & Co-Founder
Ben Backus, Chief Science Officer
Sunao Miyoshi, VP of Asia

Provider of virtual reality solutions. The company
offers services to eye clinics and also kids and
adults.

Vivotek USA BR
2050 Ringwood Ave
San Jose CA 95131
P: 408-773-8686 F: 408-773-8298 PRC:168
www.vivotek.com
Email: salesusa@vivotek.com
Estab: 2008

Roy Pangilinan, VP of Engineering
Kelly Lee, Finance & Administration Director
Alan Green, Director of Sales of North America
Stanley Yu Chih, Regional Sales Manager
David Liu, National Sales Manager

Provider of surveillance solutions. The company
specializes in manufacturing network cameras for
the network video surveillance industries.

Vlsi Research Inc HQ
2290 N First St Ste 202
San Jose CA 95131-2017
P: 408-453-8844 F: 408-437-0608 PRC:212
www.vlsiresearch.com
Email: clientservices@vlsiresearch.com
Estab: 1976

Risto Puhakka, President
Dan Hutcheson, CEO
Manjesh Singh, CTO
Lisa M. Steele, VP of Administration
Andrea Lati, VP of Market Research

Provider of chip market research, consultation,
semiconductor analysis, and data spreadsheets
and reports.

VLSI Standards Inc HQ
5 Technology Dr
Milpitas CA 95035-7916
P: 408-428-1800 F: 408-428-9555 PRC:212
www.vlsistandards.com
Email: sales.support@vlsistd.com
Estab: 1984

Lane Stump, Facilities Engineer
Yu Guan, Engineer

Manufacturer of electrical and solar energy products. The company offers calibration services to
the semiconductor industry.

VMware Inc HQ
3401 Hillview Ave
Palo Alto CA 94304
P: 650-427-1000   F: 650-475-5001   PRC:322
www.vmware.com
Estab: 1998
Sales: Over $3B

Pat Gelsinger, CEO
Robin Matlock, CMO
Ben Fathi, CTO
Rajiv Ramaswami, COO of Products & Cloud Services
Zane C. Rowe, CFO & EVP

Provider of storage, data center, application virtualization, and enterprise mobility management products.

Voce Communications HQ
55 Union St
San Francisco CA 94111
P: 415-975-2200   F: 415-975-2201   PRC:67
vocecommunications.com
Email: info@vocecomm.com
Estab: 1999

Jessica Kerr, Account Manager
June LaPore, Office Manager

Provider of marketing and communication consultancy services. The company in engaged in public relation, media marketing, and web development.

Vocera Communications HQ
525 Race St
San Jose CA 95126
P: 408-882-5600   PRC:68
www.vocera.com
Email: support@vocera.com
Estab: 2000
Sales: $100M to $300M

Brent D. Lang, Chairman & CEO
Bridget Duffy, CMO
Justin R. Spencer, EVP & CFO
Benjamin Kanter, Chief Medical Information Officer
Paul T. Johnson, EVP of Sales & Services

Provider of mobile communication solutions. The company provides voice communication, messaging, wireless networking, and technical support.

Voltage Multipliers Inc HQ
8711 W Roosevelt Ave
Visalia CA 93291
P: 559-651-1402   F: 559-651-0740   PRC:209
www.voltagemultipliers.com
Email: sales@voltagemultipliers.com
Estab: 1980

Dennis Kemp, President
Ken Haag, VP of Marketing
Karen Spano, Sales Administration Manager
Todd Cooney, Production Manager
Jorge Mejia, Engineering Manager

Manufacturer of voltage multipliers, high voltage diodes, rectifiers, opto-couplers, and power supplies.

Volume Precision Glass Inc HQ
150 Todd Rd Bldg 100
Santa Rosa CA 95407
P: 707-206-0100   F: 707-206-0105   PRC:175
www.vpglass.com
Email: info@vpglass.com
Estab: 1998

Croy Davis, President

Fabricator of optical components and thin-film coatings for photonics, military, industrial, and lighting applications.

VORTRAN Medical Technology Inc HQ
21 Goldenland Ct Ste 100
Sacramento CA 95834
P: 800-434-4034   F: 916-243-1338   PRC:189
www.vortran.com
Email: info@vortran.com
Estab: 1983

James Lee, EVP & COO
Reza Saied, VP of Engineering & RA

Developer of pulmonary modulation technology solutions. The company offers automatic disposable respiratory devices for treating pulmonary diseases.

VSP Optics Group HQ
3333 Quality Dr
Rancho Cordova CA 95670
P: 800-852-7600   PRC:170
vspglobal.com
Email: pathtopremier@vsp.com
Estab: 1955

Andy Kopitske, Product Manager
Brian Baxter, Lab Manager
Jack Murphy, Maintenance Manager
Melissa Bierer Parker, Supervisor
Tarry Loop, Senior OS Supply Chain Analyst

Provider of eye care solutions. The company offers eye care insurance, eyewear, lenses, ophthalmic technology and retail solutions.

Vulcan Inc HQ
23445 Foley St
Hayward CA 94545
P: 510-887-2495   F: 510-887-3792   PRC:78
www.vulcanwire.com
Estab: 1975

Michael Graffio, CEO & President

Focuses on the manufacture and fabrication of aluminum coiled sheets, aluminum sign blanks, and finished traffic control signs.

VytronUS Inc HQ
658 N Pastoria Ave
Sunnyvale CA 94085
P: 408-730-1333   PRC:186
www.vytronus.com
Email: info@vytronus.com
Estab: 2006

John Pavlidis, CEO
Dave Gallup, COO
Patrick Phillips, SVP of Engineering & Manufacturing
Paul Chan, VP of Finance
Dave White, VP of Manufacturing

Developer of ablation systems for the treatment of atrial fibrillation and other cardiac arrhythmias. The company deals with customizable lesions.

W E Plemons Machinery Services Inc HQ
13479 E Industrial Dr
Parlier CA 93648
P: 559-646-6630   F: 559-646-9630   PRC:80
weplemons.com
Email: pms@weplemons.com

William Plemons, President & CEO
Jeff Winters, VP

Provider of flange seals and automatic lidding attachments. The company's services include box designs and rebuilding.

WBR Inc HQ
1111A Quail St   [N]
Newport Beach CA 92660
P: 949-673-1247   F: 949-673-0846   PRC:141
www.wbrinc.com
Email: info@wbrinc.com
Estab: 1992

Craig Barrett, Contact
John Lindsey, Contact

Provider of waste transportation and disposal systems.

WM Lyles Co HQ
1210 W Olive Ave   [N]
Fresno CA 93728
P: 559-441-1900   PRC:304
www.wmlyles.com
Email: info@wmlyles.com
Estab: 1945

Dave Dawson, President & CEO
Ken Strosnider, SVP & Division Manager

Provider of infrastructure, energy and environmental construction services.

W2 Systems HQ
304 Industrial Way
Brisbane CA 94005
P: 415-468-9858   F: 415-468-9854   PRC:143
www.w2systems.com
Email: info@w2systems.com
Estab: 1986

Kirk Howard, President

Provider of customized water treatment support and solutions. The company also offers services like design, technical support, and control services.

Wachters' Organic Sea Products HQ
550 Sylvan St
Daly City CA 94014
P: 650-757-9851   F: 650-757-9858   PRC:272
wachters.com
Email: info@wachters.com
Estab: 1932

Carrie Minucianni, CEO

Manufacturer and distributor of nutritional products. The company's products include pet products, personal care, and cleaning products.

Wafer Process Systems Inc   HQ
3641 Charter Park Dr
San Jose CA 95136
P: 408-445-3010   F: 408-445-3004   PRC:124
www.waferprocess.com
Estab: 1983

Douglas H. Caldwell, President & CEO
Barbara C. Caldwell, CFO & VP of Administration
Christopher J. Schmitz, VP of Engineering
Stuart H. Lebherz, Customer Service Manager

Manufacturer of semiconductors, MEMS, and photonics. The company also focuses on RFID products, disc drives, and flat panel displays.

WaferMasters Inc   HQ
2251 Brandini Dr
Dublin CA 94568
P: 408-451-0850   PRC:204
www.wafermasters.com
Email: info@wafermasters.com
Estab: 1999

Shintaro Fujimoto, COO
Kitaek Kang, Engineer

Provider of thermal processing services. The company also focuses on diagnostic metrology and design and consulting services.

WaferNet Inc   HQ
2142 Paragon Dr
San Jose CA 95131
P: 866-749-2337   PRC:124
wafernet.com
Estab: 1988

Jon Mewes, VP
Omar Ghosheh, VP of Sales

Supplier of silicon wafers. The company serves semiconductor equipment manufacturers and universities.

WAGAN Corp   HQ
31088 San Clemente St
Hayward CA 94544
P: 510-471-9221   F: 510-489-3451   PRC:135
wagan.com
Email: customerservice@wagan.com
Estab: 1983

Alex Hsu, President

Developer and marketer of automotive accessories to mobile professionals. The company's offerings include warmers, defrosters, and heated cushions.

Walters & Wolf   BR
41450 Boscell Rd
Fremont CA 94538
P: 510-490-1115   F: 510-490-7114   PRC:80
www.waltersandwolf.com
Email: interiorsinfo@waltersandwolf.com
Estab: 1977

Rick Calhoun, President
Jeff Belzer, CFO
Mike Gross, VP
Glenn A. Radel, VP
Steve Watts, VP

Provider of cladding services. The company specializes in design, engineering, fabrication, and delivery and installation.

Walters Wholesale Electric Co   HQ
2825 Temple Ave   [N]
Signal Hill CA 90755
P: 562-988-3100   F: 562-988-3150   PRC:245
www.walterswholesale.com
Email: tools@walterswholesale.com
Emp: 501-1000   Estab: 1953

Bill Durkee, President

Wholesaler of industrial automation, low voltage, residential and commercial lighting products and much more.

Ward Systems Inc   HQ
12912 Madrona Leaf Ct
Grass Valley CA 95945
P: 530-271-1800   F: 530-271-1801   PRC:180
www.wardventures.com
Email: sales@wardventures.com

Glen Ward, President

Provider of custom automation services. The company's services include valve installation, maintenance, and reconfiguration.

Warren & Baerg Manufacturing Inc   HQ
39950 Rd 108
Dinuba CA 93618
P: 559-591-6790   F: 559-591-5728   PRC:159
warrenbaerg.com
Email: Info@warrenbaerg.com
Estab: 1966

Randy Baerg, Owner
Wendell Spray, General Manager & Sales
Woody Darren Randel, Technical Sales Manager

Manufacturer of agricultural and industrial systems. The company's services include installation, manufacturing, and technical support.

Warren Distributing Inc   HQ
8737 Dice Rd   [N]
Santa Fe Springs CA 90670
P: 562-789-3360   F: 562-789-3361   PRC:359
www.warrendist.com
Estab: 1963

Brian Weiss, President
Gary Jacobson, VP of Operations

Manufacturer and distributor of automotive parts and lubricants.

Wasco Hardfacing Co   HQ
4585 E Citron Ave
Fresno CA 93725
P: 559-485-5860   F: 559-233-4436   PRC:158
www.wascohardfacing.com
Email: info@ag1.net
Estab: 1952

Robin Messick, Owner

Manufacturer of hardfacing electrodes for steel, cement, and mining applications. The company also offers welding alloy solutions.

Watchwith Inc   HQ
301 Howard St 19th Fl
San Francisco CA 94105
P: 415-552-1552   PRC:326
www.watchwith.com
Estab: 2006

Zane Vella, Founder & CEO
Mike Dalrymple, SVP of Engineering
Susan Kalman, Corporate Controller

Provider of software and data solutions for the film and television content creators and consumer electronics manufacturers.

Waterman Industries   HQ
25500 Rd 204
Exeter CA 93221
P: 559-562-4000   F: 559-562-2277   PRC:144
watermanusa.com
Email: sales@watermanusa.com
Estab: 1912

Francisco Soto, Project Manager
John Speidel, Engineering Manager of AG & Cast Products & New Product Development
Mike Rudy, Estimating Manager
Darryl Pauls, Senior Mechanical Engineer
Steve Corter, Network Administrator

Designer and manufacturer of water-control sluice gates, penstocks, valves, and water control products.

Wave Systems Corp   HQ
1159 Sonora Ct
Sunnyvale CA 94086
P: 408-524-8630   PRC:323
www.wavesystems.com
Email: info@wavesystems.com
Estab: 1994

Bhupinder Lehga, President & CEO
Joe Luong, Staff Engineer
Muhammad Umar, Senior Software Engineer

Provider of customized software development for the law enforcement, casino, corporate security, and hospitals segments.

Wavesplitter Technologies Inc   HQ
2080 Rancho Higuera Ct
Fremont CA 94539
P: 925-596-0414   F: 408-432-8111   PRC:61
www.wavesplitter.com
Email: info@wavesplitter.com
Estab: 1996

Sheau Sheng Chen, CEO & Chairman & Founder

Manufacturer of passive devices and active optical components for enterprise and residential broadband networks.

WCR Inc   BR
4636 E Drummond Ave
Fresno CA 93725
P: 559-266-8374   F: 559-266-3354   PRC:153
www.wcrhx.com

Greg Pinasco, VP of Western Operations

Developer and manufacturer of heat exchangers. The company's products include plate heat exchangers, brazed heat exchangers, and welded heat exchangers.

Weatherflow Inc HQ
108 Whispering Pines Ste 245
Scotts Valley CA 95066
P: 800-946-3225 PRC:142
www.weatherflow.com
Email: info@weatherflow.com

Buck Lyons, CEO
Jenna Hampton, Creative Director
Marty Bell, Director of Research & Modeling
Bob LeRoyer, Project Manager & Engineer
Keith Koenig, Head of Product Marketing

Provider of modeling and forecasting technologies
for the weather forecast industry. The company
also offers wind-based and coastal forecasting.

Webenertia HQ
1570 The Alameda Ste 330
San Jose CA 95126
P: 408-246-0000 F: 408-275-0970 PRC:325
www.webenertia.com
Email: info@webenertia.com
Estab: 1999

Steve Ohanians, Founder & Director of Digital
Strategy
Margaret Nora, CMO
Annie Raygoza, Director of Client Services
Danny Halvorson, Interactive Director
Juliann Klein, Director Of Client Services

Provider of web applications and e-commerce
services. The company also focuses on motion
graphics and Internet marketing solutions.

Weber Hayes & Associates Inc HQ
120 Westgate Dr
Watsonville CA 95076
P: 831-722-3580 F: 831-722-1159 PRC:142
weber-hayes.com
Email: info@weber-hayes.com
Estab: 1974

Pat Hoban, President & Senior Geologist
Laura Garcia, CFO
Elizabeth Fisher, Administrative Support Manager
Craig Drizin, Senior Engineer
Josh Hannaleck, Staff Civil & Environmental
Engineer

Provider of hydrogeologic and environmental
engineering consulting services. The company
offers cleanup of soil, groundwater, and stormwater services.

Weichhart Stamping Company inc HQ
39 Maxwell Ct
Santa Rosa CA 95401
P: 510-562-6886 F: 510-562-6856 PRC:82
www.weichhartstamping.com
Email: rex@weichhartstamping.com
Estab: 1933

John Weichhart, Owner

Manufacturer of tools and metal stampings in
the San Francisco area. The company's offerings
include flat springs, wire forms, spring washers,
and wave washers.

Wellex Corp HQ
551 Brown Rd
Fremont CA 94539-7003
P: 510-743-1818 F: 510-743-1899 PRC:211
www.wellex.com
Email: salesmarketing_web@wellex.com
Estab: 1983

Jett Tsai, VP of Operations
Andy Chang, Director of Sales & Marketing
Susan Huang, Accounting Manager & Accounting
Manager
Daniel Shih, Program Manager
John Suh, Program Manager

Provider of printed circuit boards, cables, harness
assemblies, and wiring products. The company
is engaged in engineering and manufacturing
services.

Wellmade Products HQ
1715 Kibby Rd
Merced CA 95341
P: 209-723-9120 F: 209-723-9131 PRC:88
www.wlmd.com

David Verstoppen, VP of Sales
Steve Squires, General Manager

Manufacturer of lighting, wheelbarrows, and sheet
metal products. The company also offers photometric sheets.

WellnessFX Inc HQ
1550 Bryant St Ste 590
San Francisco CA 94103
P: 415-796-3373 PRC:325
www.wellnessfx.com
Email: support@wellnessfx.com
Estab: 2010

Paul Jacobson, CEO
Jeremy Barth, CTO
Christine Keating, Director of Customer Support
& Operations

Specializes in web-based services. The company
focuses on diagnostic testing and it serves medical practitioners.

Wells Dental Inc HQ
5860 Flynn Creek Rd
Comptche CA 95427-0106
P: 707-937-0521 F: 707-937-2809 PRC:185
wellsdental.com
Estab: 1975

Earl Wells, Founder

Supplier of dental laboratory equipment. The
company offers engine units, finishing machines,
quick chucks, and consumables.

Wellspace BR
8233 E Stockton Blvd Ste D [N]
Sacramento CA 95828
P: 916-737-5555 PRC:45
www.wellspacehealth.org/services/counsel-
ing-prevention/suicide_prevention
Email: lwick@wellspacehealth.org
Emp: 11-50

Lisa Stewart, President
Larry Maas, VP
Margie Meza, Secretary
Ruzwa Cooper, Treasurer

Provider of quality medical care, dental care, mental health, and behavioral health services.

Wema Inc HQ
1670 Zanker Rd
San Jose CA 95112
P: 408-453-5005 F: 408-453-5502 PRC:80
www.wemainc.com
Email: machining@wemainc.com
Estab: 1992

Max Ho, President & CEO

Provider of tank sensors, gauges, and smoke
detectors for automotive, marine, agricultural, and
construction equipment.

Wenteq Inc HQ
20550 E Kettleman Ln
Lodi CA 95240
P: 209-608-2374 PRC:80
www.wenteqmachine.com

Shawn Wentzel, President

Manufacturer of print, precision, machined components, and assemblies. The company serves the
automotive, racing, and boat markers.

Werlchem LLC HQ
1660 Wayne Ave
San Leandro CA 94577
P: 510-918-1896 F: 510-352-1525 PRC:53
www.werlchem.net
Email: sales@werlchem.net
Estab: 2012

Wilson Wu, Founder

Developer and manufacturer of specialty chemicals. The company's offerings include dyes,
pharmaceutical intermediates, and electronic
materials.

Weslan Systems Inc HQ
1244 Commerce Ave
Woodland CA 95776
P: 530-668-3304 F: 530-668-3414 PRC:159
www.weslan.com
Email: info@weslan.com
Estab: 1978

Rick Weston, CEO
Jim Dittrich, Production Manager of Sales

Fabricator of custom plastic products for the semiconductor industry. The company offers contract
manufacturing services.

Wessdel Inc HQ
581 Dado St
San Jose CA 95131
P: 408-496-6822 F: 408-496-0569 PRC:80
www.wessdel.com
Email: info@wessdel.com
Estab: 1974

Bob Dorricott, President & CEO
Cindy Ketchum-Ewing, Office Manager & Human
Resources

Provider of precision machining and engineering
services for the military, aerospace, defense, and
medical sectors.

West Coast Fab Inc HQ
700 S 32nd St
Richmond CA 94804
P: 510-529-0177 F: 510-233-2248 PRC:80
westcoastfabinc.com
Email: info@westcoastfabinc.com
Estab: 1973

Tom Nelson, President
Diane Burnett, Office Manager
Scott Shelby, Programmer & QC Manager

Provider of precision electronic sheet metal fabrication services. The company specializes in finished products.

West Coast Internet Inc HQ
PO Box 7598 [N]
Capistrano Beach CA 92624
P: 949-487-3307 PRC:64
www.westcoastinternet.com
Estab: 1990

Paul Quaranto, Contact

Provider of Internet services.

West Coast Magnetics HQ
4848 Frontier Way Ste 100
Stockton CA 95215
P: 800-628-1123 F: 209-944-0747 PRC:296
www.wcmagnetics.com
Email: sales@wcmagnetics.com
Estab: 1974

Weyman Lundquist, CEO
Elizabeth Menchaca, Inside Sales Manager
Lisa Reyes, Production Manager
David Harizal, Design Engineer
Melissa Gonzales, Inside Sales Representative

Provider of electrical products. The company specializes in inductor products, transformers, chokes, and planar magnetic products.

West Coast Pathology Laboratories HQ
712 Alfred Nobel Dr
Hercules CA 94547-1805
P: 510-662-5200 F: 510-662-5240 PRC:306
www.wcpl.com
Email: contact@wcpl.com
Estab: 1985

Lisa K. Helfend, Laboratory Medical Director
Nazila Hejazi, Associate Pathologist
Alfredo Asuncion, Associate Pathologist
Tracy Chang, Cytotechnologist

Providers of anatomic pathology and cytology services. The company's expertise lies with molecular genetics and diagnostics.

West Coast Surgical HQ
141 California Ave Ste 101
Half Moon Bay CA 94019
P: 650-728-8095 F: 650-728-8096 PRC:80
www.westcoastsurgical.com

Daniel Bass, Owner & Partner
William Lynn, President
Rick Townsend, Director of Nursing
Celeste Bass, Operations Manager
Andrew Le, Assistant Manager

Manufacturer of surgical devices. The company offers designing, assembling and finishing of specialty surgical equipment.

West Coast HQ
2341 Stanwell Dr
Concord CA 94520
P: 925-270-3800 PRC:41
analyticallabgroup.com
Email: info@analyticallabgroup.com
Estab: 2006

Alan Roth, CEO
Kelly Lauer, Director of Operations
Megan Cosgrove, Director of Marketing
Mimi Leong, Director of Inside Sales - ALG-West Coast
Renee Johnston, Director of Microbiology Services

Provider of contract testing laboratory services. The company offers testing laboratories, manufacturing services, and validation and calibration services.

West Yost Associates HQ
2020 Research Park Dr Ste 100
Davis CA 95618
P: 530-756-5905 F: 530-756-5991 PRC:142
www.westyost.com
Email: info@westyost.com
Estab: 1990

Charles Duncan, President & CEO
Jeff Pelz, Chairman
Ernest Liu, CFO
Polly Boissevain, Chief Engineer
Frank Helmick, VP

Provider of water, storm water, wastewater, and construction management project services. The company also offers recycling services.

Westak HQ
1272 Forgewood Ave
Sunnyvale CA 94089
P: 408-734-8686 F: 408-734-5190 PRC:211
westak.com
Email: info@westak.com
Estab: 1972

Louise Crisham, CEO
Lou George, COO
Debby Hall, Director of Business Services
Donna Hill, Quality Assurance Manager
Brian Alarid, Account Manager

Designer and manufacturer of printed circuit boards. The company offers rigid double-sided interconnects and rigid multi-layer interconnects.

Westec Plastics Corp HQ
6757-A Las Positas Rd
Livermore CA 94551
P: 925-454-3400 PRC:159
www.westecplastics.com
Estab: 1969

Tammy Barras, President
John Baker, Business Development Manager & Director of Sales
Julie Meeks, Project Manager & Purchasing Manager
Lucero Castro, QA Manager
Tina Scheck, Controller

Provider of plastics injection molding and mold making services. The company also offers customized services.

Western Allied Mechanical Inc HQ
1180 O'Brien Dr
Menlo Park CA 94025
P: 650-326-0750 F: 650-321-4946 PRC:159
www.westernallied.com
Email: info@westernallied.com
Estab: 1961

Zachary Russi, President
Angela M. Simon, CEO
Jeff Pierce, CFO
Bob Dills, VP & Treasurer
Robert Monaghan, EVP of Service Department

Designer and builder of heating and ventilation systems. The company serves the construction and energy automation industries.

Western Case Inc HQ
6400-B Sycamore Canyon Blvd [N]
Riverside CA 92507
P: 951-214-6380 F: 951-214-6387 PRC:189
www.westerncase.com
Emp: 11-50 Estab: 1981

Steve Santos, General Manager

Manufacturer of plastics products.

Western Digital Corp HQ
7999 Gateway Blvd Ste 120
Newark CA 94560
P: 510-791-7900 PRC:95
www.westerndigital.com
Estab: 2010

Siva Sivaram, President of Technology & Strategy
Stephen D. Milligan, CEO
Loris S. Sundberg, EVP & Chief Human Resource Officer
Michael C. Ray, EVP & CLO & Secretary

Provider of storage array solutions. The company focuses on desktop virtualization, server virtualization, database hosting, and file services.

Western Digital Corp HQ
5601 Great Oaks Pkwy
San Jose CA 95119
P: 408-717-6000 PRC:95
www.westerndigital.com
Estab: 1970
Sales: Over $3B

Mark Long, EVP of Strategy & Corporate Development
Roseann Schaefer, Global Mobility Programs Manager
David P. Nguyen, Credit Coordinator

Manufacturer of external storage devices. The company also focuses on network storage and backup solutions and offers technical support services.

Western Stucco Co HQ
1550 Pkwy Blvd
West Sacramento CA 95691
P: 916-372-7442 PRC:47
www.westernblended.com
Email: wsinfo@westernblended.com
Estab: 1932

Jose Gomez, General Manager
Phill Hall, Plant Manager
Walter Rozewski, Office Manager

Developer and manufacturer of exterior products for the stucco industry. The company offers both cement color coats and resin based finishes.

Western Truck Fab Inc HQ
  1923 W Winton
  Hayward CA 94545-1605
  P: 510-785-9994   F: 510-785-9986   PRC:159
  www.westerntruckfab.com
  Estab: 1984

Julie Meyers, Owner
Brett Maury, Supervisor
Ron Frost, Final QC Inspector

Provider of custom truck body fabrication services. The company's products include lift gates, compressors, and cranes.

Western Widgets CNC Inc HQ
  915 Commercial St
  San Jose CA 95112
  P: 408-436-1230   F: 408-436-7456   PRC:159
  www.westernwidgets.com

Teresa Gale, Office Manager

Manufacturer of precision milled and turned components such as computers and optical assemblies. The company deals with milling and turning services.

Westervelt Ecological Services HQ
  600 N Market Blvd Ste 3
  Sacramento CA 95834
  P: 916-646-3644   PRC:139
  www.wesmitigation.com
  Email: wesmitigation@westervelt.com
  Estab: 2006

Steve Moore, VP of Finance & Administration
Greg DeYoung, VP
Greg Sutter, EVP
Matthew Gause, Senior Ecologist & Land Manager
Sarah Correa, Business Acquisition Manager

Provider of ecological solutions. The company offers wetland mitigation and conservation banking, geographic information system analysis, and other services.

Westfab Manufacturing Inc HQ
  3370 Keller St
  Santa Clara CA 95054
  P: 408-727-0550   F: 408-727-6776   PRC:88
  www.westfab.com
  Email: sale@westfab.com
  Estab: 1986

Ashok Dadlani, Finance Manager
Nikita Shah, Accounting Manager
Rick Rey, Sales Manager

Manufacturer of simple brackets, multiple level frames, and enclosures. The company offers assembly services for power supplies, switches, and cables.

Westland Technologies Inc HQ
  107 S Riverside Dr
  Modesto CA 95354
  P: 209-571-6400   F: 209-571-6411   PRC:57
  westlandtech.com
  Email: info@westlandtech.com
  Estab: 1996

John Grizzard, President
Tom Halyburton, CEO
Keryn Leger, CFO
Andy Jessup, VP of Operations
Joe Barbano, VP of Programmer

Provider of injection and transfer molding, pressure testing, custom hand fabricating, and acid etching services.

Westpak Inc HQ
  83 Great Oaks Blvd
  San Jose CA 95119
  P: 408-224-1300   PRC:306
  www.westpak.com
  Estab: 1986

Rizwan Silat, President
Ryan Craft, CEO
Mark Escobedo, CTO
Harmony Reynolds, General Manager & Director of Operations & Engineering Services & Site Coordinator & Manager of Oper
Aaron Suarez, Director of Engineering

Provider of customized product and packaging testing services. The company also deals with packaging, material analysis, and supply chain management.

Westport Machine Works Inc HQ
  700 Houston St
  West Sacramento CA 95691
  P: 916-371-4493   PRC:76
  westportproducts.com
  Email: westportproducts@att.net
  Estab: 1957

Cindi Lou Taylor, Office Manager

Manufacturer of assembly and balancing equipment. The company's services include fixturing, installation, and technical support.

Westside Research Inc HQ
  4293 County Rd 99 W
  Orland CA 95963
  P: 530-865-5587   F: 530-865-1474   PRC:179
  www.westsideresearch.com
  Email: info@westsideresearch.com

Tim Dexter, President & Founder

Designer and manufacturer of interior and exterior automotive cargo management products. The company specializes in truck luggage product lines.

WHILL Inc BR
  285 Old County Rd Ste 6
  San Carlos CA 94070
  P: 844-699-4455   PRC:189
  whill.us
  Email: info@whill.us
  Estab: 2013

Satoshi Sugie, CEO

Manufacturer of personal electric vehicles, wheelchairs, and mobility devices. The company serves individuals and clinics.

Whipple Industries Inc HQ
  3292 N Weber Ave
  Fresno CA 93722
  P: 559-442-1261   F: 559-442-4153   PRC:159
  whipplesuperchargers.com
  Email: sales@whipplesuperchargers.com

Art Whipple, Founder & President

Provider of supercharger for vehicles. The company's products include twin-screw superchargers and accessories.

White Industries HQ
  1325 Ross St
  Petaluma CA 94954
  P: 707-769-5600   PRC:80
  whiteind.com
  Email: info@whiteind.com
  Estab: 1978

Doug White, Owner & President
Craig White, CEO
Janet King, VP of Finance
Bill McDowell, VP of Operations
Patrick Murphy, Director of Engineer

Manufacturer of bicycle components. The company's products include cranks, front hubs, brackets, pedals, and related accessories.

Whitehat Security HQ
  1741 Technology Dr Ste 300
  San Jose CA 95110
  P: 408-343-8300   F: 408-904-7142   PRC:325
  www.whitehatsec.com
  Email: whitehat.contact@whitehatsec.com
  Estab: 2001

Craig Hinkley, CEO
Tamir Hardof, CMO
Eric Sheridan, Chief Scientist
Kanthi Prasad, VP of Engineering
Kathy Fan, Senior Finance Manager

Provider of web application security solutions such as vulnerability management, threat modeling, and risk profiling.

Whizz Systems HQ
  3240 Scott Blvd
  Santa Clara CA 95054
  P: 408-980-0400   PRC:209
  www.whizzsystems.com
  Email: info@whizzsystems.com
  Estab: 1989

Muhammad Irfan, President
Manny Karim, CFO
Kelly Christensen, Business Development Manager
Fawad Munawar, Design Engineer
Asif Hassan, Senior Design Engineer

Provider of electronics design and manufacturing services for the semiconductor, defense, computing, and industrial equipment markers.

Whole You Inc HQ
  101 Metro Dr
  San Jose CA 95110
  P: 844-548-3385   PRC:189
  wholeyou.com
  Estab: 2014

Yasunori Nishiyama, CEO
Phil Costello, Sales Manager & Marketing Manager
Nid Sartnurak, Operations Manager

Provider of healthcare solutions. The company specializes in sleep, dental, movement, and vision solutions to its customers.

Wi2wi Inc HQ
1879 Lundy Ave Ste 218
San Jose CA 95131
P: 408-416-4200   F: 608-831-3343   PRC:68
www.wi2wi.com
Email: sales@wi2wi.com
Estab: 2005

Zachariah J. Mathews, President & CEO
Dawn Leeder, CFO
Barry Arneson, VP of Engineering Frequency
Control & Timing Devices
Ramesh Duvvuru, VP of Engineering
Pierre Soulard, Company Secretary

Provider of wireless system-in-package, module,
and subsystems for embedded applications
including Wi-Fi, Bluetooth, and GPS.

Wiegmann & Rose HQ
263 S Vasco Rd
Livermore CA 94551
P: 510-632-8828   F: 510-632-8920   PRC:80
www.wiegmannandrose.com

Scott E. Logan, CEO & President
Gary D. Keeler, Plant Superintendent Sales &
Engineering
Jon E. Hammons, Quality Controller
Sam Flores, Contact
Suzette I. Logan, Contact

Provider of custom heat exchangers, pressure
vessels, and weldments. The company offers
vacuum chalmers and pipe spool products.

Wiley X Inc HQ
7800 Patterson Pass Rd
Livermore CA 94550
P: 925-243-9810   F: 925-455-8860   PRC:305
wileyx.com
Estab: 1987

Myles Freeman, President of Sales & Owner
John Moore, Senior Account Manager
Karen Stevens, Manager of Information Technology
Roseann Difu, Sales Manager

Provider of high velocity protection services. The
company specializes in climate control frames,
light adjusting lenses, and polarized lenses.

Wilkman Productions Inc HQ
6160 Rodgerton Dr   [N]
Hollywood CA 90068
P: 323-461-7028   F: 323-461-0753   PRC:60
www.wilkman.com
Estab: 1971

Jon Wilkman, President
Nancy Wilkman, VP

distributor of documentaries and other non-fiction
films and videos.

Willdan Energy Solutions BR
9281 Office Park Cir Ste 135
Elk Grove CA 95758-8068
P: 916-661-3520   F: 916-478-6005   PRC:304
www.willdan.com
Email: info@willdan.com
Estab: 2003

Stacy McLaughlin, CFO
Mehdi Ganji, VP
Mike Teate, VP
Craig Owens, Director
Emily Fisher, Program Manager

Provider of energy efficiency, water conservation,
and renewable energy services. The company
serves education, utility, labs, and other sectors.

William Stucky & Associates Inc HQ
1 Embarcadero Ctr Ste 1330
San Francisco CA 94111
P: 415-788-2441   PRC:323
www.stuckynet.com
Estab: 1979

Rosanne Doyle, VP

Provider of software products and services. The
company mainly caters to the asset-based lending
industry.

Wilson Research Group LLC HQ
4209 Berrendo Dr
Sacramento CA 95864
P: 530-350-8377   F: 530-350-7567   PRC:323
www.wilsonresearch.com

Larry Wilson, President

Provider of market research products and services. The company serves publishing, embedded
systems, and high technology fields.

Wilson, Ihrig & Associates Inc BR
6001 Shellmound Ste 400   [N]
Emeryville CA 94608
P: 510-658-6719   F: 510-652-4441   PRC:139
www.wilsonihrig.com
Email: info@wiai.com

Hildegard Dodd, Manager of Marketing & Business Development
Pablo Daroux, Principal
Richard Carman, Principal
Deborah Jue, Principal
Derek Watry, Principal

Provider of noise, vibration and acoustical consulting services.

**Winbond Electronics Corporation
America** DH
2727 N First St
San Jose CA 95134
P: 408-943-6666   PRC:116
www.winbond.com
Estab: 1987

Omar Ma, Manager of DRAM Marketing
Michael Stevenson, Founding Principal
Allison Chan, Senior Associate

Provider of memory solutions and services. The
company offers Pseudo SRAM, Serial NOR Flash,
Mobile DRAM, and KGD.

Wind River Systems Inc DH
500 Wind River Way
Alameda CA 94501
P: 510-748-4100   F: 510-749-2010   PRC:319
www.windriver.com
Email: license-ec@windriver.com
Estab: 1981

Jim Douglas, President & CEO
Michael Krutz, SVP & CPO
Gareth Noyes, CSO & SVP of Strategy & Corporate Development

Provider of automotive networking solutions. The
company's products include operating systems,
development tools, and middleware technologies.

Window Solutions HQ
186 Utah Ave
S San Francisco CA 94080
P: 650-349-2257   F: 650-349-2297   PRC:279
www.windowsolutions.com
Estab: 1969

Paul Murphy, Founder
Salvatore M. Baglione, Owner
Louis Reper, Owner
David Huntamer, President
Paul Bellamy, CEO

Provider of 3M window film and tinting installation
services. The company offers services for residential, commercial, architects, and builders.

WindSpring Inc HQ
1735 N First St Ste 102
San Jose CA 95112
P: 408-452-7400   F: 408-452-7444   PRC:324
www.windspring.com
Email: info@windspring.com
Estab: 2004

Douglas Wadkins, CEO
Devanshi Patel, Software Quality Assurance
Engineer

Manufacturer of data management tools. The
company provides a framework for optimized
compressed data management in the storage and
embedded fields.

WineDirect HQ
450 Green Island Rd
American Canyon CA 94503
P: 800-819-0325   PRC:326
www.winedirect.com
Email: info@winedirect.com
Estab: 2002

Kwangbo Shim, Owner
Joe Waechter, CEO
John Gilmer, CFO
Devin Loftis, CTO
Jim Agger, VP of Sales

Provider of DTC services such as commerce,
compliance, fulfillment, marketing, and enterprise
services for wineries.

Winning Directions — HQ

1366 San Mateo Ave [N]
S San Francisco CA 94080
P: 650-875-4000 F: 650-875-1015 PRC:24
www.winningdirections.com
Estab: 1989

Tony Fazio, President & Owner
Freddy F. Sanchez, Consultant
Nancy Todd, Consultant

Provider of professional services.

Winnov LP — HQ

3910 Freedom Cir Ste 102
Santa Clara CA 95054
P: 888-315-9460 F: 408-533-8808 PRC:95
www.winnov.com
Email: info@winnov.com
Estab: 1992

Olivier Garbe, Founder & CEO

Provider of video capture and streaming solutions. The company serves education, enterprise, healthcare, and live event sectors.

Winslow Automation Inc — HQ

905 Montague Expy
Milpitas CA 95035
P: 408-262-9004 F: 408-956-0199 PRC:311
www.winslowautomation.com
Email: sales@solderquik.com
Estab: 1986

Russell T. Winslow, President
Tisha Wolf, Operations Manager
Rebecca Parent, Production Control Coordinator
Alma Ebreo, Account Executive

Provider of lead tinning products and services. The company caters to semiconductor and electrical companies.

Wintec Industries Inc — HQ

8674 Thornton Ave
Newark CA 94560
P: 510-953-7421 F: 510-953-7414 PRC:96
www.wintecind.com
Email: sales@wintecind.com

Sue Jeng, President & COO
Sanjay Bonde, CEO
Bhaskar Bhatt, CIO
Jill Horn, VP of Sales Value Chain
Brad Rawling, VP of Supply Chain

Manufacturer and distributor of memory modules and components. The company serves consumer, embedded OEM, e-commerce, and other needs.

Wipro Limited — BR

425 National Ave Ste 200
Mountain View CA 94043
P: 650-316-3555 F: 650-316-3468 PRC:325
www.wipro.com
Email: info@wipro.com
Estab: 1945

Srinivas Pallia, President of Consumer Business Unit
N. S. Bala, President of Energy Natural Resources Utilities & Construction
K. R. Sanjiv, SVP
Pallab Deb, VP & Head of Connected Enterprise Services (CES)
Partha Mukherjee, VP & Vertical Head of Hi Tech Business Unit & Head of Technology Consulting & Global Client Partner

Provider of analytics and information management, business process outsourcing, consulting, and managed and cloud services.

WK Multimedia Network Training — HQ

178 South Blvd [N]
San Mateo CA 94402
P: 415-586-1713 PRC:104
www.reachandteach.com
Estab: 1991

Craig Wiesner, Co-Founder
Derrick Kikuchi, Co-Founder
Drew Durham, Manager
Alan Kornfield, Consultant

Provider of computer training programs and services.

Wolf Metals Inc — HQ

12562 E Putnam St [N]
Whittier CA 90606
P: 562-698-5410 F: 562-698-5413 PRC:62
www.wolfmetalsinc.com
Emp: 1-10 Estab: 1999

Stephanie Sweeney, Treasurer

Manufacturer of metal products including stainless steel, aluminum, merchant bar, tubular, bright steel, and plate as well as being able to supply stamped and pressed products.

Wolfram Inc — HQ

1309 Doker Dr Ste B
Modesto CA 95351
P: 209-238-9610 F: 209-238-9615 PRC:159
wolframlights.com
Email: wolframlights@sbcglobal.net

Steve Alexander, Founder
Kyle Alexander, Sales Manager

Designer and manufacturer of metal halide lamps for the entertainment industry. The company's lamps are used for filming motion pictures.

Wolfs Precision Works Inc — HQ

3549 Haven Ave Unit F
Menlo Park CA 94025
P: 650-364-1341 F: 650-364-4386 PRC:80
www.wpw-inc.com
Email: info@wpw-inc.com
Estab: 1983

Bill Pursell, General Manager

Provider of precision machining solutions. The company's services include milling, turning, and surface gliding.

Wonder Metals Corp — HQ

4351 Caterpillar Rd
Redding CA 96003
P: 800-366-5877 F: 530-241-1738 PRC:82
www.wondermetals.com
Email: info@wondermetals.com
Estab: 1956

Viki L. Cubbage, Owner & President
Brandon Long, Operations & Project Manager

Provider of preventing environmental pollution services. The company's products include louvers, penthouses, and control dampers.

Wong Electric Inc — HQ

4067 Transport St
Palo Alto CA 94303
P: 650-813-9999 F: 650-813-9664 PRC:304
www.wongelectric.com
Emp: 70 Estab: 1978

Steven L. Wong, President
Lester Wong, VP
Veronica Condon, Office Manager
Dionisio Milo, Electrical Estimator

Provider of electrical contracting services. The company is involved in industrial and multi-family projects.

Woodland Mdm — HQ

1229 E Kentucky Ave
Woodland CA 95776
P: 530-669-1400 F: 530-669-1413 PRC:159
www.woodlandmdm.com
Email: mail@woodlandmdm.com
Estab: 1975

Rich Currie, Business Owner

Manufacturer and supplier of new and refurbished machinery products. The company offers industrial controls and automation and case handling equipment.

Woodmack Products Inc — HQ

11430 White Rock Rd
Rancho Cordova CA 95742
P: 916-853-6150 F: 916-853-6473 PRC:82
www.woodmack.com
Email: commercial@woodmack.com
Estab: 1956

Nadine Grady, Controller & Human Resource Director

Manufacturer of tubes and pipes. The company also specializes in customized designs and engineering solutions.

Woodside Electronics Corp — HQ

1311 Blue Grass Pl
Woodland CA 95776
P: 530-666-9190 F: 530-666-9428 PRC:159
wecotek.com

Lisa B., VP of Marketing

Designer and manufacturer of electronic sorters. The company serves customers in the tomato harvesters and walnut industries.

Workday Inc — HQ

2300 Geng Rd Ste 100
Palo Alto CA 94303
P: 650-528-7500 PRC:315
www.adaptiveinsights.com
Email: support@adaptiveinsights.com
Estab: 2003

Robert Hull, Founder
Tom Bogan, CEO
Fred Gewant, CRO
Connie DeWitt, CMO
Bhaskar Himatsingka, Chief Product Officer

Developers of a cloud business planning framework to enable seamless collaboration across the enterprise.

Workday Inc HQ
6110 Stoneridge Mall Rd
Pleasanton CA 94588
P: 925-951-9000 PRC:322
www.workday.com
Estab: 2005

Dave Duffield, Co-Founder & Chairman
Aneel Bhusri, Co-Founder & CEO
Carrie Varoquiers, VP of Global Impact, Workday
Inc & President of Workday Foundation
Chano Fernandez, President
Mike Stankey, Vice Chairman

Provider of software solutions for human resources management and financial management. The company specializes in SaaS based enterprise solutions.

World Products Inc HQ
19654 Eighth St E
Sonoma CA 95476
P: 707-996-5201 F: 707-996-3380 PRC:209
www.worldproducts.com
Email: sales@worldproducts.com
Estab: 1969

David Redemer, Regional Sales Manager
Leonard Drewes, Engineering Manager
Lyn Grosser, Operations Manager

Provider of electronic component solutions and services. The company offers sales, distribution, and technical support.

World Trade Printing Co HQ
12082 Western Ave [N]
Garden Grove CA 92841
P: 714-903-2500 PRC:95
www.wtpcenter.com
Email: info@wtpcenter.com
Estab: 1991

Felipe Delgado, Contact

Provider of commercial printing services.

WorldCom Consulting HQ
PO Box 2066 [N]
Murphys CA 95247
P: 209-728-0246 F: 209-728-3479 PRC:104
www.worldcomconsulting.com
Estab: 1986

Garry J. Moes, Editor

Provider of editorial services including writing, editing, desktop publishing, printing, layout and design, web design and hosting, screenplay development, and consultation and serves educational, religious and humanitarian organizations and public affairs department.

Worldwide Energy & Manufacturing USA Inc HQ
1675 Rollins Rd Unit F
Burlingame CA 94010
P: 650-692-7788 PRC:209
wwmusa.com
Email: sales@wwmusa.com
Estab: 1996

Philip Zhang, General Manager of Contract Manufacturing
Jane Xu, Senior Sales Manager

Provider of energy and manufacturing solutions. The company's products include cables, coils, PC boards, and electronic appliances.

Worldwide Environmental Products Inc HQ
1100 W Beacon St [N]
Brea CA 92821
P: 714-990-2700 F: 714-990-3100 PRC:235
www.wep-inc.com
Email: info@wep-inc.com
Estab: 1984

Bill Delaney, Founder & President & CEO
James Delaney, CFO
Stephen Alford, CIO & CISO
Michael Delaney, Chief Development Officer
Will Delaney, Director of Business Development

Provider of automotive inspection and maintenance programs.

Worth Data Inc HQ
623 Swift St
Santa Cruz CA 95060
P: 831-458-9938 F: 831-458-9964 PRC:103
www.barcodehq.com
Email: wds@barcodehq.com
Estab: 1985

Mike Luffman, Sales Engineer

Designer and manufacturer of barcode scanners and barcode software that includes barcode printing software and inventory tracking software.

WPG Americas Inc DH
5285 Hellyer Ave Ste 150
San Jose CA 95138
P: 408-392-8100 F: 408-436-9551 PRC:86
www.wpgamericas.com
Estab: 2007

Arthur Wang, CEO
Jason Lovell, Director
Pete Gamecho, Regional Sales Manager
Tonye Dreger, Program Operations Manager

Distributor of electronic products. The company's portfolio includes encoders, sensors, solid state batteries, and timing devices.

WRA Inc HQ
2169 G E Francisco Blvd
San Rafael CA 94901
P: 415-454-8868 F: 415-454-0129 PRC:142
wra-ca.com
Estab: 1981

Allen Warren, President & CEO
Sherry Maloney, CFO & Principal
Timothy DeGraff, SVP & Senior Biologist
Sundaran Gillespie, Associate GIS Analyst & Biologist
Joel Ruiz, Accountant

Provider of environmental consulting, validation, mitigation and restoration, consultation, and wetland delineation services.

Wra-Cal Industries Inc HQ
3515 Victor St
Santa Clara CA 95054
P: 408-988-4696 PRC:80
www.wra-cal.com
Email: support@wra-cal.com
Estab: 1973

Norman H. Wray, President

Manufacturer of precision machine products. The company's products include lathes, mills and grinders, drill press, and finishing equipment.

Wrex Products Inc HQ
25 Wrex Ct
Chico CA 95928
P: 530-895-3838 F: 530-893-4426 PRC:80
www.wrexproducts.com
Estab: 1960

Jim Barnett, President
Paul Rye, CEO
Joe Vasquez, Sales Manager
Steve Overlock, Leadperson

Provider of plastic injection molding, CNC machining and finishing, coating, and tool design and engineering services.

Wright Engineered Plastics HQ
3663 N Laughlin Rd
Santa Rosa CA 95403
P: 707-575-1218 PRC:80
www.wepmolding.com
Email: info@wepmolding.com
Estab: 1970

Barbara Roberts, President & CEO
Mike Nellis, EVP & COO
Karrie Bertsch, Director of Engineering
Christopher Clark, Project Development Manager
Dale Lawler, Tooling Manager

Provider of medical components and devices. The company deals with custom plastic injection molding, tooling, and assembly related services.

Wright Williams & Kelly Inc HQ
6200 Stoneridge Mall Rd 3rd Fl
Pleasanton CA 94588
P: 925-399-6246 F: 925-396-6174 PRC:323
www.wwk.com
Email: info@wwk.com
Estab: 1991

David Jimenez, Founder & Chairman
Daren Dance, VP of Technology
Alan Levine, Director

Provider of software products and consulting services. The company also offers decision tools for cost management.

WSI Smart Solutions   HQ
4435 First St Ste 355
Livermore CA 94551
P: 925-245-0216   PRC:315
wsismartsolutions.com
Estab: 1995

Ryan Kelly, COO & Owner

Provider of search engine optimization services.
The company also deals with Internet marketing
and web design solutions.

Wso2 Inc   HQ
4131 El Camino Real Ste 200
Palo Alto CA 94306
P: 408-754-7388   F: 408-689-4328   PRC:323
www.wso2.com
Email: bizdev@wso2.com
Estab: 2005

Sanjiva Weerawarana, Founder & CEO
Devaka Randeniya, CRO
Jonathan Marsh, VP of Strategy
Shammi Jayasinghe, Technical Lead & Associate
Director & Architect
Vanjikumaran Sivajothy, Senior Lead Solution
Engineer

Provider of open source middleware platforms,
security and identity gateway solutions, and enterprise integration solutions.

Wunder Mold Inc   HQ
790 Eubanks Dr
Vacaville CA 95688
P: 707-448-2349   F: 707-448-6045   PRC:163
wundermold.com
Email: sales@wundermold.com
Estab: 1996

Calvin Swesey, General Manager

Provider of ceramic injection molding services.
The company designs and produces art molded
ceramics for appliances and electronics applications.

X-Fab Texas Inc   BR
3033 Moorpark Ave
San Jose CA 95128
P: 408-844-0066   PRC:212
xfab.com
Email: sales.americas@xfab.com
Estab: 1992

Rudi De Winter, CEO
Alba Morganti, CFO
Manfred Riemer, COO
Lyon Lee, Program Manager

Provider of foundry services. The company focuses on analog and mixed signal semiconductor
applications.

X-Scan Imaging Corp   HQ
107 Bonaventura Dr
San Jose CA 95134
P: 408-432-9888   F: 408-432-9889   PRC:91
www.x-scanimaging.com
Email: sales@x-scanimaging.com
Estab: 2006

Shizu Li, Engineering Director
Nguyen Luu, Engineering Manager
Andy Doan, Mechanical Engineer
Dongri Meng, Electrical Engineer

Supplier of x-ray imaging and inspection equipment. The company also offers array detectors
and line-scan camera products.

X-Z LAB Inc   HQ
231 Market Pl Ste 728
San Ramon CA 94583
P: 925-355-5199   PRC:304
www.x-zlab.com
Email: contact@x-zlab.com
Estab: 2013

Ying Liu, Sales Marketing Manager

Provider of digital radiation detection services. The
company engages in detecting, measuring, and
monitoring radiation activities.

Xactly Corp   HQ
505 S Market St
San Jose CA 95113
P: 408-977-3132   F: 408-292-1153   PRC:322
www.xactlycorp.com
Estab: 2005

Christopher W. Cabrera, Founder & CEO
Ron Rasmussen, CTO
Evan Ellis, COO
Leanne Bernhardt, Chief Human Resource Officer
Elizabeth Salomon, CFO

Provider of web-based sales compensation applications. The company offers services to business
organizations and enterprises.

Xandex Inc   DH
1360 Redwood Way Ste A
Petaluma CA 94954
P: 707-763-7799   F: 707-763-2631   PRC:86
www.xandexsemi.com
Email: info@xandex.com

Nariman Manoochehri, VP of Operations
Kim Anderson, Marketing Communication Man-
ager
Kiumars Kaveh, Purchasing Manager
Lori Nagayama, Sales Manager
Bill Simpson, Electrical Engineer

Designer and manufacturer of products for the
semiconductor test industry. The company's
products include automated test equipment and
interface products.

Xantrex Technology Inc   BR
161 G S Vasco Rd
Livermore CA 94551
P: 408-987-6030   F: 800-994-7828   PRC:288
www.xantrex.com
Email: customerservice@xantrex.com

Jing Wang, Deputy General Manager

Manufacturer of automotive batteries. The company offers power products for trucks, cars, and
recreational vehicles.

XC2 Software LLC   HQ
122 Taylor Dr
Fairfax CA 94930
P: 800-761-4999   PRC:319
xc2software.com
Estab: 1989

Randy Engle, Owner
Bill Lease, Technical Support Manager

Provider of integrated software suite. The company's products find application in water and
wastewater utilities.

Xcell Biosciences Inc   HQ
455 Mission Bay Blvd S
San Francisco CA 94158
P: 415-937-0321   PRC:36
www.xcellbio.com
Email: info@xcellbio.com
Estab: 2012

Brian Feth, CEO & Founder
James Lim, CSO

Provider of protocols and reagent kits for primary
cell culture applications. The company specializes
in cell-based assays.

Xeltek Inc   HQ
1296 Kifer Rd Ste 605
Sunnyvale CA 94086
P: 408-530-8080   F: 408-530-0096   PRC:212
www.xeltek.com
Email: sales@xeltek.com
Estab: 1985

Sam Kim, President

Manufacturer of automated, production, and
in-system programmers, and socket adapters, and
related supplies.

XEODesign   HQ
5273 College Ave Ste 201
Oakland CA 94618
P: 510-658-8077   PRC:317
www.xeodesign.com
Email: info@xeodesign.com
Estab: 1992

Nicole Lazzaro, President

Provider of computer multimedia software, website design hosting, programming, and technical
support services.

Xetus Mortgage Corp   HQ
1325 Howard Ave Ste 527
Burlingame CA 94010
P: 650-237-1225   PRC:319
www.xetusone.com
Email: support@xetus.com
Estab: 2002

Theo Meneau, Knowledge Manager
Terence Kent, Principal software Architect
Lu Han, Java Programmer

Provider of mortgage processing services such
as documentation monitoring, data and image
capture, and reporting and audit trail.

Xia LLC   HQ
31057 Genstar Rd
Hayward CA 94544
P: 510-401-5760   F: 510-401-5761   PRC:20
www.xia.com
Email: sales@xia.com

Peter Grudberg, President
Michael Sears, VP of Production
Jackson Harris, Senior Staff Scientist
Hui Tan, Senior Research Scientist
Nicole Thomas, Administrative Assistant

Provider of x-ray and gamma-ray detector electronics, and related instruments for the research
industry.

Xicato Inc HQ
101 Daggett Dr
San Jose CA 95134
P: 866-223-8395 PRC:243
www.xicato.com
Email: info@xicato.com
Estab: 2007

Steve Workman, CFO
Roger Sexton, VP of Specified Service
John Yriberri, VP of Worldwide Application Support
Mike Peanasky, Director of Manufacturing
Jin Luo, Senior Software Engineer

Designer and manufacturer of lighting products. The company specializes in providing different types of LED modules.

Xifin Inc HQ
12225 El Camino Real [N]
San Diego CA 92130
P: 858-793-5700 PRC:319
www.xifin.com
Email: marketinginfo@xifin.com
Emp: 201-500   Estab: 1997

Doug Wheeler, CMO
James C. Malone, CFO & EVP
Michael Coats, EVP
Steve Nielson, VP of Sales
David Byrd, VP

Provider of health care related information technology services.

Xignite Inc HQ
1825 S Grant St Ste 100
San Mateo CA 94402
P: 650-655-3700 PRC:315
www.xignite.com
Email: info@xignite.com
Estab: 2006

Stephane Dubois, Founder & CEO
Kerry Langstaff, CMO
Qin Yu, VP of Engineering
Ryan Burdick, SVP & Global Head of Sales
Vijay Choudhary, VP of Product Management & Market Data Solutions

Provider of financial Data-as-a-Service (DaaS) solution to deliver market data from the AWS public cloud.

Xmatters Inc HQ
12647 Alcosta Blvd Ste 425
San Ramon CA 94583
P: 925-226-0300   F: 925-226-0310   PRC:323
www.xmatters.com
Estab: 2000

Desi Dossantos, Founder
Troy McAlpin, CEO
Doug Peete, CPO
Abbas Haider Ali, CTO
Kendra Niedziejko, CFO

Provider of voice and text alerting system software. The company serves the healthcare, telecommunications, and manufacturing industries.

XMS Corp HQ
2351 Sunset Blvd Ste 170-101
Rocklin CA 95765-4306
P: 916-435-0267   F: 916-435-0268   PRC:196
www.x-icon.com
Email: theflin@x-icon.com
Estab: 1987

Tim Heflin, Owner
Tom Marchione, President & CEO

Manufacturer and distributor of medical devices. The company specializes in cost effective, cutting edge radiation therapy equipment.

Xoft Inc HQ
101 Nicholson Ln
San Jose CA 95134
P: 408-493-1500 PRC:186
www.xoftinc.com
Estab: 1998

Michael Klein, Executive Chairman & CEO
Stacey Stevens, President
R. Scott Areglado, CFO
Rob Neimeyer, Director of X-ray Technologies
Tiffany Daugherty, Manager of Clinical Research & Project

Developer of electronic brachytherapy systems. The company's products include rigid shield, vacuum pumps, and physics kits.

Xoriant Corp HQ
1248 Reamwood Ave
Sunnyvale CA 94089
P: 408-743-4400 PRC:323
www.xoriant.com
Email: info@xoriant.com
Estab: 1990

Girish Gaitonde, Founder & CEO
Hari Haran, President & CRO
Sudhir Kulkarni, President of Digital Solutions
Subu Subramanian, CTO
Mahesh Nalavade, CFO

Provider of enterprise applications. The company also offers mobile analytics and web application development services.

Xperi Corp HQ
3025 Orchard Pkwy
San Jose CA 95134
P: 408-321-6000 PRC:79
www.xperi.com
Email: info@tessera.com
Estab: 1990
Sales: $100M to $300M

Murali Dharan, President of Tessera
Craig Mitchell, President of Invensas
Jon E. Kirchner, CEO
Kevin Doohan, CMO
Kris M. Graves, Chief Human Resource Officer

Provider of miniaturization technology services for electronic devices. The company offers micro-electronics, and imaging and optics services.

XTAL Inc HQ
97 E Brokaw Rd Ste 330
San Jose CA 95112
P: 408-642-5328 PRC:212
www.xtalinc.com
Email: contact@xtalinc.com
Estab: 2014

Zongchang Yu, CEO
Jihui Huang, CTO
Liang Wang, Software Engineering Manager
Clayton Parker, General Counsel
Jinyu Zhang, Software Engineer

Specializes in yield enhancement, software optimization and hardware implementation targeting semiconductor ecosystem.

Xtelesis Corp HQ
800 Airport Blvd Ste 417
Burlingame CA 94010
P: 650-239-1400   F: 650-239-1410   PRC:67
www.xtelesis.com
Email: info@protelesis.com
Estab: 1997

Scott Strochak, CTO
William Traenkle, CIO
Richard Foster, VP of Sales & Marketing
Christoph Pluchar, VP of Advanced Applications
Alex Vega, Director of Managed Services

Provider of voice and data solutions. The company is engaged in data networking, audio web conferencing, and managed IT services.

Xtime Inc HQ
1400 Bridge Pkwy Ste 200
Redwood City CA 94065
P: 888-463-3888 PRC:322
xtime.com
Email: insidesales@xtime.com
Estab: 2004

Tracy Noonan Fred, VP & General Manager
Adam Springer, VP of Engineering
David Foutz, VP of Sales
Candy Lucey, Senior Director of Marketing
Darrel Ferguson, Director of Performance Management

Provider of CRM solutions for automotive service operations. The company offers scheduling and marketing solutions for automotive retailers.

Yamaichi Electronics Usa Inc HQ
475 Holger Way [N]
San Jose CA 95134
P: 408-715-9100   F: 408-715-9199   PRC:31
www.yeu.com

Alfred Muranaga, Chairman of the Board
Takeshi Nishimura, Business Manager
Pat Becker, Controller

Manufacturer of electrical connectors, sockets, probe cards and much more.

Yamamoto Manufacturing USA Inc   HQ
2025 Gateway Pl Ste 220
San Jose CA 95110
P: 408-387-5250 F: 408-387-5248   PRC:211
www.yusa.com
Email: sales@yusa.com
Estab: 1945

Mike Ferem, Sales Manager North America

Manufacturer of printed circuit boards. The company has operations in regions of Japan, Korea, and China.

Yamato Scientific America Inc   HQ
925 Walsh Ave
Santa Clara CA 95050
P: 408-235-7725 F: 408-235-7730   PRC:209
www.yamato-usa.com
Email: customerservice@yamato-usa.com
Estab: 1989

Marivic Lastimosa, Marketing Manager

Provider of ovens, incubators, evaporators, and stabilizers. The company deals with sales, distribution, and installation services.

YapStone Inc   HQ
2121 N California Blvd Ste 400 [N]
Walnut Creek CA 94596
P: 866-289-5977   PRC:24
www.yapstone.com
Emp: 201-500   Estab: 1999

Matt Golis, Co-Founder & Co-Chairman of the Board
Tom Villante, Co-Founder & Chairman & CEO
David Weiss, President
Sanjay Saraf, EVP & CTO
David Durant, General Counsel & EVP & Secretary

Developer of electronic payments platform.

YC Cable   LH
44061 Nobel Dr
Fremont CA 94538
P: 510-824-2788 F: 510-824-0339   PRC:62
www.yccable.com
Email: sales@yccable.com
Estab: 1985

Grand Fang, CEO
Bill Haas, Manager of Production & Quality
Yvonne Romero, Human Resource Manager

Manufacturer of cables. The company serves industrial, computer, telecommunications, consumer, medical and other sectors.

Yellow Magic Inc   HQ
41571 Date St   [N]
Murrieta CA 92562
P: 951-506-4005 F: 951-506-1919   PRC:319
www.yellowmagic.com
Email: sales@yellowmagic.com
Estab: 1986

Ron Mintle, President & CEO
Sam Pretorius, Director of Program Development

Developer of software for the directory publishing industry.

Yenzym Antibodies LLC   HQ
100 North Hill Dr Ste 34
Brisbane CA 94005
P: 650-583-1031   PRC:249
yenzym.com
Email: customerservice@yenzym.com

Glenn Ruiz, Manager of Operations

Provider of antigen design services. The company offers rabbit antibody and antigen specific affinity purification services.

YES Yield Engineering Systems Inc   HQ
3178 Laurelview Ct
Fremont CA 94538
P: 510-954-6889 F: 925-373-8354   PRC:86
www.yieldengineering.com
Email: sales@yieldengineering.com
Estab: 1980

William A. Moffat, Founder
Ken MacWilliams, CEO
Zia Karim, SVP & CMO
Rezwan Lateef, SVP of Sales & Service
Ken Sautter, Director of Technology

Manufacturer of process equipment for the semiconductor industry. The company offers products for surface modification and photoresist treatment.

Yola Inc   HQ
548 Market St Ste 38798
San Francisco CA 94104-5401
P: 866-764-0701 F: 415-227-0208   PRC:325
www.yola.com
Email: support@yola.com
Estab: 2007

Trevor Harries-Jones, CEO
David Saxton, SVP of Business Development & Marketing

Provider of digital marketing services. The company offers mobile, facebook, and web publishing, domain names, and reliable hosting services.

York Machine Works   HQ
1401 Charter Oak Ave
St. Helena CA 94574
P: 707-963-4966 F: 707-963-8408   PRC:80
mustfabricate.com
Email: orders@yorkmachineworks.com
Estab: 1973

Alexander Mitchell, Owner

Provider of engineering services. The company's services include machining, welding, pattern burning, and engraving.

Yosemite Pathology Medical Group Inc   HQ
2625 Coffee Rd Ste S
Modesto CA 95355
P: 209-577-1200 F: 209-577-1012   PRC:306
www.ypmg.com
Email: billing@ypmg.com

Jennifer Pinasco, CEO
Megan Dooley, CAO
Angela Hiler, Director of Sales & Marketing
Max Rosemire, Director of IT Services
Anthony R. Victorio, Director of Medical

Provider of anatomic pathology services such as tissue pathology and gynecologic specimens of oncologic and nononcologic diseases.

Yotta Navigation Corp   HQ
3777 Stevens Creek Blvd
Santa Clara CA 95051-7364
P: 800-943-1220   PRC:217
www.yottanav.com
Email: support@yottanav.com

Andrew Zaydak, Senior Engineer

Manufacturer of sub-meter positioning systems and underwater precision navigation platforms. The company serves the homeland security market.

Yuhas Tooling & Machining Inc   HQ
1031 Pecten Ct
Milpitas CA 95035
P: 408-934-9196 F: 408-934-9197   PRC:80
yuhasmachining.com
Email: sales@yuhasmachining.com

Nick Buchko, CNC Programmer

Provider of tooling and machining products for the semiconductor, medical, aerospace, telecommunications, and electronics industries.

Yunsheng USA   HQ
430 N Canal St Unit 2/3 Ste 230
S San Francisco CA 94080
P: 650-827-7928 F: 650-827-7927   PRC:275
www.yunshengusa.com
Email: service@yunshengusa.com
Estab: 1996

John Ebert, Business Manager
Carlos Chou, Account Manager
Jonathan Huang, Account Manager
Cherry Yu, Account Manager
Freddy Fernandez, Sales Manager

Manufacturer of permanent magnets. The company mainly offers Neodymium and rare earth magnet products.

YY Labs Inc   HQ
PO Box 597
Fremont CA 94537
P: 510-739-6049 F: 510-405-9030   PRC:15
www.yylabs.com
Estab: 1997

Yan Yin, Researcher

Manufacturer and supplier of optical components. The company provides LN modulators, bias controllers, generators, and accessories.

Z-Plane Inc   HQ
809 Monroe St
Santa Rosa CA 95404
P: 415-309-2647   PRC:211
Estab: 2008

Timothy A. Lemke, CTO
Ralph Britton, Group VP

Provider of electronic packaging solutions for high-speed telecommunications and computing equipment, including routers, servers, and switches.

Z-Source International HQ
1181 Quarry Ln Ste 300
Pleasanton CA 94566
P: 925-401-0090 F: 925-401-0095 PRC:211
www.zsourceintl.com
Estab: 2003

Jeff Long, Owner

Manufacturer of printed circuit boards. The company provides board procurement solutions from prototypes to full production and stocking programs.

Zag Technical Services Inc HQ
645 River Oaks Pkwy Ste 106
San Jose CA 95134
P: 408-383-2000 F: 408-383-2001 PRC:320
www.zagtech.com
Email: info@zagtech.com
Estab: 1998

Greg Gatzke, President
Jim Hunton, CTO
Joey Jose, Senior Account Manager
Andrew Benjamin, Project Manager
Karl Braun, Technical Account Manager

Provider of services for server, email stability, reliability, migration, and security assessment needs.

Zalda Technology HQ
2488 Technology Dr
Hayward CA 94545
P: 510-783-4910 F: 510-783-1897 PRC:159
www.zaldatechnology.com
Email: zaldausa@zaldatechnology.com
Estab: 1991

Johnny Qiu, Manager

Fabricator of springs. The company also offers spring design, testing, and prototype assembling services.

Zander Associates HQ
4460 Redwood Hwy Ste 16-240
San Rafael CA 94903
P: 415-897-8781 F: 415-814-4125 PRC:142
zanderassociates.com
Email: mail@zanderassociates.com

Michael J. Zander, Principal Environmental scientist

Provider of environmental consulting and assessment services. The company service areas include habitat conservation planning and wetland delineation.

Zanker Road Resource Management Ltd HQ
705 Los Esteros Rd [N]
San Jose CA 95134
P: 408-263-2384 PRC:145
www.zankerrecycling.com
Email: questions@zankerrecycling.com
Estab: 1984

Rich Cristina, President
Greg Ryan, General Manager
Michael Gross, Executive Director
Jose Monarrez, Manager of Operations
Scott Beall, Manager of Operations

Provider of a concrete recycling, composting, mixed debris and debris diversion.

Zapier Inc HQ
548 Market St Ste 62411
San Francisco CA 94104-5401
P: 877-381-8743 PRC:325
zapier.com
Email: contact@zapier.com
Estab: 2011

Wade Foster, Co-Founder & CEO
Bryan Helmig, Co-Founder & CTO
Mike Knoop, Co-Founder
Jonathan Rochelle, Chief Human Resource Officer
Jenny Bloom, CFO

Developers of an integrated app that shares information within a user's collective web app automatically.

Zaxel Systems Inc HQ
1600 Wyatt Dr Ste 13
Santa Clara CA 95054
P: 408-727-6403 PRC:60
www.zaxel.com
Email: info@zaxel.com
Estab: 1998

Norihisa Suzuki, Founder & President & CEO
Mark Marrin, Chief Engineer

Manufacturer of 4k, 8k, and 16k video servers. The company's products are used in post production facilities, museums, and planetariums.

Zebra Technologies Corp BR
2833 Junction Ave Ste 100
San Jose CA 95134-2021
P: 866-230-9494 PRC:115
zebra.com
Estab: 1969

Mark Zucherman, Senior Product Manager

Provider of business and printing solutions. The company also offers printers such as desktop, industrial, mobile, and card printers.

Zendesk Inc HQ
1019 Market St Ste 300
San Francisco CA 94103
P: 415-418-7506 PRC:322
www.zendesk.com
Email: support@zendesk.com
Estab: 2007
Sales: $300M to $1 Billion

Alexander Aghassipour, Chief Product Officer & Co-Founder
Mikkel Svane, CEO & Co-Founder & Chairman
Adrian McDermott, President of Products
Toke Nygaard, Chief Creative Officer
Sam Boonin, VP of Products

Designer and developer of cloud-based customer service software. The company deals with reporting and analytics solutions.

Zenflow Inc HQ
395 Oyster Point Blvd Ste 501
S San Francisco CA 94080
P: 650-642-9658 PRC:187
www.zenflow.com
Estab: 2014

Nick Damiano, CEO
Ronald Jabba, COO
Shreya Mehta, CTO
Austin Bly, Senior Research & Development Engineer
Mandy Chen, Junior Engineer

Developer of products for the treatment of urinary obstruction related to benign prostatic hyperplasia. The company serves the medical sector.

Zentner Planning and Ecology HQ
120 A Linden St
Oakland CA 94607
P: 510-622-8110 F: 510-622-8116 PRC:142
zentner.com
Email: info@zentner.com
Estab: 1986

John Zentner, Senior Manager & Founder
Brian Davis, Partner

Provider of environmental planning and restoration services. The company is also involved in permitting services.

Zeptor Corp HQ
3087 N First St
San Jose CA 95134
P: 408-432-6001 F: 408-432-6002 PRC:209
www.zeptoco.com
Email: info@zeptoco.com
Estab: 2009

Tatsunori Suzuki, CEO
Charles Consorte, CTO
Mikito Nagata, Director of Research & Business Development
Dan Cameron, Senior Manager
Richard Fraga, Engineering Manager

Specializes in battery technologies. The company develops and manufactures light-weight electrodes that are used in lithium batteries and fuel cells.

ZigBee Alliance HQ
508 Second St Ste 206
Davis CA 95616
P: 530-564-4565 F: 530-564-4721 PRC:64
www.zigbee.org
Estab: 2002

Tobin Richardson, President & CEO

Provider of lighting solutions. The company offers LED fixtures, light bulbs, remotes and switches and serves the residential and commercial sectors.

Zilog Inc DH
1590 Buckeye Dr
Milpitas CA 95035-7418
P: 408-457-9000   F: 408-416-0223   PRC:208
www.zilog.com
Estab: 1974

Alan Shaw, VP of Operations
Steve Darrough, VP of Sales & Marketing World-
wide
David Staab, VP of Research & Development
Nathan Zommer, General Manager
Captain Zilog, Contact

Supplier of application-specific embedded system-
on-chip (SoC) solutions for the industrial and
consumer markers.

Zip-Bit Inc HQ
20640 Third St Ste 170
Saratoga CA 95070
P: 408-839-4252   PRC:304
www.zip-bit.com
Estab: 1984

John Morewood, Owner

Provider of engineering services. The company
specializes in 3D printing, 3D modeling, and 3D
scanning.

Zip-Chem Products Inc HQ
400 Jarvis Dr
Morgan Hill CA 95037
P: 408-782-2335   F: 408-782-6304   PRC:47
www.zipchem.com
Email: forinfo@zipchem.com

Chuck Pottier, President
Charles Pottier, VP

Provider of airspace maintenance materials. The
company also offers metering equipment, spray
nozzle, and spray equipment.

Zipline Medical Inc HQ
747 Camden Ave Ste A
Campbell CA 95008
P: 408-412-7228   F: 888-265-0669   PRC:195
www.ziplinemedical.com
Email: info@ziplinemedical.com
Estab: 2009

John Tighe, President & CEO
Bauback Safa, CMO
Eric Storne, VP of Marketing
Steve Lotz, Director of Sales
Dennis Thompson, Territory Manager

Developer of zip surgical skin closure devices
for cardiology, orthopedics, dermatology, plastic
reconstructive surgery, and emergency medicine.

Zircon Corp HQ
1580 Dell Ave
Campbell CA 95008
P: 408-963-4550   F: 408-963-4597   PRC:19
www.zircon.com
Email: info@zircon.com
Estab: 1975

Ennis Pipe, VP of Global Channel Management
Barry Wingate, Design Director
Kurt Chen, Director of Industrial Design
Mark Keliihanapule, Graphics Manager
Jose Lara, Purchasing Manager

Designer and manufacturer of stud finders. The
company offers electrical scanners, metal detectors, leveling tools, and accessories.

ZL Technologies Inc HQ
860 N McCarthy Blvd Ste 100
Milpitas CA 95035
P: 408-240-8989   F: 408-240-8990   PRC:322
www.zlti.com
Email: info@zlti.com
Estab: 1999

Arvind Srinivasan, Founder & CTO
Kon Leong, CEO
Matthew Davis, VP of Operations & Senior Direc-
tor of Engineering
Ian Osborn, Product Implementation Manager
Ryan Splain, Account Management Executive
& Head of Account Management & Customer
Success

Provider of electronic content archiving software
solutions such as consulting and installation, product customization, and software upgrades.

Zmanda - A Carbonite Co HQ
465 S Mathilda Ave Ste 300
Sunnyvale CA 94086
P: 408-732-3208   F: 408-830-9675   PRC:319
www.zmanda.com
Email: zsales@zmanda.com
Estab: 2010

Paddy Sreenivasan, Founder & VP of Engineering

Provider of open source backup and recovery
software solutions. The company's applications
include centralized backup of file systems and
applications.

Zoeticx HQ
90 Great Oaks Blvd
San Jose CA 95119
P: 408-622-6119   PRC:189
zoeticx.com
Email: info@zoeticx.com
Estab: 2011

Thanh Tran, CEO & Founder
Alan Shoap, VP of Marketing
Terry Glenn, VP of Business Development
Layne Allred, VP of Business Development

Provider of healthcare solutions. The company
develops care applications and offers services to
inpatients, ICU, and outpatients.

Zogenix Inc BR
5959 Horton St 5th Fl
Emeryville CA 94608
P: 858-259-1165   PRC:257
www.zogenix.com
Email: info@zogenix.com
Estab: 2006

Steve Farr, President
Gail Farfel, Chief Development Officer
A.J. Acker, VP of Global Regulatory Affairs
Robin Ash, Director of Project Management
Mike Peterson, Director of Human Resources

Developer of medicines to treat CNS disorders
and pain. The company serves clinics, physicians,
and the healthcare sector.

Zoho Corp HQ
4141 Hacienda Dr
Pleasanton CA 94588
P: 615-671-9025   F: 925-924-9600   PRC:319
www.zohocorp.com
Email: sales@zohocorp.com
Estab: 1996

Raj Sabhlok, President
Ali Shabdar, Regional Director MEA
Tonia Lecentina, Partner Manager
Vinothkumar R., Product Manager
Clarence Rozario, Program Manager

Developer and provider of IT management software, business technology solutions, and network
management framework.

Zone24x7 Inc HQ
3150 Almaden Expressway Ste 234
San Jose CA 95118
P: 408-922-9887   PRC:322
www.zone24x7.com
Email: info@zone24x7.com
Estab: 2003

Llavan Fernando, CEO & Founder
Saw-Chin Fernando, CFO
Sankalpa Gamwarige, General Manager & VP -
Engineering
Stefan Udumalagala, Innovation Specialist
Kevin Shea, Account Executive

Provider of technology innovation, business consultation, software development, hardware design,
and system integration services.

Zosano Pharma Co HQ
34790 Ardentech Ct
Fremont CA 94555
P: 510-745-1200   PRC:251
www.zosanopharma.com
Email: bd@zosanopharma.com

John P. Walker, Chairman
Steven Lo, President & CEO
Greg Kitchener, CFO
Hayley Lewis, SVP of Operations
Dushyant Pathak, SVP of Business Development

Manufacturer of biopharmaceutical products like
peptides, proteins, small molecules and vaccines
based on transdermal delivery technology.

Zscaler Inc HQ
110 Rose Orchard Way
San Jose CA 95134
P: 408-533-0288   PRC:325
www.zscaler.com
Email: info@zscaler.com
Estab: 2008
Sales: $300M to $1 Billion

Jay Chaudhry, Founder & CEO & Chairman
Amit Sinha, President of R&D Operations & Cus-
tomer Service & CTO
Dali Rajic, President of Go-To-Market & CRO
Scott Darling, President of Dell Technologies
Capital
Patrick Foxhoven, CIO & EVP of Emerging Tech-
nologies

Provider of SaaS security solutions. The company
offers cloud security solutions for mobile enterprises.

Zspace Inc HQ
490 De Guigne Dr Ste 200
Sunnyvale CA 94085
P: 408-498-4050 PRC:110
www.zspace.com
Email: sales@zspace.com
Estab: 2007

Joe Powers, CFO
Mike Harper, EVP
Amanda Austin, Marketing Director
Steve Yeung, Director of Engineering
Elizabeth Lytle, Director

Provider of solutions for viewing, manipulating, and communicating complex ideas through direct interaction with virtual-holographic simulations.

Zultys Inc HQ
785 Lucerne Dr
Sunnyvale CA 94085
P: 408-328-0450 F: 408-328-0451 PRC:68
www.zultys.com
Estab: 2001

Steve Francis, Chief Sales & Marketing Officer
Justin Bush, VP of Sales & Director of Sales in Central Region
Pavel Matsienok, VP of Cloud Operations
Michael Troflianin, VP of Manufacturing
Ahmad Haghshenas, Director of Technical Support

Manufacturer of Voice-over-IP equipment. The company mainly caters to small to medium sized businesses.

Zygo Corp BR
3350 Scott Blvd Bldg 49 Ste 1
Santa Clara CA 95054
P: 408-434-1000 F: 408-434-0759 PRC:18
www.zygo.com
Email: inquire@zygo.com
Estab: 1970

Gary Willis, CEO
Tony Allan, COO
Dan Bajuk, VP
Karla Piccolo, Director of Supply Chain
Brian Prestash, IT Manager

Supplier of optical metrology instruments. The company also specializes in high precision optical components.

Zymergen HQ
5980 Horton St Ste 105
Emeryville CA 94608
P: 415-801-8073 PRC:24
www.zymergen.com
Email: info@zymergen.com
Estab: 2013

Jed Dean, Co-Founder
Zach Serber, Chief Science Officer & Co-Founder
Richard Pieters, President
Joshua Hoffman, CEO
Aaron Kimball, CTO

Developer of engineering biology. The company is engaged in new product development and it serves the scientific market.

Zynga Inc HQ
699 Eighth St
San Francisco CA 94103
P: 800-762-2530 PRC:317
zynga.com
Emp: 1777 Estab: 2007
Sales: $1B to $3B

Alex Garden, President of Zynga Studios
Bernard Kim, President of Publishing
Don Mattrick, CEO
Clive Downie, COO
Jeff Ryan, CPO

Provider of social game services with more than 240 million monthly active users. The company's games include CityVille, Draw Something, and Hidden Chronicles.

Zypex Inc HQ
2795 E Bidwell St Ste 100-405
Folsom CA 95630
P: 916-983-9450 F: 916-983-9448 PRC:68
www.zypex.com
Email: info@zypex.com
Estab: 1992

Del Peck, President & Founder

Provider of solutions for product development. The company specializes in industrial communication products, modules, and drivers.

PRODUCT INDEX

PRODUCT CODE CATEGORIES

COMPANY NAME	PRODUCT / SERVICE	PHONE	EMP	CITY
1 = Aerospace/Aircraft & Equipment				
N C & H Testing Service LLC (HQ)	Provider of services to oil and gas production industry specializing in pressure testing and magnetic flux testing to verify pipe and tubing integrity.	661-589-4030	NA	Bakersfield
N Cummings Transportation (HQ)	Provider of trucking services.	661-746-1786	NA	Shafter
2 = Aerospace R&D/Consulting				
Airdex International Inc (BR)	Manufacturer of air freight products. The company offers lightweight, air pallets for perishables and pharmaceuticals.	702-575-0625	NA	Newport Beach
Axelsys LLC (HQ)	Provider of electronic design and manufacturing services. The company's offerings include LED and AC to DC industrial power supplies.	408-600-0871	NA	San Jose
Calabazas Creek Research Inc (HQ)	Specializes in the research and development of high power RF sources, and components. The company offers software development services.	650-312-9575	NA	San Mateo
JP Aerospace (HQ)	Developer of volunteer-based DIY space program. The company provides the PongSat, MiniCube and Airship to Orbit programs for space enthusiasts.	916-858-0185	NA	Rancho Cordova
KaiserAir Inc (BR)	Provider of aircraft management services. The company also offers business aircraft chartering services.	510-569-9622	NA	Oakland
Nasam Inc (HQ)	Distributor of electronics products. The company offers military/defense equipment, aircraft support equipment, and other products.	650-872-1155	NA	S San Francisco
Sensor Concepts Inc (HQ)	Developer of portable and integrated measurement systems. The company offers engineering, field measurement and software development services.	925-443-9001	NA	Livermore
3 = Air Training/Simulation Equipment				
Advanced Rotorcraft Technology Inc (HQ)	Designer of fixed-wing and helicopter simulation productivity tools. The company services include avionics testing and simulator integration.	408-523-5100	NA	Sunnyvale
ICON Aircraft Inc (HQ)	Manufacturer of consumer aircraft. The company specializes in giving the freedom, fun, and adventure of flying to all who have dreamed of flight.	707-564-4100	NA	Vacaville
4 = Aircraft				
N Beranek Inc (HQ)	Manufacturer of precision machined components for aerospace, military, space and communication industry.	310-328-9094	NA	Torrance
Hexcel Corp (BR)	Provider and manufacturer of advanced material solutions. The company manufactures everything from a carbon fiber to finished aircraft structures.	800-444-3923	NA	Dublin
ICON Aircraft Inc (HQ)	Manufacturer of consumer aircraft. The company specializes in giving the freedom, fun, and adventure of flying to all who have dreamed of flight.	707-564-4100	NA	Vacaville
JP Aerospace (HQ)	Developer of volunteer-based DIY space program. The company provides the PongSat, MiniCube and Airship to Orbit programs for space enthusiasts.	916-858-0185	NA	Rancho Cordova
KaiserAir Inc (BR)	Provider of aircraft management services. The company also offers business aircraft chartering services.	510-569-9622	NA	Oakland
Moller International Inc (HQ)	Designer and developer of personal vertical takeoff and landing aircraft. The company specializes in rotapower engines.	530-756-5086	NA	Dixon
N Neill Aircraft Co (HQ)	Provider of build-to-print parts, assemblies, and kitting services to the aerospace community.	562-432-7981	11-50	Long Beach
Pacific Scientific Energetic Materials Company (California) LLC (HQ)	Provider of energetic materials and services. The company offers services to the aircraft, missiles, space, and law enforcement industries.	831-637-3731	NA	Hollister
N Ramec Engineering (HQ)	Designer, engineer, and manufacturer of aerospace parts.	310-532-2573	NA	Gardena
Rolls-Royce Engine Services - Oakland Inc (BR)	Designer, manufacturer, and marketer of power systems. The company offers engines for airliners and military aircraft.	510-613-1000	NA	Oakland
N Skyspares Parts Inc (HQ)	Manufacturer of CNC precision machined parts.	951-351-0770	NA	Riverside
5 = Aircraft Parts & Auxiliary Equipment				
Aerojet Rocketdyne (HQ)	Manufacturer of missile and space propulsion components. The company also offers defense weapons and armaments.	916-355-4000	NA	Sacramento
Aerometals (HQ)	Manufacturer of heater control valve assembly, gear shafts, and fuel filler caps. The company offers water jet cutting, milling, and lathe services.	916-939-6888	NA	El Dorado Hills
Applied Systems Engineering Inc (HQ)	Provider of consulting, software, design, and testing services. The company's products cater to communication applications.	408-364-0500	NA	Campbell
N Beranek Inc (HQ)	Manufacturer of precision machined components for aerospace, military, space and communication industry.	310-328-9094	NA	Torrance
Cutting Edge Machining Inc (HQ)	Provider of contract manufacturing solutions for the medical, aerospace, and telecommunication sectors.	408-738-8677	NA	Sunnyvale
Davtron Inc (HQ)	Designer and manufacturer of avionic instruments. The company's portfolio comprises volt meters, clocks, probes, and more.	866-369-5588	NA	Emerald Hills
ICON Aircraft Inc (HQ)	Manufacturer of consumer aircraft. The company specializes in giving the freedom, fun, and adventure of flying to all who have dreamed of flight.	707-564-4100	NA	Vacaville
Matronics (HQ)	Provider of aircraft products. The company's products include return flow controllers, pulsation dampers, and governor MK III.	925-606-1001	NA	Livermore

	COMPANY NAME	PRODUCT / SERVICE	PHONE	EMP	CITY
N	Neill Aircraft Co (HQ)	Provider of build-to-print parts, assemblies, and kitting services to the aerospace community.	562-432-7981	11-50	Long Beach
	Replicraft (HQ)	Provider of World War I aircraft plan sets for modelers. The company provides plans for the aircrafts in one-fifth, one-sixth and one-tenth scales.	510-656-6039	NA	Fremont
	Seagull Solutions Inc (HQ)	Developer and manufacturer of air bearing spindles, clamps, and custom applications. The company mainly offers custom made services.	408-778-1127	NA	Morgan Hill
N	Skyspares Parts Inc (HQ)	Manufacturer of CNC precision machined parts.	951-351-0770	NA	Riverside
	Stellar Solutions (HQ)	Provider of systems engineering, mission operations, and strategic planning services. The company focuses on commercial and government programs.	650-473-9866	NA	Palo Alto
	Tavis Corp (HQ)	Provider of custom pressure transducer sensor designs. The company offers services to measurement environments.	209-966-2027	NA	Mariposa
	The Olander Company Inc (HQ)	Distributor of standard and metric fasteners and electromechanical components. The company offers tools, adhesives, and wire management products.	408-735-1850	NA	Sunnyvale
	TPS Aviation Inc (HQ)	Distributor of commercial and military aerospace fasteners and electric components. The company focuses on aerospace parts, components, and logistics.	510-475-1010	NA	Hayward
	Ultracor Inc (HQ)	Manufacturer of engineered specialty honeycomb and related supplies. The company also deals with custom designs.	209-983-3744	NA	Stockton

6 = Ground Support Equipment

	COMPANY NAME	PRODUCT / SERVICE	PHONE	EMP	CITY
	ATAC Corp (HQ)	Developer of products and services like decision aids, analysis tools, and expert consulting for aviation modeling and simulation.	408-736-2822	NA	Santa Clara

7 = Missiles/Rockets

	COMPANY NAME	PRODUCT / SERVICE	PHONE	EMP	CITY
	Aerojet Rocketdyne (RH)	Provider of propulsion and energetic to its space, missile defense, strategic, tactical missile. and armaments customers.	916-355-4000	NA	Sacramento
N	Beranek Inc (HQ)	Manufacturer of precision machined components for aerospace, military, space and communication industry.	310-328-9094	NA	Torrance
N	Neill Aircraft Co (HQ)	Provider of build-to-print parts, assemblies, and kitting services to the aerospace community.	562-432-7981	11-50	Long Beach
	Pacific Scientific Energetic Materials Company (California) LLC (HQ)	Provider of energetic materials and services. The company offers services to the aircraft, missiles, space, and law enforcement industries.	831-637-3731	NA	Hollister
N	Skyspares Parts Inc (HQ)	Manufacturer of CNC precision machined parts.	951-351-0770	NA	Riverside

8 = Other Aerospace/Aircraft Equipment

	COMPANY NAME	PRODUCT / SERVICE	PHONE	EMP	CITY
	Ameritech Industries Inc (HQ)	Provider of aircraft engines and certified and experimental engines and propellers and also offers overhaul and exchange services.	530-221-4470	NA	Redding
	Applied Aerospace Structures Corp (HQ)	Designer of space and aircraft metal structures. The company also specializes in fabrication and other services.	209-983-3314	NA	Stockton
	ATAC Corp (HQ)	Developer of products and services like decision aids, analysis tools, and expert consulting for aviation modeling and simulation.	408-736-2822	NA	Santa Clara
	Aviation Design (HQ)	Designer of aircraft interiors for commercial and private aircrafts. The company offers services to the aviation industry.	209-962-0415	NA	Groveland
	Cobham Defence Electronics (BR)	Manufacturer and designer of electrical components. The company caters to the military and commercial sectors.	888-310-0010	NA	San Jose
	Davtron Inc (HQ)	Designer and manufacturer of avionic instruments. The company's portfolio comprises volt meters, clocks, probes, and more.	866-369-5588	NA	Emerald Hills
	EA Machining Inc (HQ)	Provider of CNC turning and milling services. The company offers services to the semiconductor manufacturing equipment industry.	408-727-4962	NA	Santa Clara
	Ellison Fluid Systems Inc (HQ)	Provider of fluid systems that includes throttle body injector. The company offers fuel metering for aircrafts engines and throttle response.	877-339-3412	NA	Mission Viejo
	Hexcel Corp (BR)	Provider and manufacturer of advanced material solutions. The company manufactures everything from a carbon fiber to finished aircraft structures.	800-444-3923	NA	Dublin
	ICON Aircraft Inc (HQ)	Manufacturer of consumer aircraft. The company specializes in giving the freedom, fun, and adventure of flying to all who have dreamed of flight.	707-564-4100	NA	Vacaville
	Moller International Inc (HQ)	Designer and developer of personal vertical takeoff and landing aircraft. The company specializes in rotapower engines.	530-756-5086	NA	Dixon
	Nasam Inc (HQ)	Distributor of electronics products. The company offers military/defense equipment, aircraft support equipment, and other products.	650-872-1155	NA	S San Francisco
	Pauli Systems Inc (HQ)	Manufacturer of custom finishing systems, abrasive booths, and equipment including blast rooms for aviation, automotive, and industrial applications.	707-429-2434	NA	Fairfield
	Seagull Solutions Inc (HQ)	Developer and manufacturer of air bearing spindles, clamps, and custom applications. The company mainly offers custom made services.	408-778-1127	NA	Morgan Hill
	Stellar Solutions (HQ)	Provider of systems engineering, mission operations, and strategic planning services. The company focuses on commercial and government programs.	650-473-9866	NA	Palo Alto

COMPANY NAME	PRODUCT / SERVICE	PHONE	EMP	CITY
Tavis Corp (HQ)	Provider of custom pressure transducer sensor designs. The company offers services to measurement environments.	209-966-2027	NA	Mariposa
TPS Aviation Inc (HQ)	Distributor of commercial and military aerospace fasteners and electric components. The company focuses on aerospace parts, components, and logistics.	510-475-1010	NA	Hayward
Ultracor Inc (HQ)	Manufacturer of engineered specialty honeycomb and related supplies. The company also deals with custom designs.	209-983-3744	NA	Stockton

9 = Spacecraft/Space Systems

COMPANY NAME	PRODUCT / SERVICE	PHONE	EMP	CITY
Applied Systems Engineering Inc (HQ)	Provider of consulting, software, design, and testing services. The company's products cater to communication applications.	408-364-0500	NA	Campbell
Hera Systems Inc (HQ)	Provider of satellite information and analytics that collects images of Earth, for commercial and government organizations to monitor and make decisions.	844-437-2797	NA	San Jose
KaiserAir Inc (BR)	Provider of aircraft management services. The company also offers business aircraft chartering services.	510-569-9622	NA	Oakland
Nasam Inc (HQ)	Distributor of electronics products. The company offers military/defense equipment, aircraft support equipment, and other products.	650-872-1155	NA	S San Francisco
Pacific Scientific Energetic Materials Company (California) LLC (HQ)	Provider of energetic materials and services. The company offers services to the aircraft, missiles, space, and law enforcement industries.	831-637-3731	NA	Hollister

11 = Analytical Instruments

COMPANY NAME	PRODUCT / SERVICE	PHONE	EMP	CITY
Airxpanders Inc (HQ)	Provider of controlled tissue expander and small handheld wireless controller of breast cancer reconstructive surgery.	650-390-9000	NA	San Jose
Aqua Metrology Systems Ltd (HQ)	Developer of online and offline analytical instrumentation for determination of water contaminants and trace metals for municipal and industrial markers.	408-523-1900	NA	Sunnyvale
CenterVue Inc (BR)	Designer and manufacturer of medical devices for the diagnosis and management of ocular pathologies.	408-988-8404	NA	Fremont
EME Systems (HQ)	Designer and manufacturer of instruments for environmental science. The company also offers signal conditioners, sensors, enclosures, and batteries.	510-848-5725	NA	Berkeley
Guided Wave Inc (HQ)	Provider of online optical measurements services. The company caters to process analytical chemistry needs.	916-638-4944	NA	Rancho Cordova
Hitachi High Technologies America Inc (BR)	Seller of semiconductor manufacturing equipment and analytical instrumentation and also offers electronic devices, bio-related, and other products.	925-218-2814	NA	Pleasanton
Infrared Industries Inc (HQ)	Developer of gas analyzer instrumentation for the automotive, oil and gas, industrial, environmental, and utility industries.	510-782-8100	NA	Hayward
Lamdagen Corp (BR)	Developer of nano technology based biosensors used in research and diagnostic equipment for human and animal health testing.	650-571-5816	NA	Menlo Park
Los Gatos Research Inc (HQ)	Manufacturer of analyzers for the measurement of trace gases and isotopes. The company serves the industrial and environmental sectors.	650-965-7772	NA	San Jose
Marvac Scientific Manufacturing Co (HQ)	Provider of industrial grade belt drive vacuum pumps. The company also offers cooling system and other tools.	925-825-4636	NA	Concord
Nyad Inc (HQ)	Supplier of gas analyzers. The company's product line includes analyzers for moisture, oxygen, carbon monoxide, carbon dioxide, hydrocarbon, and transmitters.	925-270-3971	NA	Concord
Spectrex Corp (HQ)	Developer of environmental and analytical instruments. The company's offerings include detectors and personal air samplers.	650-365-6567	NA	Redwood City

12 = Counting/Recording Devices

COMPANY NAME	PRODUCT / SERVICE	PHONE	EMP	CITY
C-Scan Corp (HQ)	Manufacturer and designer of thermal recorders and printers for medical applications and the healthcare sector.	800-953-7888	NA	Los Gatos

13 = Detection/Measuring Equipment

COMPANY NAME	PRODUCT / SERVICE	PHONE	EMP	CITY
3rd Stone Design Inc (HQ)	Provider of design, product development, and engineering services. The company serves the consumer products and healthcare industries.	415-454-3005	NA	San Rafael
All Weather Inc (HQ)	Manufacturer of meteorological instruments and systems. The company is also engaged in the development of air traffic management solutions.	800-824-5873	NA	Sacramento
Arrgh!! Manufacturing Company Inc (HQ)	Manufacturer of battery chargers, controls, battery discharge alarms, microcomputer charger controls, and gas detectors.	415-897-0220	NA	Novato
Cutera Inc (HQ)	Manufacturer of aesthetic solutions such as face and body laser, light, and other energy-based aesthetic systems for hair removal and pigmented lesions.	415-657-5500	NA	Brisbane
Detention Device Systems (HQ)	Provider of design and manufacturing services for detention equipment metal fabrications. The company offers sliding door locking and other devices.	510-783-0771	NA	Hayward
Esp Safety Inc (HQ)	Manufacturer of combustible gas and flame detectors, test lamps, and multi-channel controllers for custom applications.	408-886-9746	NA	San Jose
G&R Labs (HQ)	Manufacturer, seller, and calibrator of light measurement equipment. The company is engaged in design, delivery, and installation services.	408-986-0377	NA	Santa Clara

COMPANY NAME	PRODUCT / SERVICE	PHONE	EMP	CITY
Geometrics Inc (HQ)	Manufacturer of geophysical instruments and equipment. The company also focuses on the sales and distribution.	408-954-0522	NA	San Jose
Hamamatsu Corp (BR)	Manufacturer of devices for the generation and measurement of infrared, visible, and ultraviolet light.	408-261-2022	NA	San Jose
IDEX Health & Science LLC (BR)	Provider of precision equipment for the health care industry. The company also offers detectors, fittings, and filters.	707-588-2000	NA	Rohnert Park
International Medcom Inc (BR)	Provider of radiation detection instruments and systems. The company provides technology for nuclear medicine, health physics, and public safety products.	707-823-0336	NA	Sebastopol
N International Sensor Technology Inc (HQ)	Manufacturer and distributor of both the sensors and the instrumentations.	949-452-9000	1-10	Irvine
N Irrometer Company Inc (HQ)	Manufacturer of soil moisture measuring devices.	951-682-9505	11-50	Riverside
Jan Medical Inc (HQ)	Manufacturer of portable brain sensing devices for the detection of traumatic brain injuries, including concussions.	650-316-8811	NA	Mountain View
Krytar Inc (HQ)	Provider of broadband microwave components and test equipment. The company is engaged in troubleshooting and maintenance services.	408-734-5999	NA	Sunnyvale
KWJ Engineering Inc (HQ)	Manufacturer of gas detection products. The company offers equipment to detect chlorine, carbon monoxide, ozone, and methane and propane.	510-794-4296	NA	Newark
Lucas Signatone Corp (HQ)	Manufacturer of micro-probe stations, holders, and accessories. The company's products are used in resistivity test equipment.	408-848-2851	NA	Gilroy
Micro-Vu (HQ)	Designer and manufacturer of measuring machines, including automated and manual video systems, and optical comparators.	707-838-6272	NA	Windsor
Quality Scales Unlimited (HQ)	Provider of mechanical and computer based weighing systems. The company's services include repairs, replacement, and installation.	925-634-8068	NA	Byron
N Quint Measuring Systems Inc (HQ)	Distributor of imported hand measuring and digital reading products and publisher of books, supplier of art and graphic supplies to various trades unions, and creator of sewing and quilting tools.	800-745-5043	NA	Walnut Creek
Rheosense Inc (HQ)	Designer and manufacturer of viscometers and extensional viscometers. The company offers calibration, sample testing, and maintenance services.	925-866-3801	NA	San Ramon
RKI Instruments Inc (HQ)	Manufacturer of gas detectors and monitoring systems. The company caters to refineries, utilities, and oil tankers.	510-441-5656	NA	Union City
Spectrex Corp (HQ)	Developer of environmental and analytical instruments. The company's offerings include detectors and personal air samplers.	650-365-6567	NA	Redwood City
Structural Integrity Associates Inc (HQ)	Provider of solutions for prevention and control of structural and mechanical failures and serves nuclear plants, oil and gas, and other sectors.	408-978-8200	NA	San Jose
Unimicro Technologies Inc (HQ)	Provider of chemical and biological separation and analysis with micro separation technology especially capillary electrochromatography.	925-846-8638	NA	Pleasanton

14 = Flowmeters & Counting Devices

COMPANY NAME	PRODUCT / SERVICE	PHONE	EMP	CITY
Accusplit Inc (HQ)	Provider of digital stopwatches and pedometer products. The company is also engaged in technical support services.	800-935-1996	NA	Pleasanton
Eldridge Products Inc (HQ)	Manufacturer of thermal mass flow meters and flow switches. The company focuses on sales, installation, and inspection.	831-648-7777	NA	Marina
Kurz Instruments Inc (HQ)	Designer and manufacturer of thermal mass flow transmitters. The company's products find application in industrial gases and liquids.	831-646-5911	NA	Monterey
Liberty Test Equipment (HQ)	Provider of refurbished and new test equipment and related accessories. The company deals with sales, lease, and rental services.	916-625-4228	NA	Roseville
Max Machinery Inc (HQ)	Manufacturer of precision flow meters. The company offers intermittent injection, low flow metering, and bi-directional flow measurement services.	707-433-2662	NA	Healdsburg
Proteus Industries Inc (HQ)	Developer and manufacturer of rugged and sensitive flow sensing and control instruments. The company focuses on marketing.	650-964-4163	NA	Mountain View
RCM Industries Inc (HQ)	Manufacturer of direct reading flow meters for liquid and gases. The company's products are used in chillers and satellite systems.	925-687-8363	NA	Concord
Sage Metering Inc (HQ)	Manufacturer of thermal mass flow meters. The company offers services to the environmental and industrial sectors.	831-242-2030	NA	Monterey
Sierra Instruments Inc (HQ)	Manufacturer of mass flow meters and mass flow controllers. The company serves gas, liquid, and steam applications.	831-373-0200	NA	Monterey
Thermochem Inc (HQ)	Provider of chemical engineering, laboratory analysis, geochemistry and field testing services and products to a wide range of energy industries.	707-575-1310	NA	Santa Rosa

15 = Instruments for Measuring/Testing Electricity

COMPANY NAME	PRODUCT / SERVICE	PHONE	EMP	CITY
AEHR Test Systems (HQ)	Designer and manufacturer of dynamic burn in and test systems. The company is engaged in troubleshooting and maintenance services.	510-623-9400	NA	Fremont
Calypso Systems Inc (HQ)	Developer of solid state storage test and measurement. The company specializes in test results automatically stored in the CTS MySQL database.	408-982-9955	NA	San Jose
CSBio (HQ)	Provider of automated peptide synthesis instrumentation, peptide synthesizers, and custom peptides to the life science community.	650-322-1111	NA	Menlo Park

COMPANY NAME	PRODUCT / SERVICE	PHONE	EMP	CITY
Furaxa Inc (HQ)	Designer and supplier of signal synthesis, sampling, and pulse generating technologies and products.	925-253-2969	NA	Berkeley
Incal Technology Inc (HQ)	Designer and manufacturer of test and burn in equipment and related hardware for board testing. The company serves the semiconductor industry.	510-657-8405	NA	Fremont
Liberty Test Equipment (HQ)	Provider of refurbished and new test equipment and related accessories. The company deals with sales, lease, and rental services.	916-625-4228	NA	Roseville
Micro Lambda Wireless Inc (HQ)	Supplier of remote drivers, multipliers, bench test filters, oscillators, synthesizers, and harmonic generators.	510-770-9221	NA	Fremont
Stanford Research Systems (HQ)	Manufacturer of electronic instruments, optical choppers, and temperature controllers for the research industry.	408-744-9040	NA	Sunnyvale
YY Labs Inc (HQ)	Manufacturer and supplier of optical components. The company provides LN modulators, bias controllers, generators, and accessories.	510-739-6049	NA	Fremont

17 = Navigational Equipment

COMPANY NAME	PRODUCT / SERVICE	PHONE	EMP	CITY
Ayantra Inc (HQ)	Provider of wireless communication technology services. The company is engaged in monitoring and asset tracking.	510-623-7526	NA	Fremont
N Rantec Microwave Systems Inc (HQ)	Manufacturer of microwave antennas for military and commercial applications.	818-223-5000	11-50	Westlake Village
Spirent Communications Inc (LH)	Provider of performance analysis technology services. The company also offers network equipment and data center solutions.	408-752-7100	NA	San Jose
Trimble Inc (HQ)	Developer of positioning solutions for the agriculture, construction, mining, and surveying industries.	408-481-8000	NA	Sunnyvale

18 = Optical Measuring/Testing Devices

COMPANY NAME	PRODUCT / SERVICE	PHONE	EMP	CITY
Anritsu Co (DH)	Provider of test solutions for telecommunication applications. The company also caters to microwave applications.	408-778-2000	NA	Morgan Hill
EMSL Analytical Inc (BR)	Provider of laboratory analytical testing services. The company specializes in a wide range of environmental, material and forensic testing.	510-895-3675	NA	San Leandro
Guided Wave Inc (HQ)	Provider of online optical measurements services. The company caters to process analytical chemistry needs.	916-638-4944	NA	Rancho Cordova
Inphora Inc (HQ)	Supplier of high-precision photometric and radiometric instruments. The company's products include detectors, optical filters, and LED reference standards.	925-322-5964	NA	Moraga
Roger K Sherman Co (HQ)	Provider of microscope eyepiece reticles, calibration standards, and ruled master gages for the semiconductor and magnetic head industries.	650-941-8300	NA	Los Altos
Turner Designs Inc (HQ)	Provider of industrial fluorometers and rhodamine dyes. The company's applications include oil spill response and environmental monitoring.	408-749-0994	NA	San Jose
YY Labs Inc (HQ)	Manufacturer and supplier of optical components. The company provides LN modulators, bias controllers, generators, and accessories.	510-739-6049	NA	Fremont
Zygo Corp (BR)	Supplier of optical metrology instruments. The company also specializes in high precision optical components.	408-434-1000	NA	Santa Clara

19 = Other Analytical & Testing Equipment

COMPANY NAME	PRODUCT / SERVICE	PHONE	EMP	CITY
Applied Systems Engineering Inc (HQ)	Provider of consulting, software, design, and testing services. The company's products cater to communication applications.	408-364-0500	NA	Campbell
Automated Inspection Systems (HQ)	Designer and builder of inspection equipment. The company caters to the oil and gas pipeline inspection needs.	925-335-9206	NA	Concord
Automatic Bar Controls Inc (HQ)	Provider of beverage and liquor dispensers. The company's products include beverage and food and sauce dispensers, and food preparation systems.	707-448-5151	NA	Vacaville
Calypso Systems Inc (HQ)	Developer of solid state storage test and measurement. The company specializes in test results automatically stored in the CTS MySQL database.	408-982-9955	NA	San Jose
Coretest Systems Inc (HQ)	Designer and manufacturer of core analysis equipment for the oil and gas, hydrothermal, and environmental segments.	408-778-3771	NA	Morgan Hill
Dakota Ultrasonics (HQ)	Manufacturer of industrial ultrasonic testing equipment. The company serves the aerospace, power generation, and petrochemical industries.	831-431-9722	NA	Scotts Valley
DB Design Group (HQ)	Supplier of technology solutions. The company caters to the semiconductor, solar, and medical industries.	408-834-1400	NA	Fremont
Dicon Fiberoptics Inc (HQ)	Supplier of optical components, integrated modules, and test equipment for the fiber optics industry.	510-620-5000	NA	Richmond
Furaxa Inc (HQ)	Designer and supplier of signal synthesis, sampling, and pulse generating technologies and products.	925-253-2969	NA	Berkeley
Guidetech (HQ)	Developer of time measurement instruments. The company mainly caters to the semiconductor test industry.	408-733-6555	NA	Santa Clara
Jabil Circuit Inc (BR)	Provider of global manufacturing solutions. The company serves the defense, aerospace, and industrial markers.	408-361-3200	NA	San Jose
Larson Automation Inc (HQ)	Developer of automated test solutions for telecommunication companies. The company offers board test stations and level shifters.	408-432-4800	NA	San Jose

COMPANY NAME	PRODUCT / SERVICE	PHONE	EMP	CITY
Merieux Nutrisciences Corp (BR)	Provider of public health services. The company is focused on food and pharmaceutical products, cosmetics, and consumer goods.	209-549-7508	NA	Salida
Pembroke Instruments LLC (HQ)	Manufacturer of products for scientific imaging applications. The company also focuses on optical spectroscopy needs.	415-860-4217	NA	San Francisco
Scimet LLC (HQ)	Provider of metallurgical consulting services. The company specializes in welding, brazing, soldering, bonding, and heat treating.	925-736-2915	NA	Danville
Seco (HQ)	Manufacturer of surveying and positioning equipment and accessories. The company's products also finds application in site preparation.	530-225-8155	NA	Redding
Sessco Technologies Inc (HQ)	Designer and manufacturer of tri-temperature test handlers for the commercial, industrial, automotive, and military grade circuit test applications.	408-321-7437	NA	San Jose
Sotcher Measurement Inc (HQ)	Provider of test equipment. The company provides test stations, service tags, generator test sets, and automatic test stations.	800-922-2969	NA	San Jose
Testmetrix Inc (HQ)	Manufacturer of high-throughput AVTE systems, and offers official compliance certification test services.	408-730-5511	NA	Milpitas
Tosoh Bioscience Inc (BR)	Provider of monitoring services for life threatening diseases and cancers. The company focuses on preventing epidemics and purifying water.	650-615-4970	NA	S San Francisco
YY Labs Inc (HQ)	Manufacturer and supplier of optical components. The company provides LN modulators, bias controllers, generators, and accessories.	510-739-6049	NA	Fremont
Zircon Corp (HQ)	Designer and manufacturer of stud finders. The company offers electrical scanners, metal detectors, leveling tools, and accessories.	408-963-4550	NA	Campbell

20 = Scientific/Laboratory Equipment

COMPANY NAME	PRODUCT / SERVICE	PHONE	EMP	CITY
3rd Stone Design Inc (HQ)	Provider of design, product development, and engineering services. The company serves the consumer products and healthcare industries.	415-454-3005	NA	San Rafael
ATI North America (HQ)	Manufacturer of converting equipment. The company specializes in volume manufacturing solutions, and also offers repair and upgrade services.	916-518-1445	NA	Gold River
CP Lab Safety (HQ)	Manufacturer of laboratory safety equipment to prevent fire, reduce waste emission and exposure to toxic fumes.	415-883-2600	NA	Novato
Eldex Laboratories Inc (HQ)	Manufacturer of instruments for analytical chemistry laboratories and chemical process control. The company also creates customized products.	707-224-8800	NA	Napa
Gatan Inc (HQ)	Manufacturer of instrumentation and software used to enhance and extend the operation and performance of electron microscopes.	925 463 0200	NA	Pleasanton
Gold Standard Diagnostics Corp (HQ)	Provider of laboratory diagnostic solutions. The company specializes in diagnosis of autoimmune diseases, bacterial and viral diseases.	530-759-8000	NA	Davis
Higgins Analytical Inc (HQ)	Manufacturer and marketer of laboratory equipment and supplies. The company specializes in HPLC columns, cartridges, and separations consumables.	650-988-8930	NA	Mountain View
Incelldx Inc (HQ)	Provider of molecular diagnostics to detect and monitor cervical cancer, HIV/AIDS, hepatitis, and organ transplant rejection diseases.	650-777-7630	NA	San Carlos
Labcon North America (HQ)	Manufacturer of disposable plastic products for laboratories. The company offers products for liquid handling, culture, and molecular biology.	707-766-2100	NA	Petaluma
Mettler-Toledo Rainin LLC (BR)	Provider of laboratory weighing and process analytics services. The company also focuses on industrial weighing.	800-472-4646	NA	Oakland
Sepragen Corp (HQ)	Provider of equipment, systems, and materials for the scale-up and purification of proteins, biopharmaceuticals, and nutraceuticals.	510-475-0650	NA	Union City
Tosoh Bioscience Inc (BR)	Provider of monitoring services for life threatening diseases and cancers. The company focuses on preventing epidemics and purifying water.	650-615-4970	NA	S San Francisco
Unimicro Technologies Inc (HQ)	Provider of chemical and biological separation and analysis with micro separation technology especially capillary electrochromatography.	925-846-8638	NA	Pleasanton
Xia LLC (HQ)	Provider of x-ray and gamma-ray detector electronics, and related instruments for the research industry.	510-401-5760	NA	Hayward

21 = Services, Distribution

COMPANY NAME	PRODUCT / SERVICE	PHONE	EMP	CITY
EMSL Analytical Inc (BR)	Provider of laboratory analytical testing services. The company specializes in a wide range of environmental, material and forensic testing.	510-895-3675	NA	San Leandro
Exacta Tech Inc (HQ)	Manufacturer of custom machine components and parts and provider of design, inspection and engineering services for industries.	925-443-8963	NA	Livermore

23 = Animal Biotechnology

COMPANY NAME	PRODUCT / SERVICE	PHONE	EMP	CITY
Antech Diagnostics (HQ)	Provider of diagnostic and laboratory testing services for chemistry, pathology, endocrinology, serology, hematology, and microbiology.	800-872-1001	NA	Fountain Valley
Hygeia Laboratories Inc (HQ)	Developers of vaccines using novel technology for animals. The company offers animal pharmaceuticals for dairy cattle, sheep and poultry.	530-661-1442	NA	Woodland
Single Cell Technology Inc (HQ)	Developer of cell technology solutions and also proportionary therapeutic antibody process for its clients.	408-265-9239	NA	San Jose

COMPANY NAME	PRODUCT / SERVICE	PHONE	EMP	CITY
Southall Environmental Associates Inc (HQ)	Provider of science to support conservation management. The company specializes in marine and terrestrial ecosystems.	831-661-5177	NA	Aptos
Vetequip Inc (HQ)	Developer and manufacturer of drug delivery systems. The company specializes in nasal anesthesia delivery systems.	925-463-1828	NA	Livermore

24 = Biochemicals/Biomaterials

COMPANY NAME	PRODUCT / SERVICE	PHONE	EMP	CITY
Bell Biosystems Inc (HQ)	Provider of biotechnology services. The company develops proteins targeted to kill specific bacteria but cause minimal collateral damage.	877-420-3621	NA	Berkeley
N Big Bear Visitors Bureau (HQ)	Publisher of newsletters and magazines.	909-866-7000	NA	Big Bear Lake
Biochain Institute Inc (HQ)	Provider of bio-sample preparation, analysis, and application assays accelerating the development of personalized diagnostics, therapeutics, and medicine.	510-783-8588	NA	Newark
BioConsortia Inc (HQ)	Focuses on the discovery, development, and commercialization of microbial consortia seed treatment and soil additive products.	530-564-5570	NA	Davis
Biomarker Technologies Inc (HQ)	Provider of geochemical technology services. The company offers asphaltene analysis, diamondoids, and gas chromatography analysis services.	707-829-5551	NA	Rohnert Park
Boster Biological Technology (HQ)	Provider of antibodies and ELISA kits. The company serves customers in the biochemicals and molecular biology areas.	888-466-3604	NA	Pleasanton
Butterfly Sciences (HQ)	Developer of gene therapies for HIV and aging. The company also provides consulting services for biotech investment evaluations.	415-518-8153	NA	Davis
N Cal-Disc Grinding Company Inc (HQ)	Provider of disc grinding, flat lapping and much more services.	626-444-9576	NA	South El Monte
N Del Mar Trade Shows Inc (HQ)	Provider of electronic components, fabrication, design and most aspects of electronics manufacturing.	858-459-1682	NA	La Jolla
Discoverx Corp (HQ)	Developer and marketer of innovative solutions to study major drug target classes such as GPCRs and kinases.	510-979-1415	NA	Fremont
Drawbridge Health Inc (HQ)	Provider of diagnostic testing solutions. The company offers blood testing solutions for a range of biomarker.	650-714-6791	NA	Menlo Park
Edeniq Inc (HQ)	Focuses on the production of ethanol, other biofuels, and/or biochemicals. The company combines mechanical and biological processes.	559-302-1777	NA	Visalia
N Foothill.Net Inc (HQ)	Provider of computer and technology services to companies.	530-820-1031	NA	Foresthill
Gemini Bio-Products (HQ)	Provider of supplements, reagents, and human products. The company is involved in medical research and development.	800-543-6464	NA	West Sacramento
N Internet Brands Inc (HQ)	Operator of media and e-commerce sites for "large ticket" consumer purchases, such as cars and mortgages.	310-280-4000	5001-10000	El Segundo
Microvi Biotech Inc (HQ)	Designer and developer of biotechnology solutions. The company commercializes biocatalytic solutions in the water, energy and chemical industries.	510-344-0668	NA	Hayward
Molecular Matrix Inc (HQ)	Provider of research tools for cultivating and studying stem cells. The company products provide solutions for growing cells.	916-376-9404	NA	West Sacramento
Murigenics (HQ)	Provider of preclinical in-vivo and in-vitro contract drug discovery. The company is also focused on development services.	707-561-8900	NA	Vallejo
Nvigen Inc (HQ)	Developer of multifunctional and biodegradable nanoparticles. The company is engaged in research and development services.	650-209-0268	NA	San Jose
Prothena (RH)	Focuses on the discovery, development and commercialization of protein immunotherapy programs for the treatment of diseases that involve amyloid.	650-837-8550	NA	S San Francisco
Purigen Biosystems Inc (HQ)	Provider of biotechnology such as isotachophoresis, an electric-field driven technique for extracting and quantifying DNA and RNA from biological samples.	877-787-4436	NA	Pleasanton
QB3 (HQ)	Provider of life science services. The company focuses on research facilities, internships, mentoring, and seed-stage venture fund.	415-514-9790	NA	San Francisco
RAPT Therapeutics (HQ)	Provider of immuno-oncology oral medicines designed to activate patients own immune system to eradicate cancer.	650-489-9000	NA	S San Francisco
N Sincere Design (HQ)	Provider of website design, Internet and traditional marketing, book design and production, computer graphics and communication services.	510-215-1139	NA	Point Richmond
TOMA Biosciences Inc (HQ)	Provider of sequencing solutions. The company serves laboratories and researchers to uncover clinically meaningful genomic changes in tumors.	650-691-8662	NA	Foster City
N Winning Directions (HQ)	Provider of professional services.	650-875-4000	NA	S San Francisco
N YapStone Inc (HQ)	Developer of electronic payments platform.	866-289-5977	201-500	Walnut Creek
Zymergen (HQ)	Developer of engineering biology. The company is engaged in new product development and it serves the scientific market.	415-801-8073	NA	Emeryville

25 = Bioinformatics

COMPANY NAME	PRODUCT / SERVICE	PHONE	EMP	CITY
Bell Biosystems Inc (HQ)	Provider of biotechnology services. The company develops proteins targeted to kill specific bacteria but cause minimal collateral damage.	877-420-3621	NA	Berkeley
Blade Therapeutics Inc (HQ)	Developer of biopharmaceutical products. The company specializes anti-fibrotic drug discovery and development for treatment of fibrotic disease.	650-278-4291	NA	S San Francisco

COMPANY NAME	PRODUCT / SERVICE	PHONE	EMP	CITY
Circle Pharma (HQ)	Focuses on the development of cell permeable macrocyclic peptide therapeutics. The company serves the pharmaceutical sector.	650-392-0363	NA	S San Francisco
Complete Genomics Inc (HQ)	Developer of human genome sequencing technology, research and development, clinical and consumer applications.	408-648-2560	NA	San Jose
Ekso Bionics Holdings Inc (HQ)	Developer and manufacturer of powered exoskeleton bionic devices. The company is engaged in distribution services.	510-984-1761	NA	Richmond
GRAIL Inc (HQ)	Provider of research services and clinical study programs for the detection of cancer at an early stage.	650-542-0372	NA	Menlo Park
Karius Inc (HQ)	Provider of microbial genomics diagnostics. The company focuses on transforming infectious disease diagnostics with genomics.	866-452-7487	NA	Redwood City
Novozymes Inc (BR)	Provider of industrial biotechnology solutions for the food and beverage, agriculture, textile, and pulp and paper industries.	530-757-8100	NA	Davis
Second Genome Inc (HQ)	Focuses on the development of therapeutic products. The company serves pharmaceutical and nutritional companies.	650-440-4606	NA	S San Francisco
twoXAR Inc (HQ)	Developer of drug delivery platform. The company is involved in biological data extraction, automated model generation, and feature identification.	650-382-2605	NA	Mountain View

26 = Enzyme Systems

COMPANY NAME	PRODUCT / SERVICE	PHONE	EMP	CITY
Antibody Solutions (HQ)	Provider of antibody products and services. The company serves biotechnology, diagnostic and pharmaceutical companies.	650-938-4300	NA	Sunnyvale
Bell Biosystems Inc (HQ)	Provider of biotechnology services. The company develops proteins targeted to kill specific bacteria but cause minimal collateral damage.	877-420-3621	NA	Berkeley
CryptoForensics Technologies Inc (HQ)	Provider of cybersecurity solutions to businesses, organizations, and the government. The company focuses on cyberforensics and compliance services.	510-483-1933	NA	San Leandro
Novozymes Inc (BR)	Provider of industrial biotechnology solutions for the food and beverage, agriculture, textile, and pulp and paper industries.	530-757-8100	NA	Davis

27 = Industrial

COMPANY NAME	PRODUCT / SERVICE	PHONE	EMP	CITY
Antibody Solutions (HQ)	Provider of antibody products and services. The company serves biotechnology, diagnostic and pharmaceutical companies.	650-938-4300	NA	Sunnyvale
Bell Biosystems Inc (HQ)	Provider of biotechnology services. The company develops proteins targeted to kill specific bacteria but cause minimal collateral damage.	877-420-3621	NA	Berkeley
MTI California Inc (HQ)	Specializes in designing and validating manufacturing controls. The company offers services to biotech companies.	925-937-1500	NA	Walnut Creek
Novozymes Inc (BR)	Provider of industrial biotechnology solutions for the food and beverage, agriculture, textile, and pulp and paper industries.	530-757-8100	NA	Davis

28 = Diagnostic

COMPANY NAME	PRODUCT / SERVICE	PHONE	EMP	CITY
Antibody Solutions (HQ)	Provider of antibody products and services. The company serves biotechnology, diagnostic and pharmaceutical companies.	650-938-4300	NA	Sunnyvale
Arbor Vita Corp (HQ)	Provider of protein-based molecular diagnostics that is used for the management of infectious diseases and cancer.	408-585-3900	NA	Fremont
Bell Biosystems Inc (HQ)	Provider of biotechnology services. The company develops proteins targeted to kill specific bacteria but cause minimal collateral damage.	877-420-3621	NA	Berkeley
Bio Rad Laboratories Inc (HQ)	Provider of medical products and services that advance scientific discovery and improve healthcare for life science research and clinical diagnostic.	510-724-7000	NA	Hercules
Bio Rad Laboratories Inc (BR)	Provider of life science research and clinical diagnostics products and services for pharmaceutical manufacturers and biotechnology researchers.	510-741-1000	NA	Hercules
Broncus Medical Inc (HQ)	Provider of navigation, diagnostic and therapeutic technology solutions for treating patients with lung disease.	650-428-1600	NA	San Jose
MTI California Inc (HQ)	Specializes in designing and validating manufacturing controls. The company offers services to biotech companies.	925-937-1500	NA	Walnut Creek
Novozymes Inc (BR)	Provider of industrial biotechnology solutions for the food and beverage, agriculture, textile, and pulp and paper industries.	530-757-8100	NA	Davis
Nugen Technologies Inc (HQ)	Provider of solutions for genomic analysis. The company focuses on DNA analysis and RNA analysis applications.	650-590-3600	NA	San Carlos
Pliant Therapeutics Inc (HQ)	Developer of therapeutics medicines for the treatment of fibrosis in organs and conditions, including liver, kidney, heart, and gastrointestinal tract.	650-481-6770	NA	S San Francisco
Synergenics LLC (HQ)	Provider of life science services. The company also provides financial support and shared laboratory services.	415-554-8170	NA	San Francisco
Trianni Inc (HQ)	Developer of humanized monoclonal antibody platform. The company offers services to pharmaceutical and biotechnology companies.	866-374-9314	NA	San Francisco

29 = Instruments/Equipment

COMPANY NAME	PRODUCT / SERVICE	PHONE	EMP	CITY
CryptoForensics Technologies Inc (HQ)	Provider of cybersecurity solutions to businesses, organizations, and the government. The company focuses on cyberforensics and compliance services.	510-483-1933	NA	San Leandro

COMPANY NAME	PRODUCT / SERVICE	PHONE	EMP	CITY

30 = Bionics

Allakos Inc (HQ)	Developer of therapeutic antibodies for the treatment of inflammatory and proliferative diseases such as asthma, nasal polyposis, and fibrosis.	650-597-5002	NA	Redwood City
MTI California Inc (HQ)	Specializes in designing and validating manufacturing controls. The company offers services to biotech companies.	925-937-1500	NA	Walnut Creek

31 = Lab Instruments

Biolytic Lab Performance Inc (HQ)	Provider of instrumentation and accessories for oligonucleotide, DNA synthesis and oligo purification. The company specializes in rebuilt instruments.	510-795-1142	NA	Fremont
N Celestron LLC (HQ)	Manufacturer of telescopes, binoculars, spotting scopes, microscopes and accessories.	310-328-9560	NA	Torrance
N Coast Appliance Parts Co (HQ)	Distributor of heating, ventilating, and air conditioning equipment.	626-579-1500	NA	South El Monte
CP Lab Safety (HQ)	Manufacturer of laboratory safety equipment to prevent fire, reduce waste emission and exposure to toxic fumes.	415-883-2600	NA	Novato
CPI International (HQ)	Manufacturer of microbiological testing products and analytical instrument supplies. The company serves the semi-conductor industry.	707-525-5788	NA	Santa Rosa
N House of Batteries (HQ)	Manufacturer of battery assembly and battery pack.	714-962-7600	11-50	Fountain Valley
Immuno Concepts Na Ltd (HQ)	Manufacturer and distributor of diagnostic assays. The company's products are used for systemic rheumatic diseases.	916-363-2649	NA	Sacramento
International Process Solutions (HQ)	Provider of calibration, maintenance, document generation and validation services of pharmaceutical and biotech process equipment.	650-595-7890	NA	San Carlos
N Lambda Research Optics Inc (HQ)	Manufacturer of optical components.	714-327-0600	51-200	Costa Mesa
Marvac Scientific Manufacturing Co (HQ)	Provider of industrial grade belt drive vacuum pumps. The company also offers cooling system and other tools.	925-825-4636	NA	Concord
N Metrolaser Inc (HQ)	Provider of optical and laser solutions.	949-553-0688	11-50	Laguna Hills
Meyer Sound Laboratories Inc (HQ)	Manufacturer of loudspeakers, subwoofers, stage monitors, and amplifiers. The company serves the entertainment sector.	510-486-1166	NA	Berkeley
Microsonic Systems Inc (HQ)	Provider of ultrasonic fluid processing device built with MEMS technology to biotech and pharmaceutical industries.	408-844-4980	NA	San Jose
Molecular Devices LLC (HQ)	Manufacturer of bioanalytical measurement systems. The company is engaged in life science research, pharma, and bio therapeutic development.	800-635-5577	NA	San Jose
MTI California Inc (HQ)	Specializes in designing and validating manufacturing controls. The company offers services to biotech companies.	925-937-1500	NA	Walnut Creek
Noise and Vibration Technologies LLC (HQ)	Provider of measuring, simulating, and analyzing the effects of vibration, noise, shock, and other environmental variables for various industries.	831-655-6600	NA	Monterey
Phynexus Inc (HQ)	Provider of automated and scalable solutions for the low volume protein and nucleic acid purification.	408-267-7214	NA	San Jose
ProteinSimple (HQ)	Developer of proprietary systems, immunoassay system and consumables for protein analysis and purity of protein-based therapeutics.	408-510-5500	NA	San Jose
Scigene Corp (HQ)	Develops and commercializes solutions to automate sample workflows. The company offers reagents, microarray ovens, and arrays.	408-733-7337	NA	Sunnyvale
Ted Pella Inc (HQ)	Distributor of medical supplies and microscopy products such as inverted microscope for science and industry.	530-243-2200	NA	Redding
ThermoGenesis Holdings Inc (HQ)	Manufacturer of therapeutic products and related supplies. The company is involved in cellular bioprocessing and bone marrow transplants.	916-858-5100	NA	Rancho Cordova
N Yamaichi Electronics Usa Inc (HQ)	Manufacturer of electrical connectors, sockets, probe cards and much more.	408-715-9100	NA	San Jose

32 = Lab Accessories

MTI California Inc (HQ)	Specializes in designing and validating manufacturing controls. The company offers services to biotech companies.	925-937-1500	NA	Walnut Creek
RDM Industrial Products Inc (HQ)	Provider of laboratory and industrial furniture solutions. The company offers cabinets, counters, carts, and mobile tables.	408-945-8400	NA	Milpitas

33 = Lab Media

MTI California Inc (HQ)	Specializes in designing and validating manufacturing controls. The company offers services to biotech companies.	925-937-1500	NA	Walnut Creek

34 = Biotechnology R&D

10X Genomics Inc (HQ)	Provider of gemcode, instruments, software, and applications technology for RNA and DNA analysis.	925-401-7300	NA	Pleasanton
23andme Inc (HQ)	Provider of genetic information. The company specializes in DNA analysis technologies and web-based interactive tools.	800-239-5230	NA	Sunnyvale
3Scan Inc (HQ)	Provider of automated microscopy services and supporting software for the 3D analysis of cells, tissues, and organs.	415-851-5376	NA	San Francisco

COMPANY NAME	PRODUCT / SERVICE	PHONE	EMP	CITY
4D Molecular Therapeutics LLC (HQ)	Provider of gene therapy product research and development for the treatment of genetic diseases such as diabetes, arthritis, and heart failure.	510-505-2680	NA	Emeryville
AAT Bioquest Inc (HQ)	Developer and manufacturer of bioanalytical research reagents and kits. The company focuses on photometric detections including absorption.	408-733-1055	NA	Sunnyvale
Abbott Diabetes Care (BR)	Provider of healthcare solutions. The company specializes in diagnostics, diabetes care, vision technologies, nutrition, pharmaceuticals, and animal health.	510-749-5400	NA	Alameda
Accuray Inc (HQ)	Provider of oncology treatment solutions. The company develops, manufactures and sells precise and innovative tumor treatment solutions.	888-522-3740	NA	Sunnyvale
Achaogen Inc (HQ)	Developers of antibacterial. The company discovers and develops antibacterial for the treatment of serious bacterial infections.	650-800-3636	NA	S San Francisco
Actinix (HQ)	Developer of ultraviolet light generation, long-coherence-length pulsed fiber laser systems, high energy laser systems and optical tools/ methods.	831-440-9388	NA	Felton
Acumen Pharmaceuticals Inc (HQ)	Specializes in the discovery and development of therapeutics and diagnostics related to soluble A˜ oligomers.	925-368-8508	NA	Livermore
Advanced Cell Diagnostics Inc (HQ)	Developer of biotechnological diagnostic tests. The company specializes in the identification and validation of RNA biomarkers for cancer diagnosis.	510-576-8800	NA	Newark
Aelan Cell Technologies Inc (HQ)	Provider of research, discovery, development, and commercialization of biomedical technologies for the advancement of human health.	415-991-9915	NA	San Francisco
Aemetis Inc (HQ)	Producer of biochemicals, renewable fuels, food, and feed products. The company's products include Z-Microbe, Glycerin, and edible oils.	408-213-0940	51-200	Cupertino
Ahram Biosystems Inc (HQ)	Developer of new life science tools. The company provides battery-powered, palm-size portable PCR machine.	408-645-7300	NA	San Jose
Aimmune Therapeutics (RH)	Developer of desensitization treatments. The company is engaged in clinical trials and it serves the healthcare sector.	650-614-5220	NA	Brisbane
Allakos Inc (HQ)	Developer of therapeutic antibodies for the treatment of inflammatory and proliferative diseases such as asthma, nasal polyposis, and fibrosis.	650-597-5002	NA	Redwood City
Amgen Inc (BR)	Provider of scientific applications services. The company's services include clinical trials, ethical research, biosimilars, and web resources.	650-244-2000	NA	S San Francisco
Antibody Solutions (HQ)	Provider of antibody products and services. The company serves biotechnology, diagnostic and pharmaceutical companies.	650-938-4300	NA	Sunnyvale
Apexigen (HQ)	Specializes in document management and managed print solutions. The company serves the business sector.	650-931-6236	NA	San Carlos
Applied Stemcell Inc (HQ)	Provider of stem cell characterization, gene targeting, teratoma formation, and embryoid body (EB) formation services.	408-773-8007	NA	Milpitas
Aragen Bioscience (HQ)	Provider of services such as protein expression and purification, molecular biology, immunology, and in vivo services to the biotech and pharma industries.	408-779-1700	NA	Morgan Hill
Arcadia Biosciences Inc (HQ)	Developer of agricultural products with enhanced traits. The company uses technological tools, genetic screening and genetic engineering to achieve this.	530-756-7077	NA	Davis
Ascendis Pharma A/S (BR)	Focuses on the creation of drug candidates, proteins, peptides and small molecules, suitable for either local or systemic treatment.	650-352-8389	NA	Palo Alto
Assembly Biosciences Inc (RH)	Developer of therapeutics for the treatment of hepatitis B virus (HBV) infection. The company specializes in clinical trials.	833-509-4583	NA	S San Francisco
Aziyo Biologics Inc (BR)	Manufacturer of allograft tissue products for use in orthopedic, spinal, sports medicine, and dermal applications.	855-416-0596	NA	Richmond
Bell Biosystems Inc (HQ)	Provider of biotechnology services. The company develops proteins targeted to kill specific bacteria but cause minimal collateral damage.	877-420-3621	NA	Berkeley
Benchling Inc (HQ)	Developer of integrated software solution for experiment design, note-taking, and molecular biology for industry and academia.	415-980-9932	NA	San Francisco
N Big Bear Visitors Bureau (HQ)	Publisher of newsletters and magazines.	909-866-7000	NA	Big Bear Lake
Bio Rad Laboratories Inc (HQ)	Provider of medical products and services that advance scientific discovery and improve healthcare for life science research and clinical diagnostic.	510-724-7000	NA	Hercules
Biochain Institute Inc (HQ)	Provider of bio-sample preparation, analysis, and application assays accelerating the development of personalized diagnostics, therapeutics, and medicine.	510-783-8588	NA	Newark
BioConsortia Inc (HQ)	Focuses on the discovery, development, and commercialization of microbial consortia seed treatment and soil additive products.	530-564-5570	NA	Davis
Biomarker Technologies Inc (HQ)	Provider of geochemical technology services. The company offers asphaltene analysis, diamondoids, and gas chromatography analysis services.	707-829-5551	NA	Rohnert Park
Biosearch Technologies Inc (RH)	Manufacturer of nucleic acid based products that accelerate the discovery and application of genomic information.	415-883-8400	NA	Petaluma
Blade Therapeutics Inc (HQ)	Developer of biopharmaceutical products. The company specializes anti-fibrotic drug discovery and development for treatment of fibrotic disease.	650-278-4291	NA	S San Francisco

COMPANY NAME	PRODUCT / SERVICE	PHONE	EMP	CITY
Blue Turtle Bio Technologies Inc (HQ)	Creator of therapeutic products. The company specializes in microbiome to recruit genetically malleable and easily replenishable organ in the human body.	313-806-2774	NA	San Francisco
Boster Biological Technology (HQ)	Provider of antibodies and ELISA kits. The company serves customers in the biochemicals and molecular biology areas.	888-466-3604	NA	Pleasanton
Butterfly Sciences (HQ)	Developer of gene therapies for HIV and aging. The company also provides consulting services for biotech investment evaluations.	415-518-8153	NA	Davis
Cairn Biosciences (HQ)	Provider of therapeutic solutions for treating cancer. The company is involved in biotechnical research and commercial business.	415-503-1185	NA	San Francisco
N Cal-Disc Grinding Company Inc (HQ)	Provider of disc grinding, flat lapping and much more services.	626-444-9576	NA	South El Monte
California Seed & Plant Lab Inc (HQ)	Provider of pathological and genetic testing services. The company provides services for the vegetable seed, grapevine, and strawberry industries.	916-655-1581	NA	Pleasant Grove
Cantabio Pharmaceuticals Inc (HQ)	Provider of therapeutic solutions. The company specializes in developing therapeutic proteins to prevent degenerative brain diseases.	844-200-2826	NA	Palo Alto
Caribou Biosciences Inc (HQ)	Developer of cellular engineering and analysis solutions. The company is involved in applied biological research.	510-982-6030	NA	Berkeley
Cascadia Labs (HQ)	Provider of analytical services. The company specializes in analytical, pharmaceutical, horticulture, and food science.	855-800-6890	NA	Redwood Valley
Catalyst Biosciences (HQ)	Developer of catalytic biopharmaceutical products based on engineering human proteases for hemostasis, age-related macular degeneration, and inflammation.	650-871-0761	NA	S San Francisco
Cellecta Inc (HQ)	Provider of custom and contract solutions for high-throughput genetic screening needs and also develops therapeutic targets and drugs.	650-938-3910	NA	Mountain View
Cellerant Therapeutics Inc (HQ)	Developer of novel innate and adaptive immunotherapies for oncology and blood-related disorders, including cell-based and antibody therapeutics.	650-232-2122	NA	San Carlos
Centrillion Technologies (HQ)	Provider of genomic and bioinformatics solution. The company offers genomic technology to improve sequencing performance.	650-618-0111	NA	Palo Alto
Chai (HQ)	Specializes in DNA diagnostics. The company offers services to clinics, patients, and the medical sector.	650-779-5577	NA	Santa Clara
Circle Pharma (HQ)	Focuses on the development of cell permeable macrocyclic peptide therapeutics. The company serves the pharmaceutical sector.	650-392-0363	NA	S San Francisco
Codexis Inc (HQ)	Provider of biocatalysts products such as screening kits and other accessories. The company serves the food and nutrition industries.	650-421-8100	51-200	Redwood City
Comparative Biosciences Inc (HQ)	Provider of research and development support services. The company serves the biotechnology and pharmaceutical industries.	408-738-9260	NA	Sunnyvale
Confometrx (HQ)	Developer of a platform of drug development tools. The company specializes in drug discovery technologies.	408-496-6276	NA	Santa Clara
CSBio (HQ)	Provider of automated peptide synthesis instrumentation, peptide synthesizers, and custom peptides to the life science community.	650-322-1111	NA	Menlo Park
Curiox Biosystems Inc (HQ)	Developer of assay platforms. The company specializes in surface chemistry and engineering. It focuses on automation of bioassays.	650-226-8420	NA	San Carlos
Cyagen Biosciences Inc (HQ)	Manufacturer of cell culture products. The company also focuses on animal models and molecular biology tools.	408-969-0306	NA	Santa Clara
Cytoculture International Inc (HQ)	Provider of technical consulting and microbiological laboratory services. The company specializes in biofuel project.	510-233-0102	NA	Point Richmond
Cytokinetics Inc (HQ)	Developer of cancer treatment programs for cancer and also cardiovascular patients. The company specializes in therapeutic programs.	650-624-3000	NA	S San Francisco
Dawn Reis Ecological Studies (HQ)	Provider of wildlife research and biological consulting services. The company is specialized in aquatic systems and endangered species population.	831-588-7550	NA	Watsonville
N Del Mar Trade Shows Inc (HQ)	Provider of electronic components, fabrication, design and most aspects of electronics manufacturing.	858-459-1682	NA	La Jolla
Dermira Inc (HQ)	Developer of biopharmaceutical products for the treatment of dermatology diseases such as acne, plaque psoriasis, and hyperhidrosis.	650-421-7200	NA	Menlo Park
DiaCarta Inc (HQ)	Provider of molecular diagnostics tools such as genotyping tests, colon cancer tests, DNA sample card, and gene mutation detection kits.	800-246-8878	NA	Richmond
Diagnostic Biosystems Inc (HQ)	Developer of primary and monoclonal antibodies, ancillaries, chromogens, and multiplex kits. The company serves the healthcare sector.	925-484-3350	NA	Pleasanton
Discoverx Corp (HQ)	Developer and marketer of innovative solutions to study major drug target classes such as GPCRs and kinases.	510-979-1415	NA	Fremont
DNAmito Inc (HQ)	Provider of DNA technology and cloud platform to enable cancer treatment and early prediction of chronic disease thus vastly improving patient care.	650-687-0899	NA	Palo Alto
E-Scape Bio (HQ)	Provider of therapeutic solutions. The company focuses on discovery and development of small molecule drugs for the treatment of neurodegenerative diseases.	650-431-0100	NA	S San Francisco

COMPANY NAME	PRODUCT / SERVICE	PHONE	EMP	CITY
Ekso Bionics Holdings Inc (HQ)	Developer and manufacturer of powered exoskeleton bionic devices. The company is engaged in distribution services.	510-984-1761	NA	Richmond
ESI Bio (HQ)	Provider of stem cell solutions. The company's products are used in bioprinting, stem cell analysis, and stem cell reprogramming.	510-521-3390	NA	Alameda
Exelixis Inc (HQ)	Focuses on the development and commercialization of small molecule therapies. The company is also engaged in clinical trials.	650-837-7000	NA	Alameda
Fibrogen Inc (HQ)	Developer of therapeutic products. The company is engaged in commercialization and clinical trial programs.	415-978-1200	NA	San Francisco
Five Prime Therapeutics Inc (HQ)	Developer and discovery of therapeutics products for the enhancement of lives of patients with serious diseases.	415-365-5600	NA	S San Francisco
Fluidigm Sciences Inc (HQ)	Developer and creator of technologies for life science tools designed to revolutionize biology. The company is involved in research programs.	650-871-7152	NA	S San Francisco
N Foothill.Net Inc (HQ)	Provider of computer and technology services to companies.	530-820-1031	NA	Foresthill
Formumax Scientific Inc (HQ)	Provider of contract drug delivery to pharmaceutical and biotech industries. The company specializes in injectables, liposomes, and microemulsions.	408-400-0108	NA	Sunnyvale
ForteBio (LH)	Provider of dip and read assay kits. The company's products are used in the application of kinetic characterization.	650-322-1360	NA	Fremont
GangaGen Inc (HQ)	Provider of proprietary recombinant protein for the topical prevention and treatment of Staphylococcal infections.	650-856-9642	NA	Palo Alto
Genapsys Inc (HQ)	Developer of DNA sequencing to enable a paradigm shift in genomic diagnostics. The company specializes in GENIUS system that has footprint of Apple iPad.	650-330-1096	NA	Redwood City
Genentech Inc (BR)	Provider of biotechnology services. The company uses human genetic information to develop medicines for life-threatening medical conditions.	707-454-1000	NA	Vacaville
Genentech Inc (HQ)	Focuses on the treatment of breast cancer. The company offers services to patients and medical professionals.	650-225-1000	NA	S San Francisco
General Foundry Service (HQ)	Provider of foundry services. The company engages in pattern making, precision sand casting, and rubber plastic mold.	510-297-5040	NA	San Leandro
Genomic Health Inc (HQ)	Specializes in the treatment of cancer. The company is engaged in patient management software development.	650-556-9300	NA	Redwood City
GigaGen Inc (HQ)	Provider of biotherapeutics solutions. The company offers recombinant polyclonal hyperimmune gammaglobulin.	415-978-2101	NA	S San Francisco
Globavir Biosciences Inc (HQ)	Developer of biotechnology products. The company specializes in small molecule drugs to treat cancer and infectious diseases.	650-351-4495	NA	Los Altos
GRAIL Inc (HQ)	Provider of research services and clinical study programs for the detection of cancer at an early stage.	650-542-0372	NA	Menlo Park
Graybug Vision Inc (HQ)	Developer of pharmaceutical products for the treatment of blindness, including neovascular, glaucoma, and corneal graft rejection.	650-487-2800	NA	Redwood City
IDEAYA Biosciences (HQ)	Provider of synthetic lethality medicines for the immuno oncology therapies. The company specializes in cancer biology, small molecule drug discovery, and immunology.	650-443-6209	NA	S San Francisco
Igenex Inc (HQ)	Provider of immunology laboratory services. The company offers service to private practice physicians, hospitals, and clinical reference laboratories.	650-424-1191	NA	Milpitas
Illumina Inc (BR)	Developer, manufacturer, and marketer of integrated systems for the analysis of genetic variation and biological function.	510-670-9300	NA	Hayward
Immunoscience Inc (HQ)	Provider of biotechnology research and development for diagnosis and treatment of AIDS and HIV infection. The company also offers therapeutic vaccines.	925-828-1000	NA	Pleasanton
Inscopix Inc (HQ)	Provider of instrumentation and data analytics for next generation neuroscience. The company provides brain imaging solutions and data analysis suites.	650-600-3886	NA	Palo Alto
InSilixa Inc (HQ)	Manufacturer of CMOS biosensor devices used to identify multiple targets including nucleic acids (DNA or RNA), peptides, or metabolites.	408-809-3000	NA	Sunnyvale
N International Transportation Service Inc (HQ)	Provider of terminal services such as vessel stevedoring, container yard, maintenance, repair and much more.	562-435-7781	51-200	Long Beach
N Internet Brands Inc (HQ)	Operator of media and e-commerce sites for "large ticket" consumer purchases, such as cars and mortgages.	310-280-4000	5001-10000	El Segundo
JN Biosciences LLC (HQ)	Developer of antibody-based therapeutics and antibody engineered technologies. The company specializes in single homogenous molecular species.	650-967-9486	NA	Mountain View
Karius Inc (HQ)	Provider of microbial genomics diagnostics. The company focuses on transforming infectious disease diagnostics with genomics.	866-452-7487	NA	Redwood City
Lab Sensor Solutions Inc (HQ)	Provider of real-time sensor technology on healthcare assets so customers can monitor, report and act to assure items are in right place and condition.	650-275-3101	NA	Redwood City
LakePharma Inc (BR)	Provider of contract research organization specializing in antibody and protein engineering, cell line development, and protein production.	650-288-4891	NA	Belmont

COMPANY NAME	PRODUCT / SERVICE	PHONE	EMP	CITY
Lineage Cell Therapeutics Inc (HQ)	Provider of cell-based technologies and regenerative medicine for the treatment of chronic and degenerative diseases.	510-871-4188	NA	Carlsbad
Lumen Therapeutics LLC (HQ)	Provider of therapeutic solutions. The company focuses on the proprietary drugs based on oligo-L-arginine.	650-450-4439	NA	Menlo Park
Lumiphore Inc (HQ)	Developer of proprietary lanthanide technology. The company develops and markers biological detection reagents.	510-898-1190	NA	Berkeley
MabPlex USA Inc (BR)	Developer and manufacture of biopharmaceuticals. The company also offers contract services from DNA to finished drug product.	510-830-1065	NA	Fremont
Marin Biologic Laboratories Inc (HQ)	Provider of client research services. The company serves the pharmaceutical, biotechnology, diagnostic, agricultural, and legal markers.	415-883-8000	NA	Novato
Marrone Bio Innovations Inc (HQ)	Developer of naturally derived technologies of pest management and plant health products used in agricultural, ornamental, and water treatment.	530-750-2800	NA	Davis
MedAutonomic Inc (HQ)	Developer of Brain NeuroModulator. The company specializes in creating control action potentials in individual neurons and in functional groups.	415-377-5653	NA	Concord
Medeor Therapeutics (HQ)	Developer of personalized cellular immunotherapy for the organ transplant recipients. The company specializes in cellular immunotherapy, hematology, and transplantation product development.	650-627-4531	NA	S San Francisco
MedGenome Inc (HQ)	Provider of genomics based diagnostics and research services. The company specializes in bioinformatics, computing, genomics technologies, and big data analytics.	888-440-0954	NA	Foster City
Microvi Biotech Inc (HQ)	Designer and developer of biotechnology solutions. The company commercializes biocatalytic solutions in the water, energy and chemical industries.	510-344-0668	NA	Hayward
Molecular Matrix Inc (HQ)	Provider of research tools for cultivating and studying stem cells. The company products provide solutions for growing cells.	916-376-9404	NA	West Sacramento
MTI California Inc (HQ)	Specializes in designing and validating manufacturing controls. The company offers services to biotech companies.	925-937-1500	NA	Walnut Creek
Murigenics (HQ)	Provider of preclinical in-vivo and in-vitro contract drug discovery. The company is also focused on development services.	707-561-8900	NA	Vallejo
MyoKardia Inc (HQ)	Provider of precision medicine. The company focuses on developing and commercializing therapies for treating cardiovascular diseases.	650-741-0900	NA	Brisbane
Natera Inc (HQ)	Provider of prenatal testing services. The company specializes in non-invasive prenatal testing, genetic carrier screening and paternity testing.	650-249-9090	501-1000	San Carlos
Nektar Therapeutics (HQ)	Provider of therapeutic products for the treatment of opioid-induced constipation in adult patients with chronic non-cancer pain.	415-482-5300	NA	San Francisco
Nelson Biotechnologies Inc (HQ)	Provider of oligonucleotide labeling and modification services. The company also specializes in contract research and manufacturing.	408-778-2020	NA	Morgan Hill
Neurona Therapeutics (HQ)	Developer of neuronal stem cells to transplant into the brain. The company offers services to the healthcare industry.	650-799-6465	NA	S San Francisco
Neurotrack Technologies Inc (HQ)	Provider of computer-based cognitive tests. The company offers services to Alzheimer's patients and the medical industry.	650-549-8566	NA	Redwood City
Novabay Pharmaceuticals Inc (HQ)	Manufacturer of biopharmaceuticals. The company develops non-antibiotic anti-infective products to address the eye care market.	510-899-8800	NA	Emeryville
Novozymes Inc (BR)	Provider of industrial biotechnology solutions for the food and beverage, agriculture, textile, and pulp and paper industries.	530-757-8100	NA	Davis
Nugen Technologies Inc (HQ)	Provider of solutions for genomic analysis. The company focuses on DNA analysis and RNA analysis applications.	650-590-3600	NA	San Carlos
NuMedii Inc (HQ)	Provider of big data technology such as integrative genomics and chemoinformatics to discover and de-risk new indications for safe, existing drug.	650-918-6363	NA	San Mateo
Osel Inc (HQ)	Developer of biotherapeutic products. The company focuses on treatment and prevention of conditions for women's health and infectious diseases.	650-964-1420	NA	Mountain View
Pacific Biodevelopment LLC (HQ)	Provider of biotechnology services. The company offers drug development services to allow timely and cost efficient entry of drugs into the market.	510-858-5600	NA	Emeryville
Pacific Biosciences Of California Inc (HQ)	Provider of targeted sequencing, base modifications, microbiology, and isoform sequencing detection services.	650-521-8000	NA	Menlo Park
Patz Materials & Technologies (HQ)	Manufacturer of composite materials. The company portfolio includes unidirectional tapes, fabric prepregs, composite armor systems, and cellular developments.	707-748-7577	NA	Benicia
Paxvax Inc (HQ)	Provider of vaccines to protect from infectious diseases. The company offers treatments to diseases such as typhoid, cholera, and anthrax.	650-847-1075	NA	Redwood City
Pendulum Therapeutics Inc (HQ)	Developer of microbiome interventions and diagnostics systems. The company is involved in research and development services.	415-855-0940	NA	San Francisco
Planetary Herbals (HQ)	Provider of nutritional herbal healthcare products. The company's products include Acai, Full Spectrum, Bacopa Extract, and Digestive Comfort.	831-438-1700	NA	Soquel

	COMPANY NAME	PRODUCT / SERVICE	PHONE	EMP	CITY
	Plexxikon Inc (HQ)	Developer of pharmaceuticals. The company utilizes its proprietary discovery platform to produce highly selective and targeted medicines.	510-647-4000	NA	Berkeley
	PotBotics Inc (HQ)	Developer of medical marijuana products such as potbot, brainbot, and nanopot.	650-837-0420	NA	Palo Alto
	Primity Bio Inc (HQ)	Provider of assay platforms for biological relevance. The company specializes in cell biology, flow cytometry, and molecular biology.	510-210-0605	NA	Fremont
	Progenitor Cell Therapy (BR)	Manufacturer of biotechnology products. The company develops cell therapy products on a contract basis.	650-964-6744	NA	Mountain View
	Prolynx LLC (HQ)	Developer of technology solutions for releasable linkers. The company also specializes in injectable drugs.	415-552-5306	NA	San Francisco
	ProMab Biotechnologies Inc (HQ)	Provider of cell isolation kits, custom antibodies, cancer stem cells, and recombinant protein products.	510-860-4615	NA	Richmond
	Prothena (RH)	Focuses on the discovery, development and commercialization of protein immunotherapy programs for the treatment of diseases that involve amyloid.	650-837-8550	NA	S San Francisco
	Purigen Biosystems Inc (HQ)	Provider of biotechnology such as isotachophoresis, an electric-field driven technique for extracting and quantifying DNA and RNA from biological samples.	877-787-4436	NA	Pleasanton
	Qi Medical Inc (HQ)	Manufacturer of fingertip testing, syringe filters, rinse fluids, incubators, and vial adaptors for pharmacists and nurses who handle sterile solutions.	530-272-8700	NA	Grass Valley
	Quantapore Inc (HQ)	Developer of anopore based nucleic acid sequencing technology. The company's technology is used to read human genomes.	650-321-2032	NA	S San Francisco
	RAPT Therapeutics (HQ)	Provider of immuno-oncology oral medicines designed to activate patients own immune system to eradicate cancer.	650-489-9000	NA	S San Francisco
	ReaMetrix Inc (HQ)	Provider of biotechnology services. The company develops innovative affordable diagnostic solutions.	650-226-4144	NA	Los Altos
	Rigel Pharmaceuticals Inc (HQ)	Developer novel, small-molecule drugs for the treatment of inflammatory and autoimmune diseases, immuno-oncology related diseases, and muscle disorders.	650-624-1100	NA	S San Francisco
	Ryss Lab Inc (HQ)	Provider of biotechnology and pharmaceutical development services. The company offers services to the healthcare sector.	510-477-9570	NA	Union City
	SciBac Inc (HQ)	Developer of pharmaceuticals and medicinal probiotics for the prevention and treatment of clostridium difficile. The company serves the medical sector.	650-689-5343	NA	Burlingame
	Second Genome Inc (HQ)	Focuses on the development of therapeutic products. The company serves pharmaceutical and nutritional companies.	650-440-4606	NA	S San Francisco
	Signosis Inc (HQ)	Provider of bioassays. The company focuses on the development and commercialization of plate-based analysis products.	408-747-0771	NA	Santa Clara
	Sillajen Inc (BR)	Developer of biotherapeutics specializing in cancer products. The company also focuses on marketing.	415-281-8886	NA	San Francisco
N	Sincere Design (HQ)	Provider of website design, Internet and traditional marketing, book design and production, computer graphics and communication services.	510-215-1139	NA	Point Richmond
	Single Cell Technology Inc (HQ)	Developer of cell technology solutions and also proportionary therapeutic antibody process for its clients.	408-265-9239	NA	San Jose
	SRI International (RH)	Provider of consulting, research, and development services. The company offers services to the defense, security, and energy sectors.	650-859-2000	NA	Menlo Park
	SwitchGear Genomics Inc (HQ)	Focuses on custom cloning, pathway screening, target validation, sequence variant assay, and custom mutagenesis services.	760-431-1263	NA	Carlsbad
	Synergenics LLC (HQ)	Provider of life science services. The company also provides financial support and shared laboratory services.	415-554-8170	NA	San Francisco
	System Biosciences LLC (HQ)	Provider of genome-wide analysis of the mechanisms that regulate cellular processes and biological responses.	650-968-2200	NA	Palo Alto
	Transcriptic Inc (HQ)	Specializes in scientific research and the company also supports an array of vitro molecular biology and cell biology.	650-763-8432	NA	Menlo Park
	Trellis Bioscience LLC (HQ)	Developer of human antibody therapeutics as treatment for infectious disease and oncology indications.	650-838-1400	NA	Redwood City
	Trianni Inc (HQ)	Developer of humanized monoclonal antibody platform. The company offers services to pharmaceutical and biotechnology companies.	866-374-9314	NA	San Francisco
	Tricida Inc (HQ)	Focuses on the discovery and clinical development of therapeutics to address renal, metabolic and cardiovascular diseases.	415-429-7800	NA	S San Francisco
	Twist Bioscience (HQ)	Specializes in DNA synthesis programs. The company is engaged in genome editing and drug discovery services.	800-719-0671	NA	S San Francisco
	Valitor Inc (HQ)	Developer of therapeutic protein drugs. The company's drugs are used in dermatology, ophthalmology, orthopedics, and stem cell therapy.	510-545-6062	NA	Berkeley
N	Winning Directions (HQ)	Provider of professional services.	650-875-4000	NA	S San Francisco
N	YapStone Inc (HQ)	Developer of electronic payments platform.	866-289-5977	201-500	Walnut Creek
	Zymergen (HQ)	Developer of engineering biology. The company is engaged in new product development and it serves the scientific market.	415-801-8073	NA	Emeryville

COMPANY NAME	PRODUCT / SERVICE	PHONE	EMP	CITY
35 = Catalysts				
Catalyst Biosciences (HQ)	Developer of catalytic biopharmaceutical products based on engineering human proteases for hemostasis, age-related macular degeneration, and inflammation.	650-871-0761	NA	S San Francisco
36 = Cell Culture Technology				
10X Genomics Inc (HQ)	Provider of gemcode, instruments, software, and applications technology for RNA and DNA analysis.	925-401-7300	NA	Pleasanton
4D Molecular Therapeutics LLC (HQ)	Provider of gene therapy product research and development for the treatment of genetic diseases such as diabetes, arthritis, and heart failure.	510-505-2680	NA	Emeryville
Advanced Cell Diagnostics Inc (HQ)	Developer of biotechnological diagnostic tests. The company specializes in the identification and validation of RNA biomarkers for cancer diagnosis.	510-576-8800	NA	Newark
AerospaceComputing Inc (HQ)	Provider of computer technology application services to aerospace sciences. The company also focuses on business development services.	650-988-0388	NA	Mountain View
Allcells LLC (HQ)	Provider of medical services for human primary cells. The company focuses on fields such as cell biology, oncology, and virology.	510-726-2700	NA	Alameda
Alphalyse Inc (HQ)	Provider of protein analysis services. The company focuses on support research, manufacturing, and clinical development activities.	650-543-3193	NA	Palo Alto
Alstem Inc (HQ)	Provider of virus concentration and transduction solutions. The company's offerings include assay kits, antibodies etc.	510-708-0096	NA	Richmond
Aziyo Biologics Inc (BR)	Manufacturer of allograft tissue products for use in orthopedic, spinal, sports medicine, and dermal applications.	855-416-0596	NA	Richmond
Biochain Institute Inc (HQ)	Provider of bio-sample preparation, analysis, and application assays accelerating the development of personalized diagnostics, therapeutics, and medicine.	510-783-8588	NA	Newark
Cell Technology (HQ)	Developer of assays to study cellular functions by researchers using cell preamble agents for academic, biotechnology, and pharmaceutical industries.	650-960-2170	NA	Fremont
Celltheon (HQ)	Developer of customized solutions for preclinical studies of the biotechnology and pharmaceutical industries.	510-306-2355	NA	Union City
Cerus Corp (HQ)	Manufacturer of biomedical products such as the intercept blood system and pathogen reduction system, focused in the field of blood safety.	925-288-6000	NA	Concord
Curiox Biosystems Inc (HQ)	Developer of assay platforms. The company specializes in surface chemistry and engineering. It focuses on automation of bioassays.	650-226-8420	NA	San Carlos
Cyagen Biosciences Inc (HQ)	Manufacturer of cell culture products. The company also focuses on animal models and molecular biology tools.	408-969-0306	NA	Santa Clara
Discoverx Corp (HQ)	Developer and marketer of innovative solutions to study major drug target classes such as GPCRs and kinases.	510-979-1415	NA	Fremont
DNAmito Inc (HQ)	Provider of DNA technology and cloud platform to enable cancer treatment and early prediction of chronic disease thus vastly improving patient care.	650-687-0899	NA	Palo Alto
ESI Bio (HQ)	Provider of stem cell solutions. The company's products are used in bioprinting, stem cell analysis, and stem cell reprogramming.	510-521-3390	NA	Alameda
Fluidigm Corp (HQ)	Manufacturer of life-science tools. The company's technologies are focused on microfluidics and mass cytometry.	650-266-6000	NA	S San Francisco
Gemini Bio-Products (HQ)	Provider of supplements, reagents, and human products. The company is involved in medical research and development.	800-543-6464	NA	West Sacramento
Globavir Biosciences Inc (HQ)	Developer of biotechnology products. The company specializes in small molecule drugs to treat cancer and infectious diseases.	650-351-4495	NA	Los Altos
Graybug Vision Inc (HQ)	Developer of pharmaceutical products for the treatment of blindness, including neovascular, glaucoma, and corneal graft rejection.	650-487-2800	NA	Redwood City
Histo path (HQ)	Provider of histotechnology services. The company specializes in providing tissue culture slides for dermatologists.	209-522-8240	NA	Modesto
InSilixa Inc (HQ)	Manufacturer of CMOS biosensor devices used to identify multiple targets including nucleic acids (DNA or RNA), peptides, or metabolites.	408-809-3000	NA	Sunnyvale
Karius Inc (HQ)	Provider of microbial genomics diagnostics. The company focuses on transforming infectious disease diagnostics with genomics.	866-452-7487	NA	Redwood City
LakePharma Inc (BR)	Provider of contract research organization specializing in antibody and protein engineering, cell line development, and protein production.	650-288-4891	NA	Belmont
Lineage Cell Therapeutics Inc (HQ)	Provider of cell-based technologies and regenerative medicine for the treatment of chronic and degenerative diseases.	510-871-4188	NA	Carlsbad
Maverick Therapeutics (HQ)	Provider of therapeutic solutions for the treatment of cancer. The company focuses on the research of cytotoxic T cells.	650-338-1231	NA	Brisbane
Mawi DNA Technologies LLC (HQ)	Provider of biosampling devices for non-invasive sample collection with the main objective of simplifying genomics and proteomics workflows.	510-256-5186	NA	Hayward
Micro Lithography Inc (HQ)	Manufacturer of pellicles using high end equipment for the production of frames and engineering parts, automatic anodizing lines, and chemical labs.	408-747-1769	NA	Sunnyvale

COMPANY NAME	PRODUCT / SERVICE	PHONE	EMP	CITY
Molecular Matrix Inc (HQ)	Provider of research tools for cultivating and studying stem cells. The company products provide solutions for growing cells.	916-376-9404	NA	West Sacramento
Neurona Therapeutics (HQ)	Developer of neuronal stem cells to transplant into the brain. The company offers services to the healthcare industry.	650-799-6465	NA	S San Francisco
Nugen Technologies Inc (HQ)	Provider of solutions for genomic analysis. The company focuses on DNA analysis and RNA analysis applications.	650-590-3600	NA	San Carlos
Patz Materials & Technologies (HQ)	Manufacturer of composite materials. The company portfolio includes unidirectional tapes, fabric prepregs, composite armor systems, and cellular developments.	707-748-7577	NA	Benicia
Primity Bio Inc (HQ)	Provider of assay platforms for biological relevance. The company specializes in cell biology, flow cytometry, and molecular biology.	510-210-0605	NA	Fremont
Single Cell Technology Inc (HQ)	Developer of cell technology solutions and also proportionary therapeutic antibody process for its clients.	408-265-9239	NA	San Jose
Symic Bio Inc (BR)	Developer of proprietary bioconjugates. The company offers therapeutics focused on extracellular matrix biology.	415-805-9005	NA	Emeryville
ThermoGenesis Holdings Inc (HQ)	Manufacturer of therapeutic products and related supplies. The company is involved in cellular bioprocessing and bone marrow transplants.	916-858-5100	NA	Rancho Cordova
Trellis Bioscience LLC (HQ)	Developer of human antibody therapeutics as treatment for infectious disease and oncology indications.	650-838-1400	NA	Redwood City
Trianni Inc (HQ)	Developer of humanized monoclonal antibody platform. The company offers services to pharmaceutical and biotechnology companies.	866-374-9314	NA	San Francisco
Virovek (HQ)	Provider of adeno-associated virus production and purification services. The company involves in consulting and gene cloning services.	510-887-7121	NA	Hayward
Xcell Biosciences Inc (HQ)	Provider of protocols and reagent kits for primary cell culture applications. The company specializes in cell-based assays.	415-937-0321	NA	San Francisco

37 = Consulting/Contracting Services

	COMPANY NAME	PRODUCT / SERVICE	PHONE	EMP	CITY
N	Alcon Entertainment LLC (HQ)	Provider of finance, produce, market, and distributor of entertainment that delights both its creators and its audience.	310-789-3040	NA	Los Angeles
	Dawn Reis Ecological Studies (HQ)	Provider of wildlife research and biological consulting services. The company is specialized in aquatic systems and endangered species population.	831-588-7550	NA	Watsonville
	Denise Duffy & Associates Inc (HQ)	Provider of environmental sciences, planning, and biological consulting services. The company is also focused on land use and contract planning.	831-373-4341	NA	Monterey
	Inscopix Inc (HQ)	Provider of instrumentation and data analytics for next generation neuroscience. The company provides brain imaging solutions and data analysis suites.	650-600-3886	NA	Palo Alto
	ProTrials Research Inc (HQ)	Provider of clinical research services. The company offers the ability to move a new drug or device from conception to FDA approval.	650-864-9180	NA	San Jose
	Ryss Lab Inc (HQ)	Provider of biotechnology and pharmaceutical development services. The company offers services to the healthcare sector.	510-477-9570	NA	Union City

38 = Genetic Engineering/Research

COMPANY NAME	PRODUCT / SERVICE	PHONE	EMP	CITY
4D Molecular Therapeutics LLC (HQ)	Provider of gene therapy product research and development for the treatment of genetic diseases such as diabetes, arthritis, and heart failure.	510-505-2680	NA	Emeryville
Bell Biosystems Inc (HQ)	Provider of biotechnology services. The company develops proteins targeted to kill specific bacteria but cause minimal collateral damage.	877-420-3621	NA	Berkeley
Bioneer Inc (BR)	Developer of molecular biology products and technologies for life science researchers in academia, biotech, and pharmaceutical companies.	877-264-4300	NA	Oakland
Centrillion Technology Holdings Ltd (HQ)	Developer of genomics solutions for the researchers, physicians, and consumers. The company also offers clinical testing and consumer genomics services.	650-618-0111	NA	Palo Alto
CryptoForensics Technologies Inc (HQ)	Provider of cybersecurity solutions to businesses, organizations, and the government. The company focuses on cyberforensics and compliance services.	510-483-1933	NA	San Leandro
Genapsys Inc (HQ)	Developer of DNA sequencing to enable a paradigm shift in genomic diagnostics. The company specializes in GENIUS system that has footprint of Apple iPad.	650-330-1096	NA	Redwood City
Karius Inc (HQ)	Provider of microbial genomics diagnostics. The company focuses on transforming infectious disease diagnostics with genomics.	866-452-7487	NA	Redwood City
Natera Inc (HQ)	Provider of prenatal testing services. The company specializes in non-invasive prenatal testing, genetic carrier screening and paternity testing.	650-249-9090	501-1000	San Carlos
Rainier Therapeutics (HQ)	Developer of biologic products for the treatment of metastatic bladder cancer (urothelial cell carcinoma) and achondroplasia (dwarfism).	925-413-6140	NA	San Leandro

39 = Diagnostic

COMPANY NAME	PRODUCT / SERVICE	PHONE	EMP	CITY
4D Molecular Therapeutics LLC (HQ)	Provider of gene therapy product research and development for the treatment of genetic diseases such as diabetes, arthritis, and heart failure.	510-505-2680	NA	Emeryville

COMPANY NAME	PRODUCT / SERVICE	PHONE	EMP	CITY
Advanced Cell Diagnostics Inc (HQ)	Developer of biotechnological diagnostic tests. The company specializes in the identification and validation of RNA biomarkers for cancer diagnosis.	510-576-8800	NA	Newark
Aelan Cell Technologies Inc (HQ)	Provider of research, discovery, development, and commercialization of biomedical technologies for the advancement of human health.	415-991-9915	NA	San Francisco
Bell Biosystems Inc (HQ)	Provider of biotechnology services. The company develops proteins targeted to kill specific bacteria but cause minimal collateral damage.	877-420-3621	NA	Berkeley
Biochain Institute Inc (HQ)	Provider of bio-sample preparation, analysis, and application assays accelerating the development of personalized diagnostics, therapeutics, and medicine.	510-783-8588	NA	Newark
Bioneer Inc (BR)	Developer of molecular biology products and technologies for life science researchers in academia, biotech, and pharmaceutical companies.	877-264-4300	NA	Oakland
Centrillion Technology Holdings Ltd (HQ)	Developer of genomics solutions for the researchers, physicians, and consumers. The company also offers clinical testing and consumer genomics services.	650-618-0111	NA	Palo Alto
Genapsys Inc (HQ)	Developer of DNA sequencing to enable a paradigm shift in genomic diagnostics. The company specializes in GENIUS system that has footprint of Apple iPad.	650-330-1096	NA	Redwood City
Genemed Biotechnologies Inc (HQ)	Manufacturer of diagnostic reagents. The company caters to the pharmaceutical and diagnostic sectors.	650-952-0110	NA	S San Francisco
Immuno Concepts Na Ltd (HQ)	Manufacturer and distributor of diagnostic assays. The company's products are used for systemic rheumatic diseases.	916-363-2649	NA	Sacramento
Incotec Inc (RH)	Provider of solutions in the business areas such as vegetables, field crops, ornamentals, and analytical services.	831-757-4367	NA	Salinas
Karius Inc (HQ)	Provider of microbial genomics diagnostics. The company focuses on transforming infectious disease diagnostics with genomics.	866-452-7487	NA	Redwood City
MTI California Inc (HQ)	Specializes in designing and validating manufacturing controls. The company offers services to biotech companies.	925-937-1500	NA	Walnut Creek
Natera Inc (HQ)	Provider of prenatal testing services. The company specializes in non-invasive prenatal testing, genetic carrier screening and paternity testing.	650-249-9090	501-1000	San Carlos
Personalis Inc (HQ)	Manufacturer of genome-guided medicine for the treatment of cancer. The company deals with research services.	650-752-1300	NA	Menlo Park
Transgenomic Inc (BR)	Provider of patient testing and biomarker identification services. The company specializes in high performance products.	408-432-3230	NA	San Jose
Trianni Inc (HQ)	Developer of humanized monoclonal antibody platform. The company offers services to pharmaceutical and biotechnology companies.	866-374-9314	NA	San Francisco
Twist Bioscience (HQ)	Specializes in DNA synthesis programs. The company is engaged in genome editing and drug discovery services.	800-719-0671	NA	S San Francisco

40 = Software & IT Services

COMPANY NAME	PRODUCT / SERVICE	PHONE	EMP	CITY
Aplena Inc (HQ)	Provider of technology solutions for data center services. The company offers relocation, installation, and managed services.	408-256-0030	NA	Campbell
AppEnsure (HQ)	Provider of cloud application performance and infrastructure management such as application-aware infrastructure performance management solution.	408-418-4602	NA	San Jose
Ayla Networks Inc (HQ)	Provider of Ayla's IoT cloud platform that brings connected products to market quickly and securely for manufacturers and service providers.	408-830-9844	NA	Santa Clara
Benchling Inc (HQ)	Developer of integrated software solution for experiment design, note-taking, and molecular biology for industry and academia.	415-980-9932	NA	San Francisco
Bioscience Advisors (HQ)	Provider of consulting services. The company serves the pharmaceutical and biotechnology industries concerning commercialization agreements.	925-954-1397	NA	Walnut Creek
Bitscopic (HQ)	Provider of consulting and computer-related services. The company serves businesses and industrial customers.	650-503-3120	NA	Menlo Park
Ceras Health Inc (BR)	Focuses on mobile application development. The company serves patients, hospitals, and related healthcare organizations.	415-477-9908	NA	San Francisco
Citilabs Inc (HQ)	Provider of software development services. The company designs and develops products for transportation planning.	888-770-2823	NA	Sacramento
Coffer Group LLC (HQ)	Provider of information technology solutions. The company specializes in private equity, venture capital, and hedge funds.	415-963-4382	NA	San Francisco
Dnanexus Inc (HQ)	Provider of genome informatics and data management platform. The company provides a global network to share and manage genomic data.	415-857-0158	NA	Mountain View
DrChrono Inc (HQ)	Provider of electronic health record and practice management solution which includes scheduling and clinical documentation.	844-569-8628	NA	Sunnyvale
Eon Technologies Inc (HQ)	Provider of IT and computer support services. The company's services include malware and virus removal tools and printer repair services.	510-523-3832	NA	Alameda
First Databank Inc (HQ)	Provider of healthcare solutions to hospitals, retail pharmacies, payers, drug manufacturers, and healthcare providers.	650-588-5454	NA	S San Francisco
Fluidigm Sciences Inc (HQ)	Developer and creator of technologies for life science tools designed to revolutionize biology. The company is involved in research programs.	650-871-7152	NA	S San Francisco
H5 (HQ)	Provider of investigation solutions. The company offers hosting, case preparation, and keyword consulting services.	415-625-6700	NA	San Francisco

COMPANY NAME	PRODUCT / SERVICE	PHONE	EMP	CITY
InsightRX Inc (HQ)	Developer of cloud-based platform for precision medicine and clinical analytics. The company serves individuals and healthcare organizations.	205-351-0574	NA	San Francisco
Molecular Devices LLC (HQ)	Manufacturer of bioanalytical measurement systems. The company is engaged in life science research, pharma, and bio therapeutic development.	800-635-5577	NA	San Jose
NuMedii Inc (HQ)	Provider of big data technology such as integrative genomics and chemoinformatics to discover and de-risk new indications for safe, existing drug.	650-918-6363	NA	San Mateo
Pacific Biosciences Of California Inc (HQ)	Provider of targeted sequencing, base modifications, microbiology, and isoform sequencing detection services.	650-521-8000	NA	Menlo Park
Penguin Computing (HQ)	Provider of Linux-based cloud and HPC solutions. The company's products include servers, network switches, and integrated rack solutions.	415-954-2800	NA	Fremont
Premier Biosoft International (HQ)	Specializes in software development, design, testing and maintenance services. The company serves life science companies and laboratories.	650-856-2703	NA	Palo Alto
Sentieon Inc (HQ)	Supplier and developer of bioinformatics secondary analysis tools. The company offers precision data for precision medicine.	650-282-5650	NA	San Jose
Simplificare Inc (HQ)	Provider of software solutions for patient financial care (PFC). The company offers services to patients and clinics.	800-464-5125	NA	Palo Alto

41 = Lab Services (inc testing)

COMPANY NAME	PRODUCT / SERVICE	PHONE	EMP	CITY
AEMTEK Laboratories (HQ)	Provider of testing, research, training and consulting services and sampling products for the food, environmental and pharmaceutical industries.	510-979-1979	NA	Fremont
AGS Inc (HQ)	Provider of civil, structural, and geotechnical engineering services. The company serves the water and transportation infrastructure markers.	415-777-2166	NA	San Francisco
Al & L Crop Solutions (HQ)	Provider of solutions for crops. The company specializes in disease testing services for grapevine diseases and soil pathogens.	530-387-3270	NA	Vacaville
Allakos Inc (HQ)	Developer of therapeutic antibodies for the treatment of inflammatory and proliferative diseases such as asthma, nasal polyposis, and fibrosis.	650-597-5002	NA	Redwood City
Alstem Inc (HQ)	Provider of virus concentration and transduction solutions. The company's offerings include assay kits, antibodies etc.	510-708-0096	NA	Richmond
Antibody Solutions (HQ)	Provider of antibody products and services. The company serves biotechnology, diagnostic and pharmaceutical companies.	650-938-4300	NA	Sunnyvale
Biocare Medical LLC (HQ)	Developer of automated immunohistochemistry instrumentation, reagents for IHC lab testing. The company also offer tissue diagnostic products for cancer.	925-603-8000	NA	Pacheco
Biokey Inc (HQ)	Provider of API characterization, pre-formulation studies, formulation development, and analytical method development services.	510-668-0881	NA	Fremont
California Seed & Plant Lab Inc (HQ)	Provider of pathological and genetic testing services. The company provides services for the vegetable seed, grapevine, and strawberry industries.	916-655-1581	NA	Pleasant Grove
Caredx Inc (HQ)	Provider of genomics technologies for the development of molecular diagnostic assays. The company specializes in molecular diagnostics.	415-287-2300	NA	Brisbane
Cascadia Labs (HQ)	Provider of analytical services. The company specializes in analytical, pharmaceutical, horticulture, and food science.	855-800-6890	NA	Redwood Valley
Cellmax Life (HQ)	Provider of personalized multi-biomarker technologies for non-invasive saliva and blood tests. The company is also involved in drug discovery.	650-564-3905	NA	Sunnyvale
Comp Pro Med Inc (HQ)	Provider of laboratory information systems for clinical laboratories. The company offers services to the healthcare sector.	707-578-0239	NA	Santa Rosa
Control Laboratories Inc (HQ)	Provider of agricultural analytical services such as compost, water, soil, plant, remediation and bio-fuel testing.	831-724-5422	NA	Watsonville
DNAmito Inc (HQ)	Provider of DNA technology and cloud platform to enable cancer treatment and early prediction of chronic disease thus vastly improving patient care.	650-687-0899	NA	Palo Alto
E-Scape Bio (HQ)	Provider of therapeutic solutions. The company focuses on discovery and development of small molecule drugs for the treatment of neurodegenerative diseases.	650-431-0100	NA	S San Francisco
Exagen Inc (HQ)	Developer of laboratory technology solutions. The company offers services to hospitals, clinics, and the healthcare sector.	888-452-1522	NA	Vista
Histo path (HQ)	Provider of histotechnology services. The company specializes in providing tissue culture slides for dermatologists.	209-522-8240	NA	Modesto
Igenex Inc (HQ)	Provider of immunology laboratory services. The company offers service to private practice physicians, hospitals, and clinical reference laboratories.	650-424-1191	NA	Milpitas
Immuno Concepts Na Ltd (HQ)	Manufacturer and distributor of diagnostic assays. The company's products are used for systemic rheumatic diseases.	916-363-2649	NA	Sacramento
Merieux Nutrisciences Corp (BR)	Provider of public health services. The company is focused on food and pharmaceutical products, cosmetics, and consumer goods.	209-549-7508	NA	Salida
Microsonic Systems Inc (HQ)	Provider of ultrasonic fluid processing device built with MEMS technology to biotech and pharmaceutical industries.	408-844-4980	NA	San Jose

COMPANY NAME	PRODUCT / SERVICE	PHONE	EMP	CITY
Monterey Bay Analytical Services (HQ)	Provider of laboratory testing services. The company services include sample collection, bacteria testing, and inorganic chemistry.	831-375-6227	NA	Monterey
Nanolab Technologies Inc (HQ)	Provider of cutting edge technology and expertise for failure analysis, advanced microscopy and FIB circuit edit services.	408-433-3320	NA	Milpitas
Pacific Biolabs (HQ)	Provider of biological testing services. The company offers service to the pharmaceutical, biotechnology, and medical device industries.	510-964-9000	NA	Hercules
Personalis Inc (HQ)	Manufacturer of genome-guided medicine for the treatment of cancer. The company deals with research services.	650-752-1300	NA	Menlo Park
Plant Sciences Inc (HQ)	Provider of agricultural research services. The company develops new technology to yield good plant production.	831-728-7771	NA	Watsonville
Pulver Labs Inc (HQ)	Provider of equipment evaluation and testing services. The company also offers services for information technology, industrial and medical equipment.	408-399-7000	NA	Los Gatos
Purigen Biosystems Inc (HQ)	Provider of biotechnology such as isotachophoresis, an electric-field driven technique for extracting and quantifying DNA and RNA from biological samples.	877-787-4436	NA	Pleasanton
Pyxis Laboratories Inc (HQ)	Specializes in the research, development and production of specialty reagents for the diagnostics, pharmaceutical, and environmental industries.	949-598-1978	NA	Grass Valley
Qspec Technology Inc (HQ)	Provider of surface analysis and materials characterization services. The company's applications include device processing for microelectronics.	408-541-1398	NA	Sunnyvale
Transcriptic Inc (HQ)	Specializes in scientific research and the company also supports an array of vitro molecular biology and cell biology.	650-763-8432	NA	Menlo Park
West Coast (HQ)	Provider of contract testing laboratory services. The company offers testing laboratories, manufacturing services, and validation and calibration services.	925-270-3800	NA	Concord

42 = Protein Systems

COMPANY NAME	PRODUCT / SERVICE	PHONE	EMP	CITY
Actagro LLC (HQ)	Manufacturer of agricultural products for crops such as alfalfa, almonds, blueberries, corn, tomatoes, onions, rice, strawberries, and wine grapes.	559-369-2222	NA	Biola
Alstem Inc (HQ)	Provider of virus concentration and transduction solutions. The company's offerings include assay kits, antibodies etc.	510-708-0096	NA	Richmond
BASF Venture Capital America Inc (RH)	Manufacturer of basic chemicals and intermediates such as solvents, plasticizers, and monomers. The company serves the agriculture market.	510-445-6140	NA	Fremont
Bell Biosystems Inc (HQ)	Provider of biotechnology services. The company develops proteins targeted to kill specific bacteria but cause minimal collateral damage.	877-420-3621	NA	Berkeley
Biochain Institute Inc (HQ)	Provider of bio-sample preparation, analysis, and application assays accelerating the development of personalized diagnostics, therapeutics, and medicine.	510-783-8588	NA	Newark
BlueLight Therapeutics Inc (HQ)	Developer of proteins and biological molecules for the treatment of cancer, cardiovascular, Alzheimer's, and Parkinson's diseases.	650-871-8716	NA	S San Francisco
Confometrx (HQ)	Developer of a platform of drug development tools. The company specializes in drug discovery technologies.	408-496-6276	NA	Santa Clara
Evolve Biosystems (HQ)	Focuses on the development and marketing of probiotic-based biotherapeutics. The company serves the pharmaceutical industry.	530-747-2012	NA	Davis
Five Prime Therapeutics Inc (HQ)	Developer and discovery of therapeutics products for the enhancement of lives of patients with serious diseases.	415-365-5600	NA	S San Francisco
GangaGen Inc (HQ)	Provider of proprietary recombinant protein for the topical prevention and treatment of Staphylococcal infections.	650-856-9642	NA	Palo Alto
Global Marketing Associates Inc (HQ)	Providers of nutrition supplements to health care industry. The company supply innovative and quality ingredients to health care industry.	510-887-2462	NA	Livermore
Pivot Bio Inc (HQ)	Provider of genome-scale programming of microbes. The company offers services to farmers and the agricultural sector.	877-451-1977	NA	Berkeley
Rainier Therapeutics (HQ)	Developer of biologic products for the treatment of metastatic bladder cancer (urothelial cell carcinoma) and achondroplasia (dwarfism).	925-413-6140	NA	San Leandro
Versartis Inc (HQ)	Manufacturer and developer of therapeutic proteins for the treatment of endocrine disorders. The company develops recombinant human growth hormone.	650-963-8580	NA	Menlo Park

43 = Plant Biotechnology

COMPANY NAME	PRODUCT / SERVICE	PHONE	EMP	CITY
Agri-Analysis LLC (BR)	Provider of agricultural diagnostic laboratory services. The company specializes in grapevine virus testing services.	800-506-9852	NA	Davis
Al & L Crop Solutions (HQ)	Provider of solutions for crops. The company specializes in disease testing services for grapevine diseases and soil pathogens.	530-387-3270	NA	Vacaville
California Seed & Plant Lab Inc (HQ)	Provider of pathological and genetic testing services. The company provides services for the vegetable seed, grapevine, and strawberry industries.	916-655-1581	NA	Pleasant Grove
General Hydroponics Inc (HQ)	Providers of Hydroponics. The company offer solution for commercial producers especially in non arable areas.	707-824-9376	NA	Santa Rosa
Incotec Inc (RH)	Provider of solutions in the business areas such as vegetables, field crops, ornamentals, and analytical services.	831-757-4367	NA	Salinas

COMPANY NAME	PRODUCT / SERVICE	PHONE	EMP	CITY
Milagen Inc (HQ)	Develops and manufactures healthcare products. The company offers immunohistochemistry and cytology products.	510-597-1244	NA	Emeryville
Miltenyi Biotec Inc (DH)	Developer, manufacturer, and seller of products serving the fields of cell biology, immunology, regenerative medicine, and molecular biology.	530-888-8871	NA	Auburn
Nature's Cure (HQ)	Provider of health and beauty solutions. The company offers over-the-counter products featuring natural ingredients.	877-469-9487	NA	Oakland
Pivot Bio Inc (HQ)	Provider of genome-scale programming of microbes. The company offers services to farmers and the agricultural sector.	877-451-1977	NA	Berkeley
Plant Sciences Inc (HQ)	Provider of agricultural research services. The company develops new technology to yield good plant production.	831-728-7771	NA	Watsonville
Synergenics LLC (HQ)	Provider of life science services. The company also provides financial support and shared laboratory services.	415-554-8170	NA	San Francisco

44 = Immunological Substances/Research

COMPANY NAME	PRODUCT / SERVICE	PHONE	EMP	CITY
Apexigen (HQ)	Specializes in document management and managed print solutions. The company serves the business sector.	650-931-6236	NA	San Carlos
Biochain Institute Inc (HQ)	Provider of bio-sample preparation, analysis, and application assays accelerating the development of personalized diagnostics, therapeutics, and medicine.	510-783-8588	NA	Newark
Boster Biological Technology (HQ)	Provider of antibodies and ELISA kits. The company serves customers in the biochemicals and molecular biology areas.	888-466-3604	NA	Pleasanton
Butterfly Sciences (HQ)	Developer of gene therapies for HIV and aging. The company also provides consulting services for biotech investment evaluations.	415-518-8153	NA	Davis
Guardant Health Inc (HQ)	Provider of sequencing and rare-cell diagnostics services focusing on cancer. The company serves the healthcare sector.	855-698-8887	201-500	Redwood City
JN Biosciences LLC (HQ)	Developer of antibody-based therapeutics and antibody engineered technologies. The company specializes in single homogenous molecular species.	650-967-9486	NA	Mountain View
Maverick Therapeutics (HQ)	Provider of therapeutic solutions for the treatment of cancer. The company focuses on the research of cytotoxic T cells.	650-338-1231	NA	Brisbane
Medeor Therapeutics (HQ)	Developer of personalized cellular immunotherapy for the organ transplant recipients. The company specializes in cellular immunotherapy, hematology, and transplantation product development.	650-627-4531	NA	S San Francisco
Prothena (RH)	Focuses on the discovery, development and commercialization of protein immunotherapy programs for the treatment of diseases that involve amyloid.	650-837-8550	NA	S San Francisco
Rigel Pharmaceuticals Inc (HQ)	Developer novel, small-molecule drugs for the treatment of inflammatory and autoimmune diseases, immuno-oncology related diseases, and muscle disorders.	650-624-1100	NA	S San Francisco

45 = Business Management Services

	COMPANY NAME	PRODUCT / SERVICE	PHONE	EMP	CITY
	3Q Digital Inc (BR)	Performance and digital marketing agency that provides digital media services.	650-539-4124	NA	San Francisco
	Accenture (BR)	Provider of management consulting and technology services. The company also offers application outsourcing and IT consulting services.	415-537-5000	NA	San Francisco
N	American Integrated Services Inc (HQ)	Provider of comprehensive environmental solutions through construction, remediation, demolition, abatement, industrial services, emergency and disaster response, specialty transportation, and waste management services.	310-522-1168	51-200	Wilmington
	Antedo Inc (HQ)	Provider of consulting services. The company offers international engineering and management consulting services.	408-253-1870	NA	Cupertino
	Aragon Consulting Group Inc (HQ)	Provider of software development services. The company also offers authoring, coding, consulting, and technical support solutions.	415-869-8818	NA	Cupertino
	Aravo Solutions Inc (HQ)	Provider of risk and performance management, Supplier Information Management (SIM), and related services.	415-835-7600	NA	San Francisco
	Blackhawk Network Inc (HQ)	Provider of employee engagement and customer engagement services such as gift cards, reloadable prepaid debit cards, and cash-based payment products.	925-226-9990	NA	Pleasanton
N	Brakeley Briscoe Inc (BR)	Provider of creative and comprehensive solutions to the fundraising, strategic planning, and executive search needs.	650-344-8883	11-50	San Mateo
N	Cederdahl Consulting and Coaching (HQ)	Provider of profitable business and management experience to serious individuals, quality driven companies, and future-directed government identities to improve their bottom lines, their services include planning-creating foresighted paths for financial success, financing-finding rewarding resources for spirited growth, human resources-developing meaningful relationships for additional dividends.	619-670-1122	NA	La Mesa
	Cinnabar Bridge Communications (HQ)	Provider of writing, book publishing, book design, consulting, and project and process management services.	415-975-0950	NA	San Francisco
N	CK Associates (HQ)	Provider of sales and marketing strategy for product demands to customers.	949-457-7800	11-50	Irvine
	Common Interest Management Services (BR)	Provider of homeowner association management solutions such as escrow and disclosure, maintenance, online and community services.	650-286-0292	NA	San Mateo

	COMPANY NAME	PRODUCT / SERVICE	PHONE	EMP	CITY
	CommWorld of San Francisco (HQ)	Provider of telecommunication services such as computer networking, structured cabling, project management and repair.	650-358-8700	NA	Fremont
N	Crane Consulting (HQ)	Publisher of books on management leadership and offers consulting services.	858-487-9017	1-10	San Diego
N	Development Planning and Financing Group (BR)	Provider of real estate consulting, compliance, entitlement analysis, cash flow feasibility analysis, engineering, project management, capital markets solutions and property tax appeals.	916-480-0305	NA	Sacramento
N	Dr. Revenue (HQ)	Provider of consumer durables and services, electronics, computers, information technology, education, publishing, and professional and financial services worldwide.	310-476-3355	NA	Los Angeles
N	Dudek (HQ)	Provider of environmental planning and engineering services.	760-942-5147	501-1000	Encinitas
	Emotive Brand (HQ)	Brand strategy and design firm that helps to transform the businesses.	510-496-8888	NA	Oakland
N	EnviroKinetics Inc (HQ)	Manufacturer and supplier of excellent equipment and engineering services such as incinerators for gases and liquids with or without waste heat recovery, SCR systems for NOx reduction, catalytic oxidation, and scrubbers for entrained solids and contaminant gases and manufactures burner management systems and other skid-mounted instrument and control systems.	909-621-7599	NA	Ontario
	Epsilon Strategic Systems (HQ)	Provider of management consulting and information technology services. The company offers customization, advisory, and staff development services.	650-579-5515	NA	San Mateo
N	ESOP Services Inc (BR)	Provider of preliminary assessments, decision package, and turnkey implementation solutions.	858-292-4819	NA	San Diego
N	Foodpro International Inc (BR)	Distributor of food products.	209-943-8400	NA	Stockton
N	GlobalFluency (HQ)	Provider of communications services that helps clients in shaping perceptions, developing and growing markers, expanding customer relationships and building valued brands.	408-677-5300	11-50	San Jose
N	HFE Consulting (BR)	Provider of consulting services on human factors engineering and ergonomics issues.	408-234-6903	NA	Campbell
	Hub Strategy and Communication (BR)	Provider of web design and digital advertising.	415-561-4345	NA	San Francisco
N	Laughter Works Seminars (HQ)	Provider of seminars on the positive power of humor and creativity. Programs focus on selling, customer service, leadership, education, communication and health care. Industries served: healthcare, education, high-tech, manufacturing, service and government agencies.	916-985-6570	1-10	Folsom
	Lendingclub Corp (HQ)	Provider of financial solutions. The company offers home improvement, business, pool, and consolidated debt loans.	415-632-5600	1001-5000	San Francisco
N	M.I.B. Chock LLC (HQ)	Provider of an objective, third-party view of information systems issues to support new development, due diligence review, or litigation.	310-829-1612	NA	Santa Monica
N	Norris Associates (HQ)	Publisher of books on humor and a catalog of jokes.	805-962-7703	NA	Santa Barbara
N	Powerplant Consultants Inc (HQ)	Provider of consulting services in industrial power generation including co-generation, standby emergency power, landfill and digester gas fueled engines, geothermal, solar power, fuel cells, gas turbine generators, power plant instrumentation and control systems, economic analysis of power generation systems and other energy processes.	909-986-1141	NA	Ontario
	Primepay LLC (BR)	Provider of payroll processing services, HR solutions, and insurance and benefit management services.	650-358-4555	NA	Newark
	Ray Morgan Co (BR)	Provider of document technology solutions. The company offers paperless, project management, and imaging system solutions.	530-343-6065	NA	Chico
	Rightpoint (BR)	A digital consultancy firm that designs and engineers end-to-end digital experiences to help clients succeed at the speed of innovation.	415-935-3390	NA	Oakland
N	SAS Enterprises (HQ)	Provider of human resource management solutions.	925-685-8968	NA	Concord
N	Smaato Inc (HQ)	Operator of mobile ad optimization platform.	650-286-1198	51-200	San Francisco
N	Software Systems Quality Consulting (HQ)	Provider of software process improvement, software quality assurance and testing, CMMI implementation services. It also provides education and training services for software and hardware developers, manufacturers and service providers.	408-985-4476	NA	San Jose
N	The Trinity Group Inc (HQ)	Provider of telecommunications, technology and data networking consulting services.	209-832-1293	11-50	Tracy
N	Thomas J. Payne Market Development (BR)	Provider of food marketing consultancy services.	650-340-8311	NA	San Mateo
N	Wellspace (BR)	Provider of quality medical care, dental care, mental health, and behavioral health services.	916-737-5555	11-50	Sacramento

46 = Chemicals

N	Pindler & Pindler Inc (HQ)	Designer of fabrics.	805-531-9090	NA	Moorpark

47 = Adhesives/Coatings/Sealants

COMPANY NAME	PRODUCT / SERVICE	PHONE	EMP	CITY
Acree Technologies Inc (HQ)	Provider of PVD thin film coating services for medical, defense, and other sectors. The company also specializes in R&D and sell coating systems.	925-798-5770	NA	Concord
Adhesive Products Inc (HQ)	Manufacturer of glues, adhesives, tapes, labels, and coatings. The company is engaged in sales and delivery services.	510-526-7616	NA	Albany
Advenira Enterprises Inc (HQ)	Provider of equipment and provision of services for multi functional coating deposition using nanocomposite technology solution.	408-732-3950	NA	Sunnyvale
Anresco Laboratories (HQ)	Provider of analysis and research to food and food-related industries. The company also offers solutions to support the business and analytical specifications.	415-822-1100	NA	San Francisco
Cal-West Specialty Coatings Inc (HQ)	Supplier of liquid masking and surface preparation products. The company also offers temporary protective coatings.	408-720-7440	NA	Sunnyvale
Cemex USA (BR)	Supplier of bulk cement, sand, aggregates, ready mix materials, and architectural products. The company serves the construction industry.	916-941-2800	NA	El Dorado Hills
Crystallume Pvd (HQ)	Provider of PVD coatings for functional applications. The company also specializes in infinium coatings.	916-645-3560	NA	Lincoln
Dynatex International (HQ)	Manufacturer of semiconductor, dicing equipment, and supplies. The company also offers dicing and wafer bonding services.	707-542-4227	NA	Santa Rosa
Flamort Company Inc (HQ)	Provider of fire retardant coatings. The company's products are used in restaurants, trade shows, amusement parks, and theaters.	510-357-9494	NA	San Leandro
Form & Fusion Mfg Inc (HQ)	Provider of metal fabrication services. The company mainly focuses on powder coating, metal fabrication, and assembly and packaging.	916-638-8576	NA	Rancho Cordova
HB Fuller (BR)	Manufacturer of adhesives and sealants. The company also specializes in paints and other specialty chemical products.	916-787-6000	NA	Roseville
Kelly-Moore Paint Company Inc (HQ)	Developer and manufacturer of interior and exterior paints. The company also offers painting tools and related accessories.	650-592-8337	NA	San Carlos
Materion Corp (BR)	Provider of material solutions. The company deals with fabrication, analysis, research and development, and testing services.	510-623-1500	NA	Fremont
Metacrylics (HQ)	Provider of coatings for commercial properties including material safety data sheets, data sheets, color chart, and test data.	408-280-7733	NA	Gilroy
Plasma Ruggedized Solutions (HQ)	Provider of coating and related specialty engineering services. The company specializes in plasma technologies and offers lab services.	408-954-8405	NA	San Jose
Premier Finishing Inc (HQ)	Provider of precision services. The company focuses on powder coating, liquid coating, pad printing, and light mechanical assembly.	209-982-5585	NA	Stockton
Professional Finishing (HQ)	Provider of liquid and powder coatings and finishing to the scientific and aerospace industries. The company focuses on sandblasting and silk screening.	510-233-7629	NA	Richmond
Reaction Technology Inc (HQ)	Supplier of silicon epitaxy and silicon coatings. The company caters to the semiconductor and industrial sectors.	408-970-9601	NA	Santa Clara
Reltek LLC (HQ)	Developer of analytical and empirical Accelerated Life Testing technology for military, commercial, and nuclear products.	707-284-8808	NA	Santa Rosa
Teledyne Technologies Inc (HQ)	Manufacturer of exploding bridge wire detonators. The company also manufactures electronic firing systems.	925-456-9700	NA	Tracy
UHV Sputtering Inc (HQ)	Manufacturer of semiconductor devices and vacuum equipment. The company is involved in sputtering and bonding services.	408-779-2826	NA	Morgan Hill
Ultimate Index Inc (HQ)	Manufacturer of E-beam deposition cones. The company specializes in prepared coating materials for the precision thin film coating industry.	530-878-0573	NA	Auburn
Western Stucco Co (HQ)	Developer and manufacturer of exterior products for the stucco industry. The company offers both cement color coats and resin based finishes.	916-372-7442	NA	West Sacramento
Zip-Chem Products Inc (HQ)	Provider of airspace maintenance materials. The company also offers metering equipment, spray nozzle, and spray equipment.	408-782-2335	NA	Morgan Hill

48 = Agricultural Chemicals

E.B. Stone Organics (HQ)	Supplier of garden fertilizers. The company also offers lawn maintenance, composite maker, soil, and plant aid services.	707-426-2500	NA	Suisun
N Nu-Concepts (HQ)	Publisher of lifestyle and interior decoration magazines.	909-930-6244	NA	Ontario
N Precise Industries Inc (HQ)	Manufacturer of sheet metal fab, CNC machining, cables and electronic assemblies.	714-482-2333	11-50	Brea
Valent USA Corp (HQ)	Provider of agricultural products. The company also deals with pest management solutions and serves the commercial agricultural sector.	800-682-5368	NA	Walnut Creek

49 = Explosives

Aerojet Rocketdyne (RH)	Provider of propulsion and energetic to its space, missile defense, strategic, tactical missile. and armaments customers.	916-355-4000	NA	Sacramento
Real Sensors Inc (HQ)	Manufacturer of chemical detection systems. The company also offers security solutions to government agencies and petrochemical industries.	510-785-4100	NA	Hayward
Teledyne Technologies Inc (HQ)	Manufacturer of exploding bridge wire detonators. The company also manufactures electronic firing systems.	925-456-9700	NA	Tracy

50 = Industrial Inorganic Chemicals/Gases

COMPANY NAME	PRODUCT / SERVICE	PHONE	EMP	CITY
Anaspec Inc (HQ)	Provider of integrated proteomics solutions for life science research. The company offers peptides, detection reagents, and combinatorial chemistry.	510-791-9560	NA	Fremont
Cannon Water Technology (HQ)	Manufacturer of chemical pumps, water treatment chemicals, and water treatment equipment. The company offers services to the industrial sector.	916-315-2691	NA	Rocklin
Eastar Chemical Corp (HQ)	Manufacturer of chemicals and pharmaceuticals. The company offers Venlafaxine, Usnic acid, Pentaerythritol, and Octanedinitrile.	800-898-2436	NA	Sacramento
Lightwind Corp (HQ)	Provider of semiconductor manufacturing solutions. The company also deals with chemical analysis, process assessment, and refurbishment services.	707-981-4301	NA	Petaluma
Sierra Chemical Company (HQ)	Manufacturer of aquarium supplies, degreasers, descalers, glass cleaners, and growing products. The company deals with chemical consulting.	916-371-5943	NA	West Sacramento
Valent USA Corp (HQ)	Provider of agricultural products. The company also deals with pest management solutions and serves the commercial agricultural sector.	800-682-5368	NA	Walnut Creek
Valimet Inc (HQ)	Manufacturer of spherical atomized metal powders. The company also offers aluminum silicon and aluminum bronze and special alloys.	209-444-1600	NA	Stockton

51 = Industrial Organic Chemicals/Gases

COMPANY NAME	PRODUCT / SERVICE	PHONE	EMP	CITY
A J Edmond Co (BR)	Provider of sampling and analytical services to petroleum refineries. The company's service areas include petroleum coke, coal, and gypsum.	925-521-1555	NA	Concord
Actagro LLC (HQ)	Manufacturer of agricultural products for crops such as alfalfa, almonds, blueberries, corn, tomatoes, onions, rice, strawberries, and wine grapes.	559-369-2222	NA	Biola
Enviro Tech Chemicals Inc (HQ)	Manufacturer of peracetic acid. The company focuses on the development of EPA and FDA regulated chemistries and novel solutions.	209-581-9576	NA	Modesto
Harris Industrial Gases (HQ)	Provider of specialty gases welding equipment. The company also offers services for welding supplies and safety equipment.	916-725-2168	NA	Citrus Heights
Hill Brothers Chemical Co (BR)	Provider of industrial and construction chemicals. The company also offers decking systems and seaters.	408-599-5041	NA	San Jose
Monolith Materials Inc (BR)	Manufacturer of carbon black and hydrogen for plastics, toner and printer ink, batteries and conductive inks, and tires and industrial rubber products.	650-933-4957	NA	San Carlos
Nanosyn (HQ)	Provider of design, synthesis, and analysis of small organic compounds for the pharmaceutical and biotechnology industries.	408-987-2000	NA	Santa Clara
San Joaquin Chemicals Inc (HQ)	Provider of chemicals and services for condensers, boilers, closed loops, potable water, and waste water. The company serves the healthcare industry.	559-725-1735	NA	Fresno
Trinapco Inc (HQ)	Manufacturer of organic fine chemicals specializing in 1,8-naphthyridine compounds. The company offers custom synthesis services.	510-535-1082	NA	Oakland

52 = Lubricants

COMPANY NAME	PRODUCT / SERVICE	PHONE	EMP	CITY
Amyris Inc (HQ)	Provider of renewable products. The company delivers cosmetic emollients and fragrances, fuels and lubricants, and even biopharmaceuticals.	510-450-0761	NA	Emeryville
Eureka Chemical Co (HQ)	Provider of corrosion control services. The company is involved in creating products that offers corrosion protection and lubrication for all metals.	650-761-3536	NA	S San Francisco

53 = Miscellaneous Chemicals

COMPANY NAME	PRODUCT / SERVICE	PHONE	EMP	CITY
3DTL Inc (HQ)	Provider of authentication technology services. The company develops 3D displays for medical, industrial, and military applications.	408-541-8550	NA	Sunnyvale
A J Edmond Co (BR)	Provider of sampling and analytical services to petroleum refineries. The company's service areas include petroleum coke, coal, and gypsum.	925-521-1555	NA	Concord
AB&I Foundry (HQ)	Provider of casting products and accessories. The company's products include pipes and fittings, custom castings, foundry, and recyclable materials.	510-632-3467	NA	Oakland
Advansta Inc (HQ)	Developer and manufacturer of bioresearch agents. The company focuses on protein staining, purification, and electrophoresis.	650-325-1980	NA	Menlo Park
AMPAC Fine Chemicals (DH)	Manufacturer of active pharmaceutical ingredients (APIs) and registered intermediates. The company's services include product development and scale-up.	916-357-6880	NA	Rancho Cordova
N Cosmo Bio USA Inc (HQ)	Manufacturer and distributor of antibodies, biochemical, reagents, and instruments.	760-431-4600	1-10	Carlsbad
Datalab (HQ)	Provider of analysis and certification of process tanks and printed circuit board sections. The company also offers chemical process control software.	408-943-1888	NA	San Jose
Du Pont EKC Technology Inc (BR)	Provider of science and technology solutions. The company engages in product line such as food, personal care and industrial biotechnology.	501-784-9105	NA	Hayward
Eezer Products Inc (HQ)	Designer and manufacturer of sanding tools. The company also offers handles and various finishing tools.	559-255-4140	NA	Fresno

COMPANY NAME	PRODUCT / SERVICE	PHONE	EMP	CITY
Ethylene Control Inc (HQ)	Manufacturer of ethylene and gas removal products. The company's products include filters, filtration systems, and sachets.	559-896-1909	NA	Selma
Eureka Chemical Co (HQ)	Provider of corrosion control services. The company is involved in creating products that offers corrosion protection and lubrication for all metals.	650-761-3536	NA	S San Francisco
Gemini Bio-Products (HQ)	Provider of supplements, reagents, and human products. The company is involved in medical research and development.	800-543-6464	NA	West Sacramento
Hammon Plating Inc (HQ)	Supplier of metal plating applications. The company also provides supply chain management solutions.	650-494-2691	NA	Palo Alto
Light Polymers Inc (HQ)	Developer of polymers and materials. The company formulates and develops solutions for lyotropic liquid crystals.	650-678-7733	NA	S San Francisco
Monolith Materials Inc (BR)	Manufacturer of carbon black and hydrogen for plastics, toner and printer ink, batteries and conductive inks, and tires and industrial rubber products.	650-933-4957	NA	San Carlos
Morgan Technical Ceramics (BR)	Manufacturer of cast and powder metal stainless steels. The company also focuses on other specialty alloys.	530-823-3401	NA	Auburn
Nor-Cal Perlite Inc (HQ)	Manufacturer of perlite and perlite products. The company is involved in the development of specialty grades for individual customers.	510-232-7337	NA	Richmond
Pacific Ethanol Inc (HQ)	Producer and marketer of carbonated fuel and corn oil. The company's services include ethanol sales and distribution.	916-403-2123	501-1000	Sacramento
Prism Inks Inc (HQ)	Manufacturer of inkjet printer inks to the proofing, signage, photography, arts and coding sectors. The company's products comprise UV curable and textile inks.	408-744-6710	NA	Sunnyvale
San Joaquin Chemicals Inc (HQ)	Provider of chemicals and services for condensers, boilers, closed loops, potable water, and waste water. The company serves the healthcare industry.	559-725-1735	NA	Fresno
Sierra Chemical Company (HQ)	Manufacturer of aquarium supplies, degreasers, descalers, glass cleaners, and growing products. The company deals with chemical consulting.	916-371-5943	NA	West Sacramento
Skeletal Kinetics LLC (HQ)	Developer, manufacturer and marketer of bone fixation cement designed for the treatment of trauma fractures.	408-366-5000	NA	Cupertino
Spectra Watermakers Inc (HQ)	Designer of energy recovery systems. The company specializes in manufacturing of reverse osmosis desalination systems for the ocean sailor.	415-526-2780	NA	San Rafael
Surtec Inc (HQ)	Provider of technology solutions for maintenance chemicals. The company is focused on services for the commercial and industrial cleaning industry.	209-820-3700	NA	Tracy
Technic Inc (BR)	Manufacturer of specialty chemicals, analytical control tools, and surface finishing products. The company offers electroplating and engineered powders.	408-287-3732	NA	San Jose
N Thompson Gundrilling Inc (HQ)	Provider of deep hole drilling for industries such as nuclear, injections, military weapons, space, special tubing, aircraft, oilfield, mold bases, and dies.	818-781-0973	11-50	Van Nuys
Toray International America Inc (BR)	Provider of chemicals, plastics, textiles, and IT-related products. The company offers environment, engineering, life science, and other services.	650-341-7152	NA	San Mateo
Werlchem LLC (HQ)	Developer and manufacturer of specialty chemicals. The company's offerings include dyes, pharmaceutical intermediates, and electronic materials.	510-918-1896	NA	San Leandro

54 = Petrochemicals

COMPANY NAME	PRODUCT / SERVICE	PHONE	EMP	CITY
A J Edmond Co (BR)	Provider of sampling and analytical services to petroleum refineries. The company's service areas include petroleum coke, coal, and gypsum.	925-521-1555	NA	Concord
Amyris Inc (HQ)	Provider of renewable products. The company delivers cosmetic emollients and fragrances, fuels and lubricants, and even biopharmaceuticals.	510-450-0761	NA	Emeryville
N Armite Laboratories Inc (HQ)	Provider of lubricating oil and grease products.	949-646-9035	NA	Costa Mesa
Membrane Technology & Research (HQ)	Developer and manufacturer of membrane-based separation systems. The company serves the petrochemical, natural gas, and refining industries.	650-328-2228	NA	Newark
Real Sensors Inc (HQ)	Manufacturer of chemical detection systems. The company also offers security solutions to government agencies and petrochemical industries.	510-785-4100	NA	Hayward

55 = Plastic Materials

COMPANY NAME	PRODUCT / SERVICE	PHONE	EMP	CITY
Amyris Inc (HQ)	Provider of renewable products. The company delivers cosmetic emollients and fragrances, fuels and lubricants, and even biopharmaceuticals.	510-450-0761	NA	Emeryville

56 = Specialty Cleaning Preparations

COMPANY NAME	PRODUCT / SERVICE	PHONE	EMP	CITY
Cleantec (HQ)	Provider of solutions for greenhouse gas emissions, air pollution, water conservation, and waste management.	916-791-8478	NA	Granite Bay

COMPANY NAME	PRODUCT / SERVICE	PHONE	EMP	CITY
Nugentec (HQ)	Provider of chemicals and polymers. The company offers oilfield chemicals, cleaners, and lubricants.	707-820-4080	NA	Emeryville
Synder Filtration (HQ)	Manufacturer of membranes and systems. The company offers training and performance evaluation services. It serves mining, biotech, and food industries.	707-451-6060	NA	Vacaville
Value Products Inc (HQ)	Provider of chemical compounding and packaging solutions. The company services include silk screen printing and private labeling.	209-983-4000	NA	Stockton

57 = Synthetic Resins/Rubbers

COMPANY NAME	PRODUCT / SERVICE	PHONE	EMP	CITY
Holz Rubber Company Inc (HQ)	Provider of custom molded services. The company's offerings include pump parts, slide-lag traction pads, and related supplies.	209-368-7171	NA	Lodi
N Material Fabricators Inc (HQ)	Manufacturer of gaskets, shims, washers, metal stampings and die cut electrical insulators.	805-686-5244	NA	Buellton
N O-Rings Inc (HQ)	Manufacturer and distributor of rings and custom molded rubber products.	323-343-9500	NA	Los Angeles
Performance Polymer Technologies LLC (HQ)	Manufacturer of elastomeric components for material formulation, extruding, and stamping applications.	916-677-1414	NA	Roseville
PermaDri Inc (HQ)	Provider of eco-friendly waterproofing and corrosion protection products. The company serves the marine, landscape, and industrial markers.	559-275-9620	NA	Fresno
N R & R Rubber Molding Inc (HQ)	Manufacturer of elastomeric, rubber parts, gaskets, seals and o-rings for aerospace, industry, commercial, aftermarket, military, and OEM design and specifications through the processes of injection, transfer, and compression.	626-575-8105	NA	South El Monte
N Roettele Industries Inc (HQ)	Manufacturer of non-metallic washers and gaskets.	909-606-8252	1-10	Chino
Ryss Lab Inc (HQ)	Provider of biotechnology and pharmaceutical development services. The company offers services to the healthcare sector.	510-477-9570	NA	Union City
Toray Advanced Composites USA (BR)	Manufacturer of advanced composites like adhesives, prepregs, and liquid resin systems. The company serves military, aerospace, and other sectors.	408-465-8500	NA	Morgan Hill
Westland Technologies Inc (HQ)	Provider of injection and transfer molding, pressure testing, custom hand fabricating, and acid etching services.	209-571-6400	NA	Modesto

58 = Communications Equipment/Services

COMPANY NAME	PRODUCT / SERVICE	PHONE	EMP	CITY
Campbell/Harris Security Equipment Company (HQ)	Manufacturer of busters, fiberscopes, probe kits, and personal radiation detectors. The company also focuses on distribution.	510-864-8010	NA	Alameda

59 = Alarms/Security Systems

COMPANY NAME	PRODUCT / SERVICE	PHONE	EMP	CITY
A A Networks (HQ)	Provider of Internet, networks and cabling, computer hardware and software, remote and on-site technical support services.	650-872-1998	NA	Burlingame
Allied Security Alarms (HQ)	Provider of security products such as fire and burglar alarms, video surveillance systems, motion detectors, and access controls.	650-871-8959	NA	S San Francisco
Appro Technology Inc (BR)	Manufacturer of network surveillance systems. The company's products include dome cameras, LCD monitors, and cables.	408-720-0018	NA	Sunnyvale
Aviram Networks Inc (HQ)	Provider of wire-speed IPS for recognition and visualization, access control, and other needs. The company offers consulting and training services.	408-624-1234	NA	San Jose
Dantel Inc (HQ)	Manufacturer of telecommunications instrumentation equipment. The company offers documentation support and upgrading services.	800-432-6835	NA	Fresno
Dps Telecom (HQ)	Developer of network alarm monitoring solutions. The company also focuses on publishing the SNMP Tutorial.	559-454-1600	NA	Fresno
Foster Brothers Security Systems Inc (HQ)	Provider of security systems. The company offers locks and keys, access control systems, and tools and accessories.	408-736-4500	NA	Sunnyvale
Future Fibre Technologies (US) Inc (HQ)	Provider of fiber optic based intrusion detection systems for perimeter protection and pipeline security.	877-650-8900	NA	Mountain View
Integrated Communication Systems (HQ)	Provider of communication and integration services. The company offers installation, space planning, project management, and maintenance services.	408-491-6000	NA	San Jose
iSmart Alarm Inc (HQ)	Manufacturer of home security products. The company offers alarms, cameras, sirens, and related accessories.	408-245-2551	NA	Sunnyvale
Kimberlite Corp (HQ)	Dealer of security verification systems. The company offers access control, video surveillance, fire detection, and intrusion detection systems.	559-264-9730	NA	Fresno
LAN-Power Inc (HQ)	Designer, developer, and manufacturer of break through technology for implementing surveillance and security systems.	510-275-4572	NA	Fremont
Mixed Signal Integration (HQ)	Specializes in the design, manufacture and sale of turnkey analog and mixed-signal standard products and custom ASICs.	408-434-6305	NA	San Jose
Newland North America Inc (HQ)	Designer and developer of data collector and scanning systems. The company also offers customer information terminals.	510-490-3888	NA	Fremont
PAC Integrations Inc (HQ)	Provider of security solutions. The company offers its solutions for residential, commercial, and fire and life safety applications.	800-479-4722	NA	Concord

COMPANY NAME	PRODUCT / SERVICE	PHONE	EMP	CITY
Protection Plus Security Services Inc (HQ)	Provider of installation services to the electronic security industry. The company's products include access control, video surveillance, and fire alarm systems.	510-770-9900	NA	Fremont
Raco Manufacturing & Engineering Company Inc (HQ)	Manufacturer of alarms and controllers. The company offers remote monitoring, reporting, datalogging, and control services.	510-658-6713	NA	Emeryville
Rex Key & Security (HQ)	Designer of security systems for automotive, institutional, commercial, industrial, and residential purposes.	510-527-7000	NA	Berkeley
Securematics Inc (HQ)	Provider of secure networking, security, storage products and solutions. The company focuses on demand generation and e-commerce.	888-746-6700	NA	Santa Clara
Shotspotter Inc (HQ)	Provider of gunfire detection and location technology services. The company addresses gun violence in communities.	510-794-3144	NA	Newark
Swintek Enterprises Inc (HQ)	Provider of transceivers, tactical repeaters, and surveillance solutions for the government agencies.	408-727-4889	NA	San Jose

60 = Audio/Video/Mulitmedia

COMPANY NAME	PRODUCT / SERVICE	PHONE	EMP	CITY
Access Video Productions (HQ)	Provider of production, editing, and duplication services for small and large companies, and individuals.	510-528-6044	NA	Berkeley
Aheadtek (HQ)	Supplier of magnetic head solutions. The company specializes in television broadcast, video production, and computer and data storage.	408-226-9800	NA	San Jose
Aja Video Systems Inc (HQ)	Provider of video systems and routers. The company also offers broadcast and mini converters and recording equipment.	530-274-2048	NA	Grass Valley
Aldetec Inc (HQ)	Manufacturer of microwave amplifier products. The company provides low noise amplifiers, down converters, and octave band amplifiers.	916-453-3382	NA	Sacramento
N Associated Production Music LLC (BR)	Provider of music such as various genres and categories.	323-461-3211	NA	Hollywood
N Associated Television International (HQ)	Provider of television production and syndication services.	323-556-5600	51-200	Los Angeles
Audible Magic Corp (HQ)	Developer of media identification and synchronization, content registration, and copyright compliance solutions.	408-399-6405	NA	Los Gatos
Avid Technology Inc (BR)	Manufacturer of computer automated audio mixing consoles. The company offers audio product registration and software activation services.	800-955-0960	NA	Santa Clara
BBI Engineering Inc (HQ)	Designer and installer of audiovisual, multimedia, teleconferencing and data systems for museums, aquariums, zoos, schools, and universities.	415-695-9555	NA	San Francisco
N Bryan World Productions (HQ)	Retailer of Design CDs and DVDs, books and instruction manuals.	323-856-9256	NA	Los Angeles
N Cinema Libre Studio (HQ)	Provider and distributor of independent film production.	818-349-8822	11-50	Canoga Park
Countryman Associates Inc (HQ)	Manufacturer of direct boxes and ultra-miniature microphones. The company's products include ear sets, hanging, and podium microphones.	650-364-9988	NA	Menlo Park
Day Wireless Systems (BR)	Supplier of RF, wireless, and radio communication equipment. The company's services include rentals, system integration, and marketing.	707-746-5920	NA	Benicia
Dolby Laboratories Inc (BR)	Provider of speech recognition and voice identification products. The company also offers voice control services.	408-330-3300	NA	Sunnyvale
Earthquake Sound Corp (HQ)	Manufacturer and seller of sound equipment for mobile audio, marine audio, gaming, and home audio sectors.	510-732-1000	NA	Hayward
N El Teatro Campesino (HQ)	Publisher of theatrical material.	831-623-2444	NA	San Juan Bautista
Ensemble Designs Inc (HQ)	Manufacturer of audio embedders, video converters, routers, and related products. The company serves post production, education, and other sectors.	530-478-1830	NA	Grass Valley
Ergo Direct Com (HQ)	Provider of adjustable desks, arms, and mounts. The company offers ergonomic keyboards, monitor arms, and mounting adapters.	650-654-4300	NA	San Carlos
N Erthbound Entertainment Inc (HQ)	Publisher of racing school directory, as well as CD-ROMs, DVDs and software titles.	818-884-3033	NA	Studio City
ESS Technology Inc (HQ)	Designer and marketer of video and audio semiconductors for the home, automotive, and entertainment markers.	408-643-8800	NA	Milpitas
N Gold Standard Productions (HQ)	Provider of video production, editing, DVD authoring, business meetings services.	714-544-7000	NA	Santa Ana
Harmonic Inc (HQ)	Provider of production and delivery solutions. The company serves the broadcast, media, service providers, and post production markers.	408-542-2500	201-500	San Jose
N Harvest Moon Studio (HQ)	Publisher of books and interactive media.	323-660-3444	NA	Los Angeles
Integrated Communication Systems (HQ)	Provider of communication and integration services. The company offers installation, space planning, project management, and maintenance services.	408-491-6000	NA	San Jose
Integrated Wave Technologies (HQ)	Provider of voice recognition technology services. The company offers printing calculators and electronic camera shutters.	510-353-0260	NA	Fremont
Lumens Integration Inc (RH)	Designer and developer of visual presentation solutions. The company offers document cameras, video conferencing cameras, and charging carts.	888-542-3235	NA	Fremont
Media Specialty Resources Inc (HQ)	Provider of acoustic panels for recording studios and home theaters. The company also offers noise control and soundproofing services.	415-883-8053	NA	Novato

COMPANY NAME	PRODUCT / SERVICE	PHONE	EMP	CITY
Mesa/Boogie Ltd (HQ)	Provider of guitars, bass amplifiers, and cabinetry. The company provides pedals, speakers, guitars, and accessories.	707-778-6565	NA	Petaluma
N Opamp Labs Inc (HQ)	Manufacturer of audio and video products.	323-934-3566	NA	Los Angeles
Plantronics Inc (HQ)	Provider of audio technology systems that includes headsets, telephones, audio processors, and speakerphones.	831-426-5858	NA	Santa Cruz
N Point of View Productions (HQ)	Provider of film and video production services.	415-821-0435	NA	San Francisco
N Pomeranian Pictures (HQ)	Provider of production, post-production and distribution of independent film.	818-998-1983	NA	Winnetka
Pragmatic Communications Systems Inc (HQ)	Designer, developer, and manufacturer of pragmatic products. The company offers amplifiers, security cameras, speakers, and wireless products.	408-748-1100	NA	Santa Clara
RadioMate (HQ)	Provider of radio accessories specializing in headsets. The company also offers headsets for surveillance and fire and rescue applications.	925-332-8991	NA	Concord
Rasilient Systems Inc (HQ)	Provider of technology products and services. The company offers a range of video surveillance and storage products.	408-730-2568	NA	Santa Clara
Renegade Labs (HQ)	Manufacturer of tools for the broadcast, video, and film industries. The company's products include digital audio mixers, metering and input and output systems.	530-273-7047	NA	Grass Valley
Sonoma Wire Works (HQ)	Provider of loop-based recording and collaboration software for musicians. It's products helps musicians to play, record, and share music.	650-948-2003	NA	Mountain View
Stewart Audio Inc (HQ)	Provider of network amplifiers and sound systems. The company's products include digital signal processors, mixer amplifiers, and networked accessories.	209-588-8111	NA	Sonora
Swivl Inc (HQ)	Provider of video tools for personalized teaching and learning. The company offers services to educators.	888-837-6209	NA	Menlo Park
TKO Video Communications (HQ)	Provider of video communication services. The company focuses on audio and video conferencing, satellite broadcasting, and telecommunications training.	408-557-6900	NA	San Jose
TOA Electronics Inc (DH)	Developer and manufacturer of audio and security products. The company is engaged in design, delivery, and installation services.	650-452-1200	NA	S San Francisco
Tymphany HK Ltd (HQ)	Manufacturer of acoustic products. The company's products include consumers and Pro audio, OEM transducers, and peerless catalogs.	415-887-9538	NA	San Rafael
Vandersteen (HQ)	Manufacturer and distributor of loudspeakers. The company's products include VCC-5 Center, V2W Subwoofer, VLR, and 3a Signature.	559-582-0324	NA	Hanford
N Vidcrest (HQ)	Creator of motion picture and special interest videos.	323-822-1740	NA	Los Angeles
Video Clarity Inc (HQ)	Provider of real time and broadcast quality monitoring, perceptual analysis, recording, and automating services.	408-379-6952	NA	Campbell
VITEC (BR)	Provider of digital video products. The company offers software for video encoding, decoding, and conversion.	800-451-5101	NA	Sunnyvale
N Wilkman Productions Inc (HQ)	distributor of documentaries and other non-fiction films and videos.	323-461-7028	NA	Hollywood
Zaxel Systems Inc (HQ)	Manufacturer of 4k, 8k, and 16k video servers. The company's products are used in post production facilities, museums, and planetariums.	408-727-6403	NA	Santa Clara

61 = Broadcasting/Receiving Equipment

COMPANY NAME	PRODUCT / SERVICE	PHONE	EMP	CITY
Alien Technology Corp (HQ)	Provider of UHF radio frequency identification products and services to customers in retail, consumer goods, logistics, and pharmaceutical industries.	408-782-3900	NA	San Jose
Antedo Inc (HQ)	Provider of consulting services. The company offers international engineering and management consulting services.	408-253-1870	NA	Cupertino
Ascendance Wireless LLC (HQ)	Designer and manufacturer of fixed wireless networks. The company finds application in security and surveillance needs.	530-887-8300	NA	Auburn
Atlona Inc (HQ)	Provider of technology products for classrooms, large corporations and small businesses, hospitality venues, and residences.	877-536-3976	NA	San Jose
Broadcom Inc (HQ)	Developer of digital and analog semiconductors. The company also specializes in optical communication semiconductors.	408-433-8000	NA	San Jose
California Eastern Laboratories (HQ)	Provider of RF, microwave, and optoelectronic semiconductors. The company also offers lasers, detectors, and other products.	408-919-2500	NA	Santa Clara
Carlson Wireless Technologies Inc (HQ)	Manufacturer of wireless communication products. The company also provides broadband and related services.	707-443-0100	NA	Eureka
Celadon Inc (HQ)	Provider of OEM products and services. The company's products include OEM remote controls, infrared receivers, and backlighting systems.	415-472-1177	NA	San Rafael
Ceva Inc (HQ)	Provider of digital signal processor technology. The company also specializes in offering consulting services.	650-417-7900	NA	Mountain View
Clear-Com LLC (HQ)	Manufacturer of wireless and digital matrix intercom products and related accessories. The company serves the broadcasting and commercial markers.	510-337-6600	NA	Alameda
Communications & Power Industries LLC (HQ)	Developer and manufacturer of microwave, radio frequency, power, and control solutions. The company serves medical and critical defense fields.	650-846-2900	NA	Palo Alto

COMPANY NAME	PRODUCT / SERVICE	PHONE	EMP	CITY
Corecess Global Inc (BR)	Designer, developer, and manufacturer of telecommunication equipment for the broadband access network.	408-567-5300	NA	Santa Clara
Day Wireless Systems (BR)	Supplier of RF, wireless, and radio communication equipment. The company's services include rentals, system integration, and marketing.	707-746-5920	NA	Benicia
E-Z Tel Inc (HQ)	Provider of basic and unified communication solutions. The company serves small and medium-sized organizations and enterprises.	925-449-1504	NA	Livermore
Elk Antennas (HQ)	Provider of log periodic antennas made of aluminum elements and stainless steel hardware and with gain, directivity, and front-to-back ratio.	925-330-0049	NA	Walnut Creek
Ensemble Designs Inc (HQ)	Manufacturer of audio embedders, video converters, routers, and related products. The company serves post production, education, and other sectors.	530-478-1830	NA	Grass Valley
GCT Semiconductor Inc (HQ)	Designer and supplier of 4G mobile semiconductor solutions. The company also offers wireless solutions for its clients.	408-434-6040	NA	San Jose
Guerra Technologies Inc (HQ)	Designer and manufacturer of RF technology related products. The company also offers consulting and evaluation services.	408-526-9386	NA	San Jose
InnoMedia Inc (RH)	Provider of broadband IP telephony products and solutions including TDM-PRI SIP gateways, enterprise SIP gateways cable, and element management systems.	408-432-5400	NA	Milpitas
Inovonics Inc (HQ)	Manufacturer of a wide range of equipment for radio broadcasters. The company also focuses on the marketing aspects.	831-458-0552	NA	Felton
Inphi Corp (HQ)	Provider of semiconductor solutions for the computing and telecom markers. The company's products include amplifiers, registers, buffers, and modulator drivers.	408-217-7300	NA	Santa Clara
Jampro Antennas Inc (HQ)	Supplier of antennas, combiners and filters, and radio frequency components for applications in the broadcast industry.	916-383-1177	NA	Sacramento
Lilee Systems (HQ)	Provider of integrated services that include system prediction modeling, project management, and training services for the railroad industry.	408-988-8672	NA	San Jose
M2 Antenna Systems Inc (HQ)	Manufacturer of antennas and systems. The company specializes in computer aided antenna design and simulation, and testing and prototyping services.	559-432-8873	NA	Fresno
Magnum Towers Inc (HQ)	Provider of self-supporting and guy towers, and accessories such as safety climbs, ice bridges, antenna mounts, anti-climb devices, and insulators.	916-381-5053	NA	Sacramento
Pixelworks Inc (HQ)	Designer and developer of video and pixel processing semiconductors and software for digital video applications.	408-200-9200	NA	San Jose
Redline Communications (BR)	Provider of networking and consulting solutions. The company serves the government, telecommunication, and military sectors.	866-633-6669	NA	Santa Clara
Renegade Labs (HQ)	Manufacturer of tools for the broadcast, video, and film industries. The company's products include digital audio mixers, metering and input and output systems.	530-273-7047	NA	Grass Valley
Satellite AV LLC (HQ)	Provider of broadcaster support and call center services. The company also deals with repairs, distribution, and sales.	916-677-0720	NA	Rocklin
SatPath Systems Inc (HQ)	Provider of networking solutions. The company focuses on voice communication, video and videoconferencing, banking, and other applications.	510-979-1102	NA	Fremont
Sendero Group LLC (HQ)	Provider of GPS systems and products to the visually impaired. The company focuses on documentation and technical support services.	888-757-6810	NA	Rancho Cordova
Tarana Wireless Inc (HQ)	Provider of wireless performance solutions. The company serves the residential and enterprise markers.	408-351-4085	NA	Milpitas
TCI International Inc (DH)	Provider of innovative radio frequency solutions. The company caters to spectrum monitoring and antenna applications.	510-687-6100	NA	Fremont
Telewave Inc (HQ)	Provider of wireless products such as transmitter couplers and receiver multicouplers. The company also offers antennas.	408-929-4400	NA	San Jose
Wavesplitter Technologies Inc (HQ)	Manufacturer of passive devices and active optical components for enterprise and residential broadband networks.	925-596-0414	NA	Fremont

62 = Communications Cable & Wire (Including Fiber Optic)

COMPANY NAME	PRODUCT / SERVICE	PHONE	EMP	CITY
A'n D Cable Products Inc (HQ)	Manufacturer, installer, and reseller of cable accessories. The company focuses on cable management and labeling solutions.	925-672-3005	NA	Concord
Access Communications Inc (HQ)	Provider of telecommunications cabling and audio visual solutions. The company offers audio visual integration, installation, and design services.	800-342-4439	NA	San Jose
N Alloy Tool Steel Inc (HQ)	Distributor of stainless steel, alloy tool steel, and titanium alloys.	562-921-8605	1-10	Santa Fe Springs
N Altemp Alloys Inc (HQ)	Distributor of high-temperature alloys such as inconel, hastelloy steel, and other materials.	714-279-0249	11-50	Orange
N American Voice Mail Inc (HQ)	Provider of electronic voice mail, pager, messaging, toll and long distance services.	310-478-4949	11-50	Los Angeles
Applied Interconnect Inc (HQ)	Supplier of cables and electro mechanical assemblies. The company also specializes in microwave sub-assemblies.	408-749-9900	NA	Sunnyvale
Aria Technologies Inc (HQ)	Provider of fiber optic cable assemblies and connectivity products to the data, telecom, and operator market places.	925-447-7500	NA	Livermore

	COMPANY NAME	PRODUCT / SERVICE	PHONE	EMP	CITY
	Assembly Tek (HQ)	Manufacturer of custom cables. The company offers services like design, laminating, JIT programs, and wire preparation.	831-439-0800	NA	Scotts Valley
	Bay Associates Wire Technologies Corp (HQ)	Provider of cable and cable assembly solutions. The company serves the medical, navigation, audio, and automotive markers.	510-933-3800	NA	Fremont
	Bivio Networks Inc (HQ)	Provider of cyber security and network control solutions. The company offers cyber defense systems, surveillance, flow analysis, and monitoring tools.	925-924-8600	NA	Pleasanton
	Bizlink Technology Inc (HQ)	Manufacturer and assembler of cables and harnesses. The company serves the medical devices, solar energy, and fiber optics industries.	510-252-0786	NA	Fremont
	Bravo Communications Inc (HQ)	Supplier of network surge and lightning protection products. The company also offers data line extenders and related accessories.	408-270-1547	NA	San Jose
N	Brown Metals Co (HQ)	Manufacturer and distributor of stainless steel strip, sheet, copper strip and much more.	909-484-3124	1-10	Rancho Cucamonga
	Cable Labs (BR)	Provider of cable services. The company is engaged in virtualization and network evaluation services.	669-777-9020	NA	Sunnyvale
N	Coast Aluminum and Architectural Inc (HQ)	Manufacturer and installer of switchgear control panels, test stands and specialized electrical equipment.	562-946-6061	NA	Santa Fe Springs
	Compandent Inc (HQ)	Developer of customized algorithms. The company offers digital sign processing services to telecommunications and semiconductor companies.	650-241-9231	NA	Los Altos Hills
	Compatible Cable Inc (HQ)	Manufacturer of custom cable assemblies and off-the shelf cables. The company offers services to the automotive, broadcast, and electronics industries.	888-415-1115	NA	Concord
	Cyberdata Corp (HQ)	Designer and manufacturer of USB cables. The company also offers VoIP and printed circuit board design services.	831-373-2601	NA	Monterey
	De Anza Manufacturing Services Inc (HQ)	Provider of manufacturing services. The company specializes in cable, harness, wiring, and mechanical assemblies.	408-734-2020	NA	Sunnyvale
N	Del Paso Pipe & Steel Inc (HQ)	Manufacturer of pipes, steel products such as channel iron, angle and square tubing.	916-992-6500	NA	Sacramento
N	Dix Metals Inc (HQ)	Provider of precision-ground, machine-ready metal blanks and other materials.	714-677-0800	NA	Huntington Beach
N	Ed Fagan Inc (HQ)	Manufacturer of metals and alloys for aerospace, aviation, defense, electronics, telecommunications and other sectors.	562-431-2568	NA	Los Alamitos
	Fiber Optic Cable Shop (HQ)	Provider of fiber optic cable products. The company's products include fiber optic media inverters, adapters, aerial cables, and fiber optic switches.	510-234-9090	NA	Richmond
N	Fiberoptic Systems Inc (HQ)	Manufacturer of OEM products used to measure chemical compositions, perform medical procedures, measure color properties, and quantify radiance in the UV, visible, and IR regions of the spectrum.	805-583-2088	11-50	Simi Valley
	Golden State Assembly LLC (HQ)	Provider of turnkey engineered solutions for wiring, harnessing and custom cable assembly requirements. The company serves the industrial sector.	510-226-8155	NA	Fremont
	Granite Digital (HQ)	Manufacturer of external diagnostic peripherals. The company is engaged in troubleshooting and maintenance services.	510-471-6442	NA	Union City
	InnoMedia Inc (RH)	Provider of broadband IP telephony products and solutions including TDM-PRI SIP gateways, enterprise SIP gateways cable, and element management systems.	408-432-5400	NA	Milpitas
	Kyosemi Opto America Corp (BR)	Manufacturer of opto-semiconductor devices. The company focuses on optical communication devices and photo devices for sensors.	408-492-9361	NA	Santa Clara
	LAN-Power Inc (HQ)	Designer, developer, and manufacturer of break through technology for implementing surveillance and security systems.	510-275-4572	NA	Fremont
	LightGuideOptics USA LLC (RH)	Manufacturer of diameters, bundles and probes. The company's products are used in medical and high-tech applications.	408-244-0686	NA	San Jose
	Lorom Industrial Company Ltd (BR)	Designer and manufacturer of standard and bespoke cables and cable assemblies. The company offers services to the industrial and commercial sectors.	919-535-5830	NA	Fremont
N	Merit USA (HQ)	Provider of steel processing services for steel coils.	925-427-6427	NA	Pittsburg
	Neptec Optical Solutions Inc (HQ)	Provider of quick-turn fiber optic connectivity solutions. The company also offers connector reconditioning, switches, and fiber arrays.	510-687-1101	NA	Fremont
	Nortra-Cables Inc (HQ)	Provider of discrete and flat mechanical assembly cables. The company offers design, prototyping, and manufacturing services.	408-942-1106	NA	Milpitas
	Optoplex Corp (HQ)	Supplier of cutting-edge photonic components and modules for dynamic wavelength management and signal conditioning.	510-490-9930	NA	Fremont
	Orbex Group (HQ)	Manufacturer of electronic rings. The company offers capsule slip rings, through-hole slip rings, and harsh environment slip rings.	408-945-8980	NA	Fremont
N	Pasternack Enterprises Inc (HQ)	Supplier of RF and microwave components.	949-261-1920	NA	Irvine
N	Rickard Metals Inc (HQ)	Provider of engineering and supply chain management services.	909-947-4922	NA	Ontario
N	SkyRiver (HQ)	Provider of business Internet services.	858-812-5280	NA	San Diego
N	Southbay Foundry Inc (HQ)	Manufacturer of aerial platforms, scissor lifts, excavators, wheel loaders, crushers, crawlers and much more.	619-956-2780	NA	Santee

	COMPANY NAME	PRODUCT / SERVICE	PHONE	EMP	CITY
	Sprint (BR)	Provider of telephone and voice equipment, data communication systems, and Internet related services.	559-244-3200	NA	Fresno
	SSL Industries Inc (HQ)	Designer and manufacturer of fiber optics and networking products. The company is involved in installation services.	530-644-0233	NA	Diamond Springs
	Sumitomo Electric Device Innovations USA Inc (LH)	Developer of electronic devices that includes wireless devices, optical data links, and optical devices.	408-232-9500	NA	San Jose
	Systems Studies Inc (HQ)	Supplier of cable pressurization products. The company is involved in training services and it serves the telephone industry.	831-475-5777	NA	Santa Cruz
	The Okonite Co (BR)	Manufacturer of electrical wire insulators. The company offers high and low voltage, instrumentation, and special purpose cables.	925-830-0801	NA	San Ramon
N	Totten Tubes Inc (HQ)	Distributor of steel tubing and pipes.	626-812-0113	NA	Azusa
	Valley Communications Inc (HQ)	Provider of services for network cabling infrastructure needs. The company focuses on designing and installation.	916-349-7300	NA	Sacramento
N	Wolf Metals Inc (HQ)	Manufacturer of metal products including stainless steel, aluminum, merchant bar, tubular, bright steel, and plate as well as being able to supply stamped and pressed products.	562-698-5410	1-10	Whittier
	YC Cable (LH)	Manufacturer of cables. The company serves industrial, computer, telecommunications, consumer, medical and other sectors.	510-824-2788	NA	Fremont

63 = Communications Equipment Installation & Networking

	COMPANY NAME	PRODUCT / SERVICE	PHONE	EMP	CITY
	A A Networks (HQ)	Provider of Internet, networks and cabling, computer hardware and software, remote and on-site technical support services.	650-872-1998	NA	Burlingame
	Access Communications Inc (HQ)	Provider of telecommunications cabling and audio visual solutions. The company offers audio visual integration, installation, and design services.	800-342-4439	NA	San Jose
	Alpha Omega Wireless Inc (BR)	Provider of broadband wireless network technology integration solutions. The company also focuses on wireless backhaul solutions.	800-997-9250	NA	Sacramento
	Antedo Inc (HQ)	Provider of consulting services. The company offers international engineering and management consulting services.	408-253-1870	NA	Cupertino
	Applied Systems Engineering Inc (HQ)	Provider of consulting, software, design, and testing services. The company's products cater to communication applications.	408-364-0500	NA	Campbell
	Array Networks Inc (HQ)	Developer of integrated web traffic management technology. The company focuses on load balancing and application acceleration solutions.	408-240-8700	NA	Milpitas
	Aruba (HQ)	Manufacturer of enterprise network infrastructure equipment. The company serves healthcare, government, education, and other sectors.	408-227-4500	NA	Santa Clara
	Aviram Networks Inc (HQ)	Provider of wire-speed IPS for recognition and visualization, access control, and other needs. The company offers consulting and training services.	408-624-1234	NA	San Jose
	Bivio Networks Inc (HQ)	Provider of cyber security and network control solutions. The company offers cyber defense systems, surveillance, flow analysis, and monitoring tools.	925-924-8600	NA	Pleasanton
	Broadcom Inc (HQ)	Developer of digital and analog semiconductors. The company also specializes in optical communication semiconductors.	408-433-8000	NA	San Jose
	Capitol Communications Inc (HQ)	Provider of infrastructure communication solutions for business operations. The company caters to electronics, media, and manufacturing industries.	415-861-1727	NA	San Francisco
N	Champion Industrial Contractors Inc (HQ)	Provider of industrial HVAC, plumbing and electrical services.	209-524-6601	NA	Modesto
	Connected Io Inc (HQ)	Developer of altair-based cellular module for Internet of Things applications. The company provides hardware design and development services.	669-221-6100	NA	Los Gatos
	Crime Alert (HQ)	Provider of residential, industrial, and commercial security monitoring solutions. The company focuses on IP monitoring and disaster recovery.	800-367-1094	NA	San Jose
	Dali Wireless Inc (RH)	Provider of RF router platform for healthcare, airport, education, hospitality, stadium, residential and MDU, and metros and train industries.	408-481-9400	NA	Menlo Park
	E-3 Systems Inc (HQ)	Provider of data center design and installation services. The company focuses on engineering, cable plant analysis and documentation, and maintenance.	510-487-7393	NA	Union City
	Ettus Research LLC (DH)	Provider of software defined radio systems for research, academic, industrial, and defense applications.	408-610-6399	NA	Santa Clara
	Farpointe Data Inc (HQ)	Provider of RFID electronic access control technologies for electronic access control professionals around the world.	408-731-8700	NA	San Jose
	FutureWei Technologies Inc (BR)	Provider of information and communications technology solutions. The company focuses on products such as transport network and data communication.	408-330-5000	NA	Santa Clara
	Go!Foton Corp (RH)	Supplier of optical materials and components. The company focuses on markers such as industrial, image and scanning, and biomedical research.	408-831-0131	NA	San Jose
	Grey San Francisco (BR)	Provider of advertising, planning, sports marketing solutions. The company also focuses on customer relationship management.	415-403-8000	NA	San Francisco

COMPANY NAME	PRODUCT / SERVICE	PHONE	EMP	CITY
Hypersurf Internet Services (HQ)	Provider of Internet access and Internet presence solutions such as dial-up, residential DSL, business DSL, fiber Ethernet, and web and email hosting.	408-325-0300	NA	San Jose
Integrated Communication Systems (HQ)	Provider of communication and integration services. The company offers installation, space planning, project management, and maintenance services.	408-491-6000	NA	San Jose
ITC Service Group Inc (HQ)	Provider of personnel and managed services to IT, telecom, and the CATV industry. The company offers staffing and turnkey solutions.	877-370-4482	NA	Citrus Heights
Kyosemi Opto America Corp (BR)	Manufacturer of opto-semiconductor devices. The company focuses on optical communication devices and photo devices for sensors.	408-492-9361	NA	Santa Clara
LAN-Power Inc (HQ)	Designer, developer, and manufacturer of break through technology for implementing surveillance and security systems.	510-275-4572	NA	Fremont
Maverick Networks Inc (HQ)	Provider of VoIP telephone and related communication services. The company also provides design, implementation, and training solutions.	925-931-1900	NA	Pleasanton
MeshDynamics Inc (HQ)	Provider of wireless mesh networking solutions focusing on wireless video surveillance, emergency response networks, and smart-grid multi use products.	408-373-7700	NA	Santa Clara
Modern Systems Research Inc (HQ)	Provider of telecom design and voice and data networking services. The company also focuses on power systems and systems architecture.	650-940-2000	NA	Los Altos
Peloton Technology (HQ)	Developer of truck platooning systems. The company offers services to the transportation, trucking, and railroad industries.	650-395-7356	NA	Mountain View
Ridge Communications Inc (HQ)	Provider of network deployment and project management services. The company serves the wireless carrier industry.	925-498-2340	NA	San Ramon
N Rincon Broadcasting LLC (HQ)	Broadcaster of rock music.	805-879-8300	NA	Santa Barbara
Ruckus Networks (HQ)	Designer and manufacturer of Wi-Fi products and wireless LAN systems. The company also focuses on the marketing aspects.	650-265-4200	NA	Sunnyvale
Sasken Technologies Ltd (BR)	Provider of research and development consultation, wireless software products, and software services to automotive and health care sectors.	408-730-0100	NA	Sunnyvale
Securematics Inc (HQ)	Provider of secure networking, security, storage products and solutions. The company focuses on demand generation and e-commerce.	888-746-6700	NA	Santa Clara
SentinelOne (HQ)	Developer of endpoint protection software. The company serves the healthcare, oil and gas, and financial services industries.	855-868-3733	NA	Mountain View
Socionext Inc (HQ)	Designer and developer of System-on-Chip products. The company's products are used in imaging, networking, and computing fields.	408-550-6861	NA	Santa Clara
Solonics Inc (HQ)	Manufacturer of coded backboard systems and wire management products. The company focuses on design and delivery services.	510-471-7600	NA	Hayward
Sumitomo Electric Device Innovations USA Inc (LH)	Developer of electronic devices that includes wireless devices, optical data links, and optical devices.	408-232-9500	NA	San Jose
Systems Studies Inc (HQ)	Supplier of cable pressurization products. The company is involved in training services and it serves the telephone industry.	831-475-5777	NA	Santa Cruz
TCI International Inc (DH)	Provider of innovative radio frequency solutions. The company caters to spectrum monitoring and antenna applications.	510-687-6100	NA	Fremont
N Trinity Broadcasting Network (HQ)	Operator of a broadcasting network publishing religious content.	714-665-3619	501-1000	Tustin
Tru Technical Partners Inc (HQ)	Provider of information technology services on a contract basis. The company's services include managed desktops, workstation, anti-virus, and others.	408-559-2800	NA	Campbell
Utstarcom Inc (BR)	Manufacturer of IP based, end to end networking, and telecommunications solutions. The company also focuses on integration.	408-791-6168	NA	San Jose
Versa Networks Inc (HQ)	Provider of networking solutions. The company specializes in virtualized network functions and services.	408-385-7660	NA	Santa Clara
Vivax-Metrotech Corp (HQ)	Manufacturer of mapping tools. The company specializes in tools used for underground cabling and piping works.	408-734-1400	NA	Santa Clara

64 = Data Communication Systems

COMPANY NAME	PRODUCT / SERVICE	PHONE	EMP	CITY
Actelis Networks Inc (HQ)	Provider of carrier Ethernet over copper networking equipment. The company serves government, service operators, and utilities.	510-545-1045	NA	Fremont
Airnex Communications Inc (HQ)	Provider of digital wireless telecommunications and Internet access services. The company also focuses on web hosting.	800-708-4884	NA	Pleasanton
N American Voice Mail Inc (HQ)	Provider of electronic voice mail, pager, messaging, toll and long distance services.	310-478-4949	11-50	Los Angeles
AT&T Inc (BR)	Provider of IP based communication solutions. The company offers services in the areas of broadband, Wi-Fi, wireless networks, and mobile phones.	209-556-9042	NA	Modesto
Audible Magic Corp (HQ)	Developer of media identification and synchronization, content registration, and copyright compliance solutions.	408-399-6405	NA	Los Gatos
Avaya Inc (HQ)	Provider of PBX solutions, IVR applications, IP telephony solutions, voice messaging, and consulting.	908-953-6000	NA	Santa Clara
Cisco Systems Inc (HQ)	Designer and manufacturer of IP-based networking products. The company also offers security solutions and architectures.	408-526-4000	NA	San Jose

	COMPANY NAME	PRODUCT / SERVICE	PHONE	EMP	CITY
N	Data Trace Information Services LLC (HQ)	Provider of technology services related to real estate services and solutions.	800-221-2056	NA	Irvine
	Data-Com Solutions (HQ)	Designer of data communication networks, national equipment roll outs, and network hardware installation services.	916-331-2377	NA	Roseville
	Enablence Technologies Inc (DH)	Manufacturer of silicon products for communication needs. The company's offerings include optical splitters and channel filters.	510-226-8900	NA	Fremont
	Futuredial Inc (HQ)	Developer of carrier-grade solutions and tools for mobile device recyclers, wireless operators, and mobile device manufacturers.	408-245-8880	NA	Sunnyvale
	FutureWei Technologies Inc (BR)	Provider of information and communications technology solutions. The company focuses on products such as transport network and data communication.	408-330-5000	NA	Santa Clara
	HotLava Systems Inc (HQ)	Provider of board-level solutions for servers and appliances that operates in virtualized environments.	510-531-1169	NA	Oakland
	Industrial Control Links Inc (HQ)	Designer and manufacturer of SCADA hardware and software solutions. The company focuses on monitoring, alarming, data collection, and other needs.	530-888-1800	NA	Roseville
N	InterMetro Communications Inc (HQ)	Provider of voice calling over the Internet.	805-433-8000	11-50	Simi Valley
	MeshDynamics Inc (HQ)	Provider of wireless mesh networking solutions focusing on wireless video surveillance, emergency response networks, and smart-grid multi use products.	408-373-7700	NA	Santa Clara
	Metaswitch Networks (DH)	Provider of service management solutions. The company offers original equipment manufacturer, multimedia subsystem, and hosted business services.	415-513-1500	NA	Los Altos
	O2micro USA (LH)	Provider of battery and power management products. The company also offers LED general lighting and backlighting products.	408-987-5920	NA	Santa Clara
	OJO Technology Inc (HQ)	Manufacturer of video surveillance systems. The company offers services to the education, transportation, and utility sectors.	877-306-4656	NA	Fremont
	Orion Labs (HQ)	Developer of wearable communication accessory for instant voice conversations with many people, across any distance.	415-800-2035	NA	San Francisco
	Pacific Crest (HQ)	Provider of communication solutions. The company specializes in the design and manufacture of radio controlled and spotlight data transfer systems.	408-481-8070	NA	Sunnyvale
	Peloton Technology (HQ)	Developer of truck platooning systems. The company offers services to the transportation, trucking, and railroad industries.	650-395-7356	NA	Mountain View
	Rambus (HQ)	Manufacturer of semiconductor, lighting, and IP products. The company serves the automotive and transportation markers.	408-462-8000	NA	Sunnyvale
	Relcomm Inc (HQ)	Manufacturer of computer and data communication devices. The company offers data switches, inline buffers, and current loop products.	301-924-7400	NA	Angels Camp
	Sai Technology Inc (HQ)	Designer and developer of wireless technology solutions. The company also deals with digital signage services.	408-727-1560	NA	Santa Clara
	Sentry Products Inc (HQ)	Provider of duress alarm systems. The company caters to judicial centers, emergency medical facilities, and schools.	408-727-1866	NA	Santa Clara
N	SkyRiver (HQ)	Provider of business Internet services.	858-812-5280	NA	San Diego
	Solutions Cubed LLC (HQ)	Provider of engineering solutions. The company is involved in early stage electronic prototyping to full production runs.	530-891-8045	NA	Chico
N	South Valley Internet Inc (HQ)	Provider of Internet and phone services.	408-683-4533	11-50	San Martin
	Sprint (BR)	Provider of telephone and voice equipment, data communication systems, and Internet related services.	559-244-3200	NA	Fresno
	Stonefly Inc (HQ)	Provider of storage optimization and disaster recovery protection for software solutions. The company also offers storage area networks.	510-265-1616	NA	Hayward
	Totlcom Inc (BR)	Provider of IP voice and data services and products such as IP systems, VoIP systems, and mail systems for growing companies.	916-428-5000	NA	Sacramento
N	Transvision International (HQ)	Provider of satellite network facilities and management solution services.	805-981-8740	51-200	Oxnard
	Trivad Inc (HQ)	Developer of IT solutions. The company also offers training, implementation, and infrastructure assessment services.	650-286-1086	NA	Burlingame
N	West Coast Internet Inc (HQ)	Provider of Internet services.	949-487-3307	NA	Capistrano Beach
	ZigBee Alliance (HQ)	Provider of lighting solutions. The company offers LED fixtures, light bulbs, remotes and switches and serves the residential and commercial sectors.	530-564-4565	NA	Davis

65 = Electric Signalling Equipment

	COMPANY NAME	PRODUCT / SERVICE	PHONE	EMP	CITY
N	Advanced Microtechnology Inc (HQ)	Provider of burn-in systems, burn-in boards, burn-in board testers, custom test equipment and fixtures and system design services.	408-945-9191	NA	Milpitas
	Connected Io Inc (HQ)	Developer of altair-based cellular module for Internet of Things applications. The company provides hardware design and development services.	669-221-6100	NA	Los Gatos
N	Fischer Custom Communications Inc (HQ)	Designer, developer, and manufacturer of transient protection devices and RF test equipment.	310-303-3300	11-50	Torrance
	Highland Technology Inc (HQ)	Designer and manufacturer of precision analog instrumentation. The company serves laboratory research purposes.	415-551-1700	NA	San Francisco

COMPANY NAME	PRODUCT / SERVICE	PHONE	EMP	CITY
KMIC Technology Inc (HQ)	Provider of amplifier products and solutions to the radio frequency, microwave, and millimeter wave markers.	408-240-3600	NA	San Jose
Los Gatos Research Inc (HQ)	Manufacturer of analyzers for the measurement of trace gases and isotopes. The company serves the industrial and environmental sectors.	650-965-7772	NA	San Jose
N LTX-Credence Corp (HQ)	Manufacturer of linear and digital test equipment.	408-635-4300	NA	Milpitas
OML Inc (HQ)	Provider of millimeter wave test instruments, calibration equipment and systems for radio astronomy, communication, imaging, and other sectors.	408-779-2698	NA	Morgan Hill
N Semprex Corp (HQ)	Manufacturer of instruments that measure electricity.	408-379-3230	NA	Campbell
N Sts Instruments Inc (HQ)	Provider of off the shelf solutions for quality and or defect testing of lead-acid batteries and systems for electrical test and measurement of motors, windings, electromechanical devices, coils and lead-acid batteries.	580-223-4773	NA	Irvine
Tesco Controls Inc (HQ)	Manufacturer of instrumentation, control systems, and service pedestals for water and traffic sectors. The company offers system integration services.	916-395-8800	NA	Sacramento

66 = Electronic Mail/Message Systems

COMPANY NAME	PRODUCT / SERVICE	PHONE	EMP	CITY
Frequentis California Inc (DH)	Provider of air traffic management and other e-services. The company serves the defense and public transport sectors.	831-392-0430	NA	Monterey
Landel (HQ)	Provider of telecommunication products such as MailBug, DataBug, and SurveyBug. The company is engaged in technical support services.	408-360-0490	NA	San Jose

67 = Internet Related Services

COMPANY NAME	PRODUCT / SERVICE	PHONE	EMP	CITY
A A Networks (HQ)	Provider of Internet, networks and cabling, computer hardware and software, remote and on-site technical support services.	650-872-1998	NA	Burlingame
Allied Telesis Inc (BR)	Developer of network solutions for Internet protocol surveillance. The company focuses on web hosting and programming solutions.	408-519-8700	NA	San Jose
Alpha Omega Wireless Inc (BR)	Provider of broadband wireless network technology integration solutions. The company also focuses on wireless backhaul solutions.	800-997-9250	NA	Sacramento
ARC (HQ)	Provider of document management services to the architectural, engineering, and construction industries.	925-949-5100	NA	San Ramon
Aruba (HQ)	Manufacturer of enterprise network infrastructure equipment. The company serves healthcare, government, education, and other sectors.	408-227-4500	NA	Santa Clara
AT&T Inc (BR)	Provider of IP based communication solutions. The company offers services in the areas of broadband, Wi-Fi, wireless networks, and mobile phones.	209-556-9042	NA	Modesto
Aviram Networks Inc (HQ)	Provider of wire-speed IPS for recognition and visualization, access control, and other needs. The company offers consulting and training services.	408-624-1234	NA	San Jose
Bivio Networks Inc (HQ)	Provider of cyber security and network control solutions. The company offers cyber defense systems, surveillance, flow analysis, and monitoring tools.	925-924-8600	NA	Pleasanton
Ceniom Inc (HQ)	Provider of security, network design, and data recovery services. The company is engaged in web design, hosting, and technical support.	800-403-3204	NA	Sacramento
Configure Inc (HQ)	Provider of communication consulting services. The company specializes in network design, transport service implementation, and project management.	877-408-2636	NA	San Jose
Connected Io Inc (HQ)	Developer of altair-based cellular module for Internet of Things applications. The company provides hardware design and development services.	669-221-6100	NA	Los Gatos
Criterion Network Services Inc (HQ)	Provider of network design, system integration, configuration, and remote network management services.	650-947-7755	NA	Los Altos
CSS Corp (HQ)	Provider of enterprise level support solutions for IT products. The company is involved in virtualization, storage, and archiving solutions.	650-385-3820	NA	Milpitas
N Data Trace Information Services LLC (HQ)	Provider of technology services related to real estate services and solutions.	800-221-2056	NA	Irvine
Denodo Technologies Inc (HQ)	Provider of enterprise data virtualization, data federation, and cloud data integration middleware solutions.	650-566-8833	NA	Palo Alto
Emagined Security Inc (HQ)	Provider of professional services for information security solutions. The company also focuses on compliance.	415-944-2977	NA	San Carlos
Farpointe Data Inc (HQ)	Provider of RFID electronic access control technologies for electronic access control professionals around the world.	408-731-8700	NA	San Jose
Fire2wire (HQ)	Provider of network consulting, server colocation, website hosting and design, wireless Internet, and content management services.	209-543-1800	NA	Salida
Gold Star Web (HQ)	Provider of website design and hosting, development and web marketing, technical support, and programming services.	530-891-1841	NA	Chico
Hypersurf Internet Services (HQ)	Provider of Internet access and Internet presence solutions such as dial-up, residential DSL, business DSL, fiber Ethernet, and web and email hosting.	408-325-0300	NA	San Jose

COMPANY NAME	PRODUCT / SERVICE	PHONE	EMP	CITY
InnoMedia Inc (RH)	Provider of broadband IP telephony products and solutions including TDM-PRI SIP gateways, enterprise SIP gateways cable, and element management systems.	408-432-5400	NA	Milpitas
Intermedia.net Inc (HQ)	Provider of cloud services including VoIP telephony, instant messaging, and file management to small and mid-sized businesses.	800-379-7729	NA	Sunnyvale
Internap Corp (BR)	Provider of Internet network services, colocation, hosting, content delivery, and broadband solutions.	877-843-7627	NA	Santa Clara
Internetspeech Inc (HQ)	Provider of audio Internet technology services. The company offers world-wide web and enabled services.	408-532-8460	NA	San Jose
Ionix Internet (HQ)	Provider of web hosting solutions. The company offers network security, research, high-speed access, and telecommuting services.	888-884-6649	NA	San Francisco
ITC Service Group Inc (HQ)	Provider of personnel and managed services to IT, telecom, and the CATV industry. The company offers staffing and turnkey solutions.	877-370-4482	NA	Citrus Heights
Linguastat Inc (HQ)	Provider of web based services to corporations and government agencies. The company offers optimized product descriptions for millions of landing pages.	415-814-2999	NA	San Francisco
MatrixStream Technologies Inc (HQ)	Provider of end-to-end enterprise, hospitality, embedded, and wireless Internet protocol television solutions.	650-292-4982	NA	Redwood Shores
Nimbus Design (HQ)	Provider of design services. The company specializes in website design, content management, and e-commerce tools.	650-365-7568	NA	Redwood City
NTT Global Data Centers Americas (HQ)	Provider of information technology services such as storage, backup services, monitoring, migration planning, and disaster recovery.	916-286-3000	NA	Sacramento
Numenta Inc (HQ)	Developer of biotechnology machine intelligence technologies for commercial and scientific applications.	650-369-8282	NA	Redwood City
Promptu (HQ)	Provider of voice-activated search and navigation services. The company is also engaged in engineering and product marketing.	650-859-5800	NA	Menlo Park
SatPath Systems Inc (HQ)	Provider of networking solutions. The company focuses on voice communication, video and videoconferencing, banking, and other applications.	510-979-1102	NA	Fremont
SentinelOne (HQ)	Developer of endpoint protection software. The company serves the healthcare, oil and gas, and financial services industries.	855-868-3733	NA	Mountain View
Socionext Inc (HQ)	Designer and developer of System-on-Chip products. The company's products are used in imaging, networking, and computing fields.	408-550-6861	NA	Santa Clara
SSL Industries Inc (HQ)	Designer and manufacturer of fiber optics and networking products. The company is involved in installation services.	530-644-0233	NA	Diamond Springs
Tarana Wireless Inc (HQ)	Provider of wireless performance solutions. The company serves the residential and enterprise markers.	408-351-4085	NA	Milpitas
TechBIZ Inc (RH)	Provider of custom network and server solutions. The company is involved in design and deployment services.	510-249-6800	NA	Fremont
Tru Technical Partners Inc (HQ)	Provider of information technology services on a contract basis. The company's services include managed desktops, workstation, anti-virus, and others.	408-559-2800	NA	Campbell
Unitedlayer LLC (HQ)	Provider of cloud hosting solutions. The company offers server clusters and routers, disaster recovery, infrastructure, and colocation services.	415-349-2100	NA	San Francisco
V2plus Technology Inc (HQ)	Provider of technology solutions. The company offers services for voice, data, and video over local wired and wireless communication networks.	510-226-6006	NA	Fremont
Venturi Wireless Inc (HQ)	Provider of broadband optimization services. The company mainly caters to mobile and wireless operators.	408-982-1130	NA	San Jose
Voce Communications (HQ)	Provider of marketing and communication consultancy services. The company in engaged in public relation, media marketing, and web development.	415-975-2200	NA	San Francisco
Xtelesis Corp (HQ)	Provider of voice and data solutions. The company is engaged in data networking, audio web conferencing, and managed IT services.	650-239-1400	NA	Burlingame

68 = Miscellaneous Communications Equipment/Services

COMPANY NAME	PRODUCT / SERVICE	PHONE	EMP	CITY
8x8 Inc (HQ)	Provider of cloud communications and computing solutions. The company sells IP phones, IP conference, soft, video and analog phones and accessories.	408-727-1885	NA	Campbell
Access Communications Inc (HQ)	Provider of telecommunications cabling and audio visual solutions. The company offers audio visual integration, installation, and design services.	800-342-4439	NA	San Jose
Acco Semiconductor Inc (HQ)	Provider of outsourced operations and engineering services. The company serves fabless semiconductor companies.	408-524-2600	NA	Sunnyvale
Accurate Always Inc (HQ)	Provider of digital voice and video recording services. The company also offers radio and telephone call monitoring service.	650-728-9428	NA	Half Moon Bay
Actelis Networks Inc (HQ)	Provider of carrier Ethernet over copper networking equipment. The company serves government, service operators, and utilities.	510-545-1045	NA	Fremont
Adax Inc (HQ)	Provider of packet processing, security, and telecom network infrastructure components. The company's products include gateways and controllers.	510-548-7047	NA	Oakland
Altigen Communications Inc (HQ)	Manufacturer of voice and data telecommunication equipment. The company specializes in hosted business communication solutions.	408-597-9000	NA	Milpitas

COMPANY NAME	PRODUCT / SERVICE	PHONE	EMP	CITY
Amdocs Ltd (BR)	Provider of customer management and billing solutions software. The company offers services to the industrial sector.	916-934-7000	NA	El Dorado Hills
American Broadband Services (HQ)	Provider of web, Internet connectivity, VoIP, spam and virus filtering, and technical support services.	866-827-4638	NA	Fresno
American Power Systems (BR)	Provider of power management products and services. The company's offerings include UPS, DC power, and battery testing.	209-467-8999	NA	Stockton
N AmeriTel Inc (HQ)	Provider of system design, installation and servicing of business voice and data communications systems and offers voice processing, voice over IP, video security systems, and network services and serves the healthcare, education, hospitality, legal, financial, and manufacturing industries.	818-734-7400	11-50	Northridge
Anritsu Co (DH)	Provider of test solutions for telecommunication applications. The company also caters to microwave applications.	408-778-2000	NA	Morgan Hill
Antedo Inc (HQ)	Provider of consulting services. The company offers international engineering and management consulting services.	408-253-1870	NA	Cupertino
Anybots 2.0 Inc (BR)	Provider of robotic device that acts as a personal remote avatar which can be operated remotely thus creating a virtual presence.	877-594-1836	NA	San Jose
Applied Systems Engineering Inc (HQ)	Provider of consulting, software, design, and testing services. The company's products cater to communication applications.	408-364-0500	NA	Campbell
Applied Wireless Identifications Group Inc (HQ)	Provider of communication systems for engineering applications. The company also offers modules, antennas, and accessories.	408-825-1100	NA	Morgan Hill
Appro Technology Inc (BR)	Manufacturer of network surveillance systems. The company's products include dome cameras, LCD monitors, and cables.	408-720-0018	NA	Sunnyvale
Aptible Inc (HQ)	Developer of secure, private cloud deployment platform built to automate HIPAA compliance for digital health.	866-296-5003	NA	San Francisco
ARBOR Solution Inc (RH)	Provider of embedded computing and networking solutions for the transportation, medical, automation, and military segments.	408-452-8900	NA	Fremont
Arcscale LLC (HQ)	Provider of colocation, technology integration, hosting, implementation, and telecommunication services. The company also deals with procurement.	408-476-0554	NA	San Jose
Arista Networks Inc (HQ)	Provider of cloud networking, network virtualization, high frequency trading, and government solutions for data center needs.	408-547-5500	NA	Santa Clara
Array Networks Inc (HQ)	Developer of integrated web traffic management technology. The company focuses on load balancing and application acceleration solutions.	408-240-8700	NA	Milpitas
Aruba (HQ)	Manufacturer of enterprise network infrastructure equipment. The company serves healthcare, government, education, and other sectors.	408-227-4500	NA	Santa Clara
AT&T Inc (BR)	Provider of IP based communication solutions. The company offers services in the areas of broadband, Wi-Fi, wireless networks, and mobile phones.	209-556-9042	NA	Modesto
AT&T Inc (BR)	Provider of smartphones, TV services, business solutions, wireless networks, and broadband services.	650-938-9479	NA	Mountain View
Autonet Mobile Inc (HQ)	Provider of Internet based telematics and applications service platform for the automotive transportation market.	415-223-0316	NA	Santa Rosa
Avaya Inc (HQ)	Provider of PBX solutions, IVR applications, IP telephony solutions, voice messaging, and consulting.	908-953-6000	NA	Santa Clara
Aviram Networks Inc (HQ)	Provider of wire-speed IPS for recognition and visualization, access control, and other needs. The company offers consulting and training services.	408-624-1234	NA	San Jose
Bravo Communications Inc (HQ)	Supplier of network surge and lightning protection products. The company also offers data line extenders and related accessories.	408-270-1547	NA	San Jose
C&S Telecommunications Inc (HQ)	Supplier of telephone systems and data networks. The company offers installation, training, and other services.	916-364-8636	NA	Sacramento
Calix Inc (HQ)	Provider of broadband communications access systems and software. The company offers business, fiber access, and mobile backhaul solutions.	707-766-3000	NA	Petaluma
Capitol Communications Inc (HQ)	Provider of infrastructure communication solutions for business operations. The company caters to electronics, media, and manufacturing industries.	415-861-1727	NA	San Francisco
Carlson Wireless Technologies Inc (HQ)	Manufacturer of wireless communication products. The company also provides broadband and related services.	707-443-0100	NA	Eureka
Cetecom Inc (BR)	Provider of consulting and testing services. The company focuses on the telecommunications and information technology industries.	408-586-6200	NA	Milpitas
N CHT Global (HQ)	Developer and provider of global telecommunication solutions.	408-988-1898	11-50	San Jose
Cisco Systems Inc (HQ)	Provider of networking products and services such as routers, switches, and optical and wireless networking devices.	800-553-6387	NA	San Jose
Cobham Defence Electronics (BR)	Manufacturer and designer of electrical components. The company caters to the military and commercial sectors.	888-310-0010	NA	San Jose
Codar Ocean Sensors Ltd (HQ)	Designer and manufacturer of radar systems for ocean current and wave monitoring. The company specializes in sea state monitoring.	408-773-8240	NA	Mountain View

	COMPANY NAME	PRODUCT / SERVICE	PHONE	EMP	CITY
	Cohere Technologies Inc (HQ)	Developers of wireless technology solutions. The company offers solutions for orthogonal time frequency space.	408-246-1277	NA	Santa Clara
	Computerland Of Silicon Valley (HQ)	Provider of hardware, software, and networking services. The company serves government and educational institutions.	408-519-3200	NA	San Jose
N	Comtech Xicom Technology Inc (HQ)	Supplier of amplifiers to the satellite communications sector.	408-213-3000	NA	Santa Clara
	Cyberdata Corp (HQ)	Designer and manufacturer of USB cables. The company also offers VoIP and printed circuit board design services.	831-373-2601	NA	Monterey
N	Data Trace Information Services LLC (HQ)	Provider of technology services related to real estate services and solutions.	800-221-2056	NA	Irvine
	Day Wireless Systems (BR)	Supplier of RF, wireless, and radio communication equipment. The company's services include rentals, system integration, and marketing.	707-746-5920	NA	Benicia
	Digital Products Co (HQ)	Provider of telephone line simulators. The company offers two-line telco and party-line simulators and real phone line products.	916-985-7219	NA	Folsom
	DOCOMO Innovations Inc (HQ)	Provider of products and services for businesses. The company focuses on business development, network solutions, and mobile network technology.	650-493-9600	NA	Palo Alto
	Dolby Laboratories Inc (BR)	Provider of speech recognition and voice identification products. The company also offers voice control services.	408-330-3300	NA	Sunnyvale
	E-3 Systems Inc (HQ)	Provider of data center design and installation services. The company focuses on engineering, cable plant analysis and documentation, and maintenance.	510-487-7393	NA	Union City
	E-Fab Inc (HQ)	Provider of precision manufacturing and fabrication solutions. The company offers mesh screens, etched antennas, encoder strips, and PCB jumpers.	408-727-5218	NA	Santa Clara
	E-N-G Mobile Systems Inc (HQ)	Manufacturer of specialty vehicles. The company focuses on TV vans and trucks, emergency response trailers, mobile labs, and other vehicles.	925-798-4060	NA	Concord
	E-Z Tel Inc (HQ)	Provider of basic and unified communication solutions. The company serves small and medium-sized organizations and enterprises.	925-449-1504	NA	Livermore
	Ettus Research LLC (DH)	Provider of software defined radio systems for research, academic, industrial, and defense applications.	408-610-6399	NA	Santa Clara
	Gevicam Inc (HQ)	Developer and manufacturer of industrial cameras based on Gigabit Ethernet Technology for the industrial, scientific, and homeland security markers.	408-262-5772	NA	Milpitas
	Gilsson Technologies (HQ)	Manufacturer of GPS systems and accessories. The company offers external GPS antenna mounts and GPS antenna network splitter kits.	510-940-7777	NA	Hayward
	Glowlink Communications Technology Inc (HQ)	Provider of emitters, global monitoring, and uplink power control devices. The company also offers alignment and commissioning services.	650-237-0220	NA	Mountain View
	Helium Systems Inc (HQ)	Provider of connectivity solutions for smart devices. The company offers services to individuals and businesses.	415-510-2110	NA	San Francisco
	Integrated Communication Systems (HQ)	Provider of communication and integration services. The company offers installation, space planning, project management, and maintenance services.	408-491-6000	NA	San Jose
	Intelepeer Cloud Communications (HQ)	Provider of on-demand cloud-based communication services. The company offers media peering, SIP trunking, and direct inward dialing services.	650-525-9200	NA	San Mateo
N	InterMetro Communications Inc (HQ)	Provider of voice calling over the Internet.	805-433-8000	11-50	Simi Valley
	Ionix Internet (HQ)	Provider of web hosting solutions. The company offers network security, research, high-speed access, and telecommuting services.	888-884-6649	NA	San Francisco
	Jei (HQ)	Provider of communication recorders, voice logging recorders, and audio and custom products for public and military intelligence applications.	530-677-3210	NA	Cameron Park
	Kimberlite Corp (HQ)	Dealer of security verification systems. The company offers access control, video surveillance, fire detection, and intrusion detection systems.	559-264-9730	NA	Fresno
	KMIC Technology Inc (HQ)	Provider of amplifier products and solutions to the radio frequency, microwave, and millimeter wave markers.	408-240-3600	NA	San Jose
	Kortick Manufacturing (HQ)	Manufacturer and distributor of pole line hardware. The company primarily caters to the telecom industry.	510-856-3600	NA	Hayward
	Kyosemi Opto America Corp (BR)	Manufacturer of opto-semiconductor devices. The company focuses on optical communication devices and photo devices for sensors.	408-492-9361	NA	Santa Clara
	Landel (HQ)	Provider of telecommunication products such as MailBug, DataBug, and SurveyBug. The company is engaged in technical support services.	408-360-0490	NA	San Jose
	Langineers (HQ)	Provider of VoIP phone services, video conferencing, and hosting solutions. The company offers cordless DECT phones and video conferencing phones.	650-692-2001	NA	Burlingame
	Lasertec USA Inc (HQ)	Developer and manufacturer of systems for semi-conductor applications. The company also offers systems for flat panel displays.	408-437-1441	NA	San Jose
	Lightsand Communications (BR)	Developer of SAN connectivity products. The company is engaged in troubleshooting and maintenance services.	619-865-6400	NA	Palo Alto

COMPANY NAME	PRODUCT / SERVICE	PHONE	EMP	CITY
Lorom Industrial Company Ltd (BR)	Designer and manufacturer of standard and bespoke cables and cable assemblies. The company offers services to the industrial and commercial sectors.	919-535-5830	NA	Fremont
Marymonte Systems (HQ)	Provider of bar coding, wireless, time data collection, and RFID technology. The company offers inventory control and material handling solutions.	408-927-0606	NA	San Jose
MatrixStream Technologies Inc (HQ)	Provider of end-to-end enterprise, hospitality, embedded, and wireless Internet protocol television solutions.	650-292-4982	NA	Redwood Shores
Meraki LLC (BR)	Provider of branch networking solutions. The company offers services to the education, retail, and healthcare industries.	415-432-1000	NA	San Francisco
Mobitv (HQ)	Provider of content delivery platforms. The company's products find application in mobile and broadband networks.	510-450-5000	NA	Emeryville
Modern Systems Research Inc (HQ)	Provider of telecom design and voice and data networking services. The company also focuses on power systems and systems architecture.	650-940-2000	NA	Los Altos
Moog Animatics (BR)	Provider of motion control devices. The company offers actuators, cables, power supplies, and peripherals.	650-960-4215	NA	Mountain View
N Moseley Associates Inc (HQ)	Provider of broadband, carrier, broadcast technologies and designs, manufactures, and markers digital transmission systems, radio and television broadcast services.	805-968-9621	51-200	Santa Barbara
Nady Systems Inc (HQ)	Designer and manufacturer of wireless microphones, and a full line of audio accessories. The company also focuses on marketing.	510-652-2411	NA	Richmond
OCAMPO-ESTA Corp (HQ)	Provider of engineering, design, construction management, instrumentation and controls, and project management services.	707-642-8072	NA	Vallejo
Opal Soft Inc (HQ)	Provider of communications equipment installation and networking. The company's services include application development, network management, and maintenance.	408-267-2211	NA	Sunnyvale
Orion Labs (HQ)	Developer of wearable communication accessory for instant voice conversations with many people, across any distance.	415-800-2035	NA	San Francisco
Pacific Instruments Inc (HQ)	Manufacturer of computer-automated physical measurement systems. The company specializes in signal conditioning and data acquisition equipment.	925-827-9010	NA	Concord
Plantronics Inc (HQ)	Provider of audio technology systems that includes headsets, telephones, audio processors, and speakerphones.	831-426-5858	NA	Santa Cruz
Polycom Inc (HQ)	Manufacturer and seller of teleconferencing equipment and provider of all other communications solutions.	408-586-3837	NA	San Jose
Pragmatic Communications Systems Inc (HQ)	Designer, developer, and manufacturer of pragmatic products. The company offers amplifiers, security cameras, speakers, and wireless products.	408-748-1100	NA	Santa Clara
Proxim Wireless (HQ)	Provider of Wi-Fi, point-to-point, and 4G wireless network technologies. The company's ORiNOCO product is used by service providers and enterprises.	408-383-7600	NA	San Jose
Purple Communications Inc (HQ)	Provider of communication services to deaf or hard of hearing people. The company serves the medical sector and clinics.	877-885-3172	NA	Rocklin
Raditek Inc (HQ)	Provider of solutions for the wireless and microwave telecom sector. The company offers passive components, active assemblies, and telecom systems.	408-266-7404	NA	San Jose
Raymar Information Technology Inc (HQ)	Provider of hardware supplies, network infrastructure, virtualization, disaster recovery, and managed services.	916-783-1951	NA	Sacramento
Redpine Signals Inc (HQ)	Manufacturer of wireless systems. The company offers chipset and system level products for wireless networks.	408-748-3385	NA	San Jose
Relay2 Inc (HQ)	Provider of cloud Wi-Fi Services platform which allows service providers to monetize value added Wi-Fi services.	408-380-0031	NA	Milpitas
Ridge Communications Inc (HQ)	Provider of network deployment and project management services. The company serves the wireless carrier industry.	925-498-2340	NA	San Ramon
Riverbed Technology (HQ)	Provider of WAN optimization, cloud, consolidation, disaster recovery, and network performance management solutions.	415-247-8800	NA	San Francisco
Ruckus Networks (HQ)	Designer and manufacturer of Wi-Fi products and wireless LAN systems. The company also focuses on the marketing aspects.	650-265-4200	NA	Sunnyvale
SatPath Systems Inc (HQ)	Provider of networking solutions. The company focuses on voice communication, video and videoconferencing, banking, and other applications.	510-979-1102	NA	Fremont
N Sensor Systems Inc (HQ)	Manufacturer of airplane antennas.	818-341-5366	201-500	Chatsworth
N Sierra Tel (HQ)	Provider of telecommunication, business solutions and services.	559-683-4611	51-200	Oakhurst
SNA Electronics Inc (HQ)	Provider of electronic manufacturing services. The company offers services to OEMs in the networking, medical instruments, and aerospace industries.	510-656-3903	NA	Fremont
N South Valley Internet Inc (HQ)	Provider of Internet and phone services.	408-683-4533	11-50	San Martin
Spirent Communications Inc (LH)	Provider of performance analysis technology services. The company also offers network equipment and data center solutions.	408-752-7100	NA	San Jose

COMPANY NAME	PRODUCT / SERVICE	PHONE	EMP	CITY
Sprintcom (BR)	Provider of wireline and wireless communication services. The company serves consumers, businesses, and government entities.	925-933-0142	NA	Walnut Creek
SSL Industries Inc (HQ)	Designer and manufacturer of fiber optics and networking products. The company is involved in installation services.	530-644-0233	NA	Diamond Springs
Stealth Network Communications Inc (HQ)	Provider of voice, data, security, network, and wireless solutions. The company also deals with consulting, design, and maintenance services.	925-846-7018	NA	Santa Clara
Sumitomo Electric Device Innovations USA Inc (LH)	Developer of electronic devices that includes wireless devices, optical data links, and optical devices.	408-232-9500	NA	San Jose
Terabit Radios Inc (HQ)	Manufacturer of wireless radios. The company offers IP-centric (Gigabit and Multi-Gigabit) LoS wireless IP transport technologies to its clients.	408-431-6032	NA	Milpitas
TKO Video Communications (HQ)	Provider of video communication services. The company focuses on audio and video conferencing, satellite broadcasting, and telecommunications training.	408-557-6900	NA	San Jose
Totlcom Inc (BR)	Provider of IP voice and data services and products such as IP systems, VoIP systems, and mail systems for growing companies.	916-428-5000	NA	Sacramento
N Transvision International (HQ)	Provider of satellite network facilities and management solution services.	805-981-8740	51-200	Oxnard
TRC Companies Inc (BR)	Provider of scientific and engineering software services. The company offers hydropower licensing, power delivery, and telecommunications engineering services.	415-434-2600	NA	San Francisco
N Trivec-Avant Corp (HQ)	Designer and manufacturer of advanced antenna systems for U.S. and foreign militaries as well as commercial integrators and manufacturers.	714-841-4976	51-200	Huntington Beach
Ultra-X Inc (HQ)	Provider of personal computer diagnostic solutions for developers, manufacturers, system engineers, integrators, and computer professionals.	408-261-7090	NA	Santa Clara
N Unisec Inc (HQ)	Designer and manufacturer of security equipment.	510-352-6707	NA	San Leandro
N United Security Products Inc (HQ)	Manufacturer of security alarm products.	858-413-0149	11-50	Poway
USB Promos (HQ)	Provider of USB flash drives, power banks, web keys, video brochures and digital toys and promotional items.	800-515-3990	NA	San Francisco
Utstarcom Inc (BR)	Manufacturer of IP based, end to end networking, and telecommunications solutions. The company also focuses on integration.	408-791-6168	NA	San Jose
V2plus Technology Inc (HQ)	Provider of technology solutions. The company offers services for voice, data, and video over local wired and wireless communication networks.	510-226-6006	NA	Fremont
VeEX Inc (HQ)	Developer of test and measurement solutions for next generation communication equipment and networks. The company serves the industrial sector.	510-651-0500	NA	Fremont
Venturi Wireless Inc (HQ)	Provider of broadband optimization services. The company mainly caters to mobile and wireless operators.	408-982-1130	NA	San Jose
Versa Networks Inc (HQ)	Provider of networking solutions. The company specializes in virtualized network functions and services.	408-385-7660	NA	Santa Clara
Vocera Communications (HQ)	Provider of mobile communication solutions. The company provides voice communication, messaging, wireless networking, and technical support.	408-882-5600	NA	San Jose
N West Coast Internet Inc (HQ)	Provider of Internet services.	949-487-3307	NA	Capistrano Beach
Wi2wi Inc (HQ)	Provider of wireless system-in-package, module, and subsystems for embedded applications including Wi-Fi, Bluetooth, and GPS.	408-416-4200	NA	San Jose
Zultys Inc (HQ)	Manufacturer of Voice-over-IP equipment. The company mainly caters to small to medium sized businesses.	408-328-0450	NA	Sunnyvale
Zypex Inc (HQ)	Provider of solutions for product development. The company specializes in industrial communication products, modules, and drivers.	916-983-9450	NA	Folsom

70 = Satellite/Microwave Equipment

COMPANY NAME	PRODUCT / SERVICE	PHONE	EMP	CITY
Aldetec Inc (HQ)	Manufacturer of microwave amplifier products. The company provides low noise amplifiers, down converters, and octave band amplifiers.	916-453-3382	NA	Sacramento
Anritsu Co (DH)	Provider of test solutions for telecommunication applications. The company also caters to microwave applications.	408-778-2000	NA	Morgan Hill
Aviat Networks Inc (HQ)	Provider of microwave networking solutions. The company's products are interactive 3D product models, trunking microwaves, and dual hybrid/packet microwaves.	408-941-7100	NA	Milpitas
Carlson Wireless Technologies Inc (HQ)	Manufacturer of wireless communication products. The company also provides broadband and related services.	707-443-0100	NA	Eureka
Codar Ocean Sensors Ltd (HQ)	Designer and manufacturer of radar systems for ocean current and wave monitoring. The company specializes in sea state monitoring.	408-773-8240	NA	Mountain View
Countis Laboratories (HQ)	Manufacturer of microwave components. The company also offers custom machined components for space, defense, medical and telecommunication industries.	530-272-8334	NA	Grass Valley
DB Control Corp (HQ)	Provider of high-power solutions for mission-critical applications. The company's services include repairs and contract manufacturing.	510-656-2325	NA	Fremont
DiTom Microwave Inc (HQ)	Provider of microwave components for both military and commercial applications. The company offers products such as isolators and circulators.	559-255-7045	NA	Fresno

COMPANY NAME	PRODUCT / SERVICE	PHONE	EMP	CITY
Glowlink Communications Technology Inc (HQ)	Provider of emitters, global monitoring, and uplink power control devices. The company also offers alignment and commissioning services.	650-237-0220	NA	Mountain View
Harmonic Inc (HQ)	Provider of production and delivery solutions. The company serves the broadcast, media, service providers, and post production markers.	408-542-2500	201-500	San Jose
Krytar Inc (HQ)	Provider of broadband microwave components and test equipment. The company is engaged in troubleshooting and maintenance services.	408-734-5999	NA	Sunnyvale
Kumu Networks (HQ)	Developer of wireless technology that cancels self-interference, the unwanted energy that leaks into a radio's receiver while transmitting.	408-786-9302	NA	Sunnyvale
L-3 Narda Microwave-West (HQ)	Designer and manufacturer of RF microwave components and subsystems. The company products include power dividers, filters, and linearizers.	916-351-4500	NA	Folsom
Microwave Technology Inc (HQ)	Manufacturer of RF and microwave discrete semiconductor products, GaAs and GaN RF power amplifiers, low noise pHEMT devices, and wireless amplifiers.	510-651-6700	NA	Fremont
Nextec Microwave & Rf (HQ)	Provider of microwave amplifiers and integrated frequency multipliers. The company serves the aerospace, military, and defense sectors.	408-727-1189	NA	Santa Clara
Norden Millimeter Inc (HQ)	Developer and manufacturer of amplifier products. The company specializes in millimeter wave amplifier products.	530-642-9123	NA	Placerville
PACE Engineering Inc (HQ)	Provider of civil engineering services such as water and wastewater facilities, land development, structural, electrical, geotechnical, surveying and mapping.	530-244-0202	11-50	Redding
Premier Wireless Solutions (HQ)	Provider of wireless products, design and test /certification services, network data plans, device portals, and device management middleware.	650-230-1300	NA	San Jose
Quarterwave Corp (HQ)	Manufacturer of high power traveling wave-tube amplifiers, valves, and test equipment. The company deals with installation services.	707-793-9105	NA	Rohnert Park
Satellite AV LLC (HQ)	Provider of broadcaster support and call center services. The company also deals with repairs, distribution, and sales.	916-677-0720	NA	Rocklin
Sienna Corp (BR)	Provider of electronic manufacturing services including design and process engineering, prototyping, and electromechanical assembly services.	510-440-0200	NA	Fremont
Swedcom Corp (HQ)	Designer and manufacturer of log periodic antennas, channel banks, filters, and base stations for the telecommunication sector.	650-620-9420	NA	Belmont
Terrasat Communications Inc (HQ)	Manufacturer of RF solutions. The company caters to satellite communication and digital microwave systems.	408-782-5911	NA	Morgan Hill
Vida Products Inc (HQ)	Supplier of radio frequency and microwave components and subsystems. The company provides magnetically tuned oscillators, filters, and synthesizers.	707-541-7000	NA	Rohnert Park
Wavesplitter Technologies Inc (HQ)	Manufacturer of passive devices and active optical components for enterprise and residential broadband networks.	925-596-0414	NA	Fremont

71 = Telephone/Voice Equipment

COMPANY NAME	PRODUCT / SERVICE	PHONE	EMP	CITY
8x8 Inc (HQ)	Provider of cloud communications and computing solutions. The company sells IP phones, IP conference, soft, video and analog phones and accessories.	408-727-1885	NA	Campbell
A A Networks (HQ)	Provider of Internet, networks and cabling, computer hardware and software, remote and on-site technical support services.	650-872-1998	NA	Burlingame
American Power Systems (BR)	Provider of power management products and services. The company's offerings include UPS, DC power, and battery testing.	209-467-8999	NA	Stockton
Anybots 2.0 Inc (BR)	Provider of robotic device that acts as a personal remote avatar which can be operated remotely thus creating a virtual presence.	877-594-1836	NA	San Jose
Ashby Communications (HQ)	Provider of voice and data cabling solutions. The company's services include network installation, support, spam blocking, and cloud computing.	916-960-0701	NA	Roseville
AT&T Inc (BR)	Provider of IP based communication solutions. The company offers services in the areas of broadband, Wi-Fi, wireless networks, and mobile phones.	209-556-9042	NA	Modesto
Blue Danube Systems Inc (BR)	Designer and developer of mobile wireless access solutions that increase network capacity. The company serves the industrial sector.	650-316-5010	NA	Santa Clara
C&S Telecommunications Inc (HQ)	Supplier of telephone systems and data networks. The company offers installation, training, and other services.	916-364-8636	NA	Sacramento
Cetecom Inc (BR)	Provider of consulting and testing services. The company focuses on the telecommunications and information technology industries.	408-586-6200	NA	Milpitas
Compandent Inc (HQ)	Developer of customized algorithms. The company offers digital sign processing services to telecommunications and semiconductor companies.	650-241-9231	NA	Los Altos Hills
DOCOMO Innovations Inc (HQ)	Provider of products and services for businesses. The company focuses on business development, network solutions, and mobile network technology.	650-493-9600	NA	Palo Alto
Elecraft Inc (HQ)	Provider of transceivers and accessories. The company also offers auto antenna tuners, antenna systems, microphones, wattmeter, and other products.	831-763-4211	NA	Aptos

COMPANY NAME	PRODUCT / SERVICE	PHONE	EMP	CITY
Embedur Systems Inc (HQ)	Developer of software solutions. The company also offers technical and management services for the embedded market.	510-353-9111	NA	Fremont
FutureWei Technologies Inc (BR)	Provider of information and communications technology solutions. The company focuses on products such as transport network and data communication.	408-330-5000	NA	Santa Clara
Headsets Com Inc (BR)	Provider of office telephone headsets. The company also offers cellphone, computer, and cordless phone headsets.	800-432-3738	NA	San Francisco
Ipdialog Inc (HQ)	Developer of hardware and software technology. The company creates SIP stack, user interface, and media stream handling for phones.	408-830-0800	NA	Sunnyvale
Josephson Engineering Inc (HQ)	Manufacturer of condenser microphones for studio, stage, and field sound pickup, and audio instrumentation.	831-420-0888	NA	Santa Cruz
Langineers (HQ)	Provider of VoIP phone services, video conferencing, and hosting solutions. The company offers cordless DECT phones and video conferencing phones.	650-692-2001	NA	Burlingame
Nokia Corp (BR)	Specializes in mobile network infrastructure structure and services. The company is engaged in technology development.	408-737-0900	NA	Sunnyvale
N Nortek Security & Control LLC (HQ)	Manufacturer and distributor of wired and wireless security and control systems for residential and commercial security markers.	760-438-7000	NA	Carlsbad
Shimon Systems Inc (HQ)	Manufacturer of fingerprint authentication solutions. The company's services include research and development.	650-461-9104	NA	Los Altos
Sonim Technologies Inc (HQ)	Designer and manufacturer of water-submersible mobile phones. The company's products are used in construction, security guarding, and oil and gas operations.	650-378-8100	NA	San Mateo
Sprintcom (BR)	Provider of wireline and wireless communication services. The company serves consumers, businesses, and government entities.	925-933-0142	NA	Walnut Creek
TechBIZ Inc (RH)	Provider of custom network and server solutions. The company is involved in design and deployment services.	510-249-6800	NA	Fremont

72 = Traffic Signals

COMPANY NAME	PRODUCT / SERVICE	PHONE	EMP	CITY
Intelight ITS (HQ)	Provider of electrical engineering solutions. The company offers expertise on systems, traffic products and software.	520-795-8808	NA	Carlsbad
SatPath Systems Inc (HQ)	Provider of networking solutions. The company focuses on voice communication, video and videoconferencing, banking, and other applications.	510-979-1102	NA	Fremont
Tesco Controls Inc (HQ)	Manufacturer of instrumentation, control systems, and service pedestals for water and traffic sectors. The company offers system integration services.	916-395-8800	NA	Sacramento

74 = Aerospace

COMPANY NAME	PRODUCT / SERVICE	PHONE	EMP	CITY
Cutting Edge Machining Inc (HQ)	Provider of contract manufacturing solutions for the medical, aerospace, and telecommunication sectors.	408-738-8677	NA	Sunnyvale
EA Machining Inc (HQ)	Provider of CNC turning and milling services. The company offers services to the semiconductor manufacturing equipment industry.	408-727-4962	NA	Santa Clara
Hammon Plating Inc (HQ)	Supplier of metal plating applications. The company also provides supply chain management solutions.	650-494-2691	NA	Palo Alto
MCM Engineering Inc (HQ)	Provider of aircraft ground support systems. The company offers products and services for airports and aircraft manufacturers.	650-259-9100	NA	Burlingame
Minimatics Inc (HQ)	Provider of precision machining solutions. The company offers CNC milling, manual turning, lapping, and honing services.	650-969-5630	NA	Santa Clara
Mission Tool and Manufacturing Company Inc (HQ)	Manufacturer of precision stamped and machined components. The company serves aerospace, automotive, medical, telecom, defense, and commercial sectors.	510-782-8383	NA	Hayward
Parker Hannifin Corp (DH)	Provider of fuel, air, oil, and coolant filtration systems. The company serves the transportation, marine, and oil and gas industries.	209-521-7860	NA	Modesto
SNA Electronics Inc (HQ)	Provider of electronic manufacturing services. The company offers services to OEMs in the networking, medical instruments, and aerospace industries.	510-656-3903	NA	Fremont
Sonic Manufacturing Technologies (HQ)	Provider of contract manufacturing services. The company engages in supply chain, quality assurance, and design and engineering services.	510-756-5837	NA	Fremont
South Bay Solutions Inc (HQ)	Provider of manufacturing services for the semiconductor, medical, aerospace, solar, and petroleum industries.	650-843-1800	NA	Fremont

75 = Chassis

COMPANY NAME	PRODUCT / SERVICE	PHONE	EMP	CITY
N Pacific Dualies Inc (HQ)	Designer, manufacturer, and distributor of truck wheel simulators and accessories.	310-516-9898	11-50	Gardena
N Trade Union International Inc (HQ)	Manufacturer and distributor of wheels and accessories.	909-628-7500	NA	Montclair

76 = Electrical Connectors

COMPANY NAME	PRODUCT / SERVICE	PHONE	EMP	CITY
Aras Power Technologies (HQ)	Provider of power delivery solutions. The company offers conventional, alternating current solutions, and custom power supply design services.	408-935-8877	NA	Milpitas
Assembly Tek (HQ)	Manufacturer of custom cables. The company offers services like design, laminating, JIT programs, and wire preparation.	831-439-0800	NA	Scotts Valley

COMPANY NAME	PRODUCT / SERVICE	PHONE	EMP	CITY
Bay Area Circuits Inc (HQ)	Provider of engineering services that include fabrication, layout, and design services to the original equipment manufacturers.	510-933-9000	NA	Fremont
Hirose Electric USA Inc (BR)	Manufacturer of connectors. The company provides couplers, dividers, terminators, coaxial switches, and memory cards.	408-253-9640	NA	San Jose
Lemo USA Inc (HQ)	Designer and manufacturer of precision custom connectors, cable assemblies, and related accessories. The company serves the industrial sector.	707-578-8811	NA	Rohnert Park
Leoco USA Corp (BR)	Manufacturer of interconnects. The company offers wire to board, wire to wire, board to board, and card and telecom connectors.	510-429-3700	NA	Fremont
Loadstar Sensors Inc (HQ)	Manufacturer of sensors and load cells with wireless output, used in medical device, automotive, aerospace, consumer and other industries.	510-274-1872	NA	Fremont
Onanon Inc (HQ)	Manufacturer of connector components. The company offers pin connectors, cable assemblies, and machined plastics.	408-262-8990	NA	Milpitas
Samtec (BR)	Manufacturer of high-speed assemblies, connectors, edge cards, and jumpers. The company serves the industrial sector.	812-944-6733	NA	Santa Clara
The Best Electrical Company Inc (HQ)	Provider of tenant improvement and maintenance services for the retail, commercial, industrial, and residential communities.	408-287-2040	NA	San Jose
Westport Machine Works Inc (HQ)	Manufacturer of assembly and balancing equipment. The company's services include fixturing, installation, and technical support.	916-371-4493	NA	West Sacramento

77 = Electrical Protection Equipment

COMPANY NAME	PRODUCT / SERVICE	PHONE	EMP	CITY
Compugraphics USA Inc (BR)	Designer and developer of photomasks for semiconductor, optoelectronic devices, MEMs, nanotechnology, and renewable energy sectors.	510-249-2600	NA	Fremont
Phasespace Inc (HQ)	Developer of technologies for motion tracking markers. The company focuses on motion capture for industrial research and graphic community.	510-633-2865	NA	San Leandro
Syrma Technology (BR)	Provider of entrepreneurial manufacturing services. The company's products include magnetics, memory, and RFID.	408-404-0500	NA	San Jose
V5 Systems (HQ)	Provider of outdoor security and computing platforms. The company offers services to the government, military, and law enforcement industries.	844-604-7350	NA	Fremont

78 = Electromechanical Devices

COMPANY NAME	PRODUCT / SERVICE	PHONE	EMP	CITY
Acutherm (HQ)	Manufacturer of components for heating and air conditioning systems. The company offers therma-fuser variable air volume diffusers.	510-785-0510	NA	Dublin
Areias Systems Inc (HQ)	Provider of services to the technology sector. The company focuses on design, engineering, manufacturing, and prototyping.	831-440-9800	NA	Scotts Valley
Asepco Corp (HQ)	Manufacturer of valves and magnetic mixers. The company also offers diaphragms, connectors, and actuators.	650-691-9500	NA	Milpitas
Connekt LLC (HQ)	Developer and manufacturer of mechanical engineering design solutions. The company's services include CAD, reverse engineering, and sheet metal design.	530-604-5821	NA	Grass Valley
Dicon Fiberoptics Inc (HQ)	Supplier of optical components, integrated modules, and test equipment for the fiber optics industry.	510-620-5000	NA	Richmond
Electro Diagnostic Imaging Inc (HQ)	Developer and manufacturer of products for electrophysiology. The company's services include research, sales, and marketing.	650-631-0120	NA	Redwood City
Fujitsu Components America Inc (HQ)	Provider of computing products and services. The company's products include servers, storage, scanners, and displays.	408-745-4900	NA	San Jose
Lucero (HQ)	Manufacturer of electronic products. The company's products include cables, harnesses, and electromechanical sub assemblies.	408-298-6001	NA	San Jose
Martin Sprocket & Gear Inc (BR)	Manufacturer of industrial hand tools, conveyor pulleys, and other products. The company offers power transmission and material handling products.	916-441-7172	NA	Sacramento
ResQ Manufacturing (HQ)	Provider of contract manufacturing services. The company offers cable assembly and electro-mechanical services.	916-638-6786	NA	Rancho Cordova
Ross Engineering Corp (HQ)	Designer and manufacturer of high voltage electronic and electro-mechanical devices like relays, probes, voltmeters, switches, and breakers.	408-377-4621	NA	Campbell
Shin-Etsu Polymer America Inc (HQ)	Manufacturer of electro-mechanical components such as custom made keypads and inter-connectors, decorative films, and switch devices.	510-623-1881	NA	Newark
SNA Electronics Inc (HQ)	Provider of electronic manufacturing services. The company offers services to OEMs in the networking, medical instruments, and aerospace industries.	510-656-3903	NA	Fremont
Solutions Cubed LLC (HQ)	Provider of engineering solutions. The company is involved in early stage electronic prototyping to full production runs.	530-891-8045	NA	Chico
Sonic Manufacturing Technologies (HQ)	Provider of contract manufacturing services. The company engages in supply chain, quality assurance, and design and engineering services.	510-756-5837	NA	Fremont
Stangenes Industries Inc (HQ)	Manufacturer of isolation transformers, current monitors, charging inductors, and magnetic components.	650-493-0814	NA	Palo Alto
TOA Electronics Inc (DH)	Developer and manufacturer of audio and security products. The company is engaged in design, delivery, and installation services.	650-452-1200	NA	S San Francisco

COMPANY NAME	PRODUCT / SERVICE	PHONE	EMP	CITY
Vulcan Inc (HQ)	Focuses on the manufacture and fabrication of aluminum coiled sheets, aluminum sign blanks, and finished traffic control signs.	510-887-2495	NA	Hayward
Westport Machine Works Inc (HQ)	Manufacturer of assembly and balancing equipment. The company's services include fixturing, installation, and technical support.	916-371-4493	NA	West Sacramento

79 = Electronic Enclosures/Packaging/Shielding

COMPANY NAME	PRODUCT / SERVICE	PHONE	EMP	CITY
Allvia Inc (HQ)	Provider of silicon interposer and through-silicon via foundry services to the semiconductor and optoelectronics industries.	408-212-3200	NA	Sunnyvale
Bay Area Circuits Inc (HQ)	Provider of engineering services that include fabrication, layout, and design services to the original equipment manufacturers.	510-933-9000	NA	Fremont
Casetronic Engineering Group (HQ)	Designer and manufacturer of electronic enclosures, DC converters, AC adapters, flash readers, and IPC rackmount solutions.	408-262-8588	NA	Milpitas
Dawn VME Products (HQ)	Designer and manufacturer of enclosures, backplanes, chassis and card cage. The company also offers design services and power supplies.	510-657-4444	NA	Fremont
Dualsonic Inc (HQ)	Provider of technology solutions for electronic and precision CNC machining. The company designs and manufactures PCMCIA cards and RFID housings.	408-457-8585	NA	Santa Clara
Id Technology LLC (BR)	Designer and manufacturer of custom identification systems. The company offers labeling, coding, and marketing equipment services.	559-436-8401	NA	Fresno
JSR Micro Inc (HQ)	Provider of semiconductor, life sciences, and energy material solutions. The company specializes in lithography materials and CMP consumables.	408-543-8800	NA	Sunnyvale
Milner's Anodizing (HQ)	Provider of metal finishing solutions. The company's services include anodizing, anodizing, and passivation.	707-584-1188	NA	Santa Rosa
PAC Machinery (HQ)	Manufacturer of heat sealing and packaging equipment such as tube sealers, shrink wrap systems, and skin packaging products.	415-454-4868	NA	San Rafael
Plasmaterials Inc (HQ)	Provider of materials for thin film applications. The company offers base metal alloys, backing plates, and semiconductor alloys.	925-447-4030	NA	Livermore
Syrma Technology (BR)	Provider of entrepreneurial manufacturing services. The company's products include magnetics, memory, and RFID.	408-404-0500	NA	San Jose
Tesco Controls Inc (HQ)	Manufacturer of instrumentation, control systems, and service pedestals for water and traffic sectors. The company offers system integration services.	916-395-8800	NA	Sacramento
Xperi Corp (HQ)	Provider of miniaturization technology services for electronic devices. The company offers micro-electronics, and imaging and optics services.	408-321-6000	NA	San Jose

80 = Machine Shop/Precision Fabricated Components

	COMPANY NAME	PRODUCT / SERVICE	PHONE	EMP	CITY
N	A & A Machine & Development Company Inc (HQ)	Manufacturer of CNC equipment for airspace and commercial industries.	310-532-7706	NA	Gardena
	A&D Precision Inc (HQ)	Provider of contract manufacturing, program management, electro-mechanical assembly, and precision machining services.	510-657-6781	NA	Fremont
	A-1 Jay's Machining Inc (HQ)	Provider of machining, product assembly, and finishing services. The company is engaged in vertical milling, laser Micro-machining and waterjet cutting.	408-262-1845	NA	San Jose
	A-Laser (HQ)	Provider of precision parts manufacturing services. The company specializes in laser cutting and caters to a wide range of industries.	408-954-8582	NA	Milpitas
	Accu-Swiss Inc (HQ)	Manufacturer of precision CNC and screw machined products. The company's services include engineering, milling, and threading.	209-847-1016	NA	Oakdale
	ACI Alloys Inc (HQ)	Manufacturer of purity alloys for thin film applications. The company offers evaporation and thin film materials.	408-259-7337	NA	San Jose
	Acrylic Art (HQ)	Provider of fabrication and machining services. The company focuses on painting, product finishing, anodizing, and vapor polishing.	510-654-0953	NA	Emeryville
	Acu Spec Inc (HQ)	Manufacturer of engineering products. The company offers horizontal and vertical machining, CNC turning, CAD software, and CMM inspection services.	408-748-8600	NA	Santa Clara
	Adem LLC (HQ)	Designer and manufacturer of special and automated fixtures for assembly lines, and also provides turnkey production solutions.	408-727-8955	NA	Santa Clara
	Advance Carbon Products Inc (HQ)	Manufacturer of carbon. The company offers equipment such as CNC lathes, grinders, lappers, and diamond saws.	510-293-5930	NA	Hayward
	Advanced Fabrication Technology (HQ)	Provider of metal fabricating services for the electronics, manufacturing, and semiconductor industries.	510-489-6218	NA	Hayward
N	Aero Chip Inc (HQ)	Designer and developer of complex components for the aerospace industry through machining, forming and assembling.	562-404-6300	11-50	Santa Fe Springs
	Aimer Corp (HQ)	Provider of thermal management products. The company also offers connectors, PCB boards, cables, and mechanical parts.	408-260-8588	NA	Santa Clara
	Airpoint Precision Inc (HQ)	Provider of precision machining services. The company serves the industrial needs of the community in a cost efficient and timely manner.	530-622-0510	NA	Diamond Springs
N	Alger Precision Machining LLC (HQ)	Manufacturer of screw machine products.	909-983-3351	NA	Ontario
	All Fab Precision Sheetmetal Inc (HQ)	Provider of contract manufacturing services for metal formed products. The company is involved in laser cutting, deburring, bending, and welding activities.	408-279-1099	NA	San Jose

	COMPANY NAME	PRODUCT / SERVICE	PHONE	EMP	CITY
	Alloy Metal Products (HQ)	Provider of precision CNC machining, tumbling, annealing, cutting, and packaging services. The company serves aerospace and medical device fields.	925-371-1234	NA	Livermore
N	Alltronics LLC (HQ)	Distributor of electrical and electro-mechanical parts such as automotive, computer, capacitors and more.	408-778-3868	1-10	Santa Clara
	Alta Design & Manufacturing Inc (HQ)	Manufacturer of precision-machined components. The company is engaged in production manufacturing, prototype services, and electromechanical assembly.	408-450-5394	NA	San Jose
	Alterflex Corp (HQ)	Designer and manufacturer of printed circuit boards. The company also provides engineering support services.	408-441-8688	NA	San Jose
	Alumawall Inc (HQ)	Manufacturer of metal panel and fabricator and erector of aluminum and metal composite panel systems.	408-292-6353	NA	San Jose
	American Die & Rollforming Inc (HQ)	Manufacturer of metal roofing, siding, and structural products. The company also specializes in canopies and decking.	916-652-7667	NA	Loomis
	American Portable Welding (HQ)	Provider of welding, fabrication, and engineering services. The company offers services to the industrial sector.	510-887-4279	NA	Hayward
	American Precision Spring Corp (HQ)	Designer of electronic circuits. The company specializes in the design and fabrication of printed circuit boards.	408-986-1020	NA	Santa Clara
	American Prototype And Production Inc (HQ)	Manufacturer of industrial laser cutting machines. The company focuses on industries such as CNC milling, CNC turning, and laser engraving.	650-595-4994	NA	San Carlos
	Applied Fusion Inc (HQ)	Provider of precision metal fabrication, electron beam and laser welding, and CNC machining services.	510-351-8314	NA	San Leandro
	Armorstruxx (HQ)	Provider of ballistic and blast protection solutions. The company offers armor systems design and integration services.	209-365-9400	NA	Lodi
	Austin Precision Inc (HQ)	Provider of precision machined parts. The company offers parts made from aluminum, plastics, stainless steel, and other metals.	925-449-1049	NA	Livermore
	Avocet Sales & Marketing Inc (HQ)	Provider of custom engineered mechanical component parts and sub assemblies. The company offers contract manufacturing and automation services.	510-891-0093	NA	Oakland
N	AW Die Engraving Inc (HQ)	Manufacturer of precision rotary and flat dies for labeling, printing and die cutting.	714-521-0842	NA	Buena Park
	B&H Engineering (HQ)	Supplier of assemblies, process kits, and individual parts. The company caters to the semiconductor equipment industry.	650-594-2861	NA	San Carlos
	B&Z Manufacturing Company Inc (HQ)	Provider of multi-axis milling and turning services. The company offers ultra precision components for electronic, aerospace, and computer fields.	408-943-1117	NA	San Jose
	B-Metal Fabrication Inc (HQ)	Provider of metal fabrication services. The company offers services for the commercial, residential, retail, and bio pharmaceutical industries.	650-615-7705	NA	S San Francisco
	Babbitt Bearing Company Inc (HQ)	Provider of repair and manufacturing services. The company deals in hard chrome plating, non-destructive testing, and machinery repair.	408-298-1101	NA	San Jose
	Bay Standard Manufacturing Inc (HQ)	Manufacturer of machinery components. The company offers thread, foundation bolts, u-bolts, and specialty fasteners.	800-228-8640	NA	Brentwood
	BayFab Metals Inc (HQ)	Manufacturer of custom and production parts. The company's products include Trumpf TruLaser, Trumpf Laser Cutter, and AMADA.	510-568-8950	NA	San Leandro
N	Bearing Engineering Company Inc (HQ)	Distributor of power transmission products such as bearings, belts, bushings, chains and chain drives and more.	510-596-4150	NA	San Leandro
	Benicia Fabrication & Machine Inc (HQ)	Manufacturer of industrial equipment and provider of repair and maintenance services. The company develops pressure vessels and heat exchangers.	707-745-8111	NA	Benicia
N	Bmw Precision Machining Inc (HQ)	Provider of full service fabrication and assembly for the medical, electronics and commercial industries.	760-439-6813	11-50	Oceanside
	BT Laser & Manufacturing Inc (HQ)	Provider of custom design, laser and water jet cutting, fabrication, and welding services for solar, semiconductor, and communication sectors.	408-566-0135	NA	Santa Clara
	C L Hann Industries Inc (HQ)	Provider of contract manufacturing services including CNC machining, welding, assembly and testing, and conditioning.	408-293-4800	NA	San Jose
	C&C Machining Inc (HQ)	Provider of machining services. The company specializes in magnetic alloys, expansion alloys, and shielding alloys.	510-876-8139	NA	Hayward
	Calchemist (HQ)	Provider of contract research services. The company specializes in chemical, material science and laboratory equipment testing.	650-551-1495	11-50	S San Francisco
	Callouette Fabricators Inc (HQ)	Developer of machining components for automotive, process control, biotech, plasma, instrumentation, and aviation industries.	707-746-0962	NA	Benicia
	Calmax Technology Inc (HQ)	Provider of precision machined components and electro-mechanical assemblies. The company serves semi-conductor and medical industries.	408-748-8660	NA	Santa Clara
N	Calolympic Safety (HQ)	Distributor of bandages and health-conscious ergonomic products.	951-340-2229	NA	Corona
	Capital Sheet Metal (HQ)	Manufacturer of custom countertops. The company deals with shearing, welding, laser cutting, and polishing services.	916-443-3761	NA	Sacramento
N	Carlson and Beauloye (HQ)	Manufacturer of the motorless water pump that generates its horsepower from water weight and gravity.	619-234-2256	NA	San Diego
N	Ceramic Tech Inc (HQ)	Manufacturer and fabrication of ceramic parts.	510-252-8500	NA	Fremont

COMPANY NAME	PRODUCT / SERVICE	PHONE	EMP	CITY
Clover Machine & Manufacturing (HQ)	Provider of contract manufacturing and machining services. The company supplies tooling and fixtures to its customers.	408-727-3380	NA	Santa Clara
Coast Metal Cutting (HQ)	Provider of machining and metal cutting services. The company's services include production, turning, drilling, and tapping.	650-369-9837	NA	Redwood City
Columbia Machine Works (HQ)	Provider of coining equipment and contracting services. The company offers coining presses, rimming machines, and consumable tooling.	510-568-0808	NA	Oakland
Comptech USA (HQ)	Manufacturer and fabricator of race engines. The company also offers R&D and road racing track maintenance services.	916-338-3434	NA	Sacramento
Concept Models Inc (HQ)	Provider of prototyping devices. The company specializes in surgical devices, CNC programming, tap burning, and rubber molding.	925-606-6743	NA	Livermore
Concord Sheet Metal (HQ)	Provider of architectural metal products. The company focuses on fasteners, copper gutters, and decorative chimney tops.	925-680-8723	NA	Pittsburg
Custom Gear & Machine (HQ)	Manufacturer of custom gears. The company also offers overhaul services for gearboxes and caters to industries like food and steel processing.	925-455-9985	NA	Livermore
Custom Micro Machining Inc (HQ)	Manufacturer of precision housing carriers and microwave assemblies. The company is involved in design, installation, and delivery services.	510-651-9434	NA	Fremont
Custom Product Development Co (HQ)	Developer and manufacturer of mechanical components and turnkey assembly solutions. The company specializes in developing customized products.	925-960-0577	NA	Livermore
Cutting Edge Machining Inc (HQ)	Provider of contract manufacturing solutions for the medical, aerospace, and telecommunication sectors.	408-738-8677	NA	Sunnyvale
CVM Inc (HQ)	Provider of custom machine tools. The company also offers electrical fabrication, machining, and robotic services.	925-847-8808	NA	Pleasanton
DAM Good Engineering & Manufacturing Inc (HQ)	Manufacturer of parts for microwave, telecom, and industrial sectors. The company offers gaming devices, model engine parts, and other products.	408-224-6494	NA	San Jose
Datum Technologies Inc (HQ)	Manufacturer of precision machining services. The company serves customers in the aerospace, medical device, and energy industries.	707-738-3914	NA	Santa Rosa
N Decco Graphics Inc (HQ)	Manufacturer of steel rule dies and hand assembly for printing industry.	310-534-2861	NA	Harbor City
Delong Manufacturing Company (HQ)	Provider of machining services. The company focuses on prototype development, production, engineering design, and kitting and assembly.	408-727-3348	NA	Santa Clara
Delta Machine (HQ)	Provider of precision machine components and custom parts. The company specializes in CNC milling, CNC turning, and turn key mechanical assemblies.	408-955-9140	NA	San Jose
Dentoni's (HQ)	Provider of services for trucks and trailers. The company specializes in welding, machining, ornamental iron, and springs.	209-464-4930	NA	Stockton
Dependable Precision Manufacturing Inc (HQ)	Provider of precision sheet metal fabrication services. The company serves the government and high tech sectors.	209-369-1055	NA	Lodi
Deweyl Tool Inc (HQ)	Manufacturer of bonding, large and double flat wire, and small wire bonding wedges. The company's products are used in ultrasonic applications.	707-765-5779	NA	Petaluma
N DG Industries (HQ)	Manufacturer and distributor of fastener products.	714-990-3787	11-50	Brea
Diablo Precision Inc (HQ)	Manufacturer of metal and plastic parts. The company also provides machining, milling, turning, and contract inspection services.	831-634-0136	NA	Hollister
N Dial Precision Inc (HQ)	Manufacturer of precision components.	760-947-3557	11-50	Hesperia
Diamond Tool & Die Inc (HQ)	Provider of general machine services for the high tech industry. The company serves the aerospace, construction, and food processing industries.	510-534-7050	NA	Oakland
Dinucci Corp (HQ)	Provider of computerized manufacturing and prototyping services. The company offers services to the business sector.	925-798-3946	NA	Concord
DKW Precision Machining Inc (HQ)	Manufacturer of precision machined parts and components. The company offers CNC milling and turning, prototype, and production services.	209-456-5709	NA	Manteca
Donal Machine Inc (HQ)	Provider of precision machining and sheet metal services. The company focuses on CNC machining, precision laser cutting, and welding and fabrication.	707-763-6625	NA	Petaluma
Dynatex International (HQ)	Manufacturer of semiconductor, dicing equipment, and supplies. The company also offers dicing and wafer bonding services.	707-542-4227	NA	Santa Rosa
E Enterprise Tech (HQ)	Manufacturer of machined components. The company offers CNC machining, sheetmetal, cabling, electrical, and mechanical assembly services.	408-844-8176	NA	San Jose
E&F Plastics Inc (HQ)	Provider of plastic fabricated products. The company offers bonded PVC, vapor polished polycarbonates, and vacuum formed Kydex.	408-226-6672	NA	San Jose
E-Fab Inc (HQ)	Provider of precision manufacturing and fabrication solutions. The company offers mesh screens, etched antennas, encoder strips, and PCB jumpers.	408-727-5218	NA	Santa Clara
E-M Manufacturing Inc (HQ)	Provider of prototyping and short run production machining services. The company is engaged in sheet metal design.	209-825-1800	NA	Manteca
EA Machining Inc (HQ)	Provider of CNC turning and milling services. The company offers services to the semiconductor manufacturing equipment industry.	408-727-4962	NA	Santa Clara

COMPANY NAME	PRODUCT / SERVICE	PHONE	EMP	CITY
East Bay Machine (HQ)	Provider of machining services including welding and fabrication. The company offers services to the business sector.	925-689-2421	NA	Concord
Eclipse Metal Fabrication Inc (HQ)	Provider of metal fabrication services. The company provides CNC machining, laser, and waterjet cutting services in the San Francisco Bay area.	650-298-8731	NA	Redwood City
Edmar Engineering Inc (HQ)	Manufacturer of precision machined products. The company's products include CNC mills and lathes, inspection equipment, and lathe and mill software.	707-693-0390	NA	Dixon
Electro-Coatings of California Inc (BR)	Provider of electroless nickel coating services. The company also offers industrial hard chrome and nickel metal finishing services.	510-849-4075	NA	Berkeley
Electrochem Solutions Inc (HQ)	Provider of plating, anodizing, parts cleaning services. The company caters to high technology industries.	510-476-1840	NA	Union City
Electronic Carbide Inc (HQ)	Provider of CNC precision machining, fabrication, and wire EDM services. The company serves the industrial sector.	530-272-6154	NA	Grass Valley
Elite E/M Inc (HQ)	Provider of precision machining services. The company offers prototyping, tooling, shearing, and cutting services.	408-988-3505	NA	Santa Clara
Emkay Manufacturing Inc (HQ)	Provider of precision milling and turning services. The company serves the medical, electrical, aerospace, and defense sectors.	650-365-3010	NA	Redwood City
Emtec Engineering (HQ)	Provider of precision machining and precision sheet metal fabrication services to the computer, telecommunication, and medical industries.	408-779-5800	NA	Morgan Hill
Encore Industries Inc (HQ)	Provider of technical services to engineering and procurement. The company's domain includes medical and science, consumer products, and structural.	408-416-0501	NA	San Jose
N Engineering Design Industries Inc (HQ)	Manufacturer and distributor of industrial machines.	626-443-7741	NA	South El Monte
Exacta Tech Inc (HQ)	Manufacturer of custom machine components and parts and provider of design, inspection and engineering services for industries.	925-443-8963	NA	Livermore
Expedite Precision Works Inc (HQ)	Manufacturer of diverse products involving micro and custom machining and fabrication of metal and plastic. The company also manufactures vessels and tanks.	408-573-9600	NA	San Jose
Fast Trak Fabrication (HQ)	Provider of metal fabrication services. The company's services include laser cutting, machining, forming, and welding.	559-222-4450	NA	Fresno
Ferrotec USA Corp (RH)	Manufacturer and distributor of quartz solutions and fluid sealants. The company serves business organizations and enterprises.	408-964-7700	NA	Santa Clara
FM Industries Inc (HQ)	Designer and manufacturer of precision machined components. The company also offers electro mechanical assemblies.	510-668-1900	NA	Fremont
Form & Fusion Mfg Inc (HQ)	Provider of metal fabrication services. The company mainly focuses on powder coating, metal fabrication, and assembly and packaging.	916-638-8576	NA	Rancho Cordova
Gateway Precision Inc (HQ)	Manufacturer of precision-machined components and assemblies for image equipment manufacturers, telecom, food processing, and semiconductor sectors.	408-855-8849	NA	Santa Clara
N Geiger Manufacturing Inc (HQ)	Provider of industrial equipment, fabrication, CNC milling and welding services.	209-464-7746	NA	Stockton
Gentec Manufacturing Inc (HQ)	Provider of machining services. The company also offers measuring, testing, turning, and engineering services.	408-432-6220	NA	San Jose
Geo M Martin Co (HQ)	Developer of equipment for corrugated container industry. The company offers training, field support, and technical services.	510-652-2200	NA	Emeryville
Gerlinger Steel & Supply Company (HQ)	Provider of metal products and industrial services. The company offers metalworking machinery and supplies.	530-243-1053	NA	Redding
Glaser & Associates Inc (HQ)	Manufacturer and distributor of fastening solutions. The company offers bolts, screws, rods and studs, and anchors.	925-228-3200	NA	Martinez
Grabber Construction Products Inc (BR)	Manufacturer of fasteners and machine tools. The company also specializes in distribution and other services.	800-869-1375	NA	Concord
Greenwood Machine & Fabrication Inc (HQ)	Provider of repair and fabrication services for commercial and industrial equipment. The company's customers include private companies and military contractors.	209-538-2277	NA	Ceres
Group Manufacturing Services Inc (HQ)	Manufacturer of precision sheet metal fabrication, precision machining, and design support services.	408-436-1040	NA	San Jose
H & M Precision Machining (HQ)	Provider of precision manufacturing solutions. The company offers screw machines, CNC turning, CNC milling, and sawing services.	408-982-9184	NA	Santa Clara
H P Machine & Engineering Inc (HQ)	Provider of job shop, prototype machining, CNC, and wire EDM services. The company offers services to the industrial sector.	408-383-9075	NA	San Jose
Haig Precision Manufacturing Corp (HQ)	Manufacturer of precision parts and assemblies. The company focuses on sheet metal, CNC milling and turning, stamping, welding, and powder coating.	408-378-4920	NA	San Jose
Hayward Quartz Technology Inc (HQ)	Manufacturer of machined and fabricated parts. The company exclusively caters to the semiconductor industry.	510-657-9605	NA	Fremont
Hellwig Products Company Inc (HQ)	Provider of sway control and load control products for trucks and SUV's. The company also offers fleet solution services.	559-734-7451	NA	Visalia

COMPANY NAME	PRODUCT / SERVICE	PHONE	EMP	CITY
Hof Machining Inc (HQ)	Provider of exotic geometry and prototype machining services. The company's offerings include machine shop services and machining materials.	408-526-1155	NA	San Jose
Hogan Manufacturing Inc (HQ)	Provider of steel manufacturing fabrication services. The company's products include plate weldments, alloy specialties, and waste separation equipment.	209-838-2400	NA	Escalon
Horn Machine Tools Inc (HQ)	Supplier of CNC and semi-automatic tube benders. The company offers new tube benders, rebuilt tube benders, and bender rebuilding and retro-fitting.	559-431-4131	NA	Madera
Howard Wire Cloth Co (HQ)	Provider of screening and wire fabrication products. The company offers wire cloth, stainless steel netting, security screening, and perforated metals.	510-887-8787	NA	Hayward
Howlett Machine Works (HQ)	Manufacturer of machine works and custom made tools. The company also offers custom test fixtures and test machines.	510-845-2759	NA	Berkeley
HS&S Inc (HQ)	Designer and manufacturer of machine tool and custom machine manufacturing. The company offers services like CNC conversion and contract inspection.	408-980-8909	NA	Santa Clara
Ht Precision Inc (HQ)	Provider of prototype, research, and production parts and equipment. The company serves electronics, medical, wireless, and semi-conductor industries.	408-719-1826	NA	San Jose
Hydratight (BR)	Manufacturer of flanges and mechanical connectors. The company focuses on the subsea, nuclear, wind, and mining industries.	562-531-0973	NA	Paramount
IDEX Health & Science LLC (BR)	Provider of precision equipment for the health care industry. The company also offers detectors, fittings, and filters.	707-588-2000	NA	Rohnert Park
ILM Tool Inc (HQ)	Provider of engineering and CNC machining services. The company offers precision machining services for the biotech and semiconductor industries.	510-782-0100	11-50	Hayward
IMT Precision Inc (HQ)	Provider of sheet metal machining, fabrication, inspection and assembly services to semiconductor, aerospace, biotech, and education sectors.	510-324-8926	NA	Hayward
Inland Metal Technologies (HQ)	Provider of sheet metal fabrication, manufacturing, powder coating, silk-screening, and laser cutting services.	510-785-8555	NA	Hayward
Inta Technologies (HQ)	Manufacturer of components used in instruments for environmental analysis. The company also offers ceramic-to-metal assemblies connectors.	408-748-9955	NA	Santa Clara
Integrated Tooling Inc (HQ)	Developer and manufacturer of tools, dies, and molds. The company specializes in fabricating small intricate parts for machines.	408-934-3862	NA	Milpitas
International Manufacturing (HQ)	Manufacturer of precision components for use in semiconductor equipment, medical devices, aerospace vehicles, and defense systems.	510-783-8872	NA	Hayward
Intool (HQ)	Manufacturer and designer of the machine components. The company is involved in machining, fabricating, casting and assembling services.	408-727-7575	NA	Santa Clara
Inverse Solutions Inc (HQ)	Manufacturer of custom-made machines for commercial and government markers. The company serves semiconductor, medical devices, and aerospace fields.	925-931-9500	NA	Pleasanton
Italix Company Inc (HQ)	Provider of chemical machining, etching, and metal finishing services. The company serves the aerospace, defense, and transportation markers.	408-988-2487	NA	Morgan Hill
J C Sales & Mfg Co (HQ)	Manufacturer of CNC machining metal and plastic parts. The company offers products for the semiconductor, electronics, military, aircraft, and other industries.	800-527-6347	NA	Ione
J&E Precision Machining (HQ)	Manufacturer of electromechanical turnkey fixtures, prototype tooling, and EDM services. The company serves computer, medical, and other sectors.	408-281-1195	NA	San Jose
Jarvis Manufacturing (HQ)	Manufacturer of precision machinery. The company offers CNC turning and milling, programming, and assembly and kitting services.	408-226-2600	NA	San Jose
JB Precision Inc (HQ)	Manufacturer of precision machining services. The company's services also include inspection, production control, and management.	408-866-1755	NA	Campbell
JP Machine Manufacturing (HQ)	Manufacturer of machine parts. The company offers medical, semiconductor capital equipment, robotics, lasers, fiber optics, and test equipment.	408-988-1400	NA	Santa Clara
Jwp Manufacturing (HQ)	Provider of manufacturing solutions. The company offers CNC machining, engineering, and other services.	408-970-0641	NA	Santa Clara
Kal Machining Inc (HQ)	Manufacturer of medical, aeronautic, and military machine parts. The company offers CNC turning and milling services for plastic and metal parts.	408-782-8989	NA	Morgan Hill
Kalman Manufacturing (HQ)	Provider of manufacturing and machining services. The company offers welding, shearing, cutting, and finishing services.	408-776-7664	NA	Morgan Hill
KAMET Precision Machining & Assembly (HQ)	Provider of manufacturing solutions. The company offers engineering support, project management, and supply chain management solutions.	408-522-8000	NA	Milpitas
Kennerley-Spratling Inc (HQ)	Manufacturer of custom plastic injection and compression moldings. The company is involved in design, installation, and delivery services.	510-351-8230	NA	San Leandro

COMPANY NAME	PRODUCT / SERVICE	PHONE	EMP	CITY
Kodiak Precision Inc (HQ)	Manufacturer of precision machine products. The company's products include milling and turning machines, fabricated parts, and machine support equipment.	510-234-4165	NA	Richmond
KOR-IT Inc (HQ)	Manufacturer of diamond tools and core drill machines. The company caters to the concrete cutting industry.	916-372-6400	NA	Sacramento
Krobach Manufacturing Corp (HQ)	Provider of precision machine shop and general machining services. The company focuses on turning, milling, and grinding.	510-783-9480	NA	Hayward
N Ksd Inc (HQ)	Manufacturer and distributor of flight safety parts.	951-849-7669	1-10	Banning
L&T Precision Engineering Inc (HQ)	Provider of fabrication, precision engineering assistance, and assembly services. The company serves semiconductor, medical, and other sectors.	408-441-1890	NA	San Jose
Lamar Tool & Die (HQ)	Manufacturer of die casting solutions. The company's offerings include machining and secondary operations.	209-545-5525	NA	Modesto
Lamek Industrial Corp (HQ)	Manufacturer of machined parts for the semiconductor, medical, and aeronautic sectors. The company focuses on bead blasting, tumbling and packaging.	408-734-3363	NA	Sunnyvale
Langill's General Machine Inc (HQ)	Manufacturer of precision machined components with a full array of state-of-the-art machines, operated by a highly trained workforce.	916-452-0167	NA	Sacramento
Larkin Precision Machining Inc (HQ)	Manufacturer of machined parts of precision CNC milling and turning devices specializing in assemblies, fixtures, flanges, grinding, and sawing.	831-438-2700	NA	Scotts Valley
Lawson Mechanical Contractors (HQ)	Provider of mechanical construction services. The company offers plumbing, HVAC, industrial, and process piping services.	916-381-5000	NA	Sacramento
Lazestar Inc (HQ)	Provider of laser sealing, packing, precision fabrication, and welding services. The company serves the aerospace and commercial industries.	925-443-5293	NA	Livermore
Lenz Precision Technology Inc (HQ)	Manufacturer of precision machined components and sub assemblies. The company also focuses on the sales aspects.	650-966-1784	NA	Mountain View
Lfw Manufacturing (HQ)	Manufacturer of gearboxes and gear sets. The company caters to a wide range of industrial applications.	209-465-0444	NA	Stockton
N Linear Industries Ltd (HQ)	Manufacturer and distributor of electronic and mechanical automation control products.	626-303-1130	NA	Monrovia
Lodi Iron Works Inc (HQ)	Provider of machine shop services. The company offers in-house pattern making, tooling, machining, and iron casting services.	209-368-5395	NA	Lodi
Lor-Van Manufacturing (HQ)	Provider of precision sheet metal fabrication, laser cutting, welding, and electronic chassis and card cage assembly services.	408-980-1045	NA	Santa Clara
Luna's Sheet Metal Inc (HQ)	Provider of metal fabrication and precision metal working services for the computer electronics, telecommunications, and automotive industries.	408-492-1260	NA	Santa Clara
M & M Machine (HQ)	Designer and manufacturer of machined parts and components for automotive, laser, audio and video and body building equipment manufacturers.	530-268-2112	NA	Auburn
M A R's Engineering Company Inc (HQ)	Manufacturer of screw machines. The company also offers prototyping, fabrication, and assembly services.	510-483-0541	NA	San Leandro
M&L Precision Machining Inc (HQ)	Provider of machine shop services. The company offers precision fabricated components, semiconductors, and related devices.	408-224-2138	NA	Morgan Hill
Mac Cal (HQ)	Provider of sheet metals, assembly, cables and harnesses and engineering tools. The company deals with engineering services.	408-441-1435	NA	San Jose
Machinist Group (HQ)	Manufacturer of precision machined parts. The company serves defense, IR, laser components, prototype, and production industries.	408-842-8437	NA	Gilroy
Martinek Manufacturing (HQ)	Provider of painting, plating, silk screening, sheet metal fabrication, machining, and precision welding services.	510-438-0357	NA	Fremont
N Martinez and Turek Inc (HQ)	Provider of engineering and manufacturing services.	909-820-6800	NA	Rialto
Master Precision Machining (HQ)	Provider of precision machining services. The company offers engineering, finishing, metrology, and milling services.	408-727-0185	NA	Santa Clara
Maxon Precision Motors Inc (BR)	Provider of high-precision drives and systems. The company's products include brushed DC motors, brushless DC motors, spindle drives, and gearheads.	650-524-8822	NA	Foster City
Mcintire Machine Inc (HQ)	Provider of precision machining, welding, and fabrication services. The company offers services to the industrial sector.	209-837-4409	NA	Crows Landing
McKenzie Machining Inc (HQ)	Provider of precision machining services of pre-fabricated components. The company R&D, manufacturing design, and other services.	408-748-8885	NA	Santa Clara
Mcneal Enterprises Inc (HQ)	Provider of machined, fabricated, and thermoformed plastic components. The company serves medical, semiconductor, solar, optics, and other needs.	408-922-7290	NA	San Jose
MDA Precision (HQ)	Provider of benchtop milling machine and benchtop lathe systems. The company offers micro drilling machines, benchtop manual mills, and lathes.	408-847-7796	NA	Morgan Hill
Meadows Manufacturing (HQ)	Provider of engineering, design, and manufacturing solutions. The company serves the commercial and industrial sectors.	408-988-1252	NA	San Jose

COMPANY NAME	PRODUCT / SERVICE	PHONE	EMP	CITY
Mecoptron Inc (HQ)	Provider of precision machining services. The company's services include prototype machining, production machining, and precision mechanical assembly services.	510-226-9966	NA	Fremont
Metal Fusion Inc (HQ)	Provider of thermal spray technology services. The company's portfolio includes shaft repair, roll repair, and mechanical seal.	650-368-7692	NA	Redwood City
Micro Machine Shop (HQ)	Manufacturer of micro machines for telecommunications, microwave, semiconductor equipment, valve, laser, medical, and other industries.	209-848-8760	NA	Oakdale
Millennium Lapping & Grind Engineering (HQ)	Provider of lapping and grinding for CNC machining. The company specializes in single and double sided lapping diamond polishing of copper and silver.	510-438-9908	NA	Fremont
Minitool Inc (HQ)	Manufacturer of precision instruments and small tools for microscopic investigation. The company also specializes in under-microscope precision tools.	408-395-1585	NA	Campbell
N Mission Janitorial & Abrasive Supplies (HQ)	Manufacturer and distributor of chemicals, cleaners, and detergents.	858-566-6700	11-50	San Diego
Mission Tool and Manufacturing Company Inc (HQ)	Manufacturer of precision stamped and machined components. The company serves aerospace, automotive, medical, telecom, defense, and commercial sectors.	510-782-8383	NA	Hayward
MJB Precision Machining Inc (HQ)	Manufacturer of precision and prototype machining parts and components for the defense, telecom, medical, and semiconductor manufacturing industries.	408-559-3035	NA	Campbell
Modern Ceramics Manufacturing Inc (HQ)	Supplier of ceramic materials and components. The company serves the semi-conductor and laser industries.	408-383-0554	NA	San Jose
Modern Linear Inc (HQ)	Manufacturer of guide roller products. The company mainly focuses on linear motion industry and serves commercial, packaging, and medical fields.	415-924-7938	NA	San Rafael
N MPBS Industries (HQ)	Manufacturer and distributor of equipment and supplies for food processors and food packagers in the United States and around the globe.	323-268-8514	11-50	Los Angeles
National Fabtronix Inc (HQ)	Provider of custom fabrication and precision sheet metal services for the computer and medical industries.	510-785-3135	NA	Hayward
Nevarez Machining (HQ)	Manufacturer of fabricated machined parts. The company offers welding, machining, inspection, and software machining services.	408-279-1196	NA	San Jose
New World Machining (HQ)	Manufacturer of machined parts for the semiconductor, electronic, and security sectors specializing in prototype, production, and engineering design.	408-227-3810	NA	San Jose
Noron Precision Machining Inc (HQ)	Provider of machined parts for medical, microwave, aircraft, auto, computer peripheral, telecommunications, and biotech industries.	408-739-6486	NA	Sunnyvale
Nq Engineering Inc (HQ)	Provider of engineering services. The company specializes in fabricating, materials, inspection, and quality control.	209-836-3255	NA	Tracy
O&M Industries Inc (HQ)	Provider of industrial, mechanical, structural contractors, and fabrication services. The company serves cement industries.	707-822-8800	NA	Arcata
O'hara Metal Products (HQ)	Manufacturer of metal products. The company's products include springs, stampings, sheet metals, and wires EDM's.	707-863-9090	NA	Fairfield
Odie Sheet Metal Shop (HQ)	Provider of sheet metal fabrication solutions. The company also deals with manufacturing and prototype development.	408-281-2919	NA	San Jose
Ogletree's Inc (HQ)	Provider of metal and equipment fabrication services. The company focuses on design, detailing, fabrication, and installation services.	707-963-3537	NA	St. Helena
Omega Diamond Inc (HQ)	Developer and manufacturer of diamond tools for the ultra precise semiconductor and optics industry. The company also offers power tools.	530-889-8977	NA	Newcastle
OMW Corp (HQ)	Manufacturer of CNC machined parts. The company also deals with production machining, prototyping, and support services.	415-382-1669	NA	Novato
Oryx Advanced Materials Inc (HQ)	Provider of thin film materials for PV cells. The company also offers sputtering targets and bonding services to the magnetic data storage market.	510-249-1157	NA	Fremont
P&L Specialties (HQ)	Provider of engineering and fabrication services. The company's services include waterjet cutting and harvest lug washing.	707-573-3141	NA	Santa Rosa
Pacific Powder Coating & Manufacturing (HQ)	Provider of electrostatic powder coating and metal fabrication services. The company focuses on sandblasting and silkscreening services, and logistics.	916-381-1154	NA	Sacramento
Pacific Precision Machine Inc (HQ)	Provider of precision machining solutions. The company offers CNC turning and milling, procurement and assembly, and computer programming services.	209-588-9664	NA	Sonora
Paragon Swiss Inc (HQ)	Manufacturer of medical instruments, precision shafts, optical bench fixtures, and related supplies.	408-748-1617	NA	Santa Clara
Peartech Inc (HQ)	Provider of solutions for electronic, computer, networking, and medical applications. The company offers solutions for precision machining and sheet metals.	408-542-9550	NA	Sunnyvale
PEC Manufacturing (HQ)	Provider of customized electromechanical, electronic, and mechanical solutions such as cable and harness assemblies and electro-mechanical assemblies.	408-577-1839	NA	San Jose

	COMPANY NAME	PRODUCT / SERVICE	PHONE	EMP	CITY
	Pencom (HQ)	Provider of component solutions to OEM design engineers. The company focuses on supply chain management, technical product support, and logistics.	650-593-3288	NA	San Carlos
	Peninsula Spring Corp (HQ)	Provider of precision spring products. The company offers sheet metal stampings, electrical contacts, clips, and wire forms.	408-848-3361	NA	Gilroy
	Peridot Corp (HQ)	Provider of design for manufacturing and packaging. The company also manufacturers of medical components, miniature component and general product prototypes.	925-461-8830	NA	Pleasanton
	Perry Tool & Research Inc (HQ)	Designer and manufacturer of powder metal parts for OEMs. The company specializes in pulleys, bearings, cams, sprockets, and fasteners.	510-782-9226	NA	Hayward
	Phil Wood & Co (HQ)	Manufacturer of cycling and related recreation oriented products. The company focuses to offer maintenance-free hubs for cyclists.	408-569-1860	NA	San Jose
	Plastech (HQ)	Provider of machined and fabricated plastic products for the semiconductor, biological, and medical industries.	650-568-9206	NA	Menlo Park
	Plastikon Industries Inc (HQ)	Provider of contract manufacturing services for custom designed plastic injection molding, for medical, pharmaceutical and other industries.	510-400-1010	NA	Hayward
	Platron (HQ)	Provider of selective plating services. The company caters to design engineering, electronics, mechanical, and field service applications.	510-781-5588	NA	Hayward
N	PM Machining Inc (HQ)	Provider of inspection equipment and processing equipment for various sectors.	619-449-8989	NA	Santee
N	Power Machinery Center (HQ)	Distributor of quality material handling and warehouse equipment.	805-485-0577	51-200	Oxnard
	Precise Automation Inc (HQ)	Provider of industrial automation solutions. The company's products include robots, guidance controllers, and kinematics.	408-224-2838	NA	Fremont
	Precision Identity Corp (HQ)	Manufacturer of machined components for the medical device manufacturing industries. The company offers inspection, cleaning, and support services.	408-374-2346	NA	Campbell
	Precision Swiss Products Inc (HQ)	Manufacturer of precision machined components. The company serves medical, energy, and military industries.	408-433-5880	NA	Milpitas
	Pro-Tek Manufacturing Inc (HQ)	Provider of sheet metal fabrication and machining services. The company is involved in prototyping and manufacturing.	925-454-8100	NA	Livermore
	Process Engineers Inc (HQ)	Manufacturer of stainless steel equipment. The company also specializes in installation and other services.	510-782-5122	NA	Hayward
N	Product Slingshot Inc (HQ)	Provider of business services.	760-929-9380	NA	Carlsbad
	Production Robotics Inc (HQ)	Designer and manufacturer of specialty engineered automation systems. The company serves biotech, diagnostics, microsurgery, and other sectors.	510-777-0375	NA	San Leandro
	Progressive Concepts Machining (HQ)	Provider of welding, assembly, and machining services. The company also deals with inspection solutions and serves businesses.	925-426-0400	NA	Pleasanton
	Prunella Enterprises Inc (HQ)	Provider of custom machining and sub assembly services. The company serves the telecommunication and space sectors.	831-465-1818	NA	Santa Cruz
N	Pump Engineering Co (HQ)	Distributor of pumps, fluid handling systems and much more.	562-944-4768	51-200	Santa Fe Springs
	Qualdeval International (HQ)	Supplier of high-pressure fluid flow and special core analysis equipment. The company offers PCB fabrication and assembly, and other services.	844-247-2523	NA	Fremont
	Quality Machine Engineering Inc (HQ)	Provider of precision engineering solutions. The company serves the medical, semiconductor, aerospace, and other markers.	707-528-1900	NA	Santa Rosa
	Quality Metal Spinning & Machining Inc (HQ)	Provider of metal spinning, sputtering shielding, and purity coils. The company's services include packing, shipping, and handling.	650-858-2491	NA	Palo Alto
	Quality Quartz Engineering Inc (HQ)	Designer and manufacturer of solid quartz products for solar, fiber optic, semiconductor, and lighting industries.	510-745-9200	NA	Newark
	Quartet Mechanics Inc (HQ)	Provider of LED, MEMS, photovoltaics (PV) solar and medical/lab automation systems. The company also offers wafer sorting and packing products.	408-564-8901	NA	Santa Clara
	Rago & Son Inc (HQ)	Provider of metal stamping and machining services. The company's services include stamping, complete welding, and perforated tubing.	510-536-5700	NA	Oakland
N	Ralph E. Ames Machine Works (HQ)	Manufacturer of industrial machinery.	310-320-2637	NA	Torrance
	Rapid Accu-Form Inc (HQ)	Provider of thermoforming and pressure forming services. The company specializes in tool and die and prototyping services.	707-745-1879	NA	Benicia
	Rapid Precision Manufacturing Inc (HQ)	Provider of screw machining, surface grinding, sheet metal fabrication, tooling, and inspection services.	408-617-0771	NA	San Jose
	Ray L Hellwig (HQ)	Designer and manufacturer of tools. It's products find application in mechanical, process piping, and plumbing needs.	408-727-5612	NA	Santa Clara
N	Regal Machine & Engineering Inc (HQ)	Manufacturer of structural components for the military and commercial aerospace industry.	323-773-7462	NA	Maywood
	Responsible Metal Fab Inc (HQ)	Provider of precision sheet metal fabrication services. The company offers machining, electromechanical assembly, packaging, and delivery services.	408-734-0713	NA	Sunnyvale
	Riley Plastic Manufacturing Inc (HQ)	Provider of vacuum forming, vapor polishing, and assembly services. The company serves the medical and biotech industries.	650-366-5104	NA	Menlo Park

COMPANY NAME	PRODUCT / SERVICE	PHONE	EMP	CITY
Ripon Manufacturing Company Inc (HQ)	Fabricator of steel processing equipment. The company manufactures and installs peelers, sizers, hardshell crackers, hoppers, dryers, and sorters.	209-599-2148	NA	Ripon
RM Machining Inc (HQ)	Provider of precision machining services. The company caters to the aerospace, defense, medical, and energy sectors.	650-591-4178	NA	San Carlos
RMC Engineering (HQ)	Provider of automated safety systems, resurfacing tools, blowers, and related supplies. The company offers repair and replacement services.	408-842-2525	NA	Gilroy
Rock Systems Inc (HQ)	Provider of material handling solutions. The company offers hoppers, feeders, conveyors, separators, and related accessories.	916-921-9000	NA	Sacramento
Roger K Sherman Co (HQ)	Provider of microscope eyepiece reticles, calibration standards, and ruled master gages for the semiconductor and magnetic head industries.	650-941-8300	NA	Los Altos
Rollin J Lobaugh Inc (HQ)	Manufacturer of machined components. The company mainly manufactures screws and offers supporting services.	650-583-9682	NA	Belmont
Ron Witherspoon Inc (HQ)	Manufacturer of high precision parts. The company offers milling, turning, electrical discharge machining, and grinding services.	408-370-6620	NA	Campbell
Rotometals Inc (HQ)	Distributor of non-ferrous metal elements and alloys such as aluminum, antimony, bismuth, indium and more.	888-779-1102	NA	San Leandro
Rutter Armey Inc (HQ)	Provider of precision machining services. The company focuses on industrial hard chrome plating, welding, and metal spraying services.	559-237-1866	NA	Fresno
SAE Engineering Inc (HQ)	Provider of integrated turnkey assembly, precision machining, and sheet metal fabrication services to many sectors. The company also offers software.	408-987-9950	NA	Santa Clara
Samax Precision Inc (HQ)	Manufacturer and supplier of precision machined products. The company offers services like grinding and honing. It serves military and aerospace fields.	408-245-9555	NA	Sunnyvale
SC Mech Solution (HQ)	Manufacturer of electronic parts and components. The company provides CNC milling, tooling, design, and contract manufacturing services.	408-748-3380	NA	San Jose
Sharp Dimension Inc (HQ)	Provider of production and prototype machining services. The company serves semiconductor, medical, robotics, solar, defense, and other sectors.	510-656-8938	NA	Fremont
Silicon Valley Mfg (HQ)	Manufacturer and engineer of EDM prototype and production machining. The company's services include CNC milling, CNC turning, and manual machining.	510-791-9450	NA	Newark
Silvestre Manufacturing (HQ)	Provider of custom fabrication services. The company specializes in machining and prototype production.	408-988-0937	NA	Santa Clara
SJ Die Casting & Machining Corp (HQ)	Manufacturer of castings for computer, electronic, automotive, and military sectors specializing in sandblasting, deburring, and assembly services.	408-262-6500	NA	Lincoln
Small Precision Tools Inc (BR)	Manufacturer of chip bonding tools, fine ceramic, and machining parts. The company offers necessary technical support and services.	707-762-5880	NA	Petaluma
Snowline Engineering Inc (HQ)	Provider of precision machining and fabrication services. The company also engages in sheet metal and assembly.	530-677-2675	NA	Cameron Park
Solonics Inc (HQ)	Manufacturer of coded backboard systems and wire management products. The company focuses on design and delivery services.	510-471-7600	NA	Hayward
South Bay Solutions Inc (HQ)	Provider of manufacturing services for the semiconductor, medical, aerospace, solar, and petroleum industries.	650-843-1800	NA	Fremont
SP3 Diamond Technologies (HQ)	Provider of electronics thermal management, diamond-on-silicon applications, and enhanced cutting surface solutions.	408-492-0630	NA	Santa Clara
Specialty Precision Machining (HQ)	Provider of machining services. The company also offers turning, contouring, milling, engraving, and drilling services.	209-939-0546	NA	Stockton
Specialty Products Design Inc (HQ)	Provider of exhaust components. The company focuses on exhaust fabricators, CNC header flanges, stainless bellows, and sealing flanges.	916-635-8108	NA	Rancho Cordova
Sputnik Enterprises Inc (HQ)	Provider of finishing, painting, casting, CNC machining, model making, and custom product development services.	650-363-7576	NA	Redwood City
Stewart Tool Company Inc (HQ)	Manufacturer of CNC precision machine components. The company specializes in manufacturing pressure vessels and provides field and assembly services.	916-635-8321	NA	Rancho Cordova
Stockton Tri Industries Inc (HQ)	Provider of custom rolling, bending, forming, machining, metal fabrication, and field erection services.	209-948-9701	NA	Stockton
Sun Enterprise Inc (HQ)	Provider of ceramic and quartz machining products. The company specializes in the semiconductor, solar, laser, and structural industries.	510-657-6507	NA	Fremont
T & K Machine (HQ)	Designer and manufacturer of precision machines. The company also offers services like plating, labeling, powder coat, and silkscreen.	925-344-7091	NA	Livermore
T&T Precision Inc (HQ)	Provider of precision machining services. The company specializes in electronics, automotive, and semiconductor equipment.	510-429-8088	NA	Union City
Tapemation (HQ)	Manufacturer of machined parts and tools for the aircraft, marine, electronic, solar, and space communication industries.	831-438-3069	NA	Scotts Valley
Tecdia Inc (HQ)	Manufacturer of precision machine tools and fixtures. The company also specializes in cutting and scribing tools.	408-748-0100	NA	Campbell

	COMPANY NAME	PRODUCT / SERVICE	PHONE	EMP	CITY
	Technic Inc (BR)	Manufacturer of specialty chemicals, analytical control tools, and surface finishing products. The company offers electroplating and engineered powders.	408-287-3732	NA	San Jose
	Tecma Co (HQ)	Provider of CNC and conventional precision machining solutions. The company serves the aerospace, commercial, medical, and defense industries.	916-925-8206	NA	Sacramento
	Terminal Manufacturing Company LLC (HQ)	Designer and manufacturer of vacuum chalmers, pressure vessels, truck tanks, and assorted fabrications.	510-526-3071	NA	Berkeley
N	The Bit Shop Inc (HQ)	Provider of plastics machining, drilling and other industrial services.	408-262-0713	NA	Milpitas
	The Broach Masters Inc (HQ)	Manufacturer of broaches, disc shapers, disc shaper cutters, shank shapers, shank shaper cutters, gear shaper cutters, and spline broaches.	530-885-1939	NA	Auburn
N	The Ely Company Inc (HQ)	Manufacturer and distributor of machined components for aerospace and commercial industries.	310-539-5831	NA	Torrance
	Therma (HQ)	Provider of mechanical contracting services. The company also offers design and installation of environmental systems.	408-347-3400	NA	San Jose
N	Tomi Engineering Inc (HQ)	Manufacturer of aerospace, medical, commercial and electronic products.	714-556-1474	51-200	Santa Ana
	Trans Bay Steel (HQ)	Provider of structural steel construction services. The company offers heavy bridge piling and mechanical fabrication services.	510-719-4613	NA	Richmond
	Tri Tool Inc (HQ)	Manufacturer of precision machine tools. The company also deals with products rentals, construction, and maintenance services.	916-288-6100	NA	Rancho Cordova
	Tridecs Corp (HQ)	Manufacturer of machined metal and plastic parts. The company offers prototyping, product machining, engineering, and design and drafting services.	510-785-2620	NA	Hayward
	Tschida Engineering Inc (HQ)	Provider of CNC turning and milling, machining, and fabrication services. The company serves semiconductor, defense, medical, and environmental sectors.	707-224-4482	NA	Napa
	UC Components Inc (HQ)	Manufacturer of RediVac coated and electro-polished vented screws. The company serves high vacuum applications.	408-782-1929	NA	Morgan Hill
	UHV Sputtering Inc (HQ)	Manufacturer of semiconductor devices and vacuum equipment. The company is involved in sputtering and bonding services.	408-779-2826	NA	Morgan Hill
	Ultra Clean Technology (HQ)	Manufacturer of gas panel delivery systems. The company primarily caters to the semiconductor industry.	510-576-4400	NA	Hayward
	Uni-Fab Industries Inc (HQ)	Provider of precision sheet metal fabrication services. The company's equipment services include laser, punching and cutting, machining, and sawing.	408-945-9733	NA	Milpitas
	Unico Mechanical Corp (HQ)	Provider of replacement machine parts. The company's services include welding, repairs, onsite machining, welding, and millwright.	707-745-9970	NA	Benicia
	Unitech Tool & Machine Inc (HQ)	Manufacturer of custom finished parts, tooling, and fixtures. The company is specialized in milling and lathe fabrication, mechanical design consulting.	408-566-0333	NA	Santa Clara
	United Mechanical Inc (HQ)	Provider of precision sheet metal fabrication services for semiconductor, disk drive, medical, pharmaceutical, and aerospace equipment.	510-537-4744	NA	Union City
	United Pro-Fab Manufacturing Inc (HQ)	Provider of machining and fabrication services. The company offers services for the aircraft, semiconductors, telecommunications, and biotechnology sectors.	510-651-5570	NA	Fremont
N	United Western Industries Inc (HQ)	Provider of sheet metal fabrication, prototypes, tool and die, precision machining, CNC machining, welding, stamping, laser cutting and grinding.	559-226-7236	1-10	Fresno
	USK Manufacturing Inc (HQ)	Provider of precision sheet metal and machining services. The company also focuses on mechanical assembly.	510-471-7555	NA	Union City
	V&O Machine Inc (HQ)	Manufacturer of machined parts for agri, hydraulics, food processing, and veterinary applications. The company focuses on prototyping and CNC milling.	530-662-0495	NA	Woodland
	Vanderhulst Associates Inc (HQ)	Provider of precision machining and manufacturing services. The company serves the medical, analytical, and semiconductor industries.	408-727-1313	NA	Santa Clara
	W E Plemons Machinery Services Inc (HQ)	Provider of flange seals and automatic lidding attachments. The company's services include box designs and rebuilding.	559-646-6630	NA	Parlier
	Walters & Wolf (BR)	Provider of cladding services. The company specializes in design, engineering, fabrication, and delivery and installation.	510-490-1115	NA	Fremont
	Wema Inc (HQ)	Provider of tank sensors, gauges, and smoke detectors for automotive, marine, agricultural, and construction equipment.	408-453-5005	NA	San Jose
	Wenteq Inc (HQ)	Manufacturer of print, precision, machined components, and assemblies. The company serves the automotive, racing, and boat markers.	209-608-2374	NA	Lodi
	Wessdel Inc (HQ)	Provider of precision machining and engineering services for the military, aerospace, defense, and medical sectors.	408-496-6822	NA	San Jose
	West Coast Fab Inc (HQ)	Provider of precision electronic sheet metal fabrication services. The company specializes in finished products.	510-529-0177	NA	Richmond
	West Coast Surgical (HQ)	Manufacturer of surgical devices. The company offers designing, assembling and finishing of specialty surgical equipment.	650-728-8095	NA	Half Moon Bay

COMPANY NAME	PRODUCT / SERVICE	PHONE	EMP	CITY
White Industries (HQ)	Manufacturer of bicycle components. The company's products include cranks, front hubs, brackets, pedals, and related accessories.	707-769-5600	NA	Petaluma
Wiegmann & Rose (HQ)	Provider of custom heat exchangers, pressure vessels, and weldments. The company offers vacuum chalmers and pipe spool products.	510-632-8828	NA	Livermore
Wolfs Precision Works Inc (HQ)	Provider of precision machining solutions. The company's services include milling, turning, and surface gliding.	650-364-1341	NA	Menlo Park
Wra-Cal Industries Inc (HQ)	Manufacturer of precision machine products. The company's products include lathes, mills and grinders, drill press, and finishing equipment.	408-988-4696	NA	Santa Clara
Wrex Products Inc (HQ)	Provider of plastic injection molding, CNC machining and finishing, coating, and tool design and engineering services.	530-895-3838	NA	Chico
Wright Engineered Plastics (HQ)	Provider of medical components and devices. The company deals with custom plastic injection molding, tooling, and assembly related services.	707-575-1218	NA	Santa Rosa
York Machine Works (HQ)	Provider of engineering services. The company's services include machining, welding, pattern burning, and engraving.	707-963-4966	NA	St. Helena
Yuhas Tooling & Machining Inc (HQ)	Provider of tooling and machining products for the semiconductor, medical, aerospace, telecommunications, and electronics industries.	408-934-9196	NA	Milpitas

81 = Mechanical Connectors/Mounts

COMPANY NAME	PRODUCT / SERVICE	PHONE	EMP	CITY
CKC Engineering LLC (HQ)	Provider of custom equipment solutions for clinical, manufacturing, pharmaceutical, medical device, and drug delivery industries.	415-494-8225	NA	Oakland
Custom Alloy Corp (BR)	Manufacturer of metals for seamless and welded pipe fittings and forgings. The company's products are in alloy steels, nickel alloys, and carbon steels.	530-544-2836	NA	South Lake Tahoe
Durabrake Co (HQ)	Manufacturer of automotive products. The company's products include brake drums, rotors, and hubs for the aftermarket and OEMs.	408-748-0400	NA	Santa Clara
Hydratight (BR)	Manufacturer of flanges and mechanical connectors. The company focuses on the subsea, nuclear, wind, and mining industries.	562-531-0973	NA	Paramount
Laser Mark's LLC (HQ)	Provider of laser marking and engraving job shop services. The company serves the agriculture, food processing, automotive, and medical industries.	408-433-9333	NA	San Jose
Morgan Manufacturing Inc (HQ)	Manufacturer of auto body tools and tie-down equipment. The company caters to the flat bed trucking industry.	707-763-6848	NA	Petaluma
Pipe Shields Inc (HQ)	Designer and manufacturer of pre-insulated pipe supports, slides, guides, and anchors. The company's products include hanger types, shoes, and riser clamps.	800-538-7007	NA	Fairfield
Wrex Products Inc (HQ)	Provider of plastic injection molding, CNC machining and finishing, coating, and tool design and engineering services.	530-895-3838	NA	Chico

82 = Miscellaneous Fabricated/Stamped Parts

	COMPANY NAME	PRODUCT / SERVICE	PHONE	EMP	CITY
	Accu-Swiss Inc (HQ)	Manufacturer of precision CNC and screw machined products. The company's services include engineering, milling, and threading.	209-847-1016	NA	Oakdale
	American Precision Spring Corp (HQ)	Designer of electronic circuits. The company specializes in the design and fabrication of printed circuit boards.	408-986-1020	NA	Santa Clara
N	Ameriflex Inc (HQ)	Manufacturer of precision bellows, flanges, flexible metal hose and much more products for vacuum applications.	951-737-5557	201-500	Corona
	Armorstruxx (HQ)	Provider of ballistic and blast protection solutions. The company offers armor systems design and integration services.	209-365-9400	NA	Lodi
	ASC Profiles LLC (HQ)	Supplier of building products such as panels, roofing products, and standing seams. The company serves the commercial and residential markers.	916-372-0933	NA	West Sacramento
	Bay Area Circuits Inc (HQ)	Provider of engineering services that include fabrication, layout, and design services to the original equipment manufacturers.	510-933-9000	NA	Fremont
	Billington Welding & Manufacturing Inc (HQ)	Manufacturer of food process equipment and custom products. The company serves the construction, automotive, and food processing industries.	209-526-9312	NA	Modesto
	Bulling Metal Works Inc (HQ)	Manufacturer of pressure vessels and laser cutting machinery. The company also offers other custom fabrication products.	510-351-2073	NA	San Leandro
	California Contract Company (HQ)	Provider of metal fabrication and installation services. The company focuses on aluminum, stainless steel and glass, and bronze.	510-654-9375	NA	Richmond
	Capital Sheet Metal (HQ)	Manufacturer of custom countertops. The company deals with shearing, welding, laser cutting, and polishing services.	916-443-3761	NA	Sacramento
	Chris French Metal Inc (HQ)	Provider of fabrication services. The company offers design, installation, prototyping, and repair services.	510-238-9339	NA	Oakland
	CKC Engineering LLC (HQ)	Provider of custom equipment solutions for clinical, manufacturing, pharmaceutical, medical device, and drug delivery industries.	415-494-8225	NA	Oakland
	Custom Product Development Co (HQ)	Developer and manufacturer of mechanical components and turnkey assembly solutions. The company specializes in developing customized products.	925-960-0577	NA	Livermore
	Dawn VME Products (HQ)	Designer and manufacturer of enclosures, backplanes, chassis and card cage. The company also offers design services and power supplies.	510-657-4444	NA	Fremont
N	Decco Graphics Inc (HQ)	Manufacturer of steel rule dies and hand assembly for printing industry.	310-534-2861	NA	Harbor City

COMPANY NAME	PRODUCT / SERVICE	PHONE	EMP	CITY
Delta Turnstiles LLC (HQ)	Manufacturer of optical turnstiles. The company mainly caters to the corporate sector and the government.	925-969-1498	NA	Concord
Expedite Precision Works Inc (HQ)	Manufacturer of diverse products involving micro and custom machining and fabrication of metal and plastic. The company also manufactures vessels and tanks.	408-573-9600	NA	San Jose
N Hallock Coin Jewelry (HQ)	Manufacturer of coin jewelry products.	714-635-8247	NA	Anaheim
Ironmind Enterprises Inc (HQ)	Manufacturer of medical products with flower essences. The company's offerings also include gym equipment and training gears.	530-272-3579	NA	Nevada City
J&M Manufacturing Inc (HQ)	Provider of TIG, MIG and spot welding, silk-screening, contract manufacturing, and assembly services.	707-795-8223	NA	Cotati
Kraemer & Co Manufacturing Inc (HQ)	Provider of industrial equipment. The company specializes in dyers, sprayers, storage units, and heaters.	530-865-7982	NA	Orland
KSM Corp (DH)	Manufacturer of welded metal bellows for transportation, solar, pharmaceutical, and other sectors and provides build to print assembly services.	408-514-2400	NA	San Jose
Larson Electronic Glass (HQ)	Manufacturer of glass to metal sealing products. The company offers vacuum flanges, viewports, bellows, and electrical and fiber optics feedthroughs.	650-369-6734	NA	Redwood City
Laser Mark's LLC (HQ)	Provider of laser marking and engraving job shop services. The company serves the agriculture, food processing, automotive, and medical industries.	408-433-9333	NA	San Jose
Melrose Nameplate & Label Co (HQ)	Developer and manufacturer of ID nameplates, labels, and membrane switches. The company offers touchscreen assembly and decorative nameplates.	510-732-3100	NA	Hayward
Metalfx Inc (HQ)	Provider of sheet metal fabrication services for metal and wood products. The company is engaged in engineering and quality assurance services.	800-479-9451	NA	Willits
Microform Precision LLC (HQ)	Provider of metal cutting, bending, fabrication, and coating services. The company offers shearing, punching, forming, and painting services.	916-419-0580	NA	Sacramento
Minimatics Inc (HQ)	Provider of precision machining solutions. The company offers CNC milling, manual turning, lapping, and honing services.	650-969-5630	NA	Santa Clara
N Mission Janitorial & Abrasive Supplies (HQ)	Manufacturer and distributor of chemicals, cleaners, and detergents.	858-566-6700	11-50	San Diego
Modern Linear Inc (HQ)	Manufacturer of guide roller products. The company mainly focuses on linear motion industry and serves commercial, packaging, and medical fields.	415-924-7938	NA	San Rafael
Nor-Cal Metal Fabricators (HQ)	Provider of general industrial metal fabrication and parts. The company is engaged in contract manufacturing and structural rolling.	510-833-7157	NA	Oakland
Nq Engineering Inc (HQ)	Provider of engineering services. The company specializes in fabricating, materials, inspection, and quality control.	209-836-3255	NA	Tracy
Omni Fab (HQ)	Provider of precision sheet metal fabrication services. The company caters to the high technology industry.	408-492-1331	NA	Santa Clara
Pacific Precision Machine Inc (HQ)	Provider of precision machining solutions. The company offers CNC turning and milling, procurement and assembly, and computer programming services.	209-588-9664	NA	Sonora
Precision Welding Technologies Inc (HQ)	Provider of welding systems and components. The company's service include equipment maintenance, planning and maintenance, and job shop.	530-269-1826	NA	Auburn
PTR Manufacturing Inc (HQ)	Manufacturer of machining and sheet metals. The company offers manufacturing and manufacturing presentation services.	510-477-9654	NA	Union City
Qualdeval International (HQ)	Supplier of high-pressure fluid flow and special core analysis equipment. The company offers PCB fabrication and assembly, and other services.	844-247-2523	NA	Fremont
Rapid Accu-Form Inc (HQ)	Provider of thermoforming and pressure forming services. The company specializes in tool and die and prototyping services.	707-745-1879	NA	Benicia
Sanctuary Stainless (HQ)	Provider of metal fabrication services. The company specializes in stainless and aluminum tubing and pipe fabrication.	831-633-3867	NA	Moss Landing
Scandic (HQ)	Provider of machine tools. The company offers heat treatment, plating, engineering, and raw material guidance services.	510-352-3700	NA	San Leandro
Tobar Industries Inc (HQ)	Provider of contract manufacturing services. The company offers services for computer chassis, card cages, and frames.	408-494-3530	NA	San Jose
N Veridiam Inc (HQ)	Manufacturer of tubing, special purpose tubular components, and nuclear components.	619-448-1000	51-200	El Cajon
Weichhart Stamping Company inc (HQ)	Manufacturer of tools and metal stampings in the San Francisco area. The company's offerings include flat springs, wire forms, spring washers, and wave washers.	510-562-6886	NA	Santa Rosa
West Coast Fab Inc (HQ)	Provider of precision electronic sheet metal fabrication services. The company specializes in finished products.	510-529-0177	NA	Richmond
Wonder Metals Corp (HQ)	Provider of preventing environmental pollution services. The company's products include louvers, penthouses, and control dampers.	800-366-5877	NA	Redding
Woodmack Products Inc (HQ)	Manufacturer of tubes and pipes. The company also specializes in customized designs and engineering solutions.	916-853-6150	NA	Rancho Cordova

COMPANY NAME	PRODUCT / SERVICE	PHONE	EMP	CITY
Wright Engineered Plastics (HQ)	Provider of medical components and devices. The company deals with custom plastic injection molding, tooling, and assembly related services.	707-575-1218	NA	Santa Rosa

83 = Optoelectronics

COMPANY NAME	PRODUCT / SERVICE	PHONE	EMP	CITY
Blue Sky Research Inc (HQ)	Manufacturer of laser products and micro optics. The company designs and fabricates semiconductor based lasers and fiber optic cables.	408-941-6068	NA	Milpitas
Enablence Technologies Inc (DH)	Manufacturer of silicon products for communication needs. The company's offerings include optical splitters and channel filters.	510-226-8900	NA	Fremont
Inphenix Inc (HQ)	Designer and manufacturer of active optoelectronic chips and modules. The company serves telecom, defense, biomedical, and industrial markers.	925-606-8809	NA	Livermore
Medland & Associates Inc (BR)	Manufacturer of OEM products. The company's products include AC and DC converters, power supplies, switching regulators, and cable assemblies.	408-686-0460	NA	San Martin
Meivac Inc (HQ)	Manufacturer of sputtering systems and components. The company offers throttle valves, integrators, OEM assemblies, and substrate heaters.	408-362-1000	NA	San Jose
RAF Electronics (HQ)	Provider of optical system design and related services. The company deals with sales and delivery solutions.	925-551-5361	NA	San Ramon
N Reynard Corp (HQ)	Manufacturer of custom optical thin film coatings.	949-366-8866	11-50	San Clemente
Samtec (BR)	Manufacturer of high-speed assemblies, connectors, edge cards, and jumpers. The company serves the industrial sector.	812-944-6733	NA	Santa Clara

84 = Plastic Parts/Components

COMPANY NAME	PRODUCT / SERVICE	PHONE	EMP	CITY
Acrylic Art (HQ)	Provider of fabrication and machining services. The company focuses on painting, product finishing, anodizing, and vapor polishing.	510-654-0953	NA	Emeryville
Cal-Tron Corp (HQ)	Developer and manufacturer of cell reagent tools. The company's products find application in proteomic research.	760-873-8491	NA	Bishop
Caltron Components Corp (HQ)	Distributor of electronic capacitors and resistors. The company also focuses on semiconductor products.	408-748-2140	NA	Santa Clara
Collimated Holes Inc (HQ)	Designer and manufacturer of fiber optic components, sub-assemblies, and imaging systems. The company also provides design and manufacturing services.	408-374-5080	NA	Campbell
Delta Pacific Products Inc (HQ)	Provider of plastics injection molding and mold making services. The company serves the automotive, agriculture, aerospace, and recreational sectors.	510-487-4411	NA	Union City
Expedite Precision Works Inc (HQ)	Manufacturer of diverse products involving micro and custom machining and fabrication of metal and plastic. The company also manufactures vessels and tanks.	408-573-9600	NA	San Jose
Freetech Plastics Inc (HQ)	Manufacturer of pressure thermoforming products. The company's products include medical, scientific, and telecommunication enclosures.	510-651-9996	NA	Fremont
Grandt Line Products (HQ)	Manufacturer and wholesaler of model railroad miniatures in plastics. The company's services include design and installation.	925-671-0143	NA	Concord
Kennerley-Spratling Inc (HQ)	Manufacturer of custom plastic injection and compression moldings. The company is involved in design, installation, and delivery services.	510-351-8230	NA	San Leandro
Mcneal Enterprises Inc (HQ)	Provider of machined, fabricated, and thermoformed plastic components. The company serves medical, semiconductor, solar, optics, and other needs.	408-922-7290	NA	San Jose
nexTier Networks Inc (HQ)	Provider of data security services and solutions for vertical markers and original equipment manufacturers.	408-282-3561	NA	Santa Clara
Pacific Rubber & Packing Inc (HQ)	Provider of rubber seals, custom seals, rubber gaskets and o-ring products for medical/pharmacy, automotive, solar energy, and general industries.	650-595-5888	NA	San Carlos
Plastikon Industries Inc (HQ)	Provider of contract manufacturing services for custom designed plastic injection molding, for medical, pharmaceutical and other industries.	510-400-1010	NA	Hayward
Pre Plastics Inc (HQ)	Provider of engineering and precision tooling services. The company also offers plastic injection molding and assembly services.	530-823-1820	NA	Auburn
Product Components Corp (HQ)	Manufacturer of industrial plastic fasteners. The company offers screws, washers, pipe plugs, circuit board hardware, and other products.	925-228-8930	NA	Martinez
Solonics Inc (HQ)	Manufacturer of coded backboard systems and wire management products. The company focuses on design and delivery services.	510-471-7600	NA	Hayward
South Bay Solutions Inc (HQ)	Provider of manufacturing services for the semiconductor, medical, aerospace, solar, and petroleum industries.	650-843-1800	NA	Fremont
Stratamet Inc (HQ)	Provider of precision ceramic components. The company offers engineering support, quick response, and customer support.	510-651-7176	NA	Fremont
Wrex Products Inc (HQ)	Provider of plastic injection molding, CNC machining and finishing, coating, and tool design and engineering services.	530-895-3838	NA	Chico

85 = Sales, Distribution and/or Repair

COMPANY NAME	PRODUCT / SERVICE	PHONE	EMP	CITY
Ampteks Inc (HQ)	Provider of engineering solutions. The company provides alternatives for dichromate plating and electro silver plating.	925-493-7150	NA	Livermore

COMPANY NAME	PRODUCT / SERVICE	PHONE	EMP	CITY
Aurostar Corp (HQ)	Provider of technology products and services focusing on home theater systems, consumer electronics, desktops and notebooks, and networking solutions.	510-249-9422	NA	Fremont
R&R Refrigeration And Air Conditioning Inc (HQ)	Provider of environmental technological solutions. The company also offers maintenance and repair services for process systems.	408-297-0383	NA	San Jose

86 = Semiconductors & Related Devices

COMPANY NAME	PRODUCT / SERVICE	PHONE	EMP	CITY
ABX Engineering Inc (HQ)	Manufacturer of printed circuit board assemblies and electromechanical products for medical devices, agriculture, and military electronics industries.	650-552-2300	NA	Burlingame
AccelerATE Solutions Inc (HQ)	Provider of test engineering services. The company offers device characterization, applications support, and test program development services.	408-573-6066	NA	San Jose
Acu Spec Inc (HQ)	Manufacturer of engineering products. The company offers horizontal and vertical machining, CNC turning, CAD software, and CMM inspection services.	408-748-8600	NA	Santa Clara
Addison Engineering Inc (HQ)	Supplier of silicon wafers and semiconductor process components. The company's products include ceramic packages and semiconductor equipment.	408-926-5000	NA	San Jose
Advanced Component Labs (HQ)	Manufacturer of flip chips, thermal vias, build ups, and related supplies. The company's services include drilling, lamination, and engineering.	408-327-0200	NA	Santa Clara
Allvia Inc (HQ)	Provider of silicon interposer and through-silicon via foundry services to the semiconductor and optoelectronics industries.	408-212-3200	NA	Sunnyvale
Allwin21 Corp (HQ)	Provider of high-tech equipment, related services, and technical support for the semiconductor and biomedical industries.	408-778-7788	NA	Morgan Hill
Altamont Manufacturing Inc (HQ)	Provider of precision CNC machining, welding, and fabrication services. The company offers semiconductor, aerospace, medical, and robotics components.	925-371-5401	NA	Livermore
Ambarella Inc (HQ)	Developer of high-definition video compression and image processing solutions. The company's products are used in security IP cameras and sports cameras.	408-734-8888	51-200	Santa Clara
Amerimade Technology Inc (HQ)	Manufacturer of wet processing equipment. The company's equipment include fully and semi automated benches, chemical handling equipment, and process tanks.	925-243-9090	NA	Livermore
Analogix Semiconductor Inc (HQ)	Designer of mixed-signal semiconductors. The company offers input-output display translators, timing controllers, and accessory display converters.	408-988-8848	NA	Santa Clara
Arteris Inc (HQ)	Provider of interconnect semiconductor IP solutions to system-on-chip makers and serves networking, automotive, video and mobile-phone processors.	408-470-7300	NA	Campbell
Axelsys LLC (HQ)	Provider of electronic design and manufacturing services. The company's offerings include LED and AC to DC industrial power supplies.	408-600-0871	NA	San Jose
AXT Inc (HQ)	Designer, developer, manufacturer, and distributor of high performance compound semiconductor substrates.	510-438-4700	NA	Fremont
B&H Engineering (HQ)	Supplier of assemblies, process kits, and individual parts. The company caters to the semiconductor equipment industry.	650-594-2861	NA	San Carlos
BaySand Incorporated (BR)	Developer of metal only configurable ASIC. The company uses disruptive metal configurable standard cell technology for its products.	408-669-4992	NA	San Jose
Caltron Components Corp (HQ)	Distributor of electronic capacitors and resistors. The company also focuses on semiconductor products.	408-748-2140	NA	Santa Clara
Capital Asset Exchange & Trading LLC (HQ)	Provider of secondary capital equipment. The company offers evaporators, spectrometers, residual gas analyzers, and electronic testing equipment.	650-326-3313	NA	Santa Clara
Cavendish Kinetics Inc (HQ)	Supplier of tunable components for RF circuit applications. The company offers antennas, power amps, filters, and other products.	408-457-1940	NA	San Jose
Compugraphics USA Inc (BR)	Designer and developer of photomasks for semiconductor, optoelectronic devices, MEMs, nanotechnology, and renewable energy sectors.	510-249-2600	NA	Fremont
Corning Technology Center (BR)	Provider of specialty glass and ceramics services and sells keystone components to electronics, mobile emissions control, and life science industries.	650-846-6000	NA	Sunnyvale
Crocus Technology (HQ)	Manufacturer of magnetic switches, current sensors, and embedded memory products. The company serves the automotive and industrial sectors.	408-380-8300	NA	Santa Clara
Custom Microwave Components Inc (HQ)	Manufacturer of microwave components. The company also specializes in providing attenuators with control devices.	510-651-3434	NA	Fremont
Cyclos Semiconductor (HQ)	Provider of resonant mesh semiconductor IP, design automation tools, and design consulting services to mobile, wireless, and medical sectors.	510-649-3741	NA	Berkeley
Dawn VME Products (HQ)	Designer and manufacturer of enclosures, backplanes, chassis and card cage. The company also offers design services and power supplies.	510-657-4444	NA	Fremont
Delphon Industries LLC (HQ)	Provider of materials and services to the semiconductor, medical, photonics, telecommunications, and military markers.	510-576-2220	NA	Hayward

COMPANY NAME	PRODUCT / SERVICE	PHONE	EMP	CITY
EA Machining Inc (HQ)	Provider of CNC turning and milling services. The company offers services to the semiconductor manufacturing equipment industry.	408-727-4962	NA	Santa Clara
Ecomicron Inc (HQ)	Manufacturer of semiconductor equipment. The company caters to semiconductor, photovoltaic, and hybrid industries.	408-526-1020	NA	San Jose
EG Systems LLC (HQ)	Provider of test equipment such as wafer probers, prober-based test handlers, and test floor management solutions.	408-528-3000	NA	Dublin
Einfochips (HQ)	Provider of product design services and solutions. The company offers product engineering and semiconductor services.	408-496-1882	NA	San Jose
Elevator Controls Corp (HQ)	Manufacturer of non-proprietary microprocessor based elevator controllers. The company offers technical support and field services.	916-428-1708	NA	Sacramento
Enplas Tech Solutions Inc (RH)	Distributor of engineering plastic products. The company also offers optical devices, semiconductor peripherals, and related supplies.	669-243-3600	NA	Santa Clara
ESS Technology Inc (HQ)	Designer and marketer of video and audio semiconductors for the home, automotive, and entertainment markers.	408-643-8800	NA	Milpitas
Fil-Tech West Inc (BR)	Distributor of semiconductor parts and vacuum components. The company is engaged in troubleshooting and maintenance services.	925-251-8200	NA	Pleasanton
Formfactor Inc (HQ)	Provider of product and professional services to semiconductor manufacturers. The company also offers sales and support services.	925-290-4000	1001-5000	Livermore
Fuji Electric Corp of America (BR)	Provider of electric technology services. The company offers solutions for disk media, power supply, industrial systems, and radiation.	510-440-1060	NA	Fremont
Geo Semiconductor Inc (HQ)	Provider of imaging solutions. The company specializes in the design and fabrication of image sensors and multimedia processing engines.	408-638-0400	NA	San Jose
Globalfoundries Inc (BR)	Provider of semiconductor foundry services. The company deals with design tools, IP suppliers and ASIC partners.	408-462-3900	NA	Santa Clara
HTA Photomask (HQ)	Manufacturer of photo imaged products such as precision scales, resolution targets, and micro detectors.	408-452-5500	NA	San Jose
Impulse Semiconductor Inc (HQ)	Provider of electrostatic discharge and electrical overstress products and services. The company also provides virtual components and hardware.	408-355-5018	NA	San Jose
IMT Precision Inc (HQ)	Provider of sheet metal machining, fabrication, inspection and assembly services to semiconductor, aerospace, biotech, and education sectors.	510-324-8926	NA	Hayward
Intrinsic-Id Inc (HQ)	Designer of security solutions. The company offers services to semiconductor companies and device manufacturers.	408-933-9980	NA	Sunnyvale
JEM America Corp (RH)	Manufacturer and supplier of probe cards and tester interfaces. The company offers cantilever, vertical, and special-applications probe cards.	510-683-9234	NA	Fremont
JVD Inc (HQ)	Provider of custom integrated circuit design and test services. The company is also involved in wafer characterization.	408-263-7704	NA	Scotts Valley
Kyec USA (DH)	Provider of testing services. The company offers services for testing integrated circuit (IC) packaging.	408-452-7680	NA	San Jose
Lightwind Corp (HQ)	Provider of semiconductor manufacturing solutions. The company also deals with chemical analysis, process assessment, and refurbishment services.	707-981-4301	NA	Petaluma
Makel Engineering Inc (HQ)	Developer and provider of products and services for aviation, space, military, and commercial applications.	530-895-2770	NA	Chico
Micron Technology Inc (BR)	Designer and manufacturer of semiconductor systems for computing, networking, and communications applications.	408-855-4000	NA	Milpitas
Mikpower Technologies Inc (HQ)	Provider of lighting solutions. The company offers IC products for light bulbs, light tubes, and square lights.	408-493-5903	NA	San Jose
Mission Tool and Manufacturing Company Inc (HQ)	Manufacturer of precision stamped and machined components. The company serves aerospace, automotive, medical, telecom, defense, and commercial sectors.	510-782-8383	NA	Hayward
MultiDimension Technology Company Ltd (BR)	Supplier of TMR magnetic sensors. The company mainly offers switch, linear, angle, and gear tooth sensors.	650-275-2318	NA	San Jose
N&K Technology Inc (HQ)	Manufacturer of metrology tools for the semiconductor, photomask, data storage, flat panel display, and solar cell industries.	408-513-3800	NA	San Jose
Neomagic Corp (HQ)	Developer of electronic device solutions. The company sells hardware, software, and microcontrollers for IP cameras and vehicle toll collection.	408-428-9725	NA	Milpitas
Nugentec (HQ)	Provider of chemicals and polymers. The company offers oilfield chemicals, cleaners, and lubricants.	707-820-4080	NA	Emeryville
NXP Semiconductors (BR)	Manufacturer of amplifiers, diodes, data converters, microcontrollers, and bipolar transistors for the healthcare, automotive, and computing sectors.	408-551-2215	NA	San Jose
Owens Design (HQ)	Developer of advanced technology systems for semiconductor, hard disk drive, solar, medical device, and other sectors.	510-659-1800	NA	Fremont
PCT Systems Inc (HQ)	Manufacturer of semiconductor equipment and supplies. The company offers services to the semi-conductor industry.	510-657-4412	NA	Fremont
Pentagon Technologies (HQ)	Distributor of electromechanical components. The company offers shaft couplings, seals, and cable assemblies.	800-379-3361	NA	Hayward
Persys Engineering Inc (HQ)	Provider of parts cleaning, refurbishing and manufacturing, decontamination, and maintenance of assemblies and machine parts.	831-471-9300	NA	Santa Cruz

COMPANY NAME	PRODUCT / SERVICE	PHONE	EMP	CITY
Precision Contacts Inc (HQ)	Provider of replacement contacts for handler manufacturer. The company's products include sockets, contacts, elements, and custom products.	916-939-4147	NA	El Dorado Hills
Qualitau Inc (HQ)	Supplier of test equipment and services. The company is involved in the development of electronic equipment for semiconductor process reliability.	650-282-6226	NA	Santa Clara
Quicklogic Corp (HQ)	Provider of trading solutions for stock market investors. The company offers online trading platforms for mobiles, smartphones, and tablets.	408-990-4000	NA	San Jose
RCH Associates Inc (HQ)	Provider of engineering solutions. The company specializes in equipment used in space, solar, and semiconductor industries.	510-657-7846	NA	Livermore
Samsung Semiconductor Inc (HQ)	Provider of electronics manufacturing and digital media products. The company also offers mobile services and PC software.	408-544-4000	NA	San Jose
Sempac Inc (HQ)	Developer of pre-molded open-cavity plastic packages for optoelectronic, telecom, RF, MEMS, and sensor applications.	408-400-9002	NA	Los Altos
Silicon Storage Technology Inc (HQ)	Designer and manufacturer of memory and non-memory products. The company serves Internet computing markers.	408-735-9110	NA	San Jose
Sitime Corp (HQ)	Provider of programmable oscillators and clock generators. The company also offers embedded resonators.	408-328-4400	NA	Santa Clara
SMTC Corp (BR)	Provider of electronics manufacturing services for the industrial, medical, computing, and communication markers.	510-737-0700	NA	Fremont
Solid State Optronics (HQ)	Manufacturer of miniature Solid State Relays. The company offers MOSFET drivers, specialty products, and optocouplers.	408-293-4600	NA	San Jose
Solutions Cubed LLC (HQ)	Provider of engineering solutions. The company is involved in early stage electronic prototyping to full production runs.	530-891-8045	NA	Chico
Stats Chippac Inc (DH)	Provider of semiconductor packaging design, bump, probe, assembly, test, and distribution solutions.	510-979-8000	NA	Fremont
Sunsil Inc (HQ)	Provider of total electronics manufacturing solutions. The company offers wafer fabrication, component assembly, testing, and wafer probing services.	925-648-7779	NA	Alamo
TDK Corporation of America (BR)	Distributor of electronic products including capacitors, inductors, ferrites, factory automation system, transformers, magnets, and anechoic chalmers.	408-467-5200	NA	San Jose
Ultra T Equipment Company Inc (HQ)	Manufacturer of spin coaters, developer stations, reionizers, and microelectronics cleaning systems.	510-440-3909	NA	Fremont
Vacuum Process Engineering Inc (HQ)	Provider of engineering services. The company focuses on precision brazing, diffusion bonding, heat treating, and production of precision assemblies.	916-925-6100	NA	Sacramento
Valqua America Inc (HQ)	Seller and marketer of semiconductor related products. The company also offers R&D services for high performance elastomer seals.	408-986-1425	NA	Santa Clara
Vishay Intertechnology Inc (BR)	Manufacturer of electronic components. The company's products comprises of semiconductors and passive components used across industries.	408-727-2500	NA	Santa Clara
WPG Americas Inc (DH)	Distributor of electronic products. The company's portfolio includes encoders, sensors, solid state batteries, and timing devices.	408-392-8100	NA	San Jose
Xandex Inc (DH)	Designer and manufacturer of products for the semiconductor test industry. The company's products include automated test equipment and interface products.	707-763-7799	NA	Petaluma
YES Yield Engineering Systems Inc (HQ)	Manufacturer of process equipment for the semiconductor industry. The company offers products for surface modification and photoresist treatment.	510-954-6889	NA	Fremont

87 = Sensors

COMPANY NAME	PRODUCT / SERVICE	PHONE	EMP	CITY
Acoustic Emission Consulting Inc (HQ)	Specializes in acoustic emission inspection services and testing, and acoustic emission instrumentation, sensors, and probes.	916-965-4827	NA	Fair Oaks
Analatom Inc (HQ)	Provider of materials science research services focusing on product development in the field of micro electrical mechanical systems.	408-980-9516	NA	Santa Clara
Applied Physics Systems (HQ)	Supplier of magnetic measure and other electronic equipment. The company specializes in measurement while drilling systems and magnetometers.	650-965-0500	NA	Mountain View
Azbil North America Inc (BR)	Designer, manufacturer, and supplier of medical devices. The company offers automation products, control products, and industrial automation systems.	408-245-3121	NA	Santa Clara
Banpil Photonics Inc (HQ)	Developer and manufacturer of image sensors for automotive and medical imaging systems, security and surveillance, and machine vision applications.	408-282-3628	NA	Santa Clara
Baystar Electrument Inc (HQ)	Manufacturer of pressure sensors, pressure transducers and transmitters. The company deals with digital signal processing services.	408-272-3669	NA	San Jose
C3Nano Inc (HQ)	Developer of transparent conductive ink and film such as touch sensors, OLED lighting and displays, EMI shielding for touch sensor and display industry.	510-259-9650	NA	Hayward

COMPANY NAME	PRODUCT / SERVICE	PHONE	EMP	CITY
Capella Microsystems Inc (HQ)	Developer of integrated technology solutions for IC design. The company is involved in installation and technical support.	408-988-8000	NA	Santa Clara
Cleangrow (DH)	Manufacturer of sensors for the measurement of calcium, potassium, ammonium, magnesium, and fluoride ions.	415-460-7295	NA	Sacramento
CMOS Sensor Inc (HQ)	Designer and manufacturer of electro-optical image acquisition and also surveillance solutions for the medical market.	408-366-2898	NA	Cupertino
Corning Technology Center (BR)	Provider of specialty glass and ceramics services and sells keystone components to electronics, mobile emissions control, and life science industries.	650-846-6000	NA	Sunnyvale
Excel Precision Corp (HQ)	Designer and manufacturer of laser interferometer systems for measurement and calibration. The company's products include level sensors and angular sensors.	408-727-4260	NA	Santa Clara
eze System (HQ)	Provider or monitoring and measuring solutions. The company's products include controllers, controller expansions, and sensors.	716-393-9330	NA	Folsom
Fairchild Imaging Inc (DH)	Developer and manufacturer of solid-state electronic imaging components, cameras, and systems. The company's products include image sensors and cameras.	650-479-5749	NA	San Jose
Hamamatsu Corp (BR)	Manufacturer of devices for the generation and measurement of infrared, visible, and ultraviolet light.	408-261-2022	NA	San Jose
Jan Medical Inc (HQ)	Manufacturer of portable brain sensing devices for the detection of traumatic brain injuries, including concussions.	650-316-8811	NA	Mountain View
Jr3 Inc (HQ)	Designer and manufacturer of multi-axis force-torque sensors. The company caters to robotics and other applications.	530-661-3677	NA	Woodland
Kionix Inc (BR)	Manufacturer of MEMS inertial sensors. The company offers accelerometers, gyroscopes, and combination sensors.	408-720-1900	NA	Santa Clara
Lamdagen Corp (BR)	Developer of nano technology based biosensors used in research and diagnostic equipment for human and animal health testing.	650-571-5816	NA	Menlo Park
Lightwind Corp (HQ)	Provider of semiconductor manufacturing solutions. The company also deals with chemical analysis, process assessment, and refurbishment services.	707-981-4301	NA	Petaluma
Loadstar Sensors Inc (HQ)	Manufacturer of sensors and load cells with wireless output, used in medical device, automotive, aerospace, consumer and other industries.	510-274-1872	NA	Fremont
Makel Engineering Inc (HQ)	Developer and provider of products and services for aviation, space, military, and commercial applications.	530-895-2770	NA	Chico
Mil-Ram Technology Inc (HQ)	Manufacturer of industrial gas and detection systems. The company serves the oil and gas, pulp and paper, and chemical industries.	510-656-2001	NA	Fremont
Neurosky Inc (HQ)	Manufacturer of ECG biosensors and also EEG biosensors for mobile solutions, wearable devices, and service providers.	408-200-6675	NA	San Jose
NK Technologies (HQ)	Manufacturer of current sensors and transducer products for the factory and industrial automation markers.	408-871-7510	NA	San Jose
Pasco Scientific (HQ)	Provider of technology-based solutions for hands-on science services. The company is engaged in technical support.	916-786-3800	NA	Roseville
Peloton Technology (HQ)	Developer of truck platooning systems. The company offers services to the transportation, trucking, and railroad industries.	650-395-7356	NA	Mountain View
PNI Sensor (BR)	Manufacturer of electronic sensors. The company designs and fabricates processors, three-axis controllers, and geomagnetic sensors.	707-566-2260	NA	Santa Rosa
Scepter Scientific Inc (HQ)	Provider of feasibility evaluations, electronic, optical, and mechanical engineering, and prototype development services.	925-373-4802	NA	Livermore
Seevider Inc (HQ)	Manufacturer of smart vision devices. The company's products are used in light management, parking occupancy detection, and guiding.	408-930-0852	NA	Santa Clara
Sensifree (HQ)	Manufacturer of contactless sensors for wearables. The company offers heart rate sensors, including fitness trackers, and activity monitors.	669-230-5116	NA	Cupertino
Sensys Networks Inc (HQ)	Manufacturer of wireless sensor cubes, repeaters, and related accessories. The company's services include training and technical support.	510-548-4620	NA	Berkeley
Sierra Instruments Inc (HQ)	Manufacturer of mass flow meters and mass flow controllers. The company serves gas, liquid, and steam applications.	831-373-0200	NA	Monterey
Solutions Cubed LLC (HQ)	Provider of engineering solutions. The company is involved in early stage electronic prototyping to full production runs.	530-891-8045	NA	Chico
Speedinfo (HQ)	Developer of traffic measurement solutions for broadcast media, government planning, and mobile applications.	408-446-7660	NA	San Jose
Telemakus LLC (HQ)	Provider of USB controlled RF devices. The company devices include switches, vector modulators, and digital attenuators.	916-458-6346	NA	Folsom
Toppan Printing Company Ltd (BR)	Provider of printing solutions. The company serves customers in the food, beverage, and high barrier product industries.	415-393-9839	NA	San Francisco
Vishay Intertechnology Inc (BR)	Manufacturer of electronic components. The company's products comprises of semiconductors and passive components used across industries.	408-727-2500	NA	Santa Clara
Westport Machine Works Inc (HQ)	Manufacturer of assembly and balancing equipment. The company's services include fixturing, installation, and technical support.	916-371-4493	NA	West Sacramento

88 = Sheet Metal Parts

COMPANY NAME	PRODUCT / SERVICE	PHONE	EMP	CITY
ABCO Wire & Metal Products (BR)	Designer and manufacturer of display racks. The company focuses on roller grill, drying racks, and POP displays.	510-909-5626	NA	Castro Valley
Advantage Metal Products (HQ)	Provider of sheet metal and machining services. The company offers painting and silk screening, forming, welding, and machine shop services.	925-667-2009	NA	Livermore
Aire Sheet Metal (HQ)	Provider of mechanical and architectural sheet metal services. The company is involved in the design and construction of commercial projects.	650-364-8081	NA	Redwood City
Airtronics Metal Products Inc (HQ)	Manufacturer of sheet metal fabrication and machining. The company provides custom sheets for the electronics, telecommunications and other markers.	408-977-7800	NA	Morgan Hill
All Fab Precision Sheetmetal Inc (HQ)	Provider of contract manufacturing services for metal formed products. The company is involved in laser cutting, deburring, bending, and welding activities.	408-279-1099	NA	San Jose
Angels Sheet Metal Inc (HQ)	Provider of sheet metal fabrication services. The company focuses on heating and air conditioning systems.	209-736-4541	NA	Angels Camp
Art's Sheet Metal Manufacturing Inc (HQ)	Manufacturer of flashings, vents, drainage products, tie plates, and hangers. The company also focuses on distribution aspects.	408-778-0606	NA	Morgan Hill
Asepco Corp (HQ)	Manufacturer of valves and magnetic mixers. The company also offers diaphragms, connectors, and actuators.	650-691-9500	NA	Milpitas
Cofan USA Inc (HQ)	Developer and manufacturer of products for thermal engineering. The company specializes in fans, heat sinks, and custom products.	510-490-7533	NA	Fremont
Concord Sheet Metal (HQ)	Provider of architectural metal products. The company focuses on fasteners, copper gutters, and decorative chimney tops.	925-680-8723	NA	Pittsburg
Custom Product Development Co (HQ)	Developer and manufacturer of mechanical components and turnkey assembly solutions. The company specializes in developing customized products.	925-960-0577	NA	Livermore
Group Manufacturing Services Inc (HQ)	Manufacturer of precision sheet metal fabrication, precision machining, and design support services.	408-436-1040	NA	San Jose
Inland Metal Technologies (HQ)	Provider of sheet metal fabrication, manufacturing, powder coating, silk-screening, and laser cutting services.	510-785-8555	NA	Hayward
Johnson Industrial Sheet Metal Inc (HQ)	Designer, fabricator, and installer of blowpipe systems, custom fabricated products, and packaged system projects.	916-927-8244	NA	Sacramento
Lawson Mechanical Contractors (HQ)	Provider of mechanical construction services. The company offers plumbing, HVAC, industrial, and process piping services.	916-381-5000	NA	Sacramento
Luna's Sheet Metal Inc (HQ)	Provider of metal fabrication and precision metal working services for the computer electronics, telecommunications, and automotive industries.	408-492-1260	NA	Santa Clara
M-T Metal Fabrication Inc (HQ)	Provider of sheet metal solutions. The company offers CNC laser cutting, precision welding, gaining, PEM fastening, and silk screen.	510-357-5262	NA	San Leandro
Melrose Nameplate & Label Co (HQ)	Developer and manufacturer of ID nameplates, labels, and membrane switches. The company offers touchscreen assembly and decorative nameplates.	510-732-3100	NA	Hayward
Micro Lithography Inc (HQ)	Manufacturer of pellicles using high end equipment for the production of frames and engineering parts, automatic anodizing lines, and chemical labs.	408-747-1769	NA	Sunnyvale
Oneto Metal Products Corp (HQ)	Manufacturer of fabricated sheet metal products. The company offers flashing, roof jacks, gravel stop and specialty architectural sheet metal.	916-681-6555	NA	Sacramento
PEC Manufacturing (HQ)	Provider of customized electromechanical, electronic, and mechanical solutions such as cable and harness assemblies and electro-mechanical assemblies.	408-577-1839	NA	San Jose
Pega Precision Inc (HQ)	Manufacturer and marketer of precision sheet metal and machining components. The company serves the military, semiconductor, and solar industries.	408-776-3700	NA	Morgan Hill
Peridot Corp (HQ)	Provider of design for manufacturing and packaging. The company also manufacturers of medical components, miniature component and general product prototypes.	925-461-8830	NA	Pleasanton
Photo Etch Technology (BR)	Provider of stainless steel stencils. The company offers epoxy stencils, precision metal parts, fixture pallets, mesh screens, and artwork services.	408-988-0220	NA	Santa Clara
Procurement Partners International Inc (HQ)	Provider of procurement services. The company offers mechanical components such as pins, rods, rollers, and sheet metal.	650-345-6118	NA	San Mateo
Qualdeval International (HQ)	Supplier of high-pressure fluid flow and special core analysis equipment. The company offers PCB fabrication and assembly, and other services.	844-247-2523	NA	Fremont
Responsible Metal Fab Inc (HQ)	Provider of precision sheet metal fabrication services. The company offers machining, electromechanical assembly, packaging, and delivery services.	408-734-0713	NA	Sunnyvale
SAE Engineering Inc (HQ)	Provider of integrated turnkey assembly, precision machining, and sheet metal fabrication services to many sectors. The company also offers software.	408-987-9950	NA	Santa Clara

COMPANY NAME	PRODUCT / SERVICE	PHONE	EMP	CITY
Sanctuary Stainless (HQ)	Provider of metal fabrication services. The company specializes in stainless and aluminum tubing and pipe fabrication.	831-633-3867	NA	Moss Landing
Terminal Manufacturing Company LLC (HQ)	Designer and manufacturer of vacuum chalmers, pressure vessels, truck tanks, and assorted fabrications.	510-526-3071	NA	Berkeley
United Sheetmetal Inc (BR)	Manufacturer of precision metal products. The company specializes in tooling, die casting, plastic injection, and sheet metal fabrication services.	510-257-1858	NA	Fremont
Wellmade Products (HQ)	Manufacturer of lighting, wheelbarrows, and sheet metal products. The company also offers photometric sheets.	209-723-9120	NA	Merced
Westfab Manufacturing Inc (HQ)	Manufacturer of simple brackets, multiple level frames, and enclosures. The company offers assembly services for power supplies, switches, and cables.	408-727-0550	NA	Santa Clara

89 = Computer Systems (Hardware)

Square Inc (HQ)	Builds tools to empower and enrich people and help sellers of all areas to start, run, and grow their businesses.	415-375-3176	NA	San Francisco

90 = CAD/CAM/CAE Workstations

Synapse Design (HQ)	Provider of embedded software design services. The company also offers test bench analysis and block and chip level verification services.	408-850-9527	NA	Santa Clara

91 = Computer Boards

Advantech Inc (DH)	Provider of system integration, hardware, software, embedded systems, automation products, and logistics support.	408-519-3898	NA	Milpitas
Alphaems Corp (HQ)	Provider of printed circuit board prototyping and PCB assembly production services. The company also involves in material purchasing and warehousing.	510-498-8788	NA	Fremont
DIGICOM Electronics Inc (HQ)	Provider of electronics manufacturing services. The company also deals with packing, shipping, and labeling services.	510-639-7003	NA	Oakland
Entech Electronics (BR)	Supplier of electronic equipment. The company also offers laser cut stencils, graphic decals, LCD screens, and engineering services.	408-730-2650	NA	Santa Clara
Exxact Corp (HQ)	Supplier of workstation graphic cards and solutions. The company also offers servers, HPC clusters, and computing software.	510-226-7366	NA	Fremont
FLYTECH Technology Company Ltd (BR)	Developer and manufacturer of touch screen, LCD, and other peripherals. The company also designs motherboard.	510-257-5180	NA	San Jose
Genstor Systems Inc (HQ)	Provider of customized hardware solutions for server, storage, clusters, personal computers, and workstations.	408-980-0121	NA	Santa Clara
Ibase Technology (USA) Inc (BR)	Developer of embedded products such as industrial motherboards, CPU modules, barebone systems, network appliances, and digital surveillance systems.	408-992-0888	NA	Sunnyvale
Inbus Engineering (HQ)	Manufacturer and supplier of obsolete Intel boards emulators. The company offers repair and replacement and disk transfer services.	925-454-2500	NA	Livermore
Intel Corp (HQ)	Designer, developer, and marketer of processors and motherboards. The company also focuses on tablets, laptops, desktops, and other devices.	408-765-8080	NA	Santa Clara
Jetway Computer Corp (HQ)	Manufacturer of motherboards and LCD monitors. The company also specializes in graphic cards and barebones systems.	510-857-0130	NA	Newark
Max Group Corp (HQ)	Distributor for computing devices. The company offers computer cases, fans and heatsinks, and hard drives.	888-644-4629	NA	Fremont
Murdoc Technology (HQ)	Manufacturer of electronics. The company primarily offers precision and wire harnesses and cables to various sectors.	559-497-1580	NA	Fresno
NVIDIA Corp (HQ)	Provider of visual computing solutions that include video games, movie production, product design, medical diagnosis, and scientific research.	408-486-2000	NA	Santa Clara
PFU America Inc (BR)	Provider of technology solutions. The company designs, develops, and sells computer hardware, peripheral products, and systems.	408-992-2900	NA	Sunnyvale
Synapse Design (HQ)	Provider of embedded software design services. The company also offers test bench analysis and block and chip level verification services.	408-850-9527	NA	Santa Clara
Vicom Systems Inc (HQ)	Provider of migration data services. The company is involved in offering transparent wire-speed data services for systems and storage.	408-588-1286	NA	Santa Clara
X-Scan Imaging Corp (HQ)	Supplier of x-ray imaging and inspection equipment. The company also offers array detectors and line-scan camera products.	408-432-9888	NA	San Jose

92 = Computer Terminals

ASA Computers Inc (HQ)	Manufacturer of full service custom servers and storage systems. The company also focuses on integration.	650-230-8000	NA	Mountain View
Exxact Corp (HQ)	Supplier of workstation graphic cards and solutions. The company also offers servers, HPC clusters, and computing software.	510-226-7366	NA	Fremont
Ibus Corp (HQ)	Manufacturer and provider of industrial computers. The company also specializes in prototyping and quality control.	408-450-7880	NA	Santa Clara
Max Group Corp (HQ)	Distributor for computing devices. The company offers computer cases, fans and heatsinks, and hard drives.	888-644-4629	NA	Fremont
Omni Pro Systems (HQ)	Supplier and integrator of computer systems. The company offers custom logo engraving services and deployment ready solutions.	415-648-1121	NA	San Francisco

COMPANY NAME	PRODUCT / SERVICE	PHONE	EMP	CITY
Patriot Memory Inc (HQ)	Developer of flash memory solutions. The company offers memory modules, flash cards, USB drives, gaming memory cards, and accessories.	510-979-1021	NA	Fremont
Posiflex Business Machines Inc (HQ)	Provider of point of service hardware and platform technology. The company caters to diverse markers.	510-429-7097	NA	Hayward
Spracht (HQ)	Designer and manufacturer of consumer electronic products. The company offers digital imaging, acoustics, LCD image displays, and other products.	650-215-7500	NA	Palo Alto
TRI MAP International Inc (HQ)	Manufacturer of industrial grade rack mounts and desktop computers. The company is engaged in engineering and fabrication services.	209-234-0100	NA	Stockton
Ultraview Corp (BR)	Provider of data acquisition solutions, bus extenders, synthesizers, and direct digital synthesizers.	925-253-2960	NA	Berkeley

93 = Computers (Mainframe, Micro, Mini & Personal)

COMPANY NAME	PRODUCT / SERVICE	PHONE	EMP	CITY
Acer America Corp (HQ)	Supplier of desktops, notebooks, tablets, monitors and projectors. The company also offers application and support services.	408-533-7700	NA	San Jose
Advanced Digital Solutions International Inc (HQ)	Provider of information technology solutions. The company provides backup media tapes, barcode labels, tape drives, and data center supplies.	510-490-6667	NA	Pleasanton
Advanced Micro Devices Inc (HQ)	Provider of products such as desktops, notebooks, servers, workstations, and embedded systems. The company also offers a variety of software.	408-749-4000	NA	Santa Clara
Alphaems Corp (HQ)	Provider of printed circuit board prototyping and PCB assembly production services. The company also involves in material purchasing and warehousing.	510-498-8788	NA	Fremont
American Portwell Technology Inc (DH)	Designer and manufacturer of industrial PC products. The company also offers embedded computing, network appliances, and human machine interfaces.	510-403-3399	NA	Fremont
Arista Corp (HQ)	Manufacturer of industrial computer products such as industrial rack mounts, touch screen displays, and fanless, embedded, and wall mount computers.	510-226-1800	NA	Fremont
Aurostar Corp (HQ)	Provider of technology products and services focusing on home theater systems, consumer electronics, desktops and notebooks, and networking solutions.	510-249-9422	NA	Fremont
Durabook Americas Inc (BR)	Manufacturer of portable notebook computers. The company offers rugged notebook and tablet PC, parts, and accessories.	510-492-0828	NA	Fremont
ELMA Electronic Inc (HQ)	Designer and manufacturer of electronic components and enclosures. The company is involved in design, installation, and delivery services.	510-656-3400	NA	Fremont
Elo Touch Solutions Inc (HQ)	Designer, developer, and manufacturer of touch products and technologies. The company's products include tablets, touchscreens, and touch monitors.	408-597-8000	NA	Milpitas
Landel (HQ)	Provider of telecommunication products such as MailBug, DataBug, and SurveyBug. The company is engaged in technical support services.	408-360-0490	NA	San Jose
Max Group Corp (HQ)	Distributor for computing devices. The company offers computer cases, fans and heatsinks, and hard drives.	888-644-4629	NA	Fremont
Omni Pro Systems (HQ)	Supplier and integrator of computer systems. The company offers custom logo engraving services and deployment ready solutions.	415-648-1121	NA	San Francisco
Polywell Computers (HQ)	Manufacturer of computer systems. The company specializes in desktop PCs, workstations, and servers.	650-583-7222	NA	S San Francisco
Recortec Inc (HQ)	Manufacturer of LCD monitors, KVM, keyboards, speakers, and computers. The company also offers customization services.	408-928-1480	NA	San Jose
N Shuttle Computer Group Inc (HQ)	Manufacturer and distributor of motherboards, barebones computers, complete PC systems, and monitors.	626-820-9000	11-50	City Of Industry
Super Micro Computer Inc (HQ)	Provider of server technology and computing solutions. The company offers networking, gaming, micro cloud, and AMD services.	408-503-8000	NA	San Jose
Toshiba America Inc (BR)	Manufacturer of LCD, laptop batteries, power adapters, laptop cases, and other laptop related accessories.	408-526-2400	NA	San Jose
Tyan Computer Corp (DH)	Designer and manufacturer of server/workstation platforms. The company's products are sold to OEMs, VARs, system integrators, and resellers.	510-651-8868	NA	Fremont

94 = Controllers

COMPANY NAME	PRODUCT / SERVICE	PHONE	EMP	CITY
Arcus Technology Inc (HQ)	Provider of motor controllers, stepper motors, and related accessories such as cables, encoders, and gearboxes.	925-373-8800	NA	Livermore
Automation Partners Inc (HQ)	Manufacturer of controls for control systems and regulators. The company specializes in products for fabric density measurement.	707-665-3980	NA	Rohnert Park
AverLogic Technologies Inc (HQ)	Designer and seller of integrated ICs. The company primarily caters to multimedia and video applications.	408-526-0400	NA	San Jose
Blair Electric Services Inc (HQ)	Provider of electrical contracting services. The company offers pump and well controls, PLC controls, and surveillance systems.	559-784-8658	NA	Porterville

COMPANY NAME	PRODUCT / SERVICE	PHONE	EMP	CITY
Curtis Instruments Inc (BR)	Manufacturer of hydraulic pump controllers. The company also specializes in electric steering controllers.	925-961-1088	NA	Livermore
Digital View Inc (HQ)	Developer and manufacturer of flat panel-related products. The company's offerings include media players, video flyers, and accessories.	408-782-7773	NA	Morgan Hill
Futronix Inc (HQ)	Designer and developer of energy management systems. The company provides computer line clocks, electronic cam systems, and energy control systems.	408-735-1122	NA	Santa Clara
Galil Motion Control (HQ)	Manufacturer and supplier of motion controllers and software tools. The company also offers drives and power supplies.	916-626-0101	NA	Rocklin
GCX Corp (HQ)	Provider of mounting solutions, application specific solutions, on-site services, and also technical support.	707-773-1100	NA	Petaluma
Highland Technology Inc (HQ)	Designer and manufacturer of precision analog instrumentation. The company serves laboratory research purposes.	415-551-1700	NA	San Francisco
ICS Electronics (HQ)	Provider of interfaces and controllers for assembling systems, interfacing devices, and legacy systems.	925-416-1000	NA	Hayward
Lucidport Technology Inc (HQ)	Provider of semiconductor solutions. The company offers USB and wireless USB controllers for printers, scanners, digital cameras, and TV tuners.	408-720-8800	NA	Saratoga
Modutek Corp (HQ)	Manufacturer of wet process equipment and environmental systems. The company serves the semiconductor sector and offers repair services.	408-362-2000	NA	San Jose
O2micro USA (LH)	Provider of battery and power management products. The company also offers LED general lighting and backlighting products.	408-987-5920	NA	Santa Clara

95 = Storage & Disk

COMPANY NAME	PRODUCT / SERVICE	PHONE	EMP	CITY
Addonics Technologies Inc (HQ)	Manufacturer of storage systems and products. The company's products include drive cartridge system, host controller, converter, and adapter.	408-573-8580	NA	San Jose
Ampex Data Systems (HQ)	Manufacturer of digital storage systems. The company also offers airborne and ground systems and related video solutions.	650-367-2011	NA	Hayward
ASA Computers Inc (HQ)	Manufacturer of full service custom servers and storage systems. The company also focuses on integration.	650-230-8000	NA	Mountain View
N Athana International Inc (HQ)	Provider of computer storage devices.	310-539-7280	NA	Redondo Beach
Avalanche Technology (HQ)	Provider of programmable storage solutions. The company offers services to the consumer electronics industry.	510-897-3300	NA	Fremont
BITMICRO Networks Inc (HQ)	Developer and manufacturer of flash-based SSD technology, products, and solutions. The company focuses on cloud computing and gaming applications.	888-723-0123	NA	Fremont
Chelsio Communications (HQ)	Provider of Ethernet adapters. The company offers storage routers, wire adapters, virtualization and management software, and accessories.	408-962-3600	NA	Sunnyvale
Data Distributing LLC (HQ)	Provider of solutions such as mass storage, peripheral, storage management software, import, archive, and images and data distribution.	831-457-3537	NA	Santa Cruz
DataDirect Networks Inc (BR)	Provider of storage array, file system, and object storage appliances to broadcast, biopharma, supercomputing, and financial service sectors.	408-419-2800	NA	Santa Clara
Drobo Inc (HQ)	Provider of virtualization and backup and archiving services. The company also offers disaster recovery and cloud storage solutions.	408-454-4200	NA	Sunnyvale
Exxact Corp (HQ)	Supplier of workstation graphic cards and solutions. The company also offers servers, HPC clusters, and computing software.	510-226-7366	NA	Fremont
Genstor Systems Inc (HQ)	Provider of customized hardware solutions for server, storage, clusters, personal computers, and workstations.	408-980-0121	NA	Santa Clara
Guzik Technical Enterprises (HQ)	Manufacturer of test equipment for the computer industry. The company is involved in sales, training, and software downloads.	408-752-5840	NA	Mountain View
Headway Technologies Inc (HQ)	Designer and manufacturer of hard-disk drives. The company is engaged in installation and technical support services.	408-934-5300	NA	Milpitas
Hyve Solutions (HQ)	Designer of data center serve, storage, networking and appliance solutions. The company specializes in rack integration services.	510-668-3877	NA	Fremont
Innodisk USA Corp (BR)	Provider of embedded flash and dynamic random access memory storage products and technology solutions.	510-770-9421	NA	Fremont
Intevac Inc (HQ)	Supplier of magnetic media processing systems. The company offers advanced equipment to the hard disk drive, solar, and photonics industries.	408-986-9888	NA	Santa Clara
ioSafe Inc (HQ)	Provider of disaster proof hardware. The company provides SoloPRO SSD External and ioSafe Rugged Portable.	530-820-3090	NA	Roseville
Iron Systems Inc (HQ)	Provider of network storage, hybrid cloud, and big data infrastructure solutions. The company offers OEM/ODM manufacturing services.	408-943-8000	NA	Fremont
iXsystems Inc (HQ)	Provider of hardware, software, server, and storage solutions, and services such as software development and consultation.	408-943-4100	NA	San Jose
Mixonic (HQ)	Provider of design services. The company offers custom CD and DVD duplication, disc packaging, CD production, and printing services.	888-464-9664	NA	San Francisco
Oryx Advanced Materials Inc (HQ)	Provider of thin film materials for PV cells. The company also offers sputtering targets and bonding services to the magnetic data storage market.	510-249-1157	NA	Fremont

COMPANY NAME	PRODUCT / SERVICE	PHONE	EMP	CITY
Owens Design (HQ)	Developer of advanced technology systems for semiconductor, hard disk drive, solar, medical device, and other sectors.	510-659-1800	NA	Fremont
Promise Technology Inc (HQ)	Provider of storage solutions such as cloud and surveillance storage and virtual tape library for digital home applications.	408-228-1400	NA	Milpitas
Pure Storage Inc (HQ)	Provider of flash storage solutions. The company is focused on developing flash arrays for various enterprises.	833-371-7873	NA	Mountain View
Qct LLC (HQ)	Provider of computer network services. The company also offers storage, database management, and data backup solutions.	510-270-6111	NA	San Jose
Rasilient Systems Inc (HQ)	Provider of technology products and services. The company offers a range of video surveillance and storage products.	408-730-2568	NA	Santa Clara
Siig Inc (HQ)	Manufacturer of computer connectivity products. The company is involved in increasing the bandwidth between a computer system and external devices.	510-657-8688	NA	Fremont
Super Talent Technology (HQ)	Designer and manufacturer of flash based storage solutions for enterprise servers, portable devices, personal computers, and consumer electronics.	408-934-2560	NA	San Jose
Tintri Inc (HQ)	Developer of zero management storage systems. The company focuses on building storage for virtual environments.	650-810-8200	NA	Mountain View
Viking Enterprise Solutions (HQ)	Provider of solutions for data enterpriser centers. The company also offers storage expansion product platform.	408-964-3730	NA	San Jose
Western Digital Corp (HQ)	Provider of storage array solutions. The company focuses on desktop virtualization, server virtualization, database hosting, and file services.	510-791-7900	NA	Newark
Western Digital Corp (HQ)	Manufacturer of external storage devices. The company also focuses on network storage and backup solutions and offers technical support services.	408-717-6000	NA	San Jose
Winnov LP (HQ)	Provider of video capture and streaming solutions. The company serves education, enterprise, healthcare, and live event sectors.	888-315-9460	NA	Santa Clara
N World Trade Printing Co (HQ)	Provider of commercial printing services.	714-903-2500	NA	Garden Grove

96 = Memory Systems

COMPANY NAME	PRODUCT / SERVICE	PHONE	EMP	CITY
ADLINK Technology Inc (LH)	Designer and manufacturer of products for embedded computing, test and measurement, and automation applications. The company serves various sectors.	408-360-0200	NA	San Jose
ATP Electronics Inc (RH)	Provider of NAND flash and DRAM memory modules. The company specializes in telecom, medical, automotive, and enterprise computing.	408-732-5000	NA	San Jose
Corsair Inc (HQ)	Designer of high-speed modules for mission-critical servers. The company also caters to high-end workstations.	510-657-8747	NA	Fremont
Gsi Technology (HQ)	Provider of telecommunication and networking services. The company is also engaged in sales and distribution.	408-331-8800	NA	Sunnyvale
Iron Systems Inc (HQ)	Provider of network storage, hybrid cloud, and big data infrastructure solutions. The company offers OEM/ODM manufacturing services.	408-943-8000	NA	Fremont
iXsystems Inc (HQ)	Provider of hardware, software, server, and storage solutions, and services such as software development and consultation.	408-943-4100	NA	San Jose
Lexar Media Inc (HQ)	Provider of memory product lines such as USB drives, memory cards, card readers, and dram computer memory.	408-933-1088	NA	San Jose
Macronix America Inc (LH)	Manufacturer of integrated device. The company offers application driven system solutions and non-volatile memory semiconductor solutions.	408-262-8887	NA	Milpitas
Max Group Corp (HQ)	Distributor for computing devices. The company offers computer cases, fans and heatsinks, and hard drives.	888-644-4629	NA	Fremont
Mixonic (HQ)	Provider of design services. The company offers custom CD and DVD duplication, disc packaging, CD production, and printing services.	888-464-9664	NA	San Francisco
POLYSTAK Inc (HQ)	Provider of silicon based multi chip package products as well as package stacking solutions and repair services of components and modules.	408-441-1400	NA	San Jose
Pure Storage Inc (HQ)	Provider of flash storage solutions. The company is focused on developing flash arrays for various enterprises.	833-371-7873	NA	Mountain View
Smart Modular Technologies (HQ)	Manufacturer of add on memory boards, flash, and storage products. The company serves defense, gaming, storage, and other sectors.	510-623-1231	NA	Newark
Spectra 7 Microsystems Ltd (HQ)	Manufacturer of analog semiconductor devices. The company focuses on micro-thin interconnects for consumer electronic products.	408-770-2915	NA	San Jose
Super Talent Technology (HQ)	Designer and manufacturer of flash based storage solutions for enterprise servers, portable devices, personal computers, and consumer electronics.	408-934-2560	NA	San Jose
Testmetrix Inc (HQ)	Manufacturer of high-throughput AVTE systems, and offers official compliance certification test services.	408-730-5511	NA	Milpitas
Wintec Industries Inc (HQ)	Manufacturer and distributor of memory modules and components. The company serves consumer, embedded OEM, e-commerce, and other needs.	510-953-7421	NA	Newark
N World Trade Printing Co (HQ)	Provider of commercial printing services.	714-903-2500	NA	Garden Grove

97 = Networking Equipment

COMPANY NAME	PRODUCT / SERVICE	PHONE	EMP	CITY
6WIND USA Inc (RH)	Manufacturer of virtual accelerators, routers, and related accessories. The company offers network security and network appliance solutions.	408-816-1366	NA	Santa Clara
A10 Networks Inc (HQ)	Provider of networking and security solutions such as cloud computing and virtualization and bandwidth management.	408-325-8668	NA	San Jose
Accton Technology Corp (DH)	Distributor of network connectivity products and ethernet hubs. The company focuses on home security, cloud, data center switch, and other needs.	408-747-0994	NA	Sunnyvale
Actiontec Electronics Inc (HQ)	Provider of Internet modems, networking adapters, and routers. The company offers fiber routers, powerline network kits and wireless display products.	408-752-7700	NA	Santa Clara
Alpha Networks Inc (HQ)	Designer and manufacturer of networking products. The company also focuses on computers and computer peripherals.	408-844-8850	NA	Milpitas
Alphaems Corp (HQ)	Provider of printed circuit board prototyping and PCB assembly production services. The company also involves in material purchasing and warehousing.	510-498-8788	NA	Fremont
Andover Consulting Group Inc (HQ)	Supplier of network components. The company offers data center liquidation, network security, and network equipment services.	415-537-6950	NA	San Mateo
Arcus Technology Inc (HQ)	Provider of motor controllers, stepper motors, and related accessories such as cables, encoders, and gearboxes.	925-373-8800	NA	Livermore
Athana International Inc (HQ)	Provider of computer storage devices.	310-539-7280	NA	Redondo Beach
Avaya Inc (HQ)	Provider of PBX solutions, IVR applications, IP telephony solutions, voice messaging, and consulting.	908-953-6000	NA	Santa Clara
Bivio Networks Inc (HQ)	Provider of cyber security and network control solutions. The company offers cyber defense systems, surveillance, flow analysis, and monitoring tools.	925-924-8600	NA	Pleasanton
Cermetek Microelectronics (HQ)	Manufacturer of communication modules for embedded systems. The company caters to power generation, irrigation control, and medical monitoring fields.	408-942-2200	NA	Milpitas
Ciena Corp (BR)	Provider of cloud networking, network transformation, and packet network solutions for multi-data center environments.	408-904-2100	NA	San Jose
Cpacket Networks (HQ)	Provider of solutions for network traffic monitoring and data center performance management. The company specializes in traffic monitoring switches.	650-969-9500	NA	San Jose
Edgewater Networks Inc (HQ)	Provider of enterprise session controllers for business purposes. The company also offers security and policy management services.	408-351-7200	NA	San Jose
Embedur Systems Inc (HQ)	Developer of software solutions. The company also offers technical and management services for the embedded market.	510-353-9111	NA	Fremont
Engage Communication Inc (HQ)	Developer and manufacturer of telecommunications equipment. The company focuses on encryption, mobile, and cellular backhauling solutions.	831-688-1021	NA	Aptos
Five9 Network Systems LLC (HQ)	Provider of server and storage solutions. The company serves the government, printing, cloud infrastructure, and energy markers.	650-494-2220	NA	Palo Alto
Genstor Systems Inc (HQ)	Provider of customized hardware solutions for server, storage, clusters, personal computers, and workstations.	408-980-0121	NA	Santa Clara
Greatlink International Inc (RH)	Manufacturer of cable assemblies and related products for the medical, aerospace, and automotive industries.	510-657-1667	NA	Fremont
HotLava Systems Inc (HQ)	Provider of board-level solutions for servers and appliances that operates in virtualized environments.	510-531-1169	NA	Oakland
Hyve Solutions (HQ)	Designer of data center serve, storage, networking and appliance solutions. The company specializes in rack integration services.	510-668-3877	NA	Fremont
Ibase Technology (USA) Inc (BR)	Developer of embedded products such as industrial motherboards, CPU modules, barebone systems, network appliances, and digital surveillance systems.	408-992-0888	NA	Sunnyvale
Infinera Corp (HQ)	Provider of services and solutions in optical networks. The company serves cable operators and Internet content providers.	408-572-5200	NA	Sunnyvale
Infoblox (HQ)	Provider of automated network control solutions. The company's services include training, implementation, migration, upgrade, repair, and maintenance.	408-986-4000	NA	Santa Clara
Interworking Labs Inc (HQ)	Provider of network related services. The company focuses on testing, emulation, and also offers network optimization products.	831-460-7010	NA	Scotts Valley
ioSafe Inc (HQ)	Provider of disaster proof hardware. The company provides SoloPRO SSD External and ioSafe Rugged Portable.	530-820-3090	NA	Roseville
King Star Computer Inc (HQ)	Provider of technology services to Fortune 500 companies, mid-size to small business, start-ups, and government and educational organizations.	408-736-8590	NA	Sunnyvale
Lewiz Communications Inc (HQ)	Provider of computer networking solutions. The company also offers data security, data management, and data streaming services.	408-432-6248	NA	San Jose
Linkbit Inc (HQ)	Manufacturer of network equipment. The company primarily caters to service providers and network operators.	408-969-9940	NA	Santa Clara
NETGEAR Inc (HQ)	Provider of network solutions for home and businesses. The company also offers home video monitoring systems and storage products.	408-907-8000	NA	San Jose

COMPANY NAME	PRODUCT / SERVICE	PHONE	EMP	CITY
OJO Technology Inc (HQ)	Manufacturer of video surveillance systems. The company offers services to the education, transportation, and utility sectors.	877-306-4656	NA	Fremont
Omnicor (HQ)	Provider of network testing tools, vacuum capacitors, and interrupters and IP performance test systems.	650-572-0122	NA	Foster City
Pica8 Inc (HQ)	Manufacturer of white box switches. The company specializes in traditional switches and routing protocols.	833-888-7422	NA	Palo Alto
Platina Systems Corp (HQ)	Manufacturer of network equipment including switches. The company serves industrial and commercial customers.	408-389-4268	NA	Santa Clara
Praesum Communications Inc (HQ)	Provider of switching communication products. The company offers IP cores, boards, and system level products.	707-338-0946	NA	Santa Rosa
Qct LLC (HQ)	Provider of computer network services. The company also offers storage, database management, and data backup solutions.	510-270-6111	NA	San Jose
Qulsar Inc (HQ)	Specializes in packaging, refinement, and distribution of precise time synchronization. The company serves the telecom and networking industries.	408-715-1098	NA	San Jose
R-Hub Communications Inc (HQ)	Provider of web conferencing and remote support services. The company offers services for on-premise security, branding, and integration.	408-899-2830	NA	San Jose
Raymar Information Technology Inc (HQ)	Provider of hardware supplies, network infrastructure, virtualization, disaster recovery, and managed services.	916-783-1951	NA	Sacramento
Siig Inc (HQ)	Manufacturer of computer connectivity products. The company is involved in increasing the bandwidth between a computer system and external devices.	510-657-8688	NA	Fremont
Stonefly Inc (HQ)	Provider of storage optimization and disaster recovery protection for software solutions. The company also offers storage area networks.	510-265-1616	NA	Hayward
Utstarcom Inc (BR)	Manufacturer of IP based, end to end networking, and telecommunications solutions. The company also focuses on integration.	408-791-6168	NA	San Jose
Zypcom Inc (HQ)	Designer and manufacturer of analog modems. The company mainly caters to the networking professionals.	510-324-2501	NA	Union City

98 = Power Supplies

COMPANY NAME	PRODUCT / SERVICE	PHONE	EMP	CITY
Aldetec Inc (HQ)	Manufacturer of microwave amplifier products. The company provides low noise amplifiers, down converters, and octave band amplifiers.	916-453-3382	NA	Sacramento
Applied Motion Products Inc (HQ)	Manufacturer of stepper drives and motors, gearheads, power supplies, and related accessories. The company offers technical support services.	831-761-6555	NA	Watsonville
Areias Systems Inc (HQ)	Provider of services to the technology sector. The company focuses on design, engineering, manufacturing, and prototyping.	831-440-9800	NA	Scotts Valley
Digital Power Corp (HQ)	Designer and manufacturer of switching power supplies. The company serves the industrial, military, and medical markers.	510-657-2635	NA	Milpitas
Eta-Usa (HQ)	Provider of power supplies and manufacturer of battery chargers. The company serves the communication, gaming, and computing industries.	408-778-2793	NA	Morgan Hill
Go!Foton Corp (RH)	Supplier of optical materials and components. The company focuses on markers such as industrial, image and scanning, and biomedical research.	408-831-0131	NA	San Jose
Paxcell Group (HQ)	Provider of electronic engineering and industrial design services. The company also offers contract manufacturing services.	408-945-8054	NA	Milpitas
RGB Spectrum (HQ)	Manufacturer of video and computer signal display processors. The company serves security, oil and gas, corporate, and military sectors.	510-814-7000	NA	Alameda
Silicon Mitus (BR)	Manufacturer and distributor of smart power management integrated chips solutions. The company focuses on power solutions.	408-446-3151	NA	Cupertino
Telemakus LLC (HQ)	Provider of USB controlled RF devices. The company devices include switches, vector modulators, and digital attenuators.	916-458-6346	NA	Folsom

99 = Process Control Computers

COMPANY NAME	PRODUCT / SERVICE	PHONE	EMP	CITY
ADLINK Technology Inc (LH)	Designer and manufacturer of products for embedded computing, test and measurement, and automation applications. The company serves various sectors.	408-360-0200	NA	San Jose
Cybosoft General Cybernation Group Inc (HQ)	Provider of control technology solutions for the process control, building control, and equipment control markers.	916-631-6313	NA	Rancho Cordova
Omni Pro Systems (HQ)	Supplier and integrator of computer systems. The company offers custom logo engraving services and deployment ready solutions.	415-648-1121	NA	San Francisco
Siig Inc (HQ)	Manufacturer of computer connectivity products. The company is involved in increasing the bandwidth between a computer system and external devices.	510-657-8688	NA	Fremont

100 = Repair & Maintenance

	COMPANY NAME	PRODUCT / SERVICE	PHONE	EMP	CITY
N	Data Trace Information Services LLC (HQ)	Provider of technology services related to real estate services and solutions.	800-221-2056	NA	Irvine
	Ibus Corp (HQ)	Manufacturer and provider of industrial computers. The company also specializes in prototyping and quality control.	408-450-7880	NA	Santa Clara

COMPANY NAME	PRODUCT / SERVICE	PHONE	EMP	CITY
Omni Pro Systems (HQ)	Supplier and integrator of computer systems. The company offers custom logo engraving services and deployment ready solutions.	415-648-1121	NA	San Francisco
Systemacs (HQ)	Provider of solutions for upgrading or setting up networks which include hardware, software, and routers.	650-329-9745	NA	Palo Alto
Veolia Water (BR)	Provider of water and wastewater treatment solutions. The company offers services for public authorities and industrial companies.	510-412-2001	NA	Richmond

101 = Computer Peripherals/Accessories

COMPANY NAME	PRODUCT / SERVICE	PHONE	EMP	CITY
Acadia Technology Inc (HQ)	Dealer of power supplies, water cooling kits, cases, fans and fan ducts, and digital temperature displayers.	408-737-9528	NA	Sunnyvale

102 = ATMs

COMPANY NAME	PRODUCT / SERVICE	PHONE	EMP	CITY
HP Development Company LP (HQ)	Provider of computer products that include desktops, monitors, printers and scanners, ink, toner and papers, and laptops.	650-857-1501	NA	Palo Alto
International Microsystems Inc (HQ)	Designer and manufacturer of flash memory duplication equipment. The company also offers related test equipment.	408-813-9748	NA	Fremont
Sycard Technology (HQ)	Provider of 16-bit PC card and CardBus devices. The company also offers USB and smart media development services.	408-399-8073	NA	Los Gatos

103 = Bar Code Scanners

COMPANY NAME	PRODUCT / SERVICE	PHONE	EMP	CITY
Data ID Systems (HQ)	Provider of identification management solutions. The company offers passport readers, barcode scanners, and fixed asset tracking products.	408-371-5764	NA	Campbell
Worth Data Inc (HQ)	Designer and manufacturer of barcode scanners and barcode software that includes barcode printing software and inventory tracking software.	831-458-9938	NA	Santa Cruz

104 = Computer R&D & Other Services

	COMPANY NAME	PRODUCT / SERVICE	PHONE	EMP	CITY
N	Abtech Technologies (HQ)	Provider of IT consulting and enterprise-wide solutions specializing in Hewlett-Packard, IBM, Sun Microsystems, and storage hardware and services. Professional services include: On-site support services, technical consulting, hardware and software rentals and leasing, asset recovery and disposal services.	760-827-5100	NA	Carlsbad
	Acronics (HQ)	Provider of engineering services. The company is involved in systems and mechanical design services.	408-432-0888	NA	San Jose
N	Dazeworks Inc (HQ)	Provider of solutions to help clients innovate and stand out from their competition.	415-818-8069	51-200	San Francisco
N	Eigenstate Consulting LLC (HQ)	Creator and provider of customized presentations for companies and groups, consulting services through the Internet and related technologies.	415-225-6703	NA	San Francisco
N	Everest Consulting Group Inc (BR)	Provider of customer solutions in IT project and staff augmentation areas offers technology due diligence, new application development, and product engineering.	510-494-8440	201-500	Fremont
N	General Networks Corp (HQ)	Provider of consulting and managed services for customers who need to manage and process business-critical information.	818-249-1962	51-200	Glendale
N	GeoTrust Inc (HQ)	Provider of digital certificates for secure online transactions and business over the Internet.	520-477-3110	NA	Mountain View
N	Imagine IT! (HQ)	Producer of customized interactive multimedia application developments for CD-ROM and corporate intranets. CD-ROMs produced are for employee training, business presentations, trade shows and conferences and also offers digital audio and video and DVD authoring.	818-368-2604	NA	Chatsworth
N	Innovative Concepts (HQ)	Provider of website design services.	805-545-9562	11-50	San Luis Obispo
	Micro Tech Systems (HQ)	Provider of cabling solutions. The company involves in the installation and repair of voice, data, and video network systems.	559-438-7580	NA	Fresno
	Silex Technology America Inc (HQ)	Manufacturer of print servers for network printers and fingerprint readers. The company serves security applications.	657-218-5199	NA	Santa Ana
	Skybox Security Inc (HQ)	Provider of risk analytics for cyber security. The company offers threat management and network security management solutions.	408-441-8060	NA	San Jose
N	TechMD (HQ)	Provider of cloud solutions, cyber security services, strategic consulting, and managed services.	888-883-2463	51-200	Santa Ana
	Tru Technical Partners Inc (HQ)	Provider of information technology services on a contract basis. The company's services include managed desktops, workstation, anti-virus, and others.	408-559-2800	NA	Campbell
N	TruAdvantage (HQ)	Provider of support services ranging from consultation to design, support and training for small and medium-sized companies and healthcare practices. Services include managed IT services, data backup and recovery, cloud services, VoIP services, and data and network security.	408-680-8389	11-50	San Jose
N	View by View Inc (HQ)	Provider of computer-generated architectural, medical modeling and simulations.	415-359-4494	NA	San Francisco
N	WK Multimedia Network Training (HQ)	Provider of computer training programs and services.	415-586-1713	NA	San Mateo

COMPANY NAME	PRODUCT / SERVICE	PHONE	EMP	CITY
N WorldCom Consulting (HQ)	Provider of editorial services including writing, editing, desktop publishing, printing, layout and design, web design and hosting, screenplay development, and consultation and serves educational, religious and humanitarian organizations and public affairs department.	209-728-0246	NA	Murphys

105 = Computer Supplies

COMPANY NAME	PRODUCT / SERVICE	PHONE	EMP	CITY
America Aopen Inc (HQ)	Specializes in the manufacture and marketing of personal computer (PC) components and peripherals. The company also offers speakers and bare systems.	408-586-1200	NA	San Jose
ASUSTeK Computer Inc (HQ)	Manufacturer of computer systems and hardware components such as desktops, notebooks, peripherals, motherboards, and graphic cards.	510-739-3777	NA	Fremont
Computerland Of Silicon Valley (HQ)	Provider of hardware, software, and networking services. The company serves government and educational institutions.	408-519-3200	NA	San Jose
Ergo Direct Com (HQ)	Provider of adjustable desks, arms, and mounts. The company offers ergonomic keyboards, monitor arms, and mounting adapters.	650-654-4300	NA	San Carlos
Landel (HQ)	Provider of telecommunication products such as MailBug, DataBug, and SurveyBug. The company is engaged in technical support services.	408-360-0490	NA	San Jose

106 = Computer Wire & Harness Assemblies

COMPANY NAME	PRODUCT / SERVICE	PHONE	EMP	CITY
America Aopen Inc (HQ)	Specializes in the manufacture and marketing of personal computer (PC) components and peripherals. The company also offers speakers and bare systems.	408-586-1200	NA	San Jose
Granite Digital (HQ)	Manufacturer of external diagnostic peripherals. The company is engaged in troubleshooting and maintenance services.	510-471-6442	NA	Union City
Lorom West (HQ)	Manufacturer of PCB assemblies, turnkey OEM/ODM products and custom cable and wire harnesses. The company offers industry solutions.	919-535-5830	NA	Fremont
Newnex Technology Corp (HQ)	Developer of connecting cables, controllers, and repeaters. The company's services include design, installation, and technical support.	408-986-9988	NA	Santa Clara

108 = Input/Output Devices

COMPANY NAME	PRODUCT / SERVICE	PHONE	EMP	CITY
Applied Systems Engineering Inc (HQ)	Provider of consulting, software, design, and testing services. The company's products cater to communication applications.	408-364-0500	NA	Campbell
Ergo Direct Com (HQ)	Provider of adjustable desks, arms, and mounts. The company offers ergonomic keyboards, monitor arms, and mounting adapters.	650-654-4300	NA	San Carlos
HP Inc (BR)	Provider of laptops, tablets, desktops, printers, and related accessories. The company specializes in business solutions.	650-857-1501	NA	Palo Alto
Kensington Computer Products Group (DH)	Provider of secure locking solution for laptops, portable laptop power, and mobile computing solutions.	650-572-2700	NA	San Mateo
Key Source International Inc (HQ)	Provider of disinfectant and germicidal wipes for keyboards. The company focuses on infection control and cross contamination.	510-562-5000	NA	Oakland
Max Group Corp (HQ)	Distributor for computing devices. The company offers computer cases, fans and heatsinks, and hard drives.	888-644-4629	NA	Fremont
Micro Tech Systems (HQ)	Provider of cabling solutions. The company involves in the installation and repair of voice, data, and video network systems.	559-438-7580	NA	Fresno

109 = Keyboards

COMPANY NAME	PRODUCT / SERVICE	PHONE	EMP	CITY
N Amag Technology Inc (HQ)	Designer and manufacturer of access control and video security solutions.	310-518-2380	51-200	Torrance
Ergo Direct Com (HQ)	Provider of adjustable desks, arms, and mounts. The company offers ergonomic keyboards, monitor arms, and mounting adapters.	650-654-4300	NA	San Carlos
N GarrettCom Inc (HQ)	Manufacturer of land products hubs, repeaters, concentrators, transceivers and media converters.	510-438-9071	51-200	Fremont
Kensington Computer Products Group (DH)	Provider of secure locking solution for laptops, portable laptop power, and mobile computing solutions.	650-572-2700	NA	San Mateo
Key Source International Inc (HQ)	Provider of disinfectant and germicidal wipes for keyboards. The company focuses on infection control and cross contamination.	510-562-5000	NA	Oakland
N Langan Products Inc (HQ)	Manufacturer of computer peripheral equipment and prepackaged software products.	415-567-8087	NA	San Francisco
N Marburg Technology Inc (HQ)	Designer and manufacturer of precision components and assemblies for the data storage and much more industries.	408-262-8400	NA	Milpitas
Max Group Corp (HQ)	Distributor for computing devices. The company offers computer cases, fans and heatsinks, and hard drives.	888-644-4629	NA	Fremont
N Micro Connectors Inc (HQ)	Distributor of computer peripheral equipment.	510-266-0299	1-10	Hayward
PFU America Inc (BR)	Provider of technology solutions. The company designs, develops, and sells computer hardware, peripheral products, and systems.	408-992-2900	NA	Sunnyvale
SJK Company Ltd (BR)	Manufacturer of automobile parts, smart grid products, input devices, and convergence products. The company offers customer support services.	510-573-4852	NA	Fremont

110 = Miscellaneous Computer Equipment

COMPANY NAME	PRODUCT / SERVICE	PHONE	EMP	CITY
Acronics (HQ)	Provider of engineering services. The company is involved in systems and mechanical design services.	408-432-0888	NA	San Jose
ADLINK Technology Inc (LH)	Designer and manufacturer of products for embedded computing, test and measurement, and automation applications. The company serves various sectors.	408-360-0200	NA	San Jose
Advantech Inc (DH)	Provider of system integration, hardware, software, embedded systems, automation products, and logistics support.	408-519-3898	NA	Milpitas
Alpha Networks Inc (HQ)	Designer and manufacturer of networking products. The company also focuses on computers and computer peripherals.	408-844-8850	NA	Milpitas
Alphaems Corp (HQ)	Provider of printed circuit board prototyping and PCB assembly production services. The company also involves in material purchasing and warehousing.	510-498-8788	NA	Fremont
Amber Precision Instruments Inc (HQ)	Provider of scanner products. The company specializes in electromagnetic immunity scanners and near field scanners.	408-752-0199	NA	San Jose
America Aopen Inc (HQ)	Specializes in the manufacture and marketing of personal computer (PC) components and peripherals. The company also offers speakers and bare systems.	408-586-1200	NA	San Jose
Ampex Data Systems (HQ)	Manufacturer of digital storage systems. The company also offers airborne and ground systems and related video solutions.	650-367-2011	NA	Hayward
Andes Technology USA Corp (RH)	Provider of infrastructural solutions for embedded system applications. The company serves the semiconductor industry.	408-809-2929	NA	San Jose
Antec Inc (HQ)	Supplier of computer components and accessories. The company provides enclosures, power supplies, accessories, and mobile products.	510-770-1200	NA	Fremont
APLEX Technology Inc (BR)	Manufacturer of industrial displays, heavy-duty expendables, industrial panels, and related accessories. The company serves the healthcare sector.	669-999-2500	NA	Santa Clara
ASUSTeK Computer Inc (HQ)	Manufacturer of computer systems and hardware components such as desktops, notebooks, peripherals, motherboards, and graphic cards.	510-739-3777	NA	Fremont
Atech Flash Technology Inc (HQ)	Provider of commercial and consumer products that include drive bay multiple flash card reader, portable card readers, and iPod accessories.	510-824-6868	NA	Fremont
Avermedia Technologies Inc (DH)	Designer and manufacturer of multimedia, Internet TV, and electronic products. The company provides USB, TV box, streaming server, and accessories.	510-403-0006	NA	Fremont
Copypro Inc (HQ)	Manufacturer and seller of heavy-duty desktop duplication systems such as duplicators, printers, and analyzers.	925-689-1200	NA	Concord
Efinix Inc (HQ)	Focuses on the building of programmable devices. The company serves the industrial, medical, and automotive markers.	408-789-6917	NA	Santa Clara
Exxact Corp (HQ)	Supplier of workstation graphic cards and solutions. The company also offers servers, HPC clusters, and computing software.	510-226-7366	NA	Fremont
Genesys Logic America Inc (BR)	Developer of electric circuits, semiconductors, digital communications products, computer peripherals, and other related products.	408-435-8899	NA	San Jose
HP Inc (BR)	Provider of laptops, tablets, desktops, printers, and related accessories. The company specializes in business solutions.	650-857-1501	NA	Palo Alto
International Microsystems Inc (HQ)	Designer and manufacturer of flash memory duplication equipment. The company also offers related test equipment.	408-813-9748	NA	Fremont
Jetway Computer Corp (HQ)	Manufacturer of motherboards and LCD monitors. The company also specializes in graphic cards and barebones systems.	510-857-0130	NA	Newark
Kaser Corp (HQ)	Developer and marketer of Internet and communication equipment. The company offers Internet telephony, digital television, and accessories.	510-894-6892	NA	Fremont
Kensington Computer Products Group (DH)	Provider of secure locking solution for laptops, portable laptop power, and mobile computing solutions.	650-572-2700	NA	San Mateo
Maxeler Technologies Inc (HQ)	Developer of computing solutions. The company offers services to the oil and gas, analytical, and financial sectors.	650-938-8818	NA	Mountain View
Micro Tech Systems (HQ)	Provider of cabling solutions. The company involves in the installation and repair of voice, data, and video network systems.	559-438-7580	NA	Fresno
NComputing Company Ltd (HQ)	Provider of desktop virtualization services. The company serves customers in the education, healthcare, enterprise, and enterprise sectors.	650-409-5959	NA	San Mateo
Oppo Digital Inc (HQ)	Manufacturer of Blu-ray players and UP converting DVD players. The company's services include design, installation, and delivery.	650-961-1118	NA	Menlo Park
Posiflex Business Machines Inc (HQ)	Provider of point of service hardware and platform technology. The company caters to diverse markers.	510-429-7097	NA	Hayward
Recortec Inc (HQ)	Manufacturer of LCD monitors, KVM, keyboards, speakers, and computers. The company also offers customization services.	408-928-1480	NA	San Jose
Siig Inc (HQ)	Manufacturer of computer connectivity products. The company is involved in increasing the bandwidth between a computer system and external devices.	510-657-8688	NA	Fremont
SJK Company Ltd (BR)	Manufacturer of automobile parts, smart grid products, input devices, and convergence products. The company offers customer support services.	510-573-4852	NA	Fremont

COMPANY NAME	PRODUCT / SERVICE	PHONE	EMP	CITY
SP Controls Inc (HQ)	Designer and manufacturer of projector control systems. The company also offers audio systems, mounting, signal distribution, and other products.	650-392-7880	NA	S San Francisco
Spectra 7 Microsystems Ltd (HQ)	Manufacturer of analog semiconductor devices. The company focuses on micro-thin interconnects for consumer electronic products.	408-770-2915	NA	San Jose
Sycard Technology (HQ)	Provider of 16-bit PC card and CardBus devices. The company also offers USB and smart media development services.	408-399-8073	NA	Los Gatos
Zspace Inc (HQ)	Provider of solutions for viewing, manipulating, and communicating complex ideas through direct interaction with virtual-holographic simulations.	408-498-4050	NA	Sunnyvale

111 = Modems

COMPANY NAME	PRODUCT / SERVICE	PHONE	EMP	CITY
Applied Systems Engineering Inc (HQ)	Provider of consulting, software, design, and testing services. The company's products cater to communication applications.	408-364-0500	NA	Campbell
Bivio Networks Inc (HQ)	Provider of cyber security and network control solutions. The company offers cyber defense systems, surveillance, flow analysis, and monitoring tools.	925-924-8600	NA	Pleasanton
Cermetek Microelectronics (HQ)	Manufacturer of communication modules for embedded systems. The company caters to power generation, irrigation control, and medical monitoring fields.	408-942-2200	NA	Milpitas
NComputing Company Ltd (HQ)	Provider of desktop virtualization services. The company serves customers in the education, healthcare, enterprise, and enterprise sectors.	650-409-5959	NA	San Mateo
Teledesign Systems Inc (HQ)	Provider of wireless data solutions. The company manufactures wireless industrial modems for commercial and industrial data collection applications.	408-941-1808	NA	Milpitas

112 = Monitors

COMPANY NAME	PRODUCT / SERVICE	PHONE	EMP	CITY
Atech Flash Technology Inc (HQ)	Provider of commercial and consumer products that include drive bay multiple flash card reader, portable card readers, and iPod accessories.	510-824-6868	NA	Fremont
Caltron Industries Inc (HQ)	Manufacturer of digital signage products and touch screen monitors. The company specializes in digital video signage and media advertising services.	510-440-1800	NA	Fremont
CERONIX Inc (HQ)	Manufacturer of color video touch display monitors and printed circuit boards. The company offers LCD and CRT monitor assemblies and spare parts.	530-886-6400	NA	Auburn
HP Development Company LP (HQ)	Provider of computer products that include desktops, monitors, printers and scanners, ink, toner and papers, and laptops.	650-857-1501	NA	Palo Alto
HP Inc (BR)	Provider of laptops, tablets, desktops, printers, and related accessories. The company specializes in business solutions.	650-857-1501	NA	Palo Alto
Immersion Corp (HQ)	Developer and marketer of haptic (touch feedback) technology. The company serves mobile device, wearable, automotive, medical, and other sectors.	408-467-1900	NA	San Jose
Key Source International Inc (HQ)	Provider of disinfectant and germicidal wipes for keyboards. The company focuses on infection control and cross contamination.	510-562-5000	NA	Oakland
NComputing Company Ltd (HQ)	Provider of desktop virtualization services. The company serves customers in the education, healthcare, enterprise, and enterprise sectors.	650-409-5959	NA	San Mateo
PFU America Inc (BR)	Provider of technology solutions. The company designs, develops, and sells computer hardware, peripheral products, and systems.	408-992-2900	NA	Sunnyvale
Tactus Technology Inc (HQ)	Developer of tactile user interface for touchscreen devices. The company serves the industrial and technological sectors.	510-244-3968	NA	Fremont

114 = Optical Character Recognition Equipment

COMPANY NAME	PRODUCT / SERVICE	PHONE	EMP	CITY
Data ID Systems (HQ)	Provider of identification management solutions. The company offers passport readers, barcode scanners, and fixed asset tracking products.	408-371-5764	NA	Campbell
Newland North America Inc (HQ)	Designer and developer of data collector and scanning systems. The company also offers customer information terminals.	510-490-3888	NA	Fremont

115 = Printers

COMPANY NAME	PRODUCT / SERVICE	PHONE	EMP	CITY
Braigo Labs Inc (HQ)	Developer of humanely optimized technologies such as research, design, and creation of technology-based innovations and services for marketplace.	408-850-0614	NA	Palo Alto
C-Scan Corp (HQ)	Manufacturer and designer of thermal recorders and printers for medical applications and the healthcare sector.	800-953-7888	NA	Los Gatos
Dolphin Graphics (HQ)	Provider of branding and marketing solutions. The company also offers graphics design and web design services.	510-881-0154	NA	Castro Valley
HP Development Company LP (HQ)	Provider of computer products that include desktops, monitors, printers and scanners, ink, toner and papers, and laptops.	650-857-1501	NA	Palo Alto
HP Inc (BR)	Provider of laptops, tablets, desktops, printers, and related accessories. The company specializes in business solutions.	650-857-1501	NA	Palo Alto

COMPANY NAME	PRODUCT / SERVICE	PHONE	EMP	CITY
Max Group Corp (HQ)	Distributor for computing devices. The company offers computer cases, fans and heatsinks, and hard drives.	888-644-4629	NA	Fremont
Posiflex Business Machines Inc (HQ)	Provider of point of service hardware and platform technology. The company caters to diverse markers.	510-429-7097	NA	Hayward
Prism Inks Inc (HQ)	Manufacturer of inkjet printer inks to the proofing, signage, photography, arts and coding sectors. The company's products comprise UV curable and textile inks.	408-744-6710	NA	Sunnyvale
Zebra Technologies Corp (BR)	Provider of business and printing solutions. The company also offers printers such as desktop, industrial, mobile, and card printers.	866-230-9494	NA	San Jose

116 = Storage Devices

COMPANY NAME	PRODUCT / SERVICE	PHONE	EMP	CITY
Acutrack Inc (HQ)	Provider of CD and DVD duplication and production services. The company is also engaged in kitting, assembly, and USB fulfillment.	925-579-5000	NA	Livermore
Addonics Technologies Inc (HQ)	Manufacturer of storage systems and products. The company's products include drive cartridge system, host controller, converter, and adapter.	408-573-8580	NA	San Jose
Amax Information Technologies Inc (HQ)	Manufacturer and seller of custom servers and storage solutions. The company focuses on platform design, custom branding, and supply chain management.	510-651-8886	NA	Fremont
Ampex Data Systems (HQ)	Manufacturer of digital storage systems. The company also offers airborne and ground systems and related video solutions.	650-367-2011	NA	Hayward
Arcscale LLC (HQ)	Provider of colocation, technology integration, hosting, implementation, and telecommunication services. The company also deals with procurement.	408-476-0554	NA	San Jose
Avalanche Technology (HQ)	Provider of programmable storage solutions. The company offers services to the consumer electronics industry.	510-897-3300	NA	Fremont
Exxact Corp (HQ)	Supplier of workstation graphic cards and solutions. The company also offers servers, HPC clusters, and computing software.	510-226-7366	NA	Fremont
Granite Digital (HQ)	Manufacturer of external diagnostic peripherals. The company is engaged in troubleshooting and maintenance services.	510-471-6442	NA	Union City
HP Development Company LP (HQ)	Provider of computer products that include desktops, monitors, printers and scanners, ink, toner and papers, and laptops.	650-857-1501	NA	Palo Alto
Max Group Corp (HQ)	Distributor for computing devices. The company offers computer cases, fans and heatsinks, and hard drives.	888-644-4629	NA	Fremont
Mixonic (HQ)	Provider of design services. The company offers custom CD and DVD duplication, disc packaging, CD production, and printing services.	888-464-9664	NA	San Francisco
NComputing Company Ltd (HQ)	Provider of desktop virtualization services. The company serves customers in the education, healthcare, enterprise, and enterprise sectors.	650-409-5959	NA	San Mateo
Olixir Technologies (HQ)	Provider of external hard drives and racks and towers. The company also offers video surveillance and backup solutions.	408-719-0595	NA	Milpitas
Rambus (HQ)	Manufacturer of semiconductor, lighting, and IP products. The company serves the automotive and transportation markers.	408-462-8000	NA	Sunnyvale
Samsung Semiconductor Inc (HQ)	Provider of electronics manufacturing and digital media products. The company also offers mobile services and PC software.	408-544-4000	NA	San Jose
SanDisk Corp (HQ)	Manufacturer of flash memory cards. The company's products include card readers, solid state drives, USB flash drives, and microSD cards.	408-801-1000	NA	Milpitas
Spectra 7 Microsystems Ltd (HQ)	Manufacturer of analog semiconductor devices. The company focuses on micro-thin interconnects for consumer electronic products.	408-770-2915	NA	San Jose
Super Talent Technology (HQ)	Designer and manufacturer of flash based storage solutions for enterprise servers, portable devices, personal computers, and consumer electronics.	408-934-2560	NA	San Jose
Unigen Corp (HQ)	Manufacturer and designer of custom enterprise-grade flash storage and DRAM and ARMOUR product applications serving the telecommunications industry.	510-896-1818	NA	Newark
Winbond Electronics Corporation America (DH)	Provider of memory solutions and services. The company offers Pseudo SRAM, Serial NOR Flash, Mobile DRAM, and KGD.	408-943-6666	NA	San Jose
N World Trade Printing Co (HQ)	Provider of commercial printing services.	714-903-2500	NA	Garden Grove

117 = Backup Equipment

COMPANY NAME	PRODUCT / SERVICE	PHONE	EMP	CITY
Mixonic (HQ)	Provider of design services. The company offers custom CD and DVD duplication, disc packaging, CD production, and printing services.	888-464-9664	NA	San Francisco
N World Trade Printing Co (HQ)	Provider of commercial printing services.	714-903-2500	NA	Garden Grove

120 = Computer Manufacturing Equipment

COMPANY NAME	PRODUCT / SERVICE	PHONE	EMP	CITY
Aurostar Corp (HQ)	Provider of technology products and services focusing on home theater systems, consumer electronics, desktops and notebooks, and networking solutions.	510-249-9422	NA	Fremont
Bold Data Technology Inc (HQ)	Provider of computer components and services. The company offers desktop computers, servers, notebooks, and workstations.	510-490-8296	NA	Fremont
Bravo Communications Inc (HQ)	Supplier of network surge and lightning protection products. The company also offers data line extenders and related accessories.	408-270-1547	NA	San Jose

COMPANY NAME	PRODUCT / SERVICE	PHONE	EMP	CITY
Chelsio Communications (HQ)	Provider of Ethernet adapters. The company offers storage routers, wire adapters, virtualization and management software, and accessories.	408-962-3600	NA	Sunnyvale
Polywell Computers (HQ)	Manufacturer of computer systems. The company specializes in desktop PCs, workstations, and servers.	650-583-7222	NA	S San Francisco
Quanta Computer USA Inc (LH)	Provider of design and manufacturing services for technology products. The company specializes in cloud computing solutions.	510-226-1001	NA	Fremont
Tangent Inc (HQ)	Provider of computer solutions. The company caters to healthcare, industrial, and military applications.	650-342-9388	NA	Burlingame
Variant Microsystems (HQ)	Manufacturer and reseller of data collection equipment such as barcode scanners, printers, portables.	510-440-2870	NA	Fremont

121 = Component Placement & Handling Systems

COMPANY NAME	PRODUCT / SERVICE	PHONE	EMP	CITY
Artcraft Welding Inc (HQ)	Designer and manufacturer of ultrasonic cleaning equipment. The company specializes in precision cleaning fixtures.	408-377-2725	NA	Campbell
Brooks Automation Inc (BR)	Provider of automation, vacuum, and instrumentation solutions for the semiconductor manufacturing, life sciences, and clean energy industries.	510-661-5000	NA	Fremont

122 = Diffusion/Ion Implant Equipment

COMPANY NAME	PRODUCT / SERVICE	PHONE	EMP	CITY
Artcraft Welding Inc (HQ)	Designer and manufacturer of ultrasonic cleaning equipment. The company specializes in precision cleaning fixtures.	408-377-2725	NA	Campbell
Automate Scientific Inc (HQ)	Manufacturer and distributor of biomedical equipment. The company offers amplifiers, manipulators, software, and accessories.	510-845-6283	NA	Berkeley
Los Gatos Research Inc (HQ)	Manufacturer of analyzers for the measurement of trace gases and isotopes. The company serves the industrial and environmental sectors.	650-965-7772	NA	San Jose

124 = Electronic/Photonic Manufacturing Equipment

COMPANY NAME	PRODUCT / SERVICE	PHONE	EMP	CITY
ABM-USA Inc (HQ)	Manufacturer and seller of mask aligner and exposure systems. The company also provides vacuum chucks, intensity meters, and probes.	408-226-8722	NA	San Jose
Advantage Electric Supply Inc (HQ)	Distributor of electrical and electronic components for OEM's, industrial automation, solar, and renewable energy industries.	510-324-9070	NA	Hayward
Allvia Inc (HQ)	Provider of silicon interposer and through-silicon via foundry services to the semiconductor and optoelectronics industries.	408-212-3200	NA	Sunnyvale
Bactrack (HQ)	Provider of breathalyzers. The company provides products for a wide range of personal, professional and smartphone use.	415-693-9756	NA	San Francisco
BASF Venture Capital America Inc (RH)	Manufacturer of basic chemicals and intermediates such as solvents, plasticizers, and monomers. The company serves the agriculture market.	510-445-6140	NA	Fremont
Bay Area Circuits Inc (HQ)	Provider of engineering services that include fabrication, layout, and design services to the original equipment manufacturers.	510-933-9000	NA	Fremont
CAD PROS PCB Design Inc (HQ)	Designer and manufacturer of printed circuit boards. The company offers services to the residential and commercial sectors.	408-734-9600	NA	San Jose
CLEARink Displays Inc (RH)	Developer of reflective display modules for wearables, smartphones/tablets, electronic shelf labels, and outdoor signage.	510-624-9305	NA	Fremont
Coadna Photonics Inc (HQ)	Provider of tunable fiber optic solutions for optical networks. The company's products are used in high broadband applications.	408-736-1100	NA	Sunnyvale
Cypress Envirosystems Inc (HQ)	Provider of solutions to retrofit existing commercial buildings and industrial facilities for improved asset utilization and lower maintenance costs.	800-544-5411	NA	San Jose
Eiq Energy Inc (HQ)	Designer and manufacturer of power electronics. The company provides solar cells, panels, and monitoring systems.	408-643-0020	NA	Santa Clara
Electronics Cooling Solutions Inc (HQ)	Provider of thermal management consulting services. The company serves customers in the avionics, medical, and telecommunications industries.	408-738-8331	NA	Santa Clara
Epiphotonics Corp (HQ)	Manufacturer of photonic components and subsystems. The company is engaged in design, delivery, and installation services.	408-920-7019	NA	San Jose
Excelitas Technologies Corp (BR)	Provider of opto-electronics solutions. The company serves the medical, industrial, aerospace, and defense markers.	510-979-6500	NA	Pleasanton
Expertech (HQ)	Provider of custom, new and re-manufactured thermal processing solutions. The company offers diffusion furnaces for semiconductor and solar devices.	831-439-9300	NA	Scotts Valley
Fairchild Imaging Inc (DH)	Developer and manufacturer of solid-state electronic imaging components, cameras, and systems. The company's products include image sensors and cameras.	650-479-5749	NA	San Jose
Farpointe Data Inc (HQ)	Provider of RFID electronic access control technologies for electronic access control professionals around the world.	408-731-8700	NA	San Jose
HTA Photomask (HQ)	Manufacturer of photo imaged products such as precision scales, resolution targets, and micro detectors.	408-452-5500	NA	San Jose
Infiniti Solutions USA (HQ)	Provider of electronic manufacturing services. The company specializes in burn-in board and system design and manufacturing.	408-923-7300	NA	San Jose
IPG Photonics (BR)	Provider of high power fiber lasers and amplifiers. The company's offerings include Q-switch lasers, multi-mode diodes, pulsed and direct-diode lasers.	408-492-8830	NA	Santa Clara

COMPANY NAME	PRODUCT / SERVICE	PHONE	EMP	CITY
iSmart Alarm Inc (HQ)	Manufacturer of home security products. The company offers alarms, cameras, sirens, and related accessories.	408-245-2551	NA	Sunnyvale
Jabil Circuit Inc (BR)	Provider of global manufacturing solutions. The company serves the defense, aerospace, and industrial markers.	408-361-3200	NA	San Jose
Meivac Inc (HQ)	Manufacturer of sputtering systems and components. The company offers throttle valves, integrators, OEM assemblies, and substrate heaters.	408-362-1000	NA	San Jose
Modules Technology Inc (HQ)	Provider of custom module design solutions. The company's offerings include grinders, etching systems, and thermal recorders.	408-392-0808	NA	San Jose
PSC Electronics Inc (HQ)	Distributor of magnetic, interconnect, and electro-mechanical components. The company specializes in cable assembly and modification.	408-737-1333	NA	Santa Clara
Radian Thermal Products Inc (BR)	Manufacturer of custom and radiant heat sinks. The company's services include prototyping and engineering support.	408-988-6200	NA	Santa Clara
Rainbow Electronics & Fasteners Corp (HQ)	Distributor of electronic and mechanical hardware products. The company's products include fasteners, screws, standoffs, and spacers.	510-475-9840	NA	Union City
SHASTA Electronic Manufacturing Services Inc (HQ)	Provider of electronic manufacturing services. The company's services include prototype manufacturing, testing, materials, and quality control.	408-436-1267	NA	San Jose
Shax Engineering Inc (HQ)	Provider of PCB fabrication and assembly services. The company serves original equipment manufacturers and technology companies.	408-452-1500	NA	Fremont
Silicon Mitus (BR)	Manufacturer and distributor of smart power management integrated chips solutions. The company focuses on power solutions.	408-446-3151	NA	Cupertino
Syrma Technology (BR)	Provider of entrepreneurial manufacturing services. The company's products include magnetics, memory, and RFID.	408-404-0500	NA	San Jose
Tango Systems Inc (HQ)	Supplier of cluster tools for dielectric films. The company's services include processing, thin film deposition, and quality analysis.	408-526-2330	NA	San Jose
Tdn Electric Inc (HQ)	Retailer of electrical construction services for lighting, uninterruptible power supply, fire alarm, and photovoltaic systems.	650-968-8000	NA	Mountain View
Tecdia Inc (HQ)	Manufacturer of precision machine tools and fixtures. The company also specializes in cutting and scribing tools.	408-748-0100	NA	Campbell
Wafer Process Systems Inc (HQ)	Manufacturer of semiconductors, MEMS, and photonics. The company also focuses on RFID products, disc drives, and flat panel displays.	408-445-3010	NA	San Jose
WaferNet Inc (HQ)	Supplier of silicon wafers. The company serves semiconductor equipment manufacturers and universities.	866-749-2337	NA	San Jose

125 = Production Clean Rooms and Related Equipment

COMPANY NAME	PRODUCT / SERVICE	PHONE	EMP	CITY
Air Exchange Inc (HQ)	Supplier of air purification and clean air machines, and fans. The company serves commercial facilities and public institutions.	800-300-2945	NA	Fairfield
CleanAir Solutions Inc (HQ)	Provider of stainless steel furniture and ESD curtain systems. The company serves pharmaceutical and medical device manufacturing companies.	707-864-9499	NA	Fairfield
Cleantec (HQ)	Provider of solutions for greenhouse gas emissions, air pollution, water conservation, and waste management.	916-791-8478	NA	Granite Bay
Fairchild Imaging Inc (DH)	Developer and manufacturer of solid-state electronic imaging components, cameras, and systems. The company's products include image sensors and cameras.	650-479-5749	NA	San Jose
Farpointe Data Inc (HQ)	Provider of RFID electronic access control technologies for electronic access control professionals around the world.	408-731-8700	NA	San Jose
Meran Technology (HQ)	Provider of process equipment for memory disk manufacturers. The company offers material handling equipment for fiber optic manufacturers.	510-530-5119	NA	Piedmont

126 = Semiconductor Manufacturing Equipment

COMPANY NAME	PRODUCT / SERVICE	PHONE	EMP	CITY
ABM-USA Inc (HQ)	Manufacturer and seller of mask aligner and exposure systems. The company also provides vacuum chucks, intensity meters, and probes.	408-226-8722	NA	San Jose
Addison Engineering Inc (HQ)	Supplier of silicon wafers and semiconductor process components. The company's products include ceramic packages and semiconductor equipment.	408-926-5000	NA	San Jose
Artcraft Welding Inc (HQ)	Designer and manufacturer of ultrasonic cleaning equipment. The company specializes in precision cleaning fixtures.	408-377-2725	NA	Campbell
Avalent Technologies Inc (HQ)	Provider of fabless semiconductor devices. The company's services include platform development, processor development, and analog design services.	408-657-7621	NA	Milpitas
Brooks Automation Inc (BR)	Provider of automation, vacuum, and instrumentation solutions for the semiconductor manufacturing, life sciences, and clean energy industries.	510-661-5000	NA	Fremont
C&D Semiconductor Services Inc (HQ)	Manufacturer of cleaner systems, wafer sorters, and wafer inspection systems. The company deals with inspection and processing.	408-383-1888	NA	San Jose
Corad Technology Inc (BR)	Manufacturer of load boards, probe cards, instrumentation systems, and related components. The company deals with installation services.	408-496-5511	NA	Santa Clara

COMPANY NAME	PRODUCT / SERVICE	PHONE	EMP	CITY
Corning Technology Center (BR)	Provider of specialty glass and ceramics services and sells keystone components to electronics, mobile emissions control, and life science industries.	650-846-6000	NA	Sunnyvale
Crocus Technology (HQ)	Manufacturer of magnetic switches, current sensors, and embedded memory products. The company serves the automotive and industrial sectors.	408-380-8300	NA	Santa Clara
DDRdrive LLC (HQ)	Provider of solid-state storage system. The company specializes in ZFS and ZIL acceleration.	650-804-8227	NA	Palo Alto
Dolphin Technology Inc (DH)	Provider of silicon-proven Internet protocol for memory, standard cells, input and output, memory controllers, and memory test and repair.	408-392-0012	NA	San Jose
Ecomicron Inc (HQ)	Manufacturer of semiconductor equipment. The company caters to semiconductor, photovoltaic, and hybrid industries.	408-526-1020	NA	San Jose
GLF Integrated Power Inc (HQ)	Manufacturer of power switch devices for smartphones, mobile health devices, laptops, remote sensors, wearables, SSD modules, and off batteries.	408-239-4326	NA	Santa Clara
Globalfoundries Inc (BR)	Provider of semiconductor foundry services. The company deals with design tools, IP suppliers and ASIC partners.	408-462-3900	NA	Santa Clara
Hammon Plating Inc (HQ)	Supplier of metal plating applications. The company also provides supply chain management solutions.	650-494-2691	NA	Palo Alto
JEM America Corp (RH)	Manufacturer and supplier of probe cards and tester interfaces. The company offers cantilever, vertical, and special-applications probe cards.	510-683-9234	NA	Fremont
JSR Micro Inc (HQ)	Provider of semiconductor, life sciences, and energy material solutions. The company specializes in lithography materials and CMP consumables.	408-543-8800	NA	Sunnyvale
Lasertec USA Inc (HQ)	Developer and manufacturer of systems for semi-conductor applications. The company also offers systems for flat panel displays.	408-437-1441	NA	San Jose
Microelec Technical (HQ)	Manufacturer of semiconductor, micro-electronics, and mixed signal devices. The company specializes in switches, bridge rectifiers, and transistors.	408-282-3508	NA	Santa Clara
Onchip Devices Inc (HQ)	Provider of silicon and ceramic solutions and integrated passive devices for the computing and consumer electronics industries.	408-654-9365	NA	Santa Clara
Samco Inc (RH)	Manufacturer of deposition, etching, and surface treatment systems used in the manufacturing of LED, MEMS, power and RF device, and other products.	408-734-0459	NA	Santa Clara
Semicat Inc (BR)	Provider of refurbished equipment for semiconductors. The company deals in LED, and novel emerging applications.	408-514-6900	NA	Fremont
Silicon Frontline Technology Inc (HQ)	Provider of parasitic extraction and analysis services for post layout verification. The company specializes in electrostatic discharge analysis.	408-963-6916	NA	San Jose
Silicon Genesis Corp (HQ)	Manufacturer of semiconductor and solar fabrication tools. The company offers stand-alone plasma tools and debond and cleave tools.	408-228-5858	NA	San Jose
SK hynix America Inc (BR)	Manufacturer of DRAM products. The company focuses on consumer memory, graphics memory, mobile memory, and CMOS image sensors.	408-232-8000	NA	San Jose
Solid State Optronics (HQ)	Manufacturer of miniature Solid State Relays. The company offers MOSFET drivers, specialty products, and optocouplers.	408-293-4600	NA	San Jose
TSMC North America (HQ)	Manufacturer of products for the computer, communications, and consumer electronics market segments.	408-382-8000	NA	San Jose
Uniquify Inc (HQ)	Developer and manufacturer of SoC displays and other semi-conductor products. The company offers technical support services.	408-235-8810	NA	San Jose
YES Yield Engineering Systems Inc (HQ)	Manufacturer of process equipment for the semiconductor industry. The company offers products for surface modification and photoresist treatment.	510-954-6889	NA	Fremont

127 = Wafer Fabrication/Crystal Finishing Equipment

COMPANY NAME	PRODUCT / SERVICE	PHONE	EMP	CITY
Addison Engineering Inc (HQ)	Supplier of silicon wafers and semiconductor process components. The company's products include ceramic packages and semiconductor equipment.	408-926-5000	NA	San Jose
Artcraft Welding Inc (HQ)	Designer and manufacturer of ultrasonic cleaning equipment. The company specializes in precision cleaning fixtures.	408-377-2725	NA	Campbell
Intermems Inc (HQ)	Provider of micromolding, plating, thin film deposition, anodic and wafer bonding, and related services.	408-241-0007	NA	San Jose
Loomis Industries Inc (HQ)	Provider of fabrication services. The company specializes in the design, print, and analysis of semiconductor components.	707-963-4111	NA	St. Helena
Qualitau Inc (HQ)	Supplier of test equipment and services. The company is involved in the development of electronic equipment for semiconductor process reliability.	650-282-6226	NA	Santa Clara
Scientific Coating Labs (HQ)	Provider of wafer coatings. The company specializes in coating components used in the semiconductor industry.	408-727-3296	NA	Santa Clara
Semicat Inc (BR)	Provider of refurbished equipment for semiconductors. The company deals in LED, and novel emerging applications.	408-514-6900	NA	Fremont

129 = Alternative Energy Systems

COMPANY NAME	PRODUCT / SERVICE	PHONE	EMP	CITY
Altergy Systems (HQ)	Designer and manufacturer of fuel cell power systems. The company serves telecommunication, emergency response, data center, and other fields.	916-458-8590	NA	Folsom
Blymyer Engineers Inc (HQ)	Provider of solar engineering, facility design, and related services. The company serves the food and beverage and glass manufacturing industries.	510-521-3773	NA	Alameda
Brightsource Energy Inc (HQ)	Developer of solar thermal technology for electric power, petroleum, and industrial-process markers.	510-550-8161	NA	Oakland
Ceecon Testing Inc (HQ)	Provider of soil and groundwater remediation services. The company services also include regulatory compliance and remediation equipment.	650-827-7474	NA	S San Francisco
Cooling Source Inc (HQ)	Provider of thermal design solution for LED lighting, medical, military/ aero, and test equipment industries.	925-292-1293	NA	Livermore
Eagle Shield Inc (HQ)	Provider of energy conservation and renewable energy solutions. The company offers services to homes and businesses.	800-408-2375	NA	Danville
Eeonyx Corp (HQ)	Manufacturer and provider of knitting services. The company focuses on textiles, foams, felts, and powders.	510-741-3632	NA	Pinole
National Center For Appropriate Technology (BR)	Provider of information and access services. The company's offerings include weatherizing houses, monitoring energy applications, and testing products.	530-792-7338	NA	Davis
Nexant Inc (HQ)	Developer of software for utility, energy, chemical, and other sectors and also offers power grid consulting and energy advisory, and other services.	415-369-1000	NA	San Francisco
Peninsula Engineering Solutions Inc (HQ)	Manufacturer of microwave RF repeaters. The company also specializes in cellular and PCS repeaters and related products.	925-837-2243	NA	Danville
Solar Sense PV Inc (HQ)	Provider of solar power system installation services. The company also focuses on design and serves residential, commercial, and utility applications.	888-786-4339	NA	Pleasanton
Sunperfect Solar Inc (HQ)	Provider of energy solutions. The company specializes in the design, manufacture, and installation of solar panels.	510-573-6888	NA	San Jose
Versatile Power (HQ)	Designer and manufacturer of electronic subsystems for manufacturers. The company focuses on application of radio frequency, ultrasonics, and lasers.	408-341-4600	NA	Campbell

130 = Energy Conservation/Management Systems

COMPANY NAME	PRODUCT / SERVICE	PHONE	EMP	CITY
Altergy Systems (HQ)	Designer and manufacturer of fuel cell power systems. The company serves telecommunication, emergency response, data center, and other fields.	916-458-8590	NA	Folsom
Brightsource Energy Inc (HQ)	Developer of solar thermal technology for electric power, petroleum, and industrial-process markers.	510-550-8161	NA	Oakland
N Caban Resources LLC (HQ)	Provider of health information management services and solutions, and coding services.	877-880-1600	NA	El Segundo
Ceecon Testing Inc (HQ)	Provider of soil and groundwater remediation services. The company services also include regulatory compliance and remediation equipment.	650-827-7474	NA	S San Francisco
Enlighted Inc (HQ)	Provider of lighting control systems to commercial buildings, office workspaces, and garages. The company serves facilities and development companies.	650-964-1094	NA	Santa Clara
Hench Control Inc (HQ)	Manufacturer of modular energy management systems. The company's products find application in industrial refrigeration.	510-741-8100	NA	Richmond
King-Solarman Inc (HQ)	Focuses on the sale of solar panels, power inverters, and related supplies. The company is involved in solar project financing services.	408-373-8800	NA	Fremont
Makel Engineering Inc (HQ)	Developer and provider of products and services for aviation, space, military, and commercial applications.	530-895-2770	NA	Chico
New Power Technologies (HQ)	Provider of energy solutions. The company's offerings include energynet platform and energynet solutions.	650-948-4546	NA	Los Altos Hills
Pacific Gas & Electric Co (BR)	Provider of natural gas and electric services. The company serves approximately 15 million people throughout northern and central California.	415-973-1000	NA	San Francisco
Paul Graham Drilling And Service Co (HQ)	Provider of gas drilling services with over head cranes and computer operated plasma cutting machines for top notch drilling.	707-374-5123	NA	Rio Vista
Peninsula Engineering Solutions Inc (HQ)	Manufacturer of microwave RF repeaters. The company also specializes in cellular and PCS repeaters and related products.	925-837-2243	NA	Danville
Sentient Energy Inc (HQ)	Provider of sensor devices for operational practices and engineering applications. The company also offers communication software.	650-523-6680	NA	Burlingame
N Signal Hill Petroleum Inc (HQ)	Producer and supplier of oil and gas.	562-595-6440	51-200	Signal Hill
N SPAP Company LLC (HQ)	International manufacturer representative agency.	714-960-0586	NA	Huntington Beach
Tesla (HQ)	Designer and manufacturer of electric sedans and electric SUVs. The company is engaged in the production of energy storage systems.	650-681-5000	NA	Palo Alto

131 = Energy-Related R&D

COMPANY NAME	PRODUCT / SERVICE	PHONE	EMP	CITY
Aemetis Inc (HQ)	Producer of biochemicals, renewable fuels, food, and feed products. The company's products include Z-Microbe, Glycerin, and edible oils.	408-213-0940	51-200	Cupertino

COMPANY NAME	PRODUCT / SERVICE	PHONE	EMP	CITY
Canary Instruments (HQ)	Provider of home energy monitor with colorful LED lights that provide instant feedback on the electricity use.	707-506-6611	NA	Arcata
Cooling Source Inc (HQ)	Provider of thermal design solution for LED lighting, medical, military/aero, and test equipment industries.	925-292-1293	NA	Livermore
Electric Power Research Institute Inc (HQ)	Provider of research and development services related to the generation, delivery, and use of electricity for the benefit of the public.	650-855-2000	NA	Palo Alto
Geochemical Research Laboratory (HQ)	The company uses energy dispersive x-ray fluorescence spectrometry to determine the element composition of volcanic rocks. The company specializes in archaeological geochemistry.	650-851-1410	NA	Portola Valley
New Power Technologies (HQ)	Provider of energy solutions. The company's offerings include energynet platform and energynet solutions.	650-948-4546	NA	Los Altos Hills
Nextracker Inc (HQ)	Provider of horizontal tracking services. The company focuses on solar power plants and clean technology solutions.	510-270-2500	NA	Fremont
OCSiAl (BR)	Provider of technology and material solutions. The company offers services to the nanomaterials industry.	415-906-5271	NA	Columbus
Pacific Gas & Electric Co (BR)	Provider of natural gas and electric services. The company serves approximately 15 million people throughout northern and central California.	415-973-1000	NA	San Francisco
N Signal Hill Petroleum Inc (HQ)	Producer and supplier of oil and gas.	562-595-6440	51-200	Signal Hill
Soltac Inc (HQ)	Designer and provider of solar devices. It's products find application in warming batteries, signaling, and radar locating.	650-327-7090	NA	Palo Alto

133 = Oil & Gas Field Machinery & Equipment

COMPANY NAME	PRODUCT / SERVICE	PHONE	EMP	CITY
A J Edmond Co (BR)	Provider of sampling and analytical services to petroleum refineries. The company's service areas include petroleum coke, coal, and gypsum.	925-521-1555	NA	Concord
Airgard Inc (HQ)	Manufacturer of gas scrubbers servicing epitaxial, metal etch, poly etch, and CVD process abatement applications.	408-573-0701	NA	San Jose
Altergy Systems (HQ)	Designer and manufacturer of fuel cell power systems. The company serves telecommunication, emergency response, data center, and other fields.	916-458-8590	NA	Folsom
Chevron Corp (HQ)	Provider of mobile asset tracking and management solutions. The company serves the marine, chemicals, and aviation industries.	925-842-1000	NA	San Ramon
Cogco Inc (HQ)	Provider of gas and oil well services such as perforating, thru tubing, case logging, and jet cutting.	530-666-1716	NA	Woodland
Garcia and Associates (HQ)	Provider of natural and cultural resource consultant services. The company's services include permit acquisition, agency consultation, and ecological research.	415-642-8969	NA	San Francisco
Matheson Tri-Gas Inc (BR)	Provider of industrial, electronic, medical, and specialty gases. The company also offers gas detection, purification, and control equipment.	510-793-2559	NA	Newark
Paul Graham Drilling And Service Co (HQ)	Provider of gas drilling services with over head cranes and computer operated plasma cutting machines for top notch drilling.	707-374-5123	NA	Rio Vista
Shields Harper & Co (HQ)	Provider of design assistance, testing, monitoring, fleet fuel control, and underground solutions to contractors, engineers, and designers.	510-653-9119	NA	Martinez
Silpac (HQ)	Distributor and manufacturer of specialty gas handling equipment. The company caters to markers like semiconductor, life science, and solar.	408-492-0011	NA	Santa Clara
Springboard Biodiesel LLC (HQ)	Manufacturer of automated biodiesel processors. The company also offers fuel pumps, and tanks to consumers, small businesses, and municipalities.	530-894-1793	NA	Chico

134 = Oil & Gas Recovery Equipment

COMPANY NAME	PRODUCT / SERVICE	PHONE	EMP	CITY
Aemetis Inc (HQ)	Producer of biochemicals, renewable fuels, food, and feed products. The company's products include Z-Microbe, Glycerin, and edible oils.	408-213-0940	51-200	Cupertino
Biofuel Oasis (HQ)	Producer of biodiesel and seller of urban farm supplies, poultry feed and equipment. The company specializes in biodiesel made from waste oil.	510-665-5509	NA	Berkeley
Cogco Inc (HQ)	Provider of gas and oil well services such as perforating, thru tubing, case logging, and jet cutting.	530-666-1716	NA	Woodland
Duravent Inc (HQ)	Manufacturer of pellets, pressure stacks, and special gas vents. The company is involved in condensing application installation.	800-835-4429	NA	Vacaville
Energy Recovery (HQ)	Manufacturer of energy recovery devices. The company offers pressure exchangers, chargers, pumps for desalination processes, oil and gas applications.	510-483-7370	NA	San Leandro
Pacific Gas & Electric Co (BR)	Provider of natural gas and electric services. The company serves approximately 15 million people throughout northern and central California.	415-973-1000	NA	San Francisco
Pacific Gas & Electric Co (BR)	Provider of natural gas and electric services to the areas in northern and central California. The company specializes in promoting renewable energy.	800-743-5002	NA	Sacramento
Real Environmental Products LLC (HQ)	Provider of landfill gas products. The company products include LFG well heads and 1200 series monitoring well monuments.	209-296-7900	NA	Pine Grove

135 = Solar Energy Collectors/Systems

COMPANY NAME	PRODUCT / SERVICE	PHONE	EMP	CITY
3rd Stone Design Inc (HQ)	Provider of design, product development, and engineering services. The company serves the consumer products and healthcare industries.	415-454-3005	NA	San Rafael
8minute Solar Energy (HQ)	Developer of solar PV projects. The company specializes in project development, financing, utility engineering, and business development.	916-608-9060	NA	El Dorado Hills
Armageddon Energy Inc (HQ)	Designer and manufacturer of rooftop solar systems. The company is engaged in installation services and serves homeowners.	650-641-2899	NA	Menlo Park
Beyond Oil Solar (HQ)	Provider of energy equipment products. The company offers solar panels, inverters, charge controllers, mounting systems, and water pumps.	415-388-0838	NA	Mill Valley
Blue Oak Energy (HQ)	Designer of photovoltaic solar energy systems. The company is engaged in designing, building, and maintenance of solar energy systems.	530-747-2026	NA	Davis
N Caban Resources LLC (HQ)	Provider of health information management services and solutions, and coding services.	877-880-1600	NA	El Segundo
California Solar Systems (BR)	Provider of grid-tied turn key solar electric systems. The company caters to both residential and commercial sectors.	855-227-6527	NA	Fresno
Cenergy Power (HQ)	Developer and installer of solar for the agricultural, commercial, industrial, and utility scale markers.	209-233-9777	NA	Merced
Crystal Solar Inc (HQ)	Developer of solar cells and modules. The company focuses on the conversion of feedstock gas to mono-crystalline silicon wafers.	408-490-1340	NA	Santa Clara
Diablo Solar Services (HQ)	Provider of solar pool heating and solar power photovoltaic systems. The company also offers installation services.	925-313-0600	NA	Martinez
Directnu Energy Corp (HQ)	Provider of wind-solar energy solutions with integrated storage and control systems for businesses and government entities.	408-657-3314	NA	San Jose
Eagle Shield Inc (HQ)	Provider of energy conservation and renewable energy solutions. The company offers services to homes and businesses.	800-408-2375	NA	Danville
Enerparc Inc (DH)	Developer and designer of photovoltaic systems. The company services include EPC work, EPC management, operation, and maintenance.	844-367-7272	NA	Oakland
ET Solar Inc (DH)	Provider of solar inverters and modules. The company offers design, installation, maintenance, and repair services.	925-460-9898	NA	Pleasanton
Fafco Inc (HQ)	Manufacturer of polymer heat exchangers. The company also specializes in thermal energy storage systems.	530-332-2100	NA	Chico
Fenix International (HQ)	Provider of affordable power generation, smart-storage, and distribution solutions for the 1.6 billion people living off the electricity grid.	415-754-9222	NA	San Francisco
Free Hot Water (HQ)	Manufacturer and distributor of solar thermal products. The company serves engineers, architects, developers, and business owners.	408-432-9900	NA	San Jose
Garcia and Associates (HQ)	Provider of natural and cultural resource consultant services. The company's services include permit acquisition, agency consultation, and ecological research.	415-642-8969	NA	San Francisco
Glasspoint Solar Inc (HQ)	Manufacturer of solar steam generators for the oil and gas industry. The company is engaged in design and installation services.	415-778-2800	NA	Fremont
Intevac Inc (HQ)	Supplier of magnetic media processing systems. The company offers advanced equipment to the hard disk drive, solar, and photonics industries.	408-986-9888	NA	Santa Clara
ISA Corp (HQ)	Developer and manufacturer of solar mounting systems for commercial applications. The company also offers solar thermal systems.	510-324-3755	NA	Union City
King-Solarman Inc (HQ)	Focuses on the sale of solar panels, power inverters, and related supplies. The company is involved in solar project financing services.	408-373-8800	NA	Fremont
Meline Engineering Corp (HQ)	Provider of energy efficient mechanical system design services. The company also offers mechanical engineering services.	916-366-3458	NA	Sacramento
MiaSole Hi-Tech Corp (HQ)	Manufacturer of copper indium gallium selenide thin-film photovoltaic solar panels. The company offers solar power plants for industrial needs.	408-940-9658	NA	Santa Clara
Morley Manufacturing Inc (HQ)	Designer and manufacturer of drain back water storage tanks for residential and commercial purposes. The company offers installation services.	530-477-6527	NA	Grass Valley
Natron Resources Inc (HQ)	Provider of solar system, flat-plate photovoltaic, and solar thermal design and installations services.	510-868-0701	NA	Moraga
Nextracker Inc (HQ)	Provider of horizontal tracking services. The company focuses on solar power plants and clean technology solutions.	510-270-2500	NA	Fremont
Occidental Power (HQ)	Designer and installer of commercial and residential solar electric, solar thermal, and natural gas cogeneration systems.	415-681-8861	NA	San Francisco
N Plumbing Wholesale Outlet (HQ)	Wholesaler of plumbing supplies and related accessories.	626-744-3170	11-50	Pasadena
Poco Solar Energy Inc (HQ)	Designer and installer of solar energy systems that provide electricity and heat for swimming pools.	408-970-0680	NA	Santa Clara
Redwood Renewables (HQ)	Developer and manufacturer of residential tiles and solar roofing. The company also focuses on the marketing aspects.	415-924-8140	NA	Corte Madera
Reel Solar Power Inc (HQ)	Provider of tools and materials to photovoltaic manufacturing. The company also engages in the manufacturing of cadmium telluride solar panels.	408-258-4714	NA	San Jose
Silicon Genesis Corp (HQ)	Manufacturer of semiconductor and solar fabrication tools. The company offers stand-alone plasma tools and debond and cleave tools.	408-228-5858	NA	San Jose

COMPANY NAME	PRODUCT / SERVICE	PHONE	EMP	CITY
Siva Power Inc (HQ)	Manufacturer of solar products. The company specializes in semiconductor, flat panel display, and solar devices.	408-834-7400	NA	Santa Clara
Solano Archaeological Services (HQ)	Provider of archaeological services. The company services also include cultural resource and artifact analysis and curation.	707-718-1416	NA	Suisun City
Solar Sense PV Inc (HQ)	Provider of solar power system installation services. The company also focuses on design and serves residential, commercial, and utility applications.	888-786-4339	NA	Pleasanton
Solarbos Inc (HQ)	Designer and manufacturer of electrical products. The company exclusively caters to the solar industry.	925-456-7744	NA	Livermore
Soltac Inc (HQ)	Designer and provider of solar devices. It's products find application in warming batteries, signaling, and radar locating.	650-327-7090	NA	Palo Alto
N SPAP Company LLC (HQ)	International manufacturer representative agency.	714-960-0586	NA	Huntington Beach
sPower (BR)	Provider of utility-scale solar generation and physical plant development services for landowners, utilities, and communities.	415-692-7740	NA	San Francisco
Sun First! Solar (HQ)	Provider of renewable energy services. The company offers residential and commercial solar PV and swimming pool systems.	415-458-5870	NA	San Rafael
Sunlink Corp (HQ)	Designer and manufacturer of roof and ground mounted systems for commercial and utility-scale installations.	415-925-9650	NA	Mill Valley
Sunperfect Solar Inc (HQ)	Provider of energy solutions. The company specializes in the design, manufacture, and installation of solar panels.	510-573-6888	NA	San Jose
Sunterra Solar Inc (HQ)	Designer of turnkey grid-connected solar power systems for commercial, agricultural, and governmental customers.	415-883-6800	NA	Novato
Suntrek Industries Inc (BR)	Manufacturer, designer, and installer of solar power systems for residential, commercial, and agricultural solar power applications.	925-372-8983	NA	Martinez
Sunverge Energy Inc (HQ)	Provider of power and energy services. The company focuses on solar power and combines batteries and power electronics.	209-931-5677	NA	Stockton
Trina Solar US Inc (RH)	Manufacturer of mono and multicrystalline photovoltaic (PV) modules. The company serves residential, commercial, and utility purposes.	800-696-7114	NA	San Jose
Ultrasolar Technology Inc (HQ)	Manufacturer of solar panel devices. The company specializes in residential, commercial, and utility solar arrays.	408-499-6227	NA	Santa Clara
Upsolar America Inc (BR)	Developer and producer of solar photovoltaic modules. The company's services include installation and maintenance and offers packing solutions.	415-263-9920	NA	San Francisco
WAGAN Corp (HQ)	Developer and marketer of automotive accessories to mobile professionals. The company's offerings include warmers, defrosters, and heated cushions.	510-471-9221	NA	Hayward

136 = Environmental

COMPANY NAME	PRODUCT / SERVICE	PHONE	EMP	CITY
Enviro Safetech Inc (HQ)	Provider of environmental, health, and safety consulting services. The company deals with auditing and inspections.	408-943-9090	NA	San Jose
The Cohen Group (HQ)	Provider of health and safety training, litigation support, indoor air quality, microbial contamination, and related services.	650-349-9737	NA	San Mateo

137 = Bioremediation Equipment/Systems

COMPANY NAME	PRODUCT / SERVICE	PHONE	EMP	CITY
Agra Tech Inc (HQ)	Manufacturer of greenhouses and accessories for commercial, horticultural, and agricultural growers. The company offers heating and cooling equipment.	925-432-3399	NA	Pittsburg
Bullet Guard Co (HQ)	Designer and manufacturer of bullet resistant and bullet proof products. The company serves the banking, government, and law enforcement sectors.	916-373-0402	NA	West Sacramento
Forsgren Associate Inc (DH)	Provider of civil and environmental engineering consulting services. The company specializes in planning, design, survey, and construction management.	916-638-1119	NA	Rancho Cordova
Ultra T Equipment Company Inc (HQ)	Manufacturer of spin coaters, developer stations, reionizers, and microelectronics cleaning systems.	510-440-3909	NA	Fremont

138 = Environmental Analysis Equipment

COMPANY NAME	PRODUCT / SERVICE	PHONE	EMP	CITY
Aethlabs (HQ)	Provider of black carbon monitoring equipment. The company also deals in manufacturing and assembly services.	415-529-2355	NA	San Francisco
Asbestos Tem Laboratories Inc (HQ)	Provider of laboratory services including asbestos and lead testing. The company serves geologists, contractors, and homeowners.	510-704-8930	NA	Oakland
Enviro-Tech Services Co (HQ)	Designer and manufacturer of environmental products. The company offers water sampling equipment, air monitoring equipment, and general field supplies.	800-468-8921	NA	Martinez
Etm Electromatic Inc (HQ)	Manufacturer of custom high voltage power supplies and amplifiers. The company is engaged in troubleshooting, repairs, and maintenance services.	510-797-1100	NA	Newark
Fortrend Engineering Corp (HQ)	Designer and manufacturer of mechanical handling equipment. The company also specializes in distribution services.	408-734-9311	NA	San Jose
Geosyntec Consultants Inc (BR)	Provider of consulting and engineering services. The company serves customers in the oil and gas, refining, petrochemical, and waste management industries.	916-637-8048	NA	Rancho Cordova

COMPANY NAME	PRODUCT / SERVICE	PHONE	EMP	CITY
Inta Technologies (HQ)	Manufacturer of components used in instruments for environmental analysis. The company also offers ceramic-to-metal assemblies connectors.	408-748-9955	NA	Santa Clara
Los Gatos Research Inc (HQ)	Manufacturer of analyzers for the measurement of trace gases and isotopes. The company serves the industrial and environmental sectors.	650-965-7772	NA	San Jose
Mesotech International Inc (HQ)	Provider of weather monitoring and reporting systems and software solutions. The company serves airport, defense, and agriculture industries.	916-368-2020	NA	Sacramento
Ondavia Inc (HQ)	Provider of water analysis solutions. The company offers OndaVia analysis system that enables laboratory-grade water testing.	510-576-0476	NA	Hayward
Protemp Mechanical Inc (HQ)	Provider of environmental test equipment calibration services. The company's services include preventative maintenance, chamber modifications, and consulting.	408-244-9821	NA	Santa Clara
Sierra Monitor Corp (HQ)	Manufacturer and seller of safety and environmental instrumentation. The company offers hazardous gas detection systems and site management products.	408-262-6611	NA	Milpitas
SWCA Environmental Consultants (BR)	Provider of environmental consultant services. The company focuses on environmental planning and regulatory compliance activities.	650-440-4160	NA	Half Moon Bay
Trinity Consultants Inc (BR)	Provider of environmental consulting services. The company engages in environmental outsourcing and litigation support services.	510-285-6351	NA	Oakland

139 = Environmental Analysis Services

COMPANY NAME	PRODUCT / SERVICE	PHONE	EMP	CITY
3rd Stone Design Inc (HQ)	Provider of design, product development, and engineering services. The company serves the consumer products and healthcare industries.	415-454-3005	NA	San Rafael
A&L Western Labs Inc (HQ)	Provider of analytical services to agricultural sector. The company's services include soil analysis, pathology, microbiology, and water analysis.	209-529-4080	NA	Modesto
ACC Environmental Consultants (HQ)	Provider of environmental consulting services. The company's services include moisture testing, site assessment, mold testing, and asbestos consulting.	510-638-8400	NA	Oakland
Adr Environmental Group Inc (HQ)	Provider of risk management services and due diligence services. The company's due diligence service includes engineering and structural services.	916-921-0600	NA	Sacramento
AEI Consultants (BR)	Provider of environmental and engineering services. The company's services also include industrial hygiene and construction.	916-333-4568	NA	Sacramento
Aero-Environmental Consulting (HQ)	Provider of environmental consulting solutions. The company's services include air quality assessment, regulatory compliance, and health planning.	831-394-1199	NA	Monterey
Allied Environmental Inc (HQ)	Provider of asbestos and lead abatement services. The company specializes in commercial, residential, and industrial contracting services.	510-732-1300	NA	Hayward
Aspen Environmental Group (BR)	Provider of environmental compliance, impact assessment, and mitigation services. The company's services include construction monitoring and project management.	415-955-4775	NA	San Francisco
Balance Hydrologics Inc (HQ)	Provider of hydrologic services. The company offers geomorphology, restoration design, watershed management, and wetland inspection services.	510-704-1000	NA	Berkeley
Baseline Environmental Consulting (HQ)	Provider of environmental consulting services including remediation, investigations, data management, and surveys.	510-420-8686	NA	Emeryville
Blackburn Consulting (HQ)	Provider of geotechnical engineering, geo environmental engineering, design materials engineering, forensic, and construction services.	530-887-1494	NA	Auburn
CEA Consulting (HQ)	Provider of environmental consulting services. The company's services include recruiting and organizational design services.	415-421-4213	NA	San Francisco
CHA Corp (HQ)	Developer and marketer of microwave technologies. The company offers carbon regeneration, hypergolic destruction, and emission control solutions.	916-550-5380	NA	Sacramento
Clean Earth (BR)	Provider of recycling solutions. The company acts as regulated and permitted electronics and universal waste recycler.	510-429-1129	NA	Hayward
Denele Analytical Inc (HQ)	Provider of agriculture and environmental support services. The company offers analytical services for plant tissue, manure, and wastewater needs.	209-634-9055	NA	Turlock
EGS Inc (HQ)	Provider of geothermal exploration development services. The company's services include remote sensing, geologic mapping, and subsurface visualization.	707-595-8760	NA	Santa Rosa
EM Lab P&K (BR)	Provider of indoor air quality testing services. The company offers culturable air fungi, spore trap analysis, and yeast identification services.	916-374-4483	NA	West Sacramento
Environmental Risk Communications Inc (BR)	Provider of consulting services in environmental liabilities management. The company's services include site strategic planning and project controls.	510-548-5570	NA	Oakland
Environmental Science Associates (HQ)	Provider of restoration and mitigation, regulatory permitting, compliance monitoring, and community planning services.	415-896-5900	NA	San Francisco

COMPANY NAME	PRODUCT / SERVICE	PHONE	EMP	CITY
Freshwater Environmental Svc (HQ)	Provider of environmental services. The company's services include soil investigation work plans, soil sampling reporting, sediment sampling, and monitoring.	707-839-0091	NA	Arcata
Frey Environmental Inc (BR)	Provider of geological and engineering consulting services. The company offers stormwater management, methane assessments/ mitigation, and asbestos-related services.	831-464-1634	NA	Santa Cruz
Grayland Environmental (HQ)	Provider of environmental and natural resources protections services. The company offers environmental engineering, geological and geophysical services.	530-756-1441	NA	Davis
Horizon Water and Environment LLC (HQ)	Provider of environmental consulting services. The company specializes in watershed science, environmental compliance, and water resources management.	510-986-1850	11-50	Oakland
Kaz & Associates Environmental Services (HQ)	Provider of water management consulting services. The company's services include enforcement response, and groundwater contamination investigation.	707-747-1126	NA	Benicia
Keish Environmental PC (HQ)	Provider of environmental and stormwater compliance services. The company also specializes in construction inspection services.	408-359-7248	NA	San Jose
Kings River Conservation District (HQ)	Provider of resource management solutions. The company focuses on flood protection, water supply, power generation, and other needs.	559-237-5567	NA	Fresno
Lamphier-Gregory (HQ)	Provider of urban planning services. The company provides environmental analysis, project management, and coordination services.	510-535-6690	NA	Oakland
N Marc Boogay (HQ)	Provider of phase I and II environmental site assessments, the design of remediation for contaminated soil or groundwater, monitoring progress in site remediation, asbestos surveys in buildings, designs asbestos abatements and asbestos operation management plans, building engineering inspection, seismic and probable maximum loss reports.	760-407-4000	NA	Oceanside
Moore Twining Associates Inc (HQ)	Provider of geotechnical engineering, environmental, construction inspection, materials testing, analytical chemistry, and drilling services.	559-268-7021	NA	Fresno
National Center For Appropriate Technology (BR)	Provider of information and access services. The company's offerings include weatherizing houses, monitoring energy applications, and testing products.	530-792-7338	NA	Davis
N Network Environmental Systems Inc (BR)	Provider of occupational health and safety training and environmental compliance consulting services.	800-637-2384	NA	Folsom
Northgate Environmental Management Inc (HQ)	Provider of interdisciplinary technical solutions. The company focuses on results-oriented scientific and engineering investigation and analysis.	510-839-0688	NA	Oakland
Quanta Laboratories (HQ)	Provider of environmental testing and consulting services. The company offers vibration test, shock test, and chalmers test services.	408-988-0770	NA	Santa Clara
Rincon Consultants Inc (BR)	Provider of environmental consulting services. The company specializes in land use planning, site assessment, remediation, and other services.	510-834-4455	NA	Oakland
N Sapphos Environmental Inc (BR)	Provider of business consulting services.	626-683-3547	11-50	Pasadena
SCA Environmental Inc (HQ)	Provider of environmental science, occupational health and safety, engineering, and laboratory analyses services.	415-882-1675	NA	San Francisco
Shields Harper & Co (HQ)	Provider of design assistance, testing, monitoring, fleet fuel control, and underground solutions to contractors, engineers, and designers.	510-653-9119	NA	Martinez
Stantec (BR)	Provider of environmental consulting services specializing in GIS mapping, remote sensing, permitting, and ecosystem restoration.	530-222-5347	NA	Redding
SWCA Environmental Consultants (BR)	Provider of environmental consultant services. The company focuses on environmental planning and regulatory compliance activities.	650-440-4160	NA	Half Moon Bay
Terradex Inc (HQ)	Provider of web and consulting services. The company offers dig clean, cleanup deck, and web development services.	650-227-3250	NA	Palo Alto
Terraphase Engineering (HQ)	Provider of environmental consulting services. The company offers environmental due diligence, and soil and groundwater remediation services.	510-645-1850	NA	Oakland
Test-O-Pac Industries Inc (HQ)	Provider of environmental and package testing services. The company deals with component testing, product reliability, and medical package testing.	408-436-1117	NA	San Jose
TRC Companies Inc (BR)	Provider of scientific and engineering software services. The company offers hydropower licensing, power delivery, and telecommunications engineering services.	415-434-2600	NA	San Francisco
Westervelt Ecological Services (HQ)	Provider of ecological solutions. The company offers wetland mitigation and conservation banking, geographic information system analysis, and other services.	916-646-3644	NA	Sacramento
N Wilson, Ihrig & Associates Inc (BR)	Provider of noise, vibration and acoustical consulting services.	510-658-6719	NA	Emeryville

140 = Environmental R&D

ACC Environmental Consultants (HQ)	Provider of environmental consulting services. The company's services include moisture testing, site assessment, mold testing, and asbestos consulting.	510-638-8400	NA	Oakland
Adr Environmental Group Inc (HQ)	Provider of risk management services and due diligence services. The company's due diligence service includes engineering and structural services.	916-921-0600	NA	Sacramento

COMPANY NAME	PRODUCT / SERVICE	PHONE	EMP	CITY
AEI Consultants (BR)	Provider of environmental and engineering services. The company's services also include industrial hygiene and construction.	916-333-4568	NA	Sacramento
Allied Environmental Inc (HQ)	Provider of asbestos and lead abatement services. The company specializes in commercial, residential, and industrial contracting services.	510-732-1300	NA	Hayward
Amprius Inc (HQ)	Developer and manufacturer of lithium-ion batteries. The company offers services to the industrial sectors.	800-425-8803	NA	Fremont
BASF Venture Capital America Inc (RH)	Manufacturer of basic chemicals and intermediates such as solvents, plasticizers, and monomers. The company serves the agriculture market.	510-445-6140	NA	Fremont
Blue Star Electronics (HQ)	Focuses on the resale, recycling and end of life programs for electronic equipment and components. The company offers e-waste solutions.	925-420-5593	NA	Livermore
BSK Associates (BR)	Provider of geotechnical and environmental testing services. The company also offers materials testing services.	916-853-9293	NA	Rancho Cordova
CEA Consulting (HQ)	Provider of environmental consulting services. The company's services include recruiting and organizational design services.	415-421-4213	NA	San Francisco
Daniel B Stephens & Associates Inc (BR)	Provider of services in hydrology, environmental engineering, and science. The company services include water resources and soil testing.	800-933-3105	NA	Oakland
E2C Remediation (HQ)	Provider of environmental remediation services. The company services also include soil and groundwater remediation and civil and geological engineering.	916-782-8700	NA	Roseville
Eeonyx Corp (HQ)	Manufacturer and provider of knitting services. The company focuses on textiles, foams, felts, and powders.	510-741-3632	NA	Pinole
Enviro-Tech Services Co (HQ)	Designer and manufacturer of environmental products. The company offers water sampling equipment, air monitoring equipment, and general field supplies.	800-468-8921	NA	Martinez
Environmental Products & Technologies Corp (HQ)	Developer of closed-loop, short hydraulic retention time anaerobic digesters. The company specializes in biogas technology solutions.	559-201-6484	NA	Visalia
Environmental Risk Communications Inc (BR)	Provider of consulting services in environmental liabilities management. The company's services include site strategic planning and project controls.	510-548-5570	NA	Oakland
Fruit Growers Laboratory Inc (BR)	Provider of testing and analytical services. The company performs drinking and waste water analysis, agriculture testing, and hazardous waste analysis.	209-942-0182	NA	Stockton
Grayland Environmental (HQ)	Provider of environmental and natural resources protections services. The company offers environmental engineering, geological and geophysical services.	530-756-1441	NA	Davis
Horizon Water and Environment LLC (HQ)	Provider of environmental consulting services. The company specializes in watershed science, environmental compliance, and water resources management.	510-986-1850	11-50	Oakland
Kaz & Associates Environmental Services (HQ)	Provider of water management consulting services. The company's services include enforcement response, and groundwater contamination investigation.	707-747-1126	NA	Benicia
Lacroix Davis LLC (BR)	Provider of building and environmental forensics and consulting services. The company provides support for investigation, litigation, and education.	925-299-1140	NA	Lafayette
Materials Testing Inc (HQ)	Provider of geotechnical engineering and materials testing services. The company offers geotechnical, environment, special inspection, and material testing services.	530-222-1116	NA	Redding
Millennium Consulting Associates (HQ)	Provider of environmental and industrial hygiene services. The company offers environmental engineering, consulting, and compliance services.	925-808-6700	NA	Oakland
NRC Environmental Services Inc (BR)	Provider of environmental, industrial, and emergency solutions. The company offers oil spill response, industrial cleaning, sediment remediation, and other services.	510-749-1390	NA	Alameda
Panasas Inc (HQ)	Provider of scale-out NAS storage system for most demanding workloads in life sciences, media and entertainment, energy, and education environments.	408-215-6800	NA	Sunnyvale
Panorama Environmental Inc (HQ)	Provider of environmental planning services. The company engages in regulatory permitting and geographic information systems.	650-373-1200	NA	San Francisco
Prima Environmental Inc (HQ)	Provider of laboratory testing services. The company specializes in treatability testing, technology evaluation, and scientific consulting services.	916-939-7300	NA	El Dorado Hills
Quanta Laboratories (HQ)	Provider of environmental testing and consulting services. The company offers vibration test, shock test, and chalmers test services.	408-988-0770	NA	Santa Clara
RES Environmental Services Inc (HQ)	Provider of environmental services. The company offers air-moving, contract safety, and vacuum truck services.	925-432-1755	NA	Pittsburg
Ridge to River (HQ)	Provider of hydrologic analysis and modeling services. The company is also focused on ecological restoration, erosion control, and water quality analysis.	707-357-0857	NA	Fort Bragg
SCHUTZE & Associates Inc (HQ)	Provider of environmental consulting services. The company's services include groundwater monitoring and dry cleaning remediation.	510-226-9944	NA	Fremont
Southall Environmental Associates Inc (HQ)	Provider of science to support conservation management. The company specializes in marine and terrestrial ecosystems.	831-661-5177	NA	Aptos

COMPANY NAME	PRODUCT / SERVICE	PHONE	EMP	CITY
141 = Hazardous & Other Waste Disposal or Management Services				
Baseline Environmental Consulting (HQ)	Provider of environmental consulting services including remediation, investigations, data management, and surveys.	510-420-8686	NA	Emeryville
Blackburn Consulting (HQ)	Provider of geotechnical engineering, geo environmental engineering, design materials engineering, forensic, and construction services.	530-887-1494	NA	Auburn
N California Steel Industries (HQ)	Manufacturer of steel products.	909-350-6300	501-1000	Fontana
N Monterey Regional Waste Management District (HQ)	Dealer of solid waste management.	831-384-5313	51-200	Marina
N Pleasanton Garbage Service Inc (HQ)	Provider of garbage collection services for residential and commercial sectors.	925-846-2042	NA	Pleasanton
Recology Of The Coast (HQ)	Provider of resource recovery services. The company's services include urban cleaning services, collection, sorting, transfer, recovery and landfill management.	650-355-9000	NA	Pacifica
SCA Environmental Inc (HQ)	Provider of environmental science, occupational health and safety, engineering, and laboratory analyses services.	415-882-1675	NA	San Francisco
N W.B.R. Inc (HQ)	Provider of waste transportation and disposal systems.	949-673-1247	NA	Newport Beach
142 = Other Environmental Services				
Adr Environmental Group Inc (HQ)	Provider of risk management services and due diligence services. The company's due diligence service includes engineering and structural services.	916-921-0600	NA	Sacramento
Advanced Geoenvironmental Inc (BR)	Provider of environmental consulting services. The company services include soil and groundwater remediation and water and wastewater services.	800-511-9300	NA	Santa Rosa
AEMTEK Laboratories (HQ)	Provider of testing, research, training and consulting services and sampling products for the food, environmental and pharmaceutical industries.	510-979-1979	NA	Fremont
Aero-Environmental Consulting (HQ)	Provider of environmental consulting solutions. The company's services include air quality assessment, regulatory compliance, and health planning.	831-394-1199	NA	Monterey
Agra Tech Inc (HQ)	Manufacturer of greenhouses and accessories for commercial, horticultural, and agricultural growers. The company offers heating and cooling equipment.	925-432-3399	NA	Pittsburg
N Alcon Entertainment LLC (HQ)	Provider of finance, produce, market, and distributor of entertainment that delights both its creators and its audience.	310-789-3040	NA	Los Angeles
Alisto Engineering Group Inc (HQ)	Provider of engineering and environmental consulting services. The company serves the private industry and government agencies.	925-279-5000	NA	Walnut Creek
All Power Labs (HQ)	Manufacturer of biomass fueled power generators. The company is a global leader in small scale gasification.	510-845-1500	NA	Berkeley
Allterra Environmental Inc (HQ)	Provider of environmental site remediation and compliance services. The company offerings include permitting, geologic hazards, and sustainable solutions.	831-425-2608	NA	Santa Cruz
Anamet Inc (HQ)	Provider of materials engineering analysis and lab testing services. The company focuses on product testing, failure analysis, and forensic engineering.	510-887-8811	NA	Hayward
Apex Envirotech Inc (HQ)	Provider of environmental management and remediation technology. The company also offers engineering services.	800-242-5249	NA	Gold River
Applied Earthworks Inc (HQ)	Provider of history, archaeology, paleontology, and cultural resources management and related services.	559-229-1856	NA	Fresno
APX Power Markets Inc (BR)	Provider of e-commerce services for the electrical sector. The company serves residential, commercial, and industrial properties.	408-517-2100	NA	San Jose
Aquifer Sciences Inc (HQ)	Provider of environmental assessment and remediation services. The company is also engaged in remedial design and implementation.	925-283-9098	NA	Lafayette
Area West Environmental Inc (HQ)	Provider of environmental assessment services. The company is also engaged in planning, permitting, and regulatory compliance management services.	916-987-3362	NA	Orangevale
Asian Pacific Environmental Network (HQ)	Provider of environmental services. The company engages in membership of low income immigrant and refugee communities.	510-834-8920	NA	Oakland
Atlas Engineering Services Inc (HQ)	Provider of environmental consulting services. The company offers services for aquifer testing, onsite wastewater disposal, and groundwater sanitary surveys.	831-426-1440	NA	Santa Cruz
Balance Hydrologics Inc (HQ)	Provider of hydrologic services. The company offers geomorphology, restoration design, watershed management, and wetland inspection services.	510-704-1000	NA	Berkeley
Basics Environmental Inc (HQ)	Provider of environmental engineering consulting services. The company focuses on environmental site assessments for real estate transactions.	510-834-9099	NA	Oakland
Better World Group Inc (BR)	Provider of environmental strategy consulting services. The company offers political strategy, coalition management, media, and communications.	916-498-9411	NA	Sacramento

COMPANY NAME	PRODUCT / SERVICE	PHONE	EMP	CITY
Biomax Environmental Inc (HQ)	Provider of indoor air quality assessment, sampling, industrial hygiene monitoring, auditing, and assessment services.	510-724-3100	NA	Pinole
Blackburn Consulting (HQ)	Provider of geotechnical engineering, geo environmental engineering, design materials engineering, forensic, and construction services.	530-887-1494	NA	Auburn
Blue Source LLC (BR)	Provider of services for the mining industry. The company offers project development, offset sales and marketing, consulting, and other related services.	415-399-9101	NA	San Francisco
Blymyer Engineers Inc (HQ)	Provider of solar engineering, facility design, and related services. The company serves the food and beverage and glass manufacturing industries.	510-521-3773	NA	Alameda
Brelje & Race Laboratories Inc (HQ)	Provider of water and wastewater testing services. The company analyses process include nitrate, arsenic, and volatile organics compounds.	707-544-8807	NA	Santa Rosa
Brown and Caldwell (BR)	Provider of engineering consulting services. The company specializes in contracting, pumping station design, project management, and odor control.	408-703-2528	NA	San Jose
Burleson Consulting Inc (HQ)	Provider of environmental compliance and engineering services for the clients in Southern Oregon, Northern California, and Nevada.	916-984-4651	NA	Folsom
California Transport Enterprises Inc (HQ)	Provider of transportation and trucking services.	323-357-1720	NA	South Gate
Capital Engineering Consultants Inc (HQ)	Provider of mechanical engineering, sustainable design and green engineering, building commissioning, energy modeling, and other related services.	916-851-3500	NA	Rancho Cordova
Catalyst Environmental Inc (HQ)	Provider of environmental services. The company's services comprise tank cleaning and hydro blasting services and soil and groundwater sampling.	650-642-6583	NA	San Carlos
CGI Technical Services Inc (HQ)	Provider of technical services. The company offerings include geotechnical engineering, engineering geology, and pavement design services.	530-244-6277	NA	Redding
CHA Corp (HQ)	Developer and marketer of microwave technologies. The company offers carbon regeneration, hypergolic destruction, and emission control solutions.	916-550-5380	NA	Sacramento
Chico Environmental Science & Planning (HQ)	Provider of environmental consulting services. The company offers site assessments, storm water pollution prevention plans, and environmental forensics.	530-899-2900	NA	Chico
Clean Earth (BR)	Provider of recycling solutions. The company acts as regulated and permitted electronics and universal waste recycler.	510-429-1129	NA	Hayward
Commodity Resource & Environmental Inc (BR)	Producer of silver. The company engages in silver recovery, photo solution waste disposal, and other activities.	408-501-0691	NA	San Jose
Condor Country Consulting (HQ)	Provider of natural and cultural resource supporting services. The company also provides ecological, natural resource, and cartographic services.	925-335-9308	NA	Martinez
David J Powers & Associates Inc (HQ)	Provider of environmental consulting services. The company focuses on transportation, parks, and recreation projects.	408-248-3500	NA	San Jose
Dawn Reis Ecological Studies (HQ)	Provider of wildlife research and biological consulting services. The company is specialized in aquatic systems and endangered species population.	831-588-7550	NA	Watsonville
Denise Duffy & Associates Inc (HQ)	Provider of environmental sciences, planning, and biological consulting services. The company is also focused on land use and contract planning.	831-373-4341	NA	Monterey
Diablo Green Consulting Inc (HQ)	Provider of environmental consulting services. The company specializes in site assessments, geophysical survey, and cultural resource management.	925-365-0730	NA	Danville
Dysert Environmental Inc (HQ)	Provider of environmental solutions. The company's services include wastewater sampling, project management, soil sampling, and decontamination confirmation.	650-799-9204	NA	San Carlos
Eastern Research Group Inc (BR)	Provider of performance measurement, risk assessment, event planning and facilitation, and training services.	916-635-6592	NA	Sacramento
Ecoshift Consulting LLC (HQ)	Provider of consulting services. The company offers consulting for alternative fuels, climate change, carbon reduction strategies, and carbon trading.	831-277-0167	NA	Monterey
EGS Inc (HQ)	Provider of geothermal exploration development services. The company's services include remote sensing, geologic mapping, and subsurface visualization.	707-595-8760	NA	Santa Rosa
Electro Magnetic Test Inc (HQ)	Provider of testing and consulting services. The company focuses on engineering services in wireless, wireline telecom, and safety certifications.	650-965-4000	NA	Mountain View
Enplan (HQ)	Provider of environmental and geospatial technology services. The company focuses on wetland delineation and permit processing activities.	530-221-0440	NA	Redding

COMPANY NAME	PRODUCT / SERVICE	PHONE	EMP	CITY
Enpro Solutions Inc (HQ)	Provider of environmental remediation, management, permitting, and construction services. The company also deals with process safety consulting.	925-803-8045	NA	Dublin
Enviro Survey Inc (HQ)	Provider of environmental consulting and technical services. The company provides soil and groundwater remediation and environmental safety services.	415-882-4549	NA	San Francisco
Enviro-Tech Services Co (HQ)	Designer and manufacturer of environmental products. The company offers water sampling equipment, air monitoring equipment, and general field supplies.	800-468-8921	NA	Martinez
Environmental Incentives LLC (HQ)	Provider of environmental conservation services. The company projects include Nevada conservation credit system and Colorado habitat exchange.	530-541-2980	NA	South Lake Tahoe
Environmental Remedies Inc (HQ)	Provider of asbestos abatement services. The company engages in mold remediation, lead removal, and biological containment radiation service.	925-461-3285	NA	Hayward
Environmental Sampling Services LLC (HQ)	Provider of technical services for environmental assessments needs. The company also focuses on investigation and remediation.	925-372-8108	NA	Martinez
Excelchem Laboratories Inc (HQ)	Provider of analytical consultation, on-site analysis, custom reporting, and mobile laboratory services.	916-543-4445	NA	Rocklin
Frey Environmental Inc (BR)	Provider of geological and engineering consulting services. The company offers stormwater management, methane assessments/ mitigation, and asbestos-related services.	831-464-1634	NA	Santa Cruz
Fruit Growers Laboratory Inc (BR)	Provider of testing and analytical services. The company performs drinking and waste water analysis, agriculture testing, and hazardous waste analysis.	209-942-0182	NA	Stockton
G Fred Lee & Associates (HQ)	Provider of surface and groundwater evaluation services. The company focuses on landfill impacts, eutrophication, watershed studies, and other needs.	530-753-9630	NA	El Macero
Geo-Tech Information Solutions (HQ)	Provider of concierge services in the environmental and natural hazard disclosure risk management field.	916-941-8300	NA	Sacramento
Geosyntec Consultants Inc (BR)	Provider of consulting and engineering services. The company serves customers in the oil and gas, refining, petrochemical, and waste management industries.	916-637-8048	NA	Rancho Cordova
Golder Associates Inc (BR)	Provider of ground engineering and environmental services. The company serves business organizations and the industrial sector.	408-220-9223	NA	Sunnyvale
Groundwater & Environmental Services Inc (BR)	Provider of environmental consulting services. The company serves customers in the oil and gas, government, and petroleum markers.	866-507-1411	NA	Benicia
Harris & Lee Environmental Sciences LLC (HQ)	Provider of environmental consulting services. The company's services include environmental risk management, and preliminary environmental assessment.	415-287-3007	NA	San Rafael
Helix Environmental Planning Inc (HQ)	Provider of landscape architecture, planning, environmental consulting, restoration, and regulatory permitting services.	619-462-1515	NA	La Mesa
HT Harvey & Associates (HQ)	Provider of ecological consulting services that include ecological research, impact analysis, restoration design, and park planning.	408-458-3200	NA	Los Gatos
Itrenew Inc (HQ)	Provider of information technology services. The company focuses on data eradication, server application, logistics management, and configuration.	408-744-9600	NA	Newark
JRP Historical Consulting LLC (HQ)	Provider of resources management services. The company's services include water use studies, flood control, public access history, and legislative history research.	530-757-2521	NA	Davis
Kaz & Associates Environmental Services (HQ)	Provider of water management consulting services. The company's services include enforcement response, and groundwater contamination investigation.	707-747-1126	NA	Benicia
Lacroix Davis LLC (BR)	Provider of building and environmental forensics and consulting services. The company provides support for investigation, litigation, and education.	925-299-1140	NA	Lafayette
Larry Walker Associates (HQ)	Provider of environmental engineering and consulting services. The company provides water quality solutions.	530-753-6400	NA	Davis
Live Oak Associates Inc (BR)	Provider of ecological and biological consulting services. The company is also focused on environmental permitting and planning activities.	408-224-8300	NA	San Jose
Locus Technologies (HQ)	Provider of web based environmental information management systems. The company's services include field installation, training, and technical support.	415-360-5889	NA	Mountain View
LSA Associates Inc (BR)	Provider of consulting services. The company focuses on environmental, transportation, and planning services.	510-540-7331	NA	Berkeley
Luhdorff & Scalmanini Consulting Engineers (HQ)	Provider of consulting and engineering services that include investigation, use, protection, development, and management of groundwater resources.	530-661-0109	NA	Woodland
Mako Industries (HQ)	Manufacturer of remediation systems for the environmental industry. The company is focused on field and carbon change out services.	925-209-7985	NA	Livermore
Matriscope (BR)	Provider of geotechnical and environmental engineering services. The company also provides materials testing and special inspection services.	916-375-6700	NA	Sacramento

COMPANY NAME	PRODUCT / SERVICE	PHONE	EMP	CITY
Millennium Consulting Associates (HQ)	Provider of environmental and industrial hygiene services. The company offers environmental engineering, consulting, and compliance services.	925-808-6700	NA	Oakland
Monk & Associates Inc (HQ)	Provider of environmental consulting services. The company specializes in biological constraints analyses and mitigation plans.	925-947-4867	NA	Walnut Creek
Moore Twining Associates Inc (HQ)	Provider of geotechnical engineering, environmental, construction inspection, materials testing, analytical chemistry, and drilling services.	559-268-7021	NA	Fresno
National Analytical Laboratories Inc (HQ)	Provider of environmental lab testing and consulting services. The company focuses on air monitoring, building inspection, and operations training.	916-361-0555	NA	Rancho Cordova
National Center For Appropriate Technology (BR)	Provider of information and access services. The company's offerings include weatherizing houses, monitoring energy applications, and testing products.	530-792-7338	NA	Davis
Northgate Environmental Management Inc (HQ)	Provider of interdisciplinary technical solutions. The company focuses on results-oriented scientific and engineering investigation and analysis.	510-839-0688	NA	Oakland
Northstar (HQ)	Provider of land development services, municipal infrastructure design, onsite waste water systems, and environmental consulting services.	530-893-1600	NA	Chico
NRC Environmental Services Inc (BR)	Provider of environmental, industrial, and emergency solutions. The company offers oil spill response, industrial cleaning, sediment remediation, and other services.	510-749-1390	NA	Alameda
Pangea Environmental Services Inc (HQ)	Provider of environmental consulting services. The company's services include site assessment and remediation, litigation support, and soil testing.	510-836-3700	NA	Berkeley
Panorama Environmental Inc (HQ)	Provider of environmental planning services. The company engages in regulatory permitting and geographic information systems.	650-373-1200	NA	San Francisco
Pyxis Laboratories Inc (HQ)	Specializes in the research, development and production of specialty reagents for the diagnostics, pharmaceutical, and environmental industries.	949-598-1978	NA	Grass Valley
Quanta Laboratories (HQ)	Provider of environmental testing and consulting services. The company offers vibration test, shock test, and chalmers test services.	408-988-0770	NA	Santa Clara
Recology Of The Coast (HQ)	Provider of resource recovery services. The company's services include urban cleaning services, collection, sorting, transfer, recovery and landfill management.	650-355-9000	NA	Pacifica
Ridge to River (HQ)	Provider of hydrologic analysis and modeling services. The company is also focused on ecological restoration, erosion control, and water quality analysis.	707-357-0857	NA	Fort Bragg
Rincon Consultants Inc (BR)	Provider of environmental consulting services. The company specializes in land use planning, site assessment, remediation, and other services.	510-834-4455	NA	Oakland
Safebridge Consultants Inc (HQ)	Provider of consulting services and analytical support. The company provides safety, health and environmental services.	650-961-4820	NA	Mountain View
SOMA Environmental Engineering Inc (HQ)	Provider of environmental engineering solutions. The company offers services for remediation and underground storage tanks.	925-734-6400	NA	Pleasanton
Stantec (BR)	Provider of civil construction services. The company also offers commercial program development and infrastructure management services.	916-773-8100	NA	Rocklin
Sustainable Conservation (HQ)	Provider of environmental protection services and solutions. The company focuses on clean-air farming and auto recycling projects.	415-977-0380	NA	San Francisco
SWCA Environmental Consultants (BR)	Provider of environmental consultant services. The company focuses on environmental planning and regulatory compliance activities.	650-440-4160	NA	Half Moon Bay
Tenera Environmental (HQ)	Provider of environmental consulting, stream restoration, power generation support, and minerals management services.	925-962-9769	NA	San Luis Obispo
Terradex Inc (HQ)	Provider of web and consulting services. The company offers dig clean, cleanup deck, and web development services.	650-227-3250	NA	Palo Alto
TMT Enterprises Inc (HQ)	Provider of baseball and softball playing surfaces and supplier of agricultural mixes, construction materials, organics, and aggregates.	408-432-9040	NA	San Jose
TRC Companies Inc (BR)	Provider of scientific and engineering software services. The company offers hydropower licensing, power delivery, and telecommunications engineering services.	415-434-2600	NA	San Francisco
Tric Tools Inc (HQ)	Provider of pipe-bursting systems. The company also offers installation, maintenance, and cleaning services for home-sewer systems.	510-640-8933	NA	Alameda
Trinity Consultants Inc (BR)	Provider of environmental consulting services. The company engages in environmental outsourcing and litigation support services.	510-285-6351	NA	Oakland
TSS Consultants (HQ)	Provider of energy resources management, environmental permitting, and financial assessment services.	916-600-4174	NA	Sacramento
US Hydrotech Environmental Solutions (HQ)	Provider of hydro tech environmental solutions. The company offers wash pads, containments, pressure washers, and solar thermal products.	707-793-4800	NA	Santa Rosa
Veolia (BR)	Provider of complete environmental solutions. The company focuses on energy, water treatment, and waste management.	916-379-0872	NA	Sacramento
Weatherflow Inc (HQ)	Provider of modeling and forecasting technologies for the weather forecast industry. The company also offers wind-based and coastal forecasting.	800-946-3225	NA	Scotts Valley

COMPANY NAME	PRODUCT / SERVICE	PHONE	EMP	CITY
Weber Hayes & Associates Inc (HQ)	Provider of hydrogeologic and environmental engineering consulting services. The company offers cleanup of soil, groundwater, and stormwater services.	831-722-3580	NA	Watsonville
West Yost Associates (HQ)	Provider of water, storm water, wastewater, and construction management project services. The company also offers recycling services.	530-756-5905	NA	Davis
Westervelt Ecological Services (HQ)	Provider of ecological solutions. The company offers wetland mitigation and conservation banking, geographic information system analysis, and other services.	916-646-3644	NA	Sacramento
WRA Inc (HQ)	Provider of environmental consulting, validation, mitigation and restoration, consultation, and wetland delineation services.	415-454-8868	NA	San Rafael
Zander Associates (HQ)	Provider of environmental consulting and assessment services. The company service areas include habitat conservation planning and wetland delineation.	415-897-8781	NA	San Rafael
Zentner Planning and Ecology (HQ)	Provider of environmental planning and restoration services. The company is also involved in permitting services.	510-622-8110	NA	Oakland

143 = Waste Disposal Equipment

COMPANY NAME	PRODUCT / SERVICE	PHONE	EMP	CITY
Chemical Safety Technology Inc (HQ)	Supplier of chemical processing machines. The company also offers design, manufacturing, and sheet metal fabrication services.	408-263-0984	NA	San Jose
Control Systems West Inc (HQ)	Designer and fabricator of a broad variety of custom electrical controls for industrial applications.	707-763-1108	NA	Petaluma
E2C Remediation (HQ)	Provider of environmental remediation services. The company services also include soil and groundwater remediation and civil and geological engineering.	916-782-8700	NA	Roseville
Filtration Solutions Inc (HQ)	Provider of water treatment systems. The company focuses on engineering, manufacturing, installation, and more.	530-534-1000	NA	Oroville
Forsgren Associate Inc (DH)	Provider of civil and environmental engineering consulting services. The company specializes in planning, design, survey, and construction management.	916-638-1119	NA	Rancho Cordova
Grayland Environmental (HQ)	Provider of environmental and natural resources protections services. The company offers environmental engineering, geological and geophysical services.	530-756-1441	NA	Davis
Tesco Controls Inc (HQ)	Manufacturer of instrumentation, control systems, and service pedestals for water and traffic sectors. The company offers system integration services.	916-395-8800	NA	Sacramento
W2 Systems (HQ)	Provider of customized water treatment support and solutions. The company also offers services like design, technical support, and control services.	415-468-9858	NA	Brisbane

144 = Water/Air Treatment Equipment

	COMPANY NAME	PRODUCT / SERVICE	PHONE	EMP	CITY
	A TEEM Electrical Engineering (HQ)	Provider of outreach safety training, electrical design and construction management, and control system programming services.	916-457-8144	NA	Sacramento
N	Applied Membranes Inc (HQ)	Manufacturer of water treatment membranes and systems.	800-321-9321	NA	Vista
	Control Systems West Inc (HQ)	Designer and fabricator of a broad variety of custom electrical controls for industrial applications.	707-763-1108	NA	Petaluma
	E2C Remediation (HQ)	Provider of environmental remediation services. The company services also include soil and groundwater remediation and civil and geological engineering.	916-782-8700	NA	Roseville
	Filtration Solutions Inc (HQ)	Provider of water treatment systems. The company focuses on engineering, manufacturing, installation, and more.	530-534-1000	NA	Oroville
	Forsgren Associate Inc (DH)	Provider of civil and environmental engineering consulting services. The company specializes in planning, design, survey, and construction management.	916-638-1119	NA	Rancho Cordova
	Freshwater Environmental Svc (HQ)	Provider of environmental services. The company's services include soil investigation work plans, soil sampling reporting, sediment sampling, and monitoring.	707-839-0091	NA	Arcata
	Frey Environmental Inc (BR)	Provider of geological and engineering consulting services. The company offers stormwater management, methane assessments/ mitigation, and asbestos-related services.	831-464-1634	NA	Santa Cruz
	Heron Innovators (HQ)	Provider of suspended air flotation systems. The company offers products for processing tomato, food, meat, and others.	916-408-6601	NA	Rocklin
	Horizon Water and Environment LLC (HQ)	Provider of environmental consulting services. The company specializes in watershed science, environmental compliance, and water resources management.	510-986-1850	11-50	Oakland
	Loprest Water Treatment Co (HQ)	Provider of water treatment systems design and fabricating services. The company focuses on media analysis and filter inspection.	510-799-3101	NA	Rodeo
	Maggiora Bros Drilling Inc (HQ)	Provider of water well drilling and pump installation services. The company specializes in hydrologic cycle such as evaporation and condensation.	831-724-1338	NA	Watsonville
	NDS Inc (HQ)	Provider of storm water management, efficient irrigation, and flow management solutions for residential and commercial applications.	888-825-4716	NA	Lindsay

COMPANY NAME	PRODUCT / SERVICE	PHONE	EMP	CITY
Ondavia Inc (HQ)	Provider of water analysis solutions. The company offers OndaVia analysis system that enables laboratory-grade water testing.	510-576-0476	NA	Hayward
Ozotech Inc (HQ)	Provider of water purification solutions. The company offers products such as bolted water systems, oxygen concentrators, air dries, and generators.	530-842-4189	NA	Yreka
Pionetics Corp (HQ)	Provider of water treatment products. The company's products include LNX 160 water filters, bottleless water coolers, and water treatment systems.	866-611-8624	NA	San Carlos
Process Solutions Inc (HQ)	Provider of disinfection solutions. The company is engaged in facility management services and serves the commercial sector.	408-370-6540	NA	Milpitas
Puronics Inc (HQ)	Manufacturer of water treatment equipment. The company's products include drinking water systems, water softeners, and reverse osmosis systems.	925-456-7000	NA	Livermore
Synder Filtration (HQ)	Manufacturer of membranes and systems. The company offers training and performance evaluation services. It serves mining, biotech, and food industries.	707-451-6060	NA	Vacaville
Tesco Controls Inc (HQ)	Manufacturer of instrumentation, control systems, and service pedestals for water and traffic sectors. The company offers system integration services.	916-395-8800	NA	Sacramento
Triple O Systems Inc (HQ)	Designer and manufacturer of water treatment systems. The company also offers reverse osmosis product water tanks and water store water tanks.	408-378-3002	NA	Campbell
Veolia Water (BR)	Provider of water and wastewater treatment solutions. The company offers services for public authorities and industrial companies.	510-412-2001	NA	Richmond
W2 Systems (HQ)	Provider of customized water treatment support and solutions. The company also offers services like design, technical support, and control services.	415-468-9858	NA	Brisbane
Waterman Industries (HQ)	Designer and manufacturer of water-control sluice gates, penstocks, valves, and water control products.	559-562-4000	NA	Exeter

145 = Industrial Equipment & Services

	COMPANY NAME	PRODUCT / SERVICE	PHONE	EMP	CITY
N	California Steel Industries (HQ)	Manufacturer of steel products.	909-350-6300	501-1000	Fontana
N	Kramer Metals Inc (HQ)	Distributor of scrap metals to steel mills, aluminum mills, non-ferrous foundries and vacuum filters.	323-587-2277	1-10	Los Angeles
N	Monico Alloys Inc (HQ)	Provider of scrap metal recycling services.	310-928-0168	11-50	Rancho Domin-guez
N	Riverside Scrap Iron (HQ)	Recycler of waste and scrap metals.	951-686-2129	NA	Riverside
N	Zanker Road Resource Management Ltd (HQ)	Provider of a concrete recycling, composting, mixed debris and debris diversion.	408-263-2384	NA	San Jose

146 = Actuators

COMPANY NAME	PRODUCT / SERVICE	PHONE	EMP	CITY
Moog Animatics (BR)	Provider of motion control devices. The company offers actuators, cables, power supplies, and peripherals.	650-960-4215	NA	Mountain View
Moog Csa Engineering (HQ)	Designer and manufacturer of high precision systems. The company offers positioning systems, actuators, absorbers, and test systems.	650-210-9000	NA	Mountain View
NB Corporation of America (BR)	Manufacturer of linear motion bearings, slides, ball splines, and related products. The company's products include slide guides, spindle shafts, and actuators.	510-490-1420	NA	Fremont
Oriental Motor USA Corp (DH)	Provider of optimal motion systems. The company focuses on producing fractional horsepower products for motion control applications.	310-715-3301	NA	Torrance
Precision Contacts Inc (HQ)	Provider of replacement contacts for handler manufacturer. The company's products include sockets, contacts, elements, and custom products.	916-939-4147	NA	El Dorado Hills
SMC Corporation of America (BR)	Provider of in pneumatic technology solutions that are used in diverse range of industries from automotive to life science.	408-943-9600	NA	San Jose

147 = Air Purification Equipment

COMPANY NAME	PRODUCT / SERVICE	PHONE	EMP	CITY
Donald P. Dick Air Conditioning (HQ)	Provider of air conditioning services. The company's offerings include sheet metal fabrication, ductless heating, energy recovery ventilators, and solar water heaters.	559-255-1644	NA	Fresno
Fresno Valves & Castings Inc (HQ)	Provider of water control devices used in irrigation applications. The company's products include valves, filters, air vents, fittings, gates, and lifts.	559-834-2511	NA	Selma
SMC Corporation of America (BR)	Provider of in pneumatic technology solutions that are used in diverse range of industries from automotive to life science.	408-943-9600	NA	San Jose

148 = Compressors

COMPANY NAME	PRODUCT / SERVICE	PHONE	EMP	CITY
Brooks Automation Inc (BR)	Provider of automation, vacuum, and instrumentation solutions for the semiconductor manufacturing, life sciences, and clean energy industries.	510-661-5000	NA	Fremont
CTI Controltech (HQ)	Provider of industrial process control and emission solutions. The company's services include engineering, sales, and support.	925-208-4250	NA	San Ramon

COMPANY NAME	PRODUCT / SERVICE	PHONE	EMP	CITY
Dripless Inc (HQ)	Manufacturer of utility spatulas, caulking guns, holsters, and related accessories. The company serves the painting industry.	707-568-5081	NA	Santa Rosa
Motor Guard Corp (HQ)	Designer and developer of spray equipment and tools for collision repairs. The company offers services to the automotive sector.	209-239-9191	NA	Manteca
Precision Contacts Inc (HQ)	Provider of replacement contacts for handler manufacturer. The company's products include sockets, contacts, elements, and custom products.	916-939-4147	NA	El Dorado Hills
RIX Industries (HQ)	Manufacturer of air and gas compressors. The company's products include industrial and commercial compressors, nitrogen generators, and AMS parts.	707-747-5900	NA	Benicia
Universal Audio Inc (HQ)	Manufacturer of analog recording equipment. The company's products include audio interfaces, channel strips, plug-ins, and compressors.	831-440-1176	NA	Scotts Valley
WAGAN Corp (HQ)	Developer and marketer of automotive accessories to mobile professionals. The company's offerings include warmers, defrosters, and heated cushions.	510-471-9221	NA	Hayward

149 = Cryogenic Tanks & Equipment

COMPANY NAME	PRODUCT / SERVICE	PHONE	EMP	CITY
N C & H Testing Service LLC (HQ)	Provider of services to oil and gas production industry specializing in pressure testing and magnetic flux testing to verify pipe and tubing integrity.	661-589-4030	NA	Bakersfield
N Cummings Transportation (HQ)	Provider of trucking services.	661-746-1786	NA	Shafter
E-N-G Mobile Systems Inc (HQ)	Manufacturer of specialty vehicles. The company focuses on TV vans and trucks, emergency response trailers, mobile labs, and other vehicles.	925-798-4060	NA	Concord
Morley Manufacturing Inc (HQ)	Designer and manufacturer of drain back water storage tanks for residential and commercial purposes. The company offers installation services.	530-477-6527	NA	Grass Valley

150 = Engines/Motors

COMPANY NAME	PRODUCT / SERVICE	PHONE	EMP	CITY
Aero Turbine Inc (HQ)	Provider of overhaul, repair, and testing services for turbine engines and accessories. The company also sells engine components and accessories.	209-983-1112	NA	Stockton
AKMI Corp (HQ)	Distributor of aftermarket diesel engine parts. The company provides accessory drive units, camshafts, flywheels, and exhaust manifolds.	510-670-9550	NA	Hayward
Akribis Systems Inc (RH)	Designer and manufacturer of motors, stages, and precision systems. The company's products are used in inspection and testing applications.	408-913-1300	NA	San Jose
Arcus Technology Inc (HQ)	Provider of motor controllers, stepper motors, and related accessories such as cables, encoders, and gearboxes.	925-373-8800	NA	Livermore
N Bernell Hydraulics Inc (HQ)	Provider of fluid power distributor, manufacturer, and systems designer, hydraulic repair, and services.	909-899-1751	11-50	Rancho Cucamonga
Comptech USA (HQ)	Manufacturer and fabricator of race engines. The company also offers R&D and road racing track maintenance services.	916-338-3434	NA	Sacramento
Efficient Drivetrains Inc (HQ)	Provider of vehicle developer equipment. The company also offers PHEV and CVT solutions, and hybrid vehicles.	408-624-1231	NA	Milpitas
Industrial Electrical Co (HQ)	Provider of electrical, manufacturing, and automation services for the commercial and industrial sectors.	209-527-2800	NA	Modesto
Interphase Systems (HQ)	Manufacturer of test equipment for the disc drive industry. The company offers consulting and build-to-print services.	408-315-8603	NA	Santa Clara
Lin Engineering (HQ)	Manufacturer of step motors. The company's products include BLDC motors, optical encoders, gearheads, and accessories.	408-919-0200	NA	Morgan Hill
Motion Control Engineering Inc (HQ)	Manufacturer of elevator control products. The company's products include elevator and escalator controls, complete elevators, and components and peripherals.	916-463-9200	NA	Rancho Cordova
Motor Guard Corp (HQ)	Designer and developer of spray equipment and tools for collision repairs. The company offers services to the automotive sector.	209-239-9191	NA	Manteca
Nyden Corp (HQ)	Supplier of stepper motors. The company deals with the design of semiconductor equipment, laser systems, and aerospace-related apparatus.	510-894-3633	NA	San Jose
Oriental Motor USA Corp (DH)	Provider of optimal motion systems. The company focuses on producing fractional horsepower products for motion control applications.	310-715-3301	NA	Torrance
Source Engineering Inc (HQ)	Manufacturer of motors, cables, harnesses, and motion control products. The company also provides custom modification services on motors.	408-980-9822	NA	Santa Clara

151 = Furnaces, Heating Equipment

COMPANY NAME	PRODUCT / SERVICE	PHONE	EMP	CITY
Clayborn Lab (HQ)	Developer of heat tapes, hot tubes, and custom tape heaters. The company serves the medical, transportation, and pharmaceutical sectors.	530-587-4700	NA	Truckee
Enphase Energy Inc (HQ)	Distributor of electronic products. The company offers services to the solar, telecom, networking, and software industries.	877-797-4743	NA	Petaluma
Envirocare International (HQ)	Designer of pollution control appliances. The company also specializes in manufacturing gas cooling and gas conditioning systems.	707-638-6800	NA	American Canyon
Ferreira Service Inc (HQ)	Provider of energy engineering services. The company offers heating, ventilation, and air conditioning maintenance and repair services.	800-522-6064	NA	San Ramon

COMPANY NAME	PRODUCT / SERVICE	PHONE	EMP	CITY
Heliodyne Inc (HQ)	Manufacturer of solar water heating systems for the residential and commercial sectors. The company focuses on installation, repair, and replacement.	510-237-9614	NA	Richmond
PAC Machinery (HQ)	Manufacturer of heat sealing and packaging equipment such as tube sealers, shrink wrap systems, and skin packaging products.	415-454-4868	NA	San Rafael
Rayteq LLC (HQ)	Manufacturer of energy-saving electric melting furnaces for the metal casting industry and offers electric heating systems and metal level sensors.	510-638-2000	NA	Healdsburg
Retech Systems LLC (HQ)	Designer and manufacturer of consumable electrode and furnaces, powder production, and other thermal processing equipment.	707-462-6522	NA	Ukiah
ST Johnson Co (HQ)	Manufacturer of burners. The company specializes in the design and fabrication of gas and nitrous oxide burners for industries.	510-652-6000	NA	Fairfield

152 = Generators

COMPANY NAME	PRODUCT / SERVICE	PHONE	EMP	CITY
Accsys Technology Inc (HQ)	Manufacturer of ion linear accelerator systems used in medical imaging devices, industrial applications and in research.	925-462-6949	NA	Pleasanton
Adelphi Technology Inc (HQ)	Developer and manufacturer of X-ray optics. The company serves the medical, industrial, and scientific sectors.	650-474-2750	NA	Redwood City
Clean Energy Systems Inc (HQ)	Developer and manufacturer of steam and drive gas generator units. The company is engaged in design, delivery, and installation services.	916-638-7967	NA	Rancho Cordova
Glasspoint Solar Inc (HQ)	Manufacturer of solar steam generators for the oil and gas industry. The company is engaged in design and installation services.	415-778-2800	NA	Fremont
Goodman Ball Inc (HQ)	Manufacturer of spare military equipment for the U.S. Government. The company's in-house capabilities include CNC machining and structural welding.	650-363-0113	NA	Menlo Park
Industrial Electrical Co (HQ)	Provider of electrical, manufacturing, and automation services for the commercial and industrial sectors.	209-527-2800	NA	Modesto
Longevity Welding (HQ)	Manufacturer of welding equipment. The company also offers filler rods, generators, plasma cutters, and related accessories.	877-566-4462	NA	Hayward
National Vapor Industries Inc (HQ)	Manufacturer of hydrogen generators. The company also offers marketing, installation, and other services.	925-980-7341	NA	Livermore
Telemakus LLC (HQ)	Provider of USB controlled RF devices. The company devices include switches, vector modulators, and digital attenuators.	916-458-6346	NA	Folsom

153 = Heat Exchangers/Pressure Vessels

COMPANY NAME	PRODUCT / SERVICE	PHONE	EMP	CITY
Ashlock Co (HQ)	Provider of pitting equipment. The company offers equipment such as cherry pitting, date pitting, and olive pitting machines.	510-351-0560	NA	San Leandro
Benchmark Thermal Corp (HQ)	Manufacturer of custom semiconductor products, drum and cartridge heaters, controls, and related accessories.	530-477-5011	NA	Grass Valley
Environmental Stress Systems Inc (HQ)	Manufacturer of mechanically refrigerated, cryogenically cooled, and liquid cooled thermal platforms.	209-588-1993	NA	Sonora
Johansing Iron Works (HQ)	Manufacturer of heat exchangers and metal tanks. The company also offers process equipment and pressure vessels.	707-361-8190	NA	Benicia
Melrose Metal Products Inc (HQ)	Manufacturer of melrose metal products. The company offers design and installation services for food processing and emission control systems.	510-657-8771	NA	Fremont
Morrill Industries Inc (HQ)	Manufacturer and supplier of irrigation equipment. The company also offers custom built rotating suction screens and industrial pipes.	209-838-2550	NA	Escalon
Quality Stainless Tanks (HQ)	Provider of ready-made tanks. The company offers crafted tanks, stainless winery equipment, and special application tanks.	707-837-2721	NA	Windsor
Rorze Automation Inc (DH)	Manufacturer of automation products. The company's applications include displays, semiconductors, and laboratories.	510-687-1340	NA	Fremont
Terminal Manufacturing Company LLC (HQ)	Designer and manufacturer of vacuum chalmers, pressure vessels, truck tanks, and assorted fabrications.	510-526-3071	NA	Berkeley
Thermal Press International Inc (HQ)	Manufacturer of thermal presses and heat staking machines. The company also offers heat sealing and degating machinery.	925-454-9800	NA	Livermore
Uniform Industrial Corp (DH)	Provider of systems and components for banking and retail solutions. The company also offers technology solutions and customer services.	510-438-6799	NA	Fremont
WCR Inc (BR)	Developer and manufacturer of heat exchangers. The company's products include plate heat exchangers, brazed heat exchangers, and welded heat exchangers.	559-266-8374	NA	Fresno
Wiegmann & Rose (HQ)	Provider of custom heat exchangers, pressure vessels, and weldments. The company offers vacuum chalmers and pipe spool products.	510-632-8828	NA	Livermore

154 = HVAC Equipment

COMPANY NAME	PRODUCT / SERVICE	PHONE	EMP	CITY
Acadia Technology Inc (HQ)	Dealer of power supplies, water cooling kits, cases, fans and fan ducts, and digital temperature displayers.	408-737-9528	NA	Sunnyvale
Acutherm (HQ)	Manufacturer of components for heating and air conditioning systems. The company offers therma-fuser variable air volume diffusers.	510-785-0510	NA	Dublin
Alzeta Corp (HQ)	Provider of clean air solutions and related research and development services. The company offers services to the industrial and commercial sectors.	408-727-8282	NA	Santa Clara

COMPANY NAME	PRODUCT / SERVICE	PHONE	EMP	CITY
ASI Controls (HQ)	Manufacturer of direct digital controls for HVAC and light industrial marketplace. The company also offers networking products and unitary controls.	925-866-8808	NA	Pleasanton
Baltimore Aircoil Company Inc (BR)	Provider of assembled evaporative heat rejection and thermal storage equipment. The company also offers circuit cooling towers.	559-673-9231	NA	Madera
Celsia Inc (HQ)	Designer and manufacturer of heat sinks. The company provides thermal solutions using vapor chamber, heat pipe, and hybrid designs.	650-667-1920	NA	Santa Clara
Environmental Stress Systems Inc (HQ)	Manufacturer of mechanically refrigerated, cryogenically cooled, and liquid cooled thermal platforms.	209-588-1993	NA	Sonora
Meline Engineering Corp (HQ)	Provider of energy efficient mechanical system design services. The company also offers mechanical engineering services.	916-366-3458	NA	Sacramento
Melrose Metal Products Inc (HQ)	Manufacturer of melrose metal products. The company offers design and installation services for food processing and emission control systems.	510-657-8771	NA	Fremont
MMR Technologies Inc (HQ)	Provider of micro-miniature refrigerator technology. The company offers hall measurement, optical study systems, and temperature control services.	650-962-9620	NA	San Jose
NBA Engineering Inc (HQ)	Provider of mechanical and electrical engineering design, energy conversion, and construction management services.	415-202-9840	NA	San Francisco
R&R Refrigeration And Air Conditioning Inc (HQ)	Provider of environmental technological solutions. The company also offers maintenance and repair services for process systems.	408-297-0383	NA	San Jose
Rudy's Commercial Refrigeration (HQ)	Provider of refrigeration products such as coolers and freezers, compressors, glass doors and strip curtains, and temperature alarms.	510-376-9163	NA	San Pablo
Trane (BR)	Provider of heating, ventilation and air conditioning (HVAC) systems, dehumidifying, and air cleaning products.	888-862-1619	NA	Sunnyvale

155 = Hydraulic/Pneumatic Equipment

COMPANY NAME	PRODUCT / SERVICE	PHONE	EMP	CITY
ABT-TRAC (HQ)	Provider of yacht and boat stabilizers and bow and stern thrusters. The company also offers integrated hydraulic products.	707-586-3155	NA	Rohnert Park
Cadence Design Systems Inc (HQ)	Provider of semiconductor IP and electronic design automation services. The company offers tools for logic and RF design, IC packaging, and other needs.	408-943-1234	NA	San Jose
Hydraulic Controls Inc (HQ)	Distributor of fluid power systems. The company specializes in hydraulics, pneumatics, automation, and extrusion.	510-658-8300	NA	Emeryville
Inventive Resources Inc (HQ)	Manufacturer of products for the environmental and contamination control industry. The company also focuses on distribution.	209-545-1663	NA	Salida
Power Industries (HQ)	Supplier of ready-made solutions for industrial applications. The company's products include bearings and seals, hydraulics, and pneumatics.	707-545-7904	NA	Santa Rosa
N Technical Heaters Inc (HQ)	Manufacturer of rubber, plastics hose and beltings.	800-394-9435	NA	San Fernando
V&O Machine Inc (HQ)	Manufacturer of machined parts for agri, hydraulics, food processing, and veterinary applications. The company focuses on prototyping and CNC milling.	530-662-0495	NA	Woodland

156 = Industrial Filters/Centrifuges

COMPANY NAME	PRODUCT / SERVICE	PHONE	EMP	CITY
Bazell Technologies Corp (HQ)	Manufacturer of solid wall basket centrifuges. The company also focuses on centrifugal fluid processing systems.	925-603-0900	NA	Concord
Filtration Group LLC (BR)	Provider of filtration solutions. The company supplies filtration products for the HVAC, turbine, cleanroom, and filter media markers.	707-525-8633	NA	Santa Rosa
Inventive Resources Inc (HQ)	Manufacturer of products for the environmental and contamination control industry. The company also focuses on distribution.	209-545-1663	NA	Salida
LAKOS Filtration Solutions (HQ)	Manufacturer of centrifugal separators and other filtration solutions to remove sand and other solids from water and liquids.	559-255-1601	NA	Fresno
N Pacific Consolidated Industries LLC (HQ)	Manufacturer of general industrial machinery.	951-479-0860	NA	Riverside
Parker Hannifin Corp (DH)	Provider of fuel, air, oil, and coolant filtration systems. The company serves the transportation, marine, and oil and gas industries.	209-521-7860	NA	Modesto
N Potter Roemer- Fire Protection Equipment (HQ)	Manufacturer and distributor of interior hose, standpipe equipment, cabinets, connections, extinguishers, and valves.	626-855-4890	NA	City Of Industry
N SAES Pure Gas Inc (HQ)	Manufacturer of gas purifiers for semiconductor industry.	805-541-9299	NA	San Luis Obispo
N Smith Precision Products Co (HQ)	Manufacturer and distributor of pumps and fertilizer injectors.	805-498-6616	NA	Newbury Park
Standard Metal Products (HQ)	Provider of prototype and production components and assemblies for transportation, bicycle builders, and medical device companies.	415-546-6784	NA	San Francisco
Tomopal Inc (HQ)	Manufacturer and distributor of glass syringes, scales and balances, gas filters, and other products for the laboratory and industrial markers.	916-429-7240	NA	Sacramento
Tooltek Engineering Corp (HQ)	Designer and fabricator of custom automated equipment. The company is also engaged in material handling and robotics solutions.	510-683-9504	NA	Fremont

157 = Machine Tools - Metal Cutting or Forming

COMPANY NAME	PRODUCT / SERVICE	PHONE	EMP	CITY
Acosta Sheet Metal Manufacturing Inc (HQ)	Manufacturer of HVAC and architectural products, and sheet metal building materials. The company provides gutter profile caps and conductor heads.	408-275-6370	NA	San Jose

COMPANY NAME	PRODUCT / SERVICE	PHONE	EMP	CITY
Adem LLC (HQ)	Designer and manufacturer of special and automated fixtures for assembly lines, and also provides turnkey production solutions.	408-727-8955	NA	Santa Clara
Advanced Laser & Waterjet Cutting Inc (HQ)	Provider of precision cutting services for all types of materials. The company's services include electronic shielding, fabrivision, and overnight shipping.	408-486-0700	NA	Fremont
Altair Technologies Inc (HQ)	Provider of precision furnace brazing services. The company serves the medical, defense, and semiconductor industries.	650-508-8700	NA	Fremont
Angular Machining Inc (HQ)	Provider of product manufacturing services for aerospace, telecom, and biomedical sectors and focuses on mechanical assembly and quality control.	408-954-8326	NA	San Jose
Bat Gundrilling Services Inc (HQ)	Provider of manufacturing services. The company specializes in engineering, tap extraction, gun drill tool sharpening, and deburring services.	408-727-1220	NA	Santa Clara
Bauer Engraving Company Inc (HQ)	Provider of engraving services. The company offers foil stamping dies, embossing dies, wood branding dies, and letterpress printing plates.	916-631-9800	NA	Rancho Cordova
Billington Welding & Manufacturing Inc (HQ)	Manufacturer of food process equipment and custom products. The company serves the construction, automotive, and food processing industries.	209-526-9312	NA	Modesto
Broadway Sheet Metal & Mfg (HQ)	Manufacturer of sheet metals. The company's products include hoods cartridge, sinks, tables, and mixer stands.	650-873-4585	NA	S San Francisco
CMI Manufacturing Inc (HQ)	Provider of prototype machining services. The company also focuses on 3D surfacing, production, and manufacturing engineering support.	408-982-9580	NA	San Jose
Connor Manufacturing Services Inc (HQ)	Provider of customized solutions for precision metal stamping, wire forms, springs, and integrated assembly needs.	800-968-7078	NA	San Mateo
Crown Manufacturing Company Inc (HQ)	Provider of plastic and injection molded products. The company offers insert and over molding, drilling, tapping, and heat stamping services.	510-742-8800	NA	Newark
Danco Machine (HQ)	Developer of machined components and assemblies. The company is involved in EDM, welding, sheet metal, and precision grinding.	408-988-5235	NA	Santa Clara
Demtech Services Inc (HQ)	Manufacturer of welding machines. The company also specializes in the manufacture of testing instruments for geosynthetic installers.	530-621-3200	NA	Diamond Springs
Destiny Tool (HQ)	Developer of end mills. The company offers technical support to customers in Philadelphia, Akron, Dayton, and Iowa regions.	408-988-8898	NA	Santa Clara
Donald P. Dick Air Conditioning (HQ)	Provider of air conditioning services. The company's offerings include sheet metal fabrication, ductless heating, energy recovery ventilators, and solar water heaters.	559-255-1644	NA	Fresno
Fastening Systems International Inc (HQ)	Supplier of blind fasteners and blind rivet installation tools. The company offers rivet guns, rivet nuts, pop rivets, and more.	707-935-1170	NA	Sonoma
Feeney Inc (HQ)	Provider of architectural and garden products. The company specializes in products such as rail kits, lighting, and accessories.	510-893-9473	NA	Oakland
Finishline Advanced Composites LLC (HQ)	Provider of composite repair services for production projects. The company is involved in design, development, prototyping, testing, and production.	707-747-0788	NA	Benicia
Flashpoint Machining (HQ)	Provider of precision prototype, R&D, and detail and production machining services. The company also offers industrial machined parts.	408-213-0071	NA	Santa Clara
Foamlinx LLC (HQ)	Provider of foam cutting computer numerical control machines. The company offers cutters, shredders, compactors, and cutting services.	408-454-6163	NA	Sunnyvale
Gateway Precision Inc (HQ)	Manufacturer of precision-machined components and assemblies for image equipment manufacturers, telecom, food processing, and semiconductor sectors.	408-855-8849	NA	Santa Clara
General Grinding Inc (HQ)	Provider of precision, centerless, and surface grinding services. The company serves the medical and military industries.	510-261-5557	NA	Oakland
Grabber Construction Products Inc (BR)	Manufacturer of fasteners and machine tools. The company also specializes in distribution and other services.	800-869-1375	NA	Concord
Hitachi Metals America Ltd (BR)	Manufacturer and marketer of metal products. The company offers cable systems, cutting tools, ceramics, sensors, and other materials.	408-467-8900	NA	San Jose
HS&S Inc (HQ)	Designer and manufacturer of machine tool and custom machine manufacturing. The company offers services like CNC conversion and contract inspection.	408-980-8909	NA	Santa Clara
KOR-IT Inc (HQ)	Manufacturer of diamond tools and core drill machines. The company caters to the concrete cutting industry.	916-372-6400	NA	Sacramento
Lfw Manufacturing (HQ)	Manufacturer of gearboxes and gear sets. The company caters to a wide range of industrial applications.	209-465-0444	NA	Stockton
Longevity Welding (HQ)	Manufacturer of welding equipment. The company also offers filler rods, generators, plasma cutters, and related accessories.	877-566-4462	NA	Hayward
Material Fabricators Inc (HQ)	Manufacturer of gaskets, shims, washers, metal stampings and die cut electrical insulators.	805-686-5244	NA	Buellton
Micro-Mechanics Inc (DH)	Manufacturer of precision tools, assemblies, and consumable parts used to manufacture and test semiconductors. The company offers mold pots and trims.	408-779-2927	NA	Morgan Hill
Mitsui High-tec Inc (BR)	Provider of grinder parts, precision tools, and stamping products. The company is involved in design, installation, and delivery services.	408-980-0782	NA	San Jose

N (left margin marker, Material Fabricators Inc row)

COMPANY NAME	PRODUCT / SERVICE	PHONE	EMP	CITY
MJB Precision Machining Inc (HQ)	Manufacturer of precision and prototype machining parts and components for the defense, telecom, medical, and semiconductor manufacturing industries.	408-559-3035	NA	Campbell
Morrill Industries Inc (HQ)	Manufacturer and supplier of irrigation equipment. The company also offers custom built rotating suction screens and industrial pipes.	209-838-2550	NA	Escalon
Nichols Manufacturing Inc (HQ)	Provider of product engineering and design, prototyping, and manufacturing services. The company serves the business sector.	408-945-0911	NA	Milpitas
N O-Rings Inc (HQ)	Manufacturer and distributor of rings and custom molded rubber products.	323-343-9500	NA	Los Angeles
Omega Diamond Inc (HQ)	Developer and manufacturer of diamond tools for the ultra precise semiconductor and optics industry. The company also offers power tools.	530-889-8977	NA	Newcastle
Pacific Pneumatic Tools Inc (HQ)	Manufacturer of air tools for industrial and automotive customers. The company offers wrenches, grinders, sanders, and other tools.	650-592-6116	NA	San Carlos
Precision Identity Corp (HQ)	Manufacturer of machined components for the medical device manufacturing industries. The company offers inspection, cleaning, and support services.	408-374-2346	NA	Campbell
Procurement Partners International Inc (HQ)	Provider of procurement services. The company offers mechanical components such as pins, rods, rollers, and sheet metal.	650-345-6118	NA	San Mateo
Prodigy Surface Tech Inc (HQ)	Provider of alternative to common electroplating shop. The company focuses on chem lab for analysis, blaster, and clean room.	408-492-9390	NA	Santa Clara
Promax Tools Lp (HQ)	Manufacturer of solid carbide round tools. The company offers finishing end mills, die and mold tools, and solid carbide end mills.	916-638-0501	NA	Rancho Cordova
N Quality Grinding Company Inc (HQ)	Manufacturer of precision grinding and machining products.	714-228-2100	NA	Buena Park
Reliable Rubber Products (HQ)	Provider of rubber products. The company's products include dock bumpers, duty corner guards, urethane wheel chocks, and street pads.	888-525-9750	NA	Modesto
Robbjack Corp (HQ)	Provider of tools for aerospace, aluminum tools, die mold and hard metal tools, custom end mills, and custom saws.	916-645-6045	NA	Lincoln
N Roettele Industries Inc (HQ)	Manufacturer of non-metallic washers and gaskets.	909-606-8252	1-10	Chino
Silicon Valley Precision Inc (HQ)	Provider of custom vertical and horizontal CNC machining, fabrication and assembly of parts. The company offers powder coating, painting and grinding.	925-373-8259	NA	Livermore
SJC Precision Inc (HQ)	Provider of precision machining and tool and die making services. The company designs and manufactures jigs, fixtures, and bookmolds.	408-262-1680	NA	Milpitas
T&T Precision Inc (HQ)	Provider of precision machining services. The company specializes in electronics, automotive, and semiconductor equipment.	510-429-8088	NA	Union City
Therm-X (HQ)	Provider of engineered solutions. The company serves the semiconductor, petrochemical, life sciences, and aerospace industries.	510-606-1012	NA	Hayward
N Tosco - Tool Specialty Co (HQ)	Manufacturer of carbide cutting tools.	323-232-3561	NA	Los Angeles
Tri Tool Inc (HQ)	Manufacturer of precision machine tools. The company also deals with products rentals, construction, and maintenance services.	916-288-6100	NA	Rancho Cordova
Tronex Technology Inc (HQ)	Manufacturer of precision cutting tools and pliers. The company offers hand cutters, hard wire cutters, and flat nose pliers.	909-627-2453	NA	Fairfield
US Union Tool (BR)	Designer and manufacturer of micro cutting tools for the printed circuit industry. The company engages in mold and dies and medical and aerospace parts.	714-521-6242	NA	Santa Clara
Westport Machine Works Inc (HQ)	Manufacturer of assembly and balancing equipment. The company's services include fixturing, installation, and technical support.	916-371-4493	NA	West Sacramento
Wonder Metals Corp (HQ)	Provider of preventing environmental pollution services. The company's products include louvers, penthouses, and control dampers.	800-366-5877	NA	Redding

158 = Mining Machinery

COMPANY NAME	PRODUCT / SERVICE	PHONE	EMP	CITY
Berkeley Forge & Tool Inc (HQ)	The company is engaged in the design, engineering, manufacture, and marketing of mining and commercial forging products.	510-526-5034	NA	Berkeley
Fit Bearings (HQ)	Designer and manufacturer of bearings. The company's products include seals, drive components, and agricultural and industrial wheel hubs.	510-623-1688	NA	Fremont
Materion Corp (BR)	Provider of material solutions. The company deals with fabrication, analysis, research and development, and testing services.	510-623-1500	NA	Fremont
Mclellan Industries Inc (HQ)	Manufacturer of stainless steel and mild steel tanks, hook lifts, tank kits, and related accessories.	800-445-8449	NA	Hanford
Wasco Hardfacing Co (HQ)	Manufacturer of hardfacing electrodes for steel, cement, and mining applications. The company also offers welding alloy solutions.	559-485-5860	NA	Fresno

159 = Miscellaneous Special Industry Equipment

COMPANY NAME	PRODUCT / SERVICE	PHONE	EMP	CITY
Able Design Inc (HQ)	Provider of design services that involves specialization in automated handling of small high technology devices.	650-961-8245	NA	Mountain View
ABT-TRAC (HQ)	Provider of yacht and boat stabilizers and bow and stern thrusters. The company also offers integrated hydraulic products.	707-586-3155	NA	Rohnert Park
Acosta Sheet Metal Manufacturing Inc (HQ)	Manufacturer of HVAC and architectural products, and sheet metal building materials. The company provides gutter profile caps and conductor heads.	408-275-6370	NA	San Jose

COMPANY NAME	PRODUCT / SERVICE	PHONE	EMP	CITY
AFC Finishing Systems (HQ)	Developer of air filter and spray booth products. The company offers auto and truck spray booths, air make-up units, and powder coating products.	800-331-7744	NA	Oroville
Agricultural Manufacturing Company Inc (HQ)	Manufacturer of sprayers. The company specializes in engineering agricultural spraying equipment and other products such as pumps and tanks.	559-485-1662	NA	Fresno
Air-O-Fan Products (HQ)	Developer of spray application machinery solutions. The company manufactures engine and PTO drives for orchard, vineyard, and herbicide sprayers.	559-638-6546	NA	Reedley
Allied Fire Protection (HQ)	Designer and manufacturer of fire protection sprinkler systems. The company also offers installation services.	510-533-5516	NA	Oakland
N Alltronics LLC (HQ)	Distributor of electrical and electro-mechanical parts such as automotive, computer, capacitors and more.	408-778-3868	1-10	Santa Clara
Altamont Manufacturing Inc (HQ)	Provider of precision CNC machining, welding, and fabrication services. The company offers semiconductor, aerospace, medical, and robotics components.	925-371-5401	NA	Livermore
American Cylinder Head Inc (HQ)	Provider of diesel and gas cylinder head repair and remanufacturing services. The company focuses on automotive, heavy duty, and CNG cylinder heads.	800-356-4889	NA	Oakland
N American Metal Bearing Co (HQ)	Designer and manufacturer of plain bearings for all industrial applications.	714-892-5527	11-50	Garden Grove
American Prototype And Production Inc (HQ)	Manufacturer of industrial laser cutting machines. The company focuses on industries such as CNC milling, CNC turning, and laser engraving.	650-595-4994	NA	San Carlos
Ampteks Inc (HQ)	Provider of engineering solutions. The company provides alternatives for dichromate plating and electro silver plating.	925-493-7150	NA	Livermore
Ansync Labs (HQ)	Provider of engineering and design services. The company specializes in electrical engineering, mechanical engineering, and industrial design.	916-933-2850	NA	El Dorado Hills
Applied Process Cooling Corp (HQ)	Provider of refrigeration solutions. The company's services include laser alignment, control panel retrofits, valve exercising, and condenser cleaning.	209-578-1000	NA	Modesto
Aqua Sierra Controls Inc (HQ)	Provider of instrumentation and electrical contract services. The company specializes in process control automation for industrial installations.	530-823-3241	NA	Auburn
Artec Group Inc (BR)	Developer and distributor of 3D scanners and 3D cameras. The company's products include Artec iD, Artec 3D, Viewshape, and Shapify	669-292-5611	NA	Santa Clara
Ashlock Co (HQ)	Provider of pitting equipment. The company offers equipment such as cherry pitting, date pitting, and olive pitting machines.	510-351-0560	NA	San Leandro
ASML Silicon Valley (BR)	Manufacturer of lithography systems for semiconductor industries. The company also offers customized imaging solutions.	669-265-3200	NA	San Jose
ATI North America (HQ)	Manufacturer of converting equipment. The company specializes in volume manufacturing solutions, and also offers repair and upgrade services.	916-518-1445	NA	Gold River
Aubin Industries Inc (HQ)	Designer and manufacturer of mobile wheel systems. The company serves the material handling industry.	209-833-7592	NA	Tracy
Banks Integration Group (HQ)	Developer and provider of control systems and plant automation software. The company serves biotech, food, brewery, oil and gas, and other sectors.	707-451-1100	NA	Vacaville
Bazell Technologies Corp (HQ)	Manufacturer of solid wall basket centrifuges. The company also focuses on centrifugal fluid processing systems.	925-603-0900	NA	Concord
Beahm Designs Inc (HQ)	Provider of tailor made manufacturing equipment. The company focuses on tube processing machines for catheter manufacturing.	408-395-5360	NA	Milpitas
N Bearing Engineering Company Inc (HQ)	Distributor of power transmission products such as bearings, belts, bushings, chains and chain drives and more.	510-596-4150	NA	San Leandro
Berkeley Forge & Tool Inc (HQ)	The company is engaged in the design, engineering, manufacture, and marketing of mining and commercial forging products.	510-526-5034	NA	Berkeley
Betts Spring Inc (HQ)	Manufacturer of custom precision spring products. The company offers coil and leaf springs and serves the mining, military, and trucking industries.	559-498-3304	NA	Fresno
Billington Welding & Manufacturing Inc (HQ)	Manufacturer of food process equipment and custom products. The company serves the construction, automotive, and food processing industries.	209-526-9312	NA	Modesto
Bishop-Wisecarver Corp (HQ)	Manufacturer of guide wheels and guided motion products for the medical, aerospace, electronic, and packaging industries.	925-439-8272	NA	Pittsburg
Blentech Corp (HQ)	Manufacturer of custom processing systems. The company serves the food production, pharmaceuticals, chemical, and biochemical industries.	707-523-5949	NA	Santa Rosa
C&P Microsystems LLC (HQ)	Manufacturer and seller of paper cutter control systems. The company offers microcip, cutternet, and micro facts.	707-776-4500	NA	Petaluma
Cable Moore Inc (HQ)	Manufacturer and distributor of safety and construction equipment and guy and bridge strands. The company offers wire ropes, cables, railings, and slings.	510-436-8000	NA	Oakland
California Brazing & Nevada Heat Treating (HQ)	Provider of brazing services. The company specializes in machining and heat treatment of components for the aviation industry.	510-790-2300	NA	Newark

	COMPANY NAME	PRODUCT / SERVICE	PHONE	EMP	CITY
N	California Hydroforming Company Inc (HQ)	Provider of metal forming using hydroforming presses.	626-912-0036	NA	City Of Industry
N	Calolympic Safety (HQ)	Distributor of bandages and health-conscious ergonomic products.	951-340-2229	NA	Corona
	Carando Technologies Inc (HQ)	Manufacturer of container closing tools and dies. The company fabricates drums, water heater tanks, spare parts, appliances, and container closing tools.	209-948-6500	NA	Stockton
N	Carlson and Beauloye (HQ)	Manufacturer of the motorless water pump that generates its horsepower from water weight and gravity.	619-234-2256	NA	San Diego
	Cesco Magnetics Inc (HQ)	Provider of magnetic separators. The company offers magnetic filters, magnetic plates, and sanitary valves.	877-624-8727	NA	Santa Rosa
	Chemical Safety Technology Inc (HQ)	Supplier of chemical processing machines. The company also offers design, manufacturing, and sheet metal fabrication services.	408-263-0984	NA	San Jose
	Clayborn Lab (HQ)	Developer of heat tapes, hot tubes, and custom tape heaters. The company serves the medical, transportation, and pharmaceutical sectors.	530-587-4700	NA	Truckee
	Cleasby Manufacturing Company Inc (HQ)	Provider of roofing services. The company also offers single ply, cold process, and built up roofing services.	415-822-6565	NA	San Francisco
	CMD Products (HQ)	Manufacturer of replacement heads and accessories. It's products find application in gas and electric weed trimmers.	916-434-0228	NA	Lincoln
	Cognex Corp (BR)	Supplier of barcode readers and sensor products. The company offers vision sensors, fixed mount readers, handheld readers, and mobile computers.	858-481-2469	NA	Cupertino
	Cold Ice Inc (HQ)	Manufacturer of refrigerants, insulated shipping containers and temperature monitors. The company serves the agricultural and gourmet food industries.	510-568-8129	NA	Oakland
	Cold Room Solutions Inc (HQ)	Provider of walk-in cold rooms, freezers, and warm rooms. The company focuses on preventive maintenance programs.	925-462-2500	NA	Pleasanton
	Columbia Machine Works (HQ)	Provider of coining equipment and contracting services. The company offers coining presses, rimming machines, and consumable tooling.	510-568-0808	NA	Oakland
	Compass & Anvil Sales and Engineering Inc (HQ)	Provider of engineering services. The company focuses on metal prototypes, forgings, castings, and metal stampings.	408-205-1319	NA	Los Gatos
	Computer Logistics Corp (HQ)	Provider of system and Internet integration, system design, custom programming, web design, and hosting services.	530-241-3131	NA	Redding
	Corium International Inc (HQ)	Provider of transdermal delivery systems and related technology solutions. The company is also engaged in therapeutic product development.	650-298-8255	NA	Menlo Park
N	Cp Manufacturing Inc (HQ)	Manufacturer of special industry machinery.	619-477-3175	NA	San Diego
	Crown Manufacturing Company Inc (HQ)	Provider of plastic and injection molded products. The company offers insert and over molding, drilling, tapping, and heat stamping services.	510-742-8800	NA	Newark
	Custom Gear & Machine (HQ)	Manufacturer of custom gears. The company also offers overhaul services for gearboxes and caters to industries like food and steel processing.	925-455-9985	NA	Livermore
	Data Scale (HQ)	Manufacturer of liquid net weight filling equipment. The company offers services to the food and chemical industries.	510-651-7350	NA	Fremont
	Delta Pacific Products Inc (HQ)	Provider of plastics injection molding and mold making services. The company serves the automotive, agriculture, aerospace, and recreational sectors.	510-487-4411	NA	Union City
	Detention Device Systems (HQ)	Provider of design and manufacturing services for detention equipment metal fabrications. The company offers sliding door locking and other devices.	510-783-0771	NA	Hayward
	Diamond Tech Inc (HQ)	Provider of drilling equipment and services. The company specializes in electric, core drills, hydraulic, and drill stands.	916-624-1118	NA	Rocklin
	Dieselcraft Fluid Engineering (HQ)	Provider of oil and fuel cleaning technology. The company offers services for pickup trucks, loaders, boats, and gen sets.	530-613-2150	NA	Auburn
	Doering Machines Inc (HQ)	Manufacturer of food processing equipment. The company also offers pumping systems, extruders, and conveyors.	415-526-2131	NA	San Francisco
	DPSS Lasers Inc (HQ)	Manufacturer of high power, short wavelength solid state lasers for industrial, scientific, and research applications.	408-988-4300	NA	Santa Clara
	Dripless Inc (HQ)	Manufacturer of utility spatulas, caulking guns, holsters, and related accessories. The company serves the painting industry.	707-568-5081	NA	Santa Rosa
	Dynatex International (HQ)	Manufacturer of semiconductor, dicing equipment, and supplies. The company also offers dicing and wafer bonding services.	707-542-4227	NA	Santa Rosa
	Earthquake Protection Systems (HQ)	Supplier of seismic isolators for earthquake bearings. The company offers single and triple pendulum bearings and related supplies.	707-644-5993	NA	Vallejo
	EDC Biosystems Inc (HQ)	Provider of technology solutions for biotech liquid transfer applications. The company serves the electronics, precision mechanics, and other sectors.	510-257-1500	NA	Fremont
	Electro Plating Specialties Inc (HQ)	Provider of electroplating services. The company offers parts cleaning, anodizing, electropolishing, and rust removal services.	510-786-1881	NA	Hayward

	COMPANY NAME	PRODUCT / SERVICE	PHONE	EMP	CITY
	Elliot Manufacturing (HQ)	Manufacturer of case erectors, case sealers, cartoners, and case packers. The company is engaged in sales and delivery services.	559-233-6235	NA	Fresno
	Engineering By Design (HQ)	Provider of engineering and support services. The company's products include laminators, coil and fiber winders, motors, and extrusion pullers.	408-324-1500	NA	San Jose
	Ethylene Control Inc (HQ)	Manufacturer of ethylene and gas removal products. The company's products include filters, filtration systems, and sachets.	559-896-1909	NA	Selma
	Evolve Manufacturing Technologies Inc (HQ)	Designer and manufacturer of electro-mechanical, optical, and prototyping products. The company offers testing, logistics, and documentation services.	510-690-8959	NA	Fremont
	Fil-Tech West Inc (BR)	Distributor of semiconductor parts and vacuum components. The company is engaged in troubleshooting and maintenance services.	925-251-8200	NA	Pleasanton
	Fisher Manufacturing (HQ)	Manufacturer of advanced plumbing systems. The company's products include faucets, valves, sprays, and fillers.	800-421-6162	NA	Tulare
	Flostor Engineering (HQ)	Developer of automation solutions for inventory, distribution, fulfillment, and manufacturing systems.	800-500-8256	NA	Hayward
N	Foodtools Inc (HQ)	Manufacturer of food products equipment.	805-962-8383	11-50	Santa Barbara
	Force Flow Inc (HQ)	Provider of chemical monitoring scales. The company exclusively caters to the water and wastewater industry.	925-686-6700	NA	Concord
	Fortrend Engineering Corp (HQ)	Designer and manufacturer of mechanical handling equipment. The company also specializes in distribution services.	408-734-9311	NA	San Jose
N	Fuller Manufacturing Inc (HQ)	Provider of precision products such as grinding, milling, cutting, turning, and drilling services.	209-267-5071	11-50	Sutter Creek
	g2 Engineering (BR)	Manufacturer of engineering products such as bead mounts and related accessories. The company's applications include industrial automation and controls.	650-605-4500	NA	Saratoga
	General Foundry Service (HQ)	Provider of foundry services. The company engages in pattern making, precision sand casting, and rubber plastic mold.	510-297-5040	NA	San Leandro
	General Lasertronics Corp (HQ)	Developer of scanning and control technologies that make laser ablation an alternative to traditional abrasives and solvents for removing coatings.	408-947-1181	NA	San Jose
	Gigamat Technologies (HQ)	Provider of polishers, sorters, grinders, crystal pullers, and related accessories. The company offers services to the industrial sector.	510-770-8008	NA	Fremont
	Granberg International (HQ)	Manufacturer of saw chain maintenance tools to repair and sharpen saw chain and attachments. The company offers brush attachments and cutting bars.	925-380-9400	NA	Pittsburg
N	Ground Hog Inc (HQ)	Provider of earth drills and trenchers.	909-478-5700	NA	San Bernardino
	Guntert & Zimmerman Const Div Inc (HQ)	Manufacturer of canal lining equipment, concrete batch plants, and other special equipment. The company serves the industrial sector.	209-599-0066	NA	Ripon
	Harris & Bruno International (HQ)	Provider of printing and coating solutions. The company offers web coaters, chalmers, offline coaters, pumps, and other products.	916-781-7676	NA	Roseville
	Heat & Control Inc (HQ)	Manufacturer of food processing and packaging equipment systems. The company offers inspection system, product handling equipment, and coating system.	510-259-0500	NA	Hayward
	Heatscape Inc (HQ)	Designer and manufacturer of thermal solutions. The company engages in thermal analysis, thermal testing, and finite element analysis.	408-778-4615	NA	Morgan Hill
	Heinzen Manufacturing International (HQ)	Designer and manufacturer of custom food processing equipment. The company specializes in shakers, bin dumpers, fruit equipment, and trimlines.	408-842-7233	NA	Gilroy
	Hepco Inc (HQ)	Manufacturer of electronic components. The company offers design, fabrication, analysis, and testing tools for semiconductor industries.	408-738-1880	NA	Sunnyvale
	Hesse Mechatronics Inc (LH)	Developer of equipment for heavy wire and thin wire wedge bonders. The company also focuses on the marketing aspects.	408-436-9300	NA	Fremont
	Hitachi Metals America Ltd (BR)	Manufacturer and marketer of metal products. The company offers cable systems, cutting tools, ceramics, sensors, and other materials.	408-467-8900	NA	San Jose
	Horn Machine Tools Inc (HQ)	Supplier of CNC and semi-automatic tube benders. The company offers new tube benders, rebuilt tube benders, and bender rebuilding and retro-fitting.	559-431-4131	NA	Madera
	Hydratech LLC (HQ)	Manufacturer of cylinder component, hydraulic, and pneumatic cylinder with engineering capabilities needed to build superior cylinder solutions.	559-233-0876	NA	Fresno
	Hydrofarm Inc (HQ)	Manufacturer of hydroponics equipment. The company also supplies plant care products and garden accessories.	800-634-9990	NA	Petaluma
	HyPower Hydraulics (HQ)	Manufacturer of hydraulic cylinders and related accessories. The company offers repair/rebuilding services.	209-632-2275	NA	Turlock
	Imtec Acculine Inc (HQ)	Provider of wet process modules and systems. The company also supplies quartz constant temperature baths.	510-770-1800	NA	Fremont
	Industrial Electrical Co (HQ)	Provider of electrical, manufacturing, and automation services for the commercial and industrial sectors.	209-527-2800	NA	Modesto
	Industrial Nuclear Co (HQ)	Manufacturer of industrial gamma radiography equipment and radioactive sources. The company's services include calibration and repair and leak testing.	510-352-6767	NA	San Leandro

COMPANY NAME	PRODUCT / SERVICE	PHONE	EMP	CITY
Intake Screens Inc (HQ)	Designer and manufacturer of intake screens for fish protection and filtration. The company also offers installation and maintenance services.	916-665-2727	NA	Sacramento
ITT BIW Connector Systems (HQ)	Supplier of connector systems and electrical feedthru products. The company's products include wellhead feedthroughs and power interconnect products.	707-523-2300	NA	Santa Rosa
Jackrabbit Inc (HQ)	Provider of nut harvesting systems including runner, elevator, reservoir cart, conditioner and pruning tower.	209-599-6118	NA	Ripon
James Cox & Sons Inc (HQ)	Developer of products for asphalt, concrete, and soil testing. The company is also engaged in calibration and remote support services.	530-346-8322	NA	Colfax
Johnson Manufacturing (HQ)	Developer of farm machinery equipment and utility vehicles. The company offers trailers, air compressors, electric cars and golf car parts.	530-662-1788	NA	Woodland
Juki Americas (BR)	Provider of SMT assembly machines. The company offers inline selective soldering systems, mini-wave soldering machines, and stamp soldering products.	510-249-6700	NA	Fremont
K&L Supply Co (HQ)	Manufacturer of specialty tools and shop equipment for motorcycle dealers. The company offers shop lift and wheel equipment, jacks, and other tools.	408-727-6767	NA	San Jose
Kearneys Metals Inc (HQ)	Provider of foundry services. The company specializes in stainless steel and aluminium plates, sheets, structurals and bars.	559-233-2591	NA	Fresno
N Keck-Craig Inc (HQ)	Manufacturer of custom machinery and packaging machinery.	626-584-1688	1-10	Pasadena
KEMPF Inc (HQ)	Provider of driving solutions. The company offers digital hand controls and other handicap driving aids for paraplegic drivers.	408-773-0219	NA	Sunnyvale
King Sales & Engineering (HQ)	Designer and seller of rotary fillers, labelers, and case packers. The company offers products for the tomato and fruit canning industry.	415-892-7961	NA	Novato
Kirby Manufacturing Inc (HQ)	Provider of cattle feeding equipment such as horizontal and vertical mixers, manure spreaders, freestall wagons, scale systems, and haybusters.	209-723-0778	NA	Merced
Kleenrite Equipment (HQ)	Developer and manufacturer of domestic and commercial cleaning devices. The company caters to commercial and constructional facilities.	800-241-4865	NA	Madera
Klippenstein Corp (HQ)	Manufacturer of packaging equipment. The company's products also include case formers, erectors, and sealers.	559-834-4258	NA	Fresno
KOR-IT Inc (HQ)	Manufacturer of diamond tools and core drill machines. The company caters to the concrete cutting industry.	916-372-6400	NA	Sacramento
N Kval Inc (HQ)	Manufacturer of CNC door machinery for architectural and residential applications.	707-762-0621	51-200	Petaluma
Kycon Inc (HQ)	Provider of interconnect solutions. The company offers products such as audio jacks, card edge, and modular jacks.	408-494-0330	NA	Morgan Hill
Laboratory Equipment Co (HQ)	Manufacturer of laboratory equipment. The company's products include alarm monitor systems, bedding dispensers, dryers, and ovens.	510-887-4040	NA	Hayward
LAKOS Filtration Solutions (HQ)	Manufacturer of centrifugal separators and other filtration solutions to remove sand and other solids from water and liquids.	559-255-1601	NA	Fresno
Lasertec USA Inc (HQ)	Developer and manufacturer of systems for semi-conductor applications. The company also offers systems for flat panel displays.	408-437-1441	NA	San Jose
Leadman Electronics USA Inc (HQ)	Provider of ODM/OEM, hardware engineering expertise, and custom solutions for a wide range of security, storage, server, and network applications.	408-380-4567	NA	Santa Clara
N Linear Industries Ltd (HQ)	Manufacturer and distributor of electronic and mechanical automation control products.	626-303-1130	NA	Monrovia
Liqua-Tech Corp (HQ)	Manufacturer of precision measurement systems. The company offers flow meters, gear trains, and measuring chalmers.	707-462-3555	NA	Ukiah
Longevity Welding (HQ)	Manufacturer of welding equipment. The company also offers filler rods, generators, plasma cutters, and related accessories.	877-566-4462	NA	Hayward
Malcolm Drilling Company Inc (HQ)	Provider of specialty foundation industry services. The company is engaged in deep foundations, dewatering, and design build services.	415-901-4400	NA	San Francisco
Martin Sprocket & Gear Inc (BR)	Manufacturer of industrial hand tools, conveyor pulleys, and other products. The company offers power transmission and material handling products.	916-441-7172	NA	Sacramento
Martin's Metal Fabrication & Welding Inc (HQ)	Provider of structural steel fabrication services in Northern California. The company offers laser cutting, beam line drilling, and other services.	707-678-4117	NA	Vacaville
MC Microwave Inc (HQ)	Provider of microwave and radio frequency components. The company's products are used in commercial and military applications.	408-446-4100	NA	San Jose
Mclellan Industries Inc (HQ)	Manufacturer of stainless steel and mild steel tanks, hook lifts, tank kits, and related accessories.	800-445-8449	NA	Hanford
Microelec Technical (HQ)	Manufacturer of semiconductor, micro-electronics, and mixed signal devices. The company specializes in switches, bridge rectifiers, and transistors.	408-282-3508	NA	Santa Clara
Modern Machine Company (HQ)	Provider of machining services. The company focuses on robotic welding, automatic screw machines, and CNC machining centers.	408-436-7670	NA	San Jose
N Morgan Industries Inc (HQ)	Manufacturer of special industry machinery.	562-634-4074	1-10	Long Beach

COMPANY NAME	PRODUCT / SERVICE	PHONE	EMP	CITY
Motor Guard Corp (HQ)	Designer and developer of spray equipment and tools for collision repairs. The company offers services to the automotive sector.	209-239-9191	NA	Manteca
Mountz Inc (HQ)	Manufacturer of torque analyzers, sensors, bits, sockets, and adapters. The company is engaged in installation and technical support services.	800-456-1828	NA	San Jose
N MPBS Industries (HQ)	Manufacturer and distributor of equipment and supplies for food processors and food packagers in the United States and around the globe.	323-268-8514	11-50	Los Angeles
Murray Trailers (HQ)	Designer and manufacturer of trailers. The company also offers related accessories and hauling services.	209-466-0266	NA	Stockton
NB Corporation of America (BR)	Manufacturer of linear motion bearings, slides, ball splines, and related products. The company's products include slide guides, spindle shafts, and actuators.	510-490-1420	NA	Fremont
Neptune Systems LLC (HQ)	Provider of aquarium controllers. The company also offers expansion modules and accessories and offers support services.	408-275-2205	NA	Morgan Hill
Netafim Irrigation Inc (HQ)	Provider of drip and micro irrigation products for agriculture, greenhouse and nursery, landscape and turf, mining, and wastewater applications.	559-453-6800	NA	Fresno
Nieco (HQ)	Manufacturer of automatic broilers. The company's applications include restaurants, fast food centers, and amusement parks.	707-284-7100	NA	Windsor
N Nordson MARCH (HQ)	Manufacturer of plasma cleaning and treatment equipment, plasma applications and many more.	925-827-1240	51-200	Concord
Nova Measuring Instruments Inc (BR)	Provider of metrology solutions for semiconductor manufacturing industries. The company offers integrated and stand-alone metrology platforms.	408-510-7400	NA	Fremont
NTFB Combustion Equipment USA Inc (HQ)	Manufacturer of combustion equipment. The company offers mid to large size, single and multiple burner, water tube boiler, and furnace applications.	510-443-0066	NA	Foster City
OCSiAl (BR)	Provider of technology and material solutions. The company offers services to the nanomaterials industry.	415-906-5271	NA	Columbus
Onchip Devices Inc (HQ)	Provider of silicon and ceramic solutions and integrated passive devices for the computing and consumer electronics industries.	408-654-9365	NA	Santa Clara
Orchard Machinery Corp (HQ)	Manufacturer of tree shakers and material handling systems comprising shuttles, bin carriers, conveyor carts, and elevators.	530-673-2822	NA	Yuba City
Pacific Coast Optics Inc (HQ)	Provider of optical products, services and applications. The company offers prototype, polishing, grinding, and coating.	916-789-0111	NA	Roseville
Pacific Ozone Technology Inc (HQ)	Supplier of air-cooled, integrated ozone and oxygen systems and packaged controls for industrial ozone applications.	707-747-9600	NA	Benicia
Pacific Roller Die Company Inc (HQ)	Designer and manufacturer of corrugated metal pipes, coated and lined pipes, and duct products. The company offers installation and delivery services.	510-782-7242	NA	Hayward
Pauli Systems Inc (HQ)	Manufacturer of custom finishing systems, abrasive booths, and equipment including blast rooms for aviation, automotive, and industrial applications.	707-429-2434	NA	Fairfield
PAX Scientific Inc (HQ)	Provider of engineering research and product design services. The company is also involved in the design of industrial equipment.	415-256-9900	NA	San Rafael
Pegasus Design Inc (HQ)	Provider of machine design and contract manufacturing services. The company serves the pharmaceutical instrument industry.	925-292-7567	NA	Livermore
Penhall Company (BR)	Provider of concrete cutting services. The company specializes in core drilling, diamond saw cutting, and pavement repair methods.	916-386-1589	NA	Sacramento
Phil Wood & Co (HQ)	Manufacturer of cycling and related recreation oriented products. The company focuses to offer maintenance-free hubs for cyclists.	408-569-1860	NA	San Jose
Plasma Ruggedized Solutions (HQ)	Provider of coating and related specialty engineering services. The company specializes in plasma technologies and offers lab services.	408-954-8405	NA	San Jose
Plasma Technology Systems LLC (HQ)	Provider of equipment and process development services for plasma treatment of surfaces. The company specializes in modification of polymers.	650-596-1606	NA	Hayward
Pneu Design LLC (HQ)	Provider of electronic and pneumatic filling machines for the petroleum and food processing industry.	530-676-4702	NA	Shingle Springs
N Power Machinery Center (HQ)	Distributor of quality material handling and warehouse equipment.	805-485-0577	51-200	Oxnard
N Prob-Test Inc (HQ)	Designer and developer of military training equipment such as laser transmitters, man-worn detectors, vehicle detector assembles and etc.	909-421-4444	11-50	Rialto
Process Engineers Inc (HQ)	Manufacturer of stainless steel equipment. The company also specializes in installation and other services.	510-782-5122	NA	Hayward
Proco Products Inc (HQ)	Manufacturer of expansion joints. The company serves the oil and gas, power generation, chemical, and steel industries.	209-943-6088	NA	Stockton
Prodigy Surface Tech Inc (HQ)	Provider of alternative to common electroplating shop. The company focuses on chem lab for analysis, blaster, and clean room.	408-492-9390	NA	Santa Clara
Progressive Concepts Machining (HQ)	Provider of welding, assembly, and machining services. The company also deals with inspection solutions and serves businesses.	925-426-0400	NA	Pleasanton
N Protec Arisawa America Inc (HQ)	Designer and manufacturer of fiber reinforced plastic pressure vessels for membrane filtration systems.	760-599-4800	NA	Vista

COMPANY NAME	PRODUCT / SERVICE	PHONE	EMP	CITY
N Pump Engineering Co (HQ)	Distributor of pumps, fluid handling systems and much more.	562-944-4768	51-200	Santa Fe Springs
N Quality Fabrication Inc (HQ)	Manufacturer and dealer of precision sheet metal fabrication and machining services.	818-709-8505	51-200	Chatsworth
N Quality Grinding Company Inc (HQ)	Manufacturer of precision grinding and machining products.	714-228-2100	NA	Buena Park
Quality Stainless Tanks (HQ)	Provider of ready-made tanks. The company offers crafted tanks, stainless winery equipment, and special application tanks.	707-837-2721	NA	Windsor
R&R Refrigeration And Air Conditioning Inc (HQ)	Provider of environmental technological solutions. The company also offers maintenance and repair services for process systems.	408-297-0383	NA	San Jose
Rainbow Electronics & Fasteners Corp (HQ)	Distributor of electronic and mechanical hardware products. The company's products include fasteners, screws, standoffs, and spacers.	510-475-9840	NA	Union City
Ralphs-Pugh Co (HQ)	Manufacturer of conveyor rollers and related components. The company serves the agriculture, chemical, and food processing industries.	707-745-6222	NA	Benicia
Ripon Manufacturing Company Inc (HQ)	Fabricator of steel processing equipment. The company manufactures and installs peelers, sizers, hardshell crackers, hoppers, dryers, and sorters.	209-599-2148	NA	Ripon
Rocklin Hydraulics (HQ)	Manufacturer of hydraulic products. The company offers hydraulic hoses, caps and plugs, jaw couplers, and brass fittings.	916-624-8900	NA	Rocklin
N Roscoe Moss Co (HQ)	Manufacturer of water well casings and screens.	323-263-4111	51-200	Los Angeles
N Rotometals Inc (HQ)	Distributor of non-ferrous metal elements and alloys such as aluminum, antimony, bismuth, indium and more.	888-779-1102	NA	San Leandro
Safety Equipment Corp (HQ)	Designer and manufacturer of gas cabinets, valve boxes, leaker cabinets, exhausted enclosures, and related products.	650-595-5422	NA	Belmont
San-I-Pak Pacific Inc (HQ)	Manufacturer of compactors, shredders, and sterilizer supplies. The company serves the industrial sector and enterprises.	209-836-2310	NA	Tracy
Sandvik Thermal Process Inc (DH)	Provider of thermal processing equipment. The company offers solar cells, semiconductors, and industrial heaters.	209-533-1990	NA	Sonora
Sentek Dynamics Inc (HQ)	Manufacturer of vibration test equipment, shakers, power amplifiers, and related instruments. The company offers customer support solutions.	408-200-3100	NA	Santa Clara
Serpa Packaging Solutions (HQ)	Provider of packaging solutions. The company's applications include pharmaceutical industry and bottles, vials, and ampules.	559-651-2339	NA	Visalia
Silicon Valley Mfg (HQ)	Manufacturer and engineer of EDM prototype and production machining. The company's services include CNC milling, CNC turning, and manual machining.	510-791-9450	NA	Newark
Simco-Ion (BR)	Manufacturer of static control and process control products. The company is engaged in design and installation services.	510-217-0460	NA	Alameda
Simplex Filler Co (HQ)	Manufacturer of liquid filling machines. The company offers volumetric fillers, pressure fillers, and accessories.	707-265-6801	NA	Napa
SJC Precision Inc (HQ)	Provider of precision machining and tool and die making services. The company designs and manufactures jigs, fixtures, and bookmolds.	408-262-1680	NA	Milpitas
Smart Wires Inc (HQ)	Provider of grid optimization solutions. The company is involved in load and generation, alleviate congestion, and network utilization services.	415-800-5555	NA	Union City
N Smith Food Machinery Inc (HQ)	Wholesaler of used food processing equipment and paint liquidations and plant and equipment appraisals, auction and plant liquidation services.	209-465-3688	NA	Stockton
Sonic Manufacturing Technologies (HQ)	Provider of contract manufacturing services. The company engages in supply chain, quality assurance, and design and engineering services.	510-756-5837	NA	Fremont
Source Engineering Inc (HQ)	Manufacturer of motors, cables, harnesses, and motion control products. The company also provides custom modification services on motors.	408-980-9822	NA	Santa Clara
Spintrac Systems Inc (HQ)	Manufacturer of automated resist coating equipment. The company is involved in repairs and maintenance services.	408-980-1155	NA	Santa Clara
Stage 8 (HQ)	Designer and manufacturer of mechanical locking systems. The company has more than 78 patents and trademarks.	415-485-5340	NA	San Rafael
N Stoll Metalcraft Inc (HQ)	Fabricator of precision sheet metal parts and electro-mechanical assemblies.	661-295-0401	11-50	Valencia
Storz & Bickel America Inc (HQ)	Manufacturer of vaporizers. The company specializes in the design and fabrication of solid valve and easy valve systems.	866-380-6278	NA	Oakland
N Stracon Inc (HQ)	Manufacturer and distributor of electronic equipment.	949-851-2288	11-50	Irvine
Sumiden Wire Products Corp (BR)	Supplier of wire products. The company offers nickel plated wires, stainless spring wires, and industrial alloys.	209-466-8924	NA	Stockton
Surveillance Systems Integration Inc (HQ)	Provider of security products. The company serves customers in the gaming, retail, education, and healthcare industries.	916-771-7272	NA	Rocklin
Sweco Products Inc (HQ)	Manufacturer of agricultural and construction equipment and hydraulic cylinders, and related supplies.	530-673-8949	NA	Sutter
Technavibes Inc (HQ)	Manufacturer of feeder bowls. The company specializes in vibratory bowl feeders, vibratory feeder in-line tracks, and vibratory feeder hoppers.	530-626-8093	NA	Diamond Springs
N Technical Heaters Inc (HQ)	Manufacturer of rubber, plastics hose and beltings.	800-394-9435	NA	San Fernando
Teknika Strapping Systems (HQ)	Provider of hand tools for plastic stripping. The company is engaged in repairs, replacement, and maintenance services.	408-441-9071	NA	San Jose

COMPANY NAME	PRODUCT / SERVICE	PHONE	EMP	CITY
Tesla (HQ)	Designer and manufacturer of electric sedans and electric SUVs. The company is engaged in the production of energy storage systems.	650-681-5000	NA	Palo Alto
The Lincoln Electric Co (BR)	Provider of industrial control and automation solutions. The company's offerings also include torches, welding guns, and related accessories.	916-939-8788	NA	El Dorado Hills
The Montague Co (HQ)	Provider of commercial cooking equipment. The company's products include boilers, ovens, and refrigerated bases.	510-785-8822	NA	Hayward
Therm-X (HQ)	Provider of engineered solutions. The company serves the semiconductor, petrochemical, life sciences, and aerospace industries.	510-606-1012	NA	Hayward
Thermal Press International Inc (HQ)	Manufacturer of thermal presses and heat staking machines. The company also offers heat sealing and degating machinery.	925-454-9800	NA	Livermore
N Tosco - Tool Specialty Co (HQ)	Manufacturer of carbide cutting tools.	323-232-3561	NA	Los Angeles
Transfer Flow Inc (HQ)	Manufacturer of fuel tanks. The company offers axillary, replacement, and tanks with built-in toolboxes.	530-893-5209	NA	Chico
Ultra T Equipment Company Inc (HQ)	Manufacturer of spin coaters, developer stations, reionizers, and microelectronics cleaning systems.	510-440-3909	NA	Fremont
Uniform Industrial Corp (DH)	Provider of systems and components for banking and retail solutions. The company also offers technology solutions and customer services.	510-438-6799	NA	Fremont
V&O Machine Inc (HQ)	Manufacturer of machined parts for agri, hydraulics, food processing, and veterinary applications. The company focuses on prototyping and CNC milling.	530-662-0495	NA	Woodland
Valley Tool & Manufacturing Co (HQ)	Manufacturer of agricultural equipment like flail mowers, sprayers, and shredders. The company also manufactures skid steer and excavator attachments.	800-426-5615	NA	Hughson
Vanderlans & Sons Inc (HQ)	Manufacturer of pipe and high pressure plugs, test equipment, hoses, gauges, ventilators, and related accessories.	209-334-4115	NA	Lodi
Ventex Corp (HQ)	Supplier of lithography equipment, spare parts, and services. The company also provides refurbishment and installation services.	408-436-2929	NA	San Jose
N Vest Inc (HQ)	Producer of electric welded carbon steel tubing products.	800-421-6370	11-50	Vernon
Warren & Baerg Manufacturing Inc (HQ)	Manufacturer of agricultural and industrial systems. The company's services include installation, manufacturing, and technical support.	559-591-6790	NA	Dinuba
Wasco Hardfacing Co (HQ)	Manufacturer of hardfacing electrodes for steel, cement, and mining applications. The company also offers welding alloy solutions.	559-485-5860	NA	Fresno
Waterman Industries (HQ)	Designer and manufacturer of water-control sluice gates, penstocks, valves, and water control products.	559-562-4000	NA	Exeter
Weslan Systems Inc (HQ)	Fabricator of custom plastic products for the semiconductor industry. The company offers contract manufacturing services.	530-668-3304	NA	Woodland
Westec Plastics Corp (HQ)	Provider of plastics injection molding and mold making services. The company also offers customized services.	925-454-3400	NA	Livermore
Western Allied Mechanical Inc (HQ)	Designer and builder of heating and ventilation systems. The company serves the construction and energy automation industries.	650-326-0750	NA	Menlo Park
Western Truck Fab Inc (HQ)	Provider of custom truck body fabrication services. The company's products include lift gates, compressors, and cranes.	510-785-9994	NA	Hayward
Western Widgets CNC Inc (HQ)	Manufacturer of precision milled and turned components such as computers and optical assemblies. The company deals with milling and turning services.	408-436-1230	NA	San Jose
Westport Machine Works Inc (HQ)	Manufacturer of assembly and balancing equipment. The company's services include fixturing, installation, and technical support.	916-371-4493	NA	West Sacramento
Whipple Industries Inc (HQ)	Provider of supercharger for vehicles. The company's products include twin-screw superchargers and accessories.	559-442-1261	NA	Fresno
Wolfram Inc (HQ)	Designer and manufacturer of metal halide lamps for the entertainment industry. The company's lamps are used for filming motion pictures.	209-238-9610	NA	Modesto
Woodland Mdm (HQ)	Manufacturer and supplier of new and refurbished machinery products. The company offers industrial controls and automation and case handling equipment.	530-669-1400	NA	Woodland
Woodside Electronics Corp (HQ)	Designer and manufacturer of electronic sorters. The company serves customers in the tomato harvesters and walnut industries.	530-666-9190	NA	Woodland
WPG Americas Inc (DH)	Distributor of electronic products. The company's portfolio includes encoders, sensors, solid state batteries, and timing devices.	408-392-8100	NA	San Jose
Zalda Technology (HQ)	Fabricator of springs. The company also offers spring design, testing, and prototype assembling services.	510-783-4910	NA	Hayward
Zircon Corp (HQ)	Designer and manufacturer of stud finders. The company offers electrical scanners, metal detectors, leveling tools, and accessories.	408-963-4550	NA	Campbell

160 = Pumps

N Alltronics LLC (HQ)	Distributor of electrical and electro-mechanical parts such as automotive, computer, capacitors and more.	408-778-3868	1-10	Santa Clara
Aqua Sierra Controls Inc (HQ)	Provider of instrumentation and electrical contract services. The company specializes in process control automation for industrial installations.	530-823-3241	NA	Auburn

	COMPANY NAME	PRODUCT / SERVICE	PHONE	EMP	CITY
N	Bearing Engineering Company Inc (HQ)	Distributor of power transmission products such as bearings, belts, bushings, chains and chain drives and more.	510-596-4150	NA	San Leandro
	BESST Inc (HQ)	Provider of groundwater sampling technology solutions. The company also offers customized packages for specialized applications.	415-453-2501	NA	San Rafael
	Biomicrolab (HQ)	Manufacturer of robotics based sorting and weighing systems sample management automation. The company serves bio-lab purposes.	925-689-1200	NA	Concord
N	Calolympic Safety (HQ)	Distributor of bandages and health-conscious ergonomic products.	951-340-2229	NA	Corona
N	Carlson and Beauloye (HQ)	Manufacturer of the motorless water pump that generates its horsepower from water weight and gravity.	619-234-2256	NA	San Diego
	Control Systems West Inc (HQ)	Designer and fabricator of a broad variety of custom electrical controls for industrial applications.	707-763-1108	NA	Petaluma
	Diener Precision Pumps LP (DH)	Developer of gear and piston pumps, and valves for cooling and fleshing, refrigeration, medical, biotech, and pharmaceutical industries.	209-365-0405	NA	Lodi
	IDEX Health & Science LLC (BR)	Provider of precision equipment for the health care industry. The company also offers detectors, fittings, and filters.	707-588-2000	NA	Rohnert Park
	Inoxpa USA Inc (HQ)	Manufacturer and trader of pumps and components. The company caters to industries like food processing, dairy, wine-making, and cosmetics.	707-585-3900	NA	Santa Rosa
N	Linear Industries Ltd (HQ)	Manufacturer and distributor of electronic and mechanical automation control products.	626-303-1130	NA	Monrovia
	Mclellan Industries Inc (HQ)	Manufacturer of stainless steel and mild steel tanks, hook lifts, tank kits, and related accessories.	800-445-8449	NA	Hanford
	Morrill Industries Inc (HQ)	Manufacturer and supplier of irrigation equipment. The company also offers custom built rotating suction screens and industrial pipes.	209-838-2550	NA	Escalon
N	MPBS Industries (HQ)	Manufacturer and distributor of equipment and supplies for food processors and food packagers in the United States and around the globe.	323-268-8514	11-50	Los Angeles
N	Power Machinery Center (HQ)	Distributor of quality material handling and warehouse equipment.	805-485-0577	51-200	Oxnard
	Price Pump Co (HQ)	Manufacturer of centrifugal and air operated diaphragm pumps. The company offers engineering services and serves industrial and OEM users.	707-938-8441	NA	Sonoma
	Process Engineers Inc (HQ)	Manufacturer of stainless steel equipment. The company also specializes in installation and other services.	510-782-5122	NA	Hayward
N	Pump Engineering Co (HQ)	Distributor of pumps, fluid handling systems and much more.	562-944-4768	51-200	Santa Fe Springs
	Simonds Machinery Co (HQ)	Distributor of portable pump carts, custom control panels, pressure booster systems, and related accessories.	650-589-9900	NA	S San Francisco
	Smart Products Inc (HQ)	Supplier of engineering products. The company offers valves, fittings, and pumps for the automotive, medical, and water treatment markers.	408-776-3035	NA	Morgan Hill
N	Smith Precision Products Co (HQ)	Manufacturer and distributor of pumps and fertilizer injectors.	805-498-6616	NA	Newbury Park
	SuperKlean (HQ)	Manufacturer of spray nozzles and swivel fittings. The company also offers hot and cold water mixing stations and hose racks.	650-375-7001	NA	Burlingame
	V-Power Equipment Inc (HQ)	Manufacturer and wholesaler of water well, wastewater, and construction dewatering pumps. The company provides pump repair and diagnostic services.	916-266-6743	NA	West Sacramento
	Varna Products (HQ)	Manufacturer of pump and valve solutions. The company offers oil pumps, pump controls, pressure relief valves, and check valves.	530-676-7770	NA	Cameron Park
	Vian Enterprises Inc (HQ)	Manufacturer of gerotors, gears, and broached hardware. The company also offers oil pump and complete lubrication systems.	530-885-1997	NA	Auburn

162 = Seals/Gaskets

	COMPANY NAME	PRODUCT / SERVICE	PHONE	EMP	CITY
N	Alltronics LLC (HQ)	Distributor of electrical and electro-mechanical parts such as automotive, computer, capacitors and more.	408-778-3868	1-10	Santa Clara
N	Bearing Engineering Company Inc (HQ)	Distributor of power transmission products such as bearings, belts, bushings, chains and chain drives and more.	510-596-4150	NA	San Leandro
N	Calolympic Safety (HQ)	Distributor of bandages and health-conscious ergonomic products.	951-340-2229	NA	Corona
	Campbell/Harris Security Equipment Company (HQ)	Manufacturer of busters, fiberscopes, probe kits, and personal radiation detectors. The company also focuses on distribution.	510-864-8010	NA	Alameda
N	Carlson and Beauloye (HQ)	Manufacturer of the motorless water pump that generates its horsepower from water weight and gravity.	619-234-2256	NA	San Diego
	Darcoid Nor-Cal Seal (HQ)	Provider of rubber based products. The company offers gaskets, composite and dynamic seals, molded shapes, and thermal products.	510-836-2449	NA	Oakland
	Gasket Specialties Inc (HQ)	Manufacturer of gaskets. The company engages in adhesives, assembly, and bar coding services.	510-547-7955	NA	Emeryville
	Lamons (BR)	Manufacturer of industrial gaskets. The company caters to the refinery and packing industrial sectors.	925-313-9080	NA	Martinez
N	Linear Industries Ltd (HQ)	Manufacturer and distributor of electronic and mechanical automation control products.	626-303-1130	NA	Monrovia
N	Material Fabricators Inc (HQ)	Manufacturer of gaskets, shims, washers, metal stampings and die cut electrical insulators.	805-686-5244	NA	Buellton

	COMPANY NAME	PRODUCT / SERVICE	PHONE	EMP	CITY
N	MPBS Industries (HQ)	Manufacturer and distributor of equipment and supplies for food processors and food packagers in the United States and around the globe.	323-268-8514	11-50	Los Angeles
N	O-Rings Inc (HQ)	Manufacturer and distributor of rings and custom molded rubber products.	323-343-9500	NA	Los Angeles
	Pacific States Felt & MFG Company Inc (HQ)	Manufacturer of gaskets, seals, washers, pads, and molded bumpers. The company is engaged in lamination and fabrication.	510-783-0277	NA	Hayward
	Power Industries (HQ)	Supplier of ready-made solutions for industrial applications. The company's products include bearings and seals, hydraulics, and pneumatics.	707-545-7904	NA	Santa Rosa
N	Power Machinery Center (HQ)	Distributor of quality material handling and warehouse equipment.	805-485-0577	51-200	Oxnard
	Process Engineers Inc (HQ)	Manufacturer of stainless steel equipment. The company also specializes in installation and other services.	510-782-5122	NA	Hayward
N	Pump Engineering Co (HQ)	Distributor of pumps, fluid handling systems and much more.	562-944-4768	51-200	Santa Fe Springs
N	R & R Rubber Molding Inc (HQ)	Manufacturer of elastomeric, rubber parts, gaskets, seals and o-rings for aerospace, industry, commercial, aftermarket, military, and OEM design and specifications through the processes of injection, transfer, and compression.	626-575-8105	NA	South El Monte
	RGS Industries (HQ)	Manufacturer and supplier of gaskets. The company offers seals, shielding and related materials, and die cutting services.	669-238-0632	NA	Santa Clara
N	Roettele Industries Inc (HQ)	Manufacturer of non-metallic washers and gaskets.	909-606-8252	1-10	Chino

163 = Special Dies, Tools & Molds

	COMPANY NAME	PRODUCT / SERVICE	PHONE	EMP	CITY
	Ace Seal LLC (HQ)	Manufacturer of molded rubber, seals, and o-rings. The company serves the aerospace, semiconductor, oil and gas, medical, and biotechnology sectors.	408-513-1070	NA	San Jose
	American Die & Rollforming Inc (HQ)	Manufacturer of metal roofing, siding, and structural products. The company also specializes in canopies and decking.	916-652-7667	NA	Loomis
N	AW Die Engraving Inc (HQ)	Manufacturer of precision rotary and flat dies for labeling, printing and die cutting.	714-521-0842	NA	Buena Park
	Bulling Metal Works Inc (HQ)	Manufacturer of pressure vessels and laser cutting machinery. The company also offers other custom fabrication products.	510-351-2073	NA	San Leandro
	Computer Plastics Inc (HQ)	Provider of molding services. The company offers custom plastic injection molding, engineering, assembly, and tooling services.	510-785-3600	NA	Hayward
	Concepts 2 Industries (HQ)	Manufacturer of custom injection molded plastic parts. The company serves computer, medical, telecom, and other sectors.	831-464-1111	NA	Soquel
	Crcdj LLC (HQ)	Provider of shaped bags and pouches. The company's services include rotary die cutting, steel rule die cutting, and micro-form and fill.	408-855-8909	NA	San Jose
	Crown Manufacturing Company Inc (HQ)	Provider of plastic and injection molded products. The company offers insert and over molding, drilling, tapping, and heat stamping services.	510-742-8800	NA	Newark
	Diamond Tool & Die Inc (HQ)	Provider of general machine services for the high tech industry. The company serves the aerospace, construction, and food processing industries.	510-534-7050	NA	Oakland
	Fastening Systems International Inc (HQ)	Supplier of blind fasteners and blind rivet installation tools. The company offers rivet guns, rivet nuts, pop rivets, and more.	707-935-1170	NA	Sonoma
	Finishline Advanced Composites LLC (HQ)	Provider of composite repair services for production projects. The company is involved in design, development, prototyping, testing, and production.	707-747-0788	NA	Benicia
	Foamlinx LLC (HQ)	Provider of foam cutting computer numerical control machines. The company offers cutters, shredders, compactors, and cutting services.	408-454-6163	NA	Sunnyvale
	GM Nameplate Inc (BR)	Manufacturer of die cut components. The company offers components for shielding, insulators, adhesives, and fabricated parts.	408-435-1666	NA	San Jose
	HECO Inc (HQ)	Manufacturer of planetary speed reducers. The company's applications include swing drives, wheel drives, conveyor drives, winch drives, mixers, and augers.	916-372-5411	NA	West Sacramento
	Hiebert Sculpture Works (HQ)	Provider of plastic injection molding products. The company also offers composite epoxy tooling, design assistance, and custom molds.	510-654-7488	NA	Oakland
	Jatco Inc (HQ)	Manufacture of plastic products. The company offers molding, tooling, quality control, and warehousing and distribution services.	510-487-0888	NA	Union City
	Kaman Industrial Technologies (BR)	Provider of industrial technology solutions. The company's portfolio comprises bearings, gearing, linear motion, and power transmission products.	650-589-6800	NA	Union City
N	Material Fabricators Inc (HQ)	Manufacturer of gaskets, shims, washers, metal stampings and die cut electrical insulators.	805-686-5244	NA	Buellton
	Minitool Inc (HQ)	Manufacturer of precision instruments and small tools for microscopic investigation. The company also specializes in under-microscope precision tools.	408-395-1585	NA	Campbell
	MOS Plastics Inc (HQ)	Provider of precision injection-molding, contract manufacturing, and assembly services for medical and electronics OEMs.	408-944-9407	NA	San Jose
N	O-Rings Inc (HQ)	Manufacturer and distributor of rings and custom molded rubber products.	323-343-9500	NA	Los Angeles

COMPANY NAME	PRODUCT / SERVICE	PHONE	EMP	CITY
Pacific Die Cut Industries (HQ)	Provider of custom converting services that include die cutting, laminating, and slitting. The company also offers packaging solutions.	510-732-8103	NA	Hayward
Pacmold (HQ)	Designer and manufacturer of plastic injection molds. The company has production facilities in Taiwan and China.	510-785-9882	NA	Hayward
Parmatech Corp (BR)	Supplier of metal injection molding components. The company serves the automotive, medical, industrial, and electronics industries.	707-778-2266	NA	Petaluma
PCC Structurals Inc (BR)	Manufacturer of complex metal components and products. The company caters to industrial and aerospace applications.	510-568-6400	NA	San Leandro
N Pottery Manufacturing and Distributing Inc (HQ)	Manufacturer and distributor of clay and glazed pottery.	310-323-7754	NA	Gardena
Precision Metal Tooling Inc (HQ)	Manufacturer of production tool and die manufacturing products. The company also focuses on prototype tooling, tool engineering, and custom tooling.	510-436-0900	NA	Oakland
N Product Slingshot Inc (HQ)	Provider of business services.	760-929-9380	NA	Carlsbad
N Roettele Industries Inc (HQ)	Manufacturer of non-metallic washers and gaskets.	909-606-8252	1-10	Chino
Silicon Microstructures Inc (HQ)	Developer and manufacturer of MEMS-based pressure sensors. The company's products are used in medical, industrial, and automotive applications.	408-577-0100	NA	Milpitas
SJC Precision Inc (HQ)	Provider of precision machining and tool and die making services. The company designs and manufactures jigs, fixtures, and bookmolds.	408-262-1680	NA	Milpitas
SKS Diecasting & Machining (HQ)	Manufacturer of aluminum die cast parts and related supplies. The company offers services to the high tech industry.	510-523-2541	NA	Alameda
Solonics Inc (HQ)	Manufacturer of coded backboard systems and wire management products. The company focuses on design and delivery services.	510-471-7600	NA	Hayward
SP3 Diamond Technologies (HQ)	Provider of electronics thermal management, diamond-on-silicon applications, and enhanced cutting surface solutions.	408-492-0630	NA	Santa Clara
Stack Plastics Inc (HQ)	Provider of plastic injection molding services. The company offers thermoplastics, elastomers, and resins.	650-361-8600	NA	Menlo Park
Sunset Moulding Company (HQ)	Provider of molding and millwork products. The company offers products such as interior jambs, board products, and shelving.	530-790-2700	NA	Yuba City
United Sheetmetal Inc (BR)	Manufacturer of precision metal products. The company specializes in tooling, die casting, plastic injection, and sheet metal fabrication services.	510-257-1858	NA	Fremont
N United Western Industries Inc (HQ)	Provider of sheet metal fabrication, prototypes, tool and die, precision machining, CNC machining, welding, stamping, laser cutting and grinding.	559-226-7236	1-10	Fresno
Westport Machine Works Inc (HQ)	Manufacturer of assembly and balancing equipment. The company's services include fixturing, installation, and technical support.	916-371-4493	NA	West Sacramento
Wunder Mold Inc (HQ)	Provider of ceramic injection molding services. The company designs and produces art molded ceramics for appliances and electronics applications.	707-448-2349	NA	Vacaville

164 = Speed Changers

HECO Inc (HQ)	Manufacturer of planetary speed reducers. The company's applications include swing drives, wheel drives, conveyor drives, winch drives, mixers, and augers.	916-372-5411	NA	West Sacramento

165 = Vacuum Products & Systems

AGS Plasma Systems Inc (HQ)	Manufacturer and distributor of vacuum plasma systems. The company serves microelectronics and optoelectronics industries.	408-855-8686	NA	Santa Clara
Anatech USA (HQ)	Provider of high vacuum systems with plasma technology. The company's applications include flip chips, multichip modules, and photoresist strips.	510-401-5990	NA	Union City
Ascentool (HQ)	Designer, manufacturer, and marketer of vacuum thin-film deposition systems for making solar photovoltaic devices.	510-683-9332	NA	Fremont
Brechtel Manufacturing Inc (HQ)	Provider of aerosol solutions to the government, academic, and corporate sectors. The company also supplies vacuum brazing furnaces and leak valves.	510-732-9723	NA	Hayward
Brooks Automation Inc (BR)	Provider of automation, vacuum, and instrumentation solutions for the semiconductor manufacturing, life sciences, and clean energy industries.	510-661-5000	NA	Fremont
Duniway Stockroom Corp (HQ)	Supplier of vacuum equipment. The company offers ion, diffusion, and mechanical pumps, and valves to the industrial sector.	650-969-8811	NA	Fremont
Finishline Advanced Composites LLC (HQ)	Provider of composite repair services for production projects. The company is involved in design, development, prototyping, testing, and production.	707-747-0788	NA	Benicia
Mcintire Machine Inc (HQ)	Provider of precision machining, welding, and fabrication services. The company offers services to the industrial sector.	209-837-4409	NA	Crows Landing
Nor-Cal Products Inc (HQ)	Provider of fabricating solutions for stainless steel flanges, fittings, and components. The company's services include welding, machining, and forming.	530-842-4457	NA	Yreka

COMPANY NAME	PRODUCT / SERVICE	PHONE	EMP	CITY
Plasma Technology Systems LLC (HQ)	Provider of equipment and process development services for plasma treatment of surfaces. The company specializes in modification of polymers.	650-596-1606	NA	Hayward
Sardee Industries Inc (BR)	Provider of container manufacturing equipment. The company also offers engineering and repair services for packing and filling industries.	209-466-1526	NA	Stockton
SMC Corporation of America (BR)	Provider of in pneumatic technology solutions that are used in diverse range of industries from automotive to life science.	408-943-9600	NA	San Jose
Transfer Engineering & Manufacturing Inc (HQ)	Manufacturer and marketer of loadlocks and transfer systems. The company offers precision magnetic manipulators and transporters, and other products.	510-651-3000	NA	Fremont
Trayer Engineering Corp (HQ)	Manufacturer of electronic distribution switchgears. The company's services include design, maintenance, and installation.	415-285-7770	NA	San Leandro
Vacuum Process Engineering Inc (HQ)	Provider of engineering services. The company focuses on precision brazing, diffusion bonding, heat treating, and production of precision assemblies.	916-925-6100	NA	Sacramento

166 = Valves

	COMPANY NAME	PRODUCT / SERVICE	PHONE	EMP	CITY
N	Alltronics LLC (HQ)	Distributor of electrical and electro-mechanical parts such as automotive, computer, capacitors and more.	408-778-3868	1-10	Santa Clara
	ATS Inc (HQ)	Manufacturer of fiberglass ductwork for fume exhaust systems. The company offers installation and other related services.	510-234-3173	NA	Richmond
N	Bearing Engineering Company Inc (HQ)	Distributor of power transmission products such as bearings, belts, bushings, chains and chain drives and more.	510-596-4150	NA	San Leandro
	Bowsmith Inc (HQ)	Provider of micro-irrigation equipment for agriculture, landscape, greenhouse, and heap leach mining. The company offers drip emitters and sprinklers.	559-592-9485	NA	Exeter
N	Calolympic Safety (HQ)	Distributor of bandages and health-conscious ergonomic products.	951-340-2229	NA	Corona
	Campbell/Harris Security Equipment Company (HQ)	Manufacturer of busters, fiberscopes, probe kits, and personal radiation detectors. The company also focuses on distribution.	510-864-8010	NA	Alameda
N	Carlson and Beauloye (HQ)	Manufacturer of the motorless water pump that generates its horsepower from water weight and gravity.	619-234-2256	NA	San Diego
N	CIRCOR Aerospace Inc (HQ)	Distributor of fluidic control and undercarriage components and subsystems in the aerospace and defense markers.	951-270-6200	501-1000	Corona
	Conval Inc (BR)	Manufacturer of pressure forged steel valves. The company products include globe valves, ball valves, and strainers.	530-877-5172	NA	Paradise
	Finishline Advanced Composites LLC (HQ)	Provider of composite repair services for production projects. The company is involved in design, development, prototyping, testing, and production.	707-747-0788	NA	Benicia
	Fresno Valves & Castings Inc (HQ)	Provider of water control devices used in irrigation applications. The company's products include valves, filters, air vents, fittings, gates, and lifts.	559-834-2511	NA	Selma
	Fujikin of America Inc (RH)	Manufacturer of fluid and gas flow valves and fittings. The company also offers process equipment control systems.	408-980-8269	NA	Fremont
	Gerlinger Steel & Supply Company (HQ)	Provider of metal products and industrial services. The company offers metalworking machinery and supplies.	530-243-1053	NA	Redding
	IDEX Health & Science LLC (BR)	Provider of precision equipment for the health care industry. The company also offers detectors, fittings, and filters.	707-588-2000	NA	Rohnert Park
	Inoxpa USA Inc (HQ)	Manufacturer and trader of pumps and components. The company caters to industries like food processing, dairy, wine-making, and cosmetics.	707-585-3900	NA	Santa Rosa
N	Linear Industries Ltd (HQ)	Manufacturer and distributor of electronic and mechanical automation control products.	626-303-1130	NA	Monrovia
	Mclellan Industries Inc (HQ)	Manufacturer of stainless steel and mild steel tanks, hook lifts, tank kits, and related accessories.	800-445-8449	NA	Hanford
	Microchek Inc (HQ)	Manufacturer of check valves and self-activating safety valves. The company's products include a diverse variety of valves.	209-333-5253	NA	Lodi
	Morrill Industries Inc (HQ)	Manufacturer and supplier of irrigation equipment. The company also offers custom built rotating suction screens and industrial pipes.	209-838-2550	NA	Escalon
N	MPBS Industries (HQ)	Manufacturer and distributor of equipment and supplies for food processors and food packagers in the United States and around the globe.	323-268-8514	11-50	Los Angeles
	Nor-Cal Products Inc (HQ)	Provider of fabricating solutions for stainless steel flanges, fittings, and components. The company's services include welding, machining, and forming.	530-842-4457	NA	Yreka
	Plug-It Products (HQ)	Provider of in-house products for the municipalities, maintenance contractors, underground contractors, and rental companies.	209-334-4904	NA	Lodi
N	Power Machinery Center (HQ)	Distributor of quality material handling and warehouse equipment.	805-485-0577	51-200	Oxnard
	Process Engineers Inc (HQ)	Manufacturer of stainless steel equipment. The company also specializes in installation and other services.	510-782-5122	NA	Hayward
	Proco Products Inc (HQ)	Manufacturer of expansion joints. The company serves the oil and gas, power generation, chemical, and steel industries.	209-943-6088	NA	Stockton

COMPANY NAME	PRODUCT / SERVICE	PHONE	EMP	CITY
N Pump Engineering Co (HQ)	Distributor of pumps, fluid handling systems and much more.	562-944-4768	51-200	Santa Fe Springs
N Roscoe Moss Co (HQ)	Manufacturer of water well casings and screens.	323-263-4111	51-200	Los Angeles
SAGE Instruments Inc (RH)	Provider of wireless base station test products. The company offers battery operated handhelds, portables, bench tops, and rackmount test platforms.	831-761-1000	NA	Freedom
Smart Products Inc (HQ)	Supplier of engineering products. The company offers valves, fittings, and pumps for the automotive, medical, and water treatment markers.	408-776-3035	NA	Morgan Hill
SMC Corporation of America (BR)	Provider of in pneumatic technology solutions that are used in diverse range of industries from automotive to life science.	408-943-9600	NA	San Jose
T&T Valve & Instrument Inc (HQ)	Provider of manual and automated valves to industrial, municipal water, and wastewater industries. The company focuses on project assistance.	925-484-4898	NA	Pleasanton
Transitional Systems Manufacturing Inc (HQ)	Provider of products to repair landscape sprinkler systems. The company also focuses on installation needs.	530-751-2610	NA	Browns Valley
Varna Products (HQ)	Manufacturer of pump and valve solutions. The company offers oil pumps, pump controls, pressure relief valves, and check valves.	530-676-7770	NA	Cameron Park
N Vest Inc (HQ)	Producer of electric welded carbon steel tubing products.	800-421-6370	11-50	Vernon
Waterman Industries (HQ)	Designer and manufacturer of water-control sluice gates, penstocks, valves, and water control products.	559-562-4000	NA	Exeter

168 = Cameras & Related Equipment

COMPANY NAME	PRODUCT / SERVICE	PHONE	EMP	CITY
Appro Technology Inc (BR)	Manufacturer of network surveillance systems. The company's products include dome cameras, LCD monitors, and cables.	408-720-0018	NA	Sunnyvale
ATN Corp (HQ)	Developer and manufacturer of precision night optics and thermal imaging solutions. The company serves law enforcement and military clients.	650-989-5100	NA	S San Francisco
Boly Media Communications Inc (HQ)	Supplier of trail cameras and security cameras. The company also specializes in ultrasonic motors and optical zooms.	408-533-0207	NA	Santa Clara
Cirrus Digital Systems (HQ)	Developer of single and multi-camera mapping systems for NASA applications and high altitude manned and unmanned aircraft needs.	415-608-9420	NA	Tiburon
Fairchild Imaging Inc (DH)	Developer and manufacturer of solid-state electronic imaging components, cameras, and systems. The company's products include image sensors and cameras.	650-479-5749	NA	San Jose
LG Display America Inc (BR)	Manufacturer of thin-film transistor liquid crystal display panels. The company is also focused on OLEDs and flexible displays.	408-350-0190	NA	San Jose
Meraki LLC (BR)	Provider of branch networking solutions. The company offers services to the education, retail, and healthcare industries.	415-432-1000	NA	San Francisco
Motion Capture Camera & Software Leader (HQ)	Provider of motion analyzers. The company specializes in engineering, animation, design, reality augmentation, and simulation services.	707-579-6500	NA	Rohnert Park
Ocean Presence Technologies (HQ)	Manufacturer of underwater video monitoring camera systems and offers cable systems, power systems, lighting, wireless networks, and accessories.	831-426-4678	NA	Santa Cruz
OJO Technology Inc (HQ)	Manufacturer of video surveillance systems. The company offers services to the education, transportation, and utility sectors.	877-306-4656	NA	Fremont
Pelco Inc (HQ)	Manufacturer of closed circuit TV cameras and accessories. The company's services include training, engineering, and technical development.	559-292-1981	NA	Fresno
Pragmatic Communications Systems Inc (HQ)	Designer, developer, and manufacturer of pragmatic products. The company offers amplifiers, security cameras, speakers, and wireless products.	408-748-1100	NA	Santa Clara
Seiwa Optical America Inc (HQ)	Manufacturer of optical components and photonic integrated circuits. The company offers network and access solutions.	408-844-8008	NA	Santa Clara
Sightech Vision Systems (HQ)	Manufacturer of industrial vision systems. The company offers quality vision systems, hard disk inspection, and crimp verification services.	408-282-3770	NA	Modesto
N StarDot Technologies (HQ)	Designer and manufacturer of digital cameras.	714-228-9282	NA	Buena Park
TOA Electronics Inc (DH)	Developer and manufacturer of audio and security products. The company is engaged in design, delivery, and installation services.	650-452-1200	NA	S San Francisco
Uniq Vision Inc (HQ)	Designer and manufacturer of high resolution CCD cameras for medical, scientific, industrial, and military applications.	408-330-0818	NA	Santa Clara
Videofax (HQ)	Manufacturer of cameras, recorders, players, and related accessories. The company offers technical support services.	415-641-0100	NA	San Francisco
Vivotek USA (BR)	Provider of surveillance solutions. The company specializes in manufacturing network cameras for the network video surveillance industries.	408-773-8686	NA	San Jose
X-Scan Imaging Corp (HQ)	Supplier of x-ray imaging and inspection equipment. The company also offers array detectors and line-scan camera products.	408-432-9888	NA	San Jose

169 = Displays

COMPANY NAME	PRODUCT / SERVICE	PHONE	EMP	CITY
Advanced Witness Series Inc (HQ)	Designer of electrical and mechanical components and tools. The company caters to various applications.	408-453-5070	NA	San Jose

COMPANY NAME	PRODUCT / SERVICE	PHONE	EMP	CITY
Arista Corp (HQ)	Manufacturer of industrial computer products such as industrial rack mounts, touch screen displays, and fanless, embedded, and wall mount computers.	510-226-1800	NA	Fremont
CLEARink Displays Inc (RH)	Developer of reflective display modules for wearables, smartphones/tablets, electronic shelf labels, and outdoor signage.	510-624-9305	NA	Fremont
Digital View Inc (HQ)	Developer and manufacturer of flat panel-related products. The company's offerings include media players, video flyers, and accessories.	408-782-7773	NA	Morgan Hill
Hantronix Inc (HQ)	Producer of standard character and graphic modules, notebook displays, and custom liquid crystal displays.	408-252-1100	NA	Cupertino
I-Tech Company LLC (HQ)	Manufacturer of panel mounts, server racks, industrial computers, touch screen displays, and related accessories.	510-226-9226	NA	Fremont
LG Display America Inc (BR)	Manufacturer of thin-film transistor liquid crystal display panels. The company is also focused on OLEDs and flexible displays.	408-350-0190	NA	San Jose
Medland & Associates Inc (BR)	Manufacturer of OEM products. The company's products include AC and DC converters, power supplies, switching regulators, and cable assemblies.	408-686-0460	NA	San Martin
NDS Surgical Imaging LLC (HQ)	Provider of medical imaging services. The company specializes in minimal invasive surgery viewing and diagnostic imaging.	408-776-0085	NA	San Jose
New Vision Display Inc (HQ)	Provider of display products. The company's products include LCD modules, TFT LCD and touch products.	916-786-8111	NA	Roseville
Pragmatic Communications Systems Inc (HQ)	Designer, developer, and manufacturer of pragmatic products. The company offers amplifiers, security cameras, speakers, and wireless products.	408-748-1100	NA	Santa Clara
Prysm Inc (HQ)	Provider of large format digital display solutions and software for real-time visual communication applications.	408-586-1100	NA	San Jose
RAF Electronics (HQ)	Provider of optical system design and related services. The company deals with sales and delivery solutions.	925-551-5361	NA	San Ramon
Sharp Electronics Corp (BR)	Provider of LCD, optoelectronics, imagers, and RF components. The company is involved in design and installation services.	408-452-6400	NA	San Jose
Silicon Mitus (BR)	Manufacturer and distributor of smart power management integrated chips solutions. The company focuses on power solutions.	408-446-3151	NA	Cupertino

170 = Fiber Optic Cables/Equipment

COMPANY NAME	PRODUCT / SERVICE	PHONE	EMP	CITY
AC Photonics Inc (HQ)	Manufacturer of custom-made precision optical components. The company also offers fiber optic components and modules.	408-986-9838	NA	Santa Clara
Aria Technologies Inc (HQ)	Provider of fiber optic cable assemblies and connectivity products to the data, telecom, and operator market places.	925-447-7500	NA	Livermore
Neptec Optical Solutions Inc (HQ)	Provider of quick-turn fiber optic connectivity solutions. The company also offers connector reconditioning, switches, and fiber arrays.	510-687-1101	NA	Fremont
N Nitto Denko America Inc (HQ)	Manufacturer of bonding, joining and surface protection products, sealants, anticorrosion and waterproofing, electrical insulating products, engineering plastics, medical-related, membrane, packaging, media-related, semiconductor-related, LCD-related and electronic components related products, industrial use barcode labels, flexible printed circuits, precision electronics materials.	510-445-5480	NA	Fremont
Nortra-Cables Inc (HQ)	Provider of discrete and flat mechanical assembly cables. The company offers design, prototyping, and manufacturing services.	408-942-1106	NA	Milpitas
Optiworks Inc (HQ)	Manufacturer of fiber optic components. The company's products include thin film filters, fused components, sub components, and accessories.	510-438-4560	NA	Fremont
Optowaves Inc (HQ)	Manufacturer and supplier of passive fiber optic components, attenuator, coupler, and isolator for the medical and communication industries.	408-724-5888	NA	San Jose
Pacific Coast Optics Inc (HQ)	Provider of optical products, services and applications. The company offers prototype, polishing, grinding, and coating.	916-789-0111	NA	Roseville
Pactech Inc (HQ)	Provider of computer cables, cooling items, and other components. The company also offers networking products.	408-526-9363	NA	San Jose
SPI Lasers LLC (BR)	Designer and manufacturer of fiber lasers for systems integrators, factory automation specialists, job shops, OEMs, and other academic institutions.	408-454-1170	NA	Santa Clara
Sumitomo Electric Device Innovations USA Inc (LH)	Developer of electronic devices that includes wireless devices, optical data links, and optical devices.	408-232-9500	NA	San Jose
Valdor Fiber Optics Inc (RH)	Provider of product design and development services of fiber optic products such as connectors, attenuators, couplers, splitters, and multiplexers.	510-293-1212	NA	Hayward
VSP Optics Group (HQ)	Provider of eye care solutions. The company offers eye care insurance, eyewear, lenses, ophthalmic technology and retail solutions.	800-852-7600	NA	Rancho Cordova

171 = Laser Measuring/Scanning/Aligning Equipment

COMPANY NAME	PRODUCT / SERVICE	PHONE	EMP	CITY
BMI Imaging Systems Inc (BR)	Provider of document management services. The company offers document scanning and hosting, system integration, and microfilm conversion services.	800-359-3456	NA	Sacramento

COMPANY NAME	PRODUCT / SERVICE	PHONE	EMP	CITY
Cutera Inc (HQ)	Manufacturer of aesthetic solutions such as face and body laser, light, and other energy-based aesthetic systems for hair removal and pigmented lesions.	415-657-5500	NA	Brisbane
Directed Light Inc (HQ)	Manufacturer of industrial and scientific laser components. The company offers laser welding, cutting, drilling, ablation, and marking services.	408-321-8500	NA	San Jose
Exatron Inc (HQ)	Manufacturer of automatic test equipment and IC handlers. The company also specializes in open short testers.	800-392-8766	NA	San Jose
Laserline Inc (BR)	Manufacturer of diode lasers for welding metals and plastics. The company also deals with cladding, hardening, and brazing.	408-834-4660	NA	Santa Clara
Macken Instruments Inc (HQ)	Manufacturer of devices for measuring and analyzing laser device power output. The company offers laser power and beam probes and thermal image plates.	707-566-2110	NA	Santa Rosa
Process Metrix Corp (BR)	Supplier of instruments for industrial measurement and control. The company's products are used in molten metal applications.	925-460-0385	NA	Pleasanton

172 = Lasers/Laser Related Equipment

COMPANY NAME	PRODUCT / SERVICE	PHONE	EMP	CITY
Applied Spectra Inc (HQ)	Manufacturer of analytical instrumentation. The company's products include J200 Tandem, J200 Femtosecond, Laser Ablation System, and Aurora LIBS Spectrometer.	510-657-7679	NA	Fremont
Artium Technologies Inc (HQ)	Developer of products for spray diagnostics, particulate monitoring, and cloud research applications.	408-737-2364	NA	Sunnyvale
ArtNet Pro Inc (HQ)	Provider of reused equipment. The company offers direct imaging systems, laser photo plotters, and scanners.	408-954-8383	NA	San Jose
Calmar Laser (HQ)	Manufacturer of ultrafast fiber laser and fiber amplifier solutions for the needs of industry, research institutions, and universities.	650-272-6980	NA	Palo Alto
CHECKPOiNT Technologies (HQ)	Manufacturer of optical failure analysis tools such as laser scanning microscopy, photon emission, infrascan, and solid immersion lens objectives.	408-321-9780	NA	San Jose
Coherent Inc (HQ)	Manufacturer of optics and laser instruments. The company serves the medical and research industries.	408-764-4000	NA	Santa Clara
Cutera Inc (HQ)	Manufacturer of aesthetic solutions such as face and body laser, light, and other energy-based aesthetic systems for hair removal and pigmented lesions.	415-657-5500	NA	Brisbane
Dataray Inc (HQ)	Supplier of performance beam profiling products to the photonics community. The company provides BladeCam, Beam Scope, Phase Pro, and UV converters.	530-395-2500	NA	Redding
Ellex iScience Inc (BR)	Developer and provider of technology solutions for the treatment of eye conditions. The company products include tango, eye one, eye cubed, tango reflex, and more.	510-291-1300	NA	Fremont
Femtochrome Research Inc (HQ)	Manufacturer of instruments for characterization of ultrafast laser pulses focusing on nonlinear crystal and two-photon conductivity autocorrelators.	510-644-1869	NA	Berkeley
General Lasertronics Corp (HQ)	Developer of scanning and control technologies that make laser ablation an alternative to traditional abrasives and solvents for removing coatings.	408-947-1181	NA	San Jose
Healthstar Laser Services Inc (HQ)	Provider of web-based scheduling and mobile laser services. The company serves the healthcare sector.	415-937-1942	NA	Lafayette
Imra America Inc (BR)	Developer and manufacturer of fiber lasers. The company's products are used in cutting, drilling, welding, and thin-film removal applications.	510-623-3507	NA	Fremont
IPG Photonics (BR)	Provider of high power fiber lasers and amplifiers. The company's offerings include Q-switch lasers, multi-mode diodes, pulsed and direct-diode lasers.	408-492-8830	NA	Santa Clara
Laser Mark's LLC (HQ)	Provider of laser marking and engraving job shop services. The company serves the agriculture, food processing, automotive, and medical industries.	408-433-9333	NA	San Jose
Laser Reference Inc (HQ)	Supplier of laser level products for interior and outdoor construction focusing on laser receivers and accessories including telescopic laser tripods.	408-361-0220	NA	San Jose
Laserline Inc (BR)	Manufacturer of diode lasers for welding metals and plastics. The company also deals with cladding, hardening, and brazing.	408-834-4660	NA	Santa Clara
Leica Geosystems HDS LLC (RH)	Manufacturer of surveying hardware and software solutions for measuring and modeling sites and structures with high accuracy, detail, speed, and safety.	925-790-2300	NA	San Ramon
Lumeras LLC (HQ)	Developer and manufacturer of short-wavelength laser sources for materials characterization and chemical and biological analysis.	650-575-7448	NA	Santa Cruz
Macken Instruments Inc (HQ)	Manufacturer of devices for measuring and analyzing laser device power output. The company offers laser power and beam probes and thermal image plates.	707-566-2110	NA	Santa Rosa
Microform Precision LLC (HQ)	Provider of metal cutting, bending, fabrication, and coating services. The company offers shearing, punching, forming, and painting services.	916-419-0580	NA	Sacramento
Modern Ceramics Manufacturing Inc (HQ)	Supplier of ceramic materials and components. The company serves the semi-conductor and laser industries.	408-383-0554	NA	San Jose

COMPANY NAME	PRODUCT / SERVICE	PHONE	EMP	CITY
Nuvolase Inc (HQ)	Manufacturer of the pinpointed foot laser used for the treatment of nail fungus and in nail fungus procedures.	530-809-1970	NA	Chico
Onyx Optics Inc (HQ)	Manufacturer of laser and telecom composite crystals and glasses. The company also offers products for optical finishing and other needs.	925-833-1969	NA	Dublin
Oxigraf Inc (HQ)	Supplier of oxygen analyzers and oxygen gas concentration measurement products. The company offers laser diode oxygen analyzers and OEM oxygen sensors.	650-237-0155	NA	Sunnyvale
Pavilion Integration Corp (HQ)	Designer and manufacturer of lasers, laser modules and subsystems for instrumentation. The company serves the industrial market.	408-453-8801	NA	San Jose
Spectra-Physics (HQ)	Provider of precision laser technology services. The company's products include ultrafast lasers, fiber lasers, and tunable lasers.	408-980-4300	NA	Santa Clara
Spectralus Corp (HQ)	Developer of green laser sources. The company primarily caters to the need of mobile projection applications.	408-516-4870	NA	Santa Clara
Sumitomo Electric Device Innovations USA Inc (LH)	Developer of electronic devices that includes wireless devices, optical data links, and optical devices.	408-232-9500	NA	San Jose

173 = Lenses

COMPANY NAME	PRODUCT / SERVICE	PHONE	EMP	CITY
Applied Optics Inc (HQ)	Provider of precision optical components and custom optics. The company is engaged in delivery and installation services.	925-932-5686	NA	Pleasant Hill
ATN Corp (HQ)	Developer and manufacturer of precision night optics and thermal imaging solutions. The company serves law enforcement and military clients.	650-989-5100	NA	S San Francisco
Carter Contact Lens Inc (HQ)	Manufacturer of contact lenses. The company product range include crescent bifocal, target bifocal, front bifocal, and keratoconic designs.	559-294-7063	NA	Clovis
Crystal River Optics (HQ)	Provider of custom fabrication services of optical components. The company is engaged in prototyping and offers technical support.	925-371-1309	NA	Livermore
ICU Eyewear (HQ)	Manufacturer of reading eyewear and sunglasses. The company provides metal half rim, polarized oval, and metal full aviator sunglasses.	800-435-5747	NA	Hollister
Industrial Optics Unlimited (HQ)	Provider of optical services. The company is involved in fabricating optical components for both commercial and laser applications.	530-365-1972	NA	Anderson
Micro Dicing Services (HQ)	Provider of sawing services. The company provides services to the microelectronic and optical industries.	408-321-8840	NA	San Jose
Precision Asphere Inc (HQ)	Provider of aspheric optical components fabrication services. The company offers optical surface forming, polishing, and metrology services.	510-668-1508	NA	Fremont
Seiwa Optical America Inc (HQ)	Manufacturer of optical components and photonic integrated circuits. The company offers network and access solutions.	408-844-8008	NA	Santa Clara
Sierra Precision Optics (HQ)	Manufacturer of optical products. The company's products include panels, mirrors, beam splitters, and cylindrical lenses.	530-885-6979	NA	Auburn
The Cooper Companies Inc (HQ)	Provider of healthcare solutions. The company offers health and wellness programs for women, individuals, and communities.	925-460-3600	NA	San Ramon
VSP Optics Group (HQ)	Provider of eye care solutions. The company offers eye care insurance, eyewear, lenses, ophthalmic technology and retail solutions.	800-852-7600	NA	Rancho Cordova

174 = Microscopes/Telescopes

COMPANY NAME	PRODUCT / SERVICE	PHONE	EMP	CITY
3Scan Inc (HQ)	Provider of automated microscopy services and supporting software for the 3D analysis of cells, tissues, and organs.	415-851-5376	NA	San Francisco
CHECKPOiNT Technologies (HQ)	Manufacturer of optical failure analysis tools such as laser scanning microscopy, photon emission, infrascan, and solid immersion lens objectives.	408-321-9780	NA	San Jose
Ellex iScience Inc (BR)	Developer and provider of technology solutions for the treatment of eye conditions. The company products include tango, eye one, eye cubed, tango reflex, and more.	510-291-1300	NA	Fremont
Labo America Inc (HQ)	Manufacturer and distributor of stereo, compound, surgical and digital microscopes, digital cameras and measuring software.	510-445-1257	NA	Fremont
Meiji Techno America (BR)	Manufacturer of optical microscope products. The company offers gemological, biological, and educational microscopes, and accessories.	408-226-3454	NA	San Jose
N Reynard Corp (HQ)	Manufacturer of custom optical thin film coatings.	949-366-8866	11-50	San Clemente
Seiwa Optical America Inc (HQ)	Manufacturer of optical components and photonic integrated circuits. The company offers network and access solutions.	408-844-8008	NA	Santa Clara
Stellarvue (HQ)	Designer and seller of refractor telescopes and telescope accessories. The company deals with design, delivery, and installation.	530-823-7796	NA	Auburn

175 = Optical Coatings

COMPANY NAME	PRODUCT / SERVICE	PHONE	EMP	CITY
Deposition Sciences Inc (HQ)	Manufacturer of heat resistant, optical thin film coatings, including color control, metal, optical mirror, and beam splitter coatings.	707-573-6700	NA	Santa Rosa
Dicon Fiberoptics Inc (HQ)	Supplier of optical components, integrated modules, and test equipment for the fiber optics industry.	510-620-5000	NA	Richmond
Dominar Inc (HQ)	Provider of optical and semiconductor thin-film coating services. The company serves customers in Europe, Asia, and Australia.	408-496-0508	NA	Santa Clara

COMPANY NAME	PRODUCT / SERVICE	PHONE	EMP	CITY
Foreal Spectrum Inc (HQ)	Provider of coating services for laser, biotech, and medical industries. The company also offers LED illumination and optical components.	408-436-5558	NA	San Jose
Ios Optics (HQ)	Manufacturer of custom precision optical components. The company offers coating and filter glass services. It serves avionics and life sciences fields.	408-982-9510	NA	Santa Clara
Micro Dicing Services (HQ)	Provider of sawing services. The company provides services to the microelectronic and optical industries.	408-321-8840	NA	San Jose
MLD Technologies LLC (HQ)	Supplier of optical coatings and components. The company specializes in the design, development, and manufacture of ion beam sputtered thin-films.	650-938-3780	NA	Mountain View
Pacific Coast Optics Inc (HQ)	Provider of optical products, services and applications. The company offers prototype, polishing, grinding, and coating.	916-789-0111	NA	Roseville
RAF Electronics (HQ)	Provider of optical system design and related services. The company deals with sales and delivery solutions.	925-551-5361	NA	San Ramon
Volume Precision Glass Inc (HQ)	Fabricator of optical components and thin-film coatings for photonics, military, industrial, and lighting applications.	707-206-0100	NA	Santa Rosa

176 = Optical Scanners & Other Optoelectronic Devices

COMPANY NAME	PRODUCT / SERVICE	PHONE	EMP	CITY
AC Photonics Inc (HQ)	Manufacturer of custom-made precision optical components. The company also offers fiber optic components and modules.	408-986-9838	NA	Santa Clara
Avision Labs Inc (DH)	Designer and manufacturer of network and document scanners. The company specializes in sales and installation services.	510-739-2369	NA	Newark
Bayspec Inc (HQ)	Manufacturer of mass spectrometers, microscopes, hyperspectral imagers, and OEM spectral engines for biomedical, pharmaceuticals, and food industries.	408-512-5928	NA	San Jose
BMI Imaging Systems Inc (BR)	Provider of document management services. The company offers document scanning and hosting, system integration, and microfilm conversion services.	800-359-3456	NA	Sacramento
Corning Technology Center (BR)	Provider of specialty glass and ceramics services and sells keystone components to electronics, mobile emissions control, and life science industries.	650-846-6000	NA	Sunnyvale
DigiLens Inc (HQ)	Provider of optical design, software development, electrical engineering, and illumination design services.	408-734-0219	NA	Sunnyvale
Enplas Tech Solutions Inc (RH)	Distributor of engineering plastic products. The company also offers optical devices, semiconductor peripherals, and related supplies.	669-243-3600	NA	Santa Clara
Equipment Solutions Inc (HQ)	Manufacturer and provider of actuators and motion control systems. The company offers optical scanners, servo amplifiers, and digital autocollimators.	408-245-7162	NA	Sunnyvale
Industrial Optics Unlimited (HQ)	Provider of optical services. The company is involved in fabricating optical components for both commercial and laser applications.	530-365-1972	NA	Anderson
Infinera Corp (HQ)	Provider of services and solutions in optical networks. The company serves cable operators and Internet content providers.	408-572-5200	NA	Sunnyvale
Intevac Inc (HQ)	Supplier of magnetic media processing systems. The company offers advanced equipment to the hard disk drive, solar, and photonics industries.	408-986-9888	NA	Santa Clara
Ios Optics (HQ)	Manufacturer of custom precision optical components. The company offers coating and filter glass services. It serves avionics and life sciences fields.	408-982-9510	NA	Santa Clara
Leica Geosystems HDS LLC (RH)	Manufacturer of surveying hardware and software solutions for measuring and modeling sites and structures with high accuracy, detail, speed, and safety.	925-790-2300	NA	San Ramon
Optical Structures Inc (HQ)	Provider of optical systems and services. The company's products find application in research and education sectors.	877-623-4021	NA	Rancho Cordova
Pacific Coast Optics Inc (HQ)	Provider of optical products, services and applications. The company offers prototype, polishing, grinding, and coating.	916-789-0111	NA	Roseville
N Reynard Corp (HQ)	Manufacturer of custom optical thin film coatings.	949-366-8866	11-50	San Clemente
Seiwa Optical America Inc (HQ)	Manufacturer of optical components and photonic integrated circuits. The company offers network and access solutions.	408-844-8008	NA	Santa Clara
Sharp Electronics Corp (BR)	Provider of LCD, optoelectronics, imagers, and RF components. The company is involved in design and installation services.	408-452-6400	NA	San Jose
Sight Sciences Inc (HQ)	Manufacturer and developer of surgical instruments and ophthalmic medical devices. The company serves the medical sector.	877-266-1144	NA	Menlo Park
Socket Mobile Inc (HQ)	Developer of wireless handheld and hands-free barcode scanners and other products and serves retail, logistics, automotive, and other sectors.	510-933-3000	NA	Newark
US Night Vision Corp (HQ)	Provider of night vision, thermal imaging, infrared and laser products. The company serves law enforcement agencies and US military.	800-500-4020	NA	Roseville
Visioneer Inc (HQ)	Marketer and distributor of digital imaging hardware devices. The company also offers related tools and utilities and power tools.	925-251-6399	NA	Pleasanton

177 = Photonics R&D and Services

COMPANY NAME	PRODUCT / SERVICE	PHONE	EMP	CITY
Banpil Photonics Inc (HQ)	Developer and manufacturer of image sensors for automotive and medical imaging systems, security and surveillance, and machine vision applications.	408-282-3628	NA	Santa Clara
Intevac Inc (HQ)	Supplier of magnetic media processing systems. The company offers advanced equipment to the hard disk drive, solar, and photonics industries.	408-986-9888	NA	Santa Clara
Meivac Inc (HQ)	Manufacturer of sputtering systems and components. The company offers throttle valves, integrators, OEM assemblies, and substrate heaters.	408-362-1000	NA	San Jose
SA Photonics Inc (HQ)	Developer of photonic systems. The company offers solutions for head-mounted displays, microwave sensors, mirror sense, and control systems.	408-560-3500	NA	Los Gatos
Sight Sciences Inc (HQ)	Manufacturer and developer of surgical instruments and ophthalmic medical devices. The company serves the medical sector.	877-266-1144	NA	Menlo Park

179 = Conveying Equipment

COMPANY NAME	PRODUCT / SERVICE	PHONE	EMP	CITY
Allied Crane Inc (HQ)	Provider of crane services. The company offers crane repair, installation and removal, and preventive maintenance programs.	925-427-9200	NA	Pittsburg
Compton Enterprises (HQ)	Manufacturer of moving equipment. The company specializes in rail-cars, conveyors, and truck loaders.	530-895-1942	NA	Chico
Cozad! Trailers (HQ)	Manufacturer of trailers. The company serves small and large construction companies and the military and aerospace industries.	209-931-3000	NA	Stockton
Crown Lift Trucks Ltd (BR)	Manufacturer of industrial lift trucks. The company offerings include C-5 Series IC Trucks, Hand Pallet Trucks, Tow Tractors, and Walkie Stackers.	916-373-8980	NA	West Sacramento
Distribution Technologies Inc (HQ)	Provider of design, analysis, simulation, automation, and project implementation solutions. The company also deals with technical support.	415-999-1191	NA	Tiburon
N Flory Industries (HQ)	Provider of nut-harvesting equipment for harvesting almonds, cashews, chestnuts, figs, hazelnuts, macadamia, pecans, tung nut and walnuts.	209-545-1167	51-200	Salida
Flostor Engineering (HQ)	Developer of automation solutions for inventory, distribution, fulfillment, and manufacturing systems.	800-500-8256	NA	Hayward
H J Hirtzer & Associates Inc (HQ)	Manufacturer of steel links. The company specializes in the fabrication of insulated links for shipping and defense industries.	925-931-1450	NA	Brentwood
N Kamper Fabrication Inc (HQ)	Designer of almond processing plants and manufactures equipment lines for almond shelling, hulling and finish processing.	209-599-7137	11-50	Ripon
N Kval Inc (HQ)	Manufacturer of CNC door machinery for architectural and residential applications.	707-762-0621	51-200	Petaluma
Lemo USA Inc (HQ)	Designer and manufacturer of precision custom connectors, cable assemblies, and related accessories. The company serves the industrial sector.	707-578-8811	NA	Rohnert Park
Morgan Royce Industries Inc (HQ)	Developer and manufacturer of custom cables, wire harness, and PCB assemblies. The company offers project management and quality control services.	510-440-8500	NA	Fremont
Orchard Machinery Corp (HQ)	Manufacturer of tree shakers and material handling systems comprising shuttles, bin carriers, conveyor carts, and elevators.	530-673-2822	NA	Yuba City
Powerlift Dumbwaiters Inc (HQ)	Provider of dumbwaiters that includes residential powerlifts, commercial units, and mezzanine lifts.	530-333-1953	NA	Georgetown
Ralphs-Pugh Co (HQ)	Manufacturer of conveyor rollers and related components. The company serves the agriculture, chemical, and food processing industries.	707-745-6222	NA	Benicia
N RM King Co (HQ)	Manufacturer of parts for cotton pickers overhauls cotton pickers.	559-266-0258	NA	Fresno
Rock Systems Inc (HQ)	Provider of material handling solutions. The company offers hoppers, feeders, conveyors, separators, and related accessories.	916-921-9000	NA	Sacramento
Sardee Industries Inc (BR)	Provider of container manufacturing equipment. The company also offers engineering and repair services for packing and filling industries.	209-466-1526	NA	Stockton
Screw Conveyor Corp (BR)	Manufacturer of bulk material handling equipment including screw conveyors, drag conveyors, and bucket elevators.	559-651-2131	NA	Visalia
Ultra Lift Corp (HQ)	Manufacturer of hand trucks. The company specializes in the fabrication of trucks that combine hand-power and electric drives.	408-287-9400	NA	San Jose
Westside Research Inc (HQ)	Designer and manufacturer of interior and exterior automotive cargo management products. The company specializes in truck luggage product lines.	530-865-5587	NA	Orland
Woodland Mdm (HQ)	Manufacturer and supplier of new and refurbished machinery products. The company offers industrial controls and automation and case handling equipment.	530-669-1400	NA	Woodland

180 = Elevators/Moving Stairways

COMPANY NAME	PRODUCT / SERVICE	PHONE	EMP	CITY
A Step Above (HQ)	Provider of elevator services. The company offers escalators, walks, manlifts, and traction cars and related troubleshooting, testing and service.	707-421-2917	NA	Fairfield
Benchmark Home Elevator Inc (HQ)	Provider of elevator products. The company's products include curved rail stairlifts, straight rail stairlifts, home elevators, and wheelchair lifts.	707-255-4687	NA	Napa

COMPANY NAME	PRODUCT / SERVICE	PHONE	EMP	CITY
Compton Enterprises (HQ)	Manufacturer of moving equipment. The company specializes in rail-cars, conveyors, and truck loaders.	530-895-1942	NA	Chico
Crown Lift Trucks Ltd (BR)	Manufacturer of industrial lift trucks. The company offerings include C-5 Series IC Trucks, Hand Pallet Trucks, Tow Tractors, and Walkie Stackers.	916-373-8980	NA	West Sacramento
Elevator Controls Corp (HQ)	Manufacturer of non-proprietary microprocessor based elevator controllers. The company offers technical support and field services.	916-428-1708	NA	Sacramento
Elevator Technology Inc (HQ)	Provider of elevator repair and installation services. The company specializes both in residential and commercial elevators.	916-939-4323	NA	El Dorado Hills
Escalera Inc (HQ)	Manufacturer of stair climbing trucks. The company's products include forklifts, handtrucks, and load movers.	530-673-6318	NA	Yuba City
Kone Inc (BR)	Manufacturer of moving solutions. The company offers automatic building doors, elevators and escalators, and accessories.	510-351-5141	NA	San Leandro
MEC Aerial Work Platforms (HQ)	Manufacturer of aerial work platforms. The company specializes in the design and manufacture of scissors and booms.	559-842-1500	NA	Kerman
Melrose Metal Products Inc (HQ)	Manufacturer of melrose metal products. The company offers design and installation services for food processing and emission control systems.	510-657-8771	NA	Fremont
Motion Control Engineering Inc (HQ)	Manufacturer of elevator control products. The company's products include elevator and escalator controls, complete elevators, and components and peripherals.	916-463-9200	NA	Rancho Cordova
Schindler Elevator Corp (BR)	Provider of elevators, escalators, and related services. The company creates and delivers urban mobility solutions.	510-382-2075	NA	San Leandro
thyssenkrupp Elevator Corp (BR)	Provider of elevators and elevator solutions. The company offers MRL elevators, synergy elevators, momentum elevators, and freight elevators.	510-476-1900	NA	San Leandro
Ward Systems Inc (HQ)	Provider of custom automation services. The company's services include valve installation, maintenance, and reconfiguration.	530-271-1800	NA	Grass Valley
Woodland Mdm (HQ)	Manufacturer and supplier of new and refurbished machinery products. The company offers industrial controls and automation and case handling equipment.	530-669-1400	NA	Woodland

181 = Factory Assembly Line Equipment

Big Joe Handling Systems (HQ)	Supplier of warehouse storage and material handling equipment. The company specializes in pallet and product storage systems.	510-785-6900	NA	Hayward
Ward Systems Inc (HQ)	Provider of custom automation services. The company's services include valve installation, maintenance, and reconfiguration.	530-271-1800	NA	Grass Valley

183 = Overhead Cranes

Allied Crane Inc (HQ)	Provider of crane services. The company offers crane repair, installation and removal, and preventive maintenance programs.	925-427-9200	NA	Pittsburg
Heco Pacific Manufacturing Inc (HQ)	Manufacturer and seller of industrial cranes and overhead cranes. The company offers custom engineering, maintenance, testing, and other services.	510-487-1155	NA	Union City
Malcolm Drilling Company Inc (HQ)	Provider of specialty foundation industry services. The company is engaged in deep foundations, dewatering, and design build services.	415-901-4400	NA	San Francisco
Paceco Corp (HQ)	Manufacturer of equipment to handle port cargo. The company also offers terminal operating systems and crane modification services.	510-264-9288	NA	Hayward
Rock Systems Inc (HQ)	Provider of material handling solutions. The company offers hoppers, feeders, conveyors, separators, and related accessories.	916-921-9000	NA	Sacramento

184 = Medical Equipment/Devices & Services

Edwards Lifesciences Corp (HQ)	Manufacturer of medical devices. The company specializes in technologies for structural heart diseases and critical care monitoring.	949-250-5070	NA	Irvine

185 = Dental Equipment, Supplies & Prosthetics

Chromeworks Inc (HQ)	Manufacturer of chrome frames for the dental lab industry. The company's services include shipping and delivery.	530-343-2278	NA	Chico
N DenMat Holdings LLC (HQ)	Manufacturer of dental products that includes curing and bleaching lights, impressions, instruments, restoratives, and more.	805-346-3700	NA	Lompoc
Lares Research (HQ)	Developer and manufacturer of dental handpieces and dental lasers. The company offers services to the healthcare industry.	530-345-1767	NA	Chico
MicroDental Laboratories (HQ)	Provider of laboratory-fabricated restorations and related equipment. The company serves the healthcare sector.	925-829-3611	NA	Dublin
Progressive Technology Inc (HQ)	Manufacturer of orthodontic braces. The company provides sapphire, alumina, zirconia, ceramic, and quartz braces.	916-632-6715	NA	Rocklin
The Wirebenders Orthodontic Lab (HQ)	Provider of clinical support, research, and development services. The company specializes in appliance designs.	408-265-5576	NA	San Jose
Wells Dental Inc (HQ)	Supplier of dental laboratory equipment. The company offers engine units, finishing machines, quick chucks, and consumables.	707-937-0521	NA	Comptche

186 = Medical Diagnostic/Analyzing Equipment

3rd Stone Design Inc (HQ)	Provider of design, product development, and engineering services. The company serves the consumer products and healthcare industries.	415-454-3005	NA	San Rafael

COMPANY NAME	PRODUCT / SERVICE	PHONE	EMP	CITY
Airxpanders Inc (HQ)	Provider of controlled tissue expander and small handheld wireless controller of breast cancer reconstructive surgery.	650-390-9000	NA	San Jose
ARK Diagnostics Inc (HQ)	Manufacturer of in vitro diagnostic products for the treatment of cancer, veterinary, HIV/AIDS, antifungal drugs, and epilepsy and pain management.	877-869-2320	NA	Fremont
BD Biosciences (BR)	Manufacturer of medical devices. The company provides a broad range of medical supplies, devices, laboratory equipment and diagnostic products.	877-232-8995	NA	San Jose
Biochain Institute Inc (HQ)	Provider of bio-sample preparation, analysis, and application assays accelerating the development of personalized diagnostics, therapeutics, and medicine.	510-783-8588	NA	Newark
Bioluminate Inc (HQ)	Developer of probes that provide breast cancer detection data to physicians. The company serves the medical sector.	650-743-0240	NA	San Carlos
Capnia (HQ)	Focuses on the development and commercialization of therapeutic and diagnostic products to address significant unmet healthcare needs.	650-213-8444	NA	Redwood City
CapsoVision (HQ)	Specializes in the diagnostic imaging of the gastrointestinal systems. The company offers services to hospitals and patients.	408-624-1488	NA	Saratoga
Cepheid (HQ)	Provider of molecular diagnostic testing of patient specimen on a centralized basis enabling medical providers identify and treat disease early.	408-541-4191	NA	Sunnyvale
D-EYE (BR)	Designer and manufacturer of diagnostic instruments. The company offers smartphone based retinal imaging systems for clinical assessments.	401-473-6323	NA	Truckee
Diagnostic Biosystems Inc (HQ)	Developer of primary and monoclonal antibodies, ancillaries, chromogens, and multiplex kits. The company serves the healthcare sector.	925-484-3350	NA	Pleasanton
Drawbridge Health Inc (HQ)	Provider of diagnostic testing solutions. The company offers blood testing solutions for a range of biomarker.	650-714-6791	NA	Menlo Park
DyAnsys Inc (HQ)	Provider of medical diagnostic and monitoring systems to clinicians and hospitals for patients. The company deals with research services.	888-950-4321	NA	San Mateo
EA Machining Inc (HQ)	Provider of CNC turning and milling services. The company offers services to the semiconductor manufacturing equipment industry.	408-727-4962	NA	Santa Clara
EBR Systems Inc (HQ)	Designer and developer of implantable systems for wireless tissue stimulation. The company focuses on the treatment of heart failure.	408-720-1906	NA	Sunnyvale
Eko Devices Inc (HQ)	Developer of digital stethoscope/electronic stethoscope to help confidently and quickly assess patient's heart, lung, and body sounds.	844-356-3384	NA	Berkeley
Electro Diagnostic Imaging Inc (HQ)	Developer and manufacturer of products for electrophysiology. The company's services include research, sales, and marketing.	650-631-0120	NA	Redwood City
Eneura Inc (HQ)	Provider of medical technology solutions. The company offers transcranial magnetic stimulation devices for the treatment of migraine.	408-245-6400	NA	Sunnyvale
Fresenius Medical Care (BR)	Focuses on the treatment of patients with renal and other chronic conditions. The company serves the healthcare industry.	925-947-4545	NA	Walnut Creek
Gold Standard Diagnostics Corp (HQ)	Provider of laboratory diagnostic solutions. The company specializes in diagnosis of autoimmune diseases, bacterial and viral diseases.	530-759-8000	NA	Davis
Hitachi Chemical Diagnostics Inc (HQ)	Provider of in vitro allergy diagnostics products. The company offers alternative means of diagnosing allergy.	650-961-5501	NA	Mountain View
Hologic Inc (BR)	Provider of healthcare and diagnostics. The company offers breast and skeletal healthcare and diagnostics, and GYN surgical solutions.	669-224-6420	NA	Santa Clara
InterVene Inc (HQ)	Provider of medical devices such as blueleaf endovenous valve formation system to treat severe venous disease in the legs.	650-351-6725	NA	S San Francisco
Iridex Corp (HQ)	Provider of therapeutic based laser consoles, delivery devices, and consumable instrumentation. The company serves the healthcare industry.	650-940-4700	NA	Mountain View
Iris Biotechnologies Inc (HQ)	Provider of medical informatics system. The company develops chips to precisely diagnose and identify actionable treatment choices for breast cancer.	408-867-2885	NA	Santa Clara
Kinematic Automation Inc (HQ)	Provider of manufacturing systems for the medical industry. The company also offers automation, strip cutting, rotatory slitting services.	209-532-3200	NA	Sonora
Los Gatos Research Inc (HQ)	Manufacturer of analyzers for the measurement of trace gases and isotopes. The company serves the industrial and environmental sectors.	650-965-7772	NA	San Jose
LS Biopath Inc (HQ)	Developer of medical products and technologies for the unmet need for real time imaging of excised tissue during breast cancer surgery.	408-464-4051	NA	Saratoga
Lumiquick Diagnostics Inc (HQ)	Manufacturer of diagnostic products and other raw materials. The company is engaged in distribution services.	408-855-0061	NA	Santa Clara
Micropoint Bioscience Inc (HQ)	Developer of medical products and services for treatment of vascular disease such as peripheral artery disease and venous blood clots disorders.	408-588-1682	NA	Santa Clara
Minerva Surgical Inc (HQ)	Manufacturer of medical devices. The company provides products for the treatment of abnormal uterine bleeding.	855-646-7874	NA	Redwood City
MIODx Inc (HQ)	Provider of diagnostics and biomarker expertise in a variety of cancer treatments including immuno-therapies.	866-756-4639	NA	San Jose

COMPANY NAME	PRODUCT / SERVICE	PHONE	EMP	CITY
Miramar Labs Inc (HQ)	Provider of solutions for excessive sweat. The company is engaged in clinical trials and research programs.	408-579-8700	NA	Santa Clara
Mission Bio (HQ)	Developer and deliverer of precision medicine. The company offers instruments, fixed panels, custom panels, and software for the researchers and clinicians.	415-854-0058	NA	S San Francisco
MORE Health Inc (HQ)	Specializes in collaborative diagnosis. The company serves patients, hospitals, and the medical industry.	888-908-6673	NA	San Mateo
Nanomix Inc (HQ)	Manufacturer of diagnostic systems and supplies. The company is engaged in product development services.	510-428-5300	NA	Emeryville
Nidek Inc (RH)	Manufacturer of ophthalmic devices. The company also offers refractive systems and diagnostic products to the medical industry.	800-223-9044	NA	Fremont
nVision Medical Corp (HQ)	Developer of women's health products. The company offers services to clinicians and the medical industry.	408-655-3577	NA	San Bruno
Optovue Inc (HQ)	Manufacturer of ophthalmic devices. The company leads the commercialization of new imaging modalities to develop ophthalmic diagnosis.	510-743-0985	NA	Fremont
Outset Medical (HQ)	Developer of hemodialysis systems. The company offers services to patients, families, providers and physicians.	669-231-8200	NA	San Jose
POC Medical Systems Inc (HQ)	Provider of diagnostic medical devices for the screening of life-threatening diseases like cancer, cardiovascular disorders, and infectious diseases.	925-331-8010	NA	Livermore
Prescient Surgical (HQ)	Developer of medical devices and technologies to reduce the risk of surgical site infections in patients undergoing abdominal gastrointestinal surgery.	650-999-0263	NA	San Carlos
Proxim Diagnostics Corp (HQ)	Manufacturer of diagnostics products and related supplies. The company deals with testing and research related services.	408-391-6090	NA	Mountain View
Pulsar Vascular Inc (HQ)	Manufacturer of endovascular diseases and it focuses on the treatment of complex aneurysms. The company is engaged in clinical trials.	408-260-9264	NA	San Jose
QuanDx Inc (HQ)	Developer of molecular diagnostics for personalized cancer treatment. The company offers detection kits and lung cancer assays.	650-262-4140	NA	San Jose
Quest Diagnostics Inc (BR)	Provider of diagnostic laboratory testing services. The company offers a wide range of test menu for diagnosing medical conditions.	916-927-9900	NA	Sacramento
Qview Medical (HQ)	Provider of assistance in the review of 3D automated breast ultrasound. The company offers services to the radiologists.	650-397-5174	NA	Los Altos
SMP Tech Inc (HQ)	Designer and builder of robotic DNA spotters, microfluidic devices, medical equipment, automated machinery, and electro-mechanical products.	408-776-7776	NA	Morgan Hill
Stellartech Research Corp (HQ)	Designer, developer, and manufacturer of medical devices. The company specializes in surgical probes, balloon electrode catheters, and other products.	408-331-3000	NA	Milpitas
Tricontinent Scientific Inc (BR)	Provider of liquid-handling products and instrument components for the medical diagnostics and biotechnology industries.	530-273-8888	NA	Auburn
ViOptix Inc (HQ)	Manufacturer of medical support devices. The company specializes in devices used for respiratory support and oxygen supply.	510-226-5860	NA	Newark
Vital Connect Inc (HQ)	Provider of healthcare solutions. The company focuses on biosensors, clinical-grade biometric measurements.	408-963-4600	NA	San Jose
VytronUS Inc (HQ)	Developer of ablation systems for the treatment of atrial fibrillation and other cardiac arrhythmias. The company deals with customizable lesions.	408-730-1333	NA	Sunnyvale
Xoft Inc (HQ)	Developer of electronic brachytherapy systems. The company's products include rigid shield, vacuum pumps, and physics kits.	408-493-1500	NA	San Jose

187 = Medical Monitoring and Test Equipment

COMPANY NAME	PRODUCT / SERVICE	PHONE	EMP	CITY
Aegea Medical Inc (HQ)	Developer of women healthcare solutions. The company develops a system for the treatment of excessive menstrual bleeding.	650-701-1125	NA	Menlo Park
Avinger Inc (HQ)	Designer and developer of precision medical device technology solutions. The company is engaged in manufacturing services.	800-208-2988	NA	Redwood City
Bactrack (HQ)	Provider of breathalyzers. The company provides products for a wide range of personal, professional and smartphone use.	415-693-9756	NA	San Francisco
Biocardia Inc (HQ)	Developer of clinical stage regenerative therapeutic products for the treatment of cardiovascular diseases.	650-226-0120	NA	San Carlos
Biocheck Inc (HQ)	Provider of custom immunoassay development, antibody conjugation and purification, and contract manufacturing services.	650-573-1968	NA	S San Francisco
Biogenex Laboratories Inc (HQ)	Manufacturer of automated slide-based staining instruments and histology products for cancer diagnosis, prognosis, and therapy selection.	510-824-1400	NA	Fremont
Bioluminate Inc (HQ)	Developer of probes that provide breast cancer detection data to physicians. The company serves the medical sector.	650-743-0240	NA	San Carlos
Buglab LLC (HQ)	Developer of biomass measuring equipment such as sensors, biomass monitor, and biomass multiplier involved in fermentation and microbial cultures.	925-208-1952	NA	Concord

COMPANY NAME	PRODUCT / SERVICE	PHONE	EMP	CITY
Chai (HQ)	Specializes in DNA diagnostics. The company offers services to clinics, patients, and the medical sector.	650-779-5577	NA	Santa Clara
Chronix Biomedical Inc (HQ)	Provider of molecular diagnostics laboratory services such as second opinion tests and delta dot test for screening and monitoring cancer.	408-960-2306	NA	San Jose
Cirtec Medical (HQ)	Manufacturer of complex implantable device manufacturing, medical device solutions, and smart solutions for highly complex miniaturization.	408-395-0443	NA	Los Gatos
Compact Imaging Inc (HQ)	Developer of miniature optical sensor technology. The company specializes in mobile health applications.	650-694-7801	NA	Mountain View
Cutera Inc (HQ)	Manufacturer of aesthetic solutions such as face and body laser, light, and other energy-based aesthetic systems for hair removal and pigmented lesions.	415-657-5500	NA	Brisbane
Cymed (HQ)	Provider of ostomy pouching systems. The company specializes in skin care products and serves individuals and hospitals.	800-582-0707	NA	Sacramento
DyAnsys Inc (HQ)	Provider of medical diagnostic and monitoring systems to clinicians and hospitals for patients. The company deals with research services.	888-950-4321	NA	San Mateo
EA Machining Inc (HQ)	Provider of CNC turning and milling services. The company offers services to the semiconductor manufacturing equipment industry.	408-727-4962	NA	Santa Clara
EBR Systems Inc (HQ)	Designer and developer of implantable systems for wireless tissue stimulation. The company focuses on the treatment of heart failure.	408-720-1906	NA	Sunnyvale
Echopixel Inc (HQ)	Provider of 3D medical visualization software for radiologists, cardiologists, pediatric cardiologists, and interventional neuroradiologists.	844-273-7766	NA	Santa Clara
Eneura Inc (HQ)	Provider of medical technology solutions. The company offers transcranial magnetic stimulation devices for the treatment of migraine.	408-245-6400	NA	Sunnyvale
Exploramed (HQ)	Developer of novel medical devices with cutting edge medical technology for use by major medical device manufacturing companies.	650-472-0300	NA	Mountain View
ExThera Medical Corp (HQ)	Developer of medical devices that address unmet clinical needs in the treatment of bloodstream infections and pathogen-reduction in blood banking.	925-839-2060	NA	Martinez
Fluidigm Sciences Inc (HQ)	Developer and creator of technologies for life science tools designed to revolutionize biology. The company is involved in research programs.	650-871-7152	NA	S San Francisco
GCX Corp (HQ)	Provider of mounting solutions, application specific solutions, on-site services, and also technical support.	707-773-1100	NA	Petaluma
Genapsys Inc (HQ)	Developer of DNA sequencing to enable a paradigm shift in genomic diagnostics. The company specializes in GENIUS system that has footprint of Apple iPad.	650-330-1096	NA	Redwood City
Gynesonics (HQ)	Manufacturer and developer of therapeutic devices and related supplies for the treatment of uterine fibroids in women.	650-216-3860	NA	Redwood City
Immuno Concepts Na Ltd (HQ)	Manufacturer and distributor of diagnostic assays. The company's products are used for systemic rheumatic diseases.	916-363-2649	NA	Sacramento
Intersect Ent Inc (HQ)	Provider of steroid-releasing implants that props open the sinuses for the treatment of common cold and sinusitis.	650-641-2100	201-500	Menlo Park
Intuity Medical Inc (HQ)	Provider of medical products such as blood glucose monitoring system, meter, cartridge, and data management for diabetes management.	510-946-8800	NA	Fremont
Jasper Ridge Inc (HQ)	Manufacturer of tint and lighting exam systems. The company offers services to patients and hospitals.	650-804-5040	NA	San Mateo
Lighthouse Worldwide Solutions (HQ)	Provider of dental supplies such as implants, dentures, partials, implant bars, and related accessories.	510-438-0500	NA	Fremont
Lumenis (DH)	Provider of minimally-invasive clinical solutions. The company develops and commercializes energy-based technologies.	877-586-3647	NA	San Jose
Mission Bio (HQ)	Developer and deliverer of precision medicine. The company offers instruments, fixed panels, custom panels, and software for the researchers and clinicians.	415-854-0058	NA	S San Francisco
Neurosky Inc (HQ)	Manufacturer of ECG biosensors and also EEG biosensors for mobile solutions, wearable devices, and service providers.	408-200-6675	NA	San Jose
Ocumetrics Inc (HQ)	Manufacturer of Fluorotron Master Ocular Fluorophotometers. The company deals with research services.	650-960-3955	NA	Mountain View
Optiscan Biomedical Corp (HQ)	Provider of monitoring products for measuring glucose, plasma collection, and also detection of glucose among patients.	510-342-5800	NA	Hayward
Phoenix Technology Group LLC (HQ)	Provider of research laboratory services. The company offers anterior segment imaging and retinal imaging microscope services.	925-485-1100	NA	Pleasanton
Profusa Inc (HQ)	Focuses on the development of biointegrated sensors. The company offers services to the environment sector.	415-655-9861	NA	Emeryville
Qardio Inc (HQ)	Creator of health monitoring devices such as blood pressure monitor, multiple-sensor EKG, and wireless scale and body analyzer.	855-240-7323	NA	San Francisco
Rimnetics Inc (BR)	Providers of RIM molded structural parts, enclosures, cosmetic housings, encapsulation and overmolding. The company makes molded polyurethane parts.	916-652-5555	NA	Loomis
Salutron Inc (HQ)	Providers of health care solutions. The company offers on-demand ECG accurate heart rate monitoring solutions.	510-795-2876	NA	Newark

COMPANY NAME	PRODUCT / SERVICE	PHONE	EMP	CITY
Si-Bone Inc (HQ)	Developer of medical products and technologies such as implants and titanium implant technology for SI joint pain and sacroiliac joint fusion surgery.	408-207-0700	NA	San Jose
Smart Monitor Corp (HQ)	Manufacturer of monitoring devices. The company provides automated solution for detecting unusual movements from chronic health conditions.	408-754-1695	NA	San Jose
Spectros Corp (HQ)	Manufacturer of tissue perfusion monitors and they are used in plastic surgery, critical care, and vascular surgery.	650-851-4040	NA	Campbell
Spinal Kinetics Inc (HQ)	Provider of preservation systems for treating degenerative diseases of the spine. The company serves the healthcare sector.	408-636-2500	NA	Sunnyvale
ViOptix Inc (HQ)	Manufacturer of medical support devices. The company specializes in devices used for respiratory support and oxygen supply.	510-226-5860	NA	Newark
Vital Connect Inc (HQ)	Provider of healthcare solutions. The company focuses on biosensors, clinical-grade biometric measurements.	408-963-4600	NA	San Jose
Zenflow Inc (HQ)	Developer of products for the treatment of urinary obstruction related to benign prostatic hyperplasia. The company serves the medical sector.	650-642-9658	NA	S San Francisco

188 = Medical Services

COMPANY NAME	PRODUCT / SERVICE	PHONE	EMP	CITY
Accuray Inc (HQ)	Provider of oncology treatment solutions. The company develops, manufactures and sells precise and innovative tumor treatment solutions.	888-522-3740	NA	Sunnyvale
Bell Biosystems Inc (HQ)	Provider of biotechnology services. The company develops proteins targeted to kill specific bacteria but cause minimal collateral damage.	877-420-3621	NA	Berkeley
Bioclinica Inc (HQ)	Developer of medical therapies. The company specializes in medical imaging services, cardiac safety, and enterprise eClinical platforms.	415-817-8900	NA	Newark
Channel Medsystems Inc (HQ)	Developer of cryothermic technology and streamlined delivery system for women with heavy menstrual bleeding.	510-338-9301	NA	Emeryville
Cutera Inc (HQ)	Manufacturer of aesthetic solutions such as face and body laser, light, and other energy-based aesthetic systems for hair removal and pigmented lesions.	415-657-5500	NA	Brisbane
Dendreon Pharmaceuticals LLC (HQ)	Provider of biotechnology services. The company provides therapeutics for the treatment of cancer employing active cellular immunotherapy.	877-256-4545	NA	Seal Beach
DirectGov Source Inc (HQ)	Manufacturer of personal protection kits. The company offers disposable clothing, biohazard disposal, antimicrobial sanitizers, and hand protection gloves.	530-899-3327	NA	Chico
Doctor on Demand (HQ)	Provider of urgent care doctors. The company offers lab screens for the treatment of mental health and chronic conditions.	800-997-6196	NA	San Francisco
Eargo Inc (HQ)	Creator of medical device. The company specializes in virtually invisible in-ear hearing device that is comfortable, natural sounding, and rechargeable.	650-351-7700	NA	San Jose
Endo Gastric Solutions Inc (HQ)	Provider of treatment services for gastroesophageal reflux disease. The company also focuses on training and education.	650-578-5100	NA	San Mateo
Eneura Inc (HQ)	Provider of medical technology solutions. The company offers transcranial magnetic stimulation devices for the treatment of migraine.	408-245-6400	NA	Sunnyvale
Genapsys Inc (HQ)	Developer of DNA sequencing to enable a paradigm shift in genomic diagnostics. The company specializes in GENIUS system that has footprint of Apple iPad.	650-330-1096	NA	Redwood City
N ICC Instrument Company Inc (HQ)	Provider of instrument calibration and repair services.	714-540-4966	NA	Santa Ana
Medtronic CardioVascular Inc (BR)	Provider of disease management services. The company specializes in cardiovascular, diabetes, surgical technologies, and spinal and biologics.	707-525-0111	NA	Santa Rosa
Minerva Surgical Inc (HQ)	Manufacturer of medical devices. The company provides products for the treatment of abnormal uterine bleeding.	855-646-7874	NA	Redwood City
Motive Medical Intelligence (HQ)	Developer of medical intelligence solutions. The company also offers care plans for population health management.	415-362-4007	NA	San Francisco
Plastikon Industries Inc (HQ)	Provider of contract manufacturing services for custom designed plastic injection molding, for medical, pharmaceutical and other industries.	510-400-1010	NA	Hayward
Polyphenolics (HQ)	Supplier of grape seed, grape pomace, and whole grape extracts. The company offers MegaNatural-BP, MegaNatural Red Wine Grape Extract, and MegaNatural-GL.	559-661-5556	NA	Madera
Providence Medical Technology Inc (HQ)	Developer of medical devices and technologies such as dtrax spinal systems, cavux cervical cages, and ally screw systems for cervical spine care.	415-923-9376	NA	Pleasanton
Qardio Inc (HQ)	Creator of health monitoring devices such as blood pressure monitor, multiple-sensor EKG, and wireless scale and body analyzer.	855-240-7323	NA	San Francisco
Relucent Solutions LLC (HQ)	Manufacturer of medical devices. The company is involved in laser cutting, precision manufacturing, wire crimping, and related services.	800-630-7704	NA	Santa Rosa
Sciton Inc (HQ)	Provider of laser and light source solutions. The company's products include JOULE, BBL, ClearSense, Halo, and more.	650-493-9155	NA	Palo Alto
Silk Road Medical Inc (HQ)	Specializes in the treatment of carotid artery diseases. The company is engaged in clinical trials and related services.	408-720-9002	NA	Sunnyvale
Smart Monitor Corp (HQ)	Manufacturer of monitoring devices. The company provides automated solution for detecting unusual movements from chronic health conditions.	408-754-1695	NA	San Jose

	COMPANY NAME	PRODUCT / SERVICE	PHONE	EMP	CITY
N	Ted Levine Drum Co (HQ)	Provider of repair services.	626-579-1084	11-50	South El Monte
	The Cooper Companies Inc (HQ)	Provider of healthcare solutions. The company offers health and wellness programs for women, individuals, and communities.	925-460-3600	NA	San Ramon
	Ultrasound Laboratories Inc (HQ)	Provider of non-invasive ultrasound imaging services. The company focuses on services such as health screening, carotid artery, and kidney screening.	408-829-6486	NA	Mountain View
	Viewics Inc (HQ)	Provider of consulting, custom development, and report authoring services. The company also offers packaged solutions.	415-439-0084	NA	Santa Clara

189 = Miscellaneous Medical/Hospital Equipment

	COMPANY NAME	PRODUCT / SERVICE	PHONE	EMP	CITY
	3rd Stone Design Inc (HQ)	Provider of design, product development, and engineering services. The company serves the consumer products and healthcare industries.	415-454-3005	NA	San Rafael
	A&D Engineering Inc (RH)	Supplier of electric scale balancers and blood pressure monitors. The company offers services to the business sector.	408-263-5333	NA	San Jose
	AB Medical Technologies Inc (HQ)	Manufacturer of electronic medical systems and powered surgical instruments such as surgical pumps, arthroscopy shavers and lab equipment.	530-605-2522	NA	Redding
	ABX Engineering Inc (HQ)	Manufacturer of printed circuit board assemblies and electromechanical products for medical devices, agriculture, and military electronics industries.	650-552-2300	NA	Burlingame
	Accsys Technology Inc (HQ)	Manufacturer of ion linear accelerator systems used in medical imaging devices, industrial applications and in research.	925-462-6949	NA	Pleasanton
	Accuray Inc (HQ)	Provider of oncology treatment solutions. The company develops, manufactures and sells precise and innovative tumor treatment solutions.	888-522-3740	NA	Sunnyvale
N	Advanced Vision Science Inc (HQ)	Manufacturer of ophthalmic medical devices including intraocular lenses and lens material.	805-683-3851	51-200	Goleta
N	Akra Plastic Products Inc (HQ)	Manufacturer of plastics products.	909-930-1999	1-10	Ontario
	Align Technology Inc (HQ)	Provider of medical devices such as invisalign clear aligners, itero intraoral scanners and ortho CAD digital services for orthodontic industry.	408-470-1000	NA	San Jose
	American Probe & Technologies Inc (HQ)	Manufacturer of analytical probes and accessories for the semiconductor test and measurement industry.	408-263-3356	NA	Merced
	Amgen Inc (BR)	Provider of scientific applications services. The company's services include clinical trials, ethical research, biosimilars, and web resources.	650-244-2000	NA	S San Francisco
	AQS Inc (DH)	Provider of electronic manufacturing solutions. The company offers electronic assembly, test engineering, system integration and final test services.	510-249-5800	NA	Fremont
	Avantec Vascular Corp (HQ)	Manufacturer of therapeutic medical devices such as cardio and peripheral vascular devices for cardiovascular, neurovascular, and peripheral disease.	408-329-5400	NA	Sunnyvale
	Bay Advanced Technologies (HQ)	Provider of solutions for automation and control applications. The company offers precision automation, fluid controls and fabricated materials.	510-857-0900	NA	Newark
	BD Biosciences (BR)	Manufacturer of medical devices. The company provides a broad range of medical supplies, devices, laboratory equipment and diagnostic products.	877-232-8995	NA	San Jose
	Bibbero Systems Inc (HQ)	Manufacturer of filing and office supplies including custom chart and index tab dividers, and color coded and pressboard classification file folders.	800-242-2376	NA	Petaluma
	Bio Plas Inc (HQ)	Manufacturer of laboratory disposables such as foam tube racks, biopsy bags, bacti cell spreaders, and siliconized products.	415-472-3777	NA	San Rafael
	Biocare Medical LLC (HQ)	Developer of automated immunohistochemistry instrumentation, reagents for IHC lab testing. The company also offer tissue diagnostic products for cancer.	925-603-8000	NA	Pacheco
	BioVentrix Inc (HQ)	Provider of medical devices. The company offers treatment for congestive heart failure by catheter based approaches.	925-830-1000	NA	San Ramon
	Biovision Inc (HQ)	Developer of medical products such as assay kits, antibodies, and research tools for studying apoptosis, metabolism, diabetes, and gene regulation.	408-493-1800	NA	Milpitas
	Boracchia & Associates (HQ)	Provider of consultant services and products to surgeons and medical facilities. The company offers operating room products, post-operative, and cast room products.	800-826-1690	NA	Petaluma
N	C & G Plastics (HQ)	Manufacturer of plastic products and also provides services including, injection molding, shipping and packaging, and assembly.	818-837-3773	NA	Sylmar
	C-Scan Corp (HQ)	Manufacturer and designer of thermal recorders and printers for medical applications and the healthcare sector.	800-953-7888	NA	Los Gatos
	Calcula Technologies (HQ)	Developer of medical devices for the treatment of kidney stones. The company serves the healthcare sector.	650-724-8696	NA	San Francisco
	CapsoVision (HQ)	Specializes in the diagnostic imaging of the gastrointestinal systems. The company offers services to hospitals and patients.	408-624-1488	NA	Saratoga

COMPANY NAME	PRODUCT / SERVICE	PHONE	EMP	CITY
Cardiva Medical Inc (HQ)	Developer of vascular access management products such as vascade and catalyst to facilitate rapid hemostasis following diagnostic procedures.	408-470-7170	NA	Santa Clara
CenterVue Inc (BR)	Designer and manufacturer of medical devices for the diagnosis and management of ocular pathologies.	408-988-8404	NA	Fremont
Certified Medical Testing (HQ)	Provider of engineering services. The company provides services for healthcare organizations related to piped medical gas and vacuum systems.	559-960-8756	NA	Fresno
Cibiem Inc (HQ)	Manufacturer of medical devices. The company provides solutions to treat sympathetic nervous system-mediated diseases.	650-397-6685	NA	Los Altos
Cirtec Medical (HQ)	Manufacturer of complex implantable device manufacturing, medical device solutions, and smart solutions for highly complex miniaturization.	408-395-0443	NA	Los Gatos
Claret Medical Inc (HQ)	Manufacturer of catheters to protect the patient's brain during Transcatheter Aortic Valve Implantation (TAVI) and other endovascular procedures.	707-528-7253	NA	Santa Rosa
Clinisense Corp (HQ)	Developer of technology for shelf-life monitoring. The company offers applications such as diagnostics, medical supplies, and RFID tags.	408-348-1495	NA	Los Gatos
Colema Boards Of California Inc (HQ)	Manufacturer of home enema board kits. The company's products include colema boards and cleansing kits.	530-347-5700	NA	Cottonwood
Collidion Inc (HQ)	Provider of healthcare products. The company specializes in antibiotic resistance, specific drugs to eradicate biofilms, and delivery systems.	707-668-7600	NA	Petaluma
N Convaid Products LLC (HQ)	Manufacturer of compact folding wheelchairs.	310-618-0111	NA	Torrance
Convergent Laser Technologies (HQ)	Provider of medical laser systems and fiber optic devices. The company deals with training and product support services.	510-832-2130	NA	Alameda
N Conversion Devices Inc (HQ)	Provider of medical power supply solutions.	714-898-6551	11-50	Huntington Beach
Cordis A Cardinal Health Co (HQ)	Provider of diagnostic and interventional products for healthcare devices such as catheters, balloons, stents, wires and vascular closure.	408-273-3700	NA	Santa Clara
Corium International Inc (HQ)	Provider of transdermal delivery systems and related technology solutions. The company is also engaged in therapeutic product development.	650-298-8255	NA	Menlo Park
N Cornucopia Tool & Plastics Inc (HQ)	Manufacturer and supplier plastics for medical and dental items, electronic components, business machines, food processing equipment, house ware products, and much more.	805-369-0030	NA	Paso Robles
Cosmed USA (HQ)	Developer and manufacturer of medical devices for accurate body composition assessments for infants, children, and adults.	925-676-6002	NA	Concord
Cutera Inc (HQ)	Manufacturer of aesthetic solutions such as face and body laser, light, and other energy-based aesthetic systems for hair removal and pigmented lesions.	415-657-5500	NA	Brisbane
Cymed (HQ)	Provider of ostomy pouching systems. The company specializes in skin care products and serves individuals and hospitals.	800-582-0707	NA	Sacramento
Dicom Systems Inc (HQ)	Provider of enterprise imaging, interoperability, and teleradiology solutions. The company offers services to patients.	415-684-8790	NA	Campbell
DirectGov Source Inc (HQ)	Manufacturer of personal protection kits. The company offers disposable clothing, biohazard disposal, antimicrobial sanitizers, and hand protection gloves.	530-899-3327	NA	Chico
Duke Empirical (HQ)	Provider of product development, catheter design, and manufacturing services to medical manufacturers.	831-420-1104	NA	Santa Cruz
Echopixel Inc (HQ)	Provider of 3D medical visualization software for radiologists, cardiologists, pediatric cardiologists, and interventional neuroradiologists.	844-273-7766	NA	Santa Clara
Eco Sound Medical Services (HQ)	Distributor of healthcare products and medical supplies. The company is focused on incontinence products, medical nutrients, and nursing supplies.	800-494-6868	NA	Tracy
Element Science Inc (HQ)	Developer of wearable platform solution. The company offers wearable cardioverter defibrillator for monitoring the heart of the patient.	415-872-6500	NA	San Francisco
Elixir Medical Corp (HQ)	Provider of pharmaceuticals for drug-device treatment solutions to patients. The company is engaged in drug delivery.	408-636-2000	NA	Milpitas
Emboline Inc (HQ)	Developer of cardiovascular embolic protection devices for transcatheter and surgical cardiac procedures.	831-900-5020	NA	Santa Cruz
EMED (HQ)	Manufacturer of safety medical products and specialty medical devices with a focus on infusion therapy.	916-932-0071	NA	El Dorado Hills
Endologix Inc (HQ)	Developer of endovascular grafts for the treatment of aneurysmal disease in the abdominal aorta and the thoracic aorta.	707-543-8800	NA	Santa Rosa
Exploramed (HQ)	Developer of novel medical devices with cutting edge medical technology for use by major medical device manufacturing companies.	650-472-0300	NA	Mountain View
Farlow's Scientific Glassblowing Inc (HQ)	Provider of precision drilling, boring, cutting, grinding, salvage and repair, custom tooling, metal-to-glass bonding, and related services.	530-477-5513	NA	Grass Valley
Gauss Surgical Inc (HQ)	Manufacturer of mobile devices. The company is engaged in research and development services and it serves the healthcare sector.	650-949-4153	NA	Los Altos
GCX Corp (HQ)	Provider of mounting solutions, application specific solutions, on-site services, and also technical support.	707-773-1100	NA	Petaluma

COMPANY NAME	PRODUCT / SERVICE	PHONE	EMP	CITY
GDM Electronic Medical (HQ)	Manufacturer of devices, electrical and electronics for medical, manufacturing and engineering industries.	408-945-4100	NA	San Jose
Genapsys Inc (HQ)	Developer of DNA sequencing to enable a paradigm shift in genomic diagnostics. The company specializes in GENIUS system that has footprint of Apple iPad.	650-330-1096	NA	Redwood City
General Foundry Service (HQ)	Provider of foundry services. The company engages in pattern making, precision sand casting, and rubber plastic mold.	510-297-5040	NA	San Leandro
General Vision (HQ)	Provider of hardware and software products. The company specializes in artificial intelligence and image analytics.	707-765-6150	NA	Petaluma
Halo Neuro Inc (HQ)	Developer of neurotech platform. The company offers services to athletes, elite teams, and organizations.	415-851-3338	NA	San Francisco
Hanger Prosthetics & Orthotics Inc (BR)	Provider of orthotic and prosthetic services and products. The company also offers clinically differentiated programs to its clients.	209-725-1295	NA	Merced
HeartVista Inc (HQ)	Developer of magnetic resonance imaging (MRI) applications and development tools to aid in the diagnosis of cardiovascular disease.	650-800-7937	NA	Los Altos
HMS Electronics Inc (HQ)	Manufacturer of medical device components. The company offers custom made specialty component parts for x-ray machines.	707-584-8760	NA	Santa Rosa
Hologic Inc (BR)	Provider of healthcare and diagnostics. The company offers breast and skeletal healthcare and diagnostics, and GYN surgical solutions.	669-224-6420	NA	Santa Clara
N Home Medix Inc (HQ)	Provider of wheelchairs, power chairs, scooters, walking aids and other medical equipment for patients, hospitals and others.	888-553-0051	11-50	Long Beach
Hospital Systems Inc (HQ)	Manufacturer of lighting, electrical and architectural products, and related supplies. The company is engaged in installation services.	925-427-7800	NA	Pittsburg
Inclin Inc (BR)	Provider of clinical, regulatory, and quality assurance services to pharmaceutical, biotechnology, and medical device companies.	650-376-4000	NA	San Mateo
InCube Labs (HQ)	Provider of laboratory services. The company offers medical devices and pharmaceuticals to various therapeutic areas.	408-457-3700	NA	San Jose
Intersect Ent Inc (HQ)	Provider of steroid-releasing implants that props open the sinuses for the treatment of common cold and sinusitis.	650-641-2100	201-500	Menlo Park
Intraop Medical Corp (HQ)	Manufacturer of mobetron for the treatment of cancer. The company offers services to hospitals, clinics, and patients.	408-636-1020	NA	Sunnyvale
Invuity Inc (HQ)	Manufacturer of surgical devices with cutting edge photonics technology to view surgical cavities during open, minimally invasive procedures.	415-655-2100	NA	San Francisco
Jasper Ridge Inc (HQ)	Manufacturer of tint and lighting exam systems. The company offers services to patients and hospitals.	650-804-5040	NA	San Mateo
N Jet Plastics (HQ)	Supplier of plastic products.	323-268-6706	51-200	Los Angeles
Kezar Life Sciences Inc (HQ)	Developer of small molecule therapeutics drugs targeting protein homeostasis for transformative treatments for autoimmune diseases.	650-822-5600	NA	S San Francisco
Kinematic Automation Inc (HQ)	Provider of manufacturing systems for the medical industry. The company also offers automation, strip cutting, rotary slitting services.	209-532-3200	NA	Sonora
Leaf Healthcare Inc (HQ)	Specializes in wearable healthcare technologies. The company deals with patient mobility programs and serves the medical industry.	844-826-5323	NA	Pleasanton
LimFlow Inc (BR)	Designer and developer of LimFlow percutaneous deep vein arterialization system to restore blood flow to the ischemic foot.	888-478-7705	NA	Santa Clara
LinaTech USA (HQ)	Manufacturer of medical devices and software for the treatment of cancer through radiotherapy. The company also supplies informatics software for managing cancer clinics.	408-733-2051	NA	Sunnyvale
LSVP International Inc (HQ)	Manufacturer of flexible and semi-rigid endoscopic instruments. The company's services include engineering and distribution.	650-969-1000	NA	Los Altos
Marathon Products Inc (HQ)	Manufacturer of equipment for collecting data on temperature for use in packaging and shipping industries.	510-562-6450	NA	San Leandro
Meddev Corp (HQ)	Developer, manufacturer, and marketer of medical devices for niche market segments throughout the world.	408-730-9702	NA	Sunnyvale
Medical Design Solutions (HQ)	Provider of medical design solutions. The company develops miniaturized sensors and systems used in medical device applications.	408-393-5386	NA	Milpitas
Merieux Nutrisciences Corp (BR)	Provider of public health services. The company is focused on food and pharmaceutical products, cosmetics, and consumer goods.	209-549-7508	NA	Salida
N Metro-Med Inc (HQ)	Distributor of home respiratory systems and supplies.	818-840-9090	NA	Burbank
MicroCam Inc (HQ)	Provider of medical devices. The company focuses on commercializing the plug and play micro imaging system.	415-729-9391	NA	San Rafael
Microcube (HQ)	Provider of concept development, design, rapid prototyping and IP management, market mapping, clinical trials, and regulatory submissions.	510-651-5000	NA	Fremont
Micropoint Bioscience Inc (HQ)	Developer of medical products and services for treatment of vascular disease such as peripheral artery disease and venous blood clots disorders.	408-588-1682	NA	Santa Clara
Minto Research & Development Inc (HQ)	Supplier of emergency fracture response systems.	530-222-2373	NA	Redding
Mirion Technologies Inc (DH)	Provider of solutions in radiation detection. The company serves the healthcare, nuclear power, and other industries.	925-543-0800	NA	San Ramon

	COMPANY NAME	PRODUCT / SERVICE	PHONE	EMP	CITY
N	Mission Rubber Co (HQ)	Manufacturer of rubber coupling products.	951-736-1343	201-500	Corona
	Mizuho OSI (HQ)	Designs and manufactures medical components. The company offers surgery tables, patient care kits, trauma tables, and more.	510-429-1500	NA	Union City
N	Modified Plastics Inc (HQ)	Manufacturer of thermoplastic components.	714-546-4667	1-10	Santa Ana
N	Moldex-Metric Inc (HQ)	Manufacturer and supplier of surgical appliances.	310-837-6500	NA	Culver City
N	Morgan Hill Plastics Inc (HQ)	Provider of vacuum forming, bending, polishing and much more services.	408-842-1322	11-50	Gilroy
	Motive Medical Intelligence (HQ)	Developer of medical intelligence solutions. The company also offers care plans for population health management.	415-362-4007	NA	San Francisco
	Moximed Inc (BR)	Developer of joint preserving option for patients with knee osteoarthritis. The company serves the medical industry.	510-887-3300	NA	Hayward
	Nano Precision Medical Inc (HQ)	Developer of medical devices. The company specializes in rice-grain sized implant for the treatment of type II diabetes.	415-506-8462	NA	Emeryville
	Nanomix Inc (HQ)	Manufacturer of diagnostic systems and supplies. The company is engaged in product development services.	510-428-5300	NA	Emeryville
	Natus Medical Inc (HQ)	Provider of medical devices, software, and services. The company offers products for neurology, newborn care, hearing diagnostics, and more.	650-802-0400	NA	San Carlos
N	Neotech Products Inc (HQ)	Manufacturer of medical products.	661-775-7466	NA	Valencia
	Neotract Inc (HQ)	Provider of medical devices for the treatment of benign prostatic hyperplasia and its side effects such as loss of productivity and sleep and depression.	925-401-0700	NA	Pleasanton
	Neuropace Inc (HQ)	Designer, developer, manufacturer, and marketer of implantable devices for the treatment of neurological disorders.	650-237-2700	NA	Mountain View
	Neurosky Inc (HQ)	Manufacturer of ECG biosensors and also EEG biosensors for mobile solutions, wearable devices, and service providers.	408-200-6675	NA	San Jose
N	Newby Rubber Inc (HQ)	Manufacturer and distributor of rubber products such as agriculture, food processing, waterworks, pump, and oilfield.	661-327-5137	11-50	Bakersfield
	North Coast Medical Inc (HQ)	Manufacturer of medical and rehabilitation products such as castings, clinical supplies, and other wellness supplies.	408-776-5000	NA	Morgan Hill
	Onda Corp (HQ)	Manufacturer of medical devices. The company offers ultrasound measurement instrumentation and services for scientific applications.	408-745-0383	NA	Sunnyvale
	Penumbra Inc (HQ)	Manufacturer of interventional therapy devices. The company develops products to treat challenging medical conditions.	510-748-3200	NA	Alameda
N	Pet Qwerks Inc (HQ)	Distributor of pet supplies.	949-916-3733	11-50	Irvine
	PhysioCue Inc (HQ)	Developer of therapies and focuses on the delivery of thermo-neurostimulation systems. The company serves patients.	408-524-1595	NA	San Jose
	Pickering Laboratories Inc (HQ)	Developer of post-column derivatization technology. The company specializes in manufacturing of cation-exchange columns for amino acid analysis.	650-694-6700	NA	Mountain View
N	Plasidyne Engineering & Manufacturing Inc (HQ)	Manufacturer of PTFE, Filled PTFE and precision-machined plastic parts for commercial and aerospace.	562-531-0510	NA	Long Beach
	POC Medical Systems Inc (HQ)	Provider of diagnostic medical devices for the screening of life-threatening diseases like cancer, cardiovascular disorders, and infectious diseases.	925-331-8010	NA	Livermore
N	Polymeric Technology Inc (HQ)	Distributor of cast, molded and injected urethane, polyurethane, plastic, silicone, and rubber parts.	510-895-6001	NA	San Leandro
	PONTiS Orthopaedics LLC (HQ)	Manufacturer of medical devices such as implants and instrumentation for use in upper and lower extremity bone and soft tissue repair.	415-567-8935	NA	San Francisco
N	Precise Aerospace Manufacturing Inc (HQ)	Manufacturer of plastics products.	951-898-0500	51-200	Corona
	Precise Light Surgical (HQ)	Provider of medical devices with vaporization technology for the removal of delicate tissues, reduce surgical risk, and down time in endoscopic surgery.	831-539-3323	NA	Campbell
	Prime Engineering (HQ)	Provider of standing systems products such as grandstand, kidstand, symmetry mobile, uprite, cindy lift, and the lift.	559-276-0991	NA	Fresno
	Procept Biorobotics (HQ)	Provider of healthcare services. The company primarily focuses on personalized image-guided waterjet tissue resection services.	650-232-7200	NA	Redwood City
N	Proulx Manufacturing Inc (HQ)	Manufacturer of trimmers.	909-980-0662	11-50	Rancho Cucamonga
	Providence Medical Technology Inc (HQ)	Developer of medical devices and technologies such as dtrax spinal systems, cavux cervical cages, and ally screw systems for cervical spine care.	415-923-9376	NA	Pleasanton
	Qi Medical Inc (HQ)	Manufacturer of fingertip testing, syringe filters, rinse fluids, incubators, and vial adaptors for pharmacists and nurses who handle sterile solutions.	530-272-8700	NA	Grass Valley
	Qview Medical (HQ)	Provider of assistance in the review of 3D automated breast ultrasound. The company offers services to the radiologists.	650-397-5174	NA	Los Altos
N	R.W. Smith & Co (HQ)	Provider of foodservice products and solutions.	800-942-1101	NA	San Diego
N	Rafi Systems Inc (HQ)	Manufacturer of ophthalmic goods.	909-861-6574	NA	Diamond Bar

	COMPANY NAME	PRODUCT / SERVICE	PHONE	EMP	CITY
	Rapidwerks Inc (HQ)	Manufacturer of medical equipment and devices. The company also offers accessories and semiconductor products.	925-417-0124	NA	Pleasanton
	RDM Industrial Products Inc (HQ)	Provider of laboratory and industrial furniture solutions. The company offers cabinets, counters, carts, and mobile tables.	408-945-8400	NA	Milpitas
	Recor Medical Inc (RH)	Manufacturer of ultrasound denervation products. The company is involved in clinical trials and research solutions.	650-542-7700	NA	Palo Alto
	Relucent Solutions LLC (HQ)	Manufacturer of medical devices. The company is involved in laser cutting, precision manufacturing, wire crimping, and related services.	800-630-7704	NA	Santa Rosa
	Renovorx Inc (HQ)	Manufacturer of medical devices. The company develops solutions for targeted delivery of therapeutic and diagnostic agents.	650-284-4433	NA	Los Altos
	Safe Hearing America Inc (HQ)	Provider of mobile hearing testing services and products. The company offerings include AQ Solid Plug, Sleep Plug, and Solid Plug.	707-446-0880	NA	Vacaville
N	Salter Labs (HQ)	Manufacturer of surgical and medical instruments.	661-854-3166	501-1000	Arvin
	Scientific Specialties Inc (HQ)	Manufacturer of injection molded plastic consumable and durable products such as tubes, pipette tips, and racks for life science research industry.	209-333-2120	NA	Lodi
	Sensoplex Inc (HQ)	Developer and manufacturer of wearable sensors. The company offers rechargeable batteries, displays, interfaces, and related accessories.	408-391-9019	NA	Redwood City
	Sentreheart Inc (HQ)	Developer of catheter technology solutions. The company is engaged in suture delivery and related services.	650-354-1200	NA	Redwood City
	Shifamed LLC (HQ)	Manufacturer of medical technologies and products catheters, custom balloons, painted balloon electrodes, and diagnostic and therapeutic instrumentation.	408-560-2500	NA	Campbell
	Shockwave Medical Inc (HQ)	Focuses on the production of highest performance personal submarines on the planet. The company is involved in research services.	877-775-4846	NA	Santa Clara
	Siesta Medical Inc (HQ)	Providers of medical devices. The company offers surgical implants and tools for the treatment of OSA.	408-320-9424	NA	Los Gatos
	Silicon Valley Precision Inc (HQ)	Provider of custom vertical and horizontal CNC machining, fabrication and assembly of parts. The company offers powder coating, painting and grinding.	925-373-8259	NA	Livermore
	SMC Ltd (BR)	Provider of custom packing for product sterilization. The company is engaged in supply chain management solutions.	707-303-3000	NA	Santa Rosa
	Sootheze (HQ)	Manufacturer of aromatherapy products and other products that help relieve pain and provide comfort.	844-576-6843	NA	Red Bluff
	Spineguard Inc (DH)	Specializes in spine surgery. The company offers services to patients, hospitals, and healthcare organizations.	415-512-2500	NA	San Francisco
	SST Group Inc (HQ)	Provider of medical displays, recorders, film digitizers, and related accessories. The company offers optical library support services.	408-350-3450	NA	Santa Clara
	Stellartech Research Corp (HQ)	Designer, developer, and manufacturer of medical devices. The company specializes in surgical probes, balloon electrode catheters, and other products.	408-331-3000	NA	Milpitas
	Sunmedica Inc (HQ)	Specializes in surgical orthopaedics, wound management, cold therapy and sports medicine. The company also offers surgical positioning devices.	530-229-1600	NA	Redding
	Supracor Inc (HQ)	Developer of honeycomb products. The company's offerings include sandals, saddle pads, and related supplies.	408-432-1616	NA	San Jose
N	Syneron Inc (HQ)	Manufacturer and distributor of aesthetic medical products including hair removal and wrinkle reduction.	949-716-6670	501-1000	Irvine
	The Cooper Companies Inc (HQ)	Provider of healthcare solutions. The company offers health and wellness programs for women, individuals, and communities.	925-460-3600	NA	San Ramon
	The Foundry LLC (HQ)	Focuses on product development, prototyping, market analysis, development, and pre-clinical and clinical support services.	650-326-2656	NA	Menlo Park
N	The Thomas Kinkade Co (HQ)	Publisher of art works.	888-368-1336	NA	Morgan Hill
N	TNT Plastic Molding Inc (HQ)	Provider of plastic injection molding services.	951-808-9700	51-200	Corona
	Triple Ring Technologies Inc (HQ)	Manufacturer of in vitro diagnostics and life science tools. The company offer services to the medical devices, imaging, and industrial sectors.	510-592-3000	NA	Newark
	Tusker Medical Inc (HQ)	Developer of pediatric-focused technologies. The company specializes in the placement of tubes without general anesthetics.	650-223-6900	NA	Menlo Park
	United Medical Instruments Inc (HQ)	Provider of ultrasound equipment. The company focuses on pain management, breast imaging, and pathology.	408-278-9300	NA	San Jose
	Vapore LLC (HQ)	Manufacturer of personal steam inhalers. The company's products are used for relief from sinus congestion, allergies, and discomfort from sore throat.	925-998-6116	NA	Concord
	VORTRAN Medical Technology Inc (HQ)	Developer of pulmonary modulation technology solutions. The company offers automatic disposable respiratory devices for treating pulmonary diseases.	800-434-4034	NA	Sacramento
N	Western Case Inc (HQ)	Manufacturer of plastics products.	951-214-6380	11-50	Riverside
	WHILL Inc (BR)	Manufacturer of personal electric vehicles, wheelchairs, and mobility devices. The company serves individuals and clinics.	844-699-4455	NA	San Carlos

COMPANY NAME	PRODUCT / SERVICE	PHONE	EMP	CITY
Whole You Inc (HQ)	Provider of healthcare solutions. The company specializes in sleep, dental, movement, and vision solutions to its customers.	844-548-3385	NA	San Jose
Zoeticx (HQ)	Provider of healthcare solutions. The company develops care applications and offers services to inpatients, ICU, and outpatients.	408-622-6119	NA	San Jose

190 = Orthopedics & Prosthetics

COMPANY NAME	PRODUCT / SERVICE	PHONE	EMP	CITY
Alpha Orthotics Corp (HQ)	Distributor of non-invasive orthotic products. The company provides products for catalogs, specialty foot retailers, and medical distributors.	415-389-8980	NA	Tiburon
Anchor Orthotics & Prosthetics (HQ)	Provider of orthotics and prosthetics. The company offers personal ankle bionic systems, braces and support and artificial limbs for amputees.	877-977-0448	NA	Sacramento
Bracesox The Original (HQ)	Manufacturer of bracesox, a brace cover with undersleeves and oversleeves to give brace comfort for patients.	831-479-7628	NA	Soquel
Consensus Orthopedics Inc (HQ)	Manufacturer of orthopedic medical devices. The company's products include consensus hip systems, revision knee systems, mobile bearing knee systems, and others.	916-355-7100	NA	El Dorado Hills
D Danz & Sons Inc (HQ)	Specializes in the custom fitting, designing, and manufacturing of ophthalmic prosthetics. The company deals with patient care.	559-252-1770	NA	Fresno
EPIX Orthopaedics Inc (HQ)	Developer of orthopaedic devices that improve patient outcomes, surgeon accuracy and efficiency, and reduce costs to patients and health care system.	844-710-9105	NA	Palo Alto
Hanger Prosthetics & Orthotics Inc (BR)	Provider of prosthetic and orthotic components and services. The company serves hospitals, patients, and the healthcare industry.	916-452-5724	NA	South Sacramento
Hanger Prosthetics & Orthotics Inc (BR)	Provider of orthotic and prosthetic services and products. The company also offers clinically differentiated programs to its clients.	209-725-1295	NA	Merced
LIM innovations Inc (HQ)	Designer and manufacturer of prosthetic sockets for amputees. The company offers custom-molded, adjustable, and modular prosthetic sockets.	844-888-8546	NA	San Francisco
N Luthier's Mercantile International Inc (HQ)	Distributor of exotic tone woods, professional tools and parts to stringed instrument makers.	707-687-2020	NA	Windsor
Moximed Inc (BR)	Developer of joint preserving option for patients with knee osteoarthritis. The company serves the medical industry.	510-887-3300	NA	Hayward
Ortho Group (HQ)	Designer of devices for the medical industry. The company specializes in orthopedic surgical devices.	916-859-0881	NA	Rancho Cordova
Plastikon Industries Inc (HQ)	Provider of contract manufacturing services for custom designed plastic injection molding, for medical, pharmaceutical and other industries.	510-400-1010	NA	Hayward
PONTiS Orthopaedics LLC (HQ)	Manufacturer of medical devices such as implants and instrumentation for use in upper and lower extremity bone and soft tissue repair.	415-567-8935	NA	San Francisco
Pro Lab Orthotics (HQ)	Manufacturer and supplier of orthoses products. The company's offerings include foot orthoses, pathology orthoses, and specialty orthoses.	707-257-4400	NA	Napa
Prosthetic Artists Inc (HQ)	Provider of impression-fitted, hand-sculpted, hand-painted ocular prosthesis. The company also fits thin shell prosthesis over disfigured eyes.	916-485-4249	NA	Sacramento
Prosthetic Solutions Inc (HQ)	Manufacturer of medical devices. The company improves the lives of amputees by providing them prosthesis.	831-637-0491	NA	Hollister
Pyramid Orthodontics (HQ)	Provider of orthodontics products. The company's products include clear brackets, bands, buccal tubes, and wire accessories.	877-337-3708	NA	San Rafael
Spectrum Orthotics & Prosthetics (BR)	Provider of orthotics and prosthetics products. The company serves physicians and the medical sector.	530-243-4500	NA	Redding
Steven R Young Ocularist Inc (HQ)	Provider of ocular prosthetic services. The company engages in scleral cover shells and maxillo-facial prosthetics.	510-836-2123	NA	Oakland
Sunrise Medical (US) LLC (HQ)	Distributor of folding wheelchairs, seating and positioning systems, and other mobility products to its customers.	800-333-4000	NA	Fresno
Top Shelf (BR)	Manufacturer of orthopedic bracing and appliances. The company offers products for knee, shoulder, foot and ankle, and spine.	866-592-0488	NA	Tracy

191 = R&D

COMPANY NAME	PRODUCT / SERVICE	PHONE	EMP	CITY
Accuray Inc (HQ)	Provider of oncology treatment solutions. The company develops, manufactures and sells precise and innovative tumor treatment solutions.	888-522-3740	NA	Sunnyvale
Advance Research Associates (HQ)	Developer of human bio-therapeutic platform technology solutions, drug discovery, and related support services.	650-810-1190	NA	Santa Clara
Airxpanders Inc (HQ)	Provider of controlled tissue expander and small handheld wireless controller of breast cancer reconstructive surgery.	650-390-9000	NA	San Jose
Arrayit Corp (HQ)	Focuses on the discovery, development and manufacture of proprietary life science technologies and consumables for disease prevention.	408-744-1331	NA	Sunnyvale
BD Biosciences (BR)	Manufacturer of medical devices. The company provides a broad range of medical supplies, devices, laboratory equipment and diagnostic products.	877-232-8995	NA	San Jose
Biochain Institute Inc (HQ)	Provider of bio-sample preparation, analysis, and application assays accelerating the development of personalized diagnostics, therapeutics, and medicine.	510-783-8588	NA	Newark

COMPANY NAME	PRODUCT / SERVICE	PHONE	EMP	CITY
Bionexus Inc (HQ)	Provider of biomedical products and services for research areas such as genomics, proteomics, immunology, protein expression, and cell biology.	510-625-8400	NA	Oakland
Broncus Medical Inc (HQ)	Provider of navigation, diagnostic and therapeutic technology solutions for treating patients with lung disease.	650-428-1600	NA	San Jose
Cairn Biosciences (HQ)	Provider of therapeutic solutions for treating cancer. The company is involved in biotechnical research and commercial business.	415-503-1185	NA	San Francisco
California Clinical Laboratory Association (HQ)	Provider of an Association for small and large laboratories in California. The company files suits to prevent medicare from denying coverage for lab tests.	916-446-2646	NA	Sacramento
Calithera Biosciences Inc (HQ)	Developer of small molecule drugs directed against tumor metabolism and tumor immunology targets for the treatment of cancer.	650-870-1000	NA	S San Francisco
CenterVue Inc (BR)	Designer and manufacturer of medical devices for the diagnosis and management of ocular pathologies.	408-988-8404	NA	Fremont
Channel Medsystems Inc (HQ)	Developer of cryothermic technology and streamlined delivery system for women with heavy menstrual bleeding.	510-338-9301	NA	Emeryville
Circuit Therapeutics Inc (HQ)	Focuses on drug discovery and development as well as forging direct therapeutic applications of optogenetics.	650-324-9400	NA	Menlo Park
Domino Data Lab Inc (HQ)	Provider of premise and cloud-based enterprise data science platform for analysis applications. The company serves the business sector.	415-570-2425	NA	San Francisco
Eargo Inc (HQ)	Creator of medical device. The company specializes in virtually invisible in-ear hearing device that is comfortable, natural sounding, and rechargeable.	650-351-7700	NA	San Jose
Evidation Health Inc (HQ)	Provider of digital health solutions for healthcare providers, payers, pharma/biotech, and digital health companies.	650-727-5557	NA	San Mateo
Fluidigm Sciences Inc (HQ)	Developer and creator of technologies for life science tools designed to revolutionize biology. The company is involved in research programs.	650-871-7152	NA	S San Francisco
Halo Neuro Inc (HQ)	Developer of neurotech platform. The company offers services to athletes, elite teams, and organizations.	415-851-3338	NA	San Francisco
Health Advances LLC (BR)	Provider of consulting services to the healthcare industry. The company offers clinical development, product positioning, lifecycle management, and more.	415-834-0800	NA	San Francisco
iHEAR Medical Inc (HQ)	Provider of hearing technology. The company specializes in web-enabled hearing device to fulfill the unmet needs of the hearing impaired.	510-276-4437	NA	San Leandro
InCube Labs (HQ)	Provider of laboratory services. The company offers medical devices and pharmaceuticals to various therapeutic areas.	408-457-3700	NA	San Jose
InterVene Inc (HQ)	Provider of medical devices such as blueleaf endovenous valve formation system to treat severe venous disease in the legs.	650-351-6725	NA	S San Francisco
Kodiak Sciences Inc (HQ)	Manufacturer of medicines for the treatment of patients with age-related macular degeneration and diabetic eye disease, two leading causes of blindness.	650-281-0850	NA	Palo Alto
Kucklick Design (HQ)	Designer and developer of medical illustration products. The company's portfolio includes NovaSom system, Starion devices, and Extravasate.	408-353-1508	NA	Los Gatos
Ligandal Inc (HQ)	Developer of nanotechnology for precise and high-efficiency delivery of nucleic acids to specific cells and organelles for genetic medicine.	650-866-5212	NA	San Francisco
Lineage Cell Therapeutics Inc (HQ)	Provider of cell-based technologies and regenerative medicine for the treatment of chronic and degenerative diseases.	510-871-4188	NA	Carlsbad
Medical Design Solutions (HQ)	Provider of medical design solutions. The company develops miniaturized sensors and systems used in medical device applications.	408-393-5386	NA	Milpitas
Minerva Surgical Inc (HQ)	Manufacturer of medical devices. The company provides products for the treatment of abnormal uterine bleeding.	855-646-7874	NA	Redwood City
Motive Medical Intelligence (HQ)	Developer of medical intelligence solutions. The company also offers care plans for population health management.	415-362-4007	NA	San Francisco
Nuvolase Inc (HQ)	Manufacturer of the pinpointed foot laser used for the treatment of nail fungus and in nail fungus procedures.	530-809-1970	NA	Chico
Ocellus Inc (HQ)	Provider of multidisciplinary technology and services such as nanotechnology-based solutions for aerospace, industrial, and medical applications.	925-606-6540	NA	Livermore
OrthoTrophix Inc (HQ)	Developer of therapies for medical needs of patients. The company specializes in regeneration of articular cartilage in knee and other joints.	510-488-3832	NA	Oakland
Penumbra Inc (HQ)	Manufacturer of interventional therapy devices. The company develops products to treat challenging medical conditions.	510-748-3200	NA	Alameda
Phoenix Technology Group LLC (HQ)	Provider of research laboratory services. The company offers anterior segment imaging and retinal imaging microscope services.	925-485-1100	NA	Pleasanton
PhysioCue Inc (HQ)	Developer of therapies and focuses on the delivery of thermo-neurostimulation systems. The company serves patients.	408-524-1595	NA	San Jose
Qi Medical Inc (HQ)	Manufacturer of fingertip testing, syringe filters, rinse fluids, incubators, and vial adaptors for pharmacists and nurses who handle sterile solutions.	530-272-8700	NA	Grass Valley
Rani Therapeutics (HQ)	Developer of drug molecules including peptides, proteins and antibodies. The company offers services to the pharmaceutical industry.	408-457-3700	NA	San Jose

COMPANY NAME	PRODUCT / SERVICE	PHONE	EMP	CITY
RDM Industrial Products Inc (HQ)	Provider of laboratory and industrial furniture solutions. The company offers cabinets, counters, carts, and mobile tables.	408-945-8400	NA	Milpitas
Renovorx Inc (HQ)	Manufacturer of medical devices. The company develops solutions for targeted delivery of therapeutic and diagnostic agents.	650-284-4433	NA	Los Altos
Sangamo Therapeutics (HQ)	Developer of engineered DNA-binding proteins for the regulation of gene expression and for gene modification.	510-970-6000	201-500	Richmond
Sensoplex Inc (HQ)	Developer and manufacturer of wearable sensors. The company offers rechargeable batteries, displays, interfaces, and related accessories.	408-391-9019	NA	Redwood City
Siesta Medical Inc (HQ)	Providers of medical devices. The company offers surgical implants and tools for the treatment of OSA.	408-320-9424	NA	Los Gatos
Silk Road Medical Inc (HQ)	Specializes in the treatment of carotid artery diseases. The company is engaged in clinical trials and related services.	408-720-9002	NA	Sunnyvale
SwitchGear Genomics Inc (HQ)	Focuses on custom cloning, pathway screening, target validation, sequence variant assay, and custom mutagenesis services.	760-431-1263	NA	Carlsbad
System Biosciences LLC (HQ)	Provider of genome-wide analysis of the mechanisms that regulate cellular processes and biological responses.	650-968-2200	NA	Palo Alto
Triple Ring Technologies Inc (HQ)	Manufacturer of in vitro diagnostics and life science tools. The company offer services to the medical devices, imaging, and industrial sectors.	510-592-3000	NA	Newark
ViOptix Inc (HQ)	Manufacturer of medical support devices. The company specializes in devices used for respiratory support and oxygen supply.	510-226-5860	NA	Newark
Vistagen Therapeutics Inc (HQ)	Developer of medicine to treat depression, cancer and diseases and disorders involving the central nervous system.	650-577-3600	NA	S San Francisco

192 = Reproduction-Related Equipment

COMPANY NAME	PRODUCT / SERVICE	PHONE	EMP	CITY
Airxpanders Inc (HQ)	Provider of controlled tissue expander and small handheld wireless controller of breast cancer reconstructive surgery.	650-390-9000	NA	San Jose
SST Group Inc (HQ)	Provider of medical displays, recorders, film digitizers, and related accessories. The company offers optical library support services.	408-350-3450	NA	Santa Clara

194 = Software

COMPANY NAME	PRODUCT / SERVICE	PHONE	EMP	CITY
314e Corp (HQ)	Provider of IT skills, methodologies, and cost-effective managed services for healthcare application and technical support services.	510-371-6736	NA	Pleasanton
Able Health Inc (HQ)	Provider of value-based reimbursements under MACRA, MIPS, PQRS, medicaids, and commercial programs.	805-288-0240	NA	San Francisco
AlgoMedica Inc (HQ)	Developer of medical imaging software based on artificial neural networks for abdomen/pelvis, head, and liver and pediatrics CT scans.	516-448-3124	NA	Sunnyvale
Apixio Inc (HQ)	Provider of cognitive computing platform that enables the analysis of unstructured healthcare data at individual level, providing groundbreaking insights.	877-427-4946	NA	San Mateo
Arterys Inc (HQ)	Developer of medical imaging cloud platform. The company specializes in diagnostic platform to make healthcare more accurate and data driven.	650-319-7230	NA	San Francisco
Augmedix Inc (HQ)	Provider of technology enabled documentation services for health systems and doctors.	888-669-4885	NA	San Francisco
Beyond Lucid Technologies Inc (HQ)	Developer of cloud-based software platform. The company offers services to the emergency medical, disaster management, and first response industries.	650-648-3727	NA	Concord
Bigfoot Biomedical Inc (HQ)	Developer of biomedical solution to improve the lives of people with diabetes through the application of smart technology.	408-716-5600	NA	Milpitas
Biosearch Technologies Inc (RH)	Manufacturer of nucleic acid based products that accelerate the discovery and application of genomic information.	415-883-8400	NA	Petaluma
Catalia Health Inc (HQ)	Provider of medical solutions for pharmaceuticals, healthcare systems, and home care. The company specializes in robotic aides for an aging population.	415-660-9264	NA	San Francisco
Cedaron Medical Inc (HQ)	Provider of entrepreneurial, medical, technological, marketing, and documentation software solutions for healthcare providers.	800-424-1007	NA	Davis
CellSight Technologies Inc (HQ)	Provider of imaging tools to assess immunotherapy for the clinicians. The company focuses on the development of polyethylene terephthalate tracers.	650-799-1589	NA	San Francisco
Chartware Inc (HQ)	Manufacturer of scheduler and practice management interfaces and systems. The company serves the medical sector.	800-642-4278	NA	Rohnert Park
Clinovo Inc (HQ)	Provider of resourcing solutions for pharmaceutical, biotechnology, diagnostic, medical device, and CRO customers.	866-994-3121	NA	San Jose
Compact Imaging Inc (HQ)	Developer of miniature optical sensor technology. The company specializes in mobile health applications.	650-694-7801	NA	Mountain View
Connectance Inc (HQ)	Provider of software for diagnosis in health care industry. The company offer online access too to detect a disease and offer treatment suggestion.	415-891-8872	NA	Mill Valley
Creganna Medical (BR)	Provider of medical devices. The company offers services that ranges from clinical and regulatory support to design and manufacturing services.	408-364-7100	NA	Campbell

COMPANY NAME	PRODUCT / SERVICE	PHONE	EMP	CITY
D-EYE (BR)	Designer and manufacturer of diagnostic instruments. The company offers smartphone based retinal imaging systems for clinical assessments.	401-473-6323	NA	Truckee
Dicom Systems Inc (HQ)	Provider of enterprise imaging, interoperability, and teleradiology solutions. The company offers services to patients.	415-684-8790	NA	Campbell
Doctor on Demand (HQ)	Provider of urgent care doctors. The company offers lab screens for the treatment of mental health and chronic conditions.	800-997-6196	NA	San Francisco
E*Healthlinecom Inc (HQ)	Provider of integrated health care information management software such as administration discharge transfer, bed management, and patient billing.	916-924-8092	NA	Sacramento
E-Health Records International Inc (HQ)	Provider of electronic medical record system that can manage all aspects of clinical care in a busy hospital environment.	707-284-4300	NA	Sebastopol
Eargo Inc (HQ)	Creator of medical device. The company specializes in virtually invisible in-ear hearing device that is comfortable, natural sounding, and rechargeable.	650-351-7700	NA	San Jose
EBR Systems Inc (HQ)	Designer and developer of implantable systems for wireless tissue stimulation. The company focuses on the treatment of heart failure.	408-720-1906	NA	Sunnyvale
Endpoint Clinical Inc (HQ)	Designer of response technology platforms to access data through phones, the web, and mobile devices. The company is engaged in engineering services.	415-229-1600	NA	San Francisco
First Databank Inc (HQ)	Provider of healthcare solutions to hospitals, retail pharmacies, payers, drug manufacturers, and healthcare providers.	650-588-5454	NA	S San Francisco
Gauss Surgical Inc (HQ)	Manufacturer of mobile devices. The company is engaged in research and development services and it serves the healthcare sector.	650-949-4153	NA	Los Altos
Glooko Inc (HQ)	Provider of diabetes management solution. The company offers platform to allow patients manage diabetes data and collaborate with their doctors.	650-720-5310	NA	Mountain View
Halo Neuro Inc (HQ)	Developer of neurotech platform. The company offers services to athletes, elite teams, and organizations.	415-851-3338	NA	San Francisco
Health Advances LLC (BR)	Provider of consulting services to the healthcare industry. The company offers clinical development, product positioning, lifecycle management, and more.	415-834-0800	NA	San Francisco
Imosphere Inc (BR)	Developer of healthcare analytics platform. The company offers services to healthcare professionals.	800-802-1884	NA	San Francisco
IntelaMetrix Inc (HQ)	Specializes in ultrasound technology solutions. The company offers assessment tools for the health, fitness and wellness industries.	925-606-7044	NA	Brentwood
Kenzen Inc (HQ)	Focuses on the manufacture of personal health monitors. The company serves individuals and healthcare organizations.	650-384-5140	NA	San Francisco
Kura MD Inc (HQ)	Provider of telemedicine platform enables convenient, secure, HIPAA compliant, and telehealth appointments between physicians and patients through tablet.	855-587-2220	NA	Roseville
Leaf Healthcare Inc (HQ)	Specializes in wearable healthcare technologies. The company deals with patient mobility programs and serves the medical industry.	844-826-5323	NA	Pleasanton
Lightning Bolt Solutions Inc (HQ)	Provider of medical staff scheduling software and solutions. The company's services include scheduling, keeping backups, technical support, and training.	866-678-3279	NA	S San Francisco
LinaTech USA (HQ)	Manufacturer of medical devices and software for the treatment of cancer through radiotherapy. The company also supplies informatics software for managing cancer clinics.	408-733-2051	NA	Sunnyvale
Medeanalytics Inc (HQ)	Provider of performance management, compliance, employer reporting, patient engagement, and satisfaction solutions.	510-379-3300	NA	Dublin
Motive Medical Intelligence (HQ)	Developer of medical intelligence solutions. The company also offers care plans for population health management.	415-362-4007	NA	San Francisco
mscripts LLC (HQ)	Specializes in clinical and manufacturer programs. The company offers services to patients and pharmacies.	888-672-7478	NA	San Francisco
NDS Surgical Imaging LLC (HQ)	Provider of medical imaging services. The company specializes in minimal invasive surgery viewing and diagnostic imaging.	408-776-0085	NA	San Jose
Prowess Inc (HQ)	Focuses on Windows-based treatment planning systems for radiation therapy treatment and OIS software.	925-356-0360	NA	Concord
Quantitative Medical Systems Inc (HQ)	Provider of medical systems and dialysis billing software products. The company is engaged in clinical support.	510-654-9200	NA	Emeryville
Qview Medical (HQ)	Provider of assistance in the review of 3D automated breast ultrasound. The company offers services to the radiologists.	650-397-5174	NA	Los Altos
SST Group Inc (HQ)	Provider of medical displays, recorders, film digitizers, and related accessories. The company offers optical library support services.	408-350-3450	NA	Santa Clara
TCS Healthcare Technologies (HQ)	Provider of care management solutions. The company offers software implementation and training and workflow design services.	530-886-1700	NA	Auburn
Thync Global Inc (HQ)	Provider of wearable technology solutions. The company is involved in testing and related support services.	408-484-4808	NA	Los Gatos
Viewics Inc (HQ)	Provider of consulting, custom development, and report authoring services. The company also offers packaged solutions.	415-439-0084	NA	Santa Clara

COMPANY NAME	PRODUCT / SERVICE	PHONE	EMP	CITY
Vital Connect Inc (HQ)	Provider of healthcare solutions. The company focuses on biosensors, clinical-grade biometric measurements.	408-963-4600	NA	San Jose
Vital Enterprises (HQ)	Provider of field service and manufacturing solutions. The company offers services to hospitals and R&D laboratories.	650-394-6486	NA	San Francisco
Zoeticx (HQ)	Provider of healthcare solutions. The company develops care applications and offers services to inpatients, ICU, and outpatients.	408-622-6119	NA	San Jose

195 = Surgical Instruments & Equipment

COMPANY NAME	PRODUCT / SERVICE	PHONE	EMP	CITY
AB Medical Technologies Inc (HQ)	Manufacturer of electronic medical systems and powered surgical instruments such as surgical pumps, arthroscopy shavers and lab equipment.	530-605-2522	NA	Redding
Amerex Instruments Inc (HQ)	Provider of lab equipment. The company provides shakers, top-loading autoclaves, incubators, hybridization and convection ovens and water baths.	925-299-0743	NA	Concord
BD Biosciences (BR)	Manufacturer of medical devices. The company provides a broad range of medical supplies, devices, laboratory equipment and diagnostic products.	877-232-8995	NA	San Jose
Benvenue Medical Inc (HQ)	Developer of expandable implant systems for the spine. The company focuses on cylindrical implant design.	408-454-9300	NA	Santa Clara
Bibbero Systems Inc (HQ)	Manufacturer of filing and office supplies including custom chart and index tab dividers, and color coded and pressboard classification file folders.	800-242-2376	NA	Petaluma
Bioluminate Inc (HQ)	Developer of probes that provide breast cancer detection data to physicians. The company serves the medical sector.	650-743-0240	NA	San Carlos
Boracchia & Associates (HQ)	Provider of consultant services and products to surgeons and medical facilities. The company offers operating room products, post-operative, and cast room products.	800-826-1690	NA	Petaluma
Boston Scientific (BR)	Provider of forceps, imaging systems, needles, pacemakers, snares, probes, and other related accessories.	510-440-7700	NA	Fremont
Boston Scientific Corp (BR)	Manufacturer of baskets, forceps, imaging systems, needles, pacemakers, CTO and direct visualization systems.	408-935-3400	NA	San Jose
Cardiva Medical Inc (HQ)	Developer of vascular access management products such as vascade and catalyst to facilitate rapid hemostasis following diagnostic procedures.	408-470-7170	NA	Santa Clara
Cirtec Medical (HQ)	Manufacturer of complex implantable device manufacturing, medical device solutions, and smart solutions for highly complex miniaturization.	408-395-0443	NA	Los Gatos
Convergent Laser Technologies (HQ)	Provider of medical laser systems and fiber optic devices. The company deals with training and product support services.	510-832-2130	NA	Alameda
N Conversion Devices Inc (HQ)	Provider of medical power supply solutions.	714-898-6551	11-50	Huntington Beach
Earlens Corp (HQ)	Manufacturer of medical devices such as contact hearing devices and sensorineural and conductive hearing impairment.	650-366-9000	NA	Menlo Park
Emboline Inc (HQ)	Developer of cardiovascular embolic protection devices for transcatheter and surgical cardiac procedures.	831-900-5020	NA	Santa Cruz
Hospital Systems Inc (HQ)	Manufacturer of lighting, electrical and architectural products, and related supplies. The company is engaged in installation services.	925-427-7800	NA	Pittsburg
InterVene Inc (HQ)	Provider of medical devices such as blueleaf endovenous valve formation system to treat severe venous disease in the legs.	650-351-6725	NA	S San Francisco
Lifescience Plus Inc (HQ)	Developer of wound care technology solutions and its applications include surgery, dentistry, and public safety.	650-565-8172	NA	Mountain View
LIM innovations Inc (HQ)	Designer and manufacturer of prosthetic sockets for amputees. The company offers custom-molded, adjustable, and modular prosthetic sockets.	844-888-8546	NA	San Francisco
Mid Labs Inc (HQ)	Manufacturer of ophthalmic products such as vitreous cutters, titanium forceps, and related accessories.	510-357-3952	NA	San Leandro
Neodyne Biosciences Inc (HQ)	Manufacturer of embrace devices and it helps in the concealment of scars. The company serves patients.	800-519-7127	NA	Newark
N Neotech Products Inc (HQ)	Manufacturer of medical products.	661-775-7466	NA	Valencia
NewGen Surgical Inc (HQ)	Designer of single use medical devices. The company offers skin staplers, needle counters, and procedure kit packaging trays.	855-295-4500	NA	San Rafael
Nidek Inc (RH)	Manufacturer of ophthalmic devices. The company also offers refractive systems and diagnostic products to the medical industry.	800-223-9044	NA	Fremont
Penumbra Inc (HQ)	Manufacturer of interventional therapy devices. The company develops products to treat challenging medical conditions.	510-748-3200	NA	Alameda
Prosurg Inc (HQ)	Manufacturer of medical devices. The company offers products for women's and men's healthcare, urological and gynecological disorders.	408-945-4044	NA	San Jose
Providence Medical Technology Inc (HQ)	Developer of medical devices and technologies such as dtrax spinal systems, cavux cervical cages, and ally screw systems for cervical spine care.	415-923-9376	NA	Pleasanton
Pulsar Vascular Inc (HQ)	Manufacturer of endovascular diseases and it focuses on the treatment of complex aneurysms. The company is engaged in clinical trials.	408-260-9264	NA	San Jose

COMPANY NAME	PRODUCT / SERVICE	PHONE	EMP	CITY
Qview Medical (HQ)	Provider of assistance in the review of 3D automated breast ultrasound. The company offers services to the radiologists.	650-397-5174	NA	Los Altos
Renovorx Inc (HQ)	Manufacturer of medical devices. The company develops solutions for targeted delivery of therapeutic and diagnostic agents.	650-284-4433	NA	Los Altos
N Salter Labs (HQ)	Manufacturer of surgical and medical instruments.	661-854-3166	501-1000	Arvin
Sanovas Inc (HQ)	Manufacturer of medical equipment. The company develops minimally invasive surgical tools and technologies.	415-729-9391	NA	San Rafael
Shen Wei USA Inc (HQ)	Manufacturer of disposable gloves and customizable products. The company offers services to the healthcare industry.	510-429-8692	NA	Union City
Starch Medical Inc (HQ)	Provider of hemostatic solutions. The company offers services to patients and serves the healthcare industry.	408-428-9818	NA	San Jose
Supracor Inc (HQ)	Developer of honeycomb products. The company's offerings include sandals, saddle pads, and related supplies.	408-432-1616	NA	San Jose
N Syneron Inc (HQ)	Manufacturer and distributor of aesthetic medical products including hair removal and wrinkle reduction.	949-716-6670	501-1000	Irvine
TTI Medical (HQ)	Designer and marketer of surgical instruments and medical devices. The company serves hospitals and the healthcare sector.	925-553-7828	NA	San Ramon
Tusker Medical Inc (HQ)	Developer of pediatric-focused technologies. The company specializes in the placement of tubes without general anesthetics.	650-223-6900	NA	Menlo Park
Varian Medical Systems Inc (BR)	Provider of radiation therapies for cancer. The company develops and markers different types of radiation technologies to cure various cancers.	408-321-9400	NA	Milpitas
Varian Medical Systems Inc (HQ)	Provider of radiation therapies for cancer. The company develops and markers different types of radiation technologies to cure various cancers.	650-493-4000	NA	Palo Alto
Velano Vascular Inc (HQ)	Manufacturer of needle-free devices for drawing blood from hospitalized patients. The company offers services to the medical industry.	844-835-2668	NA	San Francisco
VisionCare Ophthalmic Technologies Inc (HQ)	Manufacturer and marketer of implantable ophthalmic devices and technologies for improving vision of individuals with untreatable retinal disorders.	408-872-9393	NA	Saratoga
West Coast Surgical (HQ)	Manufacturer of surgical devices. The company offers designing, assembling and finishing of specialty surgical equipment.	650-728-8095	NA	Half Moon Bay
Zipline Medical Inc (HQ)	Developer of zip surgical skin closure devices for cardiology, orthopedics, dermatology, plastic reconstructive surgery, and emergency medicine.	408-412-7228	NA	Campbell

196 = Therapeutic Equipment

COMPANY NAME	PRODUCT / SERVICE	PHONE	EMP	CITY
Admecell Inc (HQ)	Manufacturer of ready to use products such as cell based, TRANSIL, and ELISA based assays for in-vitro therapeutic modeling and re-profiling.	510-522-4200	NA	Alameda
Alterg Inc (HQ)	Provider of new technologies and products such as anti-gravity treadmills and bionic leg for physical therapy and athletic training.	510-270-5900	NA	Fremont
Amgen Inc (BR)	Provider of scientific applications services. The company's services include clinical trials, ethical research, biosimilars, and web resources.	650-244-2000	NA	S San Francisco
Apollomics Inc (HQ)	Developer of oncology therapeutics. The company focuses on discovering therapeutics for the immune system and molecular pathways to treat cancer.	925-272-4090	NA	Foster City
ARK Diagnostics Inc (HQ)	Manufacturer of in vitro diagnostic products for the treatment of cancer, veterinary, HIV/AIDS, antifungal drugs, and epilepsy and pain management.	877-869-2320	NA	Fremont
Backproject Corp (HQ)	Manufacturer of physical therapy equipment. The company specializes in vertical physical therapy equipment for musculoskeletal pain relief.	408-730-1111	NA	Sunnyvale
Cairn Biosciences (HQ)	Provider of therapeutic solutions for treating cancer. The company is involved in biotechnical research and commercial business.	415-503-1185	NA	San Francisco
Cala Health Inc (HQ)	Provider of therapeutic solutions. The company focuses on the development of neuro peripheral therapy to treating chronic diseases.	415-890-3961	NA	Burlingame
Calithera Biosciences Inc (HQ)	Developer of small molecule drugs directed against tumor metabolism and tumor immunology targets for the treatment of cancer.	650-870-1000	NA	S San Francisco
Caribou Biosciences Inc (HQ)	Developer of cellular engineering and analysis solutions. The company is involved in applied biological research.	510-982-6030	NA	Berkeley
Circuit Therapeutics Inc (HQ)	Focuses on drug discovery and development as well as forging direct therapeutic applications of optogenetics.	650-324-9400	NA	Menlo Park
Dendreon Pharmaceuticals LLC (HQ)	Provider of biotechnology services. The company provides therapeutics for the treatment of cancer employing active cellular immunotherapy.	877-256-4545	NA	Seal Beach
Directed Light Inc (HQ)	Manufacturer of industrial and scientific laser components. The company offers laser welding, cutting, drilling, ablation, and marking services.	408-321-8500	NA	San Jose
Eigen (HQ)	Manufacturer of cardiology and radiology imaging products. The company serves urologists and radiation oncologists.	530-274-1240	NA	Grass Valley
Evidation Health Inc (HQ)	Provider of digital health solutions for healthcare providers, payers, pharma/biotech, and digital health companies.	650-727-5557	NA	San Mateo
Glycomine Inc (HQ)	Developer of therapy solutions for the treatment of orphan diseases of glycosylation. The company focuses on genetic disorders of lipid glycosylation and protein.	650-401-2016	NA	San Carlos

COMPANY NAME	PRODUCT / SERVICE	PHONE	EMP	CITY
Gynesonics (HQ)	Manufacturer and developer of therapeutic devices and related supplies for the treatment of uterine fibroids in women.	650-216-3860	NA	Redwood City
Health Advances LLC (BR)	Provider of consulting services to the healthcare industry. The company offers clinical development, product positioning, lifecycle management, and more.	415-834-0800	NA	San Francisco
N Holman Group (HQ)	Provider of behavioral healthcare programs and other services for employers and others.	818-704-1444	51-200	Northridge
Kucklick Design (HQ)	Designer and developer of medical illustration products. The company's portfolio includes NovaSom system, Starion devices, and Extravasate.	408-353-1508	NA	Los Gatos
LimFlow Inc (BR)	Designer and developer of LimFlow percutaneous deep vein arterialization system to restore blood flow to the ischemic foot.	888-478-7705	NA	Santa Clara
Lorom West (HQ)	Manufacturer of PCB assemblies, turnkey OEM/ODM products and custom cable and wire harnesses. The company offers industry solutions.	919-535-5830	NA	Fremont
Medtronic CardioVascular Inc (BR)	Provider of disease management services. The company specializes in cardiovascular, diabetes, surgical technologies, and spinal and biologics.	707-525-0111	NA	Santa Rosa
Mercator Medsystems Inc (HQ)	Developer of therapeutics for vascular disease, oncology and regenerative medicine, and treatment of hypertension.	510-614-4550	NA	Emeryville
Modulus Data Systems (HQ)	Provider digital clinical cell (tally) counters. The company's products include Diffcount III, Comp-U-Diff, and Uro-Comp.	650-365-3111	NA	Redwood City
Nanomix Inc (HQ)	Manufacturer of diagnostic systems and supplies. The company is engaged in product development services.	510-428-5300	NA	Emeryville
Nevro Corp (HQ)	Developer of new high-frequency stimulation technology for improving the role of spinal cord stimulation in the treatment of chronic pain.	650-251-0005	NA	Redwood City
OrthoTrophix Inc (HQ)	Developer of therapies for medical needs of patients. The company specializes in regeneration of articular cartilage in knee and other joints.	510-488-3832	NA	Oakland
Paramit Corp (HQ)	Manufacturer of medical devices. The company is engaged in the planning and also implementation of strategies.	408-782-5600	NA	Morgan Hill
Pelvalon Inc (HQ)	Provider of non-surgical therapy such as uninflated and inflated devices that offers immediate results for women experiencing loss of bowel control.	650-276-0130	NA	Santa Clara
Profusa Inc (HQ)	Focuses on the development of biointegrated sensors. The company offers services to the environment sector.	415-655-9861	NA	Emeryville
Pulmonx Corp (HQ)	Manufacturer of medical devices. The company focuses on developing both diagnostic and therapeutic technologies for Interventional Pulmonology.	650-364-0400	NA	Redwood City
Semi-Probes Inc (HQ)	Manufacturer and supplier of probe cards and tester interfaces. The company's services include design, installation, and delivery.	408-866-6535	NA	San Jose
Trellis Bioscience LLC (HQ)	Developer of human antibody therapeutics as treatment for infectious disease and oncology indications.	650-838-1400	NA	Redwood City
TriReme Medical LLC (RH)	Developer of differentiated therapeutic solutions. The company manufactures and distributes the chocolate and glider families of angioplasty balloons.	925-931-1300	NA	Pleasanton
Vistagen Therapeutics Inc (HQ)	Developer of medicine to treat depression, cancer and diseases and disorders involving the central nervous system.	650-577-3600	NA	S San Francisco
XMS Corp (HQ)	Manufacturer and distributor of medical devices. The company specializes in cost effective, cutting edge radiation therapy equipment.	916-435-0267	NA	Rocklin

198 = Medical Imaging and X-Ray Apparatus

COMPANY NAME	PRODUCT / SERVICE	PHONE	EMP	CITY
Accsys Technology Inc (HQ)	Manufacturer of ion linear accelerator systems used in medical imaging devices, industrial applications and in research.	925-462-6949	NA	Pleasanton
Bioclinica Inc (HQ)	Developer of medical therapies. The company specializes in medical imaging services, cardiac safety, and enterprise eClinical platforms.	415-817-8900	NA	Newark
BioTrace Medical Inc (HQ)	Manufacturer of medical devices. The company specializes in cardiac pacing device which can treat reversible symptomatic bradycardia.	650-779-4999	NA	Menlo Park
Boston Scientific Corp (BR)	Manufacturer of baskets, forceps, imaging systems, needles, pacemakers, CTO and direct visualization systems.	408-935-3400	NA	San Jose
CapsoVision (HQ)	Specializes in the diagnostic imaging of the gastrointestinal systems. The company offers services to hospitals and patients.	408-624-1488	NA	Saratoga
CenterVue Inc (BR)	Designer and manufacturer of medical devices for the diagnosis and management of ocular pathologies.	408-988-8404	NA	Fremont
D-EYE (BR)	Designer and manufacturer of diagnostic instruments. The company offers smartphone based retinal imaging systems for clinical assessments.	401-473-6323	NA	Truckee
Dicom Systems Inc (HQ)	Provider of enterprise imaging, interoperability, and teleradiology solutions. The company offers services to patients.	415-684-8790	NA	Campbell
Digital Artforms Inc (HQ)	Provider of immersive 3D interaction for specialized markers and applications including medicine, security, and military/command and control.	408-356-6169	NA	Los Gatos
El Portal Imaging Center (HQ)	Specializes in diagnostic imaging solutions. The company serves hospitals, clinics, and the healthcare sector.	209-384-4250	NA	Merced

COMPANY NAME	PRODUCT / SERVICE	PHONE	EMP	CITY
Hesco (HQ)	Provider of portable x-ray imaging services. The company offer services for power plants, bridges, dams, refineries, and more.	510-568-1380	NA	San Leandro
Interson Corp (HQ)	Manufacturer of ultrasound products. The company offers services to offices, hospitals, and clinics around the world.	925-462-4948	NA	Pleasanton
MicroCam Inc (HQ)	Provider of medical devices. The company focuses on commercializing the plug and play micro imaging system.	415-729-9391	NA	San Rafael
Micropoint Bioscience Inc (HQ)	Developer of medical products and services for treatment of vascular disease such as peripheral artery disease and venous blood clots disorders.	408-588-1682	NA	Santa Clara
Procept Biorobotics (HQ)	Provider of healthcare services. The company primarily focuses on personalized image-guided waterjet tissue resection services.	650-232-7200	NA	Redwood City
Scimage Inc (HQ)	Provider of imaging solutions. The company also deals with clinical and cloud solutions and business intelligence support.	866-724-6243	NA	Los Altos
SST Group Inc (HQ)	Provider of medical displays, recorders, film digitizers, and related accessories. The company offers optical library support services.	408-350-3450	NA	Santa Clara
Suni Medical Imaging Inc (HQ)	Manufacturer of digital radiography. The company designs, develops, manufactures and sell digital sensors for the medical field.	408-227-6698	NA	San Jose
TechniQuip (HQ)	Supplier of lighting products. The company's offerings include illuminators, fiber optics, and video equipment.	925-251-9030	NA	Pleasanton
Trufocus Corp (HQ)	Supplier of x-ray products. The company's products are used in industrial, medical, aerospace, and analytical application.	831-761-9981	NA	Watsonville
Xoft Inc (HQ)	Developer of electronic brachytherapy systems. The company's products include rigid shield, vacuum pumps, and physics kits.	408-493-1500	NA	San Jose

200 = Adapters

COMPANY NAME	PRODUCT / SERVICE	PHONE	EMP	CITY
Accusilicon USA Inc (HQ)	Manufacturer of TCXO IC chips and designer and developer of high frequency oscillators for the industrial sector.	408-256-0858	NA	Santa Clara
ADLINK Technology Inc (LH)	Designer and manufacturer of products for embedded computing, test and measurement, and automation applications. The company serves various sectors.	408-360-0200	NA	San Jose
Asteelflash (BR)	Provider of electronic manufacturing services. The company offers engineering design, contract manufacturing, and delivery services.	510-440-2840	NA	Fremont
N Capax Technologies Inc (HQ)	Designer and manufacturer of capacitors for commercial and military RF and Microwave applications.	661-257-7666	NA	Valencia
eze System (HQ)	Provider or monitoring and measuring solutions. The company's products include controllers, controller expansions, and sensors.	716-393-9330	NA	Folsom
Intilop Inc (HQ)	Provider of engineering design services. The company also develops and provides silicon IP products.	408-791-6700	NA	Milpitas
Iris AO Inc (HQ)	Manufacturer of microelectromechanical based optical systems. The company's applications include biomedical imaging and portable laser communications.	510-849-2375	NA	Berkeley
N Myers Power Products Inc (HQ)	Manufacturer of electrical distribution products, emergency power systems, medium voltage switchgear, powerhouses and much more.	909-923-1800	5001-10000	Corona
Phihong USA Corp (HQ)	Provider of power solutions in the telecom sector. The company also offers data solutions in industrial and personal electronic markers.	510-445-0100	NA	Fremont
Pragmatics Technologies Inc (HQ)	Provider of electromechanical interface solutions. The company deals with the development of custom and standard test interfaces.	408-289-8202	NA	San Jose
Quail Electronics Inc (HQ)	Manufacturer of power cord supplies for the OEM market. The company offers solutions for power cords, current cords, and adapters, and traveler kits.	925-373-6700	NA	Livermore
Quality Quartz Engineering Inc (HQ)	Designer and manufacturer of solid quartz products for solar, fiber optic, semiconductor, and lighting industries.	510-745-9200	NA	Newark
Quest Microwave Inc (HQ)	Provider of ferrite products for the microwave electronics industry. The company offers both standard and custom designs.	408-778-4949	NA	Morgan Hill
Rathbun Associates (HQ)	Distributor and reseller of converters. The company offers thermal management solutions, specialty tapes, and protective products.	510-661-0950	NA	Fremont
Schmartboard Inc (HQ)	Specializes in the production of hand soldering components. The company's products are used in sensor and USB technologies.	510-744-9900	NA	Fremont
Tamura Corporation of America (BR)	Manufacturer of DC power modules, current sensor products, telecom transformers, and LED products. The company is involved in distribution services.	760-871-2009	NA	Escondido
Ten Pao International Inc (HQ)	Manufacturer of power supply systems such as switchings, displays, and traditional linear transformers.	408-389-3560	NA	Sunnyvale

201 = Anodes/Cathodes/Electrodes

COMPANY NAME	PRODUCT / SERVICE	PHONE	EMP	CITY
Rose Electronics Distributing Company Inc (HQ)	Provider of batteries and power solutions. The company primarily serves original equipment manufacturers such as VRLA batteries and lithium ion batteries.	408-943-0200	NA	San Jose

202 = Cable & Wiring Assemblies

COMPANY NAME	PRODUCT / SERVICE	PHONE	EMP	CITY
Aimer Corp (HQ)	Provider of thermal management products. The company also offers connectors, PCB boards, cables, and mechanical parts.	408-260-8588	NA	Santa Clara
Allwire Inc (HQ)	Provider of design, analysis, and programming services for businesses. The company is also involved in web hosting and technical support.	559-665-4893	NA	Chowchilla
Andrew Ndt Engineering Corp (HQ)	Manufacturer of probes, ultrasonic transducers, diamond cutting tools, proximity sensors, cables, and offers calibration services.	408-710-0342	NA	San Jose
ASCENX Technologies Inc (HQ)	Provider of engineering services to the semiconductor industry. The company is also engaged in contract manufacturing and repair services.	408-945-1997	NA	Fremont
Assembly Tek (HQ)	Manufacturer of custom cables. The company offers services like design, laminating, JIT programs, and wire preparation.	831-439-0800	NA	Scotts Valley
Blue Danube Systems Inc (BR)	Designer and developer of mobile wireless access solutions that increase network capacity. The company serves the industrial sector.	650-316-5010	NA	Santa Clara
N Calpico Inc (HQ)	Manufacturer and distributor of underground piping products.	650-588-2241	1-10	S San Francisco
Compass Made (HQ)	Manufacturer of custom cables and harnesses and distributor of electronic components. The company also manufactures electromechanical products.	510-656-4700	NA	Fremont
N Connectec Company Inc (HQ)	Manufacturer of modeling, fabrication and tooling services.	949-252-1077	NA	Irvine
N Electro Adapter Inc (HQ)	Manufacturer of connector accessories and adapters.	818-998-1198	51-200	Chatsworth
Ettus Research LLC (DH)	Provider of software defined radio systems for research, academic, industrial, and defense applications.	408-610-6399	NA	Santa Clara
eze System (HQ)	Provider or monitoring and measuring solutions. The company's products include controllers, controller expansions, and sensors.	716-393-9330	NA	Folsom
GDM Electronic Medical (HQ)	Manufacturer of devices, electrical and electronics for medical, manufacturing and engineering industries.	408-945-4100	NA	San Jose
Greatlink International Inc (RH)	Manufacturer of cable assemblies and related products for the medical, aerospace, and automotive industries.	510-657-1667	NA	Fremont
N Hamrock Inc (HQ)	Provider of fabricated wire products.	562-944-0255	1-10	Santa Fe Springs
N Hi Rel Connectors Inc (HQ)	Designer, manufacturer and distributor of electrical connectors, interconnect systems, cables and connector accessories.	909-626-1820	NA	Claremont
Indtec Corp (HQ)	Manufacturer of printed circuit boards. The company specializes in assemblies, wires, cables, automated surface mounting, and harness services.	831-582-9388	NA	Marina
International Electronic Components Inc (RH)	Distributor of printed circuit boards, consumables, and inspection and measuring equipment. The company is engaged in installation services.	408-496-0474	NA	Santa Clara
Lorom West (HQ)	Manufacturer of PCB assemblies, turnkey OEM/ODM products and custom cable and wire harnesses. The company offers industry solutions.	919-535-5830	NA	Fremont
Mac Cal (HQ)	Provider of sheet metals, assembly, cables and harnesses and engineering tools. The company deals with engineering services.	408-441-1435	NA	San Jose
MC Electronics (HQ)	Provider of turnkey solution for contract manufacturing. The company focuses on cable and harness assembly and full system integration.	831-637-1651	NA	Hollister
Morgan Royce Industries Inc (HQ)	Developer and manufacturer of custom cables, wire harness, and PCB assemblies. The company offers project management and quality control services.	510-440-8500	NA	Fremont
Murdoc Technology (HQ)	Manufacturer of electronics. The company primarily offers precision and wire harnesses and cables to various sectors.	559-497-1580	NA	Fresno
NPI Solutions Inc (HQ)	Provider of design, engineering, and custom manufacturing solutions. The company offers on-site engineering services.	408-944-9178	NA	Morgan Hill
Pactech Inc (HQ)	Provider of computer cables, cooling items, and other components. The company also offers networking products.	408-526-9363	NA	San Jose
Pan-International (LH)	Supplier of computer cables, wiring, switch boxes, and connectors. The company is involved in design, installation, and delivery services.	510-623-3898	NA	Fremont
PEC Manufacturing (HQ)	Provider of customized electromechanical, electronic, and mechanical solutions such as cable and harness assemblies and electro-mechanical assemblies.	408-577-1839	NA	San Jose
Quail Electronics Inc (HQ)	Manufacturer of power cord supplies for the OEM market. The company offers solutions for power cords, current cords, and adapters, and traveler kits.	925-373-6700	NA	Livermore
Qualdeval International (HQ)	Supplier of high-pressure fluid flow and special core analysis equipment. The company offers PCB fabrication and assembly, and other services.	844-247-2523	NA	Fremont
Redpark Product Development (HQ)	Manufacturer of connectivity accessories for iPhone and iPad. The company's products include lightning cables and 30-pin cables.	510-594-1034	NA	Walnut Creek
Sicon International Inc (HQ)	Manufacturer of electronic components. The company specializes in the fabrication of connectors, cables, circuit boards, and molded cables.	408-954-9880	NA	San Jose
Ultra-Flex Inc (HQ)	Designer of component manufacturing solutions. The company offers springs, fasteners, castings, machined parts, and hardware items.	650-728-6060	NA	Half Moon Bay

203 = Capacitors

Aborn Electronics Inc (HQ)	Manufacturer of fiber optic systems. The company specializes in the design and manufacture of fiber optic receivers and transmitters.	408-436-5445	NA	San Jose

COMPANY NAME	PRODUCT / SERVICE	PHONE	EMP	CITY
Caltron Components Corp (HQ)	Distributor of electronic capacitors and resistors. The company also focuses on semiconductor products.	408-748-2140	NA	Santa Clara
EoPlex Inc (BR)	Creator of HVAM technology and process for advanced 3D-printed components for mobile devices, IoT, automotive, medical, and wearable applications.	408-638-5100	NA	San Jose
eze System (HQ)	Provider or monitoring and measuring solutions. The company's products include controllers, controller expansions, and sensors.	716-393-9330	NA	Folsom
NIC Components Corp (BR)	Designer, manufacturer, and supplier of passive components. The company offers ceramic capacitors, power inductors, and current sensing resistors.	669-342-3960	NA	San Jose
Omnicor (HQ)	Provider of network testing tools, vacuum capacitors, and interrupters and IP performance test systems.	650-572-0122	NA	Foster City
Pacific Capacitor Co (HQ)	Manufacturer of high voltage capacitors for the electronics industry. The company is engaged in sales and installation services.	408-778-6670	NA	Morgan Hill

204 = Chips/Substrates/Wafers

COMPANY NAME	PRODUCT / SERVICE	PHONE	EMP	CITY
Aborn Electronics Inc (HQ)	Manufacturer of fiber optic systems. The company specializes in the design and manufacture of fiber optic receivers and transmitters.	408-436-5445	NA	San Jose
Advanced Component Labs (HQ)	Manufacturer of flip chips, thermal vias, build ups, and related supplies. The company's services include drilling, lamination, and engineering.	408-327-0200	NA	Santa Clara
AG Microsystems Inc (HQ)	Provider of testing and development in the areas of micro electro mechanical systems and micro optics.	408-834-4888	NA	Santa Clara
Amulet Technologies LLC (HQ)	Provider of embedded graphical user interface solutions. The company also specializes in modules and chips.	408-374-4956	NA	Campbell
C&P Microsystems LLC (HQ)	Manufacturer and seller of paper cutter control systems. The company offers microcip, cutternet, and micro facts.	707-776-4500	NA	Petaluma
N Condor Reliability Services Inc (HQ)	Provider of innovative solutions to government and industry.	408-486-9600	51-200	Santa Clara
Dolphin Technology Inc (DH)	Provider of silicon-proven Internet protocol for memory, standard cells, input and output, memory controllers, and memory test and repair.	408-392-0012	NA	San Jose
Fortemedia Inc (HQ)	Provider of voice processing integrated circuits. The company also offers related hardware and software components.	408-861-8088	NA	Santa Clara
Intel Corp (HQ)	Designer, developer, and marketer of processors and motherboards. The company also focuses on tablets, laptops, desktops, and other devices.	408-765-8080	NA	Santa Clara
Intrinsic-Id Inc (HQ)	Designer of security solutions. The company offers services to semiconductor companies and device manufacturers.	408-933-0080	NA	Sunnyvale
LSI Design & Integration Corp (HQ)	Designer and manufacturer of custom chips. The company offers storage, communication, imaging, and memory components.	408-283-8540	NA	San Jose
Mixel Inc (HQ)	Designer and developer of mixed-signal Internet protocol cores for the semiconductor and electronics industries.	408-436-8500	NA	San Jose
Noel Technologies Inc (HQ)	Provider of lithography, thin film deposition, and water recycling solutions. The company serves MEMS, defense, life science, and other sectors.	408-374-9549	NA	Campbell
NTK Technologies Inc (HQ)	Manufacturer of bio ceramics, oxygen sensors, ceramic heater, and transistor packages for the medical and telecommunication applications.	408-727-5180	NA	Santa Clara
N Piezo-Metrics Inc (HQ)	Manufacturer and distributor of semiconductor strain gages, pressure transducers, temperature sensors and measuring systems.	805-522-4676	NA	Simi Valley
N Polyfet Rf Devices Inc (HQ)	Provider of RF amplifier design assistance, and RF mosfet transistors.	805-484-4210	11-50	Camarillo
POLYSTAK Inc (HQ)	Provider of silicon based multi chip package products as well as package stacking solutions and repair services of components and modules.	408-441-1400	NA	San Jose
Sperient Corporation Inc (HQ)	Designer and developer of electronic systems. The company's applications include telemedicine and robotic sensing.	925-447-3333	NA	Livermore
WaferMasters Inc (HQ)	Provider of thermal processing services. The company also focuses on diagnostic metrology and design and consulting services.	408-451-0850	NA	Dublin
Xperi Corp (HQ)	Provider of miniaturization technology services for electronic devices. The company offers micro-electronics, and imaging and optics services.	408-321-6000	NA	San Jose

206 = Electronic Connectors & Subsystems

COMPANY NAME	PRODUCT / SERVICE	PHONE	EMP	CITY
A'n D Cable Products Inc (HQ)	Manufacturer, installer, and reseller of cable accessories. The company focuses on cable management and labeling solutions.	925-672-3005	NA	Concord
Advanced Microwave Inc (HQ)	Manufacturer of military electronic components and subsystems. The company offers amplifiers, mixers, threshold detectors, and converter products.	408-739-4214	NA	Sunnyvale
Aimer Corp (HQ)	Provider of thermal management products. The company also offers connectors, PCB boards, cables, and mechanical parts.	408-260-8588	NA	Santa Clara
N Alloy Tool Steel Inc (HQ)	Distributor of stainless steel, alloy tool steel, and titanium alloys.	562-921-8605	1-10	Santa Fe Springs
N Altemp Alloys Inc (HQ)	Distributor of high-temperature alloys such as inconel, hastelloy steel, and other materials.	714-279-0249	11-50	Orange
N Brown Metals Co (HQ)	Manufacturer and distributor of stainless steel strip, sheet, copper strip and much more.	909-484-3124	1-10	Rancho Cucamonga
N Coast Aluminum and Architectural Inc (HQ)	Manufacturer and installer of switchgear control panels, test stands and specialized electrical equipment.	562-946-6061	NA	Santa Fe Springs

COMPANY NAME	PRODUCT / SERVICE	PHONE	EMP	CITY
N Del Paso Pipe & Steel Inc (HQ)	Manufacturer of pipes, steel products such as channel iron, angle and square tubing.	916-992-6500	NA	Sacramento
N Dix Metals Inc (HQ)	Provider of precision-ground, machine-ready metal blanks and other materials.	714-677-0800	NA	Huntington Beach
N Ed Fagan Inc (HQ)	Manufacturer of metals and alloys for aerospace, aviation, defense, electronics, telecommunications and other sectors.	562-431-2568	NA	Los Alamitos
EoPlex Inc (BR)	Creator of HVAM technology and process for advanced 3D-printed components for mobile devices, IoT, automotive, medical, and wearable applications.	408-638-5100	NA	San Jose
High Connection Density Inc (HQ)	Supplier of electronic packaging solutions and connection technologies. The company serves communications, medical, military, and aerospace fields.	408-743-9700	NA	Sunnyvale
Joy Signal Technology LLC (HQ)	Developer of PCB and differential terminators, MMCX plug assemblies, single signal carrier systems, Z-Trace connectors, and custom solutions.	530-891-3551	NA	Chico
N Merit USA (HQ)	Provider of steel processing services for steel coils.	925-427-6427	NA	Pittsburg
Neoconix Inc (HQ)	Provider of electrical interconnect solutions. The company offers LGA sockets, board-to-board interposers, and standard products.	408-530-9393	NA	San Jose
Peridot Corp (HQ)	Provider of design for manufacturing and packaging. The company also manufacturers of medical components, miniature component and general product prototypes.	925-461-8830	NA	Pleasanton
Pragmatics Technologies Inc (HQ)	Provider of electromechanical interface solutions. The company deals with the development of custom and standard test interfaces.	408-289-8202	NA	San Jose
N Rickard Metals Inc (HQ)	Provider of engineering and supply chain management services.	909-947-4922	NA	Ontario
N Southbay Foundry Inc (HQ)	Manufacturer of aerial platforms, scissor lifts, excavators, wheel loaders, crushers, crawlers and much more.	619-956-2780	NA	Santee
Ten Pao International Inc (HQ)	Manufacturer of power supply systems such as switchings, displays, and traditional linear transformers.	408-389-3560	NA	Sunnyvale
Thor Electronics of California (HQ)	Manufacturer of special connectors, molded cable assemblies and covers, harness assemblies, and electro-mechanical devices.	831-758-6400	NA	Salinas
N Totten Tubes Inc (HQ)	Distributor of steel tubing and pipes.	626-812-0113	NA	Azusa
USAPEX (HQ)	Manufacturer of fiber optic products, metal and plastic machined parts, lead free solder pastes, liquid flux, power adapters, cables, and connectors.	408-730-9800	NA	Sunnyvale
N Wolf Metals Inc (HQ)	Manufacturer of metal products including stainless steel, aluminum, merchant bar, tubular, bright steel, and plate as well as being able to supply stamped and pressed products.	562-698-5410	1-10	Whittier

207 = Electronic Design/R&D Services

COMPANY NAME	PRODUCT / SERVICE	PHONE	EMP	CITY
Altest Corp (HQ)	Provider of PCB assembly and engineering solutions. The company offers services to the aerospace and commercial industries.	408-436-9900	NA	San Jose
Ampro Systems Inc (RH)	Manufacturer of printed circuit board assemblies. The company deals with procurement services and serves the government and military industries.	510-624-9000	NA	Fremont
AmTECH Microelectronics Inc (HQ)	Provider of manufacturing solutions. The company deals with PCB fabrication, machining, and assembly services.	408-612-8888	NA	Morgan Hill
AuSIM Inc (HQ)	Developer of audio simulation technology and products for auditory displays for mission-critical applications.	650-322-8746	NA	Mountain View
Avp Technology LLC (HQ)	Provider of thin film equipment services. The company provides custom designing, remanufacturing, and field services.	510-683-0157	NA	Fremont
Batchtest Corp (HQ)	Provider of embedded solutions. The company specializes in the design and manufacturing of industrial PC products.	408-454-8378	NA	Santa Clara
Bay Area Circuits Inc (HQ)	Provider of engineering services that include fabrication, layout, and design services to the original equipment manufacturers.	510-933-9000	NA	Fremont
Bestronics (HQ)	Provider of electronics manufacturing services. The company deals with product development, system integration, and prototyping services.	408-385-7777	NA	San Jose
C&P Microsystems LLC (HQ)	Manufacturer and seller of paper cutter control systems. The company offers microcip, cutternet, and micro facts.	707-776-4500	NA	Petaluma
C3Nano Inc (HQ)	Developer of transparent conductive ink and film such as touch sensors, OLED lighting and displays, EMI shielding for touch sensor and display industry.	510-259-9650	NA	Hayward
Century Technology Inc (HQ)	Provider of PCB assembly services. The company also offers distribution, testing, and wire harness services.	650-583-8908	NA	S San Francisco
Cordova Printed Circuits Inc (HQ)	Provider of flex circuits and printed circuit boards. The company focuses on sculptured flex circuits and multilayer flex circuits.	408-942-1100	NA	Milpitas
Cupertino Signal Processing (HQ)	Specializes in analog circuit analysis and evaluation services. The company offers technical documentation.	408-725-0846	NA	Cupertino
Dawn VME Products (HQ)	Designer and manufacturer of enclosures, backplanes, chassis and card cage. The company also offers design services and power supplies.	510-657-4444	NA	Fremont
Dialog Semiconductor Inc (BR)	Creator of mixed-signal integrated circuits. The company offers products such as audio, backlight LED, wireless audio, and home automation.	408-845-8500	NA	Santa Clara

COMPANY NAME	PRODUCT / SERVICE	PHONE	EMP	CITY
Digital Dynamics Inc (HQ)	Supplier of embedded process control products. The company is also engaged in manufacturing OEM control system products.	831-438-4444	NA	Scotts Valley
Dolphin Technology Inc (DH)	Provider of silicon-proven Internet protocol for memory, standard cells, input and output, memory controllers, and memory test and repair.	408-392-0012	NA	San Jose
DVK Integrated Services Inc (HQ)	Provider of turnkey services that include prototyping services, printed circuit board design, and engineering services.	408-436-0100	NA	San Jose
Ettus Research LLC (DH)	Provider of software defined radio systems for research, academic, industrial, and defense applications.	408-610-6399	NA	Santa Clara
GC Micro Corp (HQ)	Provider of IT hardware, software, and related products to corporate and government accounts. The company specializes in information technology.	707-789-0600	NA	Petaluma
Hildy Licht Company Inc (HQ)	Provider of electric assembly and manufacturing services. The company is engaged in engineering and prototyping.	650-962-9300	NA	Mountain View
Megaforce Corporation Inc (HQ)	Provider of supply chain, materials management, and test solutions. The company serves the industrial, commercial, and automotive sectors.	408-956-9989	NA	San Jose
Open Five Inc (HQ)	Provider of IP, foundry, test, and packaging technologies. The company's services include system design, manufacturing, and program management.	408-240-5700	NA	Milpitas
Palo Alto Research Center Inc (DH)	Provider of custom research services and intellectual property to global Fortune 500 companies and government agency partners.	650-812-4000	NA	Palo Alto
Rocket EMS Inc (HQ)	Provider of electronic manufacturing services. The company caters to high growth technology sectors.	408-727-3700	NA	Santa Clara
ROHM Semiconductor USA LLC (BR)	Manufacturer of amplifiers, clocks, modules, passive components, remote control receivers, and timers.	408-720-1900	NA	Santa Clara
Scepter Scientific Inc (HQ)	Provider of feasibility evaluations, electronic, optical, and mechanical engineering, and prototype development services.	925-373-4802	NA	Livermore
Schmartboard Inc (HQ)	Specializes in the production of hand soldering components. The company's products are used in sensor and USB technologies.	510-744-9900	NA	Fremont
Surface Art Engineering Inc (HQ)	Provider of Printed Circuit Board Assembly (PCA) and mechanical assembly for prototype, pre-production and production assemblies.	408-433-4700	NA	San Jose
Tempo Automation (HQ)	Specializes in printed circuit board assemblies. The company is engaged in design and delivery services.	415-320-1261	NA	San Francisco
Vitron Electronic Services Inc (HQ)	Provider of electronics manufacturing services. The company deals with product development, system integration, and prototyping services.	408-251-1600	NA	San Jose

208 = Integrated Circuits

COMPANY NAME	PRODUCT / SERVICE	PHONE	EMP	CITY
Accusilicon USA Inc (HQ)	Manufacturer of TCXO IC chips and designer and developer of high frequency oscillators for the industrial sector.	408-256-0858	NA	Santa Clara
Advanced Component Labs (HQ)	Manufacturer of flip chips, thermal vias, build ups, and related supplies. The company's services include drilling, lamination, and engineering.	408-327-0200	NA	Santa Clara
Advanced Linear Devices Inc (HQ)	Designer and manufacturer of precision CMOS analog integrated circuits. The company serves industrial control, computer, automotive, and other sectors.	408-747-1155	NA	Sunnyvale
Aitech International Corp (HQ)	Provider of video conversion technology solutions. The company provides scan converters, wireless products, HDTV tuners, HDMI switches, and cables.	408-991-9699	NA	Sunnyvale
AKM Semiconductor Inc (HQ)	Designer and manufacturer of mixed signal integrated circuits. The company serves consumer electronics, industrial, and automotive sectors.	408-436-8580	NA	San Jose
AmTECH Microelectronics Inc (HQ)	Provider of manufacturing solutions. The company deals with PCB fabrication, machining, and assembly services.	408-612-8888	NA	Morgan Hill
Aquantia Corp (HQ)	Provider of software solutions such as signal processing, agile management, and technical support. The company serves the IT sector.	408-228-8300	NA	San Jose
Arteris Inc (HQ)	Provider of interconnect semiconductor IP solutions to system-on-chip makers and serves networking, automotive, video and mobile-phone processors.	408-470-7300	NA	Campbell
Azimuth Industrial Company Inc (HQ)	Provider of integrated circuit assembly and packaging services. The company specializes in prototyping and production.	510-441-6000	NA	Union City
Broadcom Inc (HQ)	Developer of digital and analog semiconductors. The company also specializes in optical communication semiconductors.	408-433-8000	NA	San Jose
C&P Microsystems LLC (HQ)	Manufacturer and seller of paper cutter control systems. The company offers microcip, cutternet, and micro facts.	707-776-4500	NA	Petaluma
CAD PROS PCB Design Inc (HQ)	Designer and manufacturer of printed circuit boards. The company offers services to the residential and commercial sectors.	408-734-9600	NA	San Jose
Caltron Components Corp (HQ)	Distributor of electronic capacitors and resistors. The company also focuses on semiconductor products.	408-748-2140	NA	Santa Clara
Capella Microsystems Inc (HQ)	Developer of integrated technology solutions for IC design. The company is involved in installation and technical support.	408-988-8000	NA	Santa Clara
Chrontel Inc (HQ)	Designer of mixed-signal IC products. The company's products find application in personal computer and telecom sectors.	408-383-9328	NA	San Jose

COMPANY NAME	PRODUCT / SERVICE	PHONE	EMP	CITY
Dialog Semiconductor (RH)	Manufacturer of AC/DC and LED SSL products. The company's products include home appliances, smart meters, power adapters, and backlighting devices.	408-374-4200	NA	Campbell
DVK Integrated Services Inc (HQ)	Provider of turnkey services that include prototyping services, printed circuit board design, and engineering services.	408-436-0100	NA	San Jose
EoPlex Inc (BR)	Creator of HVAM technology and process for advanced 3D-printed components for mobile devices, IoT, automotive, medical, and wearable applications.	408-638-5100	NA	San Jose
Etron Technology America Inc (RH)	Provider of integrated circuits for applications, such as storage device, display, handset, PDA, and multimedia device.	408-987-2255	NA	Santa Clara
Exatron Inc (HQ)	Manufacturer of automatic test equipment and IC handlers. The company also specializes in open short testers.	800-392-8766	NA	San Jose
Fuji Electric Corp of America (BR)	Provider of electric technology services. The company offers solutions for disk media, power supply, industrial systems, and radiation.	510-440-1060	NA	Fremont
Global Unichip Corp (HQ)	Provider of technology and embedded CPU design services. The company's services include package engineering, test engineering, and supply chain management.	408-382-8900	NA	San Jose
Infineon Technologies North American Corp (BR)	Provider of semiconductor and system solutions. The company focuses on mobile security, sensors, power management, and RF.	866-951-9519	NA	Morgan Hill
Integrated Silicon Solution Inc (HQ)	Designer and developer of high performance integrated circuits. The company also focuses on the marketing aspects.	408-969-6600	NA	Milpitas
Intel Corp (HQ)	Designer, developer, and marketer of processors and motherboards. The company also focuses on tablets, laptops, desktops, and other devices.	408-765-8080	NA	Santa Clara
Intest Ems Products (BR)	Manufacturer of semiconductors to test integrated circuits. The company also focuses on testing wafer products.	408-678-9167	NA	Fremont
Ise Labs Inc (HQ)	Provider of semiconductor services. The company offers services such as production test, test interface, and mechanical testing.	510-687-2500	NA	Fremont
Ixys Corp (HQ)	Manufacturer of power semiconductor products. The company specializes in power semiconductors, integrated circuits, and radio frequency power.	408-457-9000	NA	Milpitas
Linear Integrated Systems (HQ)	Manufacturer of semiconductor products. The company offers bipolar transistors, input protection diodes, resistors, and low leakage amplifiers.	510-490-9160	NA	Fremont
Micro Lithography Inc (HQ)	Manufacturer of pellicles using high end equipment for the production of frames and engineering parts, automatic anodizing lines, and chemical labs.	408-747-1769	NA	Sunnyvale
Mixed Signal Integration (HQ)	Specializes in the design, manufacture and sale of turnkey analog and mixed-signal standard products and custom ASICs.	408-434-6305	NA	San Jose
Mixel Inc (HQ)	Designer and developer of mixed-signal Internet protocol cores for the semiconductor and electronics industries.	408-436-8500	NA	San Jose
Mosaic Industries Inc (HQ)	Developer and manufacturer of embedded computers for instruments and automation. The company serves sensor calibration and PID control needs.	510-790-8222	NA	Newark
Nikon Precision Inc (HQ)	Manufacturer of optical lenses and precision equipment. The company is also the supplier of step-and-repeat and step-and-scan lithography systems.	650-508-4674	NA	Belmont
PDF Solutions Inc (HQ)	Provider of yield improvement technologies and services for the integrated circuit manufacturing process.	408-280-7900	NA	Santa Clara
Photo Etch Technology (BR)	Provider of stainless steel stencils. The company offers epoxy stencils, precision metal parts, fixture pallets, mesh screens, and artwork services.	408-988-0220	NA	Santa Clara
Power Integrations (HQ)	Supplier of electronic components. The company's products include AC-DC converters and LED drivers.	408-414-9200	NA	San Jose
Pyramid Semiconductor Corp (HQ)	Provider of assembly services. The company is focused in the assembly of monolithic ceramic products and multi-chip modules.	408-734-8200	NA	Sunnyvale
Qulsar Inc (HQ)	Specializes in packaging, refinement, and distribution of precise time synchronization. The company serves the telecom and networking industries.	408-715-1098	NA	San Jose
Robson Technologies Inc (HQ)	Provider of customizable hardware interfaces that bridge the gap between the test device and the measurement system.	408-779-8008	NA	Morgan Hill
Schmartboard Inc (HQ)	Specializes in the production of hand soldering components. The company's products are used in sensor and USB technologies.	510-744-9900	NA	Fremont
SiTune Corporation Inc (HQ)	Provider of integrated circuits and systems. The company offers spectrum reception and concurrent tuners.	408-324-1711	NA	San Jose
STMicroelectronics (BR)	Provider of analog, mixed signal ICs, transistor, and memories. The company also offers microcontroller products and services.	408-919-8400	NA	Santa Clara
Summit Wireless Technologies Inc (HQ)	Developer of wireless audio integrated circuits. The company specializes in semiconductors, home entertainment, and pro-audio markers.	408-627-4716	NA	San Jose
Tela Innovations Inc (HQ)	Provider of lithography optimized solutions. The company's services include design, implementation, and technical support.	408-558-6300	NA	Los Gatos

COMPANY NAME	PRODUCT / SERVICE	PHONE	EMP	CITY
Tenergy Corp (HQ)	Designer and manufacturer of batteries and chargers. The company serves medical, consumer electronics, data management, military, and other sectors.	510-687-0388	NA	Fremont
VeriSilicon Inc (HQ)	Provider of IC design services specializing in custom silicon solutions. The company also offers SOC turnkey services.	408-844-8560	NA	San Jose
Zilog Inc (DH)	Supplier of application-specific embedded system-on-chip (SoC) solutions for the industrial and consumer markers.	408-457-9000	NA	Milpitas

209 = Miscellaneous Electronic Devices

COMPANY NAME	PRODUCT / SERVICE	PHONE	EMP	CITY
Advanced Microwave Inc (HQ)	Manufacturer of military electronic components and subsystems. The company offers amplifiers, mixers, threshold detectors, and converter products.	408-739-4214	NA	Sunnyvale
Advantek Inc (BR)	Provider of packaging products. The company offers carrier and cover tapes, and tape and reel packaging products.	510-623-1877	NA	Hayward
Aitech International Corp (HQ)	Provider of video conversion technology solutions. The company provides scan converters, wireless products, HDTV tuners, HDMI switches, and cables.	408-991-9699	NA	Sunnyvale
Akon Inc (HQ)	Supplier of microwave products. The company focuses on airborne, ground, shipboard, and space applications.	408-432-8039	NA	San Jose
AM Fitzgerald & Associates LLC (HQ)	Provider of MEMS solutions. The company's products include piezoresistive cantilevers, ultrasound transducers, and infrared imagers.	650-347-6367	NA	Burlingame
Ampex Data Systems (HQ)	Manufacturer of digital storage systems. The company also offers airborne and ground systems and related video solutions.	650-367-2011	NA	Hayward
AmTECH Microelectronics Inc (HQ)	Provider of manufacturing solutions. The company deals with PCB fabrication, machining, and assembly services.	408-612-8888	NA	Morgan Hill
Andrew Ndt Engineering Corp (HQ)	Manufacturer of probes, ultrasonic transducers, diamond cutting tools, proximity sensors, cables, and offers calibration services.	408-710-0342	NA	San Jose
Anova Microsystems Inc (HQ)	Provider of rackmount server cabinets and system components. The company deals with storage and GPU solutions.	408-941-1888	NA	Los Altos
Apple Inc (HQ)	Designer and marketer of consumer electronics. The company also focuses on computer software and personal computers.	408-996-1010	NA	Cupertino
Applied Engineering (HQ)	Provider of contract electronics manufacturing services. The company also specializes in clean room assembly services.	408-286-2134	NA	San Jose
Applied Motion Products Inc (HQ)	Manufacturer of stepper drives and motors, gearheads, power supplies, and related accessories. The company offers technical support services.	831-761-6555	NA	Watsonville
N Apt Electronics Inc (HQ)	Manufacturer of automated electronics contract products and specializes in surface mount.	714-687-6760	51-200	Anaheim
ARBOR Solution Inc (RH)	Provider of embedded computing and networking solutions for the transportation, medical, automation, and military segments.	408-452-8900	NA	Fremont
N Artech Industries Inc (HQ)	Manufacturer and distributor of strain gauge load cells or force transducers.	951-276-3331	NA	Riverside
Azbil North America Inc (BR)	Designer, manufacturer, and supplier of medical devices. The company offers automation products, control products, and industrial automation systems.	408-245-3121	NA	Santa Clara
Bestronics (HQ)	Provider of electronics manufacturing services. The company deals with product development, system integration, and prototyping services.	408-385-7777	NA	San Jose
Betatron Inc (HQ)	Designer and manufacturer of PC board assemblies for the medical, telecommunication, industrial, commercial, and semiconductor markers.	408-453-1880	NA	San Jose
Brandt Electronics Inc (HQ)	Manufacturer of power supplies. The company specializes in the design and maintenance of power equipment used in military applications.	408-240-0004	NA	Milpitas
Bridgepoint Systems Inc (HQ)	Provider of security solutions such as CAC card readers, PIV card readers, and access control experts for government contractors and security integrators.	510-346-1510	NA	Berkeley
CAD PROS PCB Design Inc (HQ)	Designer and manufacturer of printed circuit boards. The company offers services to the residential and commercial sectors.	408-734-9600	NA	San Jose
Calex Manufacturing Company Inc (HQ)	Supplier of electrical instrument modules. The company also specializes in power supplies and converters.	925-687-4411	NA	Concord
Caltron Components Corp (HQ)	Distributor of electronic capacitors and resistors. The company also focuses on semiconductor products.	408-748-2140	NA	Santa Clara
Capella Microsystems Inc (HQ)	Developer of integrated technology solutions for IC design. The company is involved in installation and technical support.	408-988-8000	NA	Santa Clara
Century Technology Inc (HQ)	Provider of PCB assembly services. The company also offers distribution, testing, and wire harness services.	650-583-8908	NA	S San Francisco
Cernex Inc (HQ)	Manufacturer of microwave and millimeter-wave components and sub-assemblies. The company's products include amplifiers, converters, detectors, and cables.	408-541-9226	NA	San Jose
N Circuit Automation Inc (HQ)	Designer and manufacturer of dual-sided solder mask coating and vertical drying equipment.	714-763-4180	NA	Huntington Beach
Clustered Systems Company Inc (HQ)	Provider of cooling technology services. The company's resources include data sheets, technology, deployment, and white papers.	408-327-8100	NA	Santa Clara

COMPANY NAME	PRODUCT / SERVICE	PHONE	EMP	CITY
Cordova Printed Circuits Inc (HQ)	Provider of flex circuits and printed circuit boards. The company focuses on sculptured flex circuits and multilayer flex circuits.	408-942-1100	NA	Milpitas
Countryman Associates Inc (HQ)	Manufacturer of direct boxes and ultra-miniature microphones. The company's products include ear sets, hanging, and podium microphones.	650-364-9988	NA	Menlo Park
CTT Inc (HQ)	Manufacturer and supplier of power amplifiers, frequency converters and multipliers, and transmitters and receivers. The company serves military purposes.	408-541-0596	NA	San Jose
Daihen Advanced Component Inc (RH)	Supplier of vacuum environment material handling and RF transmission products to semiconductor, flat panel display and solar, and equipment manufacturers.	408-736-2000	NA	Sunnyvale
Data Physics Corp (HQ)	Provider of high performance test and measurement solutions for noise and vibration applications. The company offers drop testing services.	408-437-0100	NA	San Jose
Dawn VME Products (HQ)	Designer and manufacturer of enclosures, backplanes, chassis and card cage. The company also offers design services and power supplies.	510-657-4444	NA	Fremont
N Dcx-Chol Enterprises Inc (HQ)	Manufacturer of cable assemblies, wire harnesses, electromechanical devices and pneumatic signal and control mechanisms.	310-516-1692	NA	Los Angeles
Dicon Fiberoptics Inc (HQ)	Supplier of optical components, integrated modules, and test equipment for the fiber optics industry.	510-620-5000	NA	Richmond
DIGICOM Electronics Inc (HQ)	Provider of electronics manufacturing services. The company also deals with packing, shipping, and labeling services.	510-639-7003	NA	Oakland
Digital Dynamics Inc (HQ)	Supplier of embedded process control products. The company is also engaged in manufacturing OEM control system products.	831-438-4444	NA	Scotts Valley
Dolphin Technology Inc (DH)	Provider of silicon-proven Internet protocol for memory, standard cells, input and output, memory controllers, and memory test and repair.	408-392-0012	NA	San Jose
Douglas Electronics Inc (HQ)	Provider of CAD/CAM tools for personal computers. The company specializes in custom board manufacturing and electronic design software products.	510-483-8770	NA	San Leandro
DVK Integrated Services Inc (HQ)	Provider of turnkey services that include prototyping services, printed circuit board design, and engineering services.	408-436-0100	NA	San Jose
Elemental LED Inc (HQ)	Provider LED lighting accessories and products. The company's products include LED strip lights, kits, light fixtures, and dimmable lighting products.	510-379-4200	NA	Emeryville
Elevator Controls Corp (HQ)	Manufacturer of non-proprietary microprocessor based elevator controllers. The company offers technical support and field services.	916-428-1708	NA	Sacramento
ELMA Electronic Inc (HQ)	Designer and manufacturer of electronic components and enclosures. The company is involved in design, installation, and delivery services.	510-656-3400	NA	Fremont
N Elmech Inc (HQ)	Manufacturer of cables, harnesses, fan and power supply modification.	408-782-2990	51-200	Morgan Hill
Emotiv (HQ)	Provider of neuroengineering products and services. The company offers algorithms to detect subconscious emotional states and facial expressions.	415-801-0400	NA	San Francisco
Enel X e-Mobility (HQ)	Developer of electric vehicle charging technologies such as smart grid EV charging networks for residential, workplace, and commercial installation.	844-584-2329	NA	San Carlos
Equipment Solutions Inc (HQ)	Manufacturer and provider of actuators and motion control systems. The company offers optical scanners, servo amplifiers, and digital autocollimators.	408-245-7162	NA	Sunnyvale
ESS Technology Inc (HQ)	Designer and marketer of video and audio semiconductors for the home, automotive, and entertainment markers.	408-643-8800	NA	Milpitas
Essai Inc (HQ)	Provider of engineering services. The company provides solutions for the semiconductors, telecom, computer components, and automotive sectors.	510-580-1700	NA	Fremont
Eton Corp (HQ)	Manufacturer of solar energy products. The company offers products for weather alert radios, backup battery packs, and sound systems.	650-903-3866	NA	Palo Alto
Ettus Research LLC (DH)	Provider of software defined radio systems for research, academic, industrial, and defense applications.	408-610-6399	NA	Santa Clara
Fujikura America Inc (BR)	Manufacturer of fiber optics flexible printed circuits and cables. The company also offers membrane switches and printed circuit board assemblies.	408-748-6991	NA	Sunnyvale
GDM Electronic Medical (HQ)	Manufacturer of devices, electrical and electronics for medical, manufacturing and engineering industries.	408-945-4100	NA	San Jose
Giga Test Labs (HQ)	Provider of measurement and probing products for the electronics industry. The company offers test equipment and fixtures for modeling and simulation.	408-524-2700	NA	Santa Clara
Group Seven Corp (HQ)	Producer of turnkey solutions to support high mix and low volume needs. The company also offers Vendor Managed Inventory (VMI) services.	408-435-7477	NA	San Jose
H-Square Corp (HQ)	Designer and manufacturer of tools and equipment. The company caters to the wafer fabrication industry.	408-982-9108	NA	Santa Clara
Halo Electronics Inc (HQ)	Manufacturer of electromagnetic components. The company's products include DC/DC transformers, inductors, and RF transformers.	650-903-3800	NA	Santa Clara

COMPANY NAME	PRODUCT / SERVICE	PHONE	EMP	CITY
HBR Industries Inc (HQ)	Provider of electronics manufacturing services. The company offers coil solutions and services for the medical, military, and semiconductor industry.	408-988-0800	NA	San Jose
Highland Technology Inc (HQ)	Designer and manufacturer of precision analog instrumentation. The company serves laboratory research purposes.	415-551-1700	NA	San Francisco
Hildy Licht Company Inc (HQ)	Provider of electric assembly and manufacturing services. The company is engaged in engineering and prototyping.	650-962-9300	NA	Mountain View
Howlett Machine Works (HQ)	Manufacturer of machine works and custom made tools. The company also offers custom test fixtures and test machines.	510-845-2759	NA	Berkeley
Hunter Micro Kitting and Turnkey (HQ)	Provider of electronic solutions for emerging technology companies. The company offers design, distribution, and contract manufacturing services.	408-977-7000	NA	San Jose
Huntington Mechanical Laboratories Inc (HQ)	Manufacturer and designer of bellows, chalmers, motion positioning products, and roughing accessories.	530-273-4135	NA	Grass Valley
Hybrid Circuits Inc (HQ)	Provider of contract manufacturing services. The company focuses on design, prototyping, contract manufacturing, and delivery.	408-744-9080	NA	Sunnyvale
Ibase Technology (USA) Inc (BR)	Developer of embedded products such as industrial motherboards, CPU modules, barebone systems, network appliances, and digital surveillance systems.	408-992-0888	NA	Sunnyvale
Infineon Technologies North American Corp (BR)	Provider of semiconductor and system solutions. The company focuses on mobile security, sensors, power management, and RF.	866-951-9519	NA	Morgan Hill
Integrated Engineering Services (HQ)	Provider of designs for complex high-tech microelectronic needs. The company also serves the life science facilities.	408-261-3500	NA	Santa Clara
Integrated Surface Technologies Inc (BR)	Provider of supramolecular ceramic coating for water saving electronics. The company offers stiction control and surface modification services.	650-324-1824	NA	Menlo Park
Intilop Inc (HQ)	Provider of engineering design services. The company also develops and provides silicon IP products.	408-791-6700	NA	Milpitas
IPG Photonics (BR)	Provider of high power fiber lasers and amplifiers. The company's offerings include Q-switch lasers, multi-mode diodes, pulsed and direct-diode lasers.	408-492-8830	NA	Santa Clara
Iris AO Inc (HQ)	Manufacturer of microelectromechanical based optical systems. The company's applications include biomedical imaging and portable laser communications.	510-849-2375	NA	Berkeley
Ixys Corp (HQ)	Manufacturer of power semiconductor products. The company specializes in power semiconductors, integrated circuits, and radio frequency power.	408-457-9000	NA	Milpitas
Javad Electronic Manufacturing Services (HQ)	Provider of electronic components. The company specializes in products such as OEM, receivers, antennas, and accessories.	408-770-1700	NA	San Jose
Josephson Engineering Inc (HQ)	Manufacturer of condenser microphones for studio, stage, and field sound pickup, and audio instrumentation.	831-420-0888	NA	Santa Cruz
JSK Associates (HQ)	Provider of electronics, medical, and semiconductor manufacturing services. The company also offers assembly and research services.	408-980-8575	NA	Santa Clara
Kelytech Corp (HQ)	Provider of assembly solutions for PCBs, chassis, cables, and magnetic products. The company serves defense, medical, industrial, and other sectors.	408-935-0888	NA	Milpitas
Keysight Technologies Inc (HQ)	Provider of electronic measurement services. The company products include oscilloscopes, network analyzers, and digital multimeters.	800-829-4444	NA	Santa Rosa
Lee Mah Electronics Inc (HQ)	Provider of manufacturing solutions. The company serves customers in the medical, communications, and test and measurement industries.	415-394-1288	NA	Brisbane
M. K. Products Inc (HQ)	Supplier of welding apparatus.	949-863-1234	NA	Irvine
Marki Microwave Inc (HQ)	Manufacturer of microwave mixers. The company offers adapters, amplifiers, couplers, diplexers, DC blocks, and other equipment.	408-778-4200	NA	Morgan Hill
Masterwork Electronics Inc (HQ)	Provider of printed circuit boards, cables, harness assemblies, and wiring products. The company is engaged in engineering and manufacturing services.	707-588-9906	NA	Chula Vista
MaxLinear (BR)	Provider of integrated radio-frequency, analog, and mixed signal semiconductor SoC solutions. The company focuses on broadband communications applications.	669-265-6100	NA	San Jose
Media Specialty Resources Inc (HQ)	Provider of acoustic panels for recording studios and home theaters. The company also offers noise control and soundproofing services.	415-883-8053	NA	Novato
Mektec International Corp (HQ)	Manufacturer of printed circuit boards. The company deals with production, prototyping, and application engineering services.	408-392-4000	NA	San Jose
Melrose Nameplate & Label Co (HQ)	Developer and manufacturer of ID nameplates, labels, and membrane switches. The company offers touchscreen assembly and decorative nameplates.	510-732-3100	NA	Hayward
Mentor Graphics (RH)	Provider of electronic design automation software. The company focuses on mechanical analysis, system modeling, manufacturing, and verification.	510-354-7400	NA	Fremont
Mettler-Toledo Rainin LLC (BR)	Provider of laboratory weighing and process analytics services. The company also focuses on industrial weighing.	800-472-4646	NA	Oakland
Micro Lambda Wireless Inc (HQ)	Supplier of remote drivers, multipliers, bench test filters, oscillators, synthesizers, and harmonic generators.	510-770-9221	NA	Fremont

COMPANY NAME	PRODUCT / SERVICE	PHONE	EMP	CITY
Millennia Music & Media Systems (HQ)	Provider of music and media systems. The company also provides specialized tools for archival transfers and related applications.	530-647-0750	NA	Diamond Springs
Nady Systems Inc (HQ)	Designer and manufacturer of wireless microphones, and a full line of audio accessories. The company also focuses on marketing.	510-652-2411	NA	Richmond
Naprotek Inc (HQ)	Provider of electronics manufacturing services. The company serves customers in the satellites, industrial, medical, military, and other sectors.	408-830-5000	NA	San Jose
Neato Robotics Inc (HQ)	Manufacturer of robots. The company manufactures robots for cleaning and other activities.	510-795-1351	NA	Newark
Neophotonics Corp (HQ)	Designer and manufacturer of photonic integrated circuit based optoelectronic modules and subsystems for communications networks.	408-232-9200	NA	San Jose
Neurosky Inc (HQ)	Manufacturer of ECG biosensors and also EEG biosensors for mobile solutions, wearable devices, and service providers.	408-200-6675	NA	San Jose
Norden Millimeter Inc (HQ)	Developer and manufacturer of amplifier products. The company specializes in millimeter wave amplifier products.	530-642-9123	NA	Placerville
Novasentis Inc (HQ)	Creator of haptic actuator and sensor technology for the consumer electronics applications such as smart watches, jewelry, headbands, and smart glasses.	814-238-7400	NA	Berkeley
Nuvoton Technology Corporation America (DH)	Manufacturer of semiconductor products and applications. The company's offerings include microcontrollers, microprocessors and cloud computing.	408-544-1718	NA	San Jose
N Omega Leads Inc (HQ)	Manufacturer of commercial wire harness and cable assemblies.	310-394-6786	11-50	Santa Monica
Orbotech LT Solar LLC (BR)	Manufacturer of electronic devices. The company offers printed circuit boards, flat panel displays, and touch screens.	408-226-9900	NA	San Jose
N Pacific Power Source Inc (HQ)	Designer, developer and dealer of both linear and high performance PWM AC power sources.	949-251-1800	51-200	Irvine
Pelco By Schneider Electric (BR)	Developer of video surveillance and security solutions. The company also involves in camera and video management.	559-292-1981	NA	Fresno
PianoDisc (HQ)	Manufacturer of electronic reproducing systems for acoustic pianos. The company is engaged in design, delivery, and installation services.	916-567-9999	NA	Sacramento
PLX Devices Inc (HQ)	Developer of high-tech measuring instruments. The company is engaged in manufacturing, product testing, and technical support services.	408-745-7591	NA	San Jose
PowerBeam Research LLC (RH)	Provider of firmware, hardware, and software applications for video, optoelectronic systems (lasers, LEDs, photodiodes, waveguides), and robotics.	408-933-9373	NA	Mountain View
ProMediaÿAudio & Video (HQ)	Focuses on the integration of audio/video and performance audio systems. The company serves educational facilities, concert halls, and auditoriums.	510-741-2925	NA	Martinez
Promex Industries Inc (HQ)	Provider of packaging solutions. The company is engaged in onshore production process flows using process development.	408-496-0222	NA	Santa Clara
Quail Electronics Inc (HQ)	Manufacturer of power cord supplies for the OEM market. The company offers solutions for power cords, current cords, and adapters, and traveler kits.	925-373-6700	NA	Livermore
Quality Circuit Assembly (HQ)	Manufacturer of printed circuit board and cable assemblies. The company is also involved in box build and turnkey solutions.	408-441-1001	NA	San Jose
Quest Microwave Inc (HQ)	Provider of ferrite products for the microwave electronics industry. The company offers both standard and custom designs.	408-778-4949	NA	Morgan Hill
Radian Thermal Products Inc (BR)	Manufacturer of custom and radiant heat sinks. The company's services include prototyping and engineering support.	408-988-6200	NA	Santa Clara
Raditek Inc (HQ)	Provider of solutions for the wireless and microwave telecom sector. The company offers passive components, active assemblies, and telecom systems.	408-266-7404	NA	San Jose
N Regal Electronics Inc (HQ)	Supplier of electronic components.	408-988-2288	NA	San Jose
Revel Systems Inc (BR)	Provider of POS systems and related services. The company serves customers in the accounting, security, reporting, and other industries.	415-744-1433	NA	San Francisco
Robson Technologies Inc (HQ)	Provider of customizable hardware interfaces that bridge the gap between the test device and the measurement system.	408-779-8008	NA	Morgan Hill
ROD-L Electronics Inc (HQ)	Provider of electrical safety testing equipment. The company also offers hipot test loads, test probes, bond testers, and ground testers.	650-322-0711	NA	Mountain View
Rose Electronics Distributing Company Inc (HQ)	Provider of batteries and power solutions. The company primarily serves original equipment manufacturers such as VRLA batteries and lithium ion batteries.	408-943-0200	NA	San Jose
Sage Metering Inc (HQ)	Manufacturer of thermal mass flow meters. The company offers services to the environmental and industrial sectors.	831-242-2030	NA	Monterey
Schmartboard Inc (HQ)	Specializes in the production of hand soldering components. The company's products are used in sensor and USB technologies.	510-744-9900	NA	Fremont
Seco (HQ)	Manufacturer of surveying and positioning equipment and accessories. The company's products also finds application in site preparation.	530-225-8155	NA	Redding
Semi-Probes Inc (HQ)	Manufacturer and supplier of probe cards and tester interfaces. The company's services include design, installation, and delivery.	408-866-6535	NA	San Jose

COMPANY NAME	PRODUCT / SERVICE	PHONE	EMP	CITY
Sharp Electronics Corp (BR)	Provider of LCD, optoelectronics, imagers, and RF components. The company is involved in design and installation services.	408-452-6400	NA	San Jose
Soraa Inc (HQ)	Provider of lighting design and fixture lamp solutions. The company serves hotels, restaurants, theaters, and private residences.	510-456-2200	NA	Fremont
Sparqtron Corp (HQ)	Provider of electronic contract manufacturing services. The company focuses on prototyping, inspection, PCB assembly, and materials and logistics.	510-657-7198	NA	Fremont
Spectra-Mat Inc (HQ)	Manufacturer of products for electron emission and controlled expansion of thermal management materials for the microelectronics sector.	831-740-0200	NA	Watsonville
Sputtering Components Inc (BR)	Provider of rotating cathodes and magnet assemblies. The company's products find application in industrial systems.	925-606-7241	NA	Livermore
Strike Technology Inc (HQ)	Manufacturer of custom power supplies, converters and inverters.	562-437-3428	11-50	Carson
Sutter Instrument Co (HQ)	Manufacturer of microprocessors and precision electromechanical devices. The company offers technical support services.	415-883-0128	NA	Novato
Syntonic Microwave Inc (HQ)	Manufacturer of wire-band receivers, generators, translators, and related accessories. The company specializes in customization.	408-866-5900	NA	Campbell
Tactus Technology Inc (HQ)	Developer of tactile user interface for touchscreen devices. The company serves the industrial and technological sectors.	510-244-3968	NA	Fremont
Tamura Corporation of America (BR)	Manufacturer of DC power modules, current sensor products, telecom transformers, and LED products. The company is involved in distribution services.	760-871-2009	NA	Escondido
Ten Pao International Inc (HQ)	Manufacturer of power supply systems such as switchings, displays, and traditional linear transformers.	408-389-3560	NA	Sunnyvale
Teradyne Inc (BR)	Supplier of automatic test equipment. The company caters to semiconductor, electronics, and automotive sectors.	480-777-7090	NA	San Jose
Therm-X (HQ)	Provider of engineered solutions. The company serves the semiconductor, petrochemical, life sciences, and aerospace industries.	510-606-1012	NA	Hayward
Unitek Inc (HQ)	Provider of electronic manufacturing services. The company provides PCB assembly, material management, testing, and system integration services.	510-623-8544	NA	Fremont
USB Promos (HQ)	Provider of USB flash drives, power banks, web keys, video brochures and digital toys and promotional items.	800-515-3990	NA	San Francisco
Uvexs Inc (HQ)	Manufacturer of UV curing systems. The company's products find application in formulation of UV-curable inks, adhesives, and coatings.	408-734-4402	NA	Sunnyvale
Valleytek Inc (HQ)	Provider of expanded memory specification solutions, contract manufacturing services, and engineering services.	408-577-1218	NA	San Jose
Valmark Interface Solutions (HQ)	Manufacturer of labels, panel overlays, and membrane switches. The company is engaged in engineering, assembly, and installation services.	925-960-9900	NA	Livermore
Veeco Instruments Inc (BR)	Manufacturer of data storage, LED, and solar process equipment. The company serves solar, LED, data storage, wireless, optical, and other sectors.	408-321-8835	NA	San Jose
VITEC (BR)	Provider of digital video products. The company offers software for video encoding, decoding, and conversion.	800-451-5101	NA	Sunnyvale
Vitriflex Inc (HQ)	Manufacturer of ultra-barrier films for electronic applications. The company focuses on surface science and engineering.	408-468-6700	NA	San Jose
Voltage Multipliers Inc (HQ)	Manufacturer of voltage multipliers, high voltage diodes, rectifiers, opto-couplers, and power supplies.	559-651-1402	NA	Visalia
Whizz Systems (HQ)	Provider of electronics design and manufacturing services for the semiconductor, defense, computing, and industrial equipment markers.	408-980-0400	NA	Santa Clara
World Products Inc (HQ)	Provider of electronic component solutions and services. The company offers sales, distribution, and technical support.	707-996-5201	NA	Sonoma
Worldwide Energy & Manufacturing USA Inc (HQ)	Provider of energy and manufacturing solutions. The company's products include cables, coils, PC boards, and electronic appliances.	650-692-7788	NA	Burlingame
Yamato Scientific America Inc (HQ)	Provider of ovens, incubators, evaporators, and stabilizers. The company deals with sales, distribution, and installation services.	408-235-7725	NA	Santa Clara
Zeptor Corp (HQ)	Specializes in battery technologies. The company develops and manufactures light-weight electrodes that are used in lithium batteries and fuel cells.	408-432-6001	NA	San Jose

210 = Optoelectronics

COMPANY NAME	PRODUCT / SERVICE	PHONE	EMP	CITY
Aborn Electronics Inc (HQ)	Manufacturer of fiber optic systems. The company specializes in the design and manufacture of fiber optic receivers and transmitters.	408-436-5445	NA	San Jose
ESS Technology Inc (HQ)	Designer and marketer of video and audio semiconductors for the home, automotive, and entertainment markers.	408-643-8800	NA	Milpitas
Meivac Inc (HQ)	Manufacturer of sputtering systems and components. The company offers throttle valves, integrators, OEM assemblies, and substrate heaters.	408-362-1000	NA	San Jose
Stanford Photonics Inc (HQ)	Provider of electronic imaging, digital microscope cameras, and photonics technology solutions for the industrial and military markers.	650-969-5991	NA	Palo Alto

211 = Printed Circuit Boards

	COMPANY NAME	PRODUCT / SERVICE	PHONE	EMP	CITY
N	Accu-Sembly Inc (HQ)	Manufacturer of electronic assemblies for flight control electronics, navigation systems, and mechanical control components.	626-357-3447	51-200	Duarte
	Aimer Corp (HQ)	Provider of thermal management products. The company also offers connectors, PCB boards, cables, and mechanical parts.	408-260-8588	NA	Santa Clara
	Alta Manufacturing Inc (HQ)	Manufacturer of printed circuit board assemblies and offers program management, testing, material procurement, and optical inspection solutions.	510-668-1870	NA	Fremont
	Altaflex (HQ)	Developer and fabricator of touch panels and component assemblies, and circuits. The company serves the electronic sector.	408-727-6614	NA	Santa Clara
	Alterflex Corp (HQ)	Designer and manufacturer of printed circuit boards. The company also provides engineering support services.	408-441-8688	NA	San Jose
	Altest Corp (HQ)	Provider of PCB assembly and engineering solutions. The company offers services to the aerospace and commercial industries.	408-436-9900	NA	San Jose
	Anova Microsystems Inc (HQ)	Provider of rackmount server cabinets and system components. The company deals with storage and GPU solutions.	408-941-1888	NA	Los Altos
	ARBOR Solution Inc (RH)	Provider of embedded computing and networking solutions for the transportation, medical, automation, and military segments.	408-452-8900	NA	Fremont
	Ardent Systems Inc (HQ)	Provider of electronics manufacturing services and storage device test solutions. The company is engaged in material management services.	408-526-0100	NA	San Jose
	ArtNet Pro Inc (HQ)	Provider of reused equipment. The company offers direct imaging systems, laser photo plotters, and scanners.	408-954-8383	NA	San Jose
N	Astronic (HQ)	Manufacturer of electronic manufacturing devices.	949-900-6060	NA	Aliso Viejo
	Bay Area Circuits Inc (HQ)	Provider of engineering services that include fabrication, layout, and design services to the original equipment manufacturers.	510-933-9000	NA	Fremont
	Bema Electronics Inc (HQ)	Provider of manufacturing, supply chain management, material procurement, prototyping, and surface mount technology of electronic appliances.	510-490-7770	NA	Fremont
	Benchmark Electronics Inc (BR)	Provider of electronic manufacturing services to OEMs of telecommunication, computers, and related products.	925-363-1100	NA	Concord
	Beta Circuits Inc (HQ)	Manufacturer of printed circuit board. The company offers all solutions from designing to prototyping.	408-980-9938	NA	Santa Clara
	Betatron Inc (HQ)	Designer and manufacturer of PC board assemblies for the medical, telecommunication, industrial, commercial, and semiconductor markers.	408-453-1880	NA	San Jose
	Blair Electric Services Inc (HQ)	Provider of electrical contracting services. The company offers pump and well controls, PLC controls, and surveillance systems.	559-784-8658	NA	Porterville
	C Sys Labs Inc (HQ)	Designer and manufacturer of test printed circuit boards. The company is engaged in cable fabrication and failure analysis services.	530-894-7954	NA	Chico
	Cable Connection Inc (HQ)	Provider of premium PCB assemblies and turnkey OEM/ODM product. The company also specializes in cable and wire harness services.	510-249-9000	NA	Fremont
	Cadence Design Systems Inc (HQ)	Provider of semiconductor IP and electronic design automation services. The company offers tools for logic and RF design, IC packaging, and other needs.	408-943-1234	NA	San Jose
	California Integration Coordinators Inc (HQ)	Manufacturer of custom turnkey printed circuit boards. The company's services include repairs, component sourcing, fabrication, and assembly.	530-626-6168	NA	Diamond Springs
	Cirexx International Inc (HQ)	Provider of PCB design layout, fabrication, and assembly services. The company serves customers in the aerospace, military, semiconductor, and medical sectors.	408-988-3980	NA	Santa Clara
	Cordova Printed Circuits Inc (HQ)	Provider of flex circuits and printed circuit boards. The company focuses on sculptured flex circuits and multilayer flex circuits.	408-942-1100	NA	Milpitas
	CRI Design Inc (HQ)	Provider of PCB layout design, fabrication, assembly and turnkey services. The company offers services to the industrial sector.	510-770-4925	NA	Fremont
	Cyberdata Corp (HQ)	Designer and manufacturer of USB cables. The company also offers VoIP and printed circuit board design services.	831-373-2601	NA	Monterey
	Dawn VME Products (HQ)	Designer and manufacturer of enclosures, backplanes, chassis and card cage. The company also offers design services and power supplies.	510-657-4444	NA	Fremont
N	De Leon Enterprises (HQ)	Manufacturer of PCB assembly, harness assembly and chassis build.	818-252-6690	1-10	Sun Valley
	DIGICOM Electronics Inc (HQ)	Provider of electronics manufacturing services. The company also deals with packing, shipping, and labeling services.	510-639-7003	NA	Oakland
	Douglas Electronics Inc (HQ)	Provider of CAD/CAM tools for personal computers. The company specializes in custom board manufacturing and electronic design software products.	510-483-8770	NA	San Leandro
	DVK Integrated Services Inc (HQ)	Provider of turnkey services that include prototyping services, printed circuit board design, and engineering services.	408-436-0100	NA	San Jose
	Dynamic Test Solutions America Inc (BR)	Provider of design services. The company deals with gold and nickel plating, stub drilling and mixed dielectric fabrication.	408-264-8880	NA	San Jose
	Electromax Inc (HQ)	Manufacturer of heavy machinery. The company offers engineering support, materials management, prototyping and testing services.	408-428-9474	NA	San Jose
N	Electronic Surface Mounted Industries Inc (HQ)	Provider of electronic manufacturing services to original equipment and manufacturer in aerospace, military, industrial, education, telecommunication and consumer products.	858-455-1710	NA	San Diego

COMPANY NAME	PRODUCT / SERVICE	PHONE	EMP	CITY
Entech Electronics (BR)	Supplier of electronic equipment. The company also offers laser cut stencils, graphic decals, LCD screens, and engineering services.	408-730-2650	NA	Santa Clara
EoPlex Inc (BR)	Creator of HVAM technology and process for advanced 3D-printed components for mobile devices, IoT, automotive, medical, and wearable applications.	408-638-5100	NA	San Jose
FAB-9 Corp (BR)	Provider of printed circuit board fabrication, design, assembly, and manufacturing services. The company serves the business sector.	408-791-6462	NA	San Jose
Fine-Line Circuits Ltd (BR)	Manufacturer of printed circuit boards. The company specializes in models such as single sided, double sided, and standard multilayer.	877-876-3660	NA	Dublin
Flashline Electronics Inc (HQ)	Manufacturer of printed circuit boards. The company develops blind and buried vias, rigid flex, and flex PCB.	408-988-4722	NA	San Jose
Flex Interconnect Technologies Inc (HQ)	Developer of printed circuit technologies which provide solutions to organizational inter connectivity problems.	408-635-3540	NA	Milpitas
N FTG Circuits Inc (HQ)	Manufacturer and supplier of printed circuit boards.	818-407-4024	NA	Chatsworth
GDCA Inc (HQ)	Manufacturer of legacy embedded computers and single boards. The company also specializes in assurance, planning, and engineering.	925-456-9900	NA	Livermore
Golden Altos Corp (HQ)	Designer and manufacturer of burn-in boards. The company also provides post wafer fabrication services.	408-956-1010	NA	Milpitas
N Golden West Technology (HQ)	Manufacturer of electronic equipment.	714-738-3775	51-200	Fullerton
Gorilla Circuits Inc (HQ)	Provider of printed circuit engineering and fabrication solutions. The company caters to electronic companies.	408-294-9897	NA	San Jose
Guerra Technologies Inc (HQ)	Designer and manufacturer of RF technology related products. The company also offers consulting and evaluation services.	408-526-9386	NA	San Jose
Ibase Technology (USA) Inc (BR)	Developer of embedded products such as industrial motherboards, CPU modules, barebone systems, network appliances, and digital surveillance systems.	408-992-0888	NA	Sunnyvale
Indtec Corp (HQ)	Manufacturer of printed circuit boards. The company specializes in assemblies, wires, cables, automated surface mounting, and harness services.	831-582-9388	NA	Marina
Infinity Quick Turn Material Inc (HQ)	Provider of manufacturing solutions and services. The company deals with component distribution and PCB fabrication.	510-661-0555	NA	Fremont
Initio Corp (LH)	Provider of integrated circuits and solutions for storage devices. The company is involved in design, installation, and delivery services.	408-608-0060	NA	Campbell
Innovion (HQ)	Provider of foundry and ion implantation services. The company serves the microelectronics industry.	408-501-9100	NA	San Jose
International Electronic Components Inc (RH)	Distributor of printed circuit boards, consumables, and inspection and measuring equipment. The company is engaged in installation services.	408-496-0474	NA	Santa Clara
Interphasic LLC (HQ)	Manufacturer of motion control systems. The company offers product support services and it serves the industrial sector.	831-392-0708	NA	Seaside
Lee Mah Electronics Inc (HQ)	Provider of manufacturing solutions. The company serves customers in the medical, communications, and test and measurement industries.	415-394-1288	NA	Brisbane
Legend Design Technology Inc (HQ)	Provider of semiconductor IP characterization and verification tools and IC and PCB circuit simulators.	408-748-8888	NA	Santa Clara
Lenthor Engineering (HQ)	Designer and manufacturer of flexible and rigid printed circuit boards. The company serves the military, communications, medical, and other markers.	408-945-8787	NA	Milpitas
Macrotron Systems Inc (HQ)	Designer and manufacturer of memory modules. The company provides services such as electronics assembly and testing.	510-683-9600	NA	Fremont
Megaforce Corporation Inc (HQ)	Provider of supply chain, materials management, and test solutions. The company serves the industrial, commercial, and automotive sectors.	408-956-9989	NA	San Jose
Meritronics Inc (HQ)	Provider of electronics assembly, and equipment assemblies. The company specializes in PCB assembly, cable assembly, and system assembly.	408-969-0888	NA	Milpitas
Mvinix Systems Inc (HQ)	Provider of electronic and manufacturing service provider for printed circuit board assemblies. The company deals with design and testing services.	408-321-9109	NA	San Jose
Naprotek Inc (HQ)	Provider of electronics manufacturing services. The company serves customers in the satellites, industrial, medical, military, and other sectors.	408-830-5000	NA	San Jose
Network PCB Inc (HQ)	Provider of printed circuit board solutions. The company's product line includes probe cards, high density board, and impedance control board.	408-943-8760	NA	San Jose
Nexlogic (HQ)	Designer of electronic circuits. The company specializes in the design and fabrication of printed circuit boards.	408-436-8150	NA	San Jose
NRC Manufacturing Inc (HQ)	Provider of contract manufacturing and PCB assembly services. The company's services include cable assembly, box builds, and functional test.	510-438-9400	NA	Fremont
Optimum Design Associates (HQ)	Provider of printed circuit board design and layout services. The company also focuses on engineering and manufacturing services.	925-401-2004	NA	Pleasanton
Pactron/HJPC Corp (HQ)	Provider of electronics design and design development services. The company is also involved in engineering and contract manufacturing.	408-329-5500	NA	Santa Clara

COMPANY NAME	PRODUCT / SERVICE	PHONE	EMP	CITY
PalPilot International Corp (BR)	Developer of interconnect solutions. The company offers design, engineering, and manufacturing support services.	408-855-8866	NA	Milpitas
Pan-International (LH)	Supplier of computer cables, wiring, switch boxes, and connectors. The company is involved in design, installation, and delivery services.	510-623-3898	NA	Fremont
Proto Services Inc (HQ)	Provider of process verification, yield analysis, testing design, program management, and functional debugging services.	408-719-9088	NA	San Jose
Qualdeval International (HQ)	Supplier of high-pressure fluid flow and special core analysis equipment. The company offers PCB fabrication and assembly, and other services.	844-247-2523	NA	Fremont
Quality Circuit Assembly (HQ)	Manufacturer of printed circuit board and cable assemblies. The company is also involved in box build and turnkey solutions.	408-441-1001	NA	San Jose
Qualtech Circuits Inc (HQ)	Producer of printed circuit boards. The company's products include probe cards and edge plating.	408-727-4125	NA	Santa Clara
Qulsar Inc (HQ)	Specializes in packaging, refinement, and distribution of precise time synchronization. The company serves the telecom and networking industries.	408-715-1098	NA	San Jose
R F Circuits Inc (HQ)	Manufacturer of printed circuit boards and assemblies. The company is engaged in engineering and electronics manufacturing services.	408-324-1670	NA	San Jose
R&D Tech (HQ)	Provider of prototyping services. The company specializes in fabrication and assembly services.	408-761-5266	NA	Milpitas
Robson Technologies Inc (HQ)	Provider of customizable hardware interfaces that bridge the gap between the test device and the measurement system.	408-779-8008	NA	Morgan Hill
Royal Circuit Solutions Inc (HQ)	Manufacturer of printed circuit boards. The company's products are used in prototype and medium production runs and offers fabrication services.	831-636-7789	NA	Hollister
Rucker Kolls Inc (HQ)	Provider of solutions for ATE test interface products. The company's services include custom PCB design and card stiffeners and rings.	408-934-9875	NA	Milpitas
RUSH PCB Inc (RH)	Manufacturer of printed circuit boards and assemblies. The company is engaged in engineering and electronics manufacturing services.	408-496-6013	NA	San Jose
San Francisco Circuits (HQ)	Provider and manufacturer of printed circuit boards. The company also offers services like PCB design and assembly and specializes in complex circuits.	800-732-5143	NA	San Mateo
Schurter Inc (DH)	Manufacturer of fuses, connectors, and circuit breakers. The company also offers input systems and EMC products.	707-636-3000	NA	Santa Rosa
Sicon International Inc (HQ)	Manufacturer of electronic components. The company specializes in the fabrication of connectors, cables, circuit boards, and molded cables.	408-954-9880	NA	San Jose
Sierra Circuits (HQ)	Designer and manufacturer of printed circuit boards. The company's manufacturing facilities are located in California and Kansas.	408-735-7137	NA	Sunnyvale
Sigmatron International Inc (BR)	Provider of robust systems and program management support to track demand, material on order, inventory, finished goods, and shipments.	510-477-5000	NA	Union City
SMTC Corp (BR)	Provider of electronics manufacturing services for the industrial, medical, computing, and communication markers.	510-737-0700	NA	Fremont
Spire Manufacturing (HQ)	Designer and manufacturer of printed circuit boards. The company offers vertical probe cards, test sockets, and mother boards.	510-226-1070	NA	Fremont
Streamline Electronics Manufacturing Inc (HQ)	Provider of electronic manufacturing solutions and services. The company is engaged in product development and contract manufacturing.	408-263-3600	NA	Fremont
Surface Art Engineering Inc (HQ)	Provider of Printed Circuit Board Assembly (PCA) and mechanical assembly for prototype, pre-production and production assemblies.	408-433-4700	NA	San Jose
Symprotek Corp (HQ)	Provider of electronics manufacturing and engineering services. The company also focuses on procurement.	408-956-0700	NA	Milpitas
Tempo Automation (HQ)	Specializes in printed circuit board assemblies. The company is engaged in design and delivery services.	415-320-1261	NA	San Francisco
Test21 Inc (HQ)	Designer and manufacturer of printed circuit boards including probe cards for semiconductor, ATE manufacturers, and silicon wafer foundries.	510-438-0221	NA	Fremont
N Transline Technology Inc (HQ)	Manufacturer of printed circuit boards.	714-533-8300	11-50	Anaheim
TTM Technologies Inc (BR)	Manufacturer of printed circuit boards and backplane assemblies. The company's services include design, installation, and delivery.	408-486-3100	NA	Santa Clara
TUV Rheinland Of North America Inc (DH)	Provider of product testing, market access, specialty services, and management systems certification services.	925-249-9123	NA	Pleasanton
Tyan Computer Corp (DH)	Designer and manufacturer of server/workstation platforms. The company's products are sold to OEMs, VARs, system integrators, and resellers.	510-651-8868	NA	Fremont
Uni-Flex Circuits Inc (HQ)	Manufacturer of flexible circuits. The company specializes in the design and fabrication of consumer electronic connectors.	408-998-5500	NA	San Jose
Unitek Inc (HQ)	Provider of electronic manufacturing services. The company provides PCB assembly, material management, testing, and system integration services.	510-623-8544	NA	Fremont
Vector Fabrication Inc (HQ)	Manufacturer of printed circuit boards. The company offers circuit board assembly, drilling, solder mask, plating, and testing services.	408-942-9800	NA	Milpitas
Wafer Process Systems Inc (HQ)	Manufacturer of semiconductors, MEMS, and photonics. The company also focuses on RFID products, disc drives, and flat panel displays.	408-445-3010	NA	San Jose

COMPANY NAME	PRODUCT / SERVICE	PHONE	EMP	CITY
Wellex Corp (HQ)	Provider of printed circuit boards, cables, harness assemblies, and wiring products. The company is engaged in engineering and manufacturing services.	510-743-1818	NA	Fremont
Wenteq Inc (HQ)	Manufacturer of print, precision, machined components, and assemblies. The company serves the automotive, racing, and boat markers.	209-608-2374	NA	Lodi
Westak (HQ)	Designer and manufacturer of printed circuit boards. The company offers rigid double-sided interconnects and rigid multi-layer interconnects.	408-734-8686	NA	Sunnyvale
X-Scan Imaging Corp (HQ)	Supplier of x-ray imaging and inspection equipment. The company also offers array detectors and line-scan camera products.	408-432-9888	NA	San Jose
Yamamoto Manufacturing USA Inc (HQ)	Manufacturer of printed circuit boards. The company has operations in regions of Japan, Korea, and China.	408-387-5250	NA	San Jose
Z-Plane Inc (HQ)	Provider of electronic packaging solutions for high-speed telecommunications and computing equipment, including routers, servers, and switches.	415-309-2647	NA	Santa Rosa
Z-Source International (HQ)	Manufacturer of printed circuit boards. The company provides board procurement solutions from prototypes to full production and stocking programs.	925-401-0090	NA	Pleasanton

212 = Semiconductors & Related Devices

COMPANY NAME	PRODUCT / SERVICE	PHONE	EMP	CITY
Acco Semiconductor Inc (HQ)	Provider of outsourced operations and engineering services. The company serves fabless semiconductor companies.	408-524-2600	NA	Sunnyvale
Achronix Semiconductor Corp (HQ)	Manufacturer of semiconductor devices. The company's products are used for networking, edge networking, and test and measurement applications.	408-889-4100	NA	Santa Clara
Adaptive Engineering (HQ)	Provider of engineering products such as automatic mixture control, talking telemetry, and telephone-based microclimate monitors.	415-518-7131	NA	San Ramon
Advanced Component Labs (HQ)	Manufacturer of flip chips, thermal vias, build ups, and related supplies. The company's services include drilling, lamination, and engineering.	408-327-0200	NA	Santa Clara
Advanced Semiconductor Engineering Inc (DH)	Manufacturer of integrated circuits and semiconductor packaging products. The company is involved in delivery, installation, and sales.	408-636-9500	NA	Sunnyvale
Advantest America Inc (LH)	Provider of measurement systems and solutions. The company offers electronic measuring instruments, and optical sensing and imaging analysis systems.	408-456-3600	NA	San Jose
Advantiv Technologies Inc (DH)	Manufacturer and supplier of semiconductor components. The company offers wafers, solar, materials, and vacuum components.	510-490-8260	NA	Fremont
AG Microsystems Inc (HQ)	Provider of testing and development in the areas of micro electro mechanical systems and micro optics.	408-834-4888	NA	Santa Clara
AKM Semiconductor Inc (HQ)	Designer and manufacturer of mixed signal integrated circuits. The company serves consumer electronics, industrial, and automotive sectors.	408-436-8580	NA	San Jose
Alpha & Omega Semiconductor (HQ)	Designer, developer, and supplier of power semiconductors. The company's applications include notebook PCs and power supplies.	408-830-9742	NA	Sunnyvale
Alta Devices (HQ)	Provider of mobile power technology services. The company offers unmanned systems, consumer devices, and Internet technology services.	408-988-8600	NA	Sunnyvale
American Probe & Technologies Inc (HQ)	Manufacturer of analytical probes and accessories for the semiconductor test and measurement industry.	408-263-3356	NA	Merced
Amimon Inc (HQ)	Developer and manufacturer of HD wireless video modules. The company's products include Studio Link, Live Link, and View Link.	408-490-4686	NA	San Jose
Analatom Inc (HQ)	Provider of materials science research services focusing on product development in the field of micro electrical mechanical systems.	408-980-9516	NA	Santa Clara
Analog Bits Inc (HQ)	Supplier of low-power, customizable analog IP for modern CMOS digital chips. The company also offers interfaces and converters.	650-314-0200	NA	Sunnyvale
Anchor Semiconductor Inc (HQ)	Developer of software to improve IC manufacturing efficiency and chip yield. The company specializes in semiconductor hotspot pattern management.	408-986-8969	NA	Santa Clara
Anova Microsystems Inc (HQ)	Provider of rackmount server cabinets and system components. The company deals with storage and GPU solutions.	408-941-1888	NA	Los Altos
Applied Ceramics Inc (HQ)	Manufacturer of custom ceramics, quartz silicon, stainless steel, and sapphire for the semiconductor industries.	510-249-9700	NA	Fremont
Applied Engineering (HQ)	Provider of contract electronics manufacturing services. The company also specializes in clean room assembly services.	408-286-2134	NA	San Jose
Applied Materials Inc (HQ)	Provider of equipment, services, and software for the manufacture of semiconductor, flat panel display, and solar photovoltaic products.	408-727-5555	NA	Santa Clara
Arasan Chip Systems Inc (RH)	Provider of total IP solutions such as digital IP cores, protocol analyzers, and traffic generators for mobile storage and connectivity applications.	408-433-9633	NA	San Jose
Arm Ltd (RH)	Manufacturer of digital products and offers wireless, networking, and consumer entertainment solutions to imaging, automotive, and storage devices.	408-576-1500	NA	San Jose

COMPANY NAME	PRODUCT / SERVICE	PHONE	EMP	CITY
Arteris Inc (HQ)	Provider of interconnect semiconductor IP solutions to system-on-chip makers and serves networking, automotive, video and mobile-phone processors.	408-470-7300	NA	Campbell
Axelsys LLC (HQ)	Provider of electronic design and manufacturing services. The company's offerings include LED and AC to DC industrial power supplies.	408-600-0871	NA	San Jose
B & J Specialties Inc (HQ)	Manufacturer of nanometrics film thickness and CD measurement equipment. The company offers nanometrics equipment, Nanoline, and Nanospec.	831-454-0713	NA	Santa Cruz
N B.K. Thorpe Co (HQ)	Distributor of valves and fittings for commercial and industrial application such as brass appliances, ball-plex and duplex, grooved end, tilting disc check, sampling and much more.	562-595-1811	NA	Signal Hill
N Bearing Engineers Inc (HQ)	Manufacturer of semiconductor fabrication equipment, medical equipment, aerospace and robotics components.	949-586-7442	NA	Aliso Viejo
Benchmark Electronics Inc (BR)	Provider of electronic manufacturing services to OEMs of telecommunication, computers, and related products.	925-363-1100	NA	Concord
C&D Semiconductor Services Inc (HQ)	Manufacturer of cleaner systems, wafer sorters, and wafer inspection systems. The company deals with inspection and processing.	408-383-1888	NA	San Jose
Cadence Design Systems Inc (HQ)	Provider of semiconductor IP and electronic design automation services. The company offers tools for logic and RF design, IC packaging, and other needs.	408-943-1234	NA	San Jose
Cal Semi LLC (HQ)	Provider of semiconductor equipment remanufacturing services. The company specializes in products such as furnaces, cantilever, and wet sinks.	510-687-9960	NA	San Jose
Caltron Components Corp (HQ)	Distributor of electronic capacitors and resistors. The company also focuses on semiconductor products.	408-748-2140	NA	Santa Clara
Century Technology Inc (HQ)	Provider of PCB assembly services. The company also offers distribution, testing, and wire harness services.	650-583-8908	NA	S San Francisco
Champion Microelectronic Corp (RH)	Designer and manufacturer of semiconductor devices. The company's products include battery management IC, fan controller, and interface products.	408-985-1898	NA	San Jose
CHECKPOiNT Technologies (HQ)	Manufacturer of optical failure analysis tools such as laser scanning microscopy, photon emission, infrascan, and solid immersion lens objectives.	408-321-9780	NA	San Jose
Comit Systems Inc (HQ)	Provider of full service contract engineering for wireless and cleantech, methodology consulting, Soc design and verification, board design, and software.	408-988-2988	NA	Sunnyvale
N Condor Reliability Services Inc (HQ)	Provider of innovative solutions to government and industry.	408-486-9600	51-200	Santa Clara
Crossbar Inc (HQ)	Provider of 3D resistive RAM technology. The company serves customers in the automotive, connected devices, consumer, and enterprise segments.	408-884-0281	NA	Santa Clara
Cyclos Semiconductor (HQ)	Provider of resonant mesh semiconductor IP, design automation tools, and design consulting services to mobile, wireless, and medical sectors.	510-649-3741	NA	Berkeley
Delphon Industries LLC (HQ)	Provider of materials and services to the semiconductor, medical, photonics, telecommunications, and military markers.	510-576-2220	NA	Hayward
N Dhv Industries Inc (HQ)	Distributor of carbon steel, cast iron, stainless steel, and alloy gate valve products.	661-392-8948	11-50	Bakersfield
Dialog Semiconductor (RH)	Manufacturer of AC/DC and LED SSL products. The company's products include home appliances, smart meters, power adapters, and backlighting devices.	408-374-4200	NA	Campbell
Dialog Semiconductor Inc (BR)	Creator of mixed-signal integrated circuits. The company offers products such as audio, backlight LED, wireless audio, and home automation.	408-845-8500	NA	Santa Clara
Diodes Inc (BR)	Provider of electronic components for communications, lighting, motor control, and audio applications.	408-232-9100	NA	Milpitas
DisplayLink Corp (HQ)	Provider of solutions for virtual graphics connectivity between computers and displays. The company makes use of USB, wireless USB, and ethernet.	650-838-0481	NA	Palo Alto
Dolphin Technology Inc (DH)	Provider of silicon-proven Internet protocol for memory, standard cells, input and output, memory controllers, and memory test and repair.	408-392-0012	NA	San Jose
Dynamic Test Solutions America Inc (BR)	Provider of design services. The company deals with gold and nickel plating, stub drilling and mixed dielectric fabrication.	408-264-8880	NA	San Jose
Ebara Technologies Inc (HQ)	Manufacturer of vacuum pumps for the semiconductor industry. The company offers repair, training, and field and system services.	916-920-5451	NA	Sacramento
Embedur Systems Inc (HQ)	Developer of software solutions. The company also offers technical and management services for the embedded market.	510-353-9111	NA	Fremont
EME Systems (HQ)	Designer and manufacturer of instruments for environmental science. The company also offers signal conditioners, sensors, enclosures, and batteries.	510-848-5725	NA	Berkeley
EoPlex Inc (BR)	Creator of HVAM technology and process for advanced 3D-printed components for mobile devices, IoT, automotive, medical, and wearable applications.	408-638-5100	NA	San Jose

COMPANY NAME	PRODUCT / SERVICE	PHONE	EMP	CITY
Etron Technology America Inc (RH)	Provider of integrated circuits for applications, such as storage device, display, handset, PDA, and multimedia device.	408-987-2255	NA	Santa Clara
Exclara Inc (HQ)	Designer and manufacturer of high-voltage LED drivers which provide integrated-circuit and module-based solutions.	408-492-1009	NA	Santa Clara
FET Test Inc (HQ)	Manufacturer of automated test equipment. The company also offers modular analog/mixed-signal testers and test system controller software.	408-778-0234	NA	San Jose
Flex Logix Technologies Inc (HQ)	Developer of reconfigurable RTL IP cores and software.	650-851-1411	NA	Mountain View
Fortrend Engineering Corp (HQ)	Designer and manufacturer of mechanical handling equipment. The company also specializes in distribution services.	408-734-9311	NA	San Jose
Four Dimensions Inc (HQ)	Manufacturer of semiconductor probing systems. The company offers Four Point Probe, Mercury Probe CV maps, and Mercury Four Imaging systems.	510-782-1843	NA	Hayward
Furukawa Sangyo North America Inc (LH)	Provider of electric products for telecommunications and automotive needs. The company also serves energy, construction, and other sectors.	408-496-0051	NA	San Jose
Gambit Corp (HQ)	Provider of engineering parts and services. The company specializes in designing and building tools and dies.	707-588-2797	NA	Rohnert Park
GCT Semiconductor Inc (HQ)	Designer and supplier of 4G mobile semiconductor solutions. The company also offers wireless solutions for its clients.	408-434-6040	NA	San Jose
Glacier Microelectronics Inc (HQ)	Developer of mixed signal semiconductor devices. The company's products include synthesizers and RFIC devices.	408-244-0778	NA	Santa Clara
Global Unichip Corp (HQ)	Provider of technology and embedded CPU design services. The company's services include package engineering, test engineering, and supply chain management.	408-382-8900	NA	San Jose
Gooch & Housego (BR)	Manufacturer of precision optical components. The company also focuses on related subsystems and systems.	650-300-5744	NA	Fremont
Green Plug (HQ)	Developer and provider of digital controller technology solutions and products to the consumer electronics markers.	925-867-2781	NA	San Ramon
Greenliant Systems (HQ)	Developer of storage solutions for the embedded systems. The company offers solid-state storage, controllers, and specialty flash memory.	408-200-8000	NA	Santa Clara
Greenvity Communications Inc (HQ)	Designer and developer of semiconductor solutions for home gateways, electric vehicles, and lighting products.	408-935-9358	NA	San Jose
H-Square Corp (HQ)	Designer and manufacturer of tools and equipment. The company caters to the wafer fabrication industry.	408-982-9108	NA	Santa Clara
Hamamatsu Corp (BR)	Manufacturer of devices for the generation and measurement of infrared, visible, and ultraviolet light.	408-261-2022	NA	San Jose
Hana Microelectronics Inc (BR)	Provider of electronic manufacturing services. The company focuses on PCBs, circuit assembly, RFID devices, LEDs, coil windings, and other products.	408-452-7474	NA	Santa Clara
High Connection Density Inc (HQ)	Supplier of electronic packaging solutions and connection technologies. The company serves communications, medical, military, and aerospace fields.	408-743-9700	NA	Sunnyvale
Hitachi High Technologies America Inc (BR)	Seller of semiconductor manufacturing equipment and analytical instrumentation and also offers electronic devices, bio-related, and other products.	925-218-2814	NA	Pleasanton
Hoffmeyer Company Inc (HQ)	Manufacturer and distributor of conveyor belting and components, couplings, industrial and hydraulic hoses.	510-895-9955	51-200	San Leandro
HSQ Technology (HQ)	Provider of control system and energy management services, specializing in data and SCADA monitoring.	510-259-1334	NA	Hayward
Impulse Semiconductor Inc (HQ)	Provider of electrostatic discharge and electrical overstress products and services. The company also provides virtual components and hardware.	408-355-5018	NA	San Jose
Initio Corp (LH)	Provider of integrated circuits and solutions for storage devices. The company is involved in design, installation, and delivery services.	408-608-0060	NA	Campbell
Inphi Corp (HQ)	Provider of semiconductor solutions for the computing and telecom markers. The company's products include amplifiers, registers, buffers, and modulator drivers.	408-217-7300	NA	Santa Clara
Integrated Silicon Solution Inc (HQ)	Designer and developer of high performance integrated circuits. The company also focuses on the marketing aspects.	408-969-6600	NA	Milpitas
Intel Corp (HQ)	Designer, developer, and marketer of processors and motherboards. The company also focuses on tablets, laptops, desktops, and other devices.	408-765-8080	NA	Santa Clara
Intermems Inc (HQ)	Provider of micromolding, plating, thin film deposition, anodic and wafer bonding, and related services.	408-241-0007	NA	San Jose
Intermolecular Inc (HQ)	Provider of high productivity combinatorial technologies. The company serves solar device manufacturers.	408-582-5700	NA	San Jose
International Electronic Components Inc (RH)	Distributor of printed circuit boards, consumables, and inspection and measuring equipment. The company is engaged in installation services.	408-496-0474	NA	Santa Clara
Interphase Systems (HQ)	Manufacturer of test equipment for the disc drive industry. The company offers consulting and build-to-print services.	408-315-8603	NA	Santa Clara
Intevac Inc (HQ)	Supplier of magnetic media processing systems. The company offers advanced equipment to the hard disk drive, solar, and photonics industries.	408-986-9888	NA	Santa Clara

N

COMPANY NAME	PRODUCT / SERVICE	PHONE	EMP	CITY
Invensas Corp (HQ)	Provider of software solutions for computer applications. The company also offers semiconductor technologies.	408-321-6000	NA	San Jose
Ise Labs Inc (HQ)	Provider of semiconductor services. The company offers services such as production test, test interface, and mechanical testing.	510-687-2500	NA	Fremont
Ixys Corp (HQ)	Manufacturer of power semiconductor products. The company specializes in power semiconductors, integrated circuits, and radio frequency power.	408-457-9000	NA	Milpitas
Kinetic Technologies (HQ)	Designer and developer of analog and mixed-signal power management semiconductors. The company serves the consumer and communication markers.	512-694-6384	NA	San Jose
KLA-Tencor Corp (HQ)	Provider of inspection and metrology tools. The company also specializes in process control and yield management products.	408-875-3000	NA	Milpitas
Kokusai Semiconductor Equipment Corp (DH)	Provider of thermal processing solutions. The company also provides technical, installation, and retrofit services.	408-456-2750	NA	San Jose
Lam Research Corp (HQ)	Manufacturer and distributor of single wafer systems. The company primarily serves the semiconductor industry.	510-572-0200	NA	Fremont
Lattice Semiconductor (BR)	Provider of design, development, and marketing services for programmable logic devices. The company also offers related software.	408-826-6000	NA	San Jose
Light Guard Systems Inc (HQ)	Provider of traffic safety products such as controllers, signal head and base plate modules, and LED signage products.	707-542-4547	NA	Santa Rosa
Linear Integrated Systems (HQ)	Manufacturer of semiconductor products. The company offers bipolar transistors, input protection diodes, resistors, and low leakage amplifiers.	510-490-9160	NA	Fremont
Lumasense Technologies Inc (HQ)	Provider of temperature and gas sensing instruments for the energy, industrial, clean technology, and commercial markers.	408-727-1600	NA	Santa Clara
Luxience Technologies (HQ)	Provider of precision semiconductor equipment. The company specializes in design, fabrication, and supply of semiconductor equipment.	669-235-5778	NA	San Jose
Macrotron Systems Inc (HQ)	Designer and manufacturer of memory modules. The company provides services such as electronics assembly and testing.	510-683-9600	NA	Fremont
Malaster Company Inc (HQ)	Provider of packing materials. The company specializes in offering package and shipping solutions for semiconductor industries.	877-625-2783	NA	Santa Clara
Marseille Inc (HQ)	Provider of video processing solutions. The company's applications include home theaters and audio and video receivers.	408-855-9003	NA	Santa Clara
Micro-Mechanics Inc (DH)	Manufacturer of precision tools, assemblies, and consumable parts used to manufacture and test semiconductors. The company offers mold pots and trims.	408-779-2927	NA	Morgan Hill
Microchip Technology Inc (BR)	Provider of microcontroller and analog semiconductors. The company focuses on products such as amplifiers, data converters, and embedded controllers.	408-961-6400	NA	San Jose
Microsemi (DH)	Supplier of discrete military and aerospace components. The company's applications include embedded systems and power solutions.	408-986-8031	NA	Santa Clara
Mission Peak Optics Inc (HQ)	Provider of measurement solutions for semiconductor industry. The company offers thin film thickness measurement system.	510-438-0384	NA	Fremont
Mixed Signal Integration (HQ)	Specializes in the design, manufacture and sale of turnkey analog and mixed-signal standard products and custom ASICs.	408-434-6305	NA	San Jose
Mixel Inc (HQ)	Designer and developer of mixed-signal Internet protocol cores for the semiconductor and electronics industries.	408-436-8500	NA	San Jose
Monolithic Power Systems Inc (HQ)	Provider of analog semiconductor products. The company offers battery chargers, linear regulators and analog switches, voltage supervisors, and amplifiers.	408-826-0600	NA	San Jose
Multibeam Corp (HQ)	Producer of photomasks for optical lithography. The company's products are used in IC manufacturing and water defect inspection applications.	408-980-1800	NA	Santa Clara
Naprotek Inc (HQ)	Provider of electronics manufacturing services. The company serves customers in the satellites, industrial, medical, military, and other sectors.	408-830-5000	NA	San Jose
Neophotonics Corp (HQ)	Designer and manufacturer of photonic integrated circuit based optoelectronic modules and subsystems for communications networks.	408-232-9200	NA	San Jose
Neutronix Inc (HQ)	Manufacturer of contact or proximity and projection mask aligners. The company is involved in design, installation, and delivery services.	408-776-5190	NA	Morgan Hill
Nisene Technology Group Inc (HQ)	Provider of automated decapsulator technology and plastic etching services. The company offers custom design services for nonstandard gaskets.	831-761-7980	NA	Watsonville
Novasentis Inc (HQ)	Creator of haptic actuator and sensor technology for the consumer electronics applications such as smart watches, jewelry, headbands, and smart glasses.	814-238-7400	NA	Berkeley
Nuvoton Technology Corporation America (DH)	Manufacturer of semiconductor products and applications. The company's offerings include microcontrollers, microprocessors and cloud computing.	408-544-1718	NA	San Jose
Oepic Semiconductors Inc (HQ)	Provider of semiconductor fabrication services. The company's products include optical and optoelectronic components.	408-747-0388	NA	Sunnyvale
Omnivision Technologies Inc (HQ)	Developer of digital imaging solutions for consumer and commercial applications, and automotive, medical, and security imaging sectors.	408-567-3000	NA	Santa Clara

COMPANY NAME	PRODUCT / SERVICE	PHONE	EMP	CITY
Omniyig Inc (HQ)	Manufacturer of microwave devices for the defense industry. The company also offers limiters, drivers, and oscillators.	408-988-0843	NA	Santa Clara
Open Five Inc (HQ)	Provider of IP, foundry, test, and packaging technologies. The company's services include system design, manufacturing, and program management.	408-240-5700	NA	Milpitas
Optoplex Corp (HQ)	Supplier of cutting-edge photonic components and modules for dynamic wavelength management and signal conditioning.	510-490-9930	NA	Fremont
Owens Design (HQ)	Developer of advanced technology systems for semiconductor, hard disk drive, solar, medical device, and other sectors.	510-659-1800	NA	Fremont
Pactech Inc (HQ)	Provider of computer cables, cooling items, and other components. The company also offers networking products.	408-526-9363	NA	San Jose
Pactron/HJPC Corp (HQ)	Provider of electronics design and design development services. The company is also involved in engineering and contract manufacturing.	408-329-5500	NA	Santa Clara
Parallax Inc (HQ)	Manufacturer of electronic hardware and software products. The company offers microcontrollers, sensors, boards, and cables/converters.	916-624-8333	NA	Rocklin
Peninsula Engineering Solutions Inc (HQ)	Manufacturer of microwave RF repeaters. The company also specializes in cellular and PCS repeaters and related products.	925-837-2243	NA	Danville
Peridot Corp (HQ)	Provider of design for manufacturing and packaging. The company also manufacturers of medical components, miniature component and general product prototypes.	925-461-8830	NA	Pleasanton
N Piezo-Metrics Inc (HQ)	Manufacturer and distributor of semiconductor strain gages, pressure transducers, temperature sensors and measuring systems.	805-522-4676	NA	Simi Valley
N Polyfet Rf Devices Inc (HQ)	Provider of RF amplifier design assistance, and RF mosfet transistors.	805-484-4210	11-50	Camarillo
Pragmatics Technologies Inc (HQ)	Provider of electromechanical interface solutions. The company deals with the development of custom and standard test interfaces.	408-289-8202	NA	San Jose
Precision Tool Distributors Inc (HQ)	Specializes in dimensional measurement products. The company offers inspection hand tools and related accessories.	408-774-1274	NA	Fremont
Quantenna Communications Inc (HQ)	Developer of semiconductor solutions for the Wi-Fi networks. The company serves retail, home networking, consumer electronics, and enterprise needs.	669-209-5500	NA	San Jose
Quantum Semiconductor LLC (HQ)	Manufacturer of semiconductor devices. The company specializes in silicon photonic receivers and solar cells.	408-243-2262	NA	San Jose
N R.S. Hughes Company Inc (HQ)	Distributor of industrial supplies such as abrasives, adhesives and sealants, chemicals and much more.	877-774-8443	NA	Sunnyvale
Rambus (HQ)	Manufacturer of semiconductor, lighting, and IP products. The company serves the automotive and transportation markers.	408-462-8000	NA	Sunnyvale
ROHM Semiconductor USA LLC (BR)	Manufacturer of amplifiers, clocks, modules, passive components, remote control receivers, and timers.	408-720-1900	NA	Santa Clara
Roos Instruments Inc (BR)	Manufacturer of automated test equipment. The company's products include MEMs devices, radars, amplifiers, and mixers.	408-748-8589	NA	Santa Clara
Royce Instruments Inc (HQ)	Provider of bond testers and die sorters for the auto and medical electronics device manufacturers worldwide.	707-255-9078	NA	Napa
Rucker Kolls Inc (HQ)	Provider of solutions for ATE test interface products. The company's services include custom PCB design and card stiffeners and rings.	408-934-9875	NA	Milpitas
Schurter Inc (DH)	Manufacturer of fuses, connectors, and circuit breakers. The company also offers input systems and EMC products.	707-636-3000	NA	Santa Rosa
Semi-Probes Inc (HQ)	Manufacturer and supplier of probe cards and tester interfaces. The company's services include design, installation, and delivery.	408-866-6535	NA	San Jose
Semicore Equipment Inc (HQ)	Manufacturer of vacuum systems and equipment. The company's products include PVD coating systems, thermal evaporation, and sputtering equipment.	925-373-8201	NA	Livermore
Sentons USA Inc (HQ)	Provider of touch solutions. The company offers flat panel display, retail point of sale, and factory/industry automation products.	408-732-9000	NA	San Jose
Sigma Designs Inc (HQ)	Provider of system-on-chip solutions for media processing, smart TV, video encoding, AV networking, video processing, and home control systems.	510-897-0200	NA	Fremont
Silicon Frontline Technology Inc (HQ)	Provider of parasitic extraction and analysis services for post layout verification. The company specializes in electrostatic discharge analysis.	408-963-6916	NA	San Jose
Silicon Genesis Corp (HQ)	Manufacturer of semiconductor and solar fabrication tools. The company offers stand-alone plasma tools and debond and cleave tools.	408-228-5858	NA	San Jose
Silicon Light Machines (HQ)	Provider of optical micro-electro-mechanical systems. The company's applications include maskless lithography and large format digital displays.	408-240-4700	NA	Sunnyvale
Silicon Motion Inc (DH)	Designer of low-power semiconductor solutions. The company serves multimedia consumer electronic applications.	408-519-7289	NA	Milpitas
Silicon Wafer Enterprises LLC (HQ)	Provider of silicon wafers and other raw materials. The company's offerings include silicon, plate glass, pyrex, and sapphire.	916-201-6675	NA	El Dorado Hills
Silicon360 (HQ)	Supplier of semiconductors for the military, aerospace, industrial, medical, and commercial markers.	408-432-1790	NA	Milpitas

COMPANY NAME	PRODUCT / SERVICE	PHONE	EMP	CITY
Small Precision Tools Inc (BR)	Manufacturer of chip bonding tools, fine ceramic, and machining parts. The company offers necessary technical support and services.	707-762-5880	NA	Petaluma
Socionext Inc (HQ)	Designer and developer of System-on-Chip products. The company's products are used in imaging, networking, and computing fields.	408-550-6861	NA	Santa Clara
Solarius Development Inc (HQ)	Manufacturer of 3D metrology surface measurement systems. The company offers metrology services for surface form.	408-435-2777	NA	San Jose
Sperient Corporation Inc (HQ)	Designer and developer of electronic systems. The company's applications include telemedicine and robotic sensing.	925-447-3333	NA	Livermore
Statico (HQ)	Provider of ESD and static control products. The company offers test instruments, ionizers, and cleanroom products.	650-592-4733	NA	San Carlos
Surplus Process Equipment Corp (HQ)	Provider of new, used, and refurbished semiconductor equipment. The company offers ashing and etching systems.	408-654-9500	NA	San Jose
System General USA (DH)	Designer and manufacturer of device programmers and offers consultancy services in device programming and power management.	833-845-3900	NA	San Jose
Taracom Integrated Products (HQ)	Provider of multi-gigabit solutions for communications and storage applications. The company's solutions include backplane and fiber channel.	408-691-6655	NA	Santa Clara
Tazmo Inc (BR)	Manufacturer of SOG and LCD color filter coaters. The company offers SOG, SOD, polyimide coaters and developers and LCD Resist coaters.	510-438-4890	NA	Fremont
Tela Innovations Inc (HQ)	Provider of lithography optimized solutions. The company's services include design, implementation, and technical support.	408-558-6300	NA	Los Gatos
Teradyne Inc (BR)	Supplier of automatic test equipment. The company caters to semiconductor, electronics, and automotive sectors.	480-777-7090	NA	San Jose
Thermal Engineering Associates Inc (HQ)	Provider of semiconductor thermal measurement and modeling solutions. The company's products include thermal test systems, test fixtures, and test chips.	650-961-5900	NA	Santa Clara
Toppan Printing Company Ltd (BR)	Provider of printing solutions. The company serves customers in the food, beverage, and high barrier product industries.	415-393-9839	NA	San Francisco
N Trans-Cal Industries Inc (HQ)	Manufacturer of pressure altitude reporting equipment for general and military aviation markers.	818-787-1221	NA	Van Nuys
Translarity (HQ)	Specializes in wafer translation technology. The company offers device design and testing solutions to the semiconductor industry.	510-371-7900	NA	Fremont
True Circuits Inc (HQ)	Developer and marketer of phase-locked loops, delay-locked loops, and mixed-signal designs for integrated circuits.	650-949-3400	NA	Los Altos
TSMC North America (HQ)	Manufacturer of products for the computer, communications, and consumer electronics market segments.	408-382-8000	NA	San Jose
Vacuum Engineering & Materials Co (HQ)	Manufacturer and supplier of PVD materials. The company also offers services like shield cleaning, material reclaim, and consignment programs.	408-871-9900	NA	Santa Clara
Verific Design Automation Inc (HQ)	Specializes in electronic design automation solutions. The company offers services to the semiconductor industry.	510-522-1555	NA	Alameda
Versatile Power (HQ)	Designer and manufacturer of electronic subsystems for manufacturers. The company focuses on application of radio frequency, ultrasonics, and lasers.	408-341-4600	NA	Campbell
N Victory Foam Inc (HQ)	Provider of custom foam, plastic packaging and much more solutions for industry products and tools.	949-474-0690	51-200	Irvine
VIsi Research Inc (HQ)	Provider of chip market research, consultation, semiconductor analysis, and data spreadsheets and reports.	408-453-8844	NA	San Jose
VLSI Standards Inc (HQ)	Manufacturer of electrical and solar energy products. The company offers calibration services to the semiconductor industry.	408-428-1800	NA	Milpitas
Wafer Process Systems Inc (HQ)	Manufacturer of semiconductors, MEMS, and photonics. The company also focuses on RFID products, disc drives, and flat panel displays.	408-445-3010	NA	San Jose
Westfab Manufacturing Inc (HQ)	Manufacturer of simple brackets, multiple level frames, and enclosures. The company offers assembly services for power supplies, switches, and cables.	408-727-0550	NA	Santa Clara
World Products Inc (HQ)	Provider of electronic component solutions and services. The company offers sales, distribution, and technical support.	707-996-5201	NA	Sonoma
X-Fab Texas Inc (BR)	Provider of foundry services. The company focuses on analog and mixed signal semiconductor applications.	408-844-0066	NA	San Jose
X-Scan Imaging Corp (HQ)	Supplier of x-ray imaging and inspection equipment. The company also offers array detectors and line-scan camera products.	408-432-9888	NA	San Jose
Xeltek Inc (HQ)	Manufacturer of automated, production, and in-system programmers, and socket adapters, and related supplies.	408-530-8080	NA	Sunnyvale
XTAL Inc (HQ)	Specializes in yield enhancement, software optimization and hardware implementation targeting semiconductor ecosystem.	408-642-5328	NA	San Jose

213 = Transducers/Transistors/Resistors

Andrew Ndt Engineering Corp (HQ)	Manufacturer of probes, ultrasonic transducers, diamond cutting tools, proximity sensors, cables, and offers calibration services.	408-710-0342	NA	San Jose

	COMPANY NAME	PRODUCT / SERVICE	PHONE	EMP	CITY
N	B.K. Thorpe Co (HQ)	Distributor of valves and fittings for commercial and industrial application such as brass appliances, ball-plex and duplex, grooved end, tilting disc check, sampling and much more.	562-595-1811	NA	Signal Hill
	Bandwidth10 Inc (BR)	Developer of tunable, singlemode, 1550 nm long-wavelength VCSELs, and transceivers for datacom applications.	203-561-0769	NA	Berkeley
N	Bearing Engineers Inc (HQ)	Manufacturer of semiconductor fabrication equipment, medical equipment, aerospace and robotics components.	949-586-7442	NA	Aliso Viejo
	Caltron Components Corp (HQ)	Distributor of electronic capacitors and resistors. The company also focuses on semiconductor products.	408-748-2140	NA	Santa Clara
	Data Physics Corp (HQ)	Provider of high performance test and measurement solutions for noise and vibration applications. The company offers drop testing services.	408-437-0100	NA	San Jose
N	Dhv Industries Inc (HQ)	Distributor of carbon steel, cast iron, stainless steel, and alloy gate valve products.	661-392-8948	11-50	Bakersfield
N	Hoffmeyer Company Inc (HQ)	Manufacturer and distributor of conveyor belting and components, couplings, industrial and hydraulic hoses.	510-895-9955	51-200	San Leandro
	Infineon Technologies North American Corp (BR)	Provider of semiconductor and system solutions. The company focuses on mobile security, sensors, power management, and RF.	866-951-9519	NA	Morgan Hill
	Josephson Engineering Inc (HQ)	Manufacturer of condenser microphones for studio, stage, and field sound pickup, and audio instrumentation.	831-420-0888	NA	Santa Cruz
	NIC Components Corp (BR)	Designer, manufacturer, and supplier of passive components. The company offers ceramic capacitors, power inductors, and current sensing resistors.	669-342-3960	NA	San Jose
	NK Technologies (HQ)	Manufacturer of current sensors and transducer products for the factory and industrial automation markers.	408-871-7510	NA	San Jose
N	R.S. Hughes Company Inc (HQ)	Distributor of industrial supplies such as abrasives, adhesives and sealants, chemicals and much more.	877-774-8443	NA	Sunnyvale
	Tavis Corp (HQ)	Provider of custom pressure transducer sensor designs. The company offers services to measurement environments.	209-966-2027	NA	Mariposa
N	Trans-Cal Industries Inc (HQ)	Manufacturer of pressure altitude reporting equipment for general and military aviation markers.	818-787-1221	NA	Van Nuys
N	Victory Foam Inc (HQ)	Provider of custom foam, plastic packaging and much more solutions for industry products and tools.	949-474-0690	51-200	Irvine
	Voltage Multipliers Inc (HQ)	Manufacturer of voltage multipliers, high voltage diodes, rectifiers, opto-couplers, and power supplies.	559-651-1402	NA	Visalia

214 = Transformers

	COMPANY NAME	PRODUCT / SERVICE	PHONE	EMP	CITY
	Bandwidth10 Inc (BR)	Developer of tunable, singlemode, 1550 nm long-wavelength VCSELs, and transceivers for datacom applications.	203-561-0769	NA	Berkeley
	Custom Coils Inc (HQ)	Manufacturer of coils, coil assemblies, and solenoids. The company also offers other electro-magnetic devices.	707-752-8633	NA	Benicia
	Kemet Electronics Corp (BR)	Provider of relays, EMI filters, transformers, capacitors, and ferrite products. The company serves the aerospace, defense, and automotive industries.	877-695-3638	NA	Santa Clara
	Magnetic Circuit Elements (HQ)	Manufacturer of miniature transformers and inductors. The company's products include chokes, inductors, transformers, and sine wave inverters.	831-757-8752	NA	Salinas
N	Magtech & Power Conversion Inc (HQ)	Designer and manufacturer of custom magnets.	714-451-0106	11-50	Fullerton
	Pearson Electronics Inc (HQ)	Manufacturer of wide band current monitors. The company also offers high voltage pulse transformers and voltage dividers.	650-494-6444	NA	Palo Alto
	Stangenes Industries Inc (HQ)	Manufacturer of isolation transformers, current monitors, charging inductors, and magnetic components.	650-493-0814	NA	Palo Alto
	Tamura Corporation of America (BR)	Manufacturer of DC power modules, current sensor products, telecom transformers, and LED products. The company is involved in distribution services.	760-871-2009	NA	Escondido
	Tecdia Inc (HQ)	Manufacturer of precision machine tools and fixtures. The company also specializes in cutting and scribing tools.	408-748-0100	NA	Campbell

217 = Defense-Related R&D

	COMPANY NAME	PRODUCT / SERVICE	PHONE	EMP	CITY
	Axelsys LLC (HQ)	Provider of electronic design and manufacturing services. The company's offerings include LED and AC to DC industrial power supplies.	408-600-0871	NA	San Jose
	EA Machining Inc (HQ)	Provider of CNC turning and milling services. The company offers services to the semiconductor manufacturing equipment industry.	408-727-4962	NA	Santa Clara
	Yotta Navigation Corp (HQ)	Manufacturer of sub-meter positioning systems and underwater precision navigation platforms. The company serves the homeland security market.	800-943-1220	NA	Santa Clara

218 = Electronic Warfare Equipment

	COMPANY NAME	PRODUCT / SERVICE	PHONE	EMP	CITY
	TPS Aviation Inc (HQ)	Distributor of commercial and military aerospace fasteners and electric components. The company focuses on aerospace parts, components, and logistics.	510-475-1010	NA	Hayward

219 = Military Aircraft & Related Equipment

COMPANY NAME	PRODUCT / SERVICE	PHONE	EMP	CITY
Aero Precision (HQ)	Supplier of military aircraft parts for the aerospace industry. The company's services include repair, replacement, and maintenance.	925-455-9900	NA	Livermore
TPS Aviation Inc (HQ)	Distributor of commercial and military aerospace fasteners and electric components. The company focuses on aerospace parts, components, and logistics.	510-475-1010	NA	Hayward

220 = Military Search, Detection & Navigation Systems & Instruments

COMPANY NAME	PRODUCT / SERVICE	PHONE	EMP	CITY
Bridgepoint Systems Inc (HQ)	Provider of security solutions such as CAC card readers, PIV card readers, and access control experts for government contractors and security integrators.	510-346-1510	NA	Berkeley
SNA Electronics Inc (HQ)	Provider of electronic manufacturing services. The company offers services to OEMs in the networking, medical instruments, and aerospace industries.	510-656-3903	NA	Fremont

221 = Missiles & Related Equipment

COMPANY NAME	PRODUCT / SERVICE	PHONE	EMP	CITY
Yotta Navigation Corp (HQ)	Manufacturer of sub-meter positioning systems and underwater precision navigation platforms. The company serves the homeland security market.	800-943-1220	NA	Santa Clara

224 = Systems Analysis, Integration & Other Military Services

COMPANY NAME	PRODUCT / SERVICE	PHONE	EMP	CITY
Compudata Inc (HQ)	Provider of sales, accounting, and manufacturing software. The company especially caters to businesses.	415-495-3422	NA	San Francisco
Emlinux (HQ)	Developer of embedded Linux designs. The company provides marketing level definition and system architecture services.	408-249-5574	NA	San Jose
GoEngineer (BR)	Provider of solid works engineering and Oracle agile PLM products. The company offers services to the business sector.	408-213-1580	NA	Santa Clara
Immecor (HQ)	Provider of industrial computers, custom cables, and PCB assembly services. The company serves entertainment, medical, and telecom sectors.	707-636-2550	NA	Santa Rosa
InfoTech Spectrum Inc (HQ)	Provider of integrated creative IT services including IT consulting, advanced technology deployment, and product development.	408-705-2237	NA	Santa Clara
Ledger Systems Inc (HQ)	Provider of network design and support services. The company also offers accounting and e-Commerce solutions.	650-592-6211	NA	San Carlos
Nevtec Inc (HQ)	Provider of networks implementation and maintenance services. The company also focuses on workstations and the Internet.	408-292-8600	NA	San Jose
Presentek Inc (HQ)	Designer of websites and web portals. The company also offers content management systems and e-commerce handlers.	408-354-1264	NA	Los Gatos

226 = Monitoring/Controlling Equipment

COMPANY NAME	PRODUCT / SERVICE	PHONE	EMP	CITY
Pivotal Systems (HQ)	Provider of monitoring and process control technology solutions for the semiconductor manufacturing industry.	510-770-9125	NA	Fremont

227 = Automatic Regulating Controls

COMPANY NAME	PRODUCT / SERVICE	PHONE	EMP	CITY
Civil Maps (HQ)	Developer of autonomous vehicles and cognitive perception systems. The company specializes in localization technology and artificial intelligence.	415-287-9977	NA	San Francisco
Enocean Alliance Inc (HQ)	Manufacturer of wireless switches, sensors, and controls for building automation and residential property needs.	925-275-6601	NA	San Ramon
Lamphier-Gregory (HQ)	Provider of urban planning services. The company provides environmental analysis, project management, and coordination services.	510-535-6690	NA	Oakland
Martinelli Environmental Graphics (HQ)	Provide of environmental graphic designing services. The company offers fabrication, installation, and design build services.	415-468-4000	NA	San Francisco
Pivotal Systems (HQ)	Provider of monitoring and process control technology solutions for the semiconductor manufacturing industry.	510-770-9125	NA	Fremont
Trench & Traffic Supply Inc (HQ)	Provider of traffic control equipment for rent and sale. The company offers equipment for traffic control, shoring, and pipe testing.	916-920-3304	NA	Sacramento

228 = Control Panels

COMPANY NAME	PRODUCT / SERVICE	PHONE	EMP	CITY
Calcon Systems Inc (HQ)	Provider of process control, instrumentation, and automation solutions specializing in turnkey design-build system integration and support.	925-277-0665	NA	San Ramon
California Motor Controls (HQ)	Manufacturer of electrical control panels. The company offers pump controls and communication systems for municipal and commercial applications.	707-746-6255	NA	Benicia
Control Systems West Inc (HQ)	Designer and fabricator of a broad variety of custom electrical controls for industrial applications.	707-763-1108	NA	Petaluma
DST Controls (HQ)	Provider of control systems integration, industrial data management, and related enterprise solutions. The company serves the industrial sector.	800-251-0773	NA	Benicia
Interphasic LLC (HQ)	Manufacturer of motion control systems. The company offers product support services and it serves the industrial sector.	831-392-0708	NA	Seaside
Pivotal Systems (HQ)	Provider of monitoring and process control technology solutions for the semiconductor manufacturing industry.	510-770-9125	NA	Fremont
N Tayco Engineering Inc (HQ)	Designer and manufacturer of heating systems, temperature sensors, flexible cable, and other specialty products.	714-952-2240	51-200	Cypress

COMPANY NAME	PRODUCT / SERVICE	PHONE	EMP	CITY

230 = Flow Control Instruments

American Micro Detection Systems Inc (HQ)	Provider of water analysis treatments. The company deals with research, development, and monitoring services.	209-985-1705	NA	Stockton
Autoflow Products Inc (HQ)	Manufacturer of flow switches. The company specializes in designing switches for chemical analyzers, chemical injectors, and chromatographic systems.	916-626-3058	NA	Rocklin
Pivotal Systems (HQ)	Provider of monitoring and process control technology solutions for the semiconductor manufacturing industry.	510-770-9125	NA	Fremont
The Detection Group Inc (HQ)	Provider of monitoring and alarming solutions. The company offers wireless water leak detection systems for commercial buildings.	650-215-7300	NA	Sunnyvale

231 = Gas & Liquid Control Instruments

American Micro Detection Systems Inc (HQ)	Provider of water analysis treatments. The company deals with research, development, and monitoring services.	209-985-1705	NA	Stockton
Autoflow Products Inc (HQ)	Manufacturer of flow switches. The company specializes in designing switches for chemical analyzers, chemical injectors, and chromatographic systems.	916-626-3058	NA	Rocklin
Hpm Systems Inc (HQ)	Provider of gas monitoring control systems. The company's services include design, integration, installation, and maintenance.	408-615-6900	NA	Santa Clara
Picarro Inc (HQ)	Provider of environmental transformation solutions. The company provides isotope analyzers, trace gas analyzers, accessories, and peripherals.	408-962-3900	NA	Santa Clara

232 = Industrial Controllers & Relays

California Motor Controls (HQ)	Manufacturer of electrical control panels. The company offers pump controls and communication systems for municipal and commercial applications.	707-746-6255	NA	Benicia
Green Plug (HQ)	Developer and provider of digital controller technology solutions and products to the consumer electronics markers.	925-867-2781	NA	San Ramon
Motion Control Engineering Inc (HQ)	Manufacturer of elevator control products. The company's products include elevator and escalator controls, complete elevators, and components and peripherals.	916-463-9200	NA	Rancho Cordova
O2micro USA (LH)	Provider of battery and power management products. The company also offers LED general lighting and backlighting products.	408-987-5920	NA	Santa Clara
N Tayco Engineering Inc (HQ)	Designer and manufacturer of heating systems, temperature sensors, flexible cable, and other specialty products.	714-952-2240	51-200	Cypress

233 = Industrial Instruments for Measurement, Display & Control

Acosta Sheet Metal Manufacturing Inc (HQ)	Manufacturer of HVAC and architectural products, and sheet metal building materials. The company provides gutter profile caps and conductor heads.	408-275-6370	NA	San Jose
Air Monitor Corp (HQ)	Manufacturer of airflow and space pressurization control systems and offers airflow traverse probes, pressure sensors, and electronic transmitters.	707-544-2706	NA	Santa Rosa
Arista Corp (HQ)	Manufacturer of industrial computer products such as industrial rack mounts, touch screen displays, and fanless, embedded, and wall mount computers.	510-226-1800	NA	Fremont
Assay Technology Inc (HQ)	Provider of personal monitoring badges to monitor chemicals in worker's breathing zone. The company also analyzes the contents of returned samplers.	925-461-8880	NA	Livermore
Automate Scientific Inc (HQ)	Manufacturer and distributor of biomedical equipment. The company offers amplifiers, manipulators, software, and accessories.	510-845-6283	NA	Berkeley
Celadon Inc (HQ)	Provider of OEM products and services. The company's products include OEM remote controls, infrared receivers, and backlighting systems.	415-472-1177	NA	San Rafael
Control Systems West Inc (HQ)	Designer and fabricator of a broad variety of custom electrical controls for industrial applications.	707-763-1108	NA	Petaluma
CSI Forensic Supply (HQ)	Manufacturer and supplier of products for law enforcement for crime scene and crime laboratory applications.	925-686-6667	NA	Martinez
Deltatrak Inc (HQ)	Manufacturer of cold chain management systems. The company provides data loggers, chart recorders, thermometers, and timers and pH meters.	925-249-2250	NA	Pleasanton
Ekm Metering Inc (HQ)	Provider of submetering hardware and services. The company's solutions include revenue metering and data monitoring.	831-425-7371	NA	Santa Cruz
Enlighted Inc (HQ)	Provider of lighting control systems to commercial buildings, office workspaces, and garages. The company serves facilities and development companies.	650-964-1094	NA	Santa Clara
Fairbanks Scales (BR)	Provider of scales and weighing systems. The company serves the agriculture, parcel shipping, transport, and waste management industries.	916-384-1394	NA	Sacramento
Garratt-Callahan Co (HQ)	Provider of water treatment services. The company's solutions include cooling water treatment and safer chemical cleaning.	650-984-5126	NA	Burlingame

COMPANY NAME	PRODUCT / SERVICE	PHONE	EMP	CITY
Gonsel'S Machine Shop (HQ)	Provider of CNC and millwork, inspection, fabrication, and re-machining services. The company serves the food and beverage industry.	510-569-8086	NA	Oakland
HSQ Technology (HQ)	Provider of control system and energy management services, specializing in data and SCADA monitoring.	510-259-1334	NA	Hayward
Logosol Inc (BR)	Manufacturer and designer of motion control components. The company's products are used in semiconductor material handling applications.	408-744-0974	NA	El Dorado Hills
Mission Peak Optics Inc (HQ)	Provider of measurement solutions for semiconductor industry. The company offers thin film thickness measurement system.	510-438-0384	NA	Fremont
Neptune Systems LLC (HQ)	Provider of aquarium controllers. The company also offers expansion modules and accessories and offers support services.	408-275-2205	NA	Morgan Hill
Novalynx Corp (HQ)	Designer, manufacturer, and integrator of meteorological systems. The company's products are used in the industrial sector.	530-823-7185	NA	Grass Valley
Pivotal Systems (HQ)	Provider of monitoring and process control technology solutions for the semiconductor manufacturing industry.	510-770-9125	NA	Fremont
SAGE Instruments Inc (RH)	Provider of wireless base station test products. The company offers battery operated handhelds, portables, bench tops, and rackmount test platforms.	831-761-1000	NA	Freedom
Square Inc (HQ)	Builds tools to empower and enrich people and help sellers of all areas to start, run, and grow their businesses.	415-375-3176	NA	San Francisco
Takex America Inc (DH)	Manufacturer of security and industrial sensor products. The company's products include photoelectric beams, outdoor and indoor PIR, and tower enclosures.	408-747-0100	NA	Sunnyvale
United States Thermoelectric Consortium (HQ)	Manufacturer of thermal management and control systems. The company's offerings also include controllers and air and liquid cooling systems.	530-345-8000	NA	Chico
Video Clarity Inc (HQ)	Provider of real time and broadcast quality monitoring, perceptual analysis, recording, and automating services.	408-379-6952	NA	Campbell

234 = Machine Vision/Inspection Systems

CSI Forensic Supply (HQ)	Manufacturer and supplier of products for law enforcement for crime scene and crime laboratory applications.	925-686-6667	NA	Martinez

235 = Measurement & Test

Advanced Witness Series Inc (HQ)	Designer of electrical and mechanical components and tools. The company caters to various applications.	408-453-5070	NA	San Jose
Advantest America Inc (LH)	Provider of measurement systems and solutions. The company offers electronic measuring instruments, and optical sensing and imaging analysis systems.	408-456-3600	NA	San Jose
All Weather Inc (HQ)	Manufacturer of meteorological instruments and systems. The company is also engaged in the development of air traffic management solutions.	800-824-5873	NA	Sacramento
Azbil North America Inc (BR)	Designer, manufacturer, and supplier of medical devices. The company offers automation products, control products, and industrial automation systems.	408-245-3121	NA	Santa Clara
Buglab LLC (HQ)	Developer of biomass measuring equipment such as sensors, biomass monitor, and biomass multiplier involved in fermentation and microbial cultures.	925-208-1952	NA	Concord
CSI Forensic Supply (HQ)	Manufacturer and supplier of products for law enforcement for crime scene and crime laboratory applications.	925-686-6667	NA	Martinez
Dakota Ultrasonics (HQ)	Manufacturer of industrial ultrasonic testing equipment. The company serves the aerospace, power generation, and petrochemical industries.	831-431-9722	NA	Scotts Valley
Fibera Inc (HQ)	Manufacturer and designer of wavelength management products. The company also specializes in fiber optic products.	408-492-9555	NA	Santa Clara
Finishline Advanced Composites LLC (HQ)	Provider of composite repair services for production projects. The company is involved in design, development, prototyping, testing, and production.	707-747-0788	NA	Benicia
Flexline LLC (HQ)	Provider of custom solutions for manufacturing and test problems. The company also deals with automation, engineering, and production tooling.	408-295-3901	NA	San Jose
N Georg Fischer Signet LLC (HQ)	Manufacturer of piping systems and components.	626-571-2770	NA	El Monte
Horiba Instruments Inc (BR)	Provider of instruments and systems for automotive research and development, and process and environmental monitoring needs.	408-730-4772	NA	Sunnyvale
Lansmont Corp (HQ)	Provider of products such as field instruments, shock machines, vibration systems, drop testers, and package shakers.	831-655-6600	NA	Monterey
Magee Scientific Co (HQ)	Provider of measurement instruments such as aethalometers, transmissometers, and their accessories for monitoring air quality and source emissions.	510-845-2801	NA	Berkeley
Maselli Measurements Inc (BR)	Provider of liquid measuring solutions. The company manufactures and distributes refractometers and liquid analyzers for several industries.	209-474-9178	NA	Stockton
Mirion Technologies Inc (DH)	Provider of solutions in radiation detection. The company serves the healthcare, nuclear power, and other industries.	925-543-0800	NA	San Ramon

COMPANY NAME	PRODUCT / SERVICE	PHONE	EMP	CITY
Modutek Corp (HQ)	Manufacturer of wet process equipment and environmental systems. The company serves the semiconductor sector and offers repair services.	408-362-2000	NA	San Jose
Nitinol Devices & Components Inc (HQ)	Provider of rapid development and prototyping services. The company is also engaged in commercialization.	510-683-2000	NA	Fremont
Pacific Instruments Inc (HQ)	Manufacturer of computer-automated physical measurement systems. The company specializes in signal conditioning and data acquisition equipment.	925-827-9010	NA	Concord
Picarro Inc (HQ)	Provider of environmental transformation solutions. The company provides isotope analyzers, trace gas analyzers, accessories, and peripherals.	408-962-3900	NA	Santa Clara
Prysm Inc (HQ)	Provider of large format digital display solutions and software for real-time visual communication applications.	408-586-1100	NA	San Jose
N Ronan Engineering Co (HQ)	Manufacturer reliable and leading-edge instrumentation systems.	661-702-1344	NA	Valencia
Safe Hearing America Inc (HQ)	Provider of mobile hearing testing services and products. The company offerings include AQ Solid Plug, Sleep Plug, and Solid Plug.	707-446-0880	NA	Vacaville
Sentient Energy Inc (HQ)	Provider of sensor devices for operational practices and engineering applications. The company also offers communication software.	650-523-6680	NA	Burlingame
Solarius Development Inc (HQ)	Manufacturer of 3D metrology surface measurement systems. The company offers metrology services for surface form.	408-435-2777	NA	San Jose
Sotcher Measurement Inc (HQ)	Provider of test equipment. The company provides test stations, service tags, generator test sets, and automatic test stations.	800-922-2969	NA	San Jose
Telemakus LLC (HQ)	Provider of USB controlled RF devices. The company devices include switches, vector modulators, and digital attenuators.	916-458-6346	NA	Folsom
Teradyne Inc (BR)	Supplier of automatic test equipment. The company caters to semiconductor, electronics, and automotive sectors.	480-777-7090	NA	San Jose
Vanderlans & Sons Inc (HQ)	Manufacturer of pipe and high pressure plugs, test equipment, hoses, gauges, ventilators, and related accessories.	209-334-4115	NA	Lodi
Vena Engineering Corp (HQ)	Manufacturer of hard drive test equipment and environmental chalmers. The company also offers motors and power supplies.	831-724-5738	NA	Watsonville
N Worldwide Environmental Products Inc (HQ)	Provider of automotive inspection and maintenance programs.	714-990-2700	NA	Brea

236 = Pressure Instruments

COMPANY NAME	PRODUCT / SERVICE	PHONE	EMP	CITY
All Sensors Corp (HQ)	Manufacturer of MEMS piezoresistive pressure sensors and pressure transducers. The company serves the medical, industrial, and HVAC markers.	408-225-4314	NA	Morgan Hill
Altair Technologies Inc (HQ)	Provider of precision furnace brazing services. The company serves the medical, defense, and semiconductor industries.	650-508-8700	NA	Fremont
Mydax Inc (HQ)	Designer and manufacturer of temperature control systems. The company offers the elite chiller system.	530-888-6662	NA	Auburn
Paragon Controls Inc (HQ)	Designer and manufacturer of air flow and pressure measurement and control systems. The company also offers airflow sensing elements.	707-579-1424	NA	Santa Rosa
Vanderlans & Sons Inc (HQ)	Manufacturer of pipe and high pressure plugs, test equipment, hoses, gauges, ventilators, and related accessories.	209-334-4115	NA	Lodi

238 = Automatic Vending Machines

COMPANY NAME	PRODUCT / SERVICE	PHONE	EMP	CITY
Ventek International (HQ)	Manufacturer of parking revenue control systems. The company offers recreation, commuter rail, and parking access control solutions.	707-773-3373	NA	Petaluma

242 = Electric Security Systems

COMPANY NAME	PRODUCT / SERVICE	PHONE	EMP	CITY
Mil-Ram Technology Inc (HQ)	Manufacturer of industrial gas and detection systems. The company serves the oil and gas, pulp and paper, and chemical industries.	510-656-2001	NA	Fremont
QuantumScape Corp (HQ)	Provider of energy storage, electronics, and related solutions. The company offers services to the environmental sector.	408-452-2007	NA	San Jose

243 = Lighting Systems

COMPANY NAME	PRODUCT / SERVICE	PHONE	EMP	CITY
Advanced Radiation Corp (HQ)	Manufacturer of mercury-xenon, and capillary lamps. The company's services include design, installation, and delivery.	408-727-9200	NA	Santa Clara
Applied Photon Technology Inc (HQ)	Provider of precision flash lamps. The company's products include Krypton arc lamps, OEM's and APT's laser flash lamps, and specialty lamps.	510-780-9500	NA	Hayward
N Architectural Cathode Lighting Inc (HQ)	Manufacturer and distributor of neon, cold cathodes and LED lightings.	323-581-8800	NA	Huntington Park
Architectural Lighting Works (HQ)	Manufacturer of suspended, wall, and ceiling lighting products and related accessories. The company also deals with installation services.	510-489-2530	NA	Oakland
AutoCell Electronics Inc (HQ)	Manufacturer and distributor of energy efficient lighting products. The company offers compact fluorescent lamps, LED flashlights, and showerheads.	888-393-6668	NA	Elk Grove
B-K Lighting Inc (HQ)	Provider of architectural outdoor landscape lighting products. The company serves residential and commercial properties.	559-438-5800	NA	Madera
BBI Engineering Inc (HQ)	Designer and installer of audiovisual, multimedia, teleconferencing and data systems for museums, aquariums, zoos, schools, and universities.	415-695-9555	NA	San Francisco

	COMPANY NAME	PRODUCT / SERVICE	PHONE	EMP	CITY
	Blair Electric Services Inc (HQ)	Provider of electrical contracting services. The company offers pump and well controls, PLC controls, and surveillance systems.	559-784-8658	NA	Porterville
	Borden Lighting (HQ)	Provider of lighting solutions. The company provides table and floor lamps, architectural lighting, and louvers.	510-357-0171	NA	Oakland
	Boyd Lighting (HQ)	Manufacturer of lighting devices. The company offers its products in white glass, clear ribbed glass, and gloss ivory acrylic product finishes.	415-778-4300	NA	Sausalito
N	C.W. Cole & Company Inc (HQ)	Manufacturer and distributor of lighting products.	626-443-2473	NA	South El Monte
N	Capax Technologies Inc (HQ)	Designer and manufacturer of capacitors for commercial and military RF and Microwave applications.	661-257-7666	NA	Valencia
	Casella Lighting (HQ)	Retailer of lamps and chandeliers. The company also sells floor lamps, wall lamps, picture lights, and ceiling fixtures.	888-252-7874	NA	Sacramento
	Construction Electrical Products (HQ)	Provider of electrical products for the construction sector. The company offers temporary power products, extension cords, and portable lighting.	925-828-9420	NA	Livermore
	Cooling Source Inc (HQ)	Provider of thermal design solution for LED lighting, medical, military/aero, and test equipment industries.	925-292-1293	NA	Livermore
	Finelite Inc (HQ)	Manufacturer of lighting products. The company's services include design, installation, repairs and replacement, and maintenance.	510-441-1100	NA	Union City
	Flight Light Inc (HQ)	Supplier of airport lighting products. The company is a manufacturer of runway lights, taxiway lights, wind cones, and approach systems.	916-394-2800	NA	Sacramento
	Gara Inc (HQ)	Designer and manufacturer of energy efficient lighting technologies. The company also focuses on supply aspects.	530-887-1110	NA	Auburn
	HelioWorks Inc (HQ)	Manufacturer of infrared lamps. The company's products are used in non-dispersive infrared gas detectors for medical and industrial applications.	707-578-7200	NA	Santa Rosa
	Inlite Corp (HQ)	Manufacturer and distributor of directional lighting equipment. The company offers tracks and lighting components.	800-346-5932	NA	Berkeley
	Intematix Corp (HQ)	Developer of microscopy metrology tools and electronic materials. The company offers services to commercial properties.	510-933-3300	NA	Fremont
	Kateeva Inc (HQ)	Manufacturer of LED and other display products. The company specializes in the design and fabrication of OLED displays.	800-385-7802	NA	Newark
	Leotek Electronics USA LLC (HQ)	Manufacturer of light-emitting diodes and lights for traffic and transit, street and area, commercial, petroleum, and grocery and retail stores.	408-380-1788	NA	San Jose
	Light & Motion (HQ)	Provider of light and motion personal lighting system for mountain, bike, foot, camera, water, and underwater activities.	831-645-1538	NA	Marina
	Light Guard Systems Inc (HQ)	Provider of traffic safety products such as controllers, signal head and base plate modules, and LED signage products.	707-542-4547	NA	Santa Rosa
	Light Polymers Inc (HQ)	Developer of polymers and materials. The company formulates and develops solutions for lyotropic liquid crystals.	650-678-7733	NA	S San Francisco
N	Lightway Industries (HQ)	Designer, manufacturer and distributor of commercial, architectural lighting fixtures.	661-257-0286	1-10	Valencia
	Lindsley Lighting LLC (HQ)	Provider of lighting solutions focusing on design, sales, installation, and delivery. The company serves residential and commercial properties.	925-254-1860	NA	Martinez
	Lumenetix Inc (HQ)	Supplier of LED light engines, LED light modules, and LED components. The company also offers reflectors and surface mount LED light fixings.	877-805-7284	NA	Scotts Valley
	McWong International Inc (HQ)	Designer and manufacturer of lighting control equipment and related electrical components. The company offers sensors and LED drivers.	916-371-8080	NA	Sacramento
	Megmeet USA Inc (BR)	Manufacturer of electrical motors, general-used converters, and optional devices. The company offers industry automatic solutions.	408-260-7211	NA	San Jose
N	Myers Power Products Inc (HQ)	Manufacturer of electrical distribution products, emergency power systems, medium voltage switchgear, powerhouses and much more.	909-923-1800	5001-10000	Corona
	Ocean Presence Technologies (HQ)	Manufacturer of underwater video monitoring camera systems and offers cable systems, power systems, lighting, wireless networks, and accessories.	831-426-4678	NA	Santa Cruz
	Optoelectronix Inc (HQ)	Designer, developer, and manufacturer of plug-and-play and standardized LED-based landscape lighting and engines.	408-241-1222	NA	San Jose
N	Peerless Lighting (HQ)	Manufacturer of commercial and institutional lighting fixtures, linear and fluorescent.	510-845-2760	NA	Berkeley
	Phihong USA Corp (HQ)	Provider of power solutions in the telecom sector. The company also offers data solutions in industrial and personal electronic markers.	510-445-0100	NA	Fremont
	Rambus (HQ)	Manufacturer of semiconductor, lighting, and IP products. The company serves the automotive and transportation markers.	408-462-8000	NA	Sunnyvale
	Seascape Lamps (HQ)	Provider of contemporary and retro home lighting solutions. The company also specializes in printed drum lamp shades.	831-728-5699	NA	Freedom
	Soraa Inc (HQ)	Provider of lighting design and fixture lamp solutions. The company serves hotels, restaurants, theaters, and private residences.	510-456-2200	NA	Fremont
	Soundvision Inc (HQ)	Provider of home entertainment, home automation, house audio, lighting, and motorized window shades.	415-456-7000	NA	Novato
	TechniQuip (HQ)	Supplier of lighting products. The company's offerings include illuminators, fiber optics, and video equipment.	925-251-9030	NA	Pleasanton

COMPANY NAME	PRODUCT / SERVICE	PHONE	EMP	CITY
Universal Light Source Inc (HQ)	Provider of technical lighting applications. The company specializes in flash lamps and strobes, glass and window manufacturing, and PCBs.	415-864-2880	NA	San Francisco
Vision3 Lighting (HQ)	Manufacturer of landscape and exterior architectural lighting products. The company deals with design and installation services.	559-834-5749	NA	Fowler
WAGAN Corp (HQ)	Developer and marketer of automotive accessories to mobile professionals. The company's offerings include warmers, defrosters, and heated cushions.	510-471-9221	NA	Hayward
Xicato Inc (HQ)	Designer and manufacturer of lighting products. The company specializes in providing different types of LED modules.	866-223-8395	NA	San Jose

244 = Magnetic Tape/Compact Disks, etc.

COMPANY NAME	PRODUCT / SERVICE	PHONE	EMP	CITY
Owens Design (HQ)	Developer of advanced technology systems for semiconductor, hard disk drive, solar, medical device, and other sectors.	510-659-1800	NA	Fremont

245 = Miscellaneous Electrical/Electronic Products

	COMPANY NAME	PRODUCT / SERVICE	PHONE	EMP	CITY
	Applied Physics Systems (HQ)	Supplier of magnetic measure and other electronic equipment. The company specializes in measurement while drilling systems and magnetometers.	650-965-0500	NA	Mountain View
	Aqua Sierra Controls Inc (HQ)	Provider of instrumentation and electrical contract services. The company specializes in process control automation for industrial installations.	530-823-3241	NA	Auburn
	ASF Electric Inc (HQ)	Provider of electrical contracting services. The company installs fire safety systems for the retail, health care and public entities.	650-755-9032	NA	Daly City
	Associated Lighting Representatives (ALR) Inc (HQ)	Provider of lighting services. The company offers controls, emergency, indoor, LED, outdoor and pole lighting from several manufacturers.	510-638-3800	NA	Oakland
	Axelsys LLC (HQ)	Provider of electronic design and manufacturing services. The company's offerings include LED and AC to DC industrial power supplies.	408-600-0871	NA	San Jose
	Baldor (BR)	Manufacturer of electric drives. The company also offers bearings, electric motors, drives, gear assemblies, and transmission systems.	510-785-9900	NA	Hayward
	Buckles-Smith (BR)	Supplier of industrial automation equipment. The company offers signaling devices, wires and cables, enclosures, and fasteners.	408-280-7777	NA	Santa Clara
	Cable Connection Inc (HQ)	Provider of premium PCB assemblies and turnkey OEM/ODM product. The company also specializes in cable and wire harness services.	510-249-9000	NA	Fremont
N	California Electric Supply (HQ)	Distributor of electrical products such as cable ties, enclosures, hole cutting and much more.	661-324-6727	NA	Bakersfield
	California Motor Controls (HQ)	Manufacturer of electrical control panels. The company offers pump controls and communication systems for municipal and commercial applications.	707-746-6255	NA	Benicia
N	Coast Appliance Parts Co (HQ)	Distributor of heating, ventilating, and air conditioning equipment.	626-579-1500	NA	South El Monte
	CVM Inc (HQ)	Provider of custom machine tools. The company also offers electrical fabrication, machining, and robotic services.	925-847-8808	NA	Pleasanton
N	Decker Electric Company Inc (HQ)	Provider of comprehensive commercial, industrial, and institutional electrical services.	415-552-1622	NA	San Francisco
	Dunlop Manufacturing Inc (HQ)	Manufacturer of musical instruments and accessories. The company also designs amplifiers, guitar pedals, picks, capos, and strings.	707-745-2722	NA	Benicia
	Enel X e-Mobility (HQ)	Developer of electric vehicle charging technologies such as smart grid EV charging networks for residential, workplace, and commercial installation.	844-584-2329	NA	San Carlos
	Headsets Com Inc (BR)	Provider of office telephone headsets. The company also offers cellphone, computer, and cordless phone headsets.	800-432-3738	NA	San Francisco
	HelioWorks Inc (HQ)	Manufacturer of infrared lamps. The company's products are used in non-dispersive infrared gas detectors for medical and industrial applications.	707-578-7200	NA	Santa Rosa
N	House of Batteries (HQ)	Manufacturer of battery assembly and battery pack.	714-962-7600	11-50	Fountain Valley
	iSmart Alarm Inc (HQ)	Manufacturer of home security products. The company offers alarms, cameras, sirens, and related accessories.	408-245-2551	NA	Sunnyvale
	Lee Mah Electronics Inc (HQ)	Provider of manufacturing solutions. The company serves customers in the medical, communications, and test and measurement industries.	415-394-1288	NA	Brisbane
	LGE Electrical Sales Inc (HQ)	Provider of electrical distribution and transmission products. The company's products include distran packaged substation products, G&W, MGM, and TIKA.	916-563-2737	NA	Sacramento
	Lumenetix Inc (HQ)	Supplier of LED light engines, LED light modules, and LED components. The company also offers reflectors and surface mount LED light fixings.	877-805-7284	NA	Scotts Valley
	Magnetic Circuit Elements (HQ)	Manufacturer of miniature transformers and inductors. The company's products include chokes, inductors, transformers, and sine wave inverters.	831-757-8752	NA	Salinas
	Medland & Associates Inc (BR)	Manufacturer of OEM products. The company's products include AC and DC converters, power supplies, switching regulators, and cable assemblies.	408-686-0460	NA	San Martin
	Meyer Sound Laboratories Inc (HQ)	Manufacturer of loudspeakers, subwoofers, stage monitors, and amplifiers. The company serves the entertainment sector.	510-486-1166	NA	Berkeley

	COMPANY NAME	PRODUCT / SERVICE	PHONE	EMP	CITY
	Modules Technology Inc (HQ)	Provider of custom module design solutions. The company's offerings include grinders, etching systems, and thermal recorders.	408-392-0808	NA	San Jose
	Nady Systems Inc (HQ)	Designer and manufacturer of wireless microphones, and a full line of audio accessories. The company also focuses on marketing.	510-652-2411	NA	Richmond
	Orbotech LT Solar LLC (BR)	Manufacturer of electronic devices. The company offers printed circuit boards, flat panel displays, and touch screens.	408-226-9900	NA	San Jose
	Owens Design (HQ)	Developer of advanced technology systems for semiconductor, hard disk drive, solar, medical device, and other sectors.	510-659-1800	NA	Fremont
	Pentagon Technologies (HQ)	Distributor of electromechanical components. The company offers shaft couplings, seals, and cable assemblies.	800-379-3361	NA	Hayward
	PSC Electronics Inc (HQ)	Distributor of magnetic, interconnect, and electro-mechanical components. The company specializes in cable assembly and modification.	408-737-1333	NA	Santa Clara
	ROD-L Electronics Inc (HQ)	Provider of electrical safety testing equipment. The company also offers hipot test loads, test probes, bond testers, and ground testers.	650-322-0711	NA	Mountain View
	S&C Electric Co (BR)	Provider of equipment and services for electric power systems. The company is involved in design and installation services.	510-864-9300	NA	Alameda
	Sensifree (HQ)	Manufacturer of contactless sensors for wearables. The company offers heart rate sensors, including fitness trackers, and activity monitors.	669-230-5116	NA	Cupertino
	Sensoplex Inc (HQ)	Developer and manufacturer of wearable sensors. The company offers rechargeable batteries, displays, interfaces, and related accessories.	408-391-9019	NA	Redwood City
	Sienna Corp (BR)	Provider of electronic manufacturing services including design and process engineering, prototyping, and electromechanical assembly services.	510-440-0200	NA	Fremont
	Silicondust USA Inc (RH)	Provider of network connected TV tuners. The company offers global solutions to Live TV streaming in businesses, hotels, and education facilities.	925-443-4388	NA	Livermore
N	Staco Systems Inc (HQ)	Developer of illuminated panels, subsystems, switches and custom data entry solutions.	714-549-3041	51-200	Costa Mesa
	Stratedigm Inc (HQ)	Manufacturer of software products, consumables, and related accessories. The company deals with upgrades and installation.	408-512-3901	NA	San Jose
	Sumitomo Electric Device Innovations USA Inc (LH)	Developer of electronic devices that includes wireless devices, optical data links, and optical devices.	408-232-9500	NA	San Jose
	Tesla (HQ)	Designer and manufacturer of electric sedans and electric SUVs. The company is engaged in the production of energy storage systems.	650-681-5000	NA	Palo Alto
	Thync Global Inc (HQ)	Provider of wearable technology solutions. The company is involved in testing and related support services.	408-484-4808	NA	Los Gatos
N	Ushio America Inc (HQ)	Manufacturer and distributor of lighting products.	714-236-8600	51-200	Cypress
N	Walters Wholesale Electric Co (HQ)	Wholesaler of industrial automation, low voltage, residential and commercial lighting products and much more.	562-988-3100	501-1000	Signal Hill
N	Yamaichi Electronics Usa Inc (HQ)	Manufacturer of electrical connectors, sockets, probe cards and much more.	408-715-9100	NA	San Jose

246 = Timers

	COMPANY NAME	PRODUCT / SERVICE	PHONE	EMP	CITY
	Sensoplex Inc (HQ)	Developer and manufacturer of wearable sensors. The company offers rechargeable batteries, displays, interfaces, and related accessories.	408-391-9019	NA	Redwood City

248 = Anesthetics

	COMPANY NAME	PRODUCT / SERVICE	PHONE	EMP	CITY
	Aridis Pharmaceuticals LLC (HQ)	Focuses on anti-infective alternatives to conventional antibiotics. The company offers services to the pharmaceutical sector.	408-385-1742	NA	San Jose
	Credence MedSystems Inc (HQ)	Provider of pharmaceutical products. The company specializes in single-dose injectable medications in pre-filled syringes.	844-263-3797	NA	Menlo Park

249 = Anti Infective Agents

	COMPANY NAME	PRODUCT / SERVICE	PHONE	EMP	CITY
	Abbomax Inc (HQ)	Provider of antibody, peptide, and assay products and services. The company offers antibody production, fragmentation, assay development, and other services.	408-573-1898	NA	San Jose
	AbGenomics International Inc (HQ)	Specializes in the development of drug candidates for immune-mediated inflammation and cancer therapies.	650-453-3462	NA	Redwood City
	Adynxx Inc (HQ)	Developer of drugs to prevent acute post-surgical pain and the transition to persistent or chronic pain.	415-512-7740	NA	San Francisco
	Antibodies Inc (HQ)	Manufacturer of monoclonal and polyclonal antibodies, diagnostic reagents, diagnostic kits, and developer of immunoassays.	530-758-4400	NA	Davis
	Aridis Pharmaceuticals LLC (HQ)	Focuses on anti-infective alternatives to conventional antibiotics. The company offers services to the pharmaceutical sector.	408-385-1742	NA	San Jose
	Cell Marque Corp (HQ)	Producer of primary antibodies, buffers and pretreatment, ancillary reagents, and lab equipment for pathology laboratories and research facilities.	916-746-8900	NA	Rocklin
	Cerus Corp (HQ)	Manufacturer of biomedical products such as the intercept blood system and pathogen reduction system, focused in the field of blood safety.	925-288-6000	NA	Concord

COMPANY NAME	PRODUCT / SERVICE	PHONE	EMP	CITY
Cymabay Therapeutics Inc (HQ)	Developer of therapies for the treatment of metabolic diseases. The company serves the healthcare industry.	510-293-8800	NA	Newark
Cytomx Therapeutics Inc (HQ)	Developer of biomolecular therapeutics. The company specializes in antibody drug development, cancer study, clinical and translational medicine.	650-515-3185	NA	S San Francisco
Eiger Biopharmaceuticals Inc (HQ)	Developer of antiviral therapy and treatments for rare disease therapeutics. The company specializes in treatment for Hepatitis Delta.	650-282-6138	NA	Palo Alto
Exelixis Inc (HQ)	Focuses on the development and commercialization of small molecule therapies. The company is also engaged in clinical trials.	650-837-7000	NA	Alameda
Genentech Inc (HQ)	Focuses on the treatment of breast cancer. The company offers services to patients and medical professionals.	650-225-1000	NA	S San Francisco
MicuRx Pharmaceuticals Inc (HQ)	Provider of pharmaceuticals. The company develops antibiotics to combat drug-resistant bacterial infections.	510-782-2022	NA	Foster City
Perceptimed Inc (HQ)	Provider of medical technologies for dispensing and administration of prescription drugs safer, reducing injuries, and death.	650-941-7000	NA	Mountain View
Phage International Inc (HQ)	Provider of leverage bacteriophage therapy technologies. The company specializes in discovery and rediscovery of effective health care solutions.	925-984-9446	NA	Danville
Planet Biotechnology Inc (HQ)	Provider of biotechnology services. The company develops antibody-based therapeutic and preventative products through plants to meet medical needs.	510-887-1461	NA	Hayward
Presidio Pharmaceuticals Inc (HQ)	Developers of small-molecule antiviral therapeutics. The company is a clinical-stage pharmaceutical company.	415-655-7560	NA	San Francisco
Sagimet Biosciences (HQ)	Focuses on the discovery and development of therapeutic products for the treatment of oncology and infectious diseases.	650-561-8600	NA	San Mateo
Ultragenyx Pharmaceutical Inc (HQ)	Developer of products for the treatment of rare and ultra-rare diseases. The company is engaged in commercialization of products.	415-483-8800	501-1000	Novato
Yenzym Antibodies LLC (HQ)	Provider of antigen design services. The company offers rabbit antibody and antigen specific affinity purification services.	650-583-1031	NA	Brisbane

250 = Blood Products

COMPANY NAME	PRODUCT / SERVICE	PHONE	EMP	CITY
Admecell Inc (HQ)	Manufacturer of ready to use products such as cell based, TRANSIL, and ELISA based assays for in-vitro therapeutic modeling and re-profiling.	510-522-4200	NA	Alameda
Allergy Research Group LLC (BR)	Provider of nutritional products for blood sugar, brain, cardiovascular, metabolic, hormone, liver, and immune support.	510-263-2000	NA	Alameda
Cerus Corp (HQ)	Manufacturer of biomedical products such as the intercept blood system and pathogen reduction system, focused in the field of blood safety.	925-288-6000	NA	Concord
Drawbridge Health Inc (HQ)	Provider of diagnostic testing solutions. The company offers blood testing solutions for a range of biomarker.	650-714-6791	NA	Menlo Park
Hemostat Laboratories (HQ)	Provider of defibrinated sheep blood and other animal blood products for cell culture, diagnostic and veterinary applications.	800-572-6888	NA	Dixon
K-Pax Pharmaceuticals Inc (HQ)	Provider of pharmaceutical grade vitamins and nutritional health supplements for kids, women, and men's health, joints and bones, and immune support.	415-381-7565	NA	Mill Valley
Stemexpress (HQ)	Provider of immunophenotyping, DNA quantitation and viability, tissue transplant verification, and related services.	530-626-7000	NA	Folsom

251 = Biological/Botanical Products

COMPANY NAME	PRODUCT / SERVICE	PHONE	EMP	CITY
Amaranth Medical Inc (HQ)	Specializes in proprietary polymer structure and processing technology. The company's products are used in vascular and nonvascular applications.	650-965-3830	NA	Mountain View
Aridis Pharmaceuticals LLC (HQ)	Focuses on anti-infective alternatives to conventional antibiotics. The company offers services to the pharmaceutical sector.	408-385-1742	NA	San Jose
Cerus Corp (HQ)	Manufacturer of biomedical products such as the intercept blood system and pathogen reduction system, focused in the field of blood safety.	925-288-6000	NA	Concord
CPC Scientific Inc (HQ)	Provider of amino acids, cGMP, generic, catalog, modified, FRET and TR- FRET, and custom peptides to researchers and pharmaceutical companies.	408-734-3800	NA	San Jose
Exelixis Inc (HQ)	Focuses on the development and commercialization of small molecule therapies. The company is also engaged in clinical trials.	650-837-7000	NA	Alameda
Global Marketing Associates Inc (HQ)	Providers of nutrition supplements to health care industry. The company supply innovative and quality ingredients to health care industry.	510-887-2462	NA	Livermore
GS Cosmeceutical USA Inc (HQ)	Provider of custom contract manufacturing services. The company offers skin and personal care products.	925-371-5000	NA	Livermore
Iconic Therapeutics Inc (HQ)	Provider of tissue factor therapeutics. The company focuses on the solid tumors and wet age related macular degeneration.	650-437-1000	NA	S San Francisco
La Belle Inc (BR)	Manufacturer of colostrum and chelated minerals. The company also specializes in spray drying.	209-599-6605	NA	Ripon
MacroGenics Inc (BR)	Developer, manufacturer, and marketer of innovative antibody-based therapeutics for the treatment of cancer and autoimmune disorders.	650-624-2600	NA	Brisbane

COMPANY NAME	PRODUCT / SERVICE	PHONE	EMP	CITY
Marrone Bio Innovations Inc (HQ)	Developer of naturally derived technologies of pest management and plant health products used in agricultural, ornamental, and water treatment.	530-750-2800	NA	Davis
Nutribiotic (HQ)	Manufacturer of health, wellness, and fitness products. The company provides nutritional supplements and personal care products.	707-263-0411	NA	Lakeport
Sagimet Biosciences (HQ)	Focuses on the discovery and development of therapeutic products for the treatment of oncology and infectious diseases.	650-561-8600	NA	San Mateo
Silver Creek Pharmaceuticals Inc (HQ)	Provider of pharmaceuticals. The company develops regenerative medicines with an initial focus on treating cardiovascular disease.	415-978-2178	NA	San Francisco
Theralife Inc (HQ)	Manufacturer of botanical drugs. The company offer botanicals that provide symptom relief for problems related to eyes.	650-949-6080	NA	Los Altos
Zosano Pharma Co (HQ)	Manufacturer of biopharmaceutical products like peptides, proteins, small molecules and vaccines based on transdermal delivery technology.	510-745-1200	NA	Fremont

252 = Diagnostic Agents

COMPANY NAME	PRODUCT / SERVICE	PHONE	EMP	CITY
AAT Bioquest Inc (HQ)	Developer and manufacturer of bioanalytical research reagents and kits. The company focuses on photometric detections including absorption.	408-733-1055	NA	Sunnyvale
Amunix Pharmaceuticals Inc (HQ)	Developer of biomolecular therapy. The company specializes in the development of protein and peptide based therapeutic products.	650-428-1800	NA	Mountain View
Arbor Vita Corp (HQ)	Provider of protein-based molecular diagnostics that is used for the management of infectious diseases and cancer.	408-585-3900	NA	Fremont
Aridis Pharmaceuticals LLC (HQ)	Focuses on anti-infective alternatives to conventional antibiotics. The company offers services to the pharmaceutical sector.	408-385-1742	NA	San Jose
ARK Diagnostics Inc (HQ)	Manufacturer of in vitro diagnostic products for the treatment of cancer, veterinary, HIV/AIDS, antifungal drugs, and epilepsy and pain management.	877-869-2320	NA	Fremont
Assembly Biosciences Inc (RH)	Developer of therapeutics for the treatment of hepatitis B virus (HBV) infection. The company specializes in clinical trials.	833-509-4583	NA	S San Francisco
Biochain Institute Inc (HQ)	Provider of bio-sample preparation, analysis, and application assays accelerating the development of personalized diagnostics, therapeutics, and medicine.	510-783-8588	NA	Newark
Lumiquick Diagnostics Inc (HQ)	Manufacturer of diagnostic products and other raw materials. The company is engaged in distribution services.	408-855-0061	NA	Santa Clara
Neurotrack Technologies Inc (HQ)	Provider of computer-based cognitive tests. The company offers services to Alzheimer's patients and the medical industry.	650-549-8566	NA	Redwood City
Somagenics Inc (HQ)	Developer of RNA-based therapeutics and diagnostics. The company's services include detection, monitoring, testing, and analysis.	831-426-7700	NA	Santa Cruz

253 = Drugs

COMPANY NAME	PRODUCT / SERVICE	PHONE	EMP	CITY
Aridis Pharmaceuticals LLC (HQ)	Focuses on anti-infective alternatives to conventional antibiotics. The company offers services to the pharmaceutical sector.	408-385-1742	NA	San Jose
Ascendis Pharma A/S (BR)	Focuses on the creation of drug candidates, proteins, peptides and small molecules, suitable for either local or systemic treatment.	650-352-8389	NA	Palo Alto
Coherus Biosciences (HQ)	Developer of biosimilars and it serves the global marketplace. The company is engaged in delivery services.	800-794-5434	NA	Redwood City
Credence MedSystems Inc (HQ)	Provider of pharmaceutical products. The company specializes in single-dose injectable medications in pre-filled syringes.	844-263-3797	NA	Menlo Park

254 = Antineoplastic

COMPANY NAME	PRODUCT / SERVICE	PHONE	EMP	CITY
Apexigen (HQ)	Specializes in document management and managed print solutions. The company serves the business sector.	650-931-6236	NA	San Carlos
Aridis Pharmaceuticals LLC (HQ)	Focuses on anti-infective alternatives to conventional antibiotics. The company offers services to the pharmaceutical sector.	408-385-1742	NA	San Jose
Atara Biotherapeutics Inc (HQ)	Provider of biotherapeutic services. The company focuses on the treatment of cancer, kidney disease, and other illnesses.	650-278-8930	NA	S San Francisco
Biomarin Pharmaceutical Inc (HQ)	Developer of biopharmaceutical products for treatment of morquio A, phenylketonuria, mucopolysaccharidosis VI and I, and lambert-eaton myasthenic syndrome.	415-506-6700	NA	San Rafael
Biomarker Pharmaceuticals Inc (HQ)	Developer of scientifically-based aging intervention products for slowing the process of aging and delaying the onset of age-related diseases.	408-257-2000	NA	San Jose
Catalyst Biosciences (HQ)	Developer of catalytic biopharmaceutical products based on engineering human proteases for hemostasis, age-related macular degeneration, and inflammation.	650-871-0761	NA	S San Francisco
Clovis Oncology (BR)	Developer of targeted therapies for the treatment of patients with cancer. The company is involved in clinical trials.	415-409-5440	NA	San Francisco
Coherus Biosciences (HQ)	Developer of biosimilars and it serves the global marketplace. The company is engaged in delivery services.	800-794-5434	NA	Redwood City
Delmar Pharmaceuticals Inc (DH)	Developer of pharmaceutical products. The company specializes in treatment of various cancer such as lung, brain, cervical, ovarian tumors and leukemia.	604-629-5989	NA	Menlo Park

COMPANY NAME	PRODUCT / SERVICE	PHONE	EMP	CITY
Designerx Pharmaceuticals Inc (HQ)	Provider of pharmaceutical products for treatment of cancer cells from tumors such as melanoma, hepatocellular carcinoma, pancreatic, and mesothelioma.	707-451-0441	NA	Vacaville
Mateon Therapeutics Inc (HQ)	Developer and provider of therapeutics. The company focuses on the treatment of acute myeloid leukemia.	650-635-7000	NA	S San Francisco
Navire Pharma (HQ)	Developer of novel therapies. The company focuses on developing SHP2 inhibitors for treating rare cancers.	650-391-9740	NA	Palo Alto
Nuvora Inc (HQ)	Focuses on dry mouth treatment and offers products for bad breath prevention. The company offers Dentiva and Sales.	877-530-9811	NA	Santa Clara

255 = Antitussives

COMPANY NAME	PRODUCT / SERVICE	PHONE	EMP	CITY
Aridis Pharmaceuticals LLC (HQ)	Focuses on anti-infective alternatives to conventional antibiotics. The company offers services to the pharmaceutical sector.	408-385-1742	NA	San Jose
Cairn Biosciences (HQ)	Provider of therapeutic solutions for treating cancer. The company is involved in biotechnical research and commercial business.	415-503-1185	NA	San Francisco
Coherus Biosciences (HQ)	Developer of biosimilars and it serves the global marketplace. The company is engaged in delivery services.	800-794-5434	NA	Redwood City

256 = Autonomic

COMPANY NAME	PRODUCT / SERVICE	PHONE	EMP	CITY
Aridis Pharmaceuticals LLC (HQ)	Focuses on anti-infective alternatives to conventional antibiotics. The company offers services to the pharmaceutical sector.	408-385-1742	NA	San Jose
Coherus Biosciences (HQ)	Developer of biosimilars and it serves the global marketplace. The company is engaged in delivery services.	800-794-5434	NA	Redwood City
Formumax Scientific Inc (HQ)	Provider of contract drug delivery to pharmaceutical and biotech industries. The company specializes in injectables, liposomes, and microemulsions.	408-400-0108	NA	Sunnyvale

257 = CNS Drugs

COMPANY NAME	PRODUCT / SERVICE	PHONE	EMP	CITY
Antagene Inc (HQ)	Provider of custom antibody and peptide synthesis. The company is engaged in animal and histology services.	408-588-1998	NA	Santa Clara
Anthera Pharmaceuticals Inc (HQ)	Manufacturer of biopharmaceuticals that treat serious diseases like lupus, lupus with glomerulonephritis, IgA nephropathy and cystic fibrosis.	510-856-5600	NA	Hayward
Aridis Pharmaceuticals LLC (HQ)	Focuses on anti-infective alternatives to conventional antibiotics. The company offers services to the pharmaceutical sector.	408-385-1742	NA	San Jose
Astex Pharmaceuticals (HQ)	Developer of small-molecule therapeutics. The company focuses on products for treatment of cancer and central nervous system disorders.	925-560-0100	NA	Pleasanton
BASF Venture Capital America Inc (RH)	Manufacturer of basic chemicals and intermediates such as solvents, plasticizers, and monomers. The company serves the agriculture market.	510-445-6140	NA	Fremont
Biomarker Pharmaceuticals Inc (HQ)	Developer of scientifically-based aging intervention products for slowing the process of aging and delaying the onset of age-related diseases.	408-257-2000	NA	San Jose
Codexis Inc (HQ)	Provider of biocatalysts products such as screening kits and other accessories. The company serves the food and nutrition industries.	650-421-8100	51-200	Redwood City
Coherus Biosciences (HQ)	Developer of biosimilars and it serves the global marketplace. The company is engaged in delivery services.	800-794-5434	NA	Redwood City
Delpor Inc (HQ)	Developer of next generation drug delivery systems which improve the clinical and commercial value of new and existing drugs and biopharmaceuticals.	415-480-6870	NA	Brisbane
EGeen Inc (HQ)	Provider of drug development for biotech and pharmaceutical clients. The company serves clinics, hospitals, and the healthcare sector.	650-967-5010	NA	Mountain View
Monogram Biosciences Inc (HQ)	Develops and commercializes diagnostic products. The company offers products for the treatment of human immunodeficiency virus and other viral illnesses.	650-635-1100	NA	S San Francisco
Mountain View Pharmaceuticals Inc (HQ)	Provider of pharmaceutical development, protein biochemistry, immunology and polymer chemistry solutions for delivery of therapeutic proteins.	650-365-5515	1-10	Menlo Park
Numerate Inc (HQ)	Provider of data analytics and drug design technology services for the pharmaceutical and biotechnology industries.	650-472-0632	NA	San Francisco
Pharmagenesis Inc (HQ)	Developer and manufacturer of prescription pharmaceuticals from plant extracts and other organic products sourced from Chinese medical practice.	650-842-7060	NA	Redwood City
Retrotope Inc (HQ)	Focuses on the discovery of drugs and platforms for the treatment of regenerative diseases. The company offers services to the healthcare sector.	650-917-9256	NA	Los Altos
Reviva Pharmaceuticals Inc (HQ)	Developer of therapy for CNS, cardiovascular, metabolic and inflammatory diseases. The company is a clinical development pharmaceutical company.	408-816-1470	NA	Sunnyvale
Verge Analytics Inc (HQ)	Provider of treatment for brain diseases. The company is involved in drug development and research services.	415-355-4737	NA	S San Francisco
Zogenix Inc (BR)	Developer of medicines to treat CNS disorders and pain. The company serves clinics, physicians, and the healthcare sector.	858-259-1165	NA	Emeryville

258 = Cardiovascular

COMPANY NAME	PRODUCT / SERVICE	PHONE	EMP	CITY
Amaranth Medical Inc (HQ)	Specializes in proprietary polymer structure and processing technology. The company's products are used in vascular and nonvascular applications.	650-965-3830	NA	Mountain View
Aridis Pharmaceuticals LLC (HQ)	Focuses on anti-infective alternatives to conventional antibiotics. The company offers services to the pharmaceutical sector.	408-385-1742	NA	San Jose
Avantec Vascular Corp (HQ)	Manufacturer of therapeutic medical devices such as cardio and peripheral vascular devices for cardiovascular, neurovascular, and peripheral disease.	408-329-5400	NA	Sunnyvale
Coherus Biosciences (HQ)	Developer of biosimilars and it serves the global marketplace. The company is engaged in delivery services.	800-794-5434	NA	Redwood City
Lumedx Corp (HQ)	Provider of cardiovascular information and imaging systems. The company specializes in cloud-powered healthcare solutions.	800-966-0699	NA	Oakland
Lumiquick Diagnostics Inc (HQ)	Manufacturer of diagnostic products and other raw materials. The company is engaged in distribution services.	408-855-0061	NA	Santa Clara
NGM Biopharmaceuticals Inc (HQ)	Developer of novel and disease-altering biologics such as protein, peptide, and antibody drug for cancer, cardio-metabolic, and hepatic diseases.	650-243-5555	NA	S San Francisco
Pliant Therapeutics Inc (HQ)	Developer of therapeutics medicines for the treatment of fibrosis in organs and conditions, including liver, kidney, heart, and gastrointestinal tract.	650-481-6770	NA	S San Francisco
Silver Creek Pharmaceuticals Inc (HQ)	Provider of pharmaceuticals. The company develops regenerative medicines with an initial focus on treating cardiovascular disease.	415-978-2178	NA	San Francisco
West Coast Surgical (HQ)	Manufacturer of surgical devices. The company offers designing, assembling and finishing of specialty surgical equipment.	650-728-8095	NA	Half Moon Bay

259 = Gastrintestinal

COMPANY NAME	PRODUCT / SERVICE	PHONE	EMP	CITY
Aridis Pharmaceuticals LLC (HQ)	Focuses on anti-infective alternatives to conventional antibiotics. The company offers services to the pharmaceutical sector.	408-385-1742	NA	San Jose
Coherus Biosciences (HQ)	Developer of biosimilars and it serves the global marketplace. The company is engaged in delivery services.	800-794-5434	NA	Redwood City
Osel Inc (HQ)	Developer of biotherapeutic products. The company focuses on treatment and prevention of conditions for women's health and infectious diseases.	650-964-1420	NA	Mountain View

260 = Metabolic

COMPANY NAME	PRODUCT / SERVICE	PHONE	EMP	CITY
Aridis Pharmaceuticals LLC (HQ)	Focuses on anti-infective alternatives to conventional antibiotics. The company offers services to the pharmaceutical sector.	408-385-1742	NA	San Jose
Coherus Biosciences (HQ)	Developer of biosimilars and it serves the global marketplace. The company is engaged in delivery services.	800-794-5434	NA	Redwood City
Credence MedSystems Inc (HQ)	Provider of pharmaceutical products. The company specializes in single-dose injectable medications in pre-filled syringes.	844-263-3797	NA	Menlo Park
Second Genome Inc (HQ)	Focuses on the development of therapeutic products. The company serves pharmaceutical and nutritional companies.	650-440-4606	NA	S San Francisco

261 = OTC Drugs

	COMPANY NAME	PRODUCT / SERVICE	PHONE	EMP	CITY
	Aridis Pharmaceuticals LLC (HQ)	Focuses on anti-infective alternatives to conventional antibiotics. The company offers services to the pharmaceutical sector.	408-385-1742	NA	San Jose
	Bioassay Systems (HQ)	Developer and marketer of assay solutions. The company focuses on solutions for research and drug discovery.	510-782-9988	NA	Hayward
	Bioved Pharmaceuticals Inc (HQ)	Manufacturer of health care products. The company specializes in ayurvedic pharmaceutical, nutraceutical and OTC drugs from plant extracts.	408-432-4020	NA	San Jose
	Biozone Laboratories Inc (HQ)	Manufacturer of over the counter drugs, cosmetics, personal care, and nutritional supplements such as creams, gels, drops, syrups, and sun protection.	925-473-1000	NA	Pittsburg
	Coherus Biosciences (HQ)	Developer of biosimilars and it serves the global marketplace. The company is engaged in delivery services.	800-794-5434	NA	Redwood City
	Corcept Therapeutics Inc (HQ)	Focuses on the discovery of drugs. The company offers services to patients, physicians, and also hospitals.	650-327-3270	NA	Menlo Park
	Cymed (HQ)	Provider of ostomy pouching systems. The company specializes in skin care products and serves individuals and hospitals.	800-582-0707	NA	Sacramento
	EMSL Analytical Inc (BR)	Provider of laboratory analytical testing services. The company specializes in a wide range of environmental, material and forensic testing.	510-895-3675	NA	San Leandro
	InCarda Therapeutics Inc (HQ)	Developer of drugs and inhaled therapy intended to treat paroxysmal atrial fibrillation and other cardiovascular diseases.	510-422-5522	NA	Newark
	Jazz Pharmaceuticals (BR)	Developer and marketer of products for neurology and psychiatry. The company is engaged in clinical trials and research and development.	650-496-3777	NA	Palo Alto
N	McGuff Compounding Pharmacy Services Inc (HQ)	Distributor of prescription and proprietary drugs, toiletries and more.	877-444-1155	NA	Santa Ana

COMPANY NAME	PRODUCT / SERVICE	PHONE	EMP	CITY
Neilmed Pharmaceuticals Inc (HQ)	Manufacturer of large volume low pressure saline nasal irrigation systems for babies and children, first aid, dry noses, sterile saline spray, and ear care.	707-525-3784	NA	Santa Rosa
Novabay Pharmaceuticals Inc (HQ)	Manufacturer of biopharmaceuticals. The company develops non-antibiotic anti-infective products to address the eye care market.	510-899-8800	NA	Emeryville
Nu-Hope Laboratories Inc (HQ)	Manufacturer of ostomy support belts and pouches to non-adhesive ostomy systems.	818-899-7711	11-50	Pacoima
Nuvora Inc (HQ)	Focuses on dry mouth treatment and offers products for bad breath prevention. The company offers Dentiva and Sales.	877-530-9811	NA	Santa Clara
Otsuka America Inc (HQ)	Developer of pharmaceutical products for the treatment of central nervous system, ophthalmology, cardiovascular, and skin conditions.	415-986-5300	NA	San Francisco
PharmaLogic Development Inc (HQ)	Focuses on planning, drug development, and marketing services. The company serves the pharmaceutical and biomedical industries.	415-472-2181	NA	San Rafael
Relypsa Inc (HQ)	Developer of polymer technology for the treatment of patients with serious conditions. The company is engaged in drug discovery.	650-421-9500	NA	Redwood City
Rigel Pharmaceuticals Inc (HQ)	Developer novel, small-molecule drugs for the treatment of inflammatory and autoimmune diseases, immuno-oncology related diseases, and muscle disorders.	650-624-1100	NA	S San Francisco
Theraject Inc (HQ)	Developer of drug micro-needle technologies. The company is engaged in vaccine and also drug deliveries.	510-742-5832	NA	Fremont
Theron Pharmaceuticals (HQ)	Developer of long acting M3 muscarinic antagonist (LAMA) for the improved treatment of chronic respiratory diseases.	408-792-7424	NA	Sunnyvale
Tosk Inc (HQ)	Manufacturer of drugs for the treatment of debilitating and life-threatening diseases such as cancer, arthritis, and psoriasis.	408-245-6838	NA	Mountain View
Valitor Inc (HQ)	Developer of therapeutic protein drugs. The company's drugs are used in dermatology, ophthalmology, orthopedics, and stem cell therapy.	510-545-6062	NA	Berkeley

262 = Plant-based

COMPANY NAME	PRODUCT / SERVICE	PHONE	EMP	CITY
Aridis Pharmaceuticals LLC (HQ)	Focuses on anti-infective alternatives to conventional antibiotics. The company offers services to the pharmaceutical sector.	408-385-1742	NA	San Jose
Coherus Biosciences (HQ)	Developer of biosimilars and it serves the global marketplace. The company is engaged in delivery services.	800-794-5434	NA	Redwood City
Revolution Medicines Inc (HQ)	Developer of medicines for the treatment of serious diseases. The company is involved in the synthesis of original compounds.	650-481-6801	NA	Redwood City

263 = Pulmonary

COMPANY NAME	PRODUCT / SERVICE	PHONE	EMP	CITY
Aridis Pharmaceuticals LLC (HQ)	Focuses on anti-infective alternatives to conventional antibiotics. The company offers services to the pharmaceutical sector.	408-385-1742	NA	San Jose
Coherus Biosciences (HQ)	Developer of biosimilars and it serves the global marketplace. The company is engaged in delivery services.	800-794-5434	NA	Redwood City

264 = Skin/Mucous Membrane Drugs

COMPANY NAME	PRODUCT / SERVICE	PHONE	EMP	CITY
Aridis Pharmaceuticals LLC (HQ)	Focuses on anti-infective alternatives to conventional antibiotics. The company offers services to the pharmaceutical sector.	408-385-1742	NA	San Jose
Coherus Biosciences (HQ)	Developer of biosimilars and it serves the global marketplace. The company is engaged in delivery services.	800-794-5434	NA	Redwood City
Dermira Inc (HQ)	Developer of biopharmaceutical products for the treatment of dermatology diseases such as acne, plaque psoriasis, and hyperhidrosis.	650-421-7200	NA	Menlo Park
Libby Laboratories Inc (HQ)	Manufacturer of cosmetics, OTC pharmaceuticals, drugs, and devices. The company offers skin and hair products, toiletries, natural and organic products.	510-527-5400	NA	Berkeley
Retrotope Inc (HQ)	Focuses on the discovery of drugs and platforms for the treatment of regenerative diseases. The company offers services to the healthcare sector.	650-917-9256	NA	Los Altos

265 = Reproductive Organ

COMPANY NAME	PRODUCT / SERVICE	PHONE	EMP	CITY
Aridis Pharmaceuticals LLC (HQ)	Focuses on anti-infective alternatives to conventional antibiotics. The company offers services to the pharmaceutical sector.	408-385-1742	NA	San Jose
Coherus Biosciences (HQ)	Developer of biosimilars and it serves the global marketplace. The company is engaged in delivery services.	800-794-5434	NA	Redwood City

266 = Hormones/Synthetic Substitutes

COMPANY NAME	PRODUCT / SERVICE	PHONE	EMP	CITY
Advantage Pharmaceutics Inc (HQ)	Provider of pharmaceuticals specializing in compounding. The company provides compounded medicines in dosage forms for human and veterinary needs.	916-630-4960	NA	Rocklin
D Danz & Sons Inc (HQ)	Specializes in the custom fitting, designing, and manufacturing of ophthalmic prosthetics. The company deals with patient care.	559-252-1770	NA	Fresno
Tolerion Inc (HQ)	Provider of medical treatment solutions for autoimmune diseases. The company focuses on restoring the patient's immune system.	415-795-5800	NA	S San Francisco

267 = Pharmaceutical Packaging

COMPANY NAME	PRODUCT / SERVICE	PHONE	EMP	CITY
Aridis Pharmaceuticals LLC (HQ)	Focuses on anti-infective alternatives to conventional antibiotics. The company offers services to the pharmaceutical sector.	408-385-1742	NA	San Jose
BioQ Pharma Inc (HQ)	Manufacturer of proprietary products. The company is involved in the sale of infusion pharmaceuticals.	415-336-6496	NA	San Francisco
Corium International Inc (HQ)	Provider of transdermal delivery systems and related technology solutions. The company is also engaged in therapeutic product development.	650-298-8255	NA	Menlo Park

268 = Pharmaceutical R&D

COMPANY NAME	PRODUCT / SERVICE	PHONE	EMP	CITY
AcelRx Pharmaceuticals Inc (HQ)	Manufacturer of pharmaceuticals. The company provides therapies for treatment of acute and breakthrough pain.	650-216-3500	NA	Redwood City
Achaogen Inc (HQ)	Developers of antibacterial. The company discovers and develops antibacterial for the treatment of serious bacterial infections.	650-800-3636	NA	S San Francisco
Acumen Pharmaceuticals Inc (HQ)	Specializes in the discovery and development of therapeutics and diagnostics related to soluble A˜ oligomers.	925-368-8508	NA	Livermore
Adamas Pharmaceuticals Inc (HQ)	Manufacturer of health care products. The company offer products for patients with chronic disorders of the central nervous system.	510-450-3500	NA	Emeryville
Alector LLC (HQ)	Developer of therapeutics. The company specializes in cutting edge antibody technologies for treating alzheimer's disease.	415-231-5660	NA	S San Francisco
Allaccem Inc (HQ)	Manufacturer of pharmaceutical products such as dermatology, optic, and dental products for goats, dogs, and cats.	650-593-8700	NA	San Carlos
AMPAC Fine Chemicals (DH)	Manufacturer of active pharmaceutical ingredients (APIs) and registered intermediates. The company's services include product development and scale-up.	916-357-6880	NA	Rancho Cordova
Annexon Inc (HQ)	Focuses on the development of therapeutic products. The company serves patients with complement-mediated neurodegenerative disorders.	650-822-5500	NA	S San Francisco
Apneos Corp (HQ)	Developer of services for healthcare professionals. The company detects and manages sleep breathing disorders.	650-591-2895	NA	Belmont
Ardelyx Inc (HQ)	Developer of non-systemic and small molecule therapeutics that work in the GI tract to treat cardio-renal, GI, and metabolic diseases.	510-745-1700	NA	Fremont
Aridis Pharmaceuticals LLC (HQ)	Focuses on anti-infective alternatives to conventional antibiotics. The company offers services to the pharmaceutical sector.	408-385-1742	NA	San Jose
Arrayit Corp (HQ)	Focuses on the discovery, development and manufacture of proprietary life science technologies and consumables for disease prevention.	408-744-1331	NA	Sunnyvale
Ascendis Pharma A/S (BR)	Focuses on the creation of drug candidates, proteins, peptides and small molecules, suitable for either local or systemic treatment.	650-352-8389	NA	Palo Alto
Assembly Biosciences Inc (RH)	Developer of therapeutics for the treatment of hepatitis B virus (HBV) infection. The company specializes in clinical trials.	833-509-4583	NA	S San Francisco
Atomwise Inc (HQ)	Developer of artificial intelligence systems for the discovery of drugs. The company serves the healthcare sector.	650-449-7925	NA	San Francisco
Balance Therapeutics Inc (HQ)	Developer of pharmaceuticals. The company develops therapeutics to address neurological disabilities resulting from excess inhibition of the brain.	650-741-9100	NA	San Bruno
Bioassay Systems (HQ)	Developer and marketer of assay solutions. The company focuses on solutions for research and drug discovery.	510-782-9988	NA	Hayward
Biochain Institute Inc (HQ)	Provider of bio-sample preparation, analysis, and application assays accelerating the development of personalized diagnostics, therapeutics, and medicine.	510-783-8588	NA	Newark
Biokey Inc (HQ)	Provider of API characterization, pre-formulation studies, formulation development, and analytical method development services.	510-668-0881	NA	Fremont
Biomarin Pharmaceutical Inc (HQ)	Developer of biopharmaceutical products for treatment of morquio A, phenylketonuria, mucopolysaccharidosis VI and I, and lambert-eaton myasthenic syndrome.	415-506-6700	NA	San Rafael
Biomarker Pharmaceuticals Inc (HQ)	Developer of scientifically-based aging intervention products for slowing the process of aging and delaying the onset of age-related diseases.	408-257-2000	NA	San Jose
Biotium Inc (HQ)	Supplier of glowing products. The company offers enzyme substrates and kits for labeling proteins and antibodies.	510-265-1027	NA	Fremont
BlueLight Therapeutics Inc (HQ)	Developer of proteins and biological molecules for the treatment of cancer, cardiovascular, Alzheimer's, and Parkinson's diseases.	650-871-8716	NA	S San Francisco
Calysta (HQ)	Focuses on the development and manufacture of protein for commercial aquaculture and livestock feed.	650-492-6880	NA	Menlo Park
Cantabio Pharmaceuticals Inc (HQ)	Provider of therapeutic solutions. The company specializes in developing therapeutic proteins to prevent degenerative brain diseases.	844-200-2826	NA	Palo Alto
Carmot Therapeutics Inc (BR)	Provider of drug discovery to address unmet chemical needs for the treatment of oncology, inflammation, and metabolic disease.	510-828-0102	NA	San Francisco
CCS Associates Inc (HQ)	Provider of scientific services in product discovery and development for government agencies, pharmaceutical, and biotech industries.	650-691-4400	NA	Mountain View
Chemocentryx Inc (HQ)	Manufacturer of biopharmaceutical products and orally-administered therapeutics to treat autoimmune diseases, inflammatory disorders, and cancer.	650-210-2900	NA	Mountain View

COMPANY NAME	PRODUCT / SERVICE	PHONE	EMP	CITY
Circuit Therapeutics Inc (HQ)	Focuses on drug discovery and development as well as forging direct therapeutic applications of optogenetics.	650-324-9400	NA	Menlo Park
Coherus Biosciences (HQ)	Developer of biosimilars and it serves the global marketplace. The company is engaged in delivery services.	800-794-5434	NA	Redwood City
Comparative Biosciences Inc (HQ)	Provider of research and development support services. The company serves the biotechnology and pharmaceutical industries.	408-738-9260	NA	Sunnyvale
Corium International Inc (HQ)	Provider of transdermal delivery systems and related technology solutions. The company is also engaged in therapeutic product development.	650-298-8255	NA	Menlo Park
Corvus Pharmaceuticals Inc (HQ)	Focuses on the development of first-in-class agents that target the immune system. The company serves the healthcare industry.	650-900-4520	NA	Burlingame
Cytokinetics Inc (HQ)	Developer of cancer treatment programs for cancer and also cardiovascular patients. The company specializes in therapeutic programs.	650-624-3000	NA	S San Francisco
Denali Therapeutics Inc (HQ)	Provider of therapeutic solutions for the treatment of neurodegenerative diseases. The company also specializes in blood brain barrier programs.	650-866-8548	NA	S San Francisco
Dermira Inc (HQ)	Developer of biopharmaceutical products for the treatment of dermatology diseases such as acne, plaque psoriasis, and hyperhidrosis.	650-421-7200	NA	Menlo Park
Designerx Pharmaceuticals Inc (HQ)	Provider of pharmaceutical products for treatment of cancer cells from tumors such as melanoma, hepatocellular carcinoma, pancreatic, and mesothelioma.	707-451-0441	NA	Vacaville
Diablo Clinical Research (HQ)	Provider of clinical research services specializing in endocrinology, internal medicine, cardiology, and neurology.	925-930-7267	NA	Walnut Creek
DNA Bridges Inc (HQ)	Provider of corporate development services. The company offers market analysis, business plan development, patent research, and other services.	415-362-0442	NA	San Francisco
Dynavax Technologies Corp (HQ)	Developer of clinical-stage biopharmaceutical company committed to discovering and developing products to prevent and treat infectious diseases.	510-848-5100	51-200	Emeryville
Eckhart Corp (HQ)	Manufacturer of nutritional supplements. The company is engaged in product development and packaging services.	415-898-9528	NA	Novato
Escend Pharmaceuticals Inc (HQ)	Provider of therapeutic solutions. The company focuses on cancer stem cells in acute myelogenous leukemia and hematologic malignancies for drug development.	650-241-9128	NA	Menlo Park
Exelixis Inc (HQ)	Focuses on the development and commercialization of small molecule therapies. The company is also engaged in clinical trials.	650-837-7000	NA	Alameda
Fochon Pharmaceuticals Ltd (DH)	Provider of therapeutic solutions. The company focuses on research and development of small molecule drugs for health care.	510-638-8080	NA	San Leandro
Formumax Scientific Inc (HQ)	Provider of contract drug delivery to pharmaceutical and biotech industries. The company specializes in injectables, liposomes, and microemulsions.	408-400-0108	NA	Sunnyvale
Formurex Inc (HQ)	Provider of services to the biotech industry in preformulation, formulation development, stability and clinical trial materials manufacturing.	209-931-2040	NA	Stockton
Genepharm Inc (HQ)	Developer and commercialization of therapeutics for skin-related problems. The company is engaged in pre-clinical research.	408-773-1082	NA	Sunnyvale
Geron Corp (HQ)	Developer of telomerase inhibitors, imetelstat, in hematologic myeloid malignancies. The company is engaged in clinical trials.	650-473-7700	NA	Menlo Park
Gilead Sciences Inc (HQ)	Provider of medicines for the treatment of liver diseases, hematology, oncology, and other cardiovascular diseases.	650-574-3000	NA	Foster City
N Harkness Pharmaceuticals Inc (HQ)	Provider of research and development of therapies dealing with obesity.	858-550-6061	NA	San Diego
Hitachi Chemical Diagnostics Inc (HQ)	Provider of in vitro allergy diagnostics products. The company offers alternative means of diagnosing allergy.	650-961-5501	NA	Mountain View
Hopelab (HQ)	Developer of technology to improve human health and well-being. The company provides online games to help young people fight cancer.	650-569-5900	NA	San Francisco
Hygeia Laboratories Inc (HQ)	Developers of vaccines using novel technology for animals. The company offers animal pharmaceuticals for dairy cattle, sheep and poultry.	530-661-1442	NA	Woodland
Iconic Therapeutics Inc (HQ)	Provider of tissue factor therapeutics. The company focuses on the solid tumors and wet age related macular degeneration.	650-437-1000	NA	S San Francisco
Illustris Pharmaceuticals Inc (HQ)	Developer and provider of technology solutions for the delivery of large molecules through the tissue structures.	650-334-2090	NA	Irvine
InCube Labs (HQ)	Provider of laboratory services. The company offers medical devices and pharmaceuticals to various therapeutic areas.	408-457-3700	NA	San Jose
Intarcia Therapeutics Inc (BR)	Provider of therapeutic products and related supplies. The company is engaged in research and development services.	510-782-7800	NA	Hayward
Jaguar Health (HQ)	Provider of health solutions for the animals and humans. The company focuses on the development of gastrointestinal pharmaceuticals.	415-371-8300	NA	San Francisco
Kalytera Therapeutics Inc (HQ)	Developer of cannabidiol and cannabinoid therapeutics for the treatment of life threatening human disease.	888-861-2008	NA	San Rafael

COMPANY NAME	PRODUCT / SERVICE	PHONE	EMP	CITY
Kan Herb Company (HQ)	Provider of Chinese herbal products and services.	831-438-9450	NA	Santa Cruz
N Kinnetic Laboratories Inc (HQ)	Provider of environmental and oceanographic science services including field and laboratory studies.	831-457-3950	11-50	Santa Cruz
Lumen Therapeutics LLC (HQ)	Provider of therapeutic solutions. The company focuses on the proprietary drugs based on oligo-L-arginine.	650-450-4439	NA	Menlo Park
Lumiphore Inc (HQ)	Developer of proprietary lanthanide technology. The company develops and markers biological detection reagents.	510-898-1190	NA	Berkeley
MabPlex USA Inc (BR)	Developer and manufacture of biopharmaceuticals. The company also offers contract services from DNA to finished drug product.	510-830-1065	NA	Fremont
Mateon Therapeutics Inc (HQ)	Developer and provider of therapeutics. The company focuses on the treatment of acute myeloid leukemia.	650-635-7000	NA	S San Francisco
MedAutonomic Inc (HQ)	Developer of Brain NeuroModulator. The company specializes in creating control action potentials in individual neurons and in functional groups.	415-377-5653	NA	Concord
MedGenome Inc (HQ)	Provider of genomics based diagnostics and research services. The company specializes in bioinformatics, computing, genomics technologies, and big data analytics.	888-440-0954	NA	Foster City
Menlo Therapeutics (HQ)	Developer and manufacture of biopharmaceuticals. The company focuses on the commercialization and development of serlopitant for treating pruritus.	650-486-1416	NA	Redwood City
MicuRx Pharmaceuticals Inc (HQ)	Provider of pharmaceuticals. The company develops antibiotics to combat drug-resistant bacterial infections.	510-782-2022	NA	Foster City
Multispan Inc (HQ)	Provider of drug discovery services. The company also engages in compound profiling and antibody profiling services.	510-887-0817	NA	Hayward
Murigenics (HQ)	Provider of preclinical in-vivo and in-vitro contract drug discovery. The company is also focused on development services.	707-561-8900	NA	Vallejo
Napajen Pharma Inc (HQ)	Developer of novel drug delivery systems technologies for pharmaceutical and biotechnology industries.	650-685-2429	NA	Burlingame
Nature's Cure (HQ)	Provider of health and beauty solutions. The company offers over-the-counter products featuring natural ingredients.	877-469-9487	NA	Oakland
Navire Pharma (HQ)	Developer of novel therapies. The company focuses on developing SHP2 inhibitors for treating rare cancers.	650-391-9740	NA	Palo Alto
Neopeutics Inc USA (HQ)	Provider of pre clinical contract research services and product development for the private and governmental regulatory agencies.	650-624-4057	NA	S San Francisco
Neurotrack Technologies Inc (HQ)	Provider of computer-based cognitive tests. The company offers services to Alzheimer's patients and the medical industry.	650-549-8566	NA	Redwood City
NewGen Therapeutics Inc (HQ)	Provider of therapeutic solutions. The company focuses on the development and discovery of small molecule drugs for cancer treatment.	650-995-7508	NA	Menlo Park
Nitinol Devices & Components Inc (HQ)	Provider of rapid development and prototyping services. The company is also engaged in commercialization.	510-683-2000	NA	Fremont
Optimum Processing Inc (HQ)	Provider of filtration solutions and disposable bioprocess container systems. The company utilizes asymmetric morphology solutions.	415-461-7033	NA	San Rafael
Orbus Therapeutics Inc (HQ)	Developer of therapeutic products to treat rare disease such as anaplastic astrocytoma.	650-656-9440	NA	Palo Alto
ORIC Pharmaceuticals Inc (HQ)	Provider of pharmaceutical research. The company specializes in discovering and developing novel therapies for treatment-resistant cancers.	650-388-5600	NA	S San Francisco
OrthoTrophix Inc (HQ)	Developer of therapies for medical needs of patients. The company specializes in regeneration of articular cartilage in knee and other joints.	510-488-3832	NA	Oakland
Osel Inc (HQ)	Developer of biotherapeutic products. The company focuses on treatment and prevention of conditions for women's health and infectious diseases.	650-964-1420	NA	Mountain View
Phage International Inc (HQ)	Provider of leverage bacteriophage therapy technologies. The company specializes in discovery and rediscovery of effective health care solutions.	925-984-9446	NA	Danville
Pharmagenesis Inc (HQ)	Developer and manufacturer of prescription pharmaceuticals from plant extracts and other organic products sourced from Chinese medical practice.	650-842-7060	NA	Redwood City
Pharmedix (HQ)	Focuses on the repackaging of pharmaceutical products. The company offers dispensing systems and women's health products.	800-486-1811	NA	Union City
Pharmtak Inc (HQ)	Provider of pharmaceutical products and services. The company focuses on developing novel pharmaceuticals and cosmeceuticals utilizing technology.	408-954-8223	NA	San Jose
Pherin Pharmaceuticals Inc (HQ)	Developer of novel compounds for intranasal spray delivery and also deals with the treatment of neuro-psychiatric and neuroendocrine conditions.	650-636-7064	NA	Los Altos
Phoenix Pharmaceuticals Inc (DH)	Provider of peptide related products to researchers. The company specializes in obesity, cardiovascular, and diabetes.	650-558-8898	NA	Burlingame
Portola Pharmaceuticals Inc (HQ)	Focuses on the development and commercialization of therapeutic products for the treatment of hematologic disorders.	650-246-7000	201-500	S San Francisco

| --- | --- | --- | --- | --- |
Presidio Pharmaceuticals Inc (HQ)	Developers of small-molecule antiviral therapeutics. The company is a clinical-stage pharmaceutical company.	415-655-7560	NA	San Francisco
Primity Bio Inc (HQ)	Provider of assay platforms for biological relevance. The company specializes in cell biology, flow cytometry, and molecular biology.	510-210-0605	NA	Fremont
Prolynx LLC (HQ)	Developer of technology solutions for releasable linkers. The company also specializes in injectable drugs.	415-552-5306	NA	San Francisco
Protein Research (HQ)	Manufacturer of nutritional products. The company develops and formulates supplements for human nutrition in capsules, tablets, powders and premixes.	925-243-6300	NA	Livermore
Proteus Digital Health Inc (HQ)	Providers of health care service technology. The company offers health care products based on electronics technology.	650-632-4031	NA	Redwood City
ProTrials Research Inc (HQ)	Provider of clinical research services. The company offers the ability to move a new drug or device from conception to FDA approval.	650-864-9180	NA	San Jose
Relypsa Inc (HQ)	Developer of polymer technology for the treatment of patients with serious conditions. The company is engaged in drug discovery.	650-421-9500	NA	Redwood City
Retrotope Inc (HQ)	Focuses on the discovery of drugs and platforms for the treatment of regenerative diseases. The company offers services to the healthcare sector.	650-917-9256	NA	Los Altos
Revance Therapeutics Inc (HQ)	Developers of botulinum toxin products. The company develops and manufactures botulinum toxin products for aesthetic and therapeutic categories.	510-742-3400	51-200	Newark
Ryss Lab Inc (HQ)	Provider of biotechnology and pharmaceutical development services. The company offers services to the healthcare sector.	510-477-9570	NA	Union City
Sandhu Products Inc (HQ)	Provider of ayurvedic herbal dietary supplements. The company offers products containing vitamins, amino acids, minerals and medicinal plant extracts.	510-996-7199	NA	Livermore
N Sekisui Diagnostics (HQ)	Manufacturer of laboratories, biotechnology, and diagnostic healthcare products.	858-777-2600	201-500	San Diego
SFJ Pharmaceuticals Group (HQ)	Focuses on the clinical development and registration of pharmaceutical products. The company is involved in clinical trials.	925-223-6233	NA	Pleasanton
Silver Creek Pharmaceuticals Inc (HQ)	Provider of pharmaceuticals. The company develops regenerative medicines with an initial focus on treating cardiovascular disease.	415-978-2178	NA	San Francisco
Skeletal Kinetics LLC (HQ)	Developer, manufacturer and marketer of bone fixation cement designed for the treatment of trauma fractures.	408-366-5000	NA	Cupertino
Stemexpress (HQ)	Provider of immunophenotyping, DNA quantitation and viability, tissue transplant verification, and related services.	530-626-7000	NA	Folsom
Sutro Biopharma Inc (HQ)	Developer of therapeutics for cancer therapy. The company shares with select pharmaceutical and biotech companies to develop new therapeutics.	650-392-8412	51-200	S San Francisco
Teikoku Pharma USA Inc (LH)	Focuses on the drug development and delivery of treatments for CNS, pain management and oncology. The company serves the medical industry.	408-501-1800	NA	San Jose
Theravance Biopharma US Inc (HQ)	Provider of pharmaceuticals. The company develops new medicines with superior efficacy, convenience, tolerability and/or safety.	650-808-6000	NA	S San Francisco
Threshold Enterprises Ltd (HQ)	Distributor of nutritional supplements, healthcare, and beauty care products.	831-438-6851	NA	Scotts Valley
Titan Pharmaceuticals Inc (HQ)	Provider of biopharmaceuticals. The company discovers proprietary therapeutics primarily for the treatment of serious medical disorders.	650-244-4990	11-50	S San Francisco
Tolerion Inc (HQ)	Provider of medical treatment solutions for autoimmune diseases. The company focuses on restoring the patient's immune system.	415-795-5800	NA	S San Francisco
Trellis Bioscience LLC (HQ)	Developer of human antibody therapeutics as treatment for infectious disease and oncology indications.	650-838-1400	NA	Redwood City
twoXAR Inc (HQ)	Developer of drug delivery platform. The company is involved in biological data extraction, automated model generation, and feature identification.	650-382-2605	NA	Mountain View
Valitor Inc (HQ)	Developer of therapeutic protein drugs. The company's drugs are used in dermatology, ophthalmology, orthopedics, and stem cell therapy.	510-545-6062	NA	Berkeley
Vanton Research Laboratory LLC (HQ)	Specializes in the development of non-conventional drug delivery systems and integrated pharmaceutical services.	925-326-1802	NA	Concord
Vaxart Inc (HQ)	Manufacturer and developer of oral vaccines. The company is engaged in drug development and related services.	650-550-3500	NA	S San Francisco
Vaxcyte Inc (HQ)	Developer of vaccines for the treatment of infectious diseases. The company is also engaged in the production of vaccine antigens.	650-837-0111	NA	Foster City
Velocity Pharmaceutical Development LLC (HQ)	Developer of drug candidates. The company specializes in clinical development programs and serves biotechnology and pharmaceutical companies.	650-273-5748	NA	S San Francisco
Veracyte Inc (HQ)	Focuses on molecular analysis and diagnostic tests. The company serves patients and the healthcare sector.	650-243-6300	NA	S San Francisco
N ViaCyte Inc (HQ)	Provider of biomedical research.	858-455-3708	51-200	San Diego

COMPANY NAME	PRODUCT / SERVICE	PHONE	EMP	CITY
Vistagen Therapeutics Inc (HQ)	Developer of medicine to treat depression, cancer and diseases and disorders involving the central nervous system.	650-577-3600	NA	S San Francisco

269 = Pharmaceutical Services

COMPANY NAME	PRODUCT / SERVICE	PHONE	EMP	CITY
Acumen Pharmaceuticals Inc (HQ)	Specializes in the discovery and development of therapeutics and diagnostics related to soluble A˜ oligomers.	925-368-8508	NA	Livermore
Adynxx Inc (HQ)	Developer of drugs to prevent acute post-surgical pain and the transition to persistent or chronic pain.	415-512-7740	NA	San Francisco
Aimmune Therapeutics (RH)	Developer of desensitization treatments. The company is engaged in clinical trials and it serves the healthcare sector.	650-614-5220	NA	Brisbane
Allergy Research Group LLC (BR)	Provider of nutritional products for blood sugar, brain, cardiovascular, metabolic, hormone, liver, and immune support.	510-263-2000	NA	Alameda
Anthera Pharmaceuticals Inc (HQ)	Manufacturer of biopharmaceuticals that treat serious diseases like lupus, lupus with glomerulonephritis, IgA nephropathy and cystic fibrosis.	510-856-5600	NA	Hayward
Apollomics Inc (HQ)	Developer of oncology therapeutics. The company focuses on discovering therapeutics for the immune system and molecular pathways to treat cancer.	925-272-4090	NA	Foster City
Arable Corp (HQ)	Provider of products and services to health care, pharmaceutical, biotechnology and medical device companies.	408-825-4755	NA	Cupertino
Ardelyx Inc (HQ)	Developer of non-systemic and small molecule therapeutics that work in the GI tract to treat cardio-renal, GI, and metabolic diseases.	510-745-1700	NA	Fremont
Aridis Pharmaceuticals LLC (HQ)	Focuses on anti-infective alternatives to conventional antibiotics. The company offers services to the pharmaceutical sector.	408-385-1742	NA	San Jose
Biochain Institute Inc (HQ)	Provider of bio-sample preparation, analysis, and application assays accelerating the development of personalized diagnostics, therapeutics, and medicine.	510-783-8588	NA	Newark
Biokey Inc (HQ)	Provider of API characterization, pre-formulation studies, formulation development, and analytical method development services.	510-668-0881	NA	Fremont
Biomarin Pharmaceutical Inc (HQ)	Developer of biopharmaceutical products for treatment of morquio A, phenylketonuria, mucopolysaccharidosis VI and I, and lambert-eaton myasthenic syndrome.	415-506-6700	NA	San Rafael
Cantabio Pharmaceuticals Inc (HQ)	Provider of therapeutic solutions. The company specializes in developing therapeutic proteins to prevent degenerative brain diseases.	844-200-2826	NA	Palo Alto
Coherus Biosciences (HQ)	Developer of biosimilars and it serves the global marketplace. The company is engaged in delivery services.	800-794-5434	NA	Redwood City
Corium International Inc (HQ)	Provider of transdermal delivery systems and related technology solutions. The company is also engaged in therapeutic product development.	650-298-8255	NA	Menlo Park
Credence MedSystems Inc (HQ)	Provider of pharmaceutical products. The company specializes in single-dose injectable medications in pre-filled syringes.	844-263-3797	NA	Menlo Park
Denali Therapeutics Inc (HQ)	Provider of therapeutic solutions for the treatment of neurodegenerative diseases. The company also specializes in blood brain barrier programs.	650-866-8548	NA	S San Francisco
Durect Corp (HQ)	Developer of products for the treatment of chronic debilitating disease. The company specializes in biotechnology products.	408-777-1417	NA	Cupertino
Dynavax Technologies Corp (HQ)	Developer of clinical-stage biopharmaceutical company committed to discovering and developing products to prevent and treat infectious diseases.	510-848-5100	51-200	Emeryville
Eckhart Corp (HQ)	Manufacturer of nutritional supplements. The company is engaged in product development and packaging services.	415-898-9528	NA	Novato
Formumax Scientific Inc (HQ)	Provider of contract drug delivery to pharmaceutical and biotech industries. The company specializes in injectables, liposomes, and microemulsions.	408-400-0108	NA	Sunnyvale
HTD Biosystems Inc (HQ)	Focuses on the development of parenteral drugs. The company is engaged in design and product formulation services.	510-367-0528	NA	Pleasanton
Jaguar Health (HQ)	Provider of health solutions for the animals and humans. The company focuses on the development of gastrointestinal pharmaceuticals.	415-371-8300	NA	San Francisco
K-Pax Pharmaceuticals Inc (HQ)	Provider of pharmaceutical grade vitamins and nutritional health supplements for kids, women, and men's health, joints and bones, and immune support.	415-381-7565	NA	Mill Valley
Merieux Nutrisciences Corp (BR)	Provider of public health services. The company is focused on food and pharmaceutical products, cosmetics, and consumer goods.	209-549-7508	NA	Salida
Mission Bio (HQ)	Developer and deliverer of precision medicine. The company offers instruments, fixed panels, custom panels, and software for the researchers and clinicians.	415-854-0058	NA	S San Francisco
Napo Pharmaceuticals Inc (HQ)	Developer of pharmaceutical drugs. The company specializes in the development of patent pharmaceutical products.	415-963-9938	NA	San Francisco
Neopeutics Inc USA (HQ)	Provider of pre clinical contract research services and product development for the private and governmental regulatory agencies.	650-624-4057	NA	S San Francisco
Novici Biotech LLC (HQ)	Focuses on product development as well as protein engineering. The company serves the agriculture, industrial and pharmaceutical sectors.	707-446-5502	NA	Vacaville

COMPANY NAME	PRODUCT / SERVICE	PHONE	EMP	CITY
Optimum Processing Inc (HQ)	Provider of filtration solutions and disposable bioprocess container systems. The company utilizes asymmetric morphology solutions.	415-461-7033	NA	San Rafael
Perceptimed Inc (HQ)	Provider of medical technologies for dispensing and administration of prescription drugs safer, reducing injuries, and death.	650-941-7000	NA	Mountain View
Phage International Inc (HQ)	Provider of leverage bacteriophage therapy technologies. The company specializes in discovery and rediscovery of effective health care solutions.	925-984-9446	NA	Danville
Pharmedix (HQ)	Focuses on the repackaging of pharmaceutical products. The company offers dispensing systems and women's health products.	800-486-1811	NA	Union City
Pharmtak Inc (HQ)	Provider of pharmaceutical products and services. The company focuses on developing novel pharmaceuticals and cosmeceuticals utilizing technology.	408-954-8223	NA	San Jose
Pherin Pharmaceuticals Inc (HQ)	Developer of novel compounds for intranasal spray delivery and also deals with the treatment of neuro-psychiatric and neuroendocrine conditions.	650-636-7064	NA	Los Altos
Portola Pharmaceuticals Inc (HQ)	Focuses on the development and commercialization of therapeutic products for the treatment of hematologic disorders.	650-246-7000	201-500	S San Francisco
Prolynx LLC (HQ)	Developer of technology solutions for releasable linkers. The company also specializes in injectable drugs.	415-552-5306	NA	San Francisco
Proteus Digital Health Inc (HQ)	Providers of health care service technology. The company offers health care products based on electronics technology.	650-632-4031	NA	Redwood City
Qool Therapeutics Inc (HQ)	Developer of therapeutic hypothermia/temperature management therapies to preserve cells and tissues. The company serves the medical industry.	650-328-1426	NA	Mountain View
Reviva Pharmaceuticals Inc (HQ)	Developer of therapy for CNS, cardiovascular, metabolic and inflammatory diseases. The company is a clinical development pharmaceutical company.	408-816-1470	NA	Sunnyvale
Ryss Lab Inc (HQ)	Provider of biotechnology and pharmaceutical development services. The company offers services to the healthcare sector.	510-477-9570	NA	Union City
SFJ Pharmaceuticals Group (HQ)	Focuses on the clinical development and registration of pharmaceutical products. The company is involved in clinical trials.	925-223-6233	NA	Pleasanton
Somagenics Inc (HQ)	Developer of RNA-based therapeutics and diagnostics. The company's services include detection, monitoring, testing, and analysis.	831-426-7700	NA	Santa Cruz
Stemexpress (HQ)	Provider of immunophenotyping, DNA quantitation and viability, tissue transplant verification, and related services.	530-626-7000	NA	Folsom
Theraject Inc (HQ)	Developer of drug micro-needle technologies. The company is engaged in vaccine and also drug deliveries.	510-742-5832	NA	Fremont
Theravance Biopharma US Inc (HQ)	Provider of pharmaceuticals. The company develops new medicines with superior efficacy, convenience, tolerability and/or safety.	650-808-6000	NA	S San Francisco
Titan Pharmaceuticals Inc (HQ)	Provider of biopharmaceuticals. The company discovers proprietary therapeutics primarily for the treatment of serious medical disorders.	650-244-4990	11-50	S San Francisco
Tolerion Inc (HQ)	Provider of medical treatment solutions for autoimmune diseases. The company focuses on restoring the patient's immune system.	415-795-5800	NA	S San Francisco
Vaxcyte Inc (HQ)	Developer of vaccines for the treatment of infectious diseases. The company is also engaged in the production of vaccine antigens.	650-837-0111	NA	Foster City
Verseon Corp (HQ)	Focuses on the design of drug candidates. The company offers services to the pharmaceutical industry.	510-225-9000	NA	Fremont
Vetequip Inc (HQ)	Developer and manufacturer of drug delivery systems. The company specializes in nasal anesthesia delivery systems.	925-463-1828	NA	Livermore

270 = Pharmaceutical Software

COMPANY NAME	PRODUCT / SERVICE	PHONE	EMP	CITY
Arable Corp (HQ)	Provider of products and services to health care, pharmaceutical, biotechnology and medical device companies.	408-825-4755	NA	Cupertino
Atomwise Inc (HQ)	Developer of artificial intelligence systems for the discovery of drugs. The company serves the healthcare sector.	650-449-7925	NA	San Francisco
Healfies (HQ)	Developer and provider of software platform to manage health information. The company serves the healthcare sector.	415-312-4525	NA	San Francisco
HeartFlow Inc (RH)	Provider of analysis technology that creates a personalized 3D model of the coronary arteries and analyzes the impact that blockages have on blood flow.	650-241-1221	NA	Redwood City
Lumedx Corp (HQ)	Provider of cardiovascular information and imaging systems. The company specializes in cloud-powered healthcare solutions.	800-966-0699	NA	Oakland
Mission Bio (HQ)	Developer and deliverer of precision medicine. The company offers instruments, fixed panels, custom panels, and software for the researchers and clinicians.	415-854-0058	NA	S San Francisco
Molecular Devices LLC (HQ)	Manufacturer of bioanalytical measurement systems. The company is engaged in life science research, pharma, and bio therapeutic development.	800-635-5577	NA	San Jose
Prescript Pharmaceuticals Inc (HQ)	Provider of repackaging services. The company offers its products in sealed and tamper evident containers.	925-215-8608	NA	Pleasanton

COMPANY NAME	PRODUCT / SERVICE	PHONE	EMP	CITY
Veracyte Inc (HQ)	Focuses on molecular analysis and diagnostic tests. The company serves patients and the healthcare sector.	650-243-6300	NA	S San Francisco

271 = Serum/Vaccines

COMPANY NAME	PRODUCT / SERVICE	PHONE	EMP	CITY
Aridis Pharmaceuticals LLC (HQ)	Focuses on anti-infective alternatives to conventional antibiotics. The company offers services to the pharmaceutical sector.	408-385-1742	NA	San Jose
Biocheck Inc (HQ)	Provider of custom immunoassay development, antibody conjugation and purification, and contract manufacturing services.	650-573-1968	NA	S San Francisco
Biomertech (HQ)	Provider of tailor-made peptide and antibody solutions such as pepdyes and polyclonal antibody advantage for the scientific community.	925-931-0007	NA	Pleasanton
Corvus Pharmaceuticals Inc (HQ)	Focuses on the development of first-in-class agents that target the immune system. The company serves the healthcare industry.	650-900-4520	NA	Burlingame
Hygeia Laboratories Inc (HQ)	Developers of vaccines using novel technology for animals. The company offers animal pharmaceuticals for dairy cattle, sheep and poultry.	530-661-1442	NA	Woodland
Teknova (HQ)	Provider of agar plates and broths for growth of bacterial, yeast, and microbiological applications such as cloning, DNA sequencing, and immunology.	831-637-1100	NA	Hollister
Vaxart Inc (HQ)	Manufacturer and developer of oral vaccines. The company is engaged in drug development and related services.	650-550-3500	NA	S San Francisco

272 = Vitamins

COMPANY NAME	PRODUCT / SERVICE	PHONE	EMP	CITY
ABCO Laboratories Inc (HQ)	Provider of turnkey solutions. The company also offers contract manufacturing, product development and private labeling.	707-432-2200	NA	Fairfield
Allergy Research Group LLC (BR)	Provider of nutritional products for blood sugar, brain, cardiovascular, metabolic, hormone, liver, and immune support.	510-263-2000	NA	Alameda
Aridis Pharmaceuticals LLC (HQ)	Focuses on anti-infective alternatives to conventional antibiotics. The company offers services to the pharmaceutical sector.	408-385-1742	NA	San Jose
C&M Biolabs (HQ)	Provider of products and services to scientists. The company offers cloning and sequencing and antibody services.	510-691-7166	NA	Richmond
Calysta (HQ)	Focuses on the development and manufacture of protein for commercial aquaculture and livestock feed.	650-492-6880	NA	Menlo Park
Cypress Systems Inc (HQ)	Provider of natural food forms of organically bound minerals and nutritional yeast products and related supplies.	559-229-7850	NA	Madera
Cytosport Inc (HQ)	Manufacturer of health care supplements. The company specializes in fitness supplements for athletes, to strengthen muscles and bones.	888-298-6629	NA	Walnut Creek
Eckhart Corp (HQ)	Manufacturer of nutritional supplements. The company is engaged in product development and packaging services.	415-898-9528	NA	Novato
Econugenics Inc (HQ)	Manufacturer and distributor of dietary supplements and healthcare products. The company serves the medical sector.	800-521-0160	NA	Santa Rosa
Formulation Technology Inc (HQ)	Manufacturer of custom dietary supplements and OTC medications. The company focuses on contract manufacturing services.	209-847-0331	NA	Oakdale
Global Marketing Associates Inc (HQ)	Providers of nutrition supplements to health care industry. The company supply innovative and quality ingredients to health care industry.	510-887-2462	EMP	Livermore
K-Pax Pharmaceuticals Inc (HQ)	Provider of pharmaceutical grade vitamins and nutritional health supplements for kids, women, and men's health, joints and bones, and immune support.	415-381-7565	NA	Mill Valley
MusclePharm Corp (HQ)	Provider of sports supplement and nutrition products such as fish oil, energy sport zero, and coco protein for weight loss, fitness, and athletes.	800-292-3909	NA	Burbank
Nordic Naturals Inc (HQ)	Specializes in the delivery of omega oil to consumers, veterinary professionals, pharmacists, and healthcare professionals.	831-724-6200	NA	Watsonville
Nutribiotic (HQ)	Manufacturer of health, wellness, and fitness products. The company provides nutritional supplements and personal care products.	707-263-0411	NA	Lakeport
Pharmedix (HQ)	Focuses on the repackaging of pharmaceutical products. The company offers dispensing systems and women's health products.	800-486-1811	NA	Union City
Planetary Herbals (HQ)	Provider of nutritional herbal healthcare products. The company's products include Acai, Full Spectrum, Bacopa Extract, and Digestive Comfort.	831-438-1700	NA	Soquel
Pro-Form Laboratories (HQ)	Developer and producer of nutritional powders. The company also specializes in contract manufacturing services.	707-752-9010	NA	Orinda
Randal Optimal Nutrients Inc (HQ)	Manufacturer of consumer goods. The company produces dietary supplements and nutraceuticals to the health food and profession health care markers.	707-528-1800	NA	Santa Rosa
SFJ Pharmaceuticals Group (HQ)	Focuses on the clinical development and registration of pharmaceutical products. The company is involved in clinical trials.	925-223-6233	NA	Pleasanton
Source Naturals Inc (HQ)	Provider of vitamins, minerals, and nutritional supplements. The company deals with sales and delivery services.	831-438-1144	NA	Scotts Valley
Threshold Enterprises Ltd (HQ)	Distributor of nutritional supplements, healthcare, and beauty care products.	831-438-6851	NA	Scotts Valley
Wachters' Organic Sea Products (HQ)	Manufacturer and distributor of nutritional products. The company's products include pet products, personal care, and cleaning products.	650-757-9851	NA	Daly City

COMPANY NAME	PRODUCT / SERVICE	PHONE	EMP	CITY
273 = Veterinary Pharmaceuticals				
Allaccem Inc (HQ)	Manufacturer of pharmaceutical products such as dermatology, optic, and dental products for goats, dogs, and cats.	650-593-8700	NA	San Carlos
Antech Diagnostics (HQ)	Provider of diagnostic and laboratory testing services for chemistry, pathology, endocrinology, serology, hematology, and microbiology.	800-872-1001	NA	Fountain Valley
Hemostat Laboratories (HQ)	Provider of defibrinated sheep blood and other animal blood products for cell culture, diagnostic and veterinary applications.	800-572-6888	NA	Dixon
Kindred Biosciences Inc (HQ)	Provider of pharmaceutical products for treatment of anemia, cancer, allergic, autoimmune, and gastrointestinal diseases in cats, dogs, and horses.	650-701-7901	NA	Burlingame
VDx Veterinary Diagnostics and Preclinical Research Services (HQ)	Provider of histopathology and pathology support to the medical device, biotech, pharmaceutical, academic and veterinary communities.	530-753-4285	NA	Davis
275 = Advanced Materials R&D				
Carbon3D Inc (HQ)	Provider of hardware and software engineering and molecular science. The company specializes in continuous liquid interface production technology.	650-285-6307	NA	Redwood City
Davlin Coatings (HQ)	Manufacturer of coatings for architectural and industrial purposes. The company offers elastomeric waterproof coatings.	510-848-2863	NA	Berkeley
Dowd & Guild Inc (HQ)	Distributor of chemicals and containers. The company supplies resins, grinding media, oils and waxes, rheological products, and pigments.	925-820-7222	NA	San Ramon
Yunsheng USA (HQ)	Manufacturer of permanent magnets. The company mainly offers Neodymium and rare earth magnet products.	650-827-7928	NA	S San Francisco
277 = Ceramics				
N Abrisa Industrial Glass Inc (HQ)	Provider of full-service custom glass fabrication.	805-525-4902	NA	Santa Paula
Morgan Technical Ceramics (BR)	Manufacturer of cast and powder metal stainless steels. The company also focuses on other specialty alloys.	530-823-3401	NA	Auburn
NTK Technologies Inc (HQ)	Manufacturer of bio ceramics, oxygen sensors, ceramic heater, and transistor packages for the medical and telecommunication applications.	408-727-5180	NA	Santa Clara
Pacific Ceramics Inc (HQ)	Manufacturer of microwave ceramic material. The company's products include earth iron garnets, calcium vanadium garnets, lithium, and titanate dielectrics.	408-747-4600	NA	Sunnyvale
Sun Enterprise Inc (HQ)	Provider of ceramic and quartz machining products. The company specializes in the semiconductor, solar, laser, and structural industries.	510-657-6507	NA	Fremont
Toray Advanced Composites USA (BR)	Manufacturer of advanced composites like adhesives, prepregs, and liquid resin systems. The company serves military, aerospace, and other sectors.	408-465-8500	NA	Morgan Hill
278 = Composites				
Asbury Graphite Incorporated of CA (BR)	Supplier of carbon and graphite products for the chemicals, cement, rubber, and metal industries. The company's products include coals, cokes, and carbon fiber.	510-799-3636	NA	Rodeo
Toray Advanced Composites USA (BR)	Manufacturer of advanced composites like adhesives, prepregs, and liquid resin systems. The company serves military, aerospace, and other sectors.	408-465-8500	NA	Morgan Hill
279 = Laminates				
N Material Fabricators Inc (HQ)	Manufacturer of gaskets, shims, washers, metal stampings and die cut electrical insulators.	805-686-5244	NA	Buellton
N O-Rings Inc (HQ)	Manufacturer and distributor of rings and custom molded rubber products.	323-343-9500	NA	Los Angeles
N Roettele Industries Inc (HQ)	Manufacturer of non-metallic washers and gaskets.	909-606-8252	1-10	Chino
Window Solutions (HQ)	Provider of 3M window film and tinting installation services. The company offers services for residential, commercial, architects, and builders.	650-349-2257	NA	S San Francisco
280 = Miscellaneous Plastic Products				
Acrylic Art (HQ)	Provider of fabrication and machining services. The company focuses on painting, product finishing, anodizing, and vapor polishing.	510-654-0953	NA	Emeryville
BASF Venture Capital America Inc (RH)	Manufacturer of basic chemicals and intermediates such as solvents, plasticizers, and monomers. The company serves the agriculture market.	510-445-6140	NA	Fremont
Bio Plas Inc (HQ)	Manufacturer of laboratory disposables such as foam tube racks, biopsy bags, bacti cell spreaders, and siliconized products.	415-472-3777	NA	San Rafael
Carbon3D Inc (HQ)	Provider of hardware and software engineering and molecular science. The company specializes in continuous liquid interface production technology.	650-285-6307	NA	Redwood City
China Custom Manufacturing Ltd (HQ)	Provider of tooling, plastic injection molding, and sheet metal stamping services. The company focuses on the aerospace and electronics industries.	510-979-1920	NA	Fremont
Computer Plastics Inc (HQ)	Provider of molding services. The company offers custom plastic injection molding, engineering, assembly, and tooling services.	510-785-3600	NA	Hayward

COMPANY NAME	PRODUCT / SERVICE	PHONE	EMP	CITY
D & T Fiberglass Inc (HQ)	Manufacturer of fiberglass reinforced plastic bulk containers. The company's products are used for water and chemical treatment applications.	916-383-9012	NA	Sacramento
Delta Pacific Products Inc (HQ)	Provider of plastics injection molding and mold making services. The company serves the automotive, agriculture, aerospace, and recreational sectors.	510-487-4411	NA	Union City
Dependable Plastics (HQ)	Provider of vacuum and pressure forming, plastic fabrication, and turnkey operations that involve assembly, conductive coating, and painting.	707-863-4900	NA	Fairfield
Ens Technology LLC (HQ)	Provider of plating services. The company plates materials such as common metals, alloys, and refractory metals.	408-496-0740	NA	Santa Clara
Fictiv Inc (HQ)	Provider of tooling services for hardware engineers. The company specializes in distributed manufacturing of idle 3D printers from single platform.	415-580-2509	NA	San Francisco
Freetech Plastics Inc (HQ)	Manufacturer of pressure thermoforming products. The company's products include medical, scientific, and telecommunication enclosures.	510-651-9996	NA	Fremont
Golden Plastics Corp (HQ)	Provider of thermoforming services. The company specializes in part trimming, part design, and tooling.	510-569-6465	NA	Oakland
Kennerley-Spratling Inc (HQ)	Manufacturer of custom plastic injection and compression moldings. The company is involved in design, installation, and delivery services.	510-351-8230	NA	San Leandro
Macro Plastics Inc (HQ)	Provider of agricultural, food processing, and industrial bins. The company's services include recycling, design, and business development.	707-437-1200	NA	Fairfield
N Metal Surfaces Inc (HQ)	Provider of plating and polishing services.	562-927-1331	51-200	Bell Gardens
N MetalMart International Inc (HQ)	Distributor of metals and wrought magnesium.	562-692-9081	NA	Commerce
Plastikon Industries Inc (HQ)	Provider of contract manufacturing services for custom designed plastic injection molding, for medical, pharmaceutical and other industries.	510-400-1010	NA	Hayward
N PTM & W Industries Inc (HQ)	Manufacturer of laminated plastics plate and sheet.	562-946-4511	NA	Santa Fe Springs
Roplast Industries Inc (HQ)	Manufacturer of bags. The company specializes in custom designed bags made out of polyethylene films.	530-532-9500	NA	Oroville
Scribner Plastics (HQ)	Provider of shipping and packing solutions. The company also deals with custom plastics design and manufacturing services.	916-638-1515	NA	Rancho Cordova
N Swiss Productions Inc (HQ)	Provider of machining services for aerospace, electronic, automotive, defense and medical sectors.	805-654-8525	11-50	Ventura

281 = Monomers/Polymers

COMPANY NAME	PRODUCT / SERVICE	PHONE	EMP	CITY
Carbon3D Inc (HQ)	Provider of hardware and software engineering and molecular science. The company specializes in continuous liquid interface production technology.	650-285-6307	NA	Redwood City
Cobalt Polymers Inc (HQ)	Manufacturer of polymer tubing for medical device and high technology applications, with polymer chemistry, radiation science, and process engineering.	800-337-0901	NA	Cloverdale
N Foam Molders and Specialties (HQ)	Manufacturer of polyurethane, polyethylene, and EVA foams.	800-378-8987	NA	Cerritos
Pacific Rubber & Packing Inc (HQ)	Provider of rubber seals, custom seals, rubber gaskets and o-ring products for medical/pharmacy, automotive, solar energy, and general industries.	650-595-5888	NA	San Carlos

283 = Plastic Film/Sheets

COMPANY NAME	PRODUCT / SERVICE	PHONE	EMP	CITY
N Breathing Color Inc (HQ)	Designer and supplier of digital inkjet media and post-print protective coatings.	866-722-6567	11-50	Irvine
C3Nano Inc (HQ)	Developer of transparent conductive ink and film such as touch sensors, OLED lighting and displays, EMI shielding for touch sensor and display industry.	510-259-9650	NA	Hayward
N F.D.S. Manufacturing Co (HQ)	Manufacturer of packaging products for industrial and agricultural markers.	909-591-1733	NA	Pomona
N Nitto Denko America Inc (HQ)	Manufacturer of bonding, joining and surface protection products, sealants, anticorrosion and waterproofing, electrical insulating products, engineering plastics, medical-related, membrane, packaging, media-related, semiconductor-related, LCD-related and electronic components related products, industrial use barcode labels, flexible printed circuits, precision electronics materials.	510-445-5480	NA	Fremont
Procurement Partners International Inc (HQ)	Provider of procurement services. The company offers mechanical components such as pins, rods, rollers, and sheet metal.	650-345-6118	NA	San Mateo
Window Solutions (HQ)	Provider of 3M window film and tinting installation services. The company offers services for residential, commercial, architects, and builders.	650-349-2257	NA	S San Francisco

284 = Plastic Materials, Synthetic Resins & Elastomerss

COMPANY NAME	PRODUCT / SERVICE	PHONE	EMP	CITY
Acrylic Art (HQ)	Provider of fabrication and machining services. The company focuses on painting, product finishing, anodizing, and vapor polishing.	510-654-0953	NA	Emeryville
Amyris Inc (HQ)	Provider of renewable products. The company delivers cosmetic emollients and fragrances, fuels and lubricants, and even biopharmaceuticals.	510-450-0761	NA	Emeryville

COMPANY NAME	PRODUCT / SERVICE	PHONE	EMP	CITY
ATS Inc (HQ)	Manufacturer of fiberglass ductwork for fume exhaust systems. The company offers installation and other related services.	510-234-3173	NA	Richmond
Aubin Industries Inc (HQ)	Designer and manufacturer of mobile wheel systems. The company serves the material handling industry.	209-833-7592	NA	Tracy
Dependable Plastics (HQ)	Provider of vacuum and pressure forming, plastic fabrication, and turnkey operations that involve assembly, conductive coating, and painting.	707-863-4900	NA	Fairfield
N Elkay Plastics Inc (HQ)	Distributor of flexible packaging products for food, healthcare and various other sectors.	323-722-7073	NA	Commerce
Empire West Inc (HQ)	Designer and developer of envelope handling trays, custom thermoformed ceiling tiles and panels, and optic packaging solutions.	707-823-1190	NA	Graton
Finishline Advanced Composites LLC (HQ)	Provider of composite repair services for production projects. The company is involved in design, development, prototyping, testing, and production.	707-747-0788	NA	Benicia
Freetech Plastics Inc (HQ)	Manufacturer of pressure thermoforming products. The company's products include medical, scientific, and telecommunication enclosures.	510-651-9996	NA	Fremont
Interstate Plastics (BR)	Provider of plastic products. The company's products include plastic sheets, rods, tubes, and industrial accessories.	510-483-4341	NA	San Leandro
Interstate Plastics Inc (HQ)	Manufacturer and distributor of industrial plastics. The company offers plastic sheets, rods, tubing, and profiles.	916-422-3110	NA	Sacramento
Jatco Inc (HQ)	Manufacture of plastic products. The company offers molding, tooling, quality control, and warehousing and distribution services.	510-487-0888	NA	Union City
Loprest Water Treatment Co (HQ)	Provider of water treatment systems design and fabricating services. The company focuses on media analysis and filter inspection.	510-799-3101	NA	Rodeo
N Orange County Industrial Plastics Inc (HQ)	Manufacturer and distributor of plastic fabricator.	714-630-6489	11-50	Anaheim
Poly Seal Industries (HQ)	Manufacturer of molded rubber pipe gaskets for water and sewage treatment applications. The company serves the automotive and biomedical industries.	510-843-9722	NA	Berkeley
Precision Plastics Inc (HQ)	Provider of plastic fabrication services. The company is engaged in fabrication, countertops, machining, and consumer services.	916-689-5284	NA	Sacramento

285 = Polystyrene/Urethane Foams

COMPANY NAME	PRODUCT / SERVICE	PHONE	EMP	CITY
Foamlinx LLC (HQ)	Provider of foam cutting computer numerical control machines. The company offers cutters, shredders, compactors, and cutting services.	408-454-6163	NA	Sunnyvale
Gel-Pak (DH)	Provider of safety transport and product handling services from bare die to medical components, and other fragile parts.	510-576-2220	NA	Hayward
ICO Rally (HQ)	Manufacturer and supplier of heat shrinkable materials, wiring accessories, and insulation products. The company serves automotive and marine sectors.	650-856-9900	NA	Palo Alto

286 = Quartz, Silicon & Other Electronic Materials

COMPANY NAME	PRODUCT / SERVICE	PHONE	EMP	CITY
GM Associates Inc (HQ)	Manufacturer of quartz fabricated products and etch chalmers. The company offers machining, slicing, cutting, and other services.	510-430-0806	NA	Oakland
Hayward Quartz Technology Inc (HQ)	Manufacturer of machined and fabricated parts. The company exclusively caters to the semiconductor industry.	510-657-9605	NA	Fremont
LP Glass Blowing Inc (HQ)	Provider of high-precision quartz ware and glass products. The company offers research and development assistance services.	408-988-7561	NA	Santa Clara
Sun Enterprise Inc (HQ)	Provider of ceramic and quartz machining products. The company specializes in the semiconductor, solar, laser, and structural industries.	510-657-6507	NA	Fremont
Techni-Glass Inc (HQ)	Provider of glass blowing services. The company specializes in glass used for research, laser, oil, and medical services.	707-838-3325	NA	Windsor

288 = Batteries/Energy Storage Devices

COMPANY NAME	PRODUCT / SERVICE	PHONE	EMP	CITY
AA Portable Power Corp (HQ)	Manufacturer of lithium-ion batteries. The company serves the mobile, consumer electronics, energy storage, and light electric vehicle markers.	510-525-2328	NA	Richmond
Amprius Inc (HQ)	Developer and manufacturer of lithium-ion batteries. The company offers services to the industrial sectors.	800-425-8803	NA	Fremont
Ardica Technologies (HQ)	Provider of integrated power and fuel cell technology solutions for commercial and military applications.	415-568-9270	NA	San Francisco
Arrgh!! Manufacturing Company Inc (HQ)	Manufacturer of battery chargers, controls, battery discharge alarms, microcomputer charger controls, and gas detectors.	415-897-0220	NA	Novato
BASF Venture Capital America Inc (RH)	Manufacturer of basic chemicals and intermediates such as solvents, plasticizers, and monomers. The company serves the agriculture market.	510-445-6140	NA	Fremont
N Continental Motors Inc (HQ)	Manufacturer of aircraft batteries, ground power batteries, and standby power batteries.	909-793-3131	NA	Redlands
Energous Corp (HQ)	Provider of energy solutions. The company offers a wire-free charging system for portable electronic devices.	408-963-0200	NA	San Jose
Evergreen (CP) USA Inc (HQ)	Manufacturer of batteries. The company offers lithium coin cells, nickel cadmium batteries, manganese button cells, and silver oxide button cells.	650-952-8091	NA	S San Francisco

COMPANY NAME	PRODUCT / SERVICE	PHONE	EMP	CITY
Farasis Energy Inc (HQ)	Designer and developer of energy storage solutions. The company serves the transportation, consumer electronics, and power distribution markers.	510-732-6600	NA	Hayward
Fenix International (HQ)	Provider of affordable power generation, smart-storage, and distribution solutions for the 1.6 billion people living off the electricity grid.	415-754-9222	NA	San Francisco
FreeWire Technologies Inc (HQ)	Provider of mobile distributed power solutions. The company serves the business and industrial sectors.	415-779-5515	NA	San Leandro
IMC Power Sources (HQ)	Supplier of SLA batteries, power test equipment, and test loads. The company serves the industrial market.	408-924-0800	NA	San Jose
Imprint Energy (HQ)	Developer of zinc-based rechargeable batteries. The company is engaged in energy management solutions.	510-748-0233	NA	Alameda
King-Solarman Inc (HQ)	Focuses on the sale of solar panels, power inverters, and related supplies. The company is involved in solar project financing services.	408-373-8800	NA	Fremont
Mojo Mobility Inc (HQ)	Provider of mobile recharge devices such as batteries and pads for computer peripherals and headsets for medical and commercial sectors.	650-446-0004	NA	Santa Clara
Nanosys Inc (HQ)	Developer of nanotechnology products for the LCD display and battery markers. The company focuses on display backlighting and energy storage devices.	408-240-6700	NA	Milpitas
PPBC (HQ)	Engaged in the development of protected lithium metal electrodes. The company's products include lithium-sulfur batteries and protected lithium anodes.	510-841-7242	NA	Berkeley
Primus Power (HQ)	Provider of energy storage solutions. The company develops EnergyPod, energy storage batteries, and EnergyCell for industrial and consumer applications.	510-342-7600	NA	Hayward
Syrma Technology (BR)	Provider of entrepreneurial manufacturing services. The company's products include magnetics, memory, and RFID.	408-404-0500	NA	San Jose
Tenergy Corp (HQ)	Designer and manufacturer of batteries and chargers. The company serves medical, consumer electronics, data management, military, and other sectors.	510-687-0388	NA	Fremont
Top Microsystems Corp (HQ)	Provider of conversion solutions and integration services. The company offers blade, storage, and rackmount servers, medical equipment, and others.	408-980-9813	NA	Santa Clara
WAGAN Corp (HQ)	Developer and marketer of automotive accessories to mobile professionals. The company's offerings include warmers, defrosters, and heated cushions.	510-471-9221	NA	Hayward
Xantrex Technology Inc (BR)	Manufacturer of automotive batteries. The company offers power products for trucks, cars, and recreational vehicles.	408-987-6030	NA	Livermore

289 = Circuit Breakers

COMPANY NAME	PRODUCT / SERVICE	PHONE	EMP	CITY
Acronics (HQ)	Provider of engineering services. The company is involved in systems and mechanical design services.	408-432-0888	NA	San Jose
Barrington Consultants Inc (HQ)	Manufacturer of transformer monitors and temperature monitors for testing high voltage circuit breakers and offers circuit breaker simulators.	707-527-8254	NA	Santa Rosa
Mektec International Corp (HQ)	Manufacturer of printed circuit boards. The company deals with production, prototyping, and application engineering services.	408-392-4000	NA	San Jose

290 = Electric Power Control/Transmission Equipment

	COMPANY NAME	PRODUCT / SERVICE	PHONE	EMP	CITY
	A TEEM Electrical Engineering (HQ)	Provider of outreach safety training, electrical design and construction management, and control system programming services.	916-457-8144	NA	Sacramento
	Advanced Power Solutions (HQ)	Provider of power supplies. The company is involved in manufacturing, sales, and related support services.	925-456-9890	NA	Livermore
N	American Relays Inc (HQ)	Designer and manufacturer of reed relay.	562-944-0447	1-10	Norwalk
	AMtec Industries Inc (BR)	Manufacturer of industrial custom control panels. The company is engaged in design, fabrication, and installation services.	510-887-2289	NA	Pleasanton
	Aras Power Technologies (HQ)	Provider of power delivery solutions. The company offers conventional, alternating current solutions, and custom power supply design services.	408-935-8877	NA	Milpitas
	Calcon Systems Inc (HQ)	Provider of process control, instrumentation, and automation solutions specializing in turnkey design-build system integration and support.	925-277-0665	NA	San Ramon
	Capital Machine (HQ)	Provider of machining, welding, fabrication, and design services. The company also distributes steel and power transmission products.	916-443-6671	NA	Sacramento
	Communications & Power Industries LLC (HQ)	Developer and manufacturer of microwave, radio frequency, power, and control solutions. The company serves medical and critical defense fields.	650-846-2900	NA	Palo Alto
N	Dnh Industries Inc (HQ)	Manufacturer of electrical and electronic control products.	310-517-1769	NA	Harbor City
N	Hydra-Electric Co (HQ)	Manufacturer of switches and other related products.	818-843-6211	201-500	Burbank
	KG Technologies Inc (HQ)	Designer and developer of switching solutions. The company's applications include welding, brazing, and riveting.	888-513-1874	NA	Rohnert Park
	Megmeet USA Inc (BR)	Manufacturer of electrical motors, general-used converters, and optional devices. The company offers industry automatic solutions.	408-260-7211	NA	San Jose

COMPANY NAME	PRODUCT / SERVICE	PHONE	EMP	CITY
Polarity Inc (HQ)	Designer and manufacturer of power products for commercial and government entities. The company also offers supply solutions.	916-635-3050	NA	Rancho Cordova
S&C Electric Co (BR)	Provider of equipment and services for electric power systems. The company is involved in design and installation services.	510-864-9300	NA	Alameda
N Silveron Industries Inc (HQ)	Supplier of relays and industrial controls.	909-598-4533	NA	City Of Industry
Sparkle Power Inc (HQ)	Manufacturer of switching power supply devices. The company serves the PC, industrial PC, and telecommunication industries.	408-519-8888	NA	Fremont
N Technical Heaters Inc (HQ)	Manufacturer of rubber, plastics hose and beltings.	800-394-9435	NA	San Fernando
Total Environmental & Power Systems Inc (HQ)	Provider of HVAC, electrical, and telecommunication services. The company's service areas include generators, radio frequency, and fabrication.	925-681-2238	NA	Concord
Vantage Data Center Services & Solutionsÿ (HQ)	Provider of transformers, switches, generators, chillers, switch gears and security, and communication products.	855-878-2682	NA	Santa Clara
Varentec Inc (HQ)	Provider of grid control and monitoring solutions. The company also offers asset management and outage detection services.	408-433-9900	NA	Santa Clara

291 = Fuses

COMPANY NAME	PRODUCT / SERVICE	PHONE	EMP	CITY
Bentek Corp (HQ)	Provider of manufacturing and engineering services. The company's offerings include power distribution system design and mechanical manufacturing.	408-954-9600	NA	San Jose
Solarbos Inc (HQ)	Designer and manufacturer of electrical products. The company exclusively caters to the solar industry.	925-456-7744	NA	Livermore

292 = Generators

COMPANY NAME	PRODUCT / SERVICE	PHONE	EMP	CITY
Adtec Technology Inc (HQ)	Manufacturer of RF plasma generators, matching units, and power measurement devices. The company serves semiconductor and solar processing tool needs.	510-226-5766	NA	Fremont
Allmotion Inc (HQ)	Manufacturer and distributor of stepper drives, stepper controllers, servo drives, and servo controllers.	510-471-4000	NA	Union City
Empire Magnetics Inc (HQ)	Manufacturer of specialty, cryogenic, dust proof, high temperature, water proof, and radiation hardened motors.	707-584-2801	NA	Rohnert Park
Enphase Energy Inc (HQ)	Distributor of electronic products. The company offers services to the solar, telecom, networking, and software industries.	877-797-4743	NA	Petaluma
FreeWire Technologies Inc (HQ)	Provider of mobile distributed power solutions. The company serves the business and industrial sectors.	415-779-5515	NA	San Leandro
Liberty Test Equipment (HQ)	Provider of refurbished and new test equipment and related accessories. The company deals with sales, lease, and rental services.	916-625-4228	NA	Roseville
National Vapor Industries Inc (HQ)	Manufacturer of hydrogen generators. The company also offers marketing, installation, and other services.	925-980-7341	NA	Livermore
Omniyig Inc (HQ)	Manufacturer of microwave devices for the defense industry. The company also offers limiters, drivers, and oscillators.	408-988-0843	NA	Santa Clara
Top Microsystems Corp (HQ)	Provider of conversion solutions and integration services. The company offers blade, storage, and rackmount servers, medical equipment, and others.	408-980-9813	NA	Santa Clara

293 = Power & Distribution Equipment

COMPANY NAME	PRODUCT / SERVICE	PHONE	EMP	CITY
Amasco (HQ)	Distributor of products for the telecommunications, commercial, industrial, medical, and military electronics markers.	408-360-1300	NA	San Jose
Aras Power Technologies (HQ)	Provider of power delivery solutions. The company offers conventional, alternating current solutions, and custom power supply design services.	408-935-8877	NA	Milpitas
Berkeley Nucleonics Corp (HQ)	Designer and manufacturer of precision test, measurement, and nuclear instrumentation. The company mainly offers generators and analyzers.	415-453-9955	NA	San Rafael
Bloom Energy Corp (HQ)	Provider of power generation systems. The company focuses on solid oxide fuel cells and mission critical systems.	408-543-1500	NA	San Jose
Construction Electrical Products (HQ)	Provider of electrical products for the construction sector. The company offers temporary power products, extension cords, and portable lighting.	925-828-9420	NA	Livermore
Digital Power Corp (HQ)	Designer and manufacturer of switching power supplies. The company serves the industrial, military, and medical markers.	510-657-2635	NA	Milpitas
International Power Technology Inc (HQ)	Provider of operation and maintenance services for power plants. The company also focuses on engineering and field service.	408-246-9040	NA	San Jose
Kikusui America Inc (HQ)	Provider of electronic measuring instruments and power supplies. The company's products include electronic loads and power supply controllers.	310-214-0000	NA	Torrance
Knurr USA (BR)	Provider of custom enclosures, mobile equipment carriers and carts, outdoor cabinets, control room consoles, and technical furniture.	510-353-0177	NA	Milpitas
N M. K. Products Inc (HQ)	Supplier of welding apparatus.	949-863-1234	NA	Irvine
Martin Sprocket & Gear Inc (BR)	Manufacturer of industrial hand tools, conveyor pulleys, and other products. The company offers power transmission and material handling products.	916-441-7172	NA	Sacramento
Mean Well USA Inc (HQ)	Manufacturer of switching power supplies such as AC to DC converters, DC to DC converters, DC to AC inverters, and battery chargers.	510-683-8886	NA	Fremont

	COMPANY NAME	PRODUCT / SERVICE	PHONE	EMP	CITY
N	Mgm Transformer Co (HQ)	Manufacturer and dealer of transformers.	323-726-0888	51-200	Commerce
	Moog Animatics (BR)	Provider of motion control devices. The company offers actuators, cables, power supplies, and peripherals.	650-960-4215	NA	Mountain View
	NPI Solutions Inc (HQ)	Provider of design, engineering, and custom manufacturing solutions. The company offers on-site engineering services.	408-944-9178	NA	Morgan Hill
	Polarity Inc (HQ)	Designer and manufacturer of power products for commercial and government entities. The company also offers supply solutions.	916-635-3050	NA	Rancho Cordova
	Power Standards Lab (HQ)	Manufacturer of precision electronic power instruments. The company is involved in testing and calibration services.	510-522-4400	NA	Alameda
	Powertronix Corp (HQ)	Provider of in-house engineering and related services. The company offers services to the industrial sector.	650-345-6800	NA	Foster City
	Quality Transformer & Electronics (HQ)	Manufacturer and seller of transformers. The company also specializes in power supplies and other components.	408-263-8444	NA	Milpitas
	Solutions Cubed LLC (HQ)	Provider of engineering solutions. The company is involved in early stage electronic prototyping to full production runs.	530-891-8045	NA	Chico
	Sparkle Power Inc (HQ)	Manufacturer of switching power supply devices. The company serves the PC, industrial PC, and telecommunication industries.	408-519-8888	NA	Fremont
	Steven Engineering Inc (HQ)	Distributor of industrial controls and components. The company also provides contract manufacturing services.	800-258-9200	NA	S San Francisco
	Sunverge Energy Inc (HQ)	Provider of power and energy services. The company focuses on solar power and combines batteries and power electronics.	209-931-5677	NA	Stockton
	Syrma Technology (BR)	Provider of entrepreneurial manufacturing services. The company's products include magnetics, memory, and RFID.	408-404-0500	NA	San Jose
N	Technical Heaters Inc (HQ)	Manufacturer of rubber, plastics hose and beltings.	800-394-9435	NA	San Fernando
	Tenergy Corp (HQ)	Designer and manufacturer of batteries and chargers. The company serves medical, consumer electronics, data management, military, and other sectors.	510-687-0388	NA	Fremont
	Top Microsystems Corp (HQ)	Provider of conversion solutions and integration services. The company offers blade, storage, and rackmount servers, medical equipment, and others.	408-980-9813	NA	Santa Clara
	Total Environmental & Power Systems Inc (HQ)	Provider of HVAC, electrical, and telecommunication services. The company's service areas include generators, radio frequency, and fabrication.	925-681-2238	NA	Concord
	Varentec Inc (HQ)	Provider of grid control and monitoring solutions. The company also offers asset management and outage detection services.	408-433-9900	NA	Santa Clara
	Voltage Multipliers Inc (HQ)	Manufacturer of voltage multipliers, high voltage diodes, rectifiers, opto-couplers, and power supplies.	559-651-1402	NA	Visalia
	Xantrex Technology Inc (BR)	Manufacturer of automotive batteries. The company offers power products for trucks, cars, and recreational vehicles.	408-987-6030	NA	Livermore

295 = Switchgears and Switchboard Apparatus

COMPANY NAME	PRODUCT / SERVICE	PHONE	EMP	CITY
Arcus Technology Inc (HQ)	Provider of motor controllers, stepper motors, and related accessories such as cables, encoders, and gearboxes.	925-373-8800	NA	Livermore
Digital Loggers Inc (HQ)	Manufacturer of recording systems and power switches. The company offers call center recorders, radio logging systems, and recording accessories.	408-330-5599	NA	Santa Clara
KG Technologies Inc (HQ)	Designer and developer of switching solutions. The company's applications include welding, brazing, and riveting.	888-513-1874	NA	Rohnert Park
Knurr USA (BR)	Provider of custom enclosures, mobile equipment carriers and carts, outdoor cabinets, control room consoles, and technical furniture.	510-353-0177	NA	Milpitas
Martin Sprocket & Gear Inc (BR)	Manufacturer of industrial hand tools, conveyor pulleys, and other products. The company offers power transmission and material handling products.	916-441-7172	NA	Sacramento
Methode Electronics (BR)	Manufacturer of power management electronic products. The company is engaged in design, engineering, and technical support services.	510-610-5241	NA	San Jose
Norden Millimeter Inc (HQ)	Developer and manufacturer of amplifier products. The company specializes in millimeter wave amplifier products.	530-642-9123	NA	Placerville
Sparkle Power Inc (HQ)	Manufacturer of switching power supply devices. The company serves the PC, industrial PC, and telecommunication industries.	408-519-8888	NA	Fremont
Trayer Engineering Corp (HQ)	Manufacturer of electronic distribution switchgears. The company's services include design, maintenance, and installation.	415-285-7770	NA	San Leandro

296 = Transformers

COMPANY NAME	PRODUCT / SERVICE	PHONE	EMP	CITY
Delta Star Inc (BR)	Manufacturer of devices for the electrical sector. The company offers devices for the generation, transmission, and distribution of electrical energy.	800-892-8673	NA	San Carlos
Powertronix Corp (HQ)	Provider of in-house engineering and related services. The company offers services to the industrial sector.	650-345-6800	NA	Foster City
Quality Transformer & Electronics (HQ)	Manufacturer and seller of transformers. The company also specializes in power supplies and other components.	408-263-8444	NA	Milpitas

COMPANY NAME	PRODUCT / SERVICE	PHONE	EMP	CITY
Stangenes Industries Inc (HQ)	Manufacturer of isolation transformers, current monitors, charging inductors, and magnetic components.	650-493-0814	NA	Palo Alto
Steven Engineering Inc (HQ)	Distributor of industrial controls and components. The company also provides contract manufacturing services.	800-258-9200	NA	S San Francisco
West Coast Magnetics (HQ)	Provider of electrical products. The company specializes in inductor products, transformers, chokes, and planar magnetic products.	800-628-1123	NA	Stockton

297 = Turbines, Turbine Generator Sets

COMPANY NAME	PRODUCT / SERVICE	PHONE	EMP	CITY
Halus Power Systems (HQ)	Manufacturer of renewable energy products specializing in wind turbines and controls. The company offers design and remanufacturing services.	510-278-2212	NA	San Leandro
International Power Technology Inc (HQ)	Provider of operation and maintenance services for power plants. The company also focuses on engineering and field service.	408-246-9040	NA	San Jose

298 = Wire & Wiring devices

COMPANY NAME	PRODUCT / SERVICE	PHONE	EMP	CITY
Bentek Corp (HQ)	Provider of manufacturing and engineering services. The company's offerings include power distribution system design and mechanical manufacturing.	408-954-9600	NA	San Jose
Compatible Cable Inc (HQ)	Manufacturer of custom cable assemblies and off-the shelf cables. The company offers services to the automotive, broadcast, and electronics industries.	888-415-1115	NA	Concord
Custom Coils Inc (HQ)	Manufacturer of coils, coil assemblies, and solenoids. The company also offers other electro-magnetic devices.	707-752-8633	NA	Benicia
HBR Industries Inc (HQ)	Provider of electronics manufacturing services. The company offers coil solutions and services for the medical, military, and semiconductor industry.	408-988-0800	NA	San Jose
Jetronics Co (HQ)	Manufacturer of custom cable assemblies and harnesses, magnetics assemblies, sub-assembly components, front and rear panels, and chassis assemblies.	707-544-2436	NA	Santa Rosa
Leoco USA Corp (BR)	Manufacturer of interconnects. The company offers wire to board, wire to wire, board to board, and card and telecom connectors.	510-429-3700	NA	Fremont
Newnex Technology Corp (HQ)	Developer of connecting cables, controllers, and repeaters. The company's services include design, installation, and technical support.	408-986-9988	NA	Santa Clara
NPI Solutions Inc (HQ)	Provider of design, engineering, and custom manufacturing solutions. The company offers on-site engineering services.	408-944-9178	NA	Morgan Hill
Precision Contacts Inc (HQ)	Provider of replacement contacts for handler manufacturer. The company's products include sockets, contacts, elements, and custom products.	916-939-4147	NA	El Dorado Hills
The Okonite Co (BR)	Manufacturer of electrical wire insulators. The company offers high and low voltage, instrumentation, and special purpose cables.	925-830-0801	NA	San Ramon
Ulbrich Stainless Steels and Special Metals Inc (BR)	The company manufactures and sells specialty strip in stainless steel, and serves the industrial sector.	559-456-2310	NA	Fresno
Vulcan Inc (HQ)	Focuses on the manufacture and fabrication of aluminum coiled sheets, aluminum sign blanks, and finished traffic control signs.	510-887-2495	NA	Hayward

300 = Commercial Physical & Biological Research

COMPANY NAME	PRODUCT / SERVICE	PHONE	EMP	CITY
Apollomics Inc (HQ)	Developer of oncology therapeutics. The company focuses on discovering therapeutics for the immune system and molecular pathways to treat cancer.	925-272-4090	NA	Foster City
Biomedecon LLC (HQ)	Provider of health economics and outcomes research. The company caters to pharmaceutical and medical industries.	650-563-9475	NA	Moss Beach
Calchemist (HQ)	Provider of contract research services. The company specializes in chemical, material science and laboratory equipment testing.	650-551-1495	11-50	S San Francisco
Cell Marque Corp (HQ)	Producer of primary antibodies, buffers and pretreatment, ancillary reagents, and lab equipment for pathology laboratories and research facilities.	916-746-8900	NA	Rocklin
Celltheon (HQ)	Developer of customized solutions for preclinical studies of the biotechnology and pharmaceutical industries.	510-306-2355	NA	Union City
Fibrogen Inc (HQ)	Developer of therapeutic products. The company is engaged in commercialization and clinical trial programs.	415-978-1200	NA	San Francisco
Hilti Inc (BR)	Developer and manufacturer of construction equipment. The company's services include trainings, engineering, administration, and tools.	800-879-8000	NA	San Francisco
IBM Research - Almaden (BR)	Provider of computer technology services. The company engages in cloud, mobility, and security services.	408-927-1080	NA	San Jose
InSilixa Inc (HQ)	Manufacturer of CMOS biosensor devices used to identify multiple targets including nucleic acids (DNA or RNA), peptides, or metabolites.	408-809-3000	NA	Sunnyvale
Marin Biologic Laboratories Inc (HQ)	Provider of client research services. The company serves the pharmaceutical, biotechnology, diagnostic, agricultural, and legal markers.	415-883-8000	NA	Novato
Murigenics (HQ)	Provider of preclinical in-vivo and in-vitro contract drug discovery. The company is also focused on development services.	707-561-8900	NA	Vallejo
Pro-Form Laboratories (HQ)	Developer and producer of nutritional powders. The company also specializes in contract manufacturing services.	707-752-9010	NA	Orinda

COMPANY NAME	PRODUCT / SERVICE	PHONE	EMP	CITY
ProteinSimple (HQ)	Developer of proprietary systems, immunoassay system and consumables for protein analysis and purity of protein-based therapeutics.	408-510-5500	NA	San Jose
Strataglass (HQ)	Manufacturer of thin films. The company offers research and development, pilot production, and outsourced fabrication services.	650-988-1700	NA	Mountain View

301 = Consulting/Contracting Services

COMPANY NAME	PRODUCT / SERVICE	PHONE	EMP	CITY
Advanced Integrated Solutions Inc (BR)	Provider of enterprise systems management, call center, and information technology infrastructure library based service management solutions.	714-572-5600	NA	El Dorado Hills
BSK Associates (BR)	Provider of geotechnical and environmental testing services. The company also offers materials testing services.	916-853-9293	NA	Rancho Cordova
Calchemist (HQ)	Provider of contract research services. The company specializes in chemical, material science and laboratory equipment testing.	650-551-1495	11-50	S San Francisco
Capital Engineering Consultants Inc (HQ)	Provider of mechanical engineering, sustainable design and green engineering, building commissioning, energy modeling, and other related services.	916-851-3500	NA	Rancho Cordova
Prima Environmental Inc (HQ)	Provider of laboratory testing services. The company specializes in treatability testing, technology evaluation, and scientific consulting services.	916-939-7300	NA	El Dorado Hills
Ray Carlson & Associates Inc (HQ)	Provider of consulting, research, surveying, mapping, video branding, and related services. The company also offers data management products.	707-528-7649	NA	Santa Rosa
Verseon Corp (HQ)	Focuses on the design of drug candidates. The company offers services to the pharmaceutical industry.	510-225-9000	NA	Fremont

302 = Dental Laboratories

COMPANY NAME	PRODUCT / SERVICE	PHONE	EMP	CITY
Apollomics Inc (HQ)	Developer of oncology therapeutics. The company focuses on discovering therapeutics for the immune system and molecular pathways to treat cancer.	925-272-4090	NA	Foster City
Castagnolo Dental Laboratory Inc (HQ)	Provider of custom packed columns, empty synthesis columns, empty synthesis plates, and related supports.	408-446-1466	NA	Cupertino

303 = Medical Laboratories

COMPANY NAME	PRODUCT / SERVICE	PHONE	EMP	CITY
Abaxis Inc (HQ)	Provider of on-site patient testing, leading-edge point-of-care technologies for veterinary practices and laboratory services for medical professionals.	510-675-6500	NA	Union City
AEMTEK Laboratories (HQ)	Provider of testing, research, training and consulting services and sampling products for the food, environmental and pharmaceutical industries.	510-979-1979	NA	Fremont
Analytical Sciences LLC (HQ)	Provider of laboratory services. The company specializes in environmental testing and analytical chemistry.	707-769-3128	NA	Petaluma
Associated Pathology Medical Group Inc (HQ)	Provider of medical care services. The company focuses on women's health, dermatopathology, family practice, and urology areas.	408-399-5050	NA	Los Gatos
BD Biosciences (BR)	Manufacturer of medical devices. The company provides a broad range of medical supplies, devices, laboratory equipment and diagnostic products.	877-232-8995	NA	San Jose
Borsting Laboratories Inc (HQ)	Provider of histology services. The company specialize in processing skin biopsies and expert second-opinion dermato pathological interpretation.	415-883-1337	NA	Novato
California Clinical Laboratory Association (HQ)	Provider of an Association for small and large laboratories in California. The company files suits to prevent medicare from denying coverage for lab tests.	916-446-2646	NA	Sacramento
Cellmax Life (HQ)	Provider of personalized multi-biomarker technologies for non-invasive saliva and blood tests. The company is also involved in drug discovery.	650-564-3905	NA	Sunnyvale
Climax Laboratories Inc (HQ)	Provider of contract research services. The company offers bioanalytical and analytical testing services.	408-298-8630	NA	San Jose
CohBar Inc (HQ)	Developer of treatments for metabolic dysfunction that includes NASH, obesity, cancer, neurodegenerative diseases, and more.	650-446-7888	NA	Menlo Park
Concentric Analgesics Inc (HQ)	Developer of therapeutic solutions. The company focuses on discovery and development of novel, non opioid therapeutics for treating acute and chronic pain.	415-484-7921	NA	San Francisco
Diagnostic Pathology Medical Group Inc (HQ)	Specializes in identifying enzymes extracted from extremophiles for molecular biology, diagnostics, and industrial applications.	916-446-0424	NA	Sacramento
Domino Data Lab Inc (HQ)	Provider of premise and cloud-based enterprise data science platform for analysis applications. The company serves the business sector.	415-570-2425	NA	San Francisco
EMSL Analytical Inc (BR)	Provider of laboratory analytical testing services. The company specializes in a wide range of environmental, material and forensic testing.	510-895-3675	NA	San Leandro
Frontier Analytical Laboratory (HQ)	Provider of testing services for analysis of polychlorinated dibenzo dioxins and furans polychlorinated biphenyls and polyaromatic hydrocarbons.	916-934-0900	NA	El Dorado Hills

COMPANY NAME	PRODUCT / SERVICE	PHONE	EMP	CITY
Golden Pacific Laboratories LLC (HQ)	Provider of state of the art independent contract research services for agricultural, residential and occupational exposure assessments.	559-275-9091	NA	Fresno
Hand Biomechanics Lab Inc (HQ)	Provider of Biomechanics treatment devices. The company offers products like Agee Turnkey FCS, Wrist Jack, and Digit Widget.	916-923-5073	NA	Sacramento
Machaon Diagnostics Inc (HQ)	Provider of laboratory services in diagnosis, treatment and monitoring of hemostatic and thrombotic conditions.	510-839-5600	NA	Oakland
Quest Diagnostics Inc (BR)	Provider of diagnostic laboratory testing services. The company offers a wide range of test menu for diagnosing medical conditions.	916-927-9900	NA	Sacramento
Satori Labs Inc (HQ)	Provider of medical based software services. The company's offerings include FusionForm Desktop and FusionForm Mobile.	831-457-9100	NA	Scotts Valley
Stemexpress (HQ)	Provider of immunophenotyping, DNA quantitation and viability, tissue transplant verification, and related services.	530-626-7000	NA	Folsom
Transgenomic Inc (BR)	Provider of patient testing and biomarker identification services. The company specializes in high performance products.	408-432-3230	NA	San Jose
Ultrasound Laboratories Inc (HQ)	Provider of non-invasive ultrasound imaging services. The company focuses on services such as health screening, carotid artery, and kidney screening.	408-829-6486	NA	Mountain View

304 = Miscellaneous Technology-Related Engineering Services

COMPANY NAME	PRODUCT / SERVICE	PHONE	EMP	CITY
Abbomax Inc (HQ)	Provider of antibody, peptide, and assay products and services. The company offers antibody production, fragmentation, assay development, and other services.	408-573-1898	NA	San Jose
ACIES Engineering (HQ)	Provider of engineering and design development solutions. The company caters to retail, restaurant, residential and commercial sectors.	408-522-5255	NA	Santa Clara
Acon Builders Construction Inc (HQ)	Provider of scheduling, planning, change management, status reporting, zoning, and code compliance services.	408-980-1388	NA	Hayward
Actinix (HQ)	Developer of ultraviolet light generation, long-coherence-length pulsed fiber laser systems, high energy laser systems and optical tools/methods.	831-440-9388	NA	Felton
Aditazz (HQ)	Designer, manufacturer, and assembler of building components. The company is engaged in operational modeling.	650-492-7000	NA	Brisbane
Advantec MFS Inc (HQ)	Producer of filtration media and related scientific products. The company focuses on laboratory instruments and filtration products.	925-479-0625	NA	Dublin
Agra Tech Inc (HQ)	Manufacturer of greenhouses and accessories for commercial, horticultural, and agricultural growers. The company offers heating and cooling equipment.	925-432-3399	NA	Pittsburg
Alliacense (HQ)	Provider of intellectual property solutions. The company's services include broad spectrum, reverse engineering, and product reports.	408-446-4222	NA	Cupertino
American Micro Detection Systems Inc (HQ)	Provider of water analysis treatments. The company deals with research, development, and monitoring services.	209-985-1705	NA	Stockton
Anderson Pacific Engineering Construction Inc (HQ)	Provider of constructing and retrofitting pump stations, lift stations, bridges, reservoirs, treatment plants, and seismic retrofit projects.	408-970-9900	NA	Santa Clara
Anritsu Co (DH)	Provider of test solutions for telecommunication applications. The company also caters to microwave applications.	408-778-2000	NA	Morgan Hill
Ansari Structural Engineers Inc (HQ)	Provider of structural consulting services. The company focuses on remodeling, due diligence studies, equipment anchorage, and structural peer review.	415-348-8948	NA	San Francisco
Applied Engineering (HQ)	Provider of structural analysis and seismic evaluation services. The company is involved in specialty engineering and project management.	408-263-5900	NA	Milpitas
Applied Materials & Engineering Inc (HQ)	Provider of construction materials consulting services. The company focuses on petrographic and laboratory testing services.	510-420-8190	NA	Oakland
ARES Corp (HQ)	Provider of engineering, risk assessment, project management, and other services and focuses on nuclear, clean technology, space, and defense fields.	650-401-7100	NA	Burlingame
ARX PAX Labs Inc (HQ)	Developer of magnetic field architecture technology for structural isolation, recreation and entertainment, industrial automation, and transportation.	408-335-7630	NA	Los Gatos
Avp Technology LLC (HQ)	Provider of thin film equipment services. The company provides custom designing, remanufacturing, and field services.	510-683-0157	NA	Fremont
Azbil North America Inc (BR)	Designer, manufacturer, and supplier of medical devices. The company offers automation products, control products, and industrial automation systems.	408-245-3121	NA	Santa Clara
Baumbach & Piazza Inc (HQ)	Provider of design, engineering, and boundary and topography surveying, and construction staking services.	209-368-6618	NA	Lodi
Bess Mti Inc (BR)	Provider of subsurface utility engineering services. The company engages in utility locating and structural concrete scanning services.	408-988-0101	NA	Santa Clara
Bhatia Associates Inc (HQ)	Provider of design and electrical engineering consulting services to the institutional, commercial, residential, and light industrial buildings.	415-646-0050	NA	San Francisco
Bio Medical Forensics (HQ)	Provider of engineering and applied science. The company specializes in mechanism and causation of trauma and impact biomechanics.	925-376-1240	NA	Moraga

COMPANY NAME	PRODUCT / SERVICE	PHONE	EMP	CITY
BKF Engineers (BR)	Provider of civil engineering consulting, and land surveying services. The company serves business organizations.	925-940-2200	NA	Walnut Creek
BKF Engineers (BR)	Provider of civil engineering, design, surveying, design, transportation, and entitlement support services.	408-467-9100	NA	San Jose
Blankinship & Associates Inc (HQ)	Provider of environmental science and engineering services focusing on biological resources, stormwater and nitrogen management, and other needs.	530-757-0941	NA	Davis
Blymyer Engineers Inc (HQ)	Provider of solar engineering, facility design, and related services. The company serves the food and beverage and glass manufacturing industries.	510-521-3773	NA	Alameda
Carroll Engineering Inc (HQ)	Provider of civil engineering and surveying services focusing on boundary and topographic surveys, civil engineering design, and construction support.	408-261-9800	NA	San Jose
Chs Consulting Group (HQ)	Provider of transportation planning and traffic signal design services. The company also focuses on traffic safety.	415-392-9688	NA	San Francisco
CJS Labs (HQ)	Provider of electronic design, consulting, engineering, and test automation programming assistance services.	415-923-9535	NA	San Francisco
CKC Engineering LLC (HQ)	Provider of custom equipment solutions for clinical, manufacturing, pharmaceutical, medical device, and drug delivery industries.	415-494-8225	NA	Oakland
Controlco (HQ)	Provider of automation and solutions to address the Internet of Things for commercial buildings, (BIoT).	800-800-7126	NA	Pleasant Hill
Diablo Clinical Research (HQ)	Provider of clinical research services specializing in endocrinology, internal medicine, cardiology, and neurology.	925-930-7267	NA	Walnut Creek
DigiLens Inc (HQ)	Provider of optical design, software development, electrical engineering, and illumination design services.	408-734-0219	NA	Sunnyvale
DST Controls (HQ)	Provider of control systems integration, industrial data management, and related enterprise solutions. The company serves the industrial sector.	800-251-0773	NA	Benicia
Endpoint Clinical Inc (HQ)	Designer of response technology platforms to access data through phones, the web, and mobile devices. The company is engaged in engineering services.	415-229-1600	NA	San Francisco
N Engineering/Remediation Resources Group Inc (HQ)	Provider of construction engineering and construction material testing services and environmental and remediation construction including contaminated soil excavation, landfill capping and closure, storage tank removal and slope stabilization and hazardous waste transportation, decontamination, and disposal.	925-969-0750	201-500	Martinez
N Enovity Inc (HQ)	Designer and developer of building facilities.	415-974-0390	51-200	San Francisco
Ese Consulting Engineers Inc (HQ)	Provider of structural engineering design, seismic analysis and retrofitting, and peer review services.	707-747-1755	NA	Benicia
Fall Creek Engineering Inc (HQ)	Provider of civil, environmental, and water resources engineering and consulting services. The company engages in site planning and design services.	831-426-9054	NA	Santa Cruz
Finjan Holdings Inc (HQ)	Specializes in the research and development of transformative technologies for the securing of information.	650-282-3228	NA	East Palo Alto
Forell/Elsesser Engineers Inc (HQ)	Provider of structural engineering, design build, earthquake engineering, research and development, and seismic design services.	415-837-0700	NA	San Francisco
Foundation Constructors Inc (HQ)	Provider of pile solutions and shoring systems. The company also offers pile, H-beams, sheets, and concrete pile types.	925-754-6633	NA	Oakley
Function Engineering (HQ)	Provider of mechanical design and engineering services for product development. The company serves the consumer electronics and robotics industries.	650-326-8834	NA	Palo Alto
GDR Engineering Inc (HQ)	Provider of land development and infrastructure engineering services. The company also focuses on land planning and surveying.	209-538-3360	NA	Ceres
Hammett & Edison Inc (HQ)	Provider of engineering and related services to the wireless telecommunications and broadcasting industries.	707-996-5200	NA	Sonoma
Heco Pacific Manufacturing Inc (HQ)	Manufacturer and seller of industrial cranes and overhead cranes. The company offers custom engineering, maintenance, testing, and other services.	510-487-1155	NA	Union City
Hesco (HQ)	Provider of portable x-ray imaging services. The company offer services for power plants, bridges, dams, refineries, and more.	510-568-1380	NA	San Leandro
Honda Research Institute USA Inc (HQ)	Manufacturer of engines. The company focuses on material science research, computer science research, and academic outreach activities.	650-314-0400	NA	San Jose
IBM Research - Almaden (BR)	Provider of computer technology services. The company engages in cloud, mobility, and security services.	408-927-1080	NA	San Jose
IC Engineering Inc (HQ)	Provider of design and engineering services to industrial and commercial clients. The company serves food, oil, parts manufacturing, and other sectors.	925-415-0074	NA	San Ramon
Inspection Services Inc (HQ)	Provider of structural steel and welding, wood framing, anchor and dowel installation, roofing, and waterproofing services.	510-900-2100	NA	Berkeley
Integrated Science Solutions Inc (HQ)	Provider of professional services to federal and state clients. The company offers earth and environmental science and engineering services.	925-979-1535	NA	Walnut Creek

COMPANY NAME	PRODUCT / SERVICE	PHONE	EMP	CITY
JON BRODY Structural Engineers (HQ)	Provider of structural engineering services. The company focuses on construction documentation, reports and studies, and seismic retrofitting.	415-296-9494	NA	San Francisco
Kahler Engineering Inc (HQ)	Designer of instrumentation and power control systems. The company provides engineering services to power plant owners, operators, and constructors.	415-453-8836	NA	San Anselmo
KEMPF Inc (HQ)	Provider of driving solutions. The company offers digital hand controls and other handicap driving aids for paraplegic drivers.	408-773-0219	NA	Sunnyvale
LEE + RO Inc (BR)	Provider of environmental and infrastructure engineering solutions. The company is involved in design-build and construction management.	925-937-4050	NA	Walnut Creek
Makel Engineering Inc (HQ)	Developer and provider of products and services for aviation, space, military, and commercial applications.	530-895-2770	NA	Chico
Materials Testing Inc (HQ)	Provider of geotechnical engineering and materials testing services. The company offers geotechnical, environment, special inspection, and material testing services.	530-222-1116	NA	Redding
Materion Corp (BR)	Provider of material solutions. The company deals with fabrication, analysis, research and development, and testing services.	510-623-1500	NA	Fremont
Matriscope (BR)	Provider of geotechnical and environmental engineering services. The company also provides materials testing and special inspection services.	916-375-6700	NA	Sacramento
Meridian Surveying Engineering Inc (HQ)	Provider or residential, commercial, and municipal surveys. The company also deals with claims litigation services.	415-440-4131	NA	San Francisco
MGE Engineering Inc (HQ)	Provider of civil/structural engineering and construction management services. The company focuses on site development and construction inspection.	916-421-1000	NA	Sacramento
New Faze Development Inc (HQ)	Provider of construction and management development services. The company also offers project management and property management services.	916-929-6402	NA	Sacramento
NGM Biopharmaceuticals Inc (HQ)	Developer of novel and disease-altering biologics such as protein, peptide, and antibody drug for cancer, cardio-metabolic, and hepatic diseases.	650-243-5555	NA	S San Francisco
Nikon Precision Inc (HQ)	Manufacturer of optical lenses and precision equipment. The company is also the supplier of step-and-repeat and step-and-scan lithography systems.	650-508-4674	NA	Belmont
Nute Engineering (HQ)	Developer of technologies for the water, wastewater treatment, and environmental protection projects.	415-453-4480	NA	San Rafael
NV5 (BR)	Provider of technical consulting and certification services. The company serves the infrastructure, construction, and real estate markers.	916-641-9100	NA	Sacramento
OCAMPO-ESTA Corp (HQ)	Provider of engineering, design, construction management, instrumentation and controls, and project management services.	707-642-8072	NA	Vallejo
Opac Consulting Engineers Inc (HQ)	Provider of bridge and structural engineering services. The company's services are design, evaluation, and construction engineering.	415-989-4551	NA	San Francisco
Oscar Larson & Associates (HQ)	Provider of environmental planning, permitting, and related services and it specializes in residential and commercial projects.	707-445-2043	NA	Eureka
Otsuka America Inc (HQ)	Developer of pharmaceutical products for the treatment of central nervous system, ophthalmology, cardiovascular, and skin conditions.	415-986-5300	NA	San Francisco
Paradigm Strucural Engineers (HQ)	Provider of structural engineering and consulting services. The company offers schematic design, planning, and construction documentation services.	415-362-8944	NA	San Francisco
PAX Scientific Inc (HQ)	Provider of engineering research and product design services. The company is also involved in the design of industrial equipment.	415-256-9900	NA	San Rafael
PGH Wong Engineering Inc (HQ)	Provider of engineering, program and construction management, and technology services for transit projects.	415-566-0800	NA	San Francisco
Presto Engineering Inc (HQ)	Provider of semiconductor test and analysis solutions. The company also offers engineering services to the semiconductor market.	408-372-9500	NA	San Jose
Procept Biorobotics (HQ)	Provider of healthcare services. The company primarily focuses on personalized image-guided waterjet tissue resection services.	650-232-7200	NA	Redwood City
Proto Services Inc (HQ)	Provider of process verification, yield analysis, testing design, program management, and functional debugging services.	408-719-9088	NA	San Jose
Prousys Inc (HQ)	Provider of computer programming services, custom-designed software, systems development, and integration.	661-837-4001	51-200	Bakersfield
QT Ultrasound LLC (HQ)	Developer of ultrasound devices. The company is involved in software development and clinical testing services.	415-842-7250	NA	Novato
R&A Engineering Solutions Inc (HQ)	Provider of engineering consulting services. The company offers design, analysis, verification, and planning of HVAC, and plumbing system services.	916-920-5965	NA	Sacramento
Ray Carlson & Associates Inc (HQ)	Provider of consulting, research, surveying, mapping, video branding, and related services. The company also offers data management products.	707-528-7649	NA	Santa Rosa
RCB Elevator Consulting LLC (HQ)	Provider of elevator design and structural engineering services to building owners, architects, and elevator companies and offers field surveys.	415-350-0402	NA	Sonoma

N

COMPANY NAME	PRODUCT / SERVICE	PHONE	EMP	CITY
Redline Solutions Inc (HQ)	Provider of produce traceability and barcode solutions, and warehouse and inventory management systems.	408-562-1700	NA	Santa Clara
Remote Sensing Systems (HQ)	Processor of microwave data. The company collects the data with the help of special satellite microwave sensors.	707-545-2904	NA	Santa Rosa
Savari Inc (HQ)	Provider of communications technology solutions. The company focuses on connecting cars to traffic lights, pedestrians, and smartphones.	408-833-6369	NA	Santa Clara
SC Solutions Inc (HQ)	Provider of control design and implementation services. The company also focuses on structural design and software development.	408-617-4520	NA	Sunnyvale
Sebastian (HQ)	Provider of structured cabling and electrical contracting services. The company offers services to the residential and commercial sectors.	559-432-5800	NA	Fresno
SEG Inc (HQ)	Provider of consulting, design, engineering, project management, commissioning, and validation services.	408-260-8008	NA	Santa Clara
Semifab (HQ)	Supplier of process environment control systems for precise temperature, humidity, air flow, and airborne particulate management.	408-414-5928	NA	San Jose
Sensor Concepts Inc (HQ)	Developer of portable and integrated measurement systems. The company offers engineering, field measurement and software development services.	925-443-9001	NA	Livermore
Shen Milsom Wilke LLC (BR)	Provider of technology design and consulting solutions such as acoustics, medical equipment planning, audiovisual, and building security.	415-391-7610	NA	San Francisco
Sierra Engineering Company Inc (HQ)	Manufacturer of recreational vehicles. The company offers rebuilding, repair, and maintenance services.	559-855-2659	NA	Tollhouse
N SiteTech Inc (HQ)	Provider of civil engineering, surveying, and land development related services.	909-864-3180	1-10	Highland
SJ Amoroso Construction Co LLC (HQ)	Provider of construction contracting services. The company focuses on pre-construction consulting, design-build contracting and management.	650-654-1900	NA	Redwood City
N Soffa Electric Inc (HQ)	Provider of engineering services.	323-728-0230	51-200	Commerce
Solar Design & Drafting (HQ)	Designer of solar devices. The company's services include design considerations, flat rate permit packages, and other services.	415-305-3982	NA	Petaluma
SOMA Environmental Engineering Inc (HQ)	Provider of environmental engineering solutions. The company offers services for remediation and underground storage tanks.	925-734-6400	NA	Pleasanton
Stantec (BR)	Provider of civil construction services. The company also offers commercial program development and infrastructure management services.	916-773-8100	NA	Rocklin
Summit Engineering Inc (HQ)	Provider of facility planning, due diligence, design, project management, and other services to wineries, resorts, food, education, and other sectors.	707-527-0775	NA	Santa Rosa
Tennebaum-Manheim Engineers Inc (HQ)	Developer of engineering services. The company's projects include residential housing, commercial properties, and historical buildings.	415-772-9891	NA	San Francisco
Turley & Associates Mechanical Engineering Group Inc (HQ)	Provider of engineering services to health care, education, industrial, public, and retail facilities.	916-325-1065	NA	Sacramento
TUV SUD America Inc (BR)	Provider of services for testing, certification, and engineering audits. The company is focused on medical devices and e-mobility.	510-257-7823	NA	Fremont
TY Lin International Group (HQ)	Provider of engineering services such as construction management, inspection, design and planning, and surveying.	415-291-3700	NA	San Francisco
Velos LLC (HQ)	Provider of clinical research solutions. The company offers services to hospitals, academic medical centers, and also cancer centers.	510-739-4010	NA	Fremont
N W.M. Lyles Co (HQ)	Provider of infrastructure, energy and environmental construction services.	559-441-1900	NA	Fresno
Walters & Wolf (BR)	Provider of cladding services. The company specializes in design, engineering, fabrication, and delivery and installation.	510-490-1115	NA	Fremont
Willdan Energy Solutions (BR)	Provider of energy efficiency, water conservation, and renewable energy services. The company serves education, utility, labs, and other sectors.	916-661-3520	NA	Elk Grove
Wong Electric Inc (HQ)	Provider of electrical contracting services. The company is involved in industrial and multi-family projects.	650-813-9999	51-200	Palo Alto
X-Z LAB Inc (HQ)	Provider of digital radiation detection services. The company engages in detecting, measuring, and monitoring radiation activities.	925-355-5199	NA	San Ramon
Zip-Bit Inc (HQ)	Provider of engineering services. The company specializes in 3D printing, 3D modeling, and 3D scanning.	408-839-4252	NA	Saratoga

305 = Noncommercial Research Organizations

COMPANY NAME	PRODUCT / SERVICE	PHONE	EMP	CITY
Crown Bioscience Inc (HQ)	Specializes in drug discovery, clinical trials, and cardiovascular and metabolic disease research programs.	858-622-2900	NA	San Diego
N Dohmen Capital Research Institute (HQ)	Provider of investment, economic research, analysis and guidance.	310-476-6933	NA	Los Angeles
N Economic & Planning Systems (BR)	Provider of real estate development services for the public and private sector.	916-649-8010	11-50	Sacramento
Sanbio Inc (HQ)	Developer of regenerative therapies for neurological disorders. The company offers services to the healthcare sector.	650-625-8965	NA	Mountain View

COMPANY NAME	PRODUCT / SERVICE	PHONE	EMP	CITY
Vlsi Research Inc (HQ)	Provider of chip market research, consultation, semiconductor analysis, and data spreadsheets and reports.	408-453-8844	NA	San Jose
Wiley X Inc (HQ)	Provider of high velocity protection services. The company specializes in climate control frames, light adjusting lenses, and polarized lenses.	925-243-9810	NA	Livermore

306 = Testing Laboratories/Services

COMPANY NAME	PRODUCT / SERVICE	PHONE	EMP	CITY
Advantage Pharmaceutics Inc (HQ)	Provider of pharmaceuticals specializing in compounding. The company provides compounded medicines in dosage forms for human and veterinary needs.	916-630-4960	NA	Rocklin
Advantec MFS Inc (HQ)	Producer of filtration media and related scientific products. The company focuses on laboratory instruments and filtration products.	925-479-0625	NA	Dublin
AEMTEK Laboratories (HQ)	Provider of testing, research, training and consulting services and sampling products for the food, environmental and pharmaceutical industries.	510-979-1979	NA	Fremont
N Aircraft Xray Laboratories Inc (HQ)	Provider of NDT and surface treatment services.	323-587-4141	NA	Huntington Park
Amyris Inc (HQ)	Provider of renewable products. The company delivers cosmetic emollients and fragrances, fuels and lubricants, and even biopharmaceuticals.	510-450-0761	NA	Emeryville
Analytical Sciences LLC (HQ)	Provider of laboratory services. The company specializes in environmental testing and analytical chemistry.	707-769-3128	NA	Petaluma
N Anmar Metrology Inc (HQ)	Firm is a provider of calibration, testing and repair laboratory services and calibration software.	858-621-2630	11-50	San Diego
Anresco Laboratories (HQ)	Provider of analysis and research to food and food-related industries. The company also offers solutions to support the business and analytical specifications.	415-822-1100	NA	San Francisco
Antech Diagnostics (HQ)	Provider of diagnostic and laboratory testing services for chemistry, pathology, endocrinology, serology, hematology, and microbiology.	800-872-1001	NA	Fountain Valley
Antibodies Inc (HQ)	Manufacturer of monoclonal and polyclonal antibodies, diagnostic reagents, diagnostic kits, and developer of immunoassays.	530-758-4400	NA	Davis
Apex Testing Labs (HQ)	Provider of testing and inspection services. The company engages in the geotechnical engineering and inspection of construction materials.	415-550-9800	NA	San Francisco
APPL Inc (HQ)	Provider of analytical testing services. The company specializes in analysis of environmental samples for chemical pollutants.	559-275-2175	NA	Clovis
Asbestech Laboratory (HQ)	Provider of asbestos and lead testing services. The company also offers transmission electron microscopes.	016-481-8902	NA	Carmichael
N Atlas Testing Laboratories Inc (HQ)	Operator of testing laboratories.	909-373-4130	11-50	Rancho Cucamonga
N Babcock Laboratories Inc (HQ)	Provider of environmental and food product testing services including the analysis of food, beverages, drinking water, wastewater, groundwater, storm water and hazardous materials.	951-653-3351	51-200	Riverside
Bay Materials LLC (HQ)	Manufacturer of polymer products. The company offers services for spectroscopy, osmometry, viscosity, and surface measurement.	650-566-0800	NA	Fremont
Berkeley Analytical Associates LLC (HQ)	Provider of specialized chemical and flame retardant analysis and formaldehyde testing services. The company serves the flooring and textile industries.	510-236-2325	NA	Richmond
Bestek Manufacturing Inc (HQ)	Provider of supply chain services. The company engages focuses on systems manufacturing, materials management, and prototype support areas.	408-321-8834	NA	Milpitas
Beta Breakers Software Quality (HQ)	Provider of software and application testing services. The company offers functionality, compatibility, website, and mobile device testing services.	415-878-2990	NA	Novato
Biocare Medical LLC (HQ)	Developer of automated immunohistochemistry instrumentation, reagents for IHC lab testing. The company also offer tissue diagnostic products for cancer.	925-603-8000	NA	Pacheco
Biometrix Inc (HQ)	Manufacturer of pathway analysis and variant analysis products. The company specializes in web-analysis.	415-333-0522	NA	San Francisco
Blue Sky Environmental Inc (HQ)	Provider of air emissions source testing services. The company's services include alternative monitoring and validation testing.	510-525-1261	NA	Albany
Bolsa Analytical (HQ)	Provider of reliable chemical and microbiological analysis and testing of water, soil, plants and food.	831-637-4590	NA	San Jose
Brelje & Race Laboratories Inc (HQ)	Provider of water and wastewater testing services. The company analyses process include nitrate, arsenic, and volatile organics compounds.	707-544-8807	NA	Santa Rosa
Burlington Safety Laboratory Inc (BR)	Designer and manufacturer of laboratory and electrical safety equipment. The company's customers include electric utilities and contractors.	925-251-1412	NA	Pleasanton
Calchemist (HQ)	Provider of contract research services. The company specializes in chemical, material science and laboratory equipment testing.	650-551-1495	11-50	S San Francisco
Calcoast-Itl (HQ)	Provider of testing services for automotive and roadway lightings. The company offers consultation, assistance, and laboratory installation services.	510-924-7100	NA	San Leandro

COMPANY NAME	PRODUCT / SERVICE	PHONE	EMP	CITY
California Laboratory Services (HQ)	Provider of analytical testing services. The company offers a comprehensive range of soil and water testing for government and private agencies.	800-638-7301	NA	Rancho Cordova
Caltest Analytical Lab (HQ)	Provider of analyses services of wastewater, groundwater, non-radioactive water, and hazardous waste samples.	707-258-4000	NA	Napa
Ceecon Testing Inc (HQ)	Provider of soil and groundwater remediation services. The company services also include regulatory compliance and remediation equipment.	650-827-7474	NA	S San Francisco
Cellecta Inc (HQ)	Provider of custom and contract solutions for high-throughput genetic screening needs and also develops therapeutic targets and drugs.	650-938-3910	NA	Mountain View
Cellmax Life (HQ)	Provider of personalized multi-biomarker technologies for non-invasive saliva and blood tests. The company is also involved in drug discovery.	650-564-3905	NA	Sunnyvale
CKC Laboratories Inc (HQ)	Provider of electromagnetic compatibility testing, safety testing, design development and agency certification services for industries.	209-299-5240	NA	Mariposa
CKC Laboratories Inc (BR)	Provider of design and testing consultation services. The company offers design consultation, testing, training, and support services.	510-249-1170	NA	Fremont
Cureline Biopathology LLC (HQ)	Provider of human and animal tissue processing services. The company also focuses on preservation and biospecimen management.	415-468-6400	NA	Brisbane
Daniel B Stephens & Associates Inc (BR)	Provider of services in hydrology, environmental engineering, and science. The company services include water resources and soil testing.	800-933-3105	NA	Oakland
Datalab (HQ)	Provider of analysis and certification of process tanks and printed circuit board sections. The company also offers chemical process control software.	408-943-1888	NA	San Jose
Datest Corp (HQ)	Provider of testing and inspection services. The company specializes in engineering testing and counterfeit inspection for industrial products.	510-490-4600	NA	Fremont
EM Lab P&K (BR)	Provider of indoor air quality testing services. The company offers culturable air fungi, spore trap analysis, and yeast identification services.	916-374-4483	NA	West Sacramento
EMSL Analytical Inc (BR)	Provider of laboratory analytical testing services. The company specializes in a wide range of environmental, material and forensic testing.	510-895-3675	NA	San Leandro
Environmental Micro Analysis Inc (HQ)	Provider of food safety consulting services. The company specializes in pesticide residue analysis in agricultural products, processed foods and other matrices.	530-666-6890	NA	Woodland
ETS Laboratories (HQ)	Specializes in analytical tools. The company focuses on export analysis, harvest, and fuel ethanol services.	707-963-4806	NA	St. Helena
Eurofins E&E North America (BR)	Provider of electrical testing services focusing on product safety, RF testing, and others. The company serves medical, RFID, and other sectors.	408-748-3585	NA	Santa Clara
N Evans Analytical Group (HQ)	Provider of materials characterization surface analysis and much more services.	408-530-3500	NA	Sunnyvale
Exacta Tech Inc (HQ)	Manufacturer of custom machine components and parts and provider of design, inspection and engineering services for industries.	925-443-8963	NA	Livermore
Excelchem Laboratories Inc (HQ)	Provider of analytical consultation, on-site analysis, custom reporting, and mobile laboratory services.	916-543-4445	NA	Rocklin
Forensic Analytical Consulting Services Inc (HQ)	Provider of analytical testing services. The company specializes in a wide array of material testing, forensic and environmental testing.	866-637-9924	NA	Hayward
Geochemical Research Laboratory (HQ)	The company uses energy dispersive x-ray fluorescence spectrometry to determine the element composition of volcanic rocks. The company specializes in archaeological geochemistry.	650-851-1410	NA	Portola Valley
Giga Test Labs (HQ)	Provider of measurement and probing products for the electronics industry. The company offers test equipment and fixtures for modeling and simulation.	408-524-2700	NA	Santa Clara
Hahnemann Laboratories Inc (HQ)	Manufacturer of homeopathic medicines. The company offers dispensing kits, first aid kits, and also professional kits.	415-451-6978	NA	San Rafael
Harris Industrial Gases (HQ)	Provider of specialty gases welding equipment. The company also offers services for welding supplies and safety equipment.	916-725-2168	NA	Citrus Heights
Hemostat Laboratories (HQ)	Provider of defibrinated sheep blood and other animal blood products for cell culture, diagnostic and veterinary applications.	800-572-6888	NA	Dixon
IEH JL Analytical Services (HQ)	Provider of laboratory and consulting services for food microbiology, allergens, virology, and parasitology, forensics, and agricultural products.	209-538-8111	NA	Modesto
Igenex Inc (HQ)	Provider of immunology laboratory services. The company offers service to private practice physicians, hospitals, and clinical reference laboratories.	650-424-1191	NA	Milpitas
Intertek Group PLC (BR)	Provider of advisory, business consulting, risk management, outsourcing, validation, and training services.	650-463-2900	NA	Menlo Park
Invitae Corp (HQ)	Provider of genetic information. The company offers to bring genetic information into routine medical practice to improve the quality of healthcare.	415-930-4018	501-1000	San Francisco
Iometrix Inc (HQ)	Developer of next generation packet networks and solutions for telecom service providers and equipment manufacturers.	650-872-4001	NA	San Francisco
Ise Labs Inc (HQ)	Provider of semiconductor services. The company offers services such as production test, test interface, and mechanical testing.	510-687-2500	NA	Fremont

COMPANY NAME	PRODUCT / SERVICE	PHONE	EMP	CITY
Kimia Corp (HQ)	Manufacturer of chemicals and custom synthesis services. The company offers amino acids, vitamins, steroids, heptanes, and multifunctional heterocycles.	408-748-1046	NA	Santa Clara
Marin Biologic Laboratories Inc (HQ)	Provider of client research services. The company serves the pharmaceutical, biotechnology, diagnostic, agricultural, and legal markers.	415-883-8000	NA	Novato
Martin Testing Laboratories (HQ)	Provider of product assurance, failure analysis, mechanical, metallurgical, electrical, and paint and coating testing services.	916-920-4110	NA	Mcclellan
Maselli Measurements Inc (BR)	Provider of liquid measuring solutions. The company manufactures and distributes refractometers and liquid analyzers for several industries.	209-474-9178	NA	Stockton
Materials Testing Inc (HQ)	Provider of geotechnical engineering and materials testing services. The company offers geotechnical, environment, special inspection, and material testing services.	530-222-1116	NA	Redding
McCampbell Analytical Inc (HQ)	Provider of analytical tests on drinking water, effluent, soils, solids, hazardous waste, air, soil vapor, and industrial materials.	925-252-9262	NA	Pittsburg
MCLAB (HQ)	Provider of DNA sequencing services. The company's products include enzymes and biochemical reagents.	650-871-8771	NA	S San Francisco
Micro Precision Calibration Inc (HQ)	Provider of electrical and mechanical calibration services. The company also offers optical and temperature calibration services.	530-268-1860	NA	Grass Valley
MicroMed Laboratories (HQ)	Provider of regulatory consulting, microbial identification, environmental monitoring, and sterilization validation services.	707-782-0792	NA	Petaluma
Nanolab Technologies Inc (HQ)	Provider of cutting edge technology and expertise for failure analysis, advanced microscopy and FIB circuit edit services.	408-433-3320	NA	Milpitas
NEC Laboratories America Inc (BR)	Provider of technology research services. The company specializes in research departments such as integrated systems, machine learning, and media analytics.	408-863-6007	NA	Cupertino
Peak Laboratories LLC (HQ)	Designer and manufacturer of process gas chromatography systems. The company offers mercuric oxide, pulse discharge, and thermal conductivity detectors.	650-691-1267	NA	Mountain View
Pegasus Design Inc (HQ)	Provider of machine design and contract manufacturing services. The company serves the pharmaceutical instrument industry.	925-292-7567	NA	Livermore
Prestige Lens Lab (HQ)	Provider of optical laboratory services. The company specializes in prescription safety eyewear programs.	650-588-5540	NA	S San Francisco
Presto Engineering Inc (HQ)	Provider of semiconductor test and analysis solutions. The company also offers engineering services to the semiconductor market.	408-372-0500	NA	San Jose
Prima Environmental Inc (HQ)	Provider of laboratory testing services. The company specializes in treatability testing, technology evaluation, and scientific consulting services.	916-939-7300	NA	El Dorado Hills
N Primary Instruments Inc (HQ)	Provider of metrology services.	818-993-4971	NA	Chatsworth
Redwood Toxicology Laboratory (HQ)	Provider of drug and alcohol testing laboratories. The company specializes in substance abuse screening products to criminal justice and treatment markers.	707-577-7959	NA	Santa Rosa
Reliant Labs Inc (HQ)	Provider of environmental testing and reliability services. The company is also engaged in power supply evaluation.	408-737-7500	NA	Sunnyvale
Riga Analytical Lab Inc (HQ)	Provider of laboratory services specializing in electrical failure analysis, circuit extraction, latch up evaluation, and parallel and angel lapping.	408-496-6944	NA	Santa Clara
Safebridge Consultants Inc (HQ)	Provider of consulting services and analytical support. The company provides safety, health and environmental services.	650-961-4820	NA	Mountain View
Samsung Research America (DH)	Provider of commercial, physical, and biological research services. The company is involved in testing and identification solutions.	650-210-1001	NA	Mountain View
SC Labs (HQ)	Provider of medical quality assurance and safety testing services. The company's services include potency testing, pesticide testing, and microbial screening.	866-435-0709	NA	Santa Cruz
N SCST LLC (HQ)	Provider of geotechnical engineering, environmental science and engineering, special inspection and material testing, and facilities consulting services.	619-280-4321	NA	San Diego
Seatec Lab Repair (HQ)	Provider of services to analytical, biotech, and industrial laboratories. The company also focuses on equipment validation.	408-828-1815	NA	Santa Clara
Sierra Testing Service (HQ)	Provider of laboratory testing services. The company offers services such as grain testing, silage, and grain samples.	209-333-3337	NA	Acampo
Simco Electronics (HQ)	Providers of services and software to medical device manufacturers. The company specializes in biotechnology.	408-734-9750	NA	Santa Clara
Strataglass (HQ)	Manufacturer of thin films. The company offers research and development, pilot production, and outsourced fabrication services.	650-988-1700	NA	Mountain View
SunBurst Plant Disease Clinic Inc (HQ)	Provider of solutions for pathological and physiological problems in agriculture. The company focuses on soil and tissue examination and mineral analysis.	209-667-4442	NA	Turlock
N TestEdge Inc (HQ)	Provider of quality engineering testing of digital, analog, mixed-signal and RF devices.	858-451-1012	NA	San Diego
Theraject Inc (HQ)	Developer of drug micro-needle technologies. The company is engaged in vaccine and also drug deliveries.	510-742-5832	NA	Fremont

COMPANY NAME	PRODUCT / SERVICE	PHONE	EMP	CITY
Thermochem Inc (HQ)	Provider of chemical engineering, laboratory analysis, geochemistry and field testing services and products to a wide range of energy industries.	707-575-1310	NA	Santa Rosa
Trevi Systems (HQ)	Provider of desalination process services. The company focuses on osmosis system using proprietary membrane and draw solution using thermal heat.	707-792-2681	NA	Petaluma
N United Manufacturing Assembly Inc (HQ)	Provider of electronic manufacturing services to OEMs nationwide.	510-490-4680	NA	Fremont
Vector Laboratories Inc (HQ)	Provider of labeling and detection services for enzymes, antibodies and antigens, DNA and RNA by using polymer reagents.	650-697-3600	11-50	Burlingame
West Coast Pathology Laboratories (HQ)	Providers of anatomic pathology and cytology services. The company's expertise lies with molecular genetics and diagnostics.	510-662-5200	NA	Hercules
Westpak Inc (HQ)	Provider of customized product and packaging testing services. The company also deals with packaging, material analysis, and supply chain management.	408-224-1300	NA	San Jose
Yosemite Pathology Medical Group Inc (HQ)	Provider of anatomic pathology services such as tissue pathology and gynecologic specimens of oncologic and nononcologic diseases.	209-577-1200	NA	Modesto
YY Labs Inc (HQ)	Manufacturer and supplier of optical components. The company provides LN modulators, bias controllers, generators, and accessories.	510-739-6049	NA	Fremont

308 = Assembly Lines/Systems

COMPANY NAME	PRODUCT / SERVICE	PHONE	EMP	CITY
N Rotometals Inc (HQ)	Distributor of non-ferrous metal elements and alloys such as aluminum, antimony, bismuth, indium and more.	888-779-1102	NA	San Leandro

309 = Application-Specific Robotics

COMPANY NAME	PRODUCT / SERVICE	PHONE	EMP	CITY
Genmark Automation Inc (HQ)	Provider of robotics for automated manufacturing applications. The company offers services to the data storage and related industries.	510-897-3400	NA	Fremont
Kensington Laboratories LLC (HQ)	Provider of automation products for the semiconductor industry. The company is engaged in precision machining, automation, and system integration.	510-324-0126	NA	Dublin
Kespry Inc (HQ)	Developer of automated drone system and cloud that automatically uploads data in cloud for aggregates, insurance, and construction industries.	203-434-7988	NA	Menlo Park
MATTERNET (HQ)	Specializes in the creation of integrated delivery solutions. The company's products are used in healthcare, on-campus, and humanitarian applications.	650-260-2727	NA	Menlo Park
SRI International (RH)	Provider of consulting, research, and development services. The company offers services to the defense, security, and energy sectors.	650-859-2000	NA	Menlo Park

310 = Automatic Storage/Retrieval Systems

COMPANY NAME	PRODUCT / SERVICE	PHONE	EMP	CITY
Lexicon Branding Inc (HQ)	Provider of services to develop, select and evaluate brand names. The company services include trademark evaluation, name development, and consumer research.	415-332-1811	NA	Sausalito

311 = Automation Manufacturing/R&D Services

COMPANY NAME	PRODUCT / SERVICE	PHONE	EMP	CITY
3D Robotics Inc (HQ)	Manufacturer of drone systems for exploration and business applications. The company offers autopilot controllers and flight controllers.	858-225-1414	NA	Berkeley
ADCO Manufacturing (HQ)	Provider of consumer packaged goods. The company's solutions include cartoners, top load systems, case packers, sleevers, and robotic packaging.	559-875-5563	NA	Sanger
Distribution Technologies Inc (HQ)	Provider of design, analysis, simulation, automation, and project implementation solutions. The company also deals with technical support.	415-999-1191	NA	Tiburon
Genmark Automation Inc (HQ)	Provider of robotics for automated manufacturing applications. The company offers services to the data storage and related industries.	510-897-3400	NA	Fremont
Grabit Inc (HQ)	Inventor of electroadhesion technology. The company specializes in parts handling, package handling, and each pick applications.	408-642-1830	NA	San Carlos
Green Source Automation LLC (HQ)	Provider of redefining solutions for dairy industry. The company also offers technology for milking process.	209-531-9163	NA	Ceres
Hesse Mechatronics Inc (LH)	Developer of equipment for heavy wire and thin wire wedge bonders. The company also focuses on the marketing aspects.	408-436-9300	NA	Fremont
Kensington Laboratories LLC (HQ)	Provider of automation products for the semiconductor industry. The company is engaged in precision machining, automation, and system integration.	510-324-0126	NA	Dublin
Ologic (HQ)	Manufacturer of consumer electronics and toy products. The company specializes in defense and educational projects.	408-663-6638	NA	Santa Clara
Orbotech LT Solar LLC (BR)	Manufacturer of electronic devices. The company offers printed circuit boards, flat panel displays, and touch screens.	408-226-9900	NA	San Jose
Procept Biorobotics (HQ)	Provider of healthcare services. The company primarily focuses on personalized image-guided waterjet tissue resection services.	650-232-7200	NA	Redwood City
Quartet Mechanics Inc (HQ)	Provider of LED, MEMS, photovoltaics (PV) solar and medical/lab automation systems. The company also offers wafer sorting and packing products.	408-564-8901	NA	Santa Clara

COMPANY NAME	PRODUCT / SERVICE	PHONE	EMP	CITY
Rockwell Automation Inc (BR)	Provider of control systems, sensing devices, security, and other products. The company offers asset management, network, and other services.	925-242-5700	NA	San Ramon
Rorze Automation Inc (DH)	Manufacturer of automation products. The company's applications include displays, semiconductors, and laboratories.	510-687-1340	NA	Fremont
Superior Automation (HQ)	Provider of custom automation solutions. The company primarily caters to the semiconductor industry.	510-413-9790	NA	Fremont
Vantage Robotics LLC (HQ)	Developer and manufacturer of camera drones. The company serves the consumer electronics, automation, and robotics industries.	510-907-7012	NA	San Leandro
Winslow Automation Inc (HQ)	Provider of lead tinning products and services. The company caters to semiconductor and electrical companies.	408-262-9004	NA	Milpitas

312 = Material Dispensing Equipment

COMPANY NAME	PRODUCT / SERVICE	PHONE	EMP	CITY
Jackrabbit Inc (HQ)	Provider of nut harvesting systems including runner, elevator, reservoir cart, conditioner and pruning tower.	209-599-6118	NA	Ripon

313 = Programmable Controls for Factory Processes

COMPANY NAME	PRODUCT / SERVICE	PHONE	EMP	CITY
3D Robotics Inc (HQ)	Manufacturer of drone systems for exploration and business applications. The company offers autopilot controllers and flight controllers.	858-225-1414	NA	Berkeley
Distribution Technologies Inc (HQ)	Provider of design, analysis, simulation, automation, and project implementation solutions. The company also deals with technical support.	415-999-1191	NA	Tiburon
Galil Motion Control (HQ)	Manufacturer and supplier of motion controllers and software tools. The company also offers drives and power supplies.	916-626-0101	NA	Rocklin
Genmark Automation Inc (HQ)	Provider of robotics for automated manufacturing applications. The company offers services to the data storage and related industries.	510-897-3400	NA	Fremont
Ologic (HQ)	Manufacturer of consumer electronics and toy products. The company specializes in defense and educational projects.	408-663-6638	NA	Santa Clara

314 = Robotic Controllers/Manipulators/Feeders

COMPANY NAME	PRODUCT / SERVICE	PHONE	EMP	CITY
3D Robotics Inc (HQ)	Manufacturer of drone systems for exploration and business applications. The company offers autopilot controllers and flight controllers.	858-225-1414	NA	Berkeley
Biomicrolab (HQ)	Manufacturer of robotics based sorting and weighing systems sample management automation. The company serves bio-lab purposes.	925-689-1200	NA	Concord
Distribution Technologies Inc (HQ)	Provider of design, analysis, simulation, automation, and project implementation solutions. The company also deals with technical support.	415-999-1191	NA	Tiburon
Genmark Automation Inc (HQ)	Provider of robotics for automated manufacturing applications. The company offers services to the data storage and related industries.	510-897-3400	NA	Fremont
Grabit Inc (HQ)	Inventor of electroadhesion technology. The company specializes in parts handling, package handling, and each pick applications.	408-642-1830	NA	San Carlos
Idec Corp (BR)	Designer and manufacturer of automated machines for various sectors. The company also offers products for environment, safety, and other needs.	408-747-0550	NA	Sunnyvale
Intest Ems Products (BR)	Manufacturer of semiconductors to test integrated circuits. The company also focuses on testing wafer products.	408-678-9167	NA	Fremont
Keri Systems Inc (HQ)	Provider of access control and integrated security systems. The company offers technology support and training solutions.	408-435-8400	NA	San Jose
Knightscope Inc (HQ)	Provider of security technology. The company specializes in monotonous, computationally heavy, and sometimes dangerous work for security operations.	650-924-1025	NA	Mountain View
Procept Biorobotics (HQ)	Provider of healthcare services. The company primarily focuses on personalized image-guided waterjet tissue resection services.	650-232-7200	NA	Redwood City
Vantage Robotics LLC (HQ)	Developer and manufacturer of camera drones. The company serves the consumer electronics, automation, and robotics industries.	510-907-7012	NA	San Leandro

315 = Software Development/Services

COMPANY NAME	PRODUCT / SERVICE	PHONE	EMP	CITY
Actian Corp (HQ)	Provider of on-premises applications and cloud data management solutions.	650-587-5500	NA	Palo Alto
Applozic Inc (HQ)	Empowers businesses with in-app messaging solutions and all-in-one customer support solution.	310-909-7458	NA	Palo Alto
Apptimize Inc (HQ)	Providers of robust mobile experimentation and optimization solution to improve an user's mobile experience through A/B testing.	415-926-5398	NA	San Francisco
Apttus Corp (HQ)	Developers of AI revenue intelligence software.	650-445-7700	NA	San Mateo
Benevity Inc (BR)	Specializes in corporate social responsibility employee engagement software.	855-237-7875	NA	San Mateo
Branch Metrics (HQ)	Provides deep link solutions that unify user measurement across different devices, platforms, and channels.	650-209-6461	NA	Redwood City
Caspio Inc (HQ)	Builds online database applications without coding.	650-691-0900	NA	Santa Clara

COMPANY NAME	PRODUCT / SERVICE	PHONE	EMP	CITY
CitrusBits (HQ)	Designs and develops impactful mobile apps for businesses of all sizes by using augmented/virtual reality, artificial intelligence, blockchain, and The Internet of Things (IoT).	925-452-6012	NA	Pleasanton
Clari Inc (HQ)	Developers of an AI-based data capturing software that helps the marketing, sales, and customer success teams.	650-265-2111	NA	Sunnyvale
Code-N Technology Inc (HQ)	Leverages advanced semantic web technology to provide software solutions to businesses.	650-234-8400	NA	Menlo Park
Contract Room Inc (HQ)	Provides contract management software.	800-950-9101	NA	San Mateo
Corona Labs Inc (HQ)	A cross-platform framework for creating apps and games for mobile devices and desktop systems.	415-996-6877	NA	San Francisco
Coupa Software Inc (HQ)	Global technology platform for Business Spend Management (BSM) to deliver measurable value.	650-931-3200	501-1000	San Mateo
CrowdANALYTIX (HQ)	Develops and deploys AI and Data Science solutions.	866-333-4515	NA	Sunnyvale
Elasticsearch Inc (HQ)	A software company that builds self-managed and SaaS offerings that make data usable in real time.	650-458-2620	NA	Mountain View
Engagio Inc (HQ)	B2B Marketing Engagement Software that enables marketers and sellers to work as a team.	650-487-2050	NA	San Mateo
EverString Technology (HQ)	Provider of AI SaaS solution for B2B sales and marketing professionals.	650-425-3937	NA	San Mateo
Exadel Inc (HQ)	Custom software agency that produces software and mobile solutions.	925-363-9510	NA	Walnut Creek
Full Circle Insights Inc (HQ)	Delivers marketing and sales performance measurement solutions to optimize a company's marketing automation solutions.	650-641-2766	NA	San Mateo
GitHub Inc (HQ)	Provider of an online platform that allows users to learn, store and share codes with individuals.	877-448-4820	NA	San Francisco
Gong.io (HQ)	Developers of revenue intelligence platform that delivers insights at scale.	650-276-3068	NA	San Francisco
Grio (HQ)	Specializes in web, iOS, and Android development.	415-395-9525	NA	San Francisco
HackerRank (HQ)	Technology recruiting tool that helps tech recruiters and hiring managers to identify and hire talents.	415-900-4023	NA	Mountain View
Healthline Media (HQ)	Provider of health information.	415-281-3100	NA	San Francisco
Impekable LLC (HQ)	UI design and mobile development studio that helps organizations to create human-centric mobile experiences.	650-733-6006	NA	San Jose
Import.io (HQ)	Enables organizations to gain intelligence, abilities, and competing advantages from the vast amount of data on the web.	650-935-4336	NA	Saratoga
Informatica (HQ)	Provides data management software and services to help a company to achieve a competitive edge.	650-385-5000	NA	Redwood City
Intellectsoft (HQ)	Provider of impactful digital engineering solutions with latest technologies.	650-300-4335	NA	Palo Alto
Invoice2go Inc (HQ)	A mobile and web app for micro and small business owners to create invoice, track expenses and track time.	650-300-5180	NA	Palo Alto
KitApps Inc (HQ)	Provider of networking and other information-based tools to event organizers and attendees (end-users).	866-944-8678	NA	San Jose
Lob.com Inc (HQ)	Builds an API toolkit that allows organizations to innovate, move faster, and better differentiate themselves.	847-630-9275	NA	San Francisco
Mattermost Inc (HQ)	Delivers open-source messaging tools for security-conscious enterprises and developers.	650-866-5518	NA	Palo Alto
Paxata Inc (HQ)	Enables business analysts to easily absorb, analyze, and curate numerous raw data sets into consumable information in a self-service manner.	650-542-7900	NA	Redwood City
Practice Fusion Inc (HQ)	Provider of cloud-based electronic health records (EHR) platform in the U.S.	415-346-7700	NA	San Francisco
Provectus IT Inc (HQ)	Accelerates digital transformation by using Artificial Intelligence.	877-951-2224	NA	Palo Alto
Quid Inc (HQ)	Developers of artificial intelligence to help organizations make important decisions.	415-813-5300	NA	San Francisco
Redbooth (HQ)	A task and project management platform for team collaboration tasks, discussions, and file sharing.	650-521-5459	NA	San Francisco
Searchmetrics Inc (HQ)	A Search and Content Marketing Platform that uncovers the opportunities and pitfalls of online marketing.	866-411-9494	NA	San Mateo
Simplicant Inc (HQ)	Producer of modern recruitment software that also helps to track applicants.	650-285-2394	NA	Palo Alto
Splunk Inc (HQ)	Develops software for monitoring, searching, and analyzing machine-generated big data through a web-style interface.	415-848-8400	NA	San Francisco
TalkCycle LLC (HQ)	Providers of innovative sales communication software.	888-400-2220	NA	San Mateo
Thoughtbot Inc (BR)	Provider of web and mobile app design and development.	877-976-2687	NA	San Francisco
ThoughtSpot Inc (HQ)	A business intelligence platform that helps individuals to explore, analyze, and share real-time business analytics data.	800-508-7008	NA	Sunnyvale
Tivix (BR)	Focuses on the agile development of web, cloud, and mobile applications.	415-680-1299	NA	San Francisco

COMPANY NAME	PRODUCT / SERVICE	PHONE	EMP	CITY
Treasure Data Inc (HQ)	Empower enterprises by unifying data from multiple sources such as online, offline, IoT and device-generated data.	866-899-5386	NA	Mountain View
Verdafero Inc (HQ)	Offers a wide range of cloud-based software solutions that enable companies to manage their utility data and analytics.	650-206-2441	NA	San Jose
Veritas Technologies LLC (HQ)	Empowers business with a multi-cloud data management solution.	866-837-4827	NA	Santa Clara
Vidado Inc (HQ)	Designed to help organizations collect and digitize inaccessible data.	415-237-3676	NA	Oakland
Workday Inc (HQ)	Developers of a cloud business planning framework to enable seamless collaboration across the enterprise.	650-528-7500	NA	Palo Alto
WSI Smart Solutions (HQ)	Provider of search engine optimization services. The company also deals with Internet marketing and web design solutions.	925-245-0216	NA	Livermore
Xignite Inc (HQ)	Provider of financial Data-as-a-Service (DaaS) solution to deliver market data from the AWS public cloud.	650-655-3700	NA	San Mateo

316 = CAD/CAM & visualisation

COMPANY NAME	PRODUCT / SERVICE	PHONE	EMP	CITY
2ndEdison Inc (HQ)	Provider of e-Commerce applications. The company also offers business process consulting and design services.	844-432-8466	NA	Orinda
Acrylic Art (HQ)	Provider of fabrication and machining services. The company focuses on painting, product finishing, anodizing, and vapor polishing.	510-654-0953	NA	Emeryville
Ad Art Inc (HQ)	Provider of digital signage solutions. The company also offers graphic designs, animation, commercial lighting, and maintenance services.	800-675-6353	NA	San Francisco
N Air Hollywood (HQ)	Provider of aviation-themed production solutions to the motion picture, television, and commercial production industry.	818-890-0444	11-50	Pacoima
Alliance Support Partners Inc (HQ)	Provider of test solutions, instrumentation engineering, test system design, and turnkey outsourcing support services.	925-363-5382	NA	Concord
American Prototype And Production Inc (HQ)	Manufacturer of industrial laser cutting machines. The company focuses on industries such as CNC milling, CNC turning, and laser engraving.	650-595-4994	NA	San Carlos
Applied Engineering (HQ)	Provider of structural analysis and seismic evaluation services. The company is involved in specialty engineering and project management.	408-263-5900	NA	Milpitas
Aquifi Inc (HQ)	Developer of fluid technology solutions. The company is involved in computer vision and machine learning algorithms.	650-213-8535	NA	Palo Alto
Artwork Conversion Software Inc (HQ)	Developer of CAD translation programs and CAD viewers software. The company also offers plotting software and IC packaging software.	831-426-6163	NA	Santa Cruz
ASCENX Technologies Inc (HQ)	Provider of engineering services to the semiconductor industry. The company is also engaged in contract manufacturing and repair services.	408-945-1997	NA	Fremont
CAD Masters Inc (HQ)	Designer and developer of software and hardware solutions. The company focuses on drafting, engineering, plotting, and on-site project assistance.	925-939-1378	NA	Walnut Creek
Capital Engineering Consultants Inc (HQ)	Provider of mechanical engineering, sustainable design and green engineering, building commissioning, energy modeling, and other related services.	916-851-3500	NA	Rancho Cordova
N Coast Sign Inc (HQ)	Provider of project management, turnkey brand conversions and re-branding manufacturing specialized services, leasing, engineering, installation and much more services.	714-520-9144	201-500	Anaheim
CyberGlove Systems LLC (HQ)	Provider of data glove technology. The company offers system installation and integration and custom software and hardware services.	408-943-8114	NA	San Jose
Digital Anarchy (HQ)	Provider of photography and video plugins for Photoshop, elements, after effects, and final cut pro.	415-287-6069	NA	Brisbane
Engineering By Design (HQ)	Provider of engineering and support services. The company's products include laminators, coil and fiber winders, motors, and extrusion pullers.	408-324-1500	NA	San Jose
Funmobility Inc (HQ)	Provider of solutions for mobile engagement and mobile marketing. The company also offers content marketing, digital strategy, and other services.	925-598-9700	NA	San Ramon
Geofusion Inc (HQ)	Specializes in virtual reality and 3D visualization services. The company offers software development kits.	831-458-1418	NA	Santa Cruz
Global Presenter (BR)	Designer and builder of meeting room communication systems. The company is a provider of design, delivery, and system integration solutions.	408-526-0221	NA	San Jose
GoEngineer (BR)	Provider of solid works engineering and Oracle agile PLM products. The company offers services to the business sector.	408-213-1580	NA	Santa Clara
Hawk Ridge Systems (BR)	Provider of 3D design software solutions. The company offers CAD, analysis consulting, product data management, and solid works services.	510-482-6110	NA	Orinda
Imaging Visions (HQ)	Provider of design, prototyping, and visualization services that include architectural and lighting, exterior and landscape, and furnishing design.	408-358-6427	NA	Los Gatos
N InterMetro Communications Inc (HQ)	Provider of voice calling over the Internet.	805-433-8000	11-50	Simi Valley
IT Concepts LLC (BR)	Manufacturer of borescopes, videoscopes, fiberscopes, documentation solutions, and accessories for remote visual inspection needs.	925-401-0010	NA	Pleasanton
Lumina Decision Systems Inc (HQ)	Provider of analytical training and consulting services. The company is engaged in technical support services.	650-212-1212	NA	Los Gatos
McKenzie Machining Inc (HQ)	Provider of precision machining services of pre-fabricated components. The company R&D, manufacturing design, and other services.	408-748-8885	NA	Santa Clara

COMPANY NAME	PRODUCT / SERVICE	PHONE	EMP	CITY
Moon Valley Circuits (HQ)	Manufacturer of control systems for wineries. The company specializes in tank temperature, barrel-room, and refrigeration control systems.	707-996-4157	NA	Glen Ellen
MSC Software (BR)	Developer of simulation software for acoustics, thermal analysis, and other needs. The company also offers software implementation and systems design services.	714-540-8900	NA	Newport Beach
Netblaze Systems Inc (HQ)	Provider of IT, integration, and network consulting services. The company is also engaged in cloud computing, web hosting, and hosted exchange.	925-932-1765	NA	Walnut Creek
OCAMPO-ESTA Corp (HQ)	Provider of engineering, design, construction management, instrumentation and controls, and project management services.	707-642-8072	NA	Vallejo
Opac Consulting Engineers Inc (HQ)	Provider of bridge and structural engineering services. The company's services are design, evaluation, and construction engineering.	415-989-4551	NA	San Francisco
N Paleotechnics (HQ)	Publisher of how-to books on primitive technology and survival skills.	707-391-8683	NA	Boonville
Performex Machining Inc (HQ)	Provider of machining services. The company specializes in computer aided machining, designing, and fabrication.	650-595-2228	NA	San Carlos
Phasespace Inc (HQ)	Developer of technologies for motion tracking markers. The company focuses on motion capture for industrial research and graphic community.	510-633-2865	NA	San Leandro
Plastikon Industries Inc (HQ)	Provider of contract manufacturing services for custom designed plastic injection molding, for medical, pharmaceutical and other industries.	510-400-1010	NA	Hayward
Plethora (HQ)	Focuses on CNC milling with automatic manufacturing analysis. The company is also involved in prototyping services.	415-726-2256	NA	San Francisco
Shields Harper & Co (HQ)	Provider of design assistance, testing, monitoring, fleet fuel control, and underground solutions to contractors, engineers, and designers.	510-653-9119	NA	Martinez
Solutionware Corp (HQ)	Provider of design solutions. The company offers computer aided design and computer aided manufacturing services.	408-249-1529	NA	San Jose
N South Valley Internet Inc (HQ)	Provider of Internet and phone services.	408-683-4533	11-50	San Martin
SSP Data (HQ)	Developer of network solutions. The company also offers design, deployment, and in-house management services.	510-215-3400	NA	Richmond
N Transvision International (HQ)	Provider of satellite network facilities and management solution services.	805-981-8740	51-200	Oxnard
N United Sign Systems (HQ)	Provider of commercial sign services.	209-543-1320	11-50	Modesto
Warren & Baerg Manufacturing Inc (HQ)	Manufacturer of agricultural and industrial systems. The company's services include installation, manufacturing, and technical support.	559-591-6790	NA	Dinuba
N West Coast Internet Inc (HQ)	Provider of Internet services.	949-487-3307	NA	Capistrano Beach
Zspace Inc (HQ)	Provider of solutions for viewing, manipulating, and communicating complex ideas through direct interaction with virtual-holographic simulations.	408-498-4050	NA	Sunnyvale

317 = Games

COMPANY NAME	PRODUCT / SERVICE	PHONE	EMP	CITY
2K Games Inc (HQ)	Developer of interactive entertainment for console systems. The company also focuses on handheld gaming systems and personal computers.	415-479-3634	NA	Novato
Bandai Namco Entertainment America Inc (HQ)	Provider of gaming solutions. The company is engaged in technical support and it serves the entertainment industry.	408-235-2000	NA	Santa Clara
Capcom USA (LH)	Manufacturer and distributor of electronic game machines. The company specializes in resident evil, monster hunter, lost planet, and devroom games.	650-350-6500	NA	San Francisco
Chess com (HQ)	Provider of unlimited chess games and free tournaments that can be played by challenging friends and meet new players.	800-318-2827	NA	Palo Alto
Crystal Dynamics Inc (HQ)	Designer and developer of animated videos. The company also specializes in mobile gaming software products.	650-421-7600	NA	Redwood City
Devicelock Inc (HQ)	Developer of device control software solutions. The company offers contextual and content-based control for data leak prevention.	925-231-4400	NA	San Ramon
Electronic Arts Inc (HQ)	Developer, publisher, and distributor of software for video game systems, personal computers, wireless devices, and Internet.	800-314-3291	NA	Redwood City
Fingerprint Digital Inc (HQ)	Designer and developer of mobile kids network solutions. The company offers services to kids of all ages.	855-543-4263	NA	San Francisco
HyTrust Inc (HQ)	Provider of security, compliance, and control software for virtualization of information technology infrastructure.	650-681-8100	NA	Mountain View
Netxperts Inc (HQ)	Provider of unified communication solutions. The company offers services to the healthcare and transportation markers.	925-806-0800	NA	Walnut Creek
nWay (HQ)	Specializes in the development and publishing of free-to-play online multiplayer games. The company offers services to individuals.	415-778-2866	NA	San Francisco
Perfect World Company Ltd (HQ)	Provider of gaming solutions. The company is engaged in technical support and it serves the entertainment industry.	650-590-7700	NA	Redwood City
ROBLOX Corp (HQ)	Specializes in game development, monetization, and publishing services. The company serves businesses.	888-858-2569	NA	San Mateo
Rockyou Inc (HQ)	Provider of gaming solutions. The company's games include Poker, Bingo, Zoo World, and others and serves the entertainment sector.	415-580-6400	NA	San Francisco

COMPANY NAME	PRODUCT / SERVICE	PHONE	EMP	CITY
Secret Builders (HQ)	Provider of online games for children. The company also focuses on publishing writings, art, and videos.	650-204-9098	NA	San Mateo
Silvaco Inc (HQ)	Supplier of TCAD and EDA software for circuit simulation. The company also designs analog, mixed-signal, and RF integrated circuits.	408-567-1000	NA	Santa Clara
Trion Worlds Inc (HQ)	Publisher and developer of games. The company offers Defiance, RIFT, Archeage, and End of Nations games.	650-273-9618	NA	Redwood City
Vivid Vision Inc (HQ)	Provider of virtual reality solutions. The company offers services to eye clinics and also kids and adults.	877-877-0310	NA	San Francisco
XEODesign (HQ)	Provider of computer multimedia software, website design hosting, programming, and technical support services.	510-658-8077	NA	Oakland
Zynga Inc (HQ)	Provider of social game services with more than 240 million monthly active users. The company's games include CityVille, Draw Something, and Hidden Chronicles.	800-762-2530	1001-5000	San Francisco

318 = Multimedia/Audio/Video

	COMPANY NAME	PRODUCT / SERVICE	PHONE	EMP	CITY
	Ad Art Inc (HQ)	Provider of digital signage solutions. The company also offers graphic designs, animation, commercial lighting, and maintenance services.	800-675-6353	NA	San Francisco
N	Air Hollywood (HQ)	Provider of aviation-themed production solutions to the motion picture, television, and commercial production industry.	818-890-0444	11-50	Pacoima
	Anvato Inc (HQ)	Provider of video software platform to television broadcasters and offers live and on-demand video management, analytics, and tracking features.	866-246-6942	NA	Mountain View
	BRS Media Inc (HQ)	Provider of multimedia e-commerce services. The company specializes in radio and Internet applications.	415-677-4027	NA	San Francisco
	Circle Video Productions (HQ)	Provider of video production and multimedia solutions. The company offers video dispositions, editing, and duplication services.	650-619-7367	NA	San Mateo
N	Coast Sign Inc (HQ)	Provider of project management, turnkey brand conversions and re-branding manufacturing specialized services, leasing, engineering, installation and much more services.	714-520-9144	201-500	Anaheim
	Compandent Inc (HQ)	Developer of customized algorithms. The company offers digital sign processing services to telecommunications and semiconductor companies.	650-241-9231	NA	Los Altos Hills
	D-Tools Inc (HQ)	Developer and marketer of software to streamline processes which accompany the integration and installation of low-voltage systems.	925-681-2326	NA	Concord
	Dolphin Graphics (HQ)	Provider of branding and marketing solutions. The company also offers graphics design and web design services.	510-881-0154	NA	Castro Valley
	EXXIM Computing Corp (HQ)	Manufacturer of cutting-edge radiological imaging technology and equipment designed for dental, medical, and scientific and industrial industries.	925-416-1900	NA	Pleasanton
	Harmonic Inc (HQ)	Provider of production and delivery solutions. The company serves the broadcast, media, service providers, and post production markers.	408-542-2500	201-500	San Jose
	HyTrust Inc (HQ)	Provider of security, compliance, and control software for virtualization of information technology infrastructure.	650-681-8100	NA	Mountain View
	Inikosoft Inc (HQ)	Provider of web, graphic, and print design services. The company is also engaged in e-commerce development and social media marketing.	408-402-9545	NA	Los Gatos
	IntelliVision Technologies Corp (HQ)	Provider of software and solutions for security, surveillance, traffic, automotive, robotics, drones, smart home, mobile, and retail analytics solutions.	408-754-1690	NA	San Jose
	IT Concepts LLC (BR)	Manufacturer of borescopes, videoscopes, fiberscopes, documentation solutions, and accessories for remote visual inspection needs.	925-401-0010	NA	Pleasanton
	J&C Consulting Services (HQ)	Developer of consulting services. The company offers strategic planning, executive coaching, and leadership and team development solutions.	415-935-4313	NA	San Francisco
	Noble Image Inc (HQ)	Provider of website and graphic design, website development, hosting, programming, and technical support services.	916-419-3570	NA	Sacramento
	OJO Technology Inc (HQ)	Manufacturer of video surveillance systems. The company offers services to the education, transportation, and utility sectors.	877-306-4656	NA	Fremont
N	Paleotechnics (HQ)	Publisher of how-to books on primitive technology and survival skills.	707-391-8683	NA	Boonville
	Pass Laboratories Inc (HQ)	Developer of prototypes for amplifier design. The company specializes in manufacturing amplifiers and speakers.	530-878-5350	NA	Auburn
	Phasespace Inc (HQ)	Developer of technologies for motion tracking markers. The company focuses on motion capture for industrial research and graphic community.	510-633-2865	NA	San Leandro
	Qwilt Inc (HQ)	Developer of open caching, video intelligence, fixed, and mobile operators solutions. The company offers media analytics products.	866-824-8009	NA	Redwood City
	Rearden LLC (HQ)	Provider of cloud computing, motion picture, video game, consumer electronics, wireless, imaging, communications, and alternative energy technologies.	415-947-5555	NA	Mountain View
	Rollinson Advertising Design (HQ)	Provider of graphic design, traditional marketing, strategic planning, and e-mail blasting services.	925-518-6698	NA	Pleasant Hill
	Spectra 7 Microsystems Ltd (HQ)	Manufacturer of analog semiconductor devices. The company focuses on micro-thin interconnects for consumer electronic products.	408-770-2915	NA	San Jose

COMPANY NAME	PRODUCT / SERVICE	PHONE	EMP	CITY
N United Sign Systems (HQ)	Provider of commercial sign services.	209-543-1320	11-50	Modesto
Universal Audio Inc (HQ)	Manufacturer of analog recording equipment. The company's products include audio interfaces, channel strips, plug-ins, and compressors.	831-440-1176	NA	Scotts Valley
Video Clarity Inc (HQ)	Provider of real time and broadcast quality monitoring, perceptual analysis, recording, and automating services.	408-379-6952	NA	Campbell

319 = Prepackaged Software Development

COMPANY NAME	PRODUCT / SERVICE	PHONE	EMP	CITY
Abacus Solutions Inc (HQ)	Developer of SATURN, an integrated enterprise ETRM system and focuses on generation optimization, parameters estimation, and credit management.	650-941-1728	NA	Los Altos Hills
Acesis Inc (HQ)	Provider of web-based platform for overseeing healthcare quality improvement and compliance documentation, workflow, and analytics.	650-396-7540	NA	Mountain View
Actian Corp (HQ)	Provider of on-premises applications and cloud data management solutions.	650-587-5500	NA	Palo Alto
Adobe Systems Inc (HQ)	Developer of software solutions for digital media creation and editing, multimedia authoring, and web development.	408-536-6000	NA	San Jose
ADPAC Corp (HQ)	Provider of software to improve productivity and value of current application software focusing on business rule extraction, M&A, and documentation.	415-777-5400	NA	Livermore
N Advanced Lease Systems Inc (HQ)	Provider of design, development and other services in IT sector.	530-378-6868	NA	Redding
Agiloft Inc (HQ)	Provider of contract, work flow, change, and asset management services. The company offers services to armed forces and universities.	650-587-8615	NA	Redwood City
N Anotek Inc (HQ)	Developer of software and books to teach the Greek language to English speaking people.	310-450-5027	NA	Santa Monica
Apogee Software Inc (HQ)	Provider of integrated development environment for Java and C. The company offers industrial monitors and controllers.	408-369-9001	NA	Campbell
Applozic Inc (HQ)	Empowers businesses with in-app messaging solutions and all-in-one customer support solution.	310-909-7458	NA	Palo Alto
Apptimize Inc (HQ)	Providers of robust mobile experimentation and optimization solution to improve an user's mobile experience through A/B testing.	415-926-5398	NA	San Francisco
Apttus Corp (HQ)	Developers of AI revenue intelligence software.	650-445-7700	NA	San Mateo
Atheer Inc (HQ)	Developer of 3D smart glasses and productivity application for aerospace, insurance, field maintenance, oil and gas, and healthcare.	650-933-5004	NA	Santa Clara
Augmentum Inc (HQ)	Provider of software development and solution implementation services. The company focuses on Internet applications and product development outsourcing.	650-578-9221	NA	Foster City
Azul Systems Inc (HQ)	Provider of Java applications for real time businesses. The company's Zing is a JVM enterprise application.	650-230-6500	NA	Sunnyvale
Benevity Inc (BR)	Specializes in corporate social responsibility employee engagement software.	855-237-7875	NA	San Mateo
Bitglass Inc (HQ)	Provider of data protection solutions. The company focuses on cloud encryption, mobile security, and discovery solutions.	408-337-0190	NA	Campbell
Branch Metrics (HQ)	Provides deep link solutions that unify user measurement across different devices, platforms, and channels.	650-209-6461	NA	Redwood City
Buildera (HQ)	Focuses on structural crack monitoring solutions. The company deals with installation services and serves the industrial sector.	650-587-6738	NA	Redwood City
Caseware International Inc (DH)	Supplier of software solutions to accountants and auditors worldwide. The company offers working papers to accounting firms.	416-867-9504	NA	Berkeley
Centrify (HQ)	Provider of identity and access management solutions. The company offers services to pharma companies and financial institutions.	669-444-5200	NA	Santa Clara
N Ceridian Corp (BR)	Firm is a provider of human capital management solutions.	714-963-1311	NA	Fountain Valley
Champ Systems Inc (HQ)	Provider of business management and accounting software. The company offers ERP programming, training, software, and hardware services.	916-424-4066	NA	Sacramento
N Chander Software Solutions Inc (HQ)	Provider of marketing, call center, project management and technical support software and technical staffing augmentation solutions.	408-406-5624	NA	San Jose
ChannelNet (BR)	Provider of digital solutions to connect brands and customers. The company specializes in strategy development, design, and content optimization.	415-332-4704	NA	Sausalito
ChemSoft (HQ)	Provider of software consulting services. The company specializes in custom business solutions, access, excel, PowerPoint, word, and visual basic.	408-615-1001	NA	San Jose
Clari Inc (HQ)	Developers of an AI-based data capturing software that helps the marketing, sales, and customer success teams.	650-265-2111	NA	Sunnyvale
Clean Power Research (HQ)	Provider of program automation, customer engagement, and solar data and intelligence solutions. The company offers services to the solar industry.	707-258-2765	NA	Napa
Cloudtc (HQ)	Designer and developer of voice communications platform. The company specializes in business applications.	650-238-5203	NA	Palo Alto

COMPANY NAME	PRODUCT / SERVICE	PHONE	EMP	CITY
Computer Software For Professionals Inc (HQ)	Provider of law office management software and related tools. The company offers services to the legal industry.	510-547-8085	NA	Oakland
Contract Room Inc (HQ)	Provides contract management software.	800-950-9101	NA	San Mateo
Contrast Media Labs (HQ)	Provider of graphic design and software development services. The company services include android applications and digital and print media design.	415-471-1323	NA	San Francisco
Corona Labs Inc (HQ)	A cross-platform framework for creating apps and games for mobile devices and desktop systems.	415-996-6877	NA	San Francisco
Corona Labs Inc (HQ)	Developer of games, e-books, and other interactive content. The company offers services to the educational sector.	415-996-6877	NA	San Francisco
Coupa Software Inc (HQ)	Global technology platform for Business Spend Management (BSM) to deliver measurable value.	650-931-3200	501-1000	San Mateo
N Cpp Inc (HQ)	Publisher of books on psychology and distributes publications of Jossey-Bass, Harper and Row, and B and D book and reaches market through direct mail, trade sales, and distributors.	650-969-8901	NA	Sunnyvale
Cyrun Corp (HQ)	Developer of windows-based integrated software system. The company caters to public safety organizations.	831-458-0949	NA	Santa Cruz
Datavision Inc (HQ)	Provider of software solutions for accounting, supply chain, and water and utility applications. The company also offers hosting and support.	530-387-3575	NA	Cameron Park
Digital Keystone Inc (HQ)	Provider of solutions enabling content distribution to tablets, connected TVs, and other entertainment platforms with suite of software and tools.	650-938-7300	NA	Cupertino
DNN Corp (HQ)	Provider of software solutions for content management. The company also offers marketing and eCommerce and product development services.	650-288-3150	NA	San Mateo
Docsend Inc (HQ)	Provider of service that makes documents more effective communication tool with intelligence to track, optimize, and control the business documents sent.	888-258-5951	NA	San Francisco
Domico Software (HQ)	Supplier of management and accounting software for managing self storage units, tenants, and accounts.	510-841-4155	NA	Walnut Creek
N Douloi Automation Inc (HQ)	Developer of prepackaged motion control software.	408-735-6942	NA	Santa Clara
Druva Inc (RH)	Provider of cloud based data protection products. The company offers services to the manufacturing, healthcare, and education industries.	650-238-6200	NA	Sunnyvale
Dynamic Graphics Inc (HQ)	Provider of geospatial software solutions such as earth modeling, well planning, and visualization for the petroleum industries.	510-522-0700	NA	Alameda
N Eastridge Workforce Solutions (HQ)	Provider of workforce management, workforce recruitment, workforce technology and staffing solutions.	800-778-0197	201-500	San Diego
EDA Direct Inc (HQ)	Provider of EDA software products and services. The company's products include Cliosoft, MunEDA, and Mentor Graphics.	408-496-5890	NA	Santa Clara
Elasticsearch Inc (HQ)	A software company that builds self-managed and SaaS offerings that make data usable in real time.	650-458-2620	NA	Mountain View
Engagio Inc (HQ)	B2B Marketing Engagement Software that enables marketers and sellers to work as a team.	650-487-2050	NA	San Mateo
Equilar Inc (HQ)	Developer of industry-leading data and tools for public and private companies, compensation consultants, attorneys, and corporate governance leaders.	877-441-6090	NA	Redwood City
Evernote Corp (HQ)	Provider of note management and digital link services. The company also offers handwriting recognition services.	650-257-0885	NA	Redwood City
EverString Technology (HQ)	Provider of AI SaaS solution for B2B sales and marketing professionals.	650-425-3937	NA	San Mateo
Exadel Inc (HQ)	Custom software agency that produces software and mobile solutions.	925-363-9510	NA	Walnut Creek
Exxact Corp (HQ)	Supplier of workstation graphic cards and solutions. The company also offers servers, HPC clusters, and computing software.	510-226-7366	NA	Fremont
F5 Networks Inc (BR)	Provider of strategic points of control throughout the IT infrastructure for organizations to scale, adapt, and align with changing business demands.	408-273-4800	NA	San Jose
N FABNexus Inc (HQ)	Provider of application-specific machine control and SEMI-standards conformant network automation software to the semiconductor manufacturing and support industry.	650-207-8235	NA	Los Altos
FactoryWiz (HQ)	Provider of CNC Machine Tool monitoring and data collection products. The company is also involved in preventive maintenance services.	408-224-9167	NA	San Jose
Fair Isaac Corp (HQ)	Provider of analytical, software installation, and integration services. The company serves business enterprises.	408-817-9100	NA	San Jose
Financial Oxygen Inc (HQ)	Provider of cash management and fixed income products and it serves individual banks and broker-dealers.	925-465-1225	NA	San Jose
Flickerbox Inc (HQ)	Provider of marketing, design, and technology support services. The company also deals with lead generation campaigns.	415-436-9383	NA	San Francisco
ForgeRock (HQ)	Provider of identity solutions. The company serves the digital health, financial services, communication, and media industries.	415-599-1100	NA	San Francisco
N Formula Consultants Inc (HQ)	Provider of software development and consulting services.	714-778-0123	NA	Anaheim

COMPANY NAME	PRODUCT / SERVICE	PHONE	EMP	CITY
Fortemedia Inc (HQ)	Provider of voice processing integrated circuits. The company also offers related hardware and software components.	408-861-8088	NA	Santa Clara
Full Circle Insights Inc (HQ)	Delivers marketing and sales performance measurement solutions to optimize a company's marketing automation solutions.	650-641-2766	NA	San Mateo
Gong.io (HQ)	Developers of revenue intelligence platform that delivers insights at scale.	650-276-3068	NA	San Francisco
Grio (HQ)	Specializes in web, iOS, and Android development.	415-395-9525	NA	San Francisco
HackerRank (HQ)	Technology recruiting tool that helps tech recruiters and hiring managers to identify and hire talents.	415-900-4023	NA	Mountain View
Hawk Ridge Systems (BR)	Provider of 3D design software solutions. The company offers CAD, analysis consulting, product data management, and solid works services.	510-482-6110	NA	Orinda
Hawk Ridge Systems (BR)	Provider of parametric 3D product design and analysis services. The company also offers data management tools.	877-266-4469	NA	Mountain View
HyTrust Inc (HQ)	Provider of security, compliance, and control software for virtualization of information technology infrastructure.	650-681-8100	NA	Mountain View
IAR Systems Software Inc (RH)	Provider of software tools and embedded systems. The company's products include state machine tools, starter kits, and compiler and debugger tool suite.	650-287-4250	NA	Foster City
Impekable LLC (HQ)	UI design and mobile development studio that helps organizations to create human-centric mobile experiences.	650-733-6006	NA	San Jose
Increv Corp (HQ)	Developer of business and information technology solutions. The company is engaged in consulting and product development services.	408-689-2296	NA	Los Altos
Individual Software Inc (HQ)	Publisher and developer of education, business, and personal productivity software for consumers, schools, businesses, and government.	925-734-6767	NA	Livermore
Inductive Automation (HQ)	Supplier of web-based industrial automation software. The company offers solutions for end-users and integrators.	916-456-1045	NA	Folsom
Infin IT Consulting (HQ)	Designer and developer of CNC machining and billet products. The company's products include fire extinguisher brackets, shift knobs, and boat accessories.	866-364-2007	NA	Campbell
N Infoflex Inc (HQ)	Developer of accounting and 4GL software.	650-270-1019	NA	Burlingame
Infrared Industries Inc (HQ)	Developer of gas analyzer instrumentation for the automotive, oil and gas, industrial, environmental, and utility industries.	510-782-8100	NA	Hayward
Innosys Inc (HQ)	Provider of data communication solutions. The company serves airlines, travel agencies, and online travel services.	510-222-7717	NA	Walnut Creek
Intelight ITS (HQ)	Provider of electrical engineering solutions. The company offers expertise on systems, traffic products and software.	520-795-8808	NA	Carlsbad
Intelli-Touch Apps Inc (HQ)	Specializes in automating and simplifying the personal and business communications and it serves the legal industry.	925-884-1802	NA	San Ramon
Invoice2go Inc (HQ)	A mobile and web app for micro and small business owners to create invoice, track expenses and track time.	650-300-5180	NA	Palo Alto
Itrezzo Inc (HQ)	Provider of unified contact management solutions and it serves schools, agencies, and healthcare organizations.	408-540-5020	NA	San Jose
Jeda Technologies Inc (HQ)	Provider of chip based digital designs and semiconductor services. The company focuses on validation and automation solutions.	408-912-1856	NA	Santa Clara
N JRH GoldenState Software Inc (HQ)	Developer and provider of software tools and solutions that supports complete DB2 catalog query and object management.	310-544-1497	NA	Rancho Palos Verdes
Kaseya International Ltd (BR)	Provider of software solutions. The company offers cloud and network monitoring, asset management, and backup recovery services.	415-694-5700	NA	San Jose
Keri Systems Inc (HQ)	Provider of access control and integrated security systems. The company offers technology support and training solutions.	408-435-8400	NA	San Jose
KitApps Inc (HQ)	Provider of networking and other information-based tools to event organizers and attendees (end-users).	866-944-8678	NA	San Jose
KLC Enterprises (HQ)	Provider of accounting software for the construction industry. The company offers services to the commercial and industrial sectors.	415-485-0555	NA	San Anselmo
Knightscope Inc (HQ)	Provider of security technology. The company specializes in monotonous, computationally heavy, and sometimes dangerous work for security operations.	650-924-1025	NA	Mountain View
Knowme Inc (HQ)	Provider of web based customer relationship management services. The company is also engaged in call routing and web and phone integration.	800-713-9257	NA	San Francisco
Kovair Software Inc (HQ)	Provider of web-based document management applications. The company offers product support maintenance services.	408-262-0200	NA	San Ramon
Laru Technologies (HQ)	Provider of ACH and Wire transaction monitoring and control tools. The company focuses on risk management and compliance solutions.	916-458-6149	NA	Folsom
Lattice Semiconductor (BR)	Provider of design, development, and marketing services for programmable logic devices. The company also offers related software.	408-826-6000	NA	San Jose
Lattice Technology Inc (BR)	Developer of 3D and 2D software for design review purposes. The company also focuses on 3D simulation and animation needs.	720-330-3197	NA	San Francisco

	COMPANY NAME	PRODUCT / SERVICE	PHONE	EMP	CITY
	Learning In Motion Inc (HQ)	Provider of educational materials and services. The company offers content development, video production, and marketing collateral services.	831-600-6606	NA	Santa Cruz
	LiveAction (HQ)	Provider of network visibility and performance diagnostics products. The company focuses on network and security forensics.	408-217-6501	NA	Palo Alto
	Logen Solutions USA (HQ)	Provider of truck, container, pallet and carton loading and packaging software. The company offers solutions for cargo load planning.	408-519-5771	NA	San Jose
N	Lynx Media Inc (HQ)	Developer of inventory control and order entry software.	800-451-5969	NA	Valley Village
	Marin Software (HQ)	Developer of software products and provides software design and development for the architecture, engineering, and construction industries.	415-399-2580	NA	San Francisco
N	Mark-Costello Co (HQ)	Wholesaler of waste compactors.	310-637-1851	NA	Paramount
	MarkLogic Corp (HQ)	Provider of enterprise solutions. The company serves the healthcare, legal, and insurance industries.	650-655-2300	NA	San Carlos
	Matisse Software Inc (HQ)	Provider of database software and services. The company is also engaged in training, consulting, and technical support.	252-227-7013	NA	Mountain View
	Mattermost Inc (HQ)	Delivers open-source messaging tools for security-conscious enterprises and developers.	650-866-5518	NA	Palo Alto
	Mcafee Inc (HQ)	Provider of computer security solutions. The company specializes in database, web, email, network, endpoint, and mobile security services.	888-847-8766	NA	Santa Clara
	Merkle Inc (BR)	Provider of omnichannel loyalty solution. The company offers service and technology to deliver seamless and powerful customer retention solutions.	415-918-2990	NA	San Francisco
	Mindflash (HQ)	Provider of online training and related solutions. The company offers services to the software industry.	805-963-8417	NA	Palo Alto
	Mobitor Corp (HQ)	Provider of mobility software, connectivity, and information solutions. The company serves the aerospace, aviation, and manufacturing industries.	925-464-7700	NA	Walnut Creek
	Montavista Software LLC (HQ)	Developer of embedded Linux system software, development tools, and related software products. The company's products include CGE and DevRocket.	408-520-1591	NA	Santa Clara
	Multi Metrics Inc (HQ)	Provider of geometric dimensioning and tolerance technology products and services and offers training and corporate implementation services.	650-328-0200	NA	Menlo Park
	Notxperts Inc (HQ)	Provider of unified communication solutions. The company offers services to the healthcare and transportation markers.	925-806-0800	NA	Walnut Creek
N	New:Team SoftWare Inc (HQ)	Developer of software solutions.	415-461-8086	NA	Sacramento
	Nexant Inc (HQ)	Developer of software for utility, energy, chemical, and other sectors and also offers power grid consulting and energy advisory, and other services.	415-369-1000	NA	San Francisco
	Nextbus Inc (BR)	Provider of transit management solutions. The company also provides real-time passenger information solutions to organizations.	925-686-8200	NA	Concord
	Nexusguard Ltd (RH)	Provider of monitoring and DNA protection services. The company serves service providers and the entertainment sector.	415-299-8550	NA	San Francisco
	Optumsoft Inc (HQ)	Provider of distributed computing and technology based software development that includes maintenance of structured software systems.	844-361-8222	NA	Menlo Park
N	PBI Market Equipment Inc (HQ)	Distributor of meat wrappers, slicers, and digital scales.	562-595-4785	1-10	Signal Hill
	Professional Finishing (HQ)	Provider of liquid and powder coatings and finishing to the scientific and aerospace industries. The company focuses on sandblasting and silk screening.	510-233-7629	NA	Richmond
	Promptu (HQ)	Provider of voice-activated search and navigation services. The company is also engaged in engineering and product marketing.	650-859-5800	NA	Menlo Park
N	Pronto Networks (HQ)	Provider of Wi-Fi operation support system solutions for enterprises, wireless ISPs, WiMAX and satellite networks.	925-860-6200	51-200	Walnut Creek
	Provectus IT Inc (HQ)	Accelerates digital transformation by using Artificial Intelligence.	877-951-2224	NA	Palo Alto
	Pulse Secure LLC (HQ)	Provider of product, hardware, partner, and enterprise solutions. The company offers services to the financial services and healthcare industries.	408-372-9600	NA	San Jose
	Quantum Corp (HQ)	Provider of software for backup, recovery, and archiving needs. The company serves the healthcare, media, and entertainment industries.	408-944-4000	NA	San Jose
	Quantum3D Inc (HQ)	Developer and manufacturer of real-time visual simulation and computing systems for fast-jet, helicopter, refueling, and other needs.	408-600-2500	NA	Milpitas
	Readytech Corp (HQ)	Provider of virtual labs for training, certification, and also sales demonstrations. The company deals with technology support.	800-707-1009	NA	Oakland
N	REAL Software Systems LLC (HQ)	Developer of software solutions for the management of royalty, rights and revenue sharing contracts.	818-313-8000	NA	Woodland Hills
	Red Hat Inc (BR)	Provider of training, certification, consulting, cloud, application, and other technical support services.	650-567-9039	NA	Sunnyvale
	Redbooth (HQ)	A task and project management platform for team collaboration tasks, discussions, and file sharing.	650-521-5459	NA	San Francisco

COMPANY NAME	PRODUCT / SERVICE	PHONE	EMP	CITY
Robertson Precision Inc (HQ)	Manufacturer of precision metals and plastic products. The company's services include engineering support and process control.	650-363-2212	NA	Menlo Park
Rolepoint (HQ)	Focuses on talent acquisition services. The company serves small and medium businesses and Fortune 500 companies.	888-571-2851	NA	San Francisco
SAP America Inc (BR)	Developer of software applications. The company provides data and technology, custom development, and implementation services.	650-849-4000	NA	Palo Alto
Searchmetrics Inc (HQ)	A Search and Content Marketing Platform that uncovers the opportunities and pitfalls of online marketing.	866-411-9494	NA	San Mateo
Secugen Corp (HQ)	Manufacturer of fingerprint recognition devices. The company's products serve the purpose of integration into 3rd party hardware products.	408-727-7787	NA	Santa Clara
Sharpesoft Inc (HQ)	Provider of cost accounting, dispatching, and project management software. The company exclusively serves the construction sector.	530-671-6499	NA	Yuba City
Sherrill-Lubinski Corp (HQ)	Provider of monitoring and analytics solutions for middleware-powered applications. The company serves the electrical commodity market.	415-927-8400	NA	Riverside
Silicondust USA Inc (RH)	Provider of network connected TV tuners. The company offers global solutions to Live TV streaming in businesses, hotels, and education facilities.	925-443-4388	NA	Livermore
Simplicant Inc (HQ)	Producer of modern recruitment software that also helps to track applicants.	650-285-2394	NA	Palo Alto
SST Systems Inc (HQ)	Provider of solutions for piping design and analysis. The company's services include plant design and engineering.	408-452-8111	NA	San Jose
Stella Technology Inc (HQ)	Provider of integration and collaboration solutions. The company deals with technology design, development, and consulting services.	844-278-3552	NA	Milpitas
TalkCycle LLC (HQ)	Providers of innovative sales communication software.	888-400-2220	NA	San Mateo
Teamf1 Inc (HQ)	Provider of networking and security software for embedded devices. The company also offers technical support services.	510-505-9931	NA	Fremont
Telemanagement Technologies Inc (HQ)	Provider of telemanagement software products and services. The company is engaged in troubleshooting and maintenance services.	925-946-9800	NA	Walnut Creek
Thoughtbot Inc (BR)	Provider of web and mobile app design and development.	877-976-2687	NA	San Francisco
ThoughtSpot Inc (HQ)	A business intelligence platform that helps individuals to explore, analyze, and share real-time business analytics data.	800-508-7008	NA	Sunnyvale
TIBCO Software Inc (HQ)	Provider of enterprise application integration software. The company serves the government, healthcare, and insurance industries.	650-846-1000	NA	Palo Alto
N Tiger Software (HQ)	Developer of investment software.	858-273-5900	11-50	San Diego
Tivix (BR)	Focuses on the agile development of web, cloud, and mobile applications.	415-680-1299	NA	San Francisco
Tora Trading Services Ltd (BR)	Provider of products such as Compass, Clearpool, and Crosspoint for buy-side traders to specifically address the trading challenges to Asia.	650-513-6700	NA	Burlingame
Total Resolution LLC (HQ)	Developer of software for electron microscopy needs. The company provides MacTempasX and CrystalKitX.	510-527-6393	NA	Berkeley
Treasure Data Inc (HQ)	Empower enterprises by unifying data from multiple sources such as online, offline, IoT and device-generated data.	866-899-5386	NA	Mountain View
Ultra-X Inc (HQ)	Provider of personal computer diagnostic solutions for developers, manufacturers, system engineers, integrators, and computer professionals.	408-261-7090	NA	Santa Clara
Untangle (HQ)	Designer and developer of network management software. The company specializes in firewall and Internet management application.	408-598-4299	NA	San Jose
uSens Inc (HQ)	Creator of 3D human computing interaction software and hardware solutions. The company focuses on artificial intelligence.	408-564-0227	NA	San Jose
Valin Corp (HQ)	Provider of engineered solutions. The company serves the semiconductor, petrochemical, life sciences, and aerospace industries.	800-774-5630	NA	San Jose
N Ventricle Software Systems Inc (HQ)	Provider of software development for the healthcare industry.	310-948-2551	NA	Rancho Palos Verdes
Verific Design Automation Inc (HQ)	Specializes in electronic design automation solutions. The company offers services to the semiconductor industry.	510-522-1555	NA	Alameda
Veritas Technologies LLC (HQ)	Empowers business with a multi-cloud data management solution.	866-837-4827	NA	Santa Clara
Vicom Systems Inc (HQ)	Provider of migration data services. The company is involved in offering transparent wire-speed data services for systems and storage.	408-588-1286	NA	Santa Clara
Wind River Systems Inc (DH)	Provider of automotive networking solutions. The company's products include operating systems, development tools, and middleware technologies.	510-748-4100	NA	Alameda
Workday Inc (HQ)	Developers of a cloud business planning framework to enable seamless collaboration across the enterprise.	650-528-7500	NA	Palo Alto
XC2 Software LLC (HQ)	Provider of integrated software suite. The company's products find application in water and wastewater utilities.	800-761-4999	NA	Fairfax
XEODesign (HQ)	Provider of computer multimedia software, website design hosting, programming, and technical support services.	510-658-8077	NA	Oakland
Xetus Mortgage Corp (HQ)	Provider of mortgage processing services such as documentation monitoring, data and image capture, and reporting and audit trail.	650-237-1225	NA	Burlingame

	COMPANY NAME	PRODUCT / SERVICE	PHONE	EMP	CITY
N	Xifin Inc (HQ)	Provider of health care related information technology services.	858-793-5700	201-500	San Diego
N	Yellow Magic Inc (HQ)	Developer of software for the directory publishing industry.	951-506-4005	NA	Murrieta
	Zmanda - A Carbonite Co (HQ)	Provider of open source backup and recovery software solutions. The company's applications include centralized backup of file systems and applications.	408-732-3208	NA	Sunnyvale
	Zoho Corp (HQ)	Developer and provider of IT management software, business technology solutions, and network management framework.	615-671-9025	NA	Pleasanton

320 = Software Publication

COMPANY NAME	PRODUCT / SERVICE	PHONE	EMP	CITY
Asmeix Corp (HQ)	Provider of welding procedure software services such as technical support, installation, maintenance, and demo services.	877-977-7999	NA	Concord
Atypon Systems LLC (HQ)	Provider of service content delivery software for publishers. The company serves information discovery, e-commerce, and business intelligence needs.	408-988-1240	NA	Santa Clara
Bayometric (HQ)	Supplier of fingerprint scanners, single sign-on solution and access control systems. The company serves the business and industrial markers.	408-940-3955	NA	San Jose
Bodhtree Solutions Inc (BR)	Provider of information technology consulting services. The company deals with product engineering, application development, and training.	408-954-8700	NA	Fremont
BuyerLeverage (HQ)	Provider of technologies and services that allow consumers and businesses to profit and control their communications and information.	650-320-1608	NA	Palo Alto
Calyx Technology Inc (HQ)	Provider of mortgage solutions for banks and credit unions. The company also serves mortgage bankers and brokers.	214-252-5610	NA	San Jose
Certain Inc (DH)	Provider of enterprise event management solutions that include e-mail marketing, event reporting, registration, and consulting services.	888-237-8246	NA	San Francisco
Cirius Group Inc (HQ)	Designer and marketer of financial and medical software. The company serves hospitals and healthcare providers.	925-685-9300	NA	Pleasant Hill
Devicelock Inc (HQ)	Developer of device control software solutions. The company offers contextual and content-based control for data leak prevention.	925-231-4400	NA	San Ramon
DreamFactory Software Inc (HQ)	Provider of software development services. The company offers hosting, external integration, SQL, and user management services.	415-993-5877	NA	Campbell
Exatron Inc (HQ)	Manufacturer of automatic test equipment and IC handlers. The company also specializes in open short testers.	800-392-8766	NA	San Jose
Granite Horizon LLC (HQ)	Provider of content management solutions. The company offers design, development, project management, and user and developer training services.	916-647-6350	NA	Elk Grove
HyTrust Inc (HQ)	Provider of security, compliance, and control software for virtualization of information technology infrastructure.	650-681-8100	NA	Mountain View
Icube Information International (HQ)	Publisher of software work flow based management systems, documentation, inventory processing, and revision tracking services.	510-683-8928	NA	Fremont
Imaja (HQ)	Developer of computer applications. The company specializes in the development of educational tools for Macs.	510-526-4621	NA	Berkeley
Individual Software Inc (HQ)	Publisher and developer of education, business, and personal productivity software for consumers, schools, businesses, and government.	925-734-6767	NA	Livermore
Learning In Motion Inc (HQ)	Provider of educational materials and services. The company offers content development, video production, and marketing collateral services.	831-600-6606	NA	Santa Cruz
MobileFrame LLC (HQ)	Provider of enterprise mobility solutions that include mobile application development, device management, GPS tracking, and integration features.	408-885-1200	NA	Los Gatos
Netxperts Inc (HQ)	Provider of unified communication solutions. The company offers services to the healthcare and transportation markers.	925-806-0800	NA	Walnut Creek
Nexenta Systems Inc (HQ)	Provider of enterprise class storage software solutions. The company is engaged in virtualization and business continuity planning.	408-791-3300	NA	Santa Clara
Omnicia Inc (HQ)	Provider of electronic submissions for the life science sector. The company offers electronics and desktop publishing and document management services.	415-293-8553	NA	San Francisco
Onque Technologies Inc (HQ)	Provider of software tools used for the management of human resources. The company serves business organizations and enterprises.	707-569-3000	NA	Sonoma
Optumsoft Inc (HQ)	Provider of distributed computing and technology based software development that includes maintenance of structured software systems.	844-361-8222	NA	Menlo Park
Personal Tex Inc (HQ)	Publisher of PCTeX software that enables mathematicians to publish their formulas, equations, and thoughts.	415-296-7550	NA	San Francisco
Pictron Inc (HQ)	Provider of solutions for media applications in corporate communications, eLearning, broadcast production, and content based video search fields.	408-725-8888	NA	Sunnyvale
Reprise Software Inc (HQ)	Provider of license management software solutions. The company's products include Exa, Arxan, LMS, and Pace.	781-837-0884	NA	San Jose

COMPANY NAME	PRODUCT / SERVICE	PHONE	EMP	CITY
Silicon Publishing Inc (HQ)	Provider of digital publishing solutions. The company deals with template designs and personalized communications.	925-935-3899	NA	San Francisco
Trion Worlds Inc (HQ)	Publisher and developer of games. The company offers Defiance, RIFT, Archeage, and End of Nations games.	650-273-9618	NA	Redwood City
Zag Technical Services Inc (HQ)	Provider of services for server, email stability, reliability, migration, and security assessment needs.	408-383-2000	NA	San Jose

321 = Software - Related Services

COMPANY NAME	PRODUCT / SERVICE	PHONE	EMP	CITY
CryptoForensics Technologies Inc (HQ)	Provider of cybersecurity solutions to businesses, organizations, and the government. The company focuses on cyberforensics and compliance services.	510-483-1933	NA	San Leandro

322 = Application-Specific Software

	COMPANY NAME	PRODUCT / SERVICE	PHONE	EMP	CITY
	37 Degrees Inc (HQ)	Provider of technology and management consulting services for publishing, media, software technology, and beverage industries.	415-315-9380	NA	San Francisco
N	3K Technologies LLC (HQ)	Provider of IT services to finance, government and high-tech industries.	408-716-5900	NA	Milpitas
	Ablesys Corp (HQ)	Provider of financial trading software and web applications. The company focuses on portfolio and algorithmic trading solutions.	510-265-1883	NA	Newark
	Accelerate Learning & Development Inc (HQ)	Provider of design, live training, and performance support tools such as the influencer app that helps assess working style for managers.	831-291-3770	NA	Scotts Valley
	Accenture (BR)	Provider of management consulting and technology services. The company also offers application outsourcing and IT consulting services.	415-537-5000	NA	San Francisco
	Accounting Micro Systems (HQ)	Developer of accounting and business management software products. The company offers MAS500, MAS90 and MAS200, FAS Asset solutions, and SalesLogix.	415-362-5100	NA	San Francisco
	Acionyx (HQ)	Provider of systems development and engineering consulting services. The company also deals with testing and quality assurance.	408-366-2908	NA	San Jose
	Adaptive Insights (HQ)	Provider of training, consulting, and related support services. The company serves the healthcare, insurance, and manufacturing industries.	650-528-7500	NA	Palo Alto
	Addepar Inc (HQ)	Provider of investment management solutions and technology platform for data aggregation, powerful analytics, and empowering clients to excel.	855-464-6268	NA	Mountain View
N	Adtech IT Solutions (HQ)	Provider of IT solutions and services.	209-541-1111	NA	Ceres
N	Advanced Lease Systems Inc (HQ)	Provider of design, development and other services in IT sector.	530-378-6868	NA	Redding
N	Advanced Systems Group LLC (HQ)	Provider of design, consulting, value added reseller, large scale integration, software development, and much more services.	510-654-8300	NA	Emeryville
	AerospaceComputing Inc (HQ)	Provider of computer technology application services to aerospace sciences. The company also focuses on business development services.	650-988-0388	NA	Mountain View
	Agnitus (HQ)	Developer of touch enabled learning applications for iPad. The company specializes in educational games such as little bo peep and ABC hide n seek.	877-565-1460	NA	Palo Alto
	Air Worldwide Corp (BR)	Provider of software development and consulting services. The company focuses on risk modeling software and risk assessment and management consulting.	415-912-3111	NA	San Francisco
	Algo-Logic Systems (HQ)	Specializes in building networking solutions. The company also offers technological and data handling services to firms.	408-707-3740	NA	San Jose
N	Allstar Microelectronics Inc (HQ)	Distributor of computer storage devices.	949-546-0888	NA	Rancho Santa Margarita
	Amind Solutions LLC (HQ)	Provider of technology and services. The company offers enterprise mobility, quoting and ordering, product configuration, and e-Commerce services.	925-804-6139	NA	Alamo
	Amobee Inc (HQ)	Provider of marketing intelligence and cross channel, cross device advertiser, and publisher solutions for marketers, publishers, and operators.	650-353-4399	NA	Redwood City
	Anki Inc (HQ)	Provider of robotic racing products such as drive and expansion cars, starter, bottleneck and crossroad tracks, and accessories for consumers.	415-670-9488	NA	San Francisco
N	Anotek Inc (HQ)	Developer of software and books to teach the Greek language to English speaking people.	310-450-5027	NA	Santa Monica
	Apogee Software Inc (HQ)	Provider of integrated development environment for Java and C. The company offers industrial monitors and controllers.	408-369-9001	NA	Campbell
	Apple Inc (HQ)	Designer and marketer of consumer electronics. The company also focuses on computer software and personal computers.	408-996-1010	NA	Cupertino
	Applian Technologies Inc (HQ)	Provider of solutions for the capture and conversion of web video, streaming audio, and song and radio program software for Windows users.	415-480-1748	NA	San Anselmo
	Applied Expert Systems Inc (HQ)	Developer of networking solutions for business service management. The company provides virtualization and cloud computing services.	650-617-2400	NA	Palo Alto
	Apptology (HQ)	Provider of mobile application development, training, marketing, iPhone application development, and Android application development services.	877-990-2777	NA	Folsom

COMPANY NAME	PRODUCT / SERVICE	PHONE	EMP	CITY
Aptible Inc (HQ)	Developer of secure, private cloud deployment platform built to automate HIPAA compliance for digital health.	866-296-5003	NA	San Francisco
Aragon Consulting Group Inc (HQ)	Provider of software development services. The company also offers authoring, coding, consulting, and technical support solutions.	415-869-8818	NA	Cupertino
Arasan Chip Systems Inc (RH)	Provider of total IP solutions such as digital IP cores, protocol analyzers, and traffic generators for mobile storage and connectivity applications.	408-433-9633	NA	San Jose
ArcherHall (HQ)	Provider of litigation support services. The company offers forensic data collection, online document review, and e-discovery processing services.	855-839-9084	NA	Sacramento
Arterys Inc (HQ)	Developer of medical imaging cloud platform. The company specializes in diagnostic platform to make healthcare more accurate and data driven.	650-319-7230	NA	San Francisco
Artium Technologies Inc (HQ)	Developer of products for spray diagnostics, particulate monitoring, and cloud research applications.	408-737-2364	NA	Sunnyvale
Augmentum Inc (HQ)	Provider of software development and solution implementation services. The company focuses on Internet applications and product development outsourcing.	650-578-9221	NA	Foster City
Aurionpro Solutions Inc (DH)	Provider of solutions to streamline corporate banking, treasury, fraud prevention, risk management, governance and compliance needs.	925-242-0777	NA	San Ramon
Autonet Mobile Inc (HQ)	Provider of Internet based telematics and applications service platform for the automotive transportation market.	415-223-0316	NA	Santa Rosa
Avid Technology Inc (BR)	Manufacturer of computer automated audio mixing consoles. The company offers audio product registration and software activation services.	800-955-0960	NA	Santa Clara
Aviso Inc (HQ)	Creator of software to change how enterprises make critical revenue decisions and automate sales forecasting process with data science for enterprises.	650-567-5470	NA	Redwood City
Ayasdi Inc (HQ)	Provider of software applications that discovers critical intelligence in company data for right operational decisions quickly.	650-704-3395	NA	Menlo Park
Badger Maps Inc (HQ)	Provider of easy to use interface to manage our daily call routes, track visits, and update records.	415-592-5909	NA	San Francisco
Banks Integration Group (HQ)	Developer and provider of control systems and plant automation software. The company serves biotech, food, brewery, oil and gas, and other sectors.	707-451-1100	NA	Vacaville
Barracuda Networks Inc (HQ)	Developer of solutions for IT problems primarily focusing on security and storage. The company also focuses on application delivery and productivity.	408-342-5400	NA	Campbell
Bcl Technologies (HQ)	Developer of document creation, conversion, and extraction solutions. The company offers BCL easyPDF Cloud, a cloud-based PDF conversion platform.	408-557-2080	NA	San Jose
Berkeley Design Technology Inc (HQ)	Provider of analysis, advice, and engineering solutions for embedded processing technology and applications.	925-954-1411	NA	Walnut Creek
BetterDoctor Inc (HQ)	Provider of mobile apps for iPhone to find primary care, OBGYN, pediatricians, dentist, eye, and all specialties doctors.	844-668-2543	NA	San Francisco
N Birdsall Interactive (HQ)	Provider of website design.	510-385-4714	1-10	Lafayette
Birst Inc (HQ)	Provider of supply chain, marketing, human resources, financial, and sales analytics solutions for businesses.	415-766-4800	NA	San Francisco
BitTorrent Inc (HQ)	Provider of download software solutions. The company offers design, data and content management, and installation services.	415-568-9000	NA	San Francisco
Blackstone Technology Group Inc (HQ)	Provider of IT solutions, commercial, and government consulting, staffing services, and trellis natural gas transaction management web solution.	415-837-1400	NA	San Francisco
Blue Jeans Network Inc (HQ)	Provider of cloud-based video conferencing solutions. The company also offers mobile video collaboration and cloud video bridging solutions.	408-550-2828	NA	San Jose
Blunk Microsystems LLC (HQ)	Provider of turnkey packages for embedded development to customers around the world. The company also offers development tools.	408-323-1758	NA	Sacramento
Border Collie Solutions Inc (HQ)	Provider of security surveillance software products. The company focuses on security panel, energy management, and medical monitoring.	650-343-2400	NA	Burlingame
Bramasol Inc (BR)	Provider of SAP-based solution for high tech software, life science, industrial machinery and components, and Telco, wireless, and Internet services.	408-831-0046	NA	Santa Clara
California Software Systems (HQ)	Provider of graphics software solutions. The company products include DNC file server for windows and graphics software.	831-477-6843	NA	San Juan Bautista
N Carl Group Inc (HQ)	Provider of technical writing services, technical training, web development, web design and much more.	831-708-2610	NA	Aptos
Castle Rock Computing Inc (HQ)	Designer and manufacturer of SNMPC network management software. The company's product caters to a wide range of sectors.	408-366-6540	NA	Saratoga
Celestix Networks Inc (HQ)	Provider of security appliances and solutions for healthcare, legal and financial, education, commercial, small business, and public sector industries.	510-668-0700	NA	Fremont
Centric Software Inc (HQ)	Provider of product lifecycle management solution to apparel, consumer goods, luxury good, and footwear industries.	408-574-7802	NA	Campbell

COMPANY NAME	PRODUCT / SERVICE	PHONE	EMP	CITY
Centrify (HQ)	Provider of identity and access management solutions. The company offers services to pharma companies and financial institutions.	669-444-5200	NA	Santa Clara
N Ceridian Corp (BR)	Firm is a provider of human capital management solutions.	714-963-1311	NA	Fountain Valley
Certent Inc (HQ)	Provider of equity compensation management, equity compensation reporting, and disclosure management solutions.	925-730-4300	NA	Roseville
N Chander Software Solutions Inc (HQ)	Provider of marketing, call center, project management and technical support software and technical staffing augmentation solutions.	408-406-5624	NA	San Jose
Check Point Software Technologies Inc (HQ)	Developer of software technology solutions such as mobile security and next generation firewalls for retail/point of sale and financial services.	800-429-4391	NA	San Carlos
Chelsio Communications (HQ)	Provider of Ethernet adapters. The company offers storage routers, wire adapters, virtualization and management software, and accessories.	408-962-3600	NA	Sunnyvale
Chesapeake Technology Inc (HQ)	Provider of sonar mapping software as well as consulting services to the marine, geophysical, and geological survey industries.	650-967-2045	NA	Los Altos
Chess com (HQ)	Provider of unlimited chess games and free tournaments that can be played by challenging friends and meet new players.	800-318-2827	NA	Palo Alto
Chiapas Edi Technologies Inc (HQ)	Developer of electronic data interchange software for health insurance exchange brokers, MSOs, HMOs, and healthcare business data analytics services.	415-298-8166	NA	Davis
Chrometa LLC (HQ)	Provider of time keeping management software and services. The company offers products for PC, Mac, iPhone, and Android platforms.	916-546-9974	NA	Sacramento
Circle Internet Services Inc (HQ)	Provider of continuous integration and delivery solution. The company offers apps for docker, enterprise, and mobiles.	800-585-7075	NA	San Francisco
Cirius Group Inc (HQ)	Designer and marketer of financial and medical software. The company serves hospitals and healthcare providers.	925-685-9300	NA	Pleasant Hill
Citrix Systems Inc (BR)	Provider of transition to software-defining the workplace, uniting virtualization, mobility management, networking, and SaaS solutions.	408-790-8000	NA	Santa Clara
Claresco Inc (HQ)	Provider of design and implementation services for customized business software. The company serves multi-national firms.	510-528-0238	NA	Berkeley
Clean Power Research (HQ)	Provider of program automation, customer engagement, and solar data and intelligence solutions. The company offers services to the solar industry.	707-258-2765	NA	Napa
Codeobjects Inc (HQ)	Developer of insurance process management and business intelligence solutions. The company also offers claims management services.	408-432-1180	NA	Milpitas
Colabo Inc (HQ)	Provider of multi-functional software that enables professionals across all industries to achieve a number of business objectives.	650-288-6649	NA	San Carlos
Computers & Structures Inc (HQ)	Provider of integrated design, analysis, assessment, drafting of building systems, and related support services.	510-649-2200	NA	Walnut Creek
Conformiq (HQ)	Provider of automated test designing services. The company focuses on training, project implementation, change management, and executive consulting.	408-898-2140	NA	Saratoga
Corman Technologies Inc (HQ)	Provider of software development and consulting services for a variety of clients in the software industry.	707-575-7800	NA	Santa Rosa
Corona Labs Inc (HQ)	Developer of games, e-books, and other interactive content. The company offers services to the educational sector.	415-996-6877	NA	San Francisco
N Cpp Inc (HQ)	Publisher of books on psychology and distributes publications of Jossey-Bass, Harper and Row, and B and D book and reaches market through direct mail, trade sales, and distributors.	650-969-8901	NA	Sunnyvale
Crestpoint Solutions Inc (HQ)	Provider of project planning, programming, web hosting, and wireless and records management services.	925-828-6005	NA	Pleasanton
Crmantra Inc (HQ)	Developer of software for customer relationship management needs. The company also focuses on business intelligence and analysis.	415-839-9672	NA	Emeryville
CyberGlove Systems LLC (HQ)	Provider of data glove technology. The company offers system installation and integration and custom software and hardware services.	408-943-8114	NA	San Jose
Cygna Energy Services Inc (HQ)	Provider of application development, data integration, systems integration, consulting, and web services.	925-930-8377	NA	Walnut Creek
Data ID Systems (HQ)	Provider of identification management solutions. The company offers passport readers, barcode scanners, and fixed asset tracking products.	408-371-5764	NA	Campbell
Data Tech (HQ)	Developer of specialized accounting software. The company primarily caters to the agricultural industry.	800-833-8824	NA	Fresno
DataGlance Inc (HQ)	Provider of data management software that support LIVE data conversion/migration, electronic document generation and processing, and web services.	510-656-0500	NA	Fremont
DCM Infotech Limited (RH)	Provider of managed IT services. The company focuses on system administration, storage, enterprise management, and staffing services.	510-494-2321	NA	Fremont
Denodo Technologies Inc (HQ)	Provider of enterprise data virtualization, data federation, and cloud data integration middleware solutions.	650-566-8833	NA	Palo Alto
DevonWay (HQ)	Provider of enterprise software solutions for utilities and process industries. The company specializes in enterprise asset management solutions.	415-904-4000	NA	San Francisco

COMPANY NAME	PRODUCT / SERVICE	PHONE	EMP	CITY
Digital Keystone Inc (HQ)	Provider of solutions enabling content distribution to tablets, connected TVs, and other entertainment platforms with suite of software and tools.	650-938-7300	NA	Cupertino
Dogpatch Technology Inc (HQ)	Provider of digital strategy and mobile development solutions for game design and research, global media and communications, and grant writing projects.	415-663-6488	NA	San Francisco
Domico Software (HQ)	Supplier of management and accounting software for managing self storage units, tenants, and accounts.	510-841-4155	NA	Walnut Creek
N Douloi Automation Inc (HQ)	Developer of prepackaged motion control software.	408-735-6942	NA	Santa Clara
DreamFactory Software Inc (HQ)	Provider of software development services. The company offers hosting, external integration, SQL, and user management services.	415-993-5877	NA	Campbell
DSP Concepts Inc (HQ)	Provider of embedded audio processing tools and services. The company offers system design, embedded software development, and optimization services.	408-747-5200	NA	Santa Clara
N Eastridge Workforce Solutions (HQ)	Provider of workforce management, workforce recruitment, workforce technology and staffing solutions.	800-778-0197	201-500	San Diego
Elementum (HQ)	Provider of apps to manage your global supply chain. The company offers manufacturing operations, mission control, supplier, and logistics management.	650-318-1491	NA	San Mateo
Ellie Mae Inc (HQ)	Focuses on mortgage compliance services. The company offers services to banks and other financial institutions.	925-227-7000	NA	Pleasanton
Enea Openwave Inc (DH)	Provider of mobile media optimization solutions. The company is engaged in the mediation of encrypted traffic streams.	650-480-7200	NA	Redwood City
energyOrbit Inc (HQ)	Provider of cloud based platform and solution for streamline demand side management programs, projects, and relationship management for customers.	866-628-8744	NA	San Francisco
Envestnet (BR)	Provider of application software for financial service firms. The company is involved in practice and portfolio management.	866-924-8912	NA	San Jose
N Eritech International (HQ)	Wholesaler of computer hardware, digital cameras and TVs.	818-244-6242	NA	Glendale
Errigal Inc (HQ)	Designer and developer of software products and services. The company also deals with configuration management and ticketing.	415-523-9245	NA	San Francisco
Evernote Corp (HQ)	Provider of note management and digital link services. The company also offers handwriting recognition services.	650-257-0885	NA	Redwood City
Evolphin Software Inc (HQ)	Provider of digital and media asset management software for video production, game developers, media, television broadcasters, and eLearning groups.	888-386-4114	NA	San Ramon
Evolveware Inc (HQ)	Developer of products to automate and modernize IT infrastructure focusing on assessment, documentation, impact analysis, and other solutions.	408-748-8301	NA	Santa Clara
Exadel Inc (HQ)	Provider of software using technologies including mobile, cloud, and web user interfaces. The company also delivers tools and products for users.	925-363-9510	NA	Walnut Creek
Extractable Inc (HQ)	Provider of websites, applications, social and mobile experiences for transactional, educational, lead generation, and entertainment purposes.	415-426-3600	NA	San Francisco
N FABNexus Inc (HQ)	Provider of application-specific machine control and SEMI-standards conformant network automation software to the semiconductor manufacturing and support industry.	650-207-8235	NA	Los Altos
Facebook Inc (HQ)	Designer and developer of technologies to communicate with their family, friends, and also coworkers.	650-543-4800	NA	Menlo Park
Fiduciary Management Technologies Inc (HQ)	Provider of insolvency case, fiduciary case, and estate management solutions. The company offers SEC distribution fund administration services.	916-930-9900	NA	Sacramento
Five9 Inc (HQ)	Seller of call center software focusing on IVR System, an interactive voice response software, Outbound Call Center software, and Auto Dialer.	925-201-2000	NA	San Ramon
N Formula Consultants Inc (HQ)	Provider of software development and consulting services.	714-778-0123	NA	Anaheim
Foxit Corp (HQ)	Developer of software. The company offers software such as Foxit Reader, Enterprise, and Mobile Reader.	510-438-9090	NA	Fremont
Future Facilities Inc (BR)	Developer of engineering simulation software for the design and operation of electronics products. The company serves the industrial sector.	408-436-7701	NA	San Jose
Futuredial Inc (HQ)	Developer of carrier-grade solutions and tools for mobile device recyclers, wireless operators, and mobile device manufacturers.	408-245-8880	NA	Sunnyvale
G4s Secure Solutions (USA) Inc (BR)	Provider of security management solutions such as compliance and investigations, disaster and emergency, and fraud abatement.	408-453-4133	NA	San Jose
Game Your Game Inc (HQ)	Developer of digital tracking system such as automatic shot tracking and hands-free game tracking device to get the insights to improve the game.	888-245-3433	NA	San Francisco
Gatan Inc (HQ)	Manufacturer of instrumentation and software used to enhance and extend the operation and performance of electron microscopes.	925-463-0200	NA	Pleasanton
Genmark Automation Inc (HQ)	Provider of robotics for automated manufacturing applications. The company offers services to the data storage and related industries.	510-897-3400	NA	Fremont

COMPANY NAME	PRODUCT / SERVICE	PHONE	EMP	CITY
GestureTek Inc (HQ)	Provider of gesture-based user interfaces for mobile devices. The company offer services to the gaming and entertainment industries.	408-506-2206	NA	Santa Clara
Gigya Inc (HQ)	Provider of widget distribution, content sharing, and advertising platform. The company caters to the needs of social web.	650-353-7230	NA	Mountain View
Glassbeam Inc (HQ)	Provider of support solutions and it serves the medical, storage, and wireless networking industries.	408-740-4600	NA	Santa Clara
Global Cybersoft Inc (HQ)	Provider of software development and IT outsourcing services, such as systems integration and maintenance.	424-247-1226	NA	Pleasanton
Googleplex (HQ)	Provider of search engine to make world's information universally accessible. The company specializes in Internet-related services and products.	650-253-0000	NA	Mountain View
N Great Circle Associates Inc (HQ)	Provider of enterprise information technology infrastructure and networking services.	415-861-3588	NA	Alameda
Harmon.ie (HQ)	Provider of SharePoint applications for Outlook, mobile, and desktop platforms. The company offers records and knowledge management services.	408-907-1339	NA	Milpitas
Heirloom Computing Inc (HQ)	Focuses on the transformation of enterprise applications. The company offers services to the industrial sector.	510-573-3579	NA	Alamo
Highwired Inc (HQ)	Developer of multimedia and supporting products and services. The company focuses on branding, billing, and delivery solutions.	516-785-6197	NA	Redwood Valley
Hilti Inc (BR)	Developer and manufacturer of construction equipment. The company's services include trainings, engineering, administration, and tools.	800-879-8000	NA	San Francisco
HSQ Technology (HQ)	Provider of control system and energy management services, specializing in data and SCADA monitoring.	510-259-1334	NA	Hayward
HyTrust Inc (HQ)	Provider of security, compliance, and control software for virtualization of information technology infrastructure.	650-681-8100	NA	Mountain View
IAR Systems Software Inc (RH)	Provider of software tools and embedded systems. The company's products include state machine tools, starter kits, and compiler and debugger tool suite.	650-287-4250	NA	Foster City
IdeaBlade (HQ)	Provider of database application services. The company's products include DevForce, Coctail, and Breeze.	510-596-5100	NA	Orinda
Iksanika LLC (HQ)	Provider of custom software development, testing, quality assurance, porting, and re-engineering services.	408-490-0777	NA	San Jose
Imagine That Inc (HQ)	Developer of simulation software. The company offers services to the retail, healthcare, insurance, and financial services industries.	408-365-0305	NA	San Jose
Imperva Inc (HQ)	Provider of application and data security solutions. The company's products include database firewalls, management server, and monitoring software.	650-345-9000	NA	Redwood Shores
Infinera Corp (HQ)	Provider of services and solutions in optical networks. The company serves cable operators and Internet content providers.	408-572-5200	NA	Sunnyvale
N Infoflex Inc (HQ)	Developer of accounting and 4GL software.	650-270-1019	NA	Burlingame
Infostretch Corp (HQ)	Provider of mobile application development, quality assurance testing and automation, SaaS solutions, and ERP testing solutions.	408-727-1100	NA	Santa Clara
Innovative Interfaces Inc (HQ)	Provider of technology solutions and services. The company deals with training and hosting, and technical support.	510-655-6200	NA	Emeryville
Instart Logic Inc (HQ)	Provider of software-defined application delivery solutions. The company offers services to the travel and hospitality industries.	650-919-8856	NA	Palo Alto
Intapp Inc (HQ)	Provider of software and services for risk management, time management, and box management. The company's products include Intapp Time and Wall Builder.	650-852-0400	NA	Palo Alto
Integral Development Corp (HQ)	Provider of customer-branded trading solutions for brokers, dealers, banks, and fund investment managers.	650-424-4500	NA	Palo Alto
Intellicon Solutions (HQ)	Provider of intelligent consulting solutions for learning and development, performance management systems, and related social media communication.	925-377-7925	NA	Moraga
N Intelligent Computer Solutions Inc (HQ)	Manufacturer and marketer of hard drive formatting and software pre-loading systems.	818-998-5805	NA	Chatsworth
N International Electronic Enterprises Inc (HQ)	Distributor of computer spare parts, complete systems and peripheral devices including drives, controllers, SAN units and more and provider of digital storage solutions.	949-673-2943	NA	Newport Beach
Ipdialog Inc (HQ)	Developer of hardware and software technology. The company creates SIP stack, user interface, and media stream handling for phones.	408-830-0800	NA	Sunnyvale
Isomorphic Software (HQ)	Focuses on building web applications. The company is engaged in training, consulting, and technical support services.	415-222-9902	NA	San Francisco
Itrenew Inc (HQ)	Provider of information technology services. The company focuses on data eradication, server application, logistics management, and configuration.	408-744-9600	NA	Newark
IXL Learning (HQ)	Specializes in online maths practice and related lessons. The company serves educational institutions.	650-372-4040	NA	San Mateo

	COMPANY NAME	PRODUCT / SERVICE	PHONE	EMP	CITY
	Jeda Technologies Inc (HQ)	Provider of chip based digital designs and semiconductor services. The company focuses on validation and automation solutions.	408-912-1856	NA	Santa Clara
	Jitterbit Inc (HQ)	Focuses on application integration solutions for aerospace and defense, life sciences, pharmaceuticals, and financial services.	877-852-3500	NA	Alameda
	Jiva Creative LLC (HQ)	Provider of interactive design technology solutions. The company focuses on architecture, website hosting, and enterprise application development.	510-864-8625	NA	Alameda
	Jova Solutions Inc (HQ)	Developer of systems for distributed process control and data management for science and industrial sectors. The company offers USB instruments.	415-816-4482	NA	San Francisco
N	JRH GoldenState Software Inc (HQ)	Developer and provider of software tools and solutions that supports complete DB2 catalog query and object management.	310-544-1497	NA	Rancho Palos Verdes
	Junar Inc (HQ)	Provider of cloud-based open data platform. The company offers collaboration services to business organizations.	844-695-8627	NA	San Jose
	Key Performance Ideas Inc (BR)	Provider of enterprise performance management and business intelligence solutions. The company offers Oracle Hyperion and OBIEE software for this need.	855-457-4462	NA	San Francisco
	Kiefer Consulting Inc (HQ)	Provider of mobile application software services. The company also offers SharePoint, Microsoft Dynamics, and Microsoft.Net application services.	916-932-7220	NA	Folsom
	Larson Automation Inc (HQ)	Developer of automated test solutions for telecommunication companies. The company offers board test stations and level shifters.	408-432-4800	NA	San Jose
	Lattice Engines Inc (HQ)	Provider of business to business sales intelligence software. The company is engaged in web design and hosting and programming solutions.	877-460-0010	NA	San Mateo
	Lavante Inc (HQ)	Provider of on-demand strategic profit recovery solutions. The company also offers vendor information management software.	408-754-1410	NA	San Jose
	Ledger Systems Inc (HQ)	Provider of network design and support services. The company also offers accounting and e-Commerce solutions.	650-592-6211	NA	San Carlos
	LibraryWorld (HQ)	Provider of library automation software solutions. The company serves schools, healthcare, law firms, museum, and architectural firms.	800-852-2777	NA	San Jose
	Lighthouse Worldwide Solutions (HQ)	Provider of dental supplies such as implants, dentures, partials, implant bars, and related accessories.	510-438-0500	NA	Fremont
N	Lite-On Trading USA Inc (HQ)	Manufacturer and distributor of power conversion equipment, chassis, systems, keyboards and much more.	408-940-4873	NA	Milpitas
N	Livescribe Inc (HQ)	Provider and developer of mobile computing platform.	510-777-0071	51-200	Oakland
	Livevol Inc (BR)	Designer and developer of customized data solutions. The company's services include consulting and technical support.	312-786-7400	NA	San Francisco
	Lynch Marks LLC (HQ)	Provider of software development and technology solutions focused on shipping applications. The company focuses on consulting and package tracking.	510-559-7200	NA	Berkeley
N	Lynx Media Inc (HQ)	Developer of inventory control and order entry software.	800-451-5969	NA	Valley Village
	Lynx Software Technologies (HQ)	Developer of software technologies. The company offers development tools, real-time monitoring systems, and secure virtualization products.	408-979-3900	NA	San Jose
	Magnet Systems Inc (HQ)	Provider of mobile apps with software, infrastructure and tools to build enterprise-grade mobile apps. The company serves enterprises.	650-329-5904	NA	Palo Alto
	Marketo Inc (HQ)	Provider of marketing automation software services. The company offers email and social marketing, marketing software, and digital marketing services.	650-581-8001	NA	San Mateo
	Matisse Software Inc (HQ)	Provider of database software and services. The company is also engaged in training, consulting, and technical support.	252-227-7013	NA	Mountain View
	Media Net Link Inc (HQ)	Provider of web business solutions. The company focuses on application development, systems integration, website design, and project management.	866-563-5152	NA	Oakland
	Meta Integration Technology Inc (HQ)	Provider of metadata components to data modeling, data integration, business intelligence, and metadata management tool vendors.	650-273-6382	NA	Mountain View
	MetaCert (HQ)	Provider of security API for mobile app developers. The company offers content-based filtering services.	415-529-2571	NA	San Francisco
	Mobileiron Inc (HQ)	Provider of mobile security, device, and application management solutions. The company focuses on technical support services.	650-919-8100	NA	Mountain View
	Mphasis Corp (BR)	Provider of applications, infrastructure, and business process outsourcing services to the banking and healthcare sectors.	408-327-1240	NA	San Jose
	Netpace Inc (HQ)	Provider of consulting, cloud computing, database management, and proprietary development services.	925-543-7760	NA	San Ramon
	Netscout (BR)	Developer of service assurance and applications, service delivery management, network performance management software, and hardware solutions.	408-571-5000	NA	San Jose
	New Generation Software Inc (HQ)	Supplier of packaged data mart models with analytical presentations and reports for wholesale distribution, healthcare, and financial reporting.	916-920-2200	NA	Sacramento
N	New:Team SoftWare Inc (HQ)	Developer of software solutions.	415-461-8086	NA	Sacramento

COMPANY NAME	PRODUCT / SERVICE	PHONE	EMP	CITY
Newport-West Data Services Inc (HQ)	Designer and developer of minicomputer based business applications. The company specializes in installation.	925-855-1131	NA	San Ramon
Nextaxiom Technology Inc (HQ)	Provider of testing, certification, and other professional services. The company offers work management and scheduling solutions.	415-373-1890	NA	San Francisco
Nextbus Inc (BR)	Provider of transit management solutions. The company also provides real-time passenger information solutions to organizations.	925-686-8200	NA	Concord
NextInput Inc (HQ)	Provider of MEMS-based force sensing solutions for touch enabled devices in markers such as wearable, automotive, industrial, and medical applications.	650-963-9310	NA	Mountain View
NextLabs Inc (HQ)	Developer of software products. The company offers information risk management software products for enterprises.	650-577-9101	NA	San Mateo
Nobix Inc (HQ)	Provider IT management products for job scheduling, problem alerting, and notification as well as provides software engineering services.	925-659-3500	NA	San Ramon
Nomis Solutions Inc (HQ)	Provider of pricing and profitability management solutions. The company caters to the financial services.	650-588-9800	NA	Brisbane
Nova Measuring Instruments Inc (BR)	Provider of metrology solutions for semiconductor manufacturing industries. The company offers integrated and stand-alone metrology platforms.	408-510-7400	NA	Fremont
Nutanix Inc (HQ)	Focuses on the simplification of datacenter infrastructure by integrating server and storage resources into a turnkey hyper converged platform.	855-688-2649	NA	San Jose
Okta Inc (HQ)	Provider of identity and automated user management, administration, reporting, and application integration solutions.	800-219-0964	NA	San Francisco
Opal Soft Inc (HQ)	Provider of communications equipment installation and networking. The company's services include application development, network management, and maintenance.	408-267-2211	NA	Sunnyvale
Openclovis (HQ)	Provider of system infrastructure software platform. The company mainly serves the communication industry.	707-981-7120	NA	Petaluma
Oracle Corp (BR)	Developer of hardware and software systems. The company provides Oracle database, engineered systems, and enterprise manager solutions.	415-402-7200	NA	San Francisco
Orbeon Inc (HQ)	Provider of web form deployment services. The company offers basic, gold, and platinum development support, and validation services.	650-762-8184	NA	San Mateo
Organic Inc (HQ)	Provider of information technology services. The company develops websites, mobile applications, banner, and digital signage.	415-581-5300	NA	San Francisco
Originate Inc (DH)	Developer of software to integrate, network, and economically operate energy storage systems. The company is engaged in analysis services.	800-352-2292	NA	San Francisco
N Otter Computer Inc (HQ)	Designer and provider of PCB layout and assembly Services.	408-982-9358	1-10	Santa Clara
Pariveda Solutions Inc (BR)	Provider of IT consulting services and technology solutions such as custom application development, portals and enterprise content management.	844-325-2729	NA	San Francisco
PDF Solutions Inc (HQ)	Provider of yield improvement technologies and services for the integrated circuit manufacturing process.	408-280-7900	NA	Santa Clara
N Personal Data Systems Inc (HQ)	Provider of hardware and software development.	408-866-1126	NA	Campbell
Pivot Systems Inc (HQ)	Provider of software development services and related solutions for small, large and mid-size companies.	408-435-1000	NA	San Jose
PlanGrid (HQ)	Developer of construction apps which automatically syncs notes, markups, and photos to all the users' devices.	800-646-0796	NA	San Francisco
Polycom Inc (HQ)	Manufacturer and seller of teleconferencing equipment and provider of all other communications solutions.	408-586-3837	NA	San Jose
PosIQ Inc (HQ)	Provider of customer relationship management and data solutions. The company offers services to the hospitality sector.	408-676-7470	NA	San Jose
Powertest Inc (HQ)	Provider of software-related professional services. The company is also involved in load testing and application performance management.	415-778-0580	NA	S San Francisco
Presentek Inc (HQ)	Designer of websites and web portals. The company also offers content management systems and e-commerce handlers.	408-354-1264	NA	Los Gatos
Prezi Inc (HQ)	Provider of collaboration solutions. The company offers strategy and technical consulting services.	844-551-6941	NA	San Francisco
N Pronto Networks (HQ)	Provider of Wi-Fi operation support system solutions for enterprises, wireless ISPs, WiMAX and satellite networks.	925-860-6200	51-200	Walnut Creek
Prosoft Engineering Inc (HQ)	Developer of data recovery software. The company provides Drive Genius, Data Rescue, and Data Backup software.	877-477-6763	NA	Livermore
Proxim Diagnostics Corp (HQ)	Manufacturer of diagnostics products and related supplies. The company deals with testing and research related services.	408-391-6090	NA	Mountain View
Qantel Technologies (HQ)	Manufacturer of software systems. The company provides network connectivity and business software solutions.	510-731-2080	NA	Hayward
Qarbon Inc (HQ)	Publisher of presentation software and the originator of patented Viewlet technology. The company serves business, government, and education markers.	408-430-5560	NA	San Jose

COMPANY NAME	PRODUCT / SERVICE	PHONE	EMP	CITY
Qubop Inc (HQ)	Developer of applications and games for mobile platforms. The company specializes in web applications, localization, IOS, and android development.	415-891-7788	NA	San Francisco
Quest America Inc (HQ)	Provider of information technology services. The company offers solutions through strategy, consulting, and outsourcing.	408-492-1650	NA	San Jose
Quicklogic Corp (HQ)	Provider of trading solutions for stock market investors. The company offers online trading platforms for mobiles, smartphones, and tablets.	408-990-4000	NA	San Jose
Quiq Labs (HQ)	Developer of tools and solutions. The company focuses on influencing consumer behavior and engagement.	559-745-5511	NA	Fresno
Quisk Inc (HQ)	Specializes in the development of payment solutions. The company offers services to financial institutions.	408-462-6800	NA	Sunnyvale
Quizlet Inc (BR)	Provider of learning tools for students and teachers. The company offers services to the educational sector.	510-495-6550	NA	San Francisco
Quorum Technologies (HQ)	Developer of recycling and waste disposal solutions for the automotive, industrial, municipal, hospitality, and food industries.	916-669-5577	NA	Sacramento
R Systems Inc (RH)	Provider of information technology services and solutions. The company offers application, testing, BPO, and packaged services.	916-939-9696	NA	El Dorado Hills
REAL Software Systems LLC (HQ)	Developer of software solutions for the management of royalty, rights and revenue sharing contracts.	818-313-8000	NA	Woodland Hills
Retail Pro International (HQ)	Provider of software solutions. The company's services include automated retail planning and content strategy.	916-605-7200	NA	Folsom
Rightware Inc (BR)	Provider of user interface technologies serving the mobile, automotive, and other embedded industries.	832-483-7093	NA	Palo Alto
Rockliffe Systems Inc (HQ)	Provider of mobile communication software for service providers, enterprises, and consumers. The company offers design services.	408-879-5600	NA	Campbell
Rollbar Inc (HQ)	Developer of error tracking software. The company is also engaged in coding and troubleshooting services.	888-568-3350	NA	San Francisco
Runtime Design Automation (HQ)	Provider of management system software for the IC design industry. The company is engaged in documentation and technical support.	408-492-0940	NA	Santa Clara
Sancrosoft USA Inc (RH)	Provider of technology consulting, IT staffing, and recruiting services. The company offers systems integration and application development services.	916-671-5593	NA	Fair Oaks
SAP America Inc (BR)	Developer of software applications. The company provides data and technology, custom development, and implementation services.	650-849-4000	NA	Palo Alto
Searchforce (HQ)	Developer of automation software. The company offers software for automation, optimization, campaign management, and tracking.	650-235-8800	NA	San Mateo
Sherrill-Lubinski Corp (HQ)	Provider of monitoring and analytics solutions for middleware-powered applications. The company serves the electrical commodity market.	415-927-8400	NA	Riverside
Simco Electronics (HQ)	Providers of services and software to medical device manufacturers. The company specializes in biotechnology.	408-734-9750	NA	Santa Clara
Simplion Technologies (HQ)	Provider of consulting solutions. The company offers strategy development, implementation, deployment, and technical support services.	408-935-8686	NA	Milpitas
SMC Ltd (BR)	Provider of custom packing for product sterilization. The company is engaged in supply chain management solutions.	707-303-3000	NA	Santa Rosa
Solution Architects Inc (HQ)	Provider of sophisticated IT solutions for complex systems. The company's services include analysis and product development.	415-775-1656	NA	San Francisco
Sonasoft Corp (HQ)	Provider of software based solutions to simplify and automate replication, archiving, backup, recovery, and data protection operations.	408-708-4000	NA	San Jose
Speedinfo (HQ)	Developer of traffic measurement solutions for broadcast media, government planning, and mobile applications.	408-446-7660	NA	San Jose
Spirent Communications Inc (LH)	Provider of performance analysis technology services. The company also offers network equipment and data center solutions.	408-752-7100	NA	San Jose
Splunk Inc (HQ)	Provider of search engine services specializing in IT data. The company serves the government, healthcare, and telecommunication industries.	415-848-8400	NA	San Francisco
SRI International (RH)	Provider of consulting, research, and development services. The company offers services to the defense, security, and energy sectors.	650-859-2000	NA	Menlo Park
Stevens Creek Software (HQ)	Provider of software solutions for the palm computing platform. The company is involved in custom development and technical support.	408-725-0424	NA	Cupertino
Stratedigm Inc (HQ)	Manufacturer of software products, consumables, and related accessories. The company deals with upgrades and installation.	408-512-3901	NA	San Jose
Structural Integrity Associates Inc (HQ)	Provider of solutions for prevention and control of structural and mechanical failures and serves nuclear plants, oil and gas, and other sectors.	408-978-8200	NA	San Jose
Synapsense Corp (HQ)	Provider of wireless monitoring and cooling control solutions. The company also deals with data center infrastructure management.	916-294-0110	NA	Folsom
Synergex International Corp (HQ)	Provider of business application optimization solutions. The company serves the transportation, retail, and manufacturing sectors.	916-635-7300	NA	Gold River

N

	COMPANY NAME	PRODUCT / SERVICE	PHONE	EMP	CITY
	Synopsys Corporate (HQ)	Developer of synthesis technology solutions. The company is also involved in design flow deployment, physical design assistance, and related services.	650-584-5000	NA	Mountain View
	Tapjoy Inc (HQ)	Provider of advertising and targeting solutions. The company also deals with developer services such as consulting and real-time reporting.	415-766-6905	NA	San Francisco
	TechExcel Inc (HQ)	Provider of customer relationship management software applications. The company is involved in game development and hybrid agile management solutions.	925-871-3900	NA	Burlingame
	Teleresults Corp (HQ)	Provider of electronic medical record solutions and transplant software. The company's services include data conversion, interfaces, and training.	415-392-9670	NA	San Francisco
	Tenefit Corp (HQ)	Provider of software services. The company's IoT gateway is used by mobile users, marketplaces, and machines to connect and communicate in real-time.	877-522-9464	NA	San Jose
	TFD Group (BR)	Developer of analytical methods and software tools. The company caters to aerospace and defense sectors.	831-649-3800	NA	Monterey
	Thought Inc (HQ)	Provider of data management solutions. The company uses dynamic mapping and related software for this purpose.	415-836-9199	NA	San Francisco
	Three Palm Software (HQ)	Designer and developer of software products for medical imaging and information. The company also deals with data processing services.	408-356-3240	NA	Carmel
N	Tiger Software (HQ)	Developer of investment software.	858-273-5900	11-50	San Diego
	Trackdata Systems Corp (HQ)	Provider of greyhound, thoroughbred, and harness racing information. The company features up-to-date listing of racing schedules.	408-446-5595	NA	Cupertino
	Transend Corp (HQ)	Provider of email migration and conversion solutions that support email systems. The company serves business, education, reselling, and other sectors.	650-324-5370	NA	Palo Alto
	Turbo-Doc Medical Record Systems Inc (HQ)	Provider of electronic medical record systems. The company offers walkout statements, drug information handouts, and medication rewrites.	530-877-8650	NA	Paradise
	Untangle (HQ)	Designer and developer of network management software. The company specializes in firewall and Internet management application.	408-598-4299	NA	San Jose
	V-Soft Inc (HQ)	Provider of product development services. The company also specializes in mobile application development.	408-342-1700	NA	San Jose
N	Valley Agricultural Software Inc (HQ)	Developer of software for the dairy industry.	559-686-9496	NA	Tulare
	ValueLabs Inc (BR)	Provider of technology solutions and services. The company's services include digital solutions, quality assurance, and application development.	408-475-2445	NA	Sunnyvale
	Vayusphere Inc (HQ)	Developer of instant messaging applications. The company's customers include Morgan Stanley, Deutsche Bank, and others.	650-960-2900	NA	Mountain View
N	Vektrex Electronic Systems Inc (HQ)	Provider of custom computer programming services.	858-558-8282	NA	San Diego
N	Ventricle Software Systems Inc (HQ)	Provider of software development for the healthcare industry.	310-948-2551	NA	Rancho Palos Verdes
	Vertical Systems Inc (HQ)	Provider of centric solutions for the hospitality industry. The company is also engaged in mobile application and custom solutions.	408-752-8100	NA	Santa Clara
	Viscira LLC (HQ)	Manufacturer of software products. The company deals with the development of animation technology solutions.	415-848-8010	NA	San Francisco
	Vivotek USA (BR)	Provider of surveillance solutions. The company specializes in manufacturing network cameras for the network video surveillance industries.	408-773-8686	NA	San Jose
	VMware Inc (HQ)	Provider of storage, data center, application virtualization, and enterprise mobility management products.	650-427-1000	NA	Palo Alto
	Weatherflow Inc (HQ)	Provider of modeling and forecasting technologies for the weather forecast industry. The company also offers wind-based and coastal forecasting.	800-946-3225	NA	Scotts Valley
	Workday Inc (HQ)	Provider of software solutions for human resources management and financial management. The company specializes in SaaS based enterprise solutions.	925-951-9000	NA	Pleasanton
	Xactly Corp (HQ)	Provider of web-based sales compensation applications. The company offers services to business organizations and enterprises.	408-977-3132	NA	San Jose
	XC2 Software LLC (HQ)	Provider of integrated software suite. The company's products find application in water and wastewater utilities.	800-761-4999	NA	Fairfax
N	Xifin Inc (HQ)	Provider of health care related information technology services.	858-793-5700	201-500	San Diego
	Xtime Inc (HQ)	Provider of CRM solutions for automotive service operations. The company offers scheduling and marketing solutions for automotive retailers.	888-463-3888	NA	Redwood City
N	Yellow Magic Inc (HQ)	Developer of software for the directory publishing industry.	951-506-4005	NA	Murrieta
	Zendesk Inc (HQ)	Designer and developer of cloud-based customer service software. The company deals with reporting and analytics solutions.	415-418-7506	NA	San Francisco
	ZL Technologies Inc (HQ)	Provider of electronic content archiving software solutions such as consulting and installation, product customization, and software upgrades.	408-240-8989	NA	Milpitas

	COMPANY NAME	PRODUCT / SERVICE	PHONE	EMP	CITY
	Zone24x7 Inc (HQ)	Provider of technology innovation, business consultation, software development, hardware design, and system integration services.	408-922-9887	NA	San Jose

323 = Custom Software Development

	COMPANY NAME	PRODUCT / SERVICE	PHONE	EMP	CITY
	4D Inc (DH)	Developer of web and Internet applications. The company serves universities, corporations, governments, and individuals.	408-557-4600	NA	San Jose
	A10 Networks Inc (HQ)	Provider of networking and security solutions such as cloud computing and virtualization and bandwidth management.	408-325-8668	NA	San Jose
	ABBYY USA (HQ)	Provider of optical character recognition solutions. The company offers scanners, screenshot readers, document converters, and linguistic solutions.	408-457-9777	NA	Milpitas
N	Abtech Technologies (HQ)	Provider of IT consulting and enterprise-wide solutions specializing in Hewlett-Packard, IBM, Sun Microsystems, and storage hardware and services. Professional services include: On-site support services, technical consulting, hardware and software rentals and leasing, asset recovery and disposal services.	760-827-5100	NA	Carlsbad
	Accela Inc (HQ)	Provider of licensing, asset and land management, and public health and safety solutions. The company offers technical support services.	925-659-3200	NA	San Ramon
	Accenture (BR)	Provider of management consulting and technology services. The company also offers application outsourcing and IT consulting services.	415-537-5000	NA	San Francisco
	Access Business Technologies (HQ)	Provider of cloud-based software and hosting solutions for government agencies, banks, credit unions, accounting firms, and servicing companies.	888-636-5426	NA	Folsom
	Access Softek Inc (HQ)	Developer of mobile banking software solutions. The company focuses on software and product development, QA testing, user interface, and graphic design.	510-848-0606	NA	Berkeley
	Acrylic Art (HQ)	Provider of fabrication and machining services. The company focuses on painting, product finishing, anodizing, and vapor polishing.	510-654-0953	NA	Emeryville
	Ad Art Inc (HQ)	Provider of digital signage solutions. The company also offers graphic designs, animation, commercial lighting, and maintenance services.	800-675-6353	NA	San Francisco
	Addepar Inc (HQ)	Provider of investment management solutions and technology platform for data aggregation, powerful analytics, and empowering clients to excel.	855-464-6268	NA	Mountain View
N	Advanced Lease Systems Inc (HQ)	Provider of design, development and other services in IT sector.	530-378-6868	NA	Redding
	Advantech Inc (DH)	Provider of system integration, hardware, software, embedded systems, automation products, and logistics support.	408-519-3898	NA	Milpitas
	Advisor Software Inc (HQ)	Provider of planning, proposal generation, portfolio construction, rebalancing, and investment analytics services.	925-299-7782	NA	Walnut Creek
	Aechelon Technology Inc (HQ)	Developer of real time computer graphics applications in the training, simulation, and entertainment markers.	415-255-0120	NA	San Francisco
	Agile Global Solutions Inc (HQ)	Provider of business and IT solutions such as custom and enterprise application management and mobile business solutions.	916-655-7745	NA	Folsom
	AGTEK Development Company Inc (HQ)	Developer of high tech surveying, analysis, and control solutions for residential, commercial, transportation, water, energy, and government.	925-606-8197	NA	Livermore
	Aktana Inc (HQ)	Provider of decision support engine that pores through multiple data services and delivers insights and suggestions right in the rep's workflow.	888-707-3125	NA	San Francisco
	Alchemic Solutions Group Inc (HQ)	Provider of technology marketing solutions for wireless sectors. The company focuses on product management, software development, and consultation.	510-919-8105	NA	San Mateo
	Aldelo LP (HQ)	Provider of software solutions. The company offers solutions for the hospitality, retail, and payment processing industries.	925-621-2410	NA	Pleasanton
	Alert Technologies Corp (HQ)	Developer of emergency management software. The company offers professional services to assist customers in solving their information management challenges.	925-461-5934	NA	Pleasanton
	Allegro Consultants Inc (HQ)	Provider of operating system technical support for third party maintenance and multi-vendor service community.	408-252-2330	NA	Menlo Park
	Ameritechnology Group (HQ)	Provider of IT consulting, asset tracking, auditing, telecom connectivity logistics, relocation, and data recovery solutions for businesses.	916-395-6776	NA	Sacramento
	Amind Solutions LLC (HQ)	Provider of technology and services. The company offers enterprise mobility, quoting and ordering, product configuration, and e-Commerce services.	925-804-6139	NA	Alamo
	Amulet Technologies LLC (HQ)	Provider of embedded graphical user interface solutions. The company also specializes in modules and chips.	408-374-4956	NA	Campbell
	Anand Systems Inc (HQ)	Designer of custom software solutions for the hotel industry. The company also offers related hardware, website design, and surveillance systems.	209-830-1484	NA	Tracy
N	Anotek Inc (HQ)	Developer of software and books to teach the Greek language to English speaking people.	310-450-5027	NA	Santa Monica
	Anvato Inc (HQ)	Provider of video software platform to television broadcasters and offers live and on-demand video management, analytics, and tracking features.	866-246-6942	NA	Mountain View

COMPANY NAME	PRODUCT / SERVICE	PHONE	EMP	CITY
Apogee Software Inc (HQ)	Provider of integrated development environment for Java and C. The company offers industrial monitors and controllers.	408-369-9001	NA	Campbell
Apple Inc (HQ)	Designer and marketer of consumer electronics. The company also focuses on computer software and personal computers.	408-996-1010	NA	Cupertino
APX Power Markets Inc (BR)	Provider of e-commerce services for the electrical sector. The company serves residential, commercial, and industrial properties.	408-517-2100	NA	San Jose
Aragon Consulting Group Inc (HQ)	Provider of software development services. The company also offers authoring, coding, consulting, and technical support solutions.	415-869-8818	NA	Cupertino
Arcsoft Inc (HQ)	Developer of multimedia technologies and applications. The company serves both desktop and embedded platforms.	510-440-9901	NA	Fremont
Articulate Solutions Inc (HQ)	Provider of branding services such as website development, identity design, social media marketing, and search engine optimization.	408-842-2275	NA	Gilroy
Artifex Software Inc (HQ)	Provider of software solutions for host based applications. The company also focuses on embedded printer markers.	415-492-9861	NA	Novato
Artwork Conversion Software Inc (HQ)	Developer of CAD translation programs and CAD viewers software. The company also offers plotting software and IC packaging software.	831-426-6163	NA	Santa Cruz
Aspera Inc (HQ)	Developer of file transport technologies. The company provides client and server software, consoles, and mobile uploaders.	510-849-2386	NA	Emeryville
Atlassian (BR)	Provider of software development and collaboration tools. The company offers software for chats, tracking, repository management, and code hosting.	415-701-1110	NA	San Francisco
Attention Control Systems Inc (HQ)	Manufacturer of cognitive aids. The company also offers technical assistance solutions and serves the healthcare sector.	888-224-7328	NA	Mountain View
Augmentum Inc (HQ)	Provider of software development and solution implementation services. The company focuses on Internet applications and product development outsourcing.	650-578-9221	NA	Foster City
Auriga Corp (HQ)	Provider of technology consulting services for electric power, telecommunications, transportation, and information technology systems.	408-946-5400	NA	Milpitas
Autodesk Inc (BR)	Provider of 3D design, engineering, and entertainment software solutions. The company also offers technical support services.	415-356-0700	NA	San Francisco
AutoGrid Systems Inc (HQ)	Provider of grid-sensing technologies. The company focuses on energy data platform and optimized demand management services.	650-461-9038	NA	Redwood City
Avatier Corp (HQ)	Provider of identity management consulting, software development, password management, and user provisioning solutions.	925-217-5170	NA	Pleasanton
Avontus Software Corp (DH)	Creator of software for formwork, scaffolding, and shoring industries, both custom development for enterprises and packaged software for public.	800-848-1860	NA	Berkeley
Backshop Inc (HQ)	Provider of commercial real estate software for full deal-stack modeling, loan origination, asset management, and data library for customers.	415-332-1110	NA	Sausalito
Barco Inc (RH)	Manufacturer of digital scan conversion equipment and radars. The company serves healthcare, defense, media, simulation, and other needs.	888-414-7226	NA	Rancho Cordova
Beganto Inc (HQ)	Provider of web-based applications and support services. The company specializes in application, component, design, and sales engineering.	510-280-0554	NA	Santa Clara
BlackBag Technologies Inc (HQ)	Provider of Mac-based data forensic and eDiscovery solutions. The company is involved in data processing and related services.	408-844-8890	NA	San Jose
Border Collie Solutions Inc (HQ)	Provider of security surveillance software products. The company focuses on security panel, energy management, and medical monitoring.	650-343-2400	NA	Burlingame
Bradford Technologies Inc (HQ)	Developer of appraising software solutions for the real estate sector. The company offers backup and storage and digital signature scanning services.	408-360-8520	NA	San Jose
Bright Computing Inc (HQ)	Provider of software solutions for provisioning and managing HPC clusters, Hadoop clusters, and openstack private clouds.	408-300-9448	NA	San Jose
Brightidea Inc (HQ)	Provider of innovative management software solutions. The company's products include WebStorm, Switchboard, and Pipeline modules.	415-692-1912	NA	San Francisco
Brightsign LLC (HQ)	Provider of digital sign media players, software, and networking solutions for the commercial digital signage industry.	408-852-9263	NA	Los Gatos
Bromium Inc (HQ)	Provider of enterprise security solutions. The company focuses on security software development, technical support, and task introspection.	408-213-5668	NA	Cupertino
Burstorm Inc (HQ)	Provider of cloud design tools application. The company specializes in design, collaborate, quote, and implement of cloud architecture.	650-610-1480	NA	Danville
Busse Design USA Inc (HQ)	Provider of interface design services. The company's services include website design and application user interface.	415-689-8090	NA	Oakland
California Software Systems (HQ)	Provider of graphics software solutions. The company products include DNC file server for windows and graphics software.	831-477-6843	NA	San Juan Bautista
Calsoft Inc (HQ)	Designer and developer of storage, networking, and operating systems. The company deals with design, delivery, and installation.	408-834-7086	NA	San Jose
Calypso Technology Inc (HQ)	Provider of front-to-back technology solutions for the financial markers. The company offers technology platform for cross asset trading risk management.	415-530-4000	NA	San Francisco

	COMPANY NAME	PRODUCT / SERVICE	PHONE	EMP	CITY
	Carbon Five Inc (HQ)	Provider of software development services such as lean design and agile development for the web and mobile sectors.	415-546-0500	NA	San Francisco
	Casetrakker (HQ)	Developer of Windows-based case management software. The company is engaged in programming and hosting solutions.	916-757-1444	NA	Roseville
	Catalyst Business Solutions (HQ)	Provider of technology consulting services in business applications, data center, and machine-to-machine/Internet of things.	408-281-7100	NA	San Jose
	CCS Inc (HQ)	Provider of business accounting software solutions. The company is also engaged in web integration and custom software development.	949-855-9020	NA	Lincoln
	Celigo Inc (HQ)	Provider of cloud computing products and solutions. The company offers NetSuite consulting services that include implementation and optimization.	650-579-0210	NA	San Mateo
N	Ceridian Corp (BR)	Firm is a provider of human capital management solutions.	714-963-1311	NA	Fountain Valley
	Ceva Inc (HQ)	Provider of digital signal processor technology. The company also specializes in offering consulting services.	650-417-7900	NA	Mountain View
N	Chander Software Solutions Inc (HQ)	Provider of marketing, call center, project management and technical support software and technical staffing augmentation solutions.	408-406-5624	NA	San Jose
	ChannelNet (BR)	Provider of digital solutions to connect brands and customers. The company specializes in strategy development, design, and content optimization.	415-332-4704	NA	Sausalito
	ChemSoft (HQ)	Provider of software consulting services. The company specializes in custom business solutions, access, excel, PowerPoint, word, and visual basic.	408-615-1001	NA	San Jose
	Ciphercloud Inc (DH)	Provider of comprehensive cloud application discovery and risk assessment, data protection, data loss management, key management, and malware detection.	855-524-7437	NA	San Jose
	Cityspan Technologies Inc (HQ)	Developer of software for social services. The company offers software to manage grants, track clients, and evaluate outcomes.	510-665-1700	NA	Berkeley
	Claris International Inc (HQ)	Provider of database software which assists organizations in the management, analysis, and sharing of information.	408-987-7000	NA	Santa Clara
	ClearCare Inc (HQ)	Provider of front and back office software solution such as billing, payroll, and marketing management for private duty home care agencies.	800-449-0645	NA	San Francisco
	Clickatell (pty) Ltd (HQ)	Provider of SMS solutions such as SMS alerts, reminders, call centers, reservations and bookings for healthcare, marketing, and IT/software industries.	650-641-0011	NA	Redwood City
	Clinisense Corp (HQ)	Developer of technology for shelf-life monitoring. The company offers applications such as diagnostics, medical supplies, and RFID tags.	408-348-1495	NA	Los Gatos
	Cloudera Inc (HQ)	Provider of professional services that include cluster certification, descriptive analytics pilot, and security integration pilot.	650-362-0488	NA	Santa Clara
	Cloudmark Inc (HQ)	Provider of messaging infrastructure and security solutions. The company delivers scalable messaging platform, security intelligence, and filtering.	415-946-3800	NA	San Francisco
N	Coast Sign Inc (HQ)	Provider of project management, turnkey brand conversions and re-branding manufacturing specialized services, leasing, engineering, installation and much more services.	714-520-9144	201-500	Anaheim
	Cognex Corp (BR)	Supplier of barcode readers and sensor products. The company offers vision sensors, fixed mount readers, handheld readers, and mobile computers.	858-481-2469	NA	Cupertino
	Cognizant Technology Solutions (BR)	Provider of business consulting, enterprise application development, IT infrastructure, and outsourcing services.	925-790-2000	NA	San Ramon
	Colfax International (HQ)	Provider of workstations, servers, clusters, storage, and personal supercomputing solutions to accelerate business and research outcomes.	408-730-2275	NA	Sunnyvale
	Computer Deductions Inc (HQ)	Provider of software development services as a subcontractor to corporations. The company also offers management consulting services.	916-987-3600	NA	Orangevale
	Computer Presentation Systems Inc (HQ)	Designer and developer of hardware and software solutions for home builders ranging from local entrepreneurs to regional builders.	916-635-3487	NA	Rancho Cordova
	Computers & Structures Inc (HQ)	Provider of integrated design, analysis, assessment, drafting of building systems, and related support services.	510-649-2200	NA	Walnut Creek
	CompuTrust Software (HQ)	Developer and seller of software for public administrators. The company offers services to businesses and enterprises.	800-222-7947	NA	Morgan Hill
	Contrast Media Labs (HQ)	Provider of graphic design and software development services. The company services include android applications and digital and print media design.	415-471-1323	NA	San Francisco
	Corman Technologies Inc (HQ)	Provider of software development and consulting services for a variety of clients in the software industry.	707-575-7800	NA	Santa Rosa
	Corona Labs Inc (HQ)	Developer of games, e-books, and other interactive content. The company offers services to the educational sector.	415-996-6877	NA	San Francisco
	Couchbase Inc (HQ)	Developer of products and technology to meet the elastic scalability, always-on availability, and data mobility requirements of critical applications.	650-417-7500	NA	Santa Clara

	COMPANY NAME	PRODUCT / SERVICE	PHONE	EMP	CITY
N	Cpp Inc (HQ)	Publisher of books on psychology and distributes publications of Jossey-Bass, Harper and Row, and B and D book and reaches market through direct mail, trade sales, and distributors.	650-969-8901	NA	Sunnyvale
	CSRware Inc (HQ)	Developer of sustainability resource management software. The company specializes in supply chain, enterprise ERP solutions, and consulting services.	855-277-9273	NA	Mill Valley
	CSS Corp (HQ)	Provider of enterprise level support solutions for IT products. The company is involved in virtualization, storage, and archiving solutions.	650-385-3820	NA	Milpitas
	CUneXus Solutions Inc (HQ)	Provider of pre-screening lending strategy that pre-approves entire loan product portfolio for customers.	877-509-2089	NA	Santa Rosa
	Current Controls Inc (HQ)	Designer and manufacturer of control panels for OEMs in many sectors. The company also offers PLC programming, system integration, and other services.	916-630-5507	NA	Rocklin
	Cyberdata Corp (HQ)	Designer and manufacturer of USB cables. The company also offers VoIP and printed circuit board design services.	831-373-2601	NA	Monterey
	D-Tools Inc (HQ)	Developer and marketer of software to streamline processes which accompany the integration and installation of low-voltage systems.	925-681-2326	NA	Concord
	D2s Inc (HQ)	Supplier of a computational design platform to maximize eBeam technology. The company's products include TrueMask MDP and DS.	408-781-9017	NA	San Jose
	Data Path Inc (HQ)	Provider of IT services such as IT management, web design, software development, and education related data services.	209-521-0055	NA	Modesto
	DataGlance Inc (HQ)	Provider of data management software that support LIVE data conversion/migration, electronic document generation and processing, and web services.	510-656-0500	NA	Fremont
	Datameer Inc (HQ)	Provider of data analytics solution for business users. The company also focuses on integration, business analytics consulting, and training.	800-874-0569	NA	San Francisco
N	Dawn Sign Press (HQ)	Publisher of books and DVD"s for deaf peoples.	858-625-0600	NA	San Diego
N	Dazeworks Inc (HQ)	Provider of solutions to help clients innovate and stand out from their competition.	415-818-8069	51-200	San Francisco
	Delphix (HQ)	Developer of software, database, and database virtualization. The company focuses on website design and hosting and software application development.	650-494-1645	NA	Redwood City
	Deplabs Inc (HQ)	Provider of eCommerce projects. The company involves in eCommerce co-development, application development, third party integration, and back-end integration.	415-456-5600	NA	Petaluma
	Desaware Inc (HQ)	Developer of tools and components for visual studio programmers. The company offers documentation and professional services.	408-404-4760	NA	San Jose
	DesignMap (HQ)	Provider of web site and application design services. The company also specializes in research, usability studies, and visual design.	415-357-1875	NA	San Francisco
	Dhap Digital Inc (HQ)	Provider of interface that translates a desktop experience to a smartphone and go through Scion vehicle configurations without app download.	415-962-4900	NA	San Francisco
	Digipede Technologies LLC (HQ)	Provider of distributed computing solutions for academic research, entertainment, financial services, and manufacturing business applications.	510-834-3645	NA	Lafayette
	Digital Anarchy (HQ)	Provider of photography and video plugins for Photoshop, elements, after effects, and final cut pro.	415-287-6069	NA	Brisbane
	Digital Mountain Inc (HQ)	Provider of electronic discovery and computer forensic services focusing on reduplication, data management, ESI planning, and cybersecurity.	866-344-3627	NA	Santa Clara
	Direct Technology (HQ)	Provider of software application design and hosting services. The company is engaged in software application development.	916-787-2200	NA	Roseville
	DisplayLink Corp (HQ)	Provider of solutions for virtual graphics connectivity between computers and displays. The company makes use of USB, wireless USB, and ethernet.	650-838-0481	NA	Palo Alto
	DocuSign Inc (HQ)	Provider of digital transaction management platform helps to accelerate transactions, reduce costs, and delight customers, suppliers, and employees.	877-720-2040	NA	San Francisco
N	Douloi Automation Inc (HQ)	Developer of prepackaged motion control software.	408-735-6942	NA	Santa Clara
N	DreamHost (HQ)	Provider of web hosting and domain name registration; flash-based multimedia products.	714-671-9098	51-200	Brea
N	Drivers License Guide Co (HQ)	Provider of risk management and compliance programs.	650-369-4849	11-50	Redwood City
	Droisys Inc (HQ)	Provider of business solutions and offers services such as content management, enterprise resource planning, and business efficiency consulting.	408-874-8333	NA	Santa Clara
	Dt Research Inc (HQ)	Developer and manufacturer of embedded computing systems. The company serves hospitality, healthcare, and digital signage needs.	408-934-6220	NA	San Jose
	Dynamic Ventures Inc (HQ)	Provider of onsite and offsite custom software development services. The company also focuses on maintenance.	408-343-0234	NA	Cupertino
	DynEd International Inc (HQ)	Provider of computer-based English language teaching solutions. The company offers mobile solutions, analytics, testing, and monitoring tools.	650-375-7011	NA	Burlingame

	COMPANY NAME	PRODUCT / SERVICE	PHONE	EMP	CITY
N	Eastridge Workforce Solutions (HQ)	Provider of workforce management, workforce recruitment, workforce technology and staffing solutions.	800-778-0197	201-500	San Diego
	Ebusinessdesign (HQ)	Provider of technology consulting services, specializing in business analysis, architecture design, and open source development.	408-654-7900	NA	Campbell
	Ecodomus Inc (HQ)	Provider of information technology software for improved design and construction data collection, facility management, operation, and maintenance.	571-277-6617	NA	San Francisco
	eGain Corp (HQ)	Provider of custom engagement software solutions. The company offers co-browsing, email management, web self-service, and analytics services.	408-636-4500	NA	Sunnyvale
N	Eigenstate Consulting LLC (HQ)	Creator and provider of customized presentations for companies and groups, consulting services through the Internet and related technologies.	415-225-6703	NA	San Francisco
	Electric Cloud Inc (BR)	Provider of software development, information technology consulting, test automation, virtualization, and cloud computing solutions.	408-419-4300	NA	San Jose
	Elucit Inc (HQ)	Provider of hardware and software development services. The company also offers data recorders and calibration services.	707-961-1016	NA	Fort Bragg
	Emanio Inc (HQ)	Developer of products for data management, dashboarding, and reporting and predictive analysis needs. The company focuses on consulting and training.	510-849-9300	NA	Berkeley
	Endicia (HQ)	Provider of electronic postage software solutions and offers shipping and mailing services to online sellers, warehouse shippers, and office mailers.	800-576-3279	NA	Mountain View
	energyOrbit Inc (HQ)	Provider of cloud based platform and solution for streamline demand side management programs, projects, and relationship management for customers.	866-628-8744	NA	San Francisco
	Ensenta Corp (HQ)	Developer of software solutions. The company is involved in development of cloud-based imaging and self-service technology.	866-219-4321	NA	Redwood Shores
	Envestnet (BR)	Provider of application software for financial service firms. The company is involved in practice and portfolio management.	866-924-8912	NA	San Jose
	Enview Inc (HQ)	Specializes in threat prevention systems. The company deals with data analytics and remote sensing services.	415-483-5680	NA	San Francisco
	Epylon Corp (HQ)	Developer of e-procurement software and services. The company serves the government and education sectors.	925-407-1020	NA	Danville
	Etouch Systems Corp (BR)	Provider of design web engineering services. The company focuses on business process management and enterprise application integration services.	510-795-4800	NA	Fremont
N	Everest Consulting Group Inc (BR)	Provider of customer solutions in IT project and staff augmentation areas offers technology due diligence, new application development, and product engineering.	510-494-8440	201-500	Fremont
	Excelfore (HQ)	Provider of cloud applications. The company offers infotainment and telematics products for insurance, financing, and logistics sectors.	510-868-2500	NA	Fremont
	Expandable Software Inc (HQ)	Developer of enterprise software for manufacturers. The company is engaged in medical technology and general manufacturing solutions.	408-261-7880	NA	Santa Clara
	Exponent Partners (HQ)	Provider of performance and outcomes management solutions. The company's services include systems integration and custom application development.	800-918-2917	NA	San Francisco
	Extend Inc (HQ)	Developer of business software. The company also provides Internet and marketing consulting services.	925-484-0395	NA	Pleasanton
	EXXIM Computing Corp (HQ)	Manufacturer of cutting-edge radiological imaging technology and equipment designed for dental, medical, and scientific and industrial industries.	925-416-1900	NA	Pleasanton
	Eyefinity Inc (HQ)	Provider of software solutions for the eyecare industry. The company focuses on practice and revenue cycle management and electronic health records.	877-448-0707	NA	Rancho Cordova
N	FABNexus Inc (HQ)	Provider of application-specific machine control and SEMI-standards conformant network automation software to the semiconductor manufacturing and support industry.	650-207-8235	NA	Los Altos
	Fiduciary Management Technologies Inc (HQ)	Provider of insolvency case, fiduciary case, and estate management solutions. The company offers SEC distribution fund administration services.	916-930-9900	NA	Sacramento
	FileOpen Systems Inc (HQ)	Provider of digital rights management and document security solutions for corporations and governments.	831-706-2170	NA	Santa Cruz
	FireEye Inc (HQ)	Focuses on cyber security solutions. The company serves the utilities and pharmaceutical industries.	408-321-6300	NA	Milpitas
	Forio Corp (HQ)	Provider of software products for simulations, data explorations, and predictive analysis needs. The company caters to universities and corporations.	415-440-7500	NA	San Francisco
N	Formula Consultants Inc (HQ)	Provider of software development and consulting services.	714-778-0123	NA	Anaheim

COMPANY NAME	PRODUCT / SERVICE	PHONE	EMP	CITY
Fortinet Inc (HQ)	Provider of network security appliances and threat management solutions such as network security platform and reporting and authentication.	408-235-7700	NA	Sunnyvale
Franz Inc (HQ)	Provider of information technology solutions. The company offers web technology and enterprise development tools, and professional services.	510-452-2000	NA	Oakland
Gallery Systems Inc (BR)	Provider of collection management systems. The company offers procedures consulting, project management, and strategic planning services.	510-652-8950	NA	Berkeley
Game Your Game Inc (HQ)	Developer of digital tracking system such as automatic shot tracking and hands-free game tracking device to get the insights to improve the game.	888-245-3433	NA	San Francisco
N General Networks Corp (HQ)	Provider of consulting and managed services for customers who need to manage and process business-critical information.	818-249-1962	51-200	Glendale
N GeoTrust Inc (HQ)	Provider of digital certificates for secure online transactions and business over the Internet.	520-477-3110	NA	Mountain View
GestureTek Inc (HQ)	Provider of gesture-based user interfaces for mobile devices. The company offer services to the gaming and entertainment industries.	408-506-2206	NA	Santa Clara
Gigwalk (HQ)	Provider of analytics and collaboration tools and they are used in the management of mobile work force.	888-237-5896	NA	San Francisco
Glenmount Global Solutions (BR)	Provider of industrial equipment control, energy management, and other systems. The company serves automotive, food, chemical, and other sectors.	707-258-8400	NA	Vacaville
Global Infotech Corp (HQ)	Provider of software services. The company's software solutions focuses on staff augmentation, telecom, systems integration, chip design, ERP, and CRM domains.	408-567-0600	NA	San Jose
Global Software Resources (HQ)	Provider of application development, business intelligence, testing and mobile computing, and collaboration services.	925-249-2200	NA	Pleasanton
Globant (BR)	Provider of software products and solutions for cloud computing, mobile, gaming, enterprise consumerization, and data visualization.	877-215-5230	NA	San Francisco
Glyphic Technology (HQ)	Provider of software design and architecture solutions. The company focuses on Internet, server, desktop, mobile, and embedded systems.	650-964-5311	NA	Mountain View
Gracenote Inc (HQ)	Provider of music, video, and automotive solutions. The company focuses on television businesses and entertainment products.	510-428-7200	NA	Emeryville
Grandflow Inc (HQ)	Provider of e-cataloging and marketing automation solutions. The company offers print production, warehousing, and document management services.	925-443-0855	NA	Livermore
Grey San Francisco (BR)	Provider of advertising, planning, sports marketing solutions. The company also focuses on customer relationship management.	415-403-8000	NA	San Francisco
Greytrix (RH)	Provider of integration and migration solutions. The company deals in analytics, cloud, mobility, and ERP/CRM consulting.	888-221-6661	NA	San Francisco
Growing Energy Labs Inc (HQ)	Developer of software to integrate, network, and economically operate energy storage systems. The company is engaged in analysis services.	415-857-4354	NA	San Francisco
Hazelcast Inc (HQ)	Provider of training, consulting, and technical support services. The company serves the logistics and healthcare industries.	650-521-5453	NA	Palo Alto
Hcl America Inc (LH)	Provider of software and IT solutions, infrastructure, engineering, research and development, and outsourcing services.	408-733-0480	NA	Sunnyvale
Heroku Inc (HQ)	Designer and developer of cloud application platforms. The company offers services to software developers.	866-278-1349	NA	San Francisco
Highfive (HQ)	Focuses on video conferencing and re-imaging solutions. The company offers services to business organizations.	844-464-4445	NA	Redwood City
Hyperarts Web Design Development & Maintenance (HQ)	Provider of web design, development, and consulting services. The company performs SEO, SEM services, and web application development.	510-339-6084	NA	Oakland
Iksanika LLC (HQ)	Provider of custom software development, testing, quality assurance, porting, and re-engineering services.	408-490-0777	NA	San Jose
Illumio Inc (HQ)	Developer of security platform and it is also involved in data encryption and technical support services.	669-800-5000	NA	Sunnyvale
N Imagine IT! (HQ)	Producer of customized interactive multimedia application developments for CD-ROM and corporate intranets. CD-ROMs produced are for employee training, business presentations, trade shows and conferences and also offers digital audio and video and DVD authoring.	818-368-2604	NA	Chatsworth
Imaja (HQ)	Developer of computer applications. The company specializes in the development of educational tools for Macs.	510-526-4621	NA	Berkeley
Impression Technology Inc (HQ)	Provider of automated data capture solutions that meet the business objectives. The company primarily offers scanners.	925-280-0010	NA	Walnut Creek
Increv Corp (HQ)	Developer of business and information technology solutions. The company is engaged in consulting and product development services.	408-689-2296	NA	Los Altos
Individual Software Inc (HQ)	Publisher and developer of education, business, and personal productivity software for consumers, schools, businesses, and government.	925-734-6767	NA	Livermore

	COMPANY NAME	PRODUCT / SERVICE	PHONE	EMP	CITY
	Industrial Control Links Inc (HQ)	Designer and manufacturer of SCADA hardware and software solutions. The company focuses on monitoring, alarming, data collection, and other needs.	530-888-1800	NA	Roseville
	Infinite Technologies Inc (HQ)	Provider of information technology, strategic consulting, and engineering services. The company serves government and corporate entities.	916-987-3261	NA	El Dorado Hills
N	Infoflex Inc (HQ)	Developer of accounting and 4GL software.	650-270-1019	NA	Burlingame
	Infolane Inc (HQ)	Provider of web design and development and support services that includes web content management, application development, and technical improvements.	510-277-2399	NA	Emeryville
	Informatix Inc (HQ)	Provider of information technology and business solutions that include software development, document management, networking, and consulting services.	916-830-1400	NA	Sacramento
	Infoyogi LLC (HQ)	Provider of information technology solutions for software application development and systems integration.	408-850-1700	NA	Santa Clara
	Inikosoft Inc (HQ)	Provider of web, graphic, and print design services. The company is also engaged in e-commerce development and social media marketing.	408-402-9545	NA	Los Gatos
	Inmon Corp (HQ)	Developer of traffic management and monitoring products such as sFlow Trend, sFlow-RT, Hyper-V Agent, and others.	415-946-8901	NA	San Francisco
	Innominds Software Inc (HQ)	Provider of product incubation services for the technology industries. The company focuses on app development, analytics, mobility, and testing.	408-434-6463	NA	San Jose
N	Innovative Concepts (HQ)	Provider of website design services.	805-545-9562	11-50	San Luis Obispo
	Innovative Interfaces Inc (HQ)	Provider of technology solutions and services. The company deals with training and hosting, and technical support.	510-655-6200	NA	Emeryville
	Input Optics Inc (HQ)	Provider of integration solutions for dental practice. The company also offers complimentary assessments and web services.	650-969-3108	NA	Mountain View
	Inspirisys Solutions North America Inc (HQ)	Provider of software development and technology services for automotive, healthcare, life science, networking, storage, and enterprise software markers.	408-514-5199	NA	Santa Clara
	Inspironix Inc (HQ)	Provider of information technology solutions. The company offers software development, web application development, web design, and network services.	916-488-3222	NA	Sacramento
	Instant Systems Inc (HQ)	Provider of Internet based business software and services. The company's services include distribution and technical support.	415-682-6000	NA	Fremont
	InStyle Software Inc (HQ)	Provider of Enterprise Resource Planning Software solutions. The company offers services to the apparel industry.	314-631-6982	NA	Santa Rosa
	Inszoom Inc (HQ)	Focuses on immigration case management and compliance automation solutions. The company offers services to law firms.	925-244-0600	NA	Pleasanton
	Integrated Wave Technologies (HQ)	Provider of voice recognition technology services. The company offers printing calculators and electronic camera shutters.	510-353-0260	NA	Fremont
	Intelight ITS (HQ)	Provider of electrical engineering solutions. The company offers expertise on systems, traffic products and software.	520-795-8808	NA	Carlsbad
	Intelligent Inference Systems Corp (HQ)	Provider of computational intelligence services. The company primarily caters to high-tech companies.	408-390-1455	NA	Moffett Field
	Intelliswift Software Inc (HQ)	Provider of application development services for enterprises. The company also focuses on big data, cloud, web solutions, and staffing services.	510-490-9240	NA	Fremont
	Intercom Inc (HQ)	Designer and developer of communication packages. The company also focuses on user intelligence solutions.	877-595-5175	NA	San Francisco
	Interra Systems Inc (HQ)	Provider of diversified software products and services for digital media and semiconductor industries.	408-579-2000	NA	Cupertino
	Intrinsyx Technologies Corp (BR)	Provider of information technology solutions. The company caters to federal, state, and commercial stakeholders.	650-210-9219	NA	Moffett Field
	IO Informatics Inc (HQ)	Provider of software and services for data integration applications in areas such as life science and medicine.	510-705-8470	NA	Berkeley
	IO Integration Inc (HQ)	Provider of marketing technology and digital media workflow solutions. The company offers marketing automation and cross-media publishing services.	408-996-3420	NA	Cupertino
	iota Computing Inc (HQ)	Specializes in turnkey architecture. The company is engaged in building core technology for tiny edge devices.	888-440-4004	NA	Palo Alto
	Ipera Technology Inc (HQ)	Provider of multi-format video transcoder solutions for broadcast and IP multi-screen video production.	650-286-0889	NA	Cupertino
	Irislogic Inc (HQ)	Provider of global consulting services and solutions. The company specializes in custom software development, network security, cloud, and testing.	408-855-8741	NA	Santa Clara
	Iron Systems Inc (HQ)	Provider of network storage, hybrid cloud, and big data infrastructure solutions. The company offers OEM/ODM manufacturing services.	408-943-8000	NA	Fremont
	ISSE Services (HQ)	Provider of security solutions principally focusing on supporting system implementation and security testing.	916-670-1082	NA	Elk Grove
	Issio Solutions Inc (HQ)	Provider of workforce management software for surgical facilities. The company also serves ambulatory surgical centers.	888-994-7746	NA	Concord

COMPANY NAME	PRODUCT / SERVICE	PHONE	EMP	CITY
IT Flux (HQ)	Provider of custom software development services, outsourcing, and outsourced software testing services.	408-649-5642	NA	Napa
IT Systemworks (HQ)	Provider of networking and technological solutions. The company's services include installation, implementation, repair, and maintenance.	415-507-0123	NA	San Rafael
Ivalua Inc (HQ)	Designer and developer of spend management solutions. The company offers services to medium and large sized companies.	650-930-9710	NA	Redwood City
JAMIS Software Corp (HQ)	Provider of job-cost, billing, and accounting systems and solutions. The company caters to the government contractors.	800-655-2647	NA	San Diego
N JRH GoldenState Software Inc (HQ)	Developer and provider of software tools and solutions that supports complete DB2 catalog query and object management.	310-544-1497	NA	Rancho Palos Verdes
Juniper Networks Inc (HQ)	Provider of network security solutions. The company serves the government, healthcare, utilities, and manufacturing industries.	408-745-2000	NA	Sunnyvale
Keen Systems Inc (HQ)	Provider of web-to print solutions. The company offers cloud-based services to small and medium sized printing companies.	888-506-5336	NA	San Mateo
Keep IT Simple (HQ)	Provider of virtualization and information technology services. The company focuses on virtualization assessment, cloud computing, and networking.	510-403-7500	NA	Fremont
Key Solutions Inc (HQ)	Provider of software development and database management services. The company also specializes in business intelligence.	510-456-4500	NA	Fremont
KKI Corp (HQ)	Provider of web and business services and software solutions. The company is also involved in design and technical support services.	209-863-8550	NA	Modesto
KLC Enterprises (HQ)	Provider of accounting software for the construction industry. The company offers services to the commercial and industrial sectors.	415-485-0555	NA	San Anselmo
Kovair Software Inc (HQ)	Provider of web-based document management applications. The company offers product support maintenance services.	408-262-0200	NA	San Ramon
Kovarus Inc (HQ)	Provider of integrated business IT solutions. The company also deals with leasing, financing, project management, and related services.	800-454-1585	NA	San Ramon
Langtech (HQ)	Provider of information technology services. The company provides software solutions, cloud services, system integration, and consulting.	415-364-9600	NA	San Francisco
Language Quest Traveler (HQ)	Retailer of foreign language bibles, software, books, and dictionaries. The company also offers video/audio supplies.	530-918-9540	NA	Mount Shasta
LeapFILE Inc (HQ)	Provider of on-demand file transfer, delivery, and collaboration solutions for businesses. The company serves the healthcare and advertising sectors.	650-701-7241	NA	Cupertino
Lenos Software (HQ)	Provider of enterprise resource management, development of motion graphics, and value-added management services.	415-281-8828	NA	San Francisco
Lightning Bolt Solutions Inc (HQ)	Provider of medical staff scheduling software and solutions. The company's services include scheduling, keeping backups, technical support, and training.	866-678-3279	NA	S San Francisco
Lilee Systems (HQ)	Provider of integrated services that include system prediction modeling, project management, and training services for the railroad industry.	408-988-8672	NA	San Jose
Linden Research Inc (HQ)	Designer and developer of digital entertainment solutions. The company's products include Desura, Patterns, and Versu.	415-243-9000	NA	San Francisco
Linkbit Inc (HQ)	Manufacturer of network equipment. The company primarily caters to service providers and network operators.	408-969-9940	NA	Santa Clara
Livermore Software Technology Corp (HQ)	Developer of software for automotive crashworthiness, metal forming, aerospace, and other needs. The company also offers training.	925-449-2500	NA	Livermore
Lorentz Solution Inc (HQ)	Developer of electronic design automation software services. The company is engaged in modeling and electromagnetic shielding.	408-922-0765	NA	Santa Clara
N Loudhouse Creative (HQ)	Publisher of hand-drawn and letterpress printed greeting cards.	818-643-1725	NA	Burbank
N Lynx Media Inc (HQ)	Developer of inventory control and order entry software.	800-451-5969	NA	Valley Village
Lytrod Software Inc (HQ)	Provider of variable data print software products. The company's products include VisionDP Production and Automate, Proform Designer, and Office Designer.	707-422-9221	NA	Fairfield
N Market Vane Corp (HQ)	Provider of market sentiment analysis.	626-395-7436	NA	Pasadena
Marketo Inc (HQ)	Provider of marketing automation software services. The company offers email and social marketing, marketing software, and digital marketing services.	650-581-8001	NA	San Mateo
Matrix Computer Solutions Inc (HQ)	Provider of computer and technology solutions for residential and business customers. The company also offers data backup, repair, and other services.	415-331-3600	NA	Sausalito
Matrix Logic Corp (HQ)	Provider of enterprise content management solutions for law firms, businesses, and government agencies.	415-893-9897	NA	Chico
Meditab Software Inc (HQ)	Developer of physical therapy, urology, cosmetic, and plastic surgery solutions. The company serves the healthcare industry.	510-201-0130	NA	Sacramento
Medsoftware Inc (HQ)	Provider of practice management software solutions. The company's services include data conversion and repair, training, and implementation.	916-797-2363	NA	Aptos

COMPANY NAME	PRODUCT / SERVICE	PHONE	EMP	CITY
Meltwater Group (HQ)	Developer of software products such as Meltwater BUZZ, Meltwater NEWS, and Meltwater DRIVE to meet the specific needs of businesses around the world.	415-829-5900	NA	San Francisco
Memsql Inc (HQ)	Provider of technology solutions and services. The company serves the finance and digital advertising industries.	855-463-6775	NA	San Francisco
Metabyte Inc (HQ)	Provider of software solutions and related services to the government, healthcare, and retail industries.	510-494-9700	NA	Fremont
Metaswitch Networks (DH)	Provider of service management solutions. The company offers original equipment manufacturer, multimedia subsystem, and hosted business services.	415-513-1500	NA	Los Altos
MetricStream Inc (HQ)	Provider of enterprise risk, compliance, and internal audit management solutions. The company offers training services.	650-620-2900	NA	Palo Alto
MG Technologies Inc (HQ)	Provider of software services. The company offers conversion, training, installation, and tuning services.	408-255-8191	NA	Cupertino
Mirabilis Design Inc (HQ)	Provider of systems engineering solutions for performance analysis and architecture exploration of electronics and real-time software.	408-844-3234	NA	Sunnyvale
Mistral Solutions Inc (HQ)	Provider of technology design and systems engineering solutions. The company's solutions include hardware board design and embedded software development.	408-705-2240	NA	Fremont
Mobileiron Inc (HQ)	Provider of mobile security, device, and application management solutions. The company focuses on technical support services.	650-919-8100	NA	Mountain View
Mobiveil Inc (HQ)	Provider of technology solutions. The company's products include Silicon IP and COTS Modules and offers IC design and embedded software services.	408-212-9512	NA	Milpitas
Modius Inc (HQ)	Provider of performance management software. The company serves infrastructure monitoring applications.	415-655-6700	NA	San Francisco
Momentum Design Lab (HQ)	Designer of enterprise-grade software products. The company focuses on design, discovery, and development of software.	650-452-6290	NA	San Mateo
Mondee Inc (HQ)	Developer of technology for the generation of private fare distribution. The company offers services to the travel industry.	650-646-3320	NA	San Mateo
Moogsoft Inc (HQ)	Provider of collaborative situation management software solutions for Web-scale information technology (IT) operations.	415-738-2299	NA	San Francisco
Moonstone Interactive Inc (HQ)	Provider of website design services. The company offers web design and development, content management, and market visibility services.	925-736-4178	NA	San Ramon
Mountford Group Inc (HQ)	Provider of system development and web application services. The company also focuses on technical communication.	925-686-6613	NA	Concord
Mozilla Corp (HQ)	Designer and developer of web application tools and browsers. The company serves individuals and businesses.	650-903-0800	NA	Mountain View
MYCOM OSI Inc (RH)	Provider of performance management, compliance, employer reporting, patient engagement, and satisfaction solutions.	916-467-1500	NA	Folsom
NADA Technologies Inc (HQ)	Provider of enterprise Oracle applications. The company also offers business intelligence solutions.	650-678-4666	NA	Danville
Naehas Inc (HQ)	Specializes in the automation of sales and marketing services. The company offers services to finance and insurance companies.	877-262-3427	NA	Palo Alto
Navis LLC (HQ)	Provider of terminal operating solutions. The company offers solutions for container terminal operations, expert decking, and process automation.	510-267-5000	NA	Oakland
Nehanet Corp (HQ)	Provider of corporate responsibility management and sales and operation planning solutions to semiconductor and electronics component manufacturers.	888-552-4470	NA	Santa Clara
N Neil A. Kjos Music Co (HQ)	Creator of books and educational materials.	858-270-9800	11-50	San Diego
Neova Tech Solutions Inc (BR)	Provider of cloud solutions for web and mobile. The company offers mobile development and QA automation services.	781-640-0588	NA	Santa Clara
Netskope (HQ)	Provider of cloud security brokering services. The company offers services to the healthcare sector.	800-979-6988	NA	Santa Clara
Netwoven Inc (HQ)	Provider of enterprise content management and business intelligence solutions. The company also focuses on process management.	877-638-9683	NA	Milpitas
Neuron Corp (HQ)	Provider of computer and physical security products and services for the military, government, and corporate sectors.	408-540-7959	NA	San Jose
N New:Team SoftWare Inc (HQ)	Developer of software solutions.	415-461-8086	NA	Sacramento
Nice Touch Solutions Inc (HQ)	Developer of software for the heavy highway construction industry. The company focuses on products for generating extra work bills.	925-385-8321	NA	Alamo
Nova Measuring Instruments Inc (BR)	Provider of metrology solutions for semiconductor manufacturing industries. The company offers integrated and stand-alone metrology platforms.	408-510-7400	NA	Fremont
Numerify Inc (HQ)	Provider of business, service, and asset analytics services. The company offers services to information technology organizations.	408-822-9611	NA	San Jose
Objectivity Inc (HQ)	Provider of distributed, real-time, SOA-enabled service and offers embedded database management solutions.	408-992-7100	NA	San Jose
Oea International Inc (HQ)	Developer of signal integrity software. The company serves the electronic design automation industry.	408-778-6747	NA	Morgan Hill

COMPANY NAME	PRODUCT / SERVICE	PHONE	EMP	CITY
Ohanae Inc (HQ)	Provider of data and password protection and data compliance solutions. The company offers services to businesses.	888-617-7288	NA	Monte Sereno
Omnicia Inc (HQ)	Provider of electronic submissions for the life science sector. The company offers electronics and desktop publishing and document management services.	415-293-8553	NA	San Francisco
Oomnitza (HQ)	Provider of information technology asset management and related services. The company focuses on third party solutions.	650-417-3694	NA	San Francisco
Opal Soft Inc (HQ)	Provider of communications equipment installation and networking. The company's services include application development, network management, and maintenance.	408-267-2211	NA	Sunnyvale
Openclovis (HQ)	Provider of system infrastructure software platform. The company mainly serves the communication industry.	707-981-7120	NA	Petaluma
OpensourceCM (HQ)	Designer and developer of contract management software. The company also offers technical support services.	650-200-0506	NA	Foster City
Openvpn Technologies Inc (HQ)	Specializes in deploying VPN access solutions. The company is engaged in marketing and communication services.	925-399-1481	NA	Pleasanton
OPSWAT Inc (HQ)	Provider of endpoint software management, compliance, URL filtering, network monitoring, and related solutions.	415-590-7300	NA	San Francisco
Optimal Synthesis Inc (HQ)	Provider of research, algorithm development, and software design services. The company caters to a variety of engineering and science applications.	650-559-8585	NA	Los Altos
Orange Enterprises Inc (HQ)	Provider of software solutions. The company mainly focuses on payroll tracking and agriculture management.	559-229-2195	NA	Fresno
Orion Wine Software (HQ)	Developer of winery management solutions. The company is also engaged in sales and inventory management.	877-632-3155	NA	Santa Rosa
Osisoft LLC (HQ)	Developer of PI system software. The company offers software such as PI Computing Engine, Batch, Data Access, and Clients.	510-297-5800	NA	San Leandro
N OtherWorld Enterprises Inc (HQ)	Provider of web design, development and hosting services.	805-768-4638	NA	Simi Valley
OTRS Inc (BR)	Focuses on business solutions. The company offers services to the hospitality, education, and financial sectors.	408-549-1717	NA	Cupertino
Palantir Technologies Inc (HQ)	Provider of software for anti fraud, cyber security, intelligence, and other needs. The company serves government, commercial, and non-profit sectors.	650-815-0200	NA	Palo Alto
Palo Alto Networks Inc (HQ)	Provider of network and cyber security solutions. The company offers consulting and support, and solution assurance services.	408-753-4000	NA	Santa Clara
PanTerra Networks Inc (HQ)	Provider of cloud-based communications software solutions. The company is engaged in unified communication and technical support.	800-805-0558	NA	Santa Clara
Pasco Scientific (HQ)	Provider of technology-based solutions for hands-on science services. The company is engaged in technical support.	916-786-3800	NA	Roseville
PC Professional (HQ)	Provider of information technology solutions. The company focuses on cloud computing, application development, networking, and disaster recovery.	510-874-5871	NA	Oakland
Perforce Software Inc (BR)	Developer of software management tools and technology solutions. The company serves game development, banking, healthcare, and other sectors.	510-864-7400	NA	Alameda
PFU America Inc (BR)	Provider of technology solutions. The company designs, develops, and sells computer hardware, peripheral products, and systems.	408-992-2900	NA	Sunnyvale
Pivotal Labs (HQ)	Focuses on software development and related services. The company serves start-ups and Fortune 1000 companies.	415-777-4868	NA	San Francisco
Polymath Research Inc (HQ)	Developer of wave propagation and interaction, and photonic devices. The company offers FEMLAB based photonics modeling package and wavelet tools.	925-417-0609	NA	Pleasanton
Portrait Displays Inc (HQ)	Provider of extensible platforms supporting embedded control of all display technologies and monitors and operating system software.	925-227-2700	NA	Pleasanton
POS Specialists (HQ)	Provider of digital dining solutions. The company is engaged in business consultation, on-site training, and cloud services.	925-626-3930	NA	Concord
Posiflex Business Machines Inc (HQ)	Provider of point of service hardware and platform technology. The company caters to diverse markers.	510-429-7097	NA	Hayward
Presentek Inc (HQ)	Designer of websites and web portals. The company also offers content management systems and e-commerce handlers.	408-354-1264	NA	Los Gatos
Presidio Inc (BR)	Provider of IP telephony and wireless networking services. The company also deals with deployment, integration, and hardware and software development.	415-501-9020	NA	Pleasanton
ProcessWeaver Inc (BR)	Developer of multi-carrier shipping software and a provider of shipping solutions. The company also offers inbound and desktop shipping solutions.	888-932-8373	NA	Santa Clara
Progent Corp (HQ)	Provider of online technical support for small networks, and specializes in remote diagnosis, repair, and consulting services.	408-785-4781	NA	San Jose
N Pronto Networks (HQ)	Provider of Wi-Fi operation support system solutions for enterprises, wireless ISPs, WiMAX and satellite networks.	925-860-6200	51-200	Walnut Creek

COMPANY NAME	PRODUCT / SERVICE	PHONE	EMP	CITY
Prosoft Engineering Inc (HQ)	Developer of data recovery software. The company provides Drive Genius, Data Rescue, and Data Backup software.	877-477-6763	NA	Livermore
QSolv Inc (HQ)	Provider of cloud automation services. The company provides network management, gap analysis, tool evaluation, and framework implementation services.	408-962-3803	NA	Sunnyvale
Quadbase Systems Inc (HQ)	Designer of web-delivered and mobile enabled business intelligence reporting, charting, and dashboard tools.	408-982-0835	NA	Santa Clara
Quantum3D Inc (HQ)	Developer and manufacturer of real-time visual simulation and computing systems for fast-jet, helicopter, refueling, and other needs.	408-600-2500	NA	Milpitas
Qubell Inc (HQ)	Specializes in autonomic management solutions. The company focuses on e-commerce and other cloud applications.	888-855-9440	NA	Menlo Park
Quicklogic Corp (HQ)	Provider of trading solutions for stock market investors. The company offers online trading platforms for mobiles, smartphones, and tablets.	408-990-4000	NA	San Jose
R-Computer (HQ)	Provider of computer solutions for small and medium-sized companies. The company also offers lifetime product guarantees and sales consultation.	925-798-4884	NA	Concord
N R.L. Shep Publications (HQ)	Publisher of nineteenth-century costume, tailoring, and etiquette books.	707-964-8662	NA	Fort Bragg
Real Intent Inc (HQ)	Provider of electronic design automation services. The company offers techniques for automatic design verification.	408-830-0700	NA	Sunnyvale
N REAL Software Systems LLC (HQ)	Developer of software solutions for the management of royalty, rights and revenue sharing contracts.	818-313-8000	NA	Woodland Hills
Redolent Inc (HQ)	Provider of software solution in web, open source, e-commerce applications. The company also focuses on enterprise wide applications.	650-242-1195	NA	San Jose
Redwhale Software Corp (HQ)	Provider of software tools, technologies, and professional services for the design, development, and run-time management of user interfaces.	650-312-1500	NA	Redwood City
Resilient Networks Systems Inc (HQ)	Developer of Internet software products. The company serves the healthcare, media, information security, and government sectors.	415-291-9600	NA	San Francisco
Revel Systems Inc (BR)	Provider of POS systems and related services. The company serves customers in the accounting, security, reporting, and other industries.	415-744-1433	NA	San Francisco
RightITnow (HQ)	Provider of information technology operations management software. The company offers services to government agencies and business organizations.	415-350-3581	NA	San Francisco
Rocket Communications Inc (HQ)	Developer of user interface, visual, and icon design services for software and related applications.	415-863-0101	NA	San Francisco
Rockliffe Systems Inc (HQ)	Provider of mobile communication software for service providers, enterprises, and consumers. The company offers design services.	408-879-5600	NA	Campbell
RS Software Inc (BR)	Provider of business payment solutions for the risk prediction, residual management, payment gateway, and merchant boarding areas.	408-382-1200	NA	Milpitas
S2C Inc (HQ)	Provider of prototyping solutions. The company's customers include chip design and system design companies.	408-213-8818	NA	San Jose
Sanah Inc (HQ)	Provider of IT services such as IT strategy consulting, systems integration, and custom application development.	888-306-1942	NA	Sacramento
SAP America Inc (BR)	Developer of software applications. The company provides data and technology, custom development, and implementation services.	650-849-4000	NA	Palo Alto
Scimage Inc (HQ)	Provider of imaging solutions. The company also deals with clinical and cloud solutions and business intelligence support.	866-724-6243	NA	Los Altos
Sendero Group LLC (HQ)	Provider of GPS systems and products to the visually impaired. The company focuses on documentation and technical support services.	888-757-6810	NA	Rancho Cordova
Sercomm USA Inc (BR)	Provider of software and firmware for the development of broadband networking. The company also offers solutions for fixed mobile convergence.	510-870-1598	NA	Fremont
Sharper Technology Inc (HQ)	Provider of network security solutions and services. The company also offers design, implementation, and training services.	650-964-4600	NA	Palo Alto
Silex Technology America Inc (HQ)	Manufacturer of print servers for network printers and fingerprint readers. The company serves security applications.	657-218-5199	NA	Santa Ana
Silicon Publishing Inc (HQ)	Provider of digital publishing solutions. The company deals with template designs and personalized communications.	925-935-3899	NA	San Francisco
Silver Peak Systems Inc (HQ)	Provider of miscellaneous communication equipment and services. The company focuses on WAN optimization, cloud networking, and replication acceleration.	408-935-1800	NA	Santa Clara
Sitepen Inc (HQ)	Developer and provider of software products and services. The company also offers web application development and java support services.	650-968-8787	NA	Palo Alto
Smart ERP Solutions Inc (HQ)	Developer of enterprise class software. The company provides vendor management software and support services.	925-271-0200	NA	Pleasanton
Socket Mobile Inc (HQ)	Developer of wireless handheld and hands-free barcode scanners and other products and serves retail, logistics, automotive, and other sectors.	510-933-3000	NA	Newark
Sonasoft Corp (HQ)	Provider of software based solutions to simplify and automate replication, archiving, backup, recovery, and data protection operations.	408-708-4000	NA	San Jose
Sono Group Inc (HQ)	Provider of custom software and application development, training, social networking, and IT staffing services.	925-855-8552	NA	Danville

COMPANY NAME	PRODUCT / SERVICE	PHONE	EMP	CITY
Spence Engineering Services Inc (HQ)	Provider of solutions for hardware and software engineering problems. The company offers services to the technical sector.	650-571-6500	NA	San Mateo
Splunk Inc (HQ)	Provider of search engine services specializing in IT data. The company serves the government, healthcare, and telecommunication industries.	415-848-8400	NA	San Francisco
SS Papadopulos & Associates Inc (BR)	Provider of web-based applications for customized online communities. The company serves business enterprises.	415-773-0400	NA	San Francisco
SS&C Advent (HQ)	Provider of data services, portfolio, performance, research, client, margin and finance, and revenue management solutions.	415-645-1000	NA	San Francisco
Stanfield Systems Inc (HQ)	Provider of system engineering and data management services. The company also focuses on web development and technical services.	916-608-8006	NA	Folsom
Stopware Inc (HQ)	Developer of visitor management security software. The company offers hardware, badge stock, and training services.	408-367-0220	NA	Pleasanton
Stratovan Corp (HQ)	Developer of visual analysis software. It's product finds application in 3D imaging and surgical planning research.	530-746-7970	NA	Davis
STS International Inc (HQ)	Provider of information technology solutions that include infrastructure management, software application development, and systems integration.	925-479-7800	NA	Pleasanton
Succeed.Net (BR)	Provider of Internet services. The company specializes in metro Ethernet, wireless broadband, DSL service, national dial-up, and server co-location.	530-674-4200	NA	Roseville
Sun-Net Inc (HQ)	Provider of enterprise software solutions supporting outage scheduling, logging, and reporting for power, gas, and water utilities.	408-323-1318	NA	San Jose
Symplectic Engineering Corp (HQ)	Provider of custom computational mechanics solutions. The company is involved in consulting services and it serves the industrial sector.	510-528-1251	NA	Berkeley
Synaptics Inc (HQ)	Developer of human interface solutions. The company's products find application in mobile computing and entertainment devices.	408-904-1100	NA	San Jose
Synchron Networks Inc (HQ)	Developer of application and file distribution software. The company focuses on system management and digital asset delivery services.	831-461-9735	NA	Scotts Valley
Synergy Business Solutions (HQ)	Provider of technology evaluation, business process improvement, and custom software development services to a wide range of sectors.	415-263-1843	NA	San Francisco
Syntest Technologies Inc (HQ)	Provider of test solutions for the electronics industry. The company is involved in fault simulation solutions and services.	408-720-9956	NA	San Jose
SyTech Solutions Inc (HQ)	Provider of document management technology services. The company offers archive scanning, web-based document management, and data capture services.	916-381-3010	NA	Elk Grove
Talisman Systems Group Inc (HQ)	Provider of document and panel management tools. The company serves insurance companies and managed care organizations.	727-424-4261	NA	San Francisco
Tangent Inc (HQ)	Provider of computer solutions. The company caters to healthcare, industrial, and military applications.	650-342-9388	NA	Burlingame
N TCSN Inc (HQ)	Provider of Internet solutions, web hosting, website designing and much more.	805-227-7000	NA	Paso Robles
Tech Soft 3d (HQ)	Provider of software solutions. The company offers software for desktop visualization, modeling, cloud and mobile solutions, and data exchange.	510-883-2180	NA	Berkeley
N TechMD (HQ)	Provider of cloud solutions, cyber security services, strategic consulting, and managed services.	888-883-2463	51-200	Santa Ana
Tela Innovations Inc (HQ)	Provider of lithography optimized solutions. The company's services include design, implementation, and technical support.	408-558-6300	NA	Los Gatos
Terrace Consulting Inc (HQ)	Provider of custom software development services. The company focuses on eCommerce, back office, business intelligence, cloud, and other services.	415-848-7300	NA	San Francisco
Think Connected LLC (HQ)	Provider of data center, consulting, managed, and supplemental information technology services for small and medium-sized businesses.	877-684-4654	NA	San Francisco
Thinkify (HQ)	Provider of radio frequency identification technology application services. The company provides engineering services as well.	408-782-7111	NA	Morgan Hill
Third Pillar Systems (HQ)	Developer of networks and software for the commercial lending industry. The company offers implementation and integration services.	650-372-1200	NA	Burlingame
Thoughtworks Inc (BR)	Provider of system design and e-business consulting services. The company is also involved in software design and delivery and support.	415-273-1389	NA	San Francisco
N Tiger Software (HQ)	Developer of investment software.	858-273-5900	11-50	San Diego
Tom Sawyer Software Corp (HQ)	Developer of data relationship visualization and analysis software for application developers. The company offers training and consulting services.	510-208-4370	NA	Berkeley
Toolwire Inc (HQ)	Designer and developer of experiential learning solutions for higher education and corporate training institutions.	925-227-8500	NA	Pleasanton
Torian Group Inc (HQ)	Provider of computer, network, and web solutions such as virus removal, home network setup, and email.	559-733-1940	NA	Visalia
TRAXPayroll (HQ)	Specializes in payroll management solutions. The company also offers wage garnishment, worker's compensation, and tax filing solutions.	866-872-9123	NA	Hercules
Trinity Consultants Inc (BR)	Provider of environmental consulting services. The company engages in environmental outsourcing and litigation support services.	510-285-6351	NA	Oakland

	COMPANY NAME	PRODUCT / SERVICE	PHONE	EMP	CITY
N	TruAdvantage (HQ)	Provider of support services ranging from consultation to design, support and training for small and medium-sized companies and healthcare practices. Services include managed IT services, data backup and recovery, cloud services, VoIP services, and data and network security.	408-680-8389	11-50	San Jose
	TTI Inc (BR)	Distributor of passive, connector, electromechanical, and discrete components for the industrial, military, and aerospace sectors.	916-987-4600	NA	Folsom
	Ultra-X Inc (HQ)	Provider of personal computer diagnostic solutions for developers, manufacturers, system engineers, integrators, and computer professionals.	408-261-7090	NA	Santa Clara
N	United Sign Systems (HQ)	Provider of commercial sign services.	209-543-1320	11-50	Modesto
	uSens Inc (HQ)	Creator of 3D human computing interaction software and hardware solutions. The company focuses on artificial intelligence.	408-564-0227	NA	San Jose
	USWired Inc (HQ)	Provider of computer networking solutions that include cloud hosting, network design and installation, and wireless networks.	408-432-1144	NA	Campbell
	Valiantica Inc (HQ)	Provider of global IT solutions. The company's services include consulting, outsourcing, and mobile, enterprise and business application development.	408-725-2426	NA	San Jose
	Varite Inc (HQ)	Provider of custom software development, integration, deployment, and implementation services in the domains of core networking and virtualization.	408-977-0700	NA	San Jose
	Veeva Systems Inc (HQ)	Provider of cloud-based business solutions such as customer relationship management and content management for the life sciences industry.	925-452-6500	NA	Pleasanton
N	Ventricle Software Systems Inc (HQ)	Provider of software development for the healthcare industry.	310-948-2551	NA	Rancho Palos Verdes
	Versa Shore Inc (HQ)	Provider of data warehouse implementation, strategic blueprint creation, project management, and testing consulting services.	408-874-8330	NA	Campbell
	Versonix Corp (HQ)	Provider of integrated and customized software solutions. The company serves the travel and leisure industries.	408-873-3141	NA	San Jose
N	View by View Inc (HQ)	Provider of computer-generated architectural, medical modeling and simulations.	415-359-4494	NA	San Francisco
	Vistrian Inc (HQ)	Developer of software products. The company's services include escalation management, problem isolation, and remote access.	408-719-0500	NA	Milpitas
	VisualOn Inc (HQ)	Provider of software applications for the mobile handset market enabling customers to access multimedia content without dedicated hardware.	408-645-6618	NA	Campbell
	Wave Systems Corp (HQ)	Provider of customized software development for the law enforcement, casino, corporate security, and hospitals segments.	408-524-8630	NA	Sunnyvale
	William Stucky & Associates Inc (HQ)	Provider of software products and services. The company mainly caters to the asset-based lending industry.	415-788-2441	NA	San Francisco
	Wilson Research Group LLC (HQ)	Provider of market research products and services. The company serves publishing, embedded systems, and high technology fields.	530-350-8377	NA	Sacramento
N	WK Multimedia Network Training (HQ)	Provider of computer training programs and services.	415-586-1713	NA	San Mateo
	Workday Inc (HQ)	Provider of software solutions for human resources management and financial management. The company specializes in SaaS based enterprise solutions.	925-951-9000	NA	Pleasanton
N	WorldCom Consulting (HQ)	Provider of editorial services including writing, editing, desktop publishing, printing, layout and design, web design and hosting, screenplay development, and consultation and serves educational, religious and humanitarian organizations and public affairs department.	209-728-0246	NA	Murphys
	Wright Williams & Kelly Inc (HQ)	Provider of software products and consulting services. The company also offers decision tools for cost management.	925-399-6246	NA	Pleasanton
	Wso2 Inc (HQ)	Provider of open source middleware platforms, security and identity gateway solutions, and enterprise integration solutions.	408-754-7388	NA	Palo Alto
	X-Z LAB Inc (HQ)	Provider of digital radiation detection services. The company engages in detecting, measuring, and monitoring radiation activities.	925-355-5199	NA	San Ramon
N	Xifin Inc (HQ)	Provider of health care related information technology services.	858-793-5700	201-500	San Diego
	Xmatters Inc (HQ)	Provider of voice and text alerting system software. The company serves the healthcare, telecommunications, and manufacturing industries.	925-226-0300	NA	San Ramon
	Xoriant Corp (HQ)	Provider of enterprise applications. The company also offers mobile analytics and web application development services.	408-743-4400	NA	Sunnyvale
N	Yellow Magic Inc (HQ)	Developer of software for the directory publishing industry.	951-506-4005	NA	Murrieta
	Zmanda - A Carbonite Co (HQ)	Provider of open source backup and recovery software solutions. The company's applications include centralized backup of file systems and applications.	408-732-3208	NA	Sunnyvale

324 = Data Preparation & Processing Services

	COMPANY NAME	PRODUCT / SERVICE	PHONE	EMP	CITY
	314e Corp (HQ)	Provider of IT skills, methodologies, and cost-effective managed services for healthcare application and technical support services.	510-371-6736	NA	Pleasanton

COMPANY NAME	PRODUCT / SERVICE	PHONE	EMP	CITY
6connect Inc (HQ)	Provider of network resource provisioning and automation products and services such as data normalizer, pro services, and provision jumpstart.	650-646-2206	NA	San Francisco
8x8 Inc (HQ)	Provider of cloud communications and computing solutions. The company sells IP phones, IP conference, soft, video and analog phones and accessories.	408-727-1885	NA	Campbell
Accenture (BR)	Provider of management consulting and technology services. The company also offers application outsourcing and IT consulting services.	415-537-5000	NA	San Francisco
Accu-Image Inc (HQ)	Supplier of transfer document image processing equipment. The company is engaged in business process consulting and document management.	408-736-9066	NA	Santa Clara
Active Video Networks (HQ)	Designer and developer of advertising solutions. The company also provides mosaic, guide, and navigation enablement services.	408-931-9200	NA	San Jose
Advance Research Associates (HQ)	Developer of human bio-therapeutic platform technology solutions, drug discovery, and related support services.	650-810-1190	NA	Santa Clara
Advantrics LLC (HQ)	Designer and developer of Internet technologies. The company also specializes in multimedia-based products.	530-297-3660	NA	Davis
Airnex Communications Inc (HQ)	Provider of digital wireless telecommunications and Internet access services. The company also focuses on web hosting.	800-708-4884	NA	Pleasanton
Alacrinet Consulting Services Inc (HQ)	Developer of software solutions. The company offers enterprise search, web content management, business intelligence, and analytics services.	650-646-2670	NA	Palo Alto
Aldo Ventures Inc (HQ)	Provider of studies such as software technology, markers, companies, platforms, products, and investment strategies of the software industry.	831-662-2536	NA	Aptos
Alten Calsoft Labs (HQ)	Provider of breed consulting, enterprise IT, and product engineering services for enterprises in healthcare, telecom, and high-tech and retail industries.	408-755-3000	NA	Santa Clara
Altierre Corp (HQ)	Provider of digital retail services. The company offers retail integration, software support, and consulting services.	408-435-7343	NA	San Jose
Applied Computer Solutions (BR)	Provider of information technology solutions. The company offers solutions for virtualization, storage, security, and networking.	925-251-1000	NA	Pleasanton
ARC (HQ)	Provider of document management services to the architectural, engineering, and construction industries.	925-949-5100	NA	San Ramon
ArcherHall (HQ)	Provider of litigation support services. The company offers forensic data collection, online document review, and e-discovery processing services.	855-839-9084	NA	Sacramento
Asani Solutions LLC (HQ)	Provider of networking solutions and system integration services. The company also focuses on Internet and corporate consulting.	408-330-0821	NA	Santa Clara
Astreya (HQ)	Provider of staffing services. The company specializes in recruitment of systems administrators, network engineers, system, and network architects.	800-224-1117	NA	San Jose
N Atlantis Software Inc (HQ)	Provider of network management solutions.	510-796-2180	11-50	Fremont
Bitglass Inc (HQ)	Provider of data protection solutions. The company focuses on cloud encryption, mobile security, and discovery solutions.	408-337-0190	NA	Campbell
BMC Software Inc (BR)	Provider of cloud management, workforce automation, and IT service management solutions. The company serves business enterprises and service providers.	800-793-4262	NA	Santa Clara
Bromium Inc (HQ)	Provider of enterprise security solutions. The company focuses on security software development, technical support, and task introspection.	408-213-5668	NA	Cupertino
Certain Inc (DH)	Provider of enterprise event management solutions that include e-mail marketing, event reporting, registration, and consulting services.	888-237-8246	NA	San Francisco
ChannelNet (BR)	Provider of digital solutions to connect brands and customers. The company specializes in strategy development, design, and content optimization.	415-332-4704	NA	Sausalito
Climate Earth (HQ)	Provider of environmental product declarations and supply chain solutions such as supply chain, climate change risk, and natural capital management.	415-391-2725	NA	Point Richmond
Cloudpassage Inc (HQ)	Developer of software solutions. The company also offers account management, configuration security monitoring, and alerting services.	415-886-3020	NA	San Francisco
Cloverleaf Solutions Inc (HQ)	Provider of data validation and information processing computer solutions. The company caters to businesses.	916-484-4141	NA	Sacramento
Collaborative Drug Discovery Inc (HQ)	Provider of drug discovery research informatics. The company offers hosted biological and chemical database that securely manages private and external data.	650-242-5259	NA	Burlingame
Computer Methods (HQ)	Manufacturer of physical therapy testing equipment. The company's products include WebExam, PP004, WinHand, and ActivitySuite.	510-824-0252	NA	Tracy
Computerland Of Silicon Valley (HQ)	Provider of hardware, software, and networking services. The company serves government and educational institutions.	408-519-3200	NA	San Jose
Connected Marketing (HQ)	Provider of marketing services. The company also offers web development, branding, and lead generation services.	408-647-2198	NA	San Jose
Corrigo Inc (BR)	Developer of facilities management platforms. The company offers services to business organizations.	877-267-7440	NA	San Mateo

COMPANY NAME	PRODUCT / SERVICE	PHONE	EMP	CITY
CP Communications LLC (HQ)	Provider of audio visual production, website development and hosting, social media marketing, and related services.	951-694-4830	NA	San Ramon
Cybersoft (BR)	Provider of offshore business and knowledge process outsourcing services. The company specializes in title, financial, and document processing services.	415-449-7998	NA	San Francisco
Cypress Digital Media (HQ)	Provider of web design, mobile development, and online marketing for interactive agencies and marketing campaigns.	650-257-0741	NA	Mountain View
Daniel B Stephens & Associates Inc (BR)	Provider of services in hydrology, environmental engineering, and science. The company services include water resources and soil testing.	800-933-3105	NA	Oakland
Data Distributing LLC (HQ)	Provider of solutions such as mass storage, peripheral, storage management software, import, archive, and images and data distribution.	831-457-3537	NA	Santa Cruz
Database Republic (HQ)	Provider of enterprise analysis and strategy modeling services. The company also focuses on DB design and implementation.	530-692-2500	NA	Oregon House
DataGlance Inc (HQ)	Provider of data management software that support LIVE data conversion/migration, electronic document generation and processing, and web services.	510-656-0500	NA	Fremont
Dataguise (HQ)	Provider of cloud migration, auditing, and monitoring solutions. The company serves the healthcare, consumer, and retail industries.	877-632-0522	NA	Fremont
DataSafe Inc (HQ)	Provider of digital solutions. The company's services include records storage, document shredding and imaging, and rotation.	650-875-3800	NA	S San Francisco
Datastax Inc (RH)	Distributor of database management system for Internet enterprise. The company offers training and certification, expert support, and consulting services.	650-389-6000	NA	Santa Clara
Delphix (HQ)	Developer of software, database, and database virtualization. The company focuses on website design and hosting and software application development.	650-494-1645	NA	Redwood City
Device Authority Ltd (RH)	Provider of IoT security solutions for industrial, automotive, transportation, healthcare, utilities, and smart cities.	650-603-0997	NA	San Ramon
DevonWay (HQ)	Provider of enterprise software solutions for utilities and process industries. The company specializes in enterprise asset management solutions.	415-904-4000	NA	San Francisco
N DI-NO Computers Inc (HQ)	Retailer of computer hardware and offers computer repair services.	626-795-6674	51-200	Pasadena
Digital Mountain Inc (HQ)	Provider of electronic discovery and computer forensic services focusing on reduplication, data management, ESI planning, and cybersecurity.	866-344-3627	NA	Santa Clara
Direct Mail Center (HQ)	Provider of data processing, fulfillment, digital and offset printing, mail production, and logistics services.	415-252-1600	NA	San Francisco
N DreamHost (HQ)	Provider of web hosting and domain name registration; flash-based multimedia products.	714-671-9098	51-200	Brea
Elucit Inc (HQ)	Provider of hardware and software development services. The company also offers data recorders and calibration services.	707-961-1016	NA	Fort Bragg
Emagined Security Inc (HQ)	Provider of professional services for information security solutions. The company also focuses on compliance.	415-944-2977	NA	San Carlos
Equinix (HQ)	Provider of interconnection data center and global colocation services focusing on cloud, business continuity, financial, and digital media.	866-378-4649	NA	Redwood City
First Class Plus LLC (HQ)	Provider of fundraising and marketing solutions. The company deals with print production, design assistance, and pre-press services.	650-589-8346	NA	S San Francisco
Funambol Inc (HQ)	Provider of open source mobile application server software. The company offers training and technical support services.	650-701-1450	NA	Foster City
Gigamon (HQ)	Provider of traffic visibility solutions for enterprises, data centers, and the education, financial, and healthcare industries.	408-831-4000	NA	Santa Clara
Grandflow Inc (HQ)	Provider of e-cataloging and marketing automation solutions. The company offers print production, warehousing, and document management services.	925-443-0855	NA	Livermore
Greytrix (RH)	Provider of integration and migration solutions. The company deals in analytics, cloud, mobility, and ERP/CRM consulting.	888-221-6661	NA	San Francisco
Health Fidelity Inc (HQ)	Provider of natural language processing technology and inference platform to analyze vast amounts of unstructured data for clinical and financial insights.	650-727-3300	NA	San Mateo
Hydropoint Data Systems Inc (HQ)	Provider of irrigation solutions. The company specializes in site evaluations, upgrade planning, deployment, and optimization services.	800-362-8774	NA	Petaluma
Imperva Inc (HQ)	Provider of application and data security solutions. The company's products include database firewalls, management server, and monitoring software.	650-345-9000	NA	Redwood Shores
Inabyte Inc (HQ)	Manufacturer of developer tools. The company also offers solutions and services for developers and end users of PCs or workstations.	415-898-7905	NA	Novato
Infoblox (HQ)	Provider of automated network control solutions. The company's services include training, implementation, migration, upgrade, repair, and maintenance.	408-986-4000	NA	Santa Clara
Infoimage Inc (HQ)	Provider of technology solutions for job tracking and business continuity needs. The company also focuses on data integrity.	650-473-6388	NA	Menlo Park

COMPANY NAME	PRODUCT / SERVICE	PHONE	EMP	CITY
Informatica Corp (HQ)	Provider of enterprise data integration and management solutions including data migration, warehousing, identity resolution, and other needs.	650-385-5000	NA	Redwood City
IntelinAir Inc (HQ)	Provider of aerial imagery analytics such as image analysis and change detection and deep learning and neural networks for farmers.	818-445-2339	NA	San Jose
Interface Masters Technologies Inc (HQ)	Developer of technology and networking solutions. The company's products include embedded switches, adapters, and related accessories.	408-441-9341	NA	San Jose
Intuit Inc (HQ)	Provider of financial management software solutions. The company offers services to small businesses and related organizations.	800-446-8848	NA	Mountain View
Ionix Internet (HQ)	Provider of web hosting solutions. The company offers network security, research, high-speed access, and telecommuting services.	888-884-6649	NA	San Francisco
Irislogic Inc (HQ)	Provider of global consulting services and solutions. The company specializes in custom software development, network security, cloud, and testing.	408-855-8741	NA	Santa Clara
IT Concepts LLC (BR)	Manufacturer of borescopes, videoscopes, fiberscopes, documentation solutions, and accessories for remote visual inspection needs.	925-401-0010	NA	Pleasanton
JAMIS Software Corp (HQ)	Provider of job-cost, billing, and accounting systems and solutions. The company caters to the government contractors.	800-655-2647	NA	San Diego
Jiva Creative LLC (HQ)	Provider of interactive design technology solutions. The company focuses on architecture, website hosting, and enterprise application development.	510-864-8625	NA	Alameda
KalioTek (HQ)	Provider of enterprise applications. The company also specializes in technical infrastructure for companies.	408-550-8000	NA	Cupertino
Medallia Inc (HQ)	Provider of consulting, system configuration, user training, and data warehouse integration services.	650-321-3000	NA	San Mateo
Micromega Systems Inc (HQ)	Provider of database systems and e-business website design services. The company also focuses on training and installation.	415-924-4700	NA	Corte Madera
Modius Inc (HQ)	Provider of performance management software. The company serves infrastructure monitoring applications.	415-655-6700	NA	San Francisco
Moonstone Interactive Inc (HQ)	Provider of website design services. The company offers web design and development, content management, and market visibility services.	925-736-4178	NA	San Ramon
Mountford Group Inc (HQ)	Provider of system development and web application services. The company also focuses on technical communication.	925-686-6613	NA	Concord
Multimedia Consulting Services Inc (HQ)	Provider of multimedia consulting services. The company offers design, implementation, and maintenance of the information technology infrastructure.	650-578-8591	NA	Foster City
Navlink (LH)	Provider of managed data services, managed hosting services, and managed enterprise networking solutions.	650-616-4042	NA	San Bruno
Neospeech Inc (HQ)	Provider of text-to-speech software and applications for the mobile, enterprise, entertainment, and education markers.	408-914-2710	NA	Santa Clara
NetApp Inc (HQ)	Provider of virtualization, mobile information management, and cloud storage solutions. The company serves the business sector.	408-822-6000	NA	Sunnyvale
Netwoven Inc (HQ)	Provider of enterprise content management and business intelligence solutions. The company also focuses on process management.	877-638-9683	NA	Milpitas
nexTier Networks Inc (HQ)	Provider of data security services and solutions for vertical markers and original equipment manufacturers.	408-282-3561	NA	Santa Clara
Novani LLC (HQ)	Provider of disaster prevention and recovery solutions. The company also offers business continuity and virtualization solutions.	415-731-1111	NA	San Francisco
Numenta Inc (HQ)	Developer of biotechnology machine intelligence technologies for commercial and scientific applications.	650-369-8282	NA	Redwood City
Objectivity Inc (HQ)	Provider of distributed, real-time, SOA-enabled service and offers embedded database management solutions.	408-992-7100	NA	San Jose
Ordinal Technology Corp (HQ)	Provider of sorting services of massive and production data sets such as web logs for high-traffic websites, phone logs, and government agency data.	925-253-9204	NA	Orinda
N OtherWorld Enterprises Inc (HQ)	Provider of web design, development and hosting services.	805-768-4638	NA	Simi Valley
Persistent Systems Inc (BR)	Developer of software and technology products for life science, banking, and other sectors. The company offers big data, security, and cloud solutions.	408-216-7010	NA	Santa Clara
Planeteria Media (HQ)	Designer and developer of websites, applications, e-commerce, content management systems, video, and offers flash, and Internet marketing services.	707-843-3773	NA	Santa Rosa
Presidio Inc (BR)	Provider of IP telephony and wireless networking services. The company also deals with deployment, integration, and hardware and software development.	415-501-9020	NA	Pleasanton
Proofpoint Inc (RH)	Manufacturer of threat, email, social media, and information protection products. The company offers security and compliance solutions.	408-517-4710	NA	Sunnyvale
Quest America Inc (HQ)	Provider of information technology services. The company offers solutions through strategy, consulting, and outsourcing.	408-492-1650	NA	San Jose

COMPANY NAME	PRODUCT / SERVICE	PHONE	EMP	CITY
Quisk Inc (HQ)	Specializes in the development of payment solutions. The company offers services to financial institutions.	408-462-6800	NA	Sunnyvale
R Systems Inc (RH)	Provider of information technology services and solutions. The company offers application, testing, BPO, and packaged services.	916-939-9696	NA	El Dorado Hills
Radiant Logic Inc (HQ)	Provider of identity and context virtualization solutions. The company caters to identity integration and management needs.	415-209-6800	NA	Novato
SACC Inc (HQ)	Provider of enterprise resource planning, data warehousing, technology infrastructure, business process outsourcing, and staffing services.	408-755-3000	NA	Santa Clara
SAP Litmos (HQ)	Provider of learning management system solutions. The company serves the energy and engineering industries.	925-251-2220	NA	San Ramon
Sierra Data Systems Inc (HQ)	Provider of data communication systems, Internet related services, miscellaneous communications equipment, telephone, and voice equipment.	916-242-4604	NA	Grass Valley
Single Point Of Contact (HQ)	Provider of IT management, enterprise, and planning services. The company is also engaged in cloud computing, web hosting, and hosted exchange.	800-791-4300	NA	Palo Alto
Sios Technology Corp (HQ)	Provider of cloud virtualization protection solutions. The company also offers managed information technology services.	650-645-7000	NA	San Mateo
Sumo Logic (HQ)	Provider of compliance, security, monitoring, troubleshooting, and delivery solutions. The company serves security, IT, and development teams.	650-810-8700	NA	Redwood City
SyTech Solutions Inc (HQ)	Provider of document management technology services. The company offers archive scanning, web-based document management, and data capture services.	916-381-3010	NA	Elk Grove
TCSN Inc (HQ)	Provider of Internet solutions, web hosting, website designing and much more.	805-227-7000	NA	Paso Robles
Tenefit Corp (HQ)	Provider of software services. The company's IoT gateway is used by mobile users, marketplaces, and machines to connect and communicate in real-time.	877-522-9464	NA	San Jose
TextDigger Inc (HQ)	Developer of horizontal semantic solutions for search engines. The company focuses on content mining and analytics.	408-416-3142	NA	San Jose
Tom Sawyer Software Corp (HQ)	Developer of data relationship visualization and analysis software for application developers. The company offers training and consulting services.	510-208-4370	NA	Berkeley
Toolwire Inc (HQ)	Designer and developer of experiential learning solutions for higher education and corporate training institutions.	925-227-8500	NA	Pleasanton
TVU Networks Corp (HQ)	Provider of wireless electronic news gathering services. The company offers TV broadcast, web streaming, and law enforcement services.	650-969-6732	NA	Mountain View
Wilson Research Group LLC (HQ)	Provider of market research products and services. The company serves publishing, embedded systems, and high technology fields.	530-350-8377	NA	Sacramento
WindSpring Inc (HQ)	Manufacturer of data management tools. The company provides a framework for optimized compressed data management in the storage and embedded fields.	408-452-7400	NA	San Jose
Xtime Inc (HQ)	Provider of CRM solutions for automotive service operations. The company offers scheduling and marketing solutions for automotive retailers.	888-463-3888	NA	Redwood City

N appears to the left of TCSN Inc (HQ).

325 = Internet-Related Services

COMPANY NAME	PRODUCT / SERVICE	PHONE	EMP	CITY
6WIND USA Inc (RH)	Manufacturer of virtual accelerators, routers, and related accessories. The company offers network security and network appliance solutions.	408-816-1366	NA	Santa Clara
A A Networks (HQ)	Provider of Internet, networks and cabling, computer hardware and software, remote and on-site technical support services.	650-872-1998	NA	Burlingame
A3 Solutions Inc (HQ)	Developer and marketer of enterprise modeling software. The company is also engaged in unified budgeting and consolidation services.	415-356-2300	NA	San Francisco
Ablesys Corp (HQ)	Provider of financial trading software and web applications. The company focuses on portfolio and algorithmic trading solutions.	510-265-1883	NA	Newark
Accelerance Inc (HQ)	Provider of software design, development, and deployment services. The company focuses on web hosting and programming solutions.	650-472-3785	NA	Redwood City
Accellion (HQ)	Provider of web-based file transfer applications. The company also focuses on data management solutions.	650-485-4300	NA	Palo Alto
Access Softek Inc (HQ)	Developer of mobile banking software solutions. The company focuses on software and product development, QA testing, user interface, and graphic design.	510-848-0606	NA	Berkeley
Accounting Micro Systems (HQ)	Developer of accounting and business management software products. The company offers MAS500, MAS90 and MAS200, FAS Asset solutions, and SalesLogix.	415-362-5100	NA	San Francisco
Accu-Image Inc (HQ)	Supplier of transfer document image processing equipment. The company is engaged in business process consulting and document management.	408-736-9066	NA	Santa Clara
Acrylic Art (HQ)	Provider of fabrication and machining services. The company focuses on painting, product finishing, anodizing, and vapor polishing.	510-654-0953	NA	Emeryville

COMPANY NAME	PRODUCT / SERVICE	PHONE	EMP	CITY
Adaptive Insights (HQ)	Provider of training, consulting, and related support services. The company serves the healthcare, insurance, and manufacturing industries.	650-528-7500	NA	Palo Alto
Adobe Systems Inc (HQ)	Developer of software solutions for digital media creation and editing, multimedia authoring, and web development.	408-536-6000	NA	San Jose
Advancing Ideas LLC (HQ)	Provider of market research and analysis, application branding, and user interface development services.	415-625-3338	NA	San Francisco
Advisor Software Inc (HQ)	Provider of planning, proposal generation, portfolio construction, rebalancing, and investment analytics services.	925-299-7782	NA	Walnut Creek
Agari Data Inc (HQ)	Provider of email security and social engineering solutions. The company serves the healthcare, financial services, and government industries.	650-627-7667	NA	Foster City
Algo-Logic Systems (HQ)	Specializes in building networking solutions. The company also offers technological and data handling services to firms.	408-707-3740	NA	San Jose
Allied Telesis Inc (BR)	Developer of network solutions for Internet protocol surveillance. The company focuses on web hosting and programming solutions.	408-519-8700	NA	San Jose
Amdocs Ltd (BR)	Provider of customer management and billing solutions software. The company offers services to the industrial sector.	916-934-7000	NA	El Dorado Hills
American Telesource Inc (HQ)	Provider of voice and data communication applications. The company offers unified communications, wireless, and process automation solutions.	800-333-8394	NA	Emeryville
Amind Solutions LLC (HQ)	Provider of technology and services. The company offers enterprise mobility, quoting and ordering, product configuration, and e-Commerce services.	925-804-6139	NA	Alamo
Anand Systems Inc (HQ)	Designer of custom software solutions for the hotel industry. The company also offers related hardware, website design, and surveillance systems.	209-830-1484	NA	Tracy
Andover Consulting Group Inc (HQ)	Supplier of network components. The company offers data center liquidation, network security, and network equipment services.	415-537-6950	NA	San Mateo
Anomali (RH)	Specializes in the delivery of cyber security solutions. The company services to big and small organizations.	844-484-7328	NA	Redwood City
Apogee Software Inc (HQ)	Provider of integrated development environment for Java and C. The company offers industrial monitors and controllers.	408-369-9001	NA	Campbell
Apolent Corp (HQ)	Provider of business process and software technology outsourcing services focusing on niche market segments.	408-203-6828	NA	San Jose
Applied Expert Systems Inc (HQ)	Developer of networking solutions for business service management. The company provides virtualization and cloud computing services.	650-617-2400	NA	Palo Alto
ARC (HQ)	Provider of document management services to the architectural, engineering, and construction industries.	925-949-5100	NA	San Ramon
ARX Networks Corp (HQ)	Provider of IT support and maintenance and cloud services. The company also focuses on unified communications and procurement.	650-403-4000	NA	Newark
Aryaka Networks Inc (HQ)	Provider of cloud-based WAN optimization services. The company focuses on application performance, data protection, and bandwidth reduction.	888-692-7925	NA	San Mateo
Asap Systems (HQ)	Developer of inventory management and asset tracking software. The company also offers barcode scanners and printers and RFID tags.	408-227-2720	NA	San Jose
Aspire Systems Inc (BR)	Provider of product engineering, infrastructure and application support, and testing services. The company serves healthcare and education fields.	408-260-2076	NA	San Jose
Astreya (HQ)	Provider of staffing services. The company specializes in recruitment of systems administrators, network engineers, system, and network architects.	800-224-1117	NA	San Jose
Audible Magic Corp (HQ)	Developer of media identification and synchronization, content registration, and copyright compliance solutions.	408-399-6405	NA	Los Gatos
Augmentum Inc (HQ)	Provider of software development and solution implementation services. The company focuses on Internet applications and product development outsourcing.	650-578-9221	NA	Foster City
Autonomic Software Inc (HQ)	Developer of software for endpoint and security management, imaging, and other needs. The company serves government, finance, and other sectors.	925-683-8351	NA	Danville
AvantPage (HQ)	Provider of foreign language translation services for the medical, technical, healthcare, financial industries.	530-750-2040	NA	Davis
Axsen LLC (HQ)	Developer of web designs and provider of online marketing solutions. The company serves the industrial sector.	925-398-0112	NA	Pleasanton
Bcl Technologies (HQ)	Developer of document creation, conversion, and extraction solutions. The company offers BCL easyPDF Cloud, a cloud-based PDF conversion platform.	408-557-2080	NA	San Jose
Bct Consulting Inc (HQ)	Provider of computer network support, web design, application programming, and other technology services.	559-579-1400	NA	Fresno
Bear River Associates Inc (HQ)	Provider of enterprise mobile computing products and services. The company serves business services, government, high-tech, and life science sectors.	510-834-5300	NA	Oakland

COMPANY NAME	PRODUCT / SERVICE	PHONE	EMP	CITY
BitPusher LLC (HQ)	Provider of IT infrastructure management services. The company also focuses on consulting and hosted IT services.	415-751-1055	NA	San Francisco
Bitsculptor (HQ)	Provider of web design, hosting, branding and search engine positioning solutions. The company also offers SEO, photography, and consulting services.	707-263-5241	NA	Lakeport
BitTorrent Inc (HQ)	Provider of download software solutions. The company offers design, data and content management, and installation services.	415-568-9000	NA	San Francisco
BizeeBee Inc (HQ)	Provider of lightweight software solution designed to help fitness studios and other membership based businesses.	650-489-6233	NA	Palo Alto
BlackBag Technologies Inc (HQ)	Provider of Mac-based data forensic and eDiscovery solutions. The company is involved in data processing and related services.	408-844-8890	NA	San Jose
Blacksquare (HQ)	Provider of location-based, social, m-commerce, game, and video applications. The company serves Fortune 500 companies.	415-640-6339	NA	San Francisco
Blast Analytics & Marketing (HQ)	Provider of web design, e-commerce, and brand design services. The company is involved in hosting and technical support.	916-724-6701	NA	Rocklin
Blue Jeans Network Inc (HQ)	Provider of cloud-based video conferencing solutions. The company also offers mobile video collaboration and cloud video bridging solutions.	408-550-2828	NA	San Jose
Blunk Microsystems LLC (HQ)	Provider of turnkey packages for embedded development to customers around the world. The company also offers development tools.	408-323-1758	NA	Sacramento
Boardwalktech Inc (HQ)	Provider of enterprise collaboration software specializing in tax planning, cash management, and revenue forecasting solutions.	650-618-6200	NA	Cupertino
Bodhtree Solutions Inc (BR)	Provider of information technology consulting services. The company deals with product engineering, application development, and training.	408-954-8700	NA	Fremont
Boldfocus Inc (HQ)	Provider of digital communications and technology services focusing on development, content management, and search engine optimization.	650-212-2653	NA	San Mateo
Brekeke Software Inc (HQ)	Developer of session initiation protocol software products for Internet protocol network communication needs.	650-401-6633	NA	San Mateo
BrightEdge Technologies Inc (HQ)	Developer of mobile web applications, websites, and publishing platforms. The company specializes in SmartPath technology.	800-578-8023	NA	Foster City
Brighterion Inc (HQ)	Provider of products for fraud prevention, predictive intelligence, risk management, and homeland security. The company focuses on adaptive analytics.	415-986-5600	NA	San Francisco
Brightsign LLC (HQ)	Provider of digital sign media players, software, and networking solutions for the commercial digital signage industry.	408-852-9263	NA	Los Gatos
BRS Media Inc (HQ)	Provider of multimedia e-commerce services. The company specializes in radio and Internet applications.	415-677-4027	NA	San Francisco
Busse Design USA Inc (HQ)	Provider of interface design services. The company's services include website design and application user interface.	415-689-8090	NA	Oakland
Calsoft Inc (HQ)	Designer and developer of storage, networking, and operating systems. The company deals with design, delivery, and installation.	408-834-7086	NA	San Jose
N Capital Management Group (HQ)	Provider of management consulting service for small businesses.	714-439-9600	NA	Anaheim
Caseware International Inc (DH)	Supplier of software solutions to accountants and auditors worldwide. The company offers working papers to accounting firms.	416-867-9504	NA	Berkeley
Castle Rock Computing Inc (HQ)	Designer and manufacturer of SNMPC network management software. The company's product caters to a wide range of sectors.	408-366-6540	NA	Saratoga
N CBS Local Media (HQ)	Operator of TV broadcasting network.	415-765-8144	NA	San Francisco
Ccintegration (HQ)	Provider of business engagement models such as OEM and virtual OEM. The company services include design, integration, and logistics.	408-228-1314	NA	San Jose
Celestix Networks Inc (HQ)	Provider of security appliances and solutions for healthcare, legal and financial, education, commercial, small business, and public sector industries.	510-668-0700	NA	Fremont
Celigo Inc (HQ)	Provider of cloud computing products and solutions. The company offers NetSuite consulting services that include implementation and optimization.	650-579-0210	NA	San Mateo
Centrify (HQ)	Provider of identity and access management solutions. The company offers services to pharma companies and financial institutions.	669-444-5200	NA	Santa Clara
ChemSoft (HQ)	Provider of software consulting services. The company specializes in custom business solutions, access, excel, PowerPoint, word, and visual basic.	408-615-1001	NA	San Jose
Chesapeake Technology Inc (HQ)	Provider of sonar mapping software as well as consulting services to the marine, geophysical, and geological survey industries.	650-967-2045	NA	Los Altos
Cisco Systems Inc (HQ)	Provider of networking products and services such as routers, switches, and optical and wireless networking devices.	800-553-6387	NA	San Jose
Cityspan Technologies Inc (HQ)	Developer of software for social services. The company offers software to manage grants, track clients, and evaluate outcomes.	510-665-1700	NA	Berkeley
Civil Maps (HQ)	Developer of autonomous vehicles and cognitive perception systems. The company specializes in localization technology and artificial intelligence.	415-287-9977	NA	San Francisco

COMPANY NAME	PRODUCT / SERVICE	PHONE	EMP	CITY
Clare Computer Solutions (HQ)	Provider of information technology services. The company offers computer network, software consultation, visualization, and cloud computing solutions.	925-277-0690	NA	San Ramon
Claresco Inc (HQ)	Provider of design and implementation services for customized business software. The company serves multi-national firms.	510-528-0238	NA	Berkeley
Clarizen (HQ)	Provider of collaborative online project management software. The company offers work management, time tracking, and project scheduling solutions.	866-502-9813	NA	San Mateo
ClearStory Data Inc (HQ)	Provider of data analysis and collaboration solutions for food and beverage, healthcare and life services, media and entertainment, and financial services.	650-322-2408	NA	Menlo Park
Clicktime Com Inc (HQ)	Provider of web-based tools, software, and IT consulting services. The company serves the aerospace, defense, automotive, and construction industries.	415-684-1180	NA	San Francisco
CloudFlare Inc (RH)	Provider of load balancers, traffic controllers, and web optimization products. The company is engaged in analytics services.	650-319-8930	NA	San Francisco
Cloudpassage Inc (HQ)	Developer of software solutions. The company also offers account management, configuration security monitoring, and alerting services.	415-886-3020	NA	San Francisco
Cloudwords Inc (HQ)	Provider of translation management systems and content localization solutions to manage translation process, vendors, and content systems.	415-394-8000	NA	San Francisco
Coastside Net (HQ)	Provider of Internet access and technology solutions. The company also offers website services including website hosting, design, and development.	650-712-5900	NA	El Granada
CommerceNet (HQ)	Provider of Internet based research and piloting services such as Internet business, open trading networks, and Internet-user demographic surveys.	650-289-4040	NA	Los Altos
Connected Marketing (HQ)	Provider of marketing services. The company also offers web development, branding, and lead generation services.	408-647-2198	NA	San Jose
ConSol Consulting & Solutions Corp (HQ)	Provider of information technology services. The company offers software, networking, outsourcing, and monitoring solutions.	925-479-1370	NA	San Francisco
Contrast Security (HQ)	Designer and developer of self-protection software. The company is also engaged in operations support services.	888-371-1333	NA	Los Altos
Corrigo Inc (BR)	Developer of facilities management platforms. The company offers services to business organizations.	877-267-7440	NA	San Mateo
CP Communications LLC (HQ)	Provider of audio visual production, website development and hosting, social media marketing, and related services.	951-694-4830	NA	San Ramon
Crmantra Inc (HQ)	Developer of software for customer relationship management needs. The company also focuses on business intelligence and analysis.	415-839-9672	NA	Emeryville
CSS Corp (HQ)	Provider of enterprise level support solutions for IT products. The company is involved in virtualization, storage, and archiving solutions.	650-385-3820	NA	Milpitas
Customweather Inc (HQ)	Provider of industry solutions. The company offers hurricane tracking, developer tools, and marine forecasts.	415-777-3303	NA	Mill Valley
Cygna Energy Services Inc (HQ)	Provider of application development, data integration, systems integration, consulting, and web services.	925-930-8377	NA	Walnut Creek
Cypress Digital Media (HQ)	Provider of web design, mobile development, and online marketing for interactive agencies and marketing campaigns.	650-257-0741	NA	Mountain View
D-Tools Inc (HQ)	Developer and marketer of software to streamline processes which accompany the integration and installation of low-voltage systems.	925-681-2326	NA	Concord
d2m Interactive (HQ)	Provider of web development, management, and e-commerce services. The company also focuses on marketing.	408-315-6802	NA	Los Gatos
Daniel B Stephens & Associates Inc (BR)	Provider of services in hydrology, environmental engineering, and science. The company services include water resources and soil testing.	800-933-3105	NA	Oakland
Data Distributing LLC (HQ)	Provider of solutions such as mass storage, peripheral, storage management software, import, archive, and images and data distribution.	831-457-3537	NA	Santa Cruz
Data Path Inc (HQ)	Provider of IT services such as IT management, web design, software development, and education related data services.	209-521-0055	NA	Modesto
Database International (HQ)	Provider of database application development and database administration services and also offers project management and event coordination services.	650-965-9102	NA	Los Altos
Datameer Inc (HQ)	Provider of data analytics solution for business users. The company also focuses on integration, business analytics consulting, and training.	800-874-0569	NA	San Francisco
DataSafe Inc (HQ)	Provider of digital solutions. The company's services include records storage, document shredding and imaging, and rotation.	650-875-3800	NA	S San Francisco
DCM Infotech Limited (RH)	Provider of managed IT services. The company focuses on system administration, storage, enterprise management, and staffing services.	510-494-2321	NA	Fremont
Device Authority Ltd (RH)	Provider of IoT security solutions for industrial, automotive, transportation, healthcare, utilities, and smart cities.	650-603-0997	NA	San Ramon
Digipede Technologies LLC (HQ)	Provider of distributed computing solutions for academic research, entertainment, financial services, and manufacturing business applications.	510-834-3645	NA	Lafayette

COMPANY NAME	PRODUCT / SERVICE	PHONE	EMP	CITY
Digital Canvas (HQ)	Provider of web design and web application development services. The company also offers web hosting, security solutions, and services.	925-706-1700	NA	Antioch
Digital Keystone Inc (HQ)	Provider of solutions enabling content distribution to tablets, connected TVs, and other entertainment platforms with suite of software and tools.	650-938-7300	NA	Cupertino
Digital Mountain Inc (HQ)	Provider of electronic discovery and computer forensic services focusing on reduplication, data management, ESI planning, and cybersecurity.	866-344-3627	NA	Santa Clara
Digite Inc (HQ)	Provider of collaborative enterprise application software. The company's product finds application in process and portfolio management.	408-418-3834	NA	Cupertino
Docker Inc (HQ)	Provider of docker platform and docker ecosystem of contributors, partners, and adopters the way distributed applications are built, shipped, and run.	415-941-0376	NA	Palo Alto
DOCOMO Innovations Inc (HQ)	Provider of products and services for businesses. The company focuses on business development, network solutions, and mobile network technology.	650-493-9600	NA	Palo Alto
Dolcera Corp (BR)	Provider of business research, analytics, collaboration, IP patent licensing, and related support services.	650-425-6772	NA	San Mateo
N DreamHost (HQ)	Provider of web hosting and domain name registration; flash-based multimedia products.	714-671-9098	51-200	Brea
Drivesavers Inc (HQ)	Provider of data recovery services for financial institutions, healthcare providers, major film studios, government agencies, and small businesses.	415-382-2000	NA	Novato
Dropbox Inc (HQ)	Provider of data transfer and sharing services that involves sharing of files, documents, and pictures from anywhere.	415-857-6800	NA	San Francisco
Druva Inc (RH)	Provider of cloud based data protection products. The company offers services to the manufacturing, healthcare, and education industries.	650-238-6200	NA	Sunnyvale
DSP Concepts Inc (HQ)	Provider of embedded audio processing tools and services. The company offers system design, embedded software development, and optimization services.	408-747-5200	NA	Santa Clara
Dt Research Inc (HQ)	Developer and manufacturer of embedded computing systems. The company serves hospitality, healthcare, and digital signage needs.	408-934-6220	NA	San Jose
Dubberly Design Office (HQ)	Developer of software related solutions. The company offers user interface and visual design, brand development, and usability testing services.	415-648-9799	NA	San Francisco
Duda (HQ)	A web design platform offering web design services to small businesses.	866-776-1550	NA	Palo Alto
Dynamic Graphics Inc (HQ)	Provider of geospatial software solutions such as earth modeling, well planning, and visualization for the petroleum industries.	510-522-0700	NA	Alameda
N East West Investment Services (HQ)	Provider of investment brokerage services.	626-768-6000	NA	Pasadena
Effone Software Inc (HQ)	Provider of IT consulting services including software development, application integration, and staff augmentation.	408-830-1010	NA	Santa Clara
Egnyte Inc (HQ)	Provider of online storage, cloud computing, and file sharing services. The company serves the financial, banking, and pharmaceutical industries.	650-968-4018	NA	Mountain View
Elegrity Inc (HQ)	Provider of law business management software, SharePoint, virtualization, and unified communication solutions.	855-353-4462	NA	San Francisco
Emagined Security Inc (HQ)	Provider of professional services for information security solutions. The company also focuses on compliance.	415-944-2977	NA	San Carlos
Endicia (HQ)	Provider of electronic postage software solutions and offers shipping and mailing services to online sellers, warehouse shippers, and office mailers.	800-576-3279	NA	Mountain View
Enfos Inc (HQ)	Provider of business software solutions for environmental management. The company specializes in financial, compliance, and GIS data management.	650-357-0007	NA	San Mateo
Enview Inc (HQ)	Specializes in threat prevention systems. The company deals with data analytics and remote sensing services.	415-483-5680	NA	San Francisco
Equinix (HQ)	Provider of interconnection data center and global colocation services focusing on cloud, business continuity, financial, and digital media.	866-378-4649	NA	Redwood City
Errigal Inc (HQ)	Designer and developer of software products and services. The company also deals with configuration management and ticketing.	415-523-9245	NA	San Francisco
eShares Inc (HQ)	Specializes in capitalization table management and valuation software.	650-669-8381	NA	San Francisco
Esp Interactive Solutions Inc (HQ)	Provider of web design and development services such as web video creation, content management system, and social networks marketing.	510-526-2592	NA	Albany
Excelfore (HQ)	Provider of cloud applications. The company offers infotainment and telematics products for insurance, financing, and logistics sectors.	510-868-2500	NA	Fremont
Exit445 Group (HQ)	Provider of information architecture, e-Commerce, email marketing, search engine optimization, website hosting, and other services.	415-381-1852	NA	Mill Valley
Extend Inc (HQ)	Developer of business software. The company also provides Internet and marketing consulting services.	925-484-0395	NA	Pleasanton
Extractable Inc (HQ)	Provider of websites, applications, social and mobile experiences for transactional, educational, lead generation, and entertainment purposes.	415-426-3600	NA	San Francisco

COMPANY NAME	PRODUCT / SERVICE	PHONE	EMP	CITY
Eyefinity Inc (HQ)	Provider of software solutions for the eyecare industry. The company focuses on practice and revenue cycle management and electronic health records.	877-448-0707	NA	Rancho Cordova
EZB Solutions (HQ)	Provider of software, hardware, and installation services. The company also deals with training, consulting, and technical support.	408-988-8760	NA	Santa Clara
eze System (HQ)	Provider or monitoring and measuring solutions. The company's products include controllers, controller expansions, and sensors.	716-393-9330	NA	Folsom
Fab 7 Designs (HQ)	Provider of graphic designing services. The company offers website, multimedia, editorial, and package designing services.	650-462-9745	NA	Palo Alto
Farallon Geographics Inc (HQ)	Provider of strategic planning, spatial data processing, training, and web application development services.	415-227-1140	NA	San Francisco
FinancialContent Services Inc (HQ)	Provider of stock market information. The company deals with advertising, newspaper, and consulting services.	888-688-9880	NA	San Carlos
Financialforce Com (HQ)	Developer of automation software solutions. The company also deals with cloud accounting and resource planning solutions.	866-743-2220	NA	San Francisco
First Class Plus LLC (HQ)	Provider of fundraising and marketing solutions. The company deals with print production, design assistance, and pre-press services.	650-589-8346	NA	S San Francisco
Flashtalking (BR)	Provider of online advertising technologies. The company is also engaged in analytics and reporting services.	628-207-8080	NA	San Francisco
Forecross Corp (HQ)	Provider of automated migration of legacy systems. The company specializes in XML solutions, migration solutions, and integrity solutions.	415-543-1515	NA	San Francisco
Forescout Technologies Inc (HQ)	Provider of network access control and policy compliance management solutions. The company serves the business sector.	408-213-3191	NA	San Jose
Forio Corp (HQ)	Provider of software products for simulations, data explorations, and predictive analysis needs. The company caters to universities and corporations.	415-440-7500	NA	San Francisco
Fortinet Inc (HQ)	Provider of network security appliances and threat management solutions such as network security platform and reporting and authentication.	408-235-7700	NA	Sunnyvale
Foxit Corp (HQ)	Developer of software. The company offers software such as Foxit Reader, Enterprise, and Mobile Reader.	510-438-9090	NA	Fremont
FUEL Creative Group (HQ)	Provider of graphic design, branding, and signage services. The company also focuses on packaging and printing.	916-669-1591	NA	Sacramento
Funambol Inc (HQ)	Provider of open source mobile application server software. The company offers training and technical support services.	650-701-1450	NA	Foster City
Gallery Systems Inc (BR)	Provider of collection management systems. The company offers procedures consulting, project management, and strategic planning services.	510-652-8950	NA	Berkeley
Gen-9 Inc (HQ)	Provider of personal information management services. The company offers services to the industrial and commercial markers.	650-903-2235	NA	Mountain View
Genbook Inc (HQ)	Developer of online appointment scheduling software. The company is engaged in social media marketing services.	415-227-9904	NA	San Francisco
Gilmour Craves (HQ)	Provider of graphic design, advertising, media planning, strategic marketing, and print management services.	415-431-9955	NA	San Francisco
GiS Planning Inc (HQ)	Provider of geographic information systems. The company is engaged in the building of patent-protected site selection website.	415-294-4775	NA	San Francisco
Glassbeam Inc (HQ)	Provider of support solutions and it serves the medical, storage, and wireless networking industries.	408-740-4600	NA	Santa Clara
Global Cybersoft Inc (HQ)	Provider of software development and IT outsourcing services, such as systems integration and maintenance.	424-247-1226	NA	Pleasanton
GlobalSoft Inc (HQ)	Provider of software consultancy services. The company offers application development, training program management, and engineering services.	408-564-0307	NA	San Jose
Globant (BR)	Provider of software products and solutions for cloud computing, mobile, gaming, enterprise consumerization, and data visualization.	877-215-5230	NA	San Francisco
Golden Valley Systems Inc (HQ)	Provider of enterprise integration solutions. The company offers technical, IT consulting, and green energy services.	408-934-5898	NA	Milpitas
Good Dog Design (HQ)	Provider of digital designing services. The company offers web development and designing and mobile application services.	415-383-0110	NA	Mill Valley
Googleplex (HQ)	Provider of search engine to make world's information universally accessible. The company specializes in Internet-related services and products.	650-253-0000	NA	Mountain View
Granite Horizon LLC (HQ)	Provider of content management solutions. The company offers design, development, project management, and user and developer training services.	916-647-6350	NA	Elk Grove
GridGain Systems Inc (HQ)	Developer of a Java and Scala-based cloud computing middleware for a wide range of multimedia applications.	650-241-2281	NA	Foster City
GT Nexus Inc (HQ)	Provider of supply chain, transportation, and investment management solutions. The company serves retailers and manufacturers.	510-808-2222	NA	Oakland

COMPANY NAME	PRODUCT / SERVICE	PHONE	EMP	CITY
Guardian Analytics (HQ)	Provider of enterprise and community banking solutions. The company is engaged in training and applied fraud analysis services.	650-383-9200	NA	Mountain View
N Gumas Advertising (HQ)	Provider of strategic marketing, creative development and media planning and placement.	415-621-7575	NA	San Francisco
Harmon.ie (HQ)	Provider of SharePoint applications for Outlook, mobile, and desktop platforms. The company offers records and knowledge management services.	408-907-1339	NA	Milpitas
Hero Digital (HQ)	Provider of website and mobile design and development services. The company specializes in mobile marketing programs.	415-409-2400	NA	San Francisco
Hillstone Networks (RH)	Provider of security solutions for enterprises and data center networks. The company serves Fortune 500 companies and educational institutions.	408-508-6750	NA	Santa Clara
N Holland Communications Inc (HQ)	Provider of advertising and public relations firm.	818-854-6136	NA	Canoga Park
Hurd & Associates Design (HQ)	Provider of print, logo, and web design, branding, marketing, advertising, and identity management services.	925-930-8580	NA	Walnut Creek
Hyperarts Web Design Development & Maintenance (HQ)	Provider of web design, development, and consulting services. The company performs SEO, SEM services, and web application development.	510-339-6084	NA	Oakland
Iconix Inc (HQ)	Provider of business solutions such as email identity software. The company caters to brand and customer security needs.	408-727-6342	NA	San Jose
IdeaBlade (HQ)	Provider of database application services. The company's products include DevForce, Coctail, and Breeze.	510-596-5100	NA	Orinda
Identiv Inc (HQ)	Provider of security technology services. The company's products include desktop readers, terminals, modules, and development kits.	888-809-8880	NA	Fremont
Iksanika LLC (HQ)	Provider of custom software development, testing, quality assurance, porting, and re-engineering services.	408-490-0777	NA	San Jose
Imageteq Technologies Inc (HQ)	Provider of IT consulting and services. The company focuses on consulting, enterprise application, and staff augmentation.	650-403-4806	NA	Burlingame
iMiners Inc (HQ)	Provider of investor relations management tools and web-based communication platforms. The company offers website plug-ins and shareholder message boards.	925-447-6073	NA	Livermore
Imperva Inc (HQ)	Provider of application and data security solutions. The company's products include database firewalls, management server, and monitoring software.	650-345-9000	NA	Redwood Shores
Inabyte Inc (HQ)	Manufacturer of developer tools. The company also offers solutions and services for developers and end users of PCs or workstations.	415-898-7905	NA	Novato
Incentia Design Systems Inc (HQ)	Provider of advanced timing and signal integrity analysis, design closure, and logic synthesis software for nanometer designs.	408-727-8988	NA	Santa Clara
INDEC Medical Systems Inc (HQ)	Provider of hardware and software solutions for cardiovascular imaging applications such as intravascular ultrasound and angiography.	408-986-1600	NA	Los Altos
Inflection LLC (HQ)	Provider of technology solutions and software products. The company develops search engines, cloud management, and web server applications.	650-618-9910	NA	Redwood City
Infobahn Softworld Inc (HQ)	Provider of consulting, enterprise application integration, service oriented architecture, and systems integration solutions to fortune 500 companies.	408-855-9616	NA	San Jose
Infoblox (HQ)	Provider of automated network control solutions. The company's services include training, implementation, migration, upgrade, repair, and maintenance.	408-986-4000	NA	Santa Clara
Infolane Inc (HQ)	Provider of web design and development and support services that includes web content management, application development, and technical improvements.	510-277-2399	NA	Emeryville
Infostretch Corp (HQ)	Provider of mobile application development, quality assurance testing and automation, SaaS solutions, and ERP testing solutions.	408-727-1100	NA	Santa Clara
Innovative Interfaces Inc (HQ)	Provider of technology solutions and services. The company deals with training and hosting, and technical support.	510-655-6200	NA	Emeryville
Intapp Inc (HQ)	Provider of software and services for risk management, time management, and box management. The company's products include Intapp Time and Wall Builder.	650-852-0400	NA	Palo Alto
Intellicon Solutions (HQ)	Provider of intelligent consulting solutions for learning and development, performance management systems, and related social media communication.	925-377-7925	NA	Moraga
Intergraphics (HQ)	Developer of multilingual graphics. The company provides translation, typography, and other services.	650-359-3087	NA	Pacifica
Intermedia.net Inc (HQ)	Provider of cloud services including VoIP telephony, instant messaging, and file management to small and mid-sized businesses.	800-379-7729	NA	Sunnyvale
Intermedia.net Inc (HQ)	Provider of UCaaS, CCaaS, and cloud business applications that helps businesses and partners with secure solutions for communication and collaboration.	650-641-4000	NA	Sunnyvale
Internet Software Sciences (HQ)	Developer of web based applications for IT help desk, customer support, asset tracking, and facilities management needs.	650-949-0942	NA	Los Altos Hills

COMPANY NAME	PRODUCT / SERVICE	PHONE	EMP	CITY
Intertrust Technologies Corp (HQ)	Provider of security technology services such as content protection, white label video distribution, and software tamper resistance.	408-616-1600	NA	Sunnyvale
Intrinsyx Technologies Corp (BR)	Provider of information technology solutions. The company caters to federal, state, and commercial stakeholders.	650-210-9219	NA	Moffett Field
Intuit Inc (HQ)	Provider of financial management software solutions. The company offers services to small businesses and related organizations.	800-446-8848	NA	Mountain View
IT Flux (HQ)	Provider of custom software development services, outsourcing, and outsourced software testing services.	408-649-5642	NA	Napa
IT Pro Source (HQ)	Provider of on call plans, managed services, web based monitoring, and communication cabling services.	925-455-7701	NA	Livermore
Ivalua Inc (HQ)	Designer and developer of spend management solutions. The company offers services to medium and large sized companies.	650-930-9710	NA	Redwood City
JAMIS Software Corp (HQ)	Provider of job-cost, billing, and accounting systems and solutions. The company caters to the government contractors.	800-655-2647	NA	San Diego
Jelli Inc (HQ)	Developer of user-controlled radio used in iPhone and radio stations. The company's products are used in the automation of radio advertising.	855-790-8275	NA	San Mateo
Joe Kline Aviation Art (HQ)	Provider of military aircraft painting services. The company offers customized prints, helicopter paintings, fixed wing paintings, and other prints.	408-842-6979	NA	Gilroy
Jolly Technologies Inc (HQ)	Provider of secure identification, visitor management, barcode and asset tracking software services.	650-594-5955	NA	San Mateo
Jova Solutions Inc (HQ)	Developer of systems for distributed process control and data management for science and industrial sectors. The company offers USB instruments.	415-816-4482	NA	San Francisco
Joyent Inc (HQ)	Provider of cloud infrastructure services. The company's products include Compute service, Manta storage, and Private Cloud.	415-400-0600	NA	San Francisco
Juniper Networks Inc (HQ)	Provider of network security solutions. The company serves the government, healthcare, utilities, and manufacturing industries.	408-745-2000	NA	Sunnyvale
Jway Group Inc (HQ)	Retailer of web consulting and service solutions such as web application development, web design, and mobile programming services.	408-247-5929	NA	Milpitas
KalioTek (HQ)	Provider of enterprise applications. The company also specializes in technical infrastructure for companies.	408-550-8000	NA	Cupertino
Keep IT Simple (HQ)	Provider of virtualization and information technology services. The company focuses on virtualization assessment, cloud computing, and networking.	510-403-7500	NA	Fremont
Key Performance Ideas Inc (BR)	Provider of enterprise performance management and business intelligence solutions. The company offers Oracle Hyperion and OBIEE software for this need.	855-457-4462	NA	San Francisco
Kii Corp (HQ)	Provider of applications to device manufacturers and mobile network operators. The company serves enterprise, cross-platform games, and other needs.	650-577-2340	NA	San Mateo
KKI Corp (HQ)	Provider of web and business services and software solutions. The company is also involved in design and technical support services.	209-863-8550	NA	Modesto
KLH Consulting Inc (HQ)	Provider of IT consulting, cloud computing, and related business solutions. The company offers services to business executives and professionals.	707-575-9986	NA	Santa Rosa
Konicom Inc (HQ)	Provider of computer services to businesses and individuals. The company offers Internet related services such as wireless network and hotspot setup.	916-441-7373	NA	Sacramento
Kovair Software Inc (HQ)	Provider of web-based document management applications. The company offers product support maintenance services.	408-262-0200	NA	San Ramon
Kovarus Inc (HQ)	Provider of integrated business IT solutions. The company also deals with leasing, financing, project management, and related services.	800-454-1585	NA	San Ramon
KP LLC (BR)	Provider of marketing and outsourcing solutions offering digital and offset printing and mailing services.	510-351-5400	NA	San Leandro
Kreck Design Solutions (HQ)	Provider of graphic design and Internet-related services. The company focuses on corporate identity and marketing, web design, SEO, content management.	707-433-6166	NA	Santa Rosa
Langtech (HQ)	Provider of information technology services. The company provides software solutions, cloud services, system integration, and consulting.	415-364-9600	NA	San Francisco
Lastline (HQ)	Manufacturer of malware protection products. The company serves schools, restaurants, and the enterprise security industry.	877-671-3239	NA	San Mateo
Lattice Engines Inc (HQ)	Provider of business to business sales intelligence software. The company is engaged in web design and hosting and programming solutions.	877-460-0010	NA	San Mateo
Lavante Inc (HQ)	Provider of on-demand strategic profit recovery solutions. The company also offers vendor information management software.	408-754-1410	NA	San Jose
Leadman Electronics USA Inc (HQ)	Provider of ODM/OEM, hardware engineering expertise, and custom solutions for a wide range of security, storage, server, and network applications.	408-380-4567	NA	Santa Clara

COMPANY NAME	PRODUCT / SERVICE	PHONE	EMP	CITY
LekasMiller Design (HQ)	Provider of photography, printing, advertising, graphic design, mailing, and project management services.	925-934-3971	NA	Walnut Creek
Lenos Software (HQ)	Provider of enterprise resource management, development of motion graphics, and value-added management services.	415-281-8828	NA	San Francisco
LMI Net (HQ)	Provider of solar-assisted Internet connections. The company offers computer repair, IT services, web site development, and virus removal services.	510-843-6389	NA	Berkeley
Lucidworks (HQ)	Provider of commercial foundation for architecture, design, development, and deployment of search solutions built with lucid works enterprise.	415-329-6515	NA	San Francisco
Lunagraphica Inc (HQ)	Provider of Internet marketing and consulting solutions. The company offers services in graphic design, website design, and web development.	408-962-1588	NA	Sunnyvale
Mailshell Inc (HQ)	Provider of traffic reputation software engines. The company also specializes in anti-spam and anti-phishing software engines.	415-294-4242	NA	Santa Clara
Maxeler Technologies Inc (HQ)	Developer of computing solutions. The company offers services to the oil and gas, analytical, and financial sectors.	650-938-8818	NA	Mountain View
Medallia Inc (HQ)	Provider of consulting, system configuration, user training, and data warehouse integration services.	650-321-3000	NA	San Mateo
Media Flint (HQ)	Provides Internet marketing and advertising solutions to companies.	888-592-2921	NA	Mountain View
Media Net Link Inc (HQ)	Provider of web business solutions. The company focuses on application development, systems integration, website design, and project management.	866-563-5152	NA	Oakland
Medical Technology Stock Letter (HQ)	Publisher of medical technology stock letters.	510-843-1857	NA	Berkeley
Meltwater Group (HQ)	Developer of software products such as Meltwater BUZZ, Meltwater NEWS, and Meltwater DRIVE to meet the specific needs of businesses around the world.	415-829-5900	NA	San Francisco
Menlo Security (HQ)	Provider of security solutions. The company's offerings include web isolation, document, and phishing isolation services.	650-614-1705	NA	Palo Alto
Micromega Systems Inc (HQ)	Provider of database systems and e-business website design services. The company also focuses on training and installation.	415-924-4700	NA	Corte Madera
Milestone Inc (HQ)	Provider of hotel Internet marketing and website development services. The company focuses on website and social media marketing and ROI tracking.	408-492-9055	NA	Santa Clara
Mirantis Inc (HQ)	Specializes in the development and support of Kubernetes and OpenStack.	650-963-9828	NA	Campbell
MMC AD Systems (HQ)	Provider of architectural and consulting services. The company focuses on strategic planning, market research, and business and web development.	925-485-4949	NA	Pleasanton
Moonstone Interactive Inc (HQ)	Provider of website design services. The company offers web design and development, content management, and market visibility services.	925-736-4178	NA	San Ramon
Motiondsp Inc (HQ)	Provider of software products. The company serves the defense and intelligence, law enforcement, energy, and transportation markers.	650-288-1164	NA	Burlingame
Mountford Group Inc (HQ)	Provider of system development and web application services. The company also focuses on technical communication.	925-686-6613	NA	Concord
MTI California Inc (HQ)	Specializes in designing and validating manufacturing controls. The company offers services to biotech companies.	925-937-1500	NA	Walnut Creek
Multimedia Consulting Services Inc (HQ)	Provider of multimedia consulting services. The company offers design, implementation, and maintenance of the information technology infrastructure.	650-578-8591	NA	Foster City
Natural Logic (HQ)	Provider of consulting, product development, e-learning, digital content, and product support services.	510-248-4940	NA	Berkeley
Neo4j Inc (HQ)	Graph database platform that helps companies to access the business value of data connections.	855-636-4532	NA	San Mateo
Netease Inc (HQ)	Provider of web hosting services. The company offers domain registration, hosting, and dial-up services.	800-580-0932	NA	Forestville
Netwoven Inc (HQ)	Provider of enterprise content management and business intelligence solutions. The company also focuses on process management.	877-638-9683	NA	Milpitas
Nexb Inc (HQ)	Designer and developer of software tools and services. The company offers services to business enterprises and related organizations.	650-592-2096	NA	San Carlos
Nextbus Inc (BR)	Provider of transit management solutions. The company also provides real-time passenger information solutions to organizations.	925-686-8200	NA	Concord
Noble Image Inc (HQ)	Provider of website and graphic design, website development, hosting, programming, and technical support services.	916-419-3570	NA	Sacramento
Nok Nok Labs Inc (HQ)	Focuses on the development on online security solutions. The company is also involved in third party research services.	650-433-1300	NA	Palo Alto
Nomis Solutions Inc (HQ)	Provider of pricing and profitability management solutions. The company caters to the financial services.	650-588-9800	NA	Brisbane
Omnicia Inc (HQ)	Provider of electronic submissions for the life science sector. The company offers electronics and desktop publishing and document management services.	415-293-8553	NA	San Francisco

N

COMPANY NAME	PRODUCT / SERVICE	PHONE	EMP	CITY
OneLogin (HQ)	Provider of single sign-on and identity management for cloud-based applications. The company serves the industrial sector.	415-645-6830	NA	San Francisco
Onfulfillment Inc (HQ)	Provider of printing solutions. The company offers order fulfillment, online delivery, and print management services.	510-793-3009	NA	Newark
Opal Soft Inc (HQ)	Provider of communications equipment installation and networking. The company's services include application development, network management, and maintenance.	408-267-2211	NA	Sunnyvale
Opengov Inc (HQ)	Provider of financial transparency and business intelligence solutions. The company offers services to government agencies.	650-336-7167	NA	Redwood City
Oracle Corp (BR)	Developer of hardware and software systems. The company provides Oracle database, engineered systems, and enterprise manager solutions.	415-402-7200	NA	San Francisco
Orbeon Inc (HQ)	Provider of web form deployment services. The company offers basic, gold, and platinum development support, and validation services.	650-762-8184	NA	San Mateo
Ordinal Technology Corp (HQ)	Provider of sorting services of massive and production data sets such as web logs for high-traffic websites, phone logs, and government agency data.	925-253-9204	NA	Orinda
Organic Inc (HQ)	Provider of information technology services. The company develops websites, mobile applications, banner, and digital signage.	415-581-5300	NA	San Francisco
N OtherWorld Enterprises Inc (HQ)	Provider of web design, development and hosting services.	805-768-4638	NA	Simi Valley
Owler Inc (HQ)	Provider of reliable and up-to-date business information.	650-242-9253	NA	San Mateo
Pearl Lemon (BR)	Digital marketing agency that offers results-oriented SEO services.	628-214-1309	NA	San Francisco
Perforce Software Inc (BR)	Developer of software management tools and technology solutions. The company serves game development, banking, healthcare, and other sectors.	510-864-7400	NA	Alameda
Perryman Group Inc (HQ)	Provider of website design and hosting, e-commerce solutions, and networking services. The company serves business and residential customers.	916-630-7456	NA	Folsom
Pica8 Inc (HQ)	Manufacturer of white box switches. The company specializes in traditional switches and routing protocols.	833-888-7422	NA	Palo Alto
Pierce Washington (HQ)	Provider of systems integration and e-commerce solutions. The company also deals with the development of software tools.	415-431-8300	NA	San Francisco
Pinterest (HQ)	Specializes in mobile application tools. The company focuses on pinning items, creating boards, and interacting with other members.	415-762-7100	NA	San Francisco
Pipsqueak Productions LLC (HQ)	Provider of graphic design, photography, writing, editing, animation, and website development services.	415-668-4372	NA	San Francisco
Pixami Inc (HQ)	Provider of imaging technologies. The company caters to both photo-based and non-photo-based businesses.	925-465-5167	NA	Pleasanton
Planeteria Media (HQ)	Designer and developer of websites, applications, e-commerce, content management systems, video, and offers flash, and Internet marketing services.	707-843-3773	NA	Santa Rosa
N Popcorn Press and Media (HQ)	Creator of books and educational materials related to San Diego.	858-759-2779	NA	Rancho Santa Fe
Presentek Inc (HQ)	Designer of websites and web portals. The company also offers content management systems and e-commerce handlers.	408-354-1264	NA	Los Gatos
Presidio Inc (BR)	Provider of IP telephony and wireless networking services. The company also deals with deployment, integration, and hardware and software development.	415-501-9020	NA	Pleasanton
Prosoft Engineering Inc (HQ)	Developer of data recovery software. The company provides Drive Genius, Data Rescue, and Data Backup software.	877-477-6763	NA	Livermore
PubMatic Inc (HQ)	Developer of marketing automation software. The company deals with the planning of media campaigns and offers services to publishers.	650-331-3485	NA	Redwood City
Pulse Secure LLC (HQ)	Provider of product, hardware, partner, and enterprise solutions. The company offers services to the financial services and healthcare industries.	408-372-9600	NA	San Jose
Punchcut LLC (HQ)	Provider of interface designs. The company offers mid, small, large, micro, and medium screen solutions.	415-445-8855	NA	San Francisco
Qarbon Inc (HQ)	Publisher of presentation software and the originator of patented Viewlet technology. The company serves business, government, and education markers.	408-430-5560	NA	San Jose
Qualys Inc (HQ)	Provider of security and compliance solutions. The company also offers asset discovery and threat protection solutions.	650-801-6100	NA	Foster City
Quantitative Medical Systems Inc (HQ)	Provider of medical systems and dialysis billing software products. The company is engaged in clinical support.	510-654-9200	NA	Emeryville
Qubop Inc (HQ)	Developer of applications and games for mobile platforms. The company specializes in web applications, localization, IOS, and android development.	415-891-7788	NA	San Francisco
Quest Business Systems Inc (HQ)	Provider of solutions in police equipment tracking systems. The company also focuses on purchasing management.	925-634-2670	NA	Brentwood
Quorum Technologies (HQ)	Developer of recycling and waste disposal solutions for the automotive, industrial, municipal, hospitality, and food industries.	916-669-5577	NA	Sacramento

COMPANY NAME	PRODUCT / SERVICE	PHONE	EMP	CITY
Range Networks (HQ)	Provider of mobile network solutions. The company is also engaged in software and hardware solutions and services.	415-778-8700	NA	Santa Clara
Rasteroids Design (HQ)	Provider of web designing, custom programming, implementation, custom software development, and hosting services.	408-979-9138	NA	San Jose
Real-Time Innovations Inc (HQ)	Provider for real-time infrastructure software solutions. The company also offers engineering and product development services.	408-990-7400	NA	Sunnyvale
Rearden LLC (HQ)	Provider of cloud computing, motion picture, video game, consumer electronics, wireless, imaging, communications, and alternative energy technologies.	415-947-5555	NA	Mountain View
Redwhale Software Corp (HQ)	Provider of software tools, technologies, and professional services for the design, development, and run-time management of user interfaces.	650-312-1500	NA	Redwood City
Relay2 Inc (HQ)	Provider of cloud Wi-Fi Services platform which allows service providers to monetize value added Wi-Fi services.	408-380-0031	NA	Milpitas
Resilient Networks Systems Inc (HQ)	Developer of Internet software products. The company serves the healthcare, media, information security, and government sectors.	415-291-9600	NA	San Francisco
Resilinc Corp (HQ)	Provider of supply chain and risk management solutions. The company serves the life science and automotive industries.	408-883-8053	NA	Milpitas
RetailNext (HQ)	Provider of in-store analytics solutions. The company offers services to retail labs, marketing departments, and shopping centers.	408-884-2162	NA	San Jose
RevStream Inc (HQ)	Provider of enterprise revenue and billing management solutions. The company also offers advisory and technical support services.	888-738-0206	NA	Redwood Shores
Rootdesign LLC (HQ)	Provider of design solutions specializing in brand strategy, user interface design, and database development services.	415-282-2484	NA	San Francisco
Runscope Inc (HQ)	Specializes in automated performance monitoring and testing solutions. The company serves developers.	888-812-6786	NA	San Francisco
Samsara Networks Inc (HQ)	Manufacturer of flexible sensors. The company is engaged in fleet monitoring, industrial sensing, cold chain monitoring, and fleet telematics.	415-985-2400	NA	San Francisco
SDL USA (BR)	Provider of web content and structured content management, as well as e-commerce solutions, and language technologies.	408-743-3600	NA	San Jose
SE Ranking (BR)	SEO platform that allows individuals to optimize and promote a website on the web.	415-704-4387	NA	Palo Alto
Selectiva Systems Inc (HQ)	Provider of solutions for revenue reporting, customer service, and distributor management. The company serves high-tech, pharma, and other sectors.	408-297-1336	NA	San Jose
Sensory Inc (HQ)	Provider of speech recognition and voice biometric ICs. The company's products are used in toys and home electronic products.	408-625-3300	NA	Santa Clara
ShareThis Inc (HQ)	Developers of social sharing solutions for website owners.	650-323-1783	NA	Palo Alto
Sharper Technology Inc (HQ)	Provider of network security solutions and services. The company also offers design, implementation, and training services.	650-964-4600	NA	Palo Alto
Skybox Security Inc (HQ)	Provider of risk analytics for cyber security. The company offers threat management and network security management solutions.	408-441-8060	NA	San Jose
Sleepless Media (HQ)	Provider of website design and development services. The company focuses on content management, e-commerce, SEO, hosting, and brand identity.	831-427-1969	NA	Soquel
Smart ERP Solutions Inc (HQ)	Developer of enterprise class software. The company provides vendor management software and support services.	925-271-0200	NA	Pleasanton
Softsol Inc (HQ)	Provider of software solutions. The company offers software such as Intelli Court Case Management, Corporate Investigations, STIC, and PB Migration.	510-824-2000	NA	Fremont
Software AG (BR)	Provider of enterprise management and business solutions that include process intelligence and automation, and enterprise architecture.	800-823-2212	NA	Santa Clara
Soliton Systems Inc (BR)	Provider of information technology solutions. The company offers IT security, network infrastructure, cloud computing, and IT management services.	408-434-1923	NA	San Jose
Solution Architects Inc (HQ)	Provider of sophisticated IT solutions for complex systems. The company's services include analysis and product development.	415-775-1656	NA	San Francisco
Sono Group Inc (HQ)	Provider of custom software and application development, training, social networking, and IT staffing services.	925-855-8552	NA	Danville
Spence Engineering Services Inc (HQ)	Provider of solutions for hardware and software engineering problems. The company offers services to the technical sector.	650-571-6500	NA	San Mateo
Spiralinks Corp (HQ)	Provider of compensation management software products. The company offers compensation management, HR analytics, and payroll integration services.	408-608-6900	NA	Campbell
Splunk Inc (HQ)	Provider of search engine services specializing in IT data. The company serves the government, healthcare, and telecommunication industries.	415-848-8400	NA	San Francisco
SPYRUS (HQ)	Developer and marketer of hardware encryption, authentication, and digital content security products.	408-392-9131	NA	San Jose
Stanfield Systems Inc (HQ)	Provider of system engineering and data management services. The company also focuses on web development and technical services.	916-608-8006	NA	Folsom

COMPANY NAME	PRODUCT / SERVICE	PHONE	EMP	CITY
StarNet Communications Corp (HQ)	Developer of X Windows solutions for connecting computers to Unix and Linux desktops and applications.	408-739-0881	NA	Santa Clara
Stevens Creek Software (HQ)	Provider of software solutions for the palm computing platform. The company is involved in custom development and technical support.	408-725-0424	NA	Cupertino
Subrosasoft.Com Inc (HQ)	Developer of software for Mac operating systems. The company offers software such as FileSalvage, CopyCat, and ParentRemote.	510-870-7883	NA	Fremont
Succeed.Net (BR)	Provider of Internet services. The company specializes in metro Ethernet, wireless broadband, DSL service, national dial-up, and server co-location.	530-674-4200	NA	Roseville
Sumo Logic (HQ)	Provider of compliance, security, monitoring, troubleshooting, and delivery solutions. The company serves security, IT, and development teams.	650-810-8700	NA	Redwood City
Sun-Net Inc (HQ)	Provider of enterprise software solutions supporting outage scheduling, logging, and reporting for power, gas, and water utilities.	408-323-1318	NA	San Jose
SurveyMonkey Inc (HQ)	Provider of a cloud-based people-powered data platform.	650-543-8400	NA	San Mateo
Switchfly (HQ)	Provider of software solutions such as travel commerce platforms, payments engines, mobile platforms, and social media solutions.	415-541-9100	NA	Ste 215
Synack (HQ)	Provider of security intelligence solutions. The company offers services to the commercial, industrial, and business sectors.	855-796-2251	NA	Redwood City
Syncplicity LLC (HQ)	Provider of cloud-based file management solutions such as access, sync, backup and share of files from anywhere for businesses and individuals.	888-997-9627	NA	Santa Clara
Synergy Business Solutions (HQ)	Provider of technology evaluation, business process improvement, and custom software development services to a wide range of sectors.	415-263-1843	NA	San Francisco
N TCSN Inc (HQ)	Provider of Internet solutions, web hosting, website designing and much more.	805-227-7000	NA	Paso Robles
Tech Soft 3d (HQ)	Provider of software solutions. The company offers software for desktop visualization, modeling, cloud and mobile solutions, and data exchange.	510-883-2180	NA	Berkeley
Telemanagement Technologies Inc (HQ)	Provider of telemanagement software products and services. The company is engaged in troubleshooting and maintenance services.	925-946-9800	NA	Walnut Creek
Telosa Software Inc (HQ)	Provider of CRM and fundraising software for nonprofits. The company focuses on gift and grant tracking, donor and volunteer management.	800-750-6418	NA	Palo Alto
Tenefit Corp (HQ)	Provider of software services. The company's IoT gateway is used by mobile users, marketplaces, and machines to connect and communicate in real-time.	877-522-9464	NA	San Jose
Terrace Consulting Inc (HQ)	Provider of custom software development services. The company focuses on eCommerce, back office, business intelligence, cloud, and other services.	415-848-7300	NA	San Francisco
Text Analysis International Inc (HQ)	Provider of software development services for text analysis. The company focuses on project management, testing and implementation, and deployment.	650-308-9323	NA	Cupertino
TextDigger Inc (HQ)	Developer of horizontal semantic solutions for search engines. The company focuses on content mining and analytics.	408-416-3142	NA	San Jose
The Igneous Group Inc (HQ)	Provider of technology consulting services. The company focuses on web content, application development, and e-commerce.	831-469-7625	NA	Santa Cruz
The Wecker Group (HQ)	Provider of design studio and ad agency services. The company specializes in corporate identity, collateral, TV advertising, and event promotion.	831-372-8377	NA	Monterey
Thrasys Inc (HQ)	Provider of health networking solutions. The company serves patients, service centers, payers, and public health administrators.	650-449-1000	NA	San Francisco
Toolwire Inc (HQ)	Designer and developer of experiential learning solutions for higher education and corporate training institutions.	925-227-8500	NA	Pleasanton
Totango Inc (HQ)	A customer success software helps to connect customer data, monitor health changes, and proactively engage the customers by using an integrated platform.	800-634-1990	NA	San Mateo
Trackdata Systems Corp (HQ)	Provider of greyhound, thoroughbred, and harness racing information. The company features up-to-date listing of racing schedules.	408-446-5595	NA	Cupertino
Transend Corp (HQ)	Provider of email migration and conversion solutions that support email systems. The company serves business, education, reselling, and other sectors.	650-324-5370	NA	Palo Alto
Twilio Inc (HQ)	Provider of infrastructure APIs for businesses to build scalable, reliable voice, and text messaging apps.	415-390-2337	NA	San Francisco
Unisoft Corp (HQ)	Provider of broadcast, development, and testing tools specific to interactive TV standards. The company focuses on US cable and broadcast industries.	650-259-1290	NA	Millbrae
Unitedlayer LLC (HQ)	Provider of cloud hosting solutions. The company offers server clusters and routers, disaster recovery, infrastructure, and colocation services.	415-349-2100	NA	San Francisco
Untangle (HQ)	Designer and developer of network management software. The company specializes in firewall and Internet management application.	408-598-4299	NA	San Jose
UpGuard Inc (HQ)	Provider of integrity monitoring, vulnerability analysis, vendor risk assessment, and configuration differencing solutions.	888-882-3223	NA	Mountain View

COMPANY NAME	PRODUCT / SERVICE	PHONE	EMP	CITY
Upwork Global Inc (HQ)	Web based platform for remote work.	650-316-7500	NA	Santa Clara
UserTesting (HQ)	Deliver a human insight platform powered by customer experience for product teams, marketers, and advertising companies.	888-877-1882	NA	San Francisco
vArmour Inc (HQ)	Provider of cloud security, segmentation, monitoring, and deception solutions. The company serves banks and healthcare organizations.	650-564-5100	NA	Los Altos
Veeva Systems Inc (HQ)	Provider of cloud-based business solutions such as customer relationship management and content management for the life sciences industry.	925-452-6500	NA	Pleasanton
Verix Inc (HQ)	Designer and developer of precision tooling and equipment for performance engine builders and mechanists.	650-949-2700	NA	San Jose
Victorious (HQ)	Search engine optimization agency that leverages a wealth of performance data and market research to create scientifically-driven SEO strategies.	415-621-9830	NA	San Francisco
Video Clarity Inc (HQ)	Provider of real time and broadcast quality monitoring, perceptual analysis, recording, and automating services.	408-379-6952	NA	Campbell
Vien Thao Media (HQ)	Operator of multiple Christian television stations.	408-947-7517	NA	San Jose
Vindicia Inc (HQ)	Developer of marketing and analytics solutions. The company offers customer acquisition and retention and customer relationship management services.	650-264-4700	NA	San Mateo
Vintara Inc (HQ)	Provider of web-based enterprise process management solutions and services. The company caters to a number of industries.	877-846-8272	NA	Oakland
VipeCloud (HQ)	Developers of marketing CRM that helps small- and mid-sized businesses accelerate the growth.	650-308-8473	NA	Palo Alto
Visualware Inc (HQ)	Provider of solutions to measure broadband connection performance for enterprises, homes, and offices. The company offers both hardware and software.	209-262-3491	NA	Turlock
Vivante Corp (HQ)	Provider of semiconductors for graphics and multimedia. The company focuses on image and video processing services.	408-844-8560	NA	San Jose
Webenertia (HQ)	Provider of web applications and e-commerce services. The company also focuses on motion graphics and Internet marketing solutions.	408-246-0000	NA	San Jose
WellnessFX Inc (HQ)	Specializes in web-based services. The company focuses on diagnostic testing and it serves medical practitioners.	415-796-3373	NA	San Francisco
Whitehat Security (HQ)	Provider of web application security solutions such as vulnerability management, threat modeling, and risk profiling.	408-343-8300	NA	San Jose
William Stucky & Associates Inc (HQ)	Provider of software products and services. The company mainly caters to the asset-based lending industry.	415-788-2441	NA	San Francisco
WindSpring Inc (HQ)	Manufacturer of data management tools. The company provides a framework for optimized compressed data management in the storage and embedded fields.	408-452-7400	NA	San Jose
Wipro Limited (BR)	Provider of analytics and information management, business process outsourcing, consulting, and managed and cloud services.	650-316-3555	NA	Mountain View
Xtelesis Corp (HQ)	Provider of voice and data solutions. The company is engaged in data networking, audio web conferencing, and managed IT services.	650-239-1400	NA	Burlingame
Yola Inc (HQ)	Provider of digital marketing services. The company offers mobile, facebook, and web publishing, domain names, and reliable hosting services.	866-764-0701	NA	San Francisco
Zag Technical Services Inc (HQ)	Provider of services for server, email stability, reliability, migration, and security assessment needs.	408-383-2000	NA	San Jose
Zapier Inc (HQ)	Developers of an integrated app that shares information within a user's collective web app automatically.	877-381-8743	NA	San Francisco
Zscaler Inc (HQ)	Provider of SaaS security solutions. The company offers cloud security solutions for mobile enterprises.	408-533-0288	NA	San Jose
Zynga Inc (HQ)	Provider of social game services with more than 240 million monthly active users. The company's games include CityVille, Draw Something, and Hidden Chronicles.	800-762-2530	1001-5000	San Francisco

326 = Miscellaneous Software-Related Services

COMPANY NAME	PRODUCT / SERVICE	PHONE	EMP	CITY
15five Inc (HQ)	Provider of services that allow you to question and start conversations that matters to elevate performance of employees, managers, and entire organizations.	415-967-3483	NA	San Francisco
21Tech LLC (BR)	Provider of business and technology solutions such as technology consultancy, strategic sourcing/placement, and branding and creative services practice.	415-355-9090	NA	Oakland
314e Corp (HQ)	Provider of IT skills, methodologies, and cost-effective managed services for healthcare application and technical support services.	510-371-6736	NA	Pleasanton
6connex (HQ)	Provider of virtual environment space and powering virtual destinations for career fairs, corporate universities, product launches, and user conferences.	800-395-4702	NA	San Antonio
6WIND USA Inc (RH)	Manufacturer of virtual accelerators, routers, and related accessories. The company offers network security and network appliance solutions.	408-816-1366	NA	Santa Clara

COMPANY NAME	PRODUCT / SERVICE	PHONE	EMP	CITY
A A Networks (HQ)	Provider of Internet, networks and cabling, computer hardware and software, remote and on-site technical support services.	650-872-1998	NA	Burlingame
Abacus Solutions Inc (HQ)	Developer of SATURN, an integrated enterprise ETRM system and focuses on generation optimization, parameters estimation, and credit management.	650-941-1728	NA	Los Altos Hills
Accellion (HQ)	Provider of web-based file transfer applications. The company also focuses on data management solutions.	650-485-4300	NA	Palo Alto
Accenture (BR)	Provider of management consulting and technology services. The company also offers application outsourcing and IT consulting services.	415-537-5000	NA	San Francisco
Access Business Technologies (HQ)	Provider of cloud-based software and hosting solutions for government agencies, banks, credit unions, accounting firms, and servicing companies.	888-636-5426	NA	Folsom
Access Softek Inc (HQ)	Developer of mobile banking software solutions. The company focuses on software and product development, QA testing, user interface, and graphic design.	510-848-0606	NA	Berkeley
Acrylic Art (HQ)	Provider of fabrication and machining services. The company focuses on painting, product finishing, anodizing, and vapor polishing.	510-654-0953	NA	Emeryville
N Advanced Lease Systems Inc (HQ)	Provider of design, development and other services in IT sector.	530-378-6868	NA	Redding
Advanced Software Design Inc (HQ)	Provider of knowledge based engineering software and industry focused business solutions. The company offers services to the public sector.	925-975-0694	NA	Walnut Creek
Advancing Ideas LLC (HQ)	Provider of market research and analysis, application branding, and user interface development services.	415-625-3338	NA	San Francisco
Aechelon Technology Inc (HQ)	Developer of real time computer graphics applications in the training, simulation, and entertainment markers.	415-255-0120	NA	San Francisco
AerospaceComputing Inc (HQ)	Provider of computer technology application services to aerospace sciences. The company also focuses on business development services.	650-988-0388	NA	Mountain View
Agari Data Inc (HQ)	Provider of email security and social engineering solutions. The company serves the healthcare, financial services, and government industries.	650-627-7667	NA	Foster City
Agile Global Solutions Inc (HQ)	Provider of business and IT solutions such as custom and enterprise application management and mobile business solutions.	916-655-7745	NA	Folsom
Agilis Software LLC (HQ)	Developer of software licensing and software license management solution for enterprise software, embedded systems, and cloud software industries.	415-458-2614	NA	San Francisco
Air Worldwide Corp (BR)	Provider of software development and consulting services. The company focuses on risk modeling software and risk assessment and management consulting.	415-912-3111	NA	San Francisco
Aktana Inc (HQ)	Provider of decision support engine that pores through multiple data services and delivers insights and suggestions right in the rep's workflow.	888-707-3125	NA	San Francisco
Alten Calsoft Labs (HQ)	Provider of breed consulting, enterprise IT, and product engineering services for enterprises in healthcare, telecom, and high-tech and retail industries.	408-755-3000	NA	Santa Clara
Altierre Corp (HQ)	Provider of digital retail services. The company offers retail integration, software support, and consulting services.	408-435-7343	NA	San Jose
Altigen Communications Inc (HQ)	Manufacturer of voice and data telecommunication equipment. The company specializes in hosted business communication solutions.	408-597-9000	NA	Milpitas
American Telesource Inc (HQ)	Provider of voice and data communication applications. The company offers unified communications, wireless, and process automation solutions.	800-333-8394	NA	Emeryville
Andes Technology USA Corp (RH)	Provider of infrastructural solutions for embedded system applications. The company serves the semiconductor industry.	408-809-2929	NA	San Jose
Anomali (RH)	Specializes in the delivery of cyber security solutions. The company services to big and small organizations.	844-484-7328	NA	Redwood City
N Anotek Inc (HQ)	Developer of software and books to teach the Greek language to English speaking people.	310-450-5027	NA	Santa Monica
ANSYS Inc (BR)	Provider of engineering solutions. The company serves the aerospace, defense, and construction industries.	844-462-6797	NA	Berkeley
Apex Technology Management Inc (HQ)	Provider of information technology services such as business continuity planning, virtualization, and email protection.	530-248-1000	NA	Redding
AppEnsure (HQ)	Provider of cloud application performance and infrastructure management such as application-aware infrastructure performance management solution.	408-418-4602	NA	San Jose
Applied Computer Solutions (BR)	Provider of information technology solutions. The company offers solutions for virtualization, storage, security, and networking.	925-251-1000	NA	Pleasanton
Aptible Inc (HQ)	Developer of secure, private cloud deployment platform built to automate HIPAA compliance for digital health.	866-296-5003	NA	San Francisco
ArcherHall (HQ)	Provider of litigation support services. The company offers forensic data collection, online document review, and e-discovery processing services.	855-839-9084	NA	Sacramento
Artec Group Inc (BR)	Developer and distributor of 3D scanners and 3D cameras. The company's products include Artec iD, Artec 3D, Viewshape, and Shapify.	669-292-5611	NA	Santa Clara

COMPANY NAME	PRODUCT / SERVICE	PHONE	EMP	CITY
Aryaka Networks Inc (HQ)	Provider of cloud-based WAN optimization services. The company focuses on application performance, data protection, and bandwidth reduction.	888-692-7925	NA	San Mateo
Asap Systems (HQ)	Developer of inventory management and asset tracking software. The company also offers barcode scanners and printers and RFID tags.	408-227-2720	NA	San Jose
ASI Controls (HQ)	Manufacturer of direct digital controls for HVAC and light industrial marketplace. The company also offers networking products and unitary controls.	925-866-8808	NA	Pleasanton
Aspera Inc (HQ)	Developer of file transport technologies. The company provides client and server software, consoles, and mobile uploaders.	510-849-2386	NA	Emeryville
Aspire Systems Inc (BR)	Provider of product engineering, infrastructure and application support, and testing services. The company serves healthcare and education fields.	408-260-2076	NA	San Jose
Assia Inc (HQ)	Provider of broadband solution such as cloud check, technology licensing, DSL expresse, and expresse products and solution.	650-654-3400	NA	Redwood City
Assurx Inc (HQ)	Provider of quality management and regulatory compliance software solutions for biotechnology, medical devices, pharmaceutical, and energy industries.	408-778-1376	NA	Morgan Hill
Attention Control Systems Inc (HQ)	Manufacturer of cognitive aids. The company also offers technical assistance solutions and serves the healthcare sector.	888-224-7328	NA	Mountain View
AutoGrid Systems Inc (HQ)	Provider of grid-sensing technologies. The company focuses on energy data platform and optimized demand management services.	650-461-9038	NA	Redwood City
Automattic Inc (HQ)	Provider of blogging services. The company specializes in handling non-profit and open source projects.	877-273-3049	NA	San Francisco
Autonomic Software Inc (HQ)	Developer of software for endpoint and security management, imaging, and other needs. The company serves government, finance, and other sectors.	925-683-8351	NA	Danville
Aviso Inc (HQ)	Creator of software to change how enterprises make critical revenue decisions and automate sales forecasting process with data science for enterprises.	650-567-5470	NA	Redwood City
Avontus Software Corp (DH)	Creator of software for formwork, scaffolding, and shoring industries, both custom development for enterprises and packaged software for public.	800-848-1860	NA	Berkeley
Ayasdi Inc (HQ)	Provider of software applications that discovers critical intelligence in company data for right operational decisions quickly.	650-704-3395	NA	Menlo Park
Ayla Networks Inc (HQ)	Provider of Ayla's IoT cloud platform that brings connected products to market quickly and securely for manufacturers and service providers.	408-830-9844	NA	Santa Clara
Backshop Inc (HQ)	Provider of commercial real estate software for full deal-stack modeling, loan origination, asset management, and data library for customers.	415-332-1110	NA	Sausalito
Badger Maps Inc (HQ)	Provider of easy to use interface to manage our daily call routes, track visits, and update records.	415-592-5909	NA	San Francisco
BayNODE LLC (HQ)	Provider of data network solutions, outsourcing, and network security services. The company caters to the IT sector.	415-274-3100	NA	San Francisco
BCG Management Resources Inc (HQ)	Provider of enterprise software solutions and professional services such as dynamics NAV and BC solutions for food and manufacturing industry.	800-456-8474	NA	Concord
Bcl Technologies (HQ)	Developer of document creation, conversion, and extraction solutions. The company offers BCL easyPDF Cloud, a cloud-based PDF conversion platform.	408-557-2080	NA	San Jose
Bct Consulting Inc (HQ)	Provider of computer network support, web design, application programming, and other technology services.	559-579-1400	NA	Fresno
Bear River Associates Inc (HQ)	Provider of enterprise mobile computing products and services. The company serves business services, government, high-tech, and life science sectors.	510-834-5300	NA	Oakland
Bestek Manufacturing Inc (HQ)	Provider of supply chain services. The company engages focuses on systems manufacturing, materials management, and prototype support areas.	408-321-8834	NA	Milpitas
Beta Breakers Software Quality (HQ)	Provider of software and application testing services. The company offers functionality, compatibility, website, and mobile device testing services.	415-878-2990	NA	Novato
Bitglass Inc (HQ)	Provider of data protection solutions. The company focuses on cloud encryption, mobile security, and discovery solutions.	408-337-0190	NA	Campbell
Blast Analytics & Marketing (HQ)	Provider of web design, e-commerce, and brand design services. The company is involved in hosting and technical support.	916-724-6701	NA	Rocklin
Blue Jeans Network Inc (HQ)	Provider of cloud-based video conferencing solutions. The company also offers mobile video collaboration and cloud video bridging solutions.	408-550-2828	NA	San Jose
BlueChipTek Inc (HQ)	Provider of data management and protection, information life cycle management, networking, security, and data center solutions.	408-731-7700	NA	Santa Clara
BMC Software Inc (BR)	Provider of cloud management, workforce automation, and IT service management solutions. The company serves business enterprises and service providers.	800-793-4262	NA	Santa Clara

COMPANY NAME	PRODUCT / SERVICE	PHONE	EMP	CITY
Bramasol Inc (BR)	Provider of SAP-based solution for high tech software, life science, industrial machinery and components, and Telco, wireless, and Internet services.	408-831-0046	NA	Santa Clara
Brekeke Software Inc (HQ)	Developer of session initiation protocol software products for Internet protocol network communication needs.	650-401-6633	NA	San Mateo
Bright Computing Inc (HQ)	Provider of software solutions for provisioning and managing HPC clusters, Hadoop clusters, and openstack private clouds.	408-300-9448	NA	San Jose
Bright Pattern Inc (HQ)	Provider of enterprise contact center application for blended multi-channel interactions. The company offers products based on modern technology.	650-529-4099	NA	S San Francisco
Brighterion Inc (HQ)	Provider of products for fraud prevention, predictive intelligence, risk management, and homeland security. The company focuses on adaptive analytics.	415-986-5600	NA	San Francisco
Brightsign LLC (HQ)	Provider of digital sign media players, software, and networking solutions for the commercial digital signage industry.	408-852-9263	NA	Los Gatos
Bugcrowd (HQ)	Provider of security solutions. The company is engaged in pre-launch consulting, research, and testing services.	888-361-9734	NA	San Francisco
BuildingIQ Inc (HQ)	Provider of software-as-a-service solution to optimize energy use in commercial buildings such as hospitality, healthcare facilities, and utilities.	888-260-4080	NA	San Mateo
Burstorm Inc (HQ)	Provider of cloud design tools application. The company specializes in design, collaborate, quote, and implement of cloud architecture.	650-610-1480	NA	Danville
CAD Masters Inc (HQ)	Designer and developer of software and hardware solutions. The company focuses on drafting, engineering, plotting, and on-site project assistance.	925-939-1378	NA	Walnut Creek
Cadence Design Systems Inc (HQ)	Provider of semiconductor IP and electronic design automation services. The company offers tools for logic and RF design, IC packaging, and other needs.	408-943-1234	NA	San Jose
Calypso Technology Inc (HQ)	Provider of front-to-back technology solutions for the financial markers. The company offers technology platform for cross asset trading risk management.	415-530-4000	NA	San Francisco
Calyx Technology Inc (HQ)	Provider of mortgage solutions for banks and credit unions. The company also serves mortgage bankers and brokers.	214-252-5610	NA	San Jose
Capital Network Solutions Inc (HQ)	Provider of Internet security systems, phone systems, and off-site encrypted backup for small and medium sized businesses.	916-366-6566	NA	Sacramento
Capriza Inc (HQ)	Provider of codeless enterprise mobility platform. The company offers mobile-enabling business applications such as design, zaaps, manage, and security.	650-600-3661	NA	Palo Alto
Casahl Technology Inc (HQ)	Provider of collaboration and content environment optimization services. The company focuses on cloud integration and content management.	925-328-2828	NA	San Ramon
Caseware International Inc (DH)	Supplier of software solutions to accountants and auditors worldwide. The company offers working papers to accounting firms.	416-867-9504	NA	Berkeley
Catalyst Business Solutions (HQ)	Provider of technology consulting services in business applications, data center, and machine-to-machine/Internet of things.	408-281-7100	NA	San Jose
Ccintegration (HQ)	Provider of business engagement models such as OEM and virtual OEM. The company services include design, integration, and logistics.	408-228-1314	NA	San Jose
Celigo Inc (HQ)	Provider of cloud computing products and solutions. The company offers NetSuite consulting services that include implementation and optimization.	650-579-0210	NA	San Mateo
CellarStone Inc (HQ)	Provider of sales commissions and incentive compensation software and solutions. The company offers version upgrades and re-engineering services.	650-242-0008	NA	Half Moon Bay
Centrify (HQ)	Provider of identity and access management solutions. The company offers services to pharma companies and financial institutions.	669-444-5200	NA	Santa Clara
N Ceridian Corp (BR)	Firm is a provider of human capital management solutions.	714-963-1311	NA	Fountain Valley
Certain Inc (DH)	Provider of enterprise event management solutions that include e-mail marketing, event reporting, registration, and consulting services.	888-237-8246	NA	San Francisco
Certent Inc (HQ)	Provider of equity compensation management, equity compensation reporting, and disclosure management solutions.	925-730-4300	NA	Roseville
N Chander Software Solutions Inc (HQ)	Provider of marketing, call center, project management and technical support software and technical staffing augmentation solutions.	408-406-5624	NA	San Jose
Check Point Software Technologies Inc (HQ)	Developer of software technology solutions such as mobile security and next generation firewalls for retail/point of sale and financial services.	800-429-4391	NA	San Carlos
Chiapas Edi Technologies Inc (HQ)	Developer of electronic data interchange software for health insurance exchange brokers, MSOs, HMOs, and healthcare business data analytics services.	415-298-8166	NA	Davis
Chrometa LLC (HQ)	Provider of time keeping management software and services. The company offers products for PC, Mac, iPhone, and Android platforms.	916-546-9974	NA	Sacramento
Ciena Corp (BR)	Provider of cloud networking, network transformation, and packet network solutions for multi-data center environments.	408-904-2100	NA	San Jose

COMPANY NAME	PRODUCT / SERVICE	PHONE	EMP	CITY
Ciphercloud Inc (DH)	Provider of comprehensive cloud application discovery and risk assessment, data protection, data loss management, key management, and malware detection.	855-524-7437	NA	San Jose
Circle Internet Services Inc (HQ)	Provider of continuous integration and delivery solution. The company offers apps for docker, enterprise, and mobiles.	800-585-7075	NA	San Francisco
Citrix Systems Inc (BR)	Provider of transition to software-defining the workplace, uniting virtualization, mobility management, networking, and SaaS solutions.	408-790-8000	NA	Santa Clara
Clare Computer Solutions (HQ)	Provider of information technology services. The company offers computer network, software consultation, visualization, and cloud computing solutions.	925-277-0690	NA	San Ramon
Clarizen (HQ)	Provider of collaborative online project management software. The company offers work management, time tracking, and project scheduling solutions.	866-502-9813	NA	San Mateo
ClearCare Inc (HQ)	Provider of front and back office software solution such as billing, payroll, and marketing management for private duty home care agencies.	800-449-0645	NA	San Francisco
Clickatell (pty) Ltd (HQ)	Provider of SMS solutions such as SMS alerts, reminders, call centers, reservations and bookings for healthcare, marketing, and IT/software industries.	650-641-0011	NA	Redwood City
Climate Earth (HQ)	Provider of environmental product declarations and supply chain solutions such as supply chain, climate change risk, and natural capital management.	415-391-2725	NA	Point Richmond
Cloudera Inc (HQ)	Provider of professional services that include cluster certification, descriptive analytics pilot, and security integration pilot.	650-362-0488	NA	Santa Clara
Cloudmark Inc (HQ)	Provider of messaging infrastructure and security solutions. The company delivers scalable messaging platform, security intelligence, and filtering.	415-946-3800	NA	San Francisco
Cloudshare Inc (HQ)	Provider of flexible and cloud-computing platform for developing and testing IT applications, software, and systems.	888-609-4440	NA	San Francisco
Cloudwords Inc (HQ)	Provider of translation management systems and content localization solutions to manage translation process, vendors, and content systems.	415-394-8000	NA	San Francisco
Cognex Corp (BR)	Supplier of barcode readers and sensor products. The company offers vision sensors, fixed mount readers, handheld readers, and mobile computers.	858-481-2469	NA	Cupertino
Cognizant Technology Solutions (BR)	Provider of business consulting, enterprise application development, IT infrastructure, and outsourcing services.	925-790-2000	NA	San Ramon
Collaborative Drug Discovery Inc (HQ)	Provider of drug discovery research informatics. The company offers hosted biological and chemical database that securely manages private and external data.	650-242-5259	NA	Burlingame
CommerceNet (HQ)	Provider of Internet based research and piloting services such as Internet business, open trading networks, and Internet-user demographic surveys.	650-289-4040	NA	Los Altos
ComplianceEase (HQ)	Provider of intelligent business solutions to financial service institutions. The company offers automated compliance and risk management solutions.	650-373-1111	NA	Burlingame
Computer Logistics Corp (HQ)	Provider of system and Internet integration, system design, custom programming, web design, and hosting services.	530-241-3131	NA	Redding
CompuTrust Software (HQ)	Developer and seller of software for public administrators. The company offers services to businesses and enterprises.	800-222-7947	NA	Morgan Hill
Conformiq (HQ)	Provider of automated test designing services. The company focuses on training, project implementation, change management, and executive consulting.	408-898-2140	NA	Saratoga
Corecess Global Inc (BR)	Designer, developer, and manufacturer of telecommunication equipment for the broadband access network.	408-567-5300	NA	Santa Clara
Corona Labs Inc (HQ)	Developer of games, e-books, and other interactive content. The company offers services to the educational sector.	415-996-6877	NA	San Francisco
Couchbase Inc (HQ)	Developer of products and technology to meet the elastic scalability, always-on availability, and data mobility requirements of critical applications.	650-417-7500	NA	Santa Clara
CP Software Group (HQ)	Provider of capital formation, fund raising, management consulting, technical and marketing, and incubator services for startup and established companies.	916-985-4445	NA	Folsom
Cpacket Networks (HQ)	Provider of solutions for network traffic monitoring and data center performance management. The company specializes in traffic monitoring switches.	650-969-9500	NA	San Jose
N Cpp Inc (HQ)	Publisher of books on psychology and distributes publications of Jossey-Bass, Harper and Row, and B and D book and reaches market through direct mail, trade sales, and distributors.	650-969-8901	NA	Sunnyvale
CRMIT Solutions Pvt Ltd (HQ)	Provider of customer experience cloud solutions for banking, insurance education, retail, life science, energy, telecom, and financial services.	408-372-5379	NA	Milpitas
Cross-Circuit Networks Inc (HQ)	Provider of networking solutions specializing in information technology infrastructure design, systems virtual environment and consolidation.	408-654-9637	NA	San Jose

COMPANY NAME	PRODUCT / SERVICE	PHONE	EMP	CITY
CryptoForensics Technologies Inc (HQ)	Provider of cybersecurity solutions to businesses, organizations, and the government. The company focuses on cyberforensics and compliance services.	510-483-1933	NA	San Leandro
CSS Corp (HQ)	Provider of enterprise level support solutions for IT products. The company is involved in virtualization, storage, and archiving solutions.	650-385-3820	NA	Milpitas
Cubus Solutions Inc (HQ)	Provider of online banking solutions to seamlessly integrate with core system while delivering real-time, and secure, banking services to members.	925-344-5195	NA	Livermore
Cultivate Systems (HQ)	Provider of construction services. The company offers civil site work, construction, demolition, and general contracting services.	707-690-9425	NA	Napa
CUneXus Solutions Inc (HQ)	Provider of pre-screening lending strategy that pre-approves entire loan product portfolio for customers.	877-509-2089	NA	Santa Rosa
CyberGlove Systems LLC (HQ)	Provider of data glove technology. The company offers system installation and integration and custom software and hardware services.	408-943-8114	NA	San Jose
Cybersoft (BR)	Provider of offshore business and knowledge process outsourcing services. The company specializes in title, financial, and document processing services.	415-449-7998	NA	San Francisco
Databricks Inc (HQ)	Provider of platform for big data processing solutions. The company offers exploration and visualization, production pipelines, and third party apps.	866-330-0121	NA	San Francisco
DataDirect Networks Inc (BR)	Provider of storage array, file system, and object storage appliances to broadcast, biopharma, supercomputing, and financial service sectors.	408-419-2800	NA	Santa Clara
DataGlance Inc (HQ)	Provider of data management software that support LIVE data conversion/migration, electronic document generation and processing, and web services.	510-656-0500	NA	Fremont
Dataguise (HQ)	Provider of cloud migration, auditing, and monitoring solutions. The company serves the healthcare, consumer, and retail industries.	877-632-0522	NA	Fremont
Datastax Inc (RH)	Distributor of database management system for Internet enterprise. The company offers training and certification, expert support, and consulting services.	650-389-6000	NA	Santa Clara
Datest Corp (HQ)	Provider of testing and inspection services. The company specializes in engineering testing and counterfeit inspection for industrial products.	510-490-4600	NA	Fremont
DCL Inc (HQ)	Provider of fulfillment and supply chain management services. The company offers e-Commerce, retail fulfillment, and reverse logistics services.	510-651-5100	NA	Fremont
Delphix (HQ)	Developer of software, database, and database virtualization. The company focuses on website design and hosting and software application development.	650-494-1645	NA	Redwood City
Desaware Inc (HQ)	Developer of tools and components for visual studio programmers. The company offers documentation and professional services.	408-404-4760	NA	San Jose
DesignMap (HQ)	Provider of web site and application design services. The company also specializes in research, usability studies, and visual design.	415-357-1875	NA	San Francisco
Device Authority Ltd (RH)	Provider of IoT security solutions for industrial, automotive, transportation, healthcare, utilities, and smart cities.	650-603-0997	NA	San Ramon
Digital Anarchy (HQ)	Provider of photography and video plugins for Photoshop, elements, after effects, and final cut pro.	415-287-6069	NA	Brisbane
Digital Canvas (HQ)	Provider of web design and web application development services. The company also offers web hosting, security solutions, and services.	925-706-1700	NA	Antioch
Digital Keystone Inc (HQ)	Provider of solutions enabling content distribution to tablets, connected TVs, and other entertainment platforms with suite of software and tools.	650-938-7300	NA	Cupertino
Docker Inc (HQ)	Provider of docker platform and docker ecosystem of contributors, partners, and adopters the way distributed applications are built, shipped, and run.	415-941-0376	NA	Palo Alto
DocuSign Inc (HQ)	Provider of digital transaction management platform helps to accelerate transactions, reduce costs, and delight customers, suppliers, and employees.	877-720-2040	NA	San Francisco
N Douloi Automation Inc (HQ)	Developer of prepackaged motion control software.	408-735-6942	NA	Santa Clara
Drivesavers Inc (HQ)	Provider of data recovery services for financial institutions, healthcare providers, major film studios, government agencies, and small businesses.	415-382-2000	NA	Novato
Droisys Inc (HQ)	Provider of business solutions and offers services such as content management, enterprise resource planning, and business efficiency consulting.	408-874-8333	NA	Santa Clara
Dropbox Inc (HQ)	Provider of data transfer and sharing services that involves sharing of files, documents, and pictures from anywhere.	415-857-6800	NA	San Francisco
Druva Inc (RH)	Provider of cloud based data protection products. The company offers services to the manufacturing, healthcare, and education industries.	650-238-6200	NA	Sunnyvale
Dt Research Inc (HQ)	Developer and manufacturer of embedded computing systems. The company serves hospitality, healthcare, and digital signage needs.	408-934-6220	NA	San Jose
DynEd International Inc (HQ)	Provider of computer-based English language teaching solutions. The company offers mobile solutions, analytics, testing, and monitoring tools.	650-375-7011	NA	Burlingame

COMPANY NAME	PRODUCT / SERVICE	PHONE	EMP	CITY
E la Carte Inc (HQ)	Provider of digital restaurant services. The company specializes in operations, engineering, business development, and marketing.	530-377-3786	NA	Redwood City
N Eastridge Workforce Solutions (HQ)	Provider of workforce management, workforce recruitment, workforce technology and staffing solutions.	800-778-0197	201-500	San Diego
Ecodomus Inc (HQ)	Provider of information technology software for improved design and construction data collection, facility management, operation, and maintenance.	571-277-6617	NA	San Francisco
Ecrio Inc (HQ)	Provider of wireless messaging applications. The company offers video telephony, content sharing, social communications, and enterprise solutions.	408-973-7290	NA	Cupertino
EDA Direct Inc (HQ)	Provider of EDA software products and services. The company's products include Cliosoft, MunEDA, and Mentor Graphics.	408-496-5890	NA	Santa Clara
Electric Cloud Inc (BR)	Provider of software development, information technology consulting, test automation, virtualization, and cloud computing solutions.	408-419-4300	NA	San Jose
Elementum (HQ)	Provider of apps to manage your global supply chain. The company offers manufacturing operations, mission control, supplier, and logistics management.	650-318-1491	NA	San Mateo
Ellie Mae Inc (HQ)	Focuses on mortgage compliance services. The company offers services to banks and other financial institutions.	925-227-7000	NA	Pleasanton
Emanio Inc (HQ)	Developer of products for data management, dashboarding, and reporting and predictive analysis needs. The company focuses on consulting and training.	510-849-9300	NA	Berkeley
Emtrain (HQ)	Provider of learning management system such as online training platform for all levels of HR professionals, trainers, and administrators.	916-481-7474	NA	San Francisco
Enlighta (HQ)	Provider of software solutions to service organizations grappling with governance and management of global services delivery.	510-279-5820	NA	San Ramon
Ensenta Corp (HQ)	Developer of software solutions. The company is involved in development of cloud-based imaging and self-service technology.	866-219-4321	NA	Redwood Shores
ENT Networks Inc (HQ)	Provider of custom system manufacturing, database management, hardware sales, business consulting, and repair services.	925-462-7125	NA	Pleasanton
Enview Inc (HQ)	Specializes in threat prevention systems. The company deals with data analytics and remote sensing services.	415-483-5680	NA	San Francisco
Errigal Inc (HQ)	Designer and developer of software products and services. The company also deals with configuration management and ticketing.	415-523-9245	NA	San Francisco
Esp Interactive Solutions Inc (HQ)	Provider of web design and development services such as web video creation, content management system, and social networks marketing.	510-526-2592	NA	Albany
Etouch Systems Corp (BR)	Provider of design web engineering services. The company focuses on business process management and enterprise application integration services.	510-795-4800	NA	Fremont
Etrigue Corp (HQ)	Provider of marketing automation solutions such as email marketing, event management, derived data, 3-D leading scoring, and marketing database management.	408-490-2900	NA	San Jose
Evolveware Inc (HQ)	Developer of products to automate and modernize IT infrastructure focusing on assessment, documentation, impact analysis, and other solutions.	408-748-8301	NA	Santa Clara
Exabeam Inc (HQ)	Provider of software to discover attackers impersonating users and to protect against cyber attacks.	844-392-2326	NA	San Mateo
Excelfore (HQ)	Provider of cloud applications. The company offers infotainment and telematics products for insurance, financing, and logistics sectors.	510-868-2500	NA	Fremont
Exit445 Group (HQ)	Provider of information architecture, e-Commerce, email marketing, search engine optimization, website hosting, and other services.	415-381-1852	NA	Mill Valley
Experexchange Inc (HQ)	Provider of software and professional IT solutions such as web based applications, software life cycle service, embedded systems, and software testing.	510-623-7071	NA	Fremont
eze System (HQ)	Provider or monitoring and measuring solutions. The company's products include controllers, controller expansions, and sensors.	716-393-9330	NA	Folsom
N FABNexus Inc (HQ)	Provider of application-specific machine control and SEMI-standards conformant network automation software to the semiconductor manufacturing and support industry.	650-207-8235	NA	Los Altos
FactoryWiz (HQ)	Provider of CNC Machine Tool monitoring and data collection products. The company is also involved in preventive maintenance services.	408-224-9167	NA	San Jose
Famsoft (HQ)	Provider of ERP consulting and infrastructure management services such as managed support, IBM products, enterprise solution, and migration services.	408-452-1550	NA	San Jose
Farallon Geographics Inc (HQ)	Provider of strategic planning, spatial data processing, training, and web application development services.	415-227-1140	NA	San Francisco
FCS Software Solutions Ltd (HQ)	Provider of consulting, product development, e-learning, digital content, and product support services.	408-324-1203	NA	San Jose
Fidus Systems Inc (BR)	Specializes in electronic product development and consulting services. The company also deals with hardware design.	408-217-1928	NA	Fremont

COMPANY NAME	PRODUCT / SERVICE	PHONE	EMP	CITY
FileOpen Systems Inc (HQ)	Provider of digital rights management and document security solutions for corporations and governments.	831-706-2170	NA	Santa Cruz
Finjan Holdings Inc (HQ)	Specializes in the research and development of transformative technologies for the securing of information.	650-282-3228	NA	East Palo Alto
FireEye Inc (HQ)	Focuses on cyber security solutions. The company serves the utilities and pharmaceutical industries.	408-321-6300	NA	Milpitas
First Databank Inc (HQ)	Provider of healthcare solutions to hospitals, retail pharmacies, payers, drug manufacturers, and healthcare providers.	650-588-5454	NA	S San Francisco
Fluid Inc (HQ)	Provider of software solutions. The company's services include automated retail planning and content strategy.	877-343-3240	NA	Oakland
Forecross Corp (HQ)	Provider of automated migration of legacy systems. The company specializes in XML solutions, migration solutions, and integrity solutions.	415-543-1515	NA	San Francisco
Forensic Logic Inc (HQ)	Provider of software-as-a-service information technology to local, state and federal government workers and private sector organizations.	833-267-5465	NA	Walnut Creek
N Formula Consultants Inc (HQ)	Provider of software development and consulting services.	714-778-0123	NA	Anaheim
Fortinet Inc (HQ)	Provider of network security appliances and threat management solutions such as network security platform and reporting and authentication.	408-235-7700	NA	Sunnyvale
Franz Inc (HQ)	Provider of information technology solutions. The company offers web technology and enterprise development tools, and professional services.	510-452-2000	NA	Oakland
Frequentz LLC (HQ)	Designer and developer of product tracking software. The company serves the life sciences and industrial sectors.	925-824-0300	NA	San Ramon
Full Circle Crm Inc (HQ)	Specializes in response management and it offers management products. The company serves businesses.	650-641-2766	NA	San Mateo
Funmobility Inc (HQ)	Provider of solutions for mobile engagement and mobile marketing. The company also offers content marketing, digital strategy, and other services.	925-598-9700	NA	San Ramon
Futuredial Inc (HQ)	Developer of carrier-grade solutions and tools for mobile device recyclers, wireless operators, and mobile device manufacturers.	408-245-8880	NA	Sunnyvale
Gauss Surgical Inc (HQ)	Manufacturer of mobile devices. The company is engaged in research and development services and it serves the healthcare sector.	650-949-4153	NA	Los Altos
Genbook Inc (HQ)	Developer of online appointment scheduling software. The company is engaged in social media marketing services.	415-227-9904	NA	San Francisco
GestureTek Inc (HQ)	Provider of gesture-based user interfaces for mobile devices. The company offer services to the gaming and entertainment industries.	408-506-2206	NA	Santa Clara
Gigamon (HQ)	Provider of traffic visibility solutions for enterprises, data centers, and the education, financial, and healthcare industries.	408-831-4000	NA	Santa Clara
Gigwalk (HQ)	Provider of analytics and collaboration tools and they are used in the management of mobile work force.	888-237-5896	NA	San Francisco
Global Infotech Corp (HQ)	Provider of software services. The company's software solutions focuses on staff augmentation, telecom, systems integration, chip design, ERP, and CRM domains.	408-567-0600	NA	San Jose
Glyphic Technology (HQ)	Provider of software design and architecture solutions. The company focuses on Internet, server, desktop, mobile, and embedded systems.	650-964-5311	NA	Mountain View
Googleplex (HQ)	Provider of search engine to make world's information universally accessible. The company specializes in Internet-related services and products.	650-253-0000	NA	Mountain View
Greytrix (RH)	Provider of integration and migration solutions. The company deals in analytics, cloud, mobility, and ERP/CRM consulting.	888-221-6661	NA	San Francisco
GT Nexus Inc (HQ)	Provider of supply chain, transportation, and investment management solutions. The company serves retailers and manufacturers.	510-808-2222	NA	Oakland
Guardian Analytics (HQ)	Provider of enterprise and community banking solutions. The company is engaged in training and applied fraud analysis services.	650-383-9200	NA	Mountain View
Hazelcast Inc (HQ)	Provider of training, consulting, and technical support services. The company serves the logistics and healthcare industries.	650-521-5453	NA	Palo Alto
Health Gorilla Inc (HQ)	Focuses on diagnostic tests. The company offers services to clinics, patients and healthcare organizations.	844-446-7455	NA	Sunnyvale
Healthcare Systems & Technologies LLC (HQ)	Designer and developer of AC surgery software. The company offers services to corporate management companies.	800-290-4078	NA	Lafayette
Highwired Inc (HQ)	Developer of multimedia and supporting products and services. The company focuses on branding, billing, and delivery solutions.	516-785-6197	NA	Redwood Valley
Hillstone Networks (RH)	Provider of security solutions for enterprises and data center networks. The company serves Fortune 500 companies and educational institutions.	408-508-6750	NA	Santa Clara
HumanAPI (HQ)	Focuses on the integration of health data and it specializes in retrieval of health data and other healthcare applications.	650-542-9800	NA	San Mateo
Hydropoint Data Systems Inc (HQ)	Provider of irrigation solutions. The company specializes in site evaluations, upgrade planning, deployment, and optimization services.	800-362-8774	NA	Petaluma
Illumio Inc (HQ)	Developer of security platform and it is also involved in data encryption and technical support services.	669-800-5000	NA	Sunnyvale

COMPANY NAME	PRODUCT / SERVICE	PHONE	EMP	CITY
Imagine That Inc (HQ)	Developer of simulation software. The company offers services to the retail, healthcare, insurance, and financial services industries.	408-365-0305	NA	San Jose
iMaxsoft Corp (HQ)	Provider of database and application migration services. The company offers services to government agencies.	408-253-1987	NA	Cupertino
iMiners Inc (HQ)	Provider of investor relations management tools and web-based communication platforms. The company offers website plug-ins and shareholder message boards.	925-447-6073	NA	Livermore
Imperva Inc (HQ)	Provider of application and data security solutions. The company's products include database firewalls, management server, and monitoring software.	650-345-9000	NA	Redwood Shores
INDEC Medical Systems Inc (HQ)	Provider of hardware and software solutions for cardiovascular imaging applications such as intravascular ultrasound and angiography.	408-986-1600	NA	Los Altos
Infin IT Consulting (HQ)	Designer and developer of CNC machining and billet products. The company's products include fire extinguisher brackets, shift knobs, and boat accessories.	866-364-2007	NA	Campbell
Infinite Technologies Inc (HQ)	Provider of information technology, strategic consulting, and engineering services. The company serves government and corporate entities.	916-987-3261	NA	El Dorado Hills
N Infoflex Inc (HQ)	Developer of accounting and 4GL software.	650-270-1019	NA	Burlingame
InfoTech Spectrum Inc (HQ)	Provider of integrated creative IT services including IT consulting, advanced technology deployment, and product development.	408-705-2237	NA	Santa Clara
Input Optics Inc (HQ)	Provider of integration solutions for dental practice. The company also offers complimentary assessments and web services.	650-969-3108	NA	Mountain View
Insight (BR)	Provider of mobility, network, and security solutions. The company is engaged in design, integration, and implementation services.	877-776-0610	NA	Cupertino
Inspirisys Solutions North America Inc (HQ)	Provider of software development and technology services for automotive, healthcare, life science, networking, storage, and enterprise software markers.	408-514-5199	NA	Santa Clara
Instart Logic Inc (HQ)	Provider of software-defined application delivery solutions. The company offers services to the travel and hospitality industries.	650-919-8856	NA	Palo Alto
Inszoom Inc (HQ)	Focuses on immigration case management and compliance automation solutions. The company offers services to law firms.	925-244-0600	NA	Pleasanton
Interloc Solutions (HQ)	Provider of consulting services and mobile solutions. The company serves the oil and gas and transportation industries.	916-817-4590	NA	Folsom
Intermolecular Inc (HQ)	Provider of high productivity combinatorial technologies. The company serves solar device manufacturers.	408-582-5700	NA	San Jose
Intuit Inc (HQ)	Provider of financial management software solutions. The company offers services to small businesses and related organizations.	800-446-8848	NA	Mountain View
IO Informatics Inc (HQ)	Provider of software and services for data integration applications in areas such as life science and medicine.	510-705-8470	NA	Berkeley
IO Integration Inc (HQ)	Provider of marketing technology and digital media workflow solutions. The company offers marketing automation and cross-media publishing services.	408-996-3420	NA	Cupertino
Irislogic Inc (HQ)	Provider of global consulting services and solutions. The company specializes in custom software development, network security, cloud, and testing.	408-855-8741	NA	Santa Clara
iSOA Group Inc (BR)	Provider of business process management, service oriented architecture, and business analytics services to finance, energy, retail, and other sectors.	925-465-7400	NA	Walnut Creek
Issio Solutions Inc (HQ)	Provider of workforce management software for surgical facilities. The company also serves ambulatory surgical centers.	888-994-7746	NA	Concord
IT Pro Source (HQ)	Provider of on call plans, managed services, web based monitoring, and communication cabling services.	925-455-7701	NA	Livermore
IT Systemworks (HQ)	Provider of networking and technological solutions. The company's services include installation, implementation, repair, and maintenance.	415-507-0123	NA	San Rafael
Itradenetwork Inc (HQ)	Provider of supply chain management and intelligence solutions for procurement, order management, and data services.	925-660-1100	NA	Dublin
Itrezzo Inc (HQ)	Provider of unified contact management solutions and it serves schools, agencies, and healthcare organizations.	408-540-5020	NA	San Jose
N JRH GoldenState Software Inc (HQ)	Developer and provider of software tools and solutions that supports complete DB2 catalog query and object management.	310-544-1497	NA	Rancho Palos Verdes
Junar Inc (HQ)	Provider of cloud-based open data platform. The company offers collaboration services to business organizations.	844-695-8627	NA	San Jose
Keen Systems Inc (HQ)	Provider of web-to print solutions. The company offers cloud-based services to small and medium sized printing companies.	888-506-5336	NA	San Mateo
Keep IT Simple (HQ)	Provider of virtualization and information technology services. The company focuses on virtualization assessment, cloud computing, and networking.	510-403-7500	NA	Fremont
Kespry Inc (HQ)	Developer of automated drone system and cloud that automatically uploads data in cloud for aggregates, insurance, and construction industries.	203-434-7988	NA	Menlo Park

COMPANY NAME	PRODUCT / SERVICE	PHONE	EMP	CITY
Key Solutions Inc (HQ)	Provider of software development and database management services. The company also specializes in business intelligence.	510-456-4500	NA	Fremont
Key Source International Inc (HQ)	Provider of disinfectant and germicidal wipes for keyboards. The company focuses on infection control and cross contamination.	510-562-5000	NA	Oakland
Kidaptive Inc (HQ)	Provider of learning and integration solutions. The company offers services to learners and the educational sector.	650-265-2485	NA	Redwood City
KLH Consulting Inc (HQ)	Provider of IT consulting, cloud computing, and related business solutions. The company offers services to business executives and professionals.	707-575-9986	NA	Santa Rosa
Lastline (HQ)	Manufacturer of malware protection products. The company serves schools, restaurants, and the enterprise security industry.	877-671-3239	NA	San Mateo
LCS Technologies Inc (HQ)	Provider of information services for customers with Oracle software and service needs using resources such as people, hardware, and software.	855-277-5527	NA	Gold River
LeapFILE Inc (HQ)	Provider of on-demand file transfer, delivery, and collaboration solutions for businesses. The company serves the healthcare and advertising sectors.	650-701-7241	NA	Cupertino
Ledger Systems Inc (HQ)	Provider of network design and support services. The company also offers accounting and e-Commerce solutions.	650-592-6211	NA	San Carlos
Leica Geosystems HDS LLC (RH)	Manufacturer of surveying hardware and software solutions for measuring and modeling sites and structures with high accuracy, detail, speed, and safety.	925-790-2300	NA	San Ramon
Linden Research Inc (HQ)	Designer and developer of digital entertainment solutions. The company's products include Desura, Patterns, and Versu.	415-243-9000	NA	San Francisco
LiveVox Inc (HQ)	Specializes in business analytics and related services. The company serves the telecom and healthcare industries.	415-671-6000	NA	San Francisco
Locus Technologies (HQ)	Provider of web based environmental information management systems. The company's services include field installation, training, and technical support.	415-360-5889	NA	Mountain View
Logen Solutions USA (HQ)	Provider of truck, container, pallet and carton loading and packaging software. The company offers solutions for cargo load planning.	408-519-5771	NA	San Jose
Lynx Media Inc (HQ)	Developer of inventory control and order entry software.	800-451-5969	NA	Valley Village
Lynx Software Technologies (HQ)	Developer of software technologies. The company offers development tools, real-time monitoring systems, and secure virtualization products.	408-979-3900	NA	San Jose
MarkLogic Corp (HQ)	Provider of enterprise solutions. The company serves the healthcare, legal, and insurance industries.	650-655-2300	NA	San Carlos
Markmonitor Inc (HQ)	Provider of brand protection, domain management, domain advisory, anti-piracy, and managed services.	415-278-8400	NA	San Francisco
Maxta Inc (HQ)	Provider of software-defined storage, disaster recovery, and also testing and development solutions.	669-228-2800	NA	Santa Clara
Meditab Software Inc (HQ)	Developer of physical therapy, urology, cosmetic, and plastic surgery solutions. The company serves the healthcare industry.	510-201-0130	NA	Sacramento
Menlo Security (HQ)	Provider of security solutions. The company's offerings include web isolation, document, and phishing isolation services.	650-614-1705	NA	Palo Alto
Mentor Graphics (RH)	Provider of electronic design automation software. The company focuses on mechanical analysis, system modeling, manufacturing, and verification.	510-354-7400	NA	Fremont
Merkle Inc (BR)	Provider of omnichannel loyalty solution. The company offers service and technology to deliver seamless and powerful customer retention solutions.	415-918-2990	NA	San Francisco
MessageSolution Inc (HQ)	Provider of enterprise archiving, e-discovery, and migration solutions. The company deals with storage management solutions.	925-833-8000	NA	Dublin
Metis Technology Solutions Inc (HQ)	Provider of technical services. The company engages in engineering, IT, aviation, space, and earth sciences fields.	650-967-3051	NA	Sunnyvale
Michael Patrick Partners (HQ)	Provider of branding solutions. The company also offers logo design, portfolio creation, web content, and marketing services.	650-327-3185	NA	San Francisco
Mirabilis Design Inc (HQ)	Provider of systems engineering solutions for performance analysis and architecture exploration of electronics and real-time software.	408-844-3234	NA	Sunnyvale
Mixbook (HQ)	Provider of customizable photo books, cards and calendars, as well as creation of online scrapbooks on the web using design software.	855-649-2665	NA	Redwood City
Mobileiron Inc (HQ)	Provider of mobile security, device, and application management solutions. The company focuses on technical support services.	650-919-8100	NA	Mountain View
Moogsoft Inc (HQ)	Provider of collaborative situation management software solutions for Web-scale information technology (IT) operations.	415-738-2299	NA	San Francisco
MYCOM OSI Inc (RH)	Provider of performance management, compliance, employer reporting, patient engagement, and satisfaction solutions.	916-467-1500	NA	Folsom
MyVest Corp (HQ)	Provider of enterprise wealth management solutions. The company offers services to business organizations.	415-369-9511	NA	San Francisco
NADA Technologies Inc (HQ)	Provider of enterprise Oracle applications. The company also offers business intelligence solutions.	650-678-4666	NA	Danville

N

COMPANY NAME	PRODUCT / SERVICE	PHONE	EMP	CITY
Naehas Inc (HQ)	Specializes in the automation of sales and marketing services. The company offers services to finance and insurance companies.	877-262-3427	NA	Palo Alto
Natural Logic (HQ)	Provider of consulting, product development, e-learning, digital content, and product support services.	510-248-4940	NA	Berkeley
Neo Technology Inc (HQ)	Developer of enterprise applications. The company focuses on technical support and related services.	855-636-4532	NA	San Mateo
Neospeech Inc (HQ)	Provider of text-to-speech software and applications for the mobile, enterprise, entertainment, and education markers.	408-914-2710	NA	Santa Clara
Net4site LLC (HQ)	Provider of SAP solutions. The company serves customers in the enterprise mobility, business intelligence, and ERP arenas.	408-427-3004	NA	Santa Clara
Netformx Inc (HQ)	Designer and builder of solutions for the networking and service providers. The company specializes in desktop and cloud applications.	408-423-6600	NA	San Jose
Netscout (BR)	Developer of service assurance and applications, service delivery management, network performance management software, and hardware solutions.	408-571-5000	NA	San Jose
Netskope (HQ)	Provider of cloud security brokering services. The company offers services to the healthcare sector.	800-979-6988	NA	Santa Clara
Network Design Associates Inc (HQ)	Provider of engineering services for computer systems. The company's services include network design, implementation, support, and maintenance.	916-853-1632	NA	Citrus Heights
Neudesic LLC (BR)	Provider of technology services. The company focuses on social software, integration platform, and CRM solutions and offers cloud computing services.	949-754-4500	NA	Irvine
Nevtec Inc (HQ)	Provider of networks implementation and maintenance services. The company also focuses on workstations and the Internet.	408-292-8600	NA	San Jose
New:Team SoftWare Inc (HQ)	Developer of software solutions.	415-461-8086	NA	Sacramento
Nexb Inc (HQ)	Designer and developer of software tools and services. The company offers services to business enterprises and related organizations.	650-592-2096	NA	San Carlos
Nextbus Inc (BR)	Provider of transit management solutions. The company also provides real-time passenger information solutions to organizations.	925-686-8200	NA	Concord
NextLabs Inc (HQ)	Developer of software products. The company offers information risk management software products for enterprises.	650-577-9101	NA	San Mateo
Nextrials Inc (HQ)	Provider of c clinical and electronic health record tools. The company is engaged in clinical research and related services.	925-355-3000	NA	San Ramon
Nexusguard Ltd (RH)	Provider of monitoring and DNA protection services. The company serves service providers and the entertainment sector.	415-299-8550	NA	San Francisco
Nice Touch Solutions Inc (HQ)	Developer of software for the heavy highway construction industry. The company focuses on products for generating extra work bills.	925-385-8321	NA	Alamo
Nok Nok Labs Inc (HQ)	Focuses on the development on online security solutions. The company is also involved in third party research services.	650-433-1300	NA	Palo Alto
Nokia Corp (BR)	Specializes in mobile network infrastructure structure and services. The company is engaged in technology development.	408-737-0900	NA	Sunnyvale
Oea International Inc (HQ)	Developer of signal integrity software. The company serves the electronic design automation industry.	408-778-6747	NA	Morgan Hill
One Touch Systems (HQ)	Provider of virtual distance learning, training and communication systems. The company offers services to the educational sector.	408-660-8435	NA	San Jose
OneLogin (HQ)	Provider of single sign-on and identity management for cloud-based applications. The company serves the industrial sector.	415-645-6830	NA	San Francisco
Onfulfillment Inc (HQ)	Provider of printing solutions. The company offers order fulfillment, online delivery, and print management services.	510-793-3009	NA	Newark
Opengov Inc (HQ)	Provider of financial transparency and business intelligence solutions. The company offers services to government agencies.	650-336-7167	NA	Redwood City
OpensourceCM (HQ)	Designer and developer of contract management software. The company also offers technical support services.	650-200-0506	NA	Foster City
Opsol Integrators Inc (HQ)	Provider of universal messaging, data integration, and encryption products. The company serves banks, retail, telecom, and other sectors.	408-364-9915	NA	Campbell
Optimal Synthesis Inc (HQ)	Provider of research, algorithm development, and software design services. The company caters to a variety of engineering and science applications.	650-559-8585	NA	Los Altos
Oracle Corp (BR)	Developer of hardware and software systems. The company provides Oracle database, engineered systems, and enterprise manager solutions.	415-402-7200	NA	San Francisco
Outformations Inc (HQ)	Provider of consulting, application development, programming, technical support, and design services.	510-655-7122	NA	Oakland
PanTerra Networks Inc (HQ)	Provider of cloud-based communications software solutions. The company is engaged in unified communication and technical support.	800-805-0558	NA	Santa Clara
Park Computer Systems Inc (HQ)	Provider of mobile products and services. The company also offers sales content automation and staff augmentation services.	510-353-1700	NA	Newark

COMPANY NAME	PRODUCT / SERVICE	PHONE	EMP	CITY
Persistent Systems Inc (BR)	Developer of software and technology products for life science, banking, and other sectors. The company offers big data, security, and cloud solutions.	408-216-7010	NA	Santa Clara
Pivotal Labs (HQ)	Focuses on software development and related services. The company serves start-ups and Fortune 1000 companies.	415-777-4868	NA	San Francisco
Pixami Inc (HQ)	Provider of imaging technologies. The company caters to both photo-based and non-photo-based businesses.	925-465-5167	NA	Pleasanton
Planeteria Media (HQ)	Designer and developer of websites, applications, e-commerce, content management systems, video, and offers flash, and Internet marketing services.	707-843-3773	NA	Santa Rosa
Powertest Inc (HQ)	Provider of software-related professional services. The company is also involved in load testing and application performance management.	415-778-0580	NA	S San Francisco
ProcessWeaver Inc (BR)	Developer of multi-carrier shipping software and a provider of shipping solutions. The company also offers inbound and desktop shipping solutions.	888-932-8373	NA	Santa Clara
Progent Corp (HQ)	Provider of online technical support for small networks, and specializes in remote diagnosis, repair, and consulting services.	408-785-4781	NA	San Jose
Project Partners LLC (HQ)	Provider of business solutions and information technology systems. The company offers NetSuite, Oracle Fusion Applications, and Primavera.	650-712-6200	NA	Half Moon Bay
N Pronto Networks (HQ)	Provider of Wi-Fi operation support system solutions for enterprises, wireless ISPs, WiMAX and satellite networks.	925-860-6200	51-200	Walnut Creek
Proofpoint Inc (RH)	Manufacturer of threat, email, social media, and information protection products. The company offers security and compliance solutions.	408-517-4710	NA	Sunnyvale
ProPlus Design Solutions Inc (HQ)	Provider of electronic design automation solutions. The company's products include NoisePro, NanoSpice, and NanoYield.	408-459-6128	NA	San Jose
Proxio Inc (HQ)	Provider of digital real estate marketing solutions for agents, brokers and developers. The company serves businesses.	415-723-1691	NA	Santa Clara
Pulse Secure LLC (HQ)	Provider of product, hardware, partner, and enterprise solutions. The company offers services to the financial services and healthcare industries.	408-372-9600	NA	San Jose
Q Analysts LLC (HQ)	Provider of consulting, strategic advisory, and related compliance services. The company is also involved in mobile testing.	408-907-8500	NA	San Jose
Quadbase Systems Inc (HQ)	Designer of web-delivered and mobile enabled business intelligence reporting, charting, and dashboard tools.	408-982-0835	NA	Santa Clara
Quanergy Systems Inc (HQ)	Developer of smart sensing solutions. The company offers solutions for real-time 3D mapping, object detection, and tracking.	408-245-9500	NA	Sunnyvale
Quantum Corp (HQ)	Provider of software for backup, recovery, and archiving needs. The company serves the healthcare, media, and entertainment industries.	408-944-4000	NA	San Jose
Qubell Inc (HQ)	Specializes in autonomic management solutions. The company focuses on e-commerce and other cloud applications.	888-855-9440	NA	Menlo Park
QuesGen Systems Inc (HQ)	Provider of data management solutions. The company is involved in clinical research and related support services.	650-777-7617	NA	Burlingame
Quest Business Systems Inc (HQ)	Provider of solutions in police equipment tracking systems. The company also focuses on purchasing management.	925-634-2670	NA	Brentwood
Quest Inc (HQ)	Provider of technology and infrastructure management services. The company caters to a wide range of businesses.	800-326-4220	NA	Roseville
Quiq Labs (HQ)	Developer of tools and solutions. The company focuses on influencing consumer behavior and engagement.	559-745-5511	NA	Fresno
Quisk Inc (HQ)	Specializes in the development of payment solutions. The company offers services to financial institutions.	408-462-6800	NA	Sunnyvale
Qumu Inc (BR)	Provider of web casting, marketing, event, and other professional services. The company offers enterprise video solutions.	650-396-8530	NA	San Bruno
Quorum Technologies (HQ)	Developer of recycling and waste disposal solutions for the automotive, industrial, municipal, hospitality, and food industries.	916-669-5577	NA	Sacramento
R&D Logic Inc (HQ)	Developer of performance management software for R&D focused companies. The company offers implementation and training services.	650-356-9207	NA	San Mateo
RackWare Inc (HQ)	Provider of disaster prevention and recovery solutions. The company also offers business continuity and virtualization solutions.	408-430-5821	NA	San Jose
Radiant Logic Inc (HQ)	Provider of identity and context virtualization solutions. The company caters to identity integration and management needs.	415-209-6800	NA	Novato
Readytech Corp (HQ)	Provider of virtual labs for training, certification, and also sales demonstrations. The company deals with technology support.	800-707-1009	NA	Oakland
N REAL Software Systems LLC (HQ)	Developer of software solutions for the management of royalty, rights and revenue sharing contracts.	818-313-8000	NA	Woodland Hills
Real-Time Innovations Inc (HQ)	Provider for real-time infrastructure software solutions. The company also offers engineering and product development services.	408-990-7400	NA	Sunnyvale
Redis Labs Inc (HQ)	Provider of zero management, infinite scalability, and other solutions for start-ups and business enterprises.	415-930-9666	NA	Mountain View
Redline Solutions Inc (HQ)	Provider of produce traceability and barcode solutions, and warehouse and inventory management systems.	408-562-1700	NA	Santa Clara

COMPANY NAME	PRODUCT / SERVICE	PHONE	EMP	CITY
Reflektion Inc (HQ)	Focuses on personalized site search, marketing, analytics, and predictive product recommendation solutions.	650-293-0800	NA	San Mateo
Relay2 Inc (HQ)	Provider of cloud Wi-Fi Services platform which allows service providers to monetize value added Wi-Fi services.	408-380-0031	NA	Milpitas
Resilinc Corp (HQ)	Provider of supply chain and risk management solutions. The company serves the life science and automotive industries.	408-883-8053	NA	Milpitas
Retail Pro International (HQ)	Provider of software solutions. The company's services include automated retail planning and content strategy.	916-605-7200	NA	Folsom
RetailNext (HQ)	Provider of in-store analytics solutions. The company offers services to retail labs, marketing departments, and shopping centers.	408-884-2162	NA	San Jose
Revel Systems Inc (BR)	Provider of POS systems and related services. The company serves customers in the accounting, security, reporting, and other industries.	415-744-1433	NA	San Francisco
Rocket Communications Inc (HQ)	Developer of user interface, visual, and icon design services for software and related applications.	415-863-0101	NA	San Francisco
Rockyou Inc (HQ)	Provider of gaming solutions. The company's games include Poker, Bingo, Zoo World, and others and serves the entertainment sector.	415-580-6400	NA	San Francisco
Rollbar Inc (HQ)	Developer of error tracking software. The company is also engaged in coding and troubleshooting services.	888-568-3350	NA	San Francisco
RS Software Inc (BR)	Provider of business payment solutions for the risk prediction, residual management, payment gateway, and merchant boarding areas.	408-382-1200	NA	Milpitas
Runscope Inc (HQ)	Specializes in automated performance monitoring and testing solutions. The company serves developers.	888-812-6786	NA	San Francisco
Runtime Design Automation (HQ)	Provider of management system software for the IC design industry. The company is engaged in documentation and technical support.	408-492-0940	NA	Santa Clara
S2C Inc (HQ)	Provider of prototyping solutions. The company's customers include chip design and system design companies.	408-213-8818	NA	San Jose
Selectiva Systems Inc (HQ)	Provider of solutions for revenue reporting, customer service, and distributor management. The company serves high-tech, pharma, and other sectors.	408-297-1336	NA	San Jose
Sentient Energy Inc (HQ)	Provider of sensor devices for operational practices and engineering applications. The company also offers communication software.	650-523-6680	NA	Burlingame
SentinelOne (HQ)	Developer of endpoint protection software. The company serves the healthcare, oil and gas, and financial services industries.	855-868-3733	NA	Mountain View
Sercomm USA Inc (BR)	Provider of software and firmware for the development of broadband networking. The company also offers solutions for fixed mobile convergence.	510-870-1598	NA	Fremont
Shape Security (HQ)	Provider of defense solutions against malicious automated cyber-attacks on web and mobile applications.	650-399-0400	NA	Santra Clara
Sharper Technology Inc (HQ)	Provider of network security solutions and services. The company also offers design, implementation, and training services.	650-964-4600	NA	Palo Alto
Sherrill-Lubinski Corp (HQ)	Provider of monitoring and analytics solutions for middleware-powered applications. The company serves the electrical commodity market.	415-927-8400	NA	Riverside
Sierra Data Systems Inc (HQ)	Provider of data communication systems, Internet related services, miscellaneous communications equipment, telephone, and voice equipment.	916-242-4604	NA	Grass Valley
Silicon Laboratories (BR)	Provider of silicon, software, and system solutions. The company focuses on Internet infrastructure, industrial control, and consumer markers.	408-702-1400	NA	San Jose
Silicon Publishing Inc (HQ)	Provider of digital publishing solutions. The company deals with template designs and personalized communications.	925-935-3899	NA	San Francisco
Silvaco Inc (HQ)	Supplier of TCAD and EDA software for circuit simulation. The company also designs analog, mixed-signal, and RF integrated circuits.	408-567-1000	NA	Santa Clara
Sitepen Inc (HQ)	Developer and provider of software products and services. The company also offers web application development and java support services.	650-968-8787	NA	Palo Alto
Smart ERP Solutions Inc (HQ)	Developer of enterprise class software. The company provides vendor management software and support services.	925-271-0200	NA	Pleasanton
Softjourn Inc (HQ)	Provider of outsource software development services and focuses on offshore assessments, application development, and quality assurance testing.	510-744-1528	NA	Fremont
SoftNet Solutions Inc (HQ)	Provider of enterprise solutions for high performance computing and network security. The company specializes in IT consulting and cloud services.	408-542-0888	NA	Sunnyvale
Softsol Inc (HQ)	Provider of software solutions. The company offers software such as Intelli Court Case Management, Corporate Investigations, STIC, and PB Migration.	510-824-2000	NA	Fremont
Solarius Development Inc (HQ)	Manufacturer of 3D metrology surface measurement systems. The company offers metrology services for surface form.	408-435-2777	NA	San Jose
Sonasoft Corp (HQ)	Provider of software based solutions to simplify and automate replication, archiving, backup, recovery, and data protection operations.	408-708-4000	NA	San Jose

COMPANY NAME	PRODUCT / SERVICE	PHONE	EMP	CITY
SoundHound Inc (HQ)	Developer of a sound and speech responsive search engine. The company's product finds application in mobile and communication devices.	408-441-3200	NA	Santa Clara
Spiralinks Corp (HQ)	Provider of compensation management software products. The company offers compensation management, HR analytics, and payroll integration services.	408-608-6900	NA	Campbell
Stopware Inc (HQ)	Developer of visitor management security software. The company offers hardware, badge stock, and training services.	408-367-0220	NA	Pleasanton
Stratogent Corp (HQ)	Provider of hosting and critical software systems operations. The company is engaged in design and programming solutions.	650-577-2332	NA	San Mateo
Stratovan Corp (HQ)	Developer of visual analysis software. It's product finds application in 3D imaging and surgical planning research.	530-746-7970	NA	Davis
StrongKey (HQ)	Provider of enterprise key management solutions. The company serves the cloud computing, e-commerce, healthcare, finance, and other sectors.	408-331-2000	NA	Cupertino
Subrosasoft.Com Inc (HQ)	Developer of software for Mac operating systems. The company offers software such as FileSalvage, CopyCat, and ParentRemote.	510-870-7883	NA	Fremont
Sumo Logic (HQ)	Provider of compliance, security, monitoring, troubleshooting, and delivery solutions. The company serves security, IT, and development teams.	650-810-8700	NA	Redwood City
Synack (HQ)	Provider of security intelligence solutions. The company offers services to the commercial, industrial, and business sectors.	855-796-2251	NA	Redwood City
Synopsys Corporate (HQ)	Developer of synthesis technology solutions. The company is also involved in design flow deployment, physical design assistance, and related services.	650-584-5000	NA	Mountain View
Syntest Technologies Inc (HQ)	Provider of test solutions for the electronics industry. The company is involved in fault simulation solutions and services.	408-720-9956	NA	San Jose
Tamalpais Group Inc (HQ)	Provider of information technology solutions. The company offers data-centric delivery, infrastructure assessment, and IT performance services.	415-455-5770	NA	San Anselmo
Tapjoy Inc (HQ)	Provider of advertising and targeting solutions. The company also deals with developer services such as consulting and real-time reporting.	415-766-6905	NA	San Francisco
Teamf1 Inc (HQ)	Provider of networking and security software for embedded devices. The company also offers technical support services.	510-505-9931	NA	Fremont
Teleresults Corp (HQ)	Provider of electronic medical record solutions and transplant software. The company's services include data conversion, interfaces, and training.	415-392-9670	NA	San Francisco
TFD Group (BR)	Developer of analytical methods and software tools. The company caters to aerospace and defense sectors.	831-649-3800	NA	Monterey
TG Service Inc (HQ)	Producer of multimedia and Internet solutions. The company engages in microarray analysis on machines.	510-243-9931	NA	El Sobrante
Thought Inc (HQ)	Provider of data management solutions. The company uses dynamic mapping and related software for this purpose.	415-836-9199	NA	San Francisco
N Tiger Software (HQ)	Developer of investment software.	858-273-5900	11-50	San Diego
Touchpoints Inc (DH)	Provider of application development, big data engineering, and analytics solutions and it serves the public and commercial sectors.	916-878-5940	NA	Roseville
Trion Worlds Inc (HQ)	Publisher and developer of games. The company offers Defiance, RIFT, Archeage, and End of Nations games.	650-273-9618	NA	Redwood City
Trofholz Technologies Inc (HQ)	Developer of IT information and security systems. The company also specializes in communication solutions.	916-577-1903	NA	Rocklin
Turbo-Doc Medical Record Systems Inc (HQ)	Provider of electronic medical record systems. The company offers walkout statements, drug information handouts, and medication rewrites.	530-877-8650	NA	Paradise
Twilio Inc (HQ)	Provider of infrastructure APIs for businesses to build scalable, reliable voice, and text messaging apps.	415-390-2337	NA	San Francisco
Untangle (HQ)	Designer and developer of network management software. The company specializes in firewall and Internet management application.	408-598-4299	NA	San Jose
UpGuard Inc (HQ)	Provider of integrity monitoring, vulnerability analysis, vendor risk assessment, and configuration differencing solutions.	888-882-3223	NA	Mountain View
USWired Inc (HQ)	Provider of computer networking solutions that include cloud hosting, network design and installation, and wireless networks.	408-432-1144	NA	Campbell
Valiantica Inc (HQ)	Provider of global IT solutions. The company's services include consulting, outsourcing, and mobile, enterprise and business application development.	408-725-2426	NA	San Jose
Varite Inc (HQ)	Provider of custom software development, integration, deployment, and implementation services in the domains of core networking and virtualization.	408-977-0700	NA	San Jose
vArmour Inc (HQ)	Provider of cloud security, segmentation, monitoring, and deception solutions. The company serves banks and healthcare organizations.	650-564-5100	NA	Los Altos
Vayusphere Inc (HQ)	Developer of instant messaging applications. The company's customers include Morgan Stanley, Deutsche Bank, and others.	650-960-2900	NA	Mountain View

COMPANY NAME	PRODUCT / SERVICE	PHONE	EMP	CITY
Veeva Systems Inc (HQ)	Provider of cloud-based business solutions such as customer relationship management and content management for the life sciences industry.	925-452-6500	NA	Pleasanton
N Ventricle Software Systems Inc (HQ)	Provider of software development for the healthcare industry.	310-948-2551	NA	Rancho Palos Verdes
VeraCentra (HQ)	Provider of data leveraging services to brands for marketing needs and also focuses on customer intelligence, marketing execution, and consultation.	707-224-6161	NA	Napa
VinSuite (HQ)	Developer of wine software and serves the consumer sector. The company offers support services to wineries and tasting rooms.	707-253-7400	NA	Napa
Vintara Inc (HQ)	Provider of web-based enterprise process management solutions and services. The company caters to a number of industries.	877-846-8272	NA	Oakland
Viscira LLC (HQ)	Manufacturer of software products. The company deals with the development of animation technology solutions.	415-848-8010	NA	San Francisco
Vistrian Inc (HQ)	Developer of software products. The company's services include escalation management, problem isolation, and remote access.	408-719-0500	NA	Milpitas
VMware Inc (HQ)	Provider of storage, data center, application virtualization, and enterprise mobility management products.	650-427-1000	NA	Palo Alto
Watchwith Inc (HQ)	Provider of software and data solutions for the film and television content creators and consumer electronics manufacturers.	415-552-1552	NA	San Francisco
Whitehat Security (HQ)	Provider of web application security solutions such as vulnerability management, threat modeling, and risk profiling.	408-343-8300	NA	San Jose
Whizz Systems (HQ)	Provider of electronics design and manufacturing services for the semiconductor, defense, computing, and industrial equipment markers.	408-980-0400	NA	Santa Clara
WineDirect (HQ)	Provider of DTC services such as commerce, compliance, fulfillment, marketing, and enterprise services for wineries.	800-819-0325	NA	American Canyon
N Xifin Inc (HQ)	Provider of health care related information technology services.	858-793-5700	201-500	San Diego
Xmatters Inc (HQ)	Provider of voice and text alerting system software. The company serves the healthcare, telecommunications, and manufacturing industries.	925-226-0300	NA	San Ramon
N Yellow Magic Inc (HQ)	Developer of software for the directory publishing industry.	951-506-4005	NA	Murrieta
Zscaler Inc (HQ)	Provider of SaaS security solutions. The company offers cloud security solutions for mobile enterprises.	408-533-0288	NA	San Jose

327 = Programming Services

COMPANY NAME	PRODUCT / SERVICE	PHONE	EMP	CITY
4D Inc (DH)	Developer of web and Internet applications. The company serves universities, corporations, governments, and individuals.	408-557-4600	NA	San Jose
Acrylic Art (HQ)	Provider of fabrication and machining services. The company focuses on painting, product finishing, anodizing, and vapor polishing.	510-654-0953	NA	Emeryville
Alchemic Solutions Group Inc (HQ)	Provider of technology marketing solutions for wireless sectors. The company focuses on product management, software development, and consultation.	510-919-8105	NA	San Mateo
Alertenterprise Inc (HQ)	Developer of information and operational technology solutions such as identity intelligence, and enterprise access, and incident management.	510-440-0840	NA	Fremont
Alpha Research & Technology Inc (HQ)	Designer and manufacturer of airborne systems for command, communications, intelligence, surveillance, and other needs and focuses on installation.	916-431-9340	NA	El Dorado Hills
Andover Consulting Group Inc (HQ)	Supplier of network components. The company offers data center liquidation, network security, and network equipment services.	415-537-6950	NA	San Mateo
ANSYS Inc (BR)	Provider of engineering solutions. The company serves the aerospace, defense, and construction industries.	844-462-6797	NA	Berkeley
Beachhead Solutions Inc (HQ)	Provider of web-based console to enforce encryption, manage security, and give providers the ability to change policy on iPhones and android devices.	408-496-6936	NA	San Jose
BlueChipTek Inc (HQ)	Provider of data management and protection, information life cycle management, networking, security, and data center solutions.	408-731-7700	NA	Santa Clara
Boardwalktech Inc (HQ)	Provider of enterprise collaboration software specializing in tax planning, cash management, and revenue forecasting solutions.	650-618-6200	NA	Cupertino
Bugcrowd (HQ)	Provider of security solutions. The company is engaged in pre-launch consulting, research, and testing services.	888-361-9734	NA	San Francisco
Busse Design USA Inc (HQ)	Provider of interface design services. The company's services include website design and application user interface.	415-689-8090	NA	Oakland
Carbon Five Inc (HQ)	Provider of software development services such as lean design and agile development for the web and mobile sectors.	415-546-0500	NA	San Francisco
Casahl Technology Inc (HQ)	Provider of collaboration and content environment optimization services. The company focuses on cloud integration and content management.	925-328-2828	NA	San Ramon
Clustrix Inc (HQ)	Provider of a SQL database with no limits to database size, table size, query complexity, and performance.	415-501-9560	NA	San Francisco
Cognizant Technology Solutions (BR)	Provider of business consulting, enterprise application development, IT infrastructure, and outsourcing services.	925-790-2000	NA	San Ramon

COMPANY NAME	PRODUCT / SERVICE	PHONE	EMP	CITY
Connected Marketing (HQ)	Provider of marketing services. The company also offers web development, branding, and lead generation services.	408-647-2198	NA	San Jose
Contrast Security (HQ)	Designer and developer of self-protection software. The company is also engaged in operations support services.	888-371-1333	NA	Los Altos
CSRware Inc (HQ)	Developer of sustainability resource management software. The company specializes in supply chain, enterprise ERP solutions, and consulting services.	855-277-9273	NA	Mill Valley
Dogpatch Technology Inc (HQ)	Provider of digital strategy and mobile development solutions for game design and research, global media and communications, and grant writing projects.	415-663-6488	NA	San Francisco
Egnyte Inc (HQ)	Provider of online storage, cloud computing, and file sharing services. The company serves the financial, banking, and pharmaceutical industries.	650-968-4018	NA	Mountain View
Epylon Corp (HQ)	Developer of e-procurement software and services. The company serves the government and education sectors.	925-407-1020	NA	Danville
Exxact Corp (HQ)	Supplier of workstation graphic cards and solutions. The company also offers servers, HPC clusters, and computing software.	510-226-7366	NA	Fremont
Fidus Systems Inc (BR)	Specializes in electronic product development and consulting services. The company also deals with hardware design.	408-217-1928	NA	Fremont
Forescout Technologies Inc (HQ)	Provider of network access control and policy compliance management solutions. The company serves the business sector.	408-213-3191	NA	San Jose
Global Infotech Corp (HQ)	Provider of software services. The company's software solutions focuses on staff augmentation, telecom, systems integration, chip design, ERP, and CRM domains.	408-567-0600	NA	San Jose
Icube Information International (HQ)	Publisher of software work flow based management systems, documentation, inventory processing, and revision tracking services.	510-683-8928	NA	Fremont
Inabyte Inc (HQ)	Manufacturer of developer tools. The company also offers solutions and services for developers and end users of PCs or workstations.	415-898-7905	NA	Novato
Increv Corp (HQ)	Developer of business and information technology solutions. The company is engaged in consulting and product development services.	408-689-2296	NA	Los Altos
Ingenuus Software Inc (HQ)	Provider of enterprise process orchestration solutions. The company develops business process management and process optimization software.	510-824-5653	NA	Fremont
Issio Solutions Inc (HQ)	Provider of workforce management software for surgical facilities. The company also serves ambulatory surgical centers.	888-994-7746	NA	Concord
IT Pro Source (HQ)	Provider of on call plans, managed services, web based monitoring, and communication cabling services.	925-455-7701	NA	Livermore
JAMIS Software Corp (HQ)	Provider of job-cost, billing, and accounting systems and solutions. The company caters to the government contractors.	800-655-2647	NA	San Diego
Lytrod Software Inc (HQ)	Provider of variable data print software products. The company's products include VisionDP Production and Automate, Proform Designer, and Office Designer.	707-422-9221	NA	Fairfield
Marketo Inc (HQ)	Provider of marketing automation software services. The company offers email and social marketing, marketing software, and digital marketing services.	650-581-8001	NA	San Mateo
Medallia Inc (HQ)	Provider of consulting, system configuration, user training, and data warehouse integration services.	650-321-3000	NA	San Mateo
Metaswitch Networks (DH)	Provider of service management solutions. The company offers original equipment manufacturer, multimedia subsystem, and hosted business services.	415-513-1500	NA	Los Altos
Myers Network Solutions (HQ)	Provider of network solutions. The company focuses on IT consulting, disaster recovery, network assessment, and cloud computing.	408-483-1881	NA	San Jose
Nearsoft Inc (HQ)	Provider of services to grow development team in companies. The company exclusively caters to software product sectors.	408-691-1034	NA	San Jose
Nsymbio Inc (HQ)	Provider of printing services. The company is engaged in project management, graphic design, print, and online ordering system services.	650-968-2058	NA	Mountain View
Nuvation Engineering (HQ)	Provider of electronic engineering services. The company focuses on product design, embedded software development, and single integrity analysis.	408-228-5580	NA	Sunnyvale
Opal Soft Inc (HQ)	Provider of communications equipment installation and networking. The company's services include application development, network management, and maintenance.	408-267-2211	NA	Sunnyvale
Openclovis (HQ)	Provider of system infrastructure software platform. The company mainly serves the communication industry.	707-981-7120	NA	Petaluma
PC Professional (HQ)	Provider of information technology solutions. The company focuses on cloud computing, application development, networking, and disaster recovery.	510-874-5871	NA	Oakland
PeerNova Inc (HQ)	Provider of silicon valley-based technology such as distributed systems, networking solutions, big data, compiler technology, and financial services.	669-400-7800	NA	San Jose

COMPANY NAME	PRODUCT / SERVICE	PHONE	EMP	CITY
Penguin Computing (HQ)	Provider of Linux-based cloud and HPC solutions. The company's products include servers, network switches, and integrated rack solutions.	415-954-2800	NA	Fremont
Proxio Inc (HQ)	Provider of digital real estate marketing solutions for agents, brokers and developers. The company serves businesses.	415-723-1691	NA	Santa Clara
Qualys Inc (HQ)	Provider of security and compliance solutions. The company also offers asset discovery and threat protection solutions.	650-801-6100	NA	Foster City
Quanergy Systems Inc (HQ)	Developer of smart sensing solutions. The company offers solutions for real-time 3D mapping, object detection, and tracking.	408-245-9500	NA	Sunnyvale
Qumu Inc (BR)	Provider of web casting, marketing, event, and other professional services. The company offers enterprise video solutions.	650-396-8530	NA	San Bruno
R-Computer (HQ)	Provider of computer solutions for small and medium-sized companies. The company also offers lifetime product guarantees and sales consultation.	925-798-4884	NA	Concord
RackWare Inc (HQ)	Provider of disaster prevention and recovery solutions. The company also offers business continuity and virtualization solutions.	408-430-5821	NA	San Jose
RetailNext (HQ)	Provider of in-store analytics solutions. The company offers services to retail labs, marketing departments, and shopping centers.	408-884-2162	NA	San Jose
SACC Inc (HQ)	Provider of enterprise resource planning, data warehousing, technology infrastructure, business process outsourcing, and staffing services.	408-755-3000	NA	Santa Clara
SAP America Inc (BR)	Developer of software applications. The company provides data and technology, custom development, and implementation services.	650-849-4000	NA	Palo Alto
Softjourn Inc (HQ)	Provider of outsource software development services and focuses on offshore assessments, application development, and quality assurance testing.	510-744-1528	NA	Fremont
SoundHound Inc (HQ)	Developer of a sound and speech responsive search engine. The company's product finds application in mobile and communication devices.	408-441-3200	NA	Santa Clara
StrongKey (HQ)	Provider of enterprise key management solutions. The company serves the cloud computing, e-commerce, healthcare, finance, and other sectors.	408-331-2000	NA	Cupertino
Tanium Inc (HQ)	Provider of IT operations management, asset visibility, and security hygiene solutions. The company serves the healthcare and retail industries.	510-704-0202	NA	Emeryville
Tech Soft 3d (HQ)	Provider of software solutions. The company offers software for desktop visualization, modeling, cloud and mobile solutions, and data exchange.	510-883-2180	NA	Berkeley
Think Connected LLC (HQ)	Provider of data center, consulting, managed, and supplemental information technology services for small and medium-sized businesses.	877-684-4654	NA	San Francisco
uSens Inc (HQ)	Creator of 3D human computing interaction software and hardware solutions. The company focuses on artificial intelligence.	408-564-0227	NA	San Jose
V5 Systems (HQ)	Provider of outdoor security and computing platforms. The company offers services to the government, military, and law enforcement industries.	844-604-7350	NA	Fremont
Workday Inc (HQ)	Provider of software solutions for human resources management and financial management. The company specializes in SaaS based enterprise solutions.	925-951-9000	NA	Pleasanton

328 = Software Consulting & R&D

COMPANY NAME	PRODUCT / SERVICE	PHONE	EMP	CITY
Algo-Logic Systems (HQ)	Specializes in building networking solutions. The company also offers technological and data handling services to firms.	408-707-3740	NA	San Jose
Aspera Inc (HQ)	Developer of file transport technologies. The company provides client and server software, consoles, and mobile uploaders.	510-849-2386	NA	Emeryville
Assia Inc (HQ)	Provider of broadband solution such as cloud check, technology licensing, DSL expresse, and expresse products and solution.	650-654-3400	NA	Redwood City
Beachhead Solutions Inc (HQ)	Provider of web-based console to enforce encryption, manage security, and give providers the ability to change policy on iPhones and android devices.	408-496-6936	NA	San Jose
Beyond Lucid Technologies Inc (HQ)	Developer of cloud-based software platform. The company offers services to the emergency medical, disaster management, and first response industries.	650-648-3727	NA	Concord
Blue Harbors (HQ)	Provider of warehouse and transportation management, and shipping solutions. The company serves the industrial sector.	415-799-7769	NA	San Mateo
BlueChipTek Inc (HQ)	Provider of data management and protection, information life cycle management, networking, security, and data center solutions.	408-731-7700	NA	Santa Clara
BuyerLeverage (HQ)	Provider of technologies and services that allow consumers and businesses to profit and control their communications and information.	650-320-1608	NA	Palo Alto
C&P Microsystems LLC (HQ)	Manufacturer and seller of paper cutter control systems. The company offers microcip, cutternet, and micro facts.	707-776-4500	NA	Petaluma
Capriza Inc (HQ)	Provider of codeless enterprise mobility platform. The company offers mobile-enabling business applications such as design, zaaps, manage, and security.	650-600-3661	NA	Palo Alto

COMPANY NAME	PRODUCT / SERVICE	PHONE	EMP	CITY
Casahl Technology Inc (HQ)	Provider of collaboration and content environment optimization services. The company focuses on cloud integration and content management.	925-328-2828	NA	San Ramon
Clare Computer Solutions (HQ)	Provider of information technology services. The company offers computer network, software consultation, visualization, and cloud computing solutions.	925-277-0690	NA	San Ramon
Clean Power Research (HQ)	Provider of program automation, customer engagement, and solar data and intelligence solutions. The company offers services to the solar industry.	707-258-2765	NA	Napa
Crestpoint Solutions Inc (HQ)	Provider of project planning, programming, web hosting, and wireless and records management services.	925-828-6005	NA	Pleasanton
Cygna Energy Services Inc (HQ)	Provider of application development, data integration, systems integration, consulting, and web services.	925-930-8377	NA	Walnut Creek
Database Republic (HQ)	Provider of enterprise analysis and strategy modeling services. The company also focuses on DB design and implementation.	530-692-2500	NA	Oregon House
Exponent Partners (HQ)	Provider of performance and outcomes management solutions. The company's services include systems integration and custom application development.	800-918-2917	NA	San Francisco
FactoryWiz (HQ)	Provider of CNC Machine Tool monitoring and data collection products. The company is also involved in preventive maintenance services.	408-224-9167	NA	San Jose
Global Software Resources (HQ)	Provider of application development, business intelligence, testing and mobile computing, and collaboration services.	925-249-2200	NA	Pleasanton
Glyphic Technology (HQ)	Provider of software design and architecture solutions. The company focuses on Internet, server, desktop, mobile, and embedded systems.	650-964-5311	NA	Mountain View
Health Fidelity Inc (HQ)	Provider of natural language processing technology and inference platform to analyze vast amounts of unstructured data for clinical and financial insights.	650-727-3300	NA	San Mateo
IBM Research - Almaden (BR)	Provider of computer technology services. The company engages in cloud, mobility, and security services.	408-927-1080	NA	San Jose
Individual Software Inc (HQ)	Publisher and developer of education, business, and personal productivity software for consumers, schools, businesses, and government.	925-734-6767	NA	Livermore
Inductive Automation (HQ)	Supplier of web-based industrial automation software. The company offers solutions for end-users and integrators.	916-456-1045	NA	Folsom
Infin IT Consulting (HQ)	Designer and developer of CNC machining and billet products. The company's products include fire extinguisher brackets, shift knobs, and boat accessories.	866-364-2007	NA	Campbell
InfoTech Spectrum Inc (HQ)	Provider of integrated creative IT services including IT consulting, advanced technology deployment, and product development.	408-705-2237	NA	Santa Clara
iSOA Group Inc (BR)	Provider of business process management, service oriented architecture, and business analytics services to finance, energy, retail, and other sectors.	925-465-7400	NA	Walnut Creek
ISSE Services (HQ)	Provider of security solutions principally focusing on supporting system implementation and security testing.	916-670-1082	NA	Elk Grove
Key Business Solutions Inc (HQ)	Provider of software development and database management services. The company also specializes in business intelligence.	916-646-2080	NA	Sacramento
KLH Consulting Inc (HQ)	Provider of IT consulting, cloud computing, and related business solutions. The company offers services to business executives and professionals.	707-575-9986	NA	Santa Rosa
Kovarus Inc (HQ)	Provider of integrated business IT solutions. The company also deals with leasing, financing, project management, and related services.	800-454-1585	NA	San Ramon
Lanlogic (HQ)	Provider of information technology services. The company offers network management and support services.	925-273-2300	NA	Livermore
LCS Technologies Inc (HQ)	Provider of information services for customers with Oracle software and service needs using resources such as people, hardware, and software.	855-277-5527	NA	Gold River
Linden Research Inc (HQ)	Designer and developer of digital entertainment solutions. The company's products include Desura, Patterns, and Versu.	415-243-9000	NA	San Francisco
Metabiota Inc (HQ)	Provider of risk analytics that help protect global health for governments and multinationals, food risk, and financial risk insights.	415-398-4712	NA	San Francisco
Modius Inc (HQ)	Provider of performance management software. The company serves infrastructure monitoring applications.	415-655-6700	NA	San Francisco
Neudesic LLC (BR)	Provider of technology services. The company focuses on social software, integration platform, and CRM solutions and offers cloud computing services.	949-754-4500	NA	Irvine
Panasas Inc (HQ)	Provider of scale-out NAS storage system for most demanding workloads in life sciences, media and entertainment, energy, and education environments.	408-215-6800	NA	Sunnyvale
PeerNova Inc (HQ)	Provider of silicon valley-based technology such as distributed systems, networking solutions, big data, compiler technology, and financial services.	669-400-7800	NA	San Jose
Planisware (HQ)	Designer of portfolio management software solutions for product development and research and development organizations.	415-591-0941	NA	San Francisco

COMPANY NAME	PRODUCT / SERVICE	PHONE	EMP	CITY
POS Specialists (HQ)	Provider of digital dining solutions. The company is engaged in business consultation, on-site training, and cloud services.	925-626-3930	NA	Concord
Project Partners LLC (HQ)	Provider of business solutions and information technology systems. The company offers NetSuite, Oracle Fusion Applications, and Primavera.	650-712-6200	NA	Half Moon Bay
Proxio Inc (HQ)	Provider of digital real estate marketing solutions for agents, brokers and developers. The company serves businesses.	415-723-1691	NA	Santa Clara
Pulse Secure LLC (HQ)	Provider of product, hardware, partner, and enterprise solutions. The company offers services to the financial services and healthcare industries.	408-372-9600	NA	San Jose
Quest America Inc (HQ)	Provider of information technology services. The company offers solutions through strategy, consulting, and outsourcing.	408-492-1650	NA	San Jose
RackWare Inc (HQ)	Provider of disaster prevention and recovery solutions. The company also offers business continuity and virtualization solutions.	408-430-5821	NA	San Jose
Sherrill-Lubinski Corp (HQ)	Provider of monitoring and analytics solutions for middleware-powered applications. The company serves the electrical commodity market.	415-927-8400	NA	Riverside
Software AG (BR)	Provider of enterprise management and business solutions that include process intelligence and automation, and enterprise architecture.	800-823-2212	NA	Santa Clara
Space Machine Inc (HQ)	Specializes in academic research. The company focuses on the development of custom models and trading strategies.	650-669-8629	NA	Redwood Shores
Spreadsheetworld Inc (HQ)	Provider of services for application of MS Excel and VBA tools in various fields. The company focuses on science, engineering, and management.	818-995-3931	NA	June Lake
Synack (HQ)	Provider of security intelligence solutions. The company offers services to the commercial, industrial, and business sectors.	855-796-2251	NA	Redwood City
Synergy Business Solutions (HQ)	Provider of technology evaluation, business process improvement, and custom software development services to a wide range of sectors.	415-263-1843	NA	San Francisco
Tanium Inc (HQ)	Provider of IT operations management, asset visibility, and security hygiene solutions. The company serves the healthcare and retail industries.	510-704-0202	NA	Emeryville
The Igneous Group Inc (HQ)	Provider of technology consulting services. The company focuses on web content, application development, and e-commerce.	831-469-7625	NA	Santa Cruz
Think Connected LLC (HQ)	Provider of data center, consulting, managed, and supplemental information technology services for small and medium-sized businesses.	877-684-4654	NA	San Francisco
Untangle (HQ)	Designer and developer of network management software. The company specializes in firewall and Internet management application.	408-598-4299	NA	San Jose
USWired Inc (HQ)	Provider of computer networking solutions that include cloud hosting, network design and installation, and wireless networks.	408-432-1144	NA	Campbell
VIA Licensing Corp (HQ)	Provider of intellectual property programs and business solutions. The company serves technology companies, entertainment companies, and universities.	415-645-4700	NA	San Francisco
VinSuite (HQ)	Developer of wine software and serves the consumer sector. The company offers support services to wineries and tasting rooms.	707-253-7400	NA	Napa

329 = Systems Design & Integration

COMPANY NAME	PRODUCT / SERVICE	PHONE	EMP	CITY
2ndEdison Inc (HQ)	Provider of e-Commerce applications. The company also offers business process consulting and design services.	844-432-8466	NA	Orinda
Agile Global Solutions Inc (HQ)	Provider of business and IT solutions such as custom and enterprise application management and mobile business solutions.	916-655-7745	NA	Folsom
AGTEK Development Company Inc (HQ)	Developer of high tech surveying, analysis, and control solutions for residential, commercial, transportation, water, energy, and government.	925-606-8197	NA	Livermore
Alten Calsoft Labs (HQ)	Provider of breed consulting, enterprise IT, and product engineering services for enterprises in healthcare, telecom, and high-tech and retail industries.	408-755-3000	NA	Santa Clara
Altigen Communications Inc (HQ)	Manufacturer of voice and data telecommunication equipment. The company specializes in hosted business communication solutions.	408-597-9000	NA	Milpitas
Amdocs Ltd (BR)	Provider of customer management and billing solutions software. The company offers services to the industrial sector.	916-934-7000	NA	El Dorado Hills
ARBOR Solution Inc (RH)	Provider of embedded computing and networking solutions for the transportation, medical, automation, and military segments.	408-452-8900	NA	Fremont
Arterys Inc (HQ)	Developer of medical imaging cloud platform. The company specializes in diagnostic platform to make healthcare more accurate and data driven.	650-319-7230	NA	San Francisco
Artifex Software Inc (HQ)	Provider of software solutions for host based applications. The company also focuses on embedded printer markers.	415-492-9861	NA	Novato
ASI Controls (HQ)	Manufacturer of direct digital controls for HVAC and light industrial marketplace. The company also offers networking products and unitary controls.	925-866-8808	NA	Pleasanton
Asteelflash (BR)	Provider of electronic manufacturing services. The company offers engineering design, contract manufacturing, and delivery services.	510-440-2840	NA	Fremont
Audible Magic Corp (HQ)	Developer of media identification and synchronization, content registration, and copyright compliance solutions.	408-399-6405	NA	Los Gatos
Auriga Corp (HQ)	Provider of technology consulting services for electric power, telecommunications, transportation, and information technology systems.	408-946-5400	NA	Milpitas

COMPANY NAME	PRODUCT / SERVICE	PHONE	EMP	CITY
BBI Engineering Inc (HQ)	Designer and installer of audiovisual, multimedia, teleconferencing and data systems for museums, aquariums, zoos, schools, and universities.	415-695-9555	NA	San Francisco
Beganto Inc (HQ)	Provider of web-based applications and support services. The company specializes in application, component, design, and sales engineering.	510-280-0554	NA	Santa Clara
N Birdsall Interactive (HQ)	Provider of website design.	510-385-4714	1-10	Lafayette
BKF Engineers (BR)	Provider of civil engineering consulting, and land surveying services. The company serves business organizations.	925-940-2200	NA	Walnut Creek
BKF Engineers (BR)	Provider of civil engineering, design, surveying, design, transportation, and entitlement support services.	408-467-9100	NA	San Jose
Blackstone Technology Group Inc (HQ)	Provider of IT solutions, commercial, and government consulting, staffing services, and trellis natural gas transaction management web solution.	415-837-1400	NA	San Francisco
Brekeke Software Inc (HQ)	Developer of session initiation protocol software products for Internet protocol network communication needs.	650-401-6633	NA	San Mateo
Bright Pattern Inc (HQ)	Provider of enterprise contact center application for blended multi-channel interactions. The company offers products based on modern technology.	650-529-4099	NA	S San Francisco
Busse Design USA Inc (HQ)	Provider of interface design services. The company's services include website design and application user interface.	415-689-8090	NA	Oakland
CJS Labs (HQ)	Provider of electronic design, consulting, engineering, and test automation programming assistance services.	415-923-9535	NA	San Francisco
Configure Inc (HQ)	Provider of communication consulting services. The company specializes in network design, transport service implementation, and project management.	877-408-2636	NA	San Jose
Criterion Network Services Inc (HQ)	Provider of network design, system integration, configuration, and remote network management services.	650-947-7755	NA	Los Altos
Current Controls Inc (HQ)	Designer and manufacturer of control panels for OEMs in many sectors. The company also offers PLC programming, system integration, and other services.	916-630-5507	NA	Rocklin
Cybermanor (HQ)	Designer of Internet connected home electronic and networking solutions. The company also offers installation services.	408-399-3331	NA	Los Gatos
D-Tools Inc (HQ)	Developer and marketer of software to streamline processes which accompany the integration and installation of low-voltage systems.	925-681-2326	NA	Concord
d2m Interactive (HQ)	Provider of web development, management, and e-commerce services. The company also focuses on marketing.	408-315-6802	NA	Los Gatos
Diablo Analytical Inc (HQ)	Provider of system integration for analytical measuring instruments. The company is engaged in custom software development and laboratory analysis.	925-755-1005	NA	Antioch
Diamond Systems Corp (HQ)	Supplier of SBCs, embedded-ready subsystems, and system expansion modules targeting real-world applications.	650-810-2500	NA	Sunnyvale
Dorado Software Inc (HQ)	Provider of inventory, monitoring, storage management, network configuration, and mobile back hauling solutions.	916-673-1100	NA	El Dorado Hills
Douglas Electronics Inc (HQ)	Provider of CAD/CAM tools for personal computers. The company specializes in custom board manufacturing and electronic design software products.	510-483-8770	NA	San Leandro
Exxact Corp (HQ)	Supplier of workstation graphic cards and solutions. The company also offers servers, HPC clusters, and computing software.	510-226-7366	NA	Fremont
Game Your Game Inc (HQ)	Developer of digital tracking system such as automatic shot tracking and hands-free game tracking device to get the insights to improve the game.	888-245-3433	NA	San Francisco
Global Presenter (BR)	Designer and builder of meeting room communication systems. The company is a provider of design, delivery, and system integration solutions.	408-526-0221	NA	San Jose
Golden Valley Systems Inc (HQ)	Provider of enterprise integration solutions. The company offers technical, IT consulting, and green energy services.	408-934-5898	NA	Milpitas
Good Dog Design (HQ)	Provider of digital designing services. The company offers web development and designing and mobile application services.	415-383-0110	NA	Mill Valley
N Great Circle Associates Inc (HQ)	Provider of enterprise information technology infrastructure and networking services.	415-861-3588	NA	Alameda
Ibus Corp (HQ)	Manufacturer and provider of industrial computers. The company also specializes in prototyping and quality control.	408-450-7880	NA	Santa Clara
Icube Information International (HQ)	Publisher of software work flow based management systems, documentation, inventory processing, and revision tracking services.	510-683-8928	NA	Fremont
Infoyogi LLC (HQ)	Provider of information technology solutions for software application development and systems integration.	408-850-1700	NA	Santa Clara
IntelinAir Inc (HQ)	Provider of aerial imagery analytics such as image analysis and change detection and deep learning and neural networks for farmers.	818-445-2339	NA	San Jose
JAMIS Software Corp (HQ)	Provider of job-cost, billing, and accounting systems and solutions. The company caters to the government contractors.	800-655-2647	NA	San Diego
Jitterbit Inc (HQ)	Focuses on application integration solutions for aerospace and defense, life sciences, pharmaceuticals, and financial services.	877-852-3500	NA	Alameda

COMPANY NAME	PRODUCT / SERVICE	PHONE	EMP	CITY
Kovarus Inc (HQ)	Provider of integrated business IT solutions. The company also deals with leasing, financing, project management, and related services.	800-454-1585	NA	San Ramon
Matrix Computer Solutions Inc (HQ)	Provider of computer and technology solutions for residential and business customers. The company also offers data backup, repair, and other services.	415-331-3600	NA	Sausalito
Media Net Link Inc (HQ)	Provider of web business solutions. The company focuses on application development, systems integration, website design, and project management.	866-563-5152	NA	Oakland
Michael Patrick Partners (HQ)	Provider of branding solutions. The company also offers logo design, portfolio creation, web content, and marketing services.	650-327-3185	NA	San Francisco
Mirabilis Design Inc (HQ)	Provider of systems engineering solutions for performance analysis and architecture exploration of electronics and real-time software.	408-844-3234	NA	Sunnyvale
Mistral Solutions Inc (HQ)	Provider of technology design and systems engineering solutions. The company's solutions include hardware board design and embedded software development.	408-705-2240	NA	Fremont
Mobitor Corp (HQ)	Provider of mobility software, connectivity, and information solutions. The company serves the aerospace, aviation, and manufacturing industries.	925-464-7700	NA	Walnut Creek
Mobiveil Inc (HQ)	Provider of technology solutions. The company's products include Silicon IP and COTS Modules and offers IC design and embedded software services.	408-212-9512	NA	Milpitas
Mondo Media Inc (HQ)	Provider of gaming solutions. The company's store features men's and women's T-shirts, smartphone cases, and related supplies.	415-865-2700	NA	San Francisco
Monterey Computer Corp (HQ)	Provider of technology and integrated network services. The company offers networking, wireless Internet, server hosting, and surveillance services.	831-646-1147	NA	Monterey
MSC Software (BR)	Developer of simulation software for acoustics, thermal analysis, and other needs. The company also offers software implementation and systems design services.	714-540-8900	NA	Newport Beach
NADA Technologies Inc (HQ)	Provider of enterprise Oracle applications. The company also offers business intelligence solutions.	650-678-4666	NA	Danville
Netformx Inc (HQ)	Designer and builder of solutions for the networking and service providers. The company specializes in desktop and cloud applications.	408-423-6600	NA	San Jose
Netpace Inc (HQ)	Provider of consulting, cloud computing, database management, and proprietary development services.	925-543-7760	NA	San Ramon
Network Design Associates Inc (HQ)	Provider of engineering services for computer systems. The company's services include network design, implementation, support, and maintenance.	916-853-1632	NA	Citrus Heights
New Tech Solutions Inc (HQ)	Provider of technology solutions. The company caters to networking, security, and communication manufacturers.	510-353-4070	NA	Fremont
Nextaxiom Technology Inc (HQ)	Provider of testing, certification, and other professional services. The company offers work management and scheduling solutions.	415-373-1890	NA	San Francisco
Novani LLC (HQ)	Provider of disaster prevention and recovery solutions. The company also offers business continuity and virtualization solutions.	415-731-1111	NA	San Francisco
Nuvation Engineering (HQ)	Provider of electronic engineering services. The company focuses on product design, embedded software development, and single integrity analysis.	408-228-5580	NA	Sunnyvale
Office Information Systems (HQ)	Provider of computer network design and consulting services. The company serves small and medium sized organizations and law firms.	510-568-7900	NA	Oakland
Opsol Integrators Inc (HQ)	Provider of universal messaging, data integration, and encryption products. The company serves banks, retail, telecom, and other sectors.	408-364-9915	NA	Campbell
Outside Technology (HQ)	Provider of automated reservation systems. The company mainly caters to the outdoor recreation industry.	415-488-4909	NA	San Anselmo
Park Computer Systems Inc (HQ)	Provider of mobile products and services. The company also offers sales content automation and staff augmentation services.	510-353-1700	NA	Newark
Portola Systems Inc (HQ)	Provider of computer network engineering and integration services. The company also specializes in IT consultation.	707-824-8800	NA	Sebastopol
POS Specialists (HQ)	Provider of digital dining solutions. The company is engaged in business consultation, on-site training, and cloud services.	925-626-3930	NA	Concord
PubMatic Inc (HQ)	Developer of marketing automation software. The company deals with the planning of media campaigns and offers services to publishers.	650-331-3485	NA	Redwood City
Qumu Inc (BR)	Provider of web casting, marketing, event, and other professional services. The company offers enterprise video solutions.	650-396-8530	NA	San Bruno
R&D Logic Inc (HQ)	Developer of performance management software for R&D focused companies. The company offers implementation and training services.	650-356-9207	NA	San Mateo
R-Computer (HQ)	Provider of computer solutions for small and medium-sized companies. The company also offers lifetime product guarantees and sales consultation.	925-798-4884	NA	Concord
RackWare Inc (HQ)	Provider of disaster prevention and recovery solutions. The company also offers business continuity and virtualization solutions.	408-430-5821	NA	San Jose
Rocket Communications Inc (HQ)	Developer of user interface, visual, and icon design services for software and related applications.	415-863-0101	NA	San Francisco

COMPANY NAME	PRODUCT / SERVICE	PHONE	EMP	CITY
Sanah Inc (HQ)	Provider of IT services such as IT strategy consulting, systems integration, and custom application development.	888-306-1942	NA	Sacramento
Savari Inc (HQ)	Provider of communications technology solutions. The company focuses on connecting cars to traffic lights, pedestrians, and smartphones.	408-833-6369	NA	Santa Clara
Spreadsheetworld Inc (HQ)	Provider of services for application of MS Excel and VBA tools in various fields. The company focuses on science, engineering, and management.	818-995-3931	NA	June Lake
SS Papadopulos & Associates Inc (BR)	Provider of web-based applications for customized online communities. The company serves business enterprises.	415-773-0400	NA	San Francisco
Symplectic Engineering Corp (HQ)	Provider of custom computational mechanics solutions. The company is involved in consulting services and it serves the industrial sector.	510-528-1251	NA	Berkeley
Synapse Design (HQ)	Provider of embedded software design services. The company also offers test bench analysis and block and chip level verification services.	408-850-9527	NA	Santa Clara
Systemacs (HQ)	Provider of solutions for upgrading or setting up networks which include hardware, software, and routers.	650-329-9745	NA	Palo Alto
Tanium Inc (HQ)	Provider of IT operations management, asset visibility, and security hygiene solutions. The company serves the healthcare and retail industries.	510-704-0202	NA	Emeryville
Tenefit Corp (HQ)	Provider of software services. The company's IoT gateway is used by mobile users, marketplaces, and machines to connect and communicate in real-time.	877-522-9464	NA	San Jose
Tesco Controls Inc (HQ)	Manufacturer of instrumentation, control systems, and service pedestals for water and traffic sectors. The company offers system integration services.	916-395-8800	NA	Sacramento
V5 Systems (HQ)	Provider of outdoor security and computing platforms. The company offers services to the government, military, and law enforcement industries.	844-604-7350	NA	Fremont
Virtual Driver Interactive (HQ)	Manufacturer of virtual training simulators. The company serves schools, corporations, schools, and hospitals.	877-746-8332	NA	El Dorado Hills
Virtual Instruments (HQ)	Developer of storage area network and virtual infrastructure solutions. The company serves healthcare, federal, and outsourcing and hosting sectors.	408-579-4000	NA	San Jose
Zmanda - A Carbonite Co (HQ)	Provider of open source backup and recovery software solutions. The company's applications include centralized backup of file systems and applications.	408-732-3208	NA	Sunnyvale

330 = Biomaterials

COMPANY NAME	PRODUCT / SERVICE	PHONE	EMP	CITY
Antibody Solutions (HQ)	Provider of antibody products and services. The company serves biotechnology, diagnostic and pharmaceutical companies.	650-938-4300	NA	Sunnyvale
Bell Biosystems Inc (HQ)	Provider of biotechnology services. The company develops proteins targeted to kill specific bacteria but cause minimal collateral damage.	877-420-3621	NA	Berkeley
MTI California Inc (HQ)	Specializes in designing and validating manufacturing controls. The company offers services to biotech companies.	925-937-1500	NA	Walnut Creek
Novozymes Inc (BR)	Provider of industrial biotechnology solutions for the food and beverage, agriculture, textile, and pulp and paper industries.	530-757-8100	NA	Davis

331 = Sensors

COMPANY NAME	PRODUCT / SERVICE	PHONE	EMP	CITY
Allied Fire Protection (HQ)	Designer and manufacturer of fire protection sprinkler systems. The company also offers installation services.	510-533-5516	NA	Oakland
G4s Secure Solutions (USA) Inc (BR)	Provider of security management solutions such as compliance and investigations, disaster and emergency, and fraud abatement.	408-453-4133	NA	San Jose
MTI California Inc (HQ)	Specializes in designing and validating manufacturing controls. The company offers services to biotech companies.	925-937-1500	NA	Walnut Creek

332 = Hybrids

COMPANY NAME	PRODUCT / SERVICE	PHONE	EMP	CITY
4D Molecular Therapeutics LLC (HQ)	Provider of gene therapy product research and development for the treatment of genetic diseases such as diabetes, arthritis, and heart failure.	510-505-2680	NA	Emeryville
Bell Biosystems Inc (HQ)	Provider of biotechnology services. The company develops proteins targeted to kill specific bacteria but cause minimal collateral damage.	877-420-3621	NA	Berkeley
Bioneer Inc (BR)	Developer of molecular biology products and technologies for life science researchers in academia, biotech, and pharmaceutical companies.	877-264-4300	NA	Oakland
Centrillion Technology Holdings Ltd (HQ)	Developer of genomics solutions for the researchers, physicians, and consumers. The company also offers clinical testing and consumer genomics services.	650-618-0111	NA	Palo Alto
DNAmito Inc (HQ)	Provider of DNA technology and cloud platform to enable cancer treatment and early prediction of chronic disease thus vastly improving patient care.	650-687-0899	NA	Palo Alto
Genapsys Inc (HQ)	Developer of DNA sequencing to enable a paradigm shift in genomic diagnostics. The company specializes in GENIUS system that has footprint of Apple iPad.	650-330-1096	NA	Redwood City
Karius Inc (HQ)	Provider of microbial genomics diagnostics. The company focuses on transforming infectious disease diagnostics with genomics.	866-452-7487	NA	Redwood City

COMPANY NAME	PRODUCT / SERVICE	PHONE	EMP	CITY
MTI California Inc (HQ)	Specializes in designing and validating manufacturing controls. The company offers services to biotech companies.	925-937-1500	NA	Walnut Creek
Natera Inc (HQ)	Provider of prenatal testing services. The company specializes in non-invasive prenatal testing, genetic carrier screening and paternity testing.	650-249-9090	501-1000	San Carlos
SwitchGear Genomics Inc (HQ)	Focuses on custom cloning, pathway screening, target validation, sequence variant assay, and custom mutagenesis services.	760-431-1263	NA	Carlsbad

333 = Antihistamine

COMPANY NAME	PRODUCT / SERVICE	PHONE	EMP	CITY
Aridis Pharmaceuticals LLC (HQ)	Focuses on anti-infective alternatives to conventional antibiotics. The company offers services to the pharmaceutical sector.	408-385-1742	NA	San Jose
Coherus Biosciences (HQ)	Developer of biosimilars and it serves the global marketplace. The company is engaged in delivery services.	800-794-5434	NA	Redwood City
Credence MedSystems Inc (HQ)	Provider of pharmaceutical products. The company specializes in single-dose injectable medications in pre-filled syringes.	844-263-3797	NA	Menlo Park
EMSL Analytical Inc (BR)	Provider of laboratory analytical testing services. The company specializes in a wide range of environmental, material and forensic testing.	510-895-3675	NA	San Leandro
Gliamed Inc (HQ)	Provider of drugs for the regeneration of skin, cardiac muscle, cartilage, bone, brain and other tissues.	408-457-8828	NA	San Jose

334 = Laser

	COMPANY NAME	PRODUCT / SERVICE	PHONE	EMP	CITY
N	ICC Instrument Company Inc (HQ)	Provider of instrument calibration and repair services.	714-540-4966	NA	Santa Ana
	Peridot Corp (HQ)	Provider of design for manufacturing and packaging. The company also manufacturers of medical components, miniature component and general product prototypes.	925-461-8830	NA	Pleasanton
	Relucent Solutions LLC (HQ)	Manufacturer of medical devices. The company is involved in laser cutting, precision manufacturing, wire crimping, and related services.	800-630-7704	NA	Santa Rosa
	Sciton Inc (HQ)	Provider of laser and light source solutions. The company's products include JOULE, BBL, ClearSense, Halo, and more.	650-493-9155	NA	Palo Alto
N	Ted Levine Drum Co (HQ)	Provider of repair services.	626-579-1084	11-50	South El Monte